Europe

THE ROUGH GUIDE

S0-AUS-910

Rough Guide credits

Series editor:	Mark Ellingham
Text editors:	Jonathan Buckley, Martin Dunford, Graham Parker
Editorial:	John Fisher, Greg Ward, Jules Brown, Samantha Cook, Jo Mead
Production:	Susanne Hillen, Andy Hilliard, Gail Jammy, Vivien Antwi, Alan Spicer
Cartography:	Melissa Flack
Finance:	Celia Crowley
Publicity:	Richard Trillo

CONTRIBUTORS

Robert Andrews (Great Britain, Italy); Rosie Ayliffe (Turkey); Kate Baillie (France); Ian W. Ball (Ireland); Ros Belford (Italy); Jonathan Bousfield (Austria, Bulgaria, Great Britain, Romania, Slovenia, Switzerland); Jules Brown (Italy, Norway, Spain, Sweden); Emile Bruls (Netherlands); Jonathan Buckley (Great Britain; Italy); Phil Cheeseman (Great Britain); Fiona Clark (Poland); Sam Cole (Italy); Samantha Cook (Great Britain); Philip Cooper (Spain); Adam Coulter (Spain); Adrian Coyle (Ireland); Jane O.Davies (Italy); Seàn Doran (Ireland); Marc Dubin (Greece, Spain, Turkey); Martin Dunford (Belgium, Italy, Luxembourg, Netherlands); Mark Ellingham (Greece, Italy, Spain, Portugal); Richard Figueiras (Spain); John Fisher (Greece, Portugal, Spain); Geoff Garvey (Spain); John Gawthrop (Turkey); Donald Greig (Great Britain); Margaret Greenwood (Ireland); Don Grisbrook (Morocco); Emily Hatchwell (Great Britain); Hildi Hawkins (Ireland); Charles Hebbert (Hungary); Jack Holland (Germany, Netherlands); Joanna Howard (Spain); Rob Humphreys (Austria, Czech and Slovak Republics, Great Britain); Mike Ivy (Italy); Natania Jansz (Greece); Tim Jepson (Italy); Brenda Keatley (Italy); Anna van Kemenade (Netherlands); Graham Kenyon (Portugal, Spain); Phil Lee (Belgium, Great Britain, Netherlands, Spain); Mark Lewis (Ireland); Mark Lewis (Portugal); Gordon McLachlan (Germany, Great Britain, Poland); Jon Marks (Luxembourg); Alice Martin (Portugal); Shaun McVeigh (Morocco); Mike Parker (Great Britain); Clare Rendell (Great Britain); Dan Richardson (Bulgaria, Hungary, Romania); Lucy Ridout (France, Great Britain); Sally Roy (Great Britain); Tim Salmon (France); Mark Salter (Poland, Sweden); Mick Sinclair (Denmark, Finland); Tania Smith (Great Britain); Theo Taylor (France); Greg Ward (France, Spain); Sandra White (Ireland); Paul Whitfield (Denmark, Finland, Great Britain, Norway, Sweden, Switzerland); James Wilson (Spain); Celia Woolfrey (Italy); Chris Wright (Germany); Pat Yale (Great Britain).

The editors would like to **thank**: Jeanne Muchnick and David Reed for US and Canadian research; Pat Yale for proofreading; and Sam Kirby for map updates. Also the Swiss National Tourist Office; the Austrian National Tourist Office; the Italian Tourist Office; Eurotrain; Campus Travel; STA Travel; National Express; the English Youth Hostels Association; the Scottish Youth Hostel Association.

HELP US UPDATE

We've gone to a lot of effort to make sure that the **Rough Guide to Europe** is thoroughly up-to-date and accurate. However things do change, in Europe with alarming rapidity, and we'd very much appreciate any comments, corrections or additions for the next edition of the book. For the best letters, we'll send a copy of the new edition or any other Rough Guide. Please mark letters "Europe Update", and send them to:

Rough Guides, 1 Mercer Street, London WC2H 9QJ, or Rough Guides, 375 Hudson Street, 4th Floor, New York NY 10014.

Europe

THE ROUGH GUIDE

THE ROUGH GUIDES

The publishers and authors have done their best to ensure the accuracy and currency of all the information in *The Rough Guide to Europe*; however, they can accept no responsibility for any loss, injury or inconvenience sustained by any traveller as a result of information or advice contained in the guide.

This second edition published 1994 by Rough Guides Ltd, 1 Mercer Street, London WC2H 9QJ.
Distributed by the Penguin Group:
Penguin Books Ltd, 27 Wrights Lane, London W8 5TZ
Penguin Books USA Inc., 375 Hudson Street, New York 10014, USA
Penguin Books Australia Ltd, 487 Maroondah Highway, PO Box 257, Ringwood, Victoria 3134, Australia
Penguin Books Canada Ltd, 10 Alcorn Avenue, Toronto, Ontario M4V 1E4, Canada
Penguin Books (NZ) Ltd, 182–190 Wairau Road, Auckland 10, New Zealand

Previous edition published in the United States and Canada as *The Real Guide Europe*.

Typeset in Linotron Univers and Century Old Style to an original design by Andrew Oliver.
Printed in the UK by Cox & Wyman Ltd, Reading, Berks.

Illustrations in Part One by Edward Briant, and on pp. 1 & 53 by Henry Iles.

© Jonathan Buckley and Martin Dunford 1992, 1994

1312pp. Includes index.

A catalogue record for this book is available from the British Library.
ISBN 1-85828-077-X

CONTENTS

FINLAND

HELSINKI

OCKHOLM

Talinn
ESTONIA

Baltic Sea

Riga
LATVIA

Moscow

RUSSIA

LITHUANIA

Vilnius

Minsk

BELARUS

LAND

WARSAW

Kiev

Krakow

UKRAINE

OVAKIA

Chisinau

BUDAPEST

MOLDOVA

NGARY

ROMANIA

elgrade

BUCHAREST

GEORGIA

T'bilisi

Baki

AZERBAIJAN

Black Sea

ORMER

BULGARIA

ARMENIA

Yerevan

OSLAVIA

SOFIA

na

ALBANIA

Istanbul

ANKARA

GREECE

İzmir

TURKEY

IRAN

ATHENS

ean Sea

Crete

CYPRUS

SYRIA

Baghdad

Beirut

LEBANON

Damascus

IRAQ

0   500 km

LIST OF MAPS

PART ONE

THE
BASICS

INTRODUCTION

The collapse of the division between eastern and western **Europe** at the end of the 1980s, and the ever closer ties between the twelve countries of the European Community – increasingly a political and cultural as well as economic union – have made Europe a buzzword of the early Nineties, the word itself implying shared values, and, despite all the wrangling, a broad consensus of political beliefs. Some of this is, however, inevitably a superficial analysis, and despite the much-heralded Single Market and the imminent opening of the Channel Tunnel (now estimated to be in the summer of 1994), the changes are likely to be slow, and true European unity remains something of a distant dream.

Conventionally, the **geographical boundaries** of Europe are the Ural Mountains in the east, the Atlantic Coast in the north and west, the Mediterranean in the south. However, within these rough parameters Europe is massively diverse. The environment changes radically within very short distances, with bleak mountain ranges never far from broad, fertile plains, and deep, ancient forests close to scattered lake systems or river gorges. Politically and ethnically, too, it is an extraordinary patchwork: the Slav race scatters through central Europe from Poland in the north to Serbia and Bulgaria in the south; Finnish, spoken by the inhabitants of Europe's northernmost nation, bears a resemblance not to the tongues of its Scandinavian neighbours but to that of Hungary, over 1000km further south; and in parts of Switzerland some people still speak a language akin to Latin. These differences have been exacerbated of late with the rise of nationalism that coincided with the decline of communism, and borders are even now being redrawn, not always peacefully and often along nationalistic and linguistic lines.

Where you head for obviously depends on your tastes and the kind of vacation you want: you can sample mountain air and winter sports in the Alps of France, Austria or Switzerland, lie on a beach in the swanky resorts of the south of France or Italy, or view architecture and works of art in the great cities of London, Paris, Florence or Amsterdam. Suffice to say, the lifting of restrictions on travel in eastern Europe, with only a handful of countries still requiring visas and nothing like the bureaucratic regulations there were before, means that the continent really is there for the travelling – something manifest in the increasingly good-value *InterRail* card, which now covers everywhere except Albania. Although you may want to make a long hop or two by air, **rail** is indeed the way to see the continent, highlighting the diversity of the place when you cross the borders of central Europe that were until recently closed, or travel in a few hours from the cool temperatures of northern Europe to the rich and sultry climes of the Mediterranean. In fact, with the richness and diversity of its culture, climate, landscapes and peoples, there is no more exciting place to travel.

This book is a little eccentric in its **definition of Europe.** We include nothing on the Baltic states that were formerly part of the Soviet Union, or indeed the European parts of the Soviet Union itself; impoverished and still relatively inaccessible Albania has also been excluded, and only Slovenia has been included of the handful of republics being carved out of the former Yugoslavia, a country at the time of writing riven by a civil war.

On the other hand, we cover countries like Morocco and Turkey that are not strictly part of Europe, in the main because they are easy to reach on a European tour and are included by the *InterRail* pass. In future editions of the guide, as the constituent parts of the Soviet Union are drawn more into the European mainstream and the problems in the Balkans sort themselves out, this hopefully will change.

CLIMATE AND WHEN TO GO

Europe's **climate** is as variable as everything else about the continent. In **northwestern Europe** – Britain, Benelux, Denmark, southwestern Norway, most of France and parts of Germany – the climate is basically a cool temperate one, with the chance of rain all year round and no great extremes of either cold or hot weather. There is no bad time to travel in most of this part of the continent, although the winter months between November and March can be damp and miserable – especially in the upland regions – and obviously the summer period between May and September sees the most reliable and driest weather. In **eastern Europe,** on the other hand, basically to the right of a north–south line drawn roughly through the heart of Germany and extending down as far as the western edge of

Bulgaria (taking in eastern Germany, Poland, southern Sweden, the Czech and Slovak Republics, Austria, Switzerland, Hungary and Romania), the climatic conditions are more extreme, with freezing winters and sometimes sweltering summers. Here the transitional spring and autumn seasons are the most pleasant time to travel; deep midwinter, especially, can be very unpleasant, although it doesn't have the dampness you associate with the northwestern European climate. **Southern Europe**, principally the countries that border the Mediterranean and associated seas – southern France, Italy, Spain, Portugal, Greece and western Turkey – has the most hospitable climate in Europe, with a general pattern of warm, dry summers and mild winters. Travel is possible at any time of year here, although the peak summer months can be very hot and very busy and the deep winter ones can see some rain.

There are, too, within these three broad groupings, marked regional variations. As they're such large countries, inland Spain and France can, for example, see a **continental** type of weather as extreme as any in central Europe, and the **Alpine** areas of Italy, Austria and Switzerland – and other **mountain areas** like the Pyrenees, Apennines and parts of the Balkans – have a climate mainly influenced by altitude, which means extremes of cold, short summers, and long winters that always see snow. There are also, of course, the northern regions of the Scandinavian countries, which have an **arctic climate** – again, bitterly cold, though with some surprisingly warm temperatures during the short summer when much of the region is warmed by the Gulf Stream. Winter sees the sun barely rise at all in these areas, while high summer can mean almost perpetual daylight.

There are obviously other considerations when deciding **when to go**. If you're planning to visit fairly touristed areas, especially beach resorts in the Mediterranean, avoid July and August, when the weather can be too hot and the crowds at their most congested. Bear in mind, also, that in a number of countries in Europe everyone takes their **vacation** at the same time (this is certainly true in France and Italy in August, when *everyone* goes away). Find out the holiday month beforehand for the countries where you intend to travel, since you can expect the crush to be especially bad in the resorts; in the cities the only other people around will be fellow tourists, which can be miserable. In northern Scandinavia the climatic extremes are such that you'll find opening times severely restricted, even road and rail lines closed, outside the May–September period, making travel futile and sometimes impossible outside these months. In mountainous areas things stay open for the winter sports season, which lasts from December through to April, though outside the main resorts you'll again find many things closed. Mid-April to mid-June can be a quiet period in many mountain resorts, and you may have much of the mountains to yourselves.

TEMPERATURE CHART

	Jan	Feb	March	April	May	June	July	Aug	Sept	Oct	Nov	Dec
Amsterdam	31–40	31–42	34–49	40–56	46–64	51–70	55–72	55–71	50–67	44–57	38–48	33–42
Athens	44–57	44–57	46–60	52–68	61–77	68–88	73–92	73–92	67–84	60–75	53–66	47–58
Brussels	30–40	32–42	36–51	41–58	46–65	52–72	54–73	54–72	51–69	45–60	38–48	32–42
Bucharest	19–34	23–38	30–50	41–64	51–74	57–81	60–86	59–85	52–78	43–65	35–49	26–39
Budapest	24–35	28–39	35–50	44–62	52–71	58–78	62–82	60–81	53–74	44–61	38–47	30–39
Copenhagen	28–36	28–36	31–41	38–58	46–61	52–67	57–71	56–70	51–64	44–54	38–45	34–40
Helsinki	17–26	15–25	20–32	30–44	40–56	49–66	55–71	53–68	46–59	37–47	30–37	23–31
Innsbruck	20–34	24–40	30–51	39–60	46–68	52–74	55–77	54–75	49–69	40–58	30–46	24–36
Istanbul	37–46	36–47	38–51	45–60	53–69	60–77	65–82	66–82	61–76	55–68	48–59	41–51
Lisbon	46–57	47–59	50–63	53–67	55–71	60–77	63–81	63–82	62–79	58–72	52–63	47–58
London	36–43	36–44	38–50	42–56	47–62	53–69	56–71	56–71	52–65	46–58	42–50	38–45
Madrid	35–47	36–52	41–59	45–65	50–70	58–80	63–87	63–85	57–77	49–65	42–55	36–48
Marseille	35–50	36–53	41–59	46–64	52–71	58–79	63–84	63–84	58–77	51–68	43–58	37–52
Narvik	19–29	19–29	22–34	29–41	37–49	45–56	51–65	49–62	43–53	35–43	28–37	24–31
Oslo	19–28	19–30	25–39	34–50	43–61	50–68	55–72	53–70	46–60	38–48	31–38	25–32
Palermo	46–60	47–62	48–63	52–68	58–74	64–81	69–85	70–86	66–83	60–77	54–71	49–64
Paris	34–43	34–45	39–54	43–60	49–68	55–73	58–76	58–75	53–70	46–60	40–50	36–44
Prague	23–31	24–34	30–44	38–54	46–64	52–70	55–73	55–72	49–65	41–53	33–42	27–34
Rabat	46–63	47–65	49–68	52–71	55–74	60–78	63–82	64–83	62–81	58–77	53–70	48–65
Rome	40–52	42–55	45–59	50–66	56–74	63–82	67–87	67–86	62–79	55–71	49–61	44–55
Stockholm	23–30	22–30	26–37	34–47	43–58	51–67	57–71	56–68	49–60	41–49	34–40	29–35
Vienna	25–34	28–38	30–47	42–58	50–67	56–73	60–76	59–75	53–68	44–56	37–45	30–37
Warsaw	22–32	21–32	28–42	37–53	48–67	54–73	58–75	56–73	49–66	41–55	33–42	28–35
Zürich	26–36	28–41	34–51	40–59	47–67	53–73	56–76	56–75	51–69	43–57	35–45	29–39

The figures above represent minimum and maximum average daily temperatures in °F

TRAVELLING FROM NORTH AMERICA

The air space between North America and Europe is one of the most heavily travelled in the world. It is served by literally dozens of airlines, both US carriers and the national airlines of almost every European country, and there is consequently a huge range of seats at a huge range of prices. It all depends on where you're travelling from, and, of course, where you want to go. There is, however, a number of "gateway" cities into which you'll find a greater – and cheaper – choice of options.

THE BACKGROUND

As you'll find once you're in Europe as well, the best way to get a good-value fare is to shop around as much as possible. Discounts and special deals change all the time, and you should check the Sunday newspapers' travel sections, or consult a decent **travel agent** or **specialist in discount flights** – youth and student specialists like *Council* and *STA* often have the best deals, and not just for students. Another option is to contact a **discount travel club** – organizations which specialize in selling off the unsold seats of travel agents for bargain rates, often at up to half the original price, though you usually have to be a member to get the best deals. You could also try a so-called airline ticket **consolidator**, who sells the unsold seats direct from airlines, though bear in mind that discounts are usually not as high as with travel clubs and you may not get the exact flight you want; remember also that flights, particularly charters, cannot be changed at all once booked. Pay with a credit card if possible, so that if you do change your mind there's always a chance you can stop the payment going through.

Most of the airlines maintain a fare structure which peaks between mid-June and early September, with a shoulder season either side of this and the best deals during the November to March period, when fewer people are travelling. You'll often find the cheapest fare by leaving from the airline's "hub" – New York, Atlanta, Dallas, Chicago, Los Angeles, San Francisco, Seattle, Vancouver, Toronto and Montréal are the main ones; hub cities also tend to have non-stop flights, with no changes at all. You do, however, need to be flexible: London, Paris, or Amsterdam are usually the cheapest "gateway cities" in Europe simply because they are served by more flights; Milan, Rome and Frankfurt run a close second in some cases. Flying midweek rather than at the weekend is also a few dollars cheaper.

If money is no object you can, of course, fly **first class** or, slightly cheaper **business class**, which for greatly inflated prices give you extra legroom, better food and lots of other trimmings. Most people, however, fly coach or **economy class**, and the cheapest way of doing this is to buy an **Apex** ticket. These often work out quite a lot cheaper than an ordinary economy fare, but there are tight restrictions: you have to book – and pay – at least 21 days before departure; you must spend at least seven days abroad (maximum three months); and you tend to get penalized if you change your schedule – ten percent of the ticket value, for example, if you alter the return date or your outward reservation. There are also winter **Super-Apex** tickets, sometimes known as "Eurosavers" – slightly cheaper than an ordinary Apex but tending to be more restrictive, limiting stays to between 7 and 21 days. Bear in mind, too, that some airlines issue **special Apex** tickets to those under 24, often extending the maximum stay to a year.

FROM EASTERN AND CENTRAL USA

There are lots of options from most of the **eastern** hub cities, though most of the best deals are out of New York and Chicago to London, with Paris, Frankfurt, Amsterdam, Rome and Milan good second bests. The lowest off-peak fare to London from New York with the major carriers – *British Airways*, *American*, *United* and *Virgin Atlantic* – is around $400, though peak season prices are likely to be fifty percent higher. To give an idea of other alternatives, *United* fly from Chicago to London for $525 off-peak, $780 in summer; *Lufthansa* fly from Chicago to Frankfurt for around $570 off-peak, $870 in the summer; while a New York–Milan return fare with *Alitalia* is $520 during the winter as opposed to nearly $1000 in the summer season. Look out also for deals from the smaller airlines like *Tower* or *Balair* – good bets to Paris and Zürich respectively – and those from *Icelandair*, whose flights from New York or Baltimore to Luxembourg can work out the cheapest way of getting to Europe if you're not too fussy about where you arrive.

FROM THE WEST COAST

From the **West Coast** it's much the same story. The big airlines fly at least three times a week (sometimes daily) from Los Angeles, San Francisco and Seattle to main European cities. *British Airways* have plenty of flights, with fares starting at $550 to London; *Austrian Airlines* fly to Vienna from LA for around $770 return; *Lufthansa* fly to Frankfurt from LA for the same price; and *Alitalia* fly to Milan for around $770 off-peak, and $1160 in summer.

FROM CANADA

Most of the big airlines fly to the major European hubs from **Montréal** and **Toronto** at least once daily (the smaller airlines three times a week). *Air Canada* charge an Apex fare from Toronto to Rome of Can$1100 off-peak, $1500 or so in summer; *Iberia* fly to Madrid for around $900 from Toronto and Montréal, $1030 in summer; *KLM* fly from Montreal to Amsterdam for Can$540 off-peak, twice that during in summer.

PACKAGES AND ORGANIZED TOURS

Although you may want to see Europe in your own time, at your own pace, you shouldn't entirely write off the idea of a **package deal**. Many agents and airlines can put together very flexible deals, sometimes amounting to no more than a flight plus car and accommodation, and they can work out a great deal cheaper than organizing things when you arrive, especially as regards car rental, which in Europe can be very expensive on the spot. They are also great for peace for mind, even if all you're doing is taking care of the first week's accommodation on a longer tour.

There are literally hundreds – perhaps thousands – of different package operators, offering everything from fly-drive deals, sun-and-sea packages and coach tours to specialist interest holidays. It shouldn't be too hard, with the help of a travel agent, to find something to suit, but be sure to examine the small print of any deal (Europe's a long way from home if you end up with something you don't want), and to remember that everything in a brochure always *sounds* great, even if it ain't. Try also to only use an operator that is a member of the *United States Tour Operator Association* (*USTOA*) or approved by the *American Society of Travel Agents* (*ASTA*).

MAJOR AIRLINES IN NORTH AMERICA

Aer Lingus, 122 E 42nd St, New York, NY 10166 (☎212/557-1110 or 800/223-6537).

Air France, 888 Seventh Ave, New York, NY 10106 (☎212/830-4000 or 800/237-2747); 875 N Michigan Ave, Chicago, IL 60611 (☎312/440-7922); 2000 rue Mansfield, Montréal, PQ H3A 3A3 (☎514/847-1106); 151 Bloor St W, Suite 600, Toronto, ON M5S 1S4 (☎416/922-5024).

Alitalia, 666 Fifth Ave, New York, NY 10103 (☎212/582-8900 or 800/223-5730); 2055 Peel St, Montréal, PQ H3A 1V8 (☎514/842-5201); 120 Adelaide St West, Toronto, ON M5H 2E1 (☎416/363-2001).

American Airlines, PO Box 619616, Dallas/Fort Worth International Airport, Dallas, TX 75261 (☎817/267-1151 or 800/433-7300).

Austrian Airlines, 608 Fifth Ave, New York, NY 10020 (☎800/843-0002); 2 Bloor St East, Toronto, ON M4Q 1A8 (☎416/843-0002).

British Airways, 530 Fifth Ave, New York, NY 10017 (☎800/247-9297); 1501 McGill Collese Ave, Montréal, PQ H3A 3M8 (☎514/287-9282 or 800/668-1059); 112 Kent St, Ottawa, ON K1P 5P2 (☎800/668-1059); 4120 Yonge St, Suite 100, North York, ON M2P 2B8 (☎416/250-0880).

Continental Airlines, 2929 Allen Parkway, Houston, TX 77019 (☎713/821-2100 or 800/231-0856).

ČSA Czechoslovak Airlines, 545 Fifth Ave, New York, NY 10017 (☎212/682-5833 or 800/223-2365); 2020 University St, Montréal, PQ H3A 2A5 (☎514/844-4200); 401 Bay St, Toronto, ON M5H 2Y4 (☎416/363-3174).

Delta Airlines, Hartsfield Atlanta International Airport, Atlanta, GA 30320 (☎404/765-5000 or 800/221-1212).

Finnair, 10 E 40th St, New York, NY 10016 (☎212/889-7070 or 800/950-5000).

Iberia, 655 Madison Ave, 20th floor, New York, NY 10021 (☎212/644-8841 or 800/772-4642); 6300 Wilshire Blvd, Los Angeles, CA 90048 (☎800/772-4642); 2020 University St, Suite 1310, Montréal, PQ H3A 2A5 (☎514/985-5201 or 800/423-7421).

Icelandair, 360 W 31st St, New York, NY 10001 (☎212/967-8888 or 800/223-5500).

KLM, 565 Taxter Rd, Elmsford, NY 10523 (☎800/374-7747); 225 N Michigan Ave, Chicago, IL 60601 (☎312/861-9292); 1255 Green Ave, West Mount, PQ H3Z 2A4 (☎514/933-1314 or 800/361-5073).

LOT Polish Airlines, 500 Fifth Ave, New York, NY 10110 (☎212/869-1074 or 800/223-0593); 333 N Michigan Ave, Chicago, IL 60601 (☎312/236-3388); 2000 Peter Elizabeth London, Montréal, PQ H3A 2W5 (☎514/844-2674).

Lufthansa, 1640 Hempstead Turnpike, East Meadow, NY 11554 (☎718/895-1277 or 800/645-3880); 875 N Michigan Ave, Chicago, IL 60611 (☎312/686-8200); 55 Yonge St, Toronto, ON M5E 1J4 (☎416/368-4777); 2020 University St, Montréal, PQ H3A 2A5 (☎514/288-2227).

Malév Hungarian Airlines, 630 Fifth Ave, New York, NY 10111 (☎212/757-6446 or 800/223-6884); 175 Bloor St East, Toronto, ON M4W 3R8 (☎416/944-0093).

Northwest Airlines, Minneapolis/St Paul International Airport, St Paul, MN 55111 (☎612/726-1234 or 800/225-2525).

Olympic Airways, 645 Fifth Ave, New York, NY 10022 (☎212/838-3600 or 800/223-1226); 168 N Michigan Ave, Chicago, IL 60601 (☎312/329-0400 or 800/223-1226); 624 South End St, Suite 1709, Los Angeles 90017 (☎213/624-6441); 80 Bloor St West, Suite 502, Toronto, ON M5S 2V1 (☎416/920-2452).

Royal Air Maroc, 666 Fifth Ave, New York, NY 10103 (☎212/974 3850).

Sabena, 720 Fifth Ave, New York, NY 10022 (☎800/955-2000); 5959 W. Century Blvd, Los Angeles, CA 90045 (☎310/642-7735); 1001 bd de Maisonneuve Ouest, Montréal, H3A 3C8 (☎800/955-2000).

SAS, 9 Toledo Ave, Lindhurst, NJ 07071 (☎800/221-2350); Box 61, AMF, Toronto, ON L5 1A2 (☎416/672-5600 or 800/465-0569).

Swissair, 608 Fifth Ave, New York, NY 10020 (☎718/995-8400 or 800/221-4750); 2 Bloor St West, Suite 502, Toronto, ON M5S 2V1 (☎416/960-4270).

TAP Air Portugal, 399 Market St, Newark, NJ 07105 (☎201/344-4490 or 800/221-7370); 1010 Sherbrooke St West, Montréal, PQ H3A 2R7 (☎514/849-4217).

THY Turkish Airlines, 821 United Nations Plaza, 4th floor, New York, NY10017 (☎212/986-5050).

Trans World Airlines, 100 South Bedford Rd, Mount Kisco, NY 10549 (☎212/290-2141 or 800/892-4141).

United Airlines, PO Box 66100, Chicago, IL 60666 (☎708/952-4000 or 800/241-6522).

US Air, Crystal Park Four, 2345 Crystal Drive, Arlington, VA 22227 (☎703/418-7000 or 800/622-1015).

Virgin Atlantic Airways, 96 Horton St, New York, NY 10014 (☎212/206-6612 or 800/862-8621).

DISCOUNT FLIGHT AGENTS, TRAVEL CLUBS AND CONSOLIDATORS

Council Travel, 205 E 42nd St, New York, NY 10017 (☎212/661-1450). Head office of the nationwide US student travel organization. Branches in San Francisco, LA, Washington, New Orleans, Chicago, Seattle, Portland, Minneapolis, Boston, Atlanta and Dallas, to name only the larger ones.

Encore Short Notice, 4501 Forbes Blvd, Lanham, MD 20706 (☎301/459-8020 or 800/638-0830). East Coast travel club.

Interworld, 800 Douglass Rd, Miami, FL 33134 (☎305/443-4929). Southeastern US consolidator.

Last-Minute Travel Club, 132 Brookline Ave, Boston, MA 02215 (☎617/267-9800 or 800/LAST-MIN).

Moment's Notice, 425 Madison Ave, New York, NY 10017 (☎212/486-0503). Travel club that's good for last-minute deals.

Nouvelles Frontières, 12 E 33rd St, New York, NY 10016 (☎212/779-0600); 1001 Sherbrook East, Suite 720, Montréal, PQ H2L 1L3 (☎514/526-8444). Main US and Canadian branches of the French discount travel outfit. Other branches in LA, San Francisco and Quebec City.

STA Travel, 48 East 11th St, New York, NY 10003 (☎212/477-7166); 166 Geary St, Suite 702, San Francisco, CA 94108 (☎415/391-8407). Main US branches of the originally Australian and now worldwide specialist in independent and student travel. Other offices in LA, Boston and Honolulu.

Stand Buys, 311 W Superior St, Chicago, IL 60610 (☎800/548-1116). Good Midwestern travel club.

Travel Cuts, 187 College St, Toronto, ON M5T 1P7 (☎416/979-2406). Main office of the Canadian student travel organization. Also has many other offices nationwide.

Travelers Advantage, 49 Music Square West, Nashville, TN 37204 (☎800/548-1116). Reliable travel club.

Travac, 1177 N Warson Rd, St Louis, MO 63132 (☎800/872-8800). Good central US consolidator.

Travel Avenue, 180 North Des Plaines, Suite 201, Chicago, IL 60661 (☎312/876-1116 or 800/333-3335). Discount travel agent.

Unitravel, 1177 N Warson Rd, St Louis, MO 63132 (☎800/325-2222) Reliable consolidator.

Worldwide Discount Travel Club, 1674 Meridian Ave, Miami Beach, FL 33139 (☎305/534-2082).

USEFUL RAIL ADDRESSES IN NORTH AMERICA

British Rail International, 1500 Broadway, New York, NY 10036 (☎212/575-2667 or 800/677-8585).

CIE Tours International, 108 Ridgedale Ave, Morristown, NJ 07690 (☎201/292-3438 or 800/522-5258). A prime source for booking rail travel in Europe.

RailEurope, 226–230 Westchester Ave, White Plains, NY 10604 (☎914/682-2999 or 800/848-7245); and branches in Santa Monica, San Francisco, Fort Lauderdale, Chicago, Dallas, Vancouver and Montréal. Perhaps the best place to book rail tickets for Europe, including eastern Europe.

TOUR OPERATORS

American Express, World Financial Center, New York, NY 10285 (☎212/640-2000 or 800/241-1700). Packages, city breaks, etc, all over Europe.

Contiki Holidays, 300 Plaza Alicante, Suite 900, Garden Grove, CA, 92640 (☎714/740-0808 or 800/466-0610). Coach tours for under-35-year-olds.

Cosmos/Global Gateway, 92-25 Queens Blvd, Rego Park, NY 11374 (☎800/221-0090). The leading budget tour operators to Europe in the US. Bookable through travel agents only.

Europe Through the Back Door Tours, 109 Fourth Ave North, Box 2009, Edmonds, WA 98020 (☎206/771-8303). Excellent travel club which publishes a regular newsletter packed full of travel tales and advice, sells its own guides, travel accessories and *Eurail* passes, and runs good-value bus tours taking in the biggest European cities. Worth joining for the newsletter alone.

Europe Train Tours, 198 Boston Post Rd, Mamaroneck, NY 105431 (☎914/698-9426 or 800/551-2085). What it says.

Jet Vacations, 1775 Broadway, New York, NY 10019 (☎212/247-0999 or 800/JET-0999). Specializes in packages to Europe, especially France.

Mountain Travel/Sobek, 6420 Fairmont Ave, El Cerrito, CA 94530 (☎800/227-2384). Hiking specialist.

Scantours, 1535 6th St, Suite 205, Santa Monica, CA 90401 (☎310/451-0911 or 800/223-SCAN). Specialists in Scandinavia and eastern Europe.

Trafalgar Tours, 11 East 26th St, New York, NY 10010 (☎212/689-8977 or 800/854-0103). Coach tours all over Europe.

Trophy Tours, 1810 Glenville Drive, Suite 1124, Richardson, TX 75081 (☎800/527-2473). Good-value coach tours all over Europe. Good on Britain and Ireland.

TRAVELLING FROM BRITAIN

Until the completion of the Channel Tunnel, all routes from Britain to the continent involve either air or surface travel across the English Channel or North Sea. For destinations close to home, train and long-distance bus represent best value for money, but the further you go the cheaper air travel becomes, and it's normally cheaper to fly than take the train to most parts of southern Europe – although special deals on rail passes can bring prices down considerably.

BY AIR

As ever, the best way to find the cheapest **flight** is to shop around: air travel in Europe is still highly regulated, which means that the prices quoted by the airlines can usually be undercut considerably, even on Apex fares, by going to an agent. Check the ads in the London *Evening Standard* and listings magazine *Time Out*, or the classified sections of the quality Sunday newspapers. During the summer you can reach most of the countries of southern Europe – Portugal, Spain, Italy, Greece – on **charter flights**, block-booked by package holiday firms and usually having a few seats left over which they sell off cheap through selected **agents**, sometimes known as "bucket shops". Though they are inevitably rather restricted, with fixed return dates, a maximum validity of a month, and no chance of cancelling or changing your ticket once you've bought it, they can be very cheap – so much so in some cases that it's actually worth just using the outward portion if the return date doesn't suit. There are also flight agents who specialize in low-cost, discounted flights (charter and scheduled), some of them – like *STA Travel* and *Campus Travel* – concentrating on deals for youths and students, though they can be a good source of bargains for everyone. In addition, there are agents specializing in offers to a specific country or group of countries on both charters and regular scheduled departures. To give a rough idea of prices booked through agents, reckon on paying £90–160 to Spain in high season; £100–200 to Greece or Turkey; £65–110 to Paris, Brussels or Amsterdam; £130–200 to Scandinavia; £100–150 to the main Italian cities; £180–250 to the major cities of eastern Europe. Many agents also do so-called "open jaw" tickets, whereby you fly into one city and out from another, not necessarily even in the same country.

BY TRAIN

Until the Channel Tunnel is finished (estimated to be summer 1994), all **rail** journeys from Britain involve some kind of sea crossing, usually by ferry or hovercraft, sometimes by catamaran. The cost of the crossing is always included in the price of the rail ticket to any foreign destination, but bear in mind that if any of your journey is by French *TGV* train, or any similar special express, you need to make a **seat reservation** in advance. You can buy an ordinary rail ticket to most parts of Europe from *British Rail*, normally from your local station. **Return tickets** are valid for two months and allow for stopovers on the way, providing you stick to the prescribed route (there may be a choice, with different fares applicable). To give some idea of fares, London–Paris costs from £85 return, London–Zürich £147, London–Rome £189. You can also get heavily discounted **five-day return** fares to Channel ports and other reasonably close destinations. Kids under four travel free, those aged 4–15 years travel at reduced rates. Tickets may be purchased up to two months in advance of travel. During the summer, especially if you're travelling at night or a long distance, it's best to make reservations on most legs of your journey. At night, couchettes in six-berth compartments cost £11.90 per person; sleeping car charges start at around £38.40 a head. There are, of course, lots of ways of cutting costs. If you're under 26 you are entitled to all sorts of special deals, not least **BIJ fares**, which cut ordinary rail fares to around 200 destinations in Europe by up to fifty percent. They're issued by *Eurotrain*, the largest agent, *Wasteels*, and *British Rail* under the tag "Euro Youth". Again tickets are valid for two months and you can stop off en route. For other ways of saving money on train travel in Europe, principally with **rail passes**, see "Travelling in Europe" below.

When the **Channel Tunnel** finally becomes fully operational, *Le Shuttle* should run trains 24 hours a day, carrying cars, motorcycles, coaches and their passengers, and taking 35 minutes between Folkestone and Calais. At peak times, services will operate every fifteen minutes, making advance bookings unnecessary; during the quietest times of the night, services will still run hourly. Through-trains will connect London (Waterloo Station will be the first terminal completed) with Paris in just over three hours, and fares are expected to match those charged by the ferry companies.

BY LONG-DISTANCE BUS

A **long-distance bus**, although much less comfortable than the train, is at least a little cheaper. There are two main operators based in Britain: *Eurolines*, who have a network of routes spanning the continent – up as far as southern Scandinavia, and way down to the major cities of Morocco, Greece and Turkey – and *Citysprint*, part of the *Hoverspeed* group, who run services to France and Benelux. Prices can knock up to 25 percent off the equivalent train fare, and there are marginally cheaper youth fares for those up to 25 years of age – although these barely undercut BIJ under-26 rail rates for the same journey. As a rough rule of thumb, Paris costs around £55 return, Brussels a little less with both operators, while *Eurolines* will take you as far as Nice for £115 return, to Madrid for £140, and to Athens for around £220. A number of private companies also run buses, normally down to Greece, stopping off in various countries on the way. These, too, can be cheaper than the train, certainly if you're going as far as Greece, but it's a gruelling three- to four-day journey and the companies themselves are notoriously unreliable. Bear in mind, too, if you have a pre-planned itinerary, that *Eurolines* offer a series of circular tickets, taking in various European cities for a set price; see "Travelling in Europe" below.

BY CAR: THE FERRIES

If you're intent on taking your **car** to Europe, you're for the moment confined to crossing the Channel or the North Sea by **ferry**, **hovercraft** or "**Sea Cat**" catamaran. Routes are numerous, and the various fare structures confusing. Most travel agents carry the brochures of the various ferry companies, giving details of fares and frequencies. Prices vary with the month, day or even hour at certain times of the year, not to mention how long you're staying and the size of your car. Basically, the more convenient or popular the time of travel, the greater the cost; on some lines students qualify for a small discount. Although those going for a short time benefit from well-priced five-day returns and the like, price structures tend to be geared to one-way rather than round-trip travel, so the good thing is you don't necessarily have to use the same port in both directions. One other thing you should bear in mind is that some kind of sleeping accommodation is often obligatory on the longer crossings if made at night, pushing the price way above the basic rate.

Obviously the crossing you decide to take depends on where you are based in Britain, and where you're planning to head once across the water. The Brittany crossings are a bit out of the way for most of Europe, and are only really useful if you're planning to visit western France and perhaps drive down to Spain; **Dieppe** is more central, especially if you're intending to visit Paris, since it's closer than the French ports further north – **Boulogne**, **Calais**, **Dunkerque**. These three do, however, have the benefit of a much shorter crossing, and also leave you better placed for travelling through the heart of Europe, either through eastern France and down to Italy or into Belgium, Germany and eastern Europe. The same is true of Belgian Channel ports, though the crossings themselves are a little longer. The

FERRY CROSSINGS FROM BRITAIN

	Operator	Frequency	Duration	One-way fares	
				Small car 2 adults	Foot passenger
Plymouth–Santander	Brittany	2 weekly	24hr	£159–240	£44–65
Plymouth–Roscoff	Brittany	1–2 daily	6hr	£73–170	£22–37
Southampton–Cherbourg	Stena Sealink	1–2 daily	6–8hr	£84–146	£18–35
Portsmouth–Santander	Brittany	1–2 weekly	29hr	£159–240	£44–65
Portsmouth–St Malo	Brittany	1–7 weekly	9hr	£73–172	£23–40
Portsmouth–Caen	Brittany	2–3 daily	6hr	£69–165	£20–38
Portsmouth–Charbourg	P&O	1–4 daily	4hr 45min	£63–150	£20–35
Portsmouth–Le Havre	P&O	2–3 daily	5hr 45min	£69–157	£20–35
Newhaven–Dieppe	Stena Sealink	2–4 daily	4hr	£68–160	£28
Dover–Calais	Stena Sealink	6–22 daily	1hr 30min	£70–155	£24
Dover–Calais	P&O	15–25 daily	1hr 15min	£70–155	£24
Dover–Calais	Hoverspeed	7–20 daily	35–45min	£82–180	£26
Dover–Ostend	P&O	8 daily	4hr	£70–145	£24
Ramsgate–Dunkerque	Sally	5 daily	2hr 30min	£59–120	£15
Felixstowe–Zeebrugge	P&O	2 daily	5hr 45min	£70–145	£24
Folkestone–Boulogne	Hoverspeed	6 daily	1hr	£60–144	£21
Sheerness–Vlissingen	Olau	2 daily	6–8hr	£91–114	£27.50
Harwich–Hook of Holland	Stena Sealink	2 daily	6–8hr	£82–174	£30
Harwich–Hamburg	Scandinavian	1 daily	21hr	£166–247	£65–100
Harwich–Esbjerg	Scandinavian	1 daily	19–21hr	£184–287	£74–120
Harwich–Gothenburg	Scandinavian	5–6 weekly	24hr	£216–347	£90–150
Hull–Zeebrugge	North Sea	1 daily	14hr 30min	£151–179	£47–55
Hull–Rotterdam	North Sea	1 daily	14hr	£151–179	£47–55
Newcastle–Esbjerg	Scandinavian	April–Sept 2 weekly	20hr	£184–287	£74–120
Newcastle–Gothenburg	Scandinavian	June–Aug 1 weekly	24hr	£216–347	£90–150
Newcastle–Stavanger/Bergen	Color Line	2 weekly	20/27hr	£176–300	£68–100

Note: Fares and frequencies are for low season–peak season.

Dutch ports, principally **Hook of Holland** and **Vlissingen**, are only really worth choosing if you're specifically travelling to the Netherlands or perhaps Scandinavia, since the crossings are among the longest you could make, although the Hull–Rotterdam route is a useful one if you live in the north of England. The routes to the **Danish** and **Norwegian** ports are pricy and very long, but if you are taking your car to Scandinavia and don't want to take in other countries on the way, they are well worth the money and save a great deal of time in the long run.

PACKAGES AND INCLUSIVE TOURS

If you're sure of where you want to go, how long you want to spend there, and what you want to do during your time there, it's an odds-on bet there'll be a **package holiday** to suit you. Travelling this way isn't everybody's cup of tea, but it can work out cheaper, and it can also be a good idea if you're nervous of travelling alone. You can lie on a beach, take a short break in a major city, or there are any number of special interest packages available, from hiking trips to cycling deals, although perhaps the most popular choice for young people, especially those coming from Australasia or North America for the first time, is an all-in coach tour of the major sights and cities with an operator like *Top Deck* or *Contiki*, who cater for the 18–35 age range.

DISCOUNT FLIGHT AGENTS

Campus Travel, 52 Grosvenor Gardens, London SW1 (☎071/730 3402). Also with branches in Bristol, Cambridge, Oxford and Edinburgh.

Council Travel, 28a Poland St, London W1 (☎071/287 3337).

CTS, 44 Goodge St, London W1 (☎071/637 5601).

South Coast Student Travel, 61 Ditchling Rd, Brighton BN1 (☎0273/570226). A good agent with plenty to offer non-students as well.

STA Travel, 86 Old Brompton Rd, London SW7; 117 Euston Rd, London NW1 (☎071/937 9921). Also with branches in Bristol, Cambridge, Oxford and Manchester.

EUROPEAN AIRLINES

Travel Cuts, 295 Regent St, London W1 (☎071/255 1944).

Aer Lingus, 223 Regent St, London W1 (☎081/899 4747).

Air France, Colet Court, Hammersmith Rd, London W6 (☎071/499 9511).

Air UK, Stansted House, Stansted Airport, Stansted (☎0345/666777).

Alitalia, 205 Holland Park Avenue, London W11 (☎071/602 7111).

Austrian Airlines, 50–51 Conduit St, London W1 (☎071/439 0741).

Balkan and Bulgarian Airlines, 322 Regent St, London W1 (☎071/637 7637).

Britannia, Luton Airport, Luton (☎0582/424155).

British Airways, 101 Cheapside, London EC2 (☎081/897 4000).

British Midland, Donington Hall, Castle Donington, Derby DE74 (☎0332/854854).

ČSA Czechoslovak Airlines, 72 Margaret St, London W1 (☎071/255 1898).

Finnair, 14 Clifford St, London W1 (☎071/408 1222).

Iberia, 11 Haymarket, London SW1 (☎071/830 0011).

JAT Yugoslav Airlines, 37 Maddox St, London W1 (☎071/629 2007).

KLM, Terminal 4, Heathrow Airport, London (☎081/750 9000).

LOT Polish Airlines, 313 Regent St, London W1 (☎071/580 5037).

Lufthansa, 10 Old Bond St, London W1 (☎071/408 0442).

Luxair, Terminal 2, Heathrow Airport, London (☎081/745 4254).

Malév Hungarian Airlines, 10 Vigo St, London W1 (☎071/439 0577).

Olympic Airways, 11 Conduit St, London W1 (☎071/493 3965).

Royal Air Maroc, 205 Regent St, London W1 (☎ 071/439 8854).

Sabena, 36 Piccadilly, London W1 (☎071/437 6960).

SAS, 52 Conduit St, London W1 (☎071/734 4020).

Swissair, 10 Wardour St, London W1 (☎071/439 4144).

TAP Air Portugal, 19 Regent St, London SW1 (☎071/839 1031).

THY Turkish Airlines, 11 Hanover St, London W1 (☎071/499 9249).

BUS AND RAIL ADDRESSES IN BRITAIN

Belgian Railways, 439 Premier House, 10 Greycoat Place, London SW1 (☎071/233 0360).

British Rail European Travel Centre, Victoria Station, London SW1 (☎071/834 2345).

Citysprint, Maybrook House, Queens Gardens, Dover, Kent CT17 (☎0304/240 202).

Eurolines, 52 Grosvenor Gardens, London SW1 (☎071/730 8235).

Eurotrain, 52 Grosvenor Gardens, London SW1 (☎071/730 3402).

French Railways, 179 Piccadilly, London W1V 0BA (☎071/493 9731).

German Rail, Suite 4, The Sanctuary, 23 Oakhill Grove, Surbiton, Surrey KT6 6DU (☎081/399 3661).

Netherlands Railways, 25 Buckingham Gate, London SW1 (☎071/630 1735).

Wasteels, 121 Wilton Rd, London SW1 (☎071/834 7066).

*If not listed above, most **national rail companies** can be contacted through their national tourist organization.*

FERRY COMPANIES AND AGENTS IN BRITAIN

Brittany Ferries, Wharf Rd, Portsmouth PO2 (☎0705/827701); Milbay Docks, Plymouth PL1 (☎0752/221321).

Color Line, Tyne Commission Quay, Albert Edward Dock, North Shields, NE29 (☎091/296 1313).

Hoverspeed, Maybrook House, Queens Gardens, Dover, Kent CT17 (☎0304/240241).

Mediterranean Passenger Services, 9 Hanover St, W1 (☎071/499 0076). Italy–Greece ferry agent.

North Sea Ferries, King George Dock, Hedon Rd, Hull HU9 5QA (☎0482/77177).

Olau Line, Olau Line Terminal, Sheerness, Kent ME12 (☎0795/666666).

P&O European Ferries, Channel House, Channel View Rd, Dover, Kent CT17 (☎0304/223000).

Sally Line, 81 Piccadilly, London W1V (☎071/409 2240).

Scandinavian Seaways, 15 Hanover St, London W1 (☎071/409 6060).

Stena Sealink, Charter House, Park St, Ashford, Kent TN24 (☎0233/647047).

Sunquest Holidays, 9 Grand Parade, Green Lanes, London N4 (☎081/800 5455). Agent for *TML* ferries between Turkey, Italy and Greece.

Viamarie Travel, 33 Mapesbury Rd, London NW2 (☎081/452 8231). Agent for several European ferry lines.

TOUR OPERATORS

Contiki, Wells House, 15 Elmfield Rd, Bromley, BR1 (☎081/290 6422). Bus tours of Europe for under-30s.

Eurocamp, Canute Court, Toft Rd, Knutsford, Cheshire WA16 (☎0565/650022). Flexible packages for campers and caravanners, plus self-drive vacations to fixed-site tents and mobile homes.

Exodus, 9 Weir Rd, London SW12 (☎081/675 5550). Adventurous holidays in the mountains of France, Spain, Greece and eastern Europe.

Explore Worldwide, 1 Frederick St, Aldershot, Hants GU11 (☎0252/319448). Adventure holidays in southern and eastern Europe, Morocco and Turkey.

Holiday Autos, 25 Savile Row, London W1 (☎071/491 1111). Reliable car rental specialist.

Time Off, Chester Close, Chester St, London SW1 (☎071/235 8070). Specialist in European city breaks.

Top Deck Travel, 131–135 Earl's Court Rd, London SW5 (☎071/373 5117). Bus tours around Europe for young people, travelling in a converted double-decker.

Tracks, 12 Abingdon Rd, London W8 (☎071/937 3028). Youth-oriented bus tours of Europe.

Travelscene, 11–15 St Anne's Rd, Harrow, HA1 (☎081/427 8800). European city breaks.

TRAVELLING FROM AUSTRALASIA

There are **flights** from Melbourne, Sydney, Brisbane and Perth to most European capitals, and there really is not a great deal of difference in the fares to the busiest destinations – a single air fare from Sydney to London, Paris, Rome, Madrid, Athens or Frankfurt should be available for around Aus$780, with a return ticket costing minimally less than twice that, while a flight from Auckland to Europe will cost approximately NZ$1170 for a return flight. With the extremely large Greek populations of Sydney and Melbourne, there are also often bargain deals to be had to Athens on *Olympic Airways* – ring around first.

For these and other low-price tickets, the most reliable operator is *STA* (*STS* in New Zealand), who also supply packages with companies such as *Contiki* and *Top Deck*, and can issue **rail passes**. *STA* can also advise on **visa regulations** for Australian and New Zealand citizens – and for a fee will do all the paperwork for you. Bear in mind that to enter some countries your passport must be valid for at least six months after your date of arrival.

ADDRESSES IN AUSTRALIA AND NEW ZEALAND.

STA, 1a Lee St, Railway Square, Sydney, NSW 2000 (☎02/519 9866); 224 Faraday St, Carlton, Victoria 3053 (☎03/347 6911); 10 High St, Auckland (☎09/309 0458).

STS, 10 O'Connell St, Auckland (☎09/399 191).

Olympic Airways, 84 William St, Melbourne, Victoria 3000 (☎03/602 5400); 44 Pitt St, Sydney, NSW 2000 (☎02/251 1047).

·TRAVELLING IN EUROPE

It's easy enough to travel in Europe, and a number of special deals and passes can make it fairly economical too. Most of the options for air travel are detailed above (see "Travelling from Britain"), but you really appreciate the diversity of Europe best at ground level, by way of the enormous web of rail, road and ferry connections that covers the continent.

BY TRAIN

Though to some extent it depends on where you intend to spend most time, **train** is without doubt the best way to make a tour of Europe. The rail network in most countries is comprehensive, in some cases exceptionally so, and the continent boasts some of the most scenic rail journeys you could make anywhere in the world. Train travel is relatively cheap, too, even in the richer parts of northwest Europe, where apart from backward Britain trains are heavily subsidized, and prices are brought down further by the multiplicity of passes and discount cards available, both Europe-wide (*InterRail* for those based in Britain, *Eurail* for North Americans) and on an individual country basis. In some countries you'll find it makes more sense to travel by bus, but if you're travelling further afield buying a rail pass may still pay dividends. We've covered the various passes below, as well as the most important international routes and most useful addresses; full supplementary details, including frequencies and journey times of domestic services, are given throughout the guide in each country's "Travel details" section.

If you intend to do a lot of rail travel, the *Thomas Cook European Timetable* is an essential investment, detailing the main lines throughout Europe, as well as ferry connections, and updated monthly. *Thomas Cook* also publish a rail map of Europe, which may be a good supplement to our own train map overleaf.

INTERNATIONAL RAIL ROUTES

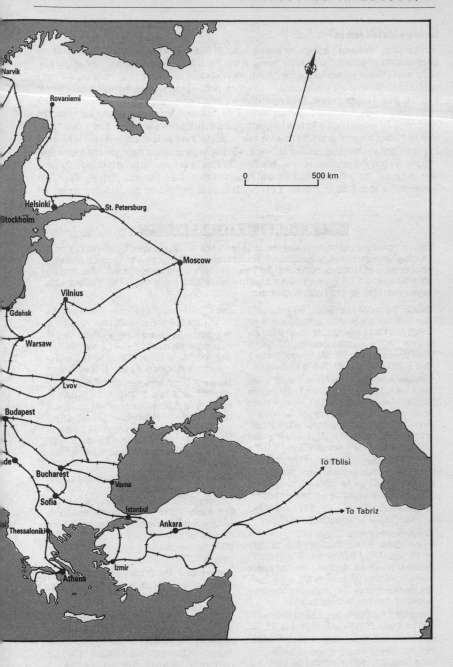

Narvik

Rovaniemi

0   500 km

Helsinki
Stockholm   St. Petersburg

Moscow

Vilnius

Gdańsk

Warsaw

Lvov

Budapest

de

Bucharest   Varna

Sofia

Istanbul

Thessaloniki   Ankara   To Tblisi

Izmir   To Tabriz

Athens

Europe-wide rail passes

Eurotrain offer **"Explorer" tickets** for anyone under 26 years old, which are valid for unlimited rail travel around a prescribed circular route, taking in, say, Paris, Amsterdam and Brussels for around £74, or the main cities of eastern Europe for £237. If you're planning on doing a lot of travelling and don't want to be tied down to one itinerary; there's also the **InterRail pass**, probably the most popular way of travelling around Europe there is. From April 1994, a zoning system applies for the European countries valid under the pass, with Zone 1 covering Britain, Zone 2 Sweden, Norway and Finland and so on. The zones you want to travel in and for how long determine the price, which starts at £179 for a Zone 1 card valid for 15 days and goes up to £249 covering 4 zones plus for a month. To qualify, you need to be under 26 years of age and have been resident in Europe or Britain for six months or more; you also need a valid passport. It's now also possible to buy an **InterRail "26-Plus" pass**, open to those over 26 for 20 countries in Europe (the excluded countries are Belgium, France, Italy, Morocco, Portugal, Spain and Switzerland). It costs £269 for a month, £209 for fifteen days. Bear in mind that, with both passes, on

NATIONAL RAIL PASSES

Some European countries provide a **national rail pass**, which can be good value if you're doing a lot of travelling within one country, or *EuroDomino*'s which you can buy before you leave. The main options are listed below: in general those quoted in £ and $ need to bought *before* you leave home, either from the office of the national rail company or national tourist office, or in the case of the US, from *RailEurope*, the general sales agent for most European railroads.

Austria The *Rabbit Card* entitles the holder to 4 days' unlimited travel within a 10-day period for ÖS700 (ÖS1130 for over-26s); the *Bundesnetzkarte* gives a month's unlimited travel for ÖS3600. A *EuroDomino* pass costs £61 (£80 for over-26s) for 3 days, £68/£89 for 5 days, £1135/176 for 10 days.

Belgium A *Belgian Tourrail* gives 5 days' unlimited travel within a month period for F1980, and the *Go Pass* allows under-26s 8 single journeys of any length in 6 months for F990. The *Half Fare Card*, is F550 a month and allows you to buy tickets at half-price. A *EuroDomino* pass is £31 (£38 for over-26s) for 3 days, £35/£44 for 5 days, £65/81 for 10 days.

Benelux A *Benelux Tourrail Card* gives 5 days' travel in a month on the Netherlands, Belgium and Luxembourg railways for F2860 (F3780 for over-26s) – £ or $ prices fluctuate with exchange rates.

Bulgaria A *EuroDomino* is £26 (£33 for over-26s) for 3 days, £33/41 for 5 days, £59/73 for 10 days.

Czech Republic A *EuroDomino* pass is £30 (£39 for over-26s) for 3 days, £40/50 for 5 days, £61/810 for 10 days. A *Rail Explorer* pass is available in London or through any *Eurotrain* agent, and allows a week's unlimited rail travel for £24 in the Czech and Slovak Republics. The *Czechoslovak Flexipass* is valid for any 5 days in 15 and costs $59.

Denmark A *EuroDomino* pass is £42 (£60 for over-26s) for 3 days, £63/£85 for 5, £85/114 for 10. For *Nordturist* and *Scandrail* passes see Scandinavia.

Finland *Finnrail* passes, purchased before you leave home, are valid for unlimited rail travel and cost 470mk (about £55) for 8 days, 730mk (£85) for 15 days and 920mk (£110) for 22 days – prices in £ or $ depend on the exchange rate of the time. A *EuroDomino* pass costs £49 (£64 for over-26s) for 3 days, £69/£92 for 5 days, £92/122 for 10 days. For *Nordturist* and *Scandrail* passes see Scandinavia.

France A *EuroDomino* pass costs £95 (£114 for over-26s) for 3 days, £131/£160 for 5 days or £205/233 for 10 days. *Carissimo* passes (bought outside France or in Paris only) give 50 percent discounts to under-26s on a specified number of journeys. The *France Railpass* for any 3 days' travel in a month and up to 6 additional rail days costs $125.

Germany The *German Rail BahnCard* gives a year of unlimited half-price travel on all trains in Germany and costs DM 220 (under-22s DM 110). The *Regional Pass* gives unlimited rail travel within a specified area for any 5 days for £51 and 10 days for £78. A *EuroDomino* pass costs £94 (£125 for over-26s) for 3 days, £104/£140 for 5 days, £155/208 for 10 days.

Great Britain The *Britrail* pass, available from *British Rail* agents outside Britain, qualifies you for unlimited rail travel throughout England, Wales and Scotland for 8, 15, 22 days or a month, and costs $219–499; there are discounts for the under-26s (*BritRail Youth* pass) and over-60s (*BritRail Senior* pass). Available in Britain, the *Young Person's Railcard* costs £16 and gives 33 percent reductions to full-time students and under-24s.

some European express trains, such as the French *TGV*, you need to pay a supplement. *InterRail* passes are available from main *British Rail* stations and *BR* agents throughout Britain. There's also the **Rail Europe Senior Card**, available to anyone over 60 who holds a *BR* Senior Citizen Railcard, which costs just £5 and gives up to fifty percent reductions on rail fares throughout Europe, thirty percent off sea crossings. There are also a number of passes giving unlimited rail travel within certain specific regions of Europe: the four main countries of Scandinavia, for example, are served by both the **Scandrail Pass** and the **Nordturist Pass**, while the **Benelux Tourrail Pass** offers unlimited travel in Belgium, the Netherlands and Luxembourg. Finally, you might find the **EuroDomino Passes** worth considering if your destination is not covered by the InterRail 26-Plus Pass; these give unlimited travel within *one* country of your choice and are available for 3, 5 or 10 days within a 30-day period.

US and Canadian citizens aren't eligible for *InterRail* passes, though they can buy *BIJ* tickets. Failing that, a **Eurail pass**, which must be bought before arrival in Europe, gives unlimited travel in seventeen countries – Austria, Belgium, Denmark, Finland, France, Germany, Greece, the Netherlands,

---

Greece A *EuroDomino* costs £34 (£44 for over-26s) for 3 days, £39/£58 for 5 days, £58/87 for 10 days.

Hungary *Eurotrain's Rail Explorer* pass gives a week's unlimited rail travel for £22. A *Hungarian Flexipass* for any 5 days in 15 is available in the US at $39. A *EuroDomino* pass costs £29 (£36 for over-26s) for 3 days, £39/52 for 5 days, £69/95 for 10 days.

Ireland *Irish Rail's Rambler Ticket* buys unlimited rail travel in the north and south on any 8 days out of 15 for IR£60 or 15 days out of 30 for IR£90. Use the *Emerald Card* on rail and bus in both north and south at IR£105 for 8 days in 15 and IR£180 for 15 days in 30. Passes for unlimited rail travel in the south cost IR£78–115 for 8 to 15 days. A *EuroDomino* pass is £36 (£38 for over-26s) for 3 days, £60/63 for 5 days, £83/90 for 10 days.

Italy The *Biglietto Turistico* gives unlimited rail travel for 8 or 12 consecutive days in 30 for £88/120. A *EuroDomino* is £79 (£105 for over-26s) for 3 days, £99/131 for 5 days, £164/219 for 10 days.

Luxembourg Passes giving unlimited rail travel cost F140 for a day, F540 for 5 days within a month-long period. A *EuroDomino* pass costs £11 (£14 for over-26s) for 3 days, £14/17 for 5 days, £23/30 for 10 days.

Morocco A *EuroDomino* is £26 (£27 for over-26s) for 3 days, £37/40 for 5 days, £72/79 for 10 days.

Netherlands *Rover* tickets give a day's unlimited travel for f63, 7 days' for f152. *EuroDomino* passes for the Netherlands cost £24 (£31 for over-26s) for 3 days, £38/51 for 5 days, £69/92 for 10 days.

Norway The *Kundekort* costs 370kr and gives 50 percent reduction on selected routes, 30 percent on others. *EuroDomino* passes for Norway cost £68 (£89 for over-26s) for 3 days, £97/126 for 5 days, £126/168 for 10 days. For *Nordturist* and *Scandrail* passes see Scandinavia below.

Poland The *Eurotrain Rail Explorer* pass gives a week's unlimited rail travel for just £20; 14 and 21 day passes are also available. *Polrail* passes cost $26 for 8 days travel ($35 for over-26s). A *EuroDomino* pass costs £28 (£33 for over-26s) for 3 days, £33/43 for 5 days, £52/69 for 10 days.

Portugal A *Tourist Pass* costs 15,200esc for a week's rail travel, 24,200esc for two weeks – not really worth it. A *Portuguese Railpass* costs $95 for 4 days' travel in 15. A *EuroDomino* pass costs £66 (£84 for over-26s) for 3 days, £81/105 for 5 days, £122/159 for 10 days.

Scandinavia The *Nordturist Pass* is valid on the rail networks of Denmark, Norway, Sweden and Finland and costs £140/$220 for 21 days' travel (£189/$300 if you're over 26). A similar *Scandrail Pass* costs £93/$155 for 4 days in 15, £151/$245 for 9 days in 21, and £217/$355 for 21 days in 30.

Slovakia A *EuroDomino* pass costs £22 (£29 for over-26s) for 3 days, £30/41 for 5 days, £49/65 for 10 days.

Slovenia A *EuroDomino* is £16 (£21 for over-26s) for 3 days, £22/32 for 5 days, £38/54 for 10 days.

Spain A *EuroDomino* is £78 (£97 for over-26s) for 3 days, £127/151 for 5 days, £204/240 for 10 days. A *Flexipass* for 3 days' travel in a month is $140.

Sweden *EuroDomino* passes for Sweden cost £68 (£92 for over-26s) for 3 days, £97/130 for 5 days, £130/173 for 10 days. *Nordturist* and *Scandrail* passes are also valid (see Scandinavia, above).

Switzerland The *Swiss Pass*, is valid for unlimited travel on rail, bus and ferry routes, and costs £97 for 8 days, £112 for 15 days. *EuroDomino* passes cost £66 (£86 for over-26s) for 3 days, £79/105 for 5 days, £105/139 for 10 days. An 8 day *Swiss Pass* costs $186.

Turkey A *EuroDomino* is £17 (£22 for over-26s) for 3 days, £26/34 for 5 days, £47/61 for 10 days.

INTERNATIONAL TRAIN ROUTES

Amsterdam–Brussels–Paris (12 daily; 3hr/6hr 30min).
Amsterdam–Cologne–Basel (6 daily; 3hr/8hr).
Amsterdam–Hannover–Berlin (2 daily; 5hr/9hr).
Basel–Cologne (hourly; 4hr 45min).
Basel–Milan–Rome (5 daily; 5hr 30min/10hr).
Basel–Vienna (3 daily; 10hr).
Berlin–Prague–Budapest (7 daily; 7hr/15hr).
Brussels–Basel (6 daily; 7hr).
Brussels–Cologne–Berlin (4 daily; 4hr/11hr).
Brussels–Hamburg (5 daily; 9hr).
Bucharest–Sofia (4 daily; 11hr).
Cologne–Vienna (6 daily; 10hr).
Cologne–Vienna–Budapest (3 daily; 10hr/17hr).
Copenhagen–Bergen (2 daily; 19hr).
Copenhagen–Gothenburg (4 daily; 4hr 30min).
Copenhagen–Helsinki (2 daily; 25hr).
Copenhagen–Oslo (3 daily; 9hr 30min).
Copenhagen–Stockholm (3 daily; 10hr).
Geneva–Paris (5 daily; 3hr 30min).
Hamburg–Vienna (4 daily; 10hr).
İstanbul–Athens (1 daily; 32–46hr).
İstanbul–Milan (1 daily; 46hr).
İstanbul–Munich (1 daily; 39hr).
İstanbul–Paris (1 daily; 52hr).
İstanbul–Rome (1 daily; 51hr).
İstanbul–Sofia (1 daily; 14hr).
İstanbul–Venice (1 daily; 41hr).
İstanbul–Vienna (1 daily; 37hr).
Ljubljana–Budapest (1 daily; 7hr 30min).
Ljubljana–Venice–Milan (2 daily; 9hr).
Ljubljana–Villach–Munich (3 daily; 6hr).
London–Ostend–Brussels–Cologne (5 daily; 5hr/6hr 30min/9hr).
London–Paris (8 daily; 8hr).
Paris–Barcelona (2 daily; 12hr).
Paris–Genoa (2 daily; 17hr).
Paris–Hamburg (6 daily; 10hr).
Paris–Lisbon (2 daily; 19–23hr).
Paris–Madrid (4 daily; 13–17hr).
Paris–Milan (5 daily; 7hr).
Paris–Munich–Vienna (5 daily; 9hr/14hr).
Paris–Turin–Rome–Naples–Messina (5 daily; 9hr/16hr/22hr/28hr).
Milan–Barcelona (4 daily; 15hr).
Milan–Nice (4 daily; 5hr).
Milan–Toulouse (2 daily; 13hr).
Munich–Bologna (8 daily; 8hr).
Munich–Prague (3 daily; 10hr).
Nürnberg–Prague (6 daily; 6hr 30min).
Rome–Nice–Barcelona (2 daily; 5hr 30min/15hr 30min).

Rome–Toulouse (2 daily; 18hr).
Sofia–Athens (2 daily; 17hr).
Sofia–Bratislava (3 daily; 20–30hr).
Sofia–Bucharest (4 daily; 11hr).
Sofia–Budapest (3 daily; 14–26hr).
Sofia–Dresden (3 daily; 35–42hr).
Sofia–İstanbul (1 daily; 12hr).
Sofia–Munich (1 daily; 33hr).
Sofia–Prague (3 daily; 27–37hr).
Sofia–Vienna (1 daily; 16hr).
Sofia–Warsaw (2 daily; 23–34hr).
Stockholm–Narvik (2–3 daily; 21hr).
Stockholm–Oslo (1–3 daily; 6hr 30min).
Stockholm–Trondheim (2 daily; 11–14hr).
Stuttgart–Zürich–Milan (6 daily; 3hr/8hr).
Vienna–Bratislava (3 daily; 2hr).
Vienna–Budapest–Bucharest (6 daily; 9hr/23hr).
Vienna–Venice (6 daily; 8hr).
Warsaw–Bucharest–Sofia (1 daily; 10hr/23hr).
Warsaw–Budapest–Sofia (1 daily; 17hr/34hr).
Zürich–Milan (hourly; 4hr 30min).
Zürich–Munich–Prague (3 daily; 4hr 30min/14hr).
Zürich–Stuttgart (7 daily; 3hr 10min).
Zürich–Vienna (4 daily; 7hr 30min).

Express trains

Amsterdam–Cologne–Munich (1 daily; 3hr 30min/10hr 30min).
Amsterdam–Hamburg (1 daily; 6hr).
Amsterdam–Nice (2 daily; 18hr).
Basel–Vienna–Budapest (1 daily; 10hr/13hr 30min).
Calais–Basel–Milan (1 daily; 9hr/15hr).
Calais–Basel–Rome (1 daily; 8hr/19hr).
Cologne–Basel–Genoa (1 daily; 5hr 30min/13hr 30min).
Cologne–Milan–Rome (1 daily; 10hr/16hr).
Dortmund–Cologne–Munich–Bolzano–Verona–Ancona (1 daily; 1hr 30min/8hr 30min/13hr 30min/15hr 30min/18hr 30min).
Frankfurt–Basel–Genoa (1 daily; 4hr 30min/12hr 30min).
Frankfurt–Milan–Rome (1 daily; 8hr 30min/14hr 30min).
Hook of Holland–Berlin–Warsaw (1 daily; 9hr 30min/21hr).
Hook of Holland–Cologne (2 daily; 4hr 20min).
Ljubljana–Vienna (1 daily; 6hr).
Madrid–Lisbon (2 daily; 7hr 30min–10hr).
Munich–Warsaw (1 daily; 21hr 30min).
Ostend–Brussels–Cologne–Berlin–Warsaw (1 daily; 1hr/4hr/12hr/22hr).

INTERNATIONAL EXPRESS TRAIN ROUTES (continued)

Ostend–Brussels–Cologne–Hamburg (1 daily; 1hr/4hr 30min/9hr 30min).

Ostend–Brussels–Cologne–Vienna (1 daily; 1hr/4hr/ 14hr 30min).

Ostend–Brussels–Luxembourg–Basel (1 daily; 1hr 30min/4hr/8hr 30min).

Paris–Cologne–Berlin–Warsaw (1 daily; 6hr 30min/ 14hr/24hr).

Paris–Cologne–Hamburg (1 daily; 6hr/11hr).

Paris–Florence (1 daily; 12hr).

Paris–Frankfurt–Prague (1 daily; 8hr 30min/18hr 30min).

Paris–Madrid (1 daily; 12hr 30min).

Paris–Munich (1 daily; 10hr 30min).

Paris–Turin–Milan (1 daily; 9hr/10hr 30min).

Paris–Turin–Rome–Naples (1 daily; 9hr/17hr 30min/ 20hr).

Paris–Turin–Rome (1 daily; 8hr/15hr 30min).

Paris–Venice (1 daily; 13hr).

Vienna–Venice–Milan (1 daily; 8hr/13hr 30min).

Vienna–Venice–Rome (1 daily; 8hr/14hr).

Warsaw–Prague (1 daily; 12hr).

Warsaw–Vienna (1 daily; 10hr 30min).

Hungary, Ireland, Italy, Luxembourg, Norway, Portugal, Spain, Sweden and Switzerland – fewer than *InterRail*, but valid for more express trains, thus saving money on supplements. There are five different kinds of pass, valid for 15 days ($460), 21 days ($598), or one ($728), two ($998) or three months ($1260). There is also the **Eurail Youth Pass**, valid for those under 26, good for one or two months and costing $508 and $698 respectively, and the **Eurail Saverpass**, allowing 15 days of unlimited first-class travel for two people for $390 each between March and October (you need 3 people to qualify between April and Sept). The **Eurail Flexipass** is more flexible, in that you choose the number of days you want to travel: 5 days' first-class travel within 15 consecutive days costs $326; 10 days within 2 months costs $496; 15 days within two months costs $676; the **Eurail Youth Flexipass**, again for under-26s, is valid for 15 days within 2 months ($496). Finally, the **Eurail Drive Pass** gives 3 days' rail travel and 3 days' car rental for $289 per person – extra days $50 each.

Australians and New Zealanders can also buy *Eurail* passes at comparable prices.

BY BUS

For most people on a tour of Europe, a **bus** is something you take when there is no train. There are some countries (Greece and Turkey are the most obvious examples) where the trains are slow and infrequent, and the bus network is more widespread. But on the whole you'll find yourself using buses for the odd trip here and there, usually locally, and long-distance bus journeys between major European cities to be a generally slower, more uncomfortable and not particularly cheap option, especially if you have a rail pass. If you have a definite itinerary, *Eurolines* offer a series of **circular tickets** originating in London and taking in several western European centres; prices for these can be good value, just undercutting rail passes, especially if you're over 26. As an example, they range from around £70 for a London–Paris–Amsterdam circuit to £220 for itineraries that take in London, Munich, Barcelona, Rome and Paris.

DRIVING AND HITCHING

In order to **drive** in Europe you need a full and up-to-date **driving licence**; in Italy you need to carry a translation of this, available from your national motoring organization or the state tourist office. In some countries you also need an **international driving permit** – something which can be a useful thing to have anyway, especially if you're thinking of renting a car. These are also available from national motoring organizations for a small fee; you'll need to show your driving licence, two passport photos and proof of age (18 or over). You should also carry your **vehicle registration document** at all times (if the named owner is not present on the trip you'll need a letter from them authorizing use of the vehicle). You should, if you're taking your own vehicle, be **insured**: your existing insurance policy may already provide third party cover for a certain period in Europe (this is frequently the case with British policies), but for some countries you will need to take out a supplementary policy. As proof of insurance cover, it's sensible to get hold of an **International Green Card** from your insurers – it's obligatory in certain countries anyway. In case of breakdown, you can take out, at extra cost, extended cover with the *AA, RAC* and *AAA*, although the motoring organizations of most countries operate some kind of reciprocal **breakdown** agreement with members of foreign motoring organizations, so if you are a member it's wise to have your membership documents with you as well. Your national organization can provide a list of countries with reciprocal arrangements. A nationality plate should be displayed on the rear of your vehicle, and a warning triangle and first aid ticket is either required or advised throughout Europe. A fire extinguisher is obligatory in Greece and Turkey. In France headlights should emit a yellow beam (you can get headlight covers from any garage), and wherever you're travelling your headlights should be adjusted for driving on the right. All the countries of Europe except Britain drive on the right-hand side of the road, and priority to the right is a common rule of the road. Pretty much every country included in this book has a decent network of main roads; only when you get onto minor roads do the differences between southern and eastern, and northwestern Europe become really apparent. In most of Europe motorways are free, but in some countries tolls are levied: in Greece, Spain and Portugal these are fairly cheap; in France they cost a little more but the primary roads there are invariably excellent; in Italy they can work out a substantial cost if you're travelling long distances. Petrol prices vary from under £2 a gallon in Greece to £3 a gallon or more in Italy and Denmark – perhaps the two most expensive countries to buy petrol.

The alternative to taking your own car is obviously to **rent** one on the spot. Compared to rates in North America, certainly, this can be expensive, and you may find it cheaper to arrange things in advance through one of the multinational chains, or by opting for some kind of fly-drive deal. If you do rent a car in Europe, rates for a small hatchback start at around £150 a week if you book in advance with a firm like *Holiday Autos*, considerably more if you rent on the spot; we've given more precise details in the relevant sections of the guide but in general costs are higher in Scandinavia and northern Europe, lower in eastern and southern Europe. Unlimited mileage deals (as opposed to those where you pay a charge per kilometre) work out better value and give more flexibility. Obviously, to rent car you need a driving licence, sometimes an international driver's permit, and you should normally be at least 21 years of age and have more than one year's driving experience, though these regulations again vary; if in doubt, check in advance with the car rental company direct or your home motoring organization, which can be a good source of all sorts of advance information, as well as maps, guides and other details.

MOTORING ORGANIZATIONS

Automobile Association, Fanum House, Basingstoke, Hants RG21 2EA (☎0256/20123).

Royal Automobile Club, PO Box 100, RAC House, Bartlett St, South Croydon CR2 (☎081/686 0088).

American Automobile Association, 1000 AAA Drive, Heathrow, FL 32746 (☎407/444-7000 or 800/566-1166).

Canadian Automobile Association, 2 Carlton St, Toronto, ON M4B 1K4 (☎416/964-3002).

Australian Automobile Association, 212 Northbourne Ave, Canberra ACT 2601 (☎61/6247-7311).

New Zealand Automobile Association, PO Box 1794, Wellington (☎64/473-8738).

Hitching

If you're not sticking to a definite itinerary – and, in some countries, even if you are – **hitching** can be as good a way to get around as any, with the added advantages of being cheaper and much more sociable – indeed, meeting people along the way is half the fun. If you're coming from Britain, getting across the Channel is cheap (day return tickets are usually the best bet), and if you don't manage to talk someone into giving you a lift on the way over, there's usually plenty of traffic heading south from the Channel ports – the Belgians tend to be better at giving lifts than the French. When hitching, it's important to choose a place where a car can see you in good time and preferably has a place to pull over if they decide to pick you up. Hitching on motorways is illegal pretty much throughout Europe, in which case you should try motorway service stations or slip roads – though success at these can be patchy. Travel as light as possible – enormous backpacks tend to put drivers off – and carry a decent road map.

Always look clean and presentable, and always, even if you have been waiting several hours for a lift, smile. Whether you use a sign or not is up to you: you may find, however, that all it does is give drivers yet another excuse not to stop. Women should be wary of hitching alone. As for when to hitch, obviously you should try and avoid hitching on Sundays and public holidays if possible, when traffic will be greatly reduced, and in general it's better to make an early start during the week, when you'll pick up most long-distance traffic. Though it might seem like cheating, there are a few countries (France and Germany most notably) which have hitchhiking organizations, whereby you pay a fee and they put you in touch with a driver going your way who wants to share petrol costs. This may seem to take the excitement out of hitching, but if you've been waiting several days for a lift it can be a godsend.

EUROPEAN FERRIES

Europe's seas and inland waterways mean that travelling by **ferry** is often the most viable – sometimes the only – way of getting from A to B, and in some countries, like Greece and Denmark, they are an essential way of reaching some of the nicest spots. The Mediterranean is the busiest stretch of water, crisscrossed by routes that connect most of the bordering countries – though some of the most useful lines, those connecting Italy and the former Yugoslavia, were out of action at the time of writing due to the troubles across the Adriatic. During the summer, most of the ferry routes here get very crowded, especially those between Italy and Greece (Brindisi–Patras is perhaps the most popular route on the continent with backpackers), and it's normally a good idea to book in advance during this time, particularly if you're travelling by car; many of the main European ferry ports (Brindisi is typical) aren't places you would want to get stuck for long. The English Channel, too, webbed by ferries between Britain and France, gets very busy, as do the lines within Greece, between the main port of Piraeus, near Athens, and the larger islands (details of these are given in the chapter on Greece). Bear in mind that *InterRail* pass holders qualify for reductions on the Brindisi–Patras route, and there are lots of reductions for *Eurail* pass holders too. Wherever you're travelling, self-catering is the best way to eat, since the food on board most ferries is mediocre and overpriced. See below for broad details of the major international routes.

INTERNATIONAL FERRY ROUTES

DENMARK

Allinge to: Malmö (1 daily in summer; 4hr).
Bagenkop to: Kiel (3 daily; 2hr 30min).
Copenhagen to: Malmö (18 hydrofoils daily – 45min; 2 boats daily – 1hr 30min); Oslo (1 daily; 16hr); Swinoujscie (2–3 weekly; 9hr 30min).
Fåborg to: Gelting (8 daily; 2hr).
Frederikshavn to: Gothenburg (8 daily; 3hr 15min); Frederikstad (5 weekly; 5hr); Oslo (1–2 daily; 10hr–13hr 30min); Larvik (1 daily; 6hr); Moss (1 daily; 7hr).
Gedser to: Warnemünde (2–4 daily; 25min); Travemünde (4 daily; 3hr 30min).
Grenå to: Varberg (1 daily in summer; 4hr); Helsingborg (1 daily in summer; 4hr 30min).
Hantsholm to: Kristiansand (1 daily in summer; 4hr); Egersund (1 daily; 6hr 30min).
Helsingør to: Helsingborg (every 15min; 25min).
Hirtshals to: Stavanger/Bergen (2 weekly; 11hr 15min/18hr); Egersund (1 weekly; 6hr 30min); Oslo (4 weekly; 9hr); Kristiansand (3 daily; 4hr 30min).

FINLAND

Helsinki to: Stockholm (2 daily; 15hr); Gdańsk (2–4 weekly; 27hr).
Kokkola to: Skellefteå (1 daily in summer; 5hr).
Kaskö to: Gävle (1 daily; 10hr).
Pietarsaari to: Skellefteå (1 daily; 5hr).
Turku to: Stockholm (2 daily; 12hr).
Vaasa to: Umeå (4 daily in summer; 4hr); Sundsvall (1 daily in winter; 8hr 30min); Örnsköldsvik (4 a week; 4hr 30min).

IRELAND

Belfast to: Liverpool (1 daily; 8hr).
Cork to: Le Havre (1 weekly June 20–Sept 1; 22hr 30min).
Dun Laoghaire to: Holyhead (4 daily; 3hr 30min).
Rosslare to: Cherbourg (1–3 weekly; 18hr); Le Havre (2–5 weekly; 22hr); Fishguard (2 daily; 3hr 15min); Pembroke (2 daily; 4hr).

INTERNATIONAL FERRY ROUTES (continued)

ITALY

Ancona to: Patras direct (2–4 weekly; 32hr 30min); Igoumenitsa/Patras/Iráklion/Kusadasi (1 weekly in summer; 25hr/33hr/60hr/80hr); Corfu/ Igoumenitsa/Patras (2–4 weekly April–Oct; 22hr 30min/24hr/34hr); Igoumenitsa/Patras (2–3 weekly; 23hr/31hr); Corfu/Piraeus/Paros/Samos/ Kusadası (1–2 weekly; 23hr/45hr/49hr 30min/57hr 30min/59hr); Bodrum (1 weekly; 68hr).

Bari to: Patras direct (3–7 weekly; 20hr); Corfu/ Igoumenitsa/Patras (3–4 weekly; 11hr/12hr 30min/20hr 30min).

Brindisi to: Patras direct (3–7 weekly; 17hr); Corfu/Igoumenitsa/Patras (6–7 weekly; 8hr 30min/ 10hr/19hr 30min).

Otranto to: Corfu/Igoumenitsa (4–6 weekly mid-June to Sept; 8hr 30min/11hr).

Venice to: Antalya (1 weekly mid-May to early Sept; 71hr); Çeşme (1 weekly late March to early Nov; 66hr).

MOROCCO

Ceuta to: Algeciras (12 daily; 1hr 30min).

Tangier to: Algeciras (4 daily; 2hr 30min); Gibraltar (3 weekly; 2hr); Sète (1 weekly; 18hr).

NETHERLANDS

Amsterdam to: Gothenburg (1–2 weekly March 21–Nov 3; 22hr 30min).

NORWAY

Egersund to: Hantsholm (3–4 weekly; 7hr 30min); Hirtshals (1 weekly; 10hr).

Fredrikstad to: Frederikshavn (1–2 daily; 7hr).

Kristiansand to: Hirtshals (1–2 daily; 4hr); Hantsholm (4 weekly; 4hr).

Larvik to: Frederikshavn (6–14 weekly; 6–8hr).

Moss to: Frederikshavn (1 daily; 7hr 30min).

Oslo to: Copenhagen (1 daily; 16hr); Frederikshavn (2 daily; 10–14hr); Hirtshals (4 weekly; 9hr); Kiel (6–7 weekly; 19hr 30min).

Stavanger to: Hirtshals (2 weekly; 11hr).

POLAND

Gdańsk to: Helsinki (2–4 weekly; 27hr); Nynäshamn (1 weekly; 19hr); Ystad (1 weekly May 12–Sept 28; 18hr).

Swinoujscie to: Copenhagen (2–3 weekly; 9hr 30min); Ystad (2–5 daily; 7–9hr).

SPAIN

Algeciras to: Tangier (4 daily; 2hr 30min); Ceuta (12 daily; 1hr 30min).

SWEDEN

Gävle to: Kaskinen (5–7 weekly; 10hr).

Gothenburg to: Frederikshavn (3–6 daily; 3hr 15min); Kiel (1 daily; 14hr).

Halmstad to: Grenå (1–2 daily; 4hr).

Helsingborg to: Helsingør (every 15–20min all day and night; 25min); Grenå (1–2 daily; 4hr).

Limhamn (Malmö) to: Dragör (hourly; 55min).

Luleå to: Jakobstad and Kokkola (May–Oct several daily; 4hr).

Malmö to: Copenhagen (6 daily; 1hr 30min).

Nynäshamn to: Gdańsk (1 weekly; 19hr).

Örnsköldsvik to: Vaasa (May to mid-June & mid-Aug to Oct 3 weekly; 5hr).

Stockholm to: Helsinki (2 daily; 15hr); Turku (4 daily; 11–13hr); Eckerö (2–3 daily; 3hr).

Sundsvall to: Vaasa (5–7 weekly; 8hr).

Umeå to: Vaasa (1–3 boats daily; 4hr; 2–3 catamarans daily; 2hr 15min).

Varberg to: Grenå (1–3 daily; 4hr).

Ystad to: Gdańsk (1 weekly May 12–Sept 28; 18hr); Swinoujscie (2–5 daily; 7–9hr).

TURKEY

Antalya to: Venice (1 weekly mid-May to early Sept; 71hr).

Ayvaljk to: Lesvos (2 daily; 2hr).

Bodrum to: Kos (1 weekly; 45min); Ancona (1 weekly; 68hr).

Çemme to: Hios (2–9 weekly; 1hr); Venice (1 weekly late March to early Nov; 66hr).

Kuşadası to: Samos (2 daily; 1hr 30min).

Marmaris to: Rhodes (3–12 weekly; 2hr 30min).

For **ferries from Britain**, see p.12.

RED TAPE AND VISAS

Since the lifting of many immigration restrictions for European Community members in January 1993, border-crossing for most EC nationals has become a much less formal procedure, with most passport-holders just having to wave their documents at border officials. As for transporting goods across borders, the Single Market has freed up certain customs restrictions, though duty-free allowances remain almost as tight as ever.

Citizens of Britain, Ireland, Australia, New Zealand, Canada and the USA need only a valid **passport** to enter many of the countries of Europe, usually for up to three months. However, there are exceptions: everyone needs a **visa** to visit Bulgaria and Romania, and everyone except UK and US citizens needs a visa to enter Poland; Australians and New Zealanders need visas to get into the Czech and Slovak Republics, and Australians need visas for France and Hungary; citizens of Britain and Ireland need visas for Turkey. Often visas are available at the point of entry to a country for a small fee; in a few other cases you need to get them stamped into your passport in advance. If in doubt about the entry requirements to any country, consult the relevant embassy before you leave home, or a decent travel agent.

A one-year British Visitor's passport, available on the spot from post offices, costs £12 and is valid for most countries in western Europe but not for those in the east. A full ten-year passport is valid everywhere and costs £18; to get one, fill in the form you get from the post office and either post it or take it in person with two passport-size photos to your nearest passport office. The main one is at Clive House, 70–78 Petty France, London SW1H 9HD (☎071/279 3434). In the USA, those applying for their first passport must do so in person at their nearest passport agency; otherwise, simply send the form along with two passport photos plus the relevant fee. In Canada you need to apply to the Passport Office, Department of External Affairs, 125 Sussex Drive, Ottawa, ON K1A 0G3. In all cases you should allow at least four weeks, sometimes longer, to receive your passport.

EUROPEAN EMBASSIES

AUSTRIA Australia 12 Talbot St, Forrest, Canberra, ACT 2603 (☎062/295-1533); **Canada** 445 Wilbrod St, Ottawa, ON K1N 6M7 (☎613/789-1444); **Great Britain** 18 Belgrave Mews, London SW1 (☎071/235 3731); **Ireland** 15 Ailesbury Apts, 93 Ailesbury Rd, Dublin 2 (☎01/694577); **New Zealand** Security Express House, 2nd Floor, 22 Garrett St, PO Box 4036, Wellington (☎04/801-9709); **USA** 3524 International Court, NW, Washington, DC 20008 (☎202/895-6700).

BELGIUM Australia 19 Arkana St, Yarralumla, Canberra, ACT 2600 (☎062/273-2502); **Canada** 85 Range Rd, Suite 601, Ottawa, ON K1N 8J6 (☎613/236-7267); **Great Britain** 103 Eaton Square, London SW1 (☎071/235 5422); **Ireland** Shrewsbury House, Shrewsbury Rd, Dublin 4 (☎01/691588); **New Zealand** Robert Jones House, 1–3 Willeston St, PO Box 3841, Wellington (☎04/729-558); **USA** 3330 Garfield St, NW, Washington, DC 20008 (☎202/333-6900).

BULGARIA Canada 325 Stewart St, Ottawa, ON K1M 6K5 (☎613/789-3215); **Great Britain** 184–186 Queens Gate SW7 (☎071/584 9400); **USA** 1621 22nd St, NW, Washington, DC 20008 (☎202/387-7969).

CZECH REPUBLIC Australia 47 Culgoa Circuit, O'Malley, Canberra, ACT 2029 (☎062/295-3713); **Canada** 50 Rideau Terrace, Ottawa, ON K1M 2A1 (☎613/749-4442); **Great Britain** 26 Kensington Palace Gdns, London W8 (☎071/243 1115); **USA** 3900 Linnnean Ave, NW, Washington, DC 20008 (☎202/363-6315).

DENMARK Australia 15 Hunter St, Yarralumla, Canberra, ACT 2600 (☎062/273-2195); **Canada** 85 Range Rd, Apt #702, Ottawa, ON K1N 8J6 (☎613/234-0704); **Great Britain** 55 Sloane St, London SW1 (☎071/235 1255); **Ireland** 121 St Stephen's Green, Dublin 2 (☎01/756404); **New Zealand** MARAC House, 105–109 The Terrace, PO Box 10035, Wellington (☎04/720-020); **USA** 3200 Whitehaven St, NW, Washington, DC 20008 (☎202/234-4300).

FINLAND Australia 10 Darwin Ave, Yarralumla, Canberra, ACT 2600 (☎062/273-3800); **Canada** 55 Metcalfe St, Suite 850, Ottawa, ON K1P 6L5 (☎613/236-2389); **Great Britain** 38 Chesham Place, London SW1 (☎071/838 6200); **New Zealand** NZI House, 25–33 Victoria St, PO Box 1201, Wellington (☎04/724-924); **USA** 3216 New Mexico Ave, NW, Washington, DC 20016 (☎202/363-2430).

FRANCE Australia 6 Perth Ave, Yarralumla, Canberra, ACT 2600 (☎062/270-5111); **Canada** 42 Sussex Drive, Ottawa, ON K1M 2C9 (☎613/789-1795); **Great Britain** 58 Knightsbridge, London SW1 (☎071/235 8080); **Ireland** 36 Ailesbury Rd, Dublin 4 (☎01/694 777); **New Zealand** Robert Jones House, 1–3 Willeston St, Wellington (☎04/720-200); **USA** 4101 Reservoir Rd, NW, Washington, DC 20007 (☎202/944-6000).

GERMANY Australia 119 Empire Circuit, Yarralumla, Canberra, ACT 2600 (☎062/270-1911); **Canada** 1 Waverly St, Ottawa, ON K2P 0T8 (☎613/232-1101); **Great Britain** 23 Belgrave Square, London SW1 (☎071/235 5033); **Ireland** 31 Trumleston Ave, Booterstow (☎01/693011); **New Zealand** 90–92 Hobson St, Thorndon, PO Box 1687, Wellington (☎04/736-063); **USA** 4645 Reservoir Rd, NW, Washington, DC 20007 (☎202/298-4000).

GREAT BRITAIN Australia Commonwealth Ave, Yarralumla, Canberra, ACT 2600 (☎062/270-6666); **Canada** 80 Elgin St, Ottawa, ON K1P 5K7 (☎613/237-1530); **Ireland** 31–33 Merrion Rd, Dublin 4 (☎01/695211); **New Zealand** Reserve Bank Bldg, 2 The Terrace, PO Box 1812, Wellington (☎04/726-049); **USA** 3100 Massachusetts Ave, NW, Washington, DC 20008 (☎202/462-1340).

GREECE Australia 9 Turrana St, Yarralumla, Canberra, ACT 2600 (☎062/273-3011); **Canada** 80 Maclaren St, Ottawa, ON K2P 0K6 (☎613/238-6271); **Great Britain** 1a Holland Park, London W11 (☎071/221 6467); **Ireland** 1 Upper Pembroke St, Dublin 2 (☎01/767254); **New Zealand** Cumberland House, 237 Willis St, PO Box 27157, Wellington (☎04/847-556); **USA** 2221 Massachusetts Ave, NW, Washington, DC 20008 (☎202/667-3168).

HUNGARY Australia 79 Hopetown Circuit, Yarralumla, Canberra, ACT 2600 (☎062/282-3226); **Canada** 7 Delaware Ave, Ottawa, K2P 0Z2 (☎613/232-1711); **Great Britain** 35 Eaton Place, London SW1 (☎071/235 4048); **USA** 3910 Shoemaker St, NW, Washington, DC 20008 (☎202/362-6733).

IRELAND Australia 20 Arkana St, Yarralumla, Canberra, ACT 2600 (☎062/273-3022); **Canada** 170 Metcalfe St, Ottawa, ON K2P 1P3 (☎613/233-6281); **Great Britain** 17 Grosvenor Place, London SW1 (☎071/235 2171); **New Zealand** Dingwall Bldg, 87 Queen St, PO Box 279, Auckland (☎09/302-2867); **USA** 2234 Massachusetts Ave, NW, Washington, DC 20008 (☎202/462-3939).

ITALY Australia 12 Grey St, Deakin, Canberra, ACT 2600 (☎062/273-3333); **Canada** 275 Slater St, Ottawa, ON K1N 5H9 (☎613/232-2403); **Great Britain** 38 Eaton Place, London SW1 (☎071/235 9371); **Ireland** 63 Northumberland Rd, Dublin 4 (☎01/601744); **New Zealand** 34 Grant Rd, Thorndon, PO Box 463, Wellington (☎04/735-339); **USA** 1601 Fuller St, NW, Washington, DC 20009 (☎202/328-5500).

LUXEMBOURG Great Britain 27 Wilton Crescent, London SW1 (☎071/235 6961); **USA** 2200 Massachusetts Ave, NW, Washington, DC 20008 (☎202/265-4171).

MOROCCO Canada 38 Range Rd, Ottawa, ON K1N 8J4 (☎613/236-7391); **Great Britain** 49 Queen's Gate Gdns, London SW7 (☎071/581 5001); **USA** 1601 21st St, NW, Washington, DC 20009 (☎202/462-7979).

NETHERLANDS Australia 120 Empire Circuit, Yarralumla, Canberra, ACT 2600 (☎062/273-3611); **Canada** 275 Slater St, 3rd floor, Ottawa, ON K1P 5H9 (☎613/237-5030); **Great Britain** 38 Hyde Park Gate, London SW7 (☎071/584 5040); **New Zealand** Investment House, 10th Floor, Ballance and Featherstone St, Wellington (☎04/738-652); **USA** 4200 Linnean Ave, NW, Washington, DC 20008 (☎202/244-5300).

NORWAY Australia 17 Hunter St, Yarralumla, Canberra, ACT 2600 (☎062/273-3444); **Canada** 90 Sparks St, Suite 532, Ottawa, ON K1P 5B4 (☎613/238-6571); **Great Britain** 25 Belgrave Square, London SW1 (☎071/235 7151); **Ireland** 69 St Stephen's Green, Dublin 2 (☎01/783133); **New Zealand** 55–67 Molesworth St, PO Box 1990, Wellington (☎04/712-503); **USA** 2720 34th St, NW, Washington, DC 20008 (☎202/333-6000).

POLAND Australia 7 Turrana St, Yarralumla, Canberra, ACT 2600 (☎062/273-1211); **Canada** 443 Daly Ave, Ottawa, ON K1N 6H3 (☎613/789-0468); **Great Britain** 47 Portland Place, London W1 (☎071/580 4324); **New Zealand** 196 The Terrace, #D, PO Box 10211, Wellington (☎04/712-456); **USA** 2640 16th St, NW, Washington, DC 20009 (☎202/234-3800).

PORTUGAL Australia 6 Campion St, 1st Floor, Deakin, Canberra, ACT 2600 (☎062/285-2084); **Canada** 645 Island Park Drive, Ottawa, ON K1Y 0B8 (☎613/729-0883); **Great Britain** 11 Belgrave Square, London SW1 (☎071/235 5331); **Ireland** Knocksinna House, Dublin 18 (☎01/893375); **New Zealand** Southpac House, 1 Victoria St, PO Box 1990, Wellington (☎04/721-677); **USA** 2125 Kalorama Rd, NW, Washington, DC 20008 (☎202/328-8610).

ROMANIA Canada 655 Lidoau St, Ottawa, ON K1N 6A3 (☎613/789-3709); **Great Britain** 4 Palace Green, London W8 (☎071/937 9666); **USA** 1607 23rd St, NW, Washington, DC 20008 (☎202/232-4747).

SLOVAK REPUBLIC Great Britain 25 Kensington Palace Gardens, London W8 (☎071/243 0803).

SLOVENIA Australia Kingston Court, 4 Tench St, Kingston ACT 2604 (☎06/295-5300); PO Box 5, Smithfield, Sydney NSW 2164 (☎02/604-5133); **Great Britain** 11–15 Wigmore St, London W1 (☎071/495 7775).

SPAIN Australia 15 Arkana St, Yarralumla, Canberra, ACT 2600 (☎062/273-3555); **Canada** 350 Spark St, Ottawa, ON K1R 7S8 (☎613/237-2193); **Great Britain** 20 Draycott Place, London SW3 (☎071/581 5921); **Ireland** 17a Merlyn Park, Dublin 4 (☎01/619640); **New Zealand** PO Box 71, Papakura, Auckland (☎09/298-5176); **USA** 2700 15th St, NW, Washington, DC 20009 (☎202/265-4939).

SWEDEN Australia 5 Turrana St, Yarralumla, Canberra, ACT 2600 (☎062/273-3033); **Canada** 377 Dalhousie St, Ottawa, ON K1N 9N8 (☎613/236-8553); **Great Britain** 11 Montagu Place, London W1 (☎071/724 2101); **Ireland** Sun Alliance House, Dawson St, Dublin 2 (☎01/715822); **New Zealand** Greenock House, 39 The Terrace, PO Box 5350, Wellington (☎04/720-909); **USA** 600 New Hampshire Ave, NW, Suite 1200, Washington, DC 20037 (☎202/944-5600).

SWITZERLAND Australia 7 Melbourne Ave, Forrest, Canberra, ACT 2603 (☎062/273-3977); **Canada** 5 Marlboro Ave, Ottawa, ON K1N 8E6 (☎613/235-1837); **Great Britain** 16–18 Montague Place, London W1 (☎071/723 0701); **Ireland** 6 Ailesbury Rd, Dublin 4 (☎01/692689); **New Zealand** Panama House, 22–24 Panama St, Wellington (☎04/721-593); **USA** 2900 Cathedral Ave, NW, Washington, DC 20008 (☎202/745-7900).

TURKEY Australia 66 Ocean St, Wollahra, Sydney, NSW 2025 (☎062/295-0227); **Canada** 197 Wurdetembourg St, Ottawa, ON K1N 8L9 (☎613/789-4044); **Great Britain** 43 Belgrave Square, London SW1 (☎071/235 5252); **Ireland** 60 Merrion Rd, Dublin 4 (☎01/685240); **New Zealand** 404 Khyber Pass Rd, Newmarket, Auckland (☎09/522-2281); **USA** 1714 Massachusetts Ave, NW, Washington, DC 20036 (☎202/387-3200).

CUSTOMS

Customs and duty-free restrictions vary throughout Europe, with subtle variations even within the European Community, at least for the moment. Since the inauguration of the EC Single Market, travellers coming into Britain directly from another EC country do not have to make a declaration to Customs at their place of entry. In other words, you can effectively bring as much duty-paid French wine or beer across the Channel as you can carry (the legal limits being 90 litres of wine or 110 of beer). However, there are still restrictions on the volume of tax- or duty-free goods you can bring into the country. In general, residents of EC countries travelling to other EC states are allowed a duty-free allowance of 200 cigarettes, one litre of spirits and five litres of wine; for non-EC residents the allowances are usually 200 cigarettes, one litre of spirits and two litres of wine. Residents of the USA and Canada can take up to 200 cigarettes and one litre of alcohol back into the country, as can Australian citizens, while New Zealanders must confine themselves to 200 cigarettes, 4.5 litres of beer or wine, and just over one litre of spirits. Again, if in doubt consult the relevant – or your own – embassy.

You'll hardly notice crossing some **borders**, especially if you're travelling by train: there are no checks between Belgium and the Netherlands, or travelling from one Scandinavian country to another, and it is likely that as Europe becomes more integrated other border checks will grow to be more relaxed. For the moment, though, while there is rarely the level of suspicion you found in the old Iron Curtain days, you are sometimes at the mercy of the good humour of the customs officer; it pays to look reasonably well turned-out, and to be polite at all times, even in the face of the most over-weening officialdom, and on entering some countries you may be asked to show a return ticket. Bear in mind also that the carrying of certain items across borders, for example any kinds of controlled drug, firearms or obscene literature, is illegal, not to mention stupid in the extreme. If you are carrying prescribed drugs of any kind, it can be a good idea to have a copy of the prescription to flash at a suspicious customs officer. Bear in mind too that the importing of food, plants or animals back into Britain, Ireland, the USA, Canada, Australia or New Zealand is prohibited.

HEALTH AND INSURANCE

As fellow members of the European Community, both Britain and Ireland have reciprocal health agreements with EC countries. These provide for free medical advice and treatment on the presentation of certificate E111, which you should apply for at least a month before leaving by filling in form CM1, available from DSS offices, post offices and travel agents. Without an E111 you won't be turned away from hospitals but you will almost certainly have to pay for any treatment or medicines. Also, in practice, some countries' doctors and hospitals charge anyway and it's up to you to claim reimbursement when you return home. Make sure you are insured for potential medical expenses, and keep copies of receipts and prescriptions.

There aren't many particular **health problems** you'll encounter travelling in most parts of Europe. You don't need to have any inoculations for any of the countries covered in this book, although in Morocco and Turkey typhoid and malaria jabs are advised. The water in most countries is drinkable, although to be on the safe side bottled mineral water is normally available; you should perhaps only avoid tap water altogether in southern Morocco and parts of Turkey. Diarrhoea and sickness from dodgy water, or – in southern Europe – food, are reasonably likely, if only in a mild form. The best thing to do is carry anti-diarrhoea tablets with you at all times. One of the biggest problems you may face if travelling in southern Europe is the sun: don't spend too much time in direct sunlight if you're not used to it, and certainly not without any kind of sun block cream; just half an hour on your first day's sunbathing is probably the limit – more than this can leave you beetroot-red and nauseous. Mosquitoes, too, are a problem Europe-wide, especially in the south and places where there's a lot of water around; the Netherlands, for example, harbours particularly virulent species. It's hard to know what to do about them: most people develop an immunity after a few days' exposure; until then an antihistamine cream like *phenergan* is the best antidote. Finally, AIDS is as much of a problem in Europe as it is in the rest of the world, and it hardly needs saying that casual sex without a condom is risky.

For **minor health problems** it's easiest to go to the local pharmacy. You'll find these pretty much everywhere and we've detailed out-of-hours ones in the text. In **more serious cases** your nearest consulate will have a list of English-speaking doctors, as will the local tourist office, and in the larger cities we've listed the most convenient casualty departments.

INSURANCE

Wherever you're travelling from, it's a very good idea to have some kind of **travel insurance**, since with this you're covered for loss of possessions and money, as well as for the cost of all medical and dental treatment. Among **British** insurers, *Endsleigh* are about the cheapest, offering a month's cover for around £30. Their policies are available from most youth/student travel specialists or direct from their offices at 97–107 Southampton Row, London WC1 (☎071/436 4451). You must make sure you keep all medical bills, and, if you have anything stolen, get a copy of the police report when you report the incident – otherwise you won't be able to claim.

In the **US and Canada** you should check the insurance policies you already have carefully before taking out a new one. You may discover that you're covered already for medical and other losses while abroad. Canadians especially are usually covered by their provincial health plans, and holders of ISIC and other academic cards are entitled to $3000-worth of accident coverage and sixty days of in-patient benefits for the period the card is valid. Students may also find their health coverage extends during vacations, and many bank and charge accounts include some form of travel cover; insurance is also sometimes included if you pay for your trip with a credit card. If you do want a specific travel insurance policy, there are numerous kinds to choose from: short-term combination policies covering everything from baggage loss to broken legs are the best bet and cost around $30 for ten days, and $60 for a month. One thing to bear in mind is that none of the currently available policies covers theft; they only cover loss while in the custody of an identifiable person – though even then you must make a report to the police and get their written statement. Two companies you might try are *Travel Guard*, 1145 Clark St, Steven Point, WI 54480 (☎715/345-0505 or 800/826-1300), or *Access America International*, 6600 West Broad St, Richmond, VA 23230 (☎800/284-8300).

INFORMATION AND MAPS

Before you leave, it's worth contacting the tourist offices of the countries you're intending to visit, since most produce copious quantities of free leaflets, maps and brochures, some of which can be quite useful, both in planning your trip and when you're travelling. This is especially true for parts of central and eastern Europe, where up-to-date maps in particular are often scarcer in the country than in their tourist offices abroad. For the rest of Europe go easy, though: much of the information these places pump out can picked up just as easily on your travels, and it can weigh a ton.

TOURIST INFORMATION OFFICES ABROAD

AUSTRIA Australia 36 Carrington St, 1st Floor, Sydney, NSW 2000 (☎02/299-3621); **Canada** 2 Bloor St East, Suite 3330, Toronto, ON M4W 1HA (☎416/967-3381); **Great Britain** 30 St George St, London W1 (☎071/629 0461); **Ireland**, The Lodge, Ardoyne House, Pembroke Park, Ballsbridge, Dublin 4 (☎01/683321); **USA** PO Box 1142, New York, NY 10108 (☎212/944-6880).

BELGIUM Great Britain 29 Princes St, London W1 (☎071/629 0230); **USA** 745 Fifth Ave, New York, NY 10151 (☎212/758-8130).

BULGARIA Great Britain 18 Princes St, London W1 (☎071/499 6988); **USA** c/o *Balkan Holidays*, 41 E 42nd St, New York, NY 10017 (☎212/573-5530).

CZECH REPUBLIC Great Britain 17–18 Bond St, London W1 (☎071/629 6058); **USA** c/o *Cedok*, 10 E 40th St, New York, NY 10016 (☎212/689-9720).

DENMARK Canada PO Box 115, Station N, Toronto, ON M8V 3S4 (☎416/823-9620); **Great Britain** Sceptre House, 169–173 Regent St, London W1 (☎071/734 2637); **USA** 655 Third Ave, New York, NY 10017 (☎212/949-2333).

FINLAND Canada 1200 Bay St, Suite 604, Toronto, ON M5R 2A5 (☎416/964-9159); **Great Britain** 66 Haymarket, London SW1 (☎071/839 4048); **USA** 655 Third Ave, New York, NY 10017 (☎212/370-5540).

FRANCE Australia Kindersley House, 33 Blight St, Sydney, NSW 2000 (☎02/231-5244); **Canada** 1 Dundas St West, Box 8, Toronto, ON N5G 1Z3 (☎416/593-4723); **Great Britain** 178 Piccadilly, London W1 (☎071/491 7622); **USA** 610 Fifth Ave, New York, NY 10020 (☎900/990-0040).

GERMANY Australia Lufthansa House, 12th Floor, 143 Macquarie St, Sydney, NSW 2000 (☎02/221-1008); **Great Britain** Nightingale House, 65 Curzon St, London W1 (☎071/495 3990); **USA** 122 E 42nd St, New York, NY 10017 (☎212/661-7200).

GREAT BRITAIN Australia 171 Clarence St, 4th Floor, Sydney, NSW 2000 (☎02/221-1008); **Canada** 111 Avenue Rd, Suite 450, Toronto, ON M5R 3J8 (☎416/925-6326); **USA** 551 Fifth Ave, New York, NY 10176 (☎212/581-0799).

GREECE **Australia** 51–57 Pitt St, Sydney, NSW 2000 (☎02/241-1663); **Canada** 1300 Bay St, Toronto, ON M5R 3K8 (☎416/968-2220); **Great Britain** 4 Conduit St, London W1 (☎071/734 5997); **USA** 645 Fifth Ave, New York, NY 10022 (☎212/421-5777).

HUNGARY **Great Britain** 6 Conduit St, London W1 (☎071/491 3588); **USA** c/o *Ibusz*, 1 Parker Plaza, Suite 1104, Fort Lee, NJ 07024 (☎204/592-8585).

IRELAND **Australia** MLC Centre, 38th Level, Martin Place, Sydney, NSW 2000 (☎02/232-7177); **Canada** 160 Bloor St East, Suite 934, Toronto, ON M4W 1B9 (☎416/929-2777); **Great Britain** 150–151 New Bond St, London W1 (☎071/493 3201); **USA** 757 Third Ave, New York, NY 10017 (☎212/418-0800).

ITALY **Canada** 1 Place Ville Marie, Suite 1914, Montreal, PQ H3B 3M9 (☎514/866-7667); **Great Britain** 1 Princes St, London W1 (☎071/408 1254); **Ireland** 47 Merrion Square, Dublin 2 (☎01/766397); **USA** 630 Fifth Ave, New York, NY 10111 (☎212/245-4822).

LUXEMBOURG **Great Britain** 122 Regent St, London W1 (☎071/434 2800); **USA** 801 Second Ave, New York, NY 10017 (☎212/370-9850).

MOROCCO **Canada** 2001 rue Université, Suite 1460, Montreal, PQ H3A 2A6 (☎514/842-8111); **Great Britain** 205 Regent St, London W1 (☎071/437 0073); **USA** 20 E 46th St, New York, NY 10017 (☎212/557-2520).

NETHERLANDS **Australia** 5 Elizabeth St, Suite 302, Sydney, NSW 2000 (☎02/276-921); **Canada** 25 Adelaide St East, Suite 710, Toronto, ON M5C 1Y2 (☎416/363-1577); **Great Britain** 25–28 Buckingham Gate, London SW1 (☎071/630 0451); **USA** 355 Lexington Ave, New York, 10020 (☎212/370-7367).

NORWAY **Great Britain** Charles House, Lower Regent St, London SW1 (☎071/839 6255); **USA** 655 Third Ave, New York, NY 10017 (☎212/949-2333).

POLAND **Great Britain** 82 Mortimer St, London W1 (☎071/636 2217); **USA** 342 Madison Ave, Suite 1512, New York, NY 10173 (☎212/867-5011).

PORTUGAL **Canada** 60 Bloor St West, Suite 10-05, Toronto, ON M4W 3B8 (☎416/921-7376); **Great Britain** 22–25a Sackville St, London W1 (☎071/494 1441); **USA** 590 Fifth Ave, New York, NY 10036 (☎212/354-4403).

ROMANIA **Great Britain** 17 Nottingham Place, London W1 (☎071/224 3692); **USA** 342 Madison Ave, Suite 210, New York, NY 10173 (☎212/697-6971).

SLOVENIA **Great Britain** Moghul House, 57 Grosvenor St, London W1 (☎071/495 4688).

SPAIN **Australia** 203 Castlereigh St, Suite 21a, PO Box A675, Sydney, NSW 2000 (☎02/264-7966); **Canada** 102 Bloor St West, Suite 1400, Toronto, ON M5S 1M8 (☎416/961-3131); **Great Britain** 57–58 St James's St, London SW1 (☎071/499 0901); **USA** 665 Fifth Ave, New York, 10022 (☎212/759-8822).

SWEDEN **Great Britain** 73 Welbeck St, London W1 (☎071/487 3135); **USA** 655 Third Ave, New York, NY 10017 (☎212/949-2333).

SWITZERLAND **Canada** 154 University Ave, Suite 610, Toronto, ON M5H 3Y9 (☎416/971-9734); **Great Britain** Swiss Centre, New Coventry St, London W1 (☎071/734 1921); **USA** 608 Fifth Ave, New York, NY 10020 (☎212/757-5944).

TURKEY **Great Britain** 170–173 Piccadilly, London W1 (☎071/734 8681); **USA** 821 UN Plaza, New York, NY 10017 (☎212/687-2194).

If your home country isn't listed here, apply to the embassy.

INFORMATION ON THE ROAD

Once you're travelling in Europe, you'll find on-the-spot information easy enough to pick up. Most countries have a well-equipped and widespread network of **tourist offices** that answer queries, dole out a range of (sometimes free) maps and brochures, and can sometimes book accommodation, or at least advise you on the best-value places if you're stuck. Tourist offices are, as you might expect, better organized in northern Europe – Scandinavia, the Netherlands, France – with branches in all but the smallest village, with mounds of information; in Greece, Turkey and eastern Europe you'll find tourist offices more infrequent and less helpful on the whole, sometimes offering no more than a couple of dog-eared brochures and a photocopied map. We've given further details, including a broad idea of opening hours, in "Basics" for each country.

MAPS

Whether you're doing a grand tour or confining yourself to one or two countries you will need a decent **map**. The best one to cover the whole continent is the *Bartholomew/RV* 1:3,500,00 version, which shows all of Europe, plus most of Turkey and northern Morocco. Although it details roads and ferry routes, however, it omits rail lines, and is probably better for a broad overview than for serious touring. For this you're better off with a map book like the *Michelin* road map of Europe, or, specifically for rail routes, the *Thomas Cook Rail Map of Europe*. In the USA and Canada good sources of maps are the *AAA*, who publish an overall Europe planning map as well as regional maps of the continent. We've recommended the best maps of individual countries throughout the book. In general, though, you'll find the best series to be either *Batholomew/RV, Kümmerley & Frey* or *Hallwag*, or, in North America, those published by *Rand McNally*. For plans of over fifty European cities, the *Falk* series of detailed, indexed maps are excellent, and they're deliberately easy to use.

Though you can often buy these (or sometimes better, locally-produced alternatives) on the spot, you may want to get them in advance to plan your trip. The best place to **buy maps** in Britain is *Stanford's*, 12–14 Long Acre, London WC2 (☎071/836 1321), who have an enormous range, taking in everything from ordinary road maps to large-scale hiking maps and detailed city plans; they also have a mail-order service and can get just about anything if they don't have it in stock. In the USA, the *Rand McNally* stores are the best source of maps. They have branches in New York at 150 E 52nd St, NY 10022 (☎212/758-7488); in Chicago at 444 N Michigan Ave, IL 60611 (☎312/321-1751); and in San Francisco at 595 Market St, CA 94105 (☎415/777-3131).

COSTS

It's hard to generalize about what you're likely to spend travelling around Europe. Some countries – Finland, Switzerland – are among the priciest places to be in the world, while in others you can live like a lord on next to nothing – Turkey, for example. The collapse of the eastern European economy means that many of the countries there appear very inexpensive if you're coming from the west. However, the absorption of a number of the previously inexpensive countries of southern Europe into the EC means that recent years have seen their costs become much more in tune with the European mainstream.

Accommodation will be the largest single cost, and can really determine where you decide to travel. For example, it's hard to find a double hotel room anywhere in Scandinavia – perhaps the most expensive part of the continent – for much under £40 a night, whereas in most parts of southern Europe, and even in France, you might be paying under half that on average. Everywhere, though, even in Scandinavia, there is some form of bottom-line accommodation available, and there's always a youth hostel on hand. In general, reckon on a minimum budget of around £10 a night per person in most parts of Europe.

Food and drink costs also vary wildly, although again in most parts of Europe you can assume that a restaurant meal will cost on average £5–10 a head, with prices at the top end of the scale in Scandinavia, at the bottom end in eastern and southern Europe. **Transport** costs are something you can pin down more exactly if you have a rail pass or are renting a car. Nowhere, though, are transport costs a major burden, except perhaps in Britain where public transport is less heavily subsidized than elsewhere. Local city transport, too, is usually good, clean and efficient, and is normally fairly cheap, even in the pricier countries of northern Europe (Britain again is an exception to all these rules). It's hard to pinpoint an average daily budget for touring the continent, but a bottom-line survival figure – camping, self-catering, hitching, etc – might be around £15 a day per person, perhaps less at a pinch; building in an investment for a rail pass, staying in hostels and eating out occasionally would bring this up to perhaps £20 a day; while staying in private rooms or hotels and eating out once a day would mean a personal daily budget of at least £25. Obviously in the more expensive countries of northern Europe you might be spending more than this, but on a wide tour this would be balanced out by spending less in southern and eastern Europe, where everything is that much cheaper.

When and where you are travelling also makes a difference. Accommodation rates tend to go up across the board in July and August, when everyone is on vacation – although paradoxically there are good deals in Scandinavia during these months. Also bear in mind that in capital cities and major resorts in the peak season everything will be a grade more expensive than anywhere else, especially if you're there when something special is going on, for example in Munich during the Beer Festival, Pamplona for the running of the bulls, Siena during the Palio. These are, in any case, times when you will be lucky to find a room at all without having booked.

As for **ways of cutting costs**, there are plenty. It makes sense, obviously, to spend less on **transport** by investing in some kind of rail pass, and if you're renting a car to do so for a week or more, thereby qualifying for cheaper rates. Always try and plan in advance. Although it's good to be flexible, buying one-off rail tickets and renting cars by the day can add a huge amount to your travel budget. The most obvious way to save on **accommodation** is to use hostels and/or camp; you can also save by planning to make some of your longer trips at night, when the cost of a couchette may undercut the cost of a night's accommodation. It's best not to be too spartan when it comes to **food** costs, but doing a certain amount of self-catering, especially at lunchtime when it's just as easy (and probably nicer) to have a picnic lunch rather than eat in a restaurant or café, will save money. Bear in mind, also, that if you're a student an **ISIC card** is well worth investing in. It can get reduced (usually 50 percent, sometimes free) entry to museums and other sights – costs which can eat their way into your budget alarmingly if you're doing a lot of sightseeing – as well as qualifying you for other discounts in certain cities. If you're not a student but are under 26, the **FIYTO card** can in some countries give much the same sort of reductions. Basically, it's worth flashing one or the other at every opportunity to see what you can get.

MONEY AND BANKS

The easiest and safest way to carry your money is in travellers' cheques, in either dollars or pounds sterling. These are available for a small commission (normally 1 percent) from any British, US or Canadian bank. You should strictly order them in advance but this isn't always necessary in larger branches. The most commonly accepted travellers' cheques are American Express, with Visa a close second, and Thomas Cook trailing third. Most cheques issued by banks will be one of these three brands. You'll usually pay commission again when you cash each cheque; this varies from country to country but is normally another 1 percent or so, or a flat rate, in which case it makes sense to cash as many as possible at once. Keep a record of the cheques as you cash them, and you can get the value of all uncashed cheques refunded immediately if you lose them.

PRICES

In the guide we've quoted **prices** in local currency wherever possible, except in those countries where the weakness of the currency and the inflation rate combine to make this a meaningless exercise. In these cases – parts of eastern Europe and Turkey – we've used either US dollars, pounds sterling or Deutschmarks, depending on which hard currency is most commonly used within that country.

For accommodation prices, we've used a standard coding system throughout the guide: see p.36 for details on this.

APPROXIMATE EXCHANGE RATES					
	£1	US$1		£1	US$1
Austrian Schilling	16.85	11.13	Netherlands Guilder	2.71	1.79
Belgian Franc	51.65	32.57	Norwegian Kroner	10.55	6.28
Danish Kroner	10.00	6.20	Portuguese Escudo	248.50	140.45
Finnish Marka	8.5	4.30	Spanish Peseta	195.50	101.63
French Franc	8.43	5.47	Swedish Kroner	12.16	5.84
German Mark	2.40	1.58	Swiss Franc	2.11	1.40
Greek Drachma	340	181.72			
Irish Punt	1.05	0.59	Exchange rates for the other currencies quoted in		
Italian Lire	2350	1260.50	this book are too volatile to estimate.		

A further option if you're travelling from Britain, and in some ways a more flexible one in the sense you don't have to budget as carefully in advance, is **Eurocheques** – available from British banks with their own cheque guarantee card. You can use your Eurochequebook in the normal way, paying for things in shops, restaurants and hotels, as well as obtaining cash in local currency from banks. You pay around 1.5 percent commission plus a small cost for the cheque card, along with a small flat fee every time you write a cheque. You can also apply for a PIN number and use your cheque card to obtain money from cash dispensers in a number of European countries.

You'll find that most hotels, shops and restaurants in Europe accept the major **credit cards** – *Access/Mastercard*, *Visa*, *American Express* and *Diners Club* – although they're less useful in eastern Europe, where you shouldn't depend on being able to use your card. You can also get cash advances from selected banks and bureaux de change on credit cards, though there will invariably be a minimum amount you can draw. This varies from one country to the next, but it's usually at least the equivalent of £50–100 in local currency.

Almost everywhere **banks** are the best places to **change money and cheques**, and we've given their opening hours in the text. Outside these times there are normally **bureaux de change**, often at train stations and airports, though rates and/or commissions will be that much less favourable. Try and avoid changing money or cheques in **hotels**, where the rates are normally rock-bottom.

If you run out of money abroad, or there is some kind of emergency, the quickest way to get **money sent out** is to contact your bank at home and have them wire the cash to the nearest bank. You can do the same thing through *Thomas Cook* or *American Express* if there is a branch nearby. Americans and Canadians can have cash sent out through *Western Union* (☎800/325-6000) to a nearby bank or post office – a process which takes 2–5 days; rates vary according to the destination. Make sure you know when it's likely to arrive, since you won't be notified by the receiving office. Though this may seem obvious, in all cases you'll need some form of identification when you pick up the money. If you have no money in your account, and there is no one you can persuade to send you any, then the options are inevitably limited. You can either find some casual, cash-in-hand work (see below), sell blood (not possible in all European countries), or, as a last resort, throw yourself on the mercy of your nearest consulate. They won't be very sympathetic or even helpful, but they may cash a cheque drawn on a home bank and supported by a cheque card. They may, if there's nothing else for it, repatriate you, though bear in mind your passport will be confiscated as soon as you set foot in your home country and you'll have to pay back all costs incurred. They rarely, if ever, lend money.

COMMUNICATIONS: POST, PHONES, THE MEDIA

Communications throughout northwestern Europe are invariably excellent: public phones are readily available and normally work, and the postal system is reasonably efficient and easy to use. In southern Europe, services are sometimes less impressive, notably in Italy where the post is notoriously awful; and in eastern Europe the infrastructure is still very poor and services consequently unpredictable.

POST

For buying stamps and, sometimes, making telephone calls, we've listed the central **post offices** in major cities, and given an idea of opening hours. Bear in mind, though, that throughout much of Europe you can avoid the queues in post offices by buying **stamps** from newsagents and the like. If you know in advance where you're going to be and when, it is possible to receive mail in advance through the **poste restante** system, whereby letters addressed "poste restante" and sent to the main post office in any town or city will be kept under your name at the relevant counter to be picked up. When collecting mail, make sure you take your passport for identification; and bear in mind, in some countries, the possibility of letters being misfiled by someone unfamiliar with your language: if there is nothing under your surname it may have been filed under your first name. If you are using **American Express** travellers' cheques, or have an *American Express* card, you can also have mail kept for you at the city centre office; again, where appropriate, we've given addresses throughout the text.

PHONES

It is often possible, especially in western Europe, to make **international calls** from a public call box, although this can often be more trouble than it's worth due to the constant need to feed in change – a number of countries (Britain, France, Portugal, to name a few) now issue phone cards, making the whole process much easier. Otherwise, you're normally better off going to a **post office**, or a special **telephone bureau**, where you can make a call from a private booth and pay afterwards. Most countries have these in one form or another, and we've listed their whereabouts in the text. Wherever possible, avoid using the telephone in your **hotel room** – it costs the earth. To dial any country in this book

INTERNATIONAL DIALLING CODES

Australia ☎61	Germany (areas formerly FDR) ☎49	Norway ☎47
Austria ☎43		Poland ☎48
Belgium ☎32	Great Britain ☎44	Portugal ☎351
Bulgaria ☎359	Greece ☎30	Romania ☎40
Canada ☎1	Hungary ☎36	Slovak Republic ☎42
Czech Republic ☎42	Ireland ☎353	Slovenia ☎38
Denmark ☎45	Italy ☎39	Spain ☎34
Finland ☎358	Luxembourg ☎352	Sweden ☎46
France ☎33	Morocco ☎212	Switzerland ☎41
Germany (areas formerly GDR) ☎37	Netherlands ☎31	Turkey ☎90
	New Zealand ☎64	USA ☎1

from Britain, dial 010, then the country code, then the city/area code less the inital zero (or in the case of Finland, Spain or Turkey the initial 9), followed by the number (bear in mind that Luxembourg has no city codes); **from the US or Canada**, the initial code is 011, **from Australia or New Zealand** 0011. To **call home** from any of these countries, dial 00, then the country code, then the city code less the initial zero, then the subscriber number.

THE MEDIA

British **newspapers and magazines** are fairly widely available in Europe, sometimes – in the Netherlands and Belgium, for example – on the day of publication, more often the day after. They do, however, cost around three times as much as they do at home. Exceptions are the *Guardian* and *Financial Times*, which print special European editions and are therefore cheaper and always available on the day of issue. You can also find the terminally dull and self-righteous *Herald Tribune* just about everywhere, as well as the plain dull *USA Today*, if you're lucky you may come across the odd *New York Times* or *Washington Post*, but don't count on it outside the major centres. What you will find is *Time* and *Newsweek* pretty much everywhere, as well as a host of British and American glossies. Finally there's the *European*, which appears in huge and slow-moving piles on newsstands all over Europe every Friday, a passable attempt at a Europe-wide newspaper in English; how long it will last is anyone's guess.

It's cheaper to get your news by tuning into the *BBC World Service* on the **radio** or one of the many local news broadcasts in English. In northern France, the Netherlands and Belgium you can pick up *BBC Radio 4* as well. The *World Service* broadcasts on short wave only, on 15575 kHz, 15070 kHz, 12095 kHz, 6195 kHz and 9410 kHz, depending on the time of day and where you are in Europe. For details of local radio programmes in English you should consult the local press. You should also be able to pick up *Voice of America*, which broadcasts on 1197 kHz all week except 8–10am on Sunday, when it uses a range of frequencies according to region (details from *VOA Europe*, PO Box 221 220, 8000 Munich 22, Germany).

With the advent of cable and satellite channels, **television** has become more of a pan-European medium than radio. *Sky TV, Superchannel, CNN, Eurosport* and the European version of *MTV* are all much more popular than they are in Britain and normally available in the better hotels. In many parts of Europe there is, in any case, a wide choice of channels (by British, if not by American standards), since a border is never far away and you can often pick up at least one other country's TV stations. This is at its most extreme in Belgium and the southern Netherlands, where as well as all the satellite and cable channels you can pick up Dutch and Belgian TV, French TV, BBC1 and BBC2, all the German stations and even the state Italian channel.

ACCOMMODATION

Although it is obviously one of the more crucial costs to consider when planning your trip, accommodation needn't be a stumbling block to a budget-conscious tour of Europe. Indeed, even in Europe's pricier reaches the hostel system means there is always an affordable place to stay, and if you're prepared to camp you can get by on very little while staying at some excellently equipped sites. The one thing you should bear in mind is that in the more popular cities and resorts – Florence, Venice, Amsterdam,

Prague, the Algarve – things can get chock-a-bloc during the peak summer months, and even if you've got plenty of money to throw around you should book in advance.

HOSTELS

The cheapest way for young people to travel around Europe is by using the extensive network of **youth hostels** that covers the continent. Some of these are **private** places, run on a one-off basis in the major cities and resorts, but by far the majority are **official hostels**, members of the *International Youth Hostel Federation* (*IYHF*), which incorporates the national youth hostel associations of each country in the world. Youth hostelling isn't the hearty, up-at-the-crack-of-dawn and early-to-bed business it once was; indeed, hostels have been keen to shed this image of late and now appeal to a wider public, and in many countries they simply represent the best-value overnight accommodation available. Most are clean, well-run places, always offering dormitory accommodation, some – especially in Scandinavia and other parts of northern Europe – offering a range of private single and double rooms, or rooms with 4–6 beds. Many hostels also either have self-catering facilities or provide low-cost meals, and the larger ones have a range of other facilities – a swimming pool, games room, common room, etc. There is no age limit (except in Bavaria), but where there is limited space priority is given to those under 27 years of age.

Strictly speaking, to use an *IYHF* hostel you have to be a member, although if there is room you can stay at most hostels by simply paying extra – and you can often join the *IYHF* on the spot. If you do intend to do a lot of hostelling, however, it is certainly worth joining, which you can do by becoming a member of your home country's hostelling association. Annual membership costs are low everywhere. As a broad guide, in Britain annual membership costs £9 if you're over 18, £3 for under-18s, and from £9–18 for family membership. In the USA membership fees range from $10 for under-18s to $25 for adults; families can join for a total fee of $35. We've detailed the hostelling situation in each country in the text, as well as giving the name and address of the relevant national hostelling organization if you want further infor-

---

ACCOMMODATION PRICE CODES

Throughout this guide, accommodation is priced on a scale of ① to ⑧, the number indicating the lowest price per night a single person could expect to pay in that establishment in high season. With hostels this is the nightly rate per person; with hotels, the price is arrived at by dividing the cost of the cheapest double room by two. The prices indicated by the codes are as follows

① = under £5 / $8   ② = £5–10 / $8–16   ③ = £10–15 / $16–24   ④ = £15–20 / $24–32

⑤ = £20–25 / $32–40   ⑥ = £25–30 / $40–48   ⑦ = £30–35 / $48–56   ⑧ = over £35 / $56

mation. The *IYHF* booklet, *Guide to Budget Accommodation*, is a good investment, too, detailing every hostel in Europe and the Mediterranean. It's available from bookstores or your national hostelling association.

YOUTH HOSTEL ASSOCIATIONS

Australia *Australian Youth Hostels Association*, Level 3, 10 Mallett St, Camperdown, NSW (☎02/565-1325).

Canada *Canadian Hostelling Association*, 1600 James Naismith Drive, Suite 608, Gloucester, ON K1B 5N4 (☎613/748-5638).

England and Wales *Youth Hostel Association* (*YHA*), Trevelyan House, 8 St Stephen's Hill, St Alban's, Herts AL1 (☎07278/45047). London shop and information: 14 Southampton St, London WC2 (☎071/836 1036).

Ireland *An Oige*, 39 Mountjoy Square, Dublin 1 (☎01/363111).

New Zealand *Youth Hostels Association of New Zealand*, PO Box 436, Christchurch 1 (☎03/799-970).

Northern Ireland *Youth Hostel Association of Northern Ireland*, 56 Bradbury Place, Belfast, BT7 (☎0232/324733).

Scotland *Scottish Youth Hostel Association*, 7 Glebe Crescent, Stirling, FK8 2JA (☎0786/51181).

USA *American Youth Hostels* (*AYH*), PO Box 37613, Washington, DC 20005 (☎202/783-6161).

HOTELS AND PENSIONS

If you've got a bit more money to spend, you may want to upgrade from hostel accommodation to something a little more comfortable and private. With **hotels** you can really spend as much or as little as you like. Most hotels in Europe are graded on some kind of star system. One- or two-star category hotels are plain and simple on the whole, usually family-run, with a number of rooms without private facilities; sometimes breakfast won't be included. In three-star hotels all the rooms will have private facilities, prices will normally include breakfast and there may well be a phone or TV in the room; while four- and five-star places will certainly have all these, perhaps on a plusher, roomier basis, perhaps also including access to other facilities – sauna, swimming pool, etc. In the really top-level places breakfast, oddly enough, isn't always included. When it is, in the Netherlands, Britain or Germany it's fairly sumptuous; in France it wouldn't amount to much anyway and it's no hardship to grab a croissant and coffee in the nearest café. We've only detailed one- and two-star hotels in the text, since for most people on a tour of Europe these are usually perfectly acceptable; in any case, it's not hard to find places above this level. The prices quoted in the text are for the cheapest option in peak season for one person – which usually works out as being the price of half a basic double room, generally without a private bathroom. Single rooms tend to be at least 75 percent of the price of a double, and for private facilities you can expect to pay around 25 percent extra in most countries. For information on the accommodation pricing codes we've used throughout the text, see opposite.

Obviously prices vary greatly, but you're rarely going to be paying less than £10 for a double room even in southern Europe, while in the Netherlands the average price is around £25, in Scandinavia somewhat higher than that. In some countries **pensions** or **bed and breakfasts** (variously known as guesthouses, *gasthausen* or numerous other names) – smaller, simpler affairs, usually with just a few rooms, that are sometimes part of a larger family house – are a cheaper alternative. In some countries these advertise with a sign in the window; in others they are bookable through the tourist office, who may demand a booking fee. There are any number of other kinds of accommodation – apartments, farmhouses, cottages, *paradors* (in Spain), *gîtes* (in France), etc – but most are geared to longer-term stays and we have only detailed them where relevant.

CAMPING

The cheapest form of accommodation is, of course, the **campsite**, either pitching your own tent or parking your caravan or camper van. Most sites make a charge per person, plus a charge per plot and another per vehicle. Obviously you'll pay less if you're travelling on foot – maybe just a couple of pounds per night between two people – but parking a car or camper van doesn't add a lot to the cost. Bear in mind also, especially in countries like France where camping is very popular, that facilities can be excellent – though the better the facilities, the pricier the site. If you're on foot you should add in the cost and inconvenience of getting to the site, since most are on the outskirts of towns, sometimes further. Although some sites can be congested and noisy, you do, however, benefit from what can sometimes be a relatively bucolic location – often a bonus after a hard day's sightseeing. Some sites have **cabins**, which you can stay in for a little extra, although these are usually fairly basic affairs, only really worth considering in regions like Scandinavia where budget options are thin on the ground.

If you're planning to do a lot of camping, an **international camping carnet** is a good investment, available from home motoring organizations, or, in Britain, from the *Camping and Caravan Club*, 32 High St, London, E15 2PF (☎081/503 0426), in the US from the *National Campers and Hikers Association*, 4804 Transit Rd, Building 2, Depew, NY 14043 (☎716/668-6242). It serves as useful identification, covers you for third party insurance when camping, and is obligatory on sites in Portugal and some Scandinavian countries. As for **camping rough**, it's a fine idea if you can get away with it – though perhaps an entire trip of rough camping is in reality too gruelling to be truly enjoyable. In some countries it's easy – indeed in parts of Scandinavia it is a legal right, and in Greece and other southern European countries you can usually find a bit of beach to pitch down on – but in others it's almost a non-starter and can get you into trouble with the law.

POLICE, TROUBLE AND SEXUAL HARASSMENT

You can expect travel in Europe to be relatively trouble-free, but like any traveller, in any part of the world, there is always the chance of petty theft. Although conditions vary greatly from, say, Scandinavia, where you're unlikely to encounter much trouble of any kind, to poorer and potentially more troublesome regions like Morocco, Turkey or southern Italy, in order to minimize the risk of having your stuff ripped off, you should take some obvious precautions.

First and perhaps most important you should try not to look too much like a tourist: appearing lost, even if you are, is to be avoided if you can; neither is it a good idea, especially in southern Europe, to walk around draped with cameras or expensive jewellery – the bands of gypsy children who tour train stations can have your watch or camera off in seconds. If you're waiting for a train, keep your eyes (and hands if necessary) on your bags at all times; if you want to sleep, put everything valuable under your head as a pillow. You should be cautious when choosing a train compartment, and a woman travelling alone should avoid sharing a compartment with a lone man. If staying in a hostel, take your valuables out with you unless there's a very secure store for them on the premises; some people even make photocopies of their more crucial documentation and leave them at home; a copy of your address book, certainly, can be a good idea.

If the worst happens and you do have something stolen, inform the **police** immediately (we've included details of the main city police stations in the text); get a statement from them detailing exactly what has been lost, which you'll need for your insurance claim back home. Generally you'll find the police sympathetic enough, sometimes able to speak English, though unwilling to do much more than make out a report for you.

As for **offences** you might commit, it's hardly necessary to state that drugs like cocaine, amphetamines, barbiturates, heroin, LSD and Ecstasy are illegal all over Europe, and although cannabis is tolerated in some countries – Spain and the Netherlands, for example – you are only allowed to possess a small amount for personal use and street-trading is strictly illegal. Everywhere, the penalties for possession of hard drugs can be severe; in certain countries, such as Greece and Morocco, even possession of cannabis can result in a hefty prison sentence, and your consulate is unlikely to plead any kind of case for you. Other, more minor misdemeanours you should be wary of committing include sleeping rough, which is more tolerated in some parts of Europe than others and should be undertaken everywhere with a certain amount of circumspection, and topless sunbathing, which is now fairly common throughout southern Europe but still often frowned upon, especially in parts of Greece, Turkey and Italy. As always, be sensitive, and err on the side of caution. If you're arrested for any kind of motoring offence, again don't expect your consulate to be very sympathetic; in any case, unless it's something really serious you'll probably get off with a spot-fine. The same goes for fare avoidance on public transport. Finally, although it's much less of an issue than it once was, avoid photography around sensitive military sites or installations – you may be arrested as a spy.

One of the major irritants for women travelling through Europe is **sexual harassment**, which in Italy, Greece, Spain and Morocco especially can be almost constant for women travelling alone or with another woman, and can put certain areas completely out of bounds. Southern European coastal areas, especially, can be a real problem, where northwestern women are often regarded as being on the look-out for sex. By far the most common kind of harassment you'll come across simply consists of street whistles and cat-calls; occasionally it's more sinister, very occasionally it can be dangerous. Indifference is often the best policy, avoiding eye contact with men and at the same time appearing as confident and purposeful as possible. If this doesn't make you feel any more comfortable, shouting a few choice phrases in the local language is a good idea; don't, however, shout in English, which often seems to encourage them. You may also come across gropers on crowded buses and trains, in which case you should complain as loudly as possible – the ensuing scene should be enough to deter your assailant. The best way of avoiding more dangerous situations is to simply be as suspicious as possible: if you're hitching, don't get into a car if you've even a hint of doubt about the driver (always ask where they are going before volunteering the information yourself); indeed, don't ever get yourself into a situation where you're alone with a man you don't know. In the larger European cities we've detailed contact points and women-only bars and cafés, so if all else fails, or you just get fed up with avoiding Neanderthals, you can always seek out a completely male-free environment.

FESTIVALS AND ANNUAL EVENTS

There is always some annual event or other happening in Europe, and some of the bigger shindigs can be reason enough alone for visiting a place, some even worth planning your entire trip around. Be warned, though, that if you're intending to visit a place during its annual festival you need to plan well in advance, since accommodation can be booked up months beforehand, especially for the larger, more internationally known events.

RELIGIOUS AND TRADITIONAL FESTIVALS

Many of the festivals and annual events you'll come across were – and in many cases still are – **religious-inspired affairs**, centring on a local miracle or saint's day. **Easter**, certainly, is celebrated throughout Europe, with most verve

and ceremony in Catholic and Orthodox Europe, where Easter Sunday or Monday are usually marked with some sort of procession; it's especially enthusiastically celebrated in Greece, where it is more important even than Christmas, though be aware that the Orthodox Church's Easter can in fact fall a week or two either side of the western festival. Earlier in the year, traditionally at the beginning of Lent in February, **Carnival** is celebrated, most conspicuously (and perhaps most stagily) in Venice, which explodes in a riot of posing and colour to become one of the country's major tourist draws at this time of year. There are smaller, perhaps more authentic carnivals in **Viareggio**, also in Italy, and in Germany, Belgium and the Netherlands, most notably in **Cologne**, **Maastricht** and tiny **Binche** in the Ardennes, where you can view some 1500 costumed *Gilles* or dancers in the streets. Also in Belgium, in mid-Lent, catch if you can the procession of white-clad *Blanc Moussis* through the streets of **Stavelot** in the Ardennes – one of Europe's oddest sights. Other religious festivals you might base a trip around include the *Festa di San Gennaro* three times a year in **Naples**, when the dried blood of the city's patron saint is supposed to liquefy to prevent disaster befalling the place – it rarely fails; the *Ommegang* procession through the heart of **Brussels** city centre to commemorate a medieval miracle; the *Heilig Bloed* procession in **Bruges**, when a much-venerated relic of Christ's blood is carried shoulder-high through the town; and, in Italy, the annual procession across **Venice**'s Grand Canal to the church of the *Madonna della Salute* to recall the deliverance of the city from a seventeenth-century plague. In Morocco and Turkey, where the predominant religion is Islam, and in the Muslim areas of Bulgaria, **Ramadan**, commemorating the revelation of the Koran to Muhammad, is observed. The most important Muslim festival, it lasts a month, during which time Muslims are supposed to fast from sunrise until sunset – although otherwise, as far as is possible, life carries on as normal.

There are, of course, other, equally long-established events which have a less obvious foundation. One of the best-known is the **April Feria** in Seville, a week's worth of flamenco music and dancing, parades and bullfights, in a frenziedly enthusiastic atmosphere. Also in Spain, for a week in early July, the **San Fermín** festival in Pamplona is if anything even more famous, its centrepiece – the running of the bulls through the streets of the city along with local macho men – drawing tourists from all over the world, though there is much more to the festival than that. Also in July, at the beginning of the month (and again in mid-August), the **Palio** in Siena is perhaps the most spectacular annual event in Italy, a bareback horse race between representatives of the different quarters of the city around the main square, its origins dating back to medieval times. It's a brutal affair, with few rules and a great sense of deeply felt rivalry, and, although there are other Palio events in Italy, it's like no other horse race you'll ever see. At least as big a deal as the Palio and San Fermín is the Munich **Oktoberfest**, a huge beer festival and fair that lasts from the last Saturday in September until the first Sunday in October. Unlike most events of its size in Europe it's less than two hundred years old, but it attracts vast numbers of people to consume gluttonous quantities of beer and food. London's **Notting Hill Carnival**, held at the end of August, is also a recent phenomenon, a predominantly Black and Caribbean celebration that's these days the biggest street festival in Europe. Other, smaller events include the great Venice **Regata Storica**, each September, a trial of skill for the city's gondoliers, and the gorgeous annual displays and processions of flowers in the Dutch **bulbfield** towns in April and May.

ARTS FESTIVALS

Festivals celebrating all or one specific aspect of the **arts** are held all over Europe throughout the year, though particularly in summer, when the weather is better suited to outdoor events. Of general international arts festivals, the one held every August in **Edinburgh** is perhaps the best-known and most enjoyable, not to mention one of the most innovative, with a mass of top-notch and fringe events in every medium, from rock to cabaret to modern experimental music and drama. For three weeks every year the whole city is given over to the festival and it's a wonderful time to be around if you don't mind the crowds and have booked somewhere to stay in advance. There is another major general arts festival in **Spoleto**, the *Festival dei Due Mondi*, held over two months each summer, which is Italy's leading international arts festival, though on a somewhat smaller scale than Edinburgh, while the midsummer **Avignon** festival in southern France is slanted towards drama but hosts plenty of other events besides and is again a great time to be in town. Smaller general arts festivals, though still attracting a variety of international names, include the **Holland Festival**, held in Amsterdam in June; the **Flanders Festival**, an umbrella title for all sorts of dramatic and musical events held mainly in the medieval buildings of Bruges and Ghent in July and August; and the **Dubrovnik Summer Festival**, with a host of musical events against the backdrop of the town's beautiful Renaissance centre – though the future of this is as uncertain as that of the country.

As regards more specialist gatherings, the **Montreux Jazz Festival** in July and the **North Sea Jazz Festival** in The Hague in mid-July are the continent's premier jazz jamborees, while the same month sees the beginning of the **Salzburg Music Festival**, perhaps the foremost – if also the most conservative – serious music festival in Europe, running through to the end of August. Florence's **Maggio Musicale** is also worth catching, a festival of opera and classical music that (confusingly) runs from late-April until early July. Less highbrow musical forms – rock, folk, etc – are celebrated, most conspicuously, at the huge **Glastonbury** festival in Britain, which – the goodwill of the site's owner permitting – will continue to happen every June; at the **Pink Pop Festival**, held every June in Geleen near Maastricht in the Netherlands; and the **Roskilde Festival** in Denmark. Look out also for the **Womad** get-togethers, a number of which are usually held each year at a variety of sites all over Europe, celebrating World, folk and roots music, and the excellent and still relatively small **Cambridge Folk Festival** in late July. For films, there is, of course, **Cannes**, though this is more of an industry affair than anything else, and the **Venice** and **Berlin** film festivals, which are more geared to the general public.

GAY EUROPE

Gays and lesbians will find most of Europe a tolerant part of the world in which to travel. Most countries have at least in part legalized homosexual relationships, and the only parts of Europe covered in this guide where homosexual acts are still against the law are Ireland and Romania. Laws still in the main apply to male homosexuality; lesbianism, it would seem, doesn't officially exist, so it is in theory legal everywhere. The homosexual age of consent is, however, usually different from the heterosexual one – on average 18 years of age as opposed to 15 or 16 years, and as high as 21 years of age in Britain. In general, the Netherlands and Scandinavia (except Finland) are the most tolerant parts of the continent, with anti-discrimination legislation, and, in Denmark and Sweden, official recognition of lesbian and gay partnerships. The least tolerant countries, with restrictions on the so-called "promotion" of homosexuality, are Austria, Finland and Great Britain.

Most cities of any size, at least in northern Europe, have a few bars or cafés frequented by **gay men**, and it's not hard to make contact with other gay people. In the major northern capitals, certainly, the gay scene is usually fairly sophisticated, with any number of bars, bookshops, clubs and gay organizations and switchboards, though things are usually firmly slanted towards gay men. The gay capital of Europe is perhaps Amsterdam, but there is plenty of interest for gay men in London, Paris, Copenhagen, and, to a lesser extent, Madrid and Barcelona. In southern Europe, things are less developed: the main cities may have the odd gay bar, but it may not advertise itself as such, and outside of the capitals there won't be many obvious places to meet at all. **Gay women** can likewise usually find somewhere to meet with other gay women in northern Europe, albeit on a much smaller scale than male gays, while elsewhere, in southern and eastern Europe, word-of-mouth is about the only course open. We've detailed the best of the gay scenes of the major cities in the text; to explore further, get hold of the *Spartacus International Gay Guide*, which gives the most up-to-date lowdown on things throughout

Europe (indeed worldwide), even if it is sometimes reduced to listing dubious outdoor cruising areas. It's available in gay bookstores or direct from *Bruno Gmünder Verlag*, at Lutzowstrasse 105/106, PO Box 30 13 45, D-1000 Berlin 30 (☎030/262 10 99), or, in the USA, 100 East Biddle St, Baltimore, MD 21202 (☎301/727-5677). Women should get hold of *Gaia's Guide*, which has all kinds of information of interest to gay women – get hold of it in Britain from 412 Archway Rd, London N6, in the USA from 147 West 42nd St, Suite 603, New York, NY 10036.

DISABLED TRAVELLERS

It's easier for a disabled person to get around in northern Europe than in the south and east, which is not surprising given the fact that this part of the continent is more developed in every other way. Access to public buildings is, however, far from the norm in many countries, as is accessibility to public transport – indeed, the only big-city underground systems that *are* accessible are those in Berlin, Amsterdam, Stockholm and Helsinki, with the rest lagging far behind; buses, too, are in general out of bounds to disabled people, although airport facilities are improving, as are those on the cross-Channel ferries. As for rail services, these vary greatly: France, for example, has very good facilities for disabled passengers, as have Belgium, Denmark and Austria, but many other countries make little, if any, provision.

It's up to you whether you decide to see Europe on a **package tour** or **independently**. There are any number of specialist tour operators, mostly catering for physically handicapped travellers, and the number of non-specialist operators who cater for disabled clients is increasing. It's also perfectly possible to go it alone, either with your own helper or by hiring one if you require assistance while away, or by joining some kind of group tour for disabled travellers.

Pressure on space means that it is impossible for us to detail access arrangements for everywhere we list in the guide; neither can we detail the best and worst of the operators, and for more **information on disabled travel abroad** you should get in touch with the *Royal Association for Disability and Rehabilitation (RADAR)*, 25 Mortimer St, London W1N 8AB (☎071/637 5400), who publish their own guide to holidays and travel abroad, as well as being a good source of all kinds of information and advice. There's also *Mobility International*, 228 Borough High St, London SE1 1JX (☎071/403 5688), who put out a quarterly newsletter that keeps up-to-date with developments in disabled travel; and the *Holiday Care Service*, 2 Old Bank Chambers, Station Rd, Horley, Surrey RH6 9HW (☎0293/774535), who publish numerous fact sheets on disabled travel abroad and deal with all sorts of queries – they also run a useful "Holiday Helpers" service. *Mobility International* also have a North American office and are contactable at PO Box 3551, Eugene, OR 97403 (☎503/343-1284). Two **other publications** to look out for are *The World Wheelchair Traveller* (AA Publications), by Susan Abbott and Mary Ann Tyrrell, which includes basic hints and advice, and our own *Nothing Ventured: Disabled People Travel the World* , by Alison Walsh, which has practical advice as well as inspiring accounts of disabled travel worldwide.

WORK AND STUDY

The opportunities for working or studying your way around Europe are almost unlimited, especially for citizens of EC nations, who benefit from the easing of restrictions on the movement of labour. You can either fix something up before you leave home and build your trip around that, or simply look out for casual labour on your travels, treating it as a way of topping up your vacation cash. Certainly the best way of discovering a country properly is to work there, learning the language if you can and discovering something about the culture. Study opportunities are a similarly good way of absorbing yourself in the local culture, but they invariably need to be fixed up in advance; check the quality newspapers for ads or contact one of the main organizations (listed below) direct.

If you're just looking to supplement your spending money while you're travelling, there are any number of jobs you can pick up on the road. It's normally not hard to pick up **bar or restaurant work**, especially in large resort areas during the summer, and your chances will be greater if you can speak the local language – although being able to speak English may be your greatest asset in the more touristy areas; you may be asked for documentation, in which case you're better off in an EC member-state, but it's unlikely. Don't be afraid to march straight in and ask, or check the noticeboards in local bars, hostels or colleges, or the local newspapers, particularly the English-language ones. Cleaning jobs, nannying and **au pair** work are also common, if not spectacularly well-paid, often just providing room and board plus pocket money, and are something you can either fix up on the spot or before you leave home. If you're staying in a place for a while, you can always place an ad or a notice yourself offering your services. The other big casual earner is farmwork, particularly **grape-picking**, which is an option in the August–October period when the vines are being harvested. The best country for this is easily France, but there's sometimes work in Germany too. Once again, you're unlikely to be asked for any kind of documentation. Also in France, along the Côte d'Azur, and in other yacht-havens like Greece and parts of southern Spain, there is sometimes **crewing** work available, though you'll obviously need some sailing experience. If this isn't up your street but you want something active to last the whole summer, tour operators are often on the lookout for **travel couriers**, though this is something better arranged from home. If you're really serious, get in touch with the companies that run bus tours for young people around Europe, who are often keen to take on new blood.

Rather better-paid, and equally widespread, if only during the September to June period, is teaching **English as a Foreign Language** (TEFL), which is something you normally (though not exclusively) need to fix up from home. Everyone is desperate to learn English right now, all over Europe, and there is plenty of this kind of work available, especially in southern Europe; you don't need to be a qualified teacher, though they may ask for some kind of TEFL qualification. Contracts are obviously longer, and you should bear in mind that if you do organize something on the spot you may have to leave the country while your employers apply for a work permit. You'll normally be paid a liveable local salary, sometimes with somewhere to live thrown in as well, and you can often supplement your income with much more lucrative private lessons. Incidentally, North Americans and Australasians might be interested to know that the TEFL teaching season is reversed in Britain, with plenty of work available during the summer in London and on the south coast for those with a little experience. It can be a good way of surviving the summer in Britain before moving on to the rest of Europe.

If you want to know more about working in Europe, a couple of **books** might come in handy: *Work your Way around the World* by Susan Griffiths (Vacation Work) and *Working Holidays*, a handbook put out by the Central Bureau for Educational Visits and Exchanges. You could also get hold of a copy of David Woodworth's *Summer Jobs Abroad* (Vacation Work), which has details of places you could try before leaving home.

Studying abroad invariably means learning a language, doing an intensive course that lasts between two weeks and three months and staying with a local family. There are plenty of places you can do this, and you should reckon on paying around £200 a week including room and board – though there are lots of options; contact the Central Bureau for full details. If you know a language well, you could also apply to do a short course in another subject at a local university; once again, scan the classified sections of the newspapers back home, and keep an eye out when you're on the spot.

USEFUL ADDRESSES

Central Bureau for Educational Visits and Exchanges, Seymour Mews House, Seymour Mews, London W1H 9PE (☎071/486 5101). The chief coordinating body in the UK for working holidays, offering advice and information on every aspect of employment abroad.

Council on International Educational Exchanges, 205 E 42nd St, New York, NY 10017 (☎212/661-1414). Worth contacting for advice on studying in Europe.

Helping Hands, 39 Rutland Avenue, Thorpe Bay, Essex SS1 2JX (☎0702/602067). Au pair agency with opportunities all over Europe.

DIRECTORY

Bargaining The only places where you need really do any bargaining when shopping are in Turkey – in the bazaars and carpet shops – and in the souks of Morocco. Everywhere else, even in the less developed parts of southern Italy and Greece, people would think it odd if you tried to haggle.

Contraceptives Condoms are available everywhere, and are normally reliable international brands like *Durex*, at least in northwestern Europe; the condoms in eastern European countries are of uncertain quality, however – best stock up in advance. The Pill is available everywhere, too, though often only on prescription; again, bring a sufficient supply.

Electric current The supply all over Europe is 220v, which means that anything on North American voltage needs an adaptor. A travel plug is also a useful thing to carry, since it adapts to most European systems.

Kids Travelling with kids is easy enough everywhere, although you'll find a marked difference in attitudes to them between northern and southern Europe. In the north you'll find people rather indifferent to children, sometimes worse – an attitude epitomized in Britain where they're regarded as something of a nuisance in public places, and barred from entry altogether to pubs, some restaurants, even some hotels. In the southern European nations, however – Italy, Spain, Turkey – children are by contrast much revered and made a fuss of in public, and, although you'll sometimes pay extra for them in hotels, they are never refused, even in restaurants or cafés. Indeed, the only problem with travelling with kids in southern Europe may be the summer heat and sun.

Left luggage Almost every train station of any size has facilities for left luggage, either lockers or a desk that's open long hours every day. We've given details in the major capital accounts.

Shops Opening hours vary from northern to southern Europe. Those in the north open Monday–Friday all day without a break (sometimes opening late one evening midweek), opening for at least half a day on Saturday and closing on Sunday almost everywhere. In the south they tend to take a break at lunchtime, during the hottest part of the day, and open again around 4pm until perhaps 8pm. They are again generally open until at least Saturday lunchtime and closed on Sunday.

Tampons In southern and western Europe you can buy tampons in all chemists and supermarkets, although in parts of eastern Europe they can still be hard to come by. If you're travelling in the east for any length of time, best bring a supply.

Time Apart from a couple of weeks in March and October, Britain is normally one hour behind the rest of Europe, two hours in the case of Greece and Turkey. Most of the countries of western Europe are five hours ahead of Eastern Standard Time, eight hours ahead of Pacific Standard Time – again add an extra hour for Greece and Turkey. Australia is between eight and ten hours ahead of Greenwich Mean Time; New Zealand is twelve hours ahead.

Tipping Although it varies from one country to the next, tipping is not really the serious business it is in North America, but in many countries it is customary to leave at least something in most restaurants and cafés, if only rounding the bill up to the next major denomination. Even in swankier establishments, a 10 percent tip is quite sufficient, and you shouldn't feel obliged to tip at all if the service was bad, certainly not if service has been included in the bill. In smarter hotels you should tip hall porters, etc.

Travel agents Most of the larger European cities have a youth/student travel specialist which is a good source of *BIJ* tickets, cheap air fares, ISIC cards, etc. We've listed the best ones throughout the text.

War Cemeteries Allied war cemeteries from both world conflicts span the continent. For information and a full list contact the Commonwealth War Graves Commission, 2 Marlow Rd, Maidenhead, Berkshire SL6 7DX (☎0628/34221).

LANGUAGE

If you're making a general tour of Europe you can't hope always to speak the language of the country you're travelling in, and in any case in Germany, Scandinavia, and especially the Netherlands and Switzerland, many people, particularly the young, speak reasonable English. That said, it is polite to know at least a few very basic words and phrases wherever you happen to be, which is why we've included the chart below, and a smattering of French or German is handy everywhere as a common language if English fails.

Perhaps the best series of **phrasebooks** you can buy are those published by Harrap in Britain, in North America by Prentice Hall. Both companies also publish a useful series of **dictionaries** to Europe's major tongues, both in pocket-size paperback form – useful as a touring reference – and much larger, more academic versions. If you want to get to grips further with any of the languages, Routledge's "Colloquial" series is the best place you could start.

GERMAN, FRENCH AND DUTCH

	German	French	Dutch
Yes	Ja	Oui	Ja
No	Nein	Non	Nee
Please	Bitte	S'il vous plaît	Alstublieft
Thank you	Danke	Merci	Dank u/Bedankt
Hello/Good Day	Güten Tag	Bonjour	Dag
Goodbye	Auf Wiedersehen	Au revoir	Tot ziens
Excuse me	Entschuldigen Sie, bitte	Pardon	Pardon
Where	Wo	Où	Waar
When	Wann	Quand	Wanneer
How	Wie	Comment	Hoe
Left	Links	Gauche	Links
Right	Rechts	Droite	Rechts
Large	Gross	Grand	Groot
Small	Klein	Petit	Klein
Good	Gut	Bon	Goed
Bad	Schlecht	Mauvais	Slecht
Near	Nah	Près	Dichtbij
Far	Weit	Loin	Ver
Cheap	Billig	Bon marché	Goedkoop
Expensive	Teuer	Cher	Duur
Open	Offen	Ouvert	Open
Closed	Geschlossen	Fermé	Dicht
Today	Heute	Aujourd'hui	Vandaag
Yesterday	Gestern	Hier	Gisteren
Tomorrow	Morgen	Demain	Morgen
Day	Tag	Jour	Dag
Week	Woche	Semaine	Week
Month	Monat	Mois	Maand
Year	Jahr	Année	Jaar
How much is....?	Wieviel kostet....?	Combien est...?	Wat kost....?
What time is it?	Wieviel Uhr ist es?	Quelle heure est-il?	Hoe laat is het?
Where is...?	Wo ist...?	Où est...?	Waar is...?
I don't understand	Ich verstehe nicht	Je ne comprends pas	Ik begrijp het niet
Do you speak English?	Sprechen Sie Englisch?	Parlez-vous anglais?	Spreekt u Engels?
Please write it down	Bitte schreiben Sie es	Veuillez me l'écrire	Wilt u het opschrijven, alstublieft
One	Eins	Un	Een
Two	Zwei	Deux	Twee
Three	Drei	Trois	Drie
Four	Vier	Quatre	Vier
Five	Fünf	Cinq	Vijf
Six	Sechs	Six	Zes
Seven	Sieben	Sept	Zeven
Eight	Acht	Huit	Acht
Nine	Neun	Neuf	Negen
Ten	Zehn	Dix	Tien

BULGARIAN, CZECH AND DANISH

	Bulgarian	Czech	Danish
Yes	Da	Ano	Ja
No	Ne	Ne	Nej
Please	Molya	Procím	Vaerså venlig
Thank you	Blagodarya	Děkuju	Tak
Hello/Good Day	Dobâr den	Dobry den/ahoj	Goddag
Goodbye	Dovizhdane	Na shledanou	Farvel
Excuse me	Izvinyavaïte	Promiňte	Undskyld
Where	Kude	Kde	Hvor
When	Koga	Kdy	Hvornår
How	Kak	Jak	Hvordan
Left	Lyavo	Vlevo	Venstre
Right	Dyasno	Vpravo	Højre
Large	Golyama	Velký	Stor
Small	Malko	Maly	Lille
Good	Dobro	Dobry	God
Bad	Plosho	Spatny	Dårlig
Near	Blizo	Blízko	Naer
Far	Daleche	Daleko	Fjern
Cheap	Eftino	Levný	Billig
Expensive	Skupo	Drahý	Dyr
Open	Otvoreno	Otevřeno	Åben
Closed	Zatvoreno	Zavřeno	Lukket
Today	Dnes	Dnes	I dag
Yesterday	Vechera	Včera	I går
Tomorrow	Utre	Zítra	I morgen
Day	Den	Den	Dag
Week	Sedmitza	Tyden	Uge
Month	Mesetz	Mesíc	Måned
Year	Godina	Rok	År
How much is....?	Kolko...?	Kolík stojí...?	Hvor koster er...?
What time is it?	Kolko e chasut?	Kolík je hodin?	Hvad er klokken?
Where is...?	Kude e	Kde je...?	Hvor er...?
I don't understand	Ne vi razbiram	Nerozumím	Jeg forstår ikke
Do you speak English?	Govorite li Angliski?	Miuvíte Anglicky?	Taler de Engelsk?
Please write it down	Molya napishete go	Prosím, napište to	Vaer venlig at skrive det
One	Edin	Jeden	En
Two	Dve	Dva	To
Three	Tri	Tri	Tre
Four	Chetiri	Ctyri	Fire
Five	Pet	Pet	Fem
Six	Shest	Sest	Seks
Seven	Sedem	Sedm	Syv
Eight	Osem	Osum	Otte
Nine	Devet	Devet	Ni
Ten	Deset	Deset	Ti

FINNISH, GREEK AND HUNGARIAN

	Finnish	Greek	Hungarian
Yes	Kyllä	Néh	Igen
No	Ei	Óhi	Nem
Please	Olkaa hyvä	Parakaló	Kérem
Thank you	Kiitos	Efharistó	Köszönöm
Hello/Good Day	Hyvää	Adío	Szia
Goodbye	Hyvästi	Hérete	Szia
Excuse me	Anteeksi	Signómi	Bocsánat
Where	Missä	Pou	Hol
When	Milloin	Póte	Mikor
How	Kuinka	Pos	Hogyan
Left	Vasen	Aristerá	Balra
Right	Oikea	Dheksiá	Jobbra
Large	Suuri	Megálo	Nagy
Small	Pieni	Mikró	Kicsi
Good	Hyvä	Kaló	Jó
Bad	Paha	Kakó	Rossz
Near	Lähellä	Kondá	Közel
Far	Kaukana	Makriá	Távol
Cheap	Halpa	Fthinós	Olcsó
Expensive	Kallis	Akrivós	Drága
Open	Avoin	Aniktós	Nyitva
Closed	Suljettu	Klistós	Zárva
Today	Tänään	Símera	Ma
Yesterday	Eilen	Khthés	Tegnap
Tomorrow	Huomenna	Ávrio	Holnap
Day	Päivä	Méra	Nap
Week	Viiko	Iméra	Hét
Month	Kuukausi	Evdomáda	Hónap
Year	Vuosi	Chrónos	Ev
How much is....?	Kuinka paljon on ...?	Póso káni...?	Mennyibe Kerül...?
What time is it?	Paljonko kello on?	Ti óra inai...?	Hány óra?
Where is...?	Missä on...?	Pou íne...?	Hol van?
I don't understand	En ymmärrä	Dhen katalavéno	Nem értem
Do you speak English?	Puhutteko Englantia?	Ksérite Angliká?	Beszél Angolul?
Please write it down	Olkaa hyvä ja karjoitta-kaa se	Parakaló grápiste to	Legyen szives, irja le
One	Yksi	Éna	Egy
Two	Kaksi	Dhío	Kettö
Three	Kolme	Tría	Három
Four	Neljä	Téseres	Négy
Five	Viisi	Pénde	Ot
Six	Kuusi	Éksi	Hayt
Seven	Seitsemän	Eftá	Hét
Eight	Kahdeksan	Októ	Nyolc
Nine	Yhdeksän	Enyá	Kilenc
Ten	Kymmenen	Dhéka	Tíz

ITALIAN, NORWEGIAN AND POLISH

	Italian	Norwegian	Polish
Yes	Si	Ja	Tak
No	No	Nei	Nie
Please	Per favore	Vaer så god	Prosze
Thank you	Grazie	Takk	Dziekuje
Hello/Good Day	Ciao/buon giorno	God dag	Dzien dobry
Goodbye	Ciao/arriverderci	Adjø	Do widzenia
Excuse me	Mi scusi/prego	Unnskyld	Przepraszam
Where	Dove	Hvor	Gdzie
When	Quando	Når	Kiedy
How	Come	Hvordan	Jak
Left	Sinistra	Venstre	Na lewo
Right	Destra	Høyre	Na prawo
Large	Grande	Stor	Wielki
Small	Piccolo	Liten	Maly
Good	Buono	God	Dobry
Bad	Cattivo	Dårlig	Zly
Near	Vicino	I naerheten	Blisko
Far	Lontano	Langt Borte	Daleko
Cheap	Buon mercato	Billig	Tani
Expensive	Caro	Dyr	Drogi
Open	Aperto	Åpen	Otwarty
Closed	Chiuso	Lukket	Zamknięty
Today	Oggi	I dag	Dzisiaj
Yesterday	Ieri	I går	Wczoraj
Tomorrow	Domani	I morgen	Jutro
Day	Giorno	Dag	Dzień
Week	Settimana	Uke	Tydzień
Month	Mese	Måned	Miesiąc
Year	Anno	År	Rok
How much is....?	Quanto è...?	Hvor mye er...?	Lle Losztuje...?
What time is it?	Che ore sono?	Hvor mange er klokken?	Która godzina?
Where is...?	Dov'è...?	Hvor er...?	Gdzie jest . . . ?
I don't understand	Non ho capito	Jeg forstår ikke	Nie rozemiem
Do you speak English?	Parla Inglese?	Snakker de Englesk?	Pani mówi po Angielsku?
Please write it down	Lo scriva, per favore	Vennligst skriv det ned?	Proszę to napisać
One	Uno	En	Jeden
Two	Due	To	Dwa
Three	Tre	Tre	Trzy
Four	Quattro	Fire	Cztery
Five	Cinque	Fem	Piec
Six	Sei	Seks	Szesc
Seven	Sette	Sju	Siedem
Eight	Otto	Åtte	Osiem
Nine	Nove	Ni	Dziewiec
Ten	Dieci	Ti	Dziesiec

PORTUGUESE, ROMANIAN AND SPANISH

	Portuguese	Romanian	Spanish
Yes	Sim	Da	Si
No	Não	Nu	No
Please	Por favor	Vă rog	Por favor
Thank you	Obrigado	Mulţumesc	Gracias
Hello/Good Day	Olá	Salut/Buna ziua	Holá
Goodbye	Adeus	La revedere	Adiós
Excuse me	Desculpe	Permiteţi-mi	Con permiso
Where	Onde	Unde	Dónde
When	Quando	Cînd	Cuándo
How	Como	Cum	Cómo
Left	Esquerda	Stînga	Izquierda
Right	Direita	Dreapta	Derecha
Large	Grande	Mare	Gran
Small	Pequeno	Mic	Pequeno
Good	Bom	Bun/Bîne	Buen
Bad	Mau	Rău	Mal
Near	Perto	Apropriat	Próximo
Far	Longe	Departe	Lejos
Cheap	Barato	Ieftin	Barato
Expensive	Caro	Scump	Caro
Open	Aberto	Închis	Abierto
Closed	Fechado	Deschis	Cerrado
Today	Hoje	Azi	Hoy
Yesterday	Ontem	Ieri	Ayer
Tomorrow	Amanhã	Mîine	Mañana
Day	Dia	Zi	Día
Week	Semana	Săptămînă	Semana
Month	Mês	Lună	Mes
Year	Ano	An	Año
How much is....?	Quanto e... ?	Cît costa...?	Cuánto costa...?
What time is it?	Que horas sao?	Ce ora este?	Tiene la hora?
Where is...?	Onde é...?	Unde este...?	Dónde estar...?
I don't understand	Não comprendo	Nu înteleg	No entiendo
Do you speak English?	Fala Inglés?	Vorbiţi Englezeste?	Habla Inglés?
Please write it down	Escreva-mo, por favor	Vă rog scrieţi	Escríbamelo, por favor?
One	Um	Unu	Un
Two	Dois	Doi	Dos
Three	Três	Trei	Tres
Four	Quatro	Patru	Cuatro
Five	Cinco	Cinci	Cinco
Six	Seis	Sase	Seis
Seven	Sete	Sapte	Siete
Eight	Oito	Opt	Ocho
Nine	Nove	Noua	Nueve
Ten	Dez	Zece	Diez

SWEDISH AND TURKISH

	Swedish	Turkish
Yes	Ja	Evet
No	Nej	Yok
Please	Var så god	Lütfen
Thank you	Tack	Tesekkür ederim
Hello/Good Day	Hej	Merhaba
Goodbye	Adjö	Allahaismarladik
Excuse me	Ursäkta mig	Pardon
Where	Var	... nerede
When	När	Ne zaman
How	Hur	Nasıl
Left	Vänster	Sol
Right	Höger	Sag
Large	Stor	Büyuk
Small	Liten	Kücük
Good	Bra	Iyi
Bad	Dalig	Kötü
Near	Nära	Yakin
Far	Avlägsen	Uzak
Cheap	Billig	Ucuz
Expensive	Dyr	Pahalı
Open	Öppen	Açık
Closed	Stängd	Kapalı
Today	I dag	Bugün
Yesterday	I går	Dün
Tomorrow	I morgon	Yarin
Day	Dag	Gün
Week	Vecka	Hafta
Month	Månad	Ay
Year	Är	Sene
How much is....?	Vad kostar det...?	Ne kadar...?
What time is it?	Hur mycket är klockan?	Saatiniz var mi?
Where is...?	Var är...?	Nerede...?
I don't understand	Jag förstår int	Anlamadim
Do you speak English?	Talar ni Engelska?	Ingilizce Biliyormusunuz?
Please write it down	Skulle ni kunna skriva det?	Onu yazarmısınız
One	Ett	Bir
Two	Två	Iki
Three	Tre	Uç
Four	Fyra	Dört
Five	Fem	Bes
Six	Sex	Alti
Seven	Sju	Yedi
Eight	Ätta	Sekiz
Nine	Nio	Dokuz
Ten	Tio	On

CLOTHING AND SHOE SIZES

Dresses

British	10	12	14	16	18	20
American	8	10	12	14	16	18
Continental	40	42	44	46	48	50

Men's suits

British	36	38	40	42	44	46
American	36	38	40	42	44	46
Continental	46	48	52	54	56	58

Men's shirts

British	14	15	16	17	18
American	14	15	16	17	18
Continental	36	38	41	43	45

Women's shoes

British	3	4	5	6	7	8
American	4	5	6	7	8	9
Continental	36	37	38	39	40	41

Men's shoes

British	6	7	8	9	10	11
American	7	8	9	10	11	12
Continental	39	40	41	42	43	44

Please note all sizes/equivalents are approximations only.

PART TWO

THE

GUIDE

CHAPTER 1

AUSTRIA

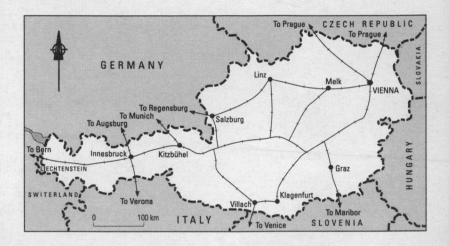

Introduction

For centuries the heart of an empire which played a pivotal role in the political and cultural destiny of continental Europe, **Austria** underwent several decades of change and uncertainty in this century – the interwar state, racked by economic problems and the slow-burning strife between right and left, falling prey to the promise of a greater Germany. But the postwar period of stability has seen the growth of a genuine patriotism, and nowadays Austrians tend to look across the frontier towards their German cousins with a mixture of amusement and condescension. The ending of the Cold War in Europe has enabled the renewal of contacts with its once-communist neighbours, and has once again put the country, and its capital Vienna, back at the heart of Europe.

The ethos of Austrian society is solidly bourgeois, although the Socialist party has been the strongest influence in government over past decades, and despite endless scandals, and the deep divisions created by the Waldheim controversy, an almost Scandinavian emphasis on social policy continues to be the guiding principle of national life. It's a consensus which derives to some extent from the current political stalemate, the Socialists sharing power with their conservative rivals in a so-called Grand Coalition ever since 1986. Neither is strong enough to live without the other, and neither wants to rock the boat to an extent that could benefit the small but vocal ultra-right Freedom Party.

Austria is primarily known for two widely contrasting attractions – the fading Imperial glories of its capital Vienna and the variety of its Alpine hinterland. **Vienna** is the gateway to much of central Europe and a good place for soaking up the culture of *Mitteleuropa* before heading towards the Magyar and Slav lands over which the city once held sway. Less renowned provincial capitals like **Graz** and **Linz** provide a similar level of culture and vitality. The most dramatic of Austria's Alpine scenery is west of here, in and around the **Tirol**, the local capital **Innsbruck** providing the best base for exploration. **Salzburg**, however, between Innsbruck and Vienna, represents urban Austria at its most picturesque, an intoxicating Baroque city, within easy striking distance of the mountains and lakes of the **Salzkammergut** to the east.

Information and Maps

Tourist offices are plentiful and come under an assortment of names, often just *Information, Verkehrsamt, Fremdenverkehrsverein* or other similar variants. All are helpful and well-organized, often hand out free maps and almost always book accommodation, sometimes for a small fee, a deposit, or both. Opening hours are all day every day in the larger cities during the summer; outside this period, and in smaller towns and remote areas, times may be restricted to a few hours on weekday mornings. Most *ÖBB* (Austrian Railways) stations now contain a travel bureau, primarily for rail enquiries but usually happy to hand out general information as well.

There are plenty of good general **maps** of Austria, one of the best the 1:500,000 *Freytag & Berndt*. The 1:200,000 *Generalkarte* series of regional maps are useful for lengthier touring, as are the more detailed 1:50,000 *Freytag & Berndt Wanderkarten* and rival *Kompas Wanderkarten*, both covering all the Alpine districts and many rural eastern areas as well.

Money and Banks

Austria's unit of **currency** is the *Schilling*, which is divided into 100 *gröschen*. There are coins for 5, 10 and 50 Gröschen, 1, 5, 10 and 20 Schillings; notes for 20, 50, 100, 500 and 1000 Schillings. Prices are usually preceded by the initials S or ÖS.

Banking hours tend to be Mon–Fri 7.45am–12.30pm and 2.15–4pm; in Vienna they're Mon–Wed and Fri 8am–3pm, Thurs 8am–5.30pm (smaller Viennese branches take an hour for lunch). Post offices charge slightly less commission on exchange transactions than banks do, and in larger cities are open longer hours.

Communications

Most **post offices** are open Mon–Fri 8am–noon and 2–6pm; in larger cities they do without the lunch break and open Sat 8–10am as well, or sometimes 24 hours. You can also buy stamps at tobacconists (*Tabak*).

ÖS1 is the smallest coin accepted in public call boxes; a couple of these should suffice for a local call; insert ÖS10 and upwards if calling longer distance or buy a *Telefonkarte* from a *Tabak* and seek out a card phone. You can make international calls from all public telephones, but it's easier from larger post offices, which have booths. Some telephones still require the user to press a red button once connected, though these are gradually being phased out. The operator number is ☎16 for domestic calls, ☎09 for international.

Getting Around

Traversing Austria by public transport is easy, and usually very scenic. Rail services cover the country fairly comprehensively, supplemented in remoter regions by buses.

■ Trains and buses

Austrian Federal Railways – *Österreichische Bundesbahnen* or *ÖBB* – run a punctual, clean and comfortable rail network, which manages to include most towns of any size. Trains marked *EC* (International expresses), *SC* or *IC* (Austrian inter-city trains), or *D* (express) are the fastest. Those designated *E* (*Eilzug*) are "semi-fast trains" stopping at most intermediate points; the slowest, local services are designated by number only. Fares are calculated according to distance, with the first 100km costing ÖS128. If you don't have an *InterRail/Eurail* pass, it might be worth buying a monthly *Bundesnetzkarte*, which gives unlimited travel on the entire network for ÖS3100. Alternatively, there's the *Rabbit Card* (ÖS950, ÖS590 for under-27s), which entitles the holder to four days' unlimited travel within a ten-day period. The *Österreichische kursbuch* (timetable), detailing the whole network, with lake and Danube transport, costs ÖS70; or timetable leaflets covering major routes are free at stations.

Austria's *Bahn-* and *Post-bus* system fills the gaps in the rail network, serving the remoter villages and otherwise inaccessible Alpine valleys. Where there is a choice, you will find trains easier and quicker, and bus fares are only slightly cheaper at ÖS112 per 100km. As a general rule, *Bahnbus* services, operated by *ÖBB*, depart from outside train stations; the *Postbus* tends to stop outside the post office.

■ Driving, hitching, cycling

Given the deals available on Austria's rail system, **driving** is not a budget option, but if you do, Austria's speed limits are 50kph in built-up areas, 100kph on normal roads, and 130kph on motor-

ways. If you break down, the *Österreichischer Automobile, Motorrad und Touring Club* has a 24-hour breakdown service (☎120). **Car rental** charges are around ÖS700 per day with unlimited mileage with the multinationals, although you may land something cheaper with smaller local firms. You need to be over 21 to rent a car.

Hitching can be difficult away from the main east–west routes, and many locals make use of the *Mitfahrzentrale*, an agency which puts potential hitchers in touch with drivers willing to take passengers for a fee – usually significantly cheaper than public transport.

Austria is very **bicycle**-friendly, with bike lanes in all major towns. All except the smallest train stations rent out bikes for ÖS80 per day, ÖS40 if you have a valid ticket. You can return them to any station.

Accommodation

Despite profiteering in tourist centres like Vienna and Salzburg, accommodation need not be expensive in Austria, and, although it can be a scramble in July and August, finding a room generally doesn't present too many problems. Most tourist offices book accommodation with little fuss, usually for a fee (around ÖS30) and deposit.

■ Hotels, pensions and private rooms

A high standard of cleanliness and comfort can usually be taken for granted in all Austrian **hotels**, although in resorts and larger towns prices can be high. Expect to pay ÖS600–800 for a double with bathroom, slightly less for rooms without private facilities. There is, however, usually good-value **bed and breakfast** accommodation available in the many small family-run hotels, known as *Gasthöfe* and *Gasthaüser*, with prices starting at ÖS400–500 for a double, and **pensions** situated in large apartment blocks offer similar prices in the larger towns and cities. Most (though not all) tourist offices also have a stock of **private rooms**, although in well-travelled rural areas where the locals depend a great deal on tourism, roadside signs offering *Zimmer frei* are fairly ubiquitous anyway. Prices hover around the ÖS300–400 mark for double rooms.

■ Hostels and student accommodation

Youth hostels (*Jugendherberge*) are fairly widespread in Austria, with around 100 in all, although

---

ACCOMMODATION PRICE CODES

Throughout this guide, accommodation is priced on a scale of ① to ⑧, the number indicating the lowest price per night a single person could expect to pay in that establishment in high season. With hostels this is the nightly rate per person; with hotels, the price is arrived at by dividing the cost of the cheapest double room by two. The prices indicated by the codes are as follows

①= under £5 / $8   ②= £5–10 / $8–16   ③= £10–15 / $16–24   ④= £15–20 / $24–32

⑤= £20–25 / $32–40   ⑥= £25–30 / $40–48   ⑦= £30–35 / $48–56   ⑧= over £35 / $56

---

standards vary, from the hearty and basic rural variety to swish, well-appointed (but crowded) hostels of the larger cities. Rates are ÖS100–170, normally including breakfast; some won't accept non-*IYHF* members. Sheet sleeping bags are obligatory, although the cost of hiring one is often included in the overnight charge. Many hostels serve other meals besides breakfast, for ÖS45–60. For more details, contact the *Österreichisches Jugendherbergswerk*, at Helferstorferstrasse 4, 1010 Wien (☎0222/533 18 33). In Vienna you may encounter **student accommodation**, made available for tourists during the summer vacation and operating under the name of *Rosenhotels* – though this is often too expensive to qualify as a true budget alternative.

■ Camping

Austria's high standards of accommodation are reflected in the country's **campsites**, the vast majority of which have laundry facilities, shops and snack bars, as well as the standard necessities. Most are open May–Sept, although a great many in the winter sports resorts of western Austria never close. Expect to pay about ÖS40–60 per person, ÖS30–60 per pitch, plus ÖS30–60 for a vehicle.

Food and Drink

Foodstuffs in Austria are more expensive than in EC countries, which for once makes eating out a marginally cheaper business than self-catering. Drinking, too, while never cheap, is affordable, and the country's bars and cafés are among its real joys.

■ Food

For ready-made snacks, try a *Konditorei* or confectioner's, which sell sweet pastries and cakes, as well as sandwiches. **Street food** centres around

the ubiquitous *Würstelstand*, which sells hot dogs, *Bratwurst* (grilled sausage), *Käsekrainer* (spicy sausage with cheese), *Bosna* (spicy beef sausage) or *Currywurst*, usually chopped up and served with a *Semmel* or bread roll, along with a *Dose* (can) of beer. *Schnell-Imbiss* or *Bufet* establishments serve similar snack fare, augmented by hamburgers and simple grills.

As for **sit-down food**, it's difficult to make hard distinctions between places to eat and places to drink, and most establishments offer snacks and main meals of some kind. Similarly, it's possible to just have a drink in most restaurants. Town centre *Kaffehaüser* or cafés tend to be the most expensive places to eat, while food served in bars can be very cheap. Light meals and snacks include pizzas from about ÖS50; and more traditional central European fare such as spicy *Serbische bohnensuppe* (Serbian bean soup) and *Gulaschsuppe* (goulash soup), both more substantial than they sound, and regular standbys on all restaurant and café menus for around ÖS30. Main dishes (*Hauptspeisen*) are dominated by veal – *Schnitzel* – often accompanied by potatoes and a vegetable or salad: *Wienerschnitzel* is fried in breadcrumbs, *Pariser* in batter, *Natur* on its own or with a creamy sauce. In general you can expect to pay ÖS80–120 for a standard main course, though lunchtime menus (*Mittagsmenü*), even in more costly establishments, always offer a wide range of cheaper dishes. Desserts (*Mehlspeisen*) include a wide range of sweets and pastries: various types of *Torte* (including the famous rich chocolate *Sachertorte*), *Apfelstrudel*, *Topfenstrudel* or cheesecake, and *Palatschinken* or pancakes, with various nut or jam fillings, are all common.

■ Drink

For urban Austrians, daytime drinking traditionally centres around the *Kaffeehaus* or **café** – relaxed old places furnished with a stock of the day's newspapers. They serve alcoholic and soft drinks, snacks and cakes, alongside a wide range of different coffees: a *Schwarzer* is small and black, a *Brauner* comes with a little milk, while a *Melange* is half coffee and half milk; a *Kurzer* is a small espresso; an *Einspänner* is a glass of black coffee topped with *Schlag*, the ubiquitous whipped cream that is offered with most pastries and cakes. A cup of coffee in a *Kaffeehaus* is, however, pricy at ÖS20–35, and numerous stand-up **coffee bars** (many part of the *Julius Meinl* or *Eduscho* chains) are a much cheaper alternative at ÖS8 a cup. Night-time drinking centres around a growing number of youthful **bars** and *Musikaffees*, although more traditional *Bierstuben* and *Weinstuben* are still thick on the ground, especially in rural areas. Austrian **beers**, while of a high standard, don't come in the infinite variety found in Germany. Most establishments serve the local brew on tap, either by the *Krügel* (half-litre, for around ÖS30) or the *Seidel* (third-litre, ÖS20–25), while also keeping a few international speciality brews in bottles. Wine, usually sold by the *Viertel* or quarter-litre, is often cheaper than other alcoholic drinks and widely consumed. The *Weinkeller* is a regular sight in Austrian towns and cities; around Vienna wine is consumed in a *Heuriger*, a traditional tavern in the vine-producing suburbs, customarily serving cold food as well. In autumn a lot of establishments serve *Sturm*, a misty, part-fermented concoction made from newly harvested grapes.

Opening Hours and Holidays

Most **shops** open Mon–Fri 9am–6pm, Sat 9am–noon. Beware of a two-hour lunch break outside major cities, and remember that everything is closed on Saturday afternoons. There are few opportunities for late-night shopping, save for basic provision stores in the larger train stations. All shops and banks will be closed on the following **public holidays**, and most museums will at least have reduced hours: Jan 1; Jan 6; Easter Monday; May 1; Ascension; Whit Monday; Corpus Christi; Aug 15; Oct 26; Nov 1; Dec 8; Dec 25 & 26.

Emergencies

Although the traditionally laid-back Austrians lack the reverence for rules and regulations shared by their German and Swiss cousins, the country is still extremely law-abiding by European standards, and is a reasonably safe place to travel. This doesn't prevent the tabloids from complaining about the increase in urban **crime**, an attitude tinged with xenophobia: Vienna in particular is suffering a rise in petty offences which the political right attributes to Austria's status as first stop on the route westward for opportunity-seeking East Europeans. Austrian **police** have a leisurely but efficient attitude to complaints, and all but the most harassed inner-city cop can be relied upon to be courteous to strangers. There are few places where female travellers will feel ill at ease, some outer districts of Vienna and Graz being notable exceptions. Remember that hitting children is technically illegal in Austria. Although everyone agrees that this is practically unenforceable, it would seem a good idea to resist the temptation to spank the little ones in public.

As for **health**, if you find yourself in need of medical treatment city hospital casualty departments will treat you and ask questions later. For prescriptions, pharmacies or *Apotheke* tend to follow normal shopping hours. A rota system covers night-time and weekend opening; each pharmacy has details of those open posted up in the window.

EMERGENCY NUMBERS
Police ☎133; ambulance ☎144; fire ☎122.

VIENNA

Most newcomers to **VIENNA** arrive with a firm image of the city already in their minds: a romantic place, full of Habsburg nostalgia and musical resonances. On a visual level it's unlikely to disappoint, an eclectic feast of architectural styles, from the high Baroque of the eighteenth century, through the monumental imperial projects of the nineteenth, to more recent experiments with modernism and enlightened municipal planning. However, the capital often seems to stand aloof from the rest of the country. Alpine Austrians look askance at Vienna, considering it an alien, eastern metropolis with an impenetrable dialect, staffed by an army of ineffectual, fund-draining bureaucrats. The city has had a tough time of it in this century, an imperial city, once at the centre of things, deprived of its hinterland by World War I, then washed up on the edges of western Europe by the arbitrary divisions which followed the last war. In a sense it's been in decline since the end of the empire, its population dropping by a quarter since 1910, its image one of melancholy and decay – though the latter is perhaps more romantic affectation than a realistic portrait of the city.

The first settlement of any substance here, Roman Vindobona, was never much more than a garrison town, and it was only with the rise of the Babenberg clan, awarded stewardship of the Ostmark by Holy Roman Emperor Otto II in the tenth century, that Vienna became an important centre, straddling the political and cultural crosscurrents of central Europe. With the eclipse of the Babenbergs, Vienna fell briefly under Bohemian influence, but with their defeat by Rudolf of Habsburg in 1278 the city was dragged back into the heart of European life. With the increasing association between the House of Habsburg and the Holy Roman Empire Vienna flourished, but had initially to compete with the likes of Prague, Linz and Graz as the imperial residence. The Turks, who first laid siege to the city under Suleyman the Magnificent in 1529, rendered Vienna constantly vulnerable, and it was only with the final removal of the Turkish threat in 1683 that the city was finally free to flourish. The court based itself here, and the great aristocratic families of the empire, many of them grown fat on the profits of the Turkish wars, flooded in to build palaces and summer residences in a frenzied period of construction that gave Vienna its Baroque character.

Despite the obvious ethnic and linguistic affinities, imperial Vienna was never a German city: the dynasty had a supranational identity and its capital epitomized the cosmopolitan nature of the empire, attracting great minds from all over central Europe. During the last imperial days the city was a breeding ground for the ideological movements of the age: nationalism, socialism, Zionism anti-Semitism all flourished here before going on to assume more extreme forms elsewhere. This turbulence was reflected in the cultural sphere, too, and the ghosts of Freud, Klimt, Schiele and Schoenberg are nowadays bigger tourist draws than old standbys like the Lippizaner horses and the Vienna Boys Choir. There is, however, more to Vienna than *fin-de-siècle* decadence, and a strong, home-grown, youthful culture, coupled with new influences from previously Iron Curtain-bound neighbours, is making it once again a city genuinely at the heart of contemporary European cultural life.

The Vienna area telephone code is ☎ 0222.

Arrival and information

Trains from the west terminate at the **Westbahnhof**, situated on the Gürtel 2km away from the centre at the top of Mariahilferstrasse, Vienna's brashest shopping street; from here trams #52 and #58 run to the Ringstrasse, which girdles the city centre. Trains

To the Freud Museum

OBERE DONAUSTRASSE

TABORSTRASSE

To Wien-Nord and the Prater

Nestroyplatz

PRATERSTRASSE

Danube Canal

FRANZ JOSEFS-KAI

Bermuda Triangle

Schwedenplatz

FLEISCHMARKT

To the Hundertwasserheus

VIENNA

ROTENTURMSTRASSE

STUBENRING

MARXERGASSE

Postsparkasse

Diocesian Museum

TUCHLAUBEN

Stephansdom

Jesuiten Kirche

WOLLZEILE

Stephansplatz

STEPHENSPL.

GRABEN

DOROTHEERGASSE

Stubentor

Figarohaus

SINGERSTRASSE

Wien-Mitte

LANDSTRASSER HAUPT

NEUER MKT

STRASSE

SEILER STÄTTE

PARKRING

Kaisergruft

Stadtpark

UNGARGASSE

Tourist Information

SCHWARZENBERGSTR.

KÄRNTNER STRASSE

SCHUBERTRING

PARKRING

AM HEUMARKT

Stadtpark

KÄRNTNER RING

AM HEUMARKT

Karlsplatz

Karlsplatz

SWARZENBERGPLATZ

Museum of the City of Vienna

Karlskirche

Soviet Monument

RENNWEG

To th Upper Belvedere & Südbahnhof

Lower Belvedere

0   200 m

from Hungary, Slovenia and stations south arrive at the **Südbahnhof**, 2km away from the centre; from here tram D goes down Prinz-Eugen-Strasse to Schwedenplatz and the Ring, or there's a *Schnellbahn* (suburban train) service to **Wien-Mitte**, a busy transport interchange just east of the Ring on Landstrasse Hauptstrasse. The city's **airport** is at Schwechat, 19km southeast; a regular bus (ÖS60) runs to the City Air Terminal under the *Hilton Hotel* every twenty minutes or so – a half-hour journey. Other buses run from the airport to both main train stations; there's also an hourly Schnellbahn rail service from the airport to Wien-Mitte. Taxis cost around ÖS350.

All points of arrival have **tourist kiosks** with accommodation booking facilities. In the city centre, the main **tourist office** is at Kärntnerstrasse 38 (daily 9am–7pm; ☎586 32 46) and has maps, brochures and a room booking service (ÖS35). There's also an **information centre** for young people at Bellariapassage (Mon–Fri noon–7pm, Sat 10am–7pm; ☎526 46 37), which sells tickets for gigs too.

City transport

Vienna is divided into numbered **districts** or *bezirke*. District 1 is the area enclosed by the Ringstrasse, the inner centre; districts 2–9 are arranged clockwise around it; beyond here, districts 10 and up are a fair way out from the city centre. All Viennese addresses begin with the number of the district, followed by the name of the street, and then the number of the house or building. So many of Vienna's attractions are within the *Innere Stadt*, or district 1, that you can do and see a great deal on foot. Otherwise **public transport** consists of a combination of **trams** – the Strassenbahn, colloquially known as *Bim* – buses, and the ultra-clean **metro** (U-Bahn), which has five lines, complemented by the Schnellbahn network of fast commuter trains. You're expected to buy your ticket in advance from the machines at station entrances and cancel it on board buses or on platforms. Fares are calculated on a zonal basis: tickets for the central zone (covering most of Vienna save the furthest suburbs) cost ÖS20 and allow any number of changes, on all modes of transport. If you're going to be using public transport a fair bit, invest in a *Netzkarte*, valid for 24 hours (ÖS45) or 72 hours (ÖS115); passes must be punched once at the beginning of the first journey. Be warned that penalties for fare-dodging are stiff. Public transport runs between 5am and midnight; at weekends, half-hourly **night buses** radiate out from Schwedenplatz. **Taxis** are notoriously difficult to hail; try the ranks outside the big hotels or main stations, or phone ☎313 00 or ☎601 60.

Accommodation

There's an abundance of **accommodation** in Vienna for those prepared to splash out. However, extreme pressure on the cheaper end of the market means that booking ahead is essential in summer, and advisable during the rest of the year. It's hard to find anything very affordable in the central area, and the cheapest double rooms within reach of the centre will set you back at least ÖS250 a head in lower-category hotels. The likeliest hunting grounds are in between the Ring and the Gürtel (districts 3–9); places here are often located on the upper floors of nineteenth-century apartment buildings, and have undeniable character. On more of a budget, Vienna's youth hostels are often full, especially during academic holidays.

The tourist offices can book **private rooms** for around ÖS300 per person (with a minimum stay of three nights), but these go quickly and are often in distant suburbs. You could also try the **Mitwohnzentrale**, 9. Kolingasse 6 (Mon–Fri 10am–6pm, Sat 10am–noon; ☎31 86 66), which tends to be a little cheaper and also offers weekly rates, or the nearby youth travel specialists *ÖKISTA*, at 9. Türkenstrasse 4–6 (Mon–Wed & Fri 9.30am–4pm, Thurs 9.30am–5.30pm; ☎34 75 26 23).

Hostels

City Hostel, 1. Seilerstätte 30 (☎512 79 23). A private hostel, open July–Sept, with no curfew. ②

Hostel Zöhrer, 8. Skodagasse 26 (☎43 07 30). A private hostel in a nice bit of town between the Ring and Gürtel. Tram #5 from U6 Josefstädter strasse. ②

Jugendgästehaus der Stadt Wien-Hütteldorf, 13. Schlossberggasse 8 (☎877 02 63). A bit far out, but pleasantly situated on the edge of Lainzer Tiergarten, and it does admit non-*IYHF* members for an extra fee. U4 to Hütteldorf. ②

Jugendgästehaus Wien-Brigittenau, 20. Friedrich-Engels-Platz 24 (☎332 82 94). The biggest and least atmospheric, but also the most likely hostel to have beds available. In a fairly unappealing part of town. U2 or U4 to Schottenring, then tram #31 or #32. Midnight curfew. ②

Jugendherberge Wien-Myrthengasse, 7. Myrthengasse 7 (☎523 63 16). The best of the bunch, conveniently placed between the Gürtel and the Ring, and with small dorms and friendly management. U6 to Thaliastrasse, then a short walk down Lerchenfelderstrasse and right into Myrthengasse. Midnight curfew. Book in advance. ②

Hotels and pensions

Aclon, 1. Dorotheergasse 6–8 (☎51 27 94 9). Pleasant pension in superb, central location. ⑤

Astra, 8. Alserstrasse 32. (☎408 22 70). A medium-sized pension out in the suburbs but within easy reach of the Ring. U6 Alserstrasse. ⑥

Bosch, 3. Keilgasse 13 (☎78 61 79). Near the Südbahnhof, in a quiet backstreet behind the Belvedere palace and gardens. ④

Esterhazy, 6. Nelkengasse 3 (☎587 51 59). Fairly basic but acceptable pension, often full of Hungarians on shopping trips to the nearby Mariahilferstrasse. ③

Falstaff, 9. Müllnergasse 5 (☎34 91 27). Highly regarded, comfortable place. ④

Geissler, 1. Postgasse 14 (☎533 28 03). Ideally placed in the centre. ⑥

Gloriette, 14. Linzerstrasse 105 (☎982 10 46). Some way out from the centre (tram #52 from the Westbahnhof) but handy for Schönbrunn. ④

Goldenes Einhorn, 5. Am Hundsturm 5 (☎55 47 55). A small family-run place where advance reservations are essential, in a residential area just within the Gürtel but with good connections with the centre. U4 Margaretengürtel. ④

Hedwig Gally, 15. Arnsteingasse 25 (☎892 90 73). Sparse, clean rooms in quiet backstreet, two stops on tram #52 or 58 from Westbahnhof. ③

Kugel, 7. Siebensterngasse 43 (☎93 33 55). Well placed just beyond the Ring (U2 Volkstheater). ④

Post, 1. Fleischmarkt 24 (☎51 583). A civilized, central hotel with big old rooms, from ÖS700. ⑤

Wild, 8. Langegasse 10 (☎43 51 74). A favourite choice, a short walk from the Ring in a student district behind the university. Booking essential. ③

Campsites

Schloss Laxenburg, Münchendorfer Strasse, Laxenburg (☎02236/713 33) Open April to Oct. The nicest of Vienna's campsites, adjacent to the grounds of Schloss Laxenburg, a former Habsburg hunting lodge. It's also the furthest out, accessible by half-hourly bus from Wien-Mitte up until 9.40pm (ask for Camping Laxenburg and the driver will stop at the gate).

Wien Süd, 23 Breitenfurter Strasse 269 (☎86 92 18). Open mid-July to Aug only, and the noisiest and most unpleasant of the sites. U6 to Philadelphiabrücke, then bus #62B.

Wien West I, 14 Hüttelbergstrasse 40 (☎94 14 49). Tram #49 from the Westbahnhof followed by a ten-minute walk. Open mid-July to Aug only.

Wien West II, 14 Hüttelbergstrasse 80. Just up the road from *Wien West I*, but larger and open all year round. It also has huts.

The City

Vienna has a compact **historical centre** or *Innere Stadt*, bound to the northeast by the Danube canal and surrounded on all other sides by the majestic cobbled sweep of the Ringstrasse. From here, the main arteries of communication radiate outwards before reaching another ring road, the Gürtel or girdle, further west. Most of the important sights are concentrated in the tourist-clogged *Innere Stadt* and along the Ring, but a lot of the essential Vienna lies outside, too, in what is an initially forbidding grid of barrack-like nineteenth-century apartment blocks: above all, some fascinating historic neighbourhoods, not to mention outlying sights such as the imperial palace at **Schönbrunn**, or the funfair and parklands of the **Prater**. With judicious use of public transport, you can see a great deal in a couple of days.

Around Stephansplatz

The obvious place to begin an exploration of Vienna is the central **Stephansplatz**, a lively pedestrianized square overlooked by the Gothic bulk of the **Stephansdom**, whose spire, nicknamed *Steffl* by the locals, together with the brightly coloured chevrons of its tiled roof, is still the dominating feature of the Vienna skyline. Once inside, the high vaulted interior is studded with Baroque detail. Immediately left of the entrance is the tomb of Prince Eugene of Savoy, hero of the campaigns against the Turks in the early eighteenth century: his capture of Belgrade in 1718 was the single most important act in making central Europe safe from the Ottomans. In the north apse is the Wiener Neustadt Altar, a masterpiece of late Gothic art, and, to its left, the tomb of Friedrich III, elected Holy Roman Emperor in 1489, after which the imperial throne remained tied to the Habsburg dynasty for the next five centuries. Highlight of the cathedral, though, is an early sixteenth-century carved stone pulpit with portraits of the four fathers of the Christian church (Saints Augustine, Gregory, Hieronymus and Ambrose), naturalistically sculpted by Anton Pilgram, who "signed" his work by showing himself peering from a window below the pulpit stairs. Other features of interest include the catacombs (daily 10–11.30am & 1.30–4.30pm; ÖS35; guided tours half-hourly), where, among other macabre remains, the entrails of illustrious Habsburgs are housed in bronze caskets; and the smaller of the cathedral's two towers, which can be ascended by elevator (daily 9am–6pm; ÖS40) for a look at the *Pummerin*, or great bell – though the 137-metre-high *Steffl* (March–Oct 9am–5.30pm; Nov–Feb 9am–4.30pm; ÖS20), a blind scramble up intestinal stairways, has better views. Finally, the seventeenth-century Archbishop's Palace on the north side of the cathedral at Stephansplatz 6 contains a **Diocesan Museum** (Tues, Wed, Fri & Sat 10am–6pm, Thurs 10am–6pm, Sun 10am–4pm; ÖS40), in which the church silver is outshone by a collection of marvellous fifteenth-century devotional paintings.

The warren of alleyways east of the cathedral preserves something of the medieval character of the city, although the architecture reflects centuries of continuous rebuilding. The medieval house on Raubensteingasse, where Mozart spent his last days, has long since disappeared, but you can still visit the composer's previous residence, the so-called **Figarohaus**, immediately behind the cathedral at Domgasse 5 (Tues–Sun 9am–12.15pm & 1–4.30pm; ÖS40), though there's little to see inside. He was only here for three years, penning at least one opera, *Der Schauspieldirector*, but not the work after which the property is named. A much more intriguing find is the **Treasury of the Order of Teutonic Knights** (Schatzkammer des Deutchen Ordens), around the corner at Singerstrasse 7 (May–Oct Mon, Thurs & Sun 10am–noon, Wed 3–5pm, Fri & Sat 10am–noon & 3–5pm; Nov–April closed Fri morning & Sun; ÖS25), where, on the first floor, you can view a varied collection of ceremonial regalia and domestic trinkets assembled by seven centuries of Grand Masters. The almost pastorally peaceful courtyard to the rear contains another of apartment-hopping Mozart's fleeting addresses; the house he died in whilst at work on his **Requiem** is now a department store, one block south of Rauhensteingasse 8 – the sports department contains a small plaque. A little further eastward, the seventeenth-century **Jesuitenkirche** on Dr-Ignaz-Seipel-Platz is a valuable piece of early Baroque architecture, much of the sumptuous interior the work of Andrea Pozzo, invited to Vienna by Leopold I in 1702 to spearhead the

city's artistic revival with an injection of Italian Jesuit style. The main reason for penetrating further in this direction is the **Postsparkasse** or Postal Savings Bank on
G.Coch-Platz (Mon–Wed & Fri 8am–3pm, Thurs 8am–5.30pm), built in 1904–06 by the
doyen of Vienna's turn-of-the-century architects, Otto Wagner. Wagner's imposing
designs broke with the nostalgic, revivalist style popular among architects at the time,
although to contemporary eyes his work seems packed with fussy ornamentation –
notably the winged figures adorning each corner of the elegant facade.

On and off Kärntnerstrasse

From Stephansplatz, Kärntnerstrasse heads southwest to join the Ring, a continuous
pedestrianized ribbon lined with gaggles of street entertainers and elegant shops. A
short way along and one block west lies **Neuer Markt**, centred on the writhing figures
of the Donner-Brunnen, a copy of an eighteenth-century fountain in which animated
nudes symbolize four of the rivers feeding into the Danube. At the southwest exit of
the square, a Capuchin church houses the **Kaisergruft** or Imperial Burial Vault (daily
9.30am–4pm; ÖS30), where Habsburg family members were interred from 1633. Maria
Theresa reputedly came here on the eighteenth of every month to commune with the
remains of her late husband Francis I; the long-suffering widow was eventually placed
beside her husband in a riotously ornamented sarcophagus of stunning proportions – a
stark contrast to the humble, unadorned coffin of her enlightened successor, Josef II.
At the head of Kärntnerstrasse, the **Staatsoper** was opened in 1869 as the first phase
of the development of the Ringstrasse. Behind, the **Albertina** (Mon, Tues & Thurs
10am–4pm, Wed 10am–6pm, Fri 10am–2pm, Sat & Sun 10am–1pm; closed Sun in July
& Aug; ÖS45) puts on constantly changing exhibitions from its stupendous assemblage
of engravings, graphics and watercolours accumulated over four centuries by enterprising Habsburgs and encompassing everything from Egyptian papyri to twentieth-
century work by the likes of Schiele. Most notable is a collection of Dürer prints
acquired by sixteenth-century Emperor Rudolf II (although these are usually only on
show in facsimile form) and paintings by Raphael, Rubens and Rembrandt.

From here Augustinerstrasse leads on to the Josefsplatz, flanked by another monument to the hoarding instincts of the Habsburgs, the **Nationalbibliotek**, whose ornate
Baroque *Prunksaal* or Great Hall (May–Oct Mon–Sat 10am–4pm, Sun 10am–1pm;
Nov–April Mon–Sat 10.30am–noon; ÖS40) on the second floor is worth a glimpse for
its frescoes, globes and gold-bound volumes. On the other side of Josefplatz, a door
leads to the imperial stables of the **Stallburg**, home to the performing white horses of
the **Spanish Riding School** – although it's difficult to see these in action and the
whole place shuts in July and August; check performance dates with the Austrian tourist office at home first if you're seriously interested (tickets range from ÖS200–700 for
a seat; ÖS160 for standing room only). Training sessions are open to the public from
mid-March to June and from September to mid-October; tickets (ÖS70) are sold on the
door on a first-come-first-served basis. Failing this, you can at least enjoy a second-hand
sighting of the prancing beasts at the video exhibition next door in **Palais Pallfy** on
Josefsplatz (daily 10am–6pm; ÖS30).

Hofburg and Maria-Therezen-Platz

On the other side of the Stallburg is Michaelerplatz, site of the **Looshaus**, built as a
department store in 1911 by another Viennese pioneer of modernism, Adolf Loos, but
representing a total break with the Jugendstil confections of Otto Wagner. Its initial
unpopularity was largely due to the fact that it was constructed directly opposite the
Michaelerplatz's main set piece, the nineteenth-century, statue-laden Michaelertor,
entrance to the city residence of the Habsburgs, the **Hofburg**. This rambling complex
of buildings has been much messed around since Rudolf I, the first Habsburg duke of
Austria, took possession of an earlier Bohemian fortress on this site in 1278. It now

contains a range of museums with imperial connections, beginning with a sumptuous but claustrophobic tour around the **Imperial Apartments** (Mon–Sat 8.30am–noon & 12.30–4pm, Sun 8.30am–12.30pm; ÖS40). On the south side of the first courtyard is the brightly painted entrance to the **Hofburgkapelle** or Palace Chapel, primarily known as the venue for Sunday Mass in the company of the Vienna Boys Choir, and the **Schatzkammer** or Imperial Treasury (10am–6pm; closed Tues; ÖS60), which holds the tenth-century crown of the Holy Roman Emperor, and the lance with which Jesus's flank was supposedly pierced (actually of ninth-century origin). Another archway leads through to the Heldenplatz, an enormous open space enclosed by the great curve of the **Neue Burg**, a grandiose neo-Renaissance building which reflects the conservative tastes of the last of the Habsburgs. This monumental piece of bombast was completed only three years before Loos's innovative edifice a few hundred metres away. Steps lead up to the **Ephesus Museum** (10am–4pm; closed Tues; ÖS60), harbouring the excellently presented finds of Austrian archeologists in Asia Minor, and collections of ancient musical instruments and arms and armour; a separate entrance leads to the Museum für Völkerkunde or Ethnographical Museum (daily except Tues 10am–4pm, ÖS30) which features the collections of Captain Cook, Aztec treasures and other temporary exhibitions.

Across the Ring from Heldenplatz, **Maria-Therezen-Platz** is framed by a museum complex designed by nineteenth-century planners to accommodate the vast imperial collections. On the left is one of the richest fine arts museums in the world, the **Kunsthistorisches Museum** (Tues–Sun 10am–6pm; ÖS95). Its ground floor is largely given over to the ancient world, with impressive Egyptian, Greek and Roman collections, and to the decorative arts, while the upstairs fine arts section is a good place to gain a perspective on the German Renaissance – the Gothic-infused canvases of Danubian painters like Altdorfer and the two Cranachs providing a link between the medieval world and the perfection of Dürer. Rubens, Caravaggio and Velasquez's paintings of the seventeenth-century Spanish court are well represented, along with two fine Rembrandt self-portraits and a portrait of the artist's mother. However, it's the unparalleled collection of Peter Bruegel the Elder that attracts most visitors, pictures such as *The Meeting of Lent and Carnival* and the famous winter scenery of the *Return of the Hunters* portraying the seasons and peasant festivities of the sixteenth-century Netherlands, which at the time were Habsburg dominions. Immediately opposite is the architecturally identical **Naturhistorisches Museum** (daily except Tues 9am–6pm; ÖS20), which, far from being a mere depository for rocks and deceased fauna, also holds a great deal of archeological interest. Many of the seventh-century BC Celtic grave finds from the Salzkammergut village of Hallstatt are here, alongside the *Venus of Willendorf*, a small stone figure carved by paleolithic inhabitants of the Danube valley some 25,000 years ago.

The Ringstrasse

This is a good place at which to begin an exploration of the **Ringstrasse**, built to fill the gap created when the last of the city's fortifications were demolished in the 1850s and lined with monumental civic buildings – "Ringstrasse Historicism" became a byword for the bad taste of the late Habsburg bourgeoisie. It's indicative of the concerns of the age that the broad sweep of the Ring wasn't just planned as an impressive symbol of imperial and municipal prestige: its very width was designed to facilitate the mobility of cannons in the event of any rebellious incursions from the proletarian districts beyond. The **Parliament building** is an imposing pastiche of Greco-Roman styles fronted by a monumental statue of Pallas Athene, while immediately to the north, spacious gardens provide luxurious frontage to the neo-Gothic **Rathaus**, parts of which are accessible on guided tours (Mon–Fri 1pm). East of here, across the Ring, **Herrengasse** was the neighbourhood the aristocracy moved into after Vienna was saved from the Turks, and is crammed with former palaces, government departments and embassies. The narrow confines of old Vienna's streets and alleyways dictated the character of the houses that were built here: the interiors were always splendid, the facades in comparison, rather dowdy and unassuming. Unfortunately, there's little chance of seeing beyond the latter, although the **Museum of Lower Austria** at no. 9 (Tues–Fri 9am–5pm, Sat 10am–noon, Sun 10am–1pm; ÖS30) contains ethnic implements along with more fine late Gothic art (including one work by Dürer) in refined surroundings.

Karlsplatz

Karlsplatz, a modern, landscaped square just beyond the Ring from the Staatsoper, is an important transport interchange from which westward explorations of the city, making use of the U4 metro line, can begin. Immediately above the station, Otto Wagner's elegant Jugendstil station pavilions, now used as an exhibition space and cafe (April–Oct Tues–Sun 9am–12.15pm & 1–4.30pm; ÖS15), were originally built for the old suburban railway system, the Stadtbahn. However, the scene is wholly dominated by the **Karlskirche**, the crowning achievement of Austria's foremost Baroque architect Fischer von Erlach, an eclectic jumble with an oval dome perched atop a colonnaded, classical front, flanked by replicas of Trajan's column in Rome, that was built by order of Emperor Charles IV to give thanks for deliverance from the plague of 1713. The **Museum of the City of Vienna** (Tues–Sun 9am– 4.30pm; ÖS30) next door includes three floors of medieval sculpture and painting, arms and armour recalling the city's struggles against the Turks, a reconstruction of Adolf Loos's ascetic living quarters, and a model of the city as it was before the Ring was built.

Immediately west of Karlsplatz across Friedrichstrasse is the **Akademie der bildenden Künste**, Schillerplatz 3 (Tues–Fri 11am–5pm, Sat & Sun 10am–4pm; ÖS30), which has an often overlooked collection, strong in Flemish works, including Bosch's *Triptych of the Last Judgement*. At the beginning of the Wienzeile, by the metro station on the other side of Karlsplatz, is the headquarters of those who broke away from the Academy in 1893, the **Sezession** (Tues–Fri 10am–6pm, Sat & Sun 10am–4pm; ÖS30). Led by Gustav Klimt, the younger generation of painters rebelled against stuffy academic historicism in favour of something more modern, although the Jugendstil (literally "youth style") they initiated was in many ways equally nostalgic, littered with symbols and themes taken from classical art and ancient mythology. The building itself is a case in point, though the "gilded cabbage" which crowns it is in a league of its own. One of Klimt's most characteristic works, the *Beethoven Frieze*, prepared for an exhibition of 1902, dominates the basement, while the rest of the building is used for contemporary exhibitions (ÖS15).

Schönbrunn and the west

The biggest attraction in the west is the imperial summer palace of **Schönbrunn** (daily April–Oct 8.30am–5pm; Nov–March 8.30am–4.30pm; ÖS50; gardens 6am–dusk), reachable by U4 to Schönbrunn or Hiezing. This was originally a royal hunting lodge until Charles VI commissioned Fischer von Erlach to draw up plans for a palace on the model of residences like Versailles. However, the plans proved too expensive, and the structure eventually put up during the reign of Charles' daughter Maria Theresa was, for all its size and elegance, far more modest than Fischer's grandiose blueprint had originally envisaged. Access is by **guided tour** only (hourly tours in English; ÖS80) and only a selection of apartments on the first floor is open. You can see Franz Josef's study, bedrooms and ceremonial hall, and any number of rooms with no obvious purpose, notably the so-called *Millionen-Zimmer*, a wood-panelled room covered from floor to ceiling with wildly irregular Rococo picture frames, each holding a Persian miniature. There's a

Coach and Carriage Museum in the right wing (April–Oct Tues–Sun 9am–6pm; Nov–March 9am–4pm; ÖS30), but you'd do better to concentrate on strolling through the palace's ornamental gardens, overlooked by the frolicking statuary of the Neptune Fountain, and the more distant Gloriette, a hill-top colonnaded monument from which you can enjoy splendid views back towards the city. The grounds also hold Vienna's **Zoo** (daily 9am–dusk; ÖS60) and the **Palmenhaus** (ÖS35), a glasshouse where you can sip an expensive cup of coffee among the tropical ferns.

On the western fringes of the city, **Lainzer Tiergarten** (April–Nov Wed–Sun 8am–dusk) is a vast game preserve in which wild boar, among other beasts, roam free. Wilder parts of the park can be reached from U4 Hütteldorf, but a more interesting point of access is the **Lainzertor** (Wed–Sun year-round), reached via U4 to Hietzing, then tram #60 to Hermestrasse, followed by either bus #60A or a twenty-minute walk. Once inside, paths lead to the **Hermesvilla** (Wed–Sun 9am–4.30pm), built for Franz Jozef's Empress Elizabeth in the 1880s and stuffed with the furnishings of the period.

South of the Ring

Immediately south of the Ring, Schwarzenbergplatz leads to the **Belvedere**, built by Lukas von Hildebrandt for Prince Eugene of Savoy between 1714 and 1723. It's in two parts, the more modest Lower Belvedere and the Upper Belvedere, separated by 500m of landscaped gardens. The whole is now home to the **Österreichische Galerie** (Tues–Sun 10am–5pm; ÖS60), a good introduction to the nation's art history, starting with the Gothic and Baroque collections in the Lower Belvedere which include the mythological subjects painted by Rottmayr, leader of the Viennese school in the early eighteenth century, the writhing contortions of his wilder, less academic successors Maulbertsch and "Kremser" Schmidt, and the grotesque caricature busts of Franz Xavier Messerschmidt. A large collection of Gothic art, a good deal of it by the Tyrolean painter Michael Pacher, is in the Orangery, while the Upper Belvedere is a good place to catch up on Jugendstil, with Klimt and Schiele each having a room to himself, as well as plenty of examples of the bourgeois and sentimental tastes of the time they rebelled against – nicknamed "Biedermeier" by a fictional art critic they invented.

Beyond the Belvedere, the area around the Südbahnhof has a distinctly Balkan feel, with scattered ethnic bars and restaurants providing a meeting place for *gastarbeiter* from the former Yugoslavia and Turkey. Heading southeast from the Südbahnhof through the Schweizer Garten are two more traditional tourist sights: the **Museum des 20 Jahrhunderts** (10am–6pm; closed Wed; ÖS30), which mounts changing exhibitions of contemporary art, and, slightly further on, the **Heeresgeschichtliches Museum** (10am–4pm; closed Fri; ÖS40), which recounts the glories of the Austrian military with weaponry and uniforms and a lot of exquisite sixteenth- and seventeenth-century engravings. One of the highlights is the car in which Archduke Ferdinand and wife Sophie Cotec were travelling in Sarajevo in June 1914 when they were assassinated; nearby lies the unfortunate heir's bloodstained uniform.

Ten minutes' walk from here (or tram #71 from Schwarzenbergplatz) is the **St Marx Cemetery**, Leberstrasse 6–8 (daily June–Aug 7am–7pm; May & Sept 7am–6pm; April & Oct 7am–5pm; Nov–March 7am–dusk), formerly the principal resting place for the dead of central Vienna. Among the shaded rows of fine nineteenth-century tombstones lies Wolfgang Amadeus Mozart, although the precise location of his grave remains a mystery due to Josef II's late eighteenth-century ban on opulent funerals. A monument marking the area in which the composer was interred was erected in 1859, but this was moved in 1891, prompting the caretaker of St Marx to assemble a new memorial – a classical column accompanied by a cherub clutching its head – out of bits and bobs he found lying around in the cemetery. The Mozart memorial was later moved to Vienna's greatest necropolis, the **Zentralfriedhof** or Central Cemetery at Simmeringer Hauptstrasse 234, further down the #71 tram line (daily; May–Aug 7am–7pm; March, April & Sept–Oct 7am–6pm; Nov–Feb 8am–5pm), in which graves of eminent Viennese are grouped together according to profession. The musicians, principally Mozart, Beethoven, Schubert, Brahms and both Strausses, are the target of most visits, and lie a short way beyond Gate 2, to the left of the central avenue. Schoenberg's uncompromisingly angular gravestone is set apart from the rest, occupying a privileged position next door to former Austrian chancellor Bruno Kreisky.

The northern suburbs

A couple of sights just to the north of the Ring merit a brief foray into district 9, the first of which is the **Freud Museum**, Berggasse 19 (daily 9am–3pm; ÖS30). Freud lived here from 1893 to 1938 and is remembered through a motley collection of photographs and artefacts, including the many ancient charms, fertility symbols and talismans with which he surrounded his desk. Three blocks further north is the early eighteenth-century Liechtenstein Palace, which is now home to the **Museum für Moderne Kunst** (10am–6pm; closed Tues; ÖS30). The parquet flooring and painted ceilings, another piece of work by Andrea Pozzo, counterpoint a representative collection of twentieth-century works including Magritte, Léger and a Picasso Harlequin, as well as the odd Klimt.

Further out, beyond the suburb of Heiligenstadt, are the vine-bearing foothills of the *Wienerwald*, or Vienna woods. The wine-producing villages of the area, especially **GRINZING**, are the traditional venue for summer evening visits to *Heurigen* or wine taverns – though Grinzing itself (tram #38 from Schottentor) is very commercialized, and **NUSSDORF** is nicer (tram D from Schottentor), with a string of pleasant and generally less expensive *Heurigen* lining the main Beethovengang. Nussdorf is also the starting point for walks up the **Kahlenberg** (although bus #38A from Heiligenstadt takes you direct to the top), a popular vantage point overlooking the Danube.

Hundertwasser, Leopoldstadt and the Danube

Hidden in the quiet backstreets east of Wien-Mitte train station is **Hundertwasser Haus**, now one of Vienna's top tourist attractions. In 1985 the hippy artist Hundertwasser was commissioned to re-design some cheap residential housing – his transformation of the dour modernist block into a higgledy-piggledy, kitsch, childlike jumble of brightly-coloured textures caught the popular imagination while enraging the architectural establishment. The residents weren't too happy either as their homes became invaded by hordes of pilgrims, so Hundertwasser obliged with an even tackier shopping arcade opposite, called **Kalke Village**, simultaneously increasing the sales outlets for his less inspiring artwork and providing a café and information centre to draw the crowds away from the flats. There's another of Hundertwasser's Gaudi-esque conversions nearby in Untere Weissegerbestrassse, but the **Kunstflaus** (daily 10am–7pm; ÖS50) has been less successful at attracting visitors, despite its permanent and temporary exhibitions on the man and his friends, another café and restaurant. If you're a convert or devotee, Hundertwasser's most recent project, the rebuilding of a rubbish incineration plant, which now looks like a giant mosque, is best viewed from the U4 line between Nussdorfstrasse and Heiligenstrasse.

Directly east of the centre across the Danube canal is district 2, or **Leopoldstadt**, for centuries the centre of a thriving Jewish community until Nazi rule deprived the area of much of its character. The district's main attraction is the **Prater** (U1 Praterstern), a large expanse of parkland which stretches for miles between the Danube canal and the river itself. Formerly the royal hunting grounds, the public were allowed access to the Prater by Josef II, who apparently walked here often himself, quixotically ordering passing members of the public not to salute him. The northern end of the Prater is the site of a long-established funfair, renowned for the **Riesenrad**, the giant ferris wheel which played a prominent part in Carol Reed's film *The Third Man*. In summer, you can take U1 east from Praterstern to the **Donauinsel**, an artificial lake in the middle of the Danube which serves as a popular bathing area. Crisscrossed by cycle paths, it's a bit sterile, and you may wish to carry on to the **Strandbad** at Gänserhäufel, 22. Moissigasse 21 (U1 to Kaisermühlen, then bus 90a).

Eating and drinking

As in the rest of Austria, the boundaries separating eating from drinking places can be pretty blurred, and recommendations inevitably overlap. The traditional venue for **eating out** in Vienna is the *Beisl*, an intimate neighbourhood place, somewhere between restaurant and pub, serving good home cooking as well as providing a cosy refuge for local beer drinkers. There are plenty of these beyond the Ring, the best places to look being the 6th, 7th and 8th districts. In the city centre, restaurants are more bland and more expensive, and you'll sometimes find cheaper and equally substantial evening meals in bars. Vienna is also the true home of the traditional Austrian *Kaffeehaus* or café – largely a venue for daytime drinking and lunchtime snacks. Those in the 1st district tend to be touristy and overpriced, but many are dripping with atmosphere and continue to be patronized by the Viennese themselves.

For **food on the move**, the *Würstelstand* is as big an institution in Vienna as anywhere else in Austria, although beware that your *Würst* tends to be priced according to weight; look out for *Leberkäse*, a slice of spicy meat sandwiched between two halves of a *Semmel*. There are plenty of lunchtime stand-up snack bars and places selling bite-size open-topped sandwiches in the city centre, one of the most famous being *Trzesniewski*, 1. Dorotheergasse 1, just around the corner from Stephansplatz. *Schwarzes Kameel*, 1. Bognergasse 5, has sandwiches and a good delicatessen, while if you want to sit down, the *Naschmarkt* chain of **self-service restaurants** has branches at 1. Schottengasse 1, and 6. Mariahilferstrasse 85. The Naschmarkt itself – the city's main fruit and veg market – is a great place to assemble a picnic, and also home to numerous cheap cafés attached to the various stalls.

Cafés

Café Central, 1. Herrengasse 14. Has an incontestable historical pedigree as the meeting place of Vienna's intelligentsia, and was reputedly Trotsky's favourite café. Today, however, little more than a skilful exercise in period reconstruction, on the original site.

Café Drechsler, 1. Linke Wienzeile 22. Opens at 4am for the stallholders of the *Naschmarkt*. A good place for breakfast after the bars and clubs close down.

Café Landtmann, 1. Karl Lueger Ring 4. The traditional haunt of politicians, civil servants and Freud, and preserving a refined, old-world ambience despite its position on a well-trodden tourist itinerary.

Café Prückel, 1. Stubenring 24. Favourite refuge of elderly Viennese matrons in between bouts of shopping.

Café Stein, 9. Währingerstrasse 6. Popular with students.

Hawelka, 1. Dorotheegasse 6. Famed for its rowdy Bohemian atmosphere, this is a popular night-time drinking venue, open until 2am. Renowned for its sweets.

Konditorei Demel, 1. Kohlmarkt 14. Vienna's most prestigious patisserie, with a café attached, and sea-food offshoot opposite.

Museum, 1. Friedrichstrasse 6. Century-old arty café, within range of both the Academy and Sezession. The sparse interior was originally designed by Adolf Loos.

Sperl, 6. Gumpendorferstrasse 11. The recently renovated turn-of-the-century interior is one of the set pieces of the Vienna coffee house scene.

Restaurants

Bizi, 1.Rotenturmstrasse. Big sit-down, self-service pizzeria. Cheap, central and quite pleasant.

Figlmüller, 1. Wollzeile 5. *The* place to eat *Wienerschnitzel* at ÖS145 a go.

Gasthaus Reinthaler, 1. Gluckgasse 5. One of few centrally located restaurants serving no-nonsense, affordable Austrian dishes.

Glacisbeisl, 7. Messeplatz. In the entrails of the Messepalast on the Ring, this is a popular venue in summer. Good vegetarian selections.

Mapitom, 1. Seitenstättergasse 5. Swish Italian late-night restaurant and bar in the Bermuda Triangle popular with young people.

Oswald und Kalb, 1 Bäckerstrasse 14. Traditional dimly-lit Gasthaus specializing in Styrian dishes. Evenings only until 2am.

Piaristenkeller, 8. Piaristengasse 45. Traditional Viennese food in an atmospheric wine cellar.

Schweizerhaus, 2. Strasse des 1 Mai 116, in the Prater. Known for its draught beer and pork specialities.

Spittelberg, 7. Spittelbergasse 12. A chic brasserie with some veggie options and delicious crepes for dessert.

Witwe Bolte, 7. Gutenberggasse 13. In the charming backstreets of Spittelberg, this serves good, cheap Viennese fare.

Wrenkh, 1. Bauernmarkt 10. Fashionable vegetarian restaurant just north of Stephansplatz. Main dishes around £10 in the evening.

Zu den 3 Hacken, 1. Singerstrasse 28. Unpretentious place serving decent, simple *Gulasch* – quite a boon in this part of the city.

Nightlife

For night-time **drinking**, the best place to head for in the centre is the so-called Bermuda Triangle, a network of alleyways centred on Rabensteig, off Rotenturmstrasse near the Danube canal; you could also try the narrow lanes around Sonnenfelsgasse and Bäckerstrasse, on the other side of Rotenturmstrasse. Beyond the Ring, the *Musikaffees* and bars of the 6th, 7th and 8th districts are well worth exploring; lively places with a youthful clientele, usually with some kind of music – you may have to pay an entrance fee if a live band is playing. Entrance to clubs and discos, and larger live venues, rarely costs over ÖS100. For details of what's on, the local listings magazine *Falter* has comprehensive details of the week's cultural programme, and is pretty easy to decipher even if you have scant German.

Late-night spots, live venues and clubs

Alt Wien, 1. Bäckerstrasse 9. Late-night imbibing in an old *Kaffeehaus* atmosphere. Good food if you can find a table.

B.A.C.H., 16. Bachgasse 21. Favourite of the alternative crowd but a bit of a trek. Occasional live bands and DJs. U6 Thaliastrasse, then three stops on tram #46.

Blue Box, 7. Richtergasse 8. Raucous place with resident DJs and a good snack menu.

Cafe Benno, 8. Alserstrasse 67. Café with a collection of puzzles and board games. Good snacks too.

Chelsea, 8. Piaristengasse 1. Punky anglophile haunt with regular live music downstairs.

Frauencafé, 8. Langegasse 11. Friendly café for women only. Open till 1am except Sun.

Jazzland, 1. Franz-Josefs-Kai 29. The main traditional jazz venue.

Krah Krah, 1. Rabensteig 8. Crowded, youthful and beery atmosphere, with occasional jazz music.

Loos Bar, 1. Kärntnerstrasse 59. Small, dark late-night bar with surprisingly rich interior by Adolf Loos. Shame about the strip club next door. Open until 5am.

Montevideo, 1. Annagasse 3a. 1970s nostalgia at Soul Train on Fridays.

Nachtasyl, 6. Stumpergasse 53. Managed by an expatriate Czech, and with a Bohemian beerhall atmosphere and occasional live music. Near Westbahnhof.

Rosa-Lila-Villa, 6. Linke Wienzeile 102. Gay and lesbian centre with late-night café. Open until 2am except Sun. U4 Pilgramgasse.

Rote Engel, 1. Rabensteig 5. Stylish bar with live jazz and blues most nights.

Szene Wien, 11. Hauftgasse 26. Run by a radical bunch of rockers from Simmering. Tram #71 from Karlsplatz.

Tunnel, 8. Florianigasse 39. Large, studenty establishment with frequent live jazz, and deservedly popular food.

U4, 12. Schönbrunnerstrasse 222. Dark, cavernous mecca of the alternative crowd; mostly rock/indie, with frequent gigs; gay and lesbian night Thurs. U4 Meidling-Hauptstrasse.

Volksgarten, 1. Volksgarten. A pavilion in the park adjoining Heldenplatz. A firm favourite with the dance crowd.

Why Not, 1. Tiefer Graben 22. Gay bar and disco of long standing, for both sexes.

Wuk, 9. Währingerstrasse 59. Old school now occupied by a sprinkling of anarchists and others. Café, live music maybe and much more.

X-Club, 1. Robert-Stolz-Platz 4. New addition to the club and live music scene, situated on the Ring.

Zwölf-Apostelkeller, 1. Sonnenfelsgasse 3. An attractive seventeenth-century building with bars housed in three levels of cellars. *The* place to drink wine, but often difficult to find a space.

Opera, ballet and classical music

You can catch high-class international **opera** and **ballet** at the *Staatsoper*, 1. Opernring 2, and Austrian opera and operetta at the *Volksoper*, 9. Währingerstrasse 78. There's a huge number of **classical music** venues, of which the principal ones are the *Musikverein*, 1. Karlsplatz 6, home of the Vienna Philharmonic, and the *Konzerthaus*, 3. Lothringerstrasse 50. Bookings can be made at *Bundestheaterkassen*, 1. Hanuschgasse 3, although you might be able to get cheap standing-room standbys at the Staatsoper by queuing up on the night of the performance.

Listings

Airlines *Austrian Airlines* 1. Kärntnerring 18 (☎ 68 00); *British Airways* 1. Kärntnerring 10 (☎65 76 91).

Bicycle rental *Radverlieh Salztorbrücke* on the Franz-Josefs-Kai near Schwedenplatz, April–Oct 9am–nightfall; *Radverlieh Hochschaubahn* next to the rollercoaster in the Prater amusement park, March–Oct Mon–Fri 10am–8pm, Sat & Sun 9am–8pm.

Books and newspapers *The British Bookshop*, 1. Singerstrasse 30, and *Shakespeare & Co*, 1. Sterngasse 2, are the best places to find English-language books; *Morawa*, 1. Wollzeile 11, is a good source of international newspapers and magazines.

Car rental *Avis*, 1. Opernring 1 (☎587 35 95); *Hertz*, 12. Kärntnerring 17 (☎512 86 77); *Interrent*, 1. Schubertring 7 (☎75 67 17).

Cinema Full listings from *Falter*. OF and OMU after the title both mean that the film is not dubbed. *Burg*, 1. Opernring 19, and *Top*, 6. Rahlgasse 1, both have regular showings of original language films.

Embassies *Australia*, 4. Mattielistrasse 2–4 (☎512 85 80); *Canada*, 1. Karl-Lueger-Ring 10 (☎533 36 91); *Great Britain*, 3. Reisnerstrasse 40 (☎ 75 61 17); *Netherlands*, 2. Untere Donaustrasse 13–15 (☎24 85 87); *New Zealand* 1. Lugeck 1 (☎52 66 36); *USA*, 1. Gartenbaupromenade 2 (☎514 51).

Exchange Outside banking hours, try the offices at the air terminal under the *Hilton* (daily 8am–12.30pm & 2–6pm), the Westbahnhof (daily 7am–10pm), or the Südbahnhof (daily 6.30am–10pm).

Hospital 24hr clinic at *Krankenhaus der Barmherzigen Brüder*, 2. Grosse Mohrengasse 9 (☎21 12 10). For a doctor, call ☎141 (7pm–7am).

Mitfahrzentrale 5. Frazengasse 11 (☎ 56 41 74).

Post office Main office at 1 Fleischmarkt 19 (Mon–Fri 8am–6pm).

Telephones At the main post office and at 1. Börseplatz 1.

Travel agent *ÖKISTA*, 9 Türkenstrasse 4–6, is best for discount flights and rail tickets.

THE DANUBE VALLEY AND LINZ

Heading west from Vienna, there are two alternatives for onward travel: to Salzburg, around three hours away, and then on to Munich or Innsbruck, or a more leisurely route following the Danube towards the **Wachau**, a tortuously winding stretch of water where vine-bearing, ruin-encrusted hills roll down to the river from the north. This is an Austria decidedly different both to cosmopolitan Vienna and the Alpine southwest, and accommodation here is generally cheaper than either place. At the eastern entrance to the Wachau, within easy reach of Vienna by train, is the historical town of **Krems**, with its older, medieval suburb of Stein; further on lies **Melk**, with its fine Benedictine monastery overlooking the river. Transport to Salzburg from Melk is pretty straightforward, although the industrialized but culturally vibrant northern city of **Linz** has enough of interest to make a further stopoff worthwhile on the way. Note that trains to Krems and Dürnstein leave from Vienna's Franz Josef Bahnhof (FJB), while Melk can be reached on the main line from Westbahnhof.

The most stylish way to travel is by **boat**. The *DDSG* line operates services between Vienna, Linz and Passau about twice a week between May and September, and the most scenic stretch between Krems and Melk has about four sailings daily in each direction (fewer in winter). The journey takes about three hours upstream, two in the opposite direction, and costs about ÖS250 each way; making your way along the river by shorter hops will work out more expensive at about ÖS100 a time, although *Eurail*-holders travel free and *InterRail* gains a fifty percent reduction.

Krems

KREMS clings to the hilly north bank of the Danube, divided between its modern centre at the eastern end and the medieval settlement of Stein (originally a city in its own right) in the west. Krems's main thoroughfare, **Landstrasse**, is a couple of blocks north of the train station, a pedestrianized shopping street studded with old buildings, including a sixteenth-century town hall. Above, a series of small squares preserves the late medieval character of this provincial wine-growing town. One of these, Pfarrplatz, is dominated by the **Pfarrkirche**, with an interior rich in fussy Baroque detail. A stairway behind it leads up to the imposing Gothic **Piaristenkirche**, with several altar-pieces by local-born Baroque artist Johann Martin Schmidt – a painter who is also celebrated in the town **Museum** (Tues–Sat 9am–noon & 2–5pm; Sun 9am–noon; ÖS20) in Körnermarkt, west of Pfarrplatz, atmospherically located in a dour Dominican church of thirteenth-century origin. There's something dark and tortured about Schmidt's work which makes it compulsive viewing. Born in nearby Grafenwörth in 1718, he trained under local artisans and set up his own workshop in Krems, eschewing the cosmopolitan art scene of the capital, and it's this attachment to provincial roots that sets his work apart from the more academic painters of the Austrian Baroque. The rest of the museum amounts to a mildly diverting trot through the history of viniculture in the region. At the western end of Landstrasse, the **Steinertor**, a monstrously belfried fifteenth-century town gate, confusingly marks the end of Krems' old town, while Kremsor Tor (a ten-minute walk away along Kasernstrasse) signals the beginning of Stein – a sequence of Renaissance town houses and crumbling old facades, opening out every hundred metres or so into small cobbled squares. Halfway along Steinerlandstrasse is the impressive shell of the thirteenth-century **Minoritenkirche** (Tues–Sun 10am–6pm; ÖS70), whose high vaulted Gothic interior presents the ideal setting for the art exhibitions it now hosts. Further along, steps climb up to the four-teenth-century **Frauenbergkirche**, now a chapel to Austrian war dead. Traces of faded medieval frescoes can still be made out on the walls.

Practicalities

The local **tourist office** is situated about halfway between Krems and Stein at Undstrasse 6 (May–Oct Mon–Fri 9am–5pm, Sat & Sun 10am–noon & 1–5pm; Nov–April Mon–Fri 8.30am–noon & 1.30–5pm). If you're planning on staying in town, there's a fairly serviceable **youth hostel** just beyond Steinertor at Kasernstrasse 6 (☎02732/842 17; ②); while *Donaucamping* just a few minutes' walk east of Landstrasse at Wiedengasse 7 (mid-April to Oct; ☎02732/84455) enjoys an idyllic riverside location. Elsewhere, signs along Steinerlandstrasse in Stein offer doubles for around ÖS500; more specially, the *Alte Post*, Obere Landstrasse 32 (☎02732/822 76; ④), has doubles overlooking an arcaded courtyard. A convenient place to **eat** in town is *Gozzoburg*, Margaretenstrasse 14, off Pfarrplatz (closed Tues), serving no-nonsense traditional dishes; *Piazza Duomo*, Margaretenstrasse 1, has more upmarket but very good Italian food.

Dürnstein and Melk

Following the river from Krems to Melk takes you first to **DÜRNSTEIN**, which sits below a rocky promontory commanding a bend in the river. The village is known primarily for the meagre ruin which overlooks the town, all that's left of the **castle** where Richard the Lionheart was famously locked up in the winter of 1192–93, after being kidnapped by Duke Leopold V of Austria. Below it stands an unmissable monastery **church**, its bright blue and white tower with gilt trimmings providing an even bigger riot of Baroque excess than is usual for this part of Austria. An accompanying bevy of sculpted saints, gesticulating in religious ecstasy, completes the scene.

Such exhibitionism was largely the result of eighteenth-century Canon Hieronymus Übelbacher's desire not to be outdone by the opulent reconstruction of the neighbouring town of **MELK**, where the monastery, perched on a bluff overlooking the river, is a dramatic sight. Traditionally a pilgrimage centre associated with the Irish missionary saint Coloman, who was revered for his powers of healing, the Benedictine foundation at Melk was transformed by the efforts of the ambitious eighteenth-century abbot Dietmayer, who dreamed of a showpiece monastery and consequently commissioned local architect Jakob Prandtauer to prepare the plans. The project was so overblown, however, that Dietmayer faced a rebellion by his own monks, dismayed by such an affront to their ascetic lifestyle, and the abbot had to prove that the monastery could afford the work before building could recommence. The end result is pretty stunning, the fanciful, monumental, coffee-cake exterior dominating the scene from whichever direction you approach, and dwarfing the town into insignificance. Highlights inside (daily Palm Sunday–Oct 9am–5/6pm; Nov–Palm Sunday guided tours only at 11am & 2pm; ÖS45–55) are the exquisite library with a cherub-infested ceiling by Troger, and the monastery church with similarly impressive work by Rottmayr. Both artists were pioneers in their day, responsible for importing high Baroque to Austria from Italy.

Melk's **river station** is situated about ten minutes' walk east of town. The **train station** is to be found at the head of Bahnhofstrasse, which will lead you directly into the old town. The **tourist office**, located on Rathausplatz (July & Aug daily 9am–6pm; mid-April to June & Sept to mid-Oct Mon–Sat 9am–noon & 3–7pm, Sun 9am–noon; mid-Oct to mid-April Mon–Fri 7am–noon & 1–4pm), has a substantial stock of **private rooms**, although you'll find that prices are a touch higher here than they are in Krems. Melk's **youth hostel** is at Abt-Karl-Strasse 42 (☎02752/26 81; ②), roughly five minutes on foot from the train station; *Camping Melk* occupies a pleasant riverside site near the river station.

Linz and around

Unfairly sidetracked by tourists, the Upper Austrian capital of **LINZ** is a pleasant Baroque city straddling the river Danube. The city has an undeserved reputation among Austrians as a workaday town, sullied by youth violence and pollution, that has to advertise in the Austrian press for prospective residents. Bearing this in mind, you may be surprised by the city's relaxed elegance. One unlikely Austrian fan of Linz, inspired by nostalgia-tinged memories of schooldays spent here at the turn of the century, was Adolf Hitler: plans for the city's reconstruction filled the last days of his life, and an architectural model of his projected urban utopia graced the Führer's bunker in Berlin.

The Town

A tour of the city should perhaps start at the fifteenth-century **Schloss**, two blocks west of Hauptplatz, the former residence of Emperor Friedrich III, who made Linz the imperial capital for four short years from 1489 (his son Maximilian later shifted the court down to Innsbruck). However, there's little dramatic to see save for a good view across the Danube and the **Schlossmuseum** (Tues–Fri 9am–5pm, Sat & Sun 10am–4pm; ÖS25), strong on weaponry and folklore, especially the work of naive village artists of the region, and with extensive Bronze Age and Roman relics on the ground floor. Below the Schloss is a pedestrianized quarter rich in Baroque houses which leads to the **Hauptplatz**, a vast windswept expanse overlooked by the **Alter Dom** or old cathedral to the southeast, an unusually stern piece of seventeenth-century architecture. The **Pfarrkirche**, around the corner to the north, is more interesting, home to a gargantuan marble slab containing Emperor Friedrich III's heart (the rest of him is in Vienna's Stephansdom). The fairly uninviting grid of streets east of Landstrasse contains a couple more museums. The **Stadtmuseum Nordico**, Bethlehemstrasse 7 (Mon–Fri 9am–6pm, Sat & Sun 3–5pm; ÖS30), is pretty unremarkable, its collections of local history usually overshadowed by bigger touring exhibitions. The **Landesgalerie**, Museumstrasse 14 (Tues–Fri 9am–6pm, Sat & Sun 10am–6pm; ÖS40), likewise plays host to temporary shows – usually prestigious selections taken from Austrian art history. Better to stroll across to the largely residential suburb of **URFAHR**, on the north bank of the river, where the **Neue Galerie** (Mon–Wed, Fri 10am–6pm, Thurs 10am–10pm, Sat 10am–1pm; ÖS25), on the first floor of the *Lentia 2000* shopping centre on Blütenstrasse, has a jewel of a collection, including a few Klimts and Schieles as well as an instructive range of paintings by lesser-known Austrians working at the same time. The only other reason to visit Urfahr is to take a ride on the **Pöstlingbergbahn**, a narrow-gauge railway which climbs to the eighteenth-century pilgrimage church of **Pöstlingberg** – a good vantage point for sweeping views of the valley. Trains leave from a twee station at the end of the #3 tram line every twenty minutes between 5am and 8pm.

Practicalities

Linz's **train station** is 2km south of the centre, on the other side of the city's main artery, Landstrasse, and connected with the central Hauptplatz by tram #3. There's a **tourist office** in the station, and a main office at Hauptplatz 34 (June–Sept Mon–Fri 8am–7pm, Sat & Sun 8–11.30am & 12.30–6pm; Oct–May Mon–Fri 8am–6pm). Affordable central **accommodation** is thin on the ground, the only feasible option the *Wilder Mann*, ten minutes' walk from the station off Landstrasse at Goetherstrasse 14 (☎0732/56 078; ③), or *Goldenes Dachl*, Hafnerstrasse 27 (☎0732/67 54 80; ③), three blocks west of Landstrasse down Langgasse. There's a small but pleasant **youth hostel** at Kapuzinerstrasse 14 (☎0732/78 27 20; non-members accepted; no curfew; ②), ten minutes west of Hauptplatz, and a bigger private **hostel** at Blütenstrasse 23 (☎0732/23 70 78; ②) in the *Lentia 2000* shopping centre across the river in Urfahr. The nearest

campsite is 10km southeast on the Pichlingersee (☎0732/30 53 14), reached by hourly bus from the Hauptbahnhof.

The **bars and restaurants** around the Hauptplatz and in the largely pedestrianized streets immediately west provide Linz with plenty of places to eat and drink. *Alte Welt*, Hauptplatz 4 (closed Sun), just off the main square, is a good place to quaff local vintages or eat an evening meal; *Klosterhof*, Landstrasse 30, serves solid Austrian food in the labyrinthine rooms of a former monastery, as well as boasting the city's largest beer garden. *Traxlmayr*, Promenade 16, southwest of Hauptplatz, a coffee house-cum-civic institution, is a good place to treat yourself to a slice of *Linzer Torte*, the local chocolate cake. The numerous *Weinkeller* along the river front in Urfahr are the best places to sample the white wines of the Mühlviertel, the vine-covered hills north of the city.

Around Linz

Of a couple of worthwhile excursions from Linz, one of the most popular is to the **Monastery of St Florian**, 7km southeast and accessible by bus (#2040 or #2042), an Augustinian foundation sponsored by the Habsburgs in the seventeenth and eighteenth centuries. Anton Bruckner was a choirboy here in the 1830s, and returned to become the monastery's organist in later life. The complex was rebuilt by Prandtauer, fresh from supervising similar work at Melk. Much of the year access is restricted to the abbey church, which has Bruckner's sarcophagus in the crypt. There are obligatory guided tours of the interior (mid-June to mid-Sept 10am, 11am, 2pm, 3pm & 4pm; April to mid-June & mid-Sept–Nov 10am, 11am, 2pm & 3.30pm; ÖS45); don't miss the *Kaisersaal* or imperial suite, with Prince Eugene's four-poster bed, an over-the-top half-Turkish, half-Rococo confection. The picture collection is extraordinarily rich in the paintings of Albrecht Altdorfer, a prolific early sixteenth-century master whose work personifies the coming together of German Gothic and Italian-inspired Renaissance styles.

Mauthausen (daily 8am–4pm; ÖS30) is also easily accessible from Linz – take the train towards Vienna and change to the local line at St Valentin. This former quarry was used by the Nazis as a concentration camp from 1938 onwards, and the sparsely furnished living quarters have been preserved much as they were during the war.

SOUTHEAST AUSTRIA

The **southeastern** corner of Austria, despite the subalpine terrain of the central province of Styria and the sun-baked plains of the Burgenland which borders on Hungary to the east, is bypassed by most visitors. The area contains a wealth of diffuse attractions, though these demand leisurely exploration, and the only obvious focus of concentrated interest is the Styrian provincial capital of Graz.

Graz

Austria's second city, **GRAZ** owes its importance to stout resistance put up in the face of invaders from the south. From the fifteenth century on, Graz was crucial to the defence of central Europe against the Turks, a city constantly under arms – a concentration of forces that rendered it far more secure than Vienna and led to a modest seventeenth-century flowering of the arts, especially the Baroque style, predating its adoption elsewhere in Austria. Later, during the last years of the empire, Graz's mild climate made it a popular retirement choice for ageing officers and civil servants, and its reputation as a conservative town swarming with pensioners has since proved hard to shake off. Nowadays, however, it is a rich and culturally varied city, with plentiful night-time diversions, partly due to the presence of a 27,000-strong student population and a highly regarded musical academy which specializes in training jazz musicians.

Arrival and accommodation

Graz's **Hauptbahnhof** is on the western edge of town, a fifteen-minute walk or short tram ride (#3 or #6) from the central Hauptplatz. There's a **tourist office** at the station and a bigger one a couple of hundred metres from Hauptplatz at Herrengasse 16 (Mon–Sat 9am–7pm, Sun 10am–3pm) which operates a helpful room-booking service – both supply city maps free of charge. The town's **youth hostel** is four blocks south of the station at Idlhofgasse 74 (☎0316/91 48 76; ③). The nearby *Hotel Strasser*, Eggenburger Gürtel 11 (☎0316/91 39 77; ③), has doubles from ÖS380 but fills quickly. More convenient for the centre is *Pension Iris*, Bergmanngasse (☎0316/320 81; ④), north of the Stadtpark.

The City

Graz is compact and easy to explore, most sights being within striking distance of **Hauptplatz**, a broad market square in the centre of which is a statue of Archduke Johann, one of the Archdukes of Inner Austria – a dynasty of second-rank Habsburgs, not in line for the imperial succession, who ruled down the town. Herrengasse leads off to the south towards the **Landhaus**, a sixteenth-century town hall with Italianate arcading in the courtyard. The next-door **Zeughaus** or armoury, Herrengasse 16 (April–Oct Mon–Fri 9am–5pm, Sat & Sun 9am–1pm; ÖS25), has endless galleries bristling with weaponry used to keep the Turks at bay. The main attraction west of Herrengasse is the **Landesmuseum Johanneum**, founded by the Archduke Johann, a vast collection housed in different locations. Entrance to the natural history section (Mon–Fri 9am–4pm, Sat & Sun 9am–noon; ÖS25) is at Raubergasse 10, two blocks west, while another block on Neutorgasse is the more interesting **Alte Galerie** (Tues–Fri 10am–5pm, Sat & Sun 10am–1pm; ÖS30), a quality collection of art rich in Gothic devotional work, much of it rescued from decay in the village churches of Styria, and credited to anonymous artists now known only by the name of the place in which their work was found. The illustrious Tyrolean Michael Pacher also puts in an appearance, with a fifteenth-century altarpiece depicting the martyrdom of Thomas à Becket, and, among other Flemish paintings, there's a grippingly macabre *Triumph of Death* by Bruegel. On the other side of Herrengasse, Stempfergasse leads into a neighbourhood of narrow alleyways that dog-leg their way up the hill towards the **Mausoleum of Ferdinand II** (11am–noon & 2–3pm; closed Sun & Fri; ÖS20), an imposing Baroque building bristling with domes that was begun in 1614 when the intended incumbent was a healthy 36 years old. It actually contains Ferdinand's mother Maria, and Ferdinand himself lies in Vienna. Next door is the originally twelfth-century **Dom-Kirche**, immediately north of which the **Burg** is an erstwhile imperial residence now given over to local government offices, although it's worth peering in the archway at the end of the first courtyard to view the unique double spiral of a fifteenth-century Gothic staircase. From here Hofgasse descends to the bustling shopping street of **Sporgasse**, where the Saurauplatz features a Turkish figure throwing himself from a small window.

A short way north of Hauptplatz, down Sackstrasse, the **Neue Galerie** (Mon–Fri 10am–6pm, Sat & Sun 10am–1pm; ÖS25), housed in the seventeenth-century Herberstein Palace, displays nineteenth- and twentieth-century works including a sprinkling of Klimts and Schieles, while the **Stadtmuseum** (Mon–Sat 10am–6pm, Sun 10am–1pm, Tues until 9pm; free) next door at no. 18 houses temporary exhibitions. From Schlossbergplatz a balustraded stone staircase zigzags up to the **Schlossberg**, a wooded hill overlooking the town (the *Schlossbergbahn* funicular, a little further along Sackstrasse, makes the same trip every 15min 9am–10pm). The Schloss from which its name derives was destroyed by Napoleon in 1811; only two prominent features survive – the sixteenth-century **Uhrturm** or clock tower, whose steep overhanging roof figures prominently in the town's tourist literature, and the more distant **Glockenturm** or bell tower of the same period. Paths descend south from the Schlossberg to the elegant sweep of the **Stadtpark**, a leafy barrier between the city and the residential suburbs beyond.

Some distance west of the town centre, at the end of tram line #1, are the luxurious state rooms of **Schloss Eggenburg**, Eggenberger Allee 90 (daily 10am–1pm & 2–5pm; ÖS40), built in 1623 for Johann Ulrich of Eggenburg, Ferdinand II's First Minister. The Schloss' historical collection is especially strong on prehistory, its most valued exhibit being the Strettweg chariot – a remarkable eighth-century wheeled platform peopled by small, weapon-wielding figures unearthed in the nearby town of Judenburg.

Eating, drinking and nightlife

Graz is foremost among Austria's provincial cities in preserving the culture of the *Kaffeehaus*. *Hofcafé Edegger Tax*, Hofgasse 8, is the sumptuous refuge of the city's more sedate citizens; the very much more modern *Operncafe*, Opernring 22, attracts a more youthful crowd and is equally popular in the evening; *Café Promenade*, in the middle of the Stadtpark, is frequented, according to one regular, by "people who think they are writers".

For something more substantial than munching a *Wurst* on Hauptplatz or visiting the fishy *Nordsee* outlet on Herrenstrasse, try *Gambrinuskeller*, Farbergasse 6–8 (closed Sun & Mon), which has a wide choice of reasonably priced food, including kebabs, stuffed peppers and other Balkan dishes. *Zur Goldenen Pastete* at Sporgasse 28 (closed Sun & Mon) is a more upmarket establishment but the food is excellent. *Mangolds*, at Griesllai 10 (closed Sun) across the river, offers self-service health food in antiseptic surroundings – though it closes at 8pm. There are more alternatives in the alleys and squares between Herrengasse and Färbergasse – *Haring*, Mehlplatz 4 (closed Sat), is one of the nicest. It's worth, too, venturing out to the cafés and bars which cluster in the streets around the university, east of the Stadtpark: *Café Harrach*, Harrachgasse 26, and *Café Wartburg*, Hälbarthgasse 14, are both student favourites, with inexpensive food; *Kulturhauskeller*, Elizabethstrasse 30, is a crowded, smoky cellar below the student cultural centre.

SALZBURG AND THE SALZKAMMERGUT

Salzburg, straddling the border with Germany, is Austria's most heavily touristed city after Vienna, a natural magnet for those seeking the best of Austria's Baroque heritage and a taste of subalpine scenery as well. The most accessible and popular of these mountain areas is the **Salzkammergut**, a region of glacier-carved lakes and craggy peaks a couple of hours by bus or train to the east.

Salzburg

The Austrian writer Thomas Bernhard, an acerbic critic of the postwar state who spent his formative years in **SALZBURG**, called his home town "a fatal illness", whose Catholicism, conservatism and sheer snobbery drove its citizens to a miserable end. The city certainly has a strong bourgeois ethos, and Salzburgers look resentfully towards the federal capital Vienna as the all-consuming metropolis of corrupt, slothful bureaucrats for whom the rest of Austria has to pay. Yet for many visitors Salzburg represents the quintessential Austria, offering the best of the country's Baroque architecture, subalpine air, and a musical heritage largely provided by the city's most famous son, Wolfgang Amadeus Mozart, whose bright-eyed visage peers from every box of the city's ubiquitous chocolate delicacy, the *Mozartkügel*.

Despite this, the city for much of its history either belonged to the Bavarian sphere or was an independent city state, only becoming part of the Habsburg domain in 1816. In the Middle Ages the city looked west, its powerful archbishops serving a see which extended over much of southern Germany, prosperous on the proceeds of the Salzkammergut salt trade. The city's High Baroque appearance is largely due to the ambition of sixteenth- and seventeenth-century Prince Archbishops Wolf Dietrich and his successor-but-one Paris Lodron, who purposefully recast Salzburg on the model of Rome, employing artists and craftsmen from south of the Alps.

Arrival and accommodation

Salzburg's **Hauptbahnhof** has a **tourist kiosk** on platform 2a (daily 8.15am–9.30pm) which sells maps, has accommodation details and books rooms for a ÖS30 fee. It's over a kilometre into town from the station, but there are regular trolleybuses covering the distance (bus #1, 2, 5, 6, 51 & 55 all go to Makartplatz on the east bank); a 24-hour *Netzkarte* costs ÖS27. The **tourist office** is at Mozartplatz 5 in the old town centre (daily July & Aug 8am–10pm; April–June, Sept & Oct 9am–7pm; Nov–March 9am–6pm). The most convenient youth hostel is *Jugendgästehaus Salzburg*, Josef-Preis-Allee 18 (☎0662/84 26 700; ②), bus #5 from the station. There's also the *Haunspergstrasse* hostel, three blocks west of the train station at Haunspergstrasse 27 (☎0662/87 50 30; midnight curfew; ②), though this is open July and August only. As for **hotels,** rooms fill quickly in summer and can be pricey. The *Schwarzes Rössl*, Priesterhausgasse 6 (☎0662/87 44 2; ④; open July–Sept only), is a marvellous, creaky old building in a good location, and there's also the *Hinterbrühl*, Schanzlgasse 12 (☎0662/84 67 98; ③). *Stadt-Camping*, Bayerhamerstrasse 14a, is the most convenient **campsite**, within walking distance of the station and town centre, open May to September.

The City

Salzburg has a compact centre and an easily walkable concentration of sights. The ensemble of archiepiscopal buildings in the centre, on the **west bank** of the river, forms a tight-knit network of alleys and squares, overlooked by the brooding presence of the medieval Hohensalzburg castle. From here it's a short hop over the river Salzach to a narrow ribbon of essential sights on the east bank.

THE WEST BANK

From the Staatsbrücke, the main bridge across the River Salzach, **Judengasse** funnels tourists up into **Mozartplatz**, home to a statue of the composer and overlooked by the **Glockenspiel**, a seventeenth-century musical clock whose chimes attract crowds at 11am and 6pm. The complex of Baroque buildings on the right exudes the ecclesiastical and temporal power wielded by Salzburg's archbishops, whose erstwhile living quarters – the **Residenz** – dominate the west side of the adjacent **Residenzplatz**. Guided tours of this (July & Aug every 20min 10am–4.40pm; Sept–June hourly 10am–3pm; ÖS40) take you through a sequence of bombastic state rooms, while one floor above, the **Residenzgalerie** (April–Oct daily 10am–5pm; Nov–March Tues–Sun 10am–5pm; ÖS40) offers a fine display of archiepiscopal acquisitions, including works by Rembrandt and Caravaggio, and a fairly comprehensive collection of Flemish works. From here arches lead through to **Domplatz**, dominated by the pale marble facade of the **Dom** – the replacement of an original Romanesque structure in 1602, put up by Archbishop Wolf Dietrich in 1628, and an impressively cavernous but otherwise undistinguished Renaissance structure. Steps descend to a modern crypt, with pieces of the medieval cathedral jutting out of the concrete and dull grey sarcophagi containing various illustrious prelates. The cathedral **museum** (mid-May to mid-Oct Mon–Sat 10am–5pm, Sun 11am–5pm; ÖS30) holds collections of pan-European bric-à-brac and treasures popular among rulers and supposedly enlightened folk in Renaissance times.

At the opposite end of the Domplatz an archway leads through to the Gothic **Franziskanerkirche**, a thirteenth-century reconstruction of an ancient eighth-century edifice that houses a fine Baroque altar by Fischer von Erlach around an earlier, Gothic *Madonna and Child* sculpted by the Tyrolean master Michael Pacher. The altar is enclosed by an arc of nine chapels, adorned in a frenzy of stucco ornamentation. Look, also, for the twelfth-century marble lion which guards the stairway to the pulpit. Around the corner is the **Rupertinum**, Wiener-Philharmonikergasse 9 (Tues–Sun 10am–5pm, Wed until 9pm; ÖS50), a picture gallery devoted to twentieth-century work and touring exhibitions, with a nice secluded café. Art exhibitions also often grace the cavernous interior of Fischer von Erlach's sizeable but somewhat graceless **Kollegienkirche** or University Church, on the adjacent Universitätsplatz. Around the back of the church, Hofstallgasse is dominated by the modern **Festspielhaus**, a principal venue for the Salzburg festival. Northeast of here, under the shadow of the Mönchberg, is the **Pferdschwemme** or horse trough, built in 1700 for the horses of the nearby Archbishop's Riding School (now part of the Festspielhaus*)* and decorated with equine motifs. A couple of hundred metres beyond, the **Museum Carolino-Augusteum**, Museumplatz 1 (Tues & Fri 9am–8pm, Wed, Thurs, Sat & Sun 9am–5pm; ÖS40), contains some Roman finds from the town centre, including a reconstructed mosaic retrieved from beneath Mozartplatz, more Gothic religious art and a room devoted to local-born painter Hans Makart, a specialist in the moralistic works of the late nineteenth century. Slightly less essential are the toys and musical instruments of the **Salzburger Museum in der Bürgerspital**, nearby at Bürgerspitalgasse 2 (Tues–Sun 9am–5pm; ÖS30). Getreidegasse leads east back towards the centre, lined with opulent boutiques and characterized by painted facades and wrought-iron shop signs. At no. 9 is **Mozart's Geburtshaus** or birthplace (daily May–Sept 9am–6.30pm; Oct–April 9am–6pm; ÖS55). Born in 1756, the musical prodigy spent most of his first 21 years in the city (at this address for the first seventeen), despite frequent absences when being touted around the courts of Europe by his father. This rather overcrowded place of pilgrimage harbours some fascinating period instruments, including one baby-sized violin used by the composer as a child.

You can get up to the **Höhensalzburg**, which commands excellent views across town from the nearby Mönchberg, by funicular from Kapitelplatz behind the cathedral, although the journey on foot isn't as hard or as time-consuming as it looks. The fortress (daily May, June & Sept 9am–5pm; July & Aug 9am–5.30pm; April, Oct 9.30am–4.30pm; Nov–Feb 9.30am–3.30pm; March 9.30am–4pm; ÖS40) was begun around 1070, its prime role to provide the archbishops with a refuge from the belligerent German princes who supported the emperor in his disputes with the pope. It was gradually transformed into a more salubrious courtly seat, although Archbishop Wolf Dietrich spent a period of less than comfortable confinement here after being imprisoned by the pope in 1612. State rooms can be visited by guided tour (ÖS30), although a roam around the ramparts and passageways of the castle is enough to gain a feel for the place. Paths lead east from the fortress to another piece of pre-Baroque Salzburg, the **Stift Nonnberg**, whose church is a largely fifteenth-century Gothic rebuilding of an earlier Romanesque structure, from which several bits of stonework can still be seen.

THE EAST BANK

Streets on the eastern bank of the river zero in on **Platzl**, a small square at the foot of the Kapuzinerberg, named after a Capuchin monastery at the summit. Neither the monastery church nor the view really warrants the stiff climb, and a more interesting walk takes you from Platzl up Linzergasse to the **Sebastianskirche** and its fascinating graveyard, home to the last resting place of Paracelsus, the Renaissance humanist and alchemist remembered among other things for introducing the word gnome into the lexicon – a creature, he suggested, which lived beneath the earth's crust – and the mausoleum of Wolf Dietrich, tiled with an almost Islamic delicacy. Two blocks north-west of Platzl is **Makartplatz**, with a **house** that Mozart's family lived in between 1773 and 1787 (daily 10am–5/6pm; ÖS35), containing more musical memorabilia, and Fischer von Erlach's **Dreifaltigkeitskirche** or Church of the Holy Trinity, notable for the elegant curve of its exterior and murky frescoes by Rottmayr inside. Dreifaltigkeltsgasse brings you shortly to the **Schloss Mirabell**, on the site of a previous palace built by Archbishop Wolf Dietrich for his mistress Salome, with whom the energetic prelate was rumoured to have sired a dozen children. Completely rebuilt by Lukas von Hildebrandt in the early eighteenth century, and having undergone further reconstruction after a fire in the nineteenth, it's now a prestigious venue for classical concerts. Its most outstanding features are the cherub-lined staircase, by Baroque master George Raphael Donner, and the ornate gardens, the rose-filled high ground of the adjoining Kurgarten offering a much-photographed view back across the city towards the Höhensalzburg. Within the gardens there's a **Barockmuseum** (Tues–Sat 9am–noon & 2–5pm, Sun 9am–noon; ÖS30), concentrating on regulars such as Donner, Rottmayr, Maulpertsch and Schmidt but also with a good deal of the second division Austrian artists overlooked elsewhere.

Eating and drinking

If you're just after a **snack**, there are plenty of outlets around Judengasse and Alter Markt offering sandwiches and suchlike. Salzburg is full of elegant cafés, the most renowned of which are *Tomasselli*, Alte Markt 9, and on the east bank *Bazar*, Schwarzstrasse 3, the latter with a nice terrace overlooking the Salzach. For **more substantial eating**, *Stiftskeller St Peter*, next to St Peter's church in the heart of old Salzburg, has a roomy, atmospheric interior but tends to fill up quickly with tourist parties. *Gablerbräu*, on Priesterhausgasse, serves good Austrian grub and has several vegetarian options too, as does *Stieglkeller*, Festungsgasse 10 (May–Sept only), which offers nice outdoor seating on the way up to the Burg. It's also a good place for drinking beer on warm evenings. *Sternbrau* is a massive beer garden and restaurant complex occupying two courtyards between Griesgasse and Getriedegasse. *Strobl Stüberl*, Rainerstrasse 11, is a smaller establishment near the station where food is served until 3am. More specifically **drinking** haunts include *Felsenkeller*, a murky wine tavern built into the cliffs behind the southern corner of the Festspielhaus; *Zum fidelen Affen*, Priesterhausgasse 8, serving excellent beer on tap and good food; and *Am Steintor*, Giselakai 17, a crowded, youthful bar which keeps going until 2am.

The Salzburg Festival

The **Salzburg Festival** has been running since 1920 and is one of the premier music festivals in Europe, beginning in the last week of July and running throughout August. Tickets are hard to come by: write to *Salzburger Festspiele*, Postfach 40, 5010 Salzburg for programme and booking details. Some standing places for the outdoor performances are available on a standby basis; check with the Festspielhaus box office on Hofstallgasse (☎0662/84 25 41).

Listings

Airport Five kilometres west of town on the Innsbrucker Bundesstrasse, linked to the Hauptbahnhof by bus #77. Information ☎0662/85 29 00.

Airlines *Austrian Airlines*, Schrannengasse 5 (☎0662/87 55 44); *British Airways* Griesgasse 29 (☎0662/84 21 08).

Amex In the main tourist office on Mozartplatz.

Car rental *Avis*, Porscherstrasse 7 (☎0662/766 74); *Hertz*, Porscherstrasse 7 (☎0662/77 27 80).

Consulates *Great Britain*, Alter Markt 4 (☎0662/84 81 33); *US*, Giselakai 51 (☎0662/286 01).

Exchange Outside banking hours in the Hauptbahnhof (daily 7am–10pm).

Hospital Mülner Hauptstrasse 48 (☎0662/315 81).
Mitfahrzentrale W. Philharmonikergasse 2 (☎0662/84 13 27).
Post office The main office at Residenzplatz 9 (Mon–Fri 7am–7pm, Sat 8am–10am) is also the best place to find phone booths.
Travel agents ÖKISTA, Hildmannplatz 1a (☎0662/84 67 89).

The Salzkammergut

Straddling the border between Land Salzburg and Upper Austria, the peaks of the **Salzkammergut** may not be as lofty as those further south, but the glacier-carved troughs that separate them make for some spectacular scenery. Most of the towns and villages in the area are modest places, quiet throughout much of the year until the annual summer influx of visitors. It's a good area for making use of plentiful private rooms and *Gasthöfe*. Natural transport and commercial hub of the region is the nineteenth-century spa town of **Bad Ischl**, 60km east of Salzburg, close by three of the most scenic of the Salzkammergut lakes, the **Wolfgangersee**, **Traunsee** and **Hallstättersee**. You can reach Bad Ischl by rail by way of a branch line off the main Salzburg–Vienna route from Attnang-Puchheim, or from Stainach-Irdning on the Graz–Salzburg route to the south. From Salzburg, a bus is the most direct route.

St Wolfgang

Hourly buses on the Salzburg–Bad Ischl route run east along the southern shores of the Wolfgangersee, though they bypass the lake's main attraction, the village of **ST WOLFGANG** itself, on the opposite shore. You can either get off at **St Gilgen** at the western end of the lake, from where regular ferries run to St Wolfgang between May and September, or continue to the village of **Strobl**, or even to Bad Ischl, and pick up a connecting bus from there. The village itself is a traditional stomping ground of middle-class, middle-aged English, and can be unpleasantly crowded in summer. But you should make a point of stopping off, if only to visit the **Pilgrimage Church** (May Mon–Sat 9am–5pm, Sun 11.30am–5pm; June–Sept Mon–Sat 9am–5.30pm, Sun 11.30am–5pm; Oct–April Mon–Sat 9am–4pm, Sun 11.30am–4pm), just above the lake shore, which contains a high altar by Michael Pacher. An extravagantly pinnacled structure measuring some twelve metres in height, the altar was probably a joint venture with Michael's brother Friedrich, and was completed some time between 1471 and 1481. Normally only the outer panels of the altar are on display, depicting scenes from the life of Saint Wolfgang, who lived as a hermit on the shores of the lake, but on Sundays the wings are opened to allow a glimpse of scenes from the life of Christ. The brightly gilded, sculpted scenes of the coronation of the Virgin, which form the altar's centrepiece, are only revealed on religious holidays and festivals. Ascents of the local peak, the **Schafberg**, by mountain railway (May–Sept; *InterRail/Eurail* concessions), are possible from a station on the western edge of town.

Bad Ischl

The elegant town houses, fountains and gardens of **BAD ISCHL** have about them an air of calm, bourgeois repose. The soothing properties of the waters here prompted the penultimate Habsburg emperor, Franz Josef, to spend each summer in the **Kaiservilla** (May–Oct daily 9am–noon & 1–5pm; ÖS60), across the river Ischl from the centre, the interior of which is crammed with the unfortunate victims of the emperor's hunting expeditions. Beyond the villa stretches a park containing the **Marmorschlössel** (April–Oct daily 9.30am–5pm; ÖS25), an exquisite marble garden retreat built for the Empress Elizabeth, now housing a small museum of photography. If you decide to stay here, the **tourist office** is to be found down near the station at Bahnhofstrasse 6 (June–Sept Mon–Fri 8am–6pm, Sat 8am–4pm, Sun 9am–11.30pm; Oct–May Mon–Fri 8am–noon &

1–5.30pm). There are a couple of **hostels**, the *Jugendgästehaus* at Am Hochensteg 5 (☎06132/65 77; ②) and the somewhat less salubrious *Pfarrholm*, on Auböckplatz (☎06132/34 83; ②).

Gmunden and the Traunsee

Despite its popularity, there's little in Bad Ischl to detain you for long, and it's best to take a train to the placid nearby lakeside resorts. Fifteen kilometres northwest, the picturesque hamlets and villages of the western shore of the **Traunsee** (accessible by short hops on the rail line) are overshadowed by the sheer grey bulk of the Traunstein, which rises majestically to the east. The main town is **GMUNDEN**, at the northern end of the lake, originally a collection centre for the salt trade that gave the region both its wealth and its name. The town's long-standing affluence manifests itself in a fine Renaissance **town hall** with a ceramic-tiled fifteenth-century clock tower, while more down-to-earth products of the local ceramic industry are highlighted in the **town museum** a block east, housed in the medieval **Kammerhof**, the former salt exchequer. The town's southern fringes are dominated by the whitewashed walls of the seventeenth-century **Schloss Ort**, situated on an island in the lake, and reached by a wooden footbridge. Gmunden's **tourist office**, the *Kurwervaltung*, is at Am Graben 2 (Mon–Fri 8am–noon & 2–6pm, Sat 9am–noon), but it's better to head south to the quieter villages along the lake. **ALTMUNSTER**, 3km beyond, has a fine Gothic altar in the church of St Benedict, and extensive lakeside walks. A further 5km down the lake is **TRAUNKIRCHEN**, built around a rocky promontory crowned by the seventeenth-century **Pfarrkirche** or parish church, famous for its eighteenth-century *Fischerkanzlei* or fisherman's pulpit, built in the shape of a boat, its net loaded with fish and dripping with silvery waters. If the local **tourist office** (May–Sept Mon–Fri 8am–noon & 2–5pm; July & Aug also Sat 10am–noon) can't find you a room (and Traunkirchen is pretty small), there may be more possibilities in **Ebensee**, a modern town marking the southern end of the lake. Its **tourist office** is at Hauptstrasse 34 (Mon–Fri 8am–noon & 1–5pm; July & Aug also Sat 9am–noon). It also has a **youth hostel**, at Rindbachstrasse 15 (☎ 06133/66 98; ②).

Hallstatt

The real jewel of the Salzkammergut is **HALLSTATT**, occupying a dramatic position 20km south of Bad Ischl on the western shores of Hallstättersee, jutting out into the lake at the base of a precipitous cliff. Before the building of the road along the western side of the lake, local transport was provided by a sharp-prowed boat known as a *Fuhr*, propelled along by a single paddle at the stern, rather like a punt, and a few of them still ply the waters of the lake, emerging from the characteristic wooden boathouses which line the shore.

Hallstatt gave its name to a distinct period of Iron Age culture after Celtic remains were discovered in the salt mines above the town. Many of the finds which made the town famous, dating back to the ninth century BC, can now be seen in the **Prehistoric Museum** (daily May–Oct 10am–6pm; Nov–April 1–5pm; ÖS20), and they include wooden mining implements, pit props and hide rucksacks used by Iron Age miners, alongside more ornamental objects such as jewellery and ornate dagger handles. The same ticket is valid for the nearby **Heimat Museum** (same hours), full of the natural historical and anthropological collections of the archeologist who worked on the Celtic sites in the 1930s, Friedrich Morton, an inveterate world traveller – and hoarder. There's also a good deal on the history of salt mining, with tableaux illustrating working conditions throughout the centuries.

Hallstatt's **Pfarrkirche**, uphill from the water's edge, has a south portal adorned with Calvary scenes painted in around 1500. Inside, a late medieval altar contains scenes from the life of Mary and the early life of Jesus, and an adjoining chapel the central panel of an earlier, mid-fifteenth-century altar, with another Crucifixion scene – the wing panels were carried off by thieves in 1987. In the graveyard outside stands a small stone structure known as the **Beinhaus**, traditionally the repository for the skulls of villagers, with their bones neatly stacked below like firewood. The skulls, some of them quite recent, are inscribed with the names of the deceased and dates of their death, and are often decorated with finely painted floral patterns as well. Paths behind the graveyard lead up to the **salt mines** that provided the area's prosperity, viewable on regular guided tours (daily June to mid-Sept 9.30am–4.30pm; May & mid-Sept to mid-Oct 9.30am–5pm; ÖS100). Between May and October you can also take the **funicular** up here from Lahn.

Hallstatt's **train station** is on the opposite side of the lake to the town, a local ferry meeting all incoming trains. However, after about 6pm trains don't stop here, continuing on to the village of OBERTRAUN a five-kilometre walk away along the shores of the lake. Hallstatt's **tourist office** is centrally located on Marktplatz (June–Sept Mon–Fri 9am–5pm, Sat & Sun 11am–3pm; Oct–May Mon–Fri 8am–noon), and has **private rooms** and can book spaces in local **guesthouses**, most of which are cheaper in the suburb of Lahn, 400m south – try *Pansion Bergfried* (☎06134/248; ③). Lahn is also the location of the town's **youth hostel** at Lahn 50 (☎06134/279; ②). There's also a **hostel** in Obertraun at Winkl 26 (☎06134/360; ②).

WESTERN AUSTRIA

West of Salzburg towards the mountain province of the **Tirol**, the grandiose scenery of Austria's Alpine heartland begins to unfold in earnest. Most of the trains from Vienna and Salzburg travel through a corner of Bavaria before joining the Inn valley and climbing back into Austria to the Tirolean capital, **Innsbruck**. A less direct but more scenic route (and one you will be more likely to follow if coming from Graz and the southeast) cuts between the Kitzbühler Alpen and the majestic **Hoher Tauern** (site of Austria's highest peak, the Grossglockner), before joining the river Inn at Wörgl. Settlements such as the exclusive resort town of **Kitzbühel** provide potential stopoffs on the way, although it's Innsbruck which offers the most convenient mix of urban sights and Alpine splendour. Further west towards Switzerland, the **Vorarlberg** is a distant, isolated extremity of Austria, though its capital, **Bregenz**, on the shores of Lake Constance (*Bodensee* in German), makes for a tranquil stop before pressing on.

Kitzbühel

KITZBÜHEL began life as a sixteenth-century copper and silver mining town, and preserves an exceedingly pretty medieval centre, despite the vast sprawl of suburbs which clutters the valley below. From the train station, head down Bahnhofstrasse and turn left at the end; the town centre is a dull fifteen-minute stroll from here. Downtown Kitz revolves around two squares, **Vorderstadt** and **Hinterstadt**. The town's mining roots are on show in an ancient twelfth-century house on the corner of Hinterstadt, which contains an excellent **museum** of mining artefacts (Mon–Sat 9am–noon; ÖS30), revealing something of the industrial grit behind the tinseltown that Kitzbühel has since become. Some of the mining wealth no doubt went into the brightly coloured facades of the town houses lining Vorderstadt, now the backdrop to a promenade of pensioners ambling endlessly up and down. Perched above are two worthwhile churches, the fifteenth-century Gothic **Pfarrkirche**, whose overhanging roof covers some medieval frescoes in the choir, and, immediately above it, the **Liebfrauenkirche**, with a monumental tower and more frescoes in the graveyard chapel.

The **tourist office** is at Hinterstadt 18 (Mon–Sat 8.30am–7.30pm, Sun 9am–5pm), and outside the winter season has plentiful **rooms** either privately or in any number of inexpensive pensions. If you do spend time in Kitzbühel, it's a good idea to escape into the beautiful highland scenery close by, something you can easily do by taking the **Hahnehkamm** chair lift at the end of Heroldstrasse, ten minutes west of Hinterstadt.

Innsbruck

Located high in the Alps, with ski resorts within easy reach, it's as a winter vacation centre that **INNSBRUCK** is primarily known. However, the city is rich in history, too: Maximilian I based the imperial court here in the 1490s, suddenly placing the provincial Alpine town at the heart of European politics and culture. It remained an imperial residence for a further century and a half, and, given Innsbruck's special associations with the Habsburg dynasty, it's perhaps not surprising that its incorporation into Bavaria (a move precipitated by the Napoleonic carve-up of Europe) produced an insurrectionary movement under the local hero after whom so many streets and squares are named – Andreas Hofer.

Arrival and accommodation

The **tourist kiosk** in Innsbruck's **Hauptbahnhof** (daily 8am–10pm) offers a speedy room booking service for a small fee and a refundable deposit. The main **tourist office** is centrally located at Burgraben 3 (Mon–Sat 8am–7pm, Sun (9am–6pm). The main **youth hostel** is the *Innsbruck* at Reichenauerstrasse 147 (☎05222/461 79; ②), reachable on bus #0 from outside the Hauptbahnhof. The *Torsten-Arneus-Schwedenhaus* hostel, Rennweg 17b (☎05222/585 814; ③), is better placed for the centre, but is only open in July and August. *Hotel-Pension Binder*, Dr Glatz-Strasse 20 (☎05222/422 360; ③), is clean and friendly, but twenty minutes from the centre; *Innrain*, Innrain 38 (☎05222/58 89 81; ③), is a small *gasthof* on the south bank of the river. *Hotel Mozart*, Müllerstrasse 15 (☎05222/595 38; ④), is a larger establishment near the Maria-Teresien-Strasse with a wide range of rooms. The only campsite is *Camping Innsbruck Kranebitten*, west of the city centre; take bus #0.

The City

Most of what you will want to see in Innsbruck is confined to the central precincts of the Altstadt, a small area bounded by the river and the Graben, following the course of the moat which used to surround the medieval town. Leading up to this, Innsbruck's main artery is **Maria-Theresien-Strasse**, famed for the view north towards the great rock wall of the Nordkette, the mountain which dominates the city. At its southern end, three blocks west of the train station down Salurnerstrasse, the triumphal arch, **Triumphpforte**, was built in advance of celebrations marking the marriage of Maria Theresa's son Leopold in 1756. The sudden death of the empress's husband Franz caused a fundamental rethink of the arch's ornamentation, turning its north face into something of a funerary monument, with macabre symbols, including an angel of death. Halfway up, the **Annasäule**, a column supporting a statue of the Virgin but named after Saint Anne, who appears at the base, was erected to commemorate the retreat of the Bavarians, who had been menacing the Tirol, on St Anne's day (July 26) 1703.

North of here, Herzog-Friedrich-Strasse leads into the centre, opening out into a plaza overlooked by the **Goldenes Dachl**, or golden roof – though the tiles which give the roof its name are actually copper, added in the 1490s to cover a window from which the imperial court could observe the square below. An alley to the right leads down to Domplatz and the **Domkirche St Jakob**, home to a valuable *Madonna and Child* by

German master Lucas Cranach the Elder, although this is hard to make out, buried as it is in the fussy Baroque detail of the altar. To the left is a monument to Archduke Maximilian III, who kneels in prayer watched over by Saint George, accompanied by a strangely subdued dragon. The adjacent **Hofburg**, entered from Rennweg, at the end of Hofgasse around the corner, has late medieval roots but was remodelled in the eighteenth century, and its Rococo state apartments are unremarkable save for the cavernous state ballroom (mid-May to mid-Oct daily 9am–5pm; mid-Oct to mid-May Mon–Sat 9am–4pm; ÖS30).

At the head of the Rennweg is the **Hofkirche**, an outwardly unassuming building which nevertheless contains the most impressive of Innsbruck's imperial monuments, the **Cenotaph of Emperor Maximilian** (May–Sept daily 9am–5pm; Oct–April Mon–Sat 9am–noon & 2–5pm, Sun 9am–noon; ÖS40), an extraordinary project intended to consummate Maximilian's special relationship with Innsbruck and bolster the prestige of the dynasty. It was originally envisaged as a series of 40 larger-than-life statues, 100 statuettes and 32 busts of Roman emperors, representing both the real and the spiritual ancestors of Maximilian, but in the end only 32 of the statuettes and 20 of the busts were completed. The resulting ensemble is still impressive, though the effect is dulled slightly by the knowledge that the emperor is actually buried at the other end of Austria in Wiener Neustadt. Upstairs is the tomb of Archduke Ferdinand II, great-grandson of Maximilian and Regent of Tirol, in the so-called *Silberkapelle* or silver chapel, named after the silver Madonna which adorns the far wall. She is faced by Ferdinand's suit of armour, suspended in a kneeling position halfway up the wall. The bones of the man himself are housed directly below.

Entrance to the Hofkirche is through the same door as the **Tiroler Volkskunstmuseum** (Mon–Sat 9am–5pm, Sun 9am–noon; ÖS40), which has an endless series of wood panelled Tirolean peasant interiors, and models of Tirolean village architecture. However, the **Tiroler Landesmuseum Ferdinandeum**, a short walk south at Museumstrasse 15 (daily 10am–5pm, Thurs also 7–9pm; ÖS40), is perhaps more engaging. It's noted for its large collection of Gothic paintings, most originating from the churches of the South Tirol now in Italy, although some are by the "Pustertal painters" based around Lienz in the East Tirol, pre-eminent among whom were Michael and Friedrich Pacher, who imported Italian Renaissance techniques into German painting and sculpture. Michael, especially, was in demand all over Austria in the late 1400s, and his work turns up in most Austrian museums of any substance, but the gallery here is the best place to get a feel for the evolution of the Pachers' art.

After that, you could take tram #3 to **Schloss Ambras** (May–Sept 10am–4pm; closed Tues; ÖS50), home of Archduke Ferdinand II, who was a great hoarder of art objects and trinkets from far-flung places; the collection is displayed very much in its original form. The Schloss also has an extensive portrait gallery, although the artists are often less interesting than the sitters, a vast array of European rulers and aristocrats across the centuries.

The quickest route to higher altitudes is the **Hungerburgbahn**, which leaves from a station at the end of Rennweg (end of tram lines #1 and #6), calling at an intermediate station for the **Alpenzoo** (daily 9am–6pm; ÖS50) – a collection of animals indigenous to mountain regions – before reaching the Hungerburg plateau itself, a good base for hikes. A three-stage sequence of cable cars continues from here to just below the summit of the **Nordkette** itself.

Eating, drinking and nightlife

The streets around the *Goldenes Dachl* are a good source of **places to eat**, packed with old coaching inns transformed into restaurants. The inexpensive *Ottoburg*, Herzog-Friedrich-Strasse 1, is one of the most atmospheric and has at least one vegetarian main dish. Ten minutes' walk north up Rennweg, the gardens of the

Löwenhaus provide a relaxed, slightly more expensive setting for outdoor eating. *Stiegelbräu*, between the old town and the station at Wilhelm-Greil-Strasse 25, has a slightly rowdier beer-garden feel. There are plenty of convivial **drinking venues** in Innsbruck's old town, but don't expect the cosmopolitanism you find further east. *Café Fuzzy*, Universitätstrasse 19 (closed Sat), is a relaxed, youthful late-night café; *Café Club Filou*, Stiftgasse, is a pricier bar (with disco), though serving an affordable range of food. Wine and beer are also consumed in large quantities in a whole string of small and intimate *gastätte* on Innstrasse, just over the river, many of which also specialize in inexpensive Austrian cooking; stroll along and take your pick.

Listings

Car rental *Avis*, Salurnerstrasse 15 (☎05222/57 17 54); *Hertz*, Südtirolerplatz 1 (☎05222/58 09 01).

Consulates *Great Britain*, Matthias-Schmidstrasse 12 (☎ 05222/58 83 20).

Exchange Out of banking hours at the main tourist office or train station.

Hiking tours Hiking tours depart daily at 8.30am (June–Sept) from Innsbruck Congress Centre, and are free to those staying in town for three nights or more; check with the tourist office for details.

Hospital *Universitätklinik*, Anichstrasse 35 (☎05222/5040).

Mitfahrzentrale Brixnerstrasse 3 (☎05222/57 23 43).

Post office 24-hr office at Maximilianstrasse 2.

Telephones At the post office.

Travel agents *ÖKISTA*, Josef-Hirn-Strasse 7 (☎05222/58 89 97).

Bregenz

Stretched along the southern shores of Lake Constance, **BREGENZ** is an obvious staging post on journeys into neighbouring Bavaria to the north, or Switzerland to the west. Like the Swiss Germans, the Vorarlbergers who live here are descended from the Aleman tribes who swept through the region during the great migrations; they speak a dialect close to Swiss German, and their relations with the rest of Austria have always been coloured by a sense of separateness. Indeed, the Vorarlbergers went so far as to declare independence in November 1918, and requested union with Switzerland – a request turned down after the Great Powers' postwar deliberations.

The Town

At first sight Bregenz is an unpleasantly disjointed town, the tranquil lakeside parks cut off from the main body of the town by the main road and rail links along the shore of Lake Constance. Most of interest is located in the old town, up the hill from the lake around **St Martinsturm**, an early seventeenth-century tower crowned by a bulbous wooden dome. There's a small museum inside containing arms and armour, and a chance to enjoy views down towards the lake. The medieval grain storehouses next door were converted into a chapel in the fourteenth century, and frescoes from the period include several figures of Christ and Saint George. Up the street from here is the seventeenth-century **town hall**, an immense half-timbered construction with a steeply inclined roof built by local architect Michael Kuen. The **Vorarlberger Landesmuseum**, Kornmarkt 1 (Tues–Sun 9am–noon & 2–5pm; ÖS30), has some outstanding paintings by sixteenth-century artists like Wolf Huber and Jörg Frosch, who had workshops in the nearby town of Feldkirch, and a selection of portraits and classical scenes by Angelika Kauffmann, a Swiss painter who achieved success in late eighteenth century London. Beyond here, leafy **parklands** line the lake, at the western end of which stands the **Festspielhaus**, a modern concert hall built to accommodate the operatic and orchestral concerts of the Bregenz Festival, usually running from the last week in July to mid-August. The most popular excursion from Bregenz, however, is to take the cable car from a station at the eastern end of town to the **Pfänder** (July–Sept 9am–10.30pm; shorter hours rest of year), a wooded hill commanding an excellent panorama of the lake.

Practicalities

The **tourist office**, Anton Schneiderstrasse 4a (July–Sept Mon–Sat 9am–7pm; Oct–June Mon–Fri 9am–noon & 2–6pm, Sat 9am–noon), can book **rooms** for ÖS250 a head plus a ÖS10 fee. Among the cheaper hotels is *Gasthof Adler*, Vorklostergasse 66 (☎05574/317 88; ③). The **youth hostel** is at Belrupstrasse 16a (☎05574/42 8 67; ②). *Seecamping*, Bodengasse 7, occupies a large site 2km west of town by the lake.

travel details

Trains

Vienna to: Attnang-Pucheim (hourly; 2hr 30min); Bregenz (8 daily; 8hr); Graz (hourly; 2hr 30min); Innsbruck (hourly; 5hr 30min); Krems (hourly; 1hr); Linz (2 an hour; 2hr 30min); Salzburg (hourly; 3hr 15min).

Attnang-Pucheim to: Bad Ischl (hourly; 1hr); Gmunden (hourly; 20min); Hallstadt (hourly; 1hr 30 min).

Bad Ischl to: St Wolfgang (hourly; 40min).

Graz to: Innsbruck (7 daily; 6hr); Linz (every 2hr; 3hr 30min); Salzburg (8 daily; 4hr 30min).

Innsbruck to: Bregenz (10 daily; 2hr).

Salzburg to: Attnang-Pucheim (hourly; 45min); Innsbruck (8 daily; 2hr 30min); Kitzbühel (hourly; 1hr 45min); Linz (hourly; 1hr 20min).

Buses

Krems to: Melk (4 daily; 1hr 5min).

Salzburg to: Bad Ischl (hourly; 1hr 30min); Ströbl (hourly; 1hr 5min).

CHAPTER 2

BELGIUM AND LUXEMBOURG

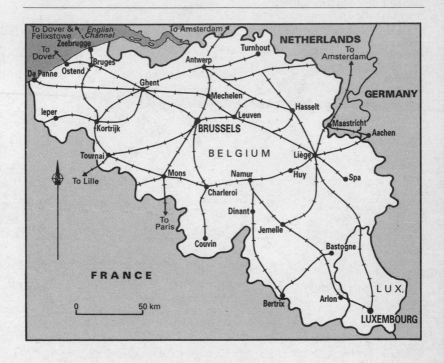

Introduction

A federal country, with three official languages and an intense regional rivalry, Belgium has a cultural mix and diversity which belies its rather dull reputation among travellers. Its population of around ten million is fairly evenly divided between Flemish-speakers (about sixty percent) and Walloons (forty percent), who speak French as their first language; there are even, in the far east of the country, a few pockets of German-speakers. Prosperity has shifted back and forth between the two communities over the centuries, and relations remain acrimonious. The line between the two cultures, officially called the "language divide" and effectively cutting the country in half, was drawn in 1962, and in response to increasing antagonism the constitution was redrawn a decade ago on a federal basis, with three separate entities – the Flemish North, Walloon South, and Brussels, which is officially bilingual (although its population is eighty percent French-speaking).

The North and South of **Belgium** are visually very different places. Marking the meeting of the two, **Brussels**, the capital, is a culturally varied city, more exciting than its reputation as bland Euro-capital would suggest. The **North**, made up of the provinces of West and East Flanders, Antwerp, Limburg and the top half of Brabant, is mainly flat, with a landscape and architecture not unlike Holland. **Antwerp** is the largest city, a bustling old port with doses of sleaze and high art in roughly equal measure. Further south, in the Flemish heartland of Flanders, are the great Belgian historic cities, **Bruges** and **Ghent**, with a stunning concentration of Flemish art and architecture. Other inland Flanders towns include the cathedral city of **Mechelen**, halfway between Brussels and Antwerp. The southern part of Brussels province, **Brabant**, is French-speaking, and merges into the solely Walloon province of **Hainaut** – rich agricultural country, dotted with ancient cities like **Tournai**. East of here lies Belgium's most scenically rewarding region, the **Ardennes**, spread across the three provinces of Namur, Liège and Luxembourg, an area of deep, wooded valleys, high elevations and dark caverns.

The Ardennes reach across the Belgian border into the northern part of the **Grand Duchy of Luxembourg**, a green landscape of rushing rivers and high hills topped with crumbling castles. **Diekirch**, **Vianden** and **Echternach** are perhaps the three best centres for touring the countryside and **Luxembourg** itself is at least worth a stop, although its population of 75,000 is still tiny by capital city standards.

Information and Maps

In both Belgium and Luxembourg there are **tourist offices** in all but the smallest villages. They often have free maps, and in the larger towns offer an accommodation service. As for **maps**, the Belgian Tourist Office gives out a decent free map of the country that incorporates basic city plans. Otherwise, the best-value general map of both countries is the 1:350,000 *Michelin*.

Money and Banks

The **currency** in both Belgium and Luxembourg is the franc, normally written as "F" or "BF" and "FLux". The Belgian and Luxembourg franc are interchangeable, with the same rate of exchange. Both currencies divide into 100 centimes, and come in **coins** worth 1, 5, 20 and 50 francs, and **notes** worth 50, 100, 500, 1000 and 5000 francs. **Banks** are the best places to change money. In Belgium they are open Mon–Fri 9am–noon & 2–4pm, in Luxembourg 9am–noon & 12.30–4.30pm; some banks also open on Saturday mornings. You can also change money in larger cities at train stations, some hotels, and bureaux de change, though the rates are less favourable; if you have a Eurocheque card with a PIN number you can use the *MISTERCASH* dispensers in Brussels and elsewhere.

Communications

In Belgium **post offices** are open Mon–Fri 9am–noon & 2–5pm and in Luxembourg Mon–Fri 8am–noon & 1.30–5pm. Some open Saturday mornings, too, and in larger centres the main offices don't shut at lunchtime. Public **phones** take F5, F20 and sometimes F50 coins, though in Belgium some also take cards, available from newsagents, post offices and train stations for F100 or F500. Calling abroad, remember that some post offices have booths where you can make your call and settle up afterwards. The operator numbers are ☎997 in Belgium, ☎0010 in Luxembourg.

Getting Around

Travelling around Belgium is rarely a problem. Distances are short, and there's an efficient and reasonably priced train service linking the major centres. Luxembourg, on the other hand, can be problematic: the train network is not extensive, and timetables often demand careful study.

■ Trains and buses

Run by the *Societé National Chemin de Fer de Belgique/Belgische Spoorwegen* (*Belgian Railways*), **Belgium**'s rail system is comprehensive and efficient, and fares are low. To cut costs further, other than *InterRail/Eurail* passes which are valid everywhere, the **Belgian Tourrail pass** gives entitlement to five days' unlimited rail travel within a month for F1980. There is also the so-called **Half-Fare Card**, which costs F550 and allows you to purchase tickets at half-price during a specified monthly period, or the **Go Pass**, valid for eight second-class journeys between two stations within six months for one or more people – price F990 for under-25s. Consider the **Benelux Tourrail Card** which gives 5 days' travel in a month for F2860 (over-26s F3780). *Belgian Railways* publish lots of **information** on their various offers and services, including national (F150) and international (F50) timetables, available from train stations.

In **Luxembourg** trains are run by *Chemins de Fer de Luxembourg – CFL*. There's one main north–south route down the middle of the country to Luxembourg City, but apart from that only a few lines branch out from the capital, and the system is mainly supplemented by **buses**. Fares are comparable, and at weekends and holidays the price of a single and return ticket are the same. There are also a number of passes available, giving unlimited train and bus travel for one day for F217; any five days within a month-long period for F658; or there's a monthly pass for F1748.

As so much of the country is covered by the rail network, **buses** in Belgium (run by *SNCV*, the national bus company) are only really used for travelling short distances, or in parts of the Ardennes where there are fewer rail lines.

■ Driving and hitching

Both countries are well covered by networks of main **roads** and (toll-free) motorways, and congestion is normally tolerable outside the major cities. You drive on the right, and the speed limit in built-up areas is 65kph, on main roads 90kph and on motorways 120kph. Seat belts in both countries are compulsory, and penalties for drunken driving stiff. Spot fines are common for some offences, and in Luxembourg it's obligatory to always carry at least F600 on you for payment of fines. The national motoring organization in Belgium is the *Touring Club Belgique* (☎02/512 78 90); in Luxembourg it's the *Automobile Club de Luxembourg* (☎45 00 45). **Car rental** in both countries is quite pricy, about F15,000 a week, though as usual there are cheaper weekend rates.

Hitching in Belgium and Luxembourg is easy: the Belgians give lifts to hitchhikers frequently, and the size of the country makes it a perfectly feasible way of getting around. Hitching on motorways is illegal, but the major towns of both countries are in any case well connected by ordinary main roads.

■ Cycling

Cycling is something of a national sport in **Belgium**, and is also a viable way of getting around, the distances and flat terrain making it a fairly effortless business. Most roads have bicycle lanes, and you can **hire** a bike from around 65 train stations, returning it to the station of your choice. Rates are cheap: F150 a day with a valid train ticket, F200 without; for a period of three days or more, the price is F100 a day. For a list of train stations offering this service, get hold of *Belgian Railways' Train & Vélo (Trein & Fiets)* leaflet. It is possible to take your **bike on the train** for F160 per journey.

In **Luxembourg** you can rent bikes throughout the country for around F250 a day, and you can take your bike on trains for F18 per journey. The Luxembourg Tourist Office issues a booklet showing cycling routes.

Accommodation

In Belgium and Luxembourg, accommodation is a major expense. Hotels, even the grottiest places, are never cheap, and hostels only provide an alternative in larger cities.

■ Hotels and private rooms

In both countries prices range from F1000–1500 for a double room in the cheapest one-star **hotel** to F4000–6000 in big city hotels – more if you go for somewhere really luxurious. In cheaper

---

ACCOMMODATION PRICE CODES

Throughout this guide, accommodation is priced on a scale of ① to ⑧, the number indicating the lowest price per night a single person could expect to pay in that establishment in high season. With hostels this is the nightly rate per person; with hotels, the price is arrived at by dividing the cost of the cheapest double room by two. The prices indicated by the codes are as follows

   ① = under £5 / $8   ② = £5–10 / $8–16   ③ = £10–15 / $16–24   ④ = £15–20 / $24 32

   ⑤ = £20–25 / $32–40   ⑥ = £25–30 / $40–48   ⑦ = £30–35 / $48–56   ⑧ = over £35 / $56

---

establishments breakfast isn't always included in the price, in which case you should add on F250 or so to the cost of the room – or, cheaper and better, use the nearest café. In summer you'd be well advised to book in advance, by either phoning direct or using the free *Belgium Tourist Reservations* service (*BTR*), Boulevard Anspach 111, Brussels B-1000 (☎02/513 74 84; fax 513 92 77). Reservations can also be made through most tourist offices, again free, though they'll often charge you a deposit which will be deducted from your final bill. The Belgian Tourist Office's guide details all the country's hotels, with prices. The Luxembourg Tourist Office also produces a booklet of approved hotels. **Private rooms** are sometimes a slightly cheaper alternative, bookable through local tourist offices at no charge. On average, reckon on spending F1000 plus a night on a double room, and expect them to sometimes be inconveniently situated.

■ Hostels, sleep-ins, student rooms

Belgium has 32 *IYHF* **youth hostels**, run by two separate organizations, one for Flanders, *Vlaamse Jeugdherbergcentrale*, Van Stralenstraat 40, B-2060 Antwerp (☎03/232 72 18), another for Wallonia, *Centrale Wallone des Auberges de la Jeunesse*, rue Van Oost 52, B-1030 Brussels (☎02/215 31 00). The Flanders hostels are large, ruthlessly organized affairs, those in Wallonia smaller and more informal. Rates run from F290 per person at the most basic places to around F380 at the better-equipped hostels, or those in Brussels which cost more. Non-members pay around F100 a night extra. Breakfast is usually included at hostels in Flanders, and not in Wallonia, where it costs about F85; charges are levied for sleeping bag hire in both regions – normally around F120. Many hostels also offer meals for F140–230. During the summer you should book in advance wherever possible.

Some of the larger cities – Antwerp and Brussels, for example – have a number of **unofficial youth hostels**. These normally charge F300–400 for a dormitory bed and are often just as comfortable. You'll also come across places known as **sleep-ins**, which offer dormitory accommodation for rock-bottom prices – sometimes as low as F250 per person. You might also find some cities offering **student accommodation** during the summer at very cheap rates.

There are about a dozen youth hostels in **Luxembourg**, all of which are members of the *Auberges de la Jeunesse de Luxembourg* (*AJL*), place d'Armes 18, Luxembourg (☎22 55 88). Rates for *IYHF* members are F300–350 per person, slightly more at the Luxembourg City hostel. Non-members pay around F100 on top. Breakfast is usually included; lunch or dinner is F110–230.

■ Camping

In view of the relatively high cost of other forms of accommodation, **camping** is an option well worth considering in both countries. There are around 400 sites in **Belgium**, most of them well-equipped and listed in the Belgian Tourist Office's *Camping* leaflet, broadly classified on a one- to four-star basis. The vast majority of sites are one-star establishments, for which you should expect to pay F40–100 per person per night, plus F50–100 for a tent, F50 for a car or motorcycle. **Luxembourg** has a little over 100 campsites, all detailed in a free booklet available from the national tourist board. Prices are usually F50–100 per person, plus F50 or so for a tent. During peak season it can be a good idea to book ahead if you're planning to arrive with a car and large tent or caravan. In Luxembourg there's also a number you can ring if you're having difficulty finding somewhere – ☎48 11 99, between 11am and 7.30pm daily.

Food and Drink

Belgian cuisine is held in high regard worldwide, and in Europe at least is regarded as second only to French in quality. The country also offers a wide range of ethnic food alternatives. The food of Luxembourg isn't as appealing or as varied, but you can still eat out well in much of the country, albeit at high prices. As for drink, beer is one of the real delights of Belgium, and Luxembourg produces some very drinkable white wines along its side of the Moselle.

■ Food

Southern Belgian cuisine is, in general, not unlike traditional French, retaining the fondness for rich sauces and ingredients that the latter has to some extent lost of late. In Flanders the food is more akin to that of Holland, though here, too, there are many interesting traditional dishes. Pork, beef and game, fish and seafood, especially mussels, are staple items, often cooked with butter, cream and herbs, or sometimes beer. Soups, too, are common: hearty affairs, especially in the south and Ardennes. The Ardennes is also well known for its smoked ham and, of course, its pâté.

In most parts of Belgium and Luxembourg you'll **start the day** in routine continental fashion with a cup of coffee and a roll or croissant. Later in the day, the most obvious **snack** is a portion of *frites* – served everywhere in Belgium from *friture* stalls, with just salt or mayonnaise, or, as in Holland, with more exotic dressings. Other street stalls, especially in the north, sell various sausages and everywhere there are stands selling waffles (*gaufres*), piping hot with jam and honey. There are also, of course, the usual burger joints, most commonly branches of the Belgian *Quick* chain.

As for sit-down food, many **bars** serve meals, at least at lunchtimes, and there is normally a host of **cafeterias** around serving up basic dishes – omelettes, steak or mussels with chips (virtually the Belgian national dish). You can expect to pay about F200 for an omelette; anything more substantial will cost F400–500, though most places have a *plat du jour* for F250–300. Though there's often a thin dividing line between the two as regards the food, **restaurants** are more expensive, and will also probably only open for the evening. Even in the cheapest restaurant, a main course will rarely cost under F400, and it's likely that prices for most things will be more like F600 upwards, particularly in Luxembourg.

Belgium is known best for its **chocolate**. The big Belgian chocolatiers, *Godiva* and *Leonidas*, have shops in the main towns and cities, and their pralines and truffles are almost worth the trip alone. Of the two, *Leonidas* is the cheaper; reckon on spending F200 or so for 500g of their chocolates.

■ Drink

The price of food in both Belgium and Luxembourg is more than compensated for by the low cost of **drinking**, especially if you like **beer**, which, in either country, is always good and comes in numerous varieties. Ask for a *bière* in a **bar** and you'll be served a roughly half-pint glass of whatever the bar has on tap. The most common Belgian brands are the Leuven-based *Stella Artois*, *Jupiler* from Liège, *Maes* and *Lamot*. In Luxembourg the most widespread brands are *Diekirch*, *Mousel* and *Bofferding*. There are also any number of **speciality beers**, usually served by the bottle but occasionally on draught. The most famous of these is perhaps *Lambic*, the generic title for beer brewed in the Brussels area which is fermented by contact with the yeast in the air. A blend of old and young lambic beers is known as *gueuze*, a cidery concoction sold in all Brussels bars. There's also *kriek* – lambic with cherries added – and *faro*, given a distinctive and refreshing flavour by adding candy sugar. Of other pilsener brands, *Duvel* stands out, not far short of the strength of wine. *De Koninck*, brewed in Antwerp, is like an English bitter but smoother, with a yeasty taste. Try also some of the strong ales brewed by the country's five Trappist monasteries, the best-known and most widely available of which is *Chimay*, brewed in Hainaut. Other examples are *Orval*, a fruitier brew from the southern province of Luxembourg, and *Westmalle*, from north of Antwerp, a rich, sweet, malty brew. **Bar prices** don't vary greatly: in both countries you'll pay around F50 for a glass of beer in all but the swankiest places, for beers like *Duvel* and *Chimay* around F90.

French **wines** are the most commonly drunk, although **Luxembourg** is a wine producer, and its white and sparkling wines, produced along the north bank of the Moselle, are very drinkable: they go for around F250 a bottle of sparkling stuff, F100–150 for ordinary white wine.

There's no national Belgian **spirit**, but all the usual kinds are available everywhere, at about F60 a glass in a bar. You will also find Dutch-style *jenever* in most bars in the north. In Luxembourg spirits are cheaper than elsewhere in Europe. You'll also come across home-produced bottles of *eau de vie*, distilled from various fruits and around fifty percent alcohol by volume.

Opening Hours and Holidays

Many **shops** are closed on Monday morning, even in major cities. Otherwise **opening hours** tend to be from 9am to 5.30 or 6pm, though certain shops stay open later on Thursday and Friday evenings. In general, things shut a little earlier on Saturday. Most museums are open, with variations, Tues–Sat 9am–4pm, and sometimes on Sunday; Monday is a common closing day. Outside the April–Sept period, many places close unless they're of prime touristic importance.

Shops and banks are closed and museums adopt Sunday hours on the following **public holidays**: Jan 1; Easter Monday; May 1; Ascension (around mid-May); Whit Monday; Aug 15; Nov 1; Nov 11; Nov 15; Dec 25 & Dec 26. In addition, June 23 is a public holiday in Luxembourg.

Emergencies

The Belgian **police force** are not quite the friendly bunch you find in the Netherlands but the country is relatively free of street crime and you shouldn't have much cause to come into contact with them. As far as **personal safety** goes, it's possible to walk anywhere in the centres of the larger cities at any time of day, though women should obviously be wary of badly lit or empty streets; parts of Brussels especially can be intimidating. If you are unlucky enough to have **something stolen**, report it immediately to the nearest police station. Get them to write a statement for your insurance claim when you get home. If you have problems you think the police can't deal with, there are a couple of organizations, primarily aimed at young people, that might be able to help: **S.O.S. Jeunes/Jeugd**, a help service that has a 24-hour emergency number available from the operator, and **Infor-Jeunes/Info Jeugd**, a nationwide information organization. Outside normal working hours, all **pharmacies** display a list of open alternatives outside. Weekend rotas are also listed in local newspapers.

> **EMERGENCY NUMBERS**
> **Belgium** Ambulance/Fire ☎100; Police ☎101.
> **Luxembourg** ☎012 for all services, including late-opening chemists, doctors, dentists, etc.

BRUSSELS

Wherever else you go in Belgium, it's likely that at some point you'll wind up in **BRUSSELS**. The city is the major air gateway for the country; it's on the main routes heading inland from the Channel ports via the Flemish art towns; and it's a convenient stopover on the train between France and the Netherlands. And, despite the city's reputation as a dull centre of commerce and diplomacy, you could do worse than stop over for a while. It has architecture and museums to rank with the best of Europe, a well-preserved medieval centre, and an energetic streetlife and night scene, especially in its immigrant quarters; indeed, the communities of European bureaucrats and business people, together with immigrants from Africa, Turkey and the Mediterranean, constitute a quarter of the population.

Brussels takes its name from Broekzele, or "village of the marsh", which grew up on the wide, shallow Senne river in the sixth century, benefiting from its position on the trade route between Cologne and the towns of Bruges and Ghent. Before long, it fell to the Dukes of Brabant, later coming under the sway of Burgundy and finally Habsburg and Spanish rule. Under the Spanish, the town flourished, eventually becoming capital of the Spanish Netherlands; later Brussels took turns with The Hague as capital of the new United Kingdom of the Netherlands, after which time, with Belgian independence, it became the capital of the new Belgian state. The nineteenth century saw the city kitted out with all the attributes of a modern European capital. The ring boulevards were built; the Senne, which had become an open sewer, was covered over in the city centre; and many slum areas were cleared and grand buildings erected. Since World War II, modernization has proceeded apace, the city's appointment as headquarters of both NATO and the EC instigating many major development projects, not least the new metro system.

The Brussels area telephone code is ☎02.

Arrival and information

Brussels has three main **train stations** – Gare Centrale, Gare du Nord and Gare du Midi – and most trains stop at all three. **Gare Centrale** is, as its name suggests, the most central, just a five-minute walk from the Grand Place; **Gare du Nord** lies in a sleazy district just north of the main ring road; and **Gare du Midi** in a depressed immigrant area to the south of the city centre. The stations are linked across the city centre by rail and underground tram. Arriving by **bus** from the UK, *Hoverspeed* coaches drop at place de la Bourse, *Eurolines* at place de Brouckère. By air, you'll land at **National Airport** in Zaventem, 12km northeast, connected by train every half-hour to the Gare du Nord and the Gare Centrale (20min; F80). Trains run until around 11.45pm; after that you'll need to take a taxi: reckon on paying around F1500 to the centre.

There's a **tourist information desk** at the airport: it has information on accommodation and transport, sells transport tickets and can make hotel reservations for you. There are two **tourist offices** in the city centre. The main one, the **TIB** in the Hôtel de Ville on the Grand Place (June–Sept daily 9am–6pm; Oct–May Mon–Sat 9am–6pm; ☎513 89 40), handles information on the city and can make hotel bookings. The **National Tourist Office**, nearby at rue Marché aux Herbes 61 (June–Sept Mon–Fri 9am–7pm, Sat & Sun 9am–1pm & 2–7pm; Oct–May Mon–Fri 9am–6pm, Sat & Sun 1–5pm; ☎504 03 90), has information on the whole of Belgium and will also make hotel reservations.

City transport

The easiest way to get around central Brussels is to **walk**, but to get from one side of the centre to the other, or to reach some of the more widely dispersed attractions, you'll need to use **public transport**. Operated by *STIB*, the system runs on a mixture of bus, tram and metro lines and covers the city comprehensively. A single flat-fare **ticket** costs F50, a strip of five F200, and a strip of ten F290, available either from tram or bus drivers, the tourist offices, metro kiosks, the *STIB* information offices in the Port de Namur, Midi and Rogier stations, or from some newsagents. A go-as-you-please *carte*, for F200, allows for 24 hours of travel on public transport. Be aware that spot fines for fare-dodging are heavy. Route maps are available free from the tourist office and from *STIB* information kiosks. Services run from 6am until midnight, after which there's a sporadic night bus service. **Taxis** don't cruise the streets but can be picked up from the ranks spread around the city – notably on Bourse, Brouckère, Grand Sablon and Porte de Namur – and at train stations. Prices start at F95. When you can't find one, phone ☎647 22 22 or ☎513 62 00.

Accommodation

Brussels has no shortage of **places to stay**, but given the number of people passing through, finding a room can be hard, particularly in summer, and it's best to book ahead at least your first night. The tourist offices can book hotel rooms on arrival, while the *Acotra* offices at the airport and in town at rue de la Madeleine 51 (☎512 55 40) will book rooms in youth hostels, though again you'd be better off doing it in advance.

Hostels

Jacques Brel, rue de la Sablonnière 30 (☎218 01 87). Official *IYHF* hostel with excellent facilities including showers in every room, bar and restaurant. Metro Madou or Botanique. ②

CHAB, rue Traversiere 8 (☎217 01 58). Spacious hostel with slightly lower prices than the official hostels. Price includes breakfast. Sinks in all rooms but shared showers and toilets. Open until 2am. Metro Botanique. Dorm beds ②, triples or quads ②, doubles ④.

Heilig Geeststraat, Heilig Geeststraat 2 (☎511 04 36). The other official hostel, more central but with shared showers. Bus #20 from Midi or bus #48 from Porte de Halle or a ten-minute walk from the Gare Centrale. ②

Maison Internationale, chaussée de Wavre 205 (☎648 97 87). Unofficial hostel with shared showers and toilets, but sinks in every room. Bus #37 or #38 from Gare Centrale, or a train to Gare du Quartier Leopold. You can camp here in summer too. ②

Sleep Well, rue de la Blanchisserie 27 (☎218 50 50). Conveniently located hostel, but it can be crowded and dirty in the height of summer. Metro Rogier. ②. As from July 1 1994, at a new address, 50m away; rue du Damier 23 (same phone).

Hotels

Bosquet, rue Bosquet 70 (☎538 52 30). A basic standard, but the price includes breakfast. Metro Hôtel des Monnaies. ④

De Boeck, rue Veydt 40 (☎537 40 33). Pleasant hotel in a pretty neighbourhood. Metro Louise. ⑦

George V, rue 't Kint 23 (☎513 50 93). Ramshackle hotel in a quiet neighbourhood. Breakfast included. Metro Bourse. ⑧

Madou, rue du Congrès 45 (☎218 83 75). A *fin-de-siècle* hotel with friendly management. All rooms have shower and toilet. Book well ahead. Metro Madou. ⑦

Osborne, rue Bosquet 67 (☎537 92 51). A hotchpotch of rooms a short walk from avenue Louise. Breakfast included in price. Metro Munthof. ⑤

Sabina, rue du Nord 78 (☎218 26 37). Spruce rooms, in a wonderful turn-of-the-century house. Metro Madou. ⑥

CENTRAL BRUSSELS

Parc de Bruxelles
Palais des Académies
Luxembourg ★
DU REGENT
Palais Royal
BOULEVARD
RUE
★ Pte. de Namur
CHAUSÉE D'IXELLES
Hôtel Bellevue
RUE DU PÉPIN
Palais des Beaux Arts
P. ROYALE
St. Jacques Condenberg
Palais d'Egmont
RUE DE STASSART
Palais des Congrès
MONT DES ARTS
Musée des Beaux Arts
RUE DE LA RÉGENCE
RUE DU GRAND SABLON
PL. DU PETIT SABLON
BOULEVARD DE WATERLOO
P. LOUISE
★ Pl. Louise
AVENUE LOUISE
P. STÉPHANIE
Gare Centrale
BLD DE L'EMPEREUR
P. DE L'ALBERTINE
Albert Library
RUE
Notre Dame du Sablon
Musée Instrumental
PL. POELAERT
Palais de Justice
VIOLETTE
Notre Dame de la Chapelle
Manneken Pis
RUE DU CHÊNE
Bruegel Youth Hostel
RUE HAUTE
RUE DE L'ÉTUVE
RUE BLAES
RUE DU POINÇON
RUE ST-GHISLAIN
QUARTIER MAROLLES
RUE DES BOGARDS
RUE DES ÉPERONNIERS
RUE DES URSULINES
RUE DES BRIGITTINES
RUE DES RENARDS
PLACE DU JEU DE BALLE
PORTE DE HAL
RUE DU MIDI
P. ROUPPE
RUE TERRE NEUVE
RUE DE LA RASIÈRE
FONTAINAS
Anneessens ★
AVENUE DE STALINGRAD
BOULEVARD M. LEMONNIER
★ Lemonnier
RUE DES FOULONS
BD. DU MIDI ZUIDLAAN
Gare du Midi

250 m
0

Windsor, place Rouppe 13 (☎511 20 14). Clean and cheerful rooms with breakfast included. Metro Anneessens. ⑦

Campsites

Grimbergen, Veldkantstraat 46, Grimbergen (☎269 25 69). North of Brussels. Take bus G from Gare du Nord to the terminus, after which it's roughly ten minutes' walk.

Paul Rosmant, Warandenberg 52, Wezembeek–Oppem (☎782 10 09). Well-equipped site east of Brussels. Metro to Kraainem (Line 1B) and from there bus #30 to place St Pierre.

The City

The centre of Brussels is enclosed within a rough pentagon of boulevards, a "petit ring" which follows the course of the fourteenth-century city walls. It is divided between the Upper and Lower Towns, the neighbourhoods generally becoming more expensive the higher you go. By far the greater part of the centre is occupied by the **Lower Town**, the medieval core of which zeroes in on the Grand Place, the unquestionable centre of Brussels and perhaps the finest preserved city square in Europe. South of here, the busy centre fades into the old working-class streets of the Marolles district and Gare du Midi, now a depressed, predominantly immigrant area; north, the shopping street of rue Neuve leads up to place Rogier and the tawdry area around the Gare du Nord. The *haute de la ville*, or **Upper Town**, is quite different in feel from the rest of the centre, with statuesque buildings lining wide, classical boulevards and squares. Appropriately, it's the home of the Belgian parliament and government departments, some of the major museums and the swishest shops.

The Lower Town

The obvious place to begin any tour of the **Lower Town** is the **Grand Place**, the commercial hub of the city since the Middle Ages – though of the square's medieval buildings only the Hôtel de Ville and one guildhouse survive, due to a 36-hour bombardment of the city by the French in 1695. The **Hôtel de Ville** (tours Tues–Fri 9.30am–12.15pm & 1.45–5pm, Sun 10am–noon & 2–4pm; F75) still dominates the proceedings, and inside, you can view various official rooms; most dazzling the sixteenth-century council chamber, decorated with gilt moulding, faded tapestries and an oak floor inlaid with ebony. On a more contemporary note, take a look at the electronic interpreting system, installed to facilitate discussion between French- and Flemish-speaking councillors. But the real glory of the Grand Place lies in the **guildhouses**, rebuilt in the early eighteenth century, their slender facades swirling with exuberant, self-publicizing carving and sculpture. The western side of the square is perhaps the most visually impressive, notably the **Maison du Renard** at no. 7, the house of the haberdashers' guild, on which cherubs in bas-relief play at haberdashery, while a gilded fox, after which the house is named, squats above the door. Next door, at no. 6, the **Maison du Cornet**, headquarters of the boatsmen's guild, is a fanciful creation of 1697 whose top storey resembles the stern of a ship; while at the end of the row, the **Roi d'Espagne**, headquarters of the guild of bakers, is named after the bust of Charles V on the facade, flanked by a Moorish and Indian prisoner to symbolize his mastery of a vast empire. Most of the northern side of the square is taken up by the sturdy neo-Gothic **Maison du Roi**, a reconstruction of a sixteenth-century building that now houses the **Musée de la Ville de Bruxelles** (Mon–Thurs 10am–12.30pm & 1.30–5pm, Sat & Sun 10am–1pm; F80), painlessly summarizing the history of Brussels with maps and models alongside displays of costumes donated to the Manneken Pis by various world leaders. On the opposite side of the square, the **Maison des Brasseurs** is the only house still owned by its original guild, the brewers, and boasts a small **Brewery Museum** (Mon–Fri 10am–noon & 2–5pm, Sat 10am–noon; F100), where you can sit over a free beer and look at various ancient bits of brewing paraphernalia. In rue Charles Buls, around the corner, the exploits of one **Everard 't Serclaes**, a fourteenth-century Brabantian hero, are commemorated by a reclining statue, whose arm is polished smooth by those who come to stroke it for good luck.

Down the street and left, rue de la Violette leads down to the **Manneken Pis**, a diminutive statue of a little boy pissing, that's supposed to embody the "irreverent spirit" of the city and is today one of Brussels' biggest tourist draws. Jerome Duquesnoy cast the original statue in the 1600s, but it was stolen several times and the current one is a copy. On the opposite side of the Grand Place, the quarter hinging on **rue des Bouchers** is the city centre's restaurant ghetto, crowded with tourists eyeing up elaborate displays of fish and seafood. Things are slightly more subdued in the nearby **Galeries St Hubert**, bisected by rue des Bouchers, which, with their refined shops, exclusive restaurants and cafés, retain an aura of sophistication.

Walking out of the Grand Place along rue du Beurre, the **Bourse**, a Neoclassical structure of 1873 caked with fruit, fronds, languishing nudes and frolicking putti, hides the view of busy boulevard Anspach beyond. Right up here is **place de Brouckère**, Brussels' modern centre, a busy traffic-choked junction surrounded by advertising hoardings, and, close by, **place de la Monnaie** – an uninteresting modern square that's home to the **Théâtre de la Monnaie**, the city opera house. From here, **rue Neuve** forges north, a gaudy pedestrianized shopping street meeting the inner ring at the junction of **place Rogier**, beyond which lies the Gare du Nord and the seedy red-light area. About a third of the way up rue Neuve, **place des Martyrs** is a cool, rational square imposed on the city by the Habsburgs that is nowadays one of its most haunting sights, a forlorn, abandoned open space, and magnet for the lonely and down-and-out. Beyond the square, the **Magasins Waucquez** at rue des Sables 20 now house the **Centre Belge de la Bande Dessinée** (Tues–Sun 10am–6pm; F150), an exhibition devoted to the history of the Belgian comic strip, focusing on a wide range of cartoonists, with specific sections on animation and, of course, Hergé and Tintin.

In the opposite direction from the Grand Place, the church of **Notre Dame de la Chapelle**, a sprawling Gothic structure, is the city's oldest church, built between 1210 and 1300. Its main claim to fame is the tomb of Pieter Bruegel the Elder in the third chapel of the south aisle, who is supposed to have lived and died around the corner at rue Haute 132. With parallel rue Blaes, rue Haute forms the spine of the **Quartier Marolles** – an earthy neighbourhood of cheap restaurants, shops and bars that grew up in the seventeenth century as a centre for artisans working on the nearby mansions of Sablon. Today, gentrification is creeping into the district, but it's got some way to go, and **place Jeu de Balle**, the heart of Marolles, is still the scene of the city's great flea market on a Sunday. Beyond, the area around the **Gare du Midi** is home to the city's many North African immigrants, a depressed quarter with an uneasy undertow by day and sometimes overtly threatening at night. The best time to go is on a Sunday morning, when a vibrant souk-like **market** is held under the arches of the station.

The Upper Town

The slopes to the **Upper Town** rise only minutes from the Grand Place, up rue de Montagne to the city's **Cathedral** (daily 7am–7pm), a Brabant-Gothic building begun in 1220 and dedicated jointly to Saint Michel and Saint Gudule, the patrons of Brussels. It was severely damaged during the Restoration and, like so much else in the city, by French shelling a century later. Napoléon later tentatively restored the building, and another major restoration is currently underway. Flooded with light from the clerestory windows, it's a fine church, though the present work means that the choir, the earliest example of the style in the Low Countries, is boarded off. There is, however, some superb sixteenth-century stained glass in the transepts – panegyrics to the Habsburgs designed by Bernard van Orley.

South of the cathedral, the so-called **Mont des Arts**, a collection of severe geometric buildings given over to a variety of arts-related activities, climbs up to the imperiously Neoclassical **place Royale** and **rue Royale**, the backbone of the Upper Town. Around the corner, the **Palais du Roi** is something of an anticlimax, a sombre 1904 conversion that isn't actually lived in by the Belgian royals and is open to the public during August. Sumptuous rooms, and tapestries designed by Goya, make a visit worthwhile, which is more than can be said for the displays in the palace annexe, **Hôtel Bellevue** (Sat–Thurs 10am–5pm; free), made up of furniture, porcelain and glass, along with an odd array of eighteenth- and nineteenth-century heart-shaped brooches, perfume bottles and ex-votos.

Opposite the Palais, the **Parc de Bruxelles** is the most central of the city's parks, while in the other direction, south, the **Musées Royaux des Beaux Arts** comprise Belgium's most satisfying all-round collection of fine art. Made up of two museums, one displaying modern art, the other older works, the galleries should really be seen on separate visits. The collections of the **Musée d'Art Ancien** (Tues–Sun 10am–noon & 1–5pm; free) are made more comprehensible by a system of colour-coded routes. The **blue route** takes in paintings of the fifteenth and sixteenth centuries, beginning with the Flemish primitives, notably several delicately realistic paintings by Rogier van der Weyden, city painter to Brussels in the fifteenth century, and the powerful *Justice of Otto* by his contemporary Dieric Bouts. There are plain, no-nonsense portraits by Hans Memling, a *Temptation of St Anthony* by Hieronymus Bosch, work by Cranach, including the sharply observed nudes of *Venus* and *Adam and Eve*, and Quentin Matsys, including a marvellous *Virgin and Child*, and Jan Mostaert's wonderfully busy *Passion*. Works by the Bruegel family, notably Pieter the Elder, are in rooms 31–34, not least the *Fall of the Rebel Angels* in the first room – actually attributed to Bosch until Bruegel's signature was discovered under the frame. Look, too, for *The Census at Bethlehem* and *Massacre of the Innocents*, with the traditionally momentous events happening among the bustle of everyday life, and, perhaps Bruegel the Elder's most haunting work, *The Fall of Icarus*. The **brown route** concentrates on work of the seventeenth and eighteenth centuries, notably some glorious canvases by Rubens. The **yellow route** of nineteenth-century works is the gallery's dullest, only redeemed by the paintings and sculptures of workers by the Belgian social realist Constantin Meunier. Revamped in the 1980s, the **Musée d'Art Moderne** (Tues–Sun 10am–1pm & 2–5pm; free) is accessible by escalator from the Ancient collection and has a grouping of works by Bonnard, Gauguin and Matisse, a Dufy *View of Marseille*, and two fanciful paintings by Chagall – though the highlight here is a series of solitary women by James Ensor. Other levels cover other movements, not least the Expressionists, Cubists and Surrealists, of which the last are the most gripping. There's a fine Dali, *The Temptation of St Anthony*, a couple of de Chirico's paintings of dressmakers' dummies, oddly erotic works by Paul Delvaux, and a small show of paintings by Magritte, whose bizarre juxtapositions aim firmly to disconcert.

From the Beaux Arts it's a short walk south to the **place du Petit Sablon**, a rectangular area off to the left that is decorated with 48 statues representing the medieval guilds, and a fountain relating the story of Counts Egmont and Hoorn, beheaded on the Grand Place for their opposition to Spanish tyranny in the 1500s. On the corner of rue de la Regence, the **Musée Instrumental** (Tues–Fri 9.30am–12.15pm & 1.45–5pm, Sun 10am–noon & 2–4pm; F75) has a fine collection of old musical instruments –exquisite keyboards and strings, and a display devoted to Adolphe Sax, the Belgian-born inventor of the saxophone. On the other side of the street, the fifteenth-century church of **Notre Dame du Sablon** began life as a chapel for the medieval guild of archers, but after a statue of Mary with powers of healing was brought by boat from Antwerp to the chapel it became a centre of pilgrimage and a proper church was built to accommodate its visitors. The statue of Mary no longer exists, but a wooden carving of a boat over the entrance and a stained-glass boat in the west window commemorate its legendary means of transport, and the occasion of its arrival is still celebrated annually in July by the Ommegang procession. Behind the church, the sloping wedge of **place du Grand Sablon** is centre of one of the city's wealthiest districts, busiest at weekends when a high-priced antique market clusters below the church. At the top end of rue de la Regence, **place Poelaert** is named after the architect who designed the immense **Palais de Justice** behind, built in 1883 and actually larger than St Peter's in Rome. A stone's throw away, **place Louise**, a chaotic traffic junction on the inner ring road, provides an unlikely setting for the city's most exclusive shopping district.

Outside the petit ring: the parks and outer boroughs

Brussels by no means ends with the petit ring. East of the inner ring road, the **Quartier Leopold** takes its name from the late nineteenth-century king of Belgium, who laid out much of the area with large boulevards and monuments and statues. It's home to the huge, winged **Berlaymont** building, headquarters of the EC, and **Parc Leopold** (metro Luxembourg or Maalbeek) – the pleasanter of the quarter's two parks. Within the park, the **Institut des Sciences Naturelles** (Tues–Sat 9.30am–4.45pm, Sun 9.30am–6pm; F120) is a rather old-fashioned natural history collection, with a great army of dinosaurs, a vivarium with some vicious-looking scorpions and a Mexican orange-kneed tarantula, and scores of stuffed animals. Just outside the park gates, at rue Vautier 62, the **Musée Wiertz** (Tues–Sun 10am–noon & 1–5pm; free) is devoted to the works of the nineteenth-century Belgian artist, responsible for vast religious and mythological canvases, and depictions of such nasty subjects as *The Burnt Child, The Thoughts and Visions of a Severed Head* and *Premature Burial*. Further east lies the larger **Parc du Cinquantenaire**, laid out for an exhibition to mark the golden anniversary of the Belgian state in 1880 and site of some of Brussels' larger museums. The **Musée Royal d'Art et d'Histoire**, in the south wing of the Palais de Cinquantenaire (Tues–Fri 9.30am–5pm, Sat & Sun 10am–5pm; free), has enormous galleries of Greek, Egyptian and Roman artefacts, displays of European applied arts and Islamic Art. Also in the south wing of the palace is **Autoworld** (daily 10am–6pm; F150), a good, if expensive, place to take the kids, although its extensive displays of vintage cars, motorcycles and fire engines should appeal to anyone. In the north wing, the collections of the **Musée Royal de l'Armée et d'Histoire Militaire** (Tues–Sun 9am–noon & 1–4.45pm; free) detail the history of the Belgian army from the eighteenth century to the present day.

Quite a way south of here, **St Gilles** is the most intriguing inner borough, a multira-cial district stretching from the refinement of avenue Louise in the east to the solidly immigrant quarters towards the Gare du Midi. Most people trek out here to see the **Musée Victor Horta**, the former home of the Art Nouveau Belgian architect at rue Americain 25 (Tues–Sun 2–5.30pm; F100), accessible by tram #92 from place Louise. From the outside it's a modest dwelling, but inside it displays all the architect's familiar trademarks: wide, bright rooms spiralling around a superbly worked staircase, stained glass, sculpture, and ornate furniture and panelling made from several different woods.

Southwest of the petit ring, **Ixelles** is another immigrant quarter, the favoured hang-out of arty types, with designer shops and a number of chic bars and restaurants join-ing the longer-established studenty and ethnic haunts. There's little to detain you by day until you reach rue J. van Volsem, where the neighbourhood's **Musée des Beaux Arts** at no. 71 (Tues–Fri 1–7.30pm, Sat & Sun 10am–5pm; free) holds a modest collec-tion of mostly French and Belgian artists – works by Magritte, Dufy, Delvaux, Toulouse-Lautrec and Meunier. There's also the **Musée Constantin Meunier**, rue de L'Abbaye 59 (Tues–Sun 10am–noon & 1–5pm; free), in the artist's old studio on the other side of avenue Louise from the **Étangs d'Ixelles**, a series of lakes at the foot of the chaussée. Further south lies the **Bois de la Cambre**, Brussels' most popular park and part of the vast **Forêt de Soignes**.

North of the ring road, **Laeken** (tram #92 from rue Royale or metro #3) is the royal suburb of Brussels. Its large public **park** – laid out in the nineteenth century by Leopold II – is best known for the **Atomium** (daily 10am–6pm; F160), a colossal model of a molecule built for the 1958 World Fair (metro Heysel). Something of a symbol of the city, it contains a museum – an unremarkable display on the peaceful uses of atomic energy – and a restaurant, but the main sensation is the disorientating feeling of travelling from sphere to sphere by escalator. Unfortunately, grey weather often obscures the views.

South of the city centre, **Anderlecht** is a dull, grimy quarter most famous for its football team. But it's worth making the effort to see the **Musée Gueuze**, rue Gheude 56 (Mon–Fri 8.30am–4.30pm, Sat 9.30am–1pm; F70), ten minutes' walk from Midi station – a mustily evocative working brewery, still brewing gueuze beer according to traditional methods. There are guided tours on Saturdays at 11am, 2pm and 3.30pm, although you can go around alone, using the excellent English-language leaflet. The beer is allowed to ferment naturally, reacting with yeasts peculiar to the Brussels air. The result is unique, as you can find out at the tasting at the end of the tour.

Eating and drinking

Brussels can be a great (and great-value) city in which to **eat**. There's a huge variety of **restaurants**, and even the most touristy places serve reasonable food for acceptable prices; the city is also among Europe's best for sampling different ethnic cuisines. For **fast food**, aside from the multinational burger and pizza chains, there are plenty of *friture* and kebab places around the Grand Place, notably on rue Marché aux Fromages, while carts around place Ste-Catherine sell hot mussels. For picnic lunches, try the city's street markets or the Italian delis around place Ste-Catherine.

For straight **drinking**, the enormous variety of bars and cafés is one of the city's real joys – sumptuous Art Nouveau cafés, traditional bars with ceilings stained brown by a century's smoke, speciality beer bars with literally hundreds of different varieties of ale, and, of course, more modern hang-outs. Many of the centrally located bars are much-frequented by tourists and ex-pats, but outside the centre, and even tucked away off the Grand Place, there are places which remain refreshingly local. A number serve meals as well as snacks, often far better value than eating in a restaurant. Bars also stay open late – most until 2 or 3am, some until dawn.

Restaurants

Le Canard à Trois Pattes, rue des Bouchers 5. Despite the very touristy location, this place serves excellent plats du jour for under F400, and menus from around F600.

Chez Léon, rue des Bouchers 18–22. Touristy but good-value restaurant near the Grand Place serving traditional Belgian fare. Most famous for its mussel dishes.

Chez Mille et Alice, rue de Flandre 101. Unpretentious neighbourhood restaurant where you can get a mountain of mussels and a large plate of chips for F360.

La Grande Porte, rue Notre–Seigneur 9. Cosy and crowded seventeenth-century *estaminet*, serving good traditional food. Main meals cost around F400.

Horta Brasserie, rue des Sables 20. The café of the recently opened *Centre Belge de la Bande Dessinée*, serving decent snacks and light meals.

't Kelderke, Grand Place 15. Boisterous, excellent-value cellar restaurant on the Grand Place, best-known for its *carbonades à la Flamande*. No reservations and you might have to queue. The new *'t Kelderke estaminet* next door has regular live music.

Le Pre Salé, rue de Flandre 16. Friendly, old-fashioned neighbourhood restaurant just off place Ste-Catherine, and a nice alternative to the swankier eateries of the district. Great mussels and other Belgian specialities.

Quartier Latin, bd General Jacques 212. Relaxed, studenty hang-out serving excellent Vietnamese food. Dim sum a speciality.

Sahbaz, chaussée de Haecht 102. Reckoned to be the city's best Turkish restaurant; cheap too – grilled meats with rice and crudités for around F200.

't Spinnekopke, place du Jardin–aux–Fleurs. Ancient restaurant and bar that serves many traditional Bruxellois dishes cooked in beer. Not especially cheap.

Stekerlapatte, rue des Prêtres 6. On the far side of the Palais de Justice, a wonderful old brasserie, usually packed with a youngish crowd, serving main meals for around F400.

Tsampa, rue de Livourne 109. Congenial Buddhist vegetarian restaurant, with daily specials for around F400. Open noon–2pm & 7–10pm, closed Sat & Sun evenings.

Bars and cafés

À la Becasse, rue Tabora 1. Spartan, old-fashioned bar not far from the Grand Place that is one of the few remaining venues for sampling *lambic*, along with simple bar snacks.

Cirio, rue de la Bourse. One of Brussels' oldest bars, sumptuously decorated in *fin-de-siècle* style.

DNA, rue Plattesteen 18. Young, lively haunt of the studenty and street-credible. Don't expect to find a seat after 10pm. Open until 3am.

't Dolle Mol, rue des Eperonniers 52. Small, predominantly Flemish-speaking bar, with a cliquey clientele and loud music. Unpretentious for such a central place.

Falstaff, rue Henri Maus 17–23. Art Nouveau café/brasserie next to the Bourse. Full of atmosphere, and usually packed. Also serves snacks and full meals – plats du jour F300.

La Fleur en Papier Doré, rue des Alexiens 53. Cluttered, cosy locals' bar, with walls covered with doodles and poems. Once the watering hole of René Magritte.

Interférences, rue de la Tête d'Or 1. Video bar which gets lively later in the evening with a mainly young crowd. Handily situated just off the Grand Place.

Moeder Lambic, rue de Savoie 68, St Gilles. Over a thousand beers on offer, including 500 Belgian varieties, and not at all expensive. Open until 4am.

À la Mort Subite, rue Montagne-aux-Herbes-Potagères 7. Popular bar with a wonderful old interior. Snacks served, or just order a plate of cheese-cubes to accompany your beer.

Les Postiers, rue Fossé aux Loups 14. Old-established and unpretentious bar neatly placed close to place de la Monnaie and serving basic snacks and light meals.

Rick's Café Americain, av Louise 344. A gathering place of resident English-speakers for close on thirty years. Full menu available, though it's most famous for its ribs.

Au Soleil, rue Marché au Charbon 86. Popular bar with a wide choice of beer, crowded until late every night with a young and trendy crowd.

Toone, petite rue des Bouchers 21. Scruffy, largely undiscovered bar belonging to the Toone puppet theatre. One of the centre's most congenial watering holes.

L'Ultieme Atome, rue Saint Boniface 14, Ixelles. Affable café serving a good range of beers and an excellent and varied menu to a youngish clientele.

De Ultieme Hallucinatie, rue Royale 316. Fanciful Art Nouveau bar done up like a Twenties train carriage. A youngish crowd sinking a good choice of beers and reasonably priced food. Live music too at weekends.

Wittamer, place du Grand Sablon 12–13. Brussels' most famous patisserie, established in 1910 and still run by the Wittamer family. Gorgeous, if pricy, pastries and cakes.

Nightlife

As far as **nightlife** goes, you may be perfectly happy to while away the evenings in one of the city's bars or restaurants. However, Brussels is also a good place to catch **live bands**; the music bars clustered around place Fernand Cocq and the lower end of the chaussée d'Ixelles are great for weekend bar-hopping. **Clubs and discos** are less impressive, but they are sometimes free, although at least one overpriced drink is usually obligatory. The best English-language source of **listings** is the weekly magazine *The Bulletin*; the Thursday pull-out in the newspaper *Le Soir* is also useful. **Tickets** for most things are available from *FNAC* in City 2, rue Neuve, or from the tourist office on the Grand Place (daily 11am–5pm) for a fee.

Concert halls

Ancienne Belgique, bd Anspach 114 (☎512 59 86). The main venue for home-grown and international indie bands. Also showcases jazz and folk.

Forest National, av du Globe 36 (☎347 03 55). Brussels' main venue for big-name international concerts, holding around 6000 people.

Palais des Beaux Arts, rue Ravenstein 23 (☎512 50 45). With a concert hall holding around 2000, the Palais is used for anything from contemporary dance to Tom Jones.

Live music bars

Le Bierodrome, place Ferdinand Cocq 21. Smoky jazz bar whose weekend gigs attract a comfortably unpretentious crowd. On other evenings it's just a nice place to drink.

Blues Corner, rue des Chapeliers 12. No-frills bar with local bands playing most nights.

Do Brasil, rue de la Caserne 88. Brazilian music and food Tues–Sat.

Machado, rue des Chapeliers 14. Jazz and Latin music until dawn.

Le Paradoxe, chaussée d'Ixelles 329. Vegetarian restaurant with an esoteric range of live jazz, folk and world music every Fri & Sat night.

Sounds, rue de la Tulipe 28. Scruffy bar serving up regular jazz and R&B.

Travers, rue Traversière 11. Informal jazz club with a reputation for showcasing up-and-coming Belgian musicians.

Clubs and discos

Le Garage, rue Duquesnoy 16. The best of the capital's large clubs, playing a frenetic mix of House, Techno and New Beat.

Le Mirano Continental, chaussée de Louvain 38. The club of the posturing media crowd, with a door policy that favours anyone who looks like a model.

The New Memphis, rue de Dublin 40. Ixelles club playing disco and funk.

The Rainbow, rue Leopold 7. Bar with disco on Sat that's patronized mainly by US school kids and UK au pairs. The music can be good, however, and it's cheap to get in.

Listings

Airlines *American Airlines*, rue de Trone 98 (☎508 77 00); *British Airways*, Centre Rogier, 9th floor (☎217 74 00); *KLM*, rue des Princes 8 (☎217 63 00); *Luxair*, av Louise 104 (☎646 03 70); *Sabena*, rue Cardinal Mercier 35 (☎511 90 30 or ☎723 60 10).

Airport enquiries ☎722 31 11 or ☎722 39 81.

American Express place Louise 2 (Mon–Fri 9am–5pm, Sat 9am–noon).

Books *WH Smith* at bd Adolphe Max 71–75 is the best central source of English-language books and magazines.

Car rental *Avis*, rue Americaine 145 (☎537 12 80); *Europcar*, av Louise 235 (☎640 94 00); *Hertz*, bd Lemonnier 8 (☎513 28 86).

Embassies *Australia*, rue Grimaud 6 (☎213 05 00); *Canada*, av de Tervuren 2 (☎735 60 40); *Great Britain*, rue Joseph II 28, Etterbeek (☎217 90 00); *Ireland*, rue du Luxembourg 19 (☎513 66 33); *New Zealand*, bd de Regent 47–48 (☎512 10 40); *USA*, bd de Regent 27 (☎513 38 30).

Exchange Outside bank hours you can change money and travellers' cheques at the Gare du Nord and Gare du Midi (daily 7am–11pm) and Gare Centrale (daily 8am–9pm). For credit cards, there's also *Best Change*, rue de la Colline 2 (daily 9am–7.45pm).

Gay and lesbian Brussels For up-to-date information on the Brussels gay scene, phone the Gay/Lesbian Line on ☎233 25 02 (daily 9am–9pm).

Hospital For medical assistance call ☎479 18 18 or ☎648 80 00, day or night.

Infor-Jeugd/Jeunes rue du Marché aux Herbes 27 (☎512 32 74). Open Mon–Fri 10am–6pm, Sat 10am–1pm.

Laundry *Salon Lavoir*, rue Haute 5.

Left luggage All three train stations have left-luggage facilities.

Post office Main office upstairs in the Centre Monnaie building on place de Brouckère (Mon–Sat 9am–5pm). There's also a 24-hour office at the Gare du Midi.

SOS-Jeugd/Jeunes rue Mercelis 27 (☎512 90 20), open 24hr.

Telephones bd de l'Impératrice 17 (daily 8am–10pm).

Train enquiries ☎219 26 40.

Travel agents *Acotra*, rue de la Madeleine 51 (☎512 55 40); *Nouvelles Frontières*, rue de la Violette 21 (☎511 80 13).

Women's contacts The English-speaking *Women's Organization for Equality* (WOE), rue Blanche 29, off av Louise (☎538 47 73), has a café. *Artemys*, Galerie Bortier, rue St Jean 8–10, is a feminist bookstore with a women's tearoom upstairs.

NORTHERN BELGIUM

North of Brussels, Belgium is entirely Flemish-speaking, the provinces of East and West Flanders, Antwerp, Limburg and North Brabant representing one-third of the Belgian federation, and the people maintaining a distinctive cultural and linguistic identity that's become a powerful political force in opposition to their Walloon neighbours. It's dull countryside on the whole, and the main attraction immediately north of the capital is **Antwerp**, a large old port with many reminders of its sixteenth-century golden age. The ecclesiastical capital of the country, **Mechelen**, also merits a brief stop, while to the west is the heartland of Flemish-speaking Belgium, a stupendously prosperous region in the Middle Ages and home to much of the modern country's industrial base. There are many reminders of the area's medieval greatness, most vivid in the ancient cloth cities of **Bruges** and **Ghent**, whose well-preserved old centres hold marvellous collections of early Flemish art.

Mechelen

Home of the Primate of Belgium, **MECHELEN** was one of the more powerful cities of medieval Flanders, and entered a brief golden age when the Burgundian prince Charles the Bold decided to base his administration here in 1473. Nowadays, though, considering its proximity to Antwerp and Brussels, Mechelen has a surprisingly provincial atmosphere.

The centre of town, **Grote Markt**, is flanked on the eastern side by the **Stadhuis**, an incoherent building that's a mixture of the medieval gabled original supplemented with an ornate sixteenth-century loggia by Rombout Keldermans. A little way west, the **Cathedral of St Rombout** (daily 9am–noon & 2–6pm; Oct–March closes 4pm; free) dominates the centre of town, a gigantic church completed in 1546. Inside, the thirteenth-century nave has all the cloistered elegance of the Brabantine Gothic style, and in the south transept hangs van Dyck's muscular *Crucifixion*, while the elaborate doors at the rear of the high altar hide the remains of Saint Rombout himself. Attached to the church, the cathedral tower contains Belgium's finest carillon, a fifteenth-century affair of 49 bells; there are regular performances on Monday evenings between June and September at 8.30pm. Guided tours of the tower leave from outside the tourist office throughout the summer (Easter–Sept Sat & Sun at 2.15pm; plus June–Sept Mon 7pm, July & Aug daily 2.15pm).

A short walk north, the church of **St Jan** (Sat 3–3.30pm; June–Sept also Sun 2–5pm) provides a nice setting for an altar triptych by Rubens, depicting the *Adoration of the Magi*, with the artist's first wife portrayed as the Virgin. Close by, the **Museum Hof van Busleyden** (daily except Tues 10am–noon & 2–5pm; F50) is housed in a splendid sixteenth-century mansion and includes a display of miscellaneous bells, a room devoted to Mechelen's guilds, a range of Gallo-Roman artefacts, and an unusual assortment of unattributed paintings. The grotesque wooden doll by the museum entrance is **Op Signoorke**, a former symbol of male irresponsibility, and later the focus of a rivalry between Antwerp and Mechelen, whose festival is held every year on the second Sunday in September – nowadays a good excuse for a long drinking session. Biest leads southeast from here to Veemarkt where the church of **St Pieter en St Paulus** (May–Sept Mon–Fri 9am–noon & 2–7pm, Sat & Sun 9.30am–noon & 2.30–5pm; Oct–April daily 9am–noon) was built for the Jesuits in the seventeenth century. The interior has an oak pulpit that pays tribute to the order's missionary work, carved in 1701 by Hendrik Verbruggen, with a globe near its base attached to represen-tations of the four continents known at the time. From here, it's a couple of minutes' walk southeast to the **Onze Lieve Vrouw over de Dijle**, on Onze Lieve Vrouwestraat (May, June & Sept Sat 2–6pm; July & Aug Wed 2–5pm), home to Rubens' exquisite *Miraculous Draught of Fishes* – a triptych painted for the fishmongers' guild in 1618.

Practicalities

Mechelen's **train station** is about fifteen minutes' walk south of the centre, straight down Hendrik Consciencestraat. The **tourist office**, in the Stadhuis on the east side of the Grote Markt (April–Sept Mon–Fri 8am–6pm, Sat & Sun 9.30am–5pm; Oct–March Mon–Fri 8am–5pm, Sat 10am–5pm), has a handful of private **rooms** for between F1500 and F1800 per double. The cheapest of several central **hotels** is *Hotel Claes*, on the south side of town at Onze Lieve Vrouwestraat 51 (☎015/41 28 66; ④). There are plenty of places to **eat** around Grote Markt and along the main streets that lead off to the south: try the seafood delicacies of the *De Gouden Vis*, by the river Dijle, off Ijzerenleen on Nauwstraat, or the good-value Spanish food at the *Madrid*, Lange Schipstraat 4. **Bars** worth trying include the lively *Lord Nelson* and *Arms of York*, on Wollemarkt, or the earthy *Den Stillen* at Nauwstraat 9.

Antwerp

Belgium's second city, **ANTWERP**, fans out from the east bank of the Scheldt about 30km north of Brussels. Most people prefer it to the capital: though not an immediately likeable place, it has a denser concentration of things to see, not least some fine churches and a varied selection of distinguished museums – reminders of its auspi-cious past as centre of a wide trading empire. It has a more clearly defined character too: a lively cultural centre, with a spirited nightlife. On the surface it's not a wealthy city – the area around the docks especially is run-down and seedy – but its diamond industry (centred behind the dusty facades around Centraal Station) is the world's larg-est. On a less contemporary note, there is also the enormous legacy of Rubens, some of whose finest works adorn Antwerp's galleries and churches.

> The Antwerp area telephone code is ☎03.

Arrival and accommodation

Most trains stop at **Centraal Station**, on the edge of the city centre about 2km east of Grote Markt, connected with the centre by tram #2 or #15 to Groenplaats from the Diamant underground station. The city's **public transport** system hinges on the streets around Centraal Station, principally Pelikaanstraat and Koningin Astridplein. The office in the Diamant underground station (Mon–Fri 8am–12.30pm & 1.30–4pm) sells tickets. A standard single fare costs F40, an eight-strip *Rittenkaart* F185, a 24-hour unlimited travel tourist card F150.

Antwerp's **tourist office** is at Grote Markt 15 (Mon–Fri 9am–6pm, Sat & Sun 9am–5pm); it has detailed city maps for F20 and free transport maps, and can make **accommodation** reservations. The two cheapest **hostels** are the *New International Youth Home*, Provinciestraat 256 (☎230 05 22; ③), just a ten-minute walk south from Centraal Station, and the nearby *Jeugdverblijfcentrum*, Stoomstraat 3–7 (☎226 46 06; ③). Another possibility is the *International Seamen's House*, a ten-minute walk north of the Grote Markt at Falconrui 21 (☎232 16 09; ④). The official **youth hostel** is 3km south of the centre at Eric Sasselaan 2 (☎238 02 73; ②), just west of the nearest **campsite**, *Vogelzang*, on Vogelzanglaan – tram #2, direction Hoboken. There's only one reasonably priced **hotel** in the city centre, the comfortable *Cammerpoorte*, at Nationalestraat 38 (☎231 97 36; ⑤). Most hotels are near Centraal Station: cheapest are the rather grim *Monico* at Koningin Astridplein 34 (☎225 00 93; ④), and the *Billard Palace* at Koningin Astridplein 40 (☎233 44 55; ⑥).

The City

The centre of Antwerp is **Grote Markt**, at the heart of which stands the **Brabo Fountain**, a haphazard pile of rocks surmounted by a bronze of Silvius Brabo, depicted flinging the hand of the giant Antigonus into the Scheldt. Legend says that Antigonus extracted tolls from all passing ships, cutting off the arms of those who refused to pay. He was eventually beaten by the valiant Brabo, who tore off his hand and threw it into the river, giving rise to the name of the city, which means literally "hand-throw". There are more realistic theories to explain the city's name, but this is the most colourful, and it certainly reflects Antwerp's early success at freeing the river from the taxes levied on shipping by neighbouring landowners. The north side of Grote Markt is lined with daintily restored sixteenth-century **guildhouses**, though they are overshadowed by the **Stadhuis**, completed in 1566 to a design by Cornelis Floris (tours Mon, Tues, Wed & Fri 9am–3pm, Sat noon–4pm; F30) and one of the most important buildings of the Northern Renaissance. Among rooms you can visit are the Leys Room, named after Baron Hendrik Leys, who painted the frescoes in the 1860s, and the Wedding Room, which has a chimneypiece decorated with two caryatids by Floris.

Southeast of Grote Markt, the **Onze Lieve Vrouwe Cathedral** (Mon–Fri 10am–5pm, Sat 10am–3pm, Sun 1–4pm; F60) is one of the finest Gothic churches in Belgium, mostly the work of Jan and Pieter Appelmans in the middle of the fifteenth century. The broad nave is notable primarily for its paintings by Rubens, of which the *Descent from the Cross*, to the right of the central crossing, is the most beautiful, painted after the artist's return from Italy and displaying an uncharacteristic realism derived from Caravaggio. A second painting, the *Assumption*, hangs over the high altar, a swirling Baroque scene full of cherubs and luxuriant drapery, while on the left of the nave is Rubens' triptych of the *Raising of the Cross*. There's another Rubens triptych in the ambulatory, a *Resurrection* painted for his friend, the printer Jan Moretus, in 1612.

Jan Moretus is further remembered by the **Plantin-Moretus Museum** (Tues–Sun 10am–5pm; F75), housed in the mansion of his father-in-law, Christopher Plantin, who was a printer here in the second half of the sixteenth century. It's one of Antwerp's most interesting museums, providing a marvellous insight into how Plantin and his offspring conducted their business. Highlights include a delightful seventeenth-century bookshop, equipped with a list of prohibited books, along with a money-balance to help identify debased coins, the old print room, and a number of examples of the work of Christopher Plantin, including the *Biblia Polyglotta*, an annotated, five-language text produced for Philip II in 1572. There are also sketches by Rubens, who occasionally worked for the family as an illustrator.

Fifteen minutes' walk south (tram #8 from Groenplaats), the **Museum voor Schone Kunsten** (Tues–Sun 10am–5pm; free) has one of the country's finest art collections. Its

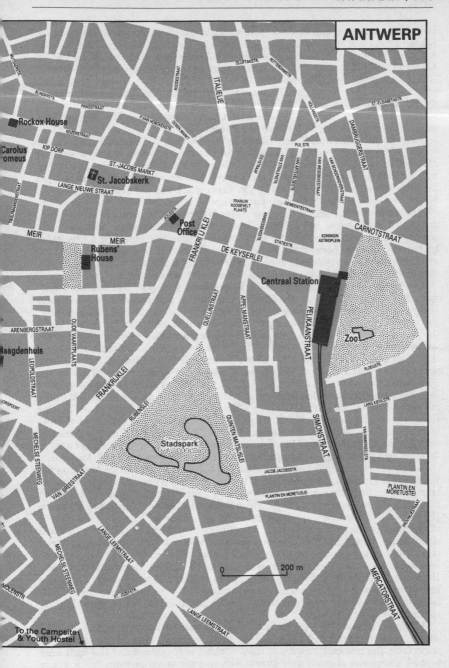

ANTWERP

Rockox House

Carolus omeus

Kip Dorp

St.-JACOBS MARKT

St. Jacobskerk

LANGE NIEUWE STRAAT

MEIR

MEIR

Rubens' House

Post Office

FRANKRIJK KLEI

DE KEYSERLEI

FRANLIN ROOSEVELT PLAATS

STATIESTR

KONINGIN ASTRIDPLEIN

CARNOTSTRAAT

Centraal Station

ARENBERGSTRAAT

OUDE VAARTPLAATS

Zoo

aagdenhuis

LEOPOLDSTRAAT

FRANKRIJKLEI

PELIKAANSTRAAT

QUELLINSTRAAT

APPELMANSTRAAT

RUBENSLEI

PLOEGSTR

LANG KIEVILSTR

MECHELSE STEENWEG

VAN BREESTRAAT

Stadspark

QUINTEN MATSIJSLEI

JACOB JACOBSSTR.

PLANTIN EN MORETUSLEI

SIMONSTRAAT

PLANTIN EN MORETUSLEI

LANGE LEEMSTRAAT

MECHELSE STEENWEG

ST. JOZEF STR.

LANGE LEEMSTRAAT

0   200 m

MERCATORSTRAAT

To the Campsite & Youth Hostel

early Flemish section includes two fine works by Jan van Eyck, a *Madonna at the Fountain* and a tiny *St Barbara*, along with works by Memling, Rogier van der Weyden and Quentin Matsys, whose triptych of the *Lamentation* was commissioned for Antwerp Cathedral in 1511. Rubens has two large rooms to himself, in which one very large canvas stands out: the *Adoration of the Magi*, a beautifully human work apparently completed in a fortnight. The museum also has a comprehensive collection of modern Belgian art, including the paintings of Paul Delvaux and James Ensor, whose subdued beginnings, such as *Afternoon at Ostend*, contrast with his piercing later works – *Skeletons Fighting for the Body of a Hanged Man*.

North, the **Maagdenhuis**, Lange Gasthuisstraat 33 (Mon & Wed–Fri 10am–5pm, Sat & Sun 1–5pm; F50), was once a home for poor children but is now part-occupied by a museum with a modest collection of art including a touching *Portrait of an Orphan Girl* by Cornelius de Vos, an overpowering *Descent from the Cross* by Jordaens and an Italianate *Adoration of the Shepherds* by Jan van Scorel. Down the street, the delightful **Mayer van den Bergh Museum**, Lange Gasthuisstraat 19 (Tues–Sun 10am–5pm; F75), contains fine examples of the applied arts, from tapestries to ceramics, silverware, illuminated manuscripts and furniture, in a crowded reconstruction of a sixteenth-century town house. There are also some excellent paintings, including a *Crucifixion* triptych by Quentin Matsys and a *St Christopher* by Jan Mostaert – though the museum's best-known work is Bruegel's *Dulle Griet* or "Mad Meg", a misogynistic allegory in which a woman, loaded down with possessions, stalks the gates of Hell.

It's a five-minute walk from here to the **Rubenshuis** at Wapper 9 (Tues–Sun 10am–5pm; F75), the former home and studio of the artist, now restored as a museum. Unfortunately, there are only one or two of his more undistinguished paintings here, and very little of the works of other artists he collected so avidly, but the restoration of the rooms is convincing, as is the spacious gallery where Rubens once displayed his favourite pictures to his friends; behind the house, the garden is laid out in the formal style of his day. Rubens died in 1640 and was buried in the **St Jacobskerk**, north of here at Lange Nieuwstraat 73 (April–Oct Mon–Sat 2–5pm; Nov–March Mon–Sat 9am–noon; F50), a structure begun in 1491 but not finished until 1659, a delay that means much of its Gothic splendour is hidden by Baroque additions. Rubens and his immediate family are buried in the chapel behind the high altar, which shows one of his last works, *Our Lady Surrounded by Saints*, in which he painted himself as Saint George, his two wives as Martha and Mary, and his father as Saint Jerome. The rest of the church is crammed with the chapels and tombs of the rich and powerful, though only the chapel next to Rubens' tomb is worth a peek, for a painting of *St Charles Borromeo* by Jacob Jordaens.

Back in the centre of the town, at the far end of Suikerrui from Grote Markt on the waterfront is the **Steen**, the remaining gatehouse and front section of what was once an impressive medieval fortress built on the site of a ninth-century fortification from which the rest of the town spread. Today the Steen houses the **National Maritime Museum** (Tues–Sun 10am–5pm; F75), whose cramped rooms feature exhibits illustrating a whole range of shipping activity from inland navigation to life on the waterfront and shipbuilding. Behind the Steen, the museum has an open-air section with a long line of tugs and barges packed in under a rickety corrugated roof. Crossing Jordaenskaai from here, it's a couple of minutes' walk east to the gabled **Vleeshuis** (Tues–Sun 10am–5pm; F75), built for the guild of butchers in 1503 and today used to display a large but rather incoherent collection of applied arts – in particular, several fine fifteenth-century wood-carvings on the ground floor and a good set of musical instruments on the uppermost level.

The streets around here were badly damaged by wartime bombing, and most of the area has been redeveloped in a twee pastiche of what went before. Cosy and respectable, the new buildings are in stark contrast to the dilapidated **red-light area** beyond, a sequence of grotty little streets with sporadic tattoo parlours that is a sure sign that you're approaching Antwerp's dockland area. A couple of minutes' walk along Vleeshouwersstraat on Veemarkt, the **St Pauluskerk** (May–Sept daily 2–5pm, F30; Oct–April daily 10am–noon, F50) is a dignified late-Gothic church of 1571 whose most prominent feature is the extraordinary mid-seventeenth-century carving of the confessionals and choir stalls, their snake-like, almost arabesque pillars the work of P. Verbrugghen the Elder. Rubens' *Disputation on the Holy Sacrament*, an early work of 1609, hangs in an altar in the south transept, opposite a series of paintings in the north aisle that includes more works by Rubens, though these aren't at their best in the gloomy church light. Outside, the **Calvaryberg** grotto clings to the buttresses of the south transept, eerily adorned with statues of Christ and other figures.

Eating and drinking

It's not difficult to **eat** cheaply and well in Antwerp, even right in the city centre. For lunches on the run, there's a baker a few doors down Hoogstraat on the right, a *friture* place almost opposite at Hoogstraat 1, as well as plenty of kebab places along Oude Koornmarkt. *Het Elfde Gebod*, on the north side of the cathedral, serves light snacks and meals in an odd, statue-filled interior. The excellent, ethno-vegetarian menu of *Den Yzeren Pot*, on Hendrik Conscienceplein, comes fairly cheap, and, opposite, *Facade* has a good small menu of dishes for F400–500. *Viskeuken* at Korte Koepoortstraat 10, on the corner of Kaaskrui and Melkmarkt, is a wonderful, unpretentious fish restaurant.

Antwerp is also a fine place to **drink**. There are loads of bars in the city centre, notably those on Groenplaats, whose terraces make a nice place to watch the world go by. More specifically, *Den Engel*, on the northwest corner of the Grote Markt, is an agreeable place, as is *Den Billekletser*, across Grote Markt at Hoogstraat 22. Just south, you could try *De Volle Mann*, Koornmarkt 7, or the more staid *De Cluyse*, across the street in an atmospheric thirteenth-century cellar. Failing that, there's the wild and wonderful *Café Pelikaan*, on the north side of the cathedral, or *De Grote Witte Arend*, around a peaceful courtyard at Reyndersstraat 18, which also serves food. For beer specialities, visit *Bierland*, a little way down Korte Nieuwestraat on the right, or the long-established *Kulminator*, five minutes' walk west of the centre at Vleminckveld 32–34.

Listings

Car rental *All-Car-Rent*, Mechelsesteenweg 141 (☎230 81 00); *Avis*, Plantin en Moretuslei 62 (☎218 94 96); *Hertz*, Mechelsesteenweg 43 (☎233 29 92).

Consulates *Great Britain*, Korte Klarenstraat 9 (☎232 6940); *USA*, Rubens Centre, Nationalestraat 5 (☎225 00 71).

Exchange There's an office at Centraal Station (daily 8.15am–11pm).

Hospital St Elizabeth Hospital, Leopoldstraat 26 (☎234 41 11).

Post office Main office at Groenplaats 42 (Mon–Fri 9am–6pm, Sat 9am–noon).

Telephones Jezusstraat 1 (daily 8am–8pm).

Train enquiries Centraal Station (Mon–Sat 8am–10pm, Sun 9am–5pm; ☎233 39 15).

Travel agents *JEST*, Sint-Katelijnevest 68 (☎232 38 71).

Ghent

The seat of the Counts of Flanders and the largest town in Western Europe during the thirteenth and fourteenth centuries, **GHENT** was at the heart of the Flemish cloth trade. By 1350, the city boasted a population of 50,000, of whom no less than 5000 were directly involved in the industry. The cloth trade began to decline in the early sixteenth century, a process which continued for several hundred years, although Ghent has picked up of late and is now the third largest Belgian city, a less immediately picturesque place than Bruges – though this can be to its advantage.

> The Ghent area telephone code is ☎09.

Arrival and accommodation

Of Ghent's three **train stations**, the most useful is **St Pieters**, 2km south of the centre and connected by **trams** #1, #10, #11 and #12. The **tourist office** is in the crypt of the town hall on Botermarkt (daily April–Oct 9.30am–6.30pm; Nov–March 9.30am–4.30pm). There are several cheap and basic **hotels** behind the station, including a couple on Sint-Denijslaan, like the *Adoma* at no. 19 (☎222 65 50; ③), and the *Trianon I* at no. 203 (☎221 39 44; ③). Closer to the centre is the *Flandria*, off Nederpolder just east of the cathedral at Barrestraat 3 (☎223 06 26; ⑤). The plush, modern *De Draecke* **youth hostel** is a few minutes' walk from the castle at Sint-Widostraat, just off Braderijstraat (☎233 70 50; ②). Between mid-July and the end of September, **student rooms** are let for F500 per person including breakfast; ask at the tourist office for further details. The best **campsite** is *Camping Blaarmeersen*, Zuiderlaan 12, west of the centre; buses #51, #52 and #53 run from the station, or you can take #38 from Bij St Jacobs.

The best way of seeing the sights is on foot, but Ghent is a large city and you may find you have to use a **tram** or **bus** at some point. Standard single fares cost F40, and a ten-journey, transferable *Rittenkaart* F230. Single tickets can be bought direct from the driver; *Rittenkaarts* are sold at shops and kiosks all over town.

The City

The best place to start exploring is at the mainly Gothic **St Baaf's Cathedral**, squeezed into the corner of St Baafsplein (April–Sept Mon–Sat 9.30am–noon & 2–6pm, Sun 1–6pm; Oct–March Mon–Sat 10am–noon & 2.30–4pm, Sun 2–5pm; free), where a small ambulatory chapel holds Ghent's greatest treasure, the altarpiece of the *Adoration of the Mystic Lamb* (F50), a seminal work of the early fifteenth century believed to be by Jan van Eyck, whose oil-painting technique and needle-sharp realism were revolutionary for their time. The cover screens display an Annunciation scene with the archangel Gabriel's wings reaching up to the timbered ceiling of a Flemish house, the streets of a town visible through the windows; on the inside – only revealed when the shutters were opened on Sundays and feast days – the upper level shows God the Father, the Virgin and John the Baptist in gleaming clarity, next to a group of singing angels who strain to read their music, while in the lower panel the Lamb is approached by various figures in paradise, seen as a sort of idealized Low Countries – look closely and you can see the cathedrals of Bruges, Utrecht and Maastricht surrounded by fastidiously detailed flora. After seeing the altarpiece, peek in at the twelfth-century crypt (F50), preserving features of the earlier Romanesque church of St John, along with murals painted between 1480 and 1540 and various bits of religious bric-a-brac.

Just west of St Baaf's, the fifteenth-century **Lakenhalle** or Cloth Hall is no more than an empty shell, whose first-floor entrance leads to the adjoining **Belfry** (tours daily every 30min, 10am–4.30pm; F100), a much-amended edifice from the fourteenth century, now a dusty ruin. A glass-sided lift climbs up to the roof for excellent views over the city centre. The Flamboyant Gothic facade of the **Stadhuis** across the street (tours May–Oct Mon–Thurs afternoon; F40) was designed by Rombout Keldermans, and each ornate niche holds a statuette – detailed carvings of the powerful and famous in characteristic poses, including Keldermans himself rubbing his chin and studying his plans for the building. Inside, the *Pacificatiezaal* was the venue of the signing of the Pacification of Ghent in 1576.

South of here, Ghent's main shopping street, **Veldstraat**, leads south from the city centre to the **Bijlokemuseum** at Godhuizenlaan 2 (Tues–Sun 9.30am–5pm; F80), an unremarkable museum of art and applied art pertaining to the Ghent region – although the old abbey buildings in which the museum is housed are some of the prettiest in the city, and the guild room, in the old dormitory, is splendid. Ten minutes' walk away to the southeast, the **Museum voor Schone Kunsten**, at Nicolaas de Liemaeckereplein 3 (same times and price), is rather better, with two main collections – a small display of modern art on the first floor and a collection of older masters on the ground floor, including Bosch's *Carrying of the Cross* and the smaller, less well-known *St Jerome at Prayer*, along with work by Pieter Bruegel the Younger, Jordaens, van Dyck and Frans Hals. West of the Stadhuis, **Korenlei** forms the western side of the harbour, home to a series of stolid merchants' houses dating from the eighteenth century; the **Graslei**, opposite, has the squat, gabled guild- and warehouses of the town's boatmen and grain-weighers, a few minutes' north of which is the sinister-looking **'s Gravensteen** (daily April–Sept 9am–6pm; Oct–March 9am–5pm; F80) or Castle of the Counts, whose interior includes an assembly room with a magnificent stone fireplace and a gruesome collection of instruments of torture with illustrations of their use. Across the canal, the **Museum voor Sierkunst**, Jan Breydelstraat 5 (Tues–Sun 9am–12.30pm & 1.30–5.30pm; F80), has a sequence of period rooms interspersed with displays of comparative furniture design. Beyond here, Braderijstraat heads east to **Lievekaai**, Ghent's second oldest harbour, across which are the lanes and alleys of the **Patershol**, a part-gentrified web of seventeenth-century terraces that is home to the **Museum voor Volkskunde**, Kraanlei 65 (Tues–Sun April–Oct 9am–12.30pm & 1.30–5.30pm; Nov–March 10am–noon & 1.30–5pm; F50), in a series of restored almshouses, made up of a delightful chain of period rooms depicting local life and work in the eighteenth and nineteenth centuries. Across Kraanlei, **Vrijdagmarkt** was the old political centre of Ghent and the site of public meetings and executions, adjacent to which is the crowded **Bij St Jacobs**, with Steendam heading off east, sprinkled with antique shops.

Eating and drinking

For **fast food**, there's a *friture* stand opposite the castle entrance. Otherwise Ghent's cheapest **sit-down eating** is at the university canteen, the *Overpoort* on Overpoortstraat (Mon–Fri 11.30am–5pm), where meals cost F300 (*ISIC*s are sometimes requested). Of fully-fledged restaurants, the busy *Du Progres*, Korenmarkt 10, does good basic fare; *Pascalino*, opposite the Stadhuis at Botermarkt 11, is a good source of cheap and substantial meals; and the *Buddhasbelly*, Hoogpoortstraat 30, does tasty vegetarian dishes. Up a notch in price, *De Hel* at Kraanlei 51 serves excellent Flemish food for F600 upwards, as do a number of more informal establishments, notably *'t Marmietje*, on the Korenlei. Among straight **bars**, try the dark and mysterious *De Tap en de Tepel* ("Tap and Nipple") on Gewad or the packed *Tolhuisje Tavern* on Graslei. *Het Waterhuis*, near the castle at Groentenmarkt 9, serves over one hundred sorts of beer in pleasant surroundings.

Bruges

"Somewhere within the dingy casing lay the ancient city," wrote Graham Greene of **BRUGES**, "like a notorious jewel, too stared at, talked of, trafficked over." And it's true that Bruges' justified reputation as one of the most perfectly preserved medieval cities in western Europe has made it the most popular tourist destination in Belgium, packed with visitors throughout the summer. Inevitably, the crowds overwhelm the town's charms, but you would be mad to come to Flanders and miss the place: its museums, to name just one attraction, hold some of the country's finest collections of Flemish art; and its intimate, winding streets, woven around a pattern of narrow canals and lined with gorgeous ancient buildings, live up to even the most inflated hype.

By the fourteenth century Bruges shared effective control of the cloth trade with its two great rivals, Ghent and Ypres, turning high-quality English wool into thousands of items of clothing that were exported all over the known world. It was an immensely profitable business, and made the city a centre of international trade: at its height, the town was a key member of the Hanseatic League, the most powerful economic alliance in medieval Europe. By the end of the fifteenth century, though, Bruges was in decline, partly because of a recession in the cloth trade, but principally because of the silting of the Zwin river – the city's trading lifeblood. By the 1490s, the stretch of water between Sluis and Damme was only navigable by smaller ships, and by the 1530s the town's sea trade had collapsed completely. Bruges simply withered away, later managing to escape damage in both world wars to emerge the perfect tourist attraction.

> The Bruges area telephone code is ☎050.

Arrival and accommodation

Bruges **train station** is twenty minutes' walk or a short bus ride southwest of the town centre. The station has a **hotel booking** service (Mon–Fri 7am–7pm, Sat & Sun 9.30am–5.30pm), as has the **tourist office** in the city centre at Burg 11 (April–Sept Mon–Fri 9.30am–6.30pm, Sat & Sun 10am–noon & 2–6.30pm; Oct–March Mon–Fri 9.30am–5pm, Sat 9.30–12.45pm & 2–5pm), where there's also a bureau de change and useful free maps. There are several **unofficial youth hostels** with dormitory beds for F300–400 per night and limited supplies of smaller rooms (③). These include the *Bauhaus International Youth Hotel*, fifteen minutes' walk east of Burg at Langestraat 135 (☎34 10 93; ②), the *Passage*, Dweersstraat 26 (☎34 02 32; ②), and *Kilroy's Garden*, Singel 12 (☎38 93 82; ②). There's an official **youth hostel** 2km south of the centre at Baron Ruzettelaan 143 (☎35 26 79; ②) – bus #2. There is a cluster of cheap **hotels** west of Markt along 't Zand, among them the *Speelmanshuys*, at no. 3 (☎33 95 52; ⑥), and the *Roosterhuys*, at no. 13 (☎33 30 35; ⑥). Alternatively, try the *Lybeer*, off 't Zand at Korte Vuldersstraat 31 (☎33 43 55; ⑥), the cosy *Cordoeanier*, Cordoeanierstraat 18 (☎33 90 51, ⑥), or the well-cared-for *Pension Geestelijk Hof*, just west of the Burg at Heilige Geeststraat 2 (☎34 25 94; ⑥). The cheapest hotel of all is the *'t Keizershof*, between the train station and the Burg at Oostmeers 126 (☎33 87 28; ⑤). The **camp-site**, *St Michiel*, is 3km southwest of the train station at Tillegemstraat 55; take bus #7 and get off at the junction of St Michielslaan and Rijselstraat.

The City

The older sections of Bruges fan out from two central squares, Markt and Burg. **Markt**, edged on three sides by gabled buildings, is the larger of the two, an impressive open space, on the south side of which the octagonal **Belfry** (daily April–Sept 9.30am–5pm; Oct–March 9.30am–12.30pm & 1.30–5pm; F100) was built in the thirteenth century when the town was at its richest and most extravagant. Inside, the staircase passes the room where the town charters were locked for safekeeping, and an eighteenth-century carillon, before emerging onto the roof. At the foot of the belfry, the **Halle** is a much-restored edifice dating from the thirteenth century, its style and structure modelled on the cloth hall at Ypres. Breidelstraat leads through to **Burg**, whose southern half is fringed by the city's finest group of buildings, one of the best being the **Heilig Bloed Basiliek** (daily 9.30/10am–noon & 2–4/6pm; free), named after a holy relic of the blood of Christ that found its way here in 1150. The basilica divides into a shadowy Lower Chapel, originally built at the beginning of the twelfth century to house another relic, that of Saint Basil, one of the great figures of the early Greek church, and, next door, an Upper Chapel – home to the rock-crystal phial of the Holy Blood, stored within a grandiose silver tabernacle in a side chapel, the gift of the King and Queen of Spain, Albert and Isabella, in 1611. After several weeks in Bruges, the relic was found to be dry, but soon after it proceeded to liquefy every Friday at 6pm until 1325. It is still venerated here on Fridays at 6pm, and, despite modern scepticism, reverence for it remains strong, not least on Ascension Day when it is carried through the town in a colourful but solemn procession, the *Helig-Bloedprocessie*. In the tiny **Treasury** (F40) you'll find the extravagant reliquary that holds the Holy Blood during the procession.

To the left of the basilica, the **Stadhuis** has a beautiful, turreted sandstone facade, a much-copied exterior that dates from 1376, though its sequence of statues of the counts and countesses of Flanders is a replacement. Inside, the magnificent Gothic Hall of 1400 (daily April–Sept 9.30am–5pm; Oct–March 9.30am–noon & 2–5pm; F60) is worth a look, with vaults depicting New Testament scenes and paintings commissioned in 1895 to illustrate the history of the town, while an adjoining room has a modest display of coins and seals, and information on the modernization of the town's harbour at the turn of the century.

Also on the square, the **Bruges Vrije Museum** (daily except Mon 10am–noon & 1.30–5pm; F20) has only one exhibit, an enormous marble and oak chimneypiece located in the province's old Magistrates' Hall, the only room to have survived from the original fifteenth-century palace. A fine example of Renaissance carving, the chimney-piece was completed in 1531 to celebrate the defeat of the French at Pavia in 1525 and the Treaty of Cambrai that followed, and is dominated by figures of the emperor Charles V and his Austrian and Spanish relatives. An arch leads south from here across the canal to the eighteenth-century **Vismarkt**, beyond which a huddle of picturesque houses make up **Huidevettersplaats**. Close by, **Dijver** follows the canal to the **Groeninge Museum** at Dijver 12 (April–Sept daily 9.30am–5pm; Oct–March daily except Tues 9.30am–12.30pm & 2–5pm; F130, F350 to include the Memling, Brangwyn & Gruuthuse Museums), which houses a superb sample of Flemish paintings from the fourteenth to the twentieth centuries, best a section of early Flemish work, including several canvases by Jan van Eyck, who lived and worked in Bruges from 1430 until his death eleven years later, and the *Judgement of Cambyses* by Gerard David, which was hung in the town hall as a sort of public apology for the imprisonment of Archduke Maximilian here in 1488. There's also work by Hieronymus Bosch, his *Last Judgement* a trio of panels crammed with mysterious beasts and scenes of awful cruelty, and the *Moreel Triptych* by Hans Memling. The museum's selection of seventeenth-century paintings is more modest, though there's a delightfully naturalistic *Peasant Lawyer* after Pieter Bruegel the Younger, a couple of riverscapes by Jan van Goyen, and a *Country Scene* by Albert Cuyp. Of modern paintings, look out for Jean Delville's enormous *De Godmens*, Paul Delvaux's *Serenity*, and the lively *Birdspark* painted in 1918 by James Ensor.

At Dijver 17 the **Gruuthuse Museum** (same times and price), sited in a rambling fifteenth-century mansion, has a varied collection of fine and applied art, including old lace, musical instruments, sixteenth- and seventeenth-century pictorial tapestries and many different types of furniture. Almost next door, the **Brangwyn Museum**, Dijver 16 (same times; F80), has a dull display of paintings, plates and pewter but is worth visiting if you're interested in the work of Frank Brangwyn, a Welsh artist born in Bruges who donated this large collection of moody etchings, studies and paintings to the town in 1936.

Beyond the Gruuthuse, the **Onze Lieve Vrouwekerk** (April–Sept Mon–Sat 10–11.30am & 2.30–5pm, Sun 2.30–5pm; Oct–March Mon–Sat 10–11.30am & 2.30–4.30pm, Sun 2.30–4.30pm; free) is a massive shambles of different dates and styles, among whose treasures is a delicate marble *Madonna and Child* by Michelangelo, an influential early work brought from Tuscany by a Flemish merchant. It is also home to the mausoleums (F30) of Charles the Bold and his daughter Mary of Burgundy, fine examples of Renaissance carving enhanced by details which give a sense of personality, from

BRUGES

500 m

To the Youth Hostel

BARON RUZETTELAAN

BUITEN KAZERNEVEST

BUITEN BONINVEST

BUITEN GENTPOORTVEST

BUITEN KATELIJNEVEST

COUPURE

COUPURE

Koningin Astridpark

Tourist Office

Brugge Vrije

Vismarkt

Post Office

Stadhuis

BURG

PHILIPSTOCKSTRAAT

HOOGSTRAAT

Brangwyn Museum

Groeninge Museum

Gruuthuse Museum

MARIA STRAAT

KATELIJNE STRAAT

OUDE GENTWEG

Minnewater Park

Minnewater

Halle and Belfry

MARKT

STEENSTRAAT

O.L. Vrouwekerk

St-Jans Hospital

Memling Museum

Begijnhof

OOSTMEERS

WESTMEERS

WAPLEIN

Sint-Salvator Kathedraal

NOORDZAND STRAAT

GELDMUNTSTR.

KOBSTRAAT

HOFFUIZER LAAN

'T ZAND

KONING ALBERTLAAN

GUIDO GEZELLELAAN

HENDRIK CONSCIENCELAAN

SINGEL

Train Station

Bus Station

To Camping St. Michiel

the helmet and gloves placed by Charles to the pair of dogs at Mary's feet. The earth beneath the mausoleums has been dug up and a couple of mirrors now reveal the original frescoes, painted on the tomb walls at the start of the sixteenth century. Opposite the church, the **St Jans Hospitaal** complex contains a well-preserved fifteenth-century dispensary and a number of partly furnished meeting rooms and old wards, as part of its **Memling Museum** (same times and price as Groeninge Museum; Oct–March closed Wed). Born in 1433, Hans Memling spent most of his working life in Bruges. Of the six paintings on display, the *Mystical Marriage of St Catherine* is perhaps the most notable, the middle panel of an altarpiece painted between 1475 and 1479, whose gently formal symmetry is in the Eyckian Realist tradition. Close by, the *Reliquary of St Ursula* is an unusual and lovely piece of work, a miniature wooden Gothic church painted with the story of Saint Ursula and the 11,000 martyred virgins. Just north of the St Jans Hospitaal, Heilige Geeststraat heads northwest to the **Kathedraal Sint Salvator** (April–Sept Mon, Tues & Thurs–Sat 10am–noon & 2–5pm, Sun 3–5pm; Oct–March Mon, Tues & Thurs–Sat 2–5pm; museum F40), a replacement for the cathedral destroyed by the French in the eighteenth century. Its thirteenth-century choir is worth a glance for the stalls, whose misericords are decorated with delightful scenes of everyday life; the cathedral's **museum** houses a vividly realistic triptych by Dieric Bouts and Hugo van der Goes entitled *The Martyrdom of St Hippolytus*. Not far south, stroll down to the **Begijnhof** (daily 9am–6pm), a circle of whitewashed houses around a tidy green, and the picturesque **Minnewater** nearby, edged by a fifteenth-century Lock Gate – a reminder of the lake's earlier use as a town harbour.

Eating and drinking

For **snacks**, the fish shops that line the Vismarkt are a good bet, with delicious prepared specialities for around F200. The *'t Mozarthuys*, Huidenvettersplein 1, has light meals and sandwiches, and its outside tables are an agreeable, if crowded, place to have lunch. The self-service *Selfi* restaurant, Steenstraat 58, has *dagschotels* for F265 and plenty for much less. Many restaurants dotted around the centre of town offer three-course menus for F400–500, and you can get cheap meals at most of the hostels – best are the *Passage* and the *Bauhaus*. The **restaurants** in the *Koffieboontje* hotel, Hallestraat 4, and the *Voermanshuys* and *Tassche* hotels on Oude Burg have menus at F400–600; *Koetse*, Oude Burg 31, does excellent mussels and herring dishes, and meat too, for F400–500; and *Malpertuus*, Eiermarkt 9, serves a fine *waterzooi* and has menus starting at F400. Check out also the seafood of *Curiosa*, Vlamingstraat 22, or those of the *Staminée de Garre*, down a narrow alley off Breidelstraat at De Garre 1. Vegetarians should head for *Zen*, a ten-minute walk west of the Markt at Beenhouwersstraat 117, which has *dagschotels* for around F200, though it closes around 8.30pm. For **drinking**, the *Uilenspiegel* bar, at the city centre end of Langestraat, is a good place for an early evening tipple, with a canalside terrace, or try *'t Traptje*, off the Markt at Wollestraat 39, with its 40-odd selection of beers; later on, the bar of the *Bauhaus* hostel is lively and has music.

SOUTHERN BELGIUM

Southwest of Brussels, the central portion of Wallonia is given over mainly to the province of Hainaut, a rolling agricultural area in its western reaches, in the east home to one of Belgium's severest belts of industry, concentrated between Mons and Charleroi. Its highlight is **Tournai** in the western part of the province, a relaxing, rather genteel place, with a number of decent museums and the finest Romanesque-Gothic cathedral in the country. East of here lie the high wooded hills of the **Ardennes**, covered by the three provinces of Namur in the west, Luxembourg in the south and Liège in the east.

The best gateway cities for the Ardennes, which are well worth exploring on the way south into Luxembourg and Germany, are the lively provincial centre of **Namur**, an hour from Brussels by train, and **Liège** – an industrial city but a pleasant one, conveniently situated on the main rail line up to Maastricht in the Netherlands.

Tournai

TOURNAI is the nearest equivalent Southern Belgium has to the Flemish "art towns" of Flanders and the north, a prosperous and bourgeois place that's a pleasant stopover for a couple of days. Along with Tongeren it's the oldest town in Belgium: Clovis, the Merovingian king, was born here in 465 and made it his capital; later it became the first capital of the Frankish kingdom, remaining in French hands for a large part of its history. Sadly, much of Tournai's beautifully preserved centre was destroyed by Allied bombing, but the town does *feel* old, and its cathedral is perhaps the finest in the country.

Most things of interest are on the southern side of the river that splits the city centre in two, grouped around or within easy walking distance of the sprawling **Grand Place**. Dominating the skyline with its distinctive five towers is Tournai's Romanesque **Cathédrale Notre-Dame** (daily April–Oct 9am–noon & 2–6pm; Nov–March 2–4.30pm; free), built out of the local slate-coloured marble. The most unusual feature of the exterior is the west facade, which has three tiers of sculptures dating from the fourteenth to seventeenth centuries, though they are currently shrouded in scaffolding, the subject of a major restoration. Inside, the nave was erected in 1171, its intricately carved capitals leading down to a choir that was the first manifestation of the Gothic style in Belgium. In front, the Renaissance rood screen is a flamboyant marble extravaganza by Cornelis Floris, although the majestic late twelfth-century transepts are probably the most impressive feature of the building, their windows holding superb sixteenth-century stained glass depicting semi-mythical scenes from Tournai's history. To the left of the entrance, a chapel holds a melodramatic *Crucifixion* by Jordaens, and there's a characteristically bold *Souls in Purgatory* by Rubens, which, newly restored, hangs in the north aisle of the choir. Be sure also to see the treasury before you leave (closed noon–2pm; F30), which houses two important thirteenth-century gilt reliquaries: the Romanesque-Gothic *châsse de Notre-Dame* by Nicolas de Verdun, and the *châsse de Saint Eleuthère* (1247).

Across from the cathedral, virtually on the corner of the Grand Place, the **Belfry** is the oldest such structure in Belgium, its lower portion dating from 1200. You can normally climb to the top for a view over the town (closed for restoration at the moment). Nearby, down an alley off the Grand Place, the **Musée de Folklore** (daily except Tues 10am–noon & 2–5pm; F50) has several floors detailing old Tournai trades and daily life in the mid-nineteenth century, although its reconstructions of various workshops and domestic rooms are not terribly spectacular, while to the north of the Grand Place, the **Musée d'Histoire et d'Archeologie**, rue des Carmes 8 (daily except Tues 10am–noon & 2–5.30pm; free), contains – as well as an attached prehistorical section – rooms devoted to the development of Tournai sculpture, a modest collection of pewterware and a good sample of porcelain from the town's own factory. In the opposite direction, on place Reine Astrid just past the belfry, the **Musée de la Tapisserie** (same hours; free) features old tapestries on the ground floor and modern works above – Tournai was among the most important pictorial tapestry centres in Belgium in the fifteenth and sixteenth centuries. Around the corner, the **Hôtel de Ville** is an eighteenth-century building, part of which now houses a small natural history museum. Behind, the **Musée des Beaux Arts** (daily except Tues 10am–noon & 2–5.30pm; F50), housed in a spacious late Twenties building by Victor Horta, has a well-displayed collection of mainly Belgian painting from the Flemish primitives to the twentieth century. There's work by Rogier van der Weyden, a native of Tournai, Pieter Bruegel the Younger and Jan Gossaert, big, fleshy pieces by Jordaens, as well as a number of French Impressionists.

Practicalities

Tournai's **train station** is on the northern edge of the town about 400m from the river. The **tourist office** at rue du Vieux Marché-aux-Poteries 14, opposite the Belfry (Mon–Fri 9am–7pm, Sat & Sun 10am–1pm & 3–6pm), has a list of **hotels**. The cheapest are on or around the Grand Place: *Aux Armes de Tournai*, five minutes' walk north of the Grand Place at place de Lille 24 (☎069/22 67 23; ⑤), is the best bet on a budget; if that's full, try the *Tour St-Georges*, behind the Halle de Draps at rue St-Georges 2 (☎069/22 53 00; ⑤). The **youth hostel** is centrally placed, five minutes' walk from the belfry at rue St-Martin 64 (April–Sept; ☎069/21 61 36; ②). The nearest **campsite** is *Camping de l'Orient*, 500m east of the ring road along rue Vieux-Chemin-de-Mons.

As for **food**, the *Bistro de la Cathédrale*, next door to the tourist office at rue Vieux Marché-aux-Potères 15, serves a number of excellent daily specials and is a good place to try the local speciality, *lapin à la Tournaissienne* (rabbit cooked in beer); the dour *À l' Bancloque* down the hill from here at rue des Chapeliers 46, serves excellent crèpes, along with a more varied menu; while, for pizza, *Le Verdé*, on the other side of the Grand Place at rue de l'Yser 2, is a simple and authentic Italian that serves great wood-fired oven pizzas.

Namur

Known as the "Gateway to the Ardennes", **NAMUR** is a logical first stop if you're heading into the region from the north or west, though without a car the dark forests and hills are still a long way off. That said, the town feels refreshingly free of the industrial belt of Hainaut, and its elegant, mansion-filled centre is the backdrop of a night scene – lent vigour by the university – that is a good antidote to the inevitably rather limited offerings of the Ardennes region beyond.

Cutting through the centre of town, **rue de l'Ange** is Namur's main shopping street, running north into the rue de Fer, where the **Musée des Arts du Namurois** (daily 10am–12.30pm & 1.30–6pm; closed Tues; F100) has displays of the work of Mosan goldsmiths and silversmiths of the eleventh to thirteenth centuries and a beautiful four-teenth-century ivory portable altarpiece. West of here, on place St-Aubain, Namur's Neoclassical **Cathédrale St-Aubain** has paintings from the School of Rubens, includ-ing one from the hand of van Dyck, and just behind, the **Musée Diocésain** (Tues–Sat 10am–noon & 2.30–6pm, Sun 2.30–6pm; F50) which displays objects from churches of Namur and Luxembourg provinces, including a golden crown reliquary with thorns from Christ's crown of thorns, a twelfth-century portable altar with ivory carvings and a silver reliquary of Saint Blaise. Down towards the river, the **Musée de Groesbeeck de Croix**, rue Saintraint 3 (daily 10am–noon & 2–5pm; visits on the hour only; F100), is a luxurious Louis XV-style palace containing seventeenth- and eighteenth-century art objects from the Namur region – clocks, marble fireplaces, furniture, ceramics and floor mosaics. A block from the river, left off mansion-lined rue des Brasseurs, the **Musée Felicien Rops** at no. 12 (daily 10am–5pm; closed Tues except July & Aug; F100) holds a collection of work by the nineteenth-century Namur illustrator, best known for his erotic drawings. West of here, the **Trésor d'Oignies**, rue Julie Billiart 19 (Mon–Sat 10am–noon & 2–5pm, Sun 2–5pm; F50), is Namur's best museum, a unique collection of the beautiful gold and silver work of local craftsman Hugo d'Oignies between 1230 and 1238. The Mosan gold and silver workers of the twelfth century were renowned, and form something of a transition between Romanesque and Gothic art, and these are beautiful devotional pieces, most holding holy relics and studded with precious and semiprecious stones, decorated with lively and realistic scenes – minute hunting scenes, or a tiny picture of the artist offering up his art to God.

Across the bridge, Namur's **Citadel** (April–June & Oct Sat & Sun 11am–6pm; July–Sept daily 11am–6pm; F180) is inevitably the city's major attraction, and deservedly so, originally constructed in medieval times to defend Namur's strategic position at the junction of the Sambre and Meuse rivers, and later extended by Vauban and the Dutchman Coheorn, by which time it was regarded as one of the most impregnable fortresses in Europe. It's a huge, sprawling place, most easily accessible by the *téléphérique* cable car (April–Sept daily 11am–7pm; Oct to mid-Nov Sat & Sun 10am–6pm) from near the car park over the Pont du Musée – an exhilarating ride. The entrance fee includes an audiovisual display on the history of the citadel, a miniature train ride around the grounds to see the various structures, and a guided tour of the deepest underground passages, as well as access to the fortress's museums – a **Musée d'Armes et d'Histoire** (Easter–Sept daily 10am–6pm), with a large collection of artefacts relating to the military history of the area, and a **Musée de la Forêt** (daily 9am–noon & 2–5pm; April–Oct closed Fri; F50), which has displays on the wildlife of the Ardennes.

Practicalities

Namur's **train station** is on the northern edge of the city centre, on avenue de la Gare, ten minutes' walk from the river and close by the **tourist office** on square de l'Europe Unie (daily summer 9am–6pm; winter 9am–5pm) at the top of rue de Fer. South of here, at the junction where the two rivers meet in the centre, there is another **information chalet** (June–Aug 9am–6pm) selling combined tickets for town sights, including the citadel and major museums. Across from here away from the city centre, at rue Notre Dame 3, is the **provincial tourist office**, with information on the whole Namur region (Mon–Fri 8am–noon & 1–6pm). Namur's cheapest **hotel** is the *Queen Victoria*, handily placed almost opposite the station at avenue de la Gare 11–12 (☎081/22 29 71; ⑥), and twenty metres further on is the *Excelsior* at no. 4 (☎081/23 13 45; ⑦). The tourist office has a stock of **private rooms**, which may work out cheaper, and there's a **youth hostel** on the far edge of town at avenue F. Rops 8 (☎081/22 36 88; ②); take bus #1, #3 or #4 from opposite the station. The nearest **campsite**, *Camping des 4 Fils Aymon*, is 10km away at chaussée de Liège 989, in Lives-sur-Meuse (April–Sept – take bus #12 from the bus station to the left of the train station, a fifteen-minute journey). Namur is a great place to eat and drink, and there are lots of places to do both in the streets between place d'Armes and place St-Aubin. On the place Marché-aux-Légumes, the *Tavern Alsacienne* serves good basic food from F350; close by, on rue de la Halle, the *Pied Boeuf* sells cheap kebabs to take away, and *Il Vesuvio* has pizzas. A couple of minutes' walk away, the *Restaurant Le Rimbaud*, rue de la Croix 58, serves excellent main courses for F400, and further down rue de la Croix is the *Brasserie Mary*, place St-Aubin 3, a bustling place to eat and drink with a simple French menu and plenty of good Belgian beer. On the other side of the centre, *Le P'tit Gris*, rue Rogier 46, is a quieter alternative, with excellent and moderately priced local cooking. Solely for **drinking**, the *Ratin Tot*, on place Marché-aux-Légumes, is the self-proclaimed oldest bar in town; *La Rhumière*, just off the square on rue St Jean, has an offbeat decor and clientele.

Liège

Though the effective capital of the Ardennes, **LIÈGE** isn't the most obvious stop on most travellers' itineraries. It's a large, grimy, industrial city, with few notable sights and little immediate appeal. However, if you're heading down this way from Holland it is hard to avoid – trains on both routes to Luxembourg, for example, pass through – and once you've got to grips with its size, Liège even has a few surprises up its sleeve.

The City

Situated on the west bank of the Meuse, the city centre divides into two parts – the **new and old towns**, which meet at **place de la République Française**, more of a roundabout than a square, fading seamlessly into tawdry **place St-Lambert**, flanked by the long sixteenth-century facade of the **Palais des Princes Evêques**. East of the palace, the open space of place St-Lambert narrows to **place du Marché**, beyond which **Feronstrée** leads east, the central spine of the so-called old town, which climbs up the sharp gradient from the river to the citadel above. The first turning left, rue des Mineurs, leads up to the **Musée de la Vie Wallonne** (Tues–Sat 10am–5pm, Sun 10am–4pm; F80), one of several museums in the area devoted to aspects of Walloon culture. Housed in the reconstruction of a former Franciscan monastery, there are lots of photographs of nineteenth-century Walloon village life, a mock-up of a typical Ardennes kitchen from days gone by, and displays of tools of various trades, including those used in traditional Ardennes industries like glass-blowing and "Dinanderie" or copper-working. Almost next door, along rue Hors Château, the **Musée d'Art Religieux et d'Art Mosan** (Tues–Sat 1–6pm, Sun 11am–4pm; F50) has a sensitively displayed assortment of Christian carvings and paintings from the Middle Ages on from Liège and the surrounding area. On the opposite side of Feronstrée, the **Musée de l'Art Wallon**, Feronstreé 86 (Tues–Sat 1–6pm, Sun 11am–4.30pm; F50), housed in a modern building by the river, comprises nineteenth- and twentieth-century work by French-speaking Belgian artists, including paintings by Constantin Meunier and Antoine Wiertz, Delvaux and Magritte. Further along Feronstrée, the **Musée d'Ansembourg** (Tues–Sun 1–6pm; F50) hosts a sumptuous collection of eighteenth-century furniture and decorations in an authentic period setting. Almost opposite, set back from the road, the church of **St-Barthélemy** (Tues–Sat 10am–noon & 2–5pm; April–Oct also Sun 1–5pm; F80) is a Romanesque structure, built at the end of the twelfth century but extensively restored, and home to one of the country's greatest treasures – a bronze baptismal font of 1118, the work of Renier de Huy, resting on ten oxen and decorated with a circular relief depicting various baptisms in progress. On the riverfront, the **Musée d'Armes** (Mon, Thurs & Sat 10am–1pm, Wed & Fri 2–5pm, 1st or 3rd Sun each month 10am–1pm; F50) has lots of beautifully engraved pistols and rifles from the eighteenth to twentieth centuries along with examples of military modelling, suits of armour and ancient swords, some dating back to the sixth century. Further along, the **Musée Curtius** is better (Mon, Thurs & Sat 2–5pm, Wed & Fri 10am–1pm, 2nd & 4th Sun each month 10am–1pm; F50). Housed in a turreted mansion from the early seventeenth century, it displays decorative arts from the environs of Liège up to the nineteenth century, notably the late tenth-century Gospel Book of Bishop Notger, and a display of glasswork that is one of the world's finest, containing over 9000 exhibits ranging from European crystal to gorgeous medieval Islamic artefacts.

In the opposite direction from place St-Lambert, the newer part of the city is in many ways a preferable area, partly pedestrianized and livelier, with the bulk of the city's shops, restaurants and nightlife. A short walk from rue Leopold, the church of **St-Denis** (daily 9am–12.15pm & 1.30–6pm), on the square of the same name, has a marvellous early sixteenth-century wooden retable, whose top – and principal – section has six panels showing the Passion of Christ, very Gothic in tone, full of drama, with assertively carved depictions of grieving, leering and abusing humanity. The bottom set of panels is later and gentler in style, with smaller figures, less sensationally observed, telling the story of Saint Denis from baptism to decapitation. From St-Denis, rue de la Cathédrale leads down to the **Cathédrale St-Paul** (daily 8am–noon & 2–5.15pm), actually only elevated to cathedral status in 1801, the replacement of an earlier building destroyed in 1794 by revolutionary French guards. The treasury (F50) in the cloisters is of most interest, its small collection including a massive 90-kilogram bust reliquary of Saint Lambert, the work of a goldsmith from Aachen, dating from 1508–12, some lovely examples of ivory work from the eleventh century, and a similarly dated missal, stained by the waters of a 1920s flood in the church.

Practicalities

You're most likely to arrive at **Gare de Guillemins**, 2km south of the city centre, with which it's connected by bus #1 or #4; tickets cost F36. There's a small **tourist office** at the station (Mon–Sat 10am–noon & 12.30–4pm) and the main office at Feronstrée 92 (Mon–Fri 9am–6pm, Sat 10am–4pm), which has maps and can advise on accommodation; there's also a **provincial tourist office** in the centre of town at boulevard de la Sauvenière 77 (Mon–Fri 8.30am–5pm, Sat 9am–1pm). Liège's most economical **hotels** are around the train station, though there's nothing especially cheap. There's the *Couronne*, dead opposite (☎041/52 21 68; ⑨), the *Univers*, on the corner at rue des Guillemins 116 (☎041/52 26 50; ⑨), the slightly cheaper *Metropole*, at rue des Guillemins 141 (☎041/52 42 93; ⑨), or the *Cygne d'Argent*, rue Beekman 46 (☎041/23 70 01; ⑨). The nearest **youth hostel** is 6km south of the city in Tilff (☎041/88 21 00; ②), five minutes' walk from the train station. The closest **campsite** is *Camping de l'Allee Verte*, in VISÉ, fifteen minutes' north by hourly train.

For **lunch**, there are lots of places in the centre of town, notably *Le Tivoli*, on rue G. Clemenceau, which has many dishes for around F200. In the old town, *Le Cheval d'Or*, rue des Mineurs 6, has menus for F400 upwards, as well as light dishes for around F200. *Au Point de Vue*, on place de la République Française, claims to be the oldest tavern in Liège and does cheap meals lunchtimes and evenings. You'll also find plenty of restaurants in the grid of streets that run north from rue Pont d'Avroy up to rue de la Casquette, the city's most popular area for **nightlife**. *L'Aquarelle*, on the corner of rue de Pot d'Or and rue Tête du Boeuf, is a youthful bar which plays good music, as does *L'Escalier*, rue St–Jean-en-Île 26; *Le Seigneur d'Amay*, at rue d'Amay 10, is a more sedate bar, with imposing wall paintings and impromptu performances at the piano. Five minutes' walk away, *Taverne St Paul*, behind the cathedral down rue St-Paul, is a well-established bar, with outside seating and bar snacks at lunchtime.

LUXEMBOURG

Across the border from the Belgian province of Luxembourg, the **Grand Duchy of Luxembourg** is one of Europe's smallest sovereign states, a tiny independent principality with a population of around 365,000. As a country, it's relatively neglected by travellers, most people tending to write it off as a dull and expensive financial centre. This is a mistake. Compared to much of Europe, its attractions are fairly low-key, and it is pricy. But it has marvellous scenery in abundance, the green hills of the Ardennes spreading over the border to form a glorious heartland of deep wooded valleys spiked with sharp craggy hilltops crowned with castles.

The capital of the country, **Luxembourg City**, is almost impossible to avoid if you're not travelling by car, a dramatically situated city that is perhaps the country's only genuinely urban environment, home to something like a fifth of the population, although you can exhaust its handful of sights and rather groggy nightlife in a couple of days. The **central** part of Luxembourg is more spectacular, rucking up into rich green hills and valleys that reach their climax in the narrowing **north** of the country around **Echternach**, a tiny town dominated by its ancient abbey, and **Vianden**, with its magnificent castle.

Luxembourg City came into being in Roman times, at the strategic junction of the trading roads between Trier and Paris, Metz and Liège. Later, its prime defensive position was exploited by Count Siegfried of Lorraine in 963, who built the city's first citadel and ruled the surrounding area from the town as a nominally independent fief-dom of the Holy Roman Empire. Luxembourg eventually became absorbed, like most of what is now Belgium, into the lands of the House of Burgundy, and its subsequent history mirrors that of its neighbour, becoming part of the Spanish and later Austrian Netherlands. The Congress of Vienna decided to create the Grand Duchy of Luxembourg, and the throne was assumed by William I of the House of Orange-Nassau, the monarch of the new united kingdom of the Netherlands. Nowadays Luxembourg is an independent constitutional monarchy, ruled by Grand Duke Jean, who came to the throne in 1964 and is married to the daughter of the previous Belgian king, Leopold II. Although everyone speaks the indigenous language, Letzeburgesch (a dialect of German that sounds a bit like Dutch), most also speak French and German; indeed, French is the official language of the government and judiciary, the one you'll see on street signs and suchlike, and is the one people most readily converse in. German is the language most used by the press, and is spoken with equal ease by all Luxembourgers.

Luxembourg City

The city of **LUXEMBOURG** is one of the most spectacularly sited capitals in Europe, the deep canyons of its two rivers, the Alzette and Pétrusse, lending it an almost perfect strategic location. It's a tiny place by capital city standards, and broadly divides into three distinct sections. The **old centre**, on the northern side of the Pétrusse valley, is not noticeably very old, but its tight grid of streets, home to most of the city's real sights, makes for a pleasant, lively area by day. On the opposite side of the Pétrusse, connected by two bridges, the Pont Adolphe and Pasarelle, lies the **modern city** – less attractive and of no real interest beyond being the location of the city's train station and cheap hotels. The **valleys** themselves, far below and most easily accessible by lift from place St-Esprit, are a curious mixture of houses, allotments and parkland, banking steeply up to the massive bastions that secure the old centre.

Arrival and accommodation

The **train station** is a fifteen-minute walk south of the city centre proper, hub of all city bus lines and close to most of the city's cheaper hotels. Luxembourg's **airport**, Findel, is 6km east of the city. Bus #9 runs every twenty minutes between the airport and the train station (30min; F35 plus F35 for any large items of luggage). There are also faster but less regular *Luxair* buses, connecting with major flights, for F120. For a taxi you'll pay about F500–600 to the station, F600–700 into the city centre.

There are branches of the **national tourist office** at the airport (daily 10am–6.30pm) and outside the station (daily 9am–noon & 2–6.30pm; ☎48 11 99). These have city maps, and can change money and book accommodation. There's also the busier **city tourist office**, in the centre on the place d'Armes (June–Sept Mon–Fri 9am–7pm, Sat 9am–1pm & 2–7pm, Sun 10am–noon & 2–6pm; Oct–May Mon–Sat 9am–1pm & 2–6pm; ☎22 809), which offers much the same facilities. There is a reasonable **public bus system**, but Luxembourg is small enough to make **walking** the best way of getting around. If you do have to take a bus, tickets cost a flat F35; day tickets are available for F140 from drivers, as are the better-value ten-ride tickets, which several people can use.

Most of the city's cheaper **hotels** are close to the train station. There are a number of reasonable options down rue Joseph Junck, immediately opposite. The *Century*, at no. 6 (☎48 94 37; ⑧), and the slightly nicer *Chemin de Fer*, next door (☎49 35 28; ⑧), are fair bets. Further down the street at no. 36, the *Zurich* (☎49 13 50; ⑦) is slightly cheaper, as is the *Axe*, across the road at no. 34 (☎49 09 53; ⑦). Other alternatives around the station include the *Bristol* at rue de Strasbourg 11 (☎48 58 29; ⑦) – though

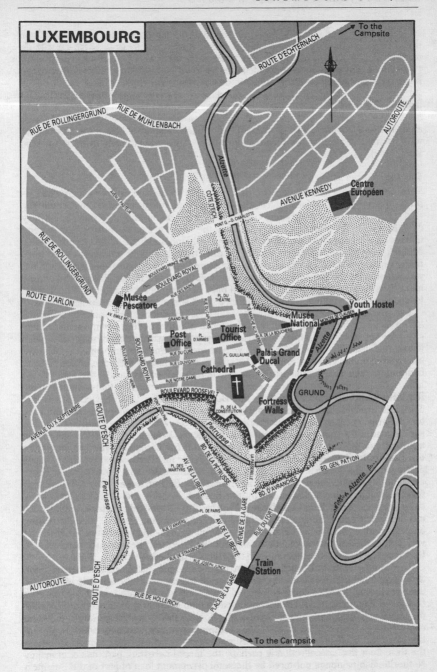

LUXEMBOURG

To the Campsite

ROUTE D'ECHTERNACH

AUTOROUTE

RUE DE ROLLINGERGRUND

RUE DE MUHLENBACH

CÔTE D'EICH

Alzette

PONT G. –D. CHARLOTTE

AVENUE KENNEDY

Centre Européen

RUE DE ROLLINGERGRUND

AVENUE PASTEUR

ROUTE D'ARLON

BOULEVARD PRINCE HENRI

BOULEVARD ROYAL

RUE DES BAINS

PL. DU THÉÂTRE

RUE DE L'EAU

RUE ALDRINGEN

AV. EMILE REUTER

Musée Pescatore

GRAND RUE

RUE DU FOSSÉ

RUE DU CURÉ

RUE BEAUMONT

Musée National

Youth Hostel

MONTÉE DE CLAUSEN

RUE DE LA BOUCHERIE

Tourist Office

PL. D'ARMES

Post Office

PL. GUILLAUME

Palais Grand Ducal

RUE LOUVIGNY

RUE NOTRE DAME

Cathedral

BOULEVARD PRINCE HENRI

BOULEVARD ROOSEVELT

Alzette

GRUND

PL. DE LA CONSTITUTION

Fortress Walls

Pétrusse

AVENUE DU X SEPTEMBRE

ROUTE D'ESCH

PL. DES MARTYRS

AV. DE LA LIBERTÉ

BD. DE LA PÉTRUSSE

LA PASSERELLE

BD. D'AVRANCHES

BD. GEN. PATTON

Vallée de l'Alzette

Pétrusse

PL. DE PARIS

AV. DE LA GARE

RUE DU FORT

RUE D'ANVERS

AUTOROUTE

ROUTE D'ESCH

RUE DE HOLLERICH

RUE DE STRASBOURG

RUE JOSEPH JUNCK

PLACE DE LA GARE

AVENUE DE LA LIBERTÉ

Train Station

To the Campsite

avoid the other hotels on this street as they (like the street) are decidedly seedy – or the *Red Lion*, slightly distanced from the station at rue Zithe 50 (☎48 17 89; ⑤) with its pleasant bar. A more centrally placed hotel is the *San Remo*, place Guillaume 8–10 (☎47 25 68; ⑥). One of the best locations in town is enjoyed by the **youth hostel**, beyond the Bock fortress on the Montée de Clausen at rue du Fort Olisy 2 (☎22 68 89; ②), close by the *Mousel* brewery. Open all year, it's reachable from the station by taking bus #9 or #16; on foot it takes twenty minutes from the station. The closest and most pleasant **campsite** is north of the centre on the edge of the Grungewald forest area, just past Dommeldange off route d'Echternach; take bus #20 or it's a forty-minute walk from the city centre. Dommeldange is also connected to the city by train (towards Ettelbruck).

The City

The centre of Luxembourg focuses on two squares, the most important of which is **place d'Armes**, a shady oblong fringed with cafés and restaurants. To the north lie the city's principal shops, mainly along **Grand Rue**, while on the southern side a small alley cuts through to the larger **place Guillaume**, the venue of Luxembourg's main general market on weekday mornings and flanked by the bland buildings of the city authorities. A block away, the Renaissance **Palais Grand-Ducal** was built originally as the town hall, a replacement for a previous Gothic structure that perished in a 1554 explosion, but was adopted by the Luxembourg royals as their residence in the nineteenth century. Nowadays it's kept for state occasions, but once the current restoration has finished the tours will be worth taking, winding through a set of sumptuous state apartments.

Left of the palace lies the oldest part of the city, the **Rocher du Bock**, where in 963 Count Siegfried built the fort that was to develop into the modern town. An ideal defensive position, it was subsequently expanded upon by just about every major European power, not least the French in 1648, who made Luxembourg into one of the most strongly defended cities in Europe. The streets here cling to the edge of the plateau, overlooking the sharp drop below, at the bottom of which nestle the slate-roofed houses of the village-like Grund – accessible by lift. Of the fortifications which remain, the largest and most accessible are the **Bock casemates** (March–Oct daily 10am–5pm; F50). Used as bomb shelters during World War II, their galleries honeycomb the long protrusion of the Bock, which slopes out into the valley. There's nothing much to see beyond a few rusty old cannons, but the views, looking out over the spires and aqueducts of the city's green heart, are fine. From the casemates you can follow the **chemin de la Corniche** to place St-Esprit and more fortifications, where the bastions of the **Citadelle du St-Esprit**, built in 1685 by Vauban, are now a grassy park. There are more casemates close by, the **Casemates de la Pétrusse** (Easter, Whitsun & July–Sept only; F50), hollowed out by the Spanish in 1674 and accessible by way of some steps off place de la Constitution. Nearby, the **Cathédrale Notre-Dame**, whose slender black spire dominates the city's puckered skyline, isn't a very interesting church, a rather perplexing building that went up in 1613–18 in a mixture of styles that varies from the Gothic vaulting of the interior to the eastern Renaissance porchway. In the crypt you'll notice the tomb of John the Blind, who died at Crécy in 1346.

The **Musée National** (Tues–Fri 10am–noon & 1–5pm, Sat 2–6pm, Sun 10am–noon & 2–6pm; free) occupies a number of converted mansions on the left side of **Marché aux Poissons**, the main square of the old town – a large and rather rambling museum that gives something of a lowdown on the city's (and country's) history. There are fragments of medieval sculpture, Roman archeological finds, prehistoric and geological collections, mock-ups of eighteenth- and nineteenth-century domestic rooms, models of the city's fortifications and a room detailing the Luxembourg royal lineage. However, the third-floor fine art collection is perhaps the most interesting part, its set of mainly Netherlandish paintings bolstered by the semi-permanent loan of part of the Bentinck-

Thyssen collection. Highlights include canvases by Cranach and Cornelisz van Haarlem, Flemish paintings by Joos van Cleve and Quentin Matsys, and later Dutch works by Bol, Hals, Jan Steen and Adriaen van Ostade. On the other side of the centre from here, across boulevard Royale, is Luxembourg's other main museum, the **Musée Pescatore**, partly occupied by the Luxembourg royals as they await completion of the palace renovations; when open, it has a modest permanent collection of fine art – though this is only displayed during July and August and the rest of the time the building is turned over to temporary exhibitions. If you're here at the right time, its small array of paintings takes in Dutch, Flemish and French artists from the seventeenth to the nineteenth century, including canvases by Dou, David Teniers and Courbet.

Eating, drinking and nightlife

Many of the city's **restaurants** are located in the tawdry station area, but they're not particularly cheaper than places across the river, where the quality is likely to be better. For lunch, the *Brasserie Chimay*, rue de Chimay 15, just off place d'Armes, serves up good-quality, filling *plats du jour* for about F300, while on the other side of place d'Armes there's a clutter of lively bars and restaurants around rue des Capuchins: the *Brasserie des Bains*, rue de Bains 23, serves good pasta dishes and wood-fired oven pizzas; *Yucatan*, rue Notre-Dame 13, is a good-value Mexican restaurant; *La Grotta*, on rue des Bains, serves pasta dishes; *Maison des Brasseurs*, Grand Rue 48, specializes in sauerkraut. *Um Dierfgen*, côte d'Eich 6, is a bar and restaurant serving main courses for F400 or so, light meals for less. A little more expensively, the bar of *Club 5*, rue de Chimay 5, is one of the trendier hang-outs, and has an excellent upstairs restaurant. Luxembourg's **nightlife** is rather tame for a capital city, but it has a positive side in some convivial bars. In the centre of the city, *Interview*, just up from the post office at rue Aldringen 21, and *Um Piquet*, around the corner at rue de la Poste 30, are two lively central watering holes. Down in the valley in **Grund**, *Scott's* by the bridge is a pubby English bar that's the haunt of Luxembourg's expats, while in **Clansen** there is *Malon*, rue de la Tour Jacob 19, a popular boho and intellectuals' hang-out, and *Pygmalion*, rue de la Tour Jacob 19, an Irish bar and open until 3am at weekends.

Listings

Airlines *British Airways*, rue Notre Dame 15 (☎22 088); *Icelandair* rue Glesener (☎40 27 272); *Luxair*, Findel airport (☎47 98 23 12); *Sabena*, Grand Rue 70 (☎21 212).

Airport enquiries ☎48 11 99.

American Express, rue Origer 6–8 (☎49 60 41; Mon–Fri 9am–1pm & 2–5pm, Sat 9am–noon).

Bicycle rental Rue Bisserwe 8, Grund. F100 per hour, F250 per half-day, F400 per day.

Car rental *Avis*, place de la Gare 2 (☎18 95 95); *Europcar*, route de Thionville 88 (☎48 76 84); *Hertz*, av de la Liberté 25 (48 54 85).

Embassies *Great Britain*, bd Roosevelt 14 (☎29 864); *Ireland*, route d'Arlon 28 (☎45 06 10); *Netherlands*, rue C.M. S.poo 5 (☎27 570); *USA*, bd E. Servais 22 (☎46 01 23).

Exchange Outside banking hours use the office on place de la Gare or inside the station itself (Mon–Sat 8.30am–9pm, Sun 9am–9pm).

Hospital The Clinique Ste-Elisabeth, av Emile Reuter 19 (☎45 05 81), is the most central hospital.

Laundry *Quick Wash*, rue de Strasbourg 31.

Left luggage At the train station (daily 6am–10pm) – F60 per item. Also lockers for F40–60.

Pharmacy Dial ☎012 for details of late-opening pharmacies.

Police rue Glesener 58–60 (☎40 91 91).

Post office Main office on place Emile Hamilius (Mon–Fri 7am–8pm, Sat 7am–7pm).

Telephones The post office has booths.

Train enquiries The office in the station is open daily 7am–8pm (☎49 24 24 or ☎499 05 72).

Travel agents *Wasteels*, place de la Gare 4 (☎48 63 63).

The Grand Duchy

Luxembourg is a city soon exhausted, and you may want to get out to see something of the rest of the **Grand Duchy**, about two-thirds of which is feasibly visited on day trips, especially with a car. To the north, the first major rail junction is **Ettelbruck**, which is not of interest in itself but gives access by bus to the first taste of the country's finest scenery and **DIEKIRCH**, 5km away. Diekirch suffered greatly during the Battle of the Bulge in the last war, an event recounted in some detail in the **Musée Historique**, 200m from the main place Guillaume, on the right up Montée de la Seitert (May–Oct daily 10am–noon & 2–6pm; F80), with photographs, dioramas – many modelled diligently after actual photographs – and a hoard of military paraphernalia. Diekirch's second museum, the **Musée Mosaïques Romaines**, is on the other side of the square (daily except Thurs; 10am–noon & 2–6pm; F20) – two rooms, basically, each holding a reasonably well preserved Roman floor mosaic, one from 150 AD, the other from around the third century, found on a site in the centre of Diekirch. The town's **tourist office** is on the corner of place Guillaume (Mon–Fri 9am–noon & 2–7pm; July & Aug also Sat & Sun 10am–noon & 2–4pm). Of **hotels**, the *Hôtel de la Paix* (④), around the corner from the tourist office on place Guillaume, is the cheapest, but it's pretty seedy. Rather nicer are two hotels opposite the bus station – the *Au Bon Accueil*, avenue de la Gare 77 (☎80 34 76; ⑦), and the *de la Gare*, avenue de la Gare 73 (☎80 33 05; ⑦). The town's two **campsites** – *de la Sûre* and *Op de Sauer* – are handily placed a few minutes' walk from the centre, by the river. For **eating**, you could try the Italian food served in the *Rialto*, Grand Rue 15, or the more traditional Luxembourg fare at the excellent *Brasserie du Commerce*, at the top end of Grand Rue on place de la Liberation.

Ten kilometres east of Diekirch, the Sûre river becomes the border between Luxembourg and Germany, edging an area known – rather optimistically – as **Petit Suisse** or "Little Switzerland", for its thickly wooded hills and rocky valleys. **ECHTERNACH** is the main centre of this region, a town of around 4000 people that grew up around an abbey founded here in 698 by one Saint Willibrord, an English missionary monk who went on to become famous for curing epilepsy and cattle – skills commemorated by the renowned hour-long dancing procession around the saint's tomb and town centre each Whit Tuesday. The centre of town is the wedge-shaped **place du Marché**, an elegant conglomeration of ancient buildings, most notable among which is the fifteenth-century turreted old **town hall**, with its Gothic loggia of 1520. The town's real attraction is, however, the **Abbey** itself, just north of place du Marché, signalled by the spires of its enormous **church**, rebuilt to a former eleventh-century plan after sustaining heavy bomb damage in 1944. Downstairs, the crypt dates from around 900, its walls bearing some unfinished frescoes and the primitive coffin of the saint himself, covered by an ornate canopy of 1906. The huge abbey complex spreads out beyond the church to a set of formal gardens by the river, its mainly eighteenth-century buildings given over to a variety of secular activities these days. One houses the **Musée de l'Abbaye** (daily 10am–noon & 2–5pm; F40), with fragments of Saint Willibrord's first convent and church and the eleventh-century *Codex Aureus* of Echternach, whose superb jewelled cover, from 990, was the work of a Trier craftsman.

The **bus station** is five minutes from the centre of town, at the end of rue de la Gare. The **tourist office** is opposite the abbey church (Mon–Fri 9am–noon & 2–5pm) and has maps and information on **accommodation**. Echternach has loads of **hotels**, many along rue de la Gare: try the *Regine* at no. 53 (☎72 077; ⑦), the *Pavillon* at no. 2 (☎72 98 09; ⑦), or the central *Petite Poète* on place du Marché (☎72 072; ⑥). There's a **campsite** 300m beyond the bus station following the river out of town, and a **youth hostel** at rue André Deutscher 9 (☎72 158; ②) – follow the road south from the corner of place du Marché and rue de la Gare. For **food**, the *Benelux* restaurant on the same corner is very reasonably priced.

Though it's not centrally placed, the best base for seeing the Luxembourg Ardennes is **VIANDEN**, close to the German border, probably the most strikingly sited of all Luxembourg's provincial towns, still surrounded by ramparts and dominated by its **castle** on the hill above (Jan & Feb Sat & Sun 10am–4pm; March daily 10am–4pm; April daily 10am–6pm; May–Aug daily 9am–7pm; Sept–Dec daily 10am–5pm; F100), recently reopened following a very thorough restoration. Originally a fifth-century structure, the present building dates mostly from the eleventh century and displays features from the Romanesque style to the Renaissance. On show are the inevitable suits of armour and suchlike, but much has just been left empty, notably the long Byzantine Room, and the octagonal upper chapel, surrounded by a narrow defensive walkway. There are exhibits on the development of the building, detailing its restoration, and on the history of the town, and some rooms that have been partly furnished in period style – the Banqueting Hall and the huge Counts' Hall, decorated with seventeenth-century tapestries. For a more authentic mustiness, peek down the well just off the old kitchen, its murky darkness lit to reveal massive depths, and leave through the unrestored Gothic dungeon. You can survey the castle from the hill above by taking the **télésiège** or cable car to its 450-metre-high summit (Easter–Oct daily 10am–6pm; F140 return) from rue du Sanatorium, just off rue Victor Hugo. At the top there's a restaurant with a terrace, and you can walk down to the castle by way of a footpath.

Buses to Vianden stop on the far eastern edge of town on the route de la Frontière, about five minutes' walk from the **tourist office** (daily except Wed 9.30am–noon & 2–6pm) on the main street by the bridge, in a house that was the part-time home of **Victor Hugo** and is now a small **museum** (July & Aug daily 9.30am–noon & 2–6pm; closed Wed rest of year; F25), with many letters and copies of original poems and manuscripts. Among the cheaper alternatives along the hotel-lined main street are *Hôtel Collette*, Grand Rue 68–70 (☎84 004; ⑤), *Hôtel Reunion*, Grand Rue 66 (☎84 155; ⑤), and the *Café de la Poste*, Grand Rue 10 (☎84 209; ⑤). Right by the river is the *Auberge de l'Our*, rue de la Gare 35 (☎84 675; ⑤), with its well-priced, popular restaurant. There's also a **youth hostel** nicely placed at the top of Grand Rue at Montée du Chateau 3 (☎84 177; ②). The nearest **campsite** is *Op dem Deich*, by the river near the bus station. Most of the hotels have **restaurants**, and these form the bulk of the eating options. The *De l'Our* hotel by the bridge serves a good array of local specialities, though its riverside terrace means it gets very busy.

travel details

Trains

Antwerp to: Bruges (hourly; hr 20min); Ghent (hourly; 1hr 20min).

Bruges to: Ostend (every 20min; 15min); Zeebrugge (hourly; 15min).

Brussels to: Antwerp (every 30min; 40min); Bruges (every 30min; 1hr); Ghent (every 30min; 40min); Liège (every 30min; 1hr 30min); Luxembourg (every 2hr; 2hr 30min); Mechelen (every 30min; 20min); Namur (hourly; 50min); Ostend (hourly; 1hr 20min); Tournai (hourly; 1hr).

Luxembourg to: Brussels (every 2hr; 2hr 30min); Diekirch (change at Ettelbruck; 8 daily; 40min); Ettelbruck (hourly; 1hr); Liège (for Maastricht; 7 daily; 2hr 30min); Namur (hourly; 1hr 50min).

Mechelen to: Liège (hourly; 1hr 10min).

Namur to: Liège (every 30min; 40min); Luxembourg (hourly; 1hr 50min).

Buses

Diekirch to: Echternach (10 daily; 35min); Vianden (hourly; 20min).

Ettelbruck to: Diekirch (every 10min; 10min); Echternach (10 daily; 45min); Vianden (12 daily; 30min).

Luxembourg to: Diekirch (8 daily; 1hr 20min); Echternach (12 daily; 1hr 10min); Vianden (2 daily; 55min).

CHAPTER 3

BULGARIA

Introduction

If Westerners have an image of **Bulgaria**, it tends to be coloured by the murky intrigues of Balkan politics, exemplified by the infamous tales of poisoned umbrellas and plots to kill the pope. From the Bulgarians' standpoint, though, the nation has come a long way since it threw off the 500-year-old yoke of the Ottoman Empire in the 1870s, and is now coping well with the aftermath of communist misrule. However, the transition to democracy has been far from smooth. After an internal Communist Party coup deposed the hardline leadership of Todor Zhivkov in November 1989, the communists deftly changed their name to the Bulgarian Socialist Party and promptly won the elections in the following spring. But popular demonstrations followed, and the main opposition coalition, the SDS, managed to force the Socialists to relinquish key cabinet posts as well as the presidency. Elections in 1991 left the power struggle unresolved.

Meanwhile, the less attractive features of the free market – inflation and rising unemployment – have made their presence felt, thus ensuring that the days of socialism will be remembered with nostalgia by some. Those that are able to afford it are jumping on the capitalist bandwagon, and Bulgarians are increasingly subjected to a flood of Western popular culture. Links with the rest of the Slav world remain strong, however, and the Russian role in Bulgaria's liberation struggle of the nineteenth century fostered a genuinely affectionate relationship between the two.

Independent travel here is not common, but there are relatively few restrictions, the costs are low, and for the committed there is much to take in. The main attractions are the mountainous scenery – offering great hiking, especially in the **Rila Mountains** of the southwest – and the web of towns with a crafts tradition, where you'll find the wonderfully romantic architecture of the National Revival era. Foremost among these are **Koprivshtitsa** in the Sredna Gora range, where the heroic April Rising started; **Plovdiv**, the second largest city; and **Veliko Târnovo**, the medieval capital. The monasteries can be startling, too – the finest, **Rila**, is on every tourist's itinerary. For urban thrills, the capital **Sofia** and the animated coastal resort of **Varna** are the places where the changes of the last four years have most taken root.

Information and Maps

Tourist information – like hotels and most tourist services – used to be exclusively under the aegis of the unpredictable **Balkantourist**. Now the *Balkantourist* empire is being broken up among new outfits, such as *Varnenski bryag* in the Varna area, and the situation can be frustratingly muddled. Nearly all main towns have an accommodation bureau responsible for handling private rooms; they might also book other forms of accommodation, and will probably have local maps and other types of information too. Though staff in Sofia and the main resorts generally speak English, their colleagues elsewhere are more likely to understand German, French or Russian.

The best **map** currently available is *Freytag and Berndt*'s map of Romania and Bulgaria. Once in the country, you're limited to much less detailed and often out-of-date maps. Street plans of Sofia and Plovdiv are widely available, but plans for other cities are often out of print – it's best to check the stock at the Bulgarian National Tourist Office in your own country before departure.

Money and Banks

Bulgaria's national currency – the **leva** – is one of the weakest in Europe, which has made Bulgaria an extremely cheap place to travel, inflation notwithstanding. The **exchange rate** offered at banks and *Balkantourist* offices is realistic enough to destroy the appeal of the black market, and new private exchange offices often have even better rates. It's best to bring a good supply of foreign currency with you, as many smaller banks and offices won't accept travellers' cheques, and credit cards are virtually useless.

Be sure to get – and keep – exchange **receipts**, since these may have to be produced when paying for accommodation in leva. Bulgarian currency comes in 1, 2, 5, 10, 20, 50, 100 and 200 leva notes, and coins of 2, 10, 20 and 50 stotinki (100 stotinki = 1 lev) and 1, 2 and 5 leva. You can change surplus leva back into hard currency in banks and exchange bureaux before leaving (you may be asked to produce your original exchange receipts), but often at a highly disadvantageous rate.

Communications

Street kiosks sell envelopes (*plika*) but stamps (*marki*) are only sold at **post offices**, usually open Mon–Sat 8.30am–5.30pm. The main *Poshta* will have a **poste restante**, but postal officers tend to return mail to sender if not claimed immediately.

Public telephones, taking 20-stotinki coins, are good only for local calls, and even then success is not assured. For calls outside the town you're in, go to a post office. The **operator number** for domestic calls is ☎121, for international calls ☎0123.

Getting Around

Public transport in Bulgaria is inexpensive, and generally hassle-free, although bear in mind that bus and train journeys are notoriously slow – a product of mountainous terrain and badly maintained roads.

■ Trains

Bulgarian State Railways (*BDZh*) can get you to most towns; trains are punctual if slow, and fares low – to the coast from Sofia for as little as £4/$6 first class. Express services (*Ekspresen*) are restricted to trunk routes, but on all except the humblest branch lines you'll find so-called Rapid (*bârz vlak*) trains. Use these rather than the snail-like *pâtnicheski* services unless you're planning to alight at some particularly insignificant halt. Long-distance/overnight trains have reasonably priced couchettes (*kushet*) and/or sleepers (*spalen vagon*). For these, on all expresses and many rapids, you need seat **reservations** (*zapazeni mesta*) as well as **tickets** (*bileti*). Be sure to ask for them, since ticket clerks seem to delight in the prospect of unwitting travellers riding in the aisles. In large towns, it's usually easier to obtain tickets and reservations from **railway booking offices** (*BDZh*) or **transport service bureaux** (*kompleksni transportni uslugi*) rather than the station, and wise to book a day in advance. Advance bookings are required for **international tickets**, handled by a separate organization, the *Rila Agency*. Bulgaria overcharges for international tickets, so it's worth buying a return outside Bulgaria if you're travelling back on the same route. Most stations have **left-luggage offices** (*garderob*). *InterRail* passes are valid in Bulgaria, but not *Eurail*.

■ Buses

Practically everywhere is accessible by **bus** (*avtobus*), though in remoter areas there may only be two or three services a day. Generally, you can buy a ticket at least an hour in advance when travelling between towns, but on some routes they're only sold when the bus arrives. On rural routes, tickets are often sold by the driver rather than at the terminal.

■ Driving and hitching

To drive in Bulgaria you'll need a current **driving licence**, third party insurance plus a Green Card – which can be bought at the border. Entering Bulgaria, your vehicle will be registered with a special "visa tag" which must be presented on leaving the country – a rule intended to prevent foreigners from flogging their cars here. Speed limits are 50–60kph in towns, 120kph on express roads, 80kph on all other roads. **Car rental** is arranged by *Balkantourist*, who reckon payment in US dollars – expect to pay $160 per week with unlimited mileage.

You'll find filling stations spaced every 30–40km apart along the highways, but petrol is constantly in short supply, so expect queues. **Breakdown assistance** is available only on the principal highways – the emergency number is ☎146.

Hitching is fair to good in most parts of Bulgaria, though given the low price of public transport, there's not much point.

Accommodation

Although foreigners are required to pay two or three times the rate charged to Bulgarians, accommodation in Bulgaria is still very cheap by Western standards. Though prices are sometimes quoted in dollars, you can pay in local currency, and only rarely are you required to produce exchange receipts to prove that you've obtained your leva legally – but it's best to keep a few just in case.

■ Hotels

Most one- or two-star hotels rent doubles for $15 a head, a little more in Sofia and Plovdiv. A small number of privately owned hotels are beginning to appear on the coast and in the busier inland spots, charging a similar amount per person for bed and breakfast. With the reorganization of

---

Balkantourist it can often be difficult to get information about these places other than from roadside advertisements. Hotel rooms in the big coastal resorts are allocated through the tourist office, which often tries to push the dearest place, so insist on being told about everything that's available. If there's a group of you, it might work out cheaper to rent a **villa** in one of the holiday villages there. **Motels** along the main highways cost roughly the same as two-star hotels.

■ Private rooms

Private rooms are available in most large towns, and are usually administered by *Balkantourist* or their regional successor – expect to pay around $6–10 for a double, more in Sofia and Plovdiv. Singles are rarely on offer, and single travellers must pay the full fee for a double. The quality varies enormously (it's rarely possible to inspect the place first), but as a rule, anywhere outside the centre of town will be in a tower block.

■ Campsites and hostels

Most towns of interest have a **campsite**, (*Kamping*), on the outskirts. The majority have two-person chalets (10–15 leva per night), though to get one on the busy coastal campsites you'll need to book through *Balkantourist*. **Camping rough** is illegal and punishable with a fine. Two further types of accommodation are mainly found in the mountains or small towns. Dirt cheap, very basic **hostels** (*Turisticheska spalnya*), run by the Bulgarian Tourist Union, lurk in the backstreets of places like Tryavna and Melnik, and sometimes admit Westerners on the quiet. In highland areas favoured by hikers there are scores of **hizhas** or alpine chalets, some primitive, others comfy hotels in all but name; most come under the aegis of the Tourist Union.

Food and Drink

Fresh fruit and vegetables have long formed the basis of Bulgarian cuisine, although you'll rarely find this reflected in restaurants, where menus have become pretty standardized and uninspiring. Grilled meats are the backbone of most Bulgarian restaurant meals, although you'll sometimes find more traditional roasted or stewed dishes.

■ Food

To escape surly service or lukewarm dishes it's usually best to opt for upmarket **restaurants**, or look for humble "family" places, patronized almost exclusively by Bulgarians – wherever you go, you're unlikely to spend more than $5 for a meal comprising main course, salad and drink. Restaurants in de luxe hotels tend to serve either "international" food, foreign cuisine or regional specialities, which are quite a lot cheaper in an inn, or **han**. Tavernas, or **mehanas**, are less predictable: although their grills and salads can be excellent, some are just for drinking. The same applies to **skara-bira joints**, lower forms of culinary life serving little more than beer and kebabs, which in rural areas, at least, are a male preserve.

Foremost among **snacks** are *kebapcheta*, grilled mincemeat served with a chunk of bread, or variations on the theme like *Shishche* (shish kebab) or *kebap*. Another favourite is the *Banitsa*, a flaky-pastry envelope with a filling – usually cheese; it's sold by street vendors in the morning and evening, to people going to and from work. Elsewhere, *hamburgeri* (basically anything placed between two halves of a bun), *sandvichi* (toasted open sandwiches, usually cheese) and *pitsi* (pizzas) dominate the fast-food repertoire. Bulgarians consider their **yoghurt** (*kiselo mlyako*) the world's finest, and hardly miss a day without consuming a glass.

Mainstay of any Bulgarian restaurant menu are the **grilled meats**, of which *kebapcheta* and *kyofte* are the most common. More substantial are chops (*pârzhola* or *kotlet*) or fillets (*file*), invariably *teleshko* (veal), or *svinsko* (pork). In the grander restaurants the main course will be accompanied by potatoes (*kartofi*) and a couple of vegetables, as well as bread: sometimes a *pitka* or small bread bun, or more rarely a *simitla*, a glazed bun made from chickpea flour. Lower down the scale, you may just get chips (*pârzheni kartofi*) and a couple of slices of a stale loaf.

Touristy folk-style restaurants are the likeliest places to find **traditional Bulgarian dishes** baked and served in earthenware pots. The best known is *gyuvech* (which literally means "earthenware dish"), a rich stew comprising peppers, aubergines and beans, to which are added either meat or meat stock. *Kavarma*, a spicy meat stew (often pork), is prepared in a similar fashion. Two other traditional receipes which you may come across if you're lucky are *sarmi*, cabbage leaves stuffed with rice and mincemeat, and *imam bayaldi*, aubergine stuffed with all manner of vegetables, meat and herbs – a Turkish dish, whose name translates as "the priest burst".

Finally, along the coast and around the highland lakes and reservoirs, there's **fish** (*riba*) – most often fried or grilled, but sometimes in a soup or stew.

Pancakes – sweet or savoury – are sometimes sold on the street and always in **patisseries** or *Sladkarnitsa*, alongside *baklava* and *revane* (nut-filled flaky pastry) and the gooey, rich *kadaif* – all of Turkish origin – plus various cakes (*torta*).

■ Drink

From having an insular **wine** industry before World War II, Bulgaria has muscled its way into the forefront of the world's export market. Amongst the **reds** are full-bodied *Cabarnet*, heavier, mellower *Melnik* and *Gâmza*, rich, dark *Mavrud*, and the smooth, strawberry-flavoured *Haskovski Merlot*. The sweeter **whites** are preferable to *Dimyat* unless you like your wine very dry; *Karlovski Misket* (Muscatel) and *Tamyanka* are widely available, the golden-coloured *Euxinovgrad* much harder to find.

Cheap native **spirits** are highly potent, drunk diluted with water in the case of *mastika* (like ouzo in Greece) or downed in one, Balkan-style, in the case of plum brandy *rakiya*. *Pliska* cognac and excellent Russian *Stolichnaya* vodka are only slightly dearer, while imported whisky is available everywhere at virtually duty-free prices. Bottled Bulgarian *bira* is pretty unexciting (save for the smooth-textured *Astika*, the country's best), and most places now serve German, Austrian or even Turkish brands.

Local equivalents of Coke or Pepsi are sold everywhere, and the Bulgarians have their own millet-based beverage, *Bozo*, which tastes like liquidized shredded wheat. Patisseries serve **coffee** (*kafe*), which if you don't specify will probably come *espresso*, though you will sometimes encounter *kapuchino* or *kafe sâs smetana* (coffee with cream). Coffee is usually drunk alongside *sok* (fruit juice), intended to counteract the strong taste. **Tea** (*chai*) is nearly always herbal.

Opening Hours and Holidays

Big city shops and supermarkets are generally **open** Mon–Sat 8.30am–6pm or later. In rural areas and small towns, a kind of unofficial siesta may prevail between noon and 3pm. All shops, offices and banks, and many museums, are closed on the following days: Jan 1; May 1 & 2; May 24; Sept 9 & 10; Nov 7; Dec 25 & 26. Museum entry charges are low, but so changeable that it is impossible to give accurate fees in the guide.

Emergencies

Most tourists have little or no contact with the Bulgarian **police** beyond an occasional request to show one's passport. **Consulates** may be helpful in some respects, but they never lend cash to nationals who've run out or been robbed. **Women** travelling alone can expect to encounter stares, comments and sometimes worse from macho types, and discos on the coast are pretty much seen as cattle-markets, but a firm response should be enough to cope with most situations.

If you need a **doctor** (*lekar*) or dentist (*zâbolekar*), go to the nearest *Poliklinika* (health centre), whose staff might well speak English or German. Emergency treatment is free of charge although you must pay for **medicines** – larger towns will have at least one 24-hour pharmacy.

EMERGENCY NUMBERS
Police ☎166; Ambulance ☎150.

SOFIA

Gone are the days when **SOFIA** resembled a kind of communist Geneva, with fresh wreaths stacked against its monuments and a police force that one could imagine club-bing litterbugs and jaywalkers. The downtown streets and parks are still fairly spruce, but the sudden emergence of free enterprise, with traders hawking Western goods from pavement stalls and privately owned cafés crammed into alleyways, has given the capital a new vigour. Now that the Party is no longer around to fulminate against drink-ing, pop music and jeans, Sofian society has loosened up considerably, with a desire to emulate the West most evident in the fashions of the capital's youth. However, their spending power is limited, and entertainment still revolves around the evening prome-nade or *korso*, followed by a coffee in one of the many outdoor cafés. Nightlife boils down to the odd disco and a few bars, plus lots of drama and serious music, especially during the Sofia Music Weeks.

The city was founded by a Thracian tribe some 3000 years ago, and various **Byzantine ruins** attest to its zenith under Constantine (306–337). The Bulgars didn't arrive on the scene until the ninth century, and with the notable exception of the thir-teenth-century Boyana Church, their cultural monuments largely disappeared during the Turkish occupation (1381–1878), of which the sole visible legacy is a couple of stately **mosques**. Sofia's finest architecture postdates Bulgaria's liberation: handsome public buildings and parks, and the magnificent Aleksandâr Nevski cathedral.

> The Sofia area telephone code is ☎02.

Arrival and information

Trains arrive at **Central Station** (*Tsentralna Gara*), a concrete barn with an unhelpful tourist bureau in its underground forecourt. Five minutes' ride along bul Knyaginya Mariya Luiza (tram #1 or #7) is Sveta Nedelya Square, within walking distance of several hotels and the main **Balkantourist** office at bul Stamboliiski 27 (7am–10pm), the best source of information. There are three main bus stations: services from points north and northeast of Sofia use the Autogara Poduyane terminal on ul Todorini Kukli (tram #20 to centre); buses from the southwest use Ovcha Kupel, halfway along bul Tsar Boris III (tram #5); buses from the southeast use the Yug terminal on bul Dragan Tsankov, beneath the flyover just beyond Borisova Gradina (tram #14). International buses arrive at a small terminal at Dame Gruev 38, ten minutes' walk west of the centre. Some privately operated express bus services, linking Sofia with major towns, operate from the car park behind the *Novotel Europa*, just opposite the train station. Bus #84, running every ten to twenty minutes, connects **Sofia Airport** with the Orlov Most, from where you can walk into the city centre; the last bus leaves the airport at midnight.

City transport

Public transport is dirt cheap and reasonably efficient. Folks get around on **buses** (*avtobus*), **trolleybuses** (*troleibus*) and, slowest of all, on **trams** (*tramvai*). Most buses run from 4am until around midnight; trams and trolleybuses stop running about an hour later. Triple-digit route numbers indicate express buses. There's a **flat fare** of 3 leva (around 10p) on all urban routes; tickets (*bileti*) are sold from street kiosks and must be punched on board the vehicle (inspections are frequent and there are spot fines for fare-dodgers). **Taxis** charge about ten leva (around 25p) per kilometre until nightfall, after which all taxi fares tend to become the subject of negotiation.

Vidin

Tsentralna Gara

Novotel Evropa

BULEVARD SLIVNITSA

LĀVOV MOST

Belgrade

Dimitrov Memorial House

ULITSA TSAR SIMEON

BULEVARD HRISTO BOTEV

Open-air Market

Hotel Edelvais

ULITSA EXZARH IOSIF

ULITSA GEORGI KIRKOV

BULEVARD KNYAGINYA MARIYA LUIZA

Banya Bashi Mosque

Hotel Iskâr

ULITSA GEORGI SAVA RAKOVSKI

BULEVARD LEVSKI

Synagogue

Hali

Turkish Baths

Balkantours

KNYAZ DONDUKOV

Restaurant Vietnam

TsUM

Party House

National Art Gallery

Russian Church

SS Cyril & Methodivs Foundation

ULITSA OPALCHENSKA

BULEVARD ALEKSANDAR STAMBOLIISKI

THE LARGO

Hotel Balkan

BULEVARD TSAR OSVOBODITEL

Aleksandâr Nevski Church

Balkantours

St Nedelya Church

US Embassy

Dimitrov Mausoleum

BALKAN (external)

National History Museum

Evropa Palace Hotel

City Garden

Hotel Slavyanska-Beseda

DAME GRUEV

ULITSA ALABIN

BALKAN (internal)

Rila Ticket Agency

ULITSA G.S. RAKOVSKI

Hotel Sevastopol

ULITSA IVAN VAZOV

International Bus terminal

ULITSA SOLUNSKA

BULEVARD VITOSHA

Central Post Office

ULITSA GENERAL GURKO

BULEVARD HRISTO BOTEV

Hotel Rodina

ULITSA GRAF IGNATIEV

BULEVARD TSAR BORIS III

GENERAL SKOBELEV

NEOFIT RILSKI

HAN ASPARUH

BULEVARD PATRIARH EVTIMII

Ovcha Kupel Bus Station, Hotel Slaviya & Boyana

Museum of Military History

1300 Years Monument

British Embassy

BULEVARD BĀLGARIA

Tihiya Kât & Zlatni Mostove

National Palace of Culture

Yuzhen Park

Hotels Vitosha & Orbita

Hotel Hemus

0   500 m

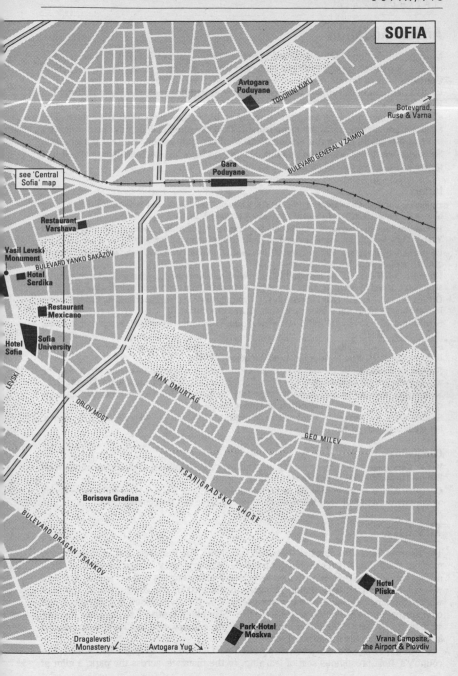

SOFIA

Avtogara
Poduyane

TODORINI KUKU

Botevgrad,
Ruse & Varna

Gara
Poduyane

BULEVARD GENERAL V ZAIMOV

see 'Central
Sofia' map

Restaurant
Varshava

Vasil Levski
Monument

BULEVARD YANKO SAKAZOV

Hotel
Serdika

Restaurant
Mexicano

Hotel
Sofia

Sofia
University

LEVSKI

ORLOV MOST

HAN OMURTAG

GEO MILEV

TSARIGRADSKO SHOSE

Borisova Gradina

BULEVARD DRAGAN TSANKOV

Hotel
Pliska

Park-Hotel
Moskva

Dragalevsti
Monastery

Avtogara Yug.

Vrana Campsite,
the Airport & Plovdiv

Accommodation

Most of Sofia's hotels are overpriced considering the level of comfort they are able to offer, so a **private room** is still the cheapest way of getting a place close to the action. Centrally located private rooms are available from *Balkantourist* at bul Stamboliiski 27 for $13 per person. A couple of independent room letting agencies – *Sofia Turist* at bul Knyaginya Mariya Luiza 79 and *Markela*, bul Knyaginyo Mariya Luiza 17 – offer slightly cheaper quarters, but they're likely to be further away from the centre. The agencies and *Balkantourist* are more reliable than the unofficial lodgings sometimes on offer to foreigners at Central Station. Sofia's official **campsites** also rent out **chalets**. Sleeping two, these are let for around $11 per night, while campers are charged just under $2 per head, and $2 for ground space.

Hotels

Bulgaria, bul Tsar Osvoboditel 4 (☎870-191). The only hotel in central Sofia with any remaining olde-worlde splendour. Treat yourself if you feel flush with cash. ⑤

Deva-Spartak, bul Arsenalski (☎661-261). Small, modern place, 2km south of the centre beyond Yuzhen Park, next to the Spartak swimming pool. Tram #6 from the station. ④

Edelvais, bul Knyaginya Mariya Luiza 79 (☎835-431). Rather run-down, basic and noisy. Despite central location, suitable for short stay only. ②

Kopitoto (☎571-256). In the foothills of Mount Vitosha above the Knyazhevo district, this chalet-style hotel is used by winter tourists; accessible by tram #5 from the centre, and then bus #62. ③

Orbita, bul Dzheimz Baucâhr 76 (☎639-3444). Typically basic and characterless, but handy for foothills of Mount Vitosha and Yuzhen Park. Tram #9 from the station. ④

Sebastopol, ul Rakovski 116 (☎875-941). Few creature comforts, but perfectly acceptable and bang in the centre. ②–③

Serdika, bul Yanko Sakâzov 2 (☎443-411). Probably the cheapest source of rooms with ensuite bathroom facilities. Near to Orlov Most and the university. ④

Slaviya, ul Sofiiski Geroi 2 (☎443-441). Comfortable modern place but in a relatively uninspiring part of town, just off the southward Tsar Boris III highway. Handy for Mount Vitosha though. ④

Slavyanska Beseda, ul Slavyanska 3 (☎880-441). Rather characterless and gloomy, but fairly central, and like the *Sedika*, an affordable mid-range choice. ④

Sredna Gora, bul Knyaginya Mariya Luiza 60 (☎835-311). Within 10 minutes' walk of the station, but seedy and decrepit. ②

Campsites

Vrana Camping. Well-equipped but big and soulless. 10km southeast of the centre on the main E80 road to Plovdiv. Bus #5 from the Orlov Most.

Cherniya Kos. A small, wooded site on the shoulders of Mount Vitosha, 11km out towards Pernik on the Tsar Boris III highway – take tram #5 to the end of the line, then bus #59 or #58.

The City

The heart of Sofia fits compactly between two rivers, the Perlovets and Vladaya, whose modest width didn't deter architects from designing a fancy bridge for each of them during the 1890s. Crowned with four ferocious-looking statues and set amidst weeping willows, the **Orlov Most** (Eagle Bridge), to the east of the centre, marks the spot where liberated prisoners of war were greeted by their victorious Russian allies and compatriots in 1878. Popular regard for the "Slav elder brother" stems from Russian support for Bulgarian liberation in the nineteenth century, and has little or no parallel in most other parts of the former Eastern Bloc.

From the bridge it's a brief stroll up bul Tsar Osvoboditel to **Sofia University**, the country's most prestigious seat of learning. In the distance, across the park, a glint of gold betrays the proximity of the **Aleksandâr Nevski** cathedral, one of the finest pieces of architecture in the Balkans. Financed by public subscription and built between 1882 and 1924 to honour the 200,000 Russian casualties of the 1877–78 War of Liberation, it's a magnificent structure, bulging with domes and semi-domes and glittering with gold leaf. Within the cavernous interior, a white-bearded God glowers down from the main cupola, an angelic sunburst covers the central vault, and as a parting shot Vasnetsov's *Day of Judgement* looms above the exit. The modern crypt, entered from outside (Wed–Sun 10.30am–6.30pm), contains a superb collection of **icons** from all over the country, mostly eighteenth- and nineteenth-century pieces – though look out for some medieval gems from the coastal towns of Nesebâr and Sozopol.

An imposing gallery on the northeastern edge of the cathedral square houses the **SS. Cyril and Methodius Foundation** (10am–6.30pm; closed Tues), an international art collection which includes an extraordinary display of eighteenth-century Japanese prints on the ground floor. Upstairs, second-division French artists take up a lot of space, though there are a couple of Delacroix sketches and a small Picasso etching. For the most part, the modern art on display reflects the tastes of Bulgaria's erstwhile socialist elite, typified by Cuban artist Carmelo Gonzales Iglesias' *Poetry, Socialism* – a still life featuring machine gun, hammer and loaf.

Heading west across the square, you'll pass two recumbent lions flanking the Tomb of the Unknown Soldier, set beside the wall of the brown-brick **Church of Sveta Sofia**. Raised during the sixth-century reign of Justinian, it follows the classic Byzantine plan of a regular cross with a dome at the intersection. Sveta Sofia means "holy wisdom", and the name of the saint was adopted by the city towards the end of the fourteenth century.

The best route from here is to cut down past the building housing the National Assembly on to **Bulevard Tsar Osvoboditel**, an attractive thoroughfare surfaced with yellow stone and partly lined with chestnut trees. West along the boulevard is the **Russian Church** (Tues–Sat 7.30am–7.30pm, Sun 7.30am–4.30pm), a zany firecracker of a building with an exuberant bright yellow tiled exterior, five gilded domes and an emerald spire, concealing a dark, candlewax-scented interior. Close by is the **Natural Science Museum** (Wed–Fri 9am–noon & 1–6pm, Sat & Sun 9am–noon & 3–6pm), which presents a thorough visual catalogue of Bulgarian and more general wildlife.

At its western end Bulevard Tsar Osvoboditel opens into **ploshtad Alexander Battenberg**, after the German aristocrat chosen to be the newly independent country's first monarch in 1878. The square was once the scene of communist rallies and parades, and is still dominated by the graffiti-daubed but empty mausoleum of Georgi Dimitrov, first leader of the People's Republic of Bulgaria. Opposite, in the former royal palace, are the uninspiring **National Art Gallery** (Tues–Sun 10am–6pm) and the more interesting **Ethnographic Museum** (Wed–Sun 10am–12.30pm & 1.30–6pm), where costumes and craft objects provide a thorough introduction to Bulgarian folklore.

Since the last war the seat of power has shifted westwards to the **Largo**. Flanked on three sides by severely monumental buildings, this elongated plaza was built on the ruins of central Sofia, pulverized by British and American bombers in the autumn of 1944. Of the complex, the white, colonnaded supertanker of the former **Party House**, originally the home of the communist hierarchy, is the most arresting structure. Protesters set fire to it in the summer of 1990 (smoke-blackened walls bear testimony to their discontent), but the Party wasn't ejected from the building until early 1992. The city authorities are undecided as to what to do with it and it's currently a cinema, showing the kind of flashy American movies that would send Bulgaria's formal moral guardians into shock. Immediately in front of the Party House, a pedestrian subway contains some **ruins of Serdica**, the ancient precursor of Sofia. The underpass gives onto the brick stumps of walls from the Byzantine fortifications, a section of original pavement and, eventually, the eastern gate of the city. Most of the ruins here, and in other parts of

Sofia, postdate the fifth-century Hun invasion; the majority are fragments of the new walls and buildings that were raised during the reign of Justinian.

South of the Largo, the *Hotel Sheraton* casts its sombre wings around a courtyard containing the fourth-century **Rotunda of St George's Church**, a brick building, under restoration for years. On the northern side of the Largo, an equally large structure houses the Council of Ministers (Bulgaria's cabinet), and Sofia's main department store, the **TsUM**. Another underpass gives access to a sunken plaza laid out with café tables, whose bright awnings contrast with the weathered brick and stone **Church of Sveta Petka Samardzhiiska** (Tues–Sat 10.30am–1pm & 3.30–6pm), containing fragmentary and much-restored frescoes. It's barely recognizable as a church and was built deliberately so by the saddlers' guild in an effort not to irritate the Turkish conquerors.

The square elongates northwards to join **Bulevard Knyaginya Mariya Luiza**, lined with greyish turn-of-the-century buildings. Here the **Banya Bashi Mosque** catches the eye, built in 1576 by Hadzhi Mimar Sonah, who also designed the great mosque at Edirne in Turkey. As the name suggests, the mosque stands in proximity to Sofia's **Mineral Baths**, occupying a stylish if tatty neo-Renaissance pile decorated with ceramics. The baths are currently semi-derelict awaiting funds for restoration, as is the market hall or **Hali** – a mass of ironwork crowned by a clocktower, standing on the other side of the road to the mosque.

The **Church of St Nedelya**, marking the southern boundary of pl Sveta Nedelya, was constructed after the liberation as the successor to a number of churches that have stood here since medieval times. South of St Nedelya, the silhouette of Mount Vitosha surmounts the rooftops of **Vitosha Bulevard**, its foothills hazy beyond the trolleybus wires and exhaust fumes.

The **National History Museum** occupies the former Palace of Justice on the western side of the boulevard (Tues–Thurs, Sat & Sun 10.30am–6.30pm, Fri 2pm–6.30pm); a superbly arranged museum, in the future it will be moved to new premises as the building reverts to its former function. On the ground floor, pride of place is given to the magnificent gold treasures of Vâlchitrân and Panagyurishte, and the 4th-century BC silver treasure of Rogozen, all of which demonstrate the achievements of Thracian civilization. Bas-reliefs, ceramics, silverware and frescoes give some idea of the artistic heights attained during the medieval era, when Pliska, Preslav and Veliko Târnovo enjoyed their heyday as capitals – although these pale before the collection of ecclesiastical art displayed upstairs. Centuries of Ottoman rule are ignored in favour of the National Revival of the eighteenth and nineteenth centuries, when progressive Bulgarians struggled for civic reforms and, ultimately, independence. The upper floor also exhibits a wonderful collection of nineteenth-century folk costumes and carpets.

Sofia's southeastern quarter is probably the liveliest part of the inner city, its **City Garden** and pavement cafés providing the focus for social life until its theatres and restaurants take over during the evening. Across the well-tended lawns, fountains splash opposite the **Ivan Vazov National Theatre**, a handsome Neoclassical building which provides a welcome contrast to the sombrely ministerial buildings along ul Vasil Levski. At the southern end of this street one comes upon ul General Gurko, where you'll find the **City Art Gallery** (daily 6am–3.30pm), a showcase for contemporary paintings, drawings and sculpture chiefly by Bulgarian artists.

Running parallel to the south, the shop-flanked **Graf Ignatiev** meanders to the **Friendship Bridge** (Most na Druzhba), one of the approaches to **Borisova Gradina** ("Boris's Garden", after Bulgaria's inter-war monarch, Tsar Boris III). The park itself is the oldest and largest in Sofia, with a rich variety of flowers and trees, and two huge football stadiums. As an evening parade ground for the city's burgeoning youth culture, Borisova Gradina is outshone by **Yuzhen Park**, at the southern end of bul Vitosha. It's dominated by the National Palace of Culture (NDK), an ultra-modern concert and congress centre, originally built in honour of Todor Zhivkov's daughter Lyudmilla.

Mount Vitosha

A wooded mass of granite 20km long and 16km wide, **Mount Vitosha** is where Sofians come for picnics, views or skiing, and the ascent of its highest peak, Cherni Vrâh, has become a traditional test of stamina. If you're seeking tranquillity, it's best to come on a weekday, or at least to get some distance from the chairlift terminals.

One approach is to take a tram #5 from behind the National History Museum to Ovcha Kupel, then change to bus #61, #62 or #107 to **BOYANA**. There, follow ul Belite Brezi uphill and you'll come to a small garden surrounding the **Boyana Church** (Mon–Fri 8.45am–5pm), home to a recently restored set of medieval frescoes. Largely executed in 1259, they anticipate the work of Giotto with their realism and rejection of the hieratic Byzantine style. The unknown artist drew on contemporary life for inspiration, clothing the saints in medieval Bulgarian dress and setting garlic, radishes and bread – the peasant staples – on the table in the *Last Supper*.

Bus #61 continues on to **KNYAZHEVO**, from where there's a cabin-lift up to the *Hotel Kopitoto*, while bus #62 ascends through the forests past the *Tihya Kât* motel to *Zlatni Mostove*, a restaurant just to the east of the so-called **Stone River**. Beneath the large boulders running down the mountainside burbles a rivulet which once attracted gold-panners – hence the village's name, which means "Golden Bridges".

Another route to the mountain runs via **DRAGALEVTSI** village, which you can reach by taking tram #2 from Graf Ignatiev or Patriarch Evtimii to the Hladilnika stop on Cherni Vrâh Blvd, and then bus #66. Climbing the road beyond the village, the bus passes three old mills now serving as the *Vodenicharski* taverna, near which begins a chair lift to the *Shtastlivetsa Hotel*. Some twenty minutes later bus #66 arrives at **ALEKO**, an expanding winter sports centre which has a range of pistes to suit all grades of skiers and operates from November through until late spring.

Eating, drinking and entertainment

Market economics and creeping westernization have made big changes in the range of food, drink and nightlife, ensuring that the Bulgarian capital is no longer the stern and joyless place it was before 1989. Indigenous grilled **snack foods** have (perhaps regrettably) been largely replaced by *hamburgeri*, *sandvichi* and *pitsi* (pizzas), from kiosks and fast-food joints throughout the city. Sofia's **restaurants** have undergone a facelift, with many dingy, unprofitable places closing down to be replaced by rather more garish, cosmopolitan places, most of which feature live musical entertainment. Menus continue to be rather one-dimensional, but if you tire of the standard Bulgarian meal of grilled meat plus salad, various restaurants offering foreign cuisine present alternative options.

Daytime **drinking** takes place in the cafés around bulevard Vitosha or around the numerous kiosks which dot the city's open spaces. **Bars** are on the increase, although many of them are hastily-built affairs stationed in the owner's basement or garage. If you're renting a room in central Sofia, you'll probably find a couple of these small and intimate drinking venues on your block: otherwise, the residential streets either side of bulevard Vitosha are the best places to look.

Restaurants

Boyansko Hanche, Boyana (☎563-016). Just below the Boyana church and so a popular stop-off with sightseers, the Hanche is a custom-built "inn" with folklore shows in the evenings. Bus #63.

Budapest, Rakovski 145 (☎872-750). Possibly the best of central Sofia's restaurants, with a comparatively varied menu of central European dishes. Elegant decor, and a selection of Danubian waltzes performed by live musicians.

Havana, bul Vitosha 27 (☎800-544). The Havana's claim to serve Cuban cuisine has now all but been dispensed with, although a certain Caribbean ambience lives on in the vaguely tropical plants surrounding the dining area. Live music.

Krim, Slavyanska 17 (☎870-131). Delicious Russian food served in a nineteenth-century mansion, although the atmosphere is quite snooty – best reserve in advance. Summer garden.

Melnik, bul Hristo Botev 48 (☎878-142). Basic *mehana* serving grills.

Mexicano, Evlogi Georgiev 1 (☎446-598). New top-class restaurant (dress smart and make a reservation) situated in the headquarters of the Union of Bulgarian Architects.

Peking, inside the *Hotel Rodina*, bul Totleben (☎516-31). Chinese restaurant with Chinese kitchen staff – so expect some reasonably authentic food.

Piccola Italia, Yanko Sakâzov 20. More of a fast-food joint than a restaurant. Tasty pizza and pasta fare at rock-bottom prices.

Pizza Palace, Vitosha 34. The best of Sofia's nascent pizza restaurants. Bright pink decor and breezy service.

Sekura, in the *Hotel Vitosha*, bul Anton Ivanov 100 (☎624-51). Top-class Japanese restaurant: a meal with sake will set you back a small fortune by any standards.

Snack Bar Thessaloniki, Serdika 18. No nonsense cafeteria-style place offering souvlaki and other Greek-style grills.

Vodenicharski Mehani, Dragalevtsi (☎671-021). Housed in three renovated mills and serving up traditional millers' nosh, such as *kachamak* (fried maize dough with meat). Bus #93.

Cafés and patisseries

Café-Bistro Croissant, ul Alabin 42. Small place serving up good breakfast patisseries.

Havana, bul Vitosha 27. Largest café on the main street, with a warren of late-night bars inside.

Moskva, pl Sveta Nedelya. Elegant, central European-style coffee house with excellent cakes and ice cream.

Panorama, NDK , 8th floor. Unparalleled views across the city, and more good ice cream.

Patisserie Osnakis, Knyaginya Mariya Luiza 36. Excellent cakeshop-cum-pavement café with an opulent selection of sweets.

Bars

Coctail Bar Sugar Johnny, Han Asparuh 18. Animated drinking haunt with seating on two levels, one block west of bul Vitosha.

Jazz Club Piano Bar, ul Kârnigradska 17. Stylish place in which to enjoy upmarket drinks to ivory-tinkling accompaniment.

Kyubcheto, Tsar Asen 14. Very chic but very, very small. Don't expect to find a seat.

Markrit, Patriarh Evtimii 61. Wicker furniture and pot plants make this the best place in central Sofia for a relaxed, intimate drink.

Sayonara, ul Alabin 27. On the first floor of an office block off bul Vitosha, but it's a relaxed place with good ice cream.

Traffic, corner of Vitosha and pl Baba Nedelya. Opposite Yuzhen Park, a popular place to watch the promenading crowds during the early evening.

Zoksim, Vitosha 13. A bit too self-consciously stylish, with prices to match – but best of the places on the main bulevard.

Discos

Angel, pl Narodno Sâbranie 9. In the Student Cultural Centre.

Dzho ("Joe"), Zimniya dvorets, studentski grad. Best of the bars and clubs catering for the population of Sofia's student complex on the southeast of town. Bus #80 from outside the university.

Orbilux, Dzheimz Bauchâr 76. Long considered the most stylish of Sofia's discos, located in the basement of the *Orbita Hotel*.

Strada, Dimitâr Polyanov 2. Tackier, slightly less pretentious nightspot.

Yalta, Aksakov 31. Relatively new, glitzy place just opposite the university.

Music

Bulgaria's annual **Jazz Festival** takes place in the second week of November, usually in Sofia's *Universiade* sports hall at ul Shipchenski Prohod 2, where **rock concerts** are also sometimes held; ask at ul Aksakov 7a for information. **Classical music** has a far higher profile, with opera at the Opera House adjoining Aleksandâr Nevski square and concerts at the *Bâlgaria* (ul Benkovski 1) and *Slaveykov* (Slaveykov Square) halls, and the NDK. Famous foreign soloists and ensembles appear during the **Sofia Music Weeks** (around May 24–June 20); the **Music Evenings** in the first week of December are primarily a showcase for native talent. **Tickets and information** can be obtained from the NDK tourist bureau or the bookings office at bul Tsar Osvoboditel 1.

Listings

Airlines *Aeroflot*, bul Tsar Osvoboditel 2 (☎879-080); *Air France*, ul Sâborna 2 (☎872-686); *Austrian Airlines*, Knyaginya Mariya Luiza 68 (☎327-057); *Lufthansa*, ul Sâborna 9 (☎882-310); *Swissair*, Knyaginya Mariya Luiza 66 (☎328-181); *Balkan*, pl Narodno Sâbranie 12 (☎880-663).

Airport information Domestic flights ☎451-113; international flights ☎722-414.

Bus tickets Information and reservations best obtained from the *Transport Service Centre* beneath the NDK building (Mon–Fri 7am–7pm, Sat 8am–2pm; ☎597-095).

Car rental *Hertz* at *Balkantours*, bul Vitosha 1 (☎874480) and at the airport (☎791-506); *Europcar* at *Interbalkan*, bul Stamboliiski 11 (☎877-788) and at the airport (☎720-157).

Embassies and consulates *Great Britain*, 65 bul Tolbuhin (☎885361); *Netherlands*, 19a ul Denkoglou (☎874-186); *USA*, bul Stamboliiski 1 (☎884-801). Australia, Canada and New Zealand have no representation in Sofia but the British Embassy might help out.

Medical emergencies Medical treatment for foreigners at ul Evgeni Pavolvski 1 (☎75-361) in the Mladost I housing estate – bus #75 from the Eagle Bridge.

Pharmacies 24-hr service at ul Alabin 29, ul Rakovski 159, Yanko Sakâzov 102 or bul Hristo Botev 123. Current information can be obtained by dialling ☎178.

Post office Ul General Gurko (daily 7am–9pm).

Telephones International calls best made from booths one block east of the main post office, behind the *Telefonska Palata*.

Train tickets The system of platform numbering at *Tsentrala Gara* is incredibly confusing, so allow plenty of time to catch your train; platforms are divided into *zapad* (west) and *istok* (east) sections, and may have two different trains departing simultaneously. To beat the queues, make advance bookings at the *Transport Service Centre*, below the NDK building.

SOUTHERN BULGARIA

Trains heading from Bulgaria to Greece follow the Struma valley south from Sofia, skirting some of the country's most grandiose mountains on the way. Formerly noted for their bandits and hermits, the Rila mountains contain Bulgaria's highest, stormiest peaks, swathed in forests and dotted with alpine lakes awaiting anyone prepared to hike or risk their car's suspension on the backroads. If time is short, the two spots to select are the most revered of Bulgarian monasteries, **Rila**, lying some 30km east of the main southbound route, and the village of **Melnik**, known both for its wine and its vernacular architecture.

Another much-travelled route heads southeast from Sofia towards Istanbul, through the Plain of Thrace, a fertile region that was the heartland of the ancient Thracians, whose culture began to emerge during the third millennium BC. The E80 road, which now links Istanbul and Sofia, essentially follows the course of the Roman Serdica to Constantinople road, past towns formerly ruled by the Ottomans for so long that foreigners used to call this "European Turkey". Of these, the most important is **Plovdiv**, Bulgaria's second city, whose old quarter is a wonderful melange of Renaissance mansions, mosques and classical remains, spread over three hills. Thirty kilometres east of Plovdiv is the **Bachkovo Monastery**, whose churches and court-yards contain some of Bulgaria's most vivid frescoes.

Rila Monastery

The best-known of Bulgaria's monasteries, famed for its architecture and mountainous setting, **Rila** receives a steady stream of visitors, many of whom come on expensive excursions from Sofia. You can treat Rila as a day trip from the capital if you catch the daily bus from the Ovcha Kupel terminal at 6.30am, but you'll have less than an hour's time to look round before boarding the return service back to Sofia. A more relaxed way of getting to the monastery – although it involves lots of changes – is to take one of the regular southbound trains to the village of Kocherinovo, then catch a local bus to Rila village, from where local minibuses run to the monastery itself, 12km further east.

The single road to the **Rila Monastery** runs above the foaming River Rilska, fed by innumerable springs from the surrounding mountains, which are covered with pines and beech beneath peaks flecked with snow. Even today there's a palpable sense of isolation, and it's easy to see why Ivan Rilski – or **John of Rila** – chose this valley to escape the savagery of feudal life and the laxity of the established monasteries at the end of the ninth century. Founded in 1335, four kilometres from John's original hermitage, the monastery was plundered during the eighteenth century and repairs had hardly begun when the whole structure burned down in 1833. Its resurrection was presented as a religious and patriotic duty: public donations poured in throughout the last century, and the east wing was built as recently as 1961 to display the treasury.

Ringed by mighty walls, the monastery has the outward appearance of a fortress, but past the west gate this impression is negated by the beauty of the interior, which even the crowds can't mar. Graceful arches surrounding the flagstoned courtyard support tiers of monastic cells, and stairways ascend to top-floor balconies which – viewed from below – resemble the outstretched petals of flowers. Bold red stripes and black and white check patterns enliven the facade, contrasting with the sombre mountains behind, and creating a harmony between the cloisters and the **church** within. Richly coloured frescoes shelter beneath the porch of the monastery church and cover much of its interior. The iconostasis is particularly splendid, almost ten metres wide and covered by a mass of intricate carvings and gold leaf.

Beside the church is **Hyrelo's Tower**, the sole remaining building from the fourteenth century. Cauldrons once used to feed pilgrims occupy the kitchen on the ground floor of the north wing, where the soot-encrusted ceiling has the shape and texture of a huge termite's nest. Things are more salubrious on the floors above, where the spartan refectory and some of the panelled guest rooms are open for inspection. The **ethnographic collection** (daily 8am–5pm) is notable for its carpets and silverware, while beneath the east wing there's a wealth of objects in the **treasury** (same hours). These include icons and medieval Gospels; Rila's charter from Tsar Ivan Shishman, written on leather and sealed with gold in 1378; and a miniature cross made by the monk Raphael during the 1970s. Containing more than 1500 human figures, each the size of a grain of rice, this took Raphael twelve years to carve with a needle, and cost him his eyesight.

Sadly, it's no longer possible for visitors to stay in Rila's cells, and the only **rooms** on offer are either at the *Turisticheska spalnya* just down the hill from the monastery's eastern gate, or at the 3-star *Hotel Rilets* (☎93754/2106; ④), a further 2km eastwards and across the Rilska river. Near the hotel is *Bor* **camping**, a fairly primitive and unsupervized site with campers lighting fires amid the rugged scenery. There's also the 2-star *Orbita* hotel (☎93754/2167; ③) back down the valley in Rila village.

For **snacks**, delicious bread can be had from the bakery (which is run by monks) that stands just outside the monastery's east gate. A *skara-bira* den and a *sladkarnitsa* are situated just a few metres up the hill, although the grilled dishes on offer at the *Bachkova Cheshma* are tastier 2km away on the road east. Slightly more pricy **restaurant fare** is available at the *Rila* restaurant just beyond the east gate, which has a disco downstairs. **Nightlife** is limited to the disco and the plush bar of the *Hotel Rilets*.

Melnik

Approaching **MELNIK** on the bus from Sandanski (served by frequent trains and buses from Sofia), you catch glimpses of the wall of mountains which allowed the townsfolk to thumb their noses at Byzantium during the eleventh century. The town hides until the last moment, encircled by hard-edged crags, scree slopes and rounded sandstone cones. With its whitewashed stone houses on timber props festooned with flowers, its cobbled alleys and its narrow courtyards, Melnik is stunning – but socially and economically it's fast becoming a fossil. In 1880 Melnik had 20,000 inhabitants, 75 churches and a thriving market on the Charshiya, the main street. The economy waned towards the end of the last century and the Balkan War of 1913 burned the town to the ground and sundered its trade routes. Nowadays there are only 570 inhabitants and the town survives on **wine-making** – the traditional standby – and tourism.

Melnik's backstreets invite aimless wandering and guarantee a succession of eye-catching details. It's oldest ruin – known as the Byzantine or **Bolyar House** – is sited on the high ground immediately east of the centre, and was clearly built with defence in mind. It was probably the residence of Melnik's thirteenth-century overlord, Alexei Slav, who invited rich Greeks to settle here. Southeast of the Bolyar House you'll see the balustraded tower of the **Church of Sveti Nikolai** (Tues–Sat 10am–noon & 2–5pm). Inside, a wooden bishop's throne decorated with light blue floral patterns offsets a fine iconostasis, on which white-bearded St Nicholas himself is prominently featured.

The houses that belonged to the town's Greek entrepreneurs, rebuilt during the National Revival, are now Melnik's most impressive buildings, and none more so than the old **Kordopulov Mansion** (Tues–Sun 8am–noon & 2–6pm) situated on the outskirts of town. Follow the track up from the river gully and you'll see the stone-walled house protruding from the hillside, its windows surveying every approach. Above the ground floor, now a *mehana*, the spacious rooms are intimate, the reception room a superb fusion of Greek and Bulgarian crafts, with an intricate lattice-work ceiling and a multitude of stained-glass windows. Another relic is the Pashov house just below the main square, which contains the **Town Museum** (same times). The creaking stairways and elegant rooms are more arresting than most of the exhibits – though photos and engravings of old Melnik manage to leap the language barrier.

You should be able to get a **private room** from the accommodation bureau on the main street or by asking around. Otherwise, there are cheap dormitory beds in the *Turisticheska spalnya* perched above the river gully, or the more salubrious rooms at the 3-star *Hotel Melnik* (☎9972-7437/272; ③), overlooking the town centre from a hillside to the south. *Kâmping Melnik*, 500m north of Melnik on the Rozhen road, is fairly basic and doesn't have any chalets. Of the half-dozen **places to eat**, the best is the *Chinarite*, a friendly *mehana* just beyond the bridge at the top end of the square – standard fare, but the place buzzes until close-down at 11pm. More restrained is the *Paskaleva Kâshta* restaurant, in a nineteenth-century house on the opposite side of the valley.

Plovdiv

The country's second largest city, **PLOVDIV** is one of its most attractive and vibrant centres – and, arguably, has more to recommend it than Sofia. The old town embodies Plovdiv's long history – Thracian fortifications subsumed by Macedonian masonry, overlaid with Byzantine walls and by great timber-framed mansions erected during the Bulgarian renaissance, symbolically looking down upon the derelict Ottoman mosques and artisans' dwellings of the lower town. But Plovdiv isn't merely a parade of antiquities: the city's arts festivals and trade fairs rival Sofia's, and its restaurants and promenade are equal to those of the capital.

Arrival and accommodation

Trains arrive at the *Tsentrala Gara* on the southern fringe of the centre, and the two bus terminals are nearby. *Rodopi*, serving the mountain resorts to the south, is just on the other side of the tracks, while *Autogara Yug*, serving the southeast, is one block east. For **information**, head for *Puldin Tour* at bul Bâlgariya 106 (daily 8.45am–12.30pm & 1.30–6.30pm) – take bus #1 or #7 from the station and alight once you've crossed the river. They can advise on the availability of hotel rooms and arrange **private rooms** for $12 a double – $15 during the second half of September, when the Trade Fair inflates the price of accommodation. The *Turisticheski Dom* at ul P.R. Slaveikov has cheap dorm beds bang in the heart of the town, but these are usually booked solid by holidaying Bulgarians. The *Bâlgariya* **hotel**, Patriarch Evtimii 13 (③; just off the main ul Knyaz Aleksandâr), is the only other source of moderately-priced rooms.

Central Plovdiv

Central Plovdiv revolves around the large **Tsentralen** square, dominated by the ponderously Stalinist *Hotel Trimontsium*. The **Freedom Park** is immediately to the west, marking the tail end of the promenade which brings hundreds of people onto ulitsa Knyaz Aleksandâr around noon and the close of the working day. Knyaz Aleksandâr is lined with shops and cinemas, and bars with terraces from which folk watch life go by. Off to the right, Gavril Genov and Stanislav Dospevski streets lead up past the lovely church of **Sveta Marina** into the old quarter (see below), which looms above the rooftops of the lower town.

Further north, Knyaz Aleksandâr gives onto the arresting **pl Stamboliiski**, surrounded by small cafés packed with students, whiskery elders and corpulent bons viveurs. The ruins of a **Roman stadium**, visible in a pit beneath the square, are but a fragment of the arena where up to 30,000 spectators watched chariot races, wrestling, athletics and other events. Among the variously styled buildings around here, the **Dzhumaiya Mosque**, with its diamond-patterned minaret and lead-sheathed domes, steals the show. It's believed that the mosque dates back to the reign of Sultan Murad II (1359–85), and its thick walls and the configuration of the prayer hall – divided by four columns into nine squares – are typical of mosques of that period. From the square, ul Raiko Daskalov continues north to meet bul Hristo Danov and two further relics of Turkish rule: the leaden domes and sturdy masonry identify the *Chifte Hamam* as an original **Turkish bath**, while the zigzag brickwork on the minaret of the **Imaret Mosque** jazzes up the ponderous bulk of the building.

Immediately west of the Imaret, opposite Milenkov's surreal monument to the union of 1885 on pl Sâedinenie, there's the **Archeological Museum** (Tues–Thurs, Sat & Sun 9am–12.30pm & 2.30–5.30pm, Fri 9am–12.30pm & 2–5pm). For many years, the star attraction was the magnificent gold treasure of Panagyurishte, beautifully worked by Thracian goldsmiths during the third century BC, but this has been claimed by Sofia's National History Museum, so visitors have to content themselves with copies of the originals. Otherwise there are a few Neolithic pots and a hoard of twelfth-century Byzantine coins to supplement a humble collection of oddments.

With its cobbled streets and orieled mansions covering one of Plovdiv's three hills (hence the town's Roman name, Trimontium), Plovdiv's **old quarter** is a painter's dream and a cartographer's nightmare. As good a route as any is to start from ul Stanislav Dospevski, beyond the **Sveta Marina** church – which has boldly coloured murals beneath its porch and beguiling creatures peeping out from the wooden foliage of its iconostasis. From Dospevski you can climb a stairway to the **Antique Theatre**. These imposing ruins are practically the only remains of an acropolis the Romans built when they made Trimontium a provincial capital in the second century. The acropolis, like the residential districts below, was devastated by Goths in 251, and later used as building material when the town revived.

Blackened **fortress walls** dating from Byzantine times can be seen around streets like Knyaz Tsertelov and Maksim Gorki, sometimes incorporated into the dozens of **National Revival-style houses** that are Plovdiv's speciality. Typically, these rest upon an incline and expand with each storey by means of timber-framed oriels – cleverly resolving the problem posed by the scarcity of groundspace. Outside and inside, the walls are frequently decorated with niches, floral motifs or false columns painted in the style known as *alafranga*, executed by itinerant artists.

At the corner of Knyaz Tsertelev and Todor Samodumov stands a large buff-coloured mansion with dozens of windows and sturdy ribs supporting the oriels. Known as the **Lamartine House** after the French poet who stayed here in 1833, it now contains a small museum (Mon, Tues & Sun 9am–noon) with pictures of the author and the places he visited on his travels through Bulgaria. For ornate facades, few houses can match **ul Kiril Nektariev 15**, embellished with swags, medallions and intricate tracery in a vivid shade of blue, and although it's not open to the public, the **House of the People's Artists**, at no. 21, sometimes is.

It's the monumental scale rather than ornamentation that makes the **Georgiadi House** at ul Starinna 1 so remarkable; built for a rich Greek in 1846, the mansion contains the **Museum of National Liberation** (Mon & Wed–Sun 9.30am–12.30pm & 2–5pm). Pride of place is given to replicas of the bell that tolled and a cannon that fired during the April Rising, during which the streets of Plovdiv were hung with corpses that the rebellious population were forbidden to bury.

A little further uphill is the rather doomy-looking **Hisar Gate**, which has been rebuilt countless times since Philip of Macedon originally had it raised to form the citadel's eastern portal. The alleyway running off between the Georgiadi House and the gate leads down to several **craft workshops** and many humbler dwellings that have yet to be renovated despite their listed status. The first stretch is overhung by four triangular oriels which protrude from the rear of Plovdiv's most photographed building – the **Kuyumdzhioglu House**. Still known after the Greek who commissioned it in 1847, the house graces a garden which you enter from Dr Chomakov street and combines Baroque and native folk motifs in its richly decorated facade, with its undulating pediment copying the line of the carrying-yoke. The **Ethnographic Museum** (Tues–Thurs, Sat & Sun 9am–noon & 1.30–5.30pm, Fri 9am–noon) in the mansion's lower rooms is mundane, but upstairs the elegant rooms opening off the grand reception hall are furnished with objects reflecting the owner's taste for Viennese and French Baroque, and filled with showcases of sumptuous jewellery and traditional peasant costumes.

The ruined **Nebet Tepé Citadel** was fortified by the Thracians as early as the fifth century BC, and was subsequently captured by Philip of Macedon in 342 BC, who ordered it to be rebuilt in tandem with the new town modestly named Philippopolis – which his son, Alexander the Great, later abandoned in search of new conquests in Asia. Over the following centuries, the inhabitants must have often resorted to the secret tunnel linking Nebet Tepé with the riverbank, as the town and citadel were sacked by Romans, Slavs, Bulgars, Byzantines and the Ottoman Empire, to name but a few.

Back on the south side of the Hisar Gate, the church of **SS. Constantine and Elena** contains a fine gilt iconostasis by Ivan Pashkula, partly decorated by the prolific nineteenth-century artist Zahari Zograf, whose work also appears in the adjacent **Museum of Icons** (Tues–Sun 9.30am–12.30pm & 2–6pm).

Eating and drinking

Several **restaurants** in the old town serve good Bulgarian food in elegant surroundings. The *Páldin*, ul Knyaz Tseretelev 3, is the most exclusive, and even then an excellent meal will set you back only $7. Both the *Alafrangite*, ul Nektariev 15, and the *Trakiiski Stan*, ul Pâldin 7, are not quite as expensive, but the latter place is very often plagued by large tour groups and folklore shows. In the new town, the *Zlatna Krusha* restaurant at Otets Paisii 28 is quiet and elegant, while ul Daskalov – awash with hamburger, doner kebab and pizza outlets – is the place to look for cheaper snack fare.

Daytime **drinking** takes place in the cafés of ul Knyaz Aleksandâr and pl Stamboliiski, while at night the more intimate bars of the old town come into their own – *Bar Valeo*, bul Gorki 21, and *Kino Klub*, ul Gorki 29, are worth sampling.

Moving on from Plovdiv

From Plovdiv there are hourly trains to **Sofia**, plus four daily expresses to **Burgas** and two to **Varna**. You can minimize queueing by buying tickets and making seat reservations at ul General Gurko 5 rather than the station itself. This same agency handles bookings to **Belgrade** (cheap fares, but a miserable 10-hour journey), and **İstanbul** – although here, problems can arise. The Bulgars charge $45 for a seat on the *Istanbul Express*, and refuse to sell travellers a cheap ticket. To avoid paying the full whack, you'll have to board the train without a ticket and hope that the conductor will let you ride to the border town of Svilengrad for around $10 – the fare for non-foreigners. Once inside Turkey you can buy a ticket to Istanbul from the guard for $8, or an equivalent sum in other hard currencies.

Bachkovo Monastery

The most attractive destination to the south of Plovdiv is **Bachkovo Monastery**, an easy day trip from the city as it lies on the route of the hourly buses that run from the *Rodopi* bus terminal in Plovdiv through to Smolyan. The fortress-like stone houses of **BACHKOVO** village, overgrown with flowers, give you no indication of the exuberance to be seen at the monastery, a kilometre or so further up the road. Founded in 1038 by two Georgians in the service of the Byzantine empire, this is Bulgaria's second largest monastery and, like Rila, has been declared a "world heritage site" by UNESCO.

A great iron-studded door admits visitors to the cobblestoned courtyard, surrounded by vine-wreathed wooden galleries and kept free of grass by sheep. Along one wall of the courtyard, frescoes provide a pictorial narrative of the monastery's history, showing Bachkovo roughly as it appears today, but watched over by God's eye and a celestial Madonna and Child. Beneath the vaulted porch of Bachkovo's principal church, **Sveta Bogoroditsa**, are frescoes expressing the horrors in store for sinners, but the entrance itself is more cheerful, overseen by the Holy Trinity. Floral motifs in a "naive" style decorate the beams of the interior, where the iconostasis bears a fourteenth-century icon of the Virgin, of Georgian origin.

The church of **St Nicholas**, originally founded during the nineteenth century and recently restored, features a fine *Last Judgement* covering the porch exterior, which includes portraits of the artist, Zahari Zograf, and of two of his colleagues in the upper left-hand corner. In the old refectory you can see *The Procession of the Miraculous Icon*, executed by Zograf's pupils, which repeats the pilgrimage scene portrayed on the wall of the courtyard. A bizarre mixture of carved spoons, broken teapots and ecclesiastical hats are lumped together with filigreed crosses, books bound in gold and the odd Thracian bas-relief inside the church **museum**, as if visitors were being invited to choose at a jumble sale. Finally, **Sveta Troitsa**, standing 300 metres from the main gate, contains a number of early medieval frescoes and life-sized portraits of Tsar Ivan Aleksandâr and the royal family, who lavishly endowed the monastery in the fourteenth century.

NORTHERN BULGARIA

Routes from Sofia to the Black Sea coast take you through the mountainous terrain of central and northern Bulgaria – a gruelling eight- or nine-hour ride that's worth interrupting to savour something of the country's heartland. For over a thousand years, the "Old Mountain" (Stara Planina) – known to foreigners as the **Balkan range** – has been the cradle of the Bulgarian nation and the cockpit of its destiny. It was here that the Khans established and ruled over the feudal realm known as the "First Kingdom". Here, too, after a period of Byzantine control, the boyars proclaimed the "Second Kingdom", and created a magnificent capital at **Veliko Târnovo** – which remains one of Bulgaria's most impressive cities. Closer to the capital, the **Sredna Gora** (Central Range) was inhabited as early as the fifth millennium BC, but for Bulgarians this forested region is best known as the "land of the April Rising", the nineteenth-century rebellion for which the highly picturesque **Koprivshtitsa** will always be remembered.

Although they lie some way off the main rail lines from Sofia, neither Veliko Târnovo nor Koprivshtitsa is difficult to reach. The former lies just south of Gorna Oryahovitsa, a major rail junction midway between Varna and Sofia, from where you can pick up a local train or bus; the latter is served by a stop on the Sofia to Burgas line, whose five daily trains in each direction are met by local buses to ferry you the 12km to the village itself.

Koprivshtitsa

Seen from a distance, **KOPRIVSHTITSA** looks almost too lovely to be real, its half-timbered houses nestled in a valley amid wooded hills. On closer inspection, however, something of the appeal begins to fade, as it's invariably full of tourists drawn by the superb architecture and Bulgarians paying homage to a landmark in their nation's history. From the Place of the Scimitar Charge to the Street of the Counter Attack, there's hardly a part of Koprivshtitsa that isn't named for an episode or participant in the **April Rising of 1876**. As neighbouring towns were burned by the Bashibazouks – the irregular troops recruited by the Turks to put the rebels in their place – refugees flooded into Koprivshtitsa, spreading panic. The rebels eventually took to the hills while the local traders bribed the Bashibazouks to spare the village – and so Koprivshtitsa survived unscathed to be admired by subsequent generations as a symbol of heroism.

You arrive at a small bus station one hundred metres south of the main square, where the **Apriltsi Mausoleum** is inscribed "Let us keep the national liberty for which the heroes of the rising of 1876 fell". Also here is the *Museum Service* office, which sells an all-in ticket for Koprivshtitsa's museum-houses. On the opposite side of the river you'll see the **Dyado Liben Inn**, occupying the beautiful Dragilska house, a few yards north of which stands the memorial house of **Lyuben Karavelov** (7.30am–12.30pm & 1.30–5.30pm; closed Tues), one of Bulgaria's main revolutionary ideologues in the last century.

A street running off to the west of the main square leads down to the **Oslekov House** (same hours), the finest in Koprivshtitsa, with pillars of cypress wood imported from Lebanon supporting the facade. Its Red Room is particularly impressive, with a vast wooden ceiling carved with geometric motifs. One of the medallions painted on the wall shows the original, symmetrical plan of the house, never realized since Oslekov's neighbours refused to sell him the necessary land. Further along, the street joins ul Debelyanov, which straddles a hill between two bridges and boasts some more lovely buildings. Near the Surlya Bridge is the birthplace of the poet **Dimcho Debelyanov** (no. 6), who is buried in the yard of the hill-top **Church of the Holy Virgin**. Built in 1817 and partly sunken into the ground to comply with Ottoman restrictions, the church contains icons by Zograf and the seventeenth-century *Rasho Gospel*.

A gate at the rear of the churchyard leads to the birthplace of **Todor Kableshkov**, leader of the local rebels. Kableshkov's house now displays the insurgents' silk banner embroidered with the Bulgarian Lion and "Liberty 'or Death!", and one of the twenty **cherry-tree cannons** secretly manufactured by the rebels. Although one bore the engraved slogan "End of the Turkish Empire, 1876", the cannons soon became a liability, as they tended to explode.

Near the **Bridge of the First Shot** – where the uprising began – stands another striking example of Bulgarian Baroque, the **Lyutov House**, built in 1854. It's best known for its wealth of murals: palaces, temples and travel scenes splashed across the walls and niches; wreaths, blossoms and nosegays in the Blue Room; and oval medallions on the ceilings. The side street running southeast away from the bridge leads past the post office, from where it's only a few minutes' walk to the **St Nikola Church**. Here, despite the dedication, the emphasis is on Saint Spiridion, whose life is told in ten medallions surrounding a figure of the saint.

Following the Kosovo stream down to the main street, and then walking up ul Dorosiev, brings you to the birthplace of another major figure in the uprising, **Georgi Benkovski**. A tailor by profession, he made the insurgents' banner and uniforms, and commanded a rebel band on Mount Eledzhik, which fought its way north until it was wiped out near Teteven.

Practicalities

A *Balkantourist* office at Anton Ivanor 42, just north of the main square, may be able to book **rooms** in some of Koprivshtitsa's old houses. Otherwise, the *Hotel Koprivshtitsa* (☎997184/2182; ③) up the hill from the main square is the only place to stay. For **eating and drinking**, the best places are the *Dyado Liben Inn*, with a restaurant upstairs and café-aperitif bar on the ground floor (Tues–Sun noon–3pm & 7–11pm), and the *April 20 Complex*, containing a restaurant and café on the main square.

Veliko Târnovo

Even the dour Prussian Field-Marshal, Von Moltke, was moved to remark that he had "never seen a town of more romantic location" than **VELIKO TÂRNOVO**, which seems poised to leap into the chasms that divide the city. Medieval fortifications add melodrama to the scene, and the huddles of antique houses seem bound to the rocks by wild lilac and vines that form picturesque reefs veined by steps and narrow streets. But for Bulgarians the city has a deeper significance. When the National Assembly met here to draft Bulgaria's first constitution in 1879, it did so in the former capital of the Second Kingdom (1185–1396), whose civilization was snuffed out by the Turks. Reclaiming this heritage was an integral part of the National Revival, and since independence archeologists have been keenly uncovering the past of Târnovo "the Great".

Arrival and accommodation

All trains between Sofia and Varna stop at Gorna Oryahovitsa, from where eight local trains daily cover the remaining 13km to Veliko Târnovo. In the middle of the day there's a large gap between these local services, so you could save time by hopping on the bus shuttle to Gorna Oryahovitsa's bus terminal, from where there's a half-hourly connection to Veliko Târnovo. The Veliko Târnovo **train station** is 2km south of the centre – buses #4, #12 and #13 run to the main thoroughfare, bul Levski, but they are so rare that it's best to start walking.

If you bear left out of the station and keep to the left for the next fifteen minutes, you'll find yourself at a footbridge from which ul Aleksandâr Stamboliiski ascends past the *Veliko Târnovo* and *Etâr* **hotels** to the Mother Bulgaria monument, which marks the northern end of bul Levski. The **Balkantourist** office inside the *Etâr* has a stock of **private rooms** in the old town, though these can be heavily booked in summer. The *Etâr* itself (☎62/26-861; ③), the *Orbita* (③), round the corner at Hristo Botev 15, and the *Yantra* (☎62/20-391; ④), in the old town at pl Velchova Zavera 1, are the cheapest **hotels** within striking distance of the sights. Close to the train station, the *Sveta Gora* **campsite** has cheap chalets.

The Town

The Mother Bulgaria monument marks the fringe of the old town: from here bul Levski heads northeast into the network of narrow streets which curve around the heights above the river Yantra. Like many of the old houses here, the immediately conspicuous **House of the Little Monkey** at ul Vâstanicheska 14 – which gets its nickname from the grimacing statuette over the balcony – sits precariously above a limited ground space, with orieled living quarters above what used to be a shop or warehouse. The former **Inn of Hadzhi Nikolai Minchev**, nearby at ul Rakovski 17, is more satisfying since it nowadays serves as an **Ethnographic Museum** (Tues–Sun 9am–noon & 1–5pm). The size of the ground-floor caravanserai, with its airy, undulating arcades, reflects Târnovo's commercial upsurge following the Crimean War, which forced the Ottoman Empire to accept Western products. Among the woodcarvings, pewter and silverwork on the first floor, the jewel-encrusted belt-clasps are outstanding.

Various restored workshops and an olde-worlde café and pastry shop make up the **bazaar** at the junction of Rakovski and pl Georgi Kirkov. It's a good place to observe craftspeople at work, and highly photogenic, too, with its wrought-iron facades and cobbled slopes, but it lacks a real bazaar's bustle and hustle. Starting from the square you can follow ul Nikolai Zlatarski up into the narrow streets of the peaceful old **Varosh quarter**, whose two nineteenth-century churches are verging on decrepitude. Should you climb onto the plateau above Varosh, you can pick up a fairly obvious two-hour trail to the beautiful **Preobrazhenski Monastery**, which was founded during the Second Kingdom but rebuilt in the last century.

Heading downhill from pl G. Kirkov instead, you can take the stairway behind the *Hotel Yantra* down to the pedestrian walkway over to **Trapezitsa**, across the gorge. Sticking to ul Ivan Vazov instead, you'll pass two churches sited on opposite sides – the **Cathedral of the Virgin**, standing aloof on a terrace, and **SS. Constantine and Elena**, skulking behind foliage at the bottom of a steep flight of steps.

More steps descend from SS. Constantine and Elena to **ul General Gurko**, where the houses – mainly dating from Ottoman times – look incredibly picturesque perched along the curve of the ravine. Don't miss the **Sarafina House** at no. 88 (Tues–Sun 9am–noon & 1–6pm), which is so contrived that only two floors are visible from General Gurko but a further three overhang the river. The interior is notable for the splendid octagonal vestibule with wrought-iron fixtures and a panelled rosette-ceiling; the inclusion of photos of old Târnovo downstairs justifies billing this as a **Museum of Nineteenth-Century Life**.

To the southeast stands a spacious blue and white edifice: the **Konak** of the Turkish governor, Ali Bey. It was here the rebels of 1876 stood trial, and it was subsequently the venue for two months of deliberations before the first Bulgarian parliament assembled. This hallowed building was reconstructed after being devastated by fire in time to allow the proclamation of People's Power from the premises on September 9, 1944 – Bulgaria's first post-communist parliament also met here briefly in summer 1990 before relocating to Sofia. Unsurprisingly, it's now occupied by a **Museum of the National Revival and the Constituent Assembly** (daily 10am–5pm), while the adjoining block mounts an **Archeological Exposition of Medieval Târnovo**. From here, ul Ivan Vazov leads directly to Tsarevets, the medieval fortress.

TSAREVETS

Approaching **Tsarevets** (daily 8am–dusk) along the stone causeway that was erected after the drawbridge collapsed beneath the Bey's harem, you can appreciate how the boyars Petâr and Asen were emboldened enough by possession of this **citadel** to lead a rebellion against Byzantium in 1185. Petâr's proclamation of the Second Kingdom occurred when the empire was preoccupied by the Seljuk Turk menace, and when a Byzantine army was finally sent in 1190 it was defeated at the Tryavna Pass. Yet by the late fourteenth century the Second Kingdom had fragmented into several semi-autonomous states which were no match for the expansionist Ottoman Turks, who besieged Târnovo for three months before plundering it in July 1393. Now restored and spotlit at night, Tsarevets conveys something of the grandeur of the Second Kingdom's heyday, when travellers deemed Târnovo "second after Constantinople".

Artisans and clerics entered Tsarevets via the **Asenova Gate** halfway along the western ramparts; foreign merchants, invited to settle here by Tsar Asen II, had their own entrance, the "Frankish" or **Frenkhisar Gate** near the southern end of the massif. Rapidly becoming a regional power, the Second Kingdom intervened to help Byzantium overthrow the first Latin Emperor of the East, Baldwin of Flanders, in 1205; the former emperor ended his days in the bastion overlooking the Frenkhisar Gate, thereafter known as **Baldwin's Tower**.

The ruins of the **Palace** seem insignificant compared to the ramparts, but it once looked splendid, with its 105-foot-long throne room adorned with green serpentine, Egyptian porphyry, pink marble and mosaics. The thirteenth-century Church of the Blessed Saviour or **Patriarchate** was the only structure permitted to surpass the palace in height. Ribbed with red brick and inset with green and orange ceramics, the church is now a favourite location for the filming of historical epics.

THE ASENOVA QUARTER, TRAPEZITSA AND SVETA GORA

To the west of Tsarevets on both banks of the Yantra lies the **Asenova quarter**, where chickens strut and children fish beside the river. During the Middle Ages this was the artisan quarter, which it remained until 1913, when it was struck by an earthquake which levelled all the medieval buildings except the churches. The **Church of the Forty Martyrs** was founded in 1230 and became the burial place of Saint Sava and several tsars. The Bulgars saw God's hand behind the collapse of the minaret built by the Turks when they transformed it into a mosque. Further north, the **Church of SS. Peter and Paul** contains several capitals carved with vine leaves and some well-preserved frescoes of which the oldest – dating back to the fourteenth century – is the *Pietà* opposite the altar.

On the other side of the river, the **Church of St Demetrius** is the best-looking of the surviving medieval churches, with its red-brick stripes and trefoil windows inlaid with orange plaques – although most of its frescoes have been painted over. **St George's Church**, further to the south, is smaller but has better-preserved frescoes. Overhead rises the massif known as **Trapezitsa**, where the boyars and leading clergy of the Second Kingdom built their mansions and some forty private churches, sixteen of which are currently being excavated.

Sveta Gora (Holy Hill), on the south bank of the Yantra, used to be a centre of monastic scholasticism and nowadays provides the site for **Cyril and Methodius University**, which can be reached by a bridge to the south of Tsarevets. Its large, copper-roofed **Art Gallery** is devoted to "Târnovo through the eyes of diverse paint-ers" – an unchallenging jumble of townscapes.

Eating and drinking

The *Samovodska Sreshta* **restaurant** at the corner of ul G. Rakovski and pl G. Kirkov is popular with locals and tourists alike, and has a varied menu. The *Suhindol*, around the corner at G. Mamarčev 14, offers cheap and filling grills as well as good draught beer. The *Grill-Restaurant Veliko Târnovo* on pl Sâedinenie – above the Museum of the National Revival – has a tiny menu but is very good value. The *Hotel Târnovo* on ul Popov has an international restaurant, occasional discos and a popular café on a terrace overlooking the river. Most evening **drinking** takes place in the numerous private **bars** in the old town – try the *Café Boyarka* at ul D. Blagoev 41, or the *Simeon i Sin*, opposite the entrance to Tsarevets.

THE COAST

It was the Soviet leader Khrushchev who first suggested that the Black Sea coastline be developed for tourism, and since then the **resorts** have mushroomed, growing increasingly sophisticated as the prototype mega-complexes have been followed by "holiday villages". With fine weather and safe bathing practically guaranteed, the selling of the coast has been a success in economic terms, but with the exception of ancient **Sozopol** and over-touristed **Nesebâr**, there's little to please the eye. Of the coast's two main towns – **Varna** and **Burgas** – the former is by far the preferable one as a base for getting to the less developed spots.

Varna

VARNA's origins go back almost five millennia, but it wasn't until seafaring Greeks founded a colony here in 585 BC that the town became a port. The modern city is an amalgam of different roles – a shipyard and port for commercial freighters and the navy, and a riviera town visited by tourists of every nationality. It's a cosmopolitan place and a nice one to stroll through: Baroque, turn-of-the-century and contemporary architecture pleasantly blended with shady promenades and a handsome seaside garden.

Social life revolves around the **pl Nezavisimost**, where the opera house and theatre provide a backdrop for an ensemble of restaurants and cafés. The square is the starting point of Varna's evening promenade, which flows eastward from here along bul Knyaz Boris I towards bul Slivnitsa and the seaside gardens. Beyond the opera house and town council, Varna's main lateral boulevard cuts through pl Varnenska Komuna, followed by a wind that rustles the trees around the domed **Cathedral of the Assumption**. Constructed in 1886 along the lines of St Petersburg's cathedral, it contains a splendid iconostasis and carved bishop's throne, and murals painted after the last war.

Exhibits in the **Varna Museum of History and Art** on the corner of Dimitâr Blagoev and Slivnitsa (Tues–Sun 10am–5pm) fill forty halls, three of them devoted to skeletons and artefacts from a necropolis where a hoard of 4500-year-old gold objects was discovered in 1972. Other halls display Greek and Roman antiquities, medieval weaponry and ecclesiastical art, and the usual arms, banners and manifestoes dating from the revolutionary and National Revival periods.

South of the centre, on ul Han Krum, you'll stumble upon the impressive second-century **Roman baths** (Tues–Sun 10am–6pm). The **Ethnographic Museum** (Tues–Sun 10am–5pm), occupying an old house just west of here on ul Panagyurishte, contains a fine display of costumes and jewellery, and a variety of "ritual loaves" – like the foot-shaped *Proshtupalnik*, which was baked to celebrate a child's first steps.

The boat responsible for the Navy's only victory – the *Drâzhki* (Intrepid) – is honourably embedded on the waterfront outside the **Navy Museum** (9am–noon & 1.30–5pm); it sank the Turkish cruiser *Hamidie* off Cape Kaliakra in 1912. The museum traces sea power and commerce on the Black Sea and the lower Danube back to its earliest days.

Practicalities

Each of the main points of arrival has good bus connections with the centre. You'll approach it from the northwest if you come in from the **bus terminal** (bus #1, #22 or #41) on bul Vladislav Varnenchik or Varna **airport** (#50), whereas travellers coming in at the **train station** (#1, #4 or #6) basically head uphill from the south.

The **Balkantourist** office at ul Musala 3 (Mon–Fri 8.30am–12.30pm & 1–6pm) has **private rooms** for $9, usually quite central. The next door *Hotel Musala* (☎052/239-25; ③), *Orbita*, Tsar Osvoboditel 25 (☎052/225-162; ③), or the more central *Odessa*, bul Primorski 4 (☎052/228-381; ④), are the cheapest of the hotels. The *Galata* **campsite** can be reached by bus #17 from bul Botev to the Galata terminal.

Most of Varna's **eating and drinking** venues are to be found along bul Knyaz Boris I and bul Slivnitsa – the latter a seemingly unbroken strip of cafés, bars and restaurants. You'll find more hot-dog and burger-eating opportunities than anywhere else in Bulgaria, as well as new fast-food joints like the *Pizzeria San Nicolo*, on the corner of ul 27 Yuli and Knyaz Boris I. For more substantial eating, *Zlantno Pile*, Slivnitsa 7, has a pretty basic chicken-and-chips menu, but the draught beer is excellent; the *Galera*, ul Dråzhki 17, offers traditional Bulgarian dishes in a rebuilt nineteenth-century house; the *Rimska Terma*, ul 8 Noemuri (just below the Roman baths) is a small privately-owned place offering good home cooking, while the *Panorama* on the top floor of the *Cherno More* hotel (corner of Knyaz Boris I and Slivnitsa) offers an affordable slap-up meal to live jazz or classical accompaniment.

The flashy bars lining bul Slivnitsa are the obvious places to drink – *Café Lauta* is one of the most popular – although places hidden away in the streets north of Knyaz Boris I can be quieter: *Black Hole*, Shipka 23 is a cellar bar, *Dalia*, Bdin 17 is more plush.

The *Festival Complex*, Slivnitsa 2, is a popular meeting-place for the town's youth, containing a café (with excellent ice cream), an art-house cinema, and a popular **disco**.

The southern coast

Heavily industrialized **BURGAS**, the south coast's prime urban centre, can be reached by train from Sofia and Plovdiv, or by bus from Varna. The town is ugly and really only worth considering for its access to the museum town of Nesebâr to the north or the more unexploited spots – like Sozopol – to the south. There are regular buses from the airport into town, and other points of arrival are clustered near the waterfront. If it's necessary to stay, private **accommodation** can be arranged by **Primoretz-tourist** at Aleksandroska 2 opposite the train station (daily 8am–8pm) – they have doubles for as little as $4.

Nesebâr

Founded by the Greeks, **NESEBÂR** – 35km northeast of Burgas – was later used by the Byzantines as a base from which to assail the First Kingdom, provoking Khan Krum to seize it in 812. Thereafter ownership alternated between Bulgaria and Byzantium until the Ottomans captured it in 1453. The town's decline to a humble fishing port under Turkish rule left Nesebâr's **Byzantine churches** reasonably intact, and nowadays the town depends on them for its tourist appeal, a constant stream of visitors crossing the slender isthmus connecting the old town with the mainland. Access to Nesebâr is easy: half-hourly buses run from Burgas to the resort of Slånchev Bryag, from where there's a shuttle bus every 10–15 minutes.

The first church you come to, the **Church of Christ the Pantokrator**, was completed during the fourteenth-century reign of Tsar Aleksandâr and its blind niches, turquoise ceramic inlays and red brick motifs are characteristic of latter-day Byzantine architecture, although the frieze of swastikas – a symbol of the sun and continual change – is unusual. Across the road on ul Mitropolitska, **St John the Baptist** also has a cruciform plan, but its undressed stone exterior dates it as a tenth- or eleventh-century building. Inside are several frescoes – the portraits of the donor and his contemporaries, on the west part of the south wall and beneath the dome, date from when the church was built.

Overhung by half-timbered houses carved with sun-signs, fish and other symbols, ul Aheloi branches off from ul Mitropolitska towards the **Church of Sveti Spas**, outwardly unremarkable, but filled with seventeenth-century frescoes. Diagonally opposite is the now ruined **Church of the Archangels Michael and Gabriel**, patterned not unlike the Pantokrator. A few steps to the east lies the ruined **Old Metropolitan Church**, dominating a plaza filled with pavement cafés, street traders and hawkers. The church itself dates back to the fifth or sixth century, and it was here that bishops officiated during the city-state's heyday. At the northern tip of the peninsula you'll stumble upon the remains of the so-called **Basilica by the Seashore**, and a keep suggesting the frequency with which this exposed church was sacked by numerous pirates and invaders.

The thirteenth-century **Church of St Theodor**, nearby, is modestly sized, and the old houses along the streets leading back into the centre are far more eye-catching. A left turn just before the end of the main street, ul Mesembriya, brings you to the **New Metropolitan Church** (also known as *Sveti Stefan*; daily 9am–1pm & 2–6pm), whose interior fresco of the *Forty Martyrs*, on the west wall, gives pride of place to the patron who financed the church's enlargement during the fifteenth century. Completing the loop through the town, there's the ruined **Church of St John Aliturgetos**, standing in splendid isolation beside the shore and representing the zenith of Byzantine architecture in Bulgaria. Its exterior decoration is strikingly varied, employing limestone, red bricks, crosses, mussel shells and ceramic plaques, with a representation of a human figure composed of limestone blocks incorporated into the north wall.

Nesebâr's **accommodation bureau** (daily 8am–7pm) is opposite the harbour, which is also where buses arrive; their **private rooms**, many of them in fine old houses, begin at a mere $6 for a double. The *Hotel Mesambria* in ul Ribarska (✆0554/3255; ③) is usually full, but has reasonable doubles for $20. There are plenty of places to get **food**, beginning with the harbour kiosks serving fresh mackerel and chips. The old town is crammed with tourist restaurants, but for more authentic fish dishes try the intimate *Stariyat Ribar* in ul Ivan Isan, or the more raucous *Kapetanska Sreshta* at the bottom of ul Ribarska. *Bar Burgas*, Meha 10, is one of the better places to enjoy an evening drink.

Sozopol
SOZOPOL, the oldest settlement on the coast, was founded in the seventh century BC by Ionian colonists from Miletus, who called the town Apollonia and prospered by trading Greek textiles and wine for honey and corn. Today it's a busy port and the favoured resort of Bulgaria's literary and artistic set, attracted here by the relative tranquillity of fishing-village life. The **Church of the Holy Virgin**, built in the nineteenth century, features a finely carved iconostasis and bishop's throne, but it's the old houses that give Sozopol its charm. With space at a premium, their upper storeys project so far out that houses on opposite sides of the narrow, cobbled streets almost meet. Sozopol's **Archeological Museum** (Mon–Fri 8am–noon & 1–5pm, Sat & Sun 9am–noon & 2–4.30pm), hidden behind the library, should not be missed, for its collection of amphoras dredged from the surrounding waters and its display of exquisitely decorated Greek vases called *kraters*.

The hourly **buses** from Burgas arrive at the southern edge of the old town opposite the main beach. Head southeast from here along ul Republikanska to reach the larger south beach and the accommodation bureau at ul Ropotamo 28; atmospheric old rooms in the old town or more roomy apartments in the new town go for about $10 a double. Otherwise, just ask around – everyone in Sozopol rents out rooms over the summer. The *Mehana Sozopol*, ul Apoloniya, and the *Vyatarna Melnitsa*, ul Morski Skali, are a couple of good **restaurants** – the latter with occasional live music. Many of the smaller, privately-owned eateries, such as *Mehana Amfora*, Kulata 2, and *Neptun*, Morski Skali, are more friendly and intimate.

travel details

Trains

Sofia to: Burgas (7 daily; 6–8hr); Gorna Oryahovitsa (hourly; 4hr 15min); Kocherinovo (5 daily; 2hr 15min–3hr); Koprivshtitsa (5 daily; 1hr 40min–2hr 20min); Plovdiv (10 daily; 2hr 30min–3hr); Sandanski (5 daily; 3hr 30min–4hr 30min); Varna (5 daily; 9hr).

Gorna Oryahovitsa to: Veliko Târnovo (8 daily; 30min).

Plovdiv to: Burgas (5 daily; 5hr); Sofia (10 daily; 2hr 30min–3hr); Veliko Târnovo (1 daily; 5hr).

Buses

Sofia to: Koprivshtitsa (1 daily; 2hr); Plovdiv (2 daily; 2hr); Rila (1 daily; 3hr); Sandanski (3 daily; 3hr); Veliko Târnovo (2 daily; 4hr).

Burgas to: Slânchev Bryag (every 30min; 50min); Sozopol (hourly; 40min); Varna (6 daily; 3hr).

Gorna Oryahovitsa to: Veliko Târnovo (every 30min; 30min).

Kocherinovo to: Rila (every 2hr; 30min).

Plovdiv to: Bachkovo (hourly; 40min); Nesebâr (1 daily; 3hr).

Sandanski to: Melnik (2 daily; 40min).

Slânchev Bryag to: Nesebâr (every 15min; 10min).

CHAPTER 4

CZECH & SLOVAK REPUBLICS

GERMANY

To Dresden

To Wroclaw

POLAND

CZECH

To Nurnberg

Karlovy PRAGUE
Vary

To Kraków

REPUBLIC

Olomouc

Pizeň

To Petersberg

Český
Krumlov

České
Budějovice

Brno

Poprad

Košice

SLOVAKIA

UKRAINE

To Lvov

To Linz

To
Vienna

BRATISLAVA

AUSTRIA

HUNGARY

0   100 km

To Budapest

ROMANIA

Introduction

Czechoslovakia's "Velvet Revolution" in November 1989 was probably the most unequivocably positive of all the anti-Communist upheavals in Eastern Europe. True to their pacifist past, the Czechs and Slovaks shrugged off forty-one years of communist rule without so much as a shot being fired. The rapid emergence of a leader of impeccably democratic and intellectual credentials helped boost the people's exhilaration in the face of an uncertain future. The euphoria and unity of those first few months evaporated more quickly than anyone could have imagined, and just three years after the revolution, against most people's predictions, the country split into two separate republics.

The two republics together span a full range of cultural influences, from the old German towns of the former Sudetenland to the Hungarian and Rusyn villages in East Slovakia. The **Czechs** who inhabit the westernmost republic – itself divided into Bohemia and Moravia – are among the most westernized Slavs in Europe: urbane, agnostic, liberal and traditionally fairly well-off. The **Slovaks**, to the east, are by contrast fervently Catholic, and, for the most part, deeply conservative. In physical terms, too, it's impossible to generalize: Bohemia's lush rolling hills couldn't be more different from the flat Danube basin of west Slovakia, or the granite alpine peaks of the High Tatras, the beech forests of the far east, or the coal basins of northern Moravia.

In contrast to the political upheavals that have plagued the region, the Czech and Slovak Republics have suffered very little physical damage. Almost utouched by this century's wars, the Czech capital, **Prague**, is justifiably the most popular destination in either republic, and is perfectly poised for exploring the gentle hills and spa towns of surrounding **Bohemia**. The country's most central province, **Moravia**, is every bit as beautiful, and less touristed. **Olomouc** is the most attractive town here, but **Brno**, the largest city, has its own peculiar pleasures, and gives access to the popular Moravian karst region and a host of nearby castles and châteaux.

Slovakia has some of Europe's highest mountains outside the Alps: they have long formed barriers to industrialization and modernization, preserving and strengthening regional differences in the face of Prague's centralizing efforts. While by no means as stunningly beautiful as Prague,

Bratislava, the Slovak capital, has a compact old town in the midst of its redevelopments, and is a lively place day and night.

Information and Maps

Prague and Bratislava have tourist offices (*PIS* in Prague and *BIS* in Bratislava) specifically set up to give information to foreign visitors. Other cities like Brno are beginning to follow suit, but in many places **ČEDOK**, the former state travel agency, is your only hope; they are generally open Mon–Fri 9am–noon & 1–5pm, plus Saturday mornings in larger places. However, worthwhile information is thin on the ground, and staff are notoriously unhelpful. This will soon change as more locally organized tourist offices start to emerge.

All kinds of **maps** are available in the country. You can buy them, often very cheaply, from bookshops and some hotels – ask for a *plán města* (town plan) or *mapa okolí* (regional map). For road maps, the 1:200,000 *Autoatlas* is the best, marking all campsites and petrol stations. For **hiking**, the 1:100,000 *turistická mapa* series details the country's complex network of footpaths – ask for the *letná mapa* (summer map), as the *zimní mapa* (winter map) concentrates on pistes, ski-lifts and other such matters.

Money and Banks

The Czech and Slovak Republics now have totally **separate currencies**, though, confusingly they are both still known as the crown and are both divided into one hundred heller. The Czech crown, or *koruna česká* (*kč*), is stronger than the Slovak crown, or *Slovenská koruna* (*Sk*), though neither is yet fully convertible – at the time of going to print, both countries were printing entirely new sets of coins and notes. Even with the constant price rises and the recent influx of tourists, both republics are likely to remain relatively inexpensive places to visit for some time to come.

Travellers' cheques in US dollars or Deutschmarks are undoubtedly the safest way of carrying your money, though it's a good idea to keep at least some hard currency in **cash** for emergencies. **Eurocheques** are unknown outside the three big cities. **Credit cards** are accepted in most hotels, upmarket restaurants and some shops. You can also get cash on your plastic at some banks and most five-star hotels (£50/$75 equivalent minimum).

Communications

Most **post offices** (*pošta*) are open Mon–Sat 7/ 8am–5/6pm. Look out for the right sign to avoid queuing unnecessarily: *známky* (stamps), *dopisy* (letters) or *balky* (parcels). You can also buy stamps from *PNS* newsagents and kiosks, though usually only for domestic mail. **Poste restante** services are available in major towns, but remember to write *Pošta 1* (the main office), followed by the name of the town.

Cheap local **phone calls** can be made from any phone box; the new booths take 1, 2 and 5kč/ Sk coins; to call outside the local area code, the minimum charge is slightly higher. Many phones have instructions in English, but if you have any problems, ring ☎0135 and ask for an English-speaking operator. **International calls** are charged at a rate of about £1/$1.50 per two minutes at telephone exchanges in most major post offices; you can also make calls from the new phone card boxes; phone cards (*telecarty*) are available from *PNS* newsagents and post offices. To reverse the charges ask for a *hovor na účet volaného*.

Getting Around

The most pleasant way of travelling around the Czech and Slovak Republics is by train. If you're in a hurry, however, buses are always quicker, more frequent and slightly cheaper.

■ Trains

Trains go just about everywhere, and the antiquated rolling stock is a pleasure to travel in. Czech Railways, *České dráhy* (*ČD*), and Slovak Railways, *železnice Slovenskej republiky* (*ŽSR*), run two main types of service: *rychlík* trains are the faster ones which stop only at major towns, costing very little per kilometre, though almost double the price of an *osobný vlak*, or local train, which stops everywhere and averages about 30km an hour. It's often better to avoid the international expresses which, although theoretically fast, occasionally get delayed at borders. **Tickets** (*jízdenka* in Czech, *lístok* in Slovak) for domestic journeys can be bought at the station (*nádraží* in Czech, *stanica* in Slovak) before or on the day of departure. Fares are cheap – a second-class single from Prague to Poprad (perhaps the longest journey you'd ever have to make) currently costs

about £4/$6 – but expect this to rise. Services marked with an "R" surrounded by a box require a **seat reservation** (*místenka*); reservations are advisable for all services at weekends on main routes if you want to be sure of a seat. The *místenka* only costs a few crowns, but you must get it at least an hour before your train leaves. *ČD* and *ŽSR* run **sleepers** (*lůžka*) to and from a number of cities, and are reasonably priced. You must, however, book as far in advance as possible and in any case no later than six hours before departure. The *Rail Explorer* pass (see *Basics*) gives unlimited travel for £24 for 7 days. *InterRail* passes are valid; *Eurail* passes are not.

■ Buses

Trains will take you most places but if you have to change a lot, it might be easier to take one of the regional **buses** (*autobus*) mostly run by the state bus company, *Československo státní automobilová doprava* (*ČSAD*), with the privately-run *ČEBUS* providing an alternative on the more popular inter-city routes. Bus stations are usually next to the train station, and if there's no separate terminal you'll have to buy your ticket from the driver. The bigger terminals are run with train-like efficiency, and it's absolutely essential to book your ticket in advance if you're travelling at the weekend or early in the morning on one of the main routes.

■ Driving, hitching and cycling

With just one in five people owning a vehicle and most of those only used at the weekend, travelling by **car** in the Czech and Slovak Republics is a relaxing way to travel. **Speed limits** are 110kph on motorways, 90kph on other roads, and 60kph in all cities, towns and villages between 5am and 11pm. (For motorbikes it's 60kph in towns and villages, and a frustrating 80kph on open roads.) **Fuel** is currently fairly cheap by European standards, but petrol stations are scarce and most are closed at lunchtimes and after 6pm (though 24-hour ones can be found in all major cities). If you **break down**, dial ☎154.

Car hire in Czechoslovakia is currently around £185/$280 per week for a Škoda with unlimited mileage. Two state firms have branches in most major cities: *Pragocar*, whose head office is at Štěpánská 42, Prague (☎02/352 825), and *Brnocar*, Solniční 6, Brno (☎05/24039), both of which charge much the same rates as the major Western firms.

Hitching in either republic is fairly good. The problem is the lack of vehicles, so to hit what rush hour there is you'll have to set out early – and that means 6–8am. "Where are you heading?" is *kam jedete?* and if you want to get out of the car, just say *já chci vystoupit / ja chem vystúpit.*

Accommodation

The accommodation situation is much better than it used to be, though it remains the most expensive aspect of travelling in the Czech and Slovak Republics. Youth hostels are scarce outside Prague and the private room network still lacks a centralized booking system. However, if you're going to one of the big cities between late spring and late summer, or over the Christmas holidays, and want to save yourself time and effort on arrival, it's sensible to arrange accommodation before you set out.

■ Hotels

Throughout the region **hotels** are priced up for foreigners and consequently fairly expensive (£12/$18 and upwards for a double) and, especially in Prague, not, in fact, the best option. The old state hotels tend to be drab, concrete affairs, often glorified high-rises on the outskirts of town, badly in need of renovation. While these places are slowly being refurbished by their new owners, many new hotels have opened up particularly in the more heavily touristed areas – in either case, however, prices tend to be even higher. Breakfast is normally not included, unless you're paying a lot for your room. Without fail, hotels also have a restaurant and/or a bar and often double as the town's nightclub.

■ Private rooms

Since 1989, there has been a huge increase in the number of **private rooms** available – in fact,

these are now your best bet in Prague, Brno and Bratislava. Elsewhere, just keep your eyes peeled for signs saying *pokoj* or, more likely, *Zimmer Frei*. Prices will start at around 250kčs per person per night, but expect to pay more than this in Prague.

■ Hostels and refuges

Prague now has numerous private **youth hostels** which offer varying degrees of discomfort. Elsewhere, there are only a handful of unofficial and official **youth hostels**; the latter, known as *Juniorhotels* and run by *Cestovní kancelář mláde že* (*CKM*), charge very little to *IYHF* members (more to non-members). *CKM* also offers cheap **student accommodation** in the big university towns during July and August. The beds, usually in dormitories, cost about 100kčs per person for students, more for non-students. In the High Tatras, there are also a fair number of **refuges** (*bouda* or *chata*) scattered about the hillsides. Some are little less than hotels and cost over £5/$8 a double, but the more isolated ones are simple wooden shelters for as little as £1 per person. These should be booked in advance – if you turn up before 6pm at the more isolated ones, you may strike lucky, but don't bank on it.

■ Campsites and bungalows

Campsites, known as *autokempink*, are plentiful all over the Czech and Slovak Republics. Many of the sites feature **bungalows** (*chata*), often out for hire for anything upwards of £5/$8 for two people. Very few sites remain open all year round, and most don't open until May at the earliest, closing mid- to late September. Even though prices have been inflated for foreigners, costs are still reasonable; two people plus car and tent weigh in at around £1–2. **Camping rough** is relatively easy in more remote parts and you would be unlucky to get any hassle from the local police.

ACCOMMODATION PRICE CODES

Throughout this guide, accommodation is priced on a scale of ① to ⑧, the number indicating the lowest price per night a single person could expect to pay in that establishment in high season. With hostels this is the nightly rate per person; with hotels, the price is arrived at by dividing the cost of the cheapest double room by two. The prices indicated by the codes are as follows

① = under £5 / $8   ② = £5–10 / $8–16   ③ = £10–15 / $16–24   ④ = £15–20 / $24–32

⑤ = £20–25 / $32–40   ⑥ = £25–30 / $40–48   ⑦ = £30–35 / $48–56   ⑧ = over £35 / $56

Food and Drink

Regional differences in food were once as great as they are in folk costumes and dialect, but outside the home forty years of intensive centralization produced a nationwide Czechoslovak cuisine, mostly derived from German-influenced Bohemian food, with a predilection for big slabs of meat served with lashings of gravy, dumplings and pickled gherkins, not to mention a good helping of sauerkraut.

■ Food

Most Czechs and Slovaks get up so early in the morning (around 5 or 6am) that they seldom start the day with anything other than a quick cup of coffee. The usual mid-morning snack at the *bufet* (stand-up canteen) is *párek*, perhaps the most ubiquitous **takeaway food** in the country, a dubious-looking frankfurter, dipped in mustard and served with a white roll (*v rohlíku*). In most towns, some wizened character will be selling *slané tyčinky* (a salted stringy cheese) on the street, a snack which the locals eat with gusto. A Czech speciality all year round is *smažený sýr* – a slab of melted cheese (and, more often than not, ham) fried in breadcrumbs and served with a roll (*v housce*), while the Slovak national dish is *bryndzové halušky*, a sort of macaroni cheese.

Like the Austrians and Hungarians who once ruled over them, the Czechs and Slovaks have a grotesquely sweet tooth, and the coffee and cake hit is part of the daily ritual. **Coffee** is drunk black and described rather hopefully as "Turkish" or *turecká*. The *cukrárna* (in Slovak *cukráreň*) or cake shop is an important part of the country's social life, particularly on Sunday mornings when it's often the only place that's open in town. People scurry through the streets with piles of boxes under their arms, containing two main types of **cake**; *dort* consist of a series of custard cream, chocolate and sponge layers, while *řez* are lighter square cakes, usually containing a bit of fruit. Whatever the season, Czechs and Slovaks have to have their daily fix of **ice cream** (*zmrzlina*), dispensed from little window kiosks in the sides of buildings. In the *cukrárna* there's generally more choice, but it's at the outlets advertising *italská zmrzlina* (actually nothing like Italian ice cream) that the longest queues form.

Sit-down *bufets* do exist, but for a better class of food, it's best to head for a fully fledged **restaurant** (*restaurace* or *reštaurácia*) which serves hot meals non-stop from about 11.30am until 9pm, rarely later. Wine cellars (*vinárna* or *vináreň*) – though not necessarily their kitchens – sometimes stay open after 11pm. Lunch (between noon and 2pm) is the main meal of the day and generally the best time to go to a restaurant as the choice of food is at its widest. Menus and prices are nearly always displayed outside.

Most menus start with the **soups**, one of the country's culinary strong points and mainly served at lunchtimes. **Main courses** are overwhelmingly based on pork or beef, but one luxury worth taking advantage of is that carp (the traditional dish at Christmas), a rare treat in Britain, is cheaply and widely offered just about everywhere. Most main courses are served with dumplings or **vegetables**, most commonly potatoes or sauerkraut, and less frequently peas or beans. **Dumplings** (*knedlíky*), though German in origin and in name, are now the mainstay of Bohemian and Moravian cooking. With the exception of *palačinky* (pancakes) filled with chocolate or fruit and cream, **desserts**, where they exist at all, will be pretty unexciting.

■ Drink

Even the most simple *bufet* in the Czech lands almost invariably has draught **beer**, but the **pivnice** (which close around 10 or 11pm) are the places where most heavy drinking goes on. *Pivnice* are traditionally male preserves – women tend to head instead for the more mixed atmosphere of the country's restaurants or **vinárna** (in Slovak *vináreň*). The latter are the traditional places in which to drink wine, have slightly later opening hours and often double as upmarket restaurants or nightclubs.

The Czech Republic lies second in the world league table of **beer** consumption, and its beer ranks among the best in the world. The most natural starting point for any beer tour is **Plzeň** (Pilsen) in West Bohemia, whose bottom-fermented local beer is the original *Pils*. The other big brewing town is **České Budějovice** (Budweis), home to *Budvar*, a mild beer for Bohemia but still leagues ahead of *Budweiser* beer, the German name for *Budvar* that was adopted by an American brewer in 1876.

Czech and Slovak **wine** will never win over as many people as Czech beer, but the republics produce a modest selection of medium-quality wines; the biggest producers and consumers by far are the Slovaks. The home-production of

brandies is a national pastime, resulting sometimes in almost terminally strong brews. The most famous is *slivovice*, a plum brandy, originally from the border hills between Moravia and Slovakia but now available just about everywhere.

Opening Hours and Holidays

Shops in the Czech and Slovak Republics are open Mon–Fri 9am–5pm, with some shops and most supermarkets staying open till 6pm or later. Smaller shops close for lunch for an hour or so sometime between noon and 2pm, while others stay open late on Thursdays. Shops that open on Saturday close at noon or 1pm. Count on all shops being closed on Sunday.

The basic **opening hours** for castles and monasteries are Tues–Sun 8am/9am–noon/1pm, & 2–5pm. In Prague the main museums open Tues–Sun 10am–6pm, though there are of course exceptions. From the end of October to the beginning of April, most castles are closed. In April and October, opening hours are often restricted to weekends and holidays. Whatever the time of year, if you want to see the interior of the building, nine times out of ten you'll be forced to go on a guided tour (nearly always in Czech or Slovak, occasionally German) that will last at least 45 minutes. Ask for an *anglický text*, an often unintentionally hilarious English resumé of the castle's history. Entrance tickets rarely cost more than £1/$1.50 – hence few prices are quoted in the text – and no proof is needed to claim student status, which chops the price in half.

As for official holidays, May Day celebrations look set to stay for the moment, as do the *slavné májové dny* (Glorious May Days): May 5, the day of the Prague Uprising in 1945, and May 8, VE Day. Other holidays include January 1, Easter Monday, July 5, the day Saints Cyril and Methodius introduced Christianity into Czechoslovakia, and July 6, the anniversary of the death of Jan Hus, October 28, the anniversary of the Foundation of the Republic, and December 24–26.

Emergencies

Public confidence in the **police** (*policie/polícia*) has suffered a severe blow due to the current level of crime which has risen rapidly in both republics since the revolution. For tourists, theft from cars and hotel rooms is the biggest worry. Try not to look too affluent and keep your valuables on you at all times. The best way to protect yourself against such disasters, of course, is to take out travel insurance. If you are unlucky enough to have something stolen, report it immediately to the nearest police station in order to get a statement detailing what you've lost for your insurance claim. Everyone is obliged to carry some form of ID and you should carry your **passport** with you at all times, though realistically you're extremely unlikely to get stopped unless you're driving.

Minor ailments can be easily dealt with by the **chemist** or *lekárna* (in Slovak *lekáreň*), but language is likely to be a major problem once you move outside the capital. If it's a repeat prescription you want, take any empty bottles or remaining pills along with you. If the chemist can't help, they'll be able to direct you to a **hospital** or *nemocnice* (in Slovak *nemocnica*). If you do have to pay for any medication, keep the receipts for claiming on your insurance once you're home.

> **EMERGENCY NUMBERS**
> Police ☎150; Ambulance ☎155; Fire ☎158.

PRAGUE

Prague (Praha) is one of the least "Eastern" European cities you could imagine. Architecturally, and in terms of city sights, it is a revelation: few other cities anywhere in Europe look so good – and no other European capital can present six hundred years of architecture so completely untouched by natural disaster or war. Hardly surprising, then, that a staggering ninety percent of Western visitors spend all their time in and around the capital and that Praguers exude an air of confidence about their city.

Prague rose to prominence in the ninth century under Prince Bořivoj, the first Christian ruler of Prague. His grandson, Prince Václav, was to become the Přemyslid dynasty's most famous member – the Good "King" Wenceslas of the Christmas carol and the country's patron saint. Under the Přemyslids the city prospered from its position on the central European trade routes, but it was after the Přemyslid dynasty died out in 1306 that Prague enjoyed its **golden age**. In just thirty years Charles IV of Luxembourg transformed this into one of the most important cities in fourteenth-century Europe, founding an entire new town, Nové Město, to accommodate the influx of students. Following the execution of the reformist preacher Jan Hus in 1415, the country became engulfed in **religious wars**, and although the Polish Jagiello dynasty brought a degree of prosperity later that century, trouble broke out again between the Protestant nobles and the Catholic Habsburgs in 1618. Then followed the period the Czechs refer to as the **dark ages**, when the full force of the Counter-Reformation was brought to bear on the city's people. Paradoxically, though, the spurt of Baroque rebuilding during the Counter-Reformation lent Prague its most striking architectural aspect. The next two centuries saw Prague become little more than a provincial town in the greater Austrian Empire. Two things dragged it out of the doldrums: the **Industrial Revolution**, and the Czech **národní obrození**, the national revival movement that led to the foundation of the **First Republic** in 1918.

After World War II, which it survived remarkably unscathed and industrially intact, Prague disappeared completely behind the Iron Curtain. The city briefly re-emerged onto the world stage during the cultural blossoming of the **Prague Spring** in 1968, but the decisive break came in November 1989, when a peaceful student demonstration, brutally broken up by the police, triggered off the **Velvet Revolution** which eventually toppled the government. Today, the mood of optimism which followed the revolution has all but evaporated, as the more distasteful side of capitalism makes itself felt, and the wrangles over the "sandpaper divorce" with Slovakia take their toll.

> The telephone code for Prague is ☎02.

Arrival and information

Prague's **airport**, Ruzyně, is 15km northwest of the city. The simplest way of getting into the centre is by **taxi**, but the cheapest is the ČSA bus or city bus #119 (both roughly every 20min), a thirty-minute ride to the Dejvická metro station at the end of metro line A. Arriving by **train** from the west, you're most likely to end up at the **Praha hlavní nádraží**, on the edge of Nové Město and Vinohrady. It's only a short walk into the centre from here, and there's also a metro station inside the station. International expresses, passing through from Berlin/Warsaw to Budapest/Vienna often stop only at **Praha-Holešovice**, north of the city centre at the end of metro line C. Some trains from Moravia and Slovakia wind up at the central **Masarykovo nádraží**, near náměstí Republiky; and provincial trains from the south usually get no further than **Praha-Smíchov**, connected to the centre by metro line B. There are lockers and left-

luggage offices (open 24hr) at all these stations. The main **bus station** is Praha-Florenc, on the eastern edge of Nové Město, on metro line B.

The best place to go for information is the **Prague Information Service**, or *PIS* (*Pražská informační služba*), which has two offices, one on Staroměstské náměsti (Mon–Fri 9am–7pm, Sat & Sun 9am–6pm) and the other at Panská 4 (opening times as above except closed on Sun); their staff speak English, and will be able to answer most enquiries, except on the subject of accommodation (see below). *PIS* also distributes an easily decipherable listings sheet called *Přehled*, and a fairly basic map. As well as *Přehled*, it's worth getting hold of the monthly *Prognosis*, an English-language newspaper that includes a guide to cultural events.

City transport

Prague is reasonably small, but to cross the city quickly, or reach some of the more widely dispersed atttractions, you'll need to use the public transport system. **Tickets** (4kč) for the metro, trams and buses are interchangeable: you use a separate ticket each time you ride (apart from changing lines on the metro), validating it on board or at the metro entrance – they are best bought in advance from a newsagent, *tabák*, street kiosk or hotel reception desk. If you're here for a few days, it's worth getting hold of a **tourist pass** (*turistická síťová jízdenka*), valid from one to five days and currently costing 30–80kč. The fast Soviet-built **metro** (daily 5am–midnight) is the most useful form of city transport. The **trams** navigate Prague's hills and cobbles with remarkable dexterity, and run every ten or twenty minutes throughout the day. Tram #22, which runs from Vinohrady to Hradčany, is a good way to get to grips with the lie of the land, and is a cheap method of sightseeing. The easiest way to pick up a **taxi** is at one of the city's many ranks – notably on Václavské náměstí, Národní and outside the Obecní dům – although it works out cheaper if you flag one down on the street. Fares are rapidly approaching Western European prices.

Accommodation

Prague hotels are extremely expensive for what you get. As a result most tourists now stay in private accommodation or youth hostels, both of which are easy to organize on arrival in Prague. At both the main international train stations and at the airport, there are numerous accommodation agencies dealing with **private rooms** (② and upwards); among the cheapest is *AVE* (☎02/236 56 60).

Hostels

Alfa Hostel, Block 3, Spartakiádní 5, Strahov. Student hostel in big sports stadium, five minutes from the Strahov monastery. ②.

Hotel Praha, Žitná 42, Nové Město. Campbeds on a gym floor. Reception 6–11am & 5pm–midnight. ①.

Hostel Roosewelt, Strojnická 7, Holešovice. Not the nicest part of town, but close to Nádraží Holešovice. ①

U Karlova mostu, Malá Veleslavínova (☎02/232 89 37). Ridiculously central and ridiculously rudimentary. ①.

Hotels

Balkán, Svornosti 28, Smíchov (☎02/54 07 77). Recently privatized but it's still reassuringly run-down. ②

Botel Albatross, Nábřeží L. Svobody, Nové Město (☎02/231 36 34). Basically, beds on a moored boat. Not really as romantic or quite as cheap as you'd expect, but the best of the city's three floating hotels. ⑥

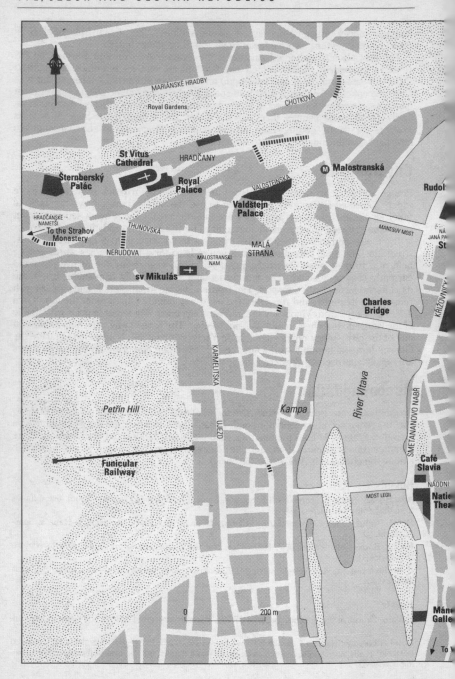

MARIÁNSKÉ HRADBY

Royal Gardens

CHOTKOVA

St Vitus Cathedral

HRADČANY

Šternberský Palác

Royal Palace

(M) **Malostranská**

VALDŠTEJNSKÁ

Rudol

Valdštejn Palace

HRADČANSKÉ NAMETŠI

THUNOVSKÁ

MANESUV MOST

NÁ JANÁ PA **St**

To the Strahov Monastery

NERUDOVA

MALÁ STRANA

MALOSTRANSKI NAM

sv Mikuláš

KRIŽOVNIC

Charles Bridge

Petřín Hill

KARMELITSKÁ

Kampa

River Vltava

SMETANOVO NABŘ

ÚJEZD

Café Slavia

Funicular Railway

NÁODNI

Nati Thea

MOST LEGII

0   200 m

Mán Galle

To ✈

PRAGUE

TNÁ
.AIN

River Vltava

NA FRANTISKU

Convent of
sv Anézka

17. LISTOPADU

RYBNÁ

REVOLCNI

Old-New Synagogue

MAISOVA

PAŘÍŽSKÁ

Klaus Synogogue
Old Jewish Cemetery

UPM
A
mèstská

RYBNÁ

NA PORICI

Masarykovo
nádraží

KAPROVA

MAISOVA

DLOUHÁ

Jan Hus
Monument

Obecni
dům

NÁM
REPUBLIKY

sv Mikuláš

STARÉ MĚSTO

STAROMÉSTSKE
NÁM

Týn
Church

CELETNÁ

Náměstí
Republiky

HYBERNSKÁ

Klementinum

Information
Office

Powder
Tower

Staroměstská
radnice

MELANTRICHOVA

OVACNÝ TRH.

KARLOVA

Stavovské
divadlo

RYTIRSKÁ

Bethlehem
Chapel

NA PŘÍKOPĚ

PÁNSKA

BETLEMSKÉ
NÁM

UHELAY
TRH.

Můstek

Hlavní nádraží

JINDRISSKÁ

Praha
hlavni
nádraží

BARTOLOMÉJSKÁ

NÁODNI

Post
Office

NÁODNI

Václavské náměsti

Národni

JUNGMANNOVA

Czech
Parliament

NOVÉ MĚSTO

VODICKOVA

SPALENA

WILSONOVA

Múzeum

ŠTEPANSKA

National
Museum

ŽITNA

ŽITNÁ

Karlovo
náměsti

ehrad

Merkur, Těšnov 9, Nové Město (☎02/231 68 40). Few mod cons here as yet, and so, for the moment, one of the few cheap, central hotels in Prague. ④.

Opera, Těšnov 13, Nové Město (☎02/231 56 09). Moderately-priced nineteenth-century hotel and remarkably pleasant considering it's right by a flyover. ④.

Campsites

Džbán, Nad lávkou 3, Vokovice. Tram #20 or #26 from Metro Dejvická; the site is 4km west of the centre, down Benešova.

Kotva Braník, U ledáren 55, Braník. Six kilometres south of the city. Open April–Sept. Tram #3, #17 or #21 along the right bank.

Troja, Trojská 171, Troja. A whole host of sites, 3km north of the centre, by the château. Hourly bus #112 from metro Holešovice, or tram #5, #17 or #25 and then a short walk.

Motol, Plzeňská, Motol. Five kilometres southwest of the centre. Open April–Sept. Tram #4 or #9 from metro Anděl.

The City

The **River Vltava** (Moldau) divides the capital into two unequal halves: the steeply inclined left bank, which accommodates the quarters of Hradčany and Malá Strana; and the more gentle, sprawling right bank, which includes Staré Město, Josefov and Nové Město. **Hradčany**, on the hill, contains the most obvious sights – the castle itself, the cathedral and the former palaces of the aristocracy. Below Hradčany, **Malá Strana**, with its narrow eighteenth-century streets, does most duty these days as the city's ministerial and diplomatic quarter, though its Baroque gardens are there for all to enjoy. Over the river, on the right bank, **Staré Město** (old town) is a web of alleys and passageways centred on the city's most beautiful square, Staroměstské náměsti. Enclosed within the boundaries of Staré Město is **Josefov**, the old Jewish quarter, now down to just a handful of synagogues and a cemetery. **Nové Město** (new town), the focus of the modern city, covers the largest area, laid out in long wide boulevards – most famously Wenceslas Square – stretching south and east of the old town. Out of the centre proper, to the south, lies the castle of **Vyšehrad**.

Hradčany

Hradčany's *raison d'être* is its **Castle**, or *hrad*, built on the site of one of the original hill settlements of the Slav tribes who migrated here in the seventh or eighth century. Viewed from the Charles Bridge, Prague Castle stands aloof from the rest of the city, protected by a sheer wall that's breached only by the great mass of **St Vitus Cathedral** (April–Oct Tues–Sun 9am–5pm; Nov–March Tues–Sun 9am–4pm; free), which was not completed until 1929 – exactly 1000 years after the death of Prince Václav (Saint Wenceslas), the first Czech to build a church within the *hrad*.

First inspiration came from Charles IV, who after his election as Holy Roman Emperor in 1346 summoned **Peter Parler**, a precocious 23-year-old from a family of great German masons, to continue the work that had just begun on the church. But the cathedral got no further than the choir and the south transept before his death in 1399, and not until the Czechs themselves began to emerge as a nation, in the nineteenth century, did building begin again in earnest. The sooty Prague air has made it hard now to differentiate between the two building periods, but the eastern section recalls the building's authentic Gothic roots and the south door, or **Zlatá brána** (Golden Gate), is also pure Parler in style.

The cathedral is the country's largest church, and, once inside, it's difficult not to be impressed by its sheer height. The grand chapel of **sv Václav**, by the south door, is easily the main attraction. Built by Parler, its rich decoration resembles the inside of a jewel casket: the gilded chapel walls are inlaid with over 1300 semiprecious stones, set around ethereal fourteenth-century Biblical frescoes, while above, the tragedy of Wenceslas unfolds in later paintings. A door in the south wall gives access to a staircase leading to the coronation chamber which houses the Bohemian crown jewels, including the gold crown of Saint Wenceslas. At the centre of the choir, within a fine Renaissance grill, cherubs lark about on the sixteenth-century marble **Imperial Mausoleum**, commissioned by Rudolf II for his grandfather, Ferdinand I, and father, Maximilian II, the first Habsburgs to wear the Bohemian crown.

Just across the courtyard from the south door of the cathedral, the **Royal Palace** (same hours) was home to the princes and kings of Bohemia from the eleventh to the seventeenth century. It's a sandwich of royal apartments, built one on top of the other by successive generations – these days you enter at the third and top floor, built at the end of the fifteenth century. The massive Vladislav Hall is where the early Bohemian kings were elected, and where every president since Masaryk has been sworn into office – including Havel on December 29, 1989.

Don't be fooled by the uninspiring red facade of the **Basilica of sv Jiří** (St George) – this is Prague's most beautiful Romanesque monument, its inside meticulously restored to recreate something like the crumble-coloured basilica which replaced the original tenth-century church in 1173. Next door, the **Convent of sv Jiří**, founded by Boleslav II in 973, now houses the National Gallery's **Old Bohemian Art Collection** (same hours), incorporating a remarkable collection of Gothic art – including the original of the bronze equestrian figure of Saint George that stands in the castle's third courtyard. Round the corner from the convent is the **Zlatá ulička** (Golden Lane), a blind alley of miniature seventeenth-century cottages in dolly-mixture colours. They were built by the twenty-four members of Rudolf II's castle guard, and the lane takes its name from the alchemists whom Rudolf summoned to his court. It remained as a kind of palace slum until 1951, when the lane was finally renovated for the tourists and converted into a line of souvenir shops. A plaque at no. 22 commemorates Franz Kafka's brief sojourn here during World War I.

North of the castle walls, across the Powder Bridge, is the entrance to the **Royal Gardens** (Královská zahrada), founded by Ferdinand I and which are still the best-kept gardens in the country, with functioning fountains and immaculately cropped lawns. At the end of the garden is Prague's most celebrated Renaissance legacy, the **Belvedere** (Královské letohrádek), a delicately arcaded summer house, now an art gallery.

TO THE STRAHOV MONASTERY

Hradčanské náměstí fans out from the castle's main gates, surrounded by the over-sized palaces of the old nobility. A passage down the side of the Archbishop's Palace leads to the early eighteenth-century **Šternberský palác**, the main building of the National Gallery (Tues–Sun 10am–6pm) – a relatively modest European art collection, which divides into three main sections. Upstairs are works from the fifteenth to the eighteenth century, the most significant of which is the *Festival of the Rosary* by Dürer. Entering the adjacent wing propels you straight into the nineteenth- and twentieth-century sections, where the most influential artist – in terms of his effect on Czech art – is Edvard Munch. The most popular bit of the gallery is the "French" section across the courtyard, featuring anyone of note who hovered around Paris in the last hundred years.

Nestling in a shallow dip to the northwest, **Nový Svět** is all that is left of the medieval slums, painted up and sanitized in the nineteenth century. Uphill from Nový Svět, Loretánské náměstí is dominated by the brutal 150-metre-long facade of the **Černín Palace**. The **Loreto Chapel's** facade (Tues–Sun 9am–noon & 1–5pm), immediately opposite, is a perfect antidote, all hot flourishes and twirls, topped by a tower which lights up like a Chinese lantern at night – and which by day clanks out a tuneless version of the hymn *We Greet Thee a Thousand Times* on its twenty-seven Dutch bells. However, the two-storey cloisters and chapels are just the outer casing for the main focus of the complex, the *Santa Casa*, a shrine that was built a century earlier. You can get some idea of the shrine's popularity with the Bohemian nobility in the **treasury**, much ransacked over the years but still stuffed full of gold. The padded ceilings and low lighting create a kind of giant jewellery box for the master exhibit, a ghastly Viennese silver monstrance studded with 6222 diamonds standing over three feet high.

A short way west up Pohořelec from Loretánské náměstí, the chunky remnants of the zigzag eighteenth-century fortifications mark the edge of the old city. Close by sits the **Strahov Monastery** (Strahovský klášter), which managed to escape the 1783 dissolution of the monasteries and continued to function until the communists closed down all religious orders in 1948. Through the cobbled courtyard, past a small church and chapel, is the monastery proper, famous for its rich collection of manuscripts and its ornate libraries. Leaving through a narrow doorway in the eastern wall, you enter the gardens and orchards of the **Strahovská zahrada**, from where you can see the whole city in perspective.

Malá Strana

More than anywhere else, **Malá Strana**, the "Little Quarter", conforms to the image of Prague as *the* Baroque city. Its narrow backstreets have changed little since Mozart walked them, while around practically every corner there's a quiet walled garden. The focus of Malá Strana is the sloping, cobbled **Malostranské náměstí**, a busy square split in two by the former Jesuit seminary and church of **sv Mikuláš** (St Nicholas), the most magnificent Baroque building in the city. Nothing of the plain west facade prepares you for the overwhelming High Baroque interior – the fresco in the nave alone covers over 1500 square metres, and portrays some of the more fanciful feats of Saint Nicholas.

Follow Tomášská north from the square and you come to the **Valdštejn Palace**. The largest palace complex in the city after the *hrad*, it was built by Albrecht von Wallenstein (Albrecht z Valdštejna), who demolished twenty-one houses to make space for a palace befitting the most powerful man in central Europe. The only part which is accessible to the public is the south wing, which contains a small exhibition on the history of Czech education; as for the rest, you'll have to make do with the view from the formal gardens (daily 9am–7pm), access to which is from a concealed entrance off Letenská.

South of the square, a continuation of Karmelitská brings you to the funicular up **Petřín Hill**, a bigger and better green space than most in Prague. It's good for a picnic, and topped by a scaled-down version of the Eiffel Tower, one of a number of sights set up in the park for the 1891 Prague Exhibition.

Staré Město

Staré Město, the "old town", founded in the early thirteenth century, is where most of the capital's markets, shops, restaurants and pubs are located. The fire of 1541, which ripped through the quarters on the other side of the river, never reached the Staré Město, yet it's still overwhelmingly Baroque, built literally on top of its Gothic predecessor to guard against the floods which plagued the former town.

The city's most familiar monument, the **Charles Bridge** – Karlův most – was begun in 1357, supervised by Peter Parler, and is named after his patron Charles IV. For all its antiquity, the bridge itself is dull. It is the statues – brilliant pieces of Jesuit propaganda added during the Counter-Reformation – that have made it renowned throughout Europe. Cross to Staré Město and you're in busy **Křížovnické náměstí**, from where the narrow, crowded **Karlova** winds past the massive **Klementinum**, the former Jesuit College, completed just before the Jesuits were turfed out of the country in 1773. It then became the university library, with over five million volumes. The entrance is inconspicuously placed just past sv Kliment church on Karlova. The first floor has temporary exhibitions of some of the library's prize possessions, while at roughly the centre of the complex is the **observatory tower** from where Johannes Kepler did his planet-gazing.

At the end of the street is **Staroměstské náměstí**, the most spectacular square in Prague and traditional heart of the city. From the eleventh century, it was Prague's main marketplace, to which all roads in Bohemia led. At its centre is the **Jan Hus Monument**, a turbulent sea of blackened bodies out of which rises the majestic moral authority of Hus himself, gazing towards the horizon. When John of Luxembourg gave Prague the right to have a town hall in 1338, the community bought a corner house on the square, gradually incorporating neighbouring buildings to form the **Staroměstská radnice** (Old Town Hall). Over the next century, the east wing was added, but only its graceful Gothic oriel and wedge-tower survived the arson of retreating Nazis. On the south facade, the central powder-red building now forms the entrance to the whole complex (tours daily on the hour March–Oct 8am–6pm; Nov–Feb 8am–5pm). You'll probably get most enjoyment from simply climbing the tower – one of the few with access for the disabled – for the panoramic sweep across Prague's spires. The greatest area of congestion is below the **Astronomical Clock**, where, every hour, tourists and Praguers watch a mechanical performance by the figures of Christ and the Apostles.

The Staré Město's most impressive Gothic structure is the mighty **Týn Church** (Panna Marie před Týnem), whose twin towers rise like giant antennae above the two arcaded houses which otherwise obscure its facade. Like the nearby Hus monument, the Týn Church is a source of Czech national pride, completed during the reign of George of Poděbrady (1436–71), the one and only Hussite King of Bohemia. Given the church's significance, it's sad that little of the interior survived its ferocious Catholicization. One exception is the fine north portal and canopy which bear the hall-mark of Peter Parler's workshop, and the fifteenth-century pulpit also stands out from the dark morass of black and gold Baroque altarpieces, its panels enhanced by some sensitive nineteenth-century icons. The pillar on the right of the chancel steps contains the marble tomb of Tycho Brahe, the famous Danish astronomer who arrived in Czechoslovakia minus his nose, which he lost in a duel in Denmark. He died of a burst bladder at one of Rudolf II's notorious binges in 1601.

JOSEFOV

Within the Staré Město lies **Josefov**, the Jewish quarter of the city until the end of the nineteenth century, when the Jews, gypsies and prostitutes were cleared out of this ghetto area in order to create a beautiful bourgeois city on Parisian lines. Kafka spent most of his life in and around Josefov, and the destruction of the Jewish quarter, which continued throughout his childhood, had a profound effect on his psyche.

All the "sights" are part of the **State Jewish Museum** (April–Oct daily except Sat 9am–6pm; Nov–March 9am–4.30pm; 80kč) and entry to them is covered by one ticket from the box office in the Klaus Synagogue, next door to the Old Jewish Cemetery on U starého hřbitova. Through the heart of the old ghetto now runs the ultimate bourgeois avenue, **Pařížská**, a riot of turn-of-the-century sculpturing, spikes and turrets. Halfway down Pařížská, on the left, is the steep brick gable of the **Old-New Synagogue** (Staronová synagoga), completed in the fourteenth century and still the religious centre of Prague's 2000-strong Jewish community. Originally it was known simply as the New Synagogue, but after several fires gutted the ghetto it became the oldest synagogue building in the quarter – hence its strange name.

Opposite the synagogue is the **Jewish Town Hall** (Židovnická radnice), founded in the sixteenth century and later turned into a creamy-pink Baroque house crowned by a wooden clocktower. In addition to the four main clocks, there's a Hebrew one stuck on the north gable, which (like the Hebrew script) goes "backwards". Next door is the **High Synagogue**, once part of the town hall, whose rich interior stands in complete contrast to its dour, grey facade; the huge vaulted hall is now used to display a mere fraction of the many hundreds of **Jewish textiles** in its possession, dating from the sixteenth to the early twentieth century.

The main reason most people visit Josefov is to see the **Old Jewish Cemetery**, which was established in the fifteenth century and was in use until 1787, by which time there were some 100,000 graves here. Get there before the crowds, and it can be a poignant reminder of the ghetto, its inhabitants subjected to inhuman overcrowding even in death. You can also enter the cemetery from the **Pinkas Synagogue** on Široká. In 1958 a chilling memorial to the 77,297 Czechoslovak Jews who were killed during the Holocaust was unveiled here – a simple menorah set against the backdrop of never-ending names carved into the stonework.

Nové Město

Nové Město, the largest and most cosmopolitan of Prague's five towns, comes over as a sprawling late nineteenth-century bourgeois quarter, but was actually founded in 1348 by Charles IV, intended as a new town which would link the southern fortress of Vyšehrad with the Staré Město. The borderline between the Staré and the Nové Město is made up by the continuous boulevards of **Národní** and **Na příkopě**, a boomerang curve which follows the course of the old moat. The city's most flamboyant Art Nouveau buildings are ranged along much of the avenue – Prague's busiest shopping street and the most expensive slice of real estate in the country. This was also the unlikely setting for the November 17 demonstration that sparked off the Velvet Revolution.

At the river end of Národní is the gold-crested **National Theatre**, proud symbol of the Czech nation. Refused money by the Austrian state, Czechs of all classes dug deep into their pockets to raise funds for the venture themselves. Opposite, the **Café Slavia** has been a favourite haunt of the city's writers and artists since the first decade of the Republic; it's been carelessly modernized since. In the opposite direction, at the top end of Na příkopě, stands the **Obecní dům**. Begun in 1903, it was decorated inside and out with the help of almost every artist connected with the Czech Secession. The best way of soaking up the hall-like interior, peppered with mosaics and pendulous brass chandeliers, is to have a beer in the *restaurace*, or a coffee in the equally cavernous *kavárna*.

Cross the boulevard at its central point and you're into the pivot of modern Prague and the political focus of the events of November 1989 – the wide, gently sloping **Václavské náměstí** (Wenceslas Square). The square's history of protest goes back to the Prague Spring of 1968: towards the top end, there's a small memorial to the victims of communism, the most famous of whom, the 21-year old student Jan Palach, set himself alight on this very spot in January 1969 in protest against the Soviet occupation.

Some of the worst town planning this century was inflicted upon the top end of Václavské náměstí, not least the building of the six-lane freeway which now effectively cuts off the square from the **National Museum** (Mon & Fri 9am–4pm, Wed, Thurs, Sat & Sun 9am–5pm). Along with the National Theatre, it's one of the great symbols of the nineteenth-century Czech national revival, with its monumental gilt-framed glass cupola, clumps of sculptural decoration and narrative frescoes from Czech history. However, unless you're a geologist or a zoologist you're likely to be unmoved by the exhibits.

Of the many roads which fan out south from Václavské náměstí, Vodičkova is probably the most impressive, running southwest for half a kilometre to **Karlovo náměstí**, Prague's biggest square. At the northern end, the **Novoměstská radnice** was once a Gothic town hall to rival that of the Staré Město, but after 1784 it was converted into a prison and criminal court.

Eating

There are two main types of establishment in Prague and elsewhere in the country where you can get something to eat: a **restaurace** (restaurant), where eating is ostensibly the main activity; and a **vinárna** (wine bar), which tends to think of itself as a touch more exclusive. Often, you'll also be able to eat in that most typical of Czech institutions, the *pivnice* (pub), though these are largely concerned with serious drinking – and are covered in the next section. In practice, these definitions are blurred, with some places having *restaurace* and *pivnice* sections under the same roof, some *vinárna* offering food, some only wine, and so on. Remember that Czechs eat early: most places pack up before 10pm.

Ali Baba, Vodiakova 5, Nové Město. Middle Eastern place serving a wicked *baba ghanoush* and other Arabic specialities.

Country Life, Melantrichova 15, Staré Město. Prague's only veggie stand-up *bufet*. Closed Sat. Cheap.

U Malířů, Maltézské náměstí 11 (☎02/53 18 83). An extremely expensive *vinárna* in Malá Strana, serving delicious French cuisine in a converted sixteenth-century house. Open Mon–Sat 11am–3pm & 6–11pm.

Reykjavík, Karlova 20, Staré Město. The owners (and the fish) really are Icelandic, though the cuisine is pretty international. Open daily 11am–11pm. Moderate to expensive.

U bílého slona, Soukenická 4. Expensive, new Thai restaurant worth the extra layout.

U čížků, Karlovo náměstí, Nové Město. Upmarket Bohemian restaurant serving traditional Bohemian food at its best.

U Govindy, Na hrazi 5, Libeň. Prague's only vegetarian restaurant run by Hare Krishnas out in the suburbs. Open daily 11am–5pm. Donations at customers' discretion.

U městské knihovny, Valentinská, Staré Město. Cheap and central restaurant in the backstreets near the Jewish Quarter.

U modré ruže, Rytířská 16, Staré Město. Pricy, but excellent new restaurant in the old town.

U Rudolfa, Maislova 5, Josefov. A good, reasonable *vinárna* in the Jewish Quarter with a meaty menu barbecued over an open grill.

U Supa, Celetná 22. Lively fourteenth-century pub serving full meals and very strong, dark *Braník 14°*, either inside or on the cobbles of its cool courtyard.

Drinking

Prague **cafés** are starting to blossom again, and the choice so far is pretty varied – from Art Nouveau relics and swish espresso bars (both of which are called *kavárna* and are licensed), to simple sugar and caffeine joints (known as *cukrárna*). For no-nonsense boozing you need to head for a **pivnice**, which invariably serves excellent beer by the half-litre, but closes around 10 to 11pm. For late-night drinking, head for one of the posh wine bars or hotel bars, which often keep going beyond midnight.

U černého vola, Loretánské náměstí 1, Hradčany. Does a brisk business providing the popular light beer *Velkopopovický kozel 12°* in huge quantities to locals. Starts and finishes early.

U dvou koček, Uhelný trh. Central, no-nonsense *Plzeňský Prazdroj* pub, which serves some cheap and basic Czech food.

Evropa, Václavské náměstí 25. *The* place to be seen on Wenceslas Square is on the *Evropa*'s summer terrace, but the Art Nouveau decor is at its best inside.

U Fleků, Křemencova 11. Famous, raucous *pivnice* where the waiters rarely bother to ask what you want, since most people are here to sample the dark *Flek 13°* beer, brewed on these premises since 1499. Despite seats for over a thousand drinkers, you may still have to fight for a bench.

U kocoura, Nerudova 2. The last surviving pub on this famous street, bought by the Beer Party in 1992 and still serving *Plzeňský Prazdroj*.

Krušovická pivnice, Široká 20. Traditional food and vast quantities of *Krušovice 12°*, which many consider to be the best Bohemian brew.

Slavia, Národní 1, Staré Město. The *Slavia* has always attracted a mixed crowd – artists, theatre-goers, old women, tourists and German trendies.

U zlatého tygra, Husova 17. Beery *pivnice* once frequented by Prague's literary crowd, including the bohemian writer Bohumil Hrabal.

Žíznivý pes, U Obecního domu, Staré Město. The "Thirsty Dog" is a raucous late-night pub dripping with American ex-pats.

Nightlife

As far as **live music** is concerned, the classical scene no longer has the edge – jazz has long been a tradition in Prague, aided by the international jazz festival held here in even-numbered years, and the home-grown rock scene is finding its feet, with new clubs opening and closing thick and fast. With the new-found freedom of the Nineties, **discos and nightclubs** are booming around Václavské náměstí, but they serve more as indoor red light districts. Predictably enough, with a playwright as president, **theatre** in Prague is thriving; without knowing the language, however, your scope is limited, though there's a tradition of innovative mime, puppetry and black theatre in the city. **Tickets** are cheap and available for most events from outlets around Václavské and Staroměstské náměstí, as well as from the venues themselves. **Listings** are best found in the English-language weeklies *Prognosis* or *Prague Post*, plus the Czech monthly, *Přehled*.

Classical music and opera

Classical concerts take place throughout the year in concert halls and churches, the biggest event being the *Pražské jaro* (Prague Spring) **international music festival**, which traditionally begins on May 12, the day of Smetana's death, with a performance of *Ma vlast*, and finishes on June 2 with a rendition of Beethoven's Ninth. As well as the main venues, watch out for concerts in the churches and palaces, especially in summer.

Stavovské divadlo, Železná 11, Staré Město. Prague's main opera house.

Smetanovo divadlo, Wilsonova, Nové Město. The former German opera house, and the city's second-choice venue for opera and ballet.

Smetanova síň, Obecní dům, náměstí Republiky, Nové Město. Beautiful Secessionist hall and home to the Czech Philharmonic Orchestra (ČF).

Jazz and rock

Bunkr, Lodecká 2, Nové Město. A converted wartime bunker (hence the name), decked out in regulation black and now an established part of the alternative scene.

Borát, Újezd 18, Malá Strana. A dark and dingy post-punk den which sprawls across three floors of a knackered old building close to the funicular railway.

Klub na Chmelnici, Koněvova 219, Žižkov. The main venue for domestic indie bands. Doubles as an alternative theatre venue too.

Press Jazz Club, Pařížská 9, Stare Město. Big new jazz venue that looks set to become the leader.

Reduta, Národní 20, Nové Město. Prague's best jazz club, anything from trad to modern. Open Mon–Fri until 2am, though the music stops at midnight.

Rock Café, Národní 22, Nové Město. Nerve centre of the underground scene.

Ubiquity, Na příkopě 22, Nové Město. The biggest club in Prague, with a team of English DJs, several dancefloors and Mexican food. The central location means more tourists than most.

Listings

Airlines *Aeroflot*, Pařížská 5, Josefov (☎26 08 62); *British Airways*, Štěpánská 63, Nové Město (☎236 03 53); *ČSA*, Revoluční 1 (☎21 46); *Lufthansa*, Pařížská 5, Josefov (☎232 74 40).

American Express, Václavské náměstí, Nové Město (Mon–Fri 6.30am–8pm, Sat 6.30am–1pm).

Car rental From *Avis/Pragocar*, Opelatova 33, Nové Město (☎34 10 97), *Budget*, Národní 17, Nové Město (☎235 28 09).

Embassies *Canada*, Mickiewiczova 6, Hradčany (☎32 69 41); *Great Britain*, Thunovská 14, Malá Strana (☎53 33 47); *USA*, Tržiště 15, Malá Strana (☎53 66 41). Nationals of Ireland, Australia and New Zealand should contact the British embassy.

Exchange There's a 24-hour exchange service at the airport.

Gay Prague For up-to-date information on the Prague gay scene, contact *Lambda Praha*, Pod Kotlářkou 14, Smíchov (☎52 73 88).

Laundry *Laundry Kings*, Dejvická 16, Dejvice; metro Hradčanská.
Pharmacy 24-hour service at Na příkopě 7, Nové Město.
Post office The main post office is at Jindřišská 14, Nové Město; there's a 24-hour service for parcels, telegrams and telephones.

BOHEMIA

Prague is the natural centre and capital of Bohemia; the rest divides easily into four geographical districts. **South Bohemia**, bordered by the Šumava mountains, is the least spoilt. The largest town by far is the brewing centre of **České Budějovice**, and its chief attraction, aside from the thickly forested hills, is a series of well-preserved medieval towns, whose undisputed gem is **Český Krumlov**. Neighbouring **West Bohemia** has a similar mix of rolling woods and hills, despite the industrial nature of its capital **Plzeň**, home of Pilsen beer and the Škoda empire. Beyond here, as you approach the German border, Bohemia's famous **Spa Region** unfolds, with magnificent resorts such as **Mariánské Lázně** and **Karlovy Vary** enjoying sparkling reputations. **North Bohemia** has real problems. Despite being similar to the lands to the south and west, it has been devastated by industrialization, rendering many parts virtually uninhabitable. **East Bohemia** has suffered indirectly from the polluting industries of its neighbour, but remains relatively blight-free. There's some great walking and climbing country here, but the only place that's an essential stop on a quick tour of the country is the silver-mining centre of **Kutná Hora**.

České Budějovice

Since its foundation in 1265, **ČESKÉ BUDĚJOVICE** (Budweis) – just two hours by train from Prague – has been a self-assured place, convinced of its own importance. Its wealth, based on medieval silver mines and its position on the salt route from Linz to Prague, was wiped out in the seventeenth century by war and fire, but the Habsburgs lavishly reconstructed most of České Budějovice in the eighteenth century. Its real renown, however, is due to its local brew *Budvar*, better known abroad under its original German name, *Budweiser*.

České Budějovice has a compact old town that's only a five-minute walk from the **train** or **bus station**, both situated to the east of the city centre, along the pedestrianized Lannova třída. The medieval grid plan leads inevitably to the magnificent central **náměstí Přemysla Otakara II**, one of Europe's largest market squares. Its buildings are elegant enough, but it's the arcades and the octagonal **Samson's Fountain** – once the only tap in town – that make the greatest impression. The 72-metre status symbol, the **Černá věž** (Black Tower), one of the few survivors of the 1641 fire, leans gently to one side of the square; its roof gallery (April–June & Sept–Nov Tues–Sun 9am–5pm; July & Aug daily) provides a superb view.

When the weather's fine people tend to promenade by the banks of the Malše, where parts of the original town walls have survived along with some of České Budějovice's oldest buildings. All that is left of the bishop's palace is the serene **garden** (daily May–Sept 8am–6pm), accessible through a small gateway in the walls. Round the corner, on Piaristické náměstí, a lively **market** spreads out in front of the thoroughly medieval **zbrojnice** (one-time arsenal), once the centre of the town's all-important salt trade.

Given České Budějovice's popularity with neighbouring Austrians and Germans, **hotel rooms** can be difficult to find even out of season. To find out what's on offer, go to the first floor of the plush *ČEDOK* offices on the main square – they can also book private rooms, of which there are a few on Panská, off Piaristické náměstí. There are no really cheap hotel options, so you might as well start your search at *Hotel Zvon* (☎038/353 61; ③), close to *ČEDOK*. In July and August rooms are available in **student hostels** – go to *CKM*, Osovobzeni 14, to get the addresses of current hostels. There's a good **campsite** at Dlouhá louka (April–Oct; bus #16 from station). The most famous hostelry in town is *Masné krámy* at Krajinská 23, which serves huge quantities of *Budvar*, and a little **food**, all day until 10pm. As for **eating**, picnic fodder can be assembled at the big supermarket on Lannova třída, or at the fruit and veg market on Piaristické náměstí. For something different, the fish restaurant, *U železné panny*, on Široká, serves carp and trout from the ponds northwest of town.

Český Krumlov

The hilly southern Bohemian town of ČESKÝ KRUMLOV (Krumau), hardly changed in the last three hundred years, ranks as one of the most beautiful in central Europe, and is currently being restored with help from UNESCO.

The **train station** is fifteen minutes' walk north of the old town, down a precipitous set of steps, while the **bus station** is closer to the heart of town, on the right bank. The twisting River Vltava divides the town into two segments: the circular Staré Město on the right bank and the Latrán quarter on the hillier left bank. For centuries, the focal point has been the **Krumlov Castle** (April–Oct Tues–Sun 8/9am–noon & 1–4/5pm) in the Latrán quarter, as good a place as any to begin a roam. The fifty-minute tour doles out rich helpings of feudal opulence, peaking at the castle's eighteenth-century Rococo theatre, due to be reopened in 1994. Another covered walkway puts you high above the town in the unexpectedly expansive **terraced gardens** (open all year). The shabby houses leaning in on Latrán lead to a wooden ramp-like bridge which connects with the Staré Město. Just before the bridge, on the left, an almost medieval scene unfolds in the cobbled courtyard of the *Krumlovská pivnice*. Head straight up the soft incline of Radniční to the main square, where a long, white Renaissance entablature connects two and a half Gothic houses to create the **Rathaus**. On the other side, the high lancet windows of the church of St Vitus rise above the ramshackle rooftops. Continuing east off the square, down Horní, the beautiful sixteenth-century Jesuit college now provides space for the *Hotel Růže*. Opposite, the local **museum** (Tues–Sat 9am–4pm, Sun 9am–noon) includes a reconstructed seventeenth-century shop interior among its exhibits; while you're there ask for directions to the new museum devoted to the painter, Egon Schiele, who moved here briefly in 1911.

The *Hotel Růže* (☎0337/22 45; ④), and the *Krumlov* on the main square (☎0337/22 55; ③) are both beautiful old **hotels** in the Staré Město. If they are full, you should find few problems getting hold of a **private room** from CTS, at Latrán 67. There's a primitive **campsite** 2km south on the road to Větřní. As far as **eating** goes, the choice has improved considerably: there's an excellent, if pricy, vegetarian restaurant, *U dvou marií*, with a riverside terrace, on Parkán, or if it's not too packed try *U hroznu* on the main square.

Plzeň

PLZEŇ (Pilsen) is the largest city in Bohemia after Prague, with a population of 175,000. The skyline is a symphony of smoke and steam, yet despite its industrial character, there are compensations – a large number of students, eclectic architecture and an unending supply of (probably) the best **beer** in the world, all of which make Plzeň a popular stopoff on the main rail line between Prague and the West. Plzeň's **train stations** are works of art in themselves: there are numerous minor ones within the city boundaries, but without doubt your likeliest point of arrival is the Hlavní nádraží (main station), east of the city centre, rather than the Jižní předměstí (south station), to the southwest. The **bus terminal** is on the west side of town. From both the bus and train station, the city centre is only a short walk away, or a few stops on tram #1 or #2.

The main square, **náměstí Republiky**, presents a full range of architectural styles, starting with the exalted heights of the Gothic church of **sv Bartoloměj**, its bile-green spire reaching up more than one hundred metres. Over the way rises the Italianate **stará radnice**, self-importantly one storey higher than the rest of the square. Here and there other old buildings survive, but the vast majority of Plzeň's buildings hail from the city's heyday during the industrial expansion around the turn of the century. In the old town, this produced some wonderful variations on neo-historical themes and Art Nouveau motifs, particularly to the north and west of the main square.

But the reason most people come to Plzeň is to sample its famous 12° *Plzeňský Prazdroj*, or **Pilsner Urquell** (its Germanized export name). Beer has been brewed in the town since it was founded in 1295, but it wasn't until 1842 that the famous *Bürgerliches Brauhaus* was built, after a near-riot by the townsfolk over the declining quality of their brew. Guided tours are available most days at the **brewery** on U Prazdroje, a glass of the real thing at the *Restaurace Prazdroj* at U Prazdroje 1. The truly dedicated can then head for the **Brewery Museum** (Tues 1–4.30pm, Wed–Sun 9am–4.30pm) at the end of the narrow, *fin-de-siècle* Veleslavínova.

Finding a vacancy in one of Plzeň's **hotels** presents few problems, though rooms don't come cheap. Besides the faded splendour of the moderate *Slovan*, Smetanovy sady 1 (☎019/335 51; ③), and the *Continental*, Zbrojnická 8 (☎019/330 60; ④), there's always the ugly *Central*, náměstí Republiky 33 (☎019/326 85; ④). **Private rooms** are available from *ČEDOK*, Prešovaká 10, for slightly less than the *Slovan*. In July and August, **student hostels** offer dorm accommodation – go to *CKM* on Dominikanská to find out the latest addresses. Bus #20 will drop you at the *Bílá hora* **campsite**, in the northern suburb of the same name. All the hotels have **restaurants** attached but for cheap meals you might as well combine your eating with your drinking. Apart from the *Restaurace Prazdroj*, you can get *Pilsner Urquell* (and cheap grub) at the *Pivnice na parkánu*, next door to the museum, and at *U kanóna*, Rooseveltova 18. *Gambrinus*, Plzeň's other main beer, is best at *U Žumbery* on Bezručova, and you can get deep-pan pizzas at *U kmatra* on Americká.

The Spa Region

The big West Bohemian spas – especially **Mariánské Lázně** and **Karlovy Vary** – were the Côte d'Azur of Habsburg Europe in the nineteenth century, attracting the great names of *Mitteleuropa*. What was the prerogative of the mega-wealthy became the right of the toiling masses after the post-war nationalization of the entire spa industry enabled every factory and trade union to receive three weeks' annual holiday at a spa pension. Nowadays, the wealthy Germans are back, but the area still has a long way to go before it catches up with the likes of Baden-Baden.

Mariánské Lázně

Once one of the most fashionable European spas, **MARIÁNSKÉ LÁZNĚ** (Marienbad) is much less exclusive today. The riotous, turn-of-the-century architecture is gradually being restored and the old state spa buildings are beginning to open up their doors to the public once again. Buses and trains stop 3km from the spa, the trolley bus #5 (pay the driver) then running up Hlavní třída to the *Hotel Excelsior*, where the pedestrianized zone begins. As far as the eye can see, sumptuous, regal spa buildings rise up from the pine-clad surrounds, most dating from the second half of the nineteenth century.

The focal point of the spa, overlooking the town, is the **Kolonáda**. Easily the most beautiful wrought-iron colonnade in Bohemia, it gently curves like a whale-ribbed railway station, the atmosphere relentlessly genteel and sober. In summer, Bohemian bands and orchestras give daily concerts here, while German tourists buy up the Bohemian crystal in the upstairs gallery. Access to the colonnade's life-giving faucets is restricted (daily 6am–noon & 4–6pm), though the spa's first and foremost spring, Křížový pramen, should shortly be reopened after a face-lift. Mariánské Lázně's altitude lends an almost subalpine freshness to the air, even at the height of summer, and **walking** is as important to "the cure" as the various specialized treatments. At the end of the Kolonáda, by the new "singing fountain", there's a map showing the various waymarked walks around the spa.

If you want to **stay**, your best bet is to visit *ČEDOK* on Třebízkého (Mon–Fri only) to enquire about vacancies. Rooms in the *Hotel Krakonoš* at Zádub 53 (☎0165/2624; ② bus #12) are cheap for *IYHF* members and students, more for others; the *Atlantic*, Hlavní třída 46 (☎0165/5911; ③), is more central and surprisingly reasonable. Otherwise there's a small **campsite** at *Motel Start* on Plzeňská (☎0165/2062). Hlavní třída is punctuated with **cafés**, shops and **restaurants**, some hinting at bygone opulence; *Café Polonia*, Hlavní třída 50, offers cakes as rich as its stucco decoration. For something different, try and get your mouth around some *vepřové po Ščchuansku* (Szechuan pork) at the *Čínský restaurace*, above the *Atlantic*.

Karlovy Vary

KARLOVY VARY (Karlsbad), king of the Bohemian spas, is one of the most cosmopolitan Czech towns. Its international clientele annually doubles the local population, which is further supplemented by thousands of able-bodied tourists in summer, when the narrow valley resounds with German and the multifarious languages of central Europe.

The **bus station** and the main **train station** are on opposing sides of the River Ohře (Eger), both in the modern part of town. The shops in this district are slightly cheaper, providing the otherwise invisible local residents with daily necessities. Half a kilometre south, the pedestrianized spa quarter stretches along the winding Teplá valley. By the time you reach the Poštovní bridge, the late nineteenth-century grandeur of Karlovy Vary is beginning to unfold. Unfortunately, many visitors' first impressions are marred by the **thermal sanatorium**, an inexcusable concrete scab for whose sake a large slice of the old town bit the dust, but a useful source of information (Mon–Fri 8am–5pm, Sat 9–11am). Behind it is the open-air spring-water **swimming pool** (Mon–Sat 2–9.30pm, Sun 9am–9.30pm; closed third Mon of month), high above the river. As the valley narrows, the river disappears under a wide terrace in front of the graceful **Mlýnská kolonáda**, each of whose four springs is more scalding than the last.

Most powerful of the town's twelve springs is the **Sprudel** (*Vřídlo* to the Czechs), which belches out over 2500 gallons every hour. The smooth marble floor of the modern **Vřídelní kolonáda** (the old one was melted down for armaments by the Nazis) allows patients to shuffle up and down contentedly, while inside the glass rotunda the geyser shoots hot water forty feet upwards. Clouds of steam obscure a view of Dientzenhofer's Baroque masterpiece, the **Church of Mary Magdalene**, pitched nearby on a precipitous site. South of the Sprudel is Karlovy Vary's most famous shopping street, the **Stará louka** (Alte Wiese). Its shops exude little of the snobbery of former days, and the tea and cakes served on marble tables at the *Elefant Café* are among the few reminders of the halcyon era. At the end of the Stará louka is the **Grand Hotel Pupp**, founded in 1701 as the greatest hotel in the world. Despite its lacklustre modernization, it can't fail to impress, and the cakes are still made to Mr Pupp's recipe.

It's best to start looking for accommodation early in the day. The taxi hut in the main train station's car park can organise **private rooms**, as can *W Privat* on náměstí

Republiky (daily 10am–7pm), near the bus station, and of course *ČEDOK* in the *Hotel Atlantic* at Tržiště 23, will do the same. Cheapest of the **hotels** is the *Národní dům*, Masarykova 24 (☎017/233 86; ②), followed by the *Turist*, dr Davida Bechera 18 (☎017/268 37; ②). One of the country's few official **youth hostels** is part of *Juniorhotel Alice*, in the woods south of the spa at Pětiletky 1 (☎017/248 48; ②); take bus #7 from behind the *Národní dům*. Just before the hostel is Karlovy Vary's **campsite** (May–Sept), which also lets out reasonable rooms. The *Francouzská restaurace* at the *Grand Hotel Pupp* is the place **to eat**, but it's not cheap and you must reserve a table. If you'd rather mix with Czechs, Slovaks and Gypsies, head for the *Národní dům*'s restaurant or check out the pizza place *Fortuna* at Zámecký vrch 14, or the vegetarian restaurant at I.P. Pavlova 25, near the *Thermal*.

Kutná Hora

Undisputed gem of the region east of Prague is **KUTNÁ HORA** (Kuttenberg), 60km from the capital and once one of the most important towns in the country. In 1308 Václav II founded the royal mint here, and the town's sudden wealth allowed it to underwrite the construction of one of the most magnificent churches in central Europe, plus a number of other prestigious monuments. By the late Middle Ages its population was equal to that of London, its shantytown suburbs straggling across what are now green fields. When the silver mines dried up at the end of the sixteenth century, Kutná Hora's importance came to an abrupt end – when the Swedes marched on the town during the Thirty Years' War, they had to be bought off with beer, not silver.

The easiest way to get here from Prague is by bus, as the main train station is several kilometres from the centre, whereas the buses stop just across the ring road. The small houses which line the town's medieval lanes give little idea of its former glories, and the same goes for **Palackého náměstí**, nominally the main square but now thoroughly provincial. A narrow alleyway on the south side of the square leads to the leafy Havlíčkovo náměstí, off which is the Vlašský dvůr (Italian Court), where Florentine workers produced Prague's silver *groschen*, a coin used throughout central Europe until the nineteenth century. The building itself has been mucked about over the centuries, though the short guided tour (daily 10am–6pm) is interesting enough. Better still, head for the **Silver Mining Museum** (April–Oct Tues–Sun 8am–noon & 1–5pm, the other side of sv Jakub, the town's oldest church. Here, you can pick up a white coat, miner's helmet and torch, and visit some of the medieval mines that were discovered beneath an old fort in the 1960s.

The Jesuits arrived too late to exploit the town's silver stocks, but with their own funds they built a **Jesuit College** on the ridge to the southwest of town. With its gallery of saints and holy men, it was a crude attempt to eclipse the astounding achievement of the neighbouring church of **sv Barbora** (Tues–Sun 8/9am–noon & 1–4/5pm). Not to be outdone by the St Vitus Cathedral in Prague, the miners of Kutná Hora financed the construction of a great cathedral of their own, dedicated to Saint Barbara, the patron saint of miners and gunners. The foundations were probably laid by Peter Parler himself in the 1380s, but work was interrupted by the Hussite wars, and the church remained unfinished. From the outside it's an incredible sight, bristling with pinnacles, finials and flying buttresses supporting a roof of three tent-like towers and unequal needle-sharp spires. Inside, cold light streams through the plain glass, lighting up a vaulted nave whose ribs form branches and petals stamped with coats of arms belonging to Václav II and the miners' guilds.

The ticket office at the Vlašský dvůr also serves as a tourist information point, and can arrange **private rooms**. Otherwise, the only hotels are the *Mědínek*, on Palackého náměstí (☎0327/2741; ③), or the small, private hotel on Barborská (②).

MORAVIA

Wedged between Bohemia and Slovakia, **Moravia** (Morava) is the smallest of the three provinces which made up Czechoslovakia, and shares characteristics with both its big brothers. Like Bohemia, much of Moravia is heavily industrialized, while the region's folk roots, traditions and even religion are as strongly felt here as in parts of Slovakia. Lying on the rail line between Prague and Bratislava, **Brno** is a once-grand nineteenth-century city, within easy striking distance of Moravia's **karst region**. In the northern half of the province, the Baroque riches of the Moravian prince-bishopric have left their mark on the old capital, **Olomouc**, now a thriving university town and the region's main attraction. The rest of the North Moravian corridor forming the gateway to Poland is a virtual rerun of North Bohemia, a black hole into which few venture voluntarily.

Brno

BRNO (Brünn) "welcomes the visitor with new constructions", as one *ČEDOK* brochure euphemistically puts it. In fact, the high-rise tenements that surround the city play a major part in discouraging travellers from stopping here. But as the second largest city in the Czech Republic, with a couple of really good museums and galleries plus a handful of other sights and a fair bit of nightlife, it's worth a day or two of anyone's time. Brno was a late developer, the first cloth factory being founded in 1766. Within fifteen years it was followed by another twenty, and at the end of the nineteenth century this was easily the largest city in Moravia. Between the wars Brno enjoyed a cultural boom, heralded by the 1928 Exhibition of Contemporary Culture which provided an impetus for much of the city's avant-garde architecture. After the war, Brno's German-speakers (one quarter of the population) were expelled to Vienna. Capital fled with the capitalists and centralized state funds were diverted to Prague and Bratislava, pushing Brno firmly into third place.

Arrival and accommodation

The fresh and creamy splendour of Brno's main **train station** – restored to commemorate the 150th anniversary of the Brno–Vienna railway – points up the decay of the rest of the city's buildings. Arriving at Brno's main **bus station**, connected to the train station by an overhead walkway, is a lot less impressive. Both stations have lockers and there's a 24hr left-luggage office at the train station. Most of Brno's sights are within easy walking distance of the train station, although **trams** will take you almost anywhere in the city within minutes. Tickets (4kč) must be bought beforehand from *PNS* newsagents, hotel lobbies or yellow ticket machines, and validated on board.

The main **tourist office** is in the Stará Radnice on Radnička (Mon–Fri 8am–6pm, Sat & Sun 9am–5pm) and there's also a smaller bureau in the train station. They will book you a private room (②) or a hotel room and can sell you a map and various guides. To get into the city **youth hostel**, Purkyňova 93, Wing C2 (②); you must book through *CKM*, Česká 11, (Mon–Fri 9am–noon & 1–5pm) though at weekends you can go straight there; it's fifteen minutes away from the centre by tram #13, #16 or#22. There's also a private hostel further out at Stamicová 11 (①) in Kohoutovice suburb. Hotels in the centre are mostly pretty expensive, the cheapest being *Pegas*, Jakobská 4 (☎422 101 04; ④), centrally located off Čestá .

Cheaper alternatives out of the centre are *Moravia*, Slovákova 12 (☎239 80; ②), *Kozák*, Honova 30 (☎74 41 89;②), or *Belvedér*, Erbenova 1 (☎57 61 41;③) on the far side of Lžanky park. Best of Brno's **campsites** is the *Obora* site (April–Oct), 10km northeast of the city on the shores of the Brno dam. A *ČSAD* bus runs hourly, and in summer you can get there by tram #3, #10, #14, #18, #20 or #21, followed by a boat across the water.

The City

From the station a steady stream of people plough up and down **Masarykova**, a hazardous cocktail of cobbles, steaming manholes and tram lines. Don't let that stop you from looking up at the five-storey mansions, some laden with a fantastic mantle of decoration, many in need of renovation. To the left as you head up Masarykova is **Zelný trh** (cabbage market), a low-key vegetable market on a sloping cobbled square, with a huge fountain by Fischer von Erlach in its centre. At the top of the square, the plain mass of the Dietrichstein Palace contains the **Moravian Museum** (Tues–Sun 9am–6pm), a worthy collection of ancient and medieval artefacts. Much more interesting, if only for their macabre value, are the **Capuchin tombs** (Tues–Sat 9–noon & 2–4.30pm, Sun 11–11.45am & 2–4.30pm) to the far south of the square, a gruesome collection of dead monks and top nobs mummified in the crypt of the Capuchin church.

Clearly visible from Zelný trh is the **Stará Radnice**. Anton Pilgram's Gothic doorway is its best feature, the thistly pinnacle above the statue of Justice symbolically twisted – Pilgram's revenge on the town aldermen who short-changed him for his work. Inside, the courtyards and passageways are jam-packed with tour groups, most of them here to see the so-called Brno dragon (actually a stuffed crocodile) and the *Brněnské kolo* (Brno wheel), made in 1636 by a cartwright from Lednice, who bet a friend that he could fell a tree, make a wheel and roll it 50km to Brno all before sunset. He won the bet, but people began to suspect that he must have been in league with the devil – his business fell off and he died in poverty. If you're still hazy on the geography of the town, the tower is worth a climb for the panorama across the red-tiled rooftops.

South of the square, the Petrov hill – on which the **dóm** stands – is one of the best places in which to make a quick escape from the choked streets below. The needle-sharp Gothic spires of Brno's dóm dominate the skyline for miles around, but close up, the crude nineteenth-century rebuilding has made it a lukewarm affair.

Back down on Masarykova, follow the flow north and you'll end up at **náměstí Svobody** – far short of magnificent but nonetheless the place where most of Brno come to do their shopping. In summer, you can sit and drink coffee under the shadow of the golden plague column erected in 1648 after the failed Swedish assault on the city. On the northeast corner of the square is the **Ethnographical Museum** (Tues–Sun 9am–6pm), which contains a large collection of Moravian stuff, as well as occasionally hosting exhibitions on other countries.

Brno's finest nineteenth-century building, the **Mahenovo divadlo**, is to the east of the square at the southern end of Rooseveltova. A forthright building exuding the municipal confidence of its German patrons, it has the distinction of being the first theatre in the Austro-Hungarian Empire to be fitted with electric light bulbs courtesy of Edison Linsey. The squat **Dům umění** is an ugly companion, but it contains one of Brno's most innovative art galleries and performance venues. A little further up Rooseveltova, the grey and unappealing **Janáčkovo divadlo** was built in the 1960s as the country's largest opera house. Across the park and a short way up Kounicova on the corner with Smetanova, there's a modest **museum** (Mon–Fri 9am–noon & 1–4pm) celebrating the life and music of **Leoš Janáček**, where you can sit back and relax to his compositions. He moved to Brno at the age of eleven and spent most of his life here, founding the Brno Conservatoire in 1882.

On the western edge of the city centre, the **Moravská galérie** on Husova (Tues–Sun 10am–6pm) contains the country's best collection of modern applied art, displaying everything from avant-garde photomontages to swirling Art Nouveau vases; it also has excellent temporary shows. Skulking in the woods above the gallery is the barely visible **Špilberk castle**, one of the worst prisons in the Habsburg empire, and later a notorious Nazi killing ground. Further west still, where the River Svratka opens onto the plain (tram #1 or #18 from the station), is the **Výstaviště Exhibition Ground**. The main buildings were laid out in 1928 for the Exhibition of Contemporary Culture, and most of the leading Czech architects of the day were involved in the scheme, which prompted a flurry of functionalist building projects across the city's burgeoning suburbs.

Eating and drinking
One of the best stand-up eateries is the new *bufet*, opposite the station. The **eating and drinking** scene has improved enormously, with a brand new brewery tap, *Pegas*, on Jakubská, and surprising ventures like the cavernous Jordanian outfit *Aladin* on Dominikanské náměstí. Surprisingly enough, the renovated Habsburg-style *restaurace* at the station is actually not a bad choice. *Špalíček*, at the top of Zelný trh, has tables outside in summer and lashings of *Gambrinus* beer from Plzeň, or you could try out the *Hotel Avion*'s roof-top café on Česká. *Kabinet múz* is a late-night theatre-café worth checking out, but the only regular nightclub venue is the post-punk dive, *Harlem*, at Spolková 8 (tram #5, #9 or #17).

Around Brno

If you're staying any amount of time in Brno, follow the advice of the local health authorities and get out of the city for a while. The most popular day trip is to the limestone caves of the **Moravský kras**, closely followed by the castle of **Pernštejn**.

The Moravský kras
Number one destination for all tour groups passing through Moravia is the limestone karst region of the **Moravský kras**, just over 25km northeast of Brno. The best approach by public transport is to get the morning train from Brno out to BLANSKO (get off at Blansko-Macocha station), and then follow the crowds to the bus terminal. If you set out early enough, you should be able to pick up a bus to the caves – if not, it's a five-kilometre hike along the green-marked path.

The **Punkevní jeskyně** is the largest cave system and the deepest part of the gorge. Daily tours run every fifteen minutes (April–Sept 7am–4.30pm; Oct–March 7.30am–2.30pm) and take around fifty minutes. A fantastic array of stalactites and stalagmites fills a series of five chambers that form a prelude to the Macocha Abyss, a 138-metre mossy chasm created when the roof of one of the caves collapsed. The two other caves open to the public are only slightly less spectacular, but the queues are appreciably smaller. The **Kateřinská jeskyně** (April–Sept 7.30am–3.30pm; Oct–March 8.30am–3.30pm), one and a half kilometres before the Punkevní jeskyně at the point where the Punkva river re-emerges, is basically one huge "cathedral" of rock formations, a hundred metres long and twenty high. The smallest system is the **Balcarka jeskyně** (same hours), which lies 2km east of the Macocha Abyss.

Pernštejn
The Gothic stronghold of **Pernštejn** is a lot of people's idea of what a medieval castle should look like, and is one of the most popular targets around Brno. The train up the Svratka valley takes over an hour, but it's a pleasant journey (you may have to change at Tišnov), making it one of the easiest and most rewarding day trips. Stepping off the platform at Nedvědice, the castle is immediately visible on the cusp of a low spur to the west. After a series of outer defences, the **castle** (April & Oct Sat & Sun 9am–4pm; May–Sept Tues–Sun 8/9am–5pm) proper is a dramatic sight, kestrels circling the dizzying walls. Built in the thirteenth century, various reconstructions have left it a jumble of angles and extras, including a death-defying wooden bridge spanning the main keeps. The hour-long guided tour is short on specific treasures, but makes up for it in atmosphere and spectacular views across the mixed woodland of the nearby hills.

Olomouc

Occupying the crucial Morava crossing point on the road to Kraków, **OLOMOUC** (pronounced "Olla-moats") was the capital of Moravia from the Middle Ages to the mid-seventeenth century and the seat of the bishopric for even longer. All this attracted the destructive attention of Swedish troops in the Thirty Years' War, though the wealth of the church and its strategic trading position kept the place going. And with a well-preserved old town, sloping cobbled squares and a plethora of Baroque fountains, not to mention a healthy quota of university students, Olomouc has a great deal going for it.

The **Staré Město** is a strange contorted shape, squeezed in the middle by an arm of the Morava. Train and bus terminals are 1.5km east of the old town, so on arrival take any tram heading west up Masarykova and get off after three or four stops (pay on board). In the western half of the Staré Město, all roads lead to the city's two central cobbled main squares, which are hinged to one another at right angles. At the centre of the upper square, the irregular **Horní náměstí**, stands the amalgamation of buildings that collectively make up the town hall or **radnice**. From its creamy rendering the occasional late Gothic or Renaissance gesture emerges – notably the handsome lanterned tower soaring to its conclusion of baubles and pinnacles. On the north side, next to the arcade of shops, is an astronomical clock which, like its more famous successor in Prague, was destroyed in the war. The remake chimes all right, but the hourly mechanical show is disappointing.

Big enough to be a chapel, the **Holy Trinity Column** to the west of the *radnice* is the country's largest plague column; many such monuments were erected as thanksgiving for deliverance from the forces of Protestantism, but few are left standing. Set into the west facade of the square is the **Divadlo Oldřicha Stibora**, where Mahler arrived as the newly appointed *Kapellmeister* in 1883; the local press took an instant dislike to him, and he lasted just three months. Olomouc makes a big fuss of its sculpture, like that adorning the Edelmann Palace (no. 28), and even more of the **fountains** that grace each of Olomouc's six ancient market squares. Náměstí Míru boasts two: Hercules, looking unusually athletic for his years, and a vigorous depiction of Julius Caesar – the fabled founder of the city – bucking on a steed which coughs water from its mouth.

Two of the city's best-looking backstreets, Školní and Michalská, lead southeast from náměstí Míru, up to the church of **sv Michal**, plain on the outside but inside clad in a masterly excess of Baroque. Firmly wedged between the two sections of the Staré Město is the obligatory **Jesuit Church**, deemed particularly necessary in a city where Protestantism had spread like wildfire in the sixteenth century. Jutting out into the road, it signals the gateway to the less hectic part of town. The great mass of the former Jesuit College, now the **Palacký University**, dominates the first square, the traffic-plagued náměstí Republiky. Opposite is the town **museum** (Tues–Sun 9am–5pm), with a pretty tame permanent display but the odd worthwhile temporary exhibition on the ground floor.

Duck down Mariánská for the peaceful, leafy **Biskupské náměstí**, closed in on by fine Baroque buildings put up after the Swedes had laid the place to waste. Further east, on the other side of 1 máje, Olomouc's **dóm** is a nineteenth-century rehash in the same vein as the dóm in Brno, but the secluded close on which it stands – Václavské náměstí – is a cut above its counterpart. Next door, the scanty remains of the twelfth-century **Přemyslid Palace** are on display in the chapterhouse.

Practicalities

ČEDOK, on Horní náměstí (Mon–Fri 8am–noon & 1–5pm, Sat 9am–noon), will book **private rooms** (②) for you. The **youth hostel**, *Milhotel*, Hamerská 46 (bus #20 from the train station; ②), is inconveniently situated in the suburbs – you'd be better off at the cheap and central *Brioni*, Riegrova 16 (☎068/296 71; ②), or in the *Narodní dům*, 8 květná 21 (☎068/251 79; ③). Rooms can be hard to come by in May when the Spring Music Festival follows the Flower Festival.

For **restaurants**, the *Hanacká* on Dolní náměstí is a cheap and traditional Moravian establishment. A good range of cakes can be found in the *cukrárna* on Náměstí Republiky. In the evenings most people head for a *pivnice* or *kavárna* like the *Opera*, by the main theatre, or *Narodní dům*, or the student café at the far end of Křížkovského. The *Múzeum umění* at Denisova 47 puts on an adventurous programme of gigs, films and video, and there are occasional gigs in the *radnice* on Horní náměstí.

SLOVAKIA

The newly-independent republic of **Slovakia** (Slovensko) consists of the long, narrow strip of land which stretches from the parched plains of the Danube basin up to the peaks of the High Tatras – perhaps Europe's most exhilarating landscape outside of the Alps. Slovak **history** is one of relentless cultural repression by the neighbouring Magyars, yet the Slovaks emerged from a millennium of punishing serfdom inside the kingdom of Hungary with their national identity pretty much intact. For the first-time visitor, perhaps the most striking cultural difference on entering Slovakia is in the attitude to religion. Catholicism is almost as strong here as in parts of Poland, the churches full to overflowing on Sundays. In other respects, though, change has come all too rapidly to parts of Slovakia, and often the new industrial and urban landscape can be depressingly similar to postwar developments all over Eastern Europe and the Soviet Union.

West Slovakia is uncharacteristically flat, and the capital, **Bratislava**, potentially disappointing, especially for those who arrive expecting a Slovak Prague, though taken on its own terms, it's a rewarding place. **Poprad** provides the transport hub for the **High Tatras**, the tallest of Slovakia's mountains, and is also the starting point for exploring the intriguing medieval towns of the **Spiš region**, East Slovakia's architectural high point.

Bratislava

BRATISLAVA has two distinct sides: on the one hand, the old quarter is a manageable and attractive slice of Habsburg Baroque, but on the other, the rest of the city has the brash, crass and butchered feel typical of the average East European metropolis. More buildings have been destroyed here since the war than were bombed out during it, with the whole Jewish quarter having been bulldozed to make way for the colossal new suspension bridge. Yet, even though the multicultural atmosphere of the prewar days is but weakly echoed in the city's smattering of Magyars, Gypsies and day-tripping Austrians, it has a cosmopolitanism with which neither Prague nor Brno can compete.

Arrival, transport and information

"East of Vienna, the Orient begins." Metternich's much-quoted aphorism rings true in the multi-ethnic chaos of Bratislava's **hlavná stanica**, where most international or long-distance **trains** pull in. Once you've arrived, go down to the big tram terminus below and, having bought your ticket from one of the machines on the platform, hop on a #1 tram into town. Some trains, particularly those heading for destinations within West Slovakia, pass through Bratislava's **Nové Mesto** station, linked to the centre by tram #6 and to the main train station by hourly train connection. **Buses** tend to arrive at the autobusová stanica on Bajkalská, also in Nové Mesto, northwest of the town centre. The best thing to do is turn right, walk 100m to the junction with Vajnorská and jump on any tram going down into town.

The best way to see Bratislava is to walk – in fact it's the only way to see the pedestrianized old town and the *hrad*, where most of the sights are concentrated. However, if you're staying outside the city centre or visiting the suburbs, you'll need to make use of the city's cheap and comprehensive **transport system**. Buy your ticket beforehand (from newsagents, kiosks, hotel lobbies or ticket machines), validate it as soon as you get on, and use a fresh ticket each time you change; if you're going to use the system a lot buy a *turistické cestovne lístok* from a *tabák*, or the central transport office on Stúrova. **Night buses** congregate at námestie SNP, every quarter to the hour.

Bratislava's **tourist office** is at Laurinská 1 (Mon–Fri 8am–6pm, Sat 8am–1pm); it's good for general queries (some English spoken) and getting hold of a map and the monthly listings magazine, *Kam v Bratislave*, but doesn't offer an accommodation service. You can buy a more detailed map from the *Deutsche Bücher* shop, two doors up from the tourist office.

Accommodation

Bratislava's proximity to Vienna means that **hotels** are more expensive even than many in Prague. For a central location, you'll have to pay through the nose: try *Perugia*, Zelená 5 (☎07/330 719; ⑥), or the kosher *Chez David*, Zámocká 13 (☎07/313 824; ⑥). *BIS* or *ČEDOK*, on Jesenského (Mon–Fri 9am–6pm, Sat 9am–noon) organize **private rooms**, or else there's a lively hostel, *Bernolák*, on Bernolákova (☎07/497 725; ①). Another option is *CKM* which lets **student hostels** in July and August ②; check addresses at the office, Hviezdoslavovo námestie 16 (Mon–Fri 9/10am–3.30/5.30pm).

Two fairly grim **campsites** are 8km northeast of the city centre, out near the lake at Zlaté Piesky (tram #4 from the station; tram #2 from town). Bungalows are on offer all year round; tent camping May to September only.

The City

Trams from the main train station offload their shoppers and sightseers behind the *Hotel Fórum* in Obchodná – literally Shop Street – which descends into Hurbanovo námestie, a busy junction on the northern edge of the Staré Mesto. Here you'll find the hefty mass of the **Trinity Church**. Despite a tired and faded air inside its single-domed nave, it's one of the city's finest churches, its exuberant *trompe l'oeil* frescoes creating a magnificent false cupola.

Opposite the Trinity Church, a footbridge passes under a tower of the city's last remaining double gateway. Below, in what used to be the city moat, is an open-air reading room (Mon–Sat 1–7pm), a tiny garden which hosts the odd literary event in amongst the modern sculpture and shrubbery. It belongs to the **Baroque Apothecary** called *U červeného raka* ("At the Red Lobster"), on your left between the towers, which now houses a **Pharmaceutical Museum** (Tues–Sun 10am–5pm), displaying everything from seventeenth-century drug grinders to reconstructed period pharmacies. The second and taller of the towers is the **Michalská brána** (daily except Tues 10am–5pm), an evocative and impressive entrance to the Staré Mesto whose outer limits are elsewhere hard to distinguish. You can climb it, giving a quick glance en route to the **Museum of Arms and Armaments**, for a great roof top view of the old town.

Michalská and Ventúrska – which make up the same street – are lined with some of Bratislava's finest Baroque palaces, and their cafés and bars are thronged with students, shoppers and arty types.

The palaces of the Austro-Hungarian aristocracy continue into Panská, starting with the **Pálffy Palace**, today a trendy **art gallery** (Tues–Sun 10am–6pm) plus a mediocre collection of European paintings from the fourteenth to the twentieth century. Further down, next to the Esterházy Palace, is the richly decorated **kaplnka Božieho tela** (Corpus Christi Chapel), packed with illuminated manuscripts, jewellery and ecclesiastical wealth.

A little east of here are the twin main squares of the Staré Mesto: **Hlavné námestie** and **Františkánske námestie**. No longer at the centre of things, they now provide a leafy respite from the city's shopping malls. Opposite the fountain is the **Stará Radnica** a lively hotchpotch of Gothic, Renaissance and nineteenth-century styles and now housing the city museum, an exhibition on viniculture and one on feudal "justice". The Counter-Reformation, which gripped the parts of Hungary not under Turkish occupation, issues forth from the square's **Jesuit Church**, filled to the brim with the usual post-Baroque kitsch. Not far from here, opposite the gaudy yellow Franciscan Church, is the **Mirbach Palace** (Tues–Fri 10am–6pm, Sat & Sun 10am–5pm; concerts Sun 10.30am), arguably the finest of Bratislava's Rococo buildings, preserving much of its original stucco decor. That said, the Baroque art inside isn't up to much, save for the wall-to-wall miniatures set into the wooden panelling and a series of seventeenth-century Dutch tapestries.

Round the back of the Stará Radnica, with the stillness of a provincial Italian piazza during siesta, is the **Primaciálne námestie**, dominated by the Neoclassical **Primate's Palace**, whose pediment frieze is topped by a 300-pound cast-iron cardinal's hat. The palace's main claim to fame is as the place where Napoleon and the Austrian emperor signed the Treaty of Pressburg in 1805.

All over the Staré Mesto, commemorative plaques make much of Bratislava's musical connections, but apart from the reflected glory of its proximity to Vienna and Budapest the city has produced only one famous composer, Johann Nepomuk Hummel (1778–1837), who was in any case very much an Austrian at heart. Still, it's as good an excuse as any for a **Hummel Museum** (Tues–Sun 10am–5pm; concerts Thurs eve), housed in the composer's birthplace, a cute apricot-coloured cottage hidden away behind two fashionable shops on Klobučnícka. Beyond the museum, at the top end of Štúrova, is **Kamenné námestie**, where the whole city seems to wind up after work, to grab a beer or takeaway from one of the many stand-up stalls, then jabber away the early evening before catching the bus or tram home.

On the side of the Staré Mesto nearest the *hrad*, the most insensitive of Bratislava's postwar developments took place. After the annihilation of the city's Jewish population by the Nazis, the communist authorities tore down virtually the whole of the **Jewish Quarter** in order to build the brutal showpiece bridge, the Most SNP. Quite apart from the devastation of the ghetto, the traffic which tears along the busy thoroughfare of Staromestská has seriously undermined the foundations of the Gothic **dóm**, coronation church of the kings and queens of Hungary for over 250 years, whose ill-proportioned steeple is topped by a tiny gilded Hungarian crown.

As you're passing under the approach road for the new bridge, you'll notice two old, thin houses standing opposite one another, both of which have now been converted into museums. The first is a **clock museum** (daily 10am–5pm; closed Tues) with a display of brilliantly kitsch Baroque and Empire clocks; the second is nominally a **folk museum** (same times) which consists of a few period dining rooms and a lot of fairly ordinary arts and crafts gear. No doubt with the hope of dispelling rumours of Slovak anti-Semitism, the authorities have sanctioned the opening of a **Museum of Jewish Culture** (daily except Sat 11am–5pm) on Židovská, with a display of Judaica and a brief history of Slovak Jews.

The **Castle** itself is an unwelcoming giant box built in the fifteenth century by the Emperor Sigismund in expectation of a Hussite attack, and burnt down by its own drunken soldiers in 1811. Recently restored, it now houses half of the uneven collections of the **Slovak National Museum** (Tues–Sun 10am–noon & 2–4pm). Numismatologists will have fun among the coins on the top floor, but most punters will probably get more out of the incredible view from outside the castle gates south across the Danube plain.

Eating, drinking and nightlife

Food is taken more seriously in Bratislava than in Prague, and despite the lack of new foreign ventures, a whole host of restaurants have recently opened up. In addition to the usual Slovak fare, Magyar cuisine finds its way onto most menus in various shapes and forms. The preference for wine over beer also lends a cosmopolitan touch to the city's many cafés and bars; draught beer is only available from a few pubs and restaurants.

Bratislava abounds in **cafés**, some of them – like the *Lýra* on Ventúrska, *Roland* on Hlavné námestie, and the student hangout *U Liszta*, by the university library just off Michalská – perfect for a quick caffeine hit. Others have outdoor tables for soaking up the streetlife; of these, perhaps the best are the *Orient* and *Sklabiňa*, grouped round the námestie SNP.

For cheap and unpretentious **food**, you could do worse than *Piváreň U Eda*, a Czech-style pub on Biela ulica. The *Stará sladovňa*, at the end of Cintorínska, is Bratislava's most famous eating and drinking establishment. It claims to be the second largest restaurant in Europe – it seats 1600 at a pinch – and the food isn't at all bad, though they stop serving around 8 or 9pm. *Arkádia*, up the Zámocké schody, is a swish new restaurant in an old Renaissance building on the way up the castle, while *chez David*, Zámocká 13, is a plush kosher restaurant serving Jewish specialities. **Wine bars**, which generally also serve food, tend to be open a bit later than ordinary restaurants; try *Veľkí františkáni* on Františkánske námestie, which features Slovak Gypsy music, or the *Kláštorná vináreň*, behind the two churches on Františkánske námestie.

Bratislava's most established **nightlife** is heavily biased towards high culture, with opera and ballet at the *Slovak National Theatre*, and orchestral concerts at the *Reduta*, as well as the varied programme put on at the modern *Dom odborov* complex (tram #4, #6 or #10 from town). Tickets for the first two are available from the box office behind the National Theatre, and for the *Dom odborov* from a box office inside the building from 3pm – many theatres close down in July and August.. The city hosts a couple of large-scale **festivals**, starting with its own Spring Music Festival in April – without the big names of Prague's, but a lot easier to get tickets for. The Bratislava Jazz Days take place in October and often headline with the same folk who've just trundled through Prague and Kraków. The best alternative venue is the multi-screen art house cinema complex, *Charlie centrum*, Spitálska 4; the entrance is one block east of the *Hotel Kyjev* on Rajská.

The High Tatras

Rising like a giant granite reef above the patchwork Poprad plain, the **High Tatras** are for many people the main reason for venturing this far into Slovakia. Yet even after all the tourist board hype, they are still an inspirational sight – a wilderness, however, they are not. All summer, visitors are shoulder to shoulder in the necklace of resorts which sit at the foot of the mountains, and things don't get that much better if you take to the hills. Yet when all's said and done, once you're above the tree line, surrounded by bare primeval scree slopes and icy blue tarns, nothing can take away the exhilaration.

The mainline train station for the Tatras is Poprad-Tatry in Poprad (the main bus station is next door). From here, cute red tram-like trains trundle across the fields, linking Poprad with the string of resorts and spas nestling at the foot of the Tatras and lying within **Tatra National Park** or **TANAP**. They're all much of a muchness, a mix of tasteless new hotels and half-timbered lodges from the last century set in eminently civilized spa gardens and pine woods – it's the mountains to which they give access that make them worth visiting. Perhaps the best to head for is **Starý Smokovec**, the central resort.

Camping in the High Tatras

Accommodation should be your first priority, since finding a place can be difficult. The cheapest option is **camping**, though all the sites are outside the boundaries of the national park, and therefore a long hike from the nearest peaks. The best one is the *Tatracamp Pod Lesom* (mid-May to Sept) in DolnÝ Smokovec (get off at Pod lesom station), with bungalows, hot showers and kitchen facilities. Two camps – *Eurocamp FICC* (all year) and *Športcamp* (June 15–Sept 15) – just south of Tatranská Lomnica (get off at Tatranská Lomnica-Eurocamp FICC station) are similarly priced but don't offer kitchen facilities. Tatranská Štrba site is the grottiest (May–Sept), while the cheapest and most basic is 1km south of Stará Lesná (June 15–Sept 15).

Poprad

POPRAD is an unprepossessing town, a great swathe of off-white housing encircling a small, scruffy old centre – but it's refreshingly free of tour groups and the pretentiousness of higher resorts. In fact, if you can get in at the refurbished *Hotel Európa* (☎092/327 44; ②), it's no bad place to stay: it's next to the train station, with a friendly, sleazy *kaviareň* and a slightly more upmarket restaurant. *Gerlach* on Hviezdoslavovo námestie (☎092/337 59; ③) is about the same price, minus the atmosphere. *ČEDOK*, on the long main square, five minutes' walk south of the train station (Mon–Fri 9am–noon & 1–6pm, Sat 9am–2pm, Sun 9am–1pm), can find **private rooms** in the area. The square is useful for picking up provisions if you're hiking. There's a good bakery and a small vegetable market on the north side, while the south side is taken up with a host of indifferent new shops, including a bookshop where you might be able to pick up relevant **maps**.

Starý Smokovec – and Tatra hikes

As far as accommodation is concerned, the best base in the Tatras is the scattered settlement of **STARÝ SMOKOVEC**, whose nucleus is the stretch of lawn between the half-timbered supermarket and the pricy *Grand Hotel* (☎0969/25 01; ⑤), the finest guesthouse around. *ČEDOK*, near the train station (Mon–Fri 8am–7pm, Sat & Sun 9.45am–3pm), deals mostly with hotel bookings in the Tatras, but can also book private rooms. Climbers and hikers wanting information on mountain **refuges** (*chata*) should go to *Slovakoturist* (Mon–Fri 8am–4pm), a couple of minutes' east of the station. The unpretentious *Tatra* **restaurant**, next door to *ČEDOK*, is the most reasonable place to eat.

If the weather's reasonably good, the most straightforward and rewarding climb is to follow the blue-marked path that leads from behind the *Grand Hotel* to the summit of **Slavkovský štít** (2452m), a return journey of nine hours. Again from behind the *Grand Hotel*, a narrow-gauge funicular climbs 250m to HREBIENOK (45min on foot), one of the lesser ski resorts on the edge of the pine forest. The smart wooden *Bilíkova chata* is a five-minute walk from the top of the funicular. Beyond the *chata*, the path continues through the wood, joining two others, from Tatranská Lesná and Tatranská Lomnica respectively, before passing the gushing waterfalls of the **Studenovodské vodopády**.

Just past the waterfall, a whole variety of trekking possibilities opens up. The right-hand fork takes you up the **Malá Studená dolina** and then zigzags above the tree line to the *Téryho chata*, set in a lunar landscape by the shores of the **Päť Spišských plies**. Following the spectacular trail over the Priečne sedlo to *Zbojnicka chata*, you can return via the Veľká studená dolina – an eight-hour round trip from Hrebienok. Another possibility is to take the left-hand fork to the *Zbojnicka chata*, and continue to Zamruznuté pleso, which sits in the shadow of **Východná Vysoká** (2428m); only a thirty-minute hike from the lake, this dishes out the best view of Gerlachovský štít – the highest of the Tatras – that a non-climber can get.

The Spiš region

The land that stretches northeast up the Poprad valley to the Polish border and east along the River Hornád towards Prešov is known as the **Spiš region**, for centuries a semi-autonomous province within the Hungarian kingdom. After the dislocation and devastation of the mid-thirteenth-century Tartar invasions, the Hungarian crown was keen to repopulate the area as a stopgap against any further incursions by the eastern hordes – and so Saxon families were encouraged to colonize the area. Today, minus its ethnic Germans, the whole of the Spiš (Zips) region shares the low living standards which are the rule throughout East Slovakia. The only glimmer of hope is in the growth of tourism, since architecturally the Spiš region has a substantial head start. The Saxon settlers had the wealth to build some wonderful Gothic churches, and later enriched almost every town and village with the distinctive touch of the Renaissance.

Kežmarok

Fourteen kilometres up the road from Poprad, **KEŽMAROK** (Käsmark) is one of the easiest Spiš towns to visit from the High Tatras. It's an odd place, combining the distinctive traits of a Teutonic town with the dozy feel of an oversized Slovak village. Kežmarok is dominated by the giant, gaudy **Lutheran Church** (daily 8am–noon & 1–5pm), built by Theophil von Hansen, the architect responsible for much of late nineteenth-century Vienna, and funded by the town's merchants. It's a seemingly random fusion of styles – Renaissance campanile, Moorish dome, classical dimensions, all dressed up in grey-green and rouge rendering. Next door is an even more remarkable wooden **Protestant church**, a work of great carpentry that's capable of seating almost 1500 people.

The old town itself is little more than two long leafy streets which fork off from the important-looking though easily missable central square. The town's Catholic church, **sv Kríž**, is tucked away in the tangle of dusty back alleys between the two prongs, once surrounded by its own line of fortifications, now protected by a Renaissance belfry whose uppermost battlements burst into sgraffito life in the best Spiš tradition. The **castle** (Tues–Sun 9am–4pm), at the end of the right-hand fork, is the main reason the odd Tatran tour group makes it here. The museum of historical artefacts which now occupies its bare rooms doesn't really justify the compulsory hour-long guided tour.

ČEDOK, on the northern edge of the old town, can book cheap **private rooms** for you; otherwise there's the *Lipa* on Toporecova (☎0968/20 37; ②), or the *Štart* (☎0968/29 15; ②), which lies in the woods to the north of the castle, a good twenty-minute walk from the train station.

Levoča and around

Twenty-five kilometres east of Poprad across the broad sweep of Spiš countryside, the walled town of **LEVOČA** (Leutschau), set on a slight incline, makes a wonderfully medieval impression. The Euclidian efficiency with which the old town is laid out means you'll inevitably end up at the main square, **námestie Majstra Pavla**. To the north is the square's least distinguished but most important building, the municipal weighhouse (now a school), which was the town's financial muscle during its trading heyday. In 1321 King Charles Robert granted the Law of Storage, an unusual medieval edict which obliged every merchant passing through the region to hole up at Levoča for at least fourteen days, pay various taxes and allow the locals first refusal on all their goods.

Of the three freestanding buildings on the main square paid for with these riches, it's the Catholic church of **sv Jakub** (May–Sept Tues–Sat 8am–5pm, Sun 1–4pm; Oct–April Tues–Sat 8am–4pm) that has the most valuable booty. Every nook and cranny is crammed with religious art, star attraction being the magnificent sixteenth-century wooden altarpiece by Master Pavol of Levoča, which, at 18.6m, is reputedly the tallest of its kind in the world. South is the **Rathaus** (same hours), built in a sturdy Renaissance style. On the first floor, there's a museum on the Spiš region, and some dubious contemporary Slovak art on the top floor. The third building in the centre of the square is the oddly squat **Protestant church**, built in an uncompromisingly Neoclassical style.

Spišský hrad

The road east from Levoča takes you to the edge of Spiš territory, clearly defined by the Branisko ridge which blocks the way to Prešov. Even if you're not going any further east, you should at least take the bus as far as **SPIŠSKÉ PODHRADIE**, for arguably the most spectacular sight in the whole country – the **Spišský hrad**. This pile of chalk-white ruins, strung out on a bleak green hill, is irresistibly photogenic and finds its way into almost every tourist hand-out in the country. Predictably enough, the ruins themselves don't quite live up to expectations close to (May–Oct Tues–Sun 9am–5pm), though the view from the top is undeniably good. *Hotel Spiš* (✆0966/8521; ②) in the village is the only nearby **accommodation** on offer.

travel details

Trains

Prague to: Bratislava (12 daily; 5hr); Brno (14 daily; 3hr); České Budějovice (6 daily; 2hr 30min); Karlovy Vary (6 daily; 4hr–5hr 30min); Kutná Hora (7 daily; 1hr); Mariánské Lázně (up to 12 daily; 3hr); Olomouc (over 25 daily; 3hr 20min–5hr 50min); Plzeň (up to 12 daily; 1hr 45min); Poprad (7 daily; 9–10hr).

Bratislava to: Brno (up to 20 daily; 2hr–3hr 30min); Poprad (9 daily; 5hr); Prague (12 daily; 5hr).

Brno to: Bratislava (12 daily; 2hr); České Budějovice (3 daily; 4hr); Olomouc (4 daily; 1hr); Prague (14 daily; 3hr).

České Budějovice to: Český Krumlov (8 daily; 1 hr); Plzeň (8 daily; 2hr–3hr 30min).

Mariánské Lázně to Karlovy Vary (8 daily; 1hr 30min).

Olomouc to: České Budějovice (1 daily; 6hr 20min); Poprad (5 daily; 6hr 30min); Prague (over 25 daily; 3hr 20min–5hr 50min).

Plzeň to: Mariánské Lázně (at least 10 daily; 1hr 15min–1hr 30min).

Poprad (Poprad-Tatry) to: Starý Smokovec (up to hourly; 45min).

Buses

Prague to: Brno (up to 13 daily; 2hr 40min); České Budějovice (up to 6 daily; 2hr 30min); Karlovy Vary (up to 14 daily; 2hr 25min–3hr 20min); Kutná Hora (up to 7 daily; 1hr 30min).

Brno to: Prague (hourly; 2hr 35min).

Plzeň to: Karlovy Vary (up to 2 hourly; 1hr 30min).

CHAPTER 5

DENMARK

To Kristiansand · To Oslo · To Larvik · To Oslo · Gothenburg
Skagen
Hirtshals
Frederikshaven
SWEDEN
To Törshavn
Hanstholm · Thisteol · Varberg
Aalborg · Kattegat
Lemvig · Viborg · Randers · Grenå · To Oslo
Silkeborg · Ebeltoft · Helsinbor
Århus · Helsingør · Hillerød
JUTLAND · COPENHAGEN
Vejle · Kalundborg · Roskilde
To Törshavn · Fredericia · Malmø
Esbjerg · Odense · Kerteminde · Ringsted
To Harwich & Newcastle · Ribe · FUNEN · Næstved · ZEALAND
Tønder · Fåborg · Svendborg
Flensberg · Gelting · Bagenkop · Rødby · Nykøbing
GERMANY · Gedser
To Kiel · To Pottgarden · To Rostock

0   50 km

Introduction

Delicately balanced between Scandinavia proper and mainland Europe, Denmark is a difficult country to pin down. In many ways it shares the characteristics of both regions: it's an EC member, and has prices and drinking laws that are broadly in line with those in the rest of Europe. But Danish social policies and the style of government in the country are distinctly Scandinavian: social benefits and the standard of living are high, and its politics are very much that of consensus.

Denmark is the easiest Scandinavian country in which to travel, both in terms of cost and distance, but the landscape itself is the region's least dramatic: very green and flat, largely farmland interrupted by innumerable pretty villages. Apart from a scattering of small islands, three main landmasses make up the country – the islands of Zealand and Funen and the peninsula of Jutland, which extends northwards from Germany.

The vast majority of visitors make for **Zealand** (*Sjælland*), and, more specifically, **Copenhagen**, the country's one large city and an exciting focal point, with a beautiful old centre, a good array of museums and a boisterous nightlife. Zealand's smaller neighbour, **Funen** (*Fyn*), has only one positive urban draw in **Odense**, and otherwise is a sedate place, renowned for its cute villages and the sandy beaches of its fragmented southern coast. Only **Jutland** (*Jylland*) is far enough away from Copenhagen to enjoy a truly individual flavour, as well as Denmark's most varied scenery, ranging from soft green hills to desolate heathlands. In **Århus**, Jutland also has the liveliest city outside the capital.

Information and Maps

All towns and some villages will have a **tourist office**, giving out free maps and sometimes able to book accommodation and change money. In large cities they also sell useful **discount cards** giving reductions on public transport, museum entry and the like. They're open long hours every day in the most popular places, but have much reduced times outside the April–September period. The best general **map** of Denmark is the *Hallwag* one.

Money and Banks

Coming from any of the other Scandinavian countries, Denmark seems remarkably cheap, with prices roughly only 10–20 percent higher than other western European countries. **Danish currency** is the *krone* (plural *kroner*), made up of 100 *øre*, and it comes in notes of 50kr, 100kr, 500kr, 1000kr, and coins of 20øre, 50øre, 1kr, 2kr, 5kr, 10kr, 20kr. **Banks** are the best places to change travellers' cheques and foreign cash; there's a uniform commission of 22kr per transaction, so change as much as possible in one go. Banking hours are Mon–Fri 9.30am–4.30pm, Thurs until 6.30pm. Most airports and ferry terminals have late-opening exchange facilities.

Communications

Most **post offices** are open Mon–Fri 9am–6pm, Sat 9am–1pm, with reduced hours in smaller communities. You can either buy stamps there or from most newsagents; mail to other parts of Europe under 20g costs 3.75kr and 5kr for the rest of the world. Danish **public telephones** come in two forms. Coin-operated ones require a minimum of 2 x 1kr for a local call (the machines irritatingly swallow one of the coins if the number is engaged), and 5kr to go international; plastic for the yellow card phones comes in denominations of 20, 50 and 100kr and works out a little cheaper. One thing to remember when dialling Danish numbers is to *always* use the area code. The international access code is ☎009; Danish directory enquiries (5kr) are on ☎118, international (also 5kr) on ☎113, with almost all operators speaking English.

Getting Around

Despite being an island country, Denmark is a swift and easy place to travel. All types of public transport – trains, buses and ferries – are punctual and efficient, and the timetables well-integrated.

■ Trains, buses and ferries

Trains are easily the best way to get about. *Danske Statsbaner* (*DSB*) – Danish State Railways – run an exhaustive and reliable network. Train types range from the large inter-city expresses (*ICs*) to smaller local trains (*persontog*). **Tickets** should be bought in advance from the station, one-way tickets allowing you to break your journey once, although travel must be completed on a single day. Fares are calculated on a zonal system: Copenhagen to Århus – probably the longest single trip you'll make – costs 161kr (201kr at weekends). Buying a return offers no savings over two singles. Seat reservations, costing 30kr from the station ticket office, are compulsory on some crossings between Zealand and Funen and on *IC* trains on Friday and Sunday afternoons (2–8pm). *InterRail* and *Eurail* passes are valid, as is the *Nordturist* pass. Available from *NSR Travel*, 21–24 Cockspur Street, London SW1Y 5DA, and throughout Scandinavia, this pass costs £189/$300 (£140/$220 for under-26s), and gives you 21 days' unlimited travel in the four main Scandinavian countries, plus free travel or large discounts on many ferry crossings and bus journeys. *NSR Travel* also sells the *Scandrail* pass, costing £93/$150 for 4 days travel in 15, £151/$240 for 9 days out of 21 and £217/$350 for 21 days travel out 30, and is again valid throughout Scandinavia. Under 26s can also buy a pass giving 14 days travel from June 20–July 4 from 435kr.

As for timings, *DSB*'s *Køreplan* (which you can pick up for 30kr from any newsagent) details all train, bus and ferry services, including the local Copenhagen S-train system and all private services; smaller timetables detailing specific routes are available free at tourist offices and station booking counters.

There are a few out-of-the-way regions trains fail to penetrate, and these can easily be crossed by **buses**, which often run in conjunction with the trains, some operated privately, some by *DSB* – on which railcards are valid. Much of Funen and the northeast of Jutland is barely touched by trains, and you can save several hours by taking the bus. There are a few long-distance bus services, too, from Copenhagen to Århus, Aalborg and Hantsholm, Esbjerg to Frederikshavn, and Odense to Nykøbing. Fares represent quite a saving over trains, but buses are much less comfortable.

Ferries link all the Danish islands, and where applicable train and bus fares include the cost of crossings (although you can also pay at the terminal and walk on); the smaller ferry crossings normally cost 10–40kr for foot passengers.

■ Driving and hitching

Given the excellence of the Danish public transport system, the size of the country and the comparatively high price of petrol, **driving** isn't really economical unless you're travelling in a group. Danes drive on the right, and there's a speed limit in towns of 50kph, 80kph in open country and 110kph on motorways. Like the other Scandinavian countries, dipped headlights have to be used during daylight hours. There are random breath tests, and the penalties for drunk driving are severe. When parking unmetered in a town, a parking-time disc must be displayed; you'll be able to get one from a tourist office, police station or bank. The national motoring organization, *Forenede Danske Motorejere*, operates a breakdown service Mon–Fri 9am–5pm, Sat 10am–1pm (☎45 93 08 00); if you find yourself stranded outside those hours, motorway assistance can be summoned from call boxes by the road – although a standard call-out fee will be charged. **Car rental** in Denmark starts at around 3500kr a week for a small hatchback with unlimited mileage. You'll need an international driving licence and must be aged at least twenty, although many firms won't rent vehicles to anyone under 25. As for **hitching**, this is illegal on motorways and difficult anywhere.

■ Cycling

Cycling is the best way to appreciate Denmark's mostly flat landscape. Most country roads have sparse vehicle traffic and all large towns have cycle tracks. Bikes can be **hired** at nearly all youth hostels and tourist offices and some train stations for 40kr per day, 75–180kr per week, although there's often a 200kr deposit. *IC* and certain regional trains (marked on timetables) won't accept bikes. On those that do, you'll have to pay 22kr or 50kr if the trip includes a ferry crossing.

Accommodation

While much less costly than it can be in other Scandinavian countries, accommodation is still going to be your major daily expense in Denmark. Hotels, however, are by no means off-limits if you are prepared to seek out the better offers, and both the youth hostels and campsites that you'll come across are plentiful and of a uniformly high standard.

ACCOMMODATION PRICE CODES

Throughout this guide, accommodation is priced on a scale of ① to ⑧, the number indicating the lowest price per night a single person could expect to pay in that establishment in high season. With hostels this is the nightly rate per person; with hotels, the price is arrived at by dividing the cost of the cheapest double room by two. The prices indicated by the codes are as follows

① = under £5 / $8   ② = £5–10 / $8–16   ③ = £10–15 / $16–24   ④ = £15–20 / $24–32

⑤ = £20–25 / $32–40   ⑥ = £25–30 / $40–48   ⑦ = £30–35 / $48–56   ⑧ = over £35 / $56

■ Hotels and private rooms

Most Danish **hotel** rooms include phone, TV and bathroom, for which you'll pay around 600kr for a double, although in most large towns you'll also find hotels offering rooms without bathrooms for as little as 350kr for a double. One advantage of staying in a hotel is the inclusive all-you-can-eat breakfast – so large you won't need to buy lunch. Only in peak season will you need to book in advance. Danish tourist offices overseas can provide a free list of hotels throughout the country, though much more accurate and extensive information can be found at local tourist offices. Tourist offices can also supply details of **private rooms** in someone's home, for which you should reckon on paying 300–500kr a double.

■ Youth hostels and sleep-ins

Youth hostels are the cheapest option under a roof. Every town has one, they're much less pricy than hotels and they have a high degree of comfort, most offering a choice of private rooms, often with toilets and showers, or dorm accommodation; nearly all have cooking facilities. Rates are around 75kr per person for a dorm bed; non-*IYHF* members pay an extra 22kr a night. It's rare for hostels other than those in major towns or ferry ports to be full, but during the summer it's still wise to phone ahead. As with all Scandinavian hostels, sleeping bags are not allowed, so you have to carry a sheet bag or hire hostel linen. If you're doing a lot of hostelling, it's worth contacting *Danmarks Vandrerhjem*, Vesterbrogade 39, DK-1620, Copenhagen V. (☎31/313612), for their hostel guide (25kr).

Sometimes cheaper still, and occasionally free, are **sleep-ins**, usually open in the main towns for a two-week period during the summer (normally late June and early July). You need your own sleeping bag, sometimes only one night's stay is permitted and there may be an age restriction. Sleep-ins come and go, however; check the current situation at a tourist office.

■ Campsites and cabins

If you don't have an International Camping Card from a camping organization at home, you'll need a Visitor's Pass to **camp** in Denmark, which costs 24kr from any campsite and is valid on all official sites until the year's end. Campsites are virtually everywhere. All sites open through the three summer months, many from April to September, while a few stay open all year. There's a rigid grading system: one-star sites have drinking water and toilets; two-stars have, in addition, showers, laundry and a food shop within a kilometre; three-stars, by far the majority, have all the above plus a TV-room, shop, cafeteria, etc. Prices vary only slightly, three-stars charging 32–42kr per person, others a few kroner less.

Many sites also have **cabin accommodation**, usually with cooking facilities, for upwards of 900kr for a six-berth affair, although these are often booked up throughout the summer. Any tourist office will give you a free leaflet listing all the sites. **Camping rough** without permission is illegal, and an on-the-spot fine may be imposed.

Food and Drink

There are plenty of ways to eat affordably and healthily in Denmark, and with plenty of variety, too. Much the same applies to drink: the only Scandinavian country free of social drinking taboos, Denmark is an imbiber's delight – both for its choice of tipples and the number of places they can be sampled.

■ Food

Traditional Danish **food** centres on meat and fish, served with potatoes and another, usually boiled, vegetable. **Breakfast** (*morgenmad*) can be the tastiest Danish meal and almost all hotels offer a sumptuous breakfast as a matter of course, as do youth hostels: a table laden with cereals, bread, cheese, boiled eggs, fruit juice, milk and tea for around 40kr. Breakfast elsewhere is less substantial: many cafés offer a basic one for 25–35kr. Later in the day, a tight budget may leave you dependent on **self-catering**. As for **snacks**, you can buy *smørrebrød* – open sandwiches heaped with meat, fish or cheese, and assorted trimmings – for 10–20kr from special shops, at least one of which will be open until 10pm. There are also **fast-food stands** (*pølsevogn*) in all main streets and at train stations, serving various hot sausages (*pølser*), toasted sandwiches (*pariser-toast*) and chips (*pomme frites*), which come in two forms: big (*store*) and small (*lille*). The size refers to the actual chips and not the portion. If you just want a cup of **coffee** or **tea**, cafés serve both; help it down with a **Danish pastry** (*wienerbrød*), tastier and much less sweet than the imitations sold under the name elsewhere.

You can find an excellent-value **lunch** (*frokost*) simply by walking around at lunchtime and reading the signs chalked up outside a café, restaurant or *bodega* (a bar which sells no-frills food). You'll often see the word *tilbud*, which refers to the "special" priced dish, or *dagens ret*, "dish of the day" – a plate of chilli con carne or lasagne for around 45kr, or a two-course set lunch for about 60kr. Some restaurants offer the Dan Menu, designed to make ordering and eating Danish food easy for tourists and comprising a two-course meal for 75kr, while many more carry a fixed price (75–90kr) three-course lunch. You can also usually get a choice of three or four *smørrebrød* for about 75kr. Elsewhere, the American **burger** franchises are commonplace, as are **pizzerias**, many of which offer special deals such as all-you-can-eat-salad with a basic pizza for 45kr. You can also get a very ordinary self-service meat, fish or omelette lunch in a **supermarket cafeteria** for 40–75kr.

Dinner (*aftensmad*) presents as much choice as does lunch, but the cost is likely to be much higher, although many youth hostels serve filling evening meals for 45–50kr. For 80–100kr you can fill up in an **ethnic restaurant**, most commonly Chinese and Middle Eastern, many of which, besides à la carte dishes, have a help-yourself table. Sadly, the same **Danish restaurants** that are promising for lunch turn into expense-account affairs at night, although a few serve the 75kr Dan Menu into the evening.

■ Drink

Although you can buy booze much more cheaply from supermarkets, the most sociable **places to drink** are pubs and cafés, where the emphasis is on beer. There are also bars and *bodegas*, in which, as a very general rule, the mood tends to favour wines and spirits and the customers are a bit older. The cheapest beer is **draught beer** (*Fadøl*), half a litre of which costs 25–35kr. Draught is a touch weaker than **bottled beer**, which costs 25–30kr for a third of a litre, and is a great deal less potent than the **export beers** (*Guldøl* or *Eksport-Øl*) costing 30–35kr a bottle. The most common brands are *Carlsberg* and *Tuborg*; *Lys Pilsner* is a very low alcohol lager, more like a soft drink. Most international **wines and spirits** are widely available, a shot of the hard stuff costing 15–20kr in a bar, a glass of wine upwards of 15kr. You should also investigate the many varieties of the schnapps-like *Akvavit*, which Danes consume as eagerly as beer; a tasty relative is the hot and strong *Gammel Dansk Bitter Dram* – Akvavit-based but made with bitters and never drunk with meals.

Opening Hours and Holidays

Shop hours are Mon–Thurs 9am–5.30pm, Fri 9am–7/8pm, Sat 9am–1/2pm. All shops and banks are **closed** on the following days, when public transport and many museums run to Sunday schedules: Jan 1; Maundy Thursday; Good Friday; Easter Monday; Prayer Day (fourth Friday after Easter); Ascension (around mid-May); Whit Monday; the afternoon of June 5; Dec 24 (afternoon only); Dec 25 and Dec 26.

Emergencies

You're likely to have little cause to trouble the Danish **police**, as street crime and hassle is minimal in Denmark – but if you do, you'll find them helpful and almost certainly able to speak English. For prescriptions, doctors' consultations and dental work – but not hospital visits – you have to pay on the spot, but to get a full refund, take your receipt, E111 and passport to the local health office.

EMERGENCY NUMBERS
Ring ☎112 for fire, police or ambulance.

COPENHAGEN AND AROUND

COPENHAGEN, as any Dane will tell you, is no introduction to Denmark; indeed, a greater contrast with the sleepy provincialism of the rest of the country would be hard to find. Despite that, the city completely dominates Denmark: it is the seat of all the nation's institutions – politics, finance, the arts – and provides the driving force for the country's social reforms. Copenhagen is also easily Scandinavia's most affordable capital, and one of Europe's most user-friendly cities, small and welcoming, with a compact, strollable centre largely given over to pedestrians. In summer, especially, there's a varied range of lively street entertainment, while at night there's a plethora of cosy bars and an intimate club and live music network that can hardly be bettered. For daytime sights, the city has first-rate collections of Danish and international art, as well as a worthy batch of smaller museums.

There was no more than a tiny fishing settlement here until the twelfth century, when Bishop Absalon oversaw the building of a castle on the site of the present Christiansborg. The settlement's prosperity grew after Erik of Pomerania granted special privileges and imposed the Sound Toll on vessels passing through the Øresund, then under Danish control, which gave the expanding city tidy profits and enabled a self-confident trading centre to flourish. Following the demise of the Hanseatic ports, the city became the Baltic's principal harbour, earning the name København ("merchant's port"), and in 1443 it was made Danish capital. A century later, Christian IV began the building programme that was the basis of the modern city: up went Rosenborg Slot, Børsen, Rundetårnet, and the districts of Nyboder and Christianshavn; and, in 1669, Frederik III graced the city with its first royal palace, Amalienborg, for his queen, Sophie Amalie.

Arrival and information

However you get to Copenhagen you'll find yourself within easy reach of the centre. Trains pull into the **Central Station**, near Vesterbrogade, where there's an *InterRail Centre* (mid-June to late Sept daily 6.30am–midnight) downstairs with left-luggage lockers, showers (10kr), cooking facilities and a message board for rail pass holders. **Long-distance buses** from other parts of Denmark each stop a short bus or S-train ride from the centre: buses from Århus stop at Valby; from Aalborg at Ryparken Station on S-train line Ii, and those from Hantsholm on Hans Knudsen Plads. **Ferries** and catamarans from Norway and Sweden dock close to Nyhavn, a few minutes' walk from the inner city. **Planes** use Kastrup Airport, 8km from the city, and connect with the Central Station every fifteen minutes by *SAS* coach (daily 5.45am–9.45pm; 20min; 28kr), and with Rådhuspladsen by the slower but cheaper city bus #32.

For maps, general information and accommodation in hotels and hostels (booking fee 13kr), head for the **tourist office**, Bernstorffsgade 1 (May Mon–Fri 9am–5pm, Sat 9am–2pm, Sun 9am–1pm; June to mid-Sept daily 9am–6pm; mid-Sept to April Mon–Fri 9am–5pm, Sat 9am–noon; ☎33.11.13.25), across the road from the train station. They also sell the **Copenhagen Card**, valid for the entire metropolitan transport system (which includes much of eastern Zealand) and giving entry to virtually every museum in the area. A one-day card costs 120kr, those for two and three days 200kr and 250kr respectively.

Far better for youth and budget-oriented help is **Use-It**, centrally placed in the *Huset* complex at Rådhusstræde 13 (mid-June to mid-Sept daily 9am–7pm; Oct–May Mon–Fri 10am–4pm), which provides a full rundown on budget accommodation, eating, drinking and entertainment, will hold mail and store luggage, has a noticeboard offering lifts, and a day old *Guardian*; in summer it also issues a useful free newspaper called *Playtime*.

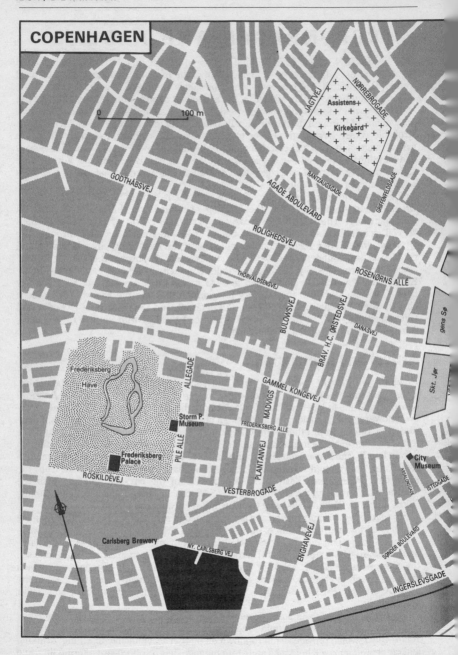

COPENHAGEN

0   100 m

JÄGTVEJ

NØRREBROGADE

Assistens+ Kirkegård

RANTZAUSGADE

GRIFFENFELDSGADE

GODTHÅBSVEJ

AGADE ÅBOULEVARD

ROLIGHEDSVEJ

ROSENØRNS ALLÉ

THORVALDSENSVEJ

BÜLOWSVEJ

BRAV. H.C. ØRSTEDSVEJ

DANASVEJ

Sct. Jør

Sterns Sø

Frederiksberg Have

ALLEGADE

GAMMEL KONGEVEJ

MADVIGS

Storm P. Museum

FREDERIKSBERG ALLÉ

PLANTANVEJ

PILE ALLÉ

Frederiksberg Palace

City Museum

RØSKILDEVEJ

VESTERBROGADE

ABSALONSGADE

ISTEDGADE

ENGHAVEVEJ

Carlsberg Brewery

NY. CARLSBERG VEJ

SØNDER BOULEVARD

INGERSLEVSGADE

City transport

An integrated network of **buses** and electric **S-trains** (*S-tog*) covers a zonal system over the whole of Copenhagen and the surrounding areas between 5am and 12.30am, after which a **night bus** (*Natbusserne*) system comes into operation. You can use *InterRail* or *Eurail* cards on the S-trains, but otherwise the best option after a Copenhagen Card is either a 2-zone (70kr) or a 3-zone (85kr) *Rabatkort*, which has ten stamps you cancel individually: one stamp on a 2-zone card gives unlimited transfers within one hour in two zones, one stamp on a 3-zone card lasts an hour and a half. Double stamping allows even longer journeys. Several people can use a *Rabatkort* simultaneously. For a single journey of less than an hour, use a *Grundbillet* (9.5kr), valid for unlimited transfers within two zones in that time. Tickets can be bought on board buses or at train stations and should be stamped when boarding the bus or in the machines on station platforms. A passenger without a valid ticket faces an instant fine of 500kr. **Route maps** cost 5kr from stations, but most free maps of the city include bus lines and a diagram of the S-train network. The basic **taxi** fare is 12kr plus 7.20kr per kilometre (9.60kr after 6pm and at weekends) – only worthwhile if several people are sharing; phone *Taxa* if you need a cab, or hail one in the street if it's showing the "Fri" sign.

Accommodation

Accommodation of all kinds is easy to come by in Copenhagen, and almost all of it is central. Only if you're going to be arriving late, or during July and August, is it necessary to book in advance. Most of the cheaper **hotels** are just outside the main centre, around Istedgade, a slightly seedy area on the far side of the train station, while there is also a good range of mid-priced hotels around Nyhavn, on the opposite side of the Indre By. Enquire at the tourist office early in the day and you may get a double room for as little as 300kr. Copenhagen has a great, though less central, selection of **hostel accommodation**, and space is only likely to be a problem in the peak summer months, when you should phone ahead or turn up as early as possible to be sure of a place.

Hostels

Bellahøj, Herbergsvejen 8 (☎31.28.97.15). Official hostel with large dorms, but more homely than its rivals, and simple to reach at fifteen minutes from the city centre on bus #2 (nightbus #902). Buses #8, #63 and #68 also stop close by. Open all year except Dec. No curfew. ②

City Public Hostel, Absalonsgade 8 (☎31.31.20.70). Only open May–Aug, but handily placed ten minutes' walk from the train station between Vesterbrogade and Istedgade. There's a noisy 60-bed dormitory on the lower floor, and less crowded conditions on other levels. No curfew. Buses #6 and #16 stop close by. ②

Copenhagen Hostel, Vejlands Allé 200 (☎31.52.29.08). Official hostel with fairly frugal and sometimes noisy 2- and 5-bed rooms. Get to it on bus #46 (daytime only), or take the C line S-train to Valby or Sjælør, then a #37 bus towards Holmens Bro, a half-hour journey. Open all year. No curfew. ②

Sleep-In, Per Henrik Lings Allé 6 (☎35.26.50.59). Open July–Aug, a vast hall divided into four-bedded compartments. Nice atmosphere, with a young staff and sporadic free gigs. Includes breakfast; sheets are 40kr if you don't have a sleeping bag. Ten minutes from the centre on S-train A, B or C, or by bus #1 towards Hellerup or #6 towards Ryvang. No curfew. ②

YWCA/Interpoint, Store Kannikestræde 19 (☎33.11.30.31). Fifteen minutes' walk from Central Station, with dorm beds for 50kr plus 25kr membership (breakfast 20kr). Open July to mid-Aug 8am–noon & 2.30–6pm & 7pm–12.30am. Mid-July to mid-Aug, there's a second *Interpoint*, a similar distance from the station at Valdermarsgade 15 (☎31.31.15.74), with the same opening hours and prices. ②

Hotels

Absalon Hotel, Helgolandsgade 19 (☎31.24.22.11). Clean and modern. ⑤

Ansgar Hotel, Colbjørnsensgade 29 (☎31.21.21.96). Compact and tidy, this place lowers its prices in high season. ⑥

Jørgensens Hotel, Rømersgade 11 (☎33.13.97.43). North of Istedgade on Isreals Plads, this is one of the cheapest hotels in town. Though not exclusively gay, it's popular with gay travellers; it also offers summer dorm accommodation at even cheaper prices. ③

Missionhotellet Nebo, Istedgade 6 (☎31.21.12.17). Small and friendly, and one of the best deals in this part of the city. ⑥

Sophie Amalie, Skt. Annæ Plads 21 (☎33.13.34.00). Large luxurious rooms right by the harbour. Good if you want to pamper yourself. ⑧

Hotel Viking, Bredgade 65 (☎33.12.45.50). Slightly faded, with an English bed and breakfast air, but quite serviceable. ④

Campsites

Absalon, 132 Korsdalsvej, Rødovre. Reasonable site about 9km to the southwest of the city and open all year. Take S-train line B to Brøndby-Øster.

Bellahøj, on Hvidkildevej, near the Bellahøj hostel. Central but grim, with long queues for the showers. Reached by bus #2. Open June–Aug.

Nærum on Ravnebakken. Quite a way from the centre but very pleasant. Take a train to Jægersborg, then private train (*InterRail* and *Eurail* not valid; *Copenhagen Card* valid) to Nærum. The site has cabins and is open mid-April to mid-Sept.

The City

Seeing Copenhagen is a doddle. Most of what you're likely to want to see can be found in the city's relatively small centre, between the long scythe of the harbour and a semi circular series of lakes. **Indre By** forms the city's inner core, an intricate maze of streets, squares and alleys. The main way into Indre By is from the buzzing open space of Rådhuspladsen, where the **Rådhus** (Mon–Fri 10am–3pm, guided tours at 3pm; 20kr) has an elegant main hall that retains many of its original turn-of-the-century features and a **bell tower** (tours at 10am, noon & 2pm; 10kr) that gives views over the city, though not madly impressive. More interesting is **Jens Olsen's World Clock** (Mon–Fri 10am–4pm, Sat 10am–1pm; 10kr), in a room close to the entrance, an astronomical timepiece which took 27 years to perfect and contains a 570,000-year calendar plotting moon and sun eclipses, solar time, local time and various planetary orbits – all with astounding accuracy.

The unbelievable thing about **Ripley's Believe It or Not** (daily 10am–9/11pm; 45kr) just across the road, is that people pay to see this continued modern-day freak show: avoid it. Beyond here, **Strøget** leads into the heart of the city, a series of streets lined by pricy stores and fast-food dives, whose appeal is in the walkers, roller-skaters and street entertainers who parade along it. The most active part is around Gammeltorv and Nytorv, two squares ("old" and "new") on either side of Strøget, where there's a morning fruit and vegetable market, jewellery and bric-a-brac stalls. A few minutes further on, the **Helligånds Kirke** (daily 11am–4pm) is one of the oldest churches in the city, founded in the fourteenth century and largely rebuilt from 1728 onwards. Its café and the art shows and exhibitions held inside provide a good excuse for a peek at the church's vaulted ceiling and its slender granite columns. The tobacco shop opposite, the **W.Ø. Larsens Tobaksmuseet** (Mon–Fri 9.30am–5pm, Sat 9am–1pm; free), has a briefly diverting clutter of vintage pipes and smoking accessories, plus paintings and drawings satirizing the rituals of smoking. At the end of Strøget, **Kongens Nytorv** is the city's largest square, with an equestrian statue of its creator, Christian V, in its centre and a couple of grandly ageing structures around two of its shallow angles, most notably **Charlottenborg** – finished in 1683, at the same time as the square itself, for a son of Frederik III. It was later sold to Queen Charlotte Amalie but since 1754 has been the home of the Royal Academy of Art, which uses some of the spacious rooms for decidedly eclectic art exhibitions.

There's more to see among the tangle of buildings and streets **west of Strøget**, not least the old university area, sometimes called the Latin Quarter, where the **Vor Frue Kirke** (Mon–Sat 9am–5pm, Sun noon–4.30pm), Copenhagen's cathedral, dates from just 1829, rising from the devastation caused by British bombardment in 1807. The weighty figure of Christ behind the altar and the solemn statues of the Apostles, some crafted by Bertel Thorvaldsen, others by his pupils, merit a quick call. Northeast, the **Rundetårnet** (Mon–Sat 10am–5/8pm, Sun noon–4/8pm; 12kr), whose summit is reached by a spiral ramp, was built by Christian IV as an observatory, and perhaps also to provide a vantage point for his subjects to admire his additions to the city. Legend has it that Tsar Peter the Great sped to the top on horseback in 1715, pursued by the Tsarina in a six-horse carriage. Close by, the **Musical History Museum**, just off Kultorvet at Åbenrå 30 (May–Sept daily except Thurs 1–4pm; 15kr), holds an impressive quantity of musical instruments and sound-making devices, spanning the globe and the last thousand years. Many musical recordings can be listened to through headphones, and guided tours take place every Wednesday at 11am. Over Nørre Voldgade, the **Workers Museum** at Rømmersgade 22 (Mon–Fri 10am–3pm, Sat & Sun 11am–4pm; Nov–June closed Mon; 25kr) is an engrossing guide to working-class life in Copenhagen from the Thirties to the Fifties using reconstructions and authentic period materials. You can walk down a bygone Copenhagen street complete with a tram and a shop window hawking the consumer durables of the day and continue, via a back yard where the washing hangs drying, through a printing works subsidized by the Marshall Plan and into a shop which sells an old-fashioned coffee and chicory blend by the cup.

North of Gothersgade

There's a profound change of mood once you cross **Gothersgade**, the road marking the northern perimeter of Indre By. The congenial alleyways and early medieval markers of the old city give way to long, broad streets and a number of proud, aristocratic structures. Running from Kongens Nytorv, a slender canal divides the two sides of **Nyhavn**, a picturesque canalside lined by eighteenth-century houses that was until recently frequented by docked sailors – who earned the area a racy reputation – but is now in the advanced stages of gentrification. Just north, the cobbled **Amalienborg Plads** focuses on a statue of Frederik V that was reputedly more expensive than the total construction cost of the four identical Rococo palaces which flank it – a mid-eighteenth-century group that introduces some welcome symmetry into the city's largely haphazard layout. Two serve as royal residences and there's a changing of the guard each day at noon when the monarch is at home. Between the square and the harbour are the lavish gardens of **Amaliehaven**, while in the opposite direction the great marble dome of **Frederikskirke**, also known as "Marmorkirken" (Mon–Fri 11am–3pm, Sat 11am–1pm, Sun noon–1pm; free guided tours Sat 11am), was modelled on St Peter's in Rome. It was begun in 1749 but because of its enormous cost remained unfinished until a century and a half later. The reward of joining a guided tour is the chance to climb to the whispering gallery and step out onto the rim of the dome itself. Further along Bredgade, at no. 62, the **Medical History Museum** (guided tours only, in English on Wed–Fri & Sun at 11am & 12.30pm) displays aborted foetuses, straitjackets, methods of syphilis treatment, amputated feet and a dissected head, while a little further on the German armoured car commandeered by Danes to bring news of the Nazi surrender marks the entrance to the **Museum of the Danish Resistance Movement** (May to mid-Sept Tues–Sat 10am–4pm, Sun 10am–5pm;

mid-Sept to April Tues–Sat 11am–3pm, Sun 11am–4pm; free), which records the growth of the organized response and has a special section on the youths from Aalborg who formed themselves into the "Churchill Club", as well as a small but moving collection of artworks and handicrafts by concentration camp inmates.

The road behind the museum crosses into the grounds of the **Kastellet** (daily 6am–sunset; free), a fortress built by Christian IV and expanded by his successors through the seventeenth century. It's now occupied by the Danish army and closed to the public, but on a nearby corner the **Little Mermaid** has, since its unveiling in 1913, been one of the city's most massive tourist targets, a bronze statue of a Hans Christian Andersen character, sculpted by Edvard Erichsen and paid for by the boss of the Carlsberg brewery. It's worth enduring the crowds for the more spectacular **Gefion Fountain**, a hundred yards away, which shows the goddess Gefion with her four sons, whom she's turned into oxen having been promised, in return, as much land as she can plough in a single night. The legend goes that she ploughed a chunk of Sweden, then picked up the piece of land (creating Lake Vänern) and tossed it into the sea – where it became Zealand.

Still north of Gothersgade, but away from the harbour across Store Kongensgade, lies **Nyboder**, a curious area of narrow streets lined with rows of compact yellow dwellings, originally built by Christian IV to encourage his sailors to live in the city. The area had at one time declined into a slum, but a recent vigorous overhaul has made the district increasingly sought-after. The oldest (and cutest) houses can be found along Skt. Pauls Gade; Baron Bolton's Court, tucked behind the corner of Gothersgade and Store Kongensgade, is a revamped precinct of eighteenth-century town houses holding shops and restaurants and hosting live jazz in summer. Across Sølvgade from Nyboder is the main entrance to **Rosenborg Slot** (June–Aug daily 10am–4pm; May, Sept & Oct daily 11am–3pm; sporadically in winter; 35kr), a Dutch Renaissance palace and one of the most elegant buildings bequeathed by Christian IV to the city. Though intended as a country residence, Rosenborg served as the main domicile of Christian IV (he died here in 1648) and, until the end of the nineteenth century, of the monarchs who succeeded him. The main building displays the rooms and furnishings used by the regal occupants, although the highlight is the downstairs treasury (separate entrance; hours as castle), which displays the rich accessories worn by Christian IV. Opposite the castle, marked by a few runic stones, is the **Geology Museum** (Tues–Sun 1–4pm; free), which has a great meteorite section and a microscopic fragment of moon rock brought back by an Apollo mission and presented by Richard Nixon to the Danish people in the name of "world peace". The neighbouring **Statens Museum for Kunst** (Tues–Sun 10am–4.30pm; 20kr) is a mammoth collection of art, with some minor Picassos and more major works by Matisse and Braque, Modigliani, Dürer and El Greco – although it's Emil Nolde, with his gross pieces showing bloated ravens, hunched figures and manic children, who manages to steal the show. Art fans will find greater things across the park behind the museum, in the **Den Hirschsprungske Samling** on Stockholmsgade (Wed–Sat 1–4pm, Sun 11am–4pm; 20kr), the collection of a late nineteenth-century tobacco baron covering twentieth-century Danish painters, including the Skagen artists.

Christiansborg

Christiansborg sits on the island of Slotsholmen, tenuously connected to Indre By by several short bridges, a mundane part of the city but historically an important one. It was here, in the twelfth century, that Bishop Absalon built the castle which instigated the city, and the drab royal palace completed in 1916 that now occupies the site is today primarily given over to government offices and the state parliament or **Folketing** (guided tours on the hour June to mid-Aug Mon–Fri & Sun 10am–4pm; mid-Aug to May Sun 10am–4pm; free). Close to the bus stop on Christiansborg Slotsplads is the doorway to the **Ruins under Christiansborg** (May–Sept daily 9.30am–3.30pm; Oct–April closed Mon & Sat; 12kr), where a staircase leads down to the remains of Absalon's original building – surprisingly absorbing, the mood enhanced by the semi-darkness and lack of external noise. In and around Christiansborg's courtyard there are a number of other, less captivating museums, including the dull **Royal Stables** (May–Sept Fri–Sun 2–4pm; Oct–April Sat & Sun 2–4pm; 10kr); a **Theatre Museum** (Wed 2–4pm, Sun noon–4pm; 20kr), housed in what was the eighteenth-century Court Theatre and displaying original costumes, set-models and the old dressing rooms and boxes; and an **Armoury Museum** (Tues–Sun 10am–4pm; 20kr), where you can view weaponry from Christian IV's arsenal and a host of crests and coats of arms.

On the far side of Slotsholmen, the **Thorvaldsens Museum** (Tues–Sun 10am–5pm; free) is the home of an enormous collection of work and memorabilia (and the body) of Denmark's most famous sculptor, who lived from 1770 to 1844. He's not a big name now outside Denmark, although in his day he enjoyed international renown and won commissions from all over Europe. Other than a selection of early works in the basement, the labels of the great, hulking statues read like a roll call of the famous and infamous: Vulcan, Adonis, Gutenberg, Pius VII and Maximilian; and the Christ Hall contains the huge casts of the Christ and Apostles statues that can be seen in Vor Frue Kirke. There's another major collection a short walk away over the Slotsholmen moat, in the **National Museum** (Tues–Sun 10am–5pm; 30kr), which has an ethnographic section in a separate wing at Ny Vestergade 10 but is really strongest on Danish history, with excellent displays on prehistory and Viking days – jewellery, sacrificial gifts, bones and even bodies, all remarkably well-preserved by Danish peat bogs.

Christianshavn and Christiania

From Christiansborg, a bridge crosses to **Christianshavn**, built by Christian IV as an autonomous new town in the early sixteenth century as housing for shipbuilding workers. It was given features more common to Dutch port towns of the time, even down to a small canal, and in parts the area is more redolent of Amsterdam than Copenhagen. On the corner of Store Søndervoldstræde, the **Danish Film Museum** (Mon, Tues, Thurs & Fri noon–4pm; until 9pm on Tues from Sept–May; free) has cameras, props and other remnants of an early film industry that before Hollywood and the talkies was among the world's best. Poking skywards on the other side of Torvegade – and clad in scaffolding until 1995 – is the blue and gold spire of **Vor Frelsers Kirke** (mid-March to Oct Mon–Sat 9am–3.30/4.30pm, Sun noon–3.30/4.30pm; rest of year Mon–Sat 10am–1:30pm, Sun noon–1.30pm; spire closed), which, with its helter-skelter-like outside staircase, was added to the otherwise plain church in the mid-eighteenth century, instantly becoming one of the more recognizable features on the city's horizon. Climbing the spire was – and hopefully will again be – fun, if a little scary with 400 steps in all, slanted and slippery and gradually becoming smaller.

A few streets from Vor Frelsers Kirke, **Christiania** is a former barracks area that was colonized by young and homeless people, finally declaring itself a "free city" in 1971 with a view to operating autonomously from Copenhagen proper, though it later became a refuge for petty crime. The place has been cleaned up since then and debate rages as to its future. The population is currently around 1000, swelled in summer by the curious and the sympathetic, although the residents ask people not to camp here, and tourists not to point cameras at the weirder-looking inhabitants. The craftshops and restaurants are, partly because of their refusal to pay any kind of tax, fairly cheap, and nearly all are good, with a couple of innovative music and performance art venues. For information, call in to *Galopperiet* (daily noon–5pm), to the left of the main entrance on the corner of Bødsmandsstræde and Prinsessegade.

Along Vesterbrogade

Hectic **Vesterbrogade** begins on the far side of Rådhuspladsen, and its first attraction is perhaps Copenhagen's most famous, the **Tivoli Gardens** (May to mid-Sept daily 10am to midnight; 38kr, 25kr before 1pm), whose opening each year on or around May 1 is taken to mark the beginning of summer. Throughout the season, the gardens feature fairground rides, fireworks, fountains, and a variety of nightly entertainment in the central arena which can include everything from acrobats and jugglers to the mid-Atlantic tones of various fixed-grin crooners. Naturally, it's overrated and overpriced, but an evening spent wandering among the revellers of all ages is an experience worth having – once. On the other side of Tietgensgade, the **Ny Carlsberg Glyptotek** (May–Aug Tues–Sun 10am–4pm; Sept–April Tues–Sat noon–3pm, Sun 10am–4pm; 15kr, free on Wed & Sun), which was opened in 1897 by the brewer Carl Jacobsen as a venue where the ordinary people of Copenhagen could see classical art exhibited in classical style, is Copenhagen's finest gallery, with a stirring array of Greek, Roman and Egyptian art and artefacts, as well as what is reckoned to be the biggest and best collection of Etruscan art outside Italy. There are, too, excellent examples of modern European art, including a complete collection of Degas casts made from the fragile working sculptures he left on his death, Manet's *Absinthe Drinker* and an antechamber with early work by Man Ray, some Chagall sketches and a Picasso plate.

The narrow streets laid out between Vesterbrogade and **Istedgade**, the other side of the train station, cradle the embers of Copenhagen's token red-light area, still gradually gaining a touch of respectability as growing numbers of students and immigrant families move into the area to take advantage of the low rents. You'll find a few pornography shops remaining, and the newer **Erotic Museum** (daily May–Sept 10am–9pm; Oct–April 11am/noon–6pm; 45kr), a mixture of titillating historical photos, sex toys and waxworks housed in a former brothel. At Vesterbrogade 59, the **City Museum** (May–Sept Tues–Sun 10am–4pm; Oct–April Tues–Sun 1–4pm; free) has reconstructed ramshackle house exteriors and tradesmen's signs from early Copenhagen and a large room recording the form Christian IV gave the city, as well as a room devoted to Søren Kierkegaard, filled with bits and bobs that form an intriguing footnote to the life of the nineteenth-century Danish writer and philosopher whose work many claim laid the foundations of existentialism. Further along Vesterbrogade, down Enghavevej and along Ny Carlsberg Vej, the tours of the **Carlsberg Brewery** (Mon–Fri 11am & 2pm; free) are well worth joining if only for the free booze provided at the end.

Eating and drinking

Whatever you feel like eating you'll find a wider choice and lower prices in Copenhagen than in any other Scandinavian capital. In the city centre, the areas around Kultorvet and along Studiestræde are loaded with great places to eat. Farther afield, Nørrebro across Peblinge Sø draws the trendy set and Vesterbrogade turns up a number of lower key places, better the further you venture. If you're **self-catering**, there are numerous *smørrebrød* outlets – *Smørrebrødskunsten*, on the corner of Magstræde at Rådhusstræde, and *Centrum Smørrebrød*, Vesterbrogade 6c, two of the most central. For more general food shopping, *Brugsen*, Axeltorv 2, and *Irma*, Vesterbrogade 1 and Borgergade 28, are cheaper than their counterparts on Strøget. An almost unchartable network of **cafés and bars** serving drinks and snacks covers Copenhagen. The best are in or close to Indre By, and it's no hardship to sample several on the same night, though bear in mind that on Fridays and Saturdays you'll probably need to queue.

Snacks and pizzerias

Alexander's Pizza House, Lille Kannikestræde 5. Does good all-you-can-eat deals for around 50kr.

Ambrosius, Niels Hemmingsensgade 32. A studenty café, good for lunch or just a drink.

Bar Bar Bar, Vesterbrogade 51. A stylish and relaxed place for a coffee, drink or light snack.

Café au Lait, Nørre Voldgade 27. Opposite the Nørreport S-train station, a pleasantly unflustered place for a coffee or snack.

Café Post Salut, 13 Rådhusstræde. Located in the *Huset* complex, this is a popular spot for breakfast from 20kr.

Italiano, Fiolstræde 2. Centrally placed and basic, selling pizzas from around 60kr.

Vagabondo's Cantina, Vesterbrogade 70. The most central of several branches of this dependable pizza chain, where hunger can be sated for less than 50kr.

Restaurants

Bali, Lille Kongensgade 4. Indonesian restaurant that does a good rice tafel for around 130kr.

Bananrepublikken A/S, Nørrebrogade 13. Ethnic foods with a modern Danish edge from around 100kr. See "Nightlife".

DSB Bistro, Banegårdspladsen 7. The city's best-value introduction to Danish food, with a massive all-you-can-eat spread for 125kr, or a smaller fish or cheese buffet for 48kr.

The Golden Temple, Blågådsgade 27. The best vegetarian Indian restaurant in the city, cheap and delicious. Bring your own booze.

Den Grønne Kælder, Klarebodene 10. A simple tiled-floor vegetarian eatery with a very filling *grøn platte* for 49kr. Mon–Sat until 9pm.

Hackenbusch, Vesterbrogade 124. Inexpensive and colourful café/bar with an inventive if short blackboard menu. Dishes (always one vegetarian) from 70kr. If this doesn't appeal, *Zugarbaby* and *Café Ludwiggen* across the road warrant checking out.

Koh I Nor, Vesterbrogade 33. A mix of Indian, Pakistani and Halal, worth hitting for the daily buffet (until 10pm), which costs 89kr.

Nyhavns Færgekro, Nyhavn 5. Unpretentious and thoroughly tasty traditional food, available either from the lunchtime fish-laden open table or the à la carte restaurant upstairs.

Pasta Basta, Valknesdorfsgade 22. Fish and meat pasta dishes, plus nine cold pasta bowls from which you can help yourself for 69kr. Open until 5am, this place is a favourite stop for late-night groovers.

Peder Ox, Gråbrødretorv 11. Especially worthwhile at lunchtime when you can get three hunks of *smørrebrød* for 78kr.

Rama, Bredgade 29. Top class Thai food; choose from set menus starting at 110kr.

Rust, Guldbergsgade 8. Fashionable bar and rock venue which also houses a good-value restaurant. 100kr buys two satisfying courses.

Spisehuset, Rådhusstræde 13. In the *Huset* building, with a varied and wholesome menu, including daily specials for 68–72kr.

Bars

Barcelona, Fælledvej 21. Chic and very much the place to be seen though you pay for the privilege.

Café Dan Turrell, Store Regnegade 3. Something of an institution with the artier student crowd and a fine place for a sociable tipple. Open 11am–2am.

Café Sommersko, Kronprinsensgade 6. Sizeable bar, crowded most nights, and with free live music on Sun afternoons.

Krasnapolsky, Vestergade 10. The Danish avant-garde art hanging on the wall reflects the trendsetting reputation of this ultra-modern watering hole. Tasty food too.

Peder Hvitfeldt, P. Hvitfeldtsstræde 15. Spit-and-sawdust place which is immensely popular. Come early if you want to sit down.

Universitetscaféen, Fiolstræde 2. A prime central location and long hours (until 5am).

Nightlife

The city is a pretty good place for **live music**. Major international names visit regularly and there are always plenty of minor gigs in cafés and bars, often free early in the week. You can get the latest on who's playing where by reading *Neon Guiden*, or *Gaffa* (free from music and record shops), or the monthly *Huset*, available from the *Huset* building at Rådhusstræde 13. If you get a craving for the dance floor, you'll find **discos** much like those in any major city, busy between midnight and 5am. Dress codes are fairly easy-going; drink prices are seldom hiked-up and admission is fairly cheap at 30–50kr.

Live music

Bananrepublikken A/S, Nørrebrogade 13. One of the best places to hear world music. See also "Restaurants".

Bar Bue, Rådhusstræde 13. Small and smoky, regularly showcasing the pick of Danish Indie bands, as well as decent discos on Fri & Sat.

Café Pavillonen, Fælledparken (near Borgmester Jensens Allé). Open-air venue for free Latin/jazz/rock concerts and sometimes movies. Barbecued food too.

Caféen Funke, Skt. Hans Torv. As the name suggests, a place to hear well-played funk, and often jazz too. Open Mon–Sat; free.

Kridthuset, Nørregade 1. Live music on weekends; Thurs nights Sixties jazz and soul.

Loppen, Bådsmansstrue 43, Christiania. Regular rock and jazz and performance artists.

The Melon, Løngangstæde 39. Late venue, its repertoire ranging from reggae to techno. 10pm–5am.

Montmartre, Nørregade 41. The city's major jazz venue, with both big names and local talent, and one of the city's better discos later on.

Musikcaféen, Rådhusstræde 13. The mainstream rock part of *Huset*, with regular live bands.

Pumpehuset, Studiestræde 52. A broad sweep of middle-strata rock, hip-hop and funk from Denmark and around the world about three times a month.

Discos

Annabell's, Lille Kongensgade 16. Comparatively upmarket but worth a fling on Fridays and Saturdays when there's a younger, brasher crowd.

U-matic, Vestergade 10. In the basement of the *Krasnapolsky* bar. With the trendiest sounds and the weirdest-dressed people, the nearest thing to a poseur's paradise in the city.

Woodstock, Vestergade 12. Pulls a large crowd with its predominantly Sixties and Seventies sounds.

Gay Copenhagen

Copenhagen has a lively **gay** scene, which includes a couple of hotels at which gays are especially welcome – *Jørgensen's*, Rømersgade 11 (☎33.13.97.43), and the *Hotel Windsor*, Frederiksborggade 30 (☎33.11.08.06). For **contacts and information**, the *National Organization for Gay Men and Women*, Knabrostræde 3 (☎33.13.19.48), offers information, a bookshop, disco and café. There's also a **gay switchboard** (☎33.13.01.12) and further information can be gleaned from *Hotside* magazine. As for **gay bars**, the *Amigo Bar*, Schønbergsgade 4, is frequented by gay men of all ages, while *Sebastian* draws a predominantly young trendy crowd. *Pan Club*, Knabrostræde 3, is part of the largest gay centre in the country and has a great disco. *After Dark*, Studiestræde 31, has a great bar and disco often featuring drag shows. The men-only *Metro* is open until very late in the same building. About the only primarily lesbian place is the café/bar *Babooshka* at Turesensgade 6.

Listings

Airlines *British Airways* Rådhuspladsen 16 (☎33.14.60.00); *SAS*, SAS Building, Hammerischgade 1–5 (☎33.15.48.77).

American Express Amagertorv 18 (☎33.12.23.01).

Books *The Book Trader*, Skindergade 23, has old and new books in English.

Car rental *Avis*, Kampmannsgade 1 (☎33.15.22.99); *Hertz*, Ved Vesterport 3 (☎33.12.77.00); *InterRent/Europcar*, Gyldenløvsgade 17 (☎33.11.62.00); *Budget*, Nyropsgade 6 (☎33.13.39.00).

Embassies *Australia*, Kristianiasgade 21 (☎35.26.22.44); *Canada*, Kristen Bernikowsgade 1 (☎33.12.22.99); *Great Britain*, Kastelsvej 40 (☎35.26.46.00); *Ireland*, Østerbanegard 21 (☎31.42.32.33); *Netherlands*, Toldbodgade 33 (☎33.15.62.93); *New Zealand* (use UK); *USA*, Dag Hammerskjölds Allé 24 (☎31.42.31.44).

Exchange The *Bank of Tivoli*, Vesterbrogade 3, is open noon–11pm between May and mid-Sept. Otherwise change money at Central Station (daily 7am–10pm).

Hospitals *Righsospitalet*, Blegdamsvej 9 (☎31.39.66.33); for a doctor (☎33.93.63.00; 9am–4pm).

Laundry Central ones are *Vascomat*, Borgergade 2, and *Møntvask*, Nansengade 39.

Left-luggage Lockers at Central Station (5.30am–1am; 20kr) and larger ones at *Use-It*.

Pharmacies 24-hour pharmacies: *Steno Apotek*, Vesterbrogade 6, and *Søndererbro Apotek*, Amagerbrogade 158.

Post office Main office at Tietgensgade 37 (Mon–Fri 10am–6pm, Sat 9am–1pm). Also at Central Station (Mon–Fri 8am–10pm, Sat 9am–4pm, Sun 10am–5pm).

Travel agent *DIS*, Skindergade 28 (☎33.11.00.44); *Kilroy Travels*, Skindergade 28 (☎33.11.00.44).

Women's movement Copenhagen's main women's centre is *Dannerhuset* (☎33.14.16.76), on Gyldenløvesgade, with a café (Mon–Wed 5–8pm) and bookshop (Mon–Fri 5–10.30pm).

Around Copenhagen: Dragør, Bakken and Louisiana

If the weather's good, take a trip to the Amager **beaches** on bus #12 along Øresundsvej. On the other side of the airport from the beaches lies the village of **DRAGØR**, an atmospheric cobbled fishing village which has good local history collections in the **Dragør Museum** (May–Sept Tues–Fri 2–5pm, Sat & Sun noon–6pm; 10kr), by the harbour, and the **Amager Museum** (June–Aug Wed–Sun noon–4pm; Sept–May Wed & Sun noon–4pm; 10kr), a few minutes' walk away. From the city, take buses #30 or #33, and pray that the construction hasn't yet started on the proposed Copenhagen–Malmö road and rail link planned to slice through the area. Failing that, if you're in the mood for an amusement park but can't afford Tivoli, venture out to **BAKKEN** (April–Aug daily 2pm–midnight; free), close to the Klampenborg stop at the end of line C on the S-train network. It's a lot more fun than its city counterpart, and besides the usual swings and rollercoasters offers pleasant walks through woods of oak and beech.

The most noteworthy attractions are a little further away from Copenhagen. A fifteen-minute walk from Runsted Kyst train station, the **Karen Blixen Museum** (May–Sept daily 10am–5pm; Oct–April Wed–Fri 1–4pm, Sat & Sun 11am–4pm; 30kr) is housed in what used to be the home of the authoress, who wrote under the name of Isak Dinesen. She gained wide international recognition when *Out of Africa*, her biographical account of running a coffee plantation in Kenya, was made into a Hollywood film. The house today is largely as she left it with the texts describing her life allowing some of her spirit and strength to shine through. In **HUMLEBÆK**, 10km further north, you'll find **Louisiana**, a modern art gallery (Mon–Fri 10am–5pm, Wed until 10pm, Sat & Sun 10am–6pm; 45kr), on the northern edge of the village at Gammel Strandvej 13, just a short walk from the train station. The museum's setting alone is worth the journey, as it harmoniously combines art, architecture and the natural landscape. The museum's American section, sited in the south corridor, stands out, with its collection of pieces by Edward Kienholz and Malcolm Morley's scintillatingly gross *Pacific Telephone Los Angeles Yellow Pages*. In addition you'll find some of Giacometti's strange gangly figures haunting a room of their own off the north corridor, and an equally affecting handful of sculptures by Max Ernst, squatting outside the windows, leering in.

ZEALAND

Even if you're only passing through Copenhagen, you should at least make a brief journey out to see how different the rest of Denmark can be. As home to the capital, **Zealand** is Denmark's most important and most visited region, and even if you don't like what you find, the swiftness of the metropolitan transport network, which covers almost half of the island, means you can be back in the capital in good time for an evening drink. North of Copenhagen, **Helsingør** is the place to cross by rail into Sweden and site of the renowned Kronborg Slot – an impressive fortification though quite unfairly stealing the spotlight from Frederiksborg Slot, at nearby **Hillerød**. West of Copenhagen, and on the main route to Funen, is **Roskilde**, a former capital with an extravagant cathedral that's still the last resting place for Danish monarchs, and with a gorgeous location on the Roskilde fjord – from where five Viking boats were salvaged and are now restored and displayed in a specially built museum. Off the S-train system, **Ringsted**, plumb in the heart of the island, is another one-time capital, a fact marked by the twelfth- and thirteenth-century royal tombs in its church.

Helsingør

First impressions of **HELSINGØR** are none too enticing, but away from the hustle of its terminals it is a quiet and likeable town. Its position on the four-kilometre strip of water linking the North Sea and the Baltic brought the town prosperity when, in 1429, the Sound Toll was imposed on passing vessels – an upturn only matched in magnitude by the severe decline following the abolition of the toll in the nineteenth century. Shipbuilding brought back some of the town's self-assurance, but today it's once again the whisker of water between Denmark and Sweden, and the ferries across it to Helsingborg, which account for most of Helsingør's through-traffic.

The town's other great tourist draw is **Kronborg Slot** (May–Sept daily 10.30am–5pm; April & Oct Tues–Sun 11am–4pm; Nov–March Tues–Sun 11am–3pm; 20kr, *Copenhagen Card* not valid), principally because of its literary associations as Elsinore Castle, whose ramparts Shakespeare's Prince Hamlet supposedly strode. Actually, the playwright never visited Helsingør, and his hero was based on Amleth, a tenth-century character shrouded in the fogs of Danish mythology and certainly predating the castle. Nevertheless, there is a thriving Hamlet souvenir business, and during the summer the numbers visiting the place make guided tours impossible. Frederik II instigated construction of the present castle in the sixteenth century on the site of an earlier fortress, commissioning the Dutch architects van Opbergen and van Paaschen, who took their ideas from the buildings of Antwerp. Various bits have been destroyed and rebuilt since, but it remains a grand affair, enhanced immeasurably by its setting and with an interior, particularly the royal chapel, that is spectacularly ornate. The body of Holger Danske, a hero from the legends of Charlemagne, is said to lie beneath the castle ready to wake again when Denmark needs him, although his tacky Viking-style statue in the labyrinthine cellars is well out of synch with their otherwise authentic decay. The castle also houses the national **Maritime Museum** (14kr, *Copenhagen Card* not valid), an uninteresting collection of model ships and nautical knick-knacks.

Moving away from Kronborg and the harbour area, Helsingør has a well-preserved **medieval quarter** which it's worth taking a walk through. **Stengade** is the main pedestrianized street, linked by a number of narrow alleyways to **Axeltorv**, the town's small market square and usually a good spot to linger over a beer. Near the corner of Stengade and Skt. Annagade, the spired **Skt. Olai's Kirke** is connected to the Karmeliter Klosteret, which contains the **Town Museum** (daily noon–4pm; 10kr). Formerly a hospital, the place prided itself on brain operations, and the unnerving tools of this craft are still here, together with diagrams of the corrective insertions made into patients' heads.

Practicalities

Buses stop outside the noisy combined **train station** and **ferry terminal**. You can pick up a free map from the **tourist office** (June–Aug Mon–Fri 9.30am–7pm, Sat 10am–6pm) across Strandgade from the train station, and you can also book **private rooms** for 250–300kr a double (25kr booking fee). The closest thing to a cheap **hotel** is *Hotel Skandia*, Bramstræde 1 (☎49.21.09.02; ⑦). More affordably, there is a **youth hostel** (☎49.21.16.40; ②) on the beach, a twenty-minute walk to the north along the coastal road (Ndr. Strandvej), or accessible on bus #340 from the station. The **campsite**, at Sundtoldvej 9, is closer to town and also by a beach, between the main road, Lappen, and the sea; take the private train (*Copenhagen Card* valid, rail passes not) to Marienlyst or bus #340. For **food**, *Kloster Caféen*, Skt. Annagade 35, is a prime lunchtime spot for its set menu and sizeable sandwiches; the well-named *Salat Cafeen*, Stengade 48, dishes up large plates for 45kr with fruit tarts to follow; or try the varied delights of *Færgegården*, Stengade 81b.

Two **ferry lines** make the twenty-minute crossing from Helsingør to Helsingborg in Sweden. The main one, and probably the best option, is the *Scandlines* boat leaving every 10–30 minutes around the clock from the main terminal by the train station and costing 30kr (rail passes valid, *Copenhagen Card* 50 percent discount). The cheaper crossing, although only by a few kroner, is with *Sundbusserne*, who operate small craft, often heavily buffeted by the choppy waters, every 15–30 minutes between 6am and 9pm for 27kr (*Copenhagen Card* 50 percent discount).

Hillerød

Half an hour by train from Helsingør and last stop on lines A and E of the S-train network from Copenhagen, **HILLERØD** has a castle which pushes the more famous Kronborg into second place: **Frederiksborg Slot** (daily May–Sept 10am–5pm; April & Oct 10am–4pm; Nov–March 11am–3pm; 30kr), which lies decorously across three small islands on an artificial lake. Buses #701, #702 and #703 run from the train station to the castle but walking only takes about twenty minutes, following the signs through town.

The castle used to be the home of Frederik II and birthplace of his son Christian IV. At the turn of the seventeenth century, under the auspices of Christian, rebuilding began in an unorthodox Dutch Renaissance style. It's the unusual aspects of the monarch's design – prolific use of towers and spires, pointed Gothic arches and flowery window ornamentation – which still stand out, despite the changes wrought by fire and restoration. Inside there's a museum of Danish history, largely funded by the Carlsberg brewery magnate Carl Jacobsen. It's a good idea to buy (25kr), or at least try and borrow, the illustrated guide to the museum, since without it the contents of the sixty-odd rooms are barely comprehensible. Many of the rooms are surprisingly free of furniture and household objects, and attention is drawn to the ranks of portraits along the walls – a motley crew of nobility, statesmen and royalty, who between them ruled and misruled Denmark for centuries. Two rooms deserve special mention: the exquisite chapel, where monarchs were annointed between 1671 and 1840, and the Great

Hall above, a reconstruction but still beautiful, bare but for the staggering wall and ceiling decorations – tapestries, wall-reliefs, portraits and a glistening black marble fireplace.

The **tourist office** at Slotsgade 52 (June–Aug Mon–Fri 9am–6pm, Sat 9am–5pm; Sept–May Mon–Fri 9am–3pm, Sat 10am–1pm) offers **private rooms** from 120kr per person (20kr booking fee). Few of Hillerød's **hotels** can match the prices you might find in Copenhagen, but if you're on a tight budget the town has a *YMCA*, Slotsgade 5 (☎42.26.01.89; ⑤). The only other budget accommodation is the **campsite**, open from Easter to mid-September, at Dyrskuepladsen, a kilometre from the centre.

Roskilde

There's very little between Copenhagen and the west Zealand coast in the way of things to explore, except for the ancient former Danish capital of **ROSKILDE**, less than half an hour by train from the capital. The arrival of Bishop Absalon in the twelfth century made the place the base of the Danish church, and as a consequence the national capital. Importance waned after the Reformation, and Roskilde came to function mainly as a market for the neighbouring rural communities – which it still is, as well as being dormitory territory for Copenhagen commuters. Its ancient centre is one of Denmark's most appealing – well worth a look on your way west to Odense.

The major pointer to the town's former status is the fabulous **Roskilde Domkirke** (May–Aug Mon–Sat 9am–4.45pm, Sun 12.30–4.45pm; Sept–April Mon–Fri 9/10am–2.45/4.45pm, Sat 11.30–2.45/4.45pm, Sun in Sept 12.30–3.45pm; 5kr), founded in 1170 and finished during the fourteenth century, although portions have been added since. The claustrophobic collection of coffins containing the regal remains of twenty kings and seventeen queens in four royal chapels is the main attraction, the most richly endowed chapel that of Christian IV, a previously austere resting place jazzed up in the early nineteenth century with bronze statues, wall-length frescoes and vast paintings of scenes from his reign. A striking contrast is provided by the simple red-brick chapel just outside the cathedral, where Frederik IX was laid in 1985 after interment against his wishes thirteen years earlier inside the cathedral.

From one end of the cathedral, a roofed passageway, the **Arch of Absalon**, feeds into the **Bishop's Palace**, housing the **Palace Collections** (daily May to mid-Sept 11am–4pm; mid-Sept to April Sat & Sun 1–3pm; 2kr), made up of paintings, furniture and other artefacts belonging to the wealthiest Roskilde families of the eighteenth and nineteenth centuries. In the same building is the **Museum of Contemporary Art** (Mon–Fri 11am–5pm, Sat & Sun noon–4pm), hosting high-standard temporary exhibitions, and a charming small sculpture garden.

The history of the town recorded in the **Roskilde Museum** at Skt. Ols Gade 18 (June–Aug daily 11am–5pm; Sept–May Mon–Sat 2–4pm, Sun 2–5pm; 5kr) is a little more enticing, with strong sections on medieval pottery and toys, although time is really better spent at the absorbing **Viking Ship Museum** (daily April–Oct 9am–5pm; Nov–March 10am–4pm; 28kr), in Strandengen on the banks of the fjord. Inside, five excellent specimens of Viking shipbuilding are proudly displayed: there's a deep sea trader, a merchant ship, a warship, a ferry and a longship, each one retrieved from the fjord where they had been sunk to block invading forces.

The gabled building near the Domkirke's main entrance houses the **tourist office** (April–Sept Mon–Fri 9am–5/7pm, Sat 9am–1/5pm, Sun in July & Aug 10am–2pm). If you decide to stay, there's a **campsite** on the wooded edge of the fjord 4km away – an appealing setting which makes it very crowded at peak times; it's open from April to September, and linked to the town centre by bus #602, Veddelev direction. The **youth hostel** is 4km away, 3km from the middle of Roskilde, at Hørhusene 61 (☎42.35.21.84; ②); buses #601 and #604 from the train station pass close by. Neither the hostel nor campsite are worth bothering with if you're here for the **Roskilde Festival**, one of the largest open-air rock events in Europe, attracting around seventy thousand people annually. The festival takes place over a weekend in early July and there's a special camping ground beside the festival site, to which shuttle buses run from the train station every ten minutes. For lunch, coffee or a game of backgammon, *Café Satchmo*, signposted off Algode, shouldn't be passed up.

FUNEN

Known as "the Garden of Denmark", partly for the lawn-like neatness of its fields, partly for the immense amounts of fruit and veg which come from them, **Funen** is the smaller of the two main Danish islands. The pastoral outlook of the place and the coastline draw many visitors, but its attractions are mainly low-profile cultural things, such as the various collections of the "Funen painters" and the birthplaces of writer Hans Christian Andersen and composer Carl Nielsen. **Odense**, Denmark's third city, is easily the island's main attraction. Close to this, the former fishing town of **Kerteminde** retains some faded charm, and is near the **Ladby Boat**, an important Viking relic.

Odense

ODENSE gained prominence in the early nineteenth century when the opening of the Odense canal linked the city to the sea and made it the major transit point for the produce of the island's farms. Nowadays it's a pleasant provincial town, with a large manufacturing sector hugging the canal bank on the northern side of the city, well out of sight of the compact old centre, which houses some fine museums and a surprisingly vigorous nightlife. Odense is also known, throughout Denmark at least, as the birthplace of Hans Christian Andersen, and, although it's all done quite discreetly, the fact is as celebrated as you might expect, souvenir shops and new hotels catering for travellers lured by the prospect of a romantic Andersen experience.

Arrival and accommodation

Long-distance **buses** and trains both terminate at the **train station**, a ten-minute walk from the city centre, where you'll find the **tourist office** (mid-June to Aug Mon–Sat 9am–7pm, Sun 11am–7pm; rest of year Mon–Fri 9am–5pm, Sat 10am–3pm) next to the bus station on the Vestergade side of the Rådhus. They sell the useful **Adventure Pass**, which for 70kr (35kr in winter) gets you into all of Odense's museums and gives unlimited travel on local buses for two days. The best bets for cheap **hotels** are the *Staldgården*, Rugårgsveg 8 (☎66.17.88.88), and the small *Kahema*, Dronningensgade 5 (☎66.12.28.21), which have doubles for 350–370kr. There's a **youth hostel** at Kragsbjergvej 121 (☎66.13.04.25) – take bus #61 or #62 south to Holluf Pile/Fraugade or Hjallese and get out along Munkebjergvej at the junction with Vissenbjergvej – and a *YWCA/InterRail Point* at Rødegårdsvej 91 (☎66.14.23.14). The closest **campsite** is at Odensevej 102, near the Funen Village, open late April to mid-September; take bus #41 from the Rådhus or station.

The Town

Save for an outlying museum, Odense is easily seen on foot, and you may as well start with the city's major collection: the **Hans Christian Andersen Museum** at Hans Jensen Stræde 37–45 (daily June–Aug 9am–6pm; April, May & Sept 10am–5pm; Oct–March 10am–3pm; 20kr), in the house where the writer was born in 1805. Oddly enough, Andersen was only really accepted in his own country towards the end of his life; his real admirers were abroad, which was perhaps why he travelled widely and often, and left Odense at the first opportunity. The son of a hard-up cobbler, Andersen had a rough upbringing in what was then one of the town's slum quarters, but few of the many less-than-fairy-tale aspects of Andersen's life are touched upon in the museum, although it is stuffed with intriguing items – bits of school reports, his certificate from Copenhagen University, early notes and manuscripts of his books, illustrations from the tales, and paraphernalia from his travels, including the piece of rope he carried to facilitate escape from hotel rooms in the event of fire. A separate gallery has headphones for listening to some of Andersen's best-known tales, and a sloppy slide-show.

The area around the museum, despite being all half-timbered houses and clean, car-free cobbled streets, lacks character; indeed, if Andersen was around he'd hardly recognize the neighbourhood, which is now one of Odense's most expensive. For far more realistic local history, head to **Møntergården**, a few streets away at Overgade 48–50 (daily 10am–4pm; 15kr), where there's an engrossing assemblage of artefacts dating from the city's earliest settlements to the Nazi occupation, plus an immense coin collection. There's more about Andersen at Monkemollestræde 3–5, between Skt. Knud Plads and Klosterbakken, in the tiny **Hans Christian Andersen's Childhood Home** (daily April–Aug 10am–5pm; Sept–March noon–3pm; 5kr), where Andersen lived from 1807 to 1819. More interesting, though, is the nearby **Skt. Knud's Domkirke** (mid-May to mid-Sept Mon–Sat 10am–5pm; June–Aug also Sun 11.30am–3.30pm; rest of year Mon–Fri 10am–4pm, Sat 10am–noon), whose crypt holds one of the most unusual and ancient finds Denmark has to offer – the skeleton of Knud II (King Canute of England). Knud was slain in 1086 by Jutish farmers, angry at the taxes he imposed on them, and laid to rest here in 1101, miracles and other events of procceding years resulting in his canonization. Close to Knud's is another coffin, thought to hold the remains of Knud's brother, Benedict; displayed alongside is the fading, but impressive, Byzantium-style silk tapestry sent as a shroud by Knud's widow, Edele. As for the cathedral itself, it's the only example of pure Gothic church architecture in the country, set off by a finely detailed sixteenth-century wooden altarpiece that's rightly regarded as one of the greatest works of the Lübeck master, Claus Berg.

The **Art Museum of Funen** situated at Jernbanegade 13 (daily 10am–4pm, Wed also 7–10pm; 15kr), just a few minutes' walk away, will give you a good idea of the region's importance to the Danish art world during the late nineteenth century, when a number of Funen-based painters abandoned portraiture for impressionistic landscapes and studies recording the lives of the peasantry. The collection contains some stirring works by Nordic greats, among them Vilhelm Hammershøi, P.S. Krøyer, Michael and Anne Ancher, and H.A. Benedekilke's enormously emotive *The Cry*.

A short walk to the east, at Claus Bergs Gade 11, the **Carl Nielsen Museum** is Odense's newest museum (daily 10am–4pm, Thurs until 8pm; 15kr). Though remembered in Denmark mostly for his popular songs, it was Nielsen's opera scores, choral pieces and symphonies which established him as a major international composer. Born in a village just outside Odense, Nielsen claimed Funen and the island's tuneful dialect as his inspiration, and in the museum you can listen to some of his work on headphones, including excerpts from his major pieces and the polka he wrote when still a child. The actual exhibits, detailing Nielsen's life and achievements, are enlivened by the accomplished sculptures of his wife, Anne Marie, many of them early studies for her equestrian statue of Christian IX, now outside the Royal Stables in Copenhagen.

South of the centre of Odense at Sejerskovvej 20 there's the **Funen Village** (June–Aug daily 10am–7.30pm; April, May & Sept to mid-Oct daily 10am–4pm; mid-Oct to March Sat & Sun 10am–4pm; 20kr), an open-air museum made up of a reconstructed nineteenth-century country village of original buildings taken from all over Funen, painstakingly reassembled and refurnished. In summer, some of the old trades are revived in the former workshops and crafthouses, and free shows are reegularly staged at the open-air theatre. Though often crowded, it's well worth a call, and you should watch out for the village-brewed beer – handed out free on special occasions. Buses #21 and #22 run to the village from the city centre, or do what the locals do and hire a boat to get there.

Eating, drinking and nightlife

There are plenty of **restaurants and snack bars** in the city centre, and some good bargains to be had. *Eventyr*, Overgade 18, is a reliable spot for sandwiches, while for more substantial eating, the best and oldest of the many pizzerias is *Pizzeria Ristorante Italiano*, Vesterbrogade 9. You might also try the Thai food of the *Asia House*, Østre Stationsvej 40, or the Mediterranean specialities of *1001 Nats*, Vindegade 57. For evening **drinking**, the no-frills *On-off*, Ny Vstergade 19, is a place for cheap draught beer; otherwise drop into the fashionable *Café Biografen*, one of many eating and drinking spots in Brandts Passage. At its entrance, *Cuckoo's Nest* is a favourite for drinks or a light snack before moving around the corner to *Cotton Club*, Pantheonsgade 5c, for swing to fusion jazz until early morning. The art centre *Badstuen*, Østre Stationsvej 26, has a café that occasionally hosts raucous live bands, as does *Rytmeposten* across the road at Østre Stationsvej 27a. There's bluesier fare to be found in the likeably scruffy *Musikkælderen*, Dronningsgengade 2B, and easier rock at *Kong Græs*, Asylgade 7.

Kerteminde

A half-hour's bus ride (#890) northeast from Odense lies **KERTEMINDE**, a sailing and holiday centre that has a prettily preserved nucleus of shops and houses around its fifteenth-century Skt. Laurentius Kirke. On Strandgade, the **Town Museum** (daily 10am–4pm; free) has five reconstructed craft workshops and a collection of fishing equipment gathered locally. On a grander note, Kerteminde was home to the "birdman of Funen", the painter Johannes Larsen, and a fairly lengthy stroll around the marina and along Møllebakken brings you to his one-time house, now the **Johannes Larsen Museum** (March–May, Sept & Oct Tues–Sun 10am–4pm; June–Aug Tues–Sun 10am–5pm; 25kr). During the late nineteenth century, Larsen produced etchings of rural locales and ornithology. The house is kept as it was when Larsen lived there, with his furnishings, knick-knacks, many of his canvases, and, in the dining room, his astonishing wall-paintings.

The **tourist office** is opposite the Skt. Laurentius Kirke, across a small alleyway (mid-June to Aug Mon–Sat 9am–5pm; Sept to mid-June Mon–Fri 9am–4pm, Sat 9am–noon). The only low-cost accommodation option is the **youth hostel** at Skovvej 46 (☎65.32.39.29; ②), a twenty-minute walk from the centre (cross the Kerteminde Fjord by the road bridge and take the first major road left and immediately right). There's also a **campsite** with cabins, open late April to August, at Hindsholmvej 80, not far from the Larsen Museum, on the main road along the seafront – a thirty-minute walk from the centre.

About 4km from Kerteminde, along the banks of the fjord at Vikingvej 123, is the **Ladby Boat** (May–Sept Tues–Sun 10am–6pm; Oct–April Tues–Sun 10am–3pm; 15kr), a vessel dredged up from the fjord and found to be the burial place of a Viking chieftain. The craft, along with the weapons, hunting dogs and horses which accompanied the deceased on his journey to Valhalla, is kept in a small purpose-built museum, and is well worth the trip out. Motorboats run out here in summer, although it's a pleasant enough walk or cycle.

JUTLAND

Long ago, the people of **Jutland**, the Jutes, were a separate tribe from the more warlike Danes who occupied the eastern islands. In pagan times, the peninsula had its own rulers and much power, and it was here that the legendary ninth-century monarch Harald Bluetooth began the process that turned the two tribes into a unified Christian nation. By the dawn of the Viking era, however, the battling Danes had spread west, absorbing the Jutes, and real power gradually shifted towards Zealand. This is where it has largely stayed, making unhurried lifestyles and rural calm the overriding impression of Jutland for most visitors; indeed, its distance from Copenhagen makes it perhaps the most distinct and interesting area in the country. In the south, Schleswig is a territory long battled over by Denmark and Germany, though beyond the immaculately restored town of **Ribe** it holds little of abiding interest. **Esbjerg**, further north, is dull too, but as a major ferry port you might well pass through. The old military stronghold of **Fredericia** is worth a brief stop before reaching **Århus** halfway up the eastern coast, Jutland's main urban centre and Denmark's second city. Further inland, the landscape is the country's most dramatic – stark heather-clad moors, dense forests and swooping gorges. Ancient **Viborg** is the best base for this, from where you can head north to vibrant **Aalborg**, on the southern bank of the Limfjord, which cuts deep into Jutland this far north – across which the landscape reaches a crescendo of storm-lashed savagery around **Skagen**, on the very tip of the peninsula. **Frederikshavn**, on the way, is the port for boats to Norway and Sweden.

Esbjerg

The only large city in southern Jutland is **ESBJERG**, home to the world's biggest fish oil factory, the stench from which matches the gloom of what must rank as Denmark's least appealing place. If this is your first view of the country, bear in mind it's an entirely untypical one: Esbjerg is a baby by Danish standards, purpose-built as a deep-water harbour during the nineteenth century.

The best way to get a sense of the city's newness is by dropping into the **Esbjerg Museum** (Tues–Sun 10am–4pm; 20kr) at Nørregade 25, with its new gallery devoted to amber along with a display recalling the so-called "American period" from the 1890s, when Esbjerg's rapid growth matched that of the US gold rush towns. Also within easy reach of the centre is the **Museum of Art** (daily 10am–4pm; 20kr), although its modern Danish artworks are fairly limp affairs, and you'd do better to visit art displays in the recently refurbished **Watertower** next door (same hours), or the **Museum of Printing** (daily 10am–4pm; 15kr), at Borgergade 6, which has an entertaining assortment of hand-, foot- and steam-operated presses as well as more recent printing machines. With more time to spare, take a bus (#21, #23 or #30 from Skolegade) to the large **Fisheries and Maritime Museum and Sealarium** on Tarphagevej (daily July & Aug 10am–8pm; mid-May to June & Sept 10am–6pm; Oct to mid-May 10am–4pm; 35kr), where you can cast an eye over the vestiges of the early Esbjerg fishing fleet and clamber around inside a spooky wartime bunker built by the Germans. The Sealarium is part of a seal research centre, which often rescues pups marooned on sandbanks, then feeds them for the public's entertainment at 11am & 2.30pm daily. A multi-entry ticket available at the above museums gets you into them all for 40kr.

The Esbjerg **tourist office** is at Skolegade 33 (Mon–Fri 9am–5pm, Sat 9am–noon; until 5pm from mid-June to Aug), on a corner of the main square. The **passenger harbour** is a twenty-minute well-signposted walk from the city centre, and trains to and from Copenhagen connect directly with the ferries, using the harbour station. The main **train station** is at the end of Skolegade. If you're staying, the cheapest **hotel** is the

Sømandshjemmet at Auktionsgade 3 (☎75.12.06.88; ④), by the harbour. The **youth hostel** is at Gammel Vardevej 80 (☎75.12.42.58; ②), 25 minutes' walk, or buses #1, #9, #11, #12 or #31, from Skolegade. Adjacent to the hostel is a **campsite** with cabins, open from mid-May to mid-September. The Esbjerg **eating** options are fairly limited if you're on a tight budget, although you can get a decent two-course lunch for around 55kr at the *Park Hotel* on Torvegade, around the corner from the tourist office, and a *dagens ret* for 35kr at *Hus Ingeborg* at 22 Kongensgade. If filling your stomach is the primary concern, then *Pizza World*, 13 Smedegade, offers as much pizza and salad as you can eat for 39kr at lunchtimes. A good place to **drink** is *Café Christian IX*, overlooking Torvet, or *Café Biographen*, Finsensgade 1, which has live music late in the week.

Ribe

Just under an hour south by train from Esbjerg, the exquisitely preserved town of **RIBE** was once a major stopover point for pilgrims on their way to Rome, as well as a significant port, until thwarted by the dual blows of the Reformation and the sanding-up of the harbour. Since then, not much appears to have changed. The surrounding marshlands, which have prevented the development of any large-scale industry, and a long-standing preservation programme, have enabled Ribe to keep the appearance and size of medieval times, and, with its wealth of minor sights around every corner, highlighted in the *Denmark's Oldest Town* leaflet, it is a delight to wander in.

From Ribe's train station, Dagmarsgade leads to Torvet and the towering **Domkirke** (May–Sept Mon–Sat 10am–5/6pm, Sun noon–5/6pm; Oct–April Mon–Sat 11am–3pm, Sun 1–3pm; 5kr; tours in summer Mon–Fri 11.30am–12.30pm; 20kr), begun around 1150, though only the "Cat's Head Door" on the south side remains from the original construction and the church's interior is not as spectacular as either its size or long history might suggest – though you can normally climb the red-brick tower and peer out over the town. Behind the cathedral, the **Weis' Stue** is a tiny inn built around 1600, from which, at 10pm each evening between May and mid-September and 8pm from June to August, the **Nightwatchman of Ribe** makes his rounds – a tourist throwback to the days when Danish towns were patrolled by guards looking for unattended candles. The watchman, dressed in a replica of the original uniform and carrying an original morning-star pike and lantern (the sharp tip doubling as a weapon), walks the narrow alleys of Ribe singing songs written by Hans Adolf Brorson (bishop of Ribe in the mid-eighteenth century, whose statue is outside the cathedral), and talking about the town's history while stopping at points of interest. It's free and can be fun.

The **tourist office** (mid-June to Aug Mon–Fri 9am–5.30pm, Sat 9am–5pm, Sun 10am–1pm; Sept to mid-June Mon–Fri 9/9.30am–4.30/5pm, Sat 10am–1pm) is behind the cathedral, opposite the Weis' Stue. If you stick around for the nightwatchman's tour, you'll probably need to spend the night. There's a **youth hostel** (☎75.42.06.20; ②), closed December and January, on the opposite side of the river from Skibbroen: cross the river bridge and turn left into Sct. Peders Gade. Failing that, there are several moderately-priced places and the *Weis' Stue* (75.42.37.00; ⑤) opposite the atmospheric *Hotel Dagmar* (☎75.42.00.33; ⑧), whose cellar bar is the best and most crowded spot for an **evening drink**. A daytime and evening alternative with food and excellent coffee is *Café Nicolaj* next to the art gallery on Sct. Nicolaj Gade. The nearest **campsite** is 2km from Ribe, along Farupvej (bus #771): it has cabins and is open all year.

Fredericia

FREDERICIA – junction of all the rail routes in east Jutland and those connecting the peninsula with Funen – has one of the oddest histories (and layouts) in Denmark. It was founded in 1650 by Frederik III, who envisaged a strategically placed reserve capital and a base from which to defend Jutland. Three nearby villages were demolished and their inhabitants forced to assist in the building of the new town. Military criteria resulted in wide streets that followed a strict grid system and low buildings enclosed by high earthen ramparts, making the town invisible to approaching armies. The train age made Fredericia a transport centre and its harbour expanded as a consequence. But it still retains a soldiering air, full of memorials to heroes and victories, and is the venue of the only military tattoo in Denmark.

The twenty-minute walk from the **train station** along Vesterbrogade toward the town centre takes you past the most impressive section of the old ramparts. They stretch for 4km and rise 15m above the streets, and walking along the top gives a good view of the layout of the town. But it's the **Landsoldaten** statue, opposite Princes Port, which best exemplifies the local spirit. The bronze figure holds a rifle in its left hand, a sprig of leaves in the right, and its left foot rests on a captured cannon. The inscription on the statue reads "6 Juli 1849", the day the town's battalion made a momentous sortie against German troops in the first Schleswig war – an anniversary celebrated as **Fredericia Day**. The downside of the battle was the 500 Danes who were killed and lie in a mass grave in the grounds of **Trinitatis Kirke** in Kongensgade. Predictably, 300 years of armed conflict also form the core of the displays at the **Fredericia Museum**, Jernbanegade 10 (mid-June to mid-Aug daily 11am–5pm; rest of year Tues–Sun noon–4pm; 10kr), along with local house interiors from the seventeenth and eighteenth centuries and a dreary selection of archeological finds.

Unless you want to laze on Fredericia's fine **beaches**, which begin at the eastern end of the ramparts, there's little reason to hang around very long. If you do want to stay, however, there's a **youth hostel** at Skovløbervænget 9 (☎75.92.12.87; ②), 2km from the train station (bus #3 from the centre). Alternatively, use the **campsite**, open April to October, on the Vejle fjord, adjacent to a public beach. You can get other information from the **tourist office** (mid-June to Aug Mon–Fri 9am–6pm, Sat 9am–5pm; Sept to mid-June Mon–Fri 9am–5pm, Sat 10am–1pm) on the corner of Dalegade and Jyllandsgade.

Århus

Geographically at the heart of the country and often regarded as Denmark's cultural capital, ÅRHUS typifies all that's good about Danish cities: it's small enough to get to know in a few hours, yet big and lively enough to fill both days and nights. Despite Viking-era origins, the city's present-day prosperity is due to its long, sheltered bay, on which the first harbour was constructed during the fifteenth century, and the more recent advent of railways, which made Århus a nationally important trade and transport centre. Easily reached by train from all the country's bigger towns, and at one end of the only direct ferry link between Jutland and Zealand, Århus also receives non-stop flights from London. There's certainly no better place for a first taste of Denmark.

Arrival and accommodation

Trains, **buses** and **ferries** all stop on the southern edge of the city centre, a short walk from the **tourist office** in Park Allé (late June–Sept daily 9am–7pm; Oct–late June Mon–Fri 9.30am–4.30pm, Sat 10am–1pm), on the ground floor of the city's Rådhus. **Airport buses** from Tirstrup connect regularly with the train station (50min; 50kr). **Getting around** is best done on foot: the city centre is compact and you'll seldom need to use the **buses** unless you're venturing out to the beaches or woods on the outskirts. If you do, the transport system divides into four zones: one and two cover all the central area, three and four reach into the country. The basic ticket costs 12.50kr from machines on board and is valid for any number of journeys during the time stamped on it (usually two hours). If you're around for several days, it's best to buy either a **tourist**

ticket, which costs 45kr for 24 hours in all four zones, or a **multi-ride ticket**, which can be used nine times and costs 70kr. These tickets can be bought at newsstands, campsites and shops displaying the Århus Sporveje sign.

With the closure of a couple of old favourites, only two reasonably-priced central **hotels** remain: Eriksens Hotel Garni, at Banegårdsgade 6 (☎86.13.62.96; ⑤), the most welcoming, and the less central Hotel Windsor, 1 Skolebakken 13 (☎86.12.23.00; ⑤) down by the harbour. Also in the centre, at Fredericks Allé 20, next to the concert hall, is the Århus Summer Sleep-in (late June to Aug; ②) with beds in school classrooms. The Århus **youth hostel**, Marienlundsvej 10 (☎86.16.72.98; ②) is rather out on a limb, though is at least close to a beach – a four-kilometre ride north on bus #1, #6, #9 or #16 from Park Allé. Of a number of **campsites**, the two most useful are Blommehaven, overlooking the bay 6km south of the city centre, open late April to mid-September and reached on bus #6 or #19; and Århus Nord, which has cabins and is open all year – accessible by bus #117 or #118 from the bus station.

The City

Århus divides into two clearly defined parts: the old section, close to the cathedral, a tight cluster of medieval streets, and, surrounding this, a less characterful modern sector. **Søndergade** is the city's main street, a pedestrianized strip that leads down into Bispetorvet and the old centre, the streets of which form a web around the **Domkirke** (Mon–Sat May–Sept 9.30am–4pm; Oct–April 10am–3pm), a massive if plain Gothic church, most of which is a fifteenth-century rebuilding after the original twelfth-century structure was destroyed by fire. At the eastern end, the altarpiece is a grand triptych by the noted Bernt Notke, one of few pre-Reformation survivors. Look also at the painted glass window behind the altar, the work of the Norwegian Emmanuel Vigeland (brother of Gustav). The area around the cathedral is a leisurely district of browsable shops and enticing cafés. On Clements Torv, across the road from the cathedral inside Unibank, the **Viking Museum** (Mon–Fri 9.30am–4pm, Thurs until 6pm; free) displays Viking finds, including sections of the original ramparts and some Viking craftsmen's tools, alongside some informative accounts of early Århus. Close by, at Domkirkeplads 5, the **Women's Museum** (Tues–Sun 10am–4/5pm; 10kr) stages temporary exhibitions on many aspects of women's lives and lifestyles past and present. West along Vestergade, the thirteenth-century **Vor Frue Kirke** (May–Aug Mon–Fri 10am–4pm, Sat 10am–2pm; Sept–April Mon–Fri 10am–2pm, Sat 10am–noon) is actually the site of three churches, most notable of which is the atmospheric eleventh-century crypt church, discovered beneath several centuries-worth of rubbish during restoration work on the main church in the 1950s. Look in, also, at the main church, for Claus Berg's detailed altarpiece, and, through the cloister remaining from the pre-Reformation monastery, now an old folks' home, for the medieval frescoes inside the third church, which depict local working people rather than Biblical scenes.

If you've visited the tourist office, you've already been inside the least interesting section of one of the modern city's major sights, the **Århus Rådhus**, a controversial structure built in the 1940s. You're free to walk in and look for yourself, but it's best to take a guided tour costing 4kr and conducted in English at 4pm on weekdays during the summer. Above the entrance hangs Hagedorn Olsen's huge mural, A Human Society, symbolically depicting the city emerging from the last war. In the council chamber, the lamps appear to hang suspended in mid-air (in fact they're held by almost invisible threads), and the shape of the council leader's chair is a distinctive curvy form mirrored in numerous smaller features throughout the building, notably the ashtrays in the lifts – though many of these have been pilfered by tourists. Perhaps most interesting of all, however, are the walls of the small civic room, covered by the intricate floral designs of the artist Albert Naur: the work took place under the Nazi occupation and in it Naur concealed various allied insignia. Finally, a lift (late June to early Sept noon & 2pm; 5kr, but included in Rådhus tour) climbs to the bell tower and a view over the city and across the bay.

It's a short walk from here to the city's best-known attraction, **Den Gamle By**, on Viborgvej (daily June–Aug 9am–6pm; April, May, Sept & Oct 10am–4/5pm; Nov–Mar 11am–3pm; 30–40kr), an open-air museum of traditional Danish life, with sixty-odd half-timbered houses from all over the country, dismantled and moved here piece by piece. Many of the craftsmen's buildings are used for their original purpose, the overall aim of the place being to give an impression of an old Danish market town, something it does very effectively. Fans of Danish art may well prefer to visit the **Århus Art Museum** (Tues–Sun 10am–5pm; 30kr) in Vennelystparken, a little way north, with works from the late eighteenth-century to the modern day, including the radiant canvases of Asger Jorn and Richard Mortensen, and Bjørn Nørgaard's sculptured version of Christian IV's tomb: the original, in Roskilde Cathedral, is stacked with riches; this one features a coffee cup, an egg and a ballpoint pen.

The Outskirts

On Sundays Århus resembles a ghost town, with most locals spending the day in the parks or beaches on the city's outskirts. The closest **beaches** are just north of the city at **Riis Skov**, easily reached with buses #6, #9 or #16. Otherwise, the **Marselisborg Skov** is the city's largest park, home to the **Marselisborg Slot**, summer residence of the Danish royals, the landscaped grounds of which can be visited when the monarch isn't staying. Further east paths run down to rarely crowded pebbly beaches, and, near the junction of Ørnerdevej and Thormsøllervej, to the **Dyrehaven** or Deer Park. A few kilometres further on, the **Moesgård Prehistoric Museum** (May to mid-Sept daily 10am–5pm; rest of year Tues–Sun 10am–4pm; 25kr), reached direct on bus #6, details Danish civilizations from the Stone Age onwards with copious finds and easy-to-follow illustrations. Its most notable exhibit is the "Grauballe Man", a skeleton dated 80 BC discovered to the west of Århus in a peat bog and thus amazingly well preserved; it was even possible to discover what the deceased had eaten for breakfast on the day of death. From the museum, a "prehistoric tramway" runs 3km to the sea, past a scattering of reassembled prehistoric dwellings, monuments and burial places. If you don't have the energy for any more walking, you can take a #19 bus back to the city from here; the stop is a hundred metres to the north.

Eating, drinking and nightlife

If cash is tight, or you're stocking up for a **picnic**, use the *Special Smørrebrød* outlet at Sønder Allé 2, or the late opening supermarket (8am–midnight) at the train station. Cruising the old town cafés and restaurants will turn up plenty of **lunchtime specials** for around 50kr; for instance *Mackie's Pizza*, 9 Skt. Clemens Torv, and around the corner on Skolegade *Pind's Café* at no. 11 which often looks shut but does excellent *smørrebrød*. *Roma*, Frederiksgade 78, is about the best pizzeria in the cheaper price range; if you have a bit more money, try *Italia*, at Åboulevarden 9. Equally good value are the Mediterranean specialities of *Kasba*, at Vestergade 50, and *Kif Kif Gallorant*, Mejlegade 41, and the highly-rated vegetarian dinners at *Den Grønne Gren*, Vestergade 7.

Århus is the only place in Denmark with a **nightlife** to match that of Copenhagen. The city has particularly wonderful **bars**, many situated in the streets close to the cathedral, including the movie-themed *Casablanca*, at Rosensgade 12, the *Carlton*, Rosensgade 23, *Englen* and *Kindrødt* on Studsgade, and *Café Eifel* at Store Torv 11, which stays open very late. The cream of Danish and international **rock** acts can be found at *Huset*, Vester Allé 15, with its restaurant and cinema; more run-of-the-mill bands at *Fatter Eskil*, Skolegade 25, and *Kulturgyngen*, Fronthuset, Mejlgade 53. *Blitz*, Klostergade 34, currently hosts the hottest club scene, while the leading **jazz** venue is the smoky, atmospheric pub *Bent J*, at Nørre Allé 66.

Listings

Airlines *SAS* ☎86.13.12.88; for domestic ☎86.13.12.11.

Car rental *Avis*, Jens Baggesens Vej 88c (☎86.16.10.99); *InterRent/Europcar*, Fredensgade 17 (☎86.13.23.33).

Hospitals Århus Kommunehospital, on Nørrebrogade. Doctor on ☎86.20.10.22 (4pm–8am) for a fee of 300kr, payable in cash only.

Pharmacy 24-hour pharmacy, *Løve Apoteket*, Store Torv 5 (☎86.12.00.22).

Police Århus Politization, Ridderstræde (☎86.13.30.00).

Post office On Banegårdpladsen, by the station (Mon–Fri 9am–5.30pm, Sat 9am–noon).

Viborg

For a long time at the junction of the major roads across Jutland, **VIBORG** was once one of the most important communities in the country. From Knud in 1027 to Christian V in 1655, all Danish kings were crowned here, and until the early nineteenth century the town was the seat of a provincial assembly. As the national administrative axis shifted towards Zealand, however, so Viborg's importance waned, and although it still has the high court of West Denmark, it's now primarily a market town for the local farming community.

The twin towers of the **Domkirke** (Mon–Fri 8/9am–4/5pm, Sat 9.30am–12.30pm) are the most visible feature of the compact town centre, and the most compelling reminder of Viborg's former glories, with an interior dominated by the brilliant frescoes of Joakim Skovgaard, an artist commemorated by the **Skovgaard Museum** (daily May–Sept 10am–5pm; Oct–April 1.30–5pm; free), inside the former Rådhus across Gammel Torv, which has a good selection of Skovgaard's paintings – although they can't fail to be anti-climactic after the works in the cathedral. For a broader perspective of Viborg's past, keep an hour spare for exploring the **District Museum** on the northern side of Hjultorvet between Vestergade and Skt. Mathias Gade (daily June–Aug 11am–5pm; Sept–May Tues–Fri 2–5pm, Sat & Sun 11am–5pm; 10kr), which has everything from prehistoric artefacts to clothes, furniture and household appliances.

The **tourist office** on Nytorv (April–Sept Mon–Fri 9am–5pm, Sat 9am–12.30/5pm; Oct–March Mon–Fri 8am–4pm, Sat 9.30am–12.30pm) can supply a handy map for exploring old Viborg and advise on **accommodation**. The best (and often reduced) rates in town are at *Palads Hotel*, 5 Sct. Mathias Gade (☎86.62.37.00; ③), or there's a **youth hostel** (☎86.67.17.81; ②) and a **campsite** with cabins, both 2km across the lake from the town centre, along Vinkelvej (bus #707).

Aalborg

The main city of north Jutland and the fourth largest in the whole country, **AALBORG**, hugging the southern bank of the Limfjord, is the most obvious place to spend a night or two before venturing into the wilder countryside beyond. It's the main transport terminus for the region, and boasts a well-preserved old centre, much of which dates from Aalborg's seventeenth-century trading heyday, an era perhaps best exemplified by the **Jens Bangs Stenhus** which stands opposite the tourist office, a grandiose five storeys in the Dutch Renaissance style, which has constantly functioned as a pharmacy since it was built. Jens Bang himself was the wealthiest merchant in the city but he was not popular with the governing elite, who conspired to keep him off the local council. The host of goblin-like figures carved on the walls is alleged to represent the councillors of the time, while another figure, said to be Bang himself, pokes out his tongue towards the former Rådhus next door. The commercial roots of the city are further evidenced by the collection of portraits of the town's merchants that hang inside the **Budolfi Domkirke** (Mon–Fri 9am–3pm, Sat 9am–noon), behind: a small but elegant specimen of sixteenth-century Gothic, built on the site of an eleventh-century wooden church, from which a few tombs remain, embedded in the walls close to the altar. Outside, across the square, the **Aalborg Historical Museum** at Aldgade 48 (Tues–Sun 10am–5pm; 10kr, Tues free) has a dramatic skeleton of a forty-year-old woman who died around 400 AD, preserved by a peat bog – though much of the rest of its displays fairly routine, apart from an impressive glasswork collection. Behind here, just off **Gammel Torv**, the fifteenth-century **Monastery of the Holy Ghost** can be viewed by way of daily guided tours (late June to Aug Mon–Fri 2pm; 20kr), which take in the monks' refectory, kept largely unchanged since the last monk left, and the small Friar's room, the only part of the monastery in which nuns (from the adjoining nunnery) were permitted. Indeed, this was one of the few monasteries where monks and nuns were allowed any contact at all, a fact which accounts for the reported hauntings of the Friar's room – reputedly by the ghost of a nun who got too friendly with a monk, and as a punishment was buried alive in a basement column. Most interesting, however, are the frescoes which cover the entire ceiling of the chapel.

On the other side of Østerå, the sixteenth-century **Aalborghus** is worth visiting for a trip round its severely gloomy **dungeon** (April–Sept Mon–Fri 8am–3.30pm; free). Outside the centre of town, the **North Jutland Art Museum** located on Kong Christians Allé (July & Aug daily 10am–5pm; Sept–May Tues–Sun 10am–5pm; 20kr), close to the junction with Vesterbro (bus #14 or a fifteen-minute walk), and housed in a building designed by the Finnish architect Alvar Aalto, is one of the country's better modern art collections, featuring, alongside numerous Danish contributions, works by Max Ernst, Andy Warhol, Le Corbusier and Claes Oldenburg. After leaving the museum, you can get a grand view over the city and the Limfjord by ascending the **Aalborg Tower** (April–Sept daily 10am–5/7pm; 15kr), on the hill just behind. Two kilometres west of the centre, the **Aalborg Shipping and Naval Museum**, Vestrefjordvej 81 (May–Aug daily 10am–6pm; March, April & Sept–Dec Wed, Sat & Sun 10am–4pm; 30kr) recalls the city's time as an important shipbuilding port. The highlight is inspecting the tight working and living conditions in "Springeren", the 54-metre-long submarine which now forms the museum's centrepiece.

Practicalities

The **tourist office** is centrally placed at Østerå 8 (mid-June to mid-Aug Mon–Fri 9am–7pm, Sat 9am–2pm, Sun 10am–1pm; rest of year Mon–Fri 9am–5pm, Sat 9am–4pm), and sells the *Aalborg Pass* (40kr), valid for three days and giving free public transport and free or reduced entry to most sights. The three cheapest **hotels** are the *Aalborg Sømandshjem*, Østerbro 27 (☎98.12.19.00; ⑤), the *Hotel Hafnia*, J.F. Kennedys Plads (☎98.13.19.00; ⑤), and *Missionshotellet Krogen*, Skibstedsvej 4 (☎98.12.17.05; ⑤). There's a large **youth hostel** (☎98.11.60.44; ②), 3km west of the town on the Limfjord bank beside the marina – take bus #1C or #8 from the centre to the end of its route – and, about 300m away, a **campsite**, *Strandparken*, open from mid-May to September. For a little more adventure, catch the half-hourly ferry (11kr) from near the campsite to Egholm, an island in Limfjord with free camping under open-sided shelters. In pursuit of **food** and **drink**, almost everybody heads for Jomfru Ane Gade, a small street close to the harbour between Bispensgade and Borgergade, on which a number of restaurants advertise daily specials: the most reliable are *Fyrtøjet*, at no. 19, and *Regensens*, no. 16, both of which generally have three-course lunches for 50–70kr. If it's Saturday, make a beeline for *Fru Jensen* at no. 13, where the herring buffet costs just 10kr and there is **live music** in the evenings. For a quieter time, try the cellar bar of the Jens Bangs Stenhus.

Frederikshavn

FREDERIKSHAVN is neither pretty nor particularly interesting, and as a ferry port it's usually full of Swedes and Norwegians taking full advantage of Denmark's liberal boozing laws. But the town is virtually unavoidable if you're heading north, being at the end of the rail route from Aalborg. If you've an international ferry to meet at Hirtshals, change to the private train (*InterRail* 50 percent reduction, *Eurail* not valid) at Hjørring.

If you have half an hour to spare, visit the squat white tower, **Krudttårnet** (April–Oct daily 10am–5pm; 10kr), near the station, which has maps detailing the harbour's seventeenth-century fortifications and a collection of military paraphernalia from the seventeenth to the nineteenth centuries. With more time, take bus #1 or #2 to Møllehuset and walk on through Bangsboparken to the **Bangsbo-Museet** (April–Oct daily 10am–5pm; Nov–March closed Mon; 20kr), where displays chart the development of Frederikshavn from the 1600s, alongside the grotesque but engrossing "Collection of Human Hairwork", and an assortment of maritime articles, distinguished only by the twelfth-century Ellingå Ship and an exhibition covering the German occupation during World War II and the rise of the Danish resistance movement.

Buses and **trains** into Frederikshavn both stop at the train station, a short walk along Skippergade and Denmarksgade from the town centre. Some continue to the **ferry terminal** near Havnepladsen, also close to the centre where *Stena Line* ferries leave for Oslo, and boats (*InterRail* 50 percent reduction) and the cheaper and much quicker sea catamarans make for Gothenburg. The **tourist office** is close by at Brotorvet 1, on the corner of Rådhus Allé and Havnepladsen (mid-June to mid-Aug Mon–Sat 8.30am–8.30pm, Sun 11am–8.30pm; April to mid-June & mid-Aug to Oct Mon–Fri 9am–4pm, Sat 9am–2pm; Nov–March Mon–Fri 9am–4pm). If you're forced to stay, the cheapest **hotels** are both central: *Discount Logi Teglgården*, Teglgårdsvej 3 (☎98.42.04.44; ④), and *Sømandshjemmet* at Tordenskjoldsgade 15b (☎98.42.09.77; ⑤). There's a **youth hostel** at Buhlsvej 6 (☎98.42.14.75; ②), 1500m from the train station, and a cabin-equipped **campsite**, *Nordstrand*, at Apholmenvej 40, 3km north of the centre off Nordre Strandvej, open April to September.

Skagen

If you have the option, skip Frederikshavn altogether in favour of **SKAGEN**, 40km north, which perches almost at the very top of Jutland amid a desolate landscape of heather-topped sand dunes. It can be reached by private bus or train (*Eurail* not valid, *InterRail* 50 percent reduction on both) roughly once an hour. The bus is the best choice if you're planning to stay at the Skagen youth hostel, as it stops outside.

Sunlight seems to gain extra brightness as it bounces off the two seas which collide off Skagen's coast, something which attracted the **Skagen artists** in the late nineteenth century, who arrived in the small fishing community during 1873 and 1874 and often met in the bar of *Brøndum's Hotel*, off Brøndumsvej, the grounds of which now house the **Skagen Museum** (June, July & Aug daily 10am–6pm; May & Sept daily 10am–5pm; April & Oct Tues–Sun 11am–4pm; Nov–March Wed–Fri 1–4pm, Sat 11am–4pm, Sun 11am–3pm; 25kr). This comprises the most comprehensive collection of the artists' work and is an impressive place, not least because so many of the canvases depict local scenes, using the town's strong natural light to capture subtleties of colour. The hotel owner's stepsister, Anna, herself a skilful painter, married one of the group's leading lights, Michael Ancher, and a few strides away, at Markvej 2, the **Anchers' Hus** (May–Sept daily 10am–5/6pm; Oct daily 11am–3pm; Nov–April Sat & Sun 11am–3pm; 25kr) was their home. This has been restored with the intention of evoking the atmosphere of their time – which, through an assortment of squeezed tubes of paint, sketches, paintings, piles of canvases, books and ornaments, it does remarkably well.

Less essential is **Drachmann's Hus** at Hans Baghsvej 21 on the junction with Skt. Laurentii Vej (June to mid-Sept daily 10am–5pm; 15kr), where another Skagen artist, Holger Drachmann, lived from 1902. Inside the house is a large collection of his paintings and sketchbooks, although it was for his lyrical poems, at the forefront of the Danish neo-Romantic movement, that he was best known.

The arrival and subsequent success of the artists made Skagen fashionable, and the town continues to be a popular holiday destination. But it still bears many marks of its tough past as a fishing community, the history of which is excellently documented in **Skagen Fortidsminder** on P.K. Nielsensvej, a fifteen-minute walk south along Skt. Laurentii Vej from the centre (daily May–Sept 10am–5pm; Oct, Nov, March & April 10am–4pm; 20kr). The museum examines local fishing techniques in its main displays and has reconstructions of the houses of both rich fishermen and their far poorer employees. Amid the dunes south of town, a further twenty minutes' walk along Skt. Laurentii Vej, Damstedvej and Gammel Kirkesti, is **Den Tilsandede Kirke**, or "the Buried Church" (June–Aug 11am–5pm; 7kr), basically the tower of a fourteenth-century church that was assaulted by vicious sandstorms during the eighteenth century. Still under the sands are the original church floor and cemetery. Although part of the tower is open to the public, the great fascination is simply looking at the thing from outside, and comprehending the incredible severity of the storms. The forces of nature can be further appreciated at **Grenen**, a lighthouse and restaurant 4km north of Skagen (hourly bus #79), along Skt. Laurentii Vej, Fyrvej and the beach, the actual meeting point of two seas – the Kattegat and Skagerrak – the spectacle of their clashing waves a powerful draw. On the way back, spare a thought for Holger Drachmann, a man so enchanted by the thrashing seas that he chose to be buried in a dune close to them. His tomb is signposted from the car park.

Practicalities

In Skagen, the combined **bus** and **train station** is on Skt. Laurentii Vej, and plays host to the **tourist office** (July & Aug Mon–Sat 9am–5.30pm, Sun 11am–2pm; Sept–May Mon–Fri 9am–4pm, Sat 10am–1pm; ☎98.44.13.77) where you can book a room from 100kr or the summer-only sleep-in for 75kr, though it is best to book ahead. Otherwise, for its artistic associations, *Brøndum's Hotel*, Anchervej 3 (☎98.44.15.55; ⑨), is by far the most atmospheric spot to stay, but book well ahead in summer. A little cheaper is *Sømandshjem*, Østre Strandvej 2 (☎98.44.21.10; ⑤), which also serves up bargain meals. The **youth hostel**, open from mid-March to October, is at Højensvej 32 in Gammel Skagen (☎98.44.13.56; ②), 3km west of Skagen (the only bus service there is the #78 to Frederikshavn). Of a number of **campsites**, the most accessible are *Grenen*, to the north along Fyrvej, which has cabins, and *Poul Eeg's*, on Batterivej, left off Oddenvej just before the town centre; both are open April to August.

travel details

Trains

Copenhagen to: Aalborg (every 2hr; 6hr 40min); Århus (12 daily; 5hr); Esbjerg (9 daily; 5hr); Helsingør (30 daily; 50min); Odense (25 daily; 3hr); Ringsted (20 daily; 55min); Roskilde (25 daily; 26min).

Århus to: Aalborg (hourly; 1hr 15min–1hr 40min); Frederikshavn (every 2hr; 3hr); Viborg (every 30min; 1hr).

Esbjerg to: Århus (hourly, change at Fredericia; 3hr 15min); Fredericia (25 daily; 1hr–1hr 10min); Ribe (hourly or better; 36min).

Fredericia to: Århus (25 daily; 1hr 22min).

Frederikshavn to: Aalborg (23 daily; 1hr–1hr 15min); Skagen (12 daily; 50min).

Helsingør to: Hillerød (hourly or better; 30min).

Odense to: Århus (30 daily; 2hr); Esbjerg (30 daily; 2hr); Nyborg (32 daily, linking with the *DSB* ferry to Korsør; 19min).

Roskilde to: Kalundborg (hourly, connects with ferry to Jutland; 1hr 15min); Korsør (25 daily, connects with ferry to Funen; 54min).

Buses

Copenhagen to: Aalborg (2 daily; 6hr); Århus (2 daily; 4hr 45min); Hantsholm (1 daily; 8hr 45min); Helsingør (30 daily; 1hr).

Århus to: Copenhagen (2–3 daily; 4hr 30min).

Frederikshavn to: Skagen (8 daily; 1hr).

Kerteminde to: Nyborg (17 daily; 33min).

Odense to: Kerteminde (42 daily; 30min); Nyborg (14 daily; 1hr 5min).

Ferries

Hundested to: Grenå (3 daily in summer; 2hr 40min).

Kalundborg to: Århus (2–8 daily; 3hr).

Korsør to: Nyborg (19–30 daily; 1hr).

CHAPTER 6

FINLAND

0   250 km

NORWAY

SWEDEN

FINLAND

RUSSIA

Arctic Circle   Rovaniemi

Tornio

Oulu

Kajaani

Vaasa   Kuopio

Jyäskylä   Joensuu

Savonlinna

Tampere   To St Petersburg

Åland   Turku   Pörvoo

To St Petersburg

HELSINKI

To   To
Stockholm   Tallinn

Introduction

Mainland Scandinavia's most culturally isolated and least understood country, **Finland** has been independent only since 1917, having been ruled for hundreds of years by imperial powers: first the Swedes and then the Tsarist Russians. Much of its history involves a struggle simply for recognition and survival, and it's not surprising that modern-day Finns have a well-developed sense of their own culture, manifest in the widely popular Golden Age paintings of Gallen-Kallela and others, the music of Sibelius, the National Romantic style of architecture, and the deeply ingrained values of rural life. These qualities are traditionally best exemplified by the small but significant proportion of Finns who come from Karelia, a large tract of land now scythed in two by the Finnish–Soviet border that was historically a homeland distinct from Finland and Russia.

Mainly flat and punctuated by huge forests and lakes, you'll need to travel around a lot to appreciate Finland's wide regional variations. **The South** contains the least dramatic scenery, but the capital, **Helsinki**, more than compensates, with its brilliant architecture and superb collections of national history and art. Stretching from the Soviet border in the east to the industrial city of **Tampere**, the vast waters of the **Lake Region** provide a natural means of transport for the timber industry – indeed, water here is a more common sight than land. Towns lie on narrow ridges between lakes, giving even major manufacturing centres green and easily accessible surrounds. North of here, Finland ranges from the flat western coast of **Ostrobothnia** to the thickly forested heartland of **Kainuu** and gradually rising fells of **Lappland**, home to Finland's most alluring terrain – and the *Same*, the semi-nomadic reindeer herders found all over northern Scandinavia. Furthermore, with the freeing-up of travel restrictions to Russia and especially Estonia, Helsinki has become a base for trips to Tallinn, St Petersburg and the former Finnish town of Viipuri now just inside Russia.

Information and Maps

Most towns have some sort of **tourist office**, with free maps and information, and which sometimes book accommodation. In summer they open every day, usually for long hours in more popular centres; in winter opening hours will be much reduced, if they open at all. The best general **map** of Finland is the *Daily Telegraph* one.

Money and Banks

Finland comes with a reputation for high expense. This is largely deserved though low inflation during the last couple of years and a devalued currency have brought travelling costs down below those of Norway and Sweden. Finnish **currency** is the *markka* (plural *markkaa*), which divides into 100 *penniä*. Notes are 10mk, 50mk, 100mk, 500mk and 1000mk; coins are 1mk, 5mk, 10p and 50p. Travellers' cheques and currency can be changed at most **banks** (Mon–Fri 9.15am–4.15pm); the charge is usually 15mk, though several people changing money together need only pay the commission charge once, and the rare *Forex* charge no commission at all. You can also change money at hotels, but normally at a much worse rate. Some banks have exchange desks at transport terminals which open to meet international arrivals. *Solo* cash machines give *Visa* (but not *MasterCard*) cash advances up to 1000mk at time.

Communications

In general, communications in Finland are dependable and quick, although in the far north and parts of the east minor delays arise due to geographical remoteness. You can buy stamps from a **post office** (normally open Mon–Fri 9am–5pm), from the street stands or *R-kioski*, and at some hotels: 2.90mk to Europe, 3.40mk to the rest of the world

An out-of-order **public phone** is virtually unheard of in Finland, although many of them, widely found on streets and at transport centres, have a dilapidated look. The minimum cost of a **local call** is 2mk. Phones take 1mk and 5mk coins, which run out rapidly, so have a supply of small change to hand. Increasingly, *Nonstop* card phones can be found taking 30, 50, 70 and 100mk. Cards are available at sites listed on the phone, usually nearby ticket offices, the post office or R-kiosks (minimum call charge 5mk). **International calls** are cheapest between 10pm and 8am. The operator numbers are ☎020 for domestic calls and ☎92020 for international calls. The international access code is 980.

Getting Around

You'll have few headaches getting around the more populated parts of Finland. The chief forms of public transport are trains, backed up, particularly on east–west journeys, by long-distance coaches. For the most part trains and buses integrate well, and you'll only need to plan with care when travelling through the remoter areas of the far north and east.

■ Trains and buses

The swiftest land link between Finland's major cities is invariably **trains**, operated by the national company, *VR*. Large, comfortable express trains (and a growing number of super-smooth Inter-City and *EP* or special express trains) serve the principal **north–south** routes several times a day. Elsewhere, especially on east–west hauls through sparsely populated regions, rail services tend to be skeletal and trains are often tiny one- or two-carriage affairs. The Arctic North is not served by trains at all.

InterRail and *Eurail* passes are valid, as is the *Nordturist* pass. Available from *NSR Travel*, 21–24 Cockspur Street, London SW1Y 5DA, and throughout Scandinavia, this pass costs £189/$300 (£140/$220 for under-26s), and gives you 21 days' unlimited travel in the four main Scandinavian countries, plus free travel or large discounts on many ferry crossings and bus journeys. *NSR Travel* also sells the *Scandrail* pass, costing £93/$150 for 4 days travel in 15, £151/$240 for 9 days out of 21 and £217/$350 for 21 days travel out 30, which is again valid throughout Scandinavia.

If you don't have one of these and are planning a lot of travelling, get a **Finnrail Pass** before arriving in Finland from either the Finnish Tourist Board or a travel agent. This costs 470mk (around £55) for 8 days, 730mk (£85) for 15 days, and 920mk (£110) for 22 days. The pass is valid for travel on the entire rail network. Ordinary **fares** are steep, although one-way tickets are valid for eight days, returns for a month and you can break your journey once in each direction, provided the ticket is stamped at the station where you stop and the total distance covered is over 75km. If there are three or more of you travelling together, group tickets, available from a train station or travel agent, can cut fares by at least twenty

percent. **Seat reservations** (compulsory on *EP* and *IC* trains), costing 15mk (25mk on *ICs*), are a good idea át weekends and holidays. **Sleeping berths** are also available on a number of routes, for 60mk sharing a 3-berth, 100mk sharing a twin. The complete **timetable** (*Suomen Kulku-neuvot*) of Finnish rail, bus, ferry and air routes costs 70mk from bookstores and kiosks, though the *Taskuaikataulu* booklet (5mk) from any tourist office or station covers the major connections.

Buses – run by local private companies but with a common ticket system – cover the whole country, and are often quicker and more frequent than trains over the shorter east–west hops. **Fares** are approximately 49mk for 100km, 167mk for a 400km journey. All types of ticket can be purchased at a bus station or at most travel agents; only ordinary one-way tickets can be bought when boarding the coach. Of **discount tickets** available, return fares are ten percent less than two singles, three or more people travelling 80km or more qualify for a **group reduction** of twenty percent; holders of *YIEE/FIYTO* cards (but not *ISIC* cards) get a thirty percent reduction on trips of similar length. A 10mk supplement is charged on express buses. **Students** can also buy a bus travel discount card for 25mk, giving 35–50 percent reductions on journeys of 75km or more. If you're going to travel a lot by bus, get a **Coach Holiday Ticket**, which gives 1000km of coach travel over any two-week period for 300mk, from any long-distance bus station. The free bus **timetable**, *Suomen Pikavuorot*, available at coach stations, lists all the routes in the country.

■ Driving and hitching

If you **bring your own car** to Finland, it's advisable (though not compulsory) to have a Green Card as proof of insurance. If you are involved in an **accident**, report it at once to the Finnish Motor Insurer's Bureau, Bulevardi 28, 00120 Helsinki (☎90/19251). Though **roads** are generally good there can be problems with melting snows, usually during April and May in the south and during June in the far north. The speed limit is 80kph, except where signposted otherwise, and on motorways, where it's 100kph. Other rules of the road include using headlights when driving outside built-up areas and the compulsory wearing of seatbelts by drivers and all passengers; as elsewhere in Scandinavia, there are severe penalties for drunk driving. **Car hire** is extremely expensive, from 165 to 300mk per day, plus 1.90–3.30mk per km. You need a valid driving licence, at least a year's driving experience, and to be aged at least 19–23, depending on the company.

Hitching is generally easy, and sometimes the quickest means of transport between two spots. Finland's large student population has helped accustom drivers to the practice, and you shouldn't have to wait too long for a ride.

Accommodation

You'll always be able to find some kind of accommodation in Finland to suit you. Prices, however, are high, and only by being aware of special offers will you be able to sleep well on a budget.

■ Hotels

Finnish **hotels** normally come with all the facilities: TV, phone and private bathroom are standard fixtures and breakfast is invariably included in the price. Costs can be formidable – frequently in excess of 500mk for a double – but planning ahead and taking advantage of various discount schemes and summer reductions can cut prices to around 300mk. Expense can also be trimmed under the *Finncheque* system, available outside Finland from the Finnish Tourist Board or a specialist travel agent, which offers an unlimited number of vouchers costing 250mk each per person, entitling two holders to a double room in hotels in participating chains between June and August – though there's often a surcharge of 75mk in more expensive hotels. The downmarket *Scanhotel* chain also offers a year-round fifty percent discount to holders of *ISIC* cards, lowering their prices to 120–160mk for a double, though the chain doesn't cover much of the country. In many towns you'll also find **tourist hotels** (*matkustajakoti*), a more basic type of hotel usually charging 150–250mk per person, although

they are often full during summer. **Summer hotels** (*kesähotelli*) are another possibility, basically accommodation in student blocks, from June to the end of August. Bookable in Finland through travel agents, they cost around 200mk per person.

■ Youth hostels

Often the cheapest option is one of the 150-odd **youth hostels** (*retkeilymaja*), though it's essential to book ahead between June and August and many hostels aren't open outside these months in any case. Hostels have been divided into three **grades**: the fairly rare two-star hostels (30–55mk per person) have basic washing and cooking facilities with beds in dormitories; three-star hostels (45–70mk) have showers, cooking facilities, serve meals – at least breakfast – and have a number of four-bedded rooms; four-star hostels, or "Finnhostels", are often identical to summer hotels, with two- and four-bedded rooms only, breakfast and bedding supplied, and prices of 55–145mk. Non-members of the *IYHF* face a 15mk supplement per night. Sleeping bags are not permitted, so bring a sheet sleeping bag: bedlinen can be hired but is expensive. The Finnish YHA's guide, *Suomen Retkeilymajat*, giving details of hostel categories is available for 30mk from *Suomen Retkeilymajajärjestö*, Yrjönkatu 38B, 00100 Helsinki (☎90/6940377), or pick up the free *Hostellit* summary from tourist offices.

■ Campsites and camping cottages

Official **campsites** (*leirintäalue*) are plentiful in Finland. Most open from May or June until August or September, although some stay open longer and a few all year. Sites are **graded** on a star system: one-star sites are in rural areas and are fairly basic; two-star sites have running water, toilets and showers; three-star sites, often on the outskirts of major towns, have hot water and full cooking and laundry facilities. The cost for two people sharing is 27–75mk depending on the

---

ACCOMMODATION PRICE CODES

Throughout this guide, accommodation is priced on a scale of ① to ⑧, the number indicating the lowest price per night a single person could expect to pay in that establishment in high season. With hostels this is the nightly rate per person; with hotels, the price is arrived at by dividing the cost of the cheapest double room by two. The prices indicated by the codes are as follows

① = under £5 / $8   ② = £5–10 / $8–16   ③ = £10–15 / $16–24   ④ = £15–20 / $24–32

⑤ = £20–25 / $32–40   ⑥ = £25–30 / $40–48   ⑦ = £30–35 / $48–56   ⑧ = over £35 / $56

rating. Many three-star sites also have **camping cottages**, from simple sleeping accommodation for 2–5 people to luxury places equipped with TV, sauna and kitchen. The cabins cost 150–400mk per day; it's advisable to book as far ahead as possible during July or August. Without an *International Camping Card* you'll need a *National Camping Card*, available at every site for 15mk and valid for a year. **Camping rough** is technically illegal without the landowner's permission.

Food and Drink

Finnish food is pricy but you can keep a grip on the expense by self-catering. Though tempered by many regulations, alcohol is more widely available than in much of the rest of Scandinavia.

■ Food

Though it may at first seem a stodgy, unsophisticated cuisine, **Finnish food** is an interesting mix of Western and Eastern influences, with Scandinavian-style fish specialities and exotic meats like reindeer and elk alongside dishes that bear a Russian stamp – pastries and casseroles, strong on cabbage and pork. If you're staying in a hotel, **breakfast** (*aamiainen*) is a sumptuous affair, a buffet of herring, eggs, cereals, cheese, salami and bread. Later in the day you can lunch on the economical **snacks** sold in ubiquitous market halls (*kauppahalli*) or in their adjoining cafeterias, where you are charged by the weight of food on your plate. Most train stations and some bus stations and supermarkets also have cafeterias proffering a selection of snacks and light meals, and the *Grilli* and *Nakkikioski* street stands turn out burgers and hot dogs for 12–18mk. Otherwise, campus cafeterias or **mensas** are the cheapest places to get a hot dish, with a choice of three menus, with bread and coffee, for 12–20mk. Theoretically you have to be a student but you are unlikely to be asked for ID, though if you can produce one, a discount is in order. In a regular restaurant or *ravintola* **lunch** (*lounas*) is the cheapest option, many places offering a lunchtime buffet table (*voileipäpöytä* or *seisova pöytä*) stacked with a choice of traditional goodies for a set price of around 75mk. A *baari*, an unlicensed restaurant with a range of Finnish dishes and snacks, is another low-cost option, although most close early – at 5 or 6pm. On Thursdays every *baari* in the country dishes up *hernekeitto ja pannukakut*, thick pea soup with

black rye bread, followed by pancakes with strawberry jam, for around 35mk. You'll get much the same fare in a *kahvila*, though these can be a little pricier, especially in larger cities. Pizzerias, too, are widespread, serving "lunch specials" for 36–45mk.

■ Drink

Finland's **alcohol laws** are as bizarre as those of Norway and Sweden, but unlike in those countries boozing is tackled enthusiastically. **Beer** (*olut*) falls into three categories: "light beer" (I-Olut) – more like a soft drink; "medium strength beer" (*Keskiolut*, III-Olut), more perceptibly alcoholic, sold in shops and cafés; and "strong beer" (A-Olut or IV-Olut), on a par with the stronger European beers, and only available at fully licensed restaurants and clubs and the offical **ALKO** shops (Mon–Thurs 10am–5pm, Fri 10am–6pm, Sat 9am–2pm; closed Sat May–Sept). Even the smallest town will have one, and prices don't vary. Strong beers like *Lapin Kulta Export*, *Karjala*, *Lahden A*, *Olvi Export*, and *Koff* porter, cost 7.90mk for a 300ml bottle. Imported beers go for 9.90–10.20mk a bottle. As for **spirits**, *Finlandia* vodka is 150mk per litre; there's also a popular rough form of vodka called *koskenkorra*, at 140mk.

Most restaurants have a full licence, and some are actually frequented more for drinking than eating. To add to the confusion, some so-called "Pubs" are not licensed. There are also **dance restaurants** (*tanssiravintola*), which serve food as well as drink, and are popular with the over-40s and charge 10–30mk admission. Sometimes you have to queue outside the most popular bars if restrictions on numbers are enforced. Only one drink per person is theoretically allowed on the table at any one time except in the case of *porter*, a stout which most Finns mix with regular beer. There's always either a doorman (*portsari*) – whom some tip (3–5mk) on leaving – or a cloakroom into which you must check your coat on arrival (again 3–5mk). Bars are usually open until midnight or 1am and service stops half an hour before the place shuts. A common order is a *tuoppi* – a half-litre glass of draught beer. Wherever you seek alcohol, you have to be eighteen to buy beer and wine, twenty for spirits.

Opening Hours and Holidays

Shops are usually open Mon–Fri 9am–6pm, Sat 9am–3pm. Some in cities keep longer hours.

Shops and banks will be closed on the following days, when most public transport and museums operate to a Sunday schedule: Jan 1; Epiphany (between Jan 6 and 12); Good Friday & Easter weekend; the Saturday before Whit Sunday; May 1; June 21; All Saint's Day (the Sat between Oct 31 and Nov 6); Dec 6; Dec 24, 25 & 26.

Emergencies

As in other Scandinavian countries, you probably won't have much cause to come into contact with the Finnish **police**, though if you do they are likely to speak English. As for **health problems**, if you're insured, you'll save time by seeing a doctor at a private health centre (*Lääkäriasema*) rather than queuing at a national health centre (*Terveyskeskus*). Medicines must be paid for at a pharmacy (*apteekki*) – although, provided you have your passport, you won't be charged more than a Finn. Hospitals charge 115mk per day.

EMERGENCY NUMBERS

Ring ☎112 for fire, police and ambulance or ☎10022 to get directly to the police.

HELSINKI AND AROUND

The southern coast of Finland makes up the most populated, industrialized and richest part of the country, with the densest concentration, not surprisingly, around the capital, **HELSINKI**. A city of half a million people, Helsinki has a character quite different from the other Scandinavian capitals, and in many ways is closer in mood – and certainly in looks – to the major cities of Eastern Europe. For years an outpost of the Russian Empire, its very shape and form is derived from its powerful neighbour. Yet through this century the city has become a showcase of independent Finland, much of its impressive architecture drawing inspiration from the dawning of Finnish nationalism and the rise of the republic. The streets have a youthful buzz, the short summer acknowledged by crowds strolling the boulevards and socializing in the outdoor cafés and restaurants. At night the pace picks up, with a great selection of pubs and clubs, free rock concerts in the numerous parks, and an impressive quota of fringe events.

The Helsinki area telephone code is ☎90.

Arrival and information

However you travel you arrive close to the city centre. The **ferry** lines, *Viking* and *Silja*, have terminals on opposite sides of the South Harbour, from where it's less than a kilometre to the centre. The **train station** is in the heart of the centre, next to one of the two bus terminals. Across Mannerheimintie and a short way up Simonkatu is the other bus terminal and the **long-distance bus station**. Helsinki's **airport**, Vantaa, is 20km to the north, connected by buses to the *Finnair* terminal under the *Inter-Continental Hotel*, halfway between the city centre and the Olympic Stadium, and to the train station (every 15–30min; 20mk). A cheaper, if slightly slower, airport connection is city bus #615, which costs 15mk and runs from the airport to the bus terminal beside the train station.

The **City Tourist Office**, at Pohjoisesplanadi 19 (mid-May to mid-Sept Mon–Fri 8.30am–6pm, Sat 8.30am–1pm; rest of year Mon 8.30am–4.30pm, Tues–Fri 8.30am–4pm; ☎90/1693757 or 174088), has free street and transport maps and useful free tourist magazines, including the glossy *Helsinki This Week*. If staying for a while, consider purchasing a **Helsinki Card**, giving unlimited travel on public transport and free entry to over forty museums. The three-day card (125mk) is the best value, although there are also two-day (105mk) and one-day (80mk) versions. For information on the rest of the country, use the **Finnish Tourist Board** across the road at Eteläesplanadi 4 (June–Aug Mon–Fri 8.30am–5pm, Sat & Sun 10am–2pm; Sept–May Mon–Fri 8.30am–4pm).

City transport

Most of the things you might want to see are within walking distance of one another. However, quick hops across the centre are easily done by way of an efficient and integrated **tram**, **bus** and small **metro** system. A single journey costs 9mk and unlimited transfers are allowed within one hour. A **multi-trip** ticket gives ten rides for 75mk. A **tourist ticket** lasts one (25mk), three (50mk) or five days (75mk), and permits travel on buses and trams displaying double arrows (effectively all of them). Single tickets are bought on board, others from the bus station, tourist office or kiosks around the centre, and **metro** tickets can be bought from the machines in the stations. Of **tram** routes, #3T, which follows a figure-of-eight route around the centre, is the most useful. **Taxis** have a basic charge of 12mk, with a further 7mk per kilometre, plus a 7mk surcharge after 6pm and on weekends, a 13mk surcharge after 10pm.

Accommodation

There's plenty of accommodation in Helsinki, but by far the bulk of it is in mid-range hotels, which go for 500–700mk for the average double – although several top-notch places drop their prices dramatically in the summer tourist season, and all have reduced rates at weekends. Otherwise there are a number of cheaper, if less luxurious tourist hotels, providing basic accommodation in private rooms without bathrooms, and a few hostels with dormitories, though there's often a limit on the length of stay during the peak summer period. Wherever you stay, you should book as far ahead as possible: the various cut-price hotel deals get snapped up quickly, and hostel space is tight in summer. If you don't have anything reserved, you can book hotel rooms and hostel beds at the **Hotel Booking Centre** at the train station (mid-May to mid-Sept Mon–Sat 9am–7pm, Sun 10am–6pm; rest of year Mon–Fri 9am–6pm).

Hostels

Academica, Hietaniemenkatu 14 (☎4020206). A well-placed summer hotel with doubles (④) on production of an *IYHF* or student card (②).

Kallion Retkeilymaja, Porthaninkatu 2 (☎7099590). Dorm beds close to Hakaniemi metro station, 2km from the centre. Trams #1, #2, #3B and #7A stop nearby. Open mid-May to Aug. ②

Stadionin Retkeilymaja, in the Olympic Stadium (☎4960710). A 3-km hike from the centre and often crowded, but cheap and open all year. Trams #3T, #4, #7 and #10 stop outside. ②

Hotels

Anna, Annankatu 1 (☎648011). Small, central and with a cosy atmosphere. ⑦

Arthur, Vuorikatu 17 (☎173441). You can save money in this good quality hotel by getting a room without a bathroom – but do it early. ⑤

Erottajanpuisto, Uudenmaankatu 9 (☎642169). Usefully positioned, and especially good for several people sharing. ③

Lönnrot, Lönnrotinkatu 16 (☎6932590). Close to the Old Church and everything central. Basic but quite endurable. ③

Finn, Kalevankatu 3b (☎640904). A modern and peaceful place, virtually in the city centre. ④

Marttahotelli, Uudenmaankatu 24 (☎646211). Recently refurbished in an enjoyable hi-tech style. ⑥

Cumulus Kaisaniemi, Kaisaniemenkatu 7 (☎172881). Well-equipped rooms that can be good value at weekends. ⑦

Omapohja, Itäinen Teatterikuja 3 (☎666211). Fairly ramshackle, but in a quiet street close to the train and bus stations. ④

Satakuntalo, Lapinrinne 1 (☎695851). Another handily located summer hotel, which doubles as an *IYHF* hostel. ③

Ursula, Paasivuorenkatu 1 (☎750311). A bit out of the way, just north of the centre close to Hakaneimentori, but well-priced. 350mk at weekends and in summer. ⑤

Campsite

Rastila, Itäkeskus. The nearer of the city's two sites, 13km east, at the end of the metro line and served by buses #90, #90A and #96. Mid-May to mid-Sept.

The City

Following a devastating fire and the city's appointment as Finland's capital in 1812, Helsinki was totally rebuilt in a style commensurate with its rank: a grid of wide streets and Neoclassical, Empire-style brick buildings, modelled on the then Russian capital, St Petersburg. It's a tribute to the vision of planner Johan Ehrenström and architect Carl Engel that from **Senate Square to Esplanadi** the grandeur has endured, often quite dramatically. The square itself is dominated by the exquisite form of the **Tuomiokirkko**

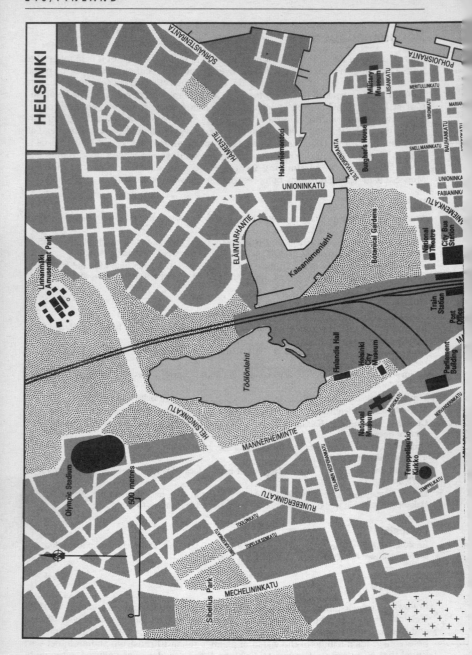

HELSINKI

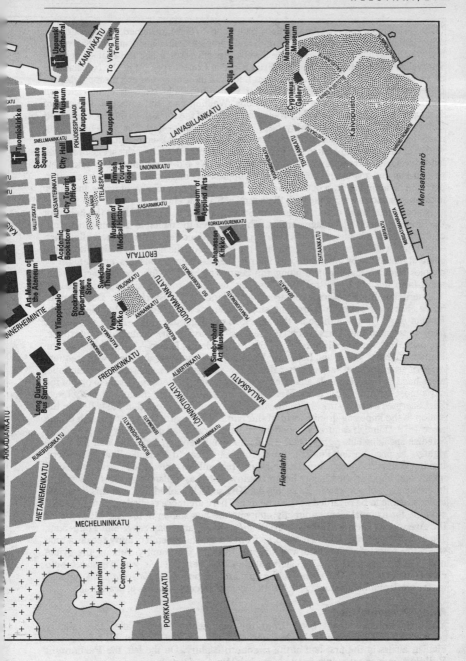

(Mon–Fri 9am–5/7pm, Sat 9am–5/6pm, Sun noon–5/6pm), designed, like most of the other buildings on the square, by Engel, and completed after his death in 1852 with a few variations, like the statues of the Twelve Apostles which line the roof – copies of Thorvaldsen's sculptures for the Vor Frue Kirke in Copenhagen. After the Neoclassical extravagances of the exterior, the spartan Lutheran interior comes as a disappointment; better is the gloomily atmospheric **crypt** (June–Aug daily 10am–4pm; entrance on Kirkkokatu), now often used for exhibitions. Walking east, the square at the end of Aleksanterinkatu is overlooked by the onion domes of the Russian Orthodox **Uspenski Cathedral** on Katajanokka (May–Sept Tues–Fri 9.30am–4pm, Sat 9am–noon, Sun noon–3pm; Oct–April Tues & Thurs 9am–2pm, Wed & Fri 2–6pm, Sun noon–3pm), a wedge of land extending out to sea between the harbours that's now the scene of a dockland development programme, converting the area's old warehouses into pricy new restaurants and apartments for Helsinki's yuppies. In contrast to its Lutheran counterpart, the cathedral is drab outside but the inside has a rich display of icons and other adornments, incense mingling with the sound of Slavonic choirs.

Across a mishmash of tram lines from South Harbour is **Esplanadi**. At the height of the Swedish/Finnish language conflict, which divided the nation in the mid-nineteenth century, this neat boulevard was where opposing factions demonstrated their allegiance – the Finns walking on the south side and the Swedes on the north. Nowadays it's dominated at lunchtime by office workers, later in the afternoon by buskers, and at night by couples strolling hand-in-hand along the central pathway to free musical accompaniment from the hut in the middle. Close by, on the corner of Aleksanterinkatu and Mannerheimintie is the brick constructivist exterior of the **Stockmann Department Store**, Europe's largest department store, selling everything from bubble gum to Persian rugs. On the fifth floor, the **Stockmann Museum** (Mon–Thurs noon–1pm; free) is a small and surprisingly interesting history of the century-old enterprise. Opposite, the **Vanha Ylioppistalo** – the old Students' House – is the home of the Finnish Students' Union and holds the **Vanhan Galleria**, a small gallery with frequent modern art events and various arty cafés. A few strides further along Mannerheimintie, steps head down to **Tunneli**, an underground complex of shops that leads to one of the city's most enjoyable structures, **Helsinki train station**, often thought of as architect Eliel Saarinen's finest work – a solid, yet graceful building erected in 1914. Beside the station is the imposing granite form of the **National Theatre**, home of Finnish drama since 1872. "Finnish culture" was considered a contradiction in terms by the governing Swedish-speaking elite right up to the mid-nineteenth century, and it was later felt (quite rightly) to pose an anti-Russian, pro-nationalist threat to Finland's Tsarist masters. Inside, Wäinö Aaltonen's bronze sculpture remembers one Aleksis Kivi, who died insane and impoverished before being acknowledged as Finland's greatest playwright. Interestingly, nobody knows for sure what Kivi actually looked like, and this imagined likeness came to be regarded as the true one. There are more reminders of the Finnish struggle for national identity directly opposite the bus station in the **Art Museum of the Ateneum** (Tues & Fri 9am–5pm, Wed & Thurs 9am–9pm, Sat & Sun 11am–5pm; 10mk), whose stirring selection of works from the late nineteenth century recalls a time when the spirit of nationalism was surging through the country. Among the prime names of the era were Akseli Gallen-Kallela and Albert Edelfelt, who translated onto canvas many of the mythic scenes of the epic Finnish poem, the *Kalevala*. Look out also for the work of Juho Rissanen, with his moody and evocative studies of peasant life.

Along Mannerheimintie

Mannerheimintie spears north from the city centre, named after the military commander and statesman C.G.E. Mannerheim, who wielded considerable influence on Finnish affairs in the first half of the twentieth century. On the left, the **Parliament Building** (guided tours July & Aug Mon–Fri 2pm, Sat 11am & noon, Sun noon & 1pm;

Sept–June Sat & Sun only; free), with its pompous columns and choking air of solemnity, was the work of J.S. Sirén, completed in 1931. North of here, the **National Museum** (daily 11am–3/4pm, Tues also 6–9pm; 10mk) is a joint effort of the three giants of Finnish architecture, Armas Lindgren, Herman Gesellius and Eliel Saarinen, its design deliberately steeped in Finnish history, drawing on the country's legacy of medieval churches and granite castles and decorated inside by Gallen-Kallela with scenes from the *Kalevala*. The museum's contents are exhaustive, and it's best to concentrate on a few specific sections. Beginning with prehistoric finds and leading through the turbulent Middle Ages to the present, exhibits include a marvellously restored seventeenth-century manor house interior and ethnographic sections exploring the characteristics of the nation's varied regions, including a *Same* department.

Directly opposite, **Finlandia Hall** (tours July at noon & 2pm; 10mk) was designed in the Seventies by the country's premier architect, Alvar Aalto, as part of a grand plan to rearrange the entire centre of Helsinki. Previously, Eliel Saarinen had planned a traffic route from the northern suburbs into a new square in the city centre, to be called Vapaudenkatu (Freedom Street) in celebration of Finnish independence. Aalto plotted a continuation of this scheme, envisaging the removal of the rail-freight yards and a fan-like terrace of new buildings to greet new arrivals, of which Finlandia was to be the first. Inside, Aalto's characteristic wave pattern (the architect's surname means "wave") and asymmetry is everywhere, from the walls and ceilings through to the lamps and vases, although the view from the foyer is still of the rail yards, and the plan for the future of Helsinki is still being discussed. Next door, the **Helsinki City Museum** (Wed–Sun 11am–5pm; 10mk), an Italian-style villa built in the 1840s, is refreshingly manageable, with a record of the growth of the city using maps and diagrams showing, above all, the impact of Ehrenström's plan and Engel's architecture. A little way north, the **Olympic Stadium** is clearly visible, originally intended for the 1940 Olympic Games, and the venue of the first postwar games in 1952. Its **tower** (Mon–Fri 9am–8pm, Sat & Sun 9am–6pm; 5mk) gives an unsurpassed view over the city and a chunk of the southern coast. Back towards the city centre, the **Hietaniemi Cemetery** houses the graves of some of the big names of Finnish history – Mannerheim, Engel and Alvar Aalto, whose witty little tombstone consisting partly of a chopped Neoclassical column is beside the main entrance; next to it is the larger marker of Gallen-Kallela, his initials woven around a painter's palette. East of here, at Lutherinkatu 3, is the late Sixties **Temppeliaukio kirkko** (daily 10am–8pm), whose odd combination of man-made and natural materials has made it a fixture on the tourist circuit. Even when crowded it's a thrill to be inside.

South of Esplanadi

Leaving Esplanadi along Kasarmikatu, the **Museum of Medical History** (Tues & Fri noon–3pm, Thurs 3–6pm; 4mk) at nos. 11–13 is housed in what was once an isolation ward, with an imposingly morbid selection of medieval folk cures, glass eyes, a mock-up of a leprosy patient's room and some vicious-looking dental instruments. A block from Kasarmikatu, the excellent **Museum of Applied Arts** (Tues–Fri 11am–5pm, Sat & Sun 11am–4pm; 20mk) traces the relationship between art and industry in Finnish history, with full explanatory texts and period exhibits, from Karelianism – the representations of peasant life from the Karelia region in eastern Finland, which dominated Finnish art and design in the years around independence – to modern movements.

West of here are the curving alleys and tall elegant buildings of **Eira**, at the centre of which is the **Vanha kirkko** or Old Church, a humble wooden structure that's another example of Engel's work, the first Lutheran church to be erected after Helsinki became the Finnish capital. A short walk south, the Sinebrychoff brewery bestows a distinctive aroma of hops to the locality and finances the **Sinebrychoff Art Museum** at Bulevardi 40 (Mon, Thurs & Fri 9am–5pm, Wed 9am–8pm, Sat & Sun 11am–5pm; 10mk), a rather precious museum housing mostly seventeenth-century Flemish and Dutch paintings, including some excellent miniatures. A few blocks from the end of Kasarmikatu is the large and rocky **Kaivopuisto** park, developed as a health resort in the 1830s, with a spa house that drew Russian nobility from St Petersburg to sample its waters, and home to the house where Gustaf Mannerheim spent the later years of his life, now maintained as the **Mannerheim Museum** (Fri–Sun 11am–4pm; 20mk). A Finnish-born Russian-trained military commander, Mannerheim led the right-wing Whites during the Civil War of 1918, and two decades later the Finnish campaigns in the Winter and Continuation Wars; his influence in the political sphere was also considerable, including a brief spell as president. The cluttered interior of the house is much as it was when he died in 1951, with an array of plunder gathered from the world over. Close by is the house of another famous Finn, Frederik Cygnaeus, filled with his outstanding collection of art, nowadays displayed as the **Cygnaeus Gallery** (Wed–Sun 11am–4pm, Wed also 6–8pm; 6mk), beautifully laid out and mainly comprising the bird and nature studies of the von Wright brothers.

Suomenlinna and Seurasaari

Built by the Swedes in 1748 to protect Helsinki from seaborne attack, the fortress of **Suomenlinna** stands on five interconnected islands that make a rewarding break from the city. Reachable by half-hourly ferry from the South Harbour, it can be visited inde-pendently or there are hour-long summer **guided walking tours** (20mk), beginning close to the ferry stage and conducted in English from June to August at 12.30pm and 2.30pm. Suomenlinna has a few museums, though none is particularly riveting. The **Nordic Arts Centre** (Mon–Sat 11am–6pm; free) has small displays of contemporary arts from the Nordic countries. The **Ehrensvärd Museum** (May–Sept daily 10am–4.30/5pm; Oct–April Sat & Sun 11am–4.30pm; 10mk) is the residence used by the first commander of the fortress, Augustin Ehrensvärd, who oversaw the building of Suomenlinna and now lies in an elaborate tomb in the grounds; his personal effects remain inside the house alongside displays on the fort's construction. The **Armfelt Museum** (mid-May to Aug daily 11am–5.30pm; Sept Sat & Sun only; 6mk) contains the eighteenth- and nineteenth-century family heirlooms of the Armfelt clan who lived in the Joensuu Manor at Halikko. Finally, the **Coastal Defence Museum** (mid-May to Aug daily 10am–5pm; Sept daily 11am–3pm; Oct to mid-May Sat & Sun 11am–3pm; 5mk) records Suomenlinna's defensive actions and, for another 5mk, lets visitors clamber around the claustrophobic World War I submarine *Vesikko*.

There are more museums a fifteen-minute tram (#4) or bus (#18, #24 or #36) ride from the city centre, close by the small wooded island of **Seurasaari**. The tram stops a few hundred metres north, at the junction of Tamminiementie and Meilahdentie, conveniently close to the **Helsinki City Art Museum** (Wed–Sun 11am–6.30pm; 15mk), one of the best, if most disorganized, collections of modern Finnish art. A few minutes' walk away, towards the Seurasaari bridge, is the long driveway leading to the **Urho Kekkonen Museum** (May to mid-Sept daily 11am–4pm; mid-Sept to April Mon–Sat 11am–3pm, Sun 11am–4pm; Thurs also 6–8pm; 10mk), the villa where the esteemed former president lived from 1956, and the former official home of all Finnish presidents. Kekkonen played a vital role in Finnish history, most significantly in continuing the work of his predecessor, Paasikivi, in the establishment of Finnish neutrality, accom-plished through delicate negotiations with Soviet leaders whose favour he would gain, legend has it, by taking them to a sauna. The feel of the place is far from institutional, filled with birchwood furniture and with large windows giving peaceful views of surrounding trees, water and wildlife. The house was given to Kekkonen on his retire-ment from office, and he lived here for six years until his death in 1981. Close by, on Seurasaari itself, is the **Open-Air Museum** (June–Aug daily 11am–5pm, Wed until 7pm; Sept–May Mon–Fri 9am–3pm, Sat & Sun 11am–5pm; 10mk), a collection of vernacular buildings assembled from all over Finland.

Eating and drinking

Eating in Helsinki, as in the rest of Finland, isn't cheap, but there is a lot of choice, and, with planning, a number of ways to stretch funds – many places offer good-value lunchtime deals and there are plenty of affordable ethnic restaurants. The stalls of the modest-sized **kauppatori** (Mon–Sat 7am–2pm; summer also Mon–Fri 3.30–8pm) are laden with fresh fruit and veg; the **kauppahalli** (Mon–Fri 8am–5pm, Sat 8am–2pm), further along, is good for snacks and reindeer kebabs. For fast food, *Jaskan Grilli*, on Töölönkatu behind the National Museum, is said to be the best of its kind in Finland; the *grill* on the corner of Fredrikinkatu and Arkadiankatu is also good, and makes its own burgers. Helsinki has several **student mensas**, two of which are centrally located at Aleksanterinkatu 5 and Hallituskatu 11–13. One or the other will be open in summer; both will be open during term time.

Drinking can be enjoyed in the city's many pub-like restaurants; on Fridays and Saturdays it's best to arrive as early as possible to get a seat without having to queue. Most drinking dives also serve food, although the grub is seldom at its best in the evening. If you want a drink but are feeling antisocial, or just very hard-up, self-service ALKO shops are located at Fabiankatu 7 and Vvorikatu 7.

Cafés

Café Ekberg, Bulevardi 9. Nineteenth-century fixtures and a deliberately *fin-de-siècle* atmosphere, with starched waitresses bringing open sandwiches and pastries to marble tables.

Café Eliel, Helsinki train station. Airy Art Nouveau interior with a good-value self-service breakfast.

Café Esplandi, corner of Mikonkatu and Esplandi. The latest place to see and be seen, sipping a cappucino at outdoor tables.

Café Fazer, Kluuvikatu 3. Helsinki's best-known bakery, justly celebrated for its pastries. Stays open late for the movie crowd.

Café Tamminiementie, Tamminiementie 8. Perhaps the city centre's nicest café, with excellent home-made cakes and countless varieties of tea.

Café Ursula, Kaivopuisto. On the beach at the edge of the Kaivopuisto park, with a wonderful view from the outdoor terrace.

Kappeli, Esplanadi Park. An elegant glasshouse often crowded but with a relaxed atmosphere. The cellar is also a great spot for an evening drink.

Restaurants

Ani, Telakkakatu 2. Turkish food from the 35mk open table at lunchtime.

Cantina West, Kasarminkatu 23. Outrageously popular Tex-Mex eatery.

Green Way, Kaisaniemenkatu 1. Wholefood restaurant with a well-stocked juice bar.

La Havanna, Erottanjankatu 7. Pioneering Cuban eatery doing great things with seafood. Eat at lunchtime because at night it is packed with boozers.

Kannu, Punavuorenkatu 12. Delicious food in an interior designed by Alvar Aalto.

Kasakka, Meritullinkatu 13. Great atmosphere and food in this old-style Russian restaurant.

Kasvisravintola, Lapinlahdenkatu 25A. One of best veggie restaurants in the city.

Kuu, Töölönkatu 27. Unpretentious place to sample inexpensive Finnish food.

Pasta Factory, Mastokatu 6. An intimate and affordable Italian food joint.

Pizza No.1, Mannerheimintie 18. Standard pizzas, but good deals at lunchtime.

Šaslik, Nertystpolku 12. pricy but delicious authentic Russian grub.

Sukhothai, Runeberginkatu 32. The least expensive and quite possibly the best of the city's new crop of Thai restaurants – try the soups.

Pubs

Angleterre, Fredrikinkatu 47. Utterly Finnish despite the Dickensian fixtures.

Bulevardia, Bulevardi 12. Art Deco decor – black furniture designed by Thirties architect Pauli Blomstedt, and birch walls.

Elite, Etläinen Hesperiankatu 22. Once the haunt of the city's artists, many of whom would settle the bill with paintings – a selection of which lines the walls. Especially good in summer, when you can drink on the terrace.

No Name Irish Bar, Töölönkatu 2. Looks like an American cocktail bar and pulls an intriguing cross-section of Finns on the razzle.

Richard's Pub, Rikhardinkatu 4. Close to the editorial offices of the major Helsinki newspapers. Usually contains a few hacks crying over lost scoops – good food too.

St Urho's Pub, Museokatu 10. One of the most popular student pubs. Guitars, a piano, etc, available for spontaneous jam sessions.

Vanhan Kahvila, Mannerheimintie 3. A self-service and comparatively cheap bar. Arrive early for a seat on the balcony overlooking the bustle of the streets below.

Vanhan Kellari, Mannerheimintie 3. Downstairs from the *Vanhan Kahvila*, its underground setting and bench-style seating help promote a cosy and smoky, if drunken, atmosphere.

Nightlife

Helsinki has a vibrant night scene, notably several venues putting on a steady diet of **live music** (costing 35–50mk) and free gigs almost every summer Sunday in Kaivopuisto park. There is also a wide range of **clubs and discos**, for which admission is usually around 35mk, half that Monday to Thursday and often free before 10pm. For details of **what's on**, read the entertainments page of *Helsingin Sanomat*, or the free fortnightly paper, *City*, found in record shops, bookshops and department stores. **Tickets** for most events can be bought at *Lippupalvelu*, Mannerheimintie 5 (Mon–Fri 9.30am–4.30pm, Sat 10am–2pm), and *Tiketti*, on the second floor of the *Forum* shopping centre, off Mannerheimintie (Mon–Fri 9am–5pm).

Clubs and venues

Berlin, Töölönkatu 3. Depending on the night, the latest acid and hip-hop sounds, heavy rock or black music specials.

Botta, Museokatu 10. Vibrant dance music of various hues most nights.

KY-Exit, Pohjoinen Rautatiekatu 21. Sometimes has foreign bands, more often lively disco nights.

Orfeus, Eerikinkatu 3. Free live jazz and blues on Thurs, Fri and Sat.

Storyville, Museokatu 8. Popular venue for nightly live jazz. Good food too.

Tavastia, Urho Kekkosenkatu 4–6. Major showcase for Finnish and Swedish bands.

Vanha Maestro, Fredrikinkatu 51–53. The place for traditional dancing. A legend among enthusiasts of *humppa*, a Finnish dance related to the waltz and tango. Entry 10–30mk.

Vanha Ylioppilastalo, Mannerheimintie 3. Main venue for international indie bands.

Listings

Airlines *British Airways*, Keskuskatu 7 (☎650677); *Finnair*, Mannerheimintie 102 (☎81881); *SAS*, Pohjoisesplanadi 23 (☎177433).

Books *Academic Bookstore*, Pohjoisesplanadi 39, has a good stock of English paperbacks.

Car rental *Avis*, Pohj. Rautatiekatu 17 (☎441155); *Budget*, Mannerheimintie 46 (☎497477); *Europcar/InterRent*, Mannerheimintie 50 (☎408443), *Hertz*, Mannerheimintie 44 (☎446910).

Doctor ☎008.

Embassies *Canada*, Pohjoisesplanadi 25B (☎171141); *Great Britain*, Itäinen Puistotie 17 (☎661293); *Netherlands*, Raatimiehenkatu 2 (☎661737); *USA*, Itäinen Puistotie 14 (☎171931).

Exchange Outside banking hours at the airport (7am–11pm); Katajanokka harbour where *Viking* and *Finnjet* dock are open daily 9–11.30am & 3.45–6pm; or *Forex* at the train station (daily 8am–9pm).

Hospital Helsinki University Central Hospital, Haartmaninkatu 4 (☎4711); bus #14 or #18.

Laundry At Punavuorenkatu 3 and Mannerheimintie 93.

Left luggage Long-distance bus station (Mon–Thurs 9am–6pm, Fri 8am–6pm); lockers at train station (daily 5.15am–midnight/1.30am).

Pharmacy 24-hour pharmacy: *Yliopiston Apteekki*, Mannerheimintie 96 (☎415778).

Police Olavinkatu 1 (☎6940633).

Post office The main office is at Mannerheimintie 11 (Mon–Fri 9am–5pm).

Women's movement The Finnish feminists' union, *Naisasialiitto Unioni*, Bulevardi 11A (☎642277), has info and a women's bookshop/café; closed July.

Around Helsinki

There's little in Helsinki's outlying area that's worth venturing out for. But a couple of places, both an easy day trip from the city, merit a visit – the home of the composer, Sibelius, at **Järvenpää**, and the evocative old town of **Porvoo**.

Järvenpää

Around 40km north of Helsinki, and easy to get to by bus or train, **JÄRVENPÄÄ**, is the site of **Ainola** (May–Sept Wed–Sun 11am–5pm; 15mk) – the house where Jean Sibelius lived from 1904 with his wife, Aino, after whom the place is named. Now regarded as one of the world's great composers, Sibelius is seen as the authentic voice of Finnish national identity. His early pieces were inspired by the Finnish folk epic, the *Kalevala*, and by the nationalist mood of the times, incurring the wrath of the country's Russian rulers when in 1899 they banned performances of his rousing *Finlandia* under any name which suggested its patriotic sentiment; to circumvent this, the piece was published as "Opus 26, No. 7". He is still revered in Finland, despite his notorious bouts of heavy drinking and an angst-ridden last few years that became known as "the silence from Järvenpää". The house is just the kind of home you'd expect, a tranquil place, close to lakes and forests, and a pilgrimage for devotees, although books, furnishings and a few paintings are all there is to see. His simple grave is in the grounds.

Porvoo

One of the oldest towns on the south coast, **PORVOO**, 50km east of Helsinki, with its narrow cobbled streets lined by small wooden buildings, gives a sense of the Finnish life which predated the capital's bold squares and Neoclassical geometry – although its elegant riverside setting and unhurried mood mean it's inevitably popular with tourists.

Close to the station, visit the preserved **Johan Ludwig Runeberg House**, Runeberginkatu 20 (May–Aug Mon–Sat 10am–4pm, Sun 11am–5pm; Sept–April Wed–Sat 10am–4pm, Sun 11am–5pm; 5mk), where the famed Finnish poet lived from 1852 while a teacher at the town school. Despite writing in Swedish, he greatly aided the nation's sense of self-esteem, and one of his poems provided the lyrics for the national anthem. Across the road, the **Walter Runeberg Gallery** (same hours; 15mk) has a collection of sculpture by Runeberg's third son, one of Finland's more celebrated sculptors. The old town is built around the hill on the other side of Mannerheimkatu, crowned by the fifteenth-century **Tuomiokirkko** (May–Sept Mon–Fri 10am–6pm, Sat 10am–2pm, Sun 2–5pm), where Alexander I proclaimed Finland a Russian Grand Duchy and convened the first Finnish Diet. This, and other aspects of the town's past, can be explored in the **Porvoo Museum** (May–Aug daily 11am–4pm; Sept–April Wed–Sun noon–4pm; 10mk) at the foot of the hill in the main square, by way of a selection of furnishings, musical instruments and oddities largely dating from the Russian rule.

Buses run all day from Helsinki to Porvoo, and a one-way trip costs around 30mk. There's also a **boat**, the *J.L.Runeberg*, which sails from Helsinki's South Harbour on Wednesdays, Fridays, Saturdays and Sundays in summer at 10am, arriving in Porvoo at

1.15pm and leaving two hours later; a one-way fare is 90mk. The **tourist office** is opposite the bus station at Rauhankatu 20 (Mon–Fri 8am–4pm, Sat 10am–2pm), and has free maps of the town, or there's an **information counter** (mid-May to mid-Aug daily 10am–6pm) on the main square. **Spending a night** in Porvoo leaves you well-placed to continue into Finland's southeastern corner, though rates are steep. There is, however, a **youth hostel**, open all year, at Linnankoskenkatu 1–3 (☎915/130012; ②), and a **campsite**, open from June to mid-August, 2km from the town centre.

THE SOUTHWEST

The area immediately west of Helsinki is probably the blandest section of the country, endless forests interrupted only by modest-sized patches of water and virtually identical villages and small towns. The far southwestern corner, however, is more interesting, with islands and inlets around a jagged shoreline and some of the country's distinctive Finland-Swedish coastal communities. The country's former capital, **Turku**, is the main target, historically and visually one of Finland's most enticing cities; indeed, many of its Swedish-speaking contingent consider Åbo – the Swedish name for Turku – the real capital and Helsinki just an upstart.

Turku

TURKU was once the national capital but lost its status in 1812, and most of its buildings in a ferocious fire in 1827. These days it's a small and highly sociable city, bristling with history and culture and with a sparkling nightlife, thanks to the boom years under Swedish rule and the students from its two universities.

Arrival and accommodation

The river Aura splits the city, its tree-lined banks forming a natural promenade as well as a useful landmark. On the northern side of the river is Turku's central grid, where you'll find the **tourist office** at Aurakatu 4 (June–Aug Mon–Fri 8.30am–7pm, Sat & Sun 10am–5pm; Sept–May Mon–Fri 8am–6pm, Sat & Sun 10am–5pm). Both the **train** and **bus station** are within easy walking distance of the river, just north of the centre. If you are making for the Stockholm ferry, you can stay on the train to the terminal 2km west or catch bus #1 on Linnankatu. Half way out there the bus passes the *InterRail Centre*, Läntinen Rantakatu 47 (July to mid-Aug Mon–Sat 8am–10pm), right by the river, where you can leave luggage, shower, rent bikes and eat cheaply.

For **accommodation**, the *Hotel Kantri*, Yliopistonkatu 29a (☎921/320921; ④), *Hotelli Aura*, Humalistonkatu 7 (☎921/651111; ④), and *Hansa Hotel*, Kristiinankatu 9 (☎921/617000; ④), offer cheap weekend and summer deals. During the week try **tourist hotels** like the *Turisti-Aula*, Käsityöläiskatu 11 (☎921/2334484; ③), *Hotel Astro*, Humalistonkatu 18 (☎921/511107; ③), or *Hotelli Kantri*, Itäienen Pitkäkatu 30b (☎921/2336666; ④), on the other side of town. Turku's **youth hostel** is at Linnankatu 39 (☎921/316578; ②), open all year and within easy walking distance of the ferry harbour. The nearest **campsite** is pleasantly sited on the island of Ruissalo, overlooking the harbour. It's open from June to August and takes fifteen minutes to reach on bus #8.

The City

Though it's not much of a taster for the actual city, **Turku Art Museum** (Mon–Sat 10am–4pm, Thurs also 6–10pm, Sun 10am–6pm; 25mk) is one of the better collections of Finnish art, with works by all the great names of the country's golden age plus a commendable stock of moderns. To get to grips with Turku itself, and its pivotal place in Finnish history, cut through the centre to the river, and the tree-framed space which before the great fire of 1879 was the bustling heart of the community, overlooked by the **Tuomiokirkko** (mid-April to mid-Sept Mon–Fri 10am–6pm, Sat 10am–3pm, Sun noon–4.30pm; mid-Sept to mid-April Mon–Sat 10am–3pm, Sun noon–3pm; free guided tours in English at 2pm, 3pm and 4pm) – Turku's cathedral, erected in the thirteenth century and still the centre of the Finnish Church. Despite repeated fires, a number of features survive, notably a deliriously ornate coffin, the tomb of one Torsten Stålhandske, commander of the Finnish cavalry during the seventeenth-century Thirty Years' War. A little further along lies Catherina Månsdotter, the wife of the Swedish King Erik XIV with whom, in the mid-sixteenth century, she was imprisoned in Turku Castle. The window behind it carries her stained-glass image – the only authentic likeness known. For 5mk, the museum upstairs gives a stronger insight into the cathedral's past, with an assortment of ancient jugs, goblets and textiles.

A short step north of the cathedral is the sleek low form of the **Sibelius Museum** (Tues–Sun 11am–3pm, Wed also 6–8pm; 15mk), which – although Sibelius had no direct connection with Turku – displays family photo albums and original manuscripts, the great man's hat, walking stick and even a final half-smoked cigar, alongside exhibits covering the musical history of the country. There is also a concert hall where you can listen to recorded requests. South of here, the engrossing **Luostarinmäki Handicrafts Museum** on Vartiovuorenkatu (daily 10am–3/6pm; 15mk) is one of the best and most authentic open-air museums in Finland, and as true a record of old Turku as exists. Following a severe fire in 1775 rigorous restrictions were imposed on new buildings but, due to a legal technicality, they didn't apply in this district. The wooden houses here were built by local working people in traditional style and they became a museum as descendants of the original owners died and the town bought them up. The chief inhabitants now are museum volunteers who dress up in period attire and demonstrate the old handicrafts.

A short walk away, on the southern bank of the river, is another worthwhile indoor collection: the **Wäinö Aaltonen Museum** (daily except Mon 11am–7pm; 15mk), a collection of work by the best-known modern Finnish sculptor, who grew up close to Turku and studied for a time at the local art school. Aaltonen dominated his field throughout the Twenties and Thirties and his influence is still felt today, his work turning up in every major town throughout the country. His pieces are imaginative and sensitive for the most part, as the exhibits here demonstrate; there's also a roomful of his paintings, some of which show why he concentrated on sculpture. Back in the direction of the cathedral, a wooden staircase runs up to the front door of the **Museum of Pharmacy and Quensel House** (daily 10am–3/6pm; 7mk), home to a seventeenth-century judge, and, later, one Professor Josef Gustaf Pipping – the "father of Finnish medicine" – and decorated with period furnishings and chemists' implements from around the country. Along Linnankatu from here, towards the mouth of the river, **Turku Castle** (same hours; 15mk) is a featureless building from the outside, a maze of cobbled courtyards, corridors and staircases within, with a bewildering array of finds and displays. The castle probably went up around 1280, and gradual expansion through the following years accounts for the patchwork effect of the architecture of the building, which was the seat of the government of the country for many centuries.

Eating and drinking

If money's very tight, *Gadolinia*, a **student mensa**, part of Åbo Akademi on Henrikenkatu, offers Turku's cheapest **food**. Otherwise the *Italia*, Linnankatu 3, produces sizeable pizzas for affordable prices. With a bit more cash, and an appetite for traditional Finnish food, go to *Brahen Kellari*, Puolankatu 1, preferably at lunchtime when you can munch through three courses for 82mk. Close by the tourist office is the **kauppatori** and the effervescent **kauppahalli** (Mon–Fri 8am–5pm, Sat 8am–2pm).

You might also eat at either of the two riverside restaurants, *Pinella*, in Porthaninkatupuisto, or *Samppalinna*, on Itäinen Rantakatu, though these do most business at night, when they're mainly used for **drinking**. Other popular imbibing venues are *Uusi Apteekki*, Kaskenkatu 1, which, true to its name, is an old pharmacy complete with ancient fittings, and *Erik XIV*, Erikenkatu 6, which also serves decent food. Consider also the pair of "English-style" pubs: *The Farmers' Inn*, Humalisonkatu 7, with its huge selection of bottled beers, and the *Green Dog*, Yliopistonkatu 29b, above which is the *Green Frog*, mostly frequented for its food.

THE LAKE REGION

About a third of Finland is consumed by the **Lake Region**, a huge area of bays, inlets and islands, interspersed with dense forests. Despite holding much of Finland's industry, it's a tranquil, verdant region, and even **Tampere**, Finland's major industrial city, enjoys a peaceful lakeside setting, as well as being easily accessible from Helsinki by train. The eastern part of the Lake Region is the most atmospheric, slender ridges furred with conifers linking the few sizeable landmasses, reached from Tampere via **Jyväskyla**, whose wealth of buildings by Alvar Aalto make it a worthwhile stopoff. Direct from Helsinki, the route goes via dull Lahti to the lakes' regional centre, **Savonlinna**, which stretches delectably across several islands and boasts a superb medieval castle. Further north, **Kuopio**, where many displaced Karelians settled after World War II, makes a decent stopoff on the way up to Kajaani.

Tampere

TAMPERE, a leafy place of parks and lakes, is Finland's biggest manufacturing centre and Scandinavia's largest inland city. Its rapid growth began just over a century ago, when Tsar Alexander I abolished taxes on local trade, encouraging the Scotsman James Finlayson to open a textile factory drawing labour from rural areas where traditional crafts were in decline. Metalwork and shoe factories soon followed, their owners paternally supplying culture to the workforce by promoting a vigorous local arts scene. Free outdoor rock and jazz concerts, lavish theatrical productions and one of the best modern art collections in Finland maintain such traditions to this day.

The City

Almost everything of consequence is within the central section, bordered on two sides by lakes Näsijärvi and Pyhäjärvi. The main streets run off either side of Hämeenkatu, which leads directly from the train station across Hämeensilta. Left off Hämeenkatu, up slender Hämeenpuisto, the Tampere Workers' Theatre and **Lenin Museum** (Mon–Fri 9am–5pm, Sat & Sun 11am–4pm; 10mk) remembers the time when, after the abortive 1905 revolution in Russia, Lenin lived in Finland and attended the Tampere conferences, held in what is now the museum. It was here that he first met Stalin, although this is barely mentioned, the two displays concentrating instead on Lenin himself and his relationship with Finland. Northwest of here there's more labour history, where some thirty homes have been preserved as the **Workers' Museum of Amuri** at Makasiininkatu 12 (mid-May to mid-Sept Tues–Sat 9am–5pm, Sun 11am–5pm; 10mk), a simple but affecting place which records the family life of working people over a hundred-year period. In each home there's a description of the inhabitants and their jobs, and authentic articles from relevant periods – from tables to family photos, newspapers and biscuit packets. Around the corner at Puutarhakatu 34, the **Art Museum of Tampere** (daily except Mon 10am–6pm; 10mk) provides an unhappy setting for mainly Finnish nineteenth-century paintings; if you're looking for

Finnish art you might be better off visiting the **Hiekka Art Gallery**, a few minutes'
walk away at Pirkankatu 6 (Wed & Sun noon–3pm; 10mk), which has sketches by
Gallen-Kallela and Helene Schjerfbeck and superb silver and other metalwork donated
by one Kustaa Heikka. Better still is the tremendous **Sara Hildén Art Museum** (daily
11am–6pm; 10mk), built on the shores of Näsijärvi (bus #16 from the bus station or the
central square), a quirky collection of Finnish and foreign modern works. Occupying
the same waterside strip as the Hildén collection is **Särkänniemi**, a tourist complex
with dolphinarium, aquarium, planetarium and observation tower, though it might be
more profitable to cross instead to the other side of the town centre to the city's
cathedral, the **Tuomikirkko**, on Satakunnankatu (May–Aug 10am–6pm; Sept–April
11am–3pm; free), decorated with gorily symbolic frescoes by Hugo Simberg including
the *Garden of Death* where skeletons happily water plants.

Practicalities

The city's **tourist office** is by the river, 500m from the **train station** at
Verkatehtaankatu 2 (June–Aug Mon–Fri 8.30am–8pm, Sat 8.30am–6pm, Sun 11.30am–
6pm; Sept–May Mon–Fri 8.30am–5pm), and a similar distance along Hatanpään from
the **bus station**. The cheapest place to stay is the **YWCA hostel** opposite the cathedral at Tuomiokirkonkatu 12a (☎931/235900; ②), though from mid-July to mid-August
the *Interpoint*, Hämeenpuisto 14 (☎931/124056; ①), marginally undercuts them. There
are dorm beds at the impersonal summer hotel, *Domus*, Pellervonkatu 9 (☎931/
550000; ②), 1km east of the train station, and more at *Uimahallinmaja*, centrally
located at Pirkankatu 10–12 (☎931/229460; ③). The nearest **campsite** is *Härmälä*,
5km south, accessible by bus #1 and open from May to late August.

The cheapest **places to eat** are the **mensas** in the university at the end of
Yliopistonkatu, just over the rail line from the city centre. Failing that, aside from
pizzerias, try the herring-laden open table at *Silakka*, or the 35mk three-course lunch
special at *Koruna*, Kauppakatu 14a. **Self-catering**, there's a *Sokos* store at Hämeenkatu
21, and a large **kauppahalli** at Hämeenkatu 19. During term time, the liveliest spot in
the **evening** is the student house, *Yo-talo*, Kauppakatu 10, which often features live
music, though in high summer *Tullikamari*, Tullikamarin Aukio 2 is often a better bet.
If you just want a drink, consider the *Tillikka* theatre by the bridge on Hämeenkatu,
frequented by students and arty types.

Savonlinna

Leisurely draped across islands, **SAVONLINNA** is one of the most relaxed towns in
Finland, a woodworking centre that also makes a decent living from tourism and its
annual opera festival in July. It's packed throughout summer, but out of peak season its
streets and beaches are uncluttered, and the town's easy-going mood – enhanced by
the slow glide of pleasure craft from its harbour – makes it a place to linger.

The best locations for soaking up the atmosphere are the **harbour** and **kauppatori**
(market square) at the end of Olavinkatu, where you can cast an eye over the grand
Seurahuone Hotel facing the **kauppahalli**. Erected in 1901, it burned down in 1947
when it was notorious as a speakeasy, selling "hard tea" laced with brandy and home-
brewed *pirtu*. While the forbidden pleasures are long gone and their current equivalents at the bar are forbiddingly expensive, you can still admire the reconstructed
Forties decor with its Art Nouveau fripperies. Follow the harbour around Linnankatu,
or better still around the sandy edge of Pihlajavesi, which brings you to atmospheric
Olavinlinna Castle (daily June to mid-Aug 10am–5pm; mid–Aug to May 10am–3pm;
14mk), perched on a small island. Catch one of the guided tours on the hour, as the
castle's excellent state of repair is matched by an intriguing history. Founded in 1475, it
witnessed a series of bloody conflicts, with ownership alternating between Sweden and

Russia during the eighteenth century, until the Russians claimed permanent possession in 1743. When Finland became a Tsarist Grand Duchy the fort was relegated to being the town jail, and the Russians added the characteristic brick extensions to the towers. Also remarkable are the brick cubicles which jut outwards from the main living rooms, possibly the first WCs in Finland; there's a drop through the pan to the river several dozen metres below. You can spend half a day here exploring two small museums. The **Orthodox Museum** has a dozen fine relics rescued from Valamo and Viipuri (both now in Russia), in June and July, you can watch rehearsals for the opera which takes place in the main courtyard. The 50mk lunches in the café are excellent too. The **Provincial Museum** (July daily 10am–8pm; Aug–June daily except Mon 11am–5pm; 12mk) occupies an old granary and displays an intriguing account of the evolution of local life, with rock paintings and a 4000-year old piece of amber with a carving of a human on it found nearby. At the end of the jetty, there are a couple of turn-of-the-century **Museum ships** (June–Aug only), which earned their keep plying the Saimaa waterways, sometimes travelling as far as St Petersburg and Lübeck.

Practicalities

Of the two **train stations**, be sure to get off at *Savonlinna-Kauppatori*, just across the main bridge from the **tourist office** at Puistokatu 1 (June daily 8am–6pm; July daily 8am–10pm; Aug–Sept Mon–Fri 9am–4pm). The **bus station** is off the main island but within easy walking distance of the town centre. Most central **accommodation** is the private hostel *Hospits*, Linnankatu 20 (☎957/22443; ③); there is an official **youth hostel**, *Malakias*, Pihlajavedenkuja 6 (June–Aug; ☎957/23283; ③), 2km west of the centre along Tulliportinkatu and then Savontie, and a summer hotel, the *Vuorilinna*, on Kasinonsaari (☎957/5750494; ③), five minutes over the bridge from the marketplace. Alternatively, you could rent a **cabin** bed (②) in the *Heinävesi* steamship in the harbour. The nearest **campsite**, 7km from the centre at Vuohimäki, is open June to August. Anything sold around the harbour is liable to be overpriced; you can find cheaper, better **food** in the pizza joints along Olavinkatu. *Majakka*, Satamakatu 11, offers good Finnish nosh at lunchtime, and *Linnakrouri*, on Linnankatu by the castle, also does good lunches and reasonably- priced drinks on the terrace.

Around Savonlinna

Savonlinna is deep in the heart of the Lake Region and boasts beautiful scenery all around, as well as being a jumping-off point for several striking places a little way beyond. Closest is the **Punkaharju Ridge**, a narrow strip of land between the Puruvesi and Pihlalavesi lakes, 28km from town. Locals say it has the healthiest air in the world, super-oxygenated by abundant conifers, and with the water never more than a few metres away on either side, this is the Lake Region at its most breathtakingly beautiful. The ridge is traversable by road and rail, both running into the town of Punkaharju and passing the incredible **Retretti Arts Centre** (daily 10am–6/7pm; 60mk, 2-day pass 65mk), situated in man-made caves gouged into three-billion-year-old rock, and with a large sculpture park outside in which fibreglass human figures by Olavi Lanu are cunningly entwined with natural forms. Buses **from Savonlinna to Punkaharju** are more expensive and less frequent than trains (8 daily in summer; 25mins; 15 mk each way), whose schedules should be checked at the tourist office. Either way, you need to make a special request to be dropped at Retretti. It's more expensive but a lot more convenient to catch one of the special direct buses to Retretti, which run from the *Finnair* office near Savonlinna's *kauppatori* (market square), about every half-hour during the summer. **Boats** run from Savonlinna harbour; 120mk for the round trip.

Kuopio

Superficially cosmopolitan with smart broad streets and modern buildings, **KUOPIO** is the only city in a vast expanse of countryside, and its earthy peasant heritage is always felt: traditional dress is common, sophistication is rare – and everything takes a back seat to unbridled revelry when the night comes.

All the sights are within the immediate central area, with one exception: the wonderful **Orthodox Church Museum** (May–Aug Tues–Sun 10am–4pm; Sept–April Mon–Fri noon–3pm, Sat & Sun noon–5pm; 15mk) on the brow of the hill, the road to which begins at the junction of Asemakatu and Puistokatu. The museum houses many objects from nearby Valamo Monastery and it's easy to spend several hours wandering around elaborate icons, gold-embossed Bibles, gowns, prayer books and other extravagant items. Back in the centre, the block formed by Kirkkokatu and Kuninkaankatu holds the **Kuopio Open-Air Museum** (mid-May to mid-Sept daily 10am–5pm, Wed also 5–7pm; mid-Sept to mid-May daily except Mon 10am–3pm; 15mk), whose buildings, still in their original locations, have interiors decked out to show housing conditions of ordinary townspeople from the late eighteenth century to the 1930s. A few streets away is another old house, **J.V. Snellman's Home**, by the corner of Snellmaninkatu and Minna Canthinkatu (mid-May to mid-Sept daily 10am–5pm, Wed until 7pm; 10mk). Snellman lived here after the Swedish-speaking ruling class expelled him from his university post in 1843, and he became head of the local school and continued his struggle to have Finnish granted the status of official language. Perhaps the best course in Kuopio, though, is to simply hang around the passenger **harbour** at the end of Kauppakatu, from where, amongst other destinations, a daily boat service makes the 11-hour trip to Savonlinna (250mk), and a day-long cruise (mid-June to mid-Aug; 210mk) gives the easiest access toValamo Monastery, the re-sited spiritual headquarters of Orthodox Karelia from the thirteenth century to the present day.

The **bus station** is at one end of Puijonkatu, which leads past the **train station** and into the **kauppatori**. The **kauppahalli** (Mon–Fri 8am–5pm, Sat 8am–1pm) adds a dash of colour and contrasts nicely with the uniform glass fronts of the encircling department stores. Opposite stands the nineteenth-century City Hall, around the side of which is the **tourist office** at Haapaniemenkatu 17 (early June to mid-Aug Mon–Fri 8am–5pm, Sat 9am–1pm; rest of year Mon–Fri 8am–5pm). The **youth hostel** is at Taivaanpankontie 14b (June to mid-August; ☎971/2822041), a thirty-minute walk or ride on bus #3 from the tourist office, or #5 from outside Kauppahalli (7mk). There are also a couple of more central private hostels – *Matkakoti Souuari*, Vuorikatu 42 (☎971/2622144; ③), and *Puijohovi*, Vuorikatu 35 (☎971/2614943; ③), straight ahead from the station – and *Hospitsi*, Myllkatu 4 (971/2614501; ③), right, then third left from the station. Away from the harbourside market, **food** is less exotic: *Restaurant Rosso*, Haapaniemenkatu 24–26, offers sizeable pizzas with help-yourself salads. *Taverna Traviata*, Kirkkokatu 40, does cheapish lunches, as does *Henry's Pub*, Kauppakatu 18, which might repay a second visit in the evening. Close to Kauppakatu is a small **market** which continues into the evening from June to August, and is the best place to sample the local speciality, *kalakukko*, a kind of bread pie of fish and pork.

Jyväskylä

JYVÄSKYLÄ is the most low-key and provincial of the main Lake Region towns, though it is well-known for its collection of buildings by **Alvar Aalto**. The legendary architect grew up here and opened his first office in the town in 1923, and his handiwork – a collection of buildings spanning his entire career including two of the town's four main museums (all daily except Mon 11am–6pm; 10mk, Fri free, combined ticket

20mk) – has greatly shaped the place. The **Alvar Aalto Museum** at Alvar Aalon Katu 7, housed in a purpose-built structure by the architect, leads off with an informative video followed by a collection of plans, photos and models, as well as a nice set of Aalto-designed furniture, and a **regional art gallery** boasting a fair display of twentieth-century paintings. Aalto also contributed to the exterior of the nearby **Museum of Central Finland**, which contains an interesting display of Jyväskylä home interiors from the nineteenth century, and designed the original core of **Jyväskylä University**, whose large campus is on the southwestern edge of the centre, right off Seminaarinkatu. The **Finnish Handicraft Museum** at Seminaarinkatu 32 is a centre for research into all kinds of crafts, with displays ranging from bell-making to jewellery, and the foursome is rounded off by the predictable and missable **National Costume Centre** at Gummeruksenkatu 3.

The **tourist office**, at Vapaudenkatu 38 (June–Aug Mon–Fri 8am–6pm, Sat & Sun 10am–6pm; Sept–May Mon–Fri 8am–5pm), is less than ten minutes' walk from the closest budget accommodation, *Amis Summerhotel*, Sepänkatu 3 (☎941/612920; ④). The **youth hostel**, Laajavuorentie 15 (☎941/253355), is a state-of-the-art affair 4km north of the centre along bus route #25 (7.5mk). The bus leaves from outside the tourist office, as does the #8 to the nearest **campsite** (June–Aug), 3km north off the E75 – take Puistokatu and then continue along Taulumäentie. **Eating** options veer from pizza establishments along the main streets through *Ravintola Elissa*, Väinönkatu 7, selling low-cost meals from one of Aalto's earliest commissions – a worker's club – to the more upmarket *Kissanviikset* ("The Cat's Whiskers") at Puistokatu 3, which serves some sizeable and just about affordable fish dishes at lunchtime. For the evening, *Alvari*, Kauppakatu 30, is a popular self-service bar, and *Becker's Book Café*, Seminaarinkatu 28, has a gay night on Wednesdays.

NORTHERN FINLAND

The three northern regions of **Ostrobothnia**, **Kainuu** and **Lappland** take up by far the largest portion of Finland, though unlike the populous south or more industrialized sections of the Lake Region, they're predominantly rural areas, a series of small communities separated by long distances. The coast of **Ostrobothnia** is home to most of the country's Swedish-speaking Finland-Swedes, a fairly affluent part of the country due to the flat and fertile farmlands, though one you're only really likely to visit in order to take a ferry to Sweden from either **Vaasa** or **Kokkola**. Even busy and expanding **Oulu**, the region's major city, has an off-putting anodyne quality, and the border town of **Tornio** to the north is mainly visited by Swedes drinking their sorrows away. **Kainuu** is the thickly forested, thinly populated heart of Finland and is traditionally peasant land, a poor area on the whole, though this is being alleviated by the marketing of the area's strong natural appeal – woods, rivers, hills and wide stretches of barely inhabited country, as well as a pleasant main centre in **Kajaani**. **Lappland**, too, is poor, remote territory, excitingly unexplored, although the bland town of **Rovaniemi**, the main gateway, shows little sign of any of this. However, it is the junction for the two major road routes into the **Arctic North**, whose wide open spaces are home to several thousand *Same*, who've lived in harmony with this special, harsh environment for millennia.

Oulu

The spick-and-span streets of OULU reflect the city's place as the national leader in computing industries, a far cry from the days when Oulu was a world centre for tar. Although the town's affluence made it a vibrant centre for business and the arts, today a handsome series of islands, a couple of highly conspicuous old buildings and the nightlife fuelled by the university are the only things bringing colour to Oulu's other-wise pallid tones. In the centre of town on Kirkkokatu, the **City Hall** retains some of the grandeur of the late nineteenth century, when it was built as a luxury hotel, and you can peek in on the wall-paintings and enclosed gardens that remain from the old days. Further along Kirkkokatu, the slight form of the **Tuomiokirkko** (summer daily 10am–7pm) seems outrageously anachronistic amidst the bulky blocks of modern Oulu. Inside the vestry, open on request, is a portrait of Johannes Messinius, the Swedish historian, supposedly painted by Cornelius Arenditz in 1611 and believed to be the oldest surviving oil portrait in Finland. Across the small canal just north of the cathedral, the **North Ostrobothnia Museum** (June–Aug Mon–Thurs 10am–6pm, Sat 10am–4pm, Sun 11am–5pm; Sept–May Mon–Thurs closes 4pm; 10mk), packed with tar-stained remnants from Oulu's past, is a large regional collection with a good *Same* section. If something more up-to-the-minute appeals, make for *Tietomaa,* a few steps away at Nakatehtaankatu 6 (April to mid-Aug daily 10am–6pm; 55mk), where experi-encing virtual reality to the strains of *Tubular Bells* is the main draw amongst all the pseudo-educational computer- and physics-related gear.

The connected **train station** and **bus station** are linked to the city centre by several parallel streets feeding to the **kauppatori** and **kauppahalli** (markets) by the water beyond. The **tourist office** is at Torikatu 10 (Mon–Fri 9am–4pm) assisted by a kiosk on Kirkkokatu (open daily). Low-cost **accommodation** in the centre is limited to the *Turisti*, Rautatienkatu 9 (✶981/375233; ④), which provides hostel-type accommodation during summer, when it takes the overspill from the official **youth hostel** at Kajaanintie 36 (June–Aug; ✶981/377707; ③), a fifteen-minute walk from the train station. Bus #5 from outside the tourist office can get you to a **campsite** with cabins at Mustassaari on Hietasaari Island, 4km from town. Budget **eating** options are mainly limited to Oulu's many pizzerias, cheapest of which are *Rosso* at Kirkkokatu 10, and, especially at lunch-time, *Lafesta*, Pakkahuoneenkatu 34, right by the train station. With a slightly deeper pocket, try the bizarre *Ravintola Franzen*, on the corner of Kirkkokatu and Kajaaninkatu, which has a quiet cellar bar decorated with bits dug up from a nearby cemetery. Best of numerous **cafés** and **pubs** is *Café Clementine* (often referred to as *Rauhala*) in the Ainola Park at Mannenkatu 1 – small and cosy with modest prices, a loud jukebox and peaceful garden. For coffee and cake, don't miss the nameless café in a tower five minutes' walk northwest of the centre along Merikosken Sillat.

Tornio

Situated on the extreme northern tip of the Gulf of Bothnia, **TORNIO** makes a living by selling booze to fugitives from Sweden's harsh alcohol laws, and catering to Finns who are here to enjoy the beach, fish, or shoot the nearby Tornionjoki Rapids. After the Swedish–Russian conflict of 1808–09, the border between Sweden and Finland was drawn around Suensaari, an oval piece of land jutting from the Swedish side into the river, on which central Tornio now sits. There's not much in the way of sights, and the dominant features of the town are its innumerable bars and restaurants. Simply stroll around Hallituskatu and Kauppakatu and drop into the ones with the most promising noises – try *Pub Tullin*, Hallituskatu 5, or *Aarninholvi*, Aarnintie 1. *Pizzeria Dar Menga*, Kauppakatu 12–14, is one of the cheapest spots for solid nourishment.

Long-distance buses terminate at Svensaari, while those replacing the train from Kemi (rail passes valid) pull up at the train station, a short walk across a bridge imme-diately opposite to get onto the island. The **tourist office** is at Lukiokatu 10 (June to mid-Aug Mon–Fri 8am–7pm, Sat & Sun 9am–7pm; mid-Aug to May Mon–Fri 8am–4pm). It's probably cheaper to sleep across the border in Haparanda, though Tornio has two summer **youth hostels**, one central at Kirkkokatu 1 (✶698/41682; ②), the other beside a **campsite** on the banks of the mainland side of the river (✶698/40146).

Kajaani

KAJAANI, 178km southeast of Oulu, could hardly be more of a contrast to the communities of the Bothnian coast. Though small and pastoral, the town is by far the biggest settlement in this very rural part of Finland and offers some insight into Finnish life away from the more prosperous regions. Fittingly, it was in Kajaani that Elias Lönnrot wrote the final parts of the *Kalevala*, the nineteenth-century collection of Finnish folk tales which extolled the virtues of traditional peasant life.

From the **train station**, Kauppakatu leads directly into Kajaani's minuscule centre. The decorative exterior of the **Kainuu Museum** at Asemakatu 4 (Tues & Thurs–Sat noon–3pm, Wed noon–8pm, Sun noon–6pm; free) holds an engrossingly ramshackle collection of local art and history that says a lot about the down-to-earth qualities of the area, as does the dramatic **Kajaani kirkko**, whose wooden frame, weird turrets and angular arches, heralded as the epitome of neo-Gothic style when the church was completed in 1896, resemble a leftover from a *Munsters* set. More historically significant, the ruined **Kajaani Castle** was built in the seventeenth century to forestall a Russian attack, and later served as a prison where troublesome Swede Johannes Messenius was incarcerated. Although schemes to rebuild it are constantly bandied about, the castle was ruined so long ago that nobody's sure what it actually looked like.

The official **youth hostel** at Oravantie 1–3 (June–Aug; ☎986/25704; ②) is on the far side of town from the train station (from Pohjolankatu turn into Sissikatu and continue through the parks); or you might try the more central hostel, *Nevalainen*, at Pohjolankatu 4 (☎986/22254; ④). The **campsite** is by the river and open from June to August. The **tourist office** is at Pohjohlankatu 16 (mid-June to mid-Aug Mon–Fri 8am–6pm, Sat 9am–2pm; rest of year Mon–Fri 8am–noon & 1–4pm).

Rovaniemi and around

Relatively easy to reach by rail from Ostrobothnia or Kainuu, **ROVANIEMI** is touted as the capital of Lappland, though it's more an administrative than cultural capital, and the tourists who arrive on day trips from Helsinki expecting sleighs and tents are normally disappointed. The wooden huts of old Rovaniemi were razed by departing Germans at the close of World War II and the town completely rebuilt during the late 1940s. Alvar Aalto's bold but impractical design has the roads forming the shape of reindeer antlers – fine if you're travelling by helicopter but making journeys on foot far longer than they need be. Rovaniemi is a likeable enough town, though most visitors only use it as a short-term stopover, or to study *Same* culture.

Aside from eating reindeer in the local restaurants, the best way to prepare yourself for what lies further north is to visit the 172m long glass tunnel of **Arktikum**, Pohjoisranta 4 (mid-June to Aug daily 10am–8pm; late-June to late July 10pm–midnight; Sept to mid-June daily except Mon 10am–6pm; 30mk), symbolically pointing north across Ounasjoki from its surrounding landscape of arctic flora. Subterranean galleries along one side house the **Provincial Museum of Lappland**, a thoughtful museum, placing genuine *Same* crafts and costumes alongside the imitations sold in souvenir shops to emphasize the romanticization of their culture. It also demonstrates the changes in the use of tools and clothing – anoraks and Wellington boots have replaced traditional apparel, which has caused a young generation of *Same* to be plagued by rheumatism and foot trouble. Without fluent Finnish or *Same*, you are reliant on an adequate synopsis borrowed from reception, a problem not experienced across the corridor in the **Arctic Centre**. This gives a thorough treatment of all things circumpolar from Invit and Alevt languages to mineral exploration and hunting from kayaks decked out in rather dashing walrus-gut waterproofs.

The remaining sights are on the south side of town near the bus and train stations, where three pristine Aalto-designed civic buildings line Hallituskatu. **Lappia House** (mid-June to mid-Aug; free guided tours Mon–Fri 10am, 1pm & 3pm) has a theatre and concert hall, and next door, the **library** (June–Aug Mon–Fri 11am–7pm, Sat 10am–4pm; Sept–May Mon–Fri 11am–8pm, Sat 10am–4pm) has a **Lappland Department**, with a staggering hoard of books in many languages covering every *Same*-related subject, a growing collection and the largest of its kind. Other attractions are few. At Kirkkotie 1, **Rovaniemi Seurakunta** church (June to mid-Sept daily 9am–8pm) repays a peek with its huge altar fresco, *Fountain of Life* by Lennart Segerstråle, an odd work pitching the struggle between good and evil into a Lappish setting. But most other things of interest are outside town, not least the **Arctic Circle**, 8km north and connected roughly hourly to the centre by bus #8 or #10 – though there's not much to see on arrival. Near the circle and served by the same buses, is **Santa Claus Village** (June–Aug daily 8am–8pm; Sept–May daily 9am–5pm; free), a large log cabin where you can meet Father Christmas all year round, contemplate reindeer grazing in the adjoining farm and leave your name for a Christmas card from Santa himself. If you've time to kill and the weather isn't too cold (Rovaniemi's prone to chilly snaps even in summer), two outdoor museums lie near each other just beyond town, accessible by buses #3 or #6, or a 4km walk. The **Ethnographical Museum Pöykkölä** (June–Aug daily except Mon noon–4pm; 5mk) is a collection of farm buildings which belonged to the Pöykkölä family from 1640 to 1910, and forms part of a pot-pourri of things pertaining to reindeer husbandry, salmon fishing and rural life in general. Five hundred metres up the road is the **Lappish Forestry Museum** (June to mid-Sept Tues–Sun noon–6pm; 10mk), where the reality of unglamorous forestry life is remembered by a reconstructed lumber camp. Although south of the Arctic Circle, the **midnight sun** is visible from town for a couple of weeks either side of mid-summer. The best spots are the striking "Lumberjack's Candlestick" bridge or 30 minutes' walk on the far side atop the conifer and mosquito-clad hill, Ounasvaara.

Practicalities

The main **tourist office** may no longer be in the town centre at Aallonkatu 1, but is sure to be well sign-posted, and open daily until 7pm or 8pm in summer. The **youth hostel** at Hallituskatu 16 (☎960/3446444; ②) is open all year but always crowded in summer – try to book in advance. Otherwise you can always fall back on the guesthouses, all within five minutes' walk of the train station: *Matka-kalle*, Asemieskatul (☎960/20130; ②), and *Outa*, Ukkoherrantie 16 (☎960/312474; ②), or *Ammattioppilaitoksksen*, Kairatie 75 (mid-June to early Aug; ☎960/392651; ②). The only other budget accommodation is the **campsite** on the far bank of Ounasjoki, facing town, a 30-minute walk from the station. *Sampo*, at Korkalonkatu 32, has a good line in inexpensive lunches and evening **meals**, their terrace bar becoming a popular spot to while away a summer evening.

travel details

Trains

Helsinki to: Jyväskylä (7 daily; 4hr); Kajaani (5 daily; 7hr 30min); Kuopio (7 daily; 5hr 30min); Oulu (7 daily; 8hr 30min); Rovaniemi (4 daily; 10hr 30min); Tampere (12 daily; 2hr 15min); Turku (7 daily; 2hr 15min).

Jyväskylä to: Tampere (7 daily; 1hr 45min).

Kokkola to: Helsinki (9 daily; 4hr); Oulu (6 daily; 2hr 30min); Tampere (9 daily; 3hr 45min).

Kuopio to: Jyväskylä (6 daily; 3hr 45min); Kajaani (4 daily; 2hr 15min).

Oulu to: Kajaani (4 daily; 2hr 45min); Rovaniemi (5 daily; 3hr); Tornio (4 daily; 2hr 15min).

Pori to: Tampere (7 daily; 2hr).

Tampere to: Helsinki (12 daily; 2hr 15min); Oulu (6 daily; 5hr 15min); Pori (6 daily; 1hr 45min); Savonlinna (1 daily; 4hr); Turku (7 daily; 2hr 15min).

Turku to: Tampere (6 daily; 2hr 30min).

Vaasa to: Helsinki (7 daily; 4hr 30min); Jyväskylä (2 daily; 5hr 30min); Oulu (4 daily; 5hr 30min); Tampere (4 daily; 2hr 30min).

Buses

Helsinki to: Jyväskylä (8 daily; 5hr); Kotka (7–9 daily; 1hr 30min); Lahti (26 daily; 1hr 30min);

Mikkeli (8 daily; 4hr); Porvoo (18 daily; 1hr); Savonlinna (3 daily; 5hr 30min); Tampere (16 daily; 3hr); Turku (21 daily; 2hr 30min).

Kuopio to: Jyväskylä (3 daily; 2hr 15min).

Savonlinna to: Kuopio (3 daily; 3hr).

Tampere to: Helsinki (5 daily; 2hr); Turku (5 daily; 2hr 30min).

Turku to: Pori (7 daily; 2hr).

CHAPTER 7

FRANCE

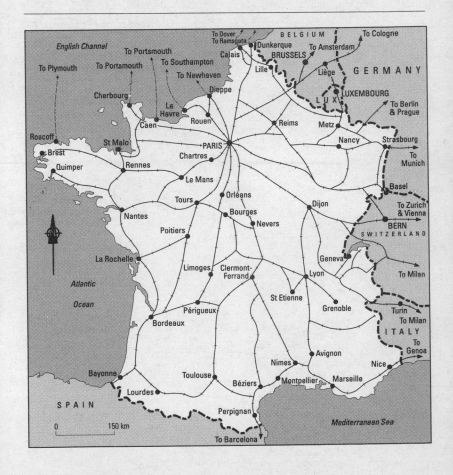

Introduction

Straddling the heart of the continent between the Iberian peninsula and the nations of eastern and southern Europe, **France** is a core country on any European tour. It is also, perhaps, its most diverse, and would be hard to exhaust in a lifetime of visits. Each area of the country looks different, feels different, has its own style of architecture and food, often its own patois or dialect, giving a strong sense of regional identity, together with an astonishing variety of things to see, whether it's the Gothic cathedrals of the north, the Romanesque churches of the centre and west, the châteaux of the Loire, the Roman monuments of the south, or the prehistoric cave-paintings of the Dordogne – not to mention the fabulous collections of paintings, many but not all of which are in Paris. The countryside, too, has its own appeal, still very rural, and, away from the urban centres, seemingly little changed for hundreds of years.

Travelling in France is easy. Budget restaurants and hotels proliferate everywhere; rail services are highly efficient, as is the road network; and the tourist information service is highly organized, with offices in practically every place in the land. As for where to go, it's hard to know where to begin. The north is perhaps the least enticing part, though you may inevitably pass through the Channel ports of **Flanders**, **Artois** and **Normandy**, and **Paris** is, of course, one of Europe's most elegant and compelling capitals. The rocky coasts of **Brittany** to the west are a possible attraction, too, as are the châteaux of the **Loire**, although most people push impatiently on south, heading for the limestone hills of **Provence**, the canyons of the **Pyrenées** and the glorious Mediterranean coastline of the **Côte d'Azur**. There are good reasons, however, for taking things more slowly, not least the Germanic towns of **Alsace** in the east, the gorgeous hills and valleys of the **Lot** and the **Dordogne**, and, more adventurously, the **Massif Central** – France's high heartland.

Information and Maps

You'll find a *Syndicat d'Initiative* or **SI** in practically every town and many villages, giving local information, including listings of things to see, bike hire, and usually free maps. They can also sometimes book accommodation anywhere in France. In larger cities and tourist resorts these will be open every day during the high season, often without a break, although times are greatly cut back in most places in the winter months.

The best **road map** of France is the *Michelin* 1:1,000,000 scale one. A useful free map for car drivers, obtainable from filling stations and traffic information kiosks in France, is the *Bison Futé*, showing alternative back routes. For more **regional detail**, the *Michelin* yellow series (scale 1:200,000) is best for the motorist. If you're planning to **walk or cycle**, check the *IGN* green (1:100,000 and 1:50,000) and purple (1:25,000) maps.

Money and Banks

French currency is the franc, which is divided into 100 centimes and comes in notes of F20, F50, F10 and F500, and coins of F1, F2, F5, F10, and 5c, 10c, 20c and 50c. The best place to change money is a bank: standard **banking hours** are 9am–noon and 2–4pm, closed on Sundays and either Monday or Saturday. Rates of exchange and commissions vary greatly; the *Banque National de Paris* often offer the best rate for the least commission. Outside of banking hours, there are **exchange counters** at the train stations of all big cities, and usually one or two in the town centre as well, though normally they offer a much worse deal.

Communications

The French term for a **post office** is either *PTT* or *Bureau de Poste*. They are generally open Mon–Fri 8am–noon and 2.30–7pm, Sat 8am–noon, although you can buy **stamps** (*timbres*) with less queuing from *tabacs*. You can make international **phone calls** from any box, and many post offices have metered booths from which you can make calls and pay afterwards. Some phones take 50c, F1, F5 and F10 coins, but most now only take **phone cards**, available for F40 from post offices and *PTT* boutiques. For calls within France – local or long distance – just dial all 8 digits of the number (which includes the former area code – displayed in every *cabine*): Paris is an exception, though: to call from Paris to anywhere else in France, you must first dial ☎16, and to call a Paris number from anywhere else, first dial ☎16–1. The operator number is ☎10.

Getting Around

With the most extensive railway network in western Europe, run by the *SNCF*, France is a country to travel by rail. The only areas not well served are the mountains, but there rail routes are replaced by *SNCF* buses. The private bus services are confusing and uncoordinated.

■ Trains and buses

SNCF **trains** are by and large clean, fast and frequent. **Fares** are reasonable, averaging – off-peak – about 70c per kilometre. The ultra-fast and ever more numerous *TGV*s (*Trains à Grande Vitesse*) require a supplement at peak times and compulsory reservation, costing around F20. The slowest trains are those marked *Autotrain* in the timetable, stopping at all stations.

The under-26 *InterRail* and all *Eurrail* **passes** are valid throughout the country, and there's also the *Eurodomino* pass, which gives unlimited travel throughout France for 3, 5 or 10 days within a month: 3 days, under 26 £84, over 26 £103; 5 days £124/141; 10 days £195/221, though you have to buy it before you enter the country. *SNCF* also offer a whole range of **discount fares**, depending on colour-coded time periods: blue, white and red, of which *période bleue* days – in effect most of the year – give the largest discounts. Under-26s can also buy a *Carissimo* pass: F190 allows travel at half-fare on 4 journeys on blue period days, F350 gives half-fares on 8 journeys. If the journeys are taken on white days the discount is 20 percent. Buying a return ticket for a total distance of over 1000km also qualifies you for a 25 percent discount (*billet séjour*), again as long as you travel on blue days. All tickets (not passes) must be stamped in the orange machines that obstruct station platforms. Rail journeys may be broken any time, anywhere, for a period of up to 24 hours. On night trains an extra F80 or so will buy you a **couchette**.

Regional **rail maps** and **timetables** are on sale at tobacconists; leaflet timetables are available free at train stations – **gares SNCF**. All but the smallest stations have an information desk and *consignes automatiques* – coin-operated left-luggage lockers. Many also rent out bicycles (see below).

Autocar at the top of a timetable column means it's an **SNCF bus service**, on which rail tickets and passes are valid. With the exception of these, the only time you'll need to take a **bus** is in cities – indeed the most frustrating thing about buses is that they rarely serve the regions outside the *SNCF* network, which is precisely where you need them. If you do need to use the bus, you'll find that the bus station – *gare routière* – in larger towns is normally next to the train station.

■ Driving, hitching and cycling

Taking a **car** gives you enormous advantages of access to remote areas, especially if you're camping. Overseas drivers' licences are valid for driving in France, and you should also carry your vehicle registration document and insurance papers. Motorways (*autoroutes*) are fairly extensive and fast, but the tolls on them are expensive; it's better to use "N" roads on the whole, which are fast enough, or, where possible, "D" roads, the next grade down. The main rule of the road to remember is that you must give way to traffic coming from your right, even when it is coming from a minor road – though on main roads there are nearly always signs to the contrary, usually a yellow diamond road sign. As for speed limits, they are 130kph on motorways, 110kph on major roads, 90kph on other roads and 60kph in towns. Fines for driving violations are exacted on the spot and only cash or a French bank account cheque are accepted. The minimum for speeding is F1300 and for exceeding the drink/driving level F2500–5000. For **information** on road conditions call *Inter Service Route* on ☎1.48.58.33.33 (24hr). In case of breakdown, there are emergency phones every 2km on the motorways. Otherwise, call the *Automobile Secours Service* (☎05.05.05.24). **Car rental** is about F2000–2500 a week for a small hatchback with unlimited mileage.

Hitching, you'll have to rely almost exclusively on car drivers, and it won't be easy – the French aren't renowned for their sympathy to hitch-hikers. On motorways the tollbooths at each major junction are the best bet for picking up long lifts. To avoid long waits, you might be better off contacting *Allostop*, a national organization with offices in Paris and a few other major towns. In return for a registration fee, they'll match you up with a driver who is going your way and wants to share petrol costs.

Keen **cyclists** are much admired in France. Traffic keeps a respectful distance (save in the big cities) and restaurants and hotels go out of their way to find a safe place for your bike, even letting you take it up to your room. You can take your bike free on some *SNCF* services – labelled *Autotrains*; on other services you have to pay F30 and hand your bike in well in advance. For details, consult the free leaflet *Train et Vélo*, available from most stations. Most *SNCF* stations also **rent bikes** for around F45F per day plus F1000–1500 deposit (or a credit card number). You can return the bike to any other specified station.

Accommodation

For most of the year it's possible to turn up in any French town and find a room or a place in a campsite. Booking a couple of nights in advance can, however, be reassuring, and is essential between July 15 and August 15, when the French take their vacations. The first weekend of August is the busiest time of all, though campsites are still usually okay unless you're travelling with a caravan.

■ Hotels

All French **hotels** are officially graded, and prices are relatively uniform. Ungraded and single-star hotels go for F80–130 per double, and are often very good; for private bath, reckon on paying around F30 more, plus sometimes F20–35 for breakfast – although there is no obligation to take this and you will nearly always do better at a café. For a room in a two-star place, which will normally always include private bath, reckon on F150–250 on average. Officially it is illegal for hotels to insist on you taking meals, but they often do and in busy resorts you may not find a room unless you agree. In country areas, in addition to standard hotels, you will come across **chambres d'hôte** – bed and breakfast accommodation in someone's house or farm. These vary in standard but are rarely an especially cheap option, usually costing the equivalent of a two-star hotel. Full **accommodation lists** for each province are available from any French Government Tourist Office or from local SIs. Travelling in peak season, especially, it is worth getting hold of these, together with a handbook for the *Logis et Auberges de France* – independent hotels, promoted together for their consistently good food and reasonably priced rooms; they're recognizable by a green and yellow logo.

■ Hostels and foyers

France boasts a wide network of official **youth hostels** or *auberges de jeunesse*, and most are of a high standard. However, their prices, while cheap – F25–80 for a dormitory bed (more in Paris) – are sometimes not much less expensive than the cheapest hotel room for a couple – particularly if you take into account fares to their sometimes inaccessible locations. Hostels do, however, sometimes allow you to cut costs by preparing your own food in their kitchens, or eating in their cheap canteens. There are two rival French youth hostel associations: the *Fédération Unie des Auberges de Jeunesse*, 27 rue Pajol, 75018 Paris (☎46.07.00.01), and the *Ligue Française pour les Auberges de Jeunesse*, 38 bd Raspail, 75007 Paris (☎45.48.69.84). *IYHF* membership covers both organizations, although only the former's hostels are detailed in their handbook.

A few large towns provide a more luxurious standard of hostel accommodation in **Foyers des Jeunes Travailleurs/euses**, residential hostels for young workers and students, charging around F60 for an individual room. They also normally have a good canteen. Bear in mind, too, in rural areas, **gîtes d'étape** – less formal than the youth hostels, often run by the local village or municipality and providing bunk beds and primitive kitchen facilities. A selective list of *gîtes* and *chambres d'hôtes* is given in the booklet *Acceuil à la Campagne*, sold by French Government tourist offices.

ACCOMMODATION PRICE CODES

Throughout this guide, accommodation is priced on a scale of ① to ⑧, the number indicating the lowest price per night a single person could expect to pay in that establishment in high season. With hostels this is the nightly rate per person; with hotels, the price is arrived at by dividing the cost of the cheapest double room by two. The prices indicated by the codes are as follows

① = under £5 / $8   ② = £5–10 / $8–16   ③ = £10–15 / $16–24   ④ = £15–20 / $24–32

⑤ = £20–25 / $32–40   ⑥ = £25–30 / $40–48   ⑦ = £30–35 / $48–56   ⑧ = over £35 / $56

■ Campsites

Practically every village and town in the country has at least one **campsite** to cater to the thousands of French people who spend their holiday under canvas. The cheapest – at F10–15 per person per night – is usually the *Camping Municipal*, normally clean, well-equipped and in a prime location. On the coast especially, there are superior categories of campsite, where you'll pay similar amounts to a hotel room for what can be extensive facilities. Inland, camping on somebody's farm is another possibility. Lists of sites are detailed in the Tourist Board's *Accueil à la Campagne* booklet. Incidentally, never **camp rough** (*camping sauvage*) on anyone's land without first asking permission. If the dogs don't get you, the guns might – farmers have been known to shoot before asking any questions.

Food and Drink

French food is as good a reason as any for a visit to France. Cooking has art status, the top chefs are stars, and dining out is a national pastime, whether it's at the local brasserie or a famed house of *haute cuisine*. It also doesn't have to cost much as long as you avoid tourist hot-spots.

■ Food

Generally the best place to eat **breakfast** is in a bar or café. Most serve buttered *baguettes* (French bread sticks) and have a basket of croissants or hard-boiled eggs on the counter, to which you can help yourself; the waiter will keep an eye on how much you've eaten and bill you accordingly. Coffee is invariably espresso and strong. *Un café* or *un express* is black; *un crème* is with milk; *un grand café* is a large cup. In the morning, ask for *café au lait* – espresso in a large cup or bowl with hot milk. Ordinary tea (*thé*) is not often drunk; to have milk with it, ask for *un peu de lait frais*. *Chocolat chaud* – hot chocolate – unlike tea, lives up to the high standards of French food and drink and can be had in any café. Every bar or café displays a full price list for drinks at the bar (*au comptoir*), sitting down (*la salle*), or on the terrace (*la terrasse*) – all progressively more expensive.

The same places are also often the best option for **lunch**, when they serve omelettes, fried eggs and various sandwiches – generally a half-*baguette* filled with cheese or meat. You may also come across *croque-monsieurs* and

madames (variations on the grilled-cheese sandwich), along with – on street stalls – *frites*, *crêpes*, *galettes* (wholewheat pancakes), *gauffres* (waffles) and Tunisian snacks like *brik à l'oeuf* (fried pastry with egg) and *merguez* (spicy sausage). For **picnic and takeaway food**, there's nothing to beat the *charcuterie* ready-made dishes – salads, meats and fully prepared main courses – also available at supermarket *charcuterie* counters. You buy by weight, or you can ask for *une tranche* (a slice), *une barquette* (a carton) or *une part* (a portion).

You can also eat lunch at a **brasserie** – like a restaurant only open all day and geared more to quicker meals; **restaurants** tend to stick to the traditional meal times of noon–2pm and 7–9.30 or 10.30pm. In major cities, town centre brasseries often serve until 11pm or midnight. Prices at both are posted outside. Normally there is a choice between one or more *menus fixes*, where the number of courses has already been determined – starting at F50 and rising to infinity – and à la carte, choosing from the menu, which is invariably more expensive than the *menu fixe* but often the only thing available after 9pm. Look out, both at lunch- and dinnertime, for the **plat du jour** (daily special), which for F35–60 in a cheap restaurant will often be the most interesting and best-value thing on the menu. *Service compris* means the service charge is included; if it's not you need to calculate an additional 15 percent. Wine (*vin*) or a drink (*boisson*) may be included; when ordering wine, ask for *un quart*, *un demi-litre* or *une carafe* (a litre). You'll normally be given the house wine unless you specify otherwise.

■ Drink

Where you can eat you can invariably drink and vice versa. **Drinking** is done at a leisurely pace whether it's a prelude to food (*apéritif*), a sequel (*digestif*) or the accompaniment, and **cafés** are the standard places to do it. **Wine** – *vin* – is drunk at just about every meal or social occasion. *Vin de table* or *vin ordinaire* – table wine – is generally drinkable and always cheap. In wine-producing areas the local table wine can be very good indeed. *AC* (*Appellation d'Origine Contrôlée*) wines are another matter. They can be excellent value at the lower end of the price scale, where favourable French taxes keep prices down to £1 or so a bottle, but move much above it and you're soon paying serious prices for serious bottles. In a café, a **glass of wine** is simply *un rouge* or *un* *blanc*. If it is an *AC* wine you may have the choice of *un ballon* (round glass) or a smaller glass (*un verre*).

The familiar Belgian and German brands account for most of the **beer** you'll find, plus brands home-grown from Alsace. Draught (*à la pression*) is the cheapest alcoholic drink you can have next to coffee and wine – ask for *un demi* (third-litre). Stronger alcohol is drunk from 5am as a pre-work fortifier, right through the day – **Cognac** or **Armagnac** brandies, dozens of *eaux de vie* (distilled from fruit) and **liqueurs**. Measures are generous, but they don't come cheap. *Pastis*, aniseed drinks such as *Pernod* or *Ricard*, are also popular, served diluted with water and ice (*glaçons*) – very refreshing and not expensive.

On the **soft drink** front, bottled fruit juices include apricot (*jus d'abricot*), blackcurrant (*cassis*) and so on. You can also get fresh orange and lemon juice (*orange/citron pressé*). Bottles of **spring water** (*eau minérale*) – either sparkling (*pétillante*) or still (*eau plate*) – abound.

Opening Hours and Holidays

The basic **working hours** in France are 8am–noon and 2–6pm. Food shops often don't reopen till halfway through the afternoon, closing around 7.30 or 8pm. Sunday and Monday are the standard **closing days**, though you'll always find at least one *boulangerie* (baker) open. **Museums** open at around 10am and close between 5 and 6pm, with reduced hours outside the mid-May to mid-September period, sometimes even outside July and August. They also usually close on Monday or Tuesday, usually the latter. Admission charges can be very off-putting, though most state-owned museums give reductions to students so always carry your ISIC card. All shops, museums and offices are closed on the following **national holidays**: Jan 1; Easter Sunday; Easter Monday; Ascension Day; Pentecost (seventh Sunday after Easter, plus the Monday); May 1; May 8; July 14; Aug 15; Nov 1; Dec 25.

Emergencies

There are two main types of French police – the **Police Nationale** and the **Gendarmeries Nationale**. For all practical purposes, they are indistinguishable; if you need to report a theft, or other incident, you can go to either. You can be stopped anywhere in France and asked to produce ID, so always carry your passport and bear in mind it's normally not worth being difficult or facetious.

Under the French Social Security system every **hospital** visit, doctor's consultation and prescribed medicine is charged, though in an emergency not upfront. Although all employed French people are entitled to a refund of 75–80 percent of their medical expenses, this can still leave a hefty shortfall, especially after a stay in hospital. In **emergencies** you will always be admitted to the **local hospital** (*Centre Hospitalier*) whether under your own power or by ambulance. To find a **doctor**, stop at any *pharmacie* and ask for an address. Consultation fees for a visit should be F75–85 and in any case you'll be given a *Feuille de Soins* (Statement of Treatment) for later documentation of insurance claims. Prescriptions should be taken to a *pharmacie*, which is also equipped – and obliged – to give first aid (for a fee). For minor illnesses pharmacists will dispense free advice and a wide range of medication.

EMERGENCY NUMBERS
Police ☎17; Ambulance ☎15; Fire ☎18.

PARIS

PARIS is the paragon of style – perhaps the most glamorous and hi-tech city in Europe. Yet it is also deeply traditional, a village-like and in parts dilapidated metropolis – consider the sleepy atmosphere of Montmartre against the cold hard lines of La Défense, the multiplicity of markets and small shops against the giant malls of Montparnasse and Les Halles. Paris has long created its own myth. Famous names and events are invested with a glamour that elevates the city and its people to a legendary realm, and it still clings to its status as an artistic, intellectual and literary pace-setter. Perhaps it is not surprising that Parisians feel they are superior to ordinary mortals.

The city's history has conspired to create this sense of being apart. From a shaky start the kings of France, whose seat was Paris, gradually extended their control over their feudal rivals, centralizing administrative, legal, financial and political power as they did so. Louis XIV consolidated this process. Supremely autocratic, he inaugurated the tradition of Paris as symbol, the glorious reflection of the pre-eminence of the State. It is a tradition his successors have been only too happy to follow, whether as king, emperor or president. Napoleon I added to the Louvre and built the Arc de Triomphe, the Madeleine and the Arc du Carrousel. Napoléon III extended the Louvre even further and had Baron Haussmann redraw the rest of the city to a plan which still determines the shape of the centre. Recent presidents have initiated the skyscrapers at La Défense, the Tour Montparnasse, Beaubourg and Les Halles shopping precinct, the space age Parc de la Villette complex, the glass pyramid entrance to the Louvre, the Musée d'Orsay, and the new Bastille opera house.

Nowadays the most tangible and immediate pleasures of Paris are to be found in its streetlife. Few cities can compete with the cafés, bars and restaurants – modern and trendy, local and traditional, humble and pretentious – that line every street and boulevard. And the city's compactness makes it possible to experience the individual feel of the different quartiers. You can move easily, even on foot, from the calm, almost small-town atmosphere of Montmartre and parts of the Latin Quarter to the busy commercial centres of the Bourse and Opéra or to the aristocratic mansions of the Marais. A grand and imposing backdrop is provided by the monumental architecture of the Arc de Triomphe, the Louvre, the Eiffel Tower, the Hôtel de Ville, the bridges and the institutions of the state. As for entertainment, the city's strong points are in film and music. Paris is a real cinema capital, and although French rock is notoriously awful, the best Parisian music encompasses jazz, avante-garde, salsa and, currently, Europe's most vibrant African music scene.

Arrival and information

The two main Paris **airports** are Roissy-Charles de Gaulle and Orly. **Charles de Gaulle**, northeast of the city, is connected with the centre by *Roissy-Rail*, a combination of airport bus and RER train to the Gare du Nord every fifteen minutes – a 35-minute journey. There's also an *Air France* **bus**, which costs F35 and departs from door 6 every fifteen minutes, terminating at the Porte Maillot métro on av MacManon, on the northwest edge of the city, 100m from the Arc de Triomphe. **Taxis** into central Paris cost F160–220, and take between 45 and 60 minutes. **Orly**, south of Paris, has a bus–rail link, *Orly-Rail*, every fifteen minutes to the Gare d'Austerlitz and other Left Bank stops. Alternatively, there are *Air France* buses to the Gare des Invalides, or *Orlybus* to the Denfert-Rochereau métro. Both leave every ten or fifteen minutes; journey time is about 35 minutes. A taxi will take about the same time, and cost between F100 and F140. Travelling by **train**, Paris has six main-line stations, all on the métro system. The Gare du Nord services trains from Boulogne, Calais, Britain, Belgium, Holland and

Scandinavia; the Gare de l'Est serves eastern France, Germany, Switzerland and Austria; Gare St-Lazare serves the UK, Dieppe and the Normandy coast; Gare de Lyon is the arrival point of trains from the Alps, the South, Italy and Greece; Gare Montparnasse is the terminus for Versailles, Chartres, Brittany and the Atlantic coast; Gare d'Austerlitz is the station for trains from the southwest and southern Atlantic coast. All long-distance **buses** except *Citysprint* use the main gare routière at Porte de la Villette, where there's a métro; *Citysprint* coaches come in at rue St-Quentin, around the corner from the Gare du Nord.

There are **tourist offices** at four of the main stations – Austerlitz, Nord, Lyon and Est – and a main office at 127 av des Champs-Élysées (Mon–Sat 8/9am–8/9pm, Sun 9am–6/8pm; ☎47.23.61.72). They have maps and leaflets, and can book last-minute accommodation for a F20–55 fee, depending on the category of hotel. There's also the **Accueil des Jeunes en France** offices at 119 rue St-Martin, opposite Centre Beaubourg (Mon–Sat 9.30am–7pm; ☎42.77.87.80), and at 139 bd St-Michel (March–Oct Mon–Fri 9.30am–6.30pm; ☎43.54.95.86), which handles youth-oriented information and can book decent low-cost accommodation.

City transport

Finding your way around is easy: central Paris is relatively small, with a public transport system that is cheap, fast and meticulously signposted. The **métro** is the simplest way of getting around: stations are widespread, and the lines are colour-coded and numbered, although they are signposted within the system with the names of the stations at the ends of the lines. Every **bus** stop displays the numbers of the buses which stop there, a map showing all the stops on the route and the times of the first and last buses. Generally speaking, buses run from 6.30am until around 9pm, while the métro operates from early morning until just after midnight, after which **night buses** run on ten routes from place du Châtelet near the Hôtel de Ville every half-hour between 1.30 and 5.30am.

Free route **maps** are available at métro stations, bus terminals and tourist offices. The same flat-fare **tickets** cost F6.50 and are valid for the bus, métro, and, within the city limits, the RER express rail lines, which also extend out into the suburbs. Single tickets can be bought in *carnets* of ten from any station or *tabac* – currently 39F. Be sure to keep your ticket until the end of the journey; you'll be fined on the spot if you can't produce one. If you are staying more than a day or two, the *Carte Orange*, obtainable at all métro stations and *tabacs* (you need a passport photo), is better value, costing F59 for a week's travel (Mon–Sun) within the city centre. Alternatively, you can buy one-day coupons for F27, or three- and five-day visitor's coupons (*Paris Visites*) for F90 and F145 respectively, available only for first-class travel. Paris **taxis** are fairly reasonable, though they'll usually take a maximum of three passengers; if you can't find a cab on the street, call ☎45.85.85.85 or ☎42.70.41.41.

Accommodation

Not surprisingly, Paris is the most expensive part of France in which to find **accommodation**. However, compared to other European capitals it's still cheap, and it is perfectly possible to find somewhere decent and centrally placed for under F250, even as low as F170, for a double room without bath, although you should always book in advance. There are also, of course, numerous places offering **hostel** accommodation. In the main you have the choice between the hostels of three organizations: the official *IYHF* hostels, hostels run by the *Accueil des Jeunes en France (AJF)*, and those run by the *Union des Centres de Rencontres Internationaux de France (UCRIF)*. IYHF rates in Paris are F86–97 a night and there's normally a maximum stay of three to four days.

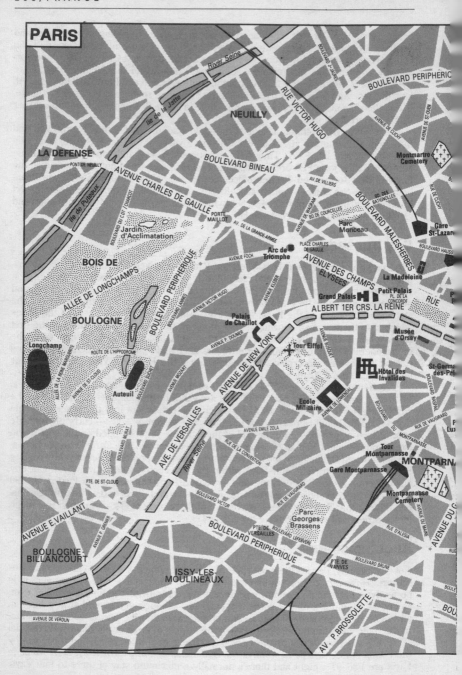

PARIS

AJF hostels, most of which are located in elegant old mansions in the Marais, charge around F105 a night and impose a maximum stay of five days; bear in mind also that you can't reserve a place in advance. *UCRIF* hostels, which are all centrally situated, charge F100 for dorm beds, rising to F160 for a private room; some do canteen meals for around F50 – again no advance bookings accepted.

IYHF hostels

D'Artagnan, 80 rue Vitruve, 20^e (☎43.61.08.75). Enormous hostel, with lots of facilities, but a fair way out on the eastern fringes of the city. M^o Porte de Bagnolet. ②

Jules Ferry, 8 bd Jules-Ferry, 11e (☎43.57.55.60). Smaller and more central than the other official *IYHF* hostel, situated in the lively area at the foot of the Belleville hill. M^o République. ②

AJF hostels

Le Fauconnier, 11 rue du Fauconnier, 4e (☎42.74.23.45). M^o St-Paul/Pont-Marie. ②

Le Fourcy, 6 rue de Fourcy, 4e (☎42.74.23.45). M^o St-Paul. ②

Maubuisson, 12 rue des Barres, 4e (☎42.72.72.09). M^o Pont-Marie/Hôtel-de-Ville. ②

Résidence Bastille, 151 av Ledru-Rollin, 11e (☎43.79.53.86). M^o Ledru-Rollin/Bastille/Voltaire. ②

UCRIF hostels

BVJ Centre International de Paris/Les Halles, 5 rue du Pélican, 1er (☎40.26.92.45). M^o Louvre/Châtelet-Les Halles/Palais-Royal. ②

BVJ Centre International de Paris/Louvre, 20 rue Jean-Jacques-Rousseau, 1er (☎42.36.88.18). M^o Louvre/Châtelet-Les Halles. ②

BVJ Centre International de Paris/Opéra, 11 rue Thérèse, 1er (☎42.60.77.23). M^o Pyramides/Palais-Royal. ②

BVJ Centre International de Paris/Quartier Latin, 44 rue des Bernardins, 5e (☎43.29.34.80). M^o Maubert-Mutualité. ②

Hotels

Hôtel des Alliés, 20 rue Berthollet, 5e (☎43.31.47.52). Simple and clean, and bargain prices. M^o Censier-Daubenton. ③

Avenir-Jonquière, 23 rue de la Jonquière, 17e (☎46.27.83.41). Clean, friendly establishment, and a good bargain. M^o Guy-Môquet. ③

Hôtel des Carmes, 5 rue des Carmes, 5e (☎43.29.78.40). Well-established and reasonable. M^o Maubert-Mutualité. ③

Castex, 5 rue Castex, 4e (☎42.72.31.52). Recently renovated building in a quiet street on the edge of the Marais. M^o Bastille. ④

Hôtel le Central, 6 rue Descartes, 5e (☎46.33.57.93). Clean and decent accommodation on top of the Montagne St-Geneviève. M^o Cardinal-Lemoine. ③

Hôtel du Centre Est, 4 rue Sibour, 10e (☎46.07.20.74). An excellent value cheapie, but you'll generally need to book. M^o Gare de l'Est. ③

Hôtel du Commerce, 14 rue de la Montagne-Ste-Geneviève, 5e (☎43.54.89.69). As cheap as you'll find, though it's pretty gloomy. M^o Maubert-Mutualité. ②

Hôtel du Dragon, 36 rue du Dragon, 6e (☎45.48.51.05). Great location and nice people: perfect if you're ready to spend a little more. M^o St-Germain-des-Prés. ④ – ⑤

Henri IV, 25 place Dauphine, 1er (☎43.54.44.53). Well-known cheapie in the beautiful place Dauphine on the Île de la Cité. Essential to book. M^o Pont-Neuf. ②

Idéal, 3 rue des Trois-Frères, 18e (☎46.06.63.63). Marvellous location on the slopes of Montmartre. A real bargain. M^o Abbesses. ③

Jeanne d'Arc, 3 rue de Jarente, 4e (☎48.87.62.11). Clean, quiet and attractive, though the Marais location means you have to reserve. M^o St-Paul. ⑤

Lévêque, 29 rue Cler, 7e (☎47.05.49.15). Clean and decent; nice people, who speak some English. Book one month ahead. M^o École-Militaire. ③

Marignan, 13 rue du Sommerard, 5ᵉ (☎43.25.31.03). One of the best bargains in town. Needs booking a month ahead in summer. Mᵒ Maubert-Mutualité. ③

Moderne, 3 rue Caron, 4ᵉ (☎48.87.97.05). Much better than the first impression of the staircase would suggest, and excellent value. Mᵒ St-Paul. ③

Oriental, 2 rue d'Arras, 5ᵉ (☎43.54.38.12). Recently refurbished, but still a good bargain for this locality – and nice people. Mᵒ Jussieu. ⑤

Pratic, 20 rue de l'Ingénieur-Keller, 15ᵉ (☎45.77.70.58). Clean and friendly. Close to the Eiffel Tower. Mᵒ Charles-Michels. ④

Tiquetonne, 6 rue Tiquetonne, 2ᵉ (☎42.36.94.58). Good value in an attractive small street. 4x Mᵒ Étienne-Marcel. ④

Tholozé, 24 rue Tholozé, 18ᵉ (☎46.06.74.83). Another real bargain – clean, friendly and quiet, in a steep street below the Moulin de la Galette. Mᵒ Blanche. ③

Campsites

The closest **campsite** to the centre of Paris is by the Seine in the Bois de Boulogne on the allée du Bord-de-l'Eau, 16e. It can get very crowded in summer and it's not especially pleasant at the best of times. It's also quite a walk from the nearest métro station at Porte Maillot. Really, it makes more sense to stay in a hostel.

The City

Paris is split into two halves by the Seine. On the north of the river, the **Right Bank** or *rive droite* is home to the grand boulevards and most monumental buildings, many dating from Haussmann's nineteenth-century redevelopment, and is where you'll spend most time, during the day at least. The top museums are here – the Louvre and Beaubourg, to name just two – as well as the the city's widest range of shops around rue de Rivoli and Les Halles; and there are also peaceful quarters like the Marais for idle strolling. The **Left Bank** (*rive gauche*) has a noticeably different feel, its very name conjuring Bohemian, dissident, intellectual connotations, and something of this atmosphere survives, in Paris' best range of bars and restaurants, some of which survive from the days when they were the haunts of Hemingway and Ezra Pound, and its most wanderable streets – the areas around St-Germain and St-Michel are full of nooks and crannies to explore. Parts of Paris, of course, don't sit easily in either category, notably the scruffier neighbourhoods of **Montmartre**, rising up immediately north of the city centre, which also trade on something of a boho tag, and the more solidly working-class districts of **eastern Paris**, with a new focus in the redevelopment of the **Parc de la Villette**, with its ground-breaking science museum. If you're planning to visit any museums, it's worth knowing that many reduce their entrance fees by up to half on Sunday.

The Voie Triomphale

As good a place as any to start exploring is along the **Voie Triomphale**, or Triumphal Way, which stretches in a dead straight line from the Louvre to the corporate skyscrapers at La Défense, 9km away, and incorporates some of the city's most famous landmarks. The best view is from the top of the **Arc de Triomphe**, Napoléon's homage to the armies of France and himself (daily 10am–5/6pm; F31), at the centre of **place de l'Étoile** – the world's first organized roundabout. From here the **Champs-Élysées** descends gracefully to the equally traffic-bound **place de la Concorde**, whose centrepiece, an obelisk from the temple of Luxor, was offered as a favour-currying gesture by the viceroy of Egypt in 1829. The symmetry continues beyond the square in the formal layout of the **Jardin des Tuileries**, which stretch down to the Louvre. Towards the river, the **Orangerie** (daily except Tues 9.45am–5.15pm; F26) displays Monet's largest water-lily paintings, as well as Cézanne's southern landscapes and portraits by van Dongen, Utrillo and Derain.

The Louvre

On the far side of the Tuileries gardens, the **Louvre** (Mon 9am–9.45pm, Wed 9am–9.45pm, Thurs–Sun 9am–6pm; F35) was first opened to the public in 1793, during the Revolution, and within a decade Napoléon had made it the largest art collection on earth with the takings from his empire. It's still a vast collection, numbingly so in fact, and it requires heroic stamina to trawl through the 300,000-odd artworks, despite the recent rearrangment of the collections. Entry is by way of I.M. Pei's controversial glass pyramid in the *Cour Napoléon*, underneath which a subterranean concourse gives onto the newly arranged sections of the museum: Sully (around the Cour Carrée), Denon (the south wing) and Richelieu (the north wing). The Sully wing holds Oriental and Egyptian antiquities, including jewellery, domestic objects, sarcophagi and dozens of examples of the delicate naturalism of Egyptian decorative technique, and statues like the pink granite *Mastaba Sphinx*. Greek and Roman antiquities divide between Denon and Sully, and include most famously the *Nike of Samothrace* and the *Venus de Milo*, one of the great sexpots of all time, both dating from the second century BC. There's applied arts, too, in the Sully and Denon wings, heavily weighted on the side of vulgar imperial opulence and ecologically catastrophic abuses such as the entire doors of tortoiseshell in the work of the renowned cabinet-maker Boulle (active round 1700), though there's relief in the smaller, less public items – Marie-Antoinette's travelling case, Limoges enamels and Byzantine ivories.

The sculpture section in Denon covers the entire development of the art in France from Romanesque to Rodin and includes Michelangelo's *Slaves*, designed for the tomb of Pope Julius II, although beyond that you may as well move on to the paintings, some of which are in Sully, some in Denon. The *Mona Lisa* in Denon is the painting most people make a beeline for, and is normally swamped with onlookers, no one paying the slightest attention to the other Leonardos in the room, including the *Virgin of the Rocks*. There is a good selection of other Italian paintings, including works by Giotto and Mantegna – a *Crucifixion* – one of Uccello's *Battle of San Romano* series, and, most strikingly, Paolo Veronese's *Marriage at Cana*, a huge work painted in 1563. Among a number of Flemish and Dutch paintings are Quentin Matsys' moralistic *Moneychanger and his Wife*, Memling's *Mystic Marriage of St Catherine*, Rembrandt's masterful *Supper at Emmaus*, and several works by Rubens, including a number of decorative canvases illustrating the life of Marie de Médici, the French queen. As for French painting, there are works here from the year dot, most notably works by Poussin and later canvases by the great French nineteenth-century artists, David, Ingres and Géricault – whose harrowing *Raft of Medusa* made his name as an artist. Look out, too, for Courbet's later *Funeral at Ornans*, perhaps the best-known Realist painting of all, its events rendered with dour, impassive precision.

The north wing of the Louvre, entered from rue de Rivoli, is given over to the **Musée des Arts Décoratifs** (Wed–Sat 12.30–6pm, Sun 11am–6pm; F25) – an enormous museum of interior design, with furnishings and fittings from the Middle Ages to the 1990s. The contemporary section is fairly meagre, but the rest of the twentieth century is fascinating, and includes a bedroom by Guimard, Jeanne Lanvin's Art Deco apartments and a salon created by Georges Hoentschel for the 1900 Expo.

The Opéra, Les Halles and the Pompidou Centre

A short walk north of the Louvre, the **Opéra** is the most preposterous building in Paris, an excessively ornate structure that covers three acres in extent, although since the completion of the Bastille opera house it has been used chiefly for ballet. You can visit the interior (daily 11am–4.30pm), including the auditorium, where the ceiling is the work of Chagall. A short walk east, the area around the former **Les Halles** was redeveloped in the Seventies amid widespread opposition, and is now promoted as the heart of trendy Paris. In truth, the multi-layered shopping precinct at its core – the **Forum des Halles** – is a tacky affair, and it's sad that so few traces of the former working-class quarter survive. It can be a tense, hassley area, too, especially at night – hence the high-profile police presence. During the day the main flow of feet is from here to the **Pompidou Centre** (Beaubourg), a little way west, a stunning design by Renzo Piano and Richard Rogers that is one of the city's most popular buildings, a seminal work that was the first public structure to manifest the hi-tech notion of wearing its innards on the outside. It's worth travelling up the escalator tubes for the views over Paris – and down on the buskers and street entertainers that congregate in the square below – and you can go inside for free to consult the ground-floor postcard and art bookshop, and the books, videos and international newspapers on the second floor, not to mention a variety of temporary art installations. The building's main attraction, however, is the **Musée National d'Art Moderne** on the fourth floor (Mon & Wed–Fri noon–10pm, Sat & Sun 10am–10pm; F30), a permanent exhibition of twentieth-century art, covering everything from the late Impressionists to late 1980s works. Early paintings include canvases by Henri Rousseau – *La Charmeuse de Serpent* – and Picasso, whose *Femme Assise* of 1909 introduces Cubism, represented in its fuller development by Braque's *L'Homme à la Guitare* and Léger's much later balancing act, *Les Acrobates en Gris*. Among abstracts, there's the sensuous rhythm of colour in Sonia Delaunay's *Prismes Electriques* and a good showing of Kandinsky at his most playful. Dalí disturbs, amuses or infuriates with *Six apparitions de Lénine sur un piano* and there are further Surreal images by Magritte and de Chirico. Moving to the section of German art, one of the most compulsive pictures is the portrait of the journalist *Sylvia von Harden* by Otto Dix, while of more recent canvases Francis Bacon's work figures prominently, as do the provocative images of the Pop Art movement – not least Warhol's *Electric Chair*.

The Marais and Île St-Louis

Just east of Beaubourg, the **Marais** is a formerly fashionable aristocratic district that until twenty years ago was one of the city centre's poorer quarters. Since then, regentrification has proceeded apace and the renovated mansions – their grandeur concealed by the narrow streets – have become museums, offices and chic apartments flanked by shops selling designer clothes and the like. A little way down the neighbourhood's main drag, rue des Francs-Bourgeois, one of the grandest Marais hôtels houses the **Musée Carnavalet** (Tues–Sun 10am–5.40pm; F26), which presents the history of Paris as viewed and lived in by royalty, aristocrats and the bourgeoisie from François I to 1900, with rooms full of sacred mementoes of the Revolution – models of the Bastille, original Declarations of the Rights of Man, tricolours, models of the guillotine and execution orders – along with displays of maps, models and plans of Paris through the ages. A short walk north, another mansion, the grandiloquent seventeenth-century Hôtel Salé at 5 rue de Thorigny, is home to the **Musée Picasso** (Wed 9.15am–10pm, Mon & Thurs–Sun 9.15am–5.15pm; F26), the largest collection of Picassos anywhere. A large proportion of the pictures were the personal property of the artist at the time of his death, and are displayed alongside paintings he bought or was given, his African masks and sculptures, photographs, letters and other personal memorabilia. Although many of the exhibits are not among Picasso's most enjoyable works, the collection leaves you with a definite sense of the man and his life, partly because these were the works he wanted to keep. The paintings of his wives, lovers and family are some of the most endearing and there are references to his political commitments, too, in his drawing entitled *Staline à la Santé* ("Here's to Stalin"), his delegate credentials for the 1948 World Congress of Peace, and the *Massacre en Corée* from 1951.

At the far end of rue des Francs-Bourgeois, off to the right, **place des Vosges** is a masterpiece of aristocratic urban planning, a vast square of stone and brick symmetry built for Henri IV and Louis XIII. Beyond, the column with the "Spirit of Liberty" on **place de la Bastille** was erected not to commemorate the surrender in 1789 of the prison but the July Revolution of 1830 – although it is the 1789 Bastille Day that France celebrates. The Bicentennial in 1989 was marked by the inauguration of the **Opéra-Bastille**, on the far side of the square, a bloated building that caused great controversy when it went up – a "hippopotamus in a bathtub", one critic called it. A short walk south, across the bridge from here, the **Île St-Louis** is one of the centre's swankier quarters, with no monuments or museums, just high houses on single-lane streets. It is, however, the most peaceful and atmospheric route through to the Île de la Cité.

Île de la Cité

The **Île de la Cité** is where Paris began, site of the Roman garrison and later of the palace of the Merovingian kings and the counts of Paris, who in 987 became kings of France. Nowadays the main lure, however, is the stupendous **Cathédrale de Notre-Dame** (daily 8am–7pm), begun in 1160 under the auspices of Bishop de Sully and completed around 1245. In the nineteenth century, Viollet-le-Duc carried out extensive renovation work, remaking most of the statuary and adding the steeple and baleful-looking gargoyles, which you can see close-up if you brave the ascent of the towers (summer 9.30am–noon & 2–6pm; winter 10am–5pm; F31). The sculpture of the west front portals is amazingly detailed, dating mainly from the twelfth and thirteenth centuries, while inside the immediately striking feature is the dramatic contrast between the darkness of the nave and the light falling on the first great clustered pillars of the choir. It is the end walls of the transepts which admit all this light, nearly two-thirds glass, including two magnificent rose windows in imperial purple – additions made in 1267.

In front of the cathedral, the **crypte archéologique** (daily 10am–5/5.30pm; F26) holds the remains of the original cathedral, as well as streets and houses of the Cité back as far as the Roman era. At the other end of the island, the dull mass of the **Palais de Justice** swallowed up the palace that was home to the French kings until the bloody revolt of 1358 frightened them into the greater security of the Louvre. The only part of the older complex that remains in its entirety is Louis IX's **Sainte-Chapelle** (April–Sept 9.30am–6.30pm; Oct–March 10am–5pm; F26), built to house a collection of holy relics and one of the finest achievements of French Gothic style, lent a fragility by its height and huge expanses of stained glass. You should also visit the **Conciergerie** (April–Sept 9.30am–6/6.30pm; Oct–March 10am–4.30pm; F26), Paris' oldest prison, where Marie-Antoinette, and, in their turn, the leading figures of the Revolution were incarcerated before execution. Its chief interest is the enormous late Gothic *Salle des Gens d'Arme*, canteen and recreation room of the royal household staff, as well as Marie-Antoinette's cell and various macabre mementoes of the guillotine's victims.

The Beaux-Quartiers, Bois de Boulogne and La Défense

South and west of the Arc de Triomphe lie the so-called **Beaux Quartiers**, the 16e and 17e *arrondissements*, in turns aristocratic and rich, bourgeois and staid districts, mainly residential, that hold little of interest save the wonderful **Musée Marmottan**, 2 rue Louis-Boilly (Tues–Sun 10am–5.30pm; F35), whose Monet paintings were bequeathed by the artist's son. Among them is the canvas entitled *Impression, Soleil Levant (Impression, Sunrise)*, an 1872 rendering of a misty sunrise over Le Havre, whose title unwittingly gave the Impressionist movement its name. There's also a dazzling collection of almost abstract canvases from Monet's last years at Giverny. Beyond the museum, the **Bois de Boulogne**, running all down the west side of the 16e, is the city centre's largest open space, supposedly modelled on Hyde Park, and offering all sorts of facilities – various museums, beautiful displays of flowers in the spring, a riding school, boating on the Lac Inférieur, wild walks in its southeast corner, and, of course, the racecourses of Longchamp and Auteuil – although it's long been known for its prodigious after-dark sexual pick-up activity.

La Défense – one RER stop on from Charles de Gaulle-Étoile – is nowadays high on the list of places to which visitors to Paris must pay homage. It's Paris' prestige business district, complete with scattered artworks by Miró and Alexander Calder, and, most impressively, **La Grande Arche**, a 112-metre tall hollow cube, clad in white marble, up which you can climb (July & Aug Sun–Thurs 10am–7pm, Fri & Sat 10am–9pm; rest of year Mon–Fri 9am–5pm, Sat & Sun 10am–7pm; F30).

The Eiffel Tower, Les Invalides and the Musée d'Orsay

A short walk south of place de l'Étoile, the **Musée d'Art Moderne de la Ville de Paris** in the Palais de Tokyo on av du Président-Wilson (Tues–Fri noon–7pm, Sat & Sun 10am–7pm; F26) displays ever-rotating examples of the schools and trends of twentieth-century art, as well as sculpture and painting by contemporary artists. Among the most spectacular works on show are Robert and Sonia Delaunay's huge whirling wheels and cogs of rainbow colour, the leaping figures of Matisse's *La Danse* and Dufy's enormous mural, *La Fée Electricité* (done for the electricity board), illustrating the story of electricity from Aristotle to thé modern power station, in 250 colourful panels. A short walk down the river, at Trocadéro, the terrace of the **Palais de Chaillot** – home to several uninteresting museums – gives splendid vistas across the river to the **Tour Eiffel**. Though no conventional beauty, this is nonetheless an amazing structure, at 300m the tallest building in the world when it was completed in 1889. Reactions to it were violent, but it stole the show at the 1889 Exposition, for which it had been constructed. It's possible to go right to the top (stages 1, 2 & 3 daily summer 9.30am–midnight; winter 10am–11pm; F18, F35, F52 respectively by lift, F10 if you walk), although the queues for the final stage can be massive during high season, and it is in any case only really worth it on an absolutely clear day.

To the west, the **Esplanade des Invalides** strikes south to the wide facade of the **Hôtel des Invalides**, built as a home for invalided soldiers on the orders of Louis XIV. One of its two churches was intended as a mausoleum for the king but now contains the mortal remains of Napoléon, enclosed within a gallery decorated with friezes of execrable taste and captioned with quotations of awesome conceit from the great man, while the main part of the building houses the vast **Musée de l'Armée** (daily 10am–5/6pm; F32). Immediately east, the **Musée Rodin**, on the corner of rue de Varenne, housed in a beautiful eighteenth-century mansion which the sculptor leased from the state in return for the gift of all his work at his death (Tues–Sun 10am–5/5.45pm; F26), represents the whole of Rodin's work. Larger projects like *Les Bourgeois de Calais* and *Balzac* are exhibited in the garden, while indoors are works in marble like *Le Baiser*, *La Main de Dieu* and *La Cathédrale*.

Along the river a little way, on quai d'Orsay, the **Musée d'Orsay** (Tues, Wed, Fri, Sat & Sun 9/10am–6pm, Thurs 9/10am–9.45pm; F32) is the newest of the city's big museums, converted from the disused gare d'Orsay in the mid-1980s and housing the painting and sculpture of the pre-modern period, 1848–1914 – bridging the gap between the Louvre and the Beaubourg. On the ground floor, there are a few canvases by Ingres and Delacroix, whose work serves to illustrate the transition from the early nineteenth century. The Symbolists and early Degas follow, while in the galleries to the left Daumier, Corot, Millet and the Realist school lead on to the first Impressionist works, including Manet's *Déjeuner sur l'Herbe*, which sent the critics into apoplexies of disgust when it appeared in 1863. On the top level there are landscapes and outdoor scenes by Renoir, Sisley, Pissarro and Monet – including his water-lilies, along with five of his Rouen cathedral series. Cézanne is also wonderfully represented, while the rest of this level is given over to Gauguin post- and pre-Tahiti, a number of *pointilliste* works by Seurat and the blinding colours of van Gogh, as well as some superb Bonnards and Vuillards and lots of Toulouse-Lautrec at his nightclubbing best – one large canvas including a gross rear view of Oscar Wilde.

The Latin Quarter, St-Germain and Montparnasse

The warren of medieval lanes around the boulevards St-Michel and St-Germain is known as the **"Quartier Latin"** because that was the language of the university sited there right up until 1789. The pivotal point of the area is **place St-Michel**, where the tree-lined **boulevard St-Michel** begins, its cafés and shops jammed with people, mainly young and in summer largely foreign. **Rue de la Huchette**, the Mecca of beats and bums in the post-World War II years, is now given over to Greek restaurants of indifferent quality and inflated price, as is the adjoining rue Xavier-Privas, with the odd *couscous* joint thrown in. Close by the St-Michel/St-Germain junction, the walls of the third-century Roman baths are visible in the garden of the Hôtel de Cluny, a sixteenth-century mansion built by the abbots of the powerful Cluny monastery as their Paris pied-à-terre and now housing the **Musée de Cluny** (daily except Tues summer 9.30am–5.15pm; winter 9.30am–12.30pm & 2–5.15pm; F26), a treasure-house of medieval art that includes some wonderful, finely detailed tapestries, best of which is *La Dame à la Licorne* – six highly symbolic medieval scenes featuring a beautiful woman flanked by a lion and a unicorn, late fifteenth-century, perhaps made in Brussels. Immediately south of here, the **Montagne St-Geneviève** slopes up to the domed **Panthéon**: Louis XIV's thankyou to Sainte Geneviève, patron saint of Paris, for curing him of illness, which was transformed during the Revolution into a mausoleum for the great (April–Sept 10am–6pm; Oct–March 10am–12.30pm & 2–5.30pm; F26). Down rue Soufflot from here, across bd St-Michel, you might prefer to while away a few hours in the elegant surrounds of the **Jardin du Luxembourg**, laid out by Marie de Médici, Henri IV's widow, to remind her of the Palazzo Pitti and Giardino di Bóboli of her native Florence. They are the chief recreation ground of the Left Bank, with tennis courts, a *boules* pitch, yachts to hire on the pond, and, in the southeast corner, a miniature orchard of elaborately espaliered pear trees.

Beyond the Luxembourg gardens, the northern half of the 6e *arrondissement* is one of the most attractive parts of the city, full of bookshops, art galleries, antique shops, cafés and restaurants. It is also, perhaps, its most culturally historic: Picasso painted *Guernica* in rue des Grands-Augustins; Delacroix painted and Balzac's printing business went bust in rue Visconti; and in the parallel rue des Beaux-Arts, Oscar Wilde died and the crazy poet Gérard de Nerval went walking with a lobster on a lead. **Place St-Germain-des-Prés**, the hub of the *quartier*, is the site of the *Deux Magots* café, renowned for the number of politico-literary backsides that have shined its seats. On the other side of the Luxembourg gardens, **Montparnasse** also trades on its association with the wild characters of the interwar artistic and literary boom, many of whom were habitués of the cafés *Select, Coupole, Dôme* and *Rotonde* on **bd du Montparnasse**. Close by, the colossal **Tour Montparnasse** has become one of the city's principal landmarks, and can be climbed for less than the Eiffel Tower (daily summer 9am–11.30pm; winter 10am–10pm; F39). A short walk down bd Edgar-Quinet, the **Cimetière Montparnasse** has plenty of illustrious names, from Baudelaire to Sartre and André Citroën to Saint-Saens.

Montmartre and eastern Paris

Montmartre lies in the middle of the largely petty-bourgeois and working-class 18e *arrondissement*, a mixture of depressing slums towards the Gare du Nord and Gare de l'Est, and respectable, almost countrified pockets around its main focus on the hill, the **Butte Montmartre**. You can get up here by **funicular** from place Suzanne-Valadon, or, for a quieter and prettier approach climb up via place des Abbesses. The **place du Tertre** is the heart of touristic Montmartre, photogenic but totally bogus, jammed with tourists, overpriced restaurants and "artists" doing quick portraits while you wait. Close by, the nineteenth-century church of **Sacré-Coeur** is, with the Eiffel Tower, one of the classics of the Paris skyline, although the best thing about it is the view from the top (daily 9am–6/7pm; F15).

North of place du Tertre, the house that holds the **Musée de Montmartre** at 12 rue Cortot (Tues–Sun 11am–5.30pm; F25) was rented at various times by Renoir, Dufy, Suzanne Valadon and her alcoholic son Utrillo, but its exhibits are disappointing. Close by, off rue Lepic, the **Moulin de la Galette** is the only survivor of Montmartre's forty odd windmills, which were immortalized by Renoir. Down the hill from here the artistic associations continue in the **Moulin Rouge** on bd de Clichy – although it's these days a mere shadow of its former self. This stretch – known as **Pigalle** – has always been a sleazy neighbourhood, the centre of the boulevard occupied by funfair sideshows while the pavements are dotted with transvestite prostitutes on the lookout. At the western end, a little way up rue Caulaincourt, the **Cimetière Montmartre** (Mon-Fri 8am–5.30pm, Sat 8am–8.30pm, Sun 8am–9pm) holds the graves of Zola, Stendhal, Berlioz, Degas, Offenbach and François Truffaut among others. Way north, on the other side of the bd Périphérique from the porte de Clignacourt, the **puces de St-Ouen** (daily 7am–7.30pm) claims to be the largest flea market in the world, although nowadays it deals mainly with expensive antiques, and what's left of the rag-and-bone element confined to the further reaches of rue Fabre and rue Lécuyer.

East of Montmartre, the **Bassin de la Villette** and the **canals** at the northeastern gate of the city were for generations the centre of a densely populated working-class district but they have recently become the subject of yet another big Paris redevelopment, whose major extravagance is the **Cité des Sciences et de l'Industrie** in the **Parc de la Villette**, built into the concrete hulk of the abandoned abattoirs on the north side of the canal de l'Ourcq (Tues–Sun 10am–6pm; F45; planetarium from 11am). Three times the size of Beaubourg, this is the most astounding monument to be added to the capital in the last decade, and is worth visiting for the interior alone – all glass and stainless steel, cantilevered platforms and suspended walkways, the different levels linked by lifts and escalators around a huge central space. Its permanent exhibition, *Explora*, on the top two floors, is the science museum to end all science museums, covering subjects such as microbes, maths, sounds, robots, flying, energy, space, information and language. The emphasis, as the name suggests, is on exploration; the means used are interactive computers, videos, holograms, animated models and games. You can intervene in stories acted out on videos, changing the behaviour of the characters to engineer a different outcome; steer robots through mazes; make music by your own movements; try out a flight simulator; watch computer-guided puppet shows and holograms of different periods' visions of the universe; and stare at two slabs of wall parting company at the rate of 2cm a year – enacting the gradual estrangement of Europe and America.

South of La Villette, Paris' **eastern** districts – Belleville, Ménilmontant – are among the poorest of the city and not on most visitors' itineraries. However, the **cimetière Père-Lachaise** draws a fair number of tourists (daily 7.30am–6pm), most of them heading for Jim Morrison's tomb, a small graffitied grave in the east of the cemetery. There are countless famous others buried here – Edith Piaf, Modigliani, Abélard and Heloïse, Sarah Bernhardt, Ingres and Corot, Delacroix and Balzac, to name only a few.

South of Père-Lachaise, the **Bois de Vincennes** is the city's other big open space, where you can spend an afternoon boating on Lac Daumesnil or feeding the ducks on Lac des Minimes on the other side of the wood (bus #112 from Vincennes métro). On the western edge, the **Musée des Arts Africains et Océaniens**, 293 av Daumesnil (Mon & Wed–Fri 10am–5.30pm, Sat & Sun 12.30–6pm; F16), is a rewarding museum, one of the least crowded in the city, a gathering of culture and creatures from the old French colonies – masks and statues, furniture, adornments and tools.

Eating

Contrary to what you might expect, **eating out** in Paris need not be an enormous extravagance. There are numerous fixed price *menus* under F80 providing simple but well-cooked fare; paying a little more than this gives you the chance to try out a greater range of dishes, and once over F150 you should be getting some gourmet satisfaction. There is a wide range of ethnic restaurants, too – North and West African, Chinese, Japanese, Vietnamese, Greek and lots more, though they are not necessarily any cheaper. Bear in mind that, in general, the latest time you can walk into a restaurant and order is about 10pm. Anyone in possession of an *ISIC* card is eligible to apply for tickets for the **university restaurants** run by *CROUS*, 39 av Georges-Bernanos, 5e. They will provide a list of addresses; tickets come in packs of ten and cost F21 each.

Snacks, sandwiches, cakes and ice cream

Angélina, 226 rue de Rivoli, 1er. A long-established gilded cage for the well-coiffed to sip the best hot chocolate in town, plus high-quality pastries and desserts.

Berthillon, 31 rue St-Louis-en-l'Île, 4e. The best ice creams and sorbets in Paris.

Drugstore Élysées, 133 av des Champs-Élysées, 8e. All-day food, along with books, newspapers, tobacco, etc. Prices are reasonable and the food much better than the decor would suggest. Other branches at 1 av Matignon, 8e, and 149 bd St-Germain, 6e.

Fauchon, 24 place de la Madeleine, 8e. Narrow counters at which to gobble wonderful *pâtisseries, plats du jour* and sandwiches – at a price.

Fleur de Lotus, 2 rue du Roi-de-Sicile, 4e. Cheap Vietnamese dishes, heated up while you wait – to take away or eat on the premises.

Jarmolinska, 272 rue St-Honoré, 1er. Polish delicatessen serving blinis, potato pancakes, etc, to eat in or take away.

Lina's Sandwiches, 50 rue Étienne-Marcel, 2e. A spacious, stylish place for your designer shopping break.

Le Loir dans la Théière, 1 rue des Rosiers, 4e. "The Dormouse in the Teapot". Sunday brunch, midday *tartes* and omelettes, fruit teas of every description and cakes all day.

Sacha Finkelsztajn, 27 rue des Rosiers, 4e: **Florence Finkelsztajn**, 24 rue des Écouffes, 4e Gorgeous East European breads, cakes, gefilte fish, blinis and borscht to take away.

Restaurants and brasseries

Aux Artistes, 63 rue Falguière, 15e. An old-time cheapie that has seen many a poor artist in its time. Still crowded and popular. Menus from F55 and F75.

Le Baptiste, 11 rue des Boulangers, 5e. Noisy, friendly and full of students. Menus from F60.

Bistro de la Sorbonne, 4 rue Toullier, 5e. Help-yourself starters and salads, good ices and *crêpes flambées*. Copious portions. F70 menu at lunchtime, F95 in the evening.

Bofinger, 3–7 rue de la Bastille, 3e. Well-established turn-of-the-century brasserie, serving the archetypal fare of *sauerkraut* and seafood. Not especially cheap, but worth it.

Chardenoux, 1 rue Jules-Vallès, 11e. An authentic oldie, with engraved mirrors dating back to 1900, that still serves solid meaty fare at very reasonable prices. Menus start at F120.

Aux Charpentiers, 10 rue Mabillon, 6e. Old-fashioned place belonging to the Carpenters' Guild. Traditional *plats du jour* are their forte, although they're not budget-priced.

Chartier, 7 rue du Faubourg-Montmartre, 9e. Good cheap food served at a run in an original turn-of-the-century soup kitchen. Closes early – at 9.30pm.

Chez Justine, 96 rue Oberkampf, 11e. Good traditional cooking at very reasonable prices. Menus at F82 and F132.

Chez Robert, 80 bd Richard-Lenoir, 11e. A leftover from the pre-Opéra days when this was a *quartier populaire*. Simple and satisfying fare, though it closes at 9pm. Menus from F56.

Le Commerce, 51 rue du Commerce, 15e. Long-established, serving nourishing and cheap food.

Drouot, 103 rue de Richelieu, 2e. Admirably cheap, good food, served at a frantic pace, in an Art Nouveau setting.

Flo, 7 cours des Petites-Écuries, 10e. Handsome old-time brasserie, where you eat elbow to elbow at long tables. Excellent food and thoroughly enjoyable atmosphere.

Germaine, 30 rue Pierre-Leroux, 7e. Cheap and good, consequently very crowded. Closes early and during Aug.

Goldenburg's, 7 rue des Rosiers, 4e. The best-known Jewish restaurant in the capital; its borscht, blinis, strudels and other central European dishes are a treat.

L'Incroyable, 26 rue de Richelieu, 1er. Hidden in a tiny *passage*, this tiny restaurant serves decent and cheap meals. Menus from F70.

Orestias, 4 rue Grégoire-de-Tours, 6e. A mixture of Greek and French cuisine. Good helpings and very cheap.

Perraudin, 157 rue St-Jacques, 5e. Well-known traditional bistro with menus from about F60.

Le Petit Prince, 12 rue Lanneau, 5e. Good food in a restaurant full of Latin Quarter charm in one of the *quartier*'s oldest lanes. Menus start at around F85.

Le Petit Ramoneur, 74 rue St-Denis, 1er. Elbow-rubbing cheapie in good bistro tradition; always crowded.

Le Petit Saint-Benoît, 4 rue Saint-Benoît, 6^e. A simple, genuine and very appealing local for the neighbourhood's chattering classes. Solid traditional fare.

Polidor, 41 rue Monsieur-le-Prince, 6^e. A traditional bistro but not as cheap as it was when James Joyce used to eat here. Good food and great atmosphere. F80–100.

Port de Pidjiguiti, 28 rue Etex, 18^e. Pleasant atmosphere and excellent food. Run by a village in Guinea-Bissau, whose inhabitants take turns in staffing the restaurant; the proceeds go to the village. Menus from F60.

Au Rendez-vous des Camioneurs, 34 rue des Plantes, 14^e. No lorry drivers any more, but good food for around F80. Wise to book.

Restaurant des Arts, 73 rue de Seine, 6^e. A small, crowded, friendly place with simple, homely fare. Menus from around F60.

Restaurant des Beaux-Arts, 11 rue Bonaparte, 6e. The traditional hang-out of the art students from across the way. The choice is wide, portions generous and the queues long.

Aux Savoyards, 14 rue des Boulangers, 5e. A delightfully friendly place, but likely to be packed. From F70.

Les Temps des Cérises, 18–20 rue de la Butte-aux-Cailles, 13e. A well-established workers' co-op with elbow-to-elbow seating and lunch menus from F52, evening menus from about F112.

Thoumieux, 79 rue St-Dominique, 7e. Large and popular establishment in this rather smart district, with a menu at around F60.

La Vallée des Bambous, 35 rue Gay-Lussac, 5e. You usually have to wait in line for this popular Chinese restaurant. The cheapest menu is excellent value.

Le Vaudeville, 29 rue Vivienne, 2e. A lively late-night brasserie – where it's often necessary to queue – with good food and an attractive marble-and-mosaic interior. Menu at F109.

Drinking

Most of Paris' main squares and boulevards have **cafés** spreading out onto the pavements, and, although these are usually the priciest places to drink, it can be worth paying the earth for a coffee for the chance to observe the streetlife. The Left Bank harbours some of the city's best-known and longest-established cafés on boulevards Montparnasse and St-Germain, while the presence of the university means there's plenty of places to drink around place de la Sorbonne and rue Soufflot. The Bastille is another good area to tour, now livelier than ever as the new Opéra and rocketing property values bring headlong development, as is Les Halles – though the latter's trade is principally among transient out-of-towners up for the bright lights. Revitalized, ironically, by the English, you'll also find **wine bars**, the best of which are long-established places serving food as well as decent wine by the glass – as well as establishments more geared to **beer**, most inspired by Belgian or British watering holes.

Académie de la Bière, 88 bd Port-Royal, 5e. Large selection of beers. Also food – good mussels and fries, Belgian cheeses and *charcuterie*.

Le Baron Rouge, 1 rue Théophile-Roussel, 12e. A crowded and popular bar, serving cheese, *charcuterie* and wines to taste at reasonable prices.

Conways, 73 rue St-Denis, 1er. New York-style bar with transatlantic food and a relaxed, friendly atmosphere.

Café Costes, 4–6 rue Berger, place des Innocents, 1er. Sparsely decorated Les Halles café designed by Philippe Starck that tries hard to be the coolest place in town.

Les Deux Magots, 170 bd St-Germain, 6e. Former haunt of J.P. Sartre and numerous famous others in the Twenties. Touristy now, inevitably, with a terrace often besieged by buskers.

Au Général Lafayette, 52 rue Lafayette, 9e. Beer-drinking hang-out with a dozen draughts, including Guinness, and many more bottled. Mixed clientele, and a pleasant, quiet feel.

La Gueuze, 19 rue Soufflot, 5e. Comfy surroundings, decent food and numerous Belgian bottles and several draughts, including cherry *kriek*.

Café de l'Industrie, 16 rue St-Sabin, 11e. Rugs on the floor around solid old wooden tables, miscellaneous objects on the walls, and a young, unpretentious crowd.

Café de la Nouvelle Mairie, 19 rue des Fossés-St-Jacques, 5e. Small, sawdusted bar in a quiet Latin Quarter street, with good wines, *saucisson* and sandwiches.

L'Oiseau Bariolé, 16 rue St-Croix-de-la-Bretonnerie, 4e. Small and friendly, surreal paintings on glass, full of Americans. *Plats du jour*, Breton cider, omelettes.

Le Piano Vache, 8 rue Laplace, 5e. Long-established student bar with canned music and relaxed atmosphere.

Le Pigalle, 22 bd de Clichy, 9e. Twenty-four-hour bar, brasserie and *tabac*. A classic, complete with 1950s decor.

Polly Magoo, 11 rue St-Jacques, 5e. A scruffy all-night bar frequented by chess addicts.

Pub Saint-Germain, 17 rue de l'Ancienne-Comédie, 6e. 21 draught beers and hundreds of bottles. Huge and crowded. Hot food at mealtimes, otherwise cold snacks. Open 24hr.

Le Rubis, 10 rue du Marché-St-Honoré, 1er. One of the oldest wine bars in Paris, with a reputation for having among the best wines, plus excellent snacks and *plats du jour*.

Le Select, 99 bd du Montparnasse, 6e. The least spoilt of the swanky Montparnasse cafés.

La Tartine, 24 rue de Rivoli, 4e. The genuine 1900s article, which still cuts across class boundaries in its clientele. A good selection of affordable wines, plus excellent cheese and snacks.

La Taverne de Nesle, 32 rue Dauphine, 6e. Vast selection of beers. Full of local nightbirds.

Tight Johnny, 55 rue Montmartre, 2e. A mostly Irish clientele at this bar that serves a reasonably priced Guinness and sometimes has impromptu Celtic bands.

Le Violon Dingue, 46 rue de la Montagne-Ste-Geneviève, 5e. A long, dark student pub, noisy and friendly.

Nightlife

Nightlife in Paris is as lively and diverse as you would expect. Its reputation for **live music** has recovered over the last decade with the growth in popularity of world music – for which Paris is a centre second to none – and there is excellent jazz in numerous St-Germain and Les Halles clubs. The tradition of *chansons*, epitomized by Edith Piaf and developed to its greatest heights by Georges Brassens and Jacques Brel, endures too, and classical music and opera takes up twice the space of "jazz-pop-folk-rock" in the listings magazines. If you're just looking for a place to dance, **clubs** come and go at as exhausting a rate as any other large city, but there are one or two long-established places that won't let you down; most clubs open around 11pm, some stay open until sunrise. For listings of **what's on** in the city, there are three weekly guides – *Pariscope, L'Officiel des Spectacles* and *7 Jours à Paris*. The best places to get **tickets** for concerts are *FNAC*, 4 place de la Bastille, and the *Virgin Megastore*, 56–60 av des Champs-Élysées.

Live music

Baiser Salé, 58 rue des Lombards, 1er. Downstairs bar and a small, crowded upstairs room with live music every night from 11pm – usually jazz or R&B.

Le Bataclan, 50 bd Voltaire, 11e. One of the best larger rock venues.

Le Caveau de la Bolée, 25 rue de l'Hirondelle, 6e. Ancient place where Parisian luminaries used to go to hear their favourite singers. Still mainly *chansons* with occasional jazz.

La Cigale, 120 bd de Rochechouart, 18e. Old-fashioned theatre with an eclectic programme of rock. Long a fixture on the Pigalle scene.

L'Escale, 15 rue Monsieur-le-Prince, 6e. Hugely popular Latin American venue.

L'Eustache, 37 rue Berger, 1er. Cheap beer and very good jazz by local musicians in this young and friendly Les Halles café. Music from 10pm.

Forum des Halles, Niveau 3, Porte Rambuteau, 15 rue de l'Équerre-d'Argent, 1er. One of the city's largest performance spaces, hosting theatre, rock, etc.

Le Gibus, 18 rue du Faubourg-du-Temple, 11e. For twenty years English rock bands on their way up have played their first Paris gig at *Gibus*. Always hot, loud and crowded.

New Morning, 7–9 rue des Petites-Écuries, 10e. The city's top jazz venue, host to regular big names, but rather sterile; no marks either for the ludicrous drink prices.

Le Petit Journal, 71 bd St-Michel, 5e. A small, smoky bar, long frequented by Left Bank student types, with good, mainly French, traditional and mainstream jazz.

Le Petit Opportun, 15 rue des Lavandières-Ste-Opportune, 1er. Dungeon-like cellar with a varied booking policy. Music from 11pm.

Phil'One, Place de la Patinoire, 3e niveau, Parvis de la Défense, 16e. One of the best venues in Paris, with a quirky musical policy encompassing African, jazz, and English and French rock.

Rex Club, 5 bd Poissonnière, 9e. Live music early on – rock, soul, raï, rap – and disco from 11pm.

Utopia, 1 rue Niepce, 14e. Good French blues singers interspersed with jazz and blues tapes.

Clubs and discos

Balajo, 9 rue de Lappe, 11e. Old-style music hall or *bal musette* with extravagant 1930s decor and music ranging from mazurkas and tangos to slurpy *chansons*.

Chapelle des Lombards, 19 rue de Lappe, 11e. Erstwhile *bal musette* that still plays the occasional waltz and tango but far more often salsa, reggae, raï and the blues.

Discophage, 11 passage du Clos-Bruneau (off 31–33 rue des Écoles), 5e. Jam-packed, tiny and under-ventilated space, but the best Brazilian sounds in Paris. Closed Aug.

La Locomotive, 90 bd de Clichy, 18e. Enormous hi-tech nightclub with two crowded dance floors.

Le Palace, 8 rue du Faubourg-Montmartre, 9e. Big, bopping club, where the clientele are an exuberant spectacle in themselves.

Whisky-a-Gogo, 57 rue de Seine, 6e. Manchester-style dance music on the site of the original *Rock'n'Roll Circus*, where Jim Morrison made his last earthly appearance.

Opera, classical and contemporary music

Paris is a stimulating environment for **classical music**, both established and contemporary. The **Cité de la Musique** project at La Villette has given Paris two new, major concert venues: the **Conservatoire**, the national music academy, on av Jean-Jaurès (☎40.40.46.46), and, next door, a new **auditorium** due to be completed in early 1995, which will become home to *L'Ensemble Inter-Contemporain*, led by Pierre Boulez, the most powerful figure on the French music scene. Otherwise, the top auditorium is the *Salle Pleyel*, 252 rue du Faubourg-St-Honoré, 8e (☎45.61.06.30), and there are regular concerts at the *Théâtre des Champs-Élysées*, 15 av Montaigne, 8e (☎49.52.50.50), and the *Théâtre Musical de Paris*, 1 place du Châtelet, 1er (☎42.33.44.44).

The new Bastille hall is the main place for **opera** (☎44.73.13.00). Tickets cost anything from F50 right up to F570 with the cheapest seats only available to personal callers; unfilled seats are sold at discount to students five minutes before the curtain goes up.

Film

There are over 350 **films** showing in Paris in any one week. Tickets cost around F40; most cinemas have lower rates on Monday, and reductions for students Monday to Thursday. Almost all of the huge selection of foreign films will be shown at some cinemas in the original – *vo* in the listings as opposed to *vf*, which means it's dubbed into French. For the committed film-freak, there are the small *cinémathèques*, which show a choice of over fifty movies a week; tickets are only F25. The *Vidéothèque de Paris* in the Forum des Halles, 2, Grande Gallerie, Porte Eustache, is an excellent-value venue for the bizarre or obscure on celluloid; their repertoires are always based around a Parisian theme. There is also the *Géode*, the mirrored globe at La Villette, which, although it shows mainly Reader's Digest views of outer space, great cities, landscapes, etc, is mightily impressive. It has several screenings a day; tickets cost F55, or F85 for the whole complex.

Gay Paris

Paris has a well-established **gay scene**, and there are numerous gay organizations. The best place for **information** is the main gay and lesbian bookshop, *Les Mots à la Bouche*, 6 rue St-Croix-de-la-Bretonnerie, 4ᵉ. Women could also try the *Maison des Femmes*, 8 Cité Prost, off rue Chanzy, 11ᵉ (☎43.48.24.91), a women's centre run by *Paris-Féministes* who produce a fortnightly bulletin and organize a wide range of events. There's also a gay switchboard, *SOS Gais* and *SOS Lesbia* (☎42.61.00.00).

Bars and clubs

Bar Hôtel Central, 33 rue Vieille-du-Temple, 4ᵉ. Quiet male bar catering mainly to over-30s.

Le BH, 7 rue du Roule, 1ᵉʳ. One of the cheapest gay discos in the city. Exclusively male.

Le Duplex, 25 rue Michel-le-Comte, 3ᵉ. Young gay bar with an arty and friendly atmosphere.

Entre Nous, 17 rue Laferrière, 9ᵉ. A small women-only club with an intimate atmosphere.

Le Monocle, 60 bd Edgar-Quinet, 14ᵉ. Lesbian club with cabaret; some men also allowed in.

Le Piano Zinc, 49 rue des Blancs-Manteaux, 4ᵉ. A happy riot of songs, music hall acts and dance, after 10pm nightly. One of the few venues patronized by both lesbians and gays.

Listings

Airlines *Air France*, 119 av des Champs-Élysées, 8ᵉ (☎45.35.61.61); *British Airways*, 12 rue de Castiglione,(☎47.78.14.14).

Airport enquiries Roissy-Charles de Gaulle ☎48.62.22.80; Orly ☎49.75.15.15.

Books English-language books from *Shakespeare & Co*, 37 rue de la Bûcherie, 5e.

Bike rental *Paris-Vélo*, 2 rue du Fer-à-Moulin, 5ᵉ (☎43.37.59.22).

Car rental *Dergi et Cie*, 60 bd St-Marcel, 5ᵉ (☎45.87.27.04); *Europcar*, 145 av de Malakoff, 16ᵉ (☎45.00.08.06); *Locabest*, 9 rue Abel, 12ᵉ (☎43.46.05.05); *Rent a Car*, 79 rue de Bercy, 12ᵉ (☎45.45.15.15).

Embassies *Australia*, 4 rue Jean-Rey, 15ᵉ (☎40.59.33.00); *Canada*, 35 av Montaigne, 8ᵉ (☎44.43.29.00); *Great Britain*, 16 rue d'Anjou, 8ᵉ (☎42.66.38.10); *Ireland*, 4 rue Rude, 16ᵉ (☎45.00.89.43); *Netherlands*, 7–9 rue Eblé, 7ᵉ (☎43.06.61.88); *New Zealand*, 7 rue Léonardo-de-Vinci, 16ᵉ (☎45.00.24.11); *USA*, 2 av Gabriel, 8ᵉ (☎42.61.80.75).

Exchange *Crédit Commercial de France*, 103 Champs-Élysées, is open on Sat until 8pm; the counters at the main stations open daily until late: Austerlitz 7am–9pm; Est 6.30am–10pm; Lyon 6.30am–11pm; Nord 6.30am–10pm; St-Lazare 8am–8pm. 24-hr cashpoint exchange at 150 av des Champs-Élysées.

Hitching *Allostop*, 84 passage Brady, 10ᵉ (☎42.46.00.66).

Hospital Call *SOS-Médecins* (☎47.07.77.77) for 24-hr medical help; ☎43.78.26.26 for 24-hour ambulance service.

Left luggage There are lockers at all train stations and *consignes* for bigger items.

Pharmacies 24-hr service at *Dhery*, 84 av des Champs-Élysées, 8e.

Police The main *Préfecture* is at 7 bd du Palais, 4ᵉ (☎42.60.33.22).

Post office Main office at 52 rue du Louvre, 1ᵉʳ (daily 8am–7pm).

Telephones The main post office is open 24hr for phone calls.

Train information ☎45.82.50.50.

Travel agents *USIT Voyages*, 6 rue de Vaugirard, 15ᵉ (☎43.29.85.00); *Nouvelles Frontières*, 66 bd St-Michel, 6ᵉ (☎41.41.58.58).

Around Paris

Like most Parisians, you may find there's enough in Paris to keep you from ever thinking about the world beyond. However, like any large city, Paris can get claustrophobic, and if it does there are one or two places in the countryside around that are worth making the trip out for. The most visited of these is undoubtedly **Versailles**, the most hyped currently **Euro Disney**, and the most rewarding is without question the cathedral at **Chartres**.

Versailles

The **Palace of Versailles** (Tues–Sun 9am–5pm; summer closes 7pm; F31) is one of the three most visited monuments in France. It is not a beautiful building by any means, its decor a grotesque homage to two of the greatest of all self-propagandists, Louis XIV and Napoléon, and it's more impressive for its size than anything else, which, by any standards, is incredible. The most amazing room is perhaps the Hall of Mirrors, although the mirrors are not the originals; you can also visit the state apartments of the king and queen, and the royal chapel, a grand structure that ranks among France's finest Baroque creations. Outside, the park is something of a relief, although it's inevitably a very ordered affair. The scenery gets better the further you go from the palace, and there are even informal groups of trees near the lesser outcrops of royal mania, the **Grand and Petit Trianons** (same times; F17 & F12 respectively). Beyond is **Le Hameau**, where Marie-Antoinette played at being a shepherdess.

To **get to Versailles**, take RER *ligne C5* to Versailles-Rive Gauche (40min). You get maps of the park from the tourist office on rue des Réservoirs to the right of the palace.

Chartres

About 35km beyond Versailles, an hour by train from Paris-Montparnasse, **CHARTRES** is a small and relatively undistinguished town. However, its **cathédrale Notre-Dame** (daily 7.30am–7.30pm) is one of the finest examples of Gothic architecture in Europe, and, built between 1194 and 1260, perhaps the quickest ever to be constructed. Its facade is dominated by two towers, which rise up above portals heavily laden with sculpture that marks the transition from the Romanesque to Gothic styles – depictions of Christ, the Apostles, and the twenty-four Elders of the book of Revelation. Inside, the chairs of the nave cover up the labyrinth on the floor, an original thirteenth-century arrangement, which traces a path over 200m long enclosed within a diameter of 13m, the same size as the rose window above the main doors. There are more than enough visible wonders to enthral: the geometry of the building, unique in being almost unaltered since its consecration; the Renaissance choir screen and the hosts of sculpted figures above each transept door; and the shining symmetries of the stained glass, 130 windows in all, virtually all of which are original, dating from the twelfth and thirteenth centuries. The oldest are those of the west front, below the rose window, which date from 1140. There's also a treasury, and it's possible to climb the north tower (daily 10–11.30am & 2–5.30pm).

Though the cathedral is why you come here, Chartres town is not entirely without appeal, with a small old quarter of mazey streets and a picturesque district of bridges and old houses down by the river Eure. The **Musée des Beaux-Arts** in the former episcopal palace just north of the cathedral (daily except Tues summer 10am–6pm; winter 10am–noon & 2–5pm; F20) has some beautiful tapestries, a room full of Vlaminck paintings, and Zurbarán's *St Lucy*, as well as good temporary exhibitions. The **tourist office** is in front of the cathedral, at 7 Cloître Notre-Dame, and can supply free maps and help with rooms if you want to stay (Mon–Sat 9.30am–6/6.45pm, Sun 10am–noon & 3–6pm; shut for lunch daily in winter). Rue du Cygne is a good place to look for **restaurants**; or, if you want to splash out, have a meal at *Henri IV*, 31 rue Soleil-d'Or, which has one of the best selections of wines in France.

Euro Disney

Around 32 kilometres east of Paris, **EURO DISNEY** is a 5000-acre slice of the USA grafted onto a bleak tract of the Bassin Parisien. The ploy was to make the Disney empire more accessible to Europeans, but it seems that many Europeans are either not interested or would rather opt for the more reliable weather and better rides of Florida's Disneyworld, which is not much more expensive a proposition. But for all the jokes about "Euro-dismal", the theatricality and professionalism of the place elevate it head and shoulders above any other theme park.

The **Magic Kingdom** is divided into four "lands" radiating out from Main Street – Fantasyland, Frontierland, Discoveryland and Adventureland. **Fantasyland** appeals to the youngest kids (Cinderella's Castle, Mad Hatter's Tea Cups, Alice in Wonderland's Maze); **Adventureland** boasts the most outlandish sets (Pirates of the Caribbean, Swiss Family Robinson Treehouse); **Frontierland** has the *Psycho*-inspired Phantom Manor and the wild-west Rustler Roundup Shootin' Gallery; and **Discoveryland**, the hi-tech 3-D Michael Jackson film *Captain EO* and a 360° Parisian exposé in Le Visionarium. The grand **parade** sallies down Main Street USA at 3pm sharp every day, and Snow White, Dumbo, Pinocchio, Roger Rabbit, Mickey et al strut their stuff with unfoundering joviality. Night-time Electrical Parades and **firework displays** take place several times a week.

The six themed Disney **hotels** may be out of many people's price range, the cheapest room off-season being 450F a night (2 adults, 2 children), rising to over F2000 peak season for a room in the *Disneyland Hotel* inside the Magic Kingdom on Main Street. The complexes are generally a mixed bag of hideous eyesores and over-ambitious kitsch, but they do offer an array of eating venues, as well as saunas, jacuzzis, golf, gyms, video games and even a children's theatre.

To enable people to commute to the park from Paris, the French government has built an RER **train station** at Marne-la-Vallée, a 40-minute journey from the Gare de Lyon and costing F62 return; by **car**, take the Serris exit on the A4.

There is talk of bringing **admission** charges more in line with the American counterparts, but at present prices are: 1-day pass F250 (under-12s F150), 2-day pass F475 (F285), 3-day pass F630 (F375).

THE NORTH

When conjuring up exotic holiday locations, **northern France** is unlikely to get a mention. Even among the French it has few adherents, including as it does some of the most industrial and densely populated parts of the country. However, it is possible that you'll both arrive and leave France via this region, and there are curiosities within easy reach of the Channel ports – of which **Boulogne** is nicest – not least two of France's finest cathedrals at **Amiens** and **Laon**. Further south, the *maisons* and vineyards of the

Champagne region are the main draw, for which the best bases are Épernay and **Reims**, the latter with another fine cathedral. Most of the champagne houses offer free visits and tastings, although beyond them the region is not the most enthralling.

Dunkerque

Frequently under a cloud of chemical smog and unstylishly resurrected from wartime devastation, **DUNKERQUE** is about as unappealing an introduction to France as could be imagined. It is the country's third largest port and a massive industrial centre, with oil refineries and steel works producing a quarter of total French output.

There is little to detain you here, but if you are stuck with time on your hands the sights include the unexpectedly brilliant **Musée d'Art Contemporain** (daily except Tues 10am–6/7pm; F6), with works by Karel Appel, Vasarely and many other stars of the postwar era, housed in a suitably serious building in a landscaped sculpture park fifteen minutes up av des Bains. Drop in, also, on the **Musée des Beaux-Arts** on place de Gaulle (daily except Tues 10am–noon & 2–6pm; F6), which has good collections of Flemish, Dutch and French painting, natural history and a display on the withdrawal of 350,000 Allied soldiers from the beaches in May 1940 after the Nazis' lightning attack.

The **ferry terminal** is 15km from the town and train station, but it's linked by a free shuttle service, dropping you in the central place Bollaert. The **tourist office** is on rue Clemenceau (Mon–Sat 9am–noon & 2–6.30pm), in the base of a medieval **belfry** that is the town's chief landmark. The grubby place de la Gare is best for inexpensive **hotels**, the cheapest of which is the *Terminus Nord* (☎28.66.54.26; ②); failing that, there's the relatively pricy *XIX Siècle* (☎28.66.79.28; ③). There's also a **youth hostel** on place Paul-Asseman, 2km east of the town centre (☎28.63.36.34; ②) – bus #3, and a 10.30pm curfew. You could do a lot worse than **eat** at the station buffet, the *Richelieu*. Other possibilities include a good pizzeria, *La Farigoule*, and the café *Aux Halles*, both in the same street. You could also try the *Hôtel Hirondelle*, 46–48 av Faidherbe (☎28.63.17.65; ④) in **MALO-LES-BAINS**, the town's eastern extension, which is a much nicer place to stay and has a decent, reasonably priced restaurant.

Calais

CALAIS is less than 40km from England – the Channel's narrowest crossing – and is the busiest French passenger port. The ferry business dominates the town, for there's not much else here. In the last war the British destroyed Calais to impede its use as a port, fearing a German invasion. Ironically, the French still refer to it as "the most English town in France", an influence which began after the battle of Crécy in 1346, when Edward III seized it for use as a beachhead in the Hundred Years' War. It remained English until 1558, and the association has been maintained across the centuries – and today eight million British travellers per year pass through, in addition to one million day-trippers. The town divides into two: **Calais-Nord**, the old town rebuilt after the war, and, separated from it by canals, **Calais-Sud**. Once you've checked out the shopping on the central place d'Armes and rue Royale, Calais-Nord's charms wear thin, though at a pinch you may enjoy the unusual lacemaking exhibition in the **Musée des Beaux-Arts** on rue Richelieu, opposite Parc Richelieu (daily except Tues 10am–noon & 2–5pm; F13). **Calais-Sud** is scarcely more significant, its focus the extravagant **Hôtel de Ville**, on the main shopping street of bd Jacquard, outside which Rodin's famous bronze **Burghers of Calais** records the self-sacrifice of these local dignitaries who offered their lives to assuage the English conqueror, Edward III. Across the street in the **Parc St-Pierre**, the **Musée de la Guerre** (mid-Feb to mid-Dec 10am–5pm; F13), installed in a former German blockhouse, records the town's wartime travails.

Don't try to walk into town. There is a free daytime bus service from the **ferry dock** at Calais-Maritime station to place d'Armes and the central Calais-Ville station in Calais-Sud; at night a taxi will cost about F40. The **tourist office** is at 12 bd Clemenceau (July & Aug Mon–Sat 9am–7.30pm, Sun 10am–1pm & 4.30–7.30pm; Sept–June Mon–Sat 9am–12.30pm & 2.30–6.30pm) and has an accommodation service, for which there is a small charge. There is a **youth hostel**, the *Maison pour Tous*, at 81 bd Jacquard (☎21.34.69.23; ②), though it's open July and August only, and a **camping municipal** at 26 av Poincaré, beyond the end of rue Royale. Affordable **hotels** include *Hôtel du Cygne*, 32 rue Jean-Jaurès (☎21.34.55.18; ②), behind the town hall, and *Le Littoral*, 71 rue Aristide-Briand (☎21.34.47.28; ②), beside Parc St-Pierre. The place d'Armes area is a good area for **restaurants**. *Le Touquet's*, 57 rue Royale, and the slightly more expensive *Le Channel* at 3 bd de la Résistance, overlooking the yacht basin, are both good.

Boulogne

BOULOGNE is the one northern Channel port that might tempt you to stay. Its **Ville Basse**, centring on place Dalton, is home to some of the best *charcuteries* and *pâtisseries* in the north, as well as an impressive array of fish restaurants, and, rising above, the **Ville Haute** is one of the gems of the northeast coast, flanked by grassy ramparts that give impressive views over the town and port. Inside the walls, the **Basilique Notre-Dame** is something of an oddity, raised in the nineteenth century without any architectural knowledge or advice by the town's vicar. Its crypt (daily 2–5pm; F10) has frescoed remains of the previous Romanesque building and relics of a Roman temple to Diana, while the main part of the church has a curious statue of the Virgin and Child on a boat-chariot, drawn here on its own wheels from Lourdes. Nearby, though less compelling, is the **Château Musée** (daily except Tues May–Oct 10am–6pm; Nov–April 10am–noon & 2–5pm; F20), which displays Egyptian items and a good collection of Greek pots.

Ferries dock within a few minutes' walk of the town centre. Arriving by **hovercraft**, a little further out, you'll be met by a free shuttle bus. The **tourist office**, over the bridge as you leave the ferry terminal (Mon–Thurs 9am–8pm, Fri & Sat 9am–10pm, Sun 10am–8pm), can advise on availability of rooms, which in summer fill early. Your best bet is probably the friendly **youth hostel**, southeast of the town walls at 36 rue de la Porte-Gayole (☎21.31.48.22; ②). Most of the cheap **hotels** enclose the port area and include the *Hamiot*, 1 rue Faidherbe (☎21.31.44.20; ②), and *Le Castel*, 51 rue Nationale (☎21.31.52.88; ②). The small *La Plage*, with an inexpensive restaurant, at 124 bd St-Beuve towards the beach (☎21.31.34.78; ③), is also worth a try. Further along bd St-Beuve, on the way to the small resort of Wimereux, is *Camping Moulin Wibert* (10min by bus). For **eating**, there are dozens of possibilities around place Dalton and the cathedral, but be selective. The brasserie *Chez Jules*, on the square, is always a good bet and serves food all day. The *Hamiot* restaurant is a basic alternative, and *La Houblonnière* on rue Monsigny has a vast international selection of brews to wash down its *plats du jour*.

Lille

By far the largest city in these northern regions, **LILLE** is the very symbol of French industry and working-class politics, a mass of suburbs and heavy industry that contains most of the problems, and assets, of contemporary France. There is some of the worst poverty and racial conflict in the country here, and a crime rate rivalled only in Paris and Marseille. There is regionalism – the Lillois sprinkle their speech with a French-Flemish patois and, to an extent, assert a Flemish identity. But there is also classic

French affluence here – the city has a lovely central heart, vibrant and prosperous, and it's a place that takes its culture and its restaurants very seriously. Though not a prime destination, if you're travelling through this region it's at least worth a night.

The busy **Grand Place** is the point to make for (also known as place du Général de Gaulle who was born here in 1890), on the southern edge of **Vieux Lille**, dominated by the old stock exchange or **Bourse**, a lavishly ornate building that now houses a flea market. The buildings around are similarly imposing, not least the strident **Opéra**, and there's a similar fascination in many of the nearby streets, most of which repay a studied wander. The **Hospice Comtesse**, roughly opposite the cathedral on rue de la Monnaie, is perhaps the main thing to see, a twelfth-century hospital that served as such right through to World War II. Its old ward, the *Salle des Malades*, can be visited (daily except Tues 10am–12.30pm & 2–6pm; F10), and at the time of writing, it was also showing a selection of Dutch, Flemish and French paintings on loan from the Musée des Beaux-Arts which is closed for restoration work until December 1994. South of the old centre lies the modern place Rihour, south of which the stylish rue de Béthune leads into café-lined **place Béthune**, and beyond to bd de la Liberté and the city's **Musée des Beaux-Arts** on place de la République.

Arriving at the **train station**, you're only a few minutes' walk from Vieux Lille. The town **tourist office** is in the old Palais Rihour on place Rihour (Mon–Sat 9am–7pm, Sun 10am–noon & 2–5pm). Most of the inexpensive **hotels** are gathered around the train station. The *Hôtel des Voyageurs*, right opposite (☎20.06.43.14; ②), is basic but reasonable, or there's the plusher *de France*, 10 rue de Béthune (☎20.57.14.78; ③), in the centre. A good fallback is the **youth hostel** at 1 av Julien-Destrée (☎20.52.98.94; ②), ten minutes' walk from the station along rue Tournai. The main area for **restaurants** is around place Rihour and place Béthune. The *Grand Café* on place Rihour is a good option for lunch, with light meals and sandwiches, though for mussels – a local speciality – the brasseries around the station are as good as any in town. *La Galetière*, 4 place Louise-de-Bettignies, is a nice crêperie, *Brasserie Jean*, on place du Théâtre, a decent all-nighter. For **drinking**, Lille students with money hang around *Le Pubstore* at 44 rue de la Halle.

Amiens

Few travellers would stop at **AMIENS** unless they were visiting its cathedral. Badly scarred during both world wars, it is not an immediately likeable place. Yet it is not uninteresting. There's a major university here, and the medieval **quartier St-Leu** north of the cathedral, cut by canals, is an oddly run-down attraction – though one that's fast being gentrified.

It is, however, the **Cathédrale Notre-Dame** that provides the city's focus, the largest Gothic building in France. Begun in 1220 and pretty well complete by the end of the century, it escaped the influence of succeeding architectural fads. The interior is a light, calm space, its only real embellishments the sixteenth-century choir stalls (guided tours only), and the sculpted panels depicting the life of Saint Firmin, Amiens' first bishop, on the right-hand side of the choir screen. Close by the cathedral, the seventeenth-century **Hôtel de Berny** (Tues–Sun 10am–12.30pm & 2–6pm; F15, includes entry to Musée de Picardie) has displays of local history collections, while another mansion five minutes' walk south of central **place Gambetta** houses the **Musée de Picardie** (same times; F15, combined ticket with Hôtel de Berny), whose star exhibit is a collection of rare sixteenth-century paintings on wood, some in their original frames, carved by the same craftsmen as worked the choir stalls. You might also be interested in visiting the **Musée Jules Verne**, devoted to the French writer who spent most of his life in this city, in his house at 2 rue Dubois (Tues–Sat 9.30am–noon & 2–6pm; F20).

Amiens' **train station** is on place Fiquet, five minutes from the cathedral. In summer there are **tourist office** kiosks in front of the cathedral and station; at other times you'll have to go to the main office at 12 rue du Chapeau de Violettes (Mon–Sat 9am–12.30pm & 2–6.30/7pm), close by the belfry about 250m west of the cathedral. If you're staying, the most affordable **hotels** are the centrally placed *Hôtel Les Touristes*, 22bis place Notre-Dame (☎22.91.33.45; ②), and *Victor Hugo*, 2 rue de l'Oratoire (☎22.91.57.91; ②). There's also a **youth hostel** (☎22.44.54.21; ②), close by a **camp-site**, though these are a good twenty-minute slog from the station along bd Alsace-Lorraine and left over the bridge. Good places to **eat** include a number of cheap brasseries in front of the station and around place Gambetta. More specifically, you might try *Le Vieil Amiens* on rue Belu, in St-Leu, and – more expensively – *Les Marissons*, on pont de la Dodane.

Laon

Looking out over the plains of Champagne from the spine of a high narrow ridge, still within its gated medieval walls, the old town of **LAON** is one of the gems of the region, dominated by the five great towers of one of the earliest and finest Gothic cathedrals in the country. To get to the upper town you can either walk – a stiff climb up the steps at the end of av Carnot – or take the cable-hauled métro which runs from the train station. The magnificent **Cathédrale de Notre-Dame** was built in the second half of the twelfth century, and was something of a trendsetter in its day, elements of its design being borrowed at Chartres, Reims and Notre-Dame in Paris. The statues on the tower ledges represent horned steers, reputedly carved in memory of the valiant beasts who lugged the cathedral's masonry up from the plains below. Inside, the effects are no less dramatic, the high white nave lit by the dense ruby, sapphire and emerald tones of the stained glass. Once you've seen the cathedral, explore the web of quiet eighteenth-century streets which rambles off to the west and some great views from the town's **ramparts**. Follow rue Pourier to the thirteenth-century **Porte d'Ardon**, which looks out over the southern part of the Ville Basse, or take rue Hermant to the little twelfth-century octagonal **Chapelle des Templiers**, set in a secluded garden by the local **museum** (daily except Tues 10am–noon & 2am–5/6pm; F8.40).

For **accommodation**, try the unprepossessing but perfectly decent *Le Vauclair* (☎23.23.02.08; ②), or *Le Welcome* (☎23.23.06.11; ②), both in the short av Carnot in front of the **train station**. In the Ville Haute, the cheapest solution is the *Maison des Jeunes*, next to the cathedral at 20 rue du Cloître (☎23.20.27.64; ②), or the *Hôtel de la Paix*, 52 rue St-Jean (☎23.23.21.95; ②), though this is closed in August. For **food**, the *Vauclair* also has a good, no-frills restaurant, or there's the Breton *Crêperie Agora* on rue des Cordeliers. The **camping municipal** is on the south side of the Ville Basse, just off N44. The **tourist office** is next door to the cathedral (daily 9am–12.30pm & 2–6.30pm).

Épernay

Though it's a pleasant enough town, the only real reason for coming to **ÉPERNAY** is to visit the champagne houses, whose free tours could keep you fully occupied for a couple of days. The largest and probably most famous is **Moët et Chandon** at 20 av de Champagne (summer Mon–Sat 9.30–11.30am & 2–4.45pm, Sun until 3.45pm; winter weekdays only), who own *Mercier, Ruinart* and a variety of other concerns. The cellars are adorned with mementoes of Napoléon, a good friend of the original M. Moët, and the vintage is named after the monastic hero of champagne history, Dom Pérignon. Tours end with a drink. Of the other *maison* visits, the most rewarding are Mercier up the road at no. 73 (Mon–Sat 9.30–11.30am & 2–4.30pm, Sun until 5.30pm; closed Tues

& Wed Dec–Feb), and Castellane, over by the station at 57 rue de Verdun (daily May–Oct 10.30am–noon & 2–6pm). Mercier's glamour relic is a giant barrel that held 200,000 bottles, taken to the Paris Exposition of 1889 with the help of twenty-four oxen – only to be upstaged by the Eiffel Tower. Visits round the cellars here are by electric train, and again climax with a *dégustation*. The Castellane tour is much less gimmicky than Mercier's or Moët's, and the *dégustation* a lot more generous.

Accommodation does not come cheap in Épernay. Your best bet is the *MJC Centre International de Séjour*, 8 rue de Reims (☎26.55.40.82; ②), a few minutes' walk from the station, with dorm beds and a cheap cafeteria. As for **hotels**, the *St-Pierre*, 1 rue Jeanne d'Arc (☎26.54.40.80; ②), is probably the cheapest alternative, followed by the *Hôtel de la Cloche* at 5 place Mendes-France (☎26.55.24.05; ③) and *Le Progrès*, 6 rue des Berceaux (☎26.55.24.75; ③). The **tourist office** is at 7 av de Champagne (Mon–Sat 9.30am–12.30pm & 1.30–7pm, Sun 11am–4pm), a short walk from the station, and has information on other options. The **campsite** is 1km north in the Parc des Sports, on the south bank of the Marne along route de Cumières. **Eating** is good and affordable at *La Terrasse*, 7 quai de Marne, across the river from the station, and there's a decent restaurant in the *de la Cloche* hotel.

Reims

Laid flat by the bombs of World War I, **REIMS** is a rather dreary city, although there are two good reasons for visiting: it's the best centre (with Épernay) for the Champagne region, and it's home to one of the most impressive Gothic cathedrals in the country, once scene of the coronations of French monarchs. Badly battered in the fighting, the west front of the **Cathédrale** is still a rare delight, with an array of restored but badly mutilated statuary – although many of the originals have been removed to the former bishops' palace (see below). Inside, the stained glass includes designs by Marc Chagall in the east chapel and glorifications of the champagne process in the south transept. Perhaps more famously, the building also preserves, in a state of somewhat absurd veneration, the paraphernalia of Charles X's coronation in 1824, a ceremony which relived the baptism of Clovis, first King of the Franks, in 496, and of the twenty-six kings who were subsequently crowned here.

Next door to the cathedral, the **Palais du Tau** (daily July & Aug 9.30am–6.30pm; Sept–June 9.30/10am–noon/12.30pm & 2–5/6pm; F26), in the bishops' palace, is worth a visit to see some of the dislodged west front figures – equally expressive at short range as in their intended positions on the cathedral. There are grinning angels, friendly-looking gargoyles and a superb Eve, shiftily clutching the monster of sin. Most of the early kings were buried in Reims' oldest building, the eleventh-century **Basilique St-Rémi** (daily 8/9am–dusk, no later than 7pm; closed during services; F5), part of a former Benedictine abbey named after the 22-year-old bishop who baptized Clovis and 3000 of his warriors. Sited 1km east of the cathedral, it's an immensely spacious building, with side naves wide enough to drive a bus through, and preserves its Romanesque choir and ambulatory chapels. You can also visit the adjacent monastic buildings, with more displays of stone sculpture and tapestries. Back near the cathedral, at 8 rue Chanzy, is the city's principal museum, the **Musée des Beaux-Arts** (daily except Tues 10am–noon & 2–6pm; F10) which, though ill-suited to its ancient building, effectively covers mainly French art from the Renaissance to the present. Few of the works are among the particular artists' best, but the collection does contain one of David's replicas of his famous Marat death scene, a set of twenty-seven Corots, two great Gauguin still lifes, and some fascinating sixteenth-century German portraits. The museum in the **Hôtel Vergeur**, a short walk north on place du Forum (daily 2–6pm; F20), is a collection that includes two sets of Dürer engravings – though to see them all you have to go through a long guided tour of the whole works.

If you're in Reims for the champagne, head to **place des Droits-des-Hommes** and **place St-Niçaise**, around which are most of the Reims *maisons*. Unlike Épernay, most charge a small fee for their tours. If you're limiting yourself to one, the **Maison Veuve Cliquot-Ponsardin**, 1 place des Droits-des-Hommes (by appointment only), is one of the least pompous and has the best video. The *caves*, with their horror-movie fungi, are old Gallo-Roman quarries. **Pommery**, too, at 5 place du Général-Gouraud (mid-March–Oct daily 10am–5.30pm; Nov to mid-March Mon–Fri 10am–noon & 2–5pm), has excavated Roman quarries for cellars. At **Tattinger**, 9 place St-Niçaise (daily 9/9.30am–noon/1pm & 2–5.30/6pm; Dec–Feb weekdays only) there are still more ancient *caves*, with statues of Saint Vincent and Saint Jean, patron saints respectively of *vignerons* and cellar hands.

Practicalities

The **train station** is on the northwest edge of the town centre, which centres on place Drouet d'Erlon. The **tourist office** is close to the cathedral at rue G-de-Machault (daily 9/9.30am–5.30/6.30/8pm). Among central **hotels**, the *Thillois*, 17 rue de Thillois (☎26.40.65.65; ②), and the *Alsace*, 6 rue Général Sarrail (☎26.47.44.08; ②), are both cheap, and there's a *Centre International de Séjour* with dorm beds at 1 chaussée Bocquaine, south of the city centre (☎26.40.52.60; ②) – twenty minutes from the station. The **camping municipal** is 1500m beyond the *maisons* on av Hoche (bus #Z). For **food**, there are a number of reasonable places on place Drouet d'Erlon; try the *Colbert* at no. 64.

NORMANDY

To the French, at least, the essence of **Normandy** is its produce. This is the land of butter and cream cuisine, famous cheeses and seafood, cider and calvados, although, oddly enough, parts of Normandy are among the most economically depressed of the whole country. The Normans themselves have a reputation for being insular and conservative, though the only sentiment they really share is a hatred of the Parisians, who use the Seine valley for their country homes and the coast for seaside weekends. There's no doubt that Normandy's Channel ports, **Dieppe** and **Le Havre**, provide a better introduction to France than their counterparts to the north; the white cliffs put on an impressive show, and there are occasional surprises, notably the Benedictine distillery at **Fécamp** and the Beaux-Arts museum in **Le Havre**. Further along the coast, you may arrive at either **Caen**, which gives good access to the town of **Bayeux** with its famous tapestry, or **Cherbourg**, to the south of which is the much-photographed monastic site of **Mont St-Michel**. It's hard to pin down specific highlights in **inland Normandy**. The pleasures lie in the feel of particular landscapes – lush meadows and orchards, half-timbered houses, and the food and drink for which the region is famous. Of urban centres, **Rouen**, the Norman capital, is by far the most compelling.

Dieppe

Crowded between high cliff headlands, **DIEPPE** is an enjoyably small-scale port, but an industrious one, its docks unloading half the bananas of the Antilles and forty percent of all shellfish destined to slither down French throats. The town was the place where Parisians used to take the sea air before fast cars took them further afield. In the centre, the streets are run-down and in continual shadow – little advertisement for the eighteenth-century town planning to which they are supposed to be a monument – but it's an appealing place nonetheless, its restaurants, if you've just arrived, providing a marvellous introduction to the delights of French cooking.

The liveliest part of town, particularly for its Saturday market, is the pedestrianized **Grande-Rue**, although the obvious place to start exploring is the medieval **castle** overlooking the seafront from the west, home of the **Musée de Dieppe** (daily June–Sept 10am–noon & 2–6pm; daily except Tues Oct–May 10am–noon & 2–5pm; F12) and two showpiece collections – a group of carved ivories plundered from Africa, and a hundred or so prints by the co-founder of Cubism, Georges Braque, who spent summers here and is buried just west of the town at Varangeville-sur-Mer. An exit from the western side of the castle takes you out on to a path up to the cliffs. On the other side, there's a flight of steps leading down to the **square du Canada**, originally a commemoration of the role played by Dieppe sailors in the colonization of Canada but since the last war dedicated to the Canadian soldiers who died in the suicidal 1942 raid on Dieppe, justified later by the Allied Command as a trial run for the 1944 Normandy landings.

The main **train station** is about 800m south of the ferry terminal; the **tourist office** is alongside the ferry terminal on Pont Ango (Easter–Sept Mon–Sat 9am–12.30pm & 1.30–7/8pm, Sun 10am–noon & 2–6pm; Oct–Easter Mon–Sat 9am–noon & 2–6pm), and can supply maps. For a **room**, try *Les Arcades*, 1–3 Arcades de la Bourse, on the curve of the port towards the ferry terminal (☎35.84.14.12; ②), or *Hôtel de Pontoise*, 10 rue Thiers (☎35.84.14.57; ③). The **youth hostel** (☎35.84.85.73; ②) is 2km to the south, on rue Louis Fromager, accessible by bus from the bus station, next to the train station. The nearest **campsite**, *du Pré St-Nicolas*, is 3km down the coastal road to Pourville. For **food**, the *Arcades* has a good restaurant and there are several others along the quaysides – try *Restaurant du Port* or *L'Armorique*.

Fécamp

About 25km kilometres west of Dieppe, **FÉCAMP** is another serious fishing port, with a seafront promenade and a **Benedictine Distillery** on rue Alexandre-le-Grand (daily 9.30–11.30am & 2–5.30pm; F25), in the narrow strip of streets running parallel to the ports towards the town centre. Tours of the distillery last 45 minutes and start with a small **museum**, set firmly in the Middle Ages beneath a nightmarish mock-Gothic roof with props of manuscripts, locks, testaments, lamps and religious paintings. The boxes of ingredients are a rare treat for the nose and there's further theatricality in the old distillery where boxes of herbs are thrown with gusto into copper vats and alembics. Finally, you are offered a *dégustation* in their bar across the road – neat, in a cocktail or on crêpes; make sure you hold on to your ticket to qualify.

The **train station** is between the port and the town centre on av Gambetta. If you're staying, there are **hotels** set back away from the sea on odd side streets, though be warned that Fécamp is popular. The *Hôtel de l'Univers*, 5 place St-Étienne (☎35.28.05.88; ③), and the *Angleterre*, 93 rue de la Plage (☎35.28.01.60; ②), are both reasonable. The **youth hostel** is east of the port along the route du Commandant Roquigny (July–Sept; ☎35.29.75.79; ②), and there's a superb **campsite**, *Camping de Renneville*, a short walk away on the western cliffs. The **tourist office** is just behind the seafront where it meets the yacht harbour (daily 10am–12.30pm & 2.30–6pm). *Le Martin*, 18 place St-Étienne, behind the post office, does good basic Norman **food**, with menus at all prices.

Le Havre

On the whole, ferry passengers move straight out from the port of **LE HAVRE**. It was conclusively destroyed during the last war, and, although it has been imaginatively rebuilt from the plans of a single architect, Auguste Perret, it is still something of a characterless urban sprawl. The port, the second largest in France after Marseille, takes up half the Seine estuary, extending far further than the town. Avenue Foch, the central street, runs east–west, looking on to the sea between the beach and the yacht harbour. On bd J. F. Kennedy, overlooking the port entrance, the **Musée des Beaux-Arts** (10am–noon & 2–6pm; closed Tues; free) is one of the best designed art galleries in the country, with one of its finest collections of nineteenth- and twentieth-century paintings – fifty canvases by Eugène Boudin and works by Corot, Courbet, Monet and Dufy, a native of Le Havre, who has a room to himself. Even if you're determined to rush off, find time for a visit. With more time to spare, you can see what old Le Havre looked like by way of the pictures and mementoes in one of the few buildings that escaped destruction, the **Musée de l'Ancien Havre** at 1 rue Jérome-Bellarmato, south of the Bassin du Commerce (Tues–Sun 10am–noon & 2–6pm; free).

The **tourist office** (daily 9am–noon & 2–7pm) is at the end of av Foch by the Hôtel de Ville. The **train station** is 1km further east along bd de Strasbourg. If you're look- ing for **accommodation**, try *Jeanne d'Arc* at 91 rue Emile-Zola (☎35.41.26.83; ②), *Séjour Fleuri*, 71 rue Emile-Zola (☎35.41.33.81; ②), *St-Michel*, 36 rue d'Ingouville (☎35.43.55.24; ②), or the municipal **hostel** at 27 rue de la Mailleraye (☎33.21.22.88; ②). The **campsite** is in the Forêt de Montgeon (bus #12 from Hôtel de Ville). If you're hungry, head for the fish **restaurant**, *Huitrère*.

Honfleur

HONFLEUR, the best-preserved of the Normandy ports, is a near-perfect seaside town, missing only a beach. It used to have one, but with the accumulation of silt from the Seine the sea has steadily withdrawn, leaving the eighteenth-century waterfront houses stranded and a little surreal. The ancient port, however, still functions – the channel to the beautiful *Vieux Bassin* is kept open by regular dredging – and although only pleasure craft now make use of the moorings in the harbour basin, fishing boats tie up alongside the pier close by, and there is usually freshly-caught fish for sale either directly from the boats or from stands on the pier. It's all highly picturesque, and not altogether different from the town that had such appeal to artists in the late nineteenth century.

It's this artistic past – and its present concentration of galleries and painters – which dominates Honfleur. It owes most to Eugène Boudin, forerunner of Impressionism, who was born and worked in the town, trained the fifteen-year-old Monet, and was joined here for various periods by Pissarro, Renoir and Cézanne. There's a good selec- tion of his work in the **Musée Eugène Boudin**, west of the port on place Erik-Satie (daily except Tues 10am–noon & 2–6pm; F14) – quite appealing here in context, partic- ularly the crayon seascapes, along with an impressive set of Dufys and Monets. Admission also gives you access to one of Monet's subjects featured in the museum, the detached belfry and church of **St-Cathérine**. These are built almost entirely of wood – supposedly due to economic restraints after the Hundred Years' War – and there is the added peculiarity of its being divided into twin naves, with one balcony running around both.

Honfleur is on the direct **bus** route #20 between Caen and Le Havre, with eight buses per day in each direction; the nearest **train station** is at Pont-l'Évêque, connected by the Lisieux bus, #50 (a 20-min ride). The **tourist office** (Mon–Sat 9am– noon & 2–6.30pm) is near the **bus station** at 33 cours des Fosses. None of the **hotels** is very affordable – the *Cascades*, 17 place Thiers (☎31.89.05.83; ②), is the best bet, or there's a **campsite** at the west end of bd Charles V on place Jean de Vienne. The most reasonable **restaurants** and **bars** are on rue Haute, on the way up to the Boudin museum. Try *Les Frères de la Côte* and *Au P'tit Marayeur*, at nos. 3 and 4.

Caen

CAEN, capital and largest city of Basse Normandie, was, like Le Havre, devastated during World War II. Its central feature is a ring of ramparts that no longer have a castle to protect, and, although there are the scattered spires and buttresses of abbeys and churches, roads and roundabouts fill the wide spaces where pre-war houses once stood. Nonetheless, the favoured residence of William the Conqueror is still impressive. The **château** ramparts are dramatically exposed, having been cleared of their medieval houses by aerial bombardment. Within are two **museums** (daily except Tues 10am–12.30pm & 2–6pm; free), devoted to Norman history and fine arts, the second of which is sadly closed until spring 1994. Amid comprehensive displays – from fifteenth-century Italian and Flemish primitives to contemporary French artists – it includes masterpieces by Poussin, Géricault, Monet and Bonnard, as well as an exceptional collection of engravings by Dürer and Rembrandt. Below the ramparts to the south is the fourteenth-century church of **St-Pierre**, its facade reconstructed since the war, which spared the magnificent Renaissance stonework of the apse. To the west and east of the town centre respectively stand two great Romanesque constructions, the **Abbaye aux Hommes** with its church of **St-Étienne**, and the **Abbaye aux Dames** with **La Trinité** church. The first was founded by William the Conqueror and designed to hold his tomb (although the Huguenots and, later, the Revolutionaries scattered his remains to the winds); the other was commissioned by his wife, Queen Matilda. Hers is the more starkly impressive, with a gloomy pillared crypt, wonderful stained glass behind the altar, and odd sculptural details like the fish curled up in the holy-water stoup.

North of Caen, at the end of av Maréchal-Montgomery, there is a brand new museum, the **Caen Memorial**, standing on a plateau beneath which the Germans had their HQ in June and July 1944 (daily July & Aug 9am–9pm; Sept–June 9am–7pm; F50). One section deals with the rise of Fascism in Germany, another with resistance and collaboration in France, while a third charts all the major battles of World War II. There's also a film documentary covering all the conflicts since 1945. Bus #12 during the week or #14 on the weekend go direct to the museum from the Tour le Roi stop in the centre of town and take about twenty minutes.

These days, most of the centre of Caen is taken up with busy new shopping developments and pedestrian precincts, and the **port**, at the end of the long canal which links Caen to the sea, is where most life goes on, at least during the summer. It is also the area where most of the **hotels** are situated, including a number of good inexpensive ones like the *Weekend* at 14 quai Vendeuvre (☎31.86.39.95; ②) and the *Bernières*, 50 rue de Bernières (☎31.86.01.26; ③). Caen's **youth hostel** is a bit further out, southwest of the train station in the *Foyer Robert-Remé* at 68bis rue E-Restout (☎31.52.19.96; open June–Sept; ②). Close by the hostel is the town's **campsite**, down beside the River Orne on route de Louvigny (bus #13). The **tourist office** is located on the central place St-Pierre (daily June–Sept 9am–7pm; Oct–May Tues–Sat 9am–noon & 2–7pm, Sun, Mon & hols 10am–noon & 2–7pm), and is connected by regular bus with the **train station** on the south side of the river. The **bus station** is a few blocks west of the train station on rue des Bras. Buses to Ouistreham, the *Brittany Ferries* **terminal**, connect with the train station and are timed to coincide with crossings to Portsmouth.

For **restaurants**, rue de Geôle, running alongside the western ramparts to place St-Pierre, is the most promising location, with some good Vietnamese and Chinese places as well as French. Another area worth trying is around the Abbaye aux Hommes. For a large traditional meal, go to *Le Boeuf Ferré* at 10 rue des Croisiers; for nouvelle cuisine try *La Mandarine* at 18 rue Froide.

Bayeux

BAYEUX's perfectly preserved medieval ensemble, magnificent cathedral and world-famous tapestry depicting scenes of the invasion of Britain make it one of the high points of Normandy. It's only fifteen minutes by train from Caen, and receives an influx of summer tourists that can make its charms pall somewhat.

The **Bayeux Tapestry** is housed in the **Centre Guillaume le Conquérant**, clearly signposted on rue de Nesmond (mid-May to mid-Sept 9am–7pm; mid-Sept to mid-May 9.30am–12.30pm & 2–6pm; F28). Visits begin with a projection of slides on swathes of canvas, before moving on to an almost full-length reproduction of the original, complete with photographic extracts and detailed commentary. Upstairs in the plush theatre there's a film (French and English versions alternate) on the general context and craft of the piece, and beyond this the tapestry itself, a 70m strip of linen embroidered with coloured wools nine centuries ago. A medieval cartoon strip in effect, it records scenes from the 1066 invasion of Britain by William the Conqueror, as well as incidental details of domestic and daily life, which run along the bottom as a counterpoint to the military scenes above. It was for the consecration in 1077 of the nearby **Cathédrale Notre-Dame** that the tapestry was commissioned – and, despite some eighteenth-century vandalism, the Romanesque plan of the church is still intact. The crypt, entirely unaltered, is a beauty, its columns graced with frescoes of angels playing trumpets and bagpipes. Otherwise, the only other sight of interest is the **Musée de la Bataille de Normandie**, whose Cold War attitudes make a sorry contrast with the tranquil dignity of the British **war cemetery** across the road.

Bayeux's **train station** is on the southern side of town, on bd Sadi Carnot. There's nothing all that cheap in the way of **accommodation**. The **tourist office**, at 1 rue des Cuisiniers (Mon–Sat 9am–noon & 2–6pm, Sun 10am–noon & 3–6pm), might be able to help. Otherwise, most affordable of the **hotels** are the *Notre-Dame*, 44 rue des Cuisiniers (☎31.92.87.24; ②), and *de la Gare*, 26 place de la Gare (☎31.92.10.70; ②). Something that calls itself the *Family Home* at 39 rue Général-du-Dais (☎31.92.15.22), north of the cathedral, doubles up as the **youth hostel** (②), and decent **food**, too. Otherwise, most of the restaurants are in the pedestrianized rue St-Jean – *La Rapière* at no. 53 is the most popular. Failing that, try the *Angevin* on rue Genas-Duhomme.

Cherbourg

Situated at the top end of the Cotentin Peninsula, the mucky metropolis of CHERBOURG may be your port of arrival, in which case you should head straight for the **train station** on av Millet – a five-minute walk from the ferry terminal behind the inner dock. The town itself is almost devoid of interest. Napoléon continued the transformation of what had been a poor but perfectly situated natural harbour into a major transatlantic port. An equestrian statue commemorates his boast that he would "recreate (in Cherbourg) the wonders of Egypt". If you're waiting for a boat, the most enjoyable way of killing time is to settle into one of the **restaurants** around quai Caligny. The *Hôtel de France*, 41 rue Maréchal-Foch, and *Café de Paris* on the quayside are both excellent.

Mont St-Michel

One place many people hurry to is the island of **Mont St-Michel**, on the far western edge of Normandy, site of a marvellous Gothic abbey. The abbey church, long known as the *Merveille*, is visible from all around the bay, and it becomes more awe-inspiring the closer you get – as Maupassant said, "the most wonderful Gothic dwelling ever made for God on this earth". The abbey's granite was sculpted to match the exact contours of the hill, and though space was always limited, the building has grown through the centuries in ever more ingenious uses of geometry. To visit, you must join a tour (English-speaking, daily 10am, 11am, noon, 1.30pm, 2.30pm, 3.30pm, 4.30pm & 5.30pm; F32); these last for about an hour, and the guides are real experts, pointing out – among much other useful information – that the current state of the stone walls is a far cry from the way the medieval monastery would have looked, brightly painted and festooned with tapestries. The base of Mont St-Michel is a jumble of overpriced postcard and souvenir shops and restaurants, maintaining the great tradition of extorting money from pilgrims. The most famous hotel, *La Mère Poulard*, uses the time-honoured legend of its fluffy omelettes to justify extortionate charges. Higher up the one twisting street, however, prices fall to surprisingly realistic levels; the *Hôtel Croix Blanche* (☎33.60.14.04; ④) has reasonably-priced rooms and an exceptional restaurant.

The nearest **train station** is at **PONTORSON**, 6km south, a forgettable town where you can hire a bike from the station or take an expensive bus to the Mont. The best budget **hotel** is the *de France*, 2 rue de Rennes (☎33.60.29.17; ③ including breakfast), next to the rail crossing; it has a late and youthful bar. Otherwise, you could stay at Avranches, where there are a number of reasonable **hotels**, including *du Jardin des Plantes* at 10 place Carnot (☎33.58.03.68; ②) and *Le Central*, 2–4 rue du Jardin-des-Plantes (☎33.58.16.59; ②). The **train station** is far below the town centre, but the views make up for that.

Rouen and around

You could spend a day wandering around **ROUEN** without realizing that the river Seine runs through the city. The war destroyed all the bridges, flattened the area between the cathedral and the *quais*, and razed much of the left bank industrial quarter. After repairing the damage, an enormous amount of money was spent on restoration to turn the centre into a largely fake medieval city. Still, the churches are extremely impressive and the whole place faintly seductive. And, as the nearest point that large container ships can get to Paris, Rouen is very much a working city too, albeit one in decline.

The nominal centre of the city, between place du Vieux-Marché and the cathedral, is the **Gros Horloge**, which spans the street named after it. It was originally on the belfry alongside but popular demand had it moved in 1529 to this more visible spot. You can climb the belfry (Easter to mid-Oct 10am–noon & 2.30–5.30pm; closed Tues & Wed am) and see the surrounding towers and spires arraying themselves in startling density. Just off here, the **Cathédrale de-Notre-Dame** remains at heart the Gothic masterpiece that was built in the twelfth and thirteenth centuries, although all kinds of vertical extensions have since been added. The west facade, intricately sculpted like the rest of the exterior, was Monet's subject for the series of celebrated studies of changing light. Inside, the carvings of the misericords in the choir provide a picture of fifteenth-century life in secular scenes of work and customs along with the usual mythical beasts. The ambulatory, with its recumbent English royals, is only accessible on guided tours.

The church of **St-Ouen**, in a park a short walk northeast, is larger than the cathedral and has far less decoration, so that the Gothic proportions have a more instant impact. Close by, the church of St-Maclou is more flamboyant, although perhaps the real interest is in its adjacent **Aître St-Maclou**, once a cemetery for plague victims and still with its original macabre decorations, together with a mummified cat. Of Rouen's museums, the most interesting is the **Musée Le Secq des Tourelles** (10am–noon & 2–6pm;

closed Tues & Wed am; F11), housed in the church of St-Laurent on rue Jacques-Villon, a brilliant collection of wrought-iron objects of all dates and descriptions. Next door, the **Musée des Beaux-Arts** (same times and price) is not tremendously enthralling but it does include a number of works by the Rouennais Géricault, Sisley and Monet, Dadaist pictures by Marcel Duchamp, and a collection of portraits by one Jacques Émile Blanche of Cocteau, Gide, Valéry, Mallarmé and others. Look in also on one of the city's smaller museums, the **Musée Flaubert et de l'Histoire de la Médicine** in the Hôpital Hôtel-Dieu on the corner of rue de Lecat and rue du Contrat-Social (Tues–Sat 10am–noon & 2–6pm; free), which is the best place to find out about Rouen's most famous novelist. Flaubert's father was chief surgeon at the medical school here, living with his family in this house within the hospital. Even during the cholera epidemic when Gustave was 11, he and his sister were not stopped from running around the wards or climbing along the garden wall to look into the lab. Some of the medical exhibits would certainly have been familiar objects to him – a phrenology model, a childbirth demonstrator like a giant rag doll, and the sets of encyclopedias.

Practicalities

The **train station** is a five-minute bus ride (#12, #15, #20) from the centre; best place to get off is the Théâtre des Arts, one block east from the **bus station**. The **tourist office**, 25 place de la Cathédrale (Mon–Sat 9am–7pm, Sun & hols 9.30am–12.30pm & 2.30–6pm), has plenty of information, though cheap and central **hotel accommodation** is in any case no problem: try the *Régent*, 128 rue Beauvoisine (☎35.71.86.03; ②), *des Flandres*, 5 rue des Bons Enfants (☎35.71.56.88; ②), or the *Saint Ouen*, 43 rue des Faulx, right alongside the church (☎35.71.46.44; ②). The **youth hostel**, south of the river at 17 rue Diderot (☎35.72.06.45; ②), is ten minutes' ride away on bus #5. The **camping municipal** is 5km northwest on rue Jules-Ferry in Déville-lès-Rouen (☎35.74.07.59), bus #2.

Rouen has a reputation for good **food**, and its most famous dish, duckling (*caneton*), can be enjoyed quite reasonably at *Pascaline*, 5 rue de la Poterne. For good basic meals, the south side of place du Vieux-Marché and the north side of St-Maclou church are both lined with good-quality restaurants. Some specific recommendations include the traditional *Le Vieux Carré* at 34 rue Ganterie, and *Walsheim* at 260 rue Martainville, next to St-Maclou, with menus from F65. The best deal in town is perhaps the *Cave Royale* at 48 rue Damiette, near St-Maclou, which serves mountains of couscous and paella for very affordable prices.

Giverny

For a complete shift of mood the best place to visit around Rouen is **GIVERNY**, and the gardens of the house Monet lived in from 1883 until his death in 1926 (Tues–Sun 10am–6pm, house 10am–noon & 2–6pm; closed Nov–March; house and gardens F35; gardens only F25), laid out by the artist himself. May and June, when the rhododendrons flower around the lily pond and the wisteria over the Japanese bridge is in bloom, are the best times to visit, but any month is overwhelmingly beautiful. Though you do get to see his famous water-lilies in real life, there aren't any paintings on show, and the house is instead filled with Monet's collection of Japanese prints. It can get very busy, and the crowds and cameras can induce a feel that seems far removed from Monet's intentions, but really there's no place like it.

Giverny isn't easy to get to from Rouen by **public transport**. Your best bet is a train to Vernon and then a ten-minute ride on the rare *Gisor* bus from the station. Nearby **accommodation** is not much easier, with a **youth hostel** in Vernon at 28 av de l'Île-de-France (☎32.51.66.48; ②).

BRITTANY

For generations the people of **Brittany** risked their lives fishing and trading on the violent seas or struggling with the arid soil of the interior, and their resilience is tinged with Celtic culture: mystical, musical, sometimes morbid, sometimes vital and inspired. Unified with France in 1532, Brittany has often been maintained as a colony by Paris; the Bretons have seen their language steadily eradicated, and the interior severely depopulated through lack of centralized aid. Today, the people still tend to treat France as a separate country, even if few of them actively support Breton nationalism much beyond putting Breizh (Breton for Brittany) stickers on their cars. The recent economic resurgence, helped partly by summer tourism, has largely been due to local initiatives, and at the same time a Celtic artistic identity has consciously been revived at festivals of traditional Breton music, poetry and dance.

For most visitors to this province, it is the **coast** that is the dominant feature. After the Côte d'Azur, this is the most popular summer resort area in France, and the attractions are obvious – white sand beaches, towering cliffs and offshore islands. Whether you approach across the Channel by ferry, or along the coast from Normandy, the Rance River, guarded by **St-Malo** on its estuary and **Dinan** 20km upstream, makes a spectacular introduction to Brittany. To the west stretches a varied coastline culminating in one of the most seductive of the islands, the Île de Bréhat; inland, most roads curl eventually to **Rennes**, the Breton capital. Brittany's **southern coast** takes in the province's (indeed Europe's) most famous prehistoric site, the alignments of **Carnac**, and although the beaches are not as spectacular as Finistère's, the water is warmer. Of the cities, **Lorient** has Brittany's most compelling **festival** and **Vannes** has one of the liveliest medieval town centres.

Rennes

Capital and power centre of Brittany, **RENNES** seems, with its Neoclassical layout and the pompous scale of its buildings, uncharacteristic of the province. It was razed in a fire of 1720 and the task of remodelling was handed out to Parisian architects – not in deference to the capital but to rival it. The city's oldest and most central quarter is bordered by the canal to the west and the river to the south. The city's one central building to survive the great fire was, symbolically enough, the **Palais de Justice**, on place du Palais, home of the old Rennes *parlement*, which fought battles with the French governor from the reign of Louis XIV up until the Revolution (tours Sat, Sun & hols 10am, 11am, 3pm, 4pm & 4.45pm; Mon & Wed–Fri contact tourist office; closed Tues; F20). The seventeenth-century chambers are opulently gilded and adorned, culminating in the debating hall hung with Gobelin tapestries depicting scenes from the history of the duchy and the province.

South of here, at 3 quai Émile-Zola, the **Musée de Bretagne** gives one of the best possible introductions to the culture and history of Brittany, and the **Musée des Beaux-Arts**, in the same building, contains an outstanding collection of pictures, from Leonardo drawings to 1960s abstracts. One room is dedicated to Brittany, with mythical and real life scenes (both daily except Tues 10am–noon & 2–6pm; F25).

The **train station** is linked with the central place de la République by buses #1, #20, #21 and #22. Nearby, on the Pont du Nemours at the point where the Vilaine River goes underground, is the provincial **tourist office** (June to mid-Sept Mon–Sat 9am–7pm; July & Aug Mon–Sun 10am–1pm & 3–5pm; mid-Sept–May Tues–Sat 10am–12.30pm & 2–6.30pm, Mon 2–6.30pm), and there's a smaller office at the train station (Mon–Fri 8am–8pm, Sat & Sun 9am–1pm & 2–6pm); further details on bikes, riding, hiking routes and waterways can be obtained at the **Association Bretonne** (*ABRI*) office at 3 rue des Portes-Mordelaise (Mon–Sat 9am–noon & 2–6pm), the last gatehouse left of the ramparts in the city's one surviving medieval quarter. **Hotels** are heavily concentrated around the place de la Gare; the *Bretagne* at no. 7 (☎99.31.48.48; ③) and the *Brest* at no. 15 (☎99.30.35.83; ③) are both reliable, but the *Tour d'Auvergne* at 20 bd de la Tour Auvergne (☎99.30.84.16; ②), five minutes' walk from the main tourist office, is the cheapest option. If you'd prefer to stay in the medieval quarter of town, try the *Rocher de Cancale*, 10 rue St-Michel (☎99.79.20.83; ③) fits the bill, ideally situated in the medieval section. The **youth hostel** is 3km out at 10–12 Canal St-Martin, on bus route #22 towards St-Gregoire (☎99.33.22.33; ②). Bus #3 takes you northeast to Gayeulles, from where it's a short walk to the city's **campsite**. The old town is the liveliest part of Rennes and stays up late, particularly in the vicinity of St-Aubin church. Good cheap **food** is to be had at *La Kalesche* on rue St-Malo, which does paella and couscous; there's an excellent *crêperie* at 5 place St-Anne. Rennes is at its best in the first ten days of July, when the **Festival des Tombées de la Nuit** takes over the whole city to celebrate Breton culture with music, theatre, film, mime and poetry.

St-Malo and around

About 50km north of Rennes, **ST-MALO**, walled and built with the same grey granite as the Mont St-Michel, presents its best face to the River Rance and the sea. If you're not planning to come here by ferry from Plymouth, it's still worth reaching it by boat – from either Dinard or Dinan. Once within the old ramparts, St-Malo can seem slightly grim and squat, and overrun by summer tourists. But away from the popular thoroughfares of the tiny **citadelle**, with its high seventeenth-century houses, random exploration is fun and you can surface to the light on the ramparts or pass through them to the nearby beaches. The **town museum**, in the castle to the right as you enter Porte St-Vincent (daily 9.30am–noon & 2–6.30pm; closed Tues Sept-May; free), glorifies on several exhausting floors St-Malo's sources of wealth and fame – colonialism, slave-trading and privateering among them. In the 1530s a St-Malo sea captain disembarked from the St Lawrence River and declared Canada to be the possession of the King of France, and the Argentinian name for the Falklands, "Las Malvinas", derives from the islands' first French colonists. But the town's proudest boast is that buried on the nearby Île de Grand (you can walk from the citadel at low tide), is the writer Châteaubriand.

Buses take you to the main city gate, the **Porte St-Vincent; trains** stop on the other side of the docks, a ten-minute walk away. It's always more difficult to find **accommodation** in the old city, despite its extraordinary number of hotels, but rooms at the *Moderne*, 10 rue Corne-du-Cerf (☎99.40.85.60; ⑤), or the *Marguerite*, 2 rue St-Benoît (☎99.40.87.03; ②), are well worth trying for. Otherwise, there's an array near the station on bd de la République, including the *Europe* at no. 44 (☎99.56.13.42; ②) and the *Vauban* at no. 7 (☎99.56.09.39; ②). In the nearby suburb of Paramé there's a **youth hostel** at 37 av Père-Umbricht (☎99.40.29.80; ②). If you have problems, the **tourist office** is in front of the Porte St-Vincent (July & Aug Mon–Sat 8.30am–8pm, Sun 10am–5.30pm; Sept–June Mon–Sat 9am–noon & 2–6pm). For **eating**, the *Étoile de Mer*, 5 rue Jacques-Cartier, is recommended.

Dinard and Dinan

Across the estuary from St-Malo, reachable by shuttle boat from below the southern wall of the citadel, **DINARD** has been transformed during this century from a simple fishing village to something along the lines of a Côte d'Azur resort, with a casino, shady villas and a glut of pricy hotels and restaurants. It's not a very welcoming place to stay, but is the start of some pleasant coastal walks, and pleasure trips by boat down the Rance to **DINAN**, whose citadel has been preserved, almost intact, within a three-kilometre circuit of walls, inside which lie street upon street of late medieval houses. It's almost too good to be true, but surprisingly not too swamped by tourists, and although there's nothing special to see, time is easily spent rambling from crêperie to café, admiring the houses on the way. Unfortunately, there's only one small stretch of the **ramparts** that you can walk along – from the gardens behind St-Sauveur to just short of the Tour Sillon – but you get a good general overview from the **Tour de l'Horloge** (daily 2–6pm; F8) or from the top of the keep guarding the town from the south, known as the **Château Duchesse Anne** (Mon–Sat 10am–noon & 2–6pm; F10). An inevitable target of any Dinan wanderings is the church of **St-Sauveur**, a real mix-up of periods, with a Romanesque porch and eighteenth-century steeple. Even its nine Gothic chapels have numerous and asymmetrical vaulting; the most complex pair, in the centre, are wonderful.

Modern Dinan is home to the **train station**, a short walk away from place Duclos. The **tourist office** is opposite the Tour de l'Horloge in the Hôtel Kératry. **Hotels** near the station are the *Hôtel de France* at 7 place du 11-Novembre (☎96.39.22.56; ③) and *Le Consigne* at 40 rue Carnot (☎96.39.00.12; ②). Within the walls there's *La Duchesse Anne* at 10 place du Guesclin (☎96.39.09.43; ③). The closest **campsite** is *La Nourais* at 103 rue Châteaubriand, which runs parallel to the western ramparts. Dinan's **youth hostel** (☎96.39.10.83; ②) is attractively set in the Moulin de Méen near the port at Taden, a two- to three-kilometre walk. The *Bar au Prélude* at 20 rue Haute-Voie is Dinan's liveliest late-night spot, with music and good basic **food**.

Roscoff

The opening of the deep-water port at **ROSCOFF** in 1973 was part of a general attempt by the government to revitalize the Breton economy. The ferry services to Plymouth and Cork are intended not just to bring tourists, but also to revive the traditional trading links that used to exist between the Celtic nations of Brittany, Ireland and southwest England. Roscoff itself has, however, remained a small resort with almost all activity confined to rue Gambetta and the old port. Until the last couple of centuries, the town made most of its money from piracy – like so many other ports along the Breton coast. There are a few reminders of that wealth in the ornate stone houses, and the **church** with its sculpted ships and protruding stone cannons, all dating from the sixteenth century.

To reach the town from the **ferry**, turn right leaving the terminal and follow the signs across a narrow promontory and down into Roscoff's harbour. Later than 9pm it may be difficult to find a restaurant still serving, but **hotels** are used to clientele arriving on late sailings. The two most reasonable are both on rue Amiral-Réveillère – *des Arcades* at no. 15 (☎98.69.70.45; ②), which has an unusually trendy bar and good food; and the quieter, more expensive *Les Chardons Bleus* at no. 4 (☎98.69.72.03; ④).

Quimper and around

QUIMPER, capital of the ancient diocese and kingdom of Cornouailles, is the oldest Breton city, founded according to legend by the original bishop of the town, Saint Corentin, who came here across the channel to the place they named Little Britain some time between the fourth and seventh centuries. It's a laid-back sort of place, with old granite buildings, two rivers and the rising woods of Mont Frugy overlooking the centre of town. There's no pressure to rush around monuments or museums and you can get to the sea in unhurried fashion on a boat down the Odet.

The town centres on the enormous Gothic **Cathédrale St-Corentin**, alongside which the bishops' palace houses a small, forgettable museum of Breton bits and pieces. More compelling is the **Musée des Beaux-Arts** next to the Hôtel de Ville (July & Aug daily 9am–7pm; Sept–June Wed–Mon 10am–noon & 2–6pm; F25), with its amazing collections of drawings by Cocteau, Max Jacob and Gustave Doré (shown in rotation) and nineteenth- and twentieth-century paintings of the Pont-Aven school. If you're interested in seeing pottery made on an industrial scale, and an exhibition of the changing styles since the first Quimper *ateliers* of the late seventeenth century, the **Faïenceries de Quimper** is another worthwhile visit. It's on place Berardier, downstream from the centre on the south bank of the Odet (tours Mon–Fri 9.30–11.30am & 1.30–5pm; free).

A short walk along the river brings you from the **train station** to the centre of town at place du Buerre. The **tourist office** is in the place de la Résistance at the western end of the rue Jean-Jaurès (Mon–Sat 9am–12.30pm & 1.30–6.30pm, Sun 9.30am–12.30pm). Budget **hotels** include the *Transvaal*, 57 rue Jean-Jaurès (☎98.90.09.91; ②), which also has a decent **restaurant**, the *Pascal* at 19 av de la Gare (☎98.90.00.81; ②), and the pleasant *Celtic*, a little way out of the centre at 13 rue de Douarnenez (☎98.55.59.35; ②). The **campsite** and **youth hostel** are downstream at 6 av des Oiseaux in the Bois du Seminaire (☎98.55.41.67; ②) – bus #1 from place de la Résistance. During the week preceding the last Sunday in July there's the **Festival Cornouailles**, a jamboree of Breton music, costume and dance; every room in the town is booked.

Boats down the Odet to the coast leave from the end of quai de l'Odet, opposite the Faïenceries, a winding journey to the upmarket resort of **BENODET**, where there's a long sheltered beach. **Hotels** are comparatively expensive, but you could try *L'Hermitage* (☎98.57.00.37; ②), and there are several large **campsites**. There are more beaches along the coast between Penmarch and Loctudy and beyond, about an hour by bus from Quimper. Another possibility is a trip to the **Pointe du Raz**, the Land's End of France, a series of plummeting fissures, filling and draining with deafening force, above which you can walk on precarious paths.

Lorient

LORIENT, Brittany's fourth largest city, is an immense natural harbour, protected from the ocean by the Île de Groix. A functional, rather depressing port, it was founded in the mid-seventeenth century for trading operations by the *Compagnie des Indes*, an equivalent of the Dutch and English East India Companies. Apart from the name, little else remains to suggest the wealth that once arrived here. During the last war, Lorient was a major target for the Allies, and the city was almost completely destroyed.

Time is more enjoyably spent on a boat trip upriver to the old walled town of **HENNEBONT**, whose imposing fortifications are marvellously preserved and give fine views over the surrounding countryside, although the overriding reason for coming to Lorient is for the **Inter-Celtic Festival**, held for ten days from the first Friday in August. This is the biggest Celtic event in Brittany, a popular celebration of cultural solidarity, with up to 250,000 people in attendance and Scotch and Guinness flowing with the French and Spanish wines and ciders. Most of the activities – which embrace music, dance and literature – happen around the central place Jules Ferry, where most people end up sleeping, too, as accommodation is pushed to the limits.

For the rest of the year, there is a huge choice of **hotels**. Among the best are the *Central*, 1 rue de Cambry (☎97.21.16.52; ③), and the *Hôtel d'Arvor*, 104 rue Lazare-Carnot (☎97.21.07.55; ②). The **youth hostel** is at 41 rue Victor-Schoelcher, 3km out on bus line #C from the **train station**, next to the River Ter (☎97.37.11.65; ②).

Carnac, Quiberon and Belle-Île

About 10km along the coast from Lorient, accessible only by way of the slightly dull town of Auray, **CARNAC** is home to one of the most important prehistoric sites in Europe, a congregation of some 2000 or so menhirs stretching for more than 4km to the north of the village, long predating Knossos, the Pyramids or Stonehenge. According to legend, the alignments are Roman soldiers turned to stone by Saint Cornely; another theory, with a certain amount of mathematical backing, says the Carnac stones were part of an observatory for the motions of the moon. The fact is, though, that no one really knows. Many have been used as ready-quarried stone, and it's impossible to say how many have disappeared, or really to prove anything from what's left. But, in spite of this, the stones remain an amazing site, and you'd be mad to miss them. Aside from strolling in wonder among them, you can get a good deal of information from the **Musée de Préhistoire** on rue du Tumulus in Carnac-Ville (July to mid-Sept daily 10am–noon & 2–6.30pm; rest of year daily except Tues 10am–noon & 2–5pm; F31), which entertainingly traces the history of the area from about 450,000 years ago.

Carnac, divided between the original **Carnac-Ville** and the more recent seaside resort of **Carnac-Plage**, is extremely popular. There is a **tourist office** at 74 av des Druides in Carnac-Plage, and this has a summer annexe in Carnac-Ville. Among the town's innumerable hotels,the *Hoty*, 15 av de Kermario (☎97.52.11.12; ③), is the best deal you'll find near the beach; in town, try the *Chez Nous*, 2 rue Poul-Person (☎97.52.07.28; ③). The best of Carnac's many **beaches** is the smallest, the **Men Dû**, just off the road towards La Trinité. If you're planning to **camp** by the sea, you should go to *L'Océan* or the *Men Dû*; otherwise, the best site is *La Grande Métairie*, opposite the stones.

South of Carnac, the **Presqu'île de Quiberon** is well worth visiting on its own merits. The town of **QUIBERON** itself is a lively port, and provides a jumping-off point for boats out to the nearby islands or simply a base for the peninsula. The ocean-facing shore, known as the **Côte Sauvage**, is a wild and unswimmable stretch, but the sheltered eastern side has safe and calm sandy beaches, and offers plenty of **campsites**. In Quiberon, Port Maria, the fishing harbour, is the most active part of town and has the best concentration of **hotels** – try the *de l'Océan* on quai de l'Océan (☎97.50.07.58; ③) or *de la Mer* on quai de Houat (☎97.50.09.05; ③). The **youth hostel**, *Les Filets Bleus*, 45 rue du Roch-Priol (☎97.50.15.54; ②), is set back from the sea close to the **train station**. A vast array of **fish restaurants** lines the seafront, of which the best is *Au Bon Accueil* on quai de Houat. The cafés by the long bathing beach are also enjoyable, especially the old-fashioned *Café du Marché*. The **tourist office** is at 7 rue de Verdun, downhill and to the left from the train station (Mon–Sat 9am–8pm, Sun 10am–noon).

Belle-Île, 45 minutes by ferry from Quiberon, has its own "Côte Sauvage" on its Atlantic coast, while the landward side is composed of more fertile, cultivated ground, interrupted by deep estuaries with tiny ports. To appreciate the island's contrasts, some form of transport is advisable – you can **hire bikes** both at the port and in the main town of **LE PALAIS**. Docking at Le Palais, the abrupt star-shaped fortifications of the island's **Citadelle** are the first thing you see. Built along stylish and ordered lines by Vauban, the complex is startling in size, filled with doorways leading to mysterious cellars and underground passages, endless sequences of rooms, dungeons and deserted cells. It only ceased being a prison in 1961, having numbered an endless succession of state enemies and revolutionaries among its inmates, including Ben Bella of Algeria. A museum (daily 9am–7pm; free) documents the island's history, in fiction as much as in fact.

Accommodation in Le Palais includes the reasonably priced *Hôtel du Commerce*, on place Hôtel-de-Ville (☎97.31.81.71; ③), a **campsite**, *Les Glacis*, and a **youth hostel** (☎97.31.81.33; ②), a short way out of town along the clifftops from the citadel. Belle-Île's second town, **SAUZON**, is set at the mouth of a long estuary 6km to the west. If you're staying any length of time, and you've got transport, it's probably a better place to base yourself. There's a good, cheap **hotel**, *du Phare* (☎97.31.60.36; ③), and two **campsites**, *Pen Prad* and *Prad Stivell*.

Vannes and the Golfe de Morbihan

VANNES is one of the most historic towns in Brittany. It was from here that the great Breton hero, Nominöe, set out to unify the region, giving the Franks a terrible beating and pushing the borders past Nantes and Rennes, where they remained up until the French Revolution nearly a millennium later. It was in Vannes, too, that the Breton assembly ratified the Act of Union with France in 1532.

The old centre of Vannes is a chaos of streets crammed around the cathedral and enclosed by ramparts and gardens, and by day at least it's this area which provides Vannes' chief source of pleasure. The building where the Act of Union was ratified, **La Cohue**, between rue des Halles and the cathedral square, has reverted after some 750 years to its original use as a marketplace, with the local **Musée des Beaux-Arts** on its top floor. Close by, the **Cathedral** is not the finest edifice in the town, but it does have one exquisite treasure, an early medieval wedding chest with beautifully painted figures (summer Mon–Sat 10am–noon & 2–5pm; F8). Nearby, on rue Noë, is the **Château Gaillard** archeology museum, with finds dating from 400,000 BC to the Roman occupation laid out with tedious precision, while around the corner, the **Hôtel de Roscannec** museum at 19 rue des Halles has an equally efficient display of stones, fossils, shells and stuffed birds (both daily except Sun summer 9.30am–noon & 2–6pm; winter 2–6pm; F20 combined ticket).

It's ten-minutes' walk south from the **train station** to the centre at place de la République. North of here is the **tourist office** at 29 rue Thiers (Mon–Sat 9am–noon & 2–6pm). Vannes has the best choice of **hotels** anywhere around the Golfe de Morbihan: two good ones are *Le Bretagne*, 34 rue du Mène (☎97.47.20.21; ②); in the old town, and *Le Marina* overlooking the port at 4 pl Gambetta (☎97.47.22.81; ③); the *Clisson* at 11 rue Olivier-de-Clisson (☎97.54.13.94; ②) is also a good standby. For **food**, the *Bistrot des Halles* on place de la Poissonnerie serves excellent fish dinners. A late-night **bar**, with a friendly atmosphere and Irish folk bands, is *Le Pandemonium* on rue de la Boucherie.

It comes as rather a surprise to discover that Vannes is on the sea. Its harbour is a channelled inlet of the ragged-edged **Golfe de Morbihan**, which lets in the tides through a narrow gap. By popular tradition, the **islands** scattered around this enclosure used to number the days of the year, though for centuries the waters have been rising and there are now fewer than one for each week. Of these, thirty are privately owned, while two – the Île aux Moines and Île d'Arz – have regular populations and ferry services and end up being crowded in summer. You can take a **boat tour** around the rest, a compelling trip through a baffling muddle of channels, megalithic ruins, stone circles and solitary menhirs on small hillocks. Full details from the Vannes tourist office.

Nantes

Though the former capital, **NANTES**, is these days not officially a part of Brittany, it remains to its inhabitants an integral part of the province. Crucial to its self-image is **Château des Ducs**, subjected to a certain amount of damage over the centuries, but still preserving the form in which it was built by two of the last rulers of independent

Brittany, François II, and his daughter Duchess Anne, who was born here in 1477. The list of famous people who have been guests or prisoners, defenders or belligerents of the castle is impressive, and includes Bluebeard, who was publicly burnt to death here in 1440, and Bonnie Prince Charlie preparing for Culloden in 1745. But the most significant act in the castle's history was the signing of the Edict of Nantes by Henri IV in 1598, which ended the Wars of Religion and granted a certain degree of toleration to the Protestants. You can walk into the courtyard and up onto the low ramparts for free, while in the grounds are three museums (10am–noon & 2–6pm; closed Tues except in July & Aug; F15). The first, the **Musée des Arts Populaires**, is a good introduction to Breton history and folklore, depicted here in a series of murals and dioramas. The **Musée des Arts Décoratifs**, in the Governor's Palace, displays a refreshingly contemporary selection of textile work, while the city's trading history is the subject of the **Musée des Salorges**, with numerous documents and objects connected with the slave trade.

In 1800 the castle's arsenal exploded, shattering the stained glass of the **Cathédrale de St-Pierre et St-Paul**, 200m away, just one of many disasters that have befallen the church. Newly restored, its soaring heights are home to the tomb of François II and his wife, Margaret. The **Musée des Beaux-Arts** on rue Clemenceau (Mon & Wed–Sat 10am–noon & 1–5.45pm, Sun 11am–5pm; F20) has a respectable collection of paintings that includes two huge canvases by Rubens. Back past the château, the so-called **Île Feydeau**, once an island, was the birthplace of Jules Verne and has a **museum** dedicated to him at 3 rue de l'Hermitage (daily except Tues 10am–noon & 2–5pm; closed Sun am; F5). It's more of an amusement for the fans of his stories than a source of any serious information, but the multitude of illustrated editions is nice.

The **train station** is on the south side of the centre, a short way east of the castle. For **places to stay**, try the *Hôtel St-Reine*, 1 rue Anatole-le-Braz (☎40.74.35.61; ②), *Hôtel de l'Océan*, 11 rue du Maréchal-de-Lattre-de-Tassigny (☎40.69.73.51; ②), or the *Fourcroy*, 11 rue Fourcroy (☎40.69.77.87; ②). Of the three **youth hostels**, the summer-only one at 2 place de la Manu (☎40.20.57.25; ②) is easiest to reach – tram #1 towards Malachère – although the other two unofficial places are preferable if you're not an *IYHF* member; they're at 1 rue Porte-Neuve (☎40.20.00.80; ②) and at 9 bd Vincent-Gache (☎40.47.91.64; ②). The **tourist office** is on place du Commerce (Mon–Fri 9am–7pm, Sat 10am–6pm), a largely pedestrian area that's a good source of **restaurants** – try the *Petit Bistrot* on rue de la Juiverie. Otherwise, the best restaurant area is among the former shipbuilders' houses on rue Kervegan on the Île Feydeau: try the *Salt and Pepper*.

THE LOIRE

Intimidated by the sheer density of châteaux, people tend to make bad use of their time spent in the Loire, which is a pity, for if you pick your castles selectively, this can be one of the most enjoyable of all French regions. The most salient features of the Loire itself are whirlpools, vicious currents and a propensity to flood. No one swims in or boats on the Loire, nor are any goods are carried along it – it's just there, the longest river in France. The stretch between Angers and Saumur is the loveliest on the lower reaches, the land on the south planted with vines and sunflowers. Other than the châteaux, the best of which are those at **Chenonceaux**, **Azay-le-Rideau** and **Loches**, the region has few other sights; the most unmissable are the tapestries in **Angers** and the gardens at **Villandry**, outside Tours. Of the other towns, **Tours** can be tedious but is good for museums, while **Saumur** is perfect for indolence but not hot on entertainment.

Angers

"Black" **ANGERS**, the capital of Anjou, gained its epithet from the slate and stone that has been quarried here since the ninth century. It is, however, an attractive, well-kept town with a lively atmosphere, worth at least a day's visit, principally for two incredible tapestries, the fourteenth-century *Apocalypse* and twentieth-century *Chant du Monde*.

The *Tapestry of the Apocalypse* is in the **Château d'Angers** (daily summer 9am–7pm; winter 9am–12.30pm & 2–6.30pm; F31), a formidable early medieval fortress with seventeen circular towers gripping the rock below the kilometre-long curtain wall. Inside, there are a few remains of the counts' royal lodgings and chapels, but the immediate and obvious focus is the tapestry, whose 100-metre length (of an original 168m) is well displayed in a modern gallery. Woven between 1375 and 1378, it takes as its text Saint John's vision of the apocalypse in the Book of Revelation; the slightly flattened medieval perspective has an hallucinatory quality, possessing an alarming power to evoke a sense of the end of the world. If you can take anything else in, there are more tapestries, of a gentler nature, in the sporadically open **Royal Lodgings** and **Governor's Lodge**, while the city's modern tapestry, *Le Chant du Monde*, is housed in the former poorhouse, **Hôpital St-Jean**, a fifteen-minute walk away on bd Arago (summer daily 10am–1pm & 2–7pm; winter Tues–Sun 10am–noon & 2–6pm; F15). It was designed, in response to the *Apocalypse*, by Jean Lurçat, who began the project in 1957 but died nine years later before its completion. It's a bright, initially overwhelming piece of work, the first frames dealing with the threat of nuclear war and finishing up with a series of images celebrating the joy of life, complete with the artist's commentary in English.

Crossing the central Pont de Verdun back to the centre, you'll see a long flight of steps leading up to the **Cathédrale St-Maurice** – an inspiring approach, giving the full benefit of the early medieval facade. Inside, the unusually wide, aisle-less nave is illuminated by twelfth-century stained glass, one window of which, in the choir, is dedicated to Thomas à Becket. The other great Gothic edifice in Angers is the chancel of the **Église St-Serge**, on av M-Talet, just north of the centre near the Jardin des Plantes. Though nothing much to look at from the outside, it has some perfect and seemingly impossible vaulting rising from the slender columns.

Practicalities

The **train station** is south of the centre across bd du Roi Reine on rue Auguste-Gaultier, a ten-minute walk from the château; or take bus #22. The **tourist office** is on place Kennedy, facing the château, and runs an accommodation service if you're thinking of staying (summer Mon–Sat 9am–7pm, Sun 10.30am–6.30pm; winter Mon–Sat 9am–12.30pm & 2–6pm). The two most central and affordable **hotels** are the *Armor*, 13 rue Bodinier (☎41.88.06.06; ②), and the *Centre*, 12 rue St-Laud (☎41.87.45.07; ②), both off rue de la Röe. There are also cheap places around the station, such as *La Coupe d'Or*, 5 rue de la Gare (☎41.88.45.02; ③). There's a summer **youth hostel**, along with a **campsite**, out on the route de Pruniers (☎41.48.57.01; ②) – bus #6 from the station. The streets around place du Ralliement and place Romain are the best for **restaurants**, among which you should try *Chez Taya*, an Oriental café on rue Pocquet de Livonnièrres serving couscous, and *Le Connétable*, 13 rue des Deux Haies, a good crêperie. For a good-quality French pig-out, *Le Meridor*, 4 rue de l'Espine, is good value.

Saumur and around

The local sparkling wines for which **SAUMUR** is best known are based outside the town – in the suburb of St-Hilaire-St-Florent – and the quiet little *ville* itself is simply peaceful and pretty, a good place to base yourself for a while, with Angers, Chinon and plenty of vineyards within easy reach. There is a **Château** (daily mid-June to mid-Sept

9am–7pm; rest of year 9am–noon & 2–6pm; closed Tues Oct–March; F32), where you can visit the dungeons and watchtower, and be guided around two museums within its walls – the **Musée des Arts Décoratifs**, with its huge collection of European china, among other things, and the **Musée du Cheval**, with bridles, saddles and stirrups. Outside the château, on av Maréchal-Foch, west of rue d'Orléans, there is another museum for horse freaks, the **Musée de la Cavalerie** (Mon–Thurs & Sat 2–5pm, Sun 9–11.30am; closed Aug; free), with uniforms, weapons, battle scenes, and a room dedicated to the cadets who held the Loire bridges between Gennes and Montsoreau against the Germans for three days in 1940, after the French government had surrendered.

Arriving at the **train station** leaves you on the north bank of the river; from here cross over the bridge to the island, then over another bridge to the main part of the town on the south bank. Saumur's main street, **rue d'Orléans**, cuts back through the south bank sector; the **tourist office** is unmissable at the foot of the second bridge, on place de la Bilange (summer Mon–Sat 9.15am–7pm, Sun 10.30am–12.30pm & 3–6.30pm; winter Mon–Sat 9.15am–12.30pm & 2–6pm). The best **hotel** is *Le Cristal*, 10 place de la République (☎41.51.09.54; ③), with river views from most rooms and very friendly proprietors; other options include *La Croix de Guerre*, 9 rue de la Petite Bilange (☎41.51.05.88; ②), the *Bretagne*, 55 rue St-Nicolas (☎41.51.26.38; ②), and *de Volney*, 1 rue Volney (☎41.51.25.41; ②). On the Île d'Offard, connected by bridges to both banks of the town, there's a good **youth hostel** at the eastern end of rue de Verden (☎41.67.45.00; ②), offering boat and bike rental, and a **campsite** next door. The best area for **eating** is around place St-Pierre: *Auberge St-Pierre*, at no. 6, has a fairly cheap menu, as does *Les Cigognes* at no. 1.

Fontévraud

The **Abbaye de Fontévraud** (daily summer 9am–7pm; winter 9.30am–12.30pm & 2–6pm; F23), 13km southeast of Saumur (bus #16), was founded in 1099 as both a nunnery and a monastery with an abbess in charge – a radical move, even if the post was filled solely by queens and princesses. The premises had to be immense to house and separate not only nuns and monks but also the sick, lepers and repentant prostitutes, and three of the original five complexes still stand. A prison from the Revolution until 1963, its most famous inmate was writer Jean Genet, but its chief significance is as the burial ground of the Plantagenet kings. Four tombstone effigies remain, of Henry II, Eleanor of Aquitaine, Richard the Lionheart and Isabelle of Angoulême (King John's wife).

Chinon

The first of the big Loire châteaux is at **CHINON** (daily July & Aug 9am–7pm; April–June & Sept 9am–6pm; Oct 9am–5pm; Nov–March 9am–noon & 2–5pm; F23). It was one of the few places in which Charles VII could stay while Henry V of England held Paris and the title to the French throne. Charles's situation changed with the arrival here in 1429 of Joan of Arc, who persuaded him to give her an army. All that remains of the scene of this encounter, the Grande Salle, is a wall and first-floor fireplace. Visits to this and to the restored royal lodgings – both guided – are not wildly exciting. More interesting is the Tour Coudray, to the west, covered with intricate thirteenth-century graffiti carved by imprisoned and doomed Templar knights. Below the castle, the town is a tacky and rather sterile place, with very few **hotels** and everything closed up long before midnight. If you're looking for a room, the two cheapest alternatives are the *Point du Jour*, 102 quai Jeanne-d'Arc (☎47.93.07.20; ②), and the *Jeanne d'Arc*, 11 rue Voltaire (☎47.93.02.85; ②). There is a **youth hostel** (☎47.93.10.48; ②) close to the **train station** on rue Descartes and a **campsite** across the river at Île-Auger. The **tourist office** is at 12 rue Voltaire (Mon–Sat 9am–7pm, Sun 10am–13.20pm). The most reasonable **restaurant** is *Les Années 30* at 78 rue Voltaire.

Azay-le-Rideau

A few kilometres upstream from Chinon, **AZAY-LE-RIDEAU** is worth visiting for its serene setting, and for its **Château** (daily July & Aug 9am–6.30pm; April–June, Sept & Oct 9.30am–5.30pm; Nov–March 10am–12.30pm & 2–5pm; F26), which is one of the Loire's loveliest, at least from the outside. Its interior, furnished in Renaissance style, doesn't add much to the experience, but the portrait gallery has the whole sixteenth-century royal Loire crew – François I, Catherine de Médici et al – and includes a fine semi-nude painting of Gabrielle d'Estrées, Henri IV's lover. There is a large **campsite** a little way upstream from the château, although **hotels** don't come cheap. A possibility if you're stuck is *Le Balzac*, 4 rue A-Richer (☎47.45.42.08; ②).

Tours and around

A little way upriver, **TOURS** is a bourgeois, rather dull city, but a large and booming one, and a reasonable base for seeing a number of châteaux. If you decide to stay, it's likely to be for these, as well as a handful of decent museums and the pleasures of the nearby vineyards. The town's main street is **rue Nationale**, a short walk down which are two of the town's most compelling collections: the **Musée de Compagnonnage** (daily except Tues 9am–noon & 2–6pm; F20), which documents the origins and militant activity of the guilds that built the châteaux, and the **Musée du Vin**, next door (same hours; F10), which gives a pretty comprehensive treatment of the history, mythology and production of the wondrous liquid. Over beside the **Cathédrale St-Gatien** – with its crumbling, Flamboyant Gothic front – the city's third museum, the **Musée des Beaux-Arts** on rue Lavoisier (daily except Tues 8am–12.45pm & 2–6pm; F30), has some beauties in its rambling collection – *Christ in the Garden of Olives* and the *Resurrection* by Mantegna, and Frans Hals' portrait of Descartes. The museum's top treasure, however, Rembrandt's *Flight into Egypt*, is difficult to see through the security glass. In the opposite direction, west of rue Nationale, Tours' **old town** crowds around place St-Pierre-le-Puellier, whose medieval half-timbered houses and bulging stairway towers are the city's showpieces.

Accommodation isn't a problem in Tours. There's an official **youth hostel** on av d'Arsonval in Parc de Grandmont (☎47.25.14.45; ②; bus #6 or #2 to Chambray), and a **hostel** for under-25s, *Le Foyer*, 16 rue Bernard-Palissy (☎47.05.38.81; ②) – call first as they may be full. The nearest **campsite**, the *Edouard Peron*, is on the north bank of the Loire (bus #6). As for **hotels**, in the unpleasant area around the station *Au Rhum* is one of the cheapest options, at 4 place des Aumônes (☎47.05.06.99; ②), while the *Mon*, nearer the cathedral at 40 rue de la Préfecture (☎47.05.67.53; ②), is similarly priced. Rue du Grand-Marché and rue de la Rôtisserie, on the periphery of old Tours, and rue Colbert – which runs down to the cathedral – are the most promising streets for **restaurants**. *Les Lionceaux* at 17 rue Jules-Favre, off rue Colbert, has the cheapest *menu fixe*, and *Le Yaki Tour*, on rue de la Rôtisserie, is a Japanese place with a F53 menu. *Le Donjon*, 7 rue de la Monnaie, has cheap and interesting international fare – good, filling stroganoff and chilli.

Villandry, Chenonceaux and Loches

The most popular attraction close to Tours is the château of **VILLANDRY**, about 13km west, where there are some extraordinary Renaissance **gardens** set out on several terraces that give marvellous views over the river (daily 9am–sunset; F24; tours of the château April–Nov 9am–6pm; F13). The château itself includes Spanish paintings and a Moorish ceiling from Toledo. There's no public transport, but if you can rent a bike it's a wonderful ride along the banks of the Cher, a tributary of the Loire.

Perhaps the finest of all the castles of the region is the river-straddling château at **CHENONCEAUX** (daily 9am–4/7pm; F35), about 15km away and connected with Tours by two daily buses. The building went up in the 1520s, and was the home of Diane de Poitiers, the lover of Henry II, until his death in 1559, when his wife Catherine de Médici had her evicted. Catherine left the château to her daughter-in-law, Louise de Lorraine, who later had the place painted black and decorated with skulls to reflect her mourning for her husband Henry III. For once you're allowed to roam around the place at will, and despite nineteenth-century restoration there is lots to see – floors of tapestries, paintings and furniture, much of it worth lingering over, not least Zurbarán's penetrating depiction of Archimedes in the Salle François I. The Salle des Gardes on the same floor houses Flemish tapestries and has beams decorated with the coat of arms of Catherine de Médici.

The château at **LOCHES**, an hour by train southeast of Tours, is visually the most impressive of the Loire fortresses, with ramparts and a huddle of houses below still partly enclosed by the outer wall of the medieval town (July & Aug daily 9am–6pm; Sept–June daily except Wed 9am–noon & 2–6pm; F26). You can climb unescorted to the top of the keep, poke around in the dungeons and torture chamber, and visit the royal lodgings in the northern end of the castle, where Charles VII and his three successors had their residence. Agnès Sorel, Charles' mistress, resided here with him, and you can see her tomb in the fifteenth-century wing, along with her portrait by Fouquet and a picture of the Virgin in her likeness.

Blois and Chambord

The **château** at **BLOIS**, 40km or so upriver from Tours (daily summer 9am–6pm; winter 9am–noon & 2–5pm; F30), was another residence of Catherine de Médici, and she died here in 1589. All six French kings of the sixteenth century spent time here; Henri III murdered the Duc de Guise and his brother here, shortly before being knocked off himself by a monk. The building, which you can tour on your own during most of the year, is a strange mixture of architectural styles. The oldest parts date from the thirteenth century, and are viewable in the Salle des États or main hall; Louis XII built the later east wing in Flamboyant Gothic style, while the early sixteenth-century north wing shows the influence of the Italian Renaissance. It also contains Beaux-Arts and archeological museums, but neither is very exciting.

Blois is a modern, uninteresting town, the château girdled by a busy road. However, if you have to stay, the **tourist office** at 3 av Jean-Laiguet (summer Mon–Sat 9am–7pm, Sun 10am–1pm & 2–7pm; winter Mon–Sat 9am–noon & 2–6pm) organizes private rooms for a small fee, and there are a few inexpensive **hotels**, including the *St-Nicolas*, 2 rue du Sermon (☎54.78.05.85; ②), and the *Hôtel du Bellay*, 12 rue des Minimes (☎54.78.23.62; ③). The closest **campsite** is 2km away across the river, on the Lac de Loire at Vineuil. There is a **youth hostel** 5km downstream at Les Grouets, 18 rue de l'Hôtel-Pasquier (☎54.78.27.21; ②); take bus #4. Best bets for **food** are *La Tosca*, 36 rue Foulérie, and *Le Maidi*, 42 rue St-Lubin.

Chambord

A few kilometres southeast of Blois, **CHAMBORD** (daily summer 9.30am–6.15pm; winter 9.30am–12.15pm & 2–5.15pm; F31), François I's little "hunting lodge", was one of the most extravagant commissions of the age – its patron's principal object was to outdo the Holy Roman Emperor Charles V, and it would, he claimed, leave him renowned as "one of the greatest builders in the universe". It was begun in 1519 and the work was executed by French masons, so the overall result is essentially French medieval, something particularly evident in the massive round towers with their conical tops and the forest of chimneys and turrets. The details, however, are pure Italian: for example the double spiral Great Staircase (attributed by some to Leonardo), panels of coloured marble, niches decorated with shell-like domes, and freestanding columns. To **get there** on public transport you'll have to use the expensive château tour buses from Blois or Tours. Cycling is a preferable option – it's a beautiful ride.

Orléans

Directly below the turned-up nose of the capital, poor **ORLÉANS** feels compelled to recuperate its faded glory from 1429, when Joan of Arc delivered the city from the English. In earlier times still, Orléans was Clovis's capital and in the days of Asterix it was one of the key Gallo-Roman cities. But now not only do Orléannais go to Paris for their evenings out, they commute to work there as well.

There is, however, enough to merit a stop. The **Cathédrale St-Croix** (daily 9am–noon & 2–6pm), battered for five and a half centuries, is wonderful, and full of Joan's presence. In the north transept, her pedestal is supported by two golden leopards (representing the English) on an altar carved with the battle scene. The late nineteenth-century stained-glass windows in the nave tell the story of Joan's life, with caricatures of the loutish Anglo-Saxons and snooty French nobles. There's more on Joan of Arc in the **Maison de Jeanne d'Arc** on place Général-de-Gaulle (Mon 2.30–5pm, Tues–Sun 9am–noon & 2–5pm; F8); it's fun for children, with good models and displays of the breaking of the Orléans siege. If you've had your fill of Joan by now, the best escape is the modern art collection in the basement of the **Musée des Beaux-Arts**, opposite the Hôtel de Ville (daily except Tues 10am–noon & 2–6pm; F15), with canvases by Picasso, Miró, Dufy, Renoir and Monet.

The **train station** and **tourist office** (daily 9am–7pm) are next door to each other on place Albert I, north of the town centre, connected by rue de la République to the central place du Martroi. There are cheap **hotels** near the station – the pleasant *Hôtel de Paris*, 29 Faubourg Bannier (☎38.53.39.58; ②), and the small and friendly *Hôtel de Trevise*, 7 rue Croix de Malte (☎38.62.69.06; ②). In the centre, you could try the *St-Jean*, 19 rue Porte-St-Jean (☎38.53.63.32; ②). The **youth hostel** is at 14 rue du Faubourg-Madeleine to the west of town (☎38.62.45.75; ②) – bus #B from place Albert I. Bus #B also goes to the nearest **campsite** at St-Jean-de-la-Ruelle, 2km out on the Blois road, rue de la Roche (☎38.88.39.39). Rue de Bourgogne, parallel to the river, has a good choice of **restaurants**. You can eat African food at *Le Dakar* at no. 24, or there's a cheap crêperie, the *Breton*, at no. 242.

Bourges

The capital of the *département* of Berry, about 50km south of Orléans, **BOURGES** has medieval links and more modern literary connections, and is an obvious stopover if you're heading towards the Massif Central. There's not much to the town, but it's a pleasant enough place to spend the night, not least for its **Cathédrale St-Étienne**, which is one of the country's most distinctive cathedrals, with five great portals opening out of its west front, adorned by thirteenth-century sculpture. Beloved of Gothic purists, the interior is impressive too: light, large and airy, double-aisled with no transepts, setting off to best effect the marvellous stained glass in the choir and apsidal chapels – the finest in France after Chartres.

Old Bourges lies within a loop of roads northwest of the cathedral. On rue Jacques-Coeur stand the head office, the stock exchange, dealing rooms, safes and the home of Charles VII's finance minister, **Jacques Coeur** (daily tours May–Oct 9–11.10am & 2.15–5.10pm; Nov–April 10–11.10am & 2–4.10pm; F15), a medieval shipping magnate, moneylender and arms dealer who dominates Bourges much as Joan of Arc does

Orléans. The visit to his palace is fun and worth while, starting with the fake windows from which very realistic sculpted figures look down. There are hardly any furnishings remaining, but the decorations on the stonework, including numerous hearts and scallop shells (*coeurs* and *coquilles St-Jacques*), clearly show the mark of the man who had it built.

The **train station** is 1km north of the centre on av P-Sémard, across the river. The **tourist office** is close by the cathedral at 21 rue Victor-Hugo (summer Mon–Sat 9am–7pm, Sun 9am–1pm & 2.30–7pm; winter Mon–Sat 9am–noon & 2–6pm). There is a **youth hostel** 2km out at 22 rue Henri-Sellier (☎48.24.58.09; ②; red bus #1), and a **campsite** across the stream from the hostel on bd de l'Industrie (bus #6 to Justices from place Cujas). Bourges' cheapest **hotel** is *Au Rendez-vous des Amis*, 6 av Marx-Dormoy (☎48.70.81.80; ②), a short walk from the station up av P-Sémard and right, while in the centre there's the *De la Poste*, 22 rue Moyenne (☎48.70.08.06; ②), and *Le Central*, 6 rue du Docteur Témoin (☎48.24.10.25; ②). The main centre for **restaurants** is place Gordaine, an attractive square where the *Lion d'Or* and *Le Compt de Paris* make reasonable options; the *Arome de Vieux Bourges* is a coffee shop selling all manner of edible delicacies – good for lunch.

POITOU-CHARENTE AND THE ATLANTIC COAST

The summer light, the warm air, the fields of sunflowers and the siesta-silent air of the farmhouses of **Poitou-Charente** give the first exciting promise of the south. The coast has great charm in places, although it remains distinctly Atlantic, with dunes, pine forests and misty mud flats, and it lacks the glamour of the Côte d'Azur. The principal port, **La Rochelle**, however, is one of the prettiest and most distinctive towns in France, and the islands of **Ré** and **Oléron**, out of season at least, are lovely, with miles of sandy beaches. **Poitiers** is a likely entry point to the region, a pleasant town with an attractive old centre. South of here, the valley of the Charente river, slow and green, epitomizes the blue-overalled, peasant France, accessible on boat trips from **Cognac**, famous for the eponymous spirit although otherwise a rather indifferent town.

Poitiers

Heading south from Tours on the *autoroute*, you'd hardly be tempted by the cluster of towers and office blocks rising from the plain, which is all you see of **POITIERS**. But go in close and things are very different. It is no seething metropolis, but a country town with a charm that comes from a long and sometimes influential history – sas seat of the Dukes of Aquitaine – discernible in the winding lines of the streets and the breadth of architectural fashions represented in its buildings.

The tree-lined **place Leclerc**, and **place de Gaulle** just a few streets north, are the two poles of communal life, flanked by cafés and bustling market stalls. Between is a warren of streets, with rue Gambetta cutting north past the **Palais de Justice**, whose nineteenth-century facade hides the twelfth-century great hall of the dukes of Aquitaine. This magnificent room, nearly 50m long, is where Jean, Duc de Berry, held his sumptuous court in the late fourteenth century, seated on the intricately carved dais at the far end of the room. In one corner, stairs give access to the old **castle keep**. Joan of Arc was once put through her ideological paces here by a committee of bishops worried about endangering their own immortal souls by endorsing a heretic. They also had her virginity checked by a posse of respectable matrons. The stairs lead out on to the roof with a fantastic view over the town.

Across from the Palais is one of the greatest and most idiosyncratic churches in France, **Notre-Dame-la-Grande**, whose west front is loaded with enthralling sculpture, typical of the Poitou brand of Romanesque (under restoration until mid-1994) – though the interior, crudely overlaid with nineteenth-century frescoes, is not nearly as interesting. There is another unusual church a little way east, literally in the middle of rue Jean-Jaurès as you head towards the river Clain. This is the mid-fourth-century **Baptistère St-Jean** (April–June & Sept–Oct daily except Tues 10.30am–12.30pm & 3–6pm; July–Aug daily 10.30am–12.30pm & 3–6pm), reputedly the oldest Christian building in France and until the seventeenth century the only place in town you could have a proper baptism; the font was the octagonal pool sunk into the floor. There are also some very ancient and faded **frescoes** on the walls, including the Emperor Constantine on horseback, and a collection of Merovingian sarcophagi. Just north, Poitiers' **Cathédrale de St-Pierre** is an enormous building, some of whose stained glass dates from the twelfth century, notably the *Crucifixion* in the centre window of the apse, in which the features of Henry II and Eleanor are supposedly discernible. Opposite, in a side street, the **Musée St-Croix** (Tues–Fri 10am–noon & 1–5pm, Sat & Sun 10am–noon & 2–6pm; F15) has a collection of local farming implements, and a good Gallo-Roman section with some handsome glass, pottery and sculpture, notably a first-century white marble Minerva.

The **train station** is at the foot of the hill which forms the kernel of the town. Among cheap **hotels** the *Renaissance*, 179 av de Nantes (☎49.58.22.27; ②), is a comfortable place, behind the train station, and the nearby *Petite Villette*, 14 bd de l'Abbé de Frémont (☎49.41.41.33; ②). It's only a short uphill walk to the town centre, where you'll pay a bit more at the attractive *Hôtel du Plat d'Étain*, 7 rue du Plat d'Étain (☎49.41.04.80; ②). There's a **youth hostel** at 17 rue de la Jeunesse (☎49.58.03.05; ②; bus #9 from the station) and a municipal **campsite** on rue du Porteau, north of the town (bus #7). The **tourist office**'s main office is at 8 rue des Grandes-Écoles (July & Aug daily 9am–7pm; Sept–June Mon–Fri 9am–noon & 1.30–6pm; Sat 9am–noon & 2–6pm), with a summer annexe by the station. As for **eating**, *Le Poitevin*, 76 rue Carnot, does regional food at reasonable prices; *Le Snooker* is a plain brasserie on rue de la Régatterie; *Pizzeria Cappuccino*, on rue de l'Université, is one of the Italians in the area.

La Rochelle and around

LA ROCHELLE is the most attractive seaside town in France, with a seventeenth- and eighteenth-century centre and waterfront that were plucked from the clutches of the developers in the 1970s. The town has a long history, as you would expect of such a sheltered Atlantic port. Eleanor of Aquitaine gave it a charter in 1199, and it rapidly became a port of major importance, trading in salt and wine, the principal terminus for trade with the French colonies in the West Indies and Canada. Indeed, many of the settlers, especially in Canada, came from this part of France.

From the visitor's point of view, everything worth seeing is in the area behind the waterfront, in effect between the harbour and place de Verdun. The heavy Gothic gateway of the **Porte de la Grosse Horloge** straddles the entrance to the old town, dominating the pleasure-boat-filled inner harbour, overlooked by two towers. Beyond the tower, steps climb up to rue Sur-les-Murs, which follows the top of the old sea wall to a third tower, the **Tour de la Lanterne** or Tour des Quatre Sergents, named after four sergeants imprisoned and executed for defying the Restoration monarchy in 1822 (9.30am–12.30pm & 2–6.30pm; closed Tues except in July & Aug; F20). From here there is a way up onto all that's left of the **city walls**, planted with unkempt greenery, beyond which is the **beach**. Through the Grosse Horloge, the main shopping street, **rue du Palais**, is lined by eighteenth-century houses and arcaded shopfronts. To the west, especially in rue de l'Escale, are the discreet residences of the eighteenth-century ship owners and chandlers, while to the east, rue du Temple leads to the **Hôtel de Ville**, begun in the reign of Henri IV, whose initials intertwined with those of Marie de Médici are carved on the ground floor gallery. It's a beautiful specimen of Frenchified Italian taste, adorned with niches and statues and coffered ceilings. There's more of this rich world in the **Musée du Nouveau Monde** on rue Fleuriau (Mon & Wed–Sat 10.30am–12.30pm & 1.30–6pm, Sun 3–6pm; closed Tues; F12), which occupies the former residence of the Fleuriau family, who, like many of their fellow-Rochelais, made fortunes from slaving and West Indian sugar, spices and coffee. Its elegantly panelled interior has a fine collection of prints, paintings and photos of the old West Indian plantations, seventeenth- and eighteenth-century maps of America and photogravures of Native Americans from around 1900, all with captions that might have been lifted from Tintin.

From the **train station**, it's ten minutes down **av de Gaulle** to the town centre. The **tourist office** is by the harbour on Quai de Gabut (June–Sept Mon–Sat 9am–8pm; Oct–May Mon–Sat 9am–12.30pm & 2–6pm), but finding **accommodation** can be a problem in season. There's a **youth hostel** in Port des Minimes to the west (☎46.44.43.11; ②) – bus #10 from the station – and two **campsites**: the *Soleil* by the hostel (May–Sept) and a municipal site on the northwestern side of town (bus #6 from Grosse Horloge). Of a handful of cheap **hotels** in the centre, the best bets are the *Bordeaux*, 43 rue St-Nicolas (☎46.41.31.22; ②), *Henri-IV*, 31 rue des Gentilshommes (☎46.41.25.79; ②), and the *Printania*, 9 rue Brave-Rondeau (☎46.41.22.86; ②). For **eating**, try the rue du Port/rue St-Sauveur area just off the waterfront and rue St-Nicolas. *Pub Lutèce* on rue St-Sauveur is a reasonably priced brasserie and *Café-Resto à la Villette*, behind the market, has good *plats du jour*; if your budget can't stretch to the inflated restaurant prices, brasseries and pubs around Grosse Horloge serve sandwiches and snacks throughout the night. For **beaches**, you're best off crossing over to the Île de Ré, a long narrow island immediately west of La Rochelle and connected by road, which is surrounded by sandy strands. Out of season it has a slow, misty charm, life in its little ports revolving around the cultivation of oysters and mussels.

Rochefort and the Île d'Oleron

A little way south of La Rochelle, **ROCHEFORT** dates from the seventeenth century, when Colbert, Louis XIII's navy minister, created it as a base to protect the coast from English raids. It is a dull place, but there is one powerful reason for visiting – the house of the novelist Julien Viaud, alias **Pierre Loti**, a native of Rochefort who stayed forty years as an officer, writing numerous bestselling romances with Oriental settings and characters. The **house**, at 141 rue Pierre-Loti (hourly tours July–Sept 10am–11am & 2–5pm; Oct–June 10am–11am & 2–4pm; closed Tues and Sun am year round; F30), is part of a row of modestly proportioned grey stone houses, outwardly a model of petty-bourgeois conformity. But inside is something of a surprise, dolled up with the exoticism that Loti so loved – a medieval banqueting hall complete with Gothic fireplace and Gobelin tapestries, a refectory with windows pinched from a ruined abbey and Damascus mosque, where a manservant would play muezzin from a miniature minaret.

Should you want to **stay**, there's a small **youth hostel** at 20 rue de la République (☎46.99.74.62; ②), and a **camping municipal** down av du Président-Wilson from the train station, about half an hour's walk. The cheapest **hotel** is the *Messageries*, by the station (☎46.99.00.90; ②). For **eating**, the *Self-Service* by the Arsenal on rue Toufaire or *l'Étalon* on the same street are adequate and convenient. If you want to **swim**, the nearby Île d'Oleron, France's largest island after Corsica, joined to the mainland by toll bridge, has miles of beautiful sandy beaches. The little towns, inevitably, have been ruined by the development of hundreds of holiday homes, and it can be a real battle in the summer season to find a place to stay, but, for all that, it's a pretty and distinctive island. With its pines, tamarisks and evergreen oaks, the stretch from Boyardville to St-Pierre – the most attractive of the towns – is the most appealing.

Cognac

Inland and southeast from Rochefort, **COGNAC** is a sunny, prosperous, self-satisfied little place, best-known for its brandy distilleries, which reveal themselves through the heady scent that pervades the place – indeed it's this which forms the main reason for coming at all. The **tourist office**, close by the central place Francois I (Mon–Sat 9am–7pm; closed for lunch off-season), has information on visiting the various cognac *chais*, most of which are situated at the end of Grand-Rue, which winds through the old quarter of town. Perhaps the best for a visit are those of **Hennessy** (9–11am & 2–5pm; closed Sun mid-June to mid-Sept, Sat & Sun mid-Sept to mid-June; free), a seventh-generation family firm of Irish origin, where tours begin with a film explaining what's what in the world of cognac. Hennessy alone keeps 180,000 barrels in stock; all are regularly checked and various blends made from barrel to barrel. Only the best is kept, a choice which depends on the tastebuds of the *maître du chais*. At Hennessy the job has been in the same family for six generations; the present heir apparent has already been sixteen years under his father's tutelage and is still said to be not yet fully qualified.

From the **train station**, take rue Mousnier, then rue Bayard, which leads you up rue du 14-Juillet – where there's a reasonably priced **restaurant**, the *Sens Unique* – to place François I. There are a couple of **cafés** and a reasonable **brasserie** on the square. Upstream from the bridge, the oak woods of the Parc François I stretch along the riverbank to the town **campsite**; the cheapest **rooms** are either at the *Tourist*, 166 av Victor-Hugo (☎45.32.09.61; ②; closed Aug), or *Le Cheval Blanc*, 6–8 place Bayard (☎45.82.09.55; ②).

AQUITAINE, THE DORDOGNE AND THE LOT

Steamy, moist and green, the **southwest** of France can feel like a kind of lower-latitude England – which is no doubt why it attracts so many urban Brits in search of the good life. In the Dordogne heartlands, the country is certainly beautiful, but the regional authorities are all too well aware of their assets, hyping up the landscape, food and medieval towns, with the result that many of more the famous spots, especially in the Dordogne valley, have become oppressively crowded in season. **Bordeaux** is a possible entry point to the region, though not really sufficiently interesting to hold your attention for long, unless you're interested in wine.

East of Bordeaux, the northern half of the Dordogne *département*, the **Périgord Blanc**, is named for the light, white colour of its rock outcrops – undulating, fertile, wooded country, rising in the north and east to the edge of the Massif Central. The regional capital is **Périgueux**, which because of its central position and relative ease of access makes the best base for the whole region, especially the cave paintings at **Les Eyzies** and around. The **Périgord Noir** is the stretch of territory from Bergerac to Brive, said to be darker in aspect than the Blanc because of the preponderance of oak woods. It's this area that people always think of when you say Dordogne, where most of the picture-book villages are, where the cuisine is at its richest and the prices at their highest. **Sarlat** is its capital and a good base for exploration. South from here lies the drier, poorer and more sparsely populated region through which the **Lot** river flows roughly parallel with the Dordogne, an ideal area to hike, bike and camp. **Cahors** has sights worth a stop, and once you're away from here you will probably have most of the region to yourself.

Bordeaux and around

The city of **BORDEAUX** is something of a disappointment for a casual visitor. It's big, with a population of nearly a quarter of a million, and obviously rich, yet the only part you could call attractive is the relatively small eighteenth-century centre. The rest is scruffy, and, even with its long history, contains far fewer sights than many a lesser place. But if you are just passing through, its regional museum is worth seeing, cheap accommodation is plentiful, and it's a good place to eat, with numerous ethnic restaurants. The surrounding countryside is not the most enticing, and you definitely need your own transport to explore it; you go for the wines rather than the landscape. More interesting are the vast pine-covered expanse of the Landes, to the south, and the huge wild Atlantic beaches.

Arrival and accommodation

Arriving by **train**, you find yourself at the **gare St-Jean**, linked to the centre of town by bus #7/8, and the heart of a convenient if insalubrious area for **accommodation**. Right outside the station, rue Charles-Domercq and cours de la Marne are full of one- and two-star **hotels** – try the *Dijon* at 22 rue Charles Dimercq (☎59.91.76.65; b), or the *San Michel* at no. 32 (☎56.91.96.40; ②). Less seedily, there's the more central *Hôtel de la Boëtie* on rue de la Boëtie (☎56.81.76.68; ②). The large **youth hostel** is here, too, to the left off cours de la Marne on cours Barbey (☎56.91.59.51; ②) – though there's an 11pm curfew. The *Maison des Étudiantes*, 50 rue Ligier (☎56.96.48.30; ②), at the end of cours de la Marne, sometimes has cheap **hostel rooms** – and, although mainly for women, will accept men in July and August. The **tourist office** is in the centre of town on the corner of Esplanade des Quinconces in the place de la Comédie (June–Sept Mon–Sat 9am–8pm, Sun 9am–3pm; Oct–May Mon–Sat 9am–6.30pm). Though the city centre is walkable, you need to take **buses** to cover longer distances; tickets, valid for half an hour, are available on board but it's cheaper to buy packs of ten from a *tabac*.

The City

The centre of the city is café-lined **place Gambetta**, a once majestic square conceived in the time of Louis XV. Its housefronts, arcaded at street level, are decorated with rows of carved masks, and in the middle an English-style garden soaks up some of the traffic fumes. In one corner, the eighteenth-century arch of the **Porte Dijeaux** spans the street. East, cours de l'Intendance, full of chic shops, leads to the impeccably classical **Grand Théâtre** on place de la Comédie, built in 1780 and faced with an immense colonnaded portico topped by Muses and Graces. From here, smart streets radiate out. Sanded and tree-lined **allées de Tourny** leads to a statue of Tourny, the eighteenth-century administrator who was prime mover of the city's golden age. **Cours du 30-juillet** leads into the bare expanse of **Esplanade des Quinconces**, said to be Europe's largest municipal square, with an enormous memorial to the Girondins, the influential local deputies to the Revolutionary Assembly of 1789, purged by Robespierre as counter-revolutionaries. Immediately south is the once-elegant part of Bordeaux – some sections have been done up while others are incongruously seedy. The most pleasing area is probably **place du Parlement** and the even more imposing **place de la Bourse**, with the old customs house and stock exchange on the riverside.

Rue St-Catherine, the city's main shopping street, leads down from place de la Comédie towards the best of the city's museums, the **Musée d'Aquitaine** at 20 cours Pasteur (daily except Mon 10am–6pm; F15, free Wed), an imaginative collection including drawings and writings that give some indication why eighteenth-century Bordeaux was compared to Paris by contemporary writers. Take a look, too, at the section on the wine trade before venturing off on a vineyard tour. A couple of blocks east is the cathedral of **St-André**, whose most eye-catching feature is the great upward sweep of the twin steeples over the north transept, an effect heightened by the adjacent fifteenth-century **Tour Pey-Berland**. The interior is not particularly interesting apart from the choir, one of the few complete examples of the Gothic Rayonnant style, but there's some fine carving in the north transept door. The surrounding square is attractive, with enticing pavement cafés and the classical **Hôtel de Ville**. A similarly handsome eighteenth-century house in neighbouring rue Bouffard houses the **Musée des Arts Décoratifs** (daily except Tues 2–6pm; F15, free Wed), whose collections include some beautiful – mainly French – porcelain and faïence, furniture, glass, miniatures and prints of the city in its maritime heyday. Just around the corner on cours d'Albret, the **Musée des Beaux-Arts** (daily except Tues 10am–6pm; F15, free Wed) has a small and unexciting collection of paintings.

Eating and drinking

There are a lot of cheap **eating** places in the station quarter, and ethnic restaurants along the left bank of the river near the station. In the centre of town, wholesome meals and terrace drinks are available from the very popular *Café des Arts* on the corner of rue St-Catherine and cours Victor-Hugo. For something a bit different, there's French Antillaise cooking at *Le Tire-Bouchon*, 15 rue des Bahutiers, and – rather cheaper – at *Les Coralies*, 76 rue du Loup, while *Aux 3 Arcades* in place du Parlement specializes in huge, unusual salads. *Baud Millet Fromagerie*, 19 rue Huguerie, offer you as much of their 100-plus cheeses as you can manage for F95 in their "tour de France des Fromages" – not after 11pm, though.

The Vineyards

With Burgundy and Champagne, the wines of Bordeaux form the Holy Trinity of French viticulture. The reds in particular – known as claret to the English – have graced the tables of the discerning for many a century. The country that produces them stretches north, east and south of the city, and is the largest quality wine district in the world. North along the west bank of the brown, island-spotted Gironde estuary are **Médoc** and **Haut-Médoc**, whose wines have a full-bodied, smoky taste and a reputation for improving with age. Across the Gironde – seven or eight ferries a day from Lamarque to Vauban-fortified Blaye – the green slopes of the *côtes* of **Bourg** and **Blaye** are home to heavier, plummier reds, cheaper than anything found on the opposite side of the river. South of the city is the domain of the great whites, the super-dry **Graves** and the sweet dessert wines of **Sauternes**, which get their flavour from grapes left to rot on the vine. East, on the other side of the River Garonne, are the **Premières Côtes de Bordeaux**, which form the first slopes of the **Entre-Deux-Mers** (by far the prettiest countryside in the Bordeaux wine region), whose wines are regarded as good but less fine than the Médocs and Graves – less fine also than the superlative reds of **Pomerol, Fronsac** and **St-Emilion**, just to the north of the River Dordogne.

The Bordeaux tourist office has a leaflet detailing all the châteaux that allow **visits and wine-tasting**. Since, however, getting to any of these places except St-Emilion without your own transport is hard work, the simplest thing is to take one of the tourist office's own **tours**, which leave daily between mid-June and mid-October. They are expensive but are generally interesting and informative and well worth the money.

The Beaches

On summer weekends the Bordelais escape to **ARCACHON**, a seaside resort forty minutes' train ride away across flat sandy forest. The beaches of white sand are magnificent but inevitably crowded, although there are lots of **campsites**. If you're stuck for a room, there's an **tourist office** to the left of the station on place Roosevelt. Arcachon's chief curiosity is the **dune de Pilat**, at 114m the highest sand dune in Europe – a veritable mountain of wind-carved sand, about 8km down the coast. Buses run there from Arcachon **train station** every half-hour in July and August; there are about five a day at other times. From the end of the line the road continues on uphill for about fifteen minutes to the inevitable group of fast-food stands and a superb view of the bay of Arcachon and the forest of the Landes stretching away to the south.

Les Landes

Travelling south from Bordeaux by road or rail, you pass for half a day through unremitting, flat, sandy pine forest – **Les Landes**. Until the nineteenth century this was a vast, infertile swamp, steadily encroached upon by the shifting sand dunes of the coast; today it supports over two million acres of trees. At **MARQUEZE**, about 15km east of Labouheyre on the N10 from Bordeaux to Bayonne, the **Parc régional des Landes de Gascogne** runs the **Écomusée** (mid-June to mid-Sept daily 10am–5.20pm; mid-Sept to mid-June Sat 2.30–4.30pm, Sun 10.15am–5.40pm; F35) to illustrate the traditional *landais* way of life, where shepherds clomped around the scrub on long stilts. *SNCF* trains stop at Labouheyre on the Facture-Bayonne run; a resuscitated steam train runs regularly between Labouheyre and Sabres, June to September, stopping at the museum.

Périgueux

PÉRIGUEUX is a busy and prosperous market town, pleasant enough but hardly compelling, though it does make a good base for seeing the best of the Dordogne's prehistoric caves. The centre of town focuses on **place Bugeaud**, a ten-minute walk from the train station. Ahead, down rue Taillefer, the **Cathédrale de St-Front**, its square, pineapple-capped belfry surging above the roofs of the surrounding medieval houses, is one of the most distinctive Romanesque churches in France, modelled on the Holy Apostles in Constantinople. Sadly, it's been spoilt by overzealous restoration, although the Byzantine influence is still evident in the interior in the Greek-cross plan, most unusual in France, and in the massive curves of the domes and their supporting arches. The big Baroque altarpiece is worth a look, too, depicting the Assumption of the Virgin. Outside, place de la Clautre gives on to Périgueux's renovated **old quarter**, with a number of fine Renaissance houses, particularly along rue Limogeanne. The **Musée du Périgord**, at the end of rue St-Front on the cours de Tourny (10am–noon & 2–5pm; closed Tues; F12), has some beautiful Gallo-Roman mosaics from local sites – Périgueux was a major provincial centre after the Roman conquest. There is an extensive but badly displayed prehistoric collection, again of local origin, and some exquisite Limoges enamels near the exit; look especially at the portraits of the twelve Caesars. For remains of the Roman heyday you have to go back to place Bugeaud and take rue du Président-Wilson to the Jardin des Arènes, which conceals the ruins of an enormous **amphitheatre**, dismantled in the third century; while over by the rail line at the end of rue Romaine, a high brick tower, the **Tour de Vésone**, is the last vestige of a temple to the city's guardian goddess.

There are some good cheap **hotels** right in front of the train station: try the *Hôtel du Midi et Terminus* (☎53.53.41.06; ②), or the *Hôtel des Charentes* (☎53.53.37.13; ②), which has an inexpensive restaurant. Alternatively, there is **hostel accommodation** at the *Foyer des Jeunes Travailleurs* off bd Lakanal (☎53.53.52.05; ②) – follow the rail track southeast from the station – and **camping** at *Barnabé-Plage* on the east bank of the River Isle. The **tourist office** is at 26 place Francheville, behind *Monoprix* on rue du Président Wilson (Mon–Fri 8am–noon & 1–7pm, Sat 9am–noon & 2–5pm). There's no shortage of good **restaurants**, though they tend to be expensive. Exceptions include *Lou Chabrol* at 22 rue Eguillerie, off place St-Louis, and *Pizzeria Les Coupoles* on rue de la Clarté, both near the cathedral. For regional dishes, try *Le Saint Front*, also on rue de la Clarté.

The Vézère Valley caves

Half an hour or so by train from Périgueux is a luxuriant cliff-cut region riddled with caves and subterranean streams. It was here that skeletons of *Homo sapiens* were first unearthed in 1868, and an incredible wealth of archeological evidence of the life of late Stone Age people has since been found here. There are various theories as to why these inaccessible spots were chosen. Most agree that if not actually places of worship, they at least had religious significance, and the cave paintings were perhaps meant to aid fertility or hunting rituals. They are remarkable not only for their great age, but also for their exquisite colouring and the skill with which they are drawn. All the caves are open to the public except the most spectacular one, at Lascaux near Montignac, which, due to deterioration from the body heat and breath of visitors, has been closed since 1963; all you can see now is a tantalizing replica.

Les Eyzies

LES EYZIES is the centre of the region, a rambling, unattractive village completely dedicated to tourism. There's a riverside **campsite**, *La Rivière*, but **hotels** are pricy and likely to ask for *demi-pension*. If you're not staying in Périgueux, try **LE BUGUE**, 10km down the River Vézère, where there's an excellent and inexpensive **hotel-restaurant** by the station on the road into town. Four **trains** run daily to Les Eyzies from Périgueux, and the Périgueux tourist office issues a sheet detailing how to get there and back in the day. For getting around the area once you've arrived, the Les Eyzies **tourist office** rents **bikes**. Worth a glance before or after visiting the caves is the **Musée National de Préhistoire** (daily except Tues 9.30am–noon & 2–5/6pm; F17), which exhibits prehistoric artefacts and art objects including copies of one of the most beautiful pieces of Stone Age art – two clay bison from the Tuc d'Audoubert cave in the Pyrenees.

Grotte de Font de Gaume

Situated just outside Les Eyzies, off the road to Sarlat, the tunnel-like **Grotte de Font de Gaume** (daily except Tues April–Sept 9am–noon & 2–6pm; Oct–March 9.30am–noon & 2–5.30pm; F31) contains dozens of polychrome paintings. Inside, the cave is a narrow twisting passage of irregular height with no lighting. When the guide finally halts and focuses her torch, you see a frieze of bison at about eye level: reddish-brown in colour, massive, full of movement, and very far from the primitive representations you might expect. Further on, in a side passage, two horses stand one behind the other, forelegs outstretched as if, as the guide suggests with a degree of relish, to attempt *un début d'accouplement* ("the beginnings of copulation"). Most miraculous of all is a frieze of five bison discovered in 1966 during cleaning operations, the colour remarkably preserved by a protective layer of calcite. Maximum group size for admission at one time is twenty and **tickets** sell out fast. To be sure of a place in season, especially on a Sunday when they're half-price, get to the ticket office at least an hour before opening.

Grotte des Combarelles

Beyond Font de Gaume is the **Grotte des Combarelles** (daily except Tues April–Sept 9am–noon & 2–6pm; Oct–March 9.30am–noon & 2–5.30pm; F25), discovered in 1910 and covered with engravings that are often superimposed, since they were drawn over a period of two thousand years. They include horses, reindeer, mammoths and crude human figures; among the finest are the heads of a horse and of a lioness. Hours are the same as Font de Gaume; unlike Font de Gaume, however, you cannot buy afternoon tickets in the morning, so you have to arrive early for both sessions.

Abri du Cap-Blanc

Not a cave but a rock shelter, **Abri du Cap-Blanc** is 7km from Les Eyzies, a steep but manageable bike ride past Grotte des Combarelles (daily mid-Feb to mid-Nov 10am–noon & 2–6pm; F23). Its sculpted frieze of horses and bison, dating from 12,000 BC, is polished and set off against a pockmarked background in extraordinary high relief – of the ten surviving prehistoric sculptures in France, this is the best.

Montignac and Lascaux

Heading up the valley of the Vézère river, northeast of Les Eyzies, **MONTIGNAC** (connected to Sarlat by bus), is more attractive than Les Eyzies but short on even moderately priced accommodation. *Hôtel de la Grotte*, 63 rue du 4-Septembre (☎53.51.80.48; b), has a couple of cheap rooms and a good cheap menu. There is also a three-star **campsite**. The **tourist office** (Mon–Sat 9.30am–noon & 2.30–5.30pm) is on place Bertran de Born, in the same building as a **museum** of local crafts. The tourist office sells the F45 tickets for the nearby cave of **Lascaux** – or rather, for a facsimile, **Lascaux II** (July & Aug daily 9.30am–7pm; Sept–Dec & Feb–June daily except Mon 10am–noon & 2–5pm), which took eleven years to construct using the same methods and materials as the original. Executed 17,000 years ago, the paintings are said to be the finest prehistoric works in existence. There are five or six identifiable styles, and subjects include the bison, mammoth and horse, plus the biggest-known prehistoric drawing in existence, a five-and-a-half-metre bull with astonishingly expressive head and face. The visit lasts forty minutes, and the commentary is in French, with English translations if requested.

Bergerac and the Dordogne Valley

Lying on the banks of the Dordogne southeast of Périgueux, **BERGERAC** is the main market centre for the surrounding maize, vine and tobacco farms. Devastated in the Wars of Religion, when most of its Protestant population fled overseas, it is essentially a modern town, yet it is still attractive. What is left of the old quarter has a lot of charm, with numerous late-medieval houses. In rue de l'Ancien-Pont the seventeenth-century Maison Peyrarède houses a **tobacco museum** (Tues–Fri 10am–noon & 2–6pm, Sat 10am–noon & 2–5pm, Sun 2.30–6.30pm; F15), detailing the history of the weed, with collections of pipes and tools of the trade. Bergerac is the mainstay of the French tobacco-growing industry, somewhat in the doldrums today since the traditional *brune* – brown cigarette tobacco – is gradually being superseded by the *blonde*, which is oven-cured and therefore a lot less labour-intensive to make. Six kilometres south of the town and perhaps best reached by bike, the small **Château de Montbazillac** (daily June–Sept 10am–12.30pm & 2–7.30pm; Oct–May 10am–noon 2–5pm; closed Mon Jan–March; F25) is a source of the well-known velvety and sweet white wine, out of fashion for many years but recently becoming popular again. **Accommodation** in Bergerac isn't hard to find: there are several small hotels, among them the *Hôtel Pozzi*, 11 rue Pozzi (☎53.57.04.68; ②), and a **campsite**. The **tourist office** is at 97 rue Neuve-d'Argenson.

To the east is **SARLAT**, capital of Périgord Noir, held in a hollow in the hills a few kilometres back from the Dordogne Valley. It has an alluring old medieval core, focusing on the central **place de la Liberté**, where you'll find the **tourist office** (mid-June to mid-Sept Mon–Sat 9am–7pm, Sun 10am–noon & 2–6pm; mid-Sept to mid-June Mon–Sat 9am–noon & 2–6pm). Although there's not much to see, it makes a good base for the surrounding countryside and trips further upstream – the tourist office has details of organized trips if you don't have your own transport. There is a **youth hostel** on the Périgueux road at 15 av de Selves (☎53.59.47.59; ②), open May to September, and a prettily sited **campsite** 2km beyond the rail viaduct. Hotels include the *Marcel*, 8 av de Selves (☎53.59.21.98; ③), which has a good restaurant, and the *Hôtel de la Mairie* on place de la Liberté (☎53.59.05.71; ③).

Among the places you might visit from Sarlat are **SOUILLAC**, further upstream, where the twelfth-century church of St-Marie has some marvellous Romanesque sculptures, and, about 10km southeast of there, **ROCAMADOUR**, wonderfully sited tucked under a cliff in a deep canyon. This has been visited for centuries by pilgrims for its miracle-working Black Madonna, housed in a votive-packed **Chapelle Miraculeuse**, to which the devout drag themselves on their knees. But be warned that it can sometimes get unbearably crowded these days, and is home to all manner of tourist junk.

Cahors and around

CAHORS, a walled backwater on the River Lot, was the capital of the old province of Quercy, and has a long and complex history dating back to its time as a Gallic settlement and Roman town. Its most remarkable sight is the fourteenth-century **Pont Valentré**, which, with its three powerful towers, guards the river crossing on the west side of town. At the far end of rue du Président-Wilson from the bridge, the other main sight is the **Cathedral**, consecrated in 1119 and the oldest and simplest in plan of the Périgord-style churches, with an aisle-less nave, no transepts and two large domes for a roof. The Gothic choir and apse are extensively but crudely painted. To their right a door opens into a delicate Flamboyant cloister, which, though damaged, retains some intricate carving. The best feature on the exterior is the elaborately decorated portal in the street on the north side, where a *Christ in Majesty* dominates the tympanum, surrounded by angels and Apostles.

The **train station** is at the end of av Jean-Jaurès, off rue du Président-Wilson which leads to the Pont Valentré. The **tourist office** is on the corner of bd Gambetta and allée Fénelon, near the cathedral. For **accommodation**, there's a **foyer** located at 20 rue Frédéric-Suisse (☎65.34.64.71; ②), a ten-minute walk from the station. Alternatively, try the **hotels** *L'Escargot* at 5 bd Gambetta (☎65.35.07.66; ③), or the *Hôtel de la Paix* on place St-Maurice by the cathedral (☎65.35.03.40; ②). The ragged **camping municipal** is to the right at the end of the Pont Louis-Philippe. For **food**, there's the convivial *La Brasérade* on rue Bergougnoux, or, a more commonplace alternative, the *Champ de Mars* at 17 bd Gambetta. Vegetarians should head for *L'Orangerie* on rue St-James.

Grotte du Pech-Merle

East of Cahors, *SNCF* buses follow the beautiful, deep-cut, twisting valley of the Lot to Conduche, from where there's a further four-kilometre walk up the tributary valley of the Célé to Cabrerets, followed by a final 1500m up to the marvellous prehistoric cave of **Pech-Merle** (April–Oct daily 9.30am–noon & 1.30–5.30pm; F42). Pech-Merle cave is larger than the Les Eyzies caves and there is normally no difficulty getting tickets. The admission charge includes admission to a **film** and excellent **museum**, where the history of prehistory is illustrated by charts, a selection of objects, beautiful slides, and the juxtaposed skulls of Neanderthals and *Homo sapiens*. The **cave** itself is more beautiful than Les Eyzies, with galleries full of spectacular stalactites and stalagmites, although the guided tours are uninspiring and tend to rush you. As well as the stunning paintings of horses and charging bison in the so-called **Chapelle des Mammouths**, there's a glorious horse panel contoured into the rock in a vast chamber, and, most chillingly, the footprints of a Stone Age adult and child preserved in a muddy pool.

THE PYRENEES

Basque-speaking and wet in the west, snowy and patois-speaking in the middle, dry and Catalan in the east, **the Pyrenees** are physically beautiful, culturally varied and a great deal less developed than the Alps. The whole range is marvellous walking country, especially the central region around the **Parc National des Pyrénées**, with its 3000-metre peaks, streams, forests, flowers and wildlife. If you're a serious hiker, it's possible to walk all the way across from Atlantic to Mediterranean between June and September, following the *GR10* or the more difficult *Haute Randonnée Pyrénéenne* – although bear in mind that these are big mountains, and to cover any of the main walks you'll need hiking boots, and, despite the southerly latitude, warm and windproof clothing. As for more conventional tourist attractions, the **Basque coast** is lovely but very popular, suffering from seaside sprawl and a massive surfeit of campsites: **St-Jean-de-Luz** is by far the prettiest of the resorts; **Bayonne** the most attractive town, with an excellent Basque museum and art gallery; **Biarritz** the most overrated. The foothill towns, on the whole, are dull, though **Pau** is worth a day or two, while **Lourdes** is a monster of kitsch that has to be seen.

Bayonne and Biarritz

Bayonne and **Biarritz** are virtual continuations of each other, but their characters are entirely different. Bayonne is a clean, sunny, southern town, workaday and very Basque; Biarritz is sophisticated and prim, redeemed only by its waves, which give some of the best surfing in Europe.

Bayonne

BAYONNE stands back some 6km from the Atlantic, a position that's protected it from any real exploitation by tourism. This is fortunate, for with its half-timbered houses, their shutters and woodwork painted in the peculiarly Basque tones of green and red, it is one of the most distinctive and enjoyable towns in France. Most travellers treat it merely as a transit point between resorts, but if you want to spend time by the sea this is as good a base as any; and it's good for a while in its own right, too.

The town is situated at the junction of the Nive and Adour rivers, with the centre grouped closely around the banks of the Nive. Close to the confluence of the two rivers, **place de la Liberté** is the main town square, full of cafés and *pâtisseries*. The **quays** nearby along the Nive are fun to wander, and on the opposite side of the river – in the area known as "Petit Bayonne" – at the corner of the second bridge, is the excellent **Musée Basque**. Unfortunately, the museum is closed at the time of writing, ostensibly because the floors are unsound, though more likely due to the petty political squabbles which are delaying a decision on its future. The latest word is that it will reopen in the fifteenth-century **Château neuf** a few blocks east, and will display exhibits illustrating Basque life through the centuries, with reconstructed farm buildings and house interiors, implements and tools. The city's second museum, the **Musée Bonnat** on nearby rue Jacques-Lafitte (daily except Tues 10am–noon & 2.30–6.30pm; summer 3–7pm; F15), is an unexpected treasury of art, with works by Rubens, Delacroix and Degas – a refreshing change from the run-of-the-mill stuff of most provincial galleries. Across the Nive, the **Cathédrale St-Marie** looks its best from a distance, its twin towers and steeple rising with airy grace above the houses. Up close, the stone reveals bad weathering, with most of the decorative detail lost, although the interior is more impressive due to the height of the nave and some stained sixteenth-century glass. On the south side is a fourteenth-century cloister with a lawn, cypress trees and begonias.

The **train station** is in the shabby quarter of **St-Esprit** on the opposite bank of the Adour, connected to the city centre by the long Pont St-Esprit. For Biarritz and the **beaches,** you can hop on a bus by the Hôtel de Ville on place Liberté, inside which is the **tourist office** (summer Mon–Sat 9am–noon & 2–7pm; winter Mon–Fri 9am–noon & 2–7pm, Sat 9am–noon). The best cheap **accommodation** is at *Hôtel des Arceaux*, 26 rue Pont-Neuf (☎59.59.15.53; ②); if that's full, try *Paris-Madrid*, by the station (☎59.55.13.98; ②), or *Hôtel des Basques*, place Paul Bert, beside St-André (☎59.59.08.02; ②). The closest and nicest **campsite** is the well-equipped *La Chêneraie*, in the St-Frédéric quarter on the north bank of the Adour, while the nearest **youth hostel** (☎59.63.86.49; ②) is at Anglet, between Bayonne and Biarritz; to get there take bus #2 or #6 from the Hôtel de Ville. The best area for **cafés and restaurants** is Petit Bayonne – try the tapas-style menu of the friendly *Xan Xan Gorri* at 9 rue des Cordeliers, or the *Bar des Amis*, 13 rue des Cordeliers, which does good cheap menus.

Biarritz

The Empress Eugénie, wife of Napoléon III, spent her childhood summers in **BIAR-RITZ** and in 1854 persuaded her husband to accompany her here, which launched the place as a resort for Europe's aristocracy. The vast, barracks-like *Hôtel du Palais* above the Grande Plage was originally their holiday home. Queen Victoria visited once, and Edward VII and the Duke of Windsor were regulars. Nowadays it is an uptight place, and its pompous, ponderous architecture gives it an unfriendly air. West of the **Grande Plage,** which is overlooked by two massive casinos, is a series of sea-girt rocks and promontories, and, beyond, the sheltered **Plage du Port-Vieux,** then the immense **Plage de la Côte des Basques** backed by grey-white cliffs. On the Plateau de l'Atalaye above the rocky promontory of the Rocher de la Vierge is a **Musée de la Mer** (daily July & Aug 9am–7pm; Sept–June 9am–noon & 2–7pm; F25), hardly a must, but with interesting exhibits to do with the fishing industry and the region's birds, and an aquarium of North Atlantic fish. A couple of good **places to stay** are *Hôtel Palym*, 7 rue du Port-Vieux (☎59.24.16.56; ④), or its neighbour the *Atlantic* (☎59.24.34.08; ②), although really you'd be better off staying in Bayonne.

St-Jean-de-Luz

ST-JEAN-DE-LUZ is by far the most attractive resort on the Basque coast. Although it gets crowded and its main seafront is undistinguished, it has a long curving beach of beautiful fine sand. It is also a thriving fishing port, the most important in France for catches of tuna and anchovy, and the old houses around the harbour, both in St-Jean and across the water in Ciboure (effectively the same town) are very picturesque.

The focus of life for visitors is **place Louis XIV** near the harbour, with its cafés, bandstand and plane trees. The seventeenth-century **house** (June–Sept daily 10.30am–noon & 3–6pm; F15) on the harbour side of the square was built by a shipowner called Lohobiague in 1635 and still belongs to the same family. It is also where Louis XIV stayed at the time of his marriage to Maria Theresa, Infanta of Castile, which took place in the town – an extravagant event at which Cardinal Mazarin alone presented the queen with 12,000 pounds of pearls and diamonds, a gold dinner service and a pair of sumptuous carriages drawn by teams of six horses. Maria Theresa lodged just along the quay in an Italianate mansion of faded pink brick. A short distance up rue Gambetta, on the town side of the square, is the church of **St-Jean-Baptiste,** the largest of the Basque churches, where Louis and Maria Theresa were married, and the door through which they left the church, on the right of the main entrance, has been walled up ever since. It is a plain, fortress-like building from the outside; inside, the barn-like nave is roofed in wood and lined on three sides with tiers of dark oak galleries, a distinctive feature of Basque churches – they were reserved for the men, while the women sat in the nave. The ex-voto model of a paddle steamer hanging from the ceiling is the Empress Eugénie's *Eagle*, which narrowly escaped wrecking near St-Jean in 1867.

The **tourist office** is in place du Maréchal-Foch (Mon–Sat 9am–12.30pm & 2–7.30pm). There are several **hotels** near the station: try *Toki-Ona*, 10 rue Marion Garay (☎59.26.11.54; ②), and *Hôtel de Verdun*, 13 av de Verdun (☎59.26.02.55; ③). There are lots of **campsites** in the vicinity, most of them grouped together a few kilometres northeast of the town; try the *Chibaou-Berria*, one of the nearest, left off the N10.

Pau and the mountains

Capital of the viscounty of Béarn, **PAU** has had a more than usually turbulent history. Like the Basque and other Pyrenean provinces which came into existence as counties and viscounties in feudal times, it held on to its separatist leanings well into the seventeenth century; even today many of the Béarnais still speak Occitan rather than French. It's a university town, good-looking, lively and, partly thanks to tourism, with a fairly buoyant prosperity. It occupies a grand natural site on a steep scarp overlooking the Gave de Pau, and from its **boulevard des Pyrénées**, the promenade which runs along the rim of the scarp, there are superb views of the higher peaks. Not surprisingly, it has become the most popular starting point for the Parc National des Pyrénées, and it's well-equipped for the purpose. As for its own sights, Pau's **Château** (daily mid-April to mid-Oct 9.30–11.45am & 2–5.45pm; mid-Oct to mid-April until 4.45pm; F25), at the west end of bd des Pyrénées, was done up by Louis-Philippe in the nineteenth century after standing empty for 200 years, and then tinkered with by Napoléon III and Eugénie – it was another of their country places. Not much remains of its original appearance except the keep, but two museums are housed there. The **Musée National** consists mainly of Napoléon III and Eugénie's weekend apartments and Henri IV memorabilia, while the **Musée Béarnais** (F6), on the top floor, has a very good collection of costumes, Pyrenean animals, birds and butterflies, and objects illustrative of the pastoral life.

From the **train station** down by the river, a free funicular shuttles you up to bd des Pyrénées. The **bus station** (for non-*SNCF* buses) is near the youth hostel on rue Michel-Houneau. The **tourist office** is at the end of place Royale (July & Aug daily 9am–6.30pm; Sept–June Mon–Sat 9am–noon & 2–6pm, Sun 10am–1pm & 2–5pm). There is a **youth hostel** at 30 rue Michel-Houneau (☎59.30.45.77; ②), and **student housing** in the Cité Universitaire at 3 av de Saragosse (☎59.02.88.46; ②) – take bus #4. For **hotels**, try the quiet and hospitable *Hôtel d'Albret*, 11 rue Jeanne d'Albret (☎59.27.81.58; ②), or the equally central *Pomme d'Or*, 11 rue Maréchal-Foch (☎59.27.78.48; ②). There are two **campsites**, a municipal site on bd du Cami-Salie, off av Sallenavem on the northern edge of town, and *Camping Le Coy* behind the station in the suburb of Bizanos. **Restaurants** are numerous, too, especially towards the château. *La Brochetterie*, 16 rue Henri-IV, has reasonably priced menus and a pleasant family atmosphere; *Le Berry* on place Clemenceau and *Le Forum* in av de la Université are a couple of brasseries popular with local students.

Into the mountains

Pau is probably the best large base for launching into the highest parts of the Pyrenees, as the **Parc National des Pyrénées Occidentales** lies to the south of the town. It is possible to hitch to the spectacular main passes of **Col d'Aubisque** and **Col du Tourmalet**, though you will find you invariably get left on the top by drivers coming up for the view and going back the same way. The **tourist office** supplies walking information and a useful pamphlet, *Randonnées Pyrénéennes*. More specialist knowledge can be gleaned from the *Club Alpin Français* on rue René Fournets (☎59.27.71.81). Various organizations run guided hikes: among them *Randonneurs Pyrénéens*, 9 rue Latapie, and *Les Amis du PNP Occidentales*, 24 rue Samonzet.

Lourdes

LOURDES, about 30km southeast of Pau, has just one function. Over six million Catholic pilgrims arrive here each year, and the town is totally given over to looking after and exploiting them. Lourdes was hardly more than a village before 1858, when Bernadette Soubirous, the fourteen-year-old daughter of an ex-miller, had the first of eighteen visions of the Virgin Mary in a spot called the Grotte de Massabielle, by the Gave de Pau. Since then Lourdes has grown a great deal, and it is now one of the biggest attractions in this part of France, many of its visitors hoping for a miraculous cure for scientifically intractable ailments.

Practically every shop is given over to the sale of religious kitsch – Bernadette in every shape and size adorning barometers, key rings, bottles, candles, plastic grottoes illuminated by coloured lights. The architecture of the **Cité Réligieuse**, by the river, which has grown up around the Gave de Pau, is scarcely any better. The **grotto** is a moisture-blackened overhang by the riverside with a statue of the Virgin in waxwork white and baby blue. Suspended in front are a row of rusting crutches, ex votos offered by the hopeful. Up above is the first church built here, dating from 1871, and below this a massive subterranean **basilica**, reputedly able to house 20,000 people at one time.

Lourdes' only secular attraction is its **Château**, poised on a rocky bluff guarding the approaches to the valleys and passes of the central Pyrénées. Briefly an English stronghold in the late fourteenth century, it later became a prison. These days, it is home to an excellent **Musée Pyrénéen** (daily 9am–noon & 2–6pm; mid-Oct to end-March closed Tues; F26), whose collections include local fauna and all sorts of fascinating pastoral and farming gear. In the rock garden outside are models of various Pyrenean house styles, as well as of the churches of St-Bertrand-de-Comminges and Luz. There is also a section on the history of Pyrenean mountaineering.

The **train station** is on the northeastern edge of town. The **tourist office** is ten minutes' walk away on place du Champ-Commun (Easter–Oct Mon–Sat 9am–noon & 2–7pm, Sun 10am–noon; Nov–Easter Mon–Sat 9am–noon & 2–6pm); turn right outside the station and then left down Chaussée Maransin: they help with **accommodation**, although Lourdes is not an ideal place to stay. There's a sprinkling of cheap hotels around the station, and more en route to the Grotte and around the castle. **Hostel** accommodation can be had at the *Centre Pax Christi* on route de la Forêt (☎62.94.00.66; ②) if you've booked ahead, and the *Camp des Jeunes*, Ferme Milhas, rue Monseigneur-Rodhain (☎62.94.03.95; ②), which has ultra-cheap dorm beds. Both places are on the western edge of town, ten minutes' walk from the centre. The nearest **campsite** is on rue de Langelle, east off the Chausée Maransin. If everything is full, consider staying in **TARBES**, twenty minutes from Lourdes by train. There's a **youth hostel** at 88 av Alsace-Lorraine (☎62.36.63.63; ②), and cheap **hotels** around the train station.

LANGUEDOC AND ROUSSILLON

Languedoc is more an idea than a geographical entity. The modern region covers only a fraction of the lands where once *Occitan* or the *langue d'oc* was spoken, which stretched south from Bordeaux and Lyon into Spain and northwest Italy. Although things are changing, the sense of being Occitanian remains strong, a regional identity that dates back to the Middle Ages, when its castles and fortified villages were the final refuges of the Cathars, a heretical religious sect.

The old Roman town of **Nîmes** is an entry point; beyond, **Montpellier** and **Sète** are good bases, though otherwise the coast is not generally noteworthy, the beaches bleak strands for the most part, windswept and cut off from their hinterland by marshy lakes. There is the bonus of relatively unpolluted and uncrowded water, but even this is under threat from development. **Narbonne** and **Béziers** are enjoyable urban diversions, as is **Toulouse**, the cultural capital, though it lies some way west. South of Languedoc, **Roussillon** maintains much of its Catalan identity, though by contrast with the Basques there is little support nowadays for political independence or reunification with Spanish Catalonia, of which it was a part until the seventeenth century. Its countryside is its best feature, its hills and valleys providing some fine walking. The coast is again something of a disappointment however, as is the region's main town, **Perpignan** – although both it and the nearby beaches and mountains are worth a brief stopover before racing on down to Spain.

Nîmes and around

NÎMES is inescapably linked to two things – denim and Rome. The latter's influence is manifest in some of the most extensive Roman remains in Europe, while the former (denim – *de Nîmes*), equally visible on the backsides of the populace, was first manufactured in the city's textile mills and exported to the southern USA in the nineteenth century to clothe the slaves.

The central part of Nîmes spreads northwest from **place de la Libération**, a few minutes from the station. The tall, narrow streets of the old town are dead ahead, while across to your left is the biggest and most spectacular edifice of all, the first-century **Arena** (daily summer 9am–7pm; winter 9am–noon & 2.30pm; F20), one of the best-preserved Roman arenas in the world, with an arcaded two-storey facade concealing massive interior vaulting that supports tiers giving a capacity of more than 20,000. When Rome's sway was broken by the barbarian invasions, the arena became a fortress and eventually a slum, home to some 2000 people when it was cleared in the early 1800s. Today it has recovered something of its former role, and is a venue for bullfighting on summer Sundays, and hosts opera and an international jazz festival. A short walk away, the **Maison Carrée** (daily mid-June to mid-Sept 9am–7pm; mid-Sept to mid-June 9am–noon & 2–5.30pm; free) is a compact little temple, built in 5 AD and celebrated for its harmony of proportion. It stands in its own small square opposite rue Auguste, where the Roman forum used to be. Around it are scattered pieces of Roman masonry, while inside are three enormous canvases donated by Julian Schnabel. The north side of place de la Maison Carrée is dominated by a brand new arts centre, *Le Carré d'Art*, designed by Norman Foster to house the *Musée d'Art Contemporain* (Tues–Sun 10am–8/10pm) and to become the Pompidou Centre of southern France.

Though already a prosperous city on the Via Domitia – the main road from Italy to Spain – Nîmes did especially well out of Augustus. He gave it its walls – remnants of which surface here and there – and its gates, as recorded in the inscription on the **Porte d'Auguste**, at the end of rue Nationale, the Roman main street. If you still have an appetite for things Roman, head for the eighteenth-century **Jardin de la Fontaine**, on the northwest edge of the centre, encircled by canals built to supplement the rather unsteady spring that gave birth to Nîmes. Fountains and nymphs and formal trees enclose the so-called **Temple of Diana** (summer daily 9am–6/7pm; free), while behind, steps climb the slope to the **Tour Magne** (9am–5.30/7pm; F10), with a terrific view over the surrounding country.

Back in the centre of town, the **Cathedral** on place aux Herbes was mutilated in the Wars of Religion and significantly altered in the last century. Alphonse Daudet was born in its shadow, as was Jean Nicot, the doctor who introduced tobacco into France from Portugal in 1560, and gave his name to nicotine. Opposite the cathedral, in the Bishop's Palace, the **Musée du Vieux Nîmes** (daily summer 9am–7pm; winter 9am–noon & 2–5pm; free) has interesting displays of Renaissance furnishings and decor, while, backing onto Grande Rue in a seventeenth-century Jesuit chapel, the **Musée Archéologique** (same hours and price) gives further background on Roman Nîmes.

Further out, across rue de la Libération, the **Musée des Beaux-Arts** on rue Cité-Foulc (same hours and price) prides itself on a huge Gallo-Roman mosaic showing the *Marriage of Admetus*.

Practicalities

The **train station** is at the end of av Feuchères, a few minutes from Esplanade de Gaulle, on the edge of the old centre; the **bus station** is opposite. The tourist office is on rue Auguste in the centre (Mon–Fri 8am–7pm, Sat 9am–noon & 2–5pm, Sun 10am–5pm), and has lots of information on what's on around town. There's a cluster of reasonable **hotels** around square de la Couronne at the beginning of bd Courbet – try *La Couronne* at no. 4 (☎66.67.51.73; ②) or the *Majestic* on rue Pradier, just off av Feuchères (☎66.29.24.14; ③). If you want to stay in the heart of things, there's *Hôtel de la Maison Carrée*, 14 rue de la Maison Carrée (☎66.67.32.89; ②). There's a **youth hostel** on chemin de la Cigale (☎66.23.25.04; ②), reached on buses #6 or #20 from the station, which also has tent space; otherwise, the main **campsite** is the *Domaine de la Bastide* on route de Générac, 4km or so from the station (bus #4 from the station). For **food**, bd de la Libération and Amiral-Courbet harbour a stock of reasonably priced brasseries and pizzerias, and the **café** scene is very lively along here. The *Tarterie Delices* on place des Herbes, by the cathedral, serves simple, affordable food, or, for something more special, there's *Ophélie* at 35 rue Fresque.

The Pont du Gard and Uzès

Several buses a day head east from Nîmes' bus station to Uzès via the **Pont du Gard**, the greatest surviving stretch of the Roman water supply system to the city, and a supreme piece of engineering. Three tiers of arches span the river, with the covered water conduit on the top waterproofed with a paint based on fig juice. You can walk across, if the height does not bother you. The whole structure narrows as it rises and is slightly bowed on the upstream side for extra resistance to flooding. A visit was a must for French journeymen masons, and many of them have left their names and home towns carved on the stone. You can also see markings of the "this-side-up" variety left on individual stones by the original builders.

UZÈS is another 17km on, an attractive old town perched on a hill above the river Alzon, a bit of a backwater until renovation put its half-dozen medieval towers and narrow lanes of Renaissance and classical houses on the tourist circuit. From **Le Portalet**, with its view out over the valley, walk past the classical church of St-Étienne into the medieval **place aux Herbes**, where there's a Sunday morning market, and up the arcaded **rue de la République**. The Gide family used to live off the square, the young André spending summer vacations with his granny there. To the right of rue de la République, the castle of **Le Duché** (daily summer 9.30am–noon & 2.30–6.30pm; winter daily except Mon 9.30am–noon & 2.30–5pm; F40), still inhabited by the same family a thousand years on, is dominated by its original keep, the Tour Bermonde. The tourist office is in av de la Libération, next to the bus station.

Montpellier

A thousand years of trade and intellect have made **MONTPELLIER** a teeming, energetic city. Benjamin of Tudela, the tireless twelfth-century Jewish traveller, reported its streets crowded with traders – Arabs from the Maghreb, merchants from Lombardy, from the kingdom of Rome, from every corner of Egypt and Greece. A few hiccups have done little more than dent this progress, and the reputation of its university, founded in the thirteenth century, has shone untarnished.

At the town's hub is **place de la Comédie** – *L'Oeuf* to the initiated – a colossal oval square, paved with cream-coloured marble and surrounded by cafés. At one end bulks the **Opéra**, an enormous, ornate nineteenth-century theatre; the other opens on to the tree-lined promenade of **Esplanade**, and, to the right, the typically French think-big urban development of the **Polygone** shopping complex. On the Esplanade, Montpellier's most trumpeted museum, the **Musée Fabre** (Tues–Sun 9am–5.30pm; F15, free Wed), has a vast collection of seventeenth- to nineteenth-century European painting, although most of it, with the exception of some Delacroix, Courbet, Impressionists and a few moderns, is of academic interest only. Behind the Opéra lie the tangled, hilly lanes of Montpellier's **oldest quarter**, full of seventeenth- and eighteenth-century mansions, a curious mix of chic restoration and squalid disorder. One of the fanciest eighteenth-century *hôtels*, the **Hôtel St-Côme**, was built as a demonstration operating theatre for medical students. On the opposite corner, rue de l'Argenterie forks up to **place Jean-Jaurès**, with its morning **market** and cafés, a short walk from two local history museums on place Petrarque: the **Musée du Vieux Montpellier** (Mon–Sat 1.30–5pm; free), concentrating on the city's history, and the more interesting **Musée du Fougau** (Wed & Thurs 3–6.30pm; free), dealing with the folk history of Languedoc. On the western edge of the centre, at the end of rue Foch, are the formal gardens of the **Promenade du Peyrou** and a vainglorious **triumphal arch** showing Louis XIV-Hercules stomping on the Austrian eagle and the English lion. The **Jardin des Plantes**, just north of here, with its alleys of exotic trees, is France's oldest botanical garden (Mon–Sat 9am–noon & 2–6pm). Opposite, on the other side of bd Henri-IV, the university medical school houses the **Musée Atger** (Mon–Fri 1.30–4.30pm; closed during school holidays; free), with an academic collection of French and Italian drawings, and the macabre **Musée Anatomique** (Mon–Fri 2.15–5pm; free).

Practicalities

The **train station** is on the southeastern edge of the centre, a short walk down rue Maguelone. The main tourist office is in the passage du Tourisme, at the top end of place de la Comédie (daily July & Aug 9am–7pm; Sept–June Mon–Fri 9am–6pm, Sat 10am–1pm & 2–6pm); there's also a desk in the station. There are numerous **hotels** between the station and place de la Comédie. The *Majestic*, 4 rue du Cheval-Blanc (☎67.66.26.85; ②), and the *Central*, rue Boussairolles/Bruyas (☎67.58.39.28; ②), are both clean and inexpensive, or there's the *Mistral*, 25 rue Boussairolles (☎67.58.45.25; ③), and its neighbour the *Imperator*, 20 rue Brussairolles (☎67.58.40.97; ③), which are a little more salubrious. The grubby and overcrowded **youth hostel** is at 2 impasse de la Petite-Corraterie (☎67.60.32.22; ②) – bus #5 from the station. There's a **camping municipal** 2km east of town on route de Mauguio (bus #15). The best general area for places to **eat** is around rue des Écoles–Laiques, and rue de l'Université. Try *Pizzeria Provençale*, 7 rue de l'École-de-Pharmacie, *Chez Marceau* or *Le Vieil Ecu* in the delightful place de la Chapelle-Neuve, or *Petit Landais*, 14 rue du Palais.

Sète and Agde

About 20km further down the coast, perched around the steep slopes of the Mont St-Clair on the edge of the Bassin de Thau, **SÈTE** has been an important port for three hundred years. Intersected by waterways lined with tall terraces and seafood restaurants, it's a lively place, and hard to beat as a base for exploring this part of the coast.

Climb up from the *vieux port* to the **Cimitière marin**, where the poet Paul Valéry is buried. A native of the town, he called Sète his "singular island", and the **Musée Valéry** above the cemetery has a room devoted to him, as well as a small but strong collection of modern French paintings. The singer-songwriter Georges Brassens has a room to himself too; the radical voice of a whole generation in France, Brassens was born and raised in Sète and is buried in the **Cimitière le Py** on the other side of the hill. If you're feeling energetic, you should keep going up the hill through the pines to the top for the view. Below the sailors' cemetery, couched neatly above the water, is Vauban's **Fort St-Pierre**, which hosts a festival of open-air theatre in August and a film festival in June. That's about it as far as sights go, though if you can it's worth being here for the **joutes nautiques** – water jousting contests held throughout the summer on the canal.

The **bus station** is awkwardly placed on quai de la République, and the **train station** further out still on quai Midi-Nord – though it is on the main bus route which circles Mont St-Clair. The tourist office main office is 60 Grand'rue Mario Roustan, and there's a summer desk at the station. The **youth hostel** (☎67.53.46.68; ②) is high up in the town on rue Général-Revest. Otherwise, try *Le Family*, 28 quai de Tassigny (☎67.74.05.03; ②), or the swankier *L'Orque Bleue*, 10 quai Aspirant-Herber (☎67.74.72.13; ④). Two **campsites** are *Les Régales* and *Le Pont-Levis*, both on the circular bus route and conveniently near a beach.

Agde and Cap d'Agde

At the other end of the Bassin de Thau, **AGDE** is, historically at least, the most interesting of the coastal towns. Originally Greek, and maintained by the Romans, it thrived for centuries but, outrun as a seaport by Sète, later degenerated into a sleazy fishing harbour. Yet today it's a major tourist centre. The heavily battlemented **cathedral** merits a brief stop; like the rest of the town it is built of the distinctive dark stone quarried from the nearby extinct volcano, Mont St-Loup. **Places to eat** are numerous, but, as with accommodation, prices in relation to quality tend to be high. If you're **camping**, there are around 25 sites in the vicinity, all lavishly equipped and usually packed.

CAP D'AGDE, reachable by bus from Agde, lies to the south of Mont St-Loup, the largest and most successful of the new resorts around here, sprawling in an excess of pseudo-traditional modern buildings that offer every type of facility and entertainment – all expensive. It is perhaps best known for its colossal **quartier naturiste**, one of the largest in France, with space for 20,000 visitors and its own (nude) restaurants, banks, post offices and shops. Access is possible, though pricy, if you're not actually staying there. But if you want to get inside for free, you can simply walk along the beach from neighbouring Marseillan-Plage, and remove fabrics en route. If you have time to fill, the **Musée de la Clape** (Tues–Sun 9am–noon & 2–7pm; free) displays local antiquities, many of them dredged from the sea, not least a beautiful little Hellenistic bronze known as the *Ephèbe d'Agde* – until recently one of the treasures of the Louvre.

Béziers

Though no longer the rich city of its nineteenth-century heyday, **BÉZIERS** is the capital of the Languedoc wine country and a focus for the Occitan movement. The fortunes of the movement and the vine have long been closely linked, for Occitan activists have helped to organize the militant local vine-growers. There were ugly events during the mid-Seventies, when blood was shed in violent confrontations with the authorities over the importation of cheap foreign wines and the low prices paid for the essentially poor-grade local product. Things are calmer now, as the conservatism of Languedoc farmers has given way to public demands for something better than the traditional table wine.

The first view of the old town as you come in from the west is spectacular. From the Pont-Neuf across the River Orb, you look upstream at the sturdy golden arches of the **Pont-Vieux**, with the **Cathedral** crowning the steep-banked hill behind, more like a castle than a church. The building is mainly Gothic, in the northern style, the original having been burnt in 1209, when most of the population was massacred for refusing to hand over about twenty Cathars. From the top of the cathedral's tower, there's a superb view out across the vine-dominated surrounding landscape, and next door an ancient **cloister** gives access to a terraced garden above the river. The narrow medieval streets make a pleasant stroll, with their mixture of sunny southern elegance and dilapidation. In rue Massol, the **Musée du Vieux-Biterrois** (Tues–Sat 9am–noon & 2–6pm, Sun 2–6pm; free) displays a variety of entertaining exhibits, ranging from Greek amphorae to nineteenth-century door-knockers and wine-presses. Centre of Béziers' life is the lively **allée Paul-Riquet**, a broad, leafy esplanade lined with cafés and restaurants. Laid out in the last century, the *allée* runs from an elaborate theatre in the north to the gorgeous little park of the **Plateau des Poètes**, designed by the creator of Paris's Bois de Boulogne.

Arriving at the **train station**, the best way into town is through the Plateau des Poètes. The tourist office is at 27 rue du 4-Septembre (July & Aug Mon–Sat 9am–7pm, Sun 10am–noon; Sept–June Mon–Sat 9am–noon & 2–6.30pm). For **hotels**, try the attractive *Hôtel des Poètes*, 80 allées Paul-Riquet (☎67.76.38.66; ②), or, if this is too expensive, either the *Champs de Mars*, 17 rue de Metz (☎67.28.35.53; ②), or the *Alma-Unic*, 41 rue Guilhemon (☎67.28.44.31; ②). **Eating**, there are several places on allées Paul-Riquet, or try the agreeable *Table d'Hôte* in place Pépézuc.

Narbonne

Capital of Rome's first colony in Gaul, **NARBONNE** was a thriving port and communications centre in classical times and again in the Middle Ages. Plague, war and the silting-up of its harbour finished it off in the fourteenth century. Today, despite the ominous presence of a nuclear power plant just 5km out of town, it's a pleasant provincial city of tree-lined walks and esplanades converging on graceful squares.

The only surviving legacy of Rome is the **horreum**, an underground storage area, at the north end of rue Rouget-de-Lisle (May–Sept daily 9.30am–12.15pm & 2–6pm; Oct–April Tues–Sun 10am–noon & 2–5pm; F10 ticket gives access to all the city's sites), an unusual site consisting of two thoroughfares lined with small shops, well preserved though now entirely underground. At the opposite end of the same street is Narbonne's other principal attraction, the enormous Gothic **Cathédrale de St-Just et St-Sauveur**, dominating the restored lanes of the old town. Despite its size, it is actually only the choir of a much more ambitious church, whose construction was halted to avoid weakening the city walls. The interior has good stained glass and imposing Aubusson tapestries. The high north tower is open for a panoramic view of the surrounding vineyards. From the place de l'Hôtel-de-Ville next door, the passage de l'Ancre leads through to the **Archbishop's Palace**, housing a tedious **museum of art** (same times) and a good **archeology museum** (same times), with interesting Roman remains, including some fine frescoes and mosaics.

The **train station** is north of the centre on av Pierre-Sémard. The tourist office has a summer annexe by the canal along Cours de la République, and a more central office next to the cathedral on place Salengro (Mon–Sat 8.30am–noon & 2–6pm, Sun 9.30am–12.30pm). Most of the cheaper **hotels** are around the station; the *Hôtel de la Gare*, 7 av Sémard (☎68.32.10.54; ②), is clean and reasonable. Alternatively, try the *Lion d'Or*, 39 av Pierre Sémard (☎68.32.06.92; ④), which has a good cheap **restaurant**.

Carcassonne

CARCASSONNE couldn't be easier to reach, sited on the main Toulouse–Montpellier train link, and for anyone travelling through this region it is a must – one of the most dramatic (if also most visited) towns in the whole of Languedoc. It owes its division into two separate "towns", the Cité and Ville Basse, to the Cathar wars of the Middle Ages. Following Simon de Montfort's capture of the town in 1209, its people tried to restore their traditional ruling family, the Trencavels, in 1240. In reprisal King Louis IX expelled them, only permitting their return on condition they built on the low ground by the River Aude.

The Ville Basse is enticing, but the main attraction is without question the **Cité**, a double-walled and turreted fortress-town crowning the hill above the Aude. Viollet-le-Duc rescued it from ruin in 1844, and his "too-perfect" restoration has been furiously debated ever since. It is, as you would expect, a real tourist trap. Yet, in spite of the chintzy cafés, arty-crafty shops and the crowds, you have to be a very stiff-necked purist not to like it at all. There is no charge for admission to the main part of the city, or the grassy *lices* (moat) between the walls. However, to see the inner fortress of the **Château Comtal**, and to walk along the walls, you have to join a guided tour (mid-May to mid-Sept 9.30am–7pm; F26); the guides point out the various phases in the construction of the fortifications, from Roman to Visigoth to Romanesque to the post-Cathar adaptations of the French kings. In addition to wandering the narrow streets, don't miss the beautiful church of **St-Nazaire** at the end of rue St-Louis, a serene combination of Romanesque nave with carved capitals and Gothic transepts and choir adorned with some of the loveliest stained glass.

The **tourist office** in the Cité is in the Porte Narbonnaise on the east side (daily July & Aug 9am–7pm; April–June, Sept & Oct 9am–12.30pm & 1.30–6pm). **Accommodation**, as you would expect, is pricy, apart from the **youth hostel** on rue du Vicomte Trencavel (☎68.25.23.16; ②), and you're better off sleeping in the Ville Basse. The tourist office here is at 15 bd Camille-Pelletan (July & Aug Mon–Sat 9am–7pm, Sun 10am–noon; April–June, Sept & Oct Mon–Sat 9am–noon & 2–7pm; Nov–March Mon–Sat 9am–noon & 2–6pm), with an annexe at the **train station**. Close to the station is the best of the cheap **hotels**, *Bonnafoux*, 40 rue de la Liberté (☎68.25.01.45; ②). The *St-Joseph*, in the same street at no. 81 (☎68.25.10.94; ②) and the *de la Poste*, 21 rue de Verdun (☎68.25.12.18; ②), are reasonable alternatives. The nearest **campsite** is *Camping de la Cité* on route de St-Hilaire below the Cité. The only affordable **restaurant** in the Cité is the excellent and cheap *L'Ostal des Troubadours* at 5 rue Viollet-le-Duc, which has menus from around F50.

Toulouse

TOULOUSE, with its beautiful historic centre, is one of the most vibrant provincial cities in France, a result of a deliberate policy to make it the centre of hi-tech industry. Always an aviation centre – St-Exupéry and Mermoz flew out from here on their pioneering flights over Africa in the 1920s – Toulouse is now home to *Aérospatiale*, the driving force behind Concorde and Airbus. Added zest comes from its 80,000 students, who make it second only to Paris as a university centre.

The City

The centre of the city is a rough hexagon clamped around a bend in the wide, brown Garonne. On the corner of rue de Metz, the **Musée des Augustins** (daily except Tues 10am–5pm; summer 10am–6pm; F20) incorporates the two cloisters of an Augustinian priory and houses collections of outstanding Romanesque and Gothic sculpture, much of it saved from the now-vanished churches of Toulouse's golden age. Outside the museum, the main shopping street, **rue Alsace-Lorraine**, runs north. West of here are the labyrinthine streets of the **old city**, lined with the ornate and arrogant *hôtels* of the merchants who grew rich on the woad trade, basis of the city's economy until the sixteenth century. The almost exclusive building material is the flat Toulousain brick, whose cheerful rosy colour gives the city its nickname of *ville rose*, and lends a small-scale, detailed finish to otherwise plain facades. Best known of these palaces is the **Hôtel Assézat**, towards the river end of rue de Metz, a vast brick extravaganza with classical columns; and there are others in the streets immediately around.

The **Hôtel du May** on rue du May houses the unexciting **Musée du Vieux-Toulouse** (June–Sept Mon–Sat 3–6pm; May & Oct Thurs only 3–6pm; F10), while a little way north, **place du Capitole** is the site of the huge classical town hall and today a great meeting place, with numerous cafés and a weekday market. North, rue du Taur leads to **place St-Sernin** and the largest Romanesque church in France, the **basilica de St-Sernin**. Begun in 1080 to accommodate the passing hordes of pilgrims, it is one of the loveliest examples of its genre, with an octagonal brick belfry with rounded and pointed arches, diamond lozenges, colonnettes and mouldings picked out in stone, and an apse of nine chapels. Inside, to get into the ambulatory you have to pay a small charge, but it's worth it for the exceptional eleventh-century marble reliefs on the end wall of the choir. Right outside is the town's archeological museum, **Musée St-Raymond** (daily winter 10am–5pm; summer 10am–6pm; F10), and on Sunday mornings an impressively shambolic flea market. West of place du Capitole, on rue Lakanal, the church of **Les Jacobins** is another ecclesiastical building you cannot miss, started in 1230 by the Dominicans who had set up here in the wake of their founding father, Saint Dominic. It's a huge fortress-like rectangle of unadorned brick, but, inside, its single space is divided by a central row of ultra-slim pillars from whose capitals spring an elegant splay of vaulting ribs. Beneath the altar lie the bones of the philosopher Saint Thomas Aquinas, while on the north side is a calming cloister.

Practicalities

By train, you arrive at the **gare Matabiau**, fifteen minutes' walk from the centre down allées Jean-Jaurés. There's an tourist office annexe here in summer, and another office in the centre of town off place du Capitole (May–Sept daily 9am–7pm; Oct–April Mon–Sat 9am–6pm). Best of the city's cheap hotels are the centrally placed *Hôtel du Grand-Balcon*, 8 rue Romiguières (☎61.21.48.08; ②), the *Hôtel des Arts*, on the corner of rue des Arts and rue Cantegril (☎61.23.36.21; ②), and the *Hôtel Anatole France*, 46 place A-France (☎61.23.19.96; ②). There's a poky but friendly **youth hostel** (☎61.80.49.93; ②) at 125 av Jean Rieux; take bus #14 from the station to place Dupuy and from there a #22. The closest **campsite** is the *Pont de Rupé*, just north of the city – bus #P from the station. When the time comes to **eat**, there are numerous places on bd de Strasbourg near place Wilson, and several popular places open for lunch only on place Victor-Hugo. In the evening, try around place Arnaud-Bernard, in the rapidly gentrifying former Arab quarter on the north edge of the centre, where *Chez Manolo*, 24 rue Trois Piliers, is a good Spanish place, with live music, and *Le Ragtime*, 14 place Amand-Bernaud, a lively jazz, salsa and blues bar. More centrally, the chic brasserie *Les Beaux-Arts*, opposite the end of the Pont Neuf, is good and reasonable, as is the nearby *La Tartina de Burgos*, 27 av de la Garonnette, with good tapas. Alternatively, there are pizzerias and brasseries aplenty on place St-Georges, behind the Musée des Augustins.

Albi

Though not itself an important centre of Catharism, **ALBI** gave its name to both the heresy and the crusade to suppress it. Today it is a small industrial town an hour's train ride northeast of Toulouse, with two unique sights. The first, the **Cathedral**, is visible the moment you arrive at the train station, dwarfing the town. It's not a conventionally beautiful building, but the sheer plainness of the exterior is impressive on this scale. Entrance is through the south portal, by contrast an extravagant piece of sixteenth-century frippery. The interior, a hall-like nave of colossal proportions, is covered in richly colourful paintings of Italian workmanship. A rood screen, delicate as lace, shuts off the choir. Opposite the east end of the cathedral, rue Mariès leads into the shopping streets of the **old town**, but the most interesting sight is next door in the powerful red-brick Palais de la Berbie, which houses Albi's other main attraction, the **Musée Toulouse-Lautrec** (April–Sept daily 10am–noon & 2–6pm; Oct–March Wed–Mon 10am–noon & 2–5pm; F20), with paintings, drawings, lithographs and posters by the artist (who was a native of the town). There is a huge range of exhibits, from the earliest work to the very last, and it's an absolute must for anyone interested in *Belle Époque* seediness and the rather offbeat style of its subject. The artist's **house** on rue Toulouse-Lautrec is also open to the public (July & Aug 9am–noon & 3–7pm).

The **tourist office** is by the cathedral (Sept–June Mon–Sat 9am–noon & 2–6pm; July & Aug Mon–Sat 9am–7pm, Sun 10.30am–12.30pm & 4.30–6.30pm). There's a scruffy **Maison des Jeunes** at 13 rue de la République (☎63.54.53.65; ②), with ultracheap dorm beds, and cheap **hotels** include the *Terminus* on place Stalingrad, by the station (☎63.54.00.99; ②), and the *Fouillade*, 12 place Pelloutin (☎63.54.21.86; ②). The closest **campsite** is the *Parc de Caussels*, about 2km east on D999. For **eating**, try the *Casa Créole* or *Auberge Saint-Loup*, both on rue Castelviel at the west end of the cathedral; the vegetarian *Le Tournesol*, in rue de l'Ort-en-Salvy, is also good.

Perpignan

PERPIGNAN is capital of French Catalonia and the only big city of the region. It's not, however, the most fascinating of places – its heyday was really during the thirteenth and fourteenth centuries, when the kings of Majorca held their court here. For most of the Middle Ages its allegiance swung back and forth between France and Aragon, until finally it became part of the French state under Louis XIV in 1659.

The centre of Perpignan is marked by the palm trees and smart cafés of **place Arago**. From here rue Alsace-Lorraine and rue de la Loge lead past the massive iron gates of the classical Hôtel de Ville to the tiny **place de la Loge**, the focus of the renovated old core, dominated by the **Loge de Mer**, a late fourteenth-century Gothic building designed to hold the city's stock exchange and a maritime court. North up rue Louis-Blanc is one of the city's few remaining fortifications, the crenellated fourteenth-century gate of **Le Castillet**, now home to the **Casa Pairal**, a fascinating **museum** of Roussillon's Catalan folk culture (daily except Tues 9.30am–11.30am & 2.30–6.30pm; free). The fourteenth-century **Cathédrale St-Jean**, reached from place de la Loge down rue St-Jean and across place Gambetta, is most interesting for its elaborate Catalan altar-pieces, shadowy in the gloom of the ill-lit nave, and for a tortured, wooden crucifix known as the *Dévôt Christ* in a side chapel to the south. Dating from around 1400, it's of Rhenish rather than local origin.

About twenty minutes away, through place des Esplanades, crowning the hill which dominates the southern part of the old town, is the **Palais des Rois de Majorque** (summer daily 10am–6pm; winter daily 9am–5pm; F20). Vauban's walls surround it now, but the two-storey palace and its great arcaded courtyard date from the late thirteenth century. Thanks to the Spanish-Moorish influence, there's a sophistication and finesse about the architecture and detailing – for instance, in the beautiful marble porch to the lower of the two chapels – which you don't often find in the heavier styles of the north.

To get to the centre from the **train station**, follow av Général-de-Gaulle to place de la Catalogne, and then continue along bd Clemenceau as far as Le Castillet; the **tourist office** is a short stroll from here, at the end of bd Wilson (June–Sept Mon–Sat 9am–7pm, Sun 9am–1pm & 3–7pm; Oct–May Mon–Sat 8.30am–noon & 2–6.30pm). For **accommodation**, the best place to look is as usual around the station: try the *Hôtel le Berry*, 6 av Général-de-Gaulle (☎68.34.59.02; ②), which is cheap and friendly. The **youth hostel** (☎68.34.63.32; ②) is about 1km from the station in Parc de la Pépinière, by the river. There are two **campsites**, *La Garrigole* on rue Maurice-Lévy (bus #2) and *Le Catalan* on route de Bompas, both signposted from the centre. The station is also a good area for inexpensive **food** – try the *Perroquet*, immediately opposite, which is excellent value.

THE MASSIF CENTRAL

Thickly forested, and sliced by numerous rivers and lakes, the **Massif Central** is geologically the oldest part of France, and culturally one of the most firmly rooted in the past. Industry and tourism have made few inroads here, and the people remain rural and taciturn, with an enduring sense of regional identity. The heart of the region is the **Auvergne**, a wild, inaccessible landscape dotted with extinct volcanic peaks known as *puys*, much of it now incorporated into the **Parc Naturel Régional des Volcans d'Auvergne**, France's largest regional park. To the southeast are the gentler wooded hills of the **Cévennes**, where Robert Louis Stevenson and his donkey made a famous literary hike. This range, too, is now part of a national park, the **Parc National des Cévennes**. Only a handful of towns have gained a foothold in this rugged terrain. **Le Puy**, spiked with jagged pinnacles of lava and with a majestic cathedral, is the most compelling, but there is appeal, too, in the elegant spa city of **Vichy** and in the provincial capital, **Clermont-Ferrand**.

Clermont-Ferrand

CLERMONT-FERRAND is an incongruous capital for rustic Auvergne, a lively, youthful place, with a major university, and a manufacturing base (it's the HQ of the Michelin organization) that has steadily been depopulating the villages of the province. As a base for this side of the Massif it's ideal, with a wide choice of rooms and some good restaurants and bars. And it is interesting in its own right too, for a well-preserved historic centre and the nearby spectacle of Puy de Dôme and the Parc des Volcans.

Clermont and neighbouring Montferrand were united in 1631 to form a single city, but you're likely to spend most of your time in the former, since what is left of Vieux Montferrand stands out on a limb to the east. Clermont's "ville-noire" aspect – so-called after the local black volcanic rock used in the construction of many of its buildings – is its most immediate feature: dark and solid, it clusters untidily around the summit of a worn-away volcanic peak. On the edge of old Clermont, the huge and soulless **place de Jaude** is by day the noisome hub of the city centre and its main shopping area. In the centre stands a rousing statue of the Gallic chieftain Vercingétorix, who in 53 BC led his people to their only – and indecisive – victory over Julius Caesar just south of the town. North from place de Jaude, **place St-Pierre** is the site of Clermont's principal marketplace, with a morning food **market**, at its liveliest on Saturdays. The nearby **Musée du Ranquet** on rue Gras (Tues–Sat 10am–noon & 2–5pm, Sun 2–5pm; free) is one of the city's best museums, with displays on local history back to Roman times. Running roughly parallel, the quarter's other main street, rue de la Boucherie, is a fragrant bazaar of tiny shops selling all kinds of food and spices.

The streets gather up to the dark and soaring **Cathédrale Notre-Dame**, whose strong volcanic stone made it possible to build vaults and pillars of unheard-of slenderness and height. Off the nave, the **Tour de la Bayette** (small charge) gives extensive views across the city, and provides some explanation as to why locals use the cathedral as a short cut – something the authorities have been trying to put a stop to for years. A short step northeast of the cathedral on place Delille stands Clermont's other great church, the **Basilique Notre-Dame du Port**: almost a century older, it's made from softer stone, which is corroding badly from exposure to Clermont's polluted air. For all that, it's a beautiful building, pure Auvergnat Romanesque with a stiff and upright Madonna and Child over the south door and inside exuding the broody mysteriousness so often generated by Romanesque; put a franc in the slot and you can light up the intricately carved ensemble of leaves, knights and Biblical figures on the church's pillars and capitals.

Practicalities

The **train station** is on av de l'URSS, east of the city centre, and is connected by regular bus with place de Jaude. The main **tourist office** is at 69 bd Gergovia (June–Sept Mon–Sat 8.30am–7pm, Sun 9am–noon & 2–6pm; Oct–May Mon–Fri 8.45am–6.30pm & Sat 9am–noon & 2–6pm), with annexes at the train station and during summer on place de Jaude. The **youth hostel** is at 55 av de l'URSS (☎73.92.26.39; ②), two minutes' walk right of the station, and a *Foyer International des Jeunes* at 12 place Regensburg (☎73.93.07.82; ②), is in the midst of a noisy housing development. The *Foyer St-Jean*, 17 rue Gaultier-de-Biauzat (☎73.37.14.31; ②), charges a little more but is much the nicest option of the three. There is a cluster of cheap **hotels** outside the station, of which the most reliable (to the left) is the *Bellevue*, 1 av de l'URSS (☎73.92.43.12; ②). For something nearer the centre there's *Hôtel Foch*, 22 rue Maréchal-Foch (☎73.93.48.40; ②). For **food**, the *Auberge Auvergnate*, 37 rue des Vieillards, is a small bistro in the old part of town with menus from F80, while the nearby *Don Camillo* at 3 rue de la Tannerie does simpler regional menus from F40; the tiny place Renoux, off rue Maréchal Joffre, and nearby place Jaude make pleasant drinking spots. **Moving on**, *Le Cévenol*, a slow train through the mountains to Nîmes, is one of the most enchanting French rail journeys you can make – so much so that during the summer *SNCF* run a *train touristique* with entertainment on board.

Puy de Dôme

Frequent buses from Clermont run to **Puy de Dôme**, a few kilometres west of Clermont, one of the tallest of the *puys*, with sweeping views back towards the town and the Parc des Volcans. Close to the summit, ruins survive of a Roman temple to Mercury, in its time considered one of the marvels of the empire, fashioned from over fifty different kinds of marble and with an enormous bronze statue of Mercury where a TV antenna now stands. Walking here from Clermont, or even Royat, be sure to allow a good half-day – and take food. The restaurant on top enjoys a monopoly and makes full use of it.

Vichy

VICHY is famous for two things: its World War II puppet government under Marshal Pétain and its curative sulphurous springs. There's nothing left to suggest that Vichy was once capital of a collaborationist Nazi state, and it's Vichy's role as one of France's foremost spa resorts that is the town's most distinctive trait. The population is largely elderly, genteel and rich, and swells several-fold in summer, and the town is almost entirely devoted to catering for them.

There's a real *fin-de-siècle* charm about the place, and a curious fascination in its continuing function. Life revolves around the **Parc des Sources**, a stately tree-shaded park that takes up most of the centre. At the north end stands the **Palais**, an enormous iron-framed greenhouse in which the various waters emerge from their spouts, people lining up to get their prescribed cupful. For a small fee you can join them, though bear in mind that only one of the five springs (the *Célestin*) is bottled and widely drunk; the others are progressively more foul and sulphurous, with the *Source de l'Hôpital*, which has its own building at the far end of the park, an almost unbelievably nasty product. All, apart from the *Célestin*, must be drunk on the spot to be efficacious – a dubious but effective way of drawing in the crowds. After the waters, Vichy's curiosities are limited. Marshal Pétain's own offices were at the *Pavillon*, while the Gestapo had their headquarters at the *Hôtel du Portugal*, but, unsurprisingly, there's nothing to commemorate either. There's a pleasant wooded riverside area, the **Parc de l'Allier**, created again for Napoléon III; and, not far from here, the old town boasts the strange **Église de St-**

Blaise, actually two churches in one, with a 1930s Baroque number built onto the original Romanesque. Inside, a Black Virgin, *Notre-Dame-des-Malades*, stands surrounded by plaques offered by the grateful healed.

Practicalities

The **train station** is on the west edge of the centre, at the end of rue de Paris. The tourist office is housed in Petain's government building, at 19 rue de Parc (Mon–Sat 9am–noon/12.30pm & 1.30/2–6.30/7pm, Sun 3–6pm). There's a **youth hostel** across the river at 19 rue du Stade (☎70.32.25.14; ②), where you'll also find a number of **campsites** – cross the pont de Bellerive from the Parc de l'Allier. Among hotels, try either the *Trianon*, 9 rue Debrest (☎70.97.95.96; ②), or the cheaper *Antilles* in the same street at no. 16 (☎70.98.27.01; ②). For **food**, the junction of rue Clemenceau, rue de Pans, rue Lucas and rue Jean-Jaurès has plenty of places; or try *Aux Éperons*, across the river in Bellerive at 5 av d'Hauterive, which has excellent menus from around F65.

Le-Puy-en-Velay

A strange town in a strange setting, **LE-PUY-EN-VELAY** sprawls across a broad basin in the mountains, a muddle of red roofs barbed with poles of volcanic rock. Capital of the Haute-Loire, it isn't easy to get to – from Clermont or Nîmes you have to change trains at St-Georges-d'Aurac – but it's well worth the effort. In medieval times it was the assembly point for pilgrims to Santiago in Spain, and amid the cobbled streets of the old town are some of the most richly endowed churches in the land. The strange surrounding countryside is an added attraction.

The **old town**, reached by climbing the steep sequence of streets and steps that terrace the town's *puy* foundation, is dominated by the **Cathedral** – almost Byzantine in style, striped with alternate layers of light and dark stone and capped with a line of small cupolas. Oddly enough, you enter from below, the nave-level being reached by clambering up yet more steps into the dull glow from the patchy gold frescoes. The Black Virgin inside is a copy of a revered original burnt during the Revolution, and is still paraded through the town every August 15. Other, lesser treasures are displayed at the back of the church in the sacristy, beyond which is the entrance to the twelfth-century cloister, patterned with the same stripes as the cathedral facade. At the highest point in the town is the giant crimson statue of **Notre-Dame-de-France**, fashioned from the metal of guns captured in the Crimean war. The nearby church of **St-Michel-d'Aiguilhe** (mid-June to mid-Sept 9am–7pm; mid-Sept to mid-June 9/10am–noon & 2–5/7pm; F8), sitting on the peak of an even steeper *puy*, is an eleventh-century construction that seems to grow out of the rock itself. It's a tough ascent, but one you should definitely make – it's a quirky little building decorated with mosaics, arabesques, and trefoil arches, its bizarre shape following that of the available flat ground. Back down below, lacemakers – a traditional, though now commercialized industry – do a fine trade, doilies and lace shawls hanging enticingly outside shops for tourists. Le Puy's maze of old lanes is uncluttered and wonderful, while in the new part of town, beyond the squat **Tour Pannessac**, **place de Breuil** and **place Michelet** form the social hub, with spacious public gardens.

Practicalities

Arriving by **bus or train** you'll find yourself on place du Maréchal-Leclerc, a ten-minute walk from place de Breuil, and within easy striking distance of some reasonably priced **hotels**, including *Hôtel des Voyageurs*, 37 bd Maréchal-Fayolle (☎71.09.05.30; ③). There is a **youth hostel** at the Centre Pierre-Cardinal, 9 rue Jule-Vallès (☎71.05.52.40; ②), and a **campsite**, *Bouthézard*, thirty minutes from the station along chemin de Roderie – bus #7. The tourist office is on place Breuil (Easter-Sept daily 8.30am–noon & 2–6pm; closed Sun rest of year). For **food**, the places around place Breuil and place Michelet are okay, and the *Cordeliers* hotel restaurant does good cheap menus. More pricily, there's the excellent *Tournayre*, 12 rue Chènbouterie, whose menus start at F95.

BURGUNDY

Peaceful, rural **Burgundy** is one of the most prosperous regions of modern France and was for a long time independent from the French state. Indeed, in the fifteenth century its dukes ruled an empire that was the best organized and richest in Europe, embracing all of Franche-Comté, Alsace and Lorraine, Belgium, the Netherlands, Picardy and Flanders, and with revenues equalled only by Venice. Everywhere there is startling evidence of this former wealth and power, both secular and religious. **Dijon**, the dukes' capital, is a slick and prosperous town with plenty of remnants of old Burgundy; to the north, the town of **Sens** is a worthy stopoff on the way into the region, as is **Avallon**, which gives access to the great abbey of **Vézelay**, just to the west. South, there are substantial Roman remains at **Autun**, and the ruins of the monastery of **Cluny**, whose influence was second only to that of Rome for a time, though wine devotees may head straight for the **vineyards**, whose produce has been a major money-maker since Louis XIV's doctor prescribed the stuff for the royal dyspepsia. **Beaune** is a good centre for sampling the best of the wine, washed down with local specialities like *escargots à la bourguignonne, boeuf bourguignon* and *coq au vin*.

Sens

SENS, though never part of the Duchy of Burgundy, feels like a typically Burgundian town. Contained within a ring of tree-lined boulevards where the city walls once stood, its ancient centre, focusing on place de la République, is still dominated by the **Cathédrale de St-Étienne**. Begun around 1130, it was the first of the great French Gothic cathedrals and is a fine example of the space and weightlessness of the genre. The architect who completed it, William of Sens, was later to rebuild the choir of Canterbury cathedral in England. Thomas à Becket spent several years in exile around Sens, and the story of his murder is told in the twelfth-century windows in the north aisle of the choir, just part of the cathedral's outstanding collection of stained glass. The treasury (daily except Tues 10am–noon & 2–5pm) is also uncommonly rich, containing Islamic, Byzantine and French vestments, jewels and embroideries. Just south is the thirteenth-century **Palais Synodal**, with its roof of Burgundian glazed tiles (tours 10am–noon & 4–6pm; F10), restored like so many other buildings in this region by Viollet-le-Duc. Its vaulted halls, originally designed to accommodate the ecclesiastical courts, now house a small **museum** of statuary from the cathedral and Gallo-Roman mosaics. Underneath is a medieval prison.

The **train station** is about ten minutes' walk from the cathedral, at the end of the main Grand Rue. The tourist office is on the north edge of the small centre, on place Jean-Jaurès (Mon–Sat 9am–noon & 2–6pm). For **accommodation**, try the *Hôtel Chemin de Fer* (☎86.65.10.27; ②) opposite the station, or in the centre, *Hôtel du Centre*, 4–8 place de la République (☎86.65.15.92; ②). The closest **campsite** is *Entre-deux-Vannes*, on route de Lyon, just out of town but not on any bus route. For **eating**, there is a cheap self-service place, *Brasserie le Senonais*, at 99 rue de la République, and a good crêperie, *Aux 4 Vents*, at 3 rue de Brennus. There are also a few affordable restaurants around place de la République, best of which is the *Roi St Louis*, which does a good cheap menu.

Avallon and Vézelay

Perched high on a ridge above the wooded valley of the River Cousin, looking out over the hilly, sparsely populated country of the Morvan national park, **AVALLON** is a small and ancient town of stone facades and cobbled streets. There's not a lot to see, but it's the closest town to Vézelay, one of Burgundy's prime tourist targets. Under the straddling arch of the **Tour de l'Horloge**, whose spire dominates the town, Grand-Rue A-Briand leads to the pilgrim church of **St-Lazare**, on whose battered Romanesque facade you can still decipher the carved signs of the zodiac and labours of the months. The tourist office is almost opposite, and a couple of hundred metres further the street passes through the city walls and out onto the lime-shaded **Promenade de la Petite Porte**, which has precipitous views across the valley of the Cousin.

For cheap **accommodation**, try *Au Bon Acceuil*, 4 rue de l'Hôpital (☎86.34.09.33; ②), or *Hôtel du Parc*, 3 place de la Gare (☎86.34.17.00; ②), both with good cheap restaurants. There is an attractive municipal **campsite** 2km away, off route de Lormes. Reasonably priced **eating** is possible at the *Cheval Blanc*, 55 rue de Lyon. The **train station** is a few minutes' walk from the centre at the end of Promenade des Capucins on rue Carnot, and is the best place to hire bikes – one way of getting to Vézelay. Alternatively, there are infrequent **buses** and **trains** to Sermizelles on the Auxerre–Avallon line, with an *SNCF* bus link on to Vézelay, 15km west of Avallon.

Vézelay

The abbey church of **La Madeleine** at **VÉZELAY** (daily sunrise–sunset), one of the seminal buildings of the Romanesque period, was saved from collapse by Viollet-le-Duc in 1840. Home – it was thought – to the bones of Mary Magdalen, the church was a major pilgrimage site, and assembly point for pilgrims heading for Santiago de Compostela in Spain. Saint Bernard preached to the Second Crusade here in 1146, and Richard the Lionheart and Philippe Auguste, King of France, made their rendezvous here before the Third Crusade in 1190. Just inside, the colossal narthex was added to the nave around 1150 to accommodate the pilgrims, and is striking for the superb sculpture on its central doorway – on the tympanum an ethereal Christ presides over a group of Apostles and ordinary people going about their business, while on the outer arch there are small-scale medallions of the zodiac signs and labours of the months. The long body of the church is vaulted by arches of alternating black and white stone, edged with fretted mouldings, and the supporting pillars are crowned with finely cut capitals, 99 in all, depicting scenes from the Bible, classical mythology, allegories and morality stories – in complete contrast to the clean, soaring lines of the early Gothic choir beyond.

The small tourist office is on the right in rue St-Pierre as you go up towards the abbey (April–Oct 10am–1pm & 2–6pm; closed Wed & Sun). Staying in Vézelay, there are a number of reasonable hotels and two **youth hostels**, both open July to September – one on rue des Écoles, the *Amis de Pax Christi* (☎86.33.26.73; ②), the other, an official hostel with camping space, about 1km along route d'Étang (☎86.33.24.18; ②).

Dijon

DIJON owes its origins to its strategic position in Celtic times on the merchant route from Britain up the Seine and across the Alps to the Adriatic. But it was as capital of the dukes of Burgundy from 1000 until the late 1400s that it knew its finest hour, under the auspices of Dukes Philippe le Hardi (the Bold), Jean sans Peur (the Fearless), Philippe le Bon (the Good) and Charles le Téméraire (the Rash). They used their tremendous wealth and power – they controlled Flanders, the industrial star of the day – to make Dijon one of the greatest centres of art, learning and science in Europe. Though it obviously lost some of this status with incorporation into the French kingdom in 1477, it has remained one of the pre-eminent provincial cities, especially since the rail and industrial boom of the mid-nineteenth century.

The City

You sense Dijon's former glory more in the lavish houses of its burghers than in the former seat of the dukes, the **Palais des Ducs**, an undistinguished building from the outside and one that has had many alterations, especially in the sixteenth and seventeenth centuries when it became the Parliament of Burgundy. In fact, the only outward reminders of the dukes' building are the fifteenth-century **Tour Philippe-le-Bon** (summer daily 9.30–11.30am & 2.30–5.30pm; F5), from whose terrace on the clearest of days they say you can see Mont Blanc, and the fourteenth- century **Tour de Bar**, which now houses Dijon's **Musée des Beaux-Arts** (Mon & Wed–Sat 10am–6pm, Sun 10am–12.30pm & 2–6pm; F11), with a collection of paintings that represents many different schools and periods, from Titian and Rubens to Monet, Manet and other Impressionists, as well as religious artefacts, ivories and tapestries. One of the most interesting exhibits is a small room devoted to the intricate woodcarving of the sixteenth-century designer and architect Hugues Sambin, whose work appears throughout the old quarter of the city in the massive doors and facades of the aristocratic *hôtels*. Visiting the museum also provides the opportunity to see the surviving portions of the ducal palace, including the vast kitchens, the magnificent Salle des Gardes, and the relocated tombs of Philippe le Hardi and of Jean sans Peur and his wife, Marguerite de Bavière. These are decorated with painted effigies of the dead, attended by angels holding their helmets and heraldic shields, and accompanied by a cortege of marvellously sculpted mourners.

The palace looks on to **place de Liberation**, a gracious semicircular space bordered by houses of honey-coloured stone, designed in the late seventeenth century. Behind the palace is a tiny, enclosed square, **place des Ducs**, and a maze of lanes flanked by beautiful old houses, best of which are those on **rue des Forges**. Parallel to rue des Forges, **rue de la Chouette** passes the north side of the impressive thirteenth-century Gothic church of **Notre-Dame**, whose north wall holds a small sculpted owl – *chouette* – which people touch for luck and which gives the street its name. The unusual west front consists of two galleries of arcades adorned with spectacular leaning gargoyles, while inside there are beautiful thirteenth-century windows, a black wooden Virgin of the twelfth century and, in the north transept, a Gobelins tapestry commemorating the 1944 liberation from the Nazis. At the end of the street is the attractive **place François-Rude**, a favourite summer hang-out, crowded with café tables. The **Cathédrale de St-Bénigne**, of similar date to Notre-Dame and with the characteristic glazed-tile roof, lies just south of here, its circular crypt part of an original tenth-century Romanesque church. Close by, the **Musée Archéologique**, 5 rue Docteur-Mare (daily except Tues June–Aug 9.30am–6pm; Sept–May 9am–noon & 2–6pm; F9.50, free Sun), has interesting Gallo-Roman funerary bas-reliefs depicting the perennial Gallic preoccupation with food and wine and a collection of ex-votos from the source of the Seine, among them the little bronze of the goddess Sequana (Seine), upright in her bird-prowed boat. Back in the town centre at 4 rue des Bons-Enfants, the **Musée Magnin** (daily except Tues June–Sept 10am–6pm; Oct–May 10am–noon & 2–6pm; F12, free Wed and Sun) is a seventeenth-century *hôtel* with its original furnishings, more interesting than its paintings. Further south, the **Musée de la Vie Bourguignonne**, 17 rue St-Anne (daily except Tues 9am–noon & 2–6pm; F9, free Wed & Sun), documents Burgundian life last century and is housed in a stark modern setting inside a former convent.

Practicalities

The **train station** is at the end of av Maréchal-Foch, five minutes from place Darcy and the main **tourist office** (daily 9am—7/9pm; closed for lunch during winter); a little east from here, the regional tourist office at 34 rue des Forges (Mon–Thurs 8am–noon & 2–6pm, Fri until 5pm) sells a cheap all-in-one ticket for the main museums and sights in the Côte d'Or region. You can also buy a general museum ticket for F14 from any of the museums. The *Foyer International d'Étudiants* on av Maréchal-Leclerc (☎80.71.51.01; ②; bus #4) is a student **hostel**, and there's an official **youth hostel** at 1 bd Champollion (☎80.71.32.12; ②), 4km from the centre – bus #5 from place Darcy. As for **hotels**, try the *Monge* at 20 rue Monge (☎80.30.55.41; ②), or in the same road, the *Hostellerie Sauvage*, 64 rue Monge (☎80.41.31.21; ③) – both excellent value. There's also the *Hôtel du Théâtre*, near the Palais des Ducs at 3 rue des Bons-Enfants (☎80.67.15.41; ②), though this gets busy. The nearest **campsite** is by the lake off bd Kir – bus #18.

There is no problem finding a good **restaurant** in this centre of *haute cuisine*, though locating affordable places is harder. The *Restaurant Buffon*, 28 rue Buffon, does good daily menus for F50; the *Coum' Chez Eux*, 68 rue J.J.-Rousseau, is an informal lunchtime option serving substantial portions. If you're prepared to spend a little more, *Le Clos des Capucines*, 3 rue Jeannin, serves excellent regional specialities. For a **drink**, the *Palais de la Bière* at the corner of rue Piron and rue Berbisey has character and is good for a daytime or early evening drink, as are the two bars, *Café de la Cathédrale* and *Café au Carillon*, popular with students, in front of the cathedral. *Le Café des Grand Ducs*, 96 rue de la Liberté, is another youthful hang-out, open until 3am.

Autun

AUTUN, today scarcely bigger than the circumference of its medieval walls, was one of the leading cities of Roman Gaul, founded by Augustus around 10 BC as part of his campaign to pacify and Romanize the broody Celts of defeated Vercingétorix. Two of the city's four **Roman gates** survive, **Porte St-André** spanning rue de la Croix-Blanche in the northeast and **Porte d'Arroux** in Faubourg d'Arroux in the northwest, while in a field just across the River Arroux stands the so-called **Temple of Janus**, a lofty section of brick wall that was probably part of the sanctuary of some Gallic deity. Off av du 2eme-Dragon are the few remains of the largest **Roman theatre** in Gaul – a measure of the importance of the settlement.

Autun's main street is av Charles-de-Gaulle, leading to the main square, **Champ de Mars**, from which the narrow streets of the **old town** spread, converging towards the **Cathédrale de St-Lazare** in the most southerly and best fortified corner. Built in the twelfth century and much altered since, the church is uniquely important for its works by Gislebertus, one of the greatest of Romanesque sculptors. The tympanum of the *Last Judgement* above the west door bears his signature beneath the feet of Christ; the sculpture was only saved from destruction during the Revolution because it had been plastered over. The interior was also decorated by Gislebertus, who himself carved most of the capitals, some of the finest of which are now in the old chapter library. There are more pieces by Gislebertus outside the cathedral in the **Musée Rolin**, an old Renaissance *hôtel* on rue des Blancs (daily except Tues April–Sept 9.30am–noon & 1.30–6pm; Oct–March 10am–noon & 2–5pm; F12), including his unashamedly sensual portrayal of Eve.

The **train station** is on av de la République, at the far end of av C. de Gaulle, on which you'll find the tourist office at no. 3 (Mon–Sat 9am–noon & 2–7pm); there's a second tourist office in front of the cathedral (daily 10am–6pm). Opposite the station, the *Hôtel de France* (☎85.52.14.00; ②) and *Hôtel Commerce et Touring* (☎85.52.17.90; ②) are both decent and inexpensive, and the latter has a very acceptable, moderately priced **restaurant**. There's a **campsite** just across the river beyond Porte d'Arroux. Of a number of places to **eat**, the *Auberge de la Bourgogne* and the brasserie *Morvandiau* on place Champ de Mars, and *Le Châteaubriant*, 14 rue Jeannin, are recommended.

Cluny

The voice of the abbot of **CLUNY**, around 50km south of Dijon, once made monarchs tremble. His power in the Christian world was second only to that of the pope, his intellectual influence arguably greater. Founded in 910, the monastery was also one of the richest in France, and it was its wealth and secular involvement that led to the decline of its spiritual influence in the wake of the reforming zeal of Saint Bernard and his Cistercians. In time, Cluny became no more than a convenient device for dressing the king's temporal machinations in a little spiritual respectability.

Sadly, practically nothing of the complex remains. The Revolution suppressed the monastery, and the eleventh-century **church**, the largest building in Christendom until St Peter's in Rome, was dismantled in 1810. All you can see now is an octagonal belfry, the south transept, and, in the granary, some capitals from its immense columns. The **Musée Ochier** (daily except Tues March–Sept 9.30am–noon & 2–6.30pm; Oct–Feb 10am–noon & 2–6pm; F13), in the fifteenth-century palace of the last abbot to be freely elected, helps flesh out the picture with reconstructions and sculpture fragments, while the Romanesque belfry of the parish church of **St-Marcel** recalls those that once adorned the abbey.

If staying in the village, the cheapest option is *Cluny Séjour,* a municipal **hostel** on rue Porte-de-Paris (☎85.59.08.93; ②), though it has a 10pm curfew, or there's a **campsite** on rue des Griottons across Pont de la Levée on the right. *Hôtel de l'Abbaye* on av de la Gare (☎85.59.11.14; ②) and *Hôtel du Commerce,* 8 place du Commerce (☎85.59.03.09; ②), have fairly cheap double rooms. *Marroniers* on av de la Gare is a reasonable **restaurant.**

The Burgundy vineyards

Burgundy's best **wines** come from a narrow strip of hillside – the **Côte d'Or**, which runs southwest from Dijon to Santenay. It is divided into two regions – Côte de Nuits and Côte de Beaune. With few exceptions, the reds of the Côte de Nuits are considered the best: they are richer, age better and cost more. Côte de Beaune is known particularly for its whites – Meursault, Montrachet and Puligny. The countryside is attractive: the steep scarp of the *côte*, wooded along the top, is cut by deep little valleys called *combes*, where local rock climbers hone their skills. The villages, strung along N74 through the town of Beaune and beyond, are sleepy and exceedingly prosperous, full of houses inhabited by well-heeled *vignerons* in expensive suits and fat-cat cars. There are numerous *caves* to taste and buy at, but as usual the former is meant to be a prelude to the latter. If you are buying, be aware that the *Hautes Côtes* (Nuits and Beaune), from the top of the slope, are cheaper, although they don't have the cachet of the big guys.

Beaune

BEAUNE, the principal town of the Côte d'Or, has many charms, but it is totally devoted to tourism. The chief attraction is the fifteenth-century hospital, the **Hôtel-Dieu** on the corner of place de la Halle (Easter to mid-Nov 9am–6.30pm; mid-Nov–Easter 9–11.30am & 2–5.30pm; F27), whose vast paved hall has an impressive painted timber roof and until quite recently continued to serve its original purpose. There's also a polyptych of the *Last Judgement,* a splendid fifteenth-century work by Rogier van der Weyden, commissioned by Nicolas Rolin, founder of the hospital. It is here that the Hospices de Beaune's wines are auctioned during the annual *Trois Glorieuses,* the prices paid setting the pattern for the season. The private residence of the dukes of Burgundy on rue d'Enfer now contains the **Musée du Vin** (daily 9.30am–6pm; F20), with giant wine presses and an interesting collection of tools of the trade. At the other end of rue d'Enfer, the church of **Notre-Dame** has five **tapestries** from the fifteenth century depicting the Life of the Virgin, also commissioned by the Rolin family.

From the **train station**, the town centre is 500 metres up av du 8-Septembre, across the boulevard, and left onto rue des Tonneliers. **Buses** leave from outside the walls at the end of rue Maufoux. The **tourist office** is opposite the Hôtel-Dieu on rue de l'Hôtel-Dieu (Easter–Oct daily 9am–10/11pm/midnight; Nov–Easter daily 9am–7.15pm) and has information on wine tours. **Accommodation** is pricy and it's cheaper to use Dijon or Chalon as a base, as both are easily accessible by train and *Transco* buses, which service all the villages down N74. But if you want to stay, *Auberge de la Gare*, 11 av des Lyonnais (☎80.22.11.13; ②), has the best value rooms and a cheap restaurant. There may be room at the *Foyer des Jeunes Travailleurs* opposite the hospital on rue Guigone-de-Salins (☎80.22.21.83; ②), and there's a **campsite**, *Les Cent Vignes*, 1km out on rue Dubois off rue du Faubourg-St-Nicolas. **Eating** can also be expensive. The best places for cheap meals are rue Monge, place Carnot and rue de Lorraine. *Le Carnot* at 18 rue Carnot is a good cafeteria, and menus at the *Brelinette*, 6 rue Madeleine, start at F58.

Chalon, Mâcon and the Beaujolais

CHALON, around 30km south of Beaune on the banks of the Saône, has long been a thriving port and industrial centre, and its old riverside quarter has an easy charm. It is not a place you want to stay very long, however, although there are numerous **hotels** and it has a riverbank **youth hostel** (②) about a ten-minute walk north of the Pont St-Laurent, the last bridge upstream. The one thing you might want to see is the **Musée Nièpce** (daily except Tues 9.30–11.30am & 2.30–5.30pm; F10), on the river quays just downstream from Pont St-Laurent. Local boy Nièpce is credited with inventing photography, and the museum possesses a fascinating range of cameras from the first ever to those taken on the *Apollo* moon mission, plus a number of 007-type spy devices.

SNCF buses go south to **MÂCON**, passing through some of the **Chalonnais** wine villages, best known for their whites. Mâcon itself is a large, modern town where again you are not likely to want to do more than stop over. The **Mâconnais** wine-producing country lies to the west. Its reds are good, but it is best known for the expensive white wines from the villages of Pouilly, Fuissé, Vinzelles and Prissé. South of here, the Mâconnais becomes the **Beaujolais**, a larger area of terraced hills producing light, fruity red wines which each November are transported to British wine bars at break-neck speeds, so they can be drunk suitably young. Of the three categories of Beaujolais, the superior *crus*, including Morgon and Fleurie, come from the northern part of the region; *Beaujolais Villages*, which produces the best nouveau, comes from the middle; and *Beaujolais Supérieur* comes from vineyards southwest of Villefranche.

ALSACE-LORRAINE

France's eastern frontier provinces, **Alsace** and **Lorraine**, were for a thousand years a battleground, disputed through the Middle Ages by independent dukes and bishops whose allegiance was endlessly contested by the kings of France and the princes of the Holy Roman Empire. They were also the scene in this century of some of the worst fighting of both world wars. The democratically-minded burghers of **Alsace** created a plethora of well-heeled semi-autonomous towns for themselves centuries before their eighteenth-century incorporation into the French state: neat, well-ordered places full of typically German fripperies on the houses – though the Alsatians remain fiercely and proudly French, despite the Germanic dialect they speak. The combination of cultures is at its most vivid in the numerous little wine towns that punctuate the so-called "Route du Vin" along the eastern margin of the wet and woody **Vosges** mountains – at **Colmar**, in **Mulhouse**, and in the great cathedral city of **Strasbourg**. By comparison, **Lorraine**, though it has suffered much the same vicissitudes, is rather wan, apart from the elegant eighteenth-century provincial capital of **Nancy**.

Nancy

NANCY, capital of Lorraine, is lighter and more southern in feel than its close neighbour Metz, with a relatively untouched eighteenth-century core that was the work of the last of the independent dukes of Lorraine, Stanislas Leczinski, dethroned King of Poland and father-in-law of Louis XV. During the twenty-odd years of his office in the middle of the eighteenth century he ordered some of the most successful urban redevelopment of the period in all France.

The centre of this is **place Stanislas**, a supremely elegant, partially enclosed square at the far end of rue Stanislas from the station, the south side of which is taken up by the **Hôtel de Ville**, its roofline topped by florid urns and lozenge-shaped lanterns dangling from the beaks of gilded cocks. On the west side of the square, the **Musée des Beaux-Arts** (Mon 2–6pm, Wed–Sun 10.30am–6pm; F30 ticket includes entry to the Musée d'École de Nancy) boasts Dufys and Matisses, but nothing outstanding. A little north, on Grand'Rue, is the **Musée Lorrain** (daily except Tues May to mid-Sept 10am–6pm; mid-Sept–April 10am–noon & 2–5/6pm; F20), devoted to Lorraine's history and with a room of etchings by the seventeenth-century artist, Jacques Callot, whose concern with social issues presaged much nineteenth- and twentieth-century art. The collection is housed in the old ducal palace, entered through an extravagant doorway surmounted by an equestrian statue of one of the dukes. Alternatively, make your way to the **Musée de l'École de Nancy**, a twenty-minute walk or #5 bus ride away at 38 rue Sergent-Blandan (daily except Tues 10am–noon & 2–5/6pm; F30 ticket includes entry to the Musée des Beaux-Arts), in a 1909 villa built for the Corbin family, founders of the big *Magasins Réunis* chain of department stores. It's an exciting collection of Art Nouveau objects, arranged as if in a private house, and evidence of Nancy's prominence in the movement – a branch of which was founded here by Émile Gallé, a local manufacturer of glass and ceramics.

The **train station** is at the end of rue Stanislas, a five-minute walk from place Stanislas, where you'll find the **tourist office** (Mon–Sat 9am–7pm; summer also Sun 10am–1pm). For cheap places to stay, there's the *Hôtel Pasteur*, 47 rue Pasteur (☎83.40.29.85; ②), and the *Jean-Jaurès*, 14 bd Jean-Jaurès (☎83.27.74.14; ②), both south of the station. There's a **youth hostel** out at the *Centre d'Accueil*, Château de Rémicourt, Villers-lès-Nancy (☎83.27.73.67; ②), a fifteen-minute #6 bus ride plus a fifteen-minute walk – curfew 10pm. *Camping de Brabois* is nearby. For **food**, Grand' Rue and rue des Maréchaux offer the best choice. At the far end of Grand' Rue, the *Caveau de la Grand' Rue* serves simple French fare in its cellar; *Le Bosphore*, further down on the opposite side, is a decent Turkish place; and if you missed out on Nancy's Art Nouveau museum, the ornate café *L'Excelsior*, across place Thiers from the train station, is a nice place for coffee, and, if you can afford it, a light meal.

Strasbourg

The capital of Alsace, **STRASBOURG** is prosperous, beautiful and modern, big enough to have a metropolitan air, but far from overwhelming. It has one of the loveliest cathedrals in France; one of the oldest and most active universities; and – ancient commercial crossroads that it is – is the current seat of the Council of Europe and part-time base of the European Parliament. You may not be planning to spend time in eastern France, but if you're around the region, it's the one city worth a detour.

The City

Strasbourg focuses on two main squares, the busy **place Kléber**, and, to the south, **place Gutenberg**, named after the pioneer of type, who lived here in the early fifteenth century. Close by, the **Cathédrale de Notre-Dame** (Mon–Sat 7–11.40am & 12.45–7pm, Sun 12.45–6pm) soars out of a huddle of medieval houses, with a spire of such delicate, flaky lightness it seems the work of confectioners rather than masons. Inside, too, it is magnificent, the high nave a model of proportion and enhanced by a glorious sequence of stained-glass windows, the finest of which are those in the south aisle next to the door, depicting the life of Christ and the Creation. On the left of the nave, the late fifteenth-century pulpit is another masterpiece of intricacy in stone, while in the south transept the slender triple-tiered thirteenth-century column, the *Pilier des Anges*, is decorated with some of the most graceful and expressive statuary of its age. Look also at the enormous and enormously complicated astrological clock built by Schwilgué of Strasbourg in 1838, a big hit with guided tours who roll up in droves to witness the clock's crowning performance of the day, striking the hour of noon with unerring accuracy at 12.31pm – noon, Strasbourg mean time.

South of the cathedral, the tree-lined **place du Château** is partly enclosed by the **Château des Rohan**, an eighteenth-century building designed for the immensely powerful Rohan family and now housing museums of **Arts Décoratifs**, **Beaux-Arts** and **Archéologique** (Mon & Wed–Sat 10am–noon & 2–6pm, Sun 11am–6pm; F15 each), none of which is especially interesting. Next door, the **Musée de l'Oeuvre Notre-Dame** (daily; same hours and price) houses the original sculptures from the cathedral exterior, damaged in the Revolution and replaced today by copies. There's also the eleventh-century *Wissembourg Christ*, said to be the oldest representation of a human figure in stained glass, from the previous cathedral, as well as the present cathedral architect's original parchment drawings for the statuary, done in fascinating detail. Among other museums, the **Musée Historique** in the old Grande Boucherie (Mon & Wed–Sat 10am–noon & 2–6pm, Sun 11am–6pm; F15) is mainly concerned with the city, though it also has an oddball collection of mechanical toys upstairs. Opposite, the **Musée d'Art Moderne** (daily 10am–noon & 2–6pm; F15) has an impressive collection featuring Monet, Klimt, Ernst, Klee and Jean Arp. There's also a **Musée Alsacien** (daily except Tues 10am–noon & 2–6pm; F15), with painted furniture and other local artefacts in a traditional house just across the Pont du Corbeau.

The area east of the cathedral is good for a stroll, too, rue des Frères leading to place St-Étienne and rue des Juifs. Just north of the old centre, across the river, **place de la République** is surrounded by vast German-Gothic edifices erected during the Imperial Prussian occupation post-1870, a few hundred metres beyond which is the **Palais de l'Europe**, home of the European Parliament and an imposing piece of contemporary architecture. The opposite edge of the city centre is more picturesque, where, around **quai Turckheim**, four square towers guard the so-called **Ponts Couverts** over a series of canals – part of the fourteenth-century city fortifications. Just upstream is a dam built by Vauban to protect the city from waterborne assault, an area known as **La Petite France**, with winding streets bordered by sixteenth- and seventeenth-century houses with carved woodwork and decked with flowers – though predictably it is something of a tourist hot spot.

Practicalities

From the **train station** take rue du Maire-Kuss and cross the river onto rue du 22-Novembre, which leads to place Kléber, from where rue des Grandes-Arcades heads south to place Gutenberg and the **tourist office** at 17 place de la Cathédrale (April–Oct daily 9am–6/7pm; Nov–March Mon–Sat 9am–12.30pm & 1.45–6pm). **Hotels** aren't cheap: close to the station there's the *Weber*, 22 bd de Nancy (☎88.32.36.47; ②), or more centrally and near the cathedral, try *Michelet* at 48 rue du Vieux Marché aux Poissons (☎88.32.47.38; ②), or the *Patricia*, 1a rue de Puits (☎88.32.14.60; ②), in the backstreets of the old town. There's a modern **youth hostel** on rue de l'Auberge-de-Jeunesse (☎88.30.36.46; ②) – take a #3, #13 or #23 bus by the next bridge upstream from Pont Kuss – and more central **hostel beds** at *CIARUS*, 7 rue Finkmatt (☎88.32.12.12; ②), which has a 1am curfew. For **food**, the *FEC* student canteen on place St-Étienne has rock-bottom prices and good meals too. Otherwise, though, eating out can be pricy. *Flam's*, 27–29 rue des Frères, serves the local speciality, *tarte flambée*, a kind of onion tart, and *L'Abécédaire* on rue de Maroquin is good. The city abounds in **wine bars** and **beer halls**: *L'Académie de la Bière*, 17 rue Adolphe Seyboth, is Strasbourg's most serious beer palace; *S'Bergerstuwel*, 10 rue de Sangier, better known as "Chez Yvonne", is a classic Alsatian *winstub*.

Colmar

A fifty-minute train ride south of Strasbourg, **COLMAR** is at first sight an unattractive sprawl, but it merits a stop for its picturesque old centre and some remarkable paintings in its **Musée d'Unterlinden**, at the end of av de la République in a former Dominican convent (April–Oct daily except Tues 9am–6pm; Nov–March daily except Tues 9am–noon & 2–5pm; F25). The most notable of these is an altarpiece for St Anthony's monastery at Isenheim, painted by Mathias Grünewald at the beginning of the sixteenth century, one of the last and most extraordinary of all Gothic paintings. Although displayed "exploded", the **Isenheim altarpiece** was designed to make a single piece. On the front was the *Crucifixion*, almost luridly expressive, with an emaciated, tortured Christ flanked by his pale fainting mother, Saint John and Mary Magdalene. It was unfolded on Sundays and feast days to reveal an *Annunciation, Resurrection* and *Virgin and Child*, and a sculpted panel depicting the saints Anthony, Augustine and Jerome.

To get there from the **train station**, go straight ahead and turn left onto av de la République. There's a **tourist office** opposite the museum (daily 9/10am–5/6pm; closed for lunch during winter). Of the **hotels** on and around av de la République, *La Chaumière* at no. 74 (☎89.41.08.99; ③), and *Hagueneck*, 83 av de Général-de-Gaulle (☎89.80.68.98; ③), are about the cheapest. There's also a reasonable **Maison des Jeunes** at 17 rue Camille-Schlumberger (☎89.41.26.87; ②), near the station. For **food**, *L'Amandine* on place de la Cathédrale has brasserie-type fare, or, for a more upmarket Alsatian experience, try *Bartholdi* at 2 rue des Boulangers, near the Dominican church.

Mulhouse

Twenty minutes down the line from Colmar, **MULHOUSE** is a large industrial city that got rich around 1800 on printed cotton fabrics and allied trades. Not having much of a centre, it is no city for strollers, but it does have three unusual museums. Closest to the **train station**, just along the canal to the right, is the **Musée de l'Impression sur Étoffes** (June to mid-Sept daily 9/10am–noon & 2–6pm; mid-Sept–May closed Tues; F27), an excellent, vast collection of the most beautiful fabrics imaginable – eighteenth-century Indian and Persian imports, silks from Turkestan, batiks from Java, Senegalese materials, some superb kimonos from Japan, and a unique display of scarves from France, Britain and the US. The other two museums are trickier to get to. The **Musée Français du Chemin de Fer** (daily 9am–5/6pm; F38), reachable by taking bus #1 to the end of the line, near the suburb of Dornach, has displays of rolling stock that include Napoléon III's ADCs' drawing-room, decorated by Viollet-le-Duc in 1856, and a luxuriously appointed 1926 diner from the *Golden Arrow*. The stars of the show are the big locomotives with their brightly painted boilers, gleaming wheels and pistons, and tangles of brass and copper piping. Finally, the exhibits at the **Musée National de l'Automobile** (daily 10am–6pm; Oct–April closed Tues; F52) – bus #2 or #7 from place de l'Europe – range from the earliest attempts at powered vehicles, like the extraordinary wooden-wheeled Jacquot steam "car" of 1878, to 1968 Porsche racing cars and contemporary factory prototypes. The largest group are the locally made Bugattis, the pride of them the Bugatti Royales, with two of the seven made on show – one Ettore Bugatti's own, with bodywork designed by his son.

Among the town's few reasonably priced **hotels**, there's the *Hôtel de Paris*, in the centre of town at 5 passage de l'Hôtel de Ville (☎89.45.21.41; ②). If it's full, the **youth hostel** (☎89.42.63.28; ②) is a little way out; take bus #4 or #6 from place de l'Europe in the city centre to the *Salle des Sports* on rue de l'Illberg. For food, the *Auberge de Vieux Mulhouse* on the main place de la Réunion is a standard Alsatian brasserie.

THE ALPS

Rousseau wrote in his *Confessions*, "I need torrents, rocks, pine trees, dark forests, mountains, rugged paths to go up and down, precipices at my elbow to give me a good fright". And these are, in essence, the principal joys of **the Alps**, made up of the *départements* of Dauphiné and Savoie. Strung in a line along their western edge, **Grenoble**, **Chambéry** and **Annecy** are the gateways to the highest parts, although you really need to spend several days here to have time to do anything more strenuous than view the peaks from your hotel window. There are four national or **regional parks** – Vanoise, Ecrins, Queyras (the least busy) and Vercors (the gentlest) – each of which is ideal walking country, and the **Grande Traversée des Alpes**, which crosses all the major massifs from St-Gingolph on Lake Geneva to Nice. But on a quick tour you're best off doing as other people do and grabbing a taster at **Chamonix**, the best base for **Mont Blanc** on the French-Italian border, or simply doing day walks from the main centres. All **routes** are clearly marked and equipped with refuge huts and *gîtes d'étape*. The *CIMES* office in Grenoble can provide detailed information on GR paths, and local tourist offices often produce detailed maps of walks in their areas. Bear in mind that anywhere above 2000m will be snowbound until the beginning of July.

Grenoble

The economic and intellectual capital of the French Alps, **GRENOBLE** is a lively, thriving city, beautifully situated on the Drac and Isère rivers. The centre of town, by the river, is marked by the sixteenth-century **Palais de Justice**, with place St-André and the church of **St-André** behind, built in the thirteenth century and heavily restored. **Place Grenette** is the favourite resort of café loungers, and nearby at 14 rue J-J-Rousseau there's a small **museum** dedicated to the French Resistance (2–5.30pm; closed Tues & Sun; free), who were particularly active in the Vercors massif. Stendhal was born in the house, though the city's **museum** of Stendhaliana is in a corner of the public gardens behind the St-André church. The **Musée de Peinture et de Sculpture** (daily except Tues 10am–noon & 2–6pm; F10), on the handsome nineteenth-century place de Verdun, is worthwhile for its collection of representative works by the big names in twentieth-century art. You should also try and visit the **Musée Dauphinois** (daily except Tues 9am–noon & 2–6pm; F10), which occupies the former convent of St-Marie-d'en-Haut, up a cobbled path opposite the Isère footbridge by the Palais de Justice. Imaginatively laid out, it is largely devoted to the history, arts and crafts of the province of Dauphiné, with exhibits on the life of the mountain people, many of whom were involved in smuggling – hence a fascinating collection of body-hugging flasks used for contraband liquor. The most unusual section is the so-called *Roman des Grenoblois*, the story of the people of Grenoble told in an excellent audiovisual presentation through the lives of various members of a representative selection of families. Finally, the one thing you shouldn't miss while in Grenoble is the trip by **téléférique** (9/11am–7.30pm/midnight; F30 return) from the riverside quai Stéphane-Jay up to **Fort de la Bastille** on the steep slopes above the north bank of the Isère. It's a hair-raising ride to an otherwise uninteresting fort, but the view is fantastic, over the surrounding mountains and valleys, as well as the nucleus of the medieval town.

Practicalities

The **train station** and **bus station** are on the western edge of the centre, at the end of av Felix-Viallet. The **tourist office** is at 14 rue de la République, near place Grenette (Mon–Sat 9am–6pm, Sun 10am–12.30pm); the hiking organization, *CIMES*, is in the same building. There are numerous **hotels** in the station area, among them the *Suisse et Bordeaux* on the corner of av Felix-Viallet (☎76.47.55.87; ③), *Alize* at 1 rue Amiral Courbet (☎76.43.12.91; ②), or, about a 10-minute walk, the very good value *Lakanal* on the corner of rue Lakanal/des Bergers (☎76.46.03.42; ②). The *Bellevue* (☎76.46.69.34; ③) has a better location, as its name suggests, on the corner of quai Stéphane-Jay and rue Belgrade. Alternatively, there's a **youth hostel** at 18 av de Grésivaudan (☎76.09.33.52; ②) in Echirolles, a ten-minute bus ride south (#8 from cours Jean-Jaurès). There is a large municipal **campsite** between rue Albert Reynier and av Beaumarchais, on the #8 bus route. For **food**, try anywhere on place St-André and place Notre-Dame, especially the *Progrès* or the *Tourneau de Diogenes*, or for something more upmarket, *La Panse* at 7 rue de la Paix, near the tourist office.

Chambéry

CHAMBÉRY lies just south of Lac du Bourget in a valley separating the Massif de la Chartreuse from the Bauges mountains, historically an important position commanding the entrance to the Alpine valleys into Italy. The present town grew up around the castle built by Count Thomas of Savoie in 1232, when Chambéry became capital of the ancient province, and flourished particularly in the fourteenth century. Although superseded as capital by Turin in 1563, it remained an important commercial and cultural centre and the emotional focus of all French Savoyards before its mid-nineteenth-century incorporation into France. This is an era well documented in the **Musée Savoisien**, just off place Métropole (daily except Tues 10am–noon & 2–6pm; F10), which has some lovely Savoyard primitive paintings and painted wood statues from various churches in the region, along with tools, carts, hay-sledges, old photos, and some very fine furniture from a house in Bessans, including a fascinating kitchen range made of wood and lined with slabs of schist. Next to the museum, in the enclosed place Métropole, is the **Cathedral**, which has a handsome though much restored Flamboyant Gothic facade and an interior painted in elaborate nineteenth-century trompe-l'œil. A passage leads from the square to rue de la Croix-d'Or, and, to the right, the long rectangular **place St-Léger**, hub of the city's social life, at the far end of which rue de Boigne leads to the castle **chapel**, dating from the early fifteenth century and really the only part worth seeing of the château (tours June & Sept daily 2.30 & 4pm; July & Aug 10.30am, 2.30, 3.30, 4.30 & 5.30pm; F20). The chapel was actually built to house the Turin Shroud, which was lodged here by the Dukes of Savoie before they took it back to Turin.

If you're **staying**, *Hôtel du Château*, rue J-P-Veyrat (☎79.69.48.78; ②), is perhaps the best-value cheap hotel. The nearest **campsite** is north of Chambéry in Bassens – take bus #C from the **SI**, which is on bd de la Colonne (Mon–Sat 9am–noon & 2–6pm). For **food**, rue Croix d'Or has numerous restaurants.

Annecy

Sited at the edge of a turquoise lake, and close to some high peaks, **ANNECY** is very much a transit-point for hikers, offering good access to the Mont Blanc area and on to Lake Geneva and the northern foothills. Historically, it enjoyed a brief flurry of importance in the early sixteenth century, when Geneva opted for the Reformation and the fugitive Catholic bishop decamped here with a train of ecclesiastics and a prosperous, cultivated, bourgeois elite.

The most interesting part of the city lies at the foot of the castle mound, a warren of lanes and passages, between which flow branches of the Canal du Thiou, which drains the lake into the River Fier. It's a picture-book pretty place, and inevitably full of tourists. Opposite the Hôtel de Ville, in the main square, is the fifteenth-century church of St-Maurice, originally built for a Dominican convent, with attractive Flamboyant windows and walls leaning outwards to an alarming degree. South of here, across the canal bridge, is the grand old Palais de l'Isle and rue St-Claire, the main street of the old town, with arcaded shops and houses. From rue de l'Isle the narrow Rampe du Château leads up to the château, former home of the Counts of Genevois and the Dukes of Nemours, a junior branch of the house of Savoy, and now housing the miscellaneous collections of the Musée du Château (daily except Tues 10am–noon & 2–6pm; F10) – archeological finds, Savoyard popular art, furniture and woodcarving, and, on the top floor, an excellent display illustrating the geology of the Alps.

The tourist office is in the Centre Bonlieu, a modern shopping centre at the end of rue Paquier (daily 9am–noon & 2–6pm). The youth hostel, 16 route de Semnoz (☎50.45.33.19; ②), is a good 45-minute walk from the old town. There are hostel beds closer in at the Centre International de Séjour at 52 rue des Marquisats (☎50.45.08.80; ②), by the lake, and the Foyer d'Evire, Montée de Novel, off rue des Martyres de la Déportation (②; bus #4) – as well as the Maison de la Jeune Fille, 1 av du Rhône (☎50.45.34.81; ②), for women only. There's a municipal campsite off bd de la Corniche – turn right up a lane opposite Chemin du Tillier and it's on the left. Hotels need to be booked in advance – it's a popular place, expecially at weekends. For somewhere close to the centre and the lake, try either the Hôtel des Alpes on rue de la Poste (☎50.45.04.56; ④), or the Rives du Lac in rue des Marquisats (☎50.51.32.85; ②). Failing these you can probably rely on Colonnes de Notre Dame, a 15-minute walk east of the station at 61 av de la Maveria (☎50.23.12.70; ②). For getting out of town, there are round-the-lake boat trips, at a reasonable price, from Compagnie des Bateaux by the mouth of the Thiou canal, and the tourist office sells a 1:50,000 map of the Annecy area with walking trails marked.

Chamonix and Mont Blanc

Mont Blanc is the biggest tourist draw in the Alps, but by walking you can soon get away from the worst of the crowds. The two approaches come together at Le Fayet, where the tramway du Mont-Blanc begins its 75-minute haul to the Nid d'Aigle, a vantage point on the northwest slope. There's more exciting access 30km further on, at CHAMONIX, although there's little else to recommend the place. The Musée Alpin off rue Whymper (June–Sept daily 2–7pm; F10) will interest mountain freaks, though it isn't as exciting as you'd expect; among various bits of equipment, documents and letters is Jacques Balmat's account of his first ascent of Mont Blanc, written in almost phonetically spelled French. The other thing you should do is take the expensive téléférique (F160 round-trip) to the Aiguille du Midi (3842m), a terrifying granite pinnacle on which the téléférique dock and a restaurant are precariously balanced. The view of Mont Blanc from here is incredible. At your feet is the snowy plateau of the Col du Midi, with the glaciers of the Vallée Blanche and Géant crawling off left at their millennial pace. To the right, a steep snowfield leads to the "easy" ridge route to the summit with its cap of ice (4807m). You must, however, go before 9am, because the summits usually cloud over towards midday and the crowds become intolerable. Be sure also to take warm clothes: even on a summer day it can be well below zero at the top.

Finding accommodation can be a big problem. The best bet is the comfortable, largely modernized and welcoming youth hostel at 127 Montée Jacques-Balmat in Les Pelerins (☎50.53.14.52; ②), just west of Chamonix proper (bus to les Houches – get off at Pèlerins École, from where the hostel is signposted). For other sporadic dormitory accommodation, ask at the tourist office near the church (daily 8.30am–7.30pm). **Campsites** are numerous, most convenient *Les Molliases* on the left of the main road, going west from Chamonix towards the Mont Blanc tunnel entrance, and *Les Arolles* on the opposite side of the road – a fifteen-minute walk from the station.

RHÔNE VALLEY AND PROVENCE

Of all the areas of France, **Provence** is the most irresistible, with attractions that range from the high mountains of the southern Alps to the wild plains of the Camargue, and one of the most visited. Yet, apart from the coast (detailed in the following section), large areas remain remarkably unscathed by development. Its complete integration into France dates only from the nineteenth century, and, although the Provençal language is rarely heard, the common accent is distinctive even to a foreign ear, and in the east the intonation is Italian. The main problem is choosing where to go. The **Rhône valley**, north–south route of ancient armies, medieval traders and modern rail and road, is nowadays fairly industrialized, and other than the big city delights of **Lyon** – not strictly in Provence but the main gateway for the region – there's not much to detain you before the Roman city of **Orange** and the old papal stronghold of **Avignon**, the latter with a brilliant summer festival. Deeper into Provence, on the edge of the flamingo-filled lagoons of the **Camargue**, **Arles** is another ancient Roman settlement, retaining a superb amphitheatre, while **Aix**, a little way east, is perhaps Provence's most sophisticated city, and for many years, home to Cézanne, for whom the nearby **Mont St-Victoire** was an enduring subject. In Eastern Provence it is the landscapes not the cities that dominate, the foothills of the Alps gradually closing in around the **Gorge du Verdon** – Europe's answer to the American Grand Canyon.

Lyon

LYON is the third largest city in France, and, viewed at high speed from the *Autoroute du Soleil,* the impression it gives is not an appealing one. In fact, it is a long-established business centre, with a prosperity built up on the back of its silk industry – a staid city, somewhat austere and very bourgeois, but not without its charms. Foremost of these is gastronomy: there are more restaurants per square foot than anywhere else on earth and the city could form a football team with its superstars of the international chef circuit. It also has all the attractions you would expect of a city of its size (around half a million): a lively nightscene and cultural life, including the famous Lyonnais puppets, all of which make a few nights here time well spent.

Arrival and accommodation

The centre of Lyon is the **Presqu'île**, the tongue of land between the rivers Saône and Rhône just before their confluence. Across the Saône is the old town, at the foot of **Fourvière**, on which the Romans built their capital of Gaul; to the north is the old silk weavers' district, **La Croix-Rousse**. Modern Lyon lies east of the Rhône, the city at its most self-assertive in the cultural and commercial centre of **La Part-Dieu**, beside the **TGV station**. Ordinary **trains** arrive at the Gare de Perrache, along with **buses**, on what was once the tip of the peninsula. The **airport**, Satolas, is off the Grenoble *autoroute*, thirty minutes by bus from La Part-Dieu. There's a **tourist office** in the Centre Perrache in front of the station, where you can pick up transport maps for Lyon's **métro, tram and bus system**, or you can just hop two stops on the métro to place Bellecour, where the central tourist office is on the southeast corner (Mon–Fri 9am–6/7pm, Sat 9am–5/6pm, Sun 10am–5/6pm). Transport tickets cost a flat F7, or you can buy them in *carnets* of six (F39) or twenty (F123). For **accommodation**, close to gare

Perrache, try the *Vaubecour*, 28 rue Vaubecour (☎78.37.44.91; ②), one block back from the Saône quays, or further north, the *Croix-Paquet*, 11 place Croix-Paquet (☎78.28.51.49; ②) has good value, fairly comfortable rooms. In Vieux Lyon, the *Celtic*, 5 place St-Paul (☎78.28.01.12; ②), is large, fairly pleasant and reasonably priced. There's a **youth hostel** 4km southeast of the centre in Venissieux, 51 rue Roger-Salengro (☎78.76.39.23; ②) – take buses #53 or #80 from Perrache or #36 from Part Dieu – and, not far away but a lot more expensive, the *Centre International de Séjour de Lyon*, 46 rue Commandant-Pégoud (☎78.01.23.45; ②); same buses. The closest **campsite** is the *Porte de Lyon* at Dardilly, a ten-minute ride by #19 bus from the Hôtel de Ville.

The City

Directly in front of the Perrache station, **place Carnot** is a green square, linked by way of the pedestrian rue Victor Hugo with the gravelly acres of the central **place Bellecour**, where even Louis XIV in the guise of a Roman emperor looks small. On rue de la Charité, which runs parallel to rue Victor-Hugo on the Rhône side, the **Musée Historique des Tissus** (Tues–Sun 10am–5.30pm; F20) is one of the city's major museums, not quite living up to its claim to cover the history of decorative cloth through the ages but with brilliant collections from specific periods, most notably sixth-century Coptic tapestries and painted linen from Egypt. There are also silks from Baghdad and carpets from Iran, Turkey, India and China, along with lovely twentieth-century pieces. From here, push straight on up rue de la République, full of people jostling back and forth between cafés and shops, past place Bellecour. To the left, at the top of quai St-Antoine, the **quartier Mercière** is the old commercial centre of the town, with sixteenth- and seventeenth-century houses lining rue Mercière, while straight ahead, the monumental nineteenth-century fountain in front of the even more monumental **Hôtel de Ville** on place des Terreaux symbolizes rivers straining to reach the ocean. The building taking up the southern side of the square is one of the four wings of Lyon's **Musée des Beaux-Arts** (Wed–Sun 10.30am–6pm; F20) and **Musée St-Pierre d'Art Contemporain** (daily except Tues noon–6pm; F20), which has a great selection of modern works – Bonnard, Monet, van Dongen – together with paintings by Rubens, El Greco, Tintoretto and a hundred others back to the Middle Ages. Downstairs are numerous objects lifted around the turn of the century from Egypt, Iran and elsewhere.

North of here, the old silk weavers' district of **La Croix-Rousse** is still a working-class area but only twenty or so people work on the computerized looms that are kept in business by the restoration and maintenance of the palaces and châteaux. You can watch the traditional looms in action at **La Maison des Canuts** at 10–12 rue d'Ivry, one block north of place de la Croix-Rousse (Mon–Fri 8.30am–noon & 2–6.30pm, Sat 9am–noon & 2–6pm; F6), but otherwise you might as well cut down through the alley-ways and narrow streets of the district to **Vieux Lyon**, across the river.

The streets pressed close together beneath the hill of Fourvière on the right bank of the Saône form an operatic set of Renaissance facades, at night brightly lit and popu-lated by a swelling chorus of well-dressed Lyonnais in search of supper. The **Musée Historique de Lyon** on place du Petit-Collège (daily except Tues 10.45am–6pm; F20) has a good collection of Nevers ceramics, although the **Musée de la Marionette** (same hours; F20) on the first floor of the same fifteenth-century mansion is more entertaining. As well as the eighteenth-century Lyonnais creations, *Guignol* and *Madelon* (the French Punch and Judy), there are glove puppets, shadow puppets and every type of rod-and-string-propelled toy actor, from Europe and the Far East.

Rue St-Jean ends at the **Cathédrale St-Jean**, a much-damaged twelfth- to fifteenth-century construction, but one whose thirteenth-century stained glass above the altar and in the rose windows of the transepts is in perfect condition. In the northern transept is a fourteenth-century clock rivalling modern digital watches for superlative functions: you can compute religious feast days until the year 2019. On the strike of noon, 1pm, 2pm and 3pm (most days), figures of the Annunciation go through an automated set piece. Just beyond the cathedral, opposite av Adolphe-Max and Pont Bonaparte, is a **funicular station**, from which you ascend to a set of **Roman remains** on rue de l'Antiquaille: consisting of two theatres and an underground museum of Lyonnais life from prehistoric times to 7 AD. There's a **Musée Gallo-Romain** at 17 rue Cléberg (Wed–Sun 9.30am–noon & 2–6pm; F20), from where it's a short walk to the late nineteenth-century **Basilique de Notre-Dame**, a miasma of multicoloured marble and mosaic. As a visual antidote, make your way to the belvedere behind and you'll probably find Lyon and its curving rivers the epitome of beauty by comparison.

Eating, drinking and nightlife

Lyon is not a vegetarian's dream, its **food** specialities revolving around the different things you can do with meat and offal, most famously in *quenelles* – a bit like dumplings. Vieux Lyon is the area with the greatest concentration of eateries, though you'll find cheaper and less busy ones between place des Jacobins and place Sathonay at the top of the Presqu'île. *Le Vieux Fourneau*, 1 rue Tramassac, has a decently priced four-course menu and a lively atmosphere; *L'Amphitryon*, 33 rue St-Jean, is open until midnight every night and gets packed, as does *La Grille*, 106 rue Sébastien-Gryphe, which is a good place to try local specialities. *La Meunière*, on rue Neuve, has a decent F80 menu, again of regional dishes, and is again normally very crowded, while the *Café des Federations*, 8 rue du Major-Martin (closed weekends), is a typical Lyon "bouchon" – a kind of wine bar with food. If you just want a **drink**, there's the *Albion Public House*, 12 rue St-Catherine, where you can play darts and listen to jazz on Saturday nights.

Orange

Around 100km south from Lyon, **ORANGE** is the first major stop in Provence proper, a pleasant town originally built by Julius Caesar for his troops as a reward for the successful conquest of Gaul. Aside from a **triumphal arch** on the north edge of town, friezed with celebrations of the campaign, the main feature of this period still left is the Roman **theatre** (April–Sept daily 9am–6.30pm; Oct–March daily 9am–noon & 1.30–5pm; F22, includes municipal museum), the best-preserved example in existence, and the only one with the stage wall still standing. The interior, though missing much of its original decoration, retains a central over-life-size statue of Augustus and the columned niches for other, lesser statues. The best view of the theatre in its entirety is from the St-Eutrope hill, into which it is built, past the remains of the forum. At the top of the hill are the ruins of the short-lived seventeenth-century **castle** of the princes of Orange. Louis XIV had it destroyed and the principality annexed to France – a small price to pay for the ruler of the Netherlands who was also to become king of England. The **municipal museum**, across the road from the theatre (same times; joint ticket), has various documents concerning the Orange dynasty, as well as an extremely unlikely collection of works by Frank Brangwyn, a Welsh painter with no connections with Orange, who learned his craft with William Morris. The pictures here are stark portrayals of British workers early this century.

The **train station** is about 1500m east of the centre, at the end of av Frédéric-Mistral; the nearest bus stop is at the bottom of rue Jean-Reboul, first left out of the station. Bus #2, direction Nogent, takes you to the ancient theatre and – the next stop – the tourist office on cours Aristide-Briand (Mon–Sat 9am–7pm, Sun 10am–6pm). If you're staying, the *Fréau*, 3 rue Ancient-Collège (☎90.34.06.26; ②), is central, immaculately kept and cheap; *St-Florent*, 4 rue de Mazeau (☎90.34.18.53; ②), is just as central but not as nice. Orange's campsite, *Le Jonquier* (March–Oct), is northwest on rue

Alexis-Carrel. For **food**, *La Fringale* on rue de Tourre does affordable *plats du jour*. *Le Yacca*, 24 place Silvian, has a generous choice of dishes in an old vaulted chamber. If it's full, try the neighbouring *Le Gallois*, or *Le Bec Fin* at 14 rue Segond-Weber.

Avignon

AVIGNON, great city of the popes and for centuries one of the major artistic centres of France, can leave you feeling rather cold, for although there's a big list of monuments and museums that can't be missed, there is no particularly cosy area of knotted medieval streets for café-lounging. Parts are good to wander around, but it's easy to feel like an outsider, unless you're here during the drama festival from mid-July to mid-August.

The Town

Central Avignon is enclosed by medieval **walls**, built by one of the nine popes that based themselves here throughout most of the fourteenth century, away from the anarchic feuding and rival popes of Rome. Avignon was a lively place when the papacy was here. Every vice flourished in the overcrowded, plague-ridden town, full of hangers-on to the papal court; according to Petrarch it was "a sewer where all the filth of the universe has gathered". The walls today do not look very convincing as a defence. When they were restored in the nineteenth century the moat could not be excavated, hence their original height is concealed. All the gates and towers are in place, however.

Centre of town is **place d'Horloge**, lined with cafés and market stalls on summer evenings, just beyond which is the monstrous **Palais des Papes** (April–Oct daily 9am–7/8pm; Nov–March daily 9am–12.45pm & 2–6pm; F51 with guide, F38 unguided). The sparse, denuded interior gives little indication of the richness of the papal court, although the building is impressive for sheer size alone. Visits take in the Consistoire, where sovereigns and ambassadors were received, with a nineteenth-century line-up of the popes, all looking very similar thanks to the one model the painter used. The adjacent Chapelle St-Jean, and the Chapelle St-Martial upstairs, were decorated by the Sienese artist Matteo Giovannetti, commissioned by Clement VI, who demanded the maximum amount of lapis lazuli, the most expensive pigment. Clement VI's secular concerns are further evident in the wonderful food-oriented murals and painted ceilings of his bedroom and study. With the study you are into the New Palace of Clement VI, in which the Grande Chapelle has the proportions of a cathedral.

The **Cathédrale Notre-Dame-des-Doms**, north of the palace, might have been a luminous Romanesque structure once, but the interior has had a bad attack of Baroque. You could ignore it and wander instead around the **Rocher des Doms** park, which gives great views over the river. The **Petit Palais**, just below (daily except Tues 9.30–11.50am & 2–6pm; F18), contains a huge and wearisome collection of paintings and sculptures, mostly Renaissance Italian. Along the river is the famous **Pont d'Avignon** of the song (April–Sept daily 9am–6.30pm; Oct–March Tues–Sun 9am–1pm & 2–5pm; F5 pr F35 including entrance to the new panoramic screen-history of Avignon). According to one theory, the words should read "Under the bridge", not "On the bridge", and refer to the trickster clientele of a tavern on the Île de la Barthelasse (which the bridge would have crossed to) dancing with glee at the arrival of more victims. Repairing the bridge from the ravages of the Rhône was finally abandoned in 1660, three and a half centuries after it was built, and only four of the original 22 arches remain.

Off rue de la République, at 65 rue Joseph-Vernet, the **Musée Calvet** (due to re-open mid-1994) is Avignon's other major museum, a varied collection and easier on the feet than the Petit Palais, with everything from an Egyptian mummy of a five-year-old boy to an anonymous sixteenth-century portrait of Henry VII of England and paintings by Utrillo, Sautine and Dufy. Across the other side of rue de la République are the pedestrian precincts of **rue des Marchands** and **rue du Vieux-Sextier**, with their complement of chapels and late-medieval mansions, and, one block south, **rue des Teinturiers**, the most atmospheric street in Avignon. Its name refers to the eighteenth- and nineteenth-century business of calico printing; the cloth was washed in the Sorgue which still runs alongside the street, turning the wheels of long-defunct mills.

Practicalities

The **train station** is beside porte de la République on bd St-Roch, on the southern edge of the centre. If you don't want to walk, you can also take bus #4 from the main PTT, on the left through porte de la République. The **tourist office** is a short walk from the station at 41 cours Jean-Jaurès (Mon–Fri 9am–1pm & 2–6pm, Sat 9am–1pm & 2–5pm) and there's another office at the Pont d'Avignon which opens on Sundays. Outside festival time, **accommodation** is not difficult to find. Off cours Jean-Jaurès between the station and the SI, rue Perdiguier has a couple of cheap hotels: *Le Parc* at no. 18bis (☎90.82.71.55; ②) and the characterless *Splendid* at no. 17 (☎90.86.14.46; ③). The *Innova*, 100 rue Joseph-Vernet (☎90.82.54.10; ②), is nicer, as is the *Mignon*, in the same street at no. 12 (☎90.82.17.30; ②). The *Foyer des Jeunes Comtadines*, 75 rue Joseph-Vernet (☎90.86.10.52; ②), is a **women's hostel**, with private rooms, and there's a small **youth hostel**, the *Centre d'Hébergement*, at 32 bd Limbert (☎90.85.27.78; ②; bus #2 from the PTT). The closest **campsite**, also with **dorm rooms**, is the *Bagatelle*, across the river on the Île de la Barthelasse – bus #10 from the PTT, or a ten-minute walk from the centre of town, across the Pont Daladier.

Eating on a budget is easy. The big brasseries on place d'Horloge all do well-priced meals and are nice places to sit outside – try *Le Venaissin* – and rue des Teinturiers is a good source of cheap restaurants. Specifically, *Le Corail*, 64 bd St Roch, serves reasonably priced Provençal dishes; *Le Petit Bédon*, 70 rue Joseph-Vernet, has perhaps the best meal under F250 to be had in the city. Vegetarians should go to *Le Pain Bis*, 6 rue Armand-de-Pontmartin. Place d'Horloge is the liveliest place to sip an early evening **drink**, though place des Corps-Saints (near the tourist office) comes a close second.

The festival

Avignon's summer festival is a great time to be in town. It's dominated by **theatre** and **film**, much of it taking place in the Palais des Papes and other interesting locations, while the streets are given over to the fringe. Around 250,000 spectators come here for the show, so doing any normal sightseeing becomes virtually impossible. The **festival headquarters** is at 8 rue de Mons (☎90.82.67.08), and, as well as providing programmes and information, shows videos and a collection of festival memorabilia dating back to its inception in 1947.

Arles

Just 25km or so south from Avignon, **ARLES** was one of the most important settlements of Gaul, providing grain for most of the western empire, as well as being a crucial port and shipbuilding centre – indeed, under Constantine it became the capital of Gaul, Britain and Spain. However, once the empire crumbled, so did Arles, with the result that the vestiges of its illustrious past have been well preserved, not least a marvellous amphitheatre.

Boulevard des Lices is the main street, along with rue Jean-Jaurès and its continuation, rue Hôtel-de-Ville. The most obvious place to start exploring is the central **place de la République**, between rue Jean-Jaurès and rue Hôtel-de-Ville, highlight of which is the **Cathédrale St-Trophime**, whose doorway is one of the most famous bits of twelfth-century Provençal carving, depicting a *Last Judgement* trumpeted by angels playing with the enthusiasm of jazz musicians. Inside, the d'Aubisson tapestries on the high nave have their lighter side – one shows mischievous dogs, a cat and a child in the scene of Mary Magdalene bathing Christ's feet – and there is more Romanesque and Gothic stone carving in the cloisters, above which there's a **Musée Necropole** displaying objects of everyday Roman life as well as coffins and urns. On the other side of the square, a deconsecrated seventeenth-century church holds the collection of the **Musée Lapidaire Paien** or pagan art (March–Oct daily 9am–12.30pm & 2–6/7pm; Nov–Feb daily 9am–noon & 2–4.30pm; F12), which has some wonderful mosaics alongside a bust of Augustus and a bas-relief from a first-century triumphal arch. Cut through the ground floor of the Hôtel de Ville on the north side of the square and turn left into rue Blaze, and there are yet more abducted stones in the **Musée Lapidaire Chrétien** (same times and price), which has a selection of sarcophagi. From a flight of stairs in the museum you can descend to the **Cryptoporticus**, a huge, dark and dank underground gallery built by the Romans as a granary. Immediately east of the cathedral, the **Théâtre-Antique** (Mar–Oct daily 9am–12.30pm & 2–6/7pm; Nov–Feb daily 9am–noon & 2–4.30pm; F12) is a fairly run-down structure, and you'd do better to stroll just beyond to the **Arènes** (same times; F17), the town's most impressive imperial structure, dating from the first century AD and originally with seating for 20,000 people. It was converted into a fortress in the eighth century, and three towers survive.

If you feel that life in Arles stopped with the Romans, you will be reassured by the **Musée Arlaten** (daily 9am–noon & 2–5/7pm; closed Mon in winter; F15) on rue de la République. Set up by Frédéric Mistral, the Nobel prize-winning local poet, its collections of costumes, documents, tools, pictures and paraphernalia of Provençal life are alternately tedious and intriguing. Another museum, the **Musée Réattu** (summer daily 9am–12.30pm & 2–7pm; winter daily 10am–12.30pm & 2–5pm; F12), opposite some Roman baths, returns you to the twentieth century, with a decent collection of modern paintings, not least a good array of work by Picasso, including sculpture and ink and crayon sketches he donated to the museum.

Practicalities

The **train station** is a few blocks north of the Arènes, close to the Porte de la Cavalerie. For **accommodation**, the *Lamartine* (☎90.96.13.83; ②) and *Regence* (☎90.96.39.85; ②), both on rue Marius Jouveau, are gloomy but adequate cheapies, as is the slightly more characterful *Le Rhône* on place Voltaire (☎90.96.43.70; ②). Perhaps the nicest choice is the *Gauguin*, also on place Voltaire (☎90.96.14.35; ②), which is comfortable, cheap and well-run. There's a **youth hostel** at 20 av Maréchal-Foch (☎90.96.18.25; ②) – take a bus from place Lamartine – and six **campsites** in the vicinity of Arles, of which the most pleasant is *La Bienheureuse*, with a restaurant, 7km out on N453 at Rapheles-lès-Arles; regular buses run there. The tourist office is opposite rue Jean-Jaurès on bd des Lices (summer Mon–Sat 9am–7/8pm & Sun 9am–1pm; winter Mon–Sat 9am–6pm), and provides a hotel booking service as well as a F44 ticket for all the monuments and museums; there's also an tourist office annexe at the gare SNCF. For a special treat, the place to **eat** is the *Hostellerie des Arènes*, 62 rue du Refuge; otherwise there are plenty of affordable brasseries on the main boulevards – try the *Van Gogh*, 28 rue Voltaire, which is good value, or *Le Tambourin*, 65 rue Amédée-Pichot, which serves fish and seafood in a pleasant atmosphere.

The Camargue

The flat, marshy delta area immediately south of Arles – the **Camargue** – is a unique area that is used as breeding-ground for the bulls used in corridas around here, along with the horses that their herdsmen ride. Neither they nor the bulls are wild, though they run in semi-liberty, and the true wildlife of the area is made up of flamingos, marsh and seabirds, and a rich flora of reeds, wild flowers and juniper trees.

If you're interested in bird-watching or walking around the lagoons, your first stop should be *La Capelière* **information centre** on the eastern side of the Étang du Vaccarès on the small road leading south off D37 from Villeneuve (Mon–Sat 9am–noon & 2–5pm). The imaginative **Musée Carmarguais**, halfway between Gimeaux and Albaron on D570, documents the traditions and livelihoods of the Camarguais people, and its main products – rice and salt (daily except Tues April–June & Sept 9am–6pm; July & Aug 9am–7pm; Oct–March 10am–5pm; F20). The town that most people head for in the Camargue is **SAINTES-MARIES-DE-LA-MER**, on the western edge, where every May 24 and 25 gypsies gather to celebrate their patron saint, Sarah, who came to an island close by after being driven out of Palestine. There's a procession from the church to the sea, carrying the statue of Sarah, with the *gardiens* in full Camargue cowboy dress accompanying them. If you're in the area, it's not to be missed.

The rest of the year Stes-Maries is a very commercialized town. However, there are miles of beaches and plenty of facilities, making it much the best resort close to Arles. The tourist office on av Van-Gogh has more details (daily 9am–1pm & 3–7pm). Of **hotels**, *Le Mediterranée*, 4 rue F-Mistral (☎90.97.82.09; ③), has some of the cheapest rooms in town, and the *Dauphin Bleu*, overlooking the sea at 31 av G-Leroy (☎90.97.80.21; ④), is pleasant too, and has a decent **restaurant**. There's a **youth hostel** at Pioch-Badet 10km along the Arles road, open March to November (☎90.97.91.72; ②). The closest **campsite** is *La Brise*, on the Vacharel road just outside the village. There's also cheap accommodation along the coast at the more down-to-earth town of Salin-de-Giraud, and you can sleep on the beach near there at the **plage de Piemançon**.

Aix-en-Provence

AIX would be the dominant city of central Provence were it not for the great metropolis of Marseille on the coast only 25km away. Aix is everything that Marseille is not, and if you take a liking to one of these cities, you are bound to hate the other. Aix, the capital of Provence from the twelfth century until the Revolution, is bourgeois, its riches based on landowning and the liberal professions. In its days as an independent fiefdom, its most mythically beloved ruler, King René of Anjou, held a brilliant court renowned for its patronage of the arts and popular festivities.

René introduced the muscat grape to the region and today he stands in stone in picture-book fashion, a bunch of grapes in his left hand, looking down the majestic seventeenth-century avenue, the **cours Mirabeau**. This is the central axis of the town, one side lined with cafés, the other with seventeenth- and eighteenth-century mansions with ornate wrought-iron balconies and Baroque decorations. **Vieil Aix** lies north of cours Mirabeau, centring on place Richelme, home to a regular market. The **Église de la Madeleine** on place des Pêcheurs, east of here, houses paintings by Van Loo, born in Aix in 1684, and Rubens. Rue Gaston-de-Saporta leads from **place de l'Hôtel-de-Ville** to the **Cathédrale St-Sauveur**, a conglomerate of fifth- to sixteenth-century building works and full of medieval art treasures, best of which is a painting commissioned by King René in 1475, *Le Buisson Ardent*. Just down from the cathedral, through place des Martyrs-de-la-Résistance, is the former **bishops' palace**, setting for part of the grandiose music festival each July and housing the **Musée des Tapisseries** (Wed–Mon 10am–noon & 2–5.45pm; F20), with a marvellous selection of both ancient and contemporary tapestries. The **Musée du Vieil Aix** at 17 rue Gaston-de-Saporta (Tues–Sun 10am–noon & 2.30–5/6pm; F10) is worth a look too. It has a set of religious marionettes, and a huge collection of Provençal crib figures.

South of the cours Mirabeau, on place St-Jean-de-Malte, the **Musée Granet** (daily except Tues 10am–noon & 2–6pm; F12) exhibits finds from the original settlement of Aix, a couple of kilometres north of the city, and a mixed bag of Italian, Dutch and

French paintings including a self-portrait by Rembrandt, a massive *Jupiter and Thetis* by Ingres, a portrait of the museum's patron by the same artist, and a wall dedicated to Paul Cézanne, who studied on the ground floor of the building, then an art school, and painted numerous studies of the Mont St-Victoire just east of town. Two of his student drawings are here as well as a handful of minor canvases such as *Bethsabée, Les Baigneuses* and *Portrait de Madame*. One of Cézanne's many studios in Aix is at what is now 9 av Paul-Cézanne, overlooking the city from the north – reachable on bus #1. The **atelier** (summer daily except Tues 10am–noon & 2–6pm; daily except Tues winter 10am–noon & 2.30–5pm; F10) is exactly as it was at the time of his death in 1906, with coat, hat, wineglass, easel and pipe, and a few letters and drawings. For a totally different experience, both visually and conceptually, you can escape to the **Vasarely Foundation** on av Marcel-Pagnol (9.30am–12.30pm & 2–5.30pm, closed Tues except July & Aug; F25) – bus #8 or #12 – itself a black-and-white Vasarely creation. There are innumerable sliding showcases, showing images related to all the themes of Vasarely's work, including his "plastic alphabet" and designs for apartment buildings, though downstairs the seven hexagonal spaces, each hung with six huge colour-wonder dimension-doubling designs, is where you'll get the immediate impact of this extraordinary man's work.

Practicalities

Aix's **train station** is on av Victor-Hugo, a #6 or #9 bus ride from the centre but easily walkable. The tourist office is at 2 place Général-de-Gaulle between av des Belges and av Victor-Hugo (mid-June to mid-Sept Mon–Sat 8am–10pm & Sun 8.30am–12.30pm; mid-Sept to mid-June Mon–Sat 8am–7pm). From mid-July to mid-August, festival time, your chances of finding an unbooked **hotel room** are pretty slim, and any time of year rates are high. The *Paul*, 10 av Pasteur (☎42.23.23.89; ③), and next door *Le Pasteur* (☎42.21.11.76; ②), are fairly comfortable. South of cours Mirabeau, there's *Des Quatre Dauphins*, 54 rue Roux-Alphéran (☎42.38.16.39; ④), and, on the western edge of town, *Vendôme* at 10 cours des Minimes (☎42.64.45.01; ②). There's a **youth hostel** at 3 av Marcel-Pagnol (☎42.20.15.99; ②) – bus #8 or #12 – with an 11pm curfew. *CROUS*, 38 av Jules-Ferry (☎42.26.33.75; ②) – bus #5 – sometimes has rooms on the university campus during July and August. The closest affordable **campsite**, *Le Félibrige*, is 5km from Aix off the N7 to Puyricard at La Calade, but it's a bother to get to (take the bus from cours Sextius). For **food**, place des Cardeurs is a good area to look – *Le Forum* at no. 20 has an excellent midday menu, as does *Le Montmartre*, 30 rue de la Verrerie. There are also some good ethnic restaurants: you can eat excellent Italian food at *Amalfi*, 5 rue d'Entrecasteaux, Egyptian at *Kéops*, 28 rue de la Verrerie, and Vietnamese at *Cay-Tam*, at no. 29.

The Grand Canyon du Verdon

Aix is the most obvious jumping-off point for the **Grand Canyon du Verdon**, 40km or so northeast, a two-kilometre-long gorge through limestone rock. You can see it by road if you have your own transport – a corniche sublime follows the canyon high to the south, while on the north side the route des Crêtes does the same, at some points looking down a sheer 800m to the sliver of water below. The entire circuit is 130km, and it's not easy cycling country. You can also discover the canyon in its depths, following the river from Rougon to Mayreste on the *Sentier Martel*; this takes two days and is not always possible, as it depends on what the French Electricity Board – who control the volume of water of the Verdon – are up to. It must be done in a group with a guide. You can do the half between Rougon and Les Malines on your own, though you should get details of the route and advice on weather conditions before you start, and take drinking water, a torch, and something to keep you warm in the cold shadows. Always stick to the path and don't cross the river.

Public transport is not brilliant. There's just one bus between Aix, La Palud and Castellane on Monday, Wednesday and Saturday from July to mid-September, the rest of the year just on Saturday; and one bus daily except Sunday between La Palud and Castellane in July and August. The best place to stay and to get information is **LA PALUD-SUR-VERDON**, on the north side of the canyon, from where the route des Crêtes loops out. The **youth hostel** has **camping** in its grounds, half a kilometre below the village (☎92.77.38.72; ②), and can help fix up guides, horses and canoes (the latter only for experts). The centre of life in La Palud is *Lou Cafetié's* bar-restaurant. There are a couple of other places to eat and a municipal **campsite** just west of the village. For **hotels** there's *Les Gorges du Verdon* (☎92.74.68.26; ④), below the youth hostel, and *L'Auberge des Crêtes* (☎92.77.38.47; ③), one kilometre east, though these tend to only be open between April and September. **CASTELLANE**, at the eastern end of the gorge, is also not short on **accommodation** – *Hostellerie du Roc*, place de l'Église (☎92.83.62.65; ③), and *Le Verdon*, bd de la République (☎92.83.62.02; ③), are good deals and there are at least sixteen **campsites**.

MARSEILLE AND THE CÔTE D'AZUR

The **Côte d'Azur** is the most built-up, overpopulated, over-eulogized, and expensive stretch of coast anywhere in the world. There are only two industries to speak of – tourism and building plus the related services of estate agents, yacht traffic wardens and Rolls-Royce valets. However, in every gap between the monstrous habitations, the remarkable beauty of the hills and coastline, the scent of the plant life, and the strange synthesis of the Mediterranean pollutants that make the water so translucent devastate the senses. The chance to see the works of innumerable artists seduced by the land and light also justifies the trip. The coast's eastern reaches are its most spectacular, the mountains breaking their fall just a few metres before levelling off to the shore. **St-Tropez** is an expensive high spot, though only **Nice** has real substance – a major city far enough away from Paris to preserve a distinctive character. At the opposite end of the coast, the squalid naval base of **Toulon** and vast, seedy sprawl of **Marseille** are quite different. There is no continuous corniche, few villas in the Grand Style, and work is geared to an annual rather than summer cycle. All the way along, the **months to avoid** are July and August, when the overflowing campsites become health hazards, all hotels are booked up, the people overworked and the vegetation at its most barren.

Marseille

The most populated city in France after Paris, **MARSEILLE** has, like the capital, prospered and been ransacked over the centuries. It has lost its privileges to French kings and foreign armies, refound its fortunes, suffered plagues, religious bigotry, republican and royalist terror and had its own Commune and Bastille storming. It was the presence of so many Marseillaise revolutionaries marching from the Rhine to Paris in 1792 that gave the name to the hymn that became the national anthem. Nowadays Marseille has every social, economic and political conflict of the country: it is a violent place and racism is rife, as is corruption and other lawlessness. Certainly it is not a glamorous city and you might not choose to live there. But it's a wonderful place to visit – a real port city with a trading history going back over two and half thousand years. It's as cosmopolitan as Paris with the advantages of being nearly 800km farther south, with more down-to-earth, informal and unstylish natives, and none of the tourist trappings of the rest of this coast.

Arrival and accommodation

Marseille's **airport**, de Marignane, is 25km northwest of the city, connected by bus every twenty minutes (F38) with the main train station, **gare St-Charles** – centrally situated on the northern edge of the 1er, around the corner from the **bus station** on place Victor-Hugo. The best way of **getting around** is to **walk**, although if you need to cover longer distances fast the **public transport** system – bus, tram and métro – is efficient enough. Tickets cost F8 each from métro stations and *RTM* kiosks. The main tourist office is at Canebière 4, down by the harbour (June–Aug daily 8am–8pm; Sept–May Mon–Sat 9am–7.15pm, Sun 10am–5pm), and offers a free **accommodation** booking service, although there are few budget **hotels**. Among cheaper places, the *Caravelle*, 5 rue Guy-Mocquet, 1er (☎91.48.44.99; ②), is friendly, quiet and close to the action; the *Edmond-Rostand*, 31 rue Dragon, 6e (☎91.37.74.95; ②), is further out but has great charm. Otherwise, the *Pilote*, 9 rue du Théâtre-Français, 1er (☎91.33.11.15; ②) is probably the best of a street full of cheapies. With more money to spend, *Le Corbusier* (☎91.77.18.15; ③), on the third floor of the architect's seminal tower block, Cité Radieuse, south of the city centre, is well worth the extra cash – bus #21 or #22. There are two official **youth hostels**: the *Bois Luzy*, 76 av de Bois-Luzy, 12^e(☎91.49.06.18; ②), is perhaps the most pleasant, housed in an old château and easy to reach on bus #8 from Centre Bourse, though it has an 11pm curfew; the other is the *Bonneveine*, 47 av J.-Vidal, impasse du Dr-Bonfils, 8e (☎91.73.21.81; ②) – bus #41, then bus #44 – which has no curfew and is near a beach. You can also **camp** at *Bois Luzy*, open March to October (get off two stops earlier), or more cheaply at *Les Vagues*, 52 av de Bonneveine, 8e, though this is fairly basic and only open June to September – métro Castellane, then bus #19.

The City

Marseille is divided into *arrondissements*, sixteen in all, which spiral out from the focal point of the city, the **Vieux Port** – a good place to indulge the sedentary pleasures of observing the city's streetlife, despite having no real claims to waterfront beauty. Two fortresses guard the entrance to the harbour, a little way south of which is the **Basilique St-Victor**, the city's oldest church, part of a monastery founded on the burial site of various third-century martyrs. It looks and feels like a fortress – the walls of the choir are almost 3m thick – and for a small fee you can visit the crypt and catacombs (Mon–Sat 10am–noon & 3–5pm, Sun 3–5pm), a warren of chapels and passages, where the atmosphere evokes the horrors of early Christianity. Saint Victor himself, a Roman soldier, was slowly ground to death between two millstones. On the other, northern side of the harbour is the former old town of Marseille, known as **Le Panier**, a densely populated area that was dynamited by the Nazis, who deported around 20,000 people from here during the entire course of the war. Nowadays it's a mainly Algerian quarter, especially over towards the train station, but it's an area that's fast being gentrified. One of the buildings that managed to survive the wartime devastation, the Maison Diamantée on rue de la Prison, now houses the **Musée de Vieux Marseille** on rue de la Prison (daily 11am–6pm; F10), which contains a hodge-podge of mementoes of old Marseille – a modelled street scene of nineteenth-century insurrectional fighting, recipes for plague antidotes, as well as pre-1943 photographs of the area. After the war, archeologists reaped the benefits of the destruction by finding remains of the Roman docks equipped with vast storage jars for food stuffs, which can be seen in situ at the **Musée des Docks Romains** on place Vivaux (daily 10am–5pm; F10). From rue Caisserie stepped passages lead up to another surviving old building, the **Hospice de la Vieille Charité** (daily 10am–6pm; F15), a seventeenth-century workhouse with a gorgeous Baroque chapel surrounded by columned arcades in pink stone. It's now a cultural centre, and hosts the city's main, rather dull archeological museum.

Down below Le Panier, **La Canebière** is the city's main street, and one which more or less separates Arab Marseille from the rest. Just north, on busy cours Belsunce, the **Centre Bourse** is a fiendish giant mall, useful for mainstream shopping and home to a museum of finds from Roman Marseille, the **Musée d'Histoire de Marseille** (Mon–Sat noon–7pm; F10), including a third-century wreck of a Roman trading vessel. At the far eastern end, the **Palais de Longchamp** (bus #80 or #41) was the grandiose conclusion of an aqueduct bringing water from the Durance to the city. Water is still pumped into the middle of the central colonnade of the building, whose north wing houses the city's **Musée des Beaux-Arts** (daily 10am–5pm; F10), a stuffy museum but with a fair share of goodies, most notably three beautiful paintings by Françoise Duparc and a room of political cartoons by the nineteenth-century Marseille satirist, Honoré Daumier, along with a famous profile of Louis XIV by Pierre Puget.

South of La Canebière are Marseille's main shopping streets, rue Paradis, rue St-Ferréol and rue de Rome, and its principal collection of twentieth-century and contemporary art, the **Musée Cantini**, 19 rue Grignan (Mon–Fri 10am–5pm, Sat & Sun noon–7pm; F15), with works by artists as diverse as Dufy, Léger, Bacon and Vasarely.

The only other thing to see while in Marseille is the **Château d'If**, the evil island fortress that figured in Dumas' great adventure story, the *Count of Monte Cristo*. No one ever escaped from here; most prisoners, incarcerated for political or religious reasons, went insane or died (usually both) before reaching the end of their sentences. The rich and blue-blooded tended to survive, having the less-fetid upper cells – inmates included Mirabeau, in for debt, and one de Niozelles who was given six years for failing to take his hat off in the presence of Louis XIV. Boats leave for the island roughly every hour, on the hour, from the quai des Belges. The journey takes twenty minutes and costs F40.

Eating, drinking and nightlife

Even the takeaway **food** is excellent in Marseille. The main boulevards, and particularly cours Belsunce, are a source of wonderful filled baguettes, and the morning **markets** – at place Sébastopol near the Palais Longchamp and place Jean-Jaurès – sell mouthwatering edibles every day except Sunday. Among **restaurants** in the old town, *Chez Angèle*, 50 rue Caisserie, has a good *menu fixe* of standard French fare, and a branch of the international vegetarian restaurant *Country Life* at 14 rue Venture, 1er, which opens Monday to Friday lunchtimes for as-much-as-you-can-eat buffets for F52. Otherwise, the best low-priced meals can be found around cours Julien and place Jean-Jaurès, where you can sample various ethnic cuisines. *Ce Cher Arwell*, 96 cours Julien, is a popular place, serving good French food in generous portions; *Saf Saf*, on rue V-Sotto, is a cheap, noisy Tunisian just off La Canebière. *Le Balthazar*, 8 rue des Trois Rois, is an intimate French restaurant with a reasonable *menu fixe*.

As for **nightlife**, the clubs around cours d'Estienne-d'Orves are for trendy kids from the upper-crust *arrondissements*, with prices to match. If you're determined to bop, *Le Seventies*, 7 rue Venture, off rue Paradis, is as good a place as any. Café-théâtre alternates with country music, rock'n'roll and R&B at *La Maison Hantée*, 10 rue Vian, while *May Be Blues*, on rue Poggioli, is a relaxed blues/jazz club, with free entry. *Le Stendhal*, 92 rue Jean-de-Bernady, is a bar with live music and a good stock of whiskies and beers. *FNAC* in the Centre Bourse or the *Virgin Megastore* (see below) are the best places to find out **what's on**, and they also sell tickets. Otherwise, check the listings of the left-wing daily, *La Marseillaise*, or pick up a copy of the free weekly *Marseille Poche*.

Listings

Airlines *Air France*, 14 La Canebière, 1er (☎91.54.92.92); *British Airways*, in the airport building (toll-free number only ☎05.12.51.25).

Beaches Best of the local beaches is the heavily landscaped plage du Prado, at the end of the Corniche du Président J. F. Kennedy – bus #83 from the Vieux Port.

Books The *Virgin Megastore*, 75 rue St-Ferréol, stocks English books.

Consulates *Canada*, 24 av du Prado, 6e (☎91.37.19.37); *Great Britain*, 24 av du Prado, 6e (☎91.53.43.32); *Ireland*, 148 rue Sainte, 1er (☎91.54.92.29); *USA*, 9 rue Armény, 6e (☎91.54.92.00).

Exchange *Thomas Cook* at gare St-Charles (Mon–Fri 6am–8pm, Sat & Sun 6am–6pm).

Hospital Hôtel-Dieu, 6 place Daviel, Le Panier, 2e, ☎91.90.61.14.

Laundry *Washmatic*, 77 rue d'Aubagne, 1er.

Pharmacy Gare St-Charles (Mon–Fri 7am–10pm, Sat 7am–8pm).

Post office Main office at 1 place de l'Hôtel-des-Postes (Mon–Fri 8am–7pm, Sat 8am–noon).

Travel agents *Nouvelle Frontières*, 11 rue Haxo, 1er (☎91.54.18.48).

Toulon

Home base to the French Mediterranean fleet and its arsenal, and until recently a major shipbuilding centre, the port of **TOULON** was half destroyed in World War II and doesn't offer much joy today. But since it is a major nexus you may well find yourself there, and it does have the advantage of being comparatively cheap for this coast. The old town, much besieged by bulldozers and planners intent on its gentrification, crams in between the main bd de Strasbourg and quai de Stalingrad, a pleasant enough place by day, though less appealing at night, especially towards the port. The **Musée d'Art** at 113 bd Maréchal-Leclerc (daily 10am–noon & 2–6pm; free) has a good collection of paintings and sculpture including work by Bruegel, Carracci, Vlaminck, Rodin and Francis Bacon. The most impressive public artwork in the city is Pierre Puget's **Atlantes**, which hold up what's left of the old town hall on quai de Stalingrad. It's thought that Puget, working in 1657, modelled these immensely strong figures on galley slaves sent here for sentences of hard labour during the nineteenth century. The best way to pass an afternoon in Toulon is to take bus #40 to bd Amiral Vence, Super Toulon, and jump on the **funicular** (Mon 2–6.30pm, Tues–Sun 9am–noon & 2–6.30pm; F30 return) to the summit of **Mont Faro**, 542m above. At the top there's a memorial **museum** to the Allied landings in Provence of August 1944 (daily 9.30–11.30am & 2.30–5.30pm; F20), with screenings of film footage.

The **train station** is on place Albert 1er. Turn left out of the station and follow bd de Tessé three blocks to the tourist office (Mon–Sat 8am–6.30pm), from which bd de Strasbourg leads down to the old town. One of the cheapest and nicest **hotels** is *Les Trois Dauphins* at 9 place des Trois Dauphins (☎94.92.65.79; ②). Close by, the *Little Palace*, 6 rue Berthelot (☎94.92.26.62; ②), is also a bargain and pleasant. *Prémar*, 19 place Monsenergue (☎94.92.27.42; ②), is on the dockside, a bit seedy but dead cheap. The **youth hostel**, open July and August only, is on rue Ernst-Renan, Quartier Mourillon (☎94.24.34.96; ②) – bus #3 from av Leclerc.

Hyères and the Îles d'Or

Walled and medieval, old **HYÈRES**, a few kilometres east of Toulon, lost out on snob appeal when the Côte clientele switched from winter convalescents to dockside strutters. Consequently it's very appealing, with a pleasant old town surrounded by strawberry fields, vines and peach orchards rather than tourist hotels. The only blight is a French air force base just north of the main port, from which test pilots play with the latest multi-million-franc exports.

The **train station** is about 1km southwest of the centre at the end of av Edith-Cavell, with frequent buses to the **bus station** on place Clemenceau, from where a medieval gatehouse opens onto rue Massillon and the old centre. For **hotels**, there's *Les Orangers* in the modern centre at 64 av des Îles-d'Or (☎94.65.07.01; ③), very comfortable and reasonably priced; the *du Portalet* on the edge of the old town at 4 rue de

Limans (94.65.39.40; ②)); or alternatively, *Le Calypso* by the sea on av de la Méditerranée (☎94.58.02.09; ③) in Hyères-Plage, some 5km from the town. There's no youth hostel in the area, but plenty of **campsites** on the coast, notably in Les Salins, due east of Hyères. The **tourist office** is on the rotunda off av de Belgique, two blocks south of place Clemenceau. For **eating and drinking** there are terraced cafés and a morning market in the spacious square at the top of rue Massillon, and in the streets below there are also several restaurants. *Les Templiers*, 2 des Écuries, has a huge choice of meat and fish dishes, and pizzas; *La Bergerie*, 16 rue de Limans, serves a marvellous range of Breton *galettes* and crêpes.

Perhaps the nicest thing to do while you're in Hyères is make a trip down to the peculiar **Presqu'île de Giens**, leashed to the mainland by a narrow isthmus, and out to the **Îles d'Or** just offshore. The largest and most accessible is **Porquerolles**, reachable by regular ferry from La Tour Fondue (bus #66) on the southeast tip of the peninsula – a twenty-minute trip. There are sandy beaches either side of the main village, much less crowded than any on the mainland, and the southern shore has some wanderable cliff paths and typically luxuriant Provençal vegetation.

St-Tropez

ST-TROPEZ is no more than a village really, gathered around a port founded by the ancient Greeks, which until recently was only easily accessible by boat. In the late nineteenth century, it became a favoured haunt of artists; later, in 1956, Roger Vadim arrived to film Brigitte Bardot in *Et Dieu Créa La Femme*, and the place has never looked back. Bardot still owns a house here, as do Elton John and Mick Jagger, although the yachts are owned more often by Manhattan banks these days. If you can save your visit for a rainy winter's day, you'll be able to separate the myth from the hype, and probably find a room and a place to eat too.

The road into St-Tropez splits in two as it enters the village, with the bus station between them and, a short distance beyond on rue de la Nouvelle-Poste, the **Musée de l'Annonciade** (June–Sept daily except Tues 10am–noon & 4–8pm; Oct–May daily except Tues 1Cam–noon & 4–6pm; F30) – a reason in itself for coming here, with works by Matisse and most of the other artists who worked here. Beyond the museum, the **Vieux Port** is the centre of the town, the dockside café clientele face to face with the yacht-deck martini-sippers, the latest fashions parading in between. Up from here, at the end of quai Jean-Jaurès, rue de la Mairie passes the town hall, with a street to the left leading down to the rocky Baie de la Glaye, and, along rue de la Ponche, the fishing port with a tiny **beach**. Both these spots are miraculously free from commercialization. Beyond the fishing port, roads lead up to the sixteenth-century **Citadelle**. Its maritime museum isn't much fun, but there are marvellous views from the ramparts.

The only vaguely affordable **hotel** is *Les Chimères*, Quartier du Pilon (☎94.97.02.90; ③), a short way back from the bus station towards La Foux, though it's likely to be booked for the summer, and you might be better off in St-Maxime, the next resort along, where the *Sarrasine* hotel/restaurant (☎94.43.67.16; ②) is pleasant and cheap. **Camping** poses similar problems. The two sites on the plage du Pampelonne are closest to St-Tropez but cost a fortune. Better is *Les Tournels* on route de Camarat, near Ramatuelle. The **tourist office**, on quai Jean-Jaurès, can help with reservations (April to mid-June daily 9am–7pm; mid-June–Sept daily 9am–8pm; Oct–March daily except Sun 9am–12.30pm & 2–6.30pm). For **eating**, *La Patate* on rue G-Clemenceau has omelettes, pasta and so forth – nothing special but it may save you from starvation. If you're prepared to go over F100, there's still no great choice, but *Lou Revelen*, near the fishing port at 4 rue des Remparts, will serve a decent meal without treating you like poor tourist scum.

St-Raphael and Fréjus

There's a better choice of accommodation in **ST-RAPHAEL**, further north, and in the adjacent town of **FRÉJUS**, 3km inland. Both were established by the Romans and various remnants of this past lie scattered around the towns, including, in Fréjus, an **amphitheatre** on rue Henri-Vardon, used in its damaged state for bullfights and rock concerts, and a **theatre** on av du XV-Corps-d'Armées. Fréjus' **Cathedral**, on place Formige, has superb twelfth-century Romanesque cloisters and a late medieval fantasy ceiling, as well as a **museum** with a complete Roman mosaic of a leopard (tours daily except Tues 9.30am–noon & 2–6pm).

St-Raphael has the better choice of **hotels**. Try *Hôtel des Templiers* on place de la République (☎94.95.38.93; ②) or the *Bellevue*, 22 bd Felix-Martin (☎94.95.00.35; ③). The tourist office is on place de la Gare, along with the **train station** and **bus station**. Between here and the seafront you'll have no trouble finding **restaurants**. Try *Les Fines Gueules*, 12 rue de la République, which does cheap *plats du jour* and a great fish paella. In Fréjus, *Le Flore*, 35 rue Grisolle (☎94.51.38.35; ③), is a cheap hotel, and there's a **youth hostel** on the route de Cannes (☎94.52.18.75; ②) – bus from Fréjus or St-Raphael station to rue Grisole, then a 1km walk. **Campsites** are ubiquitous, with at least four on the Bagnols road and one close to the youth hostel. For somewhere to eat, *Les Potiers* at 135 rue des Potiers has good seasonal menus for under F100.

Cannes

Fishing village turned millionaires' residence, **CANNES** is perhaps the most unpleasant town along the Côte d'Azur, with a fine sand beach that looks like an industrial production line for parasols. The seafront promenade, **La Croisette**, and the **Vieux Port** form the focus of Cannes life. The old town, **Le Suquet**, on the steep hill overlooking the bay from the west, masks its miserable passageways with quaint cosmetic streets; beyond Le Suquet there's another **beach**, with a better chance of not having to pay for your sand.

If you're compelled to **stay** in Cannes, the best concentration of hotels is in the centre, between the **train station** on rue Jean-Jaurès and La Croisette, around the main street of rue Antibes/Felix-Fauré. Possibilities include the unappealing *Bourgogne*, 13 rue de 24 août (☎93.38.36.73; ②), the rather nicer *Azur*, 15 rue Jean-de-Riouffe (☎93.39.52.14; ③), the adequate *National*, 8 rue Mal Joffre (☎93.39.91.92; ②), and the *Chanteclair*, 12 rue Forville (☎93.39.68.88; ③) – the last close to the old town. The nearest **campsite** is *La Grande Saule*, 24–26 bd de la Frayère, 4km west of town (bus from the Hôtel de Ville), though it's pretty exorbitant. If you're stuck, there's a **tourist office** at the train station (July & Aug daily 8am–midnight; Sept–June Mon–Fri 9am–12.30pm & 2–6.30pm) and in the Palais des Festivals on the waterfront (Mon–Sat 9am–6.30pm). Le Suquet is full of **restaurants**, which get cheaper as you reach the top. *Au Bec Fin*, at 12 rue du 24 août, has superb traditional cooking and good *plats du jour*; *La Croisette*, at 15 rue du Commandant-André, serves excellent grilled fish; and *Le Bouchon d'Objectif*, 10 rue de Constantine, is a fabulous, reasonably-priced local bistro.

Vallauris, Antibes and Biot

Just east of Cannes, **VALLAURIS**, reached by hourly bus, was home to Picasso for a while, and where he was inspired by the local craft of ceramics. The main street, av George-Clemenceau, sells nothing but pottery, much of it the garishly glazed bowls and figurines that could feature in souvenir shops anywhere; the **Madoura** pottery, where Picasso worked, is off rue 19 mars 1962, and has the sole rights on reproducing his designs. At the top of the main street, Picasso's bronze *Man with a Sheep* stands in the marketplace right opposite the **castle** courtyard, where an early medieval chapel (daily except Tues 10am–noon & 2–5/6pm; F8) was painted by the artist as *La Guerre et la Paix* in 1952 – an initially slapdash-looking work, though its pacifism is unambiguous.

A few kilometres on lies **ANTIBES**, to which Picasso returned after the war and worked in a studio that has since been converted to a museum. Picasso left much of his output while here to what is now the **Musée Picasso** (summer daily except Tues 10am–noon & 3–7pm; winter daily except Tues 10am–noon & 2–6pm; closed Nov to mid-Dec; F20); it displays numerous ceramics, still lifes of sea urchins, the wonderful *Ulysses et ses Sirènes*, and a whole room full of drawings, as well as works by contemporaries, among them Léger's tapestry of construction workers. You can see more of Léger's work beyond Antibes in the village of **BIOT**, accessible by bus, which was the home of the artist for a few years at the end of his life; the **Musée Fernand Léger** is just southeast of the village (summer daily except Tues 10am–noon & 2–6pm, winter daily except Tues 10am–noon & 2–5pm; F15).

Cagnes and Vence

A little further on from Biot, **CAGNES-SUR-MER** lies a little way inland but is walkable from the Cannes–Nice bus stop, and was home to Renoir for the last eleven years of his life. His house – *Les Collettes* – is a **museum** these days (daily except Tues June to mid-Oct 10am–noon & 2–6pm; mid-Oct–May 10am–noon & 2–5pm; F20), and his studio, north-facing to catch the late afternoon light, is arranged as if he had just popped out. The museum also displays works by Renoir's friends – Dufy, Maillol, Bonnard – and two of the artist's own bronzes, *La Maternité* and a medallion of his son Coco.

On the other side of the town, to the north, is the ancient village of **HAUT-DE-CAGNES**, where the crenellated **château** (daily except Tues July–Sept 10am–noon & 2.30–7pm; mid-Nov–June 10am–noon & 2–5pm; F5) houses a number of museums covering local history, fishing, the cultivation of olives and the **Musée d'Art Moderne Méditerranéen**. This contains changing exhibitions of the painters who have worked on the coast in the last hundred years, and the *Donation Suzy Solidor* – wonderfully diverse portraits of the cabaret star from the 1920s to the 1960s by several great painters.

The next artistic treat, and one of the best in the region, is the **Fondation Maeght** in **ST-PAUL-DE-VENCE**, reachable by taking the Nice–Vence bus from place de Gaulle in Cagnes-sur-Mer (daily July–Sept 10am–7pm; Oct–June 10am–12.30pm & 2.30–6pm; F35). It's a wonderful collection of the early works of Miró, Léger, Chagall and their contemporaries, as well as an outdoor sculpture garden featuring Giacometti at his best. **VENCE**, a few kilometres north, is the site of the **Chapelle du Rosaire** (Tues & Thurs 10–11.30am & 2.30–5.30pm; closed mid-Nov to Dec; free), built between 1949 and 1951 under the direction of Matisse, who painted the black outline figures on plain matt tiles with a brush fixed to a six-foot bamboo pole specifically to remove his own signature from the lines. Colour comes from the light diffused through green, blue and yellow windows. It was his last work, and for some is a magical creation; for others it's a grating disappointment.

Vence is a lot more affordable than St-Paul. *La Closerie des Genets*, 4 impasse Maurel (☎93.58.33.25; ③), is a reasonably priced **hotel**, and, in addition, there's a **campsite** about 3km west on the road to Tourettes-sur-Loup. For a special **meal**, try *La Fariguoule*, 15 av Henri-Isnard, or, on the same street but for half the price, *La Vieille Douve*.

Nice

NICE, the capital of the Riviera and fifth largest town in France, should be a loathsome place. It's twinned with Cape Town, South Africa, and has been run for decades by a corrupt right-wing clique. A large portion of the population are either pensioners or fat-cat businesspeople living off extortionate rents or inflated expense accounts, and it can't even boast a sandy beach. And yet it is delightful, the sun, sea and affable Niçois compensating for a multitude of sins. The city also makes the best base for visiting the 30km of the Riviera coast to the border, and west as far as Cannes.

Arrival and accommodation

The main **train station** (Nice Ville) is a relatively short step from the centre, a couple of blocks left of the top of av Jean-Médecin. The main tourist office is by the station on av Thiers (July–Sept Mon–Sat 8.45am–7pm, Sun 8.45am–12.30pm & 2–6pm; Oct–June Mon–Sat 8.45am–12.30pm & 2–6pm) and offers a good accommodation service for a small fee; it also has maps and copies of the useful weekly *7 Jours, 7 Nuits*. For **getting around the city**, you can buy a one-day or seven-day bus pass, or a *carnet* of ten tickets (reductions with *ISIC*) from *TN*, 10 av Félix-Fauré. *Carnets* can also be bought at kiosks and *tabacs*, and single tickets on the bus. The *TN* office has free bus maps.

There are lots of affordable **hotels** around the train station, including *Les Orangers*, 10bis av Durante (☎93.87.51.41; ③), popular with American students, and the light and spacious *d'Orsay*, 18 rue Alsace-Lorraine (☎93.88.45.02; ②). In the old town, you might try the well-placed but slightly dingy *Saint-François*, 3 rue St-François (☎93.85.88.69; ②). In the modern town, east of av Jean-Médecin, there's the small *Centre*, 2 rue de Suisse (☎93.88.83.85; ③). The **youth hostel** is 4km out of town on route Forestière du Mont Alban (☎93.89.23.64; ②) – take bus #14 from place Masséna. Slightly cheaper but further out, and with a 10.30pm curfew, is *Clairvallon Relais International de la Jeunesse* – north of Cimiez at 26 av Scudéri (☎93.81.27.63; ②); take bus #15 or #15A. The *Résidence Les Collinettes* is closer to the centre at 3 av R-Schuman (☎93.37.24.30; ②), though it's only open in July and August and then only for women; bus #17 from the station or #14 from the centre. Another possibility close by on the south side of the urban highway is the *MJC Magnan*, 31 rue Louis-de-Coppet (☎93.86.28.75; ②), open between June and mid-September – bus #3, #9 or #10. If you're lucky, there may be space in one of the several low-budget operations housed in the four-storey building at 22 rue Pertinax, very close to the station off av Jean-Médecin. The only **campsite** near Nice is the tiny *Camping Terry* on route de Grenoble, 6km north of the airport and not on any bus route. In summer you'll find lots of people camping on the beach – the only stretch where it's tolerated on the whole Côte.

The City

It doesn't take long to get a feel for the layout of Nice. The old town groups about the hill of Nice's former château, a previously rough but now fast-gentrifying pocket of narrow crammed streets centring on place Rosetti and the Baroque **Cathédrale St-Réparate**. Nearby is the entrance to the **parc du Château** (also reachable by lift from the eastern end of rue des Ponchettes), decked out in a mock-Grecian style harking back to the original Greek settlement of Nikea. The point of the climb, apart from the perfumed greenery, is the view stretching west and over the muddle of the old town's rooftops. The limits of the old town are marked by bd Jean-Jaurès, on which the **Musée d'Art Modern et d'Art Contemporain** (Wed–Mon 11am–6pm; free) holds a collection of Pop Art and neo-Realist work, including pieces by Andy Warhol and Roy Lichtenstein. Beyond here, place Masséna, and the spine of the centre, av Jean-Médecin, represent the commercial heart of Nice, while, a short walk south, the

promenade des Anglais was laid out by nineteenth-century English residents for their afternoon sea breeze stroll. On the far side of the centre, the **Musée des Beaux-Arts** at 33 av des Baumettes (Tues–Sun May–Sept 10am–noon & 3–6pm; Oct–April 10am–noon & 2–5pm; free), reached on bus #38, has too many whimsical canvases by Jules Chéret, who died in Nice in 1932, and far too much of G.A. Mossa, a recently deceased Nice establishment figure, whose lurid Symbolist paintings reek of misogyny. However, there are unexpected delights – a Rodin bust of Victor Hugo, a room full of works by Dufy and some very amusing van Dongens.

Up above the city centre, **Cimiez**, a posh suburb reached by bus #15 from place Masséna, was the social centre of the town's elite some seventeen centuries ago, when the city was capital of the Roman province of Alps-Maritimae. Excavations of the Roman baths are housed, along with accompanying archeological finds, in the **Musée d'Archéologie**, 160 av des Arènes (May–Sept Tues–Sat 10am–noon & 2–6pm, Sun 2–6pm; Oct–April Tues–Sat 10am–noon & 2–5pm, Sun 2–5pm; F20). Overlooking the baths, the **Musée Matisse** is home to a collection of work by the painter, who spent most of his life in Nice. The collection covers every period and includes models for the chapel in Vence and a nearly complete set of the bronze sculptures. Among the paintings are a 1905 portrait of Madame Matisse, a *Tempest in Nice*, and the 1947 *Still Life with Pomegranates*. At the foot of the hill, just off bd Cimiez on av du Docteur-Menard, there is more modern art in **Chagall's Biblical Message**, housed in a purpose-built museum opened by the artist in 1972 (July–Sept daily except Tues 10am–7pm; Oct–June daily except Tues 10am–12.30pm & 2–5.30pm; F26). The seventeen paintings are all based on the Old Testament and complemented with etchings and engravings, all perfectly set off by the light – Chagall himself contributed the stained-glass windows.

Eating, drinking and nightlife

The old town stays up the latest and is full of **restaurants**. *Café de Turin*, on place Garibaldi, is a good, basic place for mussels and clams, while *Pompeii*, 14 rue de l'Abbaye, is a decent Italian restaurant. *Le Tramway*, 11 rue Lamartine, is a good central, if pricy-ish option. Vegetarians could try *Le Moulin à Fromage*, 5 rue de Moulin, which has meat-free options on its *menu fixe*. For later carousing, *Les 3 Diables*, on cours Salaya, is a smoky, posey dive with loud music; *Scarlett O'Hara*, 22 rue Droite, is an Irish place serving decent Guinness.

Monaco

Monstrosities are common on the Côte d'Azur, but nowhere, not even Cannes, can outdo **MONACO**. This tiny independent principality has lived off gambling and class for a century and is one of the greatest property speculation sites in the world. Finding out about the workings of the regime is not easy, but it is clear that Prince Rainier is the one autocratic ruler left in Europe. A copy of every French law is sent to Monaco, reworded, and put to the prince. If he likes the law it is passed, if not, it's not. There is a parliament of limited function elected by Monagesque nationals – about sixteen per cent of the population – and no opposition to the ruling family. What the citizens and residents like so much is that they pay no income tax.

The three-kilometre-long state consists of the old town of **Monaco-Ville** around the palace on a high promontory; the new suburb and marina of **Fontvieille** in its western shadow; **La Condamine** behind the harbour on the other side of the rock; **Larvotto**, the swimming resort with artificial beaches of imported sand to the east; and **Monte Carlo** in the middle. There's little in the way of conventional sights, only the toy-town palace and assorted museums in the glacé-icing old town, where every other shop sells Prince Rainier mugs and other junk. The only real must is the **Casino**, where the

American Room is a riot of Rococo and the European Gaming Rooms have an atmosphere that's almost cathedral-like. You have to pay to get in (around F50) and you must look like a gambler, not a tourist; entrance is restricted to those over 21 and you may have to show your passport. You might also want to visit the aquarium in the basement of the **Musée Océanographique** (daily July & Aug 9am–9pm; Sept–June 9.30am–7pm; bus #1 or #2), where the fishy beings outdo the weirdest Kandinsky or Bosch creations. Less exceptional but still peculiar cacti equivalents can be viewed in the **Jardin Exotique**, high above Fontvielle (daily 9am–6/7pm).

The **train station** is on place d'Armes in La Condamine. Bus #4 takes you from the station to the Casino-Tourism stop, with the **tourist office** at 2a bd des Moulins (Mon–Sat 9am–7pm, Sun 10am–noon). If you must stay more than a day here, La Condamine is best for **hotels** – although they're expensive. You could try *Cosmopolite*, 4 rue de la Turbie (☎93.30.16.95; ③), or its neighbour *Hôtel de France* (☎93.30.24.64; ⑤). If you arrive early enough you may be able to get a dorm bed at the *Centre de Jeunesse Princesse Stéphanie*, near the station on av Prince-Pierre (☎93.50.75.05; ②). The one good free public service is the lifts, clean and efficient for north–south journeys. La Condamine and the old town are the places to look for **restaurants**, but good food and reasonable prices don't exactly match. You should be able to fill up on pizza at *Bacchus*, 13 rue de la Turbie. In Monte Carlo, try *Ramon*, 2 rue du Portier.

Menton

MENTON, the easternmost town on the French coast, is even more of a rich retirement haven than Nice, with no trace now of its revolutionary 1848 days when, with Roquebrune, it broke away from Monaco to become an independent republic before Paris sucked it in twelve years later. The pride and joy of the town is its lemon crop, which it celebrates in a citrus fruit extravaganza every February, although its real speciality is weddings. Menton is traditionally the place to come to get a French marriage certificate, and the Salles des Mariages in the **Hôtel de Ville** on the central place Ardoiono was decorated in appropriate style by Jean Cocteau (Mon–Fri 8.30am–12.30pm & 1.30–5pm; F5). On the right-hand wall a Saracen wedding party reveals a disapproving bride's mother, the spurned girlfriend of the groom and her armed revengeful brother among the cheerful guests. On the left-hand wall is the story of Orpheus and Eurydice, and on the ceiling Poetry rides Pegasus, tattered Science juggles with the planets, and Love waits with bow and arrow at the ready. There are other Cocteau works in the **museum** he set up himself in the brick bastion by quai Napoléon III, south of the old port (daily except Tues mid-June to mid-Sept 10am–noon & 3–7pm; mid-Sept to mid-June 10am–noon & 2–6pm; free); it contains more Mentonaise lovers in the *Inamorati* series, a collection of delightful *Animaux Fantastiques* and a powerful tapestry of *Judith and Holofernes*. There are also photographs, poems, a portrait by his friend Picasso and ceramics.

The **train station** is on bd Albert I, from which a short walk to the left as you come out brings you to the north–south avenues de Verdun and Boyer, divided by the Jardins Biovès. The **tourist office** is at 8 av Boyer in the Palais de l'Europe (mid-June to Aug daily 8am–8pm; Aug to mid-June daily 8.30am–noon & 2–6.30pm). The cheapest **hotel** is the *Mondial*, 12 rue Partouneaux (☎93.28.30.30; ④), or there's a **youth hostel** on Plateau St-Michel (☎93.35.93.14; ②) and a **campsite** – take bus #6 from the bus station on Esplanade de Carei, north of the rail line, or walk up a gruelling flight of steps behind the station. As you might expect, **food** doesn't come cheap. *Chez Gemaine*, 46 promenade Maréchal-Leclerc, is a gourmet fish option, while *Chez Maurice*, 17 promenade de la Mer, serves homely dishes on a balcony overlooking the sea.

CORSICA

Despite two hundred years of French rule, **Corsica** has more in common culturally with Italy than with its governing country, as testified by a profusion of Italianate churches and a language that's closely related to the Tuscan dialect. A history of repeated invasion has strengthened the cultural identity of an island whose reputation for violence and xenophobia has overshadowed the more hospitable nature of its inhabitants. Such hospitality doesn't extend to foreign property developers, however, who have been effectively kept at bay by the bombs of the burgeoning nationalist movement. This is one island that is not going to go the way of the Balearics.

Corsica, much of which is National Park, comprises an amazing diversity of landscapes: its magnificent rocky coastline is interspersed with outstanding beaches, while the inland mountains offer numerous opportunities for hiking. The extensive forests and sparkling rivers provide the islanders with a rich supply of game and fresh fish – regional specialities include wild boar, blackbird paté, cured hams and sausages.

Two French *départements* divide Corsica, each with its own capital: Napoleon's birthplace, **Ajaccio**, is a sunny elegant town on the southwest coast, while **Bastia** faces Italy in the north. At the island's core, the old capital of **Corte** is one of many fortress villages which characterize the interior. The coastal resorts are equally superbly sited: **Calvi** draws in the tourists with its massive citadel and long sandy beach, and strung out at the southernmost point lies **Bonifacio**, perched on limestone cliffs that are buffeted by the clearest water in the Mediterranean. Ajaccio, Bastia, Corte and Calvi are connected by a slender **train** service; for Bonifacio you're reliant on **buses**.

Ajaccio

Set in a magnificent bay, **AJACCIO** combines all the ingredients of the archetypal Mediterranean resort with its palm trees, spacious squares, yachts and street cafés. There may not be a great deal to see here, but as the most cosmopolitan of Corsican towns Ajaccio is a pleasant place to spend some time. The town developed around a fifteenth-century Genoese citadel and although the present castle is owned by the military and has been often restored, the streets around remain appealingly ancient. Napoléon, who was born here in 1794, gave the town fame but did little else for the place except to make it capital of Corsica for the brief period of his empire. You can visit his family house, now a museum, and you'll find the town peppered with statues and streets named after the Bonaparte family.

Arrival and accommodation

Flying into Ajaccio you'll land at Campo dell'Oro **airport**, 6km southeast of town; a bus shuttle service coincides with the flights. **Ferries** (see box below) come into the port at the town centre, but if you arrive by train from one of the other major towns you'll find yourself with about a ten-minute walk along the seafront. The **tourist office** (May–Oct Mon–Fri 9am–noon & 2–6pm, Sat 9am–noon) occupies the ground floor of the Hôtel de Ville in place Maréchal-Foch, directly opposite the port.

Cheap **accommodation** is pretty thin on the ground in Ajaccio, yet there are a few good addresses in the town centre. *Hotel Kalliste* at 41 cours Napoléon (✇95.51.34.45; ②) does a good deal whereby you can rent studios for one night, but the cheapest hotel is *Colomba* at 8 av de Paris (✇95.21.12.66; ②). Near the port there's *Le Dauphin*, 11 bd Sampiero (✇95.21.12.94; ④), and *la Pergola*, 25 av Colonna D'Ornanoé off cours Napoléon (✇95.23.36.44; ⑤). Otherwise either *Hotel Bonaparte*, 1/2 rue Étienne-Conti (✇95.21.44.19; ③), or the *Marengo*, 34 av Madame Mère (✇95.21.43.66; ⑤), are average places.

FERRIES TO CORSICA

To Ajaccio from Genoa (2 weekly; 9hr); Marseille (1 daily; 9hr); Nice (1 daily; 7hr); Toulon (2 weekly; 8hr).

To Bastia from Genoa (1 daily; 4hr); La Spezia (1 daily; 4hr); Livorno (1 daily; 3hr 30min); Marseille (1 daily; 10hr); Nice (1 daily; 8hr) Toulon (3 weekly; 10hr).

To Calvi from Genoa (2 weekly; 6hr); Marseille (4 weekly; 8hr); Nice (4 weekly; 7hr); Toulon (1 weekly; 8hr).

To Bonifacio from Sardinia (3 daily; 40min).

The Town

Cours Napoléon is the main thoroughfare of Ajaccio, running parallel to the sea and culminating in place Général-de-Gaulle, which in turn leads onto **place Maréchal-Foch**, a shady, palm-lined square bordered by cafés and restaurants and open to the sea. The most rewarding visit in Ajaccio is to the **Palais Fesch** (Tues–Sun 9am–noon & 2–6pm; 25F) the largest museum in Corsica, situated halfway down rue Fesch, an attractive winding shopping street that runs off place Foch. Apart from the **Chapelle Impériale**, where the Bonaparte family vaults have been gathered, the building is home to an important collection of Italian paintings from the fifteenth and sixteenth centuries, the legacy of Napoléon's step-uncle Cardinal Joseph Fesch. Notable among the paintings is Botticelli's *Virgin and the Garland* and Veronese's startling *Leda and the Swan*.

Admirers of Napoléon will, no doubt, head straight for the **Maison Bonaparte** (Mon 2–6pm, Tues–Sat 9am–noon & 2–6pm) located in place Laetitia, off rue Saint-Charles in the heart of the old town. A disappointingly sparse museum, its exhibits include the chair Napoléon's mother lay on when in labour, and Napoléon's bed. For dedicated Napoléon fans the **Musée Napoléonien** (Tues–Sat 9am–noon & 2–6pm) in the Hôtel de Ville houses the Bonaparte family portraits as well as other Napoléon memorabilia such as a gold replica of Napoleon's death mask. Napoléon was baptized in Ajaccio's **Cathedral**, which dominates rue Forcioli-Conti, south of place Foch. Built in 1554, the church boasts a Delacroix *Virgin* which hangs in the chapel to the left of the altar. Napoléon's dying words are inscribed on a plaque adorning the pillar to the left of the entrance, expressing his wish to be buried in Ajaccio if they wouldn't have him in Paris.

For a fascinating insight into Corsican military history, the **Musée Bandera** (May–Sept Mon–Sat 10am–noon & 3–7pm; Oct–April Wed 2–6pm; 25F) is tucked away behind place Général-de-Gaulle in rue Général Levie. Displays include an impressive collection of vendetta daggers and a room dedicated to bandits, displaying photographs and life-size models of the most notorious *bandits d'honneurs*.

Eating and drinking

Restaurants in Ajaccio vary from the simple bistro to pizzerias and expensive fish restaurants, most of which centre around the old town, east and west of place Foch. *L'Abri des Flots* at 2 place Foch does inexpensive Corsican and fish dishes, while *Pizzeria Napoli* at 9 rue Bonaparte is open very late and does excellent pizzas and Corsican specialities such as roast kid. *A Pignata*, 15 av du Roi Jerôme, is a traditional Corsican joint, serving *marcassin* (baby wild boar). Young people hang out at *Snack bar du Jetée* on the jetée de la Citadelle, overlooking the boats.

Bars and cafés take up much of the pavement space, with cocktail bars and *glaciers* lining the seafront behind the beach. Everyone goes for tea at *Bar Nord Sud* in place Général-de-Gaulle; *Café du Flore*, opposite Palais Fesch, makes a change from the traditional bar and plays jazz.

Bastia

The port of **BASTIA** is a charismatic town, with its crumbling golden-grey buildings set against a backdrop of fire-darkened hills. Now a thriving commercial port, Bastia was capital of Corsica under the Genoese, and unlike its rival Ajaccio, has remained an authentic working town which makes few concessions to tourism. The place has much to recommend it, however: the dilapidated Vieux Port, a sprinkling of lavish Baroque churches and the imposing citadel (or bastion) from which the town gets its name. A theatre and two cinemas provide some entertainment, and if you're stuck for something to do there's always the place Saint-Nicolas, a vast square lined with trees and cafés open to the sea, where you can sit and absorb the true Corsican way of life.

The most appealing part of Bastia is the **Vieux Port**, the site of the original fishing village around which the town grew, and nowadays a tranquil backwater where soaring houses seem to bend inwards towards the fishing boats glinting in the sun. Dominating the harbour are the twin towers of **Église Saint-Jean-Baptiste**, the largest but not the most interesting church in Bastia, which shoulders the place du Marché, where a half-hearted market takes place each morning. The narrow streets around are known as **Terra Vecchia**, a flaking conglomeration of tenement blocks in attractive decay.

Close by, in rue Napoléon, there are two Baroque churches whose dull facades belie their interiors. Halfway up the street stands the **Oratoire de l'Immaculée Conception**; dating from 1611 and resplendent with velvet drapery and crystal chandeliers, this little church was a Genoese showplace used for state occasions, such as the inauguration of the Anglo-Corsican parliament in the 1760s. **Oratoire Saint-Roch**, some hundred metres further up the street, was built in 1604 along the same lines. Inside there's some remarkable wooden panelling and a rare **organ** dating from 1750, which is played on festival days. Be sure not to miss the **Musée Éthnographique** (Mon–Sat 9am–noon & 2–6pm; 25F) in the old Governor's palace up in the *citadelle*. You can climb up through the Jardin Romieu at the south end of the Vieux Port to get there. Exhibits include the original Corsican **flag of independence** which Paoli's troops carried to their last battle at Ponte Novu in 1769.

Practicalities

Bastia's **airport**, Poretta, is situated 16km south of town off the RN197. Buses into the town centre stop outside the **train station** (35F); other buses stop in boulevard Paoli, the main street. **Ferries** use the Nouveau Port, just a five-minute walk from the centre. The **tourist office** in place Saint-Nicolas (Mon–Sat 9am–noon & 2–6pm) can give you bus timetables and lists of accommodation in the region.

Finding somewhere to **stay** in Bastia shouldn't be a problem even at the height of the season. About the cheapest place is the shabby but welcoming *Laetitia* at 2 bd Paoli (☎95.31.06.94; ③), or try the *Riviera* in the port at 1 rue du Nouveau Port (☎95.31.07.16; ⑤), a well-established place popular with travellers. *Hotel des Voyageurs* at 9 av du Maréchal Sebastiani (☎95.31.08.97; ④) is handy for the bus. *Hotel de la Paix*, situated high above the town at 1 bd Général Giraud (☎95.31.06.71; ⑤), commands a superb view of the Vieux Port. Also on the chic side the *Posta Vecchia* on Quai des Martyrs (☎95.32.32.38; ⑤), has a wonderful sea view.

The best **restaurants** are concentrated in and around the Vieux Port, with the emphasis on Italian food, though there are some authentic Corsican places; the best of these is *U Tianu* in rue Monsignor Roderigo, off place du Marché – they do an excellent selection of *charcuterie*. *Chez Gino*, 11 av Emile Sari, serves pizzas and authentic Italian ice cream. For cheap steaks and pasta there's *Le Paradou* in place Galetta behind the Vieux Port, and for good fish try *A Scaletta* in the Vieux Port. Also in the Vieux Port is *U Cantarettu*, where you can eat excellent pizzas to live music. For a **drink** *Bar Pascal* is the best spot in the Vieux Port, or try *Les Palmiers* in place Saint-Nicolas.

Corte

Set amidst craggy mountains and gorges, the sleepy town of **CORTE** is known as the spiritual capital of Corsica, as this is where Pascal Paoli had his seat of government during the brief period of independence in the eighteenth century. Paoli founded a university here which was reopened in the early 1980s, but despite the weekly influx of students the town lacks much vibrancy – even its inhabitants call it a *trou perdu* (a lost hole). Corte does have its attractions, however, namely its extraordinary *citadelle*, which springs from a sheer black pinnacle of rock, towering over the valley.

The main street, **cours Paoli**, runs the whole length of the small town, culminating in place Paoli, a pleasant market square. A cobbled ramp leads from the square up to the Ville Haute, where in tiny **place Gaffori** you can still see the bullet marks that were made by Genoese soldiers during the War of Independence. The vigorously pointing statue is of General Gaffori, one of Paoli's right-hand men, who led the independent army in 1756. Continuing north you'll soon come to the gates of the **Citadelle** (April–Oct daily 9am–7pm; 10F). The building comprises ramparts, army barracks and an old watchtower, known as the eagle's nest, built by Corsican overlord Vincentello d'Istria in 1420. For the best view of the tower and the town, you can climb up to the **Belvédère**, a platform opposite the tower, which affords panoramic vistas of the surrounding valley.

Corte's **train station** lies 1km out of town at the foot of the hill; **buses** to Ajaccio and Bastia stop at the north end of place Paoli. There is a small **tourist office** within the *citadelle*, which issues a map and a list of hotels and campsites. The cheapest place to **stay** in Corte is at *Hôtel de la Poste*, 2 place Padoue (☎95.46.01.37; ③), a gloomy, functional building which has no restaurant. A preferable option is to venture a kilometre out of town to the *Auberge de la Restonica*, situated along the D623 (☎95.46.20.13; ③); this sumptuous old-fashioned hunting-inn, set in the forest, overlooks a waterfall which provides its restaurant with delicious fresh trout. **Campsites** are also situated along this road: *U Sognu* (☎95.46.09.07) lies at the foot of the Restonica valley, about 500m from the town centre.

For **food** try *le Bips* in cours Paoli – traditionally a hunters' hang-out, it's popular with students these days and does delicious hearty regional food as well as pasta. Another good place is the *Gaffori* in place Gaffori, for wild boar lasagne and 45F menus. *Café de France* at 1 place Padoue is the best **café**. Corte also boasts its own **cinema**, 500m along the road to Ajaccio, just over the bridge.

Calvi

Seen from the water, the great *citadelle* of **CALVI** resembles a floating island, sharply defined against a hazy backdrop of snowcapped mountains. Corsica's third port, Calvi annually draws in thousands of tourists who come for the six kilometres of sandy beach, a semi circle of golden sand backed by a dark ribbon of pines which sweeps to the east of town. Home to the Foreign Legion and believed by many Corsicans to have been Christopher Columbus' birthplace, Calvi today is a light-hearted holiday town. Hundreds of boats, many of them huge yachts belonging to European glitterati, find a mooring in the marina, yet much of the postwar star cachet has left the place as it's become overrun by souvenir shops and raffia parasols.

Calvi started life as a Genoese stronghold, when its inhabitants were granted special privileges for being loyal citizens; their motto *Civitas Calvis Semper Fidelis* is inscribed above the gate into the *citadelle* or **Haute Ville**, a labyrinth of tortuous cobbled lanes and stairways rising from place Christophe Colomb, the square linking the two parts of town. Shops, restaurants and hotels are all found in the **Basse Ville**, which backs onto the marina, and the **beach** starts just beyond the boats.

Sainte-Cathérine **airport** is 6km south of Calvi; there are no buses into town and a taxi costs around 60F. **Trains** stop behind the marina and close by is the **tourist office** (May–Sept Mon–Sat 9am–noon & 2–7pm) which will help with accommodation for a small fee. **Ferries** come into port at the far end of the Quai Lantivy beneath the *citadelle*.

Among **hotels** in Calvi, the *Laetitia*, 5 rue Joffre (☎95.65.05.55; ③), is about the cheapest and most central, but is closed in winter. Open all year round is *Le Belvédère*, 5 place Christophe Colomb (☎95.65.01.25; ④), or try the *Balanea* at 6 rue Clemenceau (☎95.65.00.45; ④). Calvi boasts a rare **youth hostel** at 13 av de la République (☎95.65.33.72; ②), which is open all year. *La Pinède*, 1km from Calvi along the N197 (summer only; ☎95.65.17.80) is the closest **campsite**.

An abundance of **restaurants** cram the streets of the Basse Ville. *L'Abri Côtier*, 1 rue Joffre, has a terrace over the sea and serves excellent, if expensive, seafood. At the cheaper end of the range, for good pizzas and unusual pasta dishes try *Pizzeria Galère* at 6 rue des Anges. *Le Santa Marie*, 5 rue Clemenceau, next to the church, may be touristy but there's a lively ambience and it turns out some unusual Corsican specialities such as *stifatu*, a tasty blend of stuffed meats.

Bonifacio

The port of **BONIFACIO** enjoys a superbly isolated situation at Corsica's southernmost point, a narrow peninsula of dazzling white limestone creating an exceptional site for the town. A ridge of pale buildings rises from the sheer chalky cliffs, while the deep cleft between the peninsula and the mainland forms a natural harbour that is believed by some to have been one of Odysseus' landfalls. The town came into being in 828 when Count Bonifacio of Tuscany built a castle on the peninsula, but in 1194 it was taken over by the Genoese, who enticed a colony of Ligurian families here with promises of tax exemption. For five hundred years Bonifacio was a virtually independent republic, with its own laws and officers, and today a sense of detachment from the rest of Corsica persists, with many *Bonifaciens* still speaking their own dialect. Be warned, though, that the town becomes unbearably overcrowded and expensive in midsummer, as Bonifacio has become a chic holiday spot as well as a sailing centre.

The first place to head for is the **Haute Ville**, connected to the marina by a steep flight of steps at the north end of the quay. Built within the massive fortifications of the *citadelle*, it's an alluring maze of dusty streets, its houses displaying pointed arches and closed arcades unique to Bonifacio – and from the edge of the ramparts there's a glorious view across the straits to Sardinia. In rue de Palais de Garde, straight in front of the drawbrige at the top of the steps, **Église Sainte-Marie-Majeure**'s facade is hidden by the loggia where Genòese officers used to dispense justice in the thirteenth century. Inside the church, a Roman sarcophagus, on the left of the entrance, remains as the sole evidence of a nearby Roman settlement, and adorning the wall beside it is a remarkable marble tabernacle, decorated with a bas-relief of Christ supported by eight cherubs, the work of a Genoese sculptor in 1465. Whilst in the Haute Ville another essential visit is to the **Cimetière des Marins**, a captivating walled cemetery filled with elaborate mausoleums, strung out at the far end of the promontory.

Down in the marina, a worthwhile **boat excursion** (50F) to the **sea-caves**, wonderful grottoes where the rock glitters with rainbow colours and the turquoise sea is deeply translucent also takes you round the base of the cliffs for a fantastic view of the town.

The closest **beach** to town is **plage de la Catena**, a kilometre west of the port. To get there follow the road to Ajaccio, turning left at the *Araguina* campsite just beyond the marina – a ten-minute walk then brings you to the cove. Some outstanding beaches lie to the north of Bonifacio: **plage de la Rondinara**, 5km north along the road to Porto Vecchio, is an almost circular cove of white dunes and clear sea, and the **Golfe de Santa Manza**, 2km along the same road, is also sublime.

Practicalities

The nearest **airport** is Figari, 17km to the north, and as yet there's no public transport link to town. **Ferries** from Sardinia dock at the far end of the quay; **buses** from Ajaccio, the only direct public transport to Bonifacio, stop in the car park by the marina. The **tourist office** (May–Oct Mon–Fri 9am–noon & 2–7pm; Sat 9am–noon) is in the Haute Ville at the top of avenue Général-de-Gaulle. Hotels are all on the pricy side except *Les Étrangers*, 500m along the road to Ajaccio (☎95.73.00.03; ③), and *Les Voyageurs*, 15 quai Comparetti (☎95.73.00.46; ④). For those on a less tight budget *Le Royal*, 1 rue Fred Scamaroni in the Haute Ville (☎95.73.03.65; ⑦), has rooms with a fabulous view of the cliffs, and an excellent fish restaurant. **Campers** have *L'Araguina*, 500m past the marina on the road to Ajaccio (☎95.73.02.96). For **food** avoid the chintzy fish restaurants on quai Comparetti and head up to the Haute Ville where places are less pretentious and more reasonably priced. *Le Guêpier*, 7 rue Fred Scamaroni, serves inexpensive Corsican specialities such as *canelloni al brocciu*. *Pizza/Grill de la Poste*, 41 rue Fred Scamaroni, is also very popular with the locals.

travel details

Trains

Paris to: Amiens (10 daily; 1hr 10min); Bordeaux (hourly; 3hr); Boulogne (7 daily; 3hr); Caen (hourly; 2hr 15min); Calais (7 daily; 3hr 10min); Clermont-Ferrand (8 daily; 4hr); Dieppe (5 daily; 2hr 20min); Dijon (hourly; 1hr 40min); Le Havre (12 daily; 2hr 20min); Lille (13 daily; 2hr 20min); Lyon (hourly; 2hr); Marseille (12 daily; 5hr); Montpellier (4 daily; 5hr); Nancy (11 daily; 2hr 30min); Nice (9 daily; 10hr); Nîmes (3 daily; 9hr); Poitiers (hourly; 1hr 45min); Reims (8 daily; 1hr 50min); Rennes (hourly; 2hr 25min); Rouen (hourly; 1hr 15min); Strasbourg (10 daily; 4hr); Toulouse (10 daily; 5hr 30min); Tours (8 daily; 2hr 30min).

Ajaccio to: Bastia (4 daily; 4hr); Calvi (2 daily; 3hr30min); Corte (4 daily; 2hr).

Bastia to: Ajaccio (4 daily; 4hr); Calvi (2 daily; 2 daily; 3hr 30min); Corte (4 daily; 2hr).

Bergerac to: Sarlat (3 daily; 1hr 30min); Périgueux (1 daily; 1hr 50min).

Bordeaux to: Bayonne-Biarritz (11 daily; 2hr); Bergerac (6 daily; 1hr 20min); Marseille (5 daily; 6–7hr); Nice (4 daily; 9–10hr); Périgueux (11 daily; 1hr 20min); Toulouse (12 daily; 2hr).

Caen to: Rennes (2 daily; 2hr); Tours (3–6 daily; 3hr 10min).

Cahors to: Toulouse (4 daily; 1hr).

Calvi to: Ajaccio (2 daily; 3hr 30min); Bastia (2 daily; 3hr 30min); Corte (2 daily; 2hr 30 min).

Clermont-Ferrand to: Vichy (12 daily; 40min); Nimes (3 daily; 4hr 50min); Marseille (3 daily; 6hr); Toulouse (4 daily; 6hr).

Corte to: Ajaccio (4 daily; 2hr); Bastia (4 daily; 2hr); Calvi (2 daily; 2hr 30 min).

Dijon to: Lyon (14 daily; 1hr 45min); Beaune (6 daily; 25min).

Lyon to: Avignon (6 daily; 3hr); Grenoble (8–10 daily; 1hr 45min); Marseille (6 daily; 4hr); Orange (6 daily; 2hr).

Nancy to: Strasbourg (2 daily; 1hr 20min).

Narbonne to: Carcassonne (12 daily; 30min); Perpignan (hourly; 40min); Toulouse (12 daily; 1hr 30min).

Nice to: Marseille (20 daily; 2hr 30min); Menton (8 daily; 40min); St-Raphael (at least hourly; 1hr 25min).

Nîmes to: Arles (6 daily; 20min); Avignon (hourly; 30min); Clermont-Ferrand (3 daily; 5hr); Marseille (hourly; 2min).; Montpellier (hourly; 30min); Narbonne (hourly; 1hr 30hr)

Périgueux to: Les Eyzies (5 daily; 30min).

Poitiers to: Bordeaux (13 daily; 2hr); La Rochelle (8 daily; 1hr 30min).

Le Puy to: Lyon (2 daily; 2hr 30min).

Rennes to: Lorient (7 daily; 1hr 30min); Nantes (5 daily; 2hr); Quimper (7 daily; 2hr 30min); St-Malo (7 daily; 1hr 15min).

Rouen to: Amiens (3–6 daily; 1hr 30min); Caen (8 daily; 2hr); Fécamp (hourly; 1hr).

Sens to: Avallon (3–5 daily; 2hr); Dijon (7 daily; 2hr 10min).

Strasbourg to: Colmar (hourly; 30min); Mulhouse (hourly; 1hr).

Toulouse to: Albi (8 daily; 1hr); Bayonne (4 daily; 4hr); Bordeaux (12 daily; 2hr); Clermont-Ferrand (1 daily; 7hr); Lourdes (12 daily; 2hr 20min); Lyon (6 daily; 6hr); Marseille (10 daily; 4hr 30min); Pau (10 daily; 2hr 30min).

Tours to: Angers (10 daily; 1hr 30min); Azay-le-Rideau (8 daily; 30min); Bourges (4 daily; 2hr); Chinon (8 daily; 1hr); Loches (6 daily; 1hr); Lyon (5 daily; 5hr).

Buses

Ajaccio to: Bastia (2 daily; 3hr); Bonifacio (2 daily; 3hr) Corte (2 daily; 2hr).

Bastia to: Ajaccio (2 daily; 3hr); Bonifacio (2 daily; 2hr 30min); Calvi (2 daily; 3hr); Corte (2 daily; 1hr 45min).

Bonifacio to: Ajaccio (2 daily; 3hr); Bastia (2 daily; 3hr).

Calvi to: Ajaccio (2 daily; 3hr); Bastia (2 daily; 3hr).

Corte to: Ajaccio (2 daily; 2hr); Bastia (2 daily; 2hr).

CHAPTER 8

GERMANY

DENMARK

To Århus

Baltic Sea

North Sea

Lübeck

Hamburg

To Gdańsk

To Groningen

NETHERLANDS

Bremen

POLAND

Hannover

Potsdam

BERLIN

To Amsterdam

Hildesheim

Magdeburg

To Warsaw

Goslar

Münster

Meissen

To Amsterdam

Düsseldorf

Naumberg

Dresden

Cologne

Weimar

Leipzig

To Maastricht

Aachen

Bonn

Marburg

Erfurt

BELGIUM

Koblenz

To Prague

LUX

Frankfurt

Trier

Mainz

Bamberg

To Prague

Worms

Würzburg

Rothenburg

CZECH & SLOVAK

Heidelberg

Nürnberg

REPUBLICS

To Paris

Speyer

Regensburg

0   25 km

Stuttgart

To Paris

Baden Baden

Tübingen

Augsburg

Munich

FRANCE

To Vienna

Freiburg

To Vienna

Konstanz

Garmish-Partenkirchen

AUSTRIA

Basel

To Zurich

SWITZERLAND

To Innsbruck

Introduction

The stereotype of **Germany** as the great mono-lith of western Europe has always been a long way from the truth, and is especially inaccurate now that postwar division of the country has been reversed. Regional characteristics are a strong feature of German life, and there are many hangovers from the days when the country was a patchwork of independent states. To travel from the ancient ports of the north, across the open fields of the German plain, down through the Ruhr conurbation and on to the forests, moun-tains and cosmopolitan cities of the south is to experience a variety as great as any continental country can offer.

Several of Germany's cities have the air of national capitals. **Cologne**, though enmeshed in one of Europe's most intensively industrialized regions, is one of the most characterful cities in the country and the richest in historic monuments. Bavaria's capital, **Munich**, is another star attraction, boasting the best the country has to offer – whether in museums and galleries, beer, fashion or sport. **Berlin**, the nucleus of the turmoil of reunification, has an atmosphere at times electrifying, at times disturbing, while **Nürnberg** retains more than a trace of its bygone years of glory. **Frankfurt**, the economic dynamo of postwar reconstruction, looks on itself as the "real" capital of the country, but **Stuttgart** and **Düsseldorf** contest the title of champion of German success, with their corpo-rate skyscrapers and American-style consumerist buzz. In the east of the country, apart from Berlin, there's the Baroque splendour of **Dresden** to enjoy, now accessible for the first time since the 1930s.

However, because all these cities suffered considerable damage in World War II and have been subjected to some heavy-handed redevelop-ment, the smaller towns of Germany in many respects offer a richer experience. There's nowhere as well-loved in Germany as the univer-sity city of **Heidelberg**, guiding light of the Romantic movement, while **Bamberg**, **Regensburg**, **Rothenburg** and **Marburg** in the west and **Erfurt** in the east are among the many places which deserve to be regarded among the most attractive in Europe.

Among the scenic highlights are the **Bavarian Alps** (on Munich's doorstep), the **Bodensee** (Lake Constance), the **Black Forest** and the valley of the **Rhine**, whose majestic sweep has spawned a rich fund of legends and folklore.

Inevitably, the pace of change in the eastern part of the country, as with all the countries of the former Eastern Bloc, means that certain sections of this chapter will soon be out of date – prices are unpredictable, for example, and streets are reverting to their pre-communist names. But the very uncertainties of the new Germany give an edge to the experience of what was already one of the most complex countries in Europe.

Information and Maps

You'll find a **tourist office** (*Fremdenverkehrsamt*) in virtually every town in Germany. In west Germany they're almost universally friendly and very efficient, providing large amounts of often useful literature and maps. Many tourist offices in the former GDR are already as well geared-up as their counterparts in the west, but others are still stuck in a communist time-warp and tend to regard Western tourists with suspicion.

The best general **maps** are those by *RV* or *Kümmerly and Frey*, whose 1:500,000 map is the most detailed single sheet of the country availa-ble. Specialist maps marking cycling routes or alpine hikes can be bought in the relevant regions.

Money and Banks

German currency is the *Deutschmark*, which comes in notes of DM5, DM10, DM20, DM50, DM100, DM200, DM500 and DM1000; coins of DM0.01 (one *Pfennig*), DM0.02, DM0.05, DM0.10, DM0.20, DM0.50, DM1, DM2 and DM5.

Exchange facilities can be found in virtually all banks (except in the former GDR, where only major towns are dependable) as well as in post offices and commercial exchange shops called *Wechselstuben*. The *Deutsches Verkehrsbank* has branches in the train stations of most main cities which are generally open seven days a week. **Banking hours** are Mon–Fri 9am–noon & 1.30–3.30pm, with late opening on Thursday until 6pm, though these are often extended. The offices at train stations are often open until 6 or 7pm on weekdays.

Unusually, for such a consumer-oriented soci-ety, **credit cards** are little used in Germany: only the major cards will be known and accepted, and then only in large department stores or upmarket restaurants in the larger cities.

Communications

Post offices are normally open Mon–Sat 8am–6pm. **Poste restante** services are available at the main post offices in any given town: collect it from the counter marked *Postlagernde Sendungen*. Mail is usually only held for a couple of weeks. The old East German postal service has been fully amalgamated with that of the west, but as yet doesn't function as well, so expect long delays.

In the west you can **telephone abroad** from all pay phones except those marked "National"; coins of DM0.10, DM1 and DM5 are accepted, and only wholly unused ones are returned. Main post offices always have an international direct phone service facility. Phone codes in the **east** are currently being standardized, but travellers may still experience problems and inconsistencies with cities having different codes according to the place you're phoning from. Thus in the east it's always easiest to make your non-local calls from a post office, going through the operator.

The **operator number** in the west is ☎010 for domestic calls and ☎0010 for international calls; in the east, dial ☎180 for domestic calls, ☎181 for international calls.

Getting Around

While it may not be cheap, getting around Germany is quick and easy. Barely an inch of the country is untouched by an unfailingly reliable public transport system and it's a simple matter to jump from train to bus on the integrated network.

■ Trains

By far the best form of public transport in **west Germany** are **trains**, operated by the national company *Deutsche Bundesbahn* (*DB*). Fares average about DM23 per 100km, exclusive of supplements, and a return costs the same as two singles. The most luxurious service is the new 250kph **InterCityExpress** (**ICE**), which as yet only operates on the Hamburg–Frankfurt–Munich route (supplement charged according to distance travelled, but is expensive: Hannover–Frankfurt

supplement is DM28). Otherwise, the fastest and most comfortable trains are the **InterCity** (**IC**) and **EuroCity** (**EC**) (supplement of DM6-8). The new **InterRegio** (**IR**) trains offer a swift service between smaller centres (DM4 supplement for journeys of under 50km). Around major cities, the **S-Bahn** is a commuter network on which *InterRail*/*Eurail* cards are valid, as they are on all other services.

In the east, most services are still run by the *Deutsche Reichsbahn* (*DR*), though amalgamation is on the way. Fares are low, currently being calculated at DM12 for 100km, but most trains are filthy and are classified as *Personenzug*, which seem to stop at every milk churn.

If you're making a lot of rail journeys and don't have an *InterRail* or *Eurail* pass, it's sensible to buy one of the discount passes exclusively for foreigners. The **German Rail Pass** gives unlimited travel on all trains in Germany, and many buses and boats in the west; it costs £99/$170 for 5 days within any month, £149/$253 for 10 days, £179/$305 for 15 days. For under-26s, the **Junior Tourist Card** costs £69/$117, £89/$150 and £109/$185 for the same periods. Officially, these are not on sale in Germany itself, other than at frontier posts such as Aachen or Konstanz. However, provided you can prove you are not resident in Germany, you should be able to buy them at main stations in the major cities. A pass that must be bought outside Germany is the **DB Regional Rail Rover**, which gives unlimited rail travel on west German trains for any 10 days out of 21 in any of 30 specific areas; it costs £33/$56 for one person, £45/$76 for two, £55/$93 for a family group.

The colossal national **timetable** (*Kursbuch*) can be bought from stations for DM10, though it's too bulky to be easily portable. A condensed version of it (*Städteverbindungen*) can also be obtained at stations, and comes free with the German Rail Pass.

■ Buses

If you must forsake the trains for **buses** in the west, you'll find no decline in efficiency. Many are the *DB*-run *Bahnbusse*, although there are a few privately operated routes on which rail passes cannot be used. You're most likely to need buses in remote rural areas, or along designated "scenic routes" where scheduled buses take the form of luxury coaches that pause at major points of interest.

In view of the density of the train network, there's even less need to resort to buses in **the east**, although in rural areas you'll often find that they offer major savings in terms of time. Fares are broadly similar to those of the trains. Buses are operated by municipal transport authorities rather than by *DR*, so rail passes are not valid.

■ Driving and hitching

West German traffic moves fast. There are no legally enforced **speed limits** on the *Autobahnen* although there might well be soon, but there is a recommended limit of 100–130kmph. The speed limit on country roads is 80–100kmph, in towns it's generally 50kph. A national or international driving licence is valid for a year's driving. **Car rental** rates begin at around 500DM per week. The *Allgemeiner Deutscher Automobil Club* (*ADAC*) runs a 24-hour breakdown service; they can be called in the west from booths alongside the motorways or by dialling ☎19 211, with the prefix 01308 if you're outside the city limits. In the east, the *ADAC* has various numbers – so it's easiest to go through the operator.

Hitching is common practice all over Germany and with the excellent *Autobahn* network it's usually quite easy to cover long distances in a short time – though bear in mind that hitching on them or their access roads is illegal. If you can't face the uncertainty of traditional hitching, the Germans have developed an institutionalized form called *Mitfahrzentralen*, agencies that put drivers and hitchers in touch with each other for a nominal fee.

■ Cycling

Cyclists are well catered for in Germany: many smaller roads have marked cycle paths, and bike-only lanes are a common sight in cities and towns. Between April and October, the best place to rent a bike is from a railway station participat-ing in the **Fahrrad am Bahnhof** scheme (DM10 per day). You can return it to any other participating station and holders of the various rail passes get a 50 percent discount.

Accommodation

Be it high-rise city hotels or half-timbered guest-houses in the country, accommodation of all types is easy to find in Germany, and it can often be good value.

■ Hotels

An immensely complicated grading system applies to western German **hotels**, but they're all more or less the same: clean, comfortable and functional. Just take care not to turn up in a large town or city during a trade fair, or *Messe* – hotels often double their rates and still manage to get booked solid. In country areas, prices start at about DM35 for a single, DM60 for a double – at least DM10–15 extra for something similar in a city.

There's still a desperate shortage of hotel rooms in the former GDR, particularly in cities, where it can be impossible to get a bed without a reservation months in advance. Grossly inflated prices are another consequence of this failure of supply to meet demand. In holiday areas the situation is much better, thanks to the privatization of many hotels; indeed, there are many remarkable bargains on offer at the moment. Prices in the next few years are certain to be volatile, however.

■ Pensions, guesthouses and private rooms

To escape the formality of a hotel, look for one of the plentiful **pensions**, which may be rooms above a bar or restaurant or simply space in a private house; in urban areas these cost about

---

ACCOMMODATION PRICE CODES

Throughout this guide, accommodation is priced on a scale of ① to ⑧, the number indicating the lowest price per night a single person could expect to pay in that establishment in high season. With hostels this is the nightly rate per person; with hotels, the price is arrived at by dividing the cost of the cheapest double room by two. The prices indicated by the codes are as follows

① = under £5 / $8   ② = £5–10 / $8–16   ③ = £10–15 / $16–24   ④ = £15–20 / $24–32

⑤ = £20–25 / $32–40   ⑥ = £25–30 / $40–48   ⑦ = £30–35 / $48–56   ⑧ = over £35 / $56

the same as a hotel but in the countryside are usually a bit cheaper. An increasingly prevalent budget option is **bed and breakfast** accommodation in a private house (look for signs saying *Fremdenzimmer* or *Zimmer frei*). Prices vary but are usually around DM25 for a single, DM40 for a double. Particularly plentiful along the main touring routes are **country inns** or **guesthouses** (*Gasthäuser*), charging around DM55 per night for a double (more in popular areas).

The best of the budget options in the east is to get hold of a room in a **private house**, of which thousands have now become available. Prices frequently start at as little as DM10 for bed and breakfast, and seldom rise above DM30. Nearly all tourist offices will book you a room for a fee and there are also a number of private agencies that sometimes have better deals. Private rooms in the west are not as common, but can sometimes provide reasonable accommodation in rural areas.

■ Youth hostels

In Germany, you're never far away from a **youth hostel** (*Jugendherberge*), but at any time of the year (especially summer weekends) they're liable to be block-booked by school groups, so it's advisable to book as far in advance as possible. Though most staff are courteous and helpful, there's an unfortunate minority who insist on rigid regimentation.

Hostels divide into a number of **categories** according to facilities and size of rooms, ranging from Grade I hostels (basic affairs charging DM12) up to Grade VI, also known as youth guesthouses (DM26.20). *IYHF* members over 27 pay DM2–3 more per night; non-members will be charged an extra DM4 per night. Over-27s can't use the hostels in Bavaria at all, unless accompanying children.

■ Camping

Big, well-managed **campsites** are a feature all over Germany. Even the lowest grade have toilet and washing facilities and a shop, while the grandest are virtually open-air hotels with swimming pools and supermarkets. Prices are based on facilities and location, comprising a fee per person (DM3–5) and per tent (DM3–4), plus extra fees for vehicles. Many sites are full from June to September, so arrive early in the afternoon. Most close down in the winter, but those in popular skiing areas remain open all year.

Food and Drink

German food is both good value and of high quality, but it helps if you share the national penchant for solid, fatty fare accompanied by compensating fresh vegetables.

■ Food

The vast majority of German hotels and guesthouses include **breakfast** in the price of the room. Typically, you'll be offered a small platter of cold meats and cheeses, along with a selection of breads, marmalades, jams and honey, and sometimes muesli. If breakfast isn't included, you can usually do quite well by going to a local bakery – most have an area set aside for breakfast.

Elegant **cafés** are a popular and traditional institution in Germany, usually serving a choice of espresso, cappuccino and mocha to the accompaniment of cream cakes, pastries or handmade chocolates. More substantial food is available from **butcher's shops**; you can generally choose from a variety of freshly roasted meats to make up a hot sandwich. The easiest option for those in need of a quick snack is to head for the ubiquitous **Imbiss** stands and shops, serving a range of sausages, plus meatballs, hamburgers and chips; the better ones have soups, schnitzels, chops and salads as well. Spit-roasted chicken is something of an east German speciality. Among the **fast food chains**, *Kochlöffel* stands out for cleanliness and good food. The butcher's chain *Vincent Murr* sells full main courses to be eaten on your feet, costing DM5–10.

All **restaurants** display their menus and prices by the door. Hot meals are usually served throughout the day. Most of the *Gaststätte*, *Gasthaus*, *Gasthof*, *Brauhaus* or *Wirtschaft* establishments belong to a brewery and function as a social meeting point, drinking haven and cheap restaurant combined. Their style of cuisine resembles hearty German home cooking, and portions are usually very generous. Standards in west German restaurants are amazingly high, but don't expect the same to be true everywhere in the east. Main courses are overwhelmingly based on pork, usually of very high quality and served with a variety of sauces. Sausages regularly feature on the menu, and can be surprisingly tasty, with distinct regional varieties. **Vegetarians** will find east Germany extremely difficult – menus are almost exclusively for carnivores, and even an innocent-sounding item like tomato soup will have meat floating around in it.

Germany now being a multicultural society, there's a wide variety of **ethnic** eateries to choose between. Of these, the Italian are generally the best recommendations, but there are also plenty offering Balkan and Greco-Turkish cuisines. All are worth heading for if you're on a tight budget. In the east you'll find restaurants offering the cuisines of Russia and such erstwhile communist countries as Hungary and The Czech and Slovak Republics.

■ Drink

For serious **beer** drinkers, Germany is paradise. The country has around forty percent of the world's breweries, with some 800 (about half the total) in Bavaria alone. It was in this province in 1516 that the *Reinheitsgebot* (Purity Law) was formulated, laying down stringent standards of production, including a ban on chemical substitutes.

A quick beer tour of Germany would inevitably begin in **Munich**, which occupies third place in the world production league table. The city's beer gardens and beer halls are the most famous drinking dens in the country, offering a wide variety of premier products, from dark lagers through tart *Weizens* to powerful *Bocks*. **Cologne** holds the world record for the number of city breweries, all of which produce the jealously guarded *Kölsch*. **Düsseldorf** has its own distinctive brew, the dark *Alt*, but wherever you go, you can be fairly sure of getting a product made locally, often brewed in a distinctive style.

Most people's knowledge of German **wine** starts and ends with *Liebfraumilch*, a medium sweet easy-drinking wine. Sadly, its success has obscured the quality of other German wines, especially those made from the *Riesling* grape, which many consider one of the world's great white grape varieties. The vast majority of German wine is white, since the northern climate doesn't ripen red grapes regularly. If after a week or so you're pining for a glass of red, try a *Spätburgunder*.

Apart from beer and wine, there's nothing very distinctive about German drink, save for *Apfelwein*, a variant of cider. The most popular **spirits** are the fiery *Korn* and after-dinner liqueurs, which are mostly fruit-based.

Opening Hours and Holidays

By law, **shops** in Germany close at 6.30pm on weekdays (except Thursday, when it's 8.30pm), at 4pm on Saturdays in summer (2pm rest of year, but 6pm on the first Saturday of the month and in the four weeks before Christmas), and all day Sunday (except for bakers, who may open from 11am to 3pm). Exceptions are pharmacies and shops in and around train stations, which stay open late and at weekends. In east Germany the law is not rigidly enforced, so you'll find more variation there. **Museums** and **historic monuments** are, with few exceptions, closed Monday. Many museums and monuments in the former GDR still close for two days a week. Most museums offer half-price entry for students with valid ID.

Public holidays are: Jan 1; Jan 6; Good Friday; Easter Monday; May 1; Ascension Day; Whit Monday; Corpus Christi (regional); Aug 15 (regional); Assumption (regional); Oct 3; Nov 1 (regional); Day of Prayer and National Repentance (variable date in Nov); Dec 25 & 26.

Emergencies

The German **police** (*Polizei*) are not renowned for their friendliness, but they usually treat foreigners with courtesy. Reporting thefts at local police stations is straightforward, but inevitably there'll be a great deal of bureaucracy to wade through. The level of theft in the former GDR has increased dramatically with unemployment, but provided you take the normal precautions, there's no real risk. All drugs are illegal in Germany, and anyone caught with them will face either prison or deportation: consulates will not be sympathetic towards those on drug charges.

German **doctors** are likely to be able to speak English, but if you want to be certain, your consulate can provide a list of English-speaking doctors in the major cities. Pharmacies (*Apotheken*) can deal with many minor complaints and again will often speak English. In addition, in the west you'll find international *Apotheken* in most large towns, who will be able to fill a prescription in any European language. All pharmacies display a rota of 24-hour *Apotheken*.

EMERGENCY NUMBERS
Police ☎110; Ambulance & Fire ☎112.

NORTHERN GERMANY

The port of **Hamburg**, many people's introduction to Germany, is infamous for the prostitution and sleaze of the Reeperbahn, but it has plenty more to offer, not least a sparkling nightlife and a city centre composed of enjoyably contrasting neighbourhoods. In this generally physically unprepossessing northernmost region of Germany, it's another maritime city, **Lübeck**, that exerts the strongest pull. One of the main pivots of the Hanseatic League in the past, it has the same sort of visual appeal typical of the finest mercantile towns of the Low Countries. To the north, Schleswig-Holstein's countryside mix of dyke-protected marsh, peat bog and farmland holds few rewarding sights, but to the south lies the far more diverse region of Lower Saxony. **Hannover**, the capital of this Land, demands a visit for its museums and magnificent gardens, while the province's smaller towns present a fascinating contrast – **Hildesheim**, with its grandiloquent Romanesque architecture is the most outstanding from an artistic point of view, while **Goslar** is a mining town quite unlike any other in the world. Near the centre of Lower Saxony sits the Hanseatic port of **Bremen**, the largest city of this region and a Land in its own right, a continuation of its age-long tradition as a free state.

Hamburg

A stylish media centre and the third largest port in Europe, **HAMBURG** has none of the sentimental-folklore tradition of the Rhineland and the south – rather it has a certain coolness, solidity and sense of openness. Hamburg's skyline is dominated by the pale green of its copper spires and domes, but a few houses and the churches are just about all that's left from before the last century. The Great Fire of 1842 was a main cause of this loss, followed by demolition to make way for the warehouse area of the Free Port. Bombing in the last war also caused terrible devastation. Much of the subsequent rebuilding might not be especially beautiful, but at least it has preserved the human scale of the city. Two-thirds of Hamburg is occupied by parks, lakes or tree-lined canals, giving a refreshing rural feel to one of the country's major industrial centres.

Arrival and accommodation

Ferries from Harwich and Hull arrive at the St Pauli Landungsbrücken, from where it's an easy U-Bahn hop to anywhere in town. Buses run from the **airport** to the **train station** every twenty minutes, but it's a little cheaper to take the *HVV* airport bus to the U- and S-Bahn stop at Ohlsdorf, and then catch a train into town. The **tourist office** located at the station (daily 7am–11pm) has a full room-finding service. Another office is at the Hanse-Viertel's Poststr. entrance (Mon–Fri 10am–6.30pm, Sat 10am–3pm, Sun 11am–3pm). The day pass for the integrated **public transport** network makes a good investment at DM6.90, and at DM9.80 the new *Hamburg-card* gives you free travel plus free entry to eleven museums.

Near the St Pauli Landungsbrücken there's the *Auf dem Stintfang* **youth hostel**, Alfred-Wegener-Weg 5 (☎040/313 488; ②). Another hostel, the *Jugendgästehaus Horner Rennbahn*, Rennbahnstr. 100 (☎040/651 167; ③), is out in the suburb of Horn; take the S-Bahn to Horner Rennbahn. **Hotels** are not cheap in Hamburg. The pick of the lower-cost places is *Steen's Hotel*, Holzdamm 43 (☎040/244 642; ⑤), a delightful small hotel near the train station. *Annehof*, Lange Reihe 23, (☎040/243 426; ④), is a small, friendly place, and *Sarah Petersen*, just down the road at no. 50 (☎040/249 826; ④), is a good alternative. The nearest **campsite** is at Kieler Str. 374 (June–Sept); take the S-Bahn to Eidelstedt.

The City

Hamburg has no obvious centre, and it's probably best to begin an exploration in the oldest and liveliest area, the harbour. If you're arriving in Hamburg by ship, your landfall will be by the clock tower and green dome of the **St Pauli Landungsbrücken**. To the east, away from the ships and mighty cranes, is the late nineteenth-century **Speicherstadt**, whose tall, ornate warehouses belong to a bygone era of port life, but are still very much in use. You'll see bundles of oriental carpets being hoisted, and smell spices and coffee wafting on the breeze. The Speicherstadt is within the **Freihafen** (customs-free zone), which you can walk into unrestricted. It is a magical place to stroll, crisscrossing the bridges, of which Hamburg has more than Venice or Amsterdam.

Just to the north of the St Pauli Landungsbrücken is the nightlife centre of **St Pauli**, where music halls, bars and cafés sprang up in tandem with the growth of emigration to the USA. Nowadays this quarter is ruled by the sex industry, with its nerve centre on the notorious **Reeperbahn** – an ugly and unassuming street by day, ugly but sizzling with neon at night.

The main road running along the waterfront on St Pauli's edge is the **Hafenstrasse**, which runs west to the suburb of **Altona**, formerly a separate city ruled by the Holstein dukes. Its reputation for racial tolerance is one of the reasons it grew, and this part of the harbour still has a large Portuguese population – and good, very cheap Portuguese restaurants. Directly on Altona's waterfront one of Hamburg's main weekly events takes place: the **Fischmarkt**. Squeeze yourself out of bed early on a Sunday morning, or make Saturday night last, and you will find yourself in an amazing hubbub. If you want to buy bananas by the crate or an eight-foot potted palm, this is the place to do it, for the market by no means sells only fish. The bars and restaurants are in full swing by six; by ten trading has ceased; by eleven it's all over.

To all intents and purposes, Hamburg's core is the commercial and shopping district around the **Binnenalster** lake and the neo-Renaissance **Rathaus**, seat of Hamburg's government. When sessions aren't taking place you can go on a guided tour of the interior (tours in German Mon–Thurs every half-hour 10am–3pm, Fri–Sun hourly 10am–1pm; English tours fifteen minutes later than German ones); it's a magnificently pompous demonstration of the city's power and wealth in the last century. The Rathaus has one of the six towers, each well over one hundred metres tall, whose spires form a key feature of the skyline. All the other five belong to churches, two of which are a short walk to the east along Rathausstrasse: **St Petri**, the oldest building in the centre, and the far more impressive **St Jakobi**, in the late Gothic hall style typical of the Baltic regions.

Southeast of here, at the junction of Burchardstrasse and Pumpen, is Hamburg's most original building, the **Chilehaus**, designed by the Expressionist architect Fritz Höger. Rising like the prow of a huge ocean liner, the end of the Chilehaus is flanked by two small pavilions that symbolize the sea breaking against the ship. Across the street is the huge Sprinkenhof, begun by Höger immediately after the Chilehaus.

From here continue along Dovenfleet to the Gothic church of **St Katharinen**, whose Baroque tower rises high above the waterfront. Further to the west is **Deichstrasse**, one of the few surviving streets of old Hamburg. Just to the north is the tallest of the six towers, that of **St Nicolai**, while further along Ost-West-Strasse is **St Michaelis**, where the last and most imposing of the towers gives a grandstand view (Mon–Sat 9am–5pm, Sun 11.30am–6pm; DM4). Just up the Poststrasse, the old post office marks the heart of Hamburg's shopping area, where a number of classy arcades have been opened in the last few years. Architecturally they're stunning, and their exclusive shops put Bond Street in the shade: *Galleria* and the *Hanseviertel* are the ones to look out for.

Just north of the train station is the **Kunsthalle**, Hamburg's one unmissable art collection (Tues–Sun 10am–6pm, Thurs until 9pm; DM10, students DM3). Upstairs, a room is devoted to three pieces by Master Bertram, the first German painter identifiable by name, and the layout continues in a broadly chronological order. After a Renaissance display in which the major work is Cranach's *The Three Electors of Saxony*, there's a Dutch and Flemish section where everything is overshadowed by two Rembrandts. The nineteenth-century German section is one of the museum's main strengths: among the dozen works by Caspar David Friedrich are two of his most haunting creations, *Wanderer above the Mists* and *Eismeer*. Among the Expressionists, look out for two masterpieces by Munch: *Girls at the Seaside* and *Girls on the Bridge*. Pick of the twentieth-century paintings is Otto Dix's *War* triptych, a powerful anti-war statement. The **Kunstverein** next door (Tues–Sun 10am–6pm) has exhibitions of modern art.

On the other side of the train station, the **Museum für Kunst und Gewerbe** (Tues–Sun 10am–6pm, Thurs until 9pm; DM8) has excellent collections of art from ancient Egypt, Greece and Rome through to this century. The Jugendstil collection is very extensive, and also impressive are the sections dedicated to Chinese and Japanese art.

Eating, drinking and nightlife

Best places to eat are out of the city centre, in the Univiertel or the Schanzviertel around Schulterblatt and Schanzenstrasse. For snacks, the stalls in front of the Rathaus are pricy but delicious, while most café-bars (*Kneipe*) have food as well as drinks and sometimes music. Perhaps the best place for *Kaffee und Küchen* is the *Café Oertel*, Esplanade 29. The *Klett*, Grindelallee 146, is just one of a string of **café-bars** on this street in the university area; in Altona, *Eisenstein*, at Friedensallee 9, is a trendy café-bar popular with media types and serving very good food. *Aalberg*, Strandweg 33, down by the river in Blankenese, is one of the city's best **restaurants** for German dishes and fish, but main courses cost upwards of DM25. Cheaper options include *At Nali*, Rutschbahn 11, a Turkish restaurant with a large menu and friendly atmosphere; *Sagres*, Vorsetzen 42, a homely Portuguese place, popular with dock workers; *Tre Fontane*, Mundsburger Damm 45, a well-priced and intimate Italian; and the self-service *Gansemarkt Passage*, off Poststrasse.

Hamburg's **nightlife** is among the best the country has to offer – for up-to-the-minute listings, get hold of a copy of *Szene* magazine. *Grosse Freiheit*, Grosse Freiheit 36, St Pauli, is the city's main venue for **live music**, with big-name bands mostly playing at weekends. *Logo*, Grindelallee 5, hosts mainly English and American underground bands. Hamburg's latest-opening **disco** is the *Top Ten Club*, Reeperbahn 136 (10pm– 9am). Rivals include the hard-rock *Grünspan* disco, Grosse Freiheit 58, and the massive *Kaiserkeller*, in the *Grosse Freiheit* basement.

Listings

American Express Rathaus Markt 5 (☎040/331 141).

Bicycle rental From the tourist office or *Fahrrad Richter*, Barmbeker Str. 60.

Brewery tours The famous *Holstenbrauerei*, Holstenstr. 224, has regular free tours Mon–Fri except in Aug.

Consulates *Canada*, Spitalerstr. 11 (☎040/330 247); *Great Britain*, Harvestehuder Weg 8a (☎040/446 071); *Ireland*, Heilwigstr. 33 (☎040/489 250); *US*, Alsterufer 28 (☎040/441 701).

Gay Hamburg The best way to find out what's on in the lively gay scene is through the magazine *Du und Ich* and the free sheet *Gay Express*.

Hitching *Mitfahrzentrale*, Högerdamm 26a (☎040/234 123). Also, at Grindelallee 43 (☎040/450 556). there's a women's *Mitfahrzentrale*.

Post office At the Kirchenallee exit from the train station.

Women's Hamburg There are two women-only cafés: *Café Meg Donna*, Grindelallee 43, and the café in the women's bookshop *Frauenbuchladen*, Bismarck Str. 98.

Lübeck

The most enjoyable excursion from Hamburg is to the port of **LÜBECK**, just over half an hour from the city by train – but as many north and southbound trains depart from here, it's not necessary to return to Hamburg to continue your tour. What's more, Scandinavia-bound ships leave from nearby Travemünde.

Most things of interest to see are in the **Altstadt**, an egg-shaped island surrounded by the water defences of the Trave and the city moat. Left out of the train station it's only five minutes' walk to the old town, passing the twin-towered **Holstentor**, the city's emblem. Built in 1477, it leans horrifyingly these days, but that shouldn't put you off calling in at its small **Historical Museum** (Mon–Sat 10am–4/5pm; DM4) – a useful introduction to the city and Hanseatic history. On the waterfront to the right of the Holstentor is a row of lovely gabled buildings – the **Salzspeicher** (salt warehouses).

Straight ahead over the bridge and up Holstenstrasse, the first church on the right is the Gothic **Petrikirche**, one of many buildings to suffer during the Allied bombing of March 1942. A lift goes to the top of the spire (April–Oct daily 9am–6pm; DM2.50) – very useful for getting the layout of the town. Back across Holstenstrasse is the **Markt** and soaring above it the imposing **Rathaus** (tours half-hourly 10am–5pm include the Marienkirche and Buddenbrookhaus; DM5), displaying Lübeck's characteristic alternating rows of red unglazed and black glazed bricks. Opposite is the **Niederegger Haus**, renowned for its vast display of marzipan, which the town began producing in the Middle Ages; its old-style first-floor café is surprisingly affordable. Behind the north wing of the town hall is the **Marienkirche**, the earliest brick-built Gothic church in Germany. It was severely damaged in 1942, but the restored interior now makes a light and lofty backdrop for the church's treasures: a magnificent 1518 carved altar, a life-size figure of John the Evangelist dating from 1505, a beautiful Gothic gilded tabernacle and some fourteenth-century murals.

No need to go inside, but take a look at the facade of the **Katharinenkirche** on the corner of Königstrasse and Glockengiesserstrasse. The first three sculptures on the left of the west facade are by Ernst Barlach, who was commissioned to make a series of nine in the early 1930s, but had completed only these when his work was banned by the Nazis. Just north of Glockengiesser Strasse, sharing an entrance in Breitestrasse, are the **Behnhaus** and the **Drägerhaus**, two patricians' houses now converted into a museum (Tues–Sun 10am–5pm; DM3, free Fri). The Drägerhaus has impressive interiors with nineteenth-century furniture, paintings, porcelain and so forth, plus a room documenting the two literary stars of Lübeck, Thomas and Heinrich Mann. The Behnhaus displays a good collection of paintings, including works by Kirchner and Munch.

The nearby **Jakobikirche**, a sailors' church built in the thirteenth and fourteenth centuries, has Gothic wall paintings on its square pillars. On the other side of the Breite Strasse is a Renaissance house that used to belong to the fishermen's guild, the **Haus der Fischergesellschaft**. A tavern since 1535, it is decked out inside with all sorts of seagoing paraphernalia, and features on the programme of every tour group. East of here is the thirteenth-century **Heiligen-Geist-Hospital** (Tues–Sun summer 10am–5pm; winter 10am–4pm; free), one of the best-preserved hospices from this period, while if you carry on down Königstrasse you reach the **Burgtor**, an attractive square tower topped by a bell-shaped roof.

At the opposite end of the Altstadt are the **St-Annen-Museum** and the **Dom**. The museum (daily 10am–4/5pm; DM4, free Fri) has a first-rate collection reflecting domestic, civic and church art and history from the thirteenth to the eighteenth century – including a magnificent *Passion* triptych by Memling. The large brick-built Dom, founded in 1173, contains an enormous triumphal cross by Bernt Notke, a celebrity throughout the Baltic in the late fifteenth century.

Practicalities

The main **tourist office** is in the **train station** (Mon–Sat 9am–1pm & 3–7pm); there's a smaller office on the Markt (Mon–Fri 9.30am–6pm, Sat & Sun 10am–2pm), and a hotel reservation service at Breitstr. 75 opposite the Rathaus. The best **hotel** bargains in or near the centre are *Zur Burgtreppe*, Hinter der Burg 15 (☎0451/73 479; ④), and *Bahnhofshotel*, Am Bahnhof 21 (☎0451/83 883; ③). The YMCA has a central **InterRail-Point-Sleep-In** at Grosse Petersgrube 11 (☎0451/78 982; ②) which throws in breakfast. If that's full, try the **youth hostel** at Gertruden Kirchhof 4 (☎0451/33 433; ②), close to the Burgtor.

As a student town, Lübeck has a good choice of **cafés** and **eating** places. The Ratskeller serves a very good selection of vegetarian dishes, and *Schmidt's*, Dr. Julius-Leber-Str. 60–62, is a café-restaurant with a wide choice. *Tipasa*, Schlumacher Str. 14, has a great selection of cheap bistro-type dishes, highly popular with students. Opposite the station, *Belmondo*, a pleasant café with snacks, is a nice place to wait for a train. The Engelsgrube is the best street for **bars**, though the most enjoyable is probably the old, atmospheric *Zum alten Zolln*, in the centre behind *C&A*.

Bremen

Of the main north German cities, **BREMEN** is the most manageable, lacking the commercialism of Hamburg and the ugly redevelopment of Hannover. In 1949 Bremen was declared an autonomous Land, and since then it's had a reputation for being the most politically radical part of the country; in 1979 Bremen was the scene of the key breakthrough when it elected the first Green MPs.

The main area of historical interest is the **Altstadt**, on the Weser's northeast bank, reached by walking straight ahead from the train station. In Sögestrasse, Bremen's main shopping street, the single place worth stopping off for is the *Café Knigge*, but at the top is the **Liebfrauenkirche**, a lovely hall church engulfed by a flower market.

The **Marktplatz** ahead is relatively small, and is dominated by the **Rathaus**, one of the most splendid buildings in northern Germany. You can only visit the interior as part of a guided tour (Mon–Fri 10am, weekends 11am & noon; DM4), but it's worth it for the opportunity to see the extremes of Bremen's civic pride: rooms awash with gilded wallpaper and ornate carving. On the left as you face the Rathaus is a vast **statue of Roland**, erected in 1404 as a symbol of Bremen's independence from its archbishop; he now stares at the modern parliament building, one of the ugliest edifices to disgrace a German town.

On a small rise beyond the Rathaus stands the twin-towered **Dom**, its brooding interior ranging from Romanesque to late Gothic. In the eastern crypt are some fine works of art, notably an eleventh-century *Enthroned Christ* and a magnificent thirteenth-century font. Off the southeast corner is the **Bleikeller** (Mon–Fri 10am–5pm, Sat 10am–noon, Sun 2–5pm; DM2), where lead for the roofing was stored; a macabre attraction is provided by the corpses which were discovered here when the room was opened up, perfectly preserved owing to the lack of air. Surviving buildings from Bremen's Hanseatic heyday are few, but include the restored patrician houses lining much of the rest of the Marktplatz, and the **Schütting**, the ritzy, Flemish-inspired mansion where the guild of merchants convened.

Böttcherstrasse, off the south side of Marktplatz, was transformed in the 1920s by the Bremen coffee magnate Ludwig Roselius, who commissioned local artists to convert the alleyway into a Gothic-cum-Art Nouveau fantasy. Craft workshops are tucked in among the bronze reliefs, the arches and the turrets, and there's a musical clock depicting the history of transatlantic crossings. The only old house in the street is the **Roselius Haus**, now a museum of art and furniture (Mon–Thurs 10am–4pm, Sat & Sun 11am–4pm; DM2.50); the best works are paintings by the Cranachs and an alabaster statue of *Saint Barbara* by Riemenschneider. Adjoining is the **Paula-Becker-Modersohn-Haus** (Mon–Fri 10.30am–12.30pm & 3–7pm, Sat & Sun 10am–2pm), containing a number of paintings by the artist, who lived in nearby Worpswede.

Tucked away between the Dom and the river is a small, extraordinarily well-preserved area of medieval fishing houses known as the **Schnoorviertel**. Though prettified, it has managed to avoid soulless gentrification. Just east of the Schnoorviertel at Am Wall 207, the **Kunsthalle** (Tues 3–9pm, Wed–Sun 11am–5pm; DM6) houses a superb array of nineteenth- and early twentieth-century painting, including some forty works by Modersohn-Becker.

Practicalities

The **tourist office** is immediately outside the **train station** (Mon–Wed & Fri 9.30am–6.30pm, Thurs 9.30am–8.30pm, Sat 9.30am–2pm, Sun 9.30am–3.30pm). The densest and most convenient cluster of **hotels** is also near the train station, but their prices start at DM60 per person. Less costly but still fairly close to the centre is *Heinisch*, Wachmannstr. 26 (☎0421/342 925; ④); it's ten minutes' walk from the train station, on the #5 tram line. Bremen's **youth hostel** is in the western part of the old town at Kalkstr. 6 (☎0421/171 369; ②), and there's a good central **campsite**, *Internationale Campingplatz Freie Hansestadt Bremen*, Am Stadtwaldsee 1; buses #28 and #23 go in the right direction.

Bremen has a number of good **café-bars** – the *Wall Café* at Am Wall 164 has a lively atmosphere and vegetarian food, as does the *Tee Haus* in the middle of the Schnoorviertel. Bremen is home of *Beck's*, one of the most heavily exported **beers** in the country, but the products of *Haake-Beck* are the ones to go for in the city itself. Best choice of beers is at *Kleiner Ratskeller* on Hinter dem Schütting.

Hannover

HANNOVER has a closer relationship with Britain than any other German city, a consequence of the 1701 Act of Settlement, which resulted in Georg Ludwig of Hannover becoming King George I of the United Kingdom. As well as a monarch, Britain gained one of the greatest composers of all time. Anticipating the accession, the court director of music, Georg Friedrich Händel, was already well established in London by the time his employer arrived there, and it was in London that he was to write his finest works, notably the *Messiah*. Hannover's showpiece is not a great cathedral, palace or town hall, but a **series of gardens** – by far the most impressive in Germany. Add this to a number of first-class museums and there's plenty here to keep you occupied for a couple of days.

The City

Hannover has had to reconstruct itself after almost total demolition by World War II bombing, and the view on arrival at the train station isn't prepossessing, with a bland pedestrian precinct stretching ahead. Underneath runs the **Passarelle**, a sort of subterranean bazaar-cum-piazza that at night is a little disconcerting.

Standing at Hannover's most popular rendezvous, the *Café Kröpcke*, the most imposing building in view is the Neoclassical **Opernhaus**, perhaps the finest of the city's public buildings. A short distance southwest, a few streets of rebuilt half-timbered buildings convey some impression of the medieval town; most notable is the high-gabled fifteenth-century **Altes Rathaus**, its elaborate brickwork enlivened with colourful glazed tiles. Alongside is the fourteenth-century **Marktkirche**, whose bulky tower has long been the emblem of the city; inside, there's some miraculously preserved stained glass in the east windows.

Close by, at Pferdestrasse 6, the **Historical Museum** (Tues 10am–8pm, Wed–Fri 10am–4pm, Sat & Sun 10am–6pm; DM4) incorporates the sole remnant of the city walls. The displays include some state coaches, a section illustrating the changing face of Hannover, and several reconstructed interiors from farmhouses in the province.

Southwards, across the Friedrichswall, is the **Neues Rathaus**, an Art-Deco-cum-neo-Gothic extravaganza whose dome gives the best views of the city (April–Oct 9.30am–noon & 2–5pm; DM3). Next door, the **Kestner Museum** (Tues, Thurs & Fri 10am–4pm, Wed 10am–8pm, Sat & Sun 10am–6pm; DM2, free Wed) is a compact and eclectic decorative arts museum. Round the back of the Rathaus, over the road from the artificial Maschsee, is the **Landesmuseum** (Tues, Wed & Fri–Sun 10am–5pm, Thurs 10am–7pm; free), housing an excellent collection of paintings from the Middle Ages to the early twentieth century. Centre stage is taken by an exquisite *Portrait of Philipp Melanchthon* by Hans Holbein the Younger. A decent display of Italian Renaissance work includes pictures by Botticelli and Raphael, and there's a good cross-section of Dutch work, including one of Rembrandt's rare nature paintings. On the first floor, the **archeology** department's showpieces are the bodies of prehistoric men preserved in the peat bogs of Lower Saxony. The contents of several excavated graves are another highlight, along with an array of Bronze Age jewellery.

A bit further down the road, the **Sprengel Museum** (Tues 10am–10pm, Wed–Sun 10am–6pm; DM2, free weekends) is one of the most exciting modern art galleries in Germany. Much of the display space is given over to changing exhibitions of photography, graphics and experimental art forms, but there's also a first-rate permanent display of twentieth-century painting and sculpture. Focal point is a huge range of work by Hannover's own Kurt Schwitters, the landscapes and still lifes coming as a surprise if you're familiar only with the famous Dada collages.

HERRENHAUSEN

The royal gardens of **Herrenhausen**, summer residence of the Hannover court, can be reached by U-Bahn #1 or #2, but it's better to pick up the free tourist office plan of the complex and walk through it. Proceeding north from town along Nienburgerstrasse, the least remarkable of the gardens – the **Welfengarten** – lies to the right, dominated by the huge neo-Gothic **Welfenpalais**, now occupied by the university.

To the left, the dead straight Herrenhäuser Allee cuts through the **Georgengarten**, an English-style landscaped garden with an artificial lake. This garden was created as a foil to the magnificent formal **Grosser Garten** (daily summer 8am–8pm, Sat & Sun to 4.30pm only; winter 8am–4.30pm; DM2), the city's pride and joy. If possible, time your visit to coincide with the playing of the fountains (May–Sept Mon–Fri 11am–noon & 2–4pm, Sat & Sun 11am–noon & 2–5pm) or when the illuminations are switched on (May–Sept Wed, Fri & Sat at dusk). Just inside the entrance gate is one of the most striking features, the **Hedge Theatre**, a permanent amphitheatre whose hedges doubled as scenery and changing rooms. Behind the Grande Parterre, eight small plots have been laid out to illustrate different styles of landscape gardening down the centuries, while the rear section of the Grosser Garten consists of a series of radiating avenues bounded by hedges and trees, each ending at a fountain. As a centrepiece, there's the **Grosse Fontäne**, which spurts Europe's highest jet of water, reaching 82 metres. In the adjoining Georgengarten is the **Wilhelm Busch Museum** (March–Oct Tues–Sun 10am–5pm; Nov–Feb closes 4pm; DM2), which features a brilliant collection by the eponymous father of the comic-strip cartoon, as well as hosting shows of other caricaturists.

Across Herrenhäuserstrasse to the north of the Grosser Garten is the **Berggarten**, set up to tend rare and exotic plants. Some compensation for the loss of the palace in the last war is provided by a number of courtly buildings to be found to the west along Herrenhäuser Strasse. One of these, the **Fürstenhaus**, is a sort of museum of the House of Hannover (daily April–Sept 10am–6pm; Oct–March 10am–5pm; DM5).

Practicalities

The **train station** is right in the centre of town; the main **post office** is alongside the exchange bureau here. Behind is the **bus station** for long-distance routes. The **tourist office** is to the right of the train station on Ernst-August-Platz (Mon–Fri 8.30am–6pm). For DM5 the tourist office will book you into a **hotel**. As a centre of the trade fair industry (the April fair is Europe's largest), Hannover charges fancy prices. Normally the lowest rates are at *Hospiz am Bahnhof*, Joachimstr. 2 (☎0511/324 297; ④); *Flora*, Heinrichstr. 36 (☎0511/342 334; ④); *Reverey*, Aegidiendamm 8 (☎0511/883 711; ⑤); and *Gildehof*, Joachimstr. 6 (☎0511/157 424; ⑤). There's a **youth hostel** at Ferdinand-Wilhelm-Fricke-Weg 1 (☎0511/322 941; ②); take U-Bahn #3 or #7, towards Mühlenberg, and alight at Fischerhof, from where it's a five-minute walk to the left over the bridge, then right. Alongside is a **campsite**.

Hannover's major find for **snacks** is the Markthalle, where German, Italian, Spanish and Turkish stallholders sell wonderful examples of their cooking. Alternatively, there's the self-service *Mövenpick* in the shopping arcade behind the tourist office. The *Brauhaus Ernst August* on Schmiedestrasse is a brewery serving hearty German food. *Weinloch*, Burgstr. 33, and *Hannen Fass*, on the corner of Knochenhauerstrasse and Schuhstrasse, are youthful pubs serving cheap meals. Good **cafés** include *Klatsch*, Limmerstr. 58, and the celebrated *Kröpcke* on the square of the same name.

Hildesheim

Some of the finest buildings in Germany are to be found 30km southeast of Hannover at **HILDESHEIM**, where, during the eleventh century, the Romanesque style in architecture, sculpture and painting achieved its state of perfection. Much of what stands there now, however, is reconstructed: Hildesheim was bombed just a month before the German surrender in 1945, and the consequent fire caused damage which even exemplary restoration cannot disguise.

For the past decade the restorers have been at work on the town's Marktplatz, recreating what used to be Germany's most magnificent square. The fifteenth-century **Templarhaus**, the only absolutely authentic structure here, is one of the country's finest secular medieval buildings. Hildesheim's supreme monument, the serene church of **St Michael**, is about ten minutes' walk south of the train station, perched on a little hill and girded with six towers. St Michael's was very much a personal creation of Bishop Bernward, confidant of Emperor Otto II and tutor to Otto III, and bishop here from 993 to 1022. Shortly after his canonization in 1192, seven elaborately carved capitals were made for the nave, and in the west transept a choir screen was erected; only part of this remains, but its stucco carvings rank among the masterpieces of German sculpture. An even more spectacular embellishment was the painted ceiling – three-quarters of the 1300 oak panels are original.

The **Dom**, reached via Burgstrasse, is largely fake on the outside, but the interior has been restored to its eleventh-century layout. Made for St Michael's by a bronze foundry which Bernward established, the doors inside the main entrance tell the story of Adam and Eve on the left-hand side, and of Christ on the right. Soon after, the same craftsmen made a triumphal column, now in the southern transept, illustrating the lives of Jesus and John the Baptist. Almost as impressive are the huge wheel-shaped chandelier, made around 1065, and the font in the baptismal chapel, made in 1225. The cloister (Mon–Sat 10am–5pm, Sun noon–5pm; DM1) forms a protective shield round the apse, where the legendary thousand-year-old rosebush grows. In 815, Ludwig the Pious, Charlemagne's son, hung the royal chapel's relics of the Virgin on the tree while out hunting nearby. When he tried to remove them, they would not budge; taking this as divine instruction, he founded a church on the very spot. A beautiful fourteenth-century miniaturization of a Gothic cathedral, the St-Annen-Kapelle, occupies the centre of the cloister garden.

Hildesheim's **Diocesan Museum** (Tues & Thurs–Sat 10am–5pm, Wed 10am–7pm, Sun noon–5pm; DM4) contains several works dating from Bernward's time, including the *Golden Madonna* and a pair of crucifixes. Adjoining the north side of the Dom's close is the old Franciscan monastery, which now contains the archeological **Roemer-Pelizaeus Museum** (Tues–Sun 10am–4.30pm; DM3, free Sun), with a collection of Egyptian antiquities that is one of the best in Europe.

The southern part of Hildesheim was largely spared from war damage, and presents several streets of half-timbered houses as a reminder of what the whole of the old city once looked like. South of the Dom area stretches Hinterer Brühl, an almost completely preserved old street, at the end of which is **St Godehard**, built in the mid-twelfth century. East of St Godehard, Gelber Stern leads into Kesslerstrasse, arguably the most imposing of the old streets, lined with Renaissance and Baroque mansions.

The **tourist office** (Mon–Fri 9am–6pm, Sat 9am–1pm) is tucked away behind the Marktplatz on Am Ratsbauhof. Cheapest **hotel** with a decent location is *Kurth*, Küsthardtstr. 4 (☎05121/32 817; ④). The **youth hostel** is sited above Moritzberg at Schirrmannweg 4 (☎05121/42 717; ②), a good hour's walk from the centre (buses #1 and #4 go part of the way). First choice among places to **eat** and **drink** is the *Ratskeller* on the Marktplatz, which has cheap specials most lunchtimes.

Goslar

The stereotype of a mining town immediately conjures up images of grim terraced houses and louring machinery. **GOSLAR**, superbly located at the northern edge of the gentle wooded **Harz** mountains, could not be more different. For one thing, the mining here was always of a very superior nature – silver was discovered in the nearby Rammelsberg in the tenth century, and the town soon became the "treasure chest of the Holy Roman Empire". The presence of a POW hospital during World War II spared it from bombing, and Goslar can claim to have more old houses than any other town in Germany.

Although it hosts an attractive market every Tuesday and Friday morning, the central **Marktplatz** is best seen empty to fully appreciate its gorgeous visual variety, with its elegantly Gothic Rathaus and roofs of bright red tiles and contrasting grey slate. The Huldigungssaal (Hall of Homage) in the **Rathaus** contains a dazzling array of medieval wall and ceiling paintings (tours daily: June–Sept 10am–5pm; Oct–May 10am–4pm; DM3), the most valuable items hidden in altar niches and closets behind the panelling.

Just behind the Rathaus is the **Marktkirche**, facing the sixteenth-century **Brusttuch**, with its top storey crammed with satirical carvings. Goslar's half-timbered beauty begins in earnest in the streets behind the church, the oldest houses lying in the Bergstrasse and Schreiberstrasse areas. An especially fine Baroque specimen is the **Siemenshaus** (Mon–Fri 9am–noon; free) at their junction. Turning right into Bergstrasse, wind your way up to the roughly hewn **Frankenberger Kirche**, situated in tranquil solitude on the boundaries of the Altstadt. Some faint thirteenth-century frescoes compete in vain for attention against a Baroque pulpit.

Down Peterstrasse, past a variety of attractive buildings, lies the remarkable **Kaiserpfalz** (Imperial Palace). Built at the beginning of the eleventh century, the Kaiserpfalz continued to flourish until a fire gutted it in 1289 – it was rescued from disrepair by Kaiser Wilhelm I in 1868. Much of the **interior** (daily April–Oct 10am–5pm; Nov–March 10am–4pm; DM2.50) is occupied by the vast Reichssaal, decorated with romantic depictions of the emperors. Below the Kaiserpfalz, an enormous car park fills the former site of the **Dom**, pulled down in 1822 due to lack of funds for restoration. Only the entrance hall with its facade of thirteenth-century statues survived (June–Sept Tues–Sun 10am–5pm; Oct–May 11.30am–2.30pm; DM0.60). Off to the right of Hoher Weg, which leads back to the Marktplatz, is the **Goslar Museum** (Mon–Sat 10am–4/5pm; DM3.50); it contains the *Krodo* altar from the Dom – looking as if it were fashioned in the heart of Africa rather than eleventh-century Europe – and a section on mining.

A ten-minute walk northwest of Marktplatz brings you to the **Mönchehaus Museum** (Tues–Fri 10am–1pm & 3–5pm, Sun 10am–1pm; DM2.50). A black and white half-timbered building over 450 years old, it's the curious home to Goslar's modern art collection. East of here, the **Jakobikirche** contains a moving *Pietà* by the great but elusive sixteenth-century sculptor, Hans Witten. Finally, the **silver mine** in the Rammelsberg hill on the southern edge of town – the place where silver was first discovered in this vicinity – has been opened to the public as a mining museum (tours daily 9.30am–6pm; DM6).

Practicalities

The **tourist office** is at Marktplatz 7 (May–Sept Mon–Fri 9am–5pm, Sat 9am–2pm; Oct–April Mon–Fri 9am–1pm & 2–5pm, Sat 9am–2pm). Expect to pay DM50–80 for a double room in a **hotel**; the eighteenth-century *Hotel Zur Börse*, Bergstr. 53 (☎05321/22 775; ⑤), is one of the prettiest. Just a few minutes' walk from the **train station** at the northern end of town is *Gästehaus Elisabeth Möller*, Schieferweg 6 (☎05321/23 098; ④), an excellent guesthouse serving amazing breakfasts. The **youth hostel**, Rammelsbergerstr. 25 (☎05321/22 240; ②), is a bit of a trek from the centre. Nearest **camping** is the well-equipped *Sennhütte*, Clausthalerstr. 28, several kilometres along the B241 to the south – take the bus for Clausthal-Zellerfeld. As for **restaurants**, *Kontrast*, Worthstr. 10, does health-food stuff, and nearby *Worthmühle* is good for provincial cooking at very low prices. These are also the best bets if you're just looking for a place to have a **drink**.

CENTRAL GERMANY

Central Germany, the most populous region of the country, is the powerhouse of the economic miracle, and the zone of heaviest industrialization – the **Ruhrgebiet** – forms the most densely populated area in Europe. Within this conurbation, **Cologne** is the outstanding city, managing to preserve many of the splendours of its long centuries as a free state. The other city of top-class historical interest in the province of North Rhineland-Westphalia is **Aachen**, the original capital of the Holy Roman Empire, though **Münster**, formerly capital of Westphalia, boasts an extremely alluring centre. The modern seat of regional government is self-consciously cosmopolitan **Düsseldorf**, a city which inspires admiration and revulsion in roughly equal measure.

The adjoining province of Rhineland-Palatinate (Rheinland-Pfalz) is the one most overlaid by legend. The **Rhine** is seen here at its majestic best, and there's hardly a town, castle or rock along this stretch which hasn't made a distinctive contribution to its mythology. This is the land of the national epic, the *Nibelungenlied*, of the alluring Lorelei, of the robber barons who presided over tiny fiefs from lofty fortresses, and of the merchant traders who used the river routes to make the country rich. Nowadays pleasure cruisers run the length of the Rhine, through the **Rhine gorge** and past a wonderful landscape of rocks, vines, white-painted towns and ruined castles. Industry exists only in isolated pockets, and **Mainz**, the Palatinate's capital, doesn't even rank among the thirty largest cities in Germany. Its monuments, though, together with those of the two other imperial cathedral cities of **Worms** and **Speyer**, merit more than a passing glance. However, the number one city for sights is **Trier**, which preserves the finest buildings of classical antiquity this side of the Alps.

Occupying the geographical centre of the Federal Republic, the province of Hessen is focused on the American-style dynamism of **Frankfurt**. Although heavy industry still exists around the confluence of the Rhine and the Main, it's the serious money generated by banking and communications-related industries in Frankfurt that provides the region's real economic base. Of the region's historic centres, the place of particular interest is the old university town of **Marburg**.

Münster

Northern Westphalia is dominated by **MÜNSTER**, one of the most enticing cities of the German plain. Industry has been confined to the peripheries, and the centre is crowded with fashionable shops and buildings that cover the spectrum from Romanesque to Baroque – and one benefit of the large university is that bicycles rule the streets. The dominant influence on Münster has been the Church, its very name (meaning minster) deriving from the monastery of Saint Liudger, who was made bishop in 805 as part of Charlemagne's campaign to convert the Saxon tribes. Apart from an interlude of fanatical Anabaptist rule, it has remained intensely loyal to Catholicism, even during the Third Reich, when the city's bishop, Clemens August von Galen, was one of the regime's most courageous and persistent opponents.

The City

The centre of the main street, the **Prinzipalmarkt**, is occupied by the magnificently restored Gothic **Rathaus**, where in 1648 the signing of the Peace of Westphalia ended the morass of conflicts known as the Thirty Years' War. The room where it was signed, the **Friedensaal** (Peace Hall), is the only part generally open to the public (Mon–Fri 9am–5pm, Sat 9am–4pm, Sun 10am–1pm; DM1.50). Next door, the Renaissance **Stadtweinhaus** has also been returned to its former splendour, but the rest of what was once one of the handsomest main thoroughfares in Europe is more of a compromise.

At the end of Prinzipalmarkt is **St Lamberti**, with its elegant openwork spire. High up on the older section of the tower hang three iron cages, in which were displayed the bodies of the Anabaptist leader Jan van Leyden and his lieutenants after the crushing of their one-year "Reich" in 1535. The iconoclastic Anabaptists destroyed most of the sculpture of the city's medieval churches; one of the rare examples left in place is the elaborate *Tree of Jesse* over St Lamberti's south doorway.

The vast **Domplatz** is just a few strides away. Almost any point on the square gives superb views of the thirteenth-century **Dom**, built in a transitional, Romanesque–Gothic style. The inside of the porch has statues of Christ and the Apostles dating from the start of building. The interior is crammed with sculptural memorials and other works, but what really catches the eye is the **astronomical clock** in the southern arm of the ambulatory; made in the 1530s, it was decorated by the leading Münster painter of the day, Ludger tom Ring the Elder. At the far end of the cloisters, the **Domkammer** (Tues–Sat 10am–noon & 2–6pm, Sun 2–6pm; DM1) houses some beautiful religious items, pride of place going to the eleventh-century gold reliquary of Saint Paul.

Domplatz is also the city's museum centre. The **Landesmuseum** (Tues–Sun 10am–6pm; DM5, free Fri) has mainly Westphalian pieces, but it's not a parochial museum. On the ground floor is a collection of medieval sculpture, including statues smashed by the Anabaptists from the Liebfrauenkirche, and some magnificent pieces from the Dom, such as Heinrich Brabender's massive *Christ's Entry into Jerusalem*. A dimmed room is devoted to stained glass, while upstairs, the history of Westphalian painting is traced, with the Renaissance section dominated by the versatile tom Ring family. On the second floor two rooms of Expressionist paintings give a good cross-section of the movement. The similarly compendious **Westphalian Archeology Museum** (same times and prices) in the adjoining building offers a rather dry collection.

A short distance to the west is the **Liebfrauenkirche**, standing beside the Aa, Münster's tiny river. Like St Lamberti, it's a fourteenth-century hall church, with a floridly decorated tower. From here, Frauenstrasse leads to Schlossplatz with the resplendent **Schloss** of the prince bishops, now used by the university, fronting the **Botanical Gardens** (daily 8am–5pm; summer 8am–7pm).

Practicalities

The **train station** is due east of the city centre, which is reached by heading straight down Windthorststrasse; **buses** leave from Bahnhofstrasse. Directly opposite is the main **tourist office** (Mon–Fri 10am–6pm, Sat 10am–1pm; closed Sun); there's also a branch in the Rathaus (Mon–Fri 9am–5pm, Sat 9am–4pm, Sun 10am–1pm). Most convenient among the better **hotels** is *Zum Schwan*, facing the back of the station at Schillerstr. 27 (☎0251/661 166; ⑤); the pub downstairs has very reasonable meals. A central alternative is *Zur Krone*, Hammerstr. 67 (☎0251/73 868; ④). The **youth hostel** is at Bismarck Allee 31 (☎0251/43 765; ②), by the Aasee; bus #13 goes closest. There's a summer **campsite** at Dorbaumstr. 35, in the northeastern suburb of Handorf.

Münster has a wonderful choice of **bars**, **cafés** and **restaurants**. The obvious place to begin is around the Prinzipalmarkt, where *Stuhlmacher*, the city's most celebrated pub, provides a wide selection of beers – but an expensive restaurant. Across the road is the leading café, *Otto Schucan*, which is pricy but irresistible. Just down the road, *Café Kleimann*, occupying one of the finest of the old guild houses, makes a good alternative. Continuing into Roggenmarkt, you'll find one of the best **discos**, the *Elephant*, although more lively is *Byblos* on Hörsterstrasse. Another lively nightlife area is the Kuhviertel, just beyond the Liebfrauenkirche. *Pinkus Müller*, Münster's only brewery, has two places on Kreuzstrasse – the main pub-restaurant and the *Bier Galerie*. Although not the cheapest, the former is the best place in Münster for a traditional Westphalian meal.

Düsseldorf

DÜSSELDORF, Germany's richest city, is the epitome of the economic miracle – orderly, prosperous and self-confident. Never as industrialized as its Ruhr neighbours, Düsseldorf has concentrated on its role as a financial and administrative centre: one of the country's largest stock exchanges is here, as are the headquarters and offices of innumerable multinationals. At least two of these, the **Thyssen-Haus** in the heart of the city and the **Mannesmann-Haus** on the banks of the Rhine, are dominant landmarks, in the way that towers of churches and town halls were in medieval cityscapes. Even for a short visit Düsseldorf is expensive, but on the plus side the **nightlife** is among the most enjoyable in the country.

Arrival and accommodation

The **train station** is southeast of the city centre, with the shopping streets fanning out from it. S-Bahn trains leave at twenty-minute intervals for the **airport**. The **tourist office** (Mon–Fri 8am–6pm, Sat 9am–12.30pm) is on Konrad-Adenauer-Platz, facing the train station. In the same building is a **hotel reservation service** (Mon–Sat 8am–10pm, Sun 4–10pm), although their prices generally are far above the national norm. The hotels near the train station are as cheap as any, especially *Manhattan*, Graf-Adolf-Str. 39 (☎0211/370 244; ④). The **youth hostel**, at Düsseldorferstr. 1 in Oberkassel (☎0211/574 041; ③), has singles as well as dormitory beds; from the station, take bus #835 or walk down Graf-Adolf-Strasse and continue over the Rheinkniebrücke – it's the first building on the other side. There are two **campsites** (April–Sept): Oberlörick (☎0211/591 401) is reached by U-Bahn #76, #705 or #717 to Belsenplatz, then bus #828; for Unterbachsee (☎0211/899 2038), out at the eastern extremity, take bus #781.

The City

Though never one of Germany's great architectural attractions, Düsseldorf's **Altstadt** has a couple of churches to catch the eye: **St Lambertus** (Mon–Thurs 7am–5.30pm, Fri noon–5.30pm, Sat 7am–6pm, Sun 9am–6pm), a fourteenth-century brick building, is easily recognizable by its tall twisted spire, while a short walk to the east is the stuccoed **St Andreas**, mausoleum of the Electors Palatinate – the princes who elected the Holy Roman Emperor. The most popular of the Electors was Jan Wellem, commemorated in the huge open area named after him in the heart of the city, and by a masterly equestrian statue outside the Renaissance **Rathaus**. In the square immediately to the north is the **Schlossturm**, the only remnant of the old fortifications; it has been restored to house a small **Navigation Museum** (Tues–Sun 10am–5pm; DM3).

Wellem's successors employed French gardeners to transform their city with parks, canals and miscellaneous urban improvements. This culminated in the creation of the main thoroughfare, the famously chic **Königsallee**. Only the Jugendstil **Kaufhaus** has any merits as a building; diagonally opposite its rear entrance is **Wilhelm-Marx-Haus**, the earliest visible expression of Düsseldorf's infatuation with the New World, hailed as the first skyscraper in Germany when it went up in the 1920s.

The largest of the parks is the **Hofgarten**, shaped like a great stiletto-heeled shoe, now crossed by several busy streets. At its far end is **Schloss Jägerhof**, a Baroque palace which has recently been been refitted as the **Goethe Museum** (Tues–Fri & Sun 11am–5pm, Sat 1–5pm; DM3); unless you're already an avid fan, the contents will not thrill. Düsseldorf's own favourite son is another of Germany's most celebrated writers, **Heinrich Heine**, in whose honour a research institute and museum have been set up at Bilkerstrasse 14 (Tues–Sun 11am–5pm; DM2).

The two large art museums each warrant a gentle browse. Housed in an ultra-modern gallery in Grabbeplatz is the **Kunstsammlung Nordrhein-Westfalen** (Tues–Sun 10am–6pm; DM5). The collection began with an act of contrition: in atonement for the dismissal of Paul Klee from his professorship at the Düsseldorf Academy in the Nazi purges of 1933, around ninety of his works were bought by the city in 1960. Klee remains the big attraction, but later acquisitions of twentieth-century art have turned the museum into a who's who of modern painting.

The **Kunstmuseum** (Tues–Sun 11am–6pm; DM6), north of the Altstadt at Ehrenhof 5, has extensive displays on three floors. At ground level there's a fine collection of glass, much of it Art Nouveau and Art Deco. On the next floor, Rubens' altarpiece of *The Assumption* puts almost all its companions in the shade – exceptions being a *St Jerome* attributed to Ribera, and *St Francis in Meditation* by Zurbarán. Upstairs, there's a modern section that complements the Kunstsammlung, along with dull stuff from the nineteenth-century Düsseldorf Academy.

Eating, drinking and nightlife

"The longest bar in Europe" is how the tourist office describes the Altstadt: the heart of the quarter – the parallel Kurzestrasse/Andreasstrasse and Bolkerstrasse, and the streets perpendicular to them – is almost entirely given over to places of entertainment. **Eating** is one of the few things it's possible to do cheaply in Düsseldorf, thanks to the variety of the city's ethnic communities, with the ubiquitous pizzerias leading the way. For tasty **local dishes** at low prices try *Hühner-Max* in Mertensgasse. *Im Goldenen Kessel* in Bolkerstrasse is the flagship of the *Schumacher* brewery, and is equally renowned for its food. In the same street is *Zum Schlüssel*, the cavernous and popular **beer hall** of *Gatzweiler's* brewery, but perhaps the most famous house brewery in Germany is *Zum Uerige*, in Bergerstrasse. For something wilder there's *Ratinger Hof*, Ratingerstrasse, the first punk bar in Germany; on the same street is *Zum Goldenen Einhorn*, enduringly popular with the youth of the city. *Café Bernstein*, Oststrasse, is a genuine local, tucked away in the shopping area between the Altstadt and the train station – a stylish place for a nightcap. The huge *Tor 3*, Ronsdorferstr. 143 – south of the centre in the Bilk district – is the city's best **disco**.

Cologne

Currently the fourth largest city in Germany, with a population of just under a million, **COLOGNE** (Köln) is the colossus of the Rhine-Ruhr sprawl. The huge Gothic **Dom** is the country's most visited monument, while its Roman remains and medieval buildings are unsurpassed, and its museums bettered only by Berlin, Munich and Dresden. The annual **Carnival** festival in the early spring is one of Europe's major popular celebrations. The city also ranks high as a **beer** centre, with twenty-four breweries all producing the distinctive **Kölsch**.

Founded in 33 BC, Cologne owed much of its development to ecclesiastical affairs. A bishopric was established in the fourth century, and saints Severin, Gereon and Ursula were all martyred here: churches were soon dedicated to each and built over their graves. In the twelfth century Cologne acquired the relics of the Three Magi from Milan, thus increasing its standing as one of the greatest centres of pilgrimage in northern Europe. Situated on the intersection of the Rhine and several major trade routes, medieval Cologne became immensely rich – and the largest city in Germany. Later decline was partially reversed in the eighteenth century with the exploitation of an Italian recipe for distilling flower blossoms into almost pure alcohol; originally created as an aphrodisiac, it was marketed here as a toilet water, achieving worldwide fame under its new name – *Eau de Cologne*. In this century Cologne's great personality was Konrad Adenauer, deposed as mayor of the city by the Nazis, and the first chancellor of the country after the war.

Arrival and accommodation

The **train station** is immediately below the Dom; moving on is never a problem, as around a thousand trains stop here daily. The **bus station** is directly behind, with international services on the lower tier. For the **airport** take bus #170, which leaves every twenty minutes or so, and takes less than half an hour. The **tourist office** is at Unter Fettenhennen 19, in front of the Dom (May–Oct Mon–Sat 8am–10.30pm, Sun 9am–10.30pm; Nov–April Mon–Sat 8am–9pm, Sun 9.30am–7pm). It publishes a comprehensive monthly guide to what's on, *Köln-Monatsvorschau*, priced DM2.

For a **hotel room**, best advice is to pay up the DM2 the tourist office charges to find you a place. Accommodation is plentiful, but it's scattered all over the city and is mainly geared to the trade fairs. If you prefer to look yourself, the following are centrally placed: *Stapelhäuschen*, Fischmarkt 1–3 (☎0221/212 193; ⑤), *Im Kupferkessel*, Probsteigasse 6 (☎0221/135 338; ④), *Schmidt*, Elisenstr. 16 (☎0221/211 706; ⑤), *Einig*, Johanisstr. 71 (☎0221/122 128; ④), and *Alter Römer*, AM Bollwerk 23 (☎0221/212 385; ④).

There are two **youth hostels**. The more central is the dingy and claustrophobic place at Siegesstr. 5a in Deutz (☎0221/814 711; ②), about fifteen minutes' walk from the centre over the Hohenzollernbrücke. Much more enticing, and pricier, is the youth guesthouse in the northern suburb of Riehl (☎0221/767 081; ③) – take U-Bahn #5, #16 or #18 from the train station to Boltensternstrasse. The only all-year **campsite** is at Peter-Baum-Weg, in the northeastern suburb of Dünnwald.

Cologne's **public transport** network, shared with Bonn, is a mixture of buses and trams, the latter becoming the U-Bahn around the centre. Fares are high, making it better to invest in a 24-hour ticket (DM9 for Cologne only) or a three-day pass (DM17). Finally, students can get half-price admission to all Cologne's museums; if you're not eligible, it might make sense to invest in the **Museums Pass** (DM20), which allows entry to all the city collections on any three days in a week.

The City

One of the most massive Gothic buildings ever constructed, the **Dom** is built on a scale that reflects its power – the archbishop was one of the seven Electors of the Holy Roman Empire, and it remains the seat of the Primate of Germany. Impetus for its creation came with the arrival of the alleged relics of the Magi; when it came to commissioning a church of appropriate grandeur, it was decided to adopt the ethereal new Gothic style rather than the late Romanesque style still in vogue in the Rhineland. The chancel was completed in 1322, but then the ambitiousness of the plans began to take its toll. In 1560 the project was abandoned, to be resumed only in the nineteenth century. What you see today is substantially an act of homage from one age to another: taking guidance from recently discovered documents that showed the first designs for the facade, the masons continued the work in perfect imitation of the style of their precursors. Originally the **spires** were the tallest structures in the world, but were soon dwarfed by the Eiffel Tower and are no longer even the highest in Cologne. All the same, you need a fair bit of muscle to climb up the south tower for the panorama over the city and the Rhine (daily 9am–4/6pm; DM3).

From the west door your eye is immediately drawn down the length of the building to the high altar, with the spectacular golden **shrine** to the Magi, made in 1181. It's one of three masterpieces to be found here; the others are in the chapels at the entrance to the ambulatory. On the north side is the ninth-century **Gero crucifix**, the most important monumental sculpture of its period, while the corresponding chapel to the south has the greatest achievement of the fifteenth-century Cologne school of painters, the *Adoration of the Magi* by **Stefan Lochner**. Stained-glass windows are an essential component of a Gothic cathedral, and Cologne has a marvellously varied set. The oldest, dating from 1260, is in the farthest chapel of the ambulatory.

The Schatzkammer (Mon–Sat 9am–5pm, Sun 1–4pm; DM3) is far less interesting than the **Diocesan Museum**, just outside in Roncalliplatz (Mon–Wed, Fri & Sat 10am–5pm, Sun 10am–1pm; DM1). Another beautiful Lochner, *Madonna of the Violets*, forms the centrepiece.

THE WALLRAF-RICHARTZ/LUDWIG AND RÖMISCH-GERMANISCHES MUSEUMS

Housed in an ultra-modern building right next to the Dom, the **Wallraf-Richartz/ Ludwig Museum** (Tues–Thurs 10am–8pm, Fri–Sun 10am–6pm; DM8) is an amazing picture hoard, comprising three distinct sections. On the first floor, the **Wallraf-Richartz** collection is centred on the fifteenth-century Cologne school. Stefan Lochner's *Last Judgement* is an especially inventive work, but the gems of the whole display are the two large triptychs by the Master of St Bartholomew, the school's final flowering at the beginning of the sixteenth century. Displayed alongside these Cologne masters are other German paintings, including a small Dürer and several Cranach pieces. There are also a number of Flemish panels, while the rich show of seventeenth-century Dutch artists includes what is probably the last of Rembrandt's great self-portraits.

The **Ludwig Museum** of twentieth-century art occupies the remainder of the galleries, providing a jolting gear-change from fifteenth-century altarpieces to Andy Warhol, whose Brillo boxes and Campbell's cans are the centrepiece of the large Pop Art section. Among German works there's a fine group of Kirchners, a room full of Beckmanns, three superb portraits by Dix and a number of sculptures by Barlach. Two rooms are devoted to Picasso, with sculptures, ceramics and paintings from most phases of his career. The third museum, the **Agfa-Foto-Historama**, shows old photographic equipment and a selection of prints from the vast holdings of the company, whose headquarters are in nearby Leverkusen.

Germany's most important archeological museum, the neighbouring **Römisch-Germanisches Museum** (Tues & Fri–Sun 10am–5pm, Wed & Thurs 10am–8pm;

DM5), was specially constructed around its star exhibit, the **Dionysos Mosaic**. The finest work of its kind in northern Europe, it was created for the dining room of a patrician villa in about 200 AD, and covers some seventy square metres. The other main item is the adjacent **Tomb of Poblicius**; dating from about 40 AD, it stands fifteen metres high. The museum's collection of **glass** is reckoned to be the world's finest, but of more general appeal is the dazzling array of **jewellery** on the first floor, mostly dating from the so-called Dark Ages.

THE ALTSTADT

The vast **Altstadt** suffered grievous damage in the last war, and economic necessity meant that nondescript modern buildings were quickly raised to fill the bombsites. Where there wasn't a pressing need for reconstruction, as in the case of the churches, restoration projects were initiated, some of which are still going on. What has been achieved is so impressive that the Altstadt ideally requires two or three days' exploration.

For nearly 600 years, **Gross St Martin**'s tower, surrounded by four turrets, was the dominant feature of the Cologne skyline; the rest of the church seems rather truncated for such a splendid adornment, although the interior (Mon–Thurs 10am–6pm, Fri & Sun 2pm–4pm, Sat 12.30–1.30pm) has a pleasing simplicity. A short distance beyond is the Alter Markt, one of three large squares in the heart of the city. From here, you can see the irregular octagonal tower of the **Rathaus**, a real fricassee of styles; to see the historic parts of the interior you have to take an hour-long guided tour (Wed & Sat 3pm; free) – it's in German only, but you can pick up a leaflet in English. Just in front of the entrance to the Rathaus, a door leads down into the **Mikwe** (ritual bathhouse), the only remnant of the Jewish ghetto, which was razed soon after the expulsion order of 1424 (Sun 11am–1pm; during office hours ask at the Rathaus porter's desk). More subterranean sights can be found in nearby Kleine Budengasse, in the form of the **Praetorium**, the foundations of the Roman governor's palace, and the **Roman sewer**, a surprisingly elegant vaulted passageway some one hundred metres long (Tues–Sun 10am–5pm; DM3).

Proceeding south, you pass the burnt-out **Alt St Alban**, left as a war memorial, and the tower which is all that survives of **Klein St Martin**. Behind, hemmed in by modern houses, is the severe **St Maria im Kapitol**, with a majestic interior (daily 9.30am–6.30pm) – look out for the wooden doors, contemporary with the eleventh-century architecture. Its cloisters, unusually placed adjoining the facade, are the only ones left in Cologne.

Continuing in a southerly direction, go down Rheingasse to see the step-gabled **Overstolzenhaus**, the finest mansion in the city. A short walk from here is **St Maria in Lyskirchen** (Mon–Wed & Fri 10am–5.30pm, Thurs 1–5.30pm, Sat & Sun noon–5.30pm), where the vaults are covered with thirteenth-century frescoes. From here, head up Grosse Witschgasse and Georgstrasse to the eleventh-century **St Georg** (daily 8am–6pm), whose spacious interior contrasts markedly with the stumpy exterior.

The most southerly of the churches are **St Severin** (daily 9am–noon & 3–7pm), which was much altered in the Gothic era, and – northwest of it – **St Pantaleon** (daily 9am–5pm), the oldest church in the city. North up Poststrasse and Peterstrasse is **St Peter**, a Gothic church with gleaming stained-glass windows and a magnificent *Crucifixion of St Peter* by Rubens, whose childhood was spent in Cologne.

Next door, the St Cäcelien church now houses the **Schnütgen Museum** (Tues–Sun 10am–5pm, first Thurs in month 10am–8pm; DM5), a collection of all kinds of Rhineland religious art except paintings. There are some wonderful ivories, but the museum's most famous possession is a painted bust of a woman, carved by one of the Parler family and thought to be the portrait of a relative. Across the road and down Antongasse is the tiny Gothic **Antoniterkirche**, housing one of the most famous twentieth-century sculptures, Barlach's *Memorial Angel*. Around the church is the main shopping centre; the streets follow the same plan as their Roman predecessors, but almost all the buildings are modern.

A short distance west lies Neumarkt, dominated at the far end by the superb apse of **SS. Aposteln** (daily 9am–6pm), due north of which is **St Gereon** (daily 9am–noon & 3–5pm), a church without parallel in European architecture. Its kernel is an oval fourth-century chapel which, after various additions, became the basis of a four-storey decagon in the early thirteenth century – which is also when the frescoed baptistery was built.

From here you can return towards the Dom, passing a fragment of Roman wall and the Arsenal en route to the stately **St Andreas**, worth a look for its frescoes and the Maccabeus shrine, a notable piece of early sixteenth-century craftsmanship. If you then strike north you'll come to **St Ursula** (daily 9am–noon & 1–5pm), with its prominent sturdy tower; unless you're squeamish, try to get hold of the sacristan, who will show you the **Goldene Kammer**, an ornate chamber gruesomely lined with reliquaries (Mon & Wed–Sat 9am–noon & 3–5pm, Sun 3–5pm; DM2). From here the **Eigelsteintor**, an impressive survival of the medieval fortifications, is reached via the street of the same name. Dagobertstrasse then leads east to **St Kunibert**, the final fling of the Romanesque in the early thirteenth century, completed just as work began on the Dom. It's also the last church to be restored after war damage, with the nave and massive facade not yet joined up. Inside (daily 7am–noon & 3–6pm), note the stained-glass windows in the apse, which are contemporary with the architecture.

Drinking, eating and entertainment

Cologne crams over 3000 pubs, bars and cafés into a relatively small area. Their ubiquitous feature is the city's unique beer, **Kölsch**. Light and aromatically bitter, it's served in a tall, thin glass (*Stange*) which holds only a fifth of a litre – hence its rather effete image among other German beer drinkers. Best places to try it are the **Brauhäuser**, brewery-owned beer halls which although staffed by horribly matey waiters called *Köbes* are definitely worth sampling, as they offer some of the cheapest **eating** in the city. Three of the *Brauhäuser* are very close to the Dom: *Alt Köln* at Trankgasse 7–9, *Früh am Dom* at Am Hof 12–14 and *Brauhaus Sion* at Unter Taschenmacher 5. For a more authentic atmosphere and better food, you'd be better trying those a bit further away – the two called *Päffgen*, at Heumarkt 62 and Friesenstr. 64; *Haus Töller* at Weyerstr. 96; or *Zur Malzmühle* at Heumarkt 6.

Cologne's **nightspots** are concentrated in four distinct quarters. Most obvious of these is the area around Gross St Martin in the **Altstadt**, which catches the tourists and businessmen, but somehow manages to create a distinctive atmosphere in places. *Papa Joe's Klimperkasten*, Alter Markt 50, is a deservedly popular Altstadt bar for traditional live jazz; there's a cosier, smaller, equally good version called *Papa Joe's Em Streckstrumpf* at Buttermarkt 37. *Kauri*, Auf dem Rothenberg 11, is a conveniently sited disco which plays a good selection of funk and blues. Down the road from the university, in the southwestern zone, the **Quartier Lateng** is more like the real thing as far as mingling with locals is concerned, even if it has lost its trendy edge. At Zülpicher Str. 25, *Vanille* is a lovely café with kitsch decor, good food and cocktails, and occasional discos. Students make up most of the clientele at *Gilberts Pinte*, Englebertstr. 1, a bar with plenty of atmosphere. One of the most popular late-night café-bars is the *Peppermint Lounge*, Hochenstauffenring 23, springing into action around midnight, while *Weinhaus Kyffhäuser Keller*, Kyffhäuser Str. 47, is the best place in Cologne for a glass of wine. Showcase for local bands is *Juke Box*, Luxemburgerstr. 83 – it's jammed solid at weekends. The **Südstadt**, or St Severin quarter, now has the most stylish bars and cafés, and the biggest crowds. *Climax*, Ubierring 18, and *Chlodwig-Eck*, Annostr. 1, are the leaders of the pack. The more relaxed **Belgisches**

Viertel, just to the west of the centre, is nowhere near as packed or self-consciously trendy. Currently dominated by arty types, it's also a centre of the **gay scene** and has the most original **discos**. *Schulz*, Bismarckstr. 17, a very reasonably priced bar and café, is the heart of the gay scene; *Neuschwanstein Diskothek*, Mittelstr. 12, is the best disco in Cologne.

THE CARNIVAL

Though the **Carnival** season actually begins as early as November 11, the real business begins with **Weiberfastnacht** on the Thursday prior to the seventh Sunday before Easter. A ceremony at 10am in the Alter Markt leads to the official inauguration of the festival, with the mayor handing over the keys of the city to "Prinz Claus III", who assumes command for the duration. At 3pm there's the first of the great **processions** and in the evening the great series of **costume balls** begins – with singing and dancing in the streets and taverns as an authentic alternative. On the Saturday morning there's the **Funkenbiwack**, featuring the *Rote und Blaue Funken*, men dressed up in eighteenth-century military outfits who disobey every order. On Sunday the **Schull-und Veedleszög**, largely featuring children, forms a prelude to the more spectacular **Rosenmontagzug** (Rose Monday Parade). After this, the festival runs down, but there are numerous smaller parades in the suburbs on Shrove Tuesday, while the restaurants offer special fish menus on Ash Wednesday. The grandstand seats along the route are expensive for the Rose Monday Parade, but good value at DM5 on the Sunday.

Listings

Airlines *British Airways*, Marzellenstr. 1 (☎0221/135 081); *Lufthansa*, Bechergasse 2–8 (☎0221/8264).

Car rental *Avis*, Clemensstr. 29 (☎0221/234 333); *Europ-Car*, corner Gerchstr. & Christophstr. 2 (☎0221/132 071); *Hertz*, Bismarckstr. 19–21 (☎0221/515 084); *Condor*, Wilhelm-Mauserstr. 53 (☎0221/581 055).

Consulates Nearest Great Britain and US consulates are in Bonn: *Great Britain*, Friedrich-Ebert-Allee 119 (☎0228/234 061); *US*, Deichmanns Alle 29, Bad Godesberg (☎0228/3391).

Doctor ☎0221/720772.

Hitching *Mitfahrzentrale*, Saarstr. 22 (☎0221/233 464); there's a women-only branch, with a feminist bookshop, at Moltkestr. 66 (☎0221/523 152).

Post office The main office with poste restante is on An den Dominikanern, and has a 24-hour service, except for parcels, which must be sent from the depot on Marzellenstrasse. A branch at the Hauptbahnhof is open 7am–9pm, or 11am–8pm at weekends.

Aachen

Now a frontier post – it borders both Belgium and the Netherlands – **AACHEN** once played a far grander role. Around the late eighth century the city became the hub of the great empire of **Charlemagne**, a choice made partly for strategic reasons but also because of the presence of hot springs – exercising in these waters was one of the emperor's favourite pastimes.

Aachen's centre is ten minutes from the **train station** – down Bahnhofstrasse then right into Theaterstrasse. Although the surviving architectural legacy of Charlemagne is small, Aachen retains its crowning jewel in the former **Palace chapel**. Now the heart of the present-day **Dom**, its presence is enshrined in the French name for the city, Aix-la-Chapelle. As a result of the cult of Charlemagne and the possession of the so-called Great Aachen Relics (the swaddling clothes and loincloth of Christ, the gown of the Virgin and the garb of John the Baptist), pilgrims poured into the city in such numbers that the building had to be enlarged by adding the high and narrow Gothic chancel.

Some of the original furnishings survive – the bronze doors and figure of a she-wolf in the vestibule, for instance – but these are overshadowed by the embellishments added by Charlemagne's successors. Adorning the main altar is the **Pala d'Oro**, an eleventh-century altar front embossed with scenes of the Passion. Behind, and of similar date, is the ambo, a pulpit of gold-plated copper covered with precious stones, reliefs of the Evangelists and ancient Egyptian ivories. Suspended from the dome by means of a mighty iron chain is a twelfth-century chandelier so heavy that it cracked the ceiling mosaics: the present ones are a nineteenth-century recreation. At the end of the chancel, the gilded shrine of Charlemagne, finished in 1215 after fifty years' work, contains the remains of the emperor and glorifies the empire he founded. In the gallery is the **imperial throne**, perhaps made for the coronation of Otto I, which initiated the tradition of emperors being crowned at Aachen – a practice which lasted until the sixteenth century. In order to see the throne you have to join a **guided tour** (hourly in summer, at least twice daily for rest of year; DM2).

The **Schatzkammer** (Mon 10am–2pm, Tues–Sat 10am–6pm, Sun 10.30am–5pm; DM3) is the richest treasury in northern Europe. Prominent is the late tenth-century Lothair cross, studded with jewels and bearing a cameo of Augustus, and the Roman sarcophagus which served as Charlemagne's tomb for 400 years. A revealing illustration of the importance of the cult of Charlemagne is provided by the thirteenth-century shrine of the Virgin, made to house the Great Aachen Relics, but not started until Charlemagne's shrine had been completed.

Charlemagne's palace once extended across the Katsch Hof, now lined with ugly modern buildings, to the site of the fourteenth-century **Rathaus**, which incorporates two of the palace's towers. Fronting the Markt, which boasts the finest of the medieval houses left in the city, its facade is lined with the figures of fifty Holy Roman Emperors. The glory of the interior (daily 10am–6pm except Thurs 10am–8pm; DM6) is the much-restored **Kaisersaal**, repository of the crown jewels – in reproduction. The originals have been in Vienna since the early nineteenth century, when they were commandeered by the Habsburgs for their new role as emperors of Austria.

Practicalities

Pending the reappearance of the town centre **tourist office**, which has moved twice since 1992 and now vanished, the only useful branch is opposite the train station (Mon–Fri 9am–6.30pm, Sat 9am–1pm). Two of the cheaper **hotels** are near the train station: *Karls*, Leydelstr. 10 (☎0241/35 449; ④), and *Hesse*, Friedlandstr. 20 (☎0241/34 047; ④). The **youth hostel** is in a suburban park to the southwest, at Maria-Theresa-Allee 260 (☎0241/71 101; ②); take bus #2 as far as Brüsseler Ring or Ronheide. There's a **camp-site** just to the northeast of the centre at Pass Str. 85.

Many of the best places to **eat** and **drink** are found in and around the Markt. A spiced gingerbread called *Printen* is the main local speciality, and *the* place to eat it is the old coffee house *Leo van den Daele* on Büchel. The most celebrated **pub** is the *Postwagen*, built onto the end of the Rathaus, with a cheerful Baroque exterior and wonderful cramped rooms inside. For a livelier atmosphere, try *Goldener Schwan* or *Goldener Einhorn*, both on the Markt; the former has good value lunches, while the latter offers an enormous menu of German, Italian and Greek dishes.

The **student quarter** centres on Pontstrasse, where *Tangente* turns from an elegant café into a lively bar at night. *Café Kittel* is another student favourite, whereas *Labyrinth* is a more traditional beer hall, with an older, more relaxed clientele. Aachen's top **disco** is *Metropol* on Blondelstrasse on the eastern side of town, where music ranges from heavy metal to Europop until 5am on Fridays and Saturdays. It would be a pity to leave Aachen without a **swim** in the medicinal waters. Conveniently located at Buchkremerstr. 1 in the Altstadt is the **Römerbad** (Mon–Fri 7am–7pm, Sat 7am–1pm, Sun 7am–1pm; DM10) – the temperature is a constant, wonderfully refreshing 32°C.

Mainz

Situated by the confluence of the Rhine and Main, **MAINZ** developed in the eighth
century, when Saint Boniface made it the main centre of the Church north of the Alps.
Later, the local archbishop came to be one of the most powerful princes in the Holy
Roman Empire, and further prestige came through **Johannes Gutenberg**, who revolu-
tionized the art of printing here. Since the Napoleonic period it has never managed to
recover its former status, and its strategic location inevitably made it a prime target of
World War II bombers. Nonetheless, it's an agreeable mixture of old and new, and
makes a good alternative place to stay if you're flying in or out of Frankfurt, as the
airport lies on the S-Bahn line between the two cities.

Rearing high above the centre of Mainz is the red sandstone **Dom**, crowded in by
eighteenth-century houses. Choirs at both ends of the building indicate its status as an
imperial cathedral, with one area for the emperor and one for the clergy. A few years
ago it celebrated its one-thousandth anniversary, but most of what can be seen today is
twelfth-century Romanesque. The solemn and spacious interior makes a very superior
cemetery for the archbishops, whose tombs form an unrivalled panorama of sculpture
from the thirteenth century to the nineteenth. The **Diocesan Museum** (Mon–Wed &
Fri 9am–noon & 2–5pm, Thurs & Sat 9am–noon; free), off the cloisters, houses the
best sculptures of all – fragments from the demolished rood screen, created around
1240.

On Tuesday, Friday and Saturday mornings the spacious **Markt**, with its riotously
colourful fountain, is packed with market stalls and is unmissable. Dominating the
adjoining Liebfrauenplatz, the resplendent pink Haus zum Romischen Kaiser houses
the offices of the **Gutenberg Museum** (Tues–Sat 10am–6pm, Sun 10am–1pm; free) –
the actual displays are in a modern extension behind. It's a fitting tribute to one of the
greatest inventors of all time, whose pioneering development of moveable type led to
the mass-scale production of books. In 1978, the museum acquired the last Gutenberg
Bible still in private hands – made in the 1450s, it's one of only forty-odd surviving
examples.

Despite war damage, the centre of Mainz contains many fine old streets and
squares, such as the magnificent **Knebelscher Hof** north of the Dom, and
Kirschgarten and Augustinerstrasse to the south. Just off the end of Augustinerstrasse
is the sumptuous church of **St Ignaz**, in front of which a monumental *Crucifixion* by
Hans Backoffen stands over his own tomb, which is even more imposing than those he
had made for the archbishops. This marks the end of the historic quarter – beyond is
the largest red-light district in the Frankfurt conurbation.

Across Schöfferstrasse from the Dom, Ludwigstrasse runs to Schillerplatz and
Schillerstrasse, both lined with Renaissance and Baroque palaces. Up the hill by
Gaustrasse is the Gothic **St Stephan** (daily 10am–noon & 2–5pm), whose priest
persuaded Marc Chagall to make a series of stained-glass windows: symbolizing the
reconciliation between France and Germany, Christian and Jew, the nine windows
were finished in November 1984, a few months before Chagall's death. Down Grosse
Bleiche – which runs from the end of Schillerstrasse to the river – are the old imperial
stables, now home of the **Landesmuseum** (Tues–Sun 10am–5pm, Fri until 4pm; free).
The outstanding archeology department includes a hall of Roman sculptural remains,
dominated by the Jupitersäule, the most important Roman triumphal column in
Germany.

Further along is the **Schloss**, the enormous former palace of the Archbishop-
Electors, a superbly swaggering Renaissance building. The interior had to be
completely rebuilt after the war, and now contains the **Römisch-Germanisches
Museum** (Tues–Sun 10am–6pm; free), a confusing mix of original antiquities and
copies.

Practicalities

The **train station** is northwest of the city centre. A short way down Bahnhofstrasse you'll find the **tourist office** (Mon–Fri 9am–6pm, Sat 9am–1pm), situated close to many of the least expensive **hotels** – though even these tend to charge upwards of DM70 for a double. Cheaper and with a better location very near the Dom are *Stadt Coblenz*, at Rheinstr. 49 (☎06131/227 602; ④), and *Zum Schildknecht*, at Heliggrabgasse 6 (☎06131/ 225 755; ④). Alternatively, there's the **youth hostel** (☎06131/85 332; ②), situated in the wooded heights of Am Fort Weisenau and reached by bus #1 or #22.

Mainz boasts more vineyards than any other German city, and you don't need to stray far from the Dom if you fancy a **wine** crawl. Some *Weinstuben* are open in the evenings only, such as the oldest, *Alt Deutsche Weinstube* in Liebfrauenplatz, which offers cheap daily dishes. Even better food is available at *Weinhaus Schreiner*, just across Rheinstrasse. Though Mainz is a wine rather than a **beer** city, it has a traditional beer hall in *Brauhaus Zur Sonne* on Stadthausstrasse, and the excellent brewery-owned *Gastätte Zum Salvator* on Grosse Langgasse. The hottest **nightspot** is *Terminus* on Rheinallee, a former warehouse that now attracts punters from miles around.

The Rhine Gorge

North of Mainz, the Rhine bends westwards and continues its hitherto stately but undramatic journey – then suddenly, at BINGEN, the river widens and swings north into the spectacular eighty-kilometre **Rhine gorge**. This waterway may have become one of Europe's major tourist magnets, but the pleasure steamers are still outnumbered by commercial barges – a reminder of the river's crucial role in the German economy.

In summer, **accommodation** under DM30 per person is scarce and heavily booked. Spring and autumn are undoubtedly the best times to visit, and you could easily spend several days meandering. Rail and road lines lie on each side of the river and, although there are no bridges between Bingen and Koblenz, there are fairly frequent ferries, enabling you to hop from one side of the river to the other. However, it's undeniably most fun by **boat**. River cruises from Mainz depart from in front of the Rathaus, where there's also a *K-D Line* office (☎06131/24 511). Fares aren't cheap – Mainz to Koblenz costs DM69 – but day returns sometimes work out cheaper than singles, and both *Eurail* and *Deutsche Bundesbahn* train passes are valid (though not *InterRail*).

Bacharach and Kaub

At **BACHARACH**, 10km downstream from Bingen, the chunky castle of **Burg Stahleck** now houses the local **youth hostel** (☎06743/1266; ②), while cheap **hotels** are clustered in Blücherstrasse, Langstrasse and Oberstrasse. The local **campsite** is at Strandbadweg. From **KAUB**, a few kilometres on, you get a great view of the **Pfalz**, a white-walled toll fortress standing on a mid-river island which has become a famous Rhineland symbol (April–Oct 9am–noon & 1.30–5.15pm; DM1.50 plus DM2 for the boat trip). This stronghold enabled the lords of **Burg Gutenfels** above Kaub to extract a toll from passing ships until well into the nineteenth century. Burg Gutenfels as you see it today is a late nineteenth-century rebuild of the original thirteenth-century castle. There are **camping** facilities at *Am Elsleinband* on Blücherstrasse.

The Lorelei and Burg Rheinfels

On the way towards **ST GOARSHAUSEN** you'll pass the **Lorelei**, the famous outcrop of rock where the legendary siren of the Rhine lured passing sailors to watery graves. The rock is over-hyped, but there are outstanding views from the top; apart from a viewing platform, the summit has a **campsite**.

There's a regular ferry that crosses from St Goarshausen to the prettier and more touristy **ST GOAR**, over which looms the enormous **Burg Rheinfels** (daily 9am–noon & 1–5pm; DM4), that was founded back in 1245 by Count Dieter von Katzenelnbogen to secure his toll-collecting racket. St Goar has a couple of reasonable hotels: the *Rhein-Hotel*, Heerstr. 71 (☎06741/485; ④), and the *Jost*, Gründelbachtal (☎06741/314; ③). The town features a **youth hostel** at Bismarckweg 17 (☎06741/388; ②), just outside the town centre, while **camping** facilities can be found at *Friedenau*, Gründelbachstrasse 103 (☎06741/368) and the *Loreleyblick* site, An der Loreley 29–39 (☎06741 /324), both close by.

Boppard and onwards

At **BOPPARD** the valley landscape becomes a gentler one of rounded, vine-covered slopes. The town has its own share of attractions, foremost of which is the **St Severuskirche** on Marktplatz, a Romanesque-Gothic church of cathedral-like dimensions, with thirteenth-century ceiling paintings and Gothic stained glass. The **Alte Burg**, a castle and residence built by the Archbishops of Trier to consolidate their grip on the area, now houses the **Heimatmuseum** (April–Oct Tues–Fri 10am–noon & 2–4pm, Sat 10am–noon, Sun 2–4pm; free). Cheapest central **hotels** are the *Weinhaus Sonnenhof*, Kirchgasse 8 (☎06742/3223; ④), and *Weinhaus Patt*, Steinstr. 30 (☎06742/2366; ④). There are **camping** facilities just north of town right next to the Rhine.

About 10km on comes **BRAUBACH**, above which stands the **Marksburg**, the only castle on this stretch of the Rhine to escape destruction by the French. Most of the fortress was built between the twelfth and fourteenth centuries, and the interior (tours hourly: mid-March to mid-Nov 9.30am–5pm; mid-Nov to mid-March 11am–4pm; DM4) contains a very nasty assembly of medieval torture instruments as well as more conventional historical exhibits.

Next stop is **LAHNSTEIN**, which is handy for its accommodation, with a couple of **campsites** in the grounds of the castle and some reasonably priced **hotels**, including *Rheinischer Hof*, Hochstr. 47 (☎02621/2598; ⑤).

Koblenz

Packed during the tourist season and deserted when it's over, **KOBLENZ** is a town that polarizes opinion – some enjoy the relaxed and faded charm that is typical of the place, while others find it smug and boring. The Rhine and Mosel meet here, and nearby the Lahn flows in from the east, so the town lies close to the four scenic regions separated by these rivers – the Eifel, Hunsrück, Westerwald and Taunus – and thus makes an ideal touring base.

Central Koblenz is at its best in the area around the confluence at **Deutsches Eck**, close to which stands the fine Romanesque church of **St Kastor**. However, the most commanding sights are to be found across the Rhine in Ehrenbreitstein, where the Baroque **Residenz** of the Electors of Trier is overshadowed by the **Festung**. One of the largest fortresses in the world, it is now home to the **Landesmuseum** (mid-March to Oct daily 9am–5pm; DM1) and to one of the best and most popular **youth hostels** in Germany (☎0261/73 737; ②, bus #8, #9 or #10). Koblenz's main **tourist office** (Mon–Sat 8.30am–8.15pm, Sun 2–7pm) is located opposite the **train station** and **bus station**, which are a little to the southwest of the centre. **Hotel rooms** are reasonably priced in the centre: the best bargains for accommodation are the *Weinand*, Weissernonnengasse 4–6 (☎0261/32 492; ④), and *Christ*, Schützenstr. 32 (☎0261/37 702; ④). The **campsite** is at Lützel, directly opposite Deutsches Eck, where the Mosel and Rhine join (April to mid-Oct); a ferry crosses the Mosel here in summer, while another crosses the Rhine further south.

Trier

The oldest city in Germany, **TRIER** was once the capital of the Western Empire, and residence of the Emperor Constantine. Nowadays, it has the less exalted role of regional centre for the upper Mosel valley, its relaxed air a world away from the status it formerly held. Despite a turbulent history, an amazing amount of the city's past has been preserved, in particular the most impressive group of **Roman monuments** north of the Alps (daily April–Sept 9am–6pm; Oct–March 9am–5pm; Barbarathermen closed Mon all year; ticket for individual sites DM4; ticket for all DM9).

The City

The centre of modern Trier corresponds roughly to the Roman city and can easily be covered on foot. From the **train station**, it's a few minutes' walk down Theodor-Heuss-Allee to the **Porta Nigra**, northern gateway to Roman Trier, and the biggest and best preserved city gate of its period in the world. The Porta Nigra probably owes its survival to the fact that Saint Simeon chose the east tower as his refuge from the world. After his death in 1035, Porta Nigra was made into a church in his honour; the Romanesque choir and some Rococo carvings remain from post-Roman embellishments. Next door is the **Simeonstift**, a monastery built in 1037 as another memorial to Simeon; its Brunnenhof is the oldest monastery courtyard in Germany. The neighbouring **Städtisches Museum** (Tues–Fri 9am–5pm, Sat & Sun 9am–3pm; DM2) has a big selection of art from the fourteenth century to the twentieth, with the emphasis on devotional work.

From the Porta Nigra, Simeonstrasse runs down to the Hauptmarkt, roughly following the route of an old Roman street. Today it's a busy pedestrian shopping area, but can boast some outstanding medieval monuments. The most important is the thirteenth-century **Dreikönigshaus**, once a secure home in uncertain times for a rich merchant family. The **Hauptmarkt** is a real focal point, especially in summer, with stalls selling fruit and flowers, and gangs of kids and punks around the Petrusbrunnen. At the southern end of the Hauptmarkt a Baroque portal leads to the Gothic **St Gangolfskirche**, built by the burghers of Trier in an attempt to aggravate the archbishops, whose political power they resented.

If you go up Sternstrasse from the Hauptmarkt you come to the magnificent Romanesque **Dom**, standing where Constantine had a huge church built in 325. The present building was started in 1030, and the facade has not changed significantly since then. Inside, the relative austerity is enlivened by devotional and decorative features added through the centuries. Chief among these is the black Gothic sarcophagus of Archbishop Balduin, sitting in brooding splendour in the west choir. The **Schatzkammer** (Mon–Sat 10am–noon & 2–5pm, Sun 2–5pm; DM1) has many examples of the work of local goldsmiths, notably a tenth-century portable altar.

From the cloisters there's a good view of the ensemble of the Dom and the adjacent **Liebfrauenkirche**, one of Germany's first Gothic churches. From here, Liebfrauenstrasse goes past the ritzy Palais Kesselstadt to the **Konstantinbasilika**. Built as Constantine's throne hall, its dimensions are awe-inspiring: 30m high and 75m long, it has no pillars or buttresses and is completely self-supporting. It became a church for the local Protestant community in the nineteenth century, a role it still fills. Next door, the **Rococo-Palais der Kurfürsten** was built in 1756 for an archbishop who felt that the adjoining old Schloss wasn't good enough for him. Its shocking pink facade overlooks the Palastgarten, setting for the **Landesmuseum** (Mon 10am–4pm, Tues–Fri 9.30am–4pm, Sat 9.30am–1pm, Sun 9am–1pm; free). Easily the best of Trier's museums, its collection of Roman relics brings to life the sophistication and complexity of Roman civilization; prize exhibit is the famous *Neumagener Weinschiff*, a Roman sculpture of a wine ship.

At the southern end of the gardens are the **Kaiserthermen**, once one of the largest bath complexes in the Roman world. The extensive underground heating system has survived, and you can walk around the service channels and passages. From the Kaiserthermen the route to the **Amphitheatre** is well signposted. The oldest of Trier's surviving Roman buildings, it was built around 100 AD and had a capacity of 20,000. You can inspect some of the animal cages and take a look under the arena, which has an elaborate drainage system cut into its slate base.

If you go back towards the town centre down Olewiger Strasse and then head down Südallee, you'll eventually come to the **Barbarathermen**, Trier's second set of Roman baths. Built in the second century, they look more like Roman ruins should – piles of rock, vaguely defined foundations and ruined walls. Midway between the baths and the Hauptmarkt, at Brückenstrasse 10, the **Karl-Marx-Haus** (April–Oct Mon 1–6pm, Tues–Sun 10am–6pm; Nov–March Mon 3–6pm, Tues–Sun 10am–1pm & 3–6pm; DM3) explicates the life and work of Trier's most influential son in detail that verges on the excruciating.

Practicalities

Trier's **tourist office** is at An der Porta Nigra (May–Aug Mon–Sat 9am–6pm, Sun 9am–3.30pm; Sept & Oct Mon–Sat 9am–6pm; Nov–April Mon–Fri 9am–5pm, Sat 9am–1pm). Central **hotels** are *Kolpinghaus*, Dietrichstr. 42 (☎0651/75 131; ②), *Zur Glocke*, Glockenstr. 12 (☎0651/73 109; ④), and *Saarbrücker Hof*, Saarstr. 46 (☎0651/75 161; ④). The **youth hostel** is at Maarstr. 156 (☎0651/29 292; ②) on the banks of the Mosel. There's a **campsite** on the western bank of the Mosel at Luxemburger Str. 81. There are plenty of places where you can get good and inexpensive **food**, thanks to the student population. The best bet is *Asterix*, Karl-Marx-Str. 11, a big, relaxed student bar which stays open until 2am at weekends. Other student haunts are to be found in the Viehmarkplatz area. Best traditional **pub** is *Sutträng* on Jüdengasse. On Pferdemarkt are *Blaues Blut*, where the "punk's not dead" crew congregate, and *Zapotex*, hang-out of Trier's fashion victims.

Worms

Situated about 40km south of Mainz, **WORMS** achieved immense wealth during the Middle Ages and for a while was a venue for the imperial parliament. Terribly damaged in the Napoleonic Wars and the last war, it is now a medium-sized industrial town whose monuments stand out like oases amid modern rebuilding.

Foremost among the city's glories is the huge Romanesque **Dom**, with its distinctive pair of domes and four corner towers. These days the rich Gothic **Südportal** is the main entrance, but look out also for the **Kaiserportal**, on the north side of the building. As you enter the church, the sight of Balthasar Neumann's huge **high altar** – a tornado of technicolour marble and gilt – provokes a gasp. In marked contrast is the dank and eerie vault, where eight sinister sarcophagi sit in oppressive silence.

For over a millennium Worms had a large and influential Jewish population – so influential, in fact, that the city was long known as "Little Jerusalem". It all came to an end with the Nazis: in 1933 there were 1100 Jews in Worms, by 1945 all were either dead or had fled the country. The most famous and poignant reminder of the community is the **Heiliger Sand**, a short distance southwest of the Dom; the oldest Jewish cemetery in Europe, its crooked gravestones date as far back as 1076. To the southeast of the cemetery is the **Andreasstift**, comprising a Romanesque church and cloisters which now house the **Museum der Stadt Worms** (Tues–Sun 10am–noon & 2–5pm; DM2). The most significant exhibits are in the Lutherzimmer, which includes some of Luther's original writings.

The **Heylshofgarten**, just to the north of the Dom, marks the site of the now-vanished imperial palace, where an Imperial Diet was convoked in 1521 by Emperor Charles V; Luther refused to renounce his views there, and was forced into exile, setting the Reformation in motion. Within the park is the **Kunsthaus Heylshof** (May–Sept daily 9am–5pm; Oct–April Tues–Sat 2–4pm, Sun 10am–noon & 2–4pm; DM2), a fine collection of paintings, porcelain, glassware and ceramics. Beyond here lies Lutherplatz, where you'll find the **Lutherdenkmal**, a gang of bronze figures with Luther at the centre. Keep straight on and you'll come to the Romanesque **Martinskirche**; supposedly Saint Martin was once imprisoned in a dungeon underneath. Further north, around Judengasse, is the site of the old Jewish quarter. Here you'll find the Romanesque **Alte Synagoge**, re-inaugurated in 1961 following its destruction on *Kristallnacht*. In the Raschi-Haus, a former school and meeting house, is the **Judaica Museum** (Tues–Sun 10am–noon & 2–5pm; DM2), with an extensive collection detailing the history of the Jews of Worms. There's one more church worth a call, the **Pauluskirche**, in the east of the centre; a rough-hewn sandstone affair dating from about 1016, it has an unusual triple tower and a classic Romanesque circular window.

Practicalities

Worms' **tourist office** is at Neumarkt 14 (Mon–Fri 9am–noon & 2–5pm, plus Sat 9am–noon in summer). Among the **hotels** in the town centre, try *Lortze-Eck*, Schlossergasse 10–12 (☎06241/24 561; ④). There's a **youth hostel** between the Dom and the Andreasstift at Dechaneigasse 1 (☎06241/25 780; ③), and a *Naturfreundehaus* just east of the city wall at Flosshafenstr. 7 (☎06241/23 660; ③). **Camping** facilities are on the east bank of the Rhine near the Nibelungenbrücke. For typically hearty German **food**, head for *Fischereck* at Rheinstr. 54. There are also lively hang-outs on Judengasse, such as the trendy *Café Jux*, and the **bars** *Kutscherschänke* and *Schwarzer Bär*.

Speyer

SPEYER is worth visiting for an afternoon, chiefly for its Dom, one of the largest and finest Romanesque buildings in Germany. It can be reached by bus from Heidelberg or by taking the train from Worms to Ludwigshafen and catching a bus from there. From the station, head straight down Bahnhofstrasse and turn right into Maximilianstrasse, which leads straight to the centre.

The **Dom** was built in the mid-eleventh century and modified a generation later – the most significant alteration, the stone vault, was higher than any previously built. But even finer than the vaulting is the massive **crypt** – containing eight royal tombs, it has an almost Middle Eastern feel with its sandstone pillars and slabbed floor. Just to the south of the Dom, on Domplatz, is the palatial triple-towered **Historisches Museum der Pfalz** (Tue & Thurs–Sun 10am–6pm, Wed 10am–8pm; DM1.50). Currently undergoing a major restoration, it includes objects found in the Dom's imperial graves, but the most celebrated exhibit is the Bronze Age *Golden Hat of Schifferstadt*, found in a nearby town. The same building also houses the **Weinmuseum**, featuring every conceivable kind of wine-related object and what is claimed to be the oldest bottle of wine in the world, dating from 300 AD. Not far from the museum, down Judengasse, is the **Judenbad**, a twelfth-century Jewish ritual bathhouse which is the oldest and best preserved example in Germany (April–Oct daily 10am–noon & 2–5pm; DM1.50).

The **tourist office** is at Maximilianstr. 11 (Mon–Fri 9am–5pm, Sat 10am–noon). Conveniently located **hotels** include *Easthof Deutschen Kaiser*, Allerheiligenstr. 37 (☎06232/75 630; ④), and *Zur Grünen Au*, Grüner Winkel 28 (☎06232/72 196; ④). The **youth hostel** is at Leinpfad (☎06232/75 380; ②), on the Rhine south of the centre. For *Kaffee und Küchen* try *Café-Konditorei Schumacher* at Wormserstr. 23; for something more substantial, go to the atmospheric old *Wirtschaft zum Alten Engel*, Gilgenstr. 27.

Frankfurt

Straddling the Main a few kilometres before it meets the Rhine, **FRANKFURT** is a city with two faces. On the one hand it's the cutthroat financial capital of Germany, with its fulcrum in the Westend district, and on the other it's a civilized place which spends more per year on the arts than any other city in Europe. In fact, Frankfurt is a thriving recreational centre for the whole of Hessen, with a good selection of theatres and galleries, and an even better range of museums. Over half of the city, including almost all of the centre, was destroyed during the war and the rebuilders opted for innovation rather than restoration. The result is a skyline that smacks more of Chicago than of Germany.

Arrival and information

Frankfurt **airport**, one of the world's busiest, is a major point of entry into Germany, and there are regular rail links between the airport and most west German cities. Trains leave the airport approximately every ten minutes for the **train station**, from where there are even more comprehensive services. The airport is also linked to the train station by two S-Bahn lines, run by the city transport company (*FVV*), which is also responsible for bus, tram and U-Bahn services. There's a flat rate of DM3 per journey (including transfers) and you buy tickets from the blue machines for trams, S- and U-Bahns, or from the driver for buses. From the train station you can walk to the centre in fifteen minutes or take tram #11.

Frankfurt has two main **tourist offices**. There's one in the train station (Mon–Sat 8am–9/10pm, Sun 9.30am–8pm), and an office for general information at Römerberg 27 (Mon–Fri 9am–6pm, Sat & Sun 9.30am–6pm). A free listings magazine, *Frankfurter Woche*, is available at both.

Accommodation

Accommodation is pricey, thanks to the expense-account clientele. Best budget bet is the **youth hostel** at Deutschherrnufer 12 (☎069/619 058; ②), in Sachsenhausen, reached by bus #46 from the train station. As for cheap **hotels**, the few reasonably priced hotels are in the sleazy environs of the train station, close to the Kaiserstrasse red-light district. The pick of the hotels are listed below.

Atlas, Zimmerweg 1 (☎069/723 946). ④

Backer, Mendelssohnstr. 92 (☎069/747 992). Pleasant place close to the university. U-Bahn to Westend or tram #19. ⑤

Goldener Stern, Karlsruherstr. 8 (☎069/233 309). Acceptable hotel between the train station and the water. ④

Life, Weserstr. 12 (☎069/231 014). ⑤

Lohmann, Stuttgarterstr. 31 (☎069/232 534). Spacious accommodation, one block from the Goldener Stern. Closed July. ④

The City

Almost all of the city's main sights lie within the bounds of the old city walls, which have now been transformed into a stretch of narrow parkland describing an approximate semicircle; from here it's an easy matter to cross the Main into Sachsenhausen, where most of the museums are located. As good a point as any to begin your explorations is the **Römerberg**, the historical and, roughly speaking, geographical centre of the city. Charlemagne built his fort on this low hill to protect the ford which gave Frankfurt its name – *Frankonovurd* (Ford of the Franks). At the start of this century the Römerberg was still the heart of the city, and an essentially medieval quarter. All this came to an end in March 1944 when two massive air raids flattened the historic core.

The most significant survivor was the thirteenth-century St Bartholomäus or **Dom**, and even that emerged with only its main walls intact. Before the construction of the skyscrapers it was the tallest building in the city, as befitted the venue for the election and coronation of the Holy Roman Emperors. Inside, to the right of the choir, is the restored **Wahlkapelle**, where the seven Electors used to make their final choice as to who would become emperor. For a fabulous panorama, climb the 95-metre tower (April–Oct 9am–12.30pm & 2.30–6pm; DM1).

Slightly to the north, in Domstrasse, looms the newly completed **Museum für Moderne Kunst** (Tues, Thurs, Fri & Sun 10am–5pm, Wed 10am–8pm, Sat noon–7pm; DM6, free Sat), its collection featuring most of the major names in postwar American and German art, with Joseph Beuys inevitably prominent. At the opposite end of the Römerberg is the building that gave the area its name – **Römer** house, formerly the Rathaus. Its distinctive facade, with its triple-stepped gables, fronts the **Römerplatz** market square, on whose southern side stands the former court chapel, the **Nikolaikirche**. The interior is refreshingly restrained, a real refuge from the noise and rampant commercialism of the Römerplatz; though the church was given a Gothic face-lift, the lines of the original Romanesque structure are visible on the inside.

For a long time the area between the Römer and the Dom remained little more than an ugly hole in the middle of the city. In 1978 it was decided to build replicas of some of the medieval buildings that had originally occupied the site, and fill the remaining space with an ultra-modern complex. At its heart is the **Kultur-Schirn**, a general-purpose cultural centre known to the locals as the "Federal Bowling Alley".

The **Saalhof**, an amalgamation of imperial buildings now housing the **Historisches Museum**, is nearby on Mainkai, overlooking the river. Its twelfth-century chapel is all that remains of the old palace complex, which grew up in the Middle Ages. The museum (Tues & Thurs–Sat 10am–5pm, Wed 10am–8pm; free except for special exhibitions) contains an extensive local history collection, with an eye-opening section on the devastation caused by the bombing.

A short distance to the west, on Untermainkai, is the **Karmelitenkloster**, where Jerg Ratgeb's eighty-metre-long fresco cycle of the life of Jesus occupies the cloister. The southern part of the building now houses a collection devoted to early and prehistory. Just north of here, at Grosser Hirschgraben 23, is the **Goethehaus und Museum** (Mon–Sat 9am–4/6pm, Sun 10am–1pm; DM4), the house where Goethe was born and raised. It has been made to look as much as possible like it did when Goethe lived here and there are even a few objects which somehow survived the war.

A couple of minutes away on the Liebfrauenberg is the fifteenth-century **Liebfrauenkirche** – look inside for the unusual altar, a huge alabaster and gilt affair which sits well in the dusky pink interior. A little to the northwest of the Hauptwache is the **Börse**, Frankfurt's stock exchange. Appropriately enough, two of the most expensive shopping streets in the city are just around the corner. **Goethestrasse** is Frankfurt's Bond Street, all expensive jewellers and designer clothes shops, while **Grosse Bockenheimer Strasse** is home to upmarket delicatessens and smarter restaurants.

SACHSENHAUSEN

If you want to escape from the centre of Frankfurt, or have a laid-back evening out, then head for **Sachsenhausen**, the city-within-a-city on the south bank of the Main. Most people go here to eat, drink and be merry in the restaurants and bars of Alt Sachsenhausen, the network of streets around Affentorplatz, where the main attractions are the apple wine (*Ebelwei*) houses. There's entertainment of a different sort to be had on the **Museumsufer** (or Schaumainkai), which runs between the Eiserner Steg and the Friedensbrücke.

Schaumainkai's biggest draw is the **Städel** located at no. 63 (Tues–Sun 10am–5pm, until 8pm on Wed; closed Mon; DM6), one of the most comprehensive art galleries in Europe. Chronologically, the layout begins on the top floor, where virtually every big name in German art is represented: Dürer, Grünewald, both Holbeins, Cranach, Baldung and Altdorfer. One of the main strengths of the gallery is its wealth of early Netherlandish paintings, dominated by van Eyck's *Lucca Madonna*. The Madonna and Child, a frequent subject in the Netherlandish section, predominates in the Italian, where the outstanding treatment is an ethereal image by Fra Angelico; versions by Verrocchio, Perugino, Bellini, Cima and Carpaccio make fascinating comparisons. Pride of place among the collection of seventeenth-century paintings goes to Frankfurt's own Adam Elsheimer – the largest work ever painted by this master of the small-scale is the *Altarpiece of the Cross*. Poussin, Claude and Rubens, all admirers of Elsheimer, are on display in the next section, which also includes Rembrandt's *Blinding of Samson* and a glorious Vermeer. Paintings from the late eighteenth century onwards occupy the first floor. Big French names such as Courbet, Degas and Monet appear, but German artists predominate – look out for *Goethe in the Roman Campagna* by Johann Heinrich Tischbein, the most celebrated portrayal of the writer. Until the Third Reich, the Städel had perhaps the finest array of modern painting in Germany, but over 500 paintings were then removed as "degenerate art", and the collection has never recovered. However, it does include fine pieces by Beckmann, Dix, Ernst and Kirchner.

The **Museum für Kunsthandwerk**, down at no. 15 (same opening times; free), has a huge collection of applied art, divided into four sections: European, featuring a unique collection of furniture models, glassware and ceramics; Islamic, with some fine carpets; Far Eastern, with lots of jade and lacquer work plus a liberal sprinkling of porcelain and sculptures; and finally a section devoted to books and writing. Further along at no. 29, the **Museum für Völkerkunde** (same times; free) is a small ethnographical museum with an extensive collection of masks and totems from all over the world. The **Deutsches Filmmuseum**, no. 41 (Tues–Sun 11am–6.30pm; DM6), is Germany's biggest and best film museum, with its own cinema and a good little café in the basement. The **Deutsches Architekturmuseum**, no. 43 (Tues–Sun 10am–5pm, until 8pm on Wed; closed Mon; DM6), is installed in a self-consciously avant-garde conversion of a nineteenth-century villa; the highpoint is the "house within a house", which dominates the museum like an oversized dolls' house. Finally, the **Liebighaus**, no. 71 ((Tues–Sun 10am–5pm, until 8pm on Wed; closed Mon; free), is a step-by-step guide to the history of sculpture, going back to the third millennium BC.

Eating, drinking and nightlife

Not surprisingly, Frankfurt has a wealth of gastronomic possibilities, from the ultra-trendy joints found in the Westend to the cheapo Italian **restaurants** of Bockenheim, the working-class/boho/student quarter. Whether it's vegan breakfast or Japanese afternoon tea you're after, you'll be able to find it somewhere in the city – though you might have to travel some distance to get it. Frankfurt's **nightlife** is pretty eclectic too. Perhaps its best-known locale is Kleine Bockenheimer Strasse, aka *Jazzgasse* (Jazz Alley), the centre of Frankfurt's jazz scene.

CAFÉ-BARS AND CAFÉS

Café Bar, Schweizerstr. 14. The trendiest café in Sachsenhausen, all black and mirrored decor with a posey clientele.

Café Laumer, Bockenheimer Landstr. 67. One of Frankfurt's oldest cafés, halfway up the Westend's main thoroughfare.

Café Schwille, Grosse Bockenheimer Str. 50. This traditional *Kaffee und Küchen* spot is also the place for an early breakfast (opens 7am). Other branches at Rossmarkt, and next door to the Katharinenkirche.

Stattcafé, Grempstr. 21. The emphasis is on healthy eating in an informal atmosphere; popular with the Bockenheim arty crowd.

RESTAURANTS

Atschel, Wallstr. 7/Abstgäschen. One of the ubiquitous Alsace speciality places in Sachsenhausen. Fish dishes and apple wine. Closed Mon.

Aubergine, Alte Gasse 14. Good food, good service, reasonable prices by central Frankfurt standards – lunch DM20, four courses DM45. Open until 11pm.

Divan, Elbestr. 9. Turkish restaurant featuring shows with traditional music and belly dancing. 6am–1am.

Eden, Rahmhofstr. 4 . Heavy-duty vegetarian place; open until 8.30pm Mon–Sat.

Gargantua, Friesengasse 3. One of Bockenheim's best, with a three-course meal for DM40. Open until 9.30pm; closed Mon and first Sun of the month.

Die Leiter, Kaiserhofstr. 11. Classy yet not too expensive with pavement tables in the summer. DM15–25.

Mikini, Fahrgasse 93. A Japanese restaurant which makes few concessions to the west.

Nibelungen-Scänke, Niblungenallee 55. Typical Greek food at very reasonable prices. The clientele tends to be young and the place is usually open until 1am. U-bahn line #55 to Niblungenallee.

Panda, Düsseldorfer Str. 10. The cheapest good Chinese restaurant in the train station area, where there are quite a few others.

Rosa, Grüneburgweg 25. Good food for Westend types not so keen on conspicuous consumption. Closed weekends.

PUBS, WINE CELLARS AND APPLE WINE TAVERNS

Club Voltaire, Hochstr. 5. Tasty, good food with a Spanish bias, and a fairly eclectic clientele including political activists, artists and gays. One of the best-established meeting places in Frankfurt.

Haus Wertheym, Fahrtor 1. A medieval inn on the Römerberg with *Bockbier*, traditional food and a friendly atmosphere. Closed Tues.

Eichkatzerl, Dreieichstr. 29. A traditional Sachsenhausen apple wine tavern with a very popular restaurant. Closed Wed and first Thurs of every month.

MUSIC AND DISCOS

Jazz Keller, Kleine Bockenheimer Str. 18a/Goethestrasse. This atmospheric cellar is Frankfurt's premier jazz venue. Tues–Sun 9pm–3am.

Music-Hall, Voltastr. 74. Big venue northwest of the train station, with regular live music and discos. Open until 3am, with food.

Sinnkasten, Brönnerstr. 5. This place has a pool room, cabaret stage, disco and, most importantly, a concert hall where they put on everything from jazz to avant-garde and indie stuff. Open 9pm–2am; DM7.

Listings

Airlines *Air Canada*, Friedensstr. 11 (☎069/250 131); *Air New Zealand*, Rathenauplatz la (☎069/291 897); *British Airways*, Rossmarkt 23 (☎069/290 371); *Lufthansa*, Am Bahnhof 2 (☎069/25 700); *TWA*, Hamburger Allee 2-10 (☎069/770 601).

Consulates *Australia*, Gutleutstr. 85 (☎069/273 9090); *Great Britain*, Bockenheimer Landstr. 42 (☎069/170 0020); *US*, Siesmayerstr. 21 (☎069/75350).

Hitching *Mitfahrzentrale*, Gutleutstr. 125 (☎069/230 5113).

Post office The main post office is at Zeil 110.

Women's Frankfurt Frankfurt has a women's centre located at Hamburger Allee 45 (☎069/772659). The women's *Mitfahrzentrale* is to be found at Konrad-Brosswitz-Str. 11, Bockenheim (☎069/771777).

Marburg

About 80km to the north of Frankfurt, **MARBURG**, the cradle of Hessen and its original capital, clusters up the slopes of the Lahn valley in a maze of narrow streets and medieval buildings, crowned by an impressive castle. Marburg is primarily a university town and it has a relaxed and lively atmosphere. It has been touched by war less than almost any other city in the country and is one of the few Hessen towns which it is worth going out of your way to visit.

The most important building is the **Elisabethkirche** (April–Oct Mon–Sat 9am–6pm, Sun 12.30–6pm; Nov–March Mon–Sat 10am–4pm, Sun 11.15am–4pm; DM2), reached from the train station simply by following Bahnhofstrasse. The first Gothic church in Germany, it was erected to house the remains of Saint Elisabeth, who died here in 1231. Inside, the church is like a museum of German religious art, full of statues and frescoes, mainly celebrating Elisabeth's piety – her thirteenth-century shrine is in the sacristy, along with the finely carved tombs of her descendants. The church also attracts unholy pilgrims – old Nazis and their sympathizers come here to pay their respects at the tomb of **Hindenburg**, the president who appointed Hitler as chancellor in 1933. From the Elisabethkirche the Steinweg, a stepped street hemmed in by half-timbered buildings, leads up to the Marktplatz, the centre of the **Altstadt**. During term time the square is the focal point of Marburg's nightlife, but out of term it's very peaceful. The **Rathaus'** staircase tower features a statue of Elisabeth, holding a heraldic figure which is said to be the arms of the count who financed the building's completion.

From the Marktplatz make your way up Rittergasse to the thirteenth-century **Marienkirche**, just past which a flight of steps rises to the **Schloss**, towering 102 metres above the Lahn (mid-April to mid-Oct Tues–Sun 10am–6pm; mid-Oct to mid-April Tues–Sat 10am–5.30pm, Sun 2–5pm; free). The present structure was begun by Sophie, the daughter of Saint Elisabeth, but the bulk of what can be seen today dates from the fifteenth and sixteenth centuries. Look out for the Gothic **Schlosskapelle** and the Rittersaal, the largest secular Gothic hall in Germany. In October 1529 Landgrave Philipp the Magnanimous engineered a fruitless meeting between Luther and Zwingli to try to reconcile the two reformers – portraits of the Landgrave and of Luther by Lucas Cranach the Elder hang in the room where the talks took place .

As well as trying to do his bit in aid of sixteenth-century religious harmony, Philipp the Magnanimous also founded the University of Marburg, whose main buildings are situated a short way to the south of Marktplatz and whose roll call of past professors includes the Brothers Grimm and Boris Pasternak. Down the hill from the Alte Universität you come to the **Universitätsmuseum für bildende Kunst** located on Biegenstrassen (Tues–Sun 11am–1pm & 2–5pm; free), whose collection has a Cranach portrait of Luther, a Klee, a Kandinsky and a Picasso, together with a lot of fairly nondescript German stuff.

Marburg's **tourist office** (Mon–Fri 8am–12.30pm & 2–5pm; April–Sept also Sat 9.30am–noon) is found in the **train station**. The cheapest **hotel** in town is the *Rehe*, Alte Kasseler Str. 66 (☎06421/65 624; ④), no more than ten minutes' walk north of the station. The more central hotels are a little more pricey– *Gästehaus Müller*, Deutschhausstr. 29 (☎06421/65 659; ⑤), is perhaps the best of a similarly priced lot. The **youth hostel** is at Jahnstr. 1 (☎06421/23461; ②), a little to the south of the Altstadt, and **camping** facilities are over the river at Am Trojedamm. Quite a few little **pubs** are to be found on Hirschberg, the street leading off from the Marktplatz, and you could also try your luck on Untergasse. *Café Velo* on Augustinergasse is especially popular with students.

SOUTHERN GERMANY

Theodor Heuss, the first Federal President, saw Baden-Württemberg as "the model of German possibilities", and it hasn't disappointed, maintaining its ranking as the most prosperous part of the country. Being weak in natural resources, the area has had to rely on ingenuity, and ever since the motor car was invented here last century it has been at the forefront of world technology. Baden-Württemberg's largest city, **Stuttgart**, is the home of Mercedes and Porsche, and though extensively damaged in World War II it has plenty of good points apart from its shrines to these giants of the industry. The historical centre of **Freiburg im Breisgau** was also bombed, but its Münster, which ranks among Germany's greatest buildings, was spared. Germany's most famous university city, **Heidelberg**, was also hardly touched, and the spa resort of **Baden-Baden** remains wonderfully evocative of its nineteenth-century heyday as the playground of Europe's aristocracy. The scenery of the province is wonderful too: its western and southern boundaries are defined by the Rhine and its bulge into Germany's largest lake, the **Bodensee** (Lake Constance), and within the curve of the river lies the **Black Forest**, source of another of the continent's principal waterways, the Danube.

Bavaria (Bayern) is the home of all the German clichés: beer-swilling Lederhosen-clad men, sausage dogs, cowbells and Alpine villages, sauerkraut and *Wurst*. But that's only a small part of the Bavarian picture, and almost entirely restricted to the region south of the magnificent state capital **Munich**. In the state's western region, around its pristine capital **Augsburg**, things are quite different. The food is less pork and sausages and more pasta and sauces, the landscape tends to be gentle farming country ideal for camping and cycling holidays, and the only set attractions outside Augsburg are the medieval towns along the Romantic Road and the Danube. To the north lies **Nürnberg**, centre of a region of vineyards and nature parks, with hardly any of the features of traditional Bavarian culture. Eastern Bavaria is a relatively poor region – except for its regional capital, **Regensburg** – where life in the highland forests revolves around logging and workshop industries such as glass production.

One practical note: travellers over 27 are barred from using Bavarian youth hostels, but reasonable alternatives can usually be found, and you'll only be handicapped if you're on the tightest of budgets.

Heidelberg

Home to the oldest university on German soil, **HEIDELBERG** is a real-life fulfilment of the ideal German landscape, majestically set on the banks of the swift-flowing Neckar between ranges of wooded hills. Ever since the days of the Grand Tour it has seduced travellers to an extent no other German city comes close to matching.

Arrival and accommodation

First impressions are a letdown: the **train station** and **bus station** are in an anonymous quarter fifteen minutes' walk west of the centre, with the dreary Kurfürsten-Anlage leading towards town. The harassed **tourist office** is on the square outside (Mon–Sat 9am–7pm, Sun 10am–6pm; winter Mon–Sat 9am–7pm, Sun 10am–3pm), and publishes the weekly *Heidelberg diese Woche*, which gives full details of what's on.

Although a large number of **hotels** are dotted all over the city, they are often booked solid; however, there's a chart outside the tourist office to tell you where any vacancies exist. A couple of the city's budget options are the *Krokodil*, Kleinschmidstr. 12 (☎06221/24 059; ②), just a short walk in the direction of the city centre, and the *Jeske*, located in the heart of the city at Mittelbadgasse 2 (☎06221/23 733; ②). The few other

conveniently sited hotels are *Zum Weinberg*, Heliggeiststr. 1 (☎06221/21 792; ⑤), and
Elite, Bunsenstr. 15 (☎06221/25 734; ⑤). Otherwise, ask in the second-hand clothes
shop *Flic-Flac* at Unterestr. 12, where young travellers are helped to find **rooms** in
private houses. The tourist office locates private rooms for DM4 plus a five percent
deposit.

The **youth hostel** is on the north bank of the Neckar, about 4km from the centre, at
Tiergartenstr. 5 (☎06221/412 066; ②); take bus #11. Both **campsites** are east of the
city by the river – *Heide* is between Ziegelhausen and Kleingemünd; *Neckertal* is in
Schlierbach; both are served by local bus.

The Town

Centrepiece of all the views of Heidelberg is the **Schloss**, a compendium of
magnificent buildings, somehow increased in stature by its ruined condition. It was
founded at the start of the thirteenth century, but the expansion of the castle gathered
momentum in the middle of the sixteenth century, when the Electors converted to
Protestantism, and began the construction of the most splendid **Renaissance
buildings** in Germany. Friedrich V's ham-fisted attempt to establish a Protestant,
anti-Habsburg majority in the Electoral college led to the Thirty Years' War, which
devastated the country. However, it was French designs on the region in 1689 that led
to the destruction of Heidelberg and its Schloss; after this, the Electorship passed to a
Catholic branch of the family who, unable to establish a rapport with the locals,
abandoned Heidelberg.

The Schloss can be reached by funicular from the Kornmarkt for DM4.50 return,
but it's more fun to walk up via the Burgweg. At the southeastern corner is the most
romantic of the ruins, now generally known as the **Gesprengter Turm** (Blown-up
Tower); a collapsed section lies intact in the moat, leaving a clear view into the interior.
In the **Schlosshof** (acccss at all times; guided tours daily 9am–4/5pm, DM2) what
really catches your eye is the group of Renaissance palaces on the north and east sides.
In the basement of one of these is the **German Apothecary Museum** (April–Oct daily
10am–5pm; Nov–March Sat & Sun 11am–5pm; DM2), an offbeat collection featuring
reconstructed workshops from different parts of Germany. The triple loggia of the
earlier **Saalbau** forms a link to the swaggering **Friedrichsbau**, which supports a
pantheon of the House of Wittelsbach, beginning with Charlemagne, the alleged
founder of the dynasty. The statues now on view are copies; the originals can be seen
inside, along with a number of restored rooms which have been decked out in period
style. The **Fassbau** (daily April–Oct 9am–7pm; Nov–March 9am–6pm) is reached
down a passageway in front of the Schlosshof. It contains the famous **Great Vat**, said
to be the largest wine barrel in the world.

The finest surviving buildings in the **Altstadt** are grouped on Marktplatz, in the
middle of which is the red sandstone **Heiliggeistkirche**, whose domed tower is one of
the city's most prominent landmarks. Note the tiny shopping booths between its
buttresses, a feature ever since the church was built. Inside, it's light, airy and
uncluttered, but was not always so, as the church was built to house the mausoleum of
the Palatinate Electors; only one tomb remains.

Facing the church is the only mansion to survive the seventeenth-century
devastations, the **Haus zum Ritter**, so-called from the statue of St George on the
pediment. The most eye-catching Baroque building in Heidelberg is the **Alte Brücke**,
reached from the Marktplatz down Steingasse; dating from the 1780s, it was blown up
in the last war, but has been painstakingly rebuilt. The **Palais Rischer** on
Unterestrasse was the most famous venue for one of the university's more risible
traditions, the **Mensur**, or fencing match. Every vital organ was padded, but wounds
were frequent and prized as badges of courage; for optimum prestige, salt was rubbed
into them, leaving scars that would remain for life.

The **Jesuitenkirche**, across Hauptstrasse on Schulgasse, is in the sombre, classically inspired style favoured by this evangelizing order, who came here with the ill-fated intention of recapturing Heidelberg for Catholicism. Housed in its gallery and the adjoining monastery is a moderate **Museum of Sacred Art** (May–Oct Tues–Sat 10am–5pm, Sun 1–5pm; Nov–April Sat & Sun 1–5pm; DM2.50).

One side of Universitätsplatz, the heart of the old town, is occupied by the **Alte Universität**, dating back to the first quarter of the eighteenth century. The rest of the square is occupied by the Neue Universität, erected in 1931 with American funding. The oddest of Heidelberg's traditions was that its students used not to be subject to civil jurisdiction: offenders were dealt with by the university authorities, and could serve their punishment at leisure. Now a protected monument, the **Students' Prison** (Mon–Sat 10am–12.30pm & 2–5pm; Nov–Mar Mon–Fri 10am–12.30pm & 2–5pm, Sat 10am–1pm; DM1) is at the back of the Alte Universität on Augustinergasse; used from 1712 to 1914, the otherwise spartan cells are covered with graffiti.

Housed in the Palais Morass at Hauptstrasse 97, the **Kurpfälzisches Museum** (Tues & Thurs–Sun 10am–5pm, Wed 10am–9pm; DM4) has one amazing possession, the limewood *Altar of the Twelve Apostles* by Tilman Riemenschneider.

Eating and drinking

The **student taverns** in Heidelberg are a must: known for serving basic dishes at reasonable prices, they are still regularly patronized by the university fraternities, even if tourists these days make up most of the clientele. At the eastern end of Hauptstrasse are the two most famous of these hostelries – *Zum Sepp'l* at no. 213, and *Roter Ochsen* at no. 217. Less touristed is the oldest of all the taverns, *Schnookeloch*, at Haspelgasse 8. Among other traditional **restaurants**, *Perkeo* at Hauptstr. 75 is a historic inn with a Michelin rating for its food. For cheaper eating, try *Essighaus*, Plöck 97, or *Goldener Hecht*, Steingasse 2.

The *Biermuseum* at Hauptstr. 143 has 101 varieties of **beer** to choose from, while *Vetters*, Steingasse 9, has its own small house brewery. The mid-nineteenth-century *Knösel*, Haspelgasse 20, is the oldest of Heidelberg's **cafés**; its speciality is *Heidelberger Studentenkuss*, a dark chocolate filled with praline and nougat. For something more like a bistro setup, call in at the crowded *Café Journal*, Hauptstr. 162.

Stuttgart

STUTTGART breathes success. Firms like Bosch, Porsche and Daimler-Benz – whose three-pointed star beams down on the city – were in the vanguard of the German economic miracle, and have established the city at the forefront of European industry. Yet Stuttgart was slow to develop. Founded around 950 as a stud farm (Stutengarten), it became a town only in the fourteenth century, and lay in the shadow of its more venerable neighbours up to the early nineteenth century. Though not the comeliest of cities, Stuttgart has a range of superb museums, and a varied cultural and nightlife scene.

Arrival and accommodation

The **train station** is plumb in the centre of town, and immediately behind it, you'll find the **bus station**. The **airport** bus service #A runs every twenty minutes between 5am and midnight. There's a **tourist office** in front of the train station in the Klett-Passage (Mon–Fri 9.30am–8.30pm, Sat 9.30am–6pm, Sun 11am–6pm, winter 1–6pm). The integrated **public transport** network comprises buses, trams, U-Bahn, and main-line and S-Bahn trains; given that the sights are scattered, it's worth investing in a DM8.60 4-trip ticket.

Though average **hotel** rates are high, there are some bargains. Cheapest central place is *Pension Märklin*, Friedrichstr. 39 (☎0711/291 315; ④). Other budget options are *Pension Schilling*, Kernerstr. 63 (☎0711/240 860; ④), and *Schwarzwaldheim*, Fritz-Elsar-Str. 20 (☎0711/296 988; ④). Alternatively, ask the tourist office to book a room; there's no charge. The **youth hostel** is about fifteen minutes' walk east of the train station at Haussmannstr. 27 (☎0711/241 583; ① or ②, depending on dormitory size). There's also an unofficial hostel, the *Jugendwohnheim*, at Richard-Wagner-Str. 2–4a (☎0711/241 132; ③). The **campsite** is on the banks of the Neckar in Bad Cannstatt – take a main-line train, or S-Bahn #1, #2 or #3.

The City

From the train station, Königsstrasse passes the dull modern Dom and enters **Schlossplatz**, a welcome relief from the bustle, but favoured spot of Stuttgart's tramps and alcoholics. On the east side of the square, the colossal Baroque **Neues Schloss**, now used by the regional government, looks over at the Neoclassical **Königsbau**, its 135-metre facade lined with shops. At the south of the square is the Altes Schloss, which now houses the **Landesmuseum** (Tues & Thurs–Sun 10am–5pm, Wed 10am–7pm; free). Highlight of this richly varied museum is the **Kunstkammer** of the House of Württemberg, displayed in one of the corner towers: the first floor has small bronze sculptures of mainly Italian origin, while the second is laid out in the manner of a Renaissance curio cabinet. Upstairs, in the main part of the building, is a large collection of Swabian devotional sculptures, arranged thematically rather than chronologically. On the same floor, the archeology section includes excavations from Troy, Roman antiquities, the grave of a Celtic prince and Frankish jewellery. The top floor has musical instruments and a wonderful array of clocks. The nearby **Galerie der Stadt Stuttgart** (Tues & Thurs–Sun 10am–6pm, Wed 10am–8pm; free except for special exhibitions) is a poor relation of the Staatsgalerie, but does contain some superbly acerbic works by Otto Dix.

To the north of Schlossplatz, facing the straggling complex of the Staatstheater across Konrad-Adenauer-Strasse, is the **Staatsgalerie** (Tues & Thurs 10am–8pm, Wed & Fri–Sun 10am–5pm; free), completed in 1984 to the post-modern design of James Stirling – regarded by many as Britain's most accomplished living architect. The most startling work in the entire gallery is the huge, violently expressive *Herrenberg Altar* by Jerg Ratgeb, whose reputation rests almost entirely on this work. The equally idiosyncratic Hans Baldung is represented by his *Man of Sorrows* and *Portrait of Hans Jacob*. After some good examples of Cranach, Bellini, Carpaccio, Tintoretto and Tiepolo, Memling's sensual *Bathsheba at her Toilet* kicks off the Low Countries section, which also features Rembrandt's tender *Tobit Healing his Father's Blindness*. Nineteenth-century highpoints are *Bohemian Landscape* and *The Cross in the Woods* by Friedrich, and a decent cross-section of French Impressionism. The modern extension contains the finest **Picasso** collection in Germany and traces the entire progress of German art this century. Avant-garde works occupy the end halls, while major temporary exhibitions are regularly featured downstairs.

On the other side of Schlossplatz, the Altes Schloss overlooks **Schillerplatz**, Stuttgart's sole example of an old-world square. Presiding in the middle is a pensive statue of Schiller himself, erected the year after his death by the Danish sculptor Bertel Thorwaldsen. Also here are two more Renaissance buildings – the **Alte Kanzlei** and the gabled **Fruchtkasten**. The latter preserves its fourteenth-century core, which has now been converted to house the **Lapidarium** (Tues & Thurs–Sun 10am–5pm, Wed 10am–7pm; free), a collection of stone fragments from Roman times.

At the back of Schillerplatz is the **Stiftskirche**, the choir of which is lined with one of the most important pieces of German Renaissance sculpture, an ancestral gallery of the Counts and Dukes of Württemberg.

THE MERCEDES-BENZ MUSEUM

Set up in 1986 to celebrate the centenary of the invention of the motor car by Gottlieb Daimler and Carl Benz, the **Mercedes-Benz Museum** (Tues–Sun 9am–5pm; free) is an absolute must, unless you rue the day the car was invented. Even entering here is an experience – you take S-Bahn #1 to Neckarstadion, then walk; or take bus #56 to the works entrance, from where you're whisked in a sealed minibus to the museum doors. The earliest vehicle on display is the Daimler Reitwagen of 1885, the first-ever motorbike, which was capable of 12kph. The Daimler company's first Mercedes dates from 1902, its Spanish-sounding name being taken from the daughter of the firm's principal foreign agent, Emil Jellinek. Other exhibits include fire engines, motorboats, aeroplanes and buses, but the show is stolen by the luxury cars and the machines specially designed for world record attempts – so futuristic it's hard to believe they were made more than half a century ago.

THE PORSCHE MUSEUM

The **Porsche Museum**, right beside the Neuwirtshaus station on S-Bahn line #6, but using a different entrance past the main gates at the weekend (Mon–Fri 9am–4pm, Sat & Sun 9am–5pm; free), is considerably more relaxed about visitors than Daimler-Benz. Not only can you wander at will around the factory site, but there are free **guided tours** of the production lines every working day. These are generally booked solid weeks in advance, but a few extra visitors are allowed to tag on at short notice; it's still best to phone first though (☎0711/827 5685). **Ferdinand Porsche** made his name when Hitler commissioned him to create the original Volkswagen, precursor of the Beetle, the ultimate mass-market car. For his own enterprise, Porsche concentrated on the opposite end of the economic spectrum. The fifty vehicles on show illustrate all the company's cars from the 356 Roadster of 1948 to current models.

Eating, drinking and nightlife

Though fancy restaurants abound in Stuttgart, there are a number of places offering traditional Swabian dishes at low cost, with plenty of ethnic eateries to stimulate the jaded palate. First recommendations for good-quality food and drink are the numerous **Weinstuben**, archetypally German establishments that are known for their solid cooking as well as for wine. *Zur Kiste*, Kanalstr. 2, is generally agreed to be the best, but the widest choice of wines is at *Weinhaus Stetter*, Rosenstr. 32. Best restaurants in a **beer hall** setup are *Zeppelin-Stüble*, opposite the train station at Lautenschlager Str. 2, and *Ketterer*, Marienstr. 3b. The best pub in the city with an adjoining house-brewery is *Stuttgarter Lokalbrauerei*, Calwer Str. 31. *Movenpick* on Königstrasse is the best **self-service** restaurant, while the fullest range of **vegetarian** fare is at *Iden*, Ebehardstr. 1.

For **nightlife** details, get the tourist office's well-filled monthly programme, *Stuttgarter Monatsspiegel*, costing DM1.80. Alternative listings can be found in both *Stuttgart Live* and *Ketchup*, available from newsagents. *Casino*, Mörikestr. 69, is a crowded cellar bar with an underground, punkish feel; the former punk haunt of *Exil*, Filderstr. 61, now belongs to arty types, with jazz and blues in a laid-back atmosphere. Jazz also features at *Laboratorium*, Wagenburgerstr. 147, popular with the Green Party contingent. *Life*, Bolzstr. 10, is a café with live rock and occasional reggae – it serves huge cheap pizzas and excellent beer. Occupying an old rail tunnel, *Röhre*, Neckarstr. 34, platforms live bands playing everything from jazz to punk, and is also a disco patronized by fashion-conscious locals. *Café Stella*, Tübingenstrasse, is a leading **gay** hang-out.

Listings

Airlines *American Airlines*, Charlottenstr. 44 (☎0711/236 9412); *British Airways* Kriegsbergstr. 28 (☎0711/299 471); *Lufthansa*, Lautenschlagerstr. 20 (☎0711/20441); *TWA*, Sophienstr. 38 (☎0711/058 183).

Car rental *Autohansa*, Hegelstr. 25 (☎0711/693 322); *Avis*, 18 Katharinenstrasse (☎0711/241 441); *InterRent*, Friedrichstr. 28 (☎0711/221 749); *Hertz*, Hohenstaufenstr. 18 (☎0711/643 044).

Consulates *Great Britain*, Lenzhalde 65 (☎0711/220 359); *US*, Urbanstr. 7 (☎0711/210 221).

Hitching *Mitfahrzentrale*, Lerchenstr. 68 (☎0711/221 453).

Post office Main office is at the rear of the Königsbau on Schillerplatz. The branch in the train station is open until 11pm.

Tübingen

"We have a town on our campus" runs the saying in TÜBINGEN, a peaceful town sited above the willow-lined banks of the Neckar, some 30km south of Stuttgart. Over half the population of 70,000 is in some way connected with the university, and the current size of the town is due entirely to the twentieth-century boom in higher education.

The old town is a visual treat, a mixture of brightly painted half-timbered and gabled houses grouped into twisting and plunging alleys. Two large squares provide a setting for communal activities. The first, **Holzmarkt**, is dominated by the **Stiftskirche St Georg**, a gaunt late Gothic church with a stunning interior. In the chancel (April–Sept Mon–Sat 10am–noon & 2–5pm, Sun noon–5pm; Oct–March Fri 2–4pm; DM2) an outstanding series of stained-glass windows cast their reflections on the pantheon of the House of Württemberg, the thirteen tombs showing the development of Swabian sculpture in the Gothic and Renaissance periods.

Overlooking the banks of the Neckar on Bursagasse, the street immediately below, is the **Hölderlinturm** (Tues–Fri 10am–noon & 3–5pm, Sat & Sun 2–5pm; DM2). Originally part of the medieval fortifications, it's named after Friedrich Hölderlin, who lived here in the care of a carpenter's family, hopelessly but harmlessly insane, from 1807 until his death 36 years later. There's a collection of memorabilia of the poet, now regarded as one of the greatest Germany ever produced.

At the end of the street is the **Evangelisches Stift**, a Protestant seminary established in a former Augustinian monastery in 1547. From here you can continue down Neckarhalde to **Theodor Haering Haus** (Tues–Sat 1–6pm, Sun 11am–6pm; free) which contains collections on the history of the town.

The **Markt**, heart of old Tübingen, is just a short walk uphill from the Stift. It preserves many of its Renaissance mansions, along with a fountain dedicated to Neptune, around which markets are held on Mondays, Wednesdays and Fridays. Burgsteige, one of the oldest and handsomest streets in town, climbs steeply from the corner of the Markt to **Schloss Hohentübingen**, Renaissance successor to the original eleventh-century castle. You can wander around the complex, but only by taking a guided tour (April–Sept Sat 5pm, Sun 11am & 3pm; DM3) can you see the prison and the cellars, with their 18,700-gallon vat.

The northwestern part of town, lying immediately below the Schloss, has traditionally been the province of the non-academic community – especially the vine-growers. Here are some of the city's oldest and most spectacular half-timbered buildings, such as the old municipal **Kornhaus** on the alley of the same name, and the **Fruchtschranne**, formerly the storehouse for the yields of the ducal orchards, on Bachgasse.

The corresponding quarter northeast of the Markt is once more dominated by the university. Crossing Langegasse, and continuing along Metgergasse, you come to the **Nonnenhaus**, most photogenic of the half-timbered houses. Just outside the northeastern boundary of the old town are the former **Botanical Gardens**. These have been superseded by another complex, located amidst most of the modern buildings of the university, a kilometre north by the ring road (Mon–Fri 7.30am–4.45pm, Sat & Sun 10–11.45am & 1.30–4.30pm).

Practicalities

The **train station** and **bus station** are side by side, just five minutes' walk from the old town. At the edge of Eberhardsbrücke is the **tourist office** (Mon–Fri 9am–6.30pm, Sat 9am–12.30/5pm); this is the only place you can change money outside the standard banking hours. **Hotels** aren't plentiful and tend to be expensive; the best bet is *Zum Ritter*, just outside the old quarter at Am Stadtgraben 25 (☎07071/22 502; ④), or try the **youth hostel** on the banks of the Neckar, a short walk from the station at Gartenstr. 22/2 (☎07071/23 002; ②); the **tourist office** also has a list of private rooms fom DM30 per person. To reach the **campsite**, also with a riverside setting at Rappenberghalde, turn left on leaving the train station, and cross at Alleenbrücke. The best **restaurant** in the centre is *Forelle*, an old-world wine bar at Kronenstr. 8. For cheaper eating, try *Café Pfuderer* on Marktplatz, which serves Swabian specialities in a tearoom atmosphere. Also on this square is *Marktschenke*, a lively student bar.

The Black Forest Region

Stretching 170km north to south, and up to 60km east to west, the **Black Forest** (Schwarzwald) is the largest German forest and the most beautiful. As late as the 1920s, much of this area was a wilderness sunk in an eerie gloom, forming a refuge for boars and bandits. Nowadays most of the villages have been opened up as spa and health resorts, brimming with shops selling tacky souvenirs, while the old trails have become gravel paths smoothed down for pensioners and prams. Yet by no means all the modernizations are drawbacks. **Railway** fans, for example, will find several of the most spectacular lines in Europe here. It should be noted, though, that the trains tend to stick to the valleys and that **bus services** are much reduced outside the tourist season.

Most of the Black Forest is associated with the Margraviate of Baden, whose old capital of **Baden-Baden** is at the northern fringe of the forest, in a fertile orchard and vine-growing area. The only city actually surrounded by the forest is **Freiburg im Breisgau**, one of the most enticing in the country.

Baden-Baden

In the present century, the social class that made **BADEN-BADEN** the "summer capital of Europe" has almost disappeared, yet the town still has a style that no other spa in the country can quite match. Buoyed by the postwar economic prosperity, people flock here to enjoy a taste of a lifestyle their parents could only dream about. Baden is on the fast Karlsruhe to Freiburg line, but the station is 4km northwest of the centre in the suburb of Oos; take bus #1 into the centre.

The therapeutic value of Baden's hot springs was discovered by the Romans, but the town's rise to international fame only came about as a result of Napoleon's creation of the buffer state of Baden in 1806. The Grand Dukes promoted their ancestors' old seat as a modern resort, and began embellishing it with handsome buildings such as the **Kurhaus** and its integral **casino**. The easiest way to see these is to take a **guided tour** (daily 9.30–11.45am; DM3); highlight is the Winter Garden, with its glass cupola, Chinese vases and solid gold roulette table. A day ticket, with no obligation to participate, is DM5.

South of the Kurhaus runs Baden-Baden's most famous thoroughfare, the **Lichtentaler Allee**, landscaped with exotic trees and shrubs and flanked by buildings such as the Parisian-style theatre and the **Kunsthalle**, which often hosts major exhibitions of twentieth-century art. Immediately north of the Kurhaus is the **Trinkhalle**, where varieties of spring water are dispensed from a mosaic fountain, under vast frescoes illustrating legends of the town and the nearby countryside.

Little remains today of the old town, almost completely destroyed in a single day in 1689, the result of a fire started by French troops. However, halfway up the Florintinerberg is the Marktplatz, and the **Stiftskirche**, a Gothic hall church containing one of the masterpieces of European sculpture, an enormous sandstone *Crucifixion* by Nicolaus Gerhaert von Leyden. Hidden under the Stiftskirche are the remains of the Roman Imperial Baths; the more modest **Römerbad** (Easter–Oct daily 10am–noon & 1.30–4pm; DM2.50), just east on Römerplatz, was probably for soldiers. Above the ruins is the **Friedrichsbad** (Mon–Sat 9am–10pm), begun in 1869 and grand as a Renaissance palace. Speciality of the house is a two-hour "Roman-Irish Bath", which will set you back DM34, though the really broke need only fork out DM0.10 for a glass of thermal water.

From here you can climb the steep steps to the **Neues Schloss** (Tues–Sun 10am–12.30pm & 2–5pm; DM2), a mixture of Renaissance and Baroque buildings, housing displays on the history of the town. There's also the added attraction of the best view over Baden-Baden, a dramatic mix of rooftops, spires and the enveloping forest.

PRACTICALITIES

The **tourist office** is on Augustaplatz (Mon–Sat 9am–10pm, Sun 10am–10pm). Rooms are available in **private houses** for DM20 per person or even less. Main concentration of cheap **hotels** is in Oos: try *Goldener Stern*, Ooser Hauptstr. 16 (☎07221/61 509; ④), or *Zur Linde*, Sinzheimer Str. 3 (☎07221/61 519; ④). Baden-Baden's **youth hostel** is between the train station and the centre at Hardbergstr. 34 (☎07221/52 223; ②); take bus #1 to Grosse-Dollen-Strasse, from where the way is signposted. The nearest **campsite** is in the Oberbruch park on the outskirts of Bühl, three stops by slow train. Among places to **eat** and **drink**, the *Münchener Löwenbräu* on Gernsbacher Strasse makes a good choice; complete with beer garden, it's like a little corner of Bavaria, and serves excellent meals. For a trendy atmosphere, try *Leo's* on Luisenstrasse, while for solid, low-cost German food, there's *Bratwurstglöckle* on Steinstrasse.

Triberg

Heart of the central Black Forest is the little spa and health resort of **TRIBERG**, which lies at an altitude of 1000 metres on the main rail line between the Rhine and Konstanz. Prime attraction here is the **Gutach Waterfall**, which plunges in seven stages through a height of 162 metres, making it the highest in Germany. In a crass reverse of the normal German penchant for unrestricted access to nature, the cascade is sealed off, with a DM2.50 charge for admission. Ample compensation, however, is provided by the **Schwarzwald Museum** on Wallfahrtstrasse (mid-May to Sept 8am–6pm; rest of year 10am–noon & 2–5pm; DM3), which offers fascinating insights into the rural culture of the Black Forest as it was – and, to some extent, still is. Triberg's other major sight is the Baroque **Wallfahrtskirche St Maria in den Tannen** – a pilgrimage site because of miraculous powers imputed to its painting of *The Virgin of the Pines*.

There are a number of cheap **guesthouses** here: *Krone*, Schulstr. 37 (☎07722/4524; ④), which also serves excellent food; *Haus Charlotte*, Schwerstr. 12h (☎07722/4394; ④); or *Gasthaus Scwarzwaldstube*, Ober-Vogthuber-Str. 25a (☎07722/3324; ④). The **youth hostel** is high in the hills at Rohrbacher Str. 35 (☎07722/4110; ②); a bus goes as far as the waterfall, and then it's a twenty-minute climb.

Freiburg im Breisgau

"Capital" of the Black Forest, **FREIBURG IM BREISGAU** basks in a laid-back atmosphere which seems completely un-German. As a university town since 1457, it has a youthful presence that's maintained all year round with the help of a varied programme of festivals. Furthermore, the sun shines here more often, and there are more vineyards within the municipal area, than in any other city in the country.

Though it rivals any of the great European cathedrals, the dark red sandstone **Münster** was built as a mere parish church, the costs being met entirely by the local citizens. The transepts were begun in about 1200, but then one of the architects of Strasbourg cathedral took over, creating a masterly Gothic nave, resplendent with flying buttresses, gargoyles and statues. At around this time the magnificent sculptures of the west porch were created, the most important German works of their time – note the Prince of Darkness, carved where the natural light is weakest. More sculptures adorn the portals of the chancel, which was begun in the mid-fourteenth century – look out for the unusual depiction of God resting on the seventh day. From the tower (March–Nov Mon–Sat 9.30am–5pm, Sun 1–5pm; DM1.50) you get a fine panorama over the city and the forest, and of the lace-like tracery of the spire, which rounds off the tower with a bravura flourish. Inside, the transept is lit by stained-glass windows of the early thirteenth century. Most of those in the nave date from a hundred years later, and were donated by the local trades and guilds, who incorporated their coats of arms. To get a decent look at Baldung's *Coronation of the Virgin* altarpiece, you have to take a guided tour of the ambulatory chapels (DM1.50), which contain some wonderful pieces – including a retable by the two Holbeins, and a silver crucifix from the first Münster.

The spacious **Münsterplatz**, the north side of which was flattened in the last war, holds one of the most diverting daily markets in Germany. The south side of the square is dominated by the blood-red **Kaufhaus**, a sixteenth-century merchants' hall, flanked by handsome Baroque palaces.

A peculiarity of Freiburg is the system of rivulets known as the **Bächle**, which run in deep gulleys all over the city. Formerly used for watering animals, and as a fire-fighting provision, they have their purpose even today, helping to keep the city cool. Following the main channel of the Bächle southwards, you come to the **Schwaben Tor**, one of two surviving towers of the medieval fortifications. On Oberlinden, just in front, is **Zum Roten Bären**, which is generally considered to be Germany's oldest inn. Just to the west is Salzstrasse, where the **Augustiner Museum** (Tues–Fri 9.30am–5pm, Sat & Sun 10.30am–5pm; DM4) houses works of art from the Münster and a few top-class pictures, including the most important paintings by the mysterious draughtsman known as Master of the Housebook. South of here, on Marienstrasse, the **Museum of Modern Art** (same times; free) has a good cross-section of twentieth-century German painting. From here, follow Fischerau, the old fishermen's street, and you come to the other thirteenth-century tower, the **Martinstor**, in the middle of Freiburg's central axis, Kaiser-Josef-Strasse.

Back on the west side of the Münster, the **Neues Rathaus**, **Altes Rathaus**, and the plain Franciscan monastery church of **St Martin** stand around a shady chestnut-lined square. In the alley behind St Martin is the cheerful Gothic facade of the **Haus zum Wallfisch**, for two years the home of the great humanist Erasmus, who was forced to flee from Basel by the religious struggles there. A few minutes to the west, in the Columbipark opposite the tourist office, is the **Museum of Pre- and Early History** (same times; free), which has important archeological collections relating to the Black Forest region.

It's worth climbing one of the hills surrounding the city for the wonderful views. The **Schlossberg**, immediately to the east, is an easy ascent from the Schwabentor – or you could take the cable car. To the south, the **Lorettoberg** – where the stone for the Münster was quarried – makes a good afternoon or evening alternative.

PRACTICALITIES

The **train station**, with the **bus station** on its southern side, is about ten minutes' walk from the city centre. Following Eisenbahnstrasse, you come to the **tourist office** on Rotteckring (May–Oct Mon–Sat 9am–8pm, Sun 10am–noon; Nov–April Mon–Fri 9am–6pm, Sat 9am–3pm, Sun 10am–noon). For DM3, the tourist office will find you a room; if you arrive after closing time, there's an electronic noticeboard equipped with a phone, listing vacancies. Among **hotels** with a central location, the cheapest is *Schemmer*, Eschholzstr. 63 (☎0761/272 424; ④). The luxurious **youth hostel** is at Karthäuserstr. 151 (☎0761/67 656; ②), at the extreme western end of the city, reached by tram #1 to Hasemannstrasse. Nearby, slightly nearer town, is the *Hirzberg* **camp-site** (April to mid-Oct); *Möselpark* (mid-March to Oct) is on the opposite side of the river. The *St Georg* site, southwest of the centre at Basler Landstr. 62, is open all year.

Freiburg has **restaurants** for all pockets. *Oberkirchs Weinstuben* and the *Ratskeller* on Münsterplatz are two top-notch but not expensive wine cellars, and *Zur Traube* on Schusterstrasse just behind is equally good. Hearty South German cooking can be sampled at *Kleiner Meyerhof* on Rathausgasse or *Grosser Meyerhof* on Grünwälderstrasse. Currently, the trendiest place to be seen is *Uni-Café* on Universitätsecke, which serves a wide selection of coffees and has good snacks. Freiburg now ranks as one of the leading German cities for jazz, thanks to the new *Jazzhaus* on Schwenlinstrasse, which has concerts every evening.

The Southern Black Forest

The **Southern Black Forest** is especially wonderful around the two highest points, **Belchen** and **Feldberg**. Unfortunately, almost everyone in Europe knows about the beauties of this region, and in the summer months it's not unusual to find yourself sharing the sights with half a dozen coachloads.

AROUND BELCHEN

Belchen, surrounded by deep gorges some 20km south of Freiburg, is the most beautiful of the southern peaks, with wonderful views and quiet little villages in its valleys. One of these valleys is the **Münstertal**, dotted with characteristic low-roofed farms, set among lush pastures on the steep northern Belchen slopes. Some time in the seventh century, Irish missionaries came to Christianize this area; the most famous, Saint Trudpert, was murdered in 607 after three years of missionary work. The **St Trudpert Monastery** in the upper Münstertal was founded about 250 years later, and the large Baroque complex you see today forms the visual centre of the whole upper valley.

Following the Münstertal west, the foothills sink into the Rhine valley, the landscape quickly changing into gently rolling hills that sustain some of Germany's most famous vineyards and provide a lucrative living to many small and ancient towns. Of these, **STAUFEN** is particularly attractive. Situated at the bottom of the Münstertal, and surrounded by its vineyards, its location is idyllic and makes a great base for relaxed hiking tours; there are regular buses from Freiburg. The **tourist office** in the Rathaus provides accommodation lists. Cheapest option is the attractive gabled *Bahnhof-Hotel* on Bahnhofstrasse (☎07633/6190; ④).

AROUND FELDBERG

The area around the pastured slopes of **Feldberg** is one of the best hiking regions, with many beautiful trails through forests and gorges laced with romantic waterfalls and streams. One of Germany's most dramatic **train rides** is in this region too: the route from Freiburg to Feldberg-Bärental. The line winds through the narrow **Höllental** (Hell Valley) gorge to the resort of Titisee, on the lake of the same name; from there a branch line crawls up the mountainside, passing through numerous viaducts and tunnels before arriving at Feldberg-Bärental – Germany's highest station. The train then descends to the southern tip of the Schluchsee, past Schluchsee village (with a campsite, and plenty of private rooms), to the lakeside town of **SEEBRUGG**, which has a decent beach plus sailing and windsurfing facilities. There's a **youth hostel** (☎07656/494; ②) just minutes from Seebrugg's train station, along with *Pension Berger* (☎07656/238; ④).

Konstanz and the Bodensee

In the far south of the province, **KONSTANZ** lies at the tip of a tongue of land sticking out into the **Bodensee** (Lake Constance), which is really a swelling in the River Rhine. The town itself is split by the water: the **Altstadt** is a German enclave on the Swiss side of the lake, which is why it was never bombed by the Allies, who couldn't risk hitting neutral Switzerland. It's a cosy little place, with a convivial atmosphere in summer, when street cafés invite long pauses and the water is a bustle of sails.

The most prominent church is the **Münster**, set on the highest point of the Altstadt. It was here in 1417 that the papal court tried the reformer Johannes Hus for heresy – the spot on which he stood during his trial is marked in the central aisle. Konstanz's major museum is the **Rosgartenmuseum** on the street of the same name (Tues–Thurs 10am–5pm, Fri–Sun 10am–4pm; DM3), which has a fine collection of local archeological finds, plus art and craft exhibits from the Middle Ages. Everything is as it was when the museum was designed in 1871, creating a pleasantly musty atmosphere.

The **tourist office** is located alongside the train station at Bahnhofplatz 13 (May–Sept Mon–Fri 9am–8pm, Sat 10am–1pm & 4–7pm; April & Oct until 6pm on weekdays; Nov–Mar Mon–Fri 9am–noon & 2–6pm); they can book accommodation for you in private rooms, which is plentiful and cheaper than any hotel here. If you'd prefer a **hotel**, however, there's *Blauer Bock* at Hussenstr. 36 (☎07531/22 741; ④). The **youth hostel** is at Zur Allmannshöhe 18 (☎07531/32 260; ②); take bus #4 from the train station to Jugendherberge, or #1 to Post Allmannsdorf. Information on **cruises and ferries** is available from the *Bodensee-Verkehrsdienst* at Hafenstr. 6 (☎07531/281 398). Ferries regularly leave Konstanz for destinations all over the lake: perhaps the most worthwhile longer trip is to the **Rheinfall** in Switzerland – it costs DM36, but it's worth it to travel up one of the Rhine's most scenic stretches and see Europe's largest waterfall.

Lindau

At the lake's eastern edge, the Alps descend to the waters at the tiny island town of **LINDAU**, whose medieval merchants' houses create a distinctly Mediterranean ambience – strengthened by the café tables on the harbour promenade. Ferries operate on the lake in summer, or if you prefer a bit more independence, all sorts of boats, canoes and windsurfers can be rented from the marina. The stylish **Haus zum Cavazzen** on the Marktplatz contains one of the most attractive local history museums of any town in Bavaria (Tues–Sun 10am–noon & 2–5pm; DM3).

The **tourist office** (Apr–Oct Mon–Fri 8am–6pm, Sat 9am–1pm; Nov–Mar Mon–Fri 8am–noon & 2–5pm) is opposite the **train station**, and supplies free maps of Lindau and endless amounts of other publicity. **Hotels** to try are the *Inselgraben*, Hintere Metzgergasse 4–6 (☎08382/5481; ④); *Gästehaus Ladine*, In der Grub 25 (☎08382/5326; ④); and *Gästehaus Limmer*, In der Grub 16 (☎08382/5877; ③). There is a **youth hostel**, Jungendhaus Martin, at Bechtersweller 25 (☎08382/5849; ②). The **campsite** *Lindau-Zech*, by the lake, is open from April to October. You'll find the cheapest **restaurants** on the suitably named In der Grub, where there's also a welcoming bar called the *Schalldämpfer*.

Munich

Founded in 1158, **MUNICH** (München) has been the capital of Bavaria since 1503, and as far as the locals are concerned it may as well be the centre of the universe. *Münchener* pride themselves on their special status and have strong views on who exactly qualifies to be counted as one of them. Even people who have made Munich their home for most of their lives are still called *Zugereiste* (newcomers). Next to

Berlin, Munich is Germany's most popular city, with everything you'd expect in a cosmopolitan capital. Yet it's small enough to be digestible in one visit, and it's got the added bonus of a great setting, with the mountains and Alpine lakes just an hour's drive away. The best time of year to come here is from June to early October, when the beer gardens, street cafés and bars are in full swing.

Heart of the city is the **Marienplatz**; the pedestrian centre fans out from here in an approximate circle of one square kilometre. This is tourist and shopping land, with all the city's major department stores, the central market, the royal palace and the most important churches. North of Marienplatz, Ludwigstrasse and Leopoldstrasse run straight through the heart of **Schwabing**, which is the entertainment quarter and full of *Schickies* (German yuppies). It's also close to the city's main park, the **Englischer Garten**. To the west of the axis between the Marienplatz and Schwabing is the **museum quarter**, containing the most important of Munich's thirty-six museums, while to the southeast of the centre lies Haidhausen, the nearest thing Munich has to an alternative quarter.

Arrival and information

Munich's new airport, **Franz Josef Strauss Flughafen**, opened in 1992 to replace the tiny Riem airport. It is connected to the **Hauptbahnhof** by S-Bahn no. 8.

There's a **tourist desk** in the airport for general information, free maps and lists of hotels, but they can't book rooms. At the train station, the main **tourist office** (Mon–Sat 8am–11pm, Sun 1–9.30pm; ☎239 1256) is opposite platform 11. They will book rooms for a fee of DM3, and provide free brochures about the city and what's on. The **bus station** is a stone's throw from the train station.

City transport

Your best bet is to buy a **travel pass** as soon as you arrive, from the ticket office at the train station: to get there, you go down to the U-Bahn level and follow the signs to the Starnberger train station and from there to the *Zeitkartenstelle*. Twenty-four-hour validity tickets for all public transport in the city centre cost DM10, for the whole system DM20; a weekly pass covering the city centre and most of Schwabing costs DM14. Note that these passes are valid from Monday to Monday, so buying midweek means losing out. You'll need your passport and a couple of photos to buy any of the above passes. Otherwise tickets for city transport are available from ticket machines in all U-Bahn stations, at some bus and tram stops, and inside trams. If you're going longer distances across the city you will need to buy a **blue ticket** (DM10), and stamp two strips for every zone crossed – the zones are shown on maps at stations and tram and bus stops. **Red tickets** (DM8) are only for children aged four to fifteen. Tickets must be stamped before any journey – those without a validated ticket face an on-the-spot DM60 fine.

Accommodation

Cheap accommodation can be hard to find, especially during the high season in the summer, though prices are fairly constant throughout the year. If you're going to be in town during the Oktoberfest, it's essential to book your room well in advance. Details of the pick of the hotels, hostels and campsites are given below. Many pensions offer rooms with three to six beds, a much more pleasant way of saving money than hostel-type accommodation.

HOSTELS

Burg Schwaneck, Burgweg 4–6 (☎793 0643). *IYHF* hostel some way from the centre in an old castle on the river. Check-in 5pm–1am. S-Bahn #7 to Pullach, then follow signs to the *Jugendherberge*. ②

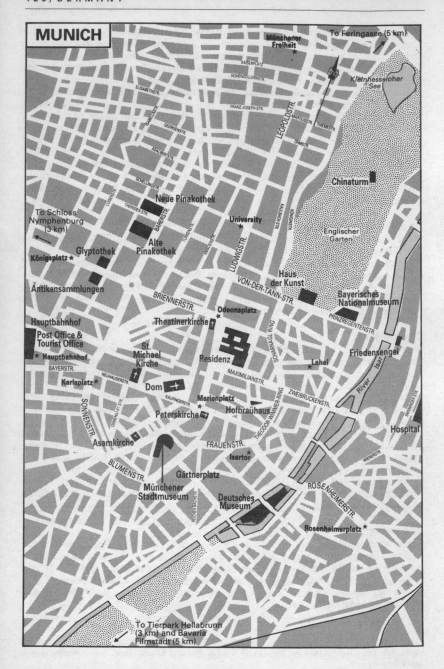

MUNICH

To Feringasee (5 km)

Münchener
Freiheit

KAISERPLATZ

HÖHENZOLLERNSTR.

Kleinhesseloher
See

ELISABETHSTR.

FRANZ-JOSEPH-STR.

LEOPOLDSTR.

MARTIUSSTR. THIEMESTR.

GEORGENSTR.

OHMSTR.

ADALBERTSTR.

Chinaturm

SCHELLINGSTR.

Neue Pinakothek

THERESIEN STR.

BARERSTR.

University

Englischer
Garten

To Schloss
Nymphenburg
(3 km)

Glyptothek

Alte
Pinakothek

LUDWIGSTR.

Königsplatz ★

Antikensammlungen

BRIENNERSTR.

VON-DER-TANN-STR.

Haus
der Kunst

Bayerisches
Nationalmuseum

Hauptbahnhof

Odeonsplatz

Theatinerkirche

Post Office &
Tourist Office

★ Hauptbahnhof

BAYERSTR.

St.
Michael
Kirche

Residenz

PRINZREGENTENSTR.

Friedensengel

MAXIMILIANSTR.

Lehel

River Isar

Karlsplatz ★

NEUHAUSERSTR.

Dom

ZWEIBRÜCKENSTR.

SONNENSTR.

Marienplatz

KAUFINGERSTR.

Peterskirche

Hofbräuhaus

Hospital

Asamkirche

FRAUENSTR.

THEODOR-WIMMER-RING

Isartor

BLUMENSTR.

Gärtnerplatz

ROSENHEIMERSTR.

Münchener
Stadtmuseum

Deutsches
Museum

Rosenheimerplatz ★

To Tierpark Hellabrunn
(3 km) and Bavaria
Filmstadt (5 km)

DJH München, Wendl-Dietrich-Strasse 20 (☎131 156). The largest, most central and most basic *IYHF* hostel, with 535 beds in dormitories. Check-in noon–1am. U-Bahn to Rotkreuzplatz. ②
DJH Jugendgästehaus, Miesingstr. 4 (☎723 6550). Smaller, more upmarket *IYHF* hostel with check-in between 7am–11pm. U-Bahn to Harras, then tram #16 to Boschetsriederstrasse. ②
Haus International, Elisabethstr. 87 (☎185 081). Centrally located in Schwabing, rooms range from five beds to singles. No age limit, no need for *IYHF* card. U-Bahn to Hohenzollernplatz, then bus #33 or tram #12 to Barbarastrasse. ④
Jugendhotel Marienberge, Goethestr. 9 (☎555 891). Very near the train station; women only, maximum age 25. ③

HOTELS AND PENSIONS

Eder, Zweigstr. 8 (☎554 560). In a quiet road between the train station and Marienplatz. ④
Frank, Schellingstr. 24 (☎281 451). Best in terms of price and atmosphere. Mainly frequented by young travellers. ④
Am Kaiserplatz, Kaiserplatz 12 (☎349 190). Very friendly, good location and big rooms, each done in a different style – from red satin to Bavarian rustic. ④
Münchener Kindl, Damenstiftstr. 16 (☎264 349). Couldn't really be closer to Marienplatz, yet is removed from the shopping mælstrom. ⑤
Steinberg, Ohmstr. 9 (☎331 011). Friendly and in a good location. ⑤
Wilhelmy, Amalienstr. 71 (☎283 971). Very quiet and well-situated. ⑤

CAMPSITES

Kapuzinerhölzl Youth Camp. 500-berth tent with showers, canteen and information bureau. Price includes blankets, air mattress and morning tea. Check-in 5pm–9am. Officially for under-23s and for a maximum of three nights, but people in charge are very flexible. Open late June to end of Aug. U-Bahn to Rotkreuzplatz, then tram #12 to the Botanischer Garten.
Obermenzing, Lochhausenerstr. 59. In a posh suburb, close to Nymphenburg. Open March 15–Oct 31. S-Bahn to Obermenzing, then bus #75 to Lochhausenerstrasse.
Thalkirchen, Zentralländerstr. 49. Most central site, in an attractive part of the Isar valley. Very popular during the Oktoberfest as it's close to the fairground. Open March 15–Oct 31. U-Bahn to Thal Kirchen.

The City

Almost nothing is left of Munich's medieval city, but three of the gates remain to mark today's city centre. Bounded by the Odeonsplatz and the Sendlinger Tor to the north and south, and the Isar Tor and Karlstor to the east and west, it's only a fifteen-minute walk across – but is so tightly packed it needs two or three days to explore thoroughly.

MARIENPLATZ AND AROUND

The central **Marienplatz** – the heart of the U-Bahn system – is always thronged, with street musicians and artists entertaining the crowds, and with local youths lounging around the central fountain. At 11am and noon, the square fills with gawping tourists and the noise of camera shutters as the tuneless **carillon** in the Rathaus tower jingles into action. The **Rathaus** itself is a neo-Gothic monstrosity built in the late nineteenth century, whose only redeeming feature is the café in its cool and breezy courtyard. To the right is the plain Gothic tower of the **Altes Rathaus**, which was rebuilt in the fifteenth-century style after being destroyed by lightning; today it houses a toy museum (Mon–Sat 10am–5.30pm, Sun 10am–6pm; DM4). Close by, the **Peterskirche** looks out across the busy Viktualienmarkt; the oldest church in Munich, it's notable for its grisly relics of Saint Munditia, patron saint of single women, and for the view from its tower (Mon–Fri 9am–7pm, Sat 8.30am–8pm, Sun 10am–7pm; DM2.50).

Almost next to the Viktualienmarkt is the **Münchener Stadtmuseum** (Tues & Thurs–Sat 10am–5pm, Wed 10am–8pm; DM5), the excellent local history museum, which also incorporates a Photo and Film Museum, a Museum of Brewing and a

Puppet Museum. The last is highly recommended: it's one of the largest collections in the world, and includes puppets ranging from Indian and Chinese paper dolls to large mechanical European creations. Southwest of here, at Sendlingerstrasse 62, stands the small **Asamkirche** – it's one of the most splendid Rococo churches in Bavaria, with its wild use of colour and gold, and countless plaster curls.

Following the pedestrian Kaufingerstrasse west from Marienplatz, you walk with the mainstream of shoppers, overlooked by the Frauenkirche or **Dom**. The red-brick Gothic cathedral is seen to its best advantage from a distance, its twin onion-domed towers forming the focus of the city's skyline. A little further up Kaufingerstrasse, the Renaissance facade of **St Michael** stands unassumingly in line with the street's other buildings. In the crypt (Mon–Fri 10am–1pm & 2–4pm, Sat 10am–3pm; DM1.50) you'll find the coffins of the Wittelsbach dynasty, including the famous castle-builder Ludwig II, a candle permanently burning at the foot of his coffin.

NORTH OF MARIENPLATZ – THE RESIDENZ

North of Marienplatz is the posh end of the city centre. **Maximilianstrasse**, the Champs-Elysées of Munich, is where the fashion houses have their shops, and the *Hotel Vierjahreszeiten* is one of the best addresses in town. When the refinement gets too much, the little Kosttor road leads straight to the **Hofbräuhaus**, Munich's largest and most famous drinking hall. Nearby is one of Munich's most regal churches: the **Theatinerkirche**, its golden-yellow towers and green copper dome adding a splash of colour to the roofscape, its Baroque facade standing proud on the Odeonsplatz.

The palace of the Wittelsbachs, the **Residenz** (Tues–Sat 10am–4.30pm, Sun 10am–1pm; DM3), stands across the square from the Theatinerkirche. One of Europe's finest Renaissance buildings, it was so badly damaged in the last war that it had to be almost totally rebuilt. To see the whole thing you have to go on two consecutive visits, as parts of the immense complex are shut in the morning and others in the afternoon. On the morning tour you see the Antiquarium, the oldest part of the palace; built in 1571 to house the ruling family's collection of antiquities, this cavernous chamber was transformed into a festive hall a generation later. The last stage of the morning tour – which can also be seen in the afternoon – includes the eight appropriately named Rich Rooms, and the Halls of the Nibelungs, in which medieval Germany's most famous epic is depicted in a series of paintings. Other rooms can be seen in the afternoon only, and include further displays of ceramics, along with the silverware collection and the Baroque Golden Hall. A separate ticket is necessary to see the fabulous treasures of the Schatzkammer (same hours; DM3); star piece of the whole display, kept in a room of its own, is the dazzling stone-encrusted statuette of St George, made around 1590. Yet another ticket has to be bought for the glorious **Cuvilliés Theatre** (Mon–Sat 2–5pm, Sun 10am–5pm; DM1.50), the Wittelsbachs' private theatre. It is named after François Cuvilliés, who began his career as court dwarf to the Elector Max Emanuel, but went on to become the state architect, developing the Rococo style in a series of stunningly original buildings, of which this is one of the finest.

ISARINSEL AND PRINZREGENTENSTRASSE

Munich's most overwhelming museum – the **Deutsches Museum** (daily 9am–5pm; DM8) – occupies much of the mid-stream island called the Isarinsel. Covering every conceivable aspect of technical endeavour, from the first flint tools to the research labs of modern industry, this is the most compendious collection of its type in Germany – which amounts to saying it's the best in Europe.

Another gargantuan collection lies close to the first bridge to the north of the Isarinsel. The **Bayerisches Nationalmuseum**, Prinzregentenstr. 3 (Tues–Sun 9.30am–5pm; DM3), is a rambling decorative arts museum, whose items of general interest are concentrated on the first floor. Alongside arms and armour, ivories and sacred objects, there's a superb display of German wood sculpture – with splendid examples of Tilman Riemenschneider's art from all phases of his career. The entrance level features Bavarian folk art and a collection of Christmas cribs, while the second floor has stained glass, crystal, ceramics, clocks and models of Bavarian towns as they appeared in the sixteenth century. Close by, the **Staatsgalerie Moderner Kunst** at Prinzregentenstr. 1 (Tues–Sun 9am–4.30pm, plus Thurs 7–9pm; DM3.50) takes up the story of twentieth-century European painting and sculpture where the Neue Pinakothek (see below) leaves off.

THE MUSEUM QUARTER

Tucked between the train station and Schwabing, the museum quarter contains enough treasures to keep you absorbed for days. All the state-owned museums are free on Sundays and public holidays.

The **Alte Pinakothek**, Barerstr. 27 (Tues–Sun 9.15am–4.30pm, plus Tues & Thurs 7–9pm; DM6, DM10 for combined ticket to Alte and Neue Pinakotheken), is one of the largest galleries in Europe and the world's finest assembly of German art, yet can still be grasped in one long visit. The most celebrated possessions are the pieces by Dürer, including the Christ-like *Self-Portrait* and the panels of *SS. Mark, John the Evangelist, Peter and Paul*, which are from the very end of his career. Other German masterpieces include Lucas Cranach the Elder's *Lucretia* and *Venus and Cupid* – the first sensually explicit nudes in German art – and Albrecht Altdorfer's *Battle of Alexander*, a heaving mass of hundreds of soldiers, each painted in minute detail. In the Italian section works by Titian steal the show, notably the *Portrait of Charles V* and *Christ Crowned with Thorns*. Centrepiece of the entire museum is the collection of works by Rubens, with sixty-two paintings displaying the scope of the artist's prodigious output. There's also a haunting *Passion Cycle* by Rembrandt, and, from an earlier period of Netherlandish art, Rogier van der Weyden's classic *Adoration of the Magi*.

The collection of eighteenth- and nineteenth-century European painting and sculpture in the **Neue Pinakothek** at Barerstr. 29 (Tues–Sun 9.15am–4.30pm, plus Tues 7–9pm; DM6, DM10 for combined ticket to Alte and Neue Pinakotheken) seems a little thin after the Alte Pinakothek, but it's nonetheless worth an hour or so. Neoclassicism, the preferred style of the age of rationalism, is beautifully embodied in the sober portrait of the *Marquise de Sourcy de Thélusson* by David, while Romanticism is represented by Carl Spitzweg, whose everyday scenes have a wry sense of humour. Of the works by French Impressionists, Manet's *Breakfast in the Studio* is probably the most famous. Turn-of-the-century art is represented by a few paintings by Cézanne, van Gogh and Gauguin, and the museum rounds off with a small selection of Art Nouveau.

The meticulously restored **Glyptothek** (Tues, Wed & Fri–Sun 10am–4.30pm, Thurs noon–8.30pm; DM5), the most striking structure on the majestically Neoclassical Königsplatz, contains a magnificent range of classical sculpture, the most striking exhibits being the ancient statuary plundered from the temple on Aegina. Facing the Glyptothek is the **Staatliche Antikensammlungen** (Tues & Thurs–Sun 10am–4.30pm, Wed noon–8.30pm; DM5, joint ticket with Glyptothek DM8), displaying Greek vases from the fifth and sixth centuries BC, as well as beautiful jewellery and small statues from Greek, Etruscan and Roman antiquity.

Situated just off Königsplatz at Luisenstrasse 30 is the **Lenbachhaus** (Tues–Sun 10am–6pm; DM5), the nineteenth-century villa that belonged to the Bavarian painter Franz von Lenbach. It's a pleasant setting for some of German art's most interesting modern painters, the highlights coming with the group known as the *Blaue Reiter*, whose members included Kandinsky, Klee, Marc and Macke. In recent years the museum has also concentrated on important temporary exhibitions of contemporary German art.

SCHWABING

Marienplatz might be the geographical centre of town but **Schwabing** is its social hub. A large part of Munich's northern sector, with Leopoldstrasse forming a straight axis through the middle, Schwabing splits into three distinct areas. Around the university and left of Leopoldstrasse, residential streets mix with student bars and restaurants. Along the centre and to its right, trendy shops and café-bars ensure permanent crowds, day and night – nightclubs are thick on the ground here, especially around the Wedekindplatz, near Münchener Freiheit station. The far north is a tidily bourgeois residential area, uninteresting for visitors apart from the **Olympiapark**, at the end of the U-Bahn. Built for the 1972 Olympics, the Olympiapark has a public swimming pool, and on weekends in July and August is the setting for free open-air rock concerts.

One diversion that unites everyone is beer drinking, especially in summer. One of the most famous beer gardens is around the Chinesischer Turm (or Chinaturm) in the **Englischer Garten**, and a couple of more peaceful gardens are not far off by the Kleinhesseloher See – the lakeside one is the more attractive. The Eisbach meadow is the city's main playground, where people come to sunbathe (often nude), picnic, swim or ride horses.

NYMPHENBURG

Schloss Nymphenburg (Tues–Sun 9am–12.30pm & 1.30–5pm; DM2.50, DM6 including the pavilions), the summer residence of the Wittelsbachs, is reached by taking the U-Bahn to Rotkreuzplatz and then tram #12. Its kernel is a small Italianate palace begun in 1664 for the Electress Adelaide, who dedicated it to the goddess Flora and her nymphs – hence the name. More enticing than the palace itself are the wonderful park and its four pavilions – all of a markedly different character. Three were designed by Joseph Effner: the **Magdalenenklause**, built to resemble a ruined hermitage; the **Pagodenburg**, used for the most exclusive parties thrown by the court; and the **Badenburg**, which, like the Pagodenburg, reflects an interest in the art of China, though both the bathing room and the banqueting hall are in the richest tradition of European Baroque. For all their charm, Effner's pavilions are overshadowed by the stunning **Amalienburg**, the hunting lodge built behind the south wing of the Schloss by his successor as court architect, François Cuvilliés. This is the supreme expression of the Rococo style, marrying a cunning design – which makes the little building seem like a full-scale palace – with the most extravagant decoration imaginable.

To the north of the Schloss, the **Botanical Gardens** (daily 9am–6/7pm, hothouses closed 11.45am–1pm; DM2) hide all manner of plants in their steamy hothouses, while the herbarium and other outdoor collections make a very fragrant landscape.

DACHAU

DACHAU, now reverted to a picturesque town on the northern edge of Munich, was site of Germany's first **concentration camp**. The motto that greeted arrivals at the gates has taken its chilling place in the history of Third Reich brutality: *Arbeit Macht Frei* – "Work Brings Freedom". There's no guided tour of the gas chamber and replica huts (Tues–Sun 9am–5pm; free) – a permanent exhibition speaks for itself. Turn up at 11.30am or 3.30pm and you can also view the short, deeply disturbing, documentary *KZ-Dachau* in English. Get there by taking bus #722 from Dachau S-Bahn station.

Eating and drinking

It's not difficult to eat well for little money in Munich. *Mensas* are the cheapest places to get a good basic meal; you're supposed to have a valid student card to eat here, but no one seems to check. The most central one is at Leopoldstr. 15 (Mon–Thurs 9am–4.45pm, Fri 9am–3.30pm), and there are two more in the main building at Schellingstrasse and at the Technical University, Arcisstr. 17. Italian restaurants are especially cheap, and the Bavarian *Gaststätten* offer filling soups, salads and sandwich-type dishes for around DM5. Not surprisingly, drinking is central to Munich social life and apart from the *Gaststätten* and beer gardens, Munich also has a lively café-bar culture, which carries on well into the early hours. The city's "alternative" district is the former working-class and immigrant quarter of **Haidhausen**, across the river to the southeast of the centre. Though tamer than Berlin's Kreuzberg and Prenzlauer Berg, it has a good mix of bars, cafés and restaurants, and makes a refreshing break from the glitz of the Schwabing nightspots.

GASTSTÄTTEN

Atzinger, Schellingstr. 98. One of the best places to pop in for a cheap lunch.

Schelling Salon, Schellingstr. 54. Good for their large cheap breakfasts and also for playing pool.

Weinbauer, Fendstr. 5. An excellent, unpretentious and cheap place in the middle of Schwabing.

CAFÉ-BARS, CAFÉS AND WINE BARS

Casino, Kellerstr. 21. Haidhausen café-bar where the real trendies hang out.

Café Kreuzkamm, Maffeistr. 4. Best and most expensive *Kaffee und Küchen* establishment.

Café Schneller, Amalienstr. 59. A basic kind of café; cosy and small.

Nachtcafé, Maximiliansplatz 5. The place to be seen in the early hours; open 8pm–5am.

Pfälzer Weinprobierstuben, Residenzstr. 1. Unpretentious place serving excellent wines.

Reitschule, Königinstr. 34. Typical haunt of the Schwabing *Schickies*.

Weintrödler, Briennerstr. 10. Late-night wine bar (5pm–6am); the last boozer to close.

RESTAURANTS

Adria, Leopoldstr. 19. Popular late-night Italian, with good food at reasonable prices.

Anti, Jahnstr. 36. Rough and ready Greek joint; good value and fun.

Bei Sülö, Rosenheimerstr. 82. Excellent kebab place in Haidhausen.

Bella Italia, Weissenburgerstr. 2. One of a chain of six Italian restaurants in Munich; a long-standing favourite.

Bernard & Bernard, Innere Wienerstr. 32. Great place for crêpes, in Haidhausen.

Bodega Dali, Augustenstr. 46. Best Spanish place in town, at lower than average Munich prices.

Bratwurstherzel, Heiliggeiststr. 3. Decent local nosh at prices that won't break the bank.

Bürgerheim, Bergmannstr. 33. Cheapish Bavarian cuisine in big portions.

Isabellahof, Isabellastr. 4. Very popular cheap Balkan restaurant in Schwabing.

Vierjahreszeiten, Sebastianplatz 9. Best vegetarian place in the centre.

BEER GARDENS

Augustiner Keller, Arnulfstr. 52, near the Hackerbrücke S-Bahn stop. A shady island of green, hidden in one of Munich's grottier quarters.

Aumeister, Sondermeierstr. 1. At the northern end of the Englischer Garten; a good place for daytime breaks.

Hofbräukeller, Innere Wienerstr. 19. Nestling under ancient chestnut trees; very popular in the evenings.

Salvator-Keller, Hochstr. 77. High up on the Nockerberg, on the east bank of the Isar; one of the oldest havens for serious beer drinkers.

Music, nightlife and festivals

Munich has a great deal to offer musically, whether you're into classical concerts or rock. Best sources for information on what's happening are the *Münchener Stadtzeitung* or *Im München*, both available at any kiosk, or the monthly *Monatsmagazin* from the tourist office. For jazz concerts – a major feature of Munich nightlife – check the monthly *Münchener Jazz-Zeitung*. Munich has three first-rate orchestras – the *Münchener Philharmonie*, the *Bayrisches Rundfunk Sinfonie Orchester* and the *Staatsorchester* – as well as eleven major theatres and numerous fringe theatres. Advance tickets for plays and concerts can be bought at the relevant box offices or commercial ticket shops such as the one located in the Marienplatz U-Bahn station. Opera tickets can be bought at the advance sales office at Maximilianstr. 11, or from the box office in the *Nationaltheater* one hour before performances begin.

ROCK AND JAZZ

Olympiapark. Free rock concerts by the lake in summer; they usually get going around 2pm at weekends.

Café Giesing, Bergstr. 5. Venue for small bands and solo artists.

Crash, Lindwurmstr. 88. Stage for heavy rock.

Domicile, Leopoldstr. 19. Mostly jazz bands with some rock.

Drehleier, Balanstr. 19. Mainly jazz on weekdays from 10.30pm.

Schwabinger Podium, Wagnerstr. 1. Chiefly Dixieland.

Unterfahrt, Kirchenstr. 96. Showcase for avant-garde jazz.

DISCOS

Cadillac, Theklastr. 1. Soul-based disco.

Nachtwerk, Landsbergerstr. 185. Draws a young crowd on Friday and Saturday.

Oly-Club, Helene-Meyer-Ring 9. Mainly student disco, generally friendlier than the others.

Sugar Shack, Herzogspitalstr. 6. A trendies' favourite.

CLASSICAL MUSIC, OPERA AND THEATRE

Cuvilliéstheater, in the Residenz. Premier venue for drama, plus the occasional chamber music recital.

Deutsches Theater, Schwanthalerstr. Home-grown and visiting spectaculars.

Gasteig Kulturzentrum, Kellerstr. One of the two main venues for classical concerts.

Herkulessaal, in the Residenz. The other big classical concert hall.

Nationaltheater, Max-Josef-Platz. Munich's answer to Covent Garden, with grand opera and ballet.

Residenztheater, Max-Josef-Platz. Traditional dramatic fare.

Staatstheater, Gärtnerplatz. Mixed programme of operetta, musicals and popular operas.

THE OKTOBERFEST AND OTHER EVENTS

The **Oktoberfest**, held on the Theresienwiese fairground from the last Saturday in September for the next sixteen days, is an orgy of beer drinking, spiced up by fairground rides that are so hairy they're banned in the USA. The proportions of the fair are so massive that the grounds are divided along four main avenues, creating a boisterous city of its own, heaving from morning till night. **Fasching**, Munich's carnival, is an excuse for parades, fancy-dress balls and general shenanigans from mid-January until the beginning of Lent. More sedate is **Auer Dult**, a traditional market that takes place on the Mariahilfplatz during the last weeks of April, July and October each year; there arer stalls selling food, craftware and antiques, and there's a fairground too.

Listings

Airlines *British Airways*, Promenadeplatz 10 (☎292 121); *Lufthansa*, Lenbachplatz 1 (☎51 130); *TWA*, Landwehrstr. 31 (☎597 643).

Airport information ☎9211 2127.

Bike rental *Aktiv-Rad*, Hans-Sachs-Str. 7.

Car rental *Europcar*, Schwanthalerstr. 10a (☎594 723). Also several firms (*Avis,* etc) have offices at the Hauptbahnhof.

Consulates *Canada*, Maximiliansplatz 9 (☎558 531); *Great Britain*, Amalienstr. 62 (☎394 015); *Ireland*, Mauerkircherstr. 1a (☎985 723); *US*, Königinstr. 5 (☎23 011).

Exchange The bank at the train station is open daily 6am–11.30pm.

Gay Munich In Bavaria there's mandatory AIDS testing of people suspected of being HIV-positive, and any HIV-positive person who does not follow the authority's guidelines on "proper behaviour" can be detained indefinitely. Openly gay lifestyles have experienced a setback in the face of these draconian laws, but there are a few bars and cafés to check out. Cafés that cater predominantly for lesbians are *Café am Gift*, St Martinstr. 1; *Frauncafé im Kofra*, Baldestr. 8; and *Mädchenpower-Café*, Baldestr. 16. The following male gay bars are well known: *Bolt*, Blumenstr. 15; *Cock*, Augsbergerstr. 21; *Colibri*, Utzschneiderstr. 8.

Hitching *Mitfahrzentrale*, Amalienstr. 87 (☎280 124).

Hospital Ismaningerstr. 22 (☎41 401).

Laundry Amalienstr. 61; Münchener Freiheit 26.

Post office Hauptbahnhofsplatz 1; open 24 hours.

Women's centre Güllstr. 3 (Mon–Fri 6–11pm; ☎725 4271).

The Bavarian Alps

It's among the picture-book scenery of the **Alps** that you'll find the Bavarian folklore and customs that are the subject of so many tourist brochures, and the region also encompasses some of the most famous places in the province, such as the Olympic ski resort of **Garmisch-Partenkirchen**, and the fantasy castle of **Neuschwanstein**, just one of the lunatic palaces built for King Ludwig II of Bavaria. The western reaches are generally cheaper and less touristy, partly because they're not so easily accessible to Munich's weekend crowds. In contrast, much of the eastern region to **Berchtesgaden** is heavily geared to the tourist trade, but if you go outside the high season of July and August, you should have a good chance of avoiding the crowds and not straining your finances.

Garmisch and Mittenwald

GARMISCH-PARTENKIRCHEN is the most famous town in the German Alps, partly because it's at the foot of the highest mountain – the **Zugspitze** (2962m) – and partly because it hosted the Winter Olympics in 1936. Garmisch has excellent facilities for skiing, skating and other winter sports, but the town is irredeemably complacent and unfriendly. The ascent of Zugspitze by rack-railway and cable car is an exhilarating expedition, but far preferable to Garmisch is **MITTENWALD**, just 15km down the road and similarly on a main rail line from Munich, which remains a community rather than a resort. The **Karwendl** mountain towering above Mittenwald is a highly popular climbing destination, and the view from the top is one of the most exhilarating and dramatic in Germany; a cable car goes there for DM25 return. There are plenty of good places to stay in the village, such as the *Haus Alpenruh*, Schillerweg 2 (☎08823/1375; ④), and *Gästehaus Bergfrühling*, Dammkarstr. 12 (☎08823/8089; ④). The nearest campsite is 3km north, on the road to Garmisch and open all year. The **tourist office**, at Dammkarrstr. 3 (Mon–Thurs & Sat 9am–noon & 2–5pm, Fri 9.30am–6pm), will reserve rooms and provide free maps of the area.

Oberammergau and Schloss Linderhof

From Murnau a branch line runs to **OBERAMMERGAU**, world-famous for its **Passion Play**, first performed in 1633 as thanks for being spared by a plague epidemic. The show takes place every ten years between May and September (next performance is in 2000), with a cast of local villagers. Many of the houses have traditional outside **frescoes** of religious or Alpine scenes, which you can see as either quaint or kitsch, and that goes for the wood carvings in the local souvenir shops too.

From here it's a short bus ride to the village of Ettal and the **Schloss Linderhof** (April–Sept 9am–noon & 12.30–5pm; DM6), one of the architectural fantasies conjured for dotty King Ludwig. Though built as a discreet private residence, it has a reception room with intricate gold-painted carvings, stucco ornamentation, and a throne canopy draped in ermine curtains. The real attraction is the delightful **park**: Italianate terraces, cascades and manicured flowerbeds give way to an English garden design that gradually blends into the forests of the mountain beyond. A number of romantic little buildings are dotted around the park, the most remarkable of which is the Venus Grotto. Based on the set for Wagner's opera *Tannhäuser* (Ludwig was the composer's principal patron), it has an illuminated lake on which floats an enormous golden conch, in which the king would sometimes take rides.

Hohenschwangau and Neuschwanstein

Lying between the Forggensee reservoir and the Ammer mountains, around 100km by rail from Munich, the adjacent towns of **FÜSSEN** and **SCHWANGAU** are the bases for visiting Bavaria's two most popular castles. **Hohenschwangau** (daily 10am–4pm; DM6), originally built in the twelfth century but heavily restored in the nineteenth, was where Ludwig spent his youth. A mark of his individualism is left in the bedroom, where he had the ceiling painted with stars that were spotlit in the evenings. **Neuschwanstein** (same times and prices), the ultimate story-book castle, was built by Ludwig a little higher up the mountain. The architectural hotchpotch ranges from a Byzantine throne hall to a Romanesque study and an artificial grotto. Left incomplete at Ludwig's death, it's a bizarre monument to a very sad and lonely man.

The nearest **youth hostel** is in Füssen, at Mariahilferstr. 5 (☎08362/7754; ②). Two **guesthouses** near the castles are the *Haus Schwansee*, Parkstr. 9 (☎08362/8353; ③), and *Pension Weiher*, Hofwiesenweg 11 (☎08362/81161; ④). The **tourist office** in Schwangau (Mon–Sat 9am–5.30pm) can book accommodation. Füssen is also the start of the much-publicized **Romantic Road** to Würzburg via Augsburg, served by innumerable special tour buses in season.

Oberstdorf

The old village of **OBERSTDORF** – 20km from Füssen at the end of a rail spur – has grown discreetly, without the high-rise aberrations found elsewhere in the mountains, but with good sports facilities and excellent opportunities for unstrenuous Alpine walking, aided by the cable cars that ascend the nearest heights. The streets around the market square have lots of friendly and busy bars, yet the agricultural life of the region makes itself felt too, with clanking cowbells waking you at daybreak. What makes Oberstdorf just about perfect is its range of cheap **accommodation**. The nearest **youth hostel** is in the neighbouring village of Kornau (bus from Oberstdorf station; ②), but there are a number of reasonably priced guesthouses near the centre: the *Alpenglühn*, Wittelsbacherstr. 4 (☎08322/4692; ④); the *Amman*, Weststr. 23 (☎08322/2961; ④); and the *Buchenberg*, Lorettostr. 6 (☎08322/2315; ④). The **campsite** at Rublingerstr. 10 is open all year. The **tourist office** is on the Marktplatz (Mon–Sat 8am–noon & 2–6pm).

Berchtesgaden

Almost entirely surrounded by mountains at Bavaria's **southeastern** extremity, the area around **BERCHTESGADEN** has a magical atmosphere, especially in the mornings, when mists rise from the lakes and swirl around lush valleys and rocky mountainsides. The town is easily reached by rail, from Munich and from Salzburg in Austria, which is just 23km to the north. Star attraction of the region is **Königssee**, Germany's highest lake, which bends around the foot of the spiky **Watzmann** to the south of the town. There are some great mountain trails to take you out of the crowds –

maps of suggested walking routes can be bought at the **tourist office** opposite the train station (Mon–Fri 8.30am–5.30pm). The area's main historical claim to fame is in its connection with Adolf Hitler. Hitler rented a house in the nearby village of Obersalzburg, which he later had enlarged into the **Berghof**, a stately retreat where he could meet foreign dignitaries. It was blown up by the Allies, and the ruins are now overgrown.

Berchtesgaden caters primarily for wealthy pensioners and families, but reasonable **guesthouse** accommodation is available at *Hansererhäusl*, Hansererweg 8 (✆08652/2523; ④), *Haus Bergwald*, Duftbachweg 3–5 (✆08652/2586; ⑤), and *Berlerlehen*, Rennweg 19 (✆08652/1590; ④). The tourist office can help with booking rooms or directing you to any of the five **campsites** in the valley.

Augsburg

Innovations, both religious and secular, have found fertile ground in AUGSBURG, 70km from Munich. Luther's reforms found their earliest support here, and in 1514 the city built the world's first housing estate for the poor, the **Fuggerei** – an institution still in use today. The citizens of Augsburg have gone to great lengths to restore the city's appearance to that of its medieval heyday, yet this isn't just a museum-piece. There's a lively cultural scene ranging from Mozart festivals to jazz and cabaret, and the university means that a thriving alternative scene keeps the place on its toes.

The City

Heart of the city is the spacious cobbled **Rathausplatz**, which turns into a massive open-air café during the summer and into a glittering market at Christmas. At the baseline of this great semicircle stands the massive **Rathaus** (daily 10am–6pm; free), perhaps Germany's finest secular Renaissance building. Inside, the spick-and-span Goldener Saal, with its gold-leaf pillars and marble floor, recalls the period when the Fugger banking dynasty made Augsburg one of the financial centres of Europe. Next to the Rathaus stands the **Perlachturm** (daily 10am–4/6pm; DM2), a good vantage point.

To the south, **Maximilianstrasse** is lined by merchants' palaces and punctuated by fountains. Soon after the Mercury fountain, the **Fugger Palais** stands proudly to the right; built in 1515 by Jacob Fugger "the Rich", it still belongs to his loaded descendants, but you can walk through the main door to see its luxurious arcaded courtyard. Opposite the Hercules fountain is the **Schaezler Palais**, through the courtyard of which is the Dominican nunnery of St Catherine and the **State Gallery** (Tues–Sun 10am–5pm; DM4), home of Dürer's portrait of Jacob Fugger. At the far end of Maximilianstrasse, Lutheran **St Ulrich** is dwarfed by the Catholic basilica of **SS. Ulrich und Afra**, resting place of Ulrich, the city's patron saint.

At the other end of the town's axis, the **Dom** stands in the grounds of the former episcopal palace, now the seat of the regional government. It was founded by Saint Ulrich in the tenth century, and the most interesting remains of its Romanesque origins are the enormous bronze doors at the southern entrance and the stained-glass windows – the oldest stained glass still in position. There are also a number of altarpieces by Hans Holbein the Elder, among the few Holbeins outside of a museum.

The town's historical museum, the **Maximilianmuseum** (Tues–Sun 10am–5pm; DM3), is housed in a merchant's house at Philippine-Welser-Strasse 24. Prehistoric and Roman remains are shown separately in the **Römisches Museum** (Tues–Sun 10am–4/5pm; DM3), which occupies the old Dominican church at Dominikanergasse 15. The light and whitewashed interior makes an excellent setting for the Roman masonry and bronzes, and the uncluttered layout is a pleasure after the usual warehouse-like museums.

For a charge of one "Our Father", one "Hail Mary" and one Creed daily, plus DM1.72 per annum, good Catholic paupers can retire to the **Fuggerei** at the age of 55. With an entrance in the Jacoberstrasse, it's a town within a town, and compared with modern housing estates is a real idyll, the cloister-like atmosphere disturbed only by the odd ringing doorbell. **Number 13** (March–Oct daily 9am–6pm; Nov Sat & Sun only; DM1) in the Mittleren Gasse is one of only two houses from the original foundation, and today it's full of furnishings that show how people lived here from the sixteenth to the eighteenth century.

On the other side of town, in Annastrasse, stands **St Anna-Kirche**, where the **Fuggerkapelle** marks the belated German debut of the full-blooded Italian Renaissance style, a spin-off of the family's extensive business interests in Italy. An effect of overwhelming richness is created by the marble pavement, stained glass, choir stalls, a sculptural group of *The Lamentation over the Dead Christ*, and memorial tablets honouring the Fugger brothers made after woodcuts designed by Dürer.

It was in St Anna that the final confrontation between the papal court and Luther took place in 1518. Luther found refuge with the Carmelites of St Anna when he was summoned to see the pope's legate, and today his room and several others in the old monastery have been turned into the **Lutherstiege** (Tues–Sun 10am–noon & 3–5pm; free), a museum of the reformer's life and times.

Practicalities

The **tourist office** (Mon–Fri 9am–6pm) is a couple of minutes from the **train station** at Bahnhofstr. 7: at weekends try the branch on Rathausplatz (Sat 10am–6pm, Sun 10am–1pm). Good **pensions** are to be found in the suburb of Lechhausen, 1.5km from the city centre and connected by three bus routes: *Bayerische Löwe*, Linke Brandstr. 2 (☎0821/702 870; ③); *Linderhof*, Aspernstr. 38 (☎0821/73 216; ③); and *Märkl*, Schillerstr. 20 (☎0821/791 499; ③). The **youth hostel** is three minutes' walk from the Dom, at Beim Pfaffenkeller 3 (☎0821/33 909; ②). The nearest **campsite** is at motorway exit Augsburg-Ost, next to the Autobahnsee.

The cheapest places for **snacks** are the market and meat halls off Annastrasse, where you'll find a couple of good *Imbiss* stands. Moving upmarket, excellent Swabian **meals** are served at the *7-Schwaben Stuben*, Am Königsplatz. For **drinking**, *Riegele*, Herman-Köhlstr. 5, is spacious and serves meals as well as drinks; *Striese*, Kirchgasse 1, is also a theatre and music venue.

Regensburg

"Regensburg surpasses every German city with its outstanding and vast buildings," drooled Emperor Maximilian I in 1517. The centre of **REGENSBURG** has changed remarkably little since then; its undisturbed medieval panorama and its stunning location on the banks of the Danube make it a great place to spend a couple of days.

Maximilianstrasse leads straight from the train station to the centre. The best view of Regensburg's medieval skyline is from the twelfth-century **Steinerne Brücke**, which was the only safe and fortified crossing along the entire length of the Danube at the time it was built, and thus had tremendous value for the city as a trading centre. On the left, just past the medieval salt depot, the **Historische Wurstküche** (daily 8am–7pm) originally functioned as the bridge workers' kitchen. It's been run by the same family for generations and serves nothing but delicious Regensburg sausages.

A short way south the **Dom** comes into full view. Bavaria's most magnificent Gothic building, it was begun around 1250, replacing a Romanesque church of which the **Eselsturm** is the only remaining part above ground. Highlights include the late thirteenth-century statues of the Annunciation and the fourteenth-century stained-glass windows in the south transept. In the cloisters – accessible only on guided tours

(May–Oct Mon–Sat 10am, 11am & 2pm, Sun noon & 2pm; Nov–April Mon–Sat 11am, Sun noon; DM3) – the Allerheiligen Kapelle still has many Romanesque frescoes. Concerts and services are a musical treat in Regensburg, as the *Domspatzen* (Cathedral Sparrows) have some of the finest choristers in the country.

Perhaps the finest of Regensburg's merchant and patrician houses are to be seen on the **Haidplatz**. The largest building on the square is the **Haus zum Goldenen Kreuz**, where Emperor Charles V used to meet a local girl called Barbara Blomberg: their son, John of Austria, was born here in 1547 and died Governor of the Netherlands in 1578. The nearby **Thon-Dittmer Palais** is one of the main cultural venues, concerts and plays being held in its courtyard in summer. Only a few minutes' walk away, the Neupfarrplatz is the centre of Regensburg's commercial life: the **Neupfarrkirche** stands rather forlorn in the middle of the car park, occupying the site of the old synagogue, which was wrecked during the 1519 expulsion of the Jews.

Apart from the Dom, the town's most important Gothic structure is the **Altes Rathaus** on the Kohlenmarkt. To appreciate its grand scale, you need to take a guided tour of the **Reichstagsmuseum** (German tours April–Oct Mon–Sat 9.30am, 10.30am, 11.30am, 2pm, 3pm & 4pm, Sun 10am, 11am & noon; English tours May–Sept Mon–Sat 3.15pm; DM3); the most significant room is the Imperial Diet Chamber, a parliamentary forum for the empire from 1663 to 1806.

On nearby Keplerstrasse, the **Kepler-Gedächtnishaus** (tours Tues–Sat 10am, 11am, 2pm & 3pm, Sun 10am & 11am; DM2.50) is dedicated to the astronomer Johann Kepler, who lived and worked in Regensburg in the early seventeenth century. Another museum worth looking into is the **Stadtmuseum** on Dachauplatz (Tues–Sat 10am–4pm, Sun 10am–1pm; DM2.50) – especially the section on Albrecht Altdorfer, who, apart from being one of Germany's greatest artists, was also a leading politician.

Schloss Thurn und Taxis (tours Mon–Fri 2pm & 3.15pm, Sat & Sun also 10am & 11.15am; DM10 combined entry to Schloss and cloisters), home of the Prince of Thurn and Taxis, is situated in the city's southern quarter. The palace isn't open to the public when the boss is at home, but when he's away a guide will show you the state rooms, with some wonderful Brussels tapestries on the walls recording the family's illustrious history. The former cloisters, now partly the library, represent some of the finest Gothic architecture to be found in Germany.

Practicalities

The **tourist office** is bang in the middle, in the Altes Rathaus (Mon–Fri 8.30am–6pm, Sat 9am–4pm, Sun 9.30am–2.30pm). Cheapest **hotel** in the town centre is the *Peterhof*, Fröhliche-Turkenstr. 12 (☎0941/57 514; ③). Just the other side of the Steinerne Brücke, the *Spitalgarten*, St Katharinen-Platz 1 (☎0941/84 774; ③), and the *Stadlerbräu*, Stadtamhof 15 (☎0941/85 682; ③), are conveniently sited next to the best beer garden. The **youth hostel**, Wöhrdstr. 60 (mid-Jan to mid-Nov; ☎0941/57 402; ②), is about five minutes' walk from the heart of things, on an island in the Danube. The **campsite** is about twenty minutes' walk from the centre, next to the Danube at Weinweg 40.

You're spoilt for places to **eat** in Regensburg. Some of the best and cheapest *schnitzel* in the world are to be eaten in *Zur Goldenen Krone*, Kepplerstr. 3. Two more *Gaststätten* with good traditional and cheap Bavarian fare are *Kneitinger*, Arnulfsplatz 3, and the *Kreuz Schenke*, Kreuzgasse 25. For more of a **bar**-type atmosphere, usually with good music, try *Namenlos*, Rote Löwengasse 10, *Jensiets*, Am Römling 1, or *Unterholz*, Silberne Fischgasse 17. Popular student hang-outs are *Schwedenkugel*, Haaggasse 15, and the *Goldene Ente*, Badstr. 32. The cosiest **wine bar** in town is *Türmchen*, Wahlenstr. 14, at the top of Regensburg's highest medieval tower. For a traditional **beer garden**, *Kneitinger Garten*, Unterer Wöhrd, Müllerstr. 1, has a great location on one of the Danube islands.

Nürnberg

Founded in the eleventh century, **NÜRNBERG** rapidly rose to become the unofficial capital of Germany, its position at the intersection of major trading routes leading to economic prosperity and political power. The arts flourished too, though the most brilliant period was not to come until the late fifteenth century, when the roll call of citizens was led by Albrecht Dürer, Germany's most complete Renaissance Man.

Like many other wealthy European cities, Nürnberg went into gradual economic and social decline once the sea routes to the Americas and Far East had been established; moreover, adoption of the Reformation cost the city the patronage of the Catholic emperors. It made a comeback in the nineteenth century, when it became the focus for the Pan-German movement, and the **Germanisches Nationalmuseum** – the most important collection of the country's arts and crafts – was founded at this time.

Nürnberg is especially enticing in the summer, when the historic centre – the Altstadt – is alive with street theatre and music, and open-air concerts liven up the parks and stadiums; but there's always a wide and varied range of nightlife.

Arrival and accommodation

The main **tourist office** (Mon–Sat 9am–7pm) is conveniently situated in the central hall of the **train station**, just outside the Altstadt. There's another office at Hauptmarkt 18, within the Altstadt (Mon–Sat 9am–1pm & 2–6pm, Sun 10am–1pm & 2–4pm). The cheapest reasonably central **hotels** are: the *Altstadt*, Hintere Ledergasse 2 (☎0911/226 102; ④), the *Humboldtklause*, Humboldtstr. 41 (☎0911/413 801; ③), and the *Melanchthon*, Melanchthonplatz 1 (☎0911/412 626; ③). A top-class **youth hostel** is located in the castle, overlooking the Altstadt (☎0911/241 352; ②). There's a **youth hotel** to the north of the city at Rathsbergstrasse 300 (☎0911/529 092; ②; no age restriction). The **campsite** is in the Volkspark, near the Dutzendteich lakes (May–Sept; tram #12).

The City

On January 2, 1945, a storm of bombs reduced ninety percent of Nürnberg's centre to ash and rubble, but you'd never guess it from the meticulous postwar rebuilding. Covering about four square kilometres, the reconstructed medieval core is surrounded by its ancient **city walls** and neatly spliced by the River Pegnitz. To walk from one end to the other takes about twenty minutes, but much of the centre, especially the area around the castle – known as the **Burgviertel** – is on a steep hill. It's not all medieval pictures, either. Significant areas of modern architecture and open spaces are nearby, ensuring a refreshing mix of old and new.

One of the highest points of the city is occupied by the **Kaiserburg** (tours daily 9/ 9.30am–noon & 12.45–4/5pm; DM3.50), whose earliest surviving part is the eastern **Fünfeckturm**, which dates back to the eleventh century. A century later, Frederick Barbarossa extended the castle to the west: his **Sinwellturm**, built directly on the rock, can be ascended for the best of all the views. Another survivor of this period is the **Kaiserkapelle**, whose upper level was reserved for the use of the emperor, with the courtiers confined to the lower tier. At the extreme east end of the complex is the **Luginslandturm**, which was erected by the city council in the fourteenth century to protect Nürnberg against the ambitious and hostile Hohenzollern family, who had inherited the oldest part of the fortress. Apart from the east wall, the Hohenstaufen residential quarters were demolished in the mid-fifteenth century and replaced by the Gothic **Palas**, which now looks rather plain and soulless inside. At the end of that century, the Luginslandturm was joined to the Fünfeckturm by the vast **Kaiserstallung** – originally a cereal warehouse and later a stable, it's now a perfect home for the youth hostel.

The area around the **Tiergärtner Tor** next to the Kaiserburg is one of the most attractive parts of the old town centre, a meeting point for summertime street vendors, artists and musicians. Virtually next door, the **Dürer Haus** (March–Oct Tues–Sun 10am–5pm, Wed to 9pm; Nov–Feb Tues, Thurs & Fri 1–5pm, Wed 1–9pm, Sat & Sun 10am–5pm; DM3.50) is where the painter, engraver, scientist, writer, traveller and politician lived from 1509 to 1528, and is one of the very few original houses still standing. Don't come here looking for original Dürer paintings, though: there are only copies, plus works by artists paying homage to the great man. (He's buried in the St Johannisfriedhof, a few minutes' walk away, along Johannisstrasse.)

Nürnberg's oldest and most important church, the twin-towered **Sebalduskirche**, is just down the road from the Fembohaus. Founded in the thirteenth century and altered a century later, it contains an astonishing array of works of art. Particularly striking are the bronze shrine of Saint Sebald, and some pieces by Veit Stoss, Nürnberg's most famous sculptor: an expressive *Crucifixion* on the pillar behind the shrine and three stone reliefs in the chancel.

The **Hauptmarkt**, commercial heart of the city and the main venue for weekly markets (and the famous Christmas market), is a couple of minutes' walk away. Its east side is bounded by the **Frauenkirche**, on whose facade a clockwork mechanism known as the *Männleinlaufen* tinkles away at noon. Also on the Hauptmarkt is a copy of the famous **Schöner Brunnen**, looking like a lost church spire.

Walking southwards from Hauptmarkt, you cross the river by Museumsbrücke, which gives you a good view of the **Fleischbrücke** to the right, and the **Heilig-Geist-Spital** – one of the largest hospitals built in the Middle Ages – on the left. Passing the oldest house in the city, the thirteenth-century **Nassauer Haus**, you shortly come to the **Lorenzkirche**, built about fifty years after the Sebalduskirche, its counterpart on the other side of the water. The nave has a resplendent rose window, while the chancel is lit by gleaming stained glass. The graceful late fifteenth-century **tabernacle**, some twenty metres high, was carved by Adam Kraft, who depicted himself as a pensive figure crouching at the base. Equally spectacular is the larger-than-life *Annunciation* by Veit Stoss, suspended above the high altar.

Further down Königstrasse in the direction of the train station is the massive and austere Renaissance **Mauthalle**, beyond which stands the Gothic **Marthakirche**, the hall of the *Meistersinger*. The distinctive form of lyric poetry known as *Meistergesang* flourished in Germany from the fourteenth century, and had a glorious final fling in Nürnberg, thanks above all to the shoemaker Hans Sachs, creator of some 6000 works.

West of the Mauthalle, the **Germanisches Nationalmuseum** occupies a fourteenth-century monastery on Kornmarkt (Tues & Thurs–Sun 10am–5pm, Wed to 9pm; DM5, free Sun). On the ground floor the displays follow a roughly chronological layout, beginning with Bronze Age items and moving on to medieval sculptures and carvings, outstanding among which are *The Seven Stations of the Cross* by Adam Kraft and works by Tilman Riemenschneider and Veit Stoss. German **painting** at its Renaissance peak dominates the first floor, with pieces by Dürer, Altdorfer, Baldung and Cranach. The following rooms focus on the diversity of Nürnberg's achievements during the Renaissance. The strong tradition of gold- and silversmithing is shown to best effect in the superb model of a three-masted ship, while the city's leading role in the fast-developing science of geography is exemplified by the first globe of the earth, made by Martin Behaim in 1491 – just before the discovery of America. This floor's south wing is entirely devoted to German folklore, and in particular to Catholic worship, notably weird votive offerings like the wax toads offered for help with women's complaints.

THE ZEPPELIN FIELD AND MARS FIELD

In virtually everyone's mind the word Nürnberg conjures up thoughts of Nazi rallies and war-crime trials. As the city council is eager to point out, the Nazis' choice of

Nürnberg had less to do with local support of Nazi ideology, and more to do with what the medieval city represented in German history. The rallies were held on the **Zeppelin and Mars fields** in the suburb of Luitpoldhain, where today Albert Speer's Stadium and Congress Hall lie derelict, used only for the occasional rock concert or car rally. The tourist board has put together a multimedia presentation called "Fascination and Force", but the atmosphere of the stadium needs little explanation. The "Nürnberg Laws" of 1935 deprived Jews of their citizenship and forbade relations between Jews and Gentiles. It was through these laws that the Nazis justified their extermination of six million Jews, 10,000 of whom came from Nürnberg. Only ten remained here after the war. It was highly significant that the war criminals of the Nazi regime were tried in the city that saw their proudest demonstrations of power.

Eating, drinking and nightlife

Nürnberg is the liveliest Bavarian city after Munich, with a wealth of *Studentenkneipen* and café-bars catering for the students. The cheapest **meals** in town are to be found in the university **mensa**, in the northeastern corner of the Altstadt. Otherwise there are plenty of *Imbiss*-type snack-joints in the pedestrian zone between St Lorenz and the Ehekarussel. In the Altstadt, good places to eat include *Bratwurst-Häusle*, Rathausplatz 1, the most celebrated of the city's sausage restaurants, and the excellent and reasonable *Nassauer Keller*, Karolinerstr. 2, installed in an atmospheric thirteenth-century cellar. In Spitalgasse, *Heilig-Geist-Spital* serves hearty fare in the setting of a medieval hospital building. The food is good at *Zum Peter*, Regensburgerstr. 51, which has a beer garden attached; *Palais Schaumburg*, Kernstr. 46, is much the same as *Zum Peter*, but a touch cheaper and better. *Altstadhof*, Bergstr. 13, is one of Germany's most famous **house breweries**. For a combination of beer haven and music bar, make for *Starclub*, Maxtorgraben 33. *Ruhestörung*, Tetzelgasse 21, is one of the most fashionable café-bars. The tiny, excellent café-bar *Meisengeige*, Innere-Laufer-Gasse 37, caters for a mixed crowd, and its small cinema shows an offbeat selection of films. The trendiest **nightclub** in Nürnberg is *Mach 1*, Kaiserstr. 1–9, with four different bars and some good lighting effects (Wed–Sun 9pm–4am; DM10). To find out what else is going on, get either the *Monatsmagazin* from the tourist office, or the *Plärrer* magazine from any kiosk.

Rothenburg ob der Tauber

The tourist itinerary known as the **Romantic Road**, which winds its way along the length of western Bavaria, runs through the most visited medieval town in Germany: **ROTHENBURG OB DER TAUBER**, 50km west of Nürnberg. To get there, *DB* buses and some trains connect with train services at Steinach, on the Augsburg–Würzburg line – and there are scores of special coaches ferrying tourists along the chain of half-timbered villages that comprise the Romantic Road.

It takes about half an hour to walk around the fourteenth-century walls of Rothenburg, the ultimate museum-piece. The promontory on the western side of town is the site of the **Burgtor** watchtower – the oldest of all the 24 towers – and the **Blasiuskapelle**, with murals from the fourteenth century. The nearby **Herrngasse** leads up to the town centre, and is the widest street in Rothenburg, being where the local nobs lived. Also on this street is the severe early Gothic **Franziskanerkirche**, which houses a startlingly realistic altarpiece showing *The Stigmatization of St Francis*.

The sloping **Marktplatz** is dominated by the arcaded front of the **Renaissance Rathaus**, which supplanted the Gothic building that stands behind it. Its sixty-metre **tower** (April–Oct daily 9.30am–12.30pm & 1–4pm; Nov–March Sun noon–3pm; DM2) is the highest point in Rothenburg and provides the best view of the town and surrounding countryside. The other main attractions on the Marktplatz are the figures on each side of the three clocks of the **Ratsherrntrinkstube**, which seven times daily re-enact an episode that occurred during the Thirty Years' War. The fearsome Johann Tilly agreed that Rothenburg should be spared if one of the councillors could drain in one draught a tankard holding over three litres of wine. A former burgomaster duly sank the contents of the so-called *Meistertrunk*, then needed three days to sleep off the effects. On the opposite side of the Marktplatz is Rothenburg's largest building, the Gothic **St Jakob-Kirche** (Easter–Oct Mon–Sat 9am–5.30pm, Sun 10.30am–5.30pm; Nov–Easter daily 10am–noon & 2–4pm; DM2), rising above the sea of red roofs like a great ship; the entrance fee is worth paying to see Tilman Riemenschneider's exquisite limewood *Heilig-Blut-Altar*.

Of the local museums, the most fascinating is the **Kriminalmuseum** at Burggasse 3 (daily March 10am–4pm; April–Oct 9.30am–6pm; Nov 2–4pm; DM5), which contains collections attesting to medieval inhumanity in the shape of torture instruments and related objects, like the beer barrels that drunks were forced to walk around in. The **Reichstadtmuseum** on Klosterhof (daily April–Oct 10am–5pm; Nov–March 1–4pm; DM3) is most interesting for its original medieval workrooms.

Two **pensions** worth trying are *Pension Schmölzer*, Rosengasse 21 (☎09861/3371; ③), and *Pension Hofmann*, Stollengasse 29 (☎09861/3371; ③). The two **youth hostels** – *Rossmühle* (☎09861/4510; ②) and *Spitalhof* (☎09861/7889; ②) – are in beautifully restored houses off the bottom of the Spitalgasse. Private rooms are the next cheapest option, charging around DM20–35 per person: details from the highly efficient **tourist office** on Marktplatz (Mon–Fri 9am–noon & 2–6pm, Sat 9am–noon).

Würzburg

Terminus of the Romantic Road, **WÜRZBURG** straddles the River Main some 60km north of Rothenburg, and can be reached either by bus from there or by train from Nürnberg, Augsburg or Munich. During the night of March 16, 1945, it got the same treatment from Allied bombers that Nürnberg had received two months earlier. Würzburg has been less successful in rebuilding itself, but a number of outstanding sights and the town's location among a landscape of vineyards easily justify a visit.

Bracketed by the river and the Residenz, the old town is focused on the **Marktplatz**, where a daily food market ensures a lively bustle. Just off the square, the **Haus zum Falken** is the city's prize example of a Rococo town house, perfectly restored to the very last stucco curl. Overlooking the Markt is the Gothic **Marienkapelle**, which has an intriguing *Annunciation* above the northern portal: a band leads from God to Mary's ear, a baby sliding towards her along its folds.

Halfway down the Kürschnerhof, leading off the Marktplatz, the **Neumünster's** dusky pink facade stands out among the postwar houses. The church was built over the graves of saints Kilian, Kolonat and Totnan, Irish missionaries martyred in 689 for trying to Christianize the region. The Kiliani festival, at the beginning of July, is the region's most important religious event, drawing thousands of pilgrims to the crypt where the saints are buried. The **Dom**, again consecrated to Saint Kilian, is virtually next door; it was burnt out in 1945, so only the exterior is true to the original Gothic.

The **Residenz** (April–Sept Tues–Sun 9am–5pm; Oct–March Tues–Sun 10am–4pm; DM4.50) was intended to show that the Würzburg bishops could hold their own among such great European courts as Versailles. Construction was left largely in the hands of the prolific Balthasar Neumann, whose famed staircase is covered by the largest fresco in the world. An allegory extolling the fame of the prince-bishops in the most immodest way imaginable, it was painted by the greatest decorator of the age, Giambattista Tiepolo. The guided tour of the palace goes through the plain stuccoed Weisser Saal, before plunging into the opulence of the Kaisersaal; once reserved for the use of the emperor, it now provides a glamorous setting for the June Mozart Festival. The marble, the gold-leaf stucco and the sparkling chandeliers produce an effect of dazzling magnificence, but finest of all are more frescoes by Tiepolo, which glorify the Holy Roman Empire and Würzburg's part within it. Built discreetly into the southwest corner of the palace in order not to spoil the symmetry, the Hofkirche is a brilliant early example of Neumann's illusionism – the interior, based on a series of ovals, appears much larger than it really is. Both side altars are by Tiepolo.

On the other side of the Dom, the twelfth-century **Alte Mainbrücke** – the oldest bridge over the Main – leads towards the **Festung Marienberg** (tours Tues–Sun April–Sept 9am–12.30pm & 1–5pm; Oct–March 10am–12.30pm & 1–4pm; DM3); if you don't fancy the climb to the castle, you can take the #9 bus from the bridge. This was home to the ruling bishops from the thirteenth century until 1750, when they shifted to the Residenz. The devastations of foreign armies – the Swedes, the Prussians, the Allies in the last war – have been so great that although much of the original structure has been restored, the interiors are largely missing. The medieval core contains the round Marienkapelle, one of Germany's oldest churches, as well as the Brunnenhaus, whose 105-metre well was chiselled through the rock in around 1200. Surrounding this are a number of other courts from different periods, and the whole Marienberg is encased by massive fortifications built after the Swedes had left. The castle's **Mainfränkisches Museum** (Tues–Sun April–Oct 10am–5pm; Nov–March 10am–4pm; DM3) contains sculptures by Riemenschneider and examples of all genres of art across the ages, as well as an interesting display on Franconian wine.

During work on the Residenz, Neumann also took time to build the **Käppele**, a pilgrimage church imperiously perched on the heights to the south of the Marienberg. Apart from the opportunity to see the interior, lavishly covered with frescoes and stucco, it's worth visiting for the **view** from the terrace – the finest in Würzburg.

Practicalities

There's a **tourist office** (Mon–Sat 8am–8pm) just outside the **train station** at the northern end of the city centre. There are plenty of reasonably priced **pensions** between the station and the centre, including *Weinhaus Schnabel*, Haugerpfarrgasse 10 (☎0931/53 314; ③), *Gasthof Kirchlein*, Textorstr. 17 (☎0931/53 014; ③), and *Pension Siegel*, Reisgrubengasse 7 (☎0931/52 941; ④). The **youth hostel**, Burkarderstr. 44 (☎0931/42 590; ②; tram #3), is situated below the Marienberg. The nearest **campsite** is about 4km south in Heidingsfeld (#16 bus from Barbarossaplatz).

Best places for Franconian **food** are *Bürgerspital*, on the corner of Theaterstrasse and Semmelstrasse, and *Juliusspital*, Juliuspromenade 19. Both were founded as homes for the needy, and financed by their vineyards – which they still do. The *Stadt Mainz*, Semmelstr. 39, though excellent, is the tourist spot in town, printing its menus in five languages. Less pretentious is the *Paulaner Bräustüberl*, Bronnbachergasse 10, which serves food until midnight. For **student bars** head to Sanderstrasse, in the south of town – *Till Eulenspiegel*, Sanderstr. 1a, is particularly good.

Bamberg

The people of **BAMBERG**, which lies 60km north of Nürnberg and 95km east of Würzburg, knock back more beer per person than any others in the country: a total of ten breweries produce thirty different kinds of ale, most notably the distinctive smoky *Rauchbier*. Bamberg's isolation has been a key factor in preserving it from the ravages of war, and it is today one of the most beautiful small towns in the world, where most European styles from the Romanesque onwards have left a mark.

Heart of the lower town is the **Maxplatz**, dominated by Balthasar Neumann's **Neues Rathaus**. A daily market is held here and on the adjoining Grüner Markt, which stands in the shadow of the huge Jesuit church of **St Martin**. On an islet anchoring the Obere Brücke to the Untere Brücke is the **Altes Rathaus**, almost too picturesque for its own good. Except for the half-timbered section overhanging the rapids, the original Gothic building was transformed into Rococo, and its walls are tattooed with exuberant frescoes. The famous **Klein-Venedig** (Little Venice) of medieval fishermen's houses is best seen from the Untere Brücke.

Uphill, the spacious, sloping **Domplatz** is lined with such a superb variety of buildings that it has no rival as Germany's finest square. The **Kaiserdom** was consecrated in 1012, but the present structure of golden sandstone is the result of a slow rebuilding that continued throughout the thirteenth century. As with the architecture, the astonishing array of sculpture was initially executed in orthodox Romanesque style, best seen in the Fürstenportal on the north side of the nave, where figures of the Apostles are carved below a *Last Judgement*. The most famous sculpture of all is inside – the enigmatic **Bamberg Rider**, one of the first equestrian statues to be made since classical antiquity. Focus of the nave is the white limestone tomb of the canonized imperial couple Heinrich II and Kunigunde; Tilman Riemenschneider laboured away for fourteen years on this sarcophagus, whose reliefs depict scenes taken from the life and times of the couple. The south transept contains a contemporaneous masterpiece, the *Nativity Altar* by Veit Stoss, made when the artist was about eighty years old.

The **Diocesan Museum** (Tues–Sun 10am–5pm; DM2), entered from the square, houses some amazing ecclesiastical vestments, notably the robes worn by Heinrich II and Kunigunde. Also here are statues of the ubiquitous emperor and his wife, in the company of the Dom's two patrons plus an erotic Adam and Eve.

Opposite the cathedral, the **Ratstube** is a Renaissance gem, now containing the **Historical Museum** (May–Oct Tues–Sun 9am–5pm; DM2), which covers local history from the Stone Age to the twentieth century, as well as Bamberg's rich art history. Adjoining it is the **Reiche Tor**, where Heinrich and Kunigunde appear once more, leading into the huge courtyard of the **Alte Hofhaltung**, the former episcopal palace. Across the street is the building which supplanted it, the huge Baroque **Neue Residenz** (daily April–Sept 9am–noon & 1.30–5pm; Oct–March to 4pm; DM3). Inside are richly decorated state rooms, and the **Staatsgalerie Bamberg**, with medieval and Baroque paintings by German masters.

From the rose garden behind the Neue Residenz is a view of Michaelsburg, crowned by a huge **Abtei**. Much of the Romanesque shell of the church remains, but the interior is an amazing hotchpotch: lavish Rococo furnishings, tombs of Bamberg bishops, and a ceiling depicting over 600 medicinal herbs. The cellars house the **Fränkisches Brauereimuseum** (Thurs–Sun 1–4pm; DM3) – even if you're not interested in beer, it's worth coming for the wonderful panorama of Bamberg's skyline and surrounding hills.

Another place for a great view is **Altenburg**, a ruined castle at the end of the very steep Altenburgerstrasse. From here, up the Untere Kaulberg and past Karmeliten-Platz, you'll find the **Karmelitenkloster**. The church is again Baroque, but the Romanesque cloister (daily 8–11am & 2–5.30pm; free), the largest in Germany, has been preserved.

Practicalities

The **train station** is fifteen minutes' walk northeast of the centre. The **tourist office** (Mon–Fri 9am–6/7pm, Sat 9am–2/6pm), at Geyerwörthstrasse 3, makes no charge for accommodation bookings, but if doing it yourself the cheapest **hotels** are *Wilder Mann*, Untere Sandstr. 9 (☎0951/56 462; ④), and *Zum Gabelmann*, Kesslerstr. 14 (☎0951/26 676; ③). Two **youth hostels** serve Bamberg: the plain but handy *Stadion* at Pödeldorferstr. 178 (☎0951/12 377; closed most of the year, so phone first; ②), reached by bus #2 from train station, and the top-class *Wolfsschlucht*, 2km south of the centre at Oberer Leinritt 70 (☎0951/56 002; ②), reached by bus #1, #7 or #11 from the train station to ZOB Promenade, then bus #18 to Regnitzufer. The local **campsite** is another 2km downriver – also reached by bus #18.

Two **restaurants** worth trying are the *Schlenkerla*, a restaurant-cum-beer hall at Dominikanerstr. 6, and *Bürgerbräu-Stübla*, Urbanstr. 18, which is good for vegetarian dishes. Three of the best **cafés** are *Am Dom*, Ringleinsgasse 2, *Michaelsberg*, Michaelsberg 10e, and the summer *Rosengarten* in the Neue Residenz. Best places to try the **local beers** are Bamberg's four beer cellar-cum-gardens: *Spezial*, on Sternwartstrasse, *Greiffenklau* at Laurenziplatz 20, *Wilde Rose* at Obere Stephansberg 49, and *Mahr* at Oberer Stephansberg 36.

BERLIN

Berlin is like no other city in Germany or the world. For over a century its political climate has mirrored or determined what has happened in the rest of Europe, and it's this sense of living in a place where all the dilemmas of contemporary Europe are embodied that gives Berlin its fascination. It was, of course, World War II that defined the shape of today's city. Bombing razed 92 percent of the shops, houses and industry here, and at the end of the war the city was split. The Allies took the west of the city, traditionally an area of bars, hotels and shops fanning out from the Kurfürstendamm and the Tiergarten Park. The Soviet zone contained what remained of imperial Berlin, centred on Unter den Linden. After the building of the Wall in 1961, which sealed the Soviet sector and consolidated its position as capital of the young German Democratic Republic, the divided sections of the city developed in different ways.

For years its isolation in the middle of the GDR meant that **western Berlin** had a pressure-cooker mentality; this, combined with the fact that many young people came here to immerse themselves in alternative lifestyles, created a vivacious nightlife and a sense of excitement on the streets. Even with the Wall gone, Berlin is still very much a city of two separate parts, with **eastern Berlin** containing constant reminders of a discarded social experiment – one whose traces the new authorities are urgently trying to erase from memory.

Arrival and information

Berlin's main train station, Zoologischer Garten – **Zoo Station** – is in the centre. Most international **coaches** stop at a station near the Funkturm, linked to the centre by #94 buses or U-Bahn from Kaiserdamm. Flights to Berlin arrive at **Tegel airport**, from where frequent #109 buses run to Zoo Station (DM3.20); or take the #109 to Jakob-Kaiser-Platz and pick up the U-Bahn. Taxis cover it in half the time and cost DM25–30.

Berlin's **tourist office**, *Verkehrsamt Berlin*, is in the Europa Center on Budapesterstrasse (Mon–Sat 8am–10.30pm, Sun 9am–9pm; ☎262 6031), with additional offices in the Zoo Station (Mon–Sat 8am–11pm, Sun 9am–9pm; ☎313 9063) and at the airport (Mon–Sat 8am–11pm, Sun 9am–9pm; ☎4101 3145). In **eastern Berlin** the **main tourist office** is at the base of the TV tower on Alexanderplatz (daily 8am–8pm; ☎242 4675); this deals mainly, but not exclusively, with the eastern part of the city. Berlin has three **listings magazines**, *Zitty* (DM3.30), *Tip* (DM3.70) and *Prinz* (DM3), which have details of events.

City transport

The **U-Bahn** underground system covers much of central Berlin and the suburbs; trains run from 4am to approximately 12.30am, an hour later on Friday and Saturday. The **S-Bahn** system is better for covering long distances fast – getting out to the Wannsee lakes, for instance. The city **bus network** – and the **trams** in eastern Berlin – covers most of the gaps in the U-Bahn system; **night buses** run at intervals of around twenty minutes, although the routes sometimes differ from daytime ones; the *BVG* (see below) will supply a map. **Tickets** can be bought from machines at U-Bahn station entrances. **Single tickets** common to all the systems cost DM3.20, and are valid for two hours. An *Einzelfahrschein Kurzstreckentarif*, or short-trip ticket, costs DM2.10 and allows you to travel up to three train or six bus stops. A **day ticket** (*Tageskarte*) costs DM12. With a passport-sized photo, you can also buy a weekly ticket (*Wochenkarte*) for DM30. There are on-the-spot fines of DM60 for those without a valid ticket or pass.

Taxis are plentiful (DM3.80 plus DM2 per km) and congregate at locations such as on Savignyplatz and by the Zoo Station in the west, and at the northern entrance to Friedrichstrasse station and the *Hotel Stadt Berlin* on Alexanderplatz in the east.

Accommodation

Accommodation in Berlin can be very hard to find, and if booking your own place in the western part it's best to call at least a couple of weeks in advance. If you turn up with nothing arranged, the tourist office in the Europa Center offers a hotel **booking service** for DM3, though their options tend to be pricey. If you're planning on a longer stay, the best way of finding a place is through one of the **Mitwohnzentrale** organizations, which can find a room, usually for a minimum of seven nights, at roughly DM30–45 per person per night. Biggest and best of the *Mitwohnzentrale* is on the third floor, Ku'damm Eck, Kurfürstendamm 227–8 (Mon–Fri 10am–7pm, Sat & Sun 11am–3pm), an easy walk from the Zoo Station.

Hostels

Bahnhofsmission, Zoo Station (☎313 8088). Dingy place with limited accommodation for rail travellers for one night only, including meagre breakfast. ②

Jugendgästehaus, Kluckstr. 3 (☎261 1097). Bus #129, direction Oranienplatz. Fairly central. 9am–noon lockout. Often full. ② for under-25s, ③ others; deposit DM10.

Jugendgästehaus am Zoo, Hardenbergstr. 9a (☎312 9410). Zoologischer Garten U- and S-Bahn. Excellent location, extremely popular. No curfew. ②

Jugendherberge Wannsee, Badweg 1 (☎803 2034). S-Bahn #3 to Nikolassee. *IYHF* hostel near the beaches of the Wannsee lakes but far from the city centre. ② for under-25s , ③ otherwise; key deposit DM20.

Hotels

Aarona, Bleibtreustr. 32 (☎881 6274). Situated behind an unusual burnt-orange mock-Gothic facade a few minutes south of the Ku'damm. ③

Alpenland, Carmerstr. 8 (☎312 9370). Well-situated and an excellent choice at this price. ⑤

Artemisia, Carmerstr. 18 (☎878 905). The city's first women-only hotel. ⑧

Biales, Carmerstr. 16 (☎312 5025). A bit bleak, but in a pretty street. ④

Bogota, Schlüterstr. 42 (☎881 5011). Pleasant luxury at sensible prices. ⑤

Centrum Pension Berlin, Kantstr. 31 (☎316 153). Great central location, and good value. ⑤

Christliches Hospiz, Auguststr. 82 (☎284 970). One of the best central hotels in this range. ⑤

Elfert, Knesebeckstr. 13–14 (☎312 1236). Slightly shabby, but worth it for a central location. ⑤

Korso am Flughaven, Templehoferdamm 2 (☎785 7077). Useful for Templehof airport, and not far from Kreuzberg's nightlife. ⑤

Neues Tor, Invalidenstr. 102 (☎282 3620). Small (only six rooms) and inexpensive. ③

Südwest, Yorckstr. 80 (☎785 8033). In a dull part of town by day; good fun at night. ⑤

Campsite

Camping Haselhorst, Pulvermühlenweg (☎334 5955). Most convenient of the Berlin sites. #110 bus in the direction of Haselhorst. Facilities include a restaurant, bar, showers and a small shop. DM6.90 per tent plus DM6 per person per night.

CENTRAL BERLIN

Plötzensee Prison

BEUSSEL STR.

KAISERIN AUGUSTA-ALLEE

ALT MOABIT

ALT

River Spree

FRANKLIN STR.

Landwehr-Kanal

ALTONAER STR.

Schloss Charlottenburg

OTTO-SUHR-ALLEE

MARCH STR.

Siegessäule

17 JUNI

Charlottenburg Museums

CHARLOTTENBURG

BISMARCK STR.

STR. DES

KAISERDAMM

HARDENBERGSTR.

Zoo Station

Zoologischer Garten

KANT STR.

KANT STR.

BUDAPESTERSTR.

Kaiser-Wilhelm-Gedächtniskirche

Europa Center Tourist Office

KURFL

KURFÜRSTENDAMM

LIETZENBURGERSTR

KLEIST

KURFÜRSTENDAMM

BRANDENBURG STR

M. LUTHER STR.

HOHENZOLLERNDAMM

BUNDES ALLEE

SCHÖNEBERG

WILMERSDORF

GRUNEWALD STR

Rathau Schöneb

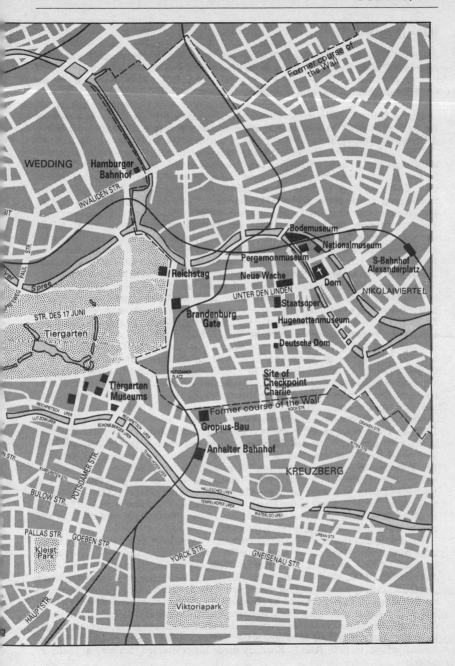

Former course of the Wall

WEDDING
Hamburger Bahnhof
INVALIDEN STR.

BIT
STR.
PAUL
Spree
SPREEWEG
STR. DES 17 JUNI
Tiergarten

Bodemuseum
Nationalmuseum
Pergamonmuseum
Reichstag
Neue Wache
S-Bahnhof Alexanderplatz
UNTER DEN LINDEN
Dom
NIKOLAIVIERTEL
Brandenburg Gate
Staatsoper
Hugenottenmuseum
Deutsche Dom

Tiergarten Museums
POTSDAMER PLATZ
Site of Checkpoint Charlie

REICHPETSCH UFER
LUTZOW UFER
SCHONEBERGER UFER
REICHETSCH UFER
Former course of the Wall
KOCH STR.
Gropius-Bau
Anhalter Bahnhof
ORANIEN STR.
RITTER STR.

TEMPELHOFER UFER
KURFURSTEN STR.
POTSDAMER STR.
BULOW STR.
HALLESCHES UFER
TEMPELHOFER UFER
WATERLOO UFER
KREUZBERG

N STR.
PALLAS STR.
GOEBEN STR.
Kleist Park
YORCK STR.
GNEISENAU STR.
URBAN STR.
HAUPTSTR.

Viktoriapark

Western Berlin

Zoo Station is at the centre of the city's maelstrom: a short walk south and you're at the eastern end of the Kurfürstendamm or **Ku'damm**, a three-and-a-half-kilometre strip of ritzy shops, cinemas, bars and cafés. The great landmark here is the **Kaiser-Wilhelm-Gedächtniskirche**, destroyed by British bombing in November 1943, and left as a reminder of wartime damage. There's little to do on the Ku'damm other than spend money, and there's only one cultural attraction, the **Käthe Kollwitz Museum** at Fasanenstr. 24 (daily except Tues 11am–6pm; DM6, students DM3), devoted to the drawings and prints of the left-wing and pacifist artist Käthe Kollwitz.

The **Zoologischer Garten** itself (daily 9am–sunset; DM8) forms the beginning of the **Tiergarten**, a restful expanse of woodland and a good place to wander along the banks of the Landwehrkanal. At the centre of Strasse des 17 Juni, the broad avenue that cuts through the Tiergarten, rises the **Siegessäule** (April–Nov Mon 3–6pm, Tues–Sun 9am–6pm; DM1.50, students DM1), a victory column celebrating Prussia's military successes; its summit offers one of Berlin's best views. Strasse des 17 Juni comes to an end at the **Brandenburg Gate**, built as a city gate-cum-triumphal arch in 1791. A little way north stands the **Reichstag**, the nineteenth-century home of the German parliament; inside is a fascinating exhibition called *Questions on German History* (Tues–Sun 10am–5pm; free). Immediately behind the Reichstag, it's just possible to make out the course of the **Berlin Wall**, which divided the city for 28 years until November 9, 1989.

The heart of Berlin used to be to the south of the Brandenburg Gate, its core formed by Potsdamer Platz. Just north of the Platz, a small hummock marks the remains of **Hitler's bunker**, where the Führer spent his last days, issuing meaningless orders as the Battle of Berlin raged above. West of Potsdamer Platz lies the **Tiergarten Complex**, a series of museums centred on the **Neue Nationalgalerie**, Potsdamerstr. 50 (Tues–Fri 9am–5pm, Sat & Sun 10am–5pm; free). It has a good collection of German paintings from the late eighteenth century on, best of which are the Berlin portraits and city-scapes of George Grosz and Otto Dix. Just north, the **Kunstgewerbemuseum** (same times; free) has a sparkling collection of European arts and crafts, from Byzantium to Bauhaus; the **Musikinstrumenten Museum** (Tues–Sat 9am–5pm, Sun 10am–5pm; free) isn't so much fun, as you can't touch any of the weird and wonderful instruments.

Southeast of here, the **Martin-Gropius-Bau** at Stresemannstr. 110 (Tues–Sun 10am–8pm; admission varies) is now a venue for prestigious art exhibitions, and home to the main part of the **Jewish Museum** (Tues–Sun 10am–10pm), a collection that documents the tragic history of Berlin's Jewish community. An adjacent exhibition, **The Topography of Terror** (Tues–Sun 10am–6pm; free), occupies the former Gestapo and SS headquarters. From here it's a ten-minute walk down Wilhelmstrasse and Kochstrasse to the site of the notorious Checkpoint Charlie; evidence of the trauma the Wall caused is still on hand in the **Haus am Checkpoint Charlie** at Friedrichstrasse 44 (daily 9am–10pm; DM7, students DM4.50), which tells the history of the Wall and the stories of those who tried to break through.

The checkpoint area marks the northern limit of **Kreuzberg**, famed for its large immi-grant community, its self-styled "alternative" inhabitants and nightlife. For most visitors the main daytime attraction is the **Berlin Museum** at Lindenstrasse 14 (Tues–Sun 10am–10pm; DM4), which illustrates the history and development of the city through paintings, prints and crafts, and also holds part of the Jewish Museum. Also of interest is the **Museum of Transport and Technology** at Trebbiner Strasse 9 (Tue–Fri 9am–5.30pm, Sat & Sun 10am–6pm; DM4, students DM2), one of the city's most entertaining museums and a button-pusher's delight. In adjoining **Schöneberg**, the other main night-life zone, the most famous attraction is the **Rathaus Schöneberg** on Martin-Luther-Strasse, where, in 1963, John F. Kennedy made his celebrated "Ich bin ein Berliner" speech.

Way over to the northwest of the Tiergarten stretches the district of **Charlottenburg**, its most significant target being the sumptuously restored **Schloss Charlottenburg** (Tues–Sun 9am–5pm; combined ticket for whole palace DM7, students DM3). Commissioned by the future Queen Sophie Charlotte in 1695, it was added to throughout the eighteenth and early nineteenth centuries, the master builder Karl Friedrich Schinkel providing the final touches. There are few better ways to idle away a morning in Berlin than to explore the museum's collection of romantic paintings and gardens (open daily till dusk). Best of the Charlottenburg museums is the **Ägyptisches Museum** at Schlossstrasse 70 (Mon–Thurs 9am–5pm, Sat & Sun 10am–5pm; DM4, students DM2; free Sun), with the famous bust of Nefertiti on the first floor. Also worth visiting, at the southwest junction of Spandauer Damm and Schlossstrasse, is the **Antikenmuseum** (Tues–Fri 9am–5pm; DM4, students DM2; free Sun), which holds Greek and Roman collections, and, just to the south, the **Bröhan-Museum** (Tues–Sun 10am–6pm; DM4, students DM2) which has a great collection of Jugendstil ceramics and furniture.

The southwestern suburb of **Dahlem**, reached by U-Bahn line #2 to Dahlem-Dorf, is home to the **Dahlem Museum** (Tues–Sun 9am–5pm; DM4, students DM2; free Sun), a museum complex that's among the best in Europe. The Picture Gallery covers the early medieval to late eighteenth-century periods, with authoritative sections on early Netherlandish painting. Best works are a beautifully lit *Madonna in the Church* by Jan van Eyck, along with works by his successors, Petrus Christus and Rogier van der Weyden. The two other major paintings from this period are both by Hugo van der Goes: the *Adoration of the Shepherds* (painted when the artist was in the first throes of madness) and the *Adoration of the Magi*. Later Dutch painting includes Vermeer's *Man and Woman Drinking Wine* and a huge collection of Rembrandts; recently, his most famous picture here, *The Man in the Golden Helmet*, was proved to be the work of his studio rather than the artist himself, though this does little to detract from the elegance and power of the portrait. There are many other medieval and Renaissance works from Germany and Italy, but if you've had enough of paintings, check out the **ethnographic** sections: rich and extensive collections from Asia, the Pacific and South Sea Islands, imaginatively laid out. Other collections within the museum include **Islamic**, **Asian**, **East Asian** and **Indian art** – dip in according to your tastes.

West of Charlottenburg, U-Bahn line #1 runs to the Olympia Stadion station; a fifteen-minute, signposted walk brings you to the vast **Olympic Stadium** itself (April–Oct daily 10am–5.30pm; DM2.50), one of the few Fascist buildings left intact in the city.

For a break from the city pressure, you could take a trip to the **Grunewald** forest and beaches on the **Havel** lakes. One possible starting point is the **Jagdschloss Grunewald** (daily except Mon April–Sept 10am–6pm; March & Oct 10am–5pm; Nov–Feb 10am–4pm; DM2.50, students DM1.50), a sixteenth-century hunting lodge reached by taking bus #115 from Fehrbelliner Platz U-Bahn to Pücklerstrasse. Near the Pücklerstrasse stop you'll find the **Brücke Museum** at Bussardsteig 9 (daily except Tues 11am–5pm; DM4, students DM2), a fine collection of works by the Die Brücke group of Expressionist painters. An alternative approach to the Grunewald is to take the #1 or #3 S-Bahn to Nikolasee station, from where it's a ten-minute walk to **Strandbad Wannsee**, a kilometre-long strip of pale sand that's the largest inland beach in Europe.

Eastern Berlin

The most atmospheric approach to eastern Berlin starts under the **Brandenburg Gate** and leads up **Unter den Linden**, a stately broad boulevard that is rapidly re-assuming its prewar role as Berlin's most important thoroughfare. Beyond the equestrian monument to Frederick the Great are gathered a host of historic buildings restored from the rubble of the war, starting with the Neoclassical Humboldt Universität, followed by the Alte Bibliothek, the flawless Deutsche Staatsoper and the domed St Hedwigs-Kathedrale, which was built for the city's Catholics in 1747. More than anyone it was Karl Friedrich Schinkel who shaped nineteenth-century Berlin and one of his most famous creations, the **Neue Wache**, can be found opposite the Staatsoper. Resembling a stylized Roman temple, this former royal guardhouse stands next door to one of eastern Berlin's finest Baroque buildings, the old Prussian arsenal, which contains the temporarily closed **Museum of German History**.

Following Charlottenstrasse south from Unter den Linden leads to the **Platz der Akademie**, much of whose appeal is derived from the **Französischer Dom** on the northern side of the square. Built as a church for Berlin's influential Huguenot community at the beginning of the eighteenth century, it today houses the **Hugenottenmuseum** (Tues, Wed & Sat 10am–5pm, Thurs 10am–6pm, Sun 11.30am–5pm; DM2, students DM1), documenting their way of life. At the southern end of the square, the **Deutscher Dom** was built around the same time for the city's Lutheran community. Schinkel's Neoclassical **Schauspielhaus** sits between the two churches.

At the eastern end of Unter den Linden is **Marx-Engels-Platz** (part of which has been renamed Lustgarten), the mid-point of a city-centre island whose northwestern part, Museumsinsel, is the location of the best of eastern Berlin's **museums**. The **Pergamonmuseum** (daily 10am–6pm; DM4, students DM2) houses the treasure trove of the German archeologists who plundered the ancient world in the nineteenth century, and includes the spectacular Pergamon Altar, which dates from 160 BC, and the huge Processional Way and Throne Room from sixth-century BC Babylon. The **Altes Museum** (Wed–Sun 10am–6pm; DM4, students DM2), perhaps Schinkel's most impressive surviving work, is now home to a collection of postwar and GDR art, and a print collection taking in artists as diverse as Botticelli, Rembrandt and Käthe Kollwitz. The **Nationalgalerie** (same hours and price) contains eastern Berlin's largest art collections, with a particularly good section of the Expressionists. In the **Bodemuseum** (same hours and price) there's the Heinrich Schliemann Collection, which consists of items unearthed by the great German archeologist on the site of ancient Troy. Elsewhere in the museum are Egyptian archeological finds and a papyrus collection, containing art and papyri from 5000 BC to the third century AD, plus mummies, friezes, weapons and jewellery. Adjacent to the Altes Museum is the **Berliner Dom**, built between 1894 and 1905 to serve the House of Hohenzollern as a family church; its vault houses ninety sarcophagi containing the remains of various members of the line.

To reach **Alexanderplatz**, the commercial hub of eastern Berlin, head along Karl-Liebknecht-Strasse past the Neptunbrunnen fountain and the thirteenth-century **Marienkirche**, Berlin's oldest parish church. Like every other building in the vicinity, the church is overshadowed by the gigantic **Fernsehturm** or TV tower (daily 8/9am–11pm; DM5, students DM3), whose observation platform offers unbeatable views of the whole city on rare clear days.

Southwest of here lies the **Nikolaiviertel**, a recent development that attempts to recreate this part of old prewar Berlin, which was razed overnight on June 16, 1944. At the centre of it all is the **Nikolaikirche** (Tues–Fri 9am–5pm, Sat 9–6pm, Sun 10–5pm; DM3, students DM1), a thirteenth-century church now housing an exhibition about medieval Berlin. Not far away on Mühlendamm is the rebuilt Rococo **Ephraim-Palais** (Tues–Fri 9am–5pm, Sat 9–5pm, Sun 10–5pm; DM3, students DM1), with a museum that details the growth of Berlin.

The one eastern *Bezirke* (district) that should on no account be missed is **Prenzlauer Berg**, radiating out from the northeastern edge of the city centre in a network of tenement-lined cobbled streets. Prenzlauer Berg, like Kreuzberg in western Berlin, has enjoyed a big influx of "alternative" lifestyle adherents and artists, a development which – coupled with the opening of various new cafés and galleries – has turned this into one of the most exciting parts of the city. The quickest way to get to Prenzlauer Berg is to take the U-Bahn from Alexanderplatz to either Dmitroffstrasse or Schönhauser Allee.

Eating, drinking and nightlife

Nowhere is more than a stone's throw from a **bar** in Berlin, and the range of **restaurants** in the west is wider than in any other German city. Cheapest way of warding off hunger is to use the **Imbiss** snack stands, or one of the **mensas**, officially for German students only but usually open to anyone who looks the part. Eating out in a proper restaurant won't break the bank, though; the prices given below are for main courses, exclusive of starters, drink or tips. Restaurants in **eastern Berlin** can still be pretty drab when compared to eating in the west. The places listed below are exceptions.

Western Berlin has four focal points for drinking: **Savignyplatz** is for conspicuous good-timers; **Kreuzberg** drinkers include political activists, punks and the Turkish community; the area around **Nollendorfplatz and Winterfeldtplatz** is the territory of sped-out all-nighters and the pushing-on-forty crew; **Schöneberg** bars are on the whole more mixed and more relaxed. Unless you're into brawling soldiers or pissed businessmen, avoid the Ku'damm and the rip-off joints around the Europa Center. In the **eastern part** of the city, don't expect the variety or gloss found in the west, but there are a number of exciting new cafés and bars, often based around squats or occupied buildings. Berlin is very much a city that wakes up when others are going to sleep – don't bother turning up before midnight for the all-night clubs in Kreuzberg and Schöneberg. (Reckon on about DM10 for admission.) For more sedate nightlife there's a number of theatres and one of Europe's great orchestras. The way to find out exactly what's on and where it's happening is to buy the listings magazines *Tip*, *Zitty* or *Prinz*, get the *Berlin Program* leaflet, or look for the fly posters about town.

Snacks

Ashoka-Imbiss, Grolmanstr. 51. Situated off Savignyplatz, this is about the best of the lot, dishing up good portions of tremendous-bargain Indian food. Daily 11am–midnight.

Ernst-Reuter-Platz Mensa, Ernst-Reuter-Platz. Small mensa of the nearby Technical University, with limited choice of meals. *ISIC* required. Mon–Fri 11.15am–2.30pm.

TU Mensa, Hardenbergstr. 34. Meals around DM4. Mon–Fri 11.15am–2.30pm.

Restaurants

Abendmahl, Muskauerstr. 9 (☎612 5170). Uniformly excellent food, a busy but congenial atmosphere, and reasonable prices (DM20) make this one of the most enjoyable places to eat in the city.

Der Ägypter, Kantstr. 26. Egyptian falafel-type meals. Spicy, filling and an adventurous alternative to the safe bets around Savignyplatz. Good vegetarian selections. DM10–15.

Algarve, Waitzstr. 11. Pleasant Portuguese restaurant with a huge variety of fish on the menu and very reasonably priced. DM12–25.

Aroma, Hochkirchstr. 8 (☎786 2989). Well above average, inexpensive Italian. One of the best places to eat in east Schöneberg, it's advisable to book after 8pm. DM8–14.

Borriquito, Wielandstr. 6. Lively, noisy Spanish restaurant that's open till 5am daily. DM18 and up.

Casa Leone, Hasenheide 69. Good-quality Italian cooking, with a varied menu and pretty terrace for sitting outside in summer. DM10–20.

Cour Carrée, Savignyplatz 5. Deservedly popular French restaurant with *fin-de-siècle* decor and garden seating. DM15–25.

Edd's Thailändisches Restaurant, Goebenstr. 20–21 (☎215 5294). Huge portions of Thai food make this a popular place: booking advised. DM10–20.

La Estancia, Bundesallee 45. Very good value for money Latin American restaurant, patronized mainly by environmentally and politically conscious Berliners. DM8–15.

Exil, Paul-Lincke-Ufer 44 (☎612 7037). Canalside place popular with the Kreuzberg arts crowd for its moderate to expensive Viennese food. Booking advisable.

Henne, Leuschnerdamm 25 (☎614 7730). Pub-style restaurant with the best chicken in Berlin. Reservation advisable. DM9–15.

India-Palace, Leibnizstr. 35. Incredible variety and low prices. DM10–14.

Kalkutta, Bleibtreustr. 17. Arguably the finest Indian restaurant in Berlin. From DM20.

Kyoto, Wilmersdorferstr. 94. Excellent Japanese with *sushi* to your heart's content. DM15–25.

La Maskera, Koburgerstr. 5. Among the best vegetarian places in town, with an Italian slant adding colour to the food and atmosphere. Wholemeal pizzas and pasta, along with egg and tofu dishes. DM8–20.

Merhaba, Hasenheide 39. Highly rated Turkish restaurant that's usually packed with locals. A selection of the starters here can be more interesting than a main course.

Osteria No.1, Kreuzbergstr. 71 (☎786 9162). Classy, inexpensive and therefore highly popular Italian run by a collective. DM10–20; booking advisable.

Pagode, Schlüterstr. 55. Claims to be Berlin's oldest Chinese restaurant; the food is certainly good quality but not cheap at DM18–25.

Petit Chinois, Spandauer Damm 82. Excellent Chinese food made from fresh ingredients. Decor is unnervingly like that of a corner *Kneipe.*

Publique, Yorckstr. 62 (☎786 9469). Friendly café-cum-restaurant serving superb food till 2am. DM16–30.

Tegernseer Tönnchen, Mommsenstr. 34. Bavarian cuisine – which means enormous dishes of *wursts* and *schnitzels* washed down with pitchers of beer. Excellent value at DM10–17.

Tres Kilos, Marheinekeplatz 3 (☎693 6044). Tex-Mex food in a drunkenly convivial atmosphere. DM12–20.

Vietnam, Suarezstr. 61. One of the city's most popular Vietnamese restaurants, quietly situated in a street of junk shops. DM10–30.

EASTERN BERLIN

Neubrandenburger Hof, Wilhelm-Pieck-Str./Borsigstr. Solid German cuisine, good value for money and fairly central. DM5–20.

Restaurant Moskau, Karl-Marx-Allee 34 (☎270 0532). Eastern Berlin's premier Russian restaurant.

Spreebuffet, Spree Ufer. Cafeteria-type eatery with stodgy portions of German food. DM5–10.

Bars

Café Adler, Friedrichstr. 206. Small café next to the site of the Checkpoint Charlie border crossing. Moderately priced breakfasts and meals.

Begine, Potsdamerstr. 139. Stylishly decorated women-only bar-bistro/gallery with limited choice of inexpensive food.

Blue Boy Bar, Eisenacherstr. 3. Tiny, convivial and relaxed gay bar.

Cazzo, Oranienstr. 187. Trendy gay bar, and a good place to sample the austere cosiness of contemporary Kreuzberg.

Estoril, Vorbergstr. 11. Chic Schöneberg bar that serves good tapas with drinks.

Fledermaus, Joachimstalerstr. 14–19. Bar and coffee shop popular with tourists as well as locals; one of the city's most relaxing gay bars.

Golgotha, Viktoriapark. Enormous and enormously popular open-air café perched near the top of Kreuzberg's hill.

Kumpelnest 3000, Lützowstr. 23. Carpeted walls and a mock-Baroque effect attract a rough-and-ready crew of under-30s to this erstwhile brothel. Gets going around 2am.

Bar am Lützowplatz, Lützowplatz 7. The longest bar in the city. A dangerously great place.

Café M, Goltzstr. 34. Berlin's favoured rendezvous for creative types and the conventionally unconventional. Usually packed, even for breakfast.

Pinguin Club, Wartburgstr. 54. Tiny and cheerful Schöneberg bar with 1950–60s America supplying its theme and background music.

Schwarzes Café, Kantstr. 148. Kantstrasse's best hang-out for the young and chic, with a relaxed atmosphere, good music and food. Open 24hr except Tues closed 8am–8pm.

Zillemarkt, Bleibtreustr. 48. Wonderful if shabby bar that attempts a *fin-de-siècle* feel.

Die Zwei, corner Martin-Lutherstr. and Motzstr. The city's best lesbian bar, but non-exclusive.

EASTERN BERLIN

Zur Letzten Instanz, Waisenstr. 14–16. Near the old city wall, this is one of the oldest city bars. Wine upstairs, beer downstairs, and in summer there's a beer garden.

Offenbachstuben, Senefelderstr./Stubbenkammerstr. Highly recommended for both food and drink. The decor has a theatrical theme and the seating niches are great for drunken late-night conversation. Also popular with the gay crowd. Closed Sun and Mon.

Silberstein, Oranienburgerstr. 27 Eastern Berlin's trendiest bar, thanks to over-the-top designer furniture and fashion-conscious clientele.

Café Westphal, Kollwitzstr. 63. One of the best new Prenzlauer Berg bars.

Discos, clubs and rock venues

Blue Note, Courbièrestr. 13. Eclectic mix of rock, Latin and (chiefly) jazz. Tues–Sun 10pm–5am.

Bronx, Wienerstr. 34. Chic and popular hip-hop disco, done out in bomb-damage decor. Daily 10pm onwards; free.

E-Werk, Wilhelmstr. Flashy techno-music in vast former east Berlin factory. Very popular and rather expensive.

K.O.B., Potsdamerstr. 157. A bar in a squatted house which on weekdays hosts interesting groups at low prices.

Quartier, Potsdamerstr. 96. Club-cum-arts-centre with acid house disco at weekends.

Tempodrom, John-Foster-Dulles-Allee. Two tents, the larger hosting bands of middling fame.

Zoo, Nürnbergerstr. 50. Hip-hop, ragamuffin and soul. Very trendy. Tues–Sun 11pm–6am.

EASTERN BERLIN

Dunckerclub, Dunckerstr. 64. Indie gigs and frequent club evenings attract a youngish local crowd. A small but atmospheric venue with open-air gigs in the back yard in summer.

Sophienclub, Sophienstr. 6. Crowded central club playing host to the best local bands and often putting on discos.

Tacheles e.V, Oranienburgerstr. 53–56. Gigs, raves and a hang-out in which a new Berlin *Szene* is taking shape.

Classical music

Philharmonie, Matthäikirchstr. 1 (☎254 880). For years classical music in Berlin meant Herbert von Karajan's Berlin Philharmonic. Since Karajan's death in 1989 Claudio Abbado has maintained the orchestra's popularity, and tickets are extremely difficult to come by.

Deutsche Oper, Bismarckstr. 34 (☎341 0249). Good classical concerts, plus opera and ballet.

Komische Oper, Behrenstr. 55–57, East Berlin (☎229 2555). The house orchestra performs classical and contemporary music, and some very good opera productions are staged here.

Schauspielhaus, Platz der Academie, East Berlin. Home to the Berlin Sinfonie Orchester and host to visting orchestras.

Theatre

Schaubühne am Lehniner Platz, Kurfürstendamm 153 (☎890 023). State-of-the-art theatre for performances of the classics and some experimental pieces.

Schiller-Theater, Bismarckstr. 110 (☎319 5236). The best state-run experimental theatre in western Berlin with three stages, but currently threatened with closure.

Berliner Ensemble, Bertolt-Brecht-Platz 1 (☎282 3160). The official Brecht theatre.

Maxim Gorki Theater, Unter den Linden, Am Festungsgraben 2 (☎207 1790). Consistently good productions of modern works.

Listings

Airlines *Air France*, Europa Center (☎261 051); *British Airways*, Europa Center (☎691 021); *EuroBerlin*, Kantstr. 165 (☎884 1920); *Lufthansa*, Kurfürstendamm 220 (☎88750).

Airport enquiries ☎410 11.

Bicycle rental *Berlin by Bike*, Möckernstr. 92 (☎216 9177). DM20 per day, DM85 per week. Deposit and passport required.

Car rental Two of the least expensive are *Mini-bus Service*, Zietenstr. 1 (☎261 6565), and *First & Second Hand Rent*, Lohmeyerstr. 7 (☎341 7076) – around DM50 daily, plus a deposit of about DM200.

Consulates *Canada*, Internationales Handelzentrum, Friedrickstr. 95 (☎261 1161); *Great Britain*, Unter den Linden 32–34 (☎220 2431); *Ireland*, Ernst-Reuter-Platz 10 (☎3480 0822); *US*, Neustadtische Kirchstr. 4–5 (☎220 2741); US visa section, Clayallee 170 (☎819 7454). New Zealand and Australia are represented by the Great Britain embassy.

Exchange At the main entrance to the Zoo Station (Mon–Sat 8am–9pm, Sun 10am–6pm).

Hitching *Mitfahrzentrale*, Kurfürstendamm 227 (☎882 7606). Women's *Mitfahrzentrale* at Potsdamerstr. 139 (☎215 3165).

Laundry Uhlandstr. 53 (6.30am–10.30pm); Hauptstr. 151 (7.30am–10.30pm). Other addresses are listed under *Wäscherei* in the yellow pages.

Left luggage Left luggage at Zoo Station (Mon–Fri 6am–midnight, Sat & Sun 6am–5.40pm & 6pm–midnight) does not accept rucksacks. In the east, there are 24-hr lockers at Friedrichstrasse and Alexanderplatz stations (DM2).

Pharmacies Outside normal hours a notice on the door of any *Apotheke* indicates the nearest one open. *Europa-Apotheke*, Tauentzienstr. 9, is open 9am–9pm daily.

Police Platz der Luftbrücke 6 (☎6990).

Post office Zoo Station, with a counter open 24 hours.

Taxi In western Berlin ☎ 69022, ☎691001 or ☎261026 (24-hour service). In eastern Berlin the number to try is ☎3644 (however, in Treptow, Köpenick, Marzahn, Hellesdorf and at Schönefeld airport, the number is ☎3366).

Women's centre Stresemannstr. 40 (☎251 0912).

EASTERN GERMANY

By the time the former German Democratic Republic was fully incorporated into the Federal Republic of Germany, just one year after the peaceful revolution of autumn 1989 (the so-called *Wende*), most vestiges of the old political system had been swept away. Yet there is a long way to go before the two parts of the country achieve parity, and the cities of **Eastern Germany** are in the process of a major social and economic upheaval. For the visitor this phase of transition is an often fascinating spectacle, but for many of the citizens of the former GDR the transformation is problematic. The post-revolution euphoria has long subsided, life in the new Germany is proving hard, and the east is troubled by rising unemployment, low incomes and increasing violence from resurgent neo-Nazi groups.

Berlin stands apart from the rest of the east, but its sense of excitement finds an echo in the two other main cities – **Leipzig**, which provided the vanguard of the revolution, and **Dresden**, the beautiful Saxon capital so ruthlessly destroyed in 1945. Equally enticing are some of the smaller places, which retain more of the appearance and atmosphere of prewar Germany than anywhere in the west, notably **Erfurt**, capital of the ancient province of Thuringia, nearby **Weimar**, the small cathedral towns of **Naumburg** and **Meissen**, and the old Prussian royal seat of **Potsdam**. Although much of eastern Germany is monotonous – its heartland was once a vast swamp – it is by no means the drab industrial landscape you might imagine.

Potsdam

Site of the colossal palace of Frederick the Great, **POTSDAM** is an easy and excellent day trip from Berlin. Bus #113 from S-Bahn station Wannsee will deposit you at **Bassinplatz** near the centre of Potsdam, or a continuation of S-Bahn line #3 from western Berlin will drop you at S-Bahn station **Potsdam Stadt**, from where it's only a few minutes' walk north over the Lange Brücke and along Friedrich-Ebert-Strasse to the central Platz der Einheit.

Park Sanssouci (9am–12.30pm & 1–3/5pm; closed first and third Mon of each month), fabled retreat of the Prussian king, stretches two kilometres west of the town centre, a beautiful spectacle in spring when trees are in leaf and flowers in bloom. These days it's too often overrun by visitors – to avoid the crowds, visit on a weekday. Frederick worked closely with his architect on designing the **Schloss Sanssouci** (tours daily March–Sept 9am–5pm; Oct & Feb 9am–4pm; Nov–Jan 9am–3pm; DM6), which was to be a place where the king could escape Berlin and his wife Elizabeth Christine, neither of whom he cared for. Begun in 1744, it's a surprisingly modest one-storey Baroque affair, topped by an oxidized green dome and ornamental statues looking out over vine terraces. Frederick loved the Schloss so much that he intended to be buried here, and had a tomb excavated for himself in front of the eastern wing; in 1991 his body was finally moved here from Garnisonkirche in Potsdam town. Inside is a frenzy of Rococo, spread through the twelve rooms where Frederick lived and entertained his guests. The most eye-catching rooms are the opulent Marble Hall and the Concert Room, where the flute-playing king had eminent musicians play his own works on concert evenings. Frederick's favourite haunt was his library where, surrounded by his two thousand volumes – mainly French translations of the classics and a sprinkling of contemporary French writings – he could oversee the work on his tomb.

West of the palace, overlooking the ornamental **Holländischer Garten**, is the **Bildergalerie** (Mid-May to mid-Oct 9am–noon & 12.45–5pm; DM4), a restrained Baroque creation that contains paintings by Rubens, van Dyck and Caravaggio. On the opposite side of the Schloss, steps lead down to the **Neue Kammern** (April–Sept 9am–12.45pm & 1–3/5pm; DM4), the architectural twin of the Bildergalerie, originally used as an orangery and later as a guesthouse. Immediately to the west of the Neue Kammern is the prim **Sizilianischer Garten**, crammed with coniferous trees and subtropical plants, complementing the **Nordische Garten** just to the north.

From the west of the Sizilianischer Garten, the Maulbeerallee cuts through the park and ascends to the **Orangerie** (mid-May to mid-Oct 9am–noon & 1–5pm; closed every fourth Mon; DM5). This Italianate Renaissance-style structure with belvedere towers is perhaps the most impressive structure in the park: a series of terraces with curved retaining walls sporting water spouts in the shape of lions' heads leads to the sandy-coloured building, whose slightly down-at-heel appearance lends it added character.

To the west through the trees rises the **Neues Palais** (April–Sept 9am–12.45pm & 1.15–5pm; Feb, March & Oct until 4pm; Nov–Jan until 3pm; closed every 2nd and 4th Mon; DM6, students DM3), another massive Rococo extravaganza from Frederick the Great's time. The main entrance to the palace is on the western facade, approached via gates flanked by stone sentry boxes. Theoretically you have to join a guided tour, but once inside you can pretty much take things at you own pace. The interior is predictably opulent, though a couple of highlights stand out: the vast and startling **Grottensaal** on the ground floor decorated entirely with shells and semi-precious stones to form images of lizards and dragons, and the equally huge **Marmorsaal**, with its beautiful floor of patterned marble slabs. The southern wing (which these days houses a small café) contains Frederick's apartments and the theatre where the king enjoyed Italian opera and French plays.

Facing the Neues Palais entrance are the **Communs**, a couple of Rococo fantasies joined by a curved colonnade. They look grandiose, but their purpose was mundane: they were built for serving and maintenance staff of the Palais.

Leipzig

Although never one of Germany's more visually appealing cities, **LEIPZIG** has always been among the most dynamic: its trade fairs have a tradition dating back to the Middle Ages and remained important during the communist years, so that there was never the degree of isolation from outside influences experienced by so many cities behind the Iron Curtain.

Arrival and accommodation

The **train station** – the largest in Europe – is at the northeastern end of the Ring, which encircles the old part of the city. Apart from the usual exchange facilities, there's a **private room agency** (Mon–Fri 8.30am–6pm, Sat 9am–noon) upstairs by the western exit. The same service is also available in the **tourist office** a short walk to the south on Sachsenplatz (Mon–Fri 9am–8pm, Sat & Sun 9.30am–2pm).

Accommodation options include the **youth hostels** at Käthe-Kollwitz-Str. 62 (☎0341/470 530; tram #1, #2 or #8) and at the far more distant Gustav-Esche-Str. 4 (☎57 189; tram #10 or #28); near the latter is the **campsite**. Most **hotels** are prohibitively priced: the trade fair means that average prices are upwards of DM60 for a single, DM90 a double. Two exceptions, both a short walk west from the train station, are *Haus-Ingeborg*, Nordstr. 58, and *Pension am Zoo*, Pfaffendorferstr. 23.

The City

Following Nikolaistrasse due south from the train station brings you to the **Nikolaikirche** (Mon–Fri 10am–6pm), one of the two main civic churches and a rallying point during the *Wende*. Although a sombre medieval structure from outside, the church's interior is a real eye-grabber, its coffered vault supported by fluted columns whose capitals sprout like palm trees. A couple of blocks to the west is the open space of the **Markt**, whose eastern side is entirely occupied by the **Altes Rathaus** (Tues–Fri 10am–6pm, Sat & Sun 10am–4pm; DM1), built in the grandest German Renaissance style with elaborate gables, an asymmetrical tower and the longest inscription to be found on any building in the world. The ground floor retains its traditional function as a covered walkway with shops; the upper storeys, long abandoned as the town hall, now house the local history museum. However, the main reason for going in is to see the 53-metre-long *Festsaal* on the first floor, with its ornate chimneypieces and haughty portraits of the local mayors and Saxon dukes. The Rathaus also contains a **museum** dedicated to the town's history: worth a look, if you're interested. On the north side of the square is another handsome public building from Renaissance times, the old weighing house or **Alte Waage**.

To the rear of the Altes Rathaus, approached by a graceful double flight of steps, is the **Alte Handelsbörse**, a Baroque gem which was formerly the trade exchange headquarters. As the trade fair expanded in the early years of this century, many historic buildings nearby were demolished to make way for the functional modern buildings which now predominate; the Altes Rathaus only escaped this fate through the casting vote of the mayor.

Following Barfussgässchen off the western side of the Markt brings you to Kleine Fleischergasse and the cheerful Baroque **Zum Coffe Baum**. One of the German pioneers in the craze for coffee which followed the Turkish invasion of Central Europe in the late seventeeth century, it gained further fame courtesy of Robert Schumann, whose came here regularly. Klostergasse leads southwards from here to the

Thomaskirche, the senior of the two big civic churches, and the place where Johann Sebastian Bach served for the last 27 years of his life. Predominantly Gothic, the church has been repeatedly altered down the centuries, notably with the addition of the galleries in line with the Protestant emphasis on preaching. However, the most remarkable feature remains its musical tradition: the *Thomanerchor*, which Bach once directed, can usually be heard on Fridays at 6pm, Saturdays at 3pm, and at the Sunday service at 9.30am. Directly across from the church is the **Bach Museum** (Tues–Sun 9am–5pm; DM2), with an extensive show of mementoes of the great man.

South along the Ring, past the bulky Neues Rathaus, you come to Georgi-Dimitroff-Platz and the supreme court of prewar Germany, the **Reichsgerichts**. The upper floor, centred on the opulent main courtroom, contains a **museum** (daily 9am–5pm; DM2) devoted to the famous trial over the Reichstag fire – the event which served as a pretext for the Nazis' clampdown on the activities of their opponents. During the trial, Georgi Dimitroff, the Bulgarian head of the Communist International, completely outwitted Hermann Göring, the chief prosecutor; this is the event commemorated in the museum, though the fall of the GDR has made its future uncertain. Downstairs is the **Museum für bildene Kunst** (Tues & Thurs–Sun 9am–5pm, Wed 1–9.30pm; DM2), which houses a collection of paintings from the Middle Ages to this century. Highlights include van der Weyden's *The Visitation*, Cranach's *Nymph at the Well*, Hals' *The Mulatto* and Friedrich's *The Steps of Life*.

The southeastern part of the Altstadt is the academic quarter. On Schillerstrasse, east of the Neues Rathaus, is a surprisingly good **Egyptian Museum** (Tues–Fri 2–6pm, Sun 10am–1pm; DM2), containing finds from nineteenth-century excavations by archeologists from Leipzig University. Beyond is a fragment of the old fortifications, the **Moritzbastei**, now occupied by the leading student club. It's completely overshadowed by the 34-storey tower of the main **University** building itself. A lift (DM1.50) ascends to the café at the top, which commands the finest view of the city. Beside it stands the **Gewandhaus**, the ultra-modern home of the oldest orchestra in the world, and still one of the best.

Crossing the Ring and following Grimmeisch Steinweg eastwards brings you to Johannisplatz and the **Grassi-Museum**, a vast complex which was once one of the most important museum complexes in Europe, but has yet to recover from war damage. In the meantime, the **Musical Instruments Museum** (Tues–Fri 9–5pm, Sat 10am–5pm, Sun 10am–1pm; DM2) and the **Ethnographical Museum** (Tues–Fri 10am–5.30pm, Sat & Sun 10am–4pm; DM2) offer reasonably complete displays; the **Decorative Arts Museum** (Tues, Thurs & Fri 10am–6pm, Wed 10am–8pm, Sat & Sun 10am–5pm; DM2) hosts temporary exhibitions but has on view only a tiny fraction of what is said to be a magnificent permanent collection.

Trams #15 and #20 run southeast to the site of the **Battle of the Nations**, where Napoleon was defeated by a combined army of Prussians, Austrians, Russians and Swedes in 1813 – a defeat that led to his exile on Elba. A colossal and tasteless monument known as the **Völkerschlachtdenkmal** (daily 10am–5pm; DM2) was erected to commemorate the centenary of the victory; it can be ascended for a sweeping view over the city and the flat countryside.

Eating and drinking

Leipzig offers a choice between traditional German taverns and the range of ethnic restaurants which are a hangover of the political allegiances of the recent past. Most of the best places are close to the Markt. *Zum Kaffeebaum*, Kleine Fleishchergasse 4, is one of the unmissable places in Leipzig, whether for *Kaffee und Küchen* or a full meal. *Café de Saxe*, Markt 11, is a new and very trendy café which also does full meals. Tucked underneath the Mädler-Passage, one of the covered shopping malls off Grimmaische Strasse at the southeastern end of the Markt, is *Auerbachs Keller*, a historic and very formal **restaurant** that was the setting for a scene in Goethe's *Faust*. However, for a hearty German meal, best choice is the rambling old *Thüringer Hof*, Burgstr. 19. *Varadero*, Barfussgässchen 8, is a popular Cuban restaurant specializing in grills and cocktails, while *Dialog*, Täubchenweg 25, has an odd jumble of German, Italian and vaguely Eastern meals. Leipzig's oldest tavern is *Burgkeller*, Naschmarkt 1, a typical German *Bierkeller*. The city is also famous for its satirical political cabaret: if your German's up to it, try the *Pfaffermühlen Club* inside the Bach Museum.

Naumburg

The old cathedral city of **NAUMBURG** is situated on the fast rail line between Leipzig and Weimar, and reachable from both in well under an hour. Rather neglected in recent decades, it has already made giant steps in scraping off the grime which had smothered its buildings, and is well on the way to reclaiming its former status as one of Germany's most beautiful and distinctive towns.

The historic part of Naumburg, set on heights overlooking the Saale valley, is dominated by the **Dom**, which shows medieval German architecture and sculpture at their peak. Though it was built as the seat of the local prince-bishop, with choirs at both ends of the building to emphasize its status as an imperial cathedral, it has been no more than a Protestant parish church since the Reformation. The thirteenth-century builders began by erecting the eastern choir, complete with its almost oriental towers, in a florid Romanesque style. However, by the time the west choir was finished – minus one of the towers, which was finally built to the original plans a century ago – Gothic had taken over completely. Pride of the interior (April–Sept Mon–Sat 8am–noon & 1–6pm; reduced hours out of season; DM3.50) is the assemblage of sculptures by the so-called **Master of Naumburg**, one of the most original masons to have worked on a great European cathedral. His rood screen, illustrating the Passion, imbues the figures with a humanity and a realism never previously found in religious art, and the twelve life-sized statues of the Dom's founders in the west choir are each given a distinctive characterization. Particularly outstanding are the couple Ekkehardt and Uta, who have come to symbolize the Germans' romantic view of their chivalric medieval past.

From the Dom, Steinweg and Herrenstrasse – each with its fair share of fine houses, often complete with wrought-iron identification signs – lead eastwards to the central **Markt**. The square is dominated by the Renaissance **Rathaus**, whose huge curved gables served as a model for other mansions in the city. Rising behind the south side of the Markt is the curiously elongated **Wenzelskirche**, which was the burghers' answer to the prince-bishop's Dom. In the Baroque period, this late Gothic church was given an interior face-lift, including the provision of a magnificent organ; look out also for two paintings by Cranach. The **tower** (April–Oct Wed–Sun 10am–6pm; DM2), which was home to a watchman until a few years ago, offers a magnificent panorama.

More fine mansions are to be seen on Jacobstrasse, which leads eastwards from the Markt. Also well worth going to see is the **Marientor**, at the edge of the inner ring road directly to the north of the Markt. This double gateway, one of the best-preserved in the country, is the only significant reminder these days of the fifteenth-century fortifications.

Naumburg's **train station** is below and northwest of the historic centre. It's fortunate that communications with Leipzig and Weimar are so fast and frequent, as accommodation is very limited, with the two hotels invariably booked out. A few overpriced **private rooms** can be booked at the **tourist office** at Lindenring 39 (Mon–Fri 9am–6pm, Sat 9am–noon) between the Dom and the Markt. Alternatively, there's a **youth hostel** way to the south of the centre at Am Tennisplatz 9 (☎03445 5316; ①). Recommendable **restaurants** include *Drei Schwannen* on Jacobstrasse and *Domklause* on Herrenstrasse.

Weimar

Despite its modest size, **WEIMAR** has played a role in the development of German culture that is unmatched: Goethe, Schiller, Herder and Nietzsche all made it their home, as did the Cranachs and Bach, and the architects and designers of the Bauhaus school. Its part in the politics of Germany is scarcely less significant: Weimar was chosen as the seat of government of the democratic republic established after World War I, a regime whose failure ended with the Nazi accession. One of the most notorious concentration camps was to be built here, and its preservation is a shocking reminder of Germany's double-edged contribution to the history of modern Europe.

The Town

Weimar preserves the appearance and atmosphere of its heyday as the capital of the Duchy of Saxe-Weimar, whose population never rose much above 100,000. The seat of power was the **Schloss** (Tues–Sun 9am–1pm & 2–6pm; DM3), set by the River Ilm at the eastern edge of the town centre, a Neoclassical complex of a size more appropriate for ruling a mighty empire. On the ground floor is a collection of old masters, including pieces by both the elder and younger Cranach, and Dürer's portraits of the Nürnberg patrician couple, Hans and Elspeth Tucher. Upstairs, some fine original interiors can be seen, along with German paintings from the Enlightenment era.

Just west of the Schloss on Herderplatz stands the **Stadtkirche SS. Peter und Paul** (Mon–Fri 10.30am–noon & 2–3.30pm, Sat & Sun 2–3pm), itself usually known as the Herderkirche in honour of the poet and folklorist who was its pastor for three decades. Inside are several impressive tombs plus a large triptych by the Cranachs –featuring portraits of Cranach the Elder and Luther as the main spectators at the Crucifixion.

South of Herderplatz is the spacious **Markt**, lined by an unusually disparate jumble of buildings, of which the most eye-catching is the green and white gabled **Cranach-Haus** on the eastern side, opposite the neo-Gothic Rathaus. Schillerstrasse snakes away from the southwest corner of the Markt to the **Schillerhaus** (9am–noon & 1–5pm; DM2), the home of the poet, dramatist and historian for the last three years of his life. Beyond lies Theaterplatz, in the centre of which is a large monument to Goethe and Schiller. The **Nationaltheater** on the west side of the square was founded and directed by Goethe, though the present building, for all its stern Neoclassical appearance, is a modern pastiche. Opposite is the **Wittumspalais** (Tues–Sun 9am–noon & 1–5pm; DM3), a Baroque palace containing some of the finest interiors of Weimar plus mementoes of the Enlightenment philosopher-poet, Christoph-Martin Wieland.

Last of the literary museums is **Goethewohnhaus und Nationalmuseum** (Tues–Sun 9am–5pm; DM5), on Frauenplan south of the Markt. Here you can see where Goethe lived for some fifty years until his death in 1832, while in the adjoining museum his range of achievement is chronicled with typically Teutonic detail. From the Goethewohnhaus, Marienstrasse continues to the **Liszthaus** (Tues–Sun 9am–noon & 1–5pm; DM3), home of the Hungarian composer and virtuoso pianist for the last seventeen years of his life, when he was director of Weimar's orchestra and opera. A couple of minutes' walk west down Geschwister-Scholl-Strasse is the **Hochschule für Architektur und Bauwesen**, where in 1919 Walter Gropius established the original Bauhaus, which had a profound impact on architecture and design throughout Europe. Further to the west is the **Alter Friedhof** or Old Cemetery, site of the Neoclassical mausoleum of Goethe and Schiller (daily except Tues 9am–1pm & 2–5pm; free).

The **Goethepark** stretches from the Schloss to the southern edge of town on both sides of the Ilm. Almost due east of the Liszthaus, on the opposite bank, is **Goethes Gartenhaus** (daily 9am–noon & 1–5pm; DM3), where the writer stayed when he first came to Weimar in 1776 as a ducal administrator. It now contains a selection of his drawings along with other exhibits concentrating on his interest in the visual arts.

Further south and back on the west bank is the ducal summer house, known as the **Römisches Haus** (Wed–Mon 9am–noon & 1–5pm; DM2). At the south edge of town, in the suburb of Oberweimar, there's the full-blown summer palace of **Schloss Belvedere** (April–Oct Wed–Sun 10am–1pm & 2–6pm; DM2.50), whose light and airy Rococo style forms a refreshing contrast to the Neoclassical solemnity of so much of the town. The orangery contains a collection of historic coaches, while the surroundings were transformed under Goethe's supervision into a *jardin anglais*.

Finally, the **Konzentratsionslager Buchenwald** (Tues–Sun 8.45am–4.30pm; free) is situated to the north of Weimar on the Ettersberg heights, and can be reached by buses which run every hour from just south of the train station. Over 240,000 prisoners were incarcerated in this concentration camp, with 65,000 dying here, among them the interwar leader of the German Communist Party, Ernst Thälmann. This gave the place a special significance for the GDR authorities, now tarnished by the emergence of evidence that the Russians used it after the war for their own political opponents.

Practicalities

Weimar's **train station**, on the main line between Leipzig and Erfurt, is a twenty-minute walk north of the main sights. The **tourist office** at Markstr. 4 (Mon–Fri 9am–7pm, Sat 9am–4pm, Sun 10am–4pm; ☎03643/21 73) can arrange accommodation in **private rooms**, but a possibly cheaper alternative is the agency *Werse & Reiseshop*, Kleine Kirchgasse 3. Cheapest **hotels** are the pension *Am Berkaer Bahnhof*, Peter-Cornelius-Str. 7 (☎2010; ④), and *Pension Savina*, Rembrandtweg 13 (☎60 0797; ④). There are **youth hostels** at Humboldtstr. 17 (☎64 4021; ②) and Carl-August-Allee 13 (☎2076; ②), plus a youth hotel at Zum Wilden Graben 12 (☎3471).

The *Galerie* at Markt 21 is a good place for a **snack**, while *Café Resi* on the adjoining Grüner Markt is recommended for coffee and cakes. For something more substantial, try other places on the Markt, such as *Schwarzer Bär* or the inevitable *Ratskeller*, or go for a fish meal at *Gastmahl des Meeres* on Herderplatz.

Erfurt

Of all Germany's large cities, it's **ERFURT**, twenty minutes from Weimar by train, which is most redolent of prewar Germany. Although it lost a couple of important monuments in bombing raids, it was otherwise relatively little damaged in World War II, while its streets of grandiose turn-of-the-century shops were saved by the communist authorities from the developers who would have demolished them had the city been on the other side of the Iron Curtain.

The vast open space of the Domplatz forms the heart of Erfurt. Imperiously set on the hill above, and reached via a monumental stairway, the **Dom** perches on a mighty fortress-like crypt. It's entered by a magnificent fourteenth-century porch which bears statues of the Apostles on one side, the Wise and Foolish Virgins on the other. Inside, the richly carved stalls and gleaming windows in the choir stand out, and the nave is jam-packed with works of art, the most notable being the so-called *Wolfram*, a Romanesque candelabrum in the shape of a man, and a spectacular font. Alongside the Dom is the **Severikirche**, a pure early Gothic example of the hall church style, containing the tomb of the saint after whom it's named, a fourteenth-century masterpiece by an anonymous sculptor whose work adorns several of the city's churches.

From Domplatz, Marktstrasse leads east to Fischmarkt, lined by handsome Renaissance mansions and the nineteenth-century Rathaus. Just beyond is Erfurt's most singular sight, the **Krämerbrücke**, which adds a welcome dash of colour. Walking along, you have the illusion of entering a narrow medieval alley; the fact that this is actually a bridge lined with shops and galleries only becomes obvious if you go down to the banks of the river.

On the west bank, to the north of the Krämerbrücke, is the imposing Gothic facade of the **University**; the rest of the building was a casualty of World War II. However, its outstanding collection of old manuscripts, housed in the Amploniana, survived, as did the academic church, the **Michaeliskirche**, which has a fine late Gothic chapel.

Across the river is the **Augustinerkloster** (tours Tues–Sat 10am–noon & 2–4pm, Sun 10.30am; DM3), one of a profusion of monasteries in Erfurt which earned it the nickname "little Rome". This one is best-known for having been where Luther served as a novice then a monk between 1505 and 1511. A visit to his cell forms part of the tour, which also includes the cloister and the typically austere church, which is enlivened by a fine stained-glass window depicting the life of Saint Augustine.

Of the other monasteries, pride of place goes to the **Predigerkirche** just south of Fischmarkt. Built by the Dominicans, it's extremely plain on the outside, but the interior is a masterpiece of spatial harmony in the purest Gothic style, and has preserved its layout and furnishings intact. Bombing wrecked the nave of the Franciscan **Barfüsserkirche**, over the river to the south, but the choir has been restored to house a small museum of religious art (Wed–Sun 2–4pm). This is a branch of the **Angermuseum** (Tues–Sun 10am–7pm, Wed 10am–8pm), in a Baroque mansion at the intersection of two of the main shopping streets, Anger and Bahnhofstrasse. Highlight here is the display of medieval artefacts, including more sculptures by the master who carved the tomb in the Severikirche. A fine collection of German painting from the Renaissance to modern times is also featured.

Practicalities

Erfurt's **train station** is situated at the southeastern corner of the city centre. At no. 37 Bahnhofstrasse, which leads to the historic quarters, is one of the two **tourist offices** (Mon–Fri 9am–6pm, Sat 10am–3pm); the other is at Krämerbrücke 3 (Mon–Fri 9am–12.30pm & 1.30–5pm, Sat & Sun 9–11am). The first of these is the place to go if you want a room in a **private house** (③); an alternative, round-the-clock telephone booking service is offered by *Zimmervermittlung Brigitte Scheel* (☎0361/413 838). **Hotels** are still thin on the ground and likely to be booked solid, so your best bet is to check the tourist office's most recent list of **pensions** (④–⑦). There's also a **youth hostel** at Hochheimerstr. 12 (☎26705; ②), southwest of the centre: take tram #5 or #51.

Erfurt's decent **restaurants** are similarly few in number, though this should improve. Try the *Etna* pizzeria on Tallinerstr., *Feuerkugel*, Michaelisstr. 3, and, if you can find a space among the tour groups, *Gildehaus* on Fischmarkt. Best selection of **beer** in town is found in *Restaurant Braugold* on Anger – a real drinkers' den.

Dresden

Generally regarded as Germany's most beautiful large city, **DRESDEN** survived World War II largely unscathed until the night of February 13, 1945. Then, in a matter of hours, it was reduced to ruins in the most savage saturation bombing ever mounted prior to Vietnam – perhaps as many as 100,000 civilians died, as the city was packed with people fleeing the advancing Red Army. With this background, it's all the more remarkable that Dresden is the one city in the former GDR which seems capable of slotting easily into the economic framework of the reunited Germany, and the post-communist authorities are now brilliantly restoring all the historic buildings left as rubble.

Arrival and accommodation

Dresden has two main **train stations** – the **Hauptbahnhof** is south of the Altstadt, while **Neustadt** is at the northwestern corner of the Neustadt district across the Elbe and only slightly further away from the main sights. The main **tourist office** is just a couple of minutes' walk from the Hauptbahnhof at Pragerstr. 10/11 (April–Sept Mon–

Sat 9am–8pm, Sun 9am–noon; Oct–March Mon–Sat 9am–6pm, Sun 9am–noon); there's also a branch in Neustadt in the underground passageway at the southern side of the Markt (Mon–Fri 9am–6pm, Sat 9am–4pm, Sun 11am–4pm; ☎53549).

Both tourist offices can book **private rooms** (③) and **pensions** (④) to the north-west of the city for a DM3 fee. For late arrivals, there's a special service offered by *Zimmervermittlung Vera Zwerg*, Zschonergrundstr. 1 (☎432 6475), on the route of tram #1. **Hotels** are typically overpriced: the only central budget options are *Stadt Rendsburg*, Kamenzerstr. 1 (☎51551; ⑤), and *Rothenburger Hof*, Rothenburgerstr. 17 (☎502 3434; ⑥). One of the two **youth hostels** is just south of the Hauptbahnhof at Hübnerstr. 11 (☎471 0667; ②); the other is well to the east at Sierksstr. 33 (☎36672; ②; bus #84). There are two **campsites** within the city boundaries, both with bungalows to rent: *Mockritz*, Boderitzerstr. 8 (tram #15 or #16, or bus #76), and *Wostra*, at Triekestrasse, on the banks of the Elbe (tram #9 or #14).

The City

If you arrive at the Hauptbahnhof, you see the worst of modern Dresden first, as the **Pragerstrasse** is an example of Stalinist planning on the grand scale – a spacious pedestrian precinct containing the standard cocktail of high-rise luxury hotels, public offices, box-like flats, soulless cafés and restaurants catering mainly for organized tour groups, with a few fountains and statues thrown in for relief. At the far end, beyond the inner ring road, is the **Altmarkt**, which was much extended after its wartime destruction; the only building of note which remains is the **Kreuzkirche**, a church which has undergone many remodellings down the centuries. The present structure mixes a Baroque body with a Neoclassical tower and a modernized interior impressive in its starkness and loftiness. On Saturdays at 6pm and at the 9.30am Sunday service you can usually hear the *Kreuzchor*, one of the world's leading church choirs.

Behind stands the Rathaus, built early this century in a lumbering historicist style complete with a belfry which rises well above that of the church. Further east is the late eighteenth-century Gewandhaus, the old cloth hall, which has been transformed into a hotel. Across the wide St-Petersburgerstrasse from here is the contemporaneous **Landhaus** (daily except Fri 10am–6pm; DM2), containing an unusually interesting museum devoted to the history of the city.

North of here, the **Albertinum** houses temporary exhibitions, the coin cabinet and the **Skulpturversammlung**, which is particularly strong in works of the classical world, including outstanding Roman copies of lost Greek originals. West of the Albertinum is the Neumarkt, formerly dominated by the **Frauenkirche**. Only a fragment of wall was left standing after the war, and the communists decided to leave it in this condition as a permanent memorial. After fierce controversy, the decision was taken in 1991 to rebuild it completely.

The colossal **Residenzschloss** of the Electors of Saxony was also wrecked in the war, and the rebuilding programme now underway is a massive task: even the projected completion date of 2006 – the city's 800th anniversary – seems optimistic. In the meantime, the **Mirror Rooms** (Mon, Tues & Fri–Sun 9am–5pm, Thurs 9am–6pm; DM5), which miraculously survived, contain the **Grünes Gewölbe** or Green Vault (Mon, Tues & Fri–Sun 9am–5pm, Wed 9am–6pm; DM5), a dazzling array of treasury items, and one of the richest in the world. Masterpieces from many periods are on view, but the most fetching works are the Baroque fancies specially created by the Saxon Electors' own jeweller, Johann Melchior Dinglinger. His *Court of Delhi on the Birthday of the Great Moghul* is a real *tour de force*, featuring 137 gilded and enamelled figures studded with 3000 diamonds, emeralds, rubies and pearls.

At the end of nearby Augustus Strasse is the Baroque **Hofkirche** – the existence of this Catholic church in a staunchly Protestant province is explained by the fact that the Saxon rulers converted in order to gain the Polish throne. The church's gleaming white interior features an ornate pulpit by the great sculptor of Dresden Baroque, Balthasar Permoser. The plush **Opernhaus** opposite was built by the leading architect of nineteenth-century Dresden, Gottfried Semper, and saw the first performances of Wagner's *The Flying Dutchman* and *Tannhäuser* and Richard Strauss's *Der Rosenkavalier*.

THE ZWINGER

Baroque Dresden's great glory was the palace known as the **Zwinger**, which was built facing the Residenzschloss; fortunately it was far less damaged in the war, and was quickly restored. It's a daringly original building: a vast open space with fountains surrounded by a single-storey gallery linking two-storey pavilions, and entered by exuberantly grandiose gateways. The effect is further enhanced by superbly expressive decoration by Permoser.

The Zwinger contains several museums. Beautifully displayed in the southeastern pavilion, entered from Sophienstrasse, is the **Porzellansammlung** (daily except Fri 9am–5pm; DM5); products from the famous Meissen factory are extensively featured. A small natural history display, the **Tierkundemuseum** (9am–4pm; closed Thurs & Fri; DM2), is housed in the southern gallery. The southwestern pavilion is known as the **Mathematisch-physikalischer Salon** (daily except Thurs 9.30am–5pm; DM3), which offers a fascinating array of globes, clocks and scientific instruments. In the northeastern part of the nineteenth-century extension is the **Historisches Museum** (daily except Wed 9am–5pm; DM3), featuring various weapons (including the sword of Elector Frederick the Valiant) and the coronation robes of Augustus the Strong.

The extension also contains the **Gemäldegalerie Alte Meister** (Tues & Thurs–Sun 9am–5pm, Wed 9am–6pm; DM7.50). The Saxon Electors' collection of old masters ranks among the dozen best in the world, and includes some of the most familiar Italian Renaissance paintings: Raphael's *Sistine Madonna*, Correggio's *Holy Night*, Giorgione's *Sleeping Venus*, Titian's *Christ and the Pharisees* and Veronese's *Marriage at Cana*. The German section includes Dürer's *Dresden Altarpiece*, Holbein's *Le Sieur de Morette* and *Thomas and John Godsalve*, and Cranach's *Duke Henry the Pious* and *Duchess Anna of Mecklenburg*, which are among the earliest full-length portraits ever painted. Van Eyck's *Madonna and Child* triptych, executed with miniaturist precision, kicks off a distinguished Low Countries section in which Rubens and Rembrandt are extensively featured. The great artists of seventeenth-century France and Spain are all represented, though the gems of this section are the set of *The Parables* by the short-lived Domenico Feti. Later highlights include one of the greatest of Romantic paintings, Friedrich's *Cross in the Mountains*. Works by most of the French Impressionists and their German contemporaries precede a section devoted to the Expressionists of the Die Brücke group, which was founded in Dresden. Of the later pictures, two pacifist works stand out: *War* by Otto Dix and *The Thousand Year Reich* by Hans Grundig, a local artist who spent four years in a concentration camp. Finally, look out for the brilliantly detailed set of views by Bernardo Bellotto showing Dresden in all its eighteenth-century splendour.

THE NEUSTADT AND SCHLOSS PILLNITZ

Across the Elbe, the **Neustadt** was a planned Baroque town and its layout is still obvious, even if few of the original buildings survive. In the centre of the Markt rises the **Goldener Reiter**, a gilded equestrian statue of the Elector Augustus the Strong – a nickname he earned by siring over three hundred children. The Neustadt's central axis, Strasse der Befreiung, preserves several Baroque houses by Pöppelmann, along with the same architect's **Dreikönigskirche**, nearing the end of its restoration following war damage. In the park overlooking the Elbe is the most esoteric creation of Dresden Baroque, the **Japanisches Palais**, which now contains a turgid archeological museum (Mon–Thurs 9am–5pm, Sun 10am–5pm; DM3). You don't have to pay to see the courtyard, a fantasy inspired by the eighteenth-century infatuation with the Orient.

Schloss Pillnitz, which lies up the Elbe at the extreme edge of the city boundary, is another Pöppelmann creation inspired by the mystique of East; it's also the only part of the city's Baroque heritage to escape war damage altogether. There are actually two summer palaces here: the **Wasserpalais** (daily except Tues 9.30am–5pm; DM3), directly above the river, contains a museum of applied arts; the **Bergpalais** (Tues–Sun 9.30am–5pm; DM3), across the courtyard, is an almost exact replica, whose apartments are themselves the main exhibits. Pillnitz can be reached by taking tram #9 or #14 to the terminus, then crossing by the ferry.

Eating, drinking and nightlife

When planning where to eat or drink in Dresden, it's worth remembering that Neustadt generally offers better value than more tourist-oriented places close to the main sights. In the old town, the city's most frequented venue is *Haus Altmarkt*, on the corner of Altmarkt and St-Petersburgerstrasse, a huge complex with a German cellar restaurant plus four cafés and bars. Also on Altmarkt, there's a classy restaurant on the second floor of the *Kulturpalast*, and, if desperate, a *McDonalds*. The *Gaststätte am Gewandhaus*, Am Gewandhaus, serving substantial German dishes, is tucked away on a quiet square. In Neustadt, *Kügelgenhaus* at Str. der Befreiung 13 is probably Dresden's best café-cum-restaurant, in a Baroque building with a beer cellar. In the same district, *Blockhaus*, Neustädter Markt 19, specializes in Russian dishes. *Am Thor*, on the corner of Str. der Befreiung and Platz der Einheit, is the place in Dresden for good beer, and also serves excellent food. As for nightlife, the *Jazzclub Tonne*, Tzschimerplatz 3, is the main jazz venue, with live music on Fridays, Saturdays and Sundays. *Bärenzwinger*, Brühlscher Garten, is a student club with a varied nightly programme of discos, films and music.

Meissen

Reachable from Dresden by a cruise down the Elbe or by S-Bahn train, the porcelain-producing town of **MEISSEN** is one of the most photogenic cities in Germany, but, unlike Dresden, it survived World War II almost unscathed. Although it has lain in Dresden's shadow since the sixteenth century, Meissen is the more ancient of the two: from the tenth century, it was one of the main outposts of Germany's medieval expansion eastwards into Slav territory. Walking towards the centre from the train station, lying on the other side of the Elbe, you can immediately see the strategic importance of the town and its commandingly sited castle. The present building, the **Albrechtsburg** (daily 9am–4pm; closed Jan; DM2), is not the original, but a late fifteenth-century combination of military fortress and residential palace. As work was nearing completion, the court decamped to Dresden, leaving it as something of a white elephant; this explains the somewhat bare feeling of most of the interior, which overenthusiastic nineteenth-century Romantic painters tried to liven up, with dubious consequences. Nonetheless, the spectacular vaulting alone justifies a look inside; you also get to walk up the beautiful external staircase, the Grosse Wendelstein, the building's other main feature.

Cocooned within the castle precinct is the **Dom** (daily 9am–4.30pm; DM3). For the most part it's a pure Gothic structure, but the distinctive openwork spires which dominate Meissen's skyline were added only in the first decade of this century. Inside, look out for the superb brass tomb plates of the Saxon dukes; the rood screen with its colourful altarpiece by Cranach; and the statues of the founders in the choir, made in the great Naumburg workshop.

Between the castle hill and the Elbe lies the atmospheric Altstadt, a series of twisting and meandering streets ideal for an aimless stroll. Centrepiece is the Markt, dominated by the Renaissance Rathaus. On its own small square to the side is the flamboyant Gothic **Frauenkirche**, whose carillon, fashioned from local porcelain, can be heard six times daily. The church's **tower** (daily except Wed 2–5pm; DM1) commands a superb view of the city and Elbe. On the terrace just above is the celebrated **Gasthaus Vinzenz Richter**, a half-timbered old tavern which preserves an eighteenth-century wine press. The wines served here have the reputation of being the best in eastern Germany. The **Staatliche Porzellan-Manufaktur Meissen** (tours 8am–noon & 1–4pm; DM1), about 1.5km south of the Markt, is easiest reached by going down Fleischer Gasse, then continuing straight down Neu Gasse; it's also close to the S-Bahn terminus, Meissen-Triebischtal. This is the latest factory to manufacture Dresden china, whose invention came about when Augustus the Strong imprisoned the alchemist Johann Friedrich Böttger in the Albrechtsburg, ordering him to produce some gold. Instead, he invented the first true European porcelain, according to a formula which remains secret. In addition to seeing the works, you can also view the **museum** (Tues–Sun 8am–4pm; DM1), which includes many of the finest achievements of the factories, most notably some gloriously over-the-top Rococo fripperies made by the most talented artist ever employed here, Joachim Kaendler.

Practicalities

Meissen's **tourist office** is near the main road bridge over the Elbe at Willi-Anker-Str. 32 (Mon–Fri 9am–noon & 1–5pm). If you're staying, the tourist office books **private rooms**, or there are several **hotels** costing far less than their Dresden counterparts: best are *Hamburger Hof*, Dresdenerstr. 9 (☎03521/2118; ③), handy for the train station, and *Goldener Löwe*, Rathenauplatz 6 (☎3304; ③), which offers an unbeatable central location. There's a **youth hostel** at Wildsrufferstr. 28 (☎3065; ②) and a **campsite** south of town on the left bank of the Elbe. For **eating** and **drinking**, the one unmissable place is the *Vinzenz Richter*; other possibilities include the *Ratskeller* and *Am Tuchmachertor* below the Frauenkirche, or, in the castle precinct, the *Domkeller* and *Burgkeller*.

travel details

Trains

Berlin to: Leipzig (hourly; 2hr 30min); Dresden (17 daily; 2hr 30min); Erfurt (4 daily; 4hr); Frankfurt (4 daily; 7–8hr); Hamburg (3 daily; 4hr 20min); Hannover (9 daily; 4–5hr); Munich (4 daily; 9–10hr); Weimar (4 daily; 3hr 40min).

Bremen to: Hannover (every 30min; 1hr).

Cologne to: Aachen (every 20min; 45min); Düsseldorf (frequent; 25min); Frankfurt (hourly; 2hr 15min); Heidelberg (hourly; 2hr 50min); Mainz (hourly; 1hr 45min); Stuttgart (hourly; 3hr 25min).

Dresden to: Bad Schandau (every 30min; 1hr); Meissen (every 30min; 40min).

Frankfurt to: Baden Baden (10 daily; 1hr 30min); Berlin (4 daily; 7–8hr); Cologne (hourly; 2hr 15min); Hamburg (hourly; 3hr 30min); Hannover (hourly; 2hr 20min); Heidelberg (every 30min; 1hr); Munich (6 daily; 4hr); Nürnberg (6 daily; 2hr); Würzburg (6 daily; 1hr).

Hamburg to: Bremen (hourly; 1hr); Hannover (every 30min; 1hr 25min); Lübeck (every 30min; 40min).

Hannover to: Goslar (hourly; 1hr 20min); Hildesheim (every 20min; 25min).

Koblenz to: Trier (hourly; 90min).

Leipzig to: Dresden (hourly; 1hr 30min); Frfurt (hourly; 50min); Meissen (5 daily; 2hr–3hr 30min); Naumburg (hourly; 1hr 40min); Weimar (hourly; 1hr 20min).

Mainz to: Koblenz (frequent; 50min); Worms (every 30min; 40min).

Munich to: Augsburg (every 20min; 30min); Nürnberg (hourly; 1hr 30min); Regensburg (hourly; 2hr); Würzburg (hourly; 2hr 20min).

Münster to: Düsseldorf (every 30min; 1hr 20min).

Nürnberg to: Bamberg (every 30min; 45min); Munich (hourly; 1hr 30min).

Stuttgart to: Freiburg (hourly; 45min); Heidelberg (every 30min; 1hr 10min); Konstanz (hourly; 2hr 40min).

CHAPTER 9

GREAT BRITAIN

To Bergen, Stavanger, Kristiansand & Gothenburg

SCOTLAND

Kyle of Lochalsh
Inverness
Skye
Fort William
Mallaig
Aberdeen
Oban
St Andrews
Glasgow Edinburgh

To Ebsjerg

NORTHERN IRELAND
Belfast
Newcastle
Durham
Ambleside

DUBLIN

IRELAND

Leeds York
Liverpool
Holyhead Manchester
Pwllheli Chester
ENGLAND

To Ebsjerg & Gothenberg

Aberystwyth
Birmingham
King's Lynn Norwich
Coventry
Cambridge
Rosslare Harbour
WALES
Stratford on Avon
Fishguard
Swansea
Cardiff
Oxford
Harwich
To Hook of Holland
Bristol
Windsor LONDON Ramsgate
To Zeebrugge
Salisbury
Brighton
Dover
Exeter
Dunkerque
Calais
Boulogna
Plymouth
Penzance
To Santander & Roscoff
To Cherbourg & Caen
To Le Havre
To Dieppe
FRANCE

0   150 km

Introduction

Though detached from the continent of Europe by just a few miles of water, **Great Britain** is permeated by a strong sense of its cultural separateness. At all levels of society, from the extravagant ceremonials of state to such humble institutions as the village pub, life in Britain retains a continuity with a past that has little in common with its economic partners across the Channel. And while Britain's government harbours doubts about the idea of European unity, many of its citizens have problems with the concept of the United Kingdom. Northern Ireland – covered in our chapter on the island as a whole – is but the most intractable aspect of national identity. Wales, long a nation in its own right, has a vividly autonomous culture, as does the equally historic nation of Scotland, whose people are famously at odds with the conservative hierarchy of London. Within England itself, regional differences are more pronounced than one might expect in a country of such modest size.

Yet the complexity of Britain is not always obvious. The high streets of its cities and towns are beginning to resemble each other more than ever before, with nationwide shops and businesses – many of them multinationals – driving out locally based firms. The tourist infrastructure is very well developed but the growth of a nostalgia-obsessed heritage industry has produced a plethora of museums and theme parks that conjure a rose-tinted simulation of the nation's past. However, the process of discovering the richness of Britain is an immensely satisfying experience. The country is rich in monuments that attest to its intricate history, from ancient hill forts and Roman villas, through a host of medieval cathedrals, to the ambitious civic projects of the Industrial Revolution. In addition, many of the national museums and art galleries are the equal of any in Europe, and most of them remain free of charge, making these stunning collections uniquely accessible.

For cultural sightseeing as for nightlife, **London** is a ceaselessly entertaining city, and inevitably it's the one place in Britain that features on everyone's itinerary. Within the heavily built-up southeast, **Brighton** and **Canterbury** offer contrasting diversions – the former an irresistibly seedy resort, the latter one of Britain's finest medieval cities. The southwest of England, with the rugged moorlands of **Devon** and the rocky coastline of **Cornwall**, is an altogether wilder region, albeit one that pulls in droves of visitors in the height of summer. In the centre of the country, the chief attractions are the university cities of **Oxford** and **Cambridge**, and Shakespeare's town, **Stratford-upon-Avon**, though the often bypassed city of **Norwich**, over in the picturesque flatlands of East Anglia, can be equally rewarding. In the north of England, the industrial cities of **Liverpool**, **Newcastle** and **Manchester** are gritty and lively places, and **York** and **Durham** have splendid historical treasures, but the landscape is again the real magnet, especially the uplands of the **Lake District** and the dales of **Yorkshire**. For true wilderness, however, you're better off heading to the mountains of **Wales** or the Scottish **Highlands**. The finest of Scotland's lochs, glens and peaks, and the magnificent scenery of the west coast **islands**, can be reached easily from the disparate cities of **Glasgow** and **Edinburgh** – itself perhaps the most attractive urban landscape in Britain.

Information and Maps

Tourist offices (usually called Tourist Information Centres) exist in virtually every British town. In high season, the average opening hours are much the same as standard shop hours, with the difference that they'll be open on a Sunday; in winter, it's usual for a tourist office to close a couple of hours earlier each day. All offer a basic range of information on accommodation, local public transport, and maps. In many cases this is free, but a growing number of offices make a small charge for an accommodation list or a town guide with an accompanying street plan. Areas designated as National Parks (such as the Lake District, Exmoor and Dartmoor) also have a fair sprinkling of National Park Information Centres, which are generally more expert in giving guidance on local walks and outdoor pursuits.

The most comprehensive series of **maps** is produced by the Ordnance Survey. The 204 maps in their 1:50,000 *Landranger* series cover the whole country and are just about detailed enough to serve as a walking and hiking aid. The more detailed 1:25,000 *Pathfinder* series is invaluable for serious walking. The best **road maps** are the *Collins* and *Ordnance Survey* road atlases.

Money and Banks

The British **pound** is divided into 100 pence; coins come in denominations of 1p, 2p, 5p, 10p, 20p, 50p and £1; notes in £5, £10, £20 and £50. A note for £1 still exists in Scotland, which issues its own banknotes. Scottish currency is legal tender throughout Britain, although some traders south of the border may be unwilling to accept it.

Normal **banking hours** are Mon–Fri 9.30am–3.30pm. Some branches stay open slightly longer on weekday afternoons, and open for a few hours on Saturday mornings, but there are few hard and fast rules about this.

Communications

Post offices are open Mon–Fri 9am–5.30pm, Sat 9am–12.30/1pm. Stamps can be bought at post offices, from vending machines outside, or from an increasing number of newsagents, although they usually only sell books of 4 or 10 stamps.

Public **payphones** are operated by *British Telecom* and by their rival *Mercury*. Most *Telecom* phones take all coins from 10p upwards, but an increasing proportion now only accept **phonecards**, available from post offices and some newsagents in denominations of £1, £2, £5 and £10; a few even accept credit cards. *Mercury* phones only accept *Mercury* cards (similar availability) and credit cards – and the *Telecom* and *Mercury* cards are not interchangeable. Inland calls are cheapest between 6pm and 8am and at weekends, and the *Mercury* rate is cheaper than *Telecom* over long distances. Reduced rate periods for most international calls are Mon–Fri 8pm–8am and all weekend, though for Australia and New Zealand it's midnight–7am and 2.30–7.30pm daily. The operator number is ☎100.

Getting Around

Most significant places in the country are accessible by train or by coach, usually by both. However **public transport** in Britain has to a large extent fallen victim to market economics, and costs can be higher than elsewhere in Europe.

■ Trains

The **British Rail** network covers most of the country, but it's a London-centric system; travelling out from London is usually extremely quick, but traversing the country from east to west can be less easy. Several parts of the network operate under different names such as Network Southeast, Scotrail, and so on, but they're all part of the same company, at least for now.

The system's main drawback is that standard fares are among the most expensive in Europe, and the pricing system can be bafflingly complicated. **Day returns** are the cheapest standard tickets, sometimes less expensive than a single; on certain major inter-city routes you also get massively reduced **Apex** and **Superapex** tickets, which have to be booked respectively a week and two weeks in advance. The price of an ordinary return depends on the day of travel, Fridays being more expensive than the rest of the week, and weekends in general being pricier than weekdays. On several main-line routes the cost of your trip depends on the time of day you travel.

The only feasible way to get around by train in Britain is to buy a special pass. In addition to *InterRail* (which gives only 30 percent discounts) there's a series of **Britrail** passes only available outside the country. For consecutive days, these begin at $179 ($145 for under-26s) for 8 days, rising to $689 ($375) for a month. Inside the UK, a **Young Person's Railcard**, from all station ticket offices for £16, allows 30 percent reductions on travel for those under 24 or in full-time study, with discounts on ferries to Ireland. There are also regional passes, like the seven-day *Freedom of Wales* and the *Highlands and Islands* passes, but these are only attractive if you're exploring these particular areas very intensively. *Eurail* passes are not valid in Britain. If travelling on routes between London and other major cities during public holidays or around Christmas it's advisable to **book a seat** a couple of days in advance. Seat reservations are free if made at the same time as purchasing a ticket, an extra £1 otherwise.

■ Buses

The long-distance **coach** services run by **National Express** duplicate many inter-city rail routes, very often at half the price or less. The frequency of service is often comparable to rail, and in many instances the difference in journey time isn't great enough to be a deciding factor. Coaches are comfortable, and longer journeys – designated *Rapide* services – often have drinks and sandwiches available on board. *National Express*'s sister company in Scotland is *Caledonian Express*, which operates services between Scotland and England and within Scotland itself. For busy routes and on any route at weekends and during holidays it's a good idea to buy a "reserved journey ticket", which guarantees you a seat. Non-UK residents are entitled to a *Britexpress* card, costing £12, which provides 30 percent reductions on fares over a 30-day period, or a **Tourist Trail Pass**, which offers unlimited travel on the *National Express* network. An 8-day pass costs £63 for students and under-23s, £90 for others; a 15-day pass £95 and £135 respectively; a 30-day pass £133 and £190.

Local bus services are run by a bewildering array of companies, some private, some not; in most cases, however, timetables and routes are well integrated. As a rule, the further away from urban areas you get, the less frequent and more expensive bus services become, but there are very few rural areas which aren't served by at least the occasional privately owned minibus.

■ Driving and hitching

Unlike continental Europe, Britain drives on the left, a situation which makes the roads around the Channel ports particularly hazardous. **Speed limits** are 30–40mph in built-up areas, 70mph on motorways and dual carriageways, 50mph on most other roads. **Car rental** costs from around £150 per week with unlimited mileage; many towns will have small companies whose rates undercut the big names, but you'll have to return the car to the place from which you rented it. The *Automobile Association* and the *Royal Automobile Club* both operate 24-hour emergency breakdown services. On motorways they can be called from roadside booths; elsewhere ring ☎0800/887766 for the *AA*, ☎0800/828282 for the *RAC* – both numbers are free.

The extensive motorway network and the density of traffic makes long-distance **hitching** relatively easy, though in rural areas you might be hanging around a long time.

Accommodation

The prevalence of bed and breakfasts and youth hostels ensures that budget **accommodation** isn't hard to come by in the UK. All tourist offices will book rooms for you, although the fee for this service varies considerably. In some areas you will merely pay a deposit, in others the office will take a percentage commission. The average is around £2, but you can pay more than twice this amount in tourist centres like London and Oxford, but only £1 or nothing at all in Scotland.

■ Hotels and bed and breakfast

Hotel accommodation in Britain is generally of a high quality but it's also expensive – in tourist cities it's difficult to find a double for less than £40. Fortunately, there's a wide range of budget accommodation in the form of **bed and breakfasts**, which often consists of a comfortable room in a family home, followed by a reasonably substantial breakfast, from around £10 a head – a few pounds more in the affluent south, and a lot more in London. The boundary separating bed and breakfasts from small hotels is a hazy one in some areas; many of the latter offer the same service for a similar price. Many B&Bs have a very small number of rooms – those listed in this guide are ones in which you stand a better chance of finding a vacancy if you arrive on spec. Even so, in summer and holiday periods several days advance booking is always advisable.

■ Hostels and camping

Britain has an extensive network of **IYHF hostels**, operated by the autonomous associations for Scotland and for England and Wales. In Scotland a bed for the night costs as little as £3.90, except in the cities, where the maximum is £6.50. In England and Wales the charge for under-18s is generally a little higher than this (a lot

---

ACCOMMODATION PRICE CODES

Throughout this guide, accommodation is priced on a scale of ① to ⑧, the number indicating the lowest price per night a single person could expect to pay in that establishment in high season. With hostels this is the nightly rate per person; with hotels, the price is arrived at by dividing the cost of the cheapest double room by two. The prices indicated by the codes are as follows

① = under £5 / $8　② = £5–10 / $8–16　③ = £10–15 / $16–24　④ = £15–20 / $24–32

⑤ = £20–25 / $32–40　⑥ = £25–30 / $40–48　⑦ = £30–35 / $48–56　⑧ = over £35 / $56

higher in London), and over-18s pay around 50 percent more than the youth tariff. Catering varies with the size of the hostel, from a set meal at a set time in the smaller ones to a cafeteria system in the bigger ones. Some of the more basic hostels – and all rural ones in Scotland – still retain a duty roster where you may be set a few cleaning chores, but generally hostels are shedding this old-fashioned image and being updated in an attempt to attract a wider public, with facilities for families and professional people. The *YHA* for England and Wales is at Trevelyan House, 8 St Stephen's Hill, St Albans, Herts AL1 2DY(☎0727/55215); the Scottish *YHA* is at 76 Glebe Crescent, Stirling FK8 2JA (☎0786/51181).

There are more than 750 official **campsites** in Britain, charging from £5 per tent per night. In the countryside farmers will let you camp in a field if you ask, sometimes charging a couple of pounds for the privilege. Camping rough is illegal in designated parkland and nature reserves.

Food and Drink

British **cuisine** does not enjoy the highest of reputations, but it's possible to eat well and cheaply in Britain thanks chiefly to the influence of immigrant communities. Social life has always focused more on drinking than eating, and the British pub is often the best introduction to a town.

■ Food

In many bed and breakfast establishments you'll be offered what's termed an **"English breakfast"**, which is basically sausage, bacon and eggs. This used to be the typical working-class breakfast, but these days the British are a nation of cereal eaters, and most places will give you this option as well. Though every major town will have its upmarket restaurant specializing in classic meat-based British food, for most customers the quintessential British meal is **fish and chips**, a dish that can vary from the succulently fresh to the indigestibly greasy. Fish and chip shops – sometimes with tables, but more often not – can be found on most high streets and main suburban thoroughfares, although in larger towns they're beginning to be outnumbered by pizza, kebab and burger outlets. Another standard feature is the so-called "greasy spoon" **café**, where the average menu will include bacon sandwiches and

cholesterol-rich variations on a sausage, beans, fried egg and chips theme. Less rudimentary meat-and-vegetable dishes form the basis of most mid-range menus – steak and kidney pie, shepherd's pie, chops and steaks being the regular staples, accompanied by boiled potatoes, carrots or some such plain veg. However, there's an increasing number of vegetarian restaurants, especially in the larger towns, and most restaurants make some attempt to cater for vegetarians.

For sit-down eating, the innumerable types of **ethnic restaurant** offer the best-value good-quality meals. In every town of any size you'll find Chinese, Indian or some other immigrant specialities, with the widest choice in London and the industrial cities of the north.

Nowadays the vast majority of **pubs** serve food of one sort or another, and although this often consists of microwaved pies and chips, the range and quality is improving all the time. Most serve food at lunchtime, with the minority keeping the kitchen open during the evening.

■ Drink

Drinking traditionally takes place in a public house, or **pub**, where a standard range of beers and lagers – sold by the pint or half-pint – generates most of the business. The drink on offer doesn't vary much from pub to pub, though imported bottled beers are becoming very fashionable and each region has its own specialist breweries, producing the so-called "real ales" that maintain the traditional flavours of English beer. A growing number of pubs now serve tea and coffee during the day. In England pubs are generally open Mon–Sat 11am–11pm (some close between about 3 & 5.30pm) and Sun 11.30am–3pm & 7–10.30pm. Hours are often longer in Scotland, while Sunday closing is common in Wales. In bigger towns there's an increasing number of wine bars, European-style cafés and brasseries in which to drink – and they also serve food.

In Scotland, the national drink is of course **whisky**, a spirit of far greater subtlety than the bland mass-marketed whiskies might lead you to believe. The best are the single malts, produced in relatively small quantities from springwater which gives each label its special taste. Only in Scotland will you find a decent choice of whiskies in a pub.

Opening Hours, Holidays and Sites

General shop hours are Mon–Sat 9am–5.30/6pm, although there's an increasing amount of Sunday and late-night shopping in big towns, and in Scotland you'll find more places open on a Sunday than in England. Many towns still retain an "early closing day" when shops close at 1pm – Wednesday is the favourite.

Public holidays in England and Wales are: Jan 1; Good Friday; Easter Monday; first Mon after May 1; last Mon in May; last Mon in August; Dec 25 & 26. In Scotland Jan1, Jan 2 and Dec 25 are the only fixed public holidays – otherwise towns are left to pick their own holidays.

Many of Britain's great national museums are free, but many stately homes and monuments are administered by the private **National Trust**, and the state-run **English Heritage**, whose entry fees can be high. Annual membership of each organization can be obtained at any of their sites and costs £24 and £17 respectively – it gives free entrance to NT and EH properties, and is worth having if you're visiting more than half a dozen of them. Wales is famous for its dramatic ruined castles and churches, many of them cared for by **Cadw**, the Welsh Historic Monuments Commission; annual membership, costing £14, is available at any Cadw property. Annual membership of **Historic Scotland**, the Scottish counterpart to Cadw, is also £14.

Emergencies

Although the traditional image of the friendly British bobby has become increasingly tarnished, **police** remain approachable and helpful. Tourists aren't a particular target for criminals except perhaps in the crowds of central London, where you should be on your guard against pickpockets. Britain's bigger conurbations all contain inner-city areas where you may feel uneasy after dark, but these are usually away from tourist sights.

Pharmacists can dispense only a limited range of drugs without a doctor's prescription. Most pharmacies are open standard shop hours, though in large towns some may stay open as late as 10pm. Local newspapers carry lists of late-opening pharmacies. Doctor's surgeries tend to be open from about 9am to noon and then for a couple of hours in the evenings; outside surgery hours, you can turn up at the casualty department of the local hospital for complaints that require immediate attention – unless it's an emergency, in which case ring for an ambulance.

EMERGENCY NUMBERS
Dial ☎999 for Fire, Police and Ambulance.

LONDON

With a population of nearly seven million, **LONDON** is by far Europe's biggest city, spreading over an area of more than 1500 square kilometres from its core on the River Thames. This is where the country's news and money is made, and as far as its inhabitants are concerned, provincial life begins beyond the circuit of the orbital motorway. Londoners' sense of superiority causes some resentment in the regions, but it's undeniable that London has an unmatched charisma, a unique aura of excitement and success. Yet despite this dominance, London is the only capital in Europe that lacks its own governing body, a symptom of a decade's political indifference to its special needs. The result is a city of ostentatious private affluence – high-rise Canary Wharf in the redeveloped Docklands is the most conspicuous new example – and increasing public squalor. At night, the doorways of the West End become the dormitories of the growing band of London's homeless, while during the day the city's commuters do battle with a public transport system that is close to breaking point.

London should be better than it is, but it is still a thrilling place. The central thoroughfares, buzzing far into the night, are interspersed with quiet squares and explorable alleyways. Contrary to many expectations, it's a very green city, with sizeable parks right in the centre – Hyde Park, Green Park and St James' – and the vast open spaces of Hampstead Heath, Greenwich and Kew on the periphery. Its museums and galleries are as varied and as rich as you'll find anywhere, and the majority of the great collections are free, even if they are now obliged to ask for voluntary donations with increasing aggression. And, of course, the city is replete with monuments of the capital's more glorious past, from its Roman origins to its role at the centre of the British Empire.

The **Ancient Romans** founded the town of Londinium on the north bank of the Thames in 43 AD, but the city's expansion didn't really begin until the eleventh century, when it became the seat of the last successful invader of Britain, the Norman duke **William II**. The first king of England to be crowned in Westminster Abbey, William was also the builder of the White Tower, the nucleus of the Tower of London. Subsequent monarchs left their imprint, especially around Whitehall, but many of the city's finest structures were destroyed in the course of a few hours in 1666, when the **Great Fire of London** eradicated over 13,000 houses and nearly 90 churches, completing a terrible cycle of destruction begun by the Great Plague of the previous year. Chief beneficiary of the blaze was Sir Christopher Wren, who was commissioned to replace much of the lost architecture, and rose to the challenge by designing such masterpieces as St Paul's Cathedral and the Naval Hospital at Greenwich. Unfortunately, only a portion of the post-Fire splendours has survived, due partly to the German bombing raids of the **Blitz** of 1940–41, and partly to some unimaginative modern development, which has lumbered London with the sort of concrete-and-glass mediocrity that has given modern architects a bad name. However, London's special atmosphere comes not from the appearance of its streets but from its people. This has been a multicultural city since at least the seventeenth century, when it was a haven for Huguenot immigrants. This century has seen the arrival of thousands from the Caribbean, the Indian subcontinent, the Mediterranean and the Far East, playing a large part in defining the character of a metropolis that is not so much a single organism as a patchwork of sub-cities.

Arrival and information

Flying into London, you'll arrive at one of the capital's three international airports, Heathrow, Gatwick or Stansted, each of which is less than an hour from the city centre.

Getting into London from **Heathrow**, twelve miles west of the city, couldn't be easier. The **Piccadilly underground line** connects the airport to central London in under an hour (£2.80), with one station serving terminals 1, 2 and 3, another serving terminal 4. There are also **Airbuses** which run from outside all Heathrow terminals to central destinations in the city: buses take about an hour and cost £5, but can be worth the money if you have a lot of luggage to haul. After midnight, the night bus #N97 runs hourly from Heathrow to Trafalgar Square. **Taxis** are plentiful, but will set you back around £30.

Gatwick Airport is thirty miles to the south, and *British Rail*'s non-stop *Gatwick Express* runs every fifteen minutes between the airport's South Terminal and Victoria (30mins; £8.70). *Flightline 777* **coaches** depart Gatwick's North and South Terminals once an hour between 5am and 10pm and cost £7.50, arriving at Victoria Coach Station approximately seventy minutes later.

The smaller **Stansted Airport** lies 34 miles northeast of the capital and is served by trains to Liverpool Street (Mon–Sat every 30min 6am–11pm, Sun hourly 7am–11pm), which take 45 minutes and cost £9.80, and by *National Express* coaches to Victoria Coach Station (hourly 8.30am–9.30pm), which take 75 minutes and cost £8.75.

Coming into London from abroad by **coach or train**, you'll almost certainly arrive at Victoria – either at the train station, which serves the English Channel ports, or at the coach station, a couple of hundred yards south down Buckingham Palace Road.

Arriving by train from elsewhere in Britain, you'll come into one of London's numerous mainline British Rail stations, all of which have adjacent underground stations that link into the city centre's tube network. (For details of train connections between other parts of Britain and the main-line stations, see P.492.)

Information

London Tourist Board (LTB) has a desk at Heathrow Airport in the underground station concourse for terminals 1, 2 and 3 (daily 8.30am–6.30pm), but the **main central office** is in the forecourt of **Victoria** station (daily 8am–7pm). Other centrally located offices can be found near Piccadilly Circus in the British Travel Centre, 12 Lower Regent St (Mon–Fri 9am–6.30pm, Sat & Sun 10am–4pm), at 35–36 Woburn Place in Bloomsbury (daily 7.30am–7.30pm), and in the basement of *Selfridges* on Oxford Street.

None of these offices will accept telephone queries – the best the LTB can manage is a service of long-winded and dull pre-recorded messages. If you want to hear what's on offer, ring ☎071/730 3488, but be warned that calls to the pre-recorded services are charged at the highest rate

City transport

The fastest way of moving around is by **Underground**, or **Tube**, as it's known to all Londoners. Operating from around 5.30am until shortly after midnight, the eleven different lines cross much of the metropolis, although London south of the river is not well covered and the reliability of certain lines (such as the notorious Northern) is often questionable. Tickets are bought from machines or from a ticket booth in the station entrance hall; the minimum for a single journey is 90p. A **travelcard**, on sale from machines and ticket booths at all tube stations, is also valid for the bus and suburban rail networks, and will quickly save a lot of money. One-day travelcards, valid on weekdays from 9.30am and all day at weekends, cost £2.60 for the central zones 1 and 2, rising to £3.50 for all six zones (which includes Heathrow). Weekly travelcards are even more economical, beginning at £11.90 for zones 1 and 2, which should cover virtually everything you'll want to see; these cards can only be bought by carriers of a **photocard**, which you can get, free of charge, from tube station ticket booths on presentation of a passport photo.

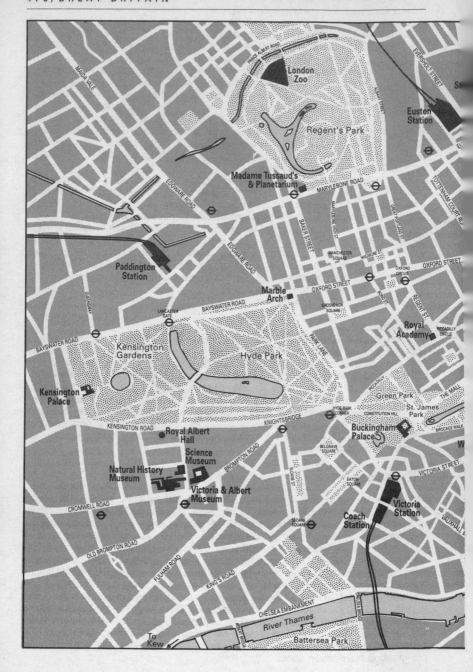

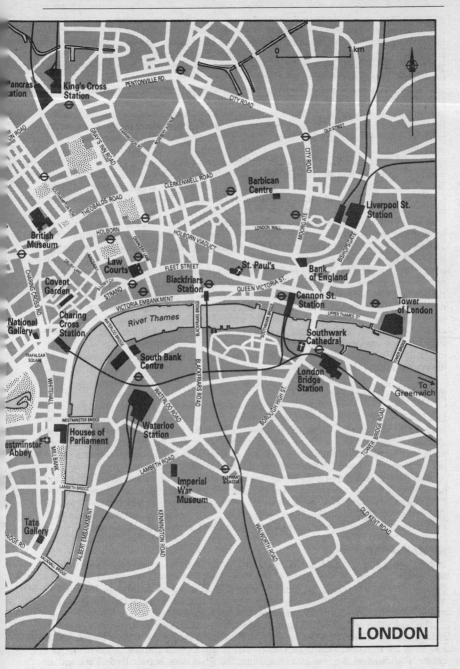

LONDON

The network of **buses** is very dense, but you will soon find that the tube is generally quicker, especially in the summer, when central London becomes a logjam. Journeys cost a minimum of 40p, but the average trip in the centre will cost around 80p; normally you pay the driver on entering, although some routes – especially those which traverse the centre – are covered by older buses with an open rear platform and staffed by a conductor. A lot of bus stops are request stops, so if you don't stick your arm out the bus will drive past. Regular buses operate between about 6am and midnight, and a network of **night buses** (prefixed with the letter "N") operates outside this period, routes radiating out from Trafalgar Square at approximately hourly intervals. Fares are twice as expensive on night buses; one-day travelcards aren't valid on them, but weekly ones are.

The principal **London Transport information office**, providing excellent free maps and details of bus and tube services, is at **Piccadilly Circus tube station** (daily 9am–6pm), and there are other desks at Euston, King's Cross, Liverpool Street, Oxford Circus, St James' Park and Victoria stations. There's also a 24-hour phone line for information on all bus and tube services (☎071/222 1234).

If you're in a group of three or more, London's metered **black cabs** can be an economical way of getting around the centre of town – a ride across the centre, from Euston to Victoria, should cost around £10. A yellow light over the windscreen tells you if the cab is available – just stick your arm out to hail it. (If you want to book one in advance, call ☎071/272 0272.) London's cabbies are the best trained in Europe – every one of them knows the shortest route between any two points in the capital, and won't rip you off by taking another route. **Minicabs** are less reliable than black cabs, as their drivers are just private individuals rather than trained professionals; however, they are often considerably cheaper, so you might want to take one back from your late-night club. There are hundreds of minicab firms in the phone book, but the best way to pick is to take the advice of the place you're at, unless you want to be certain of a woman driver, in which case call *Ladycabs* (☎071/254 3501). Not all minicabs are metered, so always ask for the fare beforehand.

Accommodation

London is a very expensive city and lower-cost **accommodation** in central London tends to be poor quality. However, the sheer size of the place means that there is little chance of failing to find a room even in midsummer, and the underground network makes accommodation outside the centre a feasible option. The capital also has plenty of **hostel** space, both in *YHA* properties and student halls.

We've given phone numbers for all our listed accommodation, but if you fail to find something you could always pay someone else to do the phoning round for you. All the LTB offices listed on P.469 operate a **room booking service**, for which they charge £5 (£1.50 for hostels), and take fifteen percent of the room fee in advance; credit card holders can also book through the LTB by phone (☎071/824 8844).

Hotels and B&Bs

In high season you should phone **hotels** as far in advance as you can if you want to stay within a couple of tube stops of the West End, and expect to pay not much less than £40 for an unexceptional double room without a private bathroom. If travelling with two or more companions, it's always worth asking the price of the family rooms, which generally sleep four and can save you a few pounds.

The best value of the central accommodation areas is **Bloomsbury** – an area which radiates out from the British Museum and the nearby B&B-filled Gower Street, and is less than ten minutes' walk from Oxford Street and Covent Garden. West of the city centre, **Paddington** is a less attractive zone, though it does border Hyde Park and, at its western edges, runs into the vibrant Notting Hill area. For cheap places in this area, check out Norfolk Square and Sussex Gardens. Slightly further from the city's main sights, but the area most favoured by budget travellers, is the network of streets around **Earl's Court** tube, which are packed with cheap, backpacker-oriented establishments – around here, head first for Penywern and Trebovir roads. The streets around **Victoria station** also harbour dozens of inexpensive B&Bs – notably along Belgrave Road and Ebury Street – though the area itself lacks the liveliness of Earl's Court and tends to go dead after the offices shut for the night.

BLOOMSBURY

Arran House Hotel, 77–79 Gower St, WC1 (☎071/636 2186). Bright, well-kept B&B; discounts in winter. Goodge St tube. ⑤

Cosmo-Bedford House Hotel, 27 Bloomsbury Square, WC1 (☎071/636 4661). Centrally located budget-conscious hotel, 150yds from the British Museum. Russell Square or Holborn tube. ⑤

Garth Hotel, 69 Gower St, WC1 (☎071/636 5761). Good value, very friendly establishment, with a small garden. Tottenham Court Road or Goodge Street tube. ④

Jesmond Hotel, 63 Gower St, WC1 (☎071/636 3199). Comfortable and spotless B&B. Goodge St tube. ④

Jesmond Dene Hotel, 27 Argyle St, WC1 (☎071/837 4654). Basic facilities, but the pleasantest of the numerous cheap places along this street near King's Cross, St Pancras and Euston BR stations. King's Cross tube. ④

Maree Hotel, 25 Gower St, WC1 (☎071/636 4868). By far the cheapest in this desirably central area; spartan but fine, with some rooms overlooking the garden. Tottenham Court Road tube. ③

Ridgemount Hotel, 65 Gower St, WC1 (☎071/636 1141). Another good budget B&B. Goodge St tube. ⑤

PADDINGTON

Classic Hotel, 92 Sussex Gardens, W2 (☎071/706 4058). The cheapest option along this tree-lined avenue stacked full of mid-range B&Bs. Large shabby rooms, with discounts for weekly stays. Paddington tube. ③

Continental Hotel, 40 Norfolk Square, W2 (☎071/723 3926). The cheapest of the dozen or so B&Bs in this pleasant leafy square close to the tube. Rooms similar to the *Classic* around the corner and just as cheap. Paddington tube. ③

Dean Court Hotel, 57 Inverness Terrace, W2 (☎071/229 2961). Very close to Hyde Park and worth considering for longer stays as they offer seven nights for the price of six. Queensway or Bayswater tube. ④

Leinster Hotel, 7–12 Leinster Sq, W2 (☎071/727 4412). Huge, budget–oriented establishment close to the lively Notting Hill area, with a variety of rooms from singles to shared 5-bed rooms. Notting Hill Gate or Bayswater tube. ②

Saint David's Hotel, 16 Norfolk Square, W2 (☎071/723 3856). Pleasant, well-appointed B&B in a quiet, attractive square. Paddington tube. ④

Talbot Hotel, 2 Talbot Square, W2 (☎071/402 7202). Nobody's idea of real comfort, but it has bags of room and it's dead cheap – especially if booked for the week or if you stay in the dormitory. Paddington tube. ②

EARL'S COURT

Albion Court Hotel, 1 Trebovir Rd, SW5 (☎071/373 0833). Well-worn but fairly inexpensive rooms in the heart of the low-budget accommodation area; dorm beds also available. Earl's Court tube. ③

Beaver Hotel, 57–59 Philbeach Gardens, SW5 (☎071/373 4553). Quiet and cosy B&B. Earl's Court tube. ④

Manor Hotel, 23 Nevern Place, SW5 (☎071/370 6018). Reasonably priced rooms just off Earl's Court Rd. Earl's Court tube. ④

Merlyn Court, 2 Barkston Gardens, SW5 (☎071/370 1640). Plain but serviceable rooms in quiet square off Earl's Court Rd. Earl's Court tube. ④

Rasool Court, 19 Penywern Rd, SW5 (☎071/373 8900). The cheapest rooms in this B&B-filled street; basic comfort, but all have satellite TV. Earl's Court tube. ③

White House Hotel, 12 Earl's Court Square, SW5 (☎071/373 5903). Basic rooms make this very popular with students. Earl's Court tube. ③

Windsor House, 12 Penywern Rd, SW5 (☎071/373 9087). Simple rooms in a large old Victorian terrace; use of garden and kitchen facilities. Earl's Court tube. ④

York House, 28 Philbeach Gardens, SW5 (☎071/373 7519). Roomy B&B that does large discounts for weekly stays. Earl's Court tube. ④

VICTORIA

Brindle House, 1 Warwick Place North, SW1 (☎071/828 0057). Small, quiet B&B off Warwick Way; all rooms have a TV. Victoria tube. ④

Chester House, 134 Ebury St, SW1 (☎071/730 3632). The cheapest of a host of B&Bs along this road, very convenient for Victoria Coach Station. Victoria tube. ④

Easton Hotel, 36-40 Belgrave Rd (☎071/834 5938). One of the biggest B&Bs in the Victoria area, so worth trying on spec in peak season; rooms adequate for the price. Victoria tube. ④

Holly House, 20 Hugh St, SW1 (☎071/834 5671). The best value B&B in the Belgrave Rd area, though some rooms overlook the railway tracks.Victoria tube. ④

Luna House, 47 Belgrave Rd, SW1 (☎071/834 5897). Inexpensive B&B that needs to be booked at least one month ahead in summer. Victoria tube. ③

Oxford House, 92–94 Cambridge St, SW1 (☎071/834 6467). Very friendly B&B with marvellous food, so booking essential. Victoria tube. ④

Stanley House, 19–21 Belgrave Rd, SW1 (☎071/834 5042). Large, friendly and well-appointed B&B offering a 10 percent discount for weekly stays; all rooms have TV. Victoria tube. ④

Windsor Guest House, 36 Alderney St, SW1 (☎071/828 7922). Homely and very reasonable. Victoria tube. ③

Hostels and camping

Most *YHA* **hostels** in London are a touch less basic and significantly more expensive than those in the provinces, but in summer you'll have to arrive as early as possible to stand a chance of getting a room, and you're usually limited to a maximum stay of four consecutive nights. Some accommodation in **student halls of residence** is available outside term time: contact the King's Campus Vacation Bureau at 552 Kings Rd, SW10 (☎071/351 6011), which has single rooms from £20 in the Kensington, Chelsea and Westminster areas, with some cheaper alternatives (from £16) in outlying Hampstead and Wandsworth. London's **campsites** are all out on the perimeters of the city, offering pitches for around £4, plus a fee of around £3 per person per night (reductions for children and out of season).

YHA HOSTELS

City of London, 36 Carter Lane, EC4 (☎071/236 4965). In the City – a desolate area at night – and with uncomfortably crowded dorms. St Paul's or Blackfriars tube. ④

Earl's Court, 38 Bolton Gardens, SW5 (☎071/373 7083). Comfortable and fairly capacious. Earl's Court tube. ④

Hampstead Heath, 4 Wellgarth Rd, NW11 (☎081/458 9054). One of the biggest and best appointed, near the wilds of Hampstead Heath. Golders Green tube. ③

Highgate Village, 84 Highgate West Hill, N6 (☎081/340 1831). Pleasant setting more than compensates for the walk and longer tube ride to the centre. Archway or Highgate tube. ③

Holland House, Holland Walk, W8 (☎071/937 0748). Nicely situated and fairly convenient for the centre. Holland Park or High Street Kensington tube. ④

Oxford St, 14 Noel St, W1 (☎071/734 1618). In the heart of the West End, but with only 90 beds, it fills up very fast. Oxford Circus or Tottenham Court Rd tube. ④

Rotherhithe, Island Yard, Salter Rd, SE16 (☎071/232 2114). Inconveniently sited on the East London tube line, but a viable option in peak season, with 320 beds available. Rotherhithe tube. ④

CAMPSITES

Crystal Palace, Crystal Palace Parade, SE19 (☎081/778 7155). All-year site, maximum one-week stay in summer, two weeks in winter. Main-line train from London Bridge to Crystal Palace or bus #2 or #3.

Hackney Camping, Millfields Rd, Hackney Marshes, E5 (☎081/ 985 7656). Big but very inconvenient, way over in the east of the city. Bus #38 or #55 from Victoria to Hackney Central, then #236 or #276. Open June–Aug

Tent City Summer Tourist Hostel, Old Oak Common Lane, W3 (☎081/743 5708). The cheapest beds in London: dorm accommodation in 14 large tents (single sex and mixed) for £5 per night, or you can pitch your own tent for the same price. Open June–Sept. East Acton tube

The City

London is not a city with a single centre. The money-markets are over in the eastern part of the inner core, in the district known, confusingly for first-time visitors, as the City of London. The heaviest spending is done around Oxford Street, a long way from the Bank of England and its attendant institutions, while the hubs of political and royal London – Parliament and Buckingham Palace – are close to neither. But the area that feels like the fulcrum is the **West End**, lying between these points and defined roughly by the neighbouring spaces of Piccadilly Circus, Leicester Square and Trafalgar Square.

It's the vigour of the streets that provides the buzz at the first two spots. **Leicester Square** is liveliest at night, with people on their way to its big-screen cinemas or to the clubs and restaurants of multi-ethnic Soho to the north. **Piccadilly Circus** is hectic throughout the day, its tarmac choked with cars and buses, its facades lurid with colossal neon advertisements. There's always a gang of wide-eyed sightseers and more desperate cases around the statue popularly referred to as Eros, although it began life as an Angel of Charity, built in honour of Victorian philanthropist Lord Shaftesbury. The street named after him curves away to the east, while to the north runs the elegant curve of Regent Street, planned by Regency architect Nash as the first phase of an avenue leading all the way to Regent's Park.

Trafalgar Square and the National Gallery

The huge traffic island of **Trafalgar Square** is dominated by Nelson's Column, a 185-foot pillar surmounted by a statue of Admiral Horatio Nelson, who died in the defeat of the French navy at the Battle of Trafalgar in 1805. Four lions designed by Victorian painter Edwin Landseer guard the column's base, and two adjacent fountains provide a magnet for overheating sightseers during the summer. At the south of the square, a small triangular traffic island bearing a statue of Charles I marks the original site of **Charing Cross**, from which all distances from the capital are measured. The place derives its name from the last of a series of crosses erected by Edward I to mark the progress of his wife Eleanor's funeral procession; the cross itself has been moved to the forecourt of Charing Cross train station, just up the Strand to the east.

The bulk of the **National Gallery** (Mon–Sat 10am–6pm, Sun 2–6pm; free except for special exhibitions), one of the world's great art collections, extends across the north side of the square. Britain may have produced few great artists of its own, and may be able to boast few enlightened patrons, but it has produced some astute and predatory collectors, especially during the eighteenth century, when many aristocrats saw the Grand Tour of Europe as a high-culture shopping spree. Consequently, London has a show of paintings from all the major European schools that matches almost any collection in the countries the artists worked in. A quick tally of the National's Italian masterpieces, for example, would include works by Piero della Francesca, Raphael, Botticelli, Uccello, Michelangelo, Caravaggio, Titian, Paolo Veronese and Mantegna. From Spain there are dazzling pieces by Velasquez (including the *Rokeby Venus*), El Greco and

Goya. From the Low Countries there's Memling, van Eyck (the *Arnolfini Marriage*), van der Weyden and Rubens, and an array of Rembrandt paintings that feature some of his most searching portraits. Poussin, Lorrain, Watteau and the only David painting in the country are the earlier highlights of a French contingent that comes right to the present century with Seurat, Cézanne and water lilies from Monet.

If you want to take the art chronologically, you should start in the new Sainsbury Wing, a timidly provocative post-modern building opened in June 1991. The compactness of the rooms makes it impossible to get a clear view of many of the pictures at peak times (Sunday afternoon is often hellish), and there's nearly always a snarl-up created by people queuing to pay reverence to the Leonardo cartoon, installed in a chapel behind his *Virgin of the Rocks*. High Renaissance and later works are displayed in the main building, but even the addition of the Sainsbury Wing hasn't created enough space for all the National's paintings to be properly exhibited – don't overlook the basement galleries, which are stacked with excellent pictures.

The western side of Trafalgar Square is occupied by the church of St Martin-in-the-Fields, James Gibbs' stately early eighteenth-century structure, which combines classical columns and pediment with a distinctly unclassical spire. Around the back of the National Gallery in St Martin's Place is the **National Portrait Gallery** (Mon–Fri 10am–5pm, Sat 10am–6pm, Sun 2–6pm; free), founded in 1856 to house uplifting depictions of the good and the great. Though it does include some fine pieces, such as Hans Holbein's larger than life drawing of Henry VIII, many of the paintings on show here are of less intrinsic interest than their subjects. Nonetheless, the museum works well both as a history of portraiture as a genre, and as a who's who of famous Brits. The collection is arranged with the Tudors on the top floor, eminent Victorians grouped by profession in the middle, and twentieth-century artists, politicians and royalty at the bottom. From time to time a part of the building is given over to a special exhibition – the photography shows are often excellent.

From Whitehall to Westminster Abbey

Trafalgar Square is joined to Parliament Square by the broad sweep of **Whitehall**, the site of the main concentration of government buildings and civil service offices. The original Whitehall was a palace built for King Henry VIII and subsequently extended, but little survived a fire of 1698. The only remnant is the supremely elegant **Banqueting House** (Mon–Sat 10am–5pm; £2.75), built by Inigo Jones for James I in the Palladian style, and decorated with vast paintings by Rubens, glorifying the Stuart dynasty. They were commissioned by James' son Charles I – who in 1649 stepped onto the executioner's scaffold from one of the building's front windows.

Current monarchical tradition is displayed at the **Horse Guards** building on the opposite side of the road. Mounted sentries of the Queen's Life Guard, in ceremonial uniform, are posted daily here from 10am to 4pm, after which they are replaced by horseless colleagues. Try and time your visit to coincide with the changing of the guard (Mon–Sat 11am, Sun 10am), when a squad of mounted troops in full livery arrive from the Parade Ground to the rear.

Further down this west side of Whitehall is the most famous street in the city, **Downing Street**. Number 10 has been the residence of the Prime Minister since the house was presented to Sir Robert Walpole by King George II in 1732. Nowadays you can only gaze at the doorway from afar, as public access has been denied since Margaret Thatcher ordered a pair of wrought-iron gates to be installed at the junction with Whitehall – a highly symbolic act, in the opinion of many. During the Blitz the government was forced to vacate Downing Street in favour of a bunker in King Charles St, which separates the Home Office from the Foreign Office. The restored **Cabinet War Rooms** (daily 10am–6pm, last admission 5.15pm; £3.80) now provide a glimpse of the claustrophobic suites from which Churchill directed wartime operations.

The **Houses of Parliament** (or Palace of Westminster to give it its proper title) stand on the site of the palace that was the seat of the English kings for five centuries before Henry VIII moved the court to Whitehall. The House of Commons, previously ensconced in the chapterhouse of Westminster Abbey, moved into Westminster soon afterwards, thus beginning the site's associations with Parliament. The jumble of buildings which made up the Palace burned down in 1834, and save for a few pieces of the original structure buried deep inside the current edifice, what one sees today is entirely nineteenth-century. Charles Barry, the architect chosen to rebuild the Palace, was told to construct something which expressed national greatness through the use of Gothic or Elizabethan styles – the resulting orgy of pinnacles and tracery is nevertheless restrained by the building's blocky symmetry. Although the angular Victoria Tower at the south end is higher, the more ornate clock tower to the north is more famous; "Big Ben", the name applied to this tower, is in fact the name of its main bell.

The Victorian love of pseudo-Gothic detail shines through in the warren of committee rooms and offices, which were largely the responsibility of Barry's assistant on the project, Augustus Pugin, who was to become the leading ideologue of the Gothic revival. Unfortunately, it's difficult to observe all this at first-hand: both the House of Commons and the House of Lords have public galleries, but entrance is granted to just a few people on a first-come first-served basis – unless you obtain tickets from your local MP or embassy in London. Debates in the Commons – the livelier house – begin at 2.30pm each weekday except Friday, when they start at 9.30am; recesses occur at Christmas, Easter, and from August to mid-October. The public entrance leads into one of the few remaining parts of the original Palace of Westminster, the eleventh-century **Westminster Hall**. This cavernous space, with its magnificent fourteenth-century oak-beamed roof, used to be the nation's law courts, and Sir Thomas More, Guy Fawkes and Charles I all passed through here on their way to the block. The last conviction was avenged when Charles II had Cromwell's exhumed head placed on the roof of the hall on the end of a pole in 1661 – where it remained for over twenty years.

Westminster Abbey (Mon, Tues, Thurs & Fri 9am–4.45pm, Wed 9am–4.45pm & 6–7.45pm, Sat 9am–2.45pm & 3.45–5.45pm, last admission always 45min before closing; Royal chapels £3, free Wed eve; chapterhouse, undercroft museum & pyx combined £2, closed Wed eve), on the western side of Parliament Square, was founded in the eighth century, then rebuilt by the eleventh-century monarch Edward the Confessor and by Henry III in the thirteenth. From William the Conqueror onwards, the Abbey has been the venue for all but two coronations, and the site of all royal burials for the half-millennium between Henry III and George II. Many of the nation's most famous citizens are honoured here, too, and the interior is crowded with monuments, reliefs and statuary. Floor plaques immediately inside commemorate Winston Churchill and the Unknown Soldier, buried in earth taken from the battlefields of World War I, although the best of the monuments lie beyond the choir. The north transept, traditionally reserved for statesmen, includes the tombs of nineteenth-century prime ministers Peel, Palmerston and Gladstone; Poet's Corner, in the south transept, contains the graves of Geoffrey Chaucer, Lord Tennyson, T.S. Eliot and many others. Behind the high altar is the chapel of Edward the Confessor, canonized in the twelfth century and still adored by pilgrims for his powers of healing. In front of Edward's tomb is the Coronation Chair, an oak monstrosity dating from around 1300 which squats above the Stone of Scone – the Scottish coronation stone until Edward I pilfered it in 1297 in a demonstration of his mastery of the north. Many of the nearby royal tombs are surmounted by superb effigies; one of the finest is the black marble sarcophagus of Henry VII and his spouse, housed at the rear of the abbey below an elaborate fan-vaulted ceiling. The ambulatory is the resting place of his granddaughters, Queen Elizabeth I and Queen Mary.

—

Doors on the south side of the nave lead to the **Great Cloister** (daily summer 10.30am–6pm; winter 10.30am–4pm; £2), at the eastern end of which are entrances to the Chapterhouse, retaining its thirteenth-century paving stones; the Chamber of the Pyx – the sacristy of Edward the Confessor's church and subsequently the royal treasury; and the Norman undercroft, now housing the Abbey museum, in which several generations of royal death masks are displayed.

The Tate Gallery

From Parliament Square the unattractive Millbank runs south along the river towards the **Tate Gallery** (Mon–Sat 10am–5.50pm, Sun 2–5.50pm; free except for temporary exhibitions), with both the national collection of British art from the sixteenth century onwards and an international display of modern art. With the exception of the roomful of glutinous Pre-Raphaelites, the quintessentially English landscapes of John Constable, and the Turner paintings crammed into the adjoining Clore Gallery – London's boldest post-modern building – the native art is not what brings the crowds in. Though underfunded by the standards of the world's top galleries, and unable to buy as much new work as it would like, the Tate has a massive stock of twentieth-century pieces, and the modern collection is re-hung every nine months to ensure a decent airing for the whole range. Thus it's difficult to predict what will be on display, but certain names survive every rearrangement: Picasso, Matisse, Degas, Miró and Pollock, to select just a few. Comprehensive assemblies of Constructivism, Surrealism, Minimal Art, Pop Art, Dada and Expressionism (both abstract and Germanic) are regular attractions, and there's nearly always a temporary exhibition in progress – ranging from modest one-artist shows to surveys of entire movements. As with the National Gallery, weekends can be a real crush, especially Sunday afternoon, a favourite slot with the coach parties.

The Mall

The southwestern exit of Trafalgar Square is marked by the imposing Admiralty Arch, built in 1910 as the eastern half of a memorial to Queen Victoria; the rest is half a mile away down the tree-lined avenue of **The Mall** in the shape of the statue of Victory in front of Buckingham Palace. Just beyond Admiralty Arch, ranged above the Mall, is Carlton House Terrace, a stretch of imposing Regency town houses built by John Nash. Part of Nash's building is now inhabited by the Institute of Contemporary Arts, or **ICA** (Mon–Sat noon–11pm, Sun noon–10.30pm; galleries only daily noon–7.30pm, Tues until 9pm; day pass £1.50), the city's main general forum for the avant-garde, with frequently changing programmes of exhibitions, films and performances.

Nash was also responsible for landscaping **St James' Park**, which stretches south of the Mall, its lake providing an inner-city reserve for wildfowl and a recreation area for the employees of Whitehall. Continuing towards Buckingham Palace, the Mall passes St James' Palace, a hospital until bon viveur Henry VIII acquired it and began the construction of yet another palace. Ambassadors to the UK are still officially known as Ambassador to the Court of St James, although the court itself has since moved down the road. The palace is closed to visitors, as is Clarence House – residence of the Queen Mother – at the end of the Mall.

Buckingham Palace has served as the monarch's permanent residence since the accession of Queen Victoria, and the building's exterior, remodelled in 1913, is as bland as it's possible to be. The palace has, however, been open to the public since August 1993 for two months of the year (daily 9.30am–5.30pm; £8); at other times there's not much to do save to await the **Changing of the Guard**, when mounted troops ride down the Mall from St James' Palace (daily May–July between 11am & 11.30am; alternate days Aug–April). Around the south side on Buckingham Gate is the **Queen's Picture Gallery** (Tues–Sat 10am–5pm, Sun 2–5pm; £2.50), a rotating selection of paintings taken from the rich royal collections, which include Reynolds, Gainsborough, Rubens, Rembrandt and masses of Canaletto.

Hyde Park and beyond

Following Constitution Hill along the north side of Buckingham Palace brings you to **Hyde Park Corner**, where a Triumphal Arch celebrates Wellington's victory at Waterloo in 1815. Wellington, mounted on his favourite horse, stands below, facing his former residence, Apsley House, on the northern corner of Piccadilly. Known during the Iron Duke's lifetime as Number One, London, the house is now a **Wellington Museum** (closed for restoration until summer 1994), which, as well as Wellington's effects, also features a curious nude statue of the vanquished Napoleon, sculpted by Italian Neoclassicist Canova.

Hyde Park itself was another piece of real estate seized by Henry VIII, who transformed it into his personal hunting ground. At the northeastern extremity of the park is **Marble Arch**, built by Nash in imitation of the arch of Constantius in Rome, and shifted here from in front of Buckingham Palace in 1851. This corner of the park is dominated by **Speaker's Corner**, a Sunday forum for soap-box orators since 1866, when riots persuaded the government to create this island of unfettered speech. Nowadays it's a place to go and enjoy a little theatre, both from the cranks who expound their views and from the often more inventive hecklers. In the middle of the park is the **Serpentine** lake, with a popular lido towards its centre; the nearby **Serpentine Gallery** (daily 10am–6pm; free) hosts contemporary art exhibitions. To the west the park merges into Kensington Gardens, leading up to **Kensington Palace** (summer Mon–Sat 9am–5.30pm, Sun 11am–5.30pm; £3.90; for winter hours call ☎071/ 937.9561), London residence of Charles and Diana, though not necessarily at the same time. The rooms you are permitted to see are a series of early nineteenth-century state apartments and a display of court costume.

A short walk north from Kensington Palace takes you into the Notting Hill district, worth visiting on August Bank Holiday for the riotous **Notting Hill Carnival**, and on any Saturday of the year for the **Portobello Road market**, where hundreds of dealers sell lorryloads of antiques and junk.

The Kensington museums

At the southern end of Kensington Gardens is the **Albert Memorial** (covered by scaffolding indefinitely), an overdecorated Gothic canopy covering a statue of Queen Victoria's much-mourned consort, who died in 1861; he's also the dedicatee of the Royal Albert Hall, home of the famous "Proms" across the road, completed in 1871 on the model of the Pantheon in Rome. To the side of the Albert Hall, Exhibition Road heads south to South Kensington and London's richest concentration of museums. Biggest is the **Victoria and Albert Museum** (Mon noon–5.50pm, Tues–Sun 10am–5.50pm; £3.50 donation requested), the world's finest collection of decorative arts. All historic periods and civilizations are represented in the V&A's eleven-kilometre maze of halls and corridors, with especially strong collections of Byzantine and medieval reliquaries, religious sculpture and other devotional items. The Raphael cartoons, a series of designs for tapestries now in the Vatican, are another highlight, while the recently opened Nehru Gallery holds one of the world's biggest assemblies of Indian sculpture. The museum's Cast Rooms are worth an afternoon in themselves, with their full-scale replicas of Michelangelo's *David*, the doors of Hildesheim cathedral, Trajan's Column, the pulpit of Pisa's cathedral and scores of other sculptural masterpieces. As if tons of exquisite silverware, ivory carvings, costumes, carpets and so forth were not enough, the V&A's temporary shows are among the best to be seen in Britain, ranging from surveys of specialized areas of craft and technology to overviews of entire cultures.

The **Natural History Museum**, across the way on Cromwell Road (Mon–Sat 10am–6pm, Sun 11am–6pm; £4.50, free after 4.30pm Mon–Fri, after 5pm Sat & Sun), usually enthrals the kids, with its massive-jawed skeletons and models of Tyrannosaurus Rex and the more grisly of his prehistoric colleagues. Inventive displays on human biology and ecology are pitched at a different audience, though there are plenty of buttons to press when the concentration flags. The same ticket gets you into the neighbouring **Geological Museum** (same times), where cabinets full of rocks are enlivened considerably by the "Story of the Earth", an audiovisual introduction to tectonic plates, volcanic eruptions, earthquakes and other acts of God. Understandably, the **Science Museum** in Exhibition Road (Mon–Sat 10am–6pm, Sun 11am–6pm; £4, free after 4.30pm) gives a lot of space to British innovation in the era of the Industrial Revolution, featuring eighteenth-century steam engines, George Stephenson's 1813 Puffing Billy, and the achievements of the likes of Humphrey Davy, Michael Faraday and Isambard Kingdom Brunel. It's far from being a chauvinstic show, however, and the museum offers some of the most stimulating interactive displays in London, as it roams through the development of information technology, space travel, medicine – in fact every conceivable area of experimental science.

Covent Garden and the British Museum

To the east of Trafalgar Square lies the area of **Covent Garden**, whose centrepiece is the splendid nineteenth-century market hall which housed London's principal fruit and vegetable market until the 1970s. The structure now shelters a gaggle of self-consciously tasteful shops and arty-crafty stalls – a microcosm of this swish district as a whole, seen at its glossiest in Floral Street. The surrounding piazza, laid out by Inigo Jones in the seventeenth century, and dominated on the western side by Jones' classical St Paul's Church, is a semi-institutionalized venue for buskers and more ambitious street performers.

From here it's a short walk northwards to the district of Bloomsbury, home to the **British Museum** on Great Russell Street (Mon–Sat 10am–5pm, Sun 2.30–6pm; free). As with the V&A, the British Museum is too big to be seen in one go – the best advice is to check the floor plans as you go in, and make for the two or three displays that interest you most. Whichever sections you pick, the exhibits will include some breathtaking items. Archeological treasures of the ancient world dominate the ground floor, where the heaviest flow of visitors winds towards the museum's most famous relics, the Elgin Marbles from the Parthenon. A whole room is devoted to these glorious sculptures, the main series of which probably depicts scenes from a procession in honour of the goddess Athena – though there's a school of thought which says it's a celebration of the victory at Marathon. Greek pottery and statuary fill a phalanx of mind-boggling rooms, one of which contains mighty fragments from two of the wonders of the ancient world, the Mausoleum at Halicarnassus – featuring a marble horse the size of an elephant – and the Temple of Diana at Ephesus.

A wander through the surrounding areas will take you past Roman mosaics and the exquisite Portland Vase; amazing Assyrian finds, including huge winged beasts with human heads from a royal palace near Nineveh; and a hoard of Egyptian antiquities that features the Rosetta Stone, whose trilingual inscription enabled scholars to decode hieroglyphs for the first time. A huge Egyptian mummy collection is located on the first floor, where a couple of preserved corpses come in for some ghoulish scrutiny – a sand-dessicated Egyptian, and the 2000-year-old Lindow Man, preserved after his sacrificial death in Cheshire bog. On the same floor, various treasure troves display some extraordinary craftwork; two of the most remarkable were found in East Anglia – Saxon pieces from Sutton Hoo, and Roman silverwork known as the Mildenhall Treasure.

The building is still the home of the **British Library**, currently in the throes of a move to a new site near St Pancras station. For the time being it occupies exhibition space in the east wing, where a selection of ancient manuscripts and precious books from its vast collection are displayed – the Magna Carta, Gutenberg Bible and the richly illustrated Lindisfarne Gospels are always on show. Visitors are admitted to the famous domed **Reading Room** on the hour every hour between 11am and 4pm; there are plans to convert the room into an exhibition space once the library's long-awaited move is finally completed.

North of the centre

The grid of streets separating Oxford Street from Regent's Park to the north hold little of interest, save for a cluster of sights along the Marylebone Road, near Baker Street tube station. **Madame Tussaud's** (Mon–Fri 10am–5.30pm, Sat & Sun 9.30am–5.30pm, sometimes earlier opening in summer; £7.40; joint ticket with Plantetarium £9.40) has been renowned for its wax approximations of the rich and famous ever since the good lady arrived in London in 1802, bearing sculpted heads of the guillotined from revolutionary France. The choice of celebrities on display fluctuates according to fashion, but permanent exhibits include the Chamber of Horrors, which panders to a fascination with mass murderers. The next-door **London Planetarium** (same times as Madame Tussaud's; shows every 45min; £4, joint ticket with Tussaud's £9.40) features illuminated displays of the heavens, projected onto the inner surface of a vast dome.

The ring around **Regent's Park** is flanked by Nash's Regency terraces, some of the most elegant residential buildings in London. At the northern end of the park is **London Zoo** (daily 10am–5.30pm; £5.30), which, despite being one of the world's oldest and most varied collections of animals, may close if further funding isn't found. The concrete hovels in which many of the beasts are housed make this a less than happy place – signs placed outside the cages of big cats ask you not to be distressed if you see them pacing up and down, as if such behaviour were quite normal in the wild.

Just five minutes' walk from the north side of the park lies trendy **Camden Town**, whose vast **weekend market** – centred on Camden Lock, beside the canal – is now less of a genuine street mart than a tourist-angled performance. The number of stalls multiplies with each month, even if the range of stuff on offer doesn't – it's mostly throwaway clothes and jewellery, and ranks of bootleg tapes.

Beyond here, there are few established tourist itineraries, although several pleasant residential neighbourhoods deserve exploration. The affluent suburb of **Hampstead** retains a small town atmosphere and excellent walking opportunities on Hampstead Heath, one of the few wild areas left within reach of central London. One major attraction northeast of Hampstead is **Highgate Cemetery**, ranged on both sides of Swains Lane (Highgate or Archway tube). Opened in 1838 as a private venture, Highgate was the preferred resting place of wealthy Victorian families, and the older, more atmospheric western cemetery (tours Mon–Fri noon, 2pm & 3pm, Sat & Sun every hour on the hour 10am–4pm; £3) is full of monuments to their vanity. Most famous denizen of the eastern cemetery (daily 10am–5pm; £2) is Karl Marx, his tomb adorned by a huge bust, placed here in 1956.

The City of London

Once the fortified heart of the capital, the **City of London** in modern times has developed as the financial and commercial district, and few people actually live here, making it a desolate place after nightfall. The area also suffered more than anywhere else from the Blitz, and soulless postwar buildings further detract from the City's appeal. An earlier conflagration, the 1666 Great Fire of London, led to an era of much more dignified rebuilding, and produced the area's finest structure, **St Paul's Cathedral** (Mon–Sat 7.30am–6pm, Sun 8am–6pm; crypt, ambulatory & galleries Mon–Sat 8.30am–4.30pm; crypt & ambulatory £2.50, galleries £2.50, combination ticket £4.50). Sir Christopher Wren was given the task of building a new structure on this site after the

Great Fire had caused irreparable damage to the Gothic St Paul's – just one of over fifty church commissions he received in the wake of the blaze. Wren's Baroque design is fronted by a double-storey colonnaded portico flanked by towers, but the most distinctive feature is the dome, second in size only to St Peter's in Rome, and still a dominating presence on the London skyline. In fact it's a triple dome, its interior cupola separated from the wooden, lead-covered outer skin by a funnel-shaped brick structure. The interior of the church is filled with funerary monuments, predominantly military figures and obscure statesmen – the only memorial to have survived from the original cathedral is an effigy of the poet John Donne, once Dean of St Paul's, in the south aisle of the choir.

A staircase in the south transept leads up to a series of galleries in the dome. The internal **Whispering Gallery** is the first, so-called because of its acoustic properties – words whispered to the wall on one side of the gallery are distinctly audible on the other. The broad Stone Gallery and the uppermost Golden Gallery both offer good panoramas of the city. Close to the entrance to the galleries is the staircase to the **Crypt**, the resting place of Wren himself; his son composed the inscription which graces his tomb – *lector, si monumentum requiris, circumspice* (reader, if you seek his monument, look around). The architect is joined by Turner, Reynolds and other artists, but the most imposing sarcophagus is the black porphyry monstrosity in the west corner of the crypt, occupied by the Duke of Wellington. Look out, too, for the marble tomb of Lord Nelson, whose body is embalmed in spirit within.

A few minutes north of St Paul's is the **Barbican**, a top-notch residential complex which incorporates an arts centre that was planned to be London's answer to the Pompidou Centre, but remains largely unloved – so unloved, in fact, that few Londoners know exactly where it is. The **Museum of London** (Tues–Sat 10am–6pm, Sun 2–6pm; £3; tickets valid for 3 months, free after 4.30pm) occupies its southern corner, offering a lot of relics from Roman London and an educative trot through subsequent epochs; the models of London in previous centuries are particularly interesting.

The **Tower of London** (April–May & Sept–Oct Mon–Sat 9am–6pm; June–Aug closes 6.30pm; Nov–March Mon–Sat 9.30am–5pm, Sun 10am–5pm; £6.70) marks the eastern extent of the old city. It's usually thought of as a place of imprisonment and death, but has variously been used as an armoury, royal residence and repository of the crown's treasure. It was also the home of the royal menagerie: the keeper of the king's leopard during the reign of Edward II was paid sixpence a day for the sustenance of the beast, one penny for himself. The Tower's oldest feature is the central White Tower, built by William the Conqueror, although the ubiquitous Christopher Wren adorned each corner with cupolas. The inner wall, with its numerous towers, was built in the time of Henry III, and a further line of fortifications was added by Edward I, so much of what's visible today was already in place by the end of the thirteenth century. Once inside, you can explore the complex on your own, although free tours of the Tower are given by Yeomen, ex-servicemen in Tudor costume, every half-hour. The **White Tower** itself holds the Royal Armouries, an immense array featuring Henry VIII's huge suit of armour, and on the second floor the Chapel of St John, London's oldest Norman church. Surrounding the White Tower is the Tower Green, where the executions took place of those traitors lucky enough to be spared the public executions on nearby Tower Hill. A stone marks the spot where Lady Jane Grey, Anne Boleyn, Catherine Howard and many others probably met their end. The Jewel House contains the Crown Jewels, the majority of which postdate the period of the Commonwealth (1649–60), when most were melted down. The three largest cut diamonds in the world are on display here; the most famous of them, the Koh-i-noor, is set into a crown made for the Queen Mother in 1937. On the south side of the complex, the Bloody Tower contains the room thought to have seen the murder of the "Princes in the Tower", Edward V and his brother, as well as the quarters where Walter Raleigh spent thirteen years of captivity writing his *History of the World.* Below lies Traitor's Gate, through which prisoners were delivered after being ferried down the Thames from the courts of justice at Westminster.

Views from the Tower are dominated by the twin towers of **Tower Bridge**, built in the 1880s and characterized by a roadway which can be raised to allow ships access to the upper reaches of the Thames. The main attraction of a visit to the bridge is a wander across the walkways linking the summits of the towers (daily April–Oct 10am–6.30pm; Nov–March 10am–4.45pm; £2.50). Intended for everyday public use when the bridge was first built, the walkways were closed due to their popularity with suicides and prostitutes.

South of the river: Waterloo to Greenwich

South London is alien territory to many who live and work north of the Thames, and just about the only spot that draws people across the river in numbers is the **South Bank Centre**. This modern arts complex embraces the National Theatre, the National Film Theatre, Hayward Gallery and a trio of concert halls, of which the largest is the Royal Festival Hall – architecturally the only ingratiating aspect of this mostly brutal concrete assembly. Two of the South Bank's attractions merit a daytime visit, though. The Museum of the Moving Image, or **MOMI** (daily 10am–6pm; £5.50), provides a history of cinema and television with various interactive displays – an extremely adroit use of a cramped site under Waterloo Bridge. The **Hayward Gallery** (daily 10am–6pm; variable price) hosts prestigious, often contemporary, travelling exhibitions.

One other national institution located south of the Thames is the **Imperial War Museum** on Lambeth Road (Lambeth North tube; daily 10am–6pm; £3.70, free after 4.30pm). Though it does feature galleries of uniforms and weaponry, this is not – contrary to the suggestion of its name – a mindless celebration of imperialistic bloodletting. The museum houses some incisive examples of war art, and uses a good deal of stagecraft to convey the miseries of combat, with recreations of World War I trenches and a simulation of bomb-ravaged wartime London.

The area stretching westward from the southern end of **London Bridge** used to be the pleasure quarter of Tudor and Stuart London, an area beyond the jurisdiction of the city authorities in which brothels and other disreputable institutions, notably theatres, could flourish. Venues associated with Shakespeare and his contemporaries, such as the Rose, the Swan and the Globe, were to be found here, although there are few reminders of that era today. **Southwark Cathedral** – the finest Gothic church in the capital after Westminster Abbey – stands at the southern end of London Bridge. Inside, the most conspicuous feature is the brightly painted tomb of poet John Gower, a contemporary of Chaucer. Clink Street leads west to the **Clink** (daily 10am–6pm; £2), a small museum on the site of a former prison of the same name, detailing the riverside lowlife which often ended up being incarcerated there. Bankside continues westward along the river towards the **Shakespeare Globe Museum** in Bear Gardens (Mon–Sat 10am–5pm, Sun 2–5.30pm; £3), which concentrates on theatrical history and features a recreation of the Globe Theatre in which many of the Bard's works were performed – though this is not the original site.

Greenwich, eight miles east of central London, is steeped in naval history and site of the Greenwich meridian. Quickest way to get here is by rail from Charing Cross, or the Docklands Light Railway from Tower Hill to Island Gardens, where a pedestrian tunnel leads under the Thames to Greenwich on the other side. Standing in a dry dock next to Greenwich pier is the **Cutty Sark** (April–Sept Mon–Sat 10am–6pm, Sun noon–6pm; Oct–March closes 5pm; £3.25), one of the last of the clippers, sail-powered cargo vessels built for speed and used on long-distance routes bringing wool, tea and other produce to London from the far-flung corners of Empire – until rendered obsolete by the arrival of steam. Next to it is Gypsy Moth IV, the vessel used in Sir Francis

Chichester's 1966 solo circumnavigation of the earth (April–Oct Mon–Sat 10am–6pm, Sun noon–6pm; closed Mon–Fri 1–2pm; Oct closes 5pm; 50p). Hugging the riverfront to the east is the extraordinary Baroque facade of the **Royal Naval College** (daily except Thurs 2.30–4.45pm; free), probably Wren's finest work after St Paul's. Across the road is the **National Maritime Museum** (April–Sept Mon–Sat 10am–6pm, Sun noon–6pm; Oct–March Mon–Sat 10am–5pm, Sun 2–5pm; £3.75), a pretty unimaginative warehouse of model ships, charts and globes. The next door **Queen's House** (same hours and price) is an impressively simple classical box built for Henrietta Maria by Inigo Jones, the first example of domestic Palladian architecture in Britain. From here Greenwich Park stretches up the hill, crowned by the **Royal Observatory** (same times as Maritime Museum), another largely Wren-inspired structure, through which the Greenwich meridian runs. The museum houses a brain-stretching display of timepieces, telescopes and navigational equipment. A day pass to all the sites costs £7.45 and allows unlimited entry up to a year after purchase.

The western outskirts: Kew to Windsor

To make the most of the Thames water buses, you could take the boat upstream from Westminster Pier to Kew Pier, disembarking for the wonderful **Royal Botanical Gardens** (daily 9.30am–dusk, glasshouses close 3.30pm; £3.50, £1.20 last hour before closing), where over 45,000 species are grown in the plantations and glasshouses of a 250-acre site.

Farther upstream, thirteen miles southwest of the centre you'll find the finest of Tudor palaces, **Hampton Court Palace** (March–Oct Mon 10.15am–6pm, Tues–Sun 9.30am–6pm; Oct–March Mon closes 4.30pm; £6.50 including maze; BR Hampton Court). Cardinal Wolsey commissioned this immense house in 1516, then handed it to Henry VIII in 1525 in a vain attempt to win back his favour. Henry enlarged and improved the palace, but it was William III who made the most radical alterations, hiring Sir Christopher Wren to remodel the buildings. **William and Mary's Apartments** are chock-full of treasures, while Henry's **Great Hall** has an astonishing hammerbeam roof. There is plenty more to see in the sixty-acre **grounds** (7am–dusk; free): the Great Vine, grown from a cutting in 1768 and now averaging about seven hundred pounds of black grapes per year; William III's Banqueting House (April–Sept only); and the Lower Orangery, a gallery for Mantegna's heroic canvases, *The Triumphs of Caesar*. The famous **maze** (daily 10am–5pm; £1.50), laid out in 1714, lies north of the palace.

Windsor, twenty-one miles west of central London, is dominated by **Windsor Castle** (March–Oct daily 10.30am–5pm; Nov–Feb 10.30am–3pm; £4), which began its days as a wooden fortress built by William the Conqueror, with numerous later monarchs having had a hand in its evolution. Some of their work was undone by a huge fire in November 1992, but most of the **State Apartments** are still open, except at Easter and in June and December, when the Queen is in residence. Highlights include Van Dyck's triptych of Charles I in the King's Drawing Room; the Queen's Ballroom, dominated by an enormous silver mirror and table, and more Van Dyck paintings; and the vast array of crested helmets and sixteenth-century armour in the Queen's Guard Chamber, which includes an etched gold suit made for Prince Hal. A separate gallery to the left of the main entrance holds exhibitions of the royal art collection – Windsor possesses the world's finest collection of drawings and notebooks by Leonardo da Vinci. A visit to the castle should take in **St George's Chapel** (summer Mon–Sat 10am–4pm, Sun 2–4pm; winter Mon–Sat 10.45am–3.45pm, Sun 2–3.45pm; £3); a glorious Perependicular structure, ranking with King's College Chapel in Cambridge, it contains the tombs of Henry VII and Edward VII.

Crossing the footbridge at the end of Thames Avenue in Windsor village brings you to **Eton**, where the *raison d'être* is of course **Eton College**, the ultra-exclusive and inexcusably powerful school founded by Henry VI in 1440.

Eating

Unlike most of the rest of Britain, London is a great place to **eat**. You can sample more or less any kind of cuisine here, and the quality will usually be good. Obviously, there are plenty of places to eat around the main tourist drags of **Soho** and **Covent Garden**. Indeed, Soho has long been one of the city's restaurant focuses, while **Chinatown**, on the other side of Shaftesbury Avenue, offers value-for-money eating right in the centre of town. But to sample the full range of possibilities you also need to get out of the West End – to the Indian restaurants of Brick Lane in the East End and Drummond Street near Euston, or to the eateries of the trendy neighbourhoods of Camden Town and Islington – a short tube ride away to the north. There are also plenty of spots to pick up a street **snack** or cheap **lunch** – and some of these quick-stop places are good standbys for an evening filler. The usual burger chains are on every corner, and there are any number of sandwich shops, which – if they have seating – may well serve hot meals too, from omelettes and fry-ups to meat-and-two-veg daily specials, normally for around £3.

Snacks and quick meals

Bar Italia, 22 Frith St, W1. A tiny café that's a Soho institution, serving coffee, sandwiches, pizza, etc until around 4am. Popular with late-night clubbers, and those here to watch the Italian league football on the giant screen. Leicester Square tube.

Café in the Crypt, St Martin-in-the-Fields church, Duncannon St, WC2. Good-quality buffet food makes this an ideal spot to fill up before hitting the West End for the evening, or after a tour of the National Gallery. Charing Cross tube.

Centrale, 16 Moor St, W1. Tiny Italian greasy spoon that serves up large plates of pasta and omelettes. You may have to wait for – or share – a table. Unlicensed. Leicester Square tube.

Food for Thought, 31 Neal St, WC2. Very small Covent Garden vegetarian restaurant – the food is good, but expect to queue and don't expect to linger. Closes around 8pm. Covent Garden tube.

Gaby's, 30 Charing Cross Rd, WC2. Café serving a wide range of home-cooked veggie and Middle Eastern specialities; famously glum staff. Leicester Square tube.

Hard Rock Café, 150 Old Park Lane, W1. The best-known burger joint in town, with permanent queue. Expensive beer. Hyde Park Corner tube.

Olive Tree, 11 Wardour St, W1. Cheap West End veggie place. Leicester Square tube.

Pho, 2 Lisle St, W1. Vietnamese fast-food café; big bowls of noodle soup. Leicester Square tube.

Pollo, 20 Old Compton St, W1. The best-value Italian food in town. Always packed, though the queues move quickly. Leicester Square tube.

Stockpot, 18 Old Compton St, W1 (Leicester Square tube); 40 Panton St, SW1 (Piccadilly Circus) and 6 Basil St, SW3 (Knightsbridge). Wholesome British grub at rock-bottom prices.

Restaurants

Café Delancey, 3 Delancey St, NW1. Comfortable Camden brasserie that's good for both a quick coffee and a snack and reasonably priced full lunches and dinners. Camden Town tube.

Café Pacifico, 5 Langley St, WC2. Rated as the best Mexican restaurant in central London, though that isn't much of a title. Fairly quiet during the day, unbelievably noisy in the evening. Good bar. Covent Garden or Leicester Square tube.

Chutneys, 124 Drummond St, NW1. One of the best of a number of cheap south Indian restaurants on this street. Euston tube.

Clifton, 126 Brick Lane, E1. One of the classiest of the Brick Lane Bangladeshi restaurants. Aldgate East tube.

Daquise, 20 Thurloe St, SW7. Something of a cult, with its gloomy Eastern Bloc decor, long-suffering staff and heartily utilitarian Polish food. Good place for a quick bite and a shot of vodka after the South Kensington museums. South Kensington tube.

Diwnana Bhel Poori House, 121 Drummond St, NW1. Unlicensed, cheap and very tasty south Indian restaurant. Euston tube.

Efes, 80 Great Titchfield St, W1. Vast Turkish kebab restaurant. Reliable and friendly. Oxford Circus tube.

Hong Kong, 6–7 Lisle St, WC2. Has probably the best vegetarian menu in Chinatown, and does excellent *dim sum*. Leicester Square tube.

India Club, 143 Strand, WC2. Their unlicensed upstairs restaurant serves authentic Indian food in faded canteen surroundings reminiscent of the "last days of the Raj" . Closes 10pm. Aldwych or Holborn tube.

Jimmy's, 23 Frith St, W1. Basement Greek restaurant that's long been part of the Soho cheap eating scene. Leicester Square tube.

Joe Allen, 13 Exeter St, WC2. London branch of the well-known American restaurant group, with the familiar chequered tablecloths and bar-room atmosphere. Burgers are excellent, but you have to ask for them – they are not on the menu. Not especially cheap, though, and always very busy. Charing Cross/Covent Garden tube.

Kettner's, 29 Romilly St, W1. Grand old place with high ceilings and a pianist, though actually part of the *Pizza Express* chain and consequently cheaper than you'd expect from the ambience. Leicester Square tube.

Lorelei, 21 Bateman St, W1. Tiny unlicensed pizza restaurant offering Soho's cheapest route to a full stomach. Tottenham Court Rd tube.

Mandeer, 21 Hanway Place, W1. It's impossible to find better vegetarian Indian food than this in the centre of town. Tottenham Court Rd tube.

Man Fu Kung, 29 Leicester Square, WC2. One of the best of this part of town's Chinese eateries, certainly the largest. Great for *dim sum*, and with a good takeaway counter out the back, opening on to Charing Cross Road.

Mille Pini, 33 Boswell St, WC1. Big portions of basic Italian food. Holborn tube.

Mr Kong, 21 Lisle St, WC2. Excellent Cantonese food in the heart of Chinatown. Go for the more adventurous "specials" menu. Leicester Square tube.

Nazrul, 130 Brick Lane, El. Though the developers are moving in, this street still has a good concentration of Bangladeshi restaurants. The unlicensed *Nazrul* is the cheapest and one of the best. Aldgate East tube.

New World, 1 Gerrard Place, W1. Though this vast Chinese restaurant is open in the evenings too, its strength is the lunchtime *dim sum*. Leicester Square tube.

Nontas, 16 Camden High St, NW1. Archetypal boisterous Greek taverna, doing all the basics well. Camden Town tube.

Pizza Express, 10 Dean St, W1; 30 Coptic St, WC1 (both Tottenham Court Rd tube); and numerous other branches all over London. Easily the best of the pizza chains, doing a good line in thincrust pizzas. The Dean Street branch has regular live jazz in the basement; the Coptic Street one is sited in a former dairy. Inexpensive.

Pizzeria Condotti, 4 Mill St, W1. Some of the capital's best pizzas. Oxford Circus tube.

Poons, 4 Leicester St and 27 Lisle St, both WC2, (both Leicester Square tube). The Lisle St branch, the original *Poons*, is a tatty café quite unlike its smarter Leicester St offspring, but many think it serves better food. There are other branches in the Whiteleys complex on Queensway (W2) and at 50 Woburn Place (WC1).

La Quercia d'Oro, 16a Endell St, WC2. Shabby, cheerful, basic Italian eatery, with big rustic portions. Covent Garden tube.

Spaghetti House, 15 Goodge St, W1. Central branch of a London-wide chain that serves excellent pasta meals and more substantial dishes for reasonable prices. Goodge St tube.

Tokyo Diner, 2 Newport Place, WC2. Brilliant Japanese diner, serving authentic food at a fraction of the cost of its rivals. Perfect service. Leicester Square tube.

Upper Street Fish Shop, 324 Upper St, N1. Classy, yuppie-ish sit-down fish and chip restaurant in the heart of trendy Islington. Angel tube.

Wagamama, 4 Streatham St, WC1. Canteen-style place, serving passable food in an austerely hi-tech setting – this must be the only restaurant in London where the waiters take your orders on hand-held computers. Tottenham Court Rd tube.

Yung's, 23 Wardour St, W1. Three-storey Cantonese serving excellent food. Open till 4am. Leicester Square tube.

Drinking

Central London is full of **pubs**, and, although you'll find much pleasanter places in the neighbourhoods further out, there are one or two watering holes that retain an element of character. Expect prices to be well above what you might have been used to paying anywhere else in Britain, but on the plus side, pub food in London is often more adventurous than outside the capital.

Albert, 52 Victoria St, SW1. Handily situated pub serving good food, including hearty breakfasts. St James' Park tube.

Argyll Arms, 18 Argyll St, W1. One of the pleasanter places in the immediate orbit of Oxford St, with original glass and wood fittings. Oxford Circus tube.

Black Friar, 174 Queen Victoria St, EC4. Art Nouveau landmark, handy for the City sights. Closes 10pm. Blackfriars tube.

Bricklayers Arms, 31 Gresse St, W1. Tucked away among harsh modern buildings just off Tottenham Court Rd, this is a real gem, with a neighbourly feel and good food. Tottenham Court Rd tube.

Buckingham Arms, 62 Petty France, SW1. Good beer within a few minutes of Buckingham Palace. St James' Park tube.

Camden Head, 2 Camden Walk, N1. A popular Islington local, handy for the Camden Passage antiques trade. Reasonable lunchtime food too. Angel tube.

Cheshire Cheese, 145 Fleet St, EC4. Famous old watering hole that's about all that's left of the journalistic Fleet Street of yore. Temple/Blackfriars tube.

Cittie of York, 22 High Holborn, WC1. Passable food is served upstairs, but the cellar bar is a more atmospheric place to savour the Sam Smith's beer. Holborn tube.

Coach & Horses, 29 Greek St, W1. Long-standing – and, for once, little-changed – haunt of the ghosts of old Soho, nightclubbers and art students from nearby St Martin's College. Leicester Square tube.

Cock & Lion, 62 Wigmore St, W1. Centrally situated pub with an old-fashioned restaurant upstairs serving wholesome English food. Oxford Circus tube.

Crown, 116 Cloudesley Rd, N1. Excellent beer in one of Islington's most welcoming pubs. Angel tube.

Dirty Dick's, 202 Bishopsgate, EC2. Very old pub with cobwebby downstairs bar. Next to Middlesex Street, for Sunday's Petticoat Lane market. Liverpool St tube.

Dog & Duck, 18 Bateman St, W1. Tiny Soho pub that retains much of its old character and has a loyal clientele. Leicester Square tube.

Flask, 14 Flask Walk, NW3. Convivial Hampstead local, close to the tube station and serving good food and real ale. Hampstead tube.

The George, 213 Strand, WC2. Various real ales and decent food. Mood of the clientele tends to reflect how their cases went in the Royal Courts of Justice, across the road. Aldwych tube.

George Inn, 77 Borough High St, SE1. Large old coaching inn, now owned by the National Trust. Borough tube.

Gordon's, Villiers St, WC2. Cavelike wine bar right next door to Charing Cross station. The excellent and varied wine list, decent buffet food and genial atmosphere make it a favourite with the neighbourhood's office workers. Open Monday to Friday. Charing Cross/Embankment tube.

King's Head, 115 Upper St, N1. Busy pub in the heart of Islington that has regular live music and a fringe theatre upstairs. For some reason the bar staff quote prices in "old money". Angel tube.

Lamb, 94 Lambs Conduit St, WC1. Pleasant pub with a marvellously well preserved Victorian interior of mirrors, old wood and "snob" screens. Russell Square tube.

Lamb & Flag, 33 Rose St, WC2. Busy and pleasantly unchanged pub tucked away down a Covent Garden alley, between Garrick Street and Floral Street. Decent food. Leicester Square tube.

Museum Tavern, 49 Great Russell St, WC1. Large and characterful old pub, right opposite the main entrance to the British Museum. Tottenham Court Rd/Russell Square tube.

Old King Lud, Ludgate Circus, EC4. Not half as cosy as its demolished predecessor on this site, but a real drinkers' pub, with 30 real ales on tap – try the Old Speckled Hen. Blackfriars tube.

Ye Olde Mitre, 1 Ely Court, Ely Place, EC1. Ancient two-bar pub, popular with City wage-slaves. Chancery Lane tube.

Paviour's Arms, Page St, SW1. Untouched Art Deco pub, close to the Tate Gallery. Pimlico tube.

Princess Louise, 208 High Holborn, WC1. Old-fashioned place, with high ceilings, lots of glass and a good range of real ales. Holborn/Chancery Lane tube.

Star, 6 Belgrave Mews West, SW1. Two-storey pub in one of London's most expensive residential areas. Fine beer and very classy food. Knightsbridge tube.

Sun, 66 Long Acre, WC2. Another reasonable Covent Garden choice, with a bustling atmosphere and fair pub grub. Covent Garden tube.

Sun, 63 Lambs Conduit St, WC1. Bareboards old pub with decent real ales and food. Russell Square tube.

Nightlife

On any night of the week London offers a vast range of things to do after dark, ranging from top-flight opera and theatre to clubs with a life span of a couple of nights. The **listings magazine** *Time Out* is essential if you want to get the most out of London, giving full details of prices and access, plus previews and reviews.

Recession has taken its toll on London's **club** scene, which used to boast seven-days-a-week party potential, but the capital has clung on to its status as **dance music** capital of Europe and favourite destination of visiting DJs from all over the world. Recent relaxations in attitudes towards late-night licensing have allowed many venues to open until 6am or even later, which has accelerated the move from illegal warehouse parties to purpose-renovated legitimate venues. Many of the best events are one-offs or itinerant clubs that rely on word-of-mouth or mailing lists for publicity – check dance magazines such as *DJ*, *Mixmag* and *Touch*, and pick up the flyers that litter the counters of record shops such as *Black Market* in D'Arblay Street, *Catch-a-Groove* in Dean Street or *Quaff* in Berwick Street (all in Soho). Prices vary enormously, with small midweek nights starting at under £5 and large weekend events charging as much as £25 – around £10–15 would be the average for a Saturday night.

After a brief flirtation with dance music, the **rock scene** is in a back-to-basics period, sparked by the success of the Seattle-based grunge phenomenon and the inexorable rise of thirtysomething soft rock. One new trend is a proliferation of acts ploughing a jazz/funk/rap furrow, and Latin music is enjoying a rise in popularity as well. Entry prices for gigs run much the same as clubs, though bar prices tend to be lower.

Though a stroll through the West End can create the impression that Lloyd-Webber musicals and revivals of clapped-out plays have a stranglehold on London's **theatres**, the capital is less staid than it might appear. Apart from the classic productions of the major repertory companies, there's a large fringe circuit, staging often provocative pieces in venues that range from proper independent auditoriums to back rooms in pubs. **Cinema** is not as adventurous as it is in some European capitals, with the number of repertory houses diminishing steadily, but there's a decent spread of screenings of general release and re-run films each night of the week. With two opera houses and several well-equipped concert halls, London's programme of **classical music** is excellent, and the annual Proms season represents Europe's most accessible festival of highbrow music. For most plays and concerts you should be able to get a seat for less than £15 in the West End, or less at venues off the main circuit.

Clubs and discos

Bar Rumba, 36 Shaftesbury Avenue, W1. New West End venue with a programme of all things Latin, jazzy and funky. Live shows too. Piccadilly Circus tube.

Busby's, 157 Charing Cross Rd, W1. Once among the hippest joints in town when it played host to the Mud Club, but now with naff nights for tourists and out-of-towners. Tottenham Court Rd tube.

Café de Paris, 3 Coventry St, WC2. Following several dark years the Café has been restored to its old glories and reopened for the city's trendy set. Leicester Square tube.

The Fridge, Town Hall Parade, Brixton, SW2. South London's big night out with a musical policy from funk to garage and featuring one of London's biggest gay nights on Tuesdays. Brixton tube.

Gardening Club, 4 Covent Garden Piazza, WC2. Small, trendy and nearly always reliable for a good night's clubbing. Covent Garden tube.

Gossips, 69 Dean St, W1. Dingy basement that seems to have been running forever. Different sounds each night of the week. Tottenham Court Rd/Leicester Sq tube.

Hippodrome, Leicester Square, WC2. London's leading neon palace and a byword for tackiness. Leicester Sq tube.

Maximus, 14 Leicester Square, WC2. Once a supertacky disco, now playing host to hip club nights. Leicester Sq tube.

Ministry of Sound, 103 Gaunt St, SE1. Large club based on New York's legendary Paradise Garage. The sound system is the best around but the crowd is becoming more touristy and suburban - and because the place opens until 10am, there's no booze. Elephant & Castle tube.

Subterrania, 12 Acklam Rd, W11. Worth a visit for its diverse (if a tad dressy) club nights on Fridays and Saturdays – if you can get in. Also has live music. Ladbroke Grove tube.

UK, Buckhold Rd, SW18. They don't advertise that this is part of Wandsworth's Arndale Centre, but nonetheless it's one of the newest big clubs in town, specializing in cutting edge British DJs. East Putney tube.

Wag, 35 Wardour St, W1. A hot spot in the mid-eighties, now in need of a major overhaul but still going strong. Piccadilly Circus tube.

Live venues

Academy, 211 Stockwell Rd, SW9. Massive Victorian hall used for concerts and club nights. Brixton tube.

Africa Centre, 38 King St, WC2. African-flavoured music in a youth club atmosphere.

Astoria, 157 Charing Cross Rd, W1. One of London's best-used venues – a large balconied theatre that has live bands and clubs. Leicester Square tube.

Bass Clef, 57 Coronet St, N1. Still one of the trendiest jazz places. Also features African and Latin music. Old St tube.

Borderline, Orange Yard, Manette St, W1. Intimate venue with diverse musical policy. Good place to catch new bands; also has club nights. Tottenham Court Rd tube.

The Forum, 9–17 Highgate Rd, NW5. Perhaps the capital's best medium-sized venue – large enough to attract established bands, but also a prime spot for newer talent. Kentish Town tube.

The Garage, 20 Highbury Corner, N1. Good for blues and R&B. Highbury and Islington tube.

Jazz Café, 5 Parkway, NW1. Slick modern jazz venue with an adventurous booking policy. Camden Town tube.

The Limelight, 136 Shaftesbury Avenue, W1. Super-trendy when it opened a few years back, now overpriced – though it has the occasional good night. Leicester Square tube.

The Marquee, 105 Charing Cross Rd, W1. Though relocated from the Wardour St site where the Rolling Stones and innumerable others made their name, this is still one of London's top venues for up-and-coming bands. Tottenham Court Rd tube.

Mean Fiddler, 28a Harlesden High St, NW10. Small venue with eclectic policy ranging from folk to rock. Willesden Junction tube.

Powerhaus, 1 Liverpool Rd, N1. A venue for small and rising acts for over a decade, under various names. Angel tube.

The Rock Garden, 6–7 Covent Garden Piazza, WC2. Mostly a stage for exceptionally obscure bands, with the odd club night. Covent garden tube.

Ronnie Scott's, 47 Frith St, W1. The most famous jazz club in London, small, smoky and rather precious. Nonetheless, it's still the place for top-line names. Leicester Square tube.

Underworld, 174 Camden High St, NW1. Good for new bands, with sporadic club nights. Camden Town tube.

ULU, Manning Hall, Malet St, W1. The best of London's university venues, with an exceptionally cheap bar. Russell Square tube.

Weavers Arms, 98 Newington Green Rd, N1. Intimate pub venue with folk, blues or country bands nightly. Highbury and Islington tube.

Wembley Arena, Empire Way. Main venue for megabands. Wembley Park tube.

100 Club, 100 Oxford St, W1. After a brief spell as a stage for punk bands, the *100 Club* is back to what is always used to be – an unpretentious and inexpensive jazz venue. Tottenham Court Rd tube.

606 Club, 90 Lots Rd, SW10. London's newest all-jazz venue, located off the untrendy part of the King's Rd. Fulham Broadway tube.

The gay and lesbian scene

The **gay scene** in London is livelier than almost anywhere else in Europe, with a vast range of venues from quiet bars to cruisy clubs and frenetic discos – Soho is the rising "gay village", focused on Old Compton Street. Apart from *Time Out*, you should check the up-to-the-minute listings in *Capital Gay*, a weekly free newspaper available in all the places listed below; most will also have the free *Backpocket Guide to Gay & Lesbian London*, a foldout map-guide to the London scene. Excellent sources of information on all aspects of gay London are the *London Lesbian and Gay Switchboard* (☎071/837 7324), which operates around-the-clock.

BARS AND CLUBS

Angel, 65 Graham St, N1. Relaxed gay café-bar. Angel tube.

The Bell, 257 Pentonville Rd, N1. Popular pub, attracting a mixed crowd with wacky Sunday night tea dance. King's Cross tube.

The Black Cap, 171 Camden High St. North London gay institution – a big cabaret venue on the drag scene. Camden Town tube.

Brompton's, 294 Old Brompton Rd, SW5. Long-established gay men's bar, pulling a mixture of tourists, local yuppies and clones. Earl's Court tube.

Compton's of Soho, 53 Old Compton St, W1. Welcoming, long-standing loud gay pub that has seen a dozen or so new gay cafés, bars and shops grow up around it. Leicester Square tube.

Club Copa, 180 Earl's Court Rd, SW5. Comfortable and atmospheric men's club, with three bars, a lounge and a pool. Earl's Court tube.

The Fridge, Town Hall Parade, Brixton, SW2. The regular Tuesday-night *Daisy Chain* is one of London's wildest gay and lesbian raves. Brixton tube.

Heaven, under the arches, Villiers St, WC2. A vast complex sprawling under Charing Cross station, this is the city's premier gay club – and has occasional mixed nights too. Charing Cross/ Embankment tube.

King William IV, 75 Hampstead High St, NW3. Long-established relaxed north London gay pub. Hampstead tube.

London Apprentice, 333 Old St, EC1. One of the best-known gay clubs in the city. Very busy, fairly cruisy, with a small dance floor downstairs. Old St tube.

Market Tavern, 1 Nine Elms Lane, SW8. Most people's choice as the best gay pub in south London, with a large dance floor out front and a quiet bar in the back. Vauxhall tube.

Paradise Club, 1 Parkfield St, N1. Large Islington gay club, with dance floors and bars on three floors. Angel tube.

The Village Soho, 81 Wardour St, W1. Chic Continental-style café-bar. Leicester Square tube.

Theatre and cinema

London's big two **theatre** companies are the **National Theatre**, performing in three theatres on the South Bank (☎071/928 2252), and the **Royal Shakespeare Company**, whose productions transfer to the two houses in the Barbican after their run in Stratford (☎071/638 8891). For a show that's had good reviews, tickets under £10 are difficult to come by at either, but it's always worth ringing their box offices for details of standby deals, which can get you the best seat in the house for as little as £5 if you're a student, otherwise £10. Similar deals are offered by many of London's scores of theatres. Venues with a reputation for challenging productions include the *Almeida, Royal Court, Young Vic, Tricycle, The Orange Tree* and the *ICA*.

A booth in Leicester Square sells half-price tickets for that day's performances at all the West End theatres, but they specialize in the top end of the price range; the Charing Cross Road and Leicester Square areas also have offices that can get tickets for virtually all shows, but the mark-up can be as high as two hundred percent. Don't buy tickets from touts – their mark-ups are outrageous, and there's no guarantee that the tickets aren't fakes.

Leicester Square and environs (Piccadilly, Haymarket, Lower Regent St) have the main concentration of big-screen **cinemas** showing new releases; seats tend to cost upwards of £7. The main repertory cinemas in the centre are the **National Film Theatre** on the South Bank and the **ICA**, both of which charge for day membership on top of the ticket price. After a spate of closures, London has very few other repertory cinemas: the *Everyman* in Hampstead has perhaps the most interesting programmes. There are, however, several excellent independent cinemas for new art-house releases – it's always worth checking what's on at the *Renoir* (Russell Square), the *Gate* (Notting Hill), the *Lumière* (St Martin's Lane) and the *Metro* (Rupert Street, near Leicester Square).

Classical music, opera and dance

For **classical concerts** the principal venue is the **South Bank Centre**, where the biggest names appear at the *Festival Hall*, with more specialized programmes being staged in the *Queen Elizabeth Hall* and *Purcell Room* (all three halls ☎071/921 6060). Programmes in the concert hall of the **Barbican Centre**, Silk St (☎071/638 8891), are too often pitched at the corporate audience, though it has the occasional classy recital; for chamber music, the **Wigmore Hall**, 36 Wigmore St (☎071/935 2141), is many people's favourite. Tickets for all these venues begin at about £5, with cheap standbys sometimes available to students on the evening of the performance.

From July to September each year the **Proms** at the **Royal Albert Hall** (☎071/589 8212) feature at least one concert daily, with hundreds of standing seats sold for just a couple of pounds on the night. The acoustics aren't the world's best, but the calibre of the performers is unbeatable, and the programme is a fascinating mix of standards and new or obscure works. The hall is so vast that only megastars like Jessye Norman can pack it out, so if you turn up half an hour before the show starts there should be little risk of being turned away.

The **Royal Opera House**, Covent Garden (☎071/240 1066), has a reputation for dull productions, expensive star names and inexcusable prices (up to £120) – though a few dozen relatively cheap seats (ie under £20) are sold from 10am on the day of the performance, which means you have to start queuing at 8am in most cases. The **English National Opera** at the *Coliseum*, St Martin's Lane (☎071/836 3161), has more radical producers and is a more democratic institution – tickets begin at £7 and any unsold seats are released on the day of the performance at greatly reduced prices. All works are sung in English at the *Coliseum*. In addition to the big two opera houses, smaller halls often stage more innovative productions by touring companies such as *Operafactory* and *Opera North* – the *Queen Elizabeth Hall* is a regular venue.

Nowadays the *Royal Opera House* has a better reputation for **ballet** than for singing, as its resident **Royal Ballet Company** can call on the talents of Darcy Bussell and Sylvie Guillem, to name just two of its most glamorous stars. Visiting classical companies also appear regularly at *Sadlers Wells* and the *Coliseum*, and less frequently at the *Royal Albert Hall*. London's **contemporary dance** scene is no less exciting – adventurous programmes are staged at the South Bank and at the *ICA*, as well as at numerous more ad hoc venues.

Listings

Airlines *American Airlines*, 421 Oxford St, W1 (☎071/572 5555); *British Airways*, 156 Regent St, W1 (☎081/897 4000); *Lufthansa*, 23 Piccadilly, W1 (☎071/408 0322); *TWA*, 200 Piccadilly, W1 (☎071/439 0707); *Virgin Atlantic*, Virgin Megastore, 14 Oxford St, W1 (☎0293/562000).

Airports Gatwick (☎0293/535 353); Heathrow (☎081/759 4321); Stansted (☎0279/680 500).

American Express 6 Haymarket, SW1 (☎071/930 4411).

Bicycle rental *On Your Bike*, 22 Duke St Hill, London Bridge, SE1 (☎071/378 6669); *Evans*, The Cut, Waterloo, SE1 (☎071/928 4785).

Books *Foyles*, 119 Charing Cross Rd, WC2, is the best-known London general bookshop but is badly stocked and chaotically organized. Neighbouring *Waterstone's* is preferable, as is *Books Etc* across the road and *Dillons*, 82 Gower St, WC1 – the university bookshop. For more radical publications, call in at *Compendium*, 234 Camden High St, NW1 (Camden Town tube). Two of London's best art bookshops are *Shipley*, 70 Charing Cross Rd, and nearby *Zwemmer's*. For maps and travel books, go to *Stanford's*, 12 Long Acre, WC2.

Bus station Long-distance coach services depart from Victoria Coach Station, Buckingham Palace Rd (Victoria tube). *National Express* ticket offices are here and at 13 Regent St (timetable info ☎071/730 0202). European services operated by *Eurolines*, 52 Grosvenor Gardens, SW1 (☎071/730 8235).

Car rental Best rates are at *Holiday Autos*, 25 Savile Row, W1 (☎071/491 1111). The big firms have outlets all over London; ring their central offices to find the nearest one: *Avis* (☎081/848 8733); *Hertz* (☎081/679 1799); *Europcar* (☎081/950 5050).

Dentist 24-hr emergency dental service (☎081/302 8106).

Embassies *Australia*, Australia House, The Strand, WC2 (☎071/379 4334); *Canada*, Canada House, Trafalgar Square, W1 (☎071/629 9492); *Ireland*, 17 Grosvenor Place, SW1 (☎071/235 2171); *Netherlands*, 38 Hyde Park Gate, SW7 (☎071/584 5040); *New Zealand*, New Zealand House, 80 Haymarket, SW1 (☎071/930 8422); *USA*, 24 Grosvenor Square, W1 (☎071/499 9000).

Exchange Shopping areas such as Oxford St and Covent Garden are littered with private exchange offices, and there are 24-hr booths at the biggest central tube stations, but their rates are always worse than the banks. Oxford St, Regent St and Piccadilly are where you'll find the major branches of all the main banks.

Hospitals The most central hospitals with 24-hr emergency units are: Guys, St Thomas St, SE1 (☎071/955 5000); St Bartholomews, West Smithfield, EC1 (☎601 8888); St Thomas's, Lambeth Palace Rd (☎071/928 9292); University College, Gower St, W1 (☎071/387 9300); and the Westminster Hospital, Dean Ryle St, SW1 (☎081/746 8000).

Left luggage Facilities at London train stations were curtailed in the wake of recent terrorist incidents, and it is impossible to predict when a full service will be resumed. The normal hours are as follows, but you should be prepared to be directed to another station: Charing Cross daily 6.30am–10.30pm; Euston 24-hr daily; Paddington daily 7am–midnight; Victoria daily 7.15am–10pm; Waterloo Mon–Sat 6.30am–11pm.

London Transport enquiries 24-hr information on ☎071/222 1234.

National Express Victoria Coach Station (☎071/730 8235).

Pharmacies *Bliss*, 5 Marble Arch W1, is open Mon–Fri 9am–midnight. The *Bliss* branch at 50–56 Willesden Lane, NW6, is open daily 9am–2am. Every police station keeps a list of emergency pharmacies in its area.

Police HQ is New Scotland Yard, Broadway (☎071/230 1212), but 10 Vine St (☎071/434 5212), just off Regent St, is the most convenient West End station.

Post offices The Trafalgar Square post office, 24–28 William IV St, WC2, has the longest opening hours: Mon–Sat 8am–8pm. Poste restante will be held by the chief post office at King Edward St, EC1, unless you specify another.

Train stations and information As a broad guide, Euston handles services to the Northwest and Glasgow; King's Cross the Northeast and Edinburgh; Liverpool St Eastern England; Paddington Western England; Victoria and Waterloo Southeast England. For information, call ☎071/928 5100 for services to Eastern and Southern England, and Eastern and Southern London; ☎071/262 6767 for the South Midlands, West England, West London and South Wales; ☎071/387 7070 for North Midlands, North Wales, Northwest England and Northwest London; and ☎071/287 2477 for Northeast England and Eastern Scotland.

Travel agents *Campus Travel*, 52 Grosvenor Gdns, SW1W 0AG (☎071/730 3402); *STA Travel*, 86 Old Brompton Rd, SW7 3LQ(☎071/937 9921); *Council Travel*, 28a Poland St, W1 (☎071/437 7767); *Trailfinders*, 42–48 Earls Court Rd, W8 (☎071/937 5400); *Travel Cuts*, 295a Regent St, W1 (☎071/255 1944).

SOUTHEAST ENGLAND

Nestling in self-satisfied prosperity, **Southeast England** is the richest part of the country, due to its agricultural wealth and proximity to the capital. Swift, frequent rail and coach services make it ideal for day trips from London. Medieval ecclesiastical power bases like **Canterbury** and **Winchester** offer an introduction to the nation's history; while on the coast you can choose between the slightly tacky hedonism of **Brighton**, London's playground by the sea, and the quieter, more traditional pleasures of the **Dover** area – also a pleasant stopover for those entering or leaving the country by ferry.

Canterbury

CANTERBURY, one of the oldest centres of Christianity in England, was home to the country's most famous martyr, archbishop Thomas à Becket, who fell victim to church-state rivalry in 1170. It was one of northern Europe's great pilgrimage sites, as Chaucer's *Canterbury Tales* attest, before Henry VIII had the martyr's shrine demolished in 1538. Today it's thronged with visitors all year round and not a little over-commercialized, but the magnificence of the cathedral is enough to make a stop rewarding.

The **Cathedral** (daily 8.45am–7pm; donation of £1.50 requested) remains the focal point of a compact town centre, which is enclosed on three sides by medieval walls. Built in stages from the eleventh century onwards, the cathedral derives its distinctive presence from the perpendicular thrust of the late Gothic towers, dominated by the central, fifteenth-century Bell Harry tower. Notable features of the high vaulted interior are the tombs of Henry IV and his wife, and the gilded effigy of the Black Prince, both in the Trinity chapel behind the main altar. The spot where Becket was killed in the northwest transept is now marked by a modern shrine, with a crude sculpture of the murder weapons suspended above. Steps from here descend to the low Romanesque arches of the **crypt**, one of the few remaining visible relics of the Norman cathedral.

Beyond the city walls east of the cathedral are the evocative ruins of **St Augustine's Abbey** (April–Sept daily 10am–6pm; Oct–March Tues–Sun 10am–4pm; £1.20), which occupies the site of a church built by Saint Augustine, who was despatched by Pope Gregory the Great to begin the conversion of the English in 597. Most of the town's other sights are located on or near the High Street. The **Eastbridge Hospital** (Mon–Sat 10am–1pm & 2–5pm, Sun opens 11am) on the other side of the street from the library, was founded in the twelfth century to provide poor pilgrims with shelter, and a thirteenth-century wall painting of Jesus is still faintly visible in the refectory upstairs. To the right as the main street crosses the River Stour are the **Weavers' Houses**, Tudor in origin although much restored. The **West Gate**, at the far end of St Peter's Street (a continuation of the High St), the only one of the town's medieval gates to survive, houses a small museum (April–Sept Mon–Fri 11am–1pm & 2–5pm; Oct–March Mon–Fri 2–4pm) containing weaponry used by the medieval city guard. The **Canterbury Tales**, St Margaret Street (daily April–Sept 9.30am–5.30pm; Oct–March Mon–Fri 10am–4.30pm; £4.25), presents the city's heritage with the recorded voices of Chaucerian characters guiding you around a series of waxwork tableaux representing various stages of the pilgrimage. **Canterbury Heritage** on the parallel Stour Street (Mon–Sat 10.30am–5pm; June–Oct also Sun 1.30–5pm; £1.40) offers similarly nostalgia-tinged simulations of Roman and medieval life.

Practicalities

Trains on the main line between London Victoria and Dover arrive at Canterbury East, from which it's a short walk into the walled town; the slower trains from Charing Cross arrive at Canterbury West, just outside the West Gate. Canterbury bus **station** is on St George's Lane; a left turn at the bottom of the forecourt brings you directly onto the High Street. The **tourist office** is just off the High Street at 34 St Margaret's Street (May–Sept daily 9.30am–5.30pm; Oct–April Mon–Sat 9.30am–5pm), and will find a B&B for a £1 fee. Otherwise, among the cheaper places you might try are: *The White House*, 6 St Peter's Lane (☎0227/464381; ④); *Wincheap Guest House*, 94 Wincheap (☎0227/762309; ④); and *Yorke Lodge*, 50 London Rd (☎0227/451243; ④). There's a *YHA* **hostel** about half a mile out of town in the Dover direction at 54 New Dover Rd (☎0227/462911; ②; bus #15, #16 or #17). There are plenty of places to **eat and drink** in the town centre. *Sweeney Todd*'s, close to the cathedral at 8 Butchery Lane, is a long-established pizzeria, popular with students, as is the *City Arms* next door, one of Canterbury's liveliest pubs. *Tapas en Las Trece*, 13 Palace St, is another possibility, close to the studenty *Bell and Crown* pub. On St Peter's St, *Marlowe's* serves standard Tex-Mex fare in huge and affordable portions, beyond which, by the Westgate Gardens, *Café des Amis* also has good Mexican food. Among other pubs, the *Miller's Arms*, on Mill Lane, is a nice place for a picturesque pint in summer; the *Jolly Sailor* is a down-to-earth haunt on Northgate.

Dover and the Kent Coast

DOVER, the port through which so much cross-Channel traffic is funnelled, is not the most appealing of seaside resorts, but it does harbour several historic attractions and provides a good base for further explorations of the Kent coast – particularly the Cinque Ports (of which Dover itself is one), the medieval maritime centres which were granted special privileges in return for providing the vulnerable kingdom with a navy. Furthermore, as night-time transport to London is poor (the last coach leaves at 7.45pm; last train at 10pm), you may be forced to stay here anyway.

Dover's main **ferry terminal** is located less than a mile east of town at the Eastern Docks (London coaches pick up and put down here); hovercraft depart from the more central Western Docks. Trains arrive at Priory Station, a ten-minute walk northwest of the centre, while the bus station is in the heart of town on Pencester Street. The **tourist office** is parallel to the rather drab seafront on Townwall Street (daily 9am–6/10pm), and staff will direct you to the numerous **B&Bs** along the Folkestone Road: recommended is *Linden* at no. 231 (☎0304/205449; ⑤). There's a crowded **youth hostel** at Charlton House, 306 London Road (☎0304/201314; ②); overspill dorms are opened at 14 Goodwyne Road in summer.

Views of Dover's famous White Cliffs are best enjoyed from a boat several miles out, although you can amble around on the grassy summit, these days cut off from town by the sweep of the main road to the ferry docks. **Dover Castle** (daily 10am–4/6pm; £5), a rambling assemblage of medieval fortifications dominated by a Norman keep, stands on a bluff between the eastern docks and the town. Inside the castle complex are the remains of a Roman lighthouse dating from the first century, and Hellfire Corner, the warren of tunnels used as a command post by the British navy during World War II. The tourist itinerary in town is dominated by the new **White Cliffs Experience** (daily 10am–3/5pm; £4.25), an extravagant stage-set of a museum which includes tableaux representing the Roman invasion (Julius Caesar landed up the coast at Deal in 55 BC), and a Dover street scene from 1944. Similarly theme-park-like is the **Town Gaol**, below the Old Town Hall on High Street (Mon–Sat 10am–4.30pm, Sun 2–4.30pm; £3), offering a taste of Victorian incarceration through a reconstructed series of courtroom, cell and exercise yard. The **Town Museum** on Market Square (Tues–Sat 10am–5pm, Sun 2–

5pm; free) has some well-displayed Roman port artefacts, and original Roman wall paintings can be seen in the nearby **Painted House**, New Street (Easter–Sept daily 10am–6pm; £1.50). The high ground to the west of the town, originally the site of a Napoleonic-era fortress, retains one interesting oddity, the **Grand Shaft** (Wed–Sun 2–5pm), a triple staircase by which troops could descend at speed to defend the port area in case of attack.

Deal and Sandwich

The more picturesque towns of the Kent coast are within easy reach of Dover by local train and bus services. The **castle** at **DEAL**, seven miles north, is a fine example of the coastal defences built by Henry VIII, although the rose-petal pattern of its terraces was as much a Tudor affectation as a defence against potential attackers (daily 10am–4/6pm; £2). The castle in Deal's neighbour **WALMER**, a mile to the south (same times; £2.70), is from the same period, but lost much of its original military character when it became the stately residence of the Lords Warden of the Cinque Ports. This had become an honorary title by the time the Duke of Wellington assumed the mantle, and rooms used both by him and the current incumbent, the Queen Mother, are on view to the public.

Twelve miles north of Dover is **SANDWICH**, an old market town on the River Stour. One of the nation's foremost ports before it became silted up, the town is now separated from the sandy beaches of Sandwich Bay by a mile of fields and golf greens. A mile and a half directly north of town are the remains of **Richborough Castle** (Easter–Sept daily 10am–6pm; Oct–Easter Tues–Sun 10am–4pm; £1.30), one of the coastal strong points built by the Romans along what became known as the Saxon Shore; amongst the relics inside the remarkably well-preserved walls are the remains of an early Saxon church. Elsewhere in town there's little to do except savour the atmosphere of provincial quiet, although if you do want to stay, Sandwich's **tourist office** in the Elizabethan Guildhall on Cattle Market (June–Sept daily 10am–2.30pm) provides a room-booking service.

Brighton

BRIGHTON is a place in which to enjoy the atmosphere of a quintessential pleasure resort rather than view historical sights or relax by the sea. The town has been a prime target for day-tripping Londoners ever since bathing in the sea first became fashionable in the late eighteenth century, and its status as the nearest convenient venue for a libidinous weekend helped provide Brighton with a racy reputation which still lingers. The wide range of nightlife owes a lot to the student population of Brighton University, the art college and Sussex University, while the summer intake of Brighton's scores of English language schools gives an international edge to the town's youthful feel.

From Brighton's **train station** it's a ten-minute straight stroll down to the seafront, four miles of shelving pebbles bordered by a balustraded promenade. If you arrive on the **coach**, you'll be put down in Pool Valley, which opens out onto the front. The **Palace Pier**, an obligatory call, is basically a half-mile amusement arcade lined with booths selling fish and chips, candyfloss and junky souvenirs. From here the antiquated locomotives of Volk's train (April–Sept), the first electric train in the country, run eastward towards the Marina and the nudist beach. Brighton's other pier, the West Pier, was severed from the mainland by gales in 1987, and now faces demolition.

A block back from the promenade are **The Lanes**, a shopping area of narrow alleys preserving the layout, but little of the ambience, of the fishing port Brighton used to be before seaside tourism took off. Inland from here, overlooking the main traffic confluence of the Old Steine, are the distinctive domes of the **Royal Pavilion** (daily 10am–5/6pm; £3.10), an Oriental pastiche built in 1817 for the future George IV. The opulently decorated interiors are Britain's most astounding example of the period's fascination with the East: look out particularly for the chinoiserie of the Music Room, the Indian-style wall paintings of the Banqueting Hall, and the kitchen's cast-iron palm trees. Brighton's **Museum and Art Gallery** (Tues–Sat 10am–5.45pm, Sun 2–5pm; free) is just around the corner on Church Street. Nondescript paintings are followed by a display of furniture through the ages, which includes some valuable Art Nouveau and Art Deco items, and a selection of local ephemera including one of the goat-drawn carts used by Victorian traders. One of the museum's more interesting features is a recreation of the "closett of curiosities" assembled by the London-based collector John Tradescant in the seventeenth century, an odd assortment of tribal implements, skulls of exotic animals and decorative trinkets from around the world.

Practicalities

The **tourist office**, at 10 Bartholomew Square in the Lanes, will book rooms for a commission (summer Mon–Fri 9am–5.30pm, Sat & Sun 10am–6pm; winter Mon–Sat 9am–5pm & Sun 10am–4pm). B&Bs are scattered all over town, with a concentration at the eastern end of town behind Marine Parade; a board at the train station gives a list of addresses and phone numbers. A few suggestions if booking ahead are *Calvaire Guest House*, 34 Upper Rock Gardens (☎0273/696899; ④), just above Marine Parade; *Cornerways*, 18–29 Caburn Rd (☎0273/731882; ④), near the station; and the *Queensbury Hotel*, 58 Regency Square (☎0273/25558; ⑤), close to the beach. Brighton's **youth hostel** at Patcham Place (☎0273/556196; ②), four miles north on the A23 to London, is not very convenient; buses #733, #107 and #137 pass nearby.

The Lanes and the surrounding streets have numerous good places to **eat**, ranging from chains like *Pizza Express* to *Wheeler's* decadent oyster-bar. Especially popular are *Food for Friends*, 41 Market Street, an inexpensive but classy vegetarian restaurant, and *Al Forno*, a cosy pizzeria tucked into a corner by the East Street entrance to the Lanes. If *Al Forno* is full, try the same management's *Al Duomo*, a bigger pizzeria by the North Street gate to the Pavilion. For straightforward drinking, the **pubs** of the Lanes are very popular, but the beer is better and the atmosphere less pushy in the pubs in Trafalgar Street, near the station – check out the *Lord Nelson* and the nearby *Prince Albert*. The *Hand in Hand*, Upper St James St, has its own brewery out the back.

Nightlife is hectic throughout the year, and there's probably more live music here than anywhere else outside London. For listings, pick up a free copy of the *Brighton Life* broadsheet from the tourist office, restaurants and pubs, or the much more substantial monthly magazine *The Punter*. Foremost among the **clubs** is *The Zap Club*, Old Ship Beach, with live events and different dance styles every night; its main rival is the *Escape Club*, 10 Marine Parade.

Chichester

CHICHESTER, a charming market town with a fine cathedral and a spate of Georgian buildings lining its central streets, is easily reached either by bus or rail from Brighton or direct from London. Both bus and train stations are at the head of Southgate Street, from where it's a ten-minute walk to the town's central Chichester Cross – an ornate stone structure built in 1501 to give shelter to market traders. Streets branch off from here at right angles, preserving the ground plan of the original Roman town.

West Street leads to the **Cathedral** (Mon–Sat 9.15am–5.15pm, Sun 10am–4pm; donation requested), largely a twelfth-century structure save for an elegant fifteenth-century bell tower, standing apart from the church to the west. The interior is renowned for its contemporary devotional art, which includes a stained-glass window by Marc Chagall. The **Town Museum** (Tues–Sat 10am–5.30pm, Sun 2–5.30pm; free) in an old corn store on Little London, just off East Street, holds a routine mishmash.

More memorable is the **Guildhall** (June–Sept Tues–Sat 1–5pm; free) at the end of Little London in Priory Park, preserving medieval frescoes in a thirteenth-century Franciscan church. The **Pallant House** (Tues–Sat 10am–5.30pm; £2.50) in the Pallant, an enclave of eighteenth-century houses, holds a wide range of modern paintings, the odd Léger and Klee among them. However, Chichester's major attraction is one and a half miles west – **Fishbourne Roman Palace** (daily 10am–6pm; Dec–Feb Sun closes 4pm; £2), the best-preserved Roman villa in the country. The home of a Romanized Celtic aristocrat, it's situated in extensive gardens which recreate the appearance of the palace grounds as they were in Roman times. A pavilion has been built over the rich floor mosaics, a mix of figurative designs (with leaping sea monsters) and intricate geometric patterns. Fishbourne can be reached by following the signs along West Street and its successors or by bus #700, asking for the Salthill Road stop.

Chichester's **tourist office** (Mon–Sat 9.30am–5.30pm) is at 29a South Street. There's no hostel here, but the tourist office should help out with room bookings – half the houses on the main roads into town seem to offer B&B. For **food**, the most filling option is *Sweeney Todd's*, 13 South St.

Winchester

WINCHESTER's rural tranquillity betrays little of its former importance as the political and ecclesiastical power base of southern England. A town of Roman foundation, Winchester rose to prominence as the capital of Wessex, where ninth-century strongman King Alfred the Great established his leadership over the fractious Anglo-Saxons, forming the nucleus of a future English kingdom. Despite the ascendancy of London, Winchester remained an important locus of power well into the Middle Ages. The shrine of Saint Swithin, tutor to King Alfred and bishop of Winchester, made the town an important destination for pilgrims, and the flow of European merchants to the annual Saint Giles' fair kept the civic coffers full.

Alfred's statue stands at the eastern end of the Broadway, the town's main thoroughfare, becoming the High Street as it progresses west. Much of the exterior of the **Cathedral**, to the south, is twelfth-century, although bits of earlier masonry show through here and there, in particular the Norman stonework of the south transept. The interior contains some fine sarcophagi, including one good example of the late medieval love of the macabre in the depiction of the wasted corpse of bishop Stephen Gardiner, who married Queen Mary to Philip of Spain here in 1554. Raised above a screen surrounding the high altar are mortuary chests holding the remains of the pre-Conquest kings of England, including the Saxon kings of Wessex as well as the Dane Canute. The Angel chapel contains sixteenth-century wall paintings of the miracles of the Virgin Mary, although a modern replica now covers the originals in order to protect them. Jane Austen is buried on the south side of the nave; the inscription on the floor slab remembers her merely as the daughter of a local clergyman, making no mention of her renown as a novelist.

Immediately outside are traces of the original Saxon cathedral, built by Cenwalh, king of Wessex, in the mid-seventh century. The true grandeur of this structure is shown by a model in the **Museum** (April–Sept Mon–Sat 10am–5pm, Sun 2–5pm; free) on the western side of the cathedral close. Other exhibits include mosaics and pottery from Roman Winchester, or Venta Belgarum – literally "market of the Belgae", a reminder that the inhabitants of Britain subjugated by the Romans were not always the "ancient Britons" of popular imagination, but often rather more recent immigrants from across the Channel. On the other side of the cathedral close is the fourteenth-century Pilgrims Hall, from where a signposted route leads through a medieval quarter to **Winchester College**, the oldest of Britain's public schools. Visitors can peer in at the school's quadrangles and visit the chapel. It's then a 25-minute walk across the Water

Meadow to the medieval almshouse of **St Cross** (April–Sept Mon–Sat 9am–12.30pm & 2–5pm; Oct–March Mon–Sat 10.30am–12.30pm & 2–3.30pm; £1), with fifteenth-century courtyards and a church containing a triptych by the Flemish painter Mabuse.

At the western end of the High Street, the **West Gate** (same hours as museum) contains artefacts relating to its seventeenth-century role as a debtors' prison. Beyond it, behind modern council offices, is the thirteenth-century **Great Hall** (daily 10am–5pm), a banqueting chamber used by successive kings of England and renowned for the thirteenth-century Round Table which now hangs from the wall. Some three centuries after its construction the table was inscribed with the names of King Arthur's knights, probably for the visit of Emperor Charles V, who was entertained here by Henry VIII in 1522.

Practicalities

Winchester **train station** is five minutes north of the West Gate. The **bus** terminal is on the High Street, just opposite the Guildhall, in which the **tourist office** is installed (May–Sept Mon–Sat 9am–5pm, plus Sun 2–5pm in summer). Winchester's affluence is reflected in both the style and prices of its **B&Bs**, most of which cluster in the streets between St Cross Road and Christchurch Road, south of town. *Brentwood* is a nice B&B in Stockbridge Road, convenient for the train station (☎0962/853536; ④). There's an atmospheric **youth hostel** in the City Mill, behind Alfred's statue (☎0962/853723; ②). For **food**, the *Baker's Arms*, 22 High St, does good pub grub, and there are a number of decent places on Jewry St; the *Wykeham Arms*, 75 Kingsgate St, is a slightly snobby pub close to Winchester College but it does decent food. Just to **drink**, the more down-to-earth *Mash Tun*, 60 Eastgate St, is good, as is the *Willow Tree*, 16 Durngate Terrace.

THE WEST COUNTRY

The **West Country** has never been a precise geographical term, and there will always be a certain amount of argument as to where it actually starts. But as a broad generalization, the cosmopolitan feel of the southeast begins to fade into a slower, rural pace of life from **Salisbury** onwards, becoming more pronounced the further west you travel. In Neolithic times a rich and powerful culture evolved here, as shown by monuments such as **Stonehenge** and **Avebury**, and the isolated moorland sites of inland **Cornwall**. The main urban attractions of western England are **Bristol**, **Exeter**, **Plymouth** and the well-preserved Regency spa town of Bath, while those in search of rural peace and quiet should head for wilder areas such as **Exmoor** or the more compelling bleakness of **Dartmoor**. The western extremities of Britain include some of the most beautiful stretches of coastline, its rugged, rocky shores battered by the Atlantic, although excellent sandy beaches make it one of the country's busiest corners over the summer. All of the region's major centres can be reached fairly easily by rail or coach direct from London. Local bus services cover most areas, although in the rural depths of Exmoor and Dartmoor they can be very sparse indeed.

Salisbury and Salisbury Plain

SALISBURY's central feature is the elegant spire of its **Cathedral** (daily 8am–6.30/8.15pm; donation requested), the tallest in the country, rising over four hundred feet above the lawns of the cathedral close. With the exception of the spire, the cathedral was almost entirely completed in the thirteenth century, and is one of the few great English churches that is not a hodge-podge of different styles. Prominent among the features of the interior are the fourteenth-century clock just inside the north porch, one of the oldest working timepieces in the country, and an exceptional Tudor memorial to the Earl of Hertford, Lady Jane Grey's brother-in-law, in the Lady Chapel at the eastern end of the church. An octagonal chapterhouse, approached via the extensive cloisters (Mon–Sat 10am–5pm, Sun 1–5pm; 30p) holds a collection of precious manuscripts, among which is one of the four original copies of the Magna Carta. For the postcard view of the cathedral immortalized by Constable, wander across the meadows and over the River Avon to **Harnham**, where you can have lunch or coffee in an old mill.

Most of Salisbury's remaining sights are grouped in a sequence of historic houses around the close, the old walled inner town around the cathedral. The **Salisbury Museum** (Mon–Sat 10am–5pm, Sun 2–5pm; £2.25), opposite the main portal of the cathedral on West Walk, is a good place to bone up on the Neolithic history of Wessex before heading out to Stonehenge and Avebury. The **Mompesson House** on North Walk (April–Oct noon–5.30pm; closed Thurs & Fri; £3.60) is a fine eighteenth-century house complete with Georgian furniture and fittings.

A ten-minute hop on local bus #3, #5, #9 or #X19 takes you to the ruins of **Old Sarum** (April–Sept daily 10am–6pm; Oct–March Tues–Sun 10am–4pm; £1.30), abandoned in the fourteenth century when the bishopric moved south to Salisbury, whereupon Old Sarum became one of the country's notorious "rotten boroughs", continuing to return two Members of Parliament until 1832 despite the absence of voters. Traces of the medieval town are visible in the outlines of its Norman cathedral and castle mound, but the ditch-encircled site is far older, populated in Iron Age, Roman and Saxon times.

Practicalities

Salisbury's train station is across the River Avon on South Western Road, a short walk northwest of town. Buses (poor London connections) terminate behind Endless Street, a block north of the **tourist office** in Fish Row, just off the Market Place (June–Sept Mon–Sat 9am–7pm, Sun 11am–4pm; Oct–May Mon–Sat 9am–5pm). There's an excellent *YHA* **hostel** at Milford Hill House, Milford Hill, five minutes east of the city centre (☎0722/327572; ②). Most **B&Bs** inhabit an arc north of town beyond the train station; if booking ahead, try the *Clovelley Guest House* on Mill Street (☎0722/322 055; ⑤), *Farthings Guest House* on Swaines Close (☎0722/330 749; ⑤), or the sixteenth-century *Old Bakery*, a B&B at 25 Bedwin St (☎0722/32100; ④). One of the best places to **eat** is *Mo's*, 62 Milford St, near the hostel; in the same street you'll find *The Oddfellows Arms*, an excellent **pub**, and the *Cathedral Hotel*, which has **live music** from time to time. The city's oldest pub is *The Hauch of Venison*, just off the market square on Minster St.

Stonehenge

The uplands northwest of Salisbury were a thriving centre of Neolithic civilization, the greatest legacy of which is **Stonehenge** (daily 10am–4/8pm; £2.70) – served by bus #3 from Salisbury four times daily or take a taxi from the train station. The monument's age is being constantly revised as research progresses, but it's known that it was built in several distinct stages and adapted to the needs of successive cultures.

The first Stonehenge probably consisted of a circular ditch dug somewhere between 2600 and 2200 BC. This was followed by the construction within the ditch of two concentric circles of sixty bluestones, thought to have originated in the Prescelly mountains of southern Wales. At least two more centuries elapsed before the outer circle and inner horseshoe were put in place, made up of local Wiltshire sarsen stones, the twenty-foot uprights topped by horizontal slabs. The way in which the sun's rays penetrate the central enclosure at dawn on midsummer's day has led to speculation about Stonehenge's role as either an astronomical observatory or a place of sun worship, but knowledge of the cultures responsible for building it is too scanty to reach any firm conclusions. Overlooking the point where the A303 and A344 meet, the stones themselves are controversially fenced off to prevent further tourist erosion, although entering the monument from the visitors' centre allows a reasonably close-up look.

Avebury

Salisbury also serves as a base for visiting the equally important – and much more atmospheric – Neolithic site at **AVEBURY**. The #6 Salisbury–Swindon bus (four daily) passes by Avebury village, and catching the 9.20am bus from Salisbury and returning from Avebury at 2pm makes a day trip feasible.

The Avebury monoliths were erected some time between 2600 and 2100 BC, and their main circle – with a diameter of some 400 metres – forms a monument bigger in scale than Stonehenge, albeit not as impressive in its architectural sophistication. Further lines of standing stones form the West Kennet Avenue, thought to be a processional way, running two miles south to the so-called Sanctuary, possibly a gathering place of religious significance, where a small circle of stones surrounds the site of a wooden hut constructed around 3000 BC. All this is best considered with a pint or two from the village pub, set right beside the main stone circle.

To walk off the beer, follow a section of the **Ridgeway**, a 4000-year old prehistoric highway, which loops northeast from Overton Hill, just south of the village; it once ran the breadth of Britain and can still be walked or cycled (it is signposted as a National Trust trail) to Streatley-on-Thames, near Reading. Avebury's little **Archeological Museum** (daily 10am–4/6.30pm; £1.20) has a display on it as well as the monoliths and other ancient sites in the vicinity. Among the most interesting and accessible are **Silbury Hill**, an enormous man-made earthwork constructed around 2800 BC, two miles southwest of the village, and **West Kennet Long Barrow** just beyond, an elongated earthen burial mound in use for over 1500 years from about 3700 BC.

Bath

The last main stop on the rail line to Bristol is the handsome town of **BATH**, an ancient Roman spa town revived by eighteenth-century high society. It's the extensive reconstruction put into effect by Neoclassicist architects John Wood and his son John Wood the Younger that gives the town its distinctive appearance, with endless terraces of weathered sandstone fringed by spindly black railings.

In the Roman era, a hot spring sacred to the Celtic goddess of the waters, Sulis, provided the centrepiece of an extensive bath complex, now restored as the **Roman Baths and Museum** (March–Oct daily 9am–6pm; Aug also 8–10pm; Nov–Feb Mon–Sat 9am–5pm, Sun 10am–5pm; £4, combined ticket with Costume Museum £5). The pools, pipes and underfloor heating are remarkable demonstrations of the ingenuity of Roman engineering. The Pump Room, built above the Roman site in the eighteenth century, is the place to sample the waters, while listening to genteel tunes from the resident chamber ensemble. The neighbouring **Abbey Church** (Mon–Sat 9am–5.30pm, Sun 1.15–2.30pm & 4.30–5.30pm) is renowned for the lofty fifteenth-century vault of its choir, and the dense carpet of gravestones and memorials which cover the floor.

The best of Bath's eighteenth-century architecture is on the high ground to the north of the town centre, where the well-proportioned urban planning of the Woods is best showcased by the elegant Circus and the adjacent **Royal Crescent**. The house at no. 1 Royal Crescent is now a museum (March–Oct Tues–Sun 10.30am–5pm; Nov to mid-Dec Tues–Sun 10.30am–4pm; £2), showing how the Crescent's houses would have looked in the Regency period. The social calendar of Bath's elite centred on John Wood the Younger's **Assembly Rooms** (March–Oct Mon–Sat 9.30am–6pm, Sun 10am–6pm; Nov–Feb Mon–Sat 10am–5pm, Sun 11am–5pm; free), just east of the Circus; recently renovated, it includes a **Museum of Costume** (same times; £2.40) in the basement. The nearby Octagon, just off Milsom Street, now houses the **National Centre of Photography** (daily 9.30am–5.30pm; £3), an impressive survey of the development of photographic technology. One small museum in this northern part of town provides a tonic after so much Georgian artifice – the **Museum of English Naive Art** in the Countess of Huntingdon Chapel, The Vineyard (April–Oct Mon–Sat 10.30am–5.30pm, Sun 2–6pm; £1.50), with its beguiling display works by itinerant painters and craftsmen.

The triple arches of Pulteney Bridge lead from the town centre across the River Avon, and up Great Pulteney Street to the **Holburne Art Museum** (end-Feb to mid-Dec Mon–Sat 11am–5pm, Sun 2.30–6pm; Nov–Easter closed Mon; £2.50), which contains silver, porcelain and furniture from the Regency period. Just south of the town centre at 19 New King Street is the **Herschel House** (March–Oct daily 2–5pm; Nov–Feb Sat & Sun only; £2), another eighteenth-century interior, housing the home-made telescope with which astronomer William Herschel first spotted Uranus in 1781.

Practicalities

Train and bus stations are both situated at the top of Manvers Street, five minutes south of the centre. The **tourist office** is in the Colonnades shopping mall just west of the Baths (June to mid-Sept Mon–Sat 9.30am–6pm, Sun 10am–4pm; mid-Sept to May Mon–Sat 9.30am–5pm). Bath's **youth hostel** is at Bathwick Hill (☎0225/465674; ②), one and a half miles east of town. Pick of Bath's **B&Bs** are *Joanna House*, 5 Pulteney Ave (☎0225/335246; ④), and *Alderney Guest House*, 3 Pulteney Rd (☎0225/312365; ④). The main tourist thoroughfares provide more tearooms than you can handle. For less delicate fare, Barton Street has a couple of good places to **eat** – *The Walrus and the Carpenter* at no. 28, and *Pasta Galore* at no. 31. The *Grapes*, Westgate Street, is a favoured student **pub**; the *Coeur de Lion*, 17 Northumberland Place, a classic watering hole, inevitably popular with tourists .

Bristol

Situated on a succession of lumpy hills just inland from the mouth of the Avon, the thriving city of **BRISTOL** grew rich on transatlantic trade – slaving, in particular – to become England's second city in the early part of the nineteenth century. It's slipped down the table since, and the docks have all but gone, but the city remains a wealthy, commercial centre, home to tobacco and aviation industries, a major university and much of the West Country's cultural life.

The city "centre" – in so much as there is one – is an elongated oval traffic interchange, built over part of the old docks. On its south side is the **Floating Harbour**, an area of waterways which formed the commercial hub of the nineteenth-century town, now the scene of a good deal of renovation. A couple of important cultural institutions are to be found in converted warehouses here: the **Arnolfini Gallery** on Narrow Quay (Mon–Sat 10am–7pm, Sun noon–7pm; free), one of Britain's best contemporary arts venues, and the **Watershed Arts Centre** , directly opposite; both have nice cafés.

Across a swing bridge from the Arnolfini, on Prince's Wharf, is the new and imaginative **Bristol Industrial Museum** (Mon–Wed, Sat & Sun 10am–1pm & 2–5pm; £2). Just east of here, at the end of Redcliffe Parade, rises the Gothic church of **St Mary Redcliffe** (daily 8am–6/8pm), described by Queen Elizabeth I as the "godliest, fairest, and most famous parish church in England". It was here that the "boy-poet" Chatterton, commemorated in the churchyard, claimed to have discovered medieval manuscripts – in reality his own compositions. To the west of the Industrial Museum, ten minutes' walk down Cumberland Road (or bus #511) and a right onto Gas Ferry Rd brings you to the **Maritime Heritage Centre** (daily 10am–5/6pm; free), celebrating Bristol's shipbuilding past and providing access to Brunel's **SS Great Britain** (£2.90), the first iron, propellor-driven ship – launched from this very dock in 1843.

Returning to the "centre", and heading uphill, past College Green – flanked by the city's **Cathedral** (not a patch on St Mary's) – you can follow Park Street to the university Wills Memorial Building, a Victorian neo-Gothic monster, endowed by the local tobacco dynasty along with the adjacent **Bristol Museum and Art Gallery** (daily 10am–5pm; £2). Beyond offerings of Egyptology, dinosaurs and giant elks, you reach a varied, half-decent art collection, predictably strongest on the Victorians and featuring Burne-Jones' *The Briar Rose* among a posy of Pre-Raphaelites. If this leaves you in need of some fresh air, take the street opposite the museum and you'll find yourself on **Brandon Hill**, topped by a splendid folly, **Cabot's Tower** (free), from which vantage point you can cast an eye over much of the city, with the old docks spread out below you to the south, the suburb of Clifton and its suspension bridge to the west.

The rest of your time is best spent wandering around **CLIFTON**, whose airy terraces, crescents and circuses give a taste of the Georgian splendours to be found in nearby Bath. It's a somewhat genteel quarter, but full of enticing pubs and with a spectacular focus in the **Clifton Suspension Bridge**, a glorious creation by the indefatigable engineer and railway builder Isambard Kingdom Brunel, spanning the limestone abyss of the Avon Gorge. It's free to cross the bridge on foot: cheap admission for generations of suicides plus the odd lunatics – like Dangerous Sports Club members, who leapt off (unscathed) on bouncing "bunjee" ropes a few years back. On a low ridge above the bridge is the **Observatory** (daily summer 10.30am–6pm; winter 11am–4pm; £1), another Victorian job, in whose dome is a *camera obscura*, encompassing views of the gorge and bridge.

Practicalities

Bristol's Temple Meads **train station** is a five-minute bus ride southeast of the centre. The **bus** station is just north of the centre on Marlborough Street. There's a **tourist office** in St Nicholas' Church beside Bristol Bridge (Mon–Fri 9am–5.15pm, Sat & Sun 9am–1pm & 2–5.15pm). There is a new, showcase **youth hostel**, 64 Prince St (☎0272/221659; ②), splendidly situated in an old wharfside building. Among the **B&Bs**, check tourist board lists for Clifton addresses, the most pleasant location: the *Oakfield Hotel*, 52 Oakfield Rd (☎0272/735556; ④), and *Naseby House Hotel*, 105 Pembroke Rd (☎0272/737859; ⑤), are two possibilities in the quarter.

For **food and drink**, Clifton again offers the best choice. First call among its pubs should be the *Coronation Tap* (on an obscure alley – ask for it by name), a classic scrumpy (cider) bar whose regulars show the effects; best value of the restaurants is *Le Franglais* at 3a Regent St. Elsewhere, pubs of note include the *Highbury Vaults*, a lively snug on St Michael's Hill (north of the centre), and two on King St (two blocks north of the Arnolfini): the ancient *Llandoger Trow* and *The Old Duke* – the latter with live jazz.

The Bristol-based listings magazine *Venue* is a vital source for details of **cultural activities and nightlife**. There's usually a lot on, with art cinemas at both the *Arnolfini* and *Watershed*, a renowned repertory company at the *Bristol Old Vic* (King St), plus a thriving local music scene. *The Lakota* on Upper York St (off Stokes Croft Rd near the bus station) is a good venue for Indie bands, as is the Anson Room in the Student Union on Queens Rd.

Wells and Glastonbury

A small town dwarfed by its extraordinary cathedral, **WELLS** is served by shoals of buses from nearby Bath and Bristol, arriving at Princes Road bus station, five minutes from the centre. Follow Cuthbert Street eastwards from here to the picturesque inn-lined Market Place, and the **tourist office** in the Town Hall (April–Oct Mon–Fri 9.30am–5.30pm, Sat & Sun 10am–5pm; Nov–March daily 10am–4pm). From here a gateway leads through to the cathedral close, bringing you face to face with an intoxicating array of Gothic statuary, mostly dating from the 1230s and 1240s. Inside, arches at the crossing form a great organic interlacing pattern – a unique arrangement devised as a means of stopping the unstable tower from corkscrewing round. South of the cathedral, a drawbridge leads across a swan-infested moat to the **Bishop's Palace** (April–Oct Tues & Thurs 11am–6pm, Sun 2–6pm; Aug daily 11am–6pm; £2), where opulently furnished rooms are watched over by portraits of former bishops. On the other side of the cathedral close are the town **Museum** (Easter–June Mon–Sat 10am–5.30pm, Sun 11am–5.30pm; July & Aug closes 3pm; Oct–Easter Wed–Sun 11am–4pm; £1) and the **Vicar's Close**, a row of fourteenth-century terraced houses. The tourist office has a list of B&Bs, but the nearest **youth hostel** is six miles west in the village of Cheddar (☎0934/742494; ②), reached on buses #126 or #826. The dramatic **Cheddar Gorge**, formed by the collapse of a cave system, is walkable from here.

Buses #163, #376 and #378 head southeast from Wells to **GLASTONBURY**, a small rural town which has attracted more mystique and speculation than any other place in England. The first layer of the Glastonbury myth stems from its status as the first Christian foundation in England, and the belief that Joseph of Arimathea, bringing the chalice of Christ's blood, was the monastery's founder. Glastonbury is also known for its Arthurian associations. The **Tor**, a natural mound overlooking the town, is identified with the Isle of Avalon, the resting place of the Once and Future King – not as ridiculous as it sounds when one remembers that the whole area was surrounded by marshes in ancient times. Cadbury Hill, facing the Tor from the opposite side of the valley, is one of the candidates for the site of Camelot. A final layer to the Glastonbury yarn comes from those who maintain that the topography of the area, both natural and man-made, corresponds to signs of the zodiac when viewed from the air. The cumulative effect of this has been to make Glastonbury a magnet for those in search of a taste of the spiritual, a process fuelled by the hippiedom of the Eighties.

The town itself is not much more than a High Street, the lower end of which, around the Market Cross, is overrun by New Age book and crystal shops. There's an intriguing **Town Museum** (Mon–Thurs 10am–4pm, Fri & Sat 10am–6pm, Sun 10am–5pm; £1) housed in the Tribunal, a fifteenth-century courthouse, which contains relics from a Celtic lake village excavated to the east of the town, including excellent examples of pottery and a wooden canoe from the period. The impressive ruins of the **Abbey** are approached around the corner from Magdalene Street (daily Sept–May 9am–6pm; June–Aug 9.30am–6pm; £1.50); this was the oldest Christian establishment in continuous use in England until Henry VIII put an end to it. A mile to the east is the Tor, at the base of which stands the natural spring known as **Chalice Well** (March–Oct 10am–6pm; Nov–Feb 1–4pm; 50p). The ferrous waters which flow from the hillside here were popularly thought to have gained their colour from the blood of Christ, supposedly flowing from the chalice buried by Joseph. On top of the Tor stands a tower, all that remains of a fourteenth-century church; the views from here are spectacular, and the Tor is a popular place from which to observe the sunrise on the morning of June 21.

By nightfall Glastonbury reverts to sleepy rural stillness – except during the summer solstice and the Glastonbury Festival, held in June most years and drawing around 80,000 people to its three-day binge of music and miscellaneous events. At other times, if you're looking for excitement it's best to press on. If you don't, the **tourist office**, housed in the Tribunal in the High Street (Mon–Thurs 10am–4pm, Fri & Sat 10am–6pm, Sun 10am–5pm; ☎0458/832954), will find a room. The nearest **youth hostel** is a basic one at The Chalet, Ivythorn Hill (☎0458/42961; ②), just outside the town of Street two miles southwest (buses include the frequent #163, as well as #131, #160, #167 and #168). Glastonbury does have a convenient **campsite**, the *Old Oak Touring Park*, at Wick Farm on the far side of the Tor (March–Oct; ☎0458/831437).

Exmoor

EXMOOR, an expanse of heather-covered moorland crossed by wooded valleys (or combes) overlooking Devon's north coast, is best approached from **MINEHEAD**, on the eastern fringes of the national park. Bus #28 runs to Minehead from the nearest railhead at Taunton, midway between Bristol and Exeter. Public transport on the moor is limited to the daily buses #300 and #X39, both covering the stretch from Minehead along the coast to Ilfracombe; #1 and #2 connect Dulverton with Lynton via Simonsbath; #13 connects Tauton to Simonsbath and Lynton; and #11 Dulverton to Minehead – but a sprinkling of youth hostels along the North Devon Coastal Path makes walking feasible. There's a basic **youth hostel** two miles south of Minehead at Alcombe Combe (April–Oct; ☎0643/702 595; ②); more appealing is the next village to the west, **PORLOCK**, with an attractive bay to the north, and Exmoor's highest peak, Dunkley Beacon, an eminently walkable four miles south. Guesthouse accommodation in Porlock can be fixed up beforehand by the tourist office in Minehead. Another twelve miles along the coast are the modern town of **LYNTON** and its more historical fishing port of Lynmouth down the hill, the two towns joined by a funicular. Either provides a good base for exploring some beautiful walking territory above the sea. Lynton's tourist office is in the town hall and there's a **hostel** at the village of Lynbridge just south of the town (☎0598/53237; ②). **ILFRACOMBE**, an old-fashioned donkeys-on-the-beach seaside resort, lies just beyond the western extremity of the national park. The town's tourist office is at The Promenade, and there's a **youth hostel** at Ashmour House, 1 Hillsborough Terrace (April–Sept; ☎0271/865337; ②). The *Earlsdale Hotel*, 51 St Brannocks Rd (☎0271/862496; ③), and *Two Ways*, 39 St Brannock's Rd (☎0271/864017; ④), are two **B&B** possibilities.

Exeter

Ranged on a hillside above the River Exe, a few miles north of where the river meets the sea, **EXETER** is no longer the busy port which made it one of England's wealthiest provincial centres in Tudor times. However, an attractive quayside provides one link with the city's maritime past, and a wide choice of nightlife provides an excuse to dally longer. Central Exeter is characterized by red sandstone – hence the name of the Norman castle of Rougemont, the brick gatehouse of which stands a block northwest of the High Street. The **Royal Albert Memorial Museum** on Queen Street, below (Tues–Sat 10am–5.30pm), holds remains from the town's Roman incarnation, and a tiger shot by King George V in 1911. On the other side of the High Street, the spacious cathedral close is dominated by the statue-filled niches of the **Cathedral's** west facade, framed by two Norman towers. Brightly painted roof bosses add colour to the nave, while the north transept's memorial to the Sylke family is overlooked by a fifteenth-century *Resurrection* and clock.

At the point where the High Street becomes Fore Street is the city's finest civic building, the **Guildhall**, originally fourteenth-century but resplendent with an Elizabethan portico. The hall itself (Tues–Fri 10am–1pm & 2–4pm, Sat 10am–12.30pm; free) merits a quick look inside for its Tudor panelling and murky portraits. A right turn off Fore Street into The Mint leads to **St Nicholas Priory** (April–Oct Tues–Sat 10am–1pm & 2–5pm; £1), preserving Tudor guest quarters and a Norman undercroft. To the southeast, occupying two sides of the dock basin, the **Maritime Museum** (April–Sept daily 10am–5pm; Oct–March Sat & Sun 10am–4pm; £3.80) maintains examples of working boats which are becoming extinct as old lifestyles die out: a Chinese junk and Indonesian fishing vessels are amongst the exhibits.

Exeter has two **train stations**: Central, north of the centre on the far side of Rougemont Castle, and Exeter St David's, further out at the end of St David's Hill. The

tourist office is in the Civic Centre on Paris Street, opposite the bus station (Mon–Fri 9am–5pm, Sat 9am–1pm & 2–5pm). The **youth hostel**, 47 Countess Wear Rd (☎0392/873329; ②), is two miles to the south (minibus K or T from the High St). Most **B&Bs** are situated between the two train stations: *Clock Tower Guest House*, 16 New North Rd (☎0392/52493; ③), and *Rhona's Guest House*, 15 Blackall Rd (☎0392/77791; ③), are both in this area.

Two historic **pubs** on the tourist itinerary, the *Turk's Head* on the High Street and the *Ship Inn* on St Martin's Lane, are good for bar lunches. *Herbie's*, 15 North St, has an extensive vegetarian menu, while *La Rosina*, 27 South Street, has a range of pasta. For evening **drinking**, there are several pubs down by the river. Two on the Quayside are *On the Waterfront* and the more cosy and traditional *Prospect*. There's a surprising array of **nightlife** on offer. *St Anne's Well Brewery* on Lower North St is a good drinking venue which sometimes has live music, the *Hothouse* on the Quay has the latest club sounds, and *Timepiece*, Little Castle St, is a club with alternative/indie leanings. The *Exeter Arts Centre*, off Candy St, programmes regular modern jazz events alongside other musical genres; *Exeter University Guild of Students*, Stocker Rd, is the place for bigger gigs.

Plymouth

PLYMOUTH owes its importance to the natural harbour of Plymouth Sound, and although most naval activity shifted westwards to the adjoining town of Devonport in the early eighteenth century, Plymouth's maritime connections remain paramount. Heavily bombed during the last war, central Plymouth has been reconstructed in sterile, concrete style; this shouldn't deter you from investigating the wealth of sights which lie near the seafront. The modern city's southern limits are bound by the grassy platform of the **Hoe**, commanding impressive panoramas of the Sound, and renowned as the venue of Sir Francis Drake's pre-battle game of bowls. The Hoe bears a statue of Drake himself, nonchalantly pawing a globe, but its dominating feature is **Smeaton's Tower** (daily Easter to mid-Sept 10.30am–5pm; 70p), the third in a series of lighthouses built to warn sailors of the Eddystone rocks on the approaches to Plymouth Sound, dismantled and brought here in 1882. Immediately below this is the **Plymouth Dome** (daily 9am–6pm; £3.30, combined ticket with Smeaton's Tower £3.80), a modern museum with audiovisual displays of maritime history.

From the Hoe, Madeira Rd winds eastward below the Citadel towards the **Barbican**, originally Plymouth's main port area and now a historic neighbourhood overlooking a thriving marina. A jetty on the waterfront itself bears the **Pilgrim Fathers' Stone**, marking their last port of call before sailing for the New World in 1620; alongside are plaques commemorating other voyagers, notably Sir Humphrey Gilbert, remembered here as "the father of British colonization", who set off from Plymouth in 1583 to claim Newfoundland. The **Elizabethan House** at 32 New Street (Easter–Sept Tues–Sat 10am–1pm & 2–5.30pm; £1) preserves the character of the harbourside dwellings in which Tudor merchants and sea captains used to live. Up the hill from the Barbican, the **Merchant's House**, 33 St Andrew's Street (April–Sept daily 10am–5.30 pm; 80p), offers glimpses of Plymouth history told through the trades of its inhabitants, and a reconstructed Victorian pharmacist's shop on the top floor. A block uphill from here is the modern reconstruction of the bombed-out Gothic church of St Andrew. Behind it is the town's oldest surviving structure, the fifteenth-century **Prysten**, or priest's house, a plain stone building holding relics from the nearby church and some interesting medieval tapestries. Plymouth's **Museum and Art Gallery**, Drake's Circus (Tues–Sat 10am–5.30pm, Sun 10am–5pm), drowns you in an ocean of porcelain, although there's an interesting collection of artefacts left by William Cottman of Ivybridge to the city in 1853, consisting of books, drawings and paintings (including a Reynolds).

Practicalities

Plymouth's **train station** is a mile north of the Hoe; the bus station is below Exeter Street to the west. The southern portion of Armada Way passes the **tourist office** in the Civic Centre (Mon–Fri 9am–5pm, Sat 9am–4pm; winter closes 12.30pm Sat). Plymouth's basic **youth hostel** is at Belmont House, Devonport Rd (☎0752/562189; ②), half a mile west of the train station. The *YWCA* houses both sexes and is just behind the Hoe at 9–13 Lockyer St (☎0752/660 321; ②). B&Bs are clustered in the streets just north of the Hoe; try *Loma Loma*, 227 Citadel Rd (0752/661859; ③), *Transatlantic Hotel*, 15 Garden Crescent (☎0752/223845; ③), or *White House*, 12 Athenaeum St (☎0752/662356; ④). Plymouth's **nightlife** centres around Union Street, a 500-yard strip running west from Royal Parade, taking in pubs, discos, clubs and fast-food joints. *The Academy*, housed in an Edwardian theatre with coloured tiles depicting the defeat of the Armada, regularly hosts clubbish discos. A swathe of similarly rowdy, but more atmospheric pubs inhabit the Barbican.

Dartmoor

Lying between Exeter and Plymouth, **Dartmoor** is one of England's most beautiful wilderness areas, an expanse of wild uplands that's home to an indigenous species of wild pony and dotted with **tors**, characteristic wind-eroded pillars of granite. The main focus for visitors in the middle of the park is **POSTBRIDGE**, easily reached by local bus from Plymouth. Famous for its medieval bridge over the East Dart river, this is a good starting point for walks in the woodlands surrounding Bellever Tor to the south. Postbridge's **tourist office**, on the main road through the village (April–Oct daily 10am–5pm; Nov–March Sat & Sun only 10am–4pm), will supply information on the national park. The nearest **youth hostel** is at Bellever, one mile south (April–Oct; ☎0822/88227; ②).

The most untamed parts of the moor, around its highest points High Willhays and Yes Tor, are above the market town of **OKEHAMPTON** – served by the four times weekly #86 bus from Plymouth or the daily #118 to Tavistock (from where there are regular buses), or the much more frequent #628 and #629 from Exeter. Despite the stark beauty of the terrain, this part of the moor is used by the Ministry of Defence as a firing range: details of times when it's safe to walk the moor are available from the National Park Information Centre on Main Street (April–Oct Mon–Sat 10am–5pm; daily in Aug; ☎0837/53020), which also operates a room-booking service. Okehampton has a couple of attractions in its own right. The **Museum of Dartmoor Life** on West St (June–Sept daily 10am–5pm; March–May, Oct & Nov closed Sun; £1.50) offers interesting anthropological insights, including a look at life in one of the Dartmoor longhouses, the stone and turf huts in which the moorland natives used to live. Surrounded by woods one mile southwest of town is the now crumbling Norman keep of **Okehampton Castle** (Easter–Sept daily 10am–6pm; Oct–Easter Tues–Sun 10am–4pm; £1.70).

Cornwall

England's westernmost county, **Cornwall** includes some of the country's most scenic stretches of coastline. Largely a rocky, rugged area, the Cornish coast also features some extensive sandy beaches, making it England's busiest seaside destination; beware of the summer crush in principal resorts like St Ives and Newquay. The Lizard peninsula and Land's End are the obvious places to gain access to the more dramatic stretches of the coast: Falmouth and Penzance respectively provide convenient bases from which to explore them. Penzance can be reached direct from London by train – Falmouth, St Ives and Newquay each require at least one change.

Falmouth and the Lizard

FALMOUTH occupies an enviable situation at the mouth of a series of estuaries, all meeting to form the perfect natural harbour of Carrick Roads. The town itself centres on the broad expanse of the Moor, site of the bus station, civic buildings and a small Art Gallery (Mon–Fri 10am–4pm), featuring local scenes by Falmouth-born Victorian painter Henry Scott-Tuke. The town's main thoroughfare, Market Street, runs parallel to the harbour towards the south, passing on the way a **Maritime Museum** (daily April–Sept 10am–4pm; Oct–March 10am–3pm) which offers a selection of dockside ephemera. More rewarding is a visit to Pendennis Point and its **Castle** (Easter–Sept daily 10am–6pm; Oct–Easter Tues–Sun 10am–4pm; £1.80), dominating the town's southern fringes. One of the best-preserved examples of Henry VIII's system of coastal forts, the castle complex retains a couple of evocative, armour-filled rooms, and the seaward panorama from the grassy ramparts makes the visit especially worthwhile. Hourly ferries leave Falmouth for the Roseland Peninsula on the opposite side of Carrick Roads, where the village of St Mawes is renowned for its lush, subtropical vegetation and another Tudor fortress (same hours; £1.30).

Falmouth's **tourist office** is at the junction of Killigrew St and the Moor (April–Oct daily 9am–6pm; Nov–March Mon–Fri 9am–5.15pm) The **youth hostel**, within the grounds of Pendennis Castle, is one of the best in the country (☎0326/311435; ②). *Bosanneth*, 1 Stracey Rd (Feb–Nov; ☎0326/314649; ④), is one of many **B&Bs** which crowd around the southern end of town, overlooking Falmouth's sandy beaches.

Bus #2 departs every two hours for Penzance, meeting a connecting service in the town of Helston for the **Lizard Peninsula**. The village of Lizard is fairly nondescript, a fifteen-minute walk from the headland itself. In each direction the clifftop path hugs a beautiful stretch of rocky coast shrouded in frequent mists, the air regularly punctuated by the stentorian tones of the lighthouse foghorn.

Penzance

The busy port of **PENZANCE** forms the natural gateway to England's westernmost extremity, the Penwith peninsula, and all the major sights of the region can be reached by day trips from here. From the train station located at the northern end of town, Market Jew Street threads its way through the town centre, culminating in the Neoclassical facade of Market House, fronted by a statue of local-born chemist and inventor Sir Humphrey Davy. A left turn into Chapel Street brings you to the **Maritime Museum** (Mon–Sat 10am–5pm; £1.50), which recreates the interior of an eighteenth-century man-of-war. West of here, a series of parks and gardens punctuate the quiet residential streets overlooking the promenade. The **Penzance and District Museum**, off Morrab Road (Mon–Fri 10.30am–4.30pm, Sat 10.30am–12.30pm; 50p), features works by members of the Newlyn school, late nineteenth-century painters of local seascapes.

More paintings of a more modern bent can be found in the **Newlyn Art Gallery** (Mon–Sat 10am–5pm), an eminently walkable mile and a half west along the coast road in Newlyn itself. A working fishing village, Newlyn is a little more authentic than its southerly neighbour, the much-visited Mousehole, a jumble of harbourside cottages easily reached by local bus (#A or #B) from Penzance.

The view east across the bay from Penzance is dominated by **St Michael's Mount**, site of a fortified medieval monastery perched on an offshore pinnacle of rock. At low tide, the Mount is joined by a cobbled causeway to the mainland village of Marazion (half-hourly buses from Penzance); at other times a regular boat shuttle links the Mount with the village. You can amble around part of the Mount's shoreline, but most of the rock lies within the grounds of the abbey and castle (April–Oct Mon–Fri 10.30am–4.45pm; Nov–March Mon, Wed & Fri 10.30am–3.45pm; £3), now a stately home belonging to Lord St Levan.

Penzance's **train and bus stations** are at the northeastern end of town, a step away from Market Jew St. The **tourist office** (Mon–Thurs 9am–5.30pm, Fri 9am–5pm, Sat 10am–1pm; ☎0736/62207) is in the bus station, and will fix up B&B **accommodation**, most of which congregates at the western end of town around Morrab Rd. The comfortable **youth hostel**, Castle Horneck, Alverton (☎0736/62666; ②), is a short walk along the Land's End road. There's also a *YMCA* in Alverton Rd (☎0736/65016; ②). For unwinding in the evening, head for town centre **pubs** like the *Star* on Market Jew St, or the more touristy *Admiral Benbow* on Chapel St, a seventeenth-century house with maritime fittings with a bar upstairs, pricy restaurant downstairs. Over the summer, look out for live folk music at the *Acorn*, Parade St.

Land's End

Land's End exerts a hold over the popular imagination that the site itself can't always live up to – especially now that a small **theme park** has been built here (daily summer 10am–6pm; winter 10am–5pm; £4). The coastal path, however, remains a public right of way, and, despite commercialization, a visit is really worthwhile, with beautiful clifftop walks overlooking some spectacular wave-carved rocks. One and a half miles north is the secluded village of Sennen Cove, overlooking the extensive sandy beaches of Whitesand Bay. Head a similar distance south for the more rugged beauty of Mill Bay.

Four miles north of Land's End is an equally spectacular stretch of coast around **Cape Cornwall**, less crowded than its more famous neighbour, although a popular venue for observing dramatic sunsets. The cape itself is a mile west of the former tin mining village of St Just; the walk here from Land's End is recommended, although it's also easily reached by bus from Penzance. St Just is also the site of the nearest **youth hostel** to Land's End at Letcha Vean, half a mile south of town (April–Oct; ☎0736/788437; ②).

St Ives

Lying across the peninsula from Penzance on Cornwall's north coast, the fishing village of **ST IVES** is the quintessential Cornish riviera resort, featuring a maze of narrow streets lined with whitewashed cottages, good sandy beaches and lush subtropical flora. The village's erstwhile tranquillity attracted several major artists earlier this century – Ben Nicholson, Barbara Hepworth and constructivist Naum Gabo among them. Insipid sunsets and other tourist fodder now fill the small galleries which cram the streets, but there's some more challenging work on show in the new **Tate Gallery** (Jun–Aug Tues & Thurs 11am–9pm; Mon, Wed & Fri 11am–7pm, Sun 1–7pm; Sept–May Tues 11am–9pm, Wed–Sat 11am–5pm, Sun 1–5pm, closed Mon; £2.50) on Porthmoor Beach, featuring the work of the various St Ives schools. The same ticket admits you to the **Barbara Hepworth Museum** (Mon–Sat 10am–4.30/6.30pm; 50p), which preserves the studio of the modernist sculptor – "a lovely girl with whom nobody would associate a hammer and chisel", according to a 1930 press cutting on display. Her photos of Cornwall quoits and landscapes provide clues to the inspiration behind her sleek monoliths, many splendid examples of which are displayed in the garden. Of the town's three beaches, the north-facing **Porthmeor** occasionally has good surf, and boards can be rented at the beach. The **tourist office** in the Guildhall, Street-an-Pol (summer Mon–Sat 9am–6pm, Sun 9am–1pm; rest of year Mon–Fri 9am–5pm; ☎0736/796297), has a room-booking service.

Newquay

Bus #57 from St Ives runs three times daily to **NEWQUAY** (also accessible from the London–Penzance rail line, changing at Par), a predominantly ugly modern resort perched on a clifftop site. A small fishing harbour at the town's western end is sheltered by the wave-battered peninsula of Towan Head, but people really come here for the beaches, especially the good surfing provided by Newquay's westernmost beach,

Fistral. *Fistral Surf Village Shop*, 1 Beacon Rd, and the *Boardwalk Surf Shop*, 17 Cliff Rd, are the best places for board rental.

The **tourist office** is a few steps away from the train station on Cliff Road (May–Sept Mon–Sat 9am–7pm, Sun 9am–1pm & 5–7pm; Oct–April Mon–Sat 9am–5pm). There's a **youth hostel** at Alexandra Court, Narrowcliff (March–Oct; ☎0637/876381; ②). **B&B** accommodation is fairly plentiful, although it's worth ringing ahead in the high season: try *The Croft*, 37 Mount Wise (☎0637/875088; ③), or *Penruddock Hotel*, 58 Tower Rd (☎0637/876677; ③).

CENTRAL AND EASTERN ENGLAND

Central England was the powerhouse of the Industrial Revolution, and although vast areas of the Midlands are greener than most people realize, it is still predominantly a region of unattractive manufacturing towns. The regional centre is **Birmingham**, hub of an industrial sprawl which encompasses some three million people – making it Britain's second largest city. Though Birmingham has the best concert hall and best orchestra in the country, the conurbation is unlikely to feature on a hurried tour of Britain. Still, two of England's essential sights are to the south of the Midlands core, and within easy reach of London: **Stratford-upon-Avon**, home of William Shakespeare, and the university town of **Oxford**, which harbours sufficient historical interest and leisure-time possibilities to merit a lengthy stay.

Eastern England is primarily known for the endless flat expanses of East Anglia, isolated from the rest of the country by the Fens, areas of wetland which were substantially drained only in recent centuries. Of the many historical towns which dot the landscape, the university town of **Cambridge** is the obvious draw, although the more workaday town of **Norwich**, further east, shouldn't be ignored, preserving a surprising amount of its medieval and Tudor heritage.

Oxford

Preconceptions about the aristocratic atmosphere of **OXFORD** are now slightly wide of the mark, for the city's university has lost much of its social exclusivity. Traditionally, as with Cambridge, its intake was dominated by students from the public schools and historic grammar schools, but the postwar era has seen the introduction of a meritocracy – students here look much the same as anywhere else, and the traditional academic dress of dark suits, white bow tie, gown and mortarboard only makes an appearance during exams and on ceremonial occasions. Yet the privileges of Oxford, embodied in its fine architecture, are what make the place an unmissable stop, and it couldn't be easier to visit – it's only ninety minutes from London's Paddington station by rail, and various bus companies make the trip from Victoria coach station, ensuring departures every twenty minutes for as little as £5 day return.

Students were originally attracted here by the scholars attached to the Oxford monasteries, before their ranks were swelled by the expulsion of English students from Paris in 1167. By the sixteenth century the collegiate system began to take shape, with students and tutors living, working and taking their meals together in the same complex of buildings – usually a couple of courtyards (or quads) with a chapel, a library and dining hall. Most Oxford colleges follow this basic pattern, forming a dense maze of historic buildings in the heart of the city. Access to many of the colleges may be restricted during term time, and they often close to visitors entirely in May and June, when exams are approaching.

The City

The main point of reference is **Carfax**, a central crossroads overlooked by the four-teenth-century St Martin's Tower (March–Oct daily 10am–6pm; £1), last surviving remnant of a church of the same name and the first of many opportunities to enjoy a panorama of the Oxford skyline.

South of Carfax, St Aldate's leads to the **Oxford Museum** (Tues–Sat 10am–5pm; free), providing an introduction to the city's history through a gruellingly detailed sequence of Roman, Saxon and medieval finds. The Museum of Modern Art, or **MOMA**, around the corner at 30 Pembroke St (Tues–Sat 10am–6pm, Sun 2–6pm; £2.50), enjoys a reputation for staging ground-breaking contemporary exhibitions. Further down St Aldate's is the biggest of Oxford's colleges, **Christ Church** (Mon–Sat 10.30am–1pm & 2–4.30pm, Sun 2–4.30pm; £1.50), traditionally maintaining the strongest links with the public schools. Christ Church's main entrance passes underneath the dome of Tom Tower, built in 1681 by Christopher Wren, before opening onto the vast expanse of Tom Quad, mostly dating from the college's foundation in the sixteenth century. Visitors must enter through the nearby Memorial Garden. The late Norman college chapel – all that's left of the priory which was demolished to make way for the college – also serves as the city's cathedral. Around the corner from the classical Peckwater Quad, the college **Picture Gallery** (Mon–Sat 10.30am–1pm & 2–4.30/5.30pm, Sun 2–5.30pm; 80p) crowds Italian Renaissance and Mannerist works into a sterile concrete bunker. Look out for an anonymous portrait of Henry VIII, who refounded Christ Church after the demise of its original patron, Cardinal Wolsey.

South of the college, Christ Church Meadow leads down to the Thames, perversely referred to hereabouts as the Isis. The narrow streets immediately east of Christ Church are occupied by a cluster of three colleges: **Oriel**, renowned for its fearsome rowing reputation and the gabled frontages of its seventeenth-century Front Quad; **Corpus Christi**, noted for its paved Front Quad and sixteenth-century sundial; and **Merton**, one of the original thirteenth-century colleges, which still preserves one court-yard of the period, Mob Quad.

At the rear of Merton College, Deadman's Walk heads east to join Rose Lane, which emerges at the eastern end of the High Street opposite **Magdalen College** (daily noon–6pm; £1), founded in 1458 and dominated by a bell tower of the same period. Fifteenth-century Cloister Quadrangle, lined with gargoyles, is the most striking of its quads. West of Magdalen along the High Street is **Queen's College** (access by tour only, arrange at the tourist office), a rare piece of English Baroque, planned by Hawksmoor. Diagonally opposite, the comparatively uninviting facade of University College conceals the **Shelley Memorial**, honouring the poet who was "sent down" (Oxford-speak for expelled) for writing a pamphlet entitled "The Necessity of Atheism".

Halfway down the High Street, **St Mary's Church** (summer 9am–7pm; winter 9.30am–dusk; spire £1) was the scene of the trial of Cranmer, Ridley and Latimer, the "Oxford Martyrs" burned at the stake by Queen Mary's counter-reforming regime in 1555. Behind the church extends an area containing many of the university's most important and imposing buildings, most dramatic of which is the Italianate **Radcliffe Camera**. Built in the 1730s by James Gibbs, it is now used as a reading room for the Bodleian Library, whose main building is immediately to the north in the Old Schools Quadrangle. A few of the Bodleian's inexhaustible supply of ancient manuscripts are selected for public display in the nearby **School of Natural Philosophy** (free; guided tours of Duke Humfrey's library, £2). Immediately to the north is the **Clarendon Building**, another Hawksmoor design, originally the headquarters of the Oxford University Press before being swallowed by the ever-expanding Bodleian. The adjacent **Sheldonian Theatre** (daily 10am–12.45pm & 2–3.45/4.45pm; 50p), a copy of the

Theatre of Marcellus in Rome, was designed by Christopher Wren as an intellectual diversion from his main profession at the time – that of Professor of Astronomy at the university. After admiring the over-the-top Baroque allegories of Robert Streeter which cover the ceiling, you can ascend to the cupola to savour views over a crowd of neighbouring spires.

To the east, a copy of Venice's Bridge of Sighs spans New College Lane, joining the two halves of Hertford College. The Lane continues to **New College** itself, founded by William of Wykeham in 1379; most of the principal buildings date from that period. West from the Sheldonian, several colleges cluster around Broad Street, which winds towards the **Ashmolean Museum** (Tues–Sat 10am–4pm, Sun 2–4pm; free) in Beaumont Street. The ground floor of the museum is strong on Egyptology, including the reconstructed inner precincts of a shrine to Amon-Ra built by Taharqa, a Nubian king who ruled in the eighth century BC. Upstairs are numerous Minoan finds unearthed by Arthur Evans, excavator of Knossos, and a fine art collection featuring early Renaissance work (look out for Paolo Uccello's *Hunt in the Forest*), some arcadian landscapes by Poussin and Lorrain, and a representative sample of French Impressionists. The Tradescant room is the museum's curio corner, displaying the stirrups of Henry VIII alongside African musical instruments and the Powhatan Mantle, the deer-skin robe of a Virginia chieftain.

The **University Museum** Parks Road, (Mon–Sat noon–5pm; free), houses a natural history collection that includes the foot and beak of a dodo. The exhibits, however, are upstaged by the building itself, with skeletal Victorian cast iron supporting a glass roof, ringed by statues of the brainy. A galleried hall at the rear of the museum holds the **Pitt Rivers** collection (Mon–Sat 1–4.30pm; free), a treasure trove of artefacts from around the globe, ranging from Egyptian mummified cats to Samurai armour and models of Indonesian fishing vessels.

Practicalities

Oxford's train station is fifteen minutes' walk west of town. The coach station is at Gloucester Green, midway between the train station and the centre. The **tourist office** is on St Aldates's, immediately south of Carfax, the town's central crossroads (Mon–Sat 9.30am–5pm, plus Sun in summer 10.30am–1pm); they will book rooms for a £2.50 fee.

There's an overloaded **youth hostel** in the eastern suburb of Headington, half an hour east of central Oxford at Jack Straws Lane (☎0865/62997; ②). Double rooms in B&Bs tend to hover between £35 and £45 in high season, and booking ahead is strongly advised. Recommended places are the *Isis Guest House*, 45–53 Iffley Rd (☎0865/248 894; ④); the *Bronte Guest House*, 282 Iffley Rd (☎0865/244594; ④); and the *Walton Guest House*, 169 Walton St (☎0865/52137; ④). The *Old Mitre Rooms*, 48 Turl St (☎0865/279821; ④), offer rooms from July to September. Nearest **campsite** is *Oxford Camping International*, 426 Abingdon Rd (☎0865/246551), a mile and a half south of the centre.

For substantial low-cost **meals**, *Browns*, Woodstock Rd, is a good choice, although its popularity with students leads to big queues. *Maxwells*, 37 Queen St, is an American-style ribs and burgers joint; while the *Gate of India*, 35 High St, is a popular venue for a post-pub curry. Amongst Oxford's more distinctive **pubs** are *The Bear*, Alfred St, long regarded as the Christ Church local; *Head of the River*, Folly Bridge, a classic summer pub with balconies overlooking the Isis; the *King's Arms*, Holywell St, a student pub with a wide choice of beers; *The Turf*, Bath Place, a small, ancient establishment; and the *Eastgate*, High St, with a lively student/town mix.

The monthly publication *What's On in Oxford* and the weekly broadsheet *Daily Information* (pinned to walls in colleges and pubs) provide details of **concerts**. For live music, *The Jericho Tavern*, Walton St, is the traditional venue for local bands. Larger visiting acts play at the *Oxford Venue*, 196 Cowley Rd.

Blenheim Palace

Half-hourly buses depart from the bus station or Cornmarket towards the village of Woodstock eight miles north, site of **Blenheim Palace** (March–Oct daily 10.30am–5.30pm; £6; park open all year 9am–4.45pm; £3 with car, 80p on foot). The palace was built by John Vanbrugh for John Churchill, the first Duke of Marlborough, whom the king wished to reward for defeating the army of Louis XIV at Blenheim in 1704. The stern exterior is an unambiguous expression of power; inside, things are marginally more homely, with opulently furnished period state rooms and a Churchill Exhibition, which includes a few of Winston's attempts at painting and a recreation of the room in which he was born. Italianate gardens are laid out to the rear of the palace, a contrast with the open spaces of Capability Brown's landscaped parkland, unlikely setting for a Butterfly House (March–Oct daily 10am–6pm).

Stratford-upon-Avon

Blessed with a higher than average sprinkling of Tudor and Jacobean half-timbered houses, **STRATFORD-UPON-AVON** would merit a visit even without the many sights associated with William Shakespeare, who was born here on April 23, 1564. There are five restored properties linked with the Bard or members of his family, three in the town proper and two within easy reach of it. If you've time to visit them all, combined tickets costing £5 for the three town properties, £7.50 for all five, may be worth considering.

Shakespeare's Birthplace (March–Oct Mon–Sat 9am–5.30pm, Sun 10am–5.30pm; Nov–Feb Mon–Sat 9.30am–4pm, Sun 10.30am–4pm; £2.50), a pale ochre half-timbered structure on Henley Street, is entered from the Shakespeare Centre just up the road. Although a bit of a crush over summer, the house provides an evocative recreation of Elizabethan life. John Shakespeare, William's father, was a glove-maker and wool dealer who served on the town council, and the rooms, although sparsely furnished, point to a lifestyle of relative comfort. A display of books suggests the kind of reading matter the young Shakespeare may have been exposed to, a 1560 translation of the Geneva Bible among them.

Prominent among the Elizabethan facades of the High Street is that of the **Harvard House** (Easter–Sept Mon–Sat 10am–4pm, Sun 2–6pm; £1.50); inside is a further taste of the living quarters of the Tudor era, but the house's real attraction lies in the intricately carved timbers of the exterior. Heading southwest, the High Street becomes Chapel Street and leads to New Place, site of the home where Shakespeare died in 1616. Sadly, the house no longer stands, demolished by a subsequent owner who was apparently tired of visitors in 1759. The Elizabethan Garden, however, has been recreated, and is entered via the next-door **Nash House** (March–Oct Mon–Sat 9.30am–5pm, Sun 10.30am–5pm; Nov–Feb Mon–Sat 10am–4pm, Sun 1.30–4pm; £1.70), home of Thomas Nash, husband of Shakespeare's granddaughter Elizabeth Hall. The half-timbered frontage is a 1911 replica, with the Tudor interior recreating the atmosphere of a middle-class seventeenth-century home, while upstairs is a small museum devoted to the town's history, with mementoes of the 1769 Shakespeare Jubilee mounted by the actor David Garrick, who did much to promote the town as a place of literary pilgrimage.

Across the road on the corner of Chapel Lane and Church Street is the **Guild Chapel**, home of the Guild of the Holy Cross, the religious institution which virtually ran medieval Stratford before being disbanded during the Reformation. Inside are some late medieval frescoes from around 1500, subsequently painted over in a fit of Puritan piousness, although it's just possible to distinguish an animated *Resurrection*. Behind the chapel is the half-timbered frontage of the King Edward VI Grammar

School, supposedly attended by the Bard. Continuing along Church Street, a left turn leads into Old Town and **Hall's Croft** (same hours and price as Nash House), home of Shakespeare's son-in-law Dr John Hall. Inside is furnished in period style, with a selection of antique medicines and herbal remedies from the doctor's dispensary. From here it's a five-minute walk to Shakespeare's last resting place, the **Holy Trinity Church** on the banks of the Avon.

About a mile and a half east of Stratford is the village of Shottery, site of **Anne Hathaway's Cottage** (same hours as the Birthplace; £2.10), home of Shakespeare's wife. Despite siring three children within five years, domesticity obviously didn't appeal to William, who abandoned family life for London and the theatre in around 1587. By the time you get to **Mary Arden's House** (same hours as Nash House; £3), three and a half miles away at Wilmcote (train from Stratford Mon–Sat), the Shakespearian connections are beginning to get a little tenuous: Mary Arden was Shakespeare's mother, but she apparently only spent a few years here as a child. That said, it's another pleasant enough site, including a **Shakespeare Countryside Museum** in which costumed wax figures stand around the cowsheds wielding period implements.

Practicalities

Stratford's train station is half a mile east of town. Coaches terminate right in the middle of things at the bottom of Bridge St, two minutes away from the **tourist office** at Bridgefoot (April–Oct Mon–Sat 9am–6pm, Sun 11am–5pm; Nov–March Mon–Sat 9am–5pm, Sun 11am–5pm; ☎0789/293127). There's a **youth hostel** in Hemmingford House, Alveston (☎0789/297093; ②), two miles east (#18 bus). The town has a wealth of **B&B** accommodation, much of it located in the southwest corner of town around Evesham Place and Evesham Rd, but rooms fill up speedily during the tourist season. First choices are *Nando's*, 18–19 Evesham Place (☎0789/204907; ②); the *Glenavon Guest House*, 6 Chestnut Walk (☎0789/292588; ③); and *Bridge House*, 190 Alcester Rd (☎0789/67723; ②).

The *Horseshoe Buttery* on Greenhill St offers cheap and filling café **food** during the daytime; *Vintners* café and wine bar on Sheep St serves meals in slightly more plush surroundings. Amongst the plentiful town centre **pubs**, the most famous is the *Black Swan* (better know as the *Dirty Duck*) on Waterside. Finally, tickets for the **Royal Shakespeare Company**, which performs in three theatres on the banks of the Avon – the main house, the smaller *Swan* and the experimental *Other Place* – begin at around £8, with standbys sometimes available. Sell-outs are very common, so book your seat as far in advance as possible (☎0789/295623).

Cambridge

Tradition has it that the University of **CAMBRIDGE** was founded by refugees from Oxford, who fled the town after one of their number was lynched by hostile townsfolk, and rivalry has existed between the two institutions ever since. On the whole, Cambridge is a quieter, more secluded place, but the famed Backs – the gardens straddling the River Cam – endow the collegiate architecture with a dramatic presence.

A logical place to begin a tour is actually not a college but the **Fitzwilliam Museum**, at the southern end of the centre on Trumpington St (Tues–Sat ground floor 10am–2pm, first floor 2–5pm; Sun both floors 2.15–5pm; donation requested). The archeological collections on the ground floor contain an imposing relief of Assyrian King Ashurnasirpal II, alongside strong Egyptian and Greek sections; upstairs, the art collection includes a couple of Titians, a Veronese, a Tintoretto, a good selection of Pre-Raphaelites and Impressionists, and a fine *Odalisque* by their Romantic predecessor Delacroix, not to mention an eclectic selection of twentieth century works.

Founded in 1284, the neighbouring **Peterhouse** is Cambridge's oldest college, but little of the original architecture survives. The college's most interesting feature is the seventeenth-century chapel, a Jacobean-Gothic structure flanked by classical colonnades. The courtyard of **Queens' College** (daily mid-March to mid-Oct; 70p) is original Tudor, but its timber-roofed Hall is a nineteenth-century medievalist construction, decorated by William Morris. The contemporaneous neo-gothic gatehouse of King's College, hogging the limelight on King's Parade, leads through to **King's College Chapel** (mid-June to Oct Mon–Fri 9.30am–4.30pm, Sun 9am–6pm; £2), one of the best examples of late medieval architecture in Britain. Begun by the college founder Henry VI in the 1450s, it boasts an extravagantly fan-vaulted ceiling, supported by a wall of stained glass on each side, and an intricately carved choir screen, added in the 1530s and probably Florentine work.

Next door to King's is the **Senate House**, an exercise in Palladian classicism by James Gibbs, the architect of St Martin-in-the-Fields in London and the Radcliffe Camera in Oxford, and the scene of graduation ceremonies in June. The nineteenth-century turreted monstrosity next door marks the southern entrance to **Gonville and Caius** (pronounced "Keys") College, hiding a fascinating series of sixteenth-century courtyards. Caius Court bears much of the personality of the college's cultured co-founder John Keys, a widely travelled philosopher and physician, who latinized his surname as was the custom with men of learning. He placed a gate on each side of the court – the Gates of Wisdom, Humility, Virtue and Honour – each representing a different stage on the path to academic enlightenment; the Gate of Honour on the south side of the court, capped with sundials, is the most ornate.

The Great Court of **Trinity College**, the largest of Cambridge's colleges, is the finest ensemble of Tudor-period buildings in the city. Another Tudor gatehouse marks the entrance to **St John's** (daily mid-June to Sept; £1) and more fine sixteenth-century courts. Standing on the corner where St John Street meets Bridge Street is the **Round Church**, built in the twelfth century on the model of the Church of the Holy Sepulchre in Jerusalem; the spire is a nineteenth-century addition, but Norman pillars remain inside. Just beyond here, Magdalene Bridge is a good place to rent boats for a leisurely punt down the river. Across the bridge, **Magdalene College** (pronounced "Mordlin"), straddles both sides of the street, the oldest parts of which are to the east. A couple of sixteenth-century courts lead through to the Pepys Library, named after the Magdalene old boy whose diary has been on display here since 1742. **Jesus College**, reached from Jesus Lane by a narrow alleyway known as the Chimney, holds a chapel which contains original medieval elements, but many of the Victorian architects engaged in the Gothic revival were involved in the chapel's reconstruction, making for an interesting hybrid. Ceiling paintings were provided by William Morris, who also – together with Burne-Jones and Ford Madox Brown – provided designs for the windows. **Christ's College**, south of Jesus on St Andrew's St, has one of Cambridge's finest Tudor gate towers, adorned with coats of arms of the Beaufort family and mythical, antelope-like beasts. The fifteenth-century stained glass in the college chapel depicts, among others, Henry VI and Henry VII.

Practicalities

Cambridge's **train station** is a dull trudge south of the centre (shuttle bus #1 runs every 8 mins until 6pm from Emmanuel St). The **bus station** on Drummer St is just a couple of blocks east of the **tourist office** on Wheeler St (Mon–Sat 9am–6pm, Sun 10.30am–3.30pm). The busy **youth hostel** is at 96 Tenison Rd (☎0223/354601; ②), not far from the train station. **B&Bs** are grouped near the station and around Chesterton Road to the north. Amongst the best are the *Six Steps Guesthouse*, 93 Tenison Rd (☎0223/353968; ③), *Dresden Villa Guest House*, 34 Cherry Hinton Rd (☎0223/247539;

④), and *Ashtrees Guest House*, 128 Perne Rd (☎0223/411233; ③). The nearest **camp-site** is *Highfield Farm*, Long Rd, Comberton (☎0223/263308; bus #118).

For **food**, *Brown's*, opposite the Fitwilliam Museum, is a vast and bustling brasserie good for both full meals or just a snack and a coffee. The *Gardenia*, 22 Mitcham's Corner, Chesterton Rd, is a decent kebab joint, and *King's Pantry*, 9a Kings Parade, is the only vegetarian restaurant in town. As for **pubs**, the *Anchor*, on Silver St overlooking the Cam, is a good place for a bar lunch or beery evening, as is the *Fort St George*, on Midsummer Common – perfect if you want to drink by the river. Others to check out are the *Champion of the Thames*, nicest of the pubs along King St, and the *Eagle*, on Bene't St. The *Junction*, Old Cattle Market, Clifton Rd, has **live music**, while the *Old Dot Jazz House*, Hobson St, is the premier jazz venue. The *Corn Exchange* in Wheeler St hosts the bigger bands. *What's On in Cambridge*, a freesheet distributed by the tourist office, has details, as does the student weekly, *Varsity*.

Norwich

NORWICH was England's second city in Tudor times, serving a vast hinterland of cloth producers in the eastern counties, whose work was exported from here to the continent. Due to its isolated position beyond the fens, Norwich often had closer cultural and trading links with the Low Countries than with London; the overland journey to the capital took far longer than crossing the Channel.

In the centre of town, the twelfth-century **Castle Keep**, the exterior of which preserves its blind arcading, a rare piece of ornamentation on a military structure, houses a **Museum and Art Gallery** (Mon–Sat 10am–5pm, Sun 2–5pm; £1.60), which contains a representative selection of landscapes by painters of the nineteenth-century Norwich School, whose outstanding figures were John Sell Cotman and John Crome. West of the castle stretches the largely pedestrianized city centre. Three blocks away on the Market Square stands a twelfth-century **Guildhall**, built from the Norfolk flint that gives a glass-like quality to many of the city's older buildings. Two blocks north of here on St Andrew's Street is the **Strangers Hall** (Mon–Fri 10am–5pm; £1), a predominantly medieval structure housing one of Norwich's most interesting museums, illustrating domestic life through the ages. The nearby **Bridewell Museum** (Mon–Sat 10am–5pm; £1) has artefacts illustrating the town's trades and professions, including a steam-powered fire engine. One block east of here, the fifteenth-century church of **St Peter Hungate** (Mon–Sat 10am–5pm) has been converted into a museum exhibiting medieval illustrated manuscripts and church brasses. Nearby, the descending cobbled lane of Elm Hill evokes something of the atmosphere of Tudor Norwich with a few half-timbered buildings. Immediately east of here is the **Cathedral** (daily 7.30am–6/7pm; donation encouraged), whose twelfth-century nave retains heavily ornamented Norman piers. Look out also for some fine examples of medieval art: the fourteenth-century *Dispenser Reredos* in St Luke's chapel and medieval frescoes in the treasury on the north side of the altar. Beyond the cathedral to the west are the best of Norwich's riverside walks, following the Wensum past the ruined Cow Tower.

A couple of hundred yards along King St, the dilapidated road south of the Castle Mound, you reach the newly restored **Dragon Hall** at no. 115–123 (April–Oct Mon–Sat 10am–4pm; Nov–March Mon–Thurs only; 50p). Built as a cloth showroom for merchant and town mayor Robert Toppes, the timber-framed Great Hall holds the brightly coloured, medieval wooden dragon which gave the place its name. A right turn up St Julian's Alley leads to **St Julian's Church** (daily 7am–6pm) and adjoining monastic cell. This was the retreat of Saint Julian, a Norwich woman who took to living here after experiencing visions of Christ in 1373; her mystical *Revelations of Divine Love* was the first widely distributed book to be written by a woman in the English language.

The University of East Anglia on the western outskirts of the city holds an important collection of modern painting in the hi-tech **Sainsbury Centre for Visual Arts** (Tues–Sun noon–5pm; £1), where Picasso and Modigliani rub shoulders with Egyptian antiquities. To get to the UEA, take bus #12, 14, 15, 23, 26, 27, 33 or 35 from Castle Meadow.

Practicalities

Norwich's train station is ten minutes away from Castle Meadow across the River Wensum to the east. Buses terminate on Surrey St, five minutes to the south of the Castle. The **tourist office** is in the Guildhall (June–Sept Mon–Sat 9.30am–5.30pm, Sun 9am–1pm; Oct–May Mon–Sat 9.30am–5pm). There's a *YHA* **hostel** at 112 Turner Rd (☎0603/627647; ②); a *YMCA* at 46–52 St Giles (☎0603/620 269; ②); and a *YWCA* at 61 Bethel St (☎0603/625982; ②). **B&B** accommodation worth trying includes the *Abbey Hotel*, 16 Stracey Rd (☎0603/612915; ④); *Arrow Hotel*, 2 Britannia Rd (☎0603/628051; ④); *Bristol House*, 80 Unthank Rd (☎0603/625729; ④); and *Chiltern House*, 2 Trafford Rd (☎0603/663033; ④). The nearest **campsite** is *Lallenham* (April–Sept; ☎ 0603/620060), a mile or so south on Martineau Lane, off King St. Centrally located places to **eat** are *Pizza One* on Tombland next to the cathedral close, and *Hector's House* on Bedford St, a livelier, place; veggies should home in on *Tree House*, above the *Rainbow* healthfood shop on Dove St. On St Benedicts St is the *Plough* and on George St the *Red Lion*, both good haunts popular with students. By way of a contrast, you could try the *Gardeners/ Murderers*, a loud maze of of a pub on Timber Hill. *Marco's* on St Andrew's St is a popular pub with regular live music in the evenings and the *Waterfront*, 139–141 King's St, is Norwich's principal club and alternative music venue.

NORTHERN ENGLAND

The main tourist draw of **northern England** is the **Lake District**, but the windswept grandeur of the Pennines, especially the upland valleys of the **Yorkshire Dales National Park**, is equally worthy of exploration. However, to restrict yourself purely to the northern outdoors would be to do a great disservice to regional cities such as **Liverpool, Manchester** and **Newcastle**. These were little more than villages until the Industrial Revolution, and their centres are alive with the ostentatious civic architecture of nineteenth-century capitalism. An entirely different angle on northern history is provided by the great medieval ecclesiastical centres of **Durham** and **York**, where famous cathedrals provide a focus for extensive medieval remains.

Liverpool

It's ironic that the city known the world over for its supreme contributions to British culture, chiefly in popular music and on the football field, should also appear the most run-down. **LIVERPOOL**, more than anywhere else, has suffered from the economic pressures of the 1980s. Yet although the docks lining the Mersey have largely fallen into disuse, the pride and aggressive wit of Liverpudlians make the city a warm and invigorating place to visit.

Liverpool's central layout is easy to assimilate: a grid of downtown streets separate Lime Street train station from the Mersey to the east. Behind the station, Mount Pleasant heads uphill towards the university and a lively student quarter. **Lime Street** itself is the scene of a fine ensemble of public buildings: immediately opposite the station, St George's Hall exemplifies the municipal classicism which spread throughout industrial Britain early last century. Immediately to the north is the **Walker Art**

Gallery (Mon–Sat 10am–5pm, Sun noon–5pm; free), one of the richest collections outside London. The odd Rubens and Rembrandt counterpoint a fairly representative jaunt through British art history, with Turner, Gainsborough, Joseph Wright of Derby and Stubbs well represented – as, inevitably, are the Pre-Raphaelites. Going down the hill from the Walker you'll pass the **Liverpool Museum** (same hours), five floors of varied exhibits featuring anthropology, stuffed beasts, a basement aquarium and a planetarium. From here it's a fairly uneventful walk eastwards to the **Pier Head** and Liverpool's waterfront. It's worth taking one of the regular ferries to Birkenhead for the views back towards the city. To the south are the great dock basins, now mostly idle, although the **Albert Dock** has been renovated as an Eighties showpiece example of urban renewal – the tacky shops and a few good eateries are just managing to ride the recession. Main focus of the dock's renovation is the **Tate Gallery** (Tues–Sun 10am–6pm; free), the provincial arm of the Tate in London, borrowing part of the capital's collection for a few months at a time. Occupying the other side of the dock is the **Maritime Museum** (daily 10.30am–5.30pm; £2.50), including models of the vessels that used to ply the Mersey and a recreation of conditions on board an emigrant ship bound for America. A ticket also gives entry to the **Museum of Liverpool Life** (same hours), which gives a poignant insight into the factors moulding the resilient and optimistic "Scouse" character. The nearby **Beatles Story**, Britannia Vaults (Easter–Oct daily 10am–6pm; £3.50), offers a disappointing recreation of the Cavern Club alongside other exploitative Fab Four memorabilia.

The major attractions to the east of Lime Street are the city's two cathedrals. The Roman Catholic **Metropolitan Cathedral of Christ the King**, ten minutes' walk up Mount Pleasant, is the sort of thing that gets modern architecture a bad name, a vast inverted funnel studded with gaudy stained glass. Opposite, Hope Street leads to the **Anglican Cathedral**, the largest in the country. Designed by Giles Gilbert Scott in 1903 while still in his early twenties, this enormous heap of pale red stone wasn't completely finished until 1978. Immediately below, in the deep trench of a former quarry, tunnelled walkways provide an interesting excursion through the cathedral graveyard.

Practicalities

Trains arrive at Lime St station on the fringes of the town centre; **coaches** currently stop around the corner, opposite the *Adelphi Hotel* on Brownlow Hill, but from summer 1994 should have a new bus station just north of Lime St. A short walk across Lime St and down Elliott St brings you to the **Merseyside Welcome Centre** in the Clayton Square shopping mall (Mon–Sat 9am–5.30pm). Another tourist office is in Albert Dock; both book accommodation without charge. There's no *YHA* hostel in Liverpool; the noisy but friendly *YMCA* is at 56–60 Mount Pleasant (☎051/709 9516; ③), though single women might be better off at the *YWCA*, 1 Rodney St (☎051/709 7791; ②). There are dormitory beds at the *Embassie Youth Hostel*, 1 Falkner Sq (☎051/707 1089; ②), or try *Feathers Hotel*, 119–125 Mount Pleasant (☎051/709 9655; ④), the best of the many hotels on that street.

There's a wide range of inexpensive ethnic **food** around Mount Pleasant, Hardman St and the grid of streets in between. The *Kismet*, 105 Bold St, and the *Everyman Bistro*, 9–11 Hope St, are both popular and cheap. The *Philharmonic Dining Rooms*, Hope St, is Liverpool's most characteristic **pub**, with a carefully recreated Victorian interior. Liverpool's music scene is not what it was, much of it now taking place in some of the late-night opening pubs popping up all over town. *Baa Bar*, 43–45 Fleet St, is the most stylish of these, though here the music is on disc. The *Picket*, 24 Hardman St, has the best selection of bands and the *Mardi Gras*, 59a Bold St, is one of the most reliable nightclubs. Bigger touring bands play at the *Royal Court*, Roe St.

Manchester

MANCHESTER has a similarly hard-bitten edge to its western neighbour, and, like Liverpool, its attractions have much to do with music and football – with the crucial differences that the Manchester music scene, though diminished from the heady *Madchester* days, is much more vibrant than its rival's, and the city's premier team, Manchester United, triumphed over the seemingly unbeatable Liverpool by winning the league in 1993.

Piccadilly Gardens, an untidy square with a bus station in the middle, passes for a central focus. The main shopping thoroughfare of Market Street runs west from here, traversing the city's heart. Turning right onto Victoria Street at Market Street's western end, it's strange to come upon the demure fifteenth-century **Cathedral**, a fine Perpendicular structure renowned for the wood carving of its choir stalls and (just to the left of the choir) a small stone bearing an eighth-century carving of an angel. From here the tedium of Deansgate leads south to the **John Rylands Library** (Mon–Fri 10am–5.30pm, Sat 10am–1pm; free), which exhibits a small and constantly changing selection of rare and ancient items, ranging from Egyptian papyri to early examples of European printing. A left turn into Brazenose Street brings you to Albert Square and the **Town Hall**, an overbearing example of the Victorian Gothic revival. Southeast of it on Peter Street is the **Free Trade Hall**, the neo-Renaissance home of northern England's best orchestra, the Hallé. A block west of the town hall on Mosely Street, the **City Art Gallery** (Mon–Sat 10am–5.45pm, Sun 2–5.45pm; free) is another temple to nineteenth-century tastes, Sir Charles Barry's Neoclassical building providing as good an indication of the predilections of the period as the paintings themselves. Amongst the latter, nostalgia for a prettified ancient world is revealed in the works of academic painters such as Alma-Tadema and Lord Leighton, while the Pre-Raphaelites pander to a yearning for a world before the factories came. Southwest of the town hall, Liverpool Road leads into the Castlefield area, where the **Museum of Science and Industry** (daily 10am–5pm; £3.50) celebrates the city of the Industrial Revolution with steam engines, textile machinery and a glimpse of the Manchester sewer system. The nearby **Granada TV Studios** on Water St (April–Sept 9.45am–7pm; Oct–March Mon–Fri 9.45am–5.30pm, Sat & Sun 9.45am–6.30pm; £10) offer tours of the *Coronation Street* set and other marvels. Manchester University on Oxford Road, southeast from the town hall, is the site of the **Manchester Museum** (Mon–Sat 10am–5.30pm), which has an extensive Egyptology collection. Further on, the **Whitworth Art Gallery** (Mon–Sat 10am–5pm, Thurs open until 9pm; free) specializes in textiles; English Tudor embroideries and elegant Indian and Far Eastern silks provide the interest.

Practicalities

Most **trains** arrive at Piccadilly station; those from the northeast terminate at Victoria, a little way northwest and linked to it by the new *Metrolink* tram system. Coaches stop at Chorlton St, close to Piccadilly. The **tourist office** is in the town hall (Mon & Sat 10am–5pm, Tues–Fri 9am–5pm). A large central **youth hostel** is due to open on Potato Wharf around August 1994, but until then the best central option is **B&B** at one of three pubs on Chapel St, Salford, reached by taking Bridge St off Deansgate. Try the *Salford Arms* at no. 146 (☎061/8347072; ④), the *Albert Vaults* at no. 169 (☎061/8344042; ④) or the *Brown Bull* at no. 187 (☎061/8344271; ④). From June to mid-September *Cavendish Hall*, Cavendish St (☎061/2471338; ③), and *Loxford Hall*, Lower Chatham St (☎061/2471334; ③), offer rooms with communal kitchens five minutes' walk south of Oxford Rd Station along Oxford Rd.

A small Chinatown in the area east of the centre around Faulkner St offers plenty of budget **eating**. In Oxford Rd, *Amigo's* at no. 14 provides plentiful Mexican food, while

On the Eighth Day at no. 111 is an excellent wholefood shop and restaurant. The *Cornerhouse Café*, in the arts centre at 70 Oxford St, has a wide range of food as well as being a fashionable place to **drink**. For details of the city's nightlife, pick up a copy of the fortnightly *City Life*. Manchester's lively club scene is going through a lot of changes at the moment, as a result of either police or gangland pressure; even the most famous venue, the *Haçienda*, 11–13 Whitworth St West, went into a few months of voluntary suspension. The nearby *Ritz* is another club of long standing, while the *Banshee*, 49a Piccadilly, is more goth-rock oriented. Bigger acts play at the *Academy* or the Manchester University Students' Union next door on Oxford Rd, or at the *G-Mex* centre on the corner of Windmill St and Mosely St.

Chester

Easily reached from Manchester or Liverpool, **CHESTER** is a compact and easily explorable town renowned for its unparalleled collection of half-timbered houses and for its complete circuit of Roman walls, resplendent in the distinctive red hues of the local sandstone. The town centre preserves the grid pattern of the Roman town, with The Cross at the centre, and Northgate, Eastgate, Bridge and Watergate streets heading off at right angles. These streets are characterized by the **Rows**, a unique series of two-tier arcaded shops, medieval buildings which perhaps owe their appearance to the need to build over existing Roman structures. The ornate timber designs of the upper storeys are quite extraordinary, although much of this is due to Victorian refurbishment. Chester's **Cathedral**, just off Northgate St, still retains the lines of a late medieval church, but is entirely faced in Victorian brick; intricately carved choir stalls and some original Norman stonework in the northern transept merit a quick look inside. To the east of Bridge Street, Pepper Street leads through Newgate Arch to the ruins of a **Roman Amphitheatre** (Easter–Sept daily 10am–6pm; Oct–Easter Tues–Sun 10am–1pm & 2–4pm; free), a shadow of the structure built to house 7000 spectators. Opposite the amphitheatre, the **Chester Visitor Centre** (daily 9am–7/9pm; free) contains more kitsch Victoriana with the reconstruction of a Row as it must have looked in the last century. Chester's history is better displayed in the archeological collections of the **Grosvenor Museum**, 27 Grosvenor St (Mon–Sat 10.30am–5pm, Sun 2–5pm; free).

There are **tourist offices** in the Town Hall on Northgate St (Mon–Sat 9am–7.30pm, Sun 10am–4pm); and also in the Visitor Centre. The **youth hostel** is at Hough Green House, 40 Hough Green (☎0244/680056; ③), one mile southwest. B&Bs offering doubles are thick on the ground around Hoole Rd and Brook St, the two roads leading up to the train station. Two good ones are the *Aplas Guest House*, 106 Brook St (☎0244/312401; ③), and *Ormonde Guest House* at no. 126 (☎0244/328816; ③).

The Lake District

The site of England's highest peaks and its biggest concentration of lakes, the glacier-carved **Lake District** is the nation's most popular walking and hiking area. The weather changes quickly here, but the sudden shifts of light on the bracken and moorland grasses, and on the slate of the local buildings, are part of the area's appeal. The most direct way of reaching the Lake District is via the London–Glasgow main line, disembarking at Lancaster, from where bus #555 (Mon–Sat hourly, Sun every 2hr) runs right through the Lake District calling at Windermere, Ambleside, Grasmere and Keswick. Alternatively, you could get off at Oxenholme, connecting with a branch line to Windermere; or Penrith, where buses #105 and #X5 (Mon–Sat only) run to Keswick. Once in the Lake District, public transport is dramatically reduced on Sundays.

Windermere and around

Largest and southernmost of the lakes, **Windermere** is also the most accessible and therefore one of the most crowded areas in summer. The town of Windermere itself is set back from the lake, and there's little to do here save stroll down to the sister town of Bowness a mile to the south on the waterfront. Windermere's **tourist office** is just outside the train station (daily 9am–5/6pm), while the nearest **hostel** is a couple of miles north, 1km from Troutbeck on the Ambleside Rd (☎05394/43543; ②). From Bowness (where there's another information office), there's a choice of **ferries**. Half a mile south of the centre, one crosses the lake, from where you can walk a steep two miles to reach the village of Near Sawrey and **Hill Top Farm** (April–Oct daily 11am–4.30pm; £3.20), home of Beatrix Potter and still crammed with her effects. The other, originating from Lakeside at the southern tip of the lake, calls at Bowness Pier right in Bowness, continuing to **AMBLESIDE** at the northern end – also served by buses #555 and #W1 from Windermere and Bowness. Thronged with visitors throughout the year, the pubs here are busier and the range of food wider than down the lake. Ambleside's most unlikely resident was German Dadaist Kurt Schwitters, who settled here in 1945; his gravestone can be seen in Ambleside cemetery. The **tourist office** is behind the bus stop on Church St (Easter–Oct daily 9am–5pm; Nov–Easter Fri & Sat 9am–5pm). Ambleside's **youth hostel** is at Waterhead, fifteen minutes south of town on the shore (☎05394/34408; ②).

Hawkshead and Coniston

Buses #505 and #506 run from Ambleside to Hawkshead and Coniston (8 daily Mon–Sat, 3 Sun), both refreshingly peaceful towns after the hurly-burly of Windermere. Six miles southwest of Ambleside, the whitewashed cottages of **HAWKSHEAD** harbour some marvellous village pubs and the school where Wordsworth was a pupil. The **Hawkshead Grammar School** (Easter–Oct Mon–Sat 10am–12.30pm & 1.30–5pm, Sun 1–5pm; £1.50) contains a desk carved with the young delinquent's name, and more ancient mementoes of the school's long history. The nearby **Beatrix Potter Gallery** (late March–Oct Mon–Fri 10.30am–4.30pm; £2.40) contains objects relating to the author's characters. A small summer **tourist office** next to the bus stop handles a range of farmhouse accommodation, but the plush, family-oriented **hostel** at Esthwaite Lodge (☎05394/36293; ②), a mile south of town, is one of the best in the country.

Four miles southwest of Hawkshead lies **Grizedale Forest**, an industrial plantation littered with intriguing wood sculptures. Straddling the only road into the forest, the Grizedale Forest Centre (daily 10am–5pm) sells trail maps for walkers and cyclists: bikes can be hired from a booth across the road for £12 a day. Walking through the forest from Hawkshead and descending towards **Lake Coniston** is a good way of reaching the village of the same name, another elegant cluster of whitewashed houses nestling beneath the target for local hikers, Coniston Old Man. There's a **hostel** north of the village at Holly How, Far End (☎05394/41323; ②), and another above Coniston on the slopes of Old Man, at Coppermines House (☎05394/41261; ②). The most popular walk from Coniston (one which can be approached from Hawkshead as well) is to **Tarn Hows**, three miles northeast, a lake surrounded by wooded high ground, with several vantage points across the hills.

The *Steam Yacht Gondola* crisscrosses the lake (4 daily April–Oct; £4 round-trip), providing the best means of getting to **Brantwood** (mid-March to mid-Nov daily 11am–5.30pm; rest of year Wed–Sun 11am–4pm; £2.80), an elegant lakeside villa once inhabited by the art historian John Ruskin. Distressed by the effects of the Industrial Revolution, Ruskin looked back on the medieval era as a golden age of pre-capitalist harmony, providing the theoretical substance for the work of the Pre-Raphaelites. The house is full of Ruskin's own drawings and sketches, as well as items relating to the painters he inspired.

Rydal and Grasmere

The trusty #555 bus connects Ambleside with the heart of Wordsworth territory, but it's an expedition which you could easily accomplish on foot. The tiny village of **RYDAL** was where Wordsworth made his home from 1813 until his death in 1850; his actual house, **Rydal Mount** (March–Oct daily 9.30am–5pm; Nov–Feb daily except Mon 10am–4pm, £2), is famous largely for the gardens laid out by Wordsworth himself. Paths on either side of Rydal Water cover the two miles to **GRASMERE**, site of Wordsworth's more famous abode, **Dove Cottage**. The cottage (daily 9.30am–5pm; £3.50) is an ascetic, cramped farmhouse, and you may have to queue before being admitted. The adjoining museum has portraits and manuscripts relating to Wordsworth, Coleridge – who regularly hiked over from Keswick to visit him here – and de Quincey, biographer of the Lake poets, who took over Dove Cottage after Wordsworth's move to Rydal. Wordsworth and sister Dorothy lie in simple graves in the churchyard of St Oswald's, in the heart of the village. Grasmere's **tourist office** is on Redbank Road just before the church (April–Oct daily 9.30am–5pm). A host of tearooms and cafés cater for the endless procession of tourists. There are two **hostels**: the nearer is at Butterslip How, ten minutes north of the village (☎05394/35316; ②); the more basic Thorney How (☎05394/35591; ②) is one mile out on the Easedale Road.

Keswick

Principal centre for the northern lakes, **KESWICK** lies on the northern fringes of **Derwentwater**, one of the few stretches of water in the area which can be walked all the way around. The main hiking attraction is **Skiddaw** to the north; inhospitable **Blencathra**, or Saddleback, five miles east, makes a more challenging day's climb. The town itself doesn't have a great many attractions: beyond a visit to the Cumberland Pencil Museum (daily 9.30am–4pm; £2), the best thing to do in Keswick is to hike a mile and a half eastwards to **Castlerigg Stone Circle**, a Neolithic monument which commands a spectacular view of the amphitheatre of mountains surrounding Thirlmere. The **tourist office** is in the Moot Hall, Market Square (daily 9.30am–5/7pm). The **youth hostel** (☎07687/72484; ②) is on Station Road by the river, or there's another on the eastern shores of Derwentwater, two miles south, in Barrow House (☎07687/77246; ②).

York

It's the medieval Minster, alleyways and ancient stone walls which draw tourists to **YORK**, but the city's character-forming experiences go back a lot further than that. It was adopted by the Romans as a base for their operations against the Brigantes, a fearsome tribe holding sway over the north from around the Humber estuary. It became the principal northern headquarters of the conquerors, and when the Emperor Severus, over here on a Scot-bashing expedition in 208, decided to split the administration of Britain into two halves, he made York one of the capitals. York's position as the north's spiritual capital dates from 627, when Edwin of Northumbria adopted Christianity – the faith of his Kentish wife. Northumbrian power crumbled in the face of a Danish invasion, the Danes sacking York in 866 and destroying one of the best libraries in western Europe in the process. By 876 one of the Danish leaders, Halfdan, had settled here with half the Viking army, beginning a century of Scandinavian rule in York, and adding another layer to a tradition of northern independence.

Without a doubt, one of the best introductions to York is to take a stroll along the city walls (open till dusk), a three-mile circuit that takes in the medieval Bars, or gates. **Bootham Bar**, adjacent to the tourist office, is as good a place as any to start, and progressing northeastwards from here will give you good views overlooking the Minster. Immediately opposite the tourist office, the **City Art Gallery** (Mon–Sat 10am–5pm, Sun 2.30–5pm; free) includes portraits of local Tudor worthies and a room devoted to the sentimental, moralizing work of local-born nineteenth-century artist William Etty. The next-door Museum Gardens lead to the ruins of the Benedictine abbey of St Mary and the **Museum of Yorkshire** (Easter–Oct daily 10am–5pm; Nov–Easter Mon–Sat 10am–5pm, Sun 1–5pm; £3), which contains much of the abbey's medieval sculpture, a Roman mosaic and a good selection of Saxon and Viking finds. In the same park are the remains of a tower built by Constantius at the end of the third century.

Ever since Edwin built a wooden chapel on the site in preparation for his baptism into the faith, **York Minster** (daily 7am–dusk) has been the centre of spiritual authority for the north of England. Most of what's visible now was built in stages between the 1220s and the 1470s, gradually blotting out an earlier Norman edifice. The straight lines of the Minster are a good example of English architecture's transition from the Gothic style of medieval Europe to the home-grown Perpendicular. Inside, the apocalyptic scenes of the East Window, completed in 1405, and the thirteenth-century *Five Sisters* window, present the finest collection of stained glass in the country. The octagonal Chapterhouse (Mon–Sat 10am–6.30pm, Sun 1–6.30pm; 60p) usually contains a few medieval manuscripts from the Minster's rich collection, while the Undercroft (same hours; £1.80) leads down to Roman relics and a Norman crypt. The finest of the cathedral towers, the Lantern (daily 10am–6pm; £2), can be ascended for sweeping views of the Vale of York.

South of the Minster, the narrow streets of the town centre have been pedestrianized and preserve much of the atmosphere of a medieval city, especially in the **Shambles**, where the overhanging upper storeys almost touch across the narrow alley.

A taste of the Viking period in the history of York is provided by the **Jorvik Viking Centre** located on Coppergate (daily 9am–5/7pm; £3.50). A remote-control dodgem car propels you through a recreation of Jorvik's streets, complete with appropriate smells and recorded sounds, while an informative commentary booms authoritatively from a loudspeaker built in behind the seat. With an eye to archeological integrity, however, the journey continues past the site of the excavations themselves, blackened shapes in the earth showing the foundations of the wattle and daub huts in which these proto-Yorkshiremen once lived.

The **Merchant Adventurers' Hall** on Fossgate (Mon–Fri 9.30am–1pm & 2–5pm; free) is a well-preserved structure dating from the fourteenth century. Despite the romantic connotations of the title, this was the guild headquarters of the solid, middle-class businessmen who controlled the local wool export trade, and whose portraits adorn the wood-panelled rooms.

Originally the keep of York castle, **Clifford's Tower** (daily 10am–4/6pm; £1.10) was the site of one of the most bizarre episodes of medieval anti-Semitism. Following a city fire, for which the Jewish community were blamed by the mob, the Jews took refuge here, then committed mass suicide in order to avoid being massacred. There's little to see in the tower itself, save for a commanding view from the top. The **Castle Museum** (Mon–Sat 9.30am–4/5.30pm, Sun 10am–4/5.30pm; £3.80) was one of the first British museums to indulge in full-scale recreations of life in bygone times, and it's still one of the best of the genre; "Kirkgate" and "Half Moon Court", reconstructed street scenes of the Victorian and Edwardian periods, are masterpieces of evocative detail. One last museum is worth a call: the **National Railway Museum**, just beyond the station on Leeman Rd (Mon–Sat 10am–6pm, Sun 11am–6pm; £3.95), contains the nation's finest collection of steam locomotives.

Practicalities

York's magnificent **train** station is east of the centre, just outside the city walls; the **bus** and coach station is at Rougier St, slightly nearer town in the same direction. Both involve a short walk down Station Rd and over Lendall Bridge, from where the next left leads to the **tourist office** in Exhibition Square (June–Sept Mon–Sat 9am–8pm, Sun 2–5pm; Oct–May Mon–Sat 9am–5pm). Rooms can be booked here for a small deposit. The *YHA*'s top-of-the-range **hostel** is twenty minutes from the centre at Haverford, Water End, Clifton (☎0904/653147; ②). *Bishophill House Hotel*, near the bus station at 11/13 Bishophill Senior (☎0904/625904; ②), also has dorm accommodation. Good **B&Bs** are concentrated in the Bootham area, to the west of the Minster; try – *Abbeyfields*, 19 Bootham Terrace (☎0904/636471; ④), *Ambleside*, 62 Bootham Crescent (☎0904/637165; ④), *Holme Lea Manor*, 18 St Peter's Grove (☎0904/623529; ④), or *St Mary's*, 17 Longfield Terrace, Bootham (☎0904/626 972; ④). Amongst York's numerous **tearooms**, *Betty's*, St Helen's Square, is the most elegant. Good places for **pub** food are the *Royal Oak*, Goodramgate; the *York Arms*, Petergate; and the *Fleece* on the Pavement.

Durham

Seen from the train, **DURHAM** presents a magnificent sight, with cathedral and castle perched atop a bluff enclosed by a loop of the River Wear, and linked to the suburbs by a series of sturdy bridges. Nowadays a quiet provincial town with a strong student presence, Durham was once one of northern England's power bases: the Bishops of Durham were virtual royal agents in the north for much of the medieval era, responsible for defending a crucial border province frequently menaced by the Scots.

The town initially owed its reputation to the possession of the remains of Saint Cuthbert, an early prior of Lindisfarne, which were evacuated to Durham in the ninth century due to Viking raids. His shrine has dominated the eastern end of the **Cathedral** ever since. The cathedral itself is the finest example of Norman architecture in England, even though the exterior has suffered a great deal from the erosion of time and the muddle-headed efforts of an eighteenth-century renovator, who began chiselling away at the stone to improve the finish. A series of intricately carved pillars, decorated with chevrons and other geometric designs, lines the nave, and medieval frescoes depicting St Cuthbert are just visible in the Galilee Chapel, which contains the remains of the Venerable Bede, brought here from Jarrow in 1020. The tombs of both Bede and Cuthbert were more colourful affairs before their destruction in the Reformation.

On the opposite side of Palace Green is the Norman **Castle** (July–Sept daily 10am–noon & 2–4.30pm; Oct–June Mon, Wed & Sat 2–4pm), taken over by the university in 1836, but preserving a solid twelfth-century chapel thought to have once served as a strongroom; look out for the naive carvings adorning the capitals of the pillars. Both cathedral and castle are surrounded by North and South Bailey, a continuous street that curves around the hillside, lined with eighteenth- and nineteenth-century buildings that are now largely the preserve of the university. Pathways along the river bank below pass the **Archeological Museum** (daily April–Oct 11am–4pm; Nov–March 12.30–3pm), with a very modest selection of prehistoric, Roman and Saxon finds.

Durham's **tourist office** is in the Market Place (June & Sept Mon–Sat 9.30am–5pm; July & Aug Mon–Sat 9.30am–6.30pm, Sun 2–5pm; Oct–May Mon–Fri 10am–4.30pm, Sat 9.30am–1pm). The **youth hostel** in Providence Row (advance booking ☎0629/825850; ②) is open only from July 18 to August 26. St Aidan's College, Windmill Hill (July–Sept; ☎091/374 3269; ②), is open slightly longer, but is often booked up by large groups. Try the smallish but excellently situated *Country View Guest House*, 40 Claypath (☎091/386 1436; ③).

Newcastle-upon-Tyne – and Hadrian's Wall

A grim, industrial city with a proud shipbuilding heritage – an industry now in severe decline – NEWCASTLE has an undeniable raw vigour and serves as a base for explorations of Hadrian's Wall, a second-century barricade that stretches from coast to coast. Your first taste of the city if arriving by rail will be the three bridges joining the city with the suburb of Gateshead, the River Tyne and the quaysides lying far below. The single steel arch of the Tyne Bridge, built in 1928, is very much the city's trademark.

The centre owes much of its character to John Dobson, who remodelled Newcastle along Neoclassical lines in the early nineteenth century. His most imposing legacy is the sweep of Grey Street, leading south from the lofty Grecian column of Grey's Monument, the city's central landmark. Newcastle's status as a border stronghold is remembered in the castle, with its Norman keep (daily April–Sept 9.30am–5.30pm; Oct–March 9.30am–4.30pm; £1), which offers good rooftop views and a succession of draughty rooms, including a Norman chapel in the basement. The city's main art collection is housed in the Laing Art Gallery on Higham Place (Tues–Fri 10am–5.30pm, Sat 10am–4.30pm, Sun 2.30–5.30pm; free). A venue for prestigious contemporary exhibitions, it also houses the usual selection of Victorian painting.

The university campus on Haymarket, on the northern fringes of the city centre, contains a trio of worthwhile museums. The Museum of Antiquities (Mon–Sat 10am–5pm; free) is a good introduction to the frontier culture of Hadrian's Wall, including a reconstruction of a Mithraeum which once stood in the nearby town of Carroburgh – a temple to the Middle Eastern deity Mithras, imported to the region by Roman soldiers serving on the Wall. The Hatton Gallery (Mon–Fri 9.30am–4.30pm, Sat in term time 10am–4.30pm) attracts touring exhibitions of contemporary art, and has a small permanent collection that includes the one surviving wall of Kurt Schwitters' barn studio in Ambleside and a wealth of African sculpture. On the second floor of the well-signposted Classics Faculty is the Greek Museum (Mon–Fri 9.30am–4.30pm; free), a small but important collection of ancient pottery, strong on the Hellenistic era and including some Etruscan finds.

Newcastle's Central Station is ten minutes directly south of the centre; the bus station, on Gallowgate, is a couple of minutes west. The tourist office in the Central Library behind Northumberland St (Tues, Wed, Fri & Sat 9am–5pm; Mon & Thurs 9.30am–8pm; ☎091/261 0691) can book accommodation. There's a hostel at 107 Jesmond Rd (☎091/281 2570; ②). Jesmond, served by Newcastle's metro system, is also the main location for B&Bs, clustered around Osborne Rd. City centre pubs and bars congregate around Bigg Market, a block east of Grey Street. Be sure to check out the Crown Posada, 31 The Side, and the nearby Barley Mow in City Road. The best-value eating in town is at Breadcrumbs, 5 St Mary's Place, and Mathers, 4 Old Eldon Square. The city's foremost live music and club venue is the Riverside, 57–59 Melbourne St; look out for other acts performing at Newcastle University Students' Union, Haymarket.

The Wall

Preserving the Pax Romana over the troublesome tribes of Britain's extremities was always a difficult task when there were more important frontiers in Europe and Asia to defend, and the Emperor Hadrian opted for containment rather than outright conquest. The turf and stone wall which bears the emperor's name was the result, punctuated by mile castles, strong points spaced at one-mile intervals, and by sixteen more substantially garrisoned forts. Regular trains and hourly buses (#685) on the Newcastle–Carlisle route pass by many of the sites: keeping your eye on the clock, you should be able to see a little of the Wall and return to Newcastle before nightfall. The best place to stop off is Bardon Mill, 35 miles west of Newcastle.

WALES

The relationship between England and **Wales** has never been entirely easy. Impatient with constant demarcation disputes, the eighth-century Saxon king Offa constructed a dyke to separate the two countries; today, a long-distance footpath running from Chepstow in the south to near Prestatyn in the north follows its route. During Edward I's reign the last of the Welsh native princes, Llewelyn ap Gruffyd, was killed, and Wales passed uneasily under English rule. Trouble flared again with the rebellion of Owain Glyndwr in the fifteenth century, but finally, when the Welsh prince Henry Tudor defeated Richard III at the Battle of Bosworth to become king of England he paved the way for the 1536 Act of Union, which joined the English and Welsh in restless but perpetual partnership.

Contact with England has watered down the indigenous Welsh culture; bricked-up, decaying chapels stand as reminders of the days when Sunday services and chapel choirs were central to community life. Harp-playing and the carving of lovespoons survive more or less courtesy of the tourism industry. Nevertheless, the Welsh language is undergoing a revival and you'll see it on bilingual road signs all over the country but are most likely to hear it spoken in north and mid Wales. Some Welsh place names have never been anglicized, but where alternative names do exist, we've given them in the text.

Much of the country, particularly the **Brecon Beacons** and **Black Mountains** in the south and **Snowdonia** in the north, is relentlessly mountainous and offers wonderful walking and climbing terrain. **Pembrokeshire** to the west also boasts a spectacular rugged coastline, dotted with offshore island nature reserves. The biggest towns, including Cardiff, Swansea, Aberystwyth and Caernarfon, cling to the coastal lowlands, but even there the mountains are no more than a bus ride away.

South Wales

Approaching from England by road via the Severn Bridge, your introduction to Wales will be **CHEPSTOW** (Cas-Gwent), encircled on three sides by thirteenth-century walls and on the fourth by the River Wye. The bridge across the Wye gives stunning views of cliff-faces soaring above the river and of the first stone castle the Normans built in Wales (March 15–Oct 15 Mon–Sat 9.30am–6.30pm, Sun 2–6.30pm; Oct 16–March 14 Mon–Sat 9.30am–4pm, Sun 2–4pm; £2.50). Opposite the castle is Gwy House, an eighteenth-century town house now home to a local **museum** (March–Oct Mon–Sat 11am–1pm & 2–5pm, Sun 2–5pm). Nothing in Chepstow itself can match the five-mile stroll along the Wye to the impossibly romantic ruins of **Tintern Abbey** (same hours as Chepstow castle; £2), built by the Cistercians in the twelfth century. The nave walls rise to such a height that, from a distance, you might think the church still stood intact beneath the overhang of the wooded cliff – only when you get close do you find the roof is long gone. If you don't fancy walking, *Red and White* bus #69 runs from Chepstow to Tintern. You can top up for the return journey in the fourteenth-century *Moon and Sixpence* by the river, which does excellent bar meals. Chepstow's **youth hostel** is in Mounton Rd (☎02912/685; ②), and *Home Farm*, Shirenewton (☎02912/334; ③), does **B&B**.

Arriving by train from London, you'll glimpse Chepstow Castle from the window, but **NEWPORT** (Casnewydd) will be the first stop; alternatively, *Red and White* bus #64 or #X73 will get you there from Chepstow. An unexciting city to linger in, it is nevertheless a useful base for exploring the nearby Roman remains – and for getting into the Brecon Beacons. **CAERLEON**, a small, traffic-bedevilled town three miles to the northeast but almost swallowed up by Newport (bus #7), preserves the extensive remains of

Roman baths, while its state-of-the-art **Legionary Museum**, in the High Street (March 15–Oct 15 Mon–Sat 10am–6pm, Sun 2–6pm; Oct 16–March 14 Mon–Sat 10am–4pm, Sun 2–4.30pm; £1.25) contains finds from all the adjacent sites. The museum stands opposite the road leading to the less dramatic remains of the barracks and amphitheatre, and sells an inclusive entrance ticket for all sites. Back in Newport, there are **beds** at *Langtree Guest House*, 49 Cardiff Rd (☎0633/440633; ④).

The Brecon Beacons

About fifteen miles north of Newport, and served by hourly trains from there, the compact town of **ABERGAVENNY** (Y Fenni) is the main base for exploring the eastern Brecon Beacons National Park. Before setting out for the mountains, pick up maps from the National Park Information Office at Swan Meadow, Cross St – and check what sort of weather you can expect, as sudden mists can play havoc. The most accessible climbing areas are the **Sugar Loaf** (1955ft), four miles to the northwest, and **Skirrid Fawr** (1595ft), three miles to the north. For **B&B** try *Belchamps Guest House*, 1 Holywell Rd (☎0873/3204; ④).

CRICKHOWELL, a small town with a fine medieval bridge five miles west of Abergavenny, is a more picturesque kicking-off point for explorations. *National Welsh* bus #21 runs an infrequent service from Abergavenny. A six-mile hike into the Black Mountains from Crickhowell takes you through remote and occasionally bleak countryside to tiny **Partrishow church**; inside, you'll find a rare rood screen complete with carved wooden loft and a mural of Father Time. To **stay** in Crickhowell try the *Dragon House Hotel* in the High St (☎0873/810362; ④).

Eight miles west, the central Brecon Beacons are accessible from **BRECON** (Aberhonddu), a sleepy little town springing to life on Tuesdays and Fridays for livestock markets. It's served by the infrequent *National Welsh* bus #21 from Crickhowell. For details of the numerous trekking routes into the Beacons, call at the National Park Information Office which shares the same building as the **tourist office** in the cattle market car park. **B&B** can be had at *Beacons Guest House*, 16 Bridge St (☎0874/3339; ③), and *Tir Bach Guest House*, 13 Alexandra Rd (☎0874/4551; ③). The Ty'n-y-Caeau **youth hostel** is one mile east of Brecon at Groesffordd (☎0874/86270; ②).

Cardiff and around

CARDIFF (Caerdydd), the Welsh capital, is rapidly picking itself up again after the collapse of the coal mining industry, and its narrow Victorian shopping arcades are interspersed with spanking new shopping centres and wide pedestrian precincts which seem to have sprung up at random. To get your bearings, pick up free maps and information at the **tourist office**, 8–14 Bridge Street, opposite the central library (summer Mon–Sat 9am–6pm, Sun 10am–6pm; winter Mon–Sat 9am–5.30pm, Sun 10am–4pm). **Cardiff Castle** (tours daily: May–Sept 10am–5.30pm; March, April & Oct 10am–4.30pm; Nov–Feb 10am–3.15pm; £3) is a good place to start your city tour. Standing on a Roman site developed by the Normans, it was embellished by William Burges in the 1860s and each room is now a wonderful example of Victorian "medieval" decoration; best of all are the Chaucer Room, the Banqueting Hall, the Arab Room and the Fairytale Nursery. Five minutes' walk away, the **National Museum of Wales** in Cathays Park (Tues–Sat 10am–5pm, Sun 2.30–5pm; £2) houses a version of Rodin's *The Kiss*, a fine collection of Impressionist paintings, and natural history and archeological exhibits.

In the **Cardiff Bay** area – reached by buses #7, #7A or #8 from Central Station – newly developed attractions include **Techniquest**, a hands-on science exhibition (Tues–Fri 9.30am–4.30pm, Sat, Sun & Bank Holidays 10.30am–5pm; £3), and the various sites of the **Welsh Industrial and Maritime Museum** (Tues–Sat & Bank

Holidays 10am–5pm, Sun 2.30–5pm; £1). The Q-Shed tells the story of seaborne passenger traffic in Wales, the Railway Gallery houses exhibits about train history and the Road Transport Collection displays horse-drawn trams and other old vehicles. Most exciting is 126 Bute Street, where a simulated dockside environment brings Cardiff's days as a coal-exporting city vividly to life again.

The **Welsh Folk Museum** at Saint Fagan's, four miles from the centre (bus #32), is a 100-acre open-air museum packed with reconstructed rural buildings from all over Wales (April–Oct daily 10am–5pm; Nov–March closed Sun; £3.50); a good time to visit is May Day when a huge fair is held here. Finally, for a revealing glimpse of coal-mining life in the valleys, catch bus #X30 to Forgeside to visit the **Blaenafon Big Pit Mining Museum** (March–Dec daily 10am–3.30pm; £4), housed in a mine which ceased production only in 1980. You descend 294 feet in a miners' cage to inspect coal-faces, underground roadways and haulage engines dating back almost 200 years.

Fans of William Burges' exquisite and elaborate style of decor shouldn't miss **Castell Coch** off the A470 at Tongwynlais (April–Oct daily 9.30am–6.30pm; Nov–March Mon–Sat 9.30am–4pm, Sun 2–4pm; £1.75). This thirteenth-century turreted castle, perched dramatically on a steep, forested hillside, was bought by the Marquis of Bute who set his favourite architect onto it, with customary lavish results.

Cardiff Central Station and the bus and coach terminal are side by side south of the city centre off Penarth Rd, although some local rail services leave from Queen St station to the west. Cardiff's **youth hostel** is in Wedal Rd (☎0222/462303; ②), or there's a **YMCA** in The Walk, Roath Park (☎0222/489101; ②). For **B&B**, try *Austin's*, 11 Coldstream Terrace (☎0222/377148; ③), just ten minutes' walk from the train station. To sample laverbread and other Welsh delicacies, head for *Celtic Cauldron* in the shopping arcade opposite the castle. Bistro-style meals can be had in *Henry's Bar* in Park Place. Real-ale lovers can sample Cardiff's own *Brain's* brew surrounded by rugby memorabilia in the *Old Arcade* in Church St.

Pembroke and the Pembrokeshire Coast National Park

PEMBROKE (Penfro), birthplace of Henry VII, is a sleepy town lying at the heart of the Pembrokeshire Coast National Park, and easily accessible by train from Cardiff. Centrepiece of the town itself is the magnificent water-surrounded **Castle** (daily 9.30am–4/6pm; £2), whose circular keep, dating from 1200, offers fine views of the countryside. The castle overshadows the high street where shops are shoehorned into an assortment of Tudor and Georgian buildings, one of them housing **Castle Hill Museum**, an eclectic collection of exhibits ranging from toys and games to fashion accessories (Easter–Oct 10.30am–5.30pm, closed Thurs & Sat; £1).

The nearest **hostels** to Pembroke are at Broad Haven, Haverfordwest (☎043783/688; ②), and Pentlepoir, Saundersfoot (☎0834/812333; ②), both a short bus hop away. In Pembroke B&B can be had at the *High Noon Guest House*, Lower Lamphey Rd (☎0646/683736; ③). Summer-only tourist information is available from the Drill Hall. Twice daily **ferries** to Rosslare leave from Pembroke Dock, taking four hours for the crossing.

The **Pembrokeshire Coast National Park** sweeps from Pendine Sands near Llansteffan to Poppit Sands near Cardigan, and the coastal path includes some of Wales' most stunning and remote scenery, offering sheer cliff-faces, panoramic sea views and excellent seabird-watching. Tricky though it may be without a car, it's worth trying to get to Saint Govan's Head – directly south of Pembroke near Broad Haven – where a chapel clings, barely credibly, to the rockface.

The other ferry port for Rosslare, with two sailings daily, is **FISHGUARD** (Abergwaub), an attractive fishing port 22 miles north of Pembroke on the rail line. The *Hamilton Guest House*, 21–23 Hamilton St (☎0348/873834; ②), and *Gorwel*, 21 Vergam Terrace (☎0348/873963; ②), are used to people arriving late or departing early.

From Fishguard bus #411 runs the thirteen miles west to **SAINT DAVID'S** (Tyddewi), where a breathtakingly beautiful **Cathedral**, delicately tinted purple, green and yellow by a combination of lichen and geology, hides in a dip behind the high street. The present building was mostly constructed between 1180 and 1522, but heavily restored in the last century. Across a thin trickle of river thousands of jackdaws congregate around the extensive remains of the fourteenth-century **Bishop's Palace** (March 15–Oct 15 Mon–Sat 9.30am–6.30pm, Sun 2–6.30pm; Oct 16–March 14 Mon–Sat 9.30am–4pm, Sun 2–4pm; £2), adding to the beauty of the setting. There's a **youth hostel** at Llaethdy, two miles west (☎0437/720345; ②), and several **B&Bs** in St David's: try *Rigsby's* (☎0437/720632; ④) or *Y Glenydd* (☎0437/720576; ④), both in Nun Street.

Mid Wales

Mid Wales, an area of wild mountain roads, hidden valleys and genteel ex-spa towns, is the least visited part of the country, perhaps because access is a little trickier. Nevertheless, it's worth making the effort, because it's here more than anywhere else that you'll discover the real Wales, in quiet towns where the pub conversation takes place in Welsh rather than English. This is also "alternative" Wales at its most hippyish – look out for health food shops and trendy bookshops, their English-speaking owners often escapees from the Midlands.

To get to Mid Wales, there's a handy **train** service **from Shrewsbury** which passes through **WELSHPOOL** (Trallwyng) and continues to Aberystwyth. Welshpool is a market town full of the distinctive black and white half-timbered houses typical of the Welsh-English borders. It's worth a stop simply to visit thirteenth-century **Powis Castle** (April–Jun & Sept–Oct Wed–Sun 11am–5pm; July–Aug Tues–Sun 11am–5pm; £5.80 castle, gardens & Clive Museum; £3.60 gardens & museum only), a gorgeous honey-coloured building that's been continuously inhabited for 500 years. It houses Wales' best collection of furniture, tapestries and pictures, as well as the Clive of India collection of Indian treasures – and Capability Brown designed the terraced gardens. If you decide to stay, **B&B** is available at *Peniarth*, 10 Cefn Hawys, Red Bank (☎0938/552324; ③).

Aberystwyth and around

ABERYSTWYTH is a lively seaside resort of neat Victorian terraces and a thriving student culture. Best place to start exploring is the **tourist office** in Terrace Rd (Easter–Oct daily 10am–6pm; Nov–Easter Mon–Thurs 10am–5pm, Fri 10am–4.30pm); upstairs, the Ceredigion Museum contains coracles once used by local fishermen and a reconstructed cottage interior. Most of the action centres on the seafront, where one of Edward I's castles bestrides a windy headland to the south. There's also a Victorian camera obscura which can be reached via an electric cliff train to the north (Easter–Sept daily 10am–6pm). For a more extended rail trip, you could take the **Vale of Rheidol** steam train service to **Devil's Bridge**, a canyon where three bridges of assorted ages and in assorted conditions span a dramatic waterfall; the return journey takes three hours, the fare is £8, and it can get very busy in the middle of the day.

Aberystwyth seafront is lined with Victorian **guesthouses**, all much of a muchness. Women might prefer to try the **YWCA** in North Parade (☎0970/871498; ②). Check out the University Arts Centre on Penglais Hill for films, plays, exhibitions and other events (closed mid-May to mid-June). *Y-Craig* at 34 Pier St is a great place to eat vegetarian **food**, and the owner is a mine of information on what's going on locally.

North of Aberystwyth the train passes through a succession of seaside resorts, some small and discreet, others large and upfront, before reaching **ABERDOVEY** (Aberdyfi), a quiet village beautifully situated at the mouth of the River Dovey. Its seafront is lined with **B&Bs** which do a roaring trade in summer: try *Brodawel Guest House*, Tywyn Rd (☎0654/767347; no singles; ④), or 1 Trefeddian Bank (☎0654/767487; ③). *Aben Café*, Smithfield St (☎0341/422460; ③), is centrally placed above a greasy caff.

Main-line trains follow the coast north to down-at-heel Barmouth, where you can catch bus #94 (7 daily, 3 Sun) inland to **DOLGELLAU**, a base for exploring **Cader Idris**. The mountain looms over the southern side of town, its summit accessible via a tough four-mile trek along Fox's Path. The **tourist office** is on Eldon Square (daily 10am–6pm). If you fancy staying, *Fronoleu Farm* a mile out on the Machynlleth road has a licensed restaurant in its converted stables as well as **B&B** (☎0341/422361; ④).

If you prefer to stick to the coast, trains from Barmouth head north to **HARLECH**, where one of the best of Edward I's great castles, later Glyndwr's residence, towers above everything else on a rocky crag overlooking the sea (April–Oct daily 9.30am–6.30pm; Nov–March Mon–Sat 9.30am–4pm, Sun 2–4pm; £2.50); the ramparts offer panoramic views over Snowdonia on one side and Tremadog Bay on the other. The town itself huddles apologetically behind the castle with little to say for itself, but if you want to stay, try the *Aris Guest House*, 4 Pen-y-Bryn (☎0766/780409; ④).

Porthmadog and Portmeirion

Even if you don't particularly want to visit **PORTHMADOG**, a somewhat gloomy Victorian town nine miles north of Harlech, you are likely to have to do so because public transport through Snowdonia converges here (see below). Anyway, it gives you the perfect excuse to visit the extraordinary village of **PORTMEIRION**, three miles southwest (bus #1, #2 or #3 or train to Minffordd), a cluster of pastel-coloured houses arrayed around a piazza in subtropical woodlands. This Italianate folly was designed by architect Sir Clough Williams-Ellis early this century, and has become the prime tourist attraction of Mid Wales. For **rooms** in Porthmadog itself, try *Owen's Hotel*, 17 High St (☎0766/512098; ④), or one of the B&Bs in Madoc St.

North Wales

Snowdonia is the glory of **North Wales**, with mountain scenery as good as anything in Scotland or the Lake District – jagged peaks, towering waterfalls and glacial lakes decorating every roadside. Not surprisingly, climbers congregate here in strength, and the villages around the area's highest peak, Snowdon, see steady tourist traffic even in the coldest, bleakest months of the year. Whatever season you're here, always check the weather forecast (☎0286/870120) and make sure you go equipped with suitable shoes, warm clothing, and food and drink to see you through any unexpected hitches. There are two main **rail routes** into North Wales: up the west coast from mid-Wales, or along the northern littoral from Chester to Caernarfon with a branch to Blaenau Ffestiniog. The main A5 road cuts through Llangollen to the heart of Snowdonia.

Blaenau Ffestiniog and Betws-y-Coed

From Porthmadog you can travel on the private Ffestiniog train as far as the slate-quarrying town of **BLAENAU FFESTINIOG**, a fourteen-mile journey through the Snowdonia National Park. On a grey day, Blaenau Ffestiniog can look particularly desolate, but it's worth a call for the **Llechwedd Slate Caverns** a mile north, reached by bus #140. A train takes visitors into the side of the mountain past an underground lake and spectacular caverns to the very bottom of the mine, on Britain's steepest train incline (daily March–Sept 10am–5.15pm; Oct–Feb 10am–4.15pm; £4.25). Should the brooding scenery have cast its spell over you, **B&B** can be had at *Afallon* in Manod Rd (☎0766/830468; ③).

You'll probably want to push on to **BETWS-Y-COED**, ten miles northeast by main-line train. A popular hiking centre for Snowdonia National Park, the town has one of the prettiest settings in Wales but is overrun with visitors in summer, many coming here just to see the **Swallow Falls** in the wooded Llugwy Valley, two miles west of town. You may want to **stay** to appreciate the wood-and-water setting after the day trippers have moved on; if so, try *Mount Pleasant*, Holyhead Rd (☎0690/710502; ③). The *Royal Oak* does excellent, value-for-money meals. From Betws-y-Coed there are trains and buses to Llandudno Junction, for train connections to the main line from Chester.

Llangollen

Hourly trains run from Chester to the almost charmless industrial town of Wrexham, where bus #94 offers a service to **LLANGOLLEN**, a delightful town ten miles southwest beside the frenetic River Dee. Its principal sight is half-timbered **Plas Newydd**, created by the oddball "Ladies of Llangollen", Eleanor Butler and Sarah Ponsonby, whose visitors – including Wordsworth and the Duke of Wellington – were expected to bring pieces of carved wood to add to the crazy decoration of the facade (May–Sept Mon–Sat 10am–7pm, Sun 10am–5pm; £1.10). Llangollen's canal offers the chance to sample the relaxing experience of travelling by horse-drawn barge – the trip to Pontcysyllte crosses Telford's aqueduct, one of the finest pieces of engineering in Britain. Afterwards, you can follow the towpath two and a half miles west to the ruins of thirteenth-century **Valle Crucis Abbey** (April–Oct Mon–Sat 9.30am–6.30pm, Sun 2–6.30pm; Nov–March Mon–Sat 9.30am–4pm, Sun 2–4pm; £1.25). From there it should be possible to hitch over the **Horseshoe Pass**, a mile along the road, which offers spectacular views.

Llangollen is best known for the **International Musical Eisteddfod**, a festival of music and dance held in July, when thousands of singers and folk dancers travel here from all around the world. For tickets and accommodation at festival time, contact the Eisteddfod office (☎0978/860236) as far in advance as you can. The **youth hostel** is in Tyndwr Hall, Tyndwr Rd (☎0978/860330; ②). **B&Bs** straggle up Hill St and along Abbey Rd, where *Glanafon* (☎0978/860725; ③) is particularly welcoming. In the evening head for *Gales*, 18 Bridge St, a bistro with 300 varieties of wine.

Conwy

From Chester twice hourly trains run along the North Wales coast, passing through a string of unappealing resorts before coming to **CONWY**, where Edward I's **Castle** (mid-March to mid-Oct daily 9.30am–6.30pm; mid-Oct to mid-March Mon–Sat 9.30am–4pm, Sun 2–4pm; £2.90) and the town walls have been listed by UNESCO as a World Heritage Site. The ramparts offer fine views of Telford's **suspension bridge** (currently being restored) over the River Conwy. For **B&B** try *Pen-y-Bryn*, 28 High St (☎0492/596445; ③), or *Mrs Salainen*, 10 Upper Gate St (☎0492/596537; ②).

Caernarfon

North coast trains converge on Bangor before heading north for Anglesey (see below). To get to **CAERNARFON** – the springboard for trips into Snowdonia from the north – you'll need bus #5A or #X5 from the bus station off Bangor High Street. Since 1301 all Princes of Wales have been invested in Caernarfon **Castle** (same hours as Conwy; £3), built in 1283 and arguably the most splendid castle in Britain. The walls completely dominate the town, but form just a shell enclosing a three-acre space. As for Caernarfon itself, time hasn't been particularly kind to it, and suburbs full of high-rise flats provide a disappointing setting for such splendour.

Tourist information is available at Oriel Pendeitsh in Castle St (daily 10am–6pm). If you can wait to escape into the Snowdonian countryside, try *Gorffwysfa Hotel*, St David's Rd (☎0286/2647; ④), or some of the hotels along North Rd for **B&B**.

Llanberis and Snowdon

Half-hourly #88 and the less frequent #11 buses run the seven miles from Caernarfon to **LLANBERIS**, a village bursting to grow into a town in the shadow of **Snowdon** (Yr Wyddfa), at 3560 feet the highest mountain in England and Wales. With the biggest concentration of guesthouses, hostels and restaurants in Snowdonia, it offers the perfect base for mountain exploration, however tentative. The longest but easiest ascent of the mountain is a signposted five-mile hike, manageable by anyone reasonably fit, although the final stretch involves a bit of a scramble. Alternatively, you can cop out and take the **Snowdon Mountain Railway** which operates from Llanberis to the summit, weather permitting, daily from mid-March to October; at the season's start and end trains may terminate at Glogwyn, three-quarters of the way up the mountain. Return tickets (£12.50) permit half an hour's viewing from the summit.

Climbers have a choice of four different **youth hostels**, all served by Gwynedd bus #11 from Llanberis, and each at the base of a footpath up Snowdon: *Llanberis*, Llwyn Celyn (☎0286/870280; ②); *Snowdon Ranger*, Rhyd Ddu (☎0286/85391; ②); *Bryn Gwyant*, Nant Gwynant (☎076686/251; ②); and *Pen-y-Pass*, Nant Gwynant (☎0286/870428; ②). The High Street is lined with small **hotels**; try *The Heights*, 74 High St (☎0286/871179; ④) which has cheaper eight-bed dorms, or *Glyn Afon* (☎0286/872528; ③). Tourist **information** is available inside the Museum of the North (daily 10am–5pm), whose displays take a Disney approach to the complexities of Welsh history.

Holyhead

The Menai Bridge was built by Telford in 1826 to connect North Wales with the island of Anglesey across the Menai Straits, but now stands forlorn as road and rail traffic flows past across the new bridge. The bridge itself is one of the two chief sights on Anglesey, the other being **Beaumaris Castle** (same hours as Conwy; £1.50), reached by bus #53 or #57 from Bangor or Menai Bridge station. The last of Edward I's masterpieces, it was built in 1295 to guard the Menai Straits and has a fairy-tale moat enclosing its twelve towers.

Most tourist traffic in this direction is heading for **HOLYHEAD**, the busiest ferry port for Ireland, with sailings at least four times a day to Dublin. If you need somewhere to stay before your boat sails, *Hendre*, Porth-y-Felin Rd (☎0407/762929; ④), *Min-y-Don*, 2 Newry Fawr (☎0407/762718; ③), and *Oakleigh*, 4 Walthew Ave (☎0407/762941; ④), are all within a few minutes' walk of the terminal.

SCOTLAND

Scotland presents a model example of how a small nation can retain its identity within the confines of a larger one. Unlike the Welsh, the Scots successfully repulsed the expansionist designs of England, and when the old enemies first formed a union in 1603, it was because King James VI of Scotland inherited the English throne. Scotland has retained its own institutions, notably distinctive legal and educational systems and the national presbyterian church, along with a radical social and political culture which stands in antithesis to the conservatism of England.

Most of the population clusters in the narrow central belt between the two principal cities: stately **Edinburgh**, the national capital, with its magnificent architecture and imperious natural setting, and earthy **Glasgow**, a powerhouse of the Industrial Revolution and still a hard-working, hard-playing place. The third city, **Aberdeen**, set in one of the rare strips of lowland in the north, is now fabulously wealthy from the proceeds of offshore oil, and its pristine granite buildings and abundant parks and gardens look even more immaculate than ever.

Yet it's the **Highlands**, severely depopulated but comprising over two-thirds of the total area, which provide most peoples' enduring image of Scotland. The dramatic landscapes are further enhanced by the volatile climate, producing an extraordinary variety of moods and colours. Here you'll find some of the last wildnernesses in Europe, though even the highest mountain, **Ben Nevis**, is an uncomplicated ascent for the average walker, while much of the finest scenery – such as the famous **lochs** Lomond and Ness and the islands of the **Hebrides** – can be enjoyed without too much effort.

Edinburgh

EDINBURGH is the showcase capital of Scotland, a well-heeled, cosmopolitan and cultured place which regularly tops the polls as Britain's best place to live. Its natural contours and stone-built houses and monuments make it visually stunning: the fairy-tale castle, perched on the summit of an extinct volcano, looks over the rooftops towards the 823-foot hill of Arthur's Seat, from where there are breathtaking vistas of hills and water. Inevitably, the city is suffering from the increasingly intrusive trappings of the tourist trade. The 430,000 population swells massively in high season, peaking during Festival time, when an estimated one million visitors come to town for the biggest arts event in Europe. Yet despite this annual invasion, and despite its proximity to the border and its integration into the transport system of the south, Edinburgh is emphatically Scottish – its richly grained and complex character typifies that of a nation which has maintained its essential autonomy despite nearly three centuries of full political union with England.

The centre has two distinct parts. The castle rock is the core of the ancient capital, where nobles and servants lived side by side for centuries within the tight defensive walls. Edinburgh earned the nickname "Auld Reekie" for the smog and smell generated by the cramped inhabitants of this **Old Town**, where the streets ran with sewage tipped out of tenement windows and disease was rife. The riddle of medieval streets and alleyways remained a run-down slum well into this century. The **New Town** was begun in the late 1700s with the announcement of a plan to develop farmland lying to the north of the castle rock. Edinburgh's wealthier worthies speculated profitably on tracts of this land, and engaged the services of eminent architects in their development. The result of their labours was an outstanding example of Georgian town planning, still largely intact.

Arrival and information

Edinburgh **airport** is eight miles west of the centre; regular bus connections operate around the clock. Waverley Station, the main **rail** terminal, is situated right in the centre: emerging from the station, a right turn will take you into the New Town and Princes Street, while to the left is the Old Town and the Castle. The **bus** terminal for local and inter-city services is on St Andrew Square, across Princes Street from Waverley; information on routes and times is available from the Lothian Region Transport Office, a hundred yards to the left of the Waverley's main entrance, at the junction of Waverley Bridge and Market Street. The main **tourist office** is at 3 Princes St, above the station on the top level of Waverley Market (July & Aug Mon–Sat 9am–8pm, Sun 11am–8pm; reduced times out of season). When the office is closed there is a 24-hour computerized information service at the door.

The Edinburgh telephone code is ☎031.

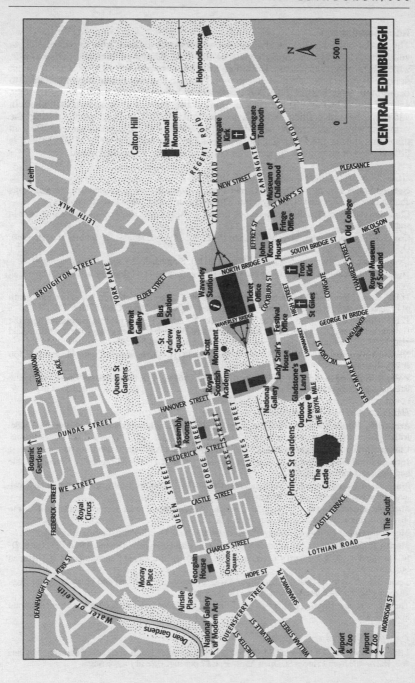

CENTRAL EDINBURGH

N

0   500 m

Holyroodhouse

Calton Hill

National Monument

REGENT ROAD

Canongate Kirk

Canongate Tolbooth

Leith

CALTON ROAD

NEW STREET

CANONGATE

Museum of Childhood

ST MARY'S ST

PLEASANCE

LEITH WALK

JEFFREY ST

John Knox House

Fringe Office

Old College

NICOLSON ST

BROUGHTON STREET

YORK PLACE

ELDER STREET

NORTH BRIDGE ST

SOUTH BRIDGE ST

CHAMBERS STREET

Royal Museum of Scotland

Waverley Station

Ticket Office

COCKBURN ST

Tron Kirk

HIGH STREET

Portrait Gallery

Bus Station

Scott Monument

WAVERLEY BRIDGE

Festival Office

St Giles

COWGATE

DRUMMOND PLACE

St Andrew Square

Royal Scottish Academy

Lady Stair's House

LAWNMARKET

GEORGE IV BRIDGE

CANDLEMAKER ROW

Queen St Gardens

HANOVER STREET

National Gallery

Gladstone's Land

Outlook Tower

THE ROYAL MILE

VICTORIA ST

DUNDAS STREET

Assembly Rooms

FREDERICK STREET

GEORGE STREET

ROSE STREET

PRINCES STREET

Princes St Gardens

The Castle

GRASSMARKET

Botanic Gardens

WE STREET

FREDERICK STREET

QUEEN STREET

CASTLE STREET

CHARLES STREET

CASTLE TERRACE

The South

Royal Circus

Moray Place

Georgian House

Charlotte Square

HOPE ST

LOTHIAN ROAD

DENHAUGH ST

KERR ST

Water of Leith

Ainslie Place

National Gallery of Modern Art

CHESTER ST

QUEENSFERRY STREET

SHANDWICK PL

Airport & Zoo

Airport & Zoo

NEVILLE ST

WILLIAM STREET

MORRISON ST

Dean Gardens

HOLYROOD ROAD

Accommodation

The tourist office has details of all grades of **accommodation**, from five-star hotels to youth hostels, and can supply copies of the free *Edinburgh Accommodation Guide*, which lists over 500 places. The office will book rooms for £3 plus a ten percent deposit. Hotel rooms and hostel accommodation in the city centre may prove hard to come by in peak season, but B&B is offered in hundreds of houses around the city, with prices as low as £10 per person, though the average is considerably higher. In addition, the universities and colleges let out student rooms, mostly during the summer, while campers are served by three sites on the fringes of the city. Bear in mind that during the Festival (last two weeks in Aug and first week of Sept) there is little chance of getting cheap accommodation unless you've booked ahead.

HOSTELS AND CAMPUS ACCOMMODATION

Belford Youth Hostel, 6–8 Douglas Gardens (☎225 6209). Housed in a redundant Arts and Crafts church near the West End of the city centre. Open all year round; dorm beds ②; doubles ③.

Christian Alliance Female Residence, 14 Coates Crescent (☎225 3608). Single rooms ④; beds in shared room ③.

Cowgate Tourist Hostel, 112 The Cowgate (☎226 2153). Basic singles ③, doubles and triples ②. Open July-Sept only.

Heriot-Watt, Riccarton Campus (☎449 5111 ext. 3113). Singles, doubles and twins year-round. ⑤

High Street Hostel, 8 Blackfriars St (☎557 3984). Popular hostel off Royal Mile. Open 24 hours, all year round. ②

IYHF Hostel Bruntsfield, 7 Bruntsfield Crescent (☎447 2994). Strictly run hostel one mile south of Princes St – take bus #11, #15 or #16 from Princes St. Open 2–11pm. Closed Jan & Feb. ②

IYHF Hostel Eglinton, 18 Eglinton Crescent (☎337 1120). To the west of the centre, near the Haymarket train station, which is the last stop before Waverley. Easier-going than the Bruntsfield place, with a 2am curfew. Includes compulsory breakfast. Closed Dec. ②

Napier University, 219 Colinton Rd (☎444 2266 ext. 4621). Single and twin rooms Easter vacation & July–Sept. ⑤

Pollock Halls of Residence, 18 Holyrood Park Rd (☎667 1971). Single rooms Easter vacation & late June to late Sept. ⑤

HOTELS AND GUESTHOUSES

Arrandale House, 28 Mayfield Gardens (☎667 6029). Friendly establishment on the south side, within easy reach of the centre by bus #50. ④

Clifton Hotel, 1 Clifton Terrace (☎337 1002). Family-run hotel opposite Haymarket station. ⑤

International Guest House, 37 Mayfield Gardens (☎667 2511). Good reputation for comfortable and clean accommodation. ④

Marrakech Guest House, 30 London Street (☎556 4444). Another family-run hotel, with an excellent Moroccan restaurant in the basement. ④

Mayfield Guest House, 15 Mayfield Gardens (☎667 8049). Pricier sister-establishment to the *Arrandale House*; £50 for a double, but worth it. ⑥

Meadows Guest House, 17 Glengyle Terrace (☎229 9559). Overlooking the Bruntsfield park. ⑤

Merith House Hotel, 2 Leith Links (☎554 5045). On Leith Links park, two miles from the centre. ④

St Bernard's, 22 St Bernard's Crescent (☎332 2339). In the elegant surroundings of Georgian Stockbridge. ⑤

Teviotdale House, 53 Grange Loan (☎667 4376). Probably the best bed and breakfast in the city – all rooms have private facilities and the food is glorious. ⑤

Thrums Private Hotel, 14 Minto St (☎667 5545). Excellent hotel with equally classy restaurant attached. ⑥

CAMPSITES

Little France, 219 Old Dalkeith Rd (☎666 2326). Three miles south of the centre, reached by bus #33, #82 or #89 from Princes St. Open April–Sept; £7 per night, £8 in July & Aug.

Mortonhall Park, 38 Mortonhall Gate, Frogston Rd East (☎664 1533). Five miles out, near the Braid Hills. Take bus #11 from Princes St. Open mid-March–Oct; £8 per night; open £9 in July & Aug, £7 otherwise.

Muirhouse Caravan Park, Marine Drive, Silverknowes (☎312 6874). Pleasant site close to the shore; a twenty-minute ride on bus #14 from North Bridge. Open April–Sept; £4.70 per night.

The City

The cobbled **Royal Mile** – composed of Castlehill, Lawnmarket, High Street and Canongate – is the busiest stretch of the tourist itinerary and the central thoroughfare of the Old Town, connecting the Palace of Holyroodhouse to the **Castle** (daily 9.30am–5.15pm; £4). For centuries the seat of kings, the castle is thought to have evolved from an Iron Age fort, the sheer rock on which it stands providing formidable defence on three sides. Within its precincts is St Margaret's Chapel, a Norman church that's probably the oldest building in the city. Also open to the public are the state apartments, including the room in which James VI of Scotland was born, the Great Hall with its magnificent hammerbeam roof, and the ancient crown jewels of Scotland. There's a large military museum here, too, and the castle esplanade provides a dramatic setting for the world-famous Military Tattoo, staged every year during the Festival.

Descending the Lawnmarket from the castle, you'll pass **Gladstone's Land**, named after the merchant who set up shop there in 1617; inside, the National Trust for Scotland has restored the painted ceilings and furnished the upper floors as they would have been during Gladstone's day (April–Oct Mon–Sat 10am–5pm, Sun 2–5pm; £2.40). **Lady Stair's Museum**, behind Gladstone's Land, is dedicated to Sir Walter Scott, Robert Burns and Robert Louis Stevenson, with memorabilia of the trio housed on three floors of the seventeenth-century building (Mon–Sat 10am–5/6pm; free).

The High Street section starts at **St Giles' Cathedral**, whose beautiful crown-shaped spire is an Edinburgh landmark. In all likelihood there's been a church here since the eighth century, but the existing building is chiefly late fourteenth and early fifteenth century, with large-scale alterations carried out in the nineteenth. At the east end of the simple and impressive interior, the Thistle Chapel, designed in 1911, is an amazing display of mock-Gothic woodcarving. The heart-shaped cobble pattern set outside the west door is known as the Heart of Midlothian – passers-by traditionally spit on it for luck. To the rear are the Neoclassical law courts, which incorporate the seventeenth-century **Parliament Hall**, under whose spectacular hammerbeam roof the Scottish parliament met until the 1707 Union with England.

South of here, the **Cowgate** provides an atmospheric flashback to old Edinburgh, and is home to the *369 Gallery*, a showcase for work by Scottish artists. A short way further south, in Chambers Street, is the **Royal Museum of Scotland** (Mon–Sat 10am–5pm, Sun noon–5pm; free); the central hall is a magnificent iron-and-glass structure, but there's a stolid worthiness to its huge collections of the decorative arts, natural history, geology, science and technology.

Back on the Royal Mile, the next stretch of the High Street takes in the **Museum of Childhood** (Mon–Sat 10am–5/6pm; free), the noisiest museum in the city, packed with games, toys and various other exhibits to prompt nostalgia in the parents and hyperactivity in the kids. Where the Royal Mile narrows to accommodate an old wellhead stands the **John Knox House**, housing an exhibition focusing on the life and times of the religious reformer (Mon–Sat 10am–4.30pm; £1.25). The adjoining *Netherbow Arts Centre* is a multimedia arts complex which offers year-round exhibitions and theatre as well as a good café.

Canongate starts at the St Mary's Street and Jeffrey Street crossroads, the original city boundary. Jeffrey Street descends towards the station and Market Street, site of the **City Art Centre** (Mon–Sat 10am–5/6pm; free). Much refurbished, the Art Centre houses the city's collection of paintings, prints, drawings and sculpture and runs a busy programme of temporary exhibitions from international blockbusters to community-based displays. Across the street, the **Fruitmarket Gallery** has an international reputation for its modern art exhibitions.

Before the New Town was built, Canongate was the chic end of the Royal Mile, where nobles and merchants established their homes. Moray House, with its balcony jutting out over the pavement, is a rare survivor, as is sixteenth-century **Huntly House** (Mon–Sat 10am–5/6pm; free), now a museum focusing on the history of the city. Across the road is **Canongate Tolbooth**, once a prison, now a museum dedicated to Edinburgh's social history; it features reconstructed interiors such as a wartime kitchen and a washhouse (same hours; free). **Canongate Kirk**, set back from the street one block down, was built in the late 1600s after the parish church in Holyrood Abbey was converted into a Catholic chapel. The simple church is used by the royal family whenever they are at Holyrood, as the coat of arms on one of the pews indicates. **Dunbar's Close**, just down from the church, conceals a reconstructed apothecary's garden, open to the public from dawn to dusk.

The **Palace of Holyroodhouse**, the Royal Family's official residence in Scotland, looks out over the Queen's Park, 650 acres of wilderness in the heart of the city. Except when the dignitaries are in residence, the public are admitted to the sumptuous state rooms and historic apartments, which include the chamber where Mary Queen of Scots, pregnant with her son James VI, witnessed the murder of her courtier David Rizzio by associates of her husband (tours April–Oct Mon–Sat 9.30am–5.15pm, Sun 10.30am–4.30pm; Nov–March Mon–Sat 9.30am–3.45pm; closed June to mid-Feb; £3). The gaunt, roofless ruins of Holyrood Abbey stand within the palace grounds; dating mainly from the turn of the thirteenth century, they were the inspiration for Mendelssohn's *Scottish Symphony*.

THE NEW TOWN

The pleasantest route from the Old Town to the Georgian grid of the New Town is to descend the Mound to the **National Gallery of Scotland** (Mon–Sat 10am–5pm, Sun 2–5pm; free), one of the best small collections in Europe. Arranged chronologically, it includes a choice selection from virtually every major European country: from Italy there's Raphael, Andrea del Sarto, Titian (including two late masterpieces), Tintoretto, Bassano, Veronese and Tiepolo; art from the Low Countries is represented by a spread that encompasses van der Goes, Rembrandt and Rubens; from Spain there's Velázquez and El Greco; and the gallery's sequence of paintings by Poussin bears comparison to that in the Louvre. The unrivalled show of Scottish artists features David Wilkie's *Pitlessie Fair*, Henry Raeburn's *The Reverend Robert Walker Skating* – a postcard favourite – and Allan Ramsay's *Portrait of Rousseau*. Opposite, the **Royal Scottish Academy** is the grandest exhibition space in the city, usually hosting a major international show during the Festival.

The Academy looks onto the broad avenue of Princes Street, the main shopping area, with homogenized chain stores crammed in cheek by jowl. A hundred yards to the east is the spire of the **Scott Monument** (Mon–Sat 10am–3/6pm; £1), decorated with figures from Sir Walter's novels; the climb to the top is demanding but rewarding. Equally conspicuous is the **National Monument** atop Calton Hill, at the far eastern end of Princes Street; it would have been a copy of the Parthenon had money not run out in 1829.

Built along a ridge parallel to Princes Street, **George Street** capitalizes on the views to the north: standing at its junction with Hanover Street you look down across the New Town, out towards the Firth of Forth and over to the hills of Fife. The **Assembly Rooms** at 54 George St are a glorious confection of ornate plasterwork and extravagant chandeliers; one of the most exciting theatre venues during the Festival, at other times they're used for a variety of purposes, from tea dances to craft fairs. At its western end George

St runs into the most elegant square in the New Town – Robert Adam's suave **Charlotte Square**. The National Trust for Scotland has restored no. 7 – the **Georgian House** (April–Oct Mon–Sat 10am–5pm, Sun 2–5pm; £2.80) – to a state of pristine perfection, stocking it with magnificent specimens from the workshops of Hepplewhite, Sheraton and Chippendale, the great names of eighteenth-century furniture.

North of George St is the broad avenue of Queen Street, at whose eastern end stands the **Scottish National Portrait Gallery** (Mon–Sat 10am–5pm, Sun 2–5pm; free). As well as a collection of portraits of prominent Scots – many of them outstanding examples of the genre – it contains a collection of photographic works from the beginnings of the art to the present day. Within the same building is the antiquities department of the **Royal Museum of Scotland** (same times; free), with priceless treasures illuminating the nation's history from prehistoric times to the eighteenth century.

STOCKBRIDGE AND LEITH

In the northwest corner of the New Town, beyond Queen Street Gardens, lies **Stockbridge**, a smart residential suburb with bohemian pretensions – especially noticeable around the atmospheric huddle of old mill buildings known as Dean Village. From here Belford Road leads up to the **Scottish National Gallery of Modern Art** (Mon–Sat 10am–5pm, Sun 2–5pm; free), where the likes of Matisse, Picasso, Giacometti and Mondrian share space with modern Scottish artists such as Paolozzi and Ian Hamilton Finlay. Although the gallery doesn't quite match the comprehensiveness of the Tate, it nonetheless has examples from most of the significant groupings of the twentieth century, from Fauvism, Cubism and Expressionism right down to Pop Art and Minimalism, while the wooded grounds make a fine setting for the sculptures of Moore, Epstein and many others.

Another luscious retreat from the city is offered by the **Royal Botanic Garden** (Mon–Sat 9am–dusk, Sun 11am–dusk; free) on the north side of Stockbridge, entered from either Arboretum Place or Inverleith Row. Covering seventy acres, the gardens support a vast array of rare plants from around the world in their landscaped grounds and magnificent hothouses.

North of Stockbridge, the Water of Leith opens out to the sea at **Leith**, the first great Scottish port – quickest reached from the city centre along Leith Walk, a broad avenue which leads off from the eastern end of Queen Street. Regular buses run down here, or it's about twenty minutes by foot. Now a yuppified suburb – dubbed Leith-sur-Mer by a local advertising agency – Leith retains a few traces of its past, such as the *King's Wark* pub on The Shore, with its Dutch-style crowstepped gables, and the sixteenth-century **Lamb's House** in Waters Close, the best large house of its date in Edinburgh. The main reasons for coming out here, though, are the sea breezes and the restaurants.

Eating and drinking

Edinburgh is well-served with **restaurants** to suit most tastes, but – as with accommodation – there's a lot of pressure on space in the better places. Whatever you plump for, be sure to book in advance for the ones for which we've given phone numbers. Unless specified otherwise, you can eat well at all our recommendations for under £10. Edinburgh's **cafés** are among the most enjoyable spots in the city – serving coffee, food and most often alcohol too, and sometimes doubling as exhibition and performance spaces during the Festival. The multitudinous **bars** of Edinburgh are among the most congenial in the country, with live music a frequent bonus.

RESTAURANTS

Brattesani's, 85 Newington Road. The fish-and-chips experts: families make a night out over fry-ups and ice cream here, but the takeaways are just as good.

Buffalo Grill, 14 Chapel St. Vegetarians have a hard time here, where the French chef's charcoal-grilled beefsteak rules. Popular and busy.

Buntom's, 9 Nelson St (☎557 4344). The first Thai restaurant in the capital, serving delicious dishes in an elegant New Town drawing room.

Chinese Home Cooking, 21 Argyle Place (☎229 4404). Cantonese and Peking style. Good family atmosphere and inexpensive food (average dish £3). Unlicensed, so bring your own bottle.

Jamdani, 4 Forrest Rd. Authentic-tasting Indian fare, good for carry-outs.

Kalpna, 2/3 St Patrick Square (☎667 9890) Prize-winning and inexpensive vegetarian Indian; delicious if small portions.

Loon Fung, 2 Warriston Place, Canonmills (☎556 1781) and 32 Grindlay St (☎229 5757). Cantonese-style, seafood a speciality. No-nonsense staff. Main dishes from £6.

Martin's, 70 Rose St, North Lane (☎225 3106). Featured in all the good food guides, has a set two-course lunch at £9.75 and an à la carte dinner menu that might set you back about £25 for three courses excluding wine.

Pierre Victoire, 10 Victoria St (☎225 1721), 38 Grassmarket (☎226 2442), 8 Union St (☎557 8451) and 5 Dock Place, Leith (☎555 6178). Excellent bargain menus presented with Gallic dash. £7–11.

Queen Street Oyster Bar, 16a Queen St (☎226 2530). Frequented by BBC staff, serves tasty dishes prepared in a postage-stamp kitchen. Stocks Belgian Trappist beers.

St James' Oyster Bar, 1 Calton Rd. Busy city-centre musicians' hang-out. Occasional live music.

San Marco, 10 Mary's Place. Family-run pasta and pizza restaurant with fun atmosphere; good value.

Le Sept, 7 Old Fishmarket Close (☎225 5428). Upstairs gets busy early, serving filling crêpes and a good vegetarian selection at reasonable prices. Downstairs is posher and pricier.

The Shore, 3 The Shore, Leith (☎553 5080). Popular haunt with a menu centred on seafood; live music every evening except Sundays.

Skipper's, 1a Dock Place, Leith (☎554 1018). Fresh seafood. Three-course fixed price dinner menu £14.50, main course lunch dishes from £4.50.

Tinelli, 139 Easter Rd (☎652 1932). A well-kept secret: small and efficient dining room serving the real North Italian thing.

Viva Mexico, 10 Anchor Close (☎226 5145) and 50 Fountainbridge (☎228 4005). Run by Mexican-Scot husband and wife team. Lavish portions and great margaritas.

BARS AND CAFÉS

Bannerman's Bar, 55 Niddry St. Rough and ready decor, good range of beers and real ales.

Bennets Bar, 8 Leven St. Next door to the *King's Theatre*; always packed out.

Café Royal, 17 West Register St, off Princes St. Beautiful horseshoe-shaped bar, original Victorian decor, frequented after office hours by city professionals.

The City Café, 19 Blair St. Retro-chic city rendezvous for the young and hip. Basic selection of bar-snack meals.

Fiddlers Arms, 9 Grassmarket. Monday night is folk night, when the impromptu music sessions start up.

Filmhouse Bar, 88 Lothian Rd. Good central meeting place attached to Edinburgh's "alternative" cinema. Art film clientele, occasional exhibitions.

Hebrides Bar, 17 Market St. Tiny old-fashioned bar near the station where Highlanders gather. Good crack, friendly service and occasional song.

Malt Shovel, 13 Cockburn St. Good beer and plenty of local colour.

Mathers, 25 Broughton St. Old-fashioned and amiable bar for serious drinkers.

The Peartree, 36 West Nicolson St. Busy pub near the university with large and popular courtyard. Efficient service and indifferent food.

Port O'Leith, 58 Constitution St, Leith. Good, honest local with excellent food.

Nightlife

Edinburgh's nightlife is as lively as that of any city in Britain, and venues change name and location with such alacrity that the only way to keep up with what's going on is to get hold of *The List* magazine, a comprehensive source of information. Live **rock** is generally the preserve of the *Playhouse* theatre on Greenside Place, the largest indoor venue in Edinburgh for touring bands. *Preservation Hall* on Victoria Street is best-known for local blues and R&B bands; the *Venue* and *Calton Studios*, both on Calton Road, present varied bills and showcase local talent, the latter staging the occasional all-night rave too. There's a good **disco** scene, with *Wilkie House* in the Cowgate a major venue. *The Network* at West Tollcross is especially popular on Saturday nights, presenting predominantly African music. Pick of the mainstream discos is *Buster Browns*, Market Street (Fri–Sun 11.30pm till late). The city's largest gay disco is the *Blue Oyster Club*, 96 Rose Street Lane North (Thurs–Sun 10pm–4am).

The Festival

The **Edinburgh Festival**, billed as the world's largest arts jamboree, was founded in 1947, and now attracts artists of all descriptions for three weeks in August and September. The show is, in fact, a multiplicity of festivals, with the official programme traditionally presenting uncontroversial highbrow fare while the frenetic Fringe presents a melange of just about everything else in the field of the performing and visual arts. In addition, there's a Film Festival focusing on the latest movies, a Jazz Festival, and – in odd-numbered years – a Book Festival. Tickets are available at the venues and from the International Festival Office at 21 Market Street (☎226 4001), and the Fringe Office at 180 High Street (☎226 5257).

Listings

Airport enquiries ☎333 1000.

Bicycle hire *Central Cycles*, 13 Lochrin Place (☎228 6333); *Sandy Gilchrist Cycles*, 1 Cadzow Place (☎652 1760).

Bus enquiries ☎556 8464.

Car rental *Arnold Clark*, Lochrin Place, Tollcross (☎228 4747); *Budget*, 111 Glasgow Rd (☎334 7740); *Hertz*, Waverley Station (☎557 5272).

Consulates *US*, 3 Regent Terrace (☎556 8315); *Australia*, 80 Hanover St (☎226 6271).

Hospital Royal Infirmary, Lauriston Place (☎229 2477).

Pharmacy *Boots* at 48 Shandwick Place is open Mon–Sat 9am–9pm, Sun 11am–4.30pm.

Police Fettes Avenue (☎311 3131).

Post office The central post office is on Waterloo Place at the east end of Princes Street; Mon–Fri 9am–5pm, Sat 9am–1pm.

Taxis *Capital Cabs* (☎220 0404), *Castle Cabs* (☎228 2555), *Central Taxis* (☎229 2468), *City Cabs* (☎228 1211).

Train enquiries ☎556 2451.

Glasgow

The largest city in Scotland, home to three-quarters of a million people, **GLASGOW** was once even more prominent than it is today. Known as the "second city of the Empire", it thrived on trade with the American colonies, on cotton production and, most famously, on the shipbuilding on the River Clyde. The civic architecture of Victorian Glasgow was as grand as any in Britain, and the West End suburbs were regarded as amongst the best designed in the country. Since this heyday, however, it has not enjoyed the best of reputations. The Gorbals area became notorious as one of the worst slums in Europe, and the city's association with violence and heavy drinking stuck to it like a curse.

Initially it can still seem a grey and depressing place, but Glasgow is undergoing another change of image nowadays; a change symbolized by the "Glasgow's Miles

Better" self-promotion campaign, by its selection as the European City of Culture in 1990, and by the opening of new shops and galleries like the slick Burrell Collection. The city is a vital mix of old and new, with a generosity of spirit which is impossible to ignore and a sense of humour that can be a tonic after the primness of Edinburgh.

Arrival and accommodation

Glasgow **airport** is eight miles west of the city, served by the half-hourly #500 bus to the central Buchanan Street **bus station** – **Prestwick** airport in Ayrshire handles a smaller number of flights; half-hourly trains, link it with Glasgow Central station. Glasgow has two central **train stations**, Queen Street and Central, the former handling traffic to Edinburgh and the north, the latter serving destinations to the south. Glasgow is easy to explore on foot – you can walk from the city centre to the West End in about half an hour. Should you tire of the pavements, the **Underground** is one of the cheapest and easiest ways to get around the centre, operating on a circular chain of fifteen stations with a flat fare of 50p. There are also various private local bus companies in the centre, most of them using the pay-as-you-enter system.

The very helpful polyglot **tourist information centre** is at the corner of George Square near the top of Buchanan Street (June–Sept Mon–Sat 9am–9pm, Sun 10am–6pm; Oct–May Mon–Sat 9am–6pm). Apart from issuing the usual glut of leaflets and maps, it can book accommodation not just in Glasgow but anywhere else in Scotland too. There's also an information centre at Glasgow airport (daily 8am–8pm).

The *IYHF* **youth hostel** is in the West End at 7–8 Park Terrace (☎041/332 3004; ②). Nearby there are also a number of reasonably priced **bed and breakfasts**, and **guesthouses**. In the centre are the comfortable and reasonably-priced *Hampton Court Hotel*, 230 Renfrew St (☎041/332 6623; ③), and the very Scottish *Babbity Bowser*, 16–18 Blackfriars St (☎041/552 5055; ④). The West End has the small, cheap *Alamo Guest House*, 46 Gray St (☎041/339 2395; ③), the busy *Argyll Lodge*, 969 Sauchiehall St (☎041/334 7802; ③), and the slightly scruffy *Smith's Hotel*, 963 Sauchiehall St (☎041/339 6363; ③), ideal for single travellers.

During the Easter and summer holidays, both Glasgow (☎041/339 5271) and Strathclyde (☎041/553 4148) universities let rooms for bed and breakfast accommodation. In addition, the *YMCA* on Petershill Drive (☎041/558 6166) has fifty self-catering flats from July to September. They sleep between four and six people and can be rented for as brief a period as one night.

The City

Glasgow's centre of gravity lies on the north bank of the Clyde, specifically around the grandiose and frenetic **George Square**. East of here on Castle Street is the **Cathedral**. Built in 1136, destroyed in 1192 and rebuilt soon after, it's the only Scottish mainland cathedral to have escaped the hands of the country's religious reformers in the sixteenth century. Their hatred of anything that smacked of idolatry wrecked many of Scotland's ancient churches, but this one survived chiefly thanks to the intervention of the city guilds. The magnificent vaulted crypt – the Laigh Kirk – is the principal remnant of the twelfth century, and contains the tomb of Saint Mungo, the city's patron. Compared to many English cathedrals, it's a modest-sized building, and it's dominated by the adjacent **Necropolis**, resting place of the magnates who made Glasgow rich. Opened in 1832, and topped by a colossal figure of arch-reformer John Knox, it's a compendium of jumbled pastiche architecture, its vaults mimicking every style from Byzantine to Gothic and Ottoman. On the other side of the cathedral is the **Provand's Lordship** (Mon–Sat 10am–5pm, Sun 2–5pm; free), the oldest house in Glasgow. Built late in the fifteenth century as a priest's dwelling, it's now furnished with items mostly dating from later centuries, complete with waxwork occupants.

If you follow Cathedral Street west to Buchanan Street and then turn right, you'll swing into Glasgow's most famous thoroughfare – the much-smartened and now pedestrianized **Sauchiehall Street**. About halfway along, one block to the north, is the **Glasgow School of Art** at 167 Renfrew Street, three of whose recent graduates – Steven Campbell, Ken Currie and Adrian Wiszniewski – are among the most fashionable names in British art. The school itself is as remarkable as anything to have emerged from it: built by Charles Rennie Mackintosh – whose distinctively streamlined Art Nouveau designs appear in jewellers, furniture outlets and various other shops in Glasgow – it's a remarkable fusion of Scottish manor house solidity and modernist refinement. The interior, making maximum use of natural light, is furnished and fitted entirely by Mackintosh, and can be seen on a guided tour (Mon–Fri 10am, 11am, 2pm & 3pm, Sat 10.30am; £2, booking advised ☎041/332 9797).

An entirely different kind of interior is on view a short distance north of here, in the **Tenement House** at 145 Buccleuch St (April–Oct daily 2–5pm; Nov–March Sat & Sun 2–4pm; £1.60). For half a century its rooms were occupied by one Agnes Toward, who seems to have been incapable of throwing anything away. Now run by the National Trust for Scotland, her home is ful of nineteenth-century furniture and bric-a-brac, from box beds and gas lamps to bars of soap – an intriguing if sanitized vision of working-class life.

Immediately west again, past the salubrious crescents of the West End, **Kelvingrove Park** has the **Glasgow Museum and Art Gallery** (Mon–Sat 10am–5pm, Sun 11am–5pm; free), a first-rate collection founded on donations from various captains of industry. Its particular strengths are pictures from Italy, the Low Countries and nineteenth-century France: Rembrandt's *Man in Armour* is perhaps the single most arresting painting, and there are notable pieces from Jordaens, Millet, van Gogh and Monet. Across the road in the Kelvin Hall on Argyle St, the **Transport Museum** (Mon–Sat 10am–5pm, Sun noon–6pm; free) boasts fleets of trams, cars and motorbikes, with models and photos celebrating the Clyde shipyards. On the northern edge of the park the campus of Glasgow university houses the **Hunterian Museum** (Mon–Sat 9.30am–5pm; free), a miscellany of things zoological and archeological, centred on one of the world's finest coin collections. It also proudly displays Scotland's solitary dinosaur. The nearby **Hunterian Art Gallery** (same hours) has works by Chardin, Stubbs and Rembrandt, plus a display of nineteenth- and twentieth-century Scottish art, but the highlights are a comprehensive survey of the output of James Abbott McNeill Whistler (only Washington has a larger collection), and the reconstructed interior of Charles Rennie Mackintosh's house (50p admission) – an astonishingly fresh creation, even half a century after his death. The Hunterian also has Scotland's best print collection, extracts from which form the exhibits in the ever-changing shows in the special print gallery.

On **Glasgow Green**, down by the river to the east of George Square, stands the **People's Palace** (Mon–Sat 10am–5pm, Sun 2–5pm; free), opened as a cultural centre for the East End in 1898. It now records the social history of the city, giving most of its space to memorabilia of Victorian Glasgow. No visit to Glasgow would be complete without a trip to the **Barras**, a huge market selling bric-a-brac, clothes, furniture, food and plants. Held every Saturday and Sunday, just off Gallowgate to the north of Glasgow Green, it starts mid-morning and runs all day, invariably drawing an enormous crowd.

Glasgow's highest-profile sight, though, is just under four miles south of the centre, in **Pollok Country Park**, which is reached by bus #45, #48 or #57 from Union St. Housed in a custom-built gallery, the **Burrell Collection** (Mon–Sat 10am–5pm, Sun 2–5pm; free) was accumulated by just one man, Sir William Burrell, who began collecting at the age of 15 and kept going until his death at 96, buying an average of two pieces a week. Though he and his brother both made substantial fortunes out of shipbuilding, his financial resources were paltry compared to those of America's industrial barons, and the richness of this assembly of paintings, tapestries, sculpture, glass and other applied arts owes as much to his canny judgement as to the size of his bank balance. Works by Memling, Cézanne, Degas, Bellini and Géricault feature among the paintings, while in adjoining galleries there are pieces from ancient Rome and Greece, medieval European arts and crafts, and a massive selection of Chinese artefacts, with outstanding ceramics, jades and bronzes. Now overshadowed by the Burrell, the nearby **Pollok House** (same hours) is a lovely eighteenth-century mansion containing Spanish paintings by such luminaries as El Greco, Goya and Murillo, in addition to some fine furniture and works by William Blake.

Eating, drinking and nightlife

For **breakfast and snacks**, one of the best and cheapest places is the *Grosvenor Café*, Ashton Lane, just off Byres Road in the West End. On Byres Road itself the *University Café* is a cheap treat, with filling chip-based meals and great ice creams. The most elegant place for a light meal is the Mackintosh-designed *Willow Tea Rooms*, at 217 Sauchiehall St. In the centre of town, the *Café Gandolfi*, Albion St, is good for medium-priced snacks, meals and drinks. Both *PJ's* in Ruthven Lane and the *Fire Station*, Ingram St, do half-price pasta dishes between 5 and 7pm seven days a week. *Balbirs Ashoka*, Elderslie St, does reasonably priced Indian meals, and its sister restaurant just along the road caters purely for vegetarians. The *Tron Theatre Café* in the Trongate also carries a good and varied menu. For the best of Scottish cooking at moderate prices, join the academics and arty set at *The Ubiquitous Chip*, 12 Ashton Lane.

Glasgow has a bewildering number of **pubs**, from watering holes which have been quenching the city's thirst for years, to new and trendy bars which spring up and often disappear swiftly. The *Riggs Bar*, Candleriggs, is one of the old school, with plenty of atmosphere. If you want to hear Gaelic spoken against a backdrop of tartan and general Scottishness, then make for the *Park Bar* on Argyle Street. Also recommended are the *Halt Bar*, Woodlands Rd (often with live music), the *Variety Bar* on the corner of Sauchiehall St and Pitt St and the *Scotia Bar* in Stockwell St (live folk music).

During the month of May, Glasgow plays host to the **Mayfest**, a carnival of formal and informal music and theatre. Details of these and all other events can be found in the *Glasgow Herald* or *Evening Times* newspapers, or the fortnightly magazine *The List* – the best source for the latest **clubs and discos**. At other times of the year, the *Tron* in Trongate and the *Citizens* in Gorbals St offer some of the most stimulating theatre in Britain, while the **Centre for Contemporary Arts** at 346–354 Sauchiehall St has a reputation for controversial exhibitions and performances. Finally, the wonderful *Glasgow Film Theatre* on Rose Street shows art **films** and old favourites.

The Borders

Scotland's **Border Country**, an upland region of rich farmland, secluded valleys, quiet villages and bustling little market towns, was for centuries the frontline between Scotland and England, and its history became an inspiration for its most famous resident, Sir Walter Scott, whose writings were to create the enduring romanticized image of Scotland. During the twelfth-century reign of King David I, four magnificent **abbeys** were built in the region as showpieces of the independent Scottish state, and these now rank among the most evocative ruins in Europe. The defensive towers which were their secular counterparts were often replaced in more peaceful times by magnificent **stately homes**, including several of Scotland's finest. No longer served by rail, the Border towns are connected to each other and to Edinburgh by plentiful **bus services**. Free timetables are available from local tourist offices, who will book **accommodation** anywhere in the region without charge – though the main places of interest can easily be visited on day trips from Edinburgh.

Melrose and around

If you've only time to visit one Border town, **MELROSE**, 37 miles south of Edinburgh, makes the obvious choice. The town is very pretty and superbly set beneath the triple-peaked Eildon Hills, with the supremely beautiful **Abbey** (April–Sept Mon–Sat 9.30am–6pm, Sun 2–6pm; Oct–March Mon–Sat 9.30am–4pm, Sun 2–4pm; £1.70). It's best seen on a bright morning, with the sun streaming through the tracery of the great east and south windows and illuminating the richly sculpted buttresses of the nave chapels.

Scott's custom-built home, **Abbotsford** (mid-March to Oct Mon–Sat 10am–5pm, Sun 2–5pm; £2.20), lies a couple of miles west of Melrose, just off the road to Galashiels. Self-consciously over-the-top, it attempts to give a physical presence to the mythical world of his novels. Details from Scotland's great ruined or unfinished buildings are aped in the architecture, while the rooms overflow with souvenirs of the military heroes of the nation's past.

Far more aesthetically pleasing is Scott's burial place, **Dryburgh Abbey** (same times as Melrose; £1.70), near the village of St Boswells, five miles southeast of Melrose. The early Gothic transept housing the writer's grave – and that of Field Marshal Earl Haig, of World War I fame – is the only part of the church to have survived, but the monastic buildings are partly intact. Best of all is the wonderfully secluded setting by the Tweed, with a spectacular array of trees and shrubs.

The Melrose **tourist office** (summer Mon–Sat 10am–7pm, Sun 1.30–7pm; shorter hours rest of year) is in a pavilion in Priorwood Gardens, on the south side of the abbey – but it's due to move during 1994. The **youth hostel** (☎089682/2521; ②) is in an old mansion, again overlooking the abbey. There's a plentiful supply of **B&Bs**, including one on High Street, a couple on Buccleuch Street, and three on Waverley Road. The old coaching inns in and around the central Market Place are a pricy accommodation option, but rather more affordable for **eating** and **drinking**: *Burt's* is the best for food.

Kelso and around

KELSO, twelve miles east of Melrose, lies at the point where the Tweed is joined by its main tributary, the Teviot. The **Abbey** (same times as Melrose; free) here was the grandest in the Borders but is now by far the most ruined: the magnificent fragment represents only the western transept and tower. Across the park to the northwest of the abbey is the eccentric octagonal **Old Parish Church** (Mon–Fri 10am–4pm); further west is the spacious Georgian **Market Square**, the largest in Scotland, dominated by the town hall and the *Cross Keys Hotel*, the most celebrated of several coaching inns in Kelso.

At the northern edge of town is **Floors Castle** (Easter, May, June & Sept Mon–Thurs & Sun 10.30am–5.30pm; July & Aug daily 10.30am–5.30pm; Oct Wed & Sun 10.30am–4pm; £3), the largest inhabited house in Scotland. William Adam's original construction was given its overloaded Romantic look by William Playfair in the 1840s, and the interior is no less rich, containing a superb set of Gobelins tapestries. An even more impressive stately home, **Mellerstain House** (Easter & May–Sept 12.30–5pm, closed Sat; £3), lies eight miles northwest of Kelso, on the route of some of the buses to Galashiels. Here Robert Adam created some of his most luxuriant interiors, including some dazzling ceilings, among which the main library's is oustanding.

Kelso's **tourist office** (summer Mon–Sat 10am–6.30pm, Sun 2–6.30pm; shorter hours rest of year) is on the Market Square. B&B **accommodation** is scattered all over town, with a couple of places on Horsemarket, just off Market Square.

Jedburgh

Situated just ten miles from the border, **JEDBURGH** is nonetheless an archetypal example of the sort of small towns which litter the map of Scotland. What makes it different from most of its counterparts is the massive sandstone **Abbey** (same times and price as Melrose), seen to best advantage from across Jed Water, just off the main road from England. Boasting an outstanding facade, the church survives almost intact save for its roof, its Romanesque features modifying into Gothic as you move from the apse to the west end.

The centre of town is the **Market Place**, dominated by the tall eighteenth-century steeple of the former Newgate prison. Castlegate, lined with impressively sober stone mansions, climbs steeply from here to the site of the castellated **Castle Jail** (April–Sept Mon–Sat 10am–5pm, Sun 1–5pm; 70p), specially constructed in the 1820s as a replacement for Newgate. Set beside well-tended gardens is the austere **Mary Queen of Scots' House** (Easter to mid-Nov daily 10am–5pm; £1.10), which takes its name from the fact that the ill-fated Mary once lodged there.

The **tourist office** is at the side of the large car park just off Canongate (summer Mon–Sat 9am–7pm, Sun 10am–7pm; shorter hours for rest of year, often closed Sun). There's a wide choice of B&B **accommodation**, with a heavy concentration on Castlegate, and rooms are available at the *Spread Eagle*, 20 High Street (☎0835/62870; ③), reputedly the oldest hotel in Scotland. The **campsite** is on Edinburgh Road (April–Oct), just to the north of town.

St Andrews

Notwithstanding a population which barely reaches five figures, **ST ANDREWS**, situated on the Fife coast 56 miles northeast of Edinburgh, has the air of a place of importance. Retaining memories of its days as medieval Scotland's academic and religious metropolis, it is still the Scottish answer to Oxford or Cambridge, with only slightly less snob appeal – you'll hear upper-class English and American accents in term time. St Andrews can be reached by **bus** from Edinburgh in just under two hours, and is a feasible day excursion. There are no longer direct **rail** services, though frequent buses connect with the station five miles away in Leuchars, where the parish church incorporates the most beautiful and intact piece of Romanesque architecture in Scotland.

The town has an exalted place in Scottish sporting history too. Entering St Andrews from the Edinburgh road, you pass no fewer than four golf links, the last of which is the **Old Course**, the most famous and – in the opinion of Jack Nicklaus – the best in the world. At the southern end of the Old Course, down towards the waterfront, is the award-winning **British Golf Museum** (Jan–Feb Mon & Thurs–Sun 11am–3pm; March–April daily except Wed 10am–5pm; May–Oct daily 10am–5.30pm; Nov daily except Wed 10am–4pm; Dec Mon & Thurs–Sun 11am–3pm; £3), where the excellent exhibition details everything you wanted to know – and more – about 500 years of golf. Immediately south of the Old Course begins North Street, one of St Andrews' two main arteries. Much of it is taken up by university buildings, with the tower of **St Salvator's College** rising proudly above all else. Together with the adjoining chapel, this dates from 1450 and is the earliest surviving part of the university. Guided tours of the academic buildings – many of them not otherwise open to the public – leave from this point (mid-June to Aug Mon–Sat 10.30am & 2.30pm; £2).

Further east, the ruined **Castle** (Mon–Sat 9.30am–4/6pm, Sun 2–4/6pm; £1) can be reached down North Castle Street. Commanding a prominent headland, it began as a fortress, but was partly transformed by the local archbishops into a Renaissance palace, of which little more than the facade survives. A short distance further along the coast is the equally ruined Gothic **Cathedral** (same times; free), the mother church of medieval Scotland and the largest and grandest ever built in the country. It's now used as a cemetery, but, even though little else survives, the intact east wall and the exposed foundations give an idea of the vast scale of what has been lost. The **museum** (same times; £1.20) contains the *St Andrews Sarcophagus*, probably ninth-century, one of the most refined products of the so-called Dark Ages. With the entrance ticket you can also ascend the austere Romanesque **tower of St Rule** – part of the priory that the cathedral replaced.

Outside the cathedral enclosure and now forming an entrance to the coastal road southwards are **the Pends**, huge fourteenth-century arches which served as the main gateway to the priory. Running westwards from the Pends is South Street, site of more historic university buildings and of **Holy Trinity** parish church (summer daily 10am-noon & 2–4pm), partly fifteenth century but much altered. Incongruously for a bastion of Presbyterianism, it contains a spectacular marble monument to Archbishop Sharp, whose attempts to change the administration of the church in Scotland led to his murder by the Presbyterian party. Further along are the elegant ruins of Blackfriars monastery, while the street terminates at the **West Port**, a well-preserved late sixteenth-century gateway that now creates a traffic bottleneck.

Practicalities

The **tourist office** at 78 South St (summer Mon–Sat 9.30am–7pm, Sun 11am–5pm; shorter hours rest of year) offers a free accommodation service – **rooms** are in short supply only when there's a big golf tournament on. A particularly dense concentration of guesthouses can be found on Murray Place and Murray Park, off North Street and close to the Old Course; prices vary from as low as £10 to as much as £25. As a summer fall-back, the **student residences** at the western entrance to town – Hamilton Hall on Golf Place (☎0334/77641) and David Russell Hall, Buchanan Gardens (☎0334/72281) – charge a flat £18.30, plus another £7 if you want dinner. There are also a number of good, but more pricy hotels on The Scores, the road leading from the Old Course to the castle, above the British Golf Museum, with good sea views. The *Golf Hotel*, 40 The Scores (☎0334/72611; ③), offers good-sized rooms with comfy beds and sofas. It also has a superb restaurant.

For **eating**, student favourites are *Brambles* on College St, the *Merchant's House* at 49 South Styand and *Ziggy's* grill-house on Murray Place. The best pubs are around the Old Course and along The Scores, although a particularly popular student place is the *Victoria Café*, 1 St Mary's Place, at the west end of Market Street. Superb ice cream is served at *Jannetta's*, 31 South St, and sumptuous cakes and handmade chocolates are sold at *Fisher & Donaldson* on Church St.

Stirling

Occupying a key strategic position between the Highlands and Lowlands at the easiest crossing of the River Forth, **STIRLING** has played a major role throughout Scottish history. Imperiously set on a rocky crag, its **Castle** (April–Sept Mon–Sat 9.30am–5.15pm, Sun 10.30am–4.45pm; Oct–March Mon–Sat 9.30am–4.20pm, Sun 12.30–3.35pm; £2.50) combined the functions of a fortress with those of a royal palace. The highlights of the extremely diverse buildings within the complex are the Gothic **Great Hall** and the Renaissance **Royal Palace**, adorned with grotesque statues outside and by magnificent oak medallions within.

The oldest part of Stirling is grouped around the streets leading up to the castle. Moving downhill, you pass first two of Scotland's most imposing Renaissance town houses – the intact **Argyll's Ludging** and the dilapidated **Mar's Wark**, with its richly decorated facade. Beyond stands the Gothic **Church of the Holy Rude** (May–Sept Mon–Fri 10am–5pm), which boasts a fine timber roof. Here the infant James VI – later the first monarch of the United Kingdom – was crowned King of Scotland in 1567. To the side of the church is the E-shaped seventeeth-century building known as the **Guildhall**, though it began life as a grand almshouse.

From here, Broad Street slopes down to the lower town. Proceeding north along Upper Bridge Street then Union Street, you come to the fifteenth-century **Old Bridge**, a replacement for the wooden construction that was the scene of Sir William Wallace's victory over the English in 1297, a crucial episode in the Wars of Independence. The Scottish hero was commemorated in Victorian times by the construction of the **Wallace Monument** (Feb, March & Oct 10am–4pm, closed Wed & Thurs; April–Sept daily 10am–5pm; July & Aug daily 9am–6pm; £2.35), about a mile further north. Though the recently refurbished building is ugly and overprominent, compensation comes in the quite stupendous views – finer even than those from the castle. In the foreground can be seen **Stirling University**, the youngest in Scotland and sometimes claimed as the most beautiful campus in the world.

The Stirling **tourist office** is located on Dumbarton Road in the lower part of town (summer Mon–Sat 9am–8pm, Sun 9am–7.30pm; shorter hours rest of year). There's the usual numerous supply of guesthouses and between June and September it's possible to stay in the university **residences** (☎0786/467140; regular buses leave from Murray Place). The new grade one **youth hostel** is on St John Street (0786/473730; ②) at the top of town. It occupies a converted church and all rooms have ensuite showers and toilets. The **campsite** is three miles east of town, off the A91 road to St Andrews (April–Oct). For **eating** and **drinking**, try *Settle Inn* on St Mary's Wynd or the *Birds and the Bees* along Easter Cornton Rd from Causewayhead.

Loch Lomond

The name of **Loch Lomond** – the largest stretch of fresh water in Britain – is almost as famous as Loch Ness, thanks to the ballad about its "bonnie, bonnie banks", which has become the epitome of the Scottish folk song. The easiest way to get to the loch is to take one of the frequent buses from Glasgow to **BALLOCH** at its southern tip, from where you can take a cruise around the thirty-three islands nearby. Above the marina is Loch Lomond's main **tourist office** (daily April–June, Sept & Oct daily 10am–5.30pm; July & Aug 9.30am–7.30pm); they'll find a **B&B** – of which there's a plentiful supply in the area – without charge. A couple of miles up the west side of the loch is Scotland's plushest **youth hostel** (☎0389/85226; ②); other hostels are in Inverbeg (☎043686/635; ②) and Rowardennan (☎036087/259; ②). There are **campsites** in all the villages mentioned in this section.

Only the **western shore** is developed, with the A82 seldom straying far from its banks. The West Highland train – the line from Glasgow to Mallaig, with a branch line to Oban – joins the loch seventeen miles north of Balloch at Tarbet, and has one other station eight miles further on at Ardlui, at the mountain-framed head of the loch. There are, however, plenty of buses down this shore from Balloch.

No buses run on the **eastern shore**, much of which can only be traversed by the footpath which forms part of the West Highland Way. The easiest access to the graceful peak of **Ben Lomond** (3192ft) is by ferry from Inverbeg (south of Tarbet) to Rowardennan. From the latter it's a straightforward three-hour hike to the top of the most southerly and popular of Scotland's great mountains.

Oban and the southern Hebrides

The southernmost of the Hebrides – notably the large island of **Mull**, the tiny sacred isle of **Iona** and the spectacular rock of **Staffa** – are among the most compelling of the entire archipelago and the easiest to reach from central Scotland. Their main point of access is **Oban**, fifty miles south of Fort William (see below). A scenic **bus** run along Loch Linnhe provides the quicker and cheaper approach from Fort William; if you're visiting Glencoe, this can be picked up at Ballachulish, not much more than a mile west of Glencoe Village. Approaching Oban **from the south** by train, you take the West Highland line to the hill-walking resort of Crianlarich, where the train divides, one part continuing north through Fort William, the other branching west to Oban.

Oban

Solidly Victorian in appearance, **OBAN** is an attractive enough place, if uncomfortably crowded for at least five months a year. It has a superb setting, the island of Kerrera providing its bay with a natural shelter, and a further distinctive note is struck by the huge circular **McCaig's Tower** on a hilltop above the town. Imitating the Colosseum in Rome, it was the brainchild of a local banker a century ago, who had the twin aims of alleviating local unemployment and creating a family mausoleum. Work never progressed further than the exterior walls, but the folly provides a wonderful seaward panorama, particularly at sunset. Equally beautiful evening views can be had by walking along the northern shore of the bay, either from or below the medieval ruins of **Dunollie Castle**. Another attraction is the **Distillery** on Stafford Street in the town centre (tours Easter–Oct Mon–Sat 9.30am–5pm).

Caledonian MacBrayne's **ferry terminal** for services to the Hebrides is just a stone's throw from the train station, which has the bus terminus on its other side. A host of private **boat operators** can be found in the harbour area, particularly along its northern side: their excursions – direct to the castles of Mull, to the seal colonies, or a combination of the two – are worth considering, particularly if you're pushed for time.

The **tourist office** (summer Mon–Sat 9.15am–8.45pm, Sun 10am–5pm; shorter hours rest of year) is tucked away on Argyll Square just to the east of the bus terminus; a £1 fee is charged for finding **accommodation**. Should you wish to look yourself, there are dozens of B&Bs in town, particularly on the central Ardconnell and Dunollie roads. Largest concentration of **hotels** is on the Esplanade, where you'll find the **youth hostel** (☎0631/62025; ②) just beyond the cathedral. **Eating** possibilities tend to be dominated by standard pub fare, but Oban's fish and chip shops are much better than average, especially *Onorio's* on George Street.

Mull

The chief appeal of **Mull** is its remarkable indented coastline – three hundred miles of it in total. Despite its proximity to the mainland, the slower pace of life is clearly apparent: most roads are single track, with only a handful of (very cheap) buses linking the main settlements. **CRAIGNURE** is the main entry point, linked to Oban by several car ferries daily, with a journey time of forty minutes. The village itself is fairly nondescript, but it offers a few guesthouses, a **campsite** and bike hire.

Both of Mull's most important historic monuments lie in the immediate vicinity. **Torosay Castle** (mid-April to mid-Oct daily 10.30am–6.30pm; £3.50) is in the full-blown Victorian Baronial style, set in a magnificent garden complete with a path lined with life-sized eighteenth-century statues. The mile and a half between Craignure and the castle can be covered by **Mull Rail**, the smallest line in Britain. A further mile and a half along the bay is **Duart Castle** (May–Sept daily 10.30am–6pm; £2), the thirteenth-century stronghold of the MacLean clan. You can peek in the dungeons and ascend to the rooftops, but the castle is seen to best advantage from the ferry.

TOBERMORY, Mull's picturesque pint-sized "capital", is 22 miles northwest of Craignure and served by up to five buses per day; there are also three sailings a week to and from Oban. The **tourist office** (summer Mon–Sat 9am–6pm, Sun 11am–5pm; shorter hours in winter) is in the *Cal-Mac* ticket office at the far northern end of the harbour. On Main Street are the island's sole bank and **youth hostel** (☎0688/2481; ②). Guesthouses are in ample supply here.

Mull's longest road (served by three buses each way Mon–Sat) is that covering the 35 miles between Craignure and Fionnphort, the port for Iona. This cuts through Glen More, past the island's highest peak, the mighty extinct volcano of **Ben More** (3169ft), then follows the shore of the long sea loch, Loch Scridain. Both Fionnphort and Bunessan, five miles to the east, have several B&B options: either is worth considering for an overnight stop, given the accommodation shortage on Iona and the beauty of the nearby coastline.

Iona and Staffa

Just three miles long and one and a half miles wide, **Iona** nevertheless manages to encapsulate all the enchantment and mystique of the Hebrides. Its chief claim to fame is as one of the cradles of British Christianity: Saint Columba arrived here from Ireland in 563 and established a monastery which was responsible for the conversion of more or less all of Scotland and northern England. Reached in a few minutes by regular ferry from Fionnphort, Iona is a feasible day excursion by public transport from Oban in summer, and in high season the island is often overrun by organized tours from the mainland. To appreciate its special atmosphere and to have time to see the whole island, including the usually overlooked west coast, it's necessary to spend at least one night either here or in Fionnphort. The two hotels are fairly expensive, but bed and breakfast **accommodation** is available in a few houses in the harbour area.

No buildings remain from Columba's time: the present **Abbey**, which dominates all views of the island, dates from a re-establishment of monasticism here by the Benedictines in around 1200. Extensively rebuilt in the fifteenth and sixteenth centuries, it fell into decay after the Reformation and was restored only in the present century, with the latest revival of religious life: the now-flourishing Iona Community. Adjoining the facade is a small chamber, traditionally assumed to be Saint Columba's grave. In front stand three delicately carved **crosses** from the eighth and ninth centuries, among the masterpieces of European sculpture of the Dark Ages. The finest of these is now represented by a copy, the original having been moved to the **museum** (Mon–Sat 9.30am–4/6pm, Sun 2–4/6pm; free) housed in the monastic infirmary.

South of the church is the simple Romanesque **St Oran's Chapel**, the oldest building on the island. Walking back to the harbour, you pass MacLean's Cross, a fifteenth-century reinterpretation of those in the abbey grounds, and the ruins of a **nunnery** founded around the same time as the Benedictine abbey.

A basaltic mass rising direct from the sea, **Staffa** is the most romantic and dramatic of Scotland's plethora of uninhabited islands. On one side, its perpendicular rockface has been cut into caverns of cathedral-like dimensions, notably **Fingal's Cave**, whose haunting noises inspired Mendelssohn's *Hebrides Overture*.

Storms and rough seas do lead to cancellations of scheduled voyages, but ultra-modern sailing craft can get to the island in conditions that used to be too difficult. The two main **operators**, both based at Iona harbour and charging around £10, are Gordon Grant (✆06817/338) and David Kirkpatrick (✆06817/373). The round trip, calling at Fionnphort, lasts about two hours, with an hour ashore and a foray into Fingal's Cave if weather permits.

Lochaber

As the **Lochaber** district contains **Ben Nevis**, Britain's highest mountain and **Glencoe**, its most famous glen, it's small wonder that it has become one of the most popular parts of the Highlands. The hub of the area is **Fort William**, which is served by buses from Glasgow and Inverness but is better approached on the **West Highland railway**, Scotland's most scenic and most brilliantly engineered rail route, crossing countryside which can otherwise be seen only from long-distance footpaths. From the junction at Crianlarich, the line climbs around Beinn Odhar on a unique horseshoe-shaped loop of viaducts, then crosses the desolate peat bogs of Rannoch Moor, where the track had to be laid on a mattress of tree roots, brushwood and thousands of tons of earth and ashes. Skirting Loch Ossian, the train descends steeply along the entire length of Loch Treig, then circumnavigates Ben Nevis to approach Fort William from the northeast, through the dramatic Monessie Gorge, Roy Bridge and the southern-most reach of the Great Glen.

Fort William and Glen Nevis

Having just celebrated its three-hundredth birthday, **FORT WILLIAM** is a mere stripling by Scottish standards. Nothing remains of the fort which preceded the town and gave it its name, nor is there anything much in the way of conventional sights – it's chiefly of use as a base for the countryside and for having the only decent shops within a radius of fifty miles. Its setting, just beyond the point where Loch Eil merges with the huge Loch Linnhe, is its strongest feature, though in the town itself you're hardly aware of the presence of the great mountain in whose lee it lies.

The **tourist office** (Mon–Fri 9am–5pm, Sat 9am–4pm) is on Cameron Square, about halfway down High Street. There are dozens of **accommodation** possibilities, with the largest concentration of B&Bs lying in and around Fassifern Road, slightly uphill from the train station. The most convenient bases for seeing the best of the scenery, however, are the **campsite** (mid-March to mid-Oct) and the **youth hostel** (☎0397/702336; ②), both located just under three miles down **Glen Nevis**. Occasional buses, terminating at the hostel, run this lovely route, departing from Middle Street, between the High Street and the loch. The easiest **walk** in the area is to continue up the glen on the road or accompanying footpath; there are wonderful and constantly changing views of Ben Nevis on one side and the peaks of Mamore Forest on the other, with the additional bonus of several waterfalls and cascades.

Top attraction, however, is the ascent of **Ben Nevis** (4406ft) itself. Although it gives the impression of being a brute of a mountain – particularly when seen from its precipitous northern side – it's actually rather a gentle climb, with a well-defined path carved out of the whaleback south side from the bridge opposite the youth hostel. Reckon on about four hours for the ascent, two for the descent and plenty of time for the vast plateau-like summit; you may have to do a fair amount of trudging through snow towards the end. The **views** are all you'd expect, though they might be better from half-way up, as the top is often shrouded in mist.

Glencoe

Easily reached by buses on the Glasgow to Fort William route, **Glencoe** stretches southeast from the shore of Loch Leven, some fifteen miles south of Fort William. Its name translates as "the Vale of Weeping", a doubly appropriate title: not only was it the site of the infamous massacre in 1692 of the MacDonalds by the Campbells, it can be drenched by rain at all seasons of the year, making its untamed scenery look all the more dramatic and menacing. The massacre, ordered by King William III as punishment for the failure of the MacDonald chief to take his oath of loyalty, took place in the vicinity of **GLENCOE VILLAGE**, which is set back from Loch Leven and in the shadow of the Pap of Glencoe, with its distinctively head-shaped summit. Here you'll find several B&Bs; most of the cheaper accommodation options – the **youth hostel** (☎08552/219; ②), and the **bunkhouse** and **campsite** (both ☎08552/256) – are down the old road southeast along the banks of the River Coe.

At the point where the old road rejoins the main A82 is the **visitor centre** of the National Trust for Scotland (April–Oct 10am–5.30pm; 30p), which owns most of Glencoe. Ask here for detailed **hiking** information: the ridges east of here are among the finest on mainland Britain, but are for experienced hill-walkers and climbers only.

From Fort William to Mallaig

For the 47-mile journey from Fort William to the Skye ferry port at Mallaig, the **train** just has the edge on the bus, even though hyper-modern commuter trains are now in use – except in summer, when a steam service operates on certain days. At Banavie, just a couple of miles after Fort William, the line crosses the Caledonian Canal and passes the spectacular flight of locks known as Neptune's Staircase. Wonderful views back towards the crushing mass of Ben Nevis come before the line reaches the northern shore of Loch Sheil, after which it passes over a mighty curved viaduct, the first concrete construction of its kind in Britain. Approaching Mallaig, the train proceeds past the rock-strewn Sound of Arisaig and along the length of Loch Eilt before passing between Loch Morar – the deepest in the country at over 1000ft – and the silver sands.

The little fishing port of **MALLAIG** is linked by ferry to Armadale in Skye (see below). In addition, *Caledonian MacBrayne* have two or three sailings a week to Kyle of Lochalsh and the "Small Isles" of the Hebrides – Muck, Eigg, Rhum and Canna. If you want to use it as a base, the village has plenty of guesthouses; if necessary, the **tourist office** by the harbour (Mon–Sat 9am–5pm) will find a room for a £1 fee.

Skye

The closest Hebridean island to the mainland, **Skye** is also the most beguiling, its richly varied scenery including Britain's most daunting mountain range, lush stretches of greenery and a coastline indented with majestic sea lochs. The tranquil present is the mirror opposite of the island's turbulent past. Throughout the Middle Ages, it was fiercely disputed by the rival MacLeods and MacDonalds, and the later conversion of the chiefs to landlords led to impoverishment for the majority of the population, provoking an armed uprising – the last in British history – in 1881.

For all its beauties, some words of warning are in order for visitors to Skye. Not for nothing is it nicknamed the "Misty Isle": the scenery is often covered from sight for days on end, even in summer – though the atmospheric light is part of Skye's charm, and the island is at its most magical when a spell of bad weather suddenly clears. Secondly, Skye isn't a place which can be seen in a hurry: many of the most beautiful spots are only accessible on foot, and are often far from the villages. Thirdly, bus services, other than on the main north–south route, are sparse as well as being the most expensive in Scotland.

Southern Skye

There are two year-round ferries making the crossing to Skye from the mainland. Boats run from Mallaig to **ARMADALE** up to four times daily except on Sundays, when there's a single service in high summer only. The **youth hostel** (☎04714/260; ②) is along the shore from the harbour; there are a few guesthouses in the adjacent village of Ardvasar. The shorter crossing is the five-minute trip from Kyle of Lochalsh to **KYLEAKIN**, which is the route used by the three or four daily buses from Glasgow to Portree (see below); boats run pretty constantly day and night, and foot passengers are carried free. Kyleakin has a picturesque harbour, dominated by the ruined Castle Moil. It also boasts the island's most luxurious **youth hostel** (☎0599/4585; ②), plus plenty of guesthouses.

That said, there seems no reason not to push on at least as far as **BROADFORD**, eight miles north. As a crossroads, it's a much better base for touring the island and offers an even wider choice of accommodation, including another **youth hostel** (☎0471/822442; ②), down the shore from the bus stop. The village has one of the two **tourist offices** on Skye (Mon–Sat 9.15am–5.30pm).

The Black Cuillins

The **Black Cuillins** in western Skye are among the great natural wonders of Europe, and although some of the peaks do require climbing skills there are other summits well within the capability of normal walkers, while wonderful views of the range can be had without expending any energy at all. One of the classic views is across the dark waters of Loch Scavaig from the beach of Elgol, fourteen miles west of Broadford via the most beautiful road in Skye; the round trip can be made by post bus on working days.

The northern starting point for exploration of the Black Cuillins is **SLIGACHAN**, sixteen miles from Broadford along the main A850 coastal road; there's little more to this hamlet than the *Sligachan* **hotel** (☎047852/204; ⑤), and a **campsite**. The most rewarding hike is down Glen Sligachan by the path to Loch Coruisk: the full return trip is a very long day's walk, though there's no need to proceed further than the Druim Hain ridge, five miles away, from which the whole of the Cuillins can be seen.

Really serious hill-walkers head for **GLENBRITTLE**, fifteen miles southwest of Sligachan by road (daily bus each way), or eight miles by footpath. The **youth hostel** (☎047842/278; ②) here is a climbing centre, and guided hikes into the Cuillins are on offer. There's also a **campsite** not too far away by the beach (☎047022/206), but other accommodation is limited to a single B&B and holiday cottages that can only be rented by the week.

Trotternish

Skye's largest peninsula is **Trotternish**, which forms the northeastern part of the island. The gateway to this is the "capital" of **PORTREE**, which from a visitor's point of view is chiefly of note for having the shops and banks which are otherwise a rare commodity in Skye. Here also is the main **tourist office** (Mon–Sat 9am–5.30/8pm), housed in the former jail overlooking the harbour. The town brims over with the island's largest choice of **B&Bs**, but there are many more congenial bases.

The most imposing scenery is to be found on the east coast of the peninsula, north of Portree – most of the buses linking Glasgow and Portree go around the island to Uig, seventeen miles away on the west coast, duplicating the route of some local buses. Some nine miles from Portree, at the edge of the Storr ridge, is a 200-foot obelisk known as the **Old Man of Storr**, which has only ever been climbed once, while a further ten miles north, rising above Staffin Bay, are the jagged pinnacles of the rest of the **Quiraing**. The straggling village of **UIG** is the ferry port for departures to the islands of the Outer Hebrides, with sailings to Tarbert in Harris and Lochmaddy in North Uist. As well as several guesthouses, there are a **youth hostel** (☎047042/211; ②) and a **campsite**, both off the Portree road at the southern end.

Northwestern Skye

DUNVEGAN, set on a sea loch between the peninsulas of Vaternish and Duirnish, some 22 miles from Portree, is the main centre of the secluded northwestern corner of Skye. Just north of the village is the **Castle** (Easter–Oct Mon–Sat 10am–5.30pm; £3.80), the stronghold of the MacLeods and by far the most notable monument on Skye. Although prettified last century, the outlines of the medieval fortress are still apparent. Inside, you can see the now rather tatty Fairy Flag, a Byzantine cloth allegedly given to a chief by his fairy wife and possessing the magic to save the clan on three occasions, two of which have already been used up. Also on show is the Dunvegan Horn, which each heir-apparent must, at the time of coming of age, fill with claret and drain in one gulp. There's the added bonus of well-tended gardens, while, between May and October, excursion boats sail from the harbour to the nearby seal colonies.

Just off the road to Portree is a **campsite** (☎047022/206); there are also several guesthouses, but prices are higher than usual for the island – starting at around £15 per person rather than £10.

Inverness and around

Capital and only large town of the Highlands, **INVERNESS** lies 160 miles north of Edinburgh, the rail line between the two traversing the gentle southern Highland countryside of Perthshire, before skirting the western fringe of the stark Cairngorms. Approaching it from the west, there's the magnificent eighty-mile train journey from Kyle of Lochalsh, a route that runs through **Wester Ross**, one of the grandest and most varied landscapes in Britain. If you're using this approach, try to travel on *The Clansman* (mid-June to Aug, departs Kyle 3.10pm), a train whose tourist provisions include an observation car.

The Town

The one asset Inverness itself has is its setting astride the River Ness at the mouth of the Beauly Firth. Despite having been a place of importance for a millennium – it was probably the capital of the Pictish kingdom and the site of Macbeth's castle – there's nothing remarkable to see, nor any particularly strong sense of character. The only attractions of historical interest are situated some six miles east of town, and can be reached by regular buses. **Culloden Moor** was the scene in 1746 of the last pitched battle on British soil, when the troops of "Butcher" Cumberland crushed Bonnie Prince Charlie's army of volunteers in just forty minutes. This ended forever Stuart ambitions of maintaining the monarchy, and marked the beginning of the break-up of the clan system which had ruled Highland society for centuries. A **visitor centre** (Feb–Oct 10am–4/5.30pm; £1.50) has displays describing the action. About a mile below the battlefield are the **Clava Cairns**, a late Neolithic burial site which is the nearest Scotland comes to a Stonehenge.

Seven miles east of Culloden lies **Cawdor Castle** (May–Oct 10am–5pm; £3.50), set in lovely gardens and parkland. The original fourteenth-century keep has grown towers, turrets and battlements over the years, and approached over its drawbridge, it's real fairy-tale stuff.

As well as the only big choice of shops, restaurants and nightlife in the Highlands, you'll find **B&Bs** by the score in Inverness. These tend to fill up in summer, so the £1 booking fee charged by the **tourist office** in Castle Wynd is a good investment (Mon–Fri 9am–5pm, Sat & Sun 10am–4pm). The official **youth hostel** is in the town centre at 1 Old Edinburgh Rd (☎0463/231771; ②); there's also a private hostel, *Inverness Student Hotel*, at 8 Culduthel Rd (☎0463/236556; ②). **Campsites** can be found at Culloden and on the road to Loch Ness, and there's a big site at Bught Parl west of the river, in Inverness itself.

Loch Ness

Loch Ness forms part of the natural fault line known as the Great Glen, which slices across the Highlands between Inverness and Fort William. Early last century, Thomas Telford linked the glen's lochs by means of the **Caledonian Canal**, which enabled ships to pass between the North Sea and the Atlantic without having to navigate Scotland's treacherous northern coast. The link having long lost its commercial significance, pleasure craft now ply the canal and its lochs. **Cruises** from Inverness provide the most straightforward way of seeing the terrain; run from Easter to October by *Jacobite Cruises*, they can be booked at the tourist office and depart from Tomnahurich Bridge, just over a mile south of the centre. The most popular trip is to Urquhart Castle, costing around £8 return.

Most visitors are hardly bothered by the scenery, hoping instead to catch a glimpse of the elusive **"Nessie"**. Tales of the monster date back at least as far as the seventh century, when it came out second best in an altercation with Saint Columba. However, the possibility that a mysterious prehistoric creature might be living in the loch only attracted worldwide attention in the 1930s, when sightings were reported during the construction of the road along its western shore. Numerous appearances have been reported since, but even the most hi-tech surveys of the loch have failed to come up with conclusive evidence.

To find out the whole story, take a bus fourteen miles to **DRUMNADROCHIT**, where you can visit the **Official Loch Ness Monster Exhibition Centre** (daily 10am–6pm; £4). There are also cruises from here, predictably focusing on "Nessie" lore. Most photographs allegedly showing the monster have been taken a couple of miles further south, around the ruined **Urquhart Castle** (daily 10am–5pm; £2), once one of Scotland's largest as well as most beautifully sited fortresses.

Aberdeen

Set on the North Sea coast between the Don and Dee rivers some 120 miles north of Edinburgh, **ABERDEEN** is the third city of Scotland, and Europe's boom town of the last two decades. Highly distinctive in appearance, it's nicknamed the "Granite City" from the solid, hard-wearing local stone used for so many of its buildings.

Until a hundred years ago, Aberdeen was two separate towns a couple of miles apart. Each community had its own university, so for more than two centuries there were the same number of universities in Aberdeen as in the whole of England. Yet while Old Aberdeen slumbered in academic and ecclesiastical tranquillity, the newer town became a major port and commercial centre, and was subject to grandiose planning schemes. The most ambitious of these, in the early nineteenth century, included the layout of spacious **Union Street**, which runs for more than a mile westwards from Castlegate, the square which fronted the long-vanished castle. Here you can see the richly carved seventeenth-century **Mercat Cross**, the finest example of this essential adornment of a Scottish burgh. Opposite stands the vast bulk of the nineteenth-century Town House, while a short way down King Street is St **Andrew's Cathedral**. This is the mother-church of the American Episcopal Church, the first American bishop having been consecrated in Aberdeen in 1784.

Proceeding along Union Street, then left down Shiprow, brings you to **Provost Ross's House**, a sixteenth-century mansion now containing the **Maritime Museum** (Mon–Sat 10am–5pm; free), which tells all about Aberdeen and its various relationships with the sea. A further short walk downhill is the bustling **harbour** area, seen at its best before 8am, when the daily fish market winds up business.

Across Union Street from Shiprow is Broad Street, dominated by **Marischal College**, the younger half of Aberdeen university. Its facade, a historicist extravaganza from the beginning of the present century, is probably the most spectacular piece of granite architecture in existence. Nestling in stranded isolation behind the hideous municipal offices opposite is the oldest surviving residential building in the city, **Provost Skene's House** (Mon–Sat 10am–5pm; free). Highlight of the interior is the sixteenth-century Painted Gallery, whose wooden ceiling is covered with depictions of religious scenes. Just west of here, standing in its own extensive grounds on the north side of Union Street, is the weird St **Nicholas Kirk** (Mon–Fri noon–4pm, Sat 1–3pm), three separate churches nestling in the shell of one, with the transept surviving from what was medieval Scotland's largest parish church. Leaving the churchyard by the northern side and continuing up Schoolhill brings you to the **Art Gallery** (Mon–Wed, Fri & Sat 10am–5pm, Thurs 10am–8pm, Sun 2–5pm; free), whose main draw is the Macdonald Collection of 92 uniform portraits of British nineteenth-century artists, many of them self-portraits. Across the road are the sunken **Union Terrace Gardens**, a fine example of Victorian urban landscaping.

Ten minutes from the centre by bus #20, **Old Aberdeen** preserves the atmosphere of a cloistered academic community. Dominating the High Street is **King's College**, the university's older half. The chapel, founded just a few years after the college at the end of the fifteenth century, boasts an outstanding crown spire; inside is a remarkably complete set of flamboyant late medieval furnishings. Closing the top end of the street is the Georgian **Old Town House**, now a public library. Over St Machar Drive lie the Chanonry, formerly a walled precinct and still with many fine houses, and **Botanical Gardens** (Oct–April Mon–Fri 9am–4.30pm; May–Sept Mon–Fri 9am–4.30pm, Sat & Sun 2–5pm; free). At the end of the Chanonry is the former cathedral, **St Machar's**, Aberdeen's first great granite construction. Its early fifteenth-century facade is a highly original, fortress-like design; equally impressive is the huge sixteenth-century heraldic ceiling covering the nave, which bears the coats of arms of the royal houses of Europe and the bishops and nobles of Scotland. A walk of about a mile through Seaton Park leads to Bridgend of Balgownie, a cluster of restored houses, beyond which is the **Brig o' Balgownie**, a graceful single-arched fourteenth-century bridge.

Practicalities

Both **bus** and **train** stations are on Guild Street, a few minutes' uphill walk from Union Street. The **tourist office** (July & Aug Mon–Fri 9am–8pm, Sat 9am–6pm, Sun 10am–6pm; reduced hours out of season) is on Broad Street, just off the eastern end of Union Street. Main concentrations of **guesthouses** are on Bon Accord Street (south from Union Street) and on the Great Western Road. At Easter and in summer, the **student residences** in Old Aberdeen (call ahead on ☎0224/273301) offer excellent value at around £8 for bed and breakfast (minimum stay two nights). The **youth hostel** can be found at 8 Queen's Road (☎0224/646988; ②), west of the centre on the route of bus #15, while the **campsite** (April–Sept) is in the suburban Hazelhead Park: take bus #4 or #14.

Top of the list for eating is *Ashvale Fish Restaurant*, 44–48 Great Western Rd, officially rated as the best **fish and chip** shop in Britain. In Guild St, *Skippers* serves massive plates of fish, chips, peas and bread at a bargain price that includes soup and dessert. Decent **pub** grub is available in most of the city's hostelries, among which the *Blue Lamp* on Gallowgate, the *Prince of Wales* on St Nicholas Lane and the *Tilted Wig* on Castlegate are particularly recommended. There are plenty of student hang-outs around Marischal College, but only one – *St Machar Bar* on High Street – in Old Aberdeen.

travel details

Trains

London to: Aberdeen (10 daily; 7hr); Bath (22 daily; 1hr 15min); Brighton (41 daily; 50min); Bristol (26 daily; 1hr 30min); Cambridge (65 daily; 1hr); Canterbury (39 daily; 1hr 20min); Cardiff (20 daily; 1hr 50min); Chester (20 daily; 2hr 40min); Dover (31 daily; 1hr 30min); Durham (hourly; 3hr); Edinburgh (17 daily; 4hr 30min); Exeter (16 daily; 2hr); Fishguard (2 daily; 4hr); Glasgow (11 daily; 5hr); Holyhead (12 daily; 4hr 30min); Inverness (7 daily; 8hr); Leeds (18 daily; 2hr 15min); Liverpool (12 daily; 2hr 25min); Manchester (17 daily; 2hr 30min); Newcastle (hourly; 3hr 15min); Norwich (20 daily; 1hr 40min); Oxford (41 daily; 55min); Pembroke (4 daily; 5hr); Penzance (8 daily; 5hr); Plymouth (16 daily; 2hr 55min); Portsmouth (38 daily; 1hr 25min); Salisbury (20 daily; 1hr 20min); York (25 daily; 2hr).

Chester to: Conwy (8 daily; 1hr); Holyhead (7 daily; 2hr); Wrexham (17 daily; 15min).

Edinburgh to: Aberdeen (hourly; 2hr 30min); Glasgow (every 30min; 45min); Inverness (6 daily; 3hr 30min); Leuchars for St Andrews (hourly; 1hr); Stirling (every 30min; 45min).

Glasgow to: Aberdeen (hourly; 2hr 30min); Fort William (3 daily; 3hr 30min); Inverness (5 daily; 3hr 30min); Oban (3 daily; 3hr); Stirling (hourly; 30min).

Aberdeen to: Inverness (11 daily; 2hr 15min); Leuchars for St Andrews (hourly; 1hr 30min); Stirling (hourly; 2hr).
Inverness to: Kyle of Lochalsh (4 daily; 2hr 30min); Stirling (15 daily; 3hr).
Fort William to: Mallaig (4 daily; 1hr 20min).

Buses

London to: Aberdeen (4 daily; 12hr); Bath (8 daily; 3hr); Bradford (9 daily; 4hr 10min); Brighton (8 daily; 2hr); Bristol (hourly; 2hr 30min); Bury St Edmunds (2 daily; 2hr 30min); Caernarfon (1 daily; 7hr 30min); Cambridge (7 daily; 2hr); Canterbury (9 daily; 1hr 50min); Cardiff (10 daily; 3hr 25min); Chester (5 daily; 5hr); Chichester (3 daily; 3hr); Dover (9 daily; 2hr 30 min); Durham (5 daily; 4hr 50min); Edinburgh (3 daily; 8hr 30min); Exeter (8 daily; 4hr); Falmouth (2 daily; 6hr 30min); Glasgow (5 daily; 7hr 30min); Keswick (2 daily; 8hr); Leeds (10 daily; 3hr 30min); Liverpool (6 daily; 4hr 30min); Manchester (6 daily; 4hr); Newcastle (7 daily; 5hr 20min); Newquay (3 daily; 6hr 15min); Norwich (5 daily; 3hr); Oxford (every 20min; 1hr 30min); Penzance (7 daily; 7hr 30min); Plymouth (8 daily; 4hr 30min); St Ives (4 daily; 7hr 30min); Salisbury (2 daily; 3hr 10min); Stratford-upon-Avon (7 daily; 3hr 20min); Windermere (2 daily; 7hr 30min); York (4 daily; 4hr 20min).

Aberdeen to: Inverness (5 daily; 3hr).
Bath to: Wells (hourly; 1hr 20min).
Bristol to: Bath (every 15min; 40min); Salisbury (hourly; 2hr 30min); Wells (hourly; 1hr).
Dover to: Canterbury (hourly; 1hr); Deal (hourly; 35min); Sandwich (hourly; 1hr).
Edinburgh to: Aberdeen (hourly; 3hr 45min); Glasgow (hourly; 1hr 15min); Inverness (hourly; 4–5hr); Jedburgh (11 daily; 2hr); Kelso (6 daily; 2hr); Stirling (hourly; 1hr); St Andrews (7 daily; 1hr 45min); Melrose (6 daily; 1hr 20min).
Exeter to: Plymouth (7 daily; 1hr 40min).
Fort William to: Oban (6 daily; 1hr 45min).
Glasgow to: Fort William (5 daily; 3hr); Glencoe (5 daily; 2hr 30min); Inverness (hourly; 4–5hr); Kyle of Lochalsh (5 daily; 5hr); Loch Lomond (hourly; 45min); Oban (3 daily; 3hr); Portree (5 daily; 6hr); Stirling (hourly; 45min).
Inverness to: Fort William (6 daily; 2hr); Kyle of Lochalsh (2 daily; 2hr); Portree (2 daily; 3hr 30 min).
Liverpool to: Manchester (9 daily; 1hr); Newcastle (6 daily; 5hr).
Oxford to: Stratford-upon-Avon (4 daily; 1hr 20min).

CHAPTER 10

GREECE

Introduction

With 166 inhabited islands and a landscape that ranges from Mediterranean to Balkan, **Greece** has enough appeal to fill months of travel. The historic sites span four millennia of civilization, encompassing the renowned – such as Mycenae, Olympia, Delphi and the Parthenon in **Athens** – and the obscure, where a visit can still seem like a personal discovery. The **beaches** are distributed along a convoluted coastline equal in length to that of France, and they range from islands where the boat calls once a week to resorts as cosmopolitan as they come.

Modern Greece is the sum of an extraordinary diversity of **influences**. Romans, Arabs, French, Venetians, Slavs, Albanians, Turks, Italians, to say nothing of the great Byzantine empire, have all been here and gone since the time of Alexander the Great. All have left their marks: the Byzantines in countless churches and monasteries, and in ghost towns like **Mystra**; the Venetians in impregnable fortifications at **Náfplio** and **Monemvassía** in the Peloponnese; the Franks in crag-top castles, again on the Peloponnese but also in the east Aegean. Most obvious, perhaps, is the heritage of 400 years of Ottoman Turkish rule which, while universally derided, exercised an inestimable influence on music, cuisine, language and the way of life. The contributions, and continued existence, of substantial minorities – Vlachs, Muslims, Jews, Gypsies – round out the list of those who have helped to make up the Hellenic identity.

The Greek people – peasants, fishermen, shepherds – created perhaps the most vigorous and truly **popular culture** in Europe, which lives on in the songs and dances, costumes, embroidery, woven bags and rugs, furniture and the white cubist houses of popular image. Its vigour may be failing rapidly under the impact of Western consumer values, but much survives, especially in remoter regions.

Of course there are formal cultural activities as well: **museums** that shouldn't be missed, in Athens, Thessaloníki and Iráklio; buildings, like the **monasteries** of the Metéora; **castles** such as those in the Dodecanese, Lésvos, central Greece and the Peloponnese; as well, of course, as the great Mycenaean, Minoan and Classical sites. The country hosts some excellent summer **festivals**, bringing international theatre groups and orchestras to perform in the ancient theatres of Epídhavros, Dodona, and Herodes Atticus in Athens – settings which in themselves are magical.

The landscape of Greece encompasses an astonishing variety: the stony deserts of the Máni, the soft theatricality of the Peloponnesian coastal hills, the poplar-studded plains of Macedonia, the resin-scented ridges of Skíathos and Sámos, the wind-tormented rocks of the central Aegean. It's the simple hedonistic pleasures of these landscapes and of the country's climate and food that make Greece special for most visitors.

Information and Maps

The National Tourist Organization of Greece (Ellinikós Organizmós Tourismoú, or **EOT**) publishes an impressive array of free regional pamphlets, a reasonable fold-out map of Greece and a large number of sheets on special interests. You will find EOT offices in most of the larger towns and resorts. Where there is no EOT office, you can try municipally-run tourist offices or the **Tourist Police**. The latter are basically a branch of the local police; they can sometimes provide you with lists of rooms to let, and in general are helpful and efficient.

The most reliable road **maps** of Greece are *Michelin* no. 980 (1:700,000) and the *Freytag-Berndt* (1:650,000). *Freytag-Berndt* also publishes a series of more detailed maps on various regions of Greece, such as the Peloponnese and Cyclades; these are issued by Efstathiadhis in Greece. Individual maps of islands are much less consistent, but are always available on the spot.

Money and Banks

Greek currency is the **drachma**, most commonly circulated in notes of 50, 100, 500, 1000 and 5000dr, and coins of 1, 2, 5, 10, 20, 50 and 100dr.

Travellers' cheques can be cashed at all banks and quite a number of hotels, agencies and tourist shops. Greek **banks** are normally open Mon–Thurs 8am–2pm and Fri 8am–1.30pm. Certain branches in the major cities and tourist centres are open extra hours in the evenings and on Saturday mornings to change money. Be prepared for at least one long queue, and possibly two. Commissions vary considerably: banks usually charge a flat 400–600dr; travel agencies may give a poorer rate, but often levy a sliding 2 percent commission, meaning you'll come out ahead on small amounts compared with banks.

For cash advances, the *Emborikí Trápeza* (Commercial Bank) handles *Visa*; the *Ethnikí Trápeza/National Bank* services *Access* customers. Some cash machines in the bigger towns, particularly those of the *Credit Bank*, also accept *Visa, Access, Barclaycard* and *American Express* cards.

Communications

Post offices are open Monday to Friday from 7.30am to 2pm or thereabouts; in big towns and important tourist centres, hours may extend into the evening and even weekends. **Stamps** (*grammatósima*) can also be purchased at a corner kiosk (*períptero*), though staff tend not to know correct rates. If you are confronted by two slots on a post box, *esoterikó* is for domestic mail, *exoterikó* for overseas. The poste restante system is reasonably efficient, especially at the post offices of larger towns. *American Express* holds mail at offices in Athens, Thessaloníki, Iráklio, Rhodes and Corfu.

In many hotel lobbies or cafés you'll find **red pay phones** which are for **local calls** only, though these may soon be replaced by **card phones**. These have recently appeared but so far are confined to Athens and the larger towns; the smallest card is 1000dr for 100 units. If you balk at this, keep in mind that phones at a *períptero* or kiosk will cost 15dr per unit.

For **international calls**, it's cheaper to visit the nearest **OTE** (*Organizmós Tiliepikinoníon tis Elládhos*) office, and you'll have to do this if you want to reverse charges. Operator-assisted calls can take over an hour to connect, but even dialling direct you should be prepared for a long wait. In major cities there is at least one branch open 24 hours; in smaller towns the OTE can close as early as 3pm; elsewhere count on service from 7am to 10pm. The **operator number** for domestic calls is ☎151, for international calls ☎162.

Getting Around

Buses are the standard means of transport in Greece. They cover just about every route on the mainland and provide a basic service on the islands. The best way to supplement buses is to hire a moped or scooter, especially on the islands, where any substantial town or resort has rental outlets.

■ Buses

Bus services on the major routes – both on the mainland and islands – are highly efficient. On secondary roads they're a lot less regular, but even the most remote villages will be connected by a school or market bus, often leaving shortly after dawn. On the islands, buses usually connect the port and main town for ferry arrivals or departures. Most of these buses are run by a syndicate of companies known as the KTEL, and charge about fifteen drachmas per kilometre.

■ Trains

The Greek **railway** network, run by OSE, is limited to the mainland, and trains are slower than the equivalent buses, except on the gowing number of showcase IC (inter-city) lines for which fares are more expensive. However, they're also much cheaper, and some of the lines are enjoyable in themselves. If you're starting a journey at the initial station of a run you can reserve a seat at no extra cost; at most intermediate points, it's first-come, first-served. Timetables are sporadically available, printed in Greek only; the best place to obtain one is the OSE office in Athens. Both *Eurail* and *InterRail* passes are valid in Greece, though holders must make reservations like other passengers.

■ Ferries

Ferries are of use primarily for travel to, and between, islands, though you may also want to make use of the routes between Athens and Monemvassía in the Peloponnese. Routes and the speed of the boats vary enormously: before buying a ticket it's wise to establish how many stops there'll be before your island, and the estimated time of arrival. Many agents act only for one specific boat, so you may have to ask around to uncover alternatives.

Schedules are notoriously erratic and out-of-season are severely reduced, with many islands served only once or twice a week. The most reliable, up-to-date information is available from the local **port police** (*limenarhío*), which maintains offices at Pireás and on most fair-sized islands.

Regular ferry tickets are, in general, best bought on the day of departure, unless you need to reserve a cabin, bunk or space for a car. There are only three periods of the year – March 23–25, Easter weekend and mid-August – when ferries need to be booked a couple of days in advance. The cheapest class of ticket, which you'll probably automatically be sold, is **deck class**. Motorbikes and cars get issued extra tickets, in the latter case up to four times as costly as simple passenger fares.

"Flying Dolphin" **hydrofoils** are roughly twice as fast and up to twice as expensive as ordinary ferries. They operate mainly among the Argo-Saronic islands close to Athens, and down the east coast of the Peloponnese to Monemvassía and Kíthira, and among the northern Sporades. There are also summer-only services in the Cyclades, the Dodecanese and between the northeast Aegean islands. If money is no object, there are now international hydrofoils between Turkey, Greece and Italy. It is only possible to buy one-way tickets on the Dolphins. In summer, if you have a tight schedule, it is worth buying your return (or onward) ticket on arrival at an island.

In season **kaíkia** (caiques) sail between adjacent islands and to a few of the more obscure ones. These are no cheaper than main services but can be useful and often very pleasant. Many depend on the whims of local boat-owners or fishermen – the only firm information is to be had on the quayside.

■ Moped and bike rental

Motorcycles, scooters, mopeds and bicycles are available for hire on many of the islands and in a few of the popular mainland resorts. Motorcycles and scooters cost from around £10/$16 a day; mopeds from £6/$10; bikes as little as £2/$3. All rates can be reduced with bargaining outside of peak season, or if you negotiate for a longer period of rental. To hire motorcycles (usually 125cc) you will need to show a driver's licence. Make sure you check them thoroughly before riding off since many are only cosmetically maintained and repaired.

■ Driving and hitching

Cars have obvious advantages for getting to the more inaccessible parts of mainland Greece. Average cost for **rental** is from £200/$320 per week with unlimited mileage, VAT and CDW included. In Greece, *InterRent*, *EuroDollar*, *Payless* and *Just* are reliable medium-sized companies with branches in many towns. Note that initial prices quoted may not include tax and

supplemental insurance premiums, and check the fine print on your contract carefully.

If you drive your own vehicle through Greece you'll need international third party insurance, and it's best to have an international driver's licence. Keep in mind that Greece has the highest accident rate in Europe after Portugal, and many of the roads, particularly if you're unfamiliar with them, can be quite perilous. Speed limits are 50kph in town, 100kph on motorways and 80kph on other roads. The *Automobile and Touring Club of Greece* (ELPA) operates a 24-hr breakdown service on major roads, and a 7am–10pm service elsewhere; the number for assistance is ☎104.

Hitching is fine in Greece as long as you're not too bothered by time. Although Greek traffic is sparse, much of it is trucks and vans which are good for thumbing. Rides are easiest to come by in remote areas where most people know that buses are scarce.

Accommodation

There are huge numbers of beds for tourists in Greece, and most of the year you can rely on turning up pretty much anywhere and finding a room. Only in July and August are you likely to experience problems. At these times, it is worth striking a little off the standard tourist routes and turning up at each new place early in the day.

■ Hotels and rooms

Hotels are officially categorized from "Luxury" down to "E-class", and all except the top category have to keep within set price limits. D- and E-class hotels are usually very reasonable, costing around £8–11/$12–17 for a double room, £6–8/$9–12 for a single. The better-value places tend to be in more remote areas, as ratings depend partly on location. In resorts and throughout the islands, you have the additional option of privately let **rooms** (*dhomátia*). These are again officially controlled and are divided into three classes (A–C). They are usually a fair deal cheaper than hotels, and are in general spotlessly clean. These days the bulk of them are in new, purpose-built low-rises but some are in people's homes, where you'll often be treated with disarming hospitality. As often as not, rooms find you: owners descend on ferry or bus arrivals to fill any space they have. In smaller places you'll often see rooms advertised, or you can just ask at the local taverna or café.

Houses or flats – and, out of season, villas – can sometimes be rented by the week or month. If you have two or three people to share costs, and want to drop roots on an island for a while, it's an option well worth considering.

■ Hostels

Greece is not exactly packed with **youth hostels** (*ksenón neotítos*) but those that there are tend to be fairly easy-going affairs. Few ever ask for an *IYHF* card, and if they do you can usually buy one on the spot, or maybe just pay a little extra for your bed. Charges are around £4/$7 a night. In Athens there are also cheap dormitory-style "**Student Houses**", non-*IYHF* hostels which despite their name are in no way limited to students. These – and sometimes rural/island tavernas – will also sometimes let roofspace, usually providing a mattress for you to lay a sleeping bag down on, or even full bedding.

■ Camping

Official **campsites** range from ramshackle compounds on the islands to highly organized EOT-run complexes. Cheap, casual places rarely cost much above £1.50/$2.50 a night per person; at the larger sites, though, it's possible for two people and a tent to add up to the price of a basic room.

Camping outside authorized campsites is such an established element of Greek travel that few people realize that it's officially forbidden, and once in a while the regulations get enforced. In effect this simply means you should exercise discretion.

■ Monasteries

Greek monasteries and convents have a tradition of putting up travellers of the appropriate sex. On the mainland, this is still customary practice; on the islands, much less so. Wherever you should always ask locally before heading out to one for the night. Also, dress modestly – shorts on either sex, and short skirts on women, are anathema – and try to arrive not later than 8pm or sunset (whichever is earlier).

Food and Drink

Greek cuisine and restaurants are simple and straightforward. There's no snobbery about eating out; everyone does it some of the time, and for foreigners with strong currencies it's reasonably priced – around £6/$10 per person for a substantial meal with house wine.

■ Food

Greeks generally don't eat **breakfast**. The only egg-and-bacon kind of places are in resorts where foreigners congregate; they're expensive compared to a taverna meal. The alternatives are the sort of bread/jam/yoghurt compromises obtainable in some *zaharoplastía* or *galaktopolía*.

Snacks can be one of the distinctive pleasures of Greek eating. Small kebabs (*souvlákia*) are on sale at bus stations, ferry crossings and all over the place in towns. The same goes for *tirópites* (cheese pies), which can almost always be found at the baker's, as can *kouloúria* (crispy baked pretzel rings sprinkled with sesame seeds). Another city staple is *yíros* (doner kebab), served in *píta* bread with garnish.

In choosing a **restaurant**, the best strategy is to go where the Greeks go – and they go late: 2 to 3pm for lunch, 9 to 11pm for dinner. There are two basic types: the *estiatório* and the *taverna*.

Estiatória specialize in the more complicated, oven-baked casserole dishes, like *moussakás* and *pastítsio*, stews like *kokinistó* and *stifádho*, *yemistá* (stuffed tomatoes or peppers), the oily vegetable casseroles called *ladherá*, and oven-baked meat and fish. The cooking is done in the morning and then left to stand, which is why the food is often lukewarm or even cold. Greeks don't mind this (most actually believe that hot food is bad for you), and in fact in summertime it hardly seems to matter. Wine will often be house bulk stuff and probably resinated.

Tavernas are much more common. The primitive ones have a very limited menu, but the more established will offer some of the main *estiatório* dishes mentioned above as well as the standard taverna fare, which essentially means *mezédhes* (hors d'œuvres) and *tis óras* (meat and fish fried or grilled to order).

The most interesting *mezédhes* are *tzatzíki* (yoghurt, garlic and cucumber dip), *melitzanosaláta* (aubergine dip), courgettes or aubergine fried in batter (*kolokithákia tiganitá, melitzánes tiganités*), *yígandes* (white haricot beans in vinaigrette sauce), small cheese and spinach pies (*tiropitákia, spanakópites*), *saganáki* (fried cheese), octopus (*okhtapódhi*) and *mavromátika* (black-eyed peas). Of meats, *souvláki* (shish kebab) and *brizóles* (chops) are reliable choices. *Keftédhes* (meatballs), *biftékia* (a sort of hamburger) and the spicy sausages called *loukánika* are cheap and good.

Seaside tavernas of course also offer fish. *Kalamarákia* (fried baby squid) are a summer staple. The choicer fish, however, such as *barboúnia* (red mullet), *tsipoúra* (gilt-head bream), *fangrí* (sea bream) and so on, are expensive. The price is quoted by the kilo, and the standard procedure is to go to the glass cooler and choose your own.

■ Drink

The *kafenío* is the traditional Greek coffee shop or café. Although its main business is Greek **coffee**, it also serves spirits such as **oúzo** (aniseed-based spirit), and brandy, beer, tea and soft drinks. Like tavernas, *kafenía* range from the plastic and sophisticated to the old-fashioned, spit-on-the-floor variety. An important institution anywhere in Greece, they are the central pivot of life in the country villages. Take your pre-dinner *oúzo* around 6pm, as the sun begins to sink and the heat of the day cools. You will be served two glasses, one with the *oúzo*, and one full of water, to be tipped into your *oúzo* until it turns a milky white.

A somewhat similar institution to the *kafenío* is the **zaharoplastío**. A cross between café and patisserie, it serves coffee, alcohol, yoghurt and a sometimes amazing variety of honey-soaked sweets. If you want a stronger slant toward the dairy products, find a **galaktopolío**, where you'll often find *rizógalo* (rice pudding), *kréma* (custard) and local *yiaoúrti* (yoghurt). Both *zaharoplastía* and *galaktopolía* are more family-oriented places than the *kafenío*, and many also serve proper (*evropaïko*) tea and different kinds of coffee.

Bars – *barákia* – are a recent transplant, confined to big cities and holiday resorts. They range from clones of Parisian cafés to seaside cocktail bars and imitation English "pabs" (sic), with videos running all day. Drinks at about £2 are invariably more expensive than at a café.

Tavernas offer a better choice of **wines**. Cambas, Boutari Rotonda or Apelia are good among the cheaper bottled ones. If you want something better, the Boutari Naoussa is hard to beat. Otherwise, go for the local wines. Retsina – pine-resinated wine, an acquired taste – is invariably better straight from the barrel.

Opening Hours and Holidays

Shops generally open between 8.30 and 9.30am, then take a long break for the hottest part of the day. Things may then reopen in the mid- to late afternoon. Tourist areas tend to adopt a more northern timetable, though, with shops and offices probably staying open right through the day. Shopping hours during the hottest months are theoretically Mon, Wed & Sat 9am–2pm, and Tues, Thurs & Fri 9am–1.30pm & 5.30–8.30pm. But there are so many exceptions to the rule that you can't count on getting anything done except from Monday to Friday from 9.30am to 1pm or so.

Opening hours for **museums and ancient sites** vary, and change with exasperating frequency; we've given optimistic high-season hours – the late weekend closing times made possible only by a grant from the Ministry of Culture. Smaller sites generally close for a long lunch and siesta (even where they're not supposed to), as do monasteries. The latter are generally open from about 9am to 1pm and 5 to 7pm for limited visits. All state-owned museums and sites are free on Sundays to EC citizens.

There's a vast range of **public holidays** and festivals. The most important, when almost everything will be closed, are: Jan 1; Jan 6; March 25; the first Monday of Lent; Easter weekend (according to the Orthodox calendar, Fri–Mon); May 1; Whit Monday (seven weeks after Easter); Aug 15; Oct 28; and several days at Christmas.

Emergencies

The most common causes of a run in with the **police** are nude bathing or sunbathing and camping outside an authorized site – though topless bathing is now acceptable on virtually all the Greek beaches. Drug offences are a serious matter. The maximum penalty for "causing the use of drugs by someone under 18", for example, is life imprisonment and a 10-million-drachma fine. Theory is by no means usual practice but foreigners caught in possession do get jail sentences of up to a year. If you get arrested for any offence you have a right to contact your consulate who will arrange a lawyer for your defence. Beyond this, there is little they can, or in most cases will, do.

For **minor medical complaints** go to the local *farmakío* (chemist). In the larger towns there'll usually be one who speaks English. If you regularly use any **prescription drug** you should bring along a copy of the prescription together with the generic name of the drug. For serious medical attention you'll find English-speaking doctors in any of the bigger towns or resorts; the tourist police or your consulate should be able to come up with some names if you have any difficulty. In emergencies, treatment – for cuts, broken bones – is given free in state hospitals though you will only get the most basic level of nursing care.

EMERGENCY NUMBERS
Police ☎110; Ambulance & Fire☎112.

ATHENS AND AROUND

Since World War II, the population of **ATHENS** (Athína) has risen from 700,000 to 3.8 million – over a third of the nation's people. The speed of this process is reflected in the city's chaotic mix of urban and rural: goats graze in yards, horse carts are pulled along streets thick with traffic, Turkish-style bazaars vie for space with outlets for Armani and Benetton. You'll find the ancient sites and the Acropolis – supreme monument though it is – only the most obvious of Athens' attractions. There are some beautiful cafés, terraced tavernas and street markets; startling views from the hills of Likavitós and Fílopáppou; and, around the foot of the Acropolis, scattered monuments of the Byzantine, medieval and nineteenth-century town. As you might expect, the city also offers the best eating to be found in Greece, as well as the most varied nightlife.

Athens has been inhabited continuously for over 7000 years. Its acropolis, supplied with springwater, protected by a ring of mountains and commanding views of all approaches from the sea, was a natural choice for prehistoric settlement and for the Mycenaeans, who established a palace-fortress on the rock. Its development into a city-state and artistic centre continued apace under the Dorians, Phoenicians and various dynastic rulers, reaching its apotheosis in the fifth century BC. This was the Classical period, when the Athenians, having launched themselves into an experiment in radical democracy, celebrated their success with a flourish of art, architecture, literature and philosophy that has pervaded Western culture ever since.

Yet, for all the claims of its ancient past, and for all its natural advantages, the city was not the first-choice capital of modern Greece. That honour went to Náfplio in the Peloponnese, where the War of Independence was masterminded by Capodistrias, and where the first Greek National Assembly met in 1828. Had Capodistrias not been assassinated the capital would most likely have remained in the Peloponnese. But following his death in 1831, the "Great Powers" of Western Europe intervened, inflicting on the Greeks a king of their own choosing – Otho, son of Ludwig I of Bavaria – and in 1834 transferring the capital to Athens.

Outside the city, the Temple of Poseidon at **Sounion** is the most popular trip, and rightly so, with its dramatic cliff-top position above the cape. **Pireás** (Piraeus), effectively an extension of Athens, is the main terminus for all domestic and international ferries, as well as for most Greek industry. The other two ports, **Rafína** and **Lávrio**, are on the east coast: the former is a useful departure point for many of the Cycladic islands, the latter serves only the islands of Kéa and Kíthnos.

> The telephone code for both Athens and Pireás is ☎01.

Arrival and information

Athens **airport** – Ellenikóu – is 16km from the centre and has two terminals: **West**, which is used by *Olympic Airways*, and **East** which is used by everyone else. Yellow #19 trolleybuses connect the two regularly from around 6am to midnight. Half-hourly **buses** run from both terminals: blue and yellow double-deckers A, A̸, B and B̸ into the central Síndagma Square and Omónia; the #19 trolley, or identically numbered blue coach, into Pireás. Buy a ticket (160dr; 200dr at night) before boarding. A **taxi** should cost around 1500dr at day rates (double that at night), but make sure the meter is working and visible from the start – double or triple overcharging of newcomers is the norm.

International **trains** arrive at the Stathmós Laríssis in the northwest of the city centre; the virtually adjacent Peloponníssou station handles traffic to and from the

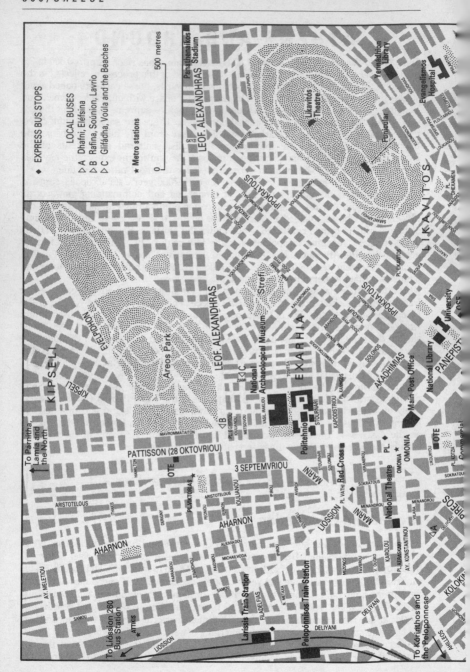

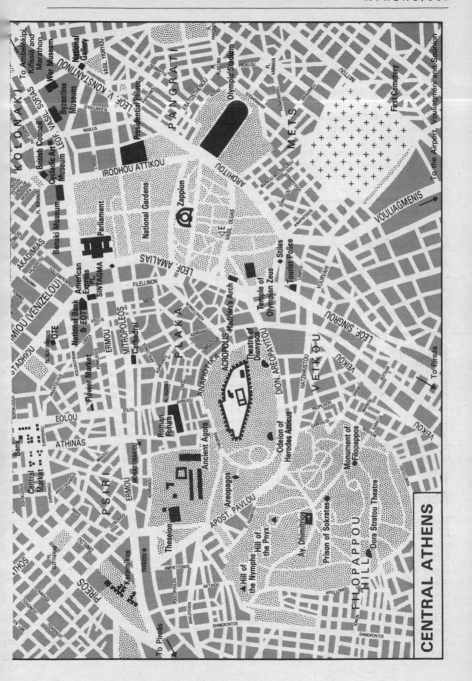

CENTRAL ATHENS

Peloponnese. The yellow trolleybus (#1), which leaves from outside Laríssis, goes to Síndagma. If you're coming into Athens **by bus from northern Greece or the Peloponnese**, you'll find yourself at **Kifissoú 100**, just a ten-minute ride from the middle of town by bus #051. Routes into the city from **central Greece** arrive rather closer to the centre at **Liossíon 260**, north of the train stations; from here you take the blue city bus #024 to Síndagma. Most **international buses** will take you to the train station or to Kifissoú 100; a few drop passengers right in the city centre. If you arrive by boat at **Pireás**, the simplest access to Athens itself is by metro to the stations at Monastiráki, Omónia or Viktorías. **Taxis** from Pireás to central Athens should cost around 1000dr.

Once you've managed to find it, **central Athens** covers a mercifully small area. **Síndagma Square** (Platía Sindágmatos, "Constitution Square") is to all intents and purposes the focus of the city, and most things you'll want to see are within thirty minutes' walk. The city's main **tourist office** is located inside the *National Bank of Greece* on the Stadhíou corner of Síndagma (Mon–Fri 8am–2pm & 3.30–6/8pm, Sat 9am–2pm).

City transport

All **public transport** systems operate from around 5am to midnight, with a skeleton service on some of the yellow trolleys in the small hours of the weekend. Athens' **bus network** is extensive but very crowded at peak times and unbearably hot in the unavoidable summer traffic jams.

The single-line **metro** is next to useless except for journeys to the termini of Pireás in the south or Kifissiá in the north; Monastiráki, Omónia and Platía Viktorías are the only central stops. You'll see ample evidence, though, of a huge extension project downtown, due to be completed sometime in 1997. The flat-fare 150dr tickets that you need for the buses are interchangeable with the metro system (75dr and 100dr, according to a zone system) and must be bought in advance from kiosks. **Taxis** in Athens are the cheapest in the EC: fares around the city will rarely come to more than 600dr. The officially licensed taxis are painted yellow with a special red number plate – beware of cowboys at the train and bus stations. Taxi drivers will often pick up a whole string of passengers along the way, each passenger (or group of passengers) paying the full fare for their journey. So if you're picked up by an already-occupied taxi, memorize the meter reading; you'll pay from then on, plus a 200dr minimum. Luggage is extra, about 50dr a piece. The only central approximation of a **taxi rank** is on the National Gardens corner of Síndagma.

Accommodation

Hotels and **hostels** can be packed to the gills in midsummer – August especially – but for most of the year there are enough beds to go around, and to suit most wallets and tastes. On the **budget level**, expect to pay around ②–③ for a double room in an E-class; as little as ① per person if you're prepared to share a three- to six-person room. If you have the money for a C-class hotel (or above) you can book through the **hotel reservations** desk beside the tourist office in the *National Bank of Greece*. For cheaper places, you're on your own, but virtually every hotel and hostel in the city will have an English-speaking receptionist.

Many of the hotels around Pláka and Omónia are victim to around-the-clock noise; if you want uninterrupted sleep, better to head for the neighbourhoods south of the Acropolis (Pangráti, Veïkoú, Koukáki) or to the north between the National Archeological Museum and the train stations.

Hostels

Athens Connection, Ioulianoú 20, just east of Patissíon (☎82 24 592). Popular student hostel with single and double rooms as well as four-bed dorms, generally knowledgeable reception, exchange and ticket-booking facilities, and a basement bar. ②

George's Guest House, Níkis 46 (☎32 26 474). One of the cheapest and most enduring of the hostel-type places, located just a block west of Síndagma. Various-sized dorms and some doubles, though bathrooms consistently sub-standard. ②

Ideal, Eólou 39, corner Voréou (☎32 13 195). Nineteenth-century building with some balconies facing the Acropolis; reasonable if somewhat decayed rooms, friendly management. ②

Iokastis' House, Aristotélous 65, corner of Ioulianoú (☎82 26 647). A similar setup to the *Athens Connection*, and very close by. ②

Joseph's House, Márkou Moussoúrou 13 (☎92 31 204). Despite new management, this elegant old building has not quite shaken off its hard-core hippie past. Kitchen facilities and one or two doubles; gloomy basement rooms. ②

XEN (YWCA), Amerikís 11 (☎36 26 970). Women-only hostel just north of Síndagma with clean, fairly quiet rooms, self-service restaurant, small library and Greek classes. The YMCA equivalent nearby, the *XAN* (Omírou 28; ☎36 24 291), is less inspiring. ②

Youth hostel #5, Damaréos 75, Pangrati (☎75 19 530). A bit out of the way but friendly, no curfew and an appealing neighbourhood; trolleys #2, #11 or #12 from downtown will get you most of the way there. ②

Budget hotels

Acropolis House, Kódhrou 6 (☎32 22 344). A very clean, well-sited pension and one that is fairly good value. ④

Pension Dioskouri, Pittákou 6 (☎32 48 165). Gloomy rooms, though well-furnished, with a garden and a good locale (one block in from Leofóros Amalías). ③

Kouros, Kódrou 11 (☎32 27 431). On the same pedestrianized street as *Acropolis House*, and more affordable, but more run-down. ②

Leto, Missaraliótou 15 (☎92 31 768). Co-managed with the *Phaedra*, but slightly cheaper. ②

Marble House, in a quiet alley off A. Zínni 35 (☎92 34 058). Probably the best value in Koukáki, with very helpful French/Greek management. Reservations essential; rooms by the month Nov–April. ③

Hotel Museum, Bouboulínas 16, corner of Tossítsa. Nicely placed hotel, right behind the National Archeological Museum. ④

Pension Myrto, Níkis 40 (☎32 27 237). Good value for its class, with baths in all rooms and a small bar. Just off Síndagma. ④

Orion, Anexartisías 5, corner Benáki, Exárhia (36 27 362). Quiet, well-run budget hotel across from the Lófos Stréfi park – a steep walk to get there. Rooftop kitchen and common area with an amazing view. ③

Hotel Orpheus, Malkokondíli 58, Platía Váthis (☎52 24 996). Recently upgraded from hostel status. ③

Phoebus, Tsátsou 12 (☎32 20 142). Probably the most characterful C-class hotel in Pláka. Three minutes' walk from Síndagma down Filellínon (Tsátsou is off Níkis). ③

Thisseus Inn, Thisséos 10 (☎32 45 960). You don't get much more central than this – three blocks west of Síndagma – nor much cheaper. ②

Tony's, Zaharítsa 26, Koukáki (☎92 36 370). Quiet and clean, slightly pricier than nearby *Marble House*, so fills last. ③

Campsites

Camping Acropolis and Camping Nea Kifissía, set a kilometre apart in the leafy suburb of Kifissía, are both good bets, with swimming pools. #528 bus from near Omónia to reach either, or (less hassle) the metro to its last stop, catching #528 behind the station for the final leg.

Dhafni Camping. Poor facilities and crowded due to its location right beside Dhafni monastery. Clearly signposted on the left of the road next to the monastery; 20min by bus #862 or #853 from Platía Eleftherías. Price is for one person, including tent fee. ②

The City

Pláka, roughly the area between Síndagma, Odhós Ermoú and the Acropolis, is the best place to begin exploring. One of the few parts of Athens with charm and architectural merit, its narrow winding streets and stairs are lined with nineteenth-century Neoclassical houses, some grand, some humble and home-made. An attractive approach to Pláka is to follow **Odhós Kidhathinéon**, a pedestrian walkway starting near the English and Russian churches on Odhós Filellínon, south of Síndagma. It leads gently downhill close by the beautiful, small **Museum of Greek Folk Art** (Tues–Sun 10am–2pm; 400dr) at Kidhathinéon 17. The first floor displays weaving, pottery and embroidery, revealing both the sophistication and a strong Middle Eastern influence on traditional Greek arts; the third and fourth levels display traditional and ceremonial costumes from almost every region of Greece. Odhós Kidhathinéon continues through café-crowded Platía Filomoúsis Eterías to Hadrian's street, **Odhós Adhriánou**, running nearly the whole length of Pláka from the Thiseion to Hadrian's Arch.

The rightward section of Adhriánoú is largely commercial – souvenir shops and sandals – as far as the Roman Forum (see below). Left, just a few metres on, there's a quiet and attractive sitting space around the fourth-century **Monument of Lysikrates**, erected to celebrate the success of a prize-winning dramatic chorus. Continuing straight ahead from the Kidhathinéon-Adhriánou intersection up **Odhós Thespídhos**, you reach the edge of the Acropolis precinct. Up to the right, the whitewashed Cycladic houses of **Anafiotiká** cheerfully proclaim an architect-free zone amidst the highest crags of the Acropolis rock.

The Forum area

The **Roman Forum** (Tues–Fri 8.30am–2.45pm; 400dr) was built as an extension of the Agora (see below) by Julius Caesar and Augustus, and its main entrance was through the relatively intact Gate of Athena Archegetis. The best preserved and easily the most intriguing of the ruins, though, is the graceful, octagonal structure known as the **Tower of the Winds**. It was designed in the first century BC by a Syrian astronomer, and served as a compass, sundial, weather vane and water clock powered by a stream from one of the Acropolis springs. Each face of the tower is adorned with a relief of a figure floating through the air, personifying the eight winds.

Bordering the east end of the site, stretching between Áreos and Eólou, stand the surviving walls of **Hadrian's Library**, an enormous building which once enclosed a cloistered court of a hundred columns. **Odhós Áreos**, alongside the library, is now mainly bamboo furniture and wickerwork shops. At its end, round behind the Roman forum, are some of the quietest, prettiest and least spoiled streets in the whole of Pláka – many of them ending in steps for the ascent to **Theorías**, the last lane below the Acropolis. Before going up, take a look at the **Kanellópoulos Museum** (Tues–Sun 8.30am–3pm; 400dr), in the topmost house under the Acropolis, a block to the left of the entrance to the hill. The bulk of eclectic exhibits are icons, but there is also Byzantine jewellery, Coptic textiles, and Cycladic, Minoan and Classical art.

The Acropolis

A craggy limestone plateau, watered by springs and rising an abrupt 100 metres out of the plain of Attica, the **Acropolis** (Mon–Fri 8am–6.45pm, Sat & Sun 8.30am–2.45pm; closes 5pm weekdays in winter; 1500dr) has been a nucleus during every phase of the city's development. The site was one of the earliest settlements in Greece, drawing a Neolithic community to its slopes around 5000 BC. In Mycenaean times it was fortified around a royal palace and temples where the cult of Athena was introduced. City and goddess were integrated by the Dorians and, with the union of Attic towns and villages in the ninth century BC, the Acropolis became the heart of the first Greek city-state. In the wake of Athenian military supremacy and a peace treaty with the Persians in 449 BC, the walls were rebuilt and architects set to draw up plans for a reconstruction worthy of the city's cultural and political position. Pericles' rebuilding plan, which produced most of the monuments you see today, was under the general direction of the architect and sculptor **Pheidias** and was completed in an incredibly short time – the Parthenon took only ten years.

Having survived more or less intact for well over two thousand years, the Acropolis buildings finally fell victim to the demands of war. In 1684 the Turks demolished the temple of Athena Nike to gain a brief tactical advantage, then three years later the Venetians, laying siege to the garrison, ignited a Turkish gunpowder magazine in the Parthenon and in the process blasted off its roof. Surpassing this destruction, at least in the minds of today's Athenians, was Lord Elgin's removal of the Parthenon's frieze in 1801; he later sold it to the British Museum.

The nineteenth-century iron clamps and supports that were used to reinforce the marble structures have since rusted and warped, causing the stones to crack. Meanwhile, earthquakes have dislodged the foundations; generations of visitors have slowly worn down the Parthenon's surfaces; and, more recently, sulphur dioxide-laden smog has been turning the marble to dust. Since 1981, visitors have been barred from the Parthenon's actual precinct, and the first phase of a major restoration scheme has recently been completed.

THE PROPYLAIA AND ATHENA NIKE TEMPLE

The Acropolis' monumental entrance, or **Propylaia**, was constructed upon completion of the Parthenon in 437 BC, and its axis and proportions aligned to balance the temple. The ancient Athenians, awed by the fact that such wealth and craftsmanship should be used for a purely secular building, ranked this as their most prestigious monument. In front of the Propylaia, the simple and elegant **Temple of Athena Nike** was begun late in the rebuilding scheme and stands on a precipitous platform overlooking Pireás and the Saronic Gulf. The temple's frieze, with more attention to realism than triumph, depicts the Athenians' victory over the Persians at Plateia. Amazingly, the whole building was reconstructed from its original blocks in the nineteenth century.

THE PARTHENON

The **Parthenon** was the first great building in Pericles' scheme. Designed by Iktinos, it utilizes all the refinements available to the Doric order of architecture to achieve an extraordinary and unequalled harmony. Built on the site of earlier temples, the Parthenon was intended as a new sanctuary for Athena and a house for her cult image, a colossal wooden statue of *Athena Polias* (Athena of the City) decked in ivory and gold plate, with precious gems as eyes and sporting an ivory gorgon death's-head on her breast. Designed by Pheidias and considered one of the Seven Wonders of the Ancient World, the sculpture was lost in ancient times but its characteristics are known through later copies – including a Roman one in the National Archeological Museum.

The name "Parthenon" means "virgins' chamber" and initially referred only to a room at the west end of the temple occupied by the priestesses of Athena. But the temple never rivalled the Erechtheion in sanctity and its role tended to remain that of treasury and artistic showcase. Originally its columns were painted and it was decorated by the finest frieze and pedimental sculpture of the Classical age. Of these, the best surviving examples are in the British Museum.

THE ERECHTHEION

To the north of the Parthenon, beyond the foundations of the Old Temple of Athena, stands the **Erechtheion**, the last of the great works of Pericles. Here, in symbolic reconciliation, Athena and the city's old patron of Poseidon-Erechtheus were both worshipped; the site, according to myth, was that on which they had contested possession of the Acropolis. Its elegant Ionic porticoes are all worth close attention, particularly the north one with its fine decorated doorway and frieze of blue Eleusinian marble. On the south side, in the Porch of the Caryatids, the Ionic line is transformed into six maidens (*caryatids*) holding the entablature on their heads. These are replicas: five of the originals are in the Acropolis Museum, a sixth was looted by Elgin.

THE ACROPOLIS MUSEUM

Placed discreetly on a level below that of the main monuments, the **Acropolis Museum** (Mon 11am–6.30pm, Tues–Fri 8am–6.30pm, Sat & Sun 8.30am–2.30pm; winter closes 5pm weekdays) contains nearly all of the portable objects removed from the Acropolis since 1834. In the first rooms to the left of the vestibule are fragments of pediment sculptures from the Old Temple of Athena, which give a good impression of the vivid colours that were used in temple decoration. Farther on is the *Moschophoros*, a painted marble statue of a young man carrying a sacrificial calf, dated 570 BC and one of the earliest examples of Greek art in marble. Room 4 displays one of the chief treasures of the building, a unique collection of Korai, or maidens, dedicated as votive offerings to Athena sometime in the sixth century BC. The only pieces of Parthenon frieze left in Greece are in Room 7, while the adjoining room contains the graceful and fluid sculpture of Athena Nike adjusting her sandals. Finally, in the last room are the authentic and semi-eroded *caryatids* from the Erechtheion, displayed in a vacuum chamber.

THE WEST SLOPE

Rock-hewn stairs immediately below the entrance to the Acropolis ascend the low hill of the **Areopagus**, the site of the court of criminal justice. Following the road or path over the flank of the Acropolis, you come out on to Leofóros Dhionissíou Areopayítou, by the Herodes Atticus theatre (see below). Turning right, a network of paths leads up **Filopáppou Hill**, its summit capped by a grandiose monument to a Roman senator and consul, Filopappos, who is depicted on its frieze driving his chariot. North, along the main path, which follows a line of truncated ancient walls, is the church of **Áyios Dhimítrios** with Byzantine frescoes. Farther to the north, above the church, rises the **Hill of the Pnyx**, an area used in Classical Athens as the meeting place for the democratic assembly. All except the most serious political issues were aired here, the hill on the north side providing a semicircular terrace from which to address the crowds of at least 6000 citizens that met more than forty times a year.

THE SOUTH SLOPE

The second-century Roman **Odeion of Herodes Atticus**, restored for performances of music and Classical drama during the summer festival, dominates the south slope of the Acropolis hill. It is open only for shows, and the main interest on the slope lies in the earlier Greek sites to the east. Pre-eminent among these is the **Theatre of Dionysus**, beside the main site entrance on Leof. Dhionissíou Areopayítou (daily 8.30am–2.30pm; 400dr). One of the most evocative locations in the city, it was here that the masterpieces of Aeschylus, Sophocles, Euripides and Aristophanes were first performed. The ruins are impressive; rebuilt in the fourth century BC, the theatre could hold some 17,000 spectators. To the west of the theatre extend the ruins of the **Asclepion**, a sanctuary devoted to the healing god Asclepius and built around a sacred spring. The curative centre was probably incorporated into the Byzantine church of the doctor-saints, Kosmas and Damian, of which there are prominent remains. Nearer to the road are the foundations of the Roman **Stoa of Eumenes**, a colonnade of stalls which stretched to the Herodes Atticus Odeion.

The Agora

Northwest of the Acropolis, the **Agora** (Tues–Sun 8.30am–2.45pm; 1000dr) was the nexus of ancient Athenian city life, where the various claims of administration, commerce, market and public assembly competed for space. The site is a confused jumble of ruins, dating from various stages of building between the sixth century BC and the fifth century AD. For some idea of what you are surveying, the place to head for is the **Museum** (same hours; included in Agora entrance fee), housed in the rebuilt Stoa of Attalos. The stoa itself is, in every respect bar one, a faithful reconstruction of the original. What is missing is colour: in Classical times the exterior would have been painted bright red and blue.

Kerameikos (Keramikós)

Still further northwest of here, the **Kerameikos** site (Tues–Sun 8.30am–3pm; 400dr), encompassing the principal cemetery of ancient Athens, provides a fascinating and quiet retreat from the Acropolis, with the Iridhanós brook lending an atmosphere of lush coolness. From the entrance at Ermoú 148, the double line of the Long Walls, which ran to the port at Pireás, can be seen. The barriers are interrupted by the great Dipylon Gate and the Sacred Gate, the latter used for the processions which followed the Sacred Way, once lined by colonnades and bronze statues, into the Agora. Between the two gates are the foundations of the Pompeion, where preparations for the processions took place and where the main vehicles were stored. Branching off from the Sacred Way is the Street of the Tombs, begun in 394 BC and now excavated along a hundred or so metres. The **Oberlaender Museum** (closed Tues) has an extensive collection of *steles*, terracotta figures, vases and sculptures from the site. Among them, that of *Ampharete Holding Her Infant Grandchild* and *The Boxer*, with a cauliflower ear and thongs of a glove tied around his wrist, in Room 1, are remarkable in their detailed execution. The terracotta figures and vases of Room 2 include some of the earliest art objects yet found in Greece.

Síndagma and the National Gardens area

All roads lead to Platía Sindágmatos – **Síndagma Square**. Geared to tourism, with the main EOT branch, post office, *American Express*, airline and travel offices grouped around, it has convenience but not much else to recommend it. At the back of the parliament buildings, the **National Gardens** provide the most refreshing spot in the whole city: not so much a flower garden, but a luxuriant tangle of trees, shrubs and creepers, whose shade, duck ponds, cafés and sparkling irrigation channels bring relief from the heat and smog of summer.

At the southern end of the park, beside one of the most hazardous road junctions in Athens, stands **Hadrian's Arch**, erected by the Roman emperor to mark the edge of the Classical city and the beginning of his own. Directly behind, the colossal pillars of the **Temple of Olympian Zeus** (Mon–Sat 9am–3pm, Sun 10am–2pm) justify his show of arrogance. The largest temple in Greece, it was dedicated by Hadrian in 131 AD, and originally had 104 columns, of which just sixteen are left standing. A walk across the National Gardens from the Olympian Zeus temple will bring you out on Leofóros Ardhittoú, across which is the pristine **Stadium**, reconstructed on Roman foundations for the modern revival of the Olympic Games in 1896.

The Benáki Museum, the Cycladic Museum and Likavitós

At the northeast corner of the National Gardens, at Koumbári 1, is the fascinating **Benáki Museum** (closed for renovation until 1995). Overlooked by ninety percent of tourists, this constantly surprising collection ranges through Chinese ceramics, Mycenaean jewellery, Greek costumes and folk artefacts, memorabilia of the Greek War of Independence – even a reconstructed Muslim palace reception hall.

Taking the second left off Vassilísis Sofías after the Benáki museum will bring you to the private **Museum of Cycladic and Ancient Greek Art** at Neofítou Dhouká 4 (Mon & Wed–Fri 10am–4pm, Sat 10am–2.45pm; 250dr), which in the quality of its display methods is streets ahead of anything else in Athens. Though the collections are restricted to covering the Cycladic civilization (third millennium BC), the pre-Minoan Bronze Age (second millennium BC), and the period from the fall of Mycenae to the beginning of historic times at around 700 BC, plus a selection of pottery, you come away having learned far more about these periods than from the equivalent sections of the National Museum.

North of the museum, past the posh shopping district of **Kolonáki**, a **funicular** begins its ascent to the summit of **Likavitós** at the corner of Dhorás Dhistría and Ploutárhou, (8am–10pm). For the more energetic, the principal path up the hill begins here, too, rambling up through the woods. On top, the chapel of Áyios Yióryios provides the main focus. There's a **café** on the adjacent terrace and another, less plastic, halfway down; both have views spectacular enough to excuse the prices and unenthusiastic service.

The National Archeological Museum

To get the most out of the treasure house of the **National Archeological Museum**, due north of the central market at Patissíon 44 (summer Mon 12.30am–7pm, Tues–Fri 8am–5/7pm, Sat & Sun 8.30am–3pm; winter Mon 11am–5pm, Tues–Fri 8am–5/7pm, Sat & Sun 8.30am–3pm; Thíra and Numismatic sections close at 3pm and 1.30pm respectively; 1500dr), buy a detailed guide before you go in, as there's little in the way of explanatory captions. The biggest crowd-puller is the **Mycenaean hall** (Room 4), facing the main entrance, with all of Schliemann's gold finds from the grave circle at Mycenae, including the so-called **Mask of Agamemnon**, as hard to see on a summer's day as the *Mona Lisa*. The Mycenaeans' consummate small-scale decoration – of rings, cups, seals, inlaid daggers – requires eye-tiring scrutiny of the packed showcases.

To the right of the Mycenaean hall, Room 6 houses a large collection of **Cycladic art** – pre-Mycenaean pieces from the islands, whose most characteristic items are folded-arm figurines, among them a near full-sized nude. Most of the rest of the ground floor is occupied by sculpture. Beginning in Room 7, on the left of the main entrance, the exhibition evolves chronologically from the Archaic through the Classical and Hellenistic periods to the Roman- and Egyptian-influenced. Room 15 heralds the **Classical art** collection, with the mid-fifth-century BC **Statue of Poseidon**, dredged from the sea off Évvia in the 1920s. The god stands poised to throw his trident, weight on the front foot, athlete's body perfectly balanced, the model of idealized male beauty. Found in the same shipwreck was the virtuoso **Little Jockey** (Room 21), but the most reproduced of all the sculptures is in Room 31: a first-century statue of a naked and indulgent **Aphrodite** about to rap Pan's knuckles for getting too fresh.

Too numerous to list, but offering fascinating glimpses of everyday life and changing styles of craftsmanship and perception of the human form, are the many **steles** or carved gravestones. Still on the ground floor, Room 32 contains the amazing **Helène Stathatos Collection** of gold jewellery from the ancient and Byzantine worlds.

Keep a reserve of energy for the reconstructed **Thíra rooms** upstairs. Discovered at Akrotiri on the island of Thíra, they date from around 1450 BC – contemporary with the Minoan civilization on Crete – and are frescoed with monkeys, antelopes and flowers, and furnished with painted wooden chairs and beds. The other upper rooms are occupied by a dizzying succession of **pottery**.

In the south wing of the museum, entered separately from Tosítsa street, is the **Numismatic Collection**, taking in over 400,000 coins from Mycenaean times to Macedonian, though only a fraction are on display.

Eating, drinking and entertainment

As you'd expect, Athens has the best and the most varied **restaurants and tavernas** in the country. If it is character you are after, Pláka's hills and lanes can still provide a pleasant evening's setting for a meal, despite the aggressive touts and tourist hype. But for good-value and good-quality fare, it's best to strike out into the ring of neighbourhoods around: to Méts, Pangráti, Exárhia, Veïkoú/Koukáki, or the more upmarket Kolonáki. None of these is more than a half-hour's walk or bus ride from the centre. The quintessentially Greek **ouzerí** are essentially bars selling *oúzo* (occasionally just *oúzo*), beer and wine, along with *mezédhes* (hors d'œuvres) to reduce the impact; in many **bars** and **pubs** you can similarly eat as well as drink. The more exciting of the city's bars, however, are music-oriented and tend to close down in the summer months. Bars, cinemas, exhibitions and nightlife venues change fast and often, so it's useful to have a copy of the monthly English-language *Athenian* magazine, the daily *Athens News* or the weekly *Athenscope* magazine, which between them have full listings of the city's clubs, galleries, concerts and films.

Restaurants

Arhaia Agora, Kalogríou 6, corner Aiolóu. Unpretentious and cheap *meze*-cafe in the tourist heart of Pláka.

Fruitopia, Soultáni 12, corner Solomoú, Exárhia district. Rare vegetarian macrobiotic restaurant; dinner only; closed August. Expensive.

Toh Kalivi, Empedhokleous 26, by Platía Varnáva, Pangráti. Excellent, traditional *mezédhes* fare. Closed June–Aug. Reasonable.

O Ilias, corner Stasínou/Telesílis (near Leofóros Konstandínou), Pangráti. A very good and very popular taverna. Tables outside in summer. Moderately priced.

Ipiros, Platía Ayíou Filíppou. Old restaurant in a great location, right at the heart of the flea market. If the food – casserole dishes – is occasionally listless, the prices and quantity are fair enough.

Ih Lefka, Mavromiháli 121, Neápoli. Traditional taverna with barrelled retsina; garden in summer. Moderate.

O Megaritis, Ferekídhou 2, corner Arátou. Cheap casserole food, barrel wine, indoor and outdoor seating.

Ta Pergoulia, Márkou Moussoúrou 16, Méts. Delicious, unusual *mezédhes* – order seven or eight and you'll have a fair-sized bill but a big meal. Closed in summer.

O Platanos, Dhioyénous 4, Pláka. Decent food served in the shade of a plane tree. Closed Sun.

Rozalia, Valetsíou 58, Exárhia. The best hors d'œuvres, plus grill fare near the triangular plaza. Supper only; garden in summer.

Vangelis, Sahíni, off Liossíon (100m up from Platía Váthis). One of the friendliest and most traditional tavernas in the city. Cheap.

Vellis, Platía Varnáva/corner Stilpónos (between Pangráti and Méts). One of the last of a dying breed of working-men's wine-with-food shops. Evenings only. Cheap.

O Virinis, Arhimídhous 11 (off Platía Plastíra). Good quality, moderately priced taverna, with its own house wine and a wide variety of *mezédhes*. Garden in summer.

O Yeros tou Morea, Arváli 4, Koukáki. Excellent home-style casserole food and *mezédhes*; bulk wine from barrels forming the main decor. Closed Sun.

Ouzerí and bars

Apotsos, Panepistimíou 10, in arcade. A lunchtime-only bar with a wide range of *mezédhes*. A landmark, frequented by journalists, politicians and writers.

Toh Athinaikon, Themistokléous, near corner with Panepistimíou. An old *ouzerí* in a new location but retaining style – marble tables, old posters, etc. Variety of good-sized *mezédhes*. Closed Sun.

Toh Dhikti, G. Olimbíou 2, Koukáki. Exotic *mezédhes* like snails and livestock bollocks; moderate to expensive. Closed Mon.

Café-Bar Dhodhoni, Sólonos 64 (parallel to Panepistimíou, 3 blocks northeast). A packed student hang-out opposite the law school. Delicious snacks.

Ouzeri Euvia, G. Olimbíou 8, Koukáki. Large portions of rich food accompany drink at this popular, reasonable place on a pedestrian street. Daily except Aug.

Toh Yerani/Kouklis/Skolarhio, Tripódhon 14, corner Epihármou, Pláka. Lively, triple-alias *mezé* bar with terrace. Open lunchtimes and evenings; moderate to pricey.

The Athens Festival

The summer **Athens Festival** has, over the years, come to encompass cultural events in just about every sphere: Classical Greek theatre most famously, but also established and contemporary dance, classical music, big-name jazz, traditional Greek music and a smattering of rock shows. As well as the Herodes Atticus theatre, which is memorable in itself on a warm summer's evening, the festival spreads to the open-air theatre on Likavitós hill, the Veákio amphitheatre in Pireás and (with special bus excursions) to the great ancient theatre at Epidaurus. The Festival runs from mid-June until mid-September, and for theatre especially, you'll have to move fast to get tickets. The main **Festival box office** is in the arcade at Stadhíou 4 (Mon–Sat 8.30am–1.30pm & 6–8.30pm; ☎32 21 459 or ☎32 23 111); theatre box offices open on the day of performance.

Listings

Airlines *Alitalia*, Níkis 10 (☎32 29 414); *British Airways*, Óthonos 10 (☎32 50 601); *Egyptair*, Óthonos 10 (☎32 33 575); *Delta*, Óthonos 4 (☎32 35 242); *El Al*, Óthonos 8 (☎32 30 116); *Kenyan*, Stadhíous 5 (☎32 47 000); *KLM*, Voulís 22 (☎32 26 011); *Olympic*, Óthonos 6 (☎92 92 555), main office at Leof. Singroú 96 (☎96 66 666); *Qantas*, Eólou 104 (☎32 39 066); *SAS*, Sína 6 (☎36 34 444); *TWA*, Xenofóndos 8 (☎32 26 451); *United*, Singroú 5 (☎92 29 186).

Bookshops *Compendium*, Níkis 28 off Síndagma, is the best organized and best value of the English-language bookstores. *Eleftheroudhakis*, Níkis 4, is probably the best for books about Greece (in English and Greek) with a good general English-language stock. *Ih Folia tou Viviou*, Panepistimíou 25, is best for fiction and social sciences.

Car rental A number of companies based along Leofóros Singroú, including *Just* (no. 43), *Europcar/InterRent* (4), *Thrifty* (24), *Ansa* (33) and *Autorent* (118); the last two give student discounts.

Embassies and consulates *Australia*, Dhimitríou Soútsou 37 (☎64 47 303); *Canada*, Ioánnou Yennadhíou 4 (☎72 39 511); *Great Britain*, Ploutárhou 1, Kolonáki (☎72 36 211); *Ireland*, Vass. Konstandínou 7 (☎72 32 771); *Netherlands*, Vass. Konstandínou 5–7 (☎72 39 701); *USA*, Vass. Sofías 91 (☎72 12 951); New Zealanders must use the UK embassy for assistance.

Emergencies In case of a medical emergency, if you can travel safely don't wait for an ambulance – get a taxi straight to the hospital address that the tourist police give you.

Exchange *National Bank of Greece* in Síndagma is open for exchange Mon–Fri 8am–2pm & 5–8pm, Sat & Sun 8am–2pm; try also the *General Bank* on the west side of the square, also with long hours.

Flight information *Olympic* ☎93 63 363; other airlines ☎96 94 666.

Laundry Angélou Yerónda 10, off Platía Fillimoussís Eterías; at Dhidhótou 46, Exárhia; and at Veïkoú 107 (below Platía Koukakíou).

Luggage storage Best arranged with your hotel. *Pacific Ltd*, Níkis 24, stores luggage for 2000dr per item per month, 700dr per week.

Pharmacies Most pharmacists speak English. The *Marinopoulos* branches in Patissíon and Panepistimíou streets are very good; ☎107 for after-hours pharmacies.

Post office The main post office, with poste restante service, is at Eólou 100, just off Omónia (Mon–Sat 7.30am–8.30pm).

Telephones 24-hr OTE office at Patissíon/Ikosiosdhóïs Oktovríou; branch at Stahíou 15 is open 7am to midnight.

Tourist police Head office at Pireós 158, corner Pétrou Rallí, near Thissío metro (☎171).

Train tickets The *OSE* office at Sína 6, by the university, gives out information and sells domestic tickets; international tickets and information at Filellínon 21 .

Travel agencies The cheapest ferry tickets to Italy are usually sold through the Irish student travel company *USIT* at Filellínon 1 (☎32 41 884), or *Magic Bus* at no. 20 of the same street. Among other agencies, *Highway Express* (Níkis 42), *Periscope* (Filellínon 22), *Himalaya* (Filellínon 7) and *Arcturus* (Apóllonos 20) are worth scanning for air deals. Cheap train tickets and rail passes for under-26s at *ISYTS*, Nikis 11, or *Transalpino*, at no. 28.

Around Athens

Attica (Attikí), the region encompassing the capital, is not much explored by tourists, with only the great romantic ruin of the **Temple of Apollo at Sounion** on the excursion circuit. The rest tends to be visited for the functional reason of escaping to the islands – from the ports of **Pireás** and **Rafína**.

Pireás (Piraeus)

PIREÁS, port of Athens since Classical times, is today a metropolis in its own right, containing much of Greater Athens' industries, as well as various commercial activities associated with a port. For most visitors it is Pireás' inter-island ferries that provide a focus and reason for coming. The easiest way there is by metro – it's the last stop.

Perhaps the most fulfilling pursuit is to check out some of the port's excellent **eating** options – you'll find several budget restaurants around the market area, back from the waterside Aktí Miaoúli/Eth. Andistáseos. For more substantial meals, there is a string of *ouzerí* and seafood tavernas along Aktí Themistokléous, west of the Zéa Marina, most of them well priced. For a real blowout, there is *Vassilenas* at Etolikoú 72, providing *mezédhes* enough to defy all appetites; it's not cheap, but so many Athenians consider it worth the drive out that most evenings you'll need to book (☎46 12 457).

If you're staying in Athens prior to heading out to the islands, it is worth calling in at the EOT office in Síndagma to pick up a schedule of departures for the current week. Most of the boats leave between 8am and 9am for the main Cycladic islands, around 1pm for the major Dodecanese islands between 5pm and 6pm for the northeast Aegean islands, and around 7pm for Crete. The best plan is to get to Pireás early and check with the various **shipping agents** around the metro station and in the quayside Platía Karaïskáki. Keep in mind that many of these act only for particular lines; for a full picture of the various boats sailing, ask at three or four outlets.

The Poseidon temple at Sounion

The seventy kilometres of coast south of Athens – the tourist-board-dubbed **"Apollo Coast"** – has some good but highly developed beaches. At weekends, when Athenians flee the city, the sands fill fast, as do the innumerable bars, restaurants and discos. If this is what you're after, then resorts like Glifádha and Vouliagméni are functional enough. But for most foreign visitors, the coast's attraction is at the end of the road, in the form of the temple at **Cape Sounion.** Half-hourly **buses** to Sounion leave from the KTEL terminal on Mavromatéon at the southwest corner of Áreos Park. They alternate between coastal (*paraliakó*) and inland (*mesoyiakó*) services, the latter slightly longer and more expensive. The coast route takes around two hours. For the main resorts there are more regular city buses from stops beside the Zappíon.

Cape Sounion – Akrí Soúnio – is one of the most imposing spots in Greece, and on its tip stands the fifth-century BC **Temple of Poseidon** (Mon–Sat 9am–sunset, Sun 10am–sunset; 600dr), built in the time of Pericles as part of a sanctuary to the sea god. In summer there is faint hope of solitude, unless you slip into the site before the tours arrive, but the temple is as evocative a ruin as Greece can offer. Doric in style, it preserves sixteen of its thirty-four columns, and the view from the temple takes in the islands of Kéa, Kíthnos and Sérifos to the southeast, Éyina and the Peloponnese to the west. Below the promontory are several **coves**, the most sheltered of which is a five-minute walk east from the car park and site entrance. The main Soúnio beach is more crowded, but has a group of tavernas at the far end – fairly reasonably priced, considering the location. There are several **campsites** near the cape: *Camping Bacchus* and *Sounion Beach Camping* are both about 5km from the temple.

Rafína

The port of **RAFÍNA** has ferries and hydrofoils to a dozen of the Cyclades, as well as nearby Évvia. It connects regularly with Athens by an hour-plus bus route from the Mavromatéon terminal through the "gap" in Mount Pendéli. Much of the town has been spoilt by seaside development, but the little fishing harbour with its line of roof-terrace seafood restaurants remains one of the most attractive spots on the Attic coast. The town's half-dozen hotels are often full; the cheapest – *Corali* (☎0294/22 477; ③), *Kymata* (☎0294/23 406; ③) and *Rafina* (☎0294/23 460; ③) – are in the Platiá Nikifórou Plastíra. The beachside **campsite** at nearby Kókkino Limaneaki is a good fall-back.

THE PELOPONNESE

The appeal of the **Peloponnese** (*Pelopónissos*) is hard to overstate. This southern penin-sula, technically an island since the cutting of the Corinth Canal, seems to have the best of almost everything Greek. Its ancient sites include the Homeric palaces of Agamemnon at **Mycenae** and of Nestor at **Pílos**; the best preserved of all Greek thea-tres at **Epidaurus**; and the sanctuary of **Olympia**, host for a millennium of the Olympic Games. The medieval remains are scarcely less rich, with the fabulous Venetian, Frankish and Turkish castles of **Náfplio** and **Kórinthos**; the strange towerhouses and churches of the **Máni**; and the extraordinary Byzantine towns of **Mystra** and **Monemvassía**. The Peloponnesian **beaches**, especially along the west coast, are among the finest and least developed in the country. And, last but by no means least, the **landscape** itself is inspiring, dominated by range after range of forested mountains, and cut by some of the lushest valleys and gorges to be imagined.

The usual approach from Athens to the Peloponnese is via **Kórinthos**; buses and trains run this way at least every hour. Alternatively – and attractively – you could go by ferry or hydrofoil, via the islands of the **Argo-Saronic**; routes run from Pireás, through the islands and then south to Monemvassía.

Kórinthos (Corinth)

The modern city of **KÓRINTHOS** was levelled by earthquakes in 1858, 1928 and again in 1981. It's a slightly grim industrial-agricultural centre, but for visitors Corinth does have the attraction of easy access to its ancient predecessor, Arhéa Kórinthos, 7km southwest and served by hourly buses and by taxis.

The centre of Kórinthos is its **park**, bordered on the longer sides by Ermoú and Ethnikís Andístassis streets. The **bus station** for Athens and most local destinations is on the Ermoú side of the park; longer-distance buses use a terminal on the other side of the park. The **train station** is a couple of blocks toward the waterside. **Hotels** are quite easy to find; two cheaper options are the badly-maintained waterside *Hotel Belle-Vue* (☎0741/22 088; ②) and the *Hotel Byron* at Dhimokratías 8, opposite the train station (☎0741/22 631; ②). If you get stuck, there's a **tourist police** post on Ermoú, just down from the bus station. Or there are a couple of unenticing **campsites** along the gulf to the west: *Corinth Beach* at Dhiavakíta and *Blue Dolphin* at Léheo. **Eating** in Kórinthos isn't spectacularly good. The few decent tavernas like *Anaxagoras* on O Moustakis, and fast-food/*souvlaki* places along the waterside, are all modestly priced.

Ancient Corinth

The ruins of the **ancient city**, which displaced Athens as capital of the Greek province in Roman times, occupy a rambling site below the acropolis hill of Acrocorinth, itself littered with medieval remains. To explore both you really need to allow`a full day, or better still, to stay close by. A modern **village** spreads back around the main archeological zone and there is a scattering of **rooms** to rent in the back streets – follow the signs or ask at the cafés. The two campsites detailed above are also within a three-kilometre walk.

Possession of Corinth gave control of trade between northern Greece and the Peloponnese, and a link between the Ionian and Aegean seas. Not surprisingly, the history of Corinth has been chequered with invasions and power struggles, but the city suffered only one break in its continuity, when the Romans razed it in 146 BC. For a century the site lay in ruins before being refounded, on a majestic scale, by Julius Caesar in 44 BC.

It is the remains of the Roman city that dominate the main excavated **site** (summer Mon–Fri 8am–6pm, Sat & Sun 8am–7pm; winter Mon–Fri 8am–5pm, Sat & Sun 8.30am–3pm; 1000dr), just behind the road where buses pull in. You enter from the south side, which leads straight into the **Roman agora**, an enormous marketplace flanked by the foundations of a huge stoa, or covered walkway. To the north is a trace of the Greek city, a **sacred spring**, covered over by a grille but with its bronze lion-head spouts still in place. More substantial is the elaborate Roman **Fountain of Peirene**, just above the starting line of the racetrack. Above the fountain, approached via a flight of steps, lies an excavated stretch of what was the main approach to the city, the **Lechaion Way**. The real focus, however, is a survival from the Classical Greek era: the fifth-century BC **Temple of Apollo**, whose seven austere Doric columns stand slightly above the level of the forum, flanked by foundations of another marketplace and baths. To the west is the site **museum**, housing a large collection of domestic pieces, some Roman mosaics and a frieze depicting the labours of Herakles.

Towering 600m above the lower town, **Acrocorinth** (Tues–Sun 8.30am–6pm; 400dr) is an amazing mass of rock still largely encircled by two kilometres of wall. During the Middle Ages the ancient acropolis of Corinth became one of Greece's most powerful fortresses, besieged by successive waves of invaders. It's a four-kilometre climb up – about an hour – but unreservedly recommended. Amid the sixty-acre site you wander through a jumble of semi-ruined chapels, mosques, houses and battlements, erected in turn by Greeks, Romans, Byzantines, Frankish Crusaders, Venetians and Turks.

Mikínes (Mycenae)

Tucked into a fold of the hills just to the east of the road from Kórinthos to Árgos is Agamemnon's citadel, "well-built **Mycenae**, rich in gold", as Homer wrote. It was uncovered in 1874 by the German archeologist Heinrich Schliemann, whose work was impelled by his belief that there was a factual basis to Homer's epics, and the brilliantly crafted gold and sophisticated architecture that he found bore out the accuracy of Homer's epithets.

Unless you have your own transport, you'll probably want to stay in the modern village of **MIKÍNES**, 2km east of the road and the train station and 2km from the ancient site. The cheapest options are the *Restaurant Iphigeneia*, halfway up the single street, which doubles up as a **youth hostel** (②), and the two **campsites**, *Camping Mycenae* and *Camping Atticus*, both fairly central. Alternatives include **rooms** to let in village houses or the C-class *Hotel Belle Hélène* (☎0751/66-255; ③), up the hill towards the site. The village has plenty of **restaurants**, all geared to the lunchtime bus-tour trade; don't expect too much in the way of first-rate cuisine.

The Site

The buildings that were unearthed by Schliemann show signs of having been occupied from around 1950 BC until 1100 BC – at which stage the town, though still prosperous, was abandoned. No coherent explanation has been found for these events, but it seems that war among the rival kingdoms was a major factor in the Mycenaean decline. The **Citadel of Mycenae** (summer Mon–Fri 8am–5pm, Sat & Sun 8am–7pm; winter Mon–Fri 8am–5pm, Sat & Sun 8.30am–3pm; 1000dr) is entered through the mighty **Lion Gate** – the motif of a pillar supported by two muscular lions was probably the symbol of the Mycenaean royal house, for a seal found on the site bears a similar device.

Inside the walls to the right is **Grave Circle A**, the royal cemetery which Schliemann believed to contain the bodies of Agamemnon and his followers, murdered on their triumphant return from Troy. In fact the burials date from at least two centuries before the Trojan war, but they were certainly royal graves, and the finds (now in Athens' National Archeological Museum) are among the richest yet unearthed. Schliemann took the extensive **South House**, beyond the grave circle, to be the Palace of Agamemnon. But a much grander building, which must have been the **Royal Palace**, was later discovered on the summit of the acropolis. Rebuilt in the thirteenth century BC, probably at the same time as the Lion Gate, it is centred – as are all Mycenaean palaces – around a **Great Court**. The small rooms to the north are believed to have been royal apartments and in one of them the remains of a red stuccoed bath have led to its fanciful identification as the spot of Agamemnon's murder. Equally evocative are the ramparts and secret cistern at their east end, near the large, stately **House of Columns**.

Outside the walls of the citadel lay the main part of the town; only the ruling elite of Mycenaean society were permitted to live within the citadel itself. The extensive remains of **merchants' houses** have been uncovered near to the road, located beside a second grave circle. On the other side of the road from the main site is the startling **Treasury of Atreus**, a royal burial vault which is entered through a majestic fifteen-metre corridor. Set above the chamber doorway is a lintel formed by two immense slabs of stone – one of which, a staggering nine metres long, is estimated to weigh 118 tons.

Tírinthos (Tiryns)

In Mycenaean times **TIRYNS** stood by the sea, commanding the coastal approaches to Árgos and Mycenae. Today the Aegean sea has receded, leaving the fortress stranded on a low hillock in the plains – alongside the region's principal modern prison. The site lies just to the west of the road from Árgos (7km away), with Náfplio 5km south. Buses will drop and pick up passengers, on request, at the café opposite.

The sophistication of the site and its unequivocally military purpose are clear as soon as you climb up the entrance ramp to the **Citadel** (Mon–Fri 8am–5pm, Sat & Sun 8.30am–2.45pm; winter may close Mon; 400dr). Wide enough to allow access to chariots, it was designed to make any invading force immediately vulnerable. Their right-hand side would be exposed the whole way, and at the top, the ramp forced a sharp turn – again surveyed by defenders from within. The gateways were considerable barriers to final access to the courtyard, the outer one similar in design to Mycenae's Lion Gate. In the thickness of the courtyard's outer wall is one of the long stone-vaulted corridors, the citadel's most dramatic feature (though currently closed to visitors due to dodgy masonry). A passage from the courtyard leads to a large forecourt and from there a staircase continues to a 21-metre-long gallery, with its numerous storage chambers. Of the **palace** itself only the limestone foundations survive, but you can gain a clear idea of its structure.

Náfplio

NÁFPLIO is a rarity amongst Greek towns. It is lively, beautifully sited and has a rather grand, fading elegance, inherited from when it was the fledgling capital of modern Greece. Today it's in danger of becoming too popular for its own good, but it remains by far the most attractive base for exploring the area and resting up for a while by the sea. Wedged between the sea and a fortress-topped headland, the town is easy to find your way around. **Buses** arrive at Ódhos Singroú, just south of the interlocking main squares, **Platía Navárhon/Platía Kapodhistrías**, in turn just west of the **train station** for the recently reinstated service from Árgos. An alternative approach to the town – or more likely a route onwards – is by the "Flying Dolphin" **hydrofoil** service; there are summer connections to Spétses and the other Argo-Saronic islands, or to Pireás and Monemvassía. In 1993 summer ferry services were introduced connecting Náfplio to various Cycladic islands; details from *Staikos Tours*, Bouboulínas 50 (☎0752/27950).

The main fort – the **Palamídhi** (summer Mon–Fri 8.30am–4.30pm, Sat & Sun 8am–7pm; winter daily 10am–3pm; 400dr) – is most directly approached by 899 stone-hewn steps from the end of Polizídhou street, by the side of a Venetian bastion. Within the walls are three self-contained castles, all built by the Venetians in the 1710s – hence the Lion of Saint Mark above the gateways. The **Íts Kalé** ("Three Castles" in Turkish), to the west, occupies the ancient acropolis, whose walls were adapted by successive medieval restorers. There's little of interest, but the hotel's service road cuts through the headland and this brings you down to a small **beach**, overcrowded in season but a nevertheless enjoyable spot to cool off. The third fort, **Boúrtzi**, occupies the islet offshore from the harbour – accessible by *kaíkia* (600dr return) in summer. In the town itself, **Platía Sindágmatos**, the main square, is the focus of most interest. On and around it survive three converted **Ottoman mosques**: one is now a cinema; another, in the southwest corner, Greece's original parliament building; the third has been reconsecrated as the cathedral of Áyios Yióryios. The **Archeological Museum** (Tues–Sun 8.30am–3pm; 400dr) occupies a Venetian mansion on the west side of Síndagma. It has some good collections, including a unique and more or less complete suit of Mycenaean armour and reconstructed frescoes from Tiryns. Equally worthwhile is the new **Folk Art Museum** (summer Tues–Sun 8.30am–3pm; winter Tues–Sun 9am–2.30pm; 400dr) on Ipsilándou, featuring superb and imaginatively displayed embroideries, costumes and traditional household tools and goods.

Practicalities

Accommodation is generally overpriced, the most reasonable being *Hotel Epidhavros* on Ipsilánoou (☎0752/27 541; ③), greatly preferable to the *Hotel Acropole*, Vasilíssis Olgas 7 (☎0752/27 796; ③) or the co-managed *Hotel King Otto* at Farmakopoúlou 3 (☎0752/27 585; ④) and *Hotel Lito* at Zigomála 28 (☎0752/28 093; ④), at the base of Íts Kalé fortress. If you're going to stay several nights, prices may work out lower in private **rooms**. Most of these cluster on the slope south of the main square, or there are a few below the *Hotel Lito*. The **youth hostel** on the corner of Vizandíou and Argonáfton (☎0752/246 720; ②) in the new town has been recently overhauled and is a good, friendly fall-back choice. For **eating**, try *Kakanarakis*, Vasillisis Ólgas 18, *Zorba* at Staïkopoúlou 30, or *O Arapakos* at Bouboulínas 81.

Epídhavros (Epidaurus)

From the sixth century BC to Roman times **EPÍDHAVROS**, some thirty kilometres east of Náfplio, was a major spa and religious centre, and its Sanctuary of Asclepius was the most famous and probably the richest of all shrines dedicated to the legendary son of Apollo. This aspect of the site, however, is for most visitors a peripheral attraction to the magnificently preserved **theatre** (summer Mon 11am–5pm, Tues–Fri 8am–5pm, Sat & Sun 8am–7pm; winter Mon–Fri 8am–5pm, Sat & Sun 8.30am–3pm; ; 1000dr), a 14,000-seat arena built in the fourth century BC that merges so well into the landscape it was rediscovered only last century. Constructed with mathematical precision, it has near-perfect acoustics – from the highest of the 54 tiers of seats you can hear coins dropped in the circular orchestra.

Close by the theatre is a small **museum** (same times; Mon opens 11am all year), which it's best to visit before exploring the somewhat obscure site of the sanctuary. This encompasses hospitals, dwellings for the priest-physicians, and hotels and amusements for the fashionable visitors. The strong significance of the serpent at Epídhavros – Asclepius was thought to assume its form – is elaborated in the circular **Tholos**, one of the best-preserved buildings on the site and designed, like the theatre, by Polycleitus. Its inner foundation walls form a labyrinth which it is believed was used as a snake pit – according to one theory, a form of shock therapy for mental patients.

Most people take in Epídhavros as a day trip (four buses daily from Náfplio – marked "Asklipion"), but if you want to stay you can **camp** near the car park. Alternatively, there's a couple of modestly priced places in Ligoúrio, 5km north – *Hotel Koronis* (☎0753/22 267; ③) and *Hotel Asklepios* (☎0753/22 251; ③). The nearest restaurant to the site is the *Oasis* on the Ligoúrio road, but *Leonidhas* in the village proper is better.

Trípoli

Unattractive **TRÍPOLI** is a major crossroads of the Peloponnese, from which most travellers either head northwest towards Olympia, or south to Spárti and Mystra, or Kalamáta. Alternatives include more direct routes to the coast – west to Kiparissía, or east to Náfplio or Ástros/Leonídhi – and the Peloponnese railway, which continues its meandering course from Kórinthos and Árgos to Kiparissía and Kalamáta. The major **bus terminal**, serving all destinations in Arcadia and the northern Peloponnese, is on Platía Kolokotrónis, one of the main squares. All other sevices – including for Spárti, Kalamáta, the Máni and Pátra – leave from the café directly oposite the **train station** at the eastern edge of town. If you need to spend a night, the E-class **hotel** *Kynouria* at Vassilísis Ólgas 79 (☎071/22 26 463; ②), is tolerable but well south of downtown, or there's a good C-class, *Hotel Alex*, at Vassiléos Yioryíou 26 (☎071/22 34 65; ③).

Spárti (Sparta)

Thucydides predicted that if Sparta were deserted, "distant ages would be very unwilling to believe its power at all equal to its fame". The city had no great temples or public buildings and during its period of greatness remained unfortified. Modern **SPÁRTI**, consequently, has few ruins to speak of, though descending through the hills into the Shangri-la fertility of the Evrótas valley you can sense how strategically located was the ancient city-state. Sparta was at the height of its powers from the eighth to the fourth century BC, the period when it established colonies around the Greek world, and a second period of prosperity came under the Romans – before decline set in as nearby Mystra became the focus of Byzantine interest.

Spárti is a good base for visiting Mystra, with a couple of cheaper **hotels** around the central square: D-class *Panhellinion* on Paleológou (☎0731/28 031; ②) and E-class *Kypros* at Leonidhíou 662 (☎0731/26 590; ②). The nearest **campsite**, 2.5km from Spárti, *Camping Mystra*, is pricy but has a swimming pool; closer to Mystra and less expensive is *Camping Castle View*. There are a couple of fair **restaurants** in Spárti: *Kali Kardia* at Ayissiláou 39, and a *psistariá* up at the north end of Stadhíou, just as it begins to bend into Tripoléos. The **main bus terminal** is on Vrassídhou, just off Stadhíou, but buses **for Mystra** leave from a stop on Leonidhíou Street, a block south of Likoúrgou.

Mistrás (Mystra)

A glorious, airy place, hugging a steep flank of Taíyettos, **MYSTRA** is arguably the most exciting site that the Peloponnese can offer – an astonishingly complete Byzantine city which once sheltered a population of some 42,000. The castle on its summit was built in 1249 by Guillaume II de Villehardouin, fourth Frankish Prince of the Morea, and together with the fortresses of Monemvassía and the Máni it guarded his territory. The Franks, however, were driven out in 1271 and an isolated triangle of land in the southeastern Peloponnese became the **Despotate of Mystra**, which through the fourteenth century and the first decades of the fifteenth was the principal cultural centre of the Byzantine world – before falling to the Turks in 1460, seven years after Constantinople.

The modern town, **Néos Mistrás**, is a small roadside community whose half-dozen tavernas are crowded with tour buses by day and revert to a low-key life at night. **Accommodation**, however, is limited to the *Hotel Byzantion* (☎0731/93-309; ④) and a small number of rooms in private houses; those of the Bakaviolos family (☎0731/93 432; ②) are especially recommended.

The Byzantine city

The site of the **Byzantine city** (summer Mon–Fri 8.30am–3pm, Sat & Sun 8am–7pm; winter Tues–Sun 8.30am–3pm; 1000dr) has two entrances on the road up from Néos Mistrás: it makes sense to take the bus to the top entrance, then explore a leisurely downhill route. Following this course, the first identifiable building that you come to is the church of **Ayía Sofía**, which served as the chapel for the Despots' Palace. The chapel's finest feature is its floor, made from polychrome marbles; its frescoes have also survived reasonably well, protected until recently by whitewash applied by the Turks, who adapted the building as a mosque. The **Kástro**, reached by a path that climbs directly from the upper gate, maintains the Frankish design of its thirteenth-century construction, though it was repaired and modified by all successive occupants.

Heading down from Ayía Sofía, there is a choice of routes. The right fork winds past the ruins of a Byzantine mansion, the **Palatáki** or "Small Palace", and **Áyios Nikólaos**, originally a Turkish building. The left fork is more interesting, passing the massively fortified **Náfplio Gate**, which was the principal entrance to the upper town, and the vast, multistoreyed complex of the **Despots' Palace**, parts of whose Gothic structures probably date to the Franks.

At the **Monemvassía Gate**, linking the upper and lower towns, go right for the **Pantánassa convent**, whose nuns were the only people allowed to stay among the ruins after the village was evacuated in 1952. The church, whose name means "Queen of All", is perhaps the finest that survives in the town, a perfectly proportioned blend of Byzantine and Gothic. Its frescoes date from various centuries, with some superb fifteenth-century work including **Scenes from the Life of Christ** in the gallery.

Farther down on this side of the lower town stands the **House of Frangopoulos**, once the home of the Despotate's chief minister. Beyond it is the diminutive **Perívleptos monastery**, whose single-domed church, partly carved out of the rock, contains Mystra's most complete cycle of frescoes, almost all of which date from the fourteenth century. Along the path leading from Perívleptos to the lower gate are a couple of minor, much-restored churches, and, just above them, the **Laskaris House**, a mansion thought to have belonged to relatives of the emperors. The **Mitrópolis**, or cathedral, immediately beyond the gateway, ranks as the oldest of Mystra's churches, built in 1309. A marble slab set in its floor is carved with the double-headed eagle of Byzantium, commemorating the spot where Constantine XI Paleologus, the last emperor, was crowned in 1448. The frescoes in the north aisle are the earliest, their comparative stiffness contrasting with the later works opposite, which date from the last great years before Mystra's fall.

Finally, a short way uphill, lies the **Vrontohión monastery**, the centre of intellectual life in the fifteenth-century town, serving as the burial place of the despots as well. There are a couple of churches attached: **Afendikó**, the farther of the two, has been beautifully restored, revealing frescoes with startlingly bold juxtapositions of colour.

Monemvassía

Set impregnably on a great eruption of rock connected to the mainland by a kilometre-long causeway, the Byzantine seaport of **MONEMVASSÍA** is a place of grand, haunted atmosphere. At the outset of the thirteenth century it was the Byzantines' sole possession in the Morea, eventually being taken by the Franks in 1249, after three years of siege. Regained by the Byzantines as part of the ransom for the captured Guillaume de Villehardouin, it served as the chief commercial port of the Despotate of the Morea. Mystra, despite the presence of the court, was never much more than a large village; Monemvassía at its peak had a population of almost 60,000.

Monemvassía can be approached by road or, more enjoyably, by sea. There is a weekly **ferry** from Pireás, and Kastélli on Crete, and more or less daily **hydrofoils** in season, linking it to the north with Leonídhi, Spétses and Pireás, to the south with Neápoli and the island of Kíthira. Buses connect with Spárti three times daily and with Yíthio twice daily in season only. The boat or hydrofoil will drop you midway down the causeway; buses arrive in the town of **YÉFIRA** on the mainland, where most accommodation is found. By the causeway there are a couple of reasonable **hotels** – *Akroyiali* (☎0732/61 202; ②) and *Aktaion* (☎0732/61 234; ②) – plus numerous pensions and **rooms**. The nearest **campsite**, *Camping Paradise*, is 3.5km south of Yéfira near a good beach. Rooms on the rock are a lot more expensive (④ and up) and in short supply.

The **Lower Town** once sheltered forty churches and over 800 homes, an incredible mass of building threaded by an intricate network of alleys. A single main street harbours most of the restored houses, plus a café, tavernas and a scattering of shops, adding much-needed life to the rock. The foremost building is the **Mitrópolis**, the cathedral built by Emperor Andronicus II Comnenus in 1293, and the largest medieval church in southern Greece. Across the square, the domed church of **Áyios Pávlos** was transformed by the Turks into a mosque and is now a small museum of local finds. Towards the sea is a third church, the **Hrissafítissa**, with its bell hanging from an old cypress tree in the courtyard. It was restored and adapted by the Venetians in the eighteenth century, when for twenty-odd years they took the Peloponnese from the Turks.

The climb to the **Upper Town** is highly worthwhile, not least for the solitude. Its fortifications, like those of the lower town, are substantially intact; within, the site is a ruin, though infinitely larger than you could imagine from below. Close to the gateway is the beautiful thirteenth-century **Ayía Sofía**, the only fully intact building. Beyond the church extend acres of ruins: the stumpy bases of Byzantine houses and public buildings, and, perhaps most striking, a vast **cistern** to ensure water in time of siege.

Yíthio and the Máni

YÍTHIO, Sparta's ancient port, is gateway to the dramatic **Máni peninsula** and one of the south's most attractive seaside towns. Its somewhat low-key harbour, with intermittent ferries or hydrofoils to Pireás, Kíthira and Crete, gives on to a graceful nineteenth-century waterside – the town has as many romantic associations as any in Greece. Out to sea, tethered by a long narrow mole, is the islet of **Marathónissi** (ancient Kranae) where Paris and Helen of Troy spent their first night after her abduction from Sparta.Buses drop you close to the centre of town and finding a **room** should be a matter of a stroll along the waterside. Just off the main square in Vassiléos Pávlou there's the D-class *Kranae* at no. 15 (☎0733/22 249; ③) and the C-class *Pantheon* at no. 33 (☎0733/22 284; ③). Four- or five-room establishments huddle by the port police; others are up the steps from the waterside and, cheapest of all, west along the seafront. If you want to **camp**, there are a couple of official summer sites at Mavrovoúni beach, which begins 3km south off the Areópoli road. For **eating**, *Petakos*, tucked against the sports stadium at the north end of town, or *Kostas*, by the bus station, tend to work out better than the obviously touristy fish tavernas on the quay.

The Máni

The southernmost peninsula of Greece, **the Máni**, stretches from Yíthio in the east and Kalamáta in the west down to Cape Ténaro, one mythical entrance to the underworld. It is a wild and arid landscape with an idiosyncratic culture and history: nowhere in Greece does a region seem so close to its medieval past. The quickest way into it is to take a bus from Yíthio to **AREÓPOLI**, gateway to the so-called Deep Máni. **Rooms** are advertised at a number of ordinary houses, mostly grouped around the cathedral; or there's *Pension Kouris* in the main square (☎0733/51 307; ③). Taxis can be hired fairly easily here, and there are daily buses south to Yerolimín in summer (three weekly out of season). More regular buses north to Khardhamíli and Kalamáta sometimes involve a change at Ítilo, 9km north.

SOUTH FROM AREÓPOLI

From Areópoli it is 8km to the village of **PÍRGOS DHIROÚ**, where the road forks off to the famed **caves**, 4km further on (daily summer 8am–6pm; winter 8am–3pm; 1500dr). They are very much a packaged attraction, with long queues for admission, but it's worthwhile for the punt around the underground waterways of the **Glifádha caves** and the tour on foot of the huge **Alepótripa caves**, where recent excavation has unearthed evidence of prehistoric occupation.

　　YEROLIMÍN has an end-of-the-world air, but despite appearances was only developed in the 1870s. There are a few shops, a couple of cafés and two very simple E-class **hotels**: the *Akroyali* (☎0733/54-204; ②) has the better restaurant, the *Akrotenaritis* (☎0733/54-205; ②) has slightly cheaper rooms. At the dock occasional boat trips are offered around Cape Ténaro, passing the pebbly bay of Asomatíi, where a small **cave** is said to be the mythical gate to Hades.

NORTH FROM AREÓPOLI

The eighty kilometres or so of road between Areópoli and Kalamáta is as dramatic and beautiful as any in Greece, a virtual corniche between Mount Taíyettos and the Gulf of Messinía. The beaches begin at **ÁYIOS NIKÓLAOS**, which has a few roadside rooms and tavernas, and extend more or less continuously through to Kardhamíli. **STOÚPA**, which has possibly the best sands, is now geared very much to tourism, with numerous **rooms** to let, several small hotels (cheapest is the C-class *Stoupa*; ☎0721/54 308; ②), a **campsite** five minutes' walk from Kalógria beach, a supermarket (which will change money and cheques) and a fair number of tavernas. **KARDHAMÍLI**, 10km north, remains a beautiful place despite its commercialization, with a long pebble beach and a ruined old tower-house quarter. Besides its ranks of pre-booked self-catering apartments, there's the *Kardamyli Beach* (☎0721/73 180; ③) hotel; **eating** is best at *Kiki's* or *Lela's* (☎0721/73 541; ③), which also has some rooms.

Kalamáta

KALAMÁTA is the largest city of the southern Peloponnese, with a long-established export trade in olives and figs and, until recently, a prospering industrial base. In 1986, however, the city was near the epicentre of a severe earthquake which killed twenty people, left 12,000 families homeless and caused 40 billion drachmas worth of damage.

Kalamáta today is not a place to linger. If you can, get transport straight through; if not, arrive early to make connections. The most regular buses run north to Megalópoli/ Trípoli and south to Koróni; the magnificent route ·over the Taíyettos to Spárti, is covered twice a day; the run to Areópoli, four times daily. Trains leave Kalamáta four times daily along the slow but enjoyable route to Kiparissía (and ultimately to Olympia) or three a day inland to Trípoli and Árgos. If you're staying, there are few central **hotels**; best value is *Galaxias* at Kolokotróni 14 (☎0721/86 002; ④). In general you'll do better down by the waterside, 3km from the centre (bus #1), where there are two places on Santarósa street: *Hotel Nevada* (☎0721/82 429; ③) and *Pension Avra* (☎0721/82 759; ③), plus the *Plaza* at nearby Navarínou 17 (③). This area has some of Kalamáta's best **eating**: *Zesti Gonia* on Satarósa, and *Meltemi* and *Akroyiali* on Navarínou.

Koróni and Methóni

At the end of the Messenian peninsula sprawling southwest of Kalamáta, **KORÓNI** and **METHÓNI** were the Venetians' longest-held possessions on the Peloponnese; today their castles shelter two attractive small resorts. Buses serve both places from Kalamáta, with a change at Pílos for Methóni, but they're linked directly only by the occasional bus in summer.Koróni's castle accents rather than dwarfs the picturesque town of tiled and pastel-painted houses spilling down to the harbour in a maze of stair-and-ramp streets. It is not undiscovered, though, the Germans having arrived in force in the 1980s, but outside summer – and the season is very long this far south – it is still a delightful place. On the opposite side of the castle from the town stretches two-kilometre **Zánga beach**. Most visitors stay in **rooms**; there are only two budget **hotels**, the *Flisvos* (☎0725/22 238; ②) and the *Diana* (☎0725/22 312; ②).

By contrast, the fortress at Methóni (Tues–Sun 8.30am–3pm; 400dr) is as imposing as they come: massively bastioned, washed on three sides by the sea, and cut off on the land side by a great moat. The village itself, dedicated more specifically to tourism than Methóni, isn't so appealing, but **accommodation** is at least reasonably priced and fairly abundant. Among less expensive hotels, *Iliodyssio* (☎0723/31 225; ③), near the moat, and *Rex* (☎0723/31 239; ③) on the beach are good choices. Behind the flat, hard-packed beach, devoted mostly to windsurfing, there's an official **campsite** (April–Oct).

Olimbía (Olympia)

The historic resonance of **OLYMPIA**, which for over a millennium hosted the Panhellenic games, is rivalled only by Delphi or Mycenae. Its site, too, ranks with this company, for although the ruins are confusing, the setting is as perfect as could be imagined: a luxuriant valley of wild olive and plane trees, beside the twin rivers of Alfiós and Kládhios, and overlooked by the pine-covered hill of Krónos. Most people arrive at Olympia **via Pírgos**, which in addition to five daily trains has sixteen bus services to the site, plus numerous buses to Pátra and a couple daily to Kalamáta/Kiparissía.

Modern **OLIMBÍA** has grown up simply to serve the excavations and tourist trade. If you're travelling alone, the **youth hostel** on the main street at Kondhíli 18 (☎0624/ 22 580; ②) is the cheapest option; between two people, **rooms** in private houses can be better value – most are signposted on the road parallel to and above Kondhíli. Among **hotels**, the cheapest is generally the D-class *Heraeum*, Kondhíli 39 (☎0624/22 539; ②) In the same price range, the pensions *Possidon* (☎0624/22 567; ②) and *Achilles* (☎0624/22 931; ②), both on Stefanoloúlou Street, are worth noting. The closest **campsite**, *Diana*, has a pool and good facilities, just off the main road. For **eating**, most of the tavernas offer standard tourist meals at mildly inflated prices; honorable exceaptions include the *Praxitelis*, a grill on Spiliopoúlou, and the *Kladeos*, an authentic taverna near the river.

The Site

The contests at Olympia probably began around the eleventh century BC, slowly developing over the next two centuries from a local festival to a major quadrennial celebration attended by states from throughout the Greek world. From the very beginning, the main **Olympic events** were athletic, but the great gathering of people expanded the games' importance: nobles and ambassadors negotiated treaties here, while merchants chased contacts, and sculptors and poets sought commissions. The games' eventual **closure** happened as a result of religious dogma rather than lack of support. In 393 AD the Emperor Theodosius, newly converted to Christianity, suspended the games as part of a general crackdown on pagan festivities. Theodosius' successor ordered the destruction of the temples, a process completed by barbarian invasion, earthquakes and, lastly, by the river Alfiós changing its course to cover the sanctuary site. There it remained, covered by seven metres of silt and sand, until the 1870s.

The entrance to the **ancient site** (summer Mon–Fri 8am–5pm, Sat & Sun 8am–7pm; winter Sat & Sun 8.30am–3pm; 1000dr) leads along the west side of the sacred precinct wall, past a group of public and official buildings, including a structure adapted as a Byzantine church. This was originally the studio of Pheidias, the fifth-century BC sculptor responsible for the great cult statue in the focus of the precinct, the great Doric **Temple of Zeus**. Built between 470 and 456 BC, it was as large as the Parthenon and its decoration rivalled the finest in Athens – partly recovered, its sculptures are now exhibited in the museum. In the *cella* was displayed the great gold and ivory cult statue by Pheidias, one of the Seven Wonders of the Ancient World. Here, too, the Olympian flame was kept alight, from the time of the games until the following spring – a tradition continued at an altar for the modern games. The smaller **Temple of Hera**, behind, was the first built here; prior to its completion in the seventh century BC, the sanctuary had only open-air altars, dedicated to Zeus and a variety of other cult gods. Rebuilt in the Doric style in the sixth century BC, it's the most complete structure on the site. Finally, though, what makes sense of Olympia is the 200-metre track of the **Stadium** itself. The start and finish lines are still there, as are the judges' thrones in the middle and seating banked to each side. The tiers here eventually accommodated up to 20,000 spectators, with a smaller number on the southern slope overlooking the **Hippodrome** where chariot races were held.

In Olympia's **museum** (summer Mon 11am–5pm, Tues–Fri 8am–5pm, Sat & Sun 8am–7pm; winter Sat & Sun 8.30am–3pm; 1000dr), a couple of hundred metres north, the centrepiece is the statuary from the Temple of Zeus, displayed in the vast main hall. Most famous of the individual sculptures is the **Hermes of Praxiteles**, dating from the fourth century BC; one of the best-preserved of all Classical sculptures, it retains traces of its original paint. The best of the smaller objects, housed in Room 4, include several fine bronzes, among them the **helmet of Miltiades**, the Athenian general at the Battle of Marathon, and a superb terracotta group of *Zeus Abducting Ganymede*.

Pátra (Patras)

PÁTRA is the largest town in the Peloponnese and, after Pireás, the major port of Greece. You can go from here to Italy and Cyprus, as well as to the Ionian islands and Crete, and the city is a key to the transport network of the mainland too. It's not the ideal holiday retreat: there are no beaches, no particular sights, the hotels are positioned on noisy streets and the restaurants are generally fairly wretched. Unless you arrive late in the day from Italy, you shouldn't need to spend more than a few hours in the city. If you do need to stay, the main concentration of low-budget **hotels** is on Ayíou Andhréou, a block back from Óthonos Keh Amalías. The cheapest is the D-class *Delphi* at no. 63 (☎061/273 050; ②), followed by the *Theoxenia* at no. 97

(☎061/222 962; ②). The main low-budget alternative to these is the **youth hostel** at Iróön Politehníou 68 (☎061/427 278; ②), a kilometre-plus walk south from the ferry terminal. **Eating** out, shun the obvious in favour of *Krini*, Pandokrátoros 57, for lunch, or *Psari* at Ayíou Dhimitríou 75 at suppertime, both well inland behind Platía Ikosipémptis Martíou.

Innumerable agents along the harbour road, Óthonos Keh Amalías, sell different **ferry** tickets to Italy. En route to Italy it is possible to make stopovers on Kefalloniá, Páxi and, most commonly, Igoumenítsa or Corfu. Individual tickets to any of these islands are also available. The **EOT** office, by the customs house at the harbour, can be helpful for information. For **money exchange**, the *National Bank of Greece*, just back from the waterside, keeps special evening hours (5.30–8pm).

The main **bus** station, midway along the waterside, has services to Athens, Killíni, Pírgos and other towns in the Peloponnese, as well as to Ioánnina. Heading to **Delphi**, take local bus #6 (from Kandakári, five blocks back from the waterside) to the Río-Andírio ferry, cross over and take another local bus to Náfpaktos and then a regular bus from there. Finally, you can reach Kórinthos in two hours by bus or half an hour longer on the frequent **trains**.

CENTRAL AND NORTHERN GREECE

Central Greece has a slightly indeterminate character: vast agricultural plains occupy much of the land, dotted with rather drab market and industrial towns. For most visitors it's an area full of highlights – **Delphi** above all, and farther to the north the unworldly rock-monasteries of the **Metéora**. Access to these monasteries is from **Kalambáka**, from where the **Katára pass** over the Píndhos mountains brings you into **Epirus** (Ípiros), the region with the strongest identity in mainland Greece. En route is **Métsovo**, perhaps the easiest location for a taste of mountain life, though becoming increasingly commercialized. Nearby **Ioánnina**, once the capital of Ali Pasha, is a town of some character, and the main transport hub for trips into the unspoilt villages of the **Zagóri** and the **Víkos gorge**. The rugged peaks, forested ravines and turbulent rivers of the Píndhos helped to protect Epirus and keep it isolated from outside influence and interference, securing it a large measure of autonomy even under Turkish rule. Because of this isolation the region's role in Greek affairs was peripheral in ancient times, so there are few archeological sites of importance: the main one is at **Dodona**, where the sanctuary includes a spectacular Classical theatre. The Epirus coast is in general disappointing: **Igoumenítsa** is a useful ferry terminal but will win few admirers, while **Párga**, the region's major resort, has been developed beyond its capacity.

The northern provinces of **Macedonia** and **Thrace** have been part of the Greek state for little more than two generations. As such, the region stands slightly apart from the rest of the nation – an impression reinforced for visitors by scenery and climate that are essentially Balkan. Macedonia is characterized by lake-speckled vistas to the west, and, to the east, moving towards Thrace, by heavily cultivated flood plains and the deltas of rivers finishing courses begun in the former Yugoslavia or Bulgaria.

The only areas to draw more than a scattering of summer visitors are **Halkidhikí** – which provides the city's beach-playground and shelters the "Monks' Republic" of Mount Áthos – and **Mount Olympus**. With a more prolonged acquaintance, the north may well grow on you. Part of its appeal lies in its vigorous day-to-day life, independent of tourism – most evident in the relaxed Macedonian capital of **Thessaloníki** and its chief port **Kavála**.

Delphi

Access to the extraordinary site of **DELPHI**, 150km northwest of Athens, is straight-forward: several buses run there from the capital daily, and services are as frequent from Livádhia, the nearest rail terminus. With its site raised on the slopes of a high mountain terrace and dwarfed by the ominous crags of Parnassós, it's easy to see why the ancients believed this to be the centre of the earth. But what confirmed its exalted status was the discovery of a rock chasm which exuded strange vapours and reduced all comers to frenzied, incoherent and prophetic mutterings. The first **oracle** estab-lished on this spot was dedicated to Gea (Mother Earth) and to Poseidon, but they were later displaced by Apollo, whose cult had been imported from Crete – legend has it that he arrived in the form of a dolphin, hence the name *Delphoi*. For over a thousand years a steady stream of pilgrims worked their way up the dangerous mountain paths to seek divine direction in matters of war, worship, love or business. The influence of the oracle spread abroad with the age of Classical colonization, reaching a peak in the sixth century BC, when it attracted powerful benefactors such as Amasis, King of Egypt, and King Croesus of Lydia. The Temple of Apollo was elaborately rebuilt in 548 BC, and the Pythian Games (named after Python, son of Gea) become one of the four great Panhellenic festivals. It was only in the fourth century AD, with the demise of paganism under Constantine and Theodosius, that the oracle became defunct.

The modern village of **DHELFÍ**, like most Greek site villages, has a quick turna-round of visitors, so finding a place to stay should present few problems. There are upwards of thirty hotels and pensions, various rooms to let, and an excellent **youth hostel** at Appollónou 29 (closed Dec–Feb; ☎0265/82 268; ①). Best value of the **pensions** are *Maniatis* at Issáia 2 (☎0265/82 134; ②) and the *Odysseus* at Fillelínon 1 (☎0265/82 235; ②). The nearest official **campsite** is the *Apollon*, 1500m west towards Ámfissa. **Eating** is best at *Taverna Vakhos*, next to the youth hostel – incredibly cheap and tasty, but only open from May to September. Otherwise, try the *Arahova Psistariá* opposite *Hotel Pan* at the west end of town, or *Stammatis* 200m further out.

The Site

The **Sacred Precinct** of Apollo (summer Mon 12.30–7pm, Tues–Fri 8am–7pm, Sat & Sun 8.30am–3pm; winter closes 5pm weekdays; 1000dr) is entered by way of a small **Agora**, enclosed by ruins of Roman porticoes and shops for the sale of votive offerings. The paved **Sacred Way** begins after a few stairs and zigzags uphill between the foun-dations of memorials and treasuries to the **Temple of Apollo**. Of the main body of the temple only the foundations stood when it was uncovered by the French in the 1890s; they have, however, re-erected six Doric columns, giving a vertical line to the ruins and providing some idea of its former dominance over the sanctuary. In the innermost part of the temple was a dark cell where the priestess of the oracle would officiate; no sign of cave or chasm has been found, but it is likely that it was closed by earthquakes. The theatre and stadium used for the main events of the Pythian games are on terraces above the temple. The **Theatre**, built in the fourth century BC with a capacity of 5000, was closely connected with Dionysus, god of the arts and wine, who reigned in Delphi over the winter months when the oracle was silent. A steep path leads up through cool pine groves to the **Stadium**, which was banked with stone seats only in Roman times – the gift, like so many other public buildings in Greece, of Herodes Atticus.

Delphi's **museum** (summer Mon 12.30–7pm, Tues–Fri 8am–7pm, Sat & Sun 8.30am–3pm; winter closes 5pm weedays; 1000dr) contains a collection of archaic sculpture, matched only by finds on the Acropolis. Its most famous exhibit is the *Charioteer*, one of the few surviving bronzes of the fifth century BC. The charioteer's eyes, made of onyx and set slightly askew, lend it a startling realism while the demure expression sets the scene as a victory lap. Other major pieces include two huge *kouroi* (archaic male figures) from the sixth century BC, large chunks of the beautifully carved Syphnian frieze, and the Hall of the Monument of Daochos, dominated by a group of three colossal dancing women.

Following the road east of the sanctuary towards Aráhova, you reach a sharp bend. To the left, marked by niches for votive offerings and the remains of an archaic fountain house, the celebrated **Castalian spring** still flows from a cleft in the cliffs, which are swathed in scaffolding to prevent collapse. Visitors to Delphi were obliged to purify themselves in its waters, usually by washing their hair, though murderers had to take the full plunge. Across and below the road from the spring is the **Marmaria** or Sanctuary of Athena (summer Mon 12.30–7pm, Tues–Fri 8am–7pm, Sat & Sun 8.30am–3pm; winter closes 5pm weekdays; free), worshipped by Delphians as the "Guardian of the Temple". The precinct's most conspicuous building is the Tholos, a fourth-century BC rotunda whose purpose is a mystery. Outside the precinct on the northwest side, above the Marmaria, is a **Gymnasium**, also built in the fourth century BC but later enlarged by the Romans, who added a running track on the now collapsed terrace.

Lamía and Vólos

LAMÍA is a busy provincial capital and an important transport junction, so you might have to stay here if you miss a connection. All **buses** – including the service from the **train** station (6km out) – arrive in the southeast quarter of the town, and most of the **hotels** are nearby. There's a pair of the cheapest places on Rozáki-Ángeli: *Thermopylae* at no. 36 (☎0231/28 840; ②) and *Athina* at no. 41 (☎0231/20 700; ②). The town's social hub is Platía Eleftherías, full of outdoor cafés and **restaurants**; a number of very cheap pasta-and-chicken restaurants can be found below Eleftherías in the vicinity of tree-shaded Platía Laoú, site of more inexpensive hotels.

Southeast of Lárissa, **VÓLOS** is Greece's fastest-growing industrial city and is not a pretty sight: a modern, concrete sprawl, rebuilt after an earthquake in 1955 and now edging to its natural limits against the Pílion foothills. That said, you may well be spending some time here, as Vólos is the gateway to the Pílion and the main **port for the northern Sporades**. Ferries leave two to four times daily for Skiáthos and Skópelos, with at least one continuing to Alónissos; hydrofoils run two to three times daily to all three, occasionally proceeding to Skíros. **Hotels** are fairly plentiful with a concentration of inexpensive places in the grid of streets behind the port. *Iason*, Pávlou Melá 1 (☎0421/26 075; ②), is about as basic as you'd want, while the nearby *Aura*, Sólonos 6 (☎0421/25 970; ③), is a bit more savoury. Two restaurants near the ferry jetty – *Ouzeri Dhelfini* – on Argonáfron 37 and *Vangelis* at K. Kortáli 4 – are recommended. If you've time to spare, the **Archeological Museum** (Tues–Sun 8.30am–6pm; 3400dr) at the east end of the waterfront has arguably the best collection of Neolithic artefacts in Europe.

The Pílion

There is something decidedly un-Greek about the **Pílion Peninsula**, with its lush fruit orchards and dense broadleaf forests. Water gurgles from crevices beside every road, and summers are a good deal cooler than the rest of central Greece. Pílion villages are idiosyncratic too, sprawling affairs due to the abundant water, with sumptuous mansions and barn-like churches lining their cobbled streets. Add to the scenery and architecture a half-dozen or so excellent beaches, and equidistance from Athens and Thessaloníki, and it's no wonder that this is a well-loved corner of Greece — especially by Greeks; avoid July and August unless you wish to camp out.

The most visited part of the peninsula lies just north and east of Vólos, with bus services biased towards the twenty-odd villages here. If your time is limited, the best single targets are the EOT-recognized showcases of Makrinítsa and Vizítsa. **MAKRINÍTSA** is becoming a bit overquaint, with expensive lodging in a bevy of restored mansions, though frequent connections to Vólos make day trips easy. Remoter **VIZÍTSA** has equally good connections, with better possibilities of **staying and eating** cheaply — try *Kalliroi Dhimou* (☎423/86 484; ③) and the taverna *O Yiorgaras*. Alternatively, the less homogeneous village of **MILIÉS**, 3km east, also has some accommodation and, down by the bus stop, the best bakery on the peninsula, cranking out every sort of pie, pasty and bread imaginable.

The largest village on the Pílion — virtually a small town — is **ZAGORÁ**, destination of fairly regular buses across the peninsula's summit. Unlike its seashore neighbours, it has a life independent of tourism, and is more appealing than first impressions suggest. You're also more likely to find a **room** here in season than down at **HOREFTÓ**, 8km below, though you can try there at the **hotels** *Votsala* (☎0426/22 001; ③) and *Erato* (☎0426/22 445; ③). There's also a good **campsite** at the south end of the main beach here; more coves beckon north of the resort.

Just before Zagorá, a junction funnels traffic southeast to **TSANGARÁDHA**, also the terminus of two daily buses from Miliés. Though nearly as large as Zagorá, it may not seem so, divided as it is into four distinct quarters along several kilometres of road. In the typical Pílion fashion, each is grouped arond a parish church and tree-shaded platía. Reasonable **rooms** are difficult to come by, though you might start at *Villa ton Rodhon* (☎0426/49 340; ③) in Ayía Paraskeví. **Eating out** is frankly uninviting; most people do so at **MOÚRESSI**, a few kilometres north, where two adjacent **tavernas** dish out Pílion specialties at fairly moderate prices. **KISSÓS**, still further towards Zagorá, is another possibility for staying and dining, with its excellent *Ksenonas Kissos* (☎0426/31 214; ③).

Most visitors, however, stay at one of several nearby beaches, the best on this shore of the peninsula. **ÁYIOS IOÁNNIS**, 6km below Kissós, is an overblown resort with sixteen hotels — most reasonable the *Armonia* (0426/31 242; ③), also with a good restaurant — and double that number of rooms establishments. If it's too busy for your tastes, head south along the sand, past its crowded campsite, to **Papaneró** beach or further still to postcard-perfect **DAMOÚHORI** with its tiny ruined castle and fishing anchorage as appetizer for a large pebble beach. The area's most scenic beach must be **Milopótamos**, reached by a winding seven-kilometre road from the south end of Tsangarádha; here a pair of pebble coves separated by a naturally tunneled monolith attract large but generally genial, multinational summer crowds.

Lárissa and Trikala

LÁRISSA stands at the heart of the Thessalian plain, a large market centre aproached across a dull landscape of wheat and corn fields. It is for the most part modern and unremarkable, but retains a few old streets which hint at its recent past as a Turkish provincial capital. As another large **road and rail junction**, the town has efficient connections with most places you'd want to reach: Vólos to the east; Tríkala and Kalambáka to the west; and Lamía to the south. Should you need to stay in Lárissa, there are numerous **hotels**. Cheapest are the three places in the square by the train station, 1km from the centre: *Diethnes* (☎041/234-210; ②), *Neon* (☎041/236-268; ②) and *Pantheon* (☎041/236 726; ②).

West from Lárissa, five daily buses follow the Piniós river to **TRÍKALA**, where you may need to change buses for Kalambáka and the Metéora. The railway makes a similar number of connections between Lárissa and Tríkala, though it loops around to the south through Kardhítsa. A lively metropolis after the agricultural plains towns of central

Thessaly, Trídkala was a centre for the nineteenth-century Turkish province and retains many of the era's houses. Downstream from the bus station, a Turkish mosque survives, too, graceful accompaniment to the town's stone churches. Around the **Fortress**, adapted by the Turks from a Byzantine structure, are some attractive gardens and the meagre remains of a **Sanctuary of Asclepius**. The cult of the healing god is, by some accounts, said to have originated here. The liveliest part of town, with numerous cafés and restaurants, is around Platía Iróön Politehníou on the riverside. Accommodation should pose few problems, with two decent budget **hotels** near the square: the E-class *Panhellinion* at Vassilísis Ólgas 2 (☎0431/27 644; ②) and the more comfortable C-class *Palladion* at Víronos 4 (☎0431/28 091; ②). Strangely, bona fide **tavernas** are scarce; good lunches can be had at *O Elatos*, corner Víronos and Asklipíou.

Kalambáka and the Metéora

There are few more exciting places to arrive at than **KALAMBÁKA**. The shabby town itself you hardly notice, for the eye is immediately drawn up in an unremitting vertical ascent to the weird grey cylinders of rock overhead. These are the outlying monoliths of the extraordinary valley of the **Metéora**. To the right you can make out the monastery of Áyios Stéfanos, firmly entrenched on a massive pedestal; beyond stretches a chaotic confusion of spikes, cones and cliffs, beaten into bizarre shapes by the action of the sea that covered the Plain of Thessaly around fifty million years ago.

The earliest religious communities in the valley emerged in the late tenth century, when hermits made their homes in the caves that score many of the rocks. In 1336 they were joined by two monks from Mount Áthos, one of whom – Athanassios – established the first monastery here. Today, put firmly on the map by appearances in such films as James Bond's *For Your Eyes Only*, the four most accessible monasteries are essentially museums. Only two, Ayía Triádha and Áyios Stéfanos, continue to function with any real monastic purpose.

Visiting the Metéora demands a full day, which means staying at least one night at Kalambáka or at the village of Kastráki, right in the shadow of the rocks. Kalambáka is a characterless but pleasant enough base, with a fairly plentiful supply of rooms. Arriving by bus or train, in season, you are likely to be offered a **room** by waiting householders; if not, there are numerous signs on the road into town from the bus station. **Hotels** are pricier, with above-usual rates. Try the C-class *Odyssion* on Kastrakioú (☎0432/22 320; ③) or the *Olympion*, Trikálon 97 (☎0432/22 792; ③).

KASTRÁKI is twenty minutes' walk out of Kalambáka. Along the way you pass the busy *Camping Vrahos*, the first of two **campsites** here; the other one, *Boufiohis*, is smaller but quieter and incomparably set under the pinnacles. The village also has a fair number of **private rooms**, as well as an extremely dilapidated E-class **hotel**, the *Kastraki* (☎0342/22 286; ②).

The Monasteries

If you want to see all the Metéora monasteries in a day, start early to take in Áyios Nikólaos, Varlaám and Méga Metéoron before 1pm (when they close for a few hours), leaving the rest of the day for the ten-kilometre walk from Kastráki to Áyios Stéfanos. Each monastery levies an admission charge of 200dr and operates a strict **dress code**: skirts for women, long trousers for men and covered arms for both sexes.

From Kastráki the road loops around between huge outcrops of rock, passing below the chapel-hermitage of **Doúpiani** before reaching a track to the left, which winds up a low rock to **Áyiou Nikólaou**. A small, recently restored monastery, this has some superb sixteenth-century frescoes in its *katholikón* (main chapel). Next to it on a needle-thin shaft is **Ayía Moní**, ruined and empty since an earthquake in 1858. Bearing off to the right, fifteen minutes or so further on, a trio of well-signed cobbled paths lead to the tiny, compact convent of **Roussánou** (or Ayía Varvára), approached across dizzying bridges from an adjacent rock. This has perhaps the most extraordinary site of all the monasteries, its walls built right on the edge of a sharp blade of rock. Its frescoes, particularly bloody scenes of martyrdom and judgement, were painted in 1660.

A short way beyond Roussánou the road divides, the left fork heading toward **Varlaám** (closed Fri), one of the oldest and most beautiful monasteries in the valley. The *katholikón* is small but glorious, supported by painted beams and with walls and pillars totally covered in frescoes. Varlaám also retains its old **Ascent Tower**: until the 1920s the only way of reaching the monasteries was by being hauled up in a net drawn by rope and windlass, or by the equally perilous retractable ladders. From Varlaám a path cuts north to **Méga Metéoron** (closed Tues). This is the grandest of the monasteries and also the highest, built 550m above the surrounding ground. Its *katholikón* is the most magnificent, a beautiful cross-in-square church surmounted by a lofty dome.

It's just under an hour's walk from here to **Ayía Triádhas** (Holy Trinity), approached up 130 steps carved into a tunnel in the rock. Although Ayía Triádha teeters above a deep ravine and its little garden ends in a precipitous drop, there is a trail at the bottom of the monastery's steps back to Kalambáka. This is about 3km long and well marked, saving a long trudge back around the circuit. **Áyios Stéfanou** (closed Mon), the last and easternmost of the monasteries, is a further twenty minutes' walk from Ayía Triádha – if you're pushed for time it's the obvious one to leave out.

The Katára pass: Kalambáka to Ioánnina

West of Kalambáka, the **Katára pass** cuts across the central range of the Píndhos to link Thessaly and Epirus. The route is one of the most spectacular in the country, and is covered by two buses daily between Tríkala and Ioánnina.

Métsovo

MÉTSOVO stands almost astride the Katára pass, a high mountain village built on two sides of a ravine and encircled by a mighty range of peaks. It is a startling site, matched by the village's traditional architecture and lifestyle – even if its popularity with the coach parties has fostered souvenir shops selling "traditional" handicrafts, some of them imported from Albania. From below the main road, the eighteenth- and nineteenth-century stone houses, with their wooden balconies and tile roofs, wind down the ravine to the main *platía*, where the old men and women loiter, magnificent in full traditional dress. The town museum occupies the **Arhondíko Tossítsas** (tours daily except Thurs 8.30am–1pm & 4–6pm; 200dr), a mansion restored to the full glory of its eighteenth-century past, with panelled rooms, rugs and a fine collection of crafts and costumes. The affiliated *Ídhrima Tositsa* down by the square also serves as a handicrafts centre, stocking what must be the most finely woven cloth, rugs and blankets in Greece – in a different class to the standard goods in the village shops.

Métsovo has quite a range of **accommodation**, and outside of the ski season or July 26, you should find little problem in getting a room. The cheapest are at the *Athinae* (☎0656/41 217; ②), near the main square, and the excellent *Acropolis* (☎0656/41 672; ②), at the top end of town, to the right of the road down from the Kalambáka-Ioánnina road. For **eating**, try *O Kostas*, under the **post office**, or the diner of the *Athinae*.

Ioánnina and around

Coming from Métsovo, you approach **IOÁNNINA** through more spectacular folds of the Píndhos mountains, emerging high above the great lake of Pamvótis. The town, once the capital of Ali Pasha, stands upon its southern edge, a rocky promontory jutting out into the water, its fortifications punctuated by towers and minarets as if to declare its history. From this base Ali, "the Lion of Ioannina", carved from the Turks a kingdom encompassing much of western Greece, an act of rebellion that portended wider defiance in the Greeks' own War of Independence.

Disappointingly, most of the city is modern and undistinguished – a testimony not so much to Ali, who burnt much of it to the ground when under siege in 1820, as to the developers of the 1950s. However, the fortifications of his citadel, the **Froúrio**, survive more or less intact, and this is an obvious point to stroll towards. Once within, signs direct you to the **Popular Art Museum** (daily 8am–3pm; 300dr), a splendidly ramshackle collection of costumes and jewellery. The museum is housed in the well-preserved Mosque of Aslan Pasha, allowing a rare glimpse in Greece of the interior of a mosque. East of Aslan Pasha sprawls the **inner citadel** of the fortress. This was used for some years by the Greek military and most of its buildings – which include Ali's palace, where Byron was entertained – have been adapted or restored past recognition.

Apart from the Froúrio, the most enjoyable quarter is the old **bazaar** area, outside the citadel's gate. This has a cluster of Turkish-era buildings, as well as a scattering of copper and silversmiths, once a mainstay of the town's economy. The heart of town lies just south of the bazaar, grouped about the central platías of Pírrou, Akaohimías and Dhimokratías. Just off the latter, beside a small park and the town's modern cathedral, is the **Archeological Museum** (Tues–Sat 8.30am–3pm; 400dr), a must if you are planning a visit to Dodona. Displayed here, along with some exceptional crafted bronze seals, is a fascinating collection of lead tablets inscribed with questions to the Dodona oracle.

The island of **Nissí**, on the polluted Lake Pamvótis, is connected by half-hourly motor-launches from the quay northwest of the Froúrio. Its village, founded in the sixteenth century by refugees from the Máni, is flanked by a beautiful group of five monasteries, providing the perfect focus for an afternoon's visit. The **Monastery of Pantelímonos**, just to the east of the village, is where Ali Pasha was assassinated in January 1822, his hiding place having been revealed to the Turks, who had finally lost patience with the wayward ruler. Stay on through the evening and you can eat at one of a string of restaurants on the waterfront, watching a superb sunset over the reed-beds.

Five kilometres north of Ioánnina, and reached by #8 bus from Platía Akadhimías, the village of Pérama boasts what are reputed to be Greece's largest **caves** – discovered during the last war by a guerrilla in hiding from the Germans. Tours are given virtually all day in summer, and until around 4pm the rest of the year.

PRACTICALITIES

If you arrive early enough in the day, it is worth heading straight out to Nissí, where the popular *Pension Della* (☎0651/73 494; ②) and adjacent *Pension Varvara* (☎0651/24 396; ②) offer the most attractive and the best-value **accommodation**. In the town, most savoury budget lodging is in the area between the bazaar and the central plazas; best to start hunting at *Metropolis*, Kristálli 2 (☎0651/26 207; ②) or *Tourist* nearby at the citadel, Kolétti 18 (☎0651/26 443; ②). The attractive *Limnopoula* campsite is 2km out of town on the road to Pérama. For **meals**, the three island tavernas are obvious choices. Back in town, more standard fare can be found in the bazaar near the Froúrio – try the *Pantheon*, or the excellent grill *Mandio*, immediately opposite the citadel gate. The main **bus station** is at Zozimádhou 4, serving most points north and west. A smaller terminal at Vizaníou 28 connects Árta, Préveza, Dodona and villages south and east. It is advisable to buy tickets the day before travelling, especially at weekends.

Dodona

At wildly mountainous **DODONA**, 22km southwest of Ioánnina, lie the ruins of the Oracle of Zeus, dominated by a vast theatre which was meticulously restored at the end of the last century. This is the oldest oracle in Greece: worship of Zeus and of the sacred oak tree of Dodona seems to have begun around 1900 BC. Entering the **ancient**

site (summer Mon–Fri 8am–7pm, Sat & Sun 8.30am–3pm; 500dr) you are immediately confronted by the massive western wall of the **Theatre**. One of the largest on the Greek mainland, it was built during the time of Pyrrhus (297–272 BC); later the Romans made adaptations necessary for their blood sports, building a protective wall over the lower seating and also a drainage channel. At the top of the auditorium, a grand entrance gate leads into the **Acropolis**, an overgrown and largely unexcavated area. Beside the theatre are the foundations of a **Bouleuterion** (council house), beyond which lie the complex ruins of the **Sanctuary of Zeus**, site of the ancient oracle. Worship centred upon Sacred Oak, within which the god was thought to dwell, and which was hacked down by Christian reformists. Remains of an early Christian **Basilica**, constructed over a Sanctuary of Herakles, are prominent nearby.

Transport to Dodona is sparse, with only two buses a day from Ioánnina, but hitching back should be feasible in summer, and a round trip by taxi from Ioánnina with an hour at the site is affordable in a group. Should you want to stay the night, there are some lovely spots to camp, a friendly if basic **taverna** in the neighbouring village, and a tiny, badly-run B-class **pension** at the site, the *Xenia Andromachi* (☎0651/91-196; ④).

Zagóri and the Víkos gorge

Few parts of Greece are more surprising or more beguiling than **Zagóri**, the wild, infertile region to the north of Ioánnina. This is the last place one would expect to find some of the most imposing architecture in Greece, yet the Zagorohória, as the 46 villages of Zagóri are called, are full of grand stone mansions, enclosed by semi-fortified walls and with deep-eaved porches opening on to immaculately cobbled streets.

In the northwest corner of the region, the awesome trench of the **Víkos gorge** – its walls nearly 1000 metres high in places – cuts through the limestone tablelands of Mount Gamíla, separating the villages of western and central Zagóri. A hike through or around Víkos is the highlight of any visit to the area, the usual starting point being the handsome village of **MONODHÉNDRI**, perched right on the rim of the gorge near its south end. There is a twice-daily bus connection with Ioánnina (except Sat & Sun), as well as a pension and various rooms to let. If these are full, there's further choice at Vítsa, fifteen minutes' walk away.

Much the clearest **path into the gorge** starts beside the church; the route is fairly straightforward, and takes under five hours to reach the point where the gorge begins to open out. From here the best option is to follow the marked 03 overland path to **MEGÁLO PÁPINGO**, two hours further on. A hillside of fifty or so houses along a tributary of the Voïdhomátis river, it has an inn with a café-grill (☎0653/41 138; ②) and a smaller inn offering just accommodation (☎0653/41 081; ②). Around half the size of its neighbour, **MIKRÓ PÁPINGO** also has a few **inns** and **tavernas**, including the sympathetic *Oi* (☎0653/41 230; ②), which provides both beds and meals. Returning to Ioánnina, there are buses four days a week from both the Pápingo villages. If there's no convenient connection, the best course is to walk to the village of Káto Klidhoniá, where there are regular buses along the Kónitsa–Ioánnina highway; the walk takes around two and a half hours.

Igoumenítsa and Párga

IGOUMENÍTSA is Greece's third passenger port after Pireás and Pátra, with almost hourly ferries to Corfu, several daily to Italy, and more sporadic connections to the Ionian islands of Páxi, Kefavloniá and Itháki. Levelled during the last war and rebuilt in a sprawling, functional style, it's a place most travellers aim to pass through in the day, but since the majority of ferries leave early in the morning, an overnight stay is often necessary. You should shop around carefully for **ferry tickets**, as prices vary greatly for similar services. Unlike sailings from Pátra, ferries from Igoumenítsa are not allowed to sell tickets with a stopover on Corfu. You can, however, take the regular Corfu ferry over and then pick up most routes from there –'a more appealing option.

If you do **stay** the night, budget hotels are plentiful if uninspiring – most are to be found either along, or just back from, the waterside. The two cheapest are generally the *Hotel Rhodos* at Kíprou 19, near the main square (☎0665/22-248; ②), and *Stavrodhromi*, Souliou 14 (☎0665/22 343; ②). The beach villages of Kalámi and Platariá, respectively 10km and 12km south, both have **campsites** and tavernas.

Párga

The best **beaches** close to Igoumenítsa are at PÁRGA (4 buses daily), a small resort with a crescent of tiered houses below a Norman-Venetian castle. Párga's beaches line three consecutive bays, split by the headland of the fortress hill. **Váltos** and **Lihnós** beaches both have **campsites**. **Rooms** are plentiful if pricey: someone will probably approach you at the bus station or ferry quay. If you want to stay in a traditional building, try the *Vassilas House* or *Petros House* **pensions**, both in the market area – but hotels are generally reserved en masse in season. For **food**, the *Restaurant Panorama* up by the castle gate is okay, and not nearly as expensive as its location would suggest.

Thessaloníki

Second city of Greece and administrative centre for the north, **THESSALONÍKI** has a very different feel from Athens: more modern, cosmopolitan and for the most part wealthier. This "modern" quality is due largely to a disastrous fire, which in 1917 levelled most of the labyrinth of Turkish lanes; the city was rebuilt eight years later on a grid plan with long central avenues running parallel to the sea.

Under Justinian's rule (527–65) **Salonica**, as it then was, became the second city of Byzantium after Constantinople, and it remained such until its sacking by Saracens in 904. It was restored to the Byzantine Empire of Nicaea in 1246, reaching a cultural "Golden Age" until Turkish conquest and occupation in 1430. Until just a few decades ago the city's population was as mixed as any in the Balkans. Besides the Turks, who had been in occupation for close on five centuries, there were Slavs, Albanians and the largest European **Jewish** community of the period – 100,000 at its peak. Numbers remained at around 70,000 up until World War II when all but a fraction were deported to the concentration camps, in the worst atrocity committed in the Balkans. You can get glimpses of "Old Salonica" in the walled **Kástra** quarter of the city, on the hillside beyond the modern grid of streets. For most visitors, however, it is Thessaloníki's excellent archeological museum that stands out, along with the unique array of churches dating from Roman times to the fifteenth century.

Arrival and accommodation

The **train station** on the west side of town is a short walk from the central grid of streets and waterfront. The new **bus terminal** is at the end of Ikosioghóis Oktouríou, (take local bus #31). Or, from the **airport**, 16km out, there's the half-hourly #78 bus.

Outside of the September to November fair and festival season, inexpensive **hotels** are reasonably easy to find – if not, as a rule, very attractive. The main concentration of D- and E-class places, along with a scattering of more upmarket hotels and the occasional bordello, are found along the busy Egnatía avenue. Congenial ones include the *Atlantis* at no. 14 (☎031/540 131; ②), the *Alexandria* at no. 18 (☎031/536 185; ②) or the *Atlas* at no. 40 (☎031/537 046; ②). If you're staying for more than a night or two, it is worth finding a more pleasant downtown location, such as the *Tourist* at Mitropóleos 21 (☎031/270 501; no singles; ②). Nearby are the *Continental* at Komnínon 5 (☎031/277 553; ③) and the *Luxembourgo* at Komnínon 6 (☎031/278 449; ②).

The *IYHF* **youth hostel** at Svólou 44 (☎031/225-946; ①) is noisy, ill-equipped and seems to be run for minimum inconvenience to the wardens. For **women**, a much better alternative is the **XAN** (YWCA) at Ayías Sofías 11 (☎031/276-144; ①), a well-run and well-maintained place, opposite the cathedral. The closest **campsites** are at the uninspiring beaches of Peréa and Ayía Triádha, 20km distant; take bus #72 from Platía Dhikastiríon or, in summer, a boat from the White Tower.

The City

The obvious place to begin a wander is the **White Tower**, a corner of the city defences; it now looks a little stagey, isolated on the seafront, but is a graceful symbol nonetheless, and you can climb to the top for the views and pleasant café. The tower is a couple of minutes' walk from the **Archeological Museum** (Mon 11am–5pm, Tues–Fri 8am–5pm, Sat & Sun 8am–7pm; winter closes 3pm weekends; 1000dr), containing almost all of the finds from the tombs of Philip II of Macedon and others at the ancient Macedonian capital of Aegae (modern Veryína). They include startling amounts of gold – masks, crowns, wreaths, pins and figurines – all of extraordinary craftsmanship.

Thessaloníki's other main museum, the **Folklife–Ethnological Museum of Macedonia** (summer Mon–Wed 9.30am–5.30pm, Tues & Fri–Sun 9.30am–2pm; winter daily except Thurs 9.30am–2pm; 2000dr), is a fifteen-minute walk east of the archeological museum at Vassilísis Ólgas 68 (#5 bus). This is the best museum of its kind in Greece, with well-written commentaries in English and Greek accompanying displays on housing, costumes, day-to-day work and crafts. There is a sharp, highly un-folkloric emphasis on context: on the role of women in the community, the clash between tradition and progress, and the cycle of agricultural and religious festivals.

The closest of the city's major churches to the White Tower is **Ayía Sofía**, built early in the eighth century on the model of its illustrious namesake in Istanbul. Its dome, ten metres in diameter, bears a splendid mosaic of *The Ascension*, currently being restored. A short distance to the northwest, the eleventh-century **Panayía Halkéon** is a classic example of the Greek cross-in-square form, but far more beautiful is the church of **Dhódheka Apóstoli** at the western end of Ayíou Dhimitríou, built three centuries later; its five domes rise in perfect symmetry above walls of fine brickwork, though its interior no longer does it justice.

Northeast of Ayía Sofía, the church of **Áyios Yióryios**, popularly known as the **Rotunda**, is the oldest and strangest of the churches. It was designed, but never used, as a Roman imperial mausoleum and converted to Christian use in the fourth century. Later it became one of the city's major mosques; the minaret remains. Sadly, the church's interior has been closed since the 1978 earthquake.

Rising in the centre of Ayíou Dhimitríou is the largest church in Greece, **Áyios Dhimítrios** (daily 8am–5/7pm). Founded in the fifth century, it's dedicated to the city's patron saint and stands on the site of his martyrdom. Amid the white plaster the few small surviving mosaics make an easy focal point. The best are grouped to the side of the iconostasis and date back to the church's second building in the late seventh century; they include the celebrated *Saint Dimitrios with the Church's Founders* and a contrastingly humane scene of the saint with two young children. The **crypt** (daily except Mon 8.30am–3pm; free) contains the *martyrion* of the saint, and was probably adapted from the original Roman baths where he was imprisoned.

Finally, tucked into the heart of the old Turkish quarter, there's the fourteenth-century **Áyios Nikólaos Orfanós** (Tues–Sun 9am–2.30pm), preserving its original frescoes. Five minutes' walk northwest, **Óssios Davíd** (daily 8am–noon & 5–7pm) is a tiny fifth-century church overzealously converted by the Turks. However, it has arguably the finest mosaic in the city, depicting a clean-shaven Christ appearing in a vision to the prophets Ezekiel and Habakkuk.

Eating, drinking and nightlife

Recently there's been an explosion of interesting places to **eat** and **drink** in Thessaloníki, few of them as obvious as the fast-food outlets dominating the city centre. Most central are the lunchtime *O Loutros*, Komninóu 23, for fish and retsina; *Tsarouhas*, Olímbou 78, a famous outlet for local specialty *patsas* (tripe and trotter soup); and *Toh Stenaki*, an *ouzeri* at Svólou 22. Up in the medieval Eptapirgíou quarter, try *Kastroperpatimata*, Steryíolu Polidhórou 15, for Cypriot-style dishes, or two grills at Graviás 2, inside the eastern gate, for carnivorous fare. Finally, for a gourmet splurge, *Ta Pringiponissia*, in the eastern part of town at Krítis 60, fits the bill with Turkish-style *mezédhes*. **Bars** and **clubs** tend to be concentrated in the narrow streets behind the quayside boulevard Níkis; good examples are *Zythos*, Katoúni 5, *Yuri's*, Pávlou Melá 2, and *Corner*, Ethnikís Amínis 6, with snacks as well. But the city's main music venue is the multi-disciplinary complex *Milos*, out in an old warehouse at Andreou Yioryíou 56 (☎031/525 968 for what's on). There are several tavernas, cafés and bars here as well as two performance halls.

Listings

Books *Molho*, Tsimíski 10; *Promitheus*, Ermoú 75.

Car rental *Ansa*, Laskárata 19; *Budget*, Angeláki 15; *Europcar/InterRent*, G. Papandhréau 5.

Consulates Great Britain and Commonwealth citizens are represented by the Honorary Consul at Venizélou 8 (☎278 006 for mandatory appointment); *Netherlands*, Komnínon 26; *USA*, Níkis 59.

Exchange The *National Bank of Greece* at Tsimíski 11 has evening and Saturday morning hours; see also under "post office" below.

Ferries In season there are "Flying Dolphin" hydrofoils to Skíathos, Skópelos and Alónissos; details and tickets from *Egnatía Tours*, Kamboínion 9 (☎031/223-811). For the three or four ferries a week to the north Aegean islands, Sporadhes, Cyclades and Crete, buy tickets at *Karaharisis*, Koundourióti 8, corner Vótsi, by the harbour gate.

Laundry *Bianca*, Antoniádhou 3; *Zerowatt*, Episkópou 2; *Canadian*, Platía Navarínou.

Phones 24-hr OTE office on Ermoú, corner Karólou Díehl.

Post office Main office at Tsimíski 45 (Mon–Fri 7.30am–8pm).

Tourist office Main EOT office at Platía Aristotélous 8 (Mon–Fri 8am–8pm, Sat 8.30am–2pm).

Train tickets For tickets and reservations, the OSE office at Aristotélous 18 is more central and more helpful than the main terminal.

Travel agents *Magic Bus* at Tsimíski 32 handles buses to İstanbul and – less recommended – to northern Europe. Flights out of Thessaloníki are not cheap, but such bucket shops as exist cluster in the side streets around Platía Eleftherías.

Pella

PELLA was the capital of Macedonia throughout its greatest period, and the first real capital of Greece after Philip II forcibly unified the country around 338 BC. It was founded some sixty years earlier by King Archelaus, and from its beginnings was a major centre of culture. The royal palace was said to be the greatest artistic showplace since the time of Classical Athens: Euripides wrote and produced his last plays at the court, and Aristotle was to tutor the young Alexander the Great – born, like his father Philip II, in this city. The site, less than 50km away, is an easy day trip from Thessaloníki: take the Édhessa-bound **bus** – they run more or less half-hourly.

The **ruins** (summer Tues–Fri 8.30am–3pm, Sat & Sun 8am–7pm; winter Tues–Sun 8.30am–3pm; 400dr) cover over one and a half square miles and as yet only a few blocks of the city have been fully excavated. To the right of the road is a grand official building, probably a government office. The three main rooms of the first court have patterned geometric floors, in the centre of which were found superb, intricate pebble-mosaics depicting scenes of a lion hunt, a griffin attacking a deer, and Dionysus riding a panther. These are now in the **museum** (summer Mon–Fri 8.30am–3pm, Sat & Sun 8am–7pm; winter Tues–Sun 8.30am–3pm; 400dr), but in the third court three mosaics have been left in situ; one of these, a stag hunt, is complete, and astounding in its dynamism and use of perspective.

Mount Olympus

Highest, most magical and most dramatic of all Greek mountains, **Mount Olympus** – the mythical seat of the gods – rears nigh on 3000 metres straight from the shores of the Thermaíkos gulf, south of Thessaloníki. Dense forests cover its slopes and its wild flowers are without parallel even by Greek standards. Equipped with decent boots and warm clothing, no special expertise is necessary to get to the top in summer, though it's a long hard pull, and at any time of year Olympus must be treated with respect: its weather is notoriously fickle and it does claim lives.

The best base for a walk up the mountain is the village of **LITÓHORO** on the eastern side. The station for trains from Thessaloníki is 9km from the village, with rare connecting buses; or you can get a bus direct from Thessaloníki. Cheapest lodgings are at the **youth hostel** (☎0352/81 311; ①) or D-class *Hotel Park* (☎0352/81 252; ②), respectively above and below the square. For a more comfortable **hotel**, well-heated in winter and only marginally more expensive, try the *Myrto* (☎0352/81 398; ③) near the main square. Best **eats** are at *Dhamaskinia*, uphill on Vassiléos Konstandínou.

Buy a proper map of the range at the youth hostel which is also the start of the well-marked scenic E4 path up the Mavrólongos canyon. Four to five hours' walk brings you to Priónia, the end of the road and last reliable water; from here begins the sharper three-hour climb along a track to the *Spílios Agapitós* refuge (May 15–Oct 31; ☎0352/81 800; ①), which perches on the edge of an abrupt spur, surrounded by huge storm-beaten trees. It's best to stay overnight here, as you need to make an early start for the three-hour ascent to **Mítikas**, the highest peak at 2917 metres – the summit frequently clouds up towards midday, to say nothing of the danger of catching one of Zeus' thunderbolts. The path continues behind the refuge, reaching a signposted fork above the tree line in about an hour. Straight on takes you to Mítikas via the ridge known as Kakí Skála, while the right goes via the *Yiósos Apostolídhis* hut in one hour (July to mid-Sept; ☎0352/82 300; ②). From the latter you can enjoyably loop down in another day's walk to the Gortsia trail head and from there back down into the Mavrólongos canyon.

Halkidhikí

The squid-shaped peninsula of Halkidhikí begins at a perforated edge of lakes east of Thessaloníki and extends into three prongs of land – Kassándhra, Sithonía and Áthos – trailing like tentacles into the Aegean sea. **Kassándhra** and **Sithonía** are Thessaloníki's beach-playground, hosting some of the fastest-growing holiday resorts in Greece. Both are connected to Thessaloníki by buses, but neither peninsula is that easy to travel around if you are dependent on public **transport.** You really have to pick a place and stay there, perhaps hiring a moped for local excursions. Sithónia is marginally less packaged, with low-key resorts at **Pórto Kouféa** and **Toróni.**

Mount Áthos, the easternmost peninsula, is in all ways separate: a "Holy Mountain" whose monastic population, semi-autonomous from the Greek state, excludes all women – even as visitors. For men who wish to experience Athonite life, a visit involves suitably Byzantine procedures – your consulate in Athens or Thessaloníki will explain the full rigmarole.

However, **boat tours** leave IERISSÓS daily in summer on a loop around the Holy Mountain – both Ierissós and Ouranópoli (see below) are served by several daily buses from Thessaloníki. Unless they are all-male parties (in which case they're allowed to dock at the monastery of Ivíron) they have to stay 500 metres from the coast, but the views of the monasteries are impressive anyway. Ierissós has many rooms to let and two **hotels** – the basic *Akanthos* (☎0377/22 359; ②) and *Marcos* (☎0377/22 518; ③).

The last settlement before you reach the monastic domains is the package resort of **OURANÓPOLI**, overrun by both Germans and Greeks in summer. **Accommodation** is plentiful, with numerous rooms and two budget hotels – the *Galini* (☎0377/71 217; ③) and *Ouranopolis* (☎0377/71 205; ③). It's from here that the most reliable ferries depart for monastic Áthos, usually by 10am. You'll need the earliest bus of the day out of Thessaloníki to coincide.

Mount Áthos

Equipped with the suitable paperwork, foreign, non-Orthodox men over the age of eighteen may stay for up to four days on the Holy Mountain, moving to a different monastery or monastic dependency each night. There are some possibilities of **moving about** by boat or bus, but walking between the communities is an integral part of the Athonite experiece, so you should be reasonably fit and self-sufficient in trail food, as **food** offered for the two meals a day tends to be spartan. Most monks tend to pay scant attention to foreigners, so you get more of an idea of the magnificent scenery and engaging architecture than of the religious life, though it's hard to avoid tangling with the disorienting daily schedule, dictated by the hours of sun and darkness.

All that said, a visit is highly recommended, though of course you can't hope to see more than a fraction of the twenty fully-fledged monasteries or their satellites in the time alotted. Choose between the "museum monasteries" of **Meyístis Lávras, Vatopedhíou, Ivíron** or **Dhioníssiou** with their wealth of treasures and art, and the more modestly endowed cloisters where the brothers will make more time for you, such as **Osíou Grigíou, Pandokratoros** and **Ayíou Pávlou**.

Kavála

KAVÁLA, backing on to the lower slopes of Mount Simbólon, is the second largest city of Macedonia and a principal port for northern Greece. Coming in through the suburbs there seems little to commend a stay, but the **Panayía** quarter above the port preserves a scattering of eighteenth- and nineteenth-century buildings, and considerable atmosphere. It is by far the most attractive part of town to explore, wandering amid the twisting wedge of lanes and up towards the citadel.

Mehmet Ali, the Pasha of Egypt and founder of the dynasty which ended with King Farouk, was born in Kavála in 1769 and his birthplace, at the corner of Pavlídhou and Méhmet Alí, is maintained as a monument. To visit its wood-panelled reception rooms, ground-floor stables and first-floor harem, ring for the caretaker. Another caretaker may escort you through the **Citadel** (daily summer 10am–7pm) so you can explore the Byzantine ramparts and dungeon; in season it hosts a few festival performances, mainly dance, in its main court.

The **Archeological Museum** (Tues–Sun 8.30am–3pm; 400dr) at the west end of the waterfront, just off Erithroú Stavroú, contains a fine dolphin mosaic, a reconstructed Macedonian funeral chamber and many terracotta figurines decorated in their original paint. Close by, on Odhós Filíppou, is the **Folk Art and Modern Art Museum** (daily 9–11am & 6–9pm), which as well as traditional costumes and household utensils has some interesting rooms devoted to the locally born sculptor Polignotos Vigis.

In the main square, Platía Eleftherías, is an **EOT** office, which can provide schedules for daily **ferries** from Kavála to Thássos and other east Aegean islands (the latter usually Wednesdays and Saturdays); tickets are sold at *Nikos Miliadhes*, Platía Karaóli Dhimitríou 36 (☎051/226 147).

Hotels are in short supply and in season it's wise to phone ahead and book. All three D-class places are in the grid of streets around Eleftherías: *Attikon*, Megaloú Alexándhrou 8 (☎051/222 257; ②), *Parthenon*, Spetsón 14 (☎051/222 205; ②), and *Rex*, Kriézi 4 (☎051/223 393; ②). Nearest **campsite** is *Camping Irini*, 2km east and reached by city bus #2. **Eating out**, it's wisest to ignore waterfront tourist traps in favour of a row of locally-favoured tavernas on Theodhórou Poulídhou, up in the Panayía district.

Alexandhroúpoli and onwards

The border town and military garrison of **ALEXANDHROÚPOLI** has little to recommend it, but it can get very crowded in season, with overland travellers and Greek holidaymakers competing for space in the few hotels and gritty beach campsites. The best places to stay are the fairly inexpensive **hotels** around the train station: the D-class *Majestic*, Platía Troúman 7 (☎0551/26 444; ②), the D-class *Metropolis* (☎0551/26 443; ②), and *Aktaeon*, Karaóli 74 (☎0551/28 078; ②). The municipal *Camping Alexandhroupoli* is a half-hour walk from the train station, or take the #5 bus. Excellent **meals** are to be had at *I Neraidha*, a couple of blocks from the train station and across from the town hall. Tickets for daily **ferries** to Samothráki are sold at a cluster of waterfront agencies opposite the dock, within sight of the train station.

CROSSING THE BORDER

There are several **buses** from here **to Istanbul**, but most start in Thessaloníki and by this stage are full. An alternative is to take a local bus to the border at **KÍPI** (6 daily). You are not allowed to cross the frontier here on foot, but it is generally no problem to get a driver to shuttle you the 500m across to the Turkish post – and possibly to give you a lift beyond. The nearest town is Ipsala (5km), but if possible get as far as Keşan (30km), from where buses to Istanbul are much more frequent. There's only one **train to Istanbul** per day from Alexandhroúpoli; services are more frequent to Kastaniés, but get an early one to ensure arrival at the frontier before it shuts at 1pm. Once over – again, no walking – there's a bus service the remaining 7km to Edirne.

There is one early morning train daily into **Bulgaria**, reaching Svilengrad in five hours. From Svilengrad, it is best to move on immediately towards Plovdiv.

THE SOUTHERN AEGEAN ISLANDS

The rocky, volcanic chain of **Argo-Saronic** islands is the nearest group to Athens and among the busiest. **Éyina** is most frenetic, but **Ídhra** and **Spétses** aren't far behind in summer: more than any other group, these islands are at their best out of season. To the east of the Argo-Saronic, the **Cyclades** is the most satisfying Greek archipelago for island-hopping. On no other group do you get such a strong feeling of each island as a microcosm with its own distinct traditions, customs and path of modern development. The majority of the islands are arid and rocky, and most share the Cycladic style of brilliant-white, cubist architecture. The extent and impact of tourism, however, is dramatically haphazard, so that although some English is spoken on most islands, a slight detour from the beaten track could have you groping for your Greek phrasebook.

Whatever the level of tourist development, there are only two Cycladic islands where it has come to completely dominate their character. These are **Íos**, the original hippie-island and still a paradise for hard-living backpackers, and **Míkonos**, by far the most visited of the group, with its teeming old town, nude beaches and highly sophisticated clubs and bars. After these, **Páros**, **Sífnos**, **Náxos** and **Thíra** are currently most popular, their beaches and main towns drastically overcrowded in July and August.

The one major ancient site worth making time for is **Delos**: the commercial and religious centre of the Classical Greek world, it's visited most easily on a day trip by *kaíki* from Míkonos. Almost all of the Cyclades are served by boats from Pireás, but there are also ferries from Rafína for Síros, Míkonos, Páros and Náxos, among others.

Further east still, the **Dodecanese** lie so close to the Turkish coast that some are almost within hailing distance of the shore. Because of this position, and their remoteness from Athens, the islands have always had a turbulent history and were only finally included in the modern Greek state in 1948 after centuries of occupation by Crusaders, Turks and Italians, a multicultural legacy which is the basis for much of the group's attraction. Medieval **Rhodes** is the most famous, but almost every island has its classical remains, its Crusaders' castle, its traditional villages and abundant grandiose public buildings. Yet the Dodecanese display a marked topographic and economic schizophrenia. The dry limestone outcrop of **Sími** has always been forced to rely on the sea for its livelihood, while the sprawling, relatively fertile giants, Rhodes and **Kós**, have recently seen their traditional agricultural economies almost totally displaced by the tourist industry. **Kárpathos** lies somewhere in between, with a once-forested north grafted on to a rocky limestone south. **Pátmos**, at the fringes of the archipelago, boasts architecture and landscapes more appropriate to the Cyclades. The main islands in the group are connected almost daily with each other, and none is hard to reach. Rhodes is another transport hub, with services to Turkey, Israel, Egypt and Cyprus, as well as connections with Crete, the northeastern Aegean islands, the Cyclades and the mainland (both Rafína and Pireás).

Éyina (Aegina)

It seems incredible today, but ancient **Aegina** was a major power in Classical times, with trade carried on to the limits of the known world. Today the island is essentially regarded as a beach annexe of Athens, and a solitary column of a Temple of Apollo beckons as your ferry steams around the point into the harbour at **ÉYINA TOWN**. The bus stop is at Platía Ethneyersías, while moped rental is also handy for a day-trip exploration of the island. There are a few ② and ③ category **hotels** scattered throughout town, particularly in the streets behind Ethneyersías – try the *Miranda* at Yimasíou 10 ☎(0297/22 266; ②). The helpful *Aegina Tourist Board* (☎0297/22334) upstairs opposite the boat jetty will book hotels and private rooms.

The **Temple of Aphaia** (summer Mon–Fri 8am–5pm, Sat & Sun 8.30am–3pm; winter closes 3pm; 600dr), dating from the fifth century BC, stands 17km east of town among pines tapped to make the excellent local retsina. To get to the temple from Éyina town you can go by bus, though the best approach is by hired bicycle; if under your own power, take the inland road which passes deserted **Paleohóra**, the island's old capital.

For such a well-visited island, Éyina is short of attractive swimming spots. The only really sandy beach is at the grossly overblown resort of **AYÍA MARÍNA**, close to the temple and mobbed due to its role as a stopoff for ferries; otherwise the best bet is in the vicinity of **PÉRDHIKA**, a fishing village twenty minutes by bus from Éyina town, with a small beach. It is certainly the best place to stay on the island besides the main town: there is a pension and a few rooms to rent. Alternatively, there are *kaíkia* from here across to **Moní Islet**, where there's an official campsite and a seasonal taverna.

Ídhra (Hydra)

The port and town of **ÍDHRA**, with its tiers of stone mansions and white, tiled houses climbing up from a perfect horseshoe harbour, is a very beautiful spectacle. Unfortunately, thousands of others think so too, and from Easter until September it's packed to the gills, with the front becoming one uninterrupted outdoor café. The town's dozens of mansions were built mostly during the eighteenth century, on the accumulated wealth of a remarkable merchant fleet of 160 ships which traded as far afield as America. By the 1820s the town's population stood at nearly 20,000, seven times what it is today. Ídhra is also reputedly hallowed by no fewer than 365 churches, the most important being the cathedral of **Panayía Mitropóleos**, built around a courtyard down by the port, and with a distinctive clock tower.

There is no shortage of inexpensive **restaurants** on the waterfront – try *Ta Tria Adhelfia* or the *Ambrosia Café* – along with a number of **pensions**, most charging thirty percent or so above usual island rates with single rooms rare. Reasonable-value places include *Leto* (☎0298/53 385; ④) and *Argo* (☎0298/52 452; ③), *Dina* (☎0298/52 248; ③) or *Sofia* (☎0298/52 313; ③), or the pleasant, unclassified *Douglas* (☎0298/52 599; ③).

The island's only sandy beach is the private one at Mandhráki, 2km east of town. On the opposite side of the harbour a coastal path leads around to a pebbly but popular stretch, just before **KAMÍNI**, where there's a good year-round taverna, *George and Anna's*. Thirty minutes' walk beyond Kamíni (or a boat ride from the port) will bring you to **VLÍHOS**, a small hamlet with **rooms** and three tavernas. **Camping** is tolerated here (the closest to town) and the swimming is good.

Spétses (Spetsai)

Spétses is very green, very small and alarmingly popular, but it absorbs its tourists with more than usual grace. The port and town of **SPÉTSES** (or Kastélli) shares with Ídhra a history of nineteenth-century mercantile prosperity, and pebble-mosaic courtyards and streets sprawl between mansions whose architecture is quite distinct from the Peloponnesian styles across the straits. Horse-drawn cabs connect the various quarters of town, spread out along the waterfront.

Most visitors stay in Spétses town, where all kinds of **accommodation** are available, from the Edwardian splendour of the *Hotel Possidonion* (☎0298/72 208; ④) to simple **rooms** in people's houses. Well worth trying also is the *Hotel Saronikos* (☎0298/72 646; ③), a lovely old inn just by the quay at Dápia, the cannon-studded main harbour. If you don't fancy pounding the streets yourself, then go to *Takis' Tourist Office*, fifty metres from the end of the jetty, and see what they can come up with. For **camping**, head out to the shade of tamarisks behind Lámpara Beach, 700m northwest of the dock. **Food and drink** can be expensive. Among cheaper places are *Ta Tzakia*, 300m south of Dápia, and *Taverna Haralambos*, on Baltíza inlet, by the smaller harbour; the only traditional taverna is *Lazaros's*, 400m inland and uphill from Dápia.

Ayii Anaryiri, on the south side of the island, is the best, if also the most popular, beach: a beautiful, long, sheltered bay of fine sand. There's a self-service taverna on the beach, and, just behind, the moderately priced *Tassos*, Spétses' finest eating establishment. It's only about an hour's walk through the woods from the town, or accessible by *káiki* from Dápia or on the island bus.

Sífnos

Sífnos does often get crowded, but on the other hand its modest size means that wherever you stay, you can reach the rest of the island by the excellent bus service to all points or on foot over a network of old stone pathways. **KAMÁRES**, the port, is tucked at the base of high bare cliffs in the west. It can be expensive – the budget option is a **room** above the *Katsoulakis Tourist Agency* close to the quay. There are other places behind the beach, including a **campsite**, and the reasonable *Hotel Stavros* (☎0284/31-641; ③), just past the church. Best meals are at the quayside *Meropi*.

An excitingly steep twenty-minute bus ride takes you up to **APOLLONÍA**, a rambling collage of flagstones, belfries and flowered courtyards. The island bank, post office and tourist police are all here, but **rooms**, though plentiful, are even more likely to be full than at Kamáres. Outside of high season, there will be vacancies at establishments lining the road to Fáros; quieter, and pricier, digs are found along the stair-street north of the main square. The **Folk Museum** (open on request only) in the square by the bus stop is also well worth a look since Sífnos produces some of the finest pottery and fabrics in Greece. As an alternative base, with a number of rooms, you could try **KÁSTRO**, a forty-minute trail walk or regular bus ride below Apollonía on the east coast. Built on a rocky outcrop with an almost sheer drop to the sea on three sides, the ancient capital of the island retains much of its medieval character.

At the southern end of the island, around 10km from Apollonía, lies the growing beach resort of **PLATÍS YIALÓS**. It has another (poor) campsite and numerous rooms to let, as well as tavernas, of which the best are *Toh Steki* and *Bus Stop*. Far less crowded sand is to be found just to the northeast at **FÁROS**, which has regular buses from Apollonía, rooms to let and good, cheap tavernas.

Perhaps the finest walk is to **VATHÍ**, around three hours from Apollonía. A fishing and pottery village on a stunning funnel-shaped bay, Vathí is the most attractive base on the island: there are **rooms** to let and summer tavernas, the best being *Okeanis*. An alternative route there is by the boat twice daily from Kamáres.

Míkonos (Mykonos)

Míkonos has become the most popular and expensive of the Cyclades, visited by nearly a million tourists a year. But if you don't mind the crowds – or you come out of season – the prosperous capital is one of the most beautiful of all island towns. Dazzlingly white, it's the archetypal postcard image, sugarcube buildings stacked around a cluster of seafront fishermen's dwellings. The labyrinthine design was intended to confuse the pirates who plagued Míkonos in the eighteenth and early nineteenth centuries and it remains effective – everyone gets lost.

If you're flying in, the **airport** is about 3km out of town, a short taxi ride away. Otherwise you'll arrive at the northern jetty, where **ferries** and cruise ships dock, to be met by a horde of owners hustling hotels and **rooms**. If you balk at the prices, be warned that a private room here is likely to be cheaper than staying in a hotel on any of the nearby beaches. As for **hotels** in town, out of season you might consider *Hotel Delfines* on Mavroyéni (☎0289/22 292; ③), *Hotel Karbonis* on Matoyiánni (☎0289/23 127; ③), *Hotel Apollon* on Mavroyénous (☎0289/22 223; ③), *Hotel Maria* at Kaloyéra 18 (☎0289/22 317; ③), *Hotel Marios* at Kaloyéra 5 (☎0289/22 704; ③), *Hotel Philippi* at Kaloyéra 32 (☎0289/22 294; ③), or *Hotel Karbonaki* at Panahrándou 21 (☎0289/23-127; ③). Otherwise there are official **campsites** at Paradise and Paránga beaches (see below), and every other bay on the island has some sort of taverna.

The harbour curves around past the dull, central Polikandhrióti beach, behind it the **bus station** for Toúrlos, Áyios Stéfanos and Áno Méra. Continue along the seafront to the southern jetty for **tourist police** and *kaíkia* to Delos. A second bus terminus, for beaches to the south of town, is right at the other end of Hóra, beyond the windmills.

The **nightlife** in town is every bit as good – and expensive – as it's cracked up to be. It's impossible to list every hot spot, but the following are worth checking out. Among the most durable are *Remezzo*, near OTE and with sunset views, or *Pierro's*, once mecca for the island's substantial gay contingent, now mixed. Around Kaloyéra is a promising area for **food**: the *Edem Garden* is a popular gay restaurant with an adventurous menu, and *El Greco* and *The Sesame Kitchen* are two other semi-reasonable eateries. Cheaper eating can be had at *Nikos*, behind the town hall, pizzas at *Rendez-Vous*, and Chinese takeaway at *Dynasty*. More drinking haunts are over in the Alefkándhra area in the south of the town – or "Little Venice" as it's known. Try *Kástro's* for an early evening cocktail, moving on later to *Montparnasse*, which is fairly swanky – to the extent of boasting a visitor's book. In K. Yiorgoúli street, off Mitropóleos, the *City Bar* is the campest spot in town; close by, *Scandinavia Bar* is a cheap, jovial and non-stop party bar. The *Famous Mykonos Dance Bar* and the *Rainbow* are young, mixed and sweaty.

The beaches

The closest decent **beach** is **ÁYIOS STÉFANOS** (4km north), connected by a very regular bus service. Other nearby, mainstream destinations are the resorts on the southwest peninsula, with fairly undistinguished beaches tucked into pretty bays at Áyios Yiannis and Órnos. Better to make for **PLATÍS YIALÓS**, 4km south, though you won't be alone. A **kaíki service** from Míkonos town connects almost all the beaches east of Platís Yialós: gorgeous, pale-sand **Piránga** beach, popular with campers; **Paradise Beach**, well sheltered by its headland, predominantly nudist, with another official campsite (April–Oct) and two tavernas; and **Super Paradise**, which has a friendly atmosphere and a couple of tavernas. Probably the best beach on Míkonos is **Elía**, the last port of call for the *kaíkia*. The longest on the island, it's a broad sandy stretch with a verdant backdrop, split in two by a rocky area. Almost exclusively nudist, it boasts an excellent restaurant, *Matheos*.

Dhílos (Delos)

The remains of ancient **Delos** (Tues–Sun 8.30am–3pm; 1000dr), though skeletal and swarming now with lizards and tourists, give some idea of the past grandeur of this sacred isle a few sea-miles west of Míkonos. The *kaíki* to Delos gives you three hours on the island – barely enough time to take in the main attractions, but it's no longer possible to stay the night.

Delos' ancient fame was due to the fact that Leto gave birth to the divine twins Artemis and Apollo on the island, and one of the first things you see is the **Sanctuary of Apollo**, while three Temples of Apollo stand in a row along the Sacred Way. To the east towards the museum you pass the **Sanctuary of Dionysus** with its marble phalli on tall pillars. To the north is the **Sacred Lake** where Leto gave birth: guarding it is a group of superb lean lions, masterfully executed in the seventh century BC. Set out in the other direction from the agora and you enter the residential area, known as the **Theatre Quarter**. Many of the walls and roads remain but there is none of the domestic detail that makes Pompeii, for example, so fascinating. Some colour is added by the mosaics: one in the **House of the Trident**, better ones in the **House of the Masks**, including a vigorous portrayal of Dionysus riding on a panther's back. The **Theatre** itself, though much ravaged, offers some fine views.

Páros and Andíparos

Páros has some of the finest beaches in the Cyclades, but to visit it for these alone, as increasing crowds seem to do every summer, is to miss much. Gently furled around a single peak, the island manages quietly and undramatically to be one of the most beautiful of the group. With a little of everything – old villages, monasteries, fishing harbour and a labyrinthine capital – Páros is a good point to begin your island wanderings, with boat connections to virtually the entire Aegean, though things are nearly as expensive and commercialized here as on Míkonos. **PARIKÍA**, the main town, sets the tone for the rest of Páros, with its ranks of typically Cycladic white houses punctuated by the occasional Venetian-style building and church domes. All ferries dock here, and the busy waterfront is jam-packed with bars, restaurants, hotels and ticket agencies.

Just outside the central clutter, the town also has one of the most interesting churches in the Aegean – the **Ekatondapilianí**, or "Church of One Hundred Gates" (daily 7am–noon & 4–8pm). The original construction was overseen in the sixth century by Isidore of Miletus but the work was carried out by his pupil Ignatius. It was so beautiful on completion that the master, consumed with jealousy, is said to have grappled with his apprentice on the rooftop, flinging them both to their deaths. They can be found today kneeling at the column bases across the courtyard: master tugging at his beard in repentance, pupil clutching a broken head. Behind Ekatondapilianí, the **Archeological Museum** (Tues–Fri 8.30am–3pm, Sat & Sun 9am–2pm) has a fair collection of antique pieces, its prize exhibit a portion of the *Parian Chronicle*, a social and cultural history of Greece up to 264 BC, recorded on marble.

Páros is fast becoming a major hub of inter-island **ferry** services. Boats dock by the windmill, which houses a summer tourist **information centre**. The bus stop is 100m or so to the left – routes extend to Náoussa in the north, Alikí in the south, and Dhríos on the island's east coast (with another very useful service between Dhríos and Náoussa). You'll be met off the ferry by locals offering **rooms**, and it's a good idea to capitulate straight away. Most of the **hotels** tend to be reserved by tour operators, and you'll have to be quick to grab space in the remaining cheaper places. Try the *Hotel Dina* near Platía Valéntza (☎0284/21 325; ③), *Oasis Rooms* (☎0284/21 227; ③) near the post office, or as a last resort, the jail-like *Hotel Kondes* behind the windmill (☎0284/21 246; ③). The best-value **food** is to be had at *I Aligaria*, inland by the dry riverbed, *Mey Tey* for modest Chinese fare, and the *Koutouki Manasis*, a couple of alleys inland from this square. There's a crowded **campsite** at the northern end of the town beach. Parikía has a wealth of **pubs, bars** and low-key **discos**, not as pretentious as on Míkonos or as raucous as on Íos, but certainly everything in between. The most popular cocktail bars extend along the seafront, tucked into a series of open squares.

The second port of Páros, **NÁOUSSA** was recently an unspoilt town, but a rash of new concrete hotels has all but swamped its character. Despite the development, the town is a good place to head for as soon as you reach Páros; it's noted for its nearby beaches, while **rooms** are marginally cheaper than in Parikía – track them down with the help of Katerini Simitzi's tourist office on the main square. Hotels are more expensive, though haggle for reduced prices out of season at the *Madaki* (☎0284/51 475; ③), the *Drossia* (☎0284/51 213; ③) and the *Stella* (☎0284/51 317; ③). There's a **campsite**, too, out of town towards Kolimbíthres, much better than the mosquito-plagued one in Parikía, and various tavernas – all of which, for a change, are pretty good, specializing in fresh fish and seafood: *Diamante* and *Limanakis* come recommended.

Some good-to-excellent **beaches** are within walking distance of Náoussa, and a summer *kaíki* service also connects them. To the west, an hour's tramping brings you to Kolimbíthres, where there are three tavernas and the wind- and sea-sculpted rock formations which give the place its Greek name. A few minutes beyond, Monastíri beach – below the abandoned Pródhromos monastery – is similarly attractive, and partly nudist. Go northeast from Náoussa and the sands are better still, the barren headland spangled with good surfing beaches: Langéri is backed by dunes; the best surfing is at Santa María, a trendy beach connected with Náoussa by road; and finally there's Platiá Ámmos, on the northeasternmost tip of the island.

In the centre of the island is perhaps the most beautiful and unspoilt village on Páros – the old capital of **LÉFKES**. Its marbled alleyways and amphitheatrical setting are unparalleled and, despite the presence of an oversized hotel, a very few rooms, a disco and a taverna on the outskirts, the area around the *platía* remains unspoilt.

Andíparos

There's little to stop for south of Parikía until **POÚNDA**, 6km away, and then only to catch the ferry to **Andíparos**. In recent years this islet has become something of an open secret – which is not to say that it's horrendously commercialized, and in high season can be very full. Most of the population of 500 live in the single northern village where the barge-ferry from Poúnda and four or five daily *kaíkia* from Parikía dock. There are a dozen tavernas, some small hotels – the cheapest are *Mandalena* (☎0284/61 206; ②) and *Anargyros* (☎0284/61 204; ②) – and a very popular campsite with a nudist beach. It's the great cave in the south of the island that is the chief attraction for day-trippers: two buses a day run there from the port, or it's a stony ninety-minute hike.

Náxos

Náxos is the largest and most fertile of the Cyclades, and with its bushy and mountainous interior seems immediately distinct from many of its neighbours. The difference is accentuated by the architecture of many of the interior villages: the Venetian occupation left towers and fortified mansions scattered throughout the island, while late medieval Cretan refugees bestowed a singular character upon the eastern settlements.

A long causeway protecting the harbour connects NÁXOS town with the islet of Palátia, where the huge stone portal of an unfinished **Temple of Apollo** still stands. Most of the town's life goes on down by the port or in the streets just behind it; stepped lanes behind lead up past crumbling balconies and through low arches to the fortified **Kástro**, from where the Venetians ruled over the Cyclades. Other brooding relics survive in the same area: a seventeenth-century Ursuline convent, the Catholic cathedral and one of Ottoman Greece's first schools, now housing an excellent **Archeological Museum** (daily except Mon 8.30am–3pm; 400dr), whose wide historical range of finds – mostly pottery – indicates that Náxos was continually occupied throughout antiquity, from Mycenaean to Roman times.

Tourism has now reached such a pitch that an annexe of purpose-built accommodation extends south of the town centre. **Rooms** downtown are uniformly poor standard and overpriced; **hotels** are better on the cooler north slope of the Kástro: best of these are the *Panorama* on Amfitrítis (☎0285/22 330; ③), the *Anixix* nearby (☎0285/22 112; ③) or the last resort *Dionysos* (☎0285/22 331; ②), with a gloomy basement hostel (①).

Much of the evening action goes on along the quayside, where cafés and restaurants are abundant enough, if a bit on the expensive side. Most traditional is *Kali Kardhia*, while *Koufopoulou* is the best waterfront grill.

The islands best **beaches** line the southwest coast a few kilometres from town, regularly served by buses. **ÁYIOS YIÓRYIOS**, a lengthy sandy bay on the south of the hotel "ghetto", is within walking distance. There are several tavernas here and you can camp officially just off the beach in the first of three organized sites on this coast. A pleasant hour's walk south through the salt marshes brings you to **PROKÓPIOS** beach (cheapish hotels and basic tavernas), whose peaceful days are again surely numbered. Or follow the tracks a little further to **AYÍA ÁNNA**, a small port where there are plenty of **rooms** to let and a few modest tavernas (plus summer *kaíkia* to Píso Livádhi on Páros). Beyond the headland stretch the five barely-developed kilometres of **PLÁKA** beach, a vegetation-fringed expanse of white sand which comfortably holds the summer crowds of nudists and campers.

Central Náxos

Although buses for Apóllon in the north link up the central Naxian villages, the core of the island – between Náxos town and Apíranthos – is best explored on moped or foot. From Sangrí the road twists northeast into the **Tragéa** region, a densely fertile area occupying a vast highland valley. It's a good jumping-off point for all sorts of exploratory rambling, and **HALKÍ** is a fine introduction to what is to come. Set high up, 16km from Hóra, it's a silent, noble town with some lovely churches. Tourists staying here are rare, but you might get a room by asking at the central store.

From Halkí a good road leads directly north to MONÍ, or for walkers a path goes there via attractive Kalóxilos. Just before Moní, you pass the sixth-century monastery of **Panayía Dhrossianí**, a group of stark grey stone buildings with some excellent frescoes; the monks allow visitors at any time, though there are coach tours too from Náxos town. The pavement continues to Kinídharos with its old marble quarry above the village, and a few kilometres beyond a signpost points you left down a rough track to **FLÉRIO**, the most interesting of Naxos' ancient marble quarries. In and above a private orchard are two famous **kouri**: idealized statues of classical youth, they were left unfinished because of flaws in the material.

At the eastern edge of the gorgeous Tragéa valley, **FILÓTI**, the largest village in the region, lies on the slopes of Mount Zás – which at 1000m is the highest point in the Cyclades. There are plenty of **rooms** and old houses to let and you could do worse than use Filóti as a base. From the village, it's a round-trip walk of 2 hours 30 minutes to the summit of Zás, a climb which provides an astounding panoramic view of virtually the whole of Náxos and its Cycladic neighbours.

Northern Náxos

The startling route to Apóllon passes through the high, remote village of **KOMIAKÍ**, the starting point for perhaps the most extraordinary walk on Náxos. Head up the mountainside and cross the ridge as far as an improbably long marble staircase which winds 300m down into the valley: the views are marvellous, the experience diminished only by repeated intersections with a new road, and the garden-hamlet at the bottom, **MIRÍSIS**, enchanting. Back on the main road, a series of slightly less hairy bends lead down a long valley to **APÓLLON** (Apóllonas). An embryonic resort, it's rather tatty so far, with the beach intermittently marred by washed-up tar. There are, however, **rooms** to let above the shops and tavernas, and one major attraction – another **kouros**, the largest of Náxos' abandoned stone figures.

Íos

No other island attracts the same vast crowds of young people as **ÍOS**, yet the island hasn't been commercialized in quite the same way as, say, Míkonos – mainly because few of the visitors have much money. You might be tempted to grab a **room** in YIALÓS as you arrive, though it's the most expensive place on the island to stay and the official campsite to the right of the harbour is the worst of the island's three. Yialós **beach**, five minutes' walk from the harbour, is backed by hotels and lodgings, but loud music seems to be accepted on the beach and obligatory in the tavernas.

Most of the cheaper **rooms** are in HÓRA, a twenty-minute walk up the mountain behind the port. There's dormitory space as well as the usual rooms and hotels – though for the latter two options, you've a better chance of getting a good deal if you're staying for several days. Every evening the streets throb to music from ranks of competing discos and clubs – mostly free or with a nominal cover charge, but drinks tend to be expensive. There are plenty of places **to eat** too: cheapest and still essentially Greek are *Folia*, near the top of the village, and *Ikoyeniaki Taverna Stani*, at the heart of town.

The most popular stop on the island's bus routes is **MILOPÓTAMOS**, site of a magnificent beach and a mini-resort. By day, bodies cover every inch of the bus-stop end of the sand – for a bit more space head the other way, where there are dunes behind the beach. There are two decently-equipped **campsites**; *Camping Stars* and *Far Out Camping*; for **rooms**, try *Draco Pension* to the right of the bus stop.

From Yialós, daily boats depart at around 10am (returning in the late afternoon) to **MANGANÁRI** on the south coast, the beach to come for serious tans. There's a better atmosphere, though, at **ÁYIOS THEODHÓTIS**, up on the northeast coast; a daily **bus** service runs from Yialós.

Thíra (Santoríni)

As the ferryboat manoeuvres into **Thíra**, gaunt, sheer cliffs loom hundreds of feet above. Nothing grows to soften the view, and the only colours are the reddish-brown, black and grey pumice striations of the cliff face. As early as 3000 BC Thíra developed as an outpost of Minoan civilisation until, around 1150 BC, the volcano island erupted; it was destroyed and, it is thought, the great Minoan civilizations on Crete fell with it.

Ferries dock at either **SKÁLA FIRÁ** or more often at the somewhat grim port of **ÓRMOS ATHINIÓS**. Half-rebuilt after a devastating earthquake in 1956, Firá lurches dementedly at the cliff's edge, and pays the price for its stunning position. Besieged by hordes of day-trippers, it's become incredibly tacky of late, the most grossly commercial spot on what can – in summer, at least – seem a grossly commercial island. If you insist on staying here, you'll have to move quickly on arrival, particularly if you want one of the better **rooms** with views over the bay: take any reasonable offer. Otherwise there are three cheap **youth hostels** in the northern part of town, the unofficial *Kamares* (②) is best of these. Firá is not a place to linger, but make time for the **Archeological Museum** (Tues–Sun 8.30am–3pm; 400dr), near the cable car to the north of town. An excellent collection, it includes a curious set of autoerotic figures.

Buses from Firá are plentiful enough to get around between the town and beaches, but if you want to see the whole island in a couple of days, hiring a **moped** is useful – try any of the firms on the main road to Ía from the bus station square.

At the northwest of the island is one of the most dramatic towns of the Cyclades, **ÍA**, a curious mix of pristine white reconstruction and tumbledown ruins clinging to the cliff face. It's also much the calmest place on Thíra, and with the recent introduction of a post office, part-time bank and bike-hire office there's no longer any reason to feel stuck in Firá. However, **rooms** aren't too easy to come by; the most reasonable choices are the *Hotel Anemones* (☎0286/71 220; ③) and the *Hotel Fregata* (☎0286/71 221; ③). Best-value eating is at the *Neptune*, or *Markozanes*, 1km east in Finikiá hamlet.

Beaches on Santoríni are bizarre: long black stretches of volcanic sand which get blisteringly hot in the afternoon sun. There's little to choose between Kamári and Périssa, the two main resorts; both have long beaches and a mass of restaurants, rooms and apartments; neither is for those seeking solitude. Périssa gets more backpackers, and has the well-run **hostel** *Anna* (②). Rough campers may be rousted by police.

Kamári and Périssa are separated by the Mésa Vounó headland, on which stood **ancient Thíra** (Tues–Sun 8.30am–3pm; free). Most of the ruins are difficult to place, but the theatre is awesome – beyond the stage there's a sheer drop to the sea.

Evidence of the Minoan colony was found at **Akrotíri** (Tues–Sun 8.30am–3pm; 1000dr), a village buried under banks of volcanic ash at the southwest tip of the island, and reached by bus from Firá or Périssa. Tunnels through the ash uncovered structures two and three storeys high; lavish frescoes adorned the walls and Cretan pottery was found stored in a chamber. The frescoes are currently exhibited in Athens, but there are plans to bring them back when a new museum is built.

Kárpathos

Kárpathos has always been something of a backwater, and despite a magnificent coastline of cliffs and rocky promontories constantly interrupted by little beaches, has succumbed surprisingly little to tourism. **PIGÁDHIA**, the capital, is now more often known simply as Kárpathos. It curves around one side of Vróndis Bay, a long sickle of sandy beach stretching north. **Hotels** such as the *Avra* (☎0245/22 388; ②) and **rooms** like at *Sofia's* (☎0245/22 154; ②) in town often get full in midsummer, but the beach to the north can be a useful campers' fall-back, particularly under the trees by the ruined fifth-century basilica of **Ayía Fotiní**.

Most, but not all ferries calling at Pigádhia stop also at **DHIAFÁNI**, the northern port, which is also served by a daily *kaíki* from Pigádhia. Although its popularity is growing, rooms in Dhiafáni are still cheap and life slow. Paths lead north to the stony Vanánda beach half an hour away and south to more isolated strands, while both road and path climb to **ÓLIMBOS**, two hours' walk into the mountains and the one essential sight on the island. The older women, in their magnificent traditional dress, dominate the village, working in the gardens, carrying goods on their shoulders, or tending mountain sheep. Ólimbos men nearly all emigrate or work outside the village, sending money home and returning only at holidays. The long-isolated villagers also speak a unique dialect, said to maintain traces of its Doric and Phrygian origins. Traditional music is still heard regularly and draws considerable crowds of visitors at festival times. There are several cheap places to stay (*Olimbos, Aphrodite* or *Posidon*; all ②) and a couple of tavernas – but it is impossible to get a room around the dates of any festival.

Ródhos (Rhodes)

It's no surprise that **RÓDHOS** is among the most visited of Greek islands. Not only is its east coast lined with sandy beaches, but the core of the capital is a beautiful and remarkably preserved medieval city. **RÓDHOS TOWN** divides neatly into two: the old walled city, and the tourist-oriented new town which has oozed out around it. The **old town** is infinitely more rewarding. First thing to meet the eye, and dominating the northeast sector of the city's fortifications, is the **Palace of the Grand Masters** (Tues–Sun 8.30am–3pm; 800dr). Destroyed by an explosion in 1856, it was reconstructed by the Italians as a summer home for Mussolini and Victor Emmanuel III, neither of whom used it much. Inside, a marble staircase leads up to rooms paved with mosaics from Kós, and the furnishings rival many a grand northern European palace.

The heavily restored **Street of the Knights** (Odhós Ippotón) leads due east from the front of the palace. The "Inns" lining it housed the Knights of St John for two centuries, and at the bottom of the slope the Knights' Hospital has been restored as the **Archeological Museum** (summer Tues–Fri 8.30am–3pm, Sat & Sun 8am–7pm; winter Tues–Sun 8.30am–3pm; 600dr), where the star exhibits are two statues of Aphrodite. Across the way is a **Byzantine Museum** (same hours and fees), housed in the knights' chapel and devoted to the island's icons and frescoes.

Leaving the Palace and heading south, it's hard to miss the most conspicuous Turkish monument in Rhodes, the candy-striped **Süleymaniye Mosque**. Downhill and east from the mosque is **Odhós Sokrátous**, once the heart of the old bazaar, and now packed with souvenir shops and milling foreigners. The most enduring civic contribution of Rhodes' Muslims is the **bathhouse** on Platía Ariónos, up in the southwest corner of the old city. One of only a couple of working public baths in Greece, it's a great place to go on an off-season day (Mon–Sat 7am–7pm; nominal charge).

Cheap **pensions** abound in Ródhos and are contained almost entirely in the quad bounded by Odhós Omírou on the south, Sokrátous on the north, Perikléos to the east and Ippodhámou in the west. Outside peak season lodging is the one thing still reasonably priced (②), but at crowded times it's wise to accept the offers of proprietors meeting the ferries. **Eating cheaply** can be more of a problem: try the little alleys and backstreets well south of Sokrátous. Here you'll find *Yiannis*, Apéllou 41, *O Meraklis* at Aristotélous 32, and *Le Bistrot*, Omírou 22.

OTE, the **post office, banks, EOT** and the **police** are all in the new town, mostly northwest of the Italian-built New Market. **Buses** for the rest of the island leave from Odhós Papágou, close to the market; services are frequent but relatively expensive.

Around the island

Heading down the east coast from Ródhos, the giant volcanic promontory of **TSAMBÍKAS**, 26km south, is the first place to seriously consider stopping – it has an excellent beach, and there's another one further south at Stégna. Best overnight base on this stretch of coast is probably **HARÁKI**, a tiny port with rooms and tavernas overlooked by an impressive castle.

LÍNDHOS, Rhodes' number-two tourist draw, erupts 12km south of here. Like Ródhos town itself, its charm is undermined by commercialism and crowds, and there are only a few places to stay that are not booked semi-permanently by tour companies. Nevertheless, if you can arrive before or after the tours, Líndhos can still be a beautiful and atmospheric place. Its **Byzantine church** is covered with eighteenth-century frescoes, and several of the older houses are open to the public; entrance is free but they tend to expect you to buy something. On the hill above the town, the scaffolding-swathed **Temple of Athena** stands inside the castle (summer Tues–Fri 8.30am–3pm, Sat & Sun 8am–7pm; winter Tues–Sun 8.30am–3pm; 800dr). Líndhos' beaches are crowded and overrated, so head for **LÁRDHOS BAY**, 10km south, which has great dunes behind its beach and the best of the island's **campsites**. Inland near here, the medieval frescoes in the village church of **ASKLIPÍO** are the best on Rhodes.

South of Lárdhos, gone are the spanking new roads and the luxury hotels, and with them most of the crowds. Gone too are most tourist facilities and public transport: only one daily bus runs along the east coast to Katavía, near Rhodes' southerly tip. It's here that you'll find the less developed beaches: often windy, but with dunes which offer shelter and plenty of scope for secluded camping. Tavernas grace the better stretches of sand but there are few places to stay except at **YENÁDHI**, where you can find rooms in the village, and **PLIMÍRI**, 20km south, where the restaurant has some basic beds. **KATAVÍA** itself has rooms and meals, and is the last inhabited outpost before the windy sandpit of **PRASSONÍSSI**, beloved of windsurfers.

Sími

Sími's great problem, lack of water, is in many ways also its greatest asset, as the island can't hope to support more than one or two large luxury hotels. Instead, hundreds of people are shipped in daily from Rhodes, relieved of their money and sent back. The island's capital consists of **Yialós**, the port, and **Horió**, on the hillside above, collectively known as **SÍMI**. Less than a century ago the town was richer and more populous than Rhodes, but the magnificent nineteenth-century mansions are now for the most part roofless and deserted, their windows gaping blankly across the harbour.

Rooms' proprietors generally meet arriving boats on a rota worked out among themselves; if you phone ahead, Katerina Tsakivis (☎0241/71 813; ③) will meet you regardless. Two budget standbys only open in high season are *Glafkos* (☎0241/71 358; ②) and *Egli* (☎0241/71 392; ②). **Eating out**, shun the north quay in favour of *O Meraklis* and *Neraidha*; in the Horió, *Georgios* is a long-standing, good-value choice. Higher up, the island **museum** contains the usual assortment of local artefacts, while at the very pinnacle a castle occupies the site of Sími's acropolis, surrounded by a dozen chapels.

Sími has no big sandy beaches, but there are plenty of pebbly stretches at the heads of the coastline's deep narrow bays. **PÉDHI**, 45 minutes' walk or a ten-minute regular bus ride from Yialós, is a hamlet in one of Sími's only farming valleys, with an average beach, some seasonal rooms and an exorbitant new hotel. Many will opt for a twenty minute walk via a goat track on the south shore to **ÁYIOS NIKÓLAOS**, stony but with fine swimming. Further afield, excursion boats tout day trips to the southeasterly bays of **MARATHOÚNDA, NANOÚ** and **ÁYIOS YIÓRYIOS DHISSÁLONA**, or the giant **Monastery of Taxiárhis Mihaél Panormítis** at the far south of the island.

Kós

After Rhodes, **Kós** is easily the most popular island in the Dodecanese, and there are remarkable similarities between the two. On Kós as on Rhodes the harbour is guarded by a castle of the Knights of St John, the waterside is lined with grandiose Italian public buildings, and minarets and palm trees punctuate extensive Greek and Roman remains. Once again, Scandinavian package tourists predominate, filling the hotels behind the beaches – in mid-season you'd be lucky to find any sort of room at all, except perhaps at the far west end of the island.

The town of **KÓS** spreads in all directions from the harbour. Around the waterside are scattered **restaurants**, with only the *Romantica* and next-door *Limnos* halfway reasonable. Among budget **hotels**, *Elena*, at Megálou Alexándhrou 5 (③), or *Pension Alexis*, Irodhótou 9 (③), are the quietest. *EOT*, next to the municipal bus stop, offers comprehensive ferry schedules; long-distance **buses** depart from beside a park 500m south of the quay. The official **campsite** is half an hour's walk along the scrappy beach to the southeast of town, served by city buses.

Apart from the **castle** (daily except Mon 8.30am–3pm; 400dr), the town's main attraction is its wealth of Hellenistic and Roman remains, the largest single section of which is the ancient **agora**, reached from the castle or the main square next to the **Archeological Museum** (same hours; free). The best pieces have been taken for safe-keeping into the castle, where most are piled up, unmarked and unnoticed. A couple of pillars, now replaced by scaffolding, formerly propped up the branches of **Hippocrates' plane tree**, which has a fair claim as one of the oldest trees in Europe.

Not only does Hippocrates have a tree named after him, but the star exhibit in the museum is his statue, and the **Asclepion** (summer Tues–Fri 8.30am–3pm, Sat & Sun 8am–7pm; winter daily except Mon 8.30am–3pm; 600dr), a temple to Asclepius and renowned centre of Hippocratic teaching, 45 minutes on foot (or briefer bus ride) from town. The road to the Asclepion passes through the bi-ethnic village of **PLATÁNI**, where the Greek Orthodox stay in their single *kafenío* while the Muslim majority hold forth at the three establishments dominating the crossroads. All of the latter serve excellent, cheap, Turkish-style food, far better than you generally get in Kós town.

If you're looking for anything resembling a deserted **beach** near the capital, you'll need to ride the urban buses again, or else hire transport. Simplest is to walk out along **Lámbi beach**, which stretches for three kilometres north of town towards Cape Skandhári, the crowds thinning progressively until you hit the off-limits military base. On the same coast, 12km west of Kós town, **TIGÁKI** is easily accessible by long-distance bus or rented bicycle, and thus crowded until evening when everyone, except for a few campers or those lucky enough to rent a room, has disappeared.

KARDHÁMENA, halfway down the southeast coast, is the island's second largest tourist playpen and runaway development has banished whatever qualities it may once have had. Continuing south, buses run as far as Kéaflos, which squats on a mesa-like hill looking back down the length of Kós. However, most visitors will have descended long before, either at **KAMÁRI**, with its plentiful accommodation, or **ÁYIOS STÉFANOS** (ditto), where the exquisite remains of a fifth-century basilica overlook tiny Kastrí islet. The beach begins at Kamári and runs five kilometres east, virtually without interruption, to cliff-framed and aptly named **Paradise beach**.

Pátmos

It was in a cave on **PÁTMOS** that Saint John the Divine wrote the Book of Revelation, and the monastery which commemorates him, founded here in 1088, dominates the island both physically and politically. While the monks no longer run the island as they did for more than 700 years, their influence has stopped most of the island going the way of Rhodes or Kós. **SKÁLA**, the port and main town, is the chief exception, crowded on summer days with excursionists from Kós and Rhodes, and by night with well-dressed cliques of French, Germans, Italians, Brits and Americans.

The boat docks are right opposite the police station, the **tourist office** just behind it. **Accommodation** here is in demand but there's a reasonable amount of it: the *Blue Bay Hotel* (☎0247/311659; ③), by the harbour, is a fine choice, or there are dozens of cheaper pensions. More likely, however, you'll end up in **rooms**, hawked vociferously as ever on the quay; they are mostly better than usual quality, though at higher than usual prices too. Among **restaurants**, try *Grigori's*, the top choice; the *Skorpios Creperie*, on the main road to Hóra; or *Platanos*, inland past the OTE on the secondary street to Hóra. North around the bay lies **Méloï Beach**, with a good, but overpriced, **campsite**; for swimming, the next beach, **Agriolivádhi** is preferable.

The **Monastery of St John** is sheltered behind massive defences in the hilltop capital of Hóra. There is a bus up, but the half-hour walk by a beautiful old cobbled path puts you in a more appropriate frame of mind. Just over halfway is the Monastery of the Apocalypse, built around the cave where Saint John heard the voice of God issuing from a cleft in the rock. This is merely a foretaste, however, of the main monastery, behind whose fortifications have been preserved a fantastic array of religious treasures dating back to the earliest days of Christianity. Opening hours are incredibly erratic – the best advice is to go any morning between 8am and noon.

HÓRA itself is a beautiful little town whose antiquated alleys shelter over forty churches and monasteries. The churches, many of them containing beautiful icons and examples of the local skill in wood carving, are almost all locked, but someone living nearby will have the key. If you're determined to stay here – and there is only a total of about fifty beds – it's best to make enquiries at the recommended taverna *Vangelis*, on Platía Levías, early in the day.

From Hóra a good road runs past the forgettable package resort of **Gríkou** to the isthmus of **Stavrós**, from where a half-hour trail leads to the much better beach, with one seasonal taverna, at **Psiliámmos** (there's also a summer *kaíki* service from Skála). More good beaches are found in the north of the island, particularly **Livádhi Yeránou**, shaded by tamarisk groves, and **Lámbi** with volcanic pebbles and two quality tavernas.

THE NORTHERN AEGEAN ISLANDS

In the northeasternmost part of the Aegean, the seven islands scattered off the coast of Asia Minor and Greece form a rather arbitrary archipelago. Despite their proximity to Turkey, members of the group bear few signs of an Ottoman heritage. There's the odd minaret or two, and some of the domestic architecture betrays obvious influences from Constantinople, Thrace and further north in the Balkans, but by and large the enduring Greekness of these islands is testimony to the 4000-year Hellenic presence in Asia Minor. International tensions are, if anything, worse than in the Dodecanese, and the resulting heavy military presence can be disconcerting. But, as in the Dodecanese, local tour operators do a thriving business shuttling passengers for absurdly high tariffs between the easternmost islands and the Turkish coast.

Sámos is the most visited of the "group", but, if you can leave the crowds behind, perhaps also the most verdant and beautiful. **Híos** is culturally interesting, but its natural beauty has been ravaged and the development of tourism has – so far – been deliberately retarded. **Lésvos** is more of an acquired taste, though once you get a feel for the island you may find it hard to leave. The appeal of **Thássos** is rather broader, with a varied offering of sandy beaches, forested mountains and minor archeological sites; cheaply accessible from the mainland, it can, however be rather overrun in high season.

The **Sporades** are a very easy group to island-hop and well connected by bus and ferry with Athens via Áyios Konstantínos or Kími, and with Vólos. The three northern Sporades – package tourist haven Skíathos, Alónissos and **Skópelos**, the pick of the trio – have good beaches, transparent waters and thick pine forests. **Skíros**, the fourth island of the archipelago, is slightly isolated from the others, less scenic, but with perhaps the most character, retaining something of its traditional culture as well as brilliant-white Cycladic-style architecture. It is only beginning to get developed, and for an uncommercialized island within six or seven hours of Athens it is hard to beat.

Sámos

Lush and seductive, Sámos was the wealthiest island in the Aegean during the seventh century, but fell on hard times thereafter; today the Samian economy is increasingly dependent on package tourism, far too much of it in places. The more rugged western part of the island has retained much of its undeveloped grandeur, but the eastern half of Sámos has surrendered to the onslaught of holiday-makers. It's a rather staid, Nordic, thirtysomething clientele, with the absence of a campsite on an island of this size clueing you in as to what sort of visitor is expected.

All main-line ferries call at both Karlóvassi in the west and Vathí, the capital, in the east; additionally there are services out of Pithagório in the south. **VATHÍ** itself lines the steep-sided shore of its namesake bay and is of minimal interest except for its hill quarter of tottering, tile-roofed houses, Áno Vathí, and an excellent **archeological museum** (Tues–Sun 8.30am–3pm; 500dr). A wealth of peculiar votive offerings balances the star exhibit: a huge, five-metre *kouros* or statue of an idealized youth.

If you want to **stay**, pensions without tour group allotments include the basic *Ionia*, Manóli Kalomíri 5 (☎0273/28 782; ②); the nearby *Trova* at no. 26 (☎0273/27 759; ②); or, moving slightly higher, the *Avli* on Lykoúrgou (☎0273/22 939; ③) and the *Pelopidas* at Roíkou 10 (☎0273/28 558; ③). **Eating out**, avoid the obvious tourist traps in favour of *Psitopolio Alekos*, in the bazaar; *Grigori's Grill,* inland near the post office; or in exchange for a bit more cash, *Ta Dhiodhia*, down at the south end of the front past the *Credit Bank*. **Bus services** off the main corridors to Kokkári and Pithagório are skimpy; you're expected to hire a **moped** or motorbike, for which there are a dozen outlets in town.

After Vathí, **PITHAGÓRIO** is the island's main resort; its views across to Turkey are more attractive than the surroundings, though the village and its relentlessly commercialized harbour retain some charm. It's built atop the ancient capital of the island, of which evidence abounds: Roman baths, an ancient aqueduct (the Evapalinio tunnel), an amphitheatre, and – 8km west – the **Sanctuary of Hera** (Tues–Sun 8.30am–3pm; 500dr), marked by a single standing column. Pithagório has little to hold you in the way of good-value accommodation or food, however, just show up for your ferry to the Dodecanese.

Heading west from Vathí, the first place of any note is the growing resort of **KOKKÁRI**, enchantingly set between twin headlands at the base of forested mountains. Nearby beaches are pebbly and exposed, prompting its role as a major windsurfers' resort. You've slightly more chance of happening on a free room here than in Pithagório; **eating out**, try the *Samia*, on the far west end of the beach strip, or *Farmers Restaurant* in the town centre. Beyond Kokkári beckon the pebble beaches of **Lemonákia, Tzamadhoú, Tzábou** and **Avlákia**, the last a low-key resort; inland a **network of hikeable trails** and jeep tracks link the villages of Vourliótes, Manolátes and Stavrinídhes, as well as the monastery of Vrondianí, with Kokkári.

KARLÓVASSI, the island's second town, divides into four, generally nondescript districts; most tourists spend their time at the harbour Limáni and the canyon-side village of Paleó Karlóvassi. Despite its lack of distinction, Karlóvassi makes an excellent base for exploring the mountains and beaches of western Sámos; in Limáni *George Moskoyannis* (☎0273/32 812; ②) and *Ioannis Feloukatzis* (☎0273/35 318; ②) are adjacent rooms establishments. Skip the overpriced harbour tavernas in favour of *Para Pende* or *Kotronis*, both 1km inland in Meséo Karlóvassi.

Less than an hour's walk west from Karlóvassi, **Potámi** is a popular beach ringed by forest and weird rock formations; for more solitude you can continue another hour or so to the two bays of **Mikró Seitáni** (pebbles) and **Megálo Seitáni** (sand). But for an actual amenitied beach resort in the west of the island, you'll need to shift south to **VOTSALÁKIA**, almost 2km of sand and pebbles lined with accommodation, under the shadow of brooding Mount Kérkis. *Emmanuel Dhespotakis* (☎0273/37 310; ③) has two premises on the westerly and more peaceful of two bays here; among tavernas, *Akroyialia* is the most reasonable and filling.

Híos

Increasing numbers of foreigners are discovering **Híos** beyond its port city – fascinating villages, an important Byzantine monument and a healthy complement of beaches. Unfortunately, there are only about 3000 guest beds on the entire island, a sobering figure when nearly that number of tourists arrive daily in season. Best, therefore, to visit out of season or stay outside the main town.

HÍOS town is always full of life, with a shambling old bazaar district, some excellent authentic tavernas, and a regular evening promenade along the waterfront. Relatively cheap **accommodation** is beginning to proliferate along the waterfront and just behind; the helpful **tourist office** at Kanári 11 has comprehensive lists. For a quick stay, the rock-bottom *Filxenia* (☎0271/22 813; ②) or the more salubrious *Apollonio* (☎0271/24 842; ③) are fine, but for a longer period such pensions as *Rooms with a View* (☎0271/20 364; ②) or *Ionia* (☎0271/22 759; ③) are preferable.

Eating out is better than the glut of fast-food places would suggest. Best of the bunch is *O Hotzas*, at the far end of the bazaar at Stefánou Tsourí 74. More centrally you can get good, cheap, cooked lunches at *Estiatorio Dhimitrakopoulos* on the corner of Sgoutá and Valtarías, a few steps from the bus terminal. At the west end of the waterside, where the big ferries dock, you'll find the *Ouzeri Theodhosiou*. The milkshops by the *Hotel Apollonio* have good puddings and breakfast yoghurts.

Green long-distance **buses** run from the terminal south of the central park to most of the villages on Híos, though services to the north are sparse. The closest good **beach** is **Karfás** (7km – very frequent blue bus), a long sweep of fine sand unfortunately overwhelmed by recent development.

Around the island

The monastery of **NÉA MONÍ**, founded by the Byzantine emperor in 1049, is the most beautiful and important medieval building on the Greek islands. Its mosaics rank among the finest artistic expressions of their age, and its setting, high in the mountains west of the port, is no less memorable. There's a direct green bus only on Wednesday mornings for mass; at other times you have to take a local blue bus as far as Karyés (7km) and walk or hitch an equal distance further. Once a community of 600 monks, Néa Moní was pillaged during Turkish atrocities in 1822 and most of its inmates put to the sword. Today the monastery, with its giant refectory and vaulted water cisterns, is maintained by just three nuns and a few lay workers.

The dry valleys of **southern Híos** are home to the mastic bush, whose resin – for centuries the base of paints and cosmetics – was the source of the island's wealth before petrochemicals came along. The towns themselves are the only settlements on Híos spared by the Turks in 1822, and at the first opportunity it's worth jumping on a bus headed for Pirgí or Mestá. **PIRGÍ**, 24km from the port, is one of the liveliest and most colourful of the villages, its houses elaborately embossed with geometric patterns cut into the plaster and then outlined with paint. On the northeast corner of the central *platía*, the fresco-embellished Byzantine church of **Áyii Apóstoli** is tucked under an arcade (erratic hours). Pirgí has a handful of rooms, a couple of tavernas, and some good beaches nearby – the closest being Eeborió, 5km from Pirgí and served by occasional buses in summer. **MESTÁ**, 11km west of Pirgí, has a more sombre feel, with its warren of stone houses doubling as the town's perimeter fortification. From the central *platía*, dominated by a church, a bewildering maze of cool, shaded lanes, provided with anti-earthquake buttresses and tunnels between the unpainted houses, wanders off in all directions. There are rooms to let here, and a few overpriced tavernas on the *platía*.

The villages of **northern Híos** never recovered from the Turkish massacres of the War of Independence, and many of the settlements are now virtually deserted. For the short-term visitor, perhaps the best target in this region is eerie **VOLISSÉS**, a large, half-inhabited village guarded by a castle. Just over a kilometre away there's **LIMNIÁ**, a lively and authentic little fishing village with two tavernas, one of which has a few rooms. One kilometre southeast, at Horí, begins an almost boundless sand-and-pebble **beach**, while the more intimate cove of Límnos is just a ten-minute walk over the headland north of the harbour. **AYÍA MARKÉLLA**, 5km further north, stars in many of the local postcards: a long, stunning beach fronting the monastery of the same name – not particularly interesting but with a summer taverna and lodging in the grounds. Most of the beaches hereabouts seem tailor-made for camping – tolerated due to the shortage of rooms – and outside of midsummer you'll have little company.

Lésvos

Lésvos, birthplace of Sappho, may not at first strike the visitor as particularly beautiful or interesting, but the rocky volcanic landscape of pine and olive groves grows on you with increased acquaintance. Despite the inroads of mass-market tourism, this is still by and large a working island, with few large hotels outside the capital, **MITILÍNI**. Moreover, buses from Mitilíni are run for the benefit of the locals, not tourists, and journeys are often slow and tortuous – it's wise to base yourself at one of the several resorts and explore its surroundings. Mitilíni itself has little to detain you, other than a good **archeological museum** (daily 8.30am–3pm; 400dr); **rooms** are expensive and restaurants substandard. Worth a detour at **VARIÁ**, 5km south, are the adjacent **Theophilos** and **Teriade museums**, with astonishing collections of folk and modern art respectively (both daily except Mon 9am–1pm & 4.30–8pm; small admission fee).

MÓLIVOS, on the northwestern coast, is easily the most attractive spot on Lésvos, a fact which is becoming better known every year. Tiers of sturdy, red-tiled houses, some standing defensively with their backs to the sea, mount the slopes between the picturesque harbour and the Genoese castle. Closer examination reveals a half-dozen weathered Turkish fountains along shady, stone-paved alleyways. There are plenty of **rooms** to let, a **tourist office** by the bus stop to help you find them if necessary, and a **campsite** east of town. The main lower road, straight past the tourist office, heads towards the picturesque harbour, where *Ta Khtapodhi* is the one affordable **taverna**; back up in town, try *Melinda's*. What with a **bank**, **post office** and **OTE** station, there's no need to move far to transact essential business.

PÉTRA, 5km due south of Mólivos, is marginally quieter, though the package companies have certainly moved in. The village spreads behind a good sand beach and a seafront *platía*, with plenty of rooms, tavernas and (for the moment) small hotels.

The island's best **beach** is **SKÁLA ERESSOÚ** on the west coast. There are rooms to let here, but sometimes not enough, so **camping** is tolerated at a quasi-official site to the west; **tavernas** with wooden terraces line the beach – best of these are *Toh Aigaion*, *Ih Paralia* and *Bennetts*, with *Aphrodite* recommended inland. Visitors include gay women paying homage to the poet **Sappho**, who supposedly lived in ancient Eressós – all that remains of the old town crumbles away atop a bluff to the east. The southeastern peninsula of Lésvos also offers its share of attractions. Foremost is the huge beach at **VATERÁ**; the equal of Skála Eressoú's and provided with a new **campsite** and good shoreline **tavernas**. Further east, **Plomári** is the island's third resort after Mólivos and Pétra, though better **beaches** and **tavernas** are at nearby **Áyios Isídhoros**. Finally, inland **Ayiássos**, north of Plomári, is a beautiful hill town famous for its August 15 festival, the liveliest of the many observed on Lésvos.

Thássos

Just twelve kilometres from the mainland, **Thássos** has long been a popular resort for northern Greeks, and in recent years has been attracting considerable numbers of foreign tourists. Without being spectacular it is a very beautiful island, its almost circular area covered in gentle slopes of pine, olive and chestnut which rise to a mountainous backbone and plunge to a line of good sand beaches.

THÁSSOS TOWN is the island capital and nexus of life, though not the main port: ferries from Kavála usually stop down the coast at Órmos Prínou, but a few each day continue to Thássos town. The largely modern town is partly redeemed by its pretty harbour and popular sand beach just east, and the substantial remains of the ancient city. If you want to stay there are several cheap **hotels** – the *Astir, Diamando, Viky* and *Angelika* (all ③) – plus reasonably plentiful rooms, though in summer you should take the first offered on arrival. **Eating out**, menus tend to be expensive and bland. There's a privately-run *Thassos Tours* **tourist information office** on the main street parallel to the seafront, and a high-season **tourist police** office near the bus station.

The main excavated area of ancient Thássos is the **agora**, entered beside the town **museum** (Tues–Sat 8.30am–3pm, Sun 9.30am–2.30pm; 400dr), a little way back from the modern harbour. Prominent are two Roman stoas but you can also make out shops, monuments, passageways and sanctuaries from the remodelled Classical city. Above the town, roughly in line with the smaller fishing port, steps spiral up to a **Hellenistic theatre**, fabulously positioned above a broad sweep of sea. Beyond the theatre, a path winds on to a **Genoese fort**, constructed out of stones from the acropolis. From here you can follow the circuit of **walls** to a high terrace supporting the foundations of a Temple of Apollo and onwards to a rock-hewn sanctuary of Pan. Below it a precarious sixth-century BC "secret stairway" descends to the outer walls and back into town.

About five **buses** per day do the full island circuit in season, and there are several more to and from different villages, with a bias towards the west coast. The south-facing coast has most of the best beaches. Above the east coast, **PANAYÍA** village, with its **accommodation** and proximity to **Hrissí Amnoudhísa Beach**, makes the best base; **KÍNIRA**, 11km south, is quieter and right on the seaside. **ALIKÍ** faces a double bay which almost pinches off a headland. The mixed sand-and-pebble spit gets too popular for its own good in high season, but the water is crystal-clear and the beachside taverna offers good food. The hamlet here has one place with rooms. At the south tip of Thássos, **ASTRÍS** has two excellent beaches set in a stunning cliffscape, but the best-appointed local resort – and virtually the only one to function outside of summer – is **POTÓS**, where there's a **campsite** plus a fine, kilometre-long sand beach facing the sunset.

Skópelos

More rugged and better cultivated than neighbouring Skíathos, **Skópelos** is also very much more attractive. Most boats call first at the small port of Loutráki, below the western village of Glóssa, but it's best to stay on board until **SKÓPELOS TOWN**, sloping down one corner of a huge, almost circular bay. **Hotels** here are ever-increasing in quantity, but occupied mainly by package tourists; tucked away on the far side of the bay, in the main body of the town there are dozens of **rooms** to let – take up one of the offers when you land. **Nightlife** is fairly subdued, though there are several discos and a dozen or so bars. The three tavernas opposite where the ferries dock are acceptable, though hardly cheap. Within the town, spread below the oddly whitewashed ruins of a Venetian **kástro**, are an enormous number of churches – 123 reputedly, though some are small enough to be mistaken for houses.

Buses cover the island's one asphalt road between Skópelos and Loutráki about six times daily, stopping at the turn-offs to all the main beaches and villages. **Stáfilos Beach**, 4km out of town, is the closest, but small, rocky and increasingly crowded – the overflow, much of it nudist, flees to Velánio, just east. Much more promising, if you're after isolation and happy to walk to a nearby beach, is **PÁNORMOS**, a pleasant little hamlet with rooms, tavernas and a **campsite**. The beach here is gravelly and steeply shelving, but there are small secluded bays close by and, slightly further on at **MILIÁ**, a tremendous, 1500m sweep of tiny pebbles beneath a bank of pines.

Skíros

Despite its closeness to Athens, Skíros was until recently a very traditional and idiosyncratic island, but it has definitely been "discovered" since 1980. Now it's very much the haunt of continental Europeans, chic Athenians and British, many of whom check into the island's "New Age" centre. The islanders, meanwhile, remain amazingly friendly and Skíros still ranks as one of the most interesting places in the Aegean. It has a long tradition of ornate woodcarving, and the older men still wear the vaguely Cretan costume of cap, vest, baggy trousers, leggings and clogs. The women favour yellow scarves and long embroidered skirts. Skíros also has some particularly lively **festivals** – notably the *Apokriatiká* (pre-Lenten) carnival's "Goat Dance", performed by masked revellers in the village streets.

The main paved road on the island connects Linariá – a functional little port with a few tourist facilities – to Hóra, the capital. The two towns are about 10km apart and there is a bus service which exists principally to meet the ferries. **HÓRA**, with its decidedly Cycladic architecture, sits on the landward side of a high rock rising precipitously from the coast. Traces of Classical walls can still be made out among the ruins of the Venetian **kástro**; just within the circuit of the walls, and dominating everything, is the crumbling, tenth-century monastery of Áyios Yióryios, its stones partly incorporated into the later *kástro*. Perhaps equally striking, and splendidly incongruous, is the **Memorial to Rupert Brooke** – a bronze nude of "Immortal Poetry" – at the north end of town. Brooke, who visited the south of the island briefly in April 1915, died shortly after of blood poisoning on a French hospital ship anchored offshore. Close to the Brooke statue there's an **Archeological Museum** (Tues–Sat 9am–3.30pm, Sun 9.30am–2.30pm) and the adjacent **Faltaitz Ethnological Museum** (daily 10am–1pm & 5.30–8pm), which has a broad selection of domestic items and rare documents.

Back in town, there are several **hotels** and plenty of **rooms to let** in private houses. The latter are preferable and you'll be met with offers as you descend from the bus. **Eating out**, you'll find most **tavernas** overpriced and mediocre, *O Glaros* being the exception. The **campsite** is down the hill from the Rupert Brooke statue, at the fishing village of **MAGAZIÁ**, with rooms and tavernas fronting the best beach on the island.

The only practical ways of getting around Skíros are on foot or by hiring a moped (there are several rental places in the main town), though in summer the whimsical bus service also visits the more popular beaches. The most rewarding walk is a four-hour traverse of the island by rough jeep track to Atsítsu on the west coast.

THE IONIAN ISLANDS

The six **Ionian islands** are both geographically and culturally a mixture of Greece and Italy. Floating on the haze of the Adriatic, their green, even lush, silhouettes come as a shock to those more used to the stark outlines of the Aegean. The islands were the Homeric realm of Odysseus and here alone of all modern Greek territory (except for Lefkádha) the Ottomans never held sway. After the fall of Byzantium, possession passed to the Venetians and the islands became a keystone in that city-state's maritime empire from 1386 until its collapse in 1797. Most of the population must have remained immune to the establishment of Italian as the official language and the arrival of Roman Catholicism, but Venetian influence remains evident and beautiful despite a series of earthquakes in the island capitals. On Corfu it is mixed with that of the British, who imposed a military "protectorate" over the Ionian islands at the close of the Napoleonic Wars before eventually ceding the archipelago to Greece in 1864.

Tourism has hit **Corfu** in a big way – so much so that it's the only island besides Crete known to locals and foreigners by different names. None of the other islands has endured anything like Corfu's scale of development, although the process seems well advanced on parts of **Zákinthos**. For a less sullied experience, the duo of **Kefalloniá** and **Itháki** is recommended.

Kérkira (Corfu)

Corfu's natural appeal remains an intense experience, if sometimes a beleaguered one, for Corfu has more package hotels and holiday villas than any other Greek island. The commercialism is apparent the moment you step ashore at the ferry dock, or cover the two kilometres from the **airport** to the city. From the latter you can walk, get a taxi, or catch the local #2 or #3 buses which leave 500m north of the terminal gates.

KÉRKIRA TOWN has a lot more going for it than first exposure to the summer crowds might indicate. The cafés on the Spianádha (Esplanade) and in the arcaded Listón have a civilized air, and the **Palace of St Michael and St George** on the Spianádha houses a large collection of Asiatic art. The Byzantine Museum and the Cathedral are also worth visiting, as is the **Archeological Museum** at Vraíla 3 (daily except Mon 8.30am–3pm; 400dr), where the small but interesting collection features a 2500-year-old gorgon's head. The island's patron saint, **Spirídhon**, is entombed in a silver-covered coffin in his own church on Odhós Vouthrótou, and four times a year, to the accompaniment of much celebration and feasting, the relics are paraded through the streets. Finally, five kilometres south of town lies one of Greece's most popular excursion targets, the postcard-picturesque **Vlahérna** island, which is capped by a small monastery and joined to the plush mainland suburb of **Kanóni** by a short causeway.

There's a very helpful **tourist office** just east of the Igoumenítsa ferry dock, next door to the tourist police. Here you can pick up free maps, bus timetables, and a list of hotels, campsites and rooms to let in private houses – the likeliest summer accommodation, though the office can't make reservations which is the province of certain agensies along Vassiléos Konstandínou. Cheaper old-town **hotels** include the *Elpis* at Parodhos Nikifórou Theotóki 4, *Kostantinoupoli* at Zavitsánou 11 and the highly visible *New York* at Ipapandís 21 – all ② out of season. **Eating out**, two authentic restaurants are *Yisdhakis* at Sólomou 20, off Theotóki, and the *Rex* on Kapodhistríou.

There are two **bus terminals**: one for blue-vehicle routes through the middle of the island on Platía San Rócco, the other for green buses to more remote destinations on Platía Néou Frouríou, just below the fort. **Mopeds** are also available nearby, and at most other main resorts.

Around the island

The coast north of the port has been remorselessly developed as far as Kassiópi and much of it is best written off. West of Kassiópi, the first substantial place to stay is **ÁYIOS SPIRÍDHON**, where there are restaurants and a few campers ignoring the "No camping" signs on the small beach. A little way on you'll see a sign to Almirós beach, start of the continuous strand that sweeps around to **RÓDHA** – once a small village but now taken over by British travel companies. The best spot on this northern coast is beyond Sidhári at **PEROULÁDHES**, a genuine, somewhat run-down village with a spectacular beach of brick-red sand below wind-eroded cliffs.

On the west coast, **PALEOKASTRÍTSA** has gone the way of all package locations, though its coves are on a beautiful stretch of coast. Expensive villas and hotels are present in abundance, plus a few **campsites**. If you just want a **room**, look uphill in the nearby villages of Lákones and Makrádhes.

The tiny village of **VÁTOS**, just inland from west-coast Ermónes, seems to be the one place within easy reach of Kérkira town that has an easy, relaxed feel to it. There are reasonable **rooms** and two **tavernas** here, both (as so often on Corfu) called *Spiro's*. Campers pitch tents down towards **Mirtiótissa Beach**, though they sometimes get encouraged to use the official site, *Vátos Camping*, near the village. The dirt track down to the sand is steep and has so far prevented development. Nearby **GLIFÁDHA** is dominated by a huge hotel and adjacent **PÉLEKAS** is likewise busy, as the main crossroads in the west-centre of the island; but it's a good alternative base, with simple **tavernas**, a **hostel** and **rooms**. Continuing south, **ÁYIOS GÓRDHIS** beach is more remote but that hasn't spared it from the crowds who come to admire the cliff-girt setting, or patronize the *Pink Palace*, a foreign-run combination holiday village/disco right on the sand.

Beyond Messongí extends the flat, sandy southern tip of Corfu. **ÁYIOS YIÓRYIOS**, on the southwest coast, consists of a developed area just before its beautiful beach. **KÁVOS**, near the cape itself, rates with its many **clubs** and **discos** as the nightlife capital of the island; for daytime solitude and swimming, you can walk to **beaches** beyond the nearby hamlets of Spartéra and Dhragotína.

Kefalloniá (Kefallinía, Cephalonia)

KEFALLONIÁ is the largest, and at first glance least glamorous, of the Ionian islands; the 1953 earthquake which rocked the archipelago was especially devastating here, with almost every town and village levelled. Couple that with the islanders' legendary eccentricity, and poor infrastructure – many roads are still unpaved – and it's no wonder tourism didn't take off until the late Eighties. Nonetheless, there's plenty here of interest: beaches to compare with the best on Corfu or Zákinthos, a good local wine, and the partly forested mass of 1632-metre Mount Énos. The island's size, skeletal bus service and persistent shortage of summer accommodation make **motorbike or car rental** a must for explorations; mopeds may not cope with some grades or surfaces.

Ferries from Pátras, other Ionian islands or overseas dock at Sámi, a drably functional port on the northeast coast; few people linger, especially when Ayía Evfimía, 10km north, makes a far more attractive base — ferries also call here from Astakós on the mainland, and you can **eat** at *Stavros Dhendhrinos*, arguably the best taverna on Kefalloniá. Between the two, 3km from Sámi, the **Melissáni cave**, a partly submerged Capri-type "blue grotto", is well worth a stop.

Southeast from Sámi you find the resorts of **POROS**, with ferries to Killíni on the Peloponnese, and **SKÁLA** whose remains of a **Roman villa** boast fine mosaics. Rooms are difficult to find here in season, being block-booked by tour operators. You may have to continue around the cape, past excellent beaches, to find accommodation in the coastal village of Lourdáta, about halfway between Skála and the island capital of Argostóli. Just inland, detour to the Venetian **castle of Áyios Yióryios**.

ARGOSTÓLI, with occasional ferries to Killíni and Zákinthos, is the bustling island capital: inevitably concrete, very Greek. The waterfront **tourist office** keeps comprehensive lists of **accommodation** and, unusually, may book private rooms for you — hotels are expensive. **Eating out**, a good if unromantically set fall-back is the *Adherfi Tzirvas*, on Vandárou near the bus station; they also have rooms to rent. Argostóli is perhaps the best place to rent your **own transport**, with a dozen agencies on the front.

Heading north from Argostóli, there's little to stop for on the west coast until you emerge, along a dizzying corniche road, above **Mírtos**, considered the best beach on the island. There are almost no facilities, though — closest place to **stay** will be almost bus-less **ÁSSOS**, a fishing port perched on a narrow isthmus linking it to a castellated headland. End of the line means **FISKÁRDHO**, with its eighteenth-century houses, notable mainly for having escaped damage in the earthquake, and exploiting this fact relentlessly. It's the most expensive place on the island, and in July free rooms are as rare as snowflakes. The main reason to come here would be for the daily **ferry** to Lefkádha island, and sometimes Itháki.

Itháki (Ithaka)

Despite its proximity to Kefalloniá, there's still very little tourist development to spoil **Itháki** (Ithaka), Odysseus' capital. There are few sandy beaches, but the island is good walking country, with a handful of small fishing villages and various pebbly coves to swim from. Ferries from Pátra, Kefalloniá, Astakós, Corfu, Igoumítsa and Italy land at the main port and the village-sized capital of **VÁTHI**, at the back of a deep bay which seems to close completely around it. **Rooms** remain fairly easy to come by except during the July music festival and the August/September theatre events; they tend, however, to be inconspicuous, and are best sought by nosing around the backstreets south of the ferry dock. There are just two mid-range **hotels** at opposite ends of the long quay, the *Odysseus* and the *Mentor* (both ③). There's more choice for **food**, with seven or eight tavernas, though all seem remarkably similar in price and fare.

In season the usual small boats shuttle tourists from the harbour to a series of tiny coves along the peninsula northeast of Váthi. The pebble-and-sand **beaches** between Cape Skinós and Sarakinikó Bay are excellent; most of those closer to town are little more than concrete diving platforms.

Three daily **buses** run north along the main road out of Váthi to **STAVRÓS**, a fair-sized village with a couple of relatively expensive tavernas and some rooms. **FRÍKES**, a half-hour walk downhill beyond Stavrós, is smaller but has a handful of tavernas, rooms and a pebbly strip of beach. This is where the seasonal ferries dock, to and from Lefkádha and Fiskárdho on northern Kefalloniá; the port is linked by bus and occasional caique to Váthi. Forty minutes' walk east, the end of the road comes at the village of **KIÓNI**, one of the more attractive bases on the island, though its few rooms seem to be booked en masse for the summer by British holiday companies.

Zákinthos (Zante)

Zákinthos, which once exceeded Corfu itself in architectural distinction, was hit hardest by the 1953 Ionian earthquake, and the island's grand old capital was completely destroyed. Although some of its beautiful Venetian churches have been restored, it's a rather sad town and the attraction for travellers lies more in the thick vineyards, orchards and olive groves of the interior, and some excellent beaches. Under two hours from Killíni on the mainland, Zákinthos now gets close to half a million visitors a year. Most tourists, though, are conveniently housed in one place, Laganás, on the south coast; if you avoid July and August, and steer clear of Laganás and the developing villages of Argássi and Tsilívi, there is still a peaceful Zákinthos to be found.

The most tangible hints of the former glory of **ZÁKINTHOS TOWN** are in **Platía Solómou**, the grand and spacious main square. At its waterside corner stands the beautiful fifteenth-century sandstone church of **Áyios Nikólaos**, whose paintings and icons, along with those from other island churches, are displayed in the imposing **Neo-Byzantine Museum** (daily except Mon 8.30am–3pm) by the town hall. The collection is exceptional, for during the seventeenth and eighteenth centuries Zante became centre of a school of painting given impetus by Cretan refugees unable to practise under Turkish rule. The large church of **Áyios Dhioníssios** was one of the few buildings left standing after the earthquake, and murals still cover the interior. If you've a couple of hours to fill, walk up the cobble path to the town's massive **Venetian fortress** (closes 8pm); en route lies the suburb village of **Boháli**, occupying a natural balcony overlooking the harbour, with a number of popular, expensive tavernas.

As there is no tourist office, the **tourist police** on Platía Solómou have information about accommodation and bus services; they're in the police station on the front. **Accommodation** in Zákinthos town is relatively plentiful and reasonably priced, but tends to be hotel-based. Cheaper **hotels** include *Nea Zakynthos* at Filíkou 7 (②) and *Oasis* at Koutózi 58 (☎0695/22 287; ②). **Restaurants** or tavernas are a bit thin on the ground. *Taverna Arekia* is strongly recommended, but it's a fair walk north along the east road. You can also work up an appetite by walking a good way in the opposite direction to the *Malavetis Restaurant* at Ayíou Dhionissíou 4. More central is the *Kalliniko*, best value of the places on the Platía Solómou.

To get to the beaches, there is a **bus service** from the station on Odhós Filitá (one block back from the *Fina* pump on the main waterside road), but since the island is mostly flat, this is an ideal place to hire a **bike**, **moped** or **motorcycle**, all available from *Motorakis* on Leofóros Dhimokratías, opposite the phone office.

Around the island

Going **north or west** from town, the road threads its way through luxuriantly fertile farmland, punctuated with tumulus-like hills. **TSILÍVI**, 4km out, is the closest beach to town worthy of the name, shallow and sandy with warm water, though the evening breeze whips up the surf. There's an official **campsite** nearby.

ORMÓS ALIKÓN, some 13km on, is a huge, gently sloping expanse of sand washed by good breakers; at its eastern end the village of **ALÍKANAS** now consists solely of villas, block-booked by tour companies, and with an alarming amount of building still going on. Nearby, however, are two excellent restaurants: *Ta Neraidha*, with a great setting on Alíkanas harbour, and *Mandalena* on the road to Alikés – arguably the best eatery on the island. Towards the northwest end of the bay, **ALIKÉS** is as busy a resort as its neighbour, with rooms, restaurants and mopeds available. *Kaïkia* sail from here to the northern tip of the island, where the **Kianóu (Blue) Caves** are terrific for snorkellers. Also in the north, the tiny port of Koríthi sees daily high-season ferries to equally miniscule Pessádha on Kefalloniá. The road **southeast** from the capital goes to **VASSILIKÓS**, untouched by the concrete merchants and with rooms to let. You'll find more rooms along the tracks which continue to the **beaches** of Pórto Róma or Yérakas.

CRETE

With its flourishing agricultural economy, **Crete** is one of the few islands which could probably support itself without tourists. Nevertheless, tourism is heavily promoted here. The northeast coast in particular is overdeveloped and, though there are parts of the south and west coasts that have not been spoiled, they are getting harder and harder to find. By contrast, the high mountains of the interior are still barely touched, and one of the best things to do is to hire a moped and explore the remoter villages.

In history Crete is distinguished above all as the home of Europe's earliest civilization, the **Minoan** which made this the centre of a maritime trading empire as early as 2000 BC. The artworks produced on Crete at this time are unsurpassed anywhere in the ancient world and it seems clear, wandering through the Minoan palaces and towns, that life on Crete in those days was good. Their culture survived for nearly 500 years – by far the longest period of peace the island has seen. Control of the island passed from Greeks to Romans to Saracens, through the Byzantine Empire to Venice, and finally to Turkey for more than two centuries. During World War II the island was occupied by the Germans and attained the dubious distinction of being the first place to be successfully invaded by paratroops. Each ruler has left some mark, and has forged for the island a personality toughened by endless struggles for independence.

Every part of Crete has its loyal devotees, but generally if you want to get away from it all you should head west, towards **Haniá** and the smaller, less well-connected places along the south and west coasts. It is in this part of the island also that the White Mountains rise, while below them yawns the famous **Samarian Gorge**. Whatever you do, the first priority is to get away from **Iráklio** as quickly as possible, having paid a visit to nearby **Knossos**. The other great Minoan sites cluster around the middle of the island as well: **Festos** and **Ayía Triádha** in the south (with Roman **Gortys** to provide contrast), **Mália** on the north coast. Almost wherever you go, though, you'll find some kind of reminder of the island's history – for many people, unexpected highlights turn out to be Crete's Venetian forts, dominant at **Réthimno**, and its Byzantine churches, most famously near **Krítsa**.

Iráklio (Heraklion)

The best way to approach **IRÁKLIO** is by sea; that way you see the city as it should be seen, with Ioúktas rising behind and the Psilorítis range to the west. As you get closer, it's the city walls which first stand out, still dominating and fully encircling the oldest part of town, and finally you sail in past the great fort defending the harbour entrance. Unfortunately, big ships no longer dock in the old port but at great modern concrete wharves alongside – which neatly sums up Iráklio itself: many of the old parts have been restored from the bottom up, but they're of no relevance to the dust and noise which characterize the city today.

Platía Eleftherías is very much the traditional heart of the city, both in terms of traffic, which swirls around it constantly, and for life in general: lined with expensive cafés and restaurants, and jammed in the evening with strolling hordes. Most of Iráklio's more expensive shops are in the streets leading off the square. The **Archeological Museum** (summer Mon 11am–5pm, Tues–Fri 8am–5pm, Sat & Sun 8am–7pm; winter Sat & Sun 8.30am–5pm; 1000dr) is also just off here, directly opposite the EOT office. Almost every important prehistoric and Minoan find on Crete is part of this fabulous, if bewilderingly large, collection. Remember to save some energy for upstairs, too, where the **Hall of the Frescoes**, with its intricately reconstructed fragments of wall paintings from Knossos and other sites, is especially wonderful.

Practicalities

Finding a **room** can be very hard in season: the best place to look is in the area below Platía Venizélou. *Rent Rooms Mary*, Hándhákos 67 (☎081/281 135; ②), *Vergina*, Hortátson 32 (☎081/242 739; ②), and *Rea*, Kalimeráki 1 (☎081/223 638; ②), are all good and are close to each other. The official **youth hostel** is at Vironos 5 (☎081/286 281; ②), and there are more dorm beds at *Yours Hostel*, Handhákos 24 (☎081/280 858). Official **camping** is at the expensive and regimented *Camping Iráklio*, about 6km west on the beach at Amoudhári (bus #6).

Places to eat are everywhere but in general are expensive. For substantial meals the best bet is Fotíou Thedhosáki, the alley off the market on Odhós 1866, leading through to Odhós Evans, which is entirely taken up with tables. The restaurant below the *Hotel Ionia*, on the corner of Evans and Yianári, is also good. Other scattered possibilities include the *Taverna Rises* at the bottom of Handhákos or the pizzeria *Tartuffo* on Odhós Dhimokratías.

Iráklio's **tourist office** is just below Platía Eleftherías, opposite the archeological museum. The **tourist police** are on Dhikeosínis, halfway between Platía Eleftherías and the market, and the **post office** is just behind here, on Platía Dhaskaloyiánni. The 24-hour **OTE** office is next to El Greco Park, in the square immediately north of Venizélou. You can find several **banks** down Ikosipémptis Avgoústou, where the **shipping and travel agents** are. You'll also find **motorbike and car hire** down here, but places off the main road offer better prices; try *Motorad* at Víronos 1 for bikes, *Ritz* at Kalimeráki 1 for cars.

Buses for all points along the coast road leave from the new station by the harbour; south and east to Áno Viános, Mírtos and Árvi, from just outside the walls on Platía Kíprou, at the end of Odhós Evans; southwest to Festos, Mátala, Léndas and Ayía Galíni, or along the old road west, from just outside the Haniá Gate. For Knossos, the #2 local bus sets off from the stop adjacent to the harbour bus station, runs up Ikosipémptis Avgoústou and out of town on Odhós Evans.

Knossos

The largest of the Minoan palaces, **KNOSSOS** reached its cultural peak over 3000 years ago, though a town of some importance persisted here until well into the Roman era. It lies on a low, largely man-made hill some 5km southeast of Iráklio amid hillsides rich in lesser remains spanning twenty-five centuries. As soon as you enter the **Palace of Knossos** (Mon–Fri 8am–5pm, Sat & Sun 8am–7pm; 1000dr) through the West Court, the ancient ceremonial entrance, it is clear how the legends of the Labyrinth of the Minotaur grew up around it. Even with a detailed plan, it's almost impossible to find your way around the site systematically – but wander around for long enough and you'll eventually stumble upon everything.

Evidence of a luxurious lifestyle is plainest in the **Queen's Suite**, off the grand **Hall of the Colonnades** at the bottom of the staircase. Here, the main living room is decorated with the celebrated dolphin fresco – a duplicate of the original now in the Iráklio archeological museum. Remember, though, that all this is speculation and some of it is pure hype – like the dolphin fresco, found in the courtyard, not the room itself. Going up the **Grand Staircase** to the floor above the Queen's domain, you come to a set of rooms in a considerably sterner vein, generally regarded as the **King's quarters**. The staircase opens into a grandiose reception chamber known as the **Hall of the Royal Guard**, its walls decorated in repeated shield patterns. Continuing to the top of the staircase you emerge on to the broad **Central Court**, which would once have been enclosed by the walls of the buildings all around. On the far side, in the northwestern corner of the courtyard, is the entrance to one of Knossos' most atmospheric survivals, the **Throne Room**, in all probability the seat of a priestess rather than a ruler.

Gortys, Festos, Ayía Triádha and Mátala

The three major sites south of Iráklio – Gortys, Festos and Ayía Triádha – can be visited on a day's tour from the city, probably with a lunchtime swim at **Mátala** thrown in. Doing it by public transport you'll be forced into a rather more leisurely pace, but there's still no reason why you shouldn't get to all three sites and reach Mátala within the day; if necessary, it's easy enough to hitch the final stretch.

GORTYS (summer Mon–Fri 8.30am–3pm, Sat & Sun 8am–7pm; winter Tues–Sun 8.30am–3pm; 400dr) is the ruined capital of the Roman province which included not only Crete but also much of North Africa. Cutting across the fields will give you some idea of the scale of this city at its zenith, approximately the third century AD; an enormous variety of other remains, including an impressive theatre, are strewn across your route. Even in the nearest village, Áyii Dhéka, you'll see Roman pillars and statues lying around in people's yards or propping up their walls. At the main entrance to the fenced site, alongside the road, is the ruinous but still impressive basilica of **Áyios Títos**, the saint who converted Crete and was also its first bishop. Beyond this is the **Odeion** which houses the most important discovery on the site, the **Law Code** – an inscription measuring about thirty feet by ten feet in all.

Despite its magnificent setting overlooking the plain of Messará, the palace at **FESTOS** (summer Mon–Fri 8am–5pm, Sat & Sun 8am–7pm; winter Sat & Sun 8.30am–3pm; 800dr) is not as arresting as those at Knossos or Mália: the plan is almost as complex as at Knossos, but there's none of the reconstruction to bolster the imagination. Oddly enough, Festos was much less ornately decorated than Knossos; there is no evidence, for example, of any dramatic Minoan wall paintings. In common with the other palaces, there is a monumental stairway to a major courtyard – from here you've the view of the mountains which prompted the palace's siting.

By contrast, some of the finest artworks in the museum at Iráklio came from **AYÍA TRIÁDHA** (daily except Mon 8.30am–3pm; 400dr), less than an hour's walk away. No one is quite sure what this site is, but the most common theory is that it was some kind of royal summer villa. Look out in particular for the row of shops in front of what was apparently a marketplace, and for the remains of the paved road which once led down to the Gulf of Messará.

MÁTALA is by far the best-known beach in Iráklio province, widely promoted and included in tours mainly because of the famous caves cut into the cliffs above its beautiful beach. These ancient tombs used to be almost permanently inhabited by a sizeable hippie community; nowadays the town is full of package tourists and tries hard to present a respectable image: the cliffs are now cleared and locked up every evening. Early afternoon, when the tour buses pull in for their swimming stop, the beach is packed to overflowing. If the crowds get too much, it's a twenty-minute clamber over the rocks to another excellent stretch of sand, known locally as "Red Beach". In the evening, when the trippers have gone, there are waterside bars and restaurants looking out over invariably spectacular sunsets. The chief remaining problem concerns prices: **rooms** are both expensive (③) and oversubscribed, food is good but also not cheap.

Mália

The resort of **MÁLIA**, 20km east of Iráklio, is very commercial, and the long sandy beach becomes extremely crowded at times, but it's fun if you're prepared to enter into the sybaritic spirit of things. There are dunes at the end of the beach where people sleep out, plus a **youth hostel** signposted just off the main road. The cheapest rooms are in the old town – the hostel has lists. Ditto for tavernas, but avoid the ones lining the road to the beach which is better as a raucous nightlife venue.

The **Palace of Mália** (daily except Mon 8.30am–3pm; 400dr) lies forty minutes' walk east of Mália town along the beach or on the main road – any bus will stop there. It's a great deal easier to comprehend than Knossos, and if you've seen the reconstructions there, it's easy to envisage this seaside palace in its days of glory. Look out for the strange indented stone in the central court, which probably held ritual offerings; for the remains of ceremonial stairways; and for the giant *pithoi* (ceramic jars) which stand like sentinels around the palace. Moving on, you should have no difficulty flagging down a bus headed towards Áyios Nikólaos.

Áyios Nikólaos and around

ÁYIOS NIKÓLAOS is set around a supposedly bottomless salt lake, now connected to the sea to form an inner harbour. It is supremely picturesque, and exploits this fact to the full. Both the lake and the port are surrounded by restaurants and bars, all of which charge well above normal, and the town itself is permanently crammed with tourists, many of whom are distinctly surprised to find themselves in a place with no decent beach. If you're after clubs, crowds and souvenirs, though, this is the place for you. Finding a cheap **room**, however, is virtually impossible in mid-season. Undeniably central, but a grim last resort, is the **youth hostel** at Stratigoú Koráka 3 (②), immediately northeast of the lake. Better to walk up the hill on one of the roads leading out northeast of town and try for rooms in all the side streets. There's also a collection of somewhat run-down places on the other side of town near the bus station. The **tourist office** at the outlet of the lake, has exhaustive accommodation lists if you have further problems.

The riviera set tends to hang out along the coast road north towards **ELOÚNDA**, a resort on a more acceptable scale. Buses cover the 8km regularly, and it's a spectacular ride with a series of impeccable views over a gulf dotted with islands and moored supertankers. From Eloúnda *kaíkia* run to the fortress-rock of **SPINALÓNGA**. As a bastion of the Venetian defence, this tiny islet withstood the Turkish invaders for 45 years after the rest of Crete had fallen; in more recent decades it served as a leper colony.

The other bus excursion everyone from Áyios Nikólaos takes goes inland to **KRITSÁ**, about 10km away. Despite the rampant commercialization it's still a good trip: the local crafts are fair value and it provides a welcome break from living in the fast lane at "Ag Nik", with the possibility of staying in **rooms** here. On the approach road some 2km before Kritsá stands the lovely Byzantine church of **Panayía Kirá** (Mon–Thurs & Sat 9am–3.15pm, Sun 9am–2pm), whose fourteenth- and fifteenth-century frescoes have been much retouched, but still make the visit worth the effort.

Sitía and Vái beach

The port and main town of the relatively unexploited eastern edge of Crete, **SITÍA** offers a plethora of waterside restaurants, a long sandy beach and a lazy lifestyle little affected even by the thousands of visitors in peak season. You pass the **youth hostel** (②) as you come into Sitía from Áyios Nikólaos on the main road, and there are a few rooms between here and the town. More pleasant options, though, can be found in the streets behind the northern stretch of the waterside, especially around the OTE. For **food**, the waterside places are expensive enough to make you careful about what you eat; there are cheaper options in the streets behind, such as *Erganos* at Dhimokrátou 4 or *Mixos* at Kornárou 117.

Vái beach features on almost every Cretan travel agent's list of excursions and for years has also been a popular hang-out for backpackers camping on the sands. This dual role has created something of a monstrosity, with the vast crowds divided into two hostile camps. The beach itself is famous above all for its palm trees, creating an illusion of a Caribbean island it's hard to dismiss. If you do sleep out, watch your belongings – this seems to be the one place on Crete with crime on any scale. All this admitted, it is a superb beach, and the trip there is an enjoyable one, passing the **Monastery of Tóplou**, which has a gorgeous flower-decked cloister and one of the masterpieces of Cretan art, the eighteenth-century icon *Lord Thou Art Great*.

Réthimno

Since the mid-1980s, **RÉTHIMNO** has seen a greater influx of tourists than perhaps anywhere else on Crete, with the development of a whole series of large hotels extending almost 10km along the beach to the east. For once, though, the middle of town has been spared, so that at its heart Réthimno remains one of the most beautiful of Crete's major cities. A wide sandy beach and palm-lined promenade border a labyrinthine tangle of Venetian and Turkish houses lining streets where many of the old men still dress proudly in high boots, baggy trousers and black head-scarves. Medieval minarets lend an exotic air to the skyline, while dominating everything from the west is the superbly preserved outline of the fortress built by the Venetians after a series of pirate raids had devastated the town.

When you get off the bus next to one of the pair of facing bus terminals, walk north toward the sea; the waterside **tourist information office** will be in front of you when you get to the beach. Most of the cheaper **rooms** are to the left as you walk down. The best bet is probably to follow Arkadhíou, the street which curves around immediately inland from the beach, and then continue towards the fortress. A couple of good possibilities among many are the *Pension Vrisinas* at Heréti 10, near the bus station (☎0831/26 092; ②), or *Pension Anna* on Kateháki, by the fortress (☎0831/25 586; ②). If you can't find a room – quite likely in midsummer – the **youth hostel** at Tombázi 41 (②) is a passable alternative, or there are two **campsites** right next to each other about 4km east along the beach, with a frequent bus service.

There's an unbroken line of **tavernas**, cafés and cocktail bars right around the waterside and into the area around the old port, but the sea view comes at a price. You'll find an assortment of better-value tavernas around the Rimóndi Fountain; or try *Soumbousakis* at Nikifórou Fóka 98. Bars and **nightlife** concentrate in the same general area, particularly towards the western end of the town beach.

South of Réthimno

South of Réthimno, there's little specifically to stop for until you reach the opposite coast, dotted with beach resorts for all tastes. **AYÍA GALÍNI** is the most overgrown, a place worth avoiding between June and September. Further west, the beaches adjacent to **PLAKIÁS** and Damnóni cove are more low-key, but only just – Plakiás in particular consists mostly of accommodation, serving as a functional base for the area.

Haniá

HANIÁ, as any of its residents will tell you, is the spiritual capital of Crete; for many it is also by far the island's most attractive city – especially if you can catch it in spring, when the Lefká Óri's snowcapped peaks seem to hover above the roofs. Although it is for the most part a modern city, the small outer harbour is surrounded by a wonderful jumble of half-derelict Venetian streets which survived the wartime bombardments.

The **bus station** is on Odhós Kidhonías, within easy walking distance of the action – turn right, then left down the side of Platía 1866 and you'll emerge at a major road junction opposite the top of Hálidhon, the main street of the old quarter. **Arriving by boat**, you'll anchor about 10km from Haniá at the port of Soúdha: there are frequent city buses which will drop you by the market on the fringes of the old town.

The **port area** is as ever the place to start, the oldest and the most interesting part of town. The little hill which rises behind the tourist office/mosque is **Kastélli**, site of the earliest habitation and core of the Venetian and Turkish towns. Beneath the hill, on the inner harbour, the arches of sixteenth-century Venetian arsenals survive alongside remains of the outer walls. Following the esplanade around in the other direction leads to a hefty bastion which now houses Crete's **Naval Museum** (Tues, Thurs & Sat 10am–2pm & 4–6pm) – not exactly riveting, but wander in anyway for a look at the seaward fortifications. Walk around the back of these restored bulwarks to a street heading inland and you'll find the best preserved stretch of the outer walls.

Behind the harbour lie the less picturesque but more lively sections of the old city. First, a short way up Hálidhon on the right is Haniá's **Archeological Museum** (Mon 11am–5pm, Tues–Fri 8am–5pm, Sat & Sun 8.30am–3pm; 400dr), housed in the Venetian-built church of San Francesco. Damaged as it is, this remains a beautiful building and a fine little display, even though there's nothing of outstanding interest. In the garden, a huge fountain and the base of a minaret survive from the period when the Turks converted the church into a mosque.

Around the nearby **Cathedral** – ordinary and relatively modern – are some of the more animated shopping areas, particularly leather-dominated **Odhós Skrídlof**, with streets leading up to the back of the market beyond. In the direction of the Spiántza quarter are ancient alleys which have yet to feel much effect of the city's modern popularity, still with tumbledown Venetian stonework and overhanging wooden balconies.

Haniá's **beaches** all lie to the west: the packed **city beach** is a ten-minute walk beyond the naval museum, but for good sand you're better off taking the local bus from the east side of Platía 1866 along the coast road to Kalamáki. In between you'll find emptier stretches if you're prepared to walk from Haniá.

Practicalities

The extremely helpful **tourist office** is in the new town at Kriari 40, fourth floor. There seem to be thousands of **rooms** on offer in Haniá; out of season the places right over the harbour are worth a try first – for example, prices are surprisingly reasonable at the *Hotel Piraeus* located on the corner of Hálidhon and Zambelíu, or the nearby *Rooms George* at Zambelíu 30. Others will be found mainly to the east of Hálidhon, around the cathedral or beyond in the run-down streets of the Spiántza area. In desperation you can almost always be sure of space at the **youth hostel** at Dhrakonianoú 33, but it's a long way out (bus labelled "Ayios Ioannis" from the corner of Yianári and Apokorónou). There are two **campsites** to the west: *Camping Hania*, just about within walking distance, and the bigger and better *Camping Ayia Marina*, 10km out in the village of the same name.

Both the inner and outer harbours are circled by **cafés, tavernas** and **bars**. One cheapish café is *Vasilis* on Platía Sindriváni, at the bottom of Hálidhon. You can eat more cheaply by avoiding the port altogether. Try up Hálidhon or on the narrow streets to the west of it, off Zambelíu: the basic *Dhíporto* diner on Skridlóf (east of Hálidhon) is famous for its multilingual menu and fried offal. At least once you'd do better to buy some of your own food, and in any event Haniá's **market**, the finest in Crete, is not to be missed.

For **nightlife**, most of the action takes place in a series of bars around the harbour, particularly near Sarpidhóna on the inner port. If it all seems a bit raunchier than you'd expect, remember that these places cater to servicemen from the nearby NATO bases at least as much as to visitors. Haniá can also be a good place to catch **local music**, especially at the *Café Kriti*, Kallérgon 22.

The Samarian Gorge

From Haniá the beautiful **Gorge of Samariá** – Europe's longest – can be visited as a day trip or as part of a longer excursion to the south. It's well worth catching the early bus at 6.15am to avoid the full heat of the day while walking through the gorge, though be warned that you will not be alone – there are often as many as four coachloads setting off before dawn for the nail-biting climb into the White Mountains.

The gorge (1000dr admission) begins at a stepped path descending steeply from the southern lip of the Omalós Plain through almost alpine scenery of pines, wild flowers and un-Cretan greenery. At an average pace with regular stops, the sixteen-kilometre walk down takes almost six hours; solid shoes are vital. There's plenty of water from springs and streams (except some years in September and October), but nothing to eat. Small churches and viewpoints dot the route, and about halfway down you pass the abandoned village of **Samariá**, now home to a wardens' station, with picnic facilities and filthy toilets. Farther down, the path levels out and the walls close in until at the narrowest point – the *Sidherespórtes* or "Iron Gates" – one can practically touch both rock faces at once, and, looking up, see them rising sheer for almost a thousand feet.

When you finally get down, the village of **AYÍA ROÚMELI** is all but abandoned until you reach the beach, a mirage of iced drinks and a cluster of expensive tavernas with equally pricy rooms to let. If you want to get back to Haniá, buy your **boat** ticket immediately, especially if you want an afternoon on the beach – the last boat tends to sell out first. You may find boats going to Soúyia rather than Hóra Sfakíon, owing to a local dispute; count your blessings, as Soúyia's a much better beach resort at which to wait for the bus to Haniá – or even stay.

Paleohóra

Several daily buses from Haniá make the trip to **PALEOHÓRA**, the main resort of southwest Crete, the route winding through the western foothills of the White Mountains. The little town is built across the base of a peninsula, its harbour on one side, the sand on the other, with Venetian ramparts standing sentinel above. These days Paleohóra is heavily developed, but if some character has been lost in recent years, the town is still enjoyable, with a main street that fills with restaurant tables in the evening. There are scores of places to **stay** and there's also a fair-sized **campsite**, east of town; sleeping on the beach is less tolerated than formerly. The town can be reached by sea, as the final stop on the Hóra Sfakíon–Ayía Roúmeli–Soúyia ferry line.

travel details

Buses

Athens to: Corfu (3 daily; 11hr); Delphi (5 daily; 3hr); Halkídha (half-hourly; 1hr 30min); Igoumenítsa (3 daily; 8hr 30min); Ioánnina (9 daily; 7hr 30min); Kefallonía (4 daily; 8hr); Kími (6 daily; 3hr 30min); Kórinthos (hourly; 1hr 30min); Lefkádha (4 daily; 5hr 30min); Mycenae (10 daily; 2hr); Náfplio (10 daily; 3hr); Olympia (4 daily; 5hr 30min); Pátra (hourly; 3hr); Pílos (2 daily; 6hr); Rafína (every 30min; 1hr 30min); Sounion (every 30min; 2hr); Spárti (7 daily; 4hr 30min); Thessaloníki (10 daily; 7hr 30min); Tríkala (7 daily; 5hr 30min); Trípoli (12 daily; 4hr); Vólos (9 daily; 5hr); Zákinthos (3 daily; 7hr).

Ioánnina to: Athens (10 daily; 7hr 30min); Igoumenítsa (10 daily; 2hr 30min); Metsovo (4 daily, 1hr 30min); Dodona (2 daily; 40min).

Igoumenítsa to: Párga (5 daily; 1hr 30min); Préveza (2 daily; 3hr).

Kalamáta to: Areópoli (4 daily; 1hr 30min); Kóroni (7 daily; 1hr 30min); Megalópoli (10 daily, 1hr); Methóni via Pílos (5 daily; 1hr 30min); Pátra (2 daily; 4hr); Pílos (8 daily; 1hr); Trípoli (10 daily, 1hr 45min).

Kórinthos to: Árgos (hourly; 1hr); Kalamáta (7 daily; 4hr); Mycenae (hourly; 30min); Náfplio (hourly; 1hr 30min); Spárti (8 daily; 4hr); Tíryn (hourly; 15min); Trípoli (9 daily; 1hr 30min).

Lamía to: Lárissa (4 daily; 3hr 30min); Tríkala, via Kardhítsa (4 daily; 3hr); Vólos (2 daily; 3hr);.

Lárissa to: Kalambáka (hourly; 30min); Litóhoro junction (almost hourly; 1hr 45min); Tríkala (every half-hour; 1hr 25min).

Náfplio to: Epidaurus (5 daily; 45min); Trípoli (6 daily; 1hr).

Pírgos to: Kalamáta (2 daily; 2hr); Kiparissía (2 daily; 1hr); Olympia (approx. hourly; 45min).

Thessaloníki to: Ierissós (7 daily; 3hr 30min); Ioánnina (4–5 daily; 7hr 30min); Kalambáka 4–5 daily; 4hr 30min); Kateríni for Mount Olympus (hourly; 1hr 30min); Ouranópoli (7 daily; 3hr 30min); Pella (hourly; 1hr); Vólos (4 daily; 4hr).

Tríkala to: Ioánnina (2 daily; 4hr); Kalambáka (hourly; 30min); Métsovo (2 daily; 2hr).

Trípoli to: Kalamáta (6 daily; 2hr); Kiparissía (2 daily; 2hr); Pílos (2 daily; 3hr); Olympia (3 daily; 5hr); Pírgos (3 daily; 3hr); Spárti (6 daily; 1hr 30min).

Vólos to: Lárissa (hourly; 1hr 30min); Makrinítsa (9 daily; 50min); Milés (6 daily; 1hr–1hr 10min); Portaría (9 daily; 40min); Thessaloníki (4 daily; 3hr 20min); Tríkala (4 daily; 2hr 30min); Vizitsu (6 daily; 1hr–1hr 10min); Zagorá (4 daily; 1hr 40min).

Trains

Athens to: Halkídha (17 daily; 1hr 30min); Kalamáta (3 daily; 7hr); Kalambáka via Pateofársala (5 daily; 5hr 30min); Kórinthos (14 daily; 1hr 30min–2hr); Mikínes (5 daily; 2hr 45min); Náfplio (5 daily; change at Árgos; 3–3hr 30min); Olympia via Pírgos (3 daily; 6–8hr with change); Pátra (9 daily; 3hr 30min–4hr); Thessaloníki (10 daily, 1 sleeper only; 6–8hr); Vólos (1 daily direct; 4hr 30min).

Thessaloníki to: Alexandhroúpoli (5 daily; 5hr 30min–7hr); Litóhoro (6 daily; 1hr 40min); Vólos (3 daily; 5hr).

Vólos to: Athens direct (1 daily; 4hr 30min); Kalambáka (4 daily; 4hr); Lárissa (13 daily; 1hr).

Ferries

Astakós to: Itháki (1 daily; 1hr 45min); Kefalloniá (2 daily; 3hr 30min).

Áyios Konstantínos to: Skópelos (7 weekly; 5hr).

Híos to: Lésvos (7 weekly; 4hr); Sámos (2–3 weekly; 4hr) .

Íos to: Náxos (at least daily; 3hr); Páros (at least 1 daily; 5hr); Thíra (at least 1 daily; 2hr).

Iráklio to: Páros (2–6 weekly; 7hr); Rhodes (2–3 weekly; 11hr).

Kavála to: northeast Aegean and Dodecanese islands (1–3 weekly); Thássos (7–11 daily).

Kefalloniá to: Zákinthos (2–4 weekly in summer).

Killíni to: Kefalloniá (1–3 daily; 1hr 30min); Zákinthos (3–7 daily; 1hr 30min).

Kími to: Skíros (1–2 daily; 2hr 30min).

Kós to: Pátmos (6 weekly; 5hr); Rhodes (9 weekly; 4hr).

Lésvos to: Híos (5–7 weekly; 4hr); Kávala (2 weekly; 15hr); Thessaloníki (2 weekly; 15hr).

Náxos to: Íos (at least 1 daily; 3hr); Iráklio (2 weekly; 6hr); Páros (at least 1 daily; 1hr); Thíra (at least 1 daily; 4hr).

Pátra to: Corfu (several daily; 7–9hr); Itháki (daily; 4–5hr); Kefalloniá (daily; 4–5hr).

Pireás to: Crete (2 daily; 12hr); Híos (8 weekly; 10hr); Íos (at least 1 daily; 10hr); Kós (9 weekly; 12hr); Lésvos (5–7 weekly; 14hr); Míkonos (at least 2 daily; 5hr); Náxos (at least 1 daily; 8hr); Páros (at least 1 daily; 7hr); Rhodes (10 weekly; 18–23hr); Sámos (5–7 weekly; 11–14hr); Sífnos (6 weekly; 6hr); Thíra (at least 1 daily; 10–12hr).

Rafína to: Míkonos, Síros, Páros, Náxos (daily; 3–7hr); Kós & Rhodes (3 weekly; 18hr total).

Rhodes to: Crete (2 weekly; 13hr); Kálimnos (9 weekly; 5hr); Kós (9 weekly; 4hr); Pátmos (6 weekly; 8hr).

Sámos to: Kálimnos (2–3 weekly; 8hr); Pátmos (2–3 weekly; 5hr).

Thessaloníki to: Híos (2 weekly; 15hr); Iráklio (2 weekly; 21hr); Lésvos (2 weekly; 15hr); Skíros (1 weekly; 7hr); Skópelos (3 weekly; 6hr).

Thíra to: Íos (at least 1 daily; 2hr); Iráklio, Crete (2–6 weekly; 5hr); Míkonos (at least 1 daily; 7hr); Náxos (at least 1 daily; 4hr); Páros (at least 1 daily; 5hr).

Vólos to: Skíathos (3–4 weekly; 3hr); Skópelos (3–4 daily; 4hr).

Zákinthos to: Killíni (3–7 daily; 1hr 30min).

CHAPTER 11

HUNGARY

SLOVAK
REPUBLIC

RUSSIA

To Prague

VIENNA

Tokaj
Miskolc

Eger

Debrecen

Szentendre

AUSTRIA

Sopron

Gyor

Esztergom

BUDAPEST

Oradea

To Bucharest

Balaton
Füred

Siófok

Lake Balaton

Keszthely

Szeged

Arad

ROMANIA

Pécs

Timişoara

Zagreb

CROATIA

0   100 km

Introduction

Visitors who refer to **Hungary** as a Balkan country risk getting a lecture on how this small, landlocked nation of 10,658,000 people differs from "all those Slavs". Natives are strongly conscious of themselves as Magyars – a race that transplanted itself from Central Asia into the heart of Europe – and as a nation that identifies with "Western values". Hungary was in the vanguard of the dissolution of communist hegemony in Eastern Europe. It's decision to open its borders in 1989 and let East Germans out to the West precipitated the fall of the repressive regimes in East Germany, Romania and Czechoslovakia.

The magnificent capital, **Budapest**, is unlikely to reinforce stereotypes of the old Eastern Bloc. It's not just the vast Gothic Parliament and other monuments of a bygone imperial era that seem to align the city with the West, but the fashions on the streets and the posters advertising things that were all the rage back home a year before. In coffee houses, Turkish baths, and the fad for Habsburg bric-a-brac, there's a strong whiff of *Mitteleuropa* – that ambient culture that welcomed Beethoven in Budapest and Hungarian-born Liszt in Vienna, a culture currently being revived in a new form by writers, film directors, artists and other media figures.

After Budapest, **Lake Balaton** and the **Danube Bend** vie for popularity. The Balaton, with its string of brash resorts, styles itself as the "Nation's Playground", and enjoys a fortuitous proximity to the Badacsony wine-producing region. The Danube Bend has more to offer in terms of scenery and historic architecture, as do the Northern Uplands and Transdanubia. **Sopron** and **Pécs** are rightfully the main attractions in Transdanubia, while in the uplands it's the famous wine centres of **Tokaj** and **Eger** that draw most visitors. On the Great Plain, the university town of **Szeged**, close to the Romanian border, is the one essential stop.

Information and Maps

A large number of photo-packed brochures, maps and leaflets are available from **IBUSZ**, the Hungarian tourist organization. The most useful are the large road map, a pamphlet detailing the year's festivals and events, and two lists of accommodation – *Hotel* and *Camping*. You'll find IBUSZ offices in most towns, along with various other tourist agencies; opening hours are generally Mon–Fri 8am–6pm and Sat 8am–1pm. In summer some offices may stay open until 8pm all week and are open Sun 8am–1pm.

Money and Banks

Hungarian **forints** (Ft) come in notes of 10, 20, 50, 100, 500, 1000 and 5000Ft, with 1, 2, 5, 10, 20, 50, 100 and 200Ft coins. The introduction of new coins means it's worth checking carefully which coins are which. Forints can't be exchanged outside the country, and importing or exporting banknotes exceeding 100Ft is illegal. You can **change money** at any *IBUSZ* or regional tourist office, or at most large hotels, campsites and **banks**. Exchange rates vary sharply, and it is best to change in banks or larger tourist offices – exchange offices in the main tourist centres are a rip off (as is American Express). The black market offers little benefit and you can easily be cheated. Keep the receipts, which are required should you wish to pay for international tickets in forints, or re-exchange forints back into hard currency. Most brands of **travellers' cheques** and Eurocheques are accepted. **Credit cards** can be used to hire cars, buy airline tickets or pay your bills directly in the fancier hotels, restaurants and tourist shops.

Communications

Post offices (*posta*) are usually open Mon–Fri 8am–6pm, Sat 8am–1pm. Mail from abroad should be addressed "*poste restante, posta*", followed by the name of the town. A more secure "drop" is the 24-hour *IBUSZ* bureau at Petőfi tér in Budapest; have letters marked "c/o American Express". It's quicker to buy stamps (*bélyeg*) at tobacconists – post offices can be full of people making complicated transactions.

Local calls can be made from public **phones** where 5Ft gets you two minutes (6min after 6pm). In some villages, long-distance calls often have to be placed by the post office or the operator; in towns, the post office might also get better results. To call direct to other parts of the country, dial ☎06, followed by the area code and subscriber number. Red phone booths and the new grey ones can be used for direct **international calls** (you need 10Ft or 20Ft coins), but it's sometimes easier to place calls through the international operator (☎09), the Telephone Bureau in Petöfi Sándor utca in Budapest, or fancy hotels in the provinces. In Budapest, there are more and more card phones – you can buy cards in post offices for 250 and 600Ft.

Getting Around

Although it doesn't break any speed records, public transport reaches most parts of Hungary, and fares remain very cheap. The only problem is *információ*, for staff rarely speak anything but Hungarian, although German is spoken around Lake Balaton.

■ Trains

The centralization of the *MÁV* rail network means that many cross-country journeys are easier if you travel via Budapest. Seat reservations are required on many *express* and *gyorsvonat* (fast trains) and all international trains, but not for *személyvonat*, which halt at every hamlet en route; reservations can be made through any *MÁV* or *Volántourist* office. Most trains have buffets and first- and second-class (*osztály*) sections; international services through Budapest have sleeping cars and couchettes (*hálókocsi* and *kusett*). **Tickets** (*jegy*) for domestic services can be bought at the station (*pályaudvar* or *vasútállomás*) on the day of departure, but it's best to buy tickets for **international trains** (*nemzetközi gyorsvonat*) at least 36 hours in advance. The tariff is 300Ft per 100km, with a 10% surcharge on expresses. You can break your journey once between the point of departure and the final destination. Most Hungarians purchase one-way tickets (*egy útra*), so specify a *retur* or *oda-vissza* if you want a return ticket.

InterRail and *Eurail* passes are both valid. *MÁV* itself issues various **season tickets**, valid on domestic lines for one week or ten days, but you'd need to travel intensively to make savings with a seven-day national *Runaround* (3700Ft). However, the *Eurotrain Explorer* (see *Basics*) gives unlimited rail travel for £22.

■ Buses

Regional *Volán* ("Wheel") companies run the bulk of Hungary's **buses**, which are often the quickest way to travel between towns. Schedules are clearly displayed in bus terminals; arrive early

to confirm the departure bay and ensure getting a seat. For long-distance services originating from Budapest or major towns, you can buy tickets with a seat booking up to half an hour before departure; after that you get them from the driver and risk standing throughout the journey. Services in rural areas may be limited to one a day, and tickets are only available on board.

■ Driving and hitching

To **drive** in Hungary you'll require an international driving licence, Green Card insurance and third-party insurance. Speed limits are 60kph in town, 80–100kph on main roads and 120kph on motorways. Accidents should be reported within a day to Hungaria Biztositó, Budapest XIV, Gvadányi ut 69 (☎1/252-6333). 24-hour breakdown assistance is available in the Budapest area from the "Yellow Angels" service (☎1/252-8000); elsewhere, you're reliant on local garages. **Car rental** costs from £235/$400 per week with unlimited mileage. Cars are available through *Avis* or *Europcar* and from hotel reception desks or certain travel agencies.

Autostop or **hitchhiking** is widely practised by young Magyars, and only forbidden on highways. A fair number of drivers seem willing to give lifts, although your prospects at weekends are pretty poor, since the small Trabants and Ladas are usually packed with families.

Accommodation

The cost of accommodation in Hungary is moderate by European standards, and finding a room to suit your tastes and budget shouldn't prove difficult. More upmarket accommodation tends to quote prices in Deutschmarks; private rooms and hostels charge in local currency. The cheapest places tend to fill up during the 'igh" season (June–Sept), so it's wise to make bookings if you're bound for somewhere with limited accommodation. You can use *IBUSZ* in Budapest to reserve hotel rooms nationwide, or regional tourist offices to reserve hotels, hostels or private rooms within their area.

■ Hotels

Three-star **hotels** (*szálló* or *szállóda*) have become the most common category, with de luxe four- and five-star establishments still confined to Budapest and major resorts, and humble one- and

ACCOMMODATION PRICE CODES

Throughout this guide, accommodation is priced on a scale of ① to ⑧, the number indicating the lowest price per night a single person could expect to pay in that establishment in high season. With hostels this is the nightly rate per person; with hotels, the price is arrived at by dividing the cost of the cheapest double room by two. The prices indicated by the codes are as follows

① = under £5 / $8   ② = £5–10 / $8–16   ③ = £10–15 / $16–24   ④ = £15–20 / $24–32

⑤ = £20–25 / $32–40   ⑥ = £25–30 / $40–48   ⑦ = £30–35 / $48–56   ⑧ = over £35 / $56

two-star joints almost extinct. Outside Budapest and Lake Balaton (where prices are 30 percent higher), a three-star hotel should charge from around DM150 for a double room with bath, TV, etc; solo travellers often have to pay this too, since singles are rare. The same goes for four-star or two-star (downwards of DM100) hotel rooms; de luxe hotels in Budapest slash their rates during winter. A similar rating system is used for **inns** (*fogadó*) and **pensions** (*pénzió* or *pánzio*), which charge a little less than hotels. Found along highways and on the outskirts of towns, many are motels in all but name.

■ Private rooms

Private rooms are a cheaper way of staying near the centre, and often quite appealing. Such accommodation (termed *Fiz*, short for *fizetővendégszolgálat*) can be arranged by local tourist offices for a small fee; dealing direct with the owner (who'll advertise *szoba kiadó* or *Zimmer frei*), you have to register with the police. Doubles range from 800Ft (in provincial towns) to 2000–3000Ft (in Budapest or around the Balaton); again, singles usually pay the same. Rooms in a town's Belváros (inner sector) are likely to be much better than those in outlying zones. It's usually impossible to take possession of the room before 5pm.

It's possible to hire whole **apartments** in some towns and resorts, while in western and southern Hungary regional tourist offices can arrange **farm accommodation** in old buildings converted into holiday homes with kitchen facilities – both are usually more expensive than private rooms.

■ Hostels

A cheaper option is **hostels**, which go under various names. In provincial towns they're called *Túristaszálló*, but in highland areas they go by the name of *Túristaház*. Both are graded "A" or "B"

and are best reserved through the regional tourist office; rates vary from 400 to 2000Ft per head. In addition to these, there's a string of not particularly cheap "hotels for young people", owned by the youth travel agency *Express*, whose local offices also rent out vacant **college dormitories** during the summer. Beds in the latter normally cost about the same as other hostels.

■ Bungalows and campsites

Throughout Hungary, campsites and bungalows come together in complexes. **Bungalows** (*faház*) proliferate around resorts and on the larger campsites; some can be hired by foreigners for 700–2500Ft, depending on their amenities and size (two to four persons). The first-class bungalows – with well-equipped kitchens, hot water and a sitting room or terrace – are excellent, while the most primitive at least have clean bedding and don't leak. **Campsites** – usually signposted *Kemping* – likewise range across the spectrum from "de luxe" to third class. The more elaborate places include a restaurant and shops and tend to be overcrowded; second- or third-class sites often have a nicer ambience. Expect to pay 400–500Ft (twice that around Lake Balaton), with reductions from September to May.

Food and Drink

For foreigners the archetypal Hungarian dish is "goulash" – historically a soup made of potatoes and whatever meat or fish was available, which was later flavoured with paprika and beefed up into a variety of stews, modified over the centuries by various foreign influences.

■ Food

As a nation of early risers, Hungarians like a calorific **breakfast** (*reggeli*) that includes cheese, eggs or salami plus bread and jam. The morning rush hour is prime time for **Tej-bár** or **Tejivó**, stand-up milk bars serving hot milk, sugary cocoa and various dunkable pastries. Though **coffee houses** are no longer at the centre of Budapest's cultural and political life, you'll find plenty of *kávéház* serving the beverage with milk (*tejeskávé*) or whipped cream (*tejszínhabbal*).

A whole range of places purvey **snacks**, including the *Csemege* or delicatessens, which display a tempting spread of salads, open sandwiches, pickles and cold meats. For sit-down nibbles, people patronize **bisztró**, which tend to offer a couple of hot dishes besides the inevitable salami rolls, and **snackbár**, superior versions of the same. Numerous **patisseries** (*cukrászda*) pander to the Magyar fondness for sweet things. Pancakes (*palacsinta*) with fillings are very popular, as are strudels (*rétes*) and a staggering array of cakes and other sticky items.

On the streets, toothless ancients preside over *kukorica* (corn on the cob) or *gesztenye* (roasted chestnuts); while fried fish (*sült hal*) shops are common in towns near rivers or lakes. *Szendvics*, *hamburger* and *gofri* (waffle) stands are mushrooming in the larger towns, and **in markets** you'll also find various greasy spoons.

Traditionally, Hungarians take their main meal at midday, so the range of dishes offered by **restaurants** is better at lunch than in the evenings. At lunchtime, some eating places offer **set menus** (*napi menü*), a very basic meal at moderate prices. Keep an eye on prices – you can pay exorbitant amounts for not very much, and gone are the days when even the top restaurants were cheap; there are still plenty of places where you can eat well and sink a few beers for 1000Ft. Note that Sunday evening is a bad night for eating out, as the menu will be limited and the bread stale – and always check your bill carefully.

You'll be asked if you want **starters** (*előételek*) – generally a soup or salad – though nobody will mind if you just have a **main course** (*ételek*). Bread is supplied almost automatically – as the old saying has it, bread is so popular that "Hungarians will even eat bread with bread". The outlook for **vegetarians** is poor: aside from cooked vegetables (notably *rántott gomba*, mushrooms in breadcrumbs), often the only meatless dishes are various permutations of eggs.

Hungarians have a variety of words implying fine distinctions among restaurants. In theory an *étterem* is a proper restaurant, while a *vendéglő* approximates to the Western notion of a bistro.

Kisvendéglő, which were originally used as youth hang-outs, are now often seedy, raucous dives. The old word for an inn, *csárda*, applies to posh places specializing in certain dishes or with rustic pretensions, besides the humbler rural establishments it originally signified.

■ Drink

Hungary's mild climate and diversity of soils is perfect for **wine** (*bor*), which is perennially cheap, whether you buy it by the bottle (*üveg*) or the glass (*pohár*). **Wine bars** (*borozó*) are ubiquitous and generally far less pretentious than in the West; while true devotees of the grape make pilgrimages to the extensive **wine cellars** (*borpince*) that honeycomb towns like Tokaj and Eger. **Spirits** are cheap, if you stick to native brands. The best-known type of **pálinka** – or brandy – is distilled from apricots (*barack*), and is a speciality of the Kecskemét region. *Szilva paliuka*, a lethal spirit produced on cottage stills in rural areas, allegedly using plums, is sometimes sold privately. Bottled **beer** (*sör*) of the lager type (*világos*) predominates, although you might find brown ale (*barna sör*) and draught beer (*csapolt sör*). Western brands are imported or brewed under licence, and the famous old Austro-Hungarian beer *Dreher* has made a comeback.

Opening Hours and Holidays

Opening times for most public buildings are Mon–Fri 8.30am–5pm, but staff at lesser institutions usually take an hour off for lunch around noon. Museums are generally open Tues–Sun 10am–6pm or 9am–5pm, and some have free admission over the weekends. **Public holidays** are: Jan 1; March 15; Easter Monday; May 1; Whitsun Monday; Aug 20; October 23; Dec 25 & 26.

Emergencies

The Hungarian **police** (*Rendőrség*) have a mild reputation, and foreign tourists are handled with kid gloves unless they're suspected of black-marketeering, drug-smuggling or driving under the influence of alcohol. Most police officers have at least a smattering of German, but rarely any other foreign language. Should you be arrested or need legal advice, ask to contact your embassy or consulate.

All towns and some villages have a **pharmacy** (*gógyszertár* or *patika*), with staff – often German-speaking – authorized to issue a wide range of drugs. However anyone requiring specific medication should bring a supply with them. Opening hours are normally Mon–Fri 9am–6pm, Sat 9am–noon/1pm; signs in the window give the location or telephone number of all-night (*éjjel*) chemists.

Tourist offices can direct you to local medical centres or doctors' surgeries (*orvosi rendelő*), while your embassy in Budapest will have the addresses of foreign-language-speaking **doctors** and **dentists**, who'll probably be in private (*magán*) practice, so you should check on prices.

EMERGENCY NUMBERS

Police ☎07; Ambulance ☎04; Fire☎05.

BUDAPEST

The importance of **BUDAPEST** to Hungary is difficult to overestimate. Over two million people – roughly one fifth of the population – live in the city, and everything converges here: wealth, political power, cultural life and transport. Surveying the city from Castle Hill, it's obvious why Budapest was dubbed the "Pearl of the Danube". Its grand buildings and sweeping bridges look magnificent, especially when floodlit or illuminated by the barrage of fireworks launched from Gellért Hill on Constitution Day. The inner city and the nineteenth-century boulevards are now under siege from Western fashions and advertising, but they retain a distinctively Hungarian character, which for visitors is highlighted by the sounds and appearance of the outlandish Magyar language.

Castle Hill (*Várhegy*) is the most prominent feature of the Buda district, a plateau one mile long laden with bastions, old mansions and a huge palace, commanding the Watertown. Its grandiosity and strategic utility have long gone hand in hand: Hungarian kings built their palaces here because it was easy to defend, a fact appreciated by the Turks, Habsburgs, Nazis and other occupiers. A war-torn legacy of bygone Magyar glories, it's been almost wholly reconstructed from the rubble of 1945, when Germans and Russians fought over the hill while the city's inhabitants hid underground.

Buda and its twin, Pest, have a surfeit of other fine sights, museums and galleries, and while nightlife isn't quite scintillating it's usually affordable. Restaurants and bars abound, and there's a wide variety of entertainments, generally well publicized by the tourist board and accessible by efficient, cheap public transport. The rhythms of life are slightly different here: people rise early and call it a day at around 10pm, interrupting their labours with breaks in patisseries and *eszpresszó* bars. Perhaps the best way to ease yourself into the life of Budapest is to wallow away an afternoon in one of the city's **thermal baths** (*gyógyfürdő*). For 2000 years people have appreciated the relaxing and curative effects of the mineral water from the Buda Hills, currently gushing at a rate of about 70,000,000 litres per day, at temperatures of up to 80°C. A basic *gyógyfürdő* ticket – costing 80–200Ft – covers three hours in the pools, *szauna* and steamrooms (*gőzfürdő*), while supplementary tickets are available for such delights as the mud baths (*iszapfürdő*).

Unless specified otherwise, Budapest's museums are open from Tuesday to Sunday, 10am to 5pm; some have a day when entry is free, and students are admitted free or half-price every day.

The Budapest telephone code is ☎1.

Arrival and information

The Danube (*Duna*) determines basic **orientation**, with Pest sprawled across the eastern plain and Buda reclining on the hilly west bank. The Belváros constitutes the city centre and the hub of Pest, while Castle Hill is the historic focal point of Buda. Each of Budapest's 22 districts (*kerületek*) is designated on maps, street signs and addresses by a Roman numeral – V is Belváros, I the Castle district. Most **points of arrival** are fifteen to thirty minutes from the centre. Keleti, Déli and Nyugati, the main **train stations**, are directly connected by metro to Deák tér in the Belváros. Across the road from Deák tér metro lies the Erzsébet tér **bus station**, where the half-hourly shuttle from **Ferihegy airport** (100/200Ft from Ferihegy Terminals 1 and 2 respectively) and international buses arrive. Pest's **Népstadion** and **Árpád híd** bus terminals are further out, but still on the metro; while **hydrofoils** from Vienna dock right alongside the Belváros embankment.

At the earliest opportunity, get hold of a proper map of the city; tourist offices supply small freebies, but far better is the **Budapest Atlas**, selling at 215Ft from newsstands in Deák tér metro, or some bookshops. Leaving aside the business of finding accommodation (see below), the main sources of practical **information** are the friendly polyglot staff of **Tourinform** (daily 8am–8pm; ☎117-9800), just around the corner from Deák tér metro at Sütő u.2. Other useful offices are those of **Budapest Tourist**, at Roosevelt tér 5 and Baross tér 3 (both Mon–Sat 8am–8pm, Sun 2–8pm). For the latest on what's on, check out the weeklies *Budapest Sun* and *Budapest Week*, the misnamed weekly *Daily News,* or *Programme* and *Where Budapest*, free guides to the month's events, available in tourist offices and hotels.

City transport

Running almost non-stop between 4.30am and 11pm, the **metro** is the easiest way of getting around. Its three lines intersect at Deák tér, and there's little risk of going astray once you've learned to recognize the *bejárat, kijárat, vonal* and *felé* signs – entrance, exit, line and towards. A yellow 25Ft ticket is valid for a journey along one line; you should punch another ticket when changing lines at Deák tér. Yellow tickets are also valid for a single journey on **buses** (*busz*), **trolley buses** (*trolibusz*), **trams** (*villamos*) and the **HÉV suburban train** as far as the city limits. Rather than queuing at a metro station, it's quicker to buy a strip of tickets from street stands, tobacconists or newsagents. Buses with red numbers make limited stops, while the prefix "E" denotes buses running non-stop between termini. Buses run every ten minutes or so during the day (like trams and trolley buses); and more or less hourly between 11pm and dawn along those routes with a **night service**. When the metro or trams are not running on a line, you'll find buses operating in their place.

A **day pass** (*Napijegy*) could save money. The yellow ones (96Ft) are valid for travel on trams, trolleybuses, *HÉV* trains and the metro; the blue ones (120Ft) for all forms of public transport. They are available from metro stations.

Taxis are a common rip off. The ones from the airport are most notorious – take an airport bus or the airport main bus service. Always go for the cab companies like *Fötaxi* (☎122-2222), *Teletaxi* (☎155-5555), or *Citytaxi* (☎153-3633), charging around 30Ft plus 30Ft per kilometre; they can also be hailed in the street.

Accommodation

Hotels are generally expensive in Budapest, and many of the better places expect payment in Deutschmarks. For hotel enquiries and bookings, you should contact *HungaroHotels*, V, Petőfi utca 16 (☎118-3393), *IBUSZ*, V, Petőfi tér 3 (☎118-5707), *Pannonia Service*, V, Kigyó utca 4/6 (☎118-3910), *Danubius Travel*, V, Martinelli tér 8 (☎117-3652), or any of the airport's tourist desks. For inexpensive **private rooms**, go to the *IBUSZ* or *Budapest Tourist* offices (see above). Another budget option is to book a **hostel** bed through the youth travel agency *Express*, at Keleti station (8am–8pm); they also deal with the hostels which operate in college dormitories during July and August.

Hostels

Citadella, I, Citadella sétány (☎166-5794). First choice hostel, with breathtaking views of the city, but you have to get there early to get a bunk. Bed in dorms ①; bed in double ③.

Donáti, I, Donáti utca 46 (☎201-1971). ①

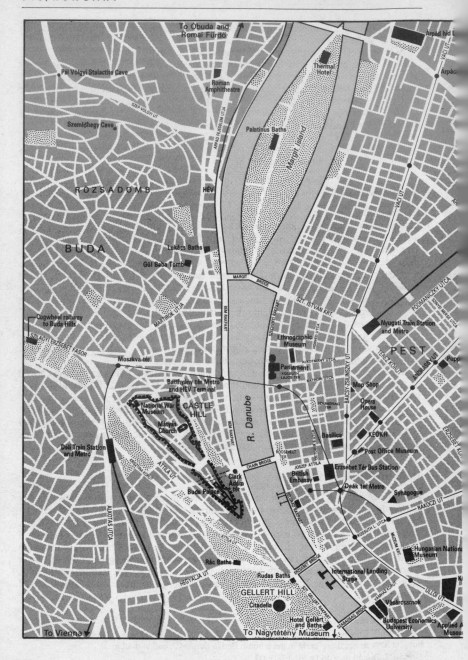

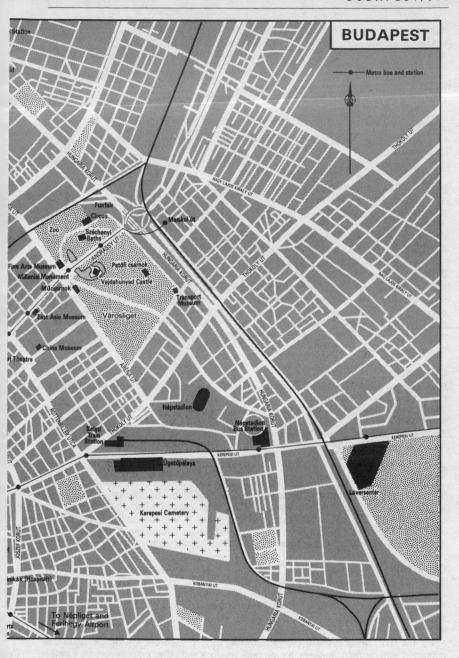

BUDAPEST

—●— Metro line and station

Station

id

THOKOLY UT

HUNGARIA KORUT

NAGY LAJOS KIRALY UT

Funfair

Circus

Mexikoi út

Zoo

Széchenyi Baths

SANDORFFY UT

HUNGARIA KORUT

THOKOLY UT

NAGY LAJOS KIRALY UT

Fine Arts Museum

Millenial Monument

Petőfi csarnok

Vajdahunyad Castle

Mücsarnok

Transport Museum

East Asia Museum

Városliget

China Museum

ARENA UT

t Theatre

ROTTENBILLER UTCA

HUNGARIA KORUT

Népstadion

Népstadion Bus Station

KEREPESI UT

Keleti Train Station

THOKOLY UT

KEREPESI UT

Ügetőpálaya

Lóversentér

+ + + + + +
+ + + + + + +
+ + + + + + +
+ Kerepesi Cemetery +
+ + + + + + +
+ + + + + + +
+ + + + + + +
+ + +

JOSZEF KORUT

inlkák (Hospitals)

KOBANYAI UT

To Népliget and Ferihegy Airport

HUNGARIA KORUT

KOBANYAI UT

rts
n

Express, XII, Beethoven utca 7–9 (☎175-2528). Three stops from Moszkva tér on tram #59. ②

Felvinci, II, Felvinci utca 8 (☎135-4983). Near Moszkva tér metro on the red line. ①

KEK Somogyi Kollégium, XI, Szüret utca 2–18 (☎185-2369). Two stops from Moricz Zigmond körter on bus #27. July & Aug only. ①

SOTE-Balassa, VIII, Tomó utca 37–41 (☎133-8916). Near Klinikák metro on the red line. ①

Hotels and pensions

Bara Panzió, Hegyalja út 34–36 (☎185-3445). Close to the centre on Gellért Hill, but on a busy road. ⑤

Dunapart, I, Szilágyi Dezso tér. Floating hotel moored upriver from the Charles Bridge on the Buda bank. ⑧

Jager Trio Panzió, XI, Ördögorom 20 (☎185-1880). Out in the Buda hills, close to the end of the bus #8 route. Open mid-March to mid-Nov. ③

Liget, VI, Aréna út 106 (☎269-5300). By the city park. ⑧

Metropol, VII, Rákoczi út 43 (☎142-1171). ④

Nemzeti, VIII, József krt 4 (☎133-9160). Splendidly revamped nineteenth-century pile on the Great Boulevard. ⑧

Orion, I, Döbröntei utea 13 (☎175-5418). Close to Castle Hill. ⑧

San Marcó Panzió, San Marcó utca 6 (☎188-9997). Small friendly pension. ②

Private rooms and apartments

Private rooms in downtown areas cost only 800–2000Ft a night – with a thirty percent surcharge for stays of three days or less. A copy of the *Budapest Atlas* is handy for checking the location of prospective sites: preferable locales are Pest's V, VI and VII districts, and the parts of Buda nearest Castle Hill. **Apartments**, hired out for 4000Ft a night, are perfect if there are several of you. They're not as common as rooms, but you should be able to find a tourist office with one on its books.

Campsites

Hárshegy, Hárshegyi út 7. Shaded site in the Buda hills run by *Budapest Tourist*. Open Easter to Oct 20; bus #22 from Moszkva tér.

Tündérhegyi-Feeberg, Szilássy út 8. All-year Buda hills site, close to the terminus of bus #28 from Moszkva tér.

Zugliget, XII, Zugligeti út 101. Occupies a disused tram cutting in the hills – the site restaurant used to be the terminus. Open March 15–Oct 15; bus #158 from Moszkva tér.

Buda

Seen from the embankments, **Buda** looks irresistibly romantic with its palatial buildings, archaic spires and outsize statues rising from rugged hills. To experience its centre – Castle Hill – at its quasi-medieval best, come in the early morning before the crowds arrive. Then you can beat them to the museums, wander off for lunch or a Turkish bath, and return to catch streetlife in full swing during the afternoon.

Castle Hill

There are several approaches to Castle Hill from Pest, starting with a breezy walk across the Chain Bridge to Clark Ádám tér, where you can ride up to the palace by the nineteenth-century funicular or **Sikló** (daily 7.30am–10pm; 60Ft). Otherwise, take the red metro line to Moszkva tér and the minibus from there; or get off at the previous stop, Batthyány tér, and start walking.

By midday, **Trinity Square** (Szentháromság tér), the heart of the Castle district, is crammed with tourists, buskers, handicrafts vendors and other entrepreneurs, a multilingual spectacle played out against the backdrop of the wildly asymmetrical **Mátyás Church** (Mátyás templom). Built in the nineteenth century, the church is a riotous recreation of the medieval spirit, grafted onto those portions of the thirteenth-century structure that survived the siege of 1686. Prior to that date the building was a mosque, whose Turkish occupants whitewashed over the religious murals – so there's more than a hint of malice in one nineteenth-century fresco, which depicts Mátyás's father Hunyadi trouncing the Turks at Belgrade in 1456. It's almost lost amid the richness of the interior: painted leaves, animals and geometric motifs run up columns and under vaulting, while shafts of light fall through rose windows onto gilded altars and statues with stunning effect.

In days gone by, the name day of Hungary's patron saint and first monarch Stephen (István) was celebrated here with a display of his "black mummified hand" and other holy relics – a ceremony now held over in Pest. An equestrian statue of **King Stephen** stands just outside the church, commemorating this ruler who forced Catholicism onto his subjects, thus aligning Hungary with the culture of western Europe. The **Fishermen's Bastion** (Halászbástya) nearby is an undulating white rampart with gargoyle-lined cloisters and seven turrets, which frames the view of Parliament across the river. By day it's besieged by diverse hustlers, surreally reflected in the copper and glass facade of the *Budapest Hilton*.

Medieval architectural features have survived along **Országház utca** (Parliament Street), at the end of which the quasi-Gothic **Mary Magdalene Tower** still lours over Kapisztrán tér, albeit gutted and transformed into an art gallery. Opposite, the **National War Museum**, on the Tóth Árpád promenade, romanticizes the nation's martial past with brilliantly coloured hussars' uniforms and revolutionary banners.

To the south of Trinity Square the street widens as it approaches the **Buda Palace**. The fortifications and dwellings built by Béla III after the thirteenth-century Mongol invasion were replaced by ever more luxurious palaces on this site, and the most recent reconstruction dates from the postwar period – the three-month siege of Buda resulted in the palace's total devastation. Grouped around two courtyards, the sombre wings of the Palace contain a clutch of museums and portions of the medieval structures discovered in the course of excavation – too much to see in one day unless you give it an unfairly cursory inspection.

The northern wing used to contain a propagandizing Museum of the Working-Class Movement, but now houses the **Ludwig Collection** (daily except Mon 10am–6pm; 80Ft, free Tues), an unexceptional collection of mainly Hungarian modern art, with the odd Picasso and Lichtenstein thrown in – and the **Museum of Contemporary History**, which hosts a variety of temporary exhibitions. The **National Gallery** (daily 10am–4/6pm; 20Ft, free Sat), occupying the central and southern wings, contains Hungarian art since the Middle Ages. In the main building, Gothic stone-carvings, altars and painted panels fill the ground floor, while nineteenth-century painting dominates the floor above. On the far side of the Lion Courtyard, much of the **Castle Museum** (Tues–Sun 10am–6pm) is installed underground, in the marbled and flagstoned halls of the Renaissance palace. Upstairs, **Two Thousand Years of Budapest** shows the evolution of the city by means of old prints, ceramics and other artefacts.

The Watertown and Gellért Hill

The busy square at the foot of Castle Hill takes its name from Adam Clark, the engineer who completed the **Chain Bridge**, which was opened in 1849 and was the first permanent bridge between Buda and Pest. The Austrians failed in their attempt to blow it up after the 1848 uprising – unlike the Germans, who wrecked it to try to slow the advancing Red Army in 1945. To the north of the bridge lies the **Watertown** (Víziváros) district, a wedge of gas-lit streets that was once a poor quarter housing fishermen, craftsmen and their families. Today it's a reclusive neighbourhood of old blocks and mansions meeting at odd angles upon the hillside, reached by alleys which mostly consist of steps rising from the main street, Fő utca. North along Fő utca stand the **Király baths**, distinguishable by the four copper cupolas shaped like tortoise shells.

To the south of Watertown, the tall Liberation Monument crowns the summit of **Gellért Hill** (Gellérthegy), named after Bishop Ghirardus, who converted the Magyars to Christianity at the behest of King Stephen. A statue of him bestrides a waterfall facing the Erzsébet Bridge, marking the spot where he was murdered in 1064 by vengeful heathens following the demise of his royal protector. Near the foot of the bridge, puffs of steam and cute little cupolas surmount the **Rudas baths**, Budapest's most atmospheric Turkish baths, whose interior has hardly changed since they were constructed in 1556. On the other side of the Hegyalja út flyover, the **Rác baths** were also built during the Turkish occupation, but largely modernized with the exception of the pool; unlike the Rudas but like the Király, it's open to women as well as men, on alternate days.

Every August 20 an amazing barrage of fireworks is launched from the hilltop **Citadella**, a low fortress built by the Habsburgs to cow Budapest's population in the aftermath of the 1848–49 revolution. Nowadays the fort (40Ft) contains nothing more sinister than a few exhibits, a tourist hostel and an overpriced restaurant. The **Liberation Monument** thrusts over a hundred feet into the sky, a stark female figure holding aloft the palm of victory. The monument was originally commissioned by Admiral Horthy, a reluctant ally of the Reich, in memory of his own son, but was adapted to suit the requirements of the Soviet liberators.

Descending the hillside through the playgrounds of Jubileumi Park, you'll see rough-hewn stone figures seemingly writhing from the massive portal of the **Gellért baths**, adjoining the *Hotel Gellért*. The best-publicized of the city's baths, they were built in 1913, and the grandeur of the entrance hall is continued in the main pool (Mon–Sat 6am–7pm, Sun 6am–4/7pm; 200Ft).

Pest

Pest is busier and more vital than Buda: the place where things are decided, made and sold. Much of the architecture and general layout dates from the late nineteenth century, when boulevards, public buildings and apartment houses were built on a scale appropriate to the Habsburg empire's second city and the capital of Hungary, which celebrated its 1000-year anniversary in 1896. The **Belváros** positively revels in its cosmopolitanism, with shops selling Nikons and French perfume, posters proclaiming the arrival of Western films and rock groups, and streets noisy with the sound of foreign cars and languages. **Ferenciek tere** is the area's centre, its approach from the Erzsébet Bridge flanked by the twin Clothild palaces, a last flourish of the empire. Overlooking the square stands a slab of gilt and gingerbread architecture, the **Párizsi udvar**, home to an ice cream parlour and a big *IBUSZ* office, but chiefly known for its "Parisian arcade" adorned with arabesques and stained glass.

To the north, **Váci utca** is thronged with people strolling past its cafés and boutiques. It's part promenade – hence its old name, the *korzó* – and part Oxford Street. Passing the *Pesti Theatre*, where twelve-year-old Liszt made his concert debut, the crowds flow onto **Vörösmarty tér**, haunt of portraitists, conjurers, violinists and other acts. While children play in the fountains, their elders congregate around the statue of Mihály Vörösmarty (1800–55) – a poet and translator whose hymn to Magyar identity, *Szózat* (Appeal), is publicly declaimed at moments of national crisis. Underfoot lies continental Europe's first underground train system, opened in 1896: the **Millennial**

Railway (metro line 1) that runs beneath Andrássy utca up to Heroes' Square. However, the most venerable institution on Vörösmarty tér is *Gerbeaud's* patisserie, the favourite of Budapest's high society since the late nineteenth century.

North of here, narrow streets lined with sombre administrative buildings lead towards the government district, whose gloom is interrupted by the verdant expanse of **Szabadság tér**, flanked by the National Bank with its bas-reliefs representing honest toil, and the equally imposing headquarters of Magyar TV. Continue northwards and Hungary's **Parliament building** (Országház) suddenly appears. Variously described as "eclectic" or "neo-Gothic" in style, it sprawls for 268 metres between the embankment and Kossuth tér, dominating the vicinity with a spiky facade embellished by 88 statues of Hungarian rulers.

Back nearer the centre of the Belváros, the facade of **Saint Stephen's Basilica** is diminished by builders' scaffolding, but the restorers have yet to reach the cavernous interior, where shadows obscure the peeling frescoes and gilding. The Basilica's dome, like that of the Parliament, is 96m high – an allusion to 896, the year of the Magyar conquest. On Saint Stephen's name day, August 20, his mummified hand and other holy relics are paraded round the building; the rest of the year, the hand is on show in a chapel behind the altar, where there's also a display on the church's construction.

To the east of the Basilica, **Andrássy út** runs dead straight for two and a half kilometres, a parade of grand buildings laden with gold leaf, dryads and colonnades. Its shops and sidewalk cafés retain some of the style that made the avenue so fashionable in the 1890s. The boulevard culminates at **Heroes' Square** (Hősök tere), erected to mark the thousandth anniversary of the Magyar conquest. Its centrepiece is the **Millennary Monument**, portraying Prince Árpád and his chieftains, half encircled by a colonnade displaying statues of Hungary's most illustrious leaders from King Stephen to Kossuth. The **Museum of Fine Arts** on the square (Tues–Sun 10am–6pm) contains Egyptian funerary relics, Greek and Roman ceramics, and paintings and drawings by European masters from the thirteenth to the twentieth centuries – including Dürer, Rembrandt, Leonardo and Picasso.

A number of side streets lead southwards towards Pest's old **Jewish quarter**. Specific "sights" here are few, but many an apartment building on Síp, Rumbach and Kazinczy streets contains a run-down yet beautiful courtyard with stained-glass panels enscribed in Hebrew characters, and sad memorial plaques naming those who perished on the "Death March" to Hegyeshalom and in the camps of Auschwitz and Bergen-Belsen. On the corner of Wesselényi and Dohány utca, just off the Little Boulevard that encircles the Belváros, restorers are hard at work on the main **Synagogue**, whose dramatic Byzantine-Moorish architecture had grown cracked and filthy from neglect. Depending on its progress, you'll be able to see at least part of the complex, and certainly the **National Jewish Museum** (Mon–Thurs 10am–3pm, Fri & Sun 10am–1pm). Magnificent exhibits dating back to the Middle Ages are opposed by a harrowing Holocaust exhibit, which casts a chill over the third section, portraying Jewish cultural life today. The museum's resurgence owes something to the World Jewish Congress of 1987, held in Budapest, which boosted the confidence of the 80,000-strong community, previously reticent to proclaim itself in a country where anti-Semitism still lingers.

South of the Synagogue, **Múzeum körút** resembles Andrássy út in miniature, with its trees, shops and grandiose stone buildings. The **National Museum** is divided into two sections – before and after the Magyar conquest – of which the latter is the more interesting. The most prestigious exhibit is the Coronation Regalia, reputedly the very crown, orb and sceptre used by King Stephen; although the crown most likely belonged to one of Stephen's successors, the regalia is nevertheless esteemed as the symbol of Hungarian statehood.

Eating and drinking

Magyar cooking naturally predominates in Budapest, but the capital has a growing number of places devoted to foreign cuisine, and it's easy to get "international" dishes and fast food. Prices by Western standards are very reasonable, and your budget should stretch to at least one binge in a top-flight place providing you're otherwise forint-conscious. The following categories – patisseries (for non-alcoholic drinks and a sweet tooth), restaurants (for eating), and taverns and brasseries (for drinking) – are to an extent arbitrary, since all restaurants serve alcohol and all bar-type places serve some food, while *eszpresszó* feature both, plus coffee and pastries.

Patisseries, coffee houses, tearooms and ice cream

Gerbeaud's, Vörösmarty tér. The flagship of the fleet, where a coffee and a *torta* will set you back around 200Ft; the same rich pastries are cheaper in *Kis Gerbeaud* around the corner, a less sumptuous annexe. Gets unbearably full in summer. Daily 9am–9pm.

Híd, IX, Ferenc krt 15. Cosy place next door to the restaurant of the same name, serving cakes prepared on the spot. Daily 7am–10pm.

Lukacs, VI, Andrássy út 70. The cakes are as good as *Gerbeaud's* but cheaper, the premises more sombre than Belle Époque, with dark old woodwork. Daily 8am–9pm.

Müvész, VI, Andrássy út 29. Another special coffee house, less crowded and again cheaper than *Gerbeaud's*. Daily 8am–midnight.

Omnia cukrászda, VIII, Rákóczi út 67. Morello cherry cake and the oddly named *Lúdláb torta* (goose-foot cake) are specialities. Mon–Sat 8am–10pm, Sun 10am–8pm.

Párizsi, VI, Andrássy út 37. Palmy stand-up patisserie with a tempting range of French ice cream.

Ruszwurm's, Szentháromság tér 7. Excellent cakes, served production-line fashion to folks taking a break from sightseeing on Castle Hill, who crowd its diminutive interior. 10am–8pm.

Fast food, self-service and snack bars

Anna Terássz, Váci utca, by Vörösmarty tér. Equally suitable for reading the papers over breakfast indoors, or observing life on Váci utca outside; but alcoholic drinks are costly.

Falafel, VI, Paulay Ede utca 53. Best of the city's falafel joints. Mon–Fri 10am–8pm.

Izes Sarok, V, Bajcsy-Zsilinszky út 1. If you don't mind standing up, a nice place to breakfast on open-faced sandwiches, coffee and juice, situated on the edge of Engels tér.

Lotto, VII, Rákóczi út 57. Cheap, basic place, 200m from Keleti station.

New York Bagels, IX, Ferenc Körút 20. Good though not cheap, open all around the clock all week.

Restaurants

Les Amis, corner of Budai L. utca and Romer Floris utca (☎135-2792). Very small place near the Margit bridge in Buda – essential to book. Wonderful cherry soup. Mon–Sat 4pm–4am.

Bohém Tanya, Paulay Ede utca 6. Popular place near Deák tér, serving traditional Hungarian food.

Csarnok, V, Hold utca 11. Excellent, unshowy and inexpensive. Close to Arany Janos on the blue metro line. Open till 11pm.

Gundels, XIV, Állatkerti krt.2. Named after the famous nineteenth-century restaurateur who founded it on the edge of City Park. Main courses over 1000Ft. Open till midnight daily.

Horgásztanya, I, Fő utca 27. Mainly into fish, on the Watertown's main street. Good food, but check your bill for errors. Noon–midnight.

Kispipa, VII, Akácfa utca 38. Stylish Hungarian restaurant with high reputation.

Marco Polo, V, Vigadó tér 3. High-quality Italian food at high prices. Open until 11pm.

Marcello, Bartok Béla út 40. Easily missed basement restaurant, with the best pizzas in town.

Robinsons, on the lake in the Városliget, by Heroes' Square. Superb waterside setting; the terrace grill has main courses from 500Ft, while the indoor room is pricier. Open till midnight daily.

Szászéves, V, Pesti Barnabás utca 2 (☎118-3608). Founded in the mid-nineteenth century, the "Hundred Years" restaurant is equally noted for its beautiful decor and flambé game dishes. Not cheap; booking essential.

Tüköry, V, Hold utca 15. Another very good cheap place, near the *Csarnok*.

Taverns, brasseries, wine bars and beer halls

Angyal, VIII, Szentkirály utca 8. Late-night bar, open from 10pm until it feels like shutting.

Apostolok, V, Kigyó utca 4–6. Just behind the *Párizsi*, this splendidly Art Nouveau-cum–Gothic establishment is also an expensive restaurant.

Biliárd fél 10 Jazz Klub, VIII, Mária utca 48. Good music and atmosphere at this bar. Pool tables too.

Fregatt, V, Molnár utca 26. Vaguely modelled on an English pub and very popular with foreign residents.

Ink and Drink, V, Király Pál utca krt 6. Blues-folk den with good crowd, tattoo parlour upstairs and music in packed small basement. Closed Sunday.

Kecskeméti borozó, corner of Retek utca and Széna tér. Real Hungarian wine bar. Open till 9pm.

Pepsi Bár, VIII, Üllői út 5. A dark little spot to swill cheap drinks until 5am, three minutes' lurch from Kálvin tér.

Picasso Point, VI, Hajos utca 31, near the Opera. Ex-pats and Magyars mix freely in one of Budapest's few ground level bars. Serves small menu and has live music.

Söröző a Két Pisztolyhoz, IX, Tompa utca 6. Another beer hall of recent origin, boasting grills including flambéed "Robbers' meat" on a spit.

Tilos as Á, VIII, Mizsáth tér. Trendy night spot by the National Museum. 70–100Ft entry; live music downstairs.

Entertainment

Star events in the capital's cultural year are the **Budapest Spring Festival** (March) and the **Autumn Music Weeks** (late Sept to late Oct), both of which attract the cream of Hungary's artists and top international acts. There's hardly less in the way of concerts and the like during the summer months, and on **Constitution Day** (Aug 20) the population lines the embankments to watch a Danube regatta and, around 8pm, a fantastic display of fireworks.

New **clubs and discos** are opening all the time, but the **Petőfi Csarnok** in the Városliget is still perhaps the main focus of Budapest's youth scene. All sorts of **events** happen here: concerts, movies and the Saturday night *Starlight Disco*, billed as Eastern Europe's largest. The 100Ft admission charge is standard at Budapest's ever-changing discos – to identify those currently active, check the fliers around Váci and Ferenciek tére.

You need a passport or ID card to enter discos at **student clubs**, where refreshments are limited to soft drinks. On the Buda side of town you'll find the *Kandó Kollegiumi klub* at Becsi út 104–108 (Fri until 1am) and three places associated with the Technological University. Both the *R-* and the *E-klub* at Egri József utca 1 (Fri & Sat 8pm–2am) are named after outlying college blocks, just around the corner from the *Új Vár klub* at Irinyi József utca 42, which swings on most summer evenings. Across the river in Pest, Budapest Economics University's *MKKE-klub* hosts a *Kalypso* disco on Tuesday, Thursday, Friday and Saturday nights.

You'll have to check the posters and listings publications for information regarding **rock concerts**. Generally, new bands play the transient clubs, bands with their foot in the door like the *E-klub* or the *Petőfi Csarnok*, and really big foreign acts merit an athletics stadium. **Tickets** for most events can be obtained through the *Central Booking Office*, VI, Andrássy út 18, or *Philharmonia*, V, Vörösmarty tér 1, for classical events and music.

Listings

Airlines *MALÉV* flights can be reserved at Roosevelt tér 2.

Bus terminals The most useful are Népstadion (metro line 2; ☎252-2096), serving areas east of the Danube; Erzsébet tér, in the Belváros, for buses to Transdanubia, Ferihegy airport and foreign countries (☎118-2122); and Árpád híd (line 3; ☎120-9229), for the Danube Bend.

Car rental *IBUSZ/Avis*, V, Martinelli tér 8 (☎118-4685) and V, Petőfi tér 3 (☎118-5707); *Főtaxi/Hertz* VII, Kertész utca 24–28 (☎122-1471); *Volántourist*, IX, Vaskapu utca 16 (☎133-4783).

Embassies/consulates *Canada*, II, Budakeszi út 32 (☎176-7312); *Great Britain*, V, Harmincad utca 6 (☎266-2888); *Netherlands*, XIV, Abonyi utca 31 (☎122-8432); *USA*, V, Szabadság tér 12 (☎112-6450).

Exchange 24-hr exchange in *IBUSZ* tourist office at V, Petőfi tér 3.

Hospital Janos korhaz, XII, Diosárok 1 (☎156-1122).

Laundry Rákoczi utca 8 & Böszörményi utca 3, near Déli station.

Mitfahrenzentrale Lifts arranged by *Kenguru*, VIII, Kofarago utca 15 (☎138-2019).

Pharmacy 24-hour service in each district – details on pharmacy doors. Central 24-hr pharmacies are opposite Déli station at Alkotás utca 1/b, and near Keleti station at Rákoczi utca 86.

Post offices Main office at V, Petőfi utca 13 (Mon–Fri 8am–6pm, Sat 8am–2pm).

Telephones International calls are best made from the telephone and telegram bureau, V, Petőfi utca 17–19 (Mon–Fri 7am–9pm, Sat 7am–8pm, Sun 8am–1pm), or, more expensively, from deluxe hotels.

Train stations Basically, Keleti is the point of departure for expresses to Austria, Germany, Switzerland, France, the Czech & Slovak Republics, Poland, Romania, Russia, the former Yugoslavia and Bulgaria. Nyugati handles traffic for Szeged, Debrecen and Nyíregyháza, and additional services to Romania, the Czech & Slovak Republics and Germany; while Déli chiefly serves Lake Balaton and Transdanubia. Bookings and international tickets should be purchased 24–36 hours in advance, preferably at the *MÁV* booking office, VI, Andrássy út 35 (Mon–Wed 9am–5pm, Thurs & Fri 9am–7pm), where queues are shorter than at the stations.

THE DANUBE BEND

Entering the Carpathian Basin, the Danube widens hugely, only to be forced by hills and mountains through a narrow, twisting valley – almost a U-turn – before parting for the length of Szentendrei Island and flowing into Budapest. To escape Budapest's humid summers, people flock to this region, known as the **Danube Bend** (Dunakanyar), where the historic attractions are Szentendre, **Esztergom** and **Visegrád**. Szentendre, forty minutes' journey by *HÉV* **train** from Batthyány tér in Budapest, is the logical place to start, though with hourly **buses** from the capital's Árpád híd terminal, you could travel directly to Visegrád or Esztergom, the heart of Hungarian Catholicism. Travelling **by boat** can be fun, but it takes five hours from Budapest to Esztergom. It's better to sail only part of the way, say between the capital and Szentendre (1hr 30min), or Visegrád and Esztergom (2hr).

Szentendre

Having cleared the bus and *HÉV* stations and found their way into its Baroque heart, visitors are seldom disappointed by **SZENTENDRE**. Ignoring the outlying housing estates and the rash of *Nosztalgia* and *Folklór* boutiques in the centre, "Saint Andrew" is a friendly maze of houses painted in autumn colours, secretive gardens and alleys leading to hilltop churches – the perfect spot for an artists' colony. Before the artists moved in during the 1900s, Szentendre owed its character largely to Serbian refugees from the Turks. Their town houses – now converted into galleries, shops and cafés – form a set piece around **Fő tér**, a stage for musicians, mimes and other events.

The **Blagovestenszka Church** – whose iconostasis by Mikhail Zivkovič suggests the richness of the Serbs' artistry and faith – is first stop on the heritage trail, while just around the corner at Vastagh Gy utca 1 stands the wonderful **Margit Kovács Museum** (Tues–Sun 9am–7pm), displaying the lifetime work of Hungary's greatest ceramicist, born in 1902. Above Fő square there's a fine view of Szentendre's steeply banked rooftops and gardens from the hilltop **Templom tér**, where frequent crafts fairs are held to help finance the restoration of the parish church. Opposite this, paintings whose fierce brush strokes and sketching were a challenge to the canons of classicism during the 1890s hang in the **Béla Czóbel Museum** (Tues–Sun April–Oct 10am–6pm; Nov–March 9am–5pm), beyond which the spire of the **Serbian Orthodox Cathedral** pokes above a walled garden. Tourists are generally not admitted, but you can see the cathedral iconostasis and treasury in the adjacent museum (Wed–Sun 10am–5.30pm).

A regular bus runs from the terminal out along Szabadságforrás út to Szentendre's **Village Museum** (April–Oct Tues–Sun 9am–5pm), which is intended eventually to include reconstructed villages from all over Hungary, and is already a fascinating place. The brochure on sale at the gate points out the finer distinctions between humble peasant dwellings like the house from Kispalad, and the cottage from Uszka formerly occupied by petty squires. During the summer on alternate weekends, people demonstrate traditional craft techniques, like pottery, baking and basket making.

While fast-food joints and **restaurants** are concentrated around the stations and the centre, **accommodation** is mainly in the north of town. Cheaper options are the *Coca Cola* at Dunakanyar körút 50 (✆26/310-410) and *Hubertus* at Tyukosdűlő 10 (✆26/310-616) – or whatever *Dunatours*, Bogdányi utca 1, can arrange in the way of **private rooms**. A lot of people end up **camping**, either on Szentendrei Island or on Pap Island to the north of town – accessible by ferry and bus respectively. Although **ferries**, leaving from the pier nearest *Dunatours*, are the coolest way of travelling north, buses are quicker and more frequent. A new road has been constructed over the hills to relieve congestion on road 11 between Szentendre and Visegrád, but most buses still take the embankment route.

Visegrád

During the fifteenth-century reign of Mátyás and Beatrice the palace at VISEGRÁD was famed throughout Europe. After the Turkish occupation Visegrád declined, gradually turning into the humble village that it is today, however the basic layout of the riverside settlement – the stunning Citadel on the hill, joined by ramparts to Soloman's Tower and the Water Bastion below – hasn't altered significantly since the thirteenth century, when Béla IV began fortifying the north against a recurrence of the Mongol invasion.

The ruins of the **Palace** are spread over four levels behind the gate of 27 Fő utca. Nothing remains of the building founded by the Angevin king Charles Robert, but the *cour d'honneur* built for his successor Louis, which provided the basis for subsequent building, is still to be seen on the second terrace. Its chief features are a Renaissance loggia and two panels from its Hercules Fountain. Reportedly, the palace's finest sight was the garden above the bath corridor, embellished by the Lion Fountain. A copy of the original bears Mátyás's raven crest and dozens of sleepy looking lions, but is no longer connected to the pipes which formerly channelled water from the Citadel.

From the decrepit **Water Bastion** just north of the main landing stage, a rampart ascends the slope to **Soloman's Tower**, a mighty hexagonal keep buttressed by concrete slabs. Inside, the tower's **Mátyás Museum** houses finds from the excavated palace including the white Anjou Fountain of the Angevins and the red marble *Visegrád Madonna*.

Visegrád's most dramatic feature is the imposing 11 **Citadel** on the mountain top; though only partly restored, it is still mightily impressive, commanding a superb view of Nagymaros and the Börzsöny Mountains on the east bank. You can reach it by the "Calvary" footpath which begins near Nagy Lajos utca, or by catching a bus from the Mátyás statue on Salamán-torony utca, which follows the scenic Panorama út. From the car park on the summit, one road leads to the luxury *Hotel Silvanus*, the other to the Nagy-Villám observation tower, where you'll get a view that stretches into the Slovak Republic.

During high summer you might have problems finding somewhere to stay – try *Fanny Reisen* (☎26/328-303), Fő utca 66. The best places to check out are the *Tourist Hostel* at Salamán-torony utca 5, the small **campsite** with bunkhouses at Széchenyi utca 7 and the *Elte Hostel* at Fő utca 117 – or ask about **private rooms** at Fő utca 107, Széchenyi utca 10 or *Dunatours* at Fő utca 3. For meals, head to the *Vár* and *Fekete Hollo* fish **restaurants** along the promenade.

Esztergom

Beautifully situated in a crook of the Danube facing the Slovak Republic, enclosed by glinting water and soft hills, **ESZTERGOM** is dominated by its great basilica, whose dome is visible for miles around. The sight is richly symbolic, for although the royal court abandoned Esztergom for Buda after the Mongol invasion, this has remained the centre of Hungarian Catholicism since 1000, when Stephen – who was born and crowned here – imposed Christianity.

Completed in 1856, Esztergom's is the largest **Basilica** in Hungary: 118m long and 40m wide, capped by a dome 71.5m high. Its nave is on a massive scale, clad in marble, gilding and mosaics, with a collection of saintly relics in the chapel to the right as you enter. A ticket is required to visit the **crypt**, which resembles a set from an old horror movie, with giant stone women flanking the stairway that descends to gloomy vaults full of prelates' tombs – including that of the conservative Cardinal Mindszenty, whose opposition to the liberalizing Kadar regime greatly embarrassed the Vatican. In May 1991 he was given a state burial by the Hungarian government, now eager to enlist the church's powers in smoothing the country's social problems. The **treasury** entrance is north of the altar, and having seen its overpowering collection of bejewelled crooks and chalices, it's almost a relief to climb the seemingly endless stairway to the **bell tower** and cupola.

On the same craggy plateau you'll find the ruins of the medieval **palace** (Tues–Sun 9am–5pm) once occupied by Béla III, the widowed Queen Beatrice and a number of sundry archbishops. You can visit the remains of a chapel with a rose window and Byzantine-style frescoes, Beatrice's suite and the study of Archbishop Vítez – known as the Hall of Virtues after its allegorical murals. Below, the Baroque streets of the Watertown are connected by the sloping Bajcsy-Zsilinszky út to the centre of down-town Esztergom, the **Rákóczi tér**. A short way south, pavement cafés are to be found around the pleasant Széchenyi tér, which also has the *Express* tourist office (no. 4) and post office.

For accommodation, private **rooms** are probably the cheapest option in town, available from *Express* and the nearby *Komturist* and *IBUSZ* bureaux, both of which you'll find in Lörinc utca; there are also student hostels in summer, or there are *panzios* in the town, like the *Ria Panzio*, Batthynny utca 11 (☎33/311-115; ④). In the centre of town is the *Fürdő Hotel*, Bajcsy-Zsilinszky utca 14 (☎33/311-688; ⑤). The nearest **campsite** is *Gran Tours*, on the central Priméas sziget. There are several decent **restaurants** on Bajcsy-Zsilinszky – pick the *Filifalatok* for economy, the *Alabárdos* for its Transylvanian roast.

WESTERN HUNGARY

The major tourist attraction to the west of the capital is **Lake Balaton**, over-romantically labelled the "Hungarian sea". Despite the fact that rising prices are push-ing out natives in favour of Austrians and Germans, this is still very much the nation's playground, with vacation resorts lining both shores. On the northern bank develop-ment has been limited to some extent by reedbanks and cooler, deeper water, giving tourism a different slant. Historic **Tihany** and the wine-producing **Badacsony Hills** offer fine sightseeing, while anyone whose social life doesn't take off in **Keszthely** can go soak themselves in the thermal lake at **Hévíz**.

More than other regions in Hungary, the western region of **Transdanubia** (Dunántúl) is a patchwork land, an ethnic and social hybrid. Its valleys and hills, forests and mud flats have been a melting pot since Roman times: settled by Magyars, Serbs, Slovaks and Germans; torn asunder and occupied by Turks and Habsburgs; and, within the last 150 years, transformed from a state of near feudalism. All the main towns display evidence of this evolution, especially **Sopron**, the most archaic, and **Pécs**, which boasts a Turkish mosque and minaret.

Lake Balaton

Given the overdevelopment of the southern shore, you'll get the best out of Lake Balaton by catching one of the **trains** from Déli station to Balatonfüred; from there they go along the northern shore until the Badacsony Hills, where they make tracks for Tapolca. Alternatively, from Budapest's Erzsébet tér you can catch **buses** to the major lakeside towns, and **hitchhiking** is feasible on all routes except the M7 motor-way. Hotels cost about the same as in Budapest, and private rooms cost from 800Ft for a double. In addition, the shore is ringed with holiday homes built for workers; it's always worth asking about spare rooms at these places, as they are often rented out at a reasonable price. Balaton **campsites** are Hungary's most expensive, though some sites drop their prices out of season.

Balatonfüred

The Romans were the first to imbibe the curative waters of **BALATONFÜRED** and nowadays some 30,000 people come every year for treatment in its sanatoria. A busy harbour and skyscraper hotels dominate Balatonfüred's approaches, but **the centre** has a sedate, convalescent atmosphere, typified by the embankment promenade, Rabindranath Tagore sétány, named after the Bengali poet who came here in 1926. The promenade opens onto Gyógy tér (Health Square), where you can drink the Kossuth spring's carbonic water at a pagoda-like structure. Four other springs feed the hospital and the adjoining mineral baths on the eastern side.

Balatonfüred's cheapest **hotels** are the *Aranycsillag* at Zsigmond utca 1 (③), *Erdei* at Koloska utca 45 (③), and *Panorama* at Kun utca 15 (③); all are a shade more expen-sive than private **rooms** from *IBUSZ*, just off Petőfi utca, the main road encircling the centre. There's a big **campsite** to the west of town, beyond the *Füred* and *Marina* hotels. For **meals**, the less touristy places are up in the old town, away from the lake – *Aranykorona* in Kossuth utca has a good reputation.

Tihany

The historic centre of **TIHANY** sits above the harbour where the ferries from Siófok and Balatonfüred pull in; you'll find it by following the winding steps up between a screen of trees, as do thousands of other people who come to rubberneck around the so-called "Pearl of the Balaton". The rail line bypasses the peninsula, so the alternative way of getting to the town is by **bus** from Balatonfüred, which stops in the touristic zone of Tihanyi-rév.

In days gone by, Tihany's tone was set by the **Benedictine Abbey**, established here at the request of Andrew I. The king's body still lies in the crypt of the rebuilt **Abbey Church**, which contains virtuoso woodcarvings by Sebestyén Stulhoff – who preserved the features of his fiancée in the face of the angel kneeling to the right of the altar of the Virgin. The adjoining monastery now contains a **museum** (Tues–Sun 9am–6pm) displaying Balaton landscapes, and an interesting collection of costumes, implements and musical instruments gathered from far-flung communities in the *taiga* beneath the Arctic Circle and in the Ural mountains – the Finno-Ugric tribes from which the Magyars originated.

Quaint adaptation à la Szentendre abounds, from the rip-off restaurant occupying the monastery stables to the Fishermen's Guild Museum down on Pisky promenade, where folkloric performances are staged in the courtyard. Around Petőfi and Csokonai street, houses are built of grey basalt tufa, with windows and doors outlined in white and porticoed terraces, including the **tourist office**. Even without a map it's easy to stumble upon **Belső-tó** lake, whose sunlit surface is visible from the abbey. From its southern bank, a path runs through vineyards, orchards and lavender fields past the Aranyház geyser cones and down to Tihanyi-rév.

Hotels in Tihanyi-rév are exorbitant – the neighbouring campsite or private rooms (from Petőfi utca 4 up in the old town) are the only affordable **accommodation**.

The Badacsony

For 30km west of Tihany the shoreline is infested with holiday homes and nondescript resorts. There's nothing worth stopping for until **the Badacsony**, a coffin-shaped hulk of rock with four villages prostrated at its feet, backed by extinct volcanoes ranged across the Taploca basin. A great semicircle of basalt columns, 210m high, forms the Badacsony's southeastern face, while Kőkapu (the Stone Gate) cleaves the northeast side, its two natural towers flanking a precipitous drop. The rich volcanic soil of the mountain's lower slopes has supported vineyards since the Avars buried grape seeds with their dead to ensure that the afterlife wouldn't lack wine.

Developments are clustered around the southern tip, where you'll find a **tourist office** behind Badacsony **station**, above the quay. From there, the trail up Lábdi út is marked by locals selling wine and jeeps shuttling tourists up to the former Bormúzeum, a large basalt hall now serving as an expensive restaurant. To escape the crowds, try the four-kilometre hike north to **Gulács-hegy**, a perfectly conical hill near the Nemesgulács train station, on the line to Tapolca. You can get **private rooms** from *Miditourist* at Park utca 53, or there's the **hostel** at Park utca 7 and the *Harsona Panzió* at Szegedi R. utca 37 (②). The **campsite** is five minutes' walk west of the tourist office.

Keszthely and around

Though you can change trains at Tapolca and ride back down to **KESZTHELY** – the Balaton's best hang-out – it's easier to continue around the southern shore by bus. Absorbing thousands of visitors gracefully, Keszthely has some good bars and restaurants, the Festetics Palace to admire, a thermal lake at nearby Hévíz, and a university to give it some life of its own. The centre is roughly ten minutes' walk from the dock (follow Erzsébet királyne útja), or from the train station at the bottom end of Mártirok útja, where some inter-city buses terminate. Most buses, however, drop passengers on Fő tér, halfway along the main drag, Kossuth utca.

Walking up from the train station you'll pass the **Balaton Museum** (daily 9/10am–5pm), whose exhibits include artefacts dating back to the first century AD, when road-building Roman imperialists disrupted the lives of the local Celtic tribes. From Fő tér, with its much-remodelled Gothic church, Kossuth utca is given over to cafés, vendors, buskers and strollers, a cheerful procession towards the **Festetics Palace**. Founded in 1745 by Count György, the palace (daily 9am–5/6pm; 75Ft) attracted the leading lights of Magyar literature from the nineteenth century onwards. The building's highlights are its gilt, mirrored ballroom and the Helikon Library, a masterpiece of joinery and carving.

Keszthely's **waterfront** has two moles (one for swimming, the other for ferries), a slew of parkland backed by plush hotels and miniature golf courses, and dozens of fast-food joints and bars. After closing time, action shifts to the centre, with a disco in the **Theatre Club** (Mon & Thurs) and **restaurants** working at full steam. *Béke* on Kossuth utca is favoured by locals for its outdoor setting and cheap meals. On Szabad nép utca, one block north of Széchenyi utca, the *Bár Picolo* is a friendly student hangout serving *Urquell* beer.

The *Helikon* **hostel** at Honvéd utca 22 (②), ten minutes' walk from the train station, has the cheapest beds, but **private rooms** are a better alternative. They are available from *IBUSZ* on Széchenyi utca (Mon–Sat 8am–6pm, plus Sun 9am–1pm in summer) and *Express* on Kossuth utca (Mon–Sat 8am–5/8pm) – or just look out for houses with *Zimmer frei* signs. **Campers** have the option of a small site just south of the station or the big and expensive *Castrum* site 1500 metres along the shore.

HÉVÍZ

Half-hourly buses from outside the train station run to **HÉVÍZ**, a spa based around Europe's largest **thermal lake**. The wooden terraces surrounding the *Tófürdő* **baths** (daily 8am–5pm; 100Ft) have a vaguely *fin-de-siècle* appearance, but the ambience is contemporary, with people sipping beer while bobbing on the lake in hired inner tubes. Otherwise, Hévíz seems to be comprised of rest homes and costly hotels, with a late-night bar and a hard-currency casino in the *Hotel Thermal*. Should you wish **to stay**, try the *Gyöngyvirag* in Felszabadulás tér, the *Piroska* at Kossuth utca 10 (☎84/312-698), or any of the **tourist offices** for private rooms – *Zalatour* at Rákoczi utca 8, a block behind the bus station, or *Express*, Petőfi utca 19.

Sopron and around

With its 240 listed buildings, **SOPRON** can legitimately claim to be "the most historic town in Hungary": north of Széchenyi tér, a few hundred metres from the station, Várkerület encircles a horseshoe-shaped inner core that contrasts starkly with the grim modern zone around it.

At the southern end of the old town, Orsolya tér features Renaissance edifices dripping with loggias and carved protrusions, a Gothic church and a **Guild Museum** (9am–5pm; closed Tues) dealing with local crafts traditions. But there's more atmosphere in the **Cezár Pince**, a cellar with oak butts and leather-aproned waiters, serving local wines and platters of *wurst*. Despite its name, **Új utca** (New Street) is one of the town's oldest thoroughfares, a gentle curve of arched dwellings painted in red, yellow and pink, with chunky cobblestones and pavements. At no. 22 stands one of the **synagogues** that flourished when the street was known as Zsidó (Jewish) utca; its collection serves as a reminder that Sopron's Jewish community survived the expulsion of 1526 only to be annihilated during World War II.

The main source of interest is up ahead on **Fő tér**, a parade of Gothic and Baroque partly overshadowed by the **Goat Church** – so called, supposedly, because its construction was financed by a goatherd whose flock unearthed a cache of loot. The Renaissance **Storno House**, once visited by King Mátyás and Count Széchenyi, now exhibits Roman, Celtic and Avar relics, plus mementoes of Liszt, while the ground floor serves as the *Corvin Pizzeria*.

North of the square rises Sopron's symbol, the **Firewatch Tower** (Tues–Sat 9am–6pm), founded upon the stones of a fortress originally laid out by the Romans, who established the town in the first century. From the top there's a stunning view of Sopron's narrow streets and weathered rooftops. Offered the choice of Austrian citizenship in 1921, the townsfolk voted to remain Magyar subjects and erected a "Gate of Loyalty" at the base of the tower to commemorate this act of patriotism. Walk through it and you'll emerge onto Előkapu (outer gate), a short street where the houses are laid out in a saw-toothed pattern. On **Várkerület** beyond, boutiques have supplanted two minor monuments: the colourfully tiled *Arany Sas* pharmacy and the former *White Horse Inn* where Haydn stayed when he wasn't enjoying the hospitality at Fertőd.

From here, Ikva híd points towards a couple more sights. Atmospheric Balfi utca leads directly to the privately owned **Zettl-Langer Collection** of porcelain, earthenware and weaponry at no. 11 (daily 10am–noon), while Pozsonyi utca wends uphill past the "House of the Two Moors" to the partly Gothic church of Saint Michael, whose gargoyles leer over the chapel of Saint Jacob decaying in the graveyard. Nearby stand the cross-less tombstones of Russians killed liberating Sopron from the Hungarian Nazi puppet-government.

Private rooms can be arranged at *IBUSZ*, Várkerület 41 (Mon–Fri 8am–4pm, Sat 8am–12.30pm), and *Ciklámen Tourist*, Ógabona tér 8 (Mon–Sat 7.30am–4pm; open till 8pm Fri & Sat in summer, plus Sun 8am–noon). They also arrange student hotel accommodation in July and August. The *Lövér* **campsite** is served by bus #12 hourly from Deák tér.

The list of places where you can sample the **local wines** include *Stefánia* at Szent György utca 12, and a couple of cellars on Fő tér, the *Cezár* and the *Gyógygödör*. Aside from hotel **restaurants** the best options are around Széchenyi tér and on Várkerület – ranging from the popular *Vörös Étterem* and *Vendéglő* (nos. 25 & 63) to the spit-and-sawdust *Finom Fatalok* grill. Új utca's *Holsten Söröző* dispenses beer and disco-beat until 10pm.

Sopron is the nearest Hungarian town to Vienna – hence the crowds of Austrian tourists strolling around town on summer weekends. Four special *GYSEV* trains leave Sopron station for Vienna daily, and there are also a dozen *Volán* buses to Vienna each week.

The Esterházy Palace

Twenty-seven kilometres from Sopron (hourly buses except on Sun) lies a monument to one of the country's most famous dynasties: the **Esterházy Palace** at **FERTŐD** (daily except Mon 8am–noon & 1-4/5pm; 80Ft). Originally of the minor nobility, the Esterházy family began its rise thanks to Nicholas I (1583–1645), who married two rich widows and sided with the Habsburgs against Transylvania during the Counter-Reformation, thereby being elevated to Count. The palace itself was begun by his grandson, Nicholas "the Ostentatious", who inherited 600,000 acres and a dukedom in 1762. Whereas his father, Paul, had been content to publish a songbook, *Harmonia Celestis*, Nicholas II boasted "Anything the Kaiser can do, I can do better!", and spent 40,000 gulden a year on pomp and entertainments.

With its 126 rooms fronted by a vast horseshoe courtyard where Hussars once pranced to the music of Haydn – Esterházy's resident maestro – the palace was intended to rival Versailles. Highlights of the guided tour include salons of blue and white chinoiserie, gilded rooms lined with mirrors, and a hall where concerts are held beneath a splendid fresco of Hermes, so contrived that from whichever angle you view it his chariot seems to be careering towards you across the sky. And, of course, there's also a room full of Haydn memorabilia.

Pécs

Strange though it might seem, the uranium mining town of **PÉCS** is not only one of Transdanubia's largest towns, but is also one of the most attractive, with its tiled roof-tops climbing the vine-laden slopes of the Mecsek range. This is also a leading centre of education, having the fifth oldest university in Europe, founded in 1367. Besides some fine museums and a great market, Pécs contains Hungary's best examples of Islamic architecture – a legacy of the long Turkish occupation.

Heading up Bajcsy-Zsilinszky ut from the bus terminal, or by bus #30 from the train station towards the centre, you'll pass Kossuth tér and Pécs's **Synagogue** (May–Oct 9am–1pm & 1.30–5pm; closed Sat). The beautiful nineteenth-century interior is a haunt-ing place, with Romantic frescoes swirling around space emptied by the murder of almost 4000 Jews – ten times the number that live in Pécs today. During the Turkish occupation (1543–1686) a similar fate befell the Christian population, whose principal church was replaced by the **Mosque of Gazi Kasim Pasha** (summer Mon–Sat 10am–4pm, Sun 11.30am–4pm; winter Mon–Sat 11am–noon, Sun 11.30am–2pm), to the north on Széchenyi tér – an otherwise modern square, with an ice cream parlour and **tourist offices**. Also on the square there's a gallery of contemporary work by local artists and an **Archeological Museum** displaying items testifying to a Roman presence between the first and fifth centuries.

From here you can follow either Káptalan or Janus Pannonius utca towards the cathedral. In the former street, Op Art hangs in the birthplace of the painter **Viktor Vasarely**, while across the road you can see equally lurid **Zsolnay porcelain**, produced by the Pécs factory that made the tiles for Budapest's applied arts museum, or be sobered by the sculptures of **Amerigo Tot**, whose *Erdély family* with its clamped grave-posts symbolizes the plight of the Magyars in Romania. The **Modern Magyar Képtár**, next door, presents a survey of Hungarian art since the School of Szentendre. Best of the museums is the **Csontváry Museum** in Janus Pannonius utca (Tues–Sun 10am–6pm), devoted to the brilliant paintings of Tivadar Csontváry Kosztka. Born in the same year as van Gogh, he was likewise largely self-taught, obsessed with follow-ing "the path of the sun" and unappreciated during his lifetime.

Though its architects have incorporated a crypt and side chapels from eleventh- to fourteenth-century churches, Pécs **Cathedral** is predominantly nineteenth-century neo-Romanesque, with four spires, three naves and a lavish decor of blue and gold and floral motifs. The site has been used for religious and funerary purposes since Roman times, and remnants of an early Christian basilica are sunk into the park-like square below Dóm tér. Behind the Bishop's Palace, a circular **Barbican** occupies a gap in the decrepit **town walls** – once a massive rampart 5500 paces long, buttressed by 87 bastions erected after the Mongol invasion. South of the barbican, Klimó György utca slopes down to meet Rákóczi út, where grubby buildings almost conceal the sixteenth-century **Jakovali Hassan Mosque** (10am–1pm; closed Wed), with friezes, a superbly carved *minbar* and Turkish carpets adorning the cool white interior.

Practicalities

Central **hotels** are expensive: central **private rooms** and student **hostel** beds from *IBUSZ* or *Mecsek Tourist* – both on Széchenyi tér – are a better deal. Bus #44 passes *Mandulás* **campsite** in the woodlands below the TV tower – be careful not to miss the turn-off at Demokcrácia út. The *Rózsakert,* opposite the Csontváry museum, and the *Minaret* on Sallai utca are both reasonably priced garden **restaurants**. Another good restaurant is the *Iparos Ház,* on Rákoczi utca by the Zsolnay monument. Király utca abounds with pizzerias and cafés; **bars** are more numerous in the western part of the Belváros, where Klimó György utca's *Barbikán Pince* is open until 2 or 3am every night.

The **Pécs Fair**, held on the morning of the first Sunday of each month, sees some hard bargaining and hard drinking, and there are smaller markets every Sunday. Bus #50 runs to the market site from outside the Domus áruház in Rákoczi utca; get a ticket before boarding from a newspaper stall or the train station.

EASTERN HUNGARY

The hilly, mountainous and forested northern region of eastern Hungary will not feature prominently in any hurried tour of the country, but nobody should overlook the famous wine-producing towns of **Eger** and **Tokaj**, whose appeal goes beyond the local beverage. Covering more than half of Hungary and awesome in its flatness, the **Great Plain** or **puszta** can shimmer like a mirage or be as drab as a farmworker's boots. Chance encounters and fleeting details are often more interesting than "sights" on the Plain, but at least one spot calls for a planned visit – **Szeged**, the most sophisticated city of the Plain, with its celebrated restaurants, buildings and festivals.

Eger

Its colourful architecture suffused by sunshine, **EGER** is a fitting place of origin for *Egri Bikavér*, the potent, throat-rasping red wine marketed as **Bull's Blood** abroad, which brings hordes of visitors to the town. Despite occasional problems with accommodation, it's a fine place to hang out and wander around, not to mention all the opportunities for drinking. There are five trains a day from Budapest; from the station, walk up the road to Deák Ferenc út, catch a #10 or #12 bus and get off when the cathedral appears.

The Neoclassical **Cathedral** – József Hild's rehearsal for the still larger Basilica at Esztergom – is approached by a flight of steps, beneath which lies the *Kazamata* restaurant, a bizarre creation that's better to look at than to eat in. Inside the cupola the City of God rises triumphantly, while Saint Rita's shrine is cluttered with supplications and testimonials. Heading towards the centre you pass several tourist offices and restaurants before reaching **Dobó István tér**. With its wine bars and action-packed statues facing a stately Minorite Church, the main square is a pleasant spot and the starting point for further sightseeing. Cross the bridge and round a corner to find Eger's most photographed structure, a slender fourteen-sided **minaret** (daily 9am–5pm; 20Ft), looking rather pathetic without its mosque, which was demolished during a nineteenth-century building boom.

Alternatively, head uphill from the square past the *Pallas Presszo* café, nestling in a strange classical courtyard, to the gates of the **Castle** (daily 9am–5pm; Tues–Sun 50Ft, Mon 20Ft, when only part is open). From the bastion overlooking the main gate, a path leads up to the ticket office and the fifteenth-century Bishop's Palace. Tapestries, ceramics, Turkish handicrafts and weaponry fill the museum upstairs in the palace, while downstairs are temporary exhibits and a Hall of Heroes (Hősök terme), where a life-size marble István Dobó lies amid a bodyguard of heroes of the siege of 1552. Ensconced in the castle under the command of Dobó, 2000 soldiers and Eger's women repulsed a Turkish force six times their number – shattering the impetus of the Ottoman advance until 1596. From the ticket office a guide will take you into the under-ground galleries, a labyrinth of sloping passageways, gun emplacements and mysterious chambers, which you can sneak off to explore.

Wine tasting and other practicalities

Local vineyards produce four types of **wine** – Muskotály (Muscatel), Bikavér (Bull's Blood), Leányka (medium dry white with a hint of herbs) and Medoc Noir (rich, dark and sweet) – all of which can be sampled in the cellars of the **Szépasszony Valley**, just west of town (100Ft by taxi). Finding the right cellar is a matter of luck and taste – but no. 38 is dry and spacious and takes its wine seriously. You can enjoy a meal beneath the vines of the *Kulacs Csárda*. The cellars tend to close by 8pm; later hours are kept in town, where the **Wine Museum**, Varosfal utca 1, gives you the chance to sample the stuff until 10pm from Tuesday to Saturday.

Eger's cheapest accommodation is the **hostel** at Dobó tér 6 (①) and the summer student hostels. Details of these and of **private rooms** are obtainable from the **tourist offices** – *Eger Tourist* at Bajcsy-Zsilinszky utca 9, *IBUSZ* in the passage behind, or *Express* on Széchenyi utca. Along from the castle is the *Tourist* motel at Mekcsey utca 2 (☎36/310-014; ①). For more comfort, there's the *Hotel Minaret*, opposite the minaret at Harangöntő utca 5 (☎36/410-020; ⑤), or the classier *Senator Hotel*, Dobó tér 11 (☎36/ 320-466; ⑥). There are two **campsites**: to the north at Rákóczi út 79 (April 15–Oct 15; bus #10 or #11), and the new *Tulipán* site in the Szépasszony Valley. The reasonable *Mecset*, opposite the minaret, is the best of Eger's **restaurants**. Standards are almost as high at the *Vadászkert*, Torony utca 1, and the *Vörös Rák* at Alkotmány u1.

Tokaj

TOKAJ is to Hungary what Champagne is to France, and this small town has become a place of pilgrimage for wine snobs. Perched beside the confluence of the rivers Bodrog and Tisza, Tokaj is a place of sloping cobbled streets and faded ochre dwellings with nesting storks and wine cellars, overlooked by lush vineyards climbing the hillside towards the "Bald Peak" and the inevitable TV transmission tower. It's fifteen minutes' walk left out of the station and left under the bridge to the old **town centre**. Tokaj has a few architectural "sights" – the old Town Hall and Rákóczi-Dessewffy mansion and a ruined castle by the river – but inevitably it's wine that attracts most people's attention.

There are three main **Tokaj wines** – the usually dry Furmint, sweet Aszú and Hárslevelű (linden leaf) – all of which derive their character from the same techniques. Heat is trapped by the volcanic soil, allowing a delayed **harvest** in October, when many over-ripe grapes have a sugar content approaching sixty percent. Their juice and pulp is added to 136-litre barrels of ordinary grapes, the volume of the addition determining the qualities of the wine. The results have collected some notable accolades: Beethoven and Schubert dedicated songs to it, and Louis XVI declared it "the wine of kings, the king of wines". The **Tokaj Museum** at Bethlen G. utca 7 (Tues–Sun 9am–3/ 5pm; 24Ft) complacently displays wine labels from Crimea, France and the Rhineland, where attempts to reproduce Tokaj all failed. The favourite place for oenophiles is the **Rákóczi cellar** at Kossuth tér 15 (daily 8am–noon & 12.30–7pm), but you can get more personal service in the small private cellars that line the hill – the **Vajtho cellar** at Rákóczi utca 4, opposite the bridge, is recommended.

If you want to indulge in a binge, **private rooms** are available at around 800Ft per double from Ovar utca 6 or Bajcsy-Zsilinszky utca 19. Also good are *Kollégium* at Bajcsy-Zsilinszky utca 15–17 (☎41/352-355; ②), from June to August and at some weekends throughout the year, and the *Hotel Tokaj*, Rákóczi utca 5 (☎41/352-344; ②). The two local campsites, *Tisza* and *Pelsőczi*, are opposite each other on the far side of the river. For **meals**, your options are the buffet by the campsite, more expensive fish dishes at *Halászcsárd*, by the bridge at Bajcsy-Zsilinszky utca 23, or the *Tokaj* hotel restaurant.

Szeged

SZEGED, straddling the Tisza like a small-scale Budapest, is as cosmopolitan a place as you'll find on the Great Plain. Much of its friendly atmosphere is due to students, while the old city's eclectic good looks have been saved by placing the ugly modern housing and industry over the river. Though the goddess-worshipping Kőrös people settled here over 4000 years ago, and the town flourished after 1225 because of its royal salt monopoly over the mines of Transylvania, Szeged's layout derives from the great flood of March 1879, which washed away all but 300 homes. The city bounced back, trumpeting its revival with huge buildings and squares where every type of architectural style got some playing time.

The result generally pleases the eye but makes initial orientation slightly harder. Tram #1 from the train station or bus #70 from the bus terminal get you to the town centre, Széchenyi tér. A few minutes' walk from here is Klauzál tér, on the other side of which lies Dugonics tér with its "Water Music" fountain – it has musical accompaniment all day. Here you'll find the **University**, Szeged's cultural mainspring, named after the poet Attila József (1905–37) – somewhat ironic in view of the fact that the university expelled him, as did the Communist Party. The illegitimate son of a washerwoman, Attila lived in extreme poverty and finally killed himself by jumping under a train.

Aside from the university and ever-larger department stores, **Dóm tér** is the main object of civic pride. Flanked by arcades with twisted columns and busts of the illustrious, the square contains a vast brown brick, neo-Romanesque **Votive Church** that the townsfolk pledged to build after the flood; it was finished – complete with a 10,180-pipe organ – in 1930. Banked opposite the church are seats for the **Szeged Weeks** arts festival (roughly July 20–Aug 20); tickets, from the office on the corner of Klauzál tér and Kiss utca, begin at a mere 100Ft. Just to the south of the square, the **Heroes' Gate** links Aradi Vértanúk tére with Boldogasszony sugárút. Though its origins are no longer publicized, the gate was raised to honour Horthy's henchmen, the "Whites", who gathered here in 1919 before they fanned out across Hungary to murder thousands of Jews and "Reds" in the "White Terror". Fascistic stone guardsmen still flank the archway, but Horthy's murals have been erased by dirt and time.

Szeged's past is mainly preserved in the **Móra Ferenc Museum** at Roosevelt tér 1–3 (Tues–Sun 10am–6pm; 12Ft), whose standard mix of local artefacts hides behind a Neoclassical facade of columns, lions and crumbling philosophers. The ruins in the park to the north once housed convicts, who laboured on the river towpaths during the eighteenth century.

Beyond its inner boulevard, Lenin körút, Szeged is shabbier and more utilitarian, but things are different across the River Tisza in **Újszeged**. On hot weekends people flock to the swimming pool to the right of the bridgehead or the grassy strand beside the river; they go in winter, too, for a wallow in the outdoor **thermal baths**.

Practicalities

Szeged Tourist, Klauzál tér 7 (July & Aug daily 9am–7pm; rest of year Mon–Fri 9am–5.30pm, Sat 8am–noon), or *IBUSZ*, Klauzál tér 7 (Mon–Fri 8am–4pm, Sat 8am–1pm), can arrange **private rooms** from 400Ft a double. The *Apáthy kollégium* student hostel is not good value; you're better off at either the *Royal* hotel, Kölcsey utca 1 (☎62/475-275; from ②), or the *Tisza*, Wesselényi utca 1 (☎ 62/478-278; ③). Cheaper than these, but rather insalubrious, is the *Sárkány Szálló*, by the train station at Indóház tér 1 (☎62/310-514; ②). Szeged's most convenient **campsite** is near the thermal baths in Újszeged (May–Sept).

For grills, stews and salads, the *Debrecen* and *Szeged* **restaurants** on the western side of Széchenyi tér are both good value; so too, for lunch, is the *Hági* around the corner from the *Hotel Royal*, which serves Brno beer and Slovak food. More expensive but still affordable are the *Tisza halászcsárda* at Roosevelt tér 12, and the *Szőke Tisza* boat-restaurant. The place the locals rate highest, though, is the riverside *Kiskörössy*, a couple of kilometres north of the centre on the road to Tape (buses and trams both go near); its fish soup is wonderful. Most of these places double as **bars**, but for a quiet drink go to the *Borkostoló* wine cellar at Somogyi utca 19. The local hot spot is the student *JATE Klub* **disco** at Toldy utca 2 (Fri & Sat 8pm–4am).

travel details

Trains

From Budapest to Esztergom (12 daily; 1hr 30min); Szentendre (every 15–30min; 45min); Balatonfüred (13 daily; 2hr–2hr 30min); Pécs (3 daily; 3hr 15min); Sopron (5 daily; 2hr 15min); Tokaj (1 daily; 2hr 45min); Szeged (2 daily; 2hr 15min).

From Esztergom to Budapest (12 daily; 1hr 30min).

From Balatonfüred to Budapest (13 daily; 2hr–2hr 30min).

From Pécs to Budapest (3 daily; 3hr 15min).

From Sopron to Budapest (5 daily; 2hr 15min).

Buses

From Budapest to Balatonfüred (1 daily); Hévíz (1 daily); Keszthely (1 daily); Sopron (2 daily); Eger (9 daily); Szeged (5 daily); Esztergom via the Danube Bend (hourly) or Dorog (every 30min); Szentendre (hourly); Visegrád (hourly).

From Esztergom to Visegrád, Szentendre & Budapest (hourly).

From Szentendre to Visegrád & Esztergom (hourly).

From Visegrád to Budapest (hourly); Esztergom (every 20–40min).

From Badacsony to Keszthely (hourly).

From Balatonfüred to Tihany (hourly).

From Keszthely to Hévíz (every 15min).

From Eger to Budapest (2–5 daily).

Hydrofoils and ferries

From Budapest to Vienna (1 or 2 daily in summer; 3 weekly in April, Sept & Oct; 5hr 30min); Esztergom (2 daily; 5hr); Szentendre (5 daily; 1hr 30min); Visegrád (3 daily; 3hr).

From Esztergom to Budapest (2 daily; 4hr); Szentendre (2 daily; 2hr 45min).

CHAPTER 12

IRELAND

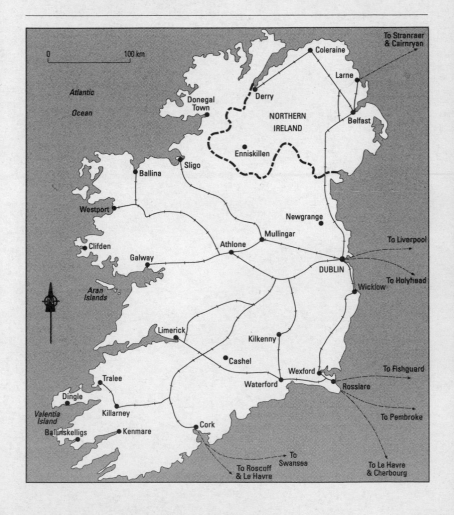

0   100 km

Atlantic
Ocean

To Stranraer
& Cairnryan

Coleraine

Larne

Donegal
Town

Derry

Belfast

NORTHERN
IRELAND

Enniskillen

Sligo

Ballina

Newgrange

Westport

Mullingar

To Liverpool

Clifden

Athlone

Galway

DUBLIN

To Holyhead

Aran
Islands

Wicklow

Limerick

Kilkenny

Cashel

Tralee

Wexford

To Fishguard

Waterford

Dingle

Rosslare

Valentia
Island

Killarney

To Pembroke

Ballinskelligs

Kenmare

Cork

To
Swansea

To Roscoff
& Le Havre

To Le Havre
& Cherbourg

Introduction

Landscape and people are what bring most visitors to **Ireland** – South and North. And once there, few are disappointed by the reality of the stock Irish images: the green, rain-hazed loughs and wild, bluff coastlines, the inspired talent for conversation, the easy pace of life. Ireland is becoming increasingly integrated with the industrial economies of western Europe, yet the modernization of the country has to date made few marks. It's a place to explore slowly, roaming through agricultural landscapes scattered with farmhouses, or along the endlessly indented coastline. In town, too, the pleasures are unhurried: evenings over Guinnesses in the snug of a pub, listening to the chat around a turf fire.

Especially in the Irish-speaking *Gaeltacht* areas, you'll be aware of the strength and continuity of the island's **oral tradition**. The speech of the country, moulded by the rhythms of the ancient tongue, has fired such twentieth-century greats as Yeats, Joyce and Beckett. **Music**, too, has always been at the centre of Irish community life, and you can expect to find traditional music sessions in the pubs of all towns of any size and along the west coast. Side by side with this is a romping rock scene, largely Dublin-based, that has spawned the Undertones, the Boomtown Rats and U2.

The area that draws most visitors is the **west coast**, whose northern reaches are characterized by the demonically daunting peninsulas and the mystical lakes and glens of **Donegal**. The midwest coastline and its offshore islands – especially the **Aran Islands** – are just as attractive, combining vertiginous cliffs, boulder-strewn wastes and violent mountains. In the south, the melodramatic peaks of the **Ring of Kerry** fall to lake-pools and seductive seascapes. In the north of the island, the principal draw is the bizarre basalt formation of the **Giant's Causeway**. The **interior** is less spectacular, but the southern pastures and low wooded hills, and the wide peat bogs of the very centre, are the classic landscapes of Ireland. Of the **inland waterways**, the most alluring is the island-studded Lough Erne, easily reached from Enniskillen.

For anyone with strictly limited time, one of the best options must be to combine a visit to **Dublin** with the mountains and monastic ruins of County Wicklow. Dublin is an extraordinary mix of youthfulness and tradition, a human-scale capital of decaying Georgian squares and vibrant pubs. **Belfast**, victim of a perennial bad press, vies with Dublin in the vitality of its pub nightlife, while the cities of **Cork**, **Waterford** and most of all, **Galway**, have a new-found energy about them.

No introduction can cope with the complexities of Ireland's **politics**, which permeate every aspect of daily life, most conspicuously in the North. Suffice it to say that, regardless of partisan politics, Irish hospitality is as warm as the brochures say, on both sides of the border.

Information and Maps

In the Republic, tourist information is handled by the **Bord Fáilte**, while in the North it's administered by the **Northern Ireland Tourist Board**. You'll find branches of one or the other almost anywhere that has a reasonable number of tourists passing through, and they'll frequently be able to assist in finding accommodation.

The best single **road map** of Ireland is the *Michelin* 1:400,000, #405. For more detail, and for walking, the *Ordnance Survey* half-inch maps are generally the best option, but are not always reliable over 1000ft. Locally produced specialist maps, such as the "Folding Landscapes" series for Connemara, the Burren and Aran Islands, may be a better bet for serious walkers.

Money and Banks

The **currency in the Republic** is the Irish pound, known as the **punt**, which is divided into 100 pence. Irish traders may well accept pounds sterling at par. The currency comes in coin denominations of 1p, 2p, 5p, 10p, 20p and IR£1, and in notes of IR£5, IR£10, IR£20, IR£50 and IR£100. Standard **bank** opening hours in the Republic are Mon–Fri 10am–12.30pm & 1.30–3pm, though many are also open through till 4pm and most have a late opening till 5pm one day a week. It makes sense to change your money while in the large towns since many small country places are served by sub-offices open only certain days of the week.

In the North the currency is the pound sterling. Banks are open Mon–Fri 10am–3.30pm in Belfast and Londonderry; elsewhere they close between 12.30–1.30pm, and in small villages the bank may not be open every day. As in the Republic, aim to get your cash in the bigger centres.

Communications

Main **post offices** in Ireland are open Mon–Fri 9am–5.30pm, Sat 9am–1pm. Stamps are sometimes available in shops selling postcards. Domestic and international calls can easily be made from pay **phones and card phones** throughout Ireland. However, in some rural areas in the Republic you may well not be able to find a modern pay phone, and so will have to make international calls from a hotel or the like – expect a hefty premium charged on top of the normal price. International calls are cheapest after 6pm on weekdays, and at weekends. The **operator number** in the Republic is ☎10 for domestic calls and ☎114 for international; in the North it's ☎100 for both.

Getting Around

Reliable, albeit infrequent and slow, public transport is run in the Republic by the state-supported train and bus companies. There are, however, anomalies – never assume that two nearby towns are necessarily going to be connected. Transport in the North is slightly more efficient.

■ Trains

In the **Republic**, *Irish Rail* (*Iarnród Éireann*) operates **trains** to many major cities and towns en route, and on direct lines it's by far the fastest way of covering long distances. In general, rail lines fan out from Dublin, with few routes running north–south across the country, so, although you can get to the West easily by train, you can't use the railways to explore the west coast. The only service **between the Republic and the North** is the non-stop Belfast–Dublin express.

Train travel is by no means cheap, but there's a complex system of peak and off-peak fares – it's always worth asking about special deals. *InterRail* and *Eurail* passes are valid in both parts of Ireland and there various other passes available. *Irish Rail's Rambler Ticket* buys unlimited rail travel on any 8 days out of 15 for IR£60 (15 days out of 30 for IR£90), and students can buy a *Travelsave stamp* for an *ISIC* card (IR£17) and get return journeys for the price of a single. A ticket allowing unlimited rail travel throughout the North and South costs IR£70 for 8 days, IR£100 for 15; the *Emerald Card* allows travel on **bus** and

train sevices in the North and the Republic and costs IR£105 for 8 days or IR£180 for 15 days.

■ Buses

The national bus company (*Dublin Bus* in the capital, *Bus Éireann* elsewhere) operates throughout the **Republic**, but routings can be complex and slow. Fares are generally far lower than the train, especially in midweek; if you travel on Tuesday, Wednesday or Thursday, ask for a *Boomerang* ticket, which will buy you the return journey free and is valid for one month. A *Rambler* ticket (around IR£26 for any 3 days out of 8; IR£90 for 15 days out of 30) gives unlimited bus travel throughout the Republic. If you are going to be using buses a lot it makes sense to buy a **timetable** from any major bus station; remote villages may only have a couple of buses a week, so knowing when they are is essential.

Private buses, which operate on many major routes, are often cheaper than *Bus Éireann*, and sometimes faster – look out for local advertisements. They're very busy at weekends, so it makes sense to book ahead; during the week you can usually pay on the bus. Prices for parts of their journeys are often negotiable, and bikes can be carried if booked with your seat.

In the **North**, *Ulsterbus* runs regular and reliable services, particularly to towns not served by the rail network. A *Freedom of Northern Ireland Ticket*, for daily (£9) or weekly (£25) unlimited travel on all scheduled *Ulsterbus* services, is available at the main bus station in Belfast.

■ Driving and hitching

Uncongested roads in the **Republic** make driving a very relaxing option – but watch out for unmarked junctions, appalling minor roads and drunk drivers late at night – despite high accident rates, the police have a lax attitude and little seems to be done about the problem. Watch out too for passing lanes or slow lanes, indicated by a broken yellow line: you are expected to pull over to the left to let someone overtake, but these lanes are best used with care since they often have poor surfaces and can suddenly come to an end with little or no warning. As in Britain you drive on the left, and most of the road signs and markings are similar. Speed limits are 30–40mph in town, 60mph outside and 70mph on motorways. **Breakdown services** are operated by the *Automobile Association* (☎01/6779481) and the *Royal Automobile Club* (☎0800/8740400 freephone).

International **car rental** companies have outlets in all major cities, airports and ferry terminals: costs are from around IR£250 a week, although smaller local firms can almost always offer better deals, and booking in advance can produce huge discounts – it's worth shopping round. Companies insist you have held a full, endorsement-free driving licence for two years, and most won't rent cars to under-23s. In the North, expect to pay around £170–200 a week.

Roads in the **North** are in general notably superior to those in the Republic. Driving is on the left, rules of the road are as in mainland Britain, and car hire costs are the same. Breakdown numbers are ☎0800/887766 (freephone) for the *AA* and ☎0800/828282 for the *RAC*. Most towns have no-parking "**control zones**" in the centre, indicated by prominent yellow or pink signs: these are to prevent car-bombs being left.

There are eighteen **approved border crossing points**, marked on all recent road maps; though it's possible to drive across in other places, you are strongly advised to use these.

The **Republic** is one of the easiest countries in Europe to **hitch** in; for locals it's almost as much a normal part of getting around as using the buses and trains. The chief problem is the lack of traffic, especially off the main roads; and if you are travelling around the tourist-swamped west you may find there's a reluctance to pick up foreigners. The best way to hitch in the **North** is to make sure you look like a tourist – and even then, it's never easy. Men travelling alone or in pairs will be viewed with suspicion, and may even find it impossible to get a lift. Men and women travelling together are at least in with a chance. Getting a lift across **the border** is very difficult.

■ Cycling

If you are lucky enough to get decent weather, cycling is one of the most enjoyable ways to see Ireland. Roads are generally empty, though very poor surfaces may slow you down. It's easy and relatively cheap to **hire a bike** in most towns in the Republic, and at a limited number of places in the North; you can't take a hired bike across the border. *Raleigh* is the biggest national operator (about IR£7 per day, IR£30–35 per week plus around IR£40 deposit; in the North £5 a day, £22

a week), but local dealers (including some hostels) are often less expensive. If you arrive with your own bike, it will cost you an extra IR£4.50 to carry it on each single bus journey or IR£3–6 on each single train journey, though bus drivers are not obliged to carry a bike and you may not be able to at peak times. To take a bike on a train in the **North**, add 25 percent extra to the price of each journey.

Accommodation

Though it's obviously the cheapest way to sleep in Ireland, camping can be hampered by tricky terrain and the possibility of continual rain. Next up in price, hostels vary a lot, but all offer the essential basics, and some are very good indeed. Above these come bed and breakfasts, guesthouses and hotels, usually – but not necessarily – officially graded by the tourist boards.

■ Bed and breakfasts and hotels

In the south, the least expensive form of comfortable accommodation is a **bed and breakfast** place. They vary enormously, but most are welcoming, warm and clean, with huge breakfasts. Registered B&Bs are generally pretty good, though it's not an absolute guarantee. Expect to pay from around IR£12 per person (from IR£10 for non-registered houses); those advertising *en suite* (ie. private shower) are usually a few pounds more expensive. Bookings for registered B&Bs can be made through tourist offices for an extra IR£1–2. Even the lowliest regular **hotels** are generally dearer, though small village hotels can cost about the same as private B&Bs. Bed and breakfast accommodation is less prominent in the **North**, and you will probably need to ring ahead if you want to guarantee somewhere to stay during the summer months.

■ Hostels

An Óige hostels – those of the official Irish Youth Hostel Association – are run like youth hostels throughout Europe, with "duties" shared out, hostels closed during the daytime, and evening curfews – at least officially. In fact, you'll find many are more flexible than the rule book would suggest, particularly in out-of-the-way places. *IYHF* membership is required at most hostels, and overnight fees for members start at IR£5. Full lists of *An Óige* places and prices are available from their HQ at 61 Mountjoy St, Dublin 7 (☎01/304555).

In the Republic, **independent hostels** are often more interesting places to stay, as each reflects the character and interests of its owner, and some are tucked away in beautiful countryside. Very often the atmosphere is cosy and informal: you can stay in all day if you want and there are no curfews or chores, though some hostels cram people in to the point of discomfort. A new tourist board approved organization of independent hostels will be in operation by summer 1994: for a free comprehensive list, write to Vary Finlay, *Bantry Independent Hostel*, Bishop Lucey Place, Bantry, Co. Cork. You may be encouraged to use a book-ahead system if you are doing a lot of hostelling; most won't let you book over the phone, but some may reserve you a bed up to a certain time in the early evening. In tourist hot spots, you may be hassled at railway stations to book a bed: there are a very small number of dangerous and disreputable hostels around, so it's a good idea to check *The Rough Guide* or ask around locally before booking in at a non-approved hostel. Expect to pay around IR£5.50 for a dormitory bed (more in Galway, Cork and Dublin), IR£6–8 per person for private rooms where available. Independent hostels are now being set up in the North as well, especially in the western part of the region.

■ Camping

The cost of staying on **organized campsites** varies from about IR£2–6 a night. In out-of-the-way places nobody minds where you pitch – the only place you definitely can't camp is in state forests. Farmers in heavily touristed areas may ask for a pound or two to use their land, but other than this you can expect to camp for free in areas where there's no official site. Some hostels will also let you camp on their land for around IR£3.

Food and Drink

One thing you won't be going to Ireland for is a wonderful gastronomic experience. The country has no real tradition of eating out, and the food you'll find as a traveller will tend to be simple and hearty at best.

■ Food

Irish food is generally highly meat-oriented. If you're staying in B&Bs, it's almost impossible to avoid the "traditional" Irish **breakfast** of sausages, bacon and eggs, although this usually comes accompanied by generous quantities of delicious soda bread. Pub **lunch** staples are usually meat and two veg, with plenty of gravy, although you can almost always get freshly made sandwiches. Most larger towns have good, simple **cafés** (open daytimes only) where you can get soup, sandwiches and cakes as well as slightly more ambitious dishes. **Hotels** are obliged to serve all comers, so you can always find a sandwich and a cup of coffee, at any reasonable hour; you can generally order a plate of sandwiches and a pot of tea in pubs, too.

The **fast-food** revolution has brought kebabs and burgers to every town of any size but old-fashioned fish and chips are a better bet, especially in coastal towns. For the occasional binge, there are some very good **seafood restaurants**, particularly along the west coast, serving fresh seafood and, often, home-grown vegetables. Irish oysters are the country's most refined and celebrated culinary treat. **Wholefood** and **vegetarian** restaurants or cafés are thin on the ground outside Dublin, Belfast and some of the more tourist-influenced areas in the west.

■ Drink

To travel through Ireland without visiting a **pub** would be to miss out on a huge chunk of Irish life.

Especially in rural areas, the pub is the social heart of the town, and often the political and cultural centre, too. Talking is an important business here, and drink is the great lubricant of social discourse. In major cities you'll find pubs heaving with life, and out in remote country villages it can be great fun drinking among the fig rolls and trifle sponges of the grocery shops-cum-bars you'll find dotted around. While women will always be treated with genuine civility, it's true to say that most bars are a predominantly male preserve. In the evening, especially, women travellers can expect occasional unwanted attention, though this rarely amounts to anything too unpleasant.

In the Republic, pub **opening hours** are Mon–Sat 10.30am–11pm (11.30pm in summer), Sun 12.30–2pm & 4–11pm; some pubs, especially in the cities, may close for a couple of hours in the afternoon. In the **North** pubs are open Mon–Sat 11am–11pm, Sun 10am–2.30pm, with many pubs in the bigger towns opening 7–10pm on Sunday, too.

The classic Irish drink is, of course, **Guinness**, which, as anybody will tell you, is simply not the same as the drink marketed as Guinness outside Ireland. It's best in Dublin, home of the brewery. "A Guinness" is a pint; if you want a half-pint of any beer, ask for "a glass". Other local stouts, like Beamish and Murphy's, make for interesting comparison: they all have their faithful adherents.

If you want a pint of English-style **bitter**, try Smithwicks, which is not so different from what you'd get in an English pub. As everywhere, of course, **lager** is also increasingly popular: mostly Harp (made by Guinness) or Heineken, though more exotic continental brews are appearing now. Whatever your tipple, you're likely to find drinking in Ireland an expensive business at around IR£1.70 a pint. Irish **whiskeys** – try Paddy's, Powers or, from the North, Bushmills – also seem expensive, but the measures are larger than those you'll get in Britain.

Opening Hours and Holidays

Business and shop **opening hours**, both North and South, are approximately Mon–Sat 9am–5.30pm, with a smattering of late openings (usually Thurs or Fri) and half-days. In the South, particularly away from the bigger towns, hours are much more flexible, with later closing times. There's no rigid pattern to the opening and closing of **museums** and the like, though most are closed at least one day a week, often Monday and many will close between 1pm and 2pm. The bigger attractions will normally be open regular shop hours, while smaller places may open only in the afternoon. Many sites away from the main tourist trails are open only during the peak summer months.

Public holidays in the Republic are: Jan 1; March 17; Good Friday & Easter Mon; first Mon in June; first Mon in Aug; last Mon in Oct; Dec 25 & 26. In the North: Jan 1; March 17; May 1; last Mon in May; July 12; last Mon in Aug; Dec 25 & 26.

Emergencies

In the Republic, people generally have a healthy indifference to law and red tape, perhaps in part a vestige of pre-Independence days, when any dealings with the police smacked of collusion with the British. The **police** – known as the **Gardai** (pronounced "gar-dee") – accordingly have a low profile. If you have any dealings with the Gardai at all, the chances are you'll find them affable enough.

In the **North**, the **Royal Ulster Constabulary** (RUC) deal with all general civic policing, and are the people you should go to if in difficulties. The North is subject to British law and heavily policed, with several "emergency measures" permanently in effect. You may well find yourself being quizzed about where you are going, what you are doing, and so forth, especially in border areas. Be cooperative and polite and you should have no difficulties. Again, whatever their reputation, you'll find that the RUC are helpful enough in matters of everyday police activity.

In the North and South, as in Britain, **pharmacists** can dispense only a limited range of drugs without a doctor's prescription. Most pharmacies are open standard shop hours, though in large towns some may stay open as late as 10pm.

EMERGENCY NUMBERS
Police, Fire and Ambulance in both North and South ☎999.

DUBLIN AND AROUND

Clustered on the banks of the River Liffey, **DUBLIN** is a splendidly monumental city, but it's also a young city. Of roughly one and a half million people in greater Dublin, about half are under 25, and with the drift of population from the countryside continuing, Dublin is bulging at the seams. Membership of the European Community has infused money into the city, and you'll see new building everywhere, but you'll also witness deprivation as bad as any in Europe. It's the collision of the old and the new, the slick and the tawdry, that makes Dublin the exciting, aggravating, energetic place it is.

Dublin really began as a Viking trading post called **Dubh Linn** (Dark Pool), which soon amalgamated with a Celtic settlement called **Baile Átha Cliath** (Town of the Hurdles) – still the Gaelic name for Dublin. Because most of the early city was built of wood, only the two cathedrals, part of the castle and one or two churches have survived from before the seventeenth century. The fabric of the city dates essentially from the Georgian period, when the military families whom the Crown had rewarded with confiscated land began to invest their income in new town houses. These mansions embodied the confidence of a ruling class that was starting to regard itself not as British, but as specifically Irish. After the Act of Union Dublin entered a long economic decline, but it was the focus of much of the agitation that eventually led to independence. In 1829 Daniel O'Connell secured a limited role for Catholics in the administration of their capital city, and Dublin was also the centre of the Gaelic League, which encouraged the formation of an Irish national consciousness through the nurturing of the native language and culture. The early years of the twentieth century saw the struggle for the establishment of trade unionism in Ireland. In 1913 this came to a head in the Great Lock-out, when forcibly unemployed workers and their families died of hunger and cold. Open violence hit the streets during Easter Week of 1916, the major uprising in the long battle for independence and an event that looms large in the consciousness of modern Dublin.

> The Dublin telephone code is ☎01.

Arrival and information

Coming in from the **airport**, six miles north of the centre, you can take the official airport bus (IR£2.50) or the city bus #41 (IR£1.10). Each takes around half an hour to reach the Central Bus Station, or **Busárus**, right by the river. If you arrive **by boat**, you'll come in at either **Dún Laoghaire** (for *StenaSealink* services), six miles out, from where the DART (Dublin Area Rapid Transport) train will whisk you into town in about twenty minutes, or at the closer **Dublin Port** (*B&I*), served by bus #53. **Trains** come in either at Heuston Station on the South Side (from Cork, Waterford, Limerick, Killarney, Tralee, Athlone, Galway, Westport, Ballina) or Connolly Station on the North Side (from Belfast, Derry, Sligo, Wexford, Rosslare Harbour). For train information call ☎363333.

Dublin's main **tourist office** is at 14 Upper O'Connell St (Mon–Fri 9am–5pm; ☎6747733); other branches are at the airport and Dún Laoghaire. The main office's room booking service costs 50p for accommodation in Dublin. The USIT office on Aston Quay, opposite O'Connell Bridge (Mon–Fri 9am–5.30pm, Sat 10am–1pm; ☎778117), not only books bed and breakfasts during the summer, but also has its own hostel and a travel agency offering student discounts on ferries and flights. For **listings** of Dublin events, the best source is the fortnightly magazine *In Dublin*.

City transport

Dublin has an extensive and reasonably priced **bus** network that makes it easy to hop around when walking the streets becomes a bit of a slog. The maximum fare is IR£1.10, a one-day bus pass is IR£2.20, a bus and rail pass (including DART) is IR£3, and a four-day bus and rail ticket costs just IR£7. Finding your way round the bus system may prove more of a problem, as there's no indication at the stops of where the buses go. Either ask a bus inspector – there usually seems to be one around – or invest in a bus timetable (50p from newsagents). The **DART** links Howth to the north of the city with Bray to the south. The maximum fare is again IR£1.10. **Taxis** in Dublin don't generally cruise the streets, but instead wait at ranks in central locations, such as outside the *Shelbourne Hotel* on St Stephen's Green. The twenty-minute ride from the airport is likely to cost around IR£10.

Accommodation

Dublin has plenty of accommodation in all price ranges, from hostels to five-star hotels. **Hotels** are generally expensive, and often no more comfortable than good guest-houses, but if you're travelling out of season it's worth checking reductions, which can be considerable – the tourist office in Upper O'Connell St will have a list. The better **B&Bs** are in the suburbs – but this is no problem, given the excellent public transport. Hostels range from the spartan *An Óige* to the comparative comfort of *Isaac's*, and there's a **campsite** within easy reach.

Hostels

An Óige, 39 Mountjoy Square (☎301766). Located in the Irish hostel association's HQ, and open all year. A supplementary hostel, *Scóil Lórcain*, opens for July & Aug at Eaton Square, Monkstown, four miles from the centre (☎801948; bus #7, #7A or #8, or DART to Seapoint). ②

Avalon House, 55 Aungier St (☎750001). Impressive red-brick Victorian building close to St Stephen's Green with a friendly café and comfortable privacy-preserving dorms. Some single and double rooms. ③

Globetrotters Tourist Hotel, 46 Lower Gardiner St (☎735893). Comfortable upper-crust hostel close to Busarus (and airport bus). Includes continental breakfast. ③

Isaac's/Dublin Tourist Hotel, 2–5 Frenchman's Lane (☎6749321). Five minutes' walk from O'Connell St; offers basic dormitory bunks and single and double rooms, plus a good, cheap restaurant and music some evenings. ③

Kinlay House USIT Hostel, 7 Anglesea St (☎6778117). Accommodation in beds in four-bedded rooms, or in more expensive twin-bedded rooms. Includes breakfast. ②

Young Traveller, St Mary's Place (☎971772). Just north of Parnell Square, with accommodation in four-berth rooms. Includes breakfast. ②

Bed and breakfast

Avondale Guest House, 40 Lower Gardiner St (☎8745200). Singles or sharing, including a good breakfast. ④

Elmar Hotel, 34 Lower Gardiner St (☎741246). Quite small but adequate rooms, with a midnight curfew. ③

Mrs R. Casey, Villa Jude, 2 Church Ave, Sandymount (☎6684982). Quiet rooms in a convenient location for the ferries. Bus #3 or DART to Sandymount. ③

Mrs O'Donoghue's, 41 Northumberland Rd (☎6681477). Big Victorian house in Ballsbridge – quite expensive, but comfortable and friendly. On bus routes #5, #6, #6A and #7. ④

Miss V. McNamara, 73 Anglesea Rd (☎6689032). About the cheapest in Ballsbridge in a well-heeled inner suburb ten minutes' brisk walk to St Stephen's Green. ③

Mrs E. Trehy, 110 Ringsend Park, Sandymount (☎6689477). Still the cheapest in Sandymount, and handy for the ferry. Served by buses #1, #2, #3 and #6. ③

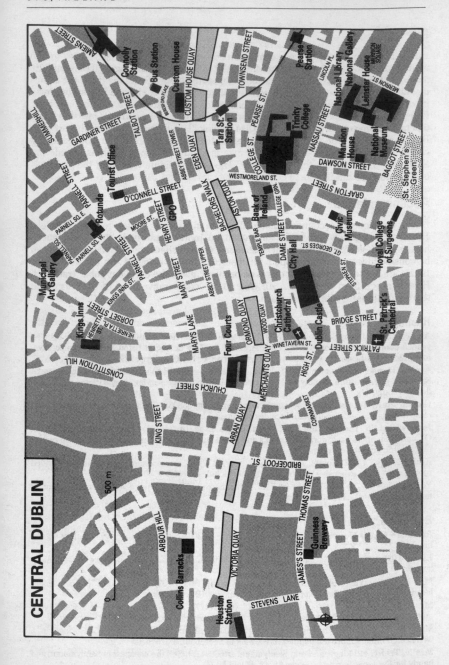

CENTRAL DUBLIN

Hotels

Central Hotel, 1–5 Exchequer St (☎6797302). Recently refurbished place, close to the lively Temple Bar area. Excellent breakfasts – and modern art on the walls. ⑦
Clarence Hotel, Wellington Quay (☎6776178). Lively and central, overlooking the Liffey; bought by U2 in 1992, it promises to become one of the hottest spots in town. ⑦
The Georgian House, 20–21 Lower Baggott St (☎6618832). Occupying a beautiful old building just five minutes' walk from St Stephen's Green. ⑥
Othello House, 74 Lower Gardiner St (☎8743460). A good budget option just off O'Connell St. ⑤
Wynn's Hotel, Lower Abbey St (☎8745131). Old-fashioned dusty establishment close to the Abbey Theatre; the downstairs bar has a dedicated if subdued following. ⑧

Campsite

Shankill. Close to the DART stop at Shankill – or take bus #45, #45A, #46 or #84. Open all year. 30p per person, IR£5.50 per tent.

The City

Two areas have a claim to be Dublin's centre of gravity – Grafton Street, the main pedestrianized shopping street which links St Stephen's Green with Trinity College, and O'Connell Street, north of the river. However, the majority of the city's historic monuments are south of the river, and College Green is as good a place as any to start.

The South Side

The Vikings sited their central meeting place and burial ground on what is now **College Green,** where **Trinity College** is the most famous landmark. Founded in 1591, it played a major role in the development of a Protestant Anglo-Irish tradition, and right up to 1966 Catholics had to get a special dispensation to study here; nowadays roughly seventy percent of the student population is Catholic. Its stern grey college buildings are ranged around cobbled quadrangles in a grander version of the arrangement at Oxford and Cambridge. The **Library** (Mon–Fri 9.30am–5pm, Sat 9.30am–12.45pm, Sun noon–4.30pm; IR£2.75, students IR£2.25, including the Dublin Experience, an audio-visual presentation of Dublin's history) contains a famous collection of priceless Irish manuscripts, with pride of place given to the eighth-century **Book of Kells,** which may actually have originated not in Ireland but in Iona, Saint Columba's first Scottish port of call. Totalling 680 pages, the Book of Kells was rebound in the 1950s into four volumes, of which two are on show at any one time, one open at a completely illuminated page, the other at a text page, itself adorned with patterns and fantastic animals inter-twined with the capitals. The **Book of Durrow** is in many ways equally interesting – it is the first of the great Irish illuminated manuscripts, dating from between 650 and 680, and has, unusually, a whole page given over to abstract ornament.

The massive **Bank of Ireland,** which faces the university obliquely across the busy traffic interchange, has played an equally central role in the history of Anglo-Irish ascendancy. When begun in 1729 it was envisaged as the parliament of independent Ireland, and it was here in 1782 that Henry Grattan – whose statue stands outside – uttered the celebrated phrase, "Ireland is now a nation". However, with the passing of the Act of Union, the building was sold to the Bank of Ireland. Sightseers are admitted during normal banking hours to be shown around the magnificent interior by ushers wearing costumes unchanged since the nineteenth century.

The streets that surround Grafton Street frame Dublin's quality shopping area – chic, sophisticated and expensive. The unmissable stop on Grafton Street is **Bewley's coffee house,** whose dark wood and marble-tabled interior is a great place to sit and watch people; there's even a small **museum** on the top floor tracing the history of this Dublin institution.

Parallel **Kildare Street** marks the point where what's left of the Georgian city gets going. The most imposing building is **Leinster House**, built in 1745 as the Duke of Leinster's town house, now the home of the Irish parliament, the **Dáil** (open, when parliament isn't in session, Tues–Sat 10am–5pm, Sun 2–5pm). It's adjoined by the National Library and the **National Museum** (Tues–Sat 10am–5pm, Sun 9am–5pm), the repository of the treasures of ancient Ireland. Entrance to the museum is free, but there's a IR£2 charge to get into the **Treasury**, housing masterpieces such as the eighth-century Ardagh Chalice and Tara Brooch, and the so-called St Patrick's Bell and the Cross of Cong, both twelfth-century. The Tara Brooch is regarded as perhaps the greatest piece of Irish metalwork and, unusually, is decorated both on the front and the back, where the intricate filigree work could be seen only by the wearer.

To discover more about the Viking tradition, go around the corner into Merrion Row for the **National Museum Annexe**, where the complexity of their culture is on show in artefacts such as eleventh-century combs and carrying cases carved from bones and antlers, and scales for weighing precious metals.

Walk to the bottom of any of these streets and you'll emerge on the north side of **St Stephen's Green**, the focus of central Dublin's city planning. The gardens, with their ornamental pond, can be a pleasant place to while away some time on a sunny day, but in terms of architecture or city life there's not a lot to see.

To the east, Merrion Square, Fitzwilliam Square and the streets immediately around them form the heart of what's left of Georgian Dublin. Nowadays the park railings on **Merrion Square** are used on Saturdays and Sundays by artists flogging their wares; the area is also a centre for most of Dublin's private galleries. At the back of Leinster House is Ireland's **National Gallery** (Mon–Sat 10am–6pm, Sun 2–5pm, open till 9pm Thurs; free), whose displays include seventeenth-century French, Italian and Spanish paintings, Dutch masters – some good Rembrandts – English watercolourists and French Impressionists. But it's the Irish paintings that are the real draw, ranging from formal portraits of the early seventeenth century and landscape paintings of the Anglo-Irish estates to the splashy creations of Jack B. Yeats.

The main thoroughfare leading west from College Green is Dame Street, immediately north of which is the area known as **Temple Bar**. With its restaurants, second-hand bookshops and bric-a-brac stores, plus the Project Arts Centre, this is one of the liveliest – and certainly the most fashionable – parts of town. **Dame Street**, focus of Dublin's banking and business, leads to **Dublin Castle**, which dates back to 1207 but was rebuilt in the eighteenth century, with only the massive stone Record Tower giving the game away. It continued as the Viceroy's seat after the Act of Union, and stands as a symbol of 700 years of British influence on Ireland. Guided tours of the castle take you around the state apartments, many of which are fitted with superb examples of craftsmanship in often dubious taste.

Nearby **St Patrick's Cathedral** (Mon–Sat 10am–12.15pm & 2–5pm, Sun 2–5pm), founded in 1172, is a much more elegant place inside than the tank-like grey exterior leads you to expect. The presence of Jonathan Swift, who was dean of the cathedral from 1713 to 1745, is inescapable: immediately to the right of the entrance are memorials to both him and Esther Johnson, the "Stella" with whom he had a passionate though apparently Platonic relationship, while the north pulpit contains Swift's writing table, chair, portrait and death mask. There are plenty of other interesting memorials in the cathedral: one of the most elaborate, at the west end, is a seventeenth-century monument to the Boyle family, teeming with painted figures of the clan, including its most famous member, the physicist Robert Boyle.

Christchurch (daily 10am–6.30pm; suggested donation IR£1), at the southern end of Patrick St, suffered like St Patrick's at the hands of Victorian restorers, but it remains a resonant historic site. Dublin's first cathedral, founded here in 1038, was demolished by Richard de Clare – Strongbow – who built the new cathedral in 1190. Strongbow himself is buried here, underneath an effigy which possibly depicts an Earl of Drogheda.

The whole area immediately to the west of Christchurch, interspersed with grim corporate housing and deserted factories, is dominated by the **Guinness Brewery**. Founded in 1759, the brewery covers 64 acres, and has the distinction of being the world's largest single beer-exporting company, exporting some 300 million pints a year. Although you can't go round the brewery, the former **Guinness Hop Store**, right in the middle of the complex in Crane St, houses an exhibition centre (Mon–Fri 10am–3pm; IR£2) where you can taste the best Guinness in Dublin. The upper floors of this airy, four-storey building are given over to exhibitions of contemporary art, and offer fine views over the city.

Plenty of buses (#24, 51, 63, 69, 78, 79, 90) ply the road out to Kilmainham and the beautiful **Kilmainham Hospital**, Ireland's first classical building, dating from 1680. The Hospital now houses the **Irish Museum of Modern Art** (Tues–Sun 11am–5.30pm; free), a controversial conversion which makes little reference to the building's past. However, the director is Declan McGonagle, whose record in commissioning and exhibiting radical art at the Orchard Gallery in Derry makes this new gallery a place to watch. Nearby, over the way from Heuston station, looms the grim mass of **Kilmainham Jail** (June–Sept daily 11am–6pm; Oct–May Mon–Fri 1–4pm, Sun 1–6pm; closed Sat; IR£1.50), whose inmates have included Parnell, Padraig Pearse and James Connolly (both executed here), and Eamon de Valera, the very last person to be incarcerated here. The guided tour climaxes in the low-lit chapel, where, at 1.30am on May 4, 1916, Joseph Plunkett, one of the leaders of the Easter Uprising, married Grace Gifford. Having been allowed precisely ten minutes in his wife's company, Plunkett was executed at 3.30am.

The North Side

Crossing O'Connell Bridge, it's easy to overlook the Georgian **Custom House**, the outstanding building on the north side of the river, as it lies in the shadow of a railway viaduct. Most things of historical interest on O'Connell Street, the main thoroughfare on this side of the river, have long since been submerged by the tide of neon and plate glass, but one major exception is the **General Post Office**, at the corner of Henry St and O'Connell St. Built in 1816, its fame stems from the fact that in 1916 it became the rebel headquarters during the Uprising; only the facade survived the fighting – you can still see the bullet scars.

At the northern end of O'Connell St lies Parnell Square, one of the first of Dublin's Georgian squares. Its plain, bright red-brick houses are broken by the grey stone mass of the **Municipal Art Gallery** (Tues–Sat 9.30am–6pm, Sun 11am–5pm; free), originally the town house of the Earl of Charlemont and the focus of fashionable Dublin before the city centre moved south of the river. The gallery was set up in 1908 and features work from the Pre-Raphaelites onwards, with an excellent section of modern Irish painters such as Jack B. Yeats and Paul Henry.

Close by at nos. 18–19 is the Dublin Writers' Museum (☎6722077; Tues–Sat 10am–5pm, Sun 1–5pm; closed Sat; IR£2.25), essentially two rooms of museum cases whisking you through Irish literary history from early Christian writings up to Samuel Beckett and Brendan Behan. The entrance fee includes an audio-guide which is a bit more enlightening; there's also a café and a well-stocked bookshop where you can browse through Swift, Yeats, Joyce and Flann O'Brien as well as some of the more recent authors not covered by the exhibition. Upstairs is a library of locked bookshelves with a fine Georgian ceiling, and a 'gallery of writers' adorned with improving messages, such as 'work is the great reality'.

Leaving Parnell Square at the northwest corner, you come to the **Black Church** in St Mary's Place, a sinister and spiky building. Legend has it that St Mary's and other similar massive Protestant churches built during the 1820s were designed so that they could be turned into defensive positions should the Catholics attack. To the west of the square, down Dorset St and Bolton St, everything speaks of urban blight: rubbish blowing in the gutters, broken glass, barred shop windows. **Henrietta Street** provides an interlude of run-down elegance, but Capel Street, once one of Dublin's most fashionable addresses, shows few signs of it now.

Down by the Liffey, the most imposing building is James Gandon's **Four Courts** – started before his Custom House but finished after. Behind the Four Courts on Church Street is **St Michan's Church** (Mon–Fri 10am–12.45pm & 2–4.45pm, Sat 10am–12.45pm; IR£1), which was founded in 1095 and is thus the oldest building on the North Side. Only the tower and a few other fragments are original – the reason it's on the tourist trail is that the crypt's combination of dry air and constant temperature has mummified the corpses in the crypt: the best preserved are on display, some over 300 years old.

Having walked through the urban confusion of the North Side, the open spaces of **Phoenix Park**, Dublin's playground, come as a welcome relief. Originally attached to a priory, then made into a royal deer park after the Reformation, the park contains Dublin's **zoo** (Mon–Sat 9.30am–6pm, Sun 11am–6pm; IR£4), the old duelling grounds or **Fifteen Acres** – now the venue for Gaelic football, cricket, soccer and polo – and the racecourse, where there's a flea market every Sunday from noon.

Howth

HOWTH – a vantage point giving views across Dublin Bay to the Wicklow Mountains and at times even as far as Wales – lies at the northernmost point of the DART line and can also be reached on the #31 bus. **Howth Head** has been a strategic point for centuries: the Gaelic chieftain Criomthain is reputedly buried under the cairn on the summit, and the Gaels in turn were succeeded by the Vikings and the Normans of Sir Almeric Tristram – whose descendants continue to live at Howth Castle today. Howth village is a sleepy, suburban place full of steep streets and sudden views. Its one monument, on a quiet site overlooking the rock-encrusted island of Ireland's Eye, is the ruined **Howth Abbey**, the first church founded by Sigtrygg, Norse king of Dublin, in 1042.

Further in towards the city is a seaside area even more readily accessible to Dubliners, **Dollymount Strand**. Designated a UNESCO Biosphere Reserve – like Booterstown Marsh further south – Dollymount is a spit of low sand dunes linked to the shore by a wooden bridge. Apart from holidaying Dubliners, it's host to thousands of wintering wildfowl and wading birds.

Eating, drinking and entertainment

Dublin may not be the gastronomic capital of the world, but there's plenty of choice for both lunchtime and evening **eating**. The cheapest fast-food outlets are centred around O'Connell Street, but are generally pretty unpleasant. Best value for lunchtime eating are Dublin's eight hundred **pubs**, where you can usually get soup and sandwiches and often much more substantial, traditional meals. For dinner, cheaper, livelier (and hipper) places are increasingly concentrated around the Temple Bar area, while around Grafton Street there are restaurants in all price ranges. The **music** scene – much of which is based in the pubs – is volatile, so it's always best to check on the latest action by reading *In Dublin* or *Hot Press*, the national music paper. **Nightclubs** are mostly pretty dire, and often directed single-mindedly at the tourist or business trade. Dublin's **theatres**, however, can hold their own with many of Europe's best.

Restaurants and cafés

Bad Ass Café, 9/11 Crown Alley. Once hip, now turning respectable; still one of the best of Dublin's many pizza joints.

Bewley's, Grafton St, Westmoreland St and South Great George's St. The one essential food experience in Dublin, serving everything from a sticky bun to a full meal. Mon–Sat 7.30am–6pm.

Cornucopia, 19 Wicklow St (☎6677583). Once Dublin's pioneering wholefood shop, now a restaurant open evenings too.

Elephant and Castle, 18 Temple Bar (☎6793121). Busy diner-brasserie with eclectic east-west cuisine; classy without being posey.

Fat Freddy's, Crow St/Temple Lane. One of the best of many pizza parlours.

Fitzers, Dawson St (☎753109). Cool, airy café/restaurant with light new-wave food and outdoor tables in summer.

Gallagher's Boxty House, 20 Temple Bar (☎6672762). Traditional Irish food and friendly atmosphere.

Irish Film Centre, 6 Eustace St (☎6678788). Excellent inventive cuisine – anything from snack to full meal– in elegantly minimal surroundings.

King Sitric's Fish Restaurant, East Pier, Howth (☎325235). Not particularly cheap, but magnificent old-fashioned seafood.

Café Kylemore, O'Connell St. A cross between *Bewley's* and a Parisian brasserie, this serves good, plain basics – chips with almost everything – and has a drinks licence.

Leo Burdock's, 2 Werburgh St (☎540366). The best fish and chips in Dublin – so good that it's best to book your table. Closed Tues & Sun.

Macoute, 21 Wicklow St. Excellent vegetarian shop and café, open until 9pm.

Nico's, 53 Dame St. Busy, unpretentious Italian restaurant.

Rudyard's, 15–16 Crown Alley. Busy restaurant and wine bar on three floors; excellent spinach pancakes at lunchtime, jazz on Saturday nights.

Tosca, 20 Suffolk St (☎66796744). Southern European food – anything from Andalucia to Athens – in elegant surroundings. Linger and read the papers.

Well Fed Café, Crow St. Radical veggie food, prepared by a workers' cooperative.

Pubs

The Bailey, 2 Duke St. Meeting point for Dublin's Literary Pub Crawls (Tues–Thurs 7.30pm in summer) and a gay venue, too.

Davy Byrne's, 21 Duke St. An object of pilgrimage for *Ulysses* fans, since Leopold Bloom stopped by for a drink. Despite the pastel-toned refit, it's still a good pub.

Doheny and Nesbitt's, 5 Lower Baggot St. Tiny, atmospheric, smoke-filled room frequented by *Irish Times* hacks.

Kehoe's, South Anne St. Wonderful snugs if you want to curl up in comparative privacy to sip your pint.

McDaid's, 3 Harry St. Excellent Guinness in Brendan Behan's former local.

Mulligan's, 8 Poolbeg St. The best Guinness in central Dublin.

Neary's, 1 Chatham St. Plenty of bevelled glass and shiny wood, plus Liberty print curtains to demonstrate a sense of style to suit the theatre people who frequent it.

Ryan's, Parkgate St, near Heuston Station. Another pub famous for its wood-lined snugs.

Stag's Head, Dame Court, almost opposite the Central Bank. Wonderfully intimate pub, all mahogany, stained glass and mirrors. Good lunches, too.

Toner's Victorian Bar, 139 Lower Baggot St. Dark, cosy and refreshingly plain.

Music pubs and venues

Bad Bob's Backstage Bar, East Essex St. Central Dublin's main late-night venue, in the Temple Bar. Live band downstairs, lounge on the middle floor, disco up top.

Brazen Head, 20 Lower Bridge St. Claims to be the oldest bar in the city; traditional music every night.

Clarence Hotel, Wellington Quay (☎6697302). Recently acquired by U2, the new club in the basement of this old-fashioned hotel looks set to become one of Dublin's hottest rock venues.

Hirschfeld, Fownes St. Gay club on three floors.

International Bar, 23 Wicklow St. Large, smoke-filled place, with mostly rock bands.

Midnight at the Olympia, 74 Dame St (☎8778962). Tinselly ex-music hall theatre; when the evening performance ends on Friday and Saturday, the place opens up for late-night rock and dancing in the aisles. Open 11.30pm–2am.

Mother Redcap's Tavern, Back Lane, off High St. Traditional and country music. Get your chips around the corner at *Burdock's*, then come here for a great Friday night.

Sides, Dame Lane. Well-designed space with wine and food bar, one of the larger dance floors, and a fair variety of music and people. Gay night on Sundays.

Slattery's, 129 Capel St, North Side. The city's best-known venue for traditional music.

The Waterfront, Sir John Rogerson's Quay (☎6778466). Music venue and restaurant filled with rock memorabilia. Check *In Dublin* for listings.

Theatre

Abbey Theatre, Lower Abbey St (☎6787222). Founded in 1904 by W. B. Yeats and Lady Gregory, the Abbey had its golden era in the days when writers like Yeats, J.M. Synge and later Sean O'Casey were its house playwrights. It's still known for its productions of older Irish plays, but does encourage younger writers. The building also houses the *Peacock Theatre*, which sometimes has more experimental shows.

Gaiety Theatre, South King St (☎6771717). Dublin's oldest theatre stages a mix of musical comedy, revues and occasional opera, plus rock music on Fridays and Sundays.

Gate Theatre, Parnell Square (☎6744045). Another of Dublin's literary institutions; a bare, rectangular room, it stages more modern Irish plays.

Project Arts Centre, East Sussex St (☎6712321). This is where you're most likely to find experimental or politically sensitive work.

Listings

Airlines *Aer Lingus*, 20 Upper O'Connell St and 42 Grafton St (☎370011); *British Airways*, 60 Dawson St (☎6610666); *British Midland*, 54 Grafton St (☎798733); *Capital*, Dublin Airport (☎6774422); *Ryanair*, 3 Dawson St (☎774422).

Airport Flight information ☎8746301.

Bicycle hire *USIT*, 58 Lower Gardiner St (Mon–Sat 9am–6pm).

Buses Buses to all parts of the country leave from the Busárus or the streets immediately around (Eden Quay/Abbey St/Talbot St). Private buses run from the Quays.

Car hire *Budget*, 29 Lower Abbey St (☎8787814); *Dan Dooley Rent-a-Car*, 5 Lyon House, Cathal Brugha St (☎8720777); *Kenning Car Hire*, 42 Westland Row (☎772723).

Embassies *Australia*, Fitzwilton House, Wilton Terrace (☎6761517); *Canada*, 65 St Stephen's Green (☎781988); *Great Britain*, 31–33 Merrion Road (☎6695211); *Netherlands*, 160 Merrion Row (☎693444); *US*, 42 Elgin Road, Ballsbridge (☎6688777).

Exchange The *Bank of Ireland* at the airport is open daily 6.45am–9/10pm.

Ferry companies *B&I*, 16 Westmoreland St (☎8724711); *StenaSealink*, 15 Westmoreland St (☎808844).

Gay Dublin Gay Switchboard Mon–Fri 8–10pm, Sat 3–6pm, Sun 7–9pm; ☎8721055.

Hospital Jervis St (☎8723355).

Laundries *Sappire*, 11 Grand St; *Powder Launderette*, 42a South Richmond St.

Left luggage At the stations: Busárus (Mon–Sat 8am–8pm, Sun 10am–6pm); Heuston (Mon–Sat 7.15am–8.35pm, Sun 8am–3pm & 5–9pm); Connolly (Mon–Sat 7.40am–9.30pm, Sun 9.15am–1pm & 5–9pm).

Pharmacy *O'Connell's*, 55 Lower O'Connell St, is open till 10pm daily.

Police The main Gardai station is in Harcourt St, just off St Stephen's Green (☎732222).

Post office General Post Office, O'Connell St (Mon–Sat 8am–8pm, Sun 10.30am–6.30pm).

Phones International booths at the General Post Office.

Taxis Taxi ranks throughout central Dublin. *National Radio Cabs* can be booked on ☎6772222, 24 hours a day.

Travel agents *USIT*, 7 Anglesea St (☎6778117), are experts in student/youth travel.

Transport information 59 Upper O'Connell St (Mon–Fri 9am–5pm, Sat 9am–1pm; ☎8787777).

Around Dublin

County Wicklow, easily accessible to the south of Dublin, has some of the wildest, most spectacular mountain scenery in Ireland, as well as some impressive monuments – the early Celtic monastery of **Glendalough** and the Neoclassical splendours of the great house of **Russborough**. To the north of the city, following the N51 to Navan, is the area known as the Brugh Na Bóinne complex, a group of forty or so prehistoric sites caught within a curve of the River Boyne between Tullyallen and Slane. The three most important of them, Dowth, Knowth and **Newgrange**, feature amazing passage graves – high round mounds raised over stone burial chambers that predate the pyramids by several centuries.

Glendalough

GLENDALOUGH, 30km south of Dublin, is one of the most important monastic sites in Ireland, with a quite tangible quality of peace and spirituality that's only marginally disturbed by the coach parties that flock here. Independent transport from the city is easy – the *St Kevin's Bus Service* leaves from St Stephen's Green at 11.30am every day and comes back in the late afternoon.

The huge **visitors' centre** features an excellent exhibition and a video show that sets Glendalough in the context of the monastic ruins elsewhere in Ireland; the admission charge (IR£1) includes a guided tour of the site itself. The **Monastery** (mid-June to mid-Sept daily 10am–6pm; mid-Sept to mid-June Tues–Sat 10am–4.30pm) was founded by Saint Kevin, a member of the royal house of Leinster, during the sixth century. As a centre of the Celtic church, it became famous throughout Europe for its learning, and despite being sacked by the Vikings in the ninth and tenth centuries and by the English in the fourteenth, monastic life at the site continued tenaciously until the sixteenth century. The **Cathedral**, which dates from the early ninth century, has an impressively ornamental east window; the saint's burial spot is marked by **St Kevin's Cross**, a massive slab of granite, carved around 1150, in the Celtic form of a cross superimposed on a wheel. Equally remarkable is the **round tower**, whose doorway is ten feet above the ground, possibly so that in times of trouble monks could pull up the ladder and turn the tower into an inaccessible treasury and refuge. Glendalough's most famous building, though, has to be the solid barrel-vaulted stone oratory of **St Kevin's Church**. Although it may well date from Saint Kevin's time, the round-tower belfry is an eleventh-century addition, and the structure has clearly been altered many times.

There are plenty more antiquities connected with the monastic life here, among the cliffs around the **Upper Lake**, many of them formerly pilgrim shrines. The site of Saint Kevin's original church, the **Temple-na-Skellig**, is on a platform approached by a flight of stone steps, accessible only by boat. **St Kevin's Bed**, a rocky ledge high up the cliff, is said to be where the holy man used to sleep in an attempt to escape the unwelcome advances of a young girl.

If you want to **stay** right in the middle of this amazing place, the *Luganure* bed and breakfast overlooks the Upper Lake. Otherwise, you've a choice between the *An Óige* hostel, about half a mile up the valley from the ruins (☎0404/5143; ②) and the independent *Mill Youth Hostel* (②), the same distance along the Rathdrum/Wexford road.

Russborough

The west of County Wicklow, away from the mountains, is less spectacular than the rest, and the main reason for coming here is to visit **Russborough House** (Easter–Oct daily 10.30am–5.30pm; IR£2.50) and its impressive art collection. Getting to Russborough is no problem – Blessington, the pleasant town it adjoins, is forty minutes from central Dublin on the Waterford bus.

A classic Palladian building whose design was subsequently repeated throughout Ireland, Russborough was constructed for Joseph Leeson, MP for Rathcormack in the days of the semi-independent Irish parliament. The house epitomizes the great flowering of Anglo-Irish confidence before the Act of Union deprived Ireland of its parliament, much of its trade and its high society. No expense was spared – the fashionable architects of the day were employed here and the plasterers, the Francini brothers, were also the best, their virtuosity demonstrated in the lunatic plasterwork on the stairs. Impressive though it is, the chief reason Russborough is so firmly on the tourist trail is its collection of paintings, which includes work by Goya, Murillo, Velázquez, Gainsborough, Rubens and Frans Hals. The snag is that security is very tight as Russborough has been burgled twice, and visitors are herded around the house with little chance to study the paintings in detail.

There's an all-year *An Óige* **youth hostel** in a tranquil location on the peninsula almost opposite Russborough (book through the Dublin main office ; ☎01/363111; ②).

Newgrange

The main N1 Belfast road and the railway provide rapid access from Dublin to Drogheda, from where it's a short bus hop to the great **Newgrange** tumulus (June–Sept daily 10am–7pm; mid-March to May daily 10am–1pm & 2–5pm; Oct to mid-March Tues–Sat 10am–4.30pm, Sun 2–4pm; IR£1.50). Raised around 5000 years ago, the mound has been so completely restored that at first sight it reminds you of a grounded flying saucer, but once you get over the initial shock, the sparkling appearance of it all serves only to heighten the wonder. The outer ring of **standing stones**, of which only twelve uprights now remain, was a feature unique among passage grave tombs, and it may have been the addition of a later civilization. There is an inner ring of 97 kerbstones all placed on their sides and touching each other, engineered perhaps as a support for the 20,000 tons of turf, loose stones, shale and boulder clay that were laid over the chambers. Perhaps the most important feature of Newgrange – again unique – is the **roof-box** several feet in from the tunnel mouth. This contains a slit through which, at the **winter solstice**, the light of the rising sun begins to penetrate as soon as its full disc appears above the horizon. The rays eventually find the back of the cruciform chamber and in minutes the chamber becomes radiant with a glow of orange light which fades as suddenly as it has blazed. The guided tour includes a "recreation" of the phenomenon, which involves a flash of orange electric light. The entry passage, about three feet wide, leads into the **central chamber** where the stones are carved with superbly intricate decorations. At the entrance to the site there's a **museum and interpretative centre** where aspects of Newgrange and other nearby prehistoric sites are more fully explored.

SOUTHERN IRELAND

The southeast of Ireland is not the most immediately attractive area of the country, but this is Ireland's sunniest and driest corner, and it does have a couple of rewarding and contrasting towns. Inland, the region's medieval and Anglo-Norman history is richly concentrated in **Kilkenny**, a bustling, quaint favourite, while on the coast there's **Waterford City**, which preserves an ancient heart but is also a thriving commercial centre, young and enjoyably lively. To the west of here, County Tipperary consists largely of prosperous, contented farming country, with little to offer visitors. At the very heart of the county there is, however, one site of outstanding interest – the **Rock of Cashel**, a spectacular natural formation topped with Christian buildings from virtually every period. Moving towards the southwest, County Cork – Ireland's largest country – is the perfect place to ease yourself into the exhilarations of the west coast, and **Cork city** manages to be both a relaxed and a spirited place.

Coming from abroad, there's ready access to the south through **Rosslare Harbour**, which serves ferries from Cherbourg (1–2 weekly), Le Havre (2–3 weekly), Fishguard (2 daily) and Pembroke (1–2 daily). At Rosslare Harbour there's a **tourist office** open for all incoming sailings in summer, and an *An Óige* **hostel** in Goulding St (☎053/ 33399; ②). Moving on from Rosslare Harbour is fairly straightforward. Trains from the pier for Wexford, Dublin and Waterford depart two to three times daily from Monday to Saturday. There are four to six buses to Dublin daily.

Kilkenny

KILKENNY is Ireland's finest medieval city, its castle set above the broad sweep of the River Nore and its narrow streets laced with carefully maintained buildings. In the mid-seventeenth century, Kilkenny became virtually the capital of Ireland, with the founding of a parliament in 1641 known as the **Confederation of Kilkenny**. This attempt to unite the resistance to English persecution of Catholicism, though powerful for a while, had greatly diminished by the time Cromwell's wreckers arrived in 1650. Kilkenny never recovered its prosperity, but enough remains to attest to its former importance.

The **bus and train stations** are a short distance north of the city, at the top of John St. Following this road over the river and climbing Rose Inn St brings you to the **tourist office** (☎056/51500; April–Sept Mon–Sat 9am–6pm, Sun 11am–1pm & 2–5pm; Oct–March Mon–Fri 9am–1pm & 2–5.15pm), housed in the sixteenth-century **Shee Alms House**, one of the very few Tudor almshouses to be found in Ireland. At the top of Rose Inn St to the left is the broad **Parade**, which leads up to the castle. To the right, the High St passes the eighteenth-century **Tholsel**, once the centre of the city's financial dealings and now the town hall. Beyond is **Parliament Street**, the main thoroughfare, where the **Rothe House** provides a unique example of an Irish Tudor merchant's home, comprising three separate houses linked by courtyards.

The highlight of this end of town is, without doubt, the thirteenth-century **St Canice's Cathedral** (Mon–Sat 9am–1pm & 2–6pm, Sun 2–6pm). Rich in carvings, it has a fine array of sixteenth-century monuments, many in black Kilkenny marble. The **round tower** next to the church (50p) is all that remains of the monastic settlement reputedly founded by Saint Canice in the sixth century; there are superb views from the top.

It's the **Castle**, though, that defines Kilkenny, an imposing building standing high and square over the river (June–Sept daily 10am–7pm; Oct–March Mon–Sat 10.30am–5pm, Sun 11am–5pm; April–May daily 10am–5pm; IR£1, students 60p, guided tours should be pre-booked). Founded in the twelfth century, the castle was radically altered by a nineteenth-century restoration – hence the folksy, pre-Raphaelite decoration on the flimsy wooden hammer-beam roof of the picture gallery. Also within the castle is the **Butler Gallery**, housing an exhibition of modern art. The castle's kitchen is a tearoom in summer.

Practicalities

Kilkenny is well served by **B&Bs**, although in the summer the city can get crowded and during festival week in August you'll need to book in advance. In the centre of town try Mrs Dempsey's at 26 James St (π056/21954; ③); Mrs O'Connell's, *St Mary's*, next door (π056/22091; ③), or one of a couple in Dean St, off Parliament St: *Church View* at number 6 above the coffee shop (π056/61734; ③), or *Dean Street House* (π056/64040; ②), which doesn't include breakfast. There's an *An Óige* **hostel** at Jenkinstown (π056/67674; ②), eight miles north along the N77 – *Buggy's* buses run to the hostel from the Parade from Monday to Saturday at 11.30am and 5.30pm. The friendly *Kilkenny Tourist Hostel*, 35 Parliament St (π056/63541; ②), is a more central independent hostel. There's **camping** at 25 Upper Patrick St, an excellent location, though without showers.

   M.L. Dore, 65 High St, serves good value hot meals till 10pm daily. There are several other good spots for bar food – *Sheni's* in John St, the *Caisléin Uícuain*, Patrick St, and *Lautrec's*, St Kieran St, the best bistro in town. **Bars** are as alluring in Kilkenny as anywhere in Ireland, and you won't be hard pushed to find music here. The *Marble City Bar* and *Jim Holland's*, both in Parliament St, are good traditional pubs; *Caisléin Uícuain* at the bottom of Patrick St, the *Pumphouse* in Parliament St and the *Arch Bar* in John St are all reliable music venues. Pick up a copy of the weekly *Kilkenny People* for information about what's on.

Waterford City

WATERFORD is basically a modern European port wrapped around an ancient Irish city. It's one of the few buoyant commercial centres of any size in the Republic, and a sign of Waterford's comparative prosperity is the number of young people the place now attracts, in strong contrast to other parts of this country bled by emigration. Alongside the city's vigorous modernity, though, there's plenty that's traditional, most obviously the place of the pub as a focal point of social activity, and the persistence of traditional music.

   Recorded history of the city starts with the **Viking** settlement founded in the mid-ninth century, and the layout of the city retains its Viking roots, the very long quays and adjacent narrow lanes forming the trading centre. The next wave of invaders to leave an imprint were the **Anglo-Normans**. When Dermot MacMurrough made his bid for the High Kingship of Ireland, he knew Waterford was vital for control of the southwest. In 1170, he called on his Welsh Anglo-Norman allies to attack the city, the most important of these being **Strongbow**. After a bloody siege, Strongbow received his reward: MacMurrough's daughter and her inheritance. The marriage took place here, and was the first such alliance between a Norman earl and an Irish king: a crucial and symbolic historical event. Waterford flourished as a European port into the eighteenth century – the period when the famous Waterford crystal was first produced – and there's plenty of architectural evidence of this period's prosperity.

   The **train and bus stations** are just across the river from the city, a good twenty minutes' walk from Waterford's most historic building – **Reginald's Tower** (April–May Mon–Fri 10am–1pm & 2–6pm, Sat 10am–1pm; June–Oct Mon–Fri 10am–8pm, Sat 10am–1pm & 2–5pm; 75p, combined ticket includes Waterford Heritage Centre IR£1), a large cylindrical late twelfth-century tower at the far end of the quays. It houses the city's **museum**, which has an impressive collection of royal charters showing the central role of Waterford's allegiance to the English crown. Wander up Bailey's New St just behind the tower and you immediately come to Waterford's other important medieval building, the ruined **French Church**, or Greyfriars. Founded by Franciscans in 1240, it served as a hospital in the sixteenth century, and from 1693 to 1815 was used as a place of worship by French Huguenot refugees. Nearby is the **Waterford Heritage Centre** (same hours as Reginald's Tower; combined ticket IR£1), a showcase for recently excavated Viking and Norman artefacts of outstanding quality and design.

Further up Bailey's New St, you enter Waterford's next significant period of church-building at **Christ Church Cathedral** (May–Sept Mon–Fri 10.30am–1pm & 2–4pm). Built in the 1770s by John Roberts, who did much work in Waterford for both Catholics and Protestants, it's a nicely proportioned Renaissance building in soothing cream and grey, with some fine monuments inside – look out for the tomb of James Rice (1482), an effigy of a corpse in an advanced state of decay. Roberts was also responsible for **Holy Trinity Cathedral** in Barron Strand St. Originally built in 1793, this was greatly altered during the nineteenth century to become the curvaceous extravaganza it is today. Christ Church Cathedral looks down over The Mall, where the **City Hall** – again by John Roberts – was once used as a merchants' exchange. By far the finest eighteenth-century architectural detail in the city, though, is the beautiful oval staircase inside the **Chamber of Commerce** in George St, yet again by John Roberts. Georgian housing continues down O'Connell St, where the *Garter Lane Arts Centre* has a gallery, a theatre and a good events noticeboard.

Practicalities

The **tourist office** (April–Sept daily 9am–6pm; Oct & March Mon–Fri 9am–5.15pm; closed Nov–Feb) is at 41 Merchants Quay. It has comprehensive lists of recommended B&Bs (③), which are concentrated along Parnell St, The Mall and O'Connell St. The *Portree Guest House* in Mary St (☎051/74574; ③) is friendly, comfortable and clean, as is *O'Connell House*, O'Connell St (☎051/74175; ③). There should be a new hostel open by summer 1994: for your own safety – especially women – we **strongly** recommend that you call at the tourist office and ask for details before approaching any places offering budget accommodation.

There are plenty of fast-food joints down Michael St and John St. *Haricot's* on O'Connell St is a cosy, reasonably priced wholefood restaurant, *Poppy's*, 18 High St, is the place to head for dearer evening meals. For **pub food** try *Egari's*, Broad St. John St has two of the city's favourite **pubs** – *Geoff's* and the *Pulpit*, both lively, young places with a good social mix, and useful for keying into what's happening in the city; after hours head for the *Preachers*, a wacky club behind the *Pulpit*. For **traditional music** there are a few regular spots: *T.H.Doolans* in George St, *Mullanes* in Newgate St, and the *Metropole*, Bridge St.

The Rock of Cashel

The town of Cashel is completely dominated by the **Rock of Cashel** (daily mid-March to mid-June 9.30am–5.30pm; mid-June to mid-Sept 9am–7.30pm; mid-Sept to mid-March 9.30am–4.30pm, last admission 40 minutes before closing), arguably the most extraordinary architectural site in Ireland. Appearing as a mirage of crenellations rising bolt upright from the vast plain, the Rock is the place where Saint Patrick is supposed to have picked a shamrock in order to explain the doctrine of the Trinity – since when the shamrock has become Ireland's unofficial emblem. It can be reached by bus from Waterford, changing at Cahir. The obvious base for a visit is one of the Cashel's **hostels**: *O'Brien's Farmhouse Hostel* (☎062/61003; ②), off the Dundnun Rd, and *Cashel Holiday Hostel*, 6 John St (☎062/62330; ②), are both a short walk from the Rock. For **B&B**, try *Abbey House*, 1 Dominic St (☎062/61104; ③), or *Maryville*, Bankplace (☎062/61098; ③). The **tourist office** in the market house in the middle of the main street will have details on more accommodation.

Approaching the Rock from Cashel town, you come first to the fifteenth-century **Hall of the Vicars**, whose vaulted undercroft today contains the original **Saint Patrick's Cross**, a uniquely simple type of high cross. Tradition has it that the cross's huge plinth was the coronation stone of the High Kings of Munster. **Cormac's**

Chapel, built in the 1130s, is the earliest and most beautiful of Ireland's Romanesque churches. Intricate carving is a feature of both the north door and the south, while the alleged sarcophagus of King Cormac, inside, has an exquisite design of interlacing serpents and ribbon decoration. The graceful limestone **Cathedral**, begun a century after Cormac's chapel, is Anglo-Norman in conception, with its Gothic arches and lancet windows. A door in the south transept gives access to the tower, and in the north transept some panels from sixteenth-century altar-tombs survive, one with an intricately carved retinue of saints. The tapering **Round Tower** is the earliest building on the Rock, perhaps dating back to the tenth century, though the officially accepted date is early twelfth century.

From the grounds of the Rock you can look down at the thirteenth-century **Hore Abbey** on the plain below. Originally a Benedictine foundation, it converted after its abbot had a wild dream that his Benedictine monks were plotting to cut his head off; he expelled them and donned the Cistercian habit in 1269. A path known as the **Bishop's Walk** leads from the Rock's rampart entrance down through the back garden of the **Palace Hotel**, built in Queen Anne style by Archbishop Theophilus Bolton – the man whose money saved the Rock's antiquities from irrevocable ruin. A further legacy is the **GPA Bolton library** (Mon–Sat 9.30am–5.30pm, Sun 2.30–5.30pm; IR£1.50, unwaged IR£1). Its ancient manuscripts, rare maps and wealth of literary treasures were principally his bequest when he died in 1744. A selection of the books and maps is on display, changing bi-monthly, and well worth viewing. If you have time, visit the **Bothàn Scóir**, a unique one-room peasant dwelling that tells the history of the common people, all passionately brought to life by the curator. Ask at the tourist office for directions.

Cork City

Everywhere in **CORK** there's evidence of the city's history as a great mercantile centre, with grey stone quaysides, old warehouses, and elegant and quirky bridges spanning the River Lee to each side of the island core. Important port though Cork remains, however, it doesn't feel overridingly commercial, and the Lee is certainly not the river of an industrial town. Cork had its origins in the seventh century when **Saint Finbarr** founded an abbey and school here. A settlement grew up around the monastic foundation, but in 820 the **Vikings** arrived and wrecked both abbey and town. They built a new settlement on one of the islands in the marshes, and eventually integrated with the native Celts. The twelfth century saw the invasion of the **Normans**, who fortified the place with massive stone walls which survived Cromwell but were destroyed by Williamite forces at the **Siege of Cork** in 1690. From this time on the city began to take on the shape recognizable today as waterborne trade brought increasing prosperity. Evidence of this wealth survives in the form of fine eighteenth-century bow-fronted houses, and the ostentatious nineteenth-century church architecture that decorates the city. More recently, Cork suffered greatly during the Anglo-Irish and Civil wars. The Black and Tans reigned here with particular terror, and were responsible for the murder of Thomas MacCurtain, the mayor of Cork, in 1920. Cork's next mayor, Terence MacSwiney, was jailed as a Republican and died in Brixton prison after a hunger strike of 74 days.

Much of the charm of the city lies in its contrasts, rather than in any great sights. Along the graceful arc of **St Patrick's Street** – which with **Grand Parade** forms the commercial heart of the centre – major chain stores exist alongside modest traditional businesses. A hundred yards north of St Patrick's St you'll find **Coal Quay market** in Cornmarket St – a flea market worthy of the name. A minute's walk from here down the ever-smarter Paul St brings still more variety in the bijou environs of French

Church St and Carey's Lane. The downstream end of the island, where many of the quays are still in use, gives the clearest sense of the old port city. In the west the island is predominantly residential, though Fitzgerald Park is the home of the **Cork Public Museum** (Mon–Sat 11am–1pm & 2.15–5pm, Sun 3–5pm; free, Sun 50p), which is primarily a museum of Republican history.

North of the River Lee is the area of **Shandon**, a reminder of Cork's eighteenth-century status as the most important port in Europe for dairy products. The most striking survival is the **Cork Butter Exchange**, stout nineteenth-century Classical buildings recently given over to craft workshops. The old **butter market** itself sits like a generously proportioned butter tub in a cobbled square; recently renovated, it now houses the **Firkin Crane** theatre. To the rear is the pleasant Georgian church of St **Anne's Shandon** (Mon–Sat 10am–4pm; June–Aug 9.30am–5pm), easily recognizable from all over the city by its weather vane – an eleven-foot salmon. The church tower (IR£1.50) gives excellent views, and an oportunity to ring the bells – a good stock of sheet tunes is provided.

To the west of here in the area known as Sunday's Well is **Cork City Gaol** (April–Oct daily 9.30am–7pm; Nov–March Sat & Sun 10am–4pm; IR£3, students IR£2), with an excellent animated taped tour that focuses on social history. From here it's possible to walk back to the town centre via the Shaky Bridge and Fitzgerald Park.

The stark precision of nineteenth-century Gothic that is repeated time and again in the city's churches may not be to everyone's taste, but undeniably gives the city an architectural cohesion. Best of all is William Burges' **St Finbarr's Cathedral**; obsessively detailed, its French Gothic spire provides a grand silhouette on the southwesterly shoulder of the city.

Practicalities

The **Bus Éireann station** is at Parnell Place alongside Merchant's Quay, while the **train station** is about one mile out of the city centre on the Lower Glanmire Road. **Ferries** from Swansea, Roscoff, St Malo and Le Havre come in at Ringaskiddy, some ten miles out, from where there's a bus into the centre.

The **tourist office** on Grand Parade will book rooms in **B&B**s for a fee of IR£1. There are plenty of B&Bs strung out along the Western Road, near the university, and along Lower Glanmire Road near the train station. *Sheila's Cork Tourist Hostel,* Belgrave Place, Wellington Rd (☎021/505562; ②), and *Isaacs,* 48 MacCurtain St (☎021/500011; ②), are both good budget options; *Kinlay House,* Shandon (☎021/508966; ②), is a little further from the stations, but another good spot. The nearest **campsite** is *Cork City Caravan and Camping Park* (Easter–Oct; #14 bus from St Patrick St or South Main St).

For **food**, the *Quay Co-op,* 24 Sullivan's Quay, offers large vegetarian meals, while the *Ivory Tower,* 35 Princes St, has a delicious, reasonably priced lunch menu. *Luciano's,* MacCurtain St, may be grotty to look at, but it makes great pizzas. *Bully's,* 40 Paul St, is a down-to-earth wine bar serving good pasta and fish dishes. Traditional Irish **music** features most nights at the *An Spailpín Fánac* pub in South Main St, and is played early in the week at *An Bodhrán* in Oliver Plunkett St. The young crowd tend to drink at trendy *An Bróg,* 78 Oliver Plunkett St, and at the quaint old *Vineyard* in Market Lane. *Gorby's,* 74 Oliver Plunkett St, and *Sir Henry's,* South Main St, form the best of Cork's **club** scene; for regular discos try *Klub Kaos,* more dressy than *Gorby's* and in the same building. The hub of artistic activity in Cork is the **Triskel Arts Centre** in Tobin St, off South Main St. It has contemporary art shows, a cinema, poetry readings, concerts and a very good wholefood café. Cork also has an **international jazz festival** towards the end of October. For the latest details about what's on, buy the *Cork Examiner,* or pick up a copy of *The Word* (Munster edition).

THE WEST COAST

If you've come to Ireland for scenery, mountains, sea and remoteness, you'll find them all in **County Kerry** – miles of mountain-moorland where the heather and the bracken are broken only by the occasional lake, smooth hills of fragrant, tussocky grass and wildflowers that fragment into jagged rocks as they reach the ocean. By far the most visited area – indeed, the most visited in the whole of Ireland – is **Killarney and the Ring of Kerry**, a route around the perimeter of the Iveragh peninsula. This region is predictably geared up for tourism,, but whether you head for the mountains or the sea, you can soon lose all contact with modern civilization. The **Dingle** peninsula, to the north, is on a smaller scale, but equally magical and peppered with ancient remains.

Across the Shannon estuary, beyond the unexciting but virtually inescapable city of Limerick, lies **County Clare**, bordered by Galway Bay to the north and the massive Lough Derg to the east. The county is sometimes glossed over as an interval between the magnificent scenery of Kerry and Galway, but Clare has its own distinctive flavour, especially on the stark and barren heights of the **Burren**.

The easiest approach to the Burren is from **Galway City**, an exceptionally enjoyable, free-spirited sort of place, and a gathering point for young travellers. The city sits at the foot of Lough Corrib, which splits County Galway in two: to the east stretches tame, fertile land which people have farmed for centuries, while to the west lies **Connemara**, a magnificently wild terrain of wind and rock and water. The **Aran Islands**, in the mouth of Galway Bay, resemble Connemara in their elemental beauty and in their culture, and offer some of the most thrilling cliff scenery in Ireland.

If you carry on up the coast you'll enter **Mayo**, where the landscape softens and the historic town of **Westport** provides the main base. Neighbouring counties **Sligo** and **Leitrim** both feature a more luscious and gentle scenery, but Sligo is the more enticing of the two, having the beautiful mountain of **Benbulben** and the enchanting **Glencar lough**. Not many people would disagree with the assertion that **County Donegal** has the richest scenery in the whole country. Second only in size to Cork, it has a spectacular two-hundred-mile coastline whose highlight is **Slieve League**, the highest cliffs in Europe.

Killarney and around

Although **KILLARNEY** has been commercialized to saturation point and has little in the way of architectural interest, its location amidst some of the best lakes, mountains and woodland in Ireland more than compensates. The town is essentially one main street and a couple of side roads, full of souvenir shops, cafés, pubs, restaurants and B&Bs. Pony traps and jaunting cars line up while their owners talk visitors into extortionate trips through the surrounding country. It's all done with bags of charm, true to Killarney's long tradition of profitably hosting the visiting masses ever since its discovery as a resort in the mid-eighteenth century.

Bed and breakfasts abound, though in high season the town fills up and it's worth calling the **tourist office** (☎064/31633), on the main street by the town hall, to make advance bookings. The **An Óige hostel** (☎064/31240; ②) is three miles out along the Killorglin road, at Aghadoe, but there are also six independent hostels in Killarney. The *Four Winds Hostel*, 43 New St (☎064/33094; ②), is extroverted and noisy; the *Neptune Town Hostel* (☎064/35255; ②) is friendly and well-equipped, and the newly opened *Railway Hostel* (☎064/35299; ②) is clean and welcoming. *The Súgan Kitchen* on Lewis Rd (☎064/33104; ②), minutes from the station, is cosier and more relaxed, with a good wholefood bistro and traditional music. The same family also runs *Bonrower House*, near Ross Castle; bookings from the *Súgan*. The *Park Hostel* (☎064/32119; ②) is up the hill off Cork Rd, opposite the petrol station. There's a **campsite** at the *Fossa*

Caravan Park, just past the Aghadoe youth hostel west of town. Places to **eat and drink** are thick on the ground: cheap dinners are available at *Sceilig* in the High St, and at *A Taste of Ireland* on College St. Evening **entertainment** is everywhere as you walk along the streets; latest news on the music venues is available from the *Súgan Kitchen*.

The real reason for coming to Killarney is, without doubt, the surrounding landscape, the three spectacular lakes – Lough Leane, Muckross Lake and the Upper Lake – forming the appetizer for MacGillycuddy's Reeks, the highest mountains in Ireland. **Cycling** is a great way of seeing the terrain, and makes good sense because local transport is sparse. *O'Callaghan Brothers* in College St are the local participants in the *Raleigh* scheme; bikes can also be rented from *O'Neill's* in Plunkett St.

Knockreer Estate

The gates of the **Knockreer Estate** are just over the road from Killarney's cathedral, and a short walk through the grounds takes you to the banks of **Lough Leane**, where tall wooded hills plunge into the water, with the peaks rising behind to the highest, **Carrintuohill** (3414ft). The main path through the estate leads to the restored four-teenth-century tower of **Ross Castle**, the last place in Munster to succumb to Cromwell's forces in 1652. From Ross Castle you can tour the lake in large glassed-over boats, but these don't make stops, and an alternative is to get a fisherman to take you out in a little craft with an outboard motor, or hire one yourself. This way, you can land on and explore the island of **Inisfallen**, the biggest and the most enchanting of the thirty-odd small islands that dot Lough Leane. Wandering around the island is a delight: heavily wooded, it's also scattered with monastic buildings – nothing from the original seventh-century foundation, but there's a small Romanesque church and an extremely ruined Augustinian priory.

Muckross and the lakes

The first place to head for in the **Muckross estate** – a mile and a half south of Killarney – is **Muckross Abbey**, not only for the ruin itself but also for its calm, contemplative location. Founded by the Franciscans in the mid-fifteenth century, it was suppressed by Henry VIII; the friars returned, but were finally driven out by Cromwell in 1652. Back at the main road, signposts direct you to **Muckross House**, a solid nine-teenth-century neo-Elizabethan mansion with a dullish crafts **museum** (March–June, Sept & Oct daily 9am–6pm; July & Aug daily 9am–7pm; Nov–Feb Tues–Sun 11am–5pm; IR£2.50, students IR£1) but wonderful gardens. The estate gives access to well-trodden paths along the shores of the Muckross Lake, and it's here that you can see one of Killarney's celebrated beauty spots, the **Meeting of Waters**. Actually a parting, it has a profusion of indigenous and flowering subtropical plants on the left of the Old Weir Bridge. Close by is the massive shoulder of Torc Mountain, shrugging off **Torc Waterfall**. The **Upper Lake** is beautiful, too, but still firmly on the tourist trail, with the main road running along one side up to **Ladies' View**, where the view is truly amazing.

The Gap of Dunloe

The **Gap of Dunloe** – a narrow defile formed by glacial overflow that cuts the mountains in two – is one of Killarney's prime tourist attractions, and expensive jaunting cars continually run here from Killarney. A better option is to walk the four miles in the late afternoon, when the cars have gone home and the light is at its most magical. **Kate Kearney's Cottage**, at the foot of the road leading up to the Gap, is the last place for food and water before Lord Brandon's Cottage, way over the other side of the valley. The road – closed to motor traffic – winds its way up the desolate valley between high rock cliffs and waterfalls, past a chain of icy loughs and tarns, up to the top, where you find yourself in what feels like one of the remotest places in the world: the **Black**

Valley. Named after its entire population perished during the potato famine, it's now inhabited by a mere handful of families, and was the very last valley in Ireland to get electricity. From here, the quick way back to Killarney is to carry on down to Lord Brandon's Cottage and take the boat across the Upper Lake.

The Ring of Kerry

Most tourists view the spectacular scenery of the 110-mile **Ring of Kerry** without ever leaving their coach or car. Consequently, anyone straying from the road or waiting until the buses knock off in the afternoon will be left to experience the slow twilights of the Atlantic seaboard in perfect seclusion. **Cycling** the Ring takes three days and a bike will let you get on to the largely deserted mountain roads. Ordinary **buses** from Killarney only go as far as Cahirciveen, but in summer flotillas of **coaches** ply the Ring in an anticlockwise direction. Most of them leave from opposite the tourist office in Killarney, and for an extra charge will drop you off somewhere along the way and pick you up the next day.

Valentia Island

At **Kells Bay** the road veers inland towards **CAHIRCIVEEN**, a long, narrow street of a town and also the main shopping centre for the western part of the peninsula, giving itself over cheerfully to the tourist trade in summer. Beyond Cahirciveen, lanes lead out to **Valentia Island**, Europe's most westerly harbour, its position on the Gulf Stream giving it a mild, balmy climate – hence the abundance of fuschias on the intensively cultivated land. Access to the island is by **ferry** from Reenard (two and a half miles from Cahirciveen) to **KNIGHTSTOWN** or via the Maurice O'Neill Bridge, at the south end of the island, thirteen miles from the main coast road and a difficult hitch. There's no public transport on the island. **Accommodation** is at a premium during the summer season, when B&Bs raise their prices to around IR£14. The Knightstown **An Óige hostel** (☎066/76154; ②) has space for forty at the Coastguard Station, but for members only, and facilities are spartan. The independent hostel on the harbour front (☎066/76144; ②) is never short of space, and midway between the bridge and Knightstown there's another independent, *Ring Lyne Hostel* (☎066/76103; ②). Knightstown is the focal village of the small island, with about a thousand houses clustering around a slate church hidden within a dark rookery. The main street has a few well-stocked shops, a post office offering free maps of the island, and a couple of bars. Uninspiring by day, these come to life after 10pm several nights a week, when accordion and pipe music accompanies rigorous Gaelic dancing. The much-touted **Grotto** – the highest point on the island – is a gaping slate cavern with a crude statue of the Virgin perched two hundred feet up, amidst dripping icy water. More exciting by far is the cliff scenery to the northwest, some of the most spectacular of the Kerry coast.

The Skellig Islands

From Valentia you get a tantalizing view across a broad strip of sea to the **Skellig Islands**. Little Skellig is a bird sanctuary where landing isn't permitted, but you can visit Great Skellig, or **Skellig Michael** as it's also called, and climb up to the ancient monastic site at the summit. To get there, enquire at shops in Knightstown about **boat trips**; these are expensive at around IR£15, but it's a dramatic voyage to the gargantuan slatey mass. From the sea there's no visible route to the summit, but from the tiny landing stage you can see steps cut into the cliff face, formerly a monks' path. Nowadays there's also a road leading to Christ's Saddle, the only patch of green on this savage island. From here, a path leads to the remains of the sixth-century **St Finian's Abbey.**

Ballinskelligs and Waterville

The stretch of coast between Valentia and Waterville is wild and almost deserted, apart from a scattering of farms and fishing villages. Sweet-smelling, tussocky grass dotted with wild flowers is raked by Atlantic winds, ending in abrupt cliffs or sandy beaches – a beguiling landscape where you can wander for days. The **An Óige hostel** (☎66/79229; ②) in **BALLINSKELLIGS** makes a good base and sells supplies. The village is something of a centre of Gaelic culture: monks from the Skellig islands retreated to Ballinskelligs Abbey in the thirteenth century, while the town itself is busy in summer with schoolchildren and students learning Gaelic. **WATERVILLE** may be touristy, but it does it with a lot of grace. Popular as a Victorian and Edwardian resort and angling centre, it still has an air of consequence that sits oddly with the wild Atlantic views. Its few bars and hotels aside, the town is chiefly notable as the best base on the Ring for exploring the coast and the mountainous country inland. The **hostel** at *Waterville Leisure Centre* (☎66/74644; ②) can supply information about surfing, mountaineering and riding in the vicinity.

Kenmare

With its delicatessens, designer boutiques and arty second-hand clothes shops, **KENMARE** is something of a cosmopolitan anomaly, where you're more likely to hear English or German tones than Irish. Kenmare was established by Sir William Petty, Cromwell's surveyor general, who laid the foundations of the mining and smelting industries in this area, encouraged fishing and founded the enormous Lansdowne estate, many of whose buildings still surround the town. Evidence of much more ancient settlement is the stone circle just outside the centre, on the banks of the river. Kenmare has two independent **hostels**: the *Fáilte* in Henry St (☎066/74644; ②), and the *Kenmare Private Hostel* (☎066/41083; ②). There are also plenty of **B&Bs**, both in and just outside town; check vacancies at the **tourist office** on Main St.

The Dingle Peninsula

The remote beauty and poverty of the **Dingle Peninsula**, and the prevalence of the Gaelic language here, have all lent fuel to romanticizing, the myth being strengthened by the wealth of Gaelic literature created on the now uninhabited Blasket Islands – and the fact that *Ryan's Daughter* was filmed here. There's one other component to the Dingle's irresistible appeal: outside the Aran Islands, the peninsula has the greatest concentration of monastic ruins in Ireland.

Dingle Town

Served by a morning bus from Killarney's train station, **DINGLE** makes the best base for exploring the peninsula. Though essentially little more than just a few streets by the side of **Dingle Bay**, Dingle has a solidity that suggests this was a place of some consequence, and the town was indeed Kerry's leading port in the fourteenth and fifteenth centuries. It later became a centre for smuggling, and at one stage during the eighteenth century – when the revenue from contraband was at its height – even minted its own coinage.

There's no shortage of **accommodation**, although a lot of Dingle's B&Bs are fairly expensive; the summer **tourist office** in Main St has an accommodation service. The *Westlodge/Westgate Hostel* (☎066/51476; ①), located just out of town on the Ventry road, is very basic; *Lovett's* hostel (☎066/51903; ②) is opposite Moran's Garage on the other side of town; the newly-opened *Marina Hostel* (☎066/51065; ①) is by the quay, and the *Rainbow Hostel* (☎066/51044; ②), probably the nicest of the bunch, is one mile out west. In addition there is haunted *Ballintaggart House Hostel* (☎066/51454; ②), one mile before Dingle Town, and the beautifully situated *Seacrest Hostel* (☎066/51390; ②)

near Lispole. All of Dingle's **restaurants**, from the cheapest through to the expense-account places, serve excellent seafood, landed just a few hundred yards away. *Greaney's*, on the corner of Dykegate and Strand St, does good cheap lunches and dinners. Life in the evenings is centred on Dingle's **pubs**, with many of them running traditional music sessions. *O'Flaherty's* in Bridge St is a good place to start – there's music most nights, and advice on where to find it elsewhere.

Cycling is the best way to explore the area beyond Dingle, as public transport in the west of the peninsula amounts to a **bus** from Dingle to Dunquin on Tuesday and Saturday at 9am and 5pm, with an extra service to Slea Head at 1pm in July and August. Mountain bikes are available from *Moriarty's* in Main St, which participates in the *Raleigh* scheme and *Paddy's* in Dykegate St.

To Slea Head – and the Blaskets

The Gaelic-speaking area west of Dingle is rich with the relics of the ancient Gaelic and early Christian cultures, and the main concentration of ancient monuments is to be found between **VENTRY**, once the main port of the peninsula, and Slea Head. First off there's the spectacular **Dun Beag** (IR£1), a scramble down from the road about four miles out from Ventry. A promontory fort, its defences include four earthen rings, with an underground escape route by the main entrance. It's a magical location, overlooking the open sea – into which some of the building has tumbled.

Between Dun Beag and Slea Head, the hillside above the road is studded with stone beehive huts, cave dwellings, souterrains, forts, churches, standing stones and crosses – over 500 of them in all. The beehive huts were being built and used for storing farm tools and produce until the late nineteenth century, but among ancient buildings like the **Fahan group** you're looking over a landscape that's remained essentially unchanged for centuries.

At **Slea Head** the view opens up to include the desolate, splintered masses of the **Blasket Islands**, which have been uninhabited since 1953. In the summer, boats bound for **Great Blasket** leave the pier just south of Dunquin every hour between 11am and 5pm, weather permitting (IR£7 return). Great Blasket's delights are simple ones: tramping the footpaths that crisscross the island, sitting on the beaches watching the seals or the amazing spectacle of the sun sinking into the ocean. Unfortunately there is no hostel but there are a few **B&Bs**, and **camping** is no problem. At the café (noon–5pm), overnighters can order good, cheap vegetarian dinners. There's an *An Óige* hostel at Dunquin (☎066/56121; ②), and B&B in *Kruger's* pub if you prefer the mainland.

Ballyferriter and around

A couple of miles around the headland from Dunquin stands **BALLYFERRITER**, where the little northward lanes will lead you to the 500-foot cliffs at Sybil Head or to Smerwick Harbour and **Dún án Óir** (Golden Fort). The single most impressive early Christian monument on the Dingle peninsula is the **Gallarus oratory**, three miles further east. It's the most perfectly preserved example of around twenty such oratories in Ireland, and is thought to have been built between the ninth and twelfth centuries. It represents a transition in styles between the round beehive huts and the later rectangular churches, an example of which is to be found a mile to the north in the rectangular church at **KILMAKEDAR**. Its nave dates from the mid-twelfth century, and the corbelled stone roof was an improvement on the unstable structure at Gallarus. The site also marks the beginning of the **Saint's Road**, dedicated to Saint Brendan, patron saint of Kerry, which leads to his shrine on the top of Brandon Mountain. The closest accommodation to Ballyferriter is the *An Bóthar Biú* hostel at Ballydavid (☎066/55109; ②).

The Burren

The Burren, a huge plateau of limestone and shale covering over a hundred square miles of northwest Clare, will come as a shock to anyone associating Ireland with all things green. Bone white in sunshine, in the rain it becomes dark and metallic, its cliffs and canyons blurred by mists. A place barely capable of sustaining human habitation, it was summed up in the words of Cromwell's surveyor Ludlow: "a savage land, yielding neither water enough to drown a man, nor a tree to hang him, nor soil enough to bury". Yet this is a botanist's delight, with an astounding variety of arctic, alpine and Mediterranean flora – a mixture that nobody can account for. The area's lack of appeal to centuries of speculators and colonizers has meant that evidence of many of the Burren's earlier inhabitants remains. The place buzzes with the prehistoric and historic past, having over sixty Stone Age burial monuments, over four hundred Iron Age ring forts, and numerous Christian churches, monasteries, round towers and high crosses.

For a quick exploration, there's a daily **Bus Éireann** service from Galway to Lisdoonvarna, where there's decent **hostel** accommodation at the *Burren Holiday Hostel* (☎065/74300; ②). Continue to the village of **DOOLIN**, lodged beside a treacherous sandy beach for a steady supply of **traditional music** all summer. Bold shelves of limestone pavement step into the sea by the pier, from where a **ferry** now runs to Inisheer (mid-April to end-Sept; 1–7 daily), the smallest of the Aran Islands. An otherwise forlorn place, Doolin has become the great centre for **music** in western Ireland, and whatever day of the week you arrive in the summer, traditional music will be playing in the bars. The village is well geared to providing **accommodation** for the devotees. Three places have cheap beds: the *Rainbow Hostel* (☎065/74415; ②), the *Aille River Hostel* (☎065/74260; ②), and the *Doolin Hostel* (☎065/74006; ②); walks and tours of the Burren are available locally; summer **campsite** by the pier.

The **Cliffs of Moher**, beginning four miles south of Doolin and stretching for five miles, are Clare's most famous tourist spot, their great bands of shale and sandstone rising 660 feet above the waves.

Galway City

The city of **GALWAY** can be difficult to leave: it has become a playground for disaffected Dubliners, and folksy young Europeans return each year with an almost religious devotion. University College Galway guarantees a high number of young people in term time, but the energy of Galway is never more evident than during its **festivals**, especially the Arts Festival in the last two weeks in July, when practitioners of theatre, music, poetry and the visual arts create a rich cultural jamboree. For the locals, however, the most important event in the social calendar is the Galway Races, usually held in the first week of August. Accommodation has to be pre-booked during these weeks.

Galway originated as a crossing point on the River Corrib, and developed as a strong Anglo-Norman colony. Granted a charter and city status in 1484 by Richard III, it was loyal to the English crown for the next two hundred years, and developed a flourishing trade with the continent, especially Spain. However, its loyalty to the monarch ensured that when Cromwellian forces arrived in 1652 the place was besieged without mercy for ninety days. The city went into a decline from then, and only recently started to revive.

Arrival and accommodation

The **bus and train stations** are off **Eyre Square**, on the northern edge of the city centre. The **tourist office** (July & Aug daily 9am–7pm; May–June Mon–Sat 9am–6pm; rest of year Mon–Fri 9am–5.45pm, Sat 9am–12.45pm) is off the south side of the square, and has an accommodation service.

You may be met by **hostel** touts at the station; there is decent budget **accommodation** available at the *Arch View Hostel*, Dominick St (☎091/66661; ②), *Corrib Villa*, 4 Waterside (☎091/62892; ②), *Woodquay Hostel*, 23–24 Woodquay (☎091/62618; ②), *Salmon Weir Hostel*, St Vincents Avenue, Woodquay (☎091/61133; ②), and *Galway City Hostel*, 25–27 Dominick St (☎091/66367; ②). There's no shortage of **B&Bs** in the centre, with several in Prospect Hill; try Joan O'Sullivan at no. 46 (☎091/66324; ③), and Brigid Quilter at no. 58 (☎091/61073; ③). There are campsites at *Ballyloughane Caravan Park* on Dublin Rd (April–Sept), and several in Salthill, the pleasantest being *Hunter's Silver Strand*, four miles west on the coast road (April–Sept).

The City

The prosperity of maritime Galway and its sense of civic dignity were expressed in the distinctive town houses of the merchant class, remnants of which are littered around the city, even though recent development is rapidly destroying the character of the place. The **Browne doorway** in Eyre Square is one such monument, a bay window and doorway with the coats of arms of the Browne and Lynch families, dated 1627. Just about the finest medieval town house in Ireland is **Lynch's Castle** in Shop St – along with Quay St, the social hub of Galway. Now housing the *Allied Irish Bank*, it dates from the fifteenth century and has a stone facade decorated with carved panels, gargoyles and a lion devouring another animal.

The city has two churches of interest: the **Collegiate Church of St Nicholas** and the **Cathedral of Our Lady Assumed into Heaven and St Nicholas**. The former, founded in 1320, is the largest medieval church in Ireland. The Cathedral, in hideous contrast, was commissioned about twenty-five years ago by the then Bishop of Galway, Michael (pronounced Me-hile) Brown – hence its nickname, "The Taj Michael". It sits on the banks of the river like a huge toad, its copper dome seeping green slime down the formica-bright limestone walls.

Down by the harbour stands the **Spanish Arch**: more evocative in name than in reality, it's a sixteenth-century structure that was used to protect galleons unloading wine and rum. Next door is housed the uninspiring **Galway Museum** (daily 10am– 1pm & 2.15–8pm; 50p), where the only things of real interest are the old photographs of the Claddagh district of the city.

SALTHILL

To the west of the city lies **SALTHILL**, Galway's seaside resort, complete with amusement arcades, discos, seasonal cafés and a fairground. The huge **Leisureland** amusement complex is used as a venue for big gigs, and also has a swimming pool (daily 10am–1pm & 2.15–8pm; 50p). **Lower Salthill** has a long promenade with a series of safe and sandy beaches, giving a great view over the glittering expanse of water to the Burren. Probably the nicest of the beaches in the vicinity is the small one at **White Strand**, nestling beneath a grassy headland immediately west of Salthill.

Eating, drinking and entertainment

If the "crack" has eluded you so far, this is where you're going to find it. The bars are the lungs of this town, and even the most abstemious travellers are going to find themselves sucked in. You are guaranteed to find music somewhere and similarly there's absolutely no problem finding places to eat. Good-value **pub food** is served around midday at *Naughton's* in Cross St and *MacSwiggan's* in Eyre St. *McDonagh's Seafood Bar* in Quay St is a must for seafood at any time of day, while *Food For Thought* in Lower Abbeygate St and in the back of the tourist office serves very cheap wholefood and vegetarian meals. *Sev'nth Heaven*, in Courthouse Lane, Quay St, serves Tex-Mex, Italian and seafood, while *Fat Freddy's*, Quay St, is a great place for pizzas.

The bars of Shop and Quay Streets offer good traditional-style bars, such as the *Quays Bar* and *Naughtons*; *Roísín Dubh*, in Dominick St, is a lively spot for bands, and on the other side of town, the *Crane Bar* is renowned for its traditional sessions. *Arus na nGael*, Dominick St, is a **club** devoted to traditional music and dance (IR£3 admission in summer, free rest of year). Galway has its fair share of **clubs** and **discos**: the *Warwick Hotel* and *Setanta*, both in Salthill, are a couple of favourites; expect to pay IR£2.50–3.50.

The Aran Islands

The **Aran Islands** – **Inishmore**, **Inishmaan** and **Inisheer** – lying thirty miles out across the mouth of Galway Bay, are spectacular settings for a wealth of pre-Christian and early Christian remains, and some of the finest archeological sites in Europe. And it's not only works in stone that have survived out here: the islands are Gaelic-speaking, and up until the early part of this century their isolation allowed the continuation of a unique, ancient culture.

With the burgeoning fascination for all things Gaelic from the 1890s onwards, the Aran Islands, along with the Blaskets, became the subject of great sociological and linguistic enquiry. In 1934 Robert Flaherty made his classic documentary *Man of Aran*, recording the life he found – the film can be seen every day during the summer in Halla Ronain, Kilronan. While the folklore and traditions in the film have massively declined, fishing and farming remain central to the way of life: look out for **currachs**, the light wood-framed boats still used for fishing and for getting ashore on the smaller islands.

Several **ferry** companies operate to the Aran Islands, a return from Galway or Rossaveal (a one hour and ten minute bus ride out of town) costing around IR£12–15. A couple of companies offer ferry-plus-hostel deals: buy one from *Island Ferries*, Victoria Place, Eyre Square (☎091/61767) if you want to stay at *Mainistir House*, Inishmore; buy one from *Aran Islands Hostel*, Kilronan, Inishmore, or *Dún Aeugus Hostel*, four miles along the island at Kilmurvey. All three islands are accessible all year – though even in summer services to Inishmaan may not operate every day. **Flights** can be booked at the *Aer Árann* desk (☎091/93034) based in the tourist office at IR£33 return, students IR£25. The alternative to the Galway approach is from **Doolin** (see above).

Inishmore

Although **Inishmore** is the most tourist-oriented of the Aran Islands, its wealth of dramatic ancient sites overrides such considerations. It's a long strip of an island, a great tilted plateau of limestone, with a scattering of villages along the sheltered northerly coast. The land slants up to the southern edge, where tremendous cliffs rip along the entire shoreline. As far as the eye can see is a tremendous patterning of stone, some of it the bare pavementing of grey rock split in bold diagonal grooves, gridded by dry-stone walls that might be contemporary, or might be pre-Christian.

The ferry comes in at **KILRONAN**, where the cheapest place to stay is the *Aran Islands Hostel* (April–Sept; ☎099/61255; ②), best booked with your ferry ticket. B&Bs can be booked through the **tourist office**, across the lane from the hostel (June to mid-Sept daily 10am–6pm). Not surprisingly, seafood is the great speciality on the island: *Dun Aonghasa* has probably the most varied menu, and is good value for anything from light snacks up to full meals; *Joe Watty's* bar serves good soups and stews, and *Peig's Café* does tasty seafood platters.

The best ways to **get about** Inishmore are cycling and walking. *Aran* **bicycle hire** is beside the ferry dock; *Costello's Bike Hire* is opposite the *American Bar* further up the lane. If you have limited time, you can take the public minibus up the island through the villages that stretch over seven miles to the west – Mainistir, Eochaill, Kilmurvey, Eoghannacht and Bun Gabhla – and walk back from any point.

Most of Aran's sites are to the northwest of Kilronan. The first hamlet in this direction is Mainistir, from where it's a short signposted walk to the simple twelfth-century church of **Teampall Chiarain**, the most interesting of the ecclesiastical sites on Inishmore. Alongside is **St Kieran's Well**, a long U-shaped spring backed by huge blocks of plant-covered stone. Back on the main road, three miles or so further is Kilmurvey, a fifteen-minute walk from the most spectacular of Aran's prehistoric sites – the fort of **Dun Aengus**. This massive ring fort, lodged on the edge of cliffs that plunge three hundred feet into the Atlantic, has an inner citadel of precise blocks of grey stone, their symmetry echoing the almost geometric regularity of the land's limestone pavementing. Nearby **Dun Eoghanachta** is a huge drum of a fort, a perfect circle of stone settled in a lonely field with the Connemara mountains as a backdrop. It's accessible by tiny lanes from Dun Aengus if you've a detailed map; otherwise retrace your steps to Kilmurvey and follow the road west for just over a mile. At the **seven churches**, just east of Eoghannacht, there are ancient slabs commemorating seven Romans who died here, testifying to the far-reaching influence of Aran's monasteries. The site is, in fact, that of two churches and several domestic buildings, dating from the eighth to the thirteenth centuries, and includes Saint Brendan's grave, adorned by an early cross with interlaced patterns. A two-mile walk **south of Kilronan** brings you to **Dun Ducathair**, the massive remains of a fort straddling an ever-shrinking headland. The eastern gateway fell into the sea early in the last century, leaving the entrance a perilous twelve inches from the sheer drop.

Inishmaan

Coming from Inishmore you are immediately struck by how much lusher **Inishmaan** is, the stone walls forming a maze that chequers off tiny fields of grass and clover. Yet at the same time it's a dour island, where farming is at subsistence level and grim cottages are overhung with soggy thatch. The island's main sight is **Dun Conchuir**: built some time between the first and seventh centuries, its massive oval wall is almost intact, and commands great views. Inishmaan's indifference to tourism means that amenities for visitors are minimal. **B&Bs** are cheaper than on the mainland; try Mrs A. Faherty (**☎**099/73012; ②). If you arrive on spec, ask at the **pub** – a warm and friendly haven, with snacks available during June and August. *An Dún* restaurant (**☎**099/73068; Mon–Sat summer only) serves lunches for around IR£4 and dinners for IR£10. Farmers will let you **camp** if you ask them.

Inisheer

Inisheer, at just under two miles across, is the smallest of the Aran Islands. Tourism has a key role here; Inisheer doesn't have the archeological wealth of Inishmore, or the wild solitude of Inishmaan, but regular day-trip ferry services from Doolin during the summer ensure an increasing flow of visitors.

A great plug of rock dominates the island, its rough, pale grey stone dripping with greenery. At the top, the fifteenth-century **O'Brien's castle** stands inside an ancient ring fort. Set around it are low fields, a small community of pubs and houses, and windswept sand dunes. Half buried in sand just south of the beach is the ancient **Church of St Kevin**, the patron saint of the island. The **tourist office** by the pier (June–Sept daily 10am–7pm) will give you a map and a list of **B&Bs**. There are a couple of **hostels**: *The Bru* (**☎**099/75024; ②), and a second tucked away behind the post office (**☎**099/70577; ②) – look out for the name "Rory" caved on the gate. The first weekend in August and Whit weekend are especially busy, but there is a **campsite** near the pier. Lunches and evening meals are available at *Radharc na Mara* (June–Sept) beside the hotel, and the *Ostan Inis Oirr* hotel (June to mid-Sept; **☎**099/75020). The hotel bar, *Tigh Ruairi*, and *Tigh Ned* have **music** during the summer.

Clifden

The great asset of **CLIFDEN** – known as the capital of Connemara – is its position, perched high above the deep sides of the boulder-strewn estuary of the Owenglin River, with the circling jumble of the Twelve Bens providing a magnificent backdrop. Clifden seems to be trying hard to cultivate the cosmopolitan atmosphere of Galway, and it attracts a fair number of young Dubliners, too, revving up the life of this rural town. There are three *Bus Éireann* services daily from Galway in summer, one daily the rest of the year.

The **tourist office** on Market St (June Mon–Sat 10am–6pm; July & Aug Mon–Sat 9am–6pm) has lists of the plentiful **B&B** accommodation in Clifden, though these can be very busy in July and August. *Corrib House*, Main St (☎095/21346; ②), is the cheapest, and very friendly. Clifden has several **hostels** in Beach Road: *Leo's Hostel* (☎095/21429; ②), the *Clifton Tourist Hostel* (☎095/21076; ②) and *Brookside* (☎095/21812; ②), 300 yards further down, are all decent. *Leo's* also has **camping** facilities.

Mannion's and *E.J. Kings* on Market St are two of the nicest **bars** for drink and music; for evening meals at IR£10 and upwards, try *O'Grady's Seafood Restaurant* or *The Old Skillet*, also in Market St. Clifden is the only real base for getting out into the Connemara countryside, and to do this you really need your own transport. There are plenty of places for **bike rental**: try *Joyce's* on Market St or *John Mannion* on Bridge St.

Westport

Set on the shores of Clew Bay at the end of a rail line from Dublin, the comfortable, relaxed town of **WESTPORT** was planned by the architect James Wyatt, and its formal layout comes as quite a surprise in the midst of the west. The money for Wyatt's scheme came from Westport's trade in linen and cotton, but after the Act of Union of 1801 Irish hand looms could not compete with Britain's industrial mills, and Westport's economy was ruined.

Its quiet Georgian beauties apart, the reason Westport is on the tourist trail nowadays is **Westport House** (Mon–Sat 10.30am–6pm, Sun 2–6pm; house only IR£5, zoo only IR£3, house and zoo IR£5.50), a mile or so out of town towards the bay. Beautifully designed in 1730 by the ubiquitous Richard Castle, this was one of the first Irish houses opened to the public – and unfortunately it's had a go at every way of making money. There's a zoo park in the grounds and horse-drawn caravans for hire, while the dungeons have gimmicks such as a trace-your-ancestor service. Inside the house there's a *Holy Family* by Rubens, a violin which used to belong to J. M. Synge, and, on the first floor, a room with lovely Chinese wallpapers dating from 1780.

For **accommodation**, you've got a choice between two independent **hostels**: the *Granary* on Quay Rd (April–Oct; ☎098/25903; ②), or the *Summerville*, a mile and a half out of town on the Louisburgh road, overlooking the bay (mid-March to mid-Oct; ☎098/25948). There are plenty of **B&Bs** about, too – check at the **tourist office** in the Mall for availability. There's a good wholefood **restaurant** in Bridge St, and another good place to eat at the entrance to Westport House – *Quay Cottage*, which serves enormous salmon salads and plenty of vegetarian food in one of a complex of refurbished waterside buildings brimming with restaurants, pubs and people.

Sligo Town and around

SLIGO, with a population of about eighteen thousand, is, after Derry, the biggest town in the northwest of Ireland and a focal point for the area. During the Famine its population fell by a third through death and emigration, but by the end of the last century things had picked up, and the upswing has continued to the present day.

The thirteenth-century **Dominican Abbey**, the town's main sight, ceased its life as a religious foundation in 1641, when the whole town was sacked. These days it makes a good place to have a picnic, as its walls still stand and the chancel and high altar, with fine carvings, are in a good state of preservation. The **Municipal Art Gallery** (Tues & Fri 10.30am–12.30pm; free), housed in the County Library on Stephen St, possesses a lot of paintings and pencil drawings by Jack Yeats. His work has a strong local flavour, and his later efforts like *The Graveyard Wall* and *The Sea and the Lighthouse* are especially potent evocations of the life and atmosphere of the area. In the same compound as the library but situated just by the entrance gate are the **Sligo County Museum** and **Yeats Memorial Museum** (daily 10.30am–12.30pm & 2.30–4.30pm; free), commemorating W.B. Yeats, not his brother. Memorabilia in the Yeats museum include photographs of his funeral, lots of letters and photos of the man himself, and the Nobel Prize medal awarded him in 1923. Before you rush out, read a bit of the long article on Michael Coleman, one of Ireland's most famous fiddle players; Fritz Kreisler, the greatest of classical violinists, wrote that even he could not attempt the kind of music Michael Coleman played, even if he practised for a thousand years.

Sligo's **tourist office**, on Temple St (July & Aug Mon–Sat 9am–8pm, Sun 10am–2pm; Sept–June Mon–Fri 9am–5pm), is the headquarters for Sligo, Donegal and Leitrim, but has little hard information to give out. In Sligo town itself **B&Bs** are the best option at around IR£10 per person: *Bridge House* on Bridge St is one of the cheaper ones. The town has a couple of **hostels** with beds from about IR£5: the *Yeats County Hostel*, on Lord Edward St (☎071/60241), beside the train station, and the more popular *White House Hostel* (☎071/22030) on Markievicz Rd, which gets overcrowded in the summer. For **bike hire**, try *Raleigh Rent-a-Bike* at the back of the *Silver Swan Hotel* in Wine St.

For **food**, *Kate's Kitchen* on Market St is very good quality and not expensive; *Beezies Dining Salon* at 45 O'Connell St is another place to try. When it comes to **pubs**, Sligo does well. *Hargadon's Pub* on O'Connell St, an exclusively male establishment until ten years ago, is a fine old talking pub, with dark recesses and shut-off rooms, and shelves of nineteenth-century earthenware jugs. *McGlynn's* on Market St is a cosy and usually crowded bar, with frequent **music** sessions. Music cognoscenti should head for the *Trades Club* on Castle St; every Tuesday the best sessions in Sligo take place here.

Drumcliff, Benbulben and Glencar Lough

Heading north from Sligo, bus #290 or #291 will take you to **DRUMCLIFF**, a monastic site probably better known as the last resting place of **W.B. Yeats**. His grave is in the grounds of an austere nineteenth-century Protestant church, within sight of Benbulben, as the poet wished. In 575 Saint Columba founded a monastery here, and you can still see the remants of a round tower on the left of the roadside and a tenth-century high cross – the only one in County Sligo – on the right. Local excavations have turned up a wealth of Iron and Bronze Age remains too.

There are **hostel** facilities at the *Yeats Tavern* (☎071/63117; ②) in Drumcliff, about a hundred yards past the church. It makes the best base for the climb of **Benbulben**, which at 1730 feet is one of the most spectacular mountains in the country, its profile changing dramatically as you round it. Access to its slopes is easy, but avoid it after dark as there are a lot of dangerous clefts.

Just to the east of Drumcliff, set into the back of Benbulben, is **Glencar Lough**, which is reached by bus #125 or #283 from Sligo. For the best of the lake, follow the road around its northern edge until you see the "Waterfall" signpost. From the nearby car park a path leads up to the waterfall itself, which is especially impressive after heavy rain. For an excellent mountain walk, continue along the road to the eastern end of the lake, where a track rises steeply northwards to the **Swiss valley**, a deep rift crowned with silver fir.

Donegal Town

A couple of buses a day connect Sligo to **DONEGAL TOWN**, whose immediate impression will be of traffic jammed around the busy **Diamond**, the old marketplace. Donegal's appeal is as a base from which to explore the stunning coastal countryside – just about the only thing to see here is the well-preserved shell of **Donegal Castle** on Tírchonaill St by the Diamond, a fine example of Jacobean architecture. On the left bank of the River Eske stand the few ruined remains of **Donegal Friary**, while on the opposite bank a woodland path known as the **Lovers Walk** offers wonderful views of stony shoreline, especially in the direction of the Blue Stack Mountains which rise at the northern end of Lough Eske.

There are dozens of **B&Bs** in town, and to avoid a lot of walking it's simplest to call at the **tourist office** on the Quay (May, June & Sept Mon–Sat 10am–1pm & 2–6pm; July & Aug Mon–Sat 9am–8pm). There are also two **hostels**, *Donegal Town Independent Hostel* (☎073/22805; ②) and *An Óige Ball Hill Hostel*, about three miles out on the north side of Donegal Bay (☎073/21174; ②), where you can also **camp**.

Eating places are plentiful: there's excellent fast-food at the *Harbour* opposite the tourist office, and the *Atlantic Café* at the town end of the Derry road is good for a substantial cheap meal. As for **pubs**, the *Old Castle Bar*, next to the castle, is fine for a quiet drink. The *Abbey Hotel* in the Diamond is the only contender for entertainment, with discos and Irish nights. **Bikes** can be hired from *O'Doherty's* on Main St, which is also useful for supplementary information about the region.

Slieve League and Glencolumbcille

To the west of Donegal Town lies one of the most stupendous landscapes in Ireland – the elementally beautiful Teelin Bay and the awesome **Slieve League cliffs**. An ideal base for exploring the region is one of the jolliest independent **hostels** in the country, the *Derrylahan Hostel* (☎073/38079; ②) between Kilcar and Carrick, which also has a campsite. The hostel is passed by the twice-daily bus that runs from Donegal Town to Glencolumbcille via Killybegs.

There are two routes up to the ridge of Slieve League: a back route following the signpost to *Baile Mór* just before you come into Teelin, and the road route from Teelin to Bunglass, which is a thousand sheer feet above the sea. The former route has you looking up continually at the ridge known as One Man's Path, on which walkers seem the size of pins, before the frontal approach swings you up to one of the most thrilling cliff scenes in the world, the **Amharc Mór** (Great View). The sea moves so far below it seems like a film that has lost its soundtrack, and the two-thousand-foot- high face of Slieve League glows with mineral deposits in tones of amber, white and red. On a good day it's possible to see one third of Ireland from the summit.

From Amharc Mór it's possible to walk via Malinbeg and Malinmore to **GLENCOLUMBCILLE** – the Glen of Saint Columbcille, the name by which Columba was known after his conversion. Approaching it by road, you cross a landscape of desolate upland moor, after which the rich verdant beauty of the Glen (as it's invariably known) comes as a welcome shock.

Glencolumbcille village has been a place of pilgrimage since the seventh century AD, in consequence of the time Saint Columba spent in the valley. Every June 9 at midnight the locals commence a three-hour barefoot itinerary of the cross-inscribed slabs that stud the valley basin, finishing up with mass at 3am in the small church. For the rest of the summer, the **Folk Village** next to the beach usually has tourists tripping over one another on the strictly guided tours (Easter–Sept Mon–Sat 10am–8pm, Sun noon–3pm; IR£1.50). There's free access to the **National School** replica and the **Sheebeen** house, where you can sample a taster of seaweed wine and other concoctions.

A path up to the left from the Folk Village leads to the *Dooey Hostel* (☎073/30130; ②) – and campsite – above the strand at the mouth of the valley. From behind the hostel, cliff walks steer off around the south side of the bay above a series of jagged drops. Rising from the opposite end of the valley mouth, the promontory of **Glen Head** is surmounted by a Martello tower. On the way out, you pass the ruins of **St Columbcille's Church**, with its "resting slab" where Saint Columba lay down exhausted from prayer. The place to **eat** in the village is the *Lace House Restaurant* on the main street above the **tourist office**. In summer, one of the nearby pastiche holiday cottages does **B&B**.

NORTHERN IRELAND

Influenced by television reports and coverage in the less than clear-eyed press, a large proportion of outsiders regard Northern Ireland as a place in which sectarian violence is the dominant factor of everyday life. While the security presence is high, you will only encounter significant army and police patrols in certain pressure points such as **Belfast** and **Derry**, cities which both merit a visit. Despite the fact that the North is generally as hospitable as the Republic, it's little frequented by tourists, even though the northern coastline of counties **Antrim** and **Derry** – expecially the weird geometry of the **Giant's Causeway** – is as spectacular as anything you will find in Ireland. Counties Tyrone and Fermanagh form the bulk of inland Northern Ireland; **Tyrone** is largely dull farming country, but **Fermanagh** has at its core the great **Lough Erne**, a huge lake complex dotted with islands and surrounded by richly beautiful countryside. **Enniskillen**, its county town, is resonant with history, as are many of the ancient sites within the waterways of Lough Erne.

Belfast

A quarter of the population of the North live in **BELFAST**, the capital of Northern Ireland, and they grab more than their share of world headlines. The "Troubles" are all too apparent, not least in the plethora of car parking pounds and the prohibition on leaving a car unattended anywhere outside them. Yet normal life continues, albeit in a way that can come as a shock to a newcomer, and the people are strikingly friendly.

Belfast began its life as a cluster of forts built to guard a ford across the River Farset, which nowadays runs beneath the High Street. However, Belfast was very slow to develop, and its history as a city doesn't really begin until 1604, when Sir Arthur Chichester was "planted" in the area by James I. By the eighteenth century the cloth trade and shipbuilding had expanded tremendously, and the population increased tenfold in a hundred years. It was then a city noted for its liberalism. In the 1790s Belfast became the centre of the **United Irishmen**, a gathering embracing Catholics and Protestants on the basis of common Irish nationality, but in the nineteenth century Presbyterian ministers began openly to attack the Catholic church, and the sectarian divide became wider and increasingly violent. Although Partition and the creation of Northern Ireland with Belfast as its capital inevitably boosted the city's status, decline has been fairly constant over recent years. Today the linen industry has disappeared altogether and shipbuilding is rapidly crumbling, but billions of pounds are being poured in from Britain and the European Community in the hope that economic revival might bring with it a more hopeful future.

The Belfast telephone code is ☎0232.

Arrival and information

Flying into Belfast you arrive either at **Belfast International Airport** (☎0649/422888), in Aldergrove, nineteen miles from the city (airport coaches to Great Victoria St Bus Station; £3.50), or less likely at **Belfast Harbour Airport**, four miles out (train from Sydenham Halt to Central Station). Of the **ferries** to Northern Ireland, only *Seacat's*, Stranraer service comes into Belfast Harbour; it's easiest to take a taxi from here, or walk through to Great George St where you can pick up buses to the centre. Other services dock at Larne, twenty miles north, connected by *Ulsterbus* to Great Victoria St and by train with Gate Station. All **trains** except those from Larne arrive at the Central Railway Station on East Bridge St, a little way east of the centre. **Buses** from the west and the Republic arrive at Great Victoria St Bus Station, whereas buses from the north and east use the equally central Oxford St.

The **Northern Ireland Tourist Board** is at 59 North St (Mon–Sat 9am–5pm; summer Mon–Fri 9am–7.30pm, Sat 9am–5pm, Sun 2–4pm; ☎246609). **Bord Fáilte**, for information about the Republic, can be found at 53 Castle St (Mon–Fri 9am–5pm, plus March–Sept Sat 9am–12.30pm; ☎327888). Both agencies operate the *Gulliver* booking system for B&Bs anywhere within Ireland.

Accommodation

Many of Belfast's numerous **B&Bs** are on the south side of the city in the university area – the tourist office can make bookings. The nearest **campsite** to the city centre is the *Belvoir Forest Site*, four miles south, for which you need a permit from the Forest Service (☎520000).

Belfast Youth Hostel, 11 Saintfield Rd (☎647865). Strictly run place with 11.30pm curfew, three miles south of the centre; bus #38 or #84 from Donegall Square East. ②

Botanic Lodge Guest House, 87 Botanic Avenue (☎327682). ③

Eglantine Guest House, 21 Eglantine Avenue (☎667585). ③

YWCA, Queen Mary's Hall, 70 Fitzwilliam St (☎240439). More comfortable than the youth hostel, and more expensive. Takes men as well as women; bus #59 from City Hall. ③

City transport

The excellent *City Bus* service covers nearly everywhere you'll want to go, with *Ulsterbus* serving the outerlying areas. Almost all buses set off from Donegall Square or the streets immediately around. City centre journeys are 65p, or you can get a multi-journey ticket (£4.70 for eight journeys, £6 for unlimited weekly pass) from newsagents and other shops. **Taxis**, based at ranks in Donegall Square and others throughout the city, charge a minimum £1.50.

The City

The **City Hall**, presiding over central **Donegall Square**, is an austere building, its civic purpose almost subservient to its role in propagating the ethics of Presbyterian power. From the main entrance Queen Victoria, portrayed as Empress, gazes maternally across the rooftops towards the Protestant Shankill area. At the northwest corner of the square stands **Linenhall Library** (Mon–Wed & Fri 9.30am–6pm, Thurs 9.30am–8.30pm, Sat 9.30am–4pm), where the Political Collection houses over 40,000 publications dealing with every aspect of Northern Irish political life since 1968. The streets leading north off Donegall Square North take you into the **city centre** proper, an area with little to offer apart from a few necessary amenities. Towards the river, along Ann St and around it, you're in the narrow alleyways known as the **Entries**. There are some great old saloon bars down here, and the docks end of the **High Street** – by the Prince Albert Memorial Clock Tower – is in places redolent of the eighteenth century. The clock tower is a good position from which to view the world's second and third largest cranes, *Goliath* and *Samson*, across the river in the *Harland & Wolff* shipyard where the *Titanic* was built.

North of the clock tower are a series of grand edifices which grew out of a similar civic vanity as that invested in the City Hall. The **Customs House**, a Corinthian-style building, is the first you'll see, but the most monolithic is the Protestant **Cathedral of St Anne** at the junction of Donegall St and York St, a neo-Romanesque basilica started in 1899. Despite a glorious west door it's almost wholly insignificant: were it not for the body of Lord Edward Henry Carson, entombed underneath the nave floor, it would be quite without interest. A Dubliner of Scots-Presbyterian background, Carson took the decision in 1910 to accept the leadership of the opposition to Home Rule, which in effect inextricably allied him to the Ulster Unionist resistance movement and made him a hero to the northern Protestants.

The university area inhabits part of the stretch of **South Belfast** now known as "The Golden Mile", starting at the Opera House on Great Victoria St. It's an area in which you're likely to find yourself spending much of your time, since it's littered with eating places, pubs and bars, B&Bs and guesthouses. Dozens of restaurants have sprung up here in the last five years, the gourmet explosion said to have been triggered by the refurbishment of the grandiose, turn-of-the-century **Opera House** in 1980, which hauls in the spenders from the suburbs.

Among the welter of attractions to be found on the Golden Mile is one of the greatest of the old Victorian **gin palaces**; the *Crown Liquor Saloon*, which has now become a National Trust property but is still open for drinking. Before heading straight into the university quarter, sidestep off Great Victoria St into **Sandy Row**, which runs parallel. A strong working-class, Protestant quarter, with the tribal pavement painting to prove it, it's one of the most glaring examples of Belfast's divided worlds, wildly different from the Golden Mile's cosmopolitan sophistication. Back on the Golden Mile, and just past the southern end of Sandy Row, three church steeples frame the entrance to the university quarter, of which **Queen's University** is the architectural centrepiece, flanked by the most satisfying example of a Georgian terrace in Belfast, University Square.

Just to the side of the University are the verdant **Botanic Gardens**, whose **Palm House** (Mon–Fri 10am–5pm, Sat 1–5pm, Sun 2–5pm; free) was the first of its kind in the world. Also in the Botanic Gardens you'll find the **Ulster Museum** (same hours; free), where the displays run from a dinosaur show, through early Irish Christian jewellery (in replica), local archeological finds, Irish wildlife and minerals, to the untold, chequered history of the post office in Ireland, waterwheels and steam engines. The various art collections are excellent: try the top floor for modern work by Francis Bacon or Henry Moore and, best of all, the Irish artists Louis le Brocquy, Paul Henry and Belfast's own most acclaimed painter, Sir John Lavery. The museum's **Girona exhibition** shows treasures from the Spanish Armada ships which foundered off the Giant's Causeway.

North Belfast's touted attractions amount to an over-restored castle and a **zoo**, next door to one another on the slopes of Cave Hill, out on the Antrim Road (daily 10am–5pm; buses #2, #3, #4, #5 or #6). **Cave Hill** itself is more rewarding: several paths lead up from the castle estate to the summit, where there's an unsurpassable overview of the whole city and lough.

Eating, drinking and entertainment

Belfast is a big city, and it's never hard to keep yourself amused in the evenings. Many of the best places to eat can be found on and around Great Victoria St, which – with the university area – also has the liveliest pubs. As so often in Ireland, the best entertainment you'll find in Belfast is music in the pubs. Some of the main sessions and venues are listed below, but you should look out for posters or check the listings in the *Belfast Telegraph* for up-to-date details.

RESTAURANTS AND CAFÉS

The Archana, Dublin Rd. Cheap Indian restaurant with good lunches.

Chez Delbart, 10 Bradbury Place. French food at good prices, though you often have to queue.

Ciro's Trattoria, Great Victoria St. Italian food in an authentic atmosphere.

Harveys Pizzas, Great Victoria St. Popular pizza joint. Loud, brash and bright.

Manor House, Donegall Pass. Reputed Cantonese fare.

Spuds, Bradbury Place. Arguably the best burgers in town.

PUBS

The Beaten Docket, Great Victoria St. Packed with fashion-conscious youngsters.

The Botanic Inn, Malone Rd. Almost entirely students, and plenty of atmosphere.

The Crown Liquor Saloon, Great Victoria St. The city's most famous pub, decked out like a spa bath, with a good range of Ulster food and Strangford oysters in season.

The Empire, Botanic Avenue. Cellar bar with a boisterous beer-hall feel. Good-value food.

Maddens, Smithfield. Unpretentious and atmospheric pub.

The Morning Star, Pottinger's Entry. Fine old-fashioned bar, busy in the day, quiet at night.

MUSIC

Errigle Inn, 320 Ormeau Road. Traditional sessions on Mon nights.

Kelly's Cellars, 30 Bank St. Folk on Sat afternoons, blues on Sat nights.

The Linenhall, Clarence St. Jazz on Mon, Wed & Sat nights; rock on Thurs.

The Liverpool, Donegall Quay. Traditional sessions on Sun evenings and some Sats.

Listings

Airlines *Aer Lingus*, 46 Castle St (☎245151); *British Airways*, 9 Fountain Centre, College St (☎899131); *British Midland*, Suite 2, Fountain Centre (☎225151).

American Express 9 North St (Mon–Fri 9am–5pm).

Bus information *City Bus* ☎246485; *Ulsterbus* ☎320011.

Car rental *Avis*, Great Victoria St (☎240404).

Exchange *Thomas Cook*, 11 Donegall Place (Mon–Sat 9am–5pm).

Ferries *Seacat* (Belfast–Stranraer) at Belfast Harbour (☎312002); *StenaSealink* (Larne–Stranraer) are on Castle Lane (☎327525); *P&O European Ferries* (Larne–Cairnryan) are based at Larne harbour (☎0574/74321); *Belfast Ferries* (Belfast–Liverpool) are at 47 Donegall Quay (☎326800).

Hospitals Belfast City Hospital, Lisburn Road (☎329241); Royal Victoria, Falls Road (☎240503).

Left luggage Due to security considerations, there is no official place to leave your luggage.

Police Main police station is in North Queen St (☎650222).

Post office General Post Office, Castle Place.

Trains Central Station information ☎230310; Gate Station information ☎741700.

Travel agents *USIT*, 31a Queen St (☎242562).

The Giant's Causeway and Dunluce

Since 1693, when the Royal Geographical Society publicized it as one of the great wonders of the natural world, the **Giant's Causeway** has been a major tourist attraction. Made up of an estimated 37,000 polygonal basalt columns, it's the result of a massive subterranean explosion some sixty million years ago, which stretched from here to Staffa, where it was responsible for the formation of Fingal's Cave. A huge mass of molten basalt spewed out onto the surface and, as it cooled, solidified into what are, essentially, massive crystals. Public transport to and from the Causeway is well organized in summer: the train line from Belfast ends at Portrush, where you can either catch the open-topped bus that originates in Coleraine, or the #172.

The Causeway's **visitor centre** (daily July & Aug 10am–7pm; rest of year 10.30am–5.30pm; closed Jan–March) is not a place to linger unless you're very cold or very wet. There's a paying exhibition that doesn't tell you a great deal, its one interesting exhibit being a tram that used to run between Portrush and the Causeway. Taking the path from the visitor centre brings you to the **Grand Causeway**, where you'll find some of the most spectacular of the blocks, and where most of the crowd lingers. If you push on, though, you'll be rewarded with relative solitude and views of some of the more impressive formations high in the cliffs. One of these, **Chimney Point**, has an appearance so bizarre that it persuaded the ships of the Spanish Armada to open fire on it, believing that they were attacking Dunluce Castle, a couple of miles further west. The **boats** that ply for trade at the Causeway will show you the caves that are inaccessible from land, including Runkerry Cave, an amazing 700 feet long and 60 high.

Dunluce Castle

A couple of miles west of the Causeway – just beyond Portballintrae, where the bus from the Causeway to Bushmills and Coleraine stops – sits sixteenth-century **Dunluce Castle** (Tues–Sat 10am–4/7pm; 70p), the most impressive ruin along this entire coastline. Sited on a fine headland high above a cave, it looks as if it only needs a roof to be perfectly habitable once again. Its history is inextricably linked with that of its original owner, **Sorley Boy MacDonnell**, whose clan ruled northeastern Ulster from Dunluce. English incursions into the area culminated in 1584 when Sir John Perrott besieged Dunluce and forced Sorley Boy to leave the castle. But as soon as Perrott departed, Sorley Boy set about repairing the castle from the proceeds of the salvaged wreckage of the Spanish Armada ship, the *Girona*. Having made his point, Sorley Boy made his peace with the English, and his son was made Viscount Dunluce and Earl of Antrim by James I. In 1639 Dunluce Castle paid the penalty for its precarious position when the kitchen, complete with cooks and dinner, fell off during a storm. Shortly afterwards the MacDonnells moved out.

Derry

Lying at the foot of Lough Foyle, immediately before the border, **DERRY** presents a beguiling picture, the city's two hillsides terraced with pastel-shaded houses punctuated by stone spires. However, the reputation of the North's second city has more to do with its politics than its scenic appeal. Until recently Derry's two-thirds Catholic majority was denied its civil rights by gerrymandering, which ensured that the Protestant minority maintained control of all important local institutions. The situation came to a head after the Protestant Apprentice Boys' March in August 1969, when the RUC attempted to storm the Catholic estates of the Bogside. For several days the area lay in a state of siege and in the mounting tension that ensued, British troops were for the first time widely deployed in the North. On January 31, 1972, the crisis reached a new pitch when British paratroopers opened fire on unarmed civilians, killing thirteen people in what became known as Bloody Sunday. Derry is now greatly changed: violence has receded here in the past five years, and a resurgence of optimism is being felt for the first time since the early 1960s. The entrance routes to the city bear the two different names – "Welcome to Londonderry, an historic city" and "Welcome to Derry, a nuclear free zone" – reflecting the changing sectarian majority on the city council.

The City

The **walls** of Derry – some of the best-preserved defences left standing in Europe – are the starting point for a walkabout of the city, and there are plans for the entire circuit of city walls to be opened to the public in 1994. A mile in length and never higher than a two-storey house, the walls are reinforced by bulwarks, bastions and a parapeted earth rampart as wide as a thoroughfare. Within their circuit, the medieval street pattern has remained, with four gateways – Shipquay, Butcher, Bishop and Ferryquay – surviving from the first construction, in slightly revised form.

You're more than likely to make your approach from the Guildhall Square, once the old quay. Most of the city's cannon are lined up here, between Shipquay and Magazine gates, their noses peering out above the ramparts. A reconstruction of the medieval **O'Doherty Castle** was built here a few years back, and is scheduled to house local history exhibits and act as an interpretive centre.

Turning left at Shipquay Gate into **Bank Place**, access to the wall promenade is pretty immediate and opens up an unhampered stretch that runs nearly to the Ferryquay Gate. On your way around you'll come across a cast-iron cruciform mould of two figures back to back. Several such sculptures have been placed at strategic points on the walls by the English artist Antony Gormley, their gaping eye sockets looking out in diametrically opposite directions from a single body – a frank comment on the city's ideological split.

Between Ferryquay and Bishop's Gate there are two sights of interest: the Protestant cathedral, just within the south section of the walls, and the Fountain, the Protestant enclave immediately outside the same stretch of walls. **St Columb's Cathedral** was built in 1633, the first cathedral to be constructed in the British Isles subsequent to the Reformation. In 1688–89 Derry played a key part in the Williamite victory over the Catholic King James II by holding out against a fifteen-week siege that cost the lives of one quarter of the city's population. The cathedral was used as a battery during the siege, its tower serving as a lookout post; today it provides the best view of the city. The present spire dates from the late Georgian period, its lead-covered wooden predecessor having been stripped to fashion bullets and cannon shot. Inside, flags brought back from various military expeditions give the interior a strong sense of the British realm and its regality. Other things to look out for are the finely sculpted reredos behind the altar, the eighteenth-century bishop's throne, and the window panels showing scenes as diverse as the relief of the city on August 12, 1689, and Saint Columba's mission to Britain.

To reach the **Fountain** area from here you'll first need to pass by the **Courthouse**, built of white sandstone in crude Greek revival style, and then cut down through a passageway tucked into the left of the Bishop Gate arch. The Fountain's political murals include a vast one reading *LONDONDERRY/WESTBANK LOYALISTS/STILL UNDER SIEGE/NO SURRENDER* – a direct reply to the more famous Catholic *FREE DERRY* mural in the Bogside, in the next valley.

Practicalities

The **tourist information** office is situated in Bishop St and contains both a *Bord Fáilte* office and a branch of the Northern Ireland Tourist Board (July–Sept Mon–Sat 9am–8pm, Sun 10am–6pm; Oct–June Mon–Thurs 9am–5.15pm, Fri 9am–5pm). There is a new *YHANI* hostel in the city centre at Oak Grove Manor, 4–6 Magazine St (☎0504/372273; ②). **B&Bs** are fairly thin on the ground within the city itself, but *Clarence House*, 15 Northland Rd (☎0504/265342; ③), has a good range of rooms.

Eating out in the city has improved dramatically over the last few years, though the choice is still not what you would call bewildering. Shipquay St has the widest variety, including *The Gallery*, which does very tasty and reasonably priced home-baked food. Even cheaper are *Anne's Hot Bread Shop* on William St and the very sociable *Leprechaun* on the Strand. For entertainment, the **pubs** once again are the best bet. The student set congregates at the *College Arms* at the bottom of the Rock Road and, of course, in the campus bar in Magee College grounds. Congenial and conversational pubs are: *Badgers Place*, 18 Orchard St, and the *Clarendon Bar*, 44 Strand Rd; livelier pubs are the *Metro*, 3 Bank Place, and the new *Monico*, Custom House St. **Traditional**

music venues that remain are grouped in and around Waterloo St, just outside the northern section of the walls. However, if you go into this area in the evenings, be aware that as a strange face you might not receive the warmest of welcomes. The *Dungloe Bar* in Waterloo St claims to be the most regular music-making place.

Enniskillen and around

ENNISKILLEN – served by regular buses from both Belfast and Dublin – is the only place of any size in Fermanagh, and although you can see all that it has to offer in a day, it makes a good base for wider exploration. The town sits on an island like an ornamental buckle, a narrow ribbon of water passing each side connecting the Lower and Upper Lough complexes. The water loops its way around the core of the town, its glassy surface lending Enniskillen a sense of calm and reflecting the mini-turrets of the **Watergate**. Rebuilt by William Cole, the man to whom the British gave Enniskillen in 1609, the Watergate houses the dull **Fermanagh County Museum** and the **Regimental Museum of the Royal Enniskillen Fusiliers** (both Tues–Fri 10am–1pm & 2–5pm, Mon 2–5pm; May–Sept also Sat & Sun 2–5pm; £1), a proud, polished display of the uniforms, flags and paraphernalia of the town's historic regiments.

Out along the Dublin road stands **Castlecoole**, the eighteenth-century home of the Earls of Belmore (July & Aug daily except Thurs 2–6pm; April, May & Sept open weekends; gardens open all year; £2.30; grounds free). A perfect Palladian building of Portland stone, with an interior of fine plasterwork and superb furnishings, it sits in a beautiful landscaped garden, whose cultivated naturalness reinforced its owners' belief that the harmony of God's creation mirrored that of society.

The **tourist office** is housed in the Lakeland Visitor Centre on Shore Rd, south of the main street (March–Oct Mon–Fri 9am–5/6.30pm; June–Sept also Sat 10am–6pm, Sun 11am–5pm; Nov–Feb Mon–Fri 9am–5pm). The office has comprehensive accommodation lists and will book rooms for a small charge. Alternatively, **B&B** is easily found across the town's western bridges, along the A46 Derrygonnelly road and along the Sligo road. The nearest **hostel** is at Castle Archdale (see below). Currently everybody's favourite place to **eat** is *Franco's* in Queen Elizabeth Rd, the northerly road that runs into East Bridge. A lot of the **bars** along the main street do decent pub food, particularly *The Vintage* and *Pat's Bar*.

Lough Erne

The earliest people to settle in this region lived on and around the two lakes of **Lough Erne**, and many of the islands here are in fact *crannogs* – Celtic artificial islands. Its myriad waterways were impenetrable to outsiders, protecting the settlers from invaders and creating an enduring cultural isolation. Evidence from stone carving suggests that Christianity was accepted far more slowly here than elsewhere: several pagan idols have been found on Christian sites, and the early Christian remains to be found on the islands show strongly the influence of pagan culture.

The easiest place to visit from Enniskillen is **Devenish Island**, two miles downstream from Enniskillen in the south of the Lower Lough – a two-hour **cruise** of Lough Erne, stopping at Devenish for half an hour, is operated by *Erne Tours* from the "Round O" pier, off the Derrygonnelly road, or you can easily rent your own boat to get there. A monastic settlement was founded here by Saint Molaise in the sixth century, and became so important during the early Christian period that it had 1500 novices attached to it. The foundation was plundered by Vikings in the ninth century and again in the twelfth, but continued to be an important religious centre up until the Plantations. It's a delightful setting, not far from the lough shore, and the ruins are considerable, spanning the entire medieval period.

To thoroughly immerse yourself in the beauty of the lough scenery, you could hardly do better than stay in the **hostel** of **Castle Archdale** (☎03656/21588; ②; closed Dec 19–Jan 19), set in a forest park near Lisnarrick on the eastern shore. A bus service runs from Enniskillen to the park once a day except during school holidays; otherwise take one of the buses to Kesh (4 daily at irregular intervals), which will put you down just a mile from the hostel. From near the hostel you can get a ferry to **White Island**, whose ruined abbey bears early Christian carvings that look eerily pagan. Found earlier this century, they are thought to be caryatids – carved supporting columns – from a monastic church of the ninth to eleventh centuries. The most disconcerting statue is the lewd female figure known as a *sheila na gig*, with bulging cheeks, a big grin, open legs and arms pointing to her genitals. This could be a female fertility figure, a warning to monks of the sins of the flesh, or an expression of the demoniacal power of women, designed to ward off evil.

travel details

Trains

Dublin to: Belfast (6 daily; 2hr 15min); Cork (6 daily; 3hr); Galway (4 daily; 3hr); Limerick Junction (8 daily; 1hr 50min); Rosslare (3 daily; 3hr); Sligo (3 daily; 3hr 15min); Waterford (3–5 daily; 2hr 30min).

Belfast to: Derry (6 daily; 2hr 20min); Dublin (6 daily; 2hr); Larne Harbour (every 30min; 45min).

Cork to: Dublin (4–7 daily; 2hr 30min–3hr).

Derry to: Belfast (6 daily; 2hr 20min); Dublin (6 daily; 2hr 20min).

Galway to: Dublin (3–5 daily; 2hr 30min).

Killarney to: Cork (3 daily; 1hr 45min); Dublin (2 daily; 3hr 30min).

Sligo to: Dublin (3 daily; 3hr 20min).

Waterford to: Dublin (3–5 daily; 3hr–3hr 30min).

Westport to: Dublin (3 daily; 3hr 45min).

Buses

Dublin to: Cork (3–4 daily; 4hr 25min); Derry (2–4 daily; 4hr 30min); Donegal (4 daily; 4hr 30min); Galway (7 daily; 3hr 45min); Waterford (2–4 daily; 3hr 45min).

Belfast to: Derry (6 daily; 1hr 30min–3hr); Dublin (4 daily; 4–5hr); Enniskillen (9 daily; 2hr 15min); Galway (4 daily; 6hr 30min); Sligo (1 daily; 4hr).

Cork to: Dublin (6 daily; 4hr 25min).

Derry to: Dublin (4 daily; 4hr 40min); Donegal (3 daily; 1hr 10min); Sligo (3 daily; 2hr 45min).

Donegal to: Dublin (4 daily; 4hr 30min).

Enniskillen to: Belfast (7 daily; 2hr 35min); Dublin (4 daily; 3hr 35min).

Galway to: Dublin (6 daily; 3hr 45min).

Sligo to: Belfast (4 daily; 4hr 10min); Galway (4 daily; 3–5hr).

CHAPTER 13

ITALY

Introduction

Of all the countries in Europe, **Italy** is perhaps the hardest to classify. It is a modern, industrialized nation; it is the harbinger of style, its designers leading the way with each season's fashions. But it is also a Mediterranean country, with all that it implies. Agricultural land covers much of the country, a lot of it, especially in the south, still owned under almost feudal conditions. In towns and villages all over the country, life stops during the middle of the day for a siesta. And it is strongly family-oriented, with an emphasis on the traditions and rituals of the Catholic church. If there is a single national characteristic, it's to embrace life to the full, manifest in the hundreds of local festivals taking place on any given day; in the importance placed on good food; and above all in the daily domestic ritual of the collective evening stroll or *passeggiata*. There is also, of course, the country's enormous cultural legacy: Tuscany alone has more classified historical monuments than any country in the world and every region retains its own relics of an artistic tradition generally acknowledged to be the world's richest.

Italy wasn't a unified state until 1861, something borne out by the regional nature of the place today. The country breaks down into nineteen often very distinct *regione*, but the sharpest division is between north and south. The north is one of the most advanced industrial societies in the world; the south, known as *il mezzogiorno*, is by contrast one of the economically most depressed areas in Europe. In the **northwest**, the regions of **Piemonte** and **Lombardy** – and the two main centres of Turin and Milan – epitomize the wealthy north. **Liguria**, the small coastal province to the south, has long been known as the "Italian Riviera" and is accordingly crowded with sun-seeking holidaymakers for much of the summer season. But it's a beautiful stretch of coast, and its capital, Genoa, is a bustling port with a long seafaring tradition. The interest of the **northeastern** regions of the **Veneto** and **Friuli-Venezia Giulia** is of course Venice itself, a unique city, and every bit as beautiful as its reputation would suggest – though this means you won't be alone in appreciating it. If the crowds are too much, there's also the arc of historic towns outside the city – Verona, Padua and Vicenza. To the south, the region of **Emilia-Romagna** has been at the heart of Italy's

postwar industrial boom. Its coast is popular among Italians, Rimini Italy's brashest seaside resort; and there are also the ancient centres of Ravenna, Ferrara, Parma and Bologna, the capital – one of Italy's liveliest but least appreciated cities. **Central Italy** perhaps represents the most commonly perceived image of the country, and **Tuscany**, with its classic rolling countryside and the art-packed towns of Florence, Pisa and Siena, is one of its most visited regions. Neighbouring **Umbria** is similar in all but its relative emptiness, though it gets fuller every year, as visitors flock into towns such as Perugia, Spoleto and Assisi – and unspoilt Urbino in adjacent **Marche**. **Lazio**, to the west, is a poor and desolate region whose real focal point is **Rome**, Italy's capital, the one city in the country which owes allegiance neither to the north nor south. Beyond Rome, Naples, capital of **Campania**, a petulant, unforgettable city, is the spiritual heart of the Italian **South**, and is close to some of Italy's finest ancient sites in Pompeii and Herculaneum, not to mention its most spectacular stretch of coast around Amalfi. **Puglia**, the "heel" of Italy, has underrated pleasures, notably the souk-like quality of its capital, Bari. As for **Sicily**, the island is really a law unto itself, a wide mixture of attractions ranging from some of the finest preserved Hellenistic treasures in Europe, to the drama of Mount Etna and one of the country's fanciest beach resorts in Taormina. **Sardinia**, too, feels far removed from the mainland, especially in its relatively undiscovered interior, though you may be content to just explore its fine beaches.

Information and Maps

Most Italian towns, major train stations and airports have a **tourist office** – usually either an *APT* (*Azienda Promozione Turistica*), an *EPT* (*Ente Provinciale per il Turismo*), a provincial branch of the state organization, an *IAT* (*Ufficio di Informazione e Accoglienza Turistica*) or an *AAST* (*Azienda Autonoma di Soggiorno e Turismo*), a smaller local outfit. Very small or out-of-the-way villages may have a tiny office known as a *Pro Loco*. All offer much the same mix of general advice and bumph, free maps and accommodation lists, though rarely do they book accommodation. Opening hours vary, but larger city offices are likely to be open Mon–Sat 9am–1pm & 4–7pm, and sometimes for a short period on Sunday mornings; smaller offices may open weekdays only.

Most tourist offices will give out **maps** of their local area for free, but if you want an indexed town plan, *Studio FMB* cover the country's towns and cities; *Falk* also sell decent plans of the major cities. For road maps, the *Automobile Club d'Italia* issue a reasonable free map, available from the State Tourist Office; the clearest and best-value large-scale commercial road map of Italy is the *Michelin* 1:1,000,000, or you have the choice between the *TCI* 1:800,000 *North* and *South* maps. *Michelin* also produce 1:400,000 maps of the north and south, as well as Sicily and Sardinia, and *TCI* do maps of the individual regions, scale 1:200,000.

Money and Banks

The Italian unit of **currency** is the *Lira* (plural *Lire*), abbreviated as L. Notes come in denominations of L1000, L2000, L5000, L10,000, L50,000 and L100,000, and coins of L50, L100, L200 and L500. The best place to change money or travellers' cheques is at a **bank**; hours are normally Mon–Fri 8.30am–1pm, and an hour in the afternoon (usually 3–4pm), though there are local variations on this. Outside banking hours, the larger hotels will change money and travellers' cheques, but if you stay in a reasonably large city the rate is invariably better at the train station exchange bureaux – normally open evenings and weekends.

Communications

Post office opening hours are usually Mon–Sat 8am–6.30pm; smaller towns won't have a service on a Saturday. If you want **stamps**, you can also buy them in *tabacchi*.

Public **telephones**, run by *SIP*, the state telephone company, come in various forms. For the most common type, you'll need L100, L200 or L500 coins, or a token known as a *gettone* (L200), available from *SIP* offices, *tabacchi*, bars and some newsstands and normally used for local calls. Other phones take *carte telefoniche* (telephone cards), available from *tabacchi* and newsstands for L5000 or L10,000. If you can't find a phone box, bars will often have a phone you can use, though these tend only to take *gettoni*. Alternatively, *SIP* (and sometimes the *AAST*) have offices where you can make a metered-call from a kiosk.

Getting Around

The easiest way of travelling around Italy is by train. The Italian train system is relatively inexpensive, reasonably comprehensive, and in the north of the country at least, fairly efficient – far preferable to the fragmented and sometimes grindingly slow buses.

■ Trains

Apart from a few private lines, Italian trains are operated by Italian State Railways, *Ferrovie dello Stato* (*FS*). There are six types of **train**. At the top of the range is the *ETR 450 Pendolino*, an exclusively first-class inter-city service whose ticket prices include reservation, newspapers and a meal. *Eurocity* trains connect the major Italian cities with centres such as Paris, Vienna, Hamburg and Barcelona, while *Intercity* trains link the major Italian centres; reservations are obligatory on both services, and a supplement of around 30 percent of the ordinary fare is payable. *Espresso* are long-distance expresses stopping at most major station, and *Diretto* routes stop at most stations; a *Locale* stops just about everywhere and is usually worth avoiding. In summer it's often worth making a seat reservation on the main routes. Fares are very reasonable, calculated by the kilometre and thus easy to work out for each journey. The single second-class fare from Milan to Bari, one of the longest journeys you're ever likely to make, currently costs about L60,000.

As with most other European countries, you can cut costs greatly by using a **rail pass**. *InterRail* and *Eurail* passes give free travel on the whole *FS* network (though you'll be liable for supplements on the fast trains), and there are specific Italian passes available. A *Euro-Domino* pass can benefit travellers from the UK with 3 days of unlimited travel for £100, 5 days for £124 or 10 days for £208. The *Biglietto Turistico Libera Circolazione* entitles you to unlimited travel on the entire network, including *Intercity* services, and for 8 days costs £88/$140, for 13 costs £110/$172, for 21 costs £126/$198, and for 30 costs £152/$240. The *Flexi-Card* is similarly valid for all trains and gives 4 days travel out of any 9 days for £66/$105, 8 days in 21 for £94/$150, and 12 in 30 for £120/$190. A *Chilométrico* ticket, valid for up to five people at once, gives 3000km worth of free travel on a maximum of 20 separate journeys and costs £90/$150. Under-26s can also buy a *Cartaverde*, which for L40,000 entitles you to 20 percent off train fares for a year; its available from any main train station in Italy. Stations also issue the *Cartargento* for people over 60, which has the same validity and price but gives a 30 percent discount. Children aged 4–12 qualify for a 50 percent discount on all journeys.

■ Buses

Almost everywhere is connected by some kind of **bus** service, but schedules can be sketchy, and are drastically reduced – sometimes non-existent – at weekends. Bear in mind also that in rural areas timetables are often designed with the working or school day in mind, making for some frighteningly early starts and occasionally no buses at all during school holidays. Even if there are plentiful buses, bear in mind that the journey will be long and full of stops and starts. Bus terminals can be anywhere in larger towns, though often they're next door to the train station. You buy tickets on the bus, though on longer hauls you can try to buy them in advance direct from the bus company; seat reservations are, however, not possible.

■ Driving and hitching

Travelling **by car** in Italy is relatively painless. The roads are good, the motorway or *autostrada* network very comprehensive, and the notorious Italian drivers rather less erratic than their reputation suggests. Most motorways are toll-roads, but rates aren't especially high: as a general reference, you'll pay just over L15,000 for a small car from Milan to Bologna. As for documentation, bringing your own car you need a valid driving licence plus an Italian translation (available from the State Tourist Office), and an International Green Card of insurance. You drive on the right, and at junctions give precedence to vehicles coming from the right. Speed limits are 50kph in built-up areas, 110kph on main roads and on motorways during the week, 130kph on motorways at weekends. If you break down, dial ☎116 and the nearest office of the *Automobile Club d'Italia* (*ACI*) will be informed.

Car rental in Italy is pricy, currently around £200 a week for a small car with unlimited mileage. Italy is also one of the most expensive countries in Europe in which to buy petrol, though if you take your own car you're entitled to petrol coupons giving a 15 percent discount and concessions on the motorway tolls; information from the State Tourist Office.

Hitchhiking is possible in Italy, though less practised in the south of the country. Getting around exclusively by hitching would be a chore, but for the odd short hop along a quiet country road, and for long hauls between major cities, it's a feasible alternative. Remember that it's illegal to hitch on motorways.

Accommodation

Accommodation in Italy is never especially cheap, but it is at least fairly reliable: hotels are star-rated and required to post their prices clearly in each room. Most tourist offices have details of hotel rates in their town or region, and you can usually expect them to be broadly accurate. In the major cities and resorts, booking ahead is often a good idea, particularly during July or August.

One peculiar Italian institution is the confusingly named *albergo diurno* or day hotel, an establishment providing bathrooms, showers, hairdressers and the like – but no accommodation. You'll often find them at train stations and they're usually open daily 6am–midnight – useful for a fast clean-up if you're on the move.

■ Hotels

Hotels in Italy come with a confusing variety of names. *Locanda* are historically the most basic option, although the word is sometimes used to denote something quite fancy these days; *pensione* too can be little differentiated from regular *alberghi* or hotels. Prices do vary greatly between the poor south and the wealthy north, but on average, you can expect to pay L40–50,000 for a double without private bathroom in a one-star hotel, and L50–60,000 with private facilities. Two-star hotels normally cost L60–80,000 a double, and with a three-star you begin to notice a difference, though you'll be paying a minimum of L100,000 a double, but rooms will have private bathrooms, and often TV and telephone as well. In very busy places it's not unusual to have to stay for a minimum of three nights, and many proprietors will add the price of breakfast to your bill whether you want it or not; try to resist this – you can eat more cheaply in a bar. Whatever happens, establish the full price of your room before you accept it.

■ Hostels and student accommodation

There are around 50 **youth hostels** in Italy, charging an average L16,000 for a dorm bed for

IYHF members, and if you're two people travelling together, they don't represent a massive saving on the cheapest double hotel room. Whether or not you're a member, you'll need to book ahead in the summer months. You can get a full list of Italian youth hostels from the *Associazione Italiana Alberghi per la Gioventù*, Via Cavour 44, 00184 Roma (☎06/487.1152). In some cities it's also possible to stay in **student accommodation** vacated by Italian students for the summer. Accommodation is generally in individual rooms and can work out cheaper than a straight hotel room. Again, you'll need to book in advance.

■ Campsites

Camping is not really as popular in Italy as it is in some other European countries, but there are plenty of sites, and most of them are well-equipped. The snag is that they're expensive, and, once you've added the cost of a tent and vehicle, don't always work out a great deal cheaper than staying in a hostel. Prices are around L6000–9000 per person daily, plus L8000–12,000 for a caravan or tent, around L5000 for a vehicle. If you're camping extensively it might be worth investing in the *TCI*'s *Campeggi e Villaggi Turistici* or the free abridged version from *Centro Internazionale Prenotazioni*, *Federcampeggio*, Castella Postale 23, 50041 Calenzano, Florence (☎055/882.391).

Food and Drink

Though it has long been popular primarily for its cheapness and convenience, Italian food is finally beginning to wrest some of the attention it deserves as one of the world's great cuisines. Indeed, there are few national cuisines that can boast so much variety in ingredients and cooking methods. Wine, too, is becoming more respected, as the Italian industry's devotion to fizzy pop and characterless plonk is replaced by a new pride and a better product.

■ Food

Most Italians start their day in a bar, their **breakfast** consisting of a coffee with hot milk, a *cappuccino*, and a *cornetto* – a jam, custard or chocolate-filled croissant. At other times of day, **sandwiches** (*panini*) can be pretty substantial. There are sandwich bars in larger towns and cities (*paninoteche*), and in smaller places grocer's shops (*alimentari*) will normally make you up whatever you want for about L2000–L4000 a sandwich. Bars may also offer *tramezzini*, ready-made sliced white bread with mixed fillings – less appetizing than the average *panino* but still tasty, and slightly cheaper at around L1500 a time. You can get hot takeaway food in a **távola calda**, a snack bar that sometimes has limited seating. The bigger towns have these, and there's often one inside larger train stations. Try also a **rosticceria**, serving spit-roast chicken, slices of pizza, chips and burgers. Italian **ice cream** (*gelato*) is justifiably famous: a cone (*un cono*) is an indispensable accessory to the evening *passeggiata*. Most bars have a fairly good selection, but for real choice go to a **gelateria**.

As for **sit-down food**, the cheapest thing you can eat is **pizza**. This is now a worldwide phenomenon but Italy remains the best place to eat it – thin and flat, and, if you're lucky, cooked in the traditional way in wood-fired ovens. **Pizzerias** range from stand-up counters selling slices (*pizza al taglio*) to fully-fledged restaurants. A basic cheese and tomato pizza (*margherita*) costs around L4000–6000, a fancier variety L6000–10,000. Full meals are generally served in a **trattoria** or a **ristorante**. Traditionally, a trattoria is a cheaper purveyor of home-style cooking, a ristorante more upmarket, though these days there's a fine line between the two. In either, pasta dishes go for around L5000–8000, and there's never any problem just having this; the main fish or meat courses will normally be L10,000–15,000. Bear in mind that almost everywhere you'll pay a cover charge on top of your food – the *pane e coperto* – of around L2000 a head. Watch out when ordering fish, which will either be served whole or by weight: 250g is usually plenty for one person. Vegetables or salads – *contorni* – are ordered separately: potatoes will invariably be chips, salads either green (*verde*) or mixed (*mista*). Afterwards you nearly always get a choice of fresh fruit (*frutta*) or a selection of desserts (*dolci*). At the **end of the meal** ask for the bill (*il conto*). As well as the cover charge, service (*servizio*) will often be added, generally about 10 percent. If service isn't included you should tip about the same amount, though trattorias outside the large cities won't necessarily expect this.

■ Drink

Although many Italian children are brought up on wine, there's not the same emphasis on dedicated drinking as there is in Britain or the US. **Bars** are less social centres than functional places for a quick coffee or beer. You pay first at the cash desk (*la cassa*), present your receipt (*scontrino*) and give your order. It's customary to leave an extra L50 or L100 on the counter for the barperson, though no one will object if you don't. Bear in mind that sitting down sometimes costs twice as much, especially if you sit outside. **Coffee** is always excellent, small and black (*espresso*, or just *caffè*), or white and frothy (*cappuccino*); try also a *granita* – cold coffee with crushed ice, usually topped with cream. If you don't like coffee, **tea** (*te*) comes with lemon (*con limone*) unless you ask for milk (*con latte*); it's also served cold (*te freddo*). As for **soft drinks**, a *spremuta* is a fresh fruit juice; there's also crushed-ice fruit *granitas*, and the usual range of fizzy drinks and concentrated juices.

    Beer (*birra*) usually comes in one-third or two-third litre bottles. Commonest and cheapest are the Italian brands, *Peroni* and *Dreher*, both of which are very drinkable; in most bars you have a choice of this or draught beer (*alla spina*). All the usual **spirits** are on sale and known mostly by their generic names, as well as Italian brandies like *Stock* and *Vecchia Romagna*. A generous shot of these costs about L2000, more for imported stuff. There's also *grappa*, made from

the leftovers from the wine-making process and something of an acquired taste. You'll also find **fortified wines** like *Martini*, *Cinzano* and *Campari* and a daunting selection of **liqueurs**. *Amaro* is a bitter after-dinner drink, *Amaretto* much sweeter with a strong taste of marzipan, *Sambuca* a sticky-sweet aniseed concoction. **Wine** is invariably drunk with meals, and is still very cheap. If you're unsure about what to order, don't be afraid to try the local stuff: sometimes served straight from the barrel, particularly down south, and often very good for just L5000 a litre. Bottled wine is pricier but still good value; expect to pay around L10,000 a bottle in a restaurant, less than half that from a shop or supermarket.

Opening Hours and Holidays

Most **shops and businesses** in Italy open Monday to Saturday from 8 or 9am until around 1pm, and from about 4pm until 7pm or 8pm, though in the north offices work to a more standard European 9am–5pm day. Everything, except bars and restaurants, closes on Sunday, though you might find fish shops in some coastal towns and *pasticcerias* or bakers open until Sunday lunchtime. Most **churches** open early morning and close around noon, opening again at 4pm until 7pm or 8pm. **Museums** generally open Tuesday to Saturday from 9am until 2pm, and from 9am to 1pm on Sunday, and are closed on Mondays. Most archeological sites open every day, 9am until late evening – usually one hour before sunset. Everything closes on the following **national holidays**: Jan 1; Jan 6; Easter Monday; April 25; May 1; Aug 15; Nov 1; Dec 8; Dec 25 & 26.

Emergencies

Despite what you hear about the Mafia, most of the **crime** you're likely to come across in Italy is of the small-time variety, prevalent in the major cities and the south of the country, where gangs of *scippatori* operate, snatching handbags, wallets, jewellery, etc. You can minimize the risk of this by being discreet, not flashing anything of value, keeping a firm hand on your camera and bag, and never leaving anything valuable in your car. If it comes to the worst, you'll be forced to have some dealings with the **police**. In Italy these come in many forms: the *Polizia Urbana/Vigili*

Urbani are mainly concerned with directing the traffic and punishing parking offences; the *Polizia Stradale* patrol motorways; the *Carabinieri*, with their military-style uniforms and white shoulder belts, deal with general crime, public order and drug control; and the *Polizia Statale* are the branch you'll perhaps have most chance of coming into contact with, since it's to them that thefts should generally be reported.

If you need medical treatment, Italian **pharmacies** (*farmacia*) are well-qualified to give you advice on minor ailments, and to dispense prescriptions, and there's generally one open all night in the bigger towns and cities. They work on a rota system; you'll find the address of the nearest open one on any *farmacia* door. If you are more seriously ill, call an ambulance or go to the *Pronto Soccorso* (casualty) section of the nearest hospital.

EMERGENCY NUMBERS
Police ☎112; Ambulance ☎113; Fire ☎115.

THE NORTHWEST

The **northwest** of Italy is many people's first experience of the country, and in many ways represents its least "Italian" corner, at least in the regions of **Piemonte** and **Val d'Aosta**, where French is still spoken by some as a first language. **Turin**, on the main rail and road route from France to Milan, is the obvious first stop, and the one place in the region that repays a lengthy visit, the first capital of Italy after the Unification in 1860 and a grand city with many remnants of its past as seat of the Savoy dukes, later the Italian royals. To the east, **Lombardy** was long viewed by northerners as the heart of Italy – emperors from Charlemagne to Napoléon came to Lombardy to be crowned – and northern European business magnates continue to take its capital, Milan, more seriously than Rome, the region's big businesses and banks wielding political as well as economic power across the nation. Lombardy's landscape has paid the price for economic success: industry chokes the peripheries of towns and even spreads its polluting tentacles into the northern lakes and mountain valleys. Nonetheless, Lombardy has its attractions. **Milan** is a natural gateway to the region, an upbeat city with plenty to see, dominating the plain that forms the southern part of Lombardy, the towns of which – for example, **Mantua** – flourished during the Middle Ages and Renaissance, and retain their historical character today. To the north, the lakes and low mountains shelter fewer historic towns, though **Brescia** and especially **Bergamo** are notable exceptions. The region of **Liguria** to the south provides light relief, an unashamedly touristy strip, and perhaps the country's most spectacular stretch of coastline. Chief town of the province is the sprawling port of **Genoa**, west of which the **Riviera del Ponente** is one long ribbon of hotels, though **Finale Ligure** is a pleasant resort. Southeast, towards Tuscany, the **Riviera del Levante** is more rugged, its mix of mountains and fishing villages "discovered" by the Romantics in the late eighteenth century, preparing the way for the first package tourists earlier this century. Now the whole area explodes into a ruck every July and August, with people coming to resorts like **Portofino** strictly for pose value – although stretches like the **Cinque Terre** are still well worth discovering.

Turin

"Do you know Turin?" wrote Nietzsche, "It is a city after my own heart . . . a princely residence of the seventeenth century, which has only one taste giving commands to everything, the court and its nobility. Aristocratic calm is preserved in everything: there are no nasty suburbs." Although **TURIN**'s traffic-choked streets are no longer calm, and its suburbs, built by the vast Fiat empire that virtually owns the city, are as nasty as any in Italy, the city centre's gracious Baroque avenues, opulent palaces, sumptuous churches and splendid collections of Egyptian antiquities and Northern European paintings are still here – a pleasant surprise to those who might have been expecting satanic factories and little else.

> The Turin area telephone code is ☎011.

Arrival and accommodation

Turin's main **train station**, Porta Nuova, is on Corso Vittorio Emanuele, at the foot of Via Roma, convenient for the city centre and hotels. There are two **tourist offices** – the main one at Via Roma 226 (Mon–Sat 9am–7pm) and a smaller one at the train station. Many of Turin's **cheap hotels** are in the sleazy quarter off Via Nizza, convenient enough but not an advisable choice for solo women. Somewhat safer, but more expensive, are the streets opposite Porta Nuova, close to Piazza Carlo Felice. There are also a number of fairly reasonably priced hotels just west of Piazza Castello. As for specific **hotels**, the *Bellavista*, Via Galliari 15 (☎668.7989; ⑤), does doubles without bath, as does the *Castagnole*, Via Berthollet 3 (☎669.8678; ④), recently refurbished and extremely clean. The *Lagrange*, Piazza Lagrange 1, just off Piazza Carlo Felice (☎538.861; ④), is good value and has a motherly owner. A little cheaper, the *Lux*, Via Galliari 9 (☎657.257; ④), is a seedy hotel, but by no means the seediest in the area. The **youth hostel** is at Via Alby 1 (☎660.2939; ②) – take bus #52 from Corso Vittorio Emanuele. If you're **camping**, the *Riviera sul Po* is the most convenient site, on the far side of the river south of the youth hostel – bus #67 from Corso Vittorio Emanuele.

The City

The grid street-plan of Turin's Baroque centre makes finding your way about easy. **Via Roma** is the city's central spine, a grand affair lined with designer shops and ritzy cafés and punctuated by the city's most elegant piazzas, most notably **Piazza San Carlo**, a little way north of Porta Nuova station – known with some justification as the parlour of Turin. This is a grand and stylish open space, flanked with symmetrical porticoed buildings housing opulent cafés and centring on an equestrian statue of the Savoy Duke, Emanuele Filiberto, its entrance guarded by the twin Baroque churches of **San Carlo** and **Santa Cristina**, whose languishing nude statues represent Turin's two rivers – the Po and the Dora. Around the corner, the **Museo Egizio** (Tues–Sun 9am–2pm; L10,000) holds a superb collection of Egyptian antiquities, gathered together in the late eighteenth century under the aegis of Carlo Emanuele III. There are gorgeously decorated mummy cases, an intriguing assortment of everyday objects and, the undoubted highlight, the Tomb of Kha, the burial chamber of a 1400 BC architect, Kha, and his wife Merit, discovered in 1906 at Deir-el-Medina. Above the museum, the **Galleria Sabauda** (Tues–Sun 9am–2pm; L6000) was built around the Savoys' private collection and is still firmly stamped with their taste – a miscellany of Italian paintings, supplemented by a fine Dutch and Flemish collection, including works by Memling, Bruegel, David Teniers Jnr and Van Dyck. Almost opposite, the **Museo del Risorgimento** (Tues–Sat 9am–6.30pm, Sun 9am–12.30pm; L5000, free Sun), housed in the double-fronted **Palazzo Carignano**, birthplace of Vittorio Emanuele II, is worth a brief visit even if you usually give such things a miss. The first meetings of the Italian parliament were held in the palace's circular chamber and the building was the power base of leaders like Cavour, who ousted the more radical Garibaldi – shown here as a scruffy, long-haired revolutionary – to an early retirement on the island of Caprera near Sardinia. The residence of Vittorio Emanuele II, the **Palazzo Reale** (tours Tues–Sun 9am–2pm; L6000) at the head of the traffic-choked **Piazza Castello**, wouldn't have impressed Garibaldi, with its comical collections of chinoiserie and vulgar Meissen porcelain – not to mention the seventeenth-century church of **San Lorenzo** behind, scalloped with chapels, and lined with multicoloured marble, frescoes and stucco festoons. Really, you'd do better to save your energy for a visit to the **Palazzo Madama**, across the square from the Palazzo Reale – an altogether more appealing building with an ornate Baroque facade by the early eighteenth-century architect, Juvarra. Inside, the originally fifteenth-century palace incorporates parts of a thirteenth-century castle and a Roman gate. Opposite is the **Armeria Reale** (Wed, Fri & Sat 9am–2pm, Tues & Thurs 2.30–7.30pm; L6000), a collection of armour and weapons spanning seven centuries and several continents started by King Carlo Alberto in 1837.

Around the corner from the Palazzo Reale, the otherwise dull fifteenth-century **Duomo** houses what has been called "the most remarkable forgery in history" – the **Turin Shroud**, a piece of cloth imprinted with the image of a man's body that has been claimed as the shroud in which Christ was wrapped after his crucifixion. One of the most famous medieval relics, it made world headlines in 1989 after carbon-dating tests concluded it was a fake, made between 1260 and 1390 – although no one is any the wiser about how the medieval forgers actually managed to create the image. You can't see the shroud itself, just a photographic reproduction; the actual shroud is kept in a locked chapel. Beyond the Duomo, the massive **Piazza della Repubblica** is another Juvarra design, though his grand plan for it is marred nowadays by seedy market buildings. The scruffy porticoes of Via Po lead down to the river, ending just before the bridge in the vast arcaded **Piazza Vittorio Veneto**. Along the river from here, the massive **Parco del Valentino** is one of Italy's largest parks, home to the **Castello e Borgo Mediovale** (Tues–Sat 9.30am–5pm, Sun 10.30am–5pm; L6000, free Fri), a synthesis of the best houses and castles of Piemonte and Val d'Aosta, built with the same materials and techniques as the originals. Further south still, the **Museo dell'Automobile** at Corso Unità d'Italia 40 (Tues–Sun 10am–6.30pm; L8000; bus #1 or #35 from Via Nizza) traces the development of the motor car, with one of the first Fiats, a bulky 1899 model, the gleaming *Isotta Franchini* driven by Gloria Swanson in *Sunset Boulevard*, and, the pride of the collection, the 1907 *Itala* which won the Peking to Paris race in the same year.

Outside the city centre, the grandiose Baroque **Basilica di Superga** gives fine views across the city to the Alps (tram #15 followed by a shuttle bus). In 1706 King Vittorio Amadeo climbed the hill in order to study the positions of the French and Spanish armies who had been besieging the city for four months, vowing that he would erect a temple to the Madonna here if aided in the coming battle. Turin was spared, and the king immediately set Juvarra to work, producing the circular basilica you see today – though many Torinese come here not to pay homage to the Virgin, nor even to the splendid tombs of the Savoys, but to visit the tomb of the 1949 Torino football team, all of whom were killed when their plane crashed into the side of the hill. The other nearby attraction is the Savoys' luxurious hunting lodge, **La Palazzina di Caccia di Stupinigi** (Tues–Thurs, Sat & Sun 10–11.50am & 3–5.30pm; L8000), out to the west of the city beyond the bleak Mirafiori suburbs. This is another Juvarra creation and perhaps his finest work, a symmetrical fantasy with a generous dash of Rococo, built in the 1730s. To get here, take bus #41 from Corso Vittorio Emanuele. Much of the exterior of the palace is rather the worse for wear, but the interior is as luxurious as it ever was, the most extravagant room, the oval Salone Centrale, a dizzying triumph of optical illusion that merges fake features with real in a superb trompe l'oeil. Other rooms are decorated with hunting motifs: Diana, goddess of hunting, bathes on bedroom ceilings, hunting scenes process across walls, and even the chapel is dedicated to Saint Hubert, patron saint of the hunt.

Eating, drinking and nightlife

There are **snack bars** and takeaways on Via Nizza, some tempting delicatessens on Via Lagrange and a superb *rosticcerie* on Corso Vittorio Emanuele for do-it-yourself lunches. *Cossolo*, Via Roma 68, does great pastries, sandwiches and other snacks. *AGM 1*, Via Lagrange 43b, is a cheap and functional self-service, and there's a branch of the quality self-service chain, *Brek*, at Piazza Carlo Felice 22. For more substantial **meals**, *Trattoria Toscana*, Via Rattazzi 5 (closed Sat), serves good food at moderate prices, as does *La Magnolia*, Via Mercanti 6 (closed Mon). *Giappone*, Via Galliari 16 (closed Wed & Thurs am), is a tiny trattoria packed with locals, and *Mamma Licia*, via Mazzini 50 (closed Mon), has good home-made food. Make sure you at least look in on one of the city's *fin-de-siècle* cafés, most of which have an atmosphere that more than compensates for the steep prices. In *Baratti* and *Milano*, on Piazza Castello, genteel Torinese sip tea in a rarefied ambience of mirrors, chandeliers and carved wood. The glitzy *Caffè San Carlo*, on Piazza San Carlo, is reputedly a favoured hang-out of politicians and industrialists. *Fiorio*, Via Po 8, was once the haunt of Cavour, and is now visited mostly for its ice cream. Later on in the evening, *ragazzi* hang out along Via Carlo Alberto, Via San

Quintino and Corso Matteotti. Otherwise try *Doctor Sax*, Mura di Lungo Po Cadorna 4, a *birreria* with music (jazz, Afro and rock), or *The Black Cat*, Via Pacchiotti 61, the most famous music place with blues, country and jazz; *La Divina Commedia*, Via San Donato 47, is another *birreria* on three floors with frequent gigs.

Milan

The dynamo behind the country's economic miracle, **MILAN** is a city like no other in Italy. It's foggy in winter, muggy in summer, and is closer in outlook as well as distance to London than Palermo, a fast-paced business city in which consumerism and the work ethic rule. Because of this most people pass straight through, and if it's summer and you're keen for sun and sea this might well be best. But at any other time of year it's worth giving Milan a bit more of a chance. It's a historic city, with enough churches and museums to keep you busy for a week, much of the city a testament to the prestige-building of the Visconti dynasty and their successors, the Sforzas, who ruled here in Renaissance times; and the contemporary aspects of the place represent the leading edge of Italy's fashion and design industry, not to mention a nightlife scene which is perhaps Italy's most varied.

> The Milan area telephone code is ☎02.

Arrival, information and city transport

Most international **trains** pull in at the monumental Stazione Centrale, northeast of the centre on Piazza Duca d'Aosta, on metro lines 2 and 3 (MM2 or MM3). International and long-distance **buses** arrive at and depart from Piazza Castello, in front of the Castello Sforzesco. Of Milan's two **airports**, Linate is the closer, 7km from the city centre, and connected with the airport bus terminal at Stazione Centrale every twenty minutes between 5.40am and 7pm, every 30 minutes from 7 to 9pm, and during August every 30 minutes all day; it's a twenty-minute journey (L3500 from ticket office, L4000 on bus). There are also ordinary **city buses** (#73) until around midnight from Linate to Piazza San Babila. The other airport, Malpensa, is 50km away towards Lago Maggiore, connected by bus with Stazione Centrale between 7.30am and 12.30pm every 30 minutes, 12.30pm to 5.30pm every hour. The journey takes an hour and costs L12,000.

Information and city maps are available from Milan's main **tourist offices**, at the Stazione Centrale and at Via Marconi 1, off Piazza Duomo (Mon–Sat 8am–8pm, Sun 9am–12.30pm & 1.30–5pm). At some point you'll want to make use of the **public transport** system – an efficient network of trams, buses and metro. The metro is the most useful, made up of three lines, the red MM1, green MM2 and yellow MM3, converging at Loreto and Cadorna. Buses, trams and the metro run from around 6am to midnight, when night buses take over, following the metro routes until 1am. Tickets, valid for 75 minutes, cost a flat L1100 from tobacconists, bars and metro station newsagents. You can also buy a *blocchetto* of 11 tickets for L10,000, or a 24-hour ticket for L3500, from the Centrale or Duomo metro stations.

Accommodation

Milan is more a business than a tourist city, and its **accommodation** is geared to the expense-account traveller. However, there are plenty of one-star **hotels**, mostly concentrated in the area around Stazione Centrale, and along Viale Vittorio Veneto and Corso Buenos Aires. Close to the station, the *Casa Mia*, Viale V. Veneto 30 (☎657.5249; ③), is the best, and *San Tomaso*, Viale Tunisia 6 (☎295.14747; ③), is a popular *pensione*; the *Arno*, Via Lazzaretto 17 (☎670.5509; ③), off Viale Tunisia not far from Stazione

Centrale, gets packed from March to July and charges extra for shower, soap and towels; at the same address is the similar *Pensione Eva* (☎670.6093; ④). The *Arthur*, Via Lazzaretto 14 (☎204.6294; ④), has clean, spacious rooms with a touch of fading splendour, and *Speronari*, Via Speronari 4 (☎864.61125; ③), is central and recommended by the *APT*; *Manzoni*, Via Senato 45, off Corso Venezia (☎760.21002; ③), is near the public gardens and very central. *Kent*, Via F. Corridon 2a (☎551.87635; ③), is just a few streets away from Duomo. The official **youth hostel**, *Piero Rotta*, Via Salmoiraghi 2 (☎392.67095; ②), out in the northwest suburbs near the San Siro stadium, is perhaps the cheapest option but has an 11.30pm curfew (MM Lotto). Failing that, *ACISJF*, Corso Garibaldi 121 (☎290.00164; ②; MM Moscova), run by nuns, is a reasonable option for women under thirty in four-bedded rooms. As for **campsites**, there's the *Autodromo* site in Monza, in the park near the renowned Formula One circuit, open May to the end of September. Take a bus from Stazione Centrale.

The City

Historic Milan lies at the centre of a web of streets zeroing in on **Piazza del Duomo**, the city's main hub, a mostly pedestrianized square that's home to the best of Milan's streetlife, and, on its eastern side, the **Duomo**, the world's largest Gothic cathedral, begun in 1386 and taking nearly five centuries to complete. From the outside it's an incredible building, notable as much for its decoration as its size and with a front that's a strange mixture of Baroque and Gothic. The gloomy interior holds, among other things, a large crucifix which contains a nail from Christ's cross, crafted to become the bit for the bridle of Emperor Constantine's horse, while close by, beneath the presbytery, the **Scurolo di San Carlo** (daily 9am–noon & 2.30–6pm; L2000) is an octagonal crypt designed to house the remains of Saint Charles Borromeo, a zealous sixteenth-century cardinal who was canonized for his work among the poor of the city. He lies here in a glass coffin, clothed and bejewelled, wearing a gold crown attributed to Cellini. Adjacent to Borromeo's resting place, the treasury has Byzantine ivory-work and heavily embroidered vestments, while, back towards the entrance, is the cathedral's fourth-century **baptistery** (Tues–Sun 10am–noon & 3–5pm), where Saint Ambrose baptized Saint Augustine in 387 AD. You can also get up to the cathedral **roof** (elevator L6000, on foot L4000), whose forest of pinnacles and statues gives fine views of the city, and on clear days even the Alps.

The **Museo del Duomo** (Tues–Sat 9.30am–12.30pm & 3–6pm; L7000), on the southern side of the piazza, holds casts of a good many of the three thousand or so statues and gargoyles that spike the duomo. You can also see how it might have ended up, in a display of entries for a nineteenth-century competition for a new facade. In the same building, the **Civico Museo di Arte Contemporanea** (Tues–Sun 9.30am–5.30pm; free) has a wide-ranging collection of twentieth-century art, with works by De Chirico, Boccioni and Morandi, as well as more recent artists. South of Piazza del Duomo, the church of **San Satiro**, on the busy shopping street of Via Torino, is a study in ingenuity, commissioned from Milan's foremost Renaissance architect, Bramante, in 1476. Originally the oratory of the adjacent ninth-century church of San Satiro, Bramante transformed it into a long-naved basilica by converting the long oblong oratory into the transept and adding a trompe l'oeil apse to the back wall. Five minutes away, just off Via Torino at Piazza Pio XI 2, the **Pinacoteca Ambrosiana** – due to open again at the end of 1993 – was founded by another member of the Borromeo family, Cardinal Federico, and is one of the largest libraries in Europe – though what you come here for now is his art collection, stamped with his taste for Jan Bruegel, sixteenth-century Venetians and some of the more kitschy followers of Leonardo. Among many mediocre works, there is a rare painting by Leonardo himself, *Portrait of a Musician*, although the museum's quirkiest exhibit is a lock of Lucrezia Borgia's hair, put for safekeeping in a glass phial ever since Byron extracted one as a keepsake.

On the opposite side of the piazza is the gaudily opulent **Galleria Vittorio Emanuele**, a cruciform glass-domed gallery designed in 1865 by Giuseppe Mengoni, who was killed when he fell from the roof a few days before the inaugural ceremony. Take a look at the circular mosaic of the zodiac beneath the cupola – it's considered good luck to stand on Taurus's testicles. The Galleria leads through to the world-famous **La Scala** opera house, opened in 1778 with an opera by Antonio Salieri. Its small **museum** (Mon–Sat 9am–noon & 2–6pm; May–Oct also Sun 9.30am–noon; L5000), with composers' death masks, plaster casts of conductors' hands and a statue of Puccini in a capacious overcoat, may be the only chance you get to see the interior. Close by on Via Manzoni, the **Museo Poldi Pezzoli** (Tues–Fri 9.30am–12.30pm & 2.30–6pm, Sat 9.30am–12.30pm & 2.30–7.30pm, Sun 9.30am–12.30pm; Oct & Nov also Sun 2.30–7.30pm; L8000) comprises pieces assembled by the nineteenth-century collector, Gian Giacomo Poldi Pezzoli, much of it dull rooms of clocks, watches, cutlery and jewellery – though the Salone Dorato upstairs contains a number of intriguing paintings, including a portrait of a portly *Saint Nicolas of Tolentino* by Piero della Francesca and two works by Botticelli, one a gentle *Madonna del Libro*, the other a mesmerizing *Deposition*, painted towards the end of his life.

North of La Scala, **Via Brera** sets the tone for the city's arty quarter with its fancy galleries and art shops, and, at its far end, Milan's most prestigious gallery, the **Pinacoteca di Brera** (Tues–Sat 9am–5.30pm, Sun 9am–12.30pm; L8000), filled with works looted from the churches and aristocratic collections of French-occupied Italy. There's a good representation of Venetian painters – works by Paolo Veronese, Tintoretto, Gentile Bellini and his follower, Carpaccio, and a *Pietà* by Gentile's more talented brother, Giovanni, deemed "one of the most moving paintings in the history of art". Look out also for Mantegna's *The Dead Christ*, an ingenious painting of Christ on a wooden slab, viewed from the soles of his feet upwards; Piero della Francesca's chill *Madonna*, perhaps the most famous painting here; and Raphael's *Marriage of the Virgin*, whose languid Renaissance mood is in sharp contrast to the grim realism of Caravaggio's *Supper at Emmaus,* painted a century later.

West of the Accademie down via Pontaccio, **Castello Sforzesco** rises imperiously from the mayhem of Foro Buonaparte, laid out by Napoléon in self-tribute as part of a grand plan for the city. An arena and triumphal arch remain from the scheme, behind the castle in the **Parco Sempione**, a notorious hang-out for junkies and prostitutes, but otherwise the red-brick castle is the main focus of interest, with its crenellated towers and fortified walls one of Milan's most striking landmarks. Begun by the Viscontis and rebuilt by their successors, the Sforzas, whose court was one of the most powerful and cultured of the Renaissance, the castle houses – along with a number of run-of-the-mill collections – the **Museo d'Arte Antica** and **Pinacoteca** (Tues–Sun 9.30am–5.30pm; free), the former including Michelangelo's *Rondanini Pietà*, which the artist worked on for the last nine years of his life. The latter contains a cycle of monochrome frescoes illustrating the Griselda story from Boccaccio's *Decameron;* one of Mantegna's last works, *Madonna in Glory among Angels and Saints*; and paintings by Vincenzo Foppa, the leading Milanese artist before Leonardo da Vinci.

South of the castle, the **Museo Archeologico** at Corso Magenta 15 (Tues–Sun 9.30am–5.30pm; free) is worth a visit for its displays of kitchen utensils and jewellery from Roman Milan, as well as a colossal head of Jove, found near the castle. But what really brings visitors into this part of town is the church of **Santa Maria delle Grazie**, an originally Gothic church, partially rebuilt by Bramante (who added the massive dome), that is famous for its mural of the *Last Supper* by Leonardo da Vinci, which covers one wall of the refectory (Tues–Sun 8.15am–1.45pm; L6,000), decayed and faded, and partly obscured by restorers' scaffolding. Leonardo spent two years on this powerful work, scouring the streets of Milan for models. When the monks complained that the face of Judas was still unfinished, Leonardo replied that he had been searching for over a year for a sufficiently evil face and that if he didn't find one he would use the face of the prior. Whether or not Judas is modelled on the prior is unrecorded, but he does seem, as Vasari wrote, "the very embodiment of treachery and inhumanity".

South of here, flanking the city's two canals, the streets of the **Navigli** quarter feel a long way from the city centre, their peeling houses and waterside views much sought after by the city's would-be Bohemians. There's not much to do other than browse in its artists' studios and antique shops, but it's a peaceful area, good for idle strolling, and at night its bars and clubs are among the city's best. Back towards the centre, the **Ticinese** is another trendy district, though as yet less a prey to the yuppie invasion than Navigli, and home to the church of **Sant'Eustorgio** on Corso di Porta Ticinese, a much-rebuilt church originally constructed in the fourth century to house the bones of the Magi, some of which are still kept in a Roman sarcophagus in the right transept. Its Portinari Chapel, commissioned from Florentine architect Michelozzi in the 1460s to house the remains of Saint Peter the Martyr, has been credited with being Milan's first building of the Renaissance, a simple geometric creation decorated with scenes from his life by Foppa and reliefs carved on the sides of the elaborate tomb. Further up the Corso, the church of **San Lorenzo** is an evocative spot, apparently considered by Leonardo da Vinci to be the most beautiful church in Milan. It was founded in the fourth century, when it was the largest centrally planned church in the western Roman Empire – though the current structure is a sixteenth-century renovation of an eleventh-century rebuilding, a shaky edifice whose most interesting feature is the partially mosaiced Cappella di San Aquilino, much of which dates from the fourth century.

Eating, drinking and nightlife

Food in workaholic Milan, at lunchtime at least, is more of a necessity than a pleasure, with the city centre dominated by *paninotece* and fast-food outlets. *Crota Piemunteisa*, Piazza Beccaria 10, has a vast array of chunky sandwiches for around L4000, and a few tables, or try out *Il Fornaio* on the opposite side of the piazza, for sandwiches and pizzas. Among **restaurants**, *Brek*, Via del Duca 5, is a good-value and central self-service place, as is *Ciao*, a citywide chain with branches on the corner of Via Dante and Via Meravigli and at Via Fabio Filzi 8, near Stazione Centrale. *Italy & Italy* is another chain, good for spaghetti and pizza, with branches at Via Lazzaro Palazzi 21/a and Corso Venezia 7. Moving upmarket a little, *Al Cantinone*, Via Agnello 19, is a famous old trattoria and bar, with home-made pasta and some choice wines; *La Bruschetta*, Piazza Beccaria 12, is one of the best city centre pizzerias, though you'll have to wait for a table. *Grand Italia*, Via Palermo 5, is cheaper and just as good. On the other side of the centre, *Artisti*, Corso di Porta Ticinese 16, is also popular, a lunchtime favourite with workers and usually crowded with locals at night. Off Corso di Porta Ticinese, *Mergellina*, Via Molino delle Armi 48, does average pizzas but the prices are hard to beat – tram #15. *Pizzeria Spontini*, Corso Buenos Aires 60 (MM Lima), serves one kind of pizza only, tomato, cheese and anchovies on a thick, soft base, to eat in or take out. Further out, there's *Da Abele*, Via della Temperenza 5 (MM Pasteur), a long-established, cosy haunt that specializes in risotto, and *Stella d'Oro*, Via Donizetti 3, an institution among Milanese cheapo restaurants – bus #60.

Milan's **nightlife** centres on two areas – the streets around the Brera gallery and the Navigli and Ticinese quarters, where there's a hip, late-night **bar** scene. *Bar Magenta*, Via Carducci 13, is extremely trendy and usually packed. *Pois*, Colonne di San Lorenzo, was once Milan's hippest bar and still tries hard. As for **live music**, *Capolinea*, Via Lodovico Il Moro 119, named after its position at the terminal of tram #19, is a long-established jazz venue that hosts top-notch performers; *Scimmie*, Via Ascanio Sforza 49, is another popular stage, small and buzzy and mainly hosting jazz. Among many **clubs**, *Plastic Killer*, Viale Umbria 120, is a Gothic hang-out; *Zimba*, Via Besenzanica 3, is a well-established club playing a wide range of music, as is *Rolling Stone*, Corso XXII Marzo, an enormous place, sometimes host to big-name rock bands. *Hollywood*, Corso Como 15, is a long-established club with an airport theme. There's also, of course, *La Scala*, one of the world's most prestigious **opera** houses, whose season runs from December to July. Although seats are expensive and can sell out months in advance, there is often a reasonable chance of picking up a seat in the gods on the day – get there an hour or so before the performance. The Wednesday or Thursday pull-outs in *Corriere della Sera* or *La Repubblica* respectively give the rundown on **what's on**. The city **information office** in the Galleria Vittorio Emanuele (Mon–Sat 8am–8pm) also has details of cultural events and can book tickets.

Listings

Airlines *Air Canada*, Piazza VIII Novembre 6 (☎295.23943); *Alitalia*, Via Albricci 5 (☎62.817); *American Airlines*, Piazza della Repubblica 30 (☎290.04919, free ☎167.865.027); *British Airways*, Corso Italia 8 (☎809.041); *Qantas*, Piazza Velasca 4 (☎865.0168).

Airport enquiries ☎748.52200.

American Express Via Brera 3 (Mon–Fri 9am–5.30pm, Sat 9am–noon).

Books Wide array of English-language books at the *American Bookstore*, Largo Cairoli.

Car rental *Avis*, Piazza Diaz 6 (☎863.494); *Europcar*, Piazza Armando Diaz 6 (☎720.22460); *Hertz*, Via Gonzaga 5 (☎720.0456).

Consulates *Australia*, Via Borgogna 2 (☎760.13330); *Canada*, Via V. Pisani 19 (☎669.7451); *Great Britain*, Via San Paolo 7 (☎723.001); *USA*, Via Principe Amadeo 2/10 (☎290.351).

Exchange Stazione Centrale office is open daily 7.30am–7pm.

Hospital 24hr casualty department at the Fatebenefratelli hospital, Corso Porta Nuova 23 (☎63.631), or Ospedale Maggiore Policlinico, Via Francesco Sforza 35 (☎551.1655) – a short walk from Piazza Duomo.

Pharmacy 24hr service in Stazione Centrale.

Police Head office at Via Fatebenefratelli 11 (☎62.261), near the Brera.

Post office Via Cordusio 4, off Piazza Cordusio (Mon–Fri 8am–8pm, Sat 8am–2pm; telephones 7am–12.45pm).

Telephones *SIP*, Galleria V. Emanuele II (daily 8am–9.30pm), or at the post office.

Train enquiries ☎67.500.

Bergamo

Just 50km north of Milan, yet much closer to the mountains in look and feel, **BERGAMO** is made up of two distinct parts – **Bergamo Bassa**, the lower, modern centre, and **Bergamo Alta**, clinging to the hill 1200 feet above the Lombardian plain. Bergamo Bassa is no great shakes, a mixture of faceless suburbs and pompous Neoclassical town planning. But Bergamo Alta is one of northern Italy's loveliest city centres, a favourite retreat for the work-weary Milanese, who flock here at weekends seeking solace in its fresh mountain air, wanderable streets and lively, easy-going pace.

You can get up to Bergamo Alta by funicular from the top end of Viale Vittorio Emanuele II, or by taking a #1 bus from the train station (L1100, valid for one hour). Its centre is **Piazza Vecchia**, a harmonious square rather enthusiastically dubbed by Stendhal "the most beautiful place on earth", and flanked by the Venetian-Gothic **Palazzo della Ragione**; to the right is the massive **Torre della Civica** (closed). Through the palazzo's arcades is the **Duomo**, and, of more interest, the church of **Santa Maria Maggiore**, an extraordinarily elaborate church, with a ceiling in the worst tradition of Baroque excess and a piece of nineteenth-century kitsch in its monument to Donizetti, the Bergamo-based composer of highly popular romantic comedies. Next door, the Renaissance **Cappella Colleoni** (Tues–Sun March–Oct 9am–noon & 2–6pm; Nov–Feb 9am–noon & 2.30–4.30pm; free), built onto the church in the 1470s, is equally extravagant, a confection of marble carved into an abundance of miniature arcades, balustrades and twisted columns, and capped with a mosque-like dome. Its opulent interior has a ceiling frescoed in the eighteenth century by Tiepolo and the ornate sarcophagus of the Venetian military hero, Bartolomeo Colleoni, topped with a gleaming gilded equestrian statue.

Leading out of Piazza Vecchia, the narrow **Via Colleoni** is the upper city's main thoroughfare, leading to the remains of Bergamo's **Cittadella**, home to museums of archeology and natural history and offering good views across to Bergamo Bassa – though for really outstanding views you should stroll (or take the funicular) up to the **Castello** on the summit of San Vigilio. In the opposite direction, down Via Porta Dipinta and through the Porta Sant'Agostino, just below the upper town, the **Accademia Carrara** (daily except Tues 9.30am–12.30pm; L3000) is among Lombardy's top quality collections of art, with portraits by Pisanello and Botticelli, works by Crivelli, Carpaccio and Lotto, the Lombard realists Foppa and Bergognone, and Venetians Titian and Palma il Vecchio.

Practicalities

The **train station** is right at the end of Bergamo Bassa's central avenue, on Piazzale Marconi. The **tourist office** at Vicolo Aquila Nera 2, off Piazza Vecchia in the upper town (daily April–Oct 9am–12.30pm & 3–6.30pm) has maps and information; the other *APT* in Bergamo Bassa is at Viale Papa Giovanni 106 (Mon–Fri 9am–12.30pm & 3–6.30pm). The **youth hostel** has been closed for renovation for several years, and the cheapest **hotel** in the upper town is the *Agnello d'Oro*, Via Gombito 22 (☎035/249.883; ⑤); otherwise most of Bergamo's cheaper hotels are in Bergamo Bassa. Closest to the upper city is *Mamma Grande*, Via N. Sauro 7 (☎035/218.413; ④) – bus #9a, #9b or #9c from Porta Nuova. Cheaper is the *Antica Trattoria della Brianza*, Via Broseto 61a (☎035/253.338; ③), a fifteen-minute walk west of the train station or bus #11 from Porta Nuova. Nearer the station, the *San Antonio*, Via Paleocapa 1 (☎035/210.284; ③), is home to the *ACLI* mensa restaurant in the basement, much the cheapest place to eat in town. Otherwise, in the upper town, the *Trattoria Bernabo*, on Via Colleoni close to Piazza Mascheroni, is excellent value, as is *Da Mimmo*, Via Colleoni 17, which serves good pizzas and a decent four-course menu for around L30,000.

Brescia and around

Famed for its arms industry, **BRESCIA** is not the kind of city that's on many travellers' itineraries – most are in a hurry to get to Venice or up to the lakes. But there is more to the town than its reputation might lead you to expect: a substantial Roman temple, a generous sprinkling of medieval and Renaissance buildings, a Romanesque cathedral – and a slick and energetic streetlife, at its best on Corso Palestro during the evening *passeggiata*. The town is also a possible base for visiting Gabriele D'Annunzio's bizarre villa and other attractions on nearby Lake Garda.

The town centre is grouped around the four piazzas beyond the main Corso Palestro, most notable of which is the marble-fringed **Piazza Vittoria**, perhaps Italy's most brutal example of Fascist town planning. The nearby **Piazza della Loggia** is prettier, with a clear Venetian influence in the fancily festooned loggia, in which both Palladio and Titian had a hand, and in the **Torre dell'Orologio**, modelled on the campanile in Venice's Piazza San Marco. A small side street leads through to **Piazza del Duomo**, one of the few squares in Italy to have two cathedrals – though, frankly, it would have been better off without the second, a heavy Mannerist monument that took over 200 years to complete. The old twelfth-century cathedral, or **Rotonda** (daily except Tues 9am–noon & 3–7pm), is quite different, a simple circular building inside which are the remains of Roman baths and the apse of an eighth-century basilica. Most interesting is the red marble tomb of Berardo Maggi, a thirteenth-century Bishop of Brescia, decorated on one side with a full-length relief of the cleric, on the other by reliefs show-ing other ecclesiasts and dignitaries processing through a lively crowd of citizens to celebrate the peace Maggi had brought to the town's rival Guelf and Ghibelline factions. Behind Piazza del Duomo, Via Mazzini leads to Via Musei, along which lie the remains of the Roman town of Brixia, though there's not a lot to see – the most substantial monument the **Capitolino** (Tues–Sun 9am–12.30pm & 2–5pm; L2000), a Roman temple built in 73 AD. There's an excellent **museum** behind, with a well displayed collection of jewellery, sculptures and bronzes, fragments of mosaic pave-ments and a life-sized winged Victory. Behind the museum, Via Piamarta climbs up the **Cydnean Hill**, the core of early Roman Brixia, crowned by the **Castello**, a monument to Brescia's various overlords, begun in the fifteenth century by Luchino Visconti and added to over the years. The result is a confusion of towers, ramparts, halls and court-yards, and holds Italy's largest museum of arms, a model railway museum and a small zoo. More appealing perhaps is Brescia's main art gallery, the **Pinacoteca Tosio-Martinengo** (Tues–Sun 9am–12.30pm & 2–5pm; L2000), though its collection is mainly made up of the works of minor local artists.

The **train station** is south of the centre, a short bus ride or fifteen-minute walk, and the **tourist office** is at Corso Zanardelli 34 (daily 9am–12.30pm & 3–6pm). For **accom-modation**, the best deals for women are the convent at Via Fratelli Bronzetti 17 (✆030/55.837; ②), though this has a 10pm curfew, or the *Paola di Rosa*, Contrada S. Croce 17 (✆030/377.2531; ②). The cheapest **hotels** are the *Calzavellia* on Via Calzavel-lia, off Corso Mameli (✆030/377.4614; ②), and the *Albergo Stazione* on Vicolo Stazione off Viale Stazione (✆030/52.128; ③); more central is the *Italia*, Via Gramsci 11 (✆030/ 375.6273/4; ④). For **eating**, there are a few pizzerias and takeaways on Corso Mameli, near the university. *Pizzeria Leonessa* in Via Laura Cereto, off Via Trieste does the city's best, and there's *Bersaglieri*, at Corso Magenta 38, too; *Ristorante Tre Merli*, Contrada del Cavalletto 8, off Corso Palestro, does a good two-course menu for L20,000, or the *Trattoria la Grotta*, Vicolo del Prezzercolo, has similarly priced good food.

Gardone Riviera and Il Vittoriale

Accessible by regular bus from Brescia, **GARDONE RIVIERA** was once the most fashionable of nearby Lake Garda's resorts, and still retains its symbols of sophistica-tion, though the elegant promenade, lush gardens and opulent villas now have to compete with more recent tourist tack. It is famous for the consistency of its climate, and has Garda's most exotic botanical garden, the **Giardino Botanico Hruska** (March–Oct daily 8.30am–6pm; closed Nov–Feb; L5000), laid out among artificial cliffs and streams – although the highlight is **Il Vittoriale** (Tues–Sun 9am–12.30pm & 2.30–6.30pm; park open daily; L15,000), home of Italy's most notorious twentieth-century writer, Gabriele D'Annunzio. Born in 1863, D'Annunzio was no ordinary writer. He did pen some exquisite poetry and a number of novels, but he was better known as a soldier and socialite, leading his own private army and indulging in much-publicized affairs with numerous aristocrats. Later, he became a fervent supporter of Mussolini, who in 1925 presented him with this villa. You have to take a **guided tour**, in Italian only, but the building really speaks for itself, D'Annunzio's personality making itself felt from the start in the two reception rooms – one a chill and formal room for guests he didn't like, the other warm and inviting for those he did. In the glitzy dining room, pride of place was given to a gilded and embalmed tortoise that had died of overeating – a warning to the greedy. In fact, D'Annunzio rarely ate with his guests, retreating instead to the Sala di Lebbroso where he would lie on a bier surrounded by leopard skins. The rest of the house is no less bizarre: the bathroom has a bathtub hemmed in by over 2000 tacky pieces of bric-à-brac, and the Sala del Mappamondo, as well as the huge globe after which it is named, contains an Austrian machine gun and books including an immense version of *The Divine Comedy*.

Mantua

Aldous Huxley called it the most romantic city in the world, and with an Arabian nights skyline rising above its three encircling lakes, **MANTUA** is undeniably evocative. It was the scene of Verdi's *Rigoletto*, and its history is one of equally operatic plots, most of them perpetuated by the Gonzagas, who ruled the town for three centuries and left two splendid palaces – the Palazzo Ducale, with Mantegna's stunning fresco of the Gonzaga court, and Palazzo del Tè, whose frescoes have entertained generations of visitors with their combination of steamy erotica and illusionistic fantasy.

The City

Historic Mantua centres on four interlinking squares. Of these, **Piazza Mantegna** is dominated by the facade of Alberti's **Sant'Andrea**, an unfinished basilica commissioned by Lodovico II Gonzaga, who felt that the existing medieval church was neither impressive enough to represent the splendour of his state, nor large enough to hold the droves of people who flocked here to see the holy relic of Christ's blood that had been found on the site. Inside, an octagonal balustrade stands above the crypt where the holy relic is kept in two vases, copies of originals designed by Cellini and stolen by the Austrians in 1846. There are also wall-paintings designed by Mantegna and executed by his students, one of whom was Correggio; Mantegna himself is buried in the church, in one of the north aisle chapels, his tomb topped with a bust that's said to be a self-portrait. Opposite Sant'Andrea and sunk below the present level of the busy **Piazza dell'Erbe**, Mantua's oldest church, the eleventh-century **Rotonda**, narrowly escaped destruction under Lodovico's city-improvement plans, and still contains traces of twelfth- and thirteenth-century frescoes.

The dark underpassage beneath the red-brick **Broletto**, or medieval town hall, leads into **Piazza Broletto**, beyond which the sombre Piazza Sordello is flanked by the Baroque facade of the **Duomo**, which conceals a rich interior designed by Giulio Romano, and the **Palazzo Ducale** (Tues–Sat 9am–12.30pm & 2.30–6pm, Sun & Mon 9am–12.30pm; L10,000), an enormous complex that was once the largest palace in Europe, with a population of over a thousand. When it was sacked by the Habsburgs in 1630, eighty carriages were needed to carry the two thousand works of art contained in its five hundred rooms. Only a proportion of these are open to visitors, and to see them you have to take a guided tour. In the Salone dei Fiume there's a trompe l'oeil garden complete with painted creepers and two ghastly fountains; the Sala dei Specchi, further on, has a notice outside signed by Monteverdi, who worked as court musician to Vincenzo I and gave frequent concerts of new works. Vincenzo also employed Rubens, whose *Adoration of the Magi* in the Salone degli Arcieri shows the Gonzaga family of 1604. However, the palace's real treasure is in the Castello di San Giorgio beyond, where you can see Mantegna's frescoes of the Gonzaga family, splendidly restored in the so-called Camera degli Sposi. In the main one Lodovico discusses a letter with a courtier while his wife looks on; their youngest daughter leans on her mother's lap, about to bite into an apple. The other fresco, *The Meeting*, shows Gonzagan retainers with dogs and a horse in attendance on Lodovico who is welcoming his son Francesco back from Rome, where he had just become the first Gonzaga to be made a cardinal.

Mantua's other main sight, the **Palazzo Tè** (Tues–Sun 10am–6pm; L10,000), was designed for Federico Gonzaga and his mistress, Isabella Boschetta, by Giulio Romano, and a tour of it is like a voyage around Giulio's imagination, a sumptuous world where very little is what it seems. In the Sala dei Cavalli, portraits of horses stand before an illusionistic background in which simulated marble, fake pilasters and mock reliefs surround views of painted landscapes through non-existent windows. The function of the Salotta di Psiche, further on, is undocumented, but the sultry frescoes, and its proximity to Federico's bedroom, might give a few clues, the ceiling paintings telling the story of Cupid and Psyche with some dizzying "sotto in su" (from the bottom up) works by Giulio. On the walls, too, are racy pieces, covered with orgiastic wedding-feast scenes, watched over by the giant Polyphemus, perched above the fireplace, while, beyond, the extraordinary Sala dei Giganti shows the destruction of the giants by the gods, with cracking pillars, toppling brickwork and screaming giants appearing to crash down into the room.

Practicalities

The city centre is a ten-minute walk from the **train station** down Via Solferino. There's an official **youth hostel**, with a **campsite** in its grounds east of the centre on Strada Legnaghese (May to mid-Oct; ☎0376/372.465; ②), though it's known for its mosquitoes and cold showers – bus #2 or #9 from Piazza Cavalotti. As for **hotels**, try *Roma Vecchia*, Via Corridoni 20 (☎0376/322.100; ③), near Piazza Martiri Belfiore, or *Rinascita*, Via Concezione 4 (☎0376/320.607; ③), about five minutes' walk from the train station. The **tourist office** (Mon–Sat 9am–noon & 3–6pm) is around the corner from Sant'Andrea, and has maps and accommodation lists. For inexpensive **food**, the cheapest place is the *Il Punto* self-service at Via Solferino 36, near the train station. Failing that, try the *Bella Napoli*, Piazza Cavalotti 14, which serves good pizza, or the *Trattoria del Lago*, Piazza Arche 5. There's the *Campeggio Sparafucile* **campsite** in Strada Legnaghese, on the lake bank (April to mid-Oct; ☎0376/372.465).

Genoa

GENOA is "a place that grows upon you every day . . . it abounds in the strangest contrasts; things that are picturesque, ugly, mean, magnificent, delightful and offensive break upon the view at every turn", wrote Dickens in 1844, and the description still fits. Genoa is a marvellously eclectic city, centring on the port that made it by the thirteenth century one of the five Italian maritime republics. Later, during the Unification era, the city was a base for radical thought. Mazzini, one of the main protagonists in Italy's unification was born here, and in 1860 Garibaldi set sail for Sicily with his "Thousand" from the city's harbour. The city is now in economic decline, but it remains a wonderfully vibrant place, with a warren-like medieval centre that has more zest than all the nearby coastal resorts put together.

> The Genoa area telephone code is ☎010.

Arrival and accommodation

Trains from the west arrive at Stazione Principe in Piazza Acquaverde, from the south and east at Stazione Brignole, Piazza Verdi; trains from the north usually stop at both, but if you have to travel between the two, take bus #37. **Ferries** arrive at the Stazione Maríttima, ten minutes' walk downhill from Stazione Principe. For **buses**, a **tourist ticket** from an *ATM* kiosk gives you an unlimited number of journeys for L3000 a day. The central **tourist office** is at Via Roma 11 (Mon–Fri 8am–1.30pm & 2–5pm, Sat 8am–1.30pm), and there are offices at the stations and airport (Mon–Sat 8am–8pm).

There are plenty of cheap **hotels** in the city centre, but many are grimy and depressing and you need to look hard to find the exceptions. Good areas to try are the roads bordering the old town, and Piazza Colombo and Via XX Settembre, near Stazione Brignole. *Pensione Mediterranee*, just north of the old town at Via Cairoli 14/4 (☎206.531; ③), is particularly good. Of the batch of places on Via XX Settembre, try the *Soana* at no. 23 (☎562.814; ④), or the *Barone*, at no. 2 (☎587.578; ③).

The City

Genoa spreads outwards from its **old town** around the port in a confusion of tiny alleyways and old palaces in which people speak the impenetrable Genoese dialect – a mixture of Neapolitan, Calabrese and Portuguese. From 1384 to 1515, except for brief periods of foreign domination, the doges ruled the city from the **Palazzo Ducale** in Piazza Matteotti, across from which the dour **Gesù** church, designed by Pellegrino Tibaldi at the end of the sixteenth century, contains Guido Reni's *Assumption* and two paintings by Rubens. Close by, the Gothic **Cattedrale di San Lorenzo** is home to the Renaissance chapel of St John the Baptist, whose remains once rested in the thirteenth-century sarcophagus. After a particularly bad storm, priests carried his casket through the city to placate the sea, and a commemorative procession takes place each June 24 to honour him. His reliquary is in the treasury (currently closed), along with a polished quartz plate on which, legend says, Salome received his severed head. Also on display is a glass dish said to have been given to Solomon by the Queen of Sheba, and used at the Last Supper. East from the adjacent Piazza Ferrari leads **Via XX Settembre**, Genoa's commercial nucleus, with big department stores and pavement cafés in the arcades.

Heading south across **Via San Bernardo**, another busy street, the mosaic spire of the church of **Sant'Agostino** marks the adjacent **Museo dell'Architettura e Scultura Ligure** (Tues–Sat 9am–7pm, Sun 9am–noon; L4000), built around the cloister of a thirteenth-century monastery, with a collection of Roman and Romanesque fragments from other churches, as well as wood-carvings and ancient maps of Genoa. Down on the waterfront, the sea once came up to the vaulted arcades of **Piazza Caricamento**, a hive of activity, fringed by café-restaurants and the stalls of its market. Customs inspectors, and subsequently the city's elected governors, set up in the **Palazzo San Giorgio** on the edge of the square, two rooms of which – the Sala dei Protettori and Sala Manica Lunga – are open to the public. Behind Piazza Caricamento is a thriving commercial zone centred on **Piazza Banchi**, formerly the heart of the medieval city, off which the long Via San Luca leads to the **Galleria Nazionale di Palazzo Spinola** (Tues–Sat 10am–7pm, Sun 9am–1pm; L4000), whose collection includes work by the Sicilian master Antonello da Messina and an *Adoration of the Magi* by Joos van Cleve.

North of here, **Via Garibaldi** is lined with Renaissance palaces, two of which have been turned into art galleries. The **Palazzo Bianco** (Tues–Sat 9am–7pm, Sun 9am–1pm; L4000) holds paintings by Genoese artists and others, including van Dyck and Rubens, and a good general gathering of Flemish art. The paintings in the **Palazzo Rosso** across the road (Tues–Sat 9am–7pm, Sun 9am–noon; L4000) include works by Titian, Caravaggio and Dürer, but it's the decor which really impresses – fantastic chandeliers, mirrors, an excess of gilding, and frescoed ceilings. Behind, Genoa heaps up the hill like the steps of an amphitheatre, a part of town best seen by way of the **funicular** from Piazza del Portello up to Sant'Anna. The view from up here is much hyped, but the trip is more absorbing than anything you'll see when you arrive.

Eating, drinking, nightlife and beaches

The cheapest places to **eat** are around the port, though these are often open only at lunchtime. For **snacks** and picnic ingredients, try the side streets around Stazione Brignole and Piazza Colombo, and the covered Mercato Orientale, halfway down Via XX Settembre in the old cloisters of an Augustinian monastery. There are stalls on Piazza Caricamento selling deep-fried seafood specialities to take away, and you'll see lots of places selling *farinata*, a kind of chickpea pancake, all over the old town. For full **meals**, *Sâ Pesta*, Via Giustiniani 16, is a well-known source of good local cooking, though it closes early. *Corona di Ferro*, Vico Inferiore del Ferro 11 (leading onto Via di

Macelli di Soziglia), is open lunchtimes and Friday and Saturday evenings for a three-course meal for L25,000–30,000, while at *Trattoria Luciano e Mimma*, Corso M. Quadrio 4 (on the edge of the port), you can eat three courses at lunchtime for L13,000. Close to here, on Salita Santa Maria di Castello, is the reasonably priced *Osteria di Castello* with its fish dishes, and there's a trattoria-pizzeria, *Florida*, just down the hill from Stazione Principe.

For a **drink**, try Via Cesearea with *All'Insieme* at no. 95 or *Lo Shaker Club* at no. 43/45, or *Cin-Cin* onVia Maragliano. If you're dying for a Guinness, hit the *Brittania Pub* in Vico Casana, just off Via San Lorenzo. *Panteca Volante* is a friendly, smoky club-cum-bar with live music most nights, hidden away at the Stazione Principe end of Via Balbi – take the set of steps just past Farmacia Pescetto up to the tiny Piazza Santa Brigida. Otherwise, head out to the suburb of **Albaro**, at the end of Corso Italia (bus #15, #41 or #43 from Stazione Principe), where people come to stroll, pose, or watch the sun set from a café table. During the day, the **beaches** at Albaro charge a small fee and provide changing areas and showers.

The Riviera di Ponente

You get the most positive impression of the coast west of Genoa – the **Riviera di Ponente** – as you speed along the *autostrada*, from where the marinas and resorts are mere specks in a panorama of glittering sea and acres of glasshouses. Close up, the seaside towns from Genoa to the French border are fairly functional places, yet they have their good points – chiefly the sandy beaches and an exceptionally mild climate, which means that flowering plants grow everywhere all year round.

With nearly a hundred hotels in and around its centre, **FINALE LIGURE**, about 40km west of Genoa, is committed to tourism, yet manages to remain an attractive place. It is well-known for its nearby Grotte delle Arene Candide, finds from which are on display at the **Museo Archeologico** in the cloisters of Santa Caterina (Tues–Sat 10am–noon & 3–6pm, Sun 9am–noon; L5000). Above all, it's a pleasant place to stay and see this part of the coast. Outstanding among the **hotels** is the friendly family-run *Cirio* on Via Pertica, in the old part of town (☎019/692.310; ③), and there's a **youth hostel** in a castle high above the train station at Via Generale Caviglia 46 (mid-March–mid-Oct; ☎019/690.515; ②). The **tourist office**, by the station at Via San Pietro 14 (Mon–Sat summer 8am–1pm & 3.30–7pm, Sun 9am–12.30pm; winter Mon–Sat closes 6.30pm), has details of plenty of other possibilities. On the food side, there's very good Ligurian fare at *Astor*, Via Roma 9, though you may need to book.

One of the other main resorts of this stretch of coast is **SAN REMO**, a grand old place whose heyday was earlier this century, when wealthy Europeans paraded up and down the Corso Imperatrice and filled the large hotels overlooking the sea. There isn't a lot in terms of things to see, and even the small **beach** by the railway station is a bit mucky, but the attraction of the place is its seediness. The **train station** is in the western corner of town and you can get assistance across the road at the **tourist office**, Via Nuvolini 1 (daily 8am–7pm). Finding a **place to stay** is no problem though, except in August. There's a concentration of hotels along Corso Mombello, five minutes' walk to the right of the station – among many choices is *Mombello* at no. 49 (☎0184/501.466; ③). The two other main streets which converge at the station are Via Roma and Corso Matteotti. Via Gioberti, between the two, is another place to look, with *Olimpia* at no. 25 (☎0184/509.628; ④); try also *La Mara*, Via Roma 93 (☎0184/533.866; ③), and *La Ginetta*, Via Marieli 18 (☎0184/570.070; ③). Up in the old town, in the first street on the right as you enter from Piazza Cassini, *Osteria della Costa* specializes in an excellent rabbit stew. At the end of the road on the right, you can't miss Piazza Eroi San Remesi, surrounded by large pizzerias with menus at L10,000 and upwards.

The Riviera di Levante

The stretch of coast east from Genoa, the **Riviera di Levante**, is not the place to come for a relaxing beach holiday. The ports which once survived on the trades of navigation, fishing and coral diving have now experienced thirty years of tourism; the coastline is still wild and beautiful in parts, but inevitably the sense of remoteness has gone.

CAMOGLI was in its day an important seafaring town, supporting a fleet of 700 vessels. But it declined in the age of steam, and these days the harbour is mostly busy with ferries along the coast to other Ligurian ports. **Punta Chiappa**, across the bay, was once famous for the "ever changing colours of the sea" but is now murky in places with rubbish from the yachts moored off the promontory. The flat rocks are still a popular place to bask, and plenty of people swim from here. It's also the starting point for trails around the edge of **Monte di Portofino**, and is accessible by ferry or by taking the path from San Rocco church, on the edge of Camogli. From Punta Chiappa it takes three hours to walk to San Fruttuoso and five to Portofino, along wild and beautiful clifftops. For **places to stay**, try *La Camogliese*, Via Garibaldi 55 (☎0185/771.402; ④), with a decent, fair-priced **restaurant**.

PORTOFINO, at the extremity of the Monte Portofino headland, manages to be both attractive and offputting at the same time, a wealthy resort but a beautiful one. The ninety-minute walk to San Fruttuoso's thirteenth-century **abbey** (March, April & Nov–Jan 10am–1pm & 2–4pm; May–Oct 10am–1pm & 2–6pm) and beach is well worth doing. Boats go from San Fruttuoso to Camogli, Portofino, Santa Margherita and Rapallo. Three kilometres out of Portofino, on the corniche road, the sparkling cove at **PARAGGI** is a good place for a swim, with a couple of bars set back from the beach, and you can take a bus to Ruta, from where you can either slog on foot to the summit of Monte Portofino or catch another bus to Portofino Vetta, from where it's twenty minutes' walk to the top. On very clear days the views are fantastic.

SANTA MARGHERITA LIGURE is a small, thoroughly attractive resort, with palm trees along the front and a minuscule pebble beach and concrete jetties to swim from – as well as plenty of cheapish accommodation, making it a convenient base for visiting Monte Portofino and the other coastal towns. The **hotels** are friendly and pleasant: try *Albergo Annabella* at Via Costasecca 10, just off Piazza Mazzini (☎0185/286.531; ③), or *Albergo Fasce*, a little further up the road at Via L. Bozzo 3 (☎0185/286.435; ⑤), which has a dozen bicycles guests may use free of charge. The **tourist office** on Via XXV Aprile (Mon–Sat 8.30–12.30pm & 3.30–7pm, Sun 9.30am–12.30pm & 3.30–6.30pm) has free footpath maps of the area.

RAPALLO crowds around the first bay along in the gulf, a highly developed though still attractive resort that used to be patronized by a number of writers, drawn here by the bay's extraordinary beauty. Caricaturist and ferocious critic of British Imperialism Max Beerbohm lived in Rapallo, attracting a vast coterie, and Ezra Pound wrote the first thirty of his *Cantos* here between 1925 and 1930. The best **places to stay** are along the front: *Pensione Bandoni*, Via Marsala 24 (☎0185/50.423; ③), *Villa Cristina*, Via P. Zupino 21 (☎0185/56.707; ②), or *Giardino*, Via Venezia 103 (☎0185/50.786; ②). There's a **campsite**, *Rapallo*, 1km before Santa Maria di Campo and the *autostrada*, at Via San Lazzaro 6. The *Il Pozzo* **restaurant**, Corso Assereto 15, offers the cheapest meal in town, or, for a more costly blowout, there's *Zi Teresa* at Corso Italia 33.

A number of paths lead down from the main Rapallo–Chiávari road to some small coves – to investigate them, take the bus and get off when you see signs pointing to the sea. **CHIÁVARI** itself faces a featureless bit of coastline, but does boast a reasonable beach. The **bus** and **train** stations are next to each other, just off the main Corso della Libertà, which bisects a grid pattern of medieval arcades. Off the Corso, at Via Costaguta 2, is the **Civico Museo Archeologico** (Tues–Thurs 9am–1pm, Fri & Sat 2–7pm;

free), with graphics explaining such matters as the triple flint arrowhead, backed by finds from a vast seventh- to eighth-century necropolis on the outskirts of town. There is an *IAT* office at Via XX Settembre 33 (☎0185/771.066), as well as others dotted throughout the city.

The road sweeps around the bay to **SESTRI LEVANTE**, one of the largest resorts this side of Genoa. It consists of two bays separated by a narrow isthmus: the "Bay of Fables" (nearer the train station), said to be so named by Hans Christian Andersen, and the "Bay of Silence". On the Bay of Fables side, the beach is wide and sandy but is packed with sunbeds and overlooked by ranks of hotels. The Bay of Silence, on the other hand, might not exactly live up to its name in high season, but is far more pleasant, with a narrow beach and lots of fishing boats. Among **places to stay** are *Villa Jolanda*, Via Pozzetto 15 (☎0185/41.354; ②), the *San Pietro* on Via Palestro (☎0185/41.279; ③), or *La Neigra*, Viale Roma 49 (☎0185/417.56; ③), near the station and with a great trattoria with a L20,000 fixed menu. Via XXV Aprile, which runs through the narrow peninsula and widens out onto Corso Colombo, is where you'll find the best places to **eat and drink**. *Polpo Mario*, at Via XXV Aprile 163, specializes in fish, and *Buon Geppin* on Corso Colombo has good antipasti.

The Cinque Terre

If you're travelling on a fast train, you'll speed through the five villages of the **Cinque Terre** without seeing much more than a few tantalizing glimpses of sheer cliff as the train dashes from one tunnel to the next. However, the stopping services on the Genoa to La Spezia line call at each one, and there is a ferry service linking them from La Spezia. Their comparative remoteness, and the drama of their position on tiny cliff-bound inlets, make a visit to the area a real attraction. **RIOMAGGIORE**, closest to La Spezia and one of the larger villages, is the best place to head, wedged impossibly into a hillside, with no two buildings on the same level. Along the cliff path which winds its way to **MANAROLA**, lemon trees flourish in every backyard, and in spring the cliffs are covered with wild flowers. From Manarola a spectacular path passes rock-cut steps leading down to the water all the way to **MONTEROSSO** (12km), largest and least charming of the villages, and the only one with a recognizable beach. **CORNIGLIA** and **VERNAZZA** are similar to Riomaggiore, but on a smaller scale. Reasonably priced **hotels** aren't too difficult to find – Monterosso and Riomaggiore present the best opportunities – or you could base yourself in **LEVANTO**, a little way west, which has plentiful reasonable accommodation and food options, including a decent **campsite**, plus a long stretch of sandy **beach** – and it's on the main rail line.

THE NORTHEAST

Italy's **northeast** is one of the country's most appealing – and versatile – regions. The appeal of **Venice** hardly needs stating: it's one of Europe's truly unique urban landscapes, and, despite its equally unique huge number of visitors, really unmissable on any European – let alone Italian – tour. The region around Venice – the **Veneto** – is a prosperous one, where virtually every acre still bears the imprint of Venetian rule. **Padua** and **Verona** are the main attractions, with their masterpieces by Giotto, Donatello and Mantegna, and a profusion of great buildings from Roman times to the Renaissance. The Palladian city of **Vicenza** also justifies the detour, though otherwise much of the countryside is dull and flat, only perking up to the north with the high peaks of the Dolomite range. East, on the former Yugoslav border, **Trieste** is capital of the partly Slav region of **Friuli-Venezia Giulia**, a Habsburg city, developed with Austrian capital to be the major port of their empire, and only finally united with Italy after the last war. South, between Lombardy and Tuscany, stretching from the Adriatic coast almost to the shores of the Mediterranean, **Emilia-Romagna** is the heartland of northern Italy, a patchwork of ducal territories formerly ruled by a handful of families, whose castles and fortresses remain in well-preserved medieval towns. Carving a dead straight route through the heart of the region, from Milan to Rimini on the coast, the Via Emilia is a central and obvious reference point, a Roman military road constructed in 187 BC that was part of the medieval pilgrim's route to Rome and the way east for crusaders to Ravenna and Venice. **Bologna**, the region's capital, is one of Italy's largest cities, but despite having one of the most beautifully preserved city centres in the country and some of its finest food, it's relatively neglected by tourists, most people passing straight through – definitely a mistake. Bologna also gives easy access to **Parma**, just an hour or so away by train, a wealthy provincial town that is worth visiting for its paintings by Parmigianino and Correggio. The coast is less interesting, and the water polluted, although **Rimini** provides a spark of interest, its oddly attractive seaside sleaze concealing a historic town centre, and, just south of the Po delta, **Ravenna** boasts probably the world's finest set of Byzantine mosaics in its churches and mausoleums. **Ferrara**, a little way inland, is, as the domain of the Este family, one of the most important Renaissance centres in Italy.

Venice

The first-time visitor to **VENICE** arrives with a heavy freight of expectations, most of which turn out to have been well-founded. It is an extraordinarily beautiful city, an urban landscape so rich that you can't walk for a minute without coming across something that's worth a stop; and the major sights like the basilica and piazza of San Marco are all they are cracked up to be, as are most of the lesser-known ones. The downside is that Venice is deluged with tourists, the annual influx exceeding the city's population two-hundredfold; and it is expensive – the price of a good meal anywhere else in Italy will get you a lousy one in Venice, and its hoteliers make the most of a situation where demand will always far outstrip supply. However, the crowds thin out beyond the magnetic field of San Marco, and in the off-season it's still possible to have parts of the centre virtually to yourself. As for keeping your costs down, there are *some* inexpensive eating places, and you *can* find a bed for the night without spending a fortune.

Venice first rose to a kind of prominence when the traders of what was then a small settlement on the lagoon signalled their independence from Byzantium through a great symbolic act – the theft from Alexandria in 828 of the body of Saint Mark, who became the city's patron. Venice later exploited the trading networks and markets of Byzantium and the East, aided by the Crusades, by the twelfth century achieving unprecedented prosperity and benefiting especially from the Sack of Constantinople in 1204, which left much of the Roman Empire under the city's sway. Following the defeat of Genoa in 1380, Venice consolidated its position as the unrivalled trading power of the region, and by the middle of the fifteenth century was in possession of a mainland empire that was to survive virtually intact for several centuries – although its eastern dominions were increasingly encroached on by the Ottomans. Decline set in in the eighteenth century, when, politically moribund and constitutionally ossified, Venice became renowned as a playground of the rich, a position consolidated in the nineteenth century with the growth of tourism and the development of the Lido as Europe's most fashionable resort. This turns out to have been a wise move, despite the drawbacks. Nowadays some 20 million people visit the city each year, around half of whom don't even stay a night. Without them, however, Venice would barely exist at all.

The Venice area telephone code is ☎041.

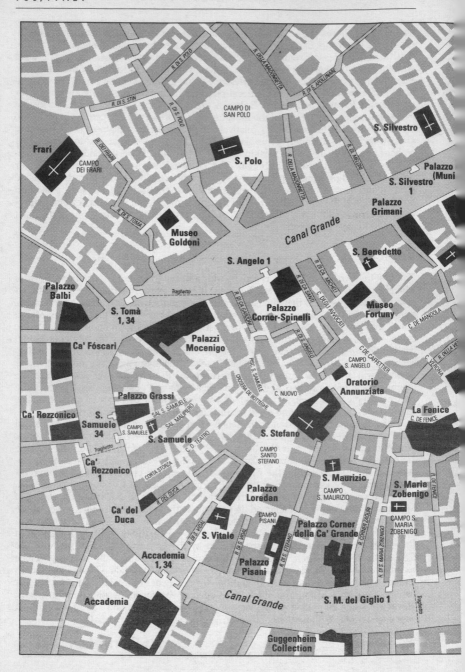

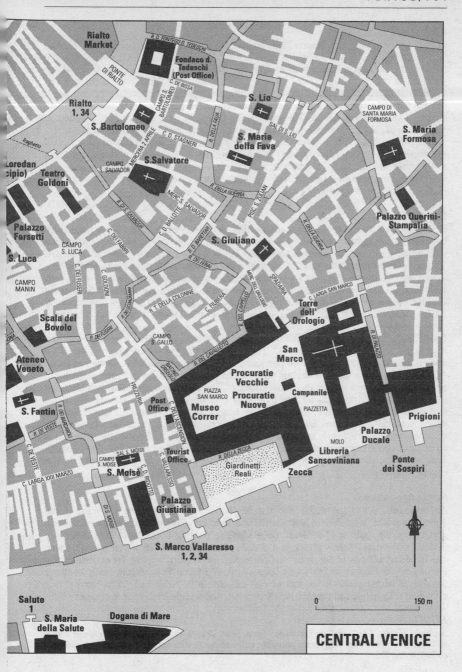

Rialto
Market

PONTE
DI RIALTO

Fondaco d.
Tedeschi
(Post Office)

R. D. FONTEBO D. TEDESCHI

C. DE BISSA

S. Lio

CAMPO DI
SANTA MARIA
FORMOSA

Rialto
1, 34

CAMPO S.
BARTOLOMEO

SAL DI S. LIO

S. Maria
Formosa

Traghetto

S. Bartolomeo

C. D. STAGNERI

R. DELLA FAVA

S. Maria
della Fava

MERCERIA 2 APRILE

S.Salvatore

CAMPO
S. SALVADOR

MERC. S. SALVADOR

R. DELLA GUERRA

Loredan
(cipio)

Teatro
Goldoni

C. DEI FABBRI

C. D. BALLOTTE

R. DE SALVADOR

R. D. BAZIETTI

S. Giuliano

PISC. S. ZULIAN

R. DELLA GIERNA

Palazzo Querini-
Stampalia

Palazzo
Farsetti

CAMPO
S. LUCA

C. DE FUSERI

S. Luca

R. DEI FERALI

CAMPO
MANIN

C. GOLDONI

C. DEI FUSERI

R. T. DELLA COLONNE

C. FUBERA

MERC. DELL'OROLOGIO

SPADARIA

C. LARGA SAN MARCO

Torre
dell'
Orologio

Scala del
Bovolo

R. DE FUSERI

CAMPO
S. GALLO

C. DEL CAPPELLO

R. DEL CAVALLETTO

San
Marco

R. DE PALAZZO

Ateneo
Veneto

PREZZERIA

BACINO
ORSEOLO

Procuratie
Vecchie

S. Fantin

R. DE BARCAROLI

Post
Office

C. DELL'ASCENSION

PIAZZA
SAN MARCO

Museo
Correr

Procuratie
Nuove

Campanile

PIAZZETTA

Prigioni

R. DE VESTE

SAL S. MOISE

Palazzo
Ducale

C. DE VESTE

CAMPO
S. MOISE

Tourist
Office

C. VALLARESSO

R. DELLA ZECCA

Giardinetti
Reali

Libreria
Sansoviniana

MOLO

Zecca

Ponte
dei Sospiri

C. LARGA XXII MARZO

S. Moisè

C. D. PIOVETTO

Palazzo
Giustinian

DI S. MOISE

S. Marco Vallaresso
1, 2, 34

N

Salute
1

S. Maria
della Salute

Dogana di Mare

0   150 m

CENTRAL VENICE

Arrival and information

Flights arrive at the city's **Marco Polo** airport, on the edge of the lagoon, linked to the city centre by *ACTV* bus #5, which runs hourly and costs just L1000. All road traffic comes into the city at **Piazzale Roma**, at the head of the Canal Grande, from where waterbus services run to the San Marco area, stopping off at Santa Lucia **train station**, the next stop along the Canal Grande. If you're coming right into Venice by **car**, you'll have to park in either the Piazzale Roma multistorey car park, or on the adjoining Tronchetto, a vast artificial island. The queues for both can be huge – a better option in summer is to park in Mestre's municipal car park, then take a bus over the causeway.

The main **tourist office** (Mon–Sat summer 8.30am–7pm; winter 8.30am–2pm) is on the edge of Piazza San Marco, at the opposite end to the Basilica, and there are desks at the train station, and, in summer, at Piazzale Roma. Pick up their free map and English-Italian magazine, *Un Ospite di Venezia*, which gives up-to-date what's on information and *vaporetto* timetables.

City transport

In most cases the speediest way of getting around Venice is **on foot**. Distances between major sights are short (you can cross the whole city in an hour), and once you've got your general bearings navigation is not as daunting a prospect as it seems. To get between two points quickly, however, it's sometimes faster to take a waterbus. There are two basic types: the slower **vaporetti**, used on the Canal Grande and other busy routes, and the smaller and faster **motoscafi**. **Tickets** are available from most landing stages and all shops displaying the *ACTV* sign. Flat-rate fares are generally L3300 for a *motoscafo*, L2200 for a *vaporetto* service. Tickets bought on board are subject to a surcharge, and the spot-fine for not having a valid ticket is L15,000, so it's a good idea to buy a block of ten (*un blochetto*). A *Biglietto Turistico* gives you unlimited travel for a 24-hour period for L12,000. There's also a *Carta Venezia*, which costs L8000 and entitles you to travel for L1000 per journey (L1200 on the *diretto*), as well as on all *ACTV* buses; take a photo and your passport to the *ACTV* office in Corte dell'Albero, near the Sant'Angelo stop on the Canal Grande. Timetables are posted at each stop, the tourist office's city map has a route plan, and *Un Ospite di Venezia* has details of the important lines. In addition, there are the **traghetti** that cross the Canale Grande, which cost L500 a trip and are the only cheap way of getting a ride on a gondola. In summer they run from early morning to around 7–9pm daily. Otherwise the **gondola** is an adjunct of the tourist industry. To hire one costs L70,000 an hour, L90,000 between 8pm and 8am, plus L35,000 for each additional 25 minutes – be sure to confirm the charge beforehand.

Accommodation

Accommodation is the major expense in Venice, although there are inexpensive options, not least a number of **hostels**, most owned by religious foundations, which are generally comfortable and well-run. Unless you're coming in the November–February period (when many hotels close), you should always book ahead; if you haven't, there are **booking offices** at the train station (daily 8am–9pm), on the Tronchetto (daily 9am–8pm), at Piazzale Roma (daily 9am–9pm), at Marco Polo airport (daily summer 9am–7pm; winter noon–7pm), and at the *autostrada's* Venice exit (8am–8pm). They only deal with hotels and take a L10,000 deposit, deductable from your first night's bill.

HOSTELS

Archie's House, Rio Terrà San Leonardo, Cannaregio 1814/b (☎720.884). Cross between hostel and *pensione*, gone downhill in recent years but still a favourite with budget travellers, especially US college types. ②

Domus Cavanis, Rio Terrà Foscarini, Dorsoduro 912 (☎528.7374). Catholic-run, so separate male and female rooms; open June–Sept. ③

Domus Civica, Calle Campazzo, San Polo 3082 (☎721.103). A student house in winter, open to women travellers June, July, Sept & Oct. 11.30pm curfew. ③

Foresteria Valdese, Santa Maria Formosa, Castello 5170 (☎528.6797). Difficult to find – go from Campo Santa Maria Formosa along Calle Lunga, and it's at the foot of the bridge at the far end. Two large dorms, and a few rooms for two to four people; open for registration 11am–1pm & 6–8.30pm. ③

Ostello Venezia, Fondementa delle Zitelle, Guidecca 86 (☎523.8211). The official *IYHF* hostel, in a superb location looking towards San Marco from the island of Giudecca. Opens at noon in summer and 4pm in winter for the 6pm registration, and it's a good idea to get there early; Oct–May you can book by phone. If it's full, don't panic: they use a local school with camp-beds as an annexe. Curfew 11.30pm. ②

HOTELS

Albergo Bernardi Semenzato, Calle dell'Oca, Cannaregio 4366 (☎522.7257). Newly renovated place with very welcoming and helpful English-speaking owners. ⑤

Antico Capon, Campo S. Margherita, Dorsoduro 3004 (☎528.5292). Situated on one of the city's most atmospheric squares, in the heart of the student district. ③

Ca' Fóscari, Calle della Frescada, Dorsoduro 3888 (☎522.5817). Tucked away in a micro-alley near San Tomà, near the university. Quiet, well decorated and relaxed. ③

Caneva, Ramo della Fava, Castello 5515 (☎522.8118). Overlooking the Rio della Fava on the approach to the busy Campo San Bartolomeo, yet very peaceful. ④

Casa Carettoni, Lista di Spagna, Cannaregio 130 (☎717.231). By a long way the most comfortable one-star in the vicinity. ③

Casa Petrarca, Calle delle Colonne, San Marco 4394 (☎520.0430). Friendly place, and the cheapest near the Piazza. Phone first, as they only have six rooms. ③

Eden, Rio Terrà Maddalena, Cannaregio 2357 (☎720.228). One to try if you're travelling alone. ⑤

Fiorita, Campiello Nuovo, San Marco 3457 (☎522.8043). Just nine rooms, so again it's important to book. Welcoming management. ③

Montin, Fondamenta di Borgo, Dorsoduro 1147 (☎522.7151). Famed for its restaurant, though the food is much pricier than the accommodation. Only seven rooms. ④

Sant'Anna, Corte del Bianco, Castello 269 (☎528.6466). A fair way out from the centre but good for families with kids, as it has rooms for 3–4 people and is near the Giardini Pubblici; a recent "find", so book in early. ⑤

Sturion, Calle del Sturion, S. Polo 679 (☎523.6243). Recently upgraded to a three-star, this hotel needs to be booked in advance as it's popular with Italian families. ⑧

Toscana-Tofanelli, Via Garibaldi, Castello 1650 (☎523.5722). Spartan hotel but a good location and excellent trattoria attached; midnight curfew. ③

CAMPSITES

There are a number of fairly expensive **campsites** along the **Litorale del Cavallino**, accessible on *vaporetto* #14 from the Riva degli Schiavoni, a forty-minute trip. Two to try are *Marina di Venezia*, Via Montello 6 (April–Sept; minimum stay 3 days; ☎966.146), and *Miramare,* Lungomare Dante Alighieri 29 (April–Sept; ☎966.150). There's an all-year site at **Fusina**, *Mestre Fusina*, on Via Moranzani – better in summer when there's a direct *vaporetto* (#16); at other times get the bus to Mestre and change there.

Self-sufficient travellers used to spread their sleeping bags in front of the train station in summer, an expedient that was banned in 1987. At that point the **Scuola San Caboto**, Cannaregio 1104/f (☎716.629), opened its doors to take in the displaced *saccopelisti*, as they're called. The school charges L5000 for sleeping in its garden, L8000 with your tent, L6500 with their tent, L10,000 dorm-style. It's open 7pm to midnight, and you have to be out by 9am; follow the signs from the Ponte delle Guglie, on the Canale di Cannaregio. Ask also at the tourist office if there's a makeshift dormitory anywhere to absorb the overspill – there normally is somewhere in the city.

The City

The 118 islands of central Venice are divided into six districts known as *sestieri*. The *sestiere* of **San Marco** is home to the majority of the essential sights, and is accordingly the most expensive and most crowded district of the city. On the east it's bordered by **Castello**, on the north by **Cannaregio** – both of which become more residential the further you go from the centre. On the other side of the Canal Grande, the largest of the *sestieri* is **Dorsoduro**, which stretches from the fashionable quarter at the southern tip of the canal to the docks in the west. **Santa Croce**, named after a now demolished church, roughly follows the curve of the Canal Grande from Piazzale Roma to a point just short of the Rialto, where it joins the smartest and commercially most active of the districts on this bank – **San Polo**.

SAN MARCO

The section of Venice enclosed by the lower loop of the Canal Grande is, in essence, the Venice of the travel brochures. The **Piazza San Marco** is the hub of most activity, signalled from most parts of the city by the **Campanile** (daily 9.30–3.30/8pm; L3000), which began life as a lighthouse in the ninth century and was modified frequently up to the early sixteenth. The present structure is in fact a reconstruction: the original tower collapsed on July 14, 1902. At 99m, it is the tallest structure in the city, and from the top you can make out virtually every building, but not a single canal. The other tower in the Piazza, the **Torre dell'Orologio**, was built between 1496 and 1506, although the panorama can't compete with the Campanile's and you can watch the Moors at the top strike the hour perfectly well from the ground; it's also currently closed for restoration. Away to the left stretches the **Procuratie Vecchie**, an early sixteenth-century structure that was converted into a palace by Napoléon, who connected the building with the other side of the piazza – the **Procuratie Nuove** – by way of a new wing for dancing. Generally known as the **Ala Napoleonica**, this short side of the Piazza is partly occupied by the **Museo Correr** (daily except Tues 9am–7pm; L5000), whose vast historical collection – coins, weapons, regalia, prints, mediocre paintings – is heavy going unless you have an intense interest in Venetian history. The **Quadreria** on the second floor is no rival for the Accademia's collection, but does set out clearly the evolution of painting in Venice from the thirteenth century to around 1500, and contains some gems – a *Pietà* by Cosmé Tura, the *Transfiguration* and *Dead Christ Supported by Angels* by Giovanni Bellini, along with a Carpaccio picture known as *The Courtesans*. There's also an appealing exhibition of applied arts, featuring a print of Jacopo de'Barbari's astonishing aerial view of Venice, engraved in 1500.

The **Basilica di San Marco** (daily 10am–5pm) is the most exotic of Europe's cathedrals, modelled on Constantinople's Church of the Twelve Apostles, finished in 1094 and embellished over the succeeding centuries with trophies brought back from abroad – proof of Venice's secular might and thus of the spiritual power of Saint Mark. The Romanesque carvings of the central door were begun around 1225 and finished in the early fourteenth century, while the mosaic above the doorway on the far left – *The Arrival of the Body of St Mark* – was made around 1260 (the only early mosaic left on the main facade) and includes the oldest known image of the Basilica. Inside, the narthex holds more mosaics, Old Testament scenes on the domes and arches, together with *The Madonna with Apostles and Evangelists* in the niches of the bay in front of the main door – dating from the 1060s, the oldest mosaics in San Marco. A steep staircase goes from the church's main door up to the **Museo Marciano** and the **Loggia dei Cavalli** (daily 9.45am–5.30pm; L2000), where you can enjoy fine views of the city and the Gothic carvings along the apex of the facade, as well as the horses in question, replicas of Roman works thieved from the Hippodrome of Constantinople (the genuine articles are inside). Downstairs, beyond the narthex, the interior proper is covered with more mosaics, most dating from the middle of the thirteenth century, although the

Sanctuary, off the south transept (Mon–Sat 9.45am–5.30pm, Sun 1.30–5.30pm; L2000), holds the most precious of San Marco's treasures, the **Pala d'Oro** or golden altar panel, commissioned in 976 in Constantinople and studded with precious stones. The **Treasury** (same times; L2000) nearby is a similarly dazzling warehouse of chalices, reliquaries and candelabra, a fair proportion pillaged from Constantinople in 1204. Look too at the **Baptistery,** altered to its present form by the fourteenth-century Doge Andrea Dandolo, whose tomb (facing the door) was thought by Ruskin to have the best monumental sculpture in the city. Back in the main body of the church, there's still more to see on the lower levels of the building. Don't overlook the **rood screen's** marble figures of *The Virgin, St Mark and the Apostles,* carved in 1394 by the dominant sculptors in Venice at that time, Jacobello and Pietro Paolo Dalle Masegne. The **pulpits** on each side of the screen were assembled in the early fourteenth century from miscellaneous panels, some from Constantinople; the new doge was presented to the people from the right-hand one. The tenth-century **Icon of the Madonna of Nicopeia** (in the chapel on the east side of the north transept) is the most revered religious image in Venice, and was one of the most revered in Constantinople.

The adjacent **Palazzo Ducale** (April to mid-Oct daily 9am–6pm; mid-Oct to March daily 9am–4pm; L8000) was the residence of the doge, as well as housing Venice's governing councils, courts, a sizeable number of its civil servants and even its prisons. Like San Marco, the Palazzo Ducale has been rebuilt many times since its foundation in the first years of the ninth century, but the earliest parts of the current structure date from 1340. The principal entrance, the **Porta della Carta,** is one of the most ornate Gothic works in the city, commissioned in 1438 by Doge Francesco Fóscari; the figures of Fóscari and his lion are replicas – the originals were pulverized in 1797 by the head of the stonemasons' guild, as a favour to Napoléon. The passage inside ends under the **Arco Fóscari,** also commissioned by Doge Fóscari but finished a few years after his death. Parts of the Palazzo Ducale can be marched through fairly briskly, its walls covered with acres of wearisome canvas, although you should linger in the **Anticollegio,** one of the palace's finest rooms and home to four pictures by Tintoretto and Veronese's characteristically benign *Rape of Europa.* The cycle of paintings on the ceiling of the adjoining Sala del Collegio is also by Veronese, and he features strongly again in the most stupendous room in the building – the Sala del Maggior Consiglio, where his ceiling panel of the *Apotheosis of Venice* is suspended over the dais from which the doge oversaw the sessions of the city assembly. The backdrop is the immense *Paradiso* painted at the end of his life by Tintoretto, with the aid of his son, Domenico. From here you descend quickly to the underbelly of the Venetian state, crossing the **Ponte dei Sospiri** (Bridge of Sighs) to the **prisons.**

Facing the Palazzo Ducale across the Piazzetta is Sansovino's masterpiece and the most consistently admired Renaissance building in the city – the **Libreria Sansoviniana,** part of which is given over to the **Museo Archeologico** (Mon–Sat 9am–2pm, Sun 9am–1pm; L4000), a collection of Greek and Roman sculpture that's best left for a rainy day.

DORSODURO

Some of the finest architecture in Venice is in the *sestiere* of **Dorsoduro,** yet for all its attractions, not many visitors wander off the strip that runs between the main sights of the area, the first of which, the **Galleria dell'Accademia** (Mon–Sat 9am–1.30pm, Sun 9am–12.30pm; L8000), is one of the finest specialist collections of European art, following the history of Venetian painting from the fourteenth to the eighteenth centuries. Housed in the church of Santa Maria della Carità and the incomplete Convento dei Canonici Lateranensi, partly built by Palladio in 1561, the gallery is laid out in roughly chronological order. The early sections include paintings by Paolo Veneziano, Carpaccio's strange and gruesome *Crucifixion and Glorification of the Ten Thousand Martyrs* *of Mount Ararat*, an exquisite *St George* by Mantegna, a series of Giovanni Bellini *Madonnas*, and one of the most mysterious of Italian paintings, Giorgione's *Tempest*. Tintoretto weighs in with the sumptuously painted *Madonna dei Camerlenghi* and three typically energetic pieces illustrating the legend of Saint Mark, and an entire wall is filled by Paolo Veronese's *Christ in the House of Levi* – called *The Last Supper* until the authorities objected to its lack of reverence. Among the most impressive pieces in the Accademia is the magnificent cycle of pictures painted around 1500 for the Scuola di San Giovanni Evangelista, of which Carpaccio's *Cure of a Lunatic* and Gentile Bellini's *Recovery of the Relic from the Canale di San Lorenzo* and *Procession of the Relic in the Piazza* stand out. There's also a cycle of pictures by Carpaccio illustrating the *Story of Saint Ursula*, painted for the Scuola di Sant'Orsola at San Zanipolo, which is one of the most unforgettable groups in the entire country. Finally, in room 24 there's Titian's *Presentation of the Virgin*, painted for the place where it hangs.

Five minutes' walk from the Accademia is the unfinished Palazzo Venier dei Leoni, home of the **Guggenheim Collection** (daily except Tues 11am–6pm, Sat closes 9pm; L7000, free Sat 6–9pm), and of Peggy Guggenheim for thirty years until her death in 1979. Her private collection is an eclectic choice of (mainly) excellent pieces from her favourite modernist movements and artists, including works by Brancusi, De Chirico, Max Ernst and Malevich. Continuing along the line of the Canal Grande, the church of Santa Maria della Salute, better known simply as the **Salute** (daily 8am–noon & 3–5pm; L1000), was built to fulfil a Senate decree of 1630 that a new church be dedicated to Mary if the city were delivered from plague. Every November 21 there's still a procession from San Marco to the church, over a specially constructed pontoon bridge, to give thanks for the city's good health, a major event on the Venetian calendar. In 1656, a hoard of Titian paintings were moved here and are now housed in the sacristy, most prominent of which is the altarpiece of *St Mark Enthroned with Saints Cosmas, Damian, Sebastian and Rocco*. The *Marriage at Cana*, with its dramatic lighting and perspective, is by Tintoretto, featuring portraits of a number of the artist's friends.

On the other side of Dorsoduro, the church of **San Sebastiano**, up by the Stazione Marittima, was built between 1505 and 1545, and was the parish church of Paolo Veronese, who provided most of its paintings and is buried here. From here it's a straightforward walk back towards the Canal Grande along Calle Avogaria and Calle Lunga San Barnaba, a route that deposits you in Campo San Barnaba, just yards from the **Ca' Rezzonico** – now the **Museo del Settecento Veneziano** (daily except Fri 9am–7pm; L5000), full of eighteenth-century Venetian applied arts and paintings in a building furnished like a wealthy house of the time. Among the paintings are Pietro Longhi's affectionate illustrations of Venetian social life and frescoes of clowns and carnival scenes painted towards the end of his life by Giandomenico Tiepolo.

SAN POLO

North of Dorsoduro is the *sestiere* of **San Polo**, on the northeastern edge of which the **Rialto** district was in former times the commercial zone of the city, home to the main Venetian banks and maritime businesses. It's the venue of the Rialto market on the far side of the Rialto Bridge, a lively affair and one of the few places in the city where it's possible to hear nothing but Italian spoken. The main reason people visit San Polo, however, is to see the mountainous brick church of the **Frari** west of here (Mon–Sat 9.30am–noon & 2.30–6pm, Sun 3–5.30pm; L1000, free Sun), whose collection of artworks includes a rare couple of paintings by Titian – his *Assumption*, painted in 1518, is a swirling piece of compositional bravura for which there was no precedent in Venetian art. Look also at the Renaissance tombs of the doges flanking the *Assumption*, dating from the late fifteenth century; the wooden *St John the Baptist*, in the chapel to the right, commissioned from Donatello in 1438; and, on the altar of the sacristy, a marvellous *Madonna and Child with Saints* by Giovanni Bellini. Titian is buried in the church, the spot marked by a bombastic nineteenth-century monument, opposite which the equally pompous Mausoleum of Canova was erected by pupils of the sculptor, following a design he himself had made for the tomb of Titian.

At the rear of the Frari is another place you should on no account miss, the **Scuola Grande di San Rocco** (daily summer 9.30am–5.30pm; winter 10am–1pm; L6000), a sixteenth-century building that is home to a cycle of more than fifty major paintings by Tintoretto. These fall into three main groups. The first, painted in 1564, adorn the upper Sala dell'Albergo – a *Glorification of St Roch*, painted for a competition, and a stupendous *Crucifixion*, which Ruskin claimed to be "above all praise". In the building's main hall, Tintoretto covered three large panels of the ceiling with Old Testament references to the alleviation of physical suffering – coded declarations of the Scuola's charitable activities – while around the walls are New Testament themes, an amazing feat of sustained inventiveness, in which every convention of perspective, lighting, colour and even anatomy is defied. The paintings on the ground floor were created between 1583 and 1587, when Tintoretto was in his late sixties, and include a turbulent *Annunciation*, a marvellous Renaissance landscape in *The Flight into Egypt* and two small paintings of *St Mary Magdalene* and *St Mary of Egypt*.

CANNAREGIO

In the northernmost section of Venice, **CANNAREGIO**, you can go from one extreme to another in a matter of minutes: it is a short distance from the bustle of the **train station** to areas which are among the quietest and prettiest parts of the whole city. The district also has the dubious distinction of containing the world's first **Ghetto**: in 1516, all the city's Jews were ordered to move to the island of the Ghetto Nuovo, an enclave which was sealed at night by Christian curfew guards and even now looks quite different from the rest of Venice, many of its buildings relatively high-rise due to the restrictions that were put on the growth of the area. A couple of the oldest synagogues – the **Scola Levantina**, founded in 1538, and the **Scola Spagnola**, founded twenty years later – are still in use and can be viewed on an informative and multilingual guided tour that leaves on the half-hour, organized by the **Jewish Museum** in Campo Ghetto Nuovo (daily 10am–7pm; L3000, with tour L7000), where you can also see a collection of silverware and embroidered and other fabric objects.

The area northeast of the Ghetto is one of the most restful parts of Venice, crossed by long straight canals and dotted with food shops, bars and trattorias. In the far eastern corner, the Gothic church of **Madonna dell'Orto** (daily summer 9am–noon & 3–7pm; winter closes 5pm) was renamed after a stone *Madonna* by Giovanni de'Santi, found discarded in a local vegetable garden, that began to work miracles. Brought inside the church in 1377, the heavily restored figure can still be seen in the Cappella di San Mauro. Also inside is the tomb of Tintoretto, in the chapel to the right of the high altar, along with those of his son and daughter, Domenico and Marietta, and a number of paintings by the artist, notably the colossal *Making of the Golden Calf* and *The Last Judgement*, which flank the main altar, plus quite a few other notable works.

CASTELLO

Northeast of San Marco, **Castello** is home among other things to the **Miracoli** church, built in the 1480s to house a painting of the Madonna which was believed to have performed a number of miracles, such as reviving a man who'd spent half an hour lying at the bottom of the Giudecca canal. The church is thought to have been designed by Pietro Lombardo, who with his two sons Tullio and Antonio oversaw the building and executed much of the carving, which ranks as some of the most intricate decorative sculpture in Venice.

East of here, the **Campo San Zanipolo** (a contraction of Santi Giovanni e Paolo) is the most impressive open space in Venice after Piazza San Marco, dominated by the huge brick church of **San Zanipolo**, founded by the Dominicans in 1246, rebuilt and enlarged from 1333 and finally consecrated in 1430. The church is perhaps best-known for the tombs and monuments around the walls, the memorials of some 25 doges, most impressive of which is perhaps the tomb of Doge Michele Morosini on the right of the chancel (daily 7am–12.30pm & 3.30–7.30pm), selected by Ruskin as "the richest monument of the Gothic period in Venice". On the square outside the church, Verrochio's statue of the Venetian military hero **Bartolomeo Colleoni** is one of the finest Renaissance equestrian mounuments in Italy, commissioned in 1481.

The other essential sight in this area is over to the east of San Marco – the **Scuola di San Giorgio degli Schiavoni** (Tues–Sat 9.30am–12.30pm & 3.30–6.30pm, Sun 11am–12.30pm; L4000), set up by Venice's Slav population in 1451. The building dates from the early sixteenth century, and its interior looks more or less as it would have then, with a superb ground-floor room decorated with a cycle painted by Vittore Carpaccio between 1502 and 1509.

THE NORTHERN ISLANDS

The major islands lying to the north of Venice – **Murano**, **Burano** and **Torcello** – can be reached by *vaporetto* from the **Fondamente Nuove**: the #5, which runs about every fifteen minutes, will take you to San Michele and Murano; for Burano and Torcello there is the *vaporetto* or steamer #12 (roughly hourly), which takes 40 minutes to Burano, from where it's a short hop to Torcello. This service can also be caught from Murano, at the Faro landing stage.

Chiefly famed as the home of Venice's glass-blowing industry, **Murano's** main *fondamente* are crowded with shops selling the mostly revolting products of the furnaces, but the process of manufacture is more interesting. There are numerous **furnaces** to visit, all free cf charge on the assumption that you will then want to buy something, though you won't be pressed too hard to do so. Many of the workshops are along Fondamenta dei Vetrai. There's also the **Museo Vetrario** in the Palazzo Giustinian (daily 9am–7pm; L5000), which displays Roman pieces and the earliest surviving examples of Murano glass, from the fifteenth century. Your entry ticket will also get you into the **Modern and Contemporary Glass Museum** on Fondamenta Manin (same hours). Other attractions include the church of **San Pietro Martire**, a Dominican Gothic church which houses an elegant *Madonna* by Giovanni Bellini, and the Veneto-Byzantine church of **Santi Maria e Donato**, founded in the seventh century and rebuilt in the twelfth (daily 8am–noon & 4–7pm), which has a beautiful mosaic floor.

Burano is still largely a fishing community, although there is also a thriving trade in **lace-making** here, and the main street is crammed with shops selling Burano-point and Venetian-point lace. Making the lace is extremely exacting work, both highly skilled and mind-bendingly repetitive, with an enormous toll on the eyesight. Each woman specializes in one particular stitch, and so each piece is passed from woman to woman during its construction. The skills are taught at the **Scuola dei Merletti** in Piazza Baldessare Galuppi (Tues–Sat 9am–6pm, Sun 10am–4pm; L5000), which also houses a small museum with work dating back as far as the sixteenth century.

The island of **Torcello** was settled as early as the fifth century, and once had a population of some 20,000. Nowadays, however, the population is about 100, and there is little visible evidence of the island's prime. The main reason that people come here today is to visit Venice's first cathedral, **Santa Maria Assunta** (daily 10am–12.30pm & 2–5pm; L1500), a Veneto-Byzantine building on the site of an original seventh- century church, only the crypt of which survives. The interior has an eleventh-century mosaic floor and a stunning twelfth-century mosaic of the Madonna and Child in the apse, resting on an eleventh-century mosaic frieze of the Apostles. Look in also on the church of **Santa Fosca**, built in the eleventh and twelfth centuries to house the body of the eponymous saint, brought to Torcello from Libya some time before 1011 and now resting under the altar. In the square outside sits the curious **chair of Attila**: sit in it and – local legend says – you will be wed within a year. Behind, the **Museo dell'Estuario** (Tues–Sun 10am–12.30pm & 2–5.30pm; L3000) displays thirteenth-century beaten gold figures, sections of mosaic heads and pieces of jewellery.

THE SOUTHERN ISLANDS

Immediately south of the Palazzo Ducale, Palladio's church of **San Giorgio Maggiore** stands on the island of the same name (daily 9am–noon & 2.30–6pm). This proved one of the most influential Renaissance church designs, and it has two pictures by Tinto-retto in the chancel – *The Fall of Manna* and *The Last Supper*, perhaps the most famous of all his images, painted as a pair in 1592–94, the last years of the artist's life. On the left of the choir a corridor leads to the **campanile**, rebuilt in 1791 after the collapse of its predecessor and one of the two best vantage points in the city. The ex-Benedictine monastery next door, now the **Fondazione Giorgio Cini**, is one of the architectural gems of Venice, incorporating a 128-metre-long dormitory designed by Giovanni Buora around 1494, and many other impressive bits and pieces by Longhena and Palladio – you may only visit by appointment (☎528.9900), except when the building is hosting an exhibition.

The long island of **La Giudecca**, to the west, was where the wealthiest aristocrats of early Renaissance Venice built their villas, and in places you can still see traces of their gardens, although the present-day suburb is a strange mixture of decrepitude and vital-ity, boatyards and fishing quays interspersed with half-abandoned factories and sheds. Unless you're staying at the *Cipriani*, the most expensive hotel in Venice, the main reason to come is the Franciscan church of the **Redentore** (daily 7.30am–noon & 3.30–7pm), designed by Palladio in 1577 in thanks for Venice's deliverance from a plague that killed a third of the population. Sadly, the church is in a bad state of repair, and a rope prevents visitors going beyond the nave, but you can see its best paintings, including a *Madonna with Child and Angels* by Alvise Vivarini, in the sacristy, as well as a curious gallery of eighteenth-century wax heads of illustrious Franciscans.

Sheltering Venice from the open sea, the thin strand of the **Lido** used to be the focus of the annual hullaballoo of Venice's "Marriage to the Sea", when the doge went out to the Porto di Lido to drop a gold ring into the brine and then disembarked for mass at San Nicolò al Lido. Later it became the smartest bathing resort in Italy, and although it's no longer as chic as it was when Thomas Mann set *Death in Venice* here, there's less room on its beaches now than ever before; indeed, unless you're staying at one of the flashy hotels on the seafront, or are prepared to pay a ludicrous fee to hire a beach hut, you won't even be allowed to get the choicest Lido sand between your toes. There are public beaches at the northern and southern ends of the island – though the water is, as you would expect, filthy.

Eating and drinking

Virtually every **restaurant** in Venice advertises a set-price *Menu Turistico*, which can be a cheap way of sampling Venetian specialities, but the quality and certainly the quantity won't be up to the mark of an à la carte meal. As a general rule, value for money tends to increase with the distance from San Marco; plenty of restaurants within a short radius of the Piazza offer menus that seem to be reasonable but you'll probably find the food unappetizing and the service abrupt. Most bars will also serve some kind of food, ranging from *tramezzini* through to more exotic nibbles called *cicheti*.

TAKEAWAYS AND PICNIC FOOD

Cip Ciap in Calle Mondo Nuovo, Castello (closed Thurs), has perhaps the city's best range of takeaway pizzas, with a wonderfully tasty spinach and ricotta variety. *Aliani Gastronomia*, Ruga Vecchia S. Giovanni, San Polo, is a good source of picnic fare, as are the fruit and veg **markets** at Santa Maria Formosa and Santa Margherita, and the general market at the Rialto, where you can buy everything you need for an impromptu feast – it's open Monday to Saturday from 8am to 1pm.

RESTAURANTS

Al Milion, Corte del Milion (behind San Giovanni Crisostomo), Castello. Mid-priced trattoria with bar serving snacks.

Alle Oche, Calle del Tintor (south side of Campo S. Giacomo dell'Orio), San Polo. Has about fifty varieties of inexpensive pizza to choose from; closed Mon.

Altanella, Calle dell'Erbe, Giudecca. Beautiful fish dishes, and a terrace overlooking the island's central canal. Good for a treat; closed Mon & Tues.

Antico Mola, Fondamenta degli Ormesini, Cannaregio. Originally a family-run, local place, but becoming trendier by the year. Good food, good value; closed Sat.

Crepizza, S. Pantalon 3757, San Polo. Pizzas, pasta dishes and crêpes that justify the slightly higher prices.

Donna Onesta, Calle della Madonna Onesta (near the Frari), San Polo. Popular and very friendly – ask about the day's special dish; closed Sun.

Frigittoria da Bruno, Calle Lunga San Barnaba, Dorsoduro. Similar to *Donna Onesta*, but a bit cheaper and more homely; closed Sat & Sun.

Paradiso Perduto, Fondamenta della Misericordia, Cannaregio. Fronted by a popular bar, with a lively relaxed atmosphere and sometimes live music. Full meals start at around L15,000; closed Wed & Sun.

Rosticceria San Bartolomeo, Calle della Bissa, San Marco. A glorified snack bar serving low-priced full meals. Good if you need to refuel quickly and cheaply but just can't face another pizza; closed Mon.

Toscana, Via Garibaldi (bottom end), Eastern Districts. Plain, with a tiny menu, but all its dishes are good and inexpensive.

BARS, CAFÉS AND PASTICCERIE

Al Volto, Calle Cavalli (near Campo S. Luca), San Marco. Stocks 1300 wines from Italy and elsewhere, some cheap, many not; good snacks, too; closed Sun.

Cantina del Vino gia Schiavi, Fondamenta Maravegie, Dorsoduro. Great wine shop and bar; closed Sun.

Do Mori, Calle Do Mori, San Polo. Narrow, standing-only bar, catering mainly for the Rialto porters and traders. Frustratingly, it is shut at lunchtime when they all nip home, but at other times it serves delicious snacks. One of the best of a number of bars in the area of the market; closed Wed pm & Sun.

Harry's Bar, Calle Vallaresso, San Marco. Long a fashionable spot, famed in equal measure for its cocktails, its sandwiches and its prices; open 3pm–1am, closed Mon.

Il Golosone, Salizzada San Lio, Castello. *Pasticceria* and bar with a glorious spread of cakes; does a delicious apple *spremute*; closed Mon.

Marchini, Ponte San Maurizio, San Marco. The most delicious and expensive of Venetian *pasticcerie*, where people come on Sunday morning to buy family treats.

Nico, Záttere ai Gesuati, Dorsoduro. Highspot of a wander in the area, celebrated for an artery-clogging creation called a *gianduiotto* – a block of praline ice cream in whipped cream; closed Thurs.

Paolin, Campo Santo Stefano, San Marco. Thought by many to be the makers of the best ice cream in Venice; the outside tables also have one of the finest settings in the city; closed Fri.

VinoVino, Ponte delle Veste, San Marco. Slightly posey bar stocking over 100 wines; open until midnight, closed Tues.

The Carnevale, Regata Storica and Biennale

Perhaps the city's most famous annual event is the **Carnevale**, which occupies the ten days leading up to Lent, finishing on Shrove Tuesday with a masked ball for the glitterati and dancing in the Piazza for the plebs. It was revived in the late Seventies, and after three years gained support from the city authorities, who now organize various pageants and performances. It's also very much a time to see and be seen: people don costumes and in the evening congregate in the squares. Masks are on sale throughout the year in Venice, but new mask and costume shops suddenly appear during Carnevale, and Campo San Maurizio sprouts a marquee with mask-making demonstrations and a variety of designs for sale. Another big event is the **Regata Storica**, held on the first Sunday in September, an annual trial of strength and skill for the city's gondoliers which starts with a procession of richly decorated historic craft along the Canal Grande course, their crews all decked out in period dress. Bystanders are expected to join in the support for the contestants in the main event, and may even be issued with appropriate colours. There's also the **Venice Biennale**, set up in 1895 as a showpiece for international contemporary art and held every odd-numbered year from June to September. Its permanent site in the Giardini Pubblici has pavilions for about forty countries, plus space for a thematic international exhibition. The *Aperto* ("Open") section, a mixed exhibition showing the work of younger or less established artists, takes over spaces all over the city, and various sites throughout the city host fringe exhibitions, installations and performances, particularly in the opening weeks.

Listings

Airlines *Alitalia*, Salizzada San Moisè, San Marco 1463 (☎520.0355); *British Airways*, Riva degli Schiavoni, Castello 4191 (☎528.5026).

Airport enquiries Marco Polo airport, ☎661.262.

Books A good general bookshop is *Goldoni*, Calle dei Fabbri, San Marco.

Car rental *Europcar*, Piazzale Roma 540 (☎523.8616).

Consulates *Great Britain* Palazzo Querini, Accademia, Dorsoduro 1051 (☎522.7207).

Exchange *American Express*, Salizzada San Moisè, San Marco (Mon–Sat 8am–8pm; ☎520.0844).

Hospital *Ospedale Civili Riunti di Venezia*, Campo Santi Giovanni e Paolo (☎520.5622).

Laundry *Lavaget*, Fondamenta Pescaria, off Rio Terrà San Leonardo, Cannaregio, and *Salizzada del Pistor*, Cannaveggio 4553, near Santi Apostoli.

Left luggage Train station left-luggage desk open 24hr; L1500 per item.

Pharmacies Call ☎192 or consult *Un Ospite di Venezia*.

Police The *Questura* is on Fondamenta San Lorenzo, Castello (☎520.3222).

Post office Central office in the Fondaco dei Tedeschi, by the Rialto Bridge (Mon–Sat 8.15am–7pm, poste restante 8.15am–6.45pm); 24hr telegram service.

Telephones 24hr booths at train station. *SIP* offices at Rialto post office (8am–8pm) and at Piazzale Roma (8am–9.30pm).

Train enquiries ☎715.555

Padua

Extensively rebuilt after damage caused by bombing in the last war, and hemmed in by the sprawl which accompanied its development as the Veneto's most important economic centre, **PADUA** is not immediately the most alluring city in northern Italy; however, it is one of the most ancient, and plentiful evidence remains of its lineage. A former Roman settlement, the city was a place of pilgrimage following the death of Saint Anthony here, and it later became an artistic and intellectual centre: Donatello and Mantegna both worked here, and in the seventeenth century Galileo researched at the university, where the medical faculty was one of the most ambitious in Europe.

The City

Just outside the city centre, through a gap in the Renaissance walls off Corso Garibaldi, the Giotto frescoes in the **Cappella degli Scrovegni** (daily summer 9am–7pm; winter 9am–5.30pm; L3000 chapel only, L8000 joint ticket with Museo Civico) are for many the reason for coming to Padua. Commissioned in 1303 by Enrico Scrovegni in atonement for his father's usury, which was so vicious that he was denied a Christian burial, the chapel's walls are covered with illustrations of the life of Mary, Jesus and the story of the Passion – a cycle, arranged in three tiers and painted against a backdrop of saturated blue, that is one of the high points in the development of European art in its innovative attention to the inner nature of its subjects. Beneath the main pictures are shown the vices and virtues in human (usually female) form, while on the wall above the door is the *Last Judgement*. Directly above the door is a portrait of Scrovegni presenting the chapel; his tomb is at the far end, behind the altar with its statues by Giovanni Pisano. The adjacent **Museo Civico** (same times) is an assembly of fourteenth- to eighteenth-century art from the Veneto, the high point being a *Crucifixion* by Giotto that was once in the Scrovegni chapel, a fine *Portrait of a Young Senator* by Bellini, and a sequence of devils overcoming angels by Guariento. After these, it's a trudge through Etruscan pot shards, dull Egyptian and Roman works, dire nineteenth-century painting, and an assortment of coins and metalwork. Nearby, the church of the **Eremitani**, built at the turn of the fourteenth century but almost completely wrecked by bombing in 1944, has been fastidiously rebuilt (Mon–Sat 8.15am–noon & 3.30–6.30pm, Sun 9am–noon & 3.30–5.30pm; winter Mon–Sat closes 5.30pm, Sun closes 5pm), although the frescoes by Mantegna that used to be here were almost totally lost, and can now be assessed only from a few fuzzy photographs and some fragments on the right of the high altar.

South of here, on the other side of the centre, the main sight of the Piazza del Santo is Donatello's **Monument to Gattamelata** ("The Honeyed Cat"), as the *condottiere* Erasmo da Narni was known. He died in 1443 and this monument was raised ten years later, the earliest large bronze sculpture of the Renaissance, and a direct precursor to Verrocchio's monument to Colleoni in Venice. On one side of the square, the basilica of San Antonio or **Il Santo** (daily 6.30am–7pm; L1000) was built to house the body of Saint Anthony, and its Cappella del Santo has a sequence of panels showing scenes from his life, carved between 1505 and 1577. Take a look, too, at Padua's finest work by Pietro Lombardo, a monument to Antonio Roselli, and the high altar's sculptures and reliefs by Donatello. The Cappella del Tesoro off the ambulatory (8am–noon & 2.30–7pm) houses the tongue and chin of Saint Anthony in a head-shaped reliquary.

Via Umberto leads you towards the **university**, established in 1221, and older than any other in Italy except Bologna. The main block is the **Palazzo del Bò**, where Galileo taught physics from 1592 to 1610, declaiming from a lectern that is still on show, though the building is currently closed for restoration and visits have to be arranged by phone (☎049/828.3111). The area west of here, around the **Piazza delle Frutta** and **Piazza dell'Erbe**, is effectively, the hub of the city. Separating the two squares is the extraordinary **Palazzo della Ragione** (Tues–Sun summer 10am–6pm; winter 10am–4pm; L4000), which, at the time of its construction in the early 1200s, sported frescoes by Giotto and his assistants. These were destroyed by fire in 1420 and most of the extant frescoes are by Nicola Miretto (1425–1440). Close by, Padua's **Duomo** (daily 7am–noon & 4–7.30pm) is an unlovely church whose design was cribbed from drawings by Michelangelo, though the adjacent Romanesque **Baptistery** is one of the unproclaimed delights of Padua (April–Sept Tues–Sun 9.30am–12.30pm & 2.30–6.30pm; Oct–March Tues–Sat 9.30am–12.30pm & 2.30–5.30pm, Sun 9.30–12.30pm; L3000), lined with some fourteenth-century frescoes by Giusto de'Menabuoi – a cycle which makes a fascinating comparison with Giotto's in the Cappella degli Scrovegni.

Practicalities

The main **tourist office** is at the **train station**, at the far end of Corso del Popolo (Mon–Sat 9am–6pm, Sun 9am–noon). Of many affordable **hotels**, *Albergo Pace*, near the Piazza della Frutta at Via Papafava 3 (☎049/875.1566; ③), and the *Verdi*, Via Dondi dell'Orologio 7 (☎049/663.450; ③) are clean and friendly. The **youth hostel** is at Via A. Aleardi 30 (☎049/875.2219; ③), and has an 11pm curfew – take bus #3, #8, #12 or #18 from the station. The nearest **campsite** is 15km away in Montegrotto Terme (Via Roma 123), served by frequent trains – a fifteen-minute trip. As for **food**, the *rosticceria* in Via Daniele Manin offers a wide variety of snacks or, if you want to sit down, there's *La Mappa*, Via Matteotti 17, with decent self-service fare (closed Sat). For a more relaxed session at only slightly greater expense, three good cheap restaurants are *Da Giovanni* at Via De Cristoforis 1, *7 Teste* at Via C. Battisti 44, and *Al Pero* on S. Lucia. On Piazza Cavour, *Pepen* (closed Sun) has a wonderful range of pizzas, with seats on the square in summer. The *Dotto*, Via Squarcione 23, is a superb mid-range restaurant – allow around L60,000 per person. Padua can also boast several really special places costing an extra L10,000 or so: *Antico Brolo*, Vicolo Cigoló 14 (☎049/664.555; closed Sun), and *El Toulà*, Via Belle Parti 11 (☎049/660.719; closed Sun & Mon).

Vicenza

Europe's largest producer of textiles and the focus of Italy's "Silicon Valley", **VICENZA** is a sleek city, although one whose centre, still partly enclosed by medieval walls, remains very well preserved. The city's numerous Gothic palaces reflect its status as a Venetian satellite, but in the latter half of the sixteenth century the city was transformed by the work of an architect who owed nothing to Venice and whose style was to influence every succeeding generation – Andrea di Pietro della Gondola, alias Palladio. The main street of Vicenza, the **Corso Andrea Palladio**, cuts through the old centre from Piazza Castello down to the Piazza Matteotti, lined with palaces and ending with one of the architect's most imperious buildings, the **Palazzo Chiericati**, now home of the **Museo Civico** (Tues–Sat 9.30am–noon & 2.30–5pm, Sun 9.30am–noon; L3000, combined ticket for Museo & Santa Corona L5000), with paintings by Memling, Tintoretto, Veronese and Tiepolo. Across the Piazza Matteotti, the **Teatro Olimpico** is the oldest indoor theatre in Europe (daily 9.30am–12.20pm & 3–5.30pm, Sun 9.30am–12.20pm & 3–4.30pm; mid-Oct to mid-March Sun am only; L5000), a covered amphitheatre derived from Palladio's reading of Vitruvius and his studies of Roman structures in Italy and France. The architect died soon after work commenced and the scheme was then overseen by Scamozzi, who added the backstage perspective of a classical city, creating the illusion of long urban vistas by tilting the "streets" at an alarming angle. The theatre opened on March 3, 1585, with an extravagant production of *Oedipus Rex*, and is still used for plays and concerts. Nearby, the church of **Santa Corona**, on the other side of the Corso Palladio (daily summer 9.30am–12.30pm & 3.30–6.30pm; winter 9.30am–12.30pm & 3–6pm), has a dull **Museo Naturalistico-Archeologico** in the cloisters (Tues–Sat 9.30am–noon & 2.30–5pm, Sun 9.30am–noon; L3000, combined ticket for Museo & Santa Corona L5000), but houses two of the three great church paintings in Vicenza – *The Baptism of Christ*, a late work by Giovanni Bellini, and *The Adoration of the Magi*, painted in 1573 by Veronese. The third of the trio is Vecchio's typically stolid and voluptuous *Madonna and Child with SS George and Lucy*, in the nearby church of **Santo Stefano** (daily 9–11am & 4–6.30pm).

South of here, the **Piazza dei Signori** is the hub of the city, and home to the most awesome of Palladio's creations – the **Basilica** (Tues–Sat 9.30am–noon & 2.30–5pm, Sun 9.30am–noon; free). Designed in the late 1540s, this was Palladio's first public project and secured his reputation. Its monumental Doric and Ionic colonnades enclose the fifteenth-century hall of the city council, an unstable structure that had defied a number of attempts to prop it up before Palladio's solution was put into effect. A late Palladio building, the unfinished **Loggia del Capitaniato**, faces the Basilica; it was built as accommodation for the city's Venetian military commander and is decorated with reliefs celebrating the victory over the Turks at Lepanto in 1571.

Practicalities

The **tourist office** is in Piazza Matteotti (Mon–Sat 9am–12.30pm & 3–6pm, Sun 9am–12.30pm), and can provide a map. When the *APT* is closed, make use of the *Digiplan* booth next to the piazza's *Bar Museo*; it looks like a public toilet, but is in fact a computerized information outlet which will print out directions, phone numbers, accommodation details and so forth, all in English. The best deal among **hotels** is the basic but central *Alpino*, Borgo Casale 33 (☎0444/505.137; ③). The *Casa San Raffaele*, Viale X Giugno 10 (☎0444/235.619; ③), has the advantage of a beautiful position on the slope of Monte Bérico but is more expensive. First recommendation for **eating** goes to the *Antica Casa della Malvasia*, Contrà delle Morette 5, an unpretentious bustling tavern just off the Piazza. Equally popular, but rather less basic, is the *Vecchia Guardia*, Contrà Pescheria Vecchia 11.

Verona

The easy-going city of **VERONA** is the largest city of the Veneto, and, with its wealth of Roman sites and streets of pink-hued medieval buildings, one of its most interesting. First settled by the Romans, it later became an independent city-state, reaching its zenith in the thirteenth century under the Scaligeri family. Ruthless in the exercise of power, the Scaligeri were at the same time energetic patrons of the arts, and many of Verona's finest buildings date from the century of their rule. With their fall, the Viscontis of Milan assumed control of the city, which was later absorbed into the Venetian empire.

The City

The city centre clusters into a deep bend in the Adige river, the main sight of its southern reaches the central hub of **Piazza Brà** and its mighty Roman **Arena** (Tues–Sun 8am–6.30pm; L6000, free first Sun of month). Dating from the first century AD, and originally with seating for some 20,000, this is the third largest surviving Roman amphitheatre, and offers a tremendous panorama from the topmost of the 44 marble tiers. North, **Via Mazzini**, a narrow traffic-free street lined with expensive shops, leads to a grouping of squares, most noteworthy of which is the **Piazza dei Signori**, flanked by the medieval **Palazzo degli Scaligeri** – the residence of the Scaligeri. At right angles to this is the fifteenth-century **Loggia del Consiglio**, the former assembly hall of the city council and Verona's outstanding early Renaissance building, while, close by, the twelfth-century **Torre dei Lamberti** (Tues–Sun 8am–6.45pm; L4000 by lift, L3000 on foot) gives dizzying views of the city. Beyond the square, in front of the Romanesque church of Santa Maria Antica, the **Arche Scaligere** are the elaborate Gothic funerary monuments of Verona's first family, in a wrought-iron palisade decorated with ladder motifs, the emblem of the Scaligeri. Mastino I ("Mastiff"), founder of the dynasty, is buried in the simple tomb against the wall of the church; Mastino II is to the left of the entrance, opposite the most florid of the tombs, that of **Cansignorio** ("Top Dog"); while over the side entrance of the church is an equestrian statue of **Cangrande I** ("Big Dog") – a copy of the original now in Verona's Castelvecchio. Towards the river from here is the church of **Sant'Anastasia**, a mainly Gothic church, completed in the late fifteenth century, with Pisanello's delicately coloured fresco of *St George and the Princess* in the sacristy. Verona's **Duomo** lies just around the river's bend, a mixture of Romanesque and Gothic styles that houses an *Assumption* by Titian in an architectural frame by Sansovino, who also designed the choir.

In the opposite direction, off Piazza delle Erbe at Via Cappello 23, is the **Casa di Giulietta**, a fourteenth-century structure that's in a fine state of preservation, though the Juliet of Shakespeare's play was, in fact, entirely fictional (Tues–Sun 8am–6.30pm; L5000). South of here, on the junction of Via Diaz and Corso Porta Borsari, the **Porta dei Borsari** is a fine Roman monument, with an inscription that dates it to 265 AD, though it's almost certainly older than that. Some way down Corso Cavour from here, the **Arco dei Gavi** is a first-century Roman triumphal arch, beyond which the **Castel-vecchio** (Tues–Sun 8am–6.30pm; L6000) houses a collection of paintings, jewellery and weapons, as well as the equestrian figure of Cangrande I, removed from his tomb, strikingly displayed on an outdoor pedestal. Outstanding among the paintings are works by Jacopo and Giovanni Bellini, a *Madonna* by Pisanello, Veronese's *Descent from the Cross*, a Tintoretto *Nativity*, and works by the two Tiepolos.

A kilometre or so northwest of here, the **Basilica di San Zeno Maggiore** is one of the most significant Romanesque churches in northern Italy, put up in the first half of the twelfth century. Its rose window, representing the Wheel of Fortune, dates from then, as does the magnificent portal, whose lintels bear sculptures representing the months while the door has bronze panels depicting scenes from the Bible and the miracles of San Zeno. The simple interior is covered with frescoes, although the church's most compulsive image is the altar's luminous *Madonna and Saints* by Mantegna.

Practicalities

The **train station** is twenty minutes outside the city centre, connected with Piazza Brà by a #1 or #8 bus. The main **tourist offices** are at Via Leoncino 61 near the Arena, outside the train station, and – in summer – Piazza delle Erbe 42 (all three summer Mon–Sat 8am–8pm; winter closes 7pm; July & Aug also Sun 9am–8pm). Of **hotels**, the *Al Castello*, Corso Cavour 43 (☎045/800.4403; ③), has recently refurbished rooms, but the best budget place is *Catullo*, Via Catullo 1 (☎045/800.2786; ③), in a central position just off Via Mazzini, or the *Aurora*, Via Pellicciai 2 (☎045/594.717; ③), with many rooms overlooking the Piazza delle Erbe. Verona's **youth hostel** is at Salita Fontana del Ferro 15 (☎045/590.360; ③), on the north side of the river behind the Teatro Romano (bus #2), close to which there's a pleasant summer **campsite**, *Campeggio Castel San Pietro*; the #20 bus stops nearby but really it's easier to walk from the centre. There's also the *Casa della Giovane*, Via Pigna 7 (☎045/596.880; ②), in the old centre, for women only.

Among **eating** options, *Pizzeria Corte Farina*, Corte Farina 4, serves good pizzas, as does *Pizzeria Arena*, Vicolo Tre Marchetti 1, and both are open until 1am; there's a *Brek* self-service on Piazza Brà; and the *Al Duca*, Via Arche Scaligiere 2/b, the best value in the city centre at around L15,000 for a full meal. Otherwise, the most plentiful source of cheap places is over the river: especially good is the *Trattoria Ropeton*, below the youth hostel at Via S. Giovanni in Valle 46. On the other side of the Teatro Romano, the *Ponte Nuovo*, Via Rocca Maggiore 8, and *Pero d'Oro*, Via Ponte Pignolo 25, serve inexpensive but genuine Veronese dishes. For evening drinks, the ultra-friendly *Bottega del Vino* in Vicolo Scudo di Francia, just off the north end of Via Mazzini, is an old **bar** frequented by German tourists, with a selection of wines from all over Italy. Try *Al Carro Armato*, Vicolo Gatto 2a, or *Osteria Al Duomo*, Via Duomo 7a. Most popular among locals and ex-pats is late-night *Vecia Veronetta* over the river at Via Scrimiari 47.

Trieste

Backed by a white limestone plateau and facing the blue Adriatic, **TRIESTE** has an idyllic setting, even by Italian standards. The city itself, however, is a strange place, its massive Neoclassical architecture and confident Baroque centre (the *borgo teresiano*) the creation of Empress Maria Theresa, who initiated the development of what was the

Habsburg empire's southern port. Lying as it does on the political and ethnic fault-line between the Latin and Slavic worlds, Trieste has long been a city of political extremes. In the last century it was a centre for the movement to "redéem" the Austrian lands of Trieste and the Trentino. Later, Yugoslavia and the Allies fought over Trieste, until in 1954 the city and a connecting strip of coast were secured for Italy, though a definitive border settlement was not reached until 1975. The neo-Fascist *MSI* party has always done well here, and there's even a local anti-Slav party, the *Lista per Trieste*.

The City

The social centre of Trieste is the huge **Piazza dell'Unità d'Italia**, opening onto the harbour and flanked by the vast bulks of the **Palazzo del Comune** and **Palazzo di Governo**. The focal point of the city's history, however, and its prime tourist site, is the hill of **San Giusto**, with its castle and cathedral, accessible on bus #24. The **Castello** (daily 8am–sunset) is a fifteenth-century Venetian fortress, built near the site of the Roman forum, whose ramparts are worth a walk and whose museum (Tues–Sun 9am–1pm; L2000) houses a collection of antique weaponry. The **Cattedrale di San Giusto** is a typically Triestine synthesis of styles, with a predominantly Romanesque facade including five Roman columns and a Gothic rose window. Inside, between Byzantine pillars, there are fine thirteenth-century frescoes of Saint Justus, a Christian martyr killed during the persecutions of Diocletian. Down the cobbled lane from the cathedral, at Via Cattedrale 15, is the **Museo di Storia ed Arte** (Tues–Sun 9am–1pm; L2000), a collection of cultural plunder that embraces Himalayan sculpture, Egyptian manuscripts and Roman glass. But Trieste's principal museum is the **Museo Revoltella** at Via Diaz 27 (Tues–Sat 9am–noon & 3–6pm, Sun 9am–noon; L2000), housed in a Viennese-style palace bequeathed to the city by the financier Baron Pasquale Revoltella in 1869 and displaying dull nineteenth-century and decent modern art collections. The nearby **Museo Sartorio**, in Largo Papa Giovanni XXIII (Tues–Sun 9am–1pm; L2000), has ceramics and icons downstairs and oppressive private rooms upstairs, all dark veneers, Gothic tracery and bad Venetian paintings. A more pleasant domestic interior is the **Museo Morpurgo**, north of San Giusto at Via Imbriani 5 (Tues–Sun 10am–1pm; L2000), a palace that was left to the city by the merchant and banker Mario Morpurgo di Nilma and hasn't really been touched since its first decoration in the 1880s. More disturbingly, on the southern side of the city, the **Risiera di San Sabba** in Via Valmaura (Tues–Sun 9am–1pm; mid-April to May & Nov closes weekdays 6pm), on the #10 bus route, was the only concentration camp in Italy. Its crematorium was installed after the German invasion of Italy in September 1943, a conversion supervised by Erwin Lambert, who had designed the death camp at Treblinka, and a permanent exhibition serves as a reminder of Fascist crimes in the region.

Practicalities

The central **train station** is on Piazza Libertà, on the northern edge of the city centre. There's a **tourist information** desk here, and a main office at Via S. Nicolo 20 (Mon–Fri 9am–1pm & 4–7pm). There are many reasonable **hotels**, nicest of which are the *Centro*, Via Roma 13 (☎040/634.408; ④), the *Rino*, Via Boccardi 5 (☎040/300.608; ③), and the *Blave Krone*, Via XXX Ottobre 12 (☎040/631.882; ③). The **youth hostel** is 8km out of the city at Viole Miramare 331 (☎040/224.102; ②) – take a #6 bus from the tourist office, then a #36. The nearest **campsite** is in nearby Obelisco, on the #4 bus route.

For **snacks and light meals**, the *Tevere Buffet* in Via Malcanton, just behind the Piazza d'Italia, is a lively place with simple food. The *Da Bepi* in Via Cassa di Risparmio is a favourite student lunch-stop, with excellent sausages and sauerkraut. Another student hang-out is *Notorious* in Via del Bosco – sandwiches and salads on the ground floor and a good cheap trattoria on the first floor. Decent pizzas can be had at *Il Barattolo* in Piazza Sant'Antonio Nuovo, and there are *Brek* self-service places in Via San

Francesco and Via Campi Elsi. For **more substantial food**, try the very popular *Trattoria All'Antica Ghiacceretta* in Via dei Fornelli, or the *Ai Due Triestini* at Via Cadorna 10. *Trattoria alla Palestra*, Via Madonna del Mare 18, has fine food at reasonable prices, and an English-speaking host. The city's favourite **café** is the *Caffè San Marco*, which has occupied its Liberty-style premises on Via G. Battisti for some eighty years. The *Caffè Tommaseo* on Piazza Tommaseo was a rendezvous for Italian nationalists in the last century and although refurbished still makes a pleasant, if pricy refuge in the summer heat. As for straight **bars**, try the *Birreria Spofford* in Via Rossetti, a youthful place attracting a student clientele, or *Osteria de Libero*, Via Risorte 8, an atmospheric place for both eating or drinking.

Bologna

The capital of Emilia-Romagna, **BOLOGNA** is a boom town of the Eighties whose computer-associated industries have brought conspicuous wealth to the old brick palaces and porticoed squares. Previously, it was best known for its food, undeniably the richest in the country, and for its politics – "Red Bologna" has been the Italian Communist party's stronghold and spiritual home since the last war. The city centre is among the best-looking in the country, still startlingly medieval in plan, and has enough curiosities for several days' leisured exploration. However, Bologna is really enjoyable just for itself, with a busy cultural life and a café and bar scene that is among northern Italy's most convivial.

> The Bologna area telephone code is ☎051.

Arrival and accommodation

Bologna's **airport** is northwest of the centre, linked to the train station by bus #91. The **train station** is on Piazza delle Medaglie d'Oro, at the end of Via dell'Indipendenza. There are **tourist information** booths at the airport and at the train station (Mon–Sat 9am–12.30pm & 2.30–6.30pm), and a main office at Piazza Maggiore 9 (Mon–Sat 9am–7pm, Sunday 9am–1pm), with what's-on booklets, maps and a hotel booking facility. In terms of **places to stay**, Bologna is not geared up for tourists, least of all for those travelling on a tight budget, and the trade fairs during high season make booking ahead imperative. The most inexpensive option, as ever, is the city's official **youth hostel**, 6km outside the centre of town at Via Viadagola 14 (☎519.202; ②), with an 11.30pm curfew. Bus #93 from Via Irnerio, a short walk southeast from the train station, takes you within 800m of the hostel. Among the few affordable **hotels** are, the *Marconi*, right out of the station at Via Marconi 22 (☎262.832; ③), the more central *Minerva*, Via De Monari 3 (☎239.652; ③), and the *Panorama*, Via Livraghi 1 (☎221.802; ③). More expensive is the *Accademia*, nicely situated at Via Belli Art 6 (☎232.318; ④), and the popular *Orologio*, Via IV Novembre 10 (☎231.253; ②), which should be booked in advance.

The City

Bologna's city centre is quite compact, with most things of interest within the main ring road. **Piazza Maggiore** is the obvious place to make for first, buzzing with an almost constant activity. On its western side, the **Palazzo Comunale** has a few galleries of paintings and ornate furniture (closed at the moment), but is mainly worth visiting for the view over the square. On the square's south side, the church of **San Petronio** is the city's largest, intended originally to have been larger than St Peter's in Rome, and one of the finest Gothic brick buildings in Italy; money and land for the side aisle were diverted by the pope's man in Bologna towards a new university, and the architect Antonio di Vicenzo's plans had to be modified. You can see the beginnings of the planned side aisle on the left of the building and there are models of what the church was supposed to look like in the museum (Mon, Wed & Fri–Sun 10am–noon); otherwise the most intriguing features are a beautiful carving of *Madonna and Child* by Jacopo della Quercia, above the central portal, and an astronomical clock – a long brass meridian line set at an angle across the floor, with a hole left in the roof for the sun to shine through on the right spot. The adjacent **Piazza Nettuno** has an extravagant **statue of Neptune** that was fashioned by Giambologna in 1566.

Across Via dell'Archiginnasio from here, the **Museo Civico Archeologico** (Tues–Fri 9am–2pm, Sat & Sun 9am–1pm & 3.30–7pm; L5000) is a rather stuffy museum but its displays of Egyptian and Roman antiquities are good ones, and the Etruscan section is one of the best outside Lazio. Down the street, Bologna's university – the **Archiginnasio** – was founded at more or less the same time as the Piazza Maggiore was laid out, predating the rest of Europe's universities, though it didn't get a special building until 1565. The most interesting part is the **Teatro Anatomico** (Mon–Sat 9am–1pm), the original medical faculty dissection theatre, whose tiers of seats surround an extraordinary professor's chair, covered with a canopy supported by figures known as "gli spellati" – "the skinned ones". South, down Via Garibaldi, **Piazza San Domenico** (daily 7am–noon & 3.30–7pm), with its strange canopied tombs holding the bones of medieval law scholars, is the site of the church of **San Domenico**, built in 1251 to house the relics of Saint Dominic. The bones rest in the so-called *Arca di San Domenico*, a fifteenth-century work that was principally the creation of Nicola Pisano – though many artists contributed to it. Pisano and his pupils were responsible for the reliefs illustrating the saint's life; the statues on top were the work of Pisano himself; Nicola dell'Arca was responsible for the canopy; and the angel and figures of saints Proculus and Petronius were the work of a very young Michelangelo.

North of here, the eastern section of Bologna's *centro storico* preserves many of the older **university** departments, housed for the most part in large seventeenth- and eighteenth-century palaces. At Piazza di Porta Ravegnana, the Torre degli Asinelli and perilously leaning Torre Gararcheolnda are together known as the **Due Torri**, the only survivors of literally hundreds of towers that were scattered across the city during the Middle Ages (daily 9am–6pm; winter closes 5pm; L3000). From here, Via San Stefano leads down past a complex of four – but originally seven – churches, collectively known as **Santo Stefano**. The striking polygonal church of **San Sepolcro**, reached through the church of **Crocifisso**, is about the most interesting: the basin in its courtyard is by tradition the one used by Pilate to wash his hands after he condemned Christ to death, while, inside, the bones of Saint Petronius provide a pleasingly kitsch focus, held in a tomb modelled on the Church of the Holy Sepulchre in Jerusalem. A doorway leads from here through to **San Vitale e Agricola**, Bologna's oldest church, built from discarded Roman fragments in the fifth century; while the fourth church, the **Trinitá**, lies across the courtyard and is home to a small museum (daily 9am–noon & 3.30–6.30pm; winter closes 5.30pm) containing a reliquary of Saint Petronius and a handful of dull paintings. One of the university buildings, the **Palazzo Poggi** at Via Zamboni 31 (Mon–Fri 9am–5pm, Sat 9am–1pm), was frescoed by the Renaissance artist Tibaldi, and also houses a small **Museo di Astronomia**, displaying a number of eighteenth-century instruments and a frescoed map of the constellations – painted just seventy years after Galileo was imprisoned for his heretical statements about the cosmos.

Close by, the **Museo di Anatomia Umana** at Via Irnerio 48 (Mon–Fri 9am–noon; free) is another oddball museum, with a collection of highly idiosyncratic but beautiful **waxworks** that were used until the nineteenth century for medical demonstrations, and are as startling as any sculpture in the city. One is a self-portrait of the creator in the midst of a brain dissection, pulling back a scalp with wispy hairs attached; other figures, unnervingly displayed in glass cases, are modelled like classical statues, one carrying a sickle, the other a scythe. More conventionally, the collection of paintings in the **Pinacoteca Nazionale** at Via Belle Arti 56 (Tues–Sat 9am–2pm, Sun 9am–1pm; L6000) includes canvases by the fourteenth-century local artist Vitale da Bologna, later works by Francia and Tibaldi, and paintings from the city's most productive artistic period, the early seventeenth century, when Annibale and Carracci, Reni and Guercino ("the cross-eyed") were active here. Among the gallery's sculptures, Nicolo dell'Arca's *Pietà*, moved here from the church of Santa Maria in Vita, is outstanding, its life-size figures suffused with emotion.

Eating, drinking and nightlife

Bologna is one of the best places in Italy to **eat**, and not just in restaurants. There are any number of places to put together delicious **picnics**, best of which is the Mercato delle Erbe, Via Ugo Bassi 2, biggest and liveliest of the city's markets. For **snacks**, the *Impero*, Via Indipendenza 39, does excellent croissants and pastries; *Altero*, at Via Indipendenza 33 or Via Ugo Bassi 10, is best for pizza by the slice; *La Torinese Salata*, under the vaults of Palazzo del Podestà in Piazza Maggiore, does quiches and stuffed vegetables. Of **restaurants**, *C'entro*, Via Indipendenza 45, and *Bassotto*, Via Ugo Bassi 8, serve quality fast food in comfortable surroundings and are open until 2am; *Boni*, Via Saragozza 88, has very good Emilian cuisine, likewise *Lamma* at Via dei Giudei 4 – a popular place with a pub atmosphere. For family-style Bolognese food, go to *Fantoni* at Via del Pratello 11, one of the oldest streets in the city. *La Mamma*, Via Zamboni 16, is a long dining room on the edge of the university quarter that serves inexpensive pizza and pasta; *Clorofilla*, Strada Maggiore 64, is a good place for vegetarians, and the self-service *Lazzarini*, Via Clabvature 1 (daily except Sun 7am–8pm), is cheap but more stylish than many self-service places.

To **drink**, there are plenty of good bars on and around Via Zamboni, in the student quarter, and plenty of *osterie* all over town – pub-like places, open late, that have been the mainstay of Bolognese **nightlife** for a few hundred years. *Matusel*, at Via Bertolini 2, close to the university, is a lively and noisy example, with reasonably priced full meals. *Dal Biassanot* at Via Piella 14 is a convivial haunt, open until 2am; *Senzanome*, Via Senzanome 42, serves good meals and has a wide choice of beers and wines. *Marione*, at Via San Felice 137, close to the city gate, is old and dark, with good wine and snacks. *Osteria dell'Infedele*, on Via Gerusalemme, has good economic food.

Parma

PARMA is about as comfortable a town as you could wish for. The measured pace of its streets, the abundance of its restaurants and the general air of provincial affluence are almost cloyingly pleasant, especially if you've arrived from the south. But it's a friendly enough place with plenty to see, not least the works of two key late Renaissance artists – Correggio and Parmigianino.

The Town

Piazza Garibaldi is the fulcrum of Parma, its packed-out cafés, along with the narrow streets and alleyways which wind south and west of the piazza, home to much of the town's nightlife. The mustard-coloured **Palazzo del Governatore** flanks the square, behind which the Renaissance church of the **Madonna della Steccata** stands, apparently using Bramante's original plan for St Peter's as a model. Inside there are frescoes by a number of sixteenth-century painters, notably Parmigianino, who spent the last ten years of his life on this work, eventually being sacked for breach of contract by the disgruntled church authorities. Five minutes' walk away the beautiful Romanesque

Duomo (daily 7am–noon & 3–7pm), dating from the eleventh century, holds earlier work by Parmigianino in its south transept, painted when the artist was a pupil of Correggio – who painted the fresco of the *Assumption* in the central cupola. Finished in 1534, this is among the most famous works of Correggio, who was paid for the painting with a sackful of small change to annoy him, since he was known to be a great miser. The story goes that he carried the sack of coins home in the heat, caught a fever and died aged forty. There's more by Correggio in the cupola of **San Giovanni Evangelista** behind the Duomo – a fresco of the *Vision of St John*. You should also visit the Duomo's octagonal **Baptistery** (daily 9am–12.30pm & 3–6pm; L3000), considered to be Benedetto Antelami's finest work, built in 1196 and bridging the gap between the Romanesque and Gothic styles. Antelami sculpted the frieze which surrounds the building, and was also responsible for the reliefs inside, including a series of fourteen statues representing the months and seasons. Take the spiral staircase to the top for a closer view of the frescoes on the ceiling; they are by an unknown thirteenth-century artist. Correggio was also responsible for the frescoes in the **Camera di San Paolo** of the former Benedictine Convent off Via Melloni, a few minutes' north; he portrayed the abbess who commissioned the work as the Goddess Diana, above the fireplace.

East of the cathedral square, the **Museo Glauco-Lombardi** at Via Garibaldi 15 (May–Sept Tues–Sat 9.30–12.30pm & 4–6pm, Sun 9.30am–1pm; Oct–April Tues–Sat 9.30–12.30pm & 3–5pm, Sun 9.30am–1pm; free), recalls later times, with a display of memorabilia relating to Marie-Louise of Austria, who reigned here after the defeat of her husband Napoléon at Waterloo, setting herself up with another suitor (much to the chagrin of her exiled spouse) and expanding the Parma violet perfume industry. Just across Piazza Marconi from here, it's hard to miss Parma's biggest monument, the **Palazzo della Pilotta**, begun for Alessandro Farnese in the sixteenth century and rebuilt after World War II bombing to house a number of Parma's museums, notably the city's main art gallery, the **Galleria Nazionale** (Tues–Sat 9am–2pm, Sun 9am–1pm; L10,000, includes admission to Teatro Farnese). The hi-tech display includes more work by Correggio and Parmigianino, and the remarkable *Apostles at the Sepulchre* and *Funeral of the Virgin* by Caracci – massive canvases suspended each side of a gantry at the top of the building. The **Teatro Farnese**, which you pass through to get to the gallery, was almost entirely destroyed in 1944 and has been virtually rebuilt. An extended semicircle of seats three tiers high, made completely of wood, it's a copy of Palladio's Teatro Olimpico at Vicenza, and as well as being (temporarily) the biggest theatre of its kind, sported Italy's first revolving stage. Up a floor, the **Museo Nazionale d'Antichita** (Tues–Sat 9am–1.30pm, Sun 9am–12.15pm; L4000) is less enticing but still worth a glance, with finds from the Etruscan city of Velleia and the prehistoric lake villages around Parma, as well as the tabletop on which the Emperor Trajan notched up a record of his gifts to the poor.

Practicalities

Parma's **train station** is fifteen minutes' walk from the central Piazza Garibaldi, or a short ride on bus #1, #6, #8, #9 or #11. The **tourist office** is on Piazza Duomo (Mon–Fri 9am–12.30pm & 3–5pm, Sat 9am–12.30pm). Finding a **place to stay** can be tricky. There's an official **youth hostel** at Parco Cittadella 5 (☎0521/581.546; ②), open April to October with an 11pm curfew; take bus #9 (after 8pm bus #E). Among **hotels** near the station, the *Brozzi*, Via Trento 11 (☎0521/272.724; ③), is reasonable; the *Leon d'Oro*, a few minutes away at Viale a. Fratti 4 (☎0521/773.182; ③), has a restaurant attached. In the centre, the *Lazzaro*, Via XX Marzo 14 (☎0521/208.944; ③), is a small *locanda*, while the *Croce di Malta*, Borgo Palmia 8 (☎0521/235.643; ③), is a restaurant in an old convent. On the other side of the river (bus #3 from Piazza Garibaldi), try *Il Sole*, Via Gramsci 15 (☎0521/995.107; ③). *Pizzeria/ristorante L'Artiste*, Via Bruno Longhi 31/a, does good pizzas and has friendly English-speaking owners, and *Trattoria San*

Ambrogio, off Strada Farini at Vicolo delle Piaghe 1, has a meaty menu that leans towards game. *Le Premier*, Borgo S. Biagio 6/d, is self-service and near the Duomo. At night, **opera** is the biggest deal; the *Teatro Regio* on Via Garibaldi (☎0521/218.678) is renowned for its discerning audiences.

Ferrara

Half an hour by train from Bologna, **FERRARA** was the residence of the Este dukes, an eccentric dynasty that ranked as a major political force throughout Renaissance times. The Este kept the main artists of the day in commissions and built a town which, despite a relatively small population, was one of the most elegant urban creations of the period. It's a popular stop for tourists travelling up from Bologna to Venice, but they rarely stay, leaving the centre enjoyably crowd-free by the evening.

Dominating the centre of town, the bulky **Castello Estense** (Tues–Sat 9.30am–12.30pm & 1.30–6.30pm, Sun 10am–6pm; L6000, price changes for exhibitions) was home to the Este court, and its rooms go some way to bringing back the days of Este magnificence, although it's a cold, draughty place on the whole, at its most evocative in the dungeons, where the numerous Este enemies were incarcerated. Just south, the **Palazzo Comunale**, built in 1243 but much altered since, holds statues of Nicolò III and his son Borso on its facade, though they're twentieth-century reproductions. A little way beyond, Ferrara's **Duomo** is a mixture of Romanesque and Gothic styles, with a carved central portal and a **museum** (Mon–Sat 10am–noon & 3.30–5.30pm; free) which has a set of bas-reliefs illustrating the labours of the months that formerly adorned the outside. There are also illuminated manuscripts, two organ shutters decorated by Cosme Turà, one of the *Annunciation*, another showing Saint George killing the dragon, and a beautiful *Madonna* by della Quercia. Corso Ercole I d'Este leads north from the castle to the **Palazzo dei Diamanti**, on the left, named after the diamond-shaped bricks that stud its facade and home to the **Pinacoteca Nazionale** (Tues–Sat 9am–2pm, Sun 9am–1pm; L6000), which holds works from the Ferrara and Bologna Schools, notably paintings by Dossi and Guercino, and a spirited *St Christopher* by Sebastian Filippo.

More Renaissance palaces lie in the southeastern quarter of the city centre, lining the wider streets above the tangled medieval district, one of which, the **Casa Romei** on Via Savaranola (Tues–Sun 10am–5pm; free) is typical of the time, with frescoes and graceful courtyards alongside artefacts rescued from various local churches. Two minutes away, the **Palazzo Schifanoia** ("Palace of Joy") on Via Scandiana (daily 9am–7pm; L5000) is one of the grandest of Ferrara's palaces. It belonged to the Este family, and Cosme Turà recorded their court in the frescoes in its Salone dei Mesi, decorated with hunting scenes, groups of musicians, signs of the zodiac and classical legends.

Practicalities

Ferrara's **train station** is just west of the city walls, ten minutes' walk (or a #1, #2 or #9 bus ride) along Viale Cavour from the centre of town. The **tourist office** at Piazza Municipale 19 (Mon–Sat 9am–1pm & 2.30–7pm, Sun 9am–1pm) has maps. Behind the duomo, the labyrinth of alleyways that makes up Ferrara's medieval quarter is the best area to look for cheap **hotels**. The best of these is the *San Paolo*, Via Baluardi 9 (☎0532/762.040; ④); if this is full there's the *Casa degli Artisti*, Via Vittoria 66 (☎0532/761.038; ③), or the *Nazionale*, Corso Porta Reno 32 (☎0532/209.604; ④). Ferrara's **campsite**, *Estense*, is off the ring road just outside the city walls in Via Gramicia (☎0532/752.396). Ferrara isn't an especially cheap place to eat. *Pizzeria-Gelateria Giuseppe* at Via Carlo Mayr 71 has decent pizzas, *Osteria Al Postiglione*, off Corso Martiri di Libertà at Vicolo Chiuso del Teatro 4, good home-made pasta and sandwiches; try *Pizzeria/ristorante Antica Ferrara* at Via Romei 51. There's also a rather dour student mensa at Corso della Giovecca 145.

Ravenna

When **RAVENNA** became capital of the Western Roman Empire fifteen hundred years ago, it was more by quirk of fate than design. The emperor Honorius, alarmed by armies invading from the north, moved his court from Rome to this obscure town on the Romagna coast because it was easy to defend, being surrounded by marshland, and situated close to the port of Classis – the biggest Roman naval base on the Adriatic. Honorius' anxiety proved well-founded – Rome was sacked by the Goths in 410 – but Ravenna's days of glory were brief, and it, too, fell in 473. Yet the Ostrogoth king Theodoric continued to beautify the city, and it wasn't long before it was taken by the Byzantines, who were responsible for Ravenna's most glorious era – the city's mosaics are generally acknowledged to be the crowning achievement of Byzantine art.

The City

The best of the mosaics are in the basilica of **San Vitale**, ten minutes northwest of the centre (daily 9am–7pm; L3000, L2500 if you have ticket to Museo Nazionale), a fairly typical Byzantine church, begun in 525 AD under Theodoric and finished in 548 under Justinian, which formed the basis for the great church of Aya Sofia in Constantinople fifteen years later. The mosaics are in the apse, arranged in a rigid hierachy, with Old Testament scenes across the semicircular lunettes of the choir, Christ, the Apostles and sons of San Vitale on the arch, and, on the semi-dome of the apse, a beardless Christ presenting a model of the church to San Vitale and Bishop Ecclesius. On the side walls of the apse are portraits of the emperor Justinian and his wife Theodora, Justinian's foot resting on that of his general, Belisarius, who defeated the Goths holding Ravenna and reclaimed the city, while Theodora looks on, her expression giving some hint of the cruelty that she was apparently notorious for.

Across from the basilica, the tiny **Mausoleo di Galla Placidia** (daily 9am–7pm; same ticket as San Vitale) was named after the half-sister of Honorius, who was responsible for much of the grandeur of Ravenna's early days, though despite the name it's unlikely that the building ever held her bones. Galla Placidia was taken hostage when the Goths sacked Rome, and created a scandal by marrying one of her kidnappers, Ataulf, going into battle with him as his army forged south. When Ataulf was assassinated, the Romans took her back for a ransom of corn, after which she was obliged to marry a Roman General, Constantius. Their son formally became the emperor Valentinian III at the age of six, and as his regent she assumed control of the Western Empire. Inside, the mosaics glow with a deep blue lustre, most in an earlier style than San Vitale's, full of Roman and naturalistic motifs. Stars around a golden cross spread across the vaulted ceiling, while at each end are representations of Saint Lawrence, with the gridiron on which he was martyred, and the Good Shepherd, with one of his flock. Adjacent to San Vitale, housed in the former cloisters of the church, the **National Museum of Antiquities** (Tues–Sun 8.30am–1.30pm; L6000) contains various items from this and later periods, most notably a sixth-century statue of Hercules capturing a stag, possibly a copy of a Greek original, and the so-called "Veil of Classis", decorated with portraits of Veronese bishops of the eighth and ninth centuries.

There are more fine mosaics east of here, on the busy Via di Roma, in the basilica of **Sant'Apollinare Nuovo** (daily 9.30am–7pm; L3000), another building of the sixth century, again built by Theodoric. These run the length of the nave and depict ceremonial processions of martyrs bearing gifts for an enthroned Christ and the Virgin through an avenue of date palms. Some of the scenery is more specific to Ravenna: you can make out what used to be the harbour at nearby Classe against the city behind, out of which rises Theodoric's palace. Five minutes' walk up Via di Roma, the **Arian Baptistery** (daily 8.30am–noon & 2.30–sunset; free) has a fine mosaic ceiling showing the twelve Apostles and the baptism of Christ. Via Diaz leads from here down to **Piazza**

del Popolo, the centre of Ravenna, a few blocks south of which the **Tomba di Dante** was put up in the eighteenth century to enclose a previous fifteenth-century tomb. Dante had been chased out of Florence by the time he arrived in Ravenna, and he was sheltered here by the Da Polenta family – then in control of the city – while he finished his *Divine Comedy*. He died in 1381 and was laid to rest in the adjoining church of **San Francesco**, a much-restored building, elements of which date from the fourth century.

A couple of minutes' away on Piazza Duomo, the **Museo Arcivescovile** (daily 9.30am–7pm; L3000) has mosaic fragments from around the city and the sixth-century Oratorio Sant'Andrea, adorned with mosaics of birds above a Christ dressed in the uniform of a Roman centurion. There are also fragments from the original cathedral (the present one is an uninteresting reconstruction), and an ornate ivory throne from Alexandria which belonged to Bishop Maximian in the sixth century. The **Neonian Baptistery** (daily 9am–7pm; same ticket as Museo Arcivescovile), next door, is a conversion from a Roman bath-house. The original floor level has sunk into the marshy ground, and you can see the remains of the previous building, three metres below.

Note that a day ticket (*biglietto giornaliero*) to all six of Ravenna's monuments plus the Ceramics Museum of Faenza costs L9000.

Practicalities

Ravenna has a compact city centre, and it's only a short walk from the **train station** on Piazza Farini, along Viale Farini and Via A. Diaz, to the central Piazza del Popolo. At Via Salara 8, the **tourist office** (daily 9.30am–1pm & 3–6pm) has maps. The slightly unsavoury district around the station is the best place for cheap **hotels** like the *Roma*, Via Candiano 26 (☎0544/421.515; ③), and *Al Giaciglio*, Via Rocca Brancaleone 42 (☎0544/39.403; ③), which has a decent restaurant, although it's further to walk. There's a **youth hostel**, the *Ostello Dante*, a ten-minute walk out of town at Via Nicolodi 12 (☎0544/420.405; ②), or take bus #1 from outside the station. Ravenna's best **places to eat** are between the duomo and Piazza San Francesco. *Ca' De Ven*, at Via C. Ricci 24, has a large selection of Emilia-Romagnan wine, and decent food. Back towards the square, on Via Mentana, *Da Renato*, and its sister restaurant next door, *Guidarello*, on Via R. Gessi, both do traditional local food. *Ristorante Scai*, Piazza Baracca 22, close to San Vitale, specializes in roast meat and game for those so inclined; it's reasonably priced and also serves pizzas in the evening. There are also mensas at the station and Via G. Oberdan 8, as well as a branch of the *Pizza Altero* chain on Via Camillo B. Cavour.

Rimini

RIMINI is the least pretentious town in Italy, the archetypal seaside city, with a reputation for good – if slightly sleazy – fun. Brash and high-rise, Rimini is a traditional family resort, to which some Italians return year after year. There's another, less savoury side to the town, however. Rimini is known across Italy for its fast-living and chancy nightlife, and there's a very active hetero- and transsexual prostitution scene.

In summer most activity is concentrated on the main seafront drag of souvenir shops, restaurants and video arcades, which stretches 9km north to the suburbs of Viserba and Torre Pedrera and 7km south to Miramare. Out of season, though, you'll find most life a little way inland in the older part of town, clustered around the main squares of **Piazza Tre Martiri** and **Piazza Cavour**. The latter is home to the Gothic **Palazzo del Podestà**, which holds a museum of ethnography (Tues–Sun 9am–1pm & 3–7pm; L8000), worth a look for its fine collection of Oceanic and pre-Colombian art, although the Roman **Ponte di Tiberio** and **Arco d'Augusto**, just inside the old town ramparts, are perhaps more interesting. Rimini's best-known monument, however, is the strange-looking **Tempio Malatestiano** on Via 4 Novembre (daily 7am–noon & 3.30–7pm), one of the masterworks of the Italian Renaissance. Originally a Gothic Franciscan church, in

1450 it was transformed for the savage Sigismondo Malatesta by Leon Battista Alberti, and is an odd mixture of private chapel and personal monument. Sigismondo treated the church as a memorial chapel to his great love, Isotta degli Atti, and their initials are linked in emblems all over the building; the Malatesta armorial emblem – the elephant – appears almost as often, alongside chubby putti, nymphs and shepherds in a decidedly unchristian celebration of excess. There are some fine artworks – one by Piero della Francesca, and a *Crucifix* attributed to Giotto – although even now you get the feeling the authorities are slightly embarassed by the place. It is, however, an appropriate attraction for a town that thrives on excess.

Practicalities

The **train station** is in the centre of Rimini, on Piazzale Cesare Battisti, ten minutes' walk from the sea and the old centre. There's a **tourist office** by the station and in the Parco dell'Indipendenza on the seafront (both daily 9am–7pm, summer closes 8pm). Both these offices can help with **accommodation**, which can be a problem during the season, when you may have to take full or half board. Try *Pensione Novella*, Via Dandolo 1 (☎0541/247.24; ⑤), in the old town, or the **youth hostel** at Via Flaminia 300 in Miramare (late-April to Sept; ☎0541/373.216; ②) – bus #9 – though it has a midnight curfew (July & Aug 1am) and you need to book. You could also **camp**: on sites next to the rail line at Viserbella (Via Colli), Torre Pedrera (Viale Tolemaide) and Rivabella (off the main road), and south towards Miramare (Viale Principe di Piemonte).

The seafront is the best place to **eat** cheaply, with hundreds of takeaway pizza places. Most of the nicer restaurants are in the old town – try *La Greppia*, at Corso d'Augusto 207, off Piazza Tre Martiri, or the *Belvedere*, on Via Molo Levante. There's also a good student mensa by the train station at Via Roma 70. Rimini's **nightlife** also happens along the seafront, out towards Riccione.

CENTRAL ITALY

The Italian heartland region of **Tuscany** represents perhaps the most archetypal image of the country – its walled towns and rolling, vineyard-covered hills the classic backdrops of Renaissance art. Of Tuscany's urban centres, few people react entirely positively to **Florence**. But however unappealing some of the central streets might look, there are plentiful compensations – the Uffizi gallery's masterpieces, the great fresco cycles in the churches, the wealth of Florentine sculpture in the city's museums. **Siena** provokes less ambiguous reactions: one of the great medieval cities of Europe, it's also the scene of Tuscany's one unmissable festival – the *Palio* – which sees bareback horse riders careering around the cobbled central square. The other major cities, **Pisa** and **Lucca**, both have medieval splendours – Pisa its Leaning Tower and cathedral ensemble, Lucca a string of Romanesque churches – and there are, of course, the smaller hill towns, of which **San Gimignano**, the "city of the towers", is the best known. The provincial capital of the upper Arno region, **Arezzo**, an hour's train ride from Florence, is also worth a stop, if only for its marvellous series of paintings by Piero della Francesca, while to the east lies **Umbria**, a beautiful region of rolling hills, woods and valleys – not unlike Tuscany but as yet less discovered. Most visitors head for the capital, **Perugia**, **Assisi** – with its extraordinary frescoes by Giotto in the Basilica di San Francesco – or **Orvieto**, where the Duomo is one of the greatest Gothic buildings in the country, though lesser-known places like **Gubbio**, ranked as the most perfect medieval centre in Italy, and **Spoleto**, for many the outstanding Umbrian town, are worth taking in, too. Further east still, the **Marche** repeats much the same sort of pleasures, the town of **Urbino** in the north of region, with its superb Renaissance ducal palace, providing a deserved highlight, and the port of **Ancona** useful ferry links to Greece.

Florence

Ever since the nineteenth-century revival of interest in the art of the Renaissance, FLORENCE has been a shrine to the cult of the beautiful. Close up, however, it does not immediately impress visitors as a beautiful city. The marble-clad Baptistery and Duomo are stupendous, of course, the architectural perfection of the latter's dome as celebrated now as it ever was. But these colourful monuments are not typical of the city as a whole: the streets of the historic centre are often narrow and dark, their palaces robust and intimidating, and few of the city's squares are places where you'd want to pass an idle hour. However, Florence is a city of incomparable indoor pleasures, its chapels, galleries and museums an inexhaustible treasure, embodying the complex, exhilarating and often elusive spirit of the Renaissance more fully than any other place in the country, and few leave completely disappointed.

Florence became the centre of artistic patronage in Italy under the Medici family, who made their fortune in banking and ruled the city as an independent state for some three centuries, most auspiciously during the years of Lorenzo de' Medici, tagged "Il Magnifico", who held fiercely onto Florentine independence in the face of papal resentment. Later, in the late eighteenth century, Florence fell under Austrian and then French rule, and in the nineteenth century was for a short time the capital of the Kingdom of Italy. The story of Florence since then has been fairly low-key, and nowadays the monuments and paintings of the city's Renaissance heyday are the basis of its survival.

> The Florence area telephone code is ☎055.

Arrival, information and city transport

The nearest major international **airport** to Florence is at Pisa, connected by a regular train service to Florence's Santa Maria Novella **train station** in the city centre; the journey takes an hour. Some flights now come into Florence's tiny Perètola airport, 5km out of the city and connected by bus to the main **bus station**, alongside Santa Maria Novella. The main **tourist offices** are at Via Cavour 1r, just north of the Duomo (Mon–Sat 8am–7pm), at Chiasso dei Baroncelli 17–19, just off Piazza della Signoria (summer daily 8am–7.30pm; winter Mon–Sat 8am–2pm), and Piazza Stazione (summer Mon–Sat 8.15am–7.15pm, Sun 8.15am–1.45pm; winter daily 8am–2pm). All have free maps and the useful *Concierge Information* booklet. **Walking** is generally the most efficient way of getting around, but if you want to cover a long distance in a hurry, take one of the orange *ATAF* **buses**; tickets, valid for sixty minutes, cost L1100 from *tabacchi* and machines all over Florence.

Accommodation

Florence's most affordable **hotels** are close to the station, in particular along and around Via Faenza and the parallel Via Fiume, and along Via della Scala and Piazza Santa Maria Novella; you could also try the slightly more salubrious Via Cavour, north of the Duomo. However, availability is a problem at most times of year, and between Easter and the start of October you're taking a risk in turning up without a pre-booked room. If you do, the *Informazioni Turistiche Alberghiere* accommodation booth at the station (daily 8.30am–9pm) can make last-minute reservations for a fee, though in high season the queues here can be a nightmare. There's normally an **emergency camping area** or *Area di Sosta*, provided by the city authorities, which at the time of writing was at the *Villa Favard*, in Via Rocca Tedalda (☎690.022), reachable by the #14a bus. Check with the accommodation office for up-to-date details.

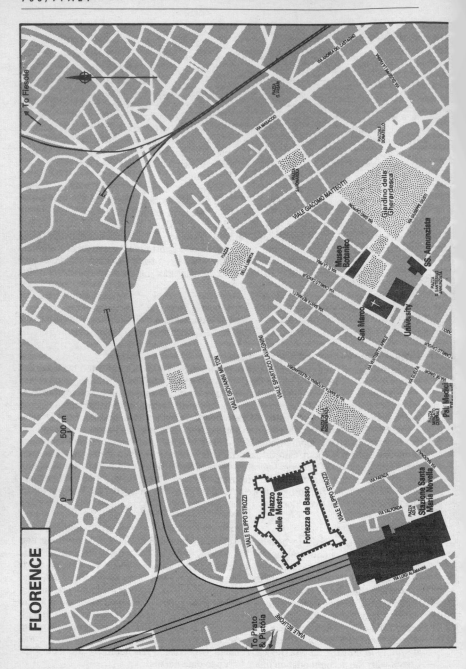

FLORENCE

To Fiesole

500 m

To Prato
& Pistóia

VIA ANDREA DEL CASTAGNO

PIAZZA
G. FALENA

VIA MAGHOLD

VIALE GIACOMO MATTEOTTI

PIAZZALE
DONATELLO

Giardino della
Gherardesca

Museo
Botanico

SS. Annunziata

PIAZZA
S. SANTISSIMO
ANNUNZIATA

San Marco

University

Pal. Medici

VIALE GIOVANNI MILTON

VIALE SPARTACO LAVAGNINI

VIALE FILIPPO STROZZI

Palazzo
delle Mostre

Fortezza da Basso

VIALE FILIPPO STROZZI

VIA FAENZA

VIA NAZIONALE

Stazione Santa
Maria Novella

VIA VALFONDA

PIAZZA
ADUA

VIA LUIGI ALAMANNI

VIALE BELFIORE

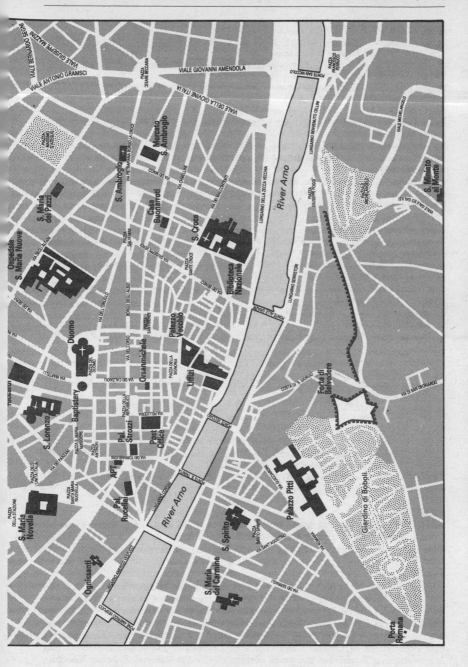

HOSTELS AND DORMITORY ACCOMMODATION

Istituto Gould, Via dei Serragli 49 (☎212.576). Over in Oltrarno, and open Mon–Fri 9am–1pm & 3–7pm & Sat 9am–1pm. It's wise to book in advance. ③

Ostello Villa Camerata, Viale Righi 2 (☎601.451). The official *IYHF* hostel lies in a beautiful park, a 30-minute journey on the #17b bus from the train station. Doors open at 2pm; if you can't be there by then, ring ahead to make sure there's space left. ②

Pio X – Artigianelli, Via dei Serragli 106 (☎225.044). The cheapest option in town, open all day year-round. Double, triple and quadruple rooms. ②

Santa Monaca, Via Santa Monaca 6 (☎268.338). In Oltrarno. Free hot showers, but an 11.30pm curfew. Very popular. ②

Suore Oblate dell'Assunzione, Via Borgo Pinti 15 (☎214.582). Not far from the Duomo, open to men and women from mid-June to the end of July and throughout September. Single and double rooms; midnight curfew. ③

Suore Oblate dello Spirito Santo, Via Nazionale 8 (☎239.8202). A few steps from the station, and open to women mid-June to Oct. Very clean and pleasant; single, double and triple rooms; 11pm curfew and minimum stay of two nights. ③

HOTELS

Alessandra, Borgo Santi Apostoli 17 (☎283.438). Occupying a sixteenth-century palazzo, a two-star hotel frequented by the fashion-show crowd. ⑤

Ausonia e Rimini, Via Nazionale 24 (☎496.547). Halfway between the train station and the market, recently refurbished and welcoming. ③

Azzi, Via Faenza 56 (☎213.806). Probably the most pleasant of six reasonably priced *pensioni* on the upper floors of this building. ③

Brunetta, Borgo Pinti 5 (☎247.8134). Cheap and central, just east of the Duomo. ③

Constantini, Via Calzaiuoli 13 (☎215.128). Friendly place on the city's main street. ⑤

Concordia, Via dell'Amorino 14 (☎213.233). Extremely convenient, right in the heart of the market area. ③

Donatello, Via Alfieri 9 (☎245.870). In a quiet area between Piazzale Donatello and Piazza d'Azeglio; strongly recommended – smartly renovated, young and friendly. ④

Mia Casa, Piazza Santa Maria Novella 23 (☎213.061). Ramshackle, with occasionally obstreperous owners but a handy, central location. ③

La Romagnola (☎211.597) and **Gigliola** (☎287.981), both at Via della Scala 40. Best of the Via della Scala hotels – midnight curfews are the only drawback. ③

Sorelle Bandini, Piazza Santo Spirito 9 (☎215.308). Across the river, vast rooms, gorgeous decor and great views make this one of Florence's most attractive options. ③

Teti and **Prestige**, Via Porta Rossa 5 (☎239.8435). Right in the thick of things between Via Tornabuoni and Piazza della Signoria. Good value and friendly. ③

Tony's Inn, Via Faenza 77 (☎284.119). Run by a Canadian woman and her Italian photographer husband. Good for homesick Anglophones. ⑤

CAMPSITES

Italiani e Stranieri, Viale Michelangelo 80 (☎681.1977). Open April–Oct, and always crowded owing to its superb hillside location. Bus #13 from the train station.

Villa Camerata, Viale Righi 2 (☎610.300). Basic site in hostel grounds, open all year.

The City

Florence sprawls along both sides of the Arno and into the hills north and south of the city, but the major sights are contained within an area that can be crossed on foot in a little over half an hour. Perhaps the most obvious place to start exploring is the **Piazza della Signoria**, a rather charmless open space, fringed on one side by the graceful late fourteenth-century **Loggia della Signoria**. Dotted with statuary, like Giambologna's equestrian statue of Cosimo I and copies of Donatello's *Judith and Holofernes* and Michelangelo's *David*, the square is dominated by the colossal **Palazzo Vecchio**,

Florence's fortress-like town hall (Mon–Fri 9am–7pm, Sun 8am–1pm; L8000, joint ticket to city museums valid for six months L10,000), begun in the last year of the thirteenth century as the home of the *Signoria*, the highest tier of the city's republican government. The Medici were only in residence here for nine years, but the layout of the palace owes much to them, notably Cosimo I, who decorated the state rooms with relentless eulogies to himself and his family. The huge Salone dei Cinquento, built at the end of the fifteenth century, is full of heroic murals by Vasari, though it is to some extent redeemed by the presence of Michelangelo's *Victory*, facing the entrance door, originally sculpted for Pope Julius II's tomb but donated to the Medici by the artist's nephew. The bizarre Studiolo di Francesco I was also created by Vasari, and decorated by several of Florence's prominent Mannerist artists as a retreat for the introverted son of Cosimo, most of the bronzes and paintings reflecting Francesco's interest in the sciences, though the best ones are those that don't fit the scheme – principally Bronzino's glacial portraits of the occupant's parents, Cosimo and Eleanor of Toledo. Bronzino also painted Eleanor's tiny chapel upstairs, and a Mannerist contemporary of Bronzino, Cecchino Salviati, produced what is widely held to be his masterpiece with the fresco cycle in the Sala d'Udienza, once the audience chamber of the Republic. The adjoining Sala dei Gigli was frescoed by Ghirlandaio, although the main focus is Donatello's recently restored *Judith and Holofernes*.

Immediately south of the piazza, the **Galleria degli Uffizi** (Tues–Sat 9am–7pm, Sun 9am–1pm; L10,000) is the greatest picture gallery in Italy, with a collection of masterpieces that is impossible to take in on a single visit. The early Renaissance is represented by three altarpieces of the *Madonna Enthroned* by Cimabue, Duccio and Giotto, and a luscious golden *Annunciation* by the fourteenth-century Sienese painter, Simone Martini. There's Uccello's *Battle of San Romano* – demonstrating the artist's obsessional interest in perspectival effects – which once hung in Lorenzo il Magnifico's bed chamber, in company with depictions of the skirmish now in the Louvre and London's National Gallery. Among plentiful works by Filippo Lippi is his *Madonna and Child with Two Angels*, one of the best-known Renaissance images of the Madonna. Close by, there's a fine *Madonna* by Botticelli, who in the next room is represented by some of his most famous works, notably *Primavera* and the *Birth of Venus*; look also at the huge *Portinari Altarpiece* by Botticelli's Flemish contemporary Hugo van der Goes, a work whose naturalism greatly influenced the artists of Florence. The Uffizi doesn't own a finished painting that's entirely by Leonardo da Vinci, but there's a celebrated *Annunciation* (mainly by him) and the angel in profile that he painted in Verrocchio's *Baptism*. Room 18, the octagonal Tribuna, where the cream of the collection used to be exhibited, houses the most important of the Medici sculptures, first among which is the *Medici Venus*, along with some chillingly precise portraits by Bronzino and Vasari's portrait of Lorenzo il Magnifico, painted long after the death of its subject. Michelangelo's *Doni Tondo* is his only completed easel painting, its contorted gestures and virulent colours studied and imitated by the Mannerist painters of the sixteenth century, as can be gauged from the nearby *Moses Defending the Daughters of Jethro* by Rosso Fiorentino, one of the pivotal figures of the movement. Separating the two Mannerist groups are a number of compositions by Raphael, including *Pope Leo X with Cardinals Giulio de' Medici and Luigi de' Rossi* – as shifty a group of ecclesiastics as ever was gathered in one frame – while Titian weighs in with his fleshily provocative *Venus of Urbino*. Later rooms include some large works by Rubens and van Dyck; Caravaggio has a cluster of pieces, including a severed head of Medusa; while another room has portraiture by Rembrandt, notably his melancholic *Self-Portrait as an Old Man*, painted five years before his death.

To get a comprehensive idea of the Renaissance achievement in Florence, you need also to visit the **Museo Nazionale del Bargello** (Tues–Sat 9am–2pm, Sun 9am–1pm; L6000), a short step north in Via del Proconsolo, where there is a full collection of sculpture from the period, housed in a thirteenth-century palace that was formerly the HQ of the city's chief of police (the *Bargello*). The first part of the collection focuses on Michelangelo, represented by among others his first major sculpture, the lurching figure of *Bacchus*, carved at the age of 22. Beyond, the more flamboyant art of Cellini and Giambologna is exhibited, notably by a huge *Bust of Cosimo I*, Cellini's first work in bronze, a sort of technical trial for the casting of the *Perseus* nearby, and Giambologna's best-known creation, the nimble figure of *Mercury*. Across the courtyard, the first-floor loggia has been turned into an aviary for Giambologna's bronze birds, imported from the Medici villa at Castello, while a nearby room displays work by Donatello – the mildly Gothic *David* and the alert figure of *St George*. His sexually ambiguous bronze *David*, the first freestanding nude figure since classical times, was cast in the early 1430s. Donatello's master, Ghiberti, is represented by his relief of *The Sacrifice of Isaac*, his successful entry in the competition for the Baptistery doors. The treatment of the theme submitted by Brunelleschi, the runner-up, is hung close by. Upstairs the Sala dei Bronzetti has Italy's best assembly of small Renaissance bronzes, with plentiful evidence of Giambologna's virtuosity, and a further room holds Renaissance portrait busts, including Mino da Fiesole's busts of *Giovanni de' Medici* and *Piero il Gottoso*, and a couple of pieces by Verrocchio, including a *David* clearly influenced by Donatello.

Parallel to Via del Proconsolo on the opposite side of Piazza della Signoria is **Via dei Calzaiuoli**, one of the city's more animated streets and home to the church of **Orsanmichele** (daily 8am–noon & 3–6pm). Its exterior is decorated by a number of early Renaissance sculptures, including, on the Via dei Calzaiuoli side, a *John the Baptist* by Ghiberti, the first life-size bronze statue of the Renaissance, and an *Incredulity of St Thomas* by Verrocchio. Inside there's a vast tabernacle by Orcagna, carved with delicate reliefs and tiny statues and studded with coloured marble and glass, framing a *Madonna* painted by Bernardo Daddi in 1347 to replace a miraculous image of the Virgin that was destroyed by a 1304 fire.

The streets west of the Signoria retain a medieval character, lined with palaces like the fourteenth-century Palazzo Davanzati on Via Porta Rossa which houses the **Museo della Casa Fiorentina Antica** (Tues–Sat 9am–2pm, Sun 9am–1pm; L4000). Inside, virtually every room of the reconstructed interior is furnished and decorated in medieval style. About 500m northwest, off Via della Scala, the church of **Santa Maria Novella** (daily 7–11.30am & 3.30–6pm) was the Florentine base of the Dominican order, a partly Gothic church that is home to an array of works of art, most notably Masaccio's extraordinary fresco of *The Trinity*, one of the earliest works in which perspective and classical proportion were rigorously employed, halfway down the left aisle of the nave. Further down the nave, the Cappella di Filippo Strozzi is covered by a fresco cycle begun by Filippino Lippi in 1486 and finished fifteen years later, after the artist's sojourn in Rome to view the ruins. Look, too, at Ghirlandaio's pictures behind the high altar, as good a chronicle of fifteenth-century life in Florence as you'll find, and at Brunelleschi's *Crucifix*, supposedly carved as a lesson to Donatello, to the left of the chancel. The church's cloisters (Mon–Thurs & Sat 9am–2pm, Sun 8am–1pm; L4000) are also richly decorated, with frescoes by Uccello and his workshop.

THE DUOMO AND AROUND

North of the Signoria on **Piazza del Duomo**, the **Duomo** (daily 10am–5.30pm) was built between the late thirteenth and mid-fifteenth centuries to an ambitious design, originally the brainchild of Arnolfo di Cambio and realized finally by Filippo Brunelleschi, who completed the majestic dome – the largest in existence until this century. The fourth largest church in the world, its ambience is more that of a great assembly hall than of a devotional building, its most conspicuous pieces of painted decoration two memorials to *condottieri* – Uccello's monument to Sir John Hawkwood, painted in 1436, and Castagno's monument to Niccolò da Tolentino, created twenty years later. Just beyond, Domenico do Michelino's *Dante Explaining the Divine Comedy*, painted in 1465, gives the recently completed dome a place only marginally less prominent than the mountain of Purgatory. Above, the fresco of *The Last Judgement* in the dome is the work of Vasari and Zuccari, below which are seven stained-glass roundels designed by Uccello, Ghiberti, Castagno and Donatello – best inspected from a gallery which forms part of the route to the top of the dome (Mon–Sat 10am–5pm; L5000). The views at the very top are as stupendous as you would expect.

Next door to the Duomo, the **Campanile** (daily 8.30am–7pm; L5000) was begun in 1334 by Giotto and continued after his death by Andrea Pisano and Francesco Talenti. The only part of the tower built exactly as Giotto designed it is the lower storey, studded with two rows of remarkable bas-reliefs, the lower one illustrating the *Creation of Man* and the *Arts and Industries* carved by Pisano. The figures of *Prophets* and *Sibyls* in the second-storey niches are by Donatello and others. Opposite, the **Baptistery** (Mon–Sat 1–6pm, Sun 9am–1pm), generally thought to date from the sixth or seventh century, is the oldest building in the city. Its most famous embellishments, the gilded bronze doors, were cast in the early fifteenth century by Lorenzo Ghiberti, and were described by Michelangelo as "so beautiful they are worthy to be the gates of Paradise". They're a primer of early Renaissance art, innovatively using perspective, gesture and sophisticated grouping of subjects to convey the human drama of each scene. Ghiberti included a self-portrait in the frame of the left-hand door – his is the fourth head from the top of the right-hand door. Inside, the Baptistery is equally stunning, with thirteenth-century mosaic floor and ceiling and the tomb of Pope John XXIII, draped by a superb marble canopy, the work of Donatello and his pupil Michelozzo.

Since the early fifteenth century the maintenance of the Duomo has been supervised from the building at Piazza del Duomo 9, nowadays housing the **Museo dell'Opera del Duomo** (summer Mon–Sat 9am–7.30pm; winter Mon–Sat 9am–6pm; L5000), the repository of the most precious and fragile works of art from the buildings around. As an overview of the sculpture of Florence it's second only to the Bargello, and is far easier to take in on a single visit. Its most arresting works include a series of sculptures by Arnolfo di Cambio, rescued from Arnolfo's unfinished facade for the Duomo; Brunelleschi's death mask; models of the dome and a variety of tools and machines devised by the architect; and, on the mezzanine level, Michelangelo's anguished late *Pietà*, intended for his own tomb. Upstairs, Donatello, the greatest of Michelangelo's forerunners, is represented by a number of figures he carved for the Campanile, the most powerful of which is that of the prophet Habbakuk. Pisano's original bas-reliefs from the Campanile are on show in one of the two adjoining rooms, while the other contains four of Ghiberti's door panels and a dazzling silver-gilt altar from the Baptistery, completed in 1480.

NORTH OF THE DUOMO

The church of **San Lorenzo** (daily 7am–noon & 3.30–6.30pm), north of the Baptistery, has good claim to be the oldest church in Florence, and for the best part of three hundred years was the city's cathedral. The Medici parish church, it inevitably benefited from the family's patronage, rebuilt in the mid-fifteenth century by Brunelleschi and, inside at least, a fine example of early Renaissance church design. Inside are two bronze pulpits by Donatello, the artist's last works and in fact completed by his pupils. Close by, a large disc of multicoloured marble marks the grave of Cosimo il Vecchio, the artist's main patron, while further pieces by Donatello adorn the neighbouring Sagrestia Vecchia by Brunelleschi – the two pairs of bronze doors, the large reliefs of *SS. Cosmas and Damian* and *SS. Lawrence and Stephen*, and the eight terracotta tondoes. At the top of the left aisle and through the cloisters, the Biblioteca Medicea–Laurenziana (Mon–Sat 9am–1pm; free) was commissioned from Michelangelo in 1524, and its most startling feature is the vestibule, a room almost filled by a flight of steps resembling a solidified lava flow. Michelangelo's most celebrated contribution to the San Lorenzo buildings, however, is the Sagrestia Nuova, part of the **Cappelle Medicee** (Tues–Sat 9am–2pm, Sun 9am–1pm; L9000). Begun in 1520, in part as a tribute to Sagrestia Vecchia, it contains the fabulous Medici tombs, carved between 1524 and 1533. To the left is the tomb of Lorenzo, Duke of Urbino, the grandson of Lorenzo il Magnifico, bearing figures of *Dawn* and *Dusk* to sum up his contemplative nature. Opposite is the tomb of Lorenzo il Magnifico's youngest son, Giuliano, his supposedly more active character symbolized by *Day* and *Night*. Their effigies were intended to face the equally grand tombs of Lorenzo il Magnifico and his brother Giuliano, though the only part of this actually realized by Michelangelo is the serene *Madonna and Child*, the last image of the Madonna he ever sculpted.

On the edge of the square in front of San Lorenzo, the **Palazzo Medici-Riccardi** (Mon, Tues & Thurs–Sat 9am–1pm & 3–5pm, Sun 9am–noon; free) was built for Cosimo il Vecchio by Michelozzo in the 1440s, though of his original scheme only the upstairs chapel remains intact, its interior covered by a colourful narrative fresco of the *Journey of the Magi*, painted around 1460 by Benozzo Gozzoli. North up Via Cavour, **Piazza San Marco** is the site of the Dominican convent and church of **San Marco**, recipient of Cosimo il Vecchio's most lavish patronage when in the 1430s he financed Michelozzo's enlargement of the buildings. As Michelozzo was altering and expanding the convent, its walls were being decorated by one of its friars, Fra Angelico, and, now deconsecrated, the church and convent today house the **Museo di San Marco** (Tues–Sat 9am–2pm, Sun 9am–1pm; L6000), in effect a museum dedicated to the art of Fra Angelico. The first part of the museum is a collection of around twenty panel paintings by him, a large number of them brought here from other churches in Florence. Across the cloister is a powerful fresco of the *Crucifixion*, painted in 1441, and there's a famous *Annunciation* at the summit of the main staircase. Around the upper floor, the 44 tiny dormitory cells were also frescoed by Angelico or by his assistants.

Just east of San Marco, the **Galleria dell'Accademia** (Tues–Sat 9am–2pm, Sun 9am–1pm; L10,000) was Europe's first school of drawing, and has an impressive collection of paintings, but most people come here to view the sculpture of Michelangelo, specifically his *David*, once the emblem of the city's republican pride and nowadays the heraldic device of touristic Florence. Finished in 1504, when Michelangelo was just 29, and carved from a gigantic block of marble, it's an incomparable show of technical bravura. The gallery also houses his remarkable unfinished **Slaves**, originally intended for the tomb of Pope Julius II but in 1564 given to the Medici, who installed them in the grotto of the Bóboli gardens. In their midst is another unfinished work, *St Matthew*, started immediately after completion of the *David* as part of a commission from the Duomo. Close by, **Piazza Santissima Annunziata** is the Florentines' favourite square, its centre marked by Giambologna's final work, the equestrian statue of **Grand Duke Ferdinando I**. Beyond, on Via della Colonna, the **Museo Archeologico** (Tues–Sat 9am–2pm, Sun 9am–1pm; L6000) has a fine showing of Etruscan finds – most notably the *Chimera*, a triple-headed monster of the fifth century BC, much admired by Cosimo I's retinue of Mannerist artists – a good Egyptian collection, and, outstanding among a number of Roman pieces, a nude known as the *Idolino*.

THE SANTA CROCE DISTRICT

Down by the river, the Franciscan church of Florence, **Santa Croce** (Mon–Sat 8am–6.30pm, Sun 8am–12.30pm & 3–6pm) was begun in 1294, possibly by the architect of the Duomo, Arnolfo di Cambio, and is full of tombstones and commemorative monuments, including Vasari's monument to Michelangelo, and, on the opposite side of the church, is the tomb of Galileo, built in 1737 when it was finally agreed to give the great scientist a Christian burial; most visitors come to see the frescoes by Giotto in the Cappella Peruzzi and the Cappella Bardi (on the right of the chancel). The former shows scenes from the lives of Saints John the Baptist and John the Evangelist; the latter, painted slightly earlier with some assistance, features the life of Saint Francis. Agnolo Gaddi was responsible for all the frescoes around and above the high altar and for the design of the stained glass in the lancet windows. At the end of the left chancel, a second Cappella Bardi houses a wooden *Crucifix* by Donatello – supposedly criticized by Brunelleschi as resembling a "peasant on the Cross". Also visit Brunelleschi's **Cappella dei Pazzi**, at the end of the first cloister (summer 10am–12.30pm & 2.30–6.30pm; winter 10am–12.30pm & 3–5pm; closed Wed; L3000), designed in the 1430s and completed in the 1470s, several years after the architect's death, with decorations by Luca della Robbia. The **Museo dell'Opera di Santa Croce**, off the first cloister (same times), also houses a miscellany of works of art, the best of which are Cimabue's flood-damaged *Crucifixion*, Gaddi's fresco of the *Last Supper and Crucifixion*, and Donatello's enormous gilded *St Louis of Toulouse*, made for Orsanmichele.

North of Santa Croce at Via Ghibellina 70, the **Casa Buonarotti** (9.30am–1.30pm; closed Tues; L8000) is enticing in name, but although Michelangelo Buonarotti did own this property he never actually lived here, and much of the space is taken up by homages to the artist, copies of works by him and portraits of him. The most exciting items are the *Madonna of the Steps*, Michelangelo's earliest known work, and the similarly unfinished *Battle of the Centaurs*, which dates from when he was living in the Medici household. There's also a torso of a *River God* intended for the Medici chapel in San Lorenzo, and a painted wooden *Crucifix* discovered in Santo Spirito in 1963.

OLTRARNO AND SAN MINIATO

Although much of the tourist traffic stays over on the north bank of the Arno, there are a number of very good reasons for crossing the river into the so-called **Oltrarno** district, not least the **Palazzo Pitti**, originally built in the mid-fifteenth century for one Luca Pitti, in a desperate attempt to go one up on his rivals, the Medici – who ironically later occupied and expanded the place. Nowadays the palace and its stupendous garden – the Giardino di Bóboli – contain six separate museums (Tues–Sat 9am–2pm, Sun 9am–1pm). Many of the paintings gathered by the Medici in the seventeenth century are now arranged in the **Galleria Palatina** (L8000), which has superb displays of the art of Raphael and Titian, including a number of Titian's most trenchant portraits. Andrea del Sarto is represented in strength, too, as is Rubens, whose *Consequences of War* packs more of a punch than most other Baroque allegories. Much of the rest of the first floor comprises the **Appartamenti Monumentali** (L8000), the Pitti's state rooms, while on the floor above, the **Galleria d'Arte Moderna** (L8000) is a chronological survey of primarily Tuscan art from the mid-eighteenth century to 1945. The Pitti's **Museo degli Argenti** (L6000), covers Costume Gallery, entered from the garden courtyard, is a collection of luxury artefacts, notably Lorenzo il Magnifico's trove of antique vases, displayed in one of the four splendidly frescoed reception rooms on the ground floor. There is also a **Galleria del Costume**, where you can admire the dress that Eleanor of Toledo was buried in, and a **Museo delle Porcellane** (closed for renovation). However, you'd be better to concentrate on the Pitti's enormous formal garden, the **Giardino di Bóboli** (Tues–Sun March, April, Sept & Oct 9am–5.30pm; May–Aug closes 6.30pm; Nov–Feb closes 4.30pm; L5000). Begun when the Medici took possession of the palace, it's full of Mannerist embellishments, the most celebrated of which is the Grotta del Buontalenti, close to the entrance to the left of the palace facade, where in amongst the fake stalactites are shepherds and sheep and replicas of Michelangelo's *Slaves*, replacing the originals that were here until 1908. In the deepest recesses of the cave stands Giambologna's *Venus*, leered at by attendant imps. The vast amphitheatre facing the palace courtyard was designed in the early seventeenth century as an arena for Medici festivities, the site having already been laid out by Ammanati as a garden in the shape of a Roman circus. A set piece of comparable scale is the fountain island called the Isolotto, approached along the central cypress avenue known as the Viottolone, many of whose statues are Roman originals. It's usually possible to leave the garden by the gate which leads to the **Forte di Belvedere** (daily 9am–8pm; free), the star-shaped fortress built on the orders of Ferdinando I in 1590.

About 500m northwest of the Palazzo Pitti, the church of **Santa Maria del Carmine** is visited for the frescoes in its Cappella Brancacci (Mon & Wed–Sat 10am–5pm, Sun 1–5pm; L5000) by Masaccio – recently, and controversially, restored. The decoration was begun by Masolino in 1425 or thereabouts, and Masaccio joined him soon after as his assistant. Within a short while the teacher was taking lessons from the pupil, whose grasp of the principles of perspective, and of the Biblical texts they were illustrating, far exceeded that of his precursors. Look, for example, at the *Expulsion of Adam and Eve* on the left of the entrance arch, which captures the desolation of the sinners so graphically. Michelangelo used to come here to make drawings of Masaccio's scenes, and had his nose broken by an irate young sculptor whom he enraged with his condescending manner. After a hiatus of about sixty years, the cycle was completed by Filippino Lippi, his most distinctive contribution being the affecting *Release of St Peter* on the right-hand side of the entrance, which portrays the trio of Alberti, Brunelleschi and Masaccio to the right of the enthroned saint.

In the opposite direction, the multicoloured facade of **San Miniato al Monte** lures troops of visitors up the hill. The oldest church building in Florence after the Baptistery, with the finest Romanesque church in Tuscany, it was erected on the spot where the corpse of one Saint Minias was seen to carry its head after martyrdom. The interior (daily 8am–noon & 2–7pm) is like no other in the city, and its general form has changed little since the mid-eleventh century, the only real structural additions the Cappella del Cardinale del Portogallo, built onto the left aisle as a memorial to Cardinal James of Lusitania, whose tomb was carved by Antonio Rossellino, and the terracotta decoration of the ceiling provided by Luca della Robbia. In the lower part of the church, don't overlook the intricately patterned panels of the pavement, from 1207, and the tabernacle between the choir stairs, designed in 1448 by Michelozzo.

Eating and drinking

Although Tuscan cuisine is distinguished by its simplicity, in recent years Florence's gastronomic reputation has suffered under the pressure of mass tourism. Certainly there's a dearth of good places to eat if you're on a limited budget, although a decent meal isn't hard to come by if you explore the remoter quarters. The best place to find **picnic food** and **snacks** is the **Mercato Centrale** (Mon–Fri 7am–2pm, Sat also 4–8pm), just east of the train station, which is full of *alimentari*, tripe sellers, greengrocers, pasta stalls and bars charging prices lower than elsewhere in the city. There are also plenty of city centre **bars**, along Via de' Panzani, Via de' Cerretani, Via Por Santa Maria and Via Guicciardini, whose snacky food offers ample compensation for their lack of character. Otherwise, try a **vinaio**, a wine cellar/snack bar that serves *crostini* and other snacks. The *vinaio* at Via Cimatori 38 is a perfect example, as is the place at Via Alfani 70, in the university area, which serves stuffed tomatoes and a range of other vegetables in addition to the traditional *crostini*. For classier snacks, try the *panini* and pasta at *Fiaschetteria*, Via de' Neri 17, or the similar fare at *Fiaschetteria da 11 Latin*, Via del Palchetti 6/r, behind Palazzo Rucellai. Another Florentine speciality is the **friggitoria**, serving *polenta*, potatoes and apple croquettes – try the one at Via Sant'Antonio 50, which also sells pizza, or the one at Volta di San Piero 5, which does burgers and salads. *Mario* is a superb *rosticceria*, with seats, at Via de' Neri 74. For **ice cream**, leader of the pack is *Vivoli*, near Santa Croce at Via Isola delle Stinche 7/r.

RESTAURANTS

Bar Santa Croce, Borgo Santa Croce 31. Good lunchtime menu and marvellous pasta.

Benvenuto, Via Mosca 16/5. off Via de' Neri. Looks more like a delicatessen than a trattoria from the street, but the groups waiting for a table give the game away; the *gnocchi* and *arista* are delicious.

Dante, Piazza Nazario Sauro 10. Busy pizzeria with around a dozen types of spaghetti on the menu too.

Da Mario, Via Rosina 2. Popular with students and market workers – be prepared to queue and share a table.

Mensa Universitaria, Via San Gallo 25a. L8000 buys a two-course meal plus fruit and drink. Mon–Sat noon–2.15pm & 6.45–8.45pm; closed mid-July to mid-Sept.

Alle Mossacce, Via del Proconsolo 55. Once the haunt of Florence's young artists; the bohemian element has since dispersed, but the food remains excellent. Closed Sun.

Palle d'Oro, Via Sant'Antonio 43. Station area eatery that's halfway between a *rosticceria* and a trattoria. Besides full meals, they do sandwiches to take away.

Dei Quattro Leoni, Via Vellutini 1. Rough-and-ready Oltrarno place; very cheap.

Trattoria Casalinga, Via Michelozzi 9r. Oltrarno restaurant that offers just about the best low-cost authentic Tuscan dishes in town. Always crowded.

Za-Za, Piazza del Mercato 26. A few tables on ground level, but a bigger canteen below.

Nightlife

Florence enjoys a reasonably vibrant **nightlife** by Italian standards. Of **places to drink**, *Rifrullo*, Via San Niccolò 55, attracts an affluent young clientele; *Dolce Vita*, on Piazza del Carmine, is a trendy hang-out that also stages small-scale art exhibitions; the nearby *Tiratoio*, on Piazza de' Nerli, is a large easy-going place, with a couple of video jukeboxes and a wide range of food. In the university district, *Video Diva*, Via San Zanobi 114, is always packed with students and serves good cocktails. For a quiet drink in a beautifully situated bar, try *Fontana* on Viale Michelangelo – pricy but worth it. Later on, *Tenax*, Via Pratese 47, is the city's biggest **disco** and one of its leading venues for new and established bands. *Yab Yum*, Via de' Sassetti 5r, is a city centre disco with a vast dance floor and the best of new dance music; *Rockafè*, Borgo Albizi 9, is a vaguely underground/avant-garde club open into the small hours every night. *Space Electronic*, Via Palazzuolo 37, is the favourite disco of young foreigners, open nightly, but *Meccanò*, Piazza Vittorio Veneto, is the "in" place to be seen. For **information** on what's on, call in at *Box Office*, Via della Pergola 10a/r (☎242.361), or consult the listings magazines *Firenze Spettacolo*, *Metró* and *Time Off*.

Listings

Airlines *Alitalia*, Lungarno Acciaioli 10–12 (☎27.881); *British Airways*, Via della Vigna Nuova 36r (☎218.655/218.659).

Airport enquiries ☎050/28.088.

American Express, Via Dante Alighieri or Via Guicciardini (Mon–Fri 9am–5.30pm, Sat 9am–12.30pm).

Books *Paperback Exchange*, Via Fiesolana 31r, carries a good stock of English books; *After Dark*, Via del Moro 86/r, is an English-language bookshop.

Car rental *Avis*, Borgognissanti 128r (☎213.629); *Hertz*, Via Maso Finiguerra 33r (☎282.260); *Maggiore*, Via Maso Finiguerra 31 (☎210.238).

Consulates *Great Britain*, Lungarno Corsini 2 (☎284.133); *USA*, Lungarno Vespucci 38 (☎239.8276).

Exchange *Esercizio Promozione Turismo*, Via Condotta 42 (Mon–Sat 10am–7pm, Sun 10am–6pm).

Hospital Santa Maria Nuova, Piazza Santa Maria Nuova 1 (☎27.581). The *Tourist Medical Service*, Via Lorenzo il Magnifico 59 (☎475.411), has English-speaking doctors on 24hr call.

Laundry *Lavanderia Manfredi*, Via Sant'Antonio 66/r, near Mercato Centrale; *Lavamatic*, Via degli Alfani 44/r, is cheapest.

Pharmacies All-night pharmacy at the train station, and *Molteni*, Via Calzaiuoli 7/r.
Police Main office at Via Zara 2 (☎49.771).
Post office Central office at Via Pellicceria (Mon–Fri 8.15am–7pm, Sat 8.15am–noon); main office at Via Pietrapiana 53–55 (same hours).
Telephones Booths at train station (8am–9.45pm; closed Sun); Via Pellicceria post office (8am–10.30pm); *Palazzo delle Poste*, Via Pietra Piana (weekdays 8am–7.45pm).
Train enquiries ☎288.785.

Fiesole

A long-established Florentine retreat from the summer heat and crowds, FIESOLE spreads over a cluster of hilltops some 8km northeast of Florence. It rivalled its neighbour until the early twelfth century, when it became favoured as a semi-rural second home for Florence's wealthier citizens. The #7 *ATAF* bus runs there every fifteen minutes from Florence's train station, a twenty-minute journey.

Fiesole's central **Piazza Mino da Fiesole** is home to the **Duomo**, in which the Cappella Salutati, right of the choir, contains two fine pieces carved by Mino da Fiesole in the mid-fifteenth century – an altar frontal of *The Madonna and Saints* and the tomb of Bishop Salutati. From here, Via San Francesco leads up to a terrace which gives a remarkable panorama of Florence, just above which the church of **Sant'Alessandro** (daily 10am–noon & 3–5pm), founded in the sixth century on the site of Etruscan and Roman temples, has a beautiful basilical interior with onion marble columns. Around the back of the duomo, in Via Marini, is the entrance to the **Teatro Romano** and **Museo Archeologico** (April–Sept Tues–Sun 9am–7pm; Oct–March Tues–Sun 10am–4pm; L4000). Built in the first century BC, the 3000-seater theatre remains in good enough repair to be used for performances during the *Estate Fiesolana* festival. Most of the museum exhibits were discovered in this area, and encompass pieces from the Bronze Age to the Roman occupation. The narrow Via Vecchia Fiesolana leads from just west of the main square to the hamlet of **SAN DOMENICO**, 1500m southwest. Fra Angelico was once prior of the Dominican **monastery** here, and the church retains a *Madonna and Angels* by him; the chapterhouse also has a Fra Angelico fresco of *The Crucifixion*. Five minutes' walk northwest from San Domenico brings you to the **Badia Fiesolana**, formerly Fiesole's cathedral and altered by Cosimo il Vecchio in the 1460s, when he left the magnificent Romanesque facade intact while transforming the interior into a superb Renaissance building.

San Gimignano

SAN GIMIGNANO – "delle Belle Torri" – is one of the best-known towns in Tuscany. Its skyline of towers has caught the tourist imagination, helped along, no doubt, by its convenience as a day trip from Florence or Siena. It is, in fact, all that it's cracked up to be: quietly monumental and well-preserved, with a fine array of religious and secular frescoes. However, from May through to October, San Gimignano is very busy, and to really get any feel for the place, beyond the level of art treasures or quaintness, you need to come out of season. If you can't, aim to spend the night here – in the evenings the town takes on a very different pace and atmosphere.

Founded around the eighth century, San Gimignano was quite a force to be reckoned with in the Middle Ages, with a population of 15,000 (twice the present number). Nowadays it's not much more than a village: you could walk across it in fifteen minutes, around the walls in an hour. The main entrance gate, facing the bus terminal on the south side of town, is **Porta San Giovanni**, from where Via San Giovanni leads to the town's interlocking main squares, Piazza della Cisterna and Piazza del Duomo. You enter the **Piazza della Cisterna** through another majestic gateway, the **Arco dei Becci**, part of the original fortifications before the town expanded in the twelfth century. The more austere **Piazza Duomo**, off to the left, is flanked by the **Collegiata** church, one of the most comprehensively frescoed churches in Tuscany, with Old Testament scenes by Bartolo di Fredi on the left wall, from around 1367, and, opposite, slightly later New Testament scenes by Barna da Siena. Look, too, at Taddeo di Bartolo's *Last Judgement* on the inner wall of the facade, one of the most gruesome depictions of a customarily lurid subject, below which is a *St Sebastian* by Benozzo Gozzoli, painted in gratitude at the end of plague in 1464. Best, though, is the fresco cycle by Ghirlandaio in the Cappella di Santa Fina, depicting the trials of a local saint – a superb work, access to which is included on a general tourist ticket (L10,000, L7500 students) that includes entry to all the town's museums. There's more work by Ghirlandaio to the left of the cathedral – a fresco of the *Annunciation* on the courtyard loggia – while the **Palazzo del Popolo**, next door (Tues–Sat summer 9.30am–5.30pm; winter 9.30am–12.30pm & 2.30–5.30pm), gives the chance to climb the **Torre Grossa**, the town's highest surviving tower and the only one you can ascend. The same building is home to a number of rooms given over to the **Museo Civico**, the first of which, frescoed with hunting scenes, is known as the Sala di Dante and houses Lippo Memmi's *Maestà*, modelled on that of Simone Martini in Siena. Search out also the delightful frescoes of wedding scenes in a small room off the stairs, completed early in the fourteenth century by the Sienese painter Memmo di Filipuccio. North from Piazza Duomo, **Via San Matteo** is one of the grandest and best preserved of the city streets, with quiet alleyways running down to the walls. The street ends at the **Porta San Matteo**, just inside which, in a corner of walls, is the large, hall church of **Sant'Agostino** (daily 8am–noon & 3–7pm), with a much-damaged fresco series of the *Life of the Virgin* by Bartolo di Fredi and a cycle of seventeen scenes of the *Life of St Augustine* by Gozzoli, behind the high altar.

Practicalities

San Gimignano's three **hotels** are expensive, and the only budget choices are the *Ristorante Il Pino*, Via San Matteo 102 (☎0577/940.41; ④), the **Convento di Sant'Agostino** (☎0577/940.383; ②), and a good new **youth hostel** at Via delle Fonti 1 (March to mid-Nov; ☎0577/941.991; ②). Accommodation lists are available from the **tourist office** on Piazza del Duomo, but from May to September you'll save a lot of frustration by using the office at Via S. Giovanni 125 (Mon–Sat summer 9.30am–7.30pm; winter 9.30am–12.30pm & 3–5pm), which arranges **private rooms** for L2000 commission. **Camping**, the nearest site is *Il Boschetto*, 3km downhill at Santa Lucia (☎0577/940.352). One of the most popular **restaurants**, a fraction cheaper than most, is *Le Vecchie Mura* on Via Piandornella, off Via San Giovanni. For **snacks**, there is pizza by the slice at Via San Giovanni 38.

Arezzo

About 50km southeast of Florence, **AREZZO** was one of the most important settlements of the Etruscan federation and a prosperous independent republic in the Middle Ages, later falling under the sway of Florence. During the Renaissance, Petrarch, Pietro Aretino and Vasari brought lasting prestige to the city, yet it was an outsider – Piero della Francesca – who gave Arezzo its permanent Renaissance monument, the glorious fresco cycle in the church of **San Francesco** (daily 7am–12.30pm & 3–6.30pm). The church to the left of Corso Italia, which leads from the lower town to the more interesting older quarter at the top of the hill, was built in the fourteenth century. A century later Piero della Francesca was commissioned to paint the choir with a cycle depicting *The Legend of the True Cross*, one of the most radiant creations of the period. He painted the series in narrative sequence, beginning on the right wall and continuing until his visit to Rome in 1459, finishing the left wall on his return with some assistance.

Further up the Corso, the twelfth-century **Pieve di Santa Maria** is one of the finest Romanesque structures in Tuscany, with some wonderful early thirteenth-century carvings of the months over the portal. The fourteenth-century campanile, known locally as "the tower of the hundred holes", has become the emblem of the town. On the other side of the church, the dramatically sloping Piazza Grande is bordered by the tiered facade of the **Palazzetto della Fraternità dei Laci**, with a Gothic ground floor and fifteenth-century upper storeys, and **Vasari's loggia**, occupied by shops that in some instances still have their original stone counters. At the highest point of the town, the large unfussy **Duomo**, begun in the late thirteenth century, has stained-glass windows from around 1520 and terracottas by the della Robbia family. Just beyond the organ is the tomb of Bishop Guido Tarlati, head of the *comune* during the early fourteenth century, the monument possibly designed by Giotto; the tiny fresco on the right-hand side of the tomb is Piero della Francesca's *Magdalene*. A short distance in the opposite direction from the duomo, the church of **San Domenico** has a dolorous *Crucifix* by Cimabue, painted when the artist would have been about twenty. Signs point the way to the nearby **Casa di Giorgio Vasari** (Tues–Sat 9am–7pm, Sun 9am–1pm; free), designed by the celebrated biographer-architect-painter for himself and coated with his own lurid frescoes. Down the slope, in Via San Lorentino, the **Museo d'Arte** (Tues–Sun 9am–7pm; L6000) has a dull collection of paintings by local artists and majolica pieces from the thirteenth to the eighteenth centuries.

Practicalities

The **tourist office** is in front of the train station (summer Mon–Sat 9am–1pm & 4–7pm, Sun 9am–1pm; winter Mon–Fri 9am–1pm & 3–6pm, Sat 9am–1pm). Rooms are hard to come by on the first weekend of every month (because of the massive antiques fair), and at the end of August and beginning of September. The most convenient affordable **hotel** is the *Milano* at Via Madonna del Prato 83 (☎0575/26.836; ③). If that's full, try *La Toscana*, Via M. Perennio 56 (☎0575/21.692; ③), on the main road coming in from the west, or *Cecco*, Corso Italia 217–17 (☎0575/20.986; ③), a very central two-star. Alternatively, there's a **youth hostel** occupying the Ostello Villa Severi, Via Redi 13 (☎0575/29.047; ②), some way out of town – take bus #4 from the train station; reception is open 8am–2pm & 5pm–midnight. For **restaurants**, the best deal is *La Scaletta*, Piazza del Popolo 11, which offers filling set meals from L25,000. *Da Guido*, Via Madonna del Prato 85, is a basic local trattoria. For pricy but high-quality Tuscan cuisine, try *La Buca di San Francesco*, by San Francesco church. An excellent place for **pizzas** in the evening is *Olga e Albano*, at Via Francesco Crispi 34.

Siena

During the Middle Ages **SIENA** was one of the major cities of Europe. It was virtually the size of Paris, controlled most of southern Tuscany and its flourishing wool industry, dominated the trade routes from France to Rome, and maintained Italy's richest pre-Medici banks. The city also developed a highly sophisticated civic life, with its own written constitution and a quasi-democratic government. Nowadays it's the perfect antidote to Florence. Self-contained and still rural in parts behind its medieval walls, its great attraction is its own cityscape – a majestic Gothic whole that could be enjoyed without venturing into a single museum. To get the most from it you'll need to stay, especially if you want to see its spectacular horse race, the *Palio* – though you'll definitely need to book during this time.

Arrival and accommodation

Arriving by **bus**, you are dropped along Via Curtatone, by the church of San Domenico; the **train station** is less convenient, 2km northeast, connected with Piazza Matteotti, at the top end of Via Curtatone, by shuttle bus. **Accommodation** is less of a struggle than in Florence, though it still pays to phone ahead. If you haven't, make your way either to the *Cooperativa* booth (Mon–Sat 9am–8pm; winter closes 7pm; ☎0577/288.084), opposite San Domenico on Via Curtatone, which can book you a room in hotels or at one of three *residenze turistico*, or to the **tourist office** at Piazza del Campo 56 (summer Mon–Sat 8.30am–7.30pm; winter Mon–Fri 9am–12.30pm & 3.30–7pm), who do rooms in private houses from L50,000 a double, and have good free maps. Otherwise, the *Locanda Garibaldi*, Via Giovanni Dupre 18 (☎0577/284.204; ④), is a good no-nonsense place, as are *Tre Donzelle* (☎0577/280.358; ③) and *Piccolo Hotel Etruria* at Via Donzelle 5 and 1 (☎0577/288.088; ④), right in the heart of town. *Cannon d'Oro*, Via Montanini 28 (☎0577/44.321; ④), is a stylish small hotel down an alleyway east of Piazza Matteotti. Alternatively, try *Santuario Casa Santa Caterina* on Via Camporegio behind San Domenico (☎0577/44.177; ④), and there's a **youth hostel** at Via Fiorentina 17 (☎0577/522.12; ①), 2km northwest of the centre; take bus #10 or #15 from Piazza Matteotti or, if you're coming from Florence, ask the bus driver to let you off at "Lo Stellino". The nearest **campsite** is the *Campeggio Siena Colleverde*, Strada di Scacciapensieri 37 (☎0577/280.044), 2km north and open mid-March to mid-November; take bus #8 from Piazza Matteotti (last one at 11.45pm).

The City

The centre of Siena is almost entirely medieval in plan and appearance, and has since the 1960s been effectively pedestrianized. At its heart, the **Campo**, with its amphitheatre curve, is an almost organic piece of city planning, and is still the focus of city life. The **Palazzo Comunale**, with its 320ft bell tower, the **Torre del Mangia** (daily 10am–5/6/7pm; mid-Nov to mid-Dec closes 1.30pm; L4000), occupies virtually its entire south side, and although it's still in use as Siena's town hall, its principal rooms have been converted into a **Museo Civico** (daily mid-Nov–mid-March 9.30am–1.45pm, Mon closes 7.45pm; mid-March–mid-Nov 9.30am–7.45pm; L6000, students L3000), a series of former public rooms, frescoed with themes integral to the secular life of the medieval city. Best of these are the Sala del Mappamondo, on the wall of which is the fabulous *Maestà* of Simone Martini, an acknowledged masterpiece of Sienese art, painted in 1315 and touched up (the site was damp) six years later, and the former Sale dei Nove, the "Room of the Nine", decorated with Lorenzetti's *Allegories of Good and Bad Government*, commissioned in 1377 to remind the councillors of the effects of their duties. Look, too, at the fine panel paintings by Lorenzetti's contemporaries, Guido da Siena and Matteo di Giovanni, displayed in the adjacent Sala della Pace. At the top end of the Campo, the fifteenth-century **Loggia di Mercanzia**, built as a dealing room for merchants, marks the intersection of the city centre's principal streets. From here Via Banchi di Sotto leads up to the **Palazzo Piccolomini**, housing the **state archive** (Mon–Fri 9am–1pm; free), which displays the painted covers of the *Tavolette di Biccherna*, the city accounts.

Further south, following Via di Pantaneto then Via Roma, the church of **Santa Maria dei Servi** houses two contrasting frescoes of the *Massacre of the Innocents* – a Gothic version by Lorenzetti, in the second chapel behind the high altar, and a Renaissance treatment by Matteo di Giovanni in the fifth chapel on the right. On the other side of the Campo, **Via di Città** cuts across the oldest, cathedral quarter of the city, fronted by some of Siena's finest private palazzi. At the end of the street, Via San Pietro leads to the **Pinacoteca Nazionale** (Tues–Sat 8.30am–2pm, Sun 8.30am–1pm; L8000), a roll call of Sienese Gothic painting housed in a fourteenth-century palace, while in the opposite direction Via di Capitano leads up to the **Duomo**, completed to virtually its present size around 1215 but subjected to constant plans for expansion throughout Siena's years of medieval prosperity. For various reasons these never came to completion, but an extension still stands at the north end of the cathedral square – a vast structure that would have created the largest church in Italy outside Rome. The Duomo is in any case a delight, its style an amazing conglomeration of Romanesque and Gothic, delineated by bands of black and white marble on its facade. This theme is continued in the *sgraffito* marble pavement, which begins with geometric patterns outside the church and takes off into a startling sequence of 56 panels within, completed between 1349 and 1547; virtually every artist who worked in the city tried his hand on a design. Many are obscure in the extreme, like Pinturicchio's *Allegory of Virtue* (a rocky island of serpents with a nude posed between a boat and the land) in the nave. The finest are reckoned to be Beccafumi's *Moses Striking Water from a Rock* and *Sacrifice of Isaac*, just beyond the dome area. The rest of the interior is equally arresting. Among the greatest individual artistic treasures are Nicola Pisano's font – completed after his commission at Pisa and more elaborate in its high relief details of the *Life of Jesus* and *Last Judgement* – and, in the north transept, a bronze Donatello statue of *St John the Baptist*. Midway along the nave, the **Libreria Piccolomini** (daily Jan to mid-March, Nov & Dec 10am–1pm & 2.30–5pm; mid-March to Oct 9am–6.30pm; L2000), signalled by Pinturicchio's brilliantly coloured fresco of the *Coronation of Pius II*, has further frescoes by Pinturicchio and his pupils (who included Raphael), illustrating scenes from Pius's life.

Behind the cathedral, the **Baptistery** (daily 9am–1pm & 3–6pm; free) houses a Renaissance font with panels illustrating John the Baptist's life by della Quercia and Donatello. Visit also the **Museo dell'Opera del Duomo** (daily Jan to mid-March, Nov & Dec 9am–1.30pm; mid-March to Sept & Oct 9am–6.30pm; L5000), which occupies part of the cathedral's planned extension and houses Pisano's original statues from the facade. Upstairs is a fine array of panels, including works by Simone Martini, Pietro Lorenzetti and Sano di Pietro, and the cathedral's original altarpiece, a haunting Byzantine icon known as the *Madonna dagli Occhi Grossi* ("Madonna of the Big Eyes"). The painting that repays a visit most, however, is the cathedral's second altarpiece, Duccio's *Maestà*, completed in 1311 and generally thought to be the climax of the Sienese style of painting. North of the cathedral, the church of **San Domenico**, founded in 1125, is closely identified with Saint Catherine of Siena, whose career, as well as encompassing innumerable miracles, was pretty extraordinary; among other things, she persuaded the pope, Gregory XI, to return to Rome from Avignon. On the right of the entrance is a kind of raised chapel, with a contemporary portrait of her by a friend, Andrea Vanni; below are steps and a niche, where she received her stigmata. Her own chapel, on the south side of the church, has frescoes of her in ecstasy by Sodoma, and a reliquary containing her head. Saint Catherine's family house, the **Casa e Sanctuario di Santa Caterina**, where she lived as a Dominican nun, is a short distance south, near the Fontebranda on Via Benincasa (daily 9am–12.30pm & 3.30–6pm; free). It's a much adapted building, with a Renaissance loggia and a series of oratories – one on the site of her cell.

Eating and drinking

Restaurants cost a bit over the odds in Siena, especially if you want to eat out in the Campo. If you just want a **snack,** there's pizza by the slice at Via delle Terme 10, and an extravagantly stocked deli, the *Pizzicheria Morbidi*, at Banchi di Sotto 27. The cheapest **sit-down** alternative is the *Mensa Universitaria*, Via Sant'Agata 1 (noon–2.30pm & 7–9pm; closed Aug), with meals for L11,000; there's another mensa at Via San Bandini 47. *Il Barbero*, Piazza Il Campo 80–81, is an honourable exception to the Campo's prices, an excellent if rather characterless self-service. *Carlo e Franca*, Via di Pantaneto

138, is an unpretentious café with pizza and pasta at fair prices; *Pizzeria Malborghetto*, on Piazza del Mercato, has impressive pizzas and great views, and *Trattoria Giorgino*, Piazza Mercato 14, serves traditional home-made food at L25,000–30,000 per person for a full meal with wine. Up a notch in price, the *Osteria Le Logge*, in an old *farmacia* in Via del Porrione 33, is a popular trattoria, as is *Cane e Gatto*, Via Pagliaresi 6 (closed Thurs), which is just the place to go for the full works – L55,000 for seven sublime courses without drinks. For **ice cream**, try *Nannini*, at the Piazza Matteotti end of Banchi di Sopra, or *Brividio*, at the corner of Via di Città and Via dei Pellegrini.

The Palio

The Siena **Palio** is the most spectacular festival event in Italy, a bareback horse race around the Campo contested twice a year (July 2 and Aug 16) between the ancient wards – or *contrade* – of the city. Each of the seventeen *contrade* has its own church, social centre and museum, and a heraldic animal motif, displayed in a modern fountain-sculpture in its individual piazza. Only ten can take part in any one race, and these are chosen by lot and their horses and jockeys assigned at random. The only rule is that riders cannot interfere with each others' reins; everything else is accepted and practised. Each *contrada* has a traditional rival, and ensuring it loses is as important as winning oneself. Jockeys may be bribed to throw the race, or whip a rival or his horse; and *contrade* have been known to drug horses and even ambush a jockey on his way to the race. Although there's a big build-up, the race itself lasts little more than a minute. Most spectators crowd (free) into the centre of the Campo; for the best view, you need to have found a position on the inner rail by 2pm and to keep it for the next six hours.

Pisa

There's no escaping the Leaning Tower in **PISA**. The medieval bell tower is one of the world's most familiar images and yet its beauty still comes as a surprise, set in chess-board formation alongside the Duomo and Baptistery on the manicured grass of the **Campo dei Miracoli** – the "Field of Miracles" – where most of the buildings belong to the city's "Golden Age" in the twelfth and thirteenth centuries, when Pisa, then still a port, was one of the great Mediterranean powers. Perhaps the strangest thing about the **Leaning Tower**, begun in 1173, is that it has always tilted; subsidence disrupted the foundations when it had reached just three of its eight storeys. For the next 180 years a succession of architects were brought in to try and correct the tilt, until around 1350 Tomasso di Andrea da Pontedera accepted the angle and completed the tower. Eight centuries on, it is thought to be nearing its limit: the overhang is over 5m and increasing each year, and the tower has been closed to the public for the last two years. The **Duomo** (daily 7.45–1pm & 3–5/7pm) was begun a century earlier, its facade – with its delicate balance of black and white marble, and tiers of arcades – setting the model for Pisa's highly distinctive brand of Romanesque. The interior continues the use of black and white marble, and with its long arcades of columns has an almost Oriental aspect. Most of the artworks are Renaissance or later, a notable exception Cimabue's mosaic of *Christ in Majesty* in the apse. Its acknowledged highlight is the Gothic pulpit by Giovanni Pisano, an astonishingly detailed work, on the base of which an inscription records that Giovanni had "the art of pure sculpture . . . and would not know how to carve ugly or base things, even if he wished to".

The third building of the Miracoli ensemble, the circular **Baptistery** (daily 8am–8pm; winter closes 5pm; L5000 or L12,000 joint ticket with Museo dell'Opera del Duomo, Museo delle Sinopie and Camposanto), is a slightly bizarre mix of Roman-esque and Gothic, embellished with statuary (now displayed in the museo) by Giovanni Pisano and his father Nicola, as well as another pulpit, sculpted by Nicola in 1260 – his first major commission. Along the north side of the Campo is the **Camposanto** (same hours; L5000, or L12,000 joint ticket), a cloistered cemetery built towards the end of the thirteenth century. Most of the cloister's frescoes were destroyed by Allied incendiary bombs in World War II, but two masterpieces survived relatively unscathed – a fourteenth-century *Triumph of Death* and *Last Judgement* in the Cappella Ammanati, a ruthless catalogue of horrors painted around the time of the Black Death. It also has a number of sculptures and numerous Roman sarcophagi – Nicola Pisano's original sources of inspiration. At the southeast corner of the Campo, a vast array of pieces from the cathedral and baptistery are displayed in the **Museo dell'Opera del Duomo** (daily summer 8am–8pm; winter 9am–5pm; L5000), a huge collection which includes statuary by each of the Pisano family and examples of *intarsia*, the art of inlaid wood.

Away from the Campo dei Miracoli, Pisa takes on a very different character, as tourists give way to students at the still-thriving university. It's nonetheless a quiet place, eerily so at night, set about a series of erratic squares and arcaded streets, and with clusters of Romanesque churches and, along the banks of the Arno, a number of fine palazzi. The **Piazza dei Cavalieri** is an obvious first stop, a large square that was the centre of medieval Pisa, before being remodelled by Vasari as the headquarters of the Knights of St Stephen, whose palace, the curving **Palazzo dei Cavalieri**, topped with busts of the Medici, faces the order's church of **San Stefano**. A short walk east along the river, the **Museo Nazionale di San Matteo** (Tues–Sat 9am–7pm, Sun 9am–1pm; L6000), housed in a twelfth-century convent, displays fourteenth-century panels by the Maestro di San Torpè, a Simon Martini polyptych and a panel of *San Paolo* by Masaccio. Also in the museum are the antique armour and wooden shields used in the annual *Gioco del Ponte* pageant.

Practicalities

Pisa's **train station** is south of the centre on Piazza della Stazione, a twenty-minute walk or #1 bus ride from the Campo dei Miracoli. From the **airport**, take the hourly Florence train. There are two **tourist offices**, one to the left of the station, another beside the Camposanto (*Station APT*, Mon–Sat 9.30am–1pm & 3.30–7pm; *Campo dei Miracoli*, Mon–Fri 9am–noon & 3–6pm, Sat 9.30am–1pm & 3.30–7pm), with map and accommodation lists. The most attractive budget **hotels** are grouped around the Campo dei Miracoli, best the elegant *Albergo Gronchi* in Piazza Arcivescovado (☎050/561.823; ②). Others include the *Locanda Galileo*, Via Santa Maria (☎050/40.621; ②), the *Hotel Giardino*, behind a self-service restaurant on Via Cammeo (☎050/562.101; ②), and *Pensione Helvetia*, Via Don G. Boschi 31, off Piazza Arcivescovado (☎050/553.084; ②). You could also try the *Serena*, Via D. Cavalca 45 (☎050/580.809; ②), or the *Rinascente*, Via del Castelleto 28 (☎050/580.460; ②), or one of a number of places in the station area, best of which is the *Albergo Milano*, Via Mascagni 14, off Piazza della Stazione (☎050/23.162; ③), or *Clio*, Via San Lorenzino 3 (☎050/28.446; ②), a spotless, friendly place at the river end of the Corso Italia. A good **women-only** alternative, five minutes' walk from the station (first right), is the *Casa della Giovane*, Via Corridoni 31 (☎050/43.061; ③). The nearest **youth hostel** is Ostello della Gioventù, Via Pietra Santina 15 (☎050/890.622; ②), 2.5km from the centre past the cemetery. The city **campsite**, *Campeggio Torre Pendente*, is 1km west of the Campo dei Miracoli at Viale delle Cascine 86 (☎050/560.665) – a large, well-maintained site, with a restaurant and shop, and open from mid-March to September.

Restaurants in the environs of the Leaning Tower are not good value, but a few blocks south, around Piazza Cavalieri and Piazza Dante, are a number of reasonably priced places. One of the most popular is *Trattoria Stelio*, Piazza Dante 11, or there's a cheaper, unnamed pizzeria on the same square. Over to the west, *Pizzeria da Cassio*, Piazza Cavallotti 14, is a good *tavola calda*, and the university building on Via Martiri, off Piazza Cavalieri, houses a student mensa (mid-Sept to mid-July Mon–Fri noon–

2.30pm & 7–9pm, Sat & Sun noon–2.30pm). The city's big traditional event is the **Gioco del Ponte**, held on the last Sunday in June, when teams from the north and south banks of the city stage a series of "battles", pushing a seven-ton carriage over the Ponte di Mezzo. The event has taken place since Medici times and continues in Renaissance costume.

Lucca

LUCCA is as graceful a provincial capital as they come, set inside a thick swathe of Renaissance walls, and with a quiet, almost entirely medieval street plan. Palazzi and the odd tower dot the streets, at intervals overlooked by a brilliantly decorated Romanesque facade. It is not exactly undiscovered, but for once the number of tourists seems to fit.

The most enjoyable way to get your bearings is to follow the path around the top of the **walls** – nearly 4km in extent, built with genuine defensive capability in the early sixteenth century, before being transformed to their present, garden aspect by the Bourbon ruler, Marie Louise. In the centre of town, just east of the main Piazza Napoleone on Piazza San Martino, the **Duomo of San Martino** (closed 3.30–6.30pm) was in part sculpted by Nicola Pisano, though sadly recent years have seen his sculptures covered for restoration, along with virtually all the high points of the great hall-like interior, which include paintings by Tintoretto, Ghirlandaio and Filippino Lippi. The most famous item, Jacopo della Quercia's *Tomb of Ilaria del Carretto*, has been restored so vigorously that one expert declared it had been ruined – prompting a libel action from the restorer. Lucca's finest sculptor was perhaps Matteo Civitali, whose *Tempietto* in the north aisle was sculpted to house the city's most famous and lucrative relic, the "Volto Santo" (Holy Face) – said to be the "true effigy of Christ" and the focus for international pilgrimage.

Northwest of the Duomo across Via Fililungo, the facade of **San Michele in Foro** church is a triumph of eccentricity, each of its loggia columns different, some twisted, others sculpted or candy-striped. The interior is relatively plain, though there's a good Andrea della Robbia terracotta and a painting by Filippino Lippi. Giacomo Puccini was born almost opposite at Via di Poggio 30, and his home, the **Casa di Puccini** (Tues–Sun 10am–4/6pm; L3000), is now a school of music with a small museum, featuring the Steinway piano on which he composed *Turandot*, along with original scores and photographs from premieres. At the end of the street in Via Galli Tassi is the seventeenth-century **Palazzo Mansi**, which houses a **Pinacoteca Nazionale** (Tues–Sat 9am–7pm, Sun 9am–2pm; L6000), an indifferent collection of pictures, although the Rococo palace itself is a sight, at its most extreme in a spectacularly gilded bridal suite.

Northeast of here, the basilica of **San Frediano** has a facade with a brilliant thirteenth-century **mosaic** of *Christ in Majesty* and fine treasures inside, most enjoyable of which is the font carved with Romanesque scenes of Moses, the Good Shepherd and Apostles; set behind it is a ceramic *Annunciation* by Andrea della Robbia.

Be sure to visit the remarkable **Piazza Anfiteatro**, a circuit of medieval buildings whose foundations are the arches of the Roman amphitheatre. Just southeast, the strangest sight in Lucca is perhaps the **Casa Guinigi**, the fifteenth-century home of Lucca's leading family, with a battlemented tower surmounted by holm oaks whose roots have grown into the room below. Much of it is being restored, but from Via San Andrea you can climb it for one of the best views over the city (daily March–Sept 9am–7.30pm; Oct 10am–6pm; Nov–Feb 10am–2.30pm; L4500). Across the narrow canal on Via della Quarquonia, the fifteenth-century **Villa Guinigi** is now the home of Lucca's major **museum** of art and sculpture (Tues–Sun 9am–2pm; L4000), with a good deal of lively Romanesque sculpture from the city and some good work by the cathedral's maestro, Matteo Civitali.

Practicalities

The **train station** is just outside the walls to the south. The **tourist office** is on the north side of Piazza Verdi (daily 9am–7pm), although **accommodation** is a problem at almost any time of year. Of **hotels**, the *Cinzia*, Via della Dogana 9 (☎0583/491.323; ②), *l'Orologio*, Via San Pierino 7 (☎0583/53.419; ②), and *La Margherita*, Via San Andrea 8 (☎0583/494.146; ④) are all good. After these the best bet is the *Moderno*, Via Civitali 38 (☎0583/558.429; ⑤). There's a **youth hostel** with **campsite** at Via del Brennero 673 (☎0583/341.811; ①), just outside the centre to the north. For **food**, try the *Trattoria da Guido*, Via C. Battisti 28, the cheapest place in town, or *Trattoria da Leo*, Via Tegrimi 1. *Trattoria da Giulio*, Via San Tommaso 29, by the Palazzo Mansi, is also good and very popular, as is *Ristorante Sergio*, Via S. Croce 44.

Perugia

The provincial capital, **PERUGIA** is the most obvious base to kick off a tour of Umbria. It's an oddly mixed town, with a medieval centre and not a little industry: *Buitoni*, the pasta people, are based here, and it's also where Italy's best chocolate, *Perugini*, is made. It can get very busy in summer, but there's a day's worth of good sightseeing to be done and the presence of the the the Italian University for Foreigners, set up by Mussolini to improve the image of Italy abroad, lends a dash of cosmopolitan style.

Perugia hinges on a single street, **Corso Vannucci**, a broad pedestrian thoroughfare constantly buzzing with action. At the far end, the austere **Piazza IV Novembre** is backed by the plain-faced **Duomo**, recently reopened after damage caused by the 1983 earthquake, although the interior, home to the so-called Virgin's "wedding ring", an unwieldy one-inch-diameter piece of agate that changes colour according to the character of the person wearing it, isn't especially interesting. The Perugians keep the ring locked up in fifteen boxes fitted into one another like Russian dolls, each opened with a key held by a different person; it's brought out for public viewing every July 30. The centrepiece of the piazza is the **Fontana Maggiore**, sculpted by the father and son team Nicola and Giovanni Pisano and describing episodes from the Old Testament, classical myth, Aesop's fables and the twelve months of the year. Opposite rises the gaunt mass of the **Palazzo dei Priori**, worth a glance inside for its frescoed **Sala dei Notari** (Tues–Sun 9am–1pm & 3–7pm; free). A few doors down the Corso is the **Collegio di Cambio** (Tues–Sun 9am–12.30pm & 2.30–5.30pm; L2000), the town's medieval money exchange, frescoed by Perugino. The palace also houses the **Galleria Nazionale di Umbria** (Tues–Sat 9am–1.45pm & 3–7pm, Sun 9am–1pm; L8000), one of central Italy's best galleries – a 33-room romp through the history of Umbrian painting, with work by Perguino and Pinturrichio along with one or two stunning Florentine masterpieces (Fra Angelico, Piero della Francesca) and early Sienese works (Duccio).

The best streets to wander around to get a feel of the old city are either side of the duomo. **Via dei Priori** is the most characteristic, leading down to Agostino di Duccio's colourful **Oratorio di San Bernardino**, whose richly embellished facade is far the best piece of sculpture in the city. From here you can wander through the northern part of the centre, along Via A. Pascoli, to the **Arco di Augusto**, whose lowest section is now one of the few remaining monuments of Etruscan Perugia. The upper remnant was added by the Romans when they captured the city in 40 BC. On the other side of town, along **Corso Cavour**, is the large church of **San Domenico**, one of whose chapels holds a superb carved arch by Agostino di Duccio, and, to the right of the altar, the tomb of Pope Benedict XI, an elegant piece by one of the period's three leading sculptors: Pisano, Lorenzo Maitini or Arnolfo di Cambio – no one knows which. There are also some impressive stained glass windows, the second biggest in Italy after those in Milan Cathedral. In the church's cloisters, the **Museo Archeologico Nazionale dell'Umbria** (Mon–Sat 9am–1.30pm & 3–7pm, Sun 9am–1pm; L4000) has one of the most extensive Etruscan collections around. Further on down the Corso Cavour, advertised by a rocket-shaped bell tower, the tenth-century basilica of **San Pietro** is the most idiosyncratic of all the town's churches. Its choir has been called the best in Italy, and there is a host of works by Perugino and others.

Practicalities

Arriving by **train**, you'll find yourself well away from the centre of Perugia on Piazza V. Veneto; buses #26, #27 and #29 run to Piazza Italia or Piazza Matteotti and you'd do well to take one rather than attempt the long walk. The friendly **tourist office**, opposite the Duomo on Piazza IV Novembre (Mon–Sat 8.30am–1.30pm & 4–7pm, Sun 9am–1pm), has a room-finding service and maps. There's an unofficial youth **hostel** two minutes from the Duomo at Via Bontempi 13 (☎075/572.2880; ③), with dorm beds. As for **hotels**, try *Rosalba* at Via del Circo 7 (☎075/572.28285; ④), *Etruria*, just off the Corso at Via della Luna 21 (☎075/572.3730; ③), or *Anna*, centrally placed at Via dei Priori 48 (☎075/573.6304; ③). On the **food** front, *Ubu Re*, Via Baldeschi 17, has no-nonsense healthy Umbrian specialities; *Lo Scalino*, on Via S. Ercolano is a decent pizzeria, as is *L'Oca Nera* in Via dei Priori. Also on Via dei Priori, *Papaia* is a good bar with plenty of seating and decent *panini*. The reasonably priced *Dal mì Cocco*, Corso Garibaldi 12, offers a student clientele and traditional cuisine near the university. *Cafe'del Cambio* at Corso Vannucci 29 is the trendiest **bar** in the centre, and does snacks and light meals at lunchtime. For **evening** entertainment, *Grand "O"*, on Via Vili, near Corso Cavour, has live music on selected nights. Nearby, the *Bratislava*, Via Fiorenzuola 12, is similar.

Gubbio

GUBBIO is the most thoroughly medieval of the Umbrian towns, an immediately likeable place that's hanging onto its charm despite an ever-increasing influx of tourists. The streets are picture-book pretty, and only the market in pricy ceramics suggests serious pandering to visitors. The first high peaks of the Apennines rising behind give the place the feel of a mountain outpost – something it's always been, in fact. The best (and most scenic) approach is by frequent bus from Perugia, or by train from Foligno to Fossato di Vico, 19km away but with an hourly connecting bus.

Centre-stage is the immense fourteenth-century **Palazzo dei Consoli** (daily 9am–12.30pm & 3–5.30pm; L4000), on the windswept Piazza della Signoria, whose crenellated outline and campanile command your attention for miles around. Inside, the cavernous Salone dell'Arengo was where council officials and leading citizens met to discuss business – the word "harangue" derives from *arengo*; the building also holds the **Museo Civico** (daily 9am–12.30pm & 3–5.30pm; L4000), unremarkable except for the famous Eugubine Tablets, Umbria's most important archeological find and the only extant record of the ancient Umbrian language. Admission to the museum also gets you into the three-roomed **Pinacoteca** upstairs, worth a look for works by the Gubbian School, notably Ottaviano Nelli – a painter who also features in the church of **San Francesco** on Piazza dei Quaranta Martiri, where he painted seventeen frescoes on the life of the Virgin. There's also an unusually lovely *Madonna del Belvedere* by him in the church of **Santa Maria Nuova**, off Corso Garibaldi. On the hillside above the town, the **Basilica of Sant'Ubaldo** is the place Gubbians drive to on Sunday mornings, a pleasant spot with a handy bar and great views, connected with the town's Porta Romana by a slightly scary **funicular** (L5000). There's not much to see in the basilica itself, except the body of the town's patron saint, Ubaldo, who's missing three fingers, hacked off by his manservant as a religious keepsake. You can't miss the big wooden pillars (*ceri*), though, featured in Gubbio's annual *Corsa dei Ceri* (May 15), a race to the basilica from the town that's second only to Siena's Palio in terms of exuberance.

You shouldn't have any problem **staying** in Gubbio, though the place does get busy. The **tourist office**, Piazza Odersi 6 (Mon–Fri 8.30am–2pm & 3.30–6.30pm, Sat 9am–1pm, Sun 9am–12.30pm), may be able to help; or try the *Galletti*, Via Piccadi 3 (☎075/927.4247; ③), or the *Grotta dell'Angelo*, Via Gioia 47 (☎075/927.3438; ④), which has an excellent restaurant. There's a good selection of **eateries**, including the pleasant workaday pizzeria, *Il Bargello*, Via dei Consoli 37, and the similarly homely *San Francesco e il Lupo*, Via Cairoli 24. Failing that, you could try the classier *Taverna del Lupo*, Via Baldassini 60. There are two **campsites** for Gubbio, both in Loc. Ottoguidone – *Villa Ortoguidone* (☎075/927.2037), open all year, and *Città di Gùbbio* (☎075/927.2037), open April to September.

Assisi

Thanks to Saint Francis, Italy's premier saint and founder of the Franciscan order, ASSISI is Umbria's best-known town, and suffers as a result, crammed with people for much for the summer season. It quietens down in the evening, and does retain some medieval hill-town charm, but you may not want to hang around.

The **Basilica di San Francesco** (daily 7am–7pm), at the end of Via San Francesco, is justly famed as Umbria's single greatest glory, and one of the most overwhelming collections of art outside a gallery anywhere in the world. Begun in 1228, two years after the saint's death, it was financed by donations that flooded in from all over Europe. The sombre **Lower Church** is the earlier of the two churches that make up the basilica, its complicated floor plan and claustrophobic vaults intended to create a mood of meditative introspection – an effect added to by brown-robed monks, strict rules on silence and no photography – Francis lies under the floor in a crypt only brought to light in 1818. Frescoes cover almost every available space, and span a century of continuous artistic development, from the anonymous early works above the altar, through Cimabue's over-restored *Madonna, Child and Angels with St Francis* in the right transept, a painting Ruskin described as the noblest depiction of the Virgin in Christendom, to work by the Sienese School painters, Simone Martini and Pietro Lorenzetti. Martini's frescoes are in the Cappella di San Martino, the first chapel on the left as you enter the nave, while Lorenzetti's works, dominated by a powerful *Crucifixion*, are in the transept and small chapel to the left of the main altar. The **Upper Church**, built to a light and airy Gothic plan, is richly decorated, too, with Giotto's dazzling frescoes on the life of Saint Francis. Giotto was still in his twenties when he accepted the commission, having been recommended for the job by Cimabue, whose own (badly damaged) frescoes fill large parts of the apse and transepts. If time allows, check out the **cloisters**, accessible from the rear of the Lower Church, and the **treasury**, which contains a rich collection of paintings, reliquaries and religious clutter.

There's not a great deal worth seeing in Assisi's small centre – only a nondescript **Museo Civico** in the central Piazza del Comune (Tues–Sun 9.30am–1pm & 3–7pm; L2500), housed in the crypt of the now defunct church of San Nicolo, whose collection includes Etruscan fragments and the so-called **Tempio di Minerva**, six columns and a pediment from a Roman temple of the first century. A short hike up the steep Via di San Rufino from here, the thirteenth-century **Duomo** has the font used to baptize Saint Francis and Saint Clare, and close by is the **Basilica di Santa Chiara**, burial place of Saint Francis's devoted early companion. Consecrated in 1265, the church is a virtual facsimile of the Basilica up the road, and is home to the macabrely blackened body of Clare herself and a Byzantine crucifix famous for having bowed to Francis and commanded him to embark on his sacred mission. Via Borgo Arentino leads outside the town centre to the church of **San Damiano** (daily 7am–noon & 2.30–7pm), one of Saint Francis's favourite spots – he is thought to have written his well-known *Canticle* *to the Sun* here. Also outside the centre, near the train station, is the vast and majestically uninspiring **Santa Maria degli Angeli**, built in the seventeenth century and rebuilt after an earthquake in 1832, with the remains of the **Porzuincola**, a tiny chapel which was effectively the first Franciscan monastery. Francis lived here after founding the order in 1208, attracted by its then remote and wooded surroundings.

Practicalities

The **train station** is 5km south of Assisi, connected to the centre by half-hourly buses. The **tourist office** is on Piazza del Comune (Mon–Fri 8am–2pm & 3.30–6.30pm, Sat 9am–1pm & 3.30–6.30pm) and has accommodation lists, including details of **private rooms**. There are plenty of cheap places to **stay** but they can get full. The functional *Italia*, off the central Piazza del Comune at Vicolo del Fortezza 2 (☎075/812.625; ③), is about the cheapest option; the *Albergo La Rocca*, Via Porta Perlici 25 (☎075/812.284; ③), is good, as is the *Antifeatro Romano*, close by at Via Antifeatro Romano 4 (☎075/ 813.025; ③). There are also pilgrim hostels – *Case Religiose di Ospitalità* – all over town, charging L18,000–35,000 depending on the type of accommodation. The *Casa del Terzario*, Piazza del Vescovado 5 (☎075/812.366; ③), is perhaps the best as far as location goes. There's a big **campsite** at Fontemaggio, 3km out on the road to the monastery of Eremo di Carceri, and an unofficial **youth hostel** (☎075/813.636; ②), 1km from the centre in Assisi Alto. For **food**, try *Il Pozzo Romano* on Via Sant'Agnese, near Santa Chiara, or *Palotta*, Via San Rufino 4, which is reasonable and friendly. The *La Rocca* hotel (see above) has a good no-frills restaurant, while *Buca di San Francesco*, Via Brizi 1, is busy but expensive.

Spoleto

SPOLETO is Umbria's most compelling town, remarkable for its extremely pretty position and several of Italy's most ancient Romanesque churches. For several centuries it was among the most influential of Italian towns, the former capital of one of the Lombards' three Italian dukedoms, which at one time stretched as far as Rome. Barbarossa flattened the city in 1155, and in 1499 the nineteen-year-old Lucrezia Borgia was appointed governor by her father, Pope Alexander VI.

Spoleto's lower town, where you arrive, was badly damaged by World War II bombing, and doesn't hold much of interest, so it's best to take a bus straight to the upper town. There's no single, central piazza, but the place to head for is **Piazza Libertà**, site of a much-restored first-century **Roman theatre**. The adjoining Piazza della Fontana has more Roman remains, best the **Arco di Druso**, built to honour the minor campaign victories of Drusus, son of Tiberius. The homely **Piazza del Mercato**, beyond, is a fine opportunity to take in some streetlife, and from there it's a short walk to the **Duomo**, whose facade of restrained elegance is one of the most memorable in the region. Inside, various Baroque embellishments are eclipsed by the superlative apse frescoes of the fifteenth-century Florentine artist Fra Lippo Lippi, dominated by his final masterpiece, a *Coronation of the Virgin*. He died shortly after their completion (amid rumours that he was poisoned for seducing the daughter of a local noble family) and was interred here in a tomb designed by his son, Filippino. You should also take the short walk out to the **Ponte delle Torri**, a picture-postcard favourite, and an astonishing piece of medieval engineering, best seen as part of a circular walk around the base of the **Rocca** – everyone's idea of a cartoon castle, with towers, crenellations and sheer walls; it served until recently as a high-security prison, home to Pope John Paul II's would-be assassin and leading members of the Red Brigade. The church of **San Pietro**, 1km or so beyond the bridge on a hillside, is also worth the walk for the splendid sculptures on its facade, among the best Romanesque carvings in Umbria.

Spoleto's **train station** is around 1km north of the town centre and the central Piazza Libertà, where you'll find the **tourist office** (Mon–Fri 9am–1pm & 4.30–7.30pm, Sat & Sun 10am–1pm & 4.30–7.30pm). If you're planning on **staying** in town, there's the reasonably priced *Pensione dell'Angelo*, Via Arco del Druso 25 (☎0743/222.385; ②). If that's full, then the only other vaguely affordable place in the upper town is the *Pensione Aurora*, off Piazza Libertà at Via dell'Apollinare 4 (☎0743/220.315; ③). The lower town is, by comparison, very much a second choice, but there are more likely to be rooms available; try first at the *Fracassa*, Via Focaroli 15 (☎0743/221.177; ②), and *Anfiteatro*, Via dell'Anfiteatro 14 (☎0743/49.853; ②). The closest **campsite** is the small *Camping Monteluco*, behind San Pietro (☎0743/220.358); tiny but very pleasant. For **food**, the best basic trattoria, always full of locals, is the *Trattoria del Festival* at Via Brignone 8. *Del Panciolle* on Largo Muzio Clemente is more upmarket, an excellent choice for a blowout. *Il Grotino*, at the end of Via Macello Vecchio off Corso Garibaldi, serves generous portions of tasty food, and *L'Angola Antica*, Via Monterone 109 (closed Mon), does a good menu of local specialities like snail, rabbit and lamb; try the more expensive *La Baraccia*, Piazza Fratelli Bandiera 3, for marvellous pasta with truffles.

In June and July Spoleto plays host to the country's leading international arts festival, the **Festival dei Due Mondi**, a great attraction if you're into live music, dance or theatre, though the place forgoes a good part of its charm as a result. On top of the crowds, ticket prices for top companies and world-class performers can be off-putting, as can the jet-set, well-heeled cut of the audiences. At the same time there's an Edinburgh-type fringe contingent and lots of film, jazz, buskers and so on. **Tickets and information** are available from the festival box office at Piazza del Duomo 9 (☎0743/44.325).

Orvieto

Out on a limb from the rest of Umbria, **ORVIETO** is flooded wth tourists in summer, most of whom are drawn by its **Duomo**, one of the greatest Gothic buildings in Italy, built, according to tradition, to celebrate the so-called Miracle of Bolsena (1263), in which a doubting priest celebrating Mass in a church on the nearby Lago di Bolsena noticed real blood dripping from the Host onto the altarcloth. The stained linen was whisked off to Pope Urban IV, who was in Orvieto to escape the heat and political hassle of Rome, and the building was constructed over the ensuing three centuries, in a surprisingly unified example of the Romanesque-Gothic style. The star turn is the facade, a riot of columns, spires, bas-reliefs, sculptures and dazzling colour, just about held together by four enormous fluted columns, the work of the master mason Lorenzo Maitini and his pupils, describing episodes from the Old and New Testaments in staggering detail. Inside, the church is surprisingly plain by comparison, mainly distinguished by Luca Signorelli's fresco of the *Last Judgement*, a realistic yet grotesque work, full of beautifully observed muscular figures, which greatly influenced Michelangelo's celebrated cycle in the Vatican's Sistine Chapel, painted forty years later. Signorelli, suitably clad in black, includes himself with Fra Angelico in the lower left-hand corner of *The Sermon of the Antichrist*, both calmly looking on as someone is garrotted at their feet. The twin Cappella del Corporale contains the sacred *corporale* (altar cloth) itself, locked away in a massive, jewel-encrusted casket (an accurate facsimile of the facade), and some appealing frescoes by local fourteenth-century painter Ugolino di Prete, describing the events of the Miracle. The same artist painted the frescoes in the apse, many of which were partly restored by Pinturicchio, who was eventually kicked off the job for "consuming too much gold, too much azure and too much wine".

Next to the duomo, the **Museo dell'Opera del Duomo** (closed for restoration at time of writing) has paintings by Martini, several important thirteenth-century sculptures by Arnolfo di Cambio and Andrea Pisano, and a lovely font filled with Escher-like carved fishes. Opposite, the **Museo Etrusco** (Mon–Sat 9am–1.30pm & 3–7pm, Sun 9am–1pm; free), features a fairly predictable collection of vases and assorted fragments excavated from local tombs. Moving north up Via del Duomo, you come to **Corso Cavour**, the town's pedestrianized main drag, at the far end of which, across Piazza Cahen, is **Il Pozzo di San Patrizio** (daily 9.30am–7pm; Aug 8.30am–8pm; L6000) the novelty act of the town, a huge cylindrical well commissioned in 1527 by Pope Clement VII to guarantee the town's water supply during an expected siege by the imperial army. It's a dank but striking piece of engineering, 62m deep, named after its supposed similarity to the Irish cave where Saint Patrick died in 493, supposedly aged 133 – though, apart from a small Etruscan tomb halfway down, it's really just an impressive hole in the ground.

Practicalities
The #1 bus makes a regular trip from the distant **train station** to Piazza XXIX Marzo, a short way north of the duomo. An alternative is the funicular up to Piazza Cahen, from where minibuses wind through the twisting streets to Piazza del Duomo. The **tourist office** is at Piazza del Duomo 24 (Mon–Fri 8am–2pm & 4–7pm, Sat 10am–1pm & 3–8pm, Sun 10am–7pm) and has an accommodation service. Of **hotels**, the *Duomo*, Via Maurizio 7 (☎0763/41.887; ④), is a good central option, as is the *Posta*, Via Luca Signorelli (☎0763/41.909; ④). Slightly pricier, the *Corso*, Corso Cavour 343 (☎0763/42.020; ④), is a pleasant hotel near Piazza Cahen. The nearest **campsite** is the *Scacco Matto*, 10km away on Lago di Corbara (bus to Baschi/Civitella de Lago/Narni). There's a group of cheap **restaurants** at the bottom of Corso Cavour, though the best-value eating is close to the duomo at *CRAMST*, Via Maitani 15, a cooperatively run canteen affair offering a choice between restaurant and self-service trattoria. *Bottegha del Buon Vino*, Via della Cave 26, is an *enoteca*/bar that's good for staples and has a few outside tables; the *Grotta*, Via Signorelli 5, off Via del Duomo, is a standard, friendly trattoria. *Da Anna*, Piazza Scalza 2, is good value too.

Urbino

For the second half of the fifteenth century, **URBINO** was one of the most prestigious courts in Europe, ruled by the remarkable Federico da Montefeltro, who employed a number of the greatest artists and architects of the time to build and decorate his palace in the town. At one time it was reckoned the most beautiful in all Italy, and it does seem from contemporary accounts that fifteenth-century Urbino was an extraordinarily civilized place, a measured and urbane society in which life was lived without indulgence.

In the centre of Urbino, the **Palazzo Ducale** is a fitting monument to Federico, home now to the **Galleria Nazionale delle Marche** (Mon–Sat 9am–2pm, Sun 9am–1pm; L8000), although it's the building itself that makes the biggest impression. Among the paintings in the Appartamento del Duca are Piero della Francesca's strange *Flagellation*, and the *Ideal City*, a famous perspective painting of a symmetrical and deserted cityscape long attributed to Piero but now thought to be by one of his followers. There's also Paolo Uccello's last work, the six-panelled *Profanation of the Host*, and, in the same room, a portrait of Federico da Montefeltro by the Spanish artist Pedro Berruguete. The most interesting and best-preserved of the palazzo's rooms is Federico's Studiolo, a triumph of illusory perspective created not with paint but *intarsia*. Shelves appear to protrude from the walls, cupboard doors seem to swing open to reveal lines of books, a letter lies in an apparently half-open drawer. Even more remarkable are the delicately hued landscapes of Urbino as it might appear from one of the surrounding hills, and the life-like squirrel perching next to a bowl of fruit.

Urbino is a lively university town, and its bustling streets – a pleasant jumble of Renaissance and medieval houses – can be a welcome antidote to the rarefied atmosphere of the Palazzo Ducale. You can wind down in one of the many bars and trattorias, or take a picnic up to the gardens within the **Fortezza Albornoz**, from where you'll get great views of the town and the countryside out to **San Bernardino**, a fine Renaissance church 2km away that is the resting place of the Montefeltros. It was long thought to have been the work of Bramante but is now attributed to Francesco di Giorgio Martini.

Urbino is notoriously difficult to reach – the best approach is by bus from Pésaro, about 30km away on the coast. Buses stop in Borgo Mercatale, at the foot of the Palazzo Ducale, which is reached either by lift or by Francesco di Giorgio Martini's recently restored spiral staircase. For **accommodation**, the cheapest options are **private rooms**, most of which are on Via Budassi – details from the **tourist office** on Piazza Rinascimento (Mon–Sat summer 9am–1pm & 3.30–6.30pm; winter 8am–2pm). The most convenient **hotels** are the *Italia*, Corso Garibaldi 32 (☎0722/2701; ③), and the *San Giovanni*, Via Barocci 13 (☎0722/2827; ③). The best deals for **food** are at the university mensa on Piazza San Filippo, or the *Self-Service Franco* on Via del Poggio. If your budget's not too tight, *Il Girarrosto*, off Via Raffaello on Piazza San Francesco, serves good traditional food.

Ancona

ANCONA is a depressing place, severely damaged by war and earthquakes, with a modern centre of bland broad avenues and palm-shaded piazzas. However, it's the mid-Adriatic's largest port, with regular ferries to Greece, and you may well pass through. Regular buses run along the seafront from the train station to the port, so it's easy enough to miss the place altogether, but if you are hanging around between connections there are a couple of things to see. The port itself is headed by a well-preserved Roman arch, the **Arco di Traiano**, raised in honour of Emperor Trajan, under whose rule Ancona first became a major port. Behind it is the **Arco Clementino**, a piece of architectural self-congratulation by Pope Clement XII, who made Ancona a free port in the eighteenth century, and thus considered himself Trajan's equal. On Via Pizzecolli is the town's **art gallery** (Tues–Sat 10am–7pm, Sun 9am–1pm; L3000, free Sun), highlights of which are Titian's *Apparition of the Virgin*, a glorious *Sacra Conversazione* by Lotto and an exquisite *Madonna and Child* by Crivelli. Further up the hill is the **Museo Nazionale delle Marche** (daily 9am–7pm; L4000), worth a visit for its frescoed ceilings by Tibaldi and a magnificent first-century gilded bronze sculpture of two Roman emperors on horseback.

As most ferry departures are at night, you're unlikely to need to stay over in Ancona. However, if you do, the most convenient **hotels** are opposite the train station – the *Dorico* (☎071/42.761; ③) and *Gino* (☎071/43.333; ④). **Bars** and **pizzerias** are plentiful along the port, or *Osteria del Pozzo*, in the old town on Via Bonda, and *Trattoria Vittoria* at Via Calatafini 2, off Piazza Cavour, are both quite reasonable.

Ferries to Greece
Ferry tickets are on sale at the Stazione Maríttima, as well as at the numerous agencies that line the road to the port. Most operators – *Minoan, GA Ferries, Anek Lines* and *Strintzis* are the main ones – run services to Igoumenitsa, Corfu and Patras; *Marlines* also go to Crete and Turkey. In peak season ferries tend to run at least daily, two to four times a week at other times of the year.

ROME

Of all Italy's historic cities, it's **ROME** which exerts the most compelling fascination. There's arguably more to see here than in any other city in the world, with the relics of a constant two thousand-plus years of population packed into its sprawling urban area; and as a contemporary European capital, it has a feel which is quite unique. Rome is, in many ways, the ideal capital of Italy, perfectly placed between Italy's warring north and south factions and heartily despised by both. For the traveller, it is the sheer weight of history in the city that is most evident, its various eras crowding in on each other to an almost breathtaking degree. There are the classical features – the Colosseum, the rubbly Forum and Palatine Hill – and relics from the early Christian period in ancient basilicas; while the fountains and churches of the Baroque period go a long way to determining the look of the city centre, most notably the work of Bernini. But these are just part of the picture, which is an almost continuous one right up to the present day, taking in Romanesque churches, Renaissance palazzi, Rococo fountains and the ponderous buildings of post-Unification, often all found within a few paces of each other.

Rome is not an easy place to absorb on one visit, and you need to approach things slowly, taking care not to try and see too much too quickly, even if you only have a few days here. On foot it's easy to lose a sense of direction in the twisting old streets, and in any case you're so likely to see something interesting that detours and stopoffs are inevitable. Stout, comfortable shoes and loose, cool clothes – Rome can get very sticky in summer – will be your greatest assets. One further thing: don't come in August, when the city centre is half closed up and the only people in town are fellow tourists.

> The Rome area telephone code is ☎06.

Arrival and information

Travelling by train, you arrive at the central **Stazione Termini**, meeting-point of the metro lines and city bus routes. Rome has two **airports**: Leonardo da Vinci, better known as Fiumicino, which handles all scheduled flights, and Ciampino, where charter flights land. From **Fiumicino**, trains run every twenty minutes or so to Stazione Ostiense, on the edge of the city centre, and link up with the Piramide stop on line B of the metro – journey time 25 minutes (L6000). You can also take bus #716 from right outside the terminal to Piazza Venezia, which is cheaper though a lot slower. A taxi will cost at least L60,000. From **Ciampino**, take a *Cotral* bus to Anagnina on metro line A (L1000), from where it's a twenty-minute ride to Termini. Taxis cost around L50,000.

There are **tourist information booths** at Fiumicino airport (Mon–Sat 8.15am–7pm) and at Termini (daily 8.15am–7.15pm), though heavy queues mean you're usually better off heading straight for the **main office** at Via Parigi 5 (Mon–Sat 8.15am–7pm; ☎488.991). They have decent free maps and can help with accommodation, as well as handing out any amount of bumph; the free booklet *Here's Rome* is useful and available in English, and the *Musei e Monumenti* pamphlet gives a listing of visitable sites. For information on Italy beyond Rome, there's the national tourist organization, the **ENIT**, to the right of Termini station as you come out, at Via Marghera 2 (Mon–Fri 9am–1pm, Mon, Wed & Fri also 4–6pm; ☎497.1282). The privately-run and more helpful *Enjoy Rome* tourist information service by the station at Via Varese 39 (Mon–Fri 9am–1pm & 3.30–6pm, Sat 8.30am–1pm; ☎445.1843) has a free hotel booking scheme and runs bus and walking tours. *Museidon Cards* are available from most sites, cost L13,000–48,000 depending on validity, and provide free entrance to selected city museums.

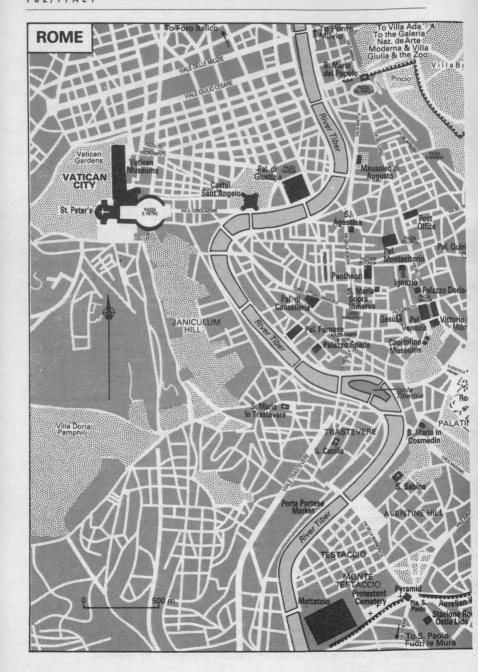

ROME

To Foro Italico

To Ponte Milvio

To Villa Ada
To the Galeria
Naz. de Arte
Moderna & Villa
Giulia & the Zoo

Villa Bo

VIALE DELLE MILIZIE

VIALE GIULIO CESARE

S. Maria del Popolo

Pincio

PIAZZA DEL POPOLO

River Tiber

Vatican Gardens

PIAZZA DEL RISORGIMENTO

Vatican Museums

VATICAN CITY

St. Peter's

PIAZZA S. PIETRO

Castel Sant'Angelo

VIA D. CONCILIAZIONE

Pal. di Giustizia

PIAZZA CAVOUR

Mausoleo di Augusto

PIAZZA DI SPAGNA

Post Office

PIAZZA COLONNA

Pal. Quiri

S. Agostina

Pal. Montecitorio

PIAZZA DI MONTANARA

Pantheon

PIAZZA ROTONDA

S. Ignazio

Palazzo Doria

CORSO VITTORIO EMANUELE

Pal. di Cancelleria

S. Maria Sopra Minerva

LARGO ARGENTINA

Gesù

Pal. Venezia

Vittorio Mon

Pel. Farnese

PIAZZA CAMPO D. FIORI

Palazzo Spada

Capitoline Museums

JANICULUM HILL

River Tiber

Isola Tiberina

Ro

PALATI

Villa Doria Pamphilj

S. Maria in Trastevere

S. Maria in Cosmedin

TRASTEVERE

S. Cecilia

VIALE TRASTEVERE

S. Sabina

Porta Portese Market

AVENTINE HILL

River Tiber

TESTACCIO

MONTE TESTACCIO

Pyramid

0   500 m

Mattatoio

Protestant Cemetery

Pta. S. Paolo

Aurelian V

Stazione Ro
Ostia Lido

To S. Paolo Fuori le Mura

Galeria Borghese
ghese
To S. Agnese & S. Constanza
Villa Torlonia
PIAZZA BOLOGNA
VIA NOMENTANA
CORSO D'ITALIA
Aurelian Walls
Pta. Pia
British Embassy
Policlinico
VIA XX SETTEMBRE
Tourist Office
Museo Nazionale Romano
Città Università
VIA TIBURTINA
Verano Cemetery
PIAZZA BARBERINI
Pal. Barberini
PIAZZA D. REPUBBLICA
Stazione Termini
S. Lorenzo Fuori le Mura
VIA NAZIONALE
S. Carlo alle Quattro Fontaine
VIA DELLE QUATTRO FONTANE
RINALE HILL
VIA CAVOUR
S. Maria Maggiore
Aurelian Walls
mphili
anuele
ment
ESQUILINE HILL
PIAZZA V. EMANUELE II
S. Pietro in Vincoli
VIA MERULANA
Colosseum
PIAZZA DI PORTA MAGGIORE
an Forum
VIA LABICANA
S. Clemente
S. Croce in Gerusalemme
HILL
SS. Giovanni e Paolo
S. Giovanni in Laterano
Pta. S. Giovanni
S. Gregorio Magno
Aurelian Walls
CELIAN HILL
Baths of Caracalla
VIA APPIA NUOVA
alle
a
Pta. S. Sebastiano
To Eur
To the Catacombs

City transport

As in most Italian cities, the best way to get around Rome is to **walk**. That said, its **bus service**, run by *ATAC*, is a good one – cheap, reliable and as quick as the clogged streets allow. Rome also has a **metro**, and although it is more directed at ferrying commuters out to the suburbs than transporting tourists around the city centre, there are a few useful stations. Flat-fare **tickets** on buses (valid for 90 mins) and the metro cost L1000 from bars with an *ATAC* sign or booths at major bus stages, and will take you as far as you want to go. You can make savings by purchasing a block of ten tickets for L6000 or a one-day ticket for L2800 from the *ATAC* booth on Piazza dei Cinquecento, where they also sell decent transport maps for L1000. The buses and the metro stop around midnight, after which a network of **night buses** clicks into service, serving most parts of the city until about 5am. **Taxis** are costly; hail one in the street, or try the ranks at Termini, Piazza Venezia, Piazza San Silvestro, or call ☎4494/88177. The meter should start at L6400.

Accommodation

In summer Rome is as crowded as you might expect, and although the city's huge number of **hotels and hostels** offers a vast capacity for absorbing visitors, you should book in advance if you can; if you can't, make straight for the tourist office to save your legs. Many of the city's cheaper hotels are handily located close to Stazione Termini, and you could do worse than hole up in one of these: the streets both sides of the station square are stacked full of cheap places. If you want to stay somewhere more central, there are hotels in the *centro storico*, some of them not that expensive, but again be warned that they might be full during the summer. For current details ask at the tourist office or contact *AIG*, Via Cavour 44 (☎487.1152).

Hostels

Ostello del Foro Italico, Viale delle Olimpiadi 61 (☎323.6279). Rome's official hostel, though not especially pleasant or central. Take bus #492 or metro line A from Termini to Ottaviano, then bus #32. ②

YWCA, Via C. Balbo 4 (☎488.3917). For women only, and more conveniently situated than the *IYHF* hostel, ten minutes' walk from Termini. Midnight curfew. ②

Hotels

Abruzzi, Piazza della Rotonda 69 (☎679.2021). Bang in front of the Pantheon, and as such you pay for the location. ③

Alimandi, Via Tunisi 8 (☎616.219). Close to the Vatican with good facilities. ③

Capitol, Via G. Amendola 77 (☎488.2617). Comfortable hotel close to the station. ②

Della Lunetta, Piazza del Paradiso 68 (☎686.1080). Close to Campo dei Fiori, an unspectacular hotel. ④

Germano, Via Calatafimi 14 (☎486.919). Friendly and cheap. ③

Katty, Via Palestro 35 (☎444.1216). One of the cheaper options east of the station. ③

Kennedy, Via F. Turati 62 (☎446.5373). Young management and well-kept. ③

Manara, Via Luciano Manara 25 (☎581.4713). The place to come if you want to be in the heart of Trastevere. ③

Marsala, Via Marsala 36 (☎444.1372). Pleasant, clean hotel 50m from the station. ⑤

Monaco, Via Flavia 84 (☎474.4335). Very welcoming and clean cheapie. ③

Navona, Via dei Sediari 8 (☎688.03802). Perfectly placed *pensione* run by an Italian-Australian couple, even though the breakfasts aren't up to much. ④

Perugia, Via del Colosseo 7 (☎679.7200). On a peaceful but central street. ③

Piccolo, Via dei Chiavari 32 (☎654.2560). Cheap hotel handily located for Piazza Navona. ⑤
Prati, Via Crescenzio 87 (☎687.5357). Two-star hotel across the river with a nice, family-run feel. ⑤
Di Rienzo, Via P. Amadeo 79 (☎446.7131). Spacious clean rooms within spitting distance of the train station. ③
Romano, Largo C. Ricci 32 (☎679.5851). Well-priced hotel in a central location. ③
Rosetta, Via Cavour 295 (☎488.1598). Nice location close to the Colosseum. ⑤
Smeraldo, Via dei Chiodaroli 11 (☎687.5929). Popular place with lovely doubles. ⑥
Sole, Via del Biscione 76 (☎688.06873). Overlooking Piazza del Campo dei Fiori, one of the nicest city centre locations. ④
Tony, Via P. Amadeo 79d (☎446.6887). Pleasant rooms. ③
Vulcania, Via Cavour 117 (☎488.4915). Good-value two-star hotel. ④

Campsites

Camping Capitol, Via Castelfusano 45. Well-equipped but a long way out, close to the sea in Ostia – take a train to Ostia Lido and a #5 bus.
Camping Flaminio, Via Flaminia Nuova. In the opposite direction, 8km north of the city; bus #202, #204 or #205 from Piazzale Flaminio, which is connected with Termini by metro line A.

The City

Piazza Venezia is a good central place to start your wanderings, flanked by the **Palazzo di Venezia** and overlooked by the hideous **Vittorio Emanuele Monument** or Altar of the Nation, erected at the turn of the century to commemorate Unification. Behind, the **Capitoline Hill**, formerly the spiritual and political centre of the Roman Empire, is home to one of Rome's most elegant squares, **Piazza del Campidoglio**, designed by Michelangelo in the 1550s for Pope Paul III, and flanked by the two branches of one of the city's most important museums of antique art – the **Capitoline Museums** (Tues–Sat 9am–1.30pm, Sun 9am–1pm; Tues also 5–8pm, Sat also 8–11pm; L10,000). On the left, the **Palazzo del Museo Capitolino** concentrates some of the best of the city's Roman and Greek sculpture into half a dozen or so rooms. There's a remarkable, controlled statue of the *Dying Gaul*, a Roman copy of a Hellenistic original; an original grappling depiction of *Eros and Psyche*; a *Satyr Resting*, after a piece by Praxiteles; and the red marble *Laughing Satyr*, another Roman copy of a Greek original. Walk through to the so-called Sala degli Imperatori, with its busts of Roman emperors and other famous names, and don't miss the coy *Capitoline Venus*, housed in a room on its own, again based on a work by Praxiteles. The same ticket will get you into the **Palazzo dei Conservatori** across the square, a larger, more varied collection, with more ancient sculpture, including the exquisite *Spinario* – a Hellenistic work from the first century BC showing a boy plucking a thorn from his foot – and the sacred Roman statue of the she-wolf suckling the twins, thought to be originally an Etruscan work. The second floor holds Renaissance painting – numerous works by Reni and Tintoretto, a vast picture by Guercino that used to hang in St Peter's, some nice small-scale work by Carracci, especially an early *Head of a Boy*, and Caravaggio's *St. John the Baptist*. Behind the square, a road skirts the Forum down to the small church of **San Giuseppe dei Falegnami** (daily 9am–noon & 2–6.30pm), built above the prison where Saint Peter is said to have been held – you can see the bars to which he was chained, along with the spring the saint is said to have created to baptize other prisoners here, and, at the top of the staircase, an imprint claimed to be of Saint Peter's head as he was tumbled down the stairs.

Via del Plebiscito forges west from Piazza Venezia past the church of **Gesù** (daily 6am–12.30pm & 4–7.30pm), a high, wide Baroque church of the Jesuit order that has served since as the model for Jesuit churches everywhere. Still well-patronized, it's notable for its size (the left transept is surmounted by the largest single piece of stone in existence) and the richness of its interior, especially the paintings of Baciccia in the dome and the ceiling's ingenious trompe l'oeil, which oozes out of its frame in a tangle of writhing bodies, flowing drapery and stucco angels. Crossing over, streets tangle down to **Piazza di Campo de' Fiori**, Rome's most appealing and unpretentious square, home to a morning market and surrounded by restaurants and bars. South of the Campo, at the end of Vicolo di Grotte, the **Galleria Spada** (Tues–Sat 9am–7pm, Sun 9am–1pm; L4000) is decorated in the manner of a Roman noble family and displays a small collection of paintings, best of which are a couple of portraits by Reni, works by the odd Italian-influenced Dutch artist (van Scorel, Honthorst), and, among bits and pieces of Roman statuary, a seated philosopher. The building itself is frilled with stucco adornments, and, left off the courtyard there's a crafty trompe l'oeil by Borromini – basically a tunnel in which the actual length is multiplied about four times through the architect's tricks with perspective. Across Via Arenula, the broad open space of **Piazza della Bocca di Verità** is home to two of the city's better-preserved Roman temples, the **Temple of Fortuna Virilis** and the circular **Temple of Vesta**, both of which date from the end of the second century BC, though the church of **Santa Maria in Cosmedin**, on the far side of the square (daily 9am–noon & 3–5pm), is more interesting, a typically Roman medieval basilica with a huge marble altar and surround and a colourful and ingenious Cosmati mosaic floor – one of the city's finest. Outside in the portico, the **Bocca di Verità** (Mouth of Truth) gives the square its name, an ancient Roman drain cover in the shape of an enormous face that in medieval times would apparently swallow the hand of anyone who hadn't told the truth.

The Centro Storico

You need to walk a little way north from the Capitoline Hill to find the real city centre of Rome, the **centro storico**, which makes up the greater part of the roughly triangular knob of land that bulges into a bend in the Tiber, above Corso Vittorio Emanuele. This area was the old Campus Martius of Roman times, outside the main body of the ancient city, a low-lying area that was mostly given over to barracks and sporting arenas, with the odd temple. Later it was the heart of the Renaissance city, and now it's the part of the town that's densest in interest, an unruly knot of narrow streets holding some of the best of Rome's classical and baroque heritage, and its street- and nightlife.

The boundary of the historic centre to the east, **Via del Corso,** is Rome's main street, holding its principal shops and cutting straight through the heart of the city centre. Walking north from Piazza Venezia, the first building on the left is the **Galleria Doria Pamphilj** (Tues & Fri–Sun 10am–1pm; L6000), one of many galleries housed in palaces belonging to Roman patrician families. Its collection includes Rome's best cache of Dutch and Flemish paintings, canvases by Caravaggio and Velásquez's painting of the Pamphilj pope, Innocent X. The next left after the palace leads into Piazza Sant'Ignazio, an odd little square dominated by the church of **Sant'Ignazio** (daily 8am–12.30pm & 4–7.15pm), which has a marvellous ceiling by Pozzo showing the entry of Saint Ignatius into paradise, employing sledgehammer trompe l'oeil effects, notably in the mock cupola painted into the dome of the crossing. Stand on the disc in the centre of the nave for the truest sense of the ingenious rendering of perspective.

Through Via di Seminario from here and you're standing in front of the **Pantheon** (Mon–Sat 9am–6pm, Sun 9am–1pm; free) on Piazza della Rotonda, the most complete ancient Roman structure in the city, finished around 125 AD. A formidable architectural achievement even now, its dome is still second largest in Rome. Inside, the dimensions of the dome and height are precisely equal, and the hole in the dome's centre is a full nine metres across; there are no visible arches or vaults to hold the whole thing up; instead, they're sunk into the concrete of the walls of the building. It would have been richly decorated, the coffered ceiling heavily stuccoed and the niches filled with statues of the gods. Now, apart from the sheer size of the place, the main thing of interest is the tomb of Raphael, inscribed by the writer and priest Bembo: "Living, great Nature feared he might outvie Her works, and dying, fears herself may die."

There's more artistic splendour on view behind the Pantheon, in the church of **Santa Maria sopra Minerva**, one of the city's art-treasure churches, crammed with the tombs and self-indulgences of wealthy Roman families. Of these, the Carafa chapel, in the south transept, is the best known, holding Filippino Lippi's recently-restored fresco of *The Assumption*, below which one painting shows a hopeful Oliviero Carafa being presented to the Virgin Mary by Thomas Aquinas; another depicts Aquinas confounding the heretics in the sight of two beautiful young boys – the future Medici popes Leo X and Clement VII. You should look, too, at the figure of *Christ bearing the Cross*, on the left-hand side of the main altar, a serene work that Michelangelo completed in 1521 especially for the church.

In the opposite direction from the Pantheon, **Piazza Navona** is in many ways the central square of Rome, an almost entirely enclosed space fringed with cafés and restaurants that actually follows the lines of the emperor Domitian's arena, site of the sports and chariot races that took place in the Campus Martius. Until the mid-fifteenth century the overgrown ruins of the arena were still here, but the square was given a face-lift in the mid-seventeenth century by Pope Innocent X building most of the grandiose palaces that surround it and commissioning Borromini to design the church of **Sant'Agnese** on the west side. The story goes that Saint Agnes was exposed naked to the public in the stadium, whereupon she miraculously grew hair to cover herself: this church, typically squeezed into the tightest of spaces by Borromini, is supposedly on the spot where it happened. The **Fontana dei Quattro Fiumi** opposite, one of three that punctuate the square, is by Borromini's arch-rival, Bernini; each figure represents one of the four great rivers of the world – the Nile, Danube, Ganges and Plate – though only the horse, symbolizing the Danube, was actually carved by Bernini himself.

North of Piazza Navona, the Renaissance facade of the church of **Sant'Agostino** is not much to look at but the church's handful of art treasures might draw you in – among them Raphael's vibrant *Isaiah*, on the third pillar on the left, Sansovino's craggy *Saint Anne, Virgin and Child*, and, in the first chapel on the left, a *Madonna and Pilgrims* by Caravaggio, though this is so dark you might well be better off buying a postcard to appreciate it best. There's more work by Caravaggio down Via della Scrofa, in the French national church of **San Luigi dei Francesi** (daily 7.30am–12.30pm & 3.30–7pm), in the last chapel on the left: early works, describing the life and martyrdom of Saint Matthew, best of which is the *Calling of St Matthew* on the left wall – Matthew is the dissolute-looking youth on the far left, illuminated by a shaft of sunlight. Caravaggio's first public commission, these paintings were actually rejected at first, partly on grounds of indecorum, and it took considerable reworking by the artist before they were finally accepted. A little way up Via della Ripetta from here, the **Ara Pacis Augustae** (summer Tues–Sat 9am–1.30pm, Tues, Thurs & Sat also 4–7pm, Sun 9am–1pm; winter Tues–Sat 9am–1.30pm, Sun 9am–1pm; L2500) was built in 13 BC to celebrate Augustus's victory over Spain and Gaul. It supports a fragmented frieze showing Augustus himself, his wife Livia, Tiberius, Agrippa, and various children clutching the togas of the elders, the last of whom is said to be the young Claudius.

At the far end of Via di Ripetta the **Piazza del Popolo** provides an impressive entrance to the city, all symmetry and grand vistas, although its real attraction is the church of **Santa Maria del Popolo**, which holds some of the best Renaissance art of any Roman church, including frescoes by Pinturicchio in the south aisle and two fine tombs by Andrea Sansovino. The penultimate chapel in the northern aisle, the Chigi chapel, was designed by Raphael for Antonio Chigi in 1516 – though most of the work was accomplished by other artists and not finished until the seventeenth century. Michelangelo's protégé, Sebastiano del Piombo, was responsible for the altarpiece; the two sculptures in the corner niches of Daniel and Habakkuk are by Bernini. Two pictures by Caravaggio get most attention – one, the *Conversion of St Paul*, showing Paul and horse bathed in a beatific radiance, the other, the *Crucifixion of St Peter*, showing Peter as an aged figure, dominated by the muscular figures hoisting him up.

East of Via del Corso

The area immediately southeast of Piazza del Popolo is travellers' Rome, historically the artistic quarter of the city, for which eighteenth- and nineteenth-century Grand Tourists would make, lending the area a distinctly cosmopolitan air, even today. At the centre of the district, **Piazza di Spagna** is a long thin square centring on the distinctive boat-shaped **Barcaccia** fountain, the last work of Bernini's father. Opposite, the **Keats-Shelley Memorial House** (Mon–Fri summer 9am–1pm & 3–6pm; winter 9am–1pm & 2.30–5pm; L5000), where John Keats died in 1821, now serves as an archive of English-language literary and historical works and a museum of literary mementoes relating to the Keats circle of the early nineteenth century – namely Keats himself, Shelley, Mary Shelley and Byron (who at one time lived across the square). Among many bits of manuscript, letters and the like, there's a silver scallop shell reliquary containing locks of Milton's and Elizabeth Barrett Browning's hair, and the poet's death mask with a resigned grimace lying in the room where he died. Beside the house, the **Spanish Steps** – a venue for international posing and fast pick-ups late into the summer nights – sweep up to the **Trinità dei Monti**, a largely sixteenth-century church that holds a couple of works by Daniel da Volterra, notably a soft flowing fresco of *The Assumption* in the third chapel on the right, which includes a portrait of his teacher Michelangelo. His *Deposition*, across the nave, is also worth a glance; it was painted from a series of cartoons by Michelangelo, and Poussin considered it the world's third greatest painting (Raphael's *Transfiguration* was, he thought, the best).

From the church, follow Via Sistina to **Piazza Barberini**, a busy traffic junction, in the centre of which is Bernini's **Fontana del Tritone**. **Via Veneto** bends north from here, its pricy bars and restaurants once the haunt of Rome's Beautiful People but now home of high-class tack and overpriced sleaze. A little way up, the Capuchin **Church of the Immaculate Conception** is not particularly notable, but is worth visiting for its Capuchin **cemetery** (daily 9am–noon & 3–6.30pm), one of the more macabre sights of Rome; here the bones of 4000 monks coat the walls of a series of chapels in abstract patterns or as fully clothed skeletons, their faces peering out of their cowls in various twisted expressions of agony, somewhere between the chilling and the ludicrous.

Retracing your steps back across Piazza Barberini, the **Palazzo Barberini** is home to the **Galleria d'Arte Antica** (Tues–Sun 9am–7pm; L6000), which displays a rich patchwork of mainly Italian art from the early Renaissance to late Baroque period. In addition to canvases by Tintoretto, Titian and El Greco, highlights include Filippo Lippi's warmly maternal *Madonna and Child*, painted in 1437, and Raphael's beguiling *Fornarina*, claimed by some experts to be the work of a pupil though Raphael's name appears clearly on the woman's bracelet. But perhaps the most impressive feature of the gallery is the building itself, the epitome of Baroque grandeur worked on at different times by the most favoured architects of the day: Bernini, Borromini and Maderno. The Salone, certainly, is guaranteed to impress, its ceiling frescoed by Pietro da Cortona in one of the best examples of exuberant Baroque trompe l'oeil work, a manic rendering of *The Triumph of Divine Providence* that almost crawls down the walls.

East down Via del Tritone from Piazza Barberini, hidden among a tight web of narrow, apparently aimless streets, is one of Rome's more surprising sights, easy to stumble upon by accident – the **Fontane di Trevi**, a huge, very Baroque gush of water over statues and rocks built onto the backside of a Renaissance palace. The fountain was originally commissioned from Bernini by Pope Urban VIII, but work didn't begin until Niccolo Salvi took up the project in 1723, and even then it took 39 years to complete. Salvi died in the process, his lungs shot by the time spent in the dank waterworks of the fountain. The Trevi fountain is now, of course, the place you come to chuck in a coin if you want to guarantee your return to Rome, and it's one of the city's most vigorous outdoor spots to hang out of an evening. A short stroll directly south from here brings you to the **Galleria Colonna**, Via della Pilotta 17 (Sat 9am–1pm; L5000), worth forty minutes or so if only for the chandelier-decked Great Hall, where a display of paintings includes Carracci's early *Bean Eater*, a *Narcissus* by Tintoretto, and a *Portrait of a Venetian Gentleman* caught in supremely confident pose by Veronese.

Five minutes from the gallery, **Via Nazionale**, Rome's main shopping street, lined with boutiques, leads up to **Piazza della Repubblica**, a stern but rather tawdry semi-circle of buildings that occupies part of the site of Diocletian's Baths, the scanty remains of which lie across the square in the church of **Santa Maria degli Angeli**. This is a huge, open building, with an interior standardized after a couple of centuries of piecemeal adaptation (started by an aged Michelangelo) by Vanvitelli in a rich eighteenth-century confection. The pink granite pillars are, however, original, and the main transept formed the main hall of the baths – though only the crescent shape of the facade remains from the original caldarium. Michelangelo is also said to have had a hand in modifying another part of the baths, the courtyard which makes up part of the **Museo Nazionale Romano** behind the church (Mon 9am–1pm, Tues–Fri 9am–2pm, Sat & Sun 9am–1pm; L3000), whose collection of Greek and Roman antiquities is second only to the Vatican's. It contains Roman sarcophagi, good mosaics and stucco-work from the ruins of an Augustan-era villa discovered in the grounds of the Villa Farnesina, and an almost complete set of frescoes from the Villa Livia on the Palatine Hill, representing an orchard dense with fruit and flowers; the museum is undergoing restoration and exhibits may be disrupted. Close by on Via XX Settembre, the church of **Santa Maria della Vittoria** was built by Carlo Maderno and its interior is one of the most elaborate examples of Baroque decoration in Rome, its ceiling and walls pitted with carving, and statues crammed into remote corners like an overstuffed attic. The church's best-known feature is Bernini's carving of the *Ecstasy of St Theresa*, the centre-piece of the sepulchral chapel of Cardinal Cornaro – a melodramatic work which poses Saint Theresa against a backdrop of theatre-boxes, from which the Cornaro cardinals watch the spectacle. The semi-visible figure on the left may well be Bernini.

South of Piazza Venezia

From Piazza Venezia **Via dei Fori Imperiali** cuts south, a soulless boulevard whose main pedestrians are tourists rooting about among the ancient sites. Just off Piazza Venezia, **Trajan's Column** was erected to celebrate the emperor's colonization of Dacia (modern-day Romania), and its reliefs illustrate the highlights of the Dacian campaign. Across the road is the main part of the **Roman Forum** (summer Mon & Wed–Sat 9am–7pm, Sun & Tues 9am–1pm; winter daily 9am–3pm; L10,000), in ancient times the centre of what was a very large city. Following the decline of the empire and the coming of Christianity, decay set in, and after the later downfall of the city to various barbarian invaders, the area was left in ruin, its relics quarried for construction in other parts of Rome during medieval and Renaissance times. Excavation of the site didn't start until the beginning of the nineteenth century, since when it has been pretty much continuous: you'll notice a fair part of the site closed off for further digs.

Running through the core of the Forum, the **Via Sacra** was the best-known street of ancient Rome. At the bottom of the Capitoline hill, the **Arch of Septimus Severus** was built in the early second century AD to commemorate the emperor's tenth anniversary in power, and the grassy, wide-open scatter of paving and beached columns in front of it was the place where most of the life of the city was carried on. Nearby, the **Curia** is one of the few whole structures here, a huge barn-like building that was begun in 80 BC, restored by Julius Caesar soon after and rebuilt by Diocletian in the third century AD. The Senate met here during the Republican period, and augurs would come to announce the wishes of the gods. On the opposite side is the **House of the Vestal Virgins**, where the six women charged with the responsibility of keeping the sacred flame of Vesta alight lived. If it should go out, the woman responsible was scourged; if she should lose her chastity, she was scourged and then buried alive (the man was merely flogged). The palace was very comfortable: four floors of rooms around a central courtyard, with the round **Temple of Vesta** at the near end. On the far side of the site, the **Basilica of Constantine and Maxentius** is, in terms of size and ingenuity, probably the Forum's most impressive remains. It's said that Michelangelo studied the hexagonal coffered arches here when grappling with the dome of St Peter's. From the basilica, the Via Sacra climbs to the **Arch of Titus** on a low arm of the Palatine Hill – although its covered for restoration – its reliefs showing the spoils of the sacking of Jerusalem being carried off by eager Romans.

Turning right at the Arch of Titus takes you up to the **Palatine Hill**, a pleasanter and greener site than the Forum. In the days of the Republic, the Palatine was the most desirable address in Rome (from it is derived our word "palace"), and the big names continued to colonize it during the Imperial era, trying to outdo each other with ever larger and more magnificent dwellings. The gargantuan **Domus Augustana** spreads to the far brink of the hill. You can look down from here onto its vast central courtyard and maze-like fountain, and wander through a handful of its bare rooms. From close by, steps lead down to the **Cryptoporticus**, a passage built by Nero to link the Palatine with his palace on the far side of the Colosseum, and decorated along part of its length with well-preserved Roman stuccowork. A left turn leads to the **House of Livia**, originally believed to have been the residence of the wife of Augustus, whose courtyard and rooms are decorated with scanty frescoes. Turn right down the passage and up some steps and you're in the **Farnese Gardens**, among the first botanical gardens in Europe, laid out by Alessandro Farnese in the mid-sixteenth century and now a tidily planted refuge from the exposed heat of the ruins. The terrace here looks back over the Forum, while the terrace at the opposite end looks down on the real centre of Rome's ancient beginning – an Iron Age hut, known as the **House of Romulus**, that is the best preserved of a ninth-century Iron Age village discovered here, and the so-called **Lupercal**, beyond, which is traditionally believed to be the cave where Romulus and Remus were suckled by the she-wolf.

Immediately outside the Forum site, the fourth-century **Arch of Constantine** marks the end of the Via Sacra. Across from here, the **Colosseum** (Mon, Tues & Thurs–Sat 9am–7pm, Sun & Wed 9am–1pm; free, L6000 for the upper levels) is Rome's most awe-inspiring ancient monument, begun by the emperor Vespasian around 72 AD and finished by his son Titus about eight years later – an event celebrated by 100 days of continuous games. The Romans flocked here for many things: gladiatorial contests were the big attraction, designed to prime soldiers for real combat, but there were other, equally cruel spectacles, pitting man against animal, animal against animal, even staging mock sea battles in an arena which could be flooded within minutes. The games were eventually outlawed in the fifth century and, pillaged over the centuries for stone to build some of Rome's grandest palaces, the Colosseum is not much more than a shell now. But the basic structure of the place is easy to see, and has served as a model for stadiums around the world ever since.

It's a short walk from here down Via San Giovanni in Laterano to the church of **San Clemente** – a light, twelfth-century basilica that encapsulates better than any other the continuity of history in the city. It's in fact a conglomeration of three places of worship. The ground-floor church is a superb example of a medieval basilica, with some fine mosaics in the apse. Downstairs (daily 9am–12.30pm & 3.30–6.30pm; L2000), there's the nave of an earlier church, dated back to 392 AD. And at the eastern end of this church, are the remains of a Roman apartment block – a labyrinthine set of rooms including a Mithraic temple of the late second century. The same street leads to the

Basilica of **San Giovanni in Laterano**, Rome's cathedral and the seat of the pope until Unification – after which the pontiff took refuge in the Vatican and only emerged when the Lateran Treaty of 1929 accorded this and the other patriarchal basilicas extra-territorial status. There has been a church on this site since the fourth century, the first established by Constantine, and the present building, reworked by Borromini in the mid-seventeenth century, evokes – like San Clemente – Rome's staggering wealth of history. The doors to the church, oddly enough, were taken from the Curia of the Roman Forum. Inside, the first pillar on the left of the right-hand aisle shows a fragment of Giotto's fresco of Boniface VIII, proclaiming the first Holy Year in 1300, while further on, a more recent monument commemorates Sylvester I, bishop of Rome during much of Constantine's reign, and incorporates part of his original tomb, said to sweat and rattle its bones when a pope is about to die. Kept secure behind the papal altar are the heads of Saint Peter and Saint Paul, the church's prize relics. Outside, the cloisters (L2000) are one of the most pleasing parts of the complex, decorated with early thirteenth-century Cosmati work. Next door to the church, the **Baptistery** is the oldest surviving baptistery in the Christian world, an octagonal structure built by Constantine and rebuilt during the fifth century, and on the other side of the church the **Scala Santa** is claimed to be the staircase from Pontius Pilate's house down which Christ walked after his trial. The 28 steps are protected by boards, and the only way you're allowed to climb them is on your knees – which pilgrims do regularly.

On the far side of the road from the Colosseum, the one feature of interest on the **Esquiline Hill** is the church of **San Pietro in Vincoli** (daily 6.30am–12.30pm & 3.30–7pm), one of Rome's most delightfully plain churches, built to house an important relic: the chains of Saint Peter from his imprisonment in Jerusalem, along with those that bound him when a prisoner in Rome. These can still be seen under the canopy in the apse, but most people come for the tomb of Pope Julius II in the southern aisle, which occupied Michelangelo on and off for much of his career and was the cause of many a dispute with Julius and his successors. He never finished the tomb, but the figure of Moses, pictured as descended from Sinai to find the Israelites worshipping the golden calf, and flanked by the gentle figures of Leah and Rachel, is one of the artist's most arresting works. Steps lead down from San Pietro to **Via Cavour**, a busy central thoroughfare which carves a route up to Termini past the basilica of **Santa Maria Maggiore** (daily 9am–6.30pm), one of the city's four great basilicas, with a broad nave fringed on both sides with strikingly well-kept mosaics, most of which date from the church's construction and tell of incidents from the Old Testament. The Sistine chapel, on the right, holds the elaborate tomb of Sixtus V, while the equally fancy Pauline chapel has a venerated twelfth-century *Madonna* topped with a panel showing the legendary tracing of the church's plan after a snowfall.

Villa Borghese

At the northern edge of the city centre, the **Villa Borghese** is made up of the grounds of the seventeenth-century palace of Cardinal Scipione Borghese – a vast area, whose woods, lakes and grass are about as near as you can get to peace in Rome without making too much effort. Apart from the tranquillity, the main attraction is the **Galleria Borghese** (Tues–Sat 9am–7pm, Sun 9am–1pm; L4000), with an assortment of works collected by Scipione Borghese. Restoration work here has been dragging on for several years, and you won't be able to see everything. But of what you can see – mainly sculpture – the work of Bernini, a protégé of Borghese, dominates. There's an *Aeneas and Anchises*, carved with his father when he was fifteen; an ingenious *Rape of Proserpine*, amid busts of Roman emperors; his dramatic *Apollo and Daphne*; and, in the next room, his *David* – a self-portrait. Paintings from the collection are on show at the **Quaderia della Galleria Borghese a San Michele**, Via di S. Michele 22 (Tues–Sat 9am–7pm; L4000).

The Villa Borghese's two other major museums are across the other side of the park, along the Viale delle Belle Arti. Of these, the **Galleria Nazionale d'Arte Moderna** (Tues–Sat 9am–7pm, Sun 9am–1pm; L8000) is probably the least compelling, housing a wide selection of nineteenth- and twentieth-century Italian names, most undistinguished; artists you might recognize include Modigliani, De Chirico, Boccione and other futurists, along with the odd Cézanne, Mondrian and Klimt. The **Villa Giulia**, ten minutes away, is more of an essential stop, a collection of courtyards, loggias and gardens that is home to the **Museo Nazionale di Villa Giulia** (Tues–Sat 9am–7pm, Sun 9am–1pm; L8000) – the world's primary collection of Etruscan treasures. Best among the sculpture is the group of *Apollo and Herakles*, from the site of Veio, north of Rome, and the remarkable *Sarcophagus of a Married Couple* from Cerveteri. Other highlights include the *Cistae* recovered from tombs around Praeneste – drum-like objects, engraved and adorned with figures, that were supposed to hold all the things needed for the care of the body after death – and marvellously intricate pieces of gold jewellery, delicately worked into tiny animals.

South of the centre

On its southern side, the Palatine Hill drops suddenly down to the **Circo Massimo**, a long green expanse that was the ancient city's main venue for chariot races. The arena could apparently hold a crowd of around 200,000 betting punters, and if it was still even half intact could no doubt have matched the Colosseum for grandeur. As it is, a litter of stones at the Viale Aventino end is all that remains. Across the far side of Piazza di Porta Capena, the **Baths of Caracalla** (Mon–Sat 9am–6pm, Sun 9am–1pm; L6000) are better preserved, and give a much better sense of the scale of Roman architecture than most of the ruins in the city. They're also still used for opera performances during summer, which is a good, if expensive, way to see them at their most evocative. It's a short walk from behind the baths down Via Gitto to the **Protestant Cemetery** (daily except Wed 8.30am–11.30am & 2.20–4.30pm; donations invited), accessible direct on metro line B, the burial place of Keats and Shelley, along with a handful of other well-known names. It's a small and surprisingly tranquil enclave, crouched behind the mossy pyramidal tomb of one Caius Cestius. Keats lies next to his friend, the painter Joseph Severn, in a corner of the old part of the cemetery near the pyramid, his stone inscribed as he wished with the words "whose name was writ in water". As for Shelley, his ashes were brought here at Mary Shelley's request and interred in the newer part of the cemetery, at the opposite end.

Two kilometres or so south, **San Paolo fuori le Mura** is one of the four patriarchal basilicas of Rome, occupying the supposed site of Saint Paul's tomb. Of the four, it has probably fared least well over the years, and the church you see is largely a nineteenth-century reconstruction. It is an huge, impressive building, and home to a handful of ancient features: in the south transept, the Paschal Candlestick is a remarkable piece of Romanesque carving, supported by half-human beasts and rising through entwined tendrils and strangely human limbs and bodies to scenes from Christ's life; the bronze doors date from 1070, and the Cosmati cloister, just behind here, is probably Rome's finest, its spiralling, mosaic-encrusted columns enclosing a peaceful rose garden.

Further south still, on the edge of the city, the **Via Appia** was the most important of all the Roman trade routes, and although it's no longer the main route south out of the city it remains an important part of early Christian Rome, its sides lined with the underground burial cemeteries or **catacombs** of the first Christians. There are around five complexes in all, dating from the first to the fourth centuries, almost entirely emptied of bodies now but still decorated with the primitive signs and frescoes that were the hallmark of the then-burgeoning Christian movement. You can get to the main grouping on bus #118 from the Colosseum (Via San Giovanni in Laterano), but the only ones of any significance are the catacombs of **San Callisto** (daily except Wed 8.30am–noon

& 2.30–5.30pm; L6000), burial place of all the third-century popes, whose tombs are preserved in the papal crypt, and the site of some well-preserved seventh- and eighth-century frescoes; and those of **San Sebastiano** (daily except Thurs 9am–noon & 2.30–5.30pm,L6000), 500m further on, situated under a basilica that was originally built by Constantine on the spot where the bodies of the Apostles Peter and Paul are said to have laid for a time. Half-hour tours take in paintings of doves and fish, a contemporary carved oil lamp and inscriptions dating the tombs themselves – although the most striking features are three pagan tombs discovered when archeologists were burrowing beneath the floor of the basilica upstairs. The nearby graffiti record the fact that this was indeed, albeit temporarily, where the Apostles Peter and Paul rested.

Trastevere

Across the Tiber from the centre of town, the district of **Trastevere** has traditionally been a place somewhat apart from the rest of the city centre, a small, tightly knit neighbourhood that was formerly the artisan quarter of the city and has since become rather gentrified, home to much of its most vibrant and youthful nightlife – and some of Rome's best and most affordable restaurants. The best time to come is on Sunday morning, when the **Porta Portese** flea market stretches down Via Portuense to Trastevere station in a congested medley of antiques, old motor spares, cheap clothing, trendy clothing and assorted junk. Afterwards, stroll north up Via Anicia to the church of **Santa Cecilia in Trastevere**, originally built here over the site of the second-century home of Saint Cecilia, who was persecuted for her Christian beliefs. The story has it that Cecilia was locked in the caldarium of her own baths for several days but refused to die, singing her way through the ordeal (Cecilia is patron saint of music). Her head was finally half hacked off with an axe, though it took several blows before she finally died. Below the high altar, Stefano Maderno's limp statue of the saint shows her incorruptible body as it was found in 1599, with three deep cuts in her neck. To the side, you can descend to the excavations of the baths, though hints at restoration have robbed these of any atmosphere. Only the caldarium itself, on the other side of the church down a small passageway off the right aisle, is clearly marked.

Santa Cecilia is situated in the quieter part of Trastevere, on the southern side of **Viale Trastevere** – the wide boulevard which cuts through the centre of the district. There's more life on the far side of here, centred around **Piazza Santa Maria in Trastevere**, named after the church of **Santa Maria in Trastevere** (daily 9.30am–12.30pm & 4–7pm) – held to be the first official church in Rome, built on a site where a fountain of oil is said to have sprung on the day of Christ's birth and sporting some of the city's most impressive mosaics. North towards the Tiber, the **Villa Farnesina** is known for its Renaissance murals, including a Raphael-designed painting of *Cupid and Psyche*, completed in 1517 by the artist's assistants. Vasari claims Raphael didn't complete the work because his infatuation with his mistress was making it impossible to concentrate, and says that Chigi arranged for her to live with the painter in the palace while he worked on the loggia. More likely, he was simply so overloaded with commissions that he couldn't possibly finish them all. He did, however, manage to finish the *Galatea* next door, which he fitted in between his Vatican commissions for Julius II; "the greatest evocation of paganism of the Renaissance," Kenneth Clark called it. The other paintings in the room are by Sebastiano del Piombo and the architect of the building, Peruzzi, who also decorated the upstairs Salone delle Prospettive, which shows trompe l'oeil views of Rome – one of the earliest examples of the technique.

Castel Sant'Angelo, St Peter's and the Vatican Museums

Across the Tiber from Rome's old centre, the **Castel Sant'Angelo** (Mon 2–6pm, Tues–Sun 9am–1pm, Sat & Sun 9am–noon; L8000) was the burial place of the emperor Hadrian. Later, the papal authorities converted the building for use as a fortress and built a passageway to link it with the Vatican as a refuge in times of siege. Inside, rooms hold swords, armour, guns and the like, while below, dungeons and storerooms are testament to the castle's grisly past as the city's most notorious Renaissance prison. Upstairs, the official papal apartments, accessible from the terrace, are extravagantly decorated with lewd frescoes amid paintings by Poussin, Jordaens and others.

Via della Conciliazione leads up from here to the **Vatican City**, a tiny territory surrounded by high walls on its far side and on the near side opening its doors to the rest of the city and its pilgrims in the form of Bernini's **Piazza San Pietro**, whose two arms extend a symbolic welcome to the lap of the Catholic church. The basilica of **San Pietro** (daily 7am–7pm; free) is the replacement of a basilica built during the time of Constantine, to a plan initially conceived at the turn of the fifteenth century by Bramante and finished off, heavily modified, over a century later by Carlo Maderno, making it something of a bridge between the Renaissance and Baroque eras. The inside is full of features from the Baroque period, although the first thing you see, on the right, is Michelangelo's *Pietà*, completed when he was just 24 and, following an attack a few years back, displayed behind glass. On the right-hand side of the nave, the bronze statue of Saint Peter was cast in the thirteenth century by Arnolfo di Cambio and has its right foot polished smooth by the attentions of pilgrims. Bronze was also the material used in Bernini's *baldachino*, the centrepiece of the sculptor's embellishment of the interior, a massive 85 feet high, said to be cast out of metal pillaged from the Pantheon roof in 1633. Despite its size, it has the odd personal touch, not least in the female faces and beaming baby carved on the plinths – said to have been done for a niece of Bernini's patron, Urban VIII, who gave birth at the same time as the sculptor was finishing the piece. Bernini's feverish sculpting decorates the apse, too, his *cattedra* enclosing the supposed chair of Saint Peter in a curvy marble and stucco throne. An entrance off the aisle leads to the **treasury** (daily 9am–6pm; L3000), which, along with more recent additions, holds artefacts left from the earlier church – principally a wall-mounted tabernacle by Donatello, and the massive, though fairly ghastly, late fifteenth-century bronze tomb of Sixtus IV by Pollaiuolo, which as a portrait is said to be very accurate. Back at the central crossing, steps lead down to the **Vatican Grottoes**, where a number of popes are buried in grandiose tombs – in the main, those not distinguished enough to be buried up above. On the opposite side of the church you can ascend to the roof and dome (without lift L5000, with lift L6000) – though you'll probably need to queue – from where the views over the city are as glorious as you'd expect.

A five-minute walk out of the northern side of the piazza takes you up to the only part of the Vatican Palace you can visit independently, the **Vatican Museums** (July–Sept Mon–Fri 9am–4pm, Sat 9am–1pm; Oct–June Mon–Sat 9am–1pm; L12,000, last Sun of month free) – quite simply, the largest, richest, most compelling museum complex in the world, stuffed with booty from every period of the city's history. There's no point in trying to see everything on one visit; you'd do far better to select what you want to see and aim to return another time if you can. It's worth also taking account of the official, colour-coded routes which are constructed for varying amounts of time and interest and can take you anything from 45 minutes to the best part of a day.

Start off at the **Raphael Stanze**, at the opposite end of the building to the entrance, a set of rooms decorated for Pope Julius II by Raphael among others. Of the two most interesting rooms, the **Stanza Eliodoro** is home to the *Expulsion of Heliodorus from the Temple*, an allusion to the military success of Julius II, depicted on the left in portrait. Not to be outdone, Leo X, Julius's successor, in the *Meeting of Atilla and Saint Leo* opposite, ordered Raphael to substitute his head for that of Julius II, turning the painting into an allegory of the Battle of Ravenna at which he was present; thus he appears twice, as pope and as the equally portly Medici cardinal just behind. In the same room, the *Mass at Bolsena* shows Julius again on the right, pictured in attendance at a famous thirteenth-century miracle in Orvieto. The next room, the **Stanza della Segnatura** or Pope's study, was decorated between 1512 and 1514, and its *School of Athens*, on the near wall as you come in, is perhaps Raphael's most renowned work, a representation of the "Triumph of Scientific Truth" in which all the great minds from antiquity are present. Plato and Aristotle discuss philosophy in the background, spread across the steps is Diogenes, lazily ignorant of all that is happening around him, while to the right Raphael cheekily added a solitary, sullen portrait of his rival Michelangelo, who was working practically next door on the Sistine Chapel at the time.

Steps lead down from the Raphael Stanze to the **Sistine Chapel**, a huge barn-like structure, built for Pope Sixtus IV in 1481, which serves as the pope's private chapel and is scene of the conclaves of cardinals for the election of each new pontiff. The **paintings** down each side wall are contemporary with the building, depictions of scenes from the lives of Moses and Christ by Perugino, Botticelli and Ghirlandaio among others. But it's the **ceiling frescoes** of Ghirlandaio's pupil, Michelangelo, depicting the *Creation*, that everyone comes to see, executed almost single-handed over a period of about four years, again for Pope Julius II. Whether the ceiling has been improved by the controversial recent restoration (financed by a Japanese TV company in return for world rights) is a moot point, but the virtuosity of the work remains stunningly impressive. Restorers have been able to chart the progress of Michelangelo as he moved across the vault; comparing the different areas of plaster, it seems the figure of Adam, in the key *Creation of Adam* scene, took just four days; God, in the same fresco, three days. Restoration work is now underway on the fresco of the *Last Judgement*, on the west wall of the chapel, painted by Michelangelo over twenty years later, and quite possibly the most inspired large-scale painting you'll ever see. Perhaps unsurprisingly, the painting offended some, and even before it was complete Rome was divided as to its merits, especially regarding the etiquette of introducing such a display of nudity into the pope's chapel; Michelangelo's response to this was unequivocal, lampooning one of his fiercer critics with ass's ears and an entwined serpent in the bottom right-hand corner of the picture. Later, the pope's zealous successor, Pius IV, objected to the painting and would have had it removed had not Michelangelo's pupil, Daniele da Volterra, appeased him by carefully adding coverings to some of the more obvious nude figures, earning himself forever the nickname of the "breeches-maker".

Having seen the Raphael rooms and the Sistine Chapel, you've barely scratched the surface of the Vatican. At the opposite end of the Vatican Palace are grouped most of the other museums. In the main body of the palace, the small **Museo Pio-Clementino** holds some of the best of the Vatican's classical statuary, including the serene *Apollo Belvedere*, a Roman copy of a fourth-century BC original, and the second-century BC *Laöcoön*, which depicts the treacherous priest of Apollo being crushed with his sons by serpents. Near the Pio-Clementino museum, the **Museo Chiaramonti** and **Braccio Nuovo** hold more classical sculpture, the **Museo Egizio** has lots of mummies, and the **Museo Gregoriano Etrusco** offers sculpture, funerary art and applied art from the sites of southern Etruria. In a separate building, the **Pinacoteca** has works from the early to High Renaissance: pieces by Crivelli, Lippi and Giotto; the rich backdrops and elegantly clad figures of the Umbrian painters Perugino and Pinturrichio; Raphael's unfinished *Transfiguration*, which hung above the artist as he lay in state, Leonardo's *St. Jerome* and Caravaggio's *Descent from the Cross* – a warts 'n' all canvas that is imitated successfully by Reni's *Crucifixion of St Peter* in the same room. Nearby, the **Museo Gregoriano Profano** holds more classical sculpture, mounted on scaffolds for all-round viewing; the adjacent **Museo Pio Cristiano** has intricate early Christian sarcophagi, and, most famously, an expressive third-century statue of the *Good Shepherd*. Finally, the **Museo Missionario Etnologico** displays art and artefacts from all over the world, collected by Catholic missionaries.

Eating and drinking

It's relatively simple to **eat** cheaply and well in Rome, certainly easier than in Venice or Florence. Prices – even in the city centre – are reasonable, and the quality remains of a fair standard. You'll find a good array of places in the *centro storico*, not all of them tourist traps by any means, and Via Cavour and up around Stazione Termini is a good source of cheaply priced restaurants – though the area isn't renowned for its food quality rating. Similarly, you can eat cheaply in the Borgo district around the Vatican. Trastevere is Rome's traditional restaurant ghetto – touristy now, inevitably, but still the home of some fine and not overpriced eateries, and Testaccio is also a popular evening place with a good selection of restaurants and pizzerias to choose from.

Snacks, cakes and ice cream

Bernasconi, Largo Argentina 1. One of the oldest and busiest *pasticcerie* in town, and also a central daytime bar.

Corso Chianti, Via del Gesù 88. Sit-down snacks or full meals in small, friendly and popular place. Arrive early.

Il Delfino, Corso V. Emanuele 67. Central and very busy cafeteria with huge choice of snacks and full meals. Good for a fast fill-up between sights.

Gelateria della Palma, Via della Maddalena 20. Designer ice cream in a choice of 104 flavours including fig, pomegranate, avocado and muesli. Currently Rome's best.

Giolitti, Via Offici del Vicaro 40. An Italian institution which once had a reputation for the country's top ice cream. Still pretty good, however, with a choice of 70 flavours.

Tre Scalini, Piazza Navona. Renowned for its absolutely remarkable *tartufo* – death by chocolate.

Restaurants

Da Augusto, Piazza de Renzi 15. Relaxed and genuine restaurant in a quiet piazza off the tourist beat. Recommended.

Da Baffetto, Via Governo Vecchio 114. Authentic pizzeria that has long been a Rome institution, though it now tends to be swamped by tourists. Amazingly, it's still good value – although service can be off-ish – but you'll always have to queue.

Il Boscaiolo, Via degli Artisti 137. Good-value pizzeria close by the Spanish Steps. Open until 2.30am.

Il Corallo, Via del Corallo 10. Friendly restaurant which attracts a lively crowd and serves way above average quality food – especially pizzas – though it ain't cheap.

La Diligenza Rossa, Via Merulana 271. Low-priced, convivial eatery full of locals.

Dragon Garden, Via del Boschetto 41. Run by an Italo/Chinese couple, and probably the best-value Chinese in the city. Slow service but worth waiting for.

Filetti di Baccala, Largo dei Librari 88. Paper-covered Formica tables, cheap wine and beer, and fried fish dishes for L3000. Recommended.

La Fraschetta, Via di San Francesco di Ripa 134. The calmer Trastevere alternative to *Ivo*, less well-known, with good pizzas and above-average desserts.

Grappola d'Oro, Piazza della Cancelleria 80. Curiously untouched place with genuine Roman cuisine and a traditional trattoria feel. Prices in upper bracket.

Hosteria Angelo, Via P. Amedeo 104. Appealing atmosphere, average prices and above average menu. Probably the best choice this side of the Termini tracks.

Hosteria l'Archetto, Via F. Turati 106. Straightforward Termini restaurant, serving decent food at decent rates.

Hosteria da Bruno, Via Varese 29. Shade more pricy than others in the Termini area, but quieter and – tellingly – with no English menu.

L'Insalata Ricca, Largo di Charivari 85. Relaxed and slightly out-of-the-ordinary place, with interesting salads and healthy Italian food.

Ivo, Via di San Francesco a Ripa 157. *The* Trastevere pizzeria. Arrive early to avoid a chaotic queue. Recommended, but in danger of becoming a caricature.

Al Leoncino, Via del Leoncino 28. Cheap and genuine city centre pizzeria, little known to out-of-towners.

Mario's, Via del Moro 53. Well-known to tourists and much-frequented Trastevere cheapie. Atmospheric and a genuine bargain, but service can be excruciatingly slow.

Il Piccolo Alpino, Via Orazio Antinori 5. Testaccio neighbourhood restaurant with good pizzas and great *spaghetti alle vongole*.

Il Piccolo Arancio, Vicolo Scanderberg 112. Handily placed restaurant just around the corner from the Trevi fountain. Excellent low-priced food and a cosy atmosphere.

Pizza Economica, Via Tiburtina 44. This well-named restaurant is a legend among the cheaper Rome eateries. The cheapest pizza in town.

Pizzeria-Steakhouse, Via Montebello 77. Despite the name, one of the best-value and friendliest of the Termini area eateries.

Popi-Popi, Via delle Fratte di Trastevere. Good place to eat in summer, when there's a number of tables outside. Not expensive either.

Remo, Piazza Santa Maria Liberatrice 44. Cheap, crowded and chaotic pizzeria in the heart of Testaccio.

Romanesca, Piazza di Campo dei Fiori 23. On the Campo, so inevitably it attracts some tourists, but it's used by market traders and retains a very Roman atmosphere.

Bars and birrerias

Antica Café della Pace, Via della Pace 5. Just off Piazza Navona, this is *the* summer bar, with outside tables full of Rome's self-consciously beautiful people.

Bar San Calisto, Piazza San Calisto 4. Basic Trastevere bar that attracts an eclectic bunch of late-night drinkers. Outside tables in summer.

Druid's, Via San Martino ai Monti 28. Appealing Irish pub with a mixed expat/Italian clientele. Cheap and lively, with occasional impromptu music.

Enoteca Cavour, Via Cavour 313. At the Forum end of Via Cavour, a handy retreat with an easy-going studenty feel, lots of wine and bottled beers and (slightly overpriced) snacks.

Fiddler's Elbow, Via dell'Omarta 43. Irish bar, roomier than *Druid's* and with a decidedly more Latin feel.

La Scala, Piazza della Scala. The most popular Trastevere birreria – big, bustling and crowded. Pub food, cheap beer and occasional (dire) music. Recommended.

Trasté, Via della Lungheretta 76. Refined meeting place for the young and cultured Trastevere crowd. Emphasis more on fancy teas then getting oiled.

La Vetrina, Via della Vetrina 20. Cocktail bar with the occasional disco, poetry reading and cabaret, popular with trendy artist types and their entourages.

Vineria, Campo de' Fiori. Small vineria which spills out into the square during the summer months.

Nightlife

Roman **nightlife** still retains some of the smart ethos satirized in Fellini's *Dolce Vita*. **Discos and clubs** cover the range: there are vast glittering palaces with stunning lights and sound systems, places that are not much more than upmarket bars with music, and other, more down-to-earth places to dance, playing a more interesting selection of music to a younger crowd, with the new *centri sociali* offering an innovative alternative to the mainstream scene. Whichever you prefer, all tend to open and close late, and some charge a heavy entrance fee, most around L20,000, the more spectacular places as much as L35,000–40,000 – though these often include one free drink. Rome's **rock scene** is a fairly limp affair, and the city is much more in its element with **jazz**, with lots of venues and a wide choice of styles performed by a healthy array of local talent. Sadly most clubs close during July and August, or move to locations on the coast; bear in mind, too, that you may have to pay a membership fee on top of the admission price. Drinks, though, are generally no more expensive than you'd pay in the average bar.

The city's best source of **listings** is the *TrovaRoma* supplement published with the Thursday edition of *La Repubblica*. For English-language information, there's *Wanted in Rome* or *Metropolitan*, and the EPT publishes *Carnet di Roma* (free). First stop for **tickets** should be *Orbis* at Piazza Esquilino 37 (☎482.7403).

Centri sociali

In the suburbs of Rome, new *centri sociali* are being opened in abandoned public buildings by squatters who offer a cheap, alternative programme of concerts, films and parties. The squatters are politically active, and work for and with newly arrived immigrants, the events they organize being among the more interesting that take place in Rome. The numerous *centri sociali* are listed in *TrovaRoma* and *Il Manifesto*.

Forte Prenestino, Via F. del Pino. One of the most established *centri* situated in an abandoned nineteenth-century fortress. Offers two big arenas for concerts and a beehive of smaller spaces used for exhibitions, cinema, a disco and a bar.

Villaggio Globale, Ex-Mattatoio. Located in the old slaughterhouse in Testaccio this *centro* works with the African community in Rome organizing concerts, parties and exhibitions, helped by a grant from local authorities.

Discos and clubs

L'Alibi, Via Monte Testaccio 44. Predominantly but not exclusively male venue that's one of Rome's best gay clubs. Downstairs cellar disco and upstairs open-air bar.

Alien, Via Velletri. Rome's trendiest club, this place is host to the best dance DJs.

Angelo Azzurro, Via Cardinale Merry del Val. Relaxed gay club with a mixed crowd.

Blue Zone, Via Campania 37. Popular disco open until 4am playing a mix of house and grunge.

Frankie Gio, Via Sciapparelli 39. Newly opened club popular with younger trendies.

Gilda, Via Mario de' Fiori 97. Slick, stylish club, the focus for the city's minor (and would-be) celebs.

Piper, Via Tagliamento 9. One of the oldest discos in Rome, with live music, videos and different nightly events.

Soul II Soul, Via dei Fienaroli 30/a. One of the few mixed clubs, playing black music from African to rap. In summer moves to outdoor locations.

Veleno, Via Sardegna 27. Happening club playing house, hip hop and soul off Via Veneto. Pricy.

Live music: rock, jazz and Latin

Alpheus, Via del Commercio 36–38. A four-roomed venue with simultaneous concerts, a disco, theatrical performances and a bar.

Big Mama's, Vicolo San Francesco a Ripa 18. Trastevere-based jazz/blues club of long standing. Closed July–Sept.

Caffè Latino, Via Monte Testaccio 96. Multi-event club in the newly hip area near the Protestant cemetery. Best at weekends when it's crowded and more atmospheric.

Fonclea, Via Crescenzio 82a. Long running jazz/salsa outfit, with live music most nights.

Melvyn's, Via Politeama 8. Roman bands of every musical shade nightly. Open until 4am.

Palladium, Piazza B. Romano 8. International groups come to this old cinema in the southern suburbs. One of the few live-music venues where dancing is encouraged.

St Louis, Via del Cardello 13a. Modern club known for serious, high-quality music. Membershoip is L20,000 a year. Live jazz, restaurant and cocktail bar. Closed July–Oct.

Yes! Brazil, Via San Francesco a Ripa 103. Brazilian-staffed bar with live Latin music nightly.

Classical music, opera and film

During the summer there are quite a few places you can hear **classical music**. The city's churches host a wide range of choral, chamber and organ recitals, many of them free. Year-round, the *Accademia di Santa Cecilia* (☎654.1044) stages concerts by its own or visiting orchestras at Via dei Greci 18 (☎678.3996) and in summer in the Piazza del Campidoglio. Rome's **opera** scene concentrates on the *Teatro dell'Opera*, on the corner of Via Torino and Piazza Beniamino Gigli (☎461.755), from November to May. Tickets go on sale two days before the performance at 10am–1pm and 5–7pm. In summer the season moves outdoors to the remains of the Roman baths at *Terme di Caracalla*, a spectacular location for what usually turn out to be epic productions. Purists should be prepared for a carnival atmosphere and plenty of unscheduled intervals. Rome's only **English-language cinema** is the *Pasquino* on Vicolo del Piede in Trastevere (☎580.3632), which shows recent general releases. Tickets are currently L4000. Other cinemas show foreign-language films on certain nights: the *Nuovo Sacher*, Largo Ascianghi 1 (☎581.8116), and *Alcazar*, Via Cardinal Merry del Val 114 (☎588.0099).

Listings

Airlines *Alitalia*, Via Bissolati 20 (☎46881); *British Airways*, Via Bissolati 54 (☎479.991); *TWA*, Via Barberini 67 (☎47211).

American Express Piazza di Spagna 38 (Mon–Fri 9am–5.30pm, Sat 9am–12.30pm; ☎72782).

Books The *Lion Bookshop*, Via del Babuino 181 (☎322.5837), is the city's biggest and best-stocked English-language bookstore. Try also the *Economy Book Center*, Via Torino 136 (☎474.6877), which has a good stock of new and used English-language paperbacks.

Car rental *Avis*, Termini Station (☎470.1219); *Europcar*, Via Lombardia 7 (☎487.1274); *Hertz*, Via Gregorio VII (☎3937.8807); *Maggiore*, Termini Station (☎488.0049).

Embassies *Australia*, Via Alessandria 215 (☎852.721); *Canada*, Via G.B. de Rossi 27 (☎841.5341); *Great Britain*, Via XX Settembre 80 (☎482.5551); *Netherlands*, Via Mercati 8 (☎322.1141); *New Zealand*, Via Zara 2 (☎440.2928); *USA*, Via V. Veneto 119 (☎46741).

Exchange Two offices at Termini station operate out of banking hours; also *Thomas Cook*, Via Barberini 21 (☎482.8082), or *Cambio Rosai*, Via Nazionale 186 (☎488.5498).

Hospital The most central hospital is the Santo Sprito, Lungotevere in Sassia 1 (☎68351). In case of emergency call ☎462.371.

Laundry Via Montebello 11.

Left luggage At Stazione Termini 7am–9pm; L1500 per item per day.

Pharmacies Call ☎1921 for a list of late-opening pharmacies in central Rome. Or try *PIRAM*, Via Nazionale 228 (☎488.0754).

Police The police station/foreign office is *Questura*, Via Genova 3 (☎4686.2987).

Post office Main office on Piazza San Silvestro (Mon–Fri 8.30am–9pm, Sat 8.30am–noon; ☎160 for information).

Telephones Phone booths at Stazione Termini (daily 8am–10.50pm); main post office (daily 8am–10.50pm).

Train enquiries ☎4775. The information booth at Termini is open daily 7am–11.30pm.

Travel agents *CTS*, Via Genova 16 (☎446.791), and Corso Vittorio Emanuele II 297 (☎687.2672); *Elsy Viaggi*,Via di Torre Argentina 80 (☎683.2097).

Women's Rome The women's bookshop, *Al Tempo Ritrovato*, on Piazza Farnese is the best place for contacts and information.

Around Rome

You may find there's quite enough of interest in Rome to keep you occupied during your stay. But Rome can be a hot and oppressive city, and you really shouldn't feel any guilt about freeing yourself from its weighty history to see something of the countryside around. Two of the main attractions visitable on a day trip are, it's true, Roman sites, but just the process of getting to them can be energizing.

Tivoli

Just 40km from Rome, **TIVOLI** has always been something of a retreat from the city. In classical days it was a retirement town for wealthy Romans; later, during Renaissance times, it again became the playground of the monied classes, attracting some of the city's most well-to-do families out here to build villas.

Most people head first for the **Villa d'Este** (daily 9am–4/7pm; L5,000), the country villa of Cardinal Ippolito d'Este, across the main square of Largo Garibaldi. It's the gardens rather than the villa itself that they come to see, peeling away down the hill in a succession of terraces – probably the most contrived gardens in Italy, interrupted at decent intervals by one playful fountain after another, unfortunately not all in working order. In their day some of these were quite ingenious – one played the organ, another imitated the call of birds – though nowadays the emphasis is on the quieter creations. There's the central *Fontana di Bicchierone* by Bernini, one of the simplest and most elegant; on the far left, the *Rometta* or "Little Rome" has reproductions of the major buildings of the city; while the *Fontana del Ovato*, on the opposite side of the garden, has statues and an arcade in which you can walk. The town's other attraction, the **Villa Gregoriana** (daily 9am–7pm; L2500), is a park with waterfalls created when Pope Gregory XVI diverted the flow of the river here in 1831 to ease periodic flooding of the town. It's less well-known than the d'Este estate, with none of the latter's conceits, its vegetation lush and overgrown, descending into a gorge over 60m deep. There are two main waterfalls – the larger *Grande Cascata* on the far side, and a small Bernini-designed one at the neck of the gorge. The path winds down to the bottom of the canyon, where you can get right up close to the pounding water, the dark shapes of the rock glowering overhead. From here the path leads up on the far side to an exit and the substantial remains of a **Temple of Vesta**, clinging to the side of the hill.

Once you've seen these two sights you've really seen Tivoli. But just outside at the bottom of the hill, fifteen minutes' walk off the main Rome road (*CAT* bus #4 from Largo Garibaldi), the **Villa Adriana** (daily 9am–1hr before sunset; L8000) casts the inventions of the Tivoli popes and cardinals very much into the shade. This was probably the largest and most sumptuous villa in the Roman empire, the retirement home of the Emperor Hadrian for a short while between 135 AD and his death three years later, and it is now one of the most soothing spots around Rome. Hadrian was a great traveller and a keen architect, and parts of the villa were inspired by buildings he had seen around the world. The massive Pecile for instance, through which you enter, is a reproduction of a building in Athens. And the Canopus, on the opposite side of the site, is a liberal copy of the sanctuary of Serapis near Alexandria, its long, elegant channel of water fringed by columns and statues. Nearby, a museum displays the latest finds from the excavations, though most of the extensive original discoveries have found their way back to Rome. Back towards the entrance, there's a fish pond with a *cryptoporticus* winding around underneath, and – perhaps the most-photographed part of the site – the Teatro Marittimo, with its island in the middle of a circular pond, to which it's believed Hadrian would retire at siesta time.

Buses leave Rome for Tivoli every half an hour from Rebiba Metro Station; tickets cost L4000 return from the office on the right –journey time 45 minutes. In Tivoli they stop at and leave from the main Largo Garibaldi, opposite the **tourist office** (Mon–Sat 9am–2pm), which has information on accommodation if you're planning to stay over.

Ostia

There are two Ostias, both reachable in around thirty minutes by regular metro from Magliana, then train: one, Lido di Ostia, is an over-visited seaside resort that is well worth avoiding; the other, the excavations of the port of **OSTIA ANTICA**, is on a par with anything you'll see in Rome itself and easily merits a half-day's outing (daily 9am–1hr before sunset; L8000). The site groups around the the town's commercial centre, otherwise known as the **Piazzale di Corporazione** for the remains of shops and trading offices that still fringe it, the mosaics in front of which denote their trade. Flanking one side of the square, the **theatre** has been much restored but is nonetheless impressive, enlarged in the second century to hold up to 4000 people. On the left of the square, the **House of Apulius** preserves mosaic floors and, beyond, a dark aisled *mithraeum* with more mosaics illustrating the cult. Behind here, the **Casa di Diana** is probably the best preserved private house in Ostia, with a dark set of rooms around a central courtyard, and again with a *mithraeum* at the back. You can climb up to its roof for a fine view of the rest of the site, afterwards crossing the road to the **Thermopolium** – an ancient Roman café, complete with seats, counter, display shelves and even wall paintings of parts of the menu. North of the Casa di Diana, the **Museum** (daily 9am–1pm & 2–6pm) holds a variety of articles from the site, including wall paintings depicting domestic life in Ostia and some fine sarcophagi and statuary. Left from here, the **Forum** centres on the **Capitol** building, reached by a wide flight of steps.

Anzio

About 40km south of Rome, **ANZIO** is much the best bet for a day by the sea if you're staying in Rome. Much of the town was damaged during a difficult Allied landing here on January 22, 1944, to which two military cemeteries (one British, one, at nearby Nettuno, American) bear testimony. But despite a pretty thorough rebuilding it's a likeable resort, still depending as much on fish as tourists for its livelihood. The town's seafood **restaurants** are reason enough to come, crowding together along the harbour and not unreasonably priced, and the **beaches**, which edge the coast on either side, don't get unbearably stuffed outside August. Anzio is also a possible route on to the islands of Ponza or Ischia, or Naples, for which **hydrofoils** leave daily in summer – ask for timings at the **tourist office** in the harbour (daily 9am–12.30pm & 5–8pm).

THE SOUTH

The Italian south or *mezzogiorno* is quite a different experience from the north; indeed, few countries are more tangibly divided into two distinct, often antagonistic, regions. While the north is rich, the south is by contrast one of the most depressed areas in Europe. Its rate of unemployment (about twenty percent) is around twice that of the north, its gross regional product about a third. Its people are dark-skinned and speak with the cadences of the Mediterranean, the dialect down here sounding almost Arabic sometimes. Indeed the south's "capital", Naples, is often compared to Cairo.

For most people, **Naples**, regional capital of **Campania** and only a couple of hours south of Rome, is the obvious focus, an utterly compelling city, dominating the region in every way. The **Bay of Naples** is dense in interest, with the ancient sites of Pompeii and Herculaneum just half an hour outside – probably Italy's best preserved and most revealing Roman remains – and the island of Cápri, swarmed over by tourists these days but so beautiful that a day there is by no means time squandered. South of Naples, **Sorrento**, at the far east end of the Bay, has all the beer 'n' chips trappings you'd expect from a major Brit package destination, but is a likeable place for all that; and the **Amalfi Coast**, across the peninsula, is probably Europe's most dramatic stretch of coastline, harbouring some enticing – if crowded – beach resorts. **Puglia** is the long strip of land that makes up the "heel" of Italy. It was for centuries a strategic province, colonized, invaded and conquered (like its near neighbours Calabria and Sicily), by just about every major power of the day. There's no escaping some of these historical influences – in the Saracenic casbah-like quarters of cities like **Bari**, and the Baroque exuberance of **Lecce** – although Puglia is still very much a province you pass through on the way elsewhere, not least to **Brindisi**, which is known and visited for its ferry connections with Greece. **Basilicata** and **Calabria**, too, are to some extent transit regions, although in many ways they represent the quintessence of the *mezzogiorno* – culturally impoverished, underdeveloped and – owing to emigration – sparsely populated. Artistically they are the most barren regions in Italy, but the combination of mountain grandeur and a relatively unspoilt coastline, often in close proximity, is a unique attraction, only now beginning to be exploited by the tourist industry.

Naples

Wherever else you travel south of Rome, the chances are that you'll wind up in **NAPLES** – capital of the whole Italian South. It's the kind of city people visit with preconceptions, and it rarely disappoints: it is filthy, large and overbearing; it is crime-infested; and it is most definitely like nowhere else in Italy – something the inhabitants will be keener than anyone to tell you. In all these things lies the city's charm. Perhaps the feeling that you're somewhere unique makes it possible to endure the noise and constant harassment, perhaps it's the feeling that you've travelled from an ordinary part of Europe to somewhere that feels like an Arab bazaar in less than three hours. One thing, though, is certain: a couple of days here and you're likely to be as staunch a defender of the place as its most devoted inhabitants. No city on earth, except perhaps New York, excites fiercer loyalties.

> The Naples area telephone code is ☎081.

Arrival and information

Naples' **Capodochino Airport** is northwest of the city centre at Viale Umberto Maddalena, connected with Piazza Garibaldi by bus #14 about every fifteen minutes. The journey takes about thirty minutes – not much more than a taxi, for which you'll pay at least L20,000; there's also a blue bus taking you straight to the port and Piazza Municipo (L3000), leaving every thirty minutes. Arriving by train, Napoli Centrale is on Piazza Garibaldi, at the main hub of all transport services. There's a **tourist office** (Mon–Sat 8.30am–8pm, Sun 8.30am–2pm) in Stazione Centrale, another at Via Partenope 10a (Mon–Sat 8.30am–2pm, Sun 8.30am–noon), on the seafront near Villa Communale, one at Capodichino Airport (7.30am–7pm), and another on Piazza del Gesù, which provides the informative *Pianto Stratificato* giving details of the different architectural periods. All have free maps of the city, information on accommodation, and copies of the free monthly booklet *Qui Napoli*, handy for current events, ferry and bus times.

City transport

The only way to really get around Naples and stay sane is to walk. However, Naples is a large, sprawling city, and its transport services extend to the bay as a whole, which means you'll definitely need to use some form of public transport sooner or later. City **buses** are much the best way of crossing the city centre: fares are a flat L1000 per journey; buy tickets in advance from tobacconists or the booth on Piazza Garibaldi; half-day tickets are also available for L1500. The bus system is supplemented by the **metropolitana**, a small underground network which crosses the centre and runs around the bay, and **funiculars** scaling the hill of the Vómero from stations at Piazzas Montesanto, Amadeo and Augusto. For **trips around the bay** in either direction, there are three rail systems, the most useful of which is the **Circumvesuviana**, which runs from its station on Corso Garibaldi around the Bay of Naples about every half-hour as far as Sorrento, which it reaches in about an hour.

Accommodation

A good many of the city's cheaper **hotels** are situated around Piazza Garibaldi, within spitting distance of the train station and not badly placed for the rest of town. The *San Pietro*, Via San Pietro ad Aram 14 (☎553.5914; ③), has clean if characterless rooms; off Piazza Garibaldi to the right is the pleasant *Casanova*, Corso Garibaldi 333 (☎268.287; ②). With a little more money, the *Odeon*, on Via Silvio Spaventa (☎285.656; ③), is a two-star hotel two minutes from the station. Enjoying a rather nicer location over in the *centro storico*, the *Imperia*, Piazza Miraglia 386 (☎459.347; ③), is a homely, clean and fairly comfortable hotel. There's a **youth hostel** in the district of Mergellina at Salita della Grotta 23 (☎761.2346; ②) – a nice location but a long way out and there's also an midnight curfew and a three-day maximum stay during July and August. Take the metropolitana to Mergellina or bus #152 from Piazza Garibaldi. The closest **campsite** is the *Vulcano Solfatara* site in nearby Pozzuoli at Via Solfatara 161 (☎ 526.7413), open between April and mid-October. Bus #152 runs right there from Piazza Garibaldi, or take the metropolitana to Pozzuoli and walk ten minutes up the hill. Out of these months, you're probably best off going to one of the other sites around the Bay – at Pompeii or Sorrento, both of which are less than an hour out from the city.

The City

Naples is a large city, with a centre that has many different focuses. The area between the vast and busy Piazza Garibaldi, where you will arrive, and Via Toledo, the main street a mile or so west, makes up the old part of the city – the **centro storico**. Buildings rise high on either side of the narrow, crowded streets, cobwebbed with washing; there's little light, not even much sense of the rest of the city outside – certainly not of the proximity of the sea. The two main drags of the *centro storico* are **Via dei Tribunali** and **Via San Biagio dei Librai** – two narrow streets, lined with old arcaded buildings, that are a maelstrom of hurrying pedestrians, revving cars and buzzing, dodging scooters. Via dei Tribunali cuts through to **Via Duomo**, a little way up which is the tucked-away **Duomo**, a Gothic building from the early thirteenth century dedicated to the patron saint of the city, San Gennaro. The church – and saint – are key reference points for Neapolitans: San Gennaro was martyred at Pozzuoli, just outside Naples, in 305 AD. When his body was transferred here, tradition has it that two phials of his blood liquefied in the bishop's hands, since which time the "miracle" has continued to repeat itself no fewer than three times a year – on the first Saturday in May (when a procession leads from the church of Santa Chiara to the cathedral) and on September 19 and December 16. Much superstition still surrounds this event: San Gennaro is seen as the saviour and protector of Naples, and if the blood refuses to liquefy – which luckily is rare – disaster is supposed to befall the city, and many still wait with bated breath to see if the miracle has occurred. The first chapel on the right as you walk into the cathedral holds the precious phials and Gennaro's skull in a silver bust-reliquary from 1305. On the other side of the church, the basilica of Santa Restituta is almost a church in its own right, officially the oldest structure in Naples, erected by Constantine in 324 and supported by columns that were taken from a temple to Apollo on this site. Downstairs, the crypt of San Gennaro is one of the finest examples of Renaissance art in Naples, founded by Cardinal Carafa and holding the tombs of both San Gennaro and Pope Innocent IV.

Across Via Duomo, Via dei Tribunali continues on into the city's busiest and most architecturally rich quarter, the so-called **Spaccanapoli** or "split-Naples" that's the heart of the old city. Cut down to its other main axis, **Via San Biagio dei Libra**, which leads west to **Piazza San Domenico Maggiore**, marked by the **Guglia di San Domenico** – one of the whimsical Baroque obelisks that pop up all over the city, built in 1737. The **church** of the same name flanks the north side of the square, an originally Gothic building from 1289, one of whose chapels holds a miraculous painting of the *Crucifixion* which is said to have spoken to Saint Thomas Aquinas during his time at the adjacent monastery. North, Via de Sanctis leads off right to one of the city's odder monuments, the **Capella Sansevero** (Mon–Sat 10am–1pm & 5–6.40pm, Sun 10am–1pm; L5000), the tomb-chapel of the di Sangro family, which was decorated by the sculptor Guiseppe Sammartino in the mid-eighteenth century with some remarkable carving – a dead *Christ*, covered with a veil of stark realism, a veiled figure of *Modesty*, and its twin *Disillusionment*, in the form of a woeful figure struggling with the marble netting of his own disenchantment. You might also want to take a look downstairs. The man responsible for the chapel, Prince Raimondo, was a well-known alchemist, and down here are the results of some of his experiments: two bodies under glass, their capillaries and most of their organs preserved by a mysterious liquid developed by the prince. Even now they make for gruesome sights.

Continuing west, the **Gesù Nuovo** church is most notable for its lava-stone facade, originally part of a fifteenth-century palace which stood here, prickled with pyramids that give it an impregnable, prison-like air. The inside is in part decorated by the Neapolitan-Spanish painter Ribera. Facing the Gesù church, the church of **Santa Chiara** is quite different, a Provençal-Gothic structure built in 1328 and rebuilt after the last war with a bare Gothic austerity that's pleasing after the excesses opposite. There's not very much to see inside, only the tombs of the Angevin monarchs, including Robert the Wise at the altar, showing the king in a monk's habit. But the attached cloister is one of the gems of the city, lushly planted and furnished with benches and walls covered with colourful majolica tiles depicting bucolic scenes of life outside.

Piazza del Municipio is a busy traffic junction that stretches down to the waterfront, dominated by the brooding hulk of the **Castel Nuovo**, erected in 1282 by the Angevins and later converted as the royal residence of the Aragon monarchs, and now containing the **Museo Civico** (daily 9am–7pm, Sun closes 1pm; L10,000) which has periodic exhibitions within a series of elaborate Gothic rooms. Saunter up to the entrance of the Castel for a look at the triumphal arch that it incorporates; built in 1454 to commemorate the taking of the city by Alfonso I, the first Aragon ruler, it shows details of his triumph topped by a rousing statue of Saint Michael. Just beyond the castle, on the left, the **Teatro San Carlo** (tours daily 9am–noon subject to rehearsals) is still the largest opera house in Italy, and one of the most distinguished in the world. Beyond, at the bottom of the main shopping street of Via Toledo, the **Palazzo Reale** (Mon–Sat 9am–7pm, Sun 9am–1pm; L6000) manages better than most of the buildings around here to retain some semblance of dignity, though it was thrown up hurriedly in 1602 to accommodate a visit by Philip II. Upstairs, the palace's first-floor rooms are decorated with gilded furniture, tromp l'oeil ceilings, great overbearing tapestries and lots and lots of undistinguished seventeenth- and eighteenth-century paintings. Best are the chapel, with its finely worked altarpiece, and the little theatre which is refreshingly restrained after the rest of the palace. Look also at the original bronze doors of the palace, at the bottom of the dwarfing main staircase, cast in 1468 and showing scenes from Ferdinand of Aragon's struggle against the local barons. The cannonball wedged in the bottom panel dates from a naval battle between the French and the Genoese that took place while the former were pillaging the doors from the palace.

Via Toledo leads north from Piazza Trieste e Trento to the **Museo Archeologico Nazionale** (daily 9am–7pm; L8000, children and over 65s free; bus #110 from Piazza Garibaldi) – perhaps Naples' most essential sight, home to the Farnese collection of antiquities from Lazio and Campania, and the best of the finds from the nearby Roman sites of Pompeii and Herculaneum. The ground floor of the museum concentrates on sculpture from the Farnese collection, displayed at its best in the mighty Great Hall, which holds imperial-era figures like the *Farnese Bull* and *Farnese Hercules* from the Baths of Caracalla in Rome – the former the largest piece of classical sculpture ever found. The mezzanine floor at the back houses the museum's collection of mosaics – remarkably preserved works all giving a superb insight into ordinary Roman customs, beliefs and humour, while upstairs, the Campanian wall paintings are the museum's other major draw, lifted from the villas of Pompeii and Herculaneum, and rich in colour and invention. Look out, too, for the group of four small pictures in the first main room, best of which is a depiction of a woman gathering flowers entitled *Primavera*. There are also actual finds from the Campanian cities – everyday items like glass, silver, ceramics, charred pieces of rope, even foodstuffs, together with a model layout of Pompeii in cork – and, on the other side of the first floor, finds from the **Villa dei Papiri** in Herculaneum – sculptures in bronze mainly, including a superb *Hermes at Rest*, a languid *Resting Satyr* and a convincingly woozy *Drunken Silenus*.

At the top of the hill is the city's other major museum, the **Palazzo Reale di Capodimonte** (daily 9am–7pm, Sun closes 1pm; L8000; buses #110 or #127 from Piazza Garibaldi, #160 or #161 from Piazza Dante), the former residence of the Bourbon King Charles III, built in 1738 and now housing the **Museo Nazionale di Capodimonte**. This has a superb collection of Renaissance paintings, including a couple of Bruegels – *The Misanthrope* and *The Blind* – canvases by Perugino and Pinturicchio, an elegant *Madonna and Child with Angels* by Botticelli and Lippi's soft, sensitive *Annunciation*. Later paintings include a room full of Titians, with a number of paintings of the shrewd Farnese Pope Paul III in various states of ageing, Raphael's austere portrait of *Leo X*, and Bellini's impressively composed *Transfiguration*.

Vómero – the district topping the hill immediately above the old city, reachable on the Montesanto funicular – also has several museums. The fourteenth-century **Certosa San Martino** has fine views over the bay and is home to the **Museo Nazionale di San Martino** (Tues–Sat 9am–2pm, Sun 9am–1pm; L6000). This features paintings by Neapolitan masters – Ribera, Stanzione, Vaccaro – and some dusty bits and pieces rescued from churches and the odd minor aristocrat, as well as historical and maritime sections displaying models of ships, documents, coins and costumes recording the era of the Kingdom of Naples. The Baroque cloisters are lovely, though rather gone to seed, and there's a display of *presepi* or Christmas cribs – the crafting of which is peculiar to the city and continued avidly today. Ten minutes' walk away, the **Villa Floridiana**, close to the Chiaia funicular, boasts lush grounds (daily 9am–7.30pm), more views and the **Duca di Martino** museum of porcelain (Tues–Sat 9am–7pm, Sun 9am–1pm; L6000) – a mixture of kitsch and restrained good taste. Go up to the star-shaped fortress of **Castel Sant'Elmo** (Mon–Sat 9am–7pm, Sun 9am–1pm; free), built in the fourteenth century and offering superb views over Naples from the parapet.

Eating

Neapolitan cuisine is among Italy's best – simple dishes cooked with fresh, healthy ingredients that have none of the richness or pretensions of the north. It's also the best place in the country to eat **pizza**, which originates from here. If you're just after a **snack**, you can pick something up from the city's **street markets** – the Forcella quarter market on the far side of Piazza Garibaldi or the fish market at Porta Nolana, off to the left – and there are plenty of snack places around Piazza Garibaldi, not to mention **restaurants**, though most of these are of indifferent quality. *O Marenaro*, at Via Casanova 101, is a good place to try one of the most delicious local specialities, *zuppa di cozze* – steamed mussels with hot pepper sauce – and it does great seafood salads, while *Da Michele*, tucked away off Corso Umberto I, at Via Cesare Sersale 1–3, is the most determinedly traditional place to eat real Naples pizza, offering just two varieties – *marinara* and *margherita*. Further into the centre, *Di Matteo*, Via dei Tribunali 94, is a cheap, unpretentious pizzeria, as is *Lombardi*, not far away at Via B. Croce 59. Next door to *Di Matteo*, *Da Carmine* is a simple trattoria with an extensive menu and low prices. *Bellini*, Via Santa Maria di Constantinopoli 80, is a good place for a splurge, one of the city's longest established restaurants, also with great pizzas. A little further on, on Piazza Dante, *Leone d'Oro* is a pleasant, centrally placed restaurant with outdoor seating and reasonably priced food. On the other side of Via Toledo, *Brandi*, Salita Sant'Anna di Palazzo 1–2, off Via Chiaia, is possibly Naples' most famous pizzeria – very friendly, and serving pasta too. *California*, Via Santa Lucia 101, is an institution of a rather different kind, with a menu that's an odd hybrid of American and Italian specialities. It's perhaps best-known for its full American breakfasts.

Listings

Airlines *Alitalia*, Via Medina 41–42 (☎542.5222); *British Airways*, Capodichino Airport (☎780.3087).

Car rental *Avis*, Via Partenope 32 (☎764.5600); *Europcar*, Via Partenope 38 (☎764.5070); *Hertz*, Via Partenope 29 (☎764.5530); *Maggiore*, Via Cervantes 92 (☎552.1900).

Consulates *Great Britain*, Via Crispi 122 (☎ 663.511); *USA*, Piazza della Repubblica (☎583.8111).

Exchange Outside banking hours at Stazione Centrale (daily 7am–9pm).

Hospital ☎751.3177 or go to the 24hr Guardia Medica Permanente in the Palazzo Municipio.

Pharmacy At Stazione Centrale Mon–Sat 8am–8pm.

Police The main station is at Via Medina 75 (☎794.1111); emergencies ☎113.

Post office Main office on Piazza Matteotti, off Via Toledo (Mon–Fri 8am–7.40pm, Sat 8.30am–noon).

Telephones *ASST* at Stazione Centrale is open 24hr, though the *ASST* at Via Depretis 40, also open 24hr, is quieter. The *SIP* office in Galleria Umberto (Mon–Sat 8am–9.30pm) is usually chaotic.

Train enquiries ☎ 554.3188 (daily 7am–midnight). The station booths are open daily 7am–10pm.

Travel agents *CTS*, Via Mezzocannone 25 (☎552.7960).

The Bay of Naples

For the Romans, the **Bay of Naples** was the land of plenty, a blessed region of mild climate, gorgeous scenery and an accessible location that made it a favourite vacation and retirement area for the city's nobility. Later, when Naples became the final stop on northerners' Grand Tours, the relics of its heady Roman period only added to the charm for most travellers. However, these days it's hard to tell where Naples ends and the countryside begins, the city sprawling around the Bay in an industrial and residential mess that is quite at odds with the region's popular image. It's only when you reach **Sorrento** in the east, or the islands that dot the bay, that you really feel free of it all. Of these, **Cápri** is the best place to visit if you're here for a short time, a place of legend, home to the mythical Sirens and a much-eulogized playground of the super-rich in the years since, though now settled down to a lucrative existence as a target for day-trippers from the mainland. There's also, of course, the ever-brooding presence of **Vesuvius**, and the incomparable Roman sites of **Herculaneum** and **Pompeii** – each of which is well worth extending your stay in the city for.

Herculaneum and Vesuvius

The first point of any interest travelling east is the town of **ERCOLANO**, the modern offshoot of the ancient site of Herculaneum, which was destroyed by the eruption of Vesuvius on August 2, 79 AD. It's worth stopping here for two reasons: to see the excavations of the site and to climb to the summit of Vesuvius – to which buses run from outside the train station. If you're planning to visit both Herculaneum and scale Vesuvius in one day, though, be sure to see Vesuvius first, and set off reasonably early – buses stop running up the mountain at lunchtime, leaving you the afternoon free to wander around the site.

Situated at the seaward end of Ercolano's main street, **Herculaneum** (daily 9am–1hr before sunset; L8000) was a residential town in Roman times, much smaller than Pompeii, and as such it's a more manageable site, less architecturally impressive but better preserved and more easily taken in on a single visit. Because it wasn't a commercial town, there is no central open space or forum, just streets of villas and shops, cut as usual by two very straight main streets. The **House of the Mosaic Atrium**, at the bottom end of the main street, Cardo IV, retains its mosaic-laid courtyard, corrugated by the force of the tufa, behind which the **House of the Deer** contains corridors decorated with richly coloured still lifes and a bawdy statue of a drunken Hercules seemingly about to piss all over the visitors. There's also a large **Thermae** or bath complex, with a domed *frigidarium* decorated with frescoes of fish and a *caldarium* containing a plunge bath at one end and a scallop-shell apse complete with washbasin and water pipes. Opposite, in the **House of the Carbonized Furniture**, there's a room with the marital bed still intact and, nearby, portraits of the gent and lady of the house – the former, in the room to the right, marked by a satyr, the latter voluptuously posed on the left-hand wall of an alcove. Close by, the dining room has pictures of Roman dishes and, on the left as you enter, there's a kitchen with an oven in the corner, and a toilet on the other side. Next door, the **House of the Neptune Mosaic** holds another sparklingly preserved mosaic floor, again including portraits of the owners of the household, and flower and vegetable frescoes which served in lieu of a garden; the concrete hatch to the right was a *vomitarium*, which allowed guests to relieve themselves of excess food before proceeding to the next course. Under the house is a wine shop, stocked with amphorae and with a coiled rope left as it lay when disaster struck.

Since its first eruption in 79 AD, when it buried the towns and inhabitants of Pompeii and Herculaneum, **Vesuvius** has dominated the lives of those who live on the Bay of Naples. It's still an active volcano, the only one on mainland Europe and there have been more than a hundred eruptions over the years, but only two of real significance: one in December 1631 that engulfed many nearby towns and killed 3000 people; and the last, in March 1944, which caused widespread devastation in the towns around, though no one was actually killed. The people who live here still fear the reawakening of Vesuvius, and with good reason – scientists calculate it should erupt every thirty years or so, and it hasn't since 1944 – though oddly enough, in this heavily populated area, there are no emergency plans as to what to do when it does.

There are two ways to make the **ascent**. *SITA* run bus services from Ercolano train station to a car park and huddle of souvenir shops and cafés close to the crater (around 6 daily; L3000 return); don't listen to the taxi drivers at the station who will try and persuade you there is no bus. If you've more energy, or have missed the bus, you can also take a local bus (#5) from the roundabout near the station to the end of the line and walk the couple of hours to the car park from there. The walk up to the crater from the car park where the *SITA* bus stops takes about half an hour, across barren gravel on marked-out paths. At the top (admission L4000), the crater is a deep, wide, jagged ashtray of red rock emitting the odd plume of smoke, though since the last eruption effectively sealed up the main crevice this is much less evident than it once was. You can walk most of the way around, but take it easy – the fences are old and rickety.

Pompeii

The other Roman town to be destroyed by Vesuvius, **Pompeii** (daily 9am–1hr before sunset; L10,000) was much larger than Herculaneum, and one of Campania's most important commercial centres. Out of a total population of 20,000, it's thought that only 2000 actually perished, asphyxiated by the toxic fumes of the volcanic debris, their homes buried in several metres of volcanic ash and pumice. In effect, the eruption froze the way of life in Pompeii as it stood at the time, and the excavations here have probably yielded more information about the life of Roman citizens during the imperial era than any other site. The full horror of their way of death is apparent in plaster casts made from the shapes their bodies left in the volcanic ash. Bear in mind, however, that most of the best mosaics and murals have found their way to the Archeological Museum in Naples.

The site covers a wide area, and seeing it properly takes half a day at least. Entering the site from the Pompeii-Villa dei Misteri side, the **Forum** is the first real feature of significance, a slim open space surrounded by the ruins of what would have been some of the town's most important official buildings. North from here, the **House of the Tragic Poet** is named for its mosaics of a theatrical production and a poet inside, though the "Cave Canem" (Beware of the Dog) mosaic by the main entrance is more eye-catching. Close by, the residents of the **House of the Faun** must have been a friendlier lot, its "Ave" (Welcome) mosaic outside beckoning you in to view the atrium and the copy of a tiny bronze dancing faun that gives the villa its name. On the street behind, the **House of the Vettii** is one of the most delightful houses in Pompeii, a merchant villa ranged around a lovely central peristyle that gives the best possible impression of the domestic environment of the city's upper middle classes. The first room on the right off the peristyle holds the best of Pompeii's murals viewable in situ: the one on the left shows the young Hercules struggling with serpents, while, through the villa's kitchen, a small room that's normally kept locked has erotic works showing various techniques of lovemaking, together with a potent-looking statue of Priapus from which women were supposed to drink to ensure fertility.

On the other side of the site, the **Grand Theatre** is very well preserved and still used for performances, as is the **Little Theatre** on its far left side. Walk up to the **Amphitheatre**, one of Italy's most intact and also its oldest, dating from 80 BC. Next door, the **Palestra** is a vast parade ground that was used by Pompeii's youth for sport and exercise. One last place you shouldn't miss is the **Villa dei Misteri**, outside the main site, a short walk from the Porta Ercolano and accessible on the same ticket. This is probably the best preserved of all Pompeii's palatial houses, and it derives its name from a series of excellently preserved paintings in one of its larger chambers: depictions of the initiation rites of a young woman into the Dionysiac Mysteries, an outlawed cult of the early imperial era.

To **reach Pompeii from Naples**, take the Circumvesuviana to Pompeii-Scavi-Villa dei Misteri (direction Sorrento) for about thirty minutes; this leaves you right outside the western entrance to the site. The Circumvesuviana also runs to Pompeii-Santuario, outside the site's eastern entrance (direction Sarno), or you can take the roughly hourly main-line train (direction Salerno) to the main Pompeii *FS* station, on the south side of the modern town. It makes most sense to see the site from Naples, and there's really no need to stay overnight, though if you get stuck or are planning to move on south after seeing Pompeii, there are plenty of **hotels** in the modern town, and a large and well-equipped **campsite** – *Zeus*, right outside the Pompeii-Villa dei Misteri station. The **tourist office** on Piazza Esedra (turn right outside Pompeii-Villa dei Misteri station) has full details and plans of the site.

Sorrento

Topping the rocky cliffs close to the end of its peninsula, **SORRENTO** is unashamedly a resort, its inspired location and mild climate having drawn foreigners from all over Europe for close on 200 years. Nowadays it's strictly package-tour territory, but really none the worse for it, a bright, lively place that retains its southern Italian roots. Cheap restaurants aren't hard to find; neither is reasonably priced accommodation; and there's really no better place outside Naples itself from which to explore the rugged Amalfi shore and the islands of the Bay.

Sorrento's centre is **Piazza Tasso**, five minutes from the train station along the busy Corso Italia, the streets around which are pedestrianized for the lively evening *passeggiata.* Strange as it may seem, Sorrento isn't particularly well provided with **beaches**: most people make do with the rocks and a tiny, crowded strip of sand at **Marina Grande** – fifteen minutes' walk or a short bus ride from Piazza Tasso – or simply use the wooden jetties. If you don't fancy this, try the beaches further along, like the tiny **Regina Giovanna** at Punta del Capo, again connected by bus from Piazza Tasso, where the ruins of the Roman Villa Pollio Felix make a unique place to bathe.

There's a **tourist office** in the large yellow *Circolo dei Foresteri* on Via de Maio, just off Piazza San Antonino (Mon–Sat 8.30am–2.30pm & 4.30–7.30pm), which has maps and details on accommodation. There's a **youth hostel** close to the station at Via Capasso 5 (☎081/878.1783; ②); turn right out of the station and it's a little way down on your left, opposite the *Carabinieri* HQ. Among a number of centrally placed **hotels**, the cheapest are the *City*, Corso Italia 221 (☎081/877.2210; ③), and the *Astoria* on Via Santa Maria delle Grazie (☎081/878.1405; ④; closed Nov–March). The cheapest and closest **campsite** is *Nube d'Argento*, ten minutes' walk from Piazza Tasso in the direction of Marina Grande at Via del Capo 12. For **eating**, the *Ristorante San Antonino*, off Piazza Antonino, is good value. For late-night boozing and **nightlife**, there are the town's English-style pubs: try the *Rover's Return*, off Piazza Tasso on Via Correale, or the *Britannia*, near the station on Corso Italia.

Cápri

Sheering out of the sea off the far end of the Sorrentine peninsula, the island of **Cápri** has long been the most sought-after part of the Bay of Naples. During Roman times Augustus retreated to the island's gorgeous cliffbound scenery to escape the cares of office; later Tiberius moved the imperial capital here, indulging himself in legendary debauched antics until his death in 37 AD. And later, the discovery of the Blue Grotto and the island's remarkable natural landscape coincided nicely with the rise of tourism; the island has attracted a steady flow of artists and writers and, more recently, inquisitive tourists, ever since. Inevitably, Cápri is a crowded and expensive place these days, and in July and August it's perhaps sensible to give it a miss. But it would be hard to find a place with more inspiring views, and it's easy enough to visit on a day trip.

From Naples, there are regular ferries to Cápri from the Molo Beverello, at the bottom of Piazza Municipio – at least six daily in summer, and the journey takes an hour and fifteen minutes; there are also regular hydrofoils from the Mergellina jetty a couple of miles north of here: these take around forty minutes but are much more expensive. You can also reach Cápri from Sorrento by hydrofoil (a twenty-minute journey). For precise timings, consult the daily newspaper, *Il Mattino*.

Ferries and hydrofoils dock at **MARINA GRANDE**, the waterside extension of Cápri town, which perches on the hill above, connected by **funicular** (L1500 one-way). There's not much to actually see, but it's very pretty, its winding, hilly alleyways converging on the dinky main square of **Piazza Umberto**. The **Certosa San Giacomo** on the far side of the town is a run-down old monastery with a handful of paintings, and the **Giardini Augustos** next door give tremendous views of the coast below and the towering jagged cliffs above. From here you can wind down to **MARINA PICCOLA**, a huddle of houses and restaurants around a few patches of pebble beach – pleasantly uncrowded out of season, though in season you might as well forget it. You can also reach the ruins of Tiberius's villa, the **Villa Jovis** (daily 9am–6pm; L4000), from Cápri town, a steep thirty-minute hike east. The site is among Cápri's most exhilarating, with incredible vistas of the Bay, although there's not much left of the villa.

The island's other main settlement, **ANACÁPRI**, is less picturesque than Cápri town, its tacky main square flanked by souvenir shops, boutiques and touristy restaurants. But during the season, a chair lift operates from here up **Monte Solaro** (9am–sunset), at 596m the island's highest point, and you can also get to the island's most famous attraction, the **Grotta Azzurra**, from here – a good 45-minute hike down Via Lo Pozzo or reachable by bus every twenty minutes from the main square. This is a bit of a rip-off, boatmen whisking visitors through the grotto in five minutes flat, but you may want to do it just to say you've been, despite the L6750 fee. In the late afternoons after the tourists have gone you can swim into the cave for nothing – change at the bar next to the entrance. It's also possible to take a boat trip to the Grotto direct from Marina Grande, though at L17,750 a head, including entrance to the cave, it's a pricy outing. Time is better spent walking in the opposite direction from Piazza Vittoria to Axel Munthe's **Villa San Michele** (daily 9am–6pm; L5000), a light, airy house that was home to the Swedish writer for a number of years, and is filled with his furniture and knick-knacks, as well as Roman artefacts ingeniously incorporated into the villa's rooms and gardens.

There are **tourist offices** in Marina Grande, on Piazza Umberto in Cápri town, and on Via G. Orlandi in Anacápri. You'd be advised not to **stay** overnight, but if keen you could try centrally placed *Quattro Stagioni*, Via Marina Piccola 1 (closed Nov–March; ☎081/837.0041; ⑥), *Stella Maris*, Via Roma 27 (☎081/837.0452; ⑤), or *Pensione Esperia*, Via Supramonte (☎081/837.0262; ③). Even if you don't stay, **eating** is an expense, and you might prefer to knock up a picnic: in Cápri town there is a supermarket and bakery a little way down Via Botteghe off Piazza Umberto, and well-stocked food stores at Via Roma 13 and 30. For sit-down food, *Di Giorgio* in Via Roma is inexpensive. For a good pizza, try *Da Gemma* in Via Madre Serafina, just off the south side of the piazza, up the steps, past the church and bearing right through the tunnel.

The Amalfi Coast

Occupying the southern side of Sorrento's peninsula, the **Amalfi Coast** lays claim to being Europe's most beautiful stretch of coast, its corniche road winding around the towering cliffs. It's an incredible ride, and if you're staying in Sorrento shouldn't be missed on any account; in any case, the towns along here hold the beaches that Sorrento lacks. It's become rather developed, but the cliffs are so steep and the towns' growth so constrained it seems unlikely that it can ever become completely spoilt.

Positano

There's not much to **POSITANO**, only a couple of decent beaches and a handful of clothing and souvenir shops. But its location, heaped up in a pyramid high above the water, has inspired a thousand picture postcards, and helped to make it a moneyed resort that runs a close second to Cápri in the celebrity stakes. The people who come here consider themselves a cut above your average sun-worshipper, and it's inevitably pricy – an overnight stay isn't recommended. But its beaches – a small one to the right of the pyramid, a larger one to the left, ringed with overpriced bars and restaurants – are rarely unpleasantly crammed. And if you can't bring yourself to get back on the bus, there are summer hydrofoil connections with Cápri, Amalfi and Salerno. For food, try the *salumeria* next to the *tabacchi* where you buy the hydrofoil tickets.

Amalfi

For affordable food and accommodation, you'd do better to push on to **AMALFI**, the largest town along this coast and an established seaside resort since Edwardian times, when the British upper classes spent their winters here. Actually, Amalfi's credentials go back much further: it was an independent republic during Byzantine times, and one of the great naval powers, with a population of some 70,000. It was finally vanquished by the Normans in 1131, and the town devastated by an earthquake in 1343, but there is still the odd remnant of Amalfi's past glories around today, and the town has a crumbly attractiveness that makes it fun to wander through.

The **Duomo**, at the top of a steep flight of steps, dominates the town's main piazza, its decorated, almost gaudy facade topped by a glazed tiled cupola that's typical of the area. Inside, it's a mixture of Saracen and Romanesque styles, though now heavily restored, with a major relic in the body of Saint Andrew buried in its crypt, though the cloister is the most appealing part of the building – oddly Arabic in feel, with its white-washed arches and palms. Close by, the **Museo Civico** displays the original *Tavoliere Amalfitane* – the book of maritime laws which governed the republic, and the rest of the Mediterranean, until 1570. Beyond these, the focus is along the busy seafront, where there's an acceptably crowded **beach**. There's a **tourist office** (daily 8am–2pm & 4.30–7pm), next door to the post office, which has maps, and a couple of fair-priced **hotels**: the *Proto*, off Via Genova (☎089/871.003; ②), and the *Vittoria*, Salita Truglio 5, also off Via Genova (☎089/871.057; ③). You could also try *A' Scalinetta*, ten minutes away on Piazza Umberto I in neighbouring Atrani (☎089/871.942; ②), which has beds in small dormitories. For **eating**, the *Green Bar*, a little way up the main street on the right, has pizza slices and the like, and a prodigious choice of beer. For something more substantial, try *Trattoria Vincola*, further up, where you can sit outside; *Trattoria Gemma*, back towards the sea on the opposite side, with a lovely terrace overlooking the street; or *Il Tari*, also on the left side of the street, a small and inexpensive eatery.

Ravello

The best views of the coast can be had inland from Amalfi, in **RAVELLO**: another renowned spot, "closer to the sky than the seashore," wrote Andre Gide – with some justification. Ravello was also an independent republic for a while, and for a time an outpost of the Amalfi city-state; now it's not much more than a large village, but its unrivalled location, spread across the top of one of the coast's mountains, makes it more than worth the thirty-minute bus ride up from Amalfi.

Buses drop off on the main **Piazza Vescovado**, outside the **Duomo**: an eleventh-century church dedicated to St. Pantaleone, a fourth-century saint whose blood – kept in a chapel on the left-hand side – is supposed to liquefy like Naples' San Gennaro's, twice a year on May 19 and August 27. It's richly decorated, with a pair of twelfth-century bronze doors, cast with 54 scenes of the Passion; inside, attention focuses on a monumental *ambo* of 1272, adorned with mosaics of dragons and birds on spiral columns, and with the coat of arms and the vivacious profiles of the Rufolo family, the donors, on each side. The Rufolos figure again on the other side of the square, where various leftovers of their **Villa Rufolo** (daily summer 9.30am–1pm & 3–7pm; winter 9.30am–1pm & 2–5.30pm; L3000, Thurs free) scatter among gardens overlooking the precipitous coastline. Ten minutes away, the gardens of the **Villa Cimbrone** (daily 8.30am–7.30pm; winter closes 5.30pm; L5000), laid out by a Yorkshire aristocrat earlier this century, spread across the furthest tip of Ravello's ridge. Most of the villa itself is not open to visitors, though it's worth peeking into the crumbly, flower-hung cloister as you go in, and the open crypt down the steps from here. Best bit of the gardens is the belvedere at the far end of the main path, giving marvellous views over the sea below.

Bari

Commercial and administrative capital of Puglia, and the second city of the *mezzogiorno*, **BARI** has its fair share of interest. But although an economically vibrant place, it harbours no pretensions about being a major tourist attraction. Primarily people come here to work, or to leave for Greece on its many ferries.

There's not a lot to the new part of the city, bar the excellent **Museo Archeologico** (Mon–Sat 9am–2pm; L3000, free Mon), which has a good selection of Greek and Puglian ceramics and a solid collection of artefacts from Puglia's earliest inhabitants. Afterwards, cut to the right for tree-lined **Corso Cavour**, Bari's main commercial street, which leads down to the waterfront and the **old city**, an entrancing labyrinth of seemingly endless passages weaving through courtyards and under arches that was originally designed to spare the inhabitants from the wind and throw invaders into a state of confusion. The **Basilica di San Nicola** (daily 9am–1pm & 5–7pm), in the heart of the old city, was consecrated in 1197 to house the relics of the saint. Inside, its twelfth-century altar canopy is one of the finest in Italy, the motifs around the capitals the work of stonemasons from Como. The twelfth-century carved doorway and the simple, striking mosaic floor of the choir are lovely, and the twelfth-century episcopal throne behind the altar is a superb piece of work, supported by small figures wheezing beneath its weight. Close by, the **Cattedrale di San Sabino** (daily 8.30am–1pm & 5–7pm), off Piazza Odegitria, was built at the end of the twelfth century, and is a plain church by contrast, home to an eighth-century icon known as the *Madonna Odegitria* that's said to be the most authentic likeness of the Madonna in existence, taken from an original sketch by Luke the Apostle. Across the piazza, the **Castello Normanno-Svevo** (Mon–Sat 8.30am–1pm & 3–7pm, Sun 8.30am–1pm; L3000) sits on the site of an earlier Roman fort. Built by Frederick II, much of it is closed to the public, but it has a vaulted hall that provides a cool escape from the afternoon sun.

Practicalities

The **tourist office** on Piazza Aldo Moro (Mon–Fri 8.30am–1pm, Sat 8.30–11am) by the train station, a kilometre south of the old city, has maps and a list of **private rooms**. All **ferries** use the Stazione Marittima, next to the old city. Finding somewhere cheap to **sleep** can be tricky: look in the streets around the station and the university, especially Via Crisanzio and Via Calefati; try *Pensione Darinka*, Via Calefati 15 (☎080/523.5049; ②), or *Pensione Giulia*, Via Crisanzio 12 (☎080/216.630; ②). If you're under thirty, you can **camp** for free between June and September at *Pineta San Francesco*, on the outskirts of the city – reachable on bus #5 from the station, bus #1 from Corso Cavour. Out of season, the nearest campsite is 6km south of the city on the SS16 – bus #12 from Teatro Petruzzelli. **Eating out**, *Le Travi de Buco*, on Largo Chiurlia in the old part of town, is good, or there's a characterful and cheap wine shop-cum-fish restaurant on the edge of the old quarter at Strada Vallisa 23.

Ferries to Greece

For details of ferry services to **Greece**, contact *Ventouris*, c/o *Pan Travel*, Via 24 Maggio 40 (☎080/521.0504), who run services to Corfu or Igoumenitsa (L50,000 one-way) and Patras (L75,000 one-way); there are daily sailings between June and September, otherwise three weekly. Travel agents around town often have a wide variety of offers on **tickets**, including *CTS*, who give a ten percent discount on student/youth fares; *InterRail* pass holders get discounts too. Once you've got your ticket, you must report to the Stazione Marittima at least two hours before departure.

Bríndisi

BRÍNDISI, about 100km southeast of Bari, was once the main crossing point between the eastern and western empires, and later, under the Normans, on the route of pilgrims heading east towards the Holy Land – and it is still strictly a place for passing through, mainly for tourists on their way to Greece. It's not a particularly pleasant place, and there's not much to see, but the old centre has a pleasant, almost Oriental flavour, with a *passeggiata* that's one of the south's best.

Ferries dock at the **Stazione Marittima** on Via del Mare, from where it's a few minutes' walk to the bottom of Corso Garibaldi, and another twenty minutes to the **train station** in Piazza Crispi. Lots of **buses** run down Corso Umberto and Corso Garibaldi (L500 a ride). There's a helpful **tourist office** on Viale Regina Margherita (Mon–Sat 8.30am–12.30pm & 4.30–7.30pm). As most ferries leave in the evening, **accommodation** isn't usually a problem: try the cental *Venezia*, Via Pisanelli 6 (☎0831/527.511; ②).

The nearest **campsite** is *Materdomin*, 5km northeast of town on the Punta Penne road, reached during the summer by local buses for the coast. There's also a **youth hostel**, 2km out of town at Via Brandi 2 (☎0831/413.123; ②) – bus #3, #4 or #5 from the train station. It's not difficult to **eat** cheaply, the whole of Corso Umberto and Corso Garibaldi (particularly the port end) being smothered in bars and restaurants in which you should be able to grab a reasonably priced if average meal. Try *Pizzeria L'Angoletto*, Via Pergola 3, just off Corso Garibaldi, which has outdoor tables and cheap local wine.

Ferries to Greece

There is a huge array of **agents** selling ferry tickets **to Greece**, and you must take care to avoid getting ripped off. The most reliable are *Hellitalia*, Via del Mare 6 (fax 0831/222.088), and *UTAC Viaggi*, Corso Garibaldi 27 (☎0831/524.921). There's usually at least one daily service to the main Greek ports throughout the year; services increase between April and September, and mid-June to August is peak season, with several sailings a day to most destinations, though you still should book in advance if possible. The most reliable ferry companies are *Adriatica*, on the first floor of the Stazione Maríttima (☎0831/523.825), who sail to Corfu, Igoumenitsa and Patras; *Hellenic Mediterranean Lines*, Corso Garibaldi 8 (☎0831/528.531), who go to the same destinations, plus Cefalonia; *Fragline*, Corso Garibaldi 88 (☎0831/568.232), with sailings to Corfu, Igoumenitsa and Patras; and *Hellenic Coastal Lines*, Corso Garibaldi 97 (☎0831/527.684), who sail to the same places, and to Cefalonia, Paxi and Ithaca, with connections for Lefkada and Zakinthos included in the price. All these companies' ferries sail at night (between 9pm and 10.30pm). **Prices** vary according to season: you're looking at around 45,000 one-way in low season to Corfu/Igoumenitsa or Patras, though less than double that for returns. *InterRail* and *Eurail* pass holders get a thirty percent discount. In general, *Adriatica* are the most expensive, *Fragline* the cheapest. Everyone pays an **embarkation tax** – currently L6000. Don't forget to stock up on **food and drink**, as there are serious mark-ups once on board. For exchanging to Greek drachmas, the most central **banks** are *Banco di Napoli* and *Credito Italiano* on Corso Garibaldi; the *Cambio* at the Stazione Marittima is open on Saturdays until 9pm.

SICILY

Coming from the Italian mainland, **Sicily** feels socially and culturally all but out of Europe. Occupying a strategically vital position, and as the largest island in the Mediterranean, Sicily's history and outlook is not that of its modern parent but of its erstwhile foreign rulers – from the Greeks who first settled the east coast in the eighth century BC, through a dazzling array of Romans, Arabs, Normans, French and Spanish, to the Bourbons seen off by Garibaldi in 1860. Substantial relics of these ages remain: temples, theatres and churches are scattered about the whole island. But there are other, more immediate hints of Sicily's unique past. A hybrid Sicilian language is still widely spoken in the countryside; the food is noticeably different, spicier and with more emphasis on fish and vegetables; and there is, of course, the Mafia – though this is not something which impinges upon the lives of tourists.

Inevitably perhaps, most points of interest are on the coast: the interior of the island is often mountainous, sparsely populated and relatively inaccessible. The capital, **Palermo**, is a memorable first stop, a bustling city with an unrivalled display of Norman art and architecture and Baroque churches. The most obvious other trips are to the chic resort of **Taormina** and the lava-built second city of **Catania**, close by which you can skirt around the foothills and even up to the craters of **Mount Etna**. To the south, the greatest draw is the grouping of temples at **Agrigento**, the best of the island's Greek remnants.

Palermo

In its own wide bay underneath the limestone bulk of Monte Pellegrino, **PALERMO** is stupendously sited. Originally a Phoenician, then a Carthaginian colony, this remarkable city was long considered a prize worth capturing, and under Saracen and Norman rule in the ninth to twelfth centuries Palermo became the greatest city in Europe, famed for the wealth of its court and peerless as a centre of learning. Nowadays it's a fast, brash and exciting city, a fascinating place to be as much for just strolling and consuming as for specific attractions. But Palermo's monuments, its unique series of Baroque and Arabo-Norman churches, the unparalleled mosaic work and excellent museums are also the equal of anything on the mainland.

Incidentally, to **get to Sicily**, you can simply take a train from the mainland – they travel across the Straits of Messina on the ferries from Villa San Giovanni and continue on the other side. Travelling by car, there are also direct ferries from Reggio di Calabria, Naples, Genoa and Livorno.

> The Palermo area telephone code is ☎091.

Arrival and accommodation

Trains all pull in at the Stazione Centrale, at the southern end of Via Roma, connected with the modern centre by almost any bus. **Ferry and hydrofoil** services dock at the Stazione Maríttima, just off Via Francesco Crispi, from where it's a ten-minute walk up Via E. Amari to Piazza Castelnuovo. There are **tourist offices** at Stazione Centrale and the Stazione Maríttima, and a main **office** at Piazza Castelnuovo 34 (Mon–Fri 8am–8pm, Sat 8am–2pm), with free maps, accommodation and entertainment guides.

You'll find getting around exclusively on foot exhausting and impractical. City **buses** are easy to use, covering every corner of Palermo and stretching out to Monreale and Mondello. There's a flat fare of L1000 and you can buy tickets from the glass booths outside Stazione Centrale, at the southern end of Viale della Libertà or from *tabacchi*. There's a built-in discount if you buy a ticket valid for the whole day for L3,000.

Most of the budget **hotel accommodation** in Palermo is on and around the southern ends of Via Maqueda and Via Roma, in the area between Stazione Centrale and Corso Vittorio Emanuele. On Via Roma, there's the *Concordia* at no. 72 (☎617.1514; ②); or off to the right, just before Corso Vittorio Emanuele, the *Olimpia* (☎616.1276; ②) has rooms overlooking Piazza Cassa di Risparmio. On Via Maqueda, in the same building at no. 8, there's the slightly smelly *Eden* (②), the *Sud* (②) and the *Vittoria* (☎616.2437; ③); and, just before Corso Vittorio Emanuele, is the atmospheric *Orientale* at no. 26 (☎616.5727; ②) – a few cavernous rooms in a marble-studded palazzo. Off Corso V. Emanuele, at Via Mottai 30, the *Letizia* (☎589.110; ②), is good, clean and safe. If you're **camping**, take bus #28 (from the Politeama theatre) out to Sferracavallo, 13km northwest of the city, where there are two sites: the *Campeggio Internazionale Trinacria* on Via Barcarello (☎530.590), open all year and with four-bedded **cabins**, and the cheaper *Matranga N.* (☎533.021), May to October only, on Via Pegaso.

The City

The heart of the old city is the dingy Baroque crossroads of the **Quattro Canti** or "Four Corners", erected in 1611, across from which is **Piazza Pretoria** and the church of **La Martorana** (daily 8.30am–1pm, also Mon–Sat 3–7pm), one of the finest survivors of the medieval city, with a slim twelfth-century campanile and a series of spectacular mosaics, animated twelfth-century Greek works. In the district southwest of here, the

Albergheria, a warren of tiny streets, the deconsecrated church of **San Giovanni degli Eremeti** (daily 9am–1pm, Tues, Wed & Fri 3–6pm) was built in 1148, and is the most obviously Arabic of the city's Norman relics, with five ochre domes topping a small church that was built upon the remains of an earlier mosque. A path leads up through citrus trees to the church, behind which lie its celebrated late thirteenth-century cloisters. From here it's a few paces north to the **Palazzo dei Normanni** whose entrance is on Piazza Indipendenza; it was originally built by the Saracens and enlarged considerably by the Normans, under whom it housed the most magnificent of medieval European courts. Sadly, there's little left from those times, and most of the interior is now taken up by the Sicilian parliament, but you can visit beautiful **Cappella Palatina** (daily 9am–noon, also Mon–Sat 3–5pm), the private royal chapel of Roger II, built between 1132 and 1143 and almost entirely covered in twelfth-century mosaics.

On the far side of Corso V. Emanuele from here, the **Cattedrale** (daily 7am–noon & 4–6.30pm) is a more substantial Norman relic, an odd building mainly because of the eighteenth-century alterations which added the dome and spoiled the fine lines of the tawny stone. Still, the triple-apsed eastern end and the lovely matching towers are all original and date from 1185; the interior is cold and Neoclassical, the only items of interest the fine portal and wooden doors and the royal tombs, containing the remains of some of Sicily's most famous monarchs. East of here, **Via Roma** is a fairly modern addition to the city, all clothes and shoe shops, beyond which is the sprawling **market** of the **Vucciria** district, its northern limit marked by the distinctive church of **San Domenico** (daily 7.30–11.30am, Sat & Sun also 5–6.30pm), with a fine eighteenth-century facade that's lit at night to great effect and an interior of tombs containing a horde of famous Sicilians. The oratory behind the church contains stuccowork by Serpotta and a masterful van Dyck altarpiece, painted in 1628 before the artist fled Palermo for Genoa to escape the plague. Just beyond, the church of **Santa Zita** on Via Squarcialupo is also known for its marvellous oratory, home to one of Serpotta's finest works – the *Battle of Lépanto* – and some rich mother-of-pearl benches.

Across Via Roma, the **Museo Archeologico Regionale** (Mon–Sat 9am–2pm, Tues & Fri also 3–6pm, Sun 9am–1pm; L2000) is a magnificent collection of artefacts, mainly from the island's Greek and Roman sites. Two cloisters hold anchors and other retrieved hardware from the sea off the Sicilian coast, and there are finds from the temple site of Selinunte, the best the Salone di Selinunte, which gathers together the rich stone carvings from the various temples. Upstairs has lead water pipes with stop-cock retrieved from a site at Termini Imerese, some 12,000 votive terracotta figures, and two bronze sculptures – the figure of an alert ram and a muscular study of Hercules subduing a stag. In the opposite direction from Santa Zita lies the depressed area around the old harbour, **La Cala**, and, across Corso V. Emanuele on Via Alloro, Sicily's **Galleria Regionale** (Mon–Sat 9am–1.30pm, Sun 9am–12.30pm; Thurs & Fri also 3–5pm; L2000), a stunning medieval art collection that includes a magnificent fifteenth-century fresco of the *Triumph of Death*, the works of fifteenth-century sculptor Francesco Laurana and paintings by Antonello da Messina.

Even if you don't have the time to see everything in the old centre, there are several targets on the outskirts of the city which warrant investigation. The third of Palermo's showpiece museums – the **Museo Etnografico Pitre** (daily except Fri 9am–1.30pm; L5000) – lies on the edge of **La Favorita**, a large park around 3km from Piazza Castelnuovo (bus #14 or #15 from Viale della Libertà). This is *the* vital exhibition of Sicilian folklore and culture on the island, with a wealth of carts painted with bright scenes from the story of the Paladins, a reconstructed puppet theatre and dozens of the expressive puppets, and a whole series of intricately worked terracotta figures, dolls and games. For real attention-grabbing stuff, take bus #27 from Corso Vittorio Emanuele southwest to Via Pindemonte (a 20-min walk), where the **Convento dei**

Cappuccini (Mon–Sat 9.30am–noon & 3–5pm) has a warren of catacombs under its church that's home to some 8000 bodies, preserved by various chemical processes and placed in niches along corridors, dressed in the suits of clothes they provided for the purpose. The rough-cut stone corridors are divided according to sex and status, different caverns reserved for men, women, the clergy, doctors, lawyers and surgeons. The bodies that aren't lined along the walls lie in stacked glass coffins, and – to say the least – it's an unnerving experience to walk among them. A sealed-off cave contains the coffin of two-year-old Rosalia Lombardo, who died in 1920 but looks simply asleep.

Eating, drinking and nightlife

For authentic Sicilian fast food, *Antica Focacceria San Francesco*, Via A. Paternostro 58 (off Corso Vittorio Emanuele), is an old-time pizzeria with marble-topped tables and pizza slices. Otherwise, the best pizzerias are *Pizzeria Italia*, Via Orologio 54, off Via Maqueda, where large queues develop quickly, and the slightly fancier *Trattoria dal Pompiere* at Via Bara 107, the next parallel street north. For full-blown **meals**, the city's best bargain is *Trattoria-Pizzeria Enzo*, Via Maurolico 17/19, close to the station. A good second choice is the small *Trattoria Azzurra*, Via dei Bottai 54 (off Corso V. Emanuele), with a long list of pasta dishes and healthy fish portions. Failing that, try *Il Cotto e il Crudo*, on Piazza Marina, with a good menu.

Come the **evening**, most young people head for the resort of **Mondello**, 11km away and connected by regular buses #3, #14 and #15. During the day it's the nearest decent place to **swim**, too. Right in the centre of Palermo, *Brinkhoff's*, on trendy Via Principe di Belmonte, is a pleasant place for a **drink**; *Pinguino*, Via Ruggero Settimo 86, has excellent ice cream, famous milk shakes and a rank of non-alcoholic cocktails.

Monreale

Sicily's most extraordinary medieval mosaics are to be seen in the Norman cathedral at **Monreale**, a small hill-town 8km southwest and accessible on buses #8/9, #8 or #9 (change at Rocca) from Piazza dell'Indipendenza, a twenty-minute journey. The **Duomo** mosaics (daily 8am–12.30pm & 3.30–7pm) represent the apex of Sicilian-Norman art, and were almost certainly executed by Greek and Byzantine craftsmen, revealing a unitary plan and inspiration: your eyes are drawn to the all-embracing figure of Christ in the central apse – an awesome and pivotal mosaic, the head and shoulders alone almost twenty metres high. Underneath sit an enthroned Virgin and Child, attendant angels and ranks of saints, each individually and subtly coloured and identified by name. No less remarkable are the nave mosaics, an animated series starting with the Creation to the right of the altar and running around the entire church. Ask at the desk by the entrance to climb the **tower** in the southwest corner of the cathedral – an unusual and precarious vantage point. It's also worth visiting the **cloisters** (daily 9am–7pm, Sun closes 1pm; L2000), part of the original Benedictine monastery here, an elegant arcaded quadrangle, with some 216 twin columns that are a riot of detail and imagination.

Taormina

TAORMINA, high on Monte Tauro and dominating two grand sweeping bays below, is Sicily's best-known resort. The outstanding remains of its classical theatre, with Mount Etna as an unparalleled backdrop, arrested passing travellers when Taormina was no more than a medieval hill village, and these days it's virtually impossible to find anywhere to stay between June and August. Despite this, Taormina retains much of its small-town charm, the main traffic-free street, Corso V. Emanuele, an unbroken line of fifteenth- to nineteenth-century palazzi and small, intimate piazzas.

The **Teatro Greco** (daily 8am–7pm; late-Sept to March closes 6pm; L2000) – signposted from just about everywhere – is the only real sight, founded by Greeks in the third century BC though most of what's left is Roman, dating from a first-century reconstruction when Taormina thrived under imperial Roman rule, although the impressive Roman scene building can only have obscured the views of Etna – presumably a major reason for the theatre's original siting; likewise, the stage and lower seats were cut back to provide room and a deep trench dug in the orchestra to accommodate the animals and fighters used in gladiatorial contests.

Trains pull up at Taormina-Giardini station, way below town, from where it's a steep thirty-minute walk up or a short bus ride to the centre of town. The **tourist office** (Mon–Fri 8am–2pm & 2.30–7.30pm, Sat 8am–noon) on Corso V. Emanuele, off Piazza Vittorio Emanuele, has free maps. There are good **accommodation** possibilities along Via Bagnoli Croce: private rooms at no. 66 (②), with incredible roof-terrace views, *Il Leone*, nos. 124–126 (☎0942/23.878; ②), and the very friendly *Villa Pompeii*, at no. 88 (☎0942/23.812; ②); and there's also the *Pensione Svizzera*, at Via Pirandello 26 (☎0942/ 23.790; ③), just up from the bus terminal. If everywhere is full, you'll have to try nearby Giardini-Naxos. The **campsite**, *San Leo*, on the cape below town is open all year; take any bus running between Taormina and the station. **Eating** can be terribly expensive – if money is tight, try a couple of unspectacular pizzerias outside Porta Messina. The only vaguely cheap trattoria is *Da Nino*, Via Pirandello 37, while *Il Baccanale* in Piazza Filea (end of Via Bagnoli Croce) has outdoor tables and similar prices.

The closest beach to town is at **MAZZARO**, with its much-photographed islet. There's a **cable car** (L2000) every fifteen minutes from Via Pirandello, and a steep path which starts just below the cable car station. The beach-bars and restaurants at **SPISONE**, north again, are also reachable by path from Taormina, this time from below the cemetery in town. From Spisone, the coast opens out and the beach gets wider. With more time, **LETOJANNI** is a little resort in its own right, with a few fishing boats on a sandy beach, two campsites and regular buses and trains back to Taormina. Roomier and better for swimming are the sands south of Taormina at **GIARDINI-NAXOS**, which is an excellent alternative source of **accommodation** and food. Prices tend to be a good bit cheaper than in Taormina and in high season it's worth trying here first. *Immobiliare Naxos*, Via V. Emanuele 58 (☎0942/51.184), can arrange apartments – good value if you're a group of four or more; recommended **hotels** include *Villa Pamar*, Via Naxos 23 (☎0942/52.448; ⑤). For **eating**, good pizzas and fresh pasta can be had at *Fratelli Marano*, Via Naxos 181. *Da Angelina*, on Via Schiso by the pier, does marvellous well-priced pizzas and has good service and great views. Also good are *Arcobaleno*, Via Naxos 169, and *Il Pescatore*, Via Naxos 96, an excellent fish restaurant.

Mount Etna

Mount Etna's massive bulk looms over much of the coastal route south of Taormina, and, if you don't have the time to reach the summit, rail services provide some alternative volcanic thrills in a ride around the base of the volcano from **GIARRE-RIPOSTO**, thirty minutes by train or bus from Taormina; *InterRail* passes are not valid, and if you make the entire trip to Catania, allow five hours; tickets cost L4600 one-way. As for the ascent, this is a spectacular trip worth every effort to make – though without your own transport that effort can be considerable. At 3323m, Etna is a fairly substantial mountain, the fact that it's also one of the world's biggest volcanoes (and still active) only adding to the draw. Some of the eruptions have been disastrous: in 1669 Catania was wrecked; this century the Circumetnea rail line has been repeatedly ruptured by lava flows, and, in 1979, nine people were killed on the edge of the main crater. This is not to say you'll be in any danger, provided you heed the warnings as you get closer to the top. There are several approaches. On public transport, you'll need to come via **NICOLOSI**, an hour from Catania by frequent bus, one of which (8.05am from Catania train station) continues on to a huddle of souvenir shops and restaurants around the **Rifugio Sapienza** (☎095/911.062; ③). Arriving on the early morning bus, you'll have enough time to make it to the top and get back for the return bus to Catania – it leaves around 4pm. To get up the volcano from the refuge, you can take the cable car up to about 2500m, or take one of the *SITAS* **minibuses** from outside the old cable car station (May–Oct; L45,000) – a two-hour return trip which gives you half an hour clambering around just below the main crater – or you can **walk**, following the rough minibus track. This will take three to four hours, the return obviously a little less. However you go, take warm clothes, good shoes and glasses to keep the flying grit out of your eyes. The highest you're allowed to get is 2900m, and though there's only a rope across the ground to prevent you from climbing further, it would be foolish to do so.

Catania

First impressions don't do much for **CATANIA**, on an initial encounter possibly the island's gloomiest spot. Built from black-grey volcanic stone, its central streets can feel suffocating. Yet fight the urge to change buses and run: Catania is one of the most intriguing and historic of Sicily's cities. Some of the island's first Greek colonists settled the site as early as 729 BC, becoming so influential that their laws were eventually adopted by all the Ionian colonies of Magna Graecia. Later, in the seventeenth century, Etna swamped the city, leading to a swift rebuilding under the architect Giovanni Vaccarini that gave the city a lofty, noble air.

Catania's main square, **Piazza del Duomo**, is a handy orientation point and one of Sicily's most attractive city squares, surrounded by fine Baroque structures, including the **Duomo**, which incorporates granite columns from Catania's Roman amphitheatre. A short way west, at the bottom of Via Crociferi, the house where the composer Vincenzo Bellini was born in 1801 now houses the **Museo Belliniano** (Mon–Fri 8am–1pm & 4–6pm, Sun 8.30am–12.30pm; free), an agreeable collection of photographs, original scores and other memorabilia; beyond it, the **Teatro Romano** (Tues–Sun 8am–1pm & 4–6pm; free) was built on the site of an earlier Greek theatre, and preserves much of its seating and underground passageways. A few minutes' walk north, the enormous **Piazza Stesicoro** marks the modern centre of Catania, one half of which is almost entirely occupied by the sunken, black remains of another Roman theatre, the **Antifeatro Romano**, dating back to the second or third century AD.

Catania's main **train station** is in Piazza Giovanni XXIII, northeast of the centre; the **Circumetnea terminus** is on Corso delle Province, off Corso Italia. There's a **tourist office** inside the train station (summer daily 8.30am–8.30pm; winter Mon–Fri 9am–1pm & 4–7pm; ☎095/373.084), with accommodation listings and maps. There are lots of **places to stay**, and some real bargains if you hunt around. One of the best is the clean and friendly *Pensione Gresi*, Via Pacini 28 (☎095/322.709; ③), and the *Rubens* at Via Etnea 196 (☎095/317.073; ④) is also good, though always busy; there's also the *Holland International*, Via V. Emanuele 8 (☎095/532.779; ②), with rooms above a courtyard in a palazzo. **Camping**, there are three sites with cabins a short way south of the city on Lungomare Kennedy; take bus #24 or #27 from the station or Via Etnea. For **eating**, the *Centrale* at Via Etnea 123 is a great place for a snack, with a superb antipasto buffet; the *Ristorante Rapido*, Via Corridoni 17, off Via Pacini, is cheap, if rather average. Worth trying, too, is the *Trattoria Calabrese*, on Via Penninello, down the steps at the end of Via Crociferi. *Le Carteria* pub, just off Piazza Bellini, is a good, untouristy place to **drink**, full of young, studenty Catanese.

Agrigento

Though it's handsome, well-sited and awash with medieval atmosphere, no one comes to **AGRIGENTO** for the town. The interest instead focuses on the substantial remains of Pindar's "most beautiful city of mortals", a couple of kilometres below. Here, strung out along a ridge facing the sea, is a series of Doric temples – the most captivating of Sicilian remains and unique outside Greece – built during the fifth century BC.

A road winds down from the modern city to the **Valle dei Templi** (daily 8am–6pm), buses dropping you at a car park between the two separate sections of archeological remains. The **eastern zone** is unenclosed, and home to scattered remains of the oldest of the temples, the **Tempio di Ercole**, probably begun in the last decades of the sixth century BC, and the better-preserved **Tempio della Concordia**, dated to around 430 BC, with fine views of the city and sea. There's also the **Tempio di Giunone**, an engaging half-ruin standing at the very edge of the ridge. The **western zone** (daily 9am–1hr before sunset; free), back along the path and beyond the car park, is less impressive, a vast tangle of stone and fallen masonry from a variety of temples. Most notable is the mammoth construction that was the **Tempio di Giove**, or Temple of Olympian Zeus, the largest Doric temple ever known, though never completed, left in ruins by the Carthaginians and further damaged by earthquakes. Via dei Templi leads back to the town from the car park via the excellent **Museo Nazionale Archeologico** (daily 9am–1pm; free) – an extraordinarily rich collection devoted to finds from the city and the surrounding area.

Trains arrive at the edge of the old town, outside which – on Piazza Marconi – buses leave for the temples. The **tourist office** (Mon–Sat 8am–2pm & 5–7pm) is in the *Banco di Sicilia* building on Piazza Marconi and has hotel listings and maps. Among **hotels** worth trying are the *Concordia*, behind the station at Piazza San Francesco 11 (☎0922/596.266; ③); the *Bella Napoli*, Piazza Lena 6 (☎0922/20.435; ③); and the *Belvedere*, Via San Vito 20 (☎0922/20.051; ②), closed November to January. You can **camp** 5km away at the coastal resort of San Leone; bus #10 from outside the train station. For **eating**, the food is excellent at *La Forchetta*, next door to the *Concordia* hotel, but not particularly cheap. If you're budgeting, the reasonable low-priced food at *La Corte degli Sfizzi* on Cortile Contarini, an alley above Via Atenea, makes up for the dreadful service.

SARDINIA

A little under 200km from the Italian mainland, slightly more than that from the North African coast at Tunisia, **Sardinia** is way off most tourist itineraries of Italy. Relatively free of large cities or heavy industry, the island boasts some of the country's cleanest, least crowded beaches, and, though not known for its cultural riches, holds some fascinating vestiges of the various civilizations that passed through. In addition to Roman and Carthaginian ruins, Genoan fortresses and a string of lovely Pisan churches, there are striking remnants of Sardinia's only significant native culture, known as the **nuraghic** civilization after the 7000-odd stone constructions which litter the landscape.

On the whole, Sardinia's smaller centres are the most attractive, but the capital, **Cágliari** – for many the arrival point – shouldn't be written off. With good facilities for eating and sleeping, it makes a useful base for exploring the southern third of the island. The other main ferry port and airport is Olbia in the north, little more than a transit town for visitors to the nearby Costa Smeralda, though budget travellers are unlikely to want to spend time in this uncomfortable mix of opulence and suburbia.

In the northwest of the island, **Sássari** and **Alghero** manifest the deepest imprint of the long Spanish presence in Sardinia, with the latter having developed into the chief package resort. Inland, **Nuoro** has impressive literary credentials and a good ethnographical museum. As Sardinia's biggest interior town, it also makes a useful stopover for visiting some of the remoter mountain areas, in particular the **Gennargentu** range, covering the heart of the island. This is where you can find what remains of the island's traditional culture, best embodied in the numerous village **festivals**.

The island boasts a good network of public transport to get you round all but the remoter areas. On the roads there is the island-wide bus network run by *ARST* and the private *PANI* for longer hauls between towns, while trains connect the major towns of Cágliari, Sássari and Olbia, with smaller lines linking with Nuoro and Alghero.

Getting to Sardinia

There are frequent daily **flights** from the Italian mainland to the island's three airports, at Cágliari, Olbia and Fertília (for Alghero and Sássari). The flights, which take about an hour, are run by *Alitalia*'s internal arm, *ATI*, and Sardinia's own *Alisarda* and *Air Sardinia*. Cheaper but slower are the overnight **ferries** from mainland Italy (Civitavecchia, Genoa, Livorno, Naples) – as well as from Sicily, Tunis, Corsica and France. If you're travelling by car, it is essential to book well in advance: sailings in July and August can be fully booked by May. Prices range from L42,000 to L150,000 per person, depending on season and type of accommodation: a berth costs a minimum of L60,000. A vehicle will cost a minimum of L70,000 for a small car in low season. Note that *Navarma* and *Sardinia Ferries* offer fifty percent discounts for vehicles on certain dates if you book your return when you buy your outward-bound ticket.

Cágliari

Rising up from its port and crowned by an old centre squeezed within a protective ring of Pisan fortifications, **CÁGLIARI** has been Sardinia's capital at least since Roman times and is still the island's biggest town. Nonetheless, its centre is easily explored on foot, and offers sophistication and charm in its raggle-taggle of narrow lanes. The main attractions here are the **museum** with its unique collection of nuraghic statuettes, the city walls, with their two **Pisan towers** looking down over the port, and the **cathedral**.

Arrival, information and accommodation

Cágliari's **port** lies in the heart of the town, opposite Via Roma. The **airport** sits beside the city's largest *stagno*, fifteen minutes' bus ride west of town. The airport has a bureau de change and a **tourist office** (Mon–Fri 9am–6pm; ☎070/240.200) with maps and information on accommodation; there's another at the Stazione Maríttima (Mon–Sat 9am–2pm; ☎070/668.352), and bigger offices at Via Mameli 97 (Mon–Sat 9am–2pm & 4–7pm; ☎070/664.195) and Piazza Defennu 9 (same hours; ☎070/663.207). A free **bus** service into town runs at least every ninety minutes from 6.20am until 8.55pm to Piazza Matteotti; otherwise a taxi ride costs around L15,000. Piazza Matteotti also has the **bus and train stations** and a tourist information kiosk (Mon–Sat 9am–2pm).

Cágliari has a good selection of budget **hotels**, though availability may be restricted in high season, and single rooms are always at a premium. In the narrow Via Sardegna, running parallel to Via Roma, try the *Centrale* at no. 4 (☎070/654.783; ②) or the nearby *La Perla* at no. 18 (☎070/669.446; ②). At the far end of Via Sardegna, the cramped but clean *Londra* at Via Regina Margherita 16 (☎070/669.083; ②) is run by a London woman who's lived seventeen years on the island. Further up from the port, the *Firenze* at Corso Vittorio Emanuele 50 (☎070/653.678; ②), like most of Cágliari's cheap hotels, lies at the top of several flights of stairs, but it's cosy and popular – and often full. The nearest **campsite** is at Quartu Sant'Elena, a 45-minute bus ride east along the coast, where the *Pini e Mare* (June–Sept; ☎070/803.107) has bungalows as well.

The City

Almost all the wandering you will want to do in Cágliari is encompassed within the old quarter. The most evocative entry to this is from the monumental **Bastione San Remy** on Piazza Costituzione. It's worth the haul up the grandiose flight of steps inside for Cágliari's best views over the port and the lagoons beyond – especially at sunset.

From the bastion, you can wander off in any direction to enter the intricate maze of Cágliari's citadel, traditionally the seat of the administration, aristocracy and highest ecclesiastical offices. It has been little altered since the Middle Ages, though the tidy Romanesque façade on the **Cattedrale** in Piazza Palazzo is in fact a fake, added in this century in the old Pisan style. The structure dates originally from the thirteenth century but has gone through what D. H. Lawrence called "the mincing machine of the ages, and oozed out Baroque and sausagey."

Inside, a couple of massive stone **pulpits** flank the main doors: they were crafted as a single piece around 1160 to grace Pisa's cathedral, but were later presented to Cágliari along with the same sculptor's set of lions, now adorning the outside of the building. Other features of the cathedral include the ornate seventeenth-century tomb of Martin II of Aragon (left transept), the presbytery, which is the entrance to a small museum, and the **crypt**. Hewn out of the rock, little of this subterranean chamber has been left undecorated, and there are carvings by Sicilian artists of Sardinian saints.

At the opposite end of Piazza Palazzo a road leads into the smaller Piazza dell'Arsenale, site of the **Museo Archeologico Nazionale** (Mon 9am–1.30pm, Tues– Sat 9am–1.30pm & 3.30–6pm, Sun 9am–12.30pm; L4000), a must for anyone interested in Sardinia's past. The island's most important Phoenician, Carthaginian and Roman finds are gathered here, but everything pales beside the museum's greatest pieces, from the Sardinia's **nuraghic** culture. Of these, the most eye-catching is a series of bronze statuettes, ranging from about six to eighteen inches in height, spindly and highly stylized, but packed with invention and quirky humour. The main source of information about this phase of the island's history, most of the figures were votive offerings, made to decorate the inside of temples, later buried to protect them from the hands of foreign predators.

Off the piazza stands the **Torre San Pancrazio**, from which it's only a short walk to Via dell'Università and the **Torre dell'Elefante**, named after the small carving of an elephant on one side. The towers were erected by Pisa after it had wrested the city from the Genoans in 1305 and formed the main bulwarks of the city's defences. Both have a half-finished look about them, with the side facing the old town completely open. Nearby, Viale Buon Cammino leads to the **Anfiteatro Romano,** normally closed to visitors, though you can see a good part just by walking round it. Cut out of solid rock in the second century AD, the amphitheatre could hold the entire city's population of 20,000.

The only item of interest in Cágliari's traffic-thronged modern quarters is the fifth-century church of **San Saturnino**, Sardinia's oldest and one of the most important surviving examples of early Christian architecture in the Mediterranean. Stranded on the busy Via Dante, and surrounded by various pieces of flotsam from the past, the basilica was erected on the spot where the Christian martyr Saturninus met his fate.

Eating and drinking

Most of Cágliari's **restaurants** are clustered around Via Sardegna. *Da Serafino*, at Via Sardegna 109, is extremely good value and popular with the locals. The *Trattoria-Pizzeria* at Via dei Mille 16 is touristy but reliable. Seafood-lovers will do well at the *Stella Marina di Montecristo*, at the end of Via Sardegna, where it meets Via Regina Margherita. Away from the port area, try *Il Gatto*, just off Piazza del Cármine at Viale Trieste 15, for seafood or meat dishes, all immaculately prepared.

For a **snack** and a beer, drop in on *Il Merlo Parlante* in Via Portascalas, an alley off Corso Vittorio Emanuele, where you can find drink, music and *panini*. Down by the port, the bars on Via Roma make good breakfast-stops, while there are several decent pizza and sandwich joints in the alleys running off it.

Su Nuraxi

If you have no time to see any other of Sardinia's ancient stone *nuraghi*, make a point of visiting SU NURAXI, the biggest and most famous of them and a good taste of the primitive grandeur of the island's only indigenous civilization. The snag is access: the site lies a kilometre outside the village of Barúmini, 50km north of Cágliari, to which there are only two daily *ARST* buses, which stop here en route to Désulo and Samugheo.

At Barúmini, turn left at the main crossroads and walk the last leg to Su Nuraxi (open daily 9am–sunset; free). Its dialect name means simply "the *nuragh*" and not only is it the biggest nuraghic complex on the island, but it's also thought to be the oldest, dating probably from around 1500 BC. Comprising a bulky fortress surrounded by the remains of a village, Su Nuraxi was a palace complex at the very least – possibly a capital city. The central tower once reached 21m (now shrunk to less than 15m), and its outer defences and inner chambers are connected by passageways and stairs. The whole complex is thought to have been covered with earth by Sards and Carthaginians at the time of the Roman conquest, which may account for its excellent state of preservation.

Nuoro and around

"There is nothing to see in Nuoro: which to tell the truth, is always a relief. Sights are an irritating bore," wrote D.H. Lawrence, though he didn't mention the town's superb position beneath the soaring peak of Monte Ortobene opposite the sheer and stark heights of Sopramonte. In many respects **NUORO** is different from the other villages of the region, but no place on the island can match its extraordinary literary fame. The best-known Sard poet, **Sebastiano Satta** (1867–1914), was Nuorese, as was the author **Grazia Deledda** (1871–1936), who won the Nobel Prize for Literature in 1927. For **Salvatore Satta** (1902–75) "Nuoro was nothing but a perch for the crows," as he wrote in his semi-autobiographical only work, *The Day of Judgment*. This century little has changed in this insular town despite the unsightly apartment blocks, administrative buildings and banks superimposed upon it.

Nuoro's **old quarter** is the most compelling part of town, spread around the pedestrianized hub of **Corso Garibaldi**, along which the *passeggiata* takes place. Otherwise the only attraction is the impressive **Museo Etnografico** (Tues–Sat 9am–1pm & 3–6/7pm, Sun 9am–1pm; free) on Via Antonio Mereu, a ten-minute walk from the Corso on the other side of Piazza Vittorio Emanuele, which contains Sardinia's most comprehensive range of local costumes, jewellery, masks, carpets and other handicrafts.

As many as three thousand of the costumes are aired at Nuoro's biggest annual **festival**, the **Sagra del Redentore**, usually taking place on the penultimate Sunday of the month and involving participants from all over the island, but especially the villages of the Barbágia. The religious festivities usually take place on August 29, when a procession from town weaves up to the 955-metre summit of **Monte Ortobene**, 8km away, where a bronze **statue** of the Redeemer stands, poised in an attitude of swirling motion with stunning views of the gorge separating Nuoro from the Sopramonte.

From Nuoro there are numerous routes weaving through Barbágia and the Gennargentu range, though the bus service is slow and sporadic. Typical of the mountain villages in this area is **ORGÓSOLO**, a straggly thirty kilometres from Nuoro, and notorious for the past exploits of its inhabitants, whose feuding and animosity towards the settled crop-farmers on Barbágia's fringes occasionally broke out into open warfare. The village's reputation has made it the destination of a constant dribble of visitors hoping to find some traces of its violent past amid the shabby collection of breeze-blocked grey houses, only to find a vivid collection of **murals**, some of them covering whole houses and shops, portraying village culture and illustrating the oppression of the landless by the landowners.

MAMOIADA, 11km west of Orgósolo, is the scene of a highly pagan carnival romp, when masked *mammuthones* representing hunted animals march through the streets, decked in sheepskin with their backs arrayed with rows of jangling goat-bells. OTTANA, on the northern fringes of the area – and reckoned to be the dead centre of Sardinia – vies with Mamoiada for its masked and horned carnival horrors. FONNI, due south of Mamoiada and at 1000m the island's highest village, has a less gruesome costumed procession in its festival of the Madonna dei Mártiri, held on the Monday following the first Sunday in June.

Practicalities

Nuoro's **train station** is a half-hour walk from the centre of town along Via La Mármora. The *PANI* buses stop at Via Brigata Sássari (parallel to Via La Marmora), while *ARST* buses stop in Piazza Vittorio Emanuele in the old town. Nuoro's few **hotels** are antiquated, grubby and usually full. The **tourist office** on Piazza Italia (Mon–Fri 9am–1pm & 4–7pm, Sat 9am–1pm) has a list of private rooms that may be the best option for a short stay. Otherwise try Signora Iacobini's unofficial hotel at Via Cedrino 31, off Piazza Italia (☎0784/30.675; ③), or the *Mini Hotel* in the centre of town, at Via Brofério 31 (☎0784/33.159; ③). The best **restaurant** is the excellent pizzeria *Da Gesuino*, at Viale Ciusa 53, on the western end of town. For a lunch-time snack, there's a handy sit-down **bar** on Via Mereu, between the museum and the Duomo.

Sássari and around

Historically, while Cágliari was Pisa's base of operations during the Middle Ages, SÁSSARI was the Genoan capital, ruled by the Doria family, whose power reached throughout the Mediterranean. Under the Aragonese it became an important centre of Spanish hegemony, and the Spanish stamp is still strong.

The **old quarter**, a network of alleys and piazzas bisected by the main Corso Vittorio Emanuele, is a good area for aimless wandering, but take a look at the **Duomo**, whose florid facade is Sardinia's most imposing example of Baroque architecture, added to a simpler Aragonese-Gothic base from the fifteenth and sixteenth centuries.

The only other item worth searching out is the late Renaissance **Fonte Rosello**, at the bottom of a flight of dilapidated steps accessible from Corso Trinità, in the northern part of the old town. The fountain is elaborately carved with dolphins and four statues representing the seasons, the work of Genoese stonemasons.

Connected by a series of squares to the old quarter, the **newer town** is centred on the grandiose Piazza Italia. Leading off the piazza is Via Roma, site of the **Museo Sanna** (Mon–Sat 9am–2pm, Sun 9am–1pm; L4000), Sardinia's second archeological museum; it's a good substitute if you've missed the main one at Cágliari, and like the Cágliari museum its most interesting exhibits are *nuraghic* sculptures.

Roughly 15km inland from Sássari, right on the main Sássari–Olbia road, the SS 597, rises the tall bell-tower of **Santa Trinità di Saccárgia**, its striking zebra-striped facade marking its Pisan origins. Built in 1116, the church owes its remote location to a divine visitation, informing the wife of the *giudice* of Logudoro that she was pregnant. It has survived remarkably well, with lovely Gothic capitals at the top of the entrance porch.

Practicalities

The **train station** is at the bottom of the old town's Corso Vittorio Emanuele. All local and *ARST* **buses** arrive at and depart from the semicircular Emiciclo Garibaldi, south of the tourist office. *PANI* buses run from Via Bellini 5, just off Via Roma. Free buses connect **Fertília airport** with the *Alitalia* office at Via Cágliari 30, scheduled to coincide with incoming and outgoing flights.

Sássari's **tourist office** is at Via Brigate Sássari 19 (Mon–Fri 8am–1.45pm & 3.30–6.30pm; ☎079/231.331), near Piazza Italia. **Staying** in Sássari can be a real problem, and you'd do well to ring ahead to ensure availability. The best budget option is the tumbledown *Pensione Famiglia* at Viale Umberto 65 (☎079/239.543; ②); otherwise try the *Giusy* (☎079/233.327; ③), conveniently near the station on Piazza Sant'Antonio. Among a range of **restaurants** in town try *Da Peppina*, in Vícolo Pigozzi, an alley off Corso Vittorio Emanuele – a good place to sample the local speciality of horsemeat.

Alghero

ALGHERO owes its predominantly Catalan flavour to a wholesale Hispanicization that followed the overthrow of the Doria family by Pedro IV of Aragon in 1354. The traces are still strong in the old town today, with its flamboyant churches, wrought-iron balconies and narrow cobbled streets named in both Italian and Catalan.

A walk around the old town should include the seven defensive **towers** which dominate Alghero's centre and surrounding walls. From the **Giardino Púbblico**, the **Porta Terra** is the first of the massive bulwarks: known as the Jewish Tower, it was erected at the expense of the prosperous Jewish community before their expulsion in 1492. Beyond is a puzzle of lanes, at the heart of which the pedestrianized Via Carlo Alberto, Via Principe Umberto and Via Roma have most of the bars and shops. At the bottom of Via Umberto stands Alghero's sixteenth-century **Cattedrale**, where Spanish viceroys stopped to take a preliminary oath before taking office in Cágliari. Its unprepossessing entrance is round the other side on Via Manno; inside, the lofty nave's alternating pillars and columns rise to an impressive octagonal dome. In fact, most of Alghero's finest architecture dates from the same period, and is built in a similar Catalan-Gothic style. Two of the best examples are a short walk away: the **Palazzo d'Albis** on Piazza Cívica, and the elegantly austere Jewish palace **Palau Reial** in Via Sant'Erasmo.

The best of the excursions you can take from the port is to **Neptune's Grotto**, with departures several times daily in summer: tickets cost L15,000, not counting the entry charge to the grotto. The ride takes you west along the coast past the long bay of Porto Conte as far as the point of **Capo Caccia**, where the spectacular sheer cliffs are riddled by deep marine caves. The most impressive is the **Grotta di Nettuno** (daily April–Sept 9am–6pm; Oct–March 9am–2pm; L9000), a long snaking passage delving far into the rock, into which half-hour tours are led, single-file, on the hour every hour, past dramatically lit and fantastical stalagmites and stalactites. A cheaper alternative to the boat tour is by bus to Capo Caccia.

Practicalities

Trains to Alghero from Sássari arrive some way out of the centre, connected to the port by shuttle buses. **Buses** arrive in Via Catalogna, on the Giardino Púbblico. Alghero's efficient **tourist office** is on the corner of the Giardino Púbblico (May–Sept daily 8am–8pm; Oct–April Mon–Sat 8am–2pm; ☎079/979.262).

The best-value **hotel** in town is the *San Francesco* (☎079.979.258; ③), in the heart of the old town at Via Machin 2, just behind San Francesco church; each of its clean, quiet rooms has a bathroom. If it's full, try the *Normandie*, on Via Enrico Mattei in the newer part of town, between Via Kennedy and Via Giovanni XXIII (☎079/975.302; ②). Two kilometres out of town, *La Mariposa* **campsite** (April–Oct; ☎079/950.480) has direct access to the beach. Alghero's *Giuliani* youth hostel (April–Oct; ☎079/930.353; ②) is actually 6km along the coast at Fertília, reachable by local bus. Ring first to check availability.

Alghero's **restaurants** are renowned for fish and seafood, always fresh, inventively prepared and well presented – spring and winter are the best seasons. The *Corsaro* on Via Columbano is excellent, as are *La Lépanto* on Via Carlo Alberto and *Da Pietro*, at Via Machin 20, though none could be described as budget places. For cheaper meals, you're better off trying the right-angled streets of the new town, like Via Mazzini, where the *Ristorante Mazzini* at no. 59 serves decent fare at modest prices and has a wood-fired oven for pizzas. For snacks, the fast-food joints by the port aren't bad.

There is an abundant supply of decent **bars** to repair to when required. The *Mill Pub* in Via Maiorca has live music nightly at 11pm, but the best venue is the vaulted *Totem* pub at Via Minerva 22, with good sounds and atmosphere.

travel details

Trains

Bari to: Bríndisi (hourly; 2hr).

Bergamo to: Brescia (19 daily; 1hr).

Bologna to: Ferrara (12 daily; 30min); Florence (hourly; 65min); Milan (hourly; 2hr 35min); Ravenna (15 daily; 1hr 25min); Rimini (hourly; 1hr 20min).

Cágliari to: Arbatax (1–2 daily; 7hr); Macomer (7 daily; 2hr); Olbia (4 daily; 5hr); Oristano (7 daily; 1hr–1hr 30 min); Sássari (4 daily; 4hr).

Ferrara to: Rimini (11 daily; 2hr 15min).

Florence to: Arezzo (hourly; 1hr); Bari (12 daily; 9hr); Bologna (hourly; 1hr 30min); Genoa (hourly; 3–4hr 30min); Lucca (hourly; 1hr 5min–1hr 50min); Milan (18 daily; 3–5hr) Naples (2 daily; 4hr); Perugia (11 daily; 2hr 10min); Pisa (every 30min; 55min); Rome (hourly; 2hr 15min–3hr 30min); Venice (hourly; 3–4hr); Verona (14 daily; 2–3hr).

Genoa to: Bologna (8 daily; 3hr); Milan (hourly; 2hr); Naples (9 daily; 8hr); Pisa (every 2hr; 2hr 30min); Rome (every 2hr; 6hr).

Milan to: Bergamo (5 daily; 50min); Bologna (hourly; 2hr); Brescia (32 daily; 45min–1hr 10min; Como (12 daily; 30min); Rome (10 daily; 4hr); Venice (every 30min; 3hr).

Naples to: Bríndisi (1 daily; 6hr); Palermo (7 daily; 10hr).

Padua to: Bologna (34 daily; 1hr 25min); Milan (25 daily; 2hr 30min); Verona (hourly; 50min); Vicenza (25 daily; 55min).

Palermo to: Agrigento: (11 daily; 2hr 30min); Catania (5 daily; 3hr 10min).

Parma to: Brescia (8 daily; 1hr 45min).

Perugia to: Assisi (hourly; 25min); Florence (4 daily; 2hr 15min); Rome (1 daily; 2hr 20min).

Pisa to: Florence (hourly; 1hr); Livorno (every 30min; 15min); Lucca (hourly; 30min).

Rome to: Ancona (8 daily; 3hr 15min–6hr); Bologna (12 daily; 3hr 20min); Florence (hourly; 2–3hr 30min); Milan (12 daily; 3hr–5hr 40min); Naples (hourly; 2hr 30min).

Sássari to: Alghero (10 daily; 50min); Cágliari (6 daily; 4hr); Macomer (6 daily; 2hr); Olbia (10 daily; 2hr); Oristano (6 daily; 3hr).

Turin to: Genoa (12 daily; 2hr); Milan (19 daily; 1hr 45min).

Venice to: Bologna (hourly; 2hr); Florence (hourly; 4hr 30min); Milan (every 30min; 3hr 30min); Padua (every 30min; 30min); Trieste (hourly; 2hr 10min); Verona (every 30min; 1hr 30min); Vicenza (every 30min; 55min).

Verona to: Milan (30 daily; 1hr 40min); Padua (25 daily; 50min); Rome (6 daily; 6hr); Venice (30 daily; 30min).

Vicenza to: Milan (every 30min; 2hr); Verona (every 30min; 30min).

Buses

Cágliari to: Macomer (5 daily; 2hr); Nuoro (4 daily; 3hr); Oristano (5 daily; 1hr); Sássari (7 daily; 3hr 15min–4hr).

Sássari to: Alghero (10 daily; 50min); Bosa (4 daily; 2hr 20min); Cágliari (5 daily; 4hr); Olbia (2 daily; 2hr); Stintino (4–5 daily; 1hr 10min).

Ferries

Arbatax to: Civitavécchia (2–3 weekly; 9hr); Genoa (2 weekly; 18hr).

Cágliari to: Civitavécchia (1 daily; 14hr); Genoa (2 weekly in summer; 20hr); Naples (1–2 weekly; 15hr); Palermo (1 weekly; 15hr); Trápani (1 weekly; 12hr); Tunis (1 weekly; 37hr).

Genoa to: Palermo (4 weekly; 23hr).

Naples to: Cápri (6 daily; 1hr 15min); Catania (1 weekly; 15hr); Palermo (1 daily; 10hr 30min); Sorrento: (3 daily ferries, 6 daily hydrofoils; 1hr 15min/40min).

Olbia to: Civitavécchia (1 daily; 8hr); Genoa (3–7 weekly; 13hr); La Spezia (1 daily; 11hr); Livorno (4–7 weekly; 9hr).

Porto: Torres to: Genoa (1 daily; 12hr); Toulon (April–Sept 1 weekly; 16hr).

Reggio di Calabria to: Catania (3 weekly; 3hr 15min); Messina (10 daily; 50min).

Santa Teresa di Gallura to: Bonifacio (2–8 daily; 1hr).

Sorrento: to: Cápri (5 daily; 50min).

Villa San Giovanni to: Messina (every 30min; 35min).

Hydrofoils

Naples to: Cápri (12 daily; 40min); Sorrento: (6 daily; 40min).

Palermo to: Naples (3 weekly; 5hr 20min).

Reggio di Calabria to: Messina (every 40min; 15min); Naples (summer 1 daily; 6hr).

Sorrento: to: Cápri (6 daily; 20min).

CHAPTER 14

MOROCCO

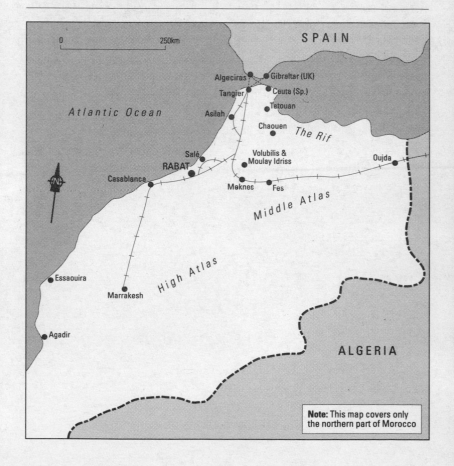

0   250km

SPAIN

Algeciras
Gibraltar (UK)
Tangier
Ceuta (Sp.)
Asilah
Tetouan

Atlantic Ocean
Chaouen
The Rif

Salé
Volubilis &
Moulay Idriss
Oujda

RABAT
Casablanca
Meknes   Fes

Middle Atlas

High Atlas

Essaouira

Marrakesh

Agadir

ALGERIA

Note: This map covers only
the northern part of Morocco

Introduction

Though just an hour's ride on the ferry from Spain, **Morocco** seems very far from Europe, with a deeply traditional Islamic culture that is almost wholly unfamiliar. Throughout the country, despite the years of French and Spanish colonial rule, a more distant past constantly makes its presence felt. Travel here is an intense and rewarding – if not always easy – experience.

Geographically, the country divides into five zones: the coast; the great cities of the plains; the Rif; the Atlas; and the oases and desert of the pre-Sahara and Sahara. Contrary to general preconceptions, it is actually the Berbers, the indigenous population of the mountains, who make up most of the population; only around ten percent of Moroccans are "pure" Arabs, although with the shift to the industrialized cities, such distinctions are becoming less significant. A more current distinction, perhaps, is the legacy of Morocco's colonial occupation over the fifty-odd years before it reasserted its independence in 1956. The country was divided into Spanish and French zones – the former contained the north and parts of the (now disputed) Western Sahara; the latter comprised the plains and the main cities, as well as the Atlas. It was the French, who ruled their "protectorate" more closely, who had the most lasting effect on Moroccan culture, Europeanizing the cities to a strong degree and firmly imposing their language, which is spoken today by all educated Moroccans (after Moroccan Arabic or the local Berber languages).

Broadly speaking, on a brief visit the coast is best enjoyed in the north at **Tangier**, beautiful and still shaped by its old "international" port status. Inland, where the real interest of Morocco lies, the outstanding cities are **Fes** and **Marrakesh**. The great imperial capitals of the country's various dynasties, they are almost unique in the Arab world for the chance they offer to witness a city life that, in patterns and appearance, remains in large part medieval. For monuments, Fes is the highlight, though Marrakesh, the "beginning of the south", is for most visitors the more enjoyable and exciting.

Travel in the south – roughly beyond a line drawn between Casablanca and **Meknes** – is, on the whole, more relaxing than in the sometimes frenetic north. This is certainly true of the **mountain ranges**. The Rif is really for hardened travellers; only **Chaouen**, on its periphery, could be counted a "holiday spot". Hiking in the **High Atlas**, especially around North Africa's highest peak, **Djebel Toubkal**, is in fact something of a growth industry. Even if you're just a casual walker, it's worth considering, with summer treks possible at all levels of experience and altitude. And, despite inroads made by commercialization, it remains essentially "undiscovered" – like the Alps must have been in the last century.

Information, Guides and Maps

There's either an **ONMT** (the Moroccan tourist board) office or **Syndicat d'Initiative** in all towns of any size or interest. Occasionally, these offices can supply you with particular local information sheets. There are also nationally produced pamphlets on the four imperial cities, the fortified towns of the coast and "La Grande Traversée des Atlas Marocains"; and there are leaflets with good maps of the other major cities and towns. But do not expect lists of local hotels – although there is a national giude of classified hotels (1993), the main use of local offices is to get you in touch with an officially recognized **guide**.

In addition to the guides trained by the government, there are scores of young Moroccans offering their services to show you around the *souks* (markets) and sights. Some of these "unofficial guides" are genuine students, who may want to earn a small fee, but may equally be interested in practising their English. Others are out-and-out hustlers. Deal with them politely at all times and do not be intimidated.

Maps of Moroccan cities are hard to obtain locally. The most functional are those in the *Rough Guide to Morocco* – beg or borrow or photocopy from travellers you meet. The best road map is the *Michelin* 1:1,000,000 sheet #969.

Money and Banks

Once you've arrived, Morocco is an inexpensive and excellent value destination, although you'll find the poverty demands some response – small tips can make a lot of difference to individual family life. Morocco's basic unit of **currency** is the **dirham** (dh). The dirham is divided into 100 **centimes** (5-, 10-, 20- and 50-centime coins are in circulation), and in markets you may well find prices written or expressed in centimes rather than dirhams. The currency is not exchangeable outside Morocco, so when you're nearing the end of your stay it's best to get down to as little Moroccan money as possible. To change money back from dirhams, you may be asked to produce exchange receipts.

For exchange purposes, by far the most useful and efficient chain of banks is the *BMCE* (*Banque Marocaine du Commerce Exterieur*). Their bureaux de change are open 8am–8pm daily. They handle travellers' cheques (3dh commission) and Eurocheques (no commission on the spot, but your bank account may be debited by between 5 and 8 percent), and give cash advances on *Visa* and *Access*. Credit cards and Eurocheques can also be used in payment at upmarket hotels, restaurants and shops, and for car hire.

Hours for banks other than the *BMCE* are normally Mon–Fri 8.30–11.30am & 3–4.30pm in winter, 8.30am–2pm in summer and during Ramadan (the Muslim month of fasting). In major resorts there is usually at least one bank that keeps flexible hours to meet tourist demand.

Communications

Stamps can often be bought alongside postcards or at tobacconists (look for the sign: three interlocking blue circles) or at a **PTT** (post office); always post letters at a PTT. Post office hours are Mon–Fri 8am–noon & 3–6pm in winter, 8am–3pm in summer. Receiving letters **poste restante** can be a bit of a lottery, as Moroccan post office workers don't always file letters under the name you might expect. The alternatives are to pick a big hotel (anything with three or more stars should be reliable) or have things sent c/o *American Express* – represented in Morocco by *Voyages Schwartz* in Tangier, Fes, Casablanca and Marrakesh.

The **public telephone section** is usually housed in the main post office, often with a separate entrance and sometimes open longer hours – 24 hours in some of the main cities. In most major towns you can also make international calls from centrally placed **phone boxes** (*cabines*). Alternatively, you can make calls through a hotel: even fairly small places will normally do this, but be sure to ask in advance about possible surcharges and the chargeable rate. **Pay phones** accept 50-centime or 1-dirham and the old, larger 5-dirham coins – a few dirhams are enough for a call within Morocco.

Getting Around

Moroccan public transport is, on the whole, pretty good. There is an efficient rail network linking the main towns of the north, the coast and Marrakesh, and elsewhere you can travel easily enough by bus or collective *grand taxi*. Hiring a car can be a good idea, at least for part of your trip, opening up routes that are time-consuming or difficult on local transport.

■ Trains

Trains cover a limited network of routes, but for travel between the major cities they are the best option – comfortable, efficient and fairly fast. **Timetables**, printed by *ONCF*, the national railway company, are usually available for a couple of dirhams at major stations.

There are three classes of **tickets** – confusingly, first, second and fourth (*economique*). **Costs** for a second-class ticket are comparable to what you'd pay for buses; on certain "express" services, which are first- and second-class only, they are around thirty percent higher. In addition, there are **couchettes** (50dh extra) available in summer on the Tangier–Marrakesh and the Tangier–Fes trains; these are worth the money for the sake of security, as passengers are locked into a carriage with a guard.

Fares follow a reasonably consistent pattern – around 1.5dh for each 10km, 2–2.5dh for an express service. *InterRail* passes are valid in Morocco, but not *Eurail*.

■ Grands taxis

Collective *grands taxis* are one of the best features of Moroccan transport. They operate on a variety of routes, are much quicker than the buses (often quicker than trains, too), and fares are very reasonable. Most business is along specific routes, the most popular routes having more or less continuous departures throughout the day. As soon as six (or, if you're willing to pay extra, five or even four) people are assembled, the taxi sets off. On established routes *grands taxis* keep to fixed **fares** for each passenger – as a general guideline, around 2dh per person for each 10km. If you want to take a non-standard route, or an excursion, it is possible to pay for a whole *grand taxi* (*une course*) for yourself or a group – bargain hard to get the price down to around 12–15dh per 10km.

■ Buses

Bus travel is marginally cheaper than taking a *grand taxi*, and there are far more regular routes. Where you can take a *grand taxi* rather than a bus, however, do so. The difference in fare is small, and all except the express buses are very much slower and less comfortable than *grands taxis*.

There are a variety of bus services and companies. Buses run by *CTM* (the national company) are usually more reliable, with numbered seats and fixed schedules. An additional service, on certain major routes, are the express buses run by the train company, *ONCF*, where there are now no trains – or never have been. These are fast and very comfortable and compare, both in terms of time and cost, with *grands taxis*. *CTM* and *ONCF* look after your luggage on airport lines.

On small private line buses, you generally have to pay for your **baggage** to be loaded onto the roof (and taken off). Moroccans pay just a small tip for this but tourists are expected to pay 2–3dh.

■ Driving, trucks and hitching

Car hire – costing from £180/$270 a week with unlimited mileage to which you must add insurance and tax (currently 19 percent) – pays obvious dividends if you are pushed for time or want to explore the south, where getting to see anything can be quite an effort if you have to rely on public transport. However, wherever buses are sporadic or even nonexistent, it is standard practice for **vans**, **lorries** and **pick-up trucks** to carry and charge passengers. You may be asked to pay a little more than the locals, and you may be expected to bargain over this price. In parts of the Atlas, the Berbers run more or less scheduled truck services to coincide with local *souks*.

Hitching is not very big in Morocco: most people, if they own any form of transport at all, have mopeds. However, it is often easy to get rides from other **tourists**, particularly if you ask around at the campsites, and for **women travel-**lers this can be an effective and positive option for getting around. Out on the road, it's inevitably a different matter – and hitching is definitely not advisable for women travelling alone.

Accommodation

Hotels in Morocco are cheap, good value and usually pretty easy to find. The only times you might find that you have any problems in getting a room are in the peak seasons (August, Christmas or Aïd el Kebir), and even then only in a handful of main cities and resorts.

■ Unclassified hotels

Unclassified hotels (charging from about £3/$4.50 for a double) are mainly to be found in the older, Arab-built parts of cities – the *medinas* – and are almost always the cheapest options on offer. At their best, unclassified *medina* hotels are beautiful, traditional houses with white-washed rooms grouped around a central patio. On the down side, they regularly have a problem with **water**. Most of the *medinas* remain substantially unmodernized, and in the hotels hot showers are a rarity and the toilets occasionally nauseating.

■ Classified hotels

Classified hotels are almost always concentrated in a town's *ville nouvelle* – the "new" or administrative quarter, built by the French and usually set slightly apart from the *medina*. Star-ratings are fairly self-explanatory and prices are reasonable for all except the 5* categories. At the lower end, there's often little difference between an officially classified 1*B and 1*A, either of which will offer you a basic double room with a washbasin for £7.25/$11. Going up to 2* and 3*, there's a definite progression in comfort, and you can find a few elegant, old hotels in these categories. However, if you're in search of a touch of luxury, you'll most likely be looking for a room with access to a swimming pool — which means, on the whole, four stars. This is going to set you back around £20–36/$30–54 for a double.

■ Hostels, refuges and campsites

At the lower price levels — though often no cheaper than a shared room in the *medina* — there are seven **youth hostels**, or *Auberges de Jeunesse*. One, in Asni in the High Atlas, is a hiking base — useful and recommended. The others are all in major cities. In the High Atlas mountains, you will also find a number of huts, or *refuges*, equipped for hikers. These provide dormitory beds and sometimes meals and/or cooking facilities.

Campsites can be worth visiting in order to find a lift or people to share car costs. Most sites are very cheap, at around 75p/$1.10 per person and per tent; the fancier places charge around double this, but offer swimming pools and better facilities on European lines.

Food and Drink

Like accommodation, food in Morocco falls into two basic categories: ordinary Moroccan meals served in the *medina* cafés (or bought from stalls), and French-influenced tourist menus in most of the hotels and *ville nouvelle* restaurants. It's best to stick largely to the *medina* places (most are cleaner than they look), with an occasional splurge in the best restaurants you can find.

■ Food

For **breakfast** or a **snack**, you can always buy a half *baguette* — plus packs of butter and jam, cheese or eggs, if you want — from many bread or grocery stores, and take it into a café to order a drink.

Basic Moroccan meals generally centre on a thick, very filling soup — most often the spicy, bean-based *harira*, which can be a meal in itself. To this you might add a plateful of kebabs and perhaps a salad, together with dates bought at a market stall. Alternatively, you could go for a *tajine* — essentially a stew, steam-cooked slowly over a charcoal fire. Either alternative will set you back about £2.50/$3.75 for a hearty meal at a hole-in-the-wall place in the *medina*.

More expensive dishes, available in some of the *medina* cafés as well as in the dearer restaurants, include **fish**, particularly on the coast, and **chicken** (*poulet*), either spit-roasted (*rôti*) or with olives and lemon (*poulet aux olives et citron*). You will sometimes find *pastilla*, too, a succulent pigeon pie, prepared with filo pastry coated with sugar and cinnamon; it is a particular speciality of Fes. And, of course, there is *couscous*, the most famous Moroccan dish, a huge bowl of steamed semolina piled with vegetables and mutton, chicken, or occasionally fish.

To supplement these standard offerings, most tourist restaurants add a few **French dishes** — steak, liver, various fish and fowl, etc — and the ubiquitous *salade marocaine*, based on a few tomatoes, cucumbers and other greens. Together with a dessert consisting either of fruit or pastry, these meals usually come to around £5/$8.

Excellent **cakes and desserts** are available in some Moroccan cafés, but more often at pastry shops or street stalls. The most common are *cornes de gazelles*, sugar-coated pastries filled with a kind of marzipan, but there are infinite variations. **Yoghurt** (*yaourt*) is also delicious, and Morocco is surprisingly rich in seasonal **fruits**. In addition to the various kinds of **dates** — sold all year but at their best fresh from the October harvests — there are grapes, melons, strawberries, peaches and figs, all advisably washed before eaten. Or for a real thirst-quencher (and a good cure for a bad stomach), you can have quantities of **prickly pear**, cactus fruit, peeled for you in the street for a couple of dirhams.

Eating in local cafés, or if invited to a home, you may find yourself using your hands rather than a knife and fork. Muslims eat only with the **right hand**, and you should do likewise. Eating from a **communal bowl** at someone's home, it is polite to take only what is immediately in front of you, unless specifically offered a piece of meat by the host.

■ Drink

The national drink is *thé à la menthe* — green tea flavoured with sprigs of mint and a with a minimum of four cubes of sugar per cup. You can also occasionally get varieties of red or amber tea — more expensive and rarely available, but delicious and well worth trying. **Coffee** (*café*) is best in French-style cafés — either *noir* (black), *cassé* (with a drop of milk), or *au lait* (white).

Wonderful, too, and easily found at cafés or street stalls, are the fresh-squeezed **juices**: *jus d'orange*, *jus d'amande* (almond), *jus des bananes* and *jus de pomme* (apple), the last three all milk-based and served chilled. *Leben* – yoghurt and water – is often sold at train and bus stations, and can do wonders for an upset stomach. **Mineral water**, which is a worthwhile investment throughout the country, is usually referred to by brand name: the ubiquitous *Sidi Harazem* , the much nicer *Sidi Ali*, or the naturally sparkling *Oulmès*.

As an Islamic nation, Morocco gives **alcohol** a low profile. It is, in fact, not generally possible to buy any alcohol at all in the *medinas*, and for beer or wine you always have to go to a tourist restaurant or hotel, or a bar in the *ville nouvelle*. Moroccan **wines**, however, can be very good, if a little heavy for drinking without a meal. Those Moroccans who drink in **bars** – a growing number in the industrial cities – tend to stick to **beer**, which should cost around 15dh a bottle in ordinary bars. Bars are totally male domains, except in tourist hotels – but even then they can be a bit rowdy.

Opening Hours and Holidays

Shops and stalls in the *souk* areas stay open just about every hour of the day, though the shop owners might be found sleeping through the midday hours. The exception to all this is Friday, when most vendors close at least for morning prayers, with some staying shut all day. **Museums** in Morocco are generally open 9am–noon & 2–6pm, closing on Friday morning. Bear in mind that non-Muslims are forbidden entry to virtually all **religious buildings**.

Islamic **religious holidays** are calculated on the lunar calendar, so their dates tend to rotate thoughout the seasons. During **Ramadan**, the ninth month of the Islamic calendar, all Muslims observe a total fast lasting from sunrise to sunset. Non-Muslims are not expected to observe Ramadan, but it is a good idea to be sensitive about not breaking the fast (particularly smoking) in public. Ramadan begins on February 11 in 1994, on January 31 in 1995 and on January 21 in 1996. The other main religious holidays in the

Islamic year are **Aïd el Kebir**, otherwise known as Aïd al Adhar (which is the celebration of Abraham's willingness to sacrifice his son Isaac), **Moharem** (the Muslim new year) and **Mouloud** (the birthday of the Prophet), each of which is usually marked by two official days off.

Secular holidays are considered less important, with most public services (except banks and offices) operating normally even during the two biggest ones – the Feast of the Throne that takes place on March 3 and Independence Day on November 18.

Emergencies

Keeping your luggage and money secure is an important consideration in Morocco – it is obviously not wise to carry large sums of cash or valuables on your person, especially in the main tourist cities. **Hotels** are generally secure for depositing money; **campsites** are considerably less secure, and many campers advise wearing a money belt even while sleeping.

There are two main types of **police**. The grey-clad **gendarmes**, who staff the road checkpoints, are the ones with whom foreigners should deal. The khaki-clad military police have limited authority and are usually none too helpful.

Moroccan **pharmacists** are well trained and dispense a wide range of drugs. If they feel you need a full diagnosis, they can usually recommend a **doctor**, or a list of English-speaking doctors in major cities can be obtained from consulates and some tourist offices.

The smoking of **kif** (hashish, *chocolaté*) has for a long time been a regular pastime of Moroccans and tourists alike. There is no real effort to stop Moroccans from using *kif*, but it is illegal nonetheless. As a tourist you are peculiarly vulnerable to the rip-offs and scams of dealers. Many have developed aggressive tactics, selling people hash (or, occasionally, even planting it) and then turning you in to the police or threatening to do so.

EMERGENCY NUMBERS
Police ☎19; Hospital ☎15.

TANGIER, MEKNES AND FES

The two chief cities of northern Morocco, Tangier and Tetouan, are by reputation difficult, with guides and hustlers preying on first-time travellers. However, it doesn't take
long to get the measure of them – and to enjoy the experience. **Tangier**, hybridized
and slightly seedy from its long European contact, has a setting and skyline the equal
of any Mediterranean resort, and is immediately compelling in its role as meeting point
of Europe and Africa. **Tetouan**, in the shadow of the wild Rif Mountains, feels more
Moroccan – its Medina a glorious labyrinth, dotted with squares, *souks* and buildings
from its seventeenth-century founding by refugees from Spanish Andalusia.

Moving on from either city, the most popular destination is the mountain town of
Chaouen – a small-scale and enjoyably laid-back place to come to terms with being in
Morocco. It is most easily reached via Tetouan. Heading south from Tangier – which
stands at the beginning of the railway lines to Fes, Rabat, Casablanca and Marrakesh –
a good place to get acclimatized is the seaside resort of **Asilah**.

Inland, **Fes** has for ten centuries been at the heart of Moroccan history and is today
unique in the Arab world, preserving the appearance and much of the life of a medieval
Islamic city. In terms of monuments, above all the intricate university *medersas*, or
colleges, Fes has as much as the other Moroccan imperial capitals together, while the
city's *souks*, extending for over a mile, maintain the whole tradition of urban crafts.
Meknes, the megalomaniac creation of Moulay Ismail, most tyrannical of all Moroccan
sultans, is also a city of lost ages, its enduring impression being that of an endless
series of walls. But Meknes is also an important modern market centre and its *souks*,
though smaller and less secretive than those of Fes, are almost as varied and generally
more authentic. There are, too, the local attractions of **Volubilis**, the best-preserved of
the country's Roman sites, and the hilltop town of **Moulay Idriss**, the most important
Moroccan shrine.

Tangier (Tanger, Tangiers)

For the first five decades of this century **TANGIER** was one of the stylish resorts of the
Mediterranean – an "International City" with its own laws and administration, plus an
eclectic community of exiles, expatriates and refugees. When Moroccan independence
was gained in 1956, however, Tangier's special status was removed. Almost overnight,
the finance and banking businesses shifted to Spain and Switzerland, and the expatriate colony dwindled as the new national government imposed bureaucratic controls.
These days there's a slight air of decay about the city, most tangible in the older hotels
and bars, and a somewhat uncertain overall identity: a city that seems halfway to
becoming a mainstream tourist resort yet still retains hints of its dubious past amid the
shambling 1930s architecture and modern high-rise apartment blocks.

Arrival and accommodation

The Gare du Port **train station** is almost directly by the **ferry terminal**; most trains
leave from here as well as the Gare de Ville, 300m past the port gates. Nearby there are
ranks for *grand* and *petit taxis*; they are best engaged here, rather than amid the hustle
of the port gates. Tangier's **airport** is about 15km outside the city; alternatives to the
very sporadic bus are to take a taxi or to walk the two kilometres to the main road,
where you can pick up the #17 or #70 bus to the Grand Socco. The **ONMT** office is at
29 bd Pasteur, just down from place de France (Mon–Sat 8am–2pm).

Tangier has dozens of **hotels and pensions**, and finding a room is never much of a
problem: if the first place you try is full, ask them to phone and reserve you a place
elsewhere – most will be happy to do so. The city does, however, get crowded during

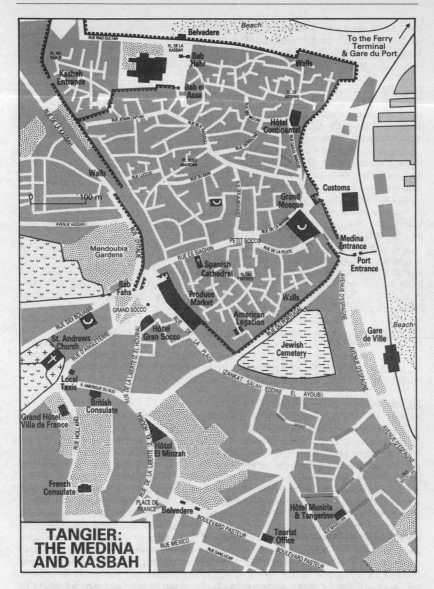

**TANGIER:
THE MEDINA
AND KASBAH**

July and August, with some of the unclassified places doubling their prices. The *Mauretania* (no ☎; ①), *Fuentes* (☎09/93.44.69; ①) and *Palace* (☎09/93.61.28; ①), all in or near the Petit Socco, are reasonable unclassified **hotels** in the Medina, while on rue Magellan in the Ville Nouvelle are the unclassified *Magellan* (☎09/93.87.26; ①) and *El Muniria* (☎09/93.53.37; ①), friendly with a late night bar (the *Tanger-Inn*). The *Miramar*, av des FAR (☎09/93.89.48; ②), with big rooms and hot showers, and the

Cecil, av d'Espagne (☎09/93.10.87; ②), over a hundred years old, but recently restored, are the best value on the seafront. The closest and most popular **campsite** is the *Miramonte* (☎09/93.71.33), 3km to the west of the centre (bus #1 from the Grand Socco). The **youth hostel**, rue el Antaki 8 (☎09/94.01.27; ①) is new, clean and well run.

The City

Together with the **beach** and the seafront **avenues d'Espagne/des FAR**, the easiest reference points are the city's three main squares – the Grand Socco, Petit Socco and place de France. The **Grand Socco** – once the main market square – offers the most straightforward approach to the **Medina**. The arch at the northwest corner of the square opens onto rue d'Italie, which becomes rue de la Kasbah, the northern entrance to the Kasbah quarter. To the right, there is an opening onto rue es Siaghin, off which are most of the *souks* and at the end of which is the **Petit Socco**, the Medina's principal landmark and square, seedy and slightly conspiratorial in feel. Heading past the Socco toward the sea walls are two small streets straddled by the Grand Mosque, which, as throughout Morocco, is strictly closed to non-Muslims. If instead you follow **rue des Chrétiens** (aka rue des Almohades) and its continuation **rue Ben Raisouli** you'll emerge, with luck, around the lower gate to the Kasbah.

The **Kasbah**, walled off from the Medina on the highest rise of the coast, has been the palace and administrative quarter since Roman times. It is a strange, somewhat sparse area of walled compounds, occasional colonnades and a number of luxurious villas built in the 1920s, when this became one of the Mediterranean's most chic residential sites. The main point of interest here is the former Sultanate Palace, or **Dar el Makhzen** (usually 9.30am–noon & 3–6pm; closed Tues), now converted to an excellent museum of crafts and antiquities. At the entrance to the main part of the palace is the **Bit el Mal**, the old treasury, and adjoining it a small private **mosque**, near to which is the entrance to the herb- and shrub-lined palace **gardens**, shaded by jacaranda trees. If you leave this way, you will come out by the stairway to the **Café-Restaurant Detroit**, set up in the early 1960s by Beat writer Brion Gysin. The café is now an overpriced tourist spot but worth the price of a mint tea for the views.

Eating, drinking and nightlife

As with most Moroccan cities, the cheapest places to **eat** are in the **Medina**. There's a choice of several hole-in-the-wall cafés on rue de Commerce and rue des Chrétiens. *Restaurant Andaluz*, rue de Commerce 7, serves impeccably fried swordfish, grilled brochettes and salad. For a little more variety, the cafés around the Grand Socco are worth a look too; most stay open all night. (Note that alcoholic drinks are not served in the Medina or Grand Socco restaurants.) In the **Ville Nouvelle**, the *Restaurant Africa*, at the lower end of rue Salah Eddine El Ayoubi is a crowded local place with inexpensive and highly recommended Moroccan dishes. *Restaurant Agadir*, rue Prince Hénetier Sidi Mohammed 21, above place de France, is small but with accomplished French and Moroccan cooking. *Raihani's*, rue Ahmed Chaoki 10 (☎90/93.48.66), and *Damascus*, av du Prince Monlay Abdallah 2, off bd Pasteur (☎09/93.22.77) serve more upmarket food – try *harira* (soup), *couscous* and *pastilla* (pigeon pie). On the seafront, many of the hotels have reliable 'continental' restaurants, but try *Hôtel-Restaurant L'Marsa*, av d'Espagne 92, for excellent pizzas and home-made ice cream to follow – with equally delicious croissants and cakes for breakfast or tea. For Spanish seafood, in vast portions, try the pricier *Romero's*, av du Prince Moulay Abdallah, off bd Pasteur (☎09/93.22.77).

For **drinking**, *Tanger-Inn* (see *Hôtel Muniria* above), rue Magellan, is an imitation Brighton pub – quite an institution, run by an ex-trooper and serving the expats for the last twenty years (daily 9pm–2am). The *Hôtel Miramar* on av des FAR is a hard-drinking seafront spot. Traditionally a gay **disco**, *Scott's* on rue El Moutanabi is worth a look for its decor; take care leaving late at night – the best idea is to tip the doorman 5dh to order you a taxi. Finally, the *Morocco Palace*, av du Prince Moulay Abdallah, is a strange, sometimes slightly manic place that puts on traditional Moroccan music for Westerners until around 1am, then a Western disco for the Moroccans.

Listings

Airlines *Royal Air Maroc*, place de France (☎09/93.47.22).

American Express Represented by *Voyages Schwartz*, 54 bd Pasteur (☎09/93.34.59). Mon–Fri 9am–noon & 3–7pm, Sat 9am–12.30pm.

Car rental Most big companies have offices along bd Pasteur/bd Mohammed V.

Chemists There are several English-speaking chemists in the place de France and along bd Pasteur.

Consulates *Great Britain*, 9 rue Amérique du Sud (☎09/93.58.97).

Exchange The *BMCE* on bd Pasteur is the most efficient (daily 8am–2pm & 4–8pm).

Moving on Travelling on within Morocco is simplest either by train (the lines run to Meknes/Fes, or Rabat/Casablanca/Marrakesh), or, if you are heading east to Tetouan, by shared *grand taxi*. Leaving the country, ferries run to Algeciras, Gibraltar and Sète (France).

Post and phones Main PTT, 33 bd Mohammed V (Mon–Sat 8.30am–noon & 2.30–6.30pm; phone section open 24hr).

Police Main station is on rue Ibn Toumert.

Asilah

The first stop on the railway beyond Tangier, **ASILAH** is one of the most elegant of the old Portuguese Atlantic ports, with its square stone ramparts flanked by palms. Its beach is also outstanding – the most popular stretches are to the north of the town. The **train station** is 2km north of the town – an easy enough walk if you miss the connecting shuttle. Arriving by **grand taxi** (1hr from Tangier), you're dropped in place Mohammed V, a small square at the edge of the Medina, about 100 metres north of the ramparts; buses drop you in an adjacent street.

The circuit of **towers and ramparts**, built by the Portuguese in the sixteenth century, are pleasant to wander around. The main keep, **El Hamra**, has been restored as a venue for the International Festival of the arts (mid-July to mid-Aug) and has the occasional exhibition at other times of the year. The newly-opened international arts centre is opposite the grand mosque. The town's focal sight – stretching over the sea at the heart of the Medina – is the **Palais de Raisuli**, built in 1909 by one Er Raisuli, a local bandit who was eventually appointed governor over practically all the tribes of northwest Morocco. It is closed outside festival times, but you may strike lucky with the caretaker. Failing that, and if you are keen, you could get a note in Arabic from the Hôtel de Ville; this should do the trick.

Asilah can be packed full during the International Festival, but most of the year **accommodation** is easy enough to find and generally inexpensive. The unclassified *Hôtel Nasr*, place Mohammed V (no ☎; ①) is pleasantly run and has the cheapest rooms. It may not be too welcoming, but rooms on a terrace above the walls overlooking the daily vegetable market make the *Asilah*, 79 av Hassan II (☎09/91.72.86; ①) an attractive alternative. *Hôtel el Makhazine*, av Melilla (☎09/91.70.90; ②), close to the seafront and with a bar, is probably the best choice if you can afford it. There is a string of **campsites** south of the train station; the closest, *Camping Echrigui* (☎09/91.71.82), is as good a choice as any. The two most obvious **restaurants**, facing each other in place Zellaca just outside the ramparts, are also generally the best: *El Oceano* and *La Alcazaba*, both have outdoor tables and Spanish-style fried fish; Further along the seafront are a couple of similar seafood restaurants: *Casa Gracia* and *El Espignon* – the latter is convenient for the campsites.

Ceuta (Sebta)

A Spanish enclave which dates back to the sixteenth century, **CEUTA** (Sebta in Arabic), is a curious political anomaly but, since the Algeciras–Ceuta ferries and hydrofoils are quicker than those going to Tangier, this drab outpost has become a popular point of entry to Morocco. Try to arrive early in the day so that you have plenty of time to move on to Tetouan or beyond. You don't officially enter Morocco until the border at **FNIDEQ**, 3km out of town, reached by local bus from the seafront. Once across, the easiest transport is a shared *grand taxi* to Tetouan; buses are infrequent, though a couple of dirhams cheaper. There are **exchange facilities** (cash only) at the frontier.

If you have to stay overnight in Ceuta, be warned that it isn't easy to find a room – and not cheap when you do. A complete list is available from the **tourist office** by the ferry dock; if it is closed you can consult the list displayed in its window. The **youth hostel** (①), at Plaza Rafael Gilbert 27, is open in July and August only.

Leaving Ceuta **by ferry** for Algeciras, you can usually turn up at the port, buy tickets, and board a ferry within a couple of hours. The one time to avoid, as at Tangier, is the last week of August. If you intend to use the quicker **hydrofoil service**, it's best to book the previous day in high season; details and tickets for the hydrofoil are available from 6 Muelle Caõnero Dato (☎0034/56.51.60.41), by the ferry terminal.

Tetouan

If you're a first-time Moroccan visitor coming from Ceuta, **TETOUAN** can be an intimidating introductory experience. The Medina seems overwhelming and totally unfamiliar, and the hustlers, often dealing large quantities of *kif* from the Rif Mountains, have the worst reputation in Morocco. Physically, though, Tetouan is strikingly beautiful, poised atop the slope of an enormous valley against a dark mass of rock. The town was hastily constructed by Andalusian refugees in the fifteenth century, and their houses, full of extravagant detail, seem more akin to the old Arab quarters of Córdoba and Seville than to other Moroccan towns.

Arriving by bus or *grand taxi*, you'll find yourself on the edge of the **Ville Nouvelle**, which follows a fairly straightforward grid. At its centre is **place Moulay el Mehdi**, with the post office and main banks. From here the grid stretches east toward **place Hassan II**, the old meeting place and market square, recently remodelled with a pavement of Islamic motifs, minaret-like floodlights and a brand new Royal Palace. The usual approach to the Medina is through **Bab el Rouah** (Gate of the Wind), the archway just south of the Royal Palace. You then find yourself on **rue Terrafin**, a relatively wide lane which, with its continuations, cuts straight across to the east gate, **Bab Okla**. To the left of rue Terrafin, a series of alleys gives access to most of the town's food and craft **souks**, packing the mass of alleys and passageways leading toward Bab Sebta, the northern gate. The quarter to the north of Bab Okla, below the Grand Mosque, was the Medina's most exclusive residential area and contains some of its finest mansions. Walking towards the gate you'll see signs for a *Palais*, one of the best of the buildings, now converted into a carpet and crafts warehouse aimed at tourists. Considerably more authentic is the **Museum of Moroccan Arts** (Mon & Wed–Fri 9am–noon & 2.30–5.30pm, Sat 9am–noon), just outside Bab Okla. A former arms bastion, the museum has one of the more impressive collections around of traditional crafts and ethnographic objects. Take a look particularly at the *zellij* – enamelled tile mosaics – and then cross the road to the **Crafts School**, where you can see craftsmen producing them in ways essentially unchanged since the fourteenth century.

Practicalities

The **tourist office** is a few metres down bd Mohammed V from place el Mehdi (Mon–Fri 8am–2pm & 3–6pm, Sat and sometimes Sun 8am–2pm); they will also change money when the banks are closed. Pick of the **classified hotels** are the comfortable *Hôtel Principe*, 20 Youssef Ibn Tachfine (☎09/96.27.95; ①), midway between the bus station and Moulay el Mehdi, and the *National*, 8 rue Mohammed Ben Larbi Torres (☎096/32.90; ①), an old-fashioned hotel with a patio bar and restaurant, which sometimes insists on full board in midsummer. Two good **unclassified** places are the tiny *Pension Iberia*, place Moulay el Mehdi (☎09/96.36.79; ①), and the slightly more expensive but spotless *Pension Cosmopolita*, 5 rue du Prince Sidi Mohammed (☎09/96.48.21; ①). The nearest **campsites** are on the coast at Martil, 11km to the east.

As ever, the cheapest **food** is to be found in the Medina, particularly the stalls inside Bab el Rouah and along rue Luneta. For variety, try one of the many places on or around bd Mohammed V/bd Mohammed Ben Larbi Torres in the Ville Nouvelle. Good choices here include *Restaurant Moderne* in Pasaje Achaach (off rue Mohammed Ben Larbi Torres) and the slightly pricier and licensed *Restaurant Zerhoun*, 7 bd Mohammed Ben Larbi Torres.

MOVING ON

There are regular **buses** from Tetouan to Chaouen, Meknes, Fes and Tangier, but heading for Tangier or Ceuta it's easiest to travel by **grand taxi**. The ONCF office on rue Achrai Mai, alongside place al Adala, sells **train** tickets that include connecting buses to the station of Tnine Sidi Lyamani, just south of Asilah.

Chaouen (Chefchaouen, Xaouen)

Shut in by a fold of mountains, **CHAOUEN** becomes visible only once you have arrived – a dramatic approach to a town which, until the arrival of Spanish troops in 1920, had been visited by just three Europeans. This whole region is sacred to Muslims due to the presence of the tomb of Moulay Abdessalam Ben Mchich – one of the "four poles of Islam" – and the town of Chaouen was itself established by one of his followers, Moulay Rachid, as a base from which to attack the Portuguese. Such was the town's isolation that when the Spanish began their occupation, they found the Jews here speaking medieval Castilian – a language extinct in Spain for nearly four hundred years.

These days, Chaouen is becoming a little over-concerned with tourism, but like Tetouan, its architecture has a strong Andalusian character, and it's a town of extraordinary light and colour, its whitewash tinted with blue and edged by golden stone walls. Pensions are among the friendliest and cheapest around, and to stay here a few days is one of the best possible introductions to Morocco.

With a population of around 20,000 – a tenth of Tetouan's – Chaouen is more like a large village in size and feel, confusing only on arrival. **Buses** and **grands taxis** drop you at the marketplace, outside the walls of the town in a vague straggle of new buildings grouped about the Mosque of Moulay Rachid. To reach the Medina, walk up across the marketplace to the tiny arched entrance, **Bab el Ain**, just above the prominent *Hôtel Magou*. Through the gate a dominant lane winds up to the main square, the elongated **place Outa el Hammam**. This is where most of the town's evening life takes place, with its cafés overhung by upper rooms – some the preserve of *kif* smokers. By day, the town's focus is the **Kasbah**, a quiet ruin with shady gardens which occupies one side of the square. Beyond, the smaller **place el Makhzen** is in some ways a continuation of the marketplace, an elegant clearing with an old fountain, and pottery stalls set up for the package tourists.

Along and just off the main route through the Medina is a series of small, **unclassified pensions**, possibly the quietest of which is the *Pension Ibn Batouta*, rue Sidi Boukhanela (☎09/98.60.44; ①), a small, basic pension with a friendly manager, signposted to the left at the near end of place Outa el Hamman. For more comfort, there is the **classified** *Hotel Salam*, 39 rue Tarik Ibn Ziad (☎09/98.62.39; ①) on the lower road; back rooms and the shady roof terrace overlook the valley. Chaouen's **campsite** is up on the hill above the town, by the modern *Hôtel Asma*; it is inexpensive but can be crowded during summer. The adjoining **youth hostel** is only worth considering if all the pensions are full.

A few of the cafés in the place Outa el Hammam serve regular Moroccan **meals**; the best is the *Restaurant Kasbah*. Better though are the two restaurants outside the Medina up from Bab el Aîn on rue Moulay Ali Ben Rachid: *Restaurant Ben Rachid* and, further up, *Restaurant Zouar*.

MOVING ON
Bus departures to Fes, and to a lesser degree, Meknes, are quite often full: try to get tickets the day before. If you can't get on a direct bus, an alternative is to take a *grand taxi* or local bus to Ouezzane and another from there, or to return to Tetouan, where most of the buses originate. For Tetouan, buses leave at least four times a day – much less of a problem – or you can share a *grand taxi*. Daily buses also run to the Ceuta border.

Meknes

Cut in two by the wide river valley of the Oued Boufekrane, **MEKNES** is a sprawling, prosperous provincial city. Monuments from its past well reward a day's exploration, as do the varied and busy *souks* of its Medina: getting a grasp of Meknes prepares you a little for the drama of Fes, and certainly helps give an idea of quality and prices for crafts shopping.

Arrival and accommodation
There are two **train stations**, both of which are situated in the Ville Nouvelle on the east bank. The smaller, more convenient one is the **Gare El Amir Abdelkadir**, a couple of blocks from the centre; all trains stop here. **Petits taxis**, **grands taxis** and **buses** arrive at the focal point of the Medina, place el Hedim. For bus connections onwards from Meknes, check at the **Syndicat d'Initiative** inside the gates at the intersection of av Hassan II and av Moulay Ismail, or at the **ONMT** tourist office on the place d'Adminstrative.

Hotels tend to be concentrated in the Ville Nouvelle, and if you're looking for comfort and proximity to bars and restaurants this is definitely the place to stay. However, it's a fairly long walk from the Ville Nouvelle to the Medina and, if you're here for only a short stay, there are more advantages in being close to the monuments and *souks*. Pick of the Medina hotels are the *Maroc*, rue Rouamazine (☎05/53.00.75; ①), and further up the street, the *Hôtel de Paris* (no ☎; ①). The best cheap choice in the Ville Nouvelle is the unclassified *Bordeaux*, 64 av de la Gare (☎05/52.23.63; ①). *Hotel Touring*, 34 av Allal Ben Abdallah (☎05/52.23.51; ①) is the best of the one-star places, followed by the *Excelsior*, 57 av des FAR (☎05/52.19.00; ①), and the friendly, old-fashioned *Majestic*, 19 av Mohammed V (☎05/52.00.35; ②), handy for the El Amir Abdelkadir rail station.

The **youth hostel**, av Okba Ibn Nafi (☎05/52.17.43; ①; reception closed 10am–noon & 4–7pm), is a bit out of the way, but well maintained and with no curfew. The town's pleasant **campsite**, *Camping Aguedal*, is a twenty-minute walk from place el Hedim, opposite the Heri as-Souani.

The City

More than any other Moroccan town, Meknes is associated with a single figure, the **Sultan Moulay Ismail**, in whose reign (1672–1727) the city was built up from a provincial centre to a spectacular capital with over fifty palaces and some fifteen miles of exterior walls. Ismail was a tyrant even by the standards of his own times – apart from battles, it is estimated that he was responsible for over 30,000 deaths – yet his reign was Morocco's last golden age. The principal remains of Ismail's creation – the imperial city of palaces and gardens, barracks, granaries and stables – sprawl below the Medina amid a confusing array of enclosures. **Place el Hedim** (the Square of Demolition and Renewal) originally formed the western corner of the Medina, but the sultan demolished the houses here to provide a grand approach to his palace quarter. Through **Bab Mansour**, and straight ahead through a second gate, you will find your-self in a large open square, on the right of which is a domed **Koubba**, once a reception hall for ambassadors to the imperial court. Below it, a stairway descends into a vast series of subterranean vaults, known as the **Prison of Christian Slaves** (10dh), though it was probably a storehouse or granary.

Ahead of the *koubba*, within the wall and at right angles to it, are two modest gates. The one on the left opens onto an apparently endless corridor of walls and, a few metres down, the entrance to **Moulay Ismail's Mausoleum** (9am–noon & 3–6pm). The fact that this has remained a shrine might seem puzzling, but his absolute tyranny of control, success in driving out the Spanish from Larache and the British from Tangier, and his extreme observance of orthodox Islam all conferred a kind of magic on him. Entering the mausoleum, you are allowed to approach the sanctuary; decorated in bright *zellij* and spiralling stuccowork, it is a fine if unspectacular series of courts and chambers.

Past the mausoleum, a gate to your left gives access to the dilapidated quarter of **Dar el Kebira**, Ismail's palace complex. The imperial structures – the legendary fifty palaces – can still be made out between and above the houses here: ogre-like creations, whose scale is hard to believe. They were completed in 1677 and dedicated at an aston-ishing midnight celebration, when the sultan personally slaughtered a wolf so that its head might be displayed at the centre of the gateway. On the opposite side of the long-walled corridor, beyond the Royal Golf Gardens, more immense buildings are spread out, making up Ismail's last great palace, the **Dar el Makhzen**. At its end, and the prin-cipal "sight" of the imperial city, is the **Heri as-Souani** – a series of storerooms and granaries that were filled with provisions for siege or drought. From the roof garden, with its café, you can gaze out across much of the Dar el Makhzen and the wonderfully still **Agdal Basin** – built as an irrigation reservoir and pleasure lake.

The Medina, although taking much of its present form and size under Moulay Ismail, bears less of his stamp. The **Dar Jamai** (9am–noon & 3–6pm; 10dh), at the back of place el Hedim, is one of the best examples of a nineteenth-century Moroccan palace. Its exhibits, some of which have been used to recreate the reception rooms, are predominantly of the same age, though some of the pieces of Fes and Meknes pottery date back to around Ismail's reign. The best display, however, is of Middle Atlas carpets, particularly those of the Beni Mguild tribe.

To get down into the **souks** from place el Hedim, follow the lane immediately behind the Dar Jamai. You will come out right in the middle of the Medina's major market street: on your left is **Souk en Nejjarin**, with the carpet *souk*; on your right, leading to the Grand Mosque and Bou Inania Medersa, are the fancier goods offered in the **Souk es Sebbat**. The **Bou Inania Medersa** (9am–noon & 3–6pm; 10dh), was constructed around 1340–50 and its most unusual feature is a ribbed dome over the entrance hall, an impressive piece of craftsmanship which extends right out into the *souk*. From the roof, to which there's generally access, you can look out to the tiled pyramids of the Grand Mosque; the *souk* is mostly obscured from view, but you can get a good, general panorama of the town.

Eating and drinking

For straight Moroccan **food** the *Restaurant Economique*, 123 rue Dar Smen, opposite Bab Djemaa en Nouar is among the best of the Medina's café-restaurants. Nearby is the *Restaurant Zitouna*, 44 rue Djemaa Zitouna, a bit fancier with good traditional food. In the Ville Nouvelle, there is *La Coupole*, on the corner of av Hassan II and Rue du Ghana, with a bar and nightclub. On rue Atlas, off av Mohammed V and near the *Hotel Majestic* are two reliable eateries: *Pizzeria Le Four* (pasta and pizzas), and the *Montana* (bar on ground floor, eat upstairs). There is also a surprising number of bars, several of them in Ville Nouvelle hotels. Freestanding are *Club de Nuit,* on the corner of av Hassan II and av des FAR, with swing doors and sawdust on the floor, and *Cabaret Oriental,* av Hassan II, which occasionally has bands into the small hours. For a quieter drink, the *Hotel Transatlantique* would be your best bet.

Volubilis and Moulay Idriss

The classic excursion from Meknes, **Volubilis** and **Moulay Idriss** embody much of Morocco's early history – Volubilis as its Roman provincial capital, Moulay Idriss as the source of the country's first Arab dynasty. The sites stand 4km apart, at either side of a deep and very fertile valley, about 30km north of Meknes. You can take in both on a leisurely day trip from Meknes by *grand taxi* or bus – non-Muslims have no choice when it comes to Moulay Idriss, as only Muslims are allowed to stay there. It is simplest to visit Volubilis first, then go on to Moulay Idriss, where you can pick up a bus or *grand taxi* returning to Meknes.

Volubilis

Visible for miles from the bends in the approach road, **VOLUBILIS** occupies the ledge of a long, high plateau. Except for a small trading post on an island off Essaouira, Volubilis was the Roman Empire's most remote base, but direct Roman rule lasted little over two centuries – the garrison withdrew in 285 AD, to ease pressure elsewhere. The city itself remained active well into the eighteenth century, when its marble was carried away by slaves for the building of Meknes. What you are able to see today, well excavated and maintained, are largely the ruins of second- and third-century AD buildings – impressive and affluent creations from its period as a colonial capital. The entrance to the site (daily, sunrise to sunset; 20dh) is through a minor gate set into the city wall, built in 168 AD following a series of Berber insurrections. Just inside the gate are the ticket office, a shaded café-bar and a small, open-air **museum** of sculpture and other fragments. The best of the finds made here – which include a superb collection of bronzes – have all been taken to the Rabat museum. Volubilis, however, has retained in situ the great majority of its **mosaics**, some thirty or so in a good state of preservation.

Moulay Idriss

MOULAY IDRISS takes its name from its founder, Morocco's most venerated saint and the creator of its first Arab dynasty. His tomb and *zaouia* (sanctuary) lie right at the heart of the town, the reason for its sacred status and the object of constant pilgrimage. Even today, now open to non-Muslims for almost seventy years, it is still a place which feels closed and introspective. Arriving in Moulay Idriss, you find yourself below an enlongated square near the base of the town; above you, almost directly ahead, stand the green-tiled pyramids of **Moulay Idriss' shrine and zaouia**. Rebuilt by Moulay Ismail, the shrine stands cordoned off from the street by a low, wooden bar to keep out Christians and beasts of burden. To get a true sense of it, you have to climb up towards one of the vantage points near the pinnacle of each quarter.

Fes

The most ancient of the imperial capitals, **FES** is a place that stimulates your senses – with haunting and beautiful sounds, infinite visual details and unfiltered odours – and seems to exist suspended somewhere between the Middle Ages and the modern world. As is usually the case, there is a French-built Ville Nouvelle, but some 200,000 of the city's approximately half-million inhabitants continue to live in an extraordinary Medina-city – Fes el Bali – which owes absolutely nothing to the West besides its electricity and its tourists. Like much of "traditional" Morocco, the city was "saved" and then re-created by the French – under the auspices of General Lyautey, the Protectorate's first Resident-General. By building a new European city nearby – the Ville Nouvelle – and then transferring Fes' economic and political functions to Rabat and the west coast, Lyautey ensured the city's eclipse along with its preservation. The decline of the city notwithstanding, **Fassis** – the people of Fes – have a reputation throughout Morocco for being successful and sophisticated, and most government ministries are headed by Fassis.

Arrival and information

The **train station** is situated in the Ville Nouvelle, ten minutes' walk from the concentration of hotels around place Mohammed V. If you prefer to stay in the Medina, either take a *petit taxi* or walk down to av Hassan II, where you can pick up the #9 bus to Dar Batha/place de l'Istiqlal, near Bab Boujeloud – the western gate to Fes el Bali. Be prepared for hustlers: Fes is possibly the worst city in Morocco in this respect, and the station is a key locale. The main **bus station** is in place Baghdadi, by Bab Boujeloud; **grands taxis** operate in and out of place Baghdadi as well.

The Medina is actually two separate cities: Fes el Bali, the oldest part, and Fes el Djedid, the "New Fes" established in the thirteenth century. Fes el Bali, where you'll want to spend most of your time, is an incredibly intricate web of lanes, blind alleys and *souks*. The free ONMT map is a useful aid, available from the **ONMT office** on place de la Résistance, in the Ville Nouvelle (Mon–Fri 8am–noon & 2–6pm, Sat 8am–noon). A half-day tour with an official guide is a useful introduction to Fes el Bali; they can be hired at the **Syndicat d'Initiative** (Mon–Sat 8am–7pm) at Bab Boujeloud, at place Mohammed V, or outside the more upmarket hotels.

Accommodation

There is a shortage of **hotel** space in all categories, so be prepared for higher than usual prices and try to phone ahead. If you are not overly concerned about the size and cleanliness of your room, then the **Medina** is the place to be, but you will be paying well over the odds for a distinctly flea-pit environment. In the **Ville Nouvelle**, there is a much wider choice of hotels – most of them adequate if unexciting, but close to the restaurants and bars, and the train station. The first three places below are in the Medina; the remainder are all in the Ville Nouvelle.

Jardin Publique, signposted down a short lane by the Boujeloud Mosque, Fes el Bali (☎05/63.30.86). Friendly and clean, with rooms around a courtyard. ①

Cascades, on the square just inside the Bab Boujeloud, Fes el Bali (☎05/63.54.68). Small, shabby rooms compensated for by a roof terrace. ①

Du Commerce, place des Alaouites, Fes el Djedid (☎05/62.22.31). Better than most Medina hotels, and facing the royal palace. ①

Jeanne d'Arc, 36 av Mohammed es Slaoui (☎05/62.12.33). Sepulchral but clean; tricky to find with a small sign hidden by trees. ①

Du Maghreb, 25 av Mohammed es Slaoui (☎05/62.59.99). Another discreet hotel near Jeanne d'Arc; reception is at the top of the stairs. ①

Kairouan, 84 rue du Sandan (☎05/62.35.90). Well-kept, well-decorated hotel. ①

Central, corner of rue Nador and bd Mohammed V (☎05/62.23.33). Cheapest of the classified hotels, therefore popular and often full. ①

Lamdaghri, 10 Kabbour el Mangad (☎05/62.03.10). Featuring bigger rooms and better service than average. ②

Olympic, rue Houman Fetouaki, off bd Mohammed V (☎05/62.45.29). A clean, reliable and functional hotel near the market. ②

Mounia, 60 rue Asilah (☎05/62.48.38). New hotel with very helpful management; bar, restaurant and the occasional disco. ②

Splendid, 9 rue Abdelkrim el Kattabi (☎05/62.21.48). Good modern hotel with pool, but relies too much on tour groups to bother with individuals. ②

Youth Hostel, 18 rue Abdeslam Serghini (☎05/62.40.85). An easy-going, friendly hostel, which rents out space on the roof if the dormitories are full. Closes 10pm. ①

Fes el Bali

The area around **Bab Boujeloud** is today the principal entrance to Fes el Bali: a place with a great concentration of cafés and stalls where people come to talk and stare. Before heading into the Medina proper, take a look at the elegant **Dar Batha** palace, designed for the reception of ambassadors and now a **Museum of Moroccan Arts and Crafts** (9–11.30am & 3–6pm; closed Tues; 10dh). The collections are probably the finest of their kind in Morocco, concentrating on local artisan tradition – and the courtyards and gardens are a good respite from the general exhaustion of the Medina.

Talâa Kebira (or rue du Grand Talâa) is the major artery of the Medina, and with its continuations runs through to the Kairaouine Mosque, lined with shops and stalls for virtually its whole length. About one hundred metres down is the most brilliant of Fes' monuments, the **Medersa Bou Inania**. Established as a rival to the Kairaouine university, and for a while the most important religious building in the city, it comes close to perfection in every aspect of its construction. In addition, it is the city's only building still in religious use that you are allowed into; you cannot enter the prayer hall but you can sit in the marble courtyard and gaze across to it (8am–5pm; closed Fri morning; 10dh).

Making your way down Talâa Kebira you will come to an arched gateway marked **Souk el Attarin** (Souk of the Spice Vendors); this is the formal heart of the city, and its richest and most sophisticated shopping district. The principal landmark to the south of the Souk el Attarin is the **Zaouia Moulay Idriss II**, one of the holiest buildings in the city. Looking in from the doorway, the tomb of Moulay Idriss II is over on the left, and a scene of intense devotion is usually going on around it.

Standing at the women's entrance to the *zaouia*, you'll see a lane off to the left – **rue du Bab Moulay Ismail** – full of stalls selling candles and silverware for devotional offerings. If you follow this lane around to the wooden bar, go under the bar (turning to the right), and then keep to your left, you should come out in the picturesque square of **place Nejjarin** (Carpenters' Square). Here is the very imposing **Nejjarin Fondouk**, built in the early eighteenth century along with a beautiful canopied fountain on one side of the square. In the alleys off the square, you'll find the **Nejjarin Souk**, easily located by the sounds and smells of the carpenters chiselling away at cedar wood. The nearby **Souk el Henna**, a tree-shaded square adjoining what was once the largest madhouse in the Merenid empire, sells henna and the usual cosmetics, as well as more esoteric ingredients for aphrodisiacs and other magical spells. Pottery stalls are gradually encroaching on the traditional pharmaceutical business.

All roads in Fes el Bali lead to **El Kairaouine**, the largest mosque in the country (until the completion of the Hassan II Mosque in Casablanca) one of the oldest universities in the world, and the fountainhead of Moroccan religious life. The mosque was founded in 857 by a Tunisian woman, a wealthy refugee from the city of Kairouan, but its present dimensions, with sixteen aisles and room for 20,000 worshippers, are essentially the product of tenth- and twelfth-century reconstructions. The mosque is enmeshed in houses and shops – the best point of reference is the Attarin Medersa, whose fairly prominent bronze door is just to the north at the far end of Souk el Attarin.

The fourteenth-century **Attarin Medersa** (daily 9am–noon & 2–6pm; closed Fri morning; 10dh) is, after the Bou Inania, the finest of the city's medieval colleges, with an incredible profusion and variety of patterning. Its lightness of feel is achieved by the relatively simple device of using pairs of symmetrical arches to join the pillars to a single lintel – a design repeated in the upper floors and mirrored in the courtyard basin.

The east gate to the Kairaouine stands right opposite the **Palais de Fes**, a nine-teenth-century mansion now converted into a restaurant and rug shop. Nearby is **place Seffarine**, almost wilfully picturesque with its faience fountain, gnarled fig trees and metalworkers hammering away. Just off the square is the entrance to the **Seffarine Medersa** (same hours; 10dh). Built around 1285, the Seffarine is unlike all the other *medersas* in that it takes the exact form of a traditional Fassi house, with an arched balcony above its courtyard.

If you're beginning to find the medieval prettiness of the central *souks* and *medersas* slightly unreal, then the region beyond the Kairaouine, with its dyers' and tanners' *souks*, should provide the antidote. The dyers' street – **Souk Sabbighin** – is directly south of the Seffarine Medersa, and is draped with fantastically coloured yarn and cloth drying in the heat. Below, workers in grey, chimney-sweep's clothes toil over ancient cauldrons of multicoloured dyes. The tanneries quarter – the **Souk Dabbaghin** – is constantly being visited by groups of tourists, with whom you could discreetly tag along for a while if you get lost. Otherwise, follow your nose or accept a guide up from the Seffarine. Inside the tanneries, water deluges through holes that were once windows of houses and hundreds of skins lie spread out on the rooftops, above vats of dye and the pigeon dung used to treat the leather.

Fes el Djedid

Unlike Fes el Bali, whose development seems to have been almost organic, **Fes el Djedid** was an entirely planned city, begun around 1273 by Sultan Abou Youssef, and completed in a manic three years. It was not an extension for the people, in any real sense, being occupied largely by the **Dar el Makhzen**, a vast royal palace, and by a series of army garrisons. Events this century, largely generated by the French Protectorate, have left Fes el Djedid greatly changed and somewhat moribund – as a "government city" it had no obvious role after the transfer of power to Rabat.

Walking down to Fes el Djedid from **Bab Boujeloud** involves a shift in scale. Gone are the labyrinthine alleyways and *souks* of the Medina, to be replaced by a massive expanse of walls. Within them, to your left, are a series of gardens: the private **Jardins Beida**, behind the Lycée, and then the public **Jardins de Boujeloud**, a vital lung for the old city. If everything gets to be too much, wander in, lounge about on the grass and spend an hour or two at the tranquil **café**, by an old waterwheel at their west corner.

Eating and drinking

Cafés are plentiful in the Ville Nouvelle, with some of the most popular around place Mohammed V, along av Mohammed es Slaoui and bd Mohammed V (both of which run between the *place* and av Hassan II). Fes el Bali has two main areas for **budget eating**: around Bab Boujeloud, and along rue Hormis (which runs up from Souk el Attarin toward Bab Guissa), but for a cheap, solid option, it's best to try one of the handful of café-restaurants near the municipal market in the Ville Nouvelle – on the left-hand side of bd Mohammed V as you walk down from the post office.

Oued de la Bière, 59 bd Mohammed V, beyond the place. An old-style French restaurant-bar which, despite its promising name, no longer serves beer or wine.

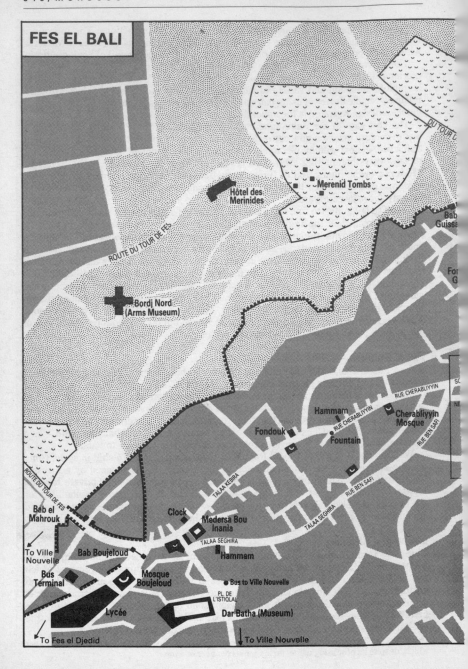

FES EL BALI

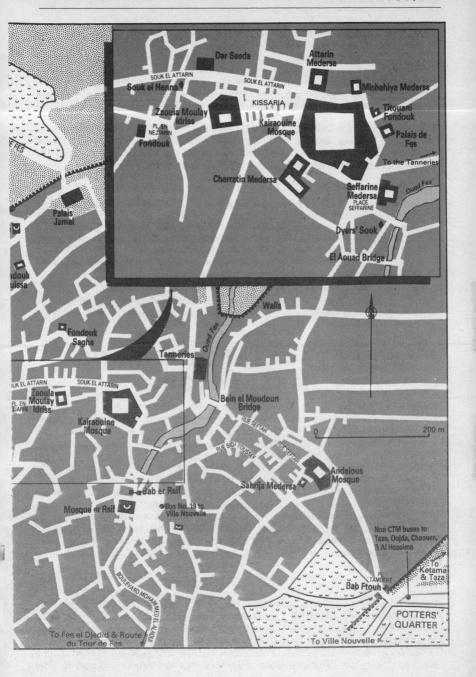

Dar Saada

Attarin
Medersa

Souk el Henna

SOUK EL ATTARIN

SOUK EL ATTARIN

Misbahiya Medersa

Zaouia Moulay
Idriss

KISSARIA

Kairaouine
Mosque

Titouani
Fondouk

Palais de
Fes

PL. EN
NEJJARIN

Fondouk

To the Tanneries

Cherratin Medersa

Oued Fes

Seffarine
Medersa

PLACE
SEFFARINE

Palais
Jamai

Dyers' Souk

ndouk
uissa

El Aouad Bridge

Fondouk
Sagha

Walls

Oued Fes

Tanneries

OUK EL ATTARIN

SOUK EL ATTARIN

Zaouia
PL. EN
JUARIN

Moulay
Idriss

Bein el Moudoun
Bridge

0   200 m

Kairaouine
Mosque

RUE SEFTAH

RUE SID YOUSSEF

RUE SEFTAH

Andalous
Mosque

Sahrija Medersa

Bab er Rsif

Mosque er Rsif

Bus No. 19 to
Ville Nouvelle

Non CTM buses to:
Taza, Oujda, Chaouen,
& Al Hoceima

To
Ketama
& Taza

BOULEVARD MOHAMMED EL AOUI

PL.
TAMDERT

Bab Ftouh

POTTERS'
QUARTER

To Fes el Djedid & Route
du Tour de Fes

To Ville Nouvelle

Restaurant Le Monnia, 11 bd Mohammed Zerktouni (near the *Hotel Splendid*). A small, welcoming restaurant with an extensive, modestly-priced menu.

Restaurant Marrakesh, 11 rue Abes Tazi (opposite *Hotel CTM*). Again small, but good and cheap.

Restaurant Chawarma, 42 rue Tetouan, off place de l'Atlas, a short walk from the town centre. Modern, without atmosphere, but very friendly; serves good Moroccan dishes at low prices.

Restaurant Courria, 29 rue Tetouan, across the street from the *Chawarma*. The patronne claims it is the only fish restaurant in Fes – and it serves fresh and very well cooked fare. Egyptian decor and music.

For **bars**, you have to look a little harder. There are the usually lively *Es Saada* on av Mohammed es Slaoui and the seedy but cheap *Dailla*, 17 bd Mohammed V. Failing those, try the hotel bars: outdoors at the *Zalagh* by the swimming pool or on the terrace with a fantastic view of old Fes, or the *Mounia* or *Splendid*.

Listings

Books The *English Bookshop*, 68 av Hassan II, has a great selection of English novels, and carries a fair number of North African writers.

Car rental *Avis*, 50 bd Chefchaouni (☎05/62.67.46); *Budget*, corner of rue Bahrein and av Hassan II (☎05/62.65.45); *Hertz*, in Hôtel de Fes, av des FAR (☎05/62.28.12); *Tourvilles*, 15 rue Houmam Fetouaki, off bd Mohammed V (☎05/62.66.35); *Zeit*, 35 av Mohammed es Slaoui (☎05/62.55.10).

Chemist *Pharmacie du Municipalité*, off place de la Résistance, on bd Moulay Youssef; open 24-hr.

Exchange The *BMCE* on place Mohammed V is the best of the banks.

Police *Commissariat Central* is on av Mohammed V (☎05/19).

Post office The main PTT is on the corner of bd Mohammed V/av Hassan II (summer 8am–2pm; winter 8.30am–noon & 2.30–6pm). Poste restante is next door to the main building; the phones section (open until 9pm) has a separate side entrance.

RABAT, CASABLANCA AND MARRAKESH

Rabat and **Casablanca** form the power base of the nation – the respective seats of government and of industry and commerce. They've acquired their preeminence almost entirely in the last fifty years, so French and post-colonial influences are dominant here. Don't show up in "Casa" (as it's popularly known) expecting it to look "Moroccan" – it doesn't; it looks very much like Marseille. Likewise Rabat, though this is one of the best places to make for as soon as you arrive in the country: the city is well connected by train with Tangier, Fes and Marrakesh, and in addition, it makes an easy cultural shift in which to gain some initial confidence. With the old port of **Salé**, facing Rabat across the estuary, it also has some of Morocco's finest and oldest monuments.

Marrakesh has always been something of a pleasure city, a marketplace where the southern tribesmen and Berber villagers bring in their goods, spend their money and find entertainment. For tourists it's an enduring fantasy, given added allure by the **High Atlas**, the grandest and most rewarding Moroccan mountain range.

Rabat

Capital of the nation since independence – and, before that, from 1912 to 1956, of the French Protectorate – **RABAT** is in many ways the city you'd expect: elegant in its spacious European grid, slightly self-conscious in its civilized modern ways, and, as an administrative centre, a little bit dull. However, Rabat's monuments punctuate the span of Moroccan history, for both the Phoenicians and Carthaginians established trading posts on modern-day Rabat's estuary site. The Arab city was largely the creation of the

Almohad Caliph Yacoub el Mansour, whose twelfth-century legacy includes the superb Oudaïa Gate, Bab er Rouah at the southwest edge of town, and the early stages of the Hassan Mosque. After Mansour's death, Rabat fell into neglect: sacked by the Portuguese, it was little more than a village when it was resettled by seventeenth-century Andalusian refugees, who rebuilt the Medina in a style reminiscent of their homes in Spanish Badajoz. Their pirate state survived until the time of Moulay Rashid, and his successor, Moulay Ismail, when Rabat finally reverted to government control.

Arrival and accommodation

The Rabat Ville **train station** is at the heart of the Ville Nouvelle, with most of the hotels situated only a few minutes' walk away. The main **bus** terminal is located in place Zerktouni, roughly 3km out from the centre; to get into the town itself, you'll have to take a local bus or compete for a *petit taxi*. An easier option, if you are coming by bus from the north, is to get off in Salé and take a *petit taxi* from there into Rabat. **Taxis** for non-local destinations operate from outside the main bus station. Those to Casa cost only a couple of dirhams more than the bus and leave more or less continuously. Local bus services radiate from bd Hassan II, where *petit taxis* can also be found.

Accommodation can be a little difficult to find in midsummer. It's perhaps best, arriving at any time of year, to concentrate your search on the **classified hotels** and, if at all possible, to make an advance reservation by phone. Unless stated otherwise, the places listed below are in the Ville Nouvelle. The nearest **campsite** is across the river at Salé.

Les Voyageurs, 8 souk Semarine, Medina (☎07/72.37.70). A cut above the other Medina hotels; worth booking in advance as it is a popular choice. ①

Dorhmi, 313 rue Mohammed V, Medina (☎07/72.38.98). Immediately on the right inside Bab Djedid. A decent hotel with a pleasant café, the *Essalem* at street level. ①

Central, 2 rue el Basra (☎07/70.73.56). A good budget choice and, with 34 rooms, likely to have space. Central location by *Hôtel Balima* and near the train station. ①

Gaulois, corner of rue Hims and av Mohammed V (☎07/72.30.22). One of a cluster of budget hotels at the bottom end of av Mohammed V. ①

Bouregreg, corner of rue Nador and bd Hassan II (☎07/72.41.10). Former *Hôtel Rex* under new management; near *grands taxis* and bus station for Salé and Plage des Nations. Recommended. ②

Splendid, 24 rue Ghazza (☎07/72.32.83). Nice old hotel which has a sense of better days; best of rooms overlook courtyard; facing is *Café-Restaurant Ghazza*, good for a meal any time. ②

D'Orsay, 11 av Moulay Youssef, on place de la Gare (☎07/76.13.19). Convenient for rail station and airport bus; friendly, helpful and efficient, a good mid-range alternative to older *Hôtel Balima*. ②

Youth Hostel, 34 bd Marrassa (☎07/72.57.69). Conveniently sited just outside the Medina walls, to the north of bd Hassan II; improved – clean, well-furnished and to be recommended. ①

The City

Rabat's **Medina** – all that there was of the city until the French arrived in 1912 – is a compact quarter, wedged on two sides by the sea and the river, on the others by the Almohad and Andalusian walls. From **bd Hassan II**, a series of streets give access to the Medina, all of them leading more or less directly through the quarter, to emerge near the Kasbah and the old cemetery. At right angles to these run the main market street, **rue Souika**, and its continuation **Souk es Sebbat**, behind which lies a residential area scattered with smaller *souks* and "parish" mosques.

North lies **Kasbah des Oudaïas**, a striking quarter whose principal gateway – **Bab el Kasbah** or Oudaïa Gate – is perhaps the most beautiful in the Moorish world. Built around 1195, the gate was the heart of the Kasbah, its chambers acting as a courthouse and staterooms, with everything important taking place within its confines. It impresses not so much by its size as by the strength and simplicity of its decoration, based on a typically Islamic rhythm which establishes a tension between the exuberant, outward expansion of the arches and the heavy, enclosing rectangle of the gate itself.

You can get into the **Kasbah** proper through the Oudaïa Gate or by means of a lower, horseshoe arch that you'll find at the base of the ceremonial stairway. This latter approach leads directly to the **Palace** built by Moulay Ismail, now housing a **Museum of Moroccan Arts** (8.30am–noon & 3–6pm; closed Tues; 10dh), which features Berber and Arab jewellery from most regions of Morocco, and traditional costumes which reveal the startling closeness of the medieval past. The adjoining **Andalusian Garden** – one of the most delightful spots in the city – was actually constructed by the French in the present century, though true to Spanish-Andalusian tradition, with deep, sunken beds of shrubs and flowering annuals. It has a pleasant Mauresque café.

The most ambitious of all Almohad buildings, the **Hassan Mosque** with its vast minaret dominates almost every view of the capital. Designed by El Mansour as the centrepiece of the new capital, the mosque seems to have been more or less abandoned at his death in 1199. It must always have seemed little more than an elaborate folly: Morocco's most important mosque, the Kairaouine in Fes, is less than half the Hassan's size, but served a much greater population. The minaret, despite its apparent simplicity, is perhaps the most complex of all Almohad structures; each facade is different, with a distinct combination of patterning, yet the whole intricacy of blind arcades and interlacing curves is based on just two formal designs. Facing the tower are the **Mosque** and **Mausoleum of Mohammed V**, begun on the sultan's death in 1961 and dedicated six years later. The mosque, extending between a pair of stark white pavilions, gives a somewhat foreshortened idea of how the Hassan Mosque must once have appeared, roofed in its traditional green tiles. The Mausoleum, with its brilliantly surfaced marbles and spiralling designs, pays homage to traditional Moroccan techniques, though fails to capture their rhythms and unity. It is, nevertheless, an important shrine for Moroccans – and one which, unusually, non-Muslims are permitted to visit.

On the opposite side of the Ville Nouvelle from the mausoleum is the **Archeological Museum** (8.30am–noon & 2.30–6pm; closed Tues; 10dh), the most important in Morocco. Although small, it has a quite exceptional and beautiful collection of Roman-era bronzes, found mainly at Volubilis, including superb figures of a guard dog and a rider, and two magnificent portrait heads, reputedly Cato the Younger and Juba II – the last significant ruler of the Romanized Berber kingdoms of Mauretania and Numidia.

The most beautiful of Moroccan ruins, the royal burial ground called the **Chellah** (sunrise to sunset; 10dh) is a startling sight as you emerge from the long avenues of the Ville Nouvelle, with its circuit of fourteenth-century walls – the legacy of **Abou el Hassan** (1331–51), the greatest of Merenid rulers. Off to the left of the main gate – whose strange turreted bastions create an almost Gothic appearance – are the partly excavated ruins of the Roman city that preceded the necropolis. The Islamic ruins are further down to the right, situated within a second inner sanctuary which is approached along a broad path through half-wild gardens. You enter directly into the courtyard of Abou Youssef's Mosque, behind which is a series of scattered royal tombs, each aligned so that the dead, dressed in white and lying on their right-hand sides, may face Mecca to await the Call of Judgement. The nearby Zaouia – a kind of monastery-shrine – is in a much better state of preservation, its long, central court enclosed by cells, with a small oratory at the end.

Eating and drinking

As ever, the cheapest **restaurants** are to be found in the Medina. Just on the edge of the quarter, down rue Mohammed V and along rue Souika, there is a string of good everyday café-restaurants – clean enough and serving regular Moroccan fare. In the Ville Nouvelle most of the restaurants are grouped around the train station and av Moulay Youssef. Thereabouts, try *Café-Restaurants de la Paix* and *Français*, and nearby *Le Clef*, all licenced. Worthwhile choices, but dearer, include the *Restaurant l'Oasis*, 7 rue Al Osquofiah (Moroccan dishes: try the chicken in honey); the slightly classier

Café-Restaurant Saadi, 81 bis av Allal Ben Abdallah, on the corner with rue el Kahira (*couscous* and *tajine*); *Le Fouquet's*, 285 av Mohammed V (fish and seafood); and the *Restaurant Saïdoune*, in the mall at 467 av Mohammed V opposite the *Hôtel Terminus*, a good Lebanese restaurant run by an Iraqi. All of these serve beer and wine with meals.

Avenues Mohammed V and Allal Ben Abdallah have some good **cafés**, but **bars** are few and far between, outside the main hotels. The one at the *Hôtel Balima* is as good a place as any. After the *Balima* has closed, late-night options include a string of disco-bars around place de Melilla and on rue Patrice Lumumba.

Listings

Airlines *Royal Air Maroc* is just down from the train station on av Mohammed V; *Air France* is on the same avenue at no. 281; *Iberia* at no. 104.

Banks Most are along av Allal Ben Abdallah and av Mohammed V. The *BMCE* (change facilities open daily 8.30am–2pm & 3–8pm) have offices at 241 av Mohammed V and at the port train station; they handle *VISA*, *Mastercard*, travellers' cheques and cash.

Car rental Cheaper deals tend to be available in Casablanca. Main companies represented in Rabat include *Avis*, 7 rue Abou Faris Al Mairini (☎07/76.97.59); *Hertz*, 467 av Mohammed V (☎07/73.44.75); *Europcar/Interent*, 25 bis rue Patrice Lumumba (☎07/72.23.21); *Tourist Cars*, 12 bd Hassan II, first floor (☎07/72.62.31).

Embassies and consulates *Australia* (representation c/o Canada); *Canada*, 13 Zankat Joafar Essadik (☎07/77.13.75); *Great Britain*, 17 bd Tour Hassan (☎07/72.09.05); *Ireland* (representation c/o Britain); *USA*, 2 av de Marrakesh (☎07/76.22.65).

Police Central office in rue Soekarno, a couple of blocks from av Mohammed V and a manned police post at Bab Djedid.

Post office The *PTT Centrale* – 24-hr a day for phones – is halfway down av Mohammed V. The poste restante section, however, is across the road from the main building.

Tourist offices *ONMT*, 22 av Al Jazair; *Syndicat d'Initiative*, rue Patrice Lumumba, opposite the *Grand Hotel*.

Salé and around

Although it is now essentially a suburb of Rabat, **SALÉ** was the pre-eminent of the two right through the Middle Ages. Today, largely neglected since the French creation of a capital in Rabat, it looks and feels very distinct. The spread of a Ville Nouvelle outside its walls has been restricted to a small area around the bus station and the north gates, and the *souks* and life within its medieval limits remain surprisingly traditional. From Rabat you can cross to Salé by **boat** or take a **bus** (#6 or #12) from bd Hassan II.

As far as buildings go, the **Grand Mosque** marks the most interesting part of town, its surrounding lanes fronting a concentration of aristocratic mansions and religious foundations. Almohad in origin, the mosque is one of the largest and oldest in Morocco, though what you can see as a non-Muslim (the gateway and minaret) are recent additions. You can, however, visit its **Medersa** (10dh), opposite the mosque's monumental main entrance. Salé's main monument, it was founded in 1341 by Sultan Abou el Hassan, and is intensely decorated in carved wood, stucco and *zellij* tilework. Close to its entrance there is a stairway up to the windowless student cells and to the roof, where, looking out across to Rabat, you sense the enormity of the Hassan Tower.

The best beach in the area is the **Plage des Nations**, 18km north and reached by taking the #28 bus to the village of BOUKNADEL and then following the crowds. Flanked by a couple of beach cafés and the four-star *Hôtel Firdaous* – a slick modern complex with a freshwater pool that's open to all for a small charge – the beach seems more Westernized than Rabat itself. The waves are big and exciting, but there are dangerous currents, hence the lifeguards along the central strip.

Casablanca

Principal city of Morocco, and capital in all but administration, **CASABLANCA** is the largest port of the Maghreb – busier even than Marseille, on which it was modelled by the French. Casa's Westernized image – with the almost total absence of women wearing veils, and its fancy beach clubs – masks what is still substantially a "first-generation" city and one which inevitably has some of Morocco's most intense social problems.

Some **trains** terminate at the **Gare des Voyageurs** (2km from the centre) rather than continuing on to the far better situated **Gare du Port**. Bus #30 runs into town from the Voyageurs – if you don't grab a seat, it's a twenty-minute walk or a *petit taxi* ride. All *CTM* **buses** arrive at the *CTM Gare Routière* on rue Léon l'Africain, off av des FAR; **grands taxis** usually stop just behind the *CTM* station.

It used to be said that Casa had not a single "real" monument. This was never quite true, but the city did undoubtedly lack any one single, great building: a position that, in part, may have prompted King Hassan II's decision to construct here the world's largest mosque. The **Hassan II Mosque** has space for 80,000 worshippers and a minaret that soars to a record 172 metres. Equally extraordinary is its cost – an estimated £320 million – and the fact that this was raised entirely by public subscription.

The French city centre and its formal colonial buildings already seem to belong to a different and distant age. Grouped around **place Mohammed V**, they served as models for administrative architecture throughout Morocco. Their style, heavily influenced by Art Deco, is known as *Mauresque* – a French idealization and "improvement" on Moorish design. If you have time to spare, visit the **New Medina** – or **Quartier Habbous** – which displays a bizarre extension of *Mauresque*. Built in the 1930s, it is an odd recreation of what the French felt domestic Moroccan architecture should be like. The **Old Medina**, lapsing into dilapidation above the port, is largely the product of the late nineteenth century, when Casa began its modest growth as a commercial centre. It has a slightly disreputable if also fairly affluent air, and is said to be the place to go to look for any stolen goods you might want to buy back.

You can get out to the beach suburb of **Aïn Diab** by bus #9 from bd de Paris, by *petit taxi* from around place des Nations Unies, or on foot. The beach starts around 3km out from the port and Old Medina, past the Hassan II Mosque, and continues for about the same distance. Aïn Diab's big attraction is not so much the sea as the **beach clubs** along its front. Each of these has one or more pools, usually filled with filtered seawater, a restaurant and a couple of snack bars.

Practicalities

Hotels are plentiful in Casa, though they run near capacity for much of the year. There are some unclassified hotels in the Medina, but there are better ones, and no dearer, in the centre: for example, *Mon Rêve*, 7 rue Chaouia (☎02/31.14.39; ①), and *Du Périgord*, 56 rue Araibi Jilali (☎02/22.10.85; ①). Next to the *Du Périgord* is *De Foucauld*, 52 rue Araibi Jilali (☎02/22.26.66; ①). Very central are two old hotels which keep up appearances and are value for money: *Excelsior*, 2 rue el Amraoui Brahim, off place des Nations Unies (☎02/20.02.63; ②), and *Plaza*, 18 bd Houphouet Boigny (☎02/22.02.26; ②).

The **youth hostel**, 6 place Amiral Philbert (☎02/22.05.51; ①), is friendly and well-maintained, just inside the Medina. The nearest **campsite** – *Camping Oasis*, av Jean Mermoz, Beauséjour (☎02/25.33.67), is 8km out on the P8 road to El Jadida (bus #31).

Casa has the reputation of being the best place to eat in Morocco, and if you can afford the fancier **restaurant** prices, this is certainly true. For anyone keeping to a budget, some of the best possibilities lie in the smaller streets off bd Mohammed V. Pricier, regular restaurants around the centre include *L'Étoile Marocaine*, 107 rue Allal Ben Abdallah; *La Corrida*, 59 rue Gay Lussac, near the PTT, an informal *tapas*-style Spanish restaurant run by a Spanish-French couple; and the stylish *Petit Poucet*, 8 bd

Mohammed V, which offers plentiful portions and has a much cheaper snack bar next door – one of the best places for some serious drinking.

Down near the Port is Centre 2000 with a group of five good ethnic restaurants serving Spanish, Italian, French, Asiatic (mainly Chinese) and Moroccan food.

Despite a scattering of more or less seedy clubs and **bars** on bd Mohammed V and bd Houphouet Boigny, nightlife in Casa is elusive. Given transport, it is better to explore the Aïn Diab coast road, bd de la Corniche. Look for *Le Balcon*, *Le Tube* and the lively *Palm Beach Club*.

Marrakesh

MARRAKESH is a city of immense beauty, low, pink and tentlike before a great shaft of mountains. It's an immediately exciting place, especially around the vast space of the Djemaa el Fna, the stage for a long-established ritual in which shifting circles of onlookers gather around groups of acrobats, drummers, pipe musicians, dancers, storytellers and comedians. Unlike Fes, for so long its rival as the nation's capital, Marrakesh exists very much in the present: its population is rising, it has a thriving industrial area and it remains the most important market and administrative centre of southern Morocco.

The **Djemaa el Fna** lies right at the heart of the Medina, and almost everything of interest is concentrated in the web of alleyways above and below it. Just to the west of the Djemaa, an unmistakable landmark, is the minaret of the great **Koutoubia** mosque – in the shadow of which begins **avenue Mohammed V**, leading out of the Medina and up the length of the new city, **Gueliz**. It is a fairly long walk between Gueliz and the Medina, but there are plenty of **petits** and **grands taxis** and a regular **bus** (#1) between the two.

Arrival and information

From the **train station**, close to Gueliz, you should take bus #3 or #8 or a *petit taxi* to get to the Djemaa. The **bus** terminal is just outside the walls of the Medina by Bab Doukkala – a 25-minute walk to the Djemaa, or again a ride on the #3 or #8 bus or *petit taxi* (6–8dh). The city's **airport** is 5km to the southwest; the #11 bus is supposed to run every half-hour to the Djemaa, but it is very erratic – *petits taxis* or *grands taxis* are a better option.

Both the **ONMT** and **Syndicat d'Initiative** are on av Mohammed V – the first is on place Abd el Moumen Benali, the second is a little way up towards the Medina, at no. 170 (both open 8.30am–noon & 3–6pm; the SI is closed Sat afternoon and Sun).

Accommodation

The Medina, as ever, has the main concentration of cheap places – most of them quite pleasant – and, unusually, has a fair number of classified hotels too. Given the attractions of the Djemaa el Fna and the *souks*, this is the first choice. The main advantages of Gueliz and Hivernage hotels are their convenience for the train station and their swimming pools, a major consideration in a city where the midday temperature can hit 130°F. At most times of year, the city has a shortage of space in the classified hotels, so **advance bookings** are a wise idea. All hotels are in the Medina unless stated otherwise.

HOTELS

La Gazelle, 12 rue Bani Marine (☎04/44.11.12). A new hotel with bright airy rooms and hot showers on a street with outdoor foodstalls. ①

De France, 197 rue Zitoun el Kedim (☎04/44.30.67). This is one of the best of the cheapies, secure and recently modernized. ①

Challa, 14 rue Zitoun el Kedim (☎04/44.29.77). Nice building and another safe bet in the quarter. Signposted on an alley off rue Zitoun el Kedim. ①

Medina, 1 Derb Sidi Bouloukat, off rue Zitoun el Kedim (no ☎). A real gem: small, clean, family run and friendly. Good value, too, with hot showers included. ①

Afriquia, 45 Derb Sidi Bouloukat (☎04/44.24.03). Decent rooms off a pleasant courtyard with orange trees. ①

Souria, 17 rue de la Recette (no ☎). Deservedly popular and perhaps the best in this listing. ①

CTM, place Djemaa el Fna (☎04/44.23.35). Located above the old bus station; decent sized rooms, as clean and cheap as many of the above – but cold showers. ①

Oukaïmeden, place Djemaa el Fna (☎04/42.23.59). Newly refurbished hotel on the north side of the square. ①

Ali, rue Moulay Ismail (☎04/44.49.79). Popular small hotel with good inexpensive Moroccan meals, usually buffet-style in the restaurant. ②

De Foucauld, av El Mouhidine (☎04/44.54.99). Rooms are on the small side, but this is a reliable choice, with friendly staff and licensed restaurant. ②

Gallia, 30 rue de la Recette (☎04/44.59.13). Pleasant building in a quiet cul-de-sac; airy and spotless rooms off two tiled courtyards. ②

Oasis, 50 av Mohammed V, Gueliz (☎04/44.71.79). Comfortable rooms; clean and well run. Also has a bar and a good restaurant. ②

Yasmine, corner of bd El Yarmouk and rue Boulaka, Hivernage (☎04/44.61.42). A new and attractive hotel, only 500m from the Djemaa el Fna, with a bar and swimming pool. ②

Imilchil, av Echonhada, Hivernage (☎04/44.76.53). One of the cheapest classified hotels in town with a full, if small, swimming pool; not too far from the Medina. ②

YOUTH HOSTEL AND CAMPSITE

Youth hostel, rue el Jahid, Gueliz (☎04/43.28.31). Quiet, clean, friendly, and a useful first-night standby; five minutes' from train station. Closes 10pm in winter, around midnight in summer. ①

Camping Municipal, av de France (☎04/43.17.07). Rather bare and unshaded site with poor facilities: just a café-restaurant and small pool (not always full). A five-minute walk from the train station; bus #3 or #8 runs from outside at the corner of av de France and av Hassan II to the Djemaa el Fna.

The City

There's nowhere in North Africa like the **Djemaa el Fna**: by day it's basically a market, with a few snake charmers and an occasional troupe of acrobats; in the evening it becomes a whole carnival of musicians, clowns and entertainers. If you get tired of the spectacle, or if things slow down, you can move over to the rooftop terraces of the *Café de France* or the *Restaurant Argana* to gaze at it all from above. The absence of any architectural feature in the Djemaa serves to emphasize the drama of the **Koutoubia Minaret**, the focus of any approach to the city. Nearly seventy metres high and visible for miles on a clear morning, it was begun shortly after the Almohad conquest of the city, around 1150. It displays many of the features that were to become widespread in Moroccan architecture – the wide band of ceramic inlay near the top, the pyramid-shaped, castellated *merlons*, and the alternation of patterning on the facades.

THE NORTHERN MEDINA

On the northern corner of Djemaa el Fna itself there is a small potters' market, but the main **souk** area begins a little further beyond this. Its entrance is initially confusing. Standing at the *Café de France*, look across the street and you'll see the *Café el Fath* and, beside it, a building with the sign "Tailleur de la place" – the lane between them will bring you out at the beginning of the crowded **Souk Smarine**, an important thoroughfare traditionally dominated by the sale of textiles. Just before the fork at its end, Souk Smarine narrows and you can get a glimpse through the passageways to its right of the **Rahba Kedima**, a small and fairly ramshackle square whose most interesting features are its apothecary stalls. At the end of Rahba Kedima, a passageway to the left gives access to another, smaller square – a bustling, carpet-draped area known as **la Criée Berbère**, which is where slave auctions used to be held.

Cutting back to **Souk el Kebir,** which by now has taken over from the Smarine, you emerge at the **kissarias,** the covered markets at the heart of the *souks. Kissarias* traditionally sell more expensive products, which today means a predominance of Western designs and imports. Off to their right is **Souk des Bijoutiers,** a modest jewellers' lane, while at the north end is a convoluted web of alleys comprising the **Souk Cherratin,** essentially a leather workers' *souk.*

If you bear left through this area and then turn right, you should arrive at the open space in front of the Mosque Ben Youssef. The **Ben Youssef Medersa** (8am–noon & 2.30–5.45pm; closed Mon & Fri morning; 10dh) – the annexe for students taking courses in the mosque – stands off a side street just to the east of the mosque, distinguishable by a series of small, grilled windows. A Merenid foundation, it was almost completely rebuilt under the Saadians, and it is this dynasty's intricate, Andalusian-influenced art that has left its mark. As with the slightly later Saadian Tombs (see below), no surface is left undecorated, and the overall quality of its craftsmanship, whether in carved wood, stuccowork or *zellij,* is startling. Parts have exact parallels in the Alhambra Palace in Granada, and it seems likely that Muslim Spanish architects were employed in its construction. After the *medersa* or the *souks,* the small **Almoravid Koubba,** just to the south of the mosque, is easy to pass by – but this, the only intact Almoravid building, is at the root of all Moroccan architecture. The motifs you've just seen in the *medersa* – the pine cones, palms and acanthus leaves – were all carved here for the first time.

THE SOUTHERN MEDINA

South of Djemaa el Fna there are two places not to be missed: the Saadian Tombs and El Badi, the ruined palace of Ahmed el Mansour. For the tombs, the simplest route from the Djemaa is to follow **rue Bab Agnaou** outside the ramparts, then aim for the conspicuous minaret of the **Kasbah Mosque** – the minaret looks gaudy and modern but is in fact contemporary with the Koutoubia and Hassan towers, and was restored to its original state in the 1960s. The narrow passageway to the tombs is well signposted at the near right-hand corner of the mosque.

Sealed up by Moulay Ismail after he had destroyed the adjoining Badi Palace, the sixteenth-century **Saadian Tombs** (9am–noon & 2–6pm; closed Fri morning; 10dh) lay half-ruined and half-forgotten at the beginning of this century. Restored, they are today the city's main "sight" – overlavish, maybe, in their decoration, but dazzling nonetheless. There are two main mausoleums in the enclosure. The finer is on the left as you come in – a beautiful group of three rooms, built to house El Mansour's own tomb and completed within his lifetime. Outside, around the garden and courtyard, are scattered the tombs of over a hundred more Saadian princes and members of the royal household. Like the privileged sixty-six given space within the mausoleums, their gravestones are brilliantly tiled and often elaborately inscribed.

Though substantially in ruins, enough remains of the **El Badi Palace** (9am–noon & 2.30–5.30pm; 3dh) to suggest that its name – "The Incomparable" – was not entirely immodest. It took Moulay Ismail over ten years of systematic work to strip the palace of everything movable or of value, and, even so, there's a lingering sense of luxury. The palace was begun shortly after Ahmed el Mansour's accession, its finance coming from the ransom paid out by the Portuguese after the Battle of the Three Kings at Ksar el Kebir in 1578. What you see today is essentially the ceremonial part of the palace complex, planned for the reception of ambassadors. To the rear extends the central court, over 130m long and nearly as wide, and built on a substructure of vaults in order to allow the circulation of water through the pools and gardens. When the pools are filled – as during the June folklore festival – they are an incredibly majestic sight.

Heading north from the El Badi, **rue Zitoun el Djedid** leads back to the Djemaa, flanked by various nineteenth-century mansions. Many of these have been converted into carpet shops or tourist restaurants, but one of them has been kept as a museum – the **Palais El Bahia** (9am–noon & 2.30–5.30pm; closed Tues; 10dh), former residence of a grand vizier. The name of the building means "The Effulgence" or "Brilliance", but after the guided tour around the rambling palace courts and apartments you might feel this to be a somewhat tall claim. There is reasonable craftsmanship in the main reception halls, and a pleasant arrangement of rooms in the harem quarter, but for the most part it is all fabulously vulgar.

Also on this route is the **Museum of Moroccan Arts** (summer 9am–noon & 4–7pm; winter 9am–noon & 2.30–6pm; closed Tues; 10dh), particularly strong on its collections of southern Berber jewellery and weapons – large, boldly designed objects of great beauty. There are also fine displays of eighteenth- and nineteenth-century carving, modern Berber rugs and a curious group of traditional wedding chairs – once widely used for carrying the bride, veiled and hidden, to her new home.

THE GARDENS

With summer temperatures peaking in excess of 100° F it seems best to devote at least the middle of a Marrakesh day to inactivity. If you want to do this in style, it means finding your way to one of the two gardens – **Agdal** and **Menara** – designed for just this purpose. Each begins near the edge of the Medina, rambles through acres of orchards and olive groves, and has, near its centre, an immense, lake-size pool. This is all – they are not flower gardens, but, cool and completely still, they are a luxurious contrast to the close city streets. To get to either, take a *petit taxi* or a horse-drawn *calèche* from the Badi palace or the Koutoubia.

A smaller garden, only twelve acres, is the meticulously-planned botanical haven, created by the French painter Jacques Majorelle (1886–1962). The entrance to the **Jardins Majorelle** is on a small cul-de-sac off av Yacoub el Mansour. Not to be missed.

Eating, drinking and entertaiment

Gueliz, naturally enough, is where you'll find French-style **cafés** and **restaurants**, and virtually all of the city's **bars** – av Mohammed V is the busiest area. In the Medina, in addition to the spectacle of the Djemaa el Fna foodstalls, there's a fair range of inexpensive café-restaurants just off the Djemaa el Fna in rue Bani Marine. More upmarket Medina options are listed below.

In the Medina, the more upmarket hotels *Ali* and the licenced *Foucauld* have justifiable popular restaurants with a range of Moroccan dishes for up to 100dh a head and pleasantly low-key musicians. The *Foucauld*'s sister hotel, the *Tazi*,on nearby rue Bab Agnaou, has a similar menu and prices but, despite generous helpings, the quality is variable. On the other hand, it has the nearest bar to Djemaa el Fna.

Around Djemaa el Fna, there's a range of restaurants from the rooftop *Argana*, with regular French-Moroccan food at around 70dh a head, and the *Hôtel du Café de France*, another superb viewpoint (the restaurant is good, but the hotel itself is wretched), to the *Restaurant Marrakesh* (✆04/42.33.77), on the corner of the road just north of *Café de France* (180dh a head for a huge meal), and, by the Police Commissariat, *Restaurant Relais Al Baraka* (✆04/44.23.41), around 350dh a head, no credit cards accepted.

Not far away from here, and facing the Koutoubia, is the *Pizzeria Venetia* on the roof terrace of the new *Hotel Islame*, 279 Mohammed V (✆04/44.00.81); the food and view are superb.

The annual two-week **Folklore Festival**, held in the Badi Palace usually in September, is almost worth planning your trip to Morocco around. It's a series of authentic, unusual performances, with groups of musicians and dancers from all over the country. Shows are held each evening from around 9pm to midnight (tickets 50dh); before they start, towards sunset, there is a **fantasia** at Bab el Djedid – a spectacle by any standard, with dozens of Berber horsemen firing their guns in the air at full gallop.

Listings

American Express c/o *Voyages Schwarz*, rue Mauritania, off av Mohammed V (☎04/43.33.21 or 43.30.22). Business hours Mon–Fri 9am–12.30pm & 3–4.30pm, but stays open until 7pm for mail.

Car rental One of the cheapest places is *Menara Tours*, 41 rue de Yugoslavie (☎04/44.66.54), which deals with a number of agencies. Other companies are concentrated on av Mohammed V.

Chemist There are several along av Mohammed V, including a good one just off place de la Liberté (or Houria), which has a doctor on call.

Doctor Dr Perez, 169 av Mohammed V (☎04/43.10.30), is reliable and speaks English.

Exchange *BMCE* is the best bet for exchange and has branches in both the Medina (place Foucauld) and Gueliz (144 bd Mohammed V), open 8am–8pm every day.

Moving on Buy bus tickets in advance for more popular destinations such as Fes and the coastal resort of Essaouira – or you could find yourself waiting for the second or third bus. *Grands taxis* can be useful for getting to Ourika or to Asni – negotiate for these by Bab er Robb (about 15dh a place to Asni). Next to flying, **trains** are the quickest and most comfortable way of getting to Casa and Rabat. If you're heading back to Tangier it's best to book a *couchette* on the night train in advance.

Post office The main *PTT* is on place 16 Novembre, midway down av Mohammed V (Mon–Sat 8am–2pm – telephone section open until 9pm).

The High Atlas

The **High Atlas**, the greatest mountain range of North Africa, is for many travellers the most beautiful and intriguing part of Morocco. A historical and physical barrier between the northern plains and the pre-Sahara, its Berber-populated valleys, kasbahs and villages are very remote from the country's mainstream or urban life. When the French began their "pacification" in the 1920s, the Atlas way of life was essentially feudal, and even today, with the region under government control through a system of local *caids*, the Atlas Berbers are not taxed, nor do they receive any national benefits or services.

The **Toubkal National Park**, a more or less roadless area enclosing the Atlas' tallest peaks, is the goal of 95 percent of people who hike in Morocco. Unless you're undertaking a particularly long or ambitious hike – or are here in winter conditions – you don't need any special equipment, nor will you need to do any actual climbing. The main physical problems you'll find are the high altitudes (3000–3700m throughout the Toubkal region), the midday heat and the tiring process of walking over long sections of scree.

Asni

The end of the line for the Marrakesh buses and *grands taxis*, **ASNI** is really little more than a roadside village and marketplace – and a spot many hikers pass straight through to get up into the mountains. If you're in a hurry, this is good reasoning, though it's no disaster if you have to stay overnight. The all-year **youth hostel** (①) has no cooking facilities and you'll need your own sleeping bag. Just beyond the hostel, a last taste of **hotel** luxury before the mountains is offered by the *Grand Hôtel du Toubkal* (②). Both hostel and hotel will store baggage for you if you want to carry a minimum load into the mountains. Getting to Imlil – a better trailhead for the ascent of Toubkal – is pretty straightforward, with pick-up vans and taxis shuttling back and forth along the 17km of road, along with larger lorries on Saturdays for the *souk*.

Imlil and the ascent of Djebel Toubkal

IMLIL comprises a small cluster of houses, along with many provisions shops, a prominent CAF refuge and several cafés. Most hikers choose to stay at the **CAF refuge**, which is open all year round and provides bunk beds, camping mattresses and blankets, as well as kitchen and washing facilities and luggage storage. In addition, Imlil now has two **hotels**, the *Étoile de Toubkal* and the more basic *Hôtel-Café Soleil*, while several houses offer **rooms**. A first stop in Imlil should be the "Shopping Centre", run

by Lahcen Esquary, an experienced Atlas guide who speaks English well. Other qualified guides are listed on the noticeboard in the square.

The ascent of **Djebel Toubkal** is a walk rather than a climb, after the snows have
cleared. The walk to the base is enjoyable in its own right, following the Mizane Valley
to the village of **Aroumd** (4km from Imlil) and thence through the hamlet of **Sidi
Chamcharouch** to the **Toubkal Refuge** (12km from Imlil – 5–6hr in all), at the foot of
Toubkal. The *gardien* is usually prepared to cook meat or vegetable *tajine* for guests,
though beware that the hut can be very busy – and crowded. Most people set out early
to mid-morning from Imlil to stay the night at Neltner, setting out at first light the next
morning for Toubkal in order to get the clearest panorama. At Neltner you're almost
bound to meet people who have just come down from Djebel Toubkal – and you should
certainly take advantage of them and the Toubkal *gardien* for a description of the
routes and the current state of the South Cirque trail to the summit.

travel details

Trains

Casablanca Port to: Fes (daily; 4hr 45min);
Meknes (2 daily; 3hr 45min); Rabat (Mon–Fri 14,
Sat 11, Sun 6; 50min–1hr).

Casablanca Voyageurs to: Marrakesh (4 daily;
3hr 30min–4hr); Meknes (5 daily; 4hr 45min);
Mohammed V airport (up to 14 daily; 30min);
Tangier (3 daily; 6hr).

Fes to: Asilah (2 daily; 5hr); Casablanca
Voyageurs (4 daily; 4hr 45min); Marrakesh (3
daily; 11hr 30min); Meknes (7 daily; 1hr), Rabat (4
daily; 3hr 45min); Sidi Kacem (1 daily; 2hr 15min);
Sidi Slimane (2 daily; 2hr 15min); Tangier (2 daily;
5hr 45min).

Marrakesh to: Casablanca (5 daily; 4hr); Fes (4
daily; 11hr 30min); Meknes (4 daily; 10hr 30min);
Rabat (5 daily; 5hr); Tangier (3 daily; 10hr–11hr
30min).

Rabat to: Casablanca Port (Mon–Fri 14, Sat 12,
Sun 8 ; 50min–1hr).

Tangier to: Asilah (3 daily, 45min); Casablanca
Port (2 daily; 6hr); Casablanca Voyageurs (2 daily;
6hr); Fes (1 daily; 5hr 45min); Marrakesh (2 daily;
11hr 30min); Meknes (4 daily; 4hr 45min); Rabat
(2 daily; 5hr); Sidi Kacem (1 daily; 3hr 30min); Sidi
Slimane (2 daily; 3hr 15min).

Buses

Casablanca to: Marrakesh (3 daily; 4hr); Rabat
(10 daily; 1hr 40min); Tangier (2 daily; 6hr 30min).

Chaouen to Al Hoceima (2 daily; 8hr); Fes (2
daily; 7hr); Ketama (2 daily; 5hr); Meknes (1 daily;
5hr 30min); Tetouan (10 daily; 3hr).

Fes to: Casablanca (8 daily; 7hr); Chaouen (2
daily; 5hr); Marrakesh (3 daily; 11hr); Rabat (6
daily; 5hr 30min); Tangier (2 daily; 6hr).

Marrakesh to: Asni (8 daily; 1hr 30min);
Casablanca (hourly; 4hr); Fes (3 daily; 11hr); Rabat
(8 daily; 5hr 30min).

Meknes to Chaouen (1 daily; 5hr 30min); Fes (1
hourly; 50min); Marrakesh (1 daily; 9hr); Rabat (3
daily; 4hr); Tangier (2 daily; 7hr).

Rabat to: Casablanca (10 daily; 1hr 40min); Fes (6
daily; 5hr 30min); Larache (4 daily; 3hr 30min);
Meknes (3 daily; 4hr); Salé (frequent; 15min);
Tangier (2 daily; 5hr).

Tangier to Asilah (7 daily; 1hr); Fes (2 daily; 8hr);
Meknes (2 daily; 7hr); Rabat (2 daily; 5hr);
Tetouan (12 daily; 1hr 30min).

Tetouan to Chaouen (10 daily; 3hr); Tangier (12
daily; 1hr 30min).

CHAPTER 15

THE
NETHERLANDS

Introduction

The Netherlands is a country partly reclaimed from the waters of the North Sea, and around half of it lies at or below sea level. Land reclamation has been the dominant motif of its history, the result a country of resonant and unique images – flat, fertile landscapes punctured by windmills and church spires; ornately gabled terraces flanking peaceful canals; and mile upon mile of grassy dune, backing onto stretches of pristine sandy beach.

A leading colonial power, its mercantile fleets once challenged the best in the world for supremacy and the country enjoyed a so-called "Golden Age" of prosperity in the seventeenth century. These days, the Netherlands is one of the most developed countries in the world, with the highest population density in Europe, its fifteen million or so inhabitants (most of whom speak English) concentrated into an area about the size of southern England.

Most people travel to **Amsterdam**, and the rest of the country, despite its relative accessibility, is comparatively undiscovered. The provinces of **North** and **South Holland**, in the west of the country, are the most populated and most historically interesting region: unrelentingly flat territory, much of it reclaimed, that has since become home to a grouping of towns known collectively as the **Randstad** (literally "rim town"). It's a good idea to forsake the capital for a day or two and investigate places like **Haarlem**, **Leiden** and **Delft** with their old canal-girded centres, the gritty port city of **Rotterdam**, or **the Hague**, stately home of the government and the Dutch royals. Outside the Randstad, life moves more slowly. The province of **Friesland**, to the north, is probably the Netherlands at its most remote, its inhabitants speaking a language, *Frysk*, neither spoken nor understood elsewhere in the country. Friesland's capital, **Leeuwarden**, is a likeable city, and neighbouring **Groningen** is one of the country's busiest cultural centres, lent verve by its large resident student population. To the south are the country's first few bumps, the landscape undulating into heathy moorland around the town of **Arnhem**, best experienced in the country's only national park, the **Hoge Veluwe**. Further south still lie the predominantly Catholic provinces of the Netherlands, and the compelling city of **Maastricht**, capital of Limburg, squeezed between the Dutch and Belgian borders.

Information and Maps

A nationwide network of **VVV offices** dispenses tourist information, usually from offices conveniently sited in the town centre or by the train station. They have plenty of information in English, maps and accommodation lists, and will book rooms for you. Most carry information on the rest of the country too. For travelling purposes, the best general **map** of the Netherlands is the *Kümmerley and Frey*. For more detailed regional maps, the Dutch motoring organization *ANWB* publishes an excellent 1:100,000 series that covers the whole country.

Money and Banks

Dutch currency is the guilder, written as "f", "fl" or "Dfl", and made up of 100 cents ("c"). It comes in coins worth 5c, tiny 10c pieces, 25c, f1, f2.50 and f5; denominations of notes are f5 (though these are being phased out), f10, f25, f50 and f100. **Banking hours** are Mon–Fri 9am–4pm; in larger cities some banks also open Thurs 7–9pm and occasionally on Saturday mornings. There are also the *GWK* exchange offices, usually at train stations, which are open late hours every day (sometimes 24hrs), change money and travellers' cheques, and give cash advances on all the major credit cards, for similar rates – though there's normally a f300 minimum. You can also change money at most VVV offices and numerous bureaux de change, though the rates will be less favourable.

Communications

Dutch post offices are usually open Mon–Fri 8.30am–5pm and in larger cities often Sat 8.30am–noon. Post boxes are everywhere, though make sure you use the correct slot for foreign destinations, marked "Overige".

Public phones are widespread. They take 25c, f1 and f2.50 coins; only wholly unused coins are returned. Phone cards are becoming more common, available from post offices and train stations – f5 for the equivalent of twenty local calls. Calling home, it might be better to use a post office, where you make your call from a booth and settle up afterwards. There is no discount rate on international calls, except to the USA and Canada, when it's cheaper to call between 7pm and 10am and (for the USA) at weekends, and to Australia and New Zealand, when the discount rate is in effect between midnight and 7am. The operator number is ☎0010 for calls within Europe, ☎0016 for all others.

Getting Around

Getting around is never a problem: distances are short, and the longest journey you'll ever make – say from Amsterdam to Maastricht – takes under three hours by train or car. Public transport in and around towns and cities, too, is efficient and cheap, running on an easy-to-understand ticketing system that covers the whole country. The bus and train networks link up together neatly, with bus terminals almost always next door to the train station.

■ Trains

The best way of travelling around Holland is to take the **train**. The system, run by *Nederlandse Spoorwegen (Netherlands Railways)*, is one of the best in Europe: trains are fast, modern and frequent, fares relatively low, and the network of lines extremely comprehensive. **Ordinary fares** are calculated by the kilometre, diminishing proportionately the further you travel. *NS* publish a booklet detailing costs and distances, so it's easy to work out how much a ticket will cost. As a rough guide, reckon on spending about f13 to travel 50km or so. With any ticket, you're also free to stop off en route and continue your journey later that day.

InterRail and *Eurail* passes are both valid, as is the **Benelux Tourrail Card** which is valid for five days unlimited travel within a specified seventeen-day period and costs f217 (f162 if you're under 26).

Of a number of ways of saving money, the **dagretour**, or day return, is the most commonly used, valid for 24 hours and costing around ten percent less than two ordinary singles. There are two kinds of domestic rail pass: **rover tickets**, which entitle the holder to unlimited travel anywhere in Holland at a cost of f63 (second-class) for one day or f152 for seven days. Optional **extras** issued in conjunction with the rover tickets are public transport link cards (f6.50 for one day, f25 for seven), which allow the additional free use of buses and trams.

Stations are well-equipped and usually have a reasonably priced restaurant and a *GWK* change office. *NS* have also devised a **treintaxi** scheme, whereby for f6 a taxi will take you anywhere within the city limits from the train station; it doesn't apply to Amsterdam, the Hague, Rotterdam or Utrecht. Vouchers for *treintaxis* must be purchased when you buy your ticket. *NS* publish mounds of **information** annually, including a free timetable detailing inter-city services, and a full timetable available from any Dutch railway station (f8.75).

■ Buses

For local transport you need to use **buses**, again very efficient, and almost always running from ranks of bus stops next to the train station. Ticketing is simple, organized on a system that covers the whole country. You need buy just one kind of ticket wherever you are, a *strippenkaart*. The country is divided into zones: the driver will cancel one strip on your *strippenkaart* for your journey plus one for each of the zones you travel through. In the larger towns and cities you'll find you only need to use two zones for the centre. Additional people can travel on the same *strippenkaart* by cancelling the requisite number of strips. You can buy 2-, 3- or 8-strip *strippenkaarts* from bus drivers, or the better-value 15-strip (f10.75) or 45-strip (f31) *strippenkaarts* in advance from train stations, tobacconists and local public transport offices.

■ Driving and hitching

The country has a good and comprehensive **road network**. You drive on the right; speed limits are 50kph in built-up areas, 80kph outside and 120kph on motorways, though some motorways have a speed limit of 100kph. Drivers and front-seat passengers are required by law to wear seatbelts, and crackdowns on drunken driving are severe. There are no toll roads, and although petrol isn't particularly cheap at around f2 a litre, once again the distances involved mean this isn't much of a factor. You need an ordinary driver's licence, and, if you bring your own car, a Green Card of insurance, though you can obtain last-minute insurance cover at border exchange offices. If you break down, the *ANWB* offers reciprocal repair and breakdown services to members of foreign motoring organizations; their nationwide number is ☎06/0888. **Car hire** is fairly expensive: reckon on paying upwards of f700 per week with unlimited mileage, or around f50 a day plus 60c per kilometre – though there are much cheaper weekend deals available. **Hitching** is feasible throughout the country: the Dutch are usually well disposed towards giving lifts. Bear in mind, though, that motorways are hard to avoid, and that it's only legal to hitch on slip roads or at the special marked places you'll find on the outskirts of some larger cities, known as *liftplaatsen*.

■ Cycling

If you're not pushed for time, **cycling** is *the* way to see the country. There's a nationwide system of well-signposted cycle paths, which often divert away from the main roads into the countryside. Bikes can be **hired** from all main train stations for f7.50 a day or f30 per week, plus a f50 deposit (f200 in larger centres); if you have a valid train ticket, it costs just f5 a day (f20 per week) with a *treinfiets* voucher. You'll also need some form of ID. The snag is that cycles must be returned to the station from which they were hired. It is possible to take your bike on trains, but it isn't encouraged; a ticket costs f9 single, f17.50 return – f15 and f25 if used on Monday or Tuesday in July and August – and you're not allowed to take your machine on board during the rush hour. Never leave your bike unlocked: most stations have somewhere you can store it for around f2 a day.

Accommodation

Accommodation is not particularly cheap in the Netherlands, though a wide network of youth hostels and well-equipped campsites can help to cut costs. Wherever you stay, you should book during the summer and over holiday periods, when places can run short.

■ Hotels and private rooms

Rates for the cheapest one- or two-star **hotel** room start at around f65 for a double without private bath or shower; count on paying upwards of f85 if you want your own facilities; three-star hotels cost f120–150. Prices usually include a reasonable breakfast. You can make reservations for free anywhere in the country through the *Netherlands Reservation Centre* (*NRC*), PO Box 404, 2260 AK Leidschendam (Mon–Fri 8am–8pm, Sat 8am–2pm; ☎070/320 50 00). You can also make reservations in person through VVV offices, for a fee of f3.50 per person.

One way of cutting costs is, wherever possible, to use **private accommodation** – rooms in private homes that are let out to visitors on a bed and breakfast basis; they're sometimes known as pensions. Prices are usually quoted per person and normally come to around f30; breakfast is usually included, but if not it will cost you about f5 extra. You have to go through the VVV to find private rooms: they will either give you a list or will insist they book the accommodation themselves and levy the appropriate fee.

■ Hostels, sleep-ins, student rooms

There are about 45 *IYHF* **youth hostels** in Holland, charging around f20 per person per night, including breakfast – f5 extra for non-members. Accommodation in these places is usually in dormitories, though some of the hostels do have single and double rooms available. Meals are also often possible – about f14 for a filling dinner – and in some hostels there are kitchens where you can self-cater. For a full list of Dutch hostels, contact the *Nederlandse Jeugdherberg Central* (*NJHC*), Prof. Tulplein 4, 1018 GX Amsterdam (☎020/551 3155). In addition to official hostels, the larger cities often have a number of **unofficial hostels** with

---

ACCOMMODATION PRICE CODES

Throughout this guide, accommodation is priced on a scale of ① to ⑧, the number indicating the lowest price per night a single person could expect to pay in that establishment in high season. With hostels this is the nightly rate per person; with hotels, the price is arrived at by dividing the cost of the cheapest double room by two. The prices indicated by the codes are as follows

① = under £5 / $8   ② = £5–10 / $8–16   ③ = £10–15 / $16–24   ④ = £15–20 / $24–32

⑤ = £20–25 / $32–40   ⑥ = £25–30 / $40–48   ⑦ = £30–35 / $48–56   ⑧ = over £35 / $56

dormitory accommodation at broadly similar prices, though standards are sometimes not as reliable. In some cities you may also come across something known as a **Sleep In** – dormitory accommodation run by the local council that's often cheaper than regular hostels and normally only open during the summer. **Student accommodation** is also sometimes open to travellers during the holidays.

■ Campsites and cabins

Camping is a serious option in Holland: there are plenty of sites, most well-equipped, and they represent a good saving on other forms of accommodation. Prices vary greatly, but you can generally expect to pay around f5 per person, plus f5–10 for a tent, and f5 or so for a car or motorcycle. There's a free tourist board (*NBT*) list of selected sites, and the *ANWB* publishes an annual guide (f16.50). Some sites also have **cabins**, spartan affairs that can house a maximum of four people for around f44 a night. Again both the *NBT* and *ANWB* can provide a list of these, and you should normally book, either direct or through the *NRC*.

Food and Drink

Holland is quite rightly not renowned for its cuisine, but although much is unimaginative it's rarely unpleasant. The country also has a good supply of ethnic restaurants, especially Indonesian and Chinese, and if you're selective prices needn't break the bank. Drinking, too, is easily affordable: Dutch beer is one of the real pleasures of the country.

■ Food

Dutch food tends to be fairly plain, mainly consisting of steak, chicken or fish, along with filling soups and stews. In all but the very cheapest hostels or most expensive hotels **breakfast** (*ontbijt*) will be included in the price of the room. Though usually nothing fancy, it's always very filling: rolls, cheese, ham, hard-boiled eggs, jam and honey or peanut butter are the principal ingredients. If you don't have a hotel breakfast, many bars and cafés serve at least rolls and sandwiches and some offer a set breakfast. The **coffee** is normally good and strong, around f2 a cup, served with a little tub of *koffiemelk* (evaporated milk). **Tea** generally comes with lemon if anything; if you want milk you have to ask for it. **Chocolate** (*chocomel*) is also popular, served hot or cold.

For the rest of the day, **fast food** options include chips – *frites* or *patat* – sprinkled with salt and smothered with mayonnaise, curry, sate, goulash or tomato sauce. If you just want salt, ask for "patat zonder"; chips with salt and mayonnaise are "patat met". Often chips are complemented with *kroketten* – spiced minced meat coated in breadcrumbs and deep fried – or *fricandel*, a frankfurter-like sausage. Tastier, and good both as a snack and a full lunch, are the fish specialities that you see being sold from street kiosks: salted raw herrings, smoked eel (*gerookte paling*), mackerel in a roll (*broodje makreel*), mussels and various kinds of deep-fried fish. A nationwide chain of fish restaurants, *Noordzee*, serves good-value fish-based sandwiches and light fish lunches. Another fast snack you'll see everywhere is *shoarma* or kebab, sold in numerous Middle Eastern restaurants and takeaways.

The majority of **bars** serve some kind of food, sometimes a full menu, in which case they may be known as an **eetcafé**. Most serve at least **sandwiches and rolls** (*boterham* and *broodjes*) – *stokbrood* if made with French bread; in winter they serve *erwtensoep*, a thick pea soup with smoked sausage, for about f6, and *uitsmijters* (literally, "bouncer"), fried eggs on buttered bread, topped with ham or roast beef for about f8. Full-blown **restaurants** tend to open in the evening only, until around 11pm. If you're on a tight budget, stick to **dagschotels** (dish of the day), for which you pay f10–15 for a meat or fish dish heavily garnished with vegetables. Otherwise, meat dishes go for f15–25, fish for f25–30. **Train station restaurants** are a good standby, as they are generally able to supply full meals for f10–15, and in university towns **student mensa restaurants** serve meals for under f10. **Vegetarian food** isn't a problem. Many *eetcafés* and restaurants have at least one meat-free item, and you'll find vegetarian restaurants in most towns, offering full-course set meals for f10–15, though they often close early. Of foreign cuisines, **Surinamese** restaurants are a good bet for food on a budget, as are **Chinese** and **Indonesian** restaurants (sometimes combined). If you're hungry, order a *rijstaffel*: rice served with a huge number of dishes for about f70 for two.

■ Drink

Most **drinking** is done either in the cosy environs of a **brown café** (*bruin kroeg*) – so named because of the colour of the walls – or in more modern-looking **bars**, usually catering to a younger crowd. Most bars open until around 1am during the week, 2am at weekends. You may also come across *proeflokaalen* or **tasting houses**, small, old-fashioned bars that only serve spirits and close around 8pm. The most commonly consumed beverage is **beer**, usually served in small measures; ask for "een pils". Prices are fairly standard; reckon on paying about f2.50 a glass pretty much everywhere. From a supermarket you'll pay f1–2 for a half-litre bottle. The most commonly seen names are *Heineken*, *Amstel*, *Oranjeboom* and *Grolsch*, though there are other regional brews and you will also come across plenty of the better-known Belgian brands. **Wine** is reasonably priced – expect to pay around f6 or so for an average bottle of French white or red. As for **spirits**, the indigenous drink is **jenever** or Dutch gin, served in small glasses and traditionally drunk straight. *Oud* (old) is smooth and mellow, *Jong* (young) packs more of a punch, though neither is extremely alcoholic. A glass in a bar costs around f2.50.

Opening Hours and Holidays

The Dutch weekend fades painlessly into the working week with many shops staying closed on Monday morning, even in major cities. Otherwise, opening hours tend to be 9am to 5.30 or 6pm, though certain shops stay open later on Thursday and Friday evenings. Outside these hours *Avondwinkels* or night shops can be found in major cities, usually opening at 6pm and closing at 1 or 2am. In general, things shut a little earlier on Saturday.

Opening times of **museums** are fairly uniform – generally Tues–Sat 10am–5pm, Sun 1/2– 5pm; entry prices for the more ordinary collections are f2–5. If you're intending to visit more than a handful of museums, it's worth investing in a

museumcard – available from the VVV or direct from museums for f25 if you're under 18, f40 otherwise, and granting free access to all state and municipally run museums and galleries for a year. An alternative is the Cultureel Jongeren Paspoort or **CJP**, which if you're under 26 gets reductions in museums and on theatre, film and concert tickets for f20 – though the discounts vary wildly. There is also the **Holland Leisure Card**, available before you leave from the *NBT* (see *Basics*, for address), which includes a museumcard in its benefits.

Shops and banks are closed and museums adopt Sunday hours on the following **public holidays**: Jan 1; Good Friday; Easter Sunday & Monday; April 30; Whit Sunday & Monday; Aug 15; Dec 5; Dec 25 & Dec 26.

Emergencies

There's little reason ever to come into contact with the **police force** in the Netherlands, and, as far as personal safety goes, it's normally possible to walk anywhere in the larger cities at any time of day, though women should obviously be wary of badly lit or empty streets. Should you find yourself in trouble, or simply need assistance of a legal nature, a nationwide organization, **JAC** (address in phone book), gives free confidential help to young people, especially foreign nationals, on work, alien status and accommodation matters. As for **drugs**, bear in mind that although it is technically legal to possess up to 28 grams of cannabis for your own consumption, the liberal attitude towards it exists only in Amsterdam and the larger cities of the Randstad. Regarding **health**, an *apoteek* or pharmacy is the place to get a prescription filled; all are open Mon–Fri 9.30am–5.30pm – outside this time there'll be a note of the nearest open pharmacy on the door.

EMERGENCY NUMBERS
Police, Ambulance and Fire ☎06 11.

AMSTERDAM

AMSTERDAM is a beguiling capital, a compact mix of the provincial and the cosmopolitan. It has a welcoming attitude towards visitors, and a uniquely youthful orientation, and it's hard not to be drawn in by the buzz of open-air summer events and the intimacy of the clubs and bars. This is more a place to wander around and soak up the atmosphere than indulge in indoor pursuits, but the city is also home to a world-class group of museums and galleries, notably the Rijksmuseum, with its collection of seventeenth-century Dutch paintings, and the Van Gogh Museum – which, for many, are reason enough alone to visit the city.

As the name suggests, Amsterdam was founded on a dam on the river Amstel, in the thirteenth century. During the wars against Spain in the sixteenth century, and the accompanying upheavals of the Reformation, it rose in stature, taking trade from Antwerp and becoming a haven for its religious refugees. Having shaken off the yoke of the Spanish, the city went from strength to strength in the seventeenth century, becoming the centre of a vast trading empire extending to the newly occupied colonies in southeast Asia, and it accommodated its expansion with the cobweb of canals that gives the city its distinctive and elegant shape today. Come the 1700s, Amsterdam went into gentle decline and never really recovered its golden days, only to emerge into prominence again in the 1960s when it became a fashionable focus for the young and alternative movements of the time – despite something of an Eighties backlash, it still is to some extent. The city retains its social attitude to soft drugs, and it remains one of Europe's best cities simply to *be*, with a streetlife second to none, not to mention one of its most beautifully preserved centres.

The area **telephone code** for Amsterdam is ☎020.

Arrival and information

Amsterdam's airport, **Schiphol**, is connected by train with the city's Centraal Station every fifteen minutes during the day, every hour at night. **Centraal Station** is at the hub of all bus and tram routes and just five minutes' walk from Dam Square. Almost all **buses** arrive here, too, except for Hoverspeed's *City Sprint* service, which terminates at Leidseplein. For **information**, the **VVV** have a main branch right outside Centraal Station (daily May–Sept 9am–9pm; Oct–April 9am–5pm; ☎06/34 03 40 66), and a smaller kiosk at Leidsestraat 106. Either can sell you a map, book accommodation and provide answers to most enquiries, though summer queues at the main office can be a nightmare. The VVV also issue a biweekly **listings guide**, *What's On In Amsterdam*, available direct from their offices for f2.75 or free from hotels, hostels and restaurants.

City transport

Amsterdam's excellent **public transport** network of **trams, buses** and a small **metro** system isn't expensive; as with the rest of the country, you can use a *strippenkaart* on all services – available from any *GVB* office, post office, selected tobacconists, at train station ticket counters, or, more expensively, from bus drivers. Since you rarely need to travel outside the central zone, cancelling two strips is normally sufficient. *Dagkaarten* – **day tickets** – are also available, valid for as many days as you need for a cost of f11.50 for one day, going up to f24.45 for four, then f3.60 for each additional day. If caught without a ticket, you're liable for a f60 spot fine. All services stop running around 12.30am, when **night buses** take over, running roughly hourly until 4am from

Centraal Station to most parts of the city. The *GVB* office in front of Centraal Station (Mon–Fri 7am–10.30pm, Sat & Sun 8am–10.30pm) has free route maps and an English guide to the ticketing system. **Taxis** are expensive, and are found in ranks on main city squares (Stationsplein, Dam Square, Leidseplein) or by phoning ☎677 77 77 – you can't hail them. **Bicycles** can be hired from Centraal Station for the usual rates or from a number of similarly priced bike hire firms scattered around town (see "Listings").

Accommodation

Unless you're camping, **accommodation** in Amsterdam can be expensive, although the city's size means that you'll inevitably end up somewhere central. At peak periods throughout the year it's advisable to book ahead.

Hostels

Bob's Youth Hostel, N. Z. Voorburgwal 92 (☎623 00 63). An old favourite of backpackers, with small, clean dorms; price includes breakfast in the ground-floor coffee shop. Curfew 3.30am; close to Centraal Station. ②

Eben Haezer, Bloemstraat 179 (☎624 47 17). Christian youth hostel providing neat, clean dormitories for rock-bottom prices, including linen and a hearty breakfast. Curfew 1am at weekends. Tram #13, #14, #17. ②

Kabul, Warmoesstraat 38–42 (☎623 71 58). There's no lockout or curfew here, and it's close to the station, with a late-opening bar attached. Breakfast f6 extra. Dorms ②; rooms ③

Keizersgracht, Keizersgracht 15 (☎625 13 64). Terrific location close to the station, with doubles and a good mixture of triples and four-bedded rooms. Breakfast is extra. Dorms ②; doubles ③

Sleep-In, 's-Gravesandestraat 51 (☎694 74 44). A little out of the centre but inexpensive and open all year. Facilities include a bar, restaurant and information centre. Weesperplein metro or tram #6. ②

Stadsdoelen, Kloveniersburgwal 97 (☎624 68 32). Official *IYHF* hostel with a restaurant that serves good-value food. Tram #4, #9, #16, #24, #25. ②

Vondel Park, Zandpad 5 (☎683 17 44). The better facilities of the two official hostels, with bar, restaurant, TV rooms and kitchen. Curfew 2am. Tram #1, #2, #5. *IYHF* members only in July and August. ②

Hotels

Acro, Jan Luykenstraat 44 (☎662 05 26). Excellent, modern hotel with stylish rooms, bar and self-service restaurant. Tram #2, #3, #5, #12. ⑥

De Admiraal, Herengracht 563 (☎626 21 50). Friendly hotel just off Rembrandtsplein. Tram #4. ④

Adolesce, Nieuwe Keizersgracht 26 (☎626 39 59). Nicely situated just off the Amstel, with a 2am curfew. Tram #7, bus #31. ⑤

Bema, Concertgebouwplein 19b (☎679 13 96). Small and welcoming, and handy for the museums. Trams #3, #5, #12. ④

Beurstraat, Beurstraat 7 (☎626 37 01). Just behind the fomer Stock Exchange in the centre of town. Very basic and very cheap. ③

Clemens, Raadhuisstraat 39 (☎624 60 89). Good value for money. Tram #13, #14, #17. ④

Crown, O. Z. Voorburgwal 21 (☎626 96 64). Friendly budget hotel in the red-light area. ⑤

Kitty, Plantage Middenlaan 40 (☎622 68 19). A little way out of the centre, but with good-sized rooms and as much breakfast as you can eat. Tram #9, #14; get off at the zoo. ④

Prinsenhof, Prinsengracht 810 (☎623 17 72). Tastefully decorated hotel with the best rooms at the back. Tram #4. ④

Ronnie, Raadhuisstraat 41 (☎624 28 21). Affable place with three-, four- and five-bed rooms; the price includes breakfast. Tram #13, #14, #17. ④

Seven Bridges, Reguliersgracht 31 (☎623 13 29). One of the city's most beautiful and best-value hotels. Tram #4. ⑤

Van Ostade, Van Ostadestraat 123 (☎679 324 52). Relaxed place that hires out bikes. Peacefully situated only five minutes' cycle out of the centre in the appealing Old South district. Tram #24, #25. ④

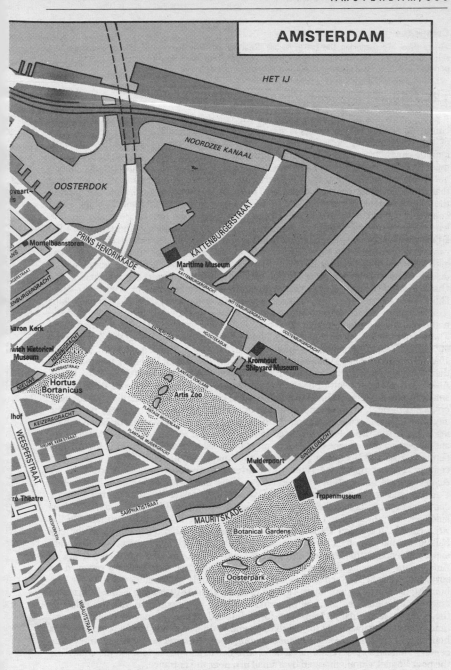

AMSTERDAM

HET IJ

NOORDZEE KANAAL

OOSTERDOK

ovaart-
is

Momelbaanstoren

PRINS HENDRIKKADE

KATTENBURGERSTRAAT

AGERSTRAAT

ENBURGERGRACHT

Maritime Museum

KATTENBURGERGRACHT

WITTENBURGERGRACHT

OOSTENBURGERGRACHT

uron Kerk

ENTREPOTDOK

HOOGTEKADIK

wich Historical
Museum

HERENGRACHT

MUIDERSTRAAT

PLANTAGE DOKLAAN

Kromhout
Shipyard Museum

NIEUWE

Hortus
Bortanicus

Artis Zoo

PLANTAGE MIDDENLAAN

lhof

KEIZERSGRACHT

PLANTAGE MUIDERGRACHT

SINGELGRACHT

NIEUW KERKSTRAAT

WEESPERSTRAAT

Muiderpoort

Tropenmuseum

ré Theatre

SARPHATISTRAAT

MAURITSKADE

WEESPERPLEIN

Botanical Gardens

Oosterpark

WIBAUTSTRAAT

Campsites

Vliegenbos, Meeuwenlaan 138 (☎636 88 55). Relaxed and friendly "youth" site, a ten-minute bus ride from Centraal Station. Facilities include a general shop and bike hire. Costs f5.75 a night per person without car. Hot showers f1.50. Bus #32, night bus #77.

The City

Amsterdam is a small city, and, although the concentric canal system can be initially confusing, finding your bearings is straightforward. The medieval core boasts the best of the city's bustling streetlife and is home to shops, many bars and restaurants, fanning south from the nineteenth-century **Centraal Station**, one of Amsterdam's most resonant landmarks and a natural focal point for urban life. Come summer there's no livelier part of the city, as street performers compete for attention with the trams that converge dangerously from all sides. From here, **Damrak** storms into the heart of the city, an unenticing avenue lined with overpriced restaurants and bobbing canal boats and flanked on the left by the **Beurs**, designed at the turn of the century by the leading light of the Dutch modern movement, H. P. Berlage, and the enormous **De Bijenkorf** department store. Left off Damrak, the **red-light district**, stretching across two canals – **Oude Zijds Voorburgwal** and **Oude Zijds Achterburgwal** – is perhaps inevitably one of the real sights of the city, thronged with people in high season just to discover how shocking it all is. A little way up **Warmoesstraat**, the precincts of the **Oude Kerk** (Mon–Sat 1–3pm, Sun 1.30–3pm; f3; tower June–Sept Wed–Sat 2–5pm; f3.50) offer a reverential peace after the excesses of the area; it's a bare, mostly fourteenth-century church with some beautifully carved misericords in the choir, and the memorial tablet of Rembrandt's first wife, Saskia van Uylenburg, who is buried here. There's nothing to stop for along Oude Zijds, only the **Amstelkring**, at the Zeedijk end, once the principal Catholic place of worship in the city and now a museum (Mon–Sat 10am–5pm, Sun 1–5pm; f4.50) commemorating the days when Catholics had to confine their worship to the privacy of their own homes. Known as "Our Dear Lord in the Attic", it occupies the loft of a wealthy merchant's house, together with those of two smaller houses behind it. Just beyond, **Zeedijk**, once haunt of Amsterdam's drug dealers, leads through to **Nieuwmarkt** where the turreted **Waag** was originally part of the city's fortifications, later becoming the civic weigh-house. **Kloveniersburgwal**, which leads south, was the outer of the three eastern canals of sixteenth-century Amsterdam, and boasts, on the left, one of the city's most impressive canal houses, built for the Trip family in 1662 and large enough to house the Rijksmuseum collection for most of last century. Further up on the right, the **Oudemanhuispoort** passage leads to O. Z. Achterburgwal, once part of an almshouse and now filled with second-hand bookstalls.

At the end of Damrak, **Dam Square**, where the Amstel was first dammed, is the centre of the city, its tusk-like **War Memorial**, filled with soil from each of the Netherlands' eleven provinces and Indonesia, serving as a meeting place for tourists. On the western side, the **Royal Palace** (daily 12.30–5pm; f5) was originally built as the city hall in the mid-seventeenth century, and the Citizen's Hall inside proclaims the pride and confidence of the seventeenth-century Golden Age, with the enthroned figure of Amsterdam surveying the world and heavens at her feet. The building received its royal monicker in 1808 when Napoléon's brother Louis commandeered it as the one building fit for a king until he was forced to abdicate in 1810, leaving behind a sizeable amount of the Empire furniture that remains. Vying for importance with the Palace is the **Nieuwe Kerk** (daily 11am–5pm; f6), a fifteenth-century structure rebuilt several times that is now used only for exhibitions and state occasions. Inside rest numerous household names from Dutch history, among them Admiral de Ruyter, seventeenth-century Holland's most valiant naval hero, who lies in an opulent tomb in the choir, and the poet Vondel, commemorated by a small urn near the entrance.

South of Dam Square, **Rokin** follows the old course of the Amstel River, lined with grandiose nineteenth-century mansions. Running parallel, **Kalverstraat** is an uninspired strip of monotonous clothes shops, halfway down which, at no. 92, a gateway forms the entrance to the former orphanage that's now the **Amsterdam Historical Museum** (Mon–Fri 10am–5pm, Sat & Sun 11am–5pm; f6.50; guided tours Wed 2pm & 3pm). This attempts to survey the city's development with artefacts, paintings and documents from the thirteenth century onwards – centring, inevitably, around the Golden Age. A large group of paintings portrays the city in its heyday and the good art collection shows how the wealthy bourgeoisie decorated their homes, while directly outside, the glassed-in Civic Guard Gallery draws passers-by with free glimpses of the large company portraits. Just around the corner off Sint Luciensteeg, the **Begijnhof** is a small court of seventeenth-century buildings originally lived in by the poor and elderly, who led a religious life here, celebrating Mass in their own, concealed **Catholic Church**. The plain and unadorned **English Reformed Church**, which takes up one side of the Begijnhof, has pulpit panels designed by the young Piet Mondrian. Close by, the **Spui** is a lively corner of town whose mixture of bookshops and packed bars centres around a small statue of a young boy – known as **'t Lieverdje** (Little Darling) – a gift to the city from a large cigarette company. Twenty years ago, this was the scene of a series of demonstrations organized by the Provos, a left-wing group that labelled the statue a monument to tomorrow's addiction to capitalism. In the opposite direction, Kalverstraat comes to an end at **Muntplein** and the **Munttoren** – originally a mint and part of the city walls, topped with a spire by Hendrik de Keyser in 1620. Across the Singel is the **Flower Market**, while in the other direction Reguliersbreestraat turns left toward the loud restaurants of **Rembrandtsplein**. To the south is **Reguliersgracht**, a broad canal of distinctive steep bridges that was to have been filled in at the beginning of the century but was saved when public outcry rose against the destruction of one of the city's more alluring stretches of water.

Across the Amstel from here, the controversial new **Muziektheater and Town Hall** flank **Waterlooplein**, to which the city's excellent **flea market** has recently returned after a few years at nearby Valkenburgstraat. You can explore backstage and get an idea of the workings of the Muziektheater on guided tours (Aug–June Wed & Sat 4pm; f8.50). Behind, **Jodenbreestraat** was once the main street of the so-called Jodenhoek, the city's Jewish quarter, and is the site of the **Rembrandt House** at no. 6 (Mon–Sat 10am–5pm, Sun 1–5pm; f5), which the painter bought at the height of his fame, living here for over twenty years and spending a fortune on furnishings – an expense that hastened his bankruptcy. The house itself is disappointing – mostly a reconstruction and with no artefacts from Rembrandt's life on exhibit – but displays a huge number of the artist's engravings. Close by, the most tangible mementoes of the Jewish community are shown in the **Portuguese Synagogue** (Sun–Fri 10am–5pm; free), completed in 1675 and once the largest synagogue in the world. Across the way, the **Jewish Historical Museum** (daily 10am–4pm; f5) is cleverly housed in a complex of Ashkenazi synagogues dating from the late seventeenth century and gives a broad and imaginative introduction to Jewish life and beliefs. Down Muiderstraat from here, the prim **Hortus Botanicus**, Plantage Middenlaan 2 (Mon–Fri 9am–4/5pm, Sat & Sun 11am–4/5pm; f6), is a pocket-sized botanical garden whose 6000 plant species make a wonderfully relaxed break from the rest of central Amsterdam; stop off for coffee and cakes in the orangery. On the far side of Plantage Middenlaan is Amsterdam's **Zoo** (daily 9am–5pm; f17.50, children F10), beyond which the **Kromhout Shipyard Museum** at Hoogte Kadijk 147 (Mon–Fri 10am–4pm; f3.50), one of the few survivors of the decline in the shipbuilding industry that flourished in the locality during the nineteenth century, is a combination of industrial monument, operating shipyard and museum, patching up ancient boats and offering a slide show. A short walk west, the **Maritime Museum** on Kattenburgerplein, housed in a fortress-like seventeenth-century arsenal (Tues–Sat 10am–5pm, Sun noon–

5pm; f10), has more marine attractions in the form of maps, navigational equipment and weapons – though most impressive are the large models of sailing ships and men-of-war.

The Main Canals

The city's expansion in the seventeenth century was designed around three new canals, **Herengracht**, **Keizersgracht** and **Prinsengracht**, which curved around the centre. Development was strictly controlled. Even the richest burgher had to conform to a set of stylistic rules when building his house, and taxes were levied according to the width of the properties, producing the loose conformity you see today – tall, narrow residences, with individualism restricted to heavy decorative gables and sometimes a gablestone to denote name and occupation. It's difficult to pick out any particular points to head for: most of the houses have been turned into offices or hotels. Rather, the appeal lies in wandering along selected stretches admiring the gables while taking in the calm of the tree-lined waterways, unusual in the centre of a modern European capital. For shops, bars, restaurants and the like, explore streets connecting the canals.

Today, Herengracht remains the city's grandest canal, especially between Leidsestraat and Vijzelstraat, a stretch known as the "Golden Bend", though to actually see the interior of one of these canal houses you should head for the **Willet-Holthuysen House**, Herengracht 605 (Mon–Fri 10am–5pm, Sat & Sun 11am–5pm; f5), splendidly decorated in Rococo style and containing Abraham Willet's collection of glass and ceramics – although, save for the well-equipped seventeenth-century kitchen, it's very much look-don't-touch territory. Perhaps more likeable, with a pleasantly down-at-heel interior of peeling stucco and shabby paintwork, is the **Van Loon House**, Keizersgracht 672 (Mon 10am–5pm, Sun 1–5pm; f5), built in 1672 for the artist Ferdinand Bol. The van Loon family bought the house in 1884, bringing with them a collection of family portraits and homely bits and pieces that stretch from 1580 to 1949.

On the corner of Keizersgracht and Leidsestraat, the designer department store, **Metz & Co**, has a top-floor coffee shop with one of the best views of the city. **Leidsestraat** itself is a long, slender passage across the main canals that broadens into **Leidseplein** at its southern end in the area that's the focus of Amsterdam's nightlife, with a concentration of bars and restaurants. On the far corner, the **Stadsschouwburg** is the city's prime performance space after the Muziektheater, while behind, and architecturally much more impressive, the fairy-castle **American Hotel** has a bar whose carefully coordinated furnishings are as fine an example of Art Nouveau as you'll find.

The area immediately north of here, around Prinsengracht, is one of the city's loveliest neighbourhoods, focusing on the gracious tower of the **Westerkerk** (daily 10am–5pm; tower Mon–Sat 10am–5pm; f3.50), designed by Hendrik de Keyser in 1631, though there's little within of special note – only a small memorial to Rembrandt, who was living nearby when he died. Directly outside the church, a statue of **Anne Frank** by the Dutch sculptor Mari Andriessen signals the fact that the house where the young diarist lived is just a few steps away at Prinsengracht 263. This is now open as the **Anne Frank House** (Mon–Sat 9am–5pm, Sun 10am–5pm; f7) and is deservedly one of the most popular tourist attractions in town. The story of Anne Frank, her family and friends is well known. They went into hiding from the Nazis in July 1942, along with a Jewish business partner and his family, staying in the annexe behind the house for two years until they were betrayed and taken away to labour camps, an experience which only Anne's father survived. Anne Frank's diary was among the few things left behind here, and was published in 1947, since when it has sold thirteen million copies worldwide. The rooms the Franks lived in are left much as they were, even down to the movie star pin-ups in Anne's bedroom and the marks on the wall recording the children's heights. A number of other rooms offer background detail on the war and occupation, one offering a video biography of Anne, another detailing the atrocities of Nazism and giving some up-to-date and pertinent examples of fascism in Europe.

Across Prinsengracht, the **Jordaan** is a beguiling area of narrow canals, narrower streets and simpler, architecturally varied houses, originally home of artisans and religious refugees, and later the inner-city enclave of Amsterdam's industrial working class – which, in spite of widespread gentrification, it to some extent remains. Other than a handful of bars and restaurants, some posh clothes shops and the odd outdoor market, there's nothing specific to see, though it's a wonderful neighbourhood to wander, focusing on **Tweede Anjelierdwarsstraat** and **Tweede Tuindwarsstraat**, which hold the bulk of the neighbourhood's trendy stores and some of its liveliest bars and cafés.

The Old South and the major museums

Immediately south of Leidseplein, the **Vondelpark** is the city's most enticing park, named after the seventeenth-century Dutch poet Joost van der Vondel and a regular forum for drama and other performance arts on summer weekends, when young Amsterdam flocks here to meet friends, laze by the lake and listen to music – in June, July and August bands give free concerts here every Sunday at 2pm. Southeast of the park is one of Amsterdam's better-heeled residential districts, with designer shops and delis along chic **P. C. Hooftstraat** and **Van Baerlestraat** and some of the city's major **museums** grouped around the grassy wedge of **Museumplein**.

The **Rijksmuseum**, Stadhouderskade 42 (Tues–Sat 10am–5pm, Sun 1–5pm; f10), is the one museum you shouldn't leave Amsterdam without visiting, with fine collections of medieval and Renaissance applied art, displays on Dutch history, a fine Asian collection, and, most importantly, an array of seventeenth-century Dutch paintings that is far and away the best in the world. Most people head straight for one of the museum's great treasures, Rembrandt's *The Night Watch*, but there are many other, perhaps more interesting examples of his work, not least the *Staalmeesters*, the late *Jewish Bride*, and some private and beautifully expressive works – a portrait of his first wife *Saskia*, a couple of his mother, a touching depiction of his son, *Titus*, and a late *Self-portrait*, caught in mid-shrug as the Apostle Paul. There are also portraits by Frans Hals, landscapes by Jan van Goyen and Jacob van Ruisdael, the riotous scenes of Jan Steen and the peaceful interiors of Vermeer and Pieter de Hooch. Look out especially for Frans Hals' expansive *Isaac Massa and His Wife*, and the *Portrait of Abraham Potter* by Carel Fabritius, a skilful work by Rembrandt's most talented student. Vermeer's *The Letter* reveals a tension between servant and mistress – the lute on the woman's lap was a well-known sexual symbol of the time – while the similarly symbolic map behind the *Young Woman Reading a Letter* hints at the far-flung places her lover is writing from. The ground floor holds later Dutch paintings, from the work of Cornelis Troost, whose eighteenth-century comic scenes earned him the dubiously deserved title of the "Dutch Hogarth", to numerous nineteenth-century landscapes, most notably those of the painters of the Hague School.

Just south, the **Rijksmuseum Vincent Van Gogh**, Paulus Potterstraat 7 (Mon–Sat 10am–5pm, Sun 1–5pm; f10), opened in 1973 and comprises the collection of the artist's art-dealer brother Theo, with drawings, notebooks and letters displayed on a rotating basis, and a collection arranged chronologically, from the early years in Holland and works like the dour *Potato Eaters*, to the brighter works he painted after moving to Paris, and, later Arles, where he produced vivid canvases like *The Yellow House* and the *Sunflowers* series. Later, more expressionistic works include the *Garden of St Paul's Hospital*, painted at the asylum in St-Rémy where van Gogh spent time after snipping off part of his ear and offering it to a local prostitute, and the final, tortured paintings done at Auvers, including *The Reaper* and *Wheatfield with Crows* – painted a few weeks before he shot and fatally wounded himself.

Further up the street at Paulus Potterstraat 13, the **Stedelijk Museum** (daily 11am–5pm; f7.50), Amsterdam's modern art museum, is a regular venue for temporary exhibitions and as such it can be hard to say what you'll see. But it has a wide permanent collection, much of which is on display in July and August, and parts of it year-round. There's normally a good showing on the first floor, starting off with drawings by Picasso, Matisse and their contemporaries, and moving on to paintings by the major Impressionists – Manet, Monet, Bonnard – and Post-Impressionists like Ensor, van Gogh and Cezanne. There's also work by Mondrian and Malevich, a good stock of Marc Chagall's paintings, and a number of American Abstract Expressionists – Mark Rothko, Ellsworth Kelly and Barnett Newman. Two additional large-scale attractions are on the ground floor: Karel Appel's *Bar* in the foyer, installed for the opening of the Stedelijk in the 1950s, and the same artist's wild daubings in the museum's restaurant.

Further along Stadhouderskade from the Rijksmuseum, the **Heineken Brewery** runs tours (Mon–Fri 9.30am, 11am, 1pm & 2.30pm; summer also 4.30pm; f2), though it recently stopped production and is in the process of being turned into a museum; afterwards you are given snacks and free beer. Beyond here, the neighbourhood is known as "De Pijp" (The Pipe) after its long, sombre canyons of brick tenements that went up in the nineteenth century as the city grew out of its canal-girded centre. De Pijp has always been one of the city's closest-knit communities, and one of its liveliest, with numerous inexpensive Surinamese and Turkish restaurants and a cheerful hub in the long slim thoroughfare of **Albert Cuypstraat**, whose daily general market is the largest in the city. Further east, off Mauritskade, the final museum you should try and visit is the **Tropenmuseum**, Linnaeusstraat 2, accessible on tram #10 (Mon–Fri 10am–5pm, Sat & Sun noon–5pm; f7.50); it's an inventive display of applied arts from all over the world, covering everything from the slum dwellings of Bombay to the destruction of the world's rainforests, the best sections being devoted to Africa, India and Indonesia, but it's really all worth seeing, even if you have little interest in ethnography.

Eating and drinking

Amsterdam may not be the culinary capital of Europe, but there's a good supply of ethnic **restaurants**, especially Indonesian and Chinese, as well as *eetcafés* and bars which serve decent, well-priced food in a relaxed and unpretentious setting. We've also listed a handful of places to get just a snack, though you can do this easily enough in many bars, as well as the best of the city's **"smoking" coffee shops**, where smoking dope is the primary pastime (all sell a range of hash and grass) to a background of video screens, loud music, etc.

Snacks and pastries

Bâton, Herengracht 82. Convivial coffee shop with a huge array of sandwiches.

J.G. Beune, Haarlemmerdijk 156. Age-old chocolatier with a tearoom attached.

Café Panini, Vijzelgracht 3–5. Coffee shop with good sandwiches and pasta dishes.

Noordzee, Kalverstraat 122. Central Amsterdam branch of a chain that specializes in cheap fish lunches and sandwiches.

Studio 2, Singel 504. Pleasantly situated, airy coffee shop that sells delicious rolls and sandwiches.

Mensas

Atrium, O. Z. Voorburgwal 237. Mon–Fri noon–2pm & 5–7pm.

De Weesper, Weesperstraat 5. Mon–Fri 5–7.25pm.

Restaurants

De Blauwe Hollander, Leidsekruisstraat 28. Long-established Dutch restaurant serving decent and affordable food in generous quantities – quite a boon in this area.

Bojo, Lange Leidsedwarsstraat 51. Perhaps the best-value Indonesian place in town, open until 6am. Expect to wait for a table, though.

Burger's Patio, 2e Tuindwarsstraat 12. Moderately priced, convivial Italian restaurant. Despite the name, not a burger in sight.

Centra, Lange Wiezel 29. Arguably the city's best Spanish restaurant.

De Eetuin, 2e Eglantiersdwarsstraat 10. Hefty portions of Dutch food, all with a salad from a serve-yourself bar for f17–24. Veggie options, too, and a delicious fish casserole.

Egg Cream, St Jacobstraat 19. Amsterdam's most famous vegetarian restaurant, with set meals for f10–15. Bear in mind the early closing time of 8pm.

Filoxenia, Berenstraat 8. Small, friendly, reasonably priced Greek restaurant.

Haesje Claes, Spuistraat 275. Dutch cuisine. Extremely popular, so get there early.

Jaya, 1e Anjeliersdwarsstraat 18. One of the smallest and best of the city's Indonesian restaurants. Bookings advised.

To Ouzeri, De Clerqstraat 106. *Eetcafé* where you can compose your own meal from the many delicious Greek dishes on offer.

Pizzeria Mimo, Lange Leidsedwarsstraat 37. Perhaps the best of the dozens of Italian restaurants along this street.

Rose's Cantina, Reguliersdwarsstraat 38. Long-established trendy restaurant, very crowded and no bookings, but the Tex-Mex food is good – from around f25.

Sisters, Nes 102. A busy vegetarian restaurant serving *dagschotels* and other main courses for around f16, as well as plenty of snack-type items. Closes 9pm.

Sluizer, Utrechtsestraat 41–43. French-orientated food in one of the city's most atmospheric restaurants.

Warung Swietie, 1e Sweelinckstraat 1. Cheap, cheerful Surinamese/Javanese *eetcafé*.

Bars

De Engelbewaarder, Kloveniersburgwal 59. Still known as the "literary café", this is a relaxed and informal bar with live jazz on Sunday afternoons.

Flying Dutchman, Martelaarsgracht 13. Principal watering hole of Amsterdam's British community, usually packed with regulars using the pool table or dartboards.

Frascati, Nes 59. Theatre bar, popular with a young, media-type crowd. Good, too, for both lunchtime and informal evening eating, with full meals for around f15. Recommended.

't Gasthuys, Grimburgwal 7. Convivial brown café often packed with students from the university across the canal. Summer seating outside by the water.

Hoppe, Spui 18. One of the city's best known and longest established bars, still hanging on despite the gentrification of the immediate surroundings.

Luxembourg, Spui 22–24. The latest watering hole of Amsterdam's advertising and media brigade, but a very elegant bar with a good, though pricy, selection of snacks.

Het Molenpad, Prinsengracht 653. Cosy and informal brown café and gallery full of bookish types from the public library just along the canal.

De Prins, Prinsengracht 124. Boisterous student bar, with a wide range of drinks and a well-priced menu that includes fondues. In a great part of town.

De Reiger, Nieuwe Leliestraat 34. The Jordaan's main meeting place, an old-style café filled with modish Amsterdammers. Affordable food, too.

De Schutter, Voetboogstraat 13–15. Likeably scruffy upstairs bar that serves well-priced food.

De Tuin, 2e Tuindwarsstraat 13. One of the best of the Jordaan's local hang-outs.

"Smoking" coffee shops

The Bulldog, Leidseplein 15, and a couple of other outlets. The oldest, biggest, and some say, still the best.

Pie in the Sky, 2e Laurierdwarsstraat 64. Beautiful canal-corner setting, great in summer.

Rusland, Rusland 16. One of the first and best Amsterdam coffee shops, a cramped, vibrant place that's a favourite with both dope fans and tea addicts (43 different kinds).

Siberië, Brouwersgracht 11. Relaxed café worth a visit whether you smoke or not.

De Tweede Kamer, Heisteeg 6. One of the few smoking coffee shops frequented by Amsterdammers: traditional decor, friendly atmosphere.

Nightlife

Amsterdam is a gathering spot for fringe performances, and buzzes with places offering a wide and often inventive range of affordable entertainment. **Rock, jazz** and **Latin American** music are well-represented in a number of small bars and clubs but the **club scene** is relatively tame: drinks prices are normally fifty percent or so more than what you pay in a bar, but entry prices are low – usually around f10 – and there's rarely any kind of door policy. Most places open around 10pm and close up around 4am or slightly later. For more highbrow entertainment, the Concertgebouw assures Amsterdam a high ranking in the **classical music** stakes, and the city has pulled itself up into the big leagues for **dance and opera** with the building of the new Muziektheater. The **Uitburo**, in the Stadsschouwburg on the corner of Marnixstraat and Leidseplein (Mon–Sat 10am–6pm, Thurs until 9pm; ☎621 12 11), is the best source of **information**, and sells **tickets** for a f2 fee; the monthly *Time Out* magazine, along with supplements in Thursday's *Het Parool* and Friday's *Volkskrant,* are also good sources of listings. Tickets can also be bought from the VVV.

Rock and jazz venues

Akhnaton, Nieuwezijds Kolk 25. Three-storey youth centre with live music at weekends – hip-hop, Latin, African and reggae. Starts around 10pm, admission around f15.

Alto Café, Korte Leidsedwarsstraat 115. Small, atmospheric jazz bar just off Leidseplein that has music every night 10pm–2.30am.

Bimhuis, Oude Schans 73–77. Excellent jazz auditorium. Concerts Thurs–Sat at 9pm (f15–25), free jazz sessions Mon & Tues at 10.30pm.

Joseph Lamm Jazz Club, Van Diemenstraat 242. Trad jazz venue with live music Sat 9pm–3am, f5; jam sessions Sun 8pm–2am, free.

Meervaart, Osdorpplein 205. A modern multi-media centre on the outskirts of town (tram #1, bus #19, #23) with a varied programme of music, film and dance. f10–25.

Melkweg, Lijnbaansgracht 234a. Probably Amsterdam's most famous entertainment venue, and these days one of the city's prime arts centres, with drama, live bands and weekend discos, films, a tearoom selling dope, and a bar and restaurant. General admission f5, plus f4 membership; concert admission f10–25. Closed Mon.

Paradiso, Weteringschans 6–8. Regular live bands from the up-and-coming to well-known names. Entrance f10–25, plus f3 membership.

PH 31, Prins Hendriklaan 31. Hard-core punk and new wave bands on Thurs, jazz and blues from 8.30pm on Sun night, other sounds during the week. Tram #2.

De Pieter, St Pieterspoortsteeg 29. Live music bar playing host to bands on Wed nights, a disco on Sat, and blaring music the rest of the week. Dark and noisy, with a mixed clientele.

Discos and clubs

Havana Club, Reguliersdwarsstraat 17–19. Very popular with a mixed clientele. Early disco on weekdays, 4pm–1am (Fri & Sat until 2am).

It, Amstelstraat 24 (☎625 01 11). Spectacular night spot and currently the city's number one gay disco, though it's also very popular with non-gays. Thurs nights free.

Mazzo, Rozengracht 114. Long-running hip disco with live music Tues & Wed.

(Op de schaal van) Richter 36, Reguliersdwarsstraat 36. Small, chic club with a fairly flexible door policy.

The Roxy, Singel 465. Housed in an old cinema, one of the city's best clubs. Thurs–Sun 11pm–5am.

Contemporary music, classical music and opera

Concertgebouw, Concertgebouwplein 2–6 (☎671 83 45). One of the most dynamic orchestras in the world in one of the finest halls. Free lunchtime concerts Sept–May. f25 and upwards.

De IJsbreker, Weesperzijde 23 (☎668 18 05). Large, varied programme of international modern, chamber and experimental music. Admission f12.50. Tram #3, #6, #7, #10.

Muziektheater, Amstel 3 (☎625 54 55). Amsterdam's fullest opera programme. Tickets cost f15–50, and sell quickly. Free lunchtime concerts, too.

Stadsschouwburg, Leidseplein 26 (☎624 23 11). Somewhat overshadowed by the Muziektheater but still a significant stage for opera and dance. Tickets f10–30.

Cinema and theatre

Cinemas in Amsterdam rarely show foreign-language films without English subtitles. There's also a resident English-language theatre, the *Stalhouderij*, 1e Bloemdwarrstraat 4 (☎626 22 82), which puts on a mixture of twentieth-century British and American plays alongside the classics at a variety of venues. The *Melkweg*, the *Shaffy Theatre*, Keizersgracht 324, and the *Mickery*, Rozengracht 117, also have regular English-language productions.

Gay Amsterdam

Amsterdam has one of the biggest and best-established **gay scenes** in Europe: attitudes are tolerant, and facilities unequalled, with a good selection of bookstores, clubs and bars catering to the needs of gay men – and, to a lesser extent, women. The nationwide gay and lesbian organization, *COC*, Rozenstraat 8 (☎623 1192), can provide on-the-spot information, and has a café and runs sporadic discos. There's a good concentration of bars around Rembrandtsplein, along the Amstel and on Reguliersdwarsstraat. The *Amstel Taveerne*, Amstel 54, is perhaps the best-established, at its most vivacious in summer when the guys spill out onto the street by the river; around the corner, *Chez Manfred*, Halvemaansteeg 10, is a tiny and similarly longtime favourite bar. *April*, Reguliersdwarsstraat 54, is a relaxed daytime hang-out, with newspapers, coffee and cakes as well as booze.

Listings

Airlines *Aer Lingus*, Heiligweg 14 (☎623 86 20); *Air UK*, Schiphol Airport (☎601 06 33); *British Airways*, Stadhouderskade 4 (☎685 22 11); *British Midland*, Stravinskylaan 1535 (☎06 022 24 26); *Canadian Pacific*, Stadhouderskade 2 (☎685 17 21); *KLM*, G. Metsustraat 2–6 (☎649 36 33); *NLM City Hopper*, Schiphol Airport (☎649 22 27); *Qantas*, Stadhouderskade 6 (☎838 08 10); *Transavia*, Schiphol Airport (☎604 65 18); *TWA*, Singel 540 (☎626 22 27).

Bicycle rental *Mac Bike*, Nieuwe Uilenburgerstraat 116 (☎620 09 85); f10 a day plus f50 deposit and passport. *Rent-a-Bike*, Pieter Jacobsdwarsstraat 17, off Damstraat (☎625 50 29); f12.50 a day plus f50 deposit and passport.

Books *Athenaeum*, Spui 14–16, is an excellent all-round bookshop and the best place to buy foreign magazines and papers.

Car rental *Budget*, Overtoom 121 (☎612 60 66); *Europcar*, Overtoom 51–53 (☎683 21 23); *Diks*, van Ostadestraat 278–280 (☎662 33 66).

Consulates *Great Britain*, Koningslaan 44 (☎676 43 43); *USA*, Museumplein 19 (☎664 56 61); *Australia*, Koninginnegracht 23, The Hague (☎070/310 82 00); *Canada*, Sophialaan 7, The Hague (☎070/361 41 11); *Ireland*, De Kuyperstraat 9, The Hague (☎070/310 82 00); *New Zealand*, Mauritskade 25, The Hague (☎070/346 93 24).

Exchange *GWK* in Centraal Station is open 24hr. *Change Express* has branches at Leidsestraat 106, Damrak 17 & 86, Kalverstraat 150 (daily until midnight).

Laundry *The Clean Brothers* is the best, at Jakob Van Lennepkade 179, Westerstraat 26, Kerkstraat 56 and Rozengracht 59 (daily until 9pm).

Left luggage Centraal Station (Mon–Fri 5am–1am, Sat & Sun 6am–1am).

Pharmacy There are no 24hr pharmacies, but every pharmacy has a sign giving the address of the nearest late-opening place.

Police station Headquarters at Elandsgracht 117 (☎559 91 11).

Post office Singel 250 (Mon–Fri 8.30am–6pm, Thurs until 8.30pm, Sat 9am–noon).

Telephones and faxes Easiest place to make calls is the *Telehouse*, Raadhuisstraat 48–50 (24hr). The *Teletalk Center*, Leidsestraat 101 (daily 10am–midnight) has phone and fax services, as well as photocopying.

Travel agents *NBBS*, Rokin 38 (☎620 50 71), and Leidsestraat 53 (☎638 17 36), is the Amsterdam branch of the nationwide youth travel organization.

Women's contacts The *Vrouwenhuis*, Nieuwe Herengracht 95 (☎625 20 66), is an organizing centre for women's activities. *Xantippe*, Prinsengracht 290, is a women's bookshop with a wide selection of titles in English. *Saarein*, Elandstraat 119, is the best-known women-only café.

THE RANDSTAD TOWNS

Historically, the provinces of North and South Holland were the richest and most influential in the Netherlands, far and away dominant in the life of the seventeenth-century Republic, and nowadays this area is the country's most populated region, a string of distinctive towns known as the **Randstad** or "rim town", situated amid a typically Dutch landscape of flat fields, cut by trenches and canals. Much of the area is easily visited by means of day trips from Amsterdam, but it's more rewarding – and not difficult – to make a proper tour. **Haarlem** is an obvious highlight, an easy day trip from Amsterdam but definitely worth treating as an overnight stop. South, the university centre of **Leiden** is a pleasant detour before the refined tranquillity of **The Hague** and the seedy lowlife of **Rotterdam**, while nearby **Delft** and **Gouda** repay visits too, the former with one of the best-preserved centres in the region. To the north, not officially part of the Randstad but still easily visited from Amsterdam, **Alkmaar** is a favourite with day-excursionists to see its rather bogus Friday cheese market.

Haarlem

Just over ten minutes from Amsterdam by train, **HAARLEM** is an easily absorbed city of around 150,000 people that sees itself as a cut above its neighbours and makes a good alternative base for exploring the province of Holland, or even Amsterdam. The Frans Hals Museum, in the almshouse where the artist spent his last years, is worth an afternoon in itself, and there are numerous beaches within easy reach, as well as some of the best of the bulbfields.

Haarlem was one of the Republic's most crucial centres, especially for the arts, and today retains an air of quiet affluence, with all the picturesque qualities of Amsterdam but little of the sleaze. The core of the city is **Grote Markt**, flanked by the gabled, originally fourteenth-century **Stadhuis** and the impressive bulk of the **Grote Kerk of St Bavo** (Mon–Sat 10am–4pm; Oct & Jan closes 3.30pm; f2). Inside, the mighty Christian Müller organ of 1738, with its 5000 pipes and razzmatazz Baroque embellishment, is said to have been played by Handel and Mozart, while, beneath, Xaverij's lovely group of draped marble figures represents Poetry and Music, offering thanks to the town patron for her generosity. In the choir there's a late fifteenth-century painting traditionally (though dubiously) attributed to Geertgen tot Sint Jans, along with memorials to painters Pieter Saenredam and Frans Hals, both of whom are buried here.

The town's real attraction is the **Frans Hals Museum** at Groot Heiligland 62 (Mon–Sat 10am–5pm, Sun 1–5pm; f6), a ten-minute stroll away in the Oudemannhuis almshouse where the aged Hals is supposed to have lived out his last years. It houses a good number of his lifelike seventeenth-century portraits, along with works by Gerard David, Jan Mostaert and the Haarlem Mannerists, including Carel van Mander, leading light of the Haarlem School and mentor of many of the others represented here – not least Cornelis Cornelisz van Haarlem, whose *Marriage of Peleus and Thetis* gives as much attention to the arrangement of elegant nudes as to his subject. Of the paintings by Hals himself, most prominent are the "Civic Guard" portraits in the west wing, which established his reputation as a portraitist and earned him a regular income. For a time, Hals himself was a member of the Company of Saint George, and in the *Officers of the Militia Company of Saint George* he appears in the top left-hand corner, a rare self-portrait. There are numerous scenes of Haarlem by Berckheyde and Saenredam, landscapes by the Ruisdaels, and the last contemplative portraits of Hals, including the *Governors of the Saint Elizabeth Gasthuis*, painted in 1641, and marvellous late portraits of the Regents and Regentesses of the Oudemannhuis itself.

On the other side of Grote Markt, the **Teylers Museum**, at Spaarne 16 (Tues–Sat 10am–5pm, Sun 1–5pm; f6.50), is the oldest museum in Holland, founded back in 1778 by wealthy local philanthropist Pieter Teyler van der Hulst. It should appeal to scientific and artistic tastes alike, containing everything from fossils, bones and crystals to weird, H.G. Wells-type technology and sketches and line drawings by Michelangelo, Raphael, Rembrandt and Claude. Look in on the rooms beyond, which are filled with work by eighteenth- and nineteenth-century Dutch painters, principally Breitner, Israëls, Weissenbruch and Wijbrand Hendriks, who was keeper of the art collection here.

Practicalities

The **train station** is on the north side of the city, about ten minutes' walk from the centre; **buses** stop right outside. The VVV, next door (April–Sept Mon–Fri 9am–5.30pm, Sat 9am–5.30pm; Oct–March Mon–Fri 9am–5.30pm, Sat 10am–4pm; ☎023/31 90 59), has maps and can book **private rooms** for around f30 a head plus a f7 reservation fee, though you'll find more choice in Zandvoort, about twenty minutes away by bus #80 (from Templierstraat) or #81 (from the rail station). The same goes for **hotels**, though Haarlem has a few reasonably priced alternatives. The *Carillon*, centrally placed at Grote Markt 27 (☎023/31 05 91; ④) is good, as is the *Waldor*, close to the station at Jansweg 40 (☎023/31 26 22; ④). There's also a **youth hostel** at Jan Gijzenpad 3 (☎023/37 37 93; ②; open March–Oct); buses #2 and #6 run frequently from the station – a ten-minute journey. Campers should try either the **campsites** among the dunes along Zeeweg out at Bloemendaal-aan-zee (bus #81), though these tend to be open during spring and summer only, or Haarlem's own site at Liewegie 17, which is open all year – bus #80 from Templierstraat.

For **lunches and snacks**, *Café Mephisto*, Grote Markt 29, is open all day and serves Dutch food for f12–20, snacks for much less. *Café 1900*, Barteljorisstraat 10, is also a good place for lunch, serving drinks and snacks in a turn-of-the-century interior. In the evening, there's *Alfonso's* Mexican restaurant at Oude Groenmarkt 8, which does Tex-Mex meals for around f19; the *Piccolo* restaurant, Riviervischmarkt 1, serves pasta and decent pizzas; or try the Indonesian food at *De Lachende Javaen*, on Frankestraat, with *rijstaffels* from f32. *Ze Crack*, at the junction of Lange Veerstraat and Kleine Houtstraat, is a dim, smoky **bar** with good music and beer by the pint.

Alkmaar

An hour from Amsterdam by train, **ALKMAAR** is typical of small-town Holland, its pretty, partly canalized centre surrounded by water and offering an undemanding provincialism which makes a pleasant change after the rigours of the big city. The town is probably best known for its **cheese market**, an ancient affair which these days ranks as one of the most extravagant tourist spectacles in Holland. Cheese has been sold on the main square here since the 1300s, and although no serious buying goes on here now, it's an institution that continues to draw crowds. If you do want to see it (mid-April to mid-Sept Fri 10am), be sure to get there early, as by opening time there's already quite a crush.

Even if you've only come for the market, it's a good idea to see something of the rest of the town before you leave. On the main square, the **Waag** was originally a chapel dedicated to the Holy Ghost, and nowadays houses the **VVV** and the **Kaasmuseum** (April–Oct Mon–Sat 10am–4pm, Fri 9am–4pm; f2), which has displays on the history of cheese and cheese-making equipment and suchlike. Across the other side of the square, the **Biermuseum de Boom**, Houttil 1 (April–Sept Tues–Sat 10am–4pm, Sun 1–4pm; Oct–March Thurs–Sun 1–4pm; f3), in the building of the old De Boom brewery, has exhibits tracing the brewing process from the malting to bottling stage, as well as a top-floor shop in which you can buy a huge range of beers and associated merchandise and a downstairs bar serving some eighty varieties of Dutch ale. The **Stedelijk Museum** (March–Dec Tues–Sat 10am–5pm, Sun 1–5pm; f2), on the other side of the town centre in Doelenstraat, displays pictures and artefacts relating to the history of the town, including a *Holy Family* by Honthorst and portraits by Maerten van Heemskerk and Caesar van Everdingen. Close by, at the far end of **Langestraat**, the town's main shopping street, the **St Laurenskerk**, a Gothic church of the late fifteenth century, is worth looking into for its huge organ, commissioned at the suggestion of Constantijn Huygens by Maria Tesselschade, local resident and friend of the Golden Age elite. It was designed by Jacob van Campen and painted by Caesar van Everdingen. In the apse is the tomb of Count Floris V, penultimate in the line of medieval counts of North Holland, who was murdered by nobles in 1296.

Practicalities

Alkmaar's **train station** is ten minutes' walk west of the centre of town on Stationsstraat. The **VVV** is five minutes on from here on Waagplein (Mon–Wed 9am–5.30pm, Thurs, Fri & Sat 9am–6pm; ☎072/11 42 84) and has **private rooms** for f25 per person. *De Nachtegaal* is the cheapest and most central **hotel**, opposite the town hall at Langestraat 100 (☎072/11 28 94; ④), or try *Pension Ida Margaretha*, Kanaaldijk 186 (☎072/61 39 89; ④). If you're **camping**, there's a site ten minutes' bus ride northwest of the town centre; take bus #168 or #169 from the station. There are quite a few decent places to eat. *Jelle's Eethuisje*, between Laat and Oude Gracht at Ridderstraat 24, is good for light lunches and cheap evening meals. *Ikan Mas*, in the old part of town at Fnidsen 101–103, is a reasonable Indonesian that does *rijstaffel* for under f30 a head, while *Rose's Cantina*, next door but one, serves Tex-Mex dishes for about f20. There are two main groupings of **bars**: one on Waagplein itself, the other on the nearby canal of Verdronken Noord, by the old Vismarkt. Of the former, *De Kaasbeurs* at 1 Houttil 30 is a lively place during the day but closes in the early evening; while *Café Corridor*, virtually next door, is a lively hang-out that plays loud music late into the night. On Verdronken Noord, *De Pilaren* is also noisy, though catering to a slightly older crowd; *Café Stapper*, next door, is a good refuge if the music gets too much.

Leiden

The home of Holland's most prestigious university, **LEIDEN** has an academic air. There's enough here to justify at least a day trip, and the town's energy, derived largely from its students, strongly counters the myth that there's nothing worth experiencing outside the capital. Leiden's museums, too, are varied and comprehensive enough to merit a visit in themselves, though the town's real charm lies in the peace and prettiness of its gabled streets and canals.

The Town

Leiden's most appealing quarter is that bordered by Witte Singel and Breestraat, focusing on Rapenburg, a peaceful area of narrow pedestrian streets and canals that is home to perhaps the city's best-known attraction, the **Rijksmuseum Van Oudheden**,

Rapenburg 25 (Tues–Sat 10am–5pm, Sun noon–5pm; f3.50, children f2), the country's principal archeological museum. You can see one of its major exhibits for free in the courtyard in front of the museum entrance – the Temple of Teffeh, a gift from the Egyptian government that dates back to the first century AD and was adapted in the fourth century to the worship of Isis. Inside the museum are more Egyptian artefacts – wall reliefs, statues, sarcophagi and mummies – along with classical Greek and Roman sculpture, and exhibits chronicling the archeological history of the country, through prehistoric, Roman and medieval times. Further along Rapenburg, at no. 73, the original home of the university is in part open as a **museum** (Wed–Fri 1–5pm; free), beyond which the **Hortus Botanicus** (Mon–Sat 9am–5pm, Sun 10am–5pm; f3.50) are supposedly among the oldest botanical gardens in Europe, planted in 1587. Across Rapenburg, a network of narrow streets converges on the **Pieterskerk** (daily 1.30–4pm; free), deconsecrated these days but still bearing the tomb of John Robinson, leader of the Pilgrim Fathers, who lived in a house on the site of what is now the **Jan Pesijn Hofje**, at Kloksteeg 21. East of here, **Breestraat** marks the edge of Leiden's commercial centre, behind which the two rivers converge at the busiest point in town, the site of a vigorous Wednesday and Saturday **market** which sprawls right over the sequence of bridges into the blandly pedestrian **Haarlemmerstraat**, the town's major shopping street. Close by, the **Burcht** (daily 10am–11pm; free) is a rather ordinary, graffiti-daubed shell of a fort perched on a mound, whose battlements you can clamber up for a view of Leiden's roofs and towers. The nearby **Hooglandsekerk** (April–Oct Tues–Sat 11am–4pm, Mon 1–3.30pm; free) is a light, lofty church with a central pillar that features an epitaph to Pieter van der Werff, the burgomaster at the time of a 1574 siege by the Spanish, who became a hero during its final days by offering his own body as a supply of food. His invitation was rejected, but – the story goes – it succeeded in instilling new determination in the flagging citizens. Across Oude Rijn from here, the **Museum Boerhaave** at Lange Agnietenstraat 10 (Tues–Sat 10am–5pm, Sun noon–5pm; f3.50) is a brief but absorbing guide to medical developments over the last three centuries, with some gruesome surgical implements, pickled brains and suchlike. Five minutes' walk away, Leiden's municipal museum, in the old **Lakenhal** at Oude Singel 28–32 (Tues–Fri 10am–5pm, Sat & Sun 1–5pm; f5), has mixed rooms of furniture, tiles, glass and ceramics, and a collection of paintings centred on Lucas van Leyden's *Last Judgement* triptych, plus canvases by Jacob van Swanenburgh, the first teacher of the young Rembrandt, by Rembrandt himself and associated Leiden painters – among them Jan Lievens (with whom he shared a studio) and Gerrit Dou, who initiated the Leiden tradition of small, minutely finished pictures. There's also a painting depicting the sixteenth-century siege that shows the heroic van der Werff in full flow. Around the corner on Molenwerf, the **Molenmuseum de Valk**, 2e Binnenvestgracht 1 (Tues–Sat 10am–5pm, Sun 1–5pm; f3), is located in a restored grain mill, one of twenty that used to surround Leiden, with living quarters furnished in simple, period style, and a slide show recounting the history of windmills in Holland. There's one other museum between here and the station, the **Rijksmuseum Voor Volkenkunde** at Steenstraat 1 (Tues–Fri 10am–5pm, Sat & Sun 1–5pm; f5), the national museum of ethnology, with complete sections on Indonesia and the Dutch colonies.

Practicalities

Leiden's **train and bus stations** are both situated on the northwest edge of town, no more than ten minutes' walk from the centre. The VVV, opposite the stations at Stationsplein 210 (Mon–Fri 9am–5.30pm, Sat 9am–4pm), has maps and leaflets, and can book **private rooms** for f35 a person. Of the few **hotels**, try the *De Ceder*, out beyond the station at Rijnsburgerweg 80 (☎071/17 59 03; ④), not including breakfast; or *De Doelen*, better placed at Rapenburg 2 (☎071/12 05 27; ⑤), with breakfast. The nearest

youth hostel is in Noordwijk, at Langevelderlaan 45 (☎02523/72920; ②) – take bus #60 from opposite the station. If you're **camping**, the closest site is the *Koningshof* in Rijnsburg, north of Leiden; take bus #40. For **lunch**, *Noroc*, just off Breestraat on Pieterskerk Choorsteeg, is a pleasant café with a light menu; *Annie's Verjaardag*, on the waterside at Hoogstraat 1a, serves main courses at reasonable prices, and *Het Huis de Bijlen*, just off Noordeinde, has even cheaper daily specials. In the **evening**, *De Brasserie*, Lange Mare 38, has Dutch food; *Eethuis de Trommelaar* is a pleasant, reasonably priced vegetarian restaurant at Apothekersdijk 22; and *Pizzeria Napoli*, Steenstraat 19, has decent pizzas.

Around Leiden: the Keukenhof Gardens and Aalsmeer

Along with Haarlem to the north, Leiden is the best base for seeing something of the Dutch **bulbfields** which flourish here in spring. The view from the train can be sufficient in itself as the line cuts directly through the main growing areas, the fields divided into stark geometric blocks of pure colour. Should you want to get closer, LISSE, home to the **Keukenhof Gardens** (late-March to May daily 8am–7.30pm; f14.50), the largest flower gardens in the world, is the best place to head for. Some seven million flowers are on show for their full flowering period, complemented, in case of especially harsh winters, by 5000 square metres of greenhouses. Special buses – #54 – run to the Keukenhof from Leiden bus station at ten and forty minutes past each hour, every day including Sunday. You can also see the industry in action in AALSMEER, 23km north of Leiden, whose flower auction, held daily in a building approximately the size of 75 football pitches (Mon–Fri 7.30–11am; f4) turns over around f1.5 billion worth of plants and flowers a year.

The Hague

With its urbane atmosphere, **THE HAGUE** is different from any other Dutch city. Since the sixteenth century it's been the Netherlands' political capital and the focus of national institutions, and its older buildings are a rather subdued collection with little of Amsterdam's flamboyance. Diplomats in dark Mercedes and the multinational businesspeople ensure that many of the city's hotels and restaurants are firmly in the expense account category, and the nightlife is similarly packaged. But, away from the mediocrity of wealth, The Hague does have cheaper and livelier bars and restaurants, as well as some excellent museums.

Arrival and accommodation

The Hague has two **train stations** – Den Haag HS and Den Haag CS, of which the latter is the more convenient, being nearer to the VVV (April–Sept Mon–Sat 9am–9pm, Sun 10am–5pm; Oct–March Mon–Sat 9am–6pm, Sun 10am–5pm; ☎070/340 35051, 50c per minute). Den Haag HS is about 1km to the south, and frequent rail services connect the two. **Accommodation** in The Hague can work out quite expensive. The VVV have a stock of **private rooms** or there's a cluster of seedy but reasonably priced **hotels** just outside Den Haag HS station: try the *Aristo*, Stationsweg 164–166 (☎070/389 08 47; ③), the *Astoria*, Stationsweg 139 (☎070/384 04 01; ④), and the *Du Commerce*, Stationsplein 64 (☎070/380 85 11; ④). The **youth hostel** *Ockenburgh* is at Monsterseweg 4 (☎070/397 001 15; ②), 10km to the west of town behind the beach at Kijkduin (bus #122, #123, #124 from Centraal Station), attached to a small hotel, and to the largest **campsite** in the area, *Camping Ockenburgh*. You could also try your luck in the resort town of Scheveningen, about 4km from the centre of The Hague, where hotels are more plentiful and a little cheaper; trams #1, #7 and #9 run there from Den Hague CS.

The City

Right in the centre, the **Binnenhof** is the home of the Dutch parliament. Count William II built a castle here in the thirteenth century, and the settlement that grew up around it became known as the "Count's Domain" – *'s Gravenhage* – which is still the city's official name. The present complex is a rather mundane affair, a small lake – the **Hof Vijver** – mirroring the symmetry of the facade; inside there's precious little to see except the **Ridderzaal**, a slender-turreted structure used for state occasions that can be viewed on regular guided tours from the information office at Binnenhof 8a (Mon–Sat 10am–4pm; July–Aug also Sun noon–4pm; f5). Immediately east, the **Royal Picture Gallery Mauritshuis**, Korte Vijverberg 8 (Tues–Sat 10am–5pm, Sun 11am–5pm; f7.50), located in a magnificent seventeenth-century mansion, is of more interest, famous for its extensive range of Flemish and Dutch paintings from the fifteenth to eighteenth centuries. Early works include paintings by Memling, Rogier van der Weyden and the Antwerp master, Quentin Matsys; there are also a number of Adriaen Brouwer's characteristically ribald canvases, work by Rubens, including a typically grand *Portrait of Isabella Brant*, his first wife, and the intriguing *Adam and Eve in Paradise* – a collaboration between Rubens, who painted the figures, and Jan Bruegel the Elder, who filled in the animals and landscape. In the same room are two examples of the work of Rubens' assistant, van Dyck, a portrait specialist who found fame at the court of Charles I. As for Dutch work, look out for the exquisite *Goldfinch* by Carel Fabritius, a pupil of Rembrandt, and, off the first-floor landing at the front of the museum, Jan Vermeer's *View of Delft*, a superb townscape of 1658. There are also numerous works by Jan Steen, and several by Rembrandt, most notably the *Anatomy Lesson of Dr Tulp* from 1632, the artist's first commission in Amsterdam.

West of the Binnenhof, the **Gevangenpoort**, Buitenhof 33, with its Prisoner's Gate Museum (Mon–Fri 10am–4pm; April–Sept also Sun 1–5pm; hourly tours only, last tour 4pm; f5), was originally part of the city fortifications. Used as a prison until the nineteenth century, it now contains an array of instruments of torture and punishment – guillotine blades, racks and gibbets – and the old cells are in a good state of preservation. Down the street at Buitenhof 35, the **Prince William V Gallery** (Tues–Sun 11am–4pm; f2.50, free with Mauritshuis ticket) has paintings by Rembrandt, Jordaens and Paulus Potter, but it's more interesting as a reconstruction of a typical eighteenth-century gallery, with paintings crammed on the walls from floor to ceiling.

Ten minutes' walk north along Noordeinde, the **Panorama Mesdag**, Zeestraat 65b (Mon–Sat 10am–5pm, Sun noon–5pm; f4), was designed in the late nineteenth century by the local painter Hendrik Mesdag. It's a depiction of Scheveningen as it would have appeared in 1881, completed in four months with help from his wife and the young G.H. Breitner, and so naturalistic that it takes a few moments for the skills of lighting and perspective to become apparent. Five minutes away at Laan van Meerdervoort 7f, the house Mesdag bought as a home and gallery today contains the **Mesdag Museum** (Tues–Sat 10am–5pm, Sun 1–5pm; f3.50), with a collection of Hague School paintings alongside works by Corot, Rousseau, Delacroix and Millet, as well as the florid and distinctive paintings of Antonio Mancini, though none of them represent the artists' best achievements. Around the corner, framing Carnegieplein, the **Peace Palace** (Mon–Fri hourly guided tours at 10am, 11am, 2pm & 3pm; May–Aug also at 4pm; f5) is home to the Court of International Justice, with tapestries, urns, marble and stained glass on show inside, the donations of various world leaders. North, the **Gemeentemuseum**, Stadhouderslaan 41 (Tues–Sun 11am–5pm; f7; bus #4 from Centraal Station), is the most diverse of The Hague's many museums, with outstanding collections of musical instruments and Islamic ceramics, and an array of modern art which attempts to outline the development of Dutch painting through the Romantic, Hague and Expressionist schools to the De Stijl movement – the museum has the world's largest collection of Mondrian's paintings. Adjacent, a modern building houses the **Museon** (Tues–Fri 10am–5pm, Sat & Sun noon–5pm; f5), a sequence of non-specialist exhibitions of human activities related to the history of the earth, and the **Omniversum** or "Space Theatre" (shows on the hour, Tues–Thurs 11am–4pm, Fri–Sun 11am–9pm; f16). Halfway between The Hague and its satellite resort of Scheveningen (reached on tram #1 or #9), the **Madurodam Miniature Town** (daily March–May 9am–10.30pm; June–Aug 9am–11pm; Sept 9am–9.30pm; Oct–Dec 9am–6pm; f12.50) is a scale model of a Dutch town, heavily plugged by the tourist authorities – though it's by no means essential unless you have kids in tow.

Eating, drinking and nightlife

For cheap food, there's a cluster of places along Herenstraat, near the Binnenhof, best of which is *De Apendans* at no. 13, a no-frills restaurant with a simple Dutch menu for f17 upwards. Other reasonably priced options include a branch of *Noordzee*, Spuistraat 44, pizzas at *Pinelli*, Dag. Groenmarkt 31, or veggie meals at *De Dageraad*, Hooikade 4. In Scheveningen, the *Big Bell*, on the seafront, serves very reasonable mounds of classic Dutch food. For **bars**, try the streets east of Lange Voorhout, where you'll find the *De Landeman* and the *Pompernickel* at Denneweg 48 and 27.

Delft

DELFT has considerable charm, its gabled red-roofed houses standing beside tree-lined canals, and the pastel colours of the pavements, brickwork and bridges giving the town a faded tranquillity – though one that is increasingly hard to find beneath the tourist onslaught during summer. The town is perhaps best known for **Delftware**, the clunky and monotonous blue and white ceramics to which the town gave its name in the seventeenth century. If you've already slogged through the vast collection in Amsterdam's Rijksmuseum, it needs no introduction, but for those sufficiently interested, **De Porceleyne Fles** at Rotterdamsweg 196, a factory producing Delftware, is open for visits (April–Oct Mon–Sat 9am–5pm, Sun 10am–4pm; Nov–March Mon–Fri 9am–5pm, Sat 10am–5pm; free), and the **Huis Lambert van Meerten Museum** at Oude Delft 199 (Tues–Sat 10am–5pm, Sun 1–5pm; f3.50) has a large collection of Delft and other tiles.

Otherwise **Markt** is the best place to start exploring, with the **Nieuwe Kerk** at one end (April–Oct Mon–Sat 9am–5pm; Nov–March Mon–Sat 11am–4pm; f2.50), recently restored and with a 100-metre tower (May to mid-June Tues–Sat 10am–4.30pm; mid-June–Aug Mon–Sat 10am–4.30pm; f3.25), giving a wonderful view of the town – although unless you're a Dutch monarchist, the interior is rather uninspiring: it contains the burial vaults of the Dutch royal family, the most recent addition being Queen Wilhelmina in 1962. Only the Mausoleum of William the Silent grabs your attention, an odd hotchpotch of styles concocted by Hendrik de Keyser, architect of the Renaissance **Stadhuis** opposite. South of here is the **Museum Tétar van Elven**, Koornmarkt 67 (May to mid-Oct Tues–Sat 1–5pm; f3), slightly drab in appearance but an authentic restoration of the eighteenth-century patrician house that was the studio and home of Paul Tétar van Elven, a provincial and somewhat forgettable artist/collector. **Wynhaven**, another old canal, leads to Hippolytusbuurt and the Gothic **Oude Kerk** (April–Oct Mon–Sat 10am–5pm; f2.50), arguably the town's finest building. Simple and unbuttressed with an unhealthily leaning tower, it has an intricately-carved pulpit dating from 1548, with figures emphasized in false perspective. Also notable is the modern stained glass, depicting and symbolizing the history of the Netherlands in the north transept. Opposite the Oude Kerk is the former Convent of Saint Agatha or **Prinsenhof** (Tues–Sat 10am–5pm, Sun 1–5pm; f3.50), housing Delft's municipal art collection (a good group of works including paintings by Aertsen and

Honthorst), and restored in the style of the late sixteenth century – an era when the building served as the base of William the Silent in his Protestant revolt against the Spanish invaders. It was also the scene of his death at the hands of a French assassin; the bullets that passed through him, each made by three pellets welded into one, left their mark on the Prinsenhof walls and can still be seen. Finally, if you have the time, the **Royal Army and Weapon Museum** (Tues–Sat 10am–5pm, Sun 1–5pm; f3.50) near the station is worth a visit, with its good display of weaponry, uniforms and military accoutrements tracing the military history of the Netherlands from the Spanish wars to the imperialist adventures of the 1950s.

Practicalities

From the train station it's a short walk into town and the VVV at Markt 85 (Mon–Fri 9am–6pm, Sat 11am–3pm; April–Sept also Sun 11am–3pm; ☎015/12 61 00), who have details of **private rooms** (③); otherwise the cheapest hotel is *Les Compagnons*, Markt 61 (☎015/14 01 02; ③). There's also a **campsite**, *De Delftse Hout*, Kortftlaan 5 (open April–Oct; bus #60 from station). For **eating**, the *Hotel Monopole*, centrally located on Markt, has pancakes, *uitsmijters* (ham or cheese with eggs), and light meals for under f10 and three-course menus for around f20; *De Koornbeurs*, close by, is a student mensa with main meals for under f10. *Locus Publicus*, Brabantse Turfmarkt 67, is a popular local hang-out, serving a staggering array of beers as well as sandwiches.

Rotterdam

ROTTERDAM lies at the heart of a maze of rivers and artificial waterways that forms the seaward outlet of the rivers Rhine and Maas. An important port as far back as the fourteenth century, it was one of the major cities of the Dutch Republic, and today, with the adjoining dockland area of Europoort, is the largest port in the world. The Germans bombed the town centre to pieces in 1940 and destroyed the harbour in 1944, since when rebuilding has produced a sterile assembly of concrete and glass. However, the city has its moments, not least one of the best and most overlooked galleries in the country.

Southeast of the station, the **Lijnbaan** was Europe's first pedestrianized shopping precinct, completed in 1953. Beyond here lies some of the city centre's more fanciful modern architecture, and the **Schielandshuis Museum** (Tues–Sat 10am–5pm, Sun 11am–5pm; f3.50), in a seventeenth-century mansion at Korte Hoogstraat 31, with a variety of displays on the history of Rotterdam. A couple of minutes south, the old city docks are enclosed by the Boompjes, a former sea dyke that's now a major freeway leading southwest to the **Euromast**, on a rather lonely park corner beside the Nieuwe Maas, where the 185-metre-high **Spacetower** (March–Oct daily 10am–6pm; Oct–Dec daily 11am–4pm; Jan & Feb Sat & Sun 11am–4pm; f13) gives spectacular views. North of here, the **Boymans-Van Beuningen Museum**, Mathenesserlaan 18–20 (Tues–Sun 11am–5pm, f6), is Rotterdam's one great attraction, accessible from Centraal Station by tram #5 or walkable from Eendrachtsplein metro. It's an enormous museum, with a fine collection of modern-era paintings, including a superb array of work by the Surrealist artists Dalí, Magritte, Ernst and de Chirico. There are also paintings by the Dutch artists Carel Willink and Charley Toorop, and, in the Van der Vorm collection on the first floor, work by Monet, van Gogh, Picasso, Gauguin, Cézanne and Munch, alongside a series of small galleries containing paintings by most of the significant artists of the Barbizon and Hague Schools. Among earlier canvases are several by Hieronymus Bosch and Jan van Scorel, Pieter Bruegel the Elder's mysterious, hazy *Tower of Babel*, and Geertgen tot Sint Jans' *Glorification of the Virgin*, as well as later work by Jan Steen, Gerrit Dou – *The Quack* – and Rembrandt, who weighs in with the intimate *Titus at his Desk*.

If nothing in the city centre can be called exactly picturesque, **Delfshaven** goes some way to make up for it. A good 45-minute walk southwest of Centraal Station – fifteen minutes by tram #4 or #6 – it was from here that the Pilgrim Fathers set sail for America in 1620, changing to the more reliable Mayflower in Plymouth. Delfshaven was only incorporated into Rotterdam in 1886 and managed to survive World War II virtually intact. Long a neglected area, the town council has recently recognized its tourist potential and has set about conserving and restoring the locality. The **Dubbelde Palmboom Museum**, Voorhaven 12 (Tues–Sun 11am–5pm; f6), once a *jenever* distillery, is now a historical museum with a wide-ranging if unexceptional collection of objects pertaining to life in the Maas delta.

Practicalities

Rotterdam's large centre is bordered by its main rail terminal, **Centraal Station**, which serves as the hub of a useful tram and metro system, though it's a seamy, hostile place late at night. There's a branch of the **VVV** here (Mon–Sat 9am–10pm, Sun 10am–10pm), which has a useful city brochure and map for f1.50, and free maps of the tram, bus and underground system. The main VVV office is ten minutes' walk away at Coolsingel 67 (Mon–Thurs 9am–5.30pm, Fri 9am–9pm, Sat 9am–5pm; April–Sept also Sun 10am–4pm; ☎010/340 340 65); both operate an **accommodation** booking service for **private rooms** (③). There's a clutch of central, reasonably priced **hotels** 1km southwest of the station, including the *Rox-Inn*, 's-Gravendijkwal 14 (☎010/436 61 09; ③; tram #1, #7 or #9; f70), and the *Heemraad*, Heemraadssingel 90 (☎010/477 54 61; ③; same trams). Immediately north of the station is the *Bagatelle*, Provenierssingel 26 (☎010/467 63 48; ③). The **youth hostel** is a fifteen-minute walk from the station at Rochussenstraat 107 (☎010/436 5763; ②; tram #4 or #6); the nearest **campsite** is north of the station at Kanaalweg 84 – bus #33. There's also a summer **Sleep In** at Mauritsweg 29b, five minutes' walk south of the station, with dormitory accommodation and breakfast for under-27s (②).

The cheapest sit-down **meal** in town is served at *Eetcafé Streetlife*, Jonker Franslaan 237; *De Eend*, Mauritsweg 28 (5.30–7.30pm), is also inexpensive, as is *De Djoek*, 's-Gravendijkwal 100–102. *De Consul*, Westersingel 28, serves a variety of dishes at reasonable prices, and vegetarians should try *Eetcafé BlaBla*, Piet Heynstraat 35 in Delfshaven. *Grand Café Dudok*, off Beursplein on Meent, is a good place to **drink**, and *Jazzcafe Dizzy*, 's-Gravendijkwal 127, and the *Harbour Jazzclub*, Delftsestraat 15, have regular **live music**.

Gouda

A pretty little place some 25km northeast of Rotterdam, **GOUDA** is almost everything you'd expect of a Dutch country town: a ring of quiet canals encircling ancient buildings and old quays. More surprisingly, its **Markt** is the largest in Holland – a reminder of the town's prominence as a centre of the medieval cloth trade, and later of its success in the manufacture of cheeses and clay pipes. The **cheese market**, held here every Thursday morning from June to August, is a shadow of its former self – and mercilessly milked by the tour operators – but out of these times the Markt is worth visiting. Slap-bang in the middle, the **Stadhuis** is an elegant Gothic building dating from 1450; on the north side is the **Waag**, a tidy seventeenth-century building decorated with a detailed relief of cheese weighing, with the remains of the old wooden scales inside. To the south, just off the square, the **St Janskerk** (Mon–Sat March–Oct 9am–5pm; Nov–Feb 10am–4pm; f2.50) was built in the sixteenth century and is famous for its magnificent stained-glass windows, the best executed between 1555 and 1571 when Holland was still Catholic. By comparison, the post-Reformation windows, dating from 1572 to 1603, adopt a more secular style, for example in the *Relief of Leiden*, which shows William the Silent retaking the town from the Spanish – though Delft and its burgomasters take prominence, no doubt because they paid for its construction. By the side of the church, the flamboyant **Lazarus Gate** of 1609 was once part of the town's leper hospital until it was moved to form the back entrance to the **Catharina Gasthuis**, now the municipal **Stedelijk Museum** (Mon–Sat 10am–5pm, Sun noon–5pm; f3.50), whose collection incorporates a fine selection of early religious art, notably a large triptych, *Life of Mary*, by Dirk Barendsz and a characteristically austere *Annunciation* by the Bruges artist Pieter Pourbus. Other highlights include a spacious hall, *Het Ruim*, dominated by two group portraits by Ferdinand Bol, and a selection of Hague and Barbizon School canvases. Gouda's other museum, **De Moriaan** (Mon–Sat 10am–5pm, Sun noon–5pm; free with Stedelijk ticket), in an old merchant's house at Westhaven 29, has a mixed bag of exhibits from clay pipes to ceramics and tiles.

Practicalities

Gouda's **train** and **bus stations** are north of the centre, ten minutes from the **VVV**, Markt 27 (Mon–Fri 9am–5pm, Sat 10am–4pm; ☎01820/13666), which has a limited supply of **private rooms** (③). Otherwise, the cheapest place is an unofficial **youth hostel**, conveniently sited at Westhaven 46 (☎01820/128 79; ②). The two most reasonably priced **hotels** are the *Het Blauwe Kruis*, Westhaven 4 (☎01820/12677; ③), and the nicer *De Utrechtse Dom*, a short stroll east of the St Janskerk at Geuzenstraat 6 (☎01820/27984; ③). For **food**, the *Borsalino*, Naalerstraat 4, serves a variety of dishes – including vegetarian – for upwards of f12.75; *'t Goudse Winkeltje*, Achter de Kerk 9a, does decent pancakes; the *Rimini*, Markt 28, cheap pizzas.

Utrecht

"I groaned with the idea of living all winter in so shocking a place", wrote Boswell in 1763, and **UTRECHT** still promises little as you approach, surrounded by shopping centres and industrial developments, although its central core, focusing on its distinctive sunken canals – whose brick cellar warehouses have been converted into chic cafés and restaurants – is one of the country's most pleasant.

The focal point of the town centre is the **Dom Tower**, which, at over 110m, is the highest church tower in the country, soaring to a delicate octagonal lantern added in 1380. A guided tour (April–Oct Mon–Fri 10am–5pm, Sat 11am–5pm, Sun noon–5pm; Nov–March Sat 11am–5pm & Sun noon–5pm; last entry one hour before closing; f3.50) takes you unnervingly near to the top, from where the gap between the tower and the Gothic **Dom Kerk** is most apparent. Only the eastern part of the great cathedral remains today, the nave having collapsed in 1674. It's worth peering inside though, (May–Sept daily 10am–5pm; Oct–April Mon–Sat 11am–4pm, Sun 2–4pm; free) to get a sense of the hangar-like space the building once had, and to wander through the **Kloostergang**, the fourteenth-century cloisters that link the cathedral to the chapterhouse, now part of the university. South of the church at Nieuwe Gracht 63, the national collection of ecclesiastical art, the **Catharijne Convent Museum** (Tues–Fri 10am–5pm, Sat & Sun 11am–5pm; f5), has a wonderfully exhibited mass of paintings, manuscripts and church ornaments from the ninth century on, including work by Geertgen tot Sint Jans, Rembrandt, Hals, and, best of all, a luminously beautiful *Virgin and Child* by van Cleve. Further along, the **Centraal Museum** at Agnietenstraat 1 (Tues–Sat 10am–5pm, Sun noon–5pm; f5) is the other main attraction of the city, and features a good collection of paintings by sixteenth- and seventeenth-century Utrecht artists. Look out for the vividly individual portraits of van Scorel's *Jerusalem Brotherhood*, which includes a depiction of the artist in the centre, and work by the Caravaggio-influenced Utrecht School, notably Honthorst's *The Procuress* and Terbrugghen's beautiful *Calling of St Matthew*.

Practicalities

Train and **bus stations** both lead into the Hoog Catharijne shopping centre. The main VVV office is at Vredenburg 90 (Mon–Fri 9am–5.30pm, Sat 9am–1.30pm; June–Sept also Sat 9am–3.30pm; ☎030/340 340 85, 50c per minute), a five-minute walk away. Of **hotels**, the *Van Ooyen*, Dantelaan 117 (☎030/93 81 90; ③), *Hotel Ouwi*, FC Donderstraat 12 (☎030/71 63 03; ③), and the *Domstad*, Parkstraat 5 (☎030/31 01 31; ③) are good; and there's a nice **youth hostel** in an old country manor house at Rhijnauwenselaan 14, Bunnik (☎03405/61277; ②), a little far out, but linked to the station by bus #40 or #43. The well-equipped **campsite** at Arienslaan 5 can be reached by a #57 bus from the station. **Restaurants** are mainly situated along Oude Gracht – the best are the *Tussen Hemel en Aarde* at no. 99 and the mostly vegetarian *De Werfkring* at no. 123. A really cheap option is to go for a *dagschotel* at *Eetcafé De Baas* at Lijnmarkt 6, and there's *Café Zeezicht* on Nobelstraat 2, with reasonably priced full meals and live music on Tuesday nights. As for the **bars**, the city's best cluster around the junction of Oude Gracht and Wed; check out the lively *De Witte Ballons* at Lijnmarkt 10–12, or the *Cafe Belgie* around the corner at Oude Gracht 196.

BEYOND THE RANDSTAD

Outside the Randstad towns, the Netherlands is relatively unknown territory to tourists. In the north, **Leeuwarden**, the provincial capital of the province of **Friesland**, is a pleasant, if sedate, town with two good museums. It also gives an opportunity to experience life in what is probably the most maverick of Dutch provinces, whose inhabitants retain their own language – although the landscape is familiar enough, dead flat and very green, dotted with black and white cattle and long, thatched farmhouses. East of Friesland, the province of **Groningen** has comparatively few attractions beyond its eponymous capital, a lively cosmopolitan place whose buzzy street- and nightlife more than make up for its shortage of historic sights. To the south, the countryside grows steadily more undulating as you head towards Germany. The town of **Arnhem** is a worthwhile stop on the way south, most famous for its bridge, a key objective in the failed Allied attack of 1944, Operation Market Garden, and a good base for the nearby **Hoge Veluwe National Park**, whose modern art museum is one of the country's best galleries. Further south, in the provinces of North Brabant and Limburg, the landscape slowly fills out, rolling into a rougher countryside of farmland and forests and eventually into the country's only hills around **Maastricht**, a city which retains a vibrant, Central European air, a world away from the clogs and canals of the north.

Leeuwarden

An old market town, **LEEUWARDEN** was the residence of the powerful Frisian Stadholders, who vied with those of Holland for control of the country during the seventeenth century. These days it's the neat and distinctly cosy provincial capital, with an air of prosperity and a smug sense of independence. It lacks the concentrated historic charm of many other Dutch towns, but it has a number of grand buildings and two outstanding museums, not to mention an appealingly compact town centre almost entirely surrounded and bisected by water.

The centre of town is **Waagplein**, a narrow open space cut by a canal and flanked by cafés and department stores. The **Waag** itself dates from 1598, but it's been converted into a restaurant and bank. Walking west, **Nieuwestad** is Leeuwarden's main shopping street, from where Kleine Kerkstraat, on the right, leads to the **Oldehoofster Kerkhof** – a large square-cum-car park near the old city walls – and the precariously leaning **Oldehove**. Something of a symbol for the city, this is part of a cathedral started in 1529 but never finished because of subsidence, a lugubrious mass of disproportion that defies all laws of gravity and geometry; those brave enough can climb it (Tues–Sat 10am–4pm; f2). **Grote Kerkstraat** leads east from here, and at no. 11 you'll pass **Het Princessehof** (Mon–Sat 10am–5pm, Sun 2–5pm; f3.50), a house from 1650 that was once the residence of the Stadholder William Friso, and now a ceramics museum with the world's largest collection of magnificent Dutch tiles; exhibits range from the fifteenth-century work of Italians based in Antwerp to later seventeenth-century pieces, and the first really mass-produced items. There is also a marvellous collection of Far Eastern ceramics, from the original Chinese porcelain of the sixteenth century, brought over by merchants, to the later western imitations that ripped the heart out of the market. Further along Grote Kerkstraat is the house where the famous World War I spy, **Mata Hari**, a native of Leeuwarden, spent her early years, now turned over to the **Frisian Literary Museum** (Mon–Fri 9am–12.30pm & 1.30–5pm), a repository for a whole range of Frisian documents together with a few derisory exhibits on Mata Hari herself – there are plans to enlarge the museum and move it down the street early in 1994. At the far end of Grote Kerkstraat, the **Grote** or **Jacobijner Kerk** (July–Sept Tues–Fri 2–4pm) is an unremarkable Gothic construction, another victim of subsidence, tilting towards the newer south aisle, where some tattered remnants of sixteenth-century frescoes are exhibited. More interesting is south of here on Turf-markt: the **Fries Museum** (Tues–Sat 10am–5pm, Sun 1–5pm; f3), one of the best regional museums in the country, with displays that trace the development of Frisian culture from prehistoric times up to the present day. As well as an extensive collection of silverware, there are rooms given over to the island of Ameland and the gaudy painted furniture of Hindeloopen, and a collection of seventeenth-century Frisian paintings, enlivened by a portrait of Rembrandt's Frisian wife, Saskia, recently found to have been from his studio, rather than by the master himself.

Practicalities

Leeuwarden's **train** and **bus** stations adjoin each other, five minutes' walk south of the town centre. The VVV at the train station (Mon–Fri 9am–5.45pm, Sat 9am–2pm) has a short list of **private rooms** (③) – the list is pinned to the office door when closed. Two reasonably priced **hotels** in town are the *De Pauw*, near the station at Stationsweg 10 (☎058/12 36 51; ③), and the more central *'t Anker*, on the north side of the centre in Eewal (☎058/12 52 16; ③). If you're **camping**, *Kleine Wielen* is about 6km out towards Dokkum, nicely sited by a lake – take bus #20, #51 or #57 from the station. One of the best places to **eat** is *Eetcafé Spinoza* on Eewal, a youthful restaurant with a good range of dishes for around f20. Try also *De Brasserie* at Wirdumerdijk 23, especially good for lunch; *Pizzeria Sardegna*, Grote Hoogstraat 28, with an extravagant variety of pizzas; or the Mexican food at *Yucatan* on St Jacobsstraat. For **drinking**, the *Spoekepolle*, on St Jacobsstraat, is a student favourite.

Groningen

Nominally a fiefdom of the Bishops of Utrecht from 1040 until 1536, the city of **GRON-INGEN** was once an important centre of trade, and capital of the Dutch province of Groningen from 1594. Heavily bombed in the last war, the city has few sights and is a jumble of architecture, but it does benefit from the presence of a large, prestigious university, lending a cosmopolitan feel quite unexpected in this part of the country.

The centre of town is **Grote Markt**, a large open space that was badly damaged by wartime bombing and has been reconstructed with little imagination. At one corner is the **Martinikerk** (June–Sept Tues–Sat noon–4pm; f1), a beacon of architectural sanity in the surrounding shambles. Though the oldest parts of the church go back to 1180, most of it dates from the mid-fifteenth century, the nave a Gothicized rebuilding undertaken to match the added choir. The vault paintings in the nave are beautifully restored, and the lofty choir holds two series of frescoes on the walled-up niches of the clerestory. Adjoining the church is the seventeenth-century tower **Martinitoren** (April–Sept daily noon–4.30pm; f2). West along A-Kerkhof NZ from Grote Markt, the **Noordelijk Scheepvaart Museum**, Brugstraat 24 (Tues–Sat 10am–5pm, Sun 1–5pm; f3.50), is one of the most comprehensive maritime museums in the country, tracing the history of northern shipping from the sixth to the twentieth centuries with displays on trade with the Indies, the development of peat canals and a series of reconstructed nautical workshops. In the same building, the smaller **Niemeyer Tabaksmuseum** is devoted to tobacco smoking from 1600 to the present day. Exhibits include a multitude of pipes and an outstanding collection of snuff paraphernalia. The city's biggest and best museum, the **Groninger Museum** (Tues–Sat 10am–5pm, Sun 1–5pm; f2) is due to reopen in a spectacular new site opposite the train station in 1994, and will house a melange of arts outlining Groningen's history, along with displays of local silverware and Far Eastern ceramics and a collection of paintings that includes Rubens' energetic *Adoration of the Magi* among a small selection of seventeenth-century works, Isaac Israels' inviting *Hoedenwinkel* from a modest sample of Hague School paintings, and a number of later works by the Expressionists of the Groningen *De Ploeg* group.

Practicalities

Groningen's **bus** and **train** stations are on the south side of town, fifteen minutes' walk from the **VVV** at Ged Kattendiep 6 (Mon–Fri 9am–5.30pm, Sat 10am–4pm); they have a short list of private rooms for about f30 per person, though few are near the city centre. Otherwise, the cheapest place to stay is the dorms of *Simplon Jongerenhotel* north of the centre at Boterdiep 73 (☎050/13 52 21; ②). Three reasonably priced **hotels** are just south of the Grote Markt: the *Garni Friesland* at Kleine Pelsterstraat 4 (☎050/12 13 07; ④); the *Garni Groningen,* Damsterdiep 94 (☎050/13 54 35; ④); and the likeable old *Weera*, Gedempte Zuiderdiep 8 (☎050/12 99 19; ④), with a decent, reasonably priced restaurant. Outside the centre, the *Bastion*, Bornhomstraat 99 (☎050/41 49 77; ④) is a little smarter and cheaper. If you're **camping**, catch bus #2 via Piezerweg from the main square for the ten-minute journey to *Camping Stadspark* (March–Oct).

For the **cheapest food** in town, head for the mensa at Oosterstraat 44 (Mon–Fri noon–1.30pm & 5–7pm) for reliable, filling canteen meals. Otherwise, the city's best places to eat and drink are concentrated around **Poelestraat**. *Bistengo*, on the western end of the street, is a decent Mexican-American restaurant with vegetarian specialities; the pizzeria next door is slightly cheaper. Around the corner on Peperstraat, *'t Pakhuis* at no. 88 has good Dutch snacks and a lively bar in an atmospheric building. On the south side of the Grote Markt is a flank of outdoor cafés, best of which are the cosy *De Witz* at no. 48, the civilized *De Drie Gezusters* at no. 29, with a great old interior, and the *Café Hooghoudt* at no.41; this last also contains a night café serving food until 4am at weekends. For veggie food, head for the excellent *Brussels Lof*, A-Kerkstraat 24.

Thanks to its large student population, Groningen has a lively **nightlife**. For live music try *De Vestibule*, Oosterstraat 24; *Vera*, in the basement below the *mensa*, at Oosterstraat 44; or *Troubadour*, Peperstraat 19. *De Spieghel* at Peperstraat 11 has live jazz nightly. Good **discos** include *Gdansk*, Poelestraat 53, and the *Palace*, Gelkinges- traat 1, which occasionally host live bands.

Arnhem and around

Way south of Groningen in the province of Gelderland, **ARNHEM** was once a wealthy resort, a watering hole to which the merchants of Amsterdam and Rotterdam would flock to idle away their fortunes. This century it's become better known as the place where thousands of British and Polish troops died in the failed Allied airborne operation of September 1944, codenamed "Operation Market Garden", which gutted the greater part of the city. What you see today is inevitably not especially enticing. But Arnhem is a lively town, with plenty going on, and is a good centre for seeing the numerous attractions scattered around its forested outskirts.

The best of old Arnhem is the northwest part of the centre, around **Korenmarkt**, a small square which escaped much of the wartime destruction and has one or two good facades. The streets which lead off Korenmarkt are full of restaurants and bars, but otherwise Arnhem deteriorates as you walk southeast towards "The Bridge too Far" – the **John Frostbrug**, named after the commander of the battalion that defended it for four days. It's just an ordinary bridge, but it remains the symbol and centre of people's remembrance of the battle to Dutch and British alike. At its north end, the characterless **Markt** is site of the reconstructed church of **St Eusabius** (mid-June to mid-Sept Tues–Sat noon–4.30pm; f1.50, tower f2.50), with the fifteenth-century **Stadhuis** tucked in behind. In the opposite direction, it's a fifteen-minute walk west from the station along Utrechtsestraat to the **Gemeentemuseum** at Utrechtseweg 87 (Tues–Sat 10am–5pm, Sun 11am–5pm; free), whose collection includes numerous archeological finds from the surrounding area, a display of Chinese, Japanese and Delft ceramics, and a modest selection of paintings, with the emphasis on views of the landscape, villages and towns of Gelderland, and canvases by the so-called magic realists.

Arnhem's **train** and **bus stations**, on the edge of the centre, are next door to the **VVV**, Stationsplein 45 (Mon–Fri 9am–5.30pm, Sat 9am–4pm), who operate an **accommodation** booking service. Among the cheaper alternatives in the town centre are the *Hotel Rijnoever*, by the river near the John Frostrug at Rijnkade 86 (☎085/45 31 94; ④), and the *Hotel Pension Parkzicht*, Apeldoornsestraat 16 (☎085/42 06 98; ③), ten minutes' walk from the station, and *Hotel Rembrandt*, Paterstraat 1 (☎085/42 01 53; ③), the second right off Apeldoornsestraat. There's a **youth hostel** 5km north at Diepenbrocklaan 27 (☎085/42 01 14; ②), reached by bus #3, and the nearest **campsite** is *Camping Warnsborn*, northwest of the centre at Bakenbergseweg 257 on bus #11. *Pizzeria Da Leone*, Korenmarkt 1, and *Nola Rae*, Marienburgstraat 2, with vegetarian specialities, are both good, cheap places to eat. For more traditional Dutch fare try the *Old Inn*, Stationsplein 40.

World War II memorials: Oosterbeek

The area around Arnhem is scattered with the graveyards of thousands of soldiers who died during **Operation Market Garden**, not least **OOSTERBEEK**, a prosperous suburb of Arnhem (4 trains hourly), where the **Airborne Cemetery** is a neat, symmetrical tribute to several hundred paratroopers whose bodies were brought here from the surrounding fields. Ten minutes south of the station, the village proper has spruce **lawns and walls** dotted with details of the battle, and the **Airborne Museum** (Mon–Sat 11am–5pm, Sun noon–5pm; f4), in the former *Hotel Hartenstein* on Utrechtseweg, where the British forces were besieged by the Germans for a week before retreating across the river, their numbers depleted from 10,005 to 2163. With the use of an English commentary, photographs, dioramas and military artefacts, the museum gives an excellent outline of the battle.

The Nederlands Openluchtmuseum

Immediately north of Arnhem, the **Nederlands Openluchtmuseum** (April–Oct Mon–Fri 9am–5pm, Sat & Sun 9.30am–5pm; f11.50) can be reached all year by bus #3 or in July and August by special bus #13, and is a huge collection of Dutch buildings taken from all over the country. Where possible, buildings have been placed in groups that resemble the traditional villages of the different regions of the Netherlands – from the farmsteads of Friesland to the peat colonies of Drenthe. There are about 120 buildings in all, including examples of every type of Dutch windmill, farmhouses, a variety of bridges and several working craft shops demonstrating traditional skills. Other parts of the museum incorporate one of the most extensive regional costume exhibitions in the country and a modest herb garden. All in all, it's an imaginative attempt to recreate the rural Dutch way of life over the past two centuries, and the museum's own guidebook explains everything with academic attention to detail.

The Hoge Veluwe National Park and Rijksmuseum Kröller-Müller

Spreading north from the Open-Air Museum is the Hoge Veluwe National Park (daily 8am–sunset; f7.50, includes museum; cars f7.50 extra), an area of heath and woodland that is much the prettiest and most accessible part of the Veluwe district of Gelderland. Formerly the private estate of wealthy local couple Anton and Helene Kröller-Müller, it has three entrances – one near the village of Otterlo on the northwest perimeter, another near Hoenderloo on the northeast edge, and a third to the south at Rijzenburg, near the village of Schaarsbergen, 10km from Arnhem.

There are a number of ways to get to the park by **bus**; easiest is to take the regular museum special from outside Arnhem train station (mid-June to Aug Tues–Sun hourly; May to mid-June, Sept & Oct Tues–Sun 3 daily; f7.25 return plus f7.50 entry ticket; pay the driver) direct to the **Visitors' Centre** (daily 10am–5pm), which has information on the park and is the place to pick up one of the white bicycles that are left out for everyone's use at no extra charge – much the best way of getting around. When the bus isn't running, you can either hire a bike at Arnhem station or take bus #107 to the entrance at Otterlo, from where it's a four-kilometre walk to the Visitors' Centre.

The main things to see are the **Jachtslot St Hubertus** (May–Nov Mon–Fri 10am–11.30am & 2–4.30pm), 3km north of the Visitors' Centre, an impressive Art Deco hunting lodge built for the Kröller-Müllers by H. P. Berlage in 1920, and the superb **Rijksmuseum Kröller-Müller** (all year-round Tues–Sat 10am–5pm; April–Oct also Sun 11am–5pm; Nov–March also Sun 1–5pm). One of the country's finest museums, it's a wide cross-section of modern European art from Impressionism to Cubism and beyond, housed in a purpose-built structure by the Belgian architect Van de Velde. There are paintings by Dutch artists like Mondrian, and Charley Toroop and her father Jan, as well as work by Fernand Léger and other Cubist-era artists. But the collection's crowning glory is its array of works by Vincent van Gogh, housed in a large room around a central courtyard and placed in context by accompanying, contemporary pictures. There are early pieces like *Head of a Peasant with a Pipe*, rough unsentimental paintings of labourers from around his parents' home in Brabant; penetrating later self-portraits; examples from the *Sunflowers* series and the joyful *Haystacks in Provence* and *Bridge at Arles*; and later, more sombre creations from his last years, such as *Prisoners Exercising* from 1890. Outside, behind the main building, there's a **Sculpture Park** (April–Oct daily 10am–4.30pm), spaciously laid out with works by Rodin, Giacometti, Jacob Epstein, Barbara Hepworth – and, most notably, Jean Debuffet's *Jardin d'Email*.

Maastricht

Situated in the corner of the thin finger of land that reaches down between Belgium and Germany, **MAASTRICHT**, the capital of the province of Limburg, is one of the most delightful cities in Holland, quite different to the twee waterland centres of the north, firmly in the heart of Europe. A cosmopolitan place, where three languages and currencies happily coexist, it's also one of the oldest towns in the country. The first settlers here were Roman, when Maastricht became an important stop on the trade route between Cologne and the coast, and the later legacy of Charlemagne – whose capital was at nearby Aachen – is manifest in two churches that are among the best surviving examples of the Romanesque in the Low Countries.

Arrival and accommodation

The centre of Maastricht is on the west bank of the river. You're likely to arrive, however, on the east bank, in the district known as **Wijk**, home to the **train and bus stations** and many of the city's hotels. The **airport** is north of the city at Beek, a twenty-minute bus journey; bus #61 runs every thirty minutes to Markt and the train station. The **VVV** (Mon–Sat 9am–6pm; July & Aug Mon–Sat 9am–7pm, Sun 11am–3pm; ☎043/25 21 21) is in the centre at Kleine Straat 1, at the end of the main shopping street, and has decent maps for f1.50 and copies of the what's on weekly *Maas en MECC*. It also does **private rooms** (③). City **hotels** include the *De la Guide* at Stationsstraat 17a (☎043/21 61 76; ④), and the more comfortable *De Poshoorn*, Stationsstraat 47 (☎043/21 73 34; ④). If you want to stay centrally there's *La Colombe*, Markt 30 (☎043/21 57 74; ④), and also a *Hotelboot* (☎043/21 90 23; ③), moored on the river on Maasboulevard, not far from the Helpoort. If you're **camping**, the *De Dousberg* site, almost in Belgium on the far western side of town, is large and well-equipped; take bus #8 from the train station and then walk for about a kilometre. There's also a **youth hostel** nearby at Dousbergweg 4 (☎043/43 44 04; ②) – again bus #8.

The Town

The busiest of Maastricht's many squares is **Markt**, at its most crowded during the Wednesday and Friday morning market. At the centre of the square, the **Stadhuis** (Mon–Fri 8.30am–12.30pm & 2–5.30pm; free) of 1664, a fairly typical slice of mid-seventeenth-century Dutch civic grandeur, was designed by Pieter Post. Just west, **Vrijthof** is a grander open space flanked by a line of café terraces on one side and on the other by the **St Servaaskerk** (Mon–Thurs, Sat & Sun 10am–5pm, Fri 10am–2pm; f3.50), the elaborate outcome of an earlier shrine dedicated to Saint Servaas, and the site of his burial in 384. Only the crypt remains of the original tenth-century church, and the rest is mostly of medieval or later construction. On the northern side of the church, the fifteenth-century Gothic cloister leads into the **treasury** (July & Aug daily 10am–6pm; Dec–March closes 4pm; April–June & Sept–Nov closes 5pm; use church entrance ticket), which holds a large collection of reliquaries and liturgical accessories, including a bust reliquary of Saint Servaas, which is carried through the town in Easter processions. There's also a coffin-reliquary of the saint from 1160, bristling with saints, stones and ornate copperwork.

The second most prominent building on the square, next door, is Maastricht's main Protestant church, the fourteenth-century **St Janskerk** (Easter to mid-Sept Mon–Sat 11am–4pm; f1.50), the baptistery of the church of St Servaas when it was a cathedral and nowadays competing for attention with its high fifteenth-century Gothic tower (f1.50). Inside are some medieval murals, but otherwise climbing the tower is the church's main appeal. The **Bonnefanten Museum** (Tues–Fri 10am–5pm, Sat & Sun 11am–5pm; f5), on the opposite corner of the square, is more engaging, home to a display of artefacts relating to Limburg and Maastricht, as well as a collection of paintings, including, among many indifferent sixteenth-century works, paintings by the Bruegels, van Mander and Bernard van Orley, and some canvases from the Italian Renaissance. Maastricht's other main church, the **Onze Lieve Vrouwe Basiliek**, is a short walk south of Vrijthof, down Bredestraat, in a small shady square crammed with café tables. Founded around 1000, it's a dark, eerily devotional place behind its unusual fortified west front, with a gorgeous galleried choir. Off the north aisle, the **treasury** (Easter to mid-Sept Mon–Sat 11am–5pm, Sun 1–5pm; f3.50) holds the usual array of ecclesiastical odd-bods, most notably the tunic of Saint Lambert – the evangelical bishop of Maastricht who was murdered at Liège in 705.

Around the corner from the square, on Plankstraat, the **Museumkelder Derlon** (Sun noon–4pm; free), in the basement of the hotel of the same name, contains one of the few remnants of Roman Maastricht – the remains of a temple to Jupiter, a well and several layers of pavement, discovered during the building of the present hotel in the mid-1980s. On the other side of the square lies another of Maastricht's most appealing quarters, narrow streets winding out to the remains of the town battlements alongside the fast-flowing river Jeker, which weaves around the various houses and ancient mills and the best surviving part of the walls, the **Helpoort** of 1229. Continuing south, the **Casemates** in the Waldeck Park (July & Aug tours at 2pm; mid-July to mid-Aug also 12.30pm; f5) are further evidence of Maastricht's once impressive fortifications, a system of galleries created through mining between 1575 and 1825 that were used in times of siege for surprise attacks on the enemy. Further south still, there are more dank passageways to explore fifteen minutes' walk away, where the flat-topped hill of **St Pietersberg** rises to a height of about 110m. Again, these aren't so much caves as galleries created by quarrying, hollowed out of the soft sandstone or marl that makes up the hill. Of two cave systems, the **Zonneberg** is probably the better, situated on the far side of the hill at Casino Slavante (guided tours in Dutch May to mid-Sept Mon–Sat hourly from 10.45am–3.45pm, Sun hourly 1.45–3.45pm; mid- to end Sept Sun at 1.30pm; Oct–April Sun at 2.30pm; f5). There is some evidence of wartime occupation, plus what everyone claims is Napoleon's signature on a graffiti-ridden wall. Also on the walls are recent charcoal drawings, usually illustrating a local story, not to mention the ten varieties of bat that inhabit the dark and cold corridors.

Eating and drinking

Eating is never a problem in Maastricht. At the bottom end of the price scale, on Graanmarkt, just off Onze Lieve Vrouweplein towards the river, *Le Chevalier* is an *eetcafé* with reasonably priced main dishes and plenty for much less. Nearby, *D'n Blind Genger*, on Koestraat, has a varied menu and a nice atmosphere. *Da Giovanni*, just off Vrijthof on Platielstraat, does a creditable plate of pasta and reasonable pizzas from f7. *Galerie*, Onze Lieve Vrouweplein 28, is rather self-consciously trendy but has good French-Dutch food. The **bars** on the east side of Vrijthof are packed in summer; *In den Ouden Vogelstruys*, on the corner of Platielstraat, is one of the nicest. Away from Vrijthof, *De Bobbel*, on Wolfstraat just off Onze Lieve Vrouweplein, is a bareboards bar, lively in the early evening; *Falstaff*, on St Amorsplein, down Platielstraat from Vrijthof, is younger and noisier, with good music and a wide range of beers.

travel details

Trains

Amsterdam to: Alkmaar (every 30min; 30min); Arnhem (every 30min; 1hr 10min); Dordrecht (every 30min; 1hr 30min); Groningen (hourly; 2hr 25min); Haarlem (every 15min; 15min); The Hague (every 15min; 33min); Leeuwarden (hourly; 2hr 25min); Leiden (every 15min; 47min); Maastricht (hourly; 2hr 30min); Rotterdam (every 30min; 1hr); Utrecht (every 20min; 20min); Vlissingen (hourly; 2hr 45min).

Alkmaar to: Hoorn (every 30min; 25min).

Arnhem to: Amsterdam (every 20min; 1hr 10min); Utrecht (7 hourly; 35min).

Haarlem to: Alkmaar (every 30min; 25min).

The Hague CS to: Delft (every 15min; 12min); Dordrecht (every 30min; 40min); Gouda (every 20min; 20min); Rotterdam (every 15min; 25min); Utrecht (every 20min; 40min).

Groningen to: Amsterdam (every 30min; 2hr 25min); Leeuwarden (every 30min; 50min).

Leeuwarden to: Amsterdam (every 30min; 2hr 25min); Groningen (every 30min; 50min).

Leiden to: Amsterdam CS (every 30min; 35min); The Hague CS (every 30min; 35min).

Maastricht to: Liège (hourly; 30min).

Rotterdam to: Gouda (every 20min; 20min); Utrecht (every 20min; 45min).

CHAPTER 16

NORWAY

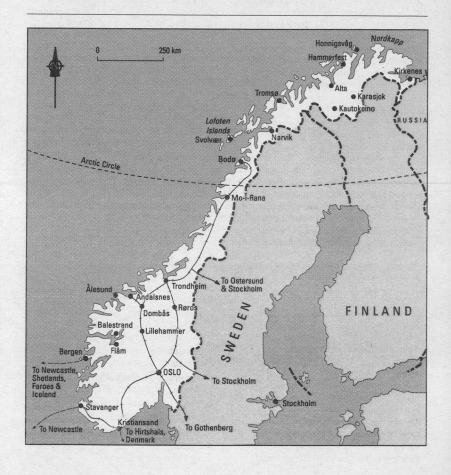

0   250 km

Nordkapp
Honnigsvåg
Hammerfest
Kirkenes
Tromsø
Alta
Karasjok
Kautokeino
RUSSIA
Lofoten Islands
Svolvær
Narvik
Arctic Circle
Bodø
Mo-i-Rana
To Ostersund & Stockholm
Ålesund
Trondheim
Andalsnes
Røros
Dombås
SWEDEN
Balestrand
Lillehammer
FINLAND
Bergen
Flåm
To Newcastle, Shetlands, Faroes & Iceland
OSLO
To Stockholm
Stockholm
Stavanger
Kristiansand
To Hirtshals, Denmark
To Gothenberg
To Newcastle

Introduction

In many ways **Norway** is still a land of unknowns. Quiet for a thousand years since the Vikings stamped their mark on Europe, the country nowadays often seems more than just geographically distant. Beyond Oslo and the famous fjords the rest of the country might as well be blank for all many visitors know – and, in a manner of speaking, large parts of it are. Vast stretches in the north and east are sparsely populated, and it is at times possible to travel for hours without seeing a soul.

Despite this isolation, Norway has had a pervasive influence. Traditionally its inhabitants were explorers, from the Vikings to more recent figures like Amundsen, Nansen and Heyerdahl; while Norse language and traditions are common to many other isolated fishing communities, not least northwest Scotland and the Shetlands. At home, too, the Norwegian people have striven to escape the charge of national provincialism, touting the disproportionate number of acclaimed artists, writers and musicians (most notably Munch, Ibsen and Grieg) who have made their mark on the wider European scene. It's also a pleasing discovery that the great outdoors – great though it is – harbours some lively historical towns.

Beyond **Oslo**, one of the world's most prettily sited capitals, the major cities of interest are medieval **Trondheim**, **Bergen** in the heart of the fjords and hilly, northern **Tromsø**. None is exactly swinging, but they are likeable, walkable cities worth time for themselves, as well as being on top of startlingly handsome countryside. The perennial draw are the **western fjords** – every bit as scenically stunning as they're cracked up to be. Dip into the region from Bergen or Åndalsnes, both accessible direct by train from Oslo, or take more time and appreciate the subtleties of the innumerable waterside towns and villages. Far to the north of here Norway grows increasingly barren, and what tourist trail there is peters out altogether. The vast lands of **Troms** and **Finnmark** were once the home of outlaws and still boast wild and untamed tracts. There are also the *Same* tribes and their herds of reindeer, which you'll see on the thin, exposed road up to the North Cape, or **Nordkapp** – the northernmost accessible point of mainland Europe, and the natural end to the long trek north.

Information and Maps

Every town has a **tourist office**, usually with a stock of free maps, timetables and other bumph. Many book private rooms and hostel beds, and rent out bikes, sell discount cards and change money. During summer they normally open daily for long hours; out of high season shop hours are more normal, while in winter many shut at weekends or close down altogether. The best general **map** of Norway is the *Terrac* 1:1,000,000 one.

Money and Banks

Though challenged by Sweden and Switzerland, Norway ranks as Europe's most expensive country, where £10 a day represents an absolute minimum expenditure, £15–20 being a more likely amount. Norwegian currency is the *krone*, one of which is divided into 100 øre. Coins in circulation are 50 øre, 1kr, 5kr and 10kr; notes are for 50, 100, 500 and 1000kr. Banks are open Monday to Friday 8am–3.30/4pm, generally staying open an hour later on Thursdays, but closing an hour earlier from June to August. Some airports, train stations and campsites have **exchange offices** open evenings and weekends, and tourist offices also change money, though all charge 10–30kr per transaction. **Credit card** cash advances should save you money here; look out for *Den Norske Creditkassen* and *ABC Bank*.

Communications

Norwegian communications are excellent, and things are made even easier by the fact that post and telephone office staff nearly all speak good English. **Post office** opening hours are usually Mon–Fri 8am–5pm, Sat 8am–1pm. **Stamps** are available from post offices, kiosks and stationers costing 4.50kr for a 20 gram letter or postcard to Europe, 5.50kr to the rest of the world. **Telephone** boxes take 1kr, 5kr and 10kr coins, and there is a minimum 2kr charge. Card phones are commonplace, the cards coming in denominations of 35kr (22 units), 98kr (65 units) and 210kr (150 units). Remember to dial all eight digits from anywhere in Norway. In Oslo and some of the larger cities there are **telephone offices**, open until late evening. The international access code is ☎095, directory enquiries ☎0180 for Scandinavian countries and 0181 otherwise.

Getting Around

Norway's transport system is comprehensive and reliable. In the winter (especially in the north), services can be cut back severely, but no part of the country is isolated for long. All the main air, train, bus and ferry services are detailed in the invaluable and free *Rutehefte for Turister*, available from most Norwegian tourist offices or in advance from the National Tourist Board. Or check the more hefty *Rutebok for Norge* (159kr from bookshops) which contains every schedule in the country. Train schedules are also included in the *NSB Togruter*, free at most stations.

■ Trains

Train services are run by *Norges Statsbaner* (*NSB*) – Norwegian State Railways – and apart from a few branch lines work on four main routes which link Oslo to Stavanger in the south, to Bergen in the west and to Trondheim and on to Bodø in the north. The nature of the country makes most of the routes engineering feats of some magnitude and worth a trip in their own right – the tiny Flåm line and sweeping Rauma run to Åndalsnes are exciting examples. *InterRail* and *Eurail* passes are valid, as is the *Nordturist* pass. Available from *NSR Travel*, 21–24 Cockspur Street, London SW1Y 5DA, and throughout Scandinavia, this pass costs £189/$300 (£140/$220 for under-26s), and gives you 21 days' unlimited travel in the four main Scandinavian countries, plus free travel or large discounts on many ferry crossings and bus journeys. *NSR Travel* also sells the *Scandrail* pass, costing £93/$150 for 4 days travel in 15, £151/$240 for 9 days out of 21 and £217/$350 for 21 days travel out 30, is again valid throughout Scandinavia. The *Kundekort*, costing 370kr and valid for a year, entitles the holder to a fifty percent reduction on so-called "green routes" at various times during each week, and thirty percent on all other journeys. Train station information offices have details of the routes, and also of the off-peak *minipris* system whereby a ticket bought at least a day in advance will cost a maximum of 470kr and give around a 20 percent discount on all routes.

Otherwise ticket prices are steep, the popular Oslo to Bergen trip, for example, costing 480kr one-way. Note that most express trains (*Ekspress* or *Hurtigtog*), and all overnight trains, require advance seat reservation (20kr, 30kr on the *ICE*

inter-city expresses) whether you have a rail pass or not. In high season it's wise to make one anyway as trains can be packed. Sleepers are reasonably priced, starting at 100kr for a bed in a three-berth compartment.

■ Buses

You'll need to use **buses** principally in the western fjords and the far north, though there are also a series of long-distance **express buses** which connect major towns. **Tickets** aren't too pricy and are usually bought on board, although travel agents sell advance tickets on the more popular routes. Information on specific routes, and timetables, are available from the local tourist offices or from *Nor-Way Bussekspress*, Karl Johans Gate 2, N–0154 Oslo 1 (☎22.33.08.62). Students and *Nordturist/InterRail* pass holders pull in a fifty percent **discount** on bus travel between the two rail termini of Fauske/Bodø and Narvik; those with *Nordturist* can also go free on the bus service between Storlien (in Sweden) and Trondheim. A long-distance coach, the **Nord-Norge Bussen**, runs between Fauske, the northernmost reach of the railway, and Kirkenes, close to the Soviet border, a 48-hour journey involving at least one stopover. The route is operated by several bus companies who combine to provide one bus daily which runs all year as far as Alta, and two daily from there to Kirkenes. Buy tickets as you go or one all-inclusive ticket in advance.

■ Ferries

It would be difficult to avoid using a **ferry** in Norway. You'll rarely pay very much to use them – say 15–30kr – and on shorter hops the ride may well be included in the bus fare. Otherwise, just walk on and pay the conductor on board. Where the ferries are part of a longer road route, they either connect with the relevant buses or there are constant daily services. Nearly all are car-ferries, which can be useful for hitch-hikers.

There's also the **Hurtigrute** (literally "rapid route"), a daily coastal steamer which links Bergen with Kirkenes, and stops off on the way. **Tickets** for short jumps are quite expensive, certainly compared with the comparable bus fares, and the full eleven-day return cruise (including a cabin and meals) goes for 8000–23,000kr. But prices are reduced outside June to August, when under-26s can buy a special **coastal pass**, which costs 1750kr for 21 days' unlimited travel. Get it on board on your first trip, at almost all travel agents or at the *Hurtigrute* company offices in Trondheim (☎73.51.51.20), Narvik (☎76.94.40.90) or Tromsø (☎77.68.60.88). Although it's a cruise ship you don't need to have a cabin: sleeping in the lounges or on deck is allowed. But plan carefully before buying your ticket, since single tickets only allow one overnight stop. The older ships are the nicest, and tend to have showers you can use on the lower corridors. Car drivers should use the new ships as the old ones only have room for five or six vehicles. Bikes travel free. A 24-hour cafeteria supplies coffee and snacks, and there's a good-value restaurant.

■ Driving and hitching

Driving, in the north especially, can be a positive adventure. On the whole, roads are good, although you'll need to take care on the winding mountain passes and in the enormous tunnels, and in winter roads like the E6 Arctic Highway are not for the ill-equipped. Your driving licence and vehicle registration papers are all that's needed, and it's recommended that you carry the international green card of insurance. You drive on the right, with dipped headlights required at all times; there's a speed limit of 50kph in built-up areas and 80kph on open roads, seatbelts are compulsory for drivers and passengers, and drunken driving is severely punished. If you **break down**, the *Norges Automobil-Forbund* (*NAF*) patrols all mountain passes between mid-June and mid-August, and there are emergency telephones along roads and motorways – look up the local number under "Redningstjeneste" in the local telephone directory. Basic breakdown help is free to *AA/RAC/AAA* members. **Car hire** is expensive: from around 3500kr a week with unlimited mileage.

In general, Norwegians don't queue up to offer lifts to **hitchers**, and most young Norwegians don't hitch at all. Short distances – the western fjords, the south coast – are your best bet for lifts, but wherever you are be prepared for some long waits.

Accommodation

Accommodation in Norway is a major expense, and you need to exercise both thought and patience to find anywhere even halfway reasonable.

■ Youth hostels

Youth hostels provide the accommodation mainstay – about ninety in all, spread right across the country. The Norwegian hostelling association, *Norske Vandrerhjem*, Dronningensgate 26, Oslo (☎22.42.14.10), puts out a free pamphlet detailing addresses, opening dates and prices. Prices vary greatly – anything from 60kr to 160kr – although the more expensive ones nearly always include a good breakfast. On average, reckon on paying 80–100kr a night for a bed, 45–50kr for breakfast and 70–80kr for a hot meal. Most hostels also have a few doubles for around 160–400kr. Non-members can use the hostels but pay an extra 25kr a night. Between June and mid-September you should, however, always ring ahead to check on space. Most hostels close between 11am and 4pm, and there's normally an 11pm/midnight curfew.

■ Campsites and cabins

Camping is the only other way of keeping accommodation costs down. There are hundreds of official sites throughout the country, and most are of a high standard; prices are usually around 70kr a tent, plus around 40kr per person. The Norwegian Tourist Board publishes an annual list. Campsites also often have **cabins**, usually

---

ACCOMMODATION PRICE CODES

Throughout this guide, accommodation is priced on a scale of ① to ⑧, the number indicating the lowest price per night a single person could expect to pay in that establishment in high season. With hostels this is the nightly rate per person; with hotels, the price is arrived at by dividing the cost of the cheapest double room by two. The prices indicated by the codes are as follows

① = under £5 / $8   ② = £5–10 / $8–16   ③ = £10–15 / $16–24   ④ = £15–20 / $24–32

⑤ = £20–25 / $32–40   ⑥ = £25–30 / $40–48   ⑦ = £30–35 / $48–56   ⑧ = over £35 / $56

four-bedded affairs with kitchen facilities and sometimes a bathroom, for upwards of 150kr. **Camping rough**, as in Sweden, is a tradition enshrined in law. You can camp anywhere in open areas as long as you are at least 150m away from houses or cabins. In all cases a good sleeping bag is essential, since even in summer it can get very cold; in the north a mosquito repellent and sun-protection cream are vital.

■ Hotels, pensions and private rooms

Hotels are generally out of the reckoning for budget travellers – the cheapest double room will set you back around 450kr a night. Still, there are bargains to be found, particularly during summer. The 50kr Fjord Pass, for example, available from the bus terminal opposite Oslo S, entitles the holder to a twenty percent discount or more on many hotels, and the larger cities' discount cards give large reductions too. Remember also that the price of a hotel room always includes breakfast. **Pensions** – *pensjonater* or *hospits* – in the more touristy towns are slightly cheaper at about 250–450kr a double; breakfast is usually extra. Failing that, tourist offices in larger towns can sometimes fix you up with a **private room** in someone's house for 250kr a double, though there's a booking fee (15–20kr) on top and the rooms are often way out of the centre.

Food and Drink

Norwegian food can, at its best, be excellent: fish is plentiful, and carnivores can have a field day trying meats like reindeer steak or elk. But once again all this costs money, and those on a tight budget may have problems varying their diet. The same can be said of drinking: buying from the supermarkets – *Rimi* and *Rema 1000* are the cheapest – and state off-licences is often the only way you'll afford a tipple.

■ Food

Breakfast (*frokost*) is a huge self-service affair of bread, crackers, cheese, eggs, preserves, cold meat and fish, washed down by unlimited tea and coffee: it's usually excellent at youth hostels, and memorable in hotels, filling you up for the day for around 50–60kr. Later in the day, **picnic food** is the best standby, although there are a number of **fast food** alternatives. The indigenous Norwegian stuff, served up from *gatekjøkken* or

street stalls, consists mainly of rubbery hot dogs (*varm pølse*), pizza slices and chicken and chips. American-style burger bars are also creeping in, including the Scandinavian *Clockburger* – hardly health food but at least the standard is consistent and they nearly always have the cheapest coffee in town. A better choice, and often no more expensive, is simply to get a sandwich, normally a huge open affair called a **smørbrød**, heaped with a variety of garnishes. You'll see them in **cafés**, or sandwich bars in larger towns.

Ice cream is a Norwegian hobby and is not at all bad, served in ice cream bars that double as hang-outs with the young. Good **coffee** is available everywhere and often free or half-price after the first cup. **Tea**, too, is ubiquitous, but the local preference is for lemon tea or a variety of flavoured infusions; if you want milk, ask for it.

The best deals for **sit-down food** are at lunchtime (*lunsj*), when self-service **kafeterias** lay on daily specials, the *dagens rett* – a fish or meat dish with potatoes and a vegetable or salad, often including a drink, sometimes bread, and occasionally coffee too, that costs around 60–70kr. Dipping into the menu is more expensive, but not cripplingly so if you stick to omelettes or cheap cutlets of meat. Most department stores and large supermarkets have surprisingly good *kafeterias*, as does every main railway station. You'll also find them above more traditional restaurants in larger towns, where they might be called *Kaffistovas*. **Restaurants**, serving dinner (*middag*) and real Norwegian food, are out of range of many budgets. Seafood is good, as are the more obscure meats, but both can be wildly expensive. Again, the best deals are at lunchtime, when many restaurants put out a *koldtbord* (the Norwegian *smörgåsbord*), where for a fixed price of around 100–150kr you can get through as much as possible during the three or four hours it's served. There are also a growing number of **ethnic restaurants**, the most affordable of which are the pizza joints in most towns; two people sharing a large pizza and a couple of small beers can expect to pay over 200kr.

■ Drink

Norwegian alcohol prices are among the highest in Europe. **Beer** is lager-like and comes in three strengths (class I, II or III), of which the strongest and most expensive is class III. **Spirits** are also way over the top in price. One local speciality worth experimenting with at least once is *akevitt*, served ice-cold in little glasses and, at forty percent proof, real headache material. In bars and cafés a half-litre of beer costs between 30kr and 45kr. Bars tend to close down at around 11pm outside the larger cities, although licensed discos and clubs stay open later.

Beer is sold in supermarkets and shops all over Norway and is about half the price you'd pay in a bar. Wines and spirits can only be purchased from the state-controlled shops known as *Vinmonopol*. There's generally one in each small town, though there are more branches in the cities; opening hours are Mon–Wed 10am–5pm, Thurs 10am–6pm, Fri 9am–5pm, Sat 9am–1pm.

Opening Hours and Holidays

Shop **opening hours** are Mon–Wed & Fri 9am–5pm, Thurs 9am–6/7pm, Sat 9am–2/3pm. Newspaper kiosks (*Narvesen*) and takeaway food stalls are open all evenings until 10 or 11pm. Everything is **closed** on the following days: Jan 1; Maundy Thursday; Good Friday; Easter Monday; May 1; May 17; Whit Monday & Tuesday; Aug 15; Dec 25 & Dec 26.

Emergencies

Like all the Scandinavian countries, Norway is in general a safe place to travel, the people friendly and helpful, and petty crime has a relatively low profile. If you have to visit the **police** you'll find them helpful and normally able to speak English. If you have something stolen, be sure to get a police report – essential for any insurance claim. As for health problems, most hotels and tourist offices have lists of local doctors and dentists. You'll pay 50–80kr for an appointment but will be reimbursed for part of the cost of any treatment; hospital stays are free. Get a receipt (*legeregning*) at the time of payment and take it and your passport to the social insurance office (*trygdekasse*) of the district where treatment was obtained. For prescriptions, most chemists (*apotek*) carry a rota in the window advising of the nearest open shop.

EMERGENCY NUMBERS
Police ☎002; Ambulance ☎003; Fire ☎001.

OSLO

Despite tourist office endeavours, OSLO retains a low profile among European cities, and even comparisons with other Scandinavian capitals are less than favourable. You'll inevitably pass through – from Oslo the main train routes head out west to the fjords, south to the coast and east to Sweden – but take heart: Oslo is definitely worth seeing. The city notches up some of Europe's best museums, fields a street-life that surprises most visitors, and helps revive travellers weary of the quiet northern wilderness.

Oslo is the oldest of the Scandinavian capital cities, founded, according to the Norse chronicler Snorre Sturlason, around 1048 by Harold Hardråde. Several decimating fires and 600 years later, Oslo upped sticks and shifted west to its present site, abandoning its old name (*os*, settlement at the mouth of the *Lo* river) in favour of Christiania – after the seventeenth-century Danish king Christian IV responsible for the move. The new city prospered and by the time of the break with Denmark in 1814, Christiania (indeed Norway as a whole) was clamouring for independence, something it achieved in 1905 – though the city didn't revert to its original name for another twenty years. The modern city centre reflects the era well: wide streets, dignified parks and gardens, solid nine-teenth-century buildings and long, consciously classical vistas combine to lend it a self-satisfied, respectable air. Seeing the city takes – and deserves – time. Its half a million inhabitants have room to spare in a city whose vast boundaries encompass huge areas of woods, sand and water, and much of the time you're as likely to be swimming or trail-walking as strolling the city centre.

Arrival and information

International and domestic **trains** use Oslo Sentralstasjonen, known as **Oslo S**, at the eastern end of the city centre. The central **bus terminal**, *Galleri Oslo* (or Oslo M), handily placed in Jernbanetorget outside Oslo S, handles all bus traffic except express buses and *Eurolines*, which drop at the *Nor-Way Busstermina* terminal on Havnegata, on the harbour side of Oslo S. **Ferries** from Copenhagen, Fredrikshavn and Hirtshals/ Harwich arrive at the quays east of Akershus Castle, a short walk from Oslo S. From Kiel you'll arrive at Hjortneskaia, some way west; tram #9 and bus #56 run into the centre. Ferries from Arendal, in southern Norway, dock at Akershus pier in front of the castle. Two **airports** serve Oslo, the larger of which, handling mainly scheduled flights, is at Fornebu, about 9km out and connected with the centre at Jernbanetorget by regular *SAS* bus (25min; 30kr); it's cheaper to walk from the airport to the main road and catch local bus #31 to the National Theatre or Jernbanetorget. The other airport, Gardermoen, 50km from Oslo, used principally by charter traffic, is also linked with the centre by bus (50min; 60kr).

If you are travelling on an *InterRail* ticket, the *InterRail Centre* (mid-June to Sept daily 7am–11pm), just inside the entrance to Oslo S, has showers, left luggage and plenty of information, including the publication put out by **Use-It**, situated at Møllergata 3, five minutes' walk away (June–Aug Mon–Fri 7.30am–6pm, Sat 9am–2pm). They provide information on accommodation, entertainment and so on for young travellers. There's also a **tourist kiosk** inside Oslo S (daily 8am–11pm; Oct–May closed 3–4.30pm Thurs–Sun), which can book rooms (20kr fee), and a main **tourist office** at Vestbaneplassen 1 (May–Sept Mon–Fri 9am–6/8pm, Sat & Sun 9am–4pm; Oct–April Mon–Fri 9am–4pm; ☎22.83.00.50). Both hand out a city plan and have free copies of various listings booklets. The tourist office sells the useful **Oslo Card**, which gives free admission to most of the museums and unlimited free travel on the transport system, including ferries, as well as useful discounts in shops and restaurants. Valid for either one, two or three days, it costs 95kr, 140kr and 170kr respectively.

City transport

Most **transport** is operated by *AS Oslo Sporveier*, whose Trafikanten information office is in Jernbanetorget outside Oslo S (Mon–Fri 7am–8pm, Sat & Sun 8am–6pm). They have a useful map and a timetable booklet, *Rutebok for Oslo*, which details every transport schedule in the city. The choice is between buses, trams, a small underground rail system, local trains and ferries. Most **buses** pass through Jernbanetorget; another common stop is outside the National Theatre (*Nationaltheatret*). Most buses stop running at around midnight, when **night buses** take over on certain routes. The fewer, slower **trams** run on seven lines from east to west, and tend to duplicate the bus routes; major terminals are Jernbanetorget and Stortorvet. The underground Tunnelbanen – **T-bane** – has eight lines, converging at Stortinget, right in the centre, though the system mainly serves commuters. Numerous **ferries** cross the fjord to connect the city with its outlying districts and archipelago: to Bygdøy and the museums they leave from the piers outside the Rådhus (May–Sept); for the islands, they go from Vippetangen quay, behind Akershus Castle (bus #29 from Jernbanetorget). It's 15kr for a flat-fare **ticket** (bought on board or at T-bane stations); a 24-hour **travel pass** costs 35kr. There is also the *Flexikort* pass, which entitles the holder to eight journeys for 100kr, and a seven-day pass for 130kr – both available from Trafikanten. **Taxis** are dear – around 100kr for up to a ten-minute ride; to get one ring *Oslo Taxicentral* (☎22.38.80.90).

Accommodation

In summer, July especially, the scramble for **budget beds** in Oslo's hostels becomes acute, and it is always worth ringing ahead to check on space, at least for the first night. You'll pay a minimum of 500kr a double in a city centre **hotel**, but at weekends and in high summer, the bigger hotels offer the *Destination Oslo* package which brings the hotel price down to as little as 295kr per person and throws in breakfast and an *Oslo card*. The **Accommodation Centre** at Oslo S (daily 8am–11pm; ☎22.17.11.24) has full accommodation lists and can make bookings for 20kr per person. They can also book **private rooms** from 260kr a double, and the supply rarely dries up; however, they tend to be out of the centre and there is a minimum two-night stay. **Pensjonater** cost from 300kr a double and can also be booked through the Accommodation Centre.

Hostels

Drammen Vandrerhjem, Korsvegen 62, Drammen (☎32.82.21.89). Outside the city, but numerous daily trains run to Drammen, a 30-min ride, then a bus to Lijordet; open end of June to mid-Aug; 90kr a bed, double rooms 210kr.

KFUM InterRail Point, Møllergata 1 (☎22.42.10.66). Most central hostel, five minutes from Oslo S. At 75kr a bed plus 20kr membership, cheapest too. Open July to mid-Aug; midnight curfew.

Oslo Haraldsheim, Haraldsheimveien 4, Grefsen (☎22.22.29.65). Best of the two *IYHF* youth hostels, 5km out of the centre but open all year. Tram #1 or #7 from Storgata to Sinsen (the end of the line) or any local train to Grefsen. The 141kr price includes breakfast and there are some double rooms for 395kr.

Oslo Holtekilen, Michelestvei 5 (☎22.53.38.53). Oslo's second official hostel 5km northeast but close to the Furuset stop on the #67 T-bane (*InterRail & Nordturist* valid). Breakfast included. ③

Pensjonater

Bella Vista, Årrundveien 11b (☎22.65.45.88). A small pension with use of kitchen facilities; open June–Aug. ④

Cochs Pensjonat, Parkveien 25 (☎22.60.48.36). Nicely sited. ④

Ellingsens Pensjonat, Holtegate 25 (☎22.60.03.59). Basic but clean, and excellent value. Tram #1 to Uranienborg. ④

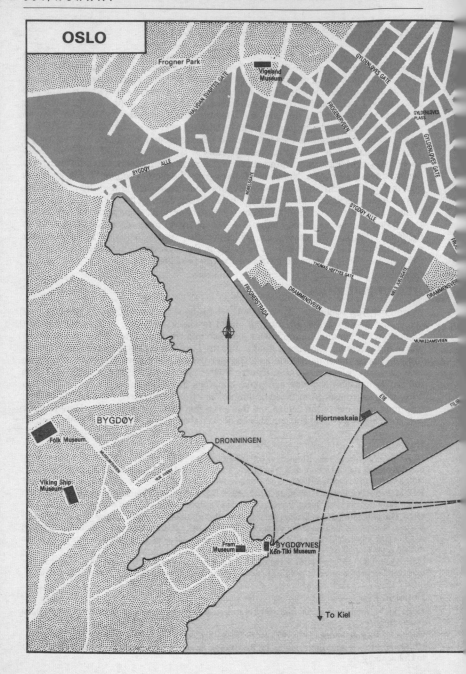

OSLO

Frogner Park

Vigeland Museum

GYLDENLØVES GATE

HALVDAN SVARTES GATE

FROGNERVEIEN

GYLDENLØVES PLASS

GYLDENLØVES GATE

BYGDØY ALLE

NOBELS GATE

BYGDØY ALLE

THOMAS HEFTYES GATE

NIELS JUELS GATE

DRAMMENSVEIEN

FRO...

FRONGSTRADA

DRAMMENSVEIEN

DRAMMENSVEIEN

MUNKEDAMSVEIEN

EIB

FILIP...

BYGDØY

Hjortneskaia

Folk Museum

DRONNINGEN

Viking Ship Museum

Fram Museum

BYGDØYNES
Kon-Tiki Museum

To Kiel

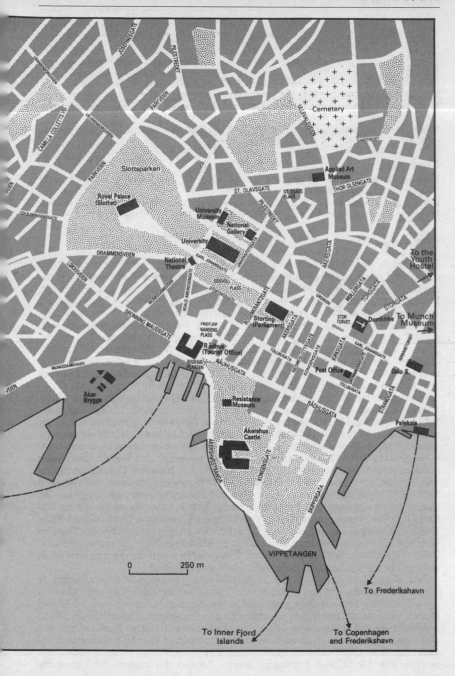

Sjømannshjemmet, Tollbugata 4 (☎22.41.20.05). Very central, and popular with seamen as the port is nearby. Scruffy but good-value doubles at 280kr. ③

Hotels

Anker Hotel, Storgaten 55 (☎22.11.40.05). A big hotel in a good location. ⑦

City Hotel, Skippergata 19 (☎22.41.36.10). Dead central popular standby with basic doubles. ⑥

Hotel Fønix, Dronningensgate 19 (☎22.42.59.57). Again, very centrally located, just around the corner from the main post office. ⑤

Munch Hotel, Munchsgate 5 (☎22.42.42.75). Well-appointed and central – lower rates at weekends. ⑧

Campsites

Ekeberg, Ekebergveien 65. Just 3km from the city centre and open June–Aug; bus #72 from the National Theatre or #24 from Jernbanetorget.

Bogstad Camp, Ankerveien 117. Larger, better equipped site, open all year, with free showers, and rooms and 4-berth cabins for around 490kr. 9km out, bus #41 from the National Theatre.

The City

Karl Johans Gate cuts west from Oslo S station through the heart of the city, Oslo's most varied street, with everything from the bars and buskers around the station to the dignified calm of the Royal Palace at the other end. The first section is pedestrianized, leading past pavement cafés to the **Domkirke** (June–Aug Mon–Fri 10am–3pm, Sat 10am–1pm; Sept–May Mon–Fri 10am–3pm), heavily restored and with few of its original late seventeenth- and early eighteenth-century fittings remaining, though with stained glass by Emmanuel Vigeland. Outside, **Stortorvet** is the main city square, guarded by a stout nineteenth-century statue of Christian IV. The curious circular cloistered building nearby, the **Basarhallene**, now beleaguered by almost continuous circles of traffic, was the city's provincial food market in the last century and has since been revived as a complex of trendy art and handicraft shops.

At the top of the hill, the **Storting** or parliament building is an imposing chunk of neo-Romanesque architecture completed in 1866. It's open to the public (July & Aug Mon–Sat 11am–1pm; free) but the obligatory tour takes in little that can't be gleaned from the outside. The park in front, **Eidsvolls Plass**, flanks Karl Johans Gate, and – along with the university gardens further down – is one of the busiest centres of night-time Oslo, usually full of jewellery hawkers and people carefully sipping overpriced drinks from the swish pavement cafés, notably that of the Neoclassical **National Theatre** on the far side. Beyond, the **Royal Palace** is a monument to Norwegian openness, built between 1825 and 1848 and still without railings and walls. Although you can't actually go into the palace, there's a snappy changing of the guard daily at 1.30pm. The statue in front is of Karl XIV Johan himself. Formerly the French General Bernadotte, he abandoned Napoléon and, elected as king of Sweden, assumed the Norwegian throne after the Treaty of Kiel, when Norway passed from Denmark to Sweden. Seemingly not content with the terms of his motto, inscribed on the statue, "The people's love is my reward", Karl Johan had this whopping palace built, only to die before its completion.

Back along Karl Johans Gate, the nineteenth-century buildings of the **University** fit well in this monumental end of the centre. The university **Aula** (July only Mon–Fri noon–2pm; free), between the symmetrical wings, has huge interior murals by Edvard Munch, controversial result of a competition held by the university authorities in 1909 to decorate their hall on the cheap. Munch had just emerged (cured) from a winter in a Copenhagen psychiatric clinic when he started the murals, and the major parts of his work, *The History*, *Sun* and *Alma Mater*, reflect a new mood in his work – confident and in tune with his beloved Norwegian nature. Around the corner, the **University**

Museums at Frederiksgate 2 (Tues–Sun 11am–3pm; free) comprise two main collections, Historical and Ethnographical, of which the **historical** section on the ground floor is much the best, with extensive Viking finds and eclectic collections of church art and runic stones. The **ethnographical** section, upstairs, is a comprehensive exhibition of art and culture from Australasia, the Middle East, North and South America, and Africa.

Norway's largest and best collection of art, the **National Gallery** (Mon, Wed, Fri & Sat 10am–4pm, Thurs 10am–8pm, Sun 11am–3pm; free, free guided tours July & Aug) is only a step away at Universitetsgata 13. An accessible collection, it ranges through sixteenth- and seventeenth-century religious works, to the gloomy icons of the Novgorod School and the Impressionists, and later pieces by the likes of Picasso and Braque. There's also a section on Norwegian painting – best the romantic works of J.C. Dahl and, the museum's highlight, a central room devoted to Munch and featuring the famous *Scream*. Still on the museum circuit, you may as well continue to the **Museum of Applied Art** at St Olav's Gate 1 (Tues–Fri 11am–3pm, Sat & Sun noon–4pm; 15kr), a multifaceted assemblage of period furniture, clothes and modern design. The protected and intricate thirteenth-century *Baldishol* tapestry is the top exhibit – perhaps the finest, and certainly the oldest tapestry in Europe. A lesser-known contender is the display of Queen Sonja's costumes, breathtaking in their opulence.

Back in the centre, you can't miss the **Rådhus** (Mon–Sat 9am–3.30pm, Sun noon–3pm; free), the modern and controversial City Hall, opened in 1950 to celebrate the 900th anniversary. Few people initially had a good word for the building; nonetheless its twin towers are a grandiose statement of civic pride and nowadays rank as the most distinctive part of waterfront Oslo. The interior (free tours 10am, noon & 2pm) was equally contentious, much of it a pictorial record of all things Norwegian. Outside you can see the old **Oslo V railway station**, now mostly closed down, and, beyond, the old warehouses of Oslo's shipyard, nowadays given over to the cavernous hi-tech shopping halls of the **Aker Brygge** development. **Rådhusgata**, running east, leads down to the other harbour, the gridded streets on either side a legacy of seventeenth-century Oslo, though sadly it's really only the layout that survives. To the south, **Akershus Castle** is the most significant memorial to medieval Oslo and quite separate from the city centre in feel, built on a plateau overlooking the harbour around 1300, though modernized in the seventeenth century by Christian IV and since then extensively rebuilt. It's now the home of the Royal Mausoleum, although many Norwegians remember it best for its role as Nazi HQ during the last war. Tours take in the chapel, underground passages and dungeons (mid- to late April & mid-Sept to Oct Sun 12.30–4pm; May to mid-Sept Mon–Sat 10am–4pm, Sun 12.30–4pm; 10kr, free guided tours Mon–Sat 11am, 1pm & 3pm), and the **park and ramparts** (daily 6am–9pm; free) have views of the harbour and the Bygdøy peninsula. There's an exhibition, too – the **Christiania Bymodell** (June–Aug Tues–Sun 10am–4pm; 10kr), tracing the development of Christian's city and including a scale model of Oslo as it appeared in 1838. Time is better spent in the nearby **Resistance Museum** (Mon–Sat 10am–3/4/5pm, Sun 11am–4/5pm; 15kr), where excellent displays document the building's past role as well as presenting a moving and factual story of occupation, resistance and eventual victory. Pressing buttons brings up extracts of Quisling's announcement of his assumption of puppet power in April 1940, while photographs show the defeated Nazis handing over their weapons.

The Bygdøy peninsula

Other than the city centre, the place you're likely to spend most time in Oslo is the **Bygdøy peninsula**, across the bay to the west, where five separate museums make up an absorbing cultural and historical display. On foot it's a long hike around the edge of the bay, but **bus #30** runs regularly from Jernbanetorget and the National Theatre, and in summer **ferries** ply between the Rådhus (every 30min 7.45am–5.15pm) and Dronningen and Bygdøynes piers.

Closest to Dronningen Pier, the **Norwegian Folk Museum** on Museumsveien (daily mid-May to mid-Sept 10am–6pm; rest of year noon–4pm; 35kr) combines vast indoor collections of furniture, china and silverware with an open-air display of reassembled period farms, houses and other buildings. Notable inside is the reconstructed nineteenth-century Norwegian parliament chamber complete with ink-wells and quills at the members' seats, and Ibsen's study, preserved from his last home in Oslo; outside, the reconstructed buildings include farms, a stave church, houses and workplaces, arranged geographically to emphasize the idea of variety and development in rural architecture. A few minutes away, the **Viking Ship Museum** (daily April & Oct 11am–4/5pm; May–Aug 9am–6pm; Sept 11am–5pm; Nov–March 11am–3pm; 20kr) contains a hoard of loot retrieved from three ritual ship burials, as well as two boats – the *Oseberg* (a royal barge) and *Gokstad* (a Viking longboat) – spectacularly restored following their late nineteenth-century discovery. Lavishly decorated and carrying bodies buried a thousand years ago, the ships were equipped with grave-furniture, textiles, solid jewellery and other implements, all of it now on display, from the ceremonial sleighs to be used in a glorious afterlife, to buttons, combs, cups and needles.

Down by the Bygdøynes pier, the marvellous **Kon-Tiki Museum** (daily Sept & April to mid-May 10.30am–5pm; mid-May to Aug 10am–6pm; Oct–March 10.30am–4pm; 20kr) displays the balsawood raft on which Thor Heyerdahl made his now legendary 1947 journey across the Pacific. Heyerdahl wanted to prove the trip could be done; he was convinced that the first Polynesian settlers had sailed from pre-Inca Peru, and rejected prevailing opinions that South American balsa rafts were unseaworthy. Looking at the flimsy raft, *Kon-Tiki*, and the later one of papyrus, *Ra II*, on which he crossed the Atlantic in 1970, you could be forgiven for agreeing with Heyerdahl's critics, although Easter Island statues and secret cave graves give further weight to his ethnological theories. Over the road, the **Fram Museum** (mid-May to Aug daily 10am–5.45pm; Sept daily 11am–4.45pm; April, Oct & Nov Mon–Fri 11am–2.45pm, Sat & Sun 11am–3.45pm; 15kr) displays the beached Polar vessel *Fram*, launched in 1893. The ship's design was unique, its sides made smooth to prevent the ice from getting a firm grip on the hull, while inside a veritable maze of beams, braces and stanchions held it all together. A veteran of three expeditions, the vessel's finest hour came in 1911 when it carried Roald Amundsen to within striking distance of the South Pole, a feat he achieved a month before Scott of the Antarctic, who died on his way back. Inside the ship, the living quarters will horrify claustrophobics. Next door, the **Norwegian Maritime Museum** (May–Sept daily 10am–7pm; Oct–April Mon, Wed & Fri–Sun 10.30am–4/5pm, Tues & Thurs until 7pm; 20kr) is a sparkling new building housing a fairly pedestrian collection of maritime artefacts. You'll probably be more taken with the café, a handy vantage point overlooking the bay, beach and city.

The Munch Museum

Also out of the centre but without question a major attraction, the **Munch Museum**, Tøyengata 53 (June to mid-Sept Mon–Sat 10am–6pm, Sun noon–6pm; mid-Sept to May Tues–Sat 10am–4pm, Thurs until 6pm, Sun noon–6pm; 40kr), is reachable on bus #29 from Jernbanetorget or by T-bane from Stortinget to Tøyen. Born in 1863, Edvard Munch is perhaps Norway's most famous painter, generally considered an initiator of Expressionism, although it wasn't until well into his career that he was fully accepted in his own country. In his will he donated all the works in his possession to Oslo city council – a mighty bequest of several thousand paintings, prints, drawings, engravings and photographs, only a small part of which can be shown at any one time. His lithographs and woodcuts are shown in one half of the gallery, a dark catalogue of swirls and fog, and in the main gallery there are early paintings, along with the great works of the 1890s, considered among Munch's finest achievements. Among many, there's *Dagny Juell*, a portrait of the Berlin socialite, Ducha, with whom both Munch and

Strindberg were infatuated, and the chilling *Virginia Creeper*, a house being consumed by the plant. Later paintings reflect a renewed interest in nature and physical work, as in the 1913 *Workers Returning Home* and the light *Children in the Street*, and *Model by the Wicker Chair*, which reveal a happier, if rather idealized, attitude to his surroundings – also evident in works like *Ploughing*, painted in 1919.

Frogner: the Vigeland Sculpture Park and Museum

On the other side of the city and reachable direct from the Munch Museum on bus #20, or tram #2 from the centre, **Frogner Park** holds more of Oslo's better cultural targets, in particular the **Vigeland Sculpture Park and Museum**, which commemorate another modern Norwegian artist of world renown, Gustav Vigeland. The **sculpture park**, which Vigeland started in 1924 and was still working on when he died in 1943, is a quite fantastic work. The central fountain, part of a separate commission begun in 1907, is an enormous bowl representing the burden of life, supported by straining, sinewy bronze Goliaths while, underneath, water tumbles out around clusters of playing and standing figures. The twenty-metre obelisk up on the stepped embankment, and the grouped granite sculptures around it, form a writhing mass which depicts the cycle of life as Vigeland saw it – an at-the-time controversial vision of humanity teaching, playing, fighting, loving, eating and sleeping, and clambering on and over each other to reach the top. At the southern corner of the park, at Nobelsgate 32, the **Vigeland Museum** (Tues–Sat noon–4/6pm; Sun noon–6/7pm; 20kr) was the artist's studio during the 1920s and traces the development of his work through a series of monumental plaster casts, drawings and woodcuts. Some of his early pieces are disturbing, not least a wall relief of emaciated figures – a far remove from the chubby characters outside. In summer, concerts and recitals are held in the courtyard.

Holmenkollen

Holmenkollen, a forested range of hills just twenty minutes' T-bane ride from the National Theatre (route #15 to the end of the line), is about the best place to get away from central Oslo's noise and traffic without actually leaving the city limits – classic Norwegian countryside, lush and peaceful. If it's a clear day, follow the signs to the **Tryvannstårnet TV Tower** (May & Sept daily 10am–5pm; June daily 10am–7pm; July daily 9am–10pm; Aug daily 9am–8pm; Oct–April Mon–Fri 10am–3pm, Sat & Sun 11am–4pm; 20kr), the views from the top of which are splendid. From here it's a fifteen-minute walk downhill to the combined **Holmenkollen Ski Museum and Ski Jump** (Jan–April & Oct–Dec Mon–Fri 10am–3pm, Sat & Sun 11am–4pm; May & Sept daily 10am–5pm; June daily 10am–7pm; July daily 9am–10pm; Aug daily 10am–8pm; 20kr each; for both 30kr; for all three 35kr), a more entertaining display than the name promises, with skis through the ages, clothes and equipment from Amundsen to the present-day, and nerve-testing views from the adjacent international ski jump.

The islands of the inner fjord

Oslo's small archipelago of **islands** in the inner fjord is the city's summer playground, popular during the day for its beaches and at night as the major party venue of Oslo's preening youth. **Ferries** (15kr one way) leave from Vippetangen quay, behind Akershus Castle: departures in summer are roughly every hour until 11pm. **Hovedøya**, the nearest and most popular island, contains the overgrown ruins of a twelfth-century Cistercian monastery built by English monks. There's a café in summer, swimming from a rocky shore and lots of shady places to lie. Nearby **Lindøya** is packed full of holiday homes and summer houses but has a few picturesque harbours and paths. The best beaches are probably those on **Gressholmen** and **Langøyene**, further south. All the islands have free **camping** in summer and at night the ferries are full of people with sleeping bags and bottles on their way to join swimming parties.

Eating and drinking

If you're on a restricted budget, the few stalls that you'll find outside the Aker Brygge development, in Jernbanetorget, or the markets at Youngstorget and Grønlands Torg (Mon–Sat 7am–2pm) are probably the best places to buy **picnic food**. For late-night food, *Jens Evesen*, situated inside the T-bane station at Grønland, remains open until 11pm. **Stand-up snacks** are on sale from the kiosks and stalls on virtually every street corner. More healthily, *Wenches* **sandwich bar** on Rådhusgata, just below Christiania Torv, features absolutely monstrous open sandwiches from 20kr (Mon–Sat 10am–5pm). For tea and **cakes**, try the *City Conditori* on Tollbugata, an old-fashioned bakery where a pot of tea and a pastry costs 25kr. Most of the cafés, restaurants and bars listed below are in the central grid-plan section of town, but it is worth a walk out along Hegdehaugsveien northeast of Slottsparken, a street lined with all manner of eating and drinking spots.

Cafés and restaurants

Café Tenerife, Dronningensgate 24. *Tapas* and Spanish dishes. Lunch deals for 50kr and main courses in the evening for not much more. Cheap beer too.

Caroline Café, Oslo Sentralstasjon. A good, cheap cafeteria, offering daily lunch deals.

Coco, Øvre Slottsgate 8. Stylish café where the slow service is compensated for by the good food – daily specials for around 69kr.

Ekebergrestauranten, Kongsveien 15. Help-yourself buffet lunches in the summer for 135kr, or a cheaper version – 80kr – served between 3 and 6pm. Ten percent discount with the Oslo Card. Tram #9 to Sjømannsskolen.

Kafé Celsius, Rådhusgata 19. Plenty of seating and an open courtyard in the summer, and Mediterranean-inspired food for around 50kr. Try the Greek stew for around 69kr. Open late.

Malik's, a chain with branches on Karl Johansgate and on Trondheimsveien. A varied menu including Wienerschnitzel for around 60kr, or cheaper burger meals.

Nador, Dronningensgate 22. A friendly Moroccan restaurant serving enormous, tasty portions of *couscous* and *tajine* dishes for around 125kr. There's also a 50kr lunch buffet.

Peppe's Pizza. Chain of pizza restaurants with branches at Stortingsgata 4 and Frognerveien 54. Huge pizzas – plenty for two – for 130–170kr, and a help-yourself salad bar for around 40kr a head.

Postcaféen, Dronningensgate 19. Hearty, averagely priced meals. Mon–Fri 8am–8pm, Sat 8am–6.30pm, Sun noon–7.30pm.

Vegeta Vertshus, Munkedamsveien 3b. Vegetarian restaurant with a help-yourself buffet. Small platefuls go for 61kr; the 98kr meal includes dessert, a drink and coffee.

Pubs and bars

Café Cappucino, Dronningensgate 27 (on Cathedral Courtyard). Coffee, light snacks and alcohol served in this daytime café in the shade of chestnut trees beneath cathedral spire.

Café Sjakk Matt, Haakon VII's Gate 5. Café open all day serving reasonably priced food for around 40–45kr a plate.

Café Stravinsky, Rosenkrantzgatan 17. Music bar that was once one of the most fashionable venues in Oslo and is still busy. Wed–Sun 9am–4am.

Lorry, corner of Parkveien and Hegdehaugsveien. Boisterous pub frequented mostly by drunk and would-be artists. Good food elbow to elbow inside or at pavement tables.

Oslo Mikrobryggeri, Bogstadveien 6 (entrance on Holegata). Male-oriented pub with home-brewed dark beer, popular with English drinkers.

Palace Grill, Solligata 2. Small American bar with a Fifties jukebox, open late and popular with everyone from yuppies to winos.

Rockall, Rosenkrantzgatan 20. On a street of cafés, this has low-cost beer before 9pm.

The Scotsman, Karl Johansgate 17. Odd Scottish-style bar with food and live Country and Western. The coffee and sandwich deal for 27kr, noon–4pm, is worth checking out.

Nightlife

Tracking down **live music** isn't too difficult, though the scene here is a lot less developed than what's on offer in Copenhagen or Stockholm. The area around Aker Brygge is a good place to look. The *Elm Street Rock Café*, Dronningensgate 32 is a popular venue; *Rockefeller*, Torggata 16, stages big-name acts, mostly from abroad; *Smuget*, Kirkegata 34, hosts live Norwegian jazz, rock and blues every night; the *New Orleans Workshop*, Christiesgate 5, has trad jazz on Thursdays from 8pm but is closed from the end of June to the beginning of August. Most Oslo **discos** are rather staid. Of the few that exist outside the larger hotels, *Barock*, Universitetsgate 26, is one of the best: a restaurant, bar and club favoured by record industry types. Other more youthful, and at weekends very busy, places to check out are *Stedet*, Torggaten 16, and *Snorre*, Rosenkrantzgaten 11. *Den Sorte Enke* is the most popular gay club. Entrance to most places will set you back around 50kr; drink prices are the same as anywhere else, closing times around 3am.

For **listings**, check out *Natt & Dag*, available free from cafés and shops, or *What's On in Oslo*, which contains a day-by-day account of everything cultural and entertaining. **Tickets** for most events can be bought from *Teatersentralen*, Youngstorget 5, or *Bilettsentralen*, on Roald Amundsensgate.

Listings

Airlines *British Airways*, Karl Johansgate 16b (☎22.33.16.00); *SAS*, Ruseløkkveien 6 (☎22.17.00.20).

Bicycle rental *Den Rustne Eike*, Enga 2; 95–145kr a day plus at least 500kr deposit.

Car rental *Avis*, Munkedamsveien 27 (☎66.84.90.60); *Bislet Bilutleie*, Pilestredet 70 (☎22.60.00.00); *Hertz*, c/o *SAS Scandinavia Hotel*, Holbergsgate 30 (☎22.20.01.21). The majors also have airport desks.

Embassies *Australia*, information office at Jerbanetorget 2 (☎22.41 44 43) – more serious matters are dealt with by Great Britain embassy; *Canada*, Oscarsgate 20 (☎22.46.69.55); *Great Britain*, Ths. Heftyesgate 8 (☎22.55.24.00); *Netherlands*, Oscarsgate 29 (☎22.60.21.93); *USA*, Drammensveien 18 (☎22.44 85 50).

Exchange Outside bank hours Oslo S has an exchange office (June–Sept daily 7am–11pm; Oct–May Mon–Fri 7am–8.30pm, Sat 10am–6pm, Sun noon–6pm). You can also change money and travellers' cheques at the main post office.

Ferry companies *Scandinavian Seaways* (to Copenhagen), Karl Johansgate 1(☎22.41.90.90); *Stena* (to Frederikshavn), Stortingsgatan 5 (☎22.30.50.00); *Color Line* (to Kiel and Hirtshals), ☎22.83.60.10.

Gay Oslo Advice and information from *Det Norske Forbundet av. 1948*, St Olavs Pass 2 (☎22.42.98.54). Gay switchboard on ☎22.42.98.54.

Hospital *Oslo Kommunale Legevakt*, Storgaten 40 (☎22.11.70.70).

Laundry *Bislett Vask og Rens*, Theresesgate 25; *Majorstua Myntvaskeri*, Vibesgate 15.

Pharmacy 24-hour service at *Jernbanetorgets Apotek*, Jernbanetorvet 46.

Police *Oslo Politikammer*, Grønlandsleiret 44 (☎22.66.99.66); bus #72 from the National Theatre.

Post office Main office at Dronningensgate 15 (Mon–Fri 8am–8pm, Sat 9am–3pm).

Telephones Kongensgate 21 (Mon–Fri 9am–8pm, Sat 10am–5pm, Sun noon–6pm), entrance on Prinsensgate.

Travel agents For discount flights, *BIJ* tickets, *ISIC* cards, etc, try *Kilroy Travels*, Nedre Slottsgate 23 (☎22.85.32.00), and out at Universitetssenteret, Blindern (Mon–Fri 8.15am–3.45pm; ☎22.85.32.00); T-bane line #13 to Blindernveien. There's also *NSB Reisebyrå*, Stortingsgata 28 (Mon–Fri 9.30am–4pm).

Women's movement The *Norsk Kvinnessaksforening*, Kvinnehuset, Rådhusgate 2 (Mon–Fri 5–10pm, Sat 11am–5pm; closed in summer; ☎22.41.28.64), can put you in touch with women's groups and provide information on events and activities.

SOUTHERN NORWAY

The half-moon bulge that is **southern Norway** is an immediately appealing region – flatlands and fells topped with a tempting coastal concentration of islands and long beaches – and as such it's the Norwegians' principal domestic holiday choice. Everyone else, though, tends to pass quickly through, and on the whole you'd do best to follow their example. The region may, of course, be your first view of Norway and it's worth spending at least some time at your point of arrival. International ferries put in to the western port of **Stavanger**, the region's major town, and central **Kristiansand**, a lively resort. Both are attractive centres in their own right, Stavanger with its medieval cathedral and small old town, and sea connections with Bergen to the north. On the way to or from Oslo, **Kongsberg** was once an important city, with a grand church that reflects its eighteenth-century role as a centre of silver production.

Stavanger – and north to Bergen

STAVANGER is something of a survivor. While other Norwegian coastal towns have fallen foul of the precarious fortunes of fishing, it has over the years grown into one of Norway's most dynamic economic power bases. Fish canning and its own merchant fleet brought initial prosperity, which shipbuilding and the oil industry have since sustained. It isn't one of Norway's most alluring cities, but it's a brash, international place, worth a little time before moving on to the fjords or Oslo.

The old centre, **Gamle Stavanger**, above the international ferry terminals, is of greatest appeal, a pristinely preserved area of tall wooden warehouses and narrow lanes that was home for seamen and visiting merchants. A note of realism is brought by the **Canning Museum**, at Øvre Strandgate 88 (mid-June to mid-Aug Tues–Sat 11am–3pm, Sun 11am–4pm; rest of year except Dec Sun 11am–4pm; 20kr), a reconstructed sardine-canning factory giving a glimpse of the industry that saved Stavanger from decay in the nineteenth century. Back towards the centre, the **Maritime Museum** at Nedre Strandgate 17 (same times; same ticket) shows the history of Stavanger. Along the length of the harbour, on **Torget**, there's a bustling daily market, while the streets around **Skagen**, on the jut of land forming the eastern side of the harbour, make up the town's shopping area, a bright mix of spidery lanes, pedestrianized streets and white-timbered houses that covers the area occupied by medieval Stavanger. The spiky **Valberg Tower** (Mon–Fri 10am–4pm, Thurs until 6pm, Sat 10am–4pm) was a nineteenth-century fire-watch, and, along with some distinctly unthrilling ceramics and textile displays, gives sweeping views of the city and its industry from the top. The only relic of medieval Stavanger is on the fringes of Torget close to **Breiavatnet** lake in the middle of the city – the twelfth-century **Domkirke** (mid-May to mid-Sept Mon–Sat 9am–6pm, Sun 1–6pm; rest of year Mon–Sat 9am–2pm), whose pointed-hat towers signal a Romanesque church altered irredeemably by modern renovation.

Practicalities

Ferries from Hirtshals and Newcastle arrive a short walk northwest from the main square, Torget; the *Kystveien* ferry from Bergen docks a little further up at Randaberg, 10km north of the city (connecting buses). **Express boats** from Bergen alight at the terminal at the bottom of Kirkegata. The **airport** is 14km south of the city at Sola: an *SAS* bus (30kr) runs into Stavanger, as do half-hourly local buses #143 and #152, dropping you at the **bus and train station** on the western side of Breiavatnet. Just up from the train station, the **tourist office** (Mon–Fri 9am–5pm, Sat 9am–2pm) sells the one, two and three day Stavanger Card, which entitles you to discounts on local buses, museum entry and the like for 95kr, 140kr and 170kr respectively.

If you need to **stay**, there's plenty of choice. The cheapest option, at 50kr per night, is the official *Mosvangen* **youth hostel**, Henrik Ibsensgate 21 (☎51.87.09.77), with beds for 110kr, double rooms 300kr; it's a thirty-minute walk from the centre, down Madlaveien and left on to the E18, from which a cycle-path leads around a lake to the hostel. Otherwise take bus #78 from the train station. Of a few **pensions**, *Bergeland Gjestgiveri*, Vikedalsgata 1a (☎51.53.41.10; ⑤), east of the train station, throws breakfast in with the price. Some of the **hotels** have summer deals between June and August: for example the *Grand Hotel*, Klubbgata 3 (☎51.53.30.20; ⑥) with bath and TV; and the *Commandør Hotel*, Valberggata 9 (☎51.52.80.00; ⑤), right in the centre. For **camping**, there's a site next to the *Mosvangen* youth hostel, open June to August, with cabins for rent. For **food**, the youth hostel serves reasonable and filling meals, as does *Cinema Paradis Bistro*, Skagen 6. The *Hong Kong Garden*, Østervåg 9, serves all-in Chinese lunches for 50kr, and *Zorba's*, Sølvberggata 14, dishes up some fine medium-priced Greek dishes.

The route to Bergen

If you're a train fanatic or already committed to a rail pass, you need to go back to Oslo to travel on to Bergen. If not, you can get there more directly by bus and ferry. For speed if not economy, the best bet is the *Hurtigbåt* or **express boat**, which runs all year. This requires advance seat reservations (☎51.52.20.90) and costs around 400kr one-way, though students, *IYHF* members and rail pass holders qualify for various discounts. The trip takes four hours. Cheaper but slower (175kr; students 120kr), the twice-daily *Kystveien* **ferry** takes about seven hours, and leaves from Randaberg, a ten-kilometre bus ride from Stavanger Marina. Another option is the **ferry from Newcastle**, which during summer continues on to Bergen and charges about 250kr (25 percent student discount) for the hop. Tickets for all are available from the terminal offices or travel agents in the city.

With more time to spare, **Route 1** or the *Kystvegen*, which cuts across the western archipelago on a succession of connecting buses and ferries, is more interesting, and more scenic. Services (on which you should pay as you go) vary, but in summer the first bus usually departs Stavanger at 9am, arriving in Bergen at around 6pm. There is also an alternative **route inland** and then north from Haugesund. One daily bus (at 9am; 133kr) makes the two-hour journey to **ODDA**, situated on a long finger of the Hardangerfjord, which also has a **youth hostel** (☎52.71.21.46; ③), from where it's a ferry and bus ride to Bergen.

Kristiansand

Founded by and named after Christian IV, **KRISTIANSAND** is the closest thing to a resort there is in Norway, a bright, energetic place which thrives on its ferry connections with England and Denmark, and its excellent, if crowded, beaches. The town has retained the seventeenth-century quadrant plan that characterized all Christian's projects and is worth a quick skirt around. Of specific sights, the squat **Christiansholm Fortress**, overlooking the colourful marina at the east harbour, these days hosts arts and crafts displays. A better bet is to take a two-hour cruise in the offshore waters on the *M/S Maarten* (mid-June to early Sept Mon–Sat 11am & 1pm; 60kr), from the fish market harbour at the end of Vestre Strandgate. This stops at several islands which have been designated free **camping** areas, so you can doss down and catch the boat back the next day. **Train, bus** and **ferry** arrivals are all fairly close to each other, by Vestre Havn, on the edge of the town grid. The **tourist office** is a few steps up at Dronningensgate 2 (summer Mon–Fri 8am–7pm, Sat 10am–7pm, Sun 1–7pm; winter Mon–Fri 8am–4pm), and can provide a handy map and information on accessible beaches and islands. The cheapest **hotels** are the *Norge*, Dronningegsgate 5 (☎38.02.00.00; ⑤), and the *Bondeheimen Hotel*, Kirkegata 15 (☎38.02.44.40; ⑤)–

though they're no real bargain even with breakfast. The **youth hostel** at Kongsgård Allé 33 (mid-June to mid-Aug; ☎38.09.53.69; ②) is 2km from the train station; cross the Lundsbroen bridge, walk up Østerveien and it's off to the right in the *Badminton Senteret*. The **campsite** (June–Aug) has a good, small stretch of beach close by; it's on Marvikveien in Roligheden, in the same direction as the youth hostel. Once across the bridge, turn right along Kuholmsveien and left along Tegelverksveien.

Kongsberg

Only an hour or so from Oslo, **KONGSBERG** is a more vital stop, the old silver mining centre of Christian IV, and in the seventeenth and eighteenth centuries the only place in the world where silver could be found in a pure form. The silver works closed in 1805, when Kongsberg began to make money out of its Royal Mint, and, a few years later, the armaments factory opened which employs people to this day. Now it's a pleasant provincial town, with a river which splashes through the centre in a series of three waterfalls.

The **silver mines** (tours mid-May to Aug; 40kr) are 7km out of town at Sølvverket, a bit of a struggle to get to without your own transport. There are buses to Notodden (June to mid-Aug Mon–Fri 3–4 daily) from the bus terminus outside the train station, or it's possible to hitch along the E76 in the Larvik direction. It's well worth the effort, since the informative tour includes a ride on a train through black tunnels to the shafts, a thrilling way to spend the afternoon. Back in town, **Kongsberg Kirke** (mid-May to Aug Mon–Fri 10am–4pm, Sat 10am–1pm; rest of year Tues–Fri 10am–noon; 10kr) is the largest and arguably most beautiful Baroque church in Norway, dating from the most prosperous mining period at the end of the eighteenth century. It's a grand affair, with a showily mock-marbled western wall, unusually comprising altar, pulpit and organ: from his place over the altar the priest would exhort the assembled workers to be more industrious in the pursuit of profit. The plush seating arrangements were hierarchically defined and determined the church's principal fixtures. On the opposite wall is the "King's Box" and boxes for the silver-works managers, while other officials sat in the glass-enclosed "cases". The pews on the ground floor were reserved for women, while the sweeping three-tiered balcony was the domain of the Kongsberg workers and petit bourgeoisie. Enthusiasts or thwarted mine-visitors might also enjoy the **Mining Museum** (mid-May to Aug daily 10am–4pm; 20kr, students free), housed in the old smelting works at the river's edge, but merely pottering around is much the most enjoyable way of spending time here.

The **tourist office** (Jan to mid-June & mid-Aug to Dec Mon–Fri 9am–4pm; mid-June to mid-Aug Mon–Sat 9am–7pm, Sun noon–4pm) is outside the **train station**, at the top of Storgaten, and can direct you to a **campsite** down by the river which has cabins for rent. Over the bridge and further up the main road towards the church is the all-year **youth hostel** (☎32.73.20.24; ③), breakfast included.

BERGEN AND THE FJORDS

The fjords are the most familiar and alluring image of Norway: huge clefts in the landscape which occur throughout the country right up to the Russian border. Wild, rugged and peaceful, these water-filled wedges of space are visually stunning; indeed, the entire fjord region elicits inordinate amounts of purple prose from tourist office handouts, and for once it's rarely overstated. Under the circumstances it seems churlish to complain of the thousands of summer visitors who tramp through the villages – quiet and isolated places the other nine months of the year. The rolling mountains are relentlessly roamed by walkers, the fjords cruised by steady flotillas of white ferries. But don't be put off: there's been little development and what there is is still not intrusive.

As for specific destinations, **Bergen**, Norway's second largest city, is a welcoming place and a handy springboard for the western fjords, notably the **Flåm Valley** and its inspiring mountain railway, which trundles down to the **Aurlandsfjord**, a tiny arm of the mighty **Sognefjord**, Norway's longest and deepest. North of the Sognefjord, there is the smaller but more varied **Nordfjord**, with patches of the **Jostedalsbreen** glacier just beyond, mainland Europe's largest ice sheet. The tiny S-shaped **Geirangerfjord**, further north again, is a marked contrast – tiny, sheer and rugged – while the northern-most **Romsdalfjord** and its many branches and inlets show signs of splintering into the scattered archipelagos which characterize the northern Norwegian coast, reaching pinnacles of isolation in the **Trollstigen** mountain highway nearby.

By rail, you can only reach Bergen in the south and Åndalsnes in the very north. For everything in between – the Nordfjord, Jostedalsbreen glacier and Sognefjord – you're confined to buses and ferries, and although they virtually all connect up with each other, it means that there is no set way to approach the fjord region, and routes are really a matter of personal choice. It's a good idea to pick up full **bus and ferry time-tables** from the local tourist offices whenever you can, and be aware that shorter bus routes are often part of a longer routing on which the buses and ferries link up. Unlike the car ferries, whose fares are proportional to distance travelled, the impressively speedy *Express boat* services are considered an extension of the train system, and hold-ers of student and rail passes qualify for fifty percent discounts.

Bergen

Though known as the rainiest place in Norway, **BERGEN** has a spectacular setting among seven hills and is one of the country's most enjoyable cities. There's plenty to see, from Bergen's fine surviving medieval buildings to a series of good museums – the best located in the atmospheric old warehouse quarter, dating from the city's days as the northernmost Hanseatic port. And it's well located for some of Norway's most spectacular scenic attractions, both around the city and further north.

Arrival and accommodation

Bergen is a busy international port and may well be your first stop in Norway. **International ferries** arrive at Skolltegrunnskaien, the quay just beyond Bergenhus fortress; **domestic ferries** line up on the opposite side of the harbour at separate quays stretching down towards Torget. The **train** and **bus station** face Strømgaten, a few minutes' walk from the centre. The **airport** is 19km south of the city and *SAS* buses (every 20 mins; 36kr) connect with the bus station. The city is also a terminal port for the *Hurti-grute* **coastal steamer** which leaves from the harbour (Frieleneskaien) behind the university.

The **tourist office** is on Bryggen (May–Sept Mon–Sat 8.30am–9pm, Sun 10am–7pm; Oct–April Mon–Sat 9am–4pm) and has free copies of the *Bergen Guide*, an exhaustive consumer's guide to the city, a city transport plan, and the useful **tourist ticket** (60kr), a 48-hour unlimited bus pass. Otherwise, each flat fare ticket is 12kr, bought on the bus and valid for an hour. Another useful link to be aware of is the **ferry** (Mon–Fri 7am–4.15pm; 7kr) across the harbour, from Carl Sundsgate to a point near Bryggen.

For **accommodation**, the **YMCA hostel**, Nedre Korskirkalm 4 (June–Aug; ☎55.31.72.52; ②), and the Christian-run *Intermission*, Kalfarveien 8 (mid-June to mid-Aug; ☎55.31.32.75; ②), behind the station, are the city's cheapest options with free show-ers, kitchen and laundry facilities. They can get full, though, in which case you should try either the *InterRail Point*, Nedre Korskirkealmenningen 4 (July to mid-Aug; ☎55.31.72.52; ②), or the enormous *Montana* **youth hostel** (May to mid-Oct; ☎55.29.29.00; ③), 5km from the centre – take bus #4 from the main post office. The tour-ist office books **private rooms** at 260–310kr a double plus a 15–20kr booking fee. There are also several **pensions** in the centre, of which *Mrs Berntsen's*, Klosteret 16 (☎55.23.35.02; ③), is best; otherwise, try the *Fagerheim* at Kalvedalsveien 49a (☎55.31.01.72; ③), beyond the station. The nearest **campsite** is *Bergenshallens Camping*, ten minutes away on bus #3 from the post office, though it gets full very quickly and is only open mid-June to mid-August. Instead, try the *Paradis Sport Centre* on the E68, close by the site of the Fantoft stave church.

The City

Founded in 1070, Bergen was the largest and most important town in medieval Norway, capital city by 1240, and later a Hanseatic port and religious centre which supported thirty churches and monasteries. Little of that era survives, although the medieval fortress – Bergenhus – still commands the entrance to the harbour. The city divides into two distinct parts: the wharf area, **Bryggen**, under the shadow of the fortress, once the working centre of the Hanseatic merchants and now the oldest part of Bergen; and the **modern centre**, which stretches from behind the main square down the long central Nordnes peninsula, taking in some of the best of Bergen's museums and shops. In between the two, the fish market at **Torget** (Mon–Sat 8am–3pm) is worth a wander, a short stroll south of which **Marken**, a hilly cobbled street of leaning wooden houses now for the most part converted into craft and clothes shops, is a refreshing change from the rest of the soulless centre, whose main attraction is really museums. The **Rasmus Meyer's Collection** on Rasmus Meyers Allé (mid-May to mid-Sept Mon–Sat 11am–4pm, Sun noon–3pm; rest of year Tues–Sun noon–3pm; 15kr) is one of the best of these, a rambling town house featuring Norwegian art with an upper floor almost entirely devoted to Munch. The **Municipal Art Museum** next door (mid-May to mid-Sept Mon–Sat 11am–4pm, Sun noon–3pm; rest of year Tues–Sun noon–3pm; 15kr), covers the last 150 years of Norwegian painting, dominated – like the period itself – by the uninspired landscapes of J.C. Dahl, although it also has an impressive cache of European moderns in an adjacent gallery. Further west, the **University Museums** on Sydneshaugen in the university grounds (daily 11am–2pm) are basically three collections – maritime, historical and natural historical – all well laid out and exhaustive; the Historical Museum (closed Fri; free) is much the most interesting, especially strong on the region's cultural history, with some outstanding displays of medieval church art and architecture, including a room full of sculpted pulpits and thirteenth-century altarpieces. Finally, there's a marvellous **Aquarium** (daily May–Sept 9am–8pm; Oct–April 10am–6pm; 25kr), the best in Norway; take bus #4 from the city centre.

The eastern side of the harbour, around **Bryggen**, is more interesting, the site of the original settlement at Bergen and now its best-preserved quarter, with the former homes and warehouses of the Hanseatic merchants who dominated life in Bergen from the early fifteenth century onwards. One of the best-preserved of the warehouses doubles as the **Hanseatic Museum** (June–Aug daily 9am–5pm; May & Sept daily 11am–2pm; Oct–May Sun, Mon, Wed & Fri 11am–2pm; 15kr), containing the possessions and documents of contemporary families. Close by, the **Bryggens Museum** (May–Aug daily 10am–5pm; Sept–April Mon–Fri 11am–3pm, Sat noon–3pm, Sun noon–4pm; 15kr) is Bergen's showpiece, containing a cultural muddle of things dug up here through the ages. The imaginative exhibitions attempt a complete reassembly of medieval life, put into context by the reconstruction in situ of the twelfth-century foundations of some of Bryggen's original boathouses and warehouses – and, outside, the scant thirteenth-century ruins of the **Lavranskirken** and **Mariagildeskålen** or guildhall. Behind the museum, the **Mariakirken** (mid-May to mid-Sept Mon–Fri 11am–4pm; mid-Sept to mid-May Tues–Fri noon–1.30pm; June–Sept 10kr) is Bergen's oldest extant building, a delightfully decorated twelfth-century treasure. Further up the quayside, past the warehouses and their narrow squeezed passages, is the **Rosenkrantz Tower** (mid-May to mid-Sept daily 10am–4pm; rest of year Sun noon–3pm; 10kr), enlarged in 1565 from its thirteenth-century foundations and used as a fortified residence by the lord of Bergenhus, Erik Rosenkrantz. There are guided tours every hour, and the winding spiral staircases, dungeon and low corridors make it an exciting half-hour's scramble.

Bryggen is bounded by **Øvregaten**, marking the extent of rows of tenements and warehouses that reached back from the quayside. Øvregaten 50, a building known as **Schøtstuene** (June–Aug daily 10am–4pm; May & Sept daily 11am–2pm; Oct–May Tues, Thurs, Sat & Sun 11am–2pm; 15kr) comprised the old Hanseatic Assembly Rooms, and exhibitions inside shed more light on daily life in the period, though if you've time, it's far better to climb the hill behind the houses for a bird's-eye view of the layout of Bryggen and surroundings, perhaps continuing up to **Mount Fløyen**. A **funicular train** (14kr each way) does it more quickly every half-hour until 11pm.

Eating and drinking

For **breakfast**, *Baker Brun* on Torget sells the city's speciality, the *skillingsboller* – a sugar-strewn bun. If you're around between the end of August and mid-June, the *Student Centre* canteen, Parkveien 1, does **snacks** and coffee, and full **meals** for under 35kr, and you don't need student ID. Otherwise you're best off at one of Bergen's assembly-line *Kaffistovas*, generally good for fish dishes – branches at Torget 1 and Strandkaien 2. You might also try the *Polar Bear* bar on Ole Bulls Plass, which serves some of the cheapest pizzas in town. There's a branch of *Peppe's Pizza* at Finnegården 2, while the *The Great India*, an Indian restaurant on Marken, near the train station, does some vegetarian meals. A little more upmarket, though also suitable for vegetarians, is the 150kr lunch buffet served at the *Grand Hotel Terminus*, King Oscars Gate 71. In the **evenings**, the sweatiest place in town is *Hulen*, a club in an old air-raid shelter at Olav Ryesvei 47 that has cheap beer, and hosts live bands midweek and discos at the weekends. *Theatercafeen*, Chr. Michelsensgate 10, is a popular pub, and *Garage Rock Club*, 14 Christiesgate, is probably the best, hosting bands towards the end of the week.

Listings

Airlines *SAS*, inside *SAS Royal Hotel* on Bryggen (☎55.23.63.00).

Consulate *Great Britain*, Carl Konowsgate 34 (☎55.34 85 05).

Car rental *Budget*, Sverresgate 12 (☎55.90 26 15); *Hertz*, Nygårdsgaten 89 (☎55.32 79 20).

Emergencies Casualty (24-hour) and emergency dental care (daily 10–11am & 7–9pm) at Lars Hillesgate 30 (☎55.32 11 20).

Pharmacy *Apoteket Nordstjernen*, at the bus station. Open 7.30am–midnight.

Post office At the junction of Olav Kyrresgate and Smastrandgate (Mon–Wed & Fri 8am–5pm, Thurs 8am–6pm, Sat 9am–2pm).

Telephones Use the Telegraph Building at Byparken (Mon–Fri 8.30am–4pm).

Train enquiries ☎55.31.96.40.

Travel agents *Norske Vandrerhjem*, Strandgaten 4 (☎55.32 68 80).

Around Bergen

There is more to Bergen than the city centre, not least a number of features just outside the city limits worth a brief look – Edvard Grieg's home is still there, but the excellent **Fantoft** stave church, reputedly the finest of its kind was burnt to the ground in 1992. Suspicions of diabolic intent are rife. Rebuilding started from scratch is underway and should be complete by summer 1994. Ask locally for details. Further out, though, the fjords beckon; if you're not journeying through the rest of the region you can get a taste by taking the train down the valley to **Flåm** and the **Aurlandsfjord** – one of the most popular of all fjord trips. The free *Sognfjorden* booklet from tourist offices is invaluable for transport and accommodation information.

Troldhaugen

The home of **Edvard Grieg**, Norway's only composer of international renown, is reached by regular bus from the bus station to Hopsbroen, a fifteen-minute journey, from where the house is a twenty-minute walk: turn right from the stop, left at Hopsvegen, and follow the signs. **Troldhaugen** (May–Sept daily 9.30am–5.30pm; 15kr) was Grieg's residence for 22 years, and he composed many of his best works here. The house is virtually as he left it, a jumble of photos, manuscripts and period furniture, and if you can bear the hagiographical atmosphere the obligatory conducted tour is quite entertaining. The composer and his wife – the singer, Nina Hagerup – are buried outside in a rockface tomb sealed with a memorial stone.

The train to Flåm

If you're short on time but want to sample a bit of fjord scenery, make the **train journey** east from Bergen, through Voss, along the main rail line as far as barren Myrdal, from where a branch line plummets 900m down into the **Flåm valley** (50kr). The track took four years to lay, and is one of the steepest anywhere in the world. You can make the trip on part of the Bergen tourist office's "Norway-in-a-Nutshell" ticket, an inclusive ticket covering the Voss–Myrdal–Flåm–Gudvangen–Voss route – cost 390kr.

FLÅM village, the train's destination, lies alongside meadows and orchards on the **Aurlandsfjord**, a matchstick-thin branch of the Sognefjord. It's a tiny village that on summer days can be packed with tourists who pour off the train, eat lunch in one of the few hotels and then head out by bus and ferry, having captured the stunning valley on film. There's not much here, but out of season, or in bad weather, or even in the early evening when the day-trippers have all moved on, Flåm can be a wonderfully restful place to spend the night. If you decide to stay, there are a couple of small **hotels**, the *Fretheim Hotell* (☎57.63.21.21; ③) and *Heimly Lodge* (☎57.63.23.00; ②), or head instead for *Flåm Camping* and the nearby **youth hostel** (☎57.63.21.21.; ②) – both are only a few minutes' signposted walk from the train station. The **tourist office** (May–Sept daily 8.45am–8.30pm), in a small wooden hut on the station platform, is handy for advance inclusive ferry/bus tickets back to Voss (90kr).

The route to Oslo

The **rail route between Bergen and Oslo** is one of the most impressive rides in the country, taking in a good number of forests, waterfalls, windswept mountains and wild valleys. You can pick the journey up at either Myrdal or **VOSS** if you've come from the north, the latter a beautifully sited but rather dull town that's mainly visited for its winter sports. Beyond here is good hiking country, and there are a couple of well-placed **youth hostels** – at Mjølfjell (☎57.51.81.11; ③), 6km from the station, and at Geilo (☎32.09.03.00; ②). The higher reaches of the rail line are desolate places even in good weather, and at Finse, the line's high point, early August snow isn't unusual.

The Sognefjord

Apart from Flåm, you'd do best to approach the **Sognefjord** from the north: it's on that bank that most of its appealing spots lie, and in any case transport connections on the south side (from Vinje) are, at best, sketchy. **BALESTRAND** is a good first stop (express boats from Bergen and Flåm), a tourist destination since the mid-nineteenth century when it was discovered by European travellers in search of cool, clear air and mountain scenery. Kaiser Wilhelm II was a frequent visitor, as were the British, and these days the village is used as a touring base for the immediate area – though farming remains the villagers' principal livelihood. Buses arrive on the quayside, where you'll find the **tourist office** (mid-June to mid-Aug Mon–Sat 8am–6pm, Sun 11am–

3pm; reduced hours a month either side). A hundred metres away, in the comfortable *Kringsjå Hotel*, the **youth hostel** (mid-June to Aug; ☎57.69.13.03; ②) does excellent-value food. There are a couple of other reasonably priced hotels in the village, and a **campsite** with cheap cabins, 1km or so past the English church.

There's not too much to see in Balestrand itself, but **DRAGSVIK**, directly across the arm of the fjord (reached by an irregular boat service, speak to the ferryman by the wharf; 15kr), now has the brand-new **Sognefjord Vikingsenter** (May–Sept 10am–6pm; April & Oct open on request; 40kr), a terrific recreation of a Viking village aimed at showing all facets of their life including the food; meals available (Wed, Fri & Sun evenings from 75kr). On the southern side of the fjord, **VIK** (reached by ferry to Vang-snes from Balestrand or nearby Hella, then bus) is home to one of the Sognefjord's several **stave churches**. This one, **Hoprekstad** (15kr), is twelfth-century and famed for the sculpted heads on its Gothic altar canopy. Otherwise, you can pick up the daily **express boat** service from Balestrand to Flåm and Gudvangen, or take one of several daily ferries across the fjord (32kr) to **FJÆRLAND**, formerly one of the most isolated spots on the Sognefjord. Sited at the end of the wild **Fjærlandsfjord**, it's a good base for visiting two arms of the **Jostedalsbreen glacier**. One or two buses daily (mid-May to mid-Sept; 65kr return) leave the village for combined visits to the Flatbreen and Bøyabreen arms, calling at the **Norsk Bremuseum**, or Norwegian Glacier Centre (June–Aug daily 9am–7pm; April, May, Sept & Oct 10am–4pm; 60kr), 3km north of Fjærland, which tells you more than you ever wanted to know about glaciers through hands-on audiovisual displays. The whole package can be organized with discounts through the tourist office in Balestrand.

The ferry from Balestrand also calls at Hella, from where it's possible to pick up the eastbound bus to **SOGNDAL** – bigger and livelier than Balestrand and a much better place to stay, and once the road is finished (scheduled Oct 1994), an alternative link to Fjærland. Its **tourist office** (June–Aug Mon–Fri 9am–8pm, Sat 10am–1pm, Sun 1–6pm; rest of year Mon–Fri 11am–4pm) is in the *Kulturhuset* next to the *K Senteret* shopping centre, and has free hiking maps of the area and **bikes** for rent. There is a comfortable **youth hostel** in the Folkehøyskolen (mid-June to mid-Aug; ☎57.67.20.33; ②), and the rooms at the *Loftesnes Pensjonat* at Fjørevegen 17 (☎57.67.15.77; ⑤) are a good deal, too.

KAUPANGER, 12km southeast of Sogndal, has a heavily restored thirteenth-century **stave church** and a **folk museum** with the usual open-air buildings. Regular buses drop you at both, just outside Kaupanger's centre, or simply follow the old Sogn-dal–Kaupanger road which skirts the fjord – a lovely three-hour hike. Kaupanger also has some important **ferry connections**, with boats leaving regularly to Gudvangen (one starting point for ferries to the Aurlandsfjord and Flåm valley) and Revsnes, from where buses make the haul over the mountains to Oslo via Fagernes.

The Nordfjord and Jostedalsbreen Glacier

STRYN, set amid the green slopes of the **Nordfjord**, is an important transport hub and may merit an overnight stop, in which case there's a **youth hostel** (mid-May to mid-Sept; ☎71.61.13.01; ②), to the right out of the bus station and signposted off to the left – a ten-minute walk up the hill. There's also a **campsite** down the hill by the main road. Several interconnected stretches of water make up the Nordfjord, all with different names but characterized by the same high surrounding mountains. With your own transport it's perhaps the most accessible of the fjords: unlike the Sognefjord, roads run along both banks and flank each branch. The most straightforward route is east, to a cluster of villages – **LOEN, OLDEN, INNVIK** and **UTVIK** – at the head of a bulbous nodule off the main fjord, easily reached by bus or on foot. They're all noted centres for hiking in the lush valleys that radiate out from the fjord, and from Loen and Olden you're within striking distance of their respective glacial lakes. Each village has at least one **campsite**, usually with cabins, and if you want more comfort, Loen has a choice of **pensions** with rooms at around 300kr.

You can't help but notice the nearby, lurking presence of the **Jostedalsbreen glacier** at some stage of your wanderings: the 800-square-kilometre ice plateau dominates the whole of the inner Nordfjord region. Lying between the eastern ends of the Nordfjord and Sognefjord, its 24 arms flowing down into the nearby valleys, it's Jostedalsbreen that gives the local rivers and glacial lakes their distinctive blue-green colouring. From Stryn a 10am bus (June to mid-Sept; 1hr; 90kr return) leaves for the most accessible arm at **BRIKSDAL**, from where it's an easy 45-minute walk to the glacier, passing waterfalls and rivers on the way. Once there, it's a simple matter to get close to the ice itself, though you can hire a pony and trap at the souvenir/café area for around 130kr. The return bus leaves at 2.15pm.

The Geirangerfjord

The **Geirangerfjord** is one of the region's smallest fjords, but also one of its most breathtaking. A convoluted branch of the Storfjord, it cuts well inland, marked by impressive waterfalls and with a tiny village at either end of the fjord's snake-like profile. You can reach the Geirangerfjord from the north or south, but you'd do best to approach from the north if you can; it's visitable on a long day trip from Åndalsnes, via the wonderful **Trollstigen Highway**, which climbs through some of the country's highest peaks before thundering down a final set of switchbacks and stopping high up on the *Ørnevegen*, the Eagle's Highway, for a first view of the fjord and the village glinting in the distance. There is little as stunning anywhere in western Norway, and it can all be seen from mid-June to August on a twice daily bus following this so-called "Golden Route" (100kr).

GEIRANGER village enjoys a commanding position at one end of the 16km S-shaped fjord, and, despite a couple of large new hotels, remains almost absurdly picturesque. Most people arrive only to take a cruise on the fjord, afterwards returning to Åndalsnes or continuing south to the Nordfjord, but you may find it difficult to tear yourself away. The **hotels** are uniformly expensive, but there is a **campsite** bang at the foot of the fjord in the village (though this gets full in summer) and another, the *Grande*, with cabins, 2km away also at the water's edge. The Geiranger **tourist office** (June–Aug daily 9am–6pm) pushes expensive sightseeing boat tours of the fjord, but you'd be better off taking the car ferry (27kr) to **HELLESYLT**, an hour's ride away through the double bend of the fjord – a former important Viking port that's now primarily a stopoff on tourist itineraries. The **tourist office** is on the quayside (June–Aug daily 9am–5.30pm) and there's a **youth hostel** (June–Aug; ☎70.26.51.28; ②) on a hill on the right of the village, with fjord-facing rooms and cabins for rent. You might want to splash out instead on the double rooms with bath at the *Grand Hotel* (☎70.26.51.00; ⑤), breakfast included. The nearest **campsite** is 2km away at Stadheimfossen (☎71.26.50.79).

The Romsdalsfjord and around

Travelling from Oslo by rail to Åndalsnes, the line splits at **DOMBÅS**, a regional hiking centre with a **youth hostel** (mid-June to mid-Aug; ☎61.24.10.45; ②); however, you might prefer to push straight on. There are two lines to choose from, both impressive: the **Dovre line** continues northwards over the fells to Oppdal, and ultimately to Trondheim, while the **Rauma line** begins a thrilling two-hour roller-coaster rattle down through the mountains to the **Romsdalsfjord**. Apart from the Sognefjord, reached from Bergen, the Romsdalsfjord is the only other Norwegian fjord accessible by train, which explains the number of backpackers wandering its principal town of

ÅNDALSNES, many people's first – sometimes only – contact with the fjord country. Despite a wonderful setting between lofty peaks and looking-glass water, the town is unexciting, and you'd do best to get out into the surroundings as soon as possible. The best and most logical route onwards is south to the Geirangerfjord, over the **Trollstigen** (see above).

With two buses a day to Geiranger to the south, several to Molde to the west and one to Ålesund to meet each train, you should have no trouble moving on, but if you need to stay there's a comfortable **youth hostel** (mid-May to mid-Sept; ☎71.22.13.82; ②), a two-kilometre hike along the E9 towards Ålesund, which rents out **bikes** – much the best form of transport for exploring the immediate area – or you can make the 9km trek out to the Trollveggen Cliff, the highest overhanging mountain wall in Europe. There's also a **campsite** (mid-May to mid-Sept) with cabins and rowboats for hire; turn first left before the hostel, 25 minutes walk in all. The **tourist office** in town (mid-June to mid-Aug Mon–Sat 9.30am–9.30pm, Sun 3.30–9.30pm; rest of year Mon–Sat 9am–6pm, Sun noon–6pm) also rents **bikes**. Otherwise, stock up in the small daily market and climb the local **mountain**, the huge shadowy mass that lurks behind the town – a steep two-hour assault.

From Åndalsnes buses head off to Molde, usually via Åfarnes, a superb route and much the best reason for making the journey. Though prettily situated, **MOLDE** itself, sheltered beneath a weighty range of snowcapped mountains, has little to offer. Many of its original features were laid waste by fire in 1916 and German bombs in 1940, and to make a visit really pay dividends you should contrive to be here during the week-long **international jazz festival**, held in the middle of July, and usually including a smattering of big names among the home-grown talent. The **tourist office** is in the Central Rådhus (June–Aug Mon–Sat 9am–6pm, Sun 9am–4pm) and will book private rooms for 250kr a double (no booking fee). The only cheap accommodation is 3km west of town (bus #10 and #40) at *Rauma Folkehøyskole*, Raumaveien 2–4 (mid-June to mid-Aug; ☎71.21.51.55; ②), and during the festival *Jazzcampen*, a **campsite** 2km west along Julsundvegen.

On the southern tip of the Romsdalsfjord, Norway's biggest fishing port, **ÅLESUND**, is immediately and distinctively different from the functional stone and brick of other modern Norwegian town centres: a conglomeration of proud grey and white facades, lavishly decorated and topped with a forest of turrets and pinnacles. In 1904, a disastrous fire left 10,000 people homeless and the town centre destroyed. A hectic reconstruction programme saw almost the entire area rebuilt by 1907 in a style which borrowed heavily from the German Jugendstil movement. Kaiser Wilhelm II, who used to holiday around Ålesund, gave assistance, and the architects ended up creating a strange hybrid of up-to-date foreign influences and folksy local elements – the buildings showing off decorative flowers, dragons, faces and fairy-tale turrets.

A stroll down **Kongensgate** reveals many of the best features of Ålesund, but most of the central streets are as decorative as each other. There's a **museum** at Rasmus Rønnebergsgate 16 (Mon–Sat 11am–3pm, Sun noon–3pm; 15kr) which records the devastation caused by the 1904 fire in a series of gloomy photographs and models. Otherwise, make a trip to the neighbouring **islands**, which have a variety of attractions including a thirteenth-century marble church (a rarity in Norway) and some Viking necropoli. The **tourist office** is in the Rådhuset (June to mid-Aug Mon–Fri 9am–6pm, Sat 9am–3pm, Sun noon–5pm; rest of year Mon–Fri 9am–4pm). The *Aarsæthergården Pensjonat* at Hellegate 6 (☎70.12.70.30; ④) has **rooms**, and there are two local **campsites**, one of which, 5km from the centre on the #10 and #22 bus routes, has good double rooms at around 150kr. For **eating**, *Skateflua Kafeteria* on the ferry quay is the cheapest place for **lunches** and large sandwiches, or try the more substantial meals (60–90kr) at *Café Hoffmann* in the **Hoffmannsgården** shopping mall on Kongensgate.

NORTHERN NORWAY

The long, thin counties of **Trøndelag** and **Nordland** mark the transition from rural southern to blustery northern Norway. The main town of Trøndelag, **Trondheim**, is easily accessible from Oslo by train, but north of here feels very far removed from the capital and travelling becomes more of a slog as the distances between places grow ever greater. In **Nordland** things get increasingly wild, though save the scenery there is little of delaying interest before the handsomely sited steel town of **Mo-i-Rana**. Just north of here you cross the **Arctic Circle**, and the land becomes ever more spectacular, not least on the offshore chain of the **Lofoten Islands**, whose idyllic fishing villages and cheap accommodation merit a stop. Back on the mainland, **Narvik** was scene of some of the fiercest fighting by the Allies and Norwegian resistance in World War II and is now a modern port handling vast quantities of iron ore amid some startling rocky surroundings. Further north still, the provinces of **Troms** and **Finnmark** are enticing lands, too, but the travelling can be harder still up here, the specific attractions well distanced and – when you reach them – subtle in their appeal. It was from **Tromsø**, northern Norway's largest urban centre and a lively university town, that the king and his government proclaimed a "Free Norway" in 1940 before fleeing into exile in Britain. The appeal of Finnmark is less obvious: much of it was laid waste during World War II by a combination of Russian bombs and the retreating German army's scorched-earth policy and it's now possible to drive for hours without coming across a building more than forty years old. Most travellers head straight for **Nordkapp** from where the Midnight Sun is visible between mid-May and the end of July, though you should also consider travelling inland to the intriguing *Same* towns of **Kautokeino** and **Karasjok** where, in the endless flat scrub plains – the *Finnmarksvidda* – winter temperatures plummet to -25°C. All this is approached from Oslo via **Lillehammer**, site of the 1994 Winter Olympics, and Røros, Norway's highest mountain town.

The **train** network reaches as far north as Fauske, **buses** making the link to Narvik, from where a separate rail line runs the few kilometres to the border and then south through Sweden. Further north, approaches are more limited, and access is either by the *Hurtigrute* steamer or bus. The *Hurtigrute* takes the best part of two days to circumnavigate the huge fjords between Harstad and Kirkenes; **bus** transport throughout the summer (and some of the winter) is efficient and regular, using the windswept E6 Arctic Highway as far as Kirkenes, branching off to Nordkapp and the *Same* towns.

Lillehammer

If you are reading this after February 1994, the Winter Olympics at **Lillehammer**, 170km north of Oslo and on the train route to Dombås and Trondheim, will be over, their legacy of new sports facilities and hotels destined to be underutilized. Outside the skiing season, a brief stop is rewarded by the attractive Swiss-style wooden architecture and the opportunity to visit the Sandvig Collection at **Maihuagen** (generally daily 10am–4pm; June–Aug 9am–6pm; 40kr; free, guided tours in English), a ten-minute walk along Anders Sandvig Gate. It's northern Europe's largest open-air museum, a resiting of around 140 buildings, including working farms complete with animals, a thirteenth-century stave church and workshop interiors decked out with authentic tools – 30,000 exhibits in all, and the work of one man, Anders Sandvig.

The **train station** and **bus terminal** are on Jernbanetorget, at the bottom of Jernbanegata, a short walk up Storgata from the **tourist office**, Lilletorget 1 (June to mid-Aug Mon–Fri 9am–8.30pm, Sat 9am–6pm, Sun 11am–6pm; mid-Aug to May Mon–Fri 9am–4pm, Sat 10am–2pm). Apart from the welter of hotels likely to be offering competitive rates, the mainstays of budget accommodation are, as ever, the **youth hostel**, 2.5km north of town at the **Smested Sommerhotell**, Smestadveien 14 (mid-June to mid-Aug; ☎61.25.09.87; ②) and its adjacent **campsite**.

Røros

RØROS, Norway's highest mountain town, is an airy, blustery place even on a summer's afternoon, and, despite a trickle of tourists, is little changed since its money-spinning days as a copper mining town. In the centre, **Røros kirke** (mid-June to Aug Mon–Sat 10am–5pm; early June & Sept Mon–Fri 2–4pm; free, frequent guided tours 12kr) is the most obvious target for a stroll, a dominant reminder of the economic power fostered by the mines in the eighteenth century. Built in 1784, and once the only stone building in the town, it's more like a theatre than a religious edifice: a huge structure capable of seating 2000 people, designed to overawe rather than inspire. A two-tiered gallery runs around the church with separate boxes for the rich, while a royal box holds commanding views from the back. Immediately below the church lies the oldest part of Røros, grass-thatched miners' cottages, storehouses and workshops in the shadow of the mountainous slagheap. **Malmplassen** (literally "ore-place") is at the heart of the old mining and working area: there's an obvious division between the bigger houses at the bottom end of town, where the owners and overseers lived, and the smaller artisans' dwellings further up, many of which have become art and craft shops. You can get a little of the flavour of the old days at the **Røros Museum**, in a reconstruction of the old smelting works (May, early June & mid-Aug to Dec Mon–Fri 11am–3.30pm, Sat & Sun 11am–2pm; early June to mid-Aug Mon–Fri 11am–6pm, Sat & Sun 11am–4pm; 30kr), while out of town the **mines** themselves (guided tours: 6 daily mid-June to mid-Aug; 1–3 daily rest of June & mid-Aug to Sept; 35kr) are open for visits. In July and early August two buses daily go there (10am & 1pm); outside that time you can hitch, or a taxi will take you there and back for 200kr – or rent a bike from the *Røros Turisthotell*.

The **train station** is at the foot of the town, a couple of minutes' walk from the **tourist office** (May–Sept Mon–Fri 9am–4pm, Sat 10am–2pm; July & Aug Mon–Sat 9am–8pm, Sat noon–6pm), where you can pick up a booklet (10kr) and town plan. The infrequent train service north and south will probably mean a night's stay in Røros. The **youth hostel**, Øraveien 25 (mid-May to mid-Sept; ☎73.41.10.89; ③), includes breakfast and has a **campsite** next door with cabins for rent.

Trondheim

Though you might not think so now, **TRONDHEIM**, an atmospheric city with much of its medieval heart intact, has been an important Norwegian power base for centuries and is now gearing up for its millennium celebrations in 1997. The early Norse parliament, or *Ting*, met here, and the city was a major pilgrimage centre. The city centre sits on a small triangle of land, a manageable place where even the main sights – bar the marvellous cathedral – have a low-key quality about them.

The City

The goal of Trondheim's pilgrims was the colossal **Nidaros Domkirke**, Scandinavia's largest medieval building, gloriously restored following the ravages of the Reformation and several fires, and still the real focal point of the city (mid-June to mid-Aug Mon–Fri 9.30am–5.30pm, Sat 9.30am–2pm, Sun 1–4pm; May to mid-June & mid-Aug to mid-Sept Mon–Fri 9.30am–2.30pm, Sat 9.30am–2pm, Sun 1–4pm; mid-Sept to late Sept Mon–Fri noon–2.30pm, Sat 11.30am–2pm, Sun 1–3pm; 10kr, tower 5kr). Tagged after Trondheim's former name, Nidaros ("mouth of the river Nid"), it's dedicated to King Olav, who was forced to flee Norway after his countrymen, disgruntled by his zealous reforms, called upon the English king, Knud (Canute), for assistance in dislodging him. Olav returned to Norway in 1030 to reclaim his inheritance but fell at the nearby battle of Stiklestad. Following a posthumous return to favour, his body was moved here and its resting place marked by the erection of a church. Over the years the church was altered and enlarged to accommodate the growing bands of medieval tourists, ultimately achieving cathedral status in 1152 and becoming the traditional burial place of Norwegian royalty. Since 1814 it has also been the place where Norwegian monarchs are crowned. The stonework on the west entrance is marvellous, massed ranks of carvings and figures peering down upon a quiet square. Inside, the gloomy half light hides much of the lofty decorative work, but the stained glass, especially the circular window above the main portal, is superb. Get there in the early morning if you can, both to miss the tourbus crowds and to see Norway's small collection of Crown Jewels.

Admission to the Domkirke also includes a visit to the heavily restored **Erkebispegården** just behind (June to mid-Aug Mon–Fri 9am–3pm, Sat 9am–2pm, Sun noon–3pm; guided tours 10kr), built in the twelfth century as the archbishop's palace and for years doubling as the city armoury. It's been thoroughly cleaned up, and many of the old weapons are now displayed in the south wing in the **Army and Resistance Museum** (June–Aug Mon–Fri 9am–1pm, Sun 11am–4pm; 5kr not included in cathedral entry). Following the river around, it's a short walk to the **old town bridge**, an elegant wooden reach with splendid views over early eighteenth-century gabled and timbered warehouses, most of which have been converted into restaurants and offices. A short walk west, the **Museum of Applied Art**, Munkegaten 5 (late-June to Aug Mon–Sat 10am–6pm, Sun noon–5pm; winter Mon–Wed, Fri & Sat 10am–3pm, Thurs 10am–7pm, Sun noon–4pm; 20kr), is a glorious exhibition of furniture, tapestries and precious metal, arranged chronologically from the Renaissance to the 1950s, and including Munch woodcuts and a Vigeland sculpture.

The broad avenues of Trondheim's centre date back to the seventeenth century, their pavement cafés and flowerbeds surrounding the tangle of narrow alleys and wooden frontages that forms the nucleus of Trondheim. The most conspicuous survivor of the town's many fires is **Stiftsgården** (June–Aug Mon–Sat 10am–3/5pm, Sun noon–4/5pm; 20kr; tours every hour 20kr), halfway up Munkegaten, a late eighteenth-century structure that claims to be the largest wooden building in northern Europe and these days is an official royal residence. More accessible are the spooky **medieval church ruins** discovered under the *Sparebanken*, around the corner on Kongensgate. Clamber down into the crypt, a semicircular cellar under the chancel where the relics of the saint were kept. Back along Kongensgate, **Torvet** is the main city square, site of the compact **Ravnkloa** fish market and looking out over the water to the fortress island of **Munkholmen**, where there's a Benedictine abbey that was converted to a fortress after the Reformation to hold eighteenth-century Norwegian political prisoners (tours 15kr). Today the island's a bathing spot, popular with the local youth, who avoid the day-tripper crowds by scrambling around the rocks on the side of the island farthest from the harbour. Ferries run between mid-May and August (10am–6pm; 25kr return). Also outside the centre is the **Museum of Musical History**, housed in the beautifully sited seventeenth-century Ringve Manor on the Lade peninsula (July to mid-Aug Mon–Sat tours in English 11am, 12.30pm, 2.30pm & 4.30pm; rest of summer less frequently; 40kr), a spectacular collection of old musical instruments, demonstrated and explained by a lengthy guided tour. Take bus #4 from Munkegaten. There's also the **Trøndelag Folk Museum** at Sverresborg (mid-May to Aug 11am–6pm, conducted tours 11.15am, 1pm, 3pm & 4.30pm; 20kr), whose collections of reconstructed and restored houses highlight the region's life and culture. Take bus #8 or #9 from Dronningensgate to Wullumsgården.

Practicalities

Trondheim is the first major northbound stop of the *Hurtigrute* **coastal steamer**, which docks behind the **train station**, where you simply cross the bridge onto the central island. Express **buses** stop at the bus station close to Torvet, where the **tourist office** (June to mid-Aug Mon–Fri 8.30am–8pm, Sat 8.30am–6pm, Sun 10am–6pm;

mid-Aug to May Mon–Fri 9am–1pm) provides the free *Trondheim Guide* and changes money. If **staying**, the tourist office books **private rooms** from 200kr a double plus a 15kr fee, and there's a **youth hostel** at Weidemannsveien 41 (☎73.53.04.90; ③), twenty-minutes' hike from the centre out past Bakke church and straight uphill; bus #63 also runs there. It's expensive but prices include breakfast. You might prefer the slightly cheaper *Singsaker Sommerhotell*, Rogertsgate 1 (☎73.52.00.92; ③), on the other side of the Kristiansten fortress, or, from early July to late August, *InterRail Centre*, Elgesetergate 1 (☎73.89.95.38; ②), which also throws in breakfast. It's a twenty-minute walk from Torvet, or take bus #41, #42, #48, #49, #52 or #63 (13kr; exact change needed) along Prinsensgate and ask for the *Studentersfundet*. The nearest **campsite**, *Sandmoen Camping*, is 10km out of town, near Heimdal on the E6, but does have cabins and rooms; take bus #44 from the bus station and get off at the last stop. For **eating**, *Pizzakjelleren*, Fjordgata 7, has good value pizzas with a 50kr all-you-can-eat deal at lunchtimes, and later *Grønn Pepper* upstairs opens for reasonably priced Mexican food in cacti-filled surroundings. *De 3 Stuer*, branches on Torget and in *Sundt* department store at Dronningensgate 11 is a good stand-by for sandwiches and hearty Norwegian meals. *Café 3b*, 3b Brattørgatan, serves snacks but is really a stylish place to drink. Due to the large student population, **nightlife** in Trondheim is quite lively. *Studentersamfunnet*, just over Elgeseter bridge, is cheap and has music and dancing, while the *Ritz* at Skansen features bands and a cheap bar; expect to pay a cover charge of around 50kr.

Mo-i-Rana

The last and only worthwhile stop before the Arctic Circle is **MO-I-RANA** or "Mo", a cosy little town at the end of the Ranafjord. There's nothing much to Mo, and the town is dominated by an enormous steel plant, but it's an ideal place to base yourself for trips to the **Svartisen ice cap**, one of whose tongues reaches down to a lake 32km north of the town. Buses run to the lake around 10am daily from outside the tourist office (100kr return); or you can catch a bus to Røssvoll airport and hitch the last 20km. Boats run across the lake hourly (late June to Aug) between 10am and 5pm and cost 50kr return, dropping you a three-kilometre hike from the glacier. Full details are available at the **tourist office** (June–Aug Mon–Fri 9am–9pm, Sat 10am–5pm, Sun 2–9pm), 4km from the **train station**. The **youth hostel** is 1km out at Finsetveien 1 (☎75.15.09.63; ②).

The Arctic Circle, Fauske and Bodø

Given its appeal as one of the last great wildernesses, crossing the **Arctic Circle** is a bit disappointing, doubly so as it is now disfigured by the brand new **Arctic Circle Centre**, right on the line 8km from Bolna (June–Aug daily 9am–10pm; May & Sept 10am–6pm; 30kr) – basically a celebration of northern Norway with a variety of multimedia displays.

Train travellers will probably cross the line without even realizing they've done so. **FAUSKE** is the northernmost point of the Norwegian rail network, and is consequently an important transport hub. Northbound travellers will almost certainly have to spend the night here in town unless they plan to make a quick change onto connecting buses. The comfortable **youth hostel** is in the centre of town at Nyveien 6 (June to mid-Aug; ☎75.64.47.06; ②), a ten-minute walk from the **train station**. The *Lundhøgda* **campsite**, open June to mid-September, is a fifty-minute walk away along Route 80.

Fauske is also the departure point of the *Nord-Norge Bussen*, the **express bus** service which carries passengers as far as Kirkenes, close to the Russian border. Get tickets from the travel agency in Fauske or buy them on the buses, which leave twice daily from the **bus station**. As on all long-distance buses to the north, there is a fifty percent discount for *InterRail/Nordturist* pass holders on the first step of the route to Narvik, a five-hour trip which is a gorgeous run past fjords, peaks and snow.

An hour west of Fauske, **BODØ** is where the trains terminate, and a stop on the *Hurtigrute* steamer route. It's also a main point of departure for the Lofoten Islands, so you might find youself here, although there's precious little to the place. The **tourist office** at Sjøgata 21, 300m from the train station (June–Aug Mon–Fri 9am–5pm or later, Sat 10am–3pm, Sun 6–8/9pm), has information on the islands. If you have to spend the night, the tourist office also books **private rooms** for 150kr a head, or there's a decent and well-priced **youth hostel**, Nordstrandveien 1 (mid-June to mid-Aug; ☎75.52.56.66; ②), ten minutes' walk from the train station. For **eating**, the *Neptun Café*, adjoining the bus station, is a good bet.

The Lofoten Islands

Stretched out in a skeletal curve across the Norwegian Sea, the **Lofoten Islands** are perfect for a simple, uncluttered few days. For somewhere so far north the weather is exceptionally mild, and there's plentiful **accommodation** in *rorbuer*, or fishermen's shacks, usually accommodating 2–6 people, rented out to tourists during the summer for 300–600kr; three youth hostels – one in Å (☎71.22.13.82; ②) in the far south of the island, the other two listed below; and plentiful campsites. The *Hurtigrute* **coastal steamer** – the only service to carry cars – calls at two ports, Stamsund and Svolvær. There are also passenger **express boats**, which work out slightly cheaper than the coastal steamer, linking both Bodø and Narvik with Svolvær. By **bus** you can leave the main E6 road at Ulvsvåg, take a connecting bus to Skutvik (47kr) and the **ferry** (47kr) from there to Svolvær. **Coming from Narvik**, buses run to Sortland, main town of the adjacent Vesterålen Islands, from where it's a quick bus ride and ferry south to the Lofotens and Svolvær.

The islands

The main town on **Austvågøy**, the largest and northernmost island of the group, is **SVOLVÆR**, a rather disappointing place, although you may find it one of the easier centres in which to stay and it's where you may arrive. The **tourist office**, located in the main town square (July Mon–Fri 8am–4pm & 5–10pm, Sat 9.30am–2pm & 5–8pm, Sun 11.30am–2pm & 4–8pm; reduced hours rest of summer), has maps, an accommodation guide and details of public transport. For **accommodation**, the youth hostel (☎76.07.07.77; ③) is in the *Vågan Folkehøgskole* and only open June to mid-August. For a more intimate experience, try instead the lovely wooden *Svolvær Sjøhuscamping* at Parkveien N. (May–Sept; ☎76.07.03.36; ④), a snug fishing house charging around 90kr a night including use of the kitchen and showers. **KABELVÅG**, 5km away (and connected by several daily buses) is home to the **Lofoten Island Museum** (daily mid-June to mid-Aug 9am–9pm; rest of year 9am–6pm; 25kr) – the definitive collection of fishing and other cultural paraphernalia on the islands. Otherwise the main attraction is the **hiking** and **climbing** in the town's delightful surroundings. The tourist office has details of routes, the most famous of which is the climb up the *Svolværgeita* ("Svolvær goat"), above the town. Daring mountaineers jump between the horns of the adjacent peaks, and the town's cemetery, 2000 feet below, is full of those who missed. You may also be cajoled into taking a **cruise** down the **Trollfjord**, an impossibly narrow stretch of water up and down which countless excursion boats inch a careful way, wringing gasps from camera-crazy tourists – though this can be pricey.

The second island of the group, **Vestvågøy**, is perhaps more interesting, due partly to the beauty of its main settlement, **STAMSUND**, which strings around its bay in a colourful jumble of wooden houses and chalets. This is the other port at which the coastal steamer docks and is much the best base for touring the island. The first place you should head for is the **youth hostel** (☎76.08.91.66; ②), situated just a little way down the road from the port, and which is made up of several *rorbuer* perched over a pin-sized rocky bay. It's open all year and very friendly; it also hires out **bikes and mopeds**, and is the best source of information. There are also *rorbuer* in the village, and the expensive *Lofoten Hotel* (☎76.08.93.00; ⑧) by the harbour. If you're **camping**, nearby Steine has an offshore archipelago with a **campsite** and several *rorbuer* (☎76.08.92.83).

Back through Stamsund, and a couple of kilometres from Leknes (administrative centre of the islands and home to their airport), is **FYGHE**, worth a stop for an excellent **museum** (Mon–Fri 11am–4pm, Sat & Sun noon–3pm; 10kr) in a restored nineteenth-century schoolhouse. Enthusiastic guides and some self-explanatory displays reveal how horribly hard life was a hundred years ago – the box-room cottage reconstructed outside just seems intimate until you realize that it slept between eight and twelve people. Head out, too, towards the western coast. At **HAUKLAND** is one of the most popular of the island's beaches, a long sandy stretch with deep green water and a **campsite** for longer stays. Around the coast, **UTAKLEIV** is a favourite spot to watch for the Midnight Sun and good for rough camping. Real isolation can be found further north at **UNSTAD**, where a rough road winds up into the hills, through a tunnel blasted out of the rock, and down to an enormous cove.

Narvik

NARVIK was established less than a century ago as an ice-free port to handle the iron ore brought by train from northern Sweden, and the **iron ore docks** are immediately conspicuous upon arrival here, slap-bang in the centre of town, the rust-coloured machinery overwhelming the whole waterfront like some huge set from a James Bond movie. There are guided tours around the **dock areas** (summer 2pm; 20kr), interesting if only for the opportunity to spend an hour inside such a hellish mess. Otherwise the town centre is rather lacking in appeal, with modern stone replacing the wooden houses and buildings flattened during the last war, when there was fierce fighting for control of the harbours and the ore supplies. Try and devote an hour or so to the **Krigsminne Museum** (Sept–March daily 11am–2pm; June–Aug Mon–Sat 10am–10pm, Sun 11am–5pm; 20kr), in the main square close to the docks. Run by the Red Cross, it documents the wartime German saturation bombing of the town, and the bitter sea and air battles in which hundreds of foreign servicemen died alongside the local population. Beyond that, a **cable car** (March–Oct), from behind the bus station, is due to restart whisking passengers up to the 700-metre height of Fagernesfjellet from June 1994. From here you can see the Midnight Sun from May 21 to July 14. The last cable car back returns after midnight, but avid Midnight Sun watchers leaving on the early morning train to Kiruna can leave their packs at the train station, take a ride up and then walk down.

The **train** and **bus stations** are close together, near to the **tourist office** at Kongensgate 66 (June to Aug Mon–Sat 9am–8pm, Sun 11am–8pm; Sept–May Mon–Fri 9am–4pm), which will book **private rooms** at 250kr double for a 15kr fee, and changes money. There's also a **youth hostel** at Havnegate 3 (☎76.94.25.98; ③), which is open all year and throws in breakfast. If the hostel's full, the cheapest *pensjonat* is the *Briedablikk* at Tore Hundsgate 41 (☎76.94.14.18; ③), or there is a **campsite** 2km north of town at Orneshaugen; turn right along the main road from the station and keep walking, or take any bus going to the airport. For **eating**, the *Havnecafé*, down the road from the hostel, has the best-value meals, or there's the *Restaurang Rosa*, over the rail bridge opposite the town square.

On from Narvik

There's a choice of several routes on from Narvik. The **rail link** (the *Ofotbana*), cut through the mountains a century ago, runs east and then south into Sweden, reaching Kiruna in three hours. **Bus** travellers can travel north to Alta along one of the most beautiful routes in the country, a succession of switchback roads, lakeside forests, high peaks and lowlands. In summer cut grass dries everywhere, stretched over wooden poles forming long lines on the hillsides like so much washing. Buses also run off the E6 to Tromsø; note that on buses south from Narvik, to either Fauske or Bodø, *InterRail* and *Nordturist* pass holders get a fifty percent discount.

Tromsø

TROMSØ was once known, rather preposterously, as the "Paris of the North", and though even the tourist office doesn't make any pretence to such grandiose titles now, the city still likes to think of itself as the capital of northern Norway. Certainly, as a base for this part of the country, it's hard to beat. It's a pleasant small city, with an above-average and affordable nightlife lent by a high-profile student population, two cathedrals and some surprisingly good museums. Throughout 1994, the city will be celebrating the bicentennial of earning its town charter, peaking with a royal visit on June 20. Finding accommodation is likely to a be a problem all summer but a multitude of activities should make booking ahead worthwhile.

You can best orient yourself by way of Tromsø's cathedrals. The **Domkirke** (mid-June to mid-Aug Tues–Sat noon–4pm; free) serves to emphasize how prosperous the town was by the nineteenth century, the result of its substantial barter trade with Russia. Completed in 1861, it's one of Norway's largest wooden churches, with some imposing fixtures in a solemn salmon-pink interior. On the other side of the water, over the spindly Tromsø Bridge, the white and modern **Arctic Cathedral** (Mon–Sat 10am–5pm, Sun 1–5pm; 5kr) is spectacularly different, made up of eleven immense triangular concrete sections representing the eleven Apostles left after the betrayal. Back in the centre of town, **Stortorget** is the main square, north of which lies old Tromsø, though a fire in 1969 left few buildings of any interest. One that did survive is the Customs House, built in 1789 and now housing the **Tromsø Bymuseum** (mid-May to mid-Sept daily 11am–3pm; rest of year Mon–Fri 11am–3pm; 10kr), with a collection of nineteenth-century artefacts. The **Polar Museum**, close by (mid-May to Aug daily 11am–6pm; rest of year daily 11am–3pm; 20kr), is better, covering trading, industrial and scientific activity through the ages in the Polar region by way of good photographs and realistic reconstructions, though its enthusiasm for hunting is unpleasant. Most rewarding is the **Tromsø Museum** (June–Aug daily 9am–9pm; Sept–May Mon–Fri 8.30am–3.30pm, Sat noon–3pm, Sun 11am–4pm; 10kr), a 25-minute walk from the centre along Strandveien (or bus #22 or #27 from Storgata; 15kr), with thoughtful zoology and botany displays, ecclesiastical bits and pieces and a *Same* exhibit.

Practicalities

The *Hurtigrute* **coastal steamer** docks in the centre of town at the bottom of Kirkegata, where there are **luggage lockers** (10kr & 15kr) open until midnight inside *Venteromskafé*; **buses** arrive and leave from the adjacent car park. The **tourist office** is on Storgata, near the Domkirke (June to mid-Aug Mon–Fri 8.30am–7pm, Sat & Sun 10am–5pm; rest of year Mon–Fri 8.30am–4pm), and sells the 24-hour tourist ticket (40kr) valid for unlimited city bus travel. The massive and comfortable **youth hostel** (☎77.68.53.19; ②), open mid-June to mid-August, demands a key-deposit of 100kr but has no curfew. It is 2km from the quay – bus #24 goes from outside the *Sparebank* on Fr. Langes Gata or else it's a steep twenty-minute walk. Alternatively, the tourist office books **private rooms** (200kr double; 25kr fee), or try one of two reasonable **pensjonater**: *Skipperhuset Pensjonat*, Storgata 112 (☎77.68.16.06; ④), or, for a few kroner more, *Hotel Nord*, Parkgata 4 (☎77.68.31.59; ④), both of which have cheap triples. The cheapest of the hotels is *Viking Hotell*, Grønnegata 18 (☎77.65.76.22; ⑤), which drops a price category in summer. The nearest **campsite**, *Tromsdalen Camping*, lies over the bridge on the mainland, and has cabins and is open all year; take bus #36 from Storgata. For **eating**, budget meals are available in the *Sagatun* in Richard Withs Plass, while *Le Mirage*, Storgata 42, past the tourist office, has reasonable pub grub. The rooftop terrace at *Paletten*, Storgata 51, is one of the more appealing and inexpensive places to eat and drink, though drinkers will find that the *Blå Rock Café*, Strandgata 14, puts up some strong competition with its CD juke box and weekend discos.

Alta and around

Strung out across a number of scattered settlements, **ALTA** is not the kind of place anyone would want to spend much time. This former *Same* town was almost entirely destroyed in the last war and is now in the grip of a comprehensive new development that has no real centre and little soul. For all that, it's an important transport junction and hard to avoid: heading to Nordkapp by road almost certainly means an overnight stop in Alta in order to catch the connecting bus to Honningsvåg the next day, and buses also head east from here along the E6 to Kirkenes and south to Kautokeino.

The town does have one remarkable feature, almost worth spending another night for: the **rock carvings at Hjemmeluft**, the most extensive area of prehistoric rock carvings in northern Europe. The site is officially only open during summer (mid-June to mid-Aug daily 8am–11pm; to 8pm two weeks either side; 25kr), but you can usually get in all year. The carvings make an extraordinarily complex tableau of ships, animals and people; they were executed between 2500 and 6000 years ago, and although the colours have been restored by scientists, they are indisputably touching in their simplicity.

Buses call at Bossekop ("whale bay"), the original settlement by the water of the Altafjord, and if you're not staying you may as well jump off here. There's a **tourist office** (June–Aug Mon–Fri 9am–7pm, Sat 9am–4pm, Sun noon–7pm) and other facilities (café, bank and post office), and you can normally leave your bag here if you just want to walk down to the carvings. If you're **staying**, you need to keep on the bus as far as Sentrum, the newest part of Alta, or a few hundred metres further to the **youth hostel**, five minutes' walk further up the E6 at Midtbakkveien 52 (mid-June to mid-Aug; ☎78.43.44.09; ②). If it's full, the *Alta Gjestestve*, Bekkefaret 3 (☎78.43.55.66; ⑤), is the cheapest hotel and serves good, cheap meals. It is opposite the petrol station in Bossekop. There are also several **campsites** in the area, one with cabins on the southern side of Bossekop, next to the rock carvings.

The Finnmarksvidda: Kautokeino and Karasjok

From Alta there are two routes into the vast plain of the **Finnmarksvidda** – south to Kautokeino, or east across the peninsula to Lakselv and then south to Karasjok. But for the steady encroachment of tourism over recent years, life has remained much the same here for centuries. The main occupations are reindeer-herding, hunting and fishing, continued by the few thousand semi-nomadic **Same** who live here in the flat plains and shallow valleys during the winter, migrating towards the coast in early May as the snow begins to melt. By October, people and deer are journeying back from their summer quarters and preparing for the great Easter festivals, when weddings and baptisms are celebrated – the best time to be here. Summer visits, on the other hand, can be disappointing, with little of the colour and activity you'll find during winter.

The easiest town to reach from Alta, **KAUTOKEINO** is, strangely enough, something of a tourist draw, principally due to the preponderance of pseudo-ethnic jewellers from the south who have set up here. During the summer, the town's main street is lined with souvenir booths which attract travellers like flies. They are not, however, selling tourist tack: *Juhl's Silvergallery* (daily summer 8.30am–10pm; winter 9am–7pm), for instance, a three-kilometre walk from the centre following the signs, is a complex of workshops and showrooms making and selling high-quality silverwork. Back in town, the **Kautokeino kirke** (July to mid-Aug 10am–8pm) is a delightful building decorated inside in bright, typically *Same* colours – seen again on Sunday in the costumes which turn out for the occasion. Nearby there is a small **open-air museum** (mid-June to mid-Aug Mon–Fri 9am–6pm, Sat & Sun 11am–4pm; 10kr) featuring a few draughty-looking dwellings: you'll see the same little turf huts and skin tents all over Finnmark, usually housing summer souvenir stalls.

Accommodation in Kautokeino is expensive: the cheapest options are *Alfreds Kro og Overnatting* (☎78.48.61.18; ④), and the cabins at *Kavtokeine Camping* (☎78.48.61.92; ⑤). Failing that, move on to **KARASJOK**, known as the "Capital of the Lapps", seat of the newly-founded Same parliament and home to a **Same Museum** (June–Aug Mon–Sat 9am–6pm, Sun 10am–6pm; Sept–May closes 3pm; 10kr), which has a mass of cultural artefacts. It is right next to the *SAS Karasjok Turisthotell* where all the buses stop – including the 9.30am service to Rovaniemi in Finland (rail passes not valid; 310kr) – and just along from the **tourist office** (June to late Aug Mon–Fri 8am–8pm, Sat & Sun 10am–8pm).

Hammerfest

As the tourist office takes great pains to point out, **HAMMERFEST** is the world's northernmost town; it was also, they add, the first town in Europe to have its streets lit by electric light. Hardly fascinating facts, but both give a glimpse of the pride that the locals take in having made the most of an inhospitable region. The harsh elements aside, the town was burnt to the ground in 1891 and, having been rebuilt, was promptly razed again, this time by retreating Germans at the end of World War II. Instead of being abandoned, Hammerfest was stubbornly rebuilt a second time and, rather than the grim industrial town you might expect, it is today a bright and rather elegant port – at least, on a sunny day when a cruise ship is in .

The town's main street, **Strandgatan**, runs parallel to the harbour, a bustling run of shops and cafés. Most action takes place down on the main quay, where the **coastal steamer** docks and the ship's tourists usually spend their hour or so on shore eating shellfish straight from the stalls along the wharf or buying souvenirs from the small summer *Same* market. The **tourist office** (June–Aug Mon–Fri 8am–7pm, Sat & Sun 9am–5pm; Sept–May Mon–Fri 8am–3pm) is a short walk left from the quay on Sjøgata and, if you are going to stay, can provide a map and information sheet. **Buses** arrive and leave from down by the quay, and there are regular, if infrequent, connections back to the E6 for Nordkapp and Alta. If you need to **stay**, the only cheap accommodation is at one of two **campsites** where you can rent cabins: the *NAF Camping Storvannet*, a fifteen-minute walk from the centre out by the sports stadium (mid-June to mid-Aug; four-bedded cabins for 230kr), and *Hammerfest Turistsenter*, 1500m from the centre (May–Sept), with slightly more pricy cabins. With more money, try the *Håja Hotel*, Storgata 9–11 (☎78.41.18.22; ⑤).

Honningsvåg and Nordkapp

A good 80km nearer the North Pole than Hammerfest, **HONNINGSVÅG** sits in the middle of a treeless windswept terrain surrounded by snow fences to protect it from avalanches. It's a fishing village primarily, but to travellers it's of more interest for its proximity to Nordkapp, 34km away – which, given the hit-and-miss nature of transport in these parts, may mean an overnight stay. Ferries from the mainland (2 hourly; 50mins; 29kr) are boarded at Kåfjord, where there is a useful **tourist office** (mid-June to Aug daily 10am–8.30pm), and dock 3km north of Honningsvåg, often met by a bus running to Nordkapp (4 daily; 50mins; 95kr return; no rail passes valid). Get the ticket countersigned by the driver if you want to return on a different day (other than the last bus back at 1.15am). Five kilometres along the road you pass the **youth hostel/ campsite** complex (☎78.47.51.13; ②), open June to mid-August, 8km out on the road to Nordkapp and accessible by the same bus. It's beautifully situated on the Skipsfjord, costs just 50kr a night and serves superb meals – usually fish fresh from the fjord – as well as life-saving breakfasts. In the other direction, Honningsvåg **tourist office** (June–Aug Mon–Fri 8.30am–4pm, Sat & Sun 11am–6pm), in *Nordkapphuset*, a community centre next to the bus station, has full details on all routes. If you need to **eat** in the village, there are several takeaway kiosks along Storgata and a couple of cafés back near the hotel. If you do stay out at the hostel, be aware of the early departure times of **onward transport**: the southbound coastal steamer leaves at 6.45am, the first bus to Lakselv at 7am – you may need to book a taxi to take you into town to pick these up.

The **coastal steamer** puts in at Honningsvåg, from where you catch a special hire-coach which gets you there and back within the two-hour stop. Hitching is a possibility, and in summer there are four daily buses (95kr return; make sure your ticket is still valid if you plan to return the next day). In winter the only option is a **taxi**, assuming the road is open – 500kr for the return trip. **Nordkapp** itself might be expected to be a bit of a disappointment. It is, after all, only a cliff with an arguable claim to being the northern-most point of Europe. But there is something about this bleak, wind-battered promon-tory that excites the senses. Originally a *Same* sacrificial site, it was named by the English explorer Richard Chancellor in 1553, as he drifted along the Norwegian coast in an attempt to find the Northeast Passage. He failed, but the trade route he opened to Russia brought the Cape to the attention of others – among them Oscar II, whose visit opened the tourist floodgates. These days **North Cape Hall** contains a post office (where you can get your letters specially stamped), souvenir shop, wide screen video show and cafeteria, though it's all really only busy when the tour buses arrive – and even then, a few minutes' walk can take you somewhere completely isolated. In 1993 entrance to the whole Nordkapp site including the hall costs 95kr, but from 1994 it is planned to restrict the charge to the hall, leaving the site cost free. The site ticket is valid for two days, and those with the equipment can easily camp nearby, using the hall's facilities. It is much quieter in the morning and if you stay two nights, you'll raise your chances of seeing the Midnight Sun, usually thirty percent during the summer. Francesco Negri, who visited Nordkapp in 1664, summed it up best: "I am now standing at North Cape, on the utmost point of Finnmark – on the very edge of the world. Here the world ends, as does my curiosity, and I shall now turn homewards, God willing . . ."

travel details

Trains

Oslo to: Åndalsnes (4 daily; 5hr 50min); Bergen (4–5 daily; 6hr 30min); Kristiansand (3–4 daily; 5hr); Røros (2 daily; 6hr); Stavanger (3 daily; 8hr); Trondheim (4 daily; 6hr 40min); Voss (4–5 daily; 5hr 15min).

Åndalsnes to: Dombås (3 daily; 2hr); Oslo (3 daily; 6–8hr).

Dombås to: Trondheim (3 daily; 2hr 30min).

Kristiansand to: Kongsberg (5 daily; 3hr 30min); Oslo (5 daily; 5hr).

Myrdal to: Flåm (June–Sept 7–8 daily; 50min).

Stavanger to: Kristiansand (3–4 daily; 3hr); Oslo (3 daily; 9hr).

Trondheim to: Bodø (2 daily; 11hr); Dombås (3 daily; 2hr 30min); Fauske (2 daily; 10hr 20min); Mo-i-Rana (2 daily; 7hr 15min); Oslo (3 daily; 6hr 45min); Røros (1–2 daily; 3hr); Stockholm (3 daily; 12hr).

Buses

Ålesund to: Bergen (1 daily except Sat; 11hr); Hellesylt (1–2 daily except Sat; 2hr 40min); Molde (4–6 daily; 2hr 15min); Stryn (1–2 daily except Sat; 4hr); Trondheim (1–2 daily; 8hr 10min).

Alta to: Hammerfest (2–4 daily; 3hr); Honningsvåg (1–2 daily; 5hr); Kautokeino (1 daily; 3hr); Tromsø (1 daily; 7hr).

Åndalsnes to: Ålesund (3–4 daily; 2hr 20min); Geiranger (June–Aug 2 daily; 3–4hr); Molde (3–7 daily; 1hr 30min).

Balestrand to: Sogndal (4–5 daily; 1hr 10min); Stryn (1 daily; 4hr).

Bergen to: Ålesund (1–2 daily; 10hr); Trondheim (1 daily; 15hr); Voss via Norheimsund (3–4 daily; 4hr); Voss (1 daily; 1hr 45min).

Fauske to: Bodø (2 daily; 1hr 10min); Narvik (2 daily; 5hr).

Hammerfest to: Alta (1–2 daily; 3hr); Honningsvåg (1–2 daily; 4hr 20min); Oslo (3 weekly; 29hr).

Kautokeino to: Alta (3 weekly; 1hr 40min); Karasjok (Mon, Wed, Fri & Sun 1 daily; 2hr 15min).

Kongsberg to: Odda (1 daily; 6hr 30min); Oslo (1 daily; 11hr 45min).

Narvik to: Alta (1 daily; 11hr); Tromsø (1–3 daily; 5–6hr).

Oslo to: Bergen (1 daily; 11hr 30min).

Stavanger to: Kristiansand (1–2 daily; 5hr).

Stryn to: Balestrand (1 daily; 4hr); Bergen (2–3 daily; 7hr); Oslo (1 daily; 8hr 30min).

Tromsø to: Alta (1 daily; 7hr); Narvik (1–3 daily; 5hr 30min); Nordkjosbotn (3–5 daily; 1hr 30min).

Trondheim to: Ålesund (1–2 daily; 8hr); Bergen (1 daily; 15hr); Molde (1–2 daily; 6hr); Røros (1–3 daily; 3hr 10min).

Voss to: Odda (1 daily; 2hr 30min); Sogndal (2–4 daily; 3hr–4hr 30min).

Ferries

Arendal to: Oslo (July to mid-Aug 1 daily; 6hr 30min).

Bergen to: Balestrand (2 daily; 4hr); Flåm (1–2 daily; 5hr 30min); Måløy (1–3 daily; 4hr); Stavanger (2–3 daily; 4hr).

Bodø to: Svolvær (1 daily except Sat; 5hr).

Narvik to: Svolvær (1 daily except Sat; 4hr).

Stavanger to: Bergen (*Kystveien* service: 1 daily; 6hr; *Hurtibåt* service: 2–3 daily; 4hr 30min).

CHAPTER 17

POLAND

Introduction

Polish images flooded the world media throughout the 1980s. Strikes and riots at the Lenin shipyards of Gdańsk and other industrial centres were the harbingers of the disintegration of communism in Eastern Europe, and throughout the years of martial law and beyond Poland maintained an exemplary momentum towards political change. The decade's end saw the establishment of a government led by the Solidarity trade union, a development followed in 1990 by the victory of union leader Lech Wałęsa in Poland's first presidential election since the 1920s.

The pattern was familiar enough through the eastern bloc, but the rebirth of democratic Poland was a uniquely Catholic revolution. The **Church** has always been the principal defender of the nation's identity, and its physical presence is inescapable in Baroque buildings, roadside shrines and images of the national icon, the Black Madonna. Encounters with the **people** are at the core of any experience of the country. On trains and buses, in the streets or the village bar, you'll never be stuck for opportunities for contact: Polish hospitality is legendary. Tourism, like every other aspect of the Polish infrastructure, is currently in a state of flux, but it's never been easier to explore the country. Foreigners are no longer subject to currency restrictions, and can travel as they please, if not always as smoothly as desired.

Unless you're driving to Poland, you're likely to begin your travels with one of the three major cities. Much of **Warsaw**, the capital, conforms to the stereotype of Eastern European greyness, but its historic centre and burgeoning street markets are diverting enough. **Kraków**, the ancient royal capital, is the real crowd puller, rivalling the Central European elegance of Prague and Vienna. The Hanseatic city of **Gdańsk**, home of the legendary shipyards, offers a dynamic brew of politics and commerce. German influences abound in the **north and southwest** of the country, in Gdańsk itself, in the austere castles and fortified settlements along the River Wisła (Vistula) and in the divided province of **Silesia**. Yet, to the north of Silesia, quintessentially Polish **Poznań** is revered as the cradle of the nation.

Despite its much-publicized pollution problems, Poland has many regions of unspoilt natural beauty, none more popular than the alpine Tatras, the most exhilarating walking terrain in the country.

Information and Maps

Poland has no national tourist board, and the provision of information through the independent tourist offices is rather diffuse. The largest of these outfits is **Orbis** (known outside the country as *Polorbis*), whose offices are able to do everything from booking rooms and tickets to processing visa extensions. **PTTK**, with its offices spread throughout Poland, has a more direct responsibility for internal tourism. **Almatur** is a student and youth travel bureau. In the major cities, municipal tourist offices also dispense information.

The easiest road **map** to follow is *Bartholomew's Europmap: Poland* (1:800,000), which is especially clear on rail lines. The *Orbis Poland: Roadmap* (1:750,000) is useful, too, and widely available in Poland. For detailed **city maps**, try to get hold of the appropriate *plan miasta*, available cheaply at local tourist offices, kiosks, street sellers and bookshops.

Money and Banks

Poland is currently one of the great travel bargains: most of the essentials are ludicrously cheap for anyone with hard currency. The Polish currency is the **złoty** (zł), which circulates in notes of 50, 100, 200, 500, 1000, 2000, 5000, 10,000, 20,000, 50,000, 100,000, 500,000, and 1,000,000 and 2,000,000zł. 50zł and 100zł notes are to be substituted with coins.

As a rule, the most competitive **exchange rates** are offered by the **banks** (usually open Mon–Fri 7.30am–5pm, Sat 7.30am–2pm), though you're almost certain to be kept waiting around for a while at the desk. A flat commission of around 20,000zł is normally deducted. *Orbis* hotels also have exchange desks, though they tend to offer poor rates and charge hefty commissions; main *Orbis* offices generally offer better rates. A host of **private banks** (*kantor* or *walut*) have sprung up, but these change cash only; US dollars and Deutschmarks are most in demand. **Travellers' cheques** can be exchanged only at main banks, *Orbis* offices and hotels, a sometimes lengthy process. Major **credit cards** are accepted by *Orbis* in payment for almost everything, and you can arrange a cash advance on most cards; an increasing number of shops also take plastic.

Communications

Post offices in Poland are identified by the name *Urząd Pocztowy* (*Poczta* for short) or by the acronym PTT. Theoretically, each city's head office has a **poste restante** facility: make sure that anyone addressing mail to you adds "No 1" (denoting the head office) after the city's name. Head office opening hours are usually Mon–Sat 7/8am–8pm; branches usually close at 6pm or earlier. Outbound mail takes up to a fortnight. Post boxes are green (local), blue (air mail) and red (all types).

Many of Poland's pay **phones** now accept *jetons*; A tokens (600zł) for local calls and C tokens (6000zł) for long distance; jetons are available from post offices and *Ruch* kiosks. Calling from city to city isn't much of a problem, but to dial a small town you'll have to queue up in a post office or *Orbis* hotel. Making **international calls** within Europe isn't too problematic these days, but for calls further afield there's little alternative but to go through an operator at an *Orbis* hotel or post office, which may entail waiting several hours (operator number ☎900). There's no facility for reversing the charges.

Getting Around

Poland has comprehensive and cheap public transport services, though they can often be overcrowded and excruciatingly slow.

■ Trains

The reasonably efficient Polish State Railways (**PKP**) runs three main types of **trains**: **express** services (*ekspresowy*) are the ones to go for if you're travelling long distances, as they stop at the main cities only; seat reservations, involving a small supplementary charge, are compulsory. So-called **fast** trains (*pośpieszne*) have far more stops, and reservations are optional. **Normal** services (*normalne* or *osobowe*) should be avoided: in rural areas they stop at every haystack. Some two dozen narrow-gauge lines are still in operation, and steam is used on some of these as well as on a few main-line routes.

Even a long cross-country haul will only set you back little more than $7.50, but it's well worth paying the fifty percent extra to travel **first-class** or make a **reservation** (*miejscówka*), as sardine-like conditions are fairly common. Most long journeys are best done overnight; second-class sleepers are a particularly good bargain at around $9 per head. Buying **tickets** in main stations can be a major hassle involving waits of upwards of an hour. Alternatively, you can buy tickets for journeys of over 100km at *Orbis* offices. The main branches of these are also the best places to book **international journeys** (hard currency only). **Rail passes** for the whole network are available in Poland for periods of seven, fourteen or twenty-one days or for a whole month, but you'd have to take an awful lot of trains to justify the outlay. However, the *Eurotrain Explorer* (see *Basics*) gives you unlimited travel for £20. *InterRail* passes are valid in Poland, but not *Eurail*.

■ Buses

Inter-city **buses** operated by **PKS**, the national bus company, are often overcrowded and slow; there are very few long-haul routes and no overnight journeys. However, in rural areas, notably the mountain regions, buses are usually the better means of getting around, scoring in the choice and greater convenience. Main bus stations are usually alongside the train station. Seat numbers are allocated when you buy tickets, though many stations cannot allocate seats for services starting from another town – in such cases you have to buy a ticket from the driver. As with trains, *Orbis* offices are the best place to go if you want to book on an **international** route.

■ Driving and hitching

Poles are not yet routine car owners and recent inflation has, if anything, cleared roads further. **Hiring a car** costs from around £80/$120 a day, £440/$640 a week (unlimited mileage). Many **petrol stations** in cities and on main international routes are open 24 hours a day, others from around 6am to 10pm. In rural areas stations can be a long way apart, so carry a fuel can. **Speed limits** are 60kph in built-up areas, 90kph on country roads, 110kph on motorways. The Polish motoring organization, *PZMot*, runs a 24-hour **car breakdown** service; the national HQ is at ul Krucza 6/14, Warsaw (☎022/293-541).

Thanks to the scarcity of private vehicles in Poland, **hitchhiking** is positively encouraged. PTTK have in fact institutionalized the practice through their *Społeczny Komitet Autostop* (Social Autostop Committee), which sells books of vouchers which can be given to drivers, qualifying them for various prizes. The head *Autostop* office is at ul Narbutta 27a, Warsaw (☎022/496-208).

Accommodation

Accommodation will almost certainly account for the majority of your costs in Poland, though there are now plenty of very cheap alternatives to the heavily touted international hotels.

■ Hotels

Orbis runs some 55 **international hotels** throughout Poland. A few of these are famous old prewar haunts, but the vast majority are in anonymous concrete style. They're extremely pricey, but they do. have consistently high standards. Minimum rates, which are based on hard currency, are around £40/$60 for a single, £70/$100 for a double rising to more than £150/$225 per head in Warsaw. Fortunately, non-guests are able to make use of their restaurants, bars and other amenities such as swimming pools.

Most **other hotels** have far more rudimentary facilities. Some highly recommendable ones charge less than £5/$7.50 for a double with bath, but you might land a tacky room without facilities for three or four times that somewhere else. Figure on paying £10/$15 a day per head as an average. The cheapest of all hotel rooms are provided by **sports hotels** (*Dom Sportowy*), charging around £3.50/$5 a head, but these are inconveniently located and likely to be booked up at weekends by visiting sports teams.

■ Hostels

Scattered throughout Poland are some 200 **official youth hostels** (*Schroniska Młodzieżowe*), but many of these are only open at the height of the summer holiday period and are liable to be booked solid, while most of the year-round hostels are still very much in line with the hair-shirt ideals of the movement's founders. Two plus points are the prices (rarely more than £2.50/$4 a head) and the locations, with many placed close to town centres. For a complete list, contact the Polish youth hostel federation (*PTSM*) at ul. Chocimska 28, Warsaw (Mon–Fri 8am–3.30pm; ☎022/498-128).

There's a network of adult **tourist hostels**, often run by PTTK and called either *Dom Turysty* or *Dom Wycieczkowy*. Found in both cities and rural locations, these are generally cheaper than any hotel, but are often a poor bargain at around £5/$7.50 for a bed in a small dorm with basic facilities. *Almatur* also organizes summer accommodation in **university hostels**; charges (including breakfast) are around £4/$6 for students and £6.50/$10 for others under 35, which is the age limit. In mountain areas, a generous number of **refuges**, which are clearly marked on hiking maps, enable you to make long-distance treks. Accommodation is in very basic dormitories, but costs are nominal and you can often get cheap and filling hot meals.

■ Private rooms

It's possible to get a **room in a private house** almost anywhere in the country. Some are pretty shabby, but it's an ideal way to find out how the Poles themselves live. All major cities have an office providing a room-finding service, usually known as the **Biuro Zakwaterowania**. The charges don't vary much: usually £6–7/$9–11 and half as much again in Warsaw. You'll be given a choice of location and category (from 1 down to 3); it makes sense not to register for too many nights ahead in case you don't like the place you're sent to. Some *Orbis* **offices** also act as agents for householders with rooms available to let. These are often a little more expensive, but the administration is far less tight. At the unofficial level, many houses in the main holiday areas hang out **signs** saying *Noclegi* (lodging) or *Pokoje* (rooms). It's up to you to bargain; £3/$4.50 is the least you can expect to pay.

ACCOMMODATION PRICE CODES

Throughout this guide, accommodation is priced on a scale of ① to ⑧, the number indicating the lowest price per night a single person could expect to pay in that establishment in high season. With hostels this is the nightly rate per person; with hotels, the price is arrived at by dividing the cost of the cheapest double room by two. The prices indicated by the codes are as follows

① = under £5 / $8   ② = £5–10 / $8–16   ③ = £10–15 / $16–24   ④ = £15–20 / $24–32

⑤ = £20–25 / $32–40   ⑥ = £25–30 / $40–48   ⑦ = £30–35 / $48–56   ⑧ = over £35 / $56

■ Camping

There are some 400 **campsites** throughout the country; for a complete list see the *Campingi w Polsce* map. Apart from main holiday areas, they can be found in most cities: the ones on the outskirts are invariably linked by bus to the centre and often have the benefit of a peaceful location and swimming pool. Most open May–Sept only. Charges usually work out at less than £2/$3 a head, a bit more if you come by car. Many sites have chalets to rent which, though spartan, are good value at around £3.50/$5 per head. **Camping rough**, outside of the national parks, is okay so long as you're discreet.

Food and Drink

Poles take their food seriously, providing snacks of feast-like proportions to the most casual visitors. The cuisine itself is a complex mix of influences: Russian, German, Ukrainian, Lithuanian and Jewish traditions all leave their mark.

■ Food

Breakfast might include fried eggs with ham, mild frankfurters, a selection of cold meats and cheese, rolls and jam. A common alternative, however, is to stop at a milk bar or self-service snack bar. Open from early morning till 5 or 6pm, **snack bars** (*samoobsługa*) are soup kitchen-type places, serving very cheap but generally uninspiring food. **Milk bars** (*bar mleczny*) are even cheaper options, offering a selection of solid, non-meat meals with the emphasis on quantity.

Traditional Polish **takeaway stands** usually sell *zapiekanki*, baguette-like pieces of bread topped with melted cheese; a less common but enjoyable version of the same thing comes with fried mushrooms. You'll also find hot dog stalls, doling out sub-frankfurter sausages in white rolls, and stalls and shops selling chips (*frytki*), accompanied by sausage (*kiełbasa*) or chicken (*kurczak*) in the tourist resorts.

All but the smartest **restaurants** (*restauracja*, sometimes *jadłodajnia*) close early, winding down around 9pm in cities, earlier in the country. Officially restaurants are graded from *kat 1* (luxury) down to *kat 4* (cheap); unless funds are very limited, stick to the top two ratings. However, many of the newer private places ignore this system, and categories are starting to disappear.

First on the menu in most places are **soups**, definitely one of Polish cuisine's strongest points,

varying from light and delicate dishes to concoctions that are virtually meals in themselves. Best known is *barszcz*, a spicy beetroot broth that's ideally accompanied by a small pastry. In better restaurants, the **hors d'œuvres** selection might include Jewish-style gefilte fish, jellied ham (*szynka w galerecie*), steak tartare (*stek tatarski*), wild rabbit paté (*pasztet zająca*), or hard-boiled eggs in mayonnaise, sometimes stuffed with vegetables (*jajka faszerowane*).

The basis of most main courses is a fried or grilled cut of **meat** in a thick sauce, commonest of which is the *kotlet schwabowy*, a fried pork cutlet. Two national specialities you'll find everywhere are *bigos* (cabbage stewed with meat and spices) and *pierogi*, dumplings stuffed with meat and mushrooms – or with cottage cheese, onion and spices in the non-meat variation (*pierogi ruskie*). **Pancakes** (*naleśniki*) often come as a main course, too, stuffed with cottage cheese (*z serem*). Fried potato pancakes (*placki ziemniaczane*) are particularly good, served in sour cream or spicy paprika sauce.

Cakes, pastries and other sweets are an integral ingredient of most Poles' daily consumption, and the **cake shops** (*cukiernia*) – which you'll find even in small villages – are as good as any in Central Europe. *Sernik* (cheesecake) is a national favourite, as are *makowiec* (poppyseed cake), *drożdówka* (a sponge cake, often topped with plums), and *babka piaskowa* (marble cake).

■ Drink

Poles' capacity for alcohol has never been in doubt, and drinking is a national pursuit. Much of the drinking goes on in **restaurants**, which in smaller towns or villages are often the only outlets selling alcohol. In the cities and larger towns, you'll come upon **hotel bars** (frequented mainly by Westerners or wealthier Poles), a growing number of **privately run bars** (*bary*), which mimic Western models, and the very different and traditional **drink bars**. The last, basic and functional, are almost exclusively male terrain and generally best avoided.

Poles can't compete with their Czech neighbours in the production and consumption of **beer** (*piwo*), but there are a number of highly drinkable Polish brands. It's with **vodka** (*wódka*) that Poles really get into their stride. Ideally it is served neat, well chilled, in measures of 25 or 50 grammes and knocked back in one go, with a mineral water chaser. Best of the clear vodkas are *Żytnia* and

Wyborowa. Of the flavoured varieties, first on most people's list is *Żubrówka*, infused with the taste of bison grass.

Opening Hours and Holidays

Most **shops** open on weekdays from around 10am to 6pm, except food stores which may open as early as 6am and close by mid-afternoon. Many shops close on Saturdays. *Ruch* kiosks, where you buy newspapers and municipal transport tickets, generally open at about 6am. Increasing numbers of street traders do business well into the evening and you can usually find the odd shop in a major city offering late-night opening throughout the week. **Museums** and **historic monuments** almost invariably close one day per week, usually Monday. **Public holidays** are: Jan 1; Easter Monday; May 1; May 3; Corpus Christi (variable May/June); Aug 15; Nov 1; Nov 11; Dec 25 & 26.

Entrance tickets cost very little but often change – hence no prices are quoted in the text.

Emergencies

The **policja** are responsible for everyday law enforcement. The biggest potential hassles are hotel room thefts, pickpocketing in the markets and car break-ins. Avoid leaving cars unattended overnight in city centres, keep valuables on you at all times; and try not to look conspicuously affluent.

For serious **health** problems you'll be directed to a **hospital** (*szpital*), where conditions will probably be pretty horrendous, with too many patients for the beds, a lack of medicines and often insanitary conditions. Doctors are heavily overworked and scandalously underpaid. If you are required to pay for medical treatment or medication, remember to keep receipts for your insurance claim when you return.

EMERGENCY NUMBERS
Police ☎997; Ambulance ☎999; Fire ☎998.

WARSAW

Likely to be most visitors' first experience of Poland, **WARSAW** makes an initial impression which is all too often negative. The years of communist rule have left no great aesthetic glories, and there's sometimes a hollowness to the faithful reconstructions of earlier eras. However, as throughout Poland, the pace of social change is tangible and fascinating, as the openings provided by the post-communist order turn the streets into a continuous marketplace, while the postwar dearth of nightlife and entertainments is gradually becoming a complaint of the past, as a plethora of new bars, restaurants and clubs establish themselves.

Warsaw became the capital of Poland in 1596, when **King Zygmunt III** moved his court two hundred miles from Kraków – a decision chiefly compelled by the shift of Poland's geographical centre after the union with Lithuania. The city was badly damaged by the Swedes during the invasion of 1655 and was then extensively reconstructed by the **Saxon kings** in the late seventeenth century – the Saxon Gardens (Ogród Saski), right in the centre, date from this period. The **Partitions** abruptly terminated this golden age, as Warsaw was absorbed into Prussia in 1795. Napoleon's arrival in 1806 gave Varsovians brief hopes of liberation, but following the 1815 Congress of Vienna, the city was integrated into the Russian-controlled **Congress Kingdom of Poland**. It was only with the outbreak of World War I that Russian control began to crumble, and in late 1914 the Germans occupied the city, remaining to the end of the war. Following the return of Polish independence, Warsaw reverted to its position as capital; but then, with the outbreak of World War II, came the progressive annihilation of the city. Hitler, infuriated by the **Warsaw Uprising**, ordered the elimination of Warsaw; by the end of the war 850,000 Varsovians – two-thirds of the city's 1939 population – were dead or missing. The task of rebuilding the city took ten years of ceaseless labour.

> The Warsaw telephone code is ☎022 for six-digit numbers, ☎02 for seven digits.

Arrival and information

Okęcie international airport is a half-hour journey by bus #175 from central Warsaw; the quicker Airport City bus (25,000zł) stops at central hotels and there's a *LOT* bus service (60,000zł) to their new terminal on al Jerozolimskie. **Warszawa Centralna**, the main **train station**, is a ten-minute bus ride (#160, #174 or #175) from the Old Town; there's a 24-hour left-luggage office here, as well as lockers. Most trains run straight through to Centralna but it's possible that you'll need to change trains at Dworzec Wschodnia (East) station, out in the Praga suburb, or Dworzec Zachodnia (West), in the Ochota district. Centralny Dworzec PKS, the main **bus station**, is across the road from Dworzec Zachodnia.

The wide open expanse of the Wisła river is the most obvious aid to **orientation**. The heart of Warsaw, the **Śródmieście** district, sits on the left bank; above it is the **Old Town** (Stare Miasto) area, with **plac Zamkowy** a useful central reference, while over on the east bank lies the **Praga** suburb.

There's still no reliable source of general **information**, though the *Informator Turystyczny* (IT) point on plac Zamkowy 1/13 (Mon–Fri 9am–6pm, Sat 10am–6pm, Sun 11am–6pm; ☎310-464) is getting better; there are rudimentary information desks in the airport arrivals lounge and the central station. The *Orbis* office at the corner of Królewska and Marszałkowska has an information desk (Mon–Fri 8am–4pm; ☎276-766), and most of the big hotels have IT points too.

City transport

Warsaw is too big to get around without using public transport. **Bus** and **tram** are the main forms of transport, and both are still very cheap for foreigners. Regular bus and tram routes close down about midnight; from 11pm to 5am **night buses** leave every thirty minutes from behind the Palace of Culture.

Tickets for both trams and buses are bought from *Ruch* counters (not from drivers), and are currently 4000zł each – but prices will certainly go up. For buses or trams numbered #1–#599 you need one ticket, for *pospieszne* (speed) buses marked #700+ and A–U you need two, and for night buses (#600–#699), three. Punch your tickets in the machines on board – inspectors will fine you 200,000zł on the spot if they catch you without a validated ticket. It's worth stocking up on Fridays, as tickets can be much harder to get hold of at weekends. Alternatively you can get day (15,000zł) or week (75,000zł) passes from the MZK at Bankowy Square.

For Westerners **taxis** are reasonable. Make sure the meter is turned on when you set off: the fare is the price displayed multiplied by the sum shown on the little sign. At night or from hotels, the airport and the train station, be prepared for drivers charging in hard currency – often at a significant mark-up on the equivalent złoty rate.

Accommodation

Warsaw has two **IYHF hostels**, and during July and August the *Almatur*-run **international student hotels** are another inexpensive possibility. The *Almatur* office at ul Kopernika 23 (Mon–Fri 9am–6pm, Sat 10am–2pm; ☎263-512) has location details and the required vouchers for those who haven't bought them beforehand. The best bet for help with hotel **bookings** is the *Informator Turystyczny*. Otherwise it's a case of phoning or calling in person – in larger hotels there'll be someone who speaks some English or German.

Hostels

Ul Karolkowa 53a (☎328-829). In the western Wola district – take tram #22 or #24 north from the main station and get off on al. Solidarności, near the *Wola* department store. Reception 5–9pm. ②

Ul Smolna 30 (☎278-952). A five-minute bus ride along al Jerozolimskie from the main station – any bus heading towards Nowy Świat will drop you at the corner of the street. Reception 4–9pm. ②

Hotels

Dom Chłopa, pl. Powstanców Warszawy 2 (☎279-251). Used by a wider clientele than its name (Farmers' House) suggests. ④

Druh, ul Niemcewicza 17 (☎6590-011). West of the main station. A young people's hotel, popular with students – more attractive option than the *Dom Turysty*; trams #7, #8, #9, #25 or bus C. ③

MDM, pl Konstytucji 1 (☎628-2526). Rooms here are quieter and pleasanter than its location and external appearance might suggest. ④

Metropol, Marsałkowska 99a (☎294-001). Sited within easy walking distance of the central station, which means this is often full. ⑤

Orzel, ul Podskarbińska 11/15 (☎105-060). By a stadium in southern Praga; bus F, then walk. ④

PTTK Dom Turysty, Krakowskie Przedmieście 4/6 (☎260-071 and ask for reception). Located just below the university campus. Tolerable doubles but messy communal bathrooms and toilets. ②

Saski, pl Bankowy 1 (☎204-611/615). Well located just off Saski park, with decent rooms and plenty of character. ②

Pensjonat Stegny, ul Inspektowa 4 (☎422-768). A sports-stadium hotel, on the way to Wilanów. Bus #130. ①

Warszawa, pl. Powstanców Warszawy 9 (☎269-421). Just off Świętokrzyska; popular with East European tourist groups. ④

Private rooms

The main source of information for **private rooms** (②) is Syrena's *biuro kwatery prywatnych* office, ul Krucza 16/22 (daily 8am–7pm; ☎628-7540/5698). Get there as early as possible – finding anything after 4pm is pushing your luck. Of the new private bureaux, the most reliable is the *Romeo i Julia*, on the second floor at Emilii Plater 30, across from the main station (Mon–Sat 9am–7pm; ☎292-993). The English-speaking proprietress guarantees to find you a decent room in central Warsaw; prices are higher than at the Syrena office.

Campsites

Camping Gromada, ul Żwirki i Wigury 32 (☎254-391). Best and most popular of the Warsaw camp-sites, on the way out to the airport – bus #136, #175 or #512.

Wisła, Wery-Kostrzewy 15/17 (☎233-748). Just south of the bus station – take bus #154 or #172. Less crowded than the *Gromada* site.

The City

Wending its way north towards Gdańsk and the Baltic Sea, the **Wisła** river divides Warsaw neatly in half: the main sights are located on the western bank, the eastern consisting predominantly of residential and business districts. Somewhat to the north of centre, the busy **Old Town** provides the historic focal point.

The Old Town

The title "Old Town" – Stare Miasto – is in some respects a misnomer for the historic nucleus of Warsaw. Forty-five years ago this compact network of streets and alleyways lay in rubble: even the cobblestones are meticulously assembled replacements. **Plac Zamkowy** (Castle Square), on the south side of the Old Town, is the obvious place to start a tour. Here the first thing to catch your eye is the bronze **statue** of Zygmunt III Waza, the king who made Warsaw the capital.

On the east side of the square is the former **Royal Castle** (Zamek Królewski), once home of the royal family and seat of the Polish parliament, now the **Castle Museum** (Tues–Sat 10am–2.30pm, Sun 10am–4.30pm). Though the structure is a replica, many of its furnishings are the originals, scooted into hiding by percipient employees during the first bombing raids. After the Chamber of Deputies, formerly the debating chamber of the parliament, the Grand Staircase leads to the most lavish section of the castle, the **Royal Apartments of King Stanisław August**. Through two smaller rooms you come to the magnificent **Canaletto Room**, with its views of Warsaw by Bernardo Bellotto, nephew of the famous Canaletto – whose name he appropriated to make his pictures sell better. Marvellous in their detail, these cityscapes provided important information for the architects rebuilding the city after the war. Next door is the richly decorated **Royal Chapel**, where an urn contains the heart – sacred to many Poles – of Tadeusz Kościuszko, swashbuckling leader of the 1794 insurrection and hero of the American War of Independence.

On Świętojańska, north of the castle, stands **St John's Cathedral**, the oldest church in Warsaw, now regaining its old official functions under the Catholic-dominated Solidarity government. A few yards away, the Old Town Square – **Rynek Starego Miasto** – is one of the most remarkable bits of postwar reconstruction anywhere in Europe. Flattened during the Warsaw Uprising, its three-storey merchants' houses have been rebuilt to their seventeenth- and eighteenth-century designs, multicoloured facades included. By day the Rynek teems with visitors, who are catered for by busk-ers, artists, cafés, moneychangers and *doroski*, the traditional horse-drawn carts that clatter tourists round the Old Town for a sizeable fee. The **Warsaw Historical**

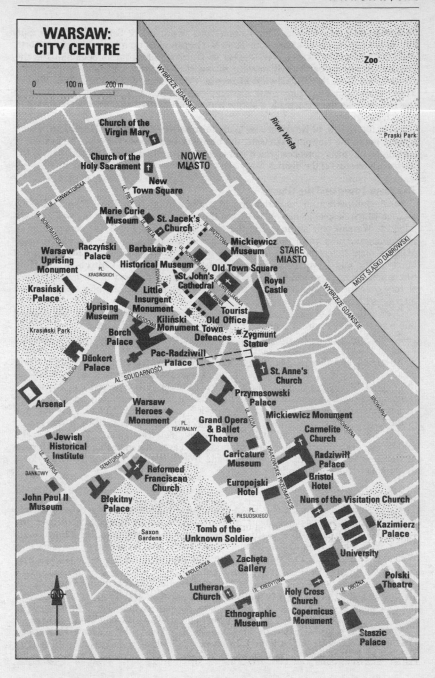

WARSAW: CITY CENTRE

0   100 m   200 m

Zoo

Praski Park

WYBRZEŻE GDAŃSKIE

River Wisła

MOST ŚLĄSKO DĄBROWSKI

WYBRZEŻE GDAŃSKIE

Church of the Virgin Mary

NOWE MIASTO

Church of the Holy Sacrament

New Town Square

UL. KONWIKTORSKA

UL. BONIFRATERSKA

UL. FRETA

Marie Curie Museum

UL. FRETA

St. Jacek's Church

UL. BRZOZOWA

Mickiewicz Museum

STARE MIASTO

Warsaw Uprising Monument

Raczyński Palace

Barbakan

Historical Museum

PL. KRASIŃSKICH

Old Town Square

Royal Castle

Krasiński Palace

Little Insurgent Monument

St. John's Cathedral

UL. PODWALE

UL. PIWNA

Uprising Museum

Krasiński Park

UL. MIODOWA

Kiliński Monument

Tourist Old Office Town Defences

Zygmunt Statue

Borch Palace

Dückert Palace

Pac-Radziwiłł Palace

AL. SOLIDARNOŚCI

St. Anne's Church

BROWARNA

Arsenal

Warsaw Heroes Monument

PL. TEATRALNY

Przymasowski Palace

Mickiewicz Monument

Grand Opera & Ballet Theatre

UL. KOZA

Carmelite Church

KRAKOWSKIE PRZEDMIEŚCIE

Jewish Historical Institute

UL. ANDERSA

PL. BANKOWY

SENATORSKA

Caricature Museum

Radziwiłł Palace

Reformed Franciscan Church

Europejski Hotel

Bristol Hotel

John Paul II Museum

Błękitny Palace

Nuns of the Visitation Church

Saxon Gardens

PL. PIŁSUDSKIEGO

Tomb of the Unknown Soldier

Kazimierz Palace

University

UL. KRÓLEWSKA

Zachęta Gallery

Polski Theatre

UL. DROŻNA

Lutheran Church

UL. KREDYTOWA

Holy Cross Church

Ethnographic Museum

Copernicus Monument

Staszic Palace

Museum (summer Tues & Thurs noon–7pm, Wed, Fri & Sat 10am–3.30pm, Sun 10.30am–4.30pm; winter closes 6pm Tues & Thurs) takes up a large part of the north side; exhibitions here cover every aspect of Warsaw's life from its beginnings to the present day, with a particularly moving chronicle of everyday resistance to the Nazis. On the east side, the **Mickiewicz Museum** (Mon, Tues & Fri 10am–3pm, Wed & Thurs 11am–6pm, Sun 11am–5pm) is a temple to the Romantic national poet; amongst the memorabilia there's actually a shrine room, with portrait and crucifix enveloped in church-like gloom.

From the Rynek, ul Nowomiejska leads to the sixteenth-century **Barbakan**, which used to guard the Nowomiejska Gate, the northern entrance to the city. The fortress is part of the old town defences, which run all the way around from plac Zamkowy to the northeastern edge of the district.

The New Town and the Ghetto

Cross the ramparts from the Barbakan and you're into the **New Town (Nowe Miasto)** district, which despite its name dates from the early fifteenth century, but was formally joined to Warsaw only at the end of the eighteenth. **Ulica Freta**, the continuation of Nowomiejska, runs north through the heart of the district to the **Rynek Nowego Miasto**, once the commercial hub of the district, now a soothing change from the bustle of the Old Town. Tucked into the eastern corner is the **Church of the Holy Sacrament**, commissioned by Queen Maria Sobieska in memory of her husband Jan's victory over the Turks at Vienna in 1683; as you might expect, highlight of the sober interior is the Sobieski funeral chapel.

Over to the west of the square is the majestic **Krasiński Palace**, its facade bearing fine sculptures by Andreas Schlüter. Behind the palace are the **gardens**, now a public park, and beyond that the Ghetto area. In 1939 there were an estimated 380,000 Jews living in and around Warsaw – one third of the total population. By May 1945, around 300 were left, and after the war Jewish Warsaw was replaced by the sprawling housing estates and tree-lined thoroughfares of the **Muranów** and **Mirów** districts, a little to the west of the city centre. However, a few traces of the Jewish presence in Warsaw do remain, and there's a small but increasingly visible Jewish community here. First stop on any itinerary of Jewish Warsaw is the **Nożyk Synagogue** on ul Twarda, the only one of the Ghetto's three synagogues still standing. Built in the early 1900s, it was gutted during the war, and reopened in 1983 after a complete restoration. Marooned in the middle of a drab square to the north of the Ghetto area, the imposing **Ghetto Heroes Monument** – unveiled in 1948 – was made from materials ordered by Hitler for a monument to the Reich's anticipated victory.

Sródmieście

The area stretching from the Old Town down towards Łazienki Park – **Sródmieście** – is the increasingly fast-paced heart of Warsaw. Of all the thoroughfares bisecting central Warsaw from north to south, the most important is the one often known as the Royal Way, which runs almost uninterrupted from plac Zamkowy to the palace of Wilanów. **Krakowskie Przedmieście**, the first part of the Royal Way, is lined with historic buildings.

Even in a city not lacking in Baroque churches, the **Church of the Nuns of the Visitation** stands out, with its columned, statue-topped facade; it's also one of the very few buildings in central Warsaw to have come through World War II unscathed. Its main claim to fame in Polish eyes is that Chopin used to play the church organ here.

Most of the rest of Krakowskie Przedmieście is taken up by **Warsaw University**. On the main campus courtyard, the **Library** stands in front of the seventeenth-century **Kazimierz Palace**, once a royal summer residence, while across the street from the gates is the former **Czapski Palace**, now home of the Academy of Fine Arts. Just south is the Baroque **Holy Cross Church** (Kosciól Świętego Krzyża), which was ruined by a two-week battle inside the building during the Warsaw Uprising; photographs of the distinctive figure of Christ left standing among the ruins became poignant emblems of Warsaw's suffering. Another factor increases local affection for this church: on a pillar to the left side of the nave there's an urn containing Chopin's heart.

Biggest among Warsaw's consistently big palaces is the early nineteenth-century **Staszic Palace**, which virtually blocks the end of Krakowskie Przedmieście. South from the Staszic, the main street becomes **Nowy Świat** (New World), an area first settled in the mid-seventeenth century. Moving down this wide boulevard, the palaces of the aristocracy give way to shops, offices and cafés.

West along al Jerozolimskie is the **National Museum** (Tues & Sun 10am–5pm, Wed, Fri & Sat 10am–4pm, Thurs noon–6pm), an impressive compendium of art and archeology. The first floor has the ancient art while the European galleries on the upper floors display a wide range of paintings and sculptures – Caravaggio, Bellini, Bruegel and Rodin included. However, most notable of the museum's collections is the display of Polish medieval altarpieces and religious sculpture, featuring some imaginative and exuberant wooden Madonnas, mainly from the Gdańsk region. The **Army Museum** next door (Wed 11am–5pm, Thurs, Fri & Sun 10am–4pm, Sat 11am–4pm) stirs pride in many Poles, but few foreigners get further than the World War II heavy armour outside.

The area below the Saxon Gardens and west of Krakowskie Przedmieście is the busiest commercial zone. **Marszałkowska**, the main road running south from the western tip of the park, is lined with department stores and privately run boutiques and workshops selling everything from jewellery to car spares. Towering over everything in this part of the city is the **Palace of Culture**, a gift from Stalin to the Polish people, and not one that could be refused. Apart from a vast conference hall, the cavernous interior contains offices, cinemas, swimming pools, some good foreign-language bookshops, and – the ultimate capitalistic revenge – a casino. The locals say that the best view of Warsaw is from the thirtieth-floor platform – the only viewpoint from which one can't see the palace (Mon–Sat 9am–7pm, Sun 10am–7pm).

Łazienki Park and Palace

Parks are one of Warsaw's distinctive and most attractive features. South of the commercial district, on the east side of al Ujazdowskie, is one of the best, the **Łazienki Park**. Once a hunting ground, the area was bought by King Stanisław August in the 1760s and turned into an English-style park with formal gardens. A few years later the slender Neoclassical **Łazienki Palace** was built across the park lake: the best memorial to the country's last and most cultured monarch.

The oak-lined promenades and pathways leading from the park entrance to the palace are a favourite with both Varsovians and tourists. On summer Sunday lunchtimes, concerts and other events take place under the watchful eye of the ponderous **Chopin Monument**, just beyond the entrance. The only way to see the **palace interior** (daily except Mon 9.30am–3pm) is on a group tour, and these get booked early in the day. Nazi damage to the rooms themselves was not irreparable, and most of the lavish furnishings, paintings and sculptures survived the war intact, having been hidden during the occupation. The stuccoed **ballroom**, the biggest ground-floor room, is a fine example of Stanisław's classicist predilections, lined with a tasteful collection of busts and classical sculptures. As the adjoining **picture galleries** demonstrate, Stanisław was a discerning art collector. Upstairs are the **king's private apartments**, most of them entirely reconstructed since the war.

Wilanów

The grandest of Warsaw's palaces, **Wilanów** makes an easy excursion from the city centre: buses #B, #122, #130 and #180 run to the town centre just over the road from the palace entrance. Sometimes called the Polish Versailles, it was the brainchild of King Jan Sobieski, who purchased the existing manor house and estate in 1677; he spent nearly twenty years turning it into his ideal country residence, which was later extended by a succession of monarchs and aristocrats. It's now a tourist favourite, and the best ways to ensure entry are either to get there early (as always), to go on a Sunday (theoretically the non-group visitors' day), or to sign up for an *Orbis* tour.

Among the sixty-odd rooms of Wilanów's **interior** (daily except Tues 9.30am–2.30pm) you'll find styles ranging from the lavish early Baroque of the apartments of Jan Sobieski and John III to the classical grace of the nineteenth-century Potocki museum rooms. Some might find the cumulative effect of all this pomp and glory rather deadening – even the official guides seem to recognize this, easing off with the facts and figures in the last part of the guided tour. If your interest hasn't flagged after the tour, there are a couple of other places of interest within the grounds. The gate on the left side beyond the main entrance opens onto the stately **palace gardens** (daily except Tues 10am till sunset), whilst to the right before you enter is the **Poster Museum** (daily except Mon 10am–4pm), a mishmash of the inspired and the bizarre from an art form which has long had major currency in Poland.

Eating and drinking

Warsaw's **cafés** have long been favoured for get-togethers, clandestine political exchanges, stand-up rows or just passing the time; **bars**, traditionally something of a low spot of Warsaw nightlife, are improving in leaps and bounds. For basic snacks, **milk bars** (*bar mleczny*) provide a good fill for under $5. As even the proudest Varsovians will admit, too many Warsaw **restaurants** are still marred by dingy surroundings, unimaginative menus and poor service. That said, there are quite a few perfectly good places to eat, and an increasing number of small, well-run private restaurants are now appearing. All the places listed below should cost under $17 a head.

Cafés

Amatorska, Nowy Śuriat 21. Modern café with a mouth-watering selection of cakes.

Boruta, Rynek Nowego Miasto. A really nice café to sit outside and write postcards while enjoying the New Town square.

Manekin, Rynek Starego Miasto 2. An enjoyable basement coffee dive on the Old Town square, with a bar at the back.

Polonia, al Jerozolimskie 45. The hotel's *cukiernia* is a nice central stopoff with a good selection of cakes, ice creams and desserts.

Milk bars and snack bars

Expresso, ul Bracka 18. Cheap central joint offering Polish-style basics. Open for breakfast.

Max, ul Pozriarísak 38. Small private bar serving good Arab nosh, particularly kebabs and *shashlik*; close to the central station.

Pod Barbakanem, ul Mostowa 29. Deservedly popular New Town milk bar near the Barbakan, where you can sit outside and watch the crowds.

Uniwersytecki, Krakowskie Przedmieście 20. Milk bar much frequented by students; just up from the university gates.

Restaurants

Gessler, Rynek Starego Miasto 21a. Low ceilings and decent Polish cuisine in an Old Town venue that's a favourite with provincial Poles bingeing it for a weekend in the capital. Open 10am–2am.

Kuźnia, Wiertnicza 2. Wilanów's restaurant. Pork dishes are a good bet, as are the peach and pear desserts. Open 10am–11pm.

Mekong, ul Wspólna 35 (☎211-881). Excellent small restaurant, owned by a Vietnamese student who stayed on. The fish dishes are definitely worth the extra twenty-minute wait. Open 10am–10pm. Booking recommended.

Pod Retmanem, ul Bednarska 9. Popular fish-oriented restaurant. Open noon to last guest.

Staropolska, ul Krakowskie Przedmieście 8. Rather gloomy decor and erratic service here is offset by a good, inevitably pork-based menu. Open 5pm–late.

Bars

Europejski, Krakowskie Przedmieście 13. In summer the hotel's terrace café is one of the nicest places in town to sit out and enjoy an early evening drink.

Pod Herbami, ul Piwna 21/23. An archetypal "drink bar" – but one that hip young Varsovians like to be seen in.

Studio M, Krakowskie Przedmieście 27. Trendy, expensive designer bar frequented by arty types – there's even a small gallery. Open till 1am.

U Fukiera, Rynek Starego Miasto 27. Smoky traditional wine bar on the square, complete with gypsy band.

U Hopfera, Krakowskie Przedmieście 55. Wine-bar-cum-restaurant that was once a favourite with students, but is now more upmarket.

Nightlife

For up-to-date **information** about what's on, check the back pages of the weekly English-language newspapers, *The Warsaw Voice*, *Welcome to Warsaw* or *Warsaw: What Where When*, or the listings in *Wik* magazine, the city's equivalent of *Time Out*, or the weekend editions of *Gazeta Wyboreza* and *Zycie Warszawy*. You can buy the latter three at most *Ruch* kiosks, and tourist offices or hotels generally supply the former. Regular Warsaw **festivals** include the excellent annual **Jazz Jamboree** in October (Miles Davis featuring among recent artists), the biannual **Warsaw Film Festival**, the **Festival of Contemporary Music** held every September, and the five-yearly **Chopin Piano Competition** – always a launch pad for a major international career.

Clubs, discos and live music

Warsaw's night scene has been feeling the economic pinch in recent years, and appearances by major bands are still a rarity. When big names do turn up, they generally play at the Dziesięciolecia Stadium in Praga. As a rule, **discos** are tacky, Europop affairs, frequented by a combination of young reticents and drunkards. Most of the clubs listed below are known as student venues.

Akwarium, ul Emilii Plater 49 (☎205-072). The only genuine jazz club in town, it has at least one good Polish or foreign act a week.

Hybrydy, ul Ztota 7/9 (☎273-763). Weekend discos with a decent beat, a "Rap-Club" and occasional live gigs.

Remont, ul Waryńskiego 12 (☎257-497). Best of the student clubs, with regular rock, folk and jazz concerts and discos.

Stodoła, ul Batorego 10 (☎256-031). Ten minutes' walk from the Piłsudski park, southwest of the centre. Lively spot at weekends, with a late disco.

Listings

Airlines The *LOT* building at al Jerozolimskie 65/79 (☎628-7580/1009) makes bookings for domestic and foreign flights, as do all the major *Orbis* offices. International airlines have offices on ul Krucza, ul Szpitalna and ul Marszałkowska, as well as desks at Okęcie airport.

Airport information International flights ☎461-731. Domestic flights ☎650-1953. *PC Express* (☎637-2461) is an English-speaking agent for leading *IATA* airlines.

Bus tickets International bus tickets are available from the main station and from the Peakaes bureaux at ul Żurawa 26 (☎213-469) and ul Świętokrzyska 30 (☎204-948). National bus tickets are available at the station.

Car rental *Orbis* rental service, ul Nowogrodzka 27 (Mon–Sat 8am–8pm; ☎211-360). *Avis Airport* (☎650-4871), *Avis Marriott Hotel* (☎630-7316); *Budget Airport* (☎467-310, *Budget Marriott Hotel* (☎630-7280).

Embassies *Australia*, ul Estońska 3/5 (☎176-081); *Canada*, ul J. Matejki 1/5 (☎298-051); *Great Britain*, al Róz 1 (☎628-1001); *Netherlands*, ul Rakowiecka 19 (☎492-351); *USA*, al Ujazdowskie 29 (☎628-3041).

Exchange *Orbis* accept travellers' cheques, but they may try to extract a ten percent commission, so the big hotels can be a better bet.

Gay Warsaw Gay nightlife has a difficult time in today's Catholic-dominated political climate. Nonetheless, the *Pink Service*, ul Warynskiego 6 (☎253-911) have English speakers and can give information on clubs, as will the central tourist office if asked specifically.

Laundry Ul Mordechaja Anielewicza, on the corner of the Ghetto monument square; bus #111 passes right by (Mon–Fri 9am–7pm, Sat 9am–1pm).

Pharmacies All-night *apteka* at ul Zielna 45, ul Freta 13, ul Leszno 38 and ul Widok 19. All *apteka* windows display the address of the nearest ones.

Post offices Main offices are at ul Świętokrzyska 31/33 and in the main train station; both open 24hr for telephones, 8am–8pm for post. Both provide poste restante: Warsaw 1 is the code number for the former, Warsaw 120 for the latter.

Train tickets For international tickets, booking at least 24hr in advance is essential, and in summer 2–3 days advance booking is the minimum. An alternative to long queues at the station is to book at *Orbis* offices, and the same goes for domestic tickets; the offices at ul Bracka 16, pl. Konstytucji 4, ul Swiętojańska 23/25 and upstairs in the *Metropol* hotel on Marszałkowska all sell tickets.

NORTHERN POLAND

Even in a country accustomed to shifts in its borders, northern Poland presents an unusually tortuous historical puzzle. Successively the domain of a Germanic crusading order, of the Hansa merchants and of the Prussians, it's only in the last forty years that the region has really become Polish. **Gdańsk, Sopot** and **Gdynia** – the **Tri-City** as their conurbation is known – dominate the area from their coastal vantage point. Like Warsaw, historic Gdańsk was obliterated in World War II but now offers some reconstructed quarters, in addition to its contemporary political interest as the birthplace of Solidarity. The most enjoyable excursions from Gdańsk are to the medieval centres of **Malbork** and **Toruń**, or to **Frombork**, chief of many towns in the region associated with the astronomer Nicolaus Copernicus.

Gdańsk

For outsiders, **GDAŃSK** is perhaps the most familiar city in Poland. The home of Lech Wałęsa, Solidarity and the former Lenin Shipyards, its images have flashed across a decade of news bulletins. Expectations formed from the newsreels are fulfilled by the industrial landscape, and suggestions of latent discontent, radicalism and future strikes are all tangible. What is more surprising, at least for those with no great knowledge of Polish history, is the cultural complexity of the place. Prewar Gdańsk – or **Danzig** as it then was – was forged by years of Prussian and Hanseatic domination, and the reconstructed city centre looks not unlike Amsterdam.

The City

The **Główne Miasto** (Main Town), the largest of the historic quarters, is the obvious starting point and is within easy walking distance of the train station. Entering it is like walking straight into a Hansa merchants' settlement, but the ancient appearance is deceptive: by May 1945 the fighting between German and Russian forces had reduced the core of Gdańsk to smouldering ruins. As with all the main streets, huge stone gateways guard both entrances to **Ulica Długa**, the main thoroughfare. Topped by a golden statue of King Zygmunt August which dominates the central skyline, the huge and well-proportioned tower of the **Town Hall** makes a powerful impact. "In all Poland there is no other, so Polish a town hall", observed one local writer, though the Dutch influences on the interior rooms might lead you to disagree. They now house the **Historical Museum** (daily except Mon 10am–5pm, last entrance 4.30pm), their lavish decorations almost upstaging the exhibits.

Past the town hall the street opens onto the wide expanses of **Długi Targ**, where the **Artus Court** (Dwór Artusa) stands out in a square filled with fine mansions. At the end of the street the archways of the **Green Gate** (Brama Zielona) open directly onto the waterfront. From the bridge over the Motława Canal you get a good view of the granaries on Spichlerze Island and to the left along the old harbour quay, now a tourist hang-out and local promenade. Halfway down is the massive and largely original fifteenth-century **Gdańsk Crane**, the biggest in medieval Europe; it now houses the **Maritime Museum** (Tues–Fri 9.30am–4pm, Sat & Sun 10am–4pm; summer closes 7pm), which features a model of every ship produced in the shipyards since 1945.

All the streets back into the town from the waterfront are worth exploring. Next up from the Green Gate is **ul Chlebnicka**, which ends at the gigantic **St Mary's Church** (Kościół Mariacka), reputedly the biggest brick church in the world. Inside, the Chapel of 11,000 Virgins has a tortured Gothic crucifix for which the artist apparently nailed his son-in-law to a cross as a model. Ulica Piwna, another street of high terraced houses west of the church entrance, ends at the monumental **Great Arsenal**, where a right turn takes you past St Nicholas' Church to the Pod Myślinksa, the main route over the canal into the Old Town.

Dominating the waterside here is the seven-storey **Great Mill** (Wielki Młyn), the biggest mill in medieval Europe – even in the 1930s it was still grinding out 200 tons of flour a day. **St Catherine's Church** (Katarżynka), the former parish church of the Old Town, to the right of the crossway, is one of the nicest in the city. Fourteenth-century – and built in brick like almost all churches in the region – it has a well-preserved and luminous interior. The most interesting part of the district is west along the canal from the mill, centred on the **Old Town Hall** (Ratusz Staromiejski), on the corner of ul Bielanska and Korzenna. Looming large in the distance are the cranes of the famous **Gdańsk shipyards** (Stocznia Gdańska) – Lenin's name was dropped in the late 1980s. With the Nowa Huta steelworks outside Kraków, this was the crucible of the political struggles of the 1980s. Ironically, the shipyards remain at the leading edge of political developments: the government is attempting to sell them to Western investors.

Stare Przedmieście – the southern part of old Gdańsk – was the limit of the original town, as testified by the ring of seventeenth-century bastions running east from plac Wałowy over the Motława. The main attraction today is the **National Art Museum** (Wed–Fri 9am–3pm, Tues & Sat 11am–5pm, Sun 9am–4pm), at Toruńska 1. There's enough local Gothic art and sculpture here to keep enthusiasts going all day, as well as a varied collection of fabrics, chests, gold and silverware – all redolent of the town's former wealth. The museum's most famous possession is Hans Memling's colossal *Last Judgement* (1473), the painter's earliest known work.

Practicalities

The main **tourist information centre**, a couple of minutes from the train station at ul Heweliusza 27 (Mon–Fri 8am–4pm; ☎058/314-355), is one of the more helpful in the country; the **Almatur office**, in the centre of town at Długi Targ 11/13 (Mon–Fri 9am–5pm, Sat 10am–3pm; ☎058/312-931), is also friendly, and employs several English-speakers; in summer they'll help you sort out accommodation in student hotels. PTTK also runs a very helpful information service from May to October in ul Dtuga 45 (daily 8am–8pm; ☎058/310-151). The **hostel** nearest the centre is the one at ul Wałowa 21 (☎058/312-313; ②), a sizeable red-brick building ten minutes' walk from the main station. Of the cheaper **hotels**, the *Jantar*, Długi Targ 19 (☎058/316-241; ②) has an excellent location in the heart of the Old Town, as does *Dom Harcerza*, ul za Murami 2/10 (☎058/313-621; ①), a downmarket place with prices to match. *Posejdon*, ul Kapliczna 30 (☎058/531-803; ⑥), halfway between Gdańsk and Sopot, is the nicest *Orbis* hotel in town. **Private rooms** can be arranged either with the efficient *Biuro Zakwaterowań* at ul Elzbietańska 10 (daily 7am–5/7pm; ☎058/312-634), or with the locals who hang about outside here and at the main train station. The most convenient campsite is at ul Jetlikowska 23 (June–Sept; ☎058/532-731), near the beach at Jetlikowo and a short walk from the terminus of trams #2 or #6, or bus #143 from Sepot station.

For **snacks**, you should check out the *Bar Neptun* at ul Długa 32/34, one of the city's classic milk bars. *Karczma Michał*, ul Jana Z. Kolna 8, is a cosy little **restaurant** close to the shipyards, serving good solid food from the owner's farm. *Retman*, ul Stągiewna 1, is a fine waterfront fish restaurant. The *Palowa* **café** underneath the town hall in Głowne Miasto, is an ideal rendezvous point, and often has a good selection of cakes too. *Zak*, ul Wały Jagiellońskie, is the best of the student **clubs**, just down from the main station.

Frombork

A little seaside town roughly 90km east along the Baltic coast from Gdańsk, **FROMBORK** was the home town of Nicolaus Copernicus, the Renaissance astronomer whose ideas overturned the earth-centred model of the universe. Most of the research for his famous *De Revolutionibus* was carried out around this town, and it was here that he died and was buried in 1543. Today it's an out-of-the-way place, almost as peaceful as it must have been in Copernicus' day. The **bus journey** from Gdańsk takes between two and three hours; for a day trip take the earlier of the two morning buses, returning late afternoon. If there's no direct bus back, take one to Elbląg and change there.

The only part of Frombork to escape unscathed from the last war was the **Cathedral Hill**, which you'll find up from the old market square in the centre of town. A compact unit surrounded by high defensive walls, its main element is the Gothic **Cathedral** (daily 9.30am–5pm), with its huge red-tiled and turreted roof. Inside, the lofty expanses of brick rise above a series of lavish altars – the high altar is a copy of the Wawel altarpiece in Kraków. To the west of the cathedral, the **Copernicus Tower** is supposed by some to have been the great man's workshop and observatory. Doubting that the local authorities would have let him make use of a part of the town defences, others maintain that he's more likely to have studied at his home, just north of the cathedral complex. The **Radziejowski Tower**, in the southwest corner of the walls, houses an assortment of Copernicus-related astronomical instruments and has an excellent view of the Wiślana lagoon. Further equipment and memorabilia are to be found in the **Copernicus Museum** across the tree-lined cathedral courtyard (Tues–Sun 9am–4.30pm). Among the exhibits are early editions of Copernicus' astronomical treatises, along with a collection of instruments, pictures and portraits.

For an overnight stay, the best of a limited choice of rooms is a decent-quality **PTTK hostel** at ul Krasickiego 3 (☎506-7252; ②). The **PTTK campsite** on ul Braniewska (May 15–Sept 15; ☎506-7368) is some way from the centre. Apart from some summer takeaway bars, the only places to **eat** are the *Pod Wzgorzem* on ul Rynek and the restaurant in the PTTK hostel.

Malbork

Following the course of the Wisła south from Gdańsk takes you into the heart of the territory once ruled by the **Teutonic Knights**. From a string of fortresses overlooking the river this religio-militaristic order controlled the medieval grain trade, and it was under their protection that merchants from the northern Hanseatic League cities established themselves on the Wisła. Their headquarters was at **MALBORK**, where the massive riverside fortress imparts a threatening atmosphere to an otherwise quiet and predominantly modern town. The **train and bus stations** are sited next to each other about ten minutes' walk south of the castle; Malbork is on the main Warsaw line, so there are plenty of trains from Gdańsk (1hr) as well as a regular bus service.

You approach the **fortress** (daily except Mon May–Sept 9am–5pm; Oct–April 9am–3pm) through the old outer castle, a zone of utility buildings which was never rebuilt after the war. Passing over the moat and through the daunting main gate, you come to the **Middle Castle**, built following the Knights' decision to move their headquarters to Malbork in 1309. Spread out around an open courtyard, this part of the complex contains the Grand Master's palace, of which the **Main Refectory** is the highlight; begun in 1330, this huge vaulted chamber shows the growing influence of the Gothic cathedral architecture developed elsewhere in Europe. Leading off from the **courtyard** are a host of dark, cavernous chambers. The largest ones contain collections of ceramics, glass, sculpture, paintings and, most importantly, a large display of Baltic **amber**, the trade in which formed the backbone of the order's fabulous wealth. From the Middle Castle a passage rises to the smaller courtyard of the **High Castle**, the oldest section of the fortress, harbouring the focus of the Knights' austere monasticism – the vast **Castle Church**.

Toruń

Poles are apt to wax lyrical on the glories of their ancient cities, and with **TORUŃ** – the biggest and most important of the Hanseatic trading centres along the Wisła – it is more than justified. Miraculously surviving the recurrent wars afflicting the region, the historic centre is one of the country's most evocative, bringing together a rich assembly of architectural styles. The principal stations are on opposite sides of the Old Town. Toruń Główny, the main **train station**, is south of the river; bus #22 and #27 run to pl Rapackiego, on the western edge of the Old Town. From the **bus station** on ul Dąbrowskiego it is a short walk south to the centre.

The westerly Old Town area is the most obvious place to start looking around – and as usual it's the mansion-lined **Rynek**, in particular the **Town Hall**, that provides the focal point. Raised in the late fourteenth century on the site of earlier cloth halls and trading stalls, this immensely elegant work is one of the finest Gothic buildings in northern Europe. The **Town Museum** (Tues–Sun 10am–4pm), which now occupies much of the building, has a gorgeous collection of the stained glass for which the city was famed and some fine sculptures – especially the celebrated "Beautiful Madonnas". On the first floor, painting takes over, a small portrait of the most famous burgher, Copernicus, basking in the limelight of a Baroque gallery. Before leaving the town hall it's also worth climbing the **tower** for a view over the city and the winding course of the Wisła.

West of here, ul Kopernika and its dingy side streets are lined with crumbling Gothic mansions and granaries, evoking a blend of past glory and shabbier contemporary reality. Halfway down Kopernika you'll find the **Copernicus Museum** (daily except Mon 10am–4pm), installed in the high brick house where the great man was born and containing a studiously assembled collection of Copernicus artefacts.

Following ul Przedzamcze north from the castle brings you onto ul Szeroka, the thoroughfare that links the Old and New Town districts. Although less grand than its mercantile neighbour, the **New Town** still boasts a number of illustrious commercial residences, most of them grouped around the **Rynek Nowomiejski**. The fourteenth-century **St James' Church**, located south of the market area of the Rynek, completes the city's collection of Gothic churches. An unusual feature of this brick basilica is its featuring of flying buttresses – a common enough sight in Western Europe but extremely rare in Poland. To the north of the square, ul Prosta leads onto Wały Sikorskego, a ring road which more or less marks the line of the old fortifications. Across it there's a small park, in the middle of which stands the former arsenal, now an **Ethnographic Museum** (Mon & Wed–Fri 9am–3pm, Tues, Sat & Sun 10am–5pm; Oct–April closes 4pm weekends) dealing with the customs and crafts of northern Poland. The displays covering historical traditions are enhanced by imaginative attention to contemporary artists, musicians and writers, whose work is actively promoted by the museum.

Practicalities

The staff in **Informacji Turystycznej**, located in the Town Hall (Mon & Sat 9am–4pm, Tues–Fri 9am–6pm; May–Aug also Sun 9am–1pm; ☎056/109-31), are exceptionally helpful. The most attractive budget **hotel** is the *Staropolski*, ul Zeglarska 12/14 (☎056/260-61; ③), well-situated just down from the Rynek. A step down in quality are the *Polonia*, pl. Teatralny 5 (☎056/230-28; ①), and the *Pod Orlem*, ul Mostowa 15 (☎056/250-24; ②), though both are in easy walking distance of the Rynek. The all-year **youth hostel** is over the river at ul Rudacka 15 (☎056/272-42; ②); bus #13 runs nearby. The *Tramp* **campsite** at ul Kujawska 14 (☎056/241-87) is a short walk west of the train station.

The town's hotels provide most of the decent places to **eat**, with the *Staropolski* restaurant offering a considerably better than average menu. **Cafés** are in good supply, with terrace places on streets such as ul Szeroka providing an opportunity to pause and enjoy the atmosphere of the Old Town. The regal *Pod Atlantem* in ul św Ducha stays open until late every evening, while at the nearby *Flisacza*, an old loggers' haunt, you can sit outside and enjoy the view over the river. Two lively new **pubs** now grace the old town: the *Piwiarnia* at no. 28 on the Rynek, and the huge *Czarna Oberza* at Rabiańska 9.

SOUTHERN POLAND

Southern Poland attracts more visitors than any other region in the country, and its attractions are clear enough from just a glance at the map. The **Tatra Mountains**, which form the border with Slovakia, are Poland's grandest and most beautiful, snowcapped for much of the year and markedly alpine in feel. **Kraków** itself is a city that ranks with Prague and Vienna as one of the architectural gems of Central Europe, but its significance for Poles goes well beyond the aesthetic, for this was the country's ancient royal capital, and the Catholic church has often looked to Kraków for guidance – Pope John Paul II was Archbishop of Kraków until his election in 1978. Equally important are the city's **Jewish roots**: until the last war, this was one of the great Jewish centres in Europe, a past whose fabric remains clear in the old ghetto area of Kazimierz, and whose culmination is starkly enshrined at the death camps of **Auschwitz-Birkenau**, west of Kraków. To the north of the city, the major attraction is the pilgrim centre of **Częstochowa**, home of the Black Madonna, the country's principal religious symbol.

Kraków

KRAKÓW was the only major city in the country to come through World War II essentially undamaged, and its assembly of monuments has now been listed by UNESCO as one of the world's twelve most significant historic sites. All the more ironic, then, that the government has had to add a further tag: that of official "ecological disaster area". The communist regime, wishing to break the hold of the university's Catholic, conservative intelligentsia, decided to graft a new working class onto the city by developing on the outskirts one of the largest steelworks in Europe, **Nowa Huta**. Consequently Kraków is faced with intractable economic and environmental problems: how to deal with the acid rain of the steelworks, how to renovate the monuments, how to maintain jobs.

Arrival and information

Kraków Główny, the central **train station**, is in walking distance of the city's historic centre; Dworzec PKS, the main **bus station**, is opposite. Kraków is bisected by the **River Wisła**, though virtually everything of interest is concentrated on the north bank; the central area is compact enough to get around on foot – indeed parts are car-free. At the heart of things, enclosed by the **Planty** – a green belt following the course of the old ramparts – is the **Stare Miasto**, the Old Town, with its great central square, the **Rynek Główny**. Just south of the Stare Miasto, looming above the river bank, is **Wawel**, the royal castle hill, beyond which lies the old Jewish quarter of **Kazimierz**.

The main **tourist office** is just down from the station at ul Pawia 8 (Mon–Fri & first Sat in month 8am–4pm; ☎226-091), with all the maps and brochures you could want. The **Almatur** office at Rynek Główny 7/8 (Mon–Fri 9am–5pm) is good for advice on nightlife. As usual, **Orbis** have information points in their hotels as well as a central office at Rynek Główny 41 (Mon–Fri 8am–7pm, Sat 8am–2pm; ☎224-035/221-157). *Dexter*, a private tourist office on the Sukiennice (Mon–Fri 9am–5pm, Sat 9am–1pm; ☎217-706), is excellent and also makes hotel reservations. Finally, for local **listings** – consult the weekly *Tyolzień w Krakowie*, or the daily newspapers, *Gazeta w Krakowie* and *Gazeta Krakowska*. The English-language *Inside Krakow* also gives monthly listings and other useful information, whilst *Welome to Crakow* is aimed more at the business market.

> The Kraków telephone code is ☎012.

Accommodation

Kraków is turning into one of Europe's prime city destinations – so you should book hotels ahead in summer. If you can't do that, be prepared to try your luck with a **private room**, which run at around £3–5/$4.50–7.50 for a double, but may well be some way out from the centre; they can be booked at the office at ul Pawia 8 (Mon–Fri 8am–9pm, Sat 9am–3pm; ☎221-921), which also deals with **hotel reservations** – prices are higher than in most Polish cities but marginally lower than Warsaw's. **Student hotels** operate from June to September, at locations which change each year. Current details are available from the **Almatur** office on the Rynek.

HOSTELS

Ul Oleandry 4 (☎338-822; fax 338-920). The main hostel is a huge concrete construction behind the *Cracovia* hotel – but still manages to get full up in summer. Open all year. ②

Ul Kościuszki 88 (☎221-951). A smaller place, housed in a former convent overlooking the river (trams #1, #2, #6, #21; bus #100). Open all year. ②

HOTELS

Monopol, św Gertrudy 6 (☎227-666). At the top end of the moderate category, but worth it for better-quality rooms. ②

Pod Kopcem, al Waszyngtona (☎222-055). Housed in an old fortress on a hill west of the centre, this is a delightfully peaceful hotel – well worth the higher prices. Bus #100 (one an hour). ③

Pollera, ul Szpitalna 30 (☎221-044). Under new management in a calm, central spot. ②

PTTK Dom Turysty, ul Westerplatte 15/16, near the station (☎229-566). Crowded with students in season; double rooms are small but decent. Self-service restaurant. ①

Saski Hotel, ul Sławkowska 3 (☎214-222). Central location and again popular with students. ③

Warszawski, ul Pawia 6 (☎220-622). Good location near the train station, but noisy. ②

Wisła, ul Reymonta 22 (☎379-782/375-575). Sports hotel, set in a pleasant park in the western Czarna Wieś district, next to the main football stadium. Buses #139, #173, #208, or trams #15 and #18 from the main bus station. ②

CAMPSITE

Krak Camping, ul Radzikowskiego 99 (☎372-122). The most popular campsite, in the northwest of the city. Buses #173 and #238, or trams #4, #12, #44.

The City

The **Rynek Główny** – the core of the Stare Miasto – was the largest square of medieval Europe: a huge expanse of flagstones, ringed by magnificent houses and towering spires. The dominant building on the square is the **Sukiennice**, rebuilt in the Renaissance and one of the most distinctive sights in the country: a vast cloth hall, topped by a sixteenth-century attic dripping with gargoyles. Its commercial traditions are perpetuated by a covered market, which bustles with tourists and street sellers at almost any time of year. The terrace cafés on either side of the hall are classic Kraków haunts, where locals idle away the afternoon over tea and *sernik*. The **Art Gallery** on the upper floor of the Sukiennice (Wed & Fri–Sun 10am–3.30pm, Thurs noon–5.30pm; free) is worth a visit for its collection of works by nineteenth-century Polish artists.

To its south is the copper-domed **St Adalbert's** (św Wojchiecha), the oldest building in the square and the first church to be founded in Kraków. The tall **tower** nearby is all that remains of the fourteenth-century town hall; it's worth the climb for an excellent overview of the city. On the east side is one of the finest Gothic structures in the country, the **Mariacki Church** (St Mary's), the taller of its towers topped by an amazing ensemble of spires, elaborated with a crown and helmet. Legend has it that during one of the Tartar raids the watchman at the top of the tower saw the invaders approaching and took up his trumpet to raise the alarm; his warning was cut short by an arrow through the throat. Every hour on the hour a lone trumpeter plays the sombre *hajnał* melody, halting abruptly at the precise point the watchman was supposed to have been hit. The national radio station broadcasts the *hajnał* live at noon every day. Walking down the nave, you'll have to pick your way past devotees kneeling in front of the fifteenth-century Chapel of Our Lady of Częstochowa, with its copy of the venerated image of the Black Madonna, which locals claim has actually been here longer than the original. Focal point of the nave is the huge stone crucifix attributed to Veit Stoss, creator of the majestic high altar at the far east end. Carved between 1477 and 1489, this huge limewood polytych is one of the finest examples of late Gothic art. The outer sides of the folded polytych feature reliefs of scenes from the lives of the Holy Family; at noon (Sundays and saints' days excluded) the altar is opened to reveal the inner panel of the *Dormition of the Virgin*, an amazing tableau of life-size figures.

NORTH OF THE RYNEK

Of the three streets leading north off the Rynek, **ul Floriańska** is the busiest and most striking, with fragments of medieval and Renaissance architecture amongst the myriad shops, cafés and restaurants. **Floriańska Gate**, at the end of the street, marks the edge of the Old Town proper. A square, robust fourteenth-century structure, it's part of a small section of fortifications saved when the old defensive walls were pulled down in the early nineteenth century. The strongest-looking defensive remnant is the **Barbakan**, just beyond Floriańska Gate. A bulbous, spiky fort, added in 1498, it's unusual in being based on Arab defensive architecture, and inaccessible behind ongoing renovation works.

Back through Floriańska Gate, a right turn down the narrow ul Pijarska brings you to the corner of ul św Jana and back down to the main square. On the way, on the left, is the **Czartoryski Palace**, housing Kraków's finest art collection (Mon, Tues, Sat & Sun 10am–3.30pm, Fri noon–5.30pm; free). The ancient art section alone contains over a thousand exhibits, from sites in Mesopotamia, Etruria, Greece and Egypt. Another intriguing highlight is the collection of trophies from the Battle of Vienna (1683), which includes sumptuous Turkish carpets, scimitars and other Oriental finery. The picture galleries offer a rich display of art and sculpture ranging from thirteenth- to eighteenth-century works, the most famous being Rembrandt's brooding *Landscape Before a Storm* and Leonardo da Vinci's *Lady with an Ermine*.

THE UNIVERSITY DISTRICT

Head west from the Rynek on any of the three main thoroughfares – ul Szczepańska, ul Szewska or ul św Anny – and you're into the **university area**, whose heart is the Gothic **Collegium Maius** building, at the intersection of ul św Anny with ul Jagiellońska. Through the passageway from the street, you find yourself in a quiet, arcaded **courtyard** with a marble fountain playing in the centre: an ensemble that, during the early 1960s, was stripped of neo-Gothic accretions and restored to something approaching its original form. The cloistered atmosphere of ancient academia makes an enjoyable break from the city in itself, though actually getting into the building is not so easy. Now the **University Museum**, the Collegium is open to guided tours only (Mon–Fri 11am–2.30pm, Sat closes 1.30pm), for which you need to book places at least a day in advance (☎220-549). If you just turn up, you might be able to talk your way onto a tour. Inside, the ground-floor rooms retain the mathematical and geographical murals once used for teaching; the Alchemy Room, with its skulls and other wizards' accoutrements, was used according to legend by the fabled magician Doctor Faustus. Stairs up from the courtyard bring you to a set of elaborately decorated reception rooms and the Treasury, where the most valued possession is the Jagiellonian globe, constructed around 1510 as the centrepiece of a clock mechanism, and featuring the earliest known illustration of America – labelled "a newly discovered land".

WAWEL HILL

The traditional route used by Polish monarchs when entering the city took them through the Floriańska Gate, down ul Floriańska to the Rynek, then southwards down ul Grodzka to **Wawel Hill**, where for over five hundred years the country's rulers lived and governed. Tourist offices can give conflicting information, but opening times are posted outside the hill itself (generally 9am–6pm).

The first **Cathedral** (summer Mon–Sat 9am–5pm, Sun 12.15–5pm; winter Mon–Sat 9am–3pm, Sun 12.15–3pm) was built here around the time King Bolesław the Brave established the Kraków bishopric in 1020, but the present brick and sandstone basilica is essentially Gothic. All bar four of Poland's forty-five monarchs are buried in the cathedral, and their tombs and side chapels are like a directory of the Central European architecture, art and sculpture of the last six centuries. Beginning from the right of the entrance, the Gothic Holy Cross Chapel (Kaplica Świętokrzyska) is the burial chamber of King Kazimierz IV Jagiełło (1447–92). The boldly coloured paintings on the walls and ceiling were completed by artists from Soviet Novgorod, while the king's marble tomb is the characteristically expressive work of Veit Stoss. Third chapel after this is the majestic Waza chapel, a Baroque mausoleum to the seventeenth-century royal dynasty, followed by the high spot of the whole cathedral, the opulent Zygmuntowska chapel, whose shining gilded cupola dominates the courtyard outside. The Gothic red Hungarian marble Tomb of King Kazimierz the Great, immediately to the right of the high altar, is a dignified tribute to the revered monarch. The Tomb of King Władysław the Short (1306–33), on the left-hand side of the altar, is the oldest in the cathedral, completed soon after his death; the coronation-robed figure lies on a white sandstone tomb edged with expressive mourning figures. The highlights of the cathedral Treasury, behind the sacristy, include Saint Maurice's spear (a present to King Bolesław the Brave from Emperor Otto), an eighth-century miniature of the four Evangelists, and King Kazimierz the Great's crown.

An ascent of the **Zygmuntowska Tower** (access again from the sacristy) gives a far-reaching panorama over the city and close-up views of the five medieval bells. The largest, known as Zygmunt, is famed for its deep, sonorous tone, which local legends claim scatters rain clouds and brings out the sun.

Back inside the cathedral proper, the **crypt** (in the left aisle) houses the remains of the poets Adam Mickiewicz and Juliusz Słowacki, while **St Leonard's Crypt**, part of a long network of vaults that can be reached from near the main entrance, contains the tombs of the national heroes Prince Józef Poniatowski and Tadeusz Kościuszko. The equally sanctified prewar independence leader Józef Piłsudski lies in a separate vault nearby.

The buildings on Wawel Hill are in the midst of a long-term renovation programme; although not too intrusive inside the cathedral, work in the **castle** (Tues, Thurs, Sat & Sun 10am–3pm, Wed & Fri 10am–4pm; free Fri), is more extensive: the Italianate courtyard is marred by scaffolding, and only some of the top-floor rooms, with their magnificent tapestries, are open for viewing.

The next thing to head for is the **Royal Treasury and Armoury** (daily except Mon 10am–3pm; free Fri) in the northeast corner of the castle (entrance on the ground floor). Much of the treasury's contents had been sold by the time of the Partitions to pay off marriage dowries and debts of state. The vaulted Gothic **Kazimierz Room** contains the finest items from a haphazard display of lesser royal possessions including the burial crown of Zygmunt August, while the prize exhibit in the next-door **Jadwiga and Jagiełło Room** is the solemnly displayed *Szczerbiec*, the thirteenth-century weapon used for centuries in the coronation of Polish monarchs.

The castle also runs exhibitions of its excellent range of Polish, British and Dutch paintings and Oriental exhibits which change every six months. The permanent **Lost Wawel** exhibition (daily except Tues 10am–3pm), beneath the old kitchens south of the cathedral, takes you past the excavated remains of the hill's most ancient buildings, including the foundations of the tenth-century **Rotunda of SS. Felix and Adauctus**, the oldest known church in Poland.

KAZIMIERZ

South from Wawel Hill lies the **Kazimierz** district, which in 1495 became the city's Jewish quarter. In tandem with Warsaw, where a **ghetto** was created around the same time, Kazimierz grew to become one of the main cultural centres of Polish Jewry, but in March 1941 the entire Jewish population of the city was crammed into a tiny ghetto over the river. After waves of deportations to the concentration camps, the ghetto was finally liquidated in March 1943, thus ending seven centuries of Jewish life in Kraków.

The tiny **Remu'h synagogue** at ul Szeroka 40 is one of two still functioning in the quarter. Built in 1557 on the site of an earlier wooden synagogue, it was ransacked by the Nazis – tombstones torn up by them have been collaged together to form a high, powerful Wailing Wall just inside the entrance. The grandest of all the Kazimierz synagogues was the **Old Synagogue** on ul Szeroka, completed in 1557 and thus the oldest surviving Jewish religious building in Poland. Since the war it's been carefully restored and turned into a **museum** of the history and culture of Kraków Jewry (Wed & Thurs 9am–3.30pm, Fri 11am–6pm, Sat & Sun 9am–3pm; closed first Sat & Sun of month, in which case it opens Mon & Tues 9am–3.30pm).

As the presence of several churches indicates, the western part of Kazimierz was where non-Jews tended to live. Despite its Baroque overlay, the interior of the Gothic **Corpus Christi** church, on the corner of ul Bożego Ciała, retains early features including stained-glass windows installed around 1420. The church looks onto **plac Wolnica**, where the rebuilt town hall now houses the largest **Ethnographic Museum** in the country (Mon 10am–6pm, Wed–Fri 10am–3pm, Sat & Sun 10am–2pm). The collection focuses on Polish folk traditions, although there's also a selection of artefacts from Siberia, Africa, Latin America and various Slav countries.

Eating, drinking and entertainment

The *cukiernia* dotted around the city centre provide delicious cakes to most Kraków cafés. However, the best of these cake shops – like *Michałek's* at ul Krupnicza 6 – sell out quickly, so go early in the day. Kraków's tourist status has given rise to a decent selection of **restaurants**, with new places springing up every week. For the better places booking is essential, and you need to turn up early too: this is not a late-night city. Recommendations within the restaurant section are in roughly ascending order of price. **Bars** are increasingly trendy and as a last resort, you can always get a drink at one of the larger hotels until around midnight.

CAFÉS

Alvorada, Rynek Główny (west side). Mouthwatering cakes at this café on the main square.

Jama Michalika, ul Floriańska 45. Historic artistic café, still redolent of old-world *Mitteleuropa*.

Mata Scena Café-Bar, ul Staswkowska 14. Black ash deco in old cellars.

Pasieka, Mały Rynek. Nice place to sit out and enjoy the atmosphere of this attractive square.

Redolfi, Rynek Główny 37 (north side). Splendid Art Nouveau remnants, and better than usual coffee.

MILK BARS AND SNACKS

PTTK Hostel, ul Westerplatte 15–16. Self-service joint near the train station, offering large portions of solid, no-nonsense meat and veg.

Żywiec, ul Floriańska 19. A reliable snack bar in a street just north of the Rynek that offers plenty of cheap places.

RESTAURANTS

Balaton, ul Grodzka 37 (☎220-469). Excellent, very busy Hungarian restaurant.

Cechowa, ul Jagiellońska 11. Handy if you're in the university area, with excellent pancakes and a fast lunchtime service.

Hawełka, Rynek Główny 34. Popular, noisy haunt serving *kasha i zrasy* (buckwheat with rolled meat) and fortified *miody pitne* wines.

Kurza Stopka, pl Wszystkich Świętych 9/10 (☎229-196). Cheap, clean and with a good reputation.

Staropolska, ul Sienna 2 (☎225-821). Deservedly popular Old Town venue with an emphasis on traditional pork and poultry dishes. Booking essential in the evening.

Wierzynek, Rynek Główny 15 (☎221-035). This stately place is Kraków's most famous restaurant, with specialities like mountain trout. For westerners prices remain very reasonable at around $25 a head; to have any chance of a table booking is essential. Open till midnight.

BARS

Galeria Krzysztofory, ul Szczepańska 2. A student hang-out with an underground atmosphere.

Maxime, ul Floriańska 32. Old established bar, open late.

Pod Strzelnicą, ul Królowej Jadwigi 184. Small private bar, with various snacks, beer and vodka.

ENTERTAINMENT

For cultural events consult *Gazeta w Krakowie* and *Inside Krakow* magazines and look in at the **Pod Baranami** at Rynek Główny 27, which serves as a clearing house for information and tickets (Room 37). For **rock** or vaguely alternative events, check posters in the university district or consult the Almatur office on the Rynek. **Pod Jaszczurami**, Rynek Główny 7/8, is a **jazz** club with occasional **discos**. Other lively **student clubs** include the *Karlik*, ul Reymonta 17, the *Forum*, ul Mikołajska 2, and the *Rotunda* out at Błonia.

Listings

Airlines *LOT*, ul Basztowa 15 (☎225-076 or 227-078); *Delta Airlines*, ul Szpitalna 36 (☎226-105).

Car rental *Hertz*, al F. Focha 1 (Mon–Sat 8am–6pm; ☎222-939); *Budget*, ul Radzikowskiego 99/100 (daily 9am–5pm; ☎370-089).

Consulates *USA*, ul Stolarska 9 (☎221-400). There is no UK representation.

Pharmacy 24-hr pharmacies change weekly. All pharmacies have a list in their window of those currently open 24 hours in the neighbourhood.

Post office Main office is at ul Wielopole 2 (Mon–Fri 7.30am–9pm, Sat 8am–2pm, Sun 9am–1pm), with 24-hr phone services; the one right opposite the station (Mon–Sat 7am–8pm, Sun 9am–4pm) is also handy.

Train tickets Available from the *Orbis* office at Rynek Główny 41 and the train station.

The outskirts – Wieliczka

Fifteen kilometres south of Kraków is the salt mine at **WIELICZKA**, described by one eighteenth-century visitor as being "as remarkable as the Pyramids and more useful". Salt deposits were discovered here as far back as the eleventh century, and from King Kazimierz's time onwards local mining rights and hence income were strictly controlled by the crown. As mining intensified over the centuries a huge network of pitfaces, rooms and tunnels proliferated – nine levels in all, extending to a depth of 327 metres. Scaled-down mining continues today, and there's a sanatorium 200 metres down, to exploit the supposedly healthy saline atmosphere. To **get to Wieliczka** take a local train – there are plenty of them. Entrance to the mine (daily 8am–6pm) is by guided tour only, in groups of thirty or so; the tour takes two hours, through nearly two miles of tunnels. The further you descend, the more spectacular and weirder the chambers get. The star attraction, **Blessed Kinga's Chapel**, comes on the bottom level: everything in the ornate fifty-metre-long chapel is carved from salt, including the stairs, bannisters, altar and chandeliers. The chapel's acoustic properties – every word uttered near the altar is audible from the gallery – has led to its use as a concert venue.

Oświęcim: Auschwitz-Birkenau

In 1940 **OŚWIĘCIM**, an insignificant town 70km west of Kraków, became the site of the Oświęcim-Brzezinka concentration camp, better known by its German name of **Auschwitz-Birkenau**. Of the many camps built by the Nazis in Poland and the other occupied countries during World War II, this was the largest and most horrific: something approaching 2 million people, 85–90 percent of them Jews, died here. If you want all the specifics on the camp, you can pick up a detailed guidebook or join a guided group, often led by former inmates. Children under thirteen are not admitted.

To get to Auschwitz-Birkenau from Kraków, you can take either of the regular bus or train services to Oświęcim station. From there it's a short bus ride to the gates of Auschwitz; there's no bus service to Birkenau, but taxis are available. Most of the Auschwitz camp buildings have been preserved as the **Museum of Martyrdom** (daily Jan, Feb & late Dec 8am–3pm; March & Nov–Dec 15 8am–4pm; April & Oct 8am–5pm; May–Sept 8am–6pm; June, July & Aug 8am–7pm). The cinema is a sobering starting point: the film was taken by the Soviet troops who liberated the camp in May 1945 – harrowing images of the survivors and the dead confirming what really happened. The bulk of the camp consists of the prison cell blocks, the first section dedicated to "exhibits" found in the camp after liberation. Despite last-minute destruction of many of the storehouses used for the possessions of murdered inmates there are rooms full of clothes and suitcases toothbrushes, dentures, glasses, shoes, and a huge mound of women's hair – 154,322 pounds of it. Many of the camp barracks are given over to national memorials, moving testimonies to the sufferings of inmates of the different countries – Poles, Russians, Czechs, Slovaks, Norwegians, Turks, French, Italians. The prison blocks terminate by the gas chambers and the ovens where the bodies were incinerated. The **Birkenau camp** (same hours) is much less visited than Auschwitz, though it was here that the majority of captives lived and died. Killing was the main goal of Birkenau, most of it carried out in the huge gas chambers at the back of the camp, damaged but not destroyed by the fleeing Nazis in 1945. Most of the victims arrived in closed trains – cattle cars mostly – to be driven directly into the gas chambers; railway line, ramp, sidings – they are all still there, just as the Nazis abandoned them.

Częstochowa

Seen from a distance, **CZĘSTOCHOWA** shows the country at its worst. Its steelworks and textile factories unleash a noxious cocktail of multicoloured fumes, while the city centre is ringed by jerry-built concrete estates. Yet all this is overshadowed by the city's status, courtesy of the monastery of **Jasna Góra** (Bright Mountain), as one of the world's greatest places of pilgrimage – its **icon of the Black Madonna** has drawn the faithful here over the past six centuries, and reproductions of it adorn almost every church in the country. On the major Marian festivals – May 3, August 15, August 26, September 8 and December 8 – up to a million pilgrims converge here.

The special position that Jasna Góra and its icon hold in the hearts and minds of the majority of Poles is due to the tenuous position Poland has held on the map of Europe. Each of Poland's non-Catholic enemies – the Swedes, the Russians and the Germans – has laid siege to Jasna Góra, yet failed to destroy it, so adding to the icon's reputation as the guarantor of Poland's very existence.

A dead straight three-kilometre-long boulevard, aleja Najświętszej Marii Panny (abbreviated as al NMP), cuts through the heart of Częstochowa, terminating at the foot of **Jasna Góra**. Inevitably, the **Chapel of the Blessed Virgin**, a separate church in its own right, is the centrepiece of the complex. Masses are said here almost constantly and you'll have to come very early or very late if you want a good view of the **Black Madonna**. Much of the time, the icon is invisible behind a screen, each raising and lowering of which is accompanied by a solemn fanfare. Even when it's on view (normally 6am–noon, 3.30–4.40pm, 7–7.45pm & 9–9.10pm) you don't get to see very much of the picture itself, as the figures are almost always decked out in crowns and robes made of diamonds and rubies. According to tradition, the Black Madonna was painted by Saint Luke on a beam from the Holy Family's house in Nazareth; tests have proved the icon cannot have been executed before the sixth century and is probably Italian in origin. At the southwestern end of the monastery is the **Arsenal** (summer Mon–Sat 9am–noon & 2.30–6pm, Sun 9am–noon & 1–6pm; closes 5pm in winter), devoted to the military history of the complex. Alongside is the **600th Anniversary Museum** (daily 11am–4.30pm), which tells the monastery's story from a religious standpoint. Exhibits include offerings from famous Poles, prominent among which is Lech Wałęsa's 1983 Nobel Peace Prize.

A day trip from Kraków will suffice for most people, but should you want to stay, the best **hotel** option is the *Mały* at ul Katedralna 18 (☎034/433-91; ①), by the train station. The all-year **youth hostel** is conveniently situated on Jasnogórska (☎034/243-121; ②).

Zakopane and the Tatras

Ask Poles to define their country's natural attractions and they often come up with the following simple definition: the Lakes, the Sea and the Mountains. "The Mountains" consist of an almost unbroken chain of ridges extending the whole length of the southern border, of which the most spectacular and most revered are the **Tatras** – or *Tatry* as they're known in Polish. Eighty kilometres long, with peaks rising to 2500m, the Polish Tatras are actually a relatively small part of the range, most of which rises across the border in the Czech Republic. As the estimated 1.5 million annual tourists show, however, the Polish section has enough to keep most people happy: high peaks for the dedicated mountaineers, excellent trails for hikers, cable cars and creature comforts for day-trippers, and ski slopes in winter.

The major resort on the fringes of the mountains is **ZAKOPANE**, a town which has succumbed whole-heartedly to tourism. It's easily reached by train or bus from Kraków, and both **stations** are a ten-minute walk east of the main street, **ul Krupówki**. A bustling pedestrian precinct, this is the focus of the town, given over to a jumble of restaurants, cafés and souvenir shops. Uphill, the street merges into ul Zamoyskiego, which runs on out of town past the fashionable *fin-de-siècle* wooden villas of the outskirts, while in the other direction it follows a rushing stream down towards Gulbałówka hill.

Trip on 23a ul Koscivszki (☎0165/122-11) is the main **information** centre and offers private rooms. The *Tatry* office at ul Chramcówki 35 (Mon–Sat 8am–7pm; ☎0165/140-00) is the first wooden hut on your right leaving the station, and has a few leaflets but mainly offers accommodation. *Orbis* at ul Krupówki 22 (Mon–Fri 8am–4pm, Sat 8am–2pm) helps with hotels, train and bus bookings and local trips, while the PTTK office across the stream from ul Krupówki has maps, guidebooks and details on mountain huts. All these tourist offices have **rooms** on offer. There's an all-year **youth hostel** at ul Nowotarska 45 (☎0165/662-03; ②) and a Juventur **student hotel** at ul Słoneczna 2a (☎0165/662-53; ②). The *Dom Turysty* at ul Zaruskiego 5 (☎0165/632-81; ①) is popular with Polish students; the laundry and showers on the second floor are handy. Mid-range, central hotels include *Gazda*, Zaruskiego 2 (☎0165/150-11; ③), and *Imperial*, ul Balzera 1 (☎0165/140-21; ①). Central **pensjonat** include *Gladiola*, ul Chramcówki 25 (☎0165/686-23; ②), *Tatry*, ul Wierchowa 4 (☎0165/660-41; ③), and *Panorama*, ul Wierchowa 6 (☎0165/150-81; ①). *Pod Krokwia* campsite (☎0165/122-56) is at the end of ul Żeromskiego on the east side of town, and another campsite at ul Za Strugium 39 (☎0165/145-66) is to the west.

If you want a fast **snack** there are plenty of cafés, milk bars, pizzerias and streetside *zapiekanki* merchants to choose from. **Restaurants** are plentiful too, with very good ones in the *Gazda* and *Giewont* hotels.

The Tatras

Most of the peaks in the **Tatras** are in the 2000–2500m range, but the unimpressive statistics belie their status and their appearance. For these are real mountains, as beautiful as any mountain landscape in northern Europe, the ascents taking you on boulder-strewn paths alongside woods and streams up to the ridges, where grand, windswept peaks rise in the brilliant alpine sunshine. Wildlife thrives here: the whole area was turned into a National Park in the 1950s and supports rare species like lynx, golden eagles and brown bear – which for once you might even glimpse.

Most foreigners can cross the Czech–Poland border with just a passport stamp, and the new political climate means that exploration of the whole Tatra region is possible for the first time since the war. A decent map of the mountains is indispensable. The best is the *Tatrzański Park Narodowy* (1:30,000), which has all the paths accurately marked and colour-coded; the *Polskie Tatry* guidebook (in Polish) is likewise invaluable. Overnighting in the eight PTTK-run huts dotted across the mountains is an experience in itself. Food is basic, but pricyfor Poles, most of whom bring their own; the huts are an ideal place to mix in, preferably over a bottle of vodka. Camping isn't allowed in the National Park area, rock-climbing only with a guide – ask at the PTTK for details.

The easiest way up to the peaks is by **cable car** from the hamlet of Kuźnice, a three-kilometre walk or bus journey south from Zakopane. The cable car ends near the summit of **Kasprowy Wierch** (1985m), where weather-beaten signs indicate the border. From here many day-trippers simply walk back down to Kuźnice through the Hala Gąsienicowa. A rather longer alternative is to strike west to the cross-topped summit of **Giewont** (1909m) and head down to Kuźnice; this is fairly easy-going and quite feasible in a day if you start out early.

East of Kasprowy Wierch the walking gets tougher. From **Świnica** (2300m), a stren-uous ninety-minute walk, experienced hikers continue along the **Orla Perć** (Eagles' Path), a challenging, exposed ridge with spectacular views. The *Pięc Stawów* **hostel** (②), in the high valley of the same name, provides overnight shelter at the end. From the hostel you can hike back down Dolina Roztoki to **Łysa Polana**, a border crossing point in the valley, and get a bus back to Zakopane. An alternative is to continue a short distance east to the **Morskie Oko Lake** (1399m). Encircled by spectacular sheer cliff faces and alpine forest, this large glacial lake is one of the Tatras' big attractions, most frequently approached on the winding forest road to Łysa Polana. Erosion problems mean that cars and buses now have to park here, the remaining distance being an 11km walk. The lakeside *Morskie Oko* **hostel** provides a base for the ascent of **Rysy** (2499m), the highest peak in the Polish Tatras.

SILESIA AND WIELKOPOLSKA

In Poland it's known as *Śląsk*, in the Czech Republic as *Sleszko*, in Germany as *Schlesien*: all three countries hold part of the frequently disputed province that's called in English **Silesia**. Since 1945, Poland has held all of it except for a few of the western-most tracts, a dominance gained as compensation for the Eastern Territories, which were incorporated into the USSR in 1939 as a result of the Nazi–Soviet pact, and never returned. Yet, although postwar Silesia has developed a strongly Polish character, people with family roots in the province are often bilingual and consider their prime loyalty to lie with Silesia rather than Poland. Heavy industry has blighted much of the region, especially in the huge **Katowice** conurbation, the largest unmodernized "black country" left in Europe. Similar problems, albeit on a smaller scale, also affect the prov-ince's chief city, **Wrocław**, holding back its potential to become a rival to Kraków, Prague and Budapest as one of central Europe's most enticing cosmopolitan centres. North of Silesia, the region known as **Wielkopolska** formed the core of the original Polish nation, and its chief interest is supplied by the regional capital of **Poznań** – famed within Poland for the 1956 riots that marked the first major revolt against communism.

Wrocław

The special nature of **WROCŁAW** comes from the fact that it contains the soul of two great cities. One of these is the city that has long stood on this spot, Slav by origin but for centuries dominated by Germans and generally known as **Breslau**. The other is **Lwów** (now L'viv), capital of the Polish Ukraine, which was annexed by the Soviets in 1939. After the war, its displaced population was encouraged to take over the severely depopulated Breslau, which had been confiscated from Germany and offered them a ready-made home. The earlier multinational influences which shaped the city are graphically reflected in its architecture: the huge Germanic brick Gothic churches that dominate the skyline are intermingled with Flemish-style Renaissance mansions, palaces and chapels of Viennese Baroque, and boldly utilitarian public buildings from the early years of this century. The tranquillity of the parks, gardens and rivers offer a ready escape from the urban bustle.

The City

Wrocław's central area is delineated by the River Odra to the north and by the bow-shaped ul Podwale – the latter following the former fortifications, whose ditch, now bordered by a shady park, still largely survives. At the centre of town is the vast space of the **Rynek**, now given over mainly to museums, restaurants, cafés, travel agencies and bookshops. The magnificent **Town Hall** dates largely to the fifteenth-century high point of local prosperity, the international mix of influences reflecting the city's status as a major European trading centre at the time. It's the **south facade** which is the real show stopper, with its huge windows, its filigree friezes of animals and foliage, and its rich statuary. Relieved of municipal duties by the adjoining nineteenth-century offices, the town hall now serves as the **Historical Museum** (Wed–Fri 10am–4pm, Sat 11am–5pm, Sun 10am–6pm). However, it's the largely unaltered interior itself which constitutes the main attraction – especially the resplendent three-aisled Knights' Hall, where the keystones of the vault feature character studies of all strata of society.

Of the mansions lining the main sides of the Rynek, those on the western side are the most distinguished and colourful. At no. 6 is the House of the Golden Sun (Pod Złotym Słońcem), home of the **Museum of the Art of Medal Making** (Wed–Sun 10am–5pm); its shop sells examples of the craft, which must be the classiest souvenirs in town. Just off the northwest corner of the Rynek are two curious Baroque houses known as **Jaś i Małgosia**, linked by a gateway giving access to the close of **St Elizabeth**, the most beautiful of Wrocław's churches – but closed off as a result of fire. Since the end of the fourteenth century its stately ninety-metre **tower**, which was under construction for 150 years, has been the city's most prominent landmark.

Southwest of the Rynek lies the maze-like former **Jewish quarter**, whose inhabitants fled or were driven from their tenements during the Third Reich. Immediately to the east of the Jewish quarter is a part of the city built in obvious imitation of the chilly classical grandeur of Berlin. Indeed, Carl Gotthard Langhans, designer of the Brandenburg Gate, had a hand in the monumental Royal Palace now housing the **Archeology Museum** (Wed & Fri 10am–4pm, Thurs 9am–4pm, Sat & Sun 10am–5pm), a dry survey of the prehistory of the region. Rather more fun is the **Ethnographical Museum** (Tues, Wed, Fri & Sat 10am–4pm, Thurs & Sun 11am–6pm) in the southern wing, a good place to visit if you have kids in tow. Its main draw is a large collection of dolls decked out in what are deemed to be traditional dresses from all around the world.

The royal flavour of this quarter is continued in a different vein with the lofty Gothic church of **St Dorothy**, which, unlike most of Wrocław's other brick churches, stayed in Catholic hands at the Reformation. Its interior was whitewashed and littered with gigantic altars in the Baroque period, giving it a very different appearance from its neighbours, which still bear the hallmarks of four centuries of Protestant sobriety.

Further east, at the northern end of pl. Dominikański, are the buildings of the **Dominican monastery**, centred on the thirteenth-century church of **St Adalbert** (św Wojciecha), which is embellished with several lavish Gothic and Baroque chapels. A couple of blocks east stands the gargantuan former **Bernardine Monastery**; severely damaged during the war, the church and cloisters have been painstakingly reconstructed to house the **Museum of Architecture** (Tues, Thurs & Fri 10am–3.30pm, Wed & Sat 10am–4pm, Sun 10am–5pm; last ticket half an hour earlier), a fascinating record of the many historic buildings in the city which perished in the war.

Wrocław's best-loved sight, the **Panorama of the Battle of Racławice** (daily except Mon summer 8am–7pm; winter 9am–6pm), is housed in a specially designed rotunda in the park nearby. This painting, 120 metres long and 15 high, was commissioned in 1894 to celebrate the centenary of the Russian army's defeat by the people's militia of Tadeusz Kościuszko near the village of Racławice, between Kraków and Kielce. Not only is it Poland's most hi-tech tourist attraction, it's also one of the most popular, an icon second only in national affection to the Black Madonna. You may have to book several hours in advance for a show lasting about 45 minutes: make sure you ask to hear the **English-language cassette** which explains all the details of the painting.

At the opposite end of the park is the ponderously Prussian neo-Renaissance home of the **National Museum** (Tues, Wed, Fri & Sat 10am–4pm, Thurs & Sun 11am–6pm), which unites the collections of Breslau and Lwów. At the moment you need to come on two consecutive days to see everything. However, one of the most important sections, **medieval stone sculpture**, is housed in the hall around the café and is open daily. Here you can see the delicately linear carving of *The Dormition of the Virgin* from the portal of St Mary Magdalene. The other major highlight is the poignant early fourteenth-century *Tomb of Henryk the Righteous*, with its group of weeping mourners. On the first floor, the most eye-catching exhibits are the colossal statues of saints from St Mary Magdalene. The foreign paintings in the opposite wing include Cranach's *Eve*, originally part of a scene showing her temptation of Adam which was cut up and repainted as two portraits of a burgher couple in the seventeenth century. One of the star pieces in the comprehensive collection of Polish paintings on the top floor is the amazingly detailed *Entry of Chancellor Jerzy Ossoliński into Rome in 1633* by Bernardo Bellotto, best known for his pictures of eighteenth-century Warsaw.

North of the Rynek the triangular-shaped university quarter, jam-packed with historic buildings, is bounded by two streets: ul Uniwersytecka to the south and ul Grodzka, which follows the Odra. Behind the fourteenth-century church of St Matthew spreads the colossal domed **Ossoliński Library**, built as a hospital at the end of the seventeenth century; one of the city's most impressive buildings, it has frequent exhibitions of items from its vast collection. However, the principal building of this district is the 171-metre-long **Collegium Maximum**, whose main assembly hall or **Aula** (daily 9.30am–3.30pm) is one of the greatest secular interiors of the Baroque age, fusing architecture, painting, sculpture and ornament into one bravura whole.

From the Market Hall, the Piaskowsky Bridge leads to the sandbank of **Wyspa Piasek** and the fourteenth-century hall church of **St Mary of the Sands** (Kościół NMP na Piasku), dull on the outside, majestically vaulted inside. The two elegant little painted bridges of Most Młyński and Most Tumski, which look as though they should belong in an ornamental garden, connect Wyspa Piasek with **Ostrów Tumski**, the city's ecclesiastical heart.

Ulica Katedralny leads past several Baroque palaces (among which priests, monks and nuns are constantly scuttling) to the twin-towered **Cathedral**. Three chapels behind the high altar make a visit to the dank and gloomy interior worthwhile: St Elizabeth's Chapel, created by followers of Bernini; the Gothic Lady Chapel, with the masterly Renaissance funerary plaque of Bishop Jan Roth; and the Corpus Christi Chapel, a perfectly proportioned and subtly decorated Baroque gem.

Practicalities

The main **train station**, Wrocław Główny – itself one of the city's sights – faces the broad boulevard of ul Marsz. Józefa Piłsudskiego, about fifteen minutes' walk south of the centre; the main **bus station** is diagonally opposite Wrocław Główny, but is due to be moved to ul Sucha, at the back of the train station. The main **tourist office** is at ul Piłsudskiego 98 (Mon–Fri 8.30am–4pm, Sat 9am–2pm; ☎071/444-101), opposite the station, and also does private rooms; a particularly helpful branch on the Stary Rynek 14 (Mon–Fri 9am–6pm, Sat 10am–4pm; ☎071/443-111) is better for leaflets. **Orbis** provides national and international train tickets on ul Piłsudskiego 62 (Mon–Fri 9am–5pm, Sat 10am–2pm). Prices for Wrocław accommodation are roughly comparable to Kraków, and a cluster of inexpensive **hotels** can be found near the main train station – best of which is the *Grand*, ul Piłsudskiego 100 (☎071/360-71; ②). On the same street are *Europejski* at no. 90 (☎071/310-71; ③) and *Polonia* at no. 66 (☎071/310-21; ②); cheaper and closer to the centre is *Hotel Damien*, at ul Kazimierza Wielkiego 45 (☎071/444-384; ②). The PTTK **tourist hostel** has an excellent location at ul Szajnochy 11 (☎071/443-073). The better of the city's **youth hostels** is close to the main station at ul Hugona Kołłątaja 20 (☎071/388-56; ②), while the better **campsite** is on the east side of town near the Olympic Stadium at al Ignacego Padarewskiego 35 (☎071/484-651) – trams #9, #12, #16 and #17 go close. Information on summer **student hostels** is available at Almatur, ul Tadeusza Kościuszki 34.

Wrocław has a good selection of places to **eat and drink**, most of which are within a relatively small area – the episcopal and university quarters are noticeably barren. The most conveniently sited of the city's **milk bars** is *Vega*, Rynek 27a; the nearby *Pod Złoty Dzbanem*, Rynek 22, is a slightly upmarket snack bar. Also on the Rynek, at no. 5, the **café** above the *Dwór Wazów* restaurant has a real palm-court atmosphere. *Tutti Frutti*, pl. Tadeusza Kościuszki 1, is the most popular rendezvous point, while the *Pod Kalamburem* café, ul Kuźnicza 29a, has beautiful Jugendstil decor yet very low prices. There are two **restaurants** called *Dwór Wazów* – the upmarket one on the Rynek and its considerably cheaper but equally good stablemate, entered from ul Kiełbaśrucza, the first street west of the Rynek. *Kambuz*, ul Ruska 58, is an excellent and reasonably priced little fish restaurant, and *KDM*, pl. Tadeusza Kościuszki 5/6, is the best choice for inexpensive traditional dishes.

Poznań

Thanks to its position on the Paris–Berlin–Moscow rail line, and as the one place where all international trains stop between the German border and Warsaw, **POZNAŃ** is many visitors' first taste of Poland. In many ways it's the ideal introduction, as no other city is more closely identified with Polish nationhood. In the ninth century the Polonians founded a castle on an island in the River Warta, and in 968 Mieszko I made this one of the two main centres of his duchy, and the seat of its first bishop. The settlement that developed here was given the name Ostrów Tumski (Cathedral Island), which it still retains. Nowadays it's a city of great diversity, its animated centre focused on one of Europe's most imposing squares, and with a dynamic business district whose trade fair is the most important in the country.

The City

For seven centuries the grandiose **Stary Rynek** has been the hub of life in Poznań, even if nowadays it has lost its position as the centre of political and economic power. The turreted **Town Hall** now houses the **Museum of the History of Poznań** (Mon, Tues & Fri 10am–4pm, Wed noon–6pm, Sun 10am–3pm); though this is less didactic than it sounds, the main reason for entering is to see the building itself. The stunner is the Renaissance **Great Hall** on the first floor, its coffered vault bearing polychrome bas-reliefs which embody the exemplary civic duties and virtues through scenes from the lives of Samson, King David, Venus and Hercules. Many a medieval and Renaissance interior lurks behind the Baroque facades of the **gabled houses** lining the outer sides of the Stary Rynek. Particularly fine are those on the eastern side, where no. 45 is the **Museum of Musical Instruments** (Tues 11am–5pm, Wed & Fri 10am–4pm, Sat 10am–5pm, Sun 10am–3pm), the only collection of its kind in Poland.

Just to the west of the Stary Rynek stands a hill with remnants of the inner circle of the medieval walls. This particular section guarded the **Castle**, which was the seat of the rulers of Wielkopolska. Modified down the centuries, it was almost completely destroyed in 1945 but has been partly restored to house the **Museum of Applied Art** (Tues, Wed, Fri & Sat 10am–4pm, Sun 10am–3pm). This features an enjoyable enough collection from medieval times to the present day, while the Gothic cellars are used for changing displays of posters, an art form taken very seriously in Poland.

From here it's only a short walk to the vast elongated space of **plac Wolności**, where the **National Museum** houses one of the few important displays of old master paintings in Poland (Tues noon–6pm, Wed, Fri & Sat 10am–4pm, Thurs 10am–5pm, Sun 10am–3pm). Dominating the gallery's small but choice Spanish section is the prize exhibit, Zurbarán's *Madonna of the Rosary*, while the extensive display of art from the Low Countries includes a regal *Adoration of the Magi* by Joos van Cleve.

To the south of the Stary Rynek is a complex of former Jesuit buildings, the finest Baroque architecture in the city. The **Parish Church** (Kościół Frany), completed just forty years before the expulsion of the Jesuits in 1773, boasts a lush interior of coloured columns, gilded capitals, monumental sculptures, large altarpieces and rich stuccowork

East of the Stary Rynek, the Bolesława Chrobrego bridge crosses to the holy island of **Ostrów Tumski**, a world away in spirit, if not in distance, from the hustle of the city. Only a small portion of the island is built upon, and a few priests and monks comprise its entire population; after 5pm the island is a ghost town. The first building you see is the late Gothic **Psalteria**, characterized by its elaborate stepped gable. Immediately behind is an earlier brick structure, the lofty and graceful **St Mary's**, while across the street is the **Archdiocesan Museum** (Mon–Sat 9am–3pm), with a homely spread of paintings, sculptures, textiles and treasury items from the Middle Ages to the present day. The streets of the island are lined by handsome eighteenth-century houses, all very much in the shadow of the **Cathedral**. Most of it was restored to its Gothic shape after wartime devastation, but a lack of documentary evidence for the eastern chapels meant that their successors had to be retained, as were the Baroque spires and the three lanterns around the ambulatory, which give a vaguely eastern touch. Inside, the crypt has been extensively excavated, uncovering remains of the pre-Romanesque and Romanesque cathedrals which stood on the site, as well as parts of the sarcophagi of the first two Polish kings, Mieszko I and Bolesław the Brave. Their current resting place is the luscious Golden Chapel on the axis of the ambulatory, representing the diverse if dubious tastes of the 1830s.

Practicalities

The main **train station**, Poznań Główny, is southwest of the historic quarter; tram #5 runs from here to the city centre. The **bus station** is five minutes' walk to the east along ul Towarowa. The main **tourist office** is at Stary Rynek 59 (Mon–Fri 9am–5pm, Sat 10am–2pm; ☎061/526-156). National and international rail tickets can be purchased from the **Orbis** office at *Hotel Poznan* on pl. Dąbrowskiego (☎061/330-221). The **Eurostop** office at Aleksandra Fredry 7 (Mon–Fri 9.30am–5pm, Sat 10am–1pm; ☎061/320-344) incorporates *Almatur* and offers an international lift-sharing service along with the usual. A monthly guide to what's on in the city and an English abridgement – both known as *iks* – are available from tourist information points. Many tourist points are now charging the *Ruch* price of 10,000zł for the paragraph of English in it.

Because of the trade fair, Poznań has plenty of **accommodation**, but hotel prices tend to be Western rather than Polish. However, the three **hotels** in the heart of the city are good value: *Rzymski*, al Karola Marcinkowskiego 22 (☎061/528-121; ②); *Wielkopolska*, ul św Marcin 67 (☎061/527-631; ③); and *Lech*, ul św Marcin 74 (☎061/530-151; ②). Poznań has three official **youth hostels**, the handiest of which is at ul Berwiniskiego 2/3 (☎061/663-680; ②), just to the southwest of the station. The **tourist hostel**, *Dom Turysty*, has an ideal location at Stary Rynek 91 (☎061/528-893; ②). For a room in a **private house**, you could try the *Biuro Zakwaterowania*, opposite the side entrance to the station at ul Głogowska 16 (Mon–Fri 7am–6pm; ☎061/663-560), but they're mainly interested in long stays. Both **campsites** entail a bus ride of some 9km. *Strzeszynek*, ul Koszalińska 15 (☎061/483-129), has a lakeside setting to the northwest and is reached by bus #95, while *Baranowo* (☎061/143-812), is on the southwest tip of Lake Kierski, served by bus #1.

In choosing somewhere to **eat and drink**, the *Orbis* hotels should always be kept in mind. Each has a restaurant and café with prices that are a bit higher than elsewhere in town but still extremely cheap; they're also among the few options if you want to eat late. *Sukiennicza*, Stary Rynek 98, serves superb coffee, cakes and ice cream in a setting reminiscent of Central Europe's pre-communist days; *Stara Ratuszowa*, Stary Rynek 55, is a conventional **café** at ground-floor level, with a wonderfully atmospheric wine bar in the medieval cellars. *Avanti*, Stary Rynek 76, is probably the cheapest and most popular snack bar in town, and two of the best **restaurants** are also on the square – *U Dylla* (no. 37) and *Club Elite* (no. 2). Best chance of some night-time action is to ask around the university buildings about **student clubs**: the largest, *Odnowa*, is at ul św Marcin 80/82.

travel details

Trains

Warsaw to: Częstochowa (9 daily; 2hr 30min–3hr 30min); Gdańsk (14 daily; 3hr 30min–4hr 30min); Gdynia 14 daily; 3hr 30min–4hr 30min); Kraków (14 daily; 3–5hr); Poznań (16 daily; 2hr 30min–3hr 30min); Toruń (3 daily; 3hr); Wrocław (9 daily; 5–6hr); Zakopane (4 daily; 6–9hr).

Częstochowa to: Kraków (7 daily; 2–4hr); Warsaw (12 daily; 3–5hr).

Gdańsk to: Częstochowa (3 daily; 6–11hr); Kraków (6 daily; 6–11hr); Poznań (5 daily; 4hr); Toruń (4 daily; 2hr 30min–3hr 30min); Warsaw (13 daily; 3hr 30min–4hr 30min); Wrocław (5 daily; 6–7hr); Zakopane (1 daily; 12hr).

Kraków to: Częstochowa (7 daily; 2hr); Gdynia (5 daily; 7–11hr 30min); Poznań (8 daily; 5–7hr 30min); Wrocław (14 daily; 4–5hr 30min); Zakopane (14 daily; 2hr 30min–4hr 30min).

Poznań to: Częstochowa (3 daily; 4hr 30min–6hr); Gdańsk (5 daily; 4hr); Kraków (6 daily; 5hr 30min–7hr); Toruń (5 daily; 2hr–2hr 30min); Warsaw (16 daily; 3–4hr 30min); Wrocław (20 daily; 2hr–3hr 30min); Zakopane (2 daily; 10hr).

Toruń to: Częstochowa (1 daily; 5hr); Gdańsk (4 daily; 3–5hr); Kraków (1 daily; 7hr 30min); Poznań (5 daily; 2–3hr); Warsaw (3 daily; 3–4hr); Wrocław (2 daily; 4hr 30min).

Wrocław to: Częstochowa (7 daily; 2hr 30min–4hr); Gdańsk (4 daily; 7–7hr); Kraków (13 daily; 4hr 30min–5hr); Poznań (19 daily; 2–3hr); Toruń (2 daily; 4hr 30min); Warsaw (9 daily; 5–7hr); Zakopane (1 daily; 7hr 30min).

Zakopane to: Częstochowa (4 daily; 5–8hr); Gdynia (1 daily; 13hr); Kraków (19 daily; 2hr 30min–4hr); Poznań (2 daily; 10hr 30min); Warsaw (4 daily; 6–9hr).

Buses

Warsaw to: Toruń (3 daily), Zakopane (1 daily).
Kraków to: Zakopane (32 daily).

CHAPTER 18

PORTUGAL

Introduction

For so small a country, **Portugal** has tremendous variety both in landscape and in its ways of life and traditions. Along the coast around Lisbon, and on the now well-developed Algarve in the south, there are highly sophisticated resorts, while Lisbon itself, in its idiosyncratic, rather old-fashioned way, has enough diversions to please most city devotees. But in its rural areas this is still a conspicuously underdeveloped country, the "Third World of Europe" as its inhabitants put it. Tourism is changing many areas, but for anyone wanting to get off the beaten track, there are limitless opportunities to experience smaller towns and countryside areas that have changed little in the past century.

In terms of population, and of customs, differences between the **north and south** are particularly striking. Above a line more or less corresponding with the course of the river Tagus, the people are of predominantly Celtic and Germanic stock. It was here, at Guimarães, that the "Lusitanian" nation was born, in the wake of the Christian reconquest from the North African Moors. South of the Tagus, where the Moorish and Roman civilizations were most established, people tend to be darker-skinned and maintain more of a "Mediterranean" lifestyle. More recent events are woven into the pattern. The 1974 **revolution** came from the south – an area of vast estates, rich landowners and a dependent workforce – while the conservative backlash of the 1980s came from the north, with its powerful religious authorities and individual smallholders wary of change. More profoundly even than the revolution, **emigration** has altered people's attitudes and the appearance of the countryside. After Lisbon, the largest Portuguese community is in Paris, and there are migrant workers spread throughout France and Germany. Returning, these emigrants have brought in modern ideas and challenged many traditional rural values.

The greatest of all Portuguese influences, however, is **the sea**. The Portuguese are very conscious of themselves as a seafaring race; mariners like Vasco da Gama led the way in the discovery of Africa and the New World, and until less than twenty years ago Portugal remained a colonial power. The colonies brought African and South American strands to the country's culture: in the distinctive music of *fado*, blues-like songs heard in Lisbon and Coimbra, for example, or in the Moorish-influenced Manueline architecture that abounds in coastal towns like Belém and Viana do Castelo.

Since Portugal is so compact, it's easy to take in something of each of its elements. Scenically, the most interesting parts of the country are in the north: the **Minho**, green, damp, and often startling in its rural customs; and the sensational gorge and valley of the **Douro**, followed along its course by the railway, off which antiquated branch lines edge into remote **Trás-os-Montes**. For contemporary interest, spend some time in both **Lisbon** and **Porto**, the only two cities of real size. And if it's monuments you're after, the whole centre of the country – above all, **Coimbra** and **Évora** – retains a faded grandeur. The **coast** is virtually continuous beach, and apart from the **Algarve** and a few pockets around Lisbon and Porto, resorts remain low-key and thoroughly Portuguese, with great stretches of deserted sands between them. Perhaps the loveliest are along the northern **Costa Verde**, around Viana do Castelo, or, for isolation, the wild beaches of **southern Alentejo**.

Information and Maps

You'll find a tourist office, or **Turismo**, in almost every town of any size. Aside from the help they can give you in finding a room, they often have local maps and leaflets. Their hours are generally Mon–Sat 9am–6pm. The National Tourist Organization can provide you with a workable map of the country. However, if you're doing any real exploration, or driving, it's worth investing in a good **road map**. The best are those put out by the *Automóvel Clube de Portugal* and the Spanish company *Plaza y Janes*, and *Michelin #437*.

Money and Banks

The Portuguese currency is the **escudo**, abbreviated as $ or **esc**. The $ sign follows the amount of escudos, with divisions after it: ie 100$00 is 100esc. Apart from their slowness, Portuguese **banks** are reasonably efficient and you'll find at least one in all but the smallest towns. Banking hours are Mon–Fri 8.30am–3pm; in Lisbon and in some of the Algarve resorts they may be open in the evening to change money. Some banks are installing **automatic exchange machines** for various currencies and denominations. These are not only more efficient, but they charge a 2 percent commission instead of the high rates often levied over the counter.

Communications

Portuguese postal services are reasonably efficient. **Post offices** (*correios*) are normally open Mon–Fri 9am–6pm, larger ones sometimes on Saturday mornings too. To buy **stamps**, stand in line for the counter marked *selos* at the post office, or go anywhere that has the sign of the red horse on a white circle over a green background and the legend *Correio de Portugal – Selos*. To receive mail **"posta restante"**, look for a counter marked *encomendas*.

International phone calls can be made direct from almost any telephone booth in the country, but in most of them you'll need a good deal of patience to get a line – making calls at a post office phone section is easier. Phone cards (750esc and 1725esc) are available from post offices. There is no cheap rate period for international calls. The operator number is ☎118.

Getting Around

Distances are small in Portugal and you can get almost everywhere easily and efficiently by either train or bus. Trains are considerably cheaper, and some lines are highly scenic, but it's almost always quicker to go by bus – especially on shorter or less obvious routes.

■ Trains

CP, the Portuguese railway company, operates all trains. About ninety percent are designated *Regional*, stop at most stations en route, and have first- and second-class cars. The next range up, *Intercidades*, are twice as fast and twice as expensive, and you should reserve a seat if using them. The fastest, most luxurious and priciest of all are the *Rápidos* (known as "Alfa"), which speed between Lisbon and Porto – sometimes they have only first-class seats. Both these latter classes involve supplements for rail pass holders. *CP* sells its own **rail passes** (valid on any train and in first class), but you'd have to do a lot of travelling to make them worthwhile. Both *InterRail* and *Eurail* passes are valid.

Be aware that stations can be some miles from the town or village they serve, and forget about trains completely on **Friday and Sunday evenings** unless you enjoy playing sardines with the Portuguese army – they're all on the move for weekend leave. Many minor lines have been replaced by buses in the last few years, but might still be marked on maps.

■ Buses

Buses can often be more flexible than trains and fares are usually competitive. The majority of buses used to be run by the state-owned *Rodoviaria Nacional* (*RN*), but the company is being broken up and privatized. Most of the former *RN* services leave from a town's central terminal. On a number of major routes – particularly Lisbon–Algarve – special **express coaches** can knock hours off the standard multiple-stop bus journeys.

■ Driving and hitching

Car rental rates in Portugal are among the lowest in Europe so it's an option worth thinking about – even for just a part of your travels. High-season rates begin at about 35000esc a week, with low-season discounts knocking up to a quarter off that. However, bear in mind that you'll have to book ahead for a car in the Algarve in summer, and that Portugal has one of the highest **accident** rates in Europe, most of them happening on the infamous Lisbon–Porto and Lisbon–Algarve motorways. August is especially lethal, when Portuguese emigrant workers return home.

If you **break down** you can get assistance from the *Automóvel Clube de Portugal* which has reciprocal arrangements with most other automobile clubs. In the north, phone their Porto service on ☎02/830 1127; in the south, phone Lisbon ☎01/560 594. Both operate 24 hours a day.

Hitching is variable. It can take hours to get out of Lisbon or Porto because there's nowhere good to stand, but most other towns are very small, their centres within easy reach of the main highways. The Portuguese are a kind, strikingly generous people and the main difficulty in a predominantly rural country is that they tend not to be driving very far.

Accommodation

In almost any town you should be able to find a single room for around 1500–2000esc, a double for 2500–3000esc. Even in mid-season you shouldn't have much problem finding a bed, except in Lisbon and the Algarve.

■ Pensions and hotels

The main budget standbys are **pensions** –*pensões* (*pensão* in the singular) – which are graded from one to three stars. Most serve meals, often in a bargain-priced, all-inclusive package, but they rarely insist that you take them. A three-star *pensão* is usually about the same price as a one-star **hotel**, and sometimes the latter can even be cheaper. Quirks abound in the official municipal grading/pricing systems and you can often pay less in a really luxurious three-star *pensão* than in a one-star pit of a hotel: similarly, some one-star pensions are far nicer than those with two or three.

Additional categories include **pousadas**, run by the state and similar to the Spanish *paradores*. These are expensive, charging at least four-star hotel prices, but they are often converted from old monasteries or castles and can be worth at least a look (or a drink) in themselves.

■ Hostels

There are only fifteen **youth hostels** (*Pousadas de Juventude*) in Portugal but in contrast to Spain they do tend to stay open all year. The price for a dormitory bed is around £5/$8 a night, a little extra if you need to rent sheets and blankets. Most have a curfew (usually 11pm or midnight) and all demand a valid *IYHF* card.

■ Private rooms

In seaside resorts there are invariably rooms (*quartos* or *dormidas*) to let in **private houses**. These are sometimes advertised, sometimes just hawked by people at the bus and train stations. They're slightly cheaper than pension rooms – especially if you haggle, as is expected in the main resorts. Tourist offices have lists.

■ Camping

Portugal has more than a hundred authorized **campsites**, most of them small, low-key and attractively located, and all of them remarkably inexpensive – it's rare that you'll end up paying more than £3/$5 a person. You can get a fairly complete map list from any Portuguese tourist office, or buy a detailed booklet guide, the *Roteiro Campista*, from bookshops or large newsstands.

With a little sensitivity you can pitch a tent for a short period almost anywhere in the countryside. The **Algarve** is different – unofficial camping is banned and campsite thefts are a regular occurrence – but over most of the country the locals are extremely honest and you can leave equipment without worrying.

Food and Drink

Portuguese food is excellent, cheap and served in quantity. Virtually all cafés, whatever their appearance, will serve you a basic meal, or at least a snack, for under £4/$6, and for a little more you have the run of most of the country's restaurants.

■ Food

Often you'll come across a whole range of dishes served at a **café** but they are much more likely to serve just **snacks and basic fare**. Favourites include *prego* (steak sandwich), usually served with a fried egg; *bifoque* (steak, chips, fried egg); *rissóis* (deep-fried meat patties); *pasteis de bacalhau* (codfish cakes); and *sandes* (sandwiches). Sometimes, too, you'll see food displayed on café counters, particularly shellfish – if you see anything that looks appealing, just ask for "*uma dose*" (a portion). "*Uma coisa destas*" (one of those) can also be a useful phrase.

Restaurant servings tend to be so enormous that you can often have a substantial meal by ordering a "*meia dose*" (half portion), or "*uma dose*" between two. Many of the cheaper *restaurantes* offer a well-priced, three-course **ementa turistica** – a soup and fish or meat dish, nearly always followed by the ubiquitous *pudim flan* (creme caramel) or *arroz doce* (rice pudding). Often **pensions** will also serve meals of this kind and, especially in the more trendy tourist resorts, they can ofetn work out the cheapest places to eat.

Regional differences aren't as great as in Spain, but it's always worth taking stock of the *prato do dia* (dish of the day) and, if you're on the coast, going for fish and seafood. If you've had enough rich food, any restaurant will fix a *salada mista* (a mixed salad), which usually has tomatoes, onions and olives as a base.

Meat is not the greatest feature of Portuguese cooking – except for pork, above all *porco á alentejana* (with clams), and smoked hams. **Soups**, everywhere, are extraordinarily cheap, and the thick vegetable soup often known as *caldo verde*, sometimes boosted with pieces of smoked sausage and black pudding, can be almost a meal in itself.

Cakes – *bolos* or *pastéis* – are often at their best in *casas de chá* (teahouses), though you'll also find them in cafés and in *pastelarias* (cake shops). Among the best are the Sintra cheesecakes (*queijadas de Sintra*), marzipan cakes from the Algarve, and the incredibly sweet egg-based *doces de ovos*.

■ Drink

In addition to food, all **cafés** serve alcohol – and they're much cheaper places to drink than **bars**, which tend to have slightly more cosmopolitan pretensions and prices. Portuguese **wines** (*tinto* for red, *branco* white) are dramatically inexpensive and of an amazing overall quality – even the standard *vinho da casa* that you get in the humblest of cafés. The fortified **port** (*vinho do Porto*) and **madeira** (*vinho da Madeira*) wines are by far the best known, and you should certainly aim to sample them both. Among **table wines**, the best of the reds come from the **Dão** region, a roughly triangular area between Coimbra, Viseu and Guarda. The light, slightly sparkling **vinhos verdes** – "green wines", in age not colour – are produced in the Minho, and are reliable.

Portuguese **brandy** is available in two varieties, *Macieiera* and *Constantino*, and like local **gin** is ridiculously cheap; if you're asking for this or any other spirits at a bar always specify you want "gin nacional", "vodka nacional", etc – it'll save you a fortune.

The most common local **beer** (*cerveja*) is *Sagres* but there are numerous other varieties – probably the best is the blue-labelled *Unica Super Bock*. Order *um fino* or *uma imperial* if you want a small glass; *uma caneca* will get you a half-litre.

Coffee (*café*) comes either black, small and espresso-strong (*uma bica*), small and with milk (*um garoto*), or large and with milk but often disgustingly weak (*um galão*). **Tea** (*chá*) is usually plain and is a big drink in Portugal – you'll find elegant *casas de chá* (tearooms) dotted around the country.

Opening Hours and Holidays

Portugal has held onto the institution of the siesta, so most shops and businesses, plus smaller museums and post offices, close for a good lunchtime break – usually from around 12.30pm to 2.30pm or 3pm. **Shops** generally open around 9am, close for lunch then keep going until 7pm. Except in the larger cities, they tend to close for the weekend at Saturday lunchtime. **Museums, churches and monuments** open from around 10am to 6pm; almost all museums and monuments, however, are closed on Mondays.

The main **public holidays** are: Jan 1; April 25; Good Friday; May 1; Corpus Christi (usually early June); June 10; Aug 15; Oct 5; Nov 1; Dec 1; Dec 8; Dec 25.

Emergencies

Portugal is a remarkably crime-free country, though there's the usual petty theft in larger tourist resorts and in Lisbon. Rented cars are always prey to thieves – leave them looking as empty as possible – and campsites in the Algarve are less reliable than elsewhere.

For your own part, violations of **drug laws** (possession of marijuana or hash is a criminal offence) carry heavy sentences. Portuguese **police**, though, are far more human than their Spanish counterparts and don't look for trouble.

For minor **health** complaints people generally go to a *farmácia* (chemist), which you'll find in almost any village; in larger towns there's usually one where English is spoken. Pharmacists are highly trained and can dispense many drugs without a prescription. In the case of serious illness, you can get the address of an English-speaking doctor from a consular office or, with luck, from the local police or tourist office.

EMERGENCY NUMBERS
All emergencies ☎115.

LISBON AND AROUND

There are few more immediately likeable capitals than **Lisbon**. A lively and varied place, it remains in some ways curiously provincial, rooted as much in the 1920s as the 1990s. Wooden trams from before World War I clank up outrageous gradients, past mosaic pavements and Art Nouveau cafés, and the medieval, village-like quarter of Alfama hangs below the city's castle. Modern Lisbon has kept an easy-going, human pace and scale, with little of the underlying violence of most cities and all ports of its size. But in other respects it's been changing – inevitably so, for its population has doubled over the present century to nearly a million, a tenth of all Portuguese.

Art and monuments are relatively thin on the ground, largely as a result of the 1755 earthquake, after which the core of the city was reconstructed on a grid pattern that still endures. But there is one building from Portugal's golden age – the **Jerónimos Monastery** at Belém – that is the equal of any monument in the country (and most in Spain). More modern developments include the **Gulbenkian Foundation** museum complex, with its superb collections of ancient and modern art, and Tómas Taveira's amazing post-modernist shopping centre at Amoreiras. The sea is close by, half an hour's journey taking you to the miles of dunes along the **Costa da Caparica**. Slightly further afield lie the lush wooded heights and royal palaces of **Sintra**, the "glorious Eden" that Byron considered "the most beautiful . . . in the world" until he found its claims surpassed by Albania. And if you become interested in Portuguese architecture, there's the monastery of **Mafra**, one of the most extraordinary buildings in the country.

> The Greater Lisbon telephone code is ☎01.

Arrival and information

From the **airport**, just twenty minutes' drive from the centre, buses #44 and #45 (140esc) run past the youth hostel to the Praça dos Restauradores and on to the Cais do Sodré (for Cascais), while the *Linha Verde* express bus (every 15min, 7.30am–10pm; 250esc) goes to the central Rossio, Praça do Comércio and Santa Apolónia. Long-distance trains use the **Santa Apolónia station**, about fifteen minutes' walk from the waterfront Praça do Comércio, or a short ride on buses #9 or #46 to the Rossio square. At the station there's a small information office and bureau de change. **Local trains** emerge at the heart of the city in the **Rossio Station**, while **trains from the Algarve and south** terminate at **Barreiro**, on the far bank of the river, where you catch a ferry (included in the price of the train ticket) to the **Fluvial** station next to the Praça do Comércio. The **bus terminal** on Avenida Casal Ribeiro (metro Saldanha) serves destinations north of Lisbon; Praça de Espanha (metro Palhavã) and Avda Cinco de Outubro 75 (bus #1 or #21 from Praça dos Restauradores) serve the south.

It could hardly be easier to get your bearings in the **Baixa**, the central city grid. At one end, opening on to the River Tagus, is the broad, arcaded **Praço do Comércio**; at the other stands Praça Dom Pedro IV, or the **Rossio**, merging with the **Praça da Figueira** and **Praça dos Restauradores**. These squares, filled with cafés, occasional street musicians, tourists and streetwise dealers, form the hub of Lisbon's daily activity. At night the focus shifts to the **Bairro Alto**, high above and to the left of the Baixa, and best reached by funicular (*Elevador da Glória*) or the great street "elevador" (*Santa Justa*) built for the city by Raul Mésnier – not, as commonly claimed, by Gustave Eiffel. East of the Baixa, the **Castelo de São Jorge**, a brooding landmark, holds a still taller hill, with the **Alfama** district – the core of the medieval city – sprawled below.

The main **tourist office** is on Praça dos Restauradores (daily 9am–8pm); they can supply maps, accommodation lists and up-to-date schedules for the plethora of bus companies operating out of Lisbon. An invaluable supplement to their information is the weekly listings paper *Se7e*.

City transport

Getting around Lisbon presents few problems. Most places of interest are within easy walking distance – and transport connections are detailed in the text for those that aren't. The bus and tram networks operate from around 6am to midnight and the metro until 1am. **Trams**, the most enjoyable way of getting around, cost 140esc per journey, as do **buses** (*carris*). The **metro** covers a few useful routes, though as a visitor to the city you're unlikely to make extensive use of it; tickets are 55esc, or a bit cheaper bought in blocks (*módulos*) of ten. All are free for children – as is Mésnier's *elevador*. If you're staying for more than a few days, the **tourist pass** for the complete public transport system might be worth considering; costing 1350esc for four days or 1900esc for seven, it is available, on production of a passport, at the booth by the Elevador Santa Justa. Lisbon's **taxis** are excellent value for trips within the city limits. All journeys are metered and should rarely cost more than 500–600esc. They can be found quite easily by day, especially around the main squares, but at night it's a different matter – if you're leaving a bar or club it's usually best to get someone to phone.

Accommodation

Lisbon has scores of small, cheap **pensions**, often grouped one on top of the other in tall tenement blocks. At Easter, and most noticeably in midsummer, however, room availability is often stretched to the limit: many single rooms are "converted" to doubles and prices may start as high as 3000esc. Fortunately, during most of the year you should have little difficulty finding a place, and for maybe a third less than the midsummer prices. For hotels costing 5000esc and up, it can save a lot of walking to use the **reservation service** at the Praça dos Restauradores tourist office or the airport; there is no commission charge. Most of the pensions listed below are one- or two-star; **addresses** – written as 53-3°, for example – specify the street number followed by the storey.

Hostels
Pousada de Juventude, Rua Andrade Corvo 46 (☎532 696). Lisbon's main hostel, a rather large, soulless place with a midnight curfew and closed 2–6pm. One block south of the Picoas metro stop, or take buses #1, #44 or #45 from Restauradores or Rossio. ②

Oeiras Youth Hostel, Forte do Catalazete (☎443 0628). Overlooking the beach at Oeiras, 20km outside the city; again closed 2–6pm. Take a slow train from Cais do Sodré and follow signs from Oeiras station. It's small, so phone before setting out. ②

Hotels
Pensão Almirante Reis, Avda Almirante Reis 98-2° (☎823 773). Cheap and cheerful. ③

Pensão Angoche, Rua dos Douradores 121-4° (☎870 711). Small, quiet, clean and friendly. In the Baixa grid. ②

Pensão Arco Bandeira, Rua Arco Bandeira 226-4° (☎342 3478). Superior pension with comfortable rooms. Close to the Rossio. ②

Hotel Borges, Rua Garrett 108 (☎361 953). Pleasant rooms with bath in a quiet hotel overlooking the elegant Chiado. ④

Pensão D Maria II, Rua Portas de Santo Antão 9-3° (☎371 128). Large airy rooms with basins and nice views over the Rossio. Good value. ②

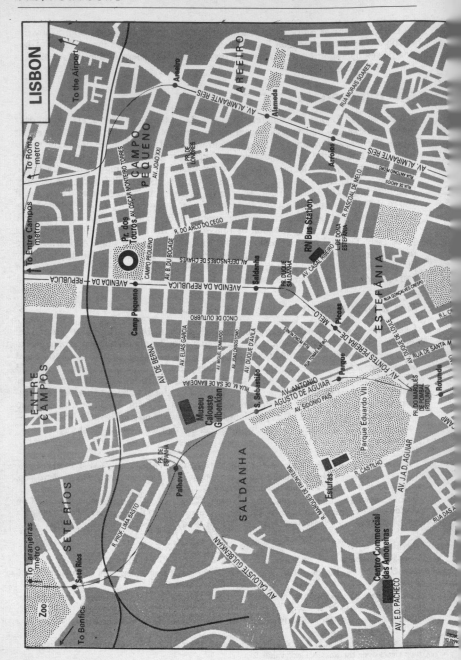

LISBON

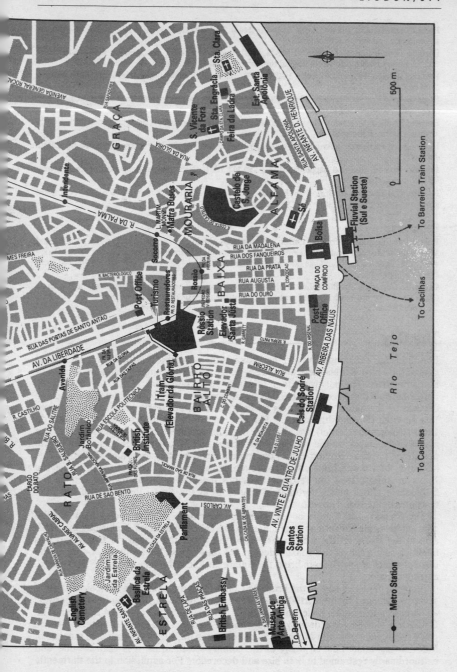

Pensão Duque, Calçada do Duque 53 (☎346 3444). Just outside the Bairro Alto nightclub zone but atmospheric and very reasonable. ①

Pensão Globo, Rua do Teixeira 37 (☎346 2279). Rooms are clean, management fine and the location, in a quiet Bairro Alto street behind the Port Wine Institute, superb. ②

Pensão Ibérica, Praça da Figueira 10-2° (☎886 7026). Good value and a superb location; ask for a front balcony room. ②

Pensão Iris, Rua da Gloria 2a-1° (☎323 157). Very basic but extremely convenient location and especially recommended for single women. ②

Pensão Moderna, Rua dos Correios 205-4° (☎346 0818). Big clean rooms, crammed with elderly furniture. In the Baixa grid. ②

Residencial Paradouro, Avda Almirante Reis 106-7° (☎815 3256). Not overpriced for its high standard. ④

Pensão Rossio, Rua dos Sapateiros 173-2° (☎342 7204). Nice rooms, bang on the Rossio, with helpful management. ②

Residencial Santa Catarina, Rua Dr Luis de Almeida e Albuquerque 6 (☎346 6106). Very good value mid-range place in Bairro Alto, with friendly staff. ③

Campsites

Parque Municipal de Tourist Office e Campismo. Main city campsite, in the Parque Florestal Monsanto, about 6km west of the centre. The entrance is on Estrada da Circunvalaçáo on the Park's west side. Take a train from Cais do Sodré to Algés, then bus #50 to the campsite, or bus #43 from Praça da Figueira.

Costa da Caparica. An alternative to Monsanto is to camp at one of the beaches along the Costa da Caparica. There are several small and lively campsites here, 30 to 50 minutes away by bus (see "Around Lisbon").

The City

For all Lisbon's cosmopolitan air, the **Baixa** is the nearest a Western European capital gets to the Third World – begging, lottery-ticket selling and shoe-shining are all growth industries here. The positive side of this, at least for outsiders, is the survival of tradition. Many of the streets in the Baixa grid maintain their crafts and businesses as devised by the autocratic Marquês de Pombal in his post-earthquake reconstruction: Rua da Prata (Silversmiths' Street), Rua dos Sapateiros (Cobblers' Street) and Rua do Ouro (Goldsmiths' Street) are all cases in point. Architecturally, the most interesting places in the Baixa are the squares – the Rossio and Praça do Comércio – and, on the periphery, the lanes leading east to the cathedral and west up towards Bairro Alto. This last area, known as **Chiado**, suffered much damage from a fire that swept across the Baixa in August 1988 but remains the city's most affluent quarter, focused on the fashionable shops and – fortunately spared from the fire – the beautiful old café-tearooms of the **Rua Garrett**.

The **Rossio** – itself more or less encircled by cafés – is very much a focus for the city, yet its single concession to grandeur is the **Teatro Nacional**, built along the north side in the 1840s. At the waterfront end of the Baixa, the **Praça do Comércio** was intended as the climax to Pombal's design, but these days it's a tawdry spot, though the town planners are working to bring the square back into the hub of city life by pedestrianizing the area.

A couple of blocks east of the Praça do Comércio is the church of **Conceição Velha**, severely damaged by the earthquake but retaining its flamboyant Manueline doorway, an early example of this style which hints at the brilliance that emerged at Belém. The **Cathedral** – or Sé – stands very stolidly above. Founded in 1150 to commemorate the city's reconquest from the Moors, it in fact occupies the site of the principal mosque of Moorish Lishbuna. Like so many of the country's cathedrals, it is Romanesque, and extraordinarily restrained in both size and decoration. For admission to the thirteenth-century cloisters you must buy a ticket, which also covers the Baroque sacristy (Tues–Sun 10am–1pm & 2–6pm; 120esc, free Sun) with its small museum of treasures – including the relics of Saint Vincent, allegedly brought to Lisbon in 1173 in a boat piloted by ravens.

From the Sé, Rua do Limoeiro winds upward towards the Castelo, past sparse ruins of a Roman theatre and the **Miradouro de Santa Luzia**, where the conquest of Lisbon and the siege of the Castelo de São Jorge are depicted in *azulejos* on the walls. At the entrance to the **Castelo** (daily 9am–9pm; free) stands a triumphant statue of Afonso Henriques, conqueror of the Moors. Of the Moorish palace that once stood here only a much-restored shell remains, in which a rather insignificant museum has been installed – but the castle as a whole is an enjoyable place to spend a couple of hours, wandering amid the ramparts and towers to look down upon the city. Crammed within the castle's outer walls is the tiny medieval quarter of **Santa Cruz**, once very much a village in itself.

The **Alfama** quarter, stumbling from the walls of the Castelo to the banks of the Tagus, is the oldest part of Lisbon. In Arab times this was the grandest part of the city but with subsequent earthquakes the new Christian nobility moved out, leaving it to the fishing community still here today. It is undergoing some commercialization, thanks to its cobbled lanes and "character", but although the antique shops and restaurants may be moving in, the quarter retains a largely traditional life of its own. The **Feira da Ladra**, Lisbon's rambling and ragged **flea market**, fills the Campo de Santa Clara, at the edge of Alfama, on Tuesday morning and all day Saturday. While at the flea market, take a look inside **Santa Engrácia**, the loftiest and most tortuously built church in the city – begun in 1682, its vast dome was finally completed in 1966. Through the tiled cloisters of nearby **São Vicente de Fora** you can visit the old monastic refectory, since 1855 the pantheon of the Bragança dynasty. Here, in more or less complete (though unexciting) sequence, are the bodies of all Portuguese kings from João IV, who restored the monarchy, to Manuel II who lost it and died in exile in England in 1932.

Mésnier's extraordinary **Elevador Santa Justa**, just off the top end of Rua do Ouro on Rua de Santa Justa, is the most obvious approach to **Bairro Alto**. Alternatively, there are the two funicular-like trams – the *Elevador da Glória* from the Praça dos Restauradores or the *Elevador da Bica* from Rua de São Paulo/Rua da Moeda. The ruined Gothic arches of the **Convento do Carmo** hang almost directly above the exit of Mésnier's *elevador*. Once the largest church in the city, this was half-destroyed by the earthquake but is perhaps even more beautiful as a result; it now houses a small archeological museum (Oct–March Mon–Sat 10am–1pm & 2–5pm; April–Sept 10am–6pm; 300esc). The church of **São Roque**, over towards the Chiado in the Largo Trindade Coelho, looks from the outside like the plainest in the city, its bleak Renaissance facade having been further simplified by the earthquake. But hang around in the gloom and the sacristan will come and escort you around, turning on lights to an incredible succession of side chapels, each lavishly crafted with *azulejos*, multicoloured marble, or Baroque painted ceilings. The climax is the Capela de São João Baptista, last on the left. It was ordered from Rome in 1742 by Dom João V to honour his patron saint and was designed using the most costly materials available, including ivory, agate, porphyry and lapis lazuli.

The Parque Eduardo VII and the Gulbenkian museum

North of the Praça dos Restauradores are the city's principal gardens, the **Parque Eduardo VII**, most easily approached by metro to Rotunda. Though there are some pleasant cafés here, the park's big attractions are the **Estufas** (daily 9am–6pm; 70esc), huge and wonderful glasshouses filled with tropical plants, flamingo pools, and endless varieties of palms and cacti.

The **Museu Calouste Gulbenkian** (Oct–May Tues–Sun 10am–5pm; June–Sept Tues, Thurs, Fri & Sun 10am–5pm, Wed & Sat 2–7.30pm; 200esc, free Sun), the great museum of Portugal, is to the north of the park in Avda de Berna – take bus #31, #41 or #46 from the Rossio, or the metro to Palhavã or São Sebastião. Established by the Armenian oil magnate Calouste Gulbenkian, the Gulbenkian Foundation runs this amazing complex – an orchestra, three concert halls and two galleries for temporary exhibitions – in the capital, and finances work in all spheres of Portuguese cultural life, in even the smallest towns. This showpiece museum is divided into two distinct parts – the first devoted to Egyptian, Greco-Roman, Islamic and Oriental arts, the second to European – and ideally you'll want to take them in on separate visits. Highlights in the former half include the entire contents of the Egyptian room, which covers almost every period of importance from the Old Kingdom (2700 BC) to the Roman period. In the European section the real strength is in the collection of paintings, featuring work from all the major schools. Ghirlandaio's *Portrait of a Young Woman* is followed by outstanding portraits by Rubens and Rembrandt, while Fragonard ushers in an excellent showing of work from France, featuring Corot, Manet and Monet. There's also a stunning room full of the Art Nouveau jewellery of René Lalique. Across the gardens, the separate **Centro de Arte Moderna** (same hours and price) has all the big names on the twentieth-century Portuguese scene, including Almada Negreiros, the founder of *modernismo*, and Paula Rego, who paints creepy kids.

Museu de Arte Antiga

The one other museum that stands up to Gulbenkian standards is the national art collection, the **Museu de Arte Antiga** (Tues–Sun 10am–1pm & 2–5pm; 250esc, free Sun am), situated on the riverfront to the west of the city at Rua das Janelas Verdes 95 (tram #19 from Praça do Comércio). Its core is formed by fifteenth- and sixteenth-century Portuguese works, the acknowledged masterpiece being Nuno Gonçalves' *St Vincent Altarpiece*, a brilliantly marshalled canvas depicting Lisbon's patron receiving homage from all ranks of its citizens. After Gonçalves and his contemporaries, the most interesting works are by Flemish and German artists (Cranach, Bosch – a fabulous *Temptation of St Anthony* – and Dürer), and miscellaneous gems by Raphael, Zurbarán and, rather oddly, Rodin.

Belém and the Monastery of Jerónimos

Even before the Great Earthquake, the **Monastery of Jerónimos** (Tues–Sun Oct–May 10am–1pm & 2.30–5pm; June–Sept 10am–6.30pm; 400esc) at **Belém** was Lisbon's finest monument: since then, it has stood quite without comparison (tram #15 or #17 from Praça do Comércio). It was from Belém in 1497 that Vasco da Gama set sail for India, and it was here, too, that he was welcomed home by Dom Manuel "the Fortunate". The monastery was funded by a levy on the fruits of his discovery – a five percent tax on all spices other than pepper, cinnamon and cloves, whose import had become the sole preserve of the crown.

Begun in 1502, this is the most ambitious achievement of Manueline architecture. The main entrance to the church is a complex, shrine-like hierarchy of figures centred around Henry the Navigator, while the church itself sets up fascinating tensions between the grand spatial design and the areas of intensely detailed ornamentation. Once you've made the analogy, it's difficult to see the six central columns as anything other than palm trunks, growing into the branches of the delicate rib-vaulting. Vaulted throughout and fantastically embellished, the cloister has a wave-like, rhythmic motion that's complemented by typically Manueline references to ropes, anchors and the sea.

The **Torre de Belém** (Tues–Sun Oct–May 10am–1pm & 2.30–5pm; June–Sept 10am–6.30pm; 400esc), guarding the entrance to the port just a couple of hundred metres from the monastery, is a multi-turreted whimsy built over the last five years of

Dom Manuel's reign. Its architect had previously worked on Portuguese fortifications in Morocco, and a Moorish influence is very strong in the delicately arched windows and balconies. The interior is unremarkable except for a "whispering gallery". Close by are a number of museums, of which the best is the **Museu de Arte Popular** (Tues–Sun 10am–1pm & 2.30–5.30pm; June–Sept 10am–1pm & 2.30–6.30pm; 400esc, free Sun), a province-by-province display of Portugal's still very diverse folk arts, housed in a shed-like building on the waterfront. Almost adjacent is the vast concrete **Monument to the Discoveries** (Tues–Sun 9.30am–7pm; 275esc), erected in 1960 to commemorate the 500th anniversary of the death of Henry the Navigator; inside, a small exhibition space has changing displays on the city's history, and there are fine views of the Tagus from the top. At the corner of Belém's other main square – Praça Afonso de Abuquerque, a few minutes' walk from the monastery along Rua de Belém – there's the **Museu dos Coches**, an interminable line of mainly eighteenth-century royal coaches, the most visited and most tedious tourist attraction in Lisbon (Tues–Sun 10am–1pm & 2.30–5.30pm; June–Sept closes 6.30pm; 400esc, free Sun).

Eating

Lisbon has some of the best-value **restaurants** of any European city – in fact, picking a place at random, outside the city centre, it's hard to go far wrong. **By day**, choices could extend through the lunchtime workers' cafés around Alfama, the fish restaurants across the Tagus at Cacilhas or down the coast at Cascais, or the multitude of set meals on offer for office employees in the Baixa. **At night** the obvious place to be is Bairro Alto, which harbours the city's most adventurous restaurants, as well as the best bars and clubs. Bear in mind that many of the places in our listings will be closed on Sundays and, especially on Saturday nights in summer, you will have to **book a table**.

For rock-bottom eating, there are stalls in the **mercado** behind Cais do Sodré station, in addition to the picnic foods on sale. Alternatively, if you're a student, the city has some of the cheapest **cantinas** (student canteens) in Europe, with full meals well under 400esc. The *cantinas* are at the junction of Rua Gomes Freire and Rua Escola de Medicina Veterinária (Picoas metro), in the centre of the university campus (Cidade Universitária metro) and on Avda das Forças Armadas (Entrecampos metro or bus #32 from Rossio).

O Barriga, Travessa da Queimada 31. One of the best deals in the Bairro Alto.

Bizarro, Rua da Atalaia 133. Excellent service and one of the cheapest joints in the Bairro Alto – under 2500esc all in.

Casa Faz Frio, Rua Dom Pedro V 96. Slightly further afield, this is an exceptionally beautiful and very traditional restaurant – not expensive if you share the vast portions.

Casa de Pasto Flores, Praça das Flores 40. Somewhat to the northwest of the heart of Bairro Alto. Good value.

Cervejaria da Trinidade, Rua Nova da Trinidade 20c. Wonderful tiled beer house, serving food until 1.30am.

O Coradinho, Rua de Sta Marta 4a. In the northward extension of Rua das Portas de Santo Antão. Very friendly and excellent value with a full *ementa turistica* for under 1500esc.

Fidalgo, Rua da Baroca 27. A no longer cheap but still trendy Bairro Alto hang-out specializing in delicious seafood creations.

Montenegro, Rua das Portas de Sto Antão 38. Cheap place worth trying.

Rio Coura, Rua de Augusto Rosa 30. A couple of hundred metres uphill from the Sé. Amazing value: soup, a skewer of squid, ham and onions with potoatoes, chocolate mousse and half a bottle of house wine for under 2000esc.

Rei dos Frangos/Bom Jardim, Travessa de Bom Jardim. Tucked into the alleyway connecting Restauradores with the Rua das Portas de Santo Antão. Usually packed out with students, this is *the* place for chicken – whole ones for under 1000esc.

Solar da Padaria, Rua da Padaria 18–20. A great restaurant in the Baixa, boasting a tempting seafood menu.

Túnel de Alfama, Rua dos Remédios 132. A more conventional restaurant than is common in Alfama, but cheap and very substantial.

Drinking and nightlife

Although there are exciting places scattered all over the city, the densest concentration of **bars and clubs** is to be found in Bairro Alto; be aware that the area is the city's sex centre, though most people up in the quarter are there just to eat, drink or listen to music. Brasher, more mainstream **discos** cluster further to the west in the quarters of Santos and the more outlying Alcântara. Tourist brochures tend to suggest that Lisbon entertainment begins and ends with **fado**, the city's traditional "blues" music, offered in thirty or so nightclubs in the Bairro Alto and elsewhere. There's no reason – except perhaps ever-rising admission prices – not to sample some *fado*, but don't miss out on other possibilities. Portuguese **jazz** can be good, **rock** an occasional surprise, and if you check out *Se7e* and the posters around Restauradores there's a good chance of catching **African music** from the former colonies.

BARS AND CLUBS
Café Targus, Rua do Diário de Notícias 40b. Slick new bar that's ideal for a quiet drink.

Cerca Moura, Largo das Portas do Sol. One of a cluster of bars on this square, with a nice view of the Tagus and a large esplanade.

Chapito, Costa do Costelo 1/7. Multimedia centre, incorporating open-air bar with a river view, circus tent, theatre and restaurant. Young, fashion-conscious – and free admission.

Finalmente, Rua Cecílio de Sousa. First-class disco with lashings of kitsch.

Fragil, Rua da Atalaia 126. Very trendy club with substantial gay following. Can be rather pretentious, but admission is free if you can get past the doorwoman.

Incognito, Rua dos Poiais de São Bento 37. Appropriately named – the only indication is the large metallic doors on the way down from Bairro Alto towards Santos. Low-lit, plush, dance floor downstairs with interesting music.

O Solar do Vinho do Porto (Port Wine Institute Bar), Rua de São Pedro de Alcântara 45. Over 300 types and vintages of port, from 150esc up. Mon–Sat 10am–midnight.

Sua Excelência O Marquês, Largo Marquês do Lavradio. Very trendy bar, behind the Sé.

Três Pastorinhos, Rua de Barroca 111–113. Ring the doorbell for entry to this fashionable club featuring current dance tracks.

Trumps, Rua da Imprensa Nacional 104 B. The biggest gay place in Lisbon. Mostly soul, rap and house. Can be cruisy.

FADO
Imagine an Afghani humming along to a Billie Holiday record and you're halfway to grasping the spirit of **fado**, the weirdest, most melancholic music in Europe. It's thought to have originated in Alfama, and Lisbon is still the best place to hear it – even though *fado* bars have inflated minimum charges (1500esc and upwards) and can be tacky. *A Severa*, Rua das Gáveas 55, *Adega Machado*, Rua do Norte 91, and *Painel do Fado*, Rua São Pedro de Alcântara 65, are the big three with the big prices. *Adega do Ribatejo*, Rua do Diário de Notícias 23, is popular with locals, and also worth considering. Before setting out, check their opening nights at the tourist office.

ROCK VENUES
Rock music is a chancier business, though there are a handful of interesting local bands. Look out for visiting Brazilian singers, who, like mainstream British or American bands, tend to play stadium gigs at the *Coliseu dos Recreios*, Rua das Portas

de Santo Antão, the *Pavilhão do Restelo*, in Restelo, or the *Pavilhão de Cascais*, out in Cascais.

CINEMAS

Lisbon and its environs have some 75 **cinemas**, virtually all of them showing original language films with Portuguese subtitles. Ticket prices are low and some of the theatres are beautiful Art Nouveau and Art Deco palaces. The national film theatre is the *Institut de Cinemateca Portuguesa* at Rua Barata Salgueiro 39, with two programmes daily. Another place for film buffs to check out is the post-modern shopping centre at **Amoreiras**, Avda Duarte Pacheco, which features no fewer than ten screens.

Listings

Airlines Most are along Avda de Liberdade – *British Airways* are at no. 36-2° (☎346 0931), *Air France* at 224a, *Air Maroc* at 225a and *TWA* at 258a. *TAP* (Air Portugal) is in the Praça Marquês de Pombal; *KLM* is at Campo Grande 220.

American Express Operated by *Top Tours Travel Agency*, Avda Duque de Loulé 108 (☎315 5885).

Banks Most head offices are in the Baixa and surrounding streets; *Banco Borges & Irmão* at Avda da Liberdade 9a is open until 7.30pm.

Car rental *Avis*, *Budget* and *Europcar* all have desks at the airport, though there are far smaller queues (and often lower prices) at smaller agencies like *Dollar* and *Budget*.

Embassies *Australia*, Avda da Liberdade 244-4° (☎523 350); *Canada*, Avda da Liberdade 144-3° (☎347 892); *Ireland*, Rua da Imprensa á Estrela 1-4° (☎396 1569); *UK*, Rua S. Domingos á Lapa 37 (☎396 1191); *Netherlands*, Rua do Sacramento á Lapa 4-1° (☎396 2306); *USA*, Avda das Forças Armadas (☎726 6600).

Hospital British Hospital, Rua Saraiva de Carvalho 49 (☎396 5067).

Laundry *Lava Neve*, at Rua de Alegría 37 in Bairro Alto, is excellent, or try the place at Rua Saraiva de Carvalho 117, a little west of Rato (bus #9 from Rossio).

Police Main station is on Rua Capelo, west of the Baixa (☎346 6141).

Post offices The main post office is on the Praça do Comércio (Mon–Fri 9am–7pm); its poste restante section has a separate entrance at Rua do Arsenal 27 (closes 2pm). Airmail leaves from a box in the Praça dos Restauradores post office (open until 11pm).

Telephones At the main post office.

Travel agencies Many firms can be found along Avda de Liberdade. Youth and budget specialists include *Intercentro*, Avda Casal de Ribeiro 18b (☎571 745), the main international bus agent, and *Abreu*, Avda da Liberdade 160 (☎347 6441), a well-established charter agent.

Around Lisbon

For escapes from the city, it's easy to get out to the beaches of **Caparica** – which the quirks of the Tagus currents have largely spared from the pollution of Lisbon – or to the architectural attractions of **Sintra** and **Mafra**. All can be visited on a day trip, but to do justice to Sintra you'll need to stay overnight.

Costa da Caparica

It takes something over an hour to reach **Costa da Caparica** from the capital, and it's here that most locals come if they want to swim or laze around on the sand. This is a thoroughly Portuguese resort, crammed with restaurants and beach cafés, yet solitude is easy enough to find, thanks to the mini-railway that runs along the 8km of dunes in summer. The most enjoyable approach is to take a **ferry** from the Fluvial station to **Cacilhas**, and then pick up the connecting bus from the dock where the boats come in. Alternatively, and more speedily, you can take a **bus** direct to Caparica from the main Praça de Espanha terminal (metro Palhavã).

At **CAPARICA** all buses stop at a dusty depot close to the beginning of the sands. If you walk along the beach to the left you come to the main square, where there's a **tourist office**, market, cinema and banks. There aren't very many hotels in Caparica but the tourist office will find you a **room** in a guesthouse. A particularly attractive place to stay is the *Hotel-Restaurante Pátio Alentejano*, Rua Professor Salazar de Sousa 17 (☎01/290 0044; ②) – just off the beach at the western end of town. **Campsites**, which range along the first few kilometres of the beach, are on the whole overcrowded and overpriced, but functional enough. A recommended **restaurant**, among dozens of fish and seafood places along the main Rua dos Pescadores, is the *Casa dos Churros* at no. 13.

Sintra
Summer residence of the kings of Portugal and of the Moorish lords of Lisbon before them, **SINTRA**'s cool, wooded heights are celebrated by the old Spanish proverb: "To see the world and leave out Sintra is to go blind about". The layout of Sintra – an amalgamation of three villages – can be confusing, but the extraordinary **Palácio Nacional** (daily tours 10am–5pm; closed Wed; 200esc), about ten minutes' walk from the station, is an obvious landmark. The palace was probably in existence under the Moors, but takes its present form from the rebuilding of Dom João I (1385–1433) and his successor, Dom Manuel, heir to Vasco da Gama's lucrative explorations. Its style is a fusion of Gothic and the latter king's Manueline additions, with their characteristically animated forms. The tours are frankly a pain unless you go very early before the groups arrive, but the palace does have four or five rooms that are well worth seeing – such as the chapel and its adjoining chamber, its floor worn by incessant pacing, where the half-mad Afonso VI was confined for six years by his brother Pedro I.

The charms of Sintra lie less in its palace buildings than in the **walks and paths** that it is able to offer, one of the best of which leads past the church of Santa Maria and up to the ruined ramparts of a **Moorish Castle**, from where the views are extraordinary. Beyond the castle, a good ninety-minute walk from town, is the lower entrance to the immense **Pena Park** (daily 10am–6pm; free), at the top end of which rears the fabulous **Palácio de Pena** (Tues–Sun 10am–5pm; 400esc). This wild fantasy of domes, towers, ramparts and walkways, approached through mock-Manueline gateways and a drawbridge that does not draw, was built in the 1840s to the specifications of Ferdinand of Saxe-Coburg-Gotha, husband of Queen Maria II, and it bears comparison with the mock-medieval castles of Ludwig of Bavaria. Inside, Pena is no less bizarre, for it has been preserved exactly as left by the royal family on their flight from Portugal in 1910. Of an original convent, founded to celebrate the first sight of Vasco da Gama's returning fleet, a chapel and genuine Manueline cloister have been retained.

After the follies of Pena, a visit to Seteais and Monserrate – the other obvious goals of a Sintra walk – comes as something of a relief. **Seteais**, just right of the Colares road, fifteen minutes' walk from town, is one of the most elegant palaces in Portugal, completed in the last years of the eighteenth century and entered through a majestic classical arch; it is now an intensely luxurious hotel and restaurant. Beyond, the road leads past a series of beautiful private estates to **Monserrate** – about an hour's walk. It's difficult to do justice to the beauty of Monserrate, whose vast **gardens** (daily 9am–5pm), filled with endless varieties of exotic trees and subtropical shrubs and plants, extend as far as the eye can see.

Finding a room at Sintra in summer can be a problem, though if you arrive early in the day you should end up with something. There are a fair number of **pensions**: best value is probably the *Adelaide* (☎01/923 0873; ②), midway between the train station and Sintra village. Alternatively, some well-priced **private rooms** can be booked through the extremely helpful **tourist office** in the centre. The nearest **campsites** are well out of town: the most convenient are at the beach-villages of Praia das Maçãs and Azenhas do Mar, both connected by bus. **Restaurants** are generally poor value, relying heavily on the tour parties. Try the *Bar Brazil* on Rua São Pedro and the two *Adega do Saloio* grillhouses, at the far end of the street. The restaurant in the *Pensão Bristol* on Rua Visconde de Monserrate also does huge, cheap menus.

Mafra

Connected by regular buses from Sintra train station and from Lisbon, **MAFRA** is dominated by one building: the vast **Palace-Convent** (10am–1pm & 2.30–5pm; closed Tues) built in emulation of Madrid's Escorial by João V, the wealthiest and most extravagant of all Portuguese monarchs. The convent was initially intended for just thirteen Franciscan friars, but as wealth poured in from Brazil, João amplified it into a massive basilica, two royal wings and monastic quarters for 300 monks and 150 novices. The sheer magnitude is what stands out: there are 5200 doorways, 2500 windows, and two bell towers each containing over 50 bells. Parts of the convent are now used by the military but one-hour guided tours take you around a sizeable portion. The highlight is the magnificent Rococo library – brilliantly lit and rivalling that of Coimbra in both design and grandeur. The basilica, which can be seen outside the tour, is no less imposing, with the multicoloured marble designs of its floor mirrored in the ceiling decoration.

CENTRAL PORTUGAL

The **Estremadura** region has played a crucial role in each phase of the nation's history – and the monuments are there to prove it. A comparatively small area, it boasts a quite extraordinary concentration of vivid architecture and engaging towns. **Alcobaça**, **Batalha** and **Tomar** – the most exciting buildings in Portugal – all lie within ninety minutes' bus ride of one another. With its fertile rolling hills, Estremadura is second in beauty only to Minho, but the adjoining bull-breeding lands of **Ribatejo** (literally "banks-of-the-Tagus") fade into the dull expanses of northwestern Alentejo, and there's no great reason to cross the river unless you're pushing on to Évora or can catch up with one of the region's traditional festivals.

North of Estremadura, life on the fertile plain of the **Beira Litoral** has been conditioned over the centuries by the twin threats of floodwaters from Portugal's highest mountains and silting by the restless Atlantic: it's an area where drainage channels have to be cut to make cultivation possible and where houses must be built on high ground. On the coast the chief attractions are **Figueira da Foz**, a lovely resort at the mouth of the Rio Mondego, and the northern town of **Aveiro**, where the production of salt and the harvesting of seaweed have become staples of the local economy. The highlight of Beira Litoral, however, is **Coimbra**, an ancient university city stacked high on the right bank of the Mondego. Less than half an hour to the north, the delightful spa town of **Luso** lies beneath the ancient **forest of Buçaco**, the most exotic of Portugal's landscapes. Further inland is the little-explored **Mountain Beiras** region, historically the heart of ancient Lusitânia, where Viriatus the Iberian rebel made his last stand against the Romans. You'll see many signs of this patriotism in the fine old town of **Viseu**, where every other place of refreshment is the *Café Viriate* or the *Restaurante Lusitânia*. At an even higher altitude stands **Guarda**, pretty diminutive for somewhere of such renown, but nonetheless bristling with life, especially on *feira* days.

Óbidos

ÓBIDOS, "The Wedding City", was the traditional bridal gift of the kings of Portugal to their queens, a custom begun in 1282 by Dom Dinis and Dona Isabel. The town – a couple of hours from Lisbon by train – can hardly have changed in appearance since then: its cobbled streets and whitewashed houses are completely enclosed by medieval walls, and steep staircases wind up to the ramparts, where you can gaze across a fable-like countryside of windmills and vineyards.

The parish church, **Igreja de Santa Maria**, in the central Praça, was chosen for the wedding of the ten-year-old child king Afonso V and his eight-year-old cousin, Isabel, in 1444. It dates mainly from the Renaissance though the interior is lined with seventeenth-century blue *azulejos* in a homely manner typical of Portuguese churches. The retable in a side chapel on the right-hand side was painted by Josefa de Óbidos, one of the finest Portuguese painters – and one of the few women artists afforded any reputation by art historians. One corner of the triangular fortifications is occupied by a massively towered **Castle** built by Dom Dinis and now converted into a *pousada* (☎062/959 105; ⑧).

Other **hotels** in Óbidos also tend to be expensive – the only reasonably priced one is *Casa de Hóspedes Madeira* on Rua Direita (②). Your cheapest option is to consult the list of private houses offering **rooms** which is posted in the **tourist office**, also on Rua Direita. It's worth staying since, as so often, the town reverts to its own life when the daytime tourists disperse. One of the better cheap places to **eat** is the *Café 1 de Dezembro*, next to the church of São Pedro.

Alcobaça

From the twelfth century until the middle of the nineteenth, the Cistercian **Abbey of ALCOBAÇA** (daily 9am–7pm; 300esc) was one of the greatest in the Christian world. Owning vast tracts of farmland, orchards and vineyards, it held jurisdiction over a dozen towns and three seaports until its ultimate dissolution in 1834. The monastery was originally founded by Dom Afonso Henriques in 1147 in celebration of the liberation of Santarém from the Moors, and is a truly vast complex – its main **Church**, modelled on the famous Cistercian abbey of Citeaux in France, the largest in Portugal. External first impressions are quite disappointing, as the Gothic facade has been superseded by unexceptional Baroque additions of the seventeenth and eighteenth centuries. Inside, however, all later adornments have been swept away, restoring the narrow soaring aisles to their original vertical simplicity. The only exception to this magnificent Gothic purity is the frothy Manueline doorway to the sacristy, hidden behind the high altar.

The abbey's most precious treasures are the fourteenth-century **tombs of Dom Pedro and Dona Inês de Castro**, each occupying one of the transepts and sculpted with phenomenal wealth of detail. The tombs are inscribed with the motto "Até o Fim do Mundo" (Until the End of the World) and in accordance with Dom Pedro's orders have been placed foot to foot so that on the Day of Judgement they may rise and immediately feast their eyes on one another. Pedro's love for Inês de Castro, the great theme of epic Portuguese poetry, was cruelly stifled by high politics. Inês, as the daughter of a Galician nobleman, was a potential source of Spanish influence over the Portuguese throne and Pedro's father, Afonso V, forbade their marriage. The ceremony nevertheless took place in secret, whereupon Afonso was persuaded to sanction his daughter-in-law's murder. When Pedro succeeded to the throne in 1357 he exhumed the corpse of his lover, forcing the entire royal circle to acknowledge her as queen by kissing her decomposing hand.

The most amazing room in the building is the **kitchen**, with its cellars and gargantuan conical chimney, supported by eight trunk-like iron columns. A stream tapped from the River Alcôa still runs straight through the room: it was used not merely for cooking and washing but also to provide a constant supply of fresh fish. The **Sala dos Reis** (Kings' Room), off the beautiful **Cloisters of Silence**, displays statues of virtually every King of Portugal down to Dom José, who died in 1777. The rest of the abbey, including four cloisters, seven dormitories and endless corridors, is closed to the public.

Alcobaça's **tourist office** is opposite the abbey on Praça 25 de Abril. *Pensão Corações Unidos* (☎062/421 142; ②), around the corner on Rua Frei António Brandão, has decent rooms. The *Quartos Alcôa* (☎062/427 27; ①) off the Praça da República, beside the abbey, is cheaper, but best of all is the *Pensão Mosteiro* (☎062/421 83; ②) on Rua Frei Estevão Martins. There's also a **campsite**, two minutes' walk from the bus station along Avda Manuel da Silva Carolino. *Restaurante Trindade*, on the Praça Afonso Henriques, and *Cervejaria Roma*, opposite the abbey, are both good-value places to eat.

Leiria

With regular bus services to the three big sites of northern Estremadura – Alcobaça, Batalha and Fátima – **LEIRIA** makes a handy centre for excursions. The chief sight in Leiria itself is the **Castle** (9am–7pm), incorporating an elegant royal palace with a magnificent balcony high above the River Lis. At the heart of the old town, Praça Rodrigues Lobo is surrounded by beautiful buildings and arcades. The **tourist office** and **bus station** are on opposite sides of a park overlooking the river in the modern city centre. The **train station** is about 4km out of town, with a connecting bus service. For accommodation, check the **pensions** and restaurants (some offering rooms) around Praça Rodrigues Lobo and on narrow side streets such as Rua Mestre Aviz and Rua Miguel Bombarda. There's also a fancy **youth hostel** with a good atmosphere, at Largo Cândido do Reis 7 (☎044/31868; ②). As for **restaurants**, try the seafood at *Jardim* (by the tourist office), or real Portuguese cuisine – slightly more expensive, but worth every penny – at *Tromba Rija* in Rua Professores Portelas, out of town on the Marrazes road.

Batalha

The **Mosteiro de Santa Maria da Vitória**, better known as the **Abbey of BATALHA** (Battle Abbey), is the finest building in Portugal and an enduring symbol of national pride, founded to commemorate the Battle of Aljubarrota (1385), which sealed Portugal's independence after decades of Spanish intrigue. It is possible to stay in the village around the abbey, but it's best to visit on a trip from Leiria (8 buses daily).

The honey-coloured abbey (Tues–Sun 9am–5pm; May–Sept closes 7pm) was transformed by Manueline additions in the late fifteenth and early sixteenth centuries, but the bulk was completed between 1388 and 1434 in a profusely ornate version of French Gothic. Within this flamboyant framework there are also strong elements of the English Perpendicular style, an influence explained by the **Capela do Fundador** (Founder's Chapel), directly to the right upon entering the church: beneath the octagonal lantern rests the tomb of Dom João I and Philippa of Lancaster, their hands clasped in the ultimate expression of harmonious relations between Portugal and England. English longbowmen played a significant role in the victory at Aljubarrota and in 1386 both countries signed the Treaty of Windsor, "an inviolable, eternal, solid, perpetual, and true league of friendship".

The four younger sons of João and Philippa are buried along the south wall of the Capela do Fundador in a row of recessed arches. Second from the right is the **Tomb of Prince Henry the Navigator**, who guided the exploration of Madeira, the Azores and the African coast as far as Sierra Leone. Maritime exploration resumed under João II (1481–95) and accelerated with the accession of Manuel I (1495–1521). The **Claustro Real** (Royal Cloister) dates from this period of burgeoning self-confidence, its intricate stone grilles being added by Diogo de Boitaca, architect of the cloisters at Belém and the prime genius of Manueline art. Off the east side opens the early fifteenth-century **Sala do Capítulo** (Chapter House), remarkable for the unsupported span of its ceiling. The Church authorities were convinced that the whole chamber would come crashing down and only employed as labourers criminals already condemned to death. The **Refectory**, on the opposite side of the cloisters, houses a military museum. From here a short passage leads into the **Claustro de Dom Afonso V**, built in a conventional Gothic style which provides a yardstick against which to measure the Manueline flamboyance of the Royal Cloister.

The **Capelas Imperfeitas** (Unfinished Chapels) form a separate structure tacked on to the east end of the church and accessible only from outside the main complex. Dom Duarte, eldest son of João and Philippa, commissioned them in 1437 as a royal mausoleum but, as with the cloisters, the original design was transformed beyond all recognition by Dom Manuel's architects. It is unique among examples of Christian architecture in its evocation of the great shrines of Islam and Hinduism: perhaps it was inspired by the tales of Indian monuments that filtered back along the eastern trade routes.

Fátima

FÁTIMA is one of the most important centres of pilgrimage in the Catholic world, a status due to the six **Apparitions of the Virgin Mary**. On May 13, 1917, three peasant children from the village were tending their parents' flock when, in a flash of lightning, they were confronted with "a lady brighter than the sun" sitting in the branches of a tree. The vision returned on the thirteenth day of the next five months, culminating in the so-called Miracle of the Sun on October 13, when a swirling ball of fire cured lifelong illnesses. Nevertheless the three children remained the only ones actually to see the Virgin, and only one of the girls – Lúcia – could communicate with her. To Lúcia were revealed the three **Secrets of Fátima**. The first was a message of peace (this was during World War I) and a vision of Hell, with anguished, charred souls plunged into an ocean of fire. The second prophesied that Russia would "spread her errors through the world, causing wars and persecution against the Church". The third secret has never been divulged – it lies in a drawer in the Vatican, read by each pope on his accession but supposedly too horrible to be revealed.

To commemorate these extraordinary events a vast white **Basílica** and gigantic esplanade have been built, more than capable of holding the crowds of 100,000 who congregate here for the main **pilgrimages** on May 12–13 and October 12–13. In the church the tombs of Jacinta and Francisco – Lúcia's fellow witnesses, neither of whom survived the European flu epidemic of 1919–20 – are the subject of constant attention in their chapels on either side of the main exit. Hospices and convents have sprung up in the shadow of the Basílica, and inevitably the fame of Fátima has resulted in its commercialization. Look out for the Fátima ballpoint pens, which reveal the Virgin in glory when tilted.

Pensions and **restaurants** abound, but there's little reason to stay except during the big pilgrimages to witness the midnight processions. Regular **bus services** to Fátima from Leiria and Tomar make a day trip easy.

Tomar

The Convento de Cristo at **TOMAR**, 34km east of Fátima, is an artistic *tour de force* which entwines the main military, religious and imperial strands in the history of Portugal. In addition, Tomar is an attractive town in its own right – especially during the *Festas dos Tabuleiros*, in the first week of July, when the place goes wild. Aim to spend a couple of days here if you can.

Built on a simple grid plan, Tomar's old quarters preserve all their traditional charm – whitewashed, terraced cottages lining narrow cobbled streets. On the central Praça da República stands an elegant seventeenth-century town hall, a ring of houses of the same period and the Manueline church of **São João Baptista**, remarkable for its octagonal belfry and elaborate doorway. Nearby, at Rua Joaquim Jacinto 73, you'll find an excellently preserved fourteenth-century **Synagogue**; in 1496 Dom Manuel ordered the expulsion or conversion of all Portuguese Jews, and the synagogue at Tomar was one of the very few to survive.

The **Convento de Cristo** (Tues–Sun 9.30am–12.30pm & 2.30–6pm; 300esc) is set among pleasant gardens with splendid views, about a quarter of an hour's walk uphill from the centre of town. Founded in 1162 by Gualdim Pais, first Master of the Knights Templar, it was the headquarters of the Order. The heart of the complex remains the **Charola**, the temple from which the knights drew their moral conviction. It is a strange place, more suggestive of the occult than of Christianity; like almost every circular church, it is ultimately based on the Church of the Holy Sepulchre in Jerusalem, for whose protection the Knights Templar were originally founded.

As the Moorish threat receded, the Knights became a challenge to the authority of European monarchs. In Spain this prompted a vicious witch-hunt and many of the Knights sought refuge in Portugal, where Dom Dinis coolly reconstituted them in 1320 under a different title: the Order of Christ. Dom Manuel succeeded to the Grand Mastership in 1492, three years before he became king, and decided to expand the convent by adding a rectangular nave to the west side of the Charola. The highlight of Tomar is the ornamentation of the windows on the main facade of its **Chapter House**, where maritime motifs form a memorial to the sailors who established the Portuguese empire. João III (1521–57) transformed the convent into a thoroughgoing monastic community, adding dormitories, kitchens and no fewer than four cloisters. The adjoining two-tiered **Great Cloisters** comprise one of the purest examples of the Renaissance style in Portugal.

Tomar has a **campsite** and at least four reasonable **pensions**: *Nun' Álvares* (☎049/ 312 873; ②), *Luz* (049/312 317; ③) and *Tomarense* (☎049/312 948; ②), all near the bus and train stations, and *Pensão Bonjardim* (☎049/313 195; ②) east of the river on Praçeta de Santo André. Each has a **restaurant**.

Coimbra

COIMBRA was Portugal's capital from 1143 to 1255 and it ranks behind only the cities of Lisbon and Porto in historic importance. Its university, founded in 1290 and finally established here in 1537 after a series of moves back and forth to Lisbon, was the only one existing in Portugal until the beginning of this century. For a provincial town it has remarkable riches, and it's an enjoyable place to be, too – lively when the students are in town, sleepy during the holidays. The best time of all to be here is in May, when the students celebrate the end of the academic year in the **Queima das Fitas**, tearing or burning their gowns and faculty ribbons. This is when you're most likely to hear the Coimbra *fado*, distinguished from the Lisbon version by its mournful pace and complex lyrics.

The City

Old Coimbra sits on a hill on the right bank of the Rio Mondego, with the university crowding its summit. The main buildings of the **Old University**, dating from the sixteenth century, are set around a courtyard dominated by a Baroque clocktower and a statue of João III looking remarkably like Henry VIII. The Chapel is covered with *azulejos* and intricate decoration, but takes second spot to the **Library** (daily 9.30am–12.30pm & 2–7pm; winter closes 5pm; 250esc), a Baroque fantasy presented to the faculty by João V in the early eighteenth century.

Below the university a good first stop is the **Museu Machado de Castro** (Tues–Sun 10am–5pm; 200esc, free Sun am), just down from the unprepossessing Sé Nova (New Cathedral). Named after an eighteenth-century sculptor, the museum is housed in the former archbishop's palace – which would be worth visiting in its own right even if it were empty. As it is, it's positively stuffed with sculpture, paintings, furniture and ceramics. The **Sé Velha** (Old Cathedral), halfway down the hill, is one of the most important Romanesque buildings in Portugal, little altered and seemingly unbowed by the years. Solid and square on the outside, it's also stolid and simple within, the decoration confined to a few giant conch shells and some unobtrusive *azulejos*.

Restraint and simplicity certainly aren't the chief qualities of the **Mosteiro de Santa Cruz** (9am–noon & 2–6pm; 150esc), at the bottom of the hill past the city gates. Although it was founded before the cathedral, nothing remains that has not been substantially remodelled. In the early sixteenth century Coimbra was the site of a major sculptural school, and the new tombs for Portugal's first kings, Afonso Henriques and Sancho I, and the elaborately carved pulpit, are among its very finest works. The Manueline theme is at its clearest in the airy arches of the Cloister of Silence, its walls decorated with bas-relief scenes from the life of Christ.

It was in Santa Cruz that Dom Pedro had his court pay homage to the corpse of Inês de Castro, which had lain in the now ruined **Convento de Santa Clara-a-Velha** across the river, alongside the convent's founder, Saint-Queen Isabel. The tombs have long since been moved away, Inês' to Alcobaça and Isabel's to the **Convento de Santa Clara-a-Nova**, higher up the hill. Two features make the climb worthwhile: the silver tomb itself and the vast cloister financed by João V, whose devotion to nuns went beyond the bounds of spiritual comfort. Between the two convents is **Portugal dos Pequeninos** (daily 9am–7pm; winter closes 5.30pm; 350esc), a park full of scale models of many of the country's great buildings, interspersed with "typical" farm houses and sections on the overseas territories, heavy with the White Man's Burden.

Practicalities

Most main-line **trains** stop at Coimbra B, from where there are frequent connecting services to Coimbra A, right at the heart of things. The main **bus station** is on Avenida Fernão de Magalhães, about fifteen minutes' walk from the centre. The **tourist office** (daily 9am–8pm) is opposite the bridge in the Largo da Portagem. Near the station, the sleazy Rua da Sota and its side streets have a few **pensions** that aren't as bad as they look – try the *Pensão Vitória* at Rua da Sota 9 (☎039/240 49; ②) or the *Pensão Flôr de Coimbra* at Rua do Poço 8 (☎039/238 65; ②), which serves extremely cheap meals to residents. *Pensão Rivoli* (☎039/255 59; ②), nearby on Praça do Comércio, has unremarkable rooms with balconies overlooking the square. Alternatively, there are several options east of the university: beneath the aqueduct, at Rua Castro Matoso 8, *Antunes* (☎039/230 48; ③) offers good service. The **youth hostel**, above the park on Rua Henrique Seco 14 (☎039/229 55; ②), is friendly and immaculately run. There's a reasonable all-year **campsite** at the municipal sports complex (☎039/712 997). To reach it, take bus #5 from Largo Portagem.

There are inexpensive **places to eat** to be found all over the centre. For really basic fare served up with loads of atmosphere, try the little dives on Beco do Forno and Rua dos Gatos, the two tiny alleys between the Largo da Portagem and Rua da Sota. Moving only a little more upmarket, *O Funchal*, near Praça do Comércio on Rua das Azeiteiras, serves, amongst other dishes, a fine chicken casserole. Be sure, also, to try one of the traditional **coffee houses** along Rua Ferreira Borges (notably the *Arcadia*) and Rua Visconde da Luz.

Figueira da Foz

FIGUEIRA DA FOZ is one of the liveliest towns on the west coast, a major resort and deep-sea fishing port at the mouth of the Mondego, only an hour by train from Coimbra. The beach is enormous: it's a good five-minute walk across the sand to the sea and unless you wear shoes or stay on the wooden walkways provided, the soles of your feet will have been burned long before you get there. It can take time to find a room in Figueira in high season, but with persistence you should be able to get something. If you need help, the **tourist office**, on the seafront promenade Avenida 25 de Abril, is even more helpful than most. For cheaper **pensions** in the town centre, check out Rua Bernardo Lopes and Rua da Liberdade: if you arrive early in the day, try the beautiful *Hotel Universal* (☎033/262 28; ④),on Rua Miguel Bombarda, or friendly *Pensão Central* (☎033/223 08; ②), just down from the casino. The nearest **campsite** (☎033/231 16) is about 2km inland.

The centre of town is packed with **places to eat**. You can get superb Goan food at *O Escondidinho*, which is hidden away on Rua Dr. F. A. Dinis. The *Restaurante Tahiti*, five minutes from the casino at Rua do Fonte 86, and the *Snack-Bar Marujo*, just up the street from the tourist office at Rua Dr. Calado 51a, both have good food and friendly staff.

Aveiro

Like Figueira da Foz, **AVEIRO** is a sizeable resort, but it's also a place of some antiquity. A thriving port throughout the Middle Ages, the town was badly hit when the mouth of the Vouga silted up in 1575, closing its harbour and creating vast fever-ridden marshes. Recovery only began in 1808 when a canal was cut through to the sea, reopening the port and draining much of the water; the shallow lagoons that were left form the backbone of an economy based on vast saltpans, fishing and the collection of seaweed for fertilizer. However, the occasional pungent odour wafting across town comes from the large paper factory nearby – this is one of Portugal's chief industries.

From the train station or bus terminal, walk straight down the broad main street in front of you and you'll eventually hit the centre of town and the **Regional Museum** (Tues–Sun 10am–12.30pm & 2–5pm) in the Convento de Jesus. The finest exhibits relate to Santa Joana, a daughter of Afonso V who lived in the convent from 1475 until her death in 1489. Her tomb and chapel are beautiful, as is the convent itself, and there's a fine collection of art and sculpture.

Finding a room isn't easy, but the **tourist office** in the central Praça da República can help. Most of the cheap places are just across the bridge on Rua José Estevão, and in the alleys around the nearby Praça 14 de Julho – try *Pensão Palmeira* (☎034/225 21; ②), just off Rua Palmeira. The main action in town is hanging around in the cafés watching life on the lagoon. Try some of the celebrated local sweets, especially *ovos moles*, candied egg yolks which come in little wooden barrels. For more substantial **food**, good standbys are *El Mercantel*, just off the Rossio, the *Zico Snack Bar* on Rua José Estevão and the **vegetarian** restaurant below the tourist office.

The Forest of Buçaco

The **Forest of Buçaco** is the country's most revered woodland, a monastic domain that was later the site of Napoléon's first significant defeat in the Peninsular War. The Benedictines established a hermitage here as early as the sixth century and the area remained in religious hands right up to the dissolution of the monasteries in 1834. Chiefly thanks to their care, there are over 700 species of tree in the forest, many of them – like the mighty Mexican Cedars – introduced from distant countries. All non-express **buses** from Coimbra to Viseu take a short detour from Luso through the forest, so you can easily stay over for a few hours on a trip in this direction, or make a day's excursion from Coimbra. Alternatively, you could camp out in the forest or spend a leisurely night in Luso, an easy walk below.

Walks are laid out everywhere in Buçaco but you can wander freely anywhere in the forest, and in many ways it is at its most attractive when it's wildest. One of the two bus stops is by the **Palace Hotel**, built on the site of the monastery as a summer retreat for royalty in the heart of the forest. An enormous imitation Manueline construction, it's dauntingly plush, but anyone can stroll in, have a drink and admire the *azulejos* depicting the Battle of Buçaco. The **Via Sacra**, a winding track lined with chapels with terracotta Stations of the Cross, leads from the hotel to the Cruz Alta, a giant cross at the summit. From here there are magnificent panoramas, even if it's not always the haven of peace the monks strove to create. In the opposite direction from the hotel, a small **military museum** near the Portas da Rainha has maps, uniforms and weapons relating to the battle. Just above it a narrow road climbs to the obelisk memorial, with vistas inland across to the Serra da Estrela; from here the **Porta de Sula** leads back into the forest.

Luso and onward

LUSO lies some 30km from Coimbra on the northwestern slope of the Serra do Buçaco. Mostly frequented by people taking the curative radioactive waters, the town is well provided with pensions and restaurants and is a pleasant place to rest up. You should have no problem finding a **room**, with excellent, inexpensive choices all over the centre. *Pensão Central* (☎031/939 254; ②) and *Pensão Astória* (☎031/939 182; ②) on Rua Emídio Navarro are good bets and the **tourist office** in the central square can help if there's any difficulty.

The **valley of the Rio Dão** east of Luso is the heart of the region where **Dão wines** – some of the finest in the country – are produced. Where they're not covered with vineyards, the slopes are thickly wooded with pine and eucalyptus, though all too often there are bare tracts where forest fires have raged. Crossing this part of the country in late summer or autumn, it's rare not to see the smudge of smoke somewhere on the horizon. The rail route that used to run along the valley has now been replaced by a *CP* bus service.

Viseu

From its high plateau, **VISEU** surveys the country around with the air of a feudal overlord, and indeed, this dignified little city is capital of all it can see. The heart of the medieval city has changed little, though it's approached now through the broad avenues of a prosperous provincial centre: parts of the walls survive and it's within their circuit, breached by two doughty gateways, that almost everything of interest lies.

At the city's highest point is the huge **Praça da Sé**, the paved square in front of the cathedral, best approached from the central Rossio through the Porta do Soar. Here, amid a line of granite buildings, stand the white Baroque facade of the **Igreja da Misericórdia** and the **Cathedral**, a weighty twin-towered Romanesque base on which a succession of generations have made their mark. The facade is stern granite, but the interior is a great hall with intricate vaulting, carved to represent twisted and knotted ropes. The cathedral's Renaissance cloister is one of the most graceful in the country; the rooms of its upper level, looking out over the tangled roofs of the oldest part of the town, house the cathedral's treasures, including a twelfth-century Bible. The greatest treasure of Viseu, though, is the adjacent **Museu Grão Vasco** (Tues–Sun 10am–5pm; 200esc, free Sat & Sun). Vasco Fernandes – known always as *Grão Vasco*, the Great Vasco – was the key figure in a school of Flemish-influenced painters which flourished here in the first half of the sixteenth century. The centrepiece of the collection is his masterly *St Peter on his Throne*; it owes considerably more to the Renaissance than some of the earlier paintings but its Flemish roots are still evident.

The **tourist office**, up from the Rossio, just off Avda 25 de Abril, is a good source of information for the region as a whole. **Accommodation** in Viseu is poor, but there are three tolerable places right in the centre: *Pensão Europa*, Rua Direita 51 (②); *Casa de Hospedes Central*, Rua do Comércio 65 (②); and *Pensão Bocage,* Travessa de São Domingos 5 (②). There's a **campsite** (☎032/261 46) in the Parque do Fontelo, about ten minutes' walk east of the centre. Some of the best **food** in the province is to be had at *Contico*, 47 Rua S. Hilário, where prices aren't too high but tables can be hard to get. **Moving on** from Viseu, there are regular buses to Lamego via Castro Daire, and to Guarda.

Guarda

GUARDA, at over 1000m, is claimed by its inhabitants to be the highest city in Europe – an assertion to be taken with a pinch of salt. It is high enough, though, to be chilly and windswept all year round and to offer endless views. The city was founded in 1197 by Dom Sancho I to guard his borders against both Moors and Spaniards, and despite the fact that castle and walls have all but disappeared it still has something of the air of a city permanently on war footing. It was known as the city of the four Fs – *Fria, Farta, Forte e Feia* – cold, rich, strong and ugly. The last is unfair: with its arcaded streets and little squares, the centre of Guarda can be distinctly picturesque.

The **train** station is miles out of town but there is, fortunately, a connecting bus that meets all the major trains; the **bus station** is about four hundred metres southeast of the cathedral, the heart of the old town. Dour and grey, the castellated facade of the **Cathedral** looks like the gateway of a castle, but around the sides the exterior is lightened by flying buttresses, pinnacles and grimacing gargoyles. Inside it's surprisingly lofty, with twisted pillars and vaulting influenced by the Manueline style. The huge carved stone retable is by João de Rouão, a leading figure in the sixteenth-century resurgence of Portuguese sculpture at Coimbra. There are modern and imaginative displays of local archeology, art and sculpture in the **Museu Regional**, a short way east. Of the **Castle**, on a bleak little hill nearby, only the square keep survives, while the **walls** are recalled by just three surviving gates. The cobbled streets of the old town, though, are fascinating in themselves – the tangled area between the **Porta da Estrela** and **Porta do Rei**, north of the cathedral, has changed little in the past four hundred years.

There is a **tourist office** (Mon–Fri 9am–12.30pm & 2–5.30pm; ☎071/222 251) behind the cathedral on Praça Luís de Camões, a good source of information for the area's many festivals. **Places to stay** are fairly easy to come by if not especially cheap: try the attractive *Pensão Moreira*, Rua Mouzinho de Albuquerque 47 (☎071/241 31; ②), or the down-at-heel *Residencial Gonçalves*, Rua Augusto Gil 17 (②), off the central square. Guarda's open-all-year **campsite** is in a park a short way from the castle; remember, though, that nights can be extremely cold. The **restaurants** between the Porta da Estrela and the church of São Vicente serve basic but good fare.

NORTHERN PORTUGAL

The economic powerhouse of the north is **Porto**, the country's second largest city and most industrious centre. It's an enticingly lively place, made especially attractive by the port-producing suburb of **Vila Nova de Gaia**, whose wines are supplied by the vine-yards of the River Douro. The **Douro valley**, a spectacular rocky gorge as it approaches the sea, is followed by a magnificent **rail route** whose branch lines run along some equally lovely valleys – along the Rio Tâmega to Amarante, along the Corgo to Vila Real, and along the Tua to **Bragança**, capital of the isolated region of **Trás-os-Montes**. The Portuguese consider the northwest province of the **Minho** to be the most beautiful part of their country, and with its river valleys, wooded hills, trailing vines and wild coastline, the attractions are obvious. A small, thoroughly rural and conservative region, its towns are often outrageously picturesque and full of quiet charm. Monuments and museums are concentrated in **Braga** and **Guimarães**, while between them lie the extensive Celtic ruins of the **Citânia de Briteiros**, the most impressive archeological site in Portugal. **Viana do Castelo**, the main town of the Minho coast, is an enjoyably low-key resort with a wonderful beach.

Porto

Capital of the north, **PORTO** is very different from Lisbon – unpretentious, inward-looking, unashamedly commercial. As the local saying goes: "Coimbra sings; Braga prays; Lisbon shows off; and Porto works." The city's fascination lies very much in the life of the place, with its prosperous business core surrounded by smart suburbs and elegant villas, side by side with a heart of cramped streets and ancient alleys.

Arrival and information

Most trains will drop you at the distant **Estação de Campanhã**; you should change here for a local train to central **São Bento** – it takes about five minutes and there should never be more than a twenty-minute wait. Certain trains from Minho (Guimarães) and the north coast (Póvoa de Varzim) use the smaller **Estação da Trindade**, from where it's a short walk down Rua da Trindade, past the town hall and into the centre. As a general rule, buses **from the south** come in around Rua Alexandre Herculano, and those **from the north** around the Praça Filipa de Lencastre.

Just a few yards north of the São Bento station lies the **Avenida dos Aliados**, Porto's main commercial centre, which culminates at Praça Gen. Humberto Delgado, site of the central post office and the main **tourist office**.

The Porto area telephone code is ☎02.

Accommodation

The **cheapest rooms** in town are on Ruas do Loureiro and Cimo do Vila, around the corner from São Bento. Be warned, though, that this is something of a red-light district. For more salubrious places, your best bet is to head for the areas west or east of Avenida dos Aliados; all the hotels listed below are to the west, except the *Norte* and *Astória*.

YOUTH HOSTEL

Pousada de Juventude, Rua Rodrigues Lobo 98 (☎606 5535). Large and clean but lacking in atmosphere. Buses #3, #20 or #52 from Praça da Liberdade – ask for Praça da Galiza; ①.

HOTELS

Pensão Astória, Rua Arnaldo Gama 56 (☎200 8175). Lovely, old-fashioned hotel behind the city wall in an un-touristy part of town; be sure to reserve in advance. ②

Residencial Continental, Rua Mouzinho da Silveira 14 (☎320 355). Good value and close to São Bento. ②

Pensão Estoril, Rua de Cedofeita 193 (☎200 2751). Wonderful value, well set-up rooms, with private baths and phones. ②

Pensão Mondariz, Rua Cimo da Vila 139 (☎200 5600). Right by São Bento and very cheap. ②

Pensão S Marino, Praça Carlos Alberto 59 (☎314 380). Efficient, friendly and set in a small pleasant square 300m from Torre dos Clérigos. Under 4000esc, breakfast and private bathroom included. ③

Pensão Norte, Rua de Fernando Tomás 579 (☎200 3503). A rambling old place with tiny wooden rooms. ②

Pensão Pão-de-Açucar, 262 Rua do Almada 262 (☎200 2425). Great value three-star with private bathrooms. ④

Residencial Vera Cruz, Rua Ramalho Ortigão (☎323 396). Smartish and conveniently located. ③

CAMPSITE

Prelada (☎812 616). Bus #6 from Praça da Liberdade until 9pm, or #54 from Praça de Lisboa until 2am.

The City

The stifled streets of the old town rarely permit any sort of overall view, so it's a good idea to climb the Baroque **Torre dos Clérigos** (10.30am–noon & 3–5pm; closed Wed) to get your bearings. There are fine views, too, from the courtyard in front of the **Sé** (daily 9am–noon & 3–6pm), an austere building standing four-square on its rocky outcrop. Inside it's depressing, even the vaunted silver altarpiece failing to make any impression in the gloom. For a small fee, however, you can escape into the cloisters, and climb to the dazzling chapterhouse, with more views over the old quarter.

Around the back, Calçada de Vandoma plunges downwards, lined with the stalls of the **flea market**. Not much goes on down at the waterfront since the big ships stopped calling here. Over to the west, a statue of Porto-born Henry the Navigator faces the pompous Bolsa (Stock Exchange) and the back of **São Francisco** (Tues–Sat 10am–12.30pm & 2.30–5pm; 250esc), perhaps the most extraordinary church in Porto. Outside it looks like an ordinary enough Gothic construction, but the interior has been transformed by an unbelievably ornate attack of eighteenth-century refurbishment. Don't miss the church's small **museum**, which consists largely of artefacts salvaged from the monastery that once stood nearby.

From here it's not far to the **Museu de Etnografia e História** (Tues–Sat 10am–noon & 2–5pm; free) in the quiet Largo de São João Novo. Occupying a beautiful house, it's a fascinating mix of jewellery, folk costumes, ancient toys and almost anything of interest that has defied easy classification. A short distance north is the **Igreja da Misericorida**, where you can see a remarkable *Crucifixion*, depicting King Manuel I with his wife Leonor and eight children kneeling before Christ. To gain admission, knock at the government offices next door and ask to see the *Sala das Sessões*.

The **Museu Nacional Soares dos Reis** at Rua de Dom Manuel II (Tues–Sun 10am–5pm; 300esc), over to the west behind the city hospital, was the first national museum in Portugal. Its collection includes glass, ceramics and a formidable array of eighteenth- and nineteenth-century paintings, as well as the late nineteenth-century sculptures of Soares dos Reis – his *O Desterro* (The Exile) is probably the best known work in Portugal. Follow the road past the museum, or take any bus from the *Cordoaria* stop except #6 and #18, and you'll come to the **Jardim do Palácio de Cristal**, a peaceful park dominated by a huge domed pavilion which now serves as an exhibition hall. In summer the park is home to a vast funfair. On the far side, across Rua Entre Quintas,

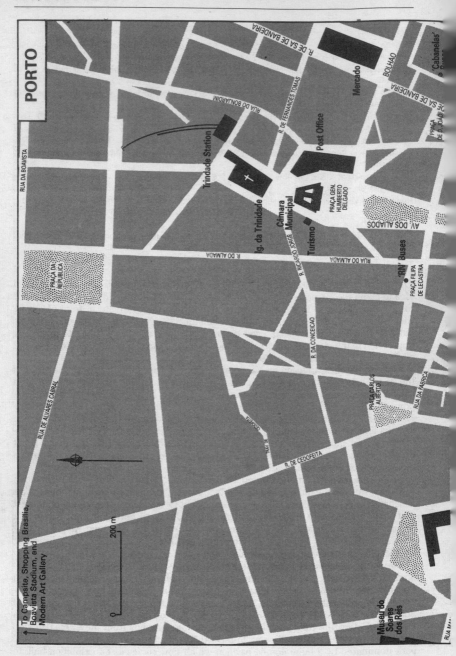

To Antas Stadium

R. DE SANTA CATARINA

R. DE PASSOS MANUEL

RUA SANTO ILDEFONSO

Turismo

PRAÇA DA BATALHA

R. A. HERCULANO

To Alameda das Fontainhas

City Wall

CAIS DA RIBEIRA

FONTE D. LUIS I

To Vila Nova da Gaia

R. DE SANTO ANTONIO (31 DE JAN)

RUA CHÃO DA VILA

R. DO LOUREIRO

AV. DE VIMIARA PERES

Mercado

R. DE D. HUGO

PRAÇA DA LIBERDADE

São Bento Station

Casa-Museu Guerra Junqueiro

Episcopal Palace

Sé

CAIS DA RIBEIRA

R. DOS CLERIGOS

R. CONDE DE VIZELA

Ig. DOS CLÉRIGOS

R. DAS FLORES

RUA MOUZINHO DA SILVEIRA

Ig. dos Grilos

R. DOS MERCADORES

R. DE S. JOAO

To see area

R. GALERIA DE PARIS

Mercado

PRAÇA DE LISBOA

Bus to Airport

Tram to see area

R. DAS CARMELITAS

FR. GOMES TEIXEIRA

Ig. da Misericórdia

R. S. BENTO DA VITORIA

R. DA VITORIA

Mercado

R. FERREIRA BORGES

R. INFANTE D. HENRIQUE

Casa do Infante

Craft Centre

Restaurants

Universidade

Jardim de Cordoaria

R. DAS TAIPAS

R. DA RESTAURAÇÃO

Hospital

Law Courts

Art Gallery

CAMPO DOS MARTIRES DA PATRIA

PASSEIO DAS VIRTUDES

Ig. de S. Pedro de Miragaia

Ig. de S. Francisco

Alfândega

To Youth Hostel

Rio Douro

Rio Douro

stands the **Solar do Vinho do Porto** (Mon–Sat 11am–midnight), where you can sample one of hundreds of varieties of **port** in air-conditioned splendour – a good prelude to visiting Vila Nova.

VILA NOVA DE GAIA

The suburb of Vila Nova de Gaia is taken over almost entirely by the port trade: the names of the various companies, spelled out in huge white letters across their roofs, dominate even the most distant view. You can walk to Gaia across the **Ponte Dom Luís**: the most direct route to the wine lodges is across the lower level from the Cais da Ribeira, but if you've a head for heights it's an amazing sensation to walk over the upper deck some 200 feet above the river. Almost all the companies offer free **tasting** and a tour of the factory: they are generally open from Monday to Saturday until 6pm. There's little pressure to buy anything – if you do, try the dry white ports, which are expensive or often unobtainable elsewhere.

A more sober visit could be made to the **Casa-Museu de Teixeira Lopes** (Tues–Sun 9am–12.30pm & 2–5.30pm; free), in the south of the suburb – take bus #36 as far as "Hospital". Lopes was Soares dos Reis' principal pupil and at the centre of an artistic set who lived in Gaia at the turn of the century – much of whose work is on show here. With its wonderful sculpture-filled courtyard, it's a good place for a picnic lunch and a couple of hours rooting around.

Eating and drinking

Porto's cafés include some elegant rivals to the turn-of-the-century places in Lisbon, while livelier places can be found down on the **waterfronts** on each side of the river – but beware that riverside cafés in Vila Nova de Gaia can be fiendishly expensive. The city's culinary speciality is *Tripas á Modo do Porto* (tripe) and its citizens are affectionately referred to by the rest of the country as *tripeiros*. Don't let this put you off – there's always plenty of choice on the menu, and there are lots of places where you can eat cheaply. At the basic level, there are **workers' cafés** galore, all with wine on tap, and often with a set menu for the day. Try the area above Rua da Fábrica and around Praça Carlos Alberto, or Rua da Picaria, or walk right up the Rua do Almada. All are busy in the middle of the day and invariably close around 7.30pm; none open on Sunday. An area that bustles later at night is down at the Cais da Ribeira where numerous cafés and restaurants have been installed under the arches of the first tier of Porto's ranks of dwellings. There are also many good cheap standbys around Praça da Batalha.

RESTAURANTS

O Assador Típico, Rua Dom Manuel II 15. Bustling cavern of a restaurant near the Museu Soares dos Reis.

Casa Filha da Mãe Preta, Cais da Ribeira 39. Bustling restaurant with excellent views over the river.

Restaurant/Snack Bar Kinary, Rua Dom João IV 8. Friendly place east of Batalha, offering a good variety of meat and fish dishes at very reasonable prices.

Majestic, Rua Santa Catarina 112. Stylish steakhouse, all mirrors and bent wood.

Montecarlo, Rua Santa Catarina 17-2°. Looks like a 1930s tearoom; has views over the Praça da Batalha and good food.

CAFÉS AND BARS

Labirinto, Rua Nossa Senhora da Fátima 334. A "bar-arcade", catering for a wide range of tastes, with exhibitions and live music. Open 9.30pm–3am.

Mercado Bar, Rua San João 36. Stylish bar featuring great dance music.

The Douro, Tâmega and Corgo lines

The valleys of the Douro and its tributaries are among the most spectacular land-scapes in Portugal, and the Douro valley itself, a narrow, winding gorge for the major-ity of its long route to the Spanish border, is the most beautiful of all. The Douro rail route, which joins the river about 60km inland and then sticks to it across the country, is one of those journeys that need no justification other than the trip itself. At present there are quite regular connections along the line as far as Peso da Régua, though you will most likely find yourself on a single carriage train; beyond Régua, there are less frequent connections to Tua and Pocinho.

The Douro line

Cete, half a dozen stations out of Porto, is just a mile away from the village of **PAÇO DE SOUSA**, a former headquarters of the Benedictines in Portugal and a popular picnic spot for Porto locals. If you're looking for a bed, it's not much further down the line to Penafiel station, connected by bus to the village itself. Split by main road traffic, **PENAFIEL** is not that enticing a place, but it has a saving grace in its fabulous local vinho verde wine, served from massive barrels in the **adega** in the central Largo do Padré Américo. The *adega* offers basic fare, washed down with pints of wine at a time; next door is the best and cheapest **hotel**, *Casa João da Liza* (☎055/251 58; ②).

At Livração, about an hour from Porto, the Tâmega line (see below) cuts off for Amarante in the mountains. Shortly after, the main line finally reaches the Douro and heads upstream until, at Mesão Frio, the valley broadens into the little plain commanded by **PESO DA RÉGUA**, the depot through which port wine must pass on its way from Pinhão – the centre of production – to Porto. The **tourist office** (Mon–Fri 9.30am–12.30pm & 2–5.30pm; ☎054/228 46) on the river bank can inform you about visits to local cellars. Apart from these alcoholic diversions, there's not much to do except wander through the upper village and along the river. If you need to stay, the high-rise *Pensão Império* at Rua José Vasques Osório 8 (②) offers good **accommodation**, breakfast and views. There are plenty of **restaurants** along the main street.

Beyond Peso da Régua begin the terraced slopes where the **port vines** are grown: they look their best in August, with the grapes ripening, and in September when the harvest has begun. The country continues in this vein, craggy and beautiful, with the softer hills of the interior fading dark green into the distance, to Tua (junction for the Tua line) and Pocinho, where buses take over for routes east towards Miranda do Douro. From there it's a straightforward hitch in summer to Zamora in Spain.

The Tâmega line

Services on the narrow-gauge **Tâmega line** run seven times a day from Livração to **AMARANTE**, half an hour up the Tâmega valley and now the terminus of the line. Set immaculately along the river, the town is a fine place to stop, with its balconied houses hanging out over the water and its riverside bars and cafés. The **Convento de São Gonçalo**, beside the elegant bridge across the Tâmega, is Amarante's most prominent monument. It forms the heart of an ancient fertility cult which persists in the grand *Festa de São Gonçalo*, celebrated on the first Saturday in June, when couples exchange phallus-shaped cakes as tokens of their love. In the church itself the saint's tomb is said to guarantee a quick marriage to anyone who touches it – his face, hands and feet have been almost worn away by hopeful suitors. **Rooms** can be scarce between June and September but are easy enough to find at other times of year. The *Hotel Silva* (☎055/432 110; ②), just past the **tourist office** on the way from the station along Rua Cândido Reis, is comfortable and pleasantly sited overlooking the river. On the other side of the river there's the *Residencial Estoril* (☎055/431 291; ③), offering smart rooms in a central location. Additionally there are a couple of **campsites**, one on the riverbank, another, newer and more spacious, a little further upstream on the right bank. Most of the pensions have **restaurants**.

The Corgo line

Five trains a day shuttle along the **Corgo line** from Régua to Vila Real, passing through a magnificent landscape where everything from cowsheds to vine posts seems to be made from granite, and where the luscious green of the vines belies the apparent barrenness of the earth. **VILA REAL** is the one break from the pastoralism of the Corgo – the largest industrial town in the northeast, it is bordered on three sides by sprawling suburbs. The setting, however, is magnificent, the twin **Serras** of **Marão** and **Alvão** forming a natural amphitheatre behind the town. The old quarter, built on a promontory above the junction of the Corgo and Cabril rivers, is attractive, though there is little to see other than the main **Avenida**, which runs down the spine of the promontory. The former palace of the Marquesses of Vila Real, no. 94 on the Avenida, now houses the **tourist office**. **Rooms** are available above the excellent *Excelsior* bar at Rua Teixeira da Sousa (②). The *Encontro* **restaurant**, no. 78 on the Avenida, also has rooms upstairs (②). The **campsite** is by the river, off the Avda 1 de Maio – if you're coming from the station, turn right after crossing the bridge.

The Tua Valley

The **Tua valley** rail line accompanies the rocky course of the river all the way from Tua (on the Douro) to Mirandela, then crawls across the Serra de Nogueira to Bragança – a total of four hours. Occasionally passengers are politely requested to step down and walk along an unstable section of track, to meet another train which takes over for the rest of the way.

Mirandela

Midway along the Tua, **MIRANDELA** is an odd little town with a medieval centre, a scattering of Baroque mansions and a brand new museum of modern art – and one of the longest **festas** in Portugal (July 25–Aug 15). The **Museu de Arte Moderna** (Mon–Fri 2.30–6pm) has two collections of paintings: one dedicated to local boy Armindo Teixeira Lopes; the other, rather more exciting, to twentieth-century Portuguese painting and print-making. In contrast to the clean lines of this modern building, the old town is in a state of decay. The chapel next to the town hall, at the summit of the ancient citadel, simply fell down six years ago. Scavengers have pilfered the most useful or attractive pieces of stonework, but there is still a pile of rubble and an altarpiece open to the skies. Mirandela's Roman bridge – renovated in the fifteenth century – is its most striking feature, stretching a good two hundred metres across the sluggish river. The **tourist office** is near the bridge. The best **pension** is the *Sá Moreno* in Avda das Amoreiras (☎078/224 34; ③), on the right coming from the station; further along the avenida is the cheaper *Residencial Flórida* (☎078/22254; ②). The *Sá Moreno* has a fair **restaurant**, too.

Bragança

On a hillock above **BRAGANÇA**, the small and remote capital of Trás-os-Montes, stands a pristine circle of walls. enclosing a medieval village that rises to a massive keep and castle. Seemingly untouched by the centuries, this extraordinary citadel – along with the fine local museum – is the principal reason for a visit to the town. The twelfth-century council chamber, the **Domus Municipalis**, stands in the heart of the **Citadel**; very few Romanesque civic buildings have survived anywhere in Europe, and no other has this pentagonal form. Next to it is the church of **Santa Maria**, with its eighteenth-century barrel-vaulted, painted ceiling – a feature common to several churches in Bragança. Towering above these two is the **Castle**, which the Portuguese royal family rejected as a residence in favour of their vast estate in the Alentejo. At its side a curious pillory rises from the back of a prehistoric granite pig (or *porca*), thought to have been a fertility idol of a prehistoric cult. Celtic-inspired medieval tombstones rub shoulders with a menagerie of *porcas* in the gardens of **Museu do Abade de Baçal**, between the citadel and cathedral in Rua Abílio Beça (Tues–Sun 10am–12.30pm & 2–5pm). Inside, a collection of sacred art and the watercolours of Alberto Souza are the highlights, along with displays of local costumes.

The helpful **tourist office** is on Avda Cidade de Zamora, a couple of hundred metres north of the cathedral. Cheapest **pension** in town is the *Transmontano*, opposite the station at Avda João da Cruz 168 (☎073/228 99; ②); you'd be better advised to pay a little more and stay at *Residencial Poças*, Rua Combatentes da G. Guerra 200 (☎073/224 28; ②). The **campsite** is 6km out of town on the França road – but there are plenty of open spaces beyond the walls of the upper town. As for **restaurants**, two favourites are *O Bolha*, behind the cathedral in Jardim Dr. António José de Almeida, and the disarmingly friendly *Machado Cure* in Rua Almirante Reis, on the other side of the cathedral.

CROSSING THE BORDER

From Bragança the most obvious route into Spain is via Quintanilha (34km), the nearest town to the **SAN MARTIN** border post. There's one direct bus daily, but any bus to Miranda do Douro will take you to a crossroads from where you can hitch the 12km to the border. You can stay here above the *Evaristo*, San Martin's only shop, restaurant and **pension**. At 7am there is a bus to Zamora, connected to Madrid by road and rail. In Bragança there's also the possibility of reserving a seat on the *Internorte* **express bus** to Zamora which passes through daily Tuesday to Saturday.

Braga and around

BRAGA, the tourist office pamphlet claims, is the Portuguese Rome. This clearly is going over the top – though it illustrates the city's ecclesiastical pretensions. Founded by the Romans in 279 BC, Braga was a bishopric before being occupied by the Moors. It was reconquered early on and by the end of the eleventh century its archbishops were pressing for recognition as "Primate of the Spains", a title they disputed with Toledo over the next six centuries. It is still Portugal's religious capital – the scene of spectacular **Easter celebrations** with torchlit processions and weirdly hooded penitents.

You won't be able to miss the **Archbishop's Palace**, a great fortress-like building, right at the centre of the old town. In medieval times it covered a tenth of the city and today easily accommodates the municipal library and various faculties of the university. Immediately opposite is the **Sé**, which like the palace encompasses Gothic, Renaissance and Baroque styles. It was founded in 1070 and its south doorway is a survival from this earliest building; its most striking element, however, is the intricate ornamentation of the roofline, executed by João de Castilho, later the architect of Lisbon's Jerónimos Monastery. A guided tour of the interior (9–11.30am & 2–5.30pm) takes you through three Gothic chapels, of which the outstanding specimen is the **Capela dos Reis** (King's Chapel), built to house the tombs of Henry of Burgundy and his wife Teresa, the cathedral's founders and the parents of Afonso Henriques, founder of the kingdom. Beyond the chapels is the cathedral **museum** – one of the richest collections in Portugal, but displayed like a junk shop.

The Art Deco **tourist office** at the corner of Avda Central has copies of the local *Correio do Minho*, good for advice on most events in the region. Two **hotels** offering excellent value are the *Residencial Inácio Filho*, Rua Francisco Sanchez 42 (☎053/238 49; ②), and the well-located *Grande Residencia Avenida*, Avda da Liberdade 738 (☎053/229 55; ②). Braga's well-equipped **youth hostel** is at Rua Santa Margarida 6 (☎053/616 163; ①), off Avda Central; the **campsite** is a fairly long walk along the Guimarães road – but very cheap and right next to the municipal swimming pool. The *Café Talismâ*, Rua do Souto, serves good cheap **food** in generous quantities, as does the *Restaurante Moçambicana* at Rua Andrade Corvo 8, one of several excellent cheap restaurants grouped around the Arco da Porta Nova. *Café Astória*, Avda da Liberdade, is by far the best of the old **coffee houses**, mahogany-panelled and with cut-glass windows. *Locomotiva*, beneath the *Hotel Turismo* on Avda da Liberdade, is Braga's most fashionable club, with a reputation that stretches as far as Lisbon; *A Salsa*, just around the corner, is the obvious retreat if the trendies get too much.

Bom Jesus

BOM JESUS, 3km outside Braga, is one of Portugal's best-known images, as much concept as building, a monumental place of pilgrimage created by Braga's archbishop in the first decades of the eighteenth century. It is a vast ornamental stairway of granite and white plaster cut into a densely wooded mount high above the city. There is no particular reason for its presence, no miracle or vision, yet it remains the object of devoted pilgrimage, penitents often climbing on their knees. **Buses** run from the Braga post office to the foot of the stairway about every half-hour, more frequently at weekends when half the city piles up there to picnic.

If you resist the temptation of the funicular and climb up the stairway, Bom Jesus' simple allegory unfolds. Each landing has a fountain: the first symbolizes the wounds of Christ, the next five the Senses, and the final three represent the Virtues. At each corner are chapels with mouldering wooden, larger-than-life tableaux of the life of Christ, leading to the Crucifixion at the altar of the church. Beyond the church there are wooded gardens, grottoes and miniature boating pools, and several cheap, lively **restaurants** – filled on Saturdays with a constant stream of wedding parties.

Citânia de Briteiros

Citânias – Celtic hill settlements – lie scattered throughout the Minho. The **Citânia de Briteiros** (daily 9am–dusk), midway betwen Braga and Guimarães, is the most spectacular, and is reputed to have been a last stronghold against the Romans. It's an impressive and exciting site, including the foundations of over 150 huts, a couple of which have been rebuilt to give a sense of their scale and design. There's a clear network of paved streets and paths, two circuits of town walls, cisterns, stone guttering and a public fountain. Don't miss the funerary chamber – a fair walk down the hill to the left of the settlement – with its geometrically patterned stone doorway. There are just two daily **buses** direct to Briteiros from Braga. Otherwise you have to **hitch or walk**: either from Bom Jesus or from Caldas das Taipas, on the Braga–Guimarães bus route (6km).

Guimarães

Birthplace of Afonso Henriques and first capital of medieval Portucale, **GUIMARÃES** remains one of the most interesting small towns in the country and one of the liveliest provincial centres. The **bus station** is located on the west side of town, near the football stadium; the **train station** is to the south – you'll pass the **tourist office** as you walk from the station to the centre.

The place to head first is the **Castelo** (Tues–Sun 9am–12.30pm & 2.30–5.30pm; free), whose great square keep and seven towers are an enduring symbol of the emergent Portuguese nation. Built by Henry of Burgundy, it became the stronghold of his son, Afonso Henriques. From here began the Reconquest and the creation of a kingdom which, within a century of Afonso's death, was to stretch to its present borders. Afonso is said to have been born in the keep, and was probably baptized in the font of the Romanesque chapel of **São Miguel** on the grassy slope below. The third building here, the **Paço dos Duques**, was once the palace of the Dukes of Bragança, but under the Salazar dictatorship was "restored" as an official residence. Looking like a mock-Gothic Victorian folly, it now houses dull collections of portraits, furniture and porcelain.

The other two museums in Guimarães are, in contrast, among the best outside Lisbon. The **Museu Alberto Sampaio**, ten minutes' walk south of the castle (Tues–Sun 10am–12.30pm & 2–5.30pm; 200esc), is mostly the treasury of the adjoining Colegiada church and the monastery that used to be here. The highlight is a silver-gilt *Triptych of the Nativity*, said to have been found in the King of Castile's tent after the Portuguese victory at Aljubarrota. Like Batalha, the **Colegiada** itself was built in honour of a vow made by João I before that decisive battle. In front of it stands a Gothic canopy-shrine that marks the spot where Wamba, unwillingly elected king of the Visigoths, drove a pole into the ground swearing that he would not reign until it blossomed. Naturally it sprouted immediately. João, feeling this a useful precedent of divine favour, set out to meet the Castilians from this very point.

Finds from various *citânias* are displayed in the **Museu Martins Sarmento** (Tues–Sun 9.30am–12.30pm & 2–5pm), housed in the former convent of São Domingo to the south of the bus station. They include a remarkable series of bronze votive offerings, ornately patterned stones and – most spectacularly – the two *Pedras Formosas* and the *Colossus of Pedralva*. The *Pedras* (literally, "beautiful stones") are the portals to funerary monuments like that at Briteiros. The colossus is more enigmatic and considerably more ancient, a vast granite hulk with arm raised aloft and an outsized phallus; it shares the bold, powerfully hewn appearance of the stone boars found in Trás-os-Montes and like them may date from pre-Celtic fertility cults.

The finest church in town is **São Francisco**, a short distance east of the tourist office, with its huge eighteenth-century *azulejos* of Saint Francis preaching to the fishes, and elegant Renaissance cloister and fountain.

Practicalities

The choice of **accommodation** is not extensive. The neat and professional *São Mamede*, Rua de São Gonçalo 1 (☎053/513 092; ③), is perhaps the best of the pensions, and there are rooms available over the *Imperial* restaurant on Alameda S. Dâmaso (☎053/415 163; ①). The town's **campsite** is 6km away at Penha, a pilgrimage mount and chapel; buses leave every half-hour between 6am and 10pm (8pm Sun). Apart from the *Imperial*, good places to **eat** include the *Alameda* and *Juncal*, both in Largo da Condessa do Juncal, and the excellent *Bom Retiro* on Rua de Avelino Germano.

Barcelos

It's worth a little planning to arrive in **BARCELOS** for the great Thursday market, the **Feira de Barcelos**. The big weekly event of southern Minho, it takes place from around dawn until mid-afternoon on the central **Campo da República**. The **market** is both a spectacle and a crash course in the region's economics – and now something of a tourist attraction. Minho is made up of hundreds of tiny, walled smallholdings, rarely more than allotments, so most people here are just selling a few vegetables, some fruit, eggs, and maybe even cheese from the family cow.

Apart from produce, the *feira*'s other big feature is its local **pottery** and handicrafts. The crockery, or *louça de Barcelos*, which is brown with distinctive yellow dots, has been well known in the region for some time, but the town was put on the map in the 1950s by Rosa Ramalho, whose work can be seen in the town's ceramics museum. There's also a permanent display in the old town **keep** near the corner of the square, which houses a shop and **tourist office**.

Whichever way you walk from the campo you'll soon end up at the **River Cávado**, as beautiful as any in the Minho, overhung by willows, fronted by gardens and spanned by a fifteenth-century bridge. Just above it loom the ruins of the **Palace of the Counts of Barcelos**, wrecked by the Great Earthquake of 1755 and now providing a shell for the **Ceramics Museum** and **Archeological Museum** (daily 10am–noon & 2–6pm). The latter, a miscellaneous assembly of stone crosses, includes a fourteenth-century crucifix that depicts the legend of the *Galo de Barcelos* (Barcelos Cock). This miraculous roast fowl rose from the table of a judge to proclaim the innocence of a wrongly condemned man, and has become a national symbol.

The *Bagoeira*, on the side of the campo at Avda Sidónio Pais 57 (✆053/811 236; ③), is the most attractive **pension**, a real old market inn, with spotless rooms. If you're on a tighter budget, stay at the *Arantes*, across the square at Avda de Liberdade 32 (✆053/ 811 326; ②), which is the cheapest place in town. On market days, be sure to have lunch at the *Bagoeira*, which sees a constant stream of stallholders bringing in pots, pans and containers for takeaways. Another fine place to eat is the *Dom António* in Rua Dom António Barroso.

Viana do Castelo

VIANA DO CASTELO is the one town in the Minho you could describe as a resort. Beautifully positioned on the north bank of the Lima estuary, it has a stylish old centre, an active fishing harbour, above-average restaurants and, some distance from the town itself, one of the best beaches in the north. What's more, Viana's **Romaria** is the biggest and most exciting fair in the Minho, three days of festivities over the weekend nearest to August 20. Viana produced some of Portugal's greatest seafarers under Dom Manuel, and many of the buildings reflect these times – unusually for the north, you'll notice Manueline mouldings on Viana's mansions. The **tourist office** by the central Praça da Erva is next door to a fine example and makes a good first stop. Close by is the beautiful **Praça da República**. You'll see copies of its Renaissance fountain throughout the Minho, but few buildings as elegant as the old **Misericórdia** (almshouse) that lines one side. Built in 1598, this is one of the most original buildings of the Portuguese Renaissance, its upper storeys supported by primitive-looking caryatids.

The ugly modern basilica of **Monte de Santa Luzia** glowers over the town like an evil eye. The views from the top are fabulous, though, and it's a great walk through the pines and eucalyptus trees – or you can be hauled up by an old funicular from just above the train station. Amid the woods here, just below a luxury hotel, lie ruins of a Celto-Iberian **citânia**, including the foundations of dozens of small, circular stone huts, a thick village wall and partly paved streets.

Praia do Cabedelo, Viana's beach, is connected by a seasonal and very rickety six-seater ferry that leaves from the Largo 5 de Outubro. The beach is an impressive sight – a low curving bay with good breakers, and an expanse of sand that extends northwards, virtually unbroken, to the border at Caminha, and south to Póvoa do Varzim.

Pensions are easy enough to find, but some are very pricy; most have restaurants beneath. *Residencial Magalhães*, Rua Manuel Espregueira 62 (✆058/823 293; ②), is furnished in best Minho tradition with dark, carved headboards on the beds. Spotless, well-furnished rooms make the *Residencial Jardim*, Largo 5 de Outubro 68 (✆058/828 915; ③), a good option. Slightly cheaper, the *Pensão Laranjeira*, Rua General Luís do

Rego 45 (☎058/822 261; ②), is friendly, fresh and comfortable, and has a bargain priced annex nearby at Rua Manuel Espregueira 24 (☎058/822 258; ②). In addition, **rooms** are advertised in the windows of private houses. The two official **campsites** by the Cabedelo beach are overpriced and overcrowded. Among the **restaurants**, *Os Tres Arcos*, Largo João Tomás da Corta 25, has excellent food and a full list of vinhos verdes, and a bar where you can eat from the same menu much more cheaply. Also highly recommended are the *Restaurante A Marisqueira*, Rua Gen. Luis do Rego 36–38, and the *Casa de Pasto Trasmontano*, Rua Gago Coutinho 12, an incredibly low-cost establishment, behind the old town hall.

SOUTHERN PORTUGAL

The huge, sparsely populated plains of the **Alentejo**, to the southeast of Lisbon, are overwhelmingly agricultural, dominated by vast cork plantations well suited to the low rainfall, sweltering heat and poor soil. This impoverished province is divided into vast estates which provide nearly half of the world's cork but only a sparse living for the mass of the agricultural workforce. Visitors to the Alentejo generally head for **Évora**, the province's dominant and most historic city. The plains south of Évora are rather dull, but the Alentejo coastline more than compensates for the lack of urban pleasures and the tedium of the inland landscape.

With its long, sandy beaches and picturesque rocky coves, the southern coastal region of the **Algarve** has attracted more tourist development than the rest of the country put together. The coastline has two different characters. To the **west of Faro** you'll find the classic postcard images of the province – a series of tiny bays and coves, broken up by weird rocky outcrops and fantastic grottoes. They're at their most exotic around the resort of **Lagos**, but if you're looking for more space, and above all if you want to camp, head instead to the historic cape of **Sagres**. **East of Faro** you encounter the first of a series of sandy offshore islets, **the Ilhas**, which front the coastline for some twenty-five miles. Not only is this the quieter section of the coast but it has the bonus of much warmer water than further west. Throughout the Algarve **accommodation** can be a major problem in summer, with hotels block-booked by package companies and pensions filling up early in the day; private rooms or campsites help fill in the gaps, but if you're unlucky you might find yourself sleeping out for the odd night.

Évora

ÉVORA is one of the most impressive cities in Portugal, its provincial atmosphere the perfect setting for a range of memorable and often intriguing monuments. The Romans were in occupation for four centuries and the Moors, who were here for just as long, have left their stamp in the tangle of narrow alleys which rise steeply among the white-washed houses. Most of the monuments, however, date from the fourteenth to the sixteenth century, when with royal encouragement the city was one of the leading centres of Portuguese art and architecture.

Used as a slaughterhouse until 1870, the **Temple of Diana** in the central square is the best preserved Roman temple in Portugal, its stark remains consisting of a small platform supporting more than a dozen granite columns with a marble entablature. Directly opposite, the former **Convento dos Lóios**, now converted into a government-owned *pousada*, has been partly attributed to Francisco de Arruda, architect of the Tower of Belém in Lisbon. To the left of the *pousada* lies the church of the convent, dedicated to **São João Evangelista**. This is the private property of the ducal Cadaval family who still occupy a wing or two of their adjacent ancestral palace. Ring the bell and you should be admitted (for a fee) to see its *azulejos*.

The Sé was begun in 1186, about twenty years after the reconquest of Évora from the Moors, and the Romanesque solidity of its two huge square towers and battlemented roofline contrasts sharply with the pointed Gothic arches of the porch and central window. The interior is more straightforwardly Gothic, although the choir and high altar were remodelled in the eighteenth century. Adjacent is the excellent **Museu de Évora** (Tues–Sun 10am–12.30pm & 2–5pm), housing important collections of fifteenth- and sixteenth-century Flemish and Portuguese paintings assembled from the city's churches and convents. These give a good illustration of the significance of Flemish artists in the development of Portuguese art, and reflect the strong trade links between the two countries.

Perhaps the most memorable sight in Évora is the **Capela dos Ossos** (Chapel of Bones) in the church of **São Francisco**, close to the bus station. A gruesome reminder of mortality, the walls and pillars of this chilling chamber are entirely covered with the bones of more than 5000 monks. A rhyming inscription over the door reads "Nós ossos que aqui estamos, Pelos vossos esperamos" (We bones here are waiting for your bones). Another interesting feature of this church is its large porch, which combines pointed, rounded and horseshoe arches in a manner typical of Manueline architecture. Appropriately enough, the restored **Palácio de Dom Manuel** – the king who gave his name to the style – lies no more than a minute's walk away, in the Jardim Público.

Directly opposite São Francisco, on the Praça 1 de Maio, the rich craft traditions of the Évora district are well displayed in the **Museu do Artesanato Regional** (daily 10am–noon & 2–5pm). The collections include pottery, weaving, tapestry and carvings in wood, cork and bone, and modern pieces are on sale too. For purchases, however, it's a lot more fun to make your way to the **city market** (Tues & Sat am), five minutes down the hill.

Practicalities

The **Praça do Giraldo**, a short distance west of the Sé, is the centre of Évora's low-key social scene. Here you can find the **tourist office** (daily 9am–12.30pm & 2–7pm) and a couple of outdoor cafés. All the cheaper **places to stay** are within five minutes' walk, but Évora's tourist appeal pushes prices way over the norm. Cheapest options are *Os Manuéis*, just west of the square at Rua do Raimundo 35a (☎066/228 61; ②); *Casa Portalegre*, Travessa do Barão 18, off Rua do Raimundo (②), and *Pensão Giraldo* at Rua dos Mercadores 15 (☎066/258 33; ③). If you're stuck for a room, the tourist office will sometimes arrange accommodation in private homes. The **campsite** (☎066/251 90) is a couple of kilometres out of town on the Alcáçovas road; there's no reliable bus service. There's no shortage of **restaurants** in the centre. *A Choupana*, Rua dos Mercadores 20, is recommended, as is *O Túnel* at Alcárcova de Baixo 59, just off Rua de Misericórdia.

The Alentejo Coast

The coast south of Lisbon features towns and beaches as inviting as those of the Algarve. Admittedly, it's exposed to the winds and waves of the Atlantic and the waters are colder than those of the eastern Algarve, but it's fine for summer swimming and far quieter. Access is straightforward, with local bus services and the twice-daily *Zambujeira Express* from Lisbon, which takes you within easy range of the whole coastline and stops at the beaches of Vila Nova de Milfontes and Zambujeira do Mar.

Four buses a day run from Lisbon to Alcacer, from where there are reasonable connections south to **SANTIAGO DO CACÉM**, a pleasant little town overlooked by a castle. In turn, there are seven buses a day from Santiago to **Lagoa de Santo André** and the adjoining **Lagoa de Melides**, with two of the best beaches in the country.

Each of these lagoons has its own small summer community entirely devoted to having a good time on the beach. The **campsites** at both places are of a high standard and there are masses of signs offering rooms, chalets and whole houses to let. Beyond the beach-cafés and ice-cream stalls miles and miles of sand stretch all the way to Comporta in the north and Sines in the south. The sea is very enticing with high waves and good surf, but take local advice on water conditions, as the undertow can be fierce. If you want to base yourself at Santiago rather than at the beaches, there's no shortage of good **food and accommodation**. The *Restaurante Covas*, by the bus station at Rua Cidade de Setúbal 10 (☎069/226 75; ②), is recommended both for its **rooms** and for its meals. There are plenty of other places around town advertising rooms, and another great **restaurant** – *O Grelhador* at Rua de Camilo Castelo Branco 26.

On the southern half of the Alentejo coast, **ODEMIRA** is the main inland base. A quiet, unspoiled country town, it has eight daily bus connections to the beach at Vila Nova de Milfontes and two to Zambujeira do Mar. Unless you're camping, you're unlikely to find anywhere to spend the night in these resorts from June to August, so it's not a bad idea to stay in Odemira and take day trips to the seaside. The town has several restaurants and **pensions**, including *Residencial Rita* (②) and *Residencial Idálio* (②), just to the left when you come out of the bus station. Among the **restaurants**, try the cheap and reasonable *O Escondidinho*, at the lower end of town.

VILA NOVA DE MILFONTES lies on the estuary of the Rio Mira, whose sandy banks gradually expand and merge into the coastline. This is generally the most crowded and popular resort in the Alentejo, with lines of villas radiating from the centre of the old village. It's a pretty place, though, with a handsome little castle and an ancient port, reputed to have harboured Hannibal and his Carthaginians during a storm. All the pensions are fully booked in summer, but there's a large **campsite** just to the north of the village. At **ZAMBUJEIRA DO MAR** a large cliff provides a dramatic backdrop to the beach, more than compensating for the winds. There's only one small pension, a few *dormidas* and a couple of bars, but a reasonable **campsite** is being redeveloped.

Faro

FARO, a sleepy provincial town twenty years ago, now has all the facilities of a modern European city, with a bustling shopping area, chic restaurants and fashionable hotels. Excellent **beaches**, too, are within easy reach, and in summer there's quite a nightlife scene, as thousands of travellers pass through on their way to and from the airport, 6km west of the town. Arriving by bus or train is more straightforward, as both terminals are centrally located.

Sacked and burned by the Earl of Essex in 1596, and devastated by the Great Earthquake of 1755, the town has few historic buildings. By far the most curious sight is the Baroque **Igreja do Carmo** (Mon–Sat 10am–noon & 3–5pm) near the central post office on Largo do Carmo. A door to the right of the altar leads to a macabre **Capela dos Ossos** (Chapel of the Bones), its walls decorated with bones disinterred from the adjacent cemetery. This aside, the most interesting buildings are all in the old, semi-walled quarter on the south side of the harbour, centred around the majestic **Largo da Sé** and entered through the eighteenth-century **Arco da Vila**. The Largo is flanked by the bishop's palace and **Sé** (Mon–Fri 10am–noon, Sat evening service only, Sun 8am–1pm), a miscellany of Gothic, Renaissance and Baroque styles, heavily remodelled after the Great Earthquake. More impressive is the nearby **Museu de Arqueologia** (Mon–Fri 9am–noon & 2–5pm), installed in a fine sixteenth-century convent. The most striking exhibit is a third-century Roman mosaic of Neptune and the four winds, unearthed near Faro train station.

Faro marks a geographical boundary on the Algarve. The whole coastline east from here to Manta Rota, near the Spanish border, is protected by thin stretches of mud flats, fringed in their turn by a chain of long and magnificent sandbanks. The "town beach", **Praia de Faro**, is typical of these sandspit beaches – but atypical in that it's both over-crowded and overdeveloped; bus #16 goes there.

Practicalities

In the season, **places to stay** in Faro can be very thin on the ground. The best bet is to head for the **tourist office** (daily 9.30am–8pm; ☎089/803 604) on the harbour front at Rua da Misericórdia 8; they have an efficient system of *quartos* allocation and a full list of pensions and hotels. **Pensions** are concentrated just north of the harbour along Conselheiro Bivar and Infante D. Henrique, and around Praça Ferreira de Almeida on Rua Vasco da Gama, Rua Filipe Alistão and Rua do Alportel. One of the better places is the increasingly upmarket *Pensão Madalena* (☎089/805 806; ③) on Rua C. Bivar; the *Pensão Nautilus* (☎089/822 557; ②) on the same street, is fine, friendly and much cheaper. Also excellent value is *Pensão Dandy*, F. Alistão 62 (☎089/824 791; ②). There are **restaurants** to meet most budgets. The *Restaurant Dois Irmãos* on Praça Almeida is good and inexpensive, while the *Esplanada-Bar As Parreiras*, Rebelo da Silva 22, serves fine seafood at affordable prices. Another street with a number of likely options is Rua Cruz de Mestras, leading east from the Largo de São Pedro. The town's nightlife street is Rua do Prior, a cobbled alley full of bars and discos.

Olhão

OLHÃO, 8km east of Faro, is the largest fishing port on the Algarve and an excellent base for visiting the sandbank *ilhas*. The **tourist office** on the main shopping street, Rua do Comércio (July & Aug Mon–Fri 9am–7pm, Sat & Sun 9am–noon & 2.30–5pm; Sept–June Mon–Fri 9am–noon & 2.30–5pm, Sat 9am–noon), will provide a town map and advice on rooms. For **accommodation**, try the highly rated *Pensão Bela Vista* (☎089/702 538; ②), left out of the tourist office then first left, or the two-star *Pensão Bicuar* at Rua Vasco da Gama 5 (☎089/714 816; ②). The nearest **campsite** is at Marim, 3km east. There are clusters of **restaurants** and **bars** around Rua do Comércio and along the seafront, the best of which are *Restaurante Isidro*, Avda 5 de Outubro 68, and *Restaurante O Aquârio* at Rua Dr João Lucio 8.

Ferries leave for the **Ilhas of Armona** and **Culatra** from the jetty at the far end of Olhão's municipal gardens, five minutes from the tourist office. The service to **ARMONA** drops you off at a long strip of holiday chalets and huts that stretches right across the island on either side of the main path. On the ocean side the beach disappears into the distance and a short walk will take you to totally deserted stretches of sand and dune. The beach facing the mainland is smaller and tends to get very crowded in summer, but the water here is always warm and calm. Boats to the more distant **Ilha of Culatra** call first at unattractive Culatra town then at **FAROL**, an untidy village of holiday homes, but edged by beautiful beaches on the ocean side.

Tavira

TAVIRA is a clear winner if you are looking for an urban base on the eastern stretch. It's a good-looking little town with superb island beaches in easy reach, yet despite ever-increasing visitors it continues to make its living as a tuna-fishing port. **Buses** pull up at the new terminal by the river, a two-minute walk from the central square, the Praça da República; the **train station** is 1km from the centre of town, straight up the Rua da Liberdade. Boats cross from Quatro Águas, 2km east of town, to the eastern end of the

Ilha de Tavira, which stretches west almost as far as Fuzeta some 14km away. If you're after isolation, it's better to take one of the regular buses to **PEDRAS D'EL REI**, 4km west, from where a miniature railway shuttles across the mud flats to the beach of **BARRIL** on the *ilha*. It's a few minutes' walk to escape the tourist facilities at the terminal and get onto the peaceful, dune-fringed beach.

The best place **to stay** in Tavira is the *Residencial Lagoas*, north of the river at Rua Almirante Cândido dos Reis 24 (☎081/222 52; ②), with the bonus of the top-notch budget eatery, the *Bica*, below. Alternatives include the *Pensão do Castelo* (☎081/239 42; ②) in the main square, the *Residencial Mirante* at Rua da Liberdade 83 (☎081/222 55; ②), and the Mendonça family's *residencial* on Rua dos Bombeiros Municipales (☎081/ 81743; ③). If these options fail to produce a bed, the **tourist office** in the Praça (May– Sept daily 9am–8pm; Oct–April Mon–Sat 9am–12.30pm & 2.30–5pm; ☎081/225 11) may be able to find a private **room**. A succession of **bars and restaurants** line the gardens along the bank of the Rio Gilão, which flows through the centre of town. Probably the best of the restaurants is the *Imperial*, which serves some of the finest seafood in the Algarve, at fairly reasonable prices. Also good are *Pastelaria Anazu*, Rua Jacques Pessoa 13, and the *Aquasul Restaurante*, Rua Dr Augusto Da Silva Carvalho 3. The *Arco*, at Almirante Candido dos Reis 67, is a friendly, laid-back **bar**.

Portimão and around

PORTIMÃO, the first tolerable place to the west of Faro, is a sprawling port, a major sardine-canning centre and a base for the construction industries spawned by the tourist boom. The best part is the riverfront – a hive of activity with its bars, restaurants and fishing port. The **train station** is inconveniently located at the northern tip of town; there's no bus connection, so it's a twenty-minute walk. Inter-town **buses** stop by the waterfront on Largo do Dique, a couple of minutes' walk from the **tourist office** on Rua Dr. João Vitorino Mealha (daily summer 9.30am–8pm; winter closes 7pm). They will help you find a private **room** for about 2500esc, or provide a list of **pensions**. Good bets include the *Pensão O Pátio* (☎082/242 88; ③), down from the tourist office at no. 5, *Residencias Roma* at Rua Júdice Fiarho 34 (☎082/238 21; ②), and the spick-and-span and more expensive *Pensão Arabi* (☎082/260 06; ③) on Praça Manuel Teixeira Gomes. *Kómaaqui*, Rua Infanta D. Henrique 136, is the town's most original **restaurant**, very popular for its African specialities. The *Palco Bar* on Avda 25 de Abril is best for **nightlife**, with African bands on Friday and Saturday.

PRAIA DA ROCHA, 3km south of Portimão and served by half-hourly buses, was one of the first Algarve tourist developments and has since become one of the most upmarket. The **beach** is among the most beautiful on the entire coast, a wide expanse of sand framed by jagged cliffs and the walls of an old fort (now a restaurant) that once protected the mouth of the river Arade. **Accommodation** is rarely hard to find and cheaper than you might imagine – the **tourist office**, near the fort, will readily find you a room (Mon–Fri 9am–7pm, Sat & Sun 9am–12.30pm & 2.30–5pm).

Silves

Capital of the Moorish kings of the al-Gharb, **SILVES** is still an imposing place and one of the few towns of inland Algarve that merits a detour. The **train station** – an easy approach from Lagos or Faro – lies 2km outside the town; there is a connecting bus, but it's better to walk, allowing the town and its fortress to appear slowly as you emerge from the wooded hills. Under the Moors Silves was a place of grandeur and industry, described in contemporary accounts as being "of shining brightness" within its triple circuit of walls. In 1189 an army led by Sancho I put an end to this splendour, killing some 6000 Moors in the process. The impressively complete sandstone walls of the

Moorish **fortress** retain their towers and elaborate communication system, but the inside is disappointing: apart from the great vaulted water cisterns that still serve the town, there's nothing left of the old citadel. Just below the fortress is Silves' s **Cathedral**, built on the site of the mosque in the thirteenth century. Flanked by two broad Gothic towers, it has a suitably defiant and military appearance, though the Great Earthquake of 1755 and centuries of impoverished restoration have left their mark inside.

The **tourist office**, in the heart of the town on Rua 25 de Abril (Mon–Thurs 9am–8pm, Fri 9am–12.30pm & 2.30–7pm, Sat & Sun 9am–12.30pm & 2.30–5pm; ☎082/442 255), will help you find a **room**. Promising options are the *Residencial Sousa* at Rua Samora Barros 17 (☎082/442 502; ②), and the rooms with Isabel Maria da Silva at Rua Cândido dos Reis 36 (☎082/442 667; ②).

Lagos

Once a quiet little town, **LAGOS** now attracts the whole gamut of tourists to its extraordinary beaches. It became a favoured residence of Henry the Navigator, who used Lagos as a base for the new African trade – which explains the formation in 1441 of the town's slave market, held under the arches of the **Customs House** that still stands in the Praça da República near the waterfront. In this same square is the church of **Santa Maria**, from whose whimsical Manueline windows the youthful Dom Sebastião is said to have roused his troops before the ill-fated Moroccan expedition of 1578 – he was to perish at Alcácer-Quibir with almost the entire Portuguese nobility. He's commemorated in the centre of Lagos by a fantastically dreadful statue. On the waterfront and to the rear of the town are the remains of Lagos' once impregnable fortifications, devastated by the Great Earthquake. One rare and beautiful church which did survive for restoration was the **Igreja de Santo António**; decorated around 1715, its gilt and carved interior is wildly obsessive, every inch filled with a private fantasy of cherubic youths struggling with animals and fish. Next door is the **Museu Municipal** (Tues–Sun 9.30am–12.30pm & 2.30–5.30pm; 200esc), a bizarre display ranging from Roman mosaics and folk costumes to misshapen animal foetuses.

The promontory **south** of Lagos is fringed by extravagantly eroded cliff faces that shelter a series of tiny **cove beaches**. All are within easy walking distance of the old town, but the headland is now cut up by campsites, hotels, roads and a multitude of tracks, and the beaches all tend to be overcrowded. Nearest is the **Praia do Pinhão**, just opposite the fire station, and close to the **Praia de Dona Ana** – one of the most photogenic of all Algarve beaches. The path leads all the way to **Praia Camilo** and, right at the point, the **Ponta da Piedade**, where a palm-bedecked lighthouse makes a great vantage point for the sunset.

Practicalities

It's a fifteen-minute walk south from the **bus** or **train terminal** to the **tourist office** in Largo Marquês de Pombal (daily 9.30am–7.30pm; winter closes 5.30pm); they may phone and find you a room. Two of the more convenient and pleasant **pensions** are just by the tourist office – the *Pensão Caravela* (☎082/763 361; ②) and the *Residencial Mar Azul* (☎082/769 749; ②), at Rua 25 de Abril 14 and 13 respectively. Lagos has two **campsites**, close to each other on the main Sagres road – the *Campismo da Trindade* (☎082/ 763 892) and the more attractive *Imulagos: Parque de Campismo* (☎082/760 031). In season a regular bus service marked "D. Ana/Porto de Mós" connects the bus station with both, and *Imulagos* provides its own free transport from the train station.

The whole centre of town is packed with **restaurants**. Some of the better ones are the cheap, good-quality fish and shellfish places by the market, where Rua das Portas de Portugal meets the waterfront. *O Cantinho Algarvio*, Rua Afonso d'Almeida 17, has a wide range of Algarve dishes at good prices; in the same street, *Casa do Pasto O Coelho* is more limited but cheaper and just as good for seafood. *Cevejaria O Sol do Algarve*, Rua Infante de Sagres 56, is an unpretentious out-of-the-way place, with great *prato do dia* bargains. *Mullens* **bar**, Rua Candido dos Reis 86, serves meals until 10pm, plays jazz on the sound system and stays open until 2am. *Adega Portuguesa*, Travessa dos Tanoeiros, just off Rua 25 de Abril, is a cosily atmospheric bar, also open till 2am. The *Eléctrico* **club**, inside the *Imulagos* campsite, seethes nightly with tourists and locals.

Lagos is the western terminus of the Algarve rail line, so for Sagres take one of the nine daily **buses**. Many of them call at the train station just after the arrival of the trains.

Sagres and around

Wild and windswept, **SAGRES** was considered by the Portuguese to be the limit of the ancient and medieval worlds. It was here in the fifteenth century that Henry the Navigator set up a maritime school, gathering the greatest astronomers, cartographers and adventurers of his age – Magellan and Vasco da Gama among them. After Henry's death in 1460, the centre of maritime studies moved to Lisbon, and Sagres slipped back into the obscurity from which he'd brought it. The **village** of Sagres, rebuilt in the nine-teenth century over the earthquake ruins of Henry's town, is little more than a long single street connecting the harbour with the square. The main road, built to transport tourists straight to the headlands, runs parallel, trailing a series of drab villas off to the east. At the end of this road, dominating the whole scene near the village, is a remnant of the **Fortaleza**, whose immense walls once surrounded the shelf-like promontory.

There are five **beaches** within easy walking distance. Three are on the more shel-tered coastline east of the Fortaleza: **Praia da Mareta** is just below the square, and the grubby **Praia da Baleeira** is by the harbour, from where it's a five-minute walk to the longest and best beach, the **Praia do Martinhal**. The **Cabo de São Vicente**, across the bay, was sacred to the Romans, who believed the sun sank into the water beyond here every night; then it became a Christian shrine when the relics of Saint Vincent arrived in the eighth century. It was almost certainly here that Henry established his School of Navigation, but today only a **lighthouse**, flanked by the ruins of a convent, is to be seen. It is, though, a dramatic and exhilarating six-kilometre walk from Sagres, skirting the tremendous cliffs for much of the way.

Sagres's combination of wild terrain and an oddball mix of visitors can make it a great place to stay. Pick of the **accommodation** is the *Aparthotel Orquídea* (③), overlooking the fishing port and with fine views up the coast, but the *Residencial Dom Henrique* (☎082/641 33; ④), on the square, is perfectly adequate. Alternatively, the **tourist office** at the fort (daily summer 9.30am–7.30pm; winter 9.30am–6.30pm) will fix up *quartos* for you. The nearest **campsite** is 2km east along the main road, convenient for Praia do Martinhal. In the evening the place to be is either *A Rosa dos Ventos*, a loud and drunken **bar** on the square, or the *Last Chance Saloon*, around the corner, overlooking the sea. When they close, people move on to the *Topas* or *Caravelo* discos. If you want classier **food** than the snacks at *Rosa's* and *Last Chance*, the *Atlântico Restaurant* on the main street is excellent, and *A Tasca*, down by the fishing boats, serves marvellous seafood.

travel details

Trains

Lisbon to: Aveiro (10 daily; 3hr); Braga (2 daily; 5hr 15min); Coimbra (10 daily; 2hr 30min); Évora (3 daily; 3hr); Faro (3 daily; 5hr); Guarda (5 daily; 7hr); Óbidos (7 daily; 2hr); Porto (10 daily; 4hr); Sintra (every 15min; 50min); Tavira (3 daily; 6hr).

Figueira da Foz to: Leira (6 daily; 1hr 15min); Lisbon (6 daily; 4hr 45min); Óbidos (6 daily; 2hr 45min).

Guarda to: Coimbra (5 daily; 3hr 30min); Lisbon (5 daily; 6hr 30min); Luso-Buçaco (5 daily; 2hr 40min).

Lagos to: Aljezur (2 daily; 1hr); Burgau (5 daily; 20min); Faro (9 daily; 50min); Luz (5 daily; 15min); Odemira (2 daily; 1hr 45min); Olhão (9 daily; 1hr 10min); Portimão (13 daily; 40min); Sagres (9 daily; 1hr 5min); Salema (5 daily; 50min); Silves (13 daily; 1hr); Tavira (9 daily; 1hr 50min); Tunes (13 daily; 1hr 20min).

Livração to: Amarante (7 daily; 1hr 30min).

Peso da Régua to: Vila Real (5 daily; 1hr).

Porto to: Aveiro (5 daily; 60–75min); Barcelos (12 daily; 2hr); Coimbra (5 daily; 2–3hr); Guimarães (hourly; 1hr 45min); Lisbon (5 daily; 4–6hr); Livração (4 daily; 1hr 30min); Peso da Régua (4 daily; 12hr 30min); Tua (4 daily; 3hr 30min); Viana do Castelo (12 daily; 2hr).

Tua to: Bragança (5 daily; 3hr 40min); Mirandela (5 daily; 1hr 40min).

Buses

Lisbon to: Évora (6 daily; 3hr 30min); Leiria (8 daily; 2hr 30min); frequent summer express coaches to Faro (5hr); Mafra (10 daily; 1hr 30min).

Aveiro to: Porto (hourly; 1hr); Viseu (4 daily; 3–4hr).

Braga to: Barcelos (7 daily; 45min); Guimarães (every 30min; 45min); Viana do Castelo (7 daily; 1hr).

Coimbra to: Castelo Branco (3 daily; 5hr); Guarda (2 daily; 4hr); Viseu (3 daily; 3hr).

Évora to: Braga (2 daily; 9hr); Lisbon (6 daily; 3hr); Porto (2 daily; 7hr 35min).

Lagos to: Portimão (12 daily; 40min); Sagres (9 daily; 1hr 5min).

Leiria to: Alcobaça (8 daily; 50min); Amarante (hourly; 1hr 30min); Batalha (8 daily; 20min); Coimbra (hourly; 1hr 40min); Fátima (4 daily; 50min); Tomar (4 daily; 2hr).

Porto to: Braga (hourly; 1hr 20min); Coimbra (4 daily; 2hr 30min); Guimarães (5 daily; 1hr); Porto (hourly; 1hr 20min); Viana do Castelo (8 daily; 2hr); Vila Real (6 daily; 3hr 40min); Viseu (3 daily; 2–4hr).

Portimão to: Silves (6 daily; 20min).

Viseu to: Porto (2 daily; 5hr).

CHAPTER 19

ROMANIA

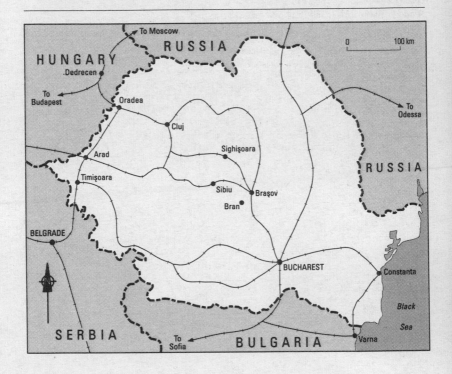

To Moscow

RUSSIA

HUNGARY

.Dedrecen

To
Budapest

Oradea

Cluj

Sighişoara

To
Odessa

RUSSIA

Arad

Timişoara

Sibiu   Braşov

Bran

BELGRADE

BUCHAREST

Constanta

Black

Sea

N

SERBIA

To
Sofia

BULGARIA

Varna

0   100 km

Introduction

Travel in **Romania** is as rewarding as it is challenging. The country's mountain scenery and great diversity of wildlife, its various cultures and its people leave few who visit unaffected. However, unless you visit on a package, it is undeniably the hardest country of the former Eastern Bloc to cope with. The regime of Nicolae Ceauşescu left Romania on the verge of bankruptcy, and the semi-reformed economy that has since emerged seems to be characterized by hustle and sharp practice.

Romanians trace their ancestry back to the Romans, and it's not unfair to say that "Latin" traits prevail. The people are generally warm, spontaneous, anarchic, and appreciative of style and life's pleasures. In addition to ethnic Romanians, there are communities from half a dozen other races and cultures: Transylvanian Germans (Saxons) reside around the fortified towns and churches built to guard the mountain passes during the Middle Ages; so do some two million Magyars, many of whom pursue an archaic lifestyle long since vanished in Hungary; and along the coast and in the Danube Delta there's a mixture of Ukrainians, Serbs, Bulgars, Gypsies, Turks and Tartars.

The capital, **Bucharest**, would not be a highlight of anyone's European tour, but the recent revolution has given parts of this once beautiful city a certain voyeuristic appeal. More attractive by far – and easily accessible even on Romania's dilapidated public transport system – are the towns of **Transylvania**, a savagely beautiful and historically fascinating region.

Information and Maps

Romania's national tourist office – the **ONT**, sometimes known as the *Carpaţi* – nowadays concentrates on selling package holidays to the locals rather than helping out foreign visitors. Maps and brochures about Romania are in particularly short supply, but even so, *ONT's* largely English-speaking staff may still be a source of good advice. You'll find offices in evey town, plus regional tourist offices (*OJT*) – equally hopeless when it comes to providing hard facts, but a reasonable source of local knowlege all the same.

It's always worth asking offices or hotel receptions for town **maps** – *plan oraşului* – including those of other towns, since these may be unobtainable once you get there. In the case of Bucharest, recently published town plans are sporadically available from street vendors, but it's worth getting the *Falk* map before you go. Bear in mind, though, that street names are changing all the time in post-communist Romania, so all maps will be out of date to some degree.

Money and Banks

The **lei** (singular *leu*), Romania's currency, comes in notes of 100, 200, 500, 1000 and 5,000 lei, with coins of 1, 3, 5, 10, 20, 50 and 100 lei; plus fiddly little 5, 10, 15 and 25-*bani* coins (100 bani = 1 leu). You can use lei for minor transactions, including hotel and restaurant bills, but bear in mind that Deutschmarks or dollars can sometimes be used (and may indeed be requested) to obtain a higher leverl of service – whether in restaurants, luxury goods shops or taxis.

Exchanging money in hotels, *ONJ* offfices or privately-owned exchange bureaux involves less hassle than banks. Don't succumb to the temptation to change money on the black market: rates are not a lot higher and the characters who operate it are a risky crew, expecially in Bucharest and Braşov.

This is a country where cash is king, so take along a stash of **dollar bills**, preferably in small denominations. However, it's wise to carry the bulk of your money in **travellers' cheques**, chiefly as a safeguard against theft. The only brand of travellers' cheques that guarantees a refund in the event of loss is *American Express*, whose Romanian agent is the main *ONT* office in Bucharest.

Romania's standard of living is abysmal, and although hotel accommodation tends to be overpriced, independent travellers will find **costs** very low. However, prices are volatile, as are the attitudes of Romanians towards bargaining – some will negotiate for hard currency, others will tell you to take it or leave it.

Communications

Post offices in towns are open Mon–Sat 7am–8.30pm, Sun 8am–noon, and, like the yellow-painted post boxes, are marked *Poşta*. It's easier to buy stamps (*timbru*) and envelopes (*plic*) at tobacconists, bookshops or hotels rather than queue for them in post offices. Sending letters to Romania is too unpredictable a process to be recommended.

If the electricity is flowing, it's feasible to make local **telephone calls** using public booths (taking 1 and 3 lei coins; the rate is 3min per leu), but long-distance calls can only be made from a post office or telephone exchange – and even then you'll be lucky to get through. In theory, you can call abroad directly; in reality, you're more likely to get through via the operator (☎071 for international calls), or by phoning from a "de luxe" hotel. Using hotel facilities inevitably means a service charge, which can be high, so ask the price beforehand.

Getting Around

All forms of public transport in Romania are cheap but slow and fairly primitive. Driving is the only speedy way of getting around, but petrol availability is a problem here.

■ Trains

Trains are often the only feasible way of covering distances of over 100km on public transport. Consequently, they're usually crowded, so seat **reservations** are virtually a necessity. Travelling first class (*casa întîi-a*) is one (affordable) way of avoiding the crush. Carriages tend to be unheated, but many routes are extremely scenic – particularly in Transylvania – and journeys are good occasions to strike up conversation with Romanians. *Rapid* services, halting only at major towns, are the most expensive type of train (though still cheap by Western standards), while *Accelerat* are slightly cheaper and slower, with more frequent stops. The excruciatingly slow *Personal* and *Cursa* trains should be avoided.

All long-distance trains in Romania have **sleeping cars** (*vagon de dormit*) and **couchettes** (*cușete*), for which a surcharge of about £2–3 is levied. On most such trains a seat reservation is obligatory. Rather than queue at the station, you're better off booking tickets at the local **Agenția CFR** at least 24 hours in advance. Most offices function Mon–Sat 8am–8pm, Sun 8am–1pm. Return tickets (*bilet dus și întors*) are rarely issued except for international services. *InterRail* cards are valid in Romania, but not *Eurail*.

■ Buses

Inter-city and rural **bus services** have been restored to a large extent since the revolution, though on many routes there are just one or two services daily. In the countryside, knowing when and where to wait for the day's bus is a local art form, and on Sundays many regions have no public transport at all. The same unfortunate truth applies in towns, where bus stops (*stație autobuz*) are prone to mysteriously changing their location, and the schedules fluctuate wildly. There, too, you'll find **trams and trolleybuses** (*tramvai* and *troleibuz*), which at least stick to their routes.

■ Driving and Hitching

Given the state of public transport, it makes sense to travel by **car** – although lead-free petrol is all but unobtainable. A national driving **licence** suffices, and if you don't have Green Card **insurance**, a month's cover can be purchased at the border. Foreign motorists belonging to organizations affiliated to the **ACR** (Romanian Automobile Club) receive free or cut-price technical **assistance**; and you can get motoring information from their head office in Bucharest at 27 Str Beloiannis (☎59-50-80). Roads are badly maintained, and driving at night can be very hairy. The complexities of **car rental** in Romania make it a cheaper option to just find someone to drive you around for a fee – tourist offices may well be able to suggest a few names to try.

Hitchhiking (*autostop*) is legal on all Romanian roads with the exception of the *Autostradă*. It's accepted practice to pay for lifts. Advertising some kind of inducement – such as a packet of Kent cigarettes – can dramatically increase your chances of snagging a driver, whom you should then ask: *cît costă pînă la . . .?* (How much to . . .?). Other useful phrases include *Doresc să cobor la . . .* (I want to get off at . . .); *Opriți la . . .* (Stop at . . .); and *Opriți aici* (Stop here).

Accommodation

Accommodation rarely comes cheap in Romania, and the general standard is perhaps the worst in Europe. Beds can be booked through *ONT* or *OJT*, but they'll direct you towards the more expensive options and charge you a hefty fee in the process.

ACCOMMODATION PRICE CODES

Throughout this guide, accommodation is priced on a scale of ① to ⑧, the number indicating the lowest price per night a single person could expect to pay in that establishment in high season. With hostels this is the nightly rate per person; with hotels, the price is arrived at by dividing the cost of the cheapest double room by two. The prices indicated by the codes are as follows

① = under £5 / $8   ② = £5–10 / $8–16   ③ = £10–15 / $16–24   ④ = £15–20 / $24–32

⑤ = £20–25 / $32–40   ⑥ = £25–30 / $40–48   ⑦ = £30–35 / $48–56   ⑧ = over £35 / $56

Hotels come graded as "de luxe", first or second class. Given the frequency of power and water cuts, it's hardly worth paying the extra – and the upmarket places are invariably infested with hookers and racketeers. In the cheapest second-class hotel (the lowest tolerable standard), a bed in a double room should cost $15–20; a private shower (*cu duş*) adds another $5–10 to the bill. Prices rarely include breakfast.

The provision of accommodation in **private houses** (*cazare la persoane particulare*) is pretty much in its infancy in Romania. In rare cases, private rooms are offered by *ONT* (most notably in Bucharest), while elsewhere in the country independent room-letting agencies are coming into being. Occasionally, you'll be approached by individuals at train stations. It's a reasonable assumption that a private room will be cheaper and more comfortable than a hotel room. $10 per person per night seems to be the going rate.

In towns with a sizeable student population, vacant college rooms – **caminul de studenti** – may be rented out between July 15 and August 31. The youth travel agency **BTT** is responsible for bookings, but prefers groups to individuals, and seems to be on the verge of extinction anyway. However, in student towns you're quite likely to receive invitations to stay in private houses.

There are more than 100 **campsites** all over the country, costing around $2.50 for tent space, and $2.50 per head. Third-class is not much more than a field with a tap and a loo, and second- and first-class sites may not be a lot better.

Food and Drink

During the Ceauşescu years **food** became a precious commodity in what used to be known as the breadbasket of Eastern Europe. The situation is now better, but supplies are still unreliable, and certain produce is still rationed, so be prepared for

austerity and carry a reserve of food with you. **Breakfast** (*micul dejun*) is typically a light meal, featuring rolls and butter (*chifle şi unt*) and an *omleta* – or long, unappealing-looking sausages (*patriciani*) – washed down with a large white coffee (*cafea mare cu lapte*) or tea (*ceai*). As for **snacks** – known as *gustări* – the most common are flaky pastries (*pateuri*) filled with cheese (*cu brînză*) or meat (*cu carne*), often dispensed through hatches in the walls of bakeries; sandwiches (*sandvici* or *tartină*); and a variety of spicy grilled sausages and meatballs called *mititei* and *chiftele* which are normally sold by street vendors.

For **sit-down meals** it's best to go upmarket, since the choice and quality of dishes in restaurants is way above the grisly stuff dished out in the drab, self-service *Autoservire* canteens. If your budget is tight, it's preferable to look out for *Lacto-Vegetarian* restaurants (most towns have one) rather than the *Autoservire*; they tend to be less crowded and generally offer better food. The menus of most Romanian restaurants concentrate on grilled meats: *friptura*, *pîrjola* and *cotlet de porc* are all forms of pork chop; while *muşchi de vacă* denotes fillet of beef. Dishes usually arrive with a garnish of chips, a couple of vegetables (when available) and a side salad. Many restaurants are beginning to offer a *program* or cabaret – usually involving dancing girls and a couple of singing acts – as a way of drumming up custom. Expect to pay a small admission charge.

At smarter **restaurants** and places with an olde-worlde decor, known as *han*, there's a fair likelihood of finding traditional Romanian dishes, which can be delicious. The best-known of these is *samarle* – bitter cabbage stuffed with rice, meat and herbs, usually served (or sometimes baked) with sour cream. Stews (*tocane*) and other dishes often feature a sclerotic combination of meat and dairy products. "Shepherd's Delight" (*muşchi ciobanesc*) is pork stuffed with ham, covered in cheese and served with mayonnaise, cucumber and herbs; while *muşchi poiana* is beef stuffed with mushrooms, bacon, pepper and paprika, served in a vegetable purée and tomato sauce.

Vegetarians in ordinary restaurants could try asking for *caşcaval pane* (hard cheese fried in breadcrumbs); *ghiveci* (mixed fried veg); *ardei umpluţi* (stuffed peppers); eggs with a spicy filling (*ouă umplute picante*) or mushroom stuffing (*ouă umplute cu ciuperci*); poached eggs (*ouă româneşti*); or vegetables and salads (see below). When in doubt, stipulate something *fără carne*, *vă rog* (without meat), or enquire *este cu carne?* (does it contain meat?).

Establishments called *cofetărie* serve coffee and cakes, and sometimes ice cream. Coffee, whether *cafea naturală* (finely ground and cooked Turkish fashion) or *nes* (Nescafé or any other instant coffee) is usually drunk black or sweet; ask for it *cu lapte* or *fără zahăr* if you prefer it with milk or without sugar. The *cofetărie* is a good place to pick up daytime snacks: *cornuiri* are croissants, *chifle* bread rolls, and *prăjitui* sweet buns. Cakes and desserts are sticky and sweet, as throughout the Balkans. Romanians enjoy pancakes (*clătite*) and pies (*plăcintă*) with various fillings; Turkish-influenced *baclava* and *cataif cu frisca* (crisp pastry soaked in syrup, filled with whipped cream); and the traditional *dulceaţă*, or glass of jam.

Evening **drinking** takes place in outdoor beer gardens (the roughest of which are pretty much all-male preserves), restaurants (where boozers often outnumber the diners), and in a growing number of Western European-style cafés and bars. As an aperitif, and to finish their meals, people like to drink *ţuică*, a tasty, powerful brandy made of plums, taken neat. In rural areas, home-made **spirits** can be fearsome stuff, often twice distilled to yield *rachia*, much rougher than grape brandy, or *rachiu*, called *coniac* by urban sophisticates. Most **beer** (*bere*) is like lager,

although you're much more likely to see imported German and Hungarian brands than local brews. Romania's best **wine** is exported or reserved for the ruling class, but most restaurants should be able to conjure up a bottle – *Cotnari* dessert wine is particularly palatable. Mineral water (*apă minerală*), as well as international *soft drinks* like Coke, Pepsi and 7-Up, are all fairly ubiquitous.

Opening Hours and Holidays

Like so many things in Romania, opening hours are in a state of flux. At the moment most **shops** are open Mon–Fri from around 9am to around 6pm, with some staying open as late as 8pm and food shops often opening a couple of hours earlier. Most are open on Saturday morning, and a few are also open on Sunday morning. **National holidays** are: Jan 1; Jan 2; May 1; May 2; Aug 23 & Aug 24.

Emergencies

There's a high incidence of **petty theft** in Romania. If your passport goes missing while in Bucharest, telephone your consulate immediately; anywhere else, contact the **police** (*Miliţia*), who'll issue a temporary visa. Don't expect the police to do anything more though.

In the event of a **health emergency**, dial the number given below or ask someone to contact the local *staţia de salvare* or *prim ajutor* – the casualty and first aid stations – which may or may not have ambulances. Don't go to Romania without good health insurance cover, and if you develop any complaint that might require hospital treatment, you should try to get out of the country. If you need medication on a regular basis, take a supply with you.

EMERGENCY NUMBERS
Police ☎055; Ambulance ☎061.

TRANSYLVANIA

The likeliest approach to Romania is by train from adjoining Hungary, from where the two main rail routes take you through **Transylvania**. Whether you take the line through Cluj and Braşov or the less popular one through Timişoara and Sibiu, you should disembark before reaching Bucharest to see the best of the country. Thanks to Bram Stoker and Hollywood, Transylvania is famed abroad as the homeland of Dracula: a mountainous place where storms lash medieval hamlets, while wolves – or werewolves – howl from the woods. Happily, the fictitious image is accurate, up to a point. The scenery is dramatic, there are spooky Gothic citadels, and one Vlad – born in Sighişoara – did style himself **Dracula** and earn the grim nickname "The Impaler". But the Dracula image is just one element of Transylvania, whose 99,837 square kilometres take in icecaps, caves, alpine meadows, dense forests sheltering bears and wild boars, and lowland valleys where buffalo cool off in the rivers.

The **population** is a jigsaw of Romanians, Magyars, Germans, Gypsies and others, formed over centuries of migration and colonization. Since the Treaty of Trianon (1920) which placed Transylvania firmly within the Romanian state, the balance of power has shifted sharply in favour of the Romanian majority, but Transylvania's history is still often disputed along nationalist lines, and popular feelings concerning the region run high inside Hungary and Romania. Though modernization and Romanianization have eroded the sharp distinctions of earlier times, the character of many towns still reflects past patterns of ethnic settlement and domination. **Cluj**, for example, is strongly Hungarian-influenced, but most striking of all are the *stuhls* – the former seats of Saxon power – with their medieval streets, defensive towers and fortified churches. **Sighişoara**, the most picturesque, could almost be the Saxons' cenotaph: their *kultur* has evaporated here, leaving only their citadels and churches, as it threatens to do in **Braşov** and **Sibiu**, and in the old German settlements roundabouts. A similarly complex ethnic mix is found in the Banat, the westernmost region of Romania, whose chief town, **Timişoara**, was the crucible of the 1989 revolution.

Timişoara

TIMIŞOARA grew up around a Magyar fortress at the marshy confluence of the Timiş and Bega, and from the fourteenth century onwards functioned as the capital of the Banat. It played a crucial role during Christian warlord János Hunyadi's campaigns against the Turks, who subsequently conquered the town, whence they ruled the surrounding terrain until 1716. The Habsburgs who ejected them proved to be relatively benign masters over the next two hundred years, and during the late nineteenth century the municipality rode a wave of progress, becoming one of the first towns in the world to have horse-drawn trams and to install electric street-lighting. This was also the period when Temeschwar (as it was then called) acquired many of its current features, a prime example being the **Bega Canal**, which cups the southern side of the historic centre and is flanked by a procession of stately **parks**. Dug to drain the surrounding marshes and permit the shipment of grain to the Danube, the canal has outlasted both requirements but continues to lend a pleasant ambience to neighbouring parts of town.

Timişoara's fame abroad rests on its crucial role in the overthrow of the Ceauşescu regime. The figure who triggered it all off was a local Hungarian priest, Laszlo Tökes, whose bishop ordered his eviction for his provocative stand on the rights of the Hungarian community here. When the police came to turf the priest out of his house on December 16, 1989, his parishioners barred their way, an act of defiance to which the Securitate responded by opening fire on the crowd. Before long the entire town had turned out, starting a five-day battle that ended when workers at the oil refinery forced the withdrawal of the troops by threatening to blow the place sky-high. Events at Timişoara provided crucial inspiration for the people of Bucharest, and Timişoara regards itself as the guardian of the revolution – memorials around town mark the places where the democratic martyrs fell, and streets are constantly being renamed in their honour.

Approaching from the train station along Bulevard Republicii, the town's architectural assets don't become evident until one enters the centre, with its carefully planned streets and squares. On Piaţa Huniade, just beyond the plush **Opera House**, you'll find the **Museum of the Banat** (Tues–Sun 11am–6pm) occupying the castle once extended by Hunyadi. Warlords and rebels figure prominently in the large historical section, as does the great strike of 1920 in support of the Banat's union with Romania; the museum also exhibits 21,000 stuffed birds and mounted butterflies.

The central Piaţa Libertăţii boasts as fine a Baroque town hall as any municipality could wish for, but the edifice is modest compared to the huge **Dicasterial Palace**, a short way north at one end of Str Ceahlău. A complex of 450 rooms built for the Habsburg bureaucracy, its sheer bulk is redolent of the state's power. One block north of the palace, Piaţa Unirii's **Museum of Fine Arts**, displaying work by minor Italian, German and Flemish masters, is overshadowed by the monumental Roman Catholic and Serbian Orthodox **Cathedrals**. Built between 1736 and 1773, the former is a fine example of Austrian Baroque, designed by von Erlach of Vienna. The latter is roughly contemporaneous and equally impressive. The **Romanian Orthodox Cathedral** is located on the other side of town, between the main square and the canal. Completed in 1946, it blends neo-Byzantine and Moldavian architectural elements and exhibits a collection of icons in its basement.

In 1868 the municipality purchased the redundant citadel from the Habsburgs, and demolished all but one section, the **Bastion**, to the east of the Serbian cathedral. The entrance at 2 Str Hector admits you to a portion that's been converted into a pâtisserie and bar, whilst further to the north another section is occupied by an **Ethnographic Museum** (Tues–Sun 10am–6pm). Varied folk costumes and coloured charts illustrate the region's ethnic diversity effectively, but in an anodyne fashion – for example, there's no mention of the thousands of Serbs exiled when the Party turned hostile towards Tito's Yugoslavia, which radically altered the Banat's ethnic make-up. In addition, the museum has an **open-air section** just outside town, where old Banat homesteads and workshops have been reassembled in the **Pădurea Verde** or Green Forest.

Practicalities

The most reasonable **hotels** are the *Parc* at 11 Blvd Republicii (③) and *Bega* at 12 Splaiul Titulescu (③) but, of all Romanian towns, this is the one where you're likeliest to be invited to stay in someone's house or be approached by private operators – always a better option. The **tourist office** at 6 Blvd Republicii might well direct you to private accommodation. Best of the **restaurants** are the *Cina* at 4 Str Piatra Craiului, and the ones in the hotels *Continental*, 2 Blvd 23 August, *Timişoara*, 1 Str Mărăşeşti, and *Central*, 6 Str Leanu. Folks who can afford it frequent **pâtisseries** such as *Violeta*, Blvd 30 Decembrie, *Trandafirul*, 5 Str Eminescu, or the place in the Bastion, which conveniently adjoins a couple of **bars**.

Sibiu

"I rubbed my eyes in amazement," wrote Walter Starkie of **SIBIU** in 1929. "The town where I found myself did not seem to be in Transylvania . . . the narrow streets and old gabled houses made me think of Nuremberg." Nowadays the illusion is harder to sustain, but Sibiu's older quarters could still serve to illustrate the Brothers Grimm. Many people here speak German and cherish links with faraway Germany, calling

Sibiu **Hermannstadt**, the name given by the Transylvanian **Saxons** to their chief city. Like Braşov, it was founded by Germans whom the Hungarian King Géza II invited to colonize strategic regions of Transylvania in 1143. Its inhabitants prospered and came to dominate trade in Transylvania and Wallachia, forming exclusive guilds under royal charter. Mindful of the destruction of their first citadel by the Tartars in 1241, the townsfolk surrounded themselves with walls and forty towers during the fifteenth century; built of brick, they were so mighty as to withstand the Turks, who dubbed Sibiu the "Red Town" for the colour of its walls and the blood shed in attempting to breach them. Alas for the Saxons, their citadels were no protection against the tide of history, which eroded their influence after the eighteenth century. Within the last five years almost the entire remnant of the Saxon community has left Romania.

To reach the centre from the main train and bus terminals, cross Piaţa Gării and follow Str Gen. Magheru until you hit the **Piaţa Mare**. Traditionally the hub of public life, it's surrounded by the premises of sixteenth- and seventeenth-century merchants, whose acumen and thrift were proverbial. On the north side, the **Councillors' Tower** contains Sibiu's **history museum** (May–Oct Tues–Sun 9am–5pm), no rival for the **Brukenthal Museum** (Tues–Sun 9am–6pm) on the opposite side. Besides the best of local silverware, pottery and furniture, the Brukenthal has an evocative collection of works by Transylvanian painters – romantic depictions of peasant life, crumbling castles and wild landscapes.

The Councillors' Tower forms a phalanx with a Catholic church, partly blocking access to the Piaţa Mică (Little Square). Just beyond on Piaţa Griviţei, the **Evangelical Cathedral** (Mon–Fri 9am–1pm) – a massive hall church raised during the fourteenth and fifteenth centuries – dominates its neighbours, confirming Sibiu's pre-eminence as a centre of the Lutheran faith, to which about 150,000 Transylvanians belong. The crypt contains the tomb of Mihnea the Bad, Dracula's son, who was stabbed to death outside in 1510.

Nearby, an alley sneaks off to join the **Passage of Stairs** behind the hill, which descends into the lower town overshadowed by arches and the medieval citadel wall. Piaţa 6 Martie – the Little Square's northern extension – bumps up against the old Town Hall, where an adjoining gate-tower leads through into **Str Iancu**, a street pockmarked with medieval windows, doorways and turrets. Just to the east, Str Ocnei runs down through a kind of miniature urban canyon spanned by the elegant wrought-iron **Liars' Bridge** – so called because of the legend that no one can tell a lie whilst standing upon it without the structure collapsing. Down in the rambling **lower town** is the octagonal-based **Tanners' Tower** (Str Pulberăriei), a tower from the now-demolished Ocna Gate. Also in the lower town, on Piaţa Cibin, there's a new and unusually thriving market, selling pottery, jewellery and food.

Sibiu's promenade takes place between Piaţa Mare and the Piaţa Unirii, mainly along **Str N. Bălcescu**. The town's militaristic architecture is exemplified by the **ramparts** and bastions along the length of Str Cetăţii to the southeast, where three mighty **towers** were once manned by the carpenters', potters' and crossbow-makers' guilds.

North of Str Bălcescu, on Str Mitropolei, you can't miss the **Orthodox Cathedral**, a twentieth-century copy of the Aya Sofia, embellished with all manner of neo-Byzantine flourishes and frescoes. It's worth visiting both the Evangelical and Orthodox churches during Sunday morning services to compare the different choral styles – but do so discreetly.

Practicalities

There's a rather hopeless **tourist office** (Mon–Fri 9am–5pm) inside *Hotel Bulevard* on Piaţa Unirii, but a more likely source of **private rooms** is *Exo*, in an alleyway behind 1 Str Nicolae Bălcescu, that will fix you up with Sibiu's suburban landladies for about $10 a head. Cheapest of the **hotels** is the new, privately-run *Podul Minciupilor*, 1 Str

Azilului (②), just beyond the Liars' Bridge, although it's no more than a converted house and soon fills up. Alternatives are uninspiring grey high-rise establishments like *Bulevard*, Piața Unirii (③); *Continental*, Calea Dumbravei (④); or the palatial *Împăratul Romanilor*, 2 Str Nicolae Bălcescu (⑤). There's a **campsite** in the forests to the south-west of town – it's at the end of the route of trolley bus #T-1 from the train station.

Places **to eat and drink** are clustered around the Piața Mare and Str Bălcescu. *Ceainăria Aroma* at 1 Str Nicolae Bălcescu serves tasty sandwiches and snacks as well as providing a bolt hole for daytime drinkers, while *Pâtisserie Eugen* on Str Avram Iancu has the best selection of pastries, cakes and ice cream. *La Turn*, on the corner of the Piața Mare and Str Avram Iancu, and the terrace of the *Hotel Bulevard*, are both popular outdoor beer drinking venues. Both the *Bulevard* and the *Continental* have **restaurants**, but are eclipsed by the sumptuous dining room of the *Hotel Împăratul*, where you can enjoy top-notch food and a rowdy floor show for about £5 a head.

Cluj

With its cupolas, Baroque outcroppings and weathered *fin-de-siècle* backstreets, down-town **CLUJ** looks like a Hungarian provincial capital – which in a sense it once was. In Hungary and (more circumspectly) within Transylvania itself, many people still regret the passing of Kolozsvár, fondly recalled as a city that embodied the Magyar *belle époque*. Modern Cluj has scores of factories and over 300,000 inhabitants, but the city has retained something of the languor and raffish undercurrent that characterized it in the olden days – not to mention cultural fixtures like its opera and university. Compared to other large Romanian towns, the restaurants and bars seem livelier, and the contents of *alimentarie* more varied.

The Town

Arriving in Cluj, take a trolleybus #3 or #4 from the train station to the centre, where the pivot of the town is the **Piața Unirii**. The square's centrepiece is the vast **St Michael's Church**, founded in the mid-fourteenth century, when the Catholic Magyar nobility ruled unchallenged over Cluj. Dwarfing the congregation in the bare nave, mighty pillars curve into vaulting like the roof of a forest. St Michael's Gothic phase of construction ended three years before the death of **Mátyás Corvinus**, whose formidable "Black Army" kept the Kingdom of Hungary safe from lawlessness and invasion for much of his reign (1458–90), and whose patronage brought the culture of Renaissance Italy to this region – an achievement for which his wife, Beatrix of Naples, should share the credit. Outside the church an imposing equestrian statue of the king accepts the homage of four dignitaries, with the crescent banner of the Turks trampled under hoof. Mátyás' birthplace was the small mansion at 6 Str Matei Corvin, up a side street leading off the square.

On the east side of the square, the **Art Museum** collection (Tues–Sun 10am–6pm) has icons, weaponry, carpets, a superbly carved sixteenth-century altar from Jimbov and paintings by Transylvanian artists. Many of the items were expropriated from Magyar aristocracy, in particular the Bánffy family, whose mansion this building once was.

Just to the north of the main square, at 2 Str Isac, the **History Museum of Transylvania** (Tues–Sun 9am–5pm), is largely given over to charting the progress from the Neolithic and Bronze Ages to the rise of the Dacian civilization, which peaked between the second century BC and the first AD. The **Dacii** were subdued by Roman legions, and the two races subsequently intermingled to form the ancestors of today's Romanians – or so the official version of Romanian history goes. An alternative theory, promulgated by those who insist on the Hungarian identity of this region, is that the Dacii died out completely, and that the Magyars took possession of a region that had no other legitimate claimants.

West of the square, at 21 Str Memorandumului, Cluj's **Ethnographic Museum** (Tues–Sun 9am–5pm) contains what is probably Romania's finest collection of carpets and folk costumes, demonstrating the country's various styles of weaving – from the dark herringbone patterns of the Pădureni region to the bold yellow, black and red stripes of Maramureş – and an even greater variety of clothing and headgear. While blouses and leggings might be predominantly black or white, women's apron-skirts and the waistcoats worn by both sexes for special occasions are brilliantly coloured. Peacock feathers serve as fans or plumes, and the love of complicated designs spills over onto cups and other everyday objects. Three neat wooden churches and other specimens of rural architecture have been assembled at the open-air **Village Museum** in a park in the northwest part of town, and a visit there will help to put the costumes in perspective.

The university quarter lies to the south of the square, with Str Universităţii heading southwards to **Babeş-Bolyai University**. Since its foundation in 1872 the university has produced scholars of the calibre of Edmund Bordeaux Székely, translator of the Dead Sea Scrolls, but also served as an instrument of cultural oppression. Long denied an education in their own language, the Romanians promptly proscribed teaching in Hungarian once they gained the upper hand in 1918. Hungarians nowadays account for about forty percent of Cluj's population, yet despite postwar reforms the provision for higher education in Hungarian is still a cause of grievance.

At the far end of Str Kogălniceanu, east of the university blocks, the restored **Tailors' Bastion** is an outcrop of the fortifications that once extended from the fifteenth-century **citadel**, which surrounds the *Belvedere Hotel* on the north of the river. Walk northwards from the bastion and you'll find yourself on an elongated square, in the southern half of which stands the neat yellow and white **Romanian National Theatre and Opera**, while the northern end is embellished with a huge and startling **Orthodox Cathedral**. Looking like a chunk of Constantinople, it was in fact founded during the 1920s, like many other grandiose structures raised to celebrate the Romanians' triumph in Transylvania, and the neo-Byzantine stone facade conceals a concrete structure. Inside, the frescoes bear the heavy-handedness characteristic of the 1950s, when Socialist Realism was the prescribed mode. From here, the direct route back to the centre is along Str Iuliu Maniu.

Practicalities

Neither the official *OJT* office west of the main square at 2 Str Şincai (Mon–Fri 8am–5pm) nor the independent *KMO* tourist office at Piaţa Unirii 10 (Mon–Fri 8am–8pm, Sat 10am–2pm) have much in the way of maps or info about private rooms as yet, but it may be worth calling in to ask. Cheapest of the **hotels** is *Pax*, opposite the railway station (③), but it's sleazy, cramped and soon fills up. Slightly better are the *Astoria*, 3 Str Horea (③), midway between the railway station and the centre, the *Uladeasa*, 20 Str Doja (③), and the *Melody* on Piaţa Unirii (③). Cheapest of the class I hotels is the relatively clean and quiet *Siesta*, 4 Str Şincai (④). There's a **campsite** in the Făget hills to the southeast – reached by bus #35 or #46 from behind the National Theatre.

Plenty of **eating and drinking** venues are clustered around Piaţa Unirii or the streets leading off it. The *Cofetăria Carpaţi* on the south side of the *piaţa* has the best cakes and coffee in town, while the *Someşul* on the east side has a plush restaurant inside. *P & P Ristorante* at 14 blvd Eroilor offers pizzas, while the *Gradina de Vara Boema* beer garden at 34 Str Iuliu Maniu features grills, and often a singer in the evenings. Traditional Transylvanian meats and stews can be sampled at *Humbertus*, 22 Str 22 Decembrie.

Several **student hang-outs** line Str Universităţii, including *Disco Bar Ciao*, a popular nighttime haunt. Gigs and discos also take place at the student cultural centre on Piaţa Păcii, at the western end of Str Napoca.

Sighişoara

A forbidding silhouette of battlements and needle spires looms over SIGHIŞOARA as the sun descends behind the hills of the Tîrnave Mare valley, and it seems fitting that this was the birthplace of Vlad Ţepeş – the man known to posterity as **Dracula**. Sighişoara makes the perfect introduction to Transylvania, especially as the *Pannonia*, *Orient* and *Balt-Orient* express trains stop here during daylight, enabling travellers to break the long journey between Budapest and Bucharest.

The road from the station to the centre passes close to the Romanian **Orthodox Cathedral**, its gleaming white, multifaceted facade a striking contrast to the dark interior, where blue and orange hues dominate the small panels of the iconostasis. Across the Tîrnave Mare river, the **Citadel** dominates the old town from a rocky massif whose slopes support a jumble of ancient, leaning houses, their windows sited to cover the steps leading up from **Piaţa Hermann Oberth** to the main gateway. Above the gateway rises the mighty **Clock Tower** where, at the stroke of midnight, a wooden figure emerges from the belfry to mark the change of day. The tower was founded in the fourteenth century when Sighişoara became a free town controlled by craft guilds – each of which had to finance the construction of a bastion and defend it during wartime – and rebuilt after earthquakes and fire in the 1670s. Sighişoara waxed rich on the proceeds of trade with Moldavia and Wallachia, as the regalia and strongboxes in the tower's **museum** attest (Tues–Sun 9am–3.30pm).

In 1431 or thereabouts, the child later known as **Dracula** was born in a two-storey house within the shadow of the clock tower at 6 Str Museului. At the time his father – Vlad Dracul – was commander of the mountain passes into Wallachia, but in 1436 he moved his family to the court at Tărgovişte. The younger Vlad's privileged childhood ended eight years later, when he and his brother Radu were sent to Anatolia as hostages for their father's good behaviour. There Vlad observed the Turks' use of terror, which he would later turn against them, earning the nickname of "The Impaler". Nowadays, Vlad's birthplace is a restaurant, although the next-door **museum of armaments** at no. 4 (Tues–Sun 10am–3.30pm) has a small *Dracula Exhibition*. A meagre display of pictures and texts in Romanian show the local ambivalence towards Sighişoara's most notorious son. The accent is on his patriotic anti-Turkish deeds, while his subsequent reputation for cruelty is portrayed as the invention of hostile Saxon propagandists.

Churches are monuments to social identity here, as in many old Transylvanian towns. The Germans raised one opposite the clock tower; its stark, whitewashed interior is hung with colourful carpets, as in the Black Church at Braşov. Their other church, the **Bergkirche** (Church on the Hill), is approached by an impressive **covered wooden stairway** which ascends steeply from the far end of Str Şcolii. Ivy-grown and massively buttressed, Bergkirche has a roomy interior that seems austere despite the blue and canary yellow vaulting. Some lovely stone tombs near the entrance are a harbinger of the **German cemetery**, a melancholy, weed-choked mass of graves spilling over the hill beside the ruined citadel walls – nine of whose fourteen **towers** survive.

The **lower town** is less appealing than the citadel, but there's a nice ambience around the shabby centre – consisting of Piaţa Hermann Oberth and Str 1 Decembrie – where townsfolk gather to consume grilled sausages and watery beer, conversing in Romanian, Magyar and antiquated German. *ONT* at 10 Str 1 Decembrie (Mon–Fri 8am–3pm, Sat 9am–1pm) has a stock of **private rooms** in the lower town for just under $10 per person per night, although they prefer it if you stay for three nights or more. Virtually next door is the town's only **hotel**, the *Steaua* (③).

The cafés and bars flanking Piaţa Hermann Oberth provide plenty of daytime **eating and drinking** venues. For more substantial fare, try the *Pizzeria Perla*, on the corner of Piaţa Hermann Oberth and Str 1 Decembri, the restaurant and beer cellar in Dracula's birthplace or the restaurant in the *Hotel Steaua*.

Braşov and around

With an eye for trade and invasion routes, the medieval Saxons sited their largest settlements within a day's journey of Transylvania's mountain passes. BRAŞOV, which they called Kronstadt, grew prosperous as a result, and for centuries the Saxons constituted an élite whose economic power long outlasted its feudal privileges. Postwar governments, wanting to create their "own" skilled working class, to this end brought thousands of Moldavian villagers to Braşov, where they were trained to work in the new factories and given modern housing during the 1960s. As a result, there are two parts to Braşov: the quasi-Gothic bit coiled beneath Mount Tîmpa and Mount Postăvaru, which looks great, and the surrounding sprawl of flats and factories, which doesn't. Old Braşov is worth at least a day's sightseeing, and the proximity of "Dracula's Castle" at Bran makes the city a must.

From the train station trolleybus #4 lurches down to central park, where you'll find a pretty useless ONT tourist office in the lobby of the exorbitant Hotel Aro Palace on Bulevard Eroilor. The boulevard meets the lowest point of the Str Republicii, the hub of Braşov's social life, with strollers dropping into the coffee houses or settling down to lengthy sessions with beer and sausages on the terrace of the Cerbul Carpatin. At the top of Str Republicii, sturdy buildings line the main square – the Piaţa Sfatului – as if on parade, presenting their shopfronts to the fifteenth-century council house, which has now been relegated to the role of History Museum (Tues–Sun 10am–5pm). As can be guessed from the exhibits, Braşov used to be dominated by Saxon guilds, whose main hang-out was the Merchants' Hall, built in the "Transylvanian Renaissance" style of the sixteenth century. Within sight of its terrace is the town's most famous landmark, the Black Church (Mon–Sat 9am–3.30pm), which stabs upwards like a series of daggers. An endearingly monstrous hall church that took almost a century to complete (1385–1477), the Biserica Neagră is so called for its soot-blackened walls, the result of a great fire that swept through Braşov in 1689. Inside, by contrast, the church is startlingly white, with Oriental carpets hung in splashes of colour along the walls of the nave.

When Turkish expansion became a threat in the fifteenth century, the inhabitants began to fortify Braşov, assigning the defence of each bastion or rampart to a particular guild. A length of fortress wall runs along the foot of Mount Tîmpa, beneath a maze of paths and a cable car running up to the summit. Of the original seven bastions the best-preserved is that of the weavers, on Str Coşbuc. This complex of wooden galleries and bolt holes now contains the Museum of the Bîrsa Land Fortifications (Tues–Sun 10am–4pm). Inside are models, pictures and weaponry recalling the bad old days when the surrounding region was repeatedly attacked by Tartars, Turks and, on a couple of occasions, by Dracula – who impaled hundreds of captives along the heights of St Jacob's Hill to terrorize the townsfolk.

Practicalities

Braşov is the kind of place where you're more than likely to be offered private rooms by those individuals hanging around the railway station. If you don't really fancy negotiating with freelancers, you should make your way to Exo, a room-letting agency at Str Postăvrului 6 (Mon–Fri 10am–2pm & 4–10pm, Sat 10am–2pm) who will do their best to fix you up. Cheapest and most basic of the hotels is the Aro Sport (③), behind the Aro Palace at 3 Str Sfîntul Ioan. More comfortable but pricy is the Hotel Postăvarul on Str Republicii (④).

The best campsite is Dîrste, out along the Bucharest road: take tram #101 to the Autocamioane factory from opposite the train station (or trolleybus #3 or #5 from the centre), then bus #17 until it turns off the Bucharest highway – the site is 500m along. This is the best campsite in the country, with permanent hot water – doubtless because of its previous popularity with Securitate campers. The *Hotel Postâvrul* has a good **restaurant**, while the central Piaţa Sfatului is awash with cafés and bars. The flashiest restaurant is the new *Orient* on the corner of Piaţa Sfatului and Str Republicii, serving excellent Chinese food. Next door is the *Casata*, dishing out good ice cream on its terrace, while the *Stradivari*, corner of Piaţa Sfatului and Str Mureşenilor serves good pizzas.

Dracula's Castle

The small town of **BRAN**, situated 28km from Braşov in the middle of the beautiful Bîrsa depression, is most conveniently reached by taking the bus that leaves at 11am from the terminal on Strada Avram Iancu, which in turn is best reached by trolleybus #5 from the centre. What's now billed as **Dracula's Castle** (Tues–Sun 10am–5pm) has only tenuous associations with Vlad the Impaler – it's quite likely that he attacked it during one of his raids – but the hyperbole is forgivable as Bran really does look like a vampire count's residence. The castle was built in 1377 to safeguard what used to be the main route into Wallachia until the opening of the Predeal Pass, and it rises in tiers of towers and ramparts from amongst the woods, against a glorious mountain background. A warren of spiral stairs, nooks and secret chambers overhangs the courtyard, filled with elaborately carved four-poster beds, throne-like chairs and portraits of grim-faced boyars. Despite its medieval aspect, most of the interior dates from a conversion job early this century, the work of a crazed old architect hired by Edinburgh-born Queen Marie of Romania. Marie called Bran a "pugnacious little fortress", but her alterations made it a rather welcoming abode, at odds with its forbidding exterior. The "restoration" work now in progress is making it even more suburban, with patio windows and buckets of white paint. In the grounds are some old peasant buildings and the **Museum of the Bran Pass**, displaying folk costumes, many of them from Marie's wardrobe. If you want a more authentically medieval experience, jump off the Braşov bus in the nearby village of Rîşnov, where the peasants' citadel on the hilltop at the edge of town has been restored with greater tact than the castle at Bran.

BUCHAREST

BUCHAREST (Bucureşti) is the least ingratiating of Europe's capitals. The parlous condition of Romania's economy is completely inescapable here: power cuts are still plunging Bucharest into semi-darkness, the water mains are still being turned off for hours on end, and the heating levels are reduced each winter, when the temperature can fall to minus 20°C. Parts of the city, especially around the train station, are awash with hustlers out to grab as many dollars as they can, while the lobbies of the fancier hotels are cruised by a range of low-life characters. Foreign visitors who aren't cocooned in the lap of a tour group usually find the city bewildering, if not horrendously frustrating.

What charm Bucharest possesses lies in its patchwork of different quarters, green with lime and horse chestnut trees. Much of the old city, however, was demolished on Ceauşescu's orders, to create a Civic Centre worthy of the "capital of the New Socialist Man". His megalomaniacal scheme, which required the demolition of around 9500 houses and some fifteen churches – the cathedral included – is undoubtedly the city's major sight, an extraordinary construction that is one of Europe's most potent political symbols. For the old atmosphere, you now need to wander towards the northern stretches of the Calea Victoriei and between Cişmigiu Gardens and the Gara de Nord, where discreet bourgeois households slowly give ground to the proletarians and the Gypsies, and life retains a village-like slowness and intimacy.

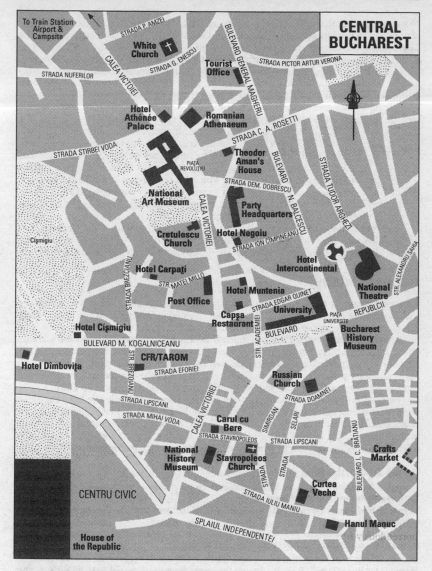

CENTRAL BUCHAREST

To Train Station Airport & Campsite

STRADA P. AMZEI

White Church

STRADA G. ENESCU

Tourist Office

STRADA NUFERILOR

CALEA VICTORIEI

BULEVARD GENERAL MAGHERU

STRADA PICTOR ARTUR VERONA

Hotel Athénée Palace

Romanian Athenaeum

STRADA C. A. ROSETTI

STRADA STIRBEI VODA

PIAȚA REVOLUȚIEI

Theodor Aman's House

BULEVARD N. BALCESCU

National Art Museum

STRADA DEM. DOBRESCU

Cișmigiu

Cretulescu Church

CALEA VICTORIEI

Party Headquarters

STRADA TUDOR ARGHEZI

Hotel Negoiu

STRADA ION CIMPINEANU

Hotel Carpați

STRADA BREZOIANU

STR. MATEI MILLO

Hotel Intercontinental

STR. ALEXANDRU SAHIA

Post Office

Hotel Muntenia

National Theatre

Hotel Cișmigiu

Capșa Restaurant

STRADA EDGAR QUINET

University

PIAȚA UNIVERSITE

REPUBLCII

BULEVARD M. KOGALNICEANU

STR. ACADEMIEI

BULEVARD

Bucharest History Museum

Hotel Dîmbovița

STR. BREZOIANU

CFR/TAROM

STRADA EFORIEI

Russian Church

STRADA LIPSCANI

CALEA VICTORIEI

STRADA DOAMNEI

STRADA MIHAI VODA

SIMIRDAN

SELARI

Carul cu Bere

STRADA STAVROPOLEOS

STRADA LIPSCANI

National History Museum

Stavropoleos Church

STRADA

STRADA

BULEVARD I. C. BRATIANU

Crafts Market

CENTRU CIVIC

STRADA IULIU MANIU

Curtea Veche

SPLAIUL INDEPENDENTEI

Hanul Manuc

House of the Republic

Arrival, information and transport

Passengers on **international flights**, which arrive at the **Otopeni Airport** will find that they face a highly variable wait for the *TAROM* coaches or taxis to carry them the 20km or so into the centre. Taxi drivers are completely unregulated, so you'll have to negotiate the fare, expecting to pay somewhere between $10 and $25. All the international and most of the domestic **train** services terminate at the hellish **Gara de**

Nord, a squalid hive with queues for everything. Be careful of pickpockets at the station and in the busier parts of the city, and steer well clear of the black marketeers. There's an *ONT* bureau at the Gara de Nord (Mon–Fri 7.30am–8pm, Sat 7.30am–3pm, Sun 7.30am–2pm), and a bigger tourist office at 7 blvd General Magheru (same times). The former is pretty useful for booking private rooms (see "Accommodation" below) and for buying the sporadically available maps, while the latter office seems to be more interested in changing money, renting cars and arranging "programmes".

Walking in this green city is no hardship, which is just as well. The **metro** system has three lines, of which the most useful are the east–west M1 line and the north–south M2, which serves the central squares. It operates from 5am until 11.30pm, with a flat fare of 100 lei per line. **Public transport** above ground is a-mess. Chronically overcrowded vehicles seem set to rattle themselves to pieces, and bus stops and timetables change with no warning. There are flat fares on all **trolleybuses** (50 lei), **buses** (40 lei) and **trams** (20 lei), which hit the streets around dawn and fade out by midnight. Except on green-liveried express buses, where one pays the driver, passengers cancel their own **tickets**, which are sold from street kiosks, open from 5am to 8pm. Always buy enough for a few journeys.

Hotel receptionists can phone for a cab if you don't want to walk to the Gara de Nord or the *Intercontinental* hotel, favourite spots for **taxis**. Drivers will occasionally ask for dollars, especially if they know you're new to the city, and all rates are negotiable.

Accommodation

Visitors' options for accommodation in Bucharest are pretty dire. The city is well served with crumbling pre-World War II **hotels**, but the majority of them are to some extent run-down and overpriced – although competition between them prevents rates from becoming too outrageous. Plenty of class II hotels are clustered around the Gara de Nord. Although exceptionally grotty by west European standards, they're conveniently sited for getting settled in and away again quickly, and are within striking distance of the parks and leafy suburbs of northern Bucharest. Hotels in the downtown area are by and large more expensive, but offer slightly higher standards of cleanliness in return.

The *ONT* in the Gara de Nord provides **private rooms** either in the town centre or the suburbs, depending on your preferences. Doubles cost around $20, and single travellers should expect to pay the full amount. If you're offered rooms unofficially by touts at the station, you'll basically have to trust your instinct. If you're tempted to take the offer, be sure to find out exactly where the house is; expect to pay around $10 per night.

Hotels around the Gara de Nord

Bucegi, 2 Str Witing (☎37 50 30; ②). Immediately on your right as you leave the Gara de Nord. Bucharest at its most cheap and basic.

Cerna, 29 blvd Dinicu Golescu (☎37 40 87; ②). Across the road from the Bucegi, relatively clean but with brusque staff.

Dunărea, 140 Calea Griviței (☎17 32 20; ③). Art Deco hotel opposite the train station, with some pleasant rooms and friendly, English-speaking management.

Grivița, 130 Calea Griviței (☎50 23 27; ③). Elegant old building with shady clients and rude staff.

Marna, 3 Str Buzești (☎50 26 75; ③). Around the corner from the Calea Griviței, and likely to have vacancies if places nearer the station are full. Gloomy and tatty.

Hotels in the town centre

Carpați, 16 Str Matei Millo (☎15 76 90; ④). Recently renovated and comparatively clean. A couple of blocks away from the main Calea Victoriei.

Dinbovița, 6 Str Schitu Măgureanu (☎15 62 44; ④). Within a few minutes of both Ceaușescu's palace and the Cișmigiu Gardens. Small and grubby.

Hanul Manuc, 62–64 Str Iuliu Maniu (☎13 14 15; ⑥). A good choice if you want to treat yourself to a category I hotel. Rooms overlook the galleried courtyard of an old inn, situated in the Lipscani quarter – central Bucharest's most picturesque.

Muntenia, 21 Str Academiei (☎14 60 10; ④). Comparatively modern, clean and comfortable. A good place to base yourself if sticking around for a while.

Negoiu, 16 Str Ion Câmpineanu (☎15 52 50; ③). Although its turn-of-the-century decor has considerably faded, the Negoiu has some of the cheapest rooms in the centre. Just off the Calea Victoriei.

Campsite

Bǎneasa. Situated out towards Otopeni Airport – take trolleybus #81, tram #33 or bus #131 or #134 from the Gara de Nord to Piața Presei Libre, then bus #148 (#149 on Sun). Ludicrously overpriced – $20 for a chalet that's like a garden shed. Tents have to be pitched on pebbles.

The City

"A savage hotch-potch" was Ferdinand Lasalle's verdict on Bucharest between the wars, with its nightlife and boulevards, its slums and beggars, its aristocratic mansions and crumbling Orthodox churches. The extremes of wealth and poverty have been mitigated, but otherwise the city has retained many of its old characteristics. Woodlands and a girdle of **lakes** freshen its northern outskirts, beyond a triumphal arch and a tree-lined avenue extending from Bucharest's main thoroughfare, the **Calea Victoriei.** The majority of inner-city sights are within walking distance of the Calea; unless stated otherwise, museum **opening hours** are 9am to 5pm or 10am to 6pm from Tuesday to Sunday – but bear in mind that random changes are common.

The **Calea Victoriei** (Street of Victory) is a place of vivid contrasts. At its verdant northern end near the Piața Victoriei, it has touches of *ancien régime* elegance, but a change occurs near the **Ceramics and Glass Museum** at no. 107, beyond which the street becomes an eclectic jumble of apartment blocks, glass and steel facades and cake shops. The splendidly furnished museum contains pieces from the pre-Christian era, Romanian work from Cluj and Bistrița, plus Turkish and Iranian tiles, European, Japanese and Chinese porcelain, and lovely Art Deco pieces.

Fulcrum of the Calea is the large **Piața Revoluței,** created during the 1930s on Carol II's orders to ensure a field of fire around his new **Royal Palace** on the western side of the square. The northern wing of the palace now contains the **National Art Museum,** which is entered from Str Știrbei Vodă. Beginning with a splendid Transylvanian diptych, the collection works through halls of embroidered boyars' garments and iconostases to the exhibition of paintings upstairs, where Nicolae Grigorescu (1838–1907) gets star billing for his dark portraits and impressionistic landscapes. The top floor features Oriental carpets, Chinese and Dutch porcelain, French furniture and tapestries, and minor works by Rembrandt, Cranach, the Bruegels, Renoir and others.

North of the palace, the contemporaneous **Athénée Palace Hotel** has always been a hive of intrigue, but was refurbished as a hotel and an "intelligence factory" in the 1950s, with bugged rooms, tapped phones and informers everywhere. The tawdrily plush interior has an expensive nightclub with a sub-*Folies Bérgères* troupe, and like all top-range hotels it's overrun with hookers. In the centre of the Piața stands the forlorn, burnt-out shell of the **University Library,** allegedly torched by the Securitate in the confused days which followed the 1989 revolution. The long white colonnaded building just to the south is the **Communist Central Party Committee** headquarters, from where Ceaușescu addressed the populace for last time on December 21, 1989. Eight minutes into his speech the booing started, and moments later the TV screens went blank, an unambiguous sign that it was all over for Nicolae. He just managed to escape from the building the following morning, lifted from the roof in a helicopter so overloaded that a few lackeys were jettisoned to get the thing into the air.

Close by, the battered eighteenth-century **Crețulescu Church** fronts a tangle of streets wending west towards **Cișmigiu Gardens**, Bucharest's oldest park. The gardens originally belonged to a Turkish water inspector, and fittingly contain a serpentine lake upon which small rowing boats glide, hired by couples seeking solitude amongst the weeping willows. The residential area between Cișmigiu and the Gara de Nord has a real urban-village character, devout women genuflecting as they pass tiny street-corner churches while neighbours gossip outside the dimly lit workshops.

Beyond the Crețulescu church the Calea continues southwards past the burned-out multistorey ex-headquarters of the police; when it was stormed in July 1990 the government responded by calling in the miners to restore order. Many people think the siege was a put-up job to provide a pretext for intervention. Directly opposite is the elegant **Pasajul Villacros** arcade, one of the few remnants of the Bucharest that used to be known as the "Paris of the Balkans". Beyond the junction with Bulevard M. Kogălniceanu, Bucharest's main east–west boulevard, the Calea crosses **Stradă Lipscani**, a shabby, shifty marketplace where you can probably buy anything if you know the people to ask. Nearing the river, the **National History Museum** looms up at no. 15 – the place to see some fine treasures. A downstairs vault holds gold and silverware left by Romania's pre-Christian inhabitants, the Dacians. Look out in particular for the fourth century BC "golden helmut of Coțofenești", an ornate piece of headgear decorated with horsemen figures hunting mythical beasts. Nearby, a vast hall contains life-size copies of the friezes surrounding Trajan's column in Rome – a self-conscious demonstration of Romania's Latin roots.

To the east of here stands the small **Stavropoleos Church**; built in the 1720s, it has gorgeous, almost arabesque, mouldings and patterns decorating its facade, and a columned portico carved with delicate tracery. To the south of the church, a maze of streets and pleasantly decrepit houses surrounds the historical centre of Bucharest, where Vlad the Impaler built a citadel in the fifteenth century. The remains of the **Curtea Veche** (Old Court) are pretty modest: a few rooms, arches and shattered columns, and a cellar containing a **museum** where the skulls of boyars whom Dracula had decapitated are lovingly displayed (Tues–Sun 9am–5pm).

A few doors along from the antiquarian bookshop opposite the Curtea Veche, an austere white building with barred windows conceals Bucharest's most famous establishment, **Manuc's Inn** – *Hanul Manuc*. Originally a caravanserai founded by a wealthy Armenian, the building contains a restaurant and wine cellar, and admits sightseers to its elegant courtyard (daily 9–11am & 5–7pm). The inn's southern wall forms one side of the **Piața Unirii**, or Square of Union, the site of a large market where all kinds of Romanians congregate, including the capital's Gypsy flower-sellers and hawkers.

Heading northwards up along the **Bulevard Anul 1848**, you'll see the **Hotel Intercontinental** towering above the **Piața Universitații**, a nexus for city life and traffic. This is where the students pitched their post-revolution City of Peace, an encampment broken up by the miners in September 1990. When the miners returned to Bucharest in 1991, this time in protest against the government rather than as its stormtroopers, they camped out here before being rooted out by the police with the same violence they had earlier dispensed.

Just to the east rises the new **National Theatre**, a pet project of Elena Ceaușescu's, resembling an Islamicized reworking of the Colosseum. Further to the west, **Bucharest University** occupies the first block on the Bulevard Republicii, its forecourt thronged with students and snack stands, whilst statues of illustrious pedagogues and statesmen gaze blindly at the crowds. The small, bulbous domes of the **Russian Church** appear through a gap in the domed buildings lining the southern side of the boulevard. Faced with yellow brick, Art Nouveau green tiling and pixie-faced nymphs, the church has a small interior, with frescoes so blackened with age and smoke that only the saintly haloes glow like golden horseshoes around Christ.

Between 1984 and 1989 acres of Bucharest – including thousands of houses and dozens of historic monuments – were demolished to create the **Centru Civic**, intended to comprise scores of tower blocks lining a six-lane, quarter-mile-long **Victory of Socialism Boulevard** – now Bulevard Unirii. At the lower end, a circle of fifty fountains awaits sufficient water pressure, while at the other, ministries and high functionaries' apartments are to be relocated within the vast **House of the Republic**, allegedly the most capacious single building in the world. A workforce of 12,000 laboured on it around the clock from 1984, hundreds dying as work continued through lethal winters. Having some 7000 rooms, with eight subterranean levels, it's linked to a network of tunnels connecting army bases and ministerial buildings. Briefly opened to the press in the immediate aftermath of the revolution, it's now back in government use. The politicos occupy marble-clad blocks near the House of the Republic, but some of the farther-flung apartments – jerry-built skeletons awaiting the pseudo-classical dressing – have been squatted by people whose homes were razed to make room for the Centru Civic.

The northern suburbs

The **Şoseaua Kiseleff**, a long avenue lined with lime trees extending northwards from the Piaţa Victoriei, is a manifestation of the Francophilia that swept Romania's educated classes during the nineteenth century, and has a triumphal arch halfway along to rub the comparison home. Ignored by hooting traffic, the **Arc de Triumpf** was originally a jerry-built structure raised to commemorate Romania's intervention on the side of the Anglo-French *entente* during World War I, but in 1935 was rebuilt in stone along the lines of the Arc de Triomphe in Paris. Beyond, trees screen the **Village Museum** adjoining Lake Herăstrău, the largest of a dozen lakes which form a continuous line across the northern suburbs. Established in 1936, this fascinating ensemble of nearly three hundred peasant houses and other structures from every region of Romania shows the extreme diversity of folk architecture: oaken houses from Maramureş with their "rope motif" carvings and shingled roofing; gateways carved with suns, moons, the Tree of Life, Adam and Eve, animals and hunting scenes; dug-out homes from Drăghiceni, with vegetables growing on the roof; and windmills from Tulcea in the Delta.

Despite a new name, hackneyed propaganda still emanates from the immense **Casa Presei Libere**, overlooking the Şoseaua's junction with Băneasa highway. The plinth of the now removed nineteen-ton statue of Lenin stands outside, daubed in slogans and draped in wreaths, while to the west you'll see the domed Exposition Pavilion, built for Bucharest's annual International Trade Fair but normally used to hold rallies.

Further out along the Şos Băneasa stand the **Museum of Popular Art** and the **Feudal Arts Museum**, a pair of villas built to hold the collection of one Dr Minovici, a successful engineer. The large, dark rooms of the Popular Art Museum contain woven blankets, Transylvanian pottery, spinning wheels, musical instruments, furniture and beautiful peasant garments. The other building is a bizarre fusion of Tudor, Italian Renaissance and fortress architecture, filled with hunting trophies and weapons, Flemish tapestries, Florentine furniture, and German and Swiss stained glass.

Eating

Hamburger bars and hot dog stalls are beginning to dominate the **snack food** scene, although you can still find places serving more traditional fast food – grilled meats and pastries – around bulevard M. Kogălniceanu and Str Lipscani.

The capital's **restaurants** are pricy but not exorbitant. There's a wider choice of traditional Romanian dishes than elsewhere in the country, and many older establishments have opulent turn-of-the-century interiors. At the height of summer people tend to favour the open-air restaurants in Bucharest's many parks. Most restaurants treat diners to music or cabaret-style entertainment: expect to pay a small cover charge for this.

Bucur, Str Apolidor 7. An old mansion on the edge of the Centru Civic. Slightly more down to earth than other city centre places.
Capşa, Str Edgar Quinet 4. Most elegant and expensive of Bucharest's restaurants.
Caru cu Bere, Str Stavropoleos 5. Literally the "beer cart", known for its neo-Gothic interior.
Doina, Şoseaua Kiseleff 4. Traditional Romanian cuisine, situated under the trees of Kiseleff Park.
Hanul Manuc, Str Iuliu Maniu 62. In the historic surroundings of an old coaching inn: a favourite venue for Godfatherish banquets.
Monte Carlo, Cişmigiu Gardens. Occupying a terrace overlooking the boating lake, although you may be less than titillated by the "sexy show" to which evening diners are treated.
Pescarus, Herastrau Park. Restaurant with fish specialities in the city's northernmost park.
Pizzeria Julia, bul Nicolae Titulescu 40. Between the Gara de Nord and Piaţa Victoriei. A wide choice of authentic pizzas, although one wonders what inspired the fiery *pizza serbeasca* ("Serbian pizza").
Spring Time, corner of Nicolae Titulescu and Piaţa Victoriei. Popular fast food restaurant serving burgers, chips and, for the really homesick – HP sauce.

Drinking and nightlife

For daytime **drinking**, folks congregate in the pavement cafés and *cofetării* of central Bucharest, although these tend to be quite expensive. The courtyard of *Hanul Manuc*, Iuliu Maniu 62, is as good an outdoor drinking venue as any; the *Cafenarea Veche*, corner of Str Sepcari and Str Covaci, has a relaxing central-European-coffee-house ambience, while the café in the *Athenée Palace Hotel*, on the corner of Str Episcopiei and Calea Victoriei, is noted for its ice cream.

Downtown **bars** tend to be very tacky, often featuring electronic slot machines and on-stage strippers. Locals tend to drink in restaurants or in small neighbourhood bars in the suburbs; if you're renting a room outside central Bucharest you're sure to find a convivial drinking hole somewhere on your block. One good local bar is the *Şarpeltu Roşu*, east of the Piaţa Română on the corner of bulevard Dacia and Str Icoanei, which serves good food from the surrounding countryside.

Bucharest's **nightlife** is hardly scintillating; the *Students' Club* at Calea Plevnei 61 has occasional discos and is the place to ask about other events at the university, while *Disco Vox Maris*, bul Mihail Kogălniceanu 2, is the best of the flashy new downtown clubs.

Listings

Airlines *Aeroflot*, 35 Nicolae Bălcescu (☎14 89 72); *Air France*, 35 Nicolae Bălcescu (☎14 13 41); *Lufthansa*, 18 Gheorghe Magheru (☎50 67 66); *Swissair*, 18 Gheorge Magheru (☎50 74 30); *TAROM*, 10 Str Ion Brezoianu (☎15 04 99) and 14 Str D.I. Mendeleev (☎59 41 25).

Car rental See *ONT* at 7 B-dul Magheru or in the de luxe hotels.

Embassies and consulates *Great Britain*, 24 Str Jules Michelet (☎12 03 03); *Canada*, 36 Str Nicolae Iorga (☎50 61 40); *Netherlands*, Str Atena 18 (☎63 32 292); *USA*, 7–9 Str Tudor Arghezi (☎12 40 40). *Australia* and *New Zealand* handled by the British Embassy.

Hospitals The *Clinica Batiştei* at 28 Str Arghezi (☎49 70 30), behind the *Intercontinental*, and the *Spitalul Clinic Municipal* at 169 Splaiul Independenţei are both used to dealing with foreigners, but for emergency treatment you should go to the *Spitalul Clinic de Urgenţa* at 8 Calea Floreasca. Your embassy can recommend doctors speaking foreign languages.

Pharmacies 24-hour pharmacy at 18–20 B-dul Magheru and 345 B-dul 1 Mai.

Post office Main office at 10 Str Matei Millo (daily 7am–midnight).

Train tickets If you don't fancy queuing at the station, go to the *Agenţie CFR* at 10 Str Ion Brezoianu (Mon–Fri 7.30am–7pm, Sat 7.30am–noon) and 139 Calea Griviţei (same hours), where you should book at least 24 hours in advance, being sure to get a seat reservation. For tickets to destinations abroad, expect to be asked to pay in hard currency.

travel details

Trains

Bucharest to: Braşov (14 daily; 2hr 45min–3hr 45min); Cluj (1 daily; 7hr); Timişoara (2 daily; 8hr).

Braşov to: Bucharest (14 daily; 2hr 45min–3hr 45min); Cluj (5 daily; 4hr 45min); Sibiu (4 daily; 1hr 45min–3hr 30min).

Cluj to: Braşov (5 daily; 4hr 45min); Bucharest (1 daily; 7hr); Sighişoara (5 daily; 3hr–4hr 30min).

Sighişoara to: Cluj (5 daily; 3hr–4hr 30min).

Timişoara to: Bucharest (2 daily; 8hr).

CHAPTER 20

SLOVENIA

Introduction

The initial impression for many visitors arriving from western Europe, is that **Slovenia** – formerly the northernmost and wealthiest republic of what was once Yugoslavia – seems especially distinct from Croatia and Hungary on its borders; indeed both historically and culturally, the Slovenes for years saw themselves as a people somehow apart from much of the rest of the former Yugoslavia. For centuries, while much of the region was under Turkish control, what now comprises Slovenia was a separate feudal state administered by Austrian and German overlords, which was eventually to become part of the Austro-Hungarian Empire. The Slovenes absorbed the culture of their captors during this period while managing to retain a strong sense of ethnic identity through the Slav-rooted Slovene language, although this is to this day somewhat different from Serbo-Croat. Economically and industrially, too, Slovenia was always streets ahead of the rest of Yugoslavia, able to offer higher wages, with lower levels of unemployment and a more westernized lifestyle; it's a distinction which, with the break-up of the country, has only grown: the shops are well stocked throughout the country and tourist facilities are developing; and since it has achieved true independence Slovenia has been increasingly keen to pull away from its Slav neighbours towards Austria and even towards potential membership of the European Community, though the loss of a captive economic hinterland in Yugoslavia for the electrical and technical goods it manufactures has caused problems.

On a more superficial level, the landscape is as varied as it is beautiful: along the Austrian border the **Julian Alps** provide stunning mountain scenery, most accessibly at lake **Bled** and lake **Bohinj**; further to the south, the brittle karst scenery is riddled with spectacular caves like those at **Postojna**. Slovenia's capital **Ljubljana** is easily the best of the cities, a vital, youthful place, manageably small, and cluttered with Baroque and Hapsburg buildings, while the short stretch of Slovenia **coast**, along the northern edge of the Istrian peninsula, is punctuated by a couple of towns that were among the most attractive resorts of the former Yugoslavia – **Piran** and **Portorož** – not to mention the port of **Koper**, with its appealingly ancient centre.

Information and Maps

The larger towns and well-touristed places usually have a **tourist information centre** run by the local authority and doling out information and local maps, and usually acting as an agency for private rooms (see below). Elsewhere, travel agencies (*Globtour*, *Alpetour*, *Generaltourist*, *Slovenijaturist* and *Kompas* are the biggest selling chains) can be a useful source of information, although they understandably concentrate on selling you tours and changing your money.

There's a good new 1:300,000 **map** of Slovenia published by *Freytag & Berndt*, otherwise, plenty of old maps of the former Yugoslavia are still sold. Excellent small-scale hiking maps are published by the Slovene Alpine Association (*Planinska zveza Slovenije*) and are widely available in bookshops once in Slovenia itself, or from *Stanfords* at 12–14 Long Acre, London WC2 before you travel.

Money and Banks

Slovenia's unit of **currency** is the *tolar*, which is divided into 100 (virtually worthless) *stotini*. Coins come in denominations of 50 stotini, 1, 2 and 5 tolars; and there are notes of 10, 20, 50, 100, 200, 500, 1000 and 5000 tolars. Prices are usually preceded by the initials *SLT*.

Banks (*banka*) are generally open Monday to Friday 7am–6pm and Saturday 7am–11pm, and at least one bank in each major centre will be open for a few hours on Sunday morning. Money can also be changed in tourist offices, travel agencies and exchange bureaux (*menjalnica*), all of which have more flexible hours. Travellers' cheques and credit cards are widely accepted; and you can use credit cards to get cash advances in the bigger banks.

Inflation is an ever-present problem here, so much so that the locals often quote prices of more important goods and services in a more stable currency ie the Deutschmark – even though payment is still made in tolars.

Communications

Most **post offices** (*pošta* or *PTT*) are open Mon–Fri 8am–6pm and Sat 8am–1pm. In big towns and resorts, some offices are open for a few hours on Sunday too. Stamps (*marke*) can also be bought at newsstands.

Public call boxes use tokens (*žetoni*), or magnetic cards (*telekartice*) which you can pick up from post offices or newspaper kiosks. When making long distance and international calls it's usually easier to go to the post office, where you're assigned to a cabin and given the bill afterwards.

Getting Around

Traversing Slovenia by any kind of public transport is easy, cheap and usually very scenic. Generally speaking, trains provide the fastest means of travelling on the main routes linking the capital with Maribor and Koper, or with Austria and Italy. Everywhere else, buses are far more convenient.

■ Trains and buses

Slovene railways (*Slovenske železnice*) seem to have done well out of Yugoslavia's break-up, inheriting the best carriages and engines, and they run a smooth and efficient service.

Trains (*vlaki*) are divided into *potniski* (slow ones which stop at every conceivable halt) and *IC* (inter-city trains which are faster and slightly more expensive). Some of the latter, colloquially known as *zeleni vlaki* (green trains), are designated on timetable by the initials *ICZV*, and are express services on which prior seat reservations (*rezervacije*) are obligatory. Timetable leaflets (*vozni red*) are sometimes available, otherwise you'll have to decipher the boards displayed on station platforms – *odhodi* are departures, *prihodi* arrivals. Both *Eurail* and *InterRail* are valid for Slovenia.

Slovenia's **bus** network consists of a confusing array of small local companies, but their services are well co-ordinated. Big towns such as Ljubljana, Maribor and Koper have big bus stations with computerized booking facilities where you can buy your tickets hours (if not days) in advance – recommended if you're travelling between Ljubljana and the coast at the height of summer. Elsewhere, simply pile onto the bus and pay the driver or his mate. You'll be charged extra for cumbersome items of baggage, which must be stored in the hold.

■ Driving, hitching and cycling

The road system is both comprehensive and of reasonable quality. Stretches of the main Ljubljana–Postojna, Ljubljana–Maribor and Ljubljana–Jesenice routes are classed as motorways (*autoceste*) and parts of them converted to dual carriageway (tolls are levied on these routes); elsewhere main roads soon get clogged up with summer traffic. Speed limits on Slovene roads are 60kph in built-up areas, 80kph on normal roads, 100kph on highways and 120kph on motorways. If you break down, the Slovene Automobile Club (*AMZS*) has a 24-hr emergency service (☎987). **Car rental** charges are about £40 a day for a Renault or Golf-type car with unlimited mileage.

Hitching is pretty common on the main Ljubljana–Maribor and Ljubljana–Koper routes, although you should be prepared to wait a long time for a lift, and remember that hitching is forbidden on anything classified as a motorway (recognizable by the green road signs). Elsewhere in the country, prospects for hitching are fairly bad.

Accommodation

Slovenia always was the most developed corner of former Yugoslavia, and had prices to match. Consequently, while tourist accommodation is universally clean and good quality, it doesn't come much cheaper than in neighbouring Italy or Austria.

ACCOMMODATION PRICE CODES

Throughout this guide, accommodation is priced on a scale of ① to ⑧, the number indicating the lowest price per night a single person could expect to pay in that establishment in high season. With hostels this is the nightly rate per person; with hotels, the price is arrived at by dividing the cost of the cheapest double room by two. The prices indicated by the codes are as follows

① = under £5 / $8   ② = £5–10 / $8–16   ③ = £10–15 / $16–24   ④ = £15–20 / $24–32

⑤ = £20–25 / $32–40   ⑥ = £25–30 / $40–48   ⑦ = £30–35 / $48–56   ⑧ = over £35 / $56

■ Hotels, guesthouses and private rooms

Apart from a couple of atmospheric turn-of-the-century establishments in Ljubljana, **hotels** in Slovene towns tend to be multi-storey concrete affairs built since World War II, providing the expected modern comforts but offering little in the way of character. Slovene hotels are classified by letter: generally speaking, C-class hotels tend to have rooms with shared bath or shower, B-class hotels have rooms with en-suite bathrooms, A-class hotels are business class and L-class are in the international luxury league. Expect to pay £25 a double upwards for C-class hotels, £35 a double upwards for B-class. The encouragement of private enterprise in recent years has seen a growth in the number of traditional family-run guesthouses (usually called *gostilne*, or inns, although beware that the term *gostilna* also applies to any small rural restaurant or bar whether it offers rooms or not). Some *gostilne* are slightly cheaper than hotels and certainly less impersonal, although they tend to be found well away from city centres and are therefore hard to find unless you have your own transport.

Private rooms (*zasebne sobe*) are available throughout Slovenia, with bookings administered by tourist information centres in places like Ljubljana and Maribor, or by travel agents like *Slovenijatourist* or *Kompas* elsewhere. Although private rooms initially look like excellent value at about £12–15 a double, bear in mind that some agents charge a booking fee of up to £10, and that stays of 3 nights or under are invariably subject to a 50 percent surcharge. Some tourist offices advertise private rooms in rural areas under the name *kmečki turizem* (village tourism), where for a similar price you get to stay with a local family in a farmhouse.

■ Hostels and campsites

There's no big network of **youth hostels** in Slovenia, but the prevalence of **student accommodation** provides a good alternative. In Ljubljana and Maribor rooms in student halls of residence (*dijaški dom*) are let out cheap to travellers during the summer vacation – usually mid-July to the end of August. Ask the local tourist information centre about vacancies, and expect to pay about £5–8 per person per night.

Campsites are plentiful in the mountains and on the coast, and are on the whole large-scale well-organized affairs with plentiful facilities, restaurants and shops. Two people travelling with a tent can expect to pay £8–10; add another £1–2 for a vehicle. Camping rough without permission is punishable by a spot fine.

Serious hikers planning an assault on the peaks of Slovenia's Julian Alps can make use of **mountain huts** (*planinske koče*). The ones on the way up Mount Tirglav are little less than hotels; elsewhere they are much more basic. Book in advance or arrive early.

Food and Drink

Slovene cuisine is very varied, occupying as it does the meeting point between German and Italian infulences from the north and west, and Balkan influence from the south. There's a native Slovene tradition, too, based on age-old peasant receipes, although this is gradually losing out as restaurants and cafés become increasingly internationalized.

■ Food

Slovenia's well-stocked supermarkets and *delikatesa* are good places to stock up on sandwich and picnic ingredients, like local cheese (*sir*) and salami (*salama*); buy fresh fruit and vegetable (*sadje in zelenjava*) from outdoor markets or roadside stalls. A *pekarna* (bakery) is the place to buy *kruh* (bread).

For breakfasts and quick snacks, *okrepčevalnice* (snack bars) and street kiosks dole out *burek*, a flaky pastry filled with cheese (*sa sirom*) or meat (*sa mesom*), or *klobase* (sausage). The latter come in various forms, most commonly hot dogs, *hrenovke* (Slovene frankfurters), or *kranjska klobasa* (big spicy sausages of local provenance).

Menus in a Slovene *restavracija* (restaurant) or *gostilna* (inn) are dominated by grilled meats and schnitzel-type dishes in which pork (*svijina*) and veal (*teletina*) predominate, although the frequency of items like *jetra* (liver) and *možgani* (grilled or fried brains) reveals a typically Slovene unsqueamishness when it comes to offal. *Golaž* or goulasch is a popular main course dish found almost everywhere; *segedin* is goulasch with lashings of sauerkraut. Two traditional Slovene dishes are *zlikrofi*, ravioli filled with potato, onion and bacon; and *žganci*, once the staple diet of rural Slovenes, a buckwheat porridge sprinkled with port crackling. On the coast you'll find plenty of *riba* (fish), *školjke* (mussels) and *kalamari* (squid). Italian pasta dishes appear on most restaurant menus, and no Slovene high street is without at least one pizzeria.

Typical desserts include several solid central European favourites: strudel, filled with apple or rhubarb; *štruklji*, dumplings with fruit filling; *potica*, a doughy roll filled with nuts and honey; and *pohorska gibanica*, a delicious local cheese-cake-type dish. *Sladoled* (ice cream) is consumed with relish everywhere.

■ Drink

Daytime drinking takes place in small café-bars, or in a *kavarna*, Slovenia's version of the central European coffee house, where a range of cakes, pastries and ice cream are usually on offer. Coffee (*kava*) is usually served black unless specified otherwise – *mleko* is milk, *šlag* means cream – and often drunk alongside a glass of mineral water (*mineralna voda*). *Čaj sa limono* or lemon tea is increasingly popular. Familiar brands of non-alcoholic drinks (*brezalkoholne pijace*) such as Coca Cola, Pepsi and Sprite are all fairly ubiquitous.

Evening drinking centres on small European-style bars or the more traditional *pivnica* (beer hall) or *vinarna* (wine cellar). Slovene beer (*pivo*) is of the central European Pilsneresque variety and is usually excellent. In Ljubljana look out for *črni baron*, a dark Guinness-like stout made by the local *Union* brewery; elsewhere in Slovenia, the lighter *Laško Zlatorog* is regarded as the best. The local wine (*vino*) is either *črno* (red) or *belo* (white) and has an international reputation: dry whites like *Laški rizling* and *Ljutomer* are regu-

larly found on western supermarket shelves; the less common and more refined *Sipon* and *Halozan* are well worth seeking out while you're here. Favourite aperitifs include the fiery *sadjevec*, a brandy made from various fermented fruits, and the gin-like juniper-based *brinovec*.

Opening Hours and Holidays

Most **shops** open Monday to Friday 9am–6pm and Saturday 9am–1pm. **Museum** times differ from place to place, but they're usually closed on Mondays.

All shops and banks will be closed on the following **public holidays**: January 1 and 2; Easter Monday; April 27 (Resistance Day); May 1, June 25 (Day of Slovene Statehood); August 15 (Assumption); and December 25.

Emergencies

Slovenia's crime rate is low and you're unlikely to have much contact with Slovene **police** (*policija*); if you do, they're generally easy-going and helpful, but unlikely to speak English. As far as health is concerned, citizens of the UK are entitled to free health care. **Pharmacies** (*lekarna*) tend to follow normal shopping hours, and a rota system covers night-time and weekend opening; details are posted in the window of each pharmacy.

EMERGENCY NUMBERS
Police ☎92; Ambulance ☎94; Fire ☎93.

LJUBLJANA AND AROUND

LJUBLJANA curls under its castle-topped hill, an old centre marooned in the shapeless modernity that stretches out across the plain, a vital and self-consciously growing capital of Slovenia. At first glance it seems Austrian, a few strands of Vienna pulled out of place, typically exuberant and refined; but really Ljubljana is Slovenian through and through, outside influences absorbed and tinkered with over the years. The city's sights are only part of the picture; first and foremost Ljubljana is a place to meet people, to get involved in the nightlife; the buildings just provide the backdrop.

The Ljubljana area telephone code is ☎061.

Arrival, information and city transport

Your likely point of arrival (and drop-off point for buses from Brnik airport), is the main **train and bus station**, ten minutes' walk to the north and east of Slovenska Cesta on Trg Osvobodilne Fronte. In the train station there's an **information office** run by *Slovenijaturist* (daily 6am–10pm), only good for getting a town plan, changing money or buying international rail tickets. Far better to head straight for the **Tourist Information Centre** (TIC) at Slovenska Cesta 35 (April–Sept Mon–Fri 8am–9pm, Sat & Sun 8am–noon & 5–9pm; Oct–March Mon–Fri 8am–7pm, Sat & Sun 8am–noon & 4–7pm; ☎224-222 or ☎215-412), a short #2 or #9 bus ride or fifteen-minute walk away. Ljubljana's **buses** are cheap, frequent and usually overcrowded. Payment is by thrusting a wad of notes into a box next to the driver (the price of a flat fare is constantly rising but clearly marked), or by using slightly cheaper **tokens** (*žetoni*) available from most kiosks.

Accommodation

The TIC can provide **private rooms** for $10–15 a double, though these tend to be in high-rise estates well out of the centre of town; a much better option, from the beginning of July to the end of August, is to utilize rooms in **student hostels**, where a bed can cost as little as £5 a night. The main venue for these is usually the *Studentsko Naselje* (Student Village) at Cesta 27 Aprila 31 (☎223-811; bus #14 or a twenty-minute walk), in a suburb to the west of town. It's important that you check at the TIC first, as venues change regularly.

Further out in the same direction, the **campsite** can be reached by taking bus #8 north along Dunajska Cesta until it reaches its terminus at Ježica (☎371-382; May–Sept; £4 per person). It's situated in a pleasant recreation area and has a few bungalows with double rooms for £25.

Hotels

Should you arrive out of the season for student rooms, or fancy something a little more luxurious, Ljubljana is well stocked with hotels.

Bellevue, Pod Gozdom 12 (☎313-133). Very small, and with few amenities, but occupying a beautiful old building above Tivoli Park with a breathtaking view across Ljubljana. ⑥

Ilirija, Trg Prekomorskih Brigad 4 (☎551-162). Basic no-frills accommodation 2.5km northwest of the city centre off Celovska Cesta; check with the TIC for directions and room availability. ⑤

Park, Tabor 9 (☎316-777). Cheapest of the big multi-storey business hotels, a few blocks east of the station. ⑤

Pansion Mrak, Rimska 4 (☎223-412). Cheapest place in the centre, small and friendly. ⑥

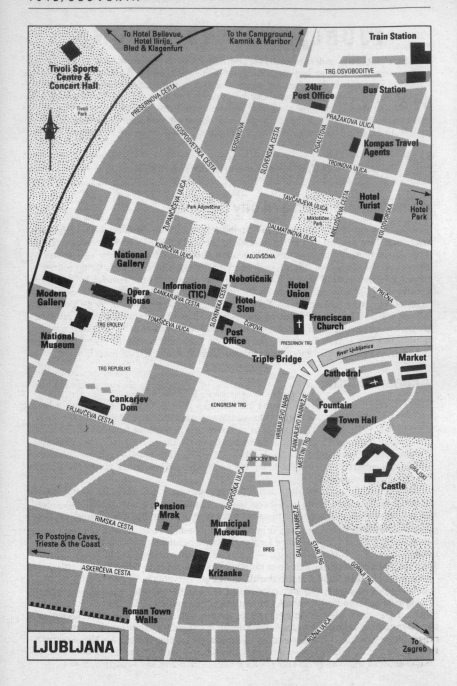

To Hotel Bellevue, Hotel Ilirija, Bled & Klagenfurt

To the Campground, Kamnik & Maribor

Train Station

TRG OSVOBODITVE

Tivoli Sports Centre & Concert Hall

Tivoli Park

PREŠERNOVA CESTA

24hr Post Office

Bus Station

KERSNIKOVA

GOSPOSVETSKA CESTA

SLOVENSKA CESTA

PRAŽAKOVA ULICA

CIGALETOVA

Kompas Travel Agents

TRDINOVA ULICA

ŽUPANČIČEVA ULICA

Park Adjovščina

TAVČARJEVA ULICA

MIKLOŠIČEVA CESTA

Hotel Turist

To Hotel Park

KIDRIČEVA ULICA

Miklošičev Park

DALMATINOVA ULICA

KOLODVORSKA

National Gallery

ADJOVŠČINA

Nebotičnik

Information (TIC)

CANKARJEVA CESTA

SLOVENSKA CESTA

Hotel Union

PREČNA

Modern Gallery

Opera House

Hotel Slon

ČOPOVA

Franciscan Church

TOMŠIČEVA ULICA

TRG EROLEV

Post Office

PREŠERNOV TRG

National Museum

TRG REPUBLIKE

Triple Bridge

River Ljubljanica

Market

Cathedral

Cankarjev Dom

KONGRESNI TRG

Fountain

Town Hall

ERJAVČEVA CESTA

HRIBARJEVO NABR.

CANKARJEVO NABREŽJE

MESTNI TRG

JURIČEV TRG

Castle

GRAJSKI

GOSPOSKA ULICA

Pension Mrak

RIMSKA CESTA

Municipal Museum

GALUSOVO NABREŽJE

STARI TRG

To Postojna Caves, Trieste & the Coast

BREG

 AŠKERČEVA CESTA

Križanke

GORNJI TRG

Roman Town Walls

ROŽNA ULICA

To Zagreb

LJUBLJANA

Slon, Titova 10 (☎211-232). Central hotel with good atmosphere. ⑧
Turist, Dalmatinova 13 (☎322-043). Situated near the heart of things, but a little bland. ⑧
Union, Miklošičeva 1 (☎212-133). B category hotel that retains a little of the old Central European atmosphere. ⑨

The City

Ljubljana's main point of reference is **Slovenska Cesta**, a busy north–south thorough-fare that slices the city down the middle. Most of the sights are within easy walking distance from here, with the **Old Town** straddling the River Ljubljanica to the south and east with its castle and cathedral; the bustling modern area lies around Slovenska Cesta at the heart of modern Ljubljana, and the ninetenth century quarter to the west, where the principal museums and galleries are to be found.

The Old Town

From the bus and train stations, walk south down Slovenska Cesta, cut left down Čopova and you're on **Prešernov Trg**, the hub around which everything in Ljubljana's **Old Town** revolves. Overlooking all, the seventeenth-century **Franciscan Church** blushes a sandy red above the bustling square and the River Ljubljanica: in its tired-feeling interior the old wall paintings look like faded photographs, and even Francesco Robba's Baroque high altar seems a little weary. Robba was an Italian architect and sculptor brought in to remodel the city in its eighteenth-century heyday. Ljubljana lay between Austria and Italy on one side, Central Europe and the East on the other, so when traders passed through and stopped off, Ljubljana got rich. So rich, in fact, that by the eighteenth century it could afford to indulge itself in Baroque excesses. Across the turn-of-the-century *Tromostovje* ("triple bridge") a **fountain**, also by Robba, symbol-izes the meeting of the rivers Sava, Krka and Ljubljanica (he stole the idea from Bernini's fountain in Rome), and the whole stretch down from Prešernov Trg west of the river is decaying Baroque grandeur. East of the river along Gallusovo Nabrežje most of the houses are ramshackle and medieval, occasionally slicked up as clothes shops and stores but mainly high, dark and crumbling – memories of an earlier, less fanciful past.

Opposite Robba's fountain is the **Magistrat** (Town Hall) on Mestni Trg – an undis-tinguished Baroque building around a courtyard (which contains another, more modest fountain by Robba), and the scene each year for the **"Country Weddings"**. This mass wedding ceremony conducted in peasant costume takes place towards the end of June: its origins are ancient, but nowadays the event has been dragged out to over a week by the ever-keen tourist authorities to form a convenient "folklore" attrac-tion. In the days preceding the ceremony events take place throughout Slovenia, usually in the presence of the betrothed couples, culminating in a procession through Ljubljana and the ceremony itself outside the Magistrat. It's undeniably colourful and good-natured, with much dancing, drinking and folk music concerts: yet you can't help but feel it's all a fraud, laid on more for the camcorder-clutching tourists than the unfor-tunate couples. If you're interested – and it *is* worth catching if you happen to be around – the *TIC* has exact dates and details.

A little east of the Magistrat the **Stolna Cerkev Sv Nikolaja** (St Nikolas' Cathedral) on Ciril-Metodov Trg is, depending on your tastes, the most sumptuous or overblown of Ljubljana's Baroque statements, all whimsical ostentation and elaborate embellish-ment, its size more than anything inducing hushed reverence as you enter. Designed by Andrea Pozzo (architect also of Dubrovnik's Jesuit Church), this is the best preserved of the city's ecclesiastical buildings. Adjoining the cathedral is the **Bishop's Palace**, and to the north a **Seminary**, with a dramatic doorway known as the *Portal of the Giants*, also the work of Pozzo.

Just to the west of the cathedral buildings you can't fail to miss the **general market** (Mon–Sat) on Vodnikov Trg, a brash free-for-all as everyone competes to sell their particular produce. Lining the river side, the herb sellers have a bewildering Macbethian selection – stock up on what you can identify as prices are minimal. As a sort of unofficial adjunct, old women sell poisonous-looking medicinal mushrooms. Purchase at your peril.

Opposite the market Studentska winds up the thickly wooded hillside to the **castle**, visible from everywhere in town and currently being restored to the glory it had when protecting Ljubljana's defensive position in earlier times – what's left today dates mainly from a sixteenth-century rebuilding. Climb the clock tower (10am–dusk) for a wide and superlative view of the old town crowded below, the urban sprawl of high-rises beyond and the Kamniški Alps to the north. Best time to be here is towards sunset, when the haze across the plains burns red and golden, suffusing the town in luxurious light.

Central Ljubljana and beyond

Back on the western side of the river, the broad slash of **Slovenska Cesta** forms the commercial heart of Ljubljana. Dominated by grimy nineteenth- and twentieth-century shops and offices, it's a place to do business rather than sightsee – save perhaps for its only real landmark, **Nebotičnik**: a gaudily painted provincial response to the American Art Deco skyscrapers of the 1930s. Nebotičnik's rather humble fourteen storeys are crowned with a penthouse café and an excellent view.

At Titova's southern end, the modern concrete expanse of **Trg Republike,** a few steps away to the west, is something of a monument to the postwar order, with the **Skupščina**, the Slovene parliament building, crouching on one side (the sculpted relief of the entrance is a fine example of 1950s Socialist Realism), and two symbols of the Republic's financial and economic power – the HQ of the Ljubljanska Banka and the industrial giant Iskra – towering above it on the other. Below, the chic matt-black exterior of the **Maximart department store** does its best to pander to Ljubljana's nascent consumerism.

Returning across Slovenska Cesta, the grubby park of Kongresni Trg leads back down towards the river. The eye-grabbing building at the Trg's western end is the early-eighteenth-century **Ursulinska Cerkev** or Ursuline church, whose looming Baroque coffee-cake exterior is one of the city's most imposing: should you manage to gain entry there's another florid high altar by Robba. Lower down, by the side of the main university building, Vegova Ulica leads southwards from Kongresni Trg towards Trg Francoske Revolucije, passing on the way the chequered pink, green and grey brickwork of the University Library. This was designed in the late 1930s by **Jože Plečnik**, the architect who more than any other determined the appearance of present-day Ljubljana: his lasting contribution to the image of the city was in the form of renovation carried out during the 1930s; a tidying up operation for a town still showing the effects of an 1895 earthquake. The whole atmosphere around the River Ljubljanica, including the riverbanks and several bridges, is the result of rebuilding work by Plečnik. His legacy, in the shape of Neoclassical columns, pillars and minature brick pyramids scattered all over the city, is impossible to avoid.

One such oddity is the **Illyrian Monument** on Trg Francoske Revolucije, erected in 1930 in belated recognition of Napoléon's short-lived attempt to create a fiefdom of the same name centred on Ljubljana. Virtually next door is the seventeenth-century monastery complex of **Križanke**: originally the seat of a thirteenth-century order of Teutonic Knights, its delightful colonnaded courtyard was restored by Plečnik to form a permanent venue for the Ljubljana Summer Festival. The beer cellar atmosphere of the aptly-named café *Plečnikov Hram*, inside the ivy-covered courtyard, is a good place to sit back and admire the man's handiwork. Across Gosposka, at no. 15, a seventeenth-century palace contains the **Municipal Museum** (Tues & Thurs 9am–noon & 4–6pm, Sun 9am–noon), which has dull furniture and duller statuary.

Beyond Trg Francoske Revolucije there's little of importance to see, except for a remaining stretch of the town's **Roman Walls** (again rearranged by Plečnik) on Mirje, and, a little further on, Plečnik's old house – now an **Architectural Museum** (Karunova 4; Tues & Thurs 10am–2pm), where you can wander around Plečnik's ascetic living quarters.

West of Titova: Museums and Tivoli Park

West of Slovenska, Cankarjeva heads down towards a neatly ordered corner of town that contains the city's most important **museums**. While under Austrian control, all attempts by the town to make itself the cultural and political capital of Slovenia were repressed, leaving it with an enforced provincialism that took years to wear off. Another post-imperial legacy was the sedate Neoclassical mansions the Austrians built: two of the three museums are housed in buildings of this period. The **National Museum**, Trg Herojev 1 (Tues–Sat 10am–6pm, Sun 10am–1pm; free) contains numerous dim halls of archeological objects, most famous of which is the **Vač Situla**, a locally-found Iron Age cauldron decorated with scenes of ritual feasting. The museum's natural history section is notable only for having the one complete mammoth skeleton found in Europe. The **National Gallery**, Cankarjeva 20 (Tues–Sat 10am–6pm, Sun 10am–1pm; free) is housed in a building of some historic interest; formerly the *Narodni Dom* it was built in the 1890s to accommodate Slovene cultural institutions in defiance of the Hapsburgs. Today, the whole question of Ljubljana's long-standing provincialism can be reviewed in the last few rooms of the gallery's collection, which are devoted to the Slovene Impressionists Rihard Jakopič, Ivan Grohar, Matija Jama and Matej Sternen. Although they were painting Impressionist works some thirty years after the French artists they emulated, the movement they represented nevertheless had considerable importance for the development of the Slovene national consciousness, extolling the virtues of rural Slovene peasantry and elevating them to the status of a subject fit for art. Just opposite, the **Modern Gallery** at Cankarjeva 15 (Tues–Sat 10am–6pm, Sun 10am–1pm; free) is pretty uninspiring save for interwar works by the Kralj brothers, and paintings from the 1980s by Irwin – a group of artists whose mixing of Slovene folkloric imagery with totalitarian symbols earned them considerable notoriety.

Beyond the National and Modern Art galleries, Cankarjeva leads you past an unobtrusive twentieth-century Serbian Orthodox church to **Tivoli Park**, an expanse of lawns and tree-lined walkways laid out by the ubiquitous Plečnik. Most of Ljubljana's recreational and sporting facilities can be found in the sports centre at the northern end of the park. A villa to one side contains the **Museum of Contemporary History** (Tues–Sun 10am–6pm), formerly a grim museum of the Socialist revolution, but nowadays given over to changing exhibitions relating to the events of the past few years.

At the top of the park's main avenue, the puce nineteenth-century **Villa Tivolski Grad** is now the centre of an international graphic arts association, and, during summers of odd-numbered years, plays host to the winners of the Ljubljana **Graphics Biennial**, the one event that puts the city on the European arts map. From here a succession of pathways winds up into the **Rožnik Hills** – a beautiful, tranquil region of woodland no more than ten minutes from the city centre. There are a number of tracks leading to the not-too-distant summit of Cankarjev Vrh, where you'll find a small **inn** (1–8pm, often closed in August) and a memorial room dedicated to the turn-of-the-century novelist **Ivan Cankar** (summer only, 10am–2pm). Other pathways through the wood lead north to the *Bellevue* hotel, whose terrace café commands a panoramic view of the city.

Eating

Eating in Ljubljana can be a memorable experience, with a wide selection of restaurants offering plenty of culinary diversity at very reasonable prices. There is a handful of good fish restaurants and many offering traditional Slovene variations, and given Lubljana's proximity to Italy, Austria, Hungary and the Adriatic coast, the range is impressive. Although café society is not what it was, you can still ferret out a couple of classy old-world places around Slovenska to take tea and typically sweet Balkan pastries.

Snacks and lunches

For **snacks**, the numerous *burek* kiosks near the station, along with the stands you'll come across throughout town which sell hot dogs and the local *gorenjska* sausages, are the quickest and cheapest choice for on-your-feet eating. The quality of Ljubljana's **delicatessens** makes them a good option for putting together picnics from locally produced cheeses, sausages and hams, washed down with a bottle of decent Slovene wine.

A cheap if rather uninspiring self-service or "express" restaurant is *Dairy Queen*, a palace of junk food on the corner of Slovenska and Cankarjeva, and there's a local version of *McDonald's*, *Ham Ham Rio*, at Slovenska 4.

For **lunches**, there's a wealth of inexpensive and reasonably decent pizza places: *Parma*, underneath *Maximarket*, is popular, lively and quick; *Mercator Pizzeria and Konditorei* halfway down Čopova, is very cheap and has a mouthwatering selection of cakes.

Restaurants

As befits its sophisticated, cosmopolitan image, Ljubljana is able to boast a tight concentration of restaurants, most of which offer excellent value for money. The compact nature of Ljubljana's centre means that interesting options are always close to hand.

Figovec, Gosposvetska 1. No-nonsense beer hall serving local specialities, including (yum yum) horsemeat.

Ljubljanski Dvor, Dvorni Trg. Inexpensive, atmospheric pizza restaurant with outdoor seating on a square overlooking the River Ljubljanica.

Maček, Cankarjevo Nabrežje 15. The best and most expensive (though by no means prohibitively so) of the city's fish restaurants. Traditional decor, good service; closed Sun.

Maxim, located underneath the *Maximarket* store on Trg Republike. Wide range of expensive international cuisine; a place for impressing guests and doing business. Closed Sat evening and all day Sun.

Operna Klet, Zupančičeva 2. Lurking behind an uninviting doorway opposite the Opera House, but one of the city's better restaurants specializing in fish dishes. Closed Sun.

Pizza Napoli, Prečna 1. Enormous, reasonably authentic and very cheap pizzas in a lively meeting place.

Pri Mraku, Rimska 4. In an unfashionable part of town and rather drab in decor, but with a good reputation for its Slovene dishes. Closed Sun.

Pri Vitezu, Breg 18–20. Popular riverside location with outdoor seating. A mixed menu, but more authentically Slovene than the others in town.

Sechuan, Gorni Trg 23. First-rate Szechwan Chinese restaurant, and a popular meeting place for a youngish crowd.

Union Klet, Miklošičeva 1. Hotel restaurant with a good selection of wines and an interesting menu of meats – it occasionally serves bear.

Zlata Ribica, Cankarjevo Nabrezje. Next door to *Maček* (see above) and not quite as stylish – or as pricy.

Cafés and patisseries

There's little of *Mitteleuropa* café society left in Ljubljana, but a few places on and around Slovenska present a convenient daytime refuge from the city centre's noise and bustle. *Evropa*, on the corner of Slovenska and Gosposvetska, serves pizzas and drinks along with sweets and ice creams, and is indecently plush and palatial like a nineteenth-century ballroom. The *Slon* hotel on the corner of Slovenska and Čopova has a couple of street-level café areas as well as a swish restaurant, but the kitsch atmosphere detracts from the undoubted quality of the cake trolley. The café-patisserie *Tivoli*, at Cankarjeva 6, has a cool dark marble interior and an extensive selection of pastries.

Nightlife

On summer evenings the cafés and bars of Ljubljana's old town spill out onto the streets with the hectic atmosphere of a mass open-air bar. In fact, there actually is one open-air bar, *Pri Konjskem Repu*, which you'll find on Prešemov Trg beside the triple bridge – a good place to get into conversation with the locals or just to hang out and watch the world go by. From here, a wander up and down the banks of the River Ljubljanica and along Stari Trg and Mestni Trg will yield an interesting locale every fifty yards or so.

Most of these places tend to close down for the night at around 11pm, after which there's a modest selection of clubs and discos to choose from. Many owe their atmosphere to the fact that Ljubljana used to be Yugoslavia's capital of alternative music, although things are a little quieter now, with today's young Slovenes preferring Madonna to Indie rock.

Some clubs double up as venues for home-grown rock bands and occasional foreign groups. Otherwise, the bigger acts play in the main hall of the *Tivoli* sports centre in Tivoli Park. Other gig venues are *KUD France Prešeren* at Karunova 14, the *Cankarjev Dom* Congress Centre on Trg Republike, or the open-air stage at *Križanke*,Trg Francoske Revolucije. Look out for street posters or the listings pages of local newspapers for news of forthcoming events.

Bars

Bistro Romeo, Stari Trg 6. Popular and elegant bar which degenerates into a crush of bodies by nightfall. Serves Italian food, ice cream and cocktails

Cantine, Zrinjskega. New and rather exclusive venue with Latin American decor and nibbles. Ring doorbell and negotiate bouncer to gain admission.

Casablanca, Cankarjevo Nabrežje. A thoroughly relaxing place with an outdoor terrace overlooking the River Ljubljanica, and a tranquil plush interior complete with deep wicker armchairs and leafy plants.

Galerija ŠKUC, Stari Trg 21. An avant-garde art gallery which turns into a bar during the evening.

Holiday's Pub, Slovenska. Central European approximation of a pub on Ljubljana's main shopping street.

Pivnica Kra Kra, Slovenska. Beer cellar offering a selection of local brews on draught located in the arcade behind Kavarna Evropa.

Rio, Slovenska 28. An absolutely massive beer garden in cobbled courtyard usually packed with a noisy cross-section of locals. Turns into an open-air cinema on some nights. Serves cheap grilled food too.

Rotovž, Mestni Trg. A chic venue for outdoor eating and drinking just next door to the Magistrat. Little to choose between this café-bar and *Valvasor* or *Pri Veijici* further south along the same street.

Sax Pub, Eipprova 7. Lively, youthful and gaudily-painted bar beside the willow-lined banks of the Gradascica canal.

Clubs and discos

Babilon, Wolfova 12. Upper-class disco for Slovenia's emergent bourgeoisie. Dress restrictions.

Disco Turist, Dalmatinova 15 (below *Hotel Turist*). Probably the best introduction to Ljubljana nightlife, because of the wide range of people who come here and the variety of different music on offer on any given night.

Drama, Erjavčeva 1. Located in the home of the Slovene National Theatre, slightly arty and self-conscious clientele.

K4, Keršinikova 4. Mecca of Ljubljana's alternative scene, offering different styles of music on different nights – including at least one gay night; pick up a copy of the weekly schedule on the door. Good place to check out local live bands.

Palma, Celovška 25 (beneath the *Tivoli Sports Centre*). Varied programme of music – including reggae, rock, Latin – on different nights of the week – and occasional gigs.

Classical music, opera and ballet

For a relatively small city, Ljubljana offers a surprisingly rich diet of classical culture. The *Cankarjev Dom*, Trg Republike (ticket office Mon–Fri 1–8pm, Sat 9am–2pm; ☎222-815), is the scene of major orchestral and theatrical events, as well as occasional folk and jazz concerts. Ljubljana's energetic **symphony orchestra**, the *Slovenska Filharmonia*, performs at Kongresni Trg 9, while the Republic's **opera and ballet** companies are housed in the *Slovensko Narodno Gledališče* (Slovene National Theatre), a sumptuous nineteenth-century Neoclassical building at Zupančičeva 1 (ticket office 11am–1pm and one hour before each performance; ☎331-950). Two big music festivals take place throughout July and August: the Ljubljana **Summer Festival** features orchestral concerts by international artistes at *Križanke* (festival box office 11am–1pm & 6–7pm; ☎226-544), while **Summer in Old Ljubljana** concentrates on chamber music in a number of venues scattered throughout the old town. The quarterly booklet *Kam?*, available from the Tourist Information Centre, has complete cultural listings.

Listings

Airline offices *Adria*, Gosposvetska 6 (☎313-312); *Lufthansa*, Slovenska 54 (☎326-662); *Swissair*, Hotel Lev, Vošnjakova 1 (☎317-647).

Airport Brnik, 20km north of the city (information ☎064/22-844). The *Adria* coach from the bus station takes the best part of an hour to reach it.

American Center Cankarjeva Cesta 11 (Mon, Wed & Fri 9am–4pm, Tues & Thurs 10am–5pm) has up-to-date US newspapers and magazines, and a well stocked library.

American Express *Atlas*, Mestni Trg 8 (Mon–Fri 8am–7pm; ☎222-711) will hold mail but does not offer cash advance services.

British Council Library Štefanova 1 (Mon, Wed & Fri 11am–1pm, Tues & Thurs 3–7pm).

Car rental *Avis*, Gosposvetska 7 (☎156-130); *Budget Glotour*, Štefanova 13 (☎213-992); *Kompas Hertz*, Miklošičeva 11 (☎311-241). *Avis* and *Hertz* both have counters at Brnik Airport.

Embassies and consulates *Great Britain*, Ilica 12, Zagreb, Croatia (☎041/424-888); *USA*, Brače Kavuriča, Zagreb, Croatia (☎041/444-800).

Launderette *Miele*, Vrtača 1 (daily 7am–3pm; service washes must be left overnight).

Medical assistance ☎323-060.

Motoring information *Auto-Motorska Zveza Slovenije* (*AMZS*, the Slovene Motoring Association), Titova 138 (☎342-378).

Pharmacies *Centralna Iekarna*, Prešernov Trg 5 has a 24hr emergency service.

Police Emergency number ☎92. Headquarters at Prešernov 18.

Post office Main office at Slovenska 32 (Mon–Fri 7am–8pm, Sat 7am–1pm). 24-hour service at Cigaletova 15.

Slovene Alpine Association (*Planinska Zveza Slovenije*), Dvoržakova 9 (☎312-556). Useful source of info if you're heading up into the Julian Alps: their detailed hiking and mountaineering maps are also widely available in Ljubljana's bookshops.

Taxis ☎9700, ☎9701, ☎9702 or ☎9703.
Telephones At post offices (see above).
Tours Guided walking tours of central sights depart from the town hall steps every day from July 1 to Aug 31 at 5pm.
Travel Agents *Atlas*, Mestni Trg 8; *Kompas*, Miklošičeva 11; *Slovenijaturist*, Slovenska 58.

Around Ljubljana

Emphatically not to be missed while you're in Ljubljana is a visit to the **Postojna Caves** – easily managed either as a day trip or en route to Koper, Opatija or Trieste in Italy, and the **Škocjanska** cave, debatably the most spectacular in the system and certainly less touristy than its better-known Postojna counterpart. A lower key alternative to the cave stop-offs is **Lipica**, where the celebrated Viennese Riding School horses are bred, or **Predjamski Grad**, near Postojna, an atmospherically sombre castle high against a cave entrance in the midst of a dramatic landscape.

Postojna

POSTOJNA is on the main rail route between Ljubljana and Trieste, but as the walk to the caves from Postojna train station is further than from the bus stop, most people go by one of the regular buses. Once in the town, signs direct you to the **caves** and their suitably cavernous entrance (tours half-hourly, last tours: May–Sept 6pm, April & Oct 5pm, Nov–March weekdays 1pm, Sat & Sun 3pm; £10/$15); inside a railway whizzes you helter-skelter through 2km of preliminary systems before the guided tour starts. It's little use trying to describe the vast and fantastic jungles of rock formations; the point is to see them for yourself – breathtaking stuff. Postojna's caves are about four million years old and provide a chilly home for *Proteus anguineus*, a weird creature that looks like a cross between a bloated sperm and a prawn. Actually it's a sort of salamander; one of whose odd capabilities is to give birth to live young in temperatures above 16°F but lay eggs if it's colder. They live their seventy-year lives down here in total darkness and hence are blind – and very confused at being put on display to inquisitive tourists.

Discovered in 1818, Postojna's 27-kilometre system wasn't explored for years, and large sections are still uncharted. During the last war Italian occupying forces used the entrance caves as a fuel dump without having a map of the system; the local Partisans, however, did, and worked their way through a side passage to blow up the stores – you can still see the walls blackened by the explosion. Do dress warmly as tours can be a chilling experience.

The **tourist office** at Tržaška 4 can book private **rooms** and give directions to the local **campsite**. The cheapest hotel is the *Pansion Erazem* (☎067/59-185; ④). Best places to eat are those in the town used by locals – anything near the cave entrance or plastered with credit card stickers is tourist-geared and, not surprisingly, overpriced.

Predjamski Grad

The other site you're steered to near Postojna is **PREDJAMSKI GRAD**, a castle 9km from Ljubljana and only reached with your own transport or on an organized trip. Pushed up high against a cave entrance in the midst of karst landscape, the sixteenth-century castle is damp and melancholy, unimproved by a lacklustre collection of odds and ends from this and an earlier castle that stood nearby. The previous castle was the home of one **Erazem**, a colourful brigand knight of the fifteenth century who spent his days waylaying the merchant caravans that passed through the region. Sheriff of Nottingham to his Robin Hood was the Governor of Trieste, who laid exasperated siege to the castle for over a year. Secure in his defensive position and supplied by a secret passage to the outside world, Erazem taunted the governor by tossing fresh cherries and the occasional roast ox over the wall to show he was far from beaten.

Such hubris couldn't go unnoticed, and Erazem finally met with one of the more ignominious deaths on record: blown to bits by a cannonball while sitting on the castle loo.

The Škocjanska and other caves

Caves abound in the limestone karst around Postojna. A seven-kilometre bus trip away, the **PLANINA** caves are little visited and provide a good contrast to Postojna – fewer rock formations but dramatic arched river passages. Four kilometres from Postojna, **PIVKA** is the cave nearest the only campsite in the area. Nothing like as dramatic as Postojna and considerably smaller, should you be passing it's just about worth going on one of the two tours a day that include entrance to the **Crna** cave.

Thirty-three kilometres southwest of Postojna the **ŠKOCJANSKA** cave (tours June–Sept daily 10am, 11.30am, 1pm, 2pm, 3.30pm & 5pm; April, May & Oct daily 2 tours; Nov–March Sun 2 tours; 90mins; £10/$15) is arguably the most magnificent in the area, though as it's little-advertised and considerably more difficult to reach by public transport, it's a far quieter, more relaxed alternative to joining the scrum at Postojna. From Divaca, the nearest town, turn right out of the combined bus and train station (it's on the Ljubljana–Koper rail route), along the road parallel to the rail lines as far as the bridge. Take the main road to Koper, and after about a kilometre the caves are signposted; all told, it's around a five-kilometre walk.

Beginning with the **Tiha Jama** ("Quiet Cave"), filled with monstrous stalactites and stalagmites, you cross over the nerve-testingly narrow and rickety **Hankarjev Bridge** towards the source of the River Reka, which plunges down, via a waterfall, to a lake, before disappearing to emerge 50km southeast in the Bay of Trieste.

The most important point is a negative one: there's no **accommodation** at the Škocjanska caves; the nearest is at Postojna, so you'll need to time your visit carefully. All the **information bureau** outside the entrance to the caves can do is give help on tour times. If you've worked up an appetite underground there's a **gostilna**, again near the entrance.

Lipica

A less spectacular alternative to the cave stopoff is **LIPICA**, near the Italian border; buses run from Divača, or tourist coaches ply the route from the coast. Very much the "oasis in the barren karst", as it's always described, Lipica gave its name to the **Lippizaner** horses that are associated with the Spanish Riding School of Vienna. There are three hundred horses here, the results of fastidious breeding that can be dated back two centuries. The Austrian Archduke Charles established the stud farm in 1580, adding Spanish and Arab blood to the Lippizaner strain that was first used by the Romans for chariot races, and it's been breeding the graceful white horses ever since. Though the school is nothing so grand as that at Vienna, tours are given round the **stud farm** (8.30am–5pm: mornings half-hourly, afternoons hourly), and twice a day the horses give the elegant displays for which they're famous (Mon–Fri 11am and 2.30pm; Sat & Sun 3pm), with a more elaborate display daily at 11am in July and August. If you've any horseriding ability, it's also possible to go on rides around the region – a wonderfully relaxing way to explore. A week's riding costs around £120/$180, and there are also beginners' and advanced riding courses. Neither of the local **hotels**; the *Club* (☎067/73-597; ⑥) or *Maestoso* (☎067/73-541; ⑥), is cheap.

Bled and Bohinj

At the tail end of the Julian Alps and within easy reach of Ljubljana, the **mountain lakes** of **Bled** and **Bohinj** are Slovenia's number one tourist attraction. And for good reason: all the delights and trappings of their Austrian and Italian neighbours are here – but at affordable prices. Tour operators have been quick to include the lakes in their brochures, and while Bled, surrounded by Olympian mountains and oozing charm, lives up to expectations it's also chock-full with English and German tourists, which can't help but temper its delights. Bohinj, in contrast, is less visited, more beautiful and cheaper – and, should you want to explore the imposing and exhilarating mountains around Mt Triglav, at 2864m the former Yugoslavia's highest peak, this is the place to go.

Buses are the easiest way to reach both Bled and Bohinj: they're frequent (hourly from Ljubljana; journey time 1hr to Bled, 2hr to Bohinj), reliable and cheap, and link most of the small villages in the area. **Rail** access to the region is via a branch line which leaves the main Ljubljana–Villach route at Jesenice and crosses the mountains towards Italy and the coast, calling at Bled, Jezero and Bohinjsko Jezero on the way. The trip from Jesenice, chugging steadily through the mountains and karst, is as impressive as you'd imagine. Train buffs should note that a **steam train**, the *Old Timer*, is laid on in summer months, at considerable additional expense.

Bled

There's no denying that **BLED** has all the right ingredients to make up a memorable visit– a placid mirror lake with romantic island, a fairy-tale castle high on a bluff, leafy lakeside lanes and a backdrop of snow-tipped mountains. As such it's worth a day of anyone's time, and one advantage of the tourist trade is that everything is efficiently packaged. In summer the lake, fed by warm water springs that take the water temperature up to 76°F, forms the setting for a whole host of water sports – major rowing contests are held here throughout summer, and in winter the surface becomes a giant skating rink.

Even if you don't stay there it's a good idea to observe the youth hostel's curfew: rise early while the hotels are still sleeping and Bled is all yours at its most atmospheric. A path just behind the youth hostel runs up to the fairy-tale **Bled Castle** (daily 8am–8pm) – which at a closer look turns out to be a pricy restaurant with a fine view and a very ordinary museum, its only surprise a small sixteenth-century chapel. The castle was founded in the eleventh century and for the next 800 years was the seat of the bishops in whose South Tyrol see Bled stood. Ignac Novak, one of Bled's more enterprising sons, was castellan here in the eighteenth century; his great plan was to drain the lake and use the residual clay as raw material for a brick factory he intended to build on the shore. With an astute eye to tourism even then, the council turned him down.

During the day a constant relay of stretched gondolas leave from below the *Park Hotel* or the bathing resort below the castle, ferrying tourists back and forth to Bled's intensely picturesque **island** (£2/$3 return). With an early start (and by hiring your own rowing boat or canoe from the same places as the gondolas) you can beat them to it. Crowning the island, the natty Baroque-decorated **Church of Sv Marika Božja**, is the last in a line of churches on a spot that's long held religious significance for the people around the lake: under the present building are remains of early graves and, below the north chapel, a very early (pre-Roman) temple. As soon as the tourist boats start up, the peace of the island is wrecked by over-amplified disco noise from a restaurant – so get here early. In summer months it's feasible to swim from the western end of the lake to the island, but remember to bring some light clothes in a watertight bag if you want to get into the church. During winter, under the snug muffle of alpine snow, you can walk or skate across.

The best options for accommodation in Bled are private **rooms** from the **tourist office** at Ljubljanska 7 (Mon–Sat 8am–5pm) or *Globustour*, Cesta Svobode 9 (stays under 3 nights £13/$20, otherwise £10/$15). The slightly cheaper **youth hostel** (③) is straight up Grajska from the bus station, past farmyards and a small shrine till you reach the hostel at Grajska 17 – where dormitory accommodation and a strict 10.30pm curfew/lockout may persuade you to reconsider a private room. The nearest **campsite**, *Zaka*, is beautifully placed, sheltered at the western end of the lake amid the pines and with its own stretch of beach; catch a bus towards Bohinj and get off at the Kidričeva street stop. Should the campsite be full, head for the *Šobec* site, 2km east of Bled on the road to Lesce; note that it's strictly illegal to camp anywhere other than an official site – a rule that's rigorously upheld by the local police. Another rustic alternative, at prices broadly similar to private rooms, is accommodation in a local **farmhouse**; bookings are handled exclusively by the tourist office. The majority of the **hotels** in Bled are block-booked and overpriced: if you do need to stay in one, *Hotel Krim* (⑨) and *Hotel Lovec* (⑨) are the least expensive. Out of the summer and winter seasons, it's worth asking at the tourist office for any bargains or "special prices".

One downside of the all-embracing tourist industry around here is that there are few cheap places **to eat** in Bled – the only budget options are the earthy *Gostilna* at the bottom of Grajska, the *Hram* pizzeria next to the *Park Hotel* at the eastern end of the lake, or hit the supermarkets for picnic ingredients. Of the restaurants, *Okarina*, Rikljeva 9, at the back of the castle, has the reputation of being one of the best in the country, and at £15 and up for a meal it's one of the most expensive; but if you feel like a blowout this is the place to do it, and its excellent menu includes vegetarian options.

Lake Bohinj

It's 30km from Bled to Lake Bohinj and buses run every half hour through the **Sava Bohinjka valley** – dense, verdant and often laden with mist and low cloud. Along its sides are dotted several examples of the *kozolec*, a wooden frame for drying hay and wheat found all over Slovenia: on the damp alpine ground crops don't dry well: hanging them on a *kozolec* lets the sharp winds do the work. Around Bohinj the double *kozolec* with workroom above and high-pitched roof is usual; further northwest they become much more decorative, with patterned animals and figures cut into the weatherboards; near Ljubljana long ranks of single *kozolci* are common.

In appearance and character **Lake Bohinj** is utterly different from Bled: the lake crooks a narrow finger under the wild mountains, woods slope gently down to the water enclosing it in secretive tranquillity and a lazy stillness hangs over all – in comparison to Bled it feels almost uninhabited.

A number of places take their name from the lake. **Bohinjska Bistrica**, 4km before Bohinj on the Bled–Bohinj bus route, has little except a few rooms. **Bohinjsko Jezero** (often just referred to as Jezero), at the eastern end of the lake, is where most facilities are based, including the **tourist office** (Sept–June Mon–Fri 7am–6pm; July & Aug daily 7am–8pm), which offers rooms, apartments and bike hire. Pride of place here goes to the **Church of Sv Janez** (July & Aug daily, 9am–noon & 3–6pm) a solid-looking structure whose nave and frescoes date back to the fourteenth century: but once you've seen this and sorted out a room there's no reason to hang about. To the west of the lake is the area known as **Zlatorog**, named after "Goldenhorn", a fearsome immortal chamois goat of local legend who guards the golden treasure of Mount Triglav. The Zlatorog **campsite** is at this end of the lake and there are a limited number of private **rooms** – try asking around or at the reception of the *Zlatorog Hotel* (☎064/723-331; ⑦), which is also a convenient place to eat and drink.

An easy walk back east takes you to the **cable car** (daily 7.30am–6pm, every half hour) at the foot of **Mt Vogel** (1540m). If the Alps look dramatic from the lakeside, from Vogel's summit they're breathtaking. As the cable car briskly climbs the 1000m drop – not for fainthearts this – the panorama is gradually revealed, with Triglav the crest of a line of pale red mountains, more like a clenched claw than the three-headed god after which it's named. Finally, if you're around at the end of September, the return of the cattle from the higher alpine pastures is celebrated in the mass booze-up called the *Kravji Bal* or "Cow Dance". This is a great opportunity to meet local people, most of whom still make their living off the land.

An hour's walk north from Zlatorog, the **Savica Waterfalls** make a good hiking target, a photogenic ribbon of water falling into the lake that marks the beginnings of the River Sava, which flows southwards through Croatia and Serbia before joining the Danube at Belgrade. Set in the foothills of the the Triglav range are the beginnings of a spectacular beech- and fir-packed National Park known as the **Valley of the Seven Lakes**. From here, armed with a copy of *How to Climb Triglav* (an English language booklet available in Ljubljana's bookshops) and a guide, you could begin your ascent of Triglav. It's a comparatively easy (if strenuous) hike amid magnificent scenery. When you reach the top, expect your companions to indulge in a little mild flagellation – tradition has it that on first scaling the summit of Triglav initiates have to be beaten on the bottom with a birch stick.

Maribor

Frequent buses and trains run from Ljubljana to **MARIBOR**, which began life as the eleventh-century castle of Marchburg, defending the German Empire's lonely south-eastern frontier against incursions by belligerent Magyars. The town came into its own in the eighteenth century, when the Austrian Emperor Charles VI decided to build a new road to Trieste; it then replaced Varaždin as the main beneficiary of Vienna's trade route to the Adriatic.

Nowadays Slovenia's second city is largely industrial, but a compact, Austrianate centre and a lively riverfront make it a worthwhile stopoff.

The Town

From the bus and rail stations on the east of town, a ten-minute walk down Partizanska brings you face to face with the forbidding red-brick bulk of the **Franciscan Church** – fortunately a reasonably pretty town centre lies behind it. Immediately beyond the church – past a disturbingly ugly war memorial – **Grajski Trg** is home to an eight-eenth-century castle that today contains the **Regional Museum** (*Pokrajnski Muzej*, Grajski 2; Tues–Fri 10am–6pm, Sat & Sun 10am–noon). It's a large collection with a little of everything, including costumes used in the *Korenti* dances of Ptuj (of which more later) and one of the most inept ceiling paintings in Europe.

Opposite the museum, Grajski Trg funnels into the largely pedestrianized **Old Town**, with the dark, narrow streets of Vetrinjska, Jurčičeva and Gosposka forming the core. A few steps away to the west is the lumpish, largely sixteenth-century Gothic **Cathedral** on Slomškov Trg – its mostly Baroque interior unremarkable save for some surviving Gothic stone pews. From here, Poštna leads down to **Glavni Trg**, a pleasing Renaissance square with a sixteenth-century town hall and a Baroque plague column. Beyond Glavni Trg, steps lead down to the river: there's not much to see on the water-front save for the town's two remaining medieval landmarks: the curious whitewashed fifteenth-century **Sodni Stolp** (judge's tower), 200m to the right, and the sixteenth-century **Vodni Stolp** (water tower), now a *vinoteka* where you can sample local wines. For the rest, there's little save for a couple of uninspiring **museums**: the **Museum of National Liberation**, Heroja Tomsica 5 (Mon–Fri 8am–1pm), is a waste of a fine nine-teenth-century mansion, and the **Art Gallery** (*Umetnostna Galerija*), Strossmayerjeva 6, two blocks west of Slomškov Trg (Tues–Sat 9am–1pm & 3–6pm, Sun 9am–3pm), has a modest collection of modern works by local artists.

One relaxing place to explore if you've got time on your hands is the **town park**, due north from the museum along Grajska. Even so it's an oddly sterile place, with well-regimented stretches of lawn bisected by concrete strips of pathway. Things get marginally better as the park climbs up into the foothills of the **Mariborske Gorice**, with vineyards rolling down into the town's northern suburbs.

Practicalities

The helpful **Maribor Tourist Information Centre** (*MATIC*, Grajski Trg 1; Mon–Fri 8am–7pm, Sat 8am–1pm) distributes maps, and will seek out private **rooms** (usually well out of the centre) or, from beginning of July to the end of August, organize you a place at one of the **student hostels**. Of central **hotels**, *Zamorec*, Gosposka (☎062/26-171; ⑨), is the cheapest and most basic. There's also a **campsite and motel** at Jezero (☎062/621-103), way out on the road to Dravograd near the village of Bresternica.

Virtually all the **restaurants** in central Maribor are owned by the same monolithic hotel and catering organization, *Pohorje*, and as such tend to be characterless places run by uninterested staff. Most locals wisely head for inns in outlying villages. Hence Maribor doesn't have much of an outdoor eating and drinking scene, although the café in the courtyard behind the town hall is adequate; the terrace of the *Hotel Orel* on Grajski Trg comes close to being a pavement café-restaurant. One restaurant with a reasonable reputation is *Novi Svet* at Jurčičeva 7, with quite expensive fish specialities and a predominantly Austrian clientele. Otherwise, the privately run bistro and bar *Amadeus* on Slovenska (the main road leading westward from Grajski Trg) appears to be the only sign of life in the centre.

Far better to head straight for the banks of the River Drava below Glavni Trg, where a string of five or six privately owned **bars** (with names such as *Capucino*, *Brut* and *Picolo*) occupy a short stretch of the recently renovated riverfront – it's here that the local youth congregate.

The best time to be in Maribor is mid-September, when the grape harvest is marked by a ten-day festival known as *Vesela Jesen* – "merry autumn". Usually running from September 14 to 25, this is the one event guaranteed to breathe life into Maribor and its normally comatose citizens.

Ptuj and around

Twenty-five kilometres down the road and an easy local bus ride from Maribor, **PTUJ** is the antidote to all this. Usually billed as the oldest town in Slovenia, it's about the most attractive as well, rising up from the Drava valley in a flutter of red roofs and topped by a friendly-looking castle. But the best thing is its streets, scaled-down mansions standing shoulder to shoulder on scaled-down boulevards, medieval fantasies crumbling next to Baroque extravagances. Out of the windows hang plants and the locals; watching the world go by is a major occupation here.

The Town

The town doesn't have a centre as such, but if it did it would be **Trg Mladinskih Brigad**, with an Austrian-style town hall at one end, and the **Priory Church** (open mornings only) at the other. Begun in the twelfth century, this is mainly Gothic, though splashed with Baroque; there's a fine carved choir of 1446. Nearby, its rather unambitious **tower** started life in the sixteenth century as a bell tower, became city watchtower in the seventeenth century and was retired in the eighteenth, when it was given an onion bulb spire for decoration. Roman tombstones have been embedded in its lower reaches, but a more noticeable leftover of Roman times is the **tablet** that stands below like an oversize tooth, actually a funeral monument to a Roman mayor. It's just possible to make out its carvings of Orpheus entertaining assembled fauna. In medieval times local ne'er-do-wells and petty criminals were chained to the tablet and publicly humiliated.

Right at the other end of the street the **Archeological Museum** (April–Nov daily 9am–3pm) lives in what was once a Dominican Monastery, a mustardy building gutted in the eighteenth century and now hung with spidery decoration, and worth a look for the carvings and statuary around its likeably dishevelled cloisters.

A path opposite the monastery winds up to the **Castle** (mid-April–Nov daily obligatory guided tours on the hour 9am–6pm). There's been a castle of sorts here for as long as there's been a town, since Ptuj was the only bridging point across the Drava for miles around, holding the defences against the tribes of the north. The Romans maintained a large base here and the fleeing Slavs fought off the Hungarians in the sixth-century migrations. An agglomeration of styles from the fourteenth to the eighteenth centuries, the castle was home to a succession of noble families who made it rich in the town. Most prominent were the Herbensteins, Austrian aristocrats who made their fortune in the Habsburg Empire's sixteenth- and seventeenth-century wars against the Turks. Their portraits hang on the walls of the **museum** the castle now holds, a collection mixed in theme and quality: on the first floor you will find period rooms, the usual stuff, with original tapestries and wallpaper; on the second are a few excellent pieces of medieval carving – St George unconcernedly killing a rather homely dragon, SS. Barbara and Catherine delicately and exquisitely crafted. There's also armour, furniture and, if you're interested, a collection of musical instruments, all of which seem to have twanged or tooted their last.

At Shrovetide (late February/early March) Ptuj is venue to one of the oldest and most unusual customs in Slovenia. The **Kurenti processions** are a sort of fertility rite and celebration of the dead confused together: participants wear sinister masks of sheepskin and feathers with a coloured beak for a nose and white beads for teeth, and possibly represent ancestral spirits – have a look at a picture and you'll see that there is something deeply and primitively frightening about them. So dressed, the *Kurenti* move in hopping procession from house to house, scaring off evil spirits with the din from the cowbells tied to their costumes. At the head of the procession is the Devil, wrapped in a net to symbolize his capture: behind the *Kurenti*, the *Orači* – "the ploughers" – pull a small wooden plough, scattering sand around to represent the sowing of seed, and housewives smash clay pots at their feet – possibly the leftovers of a sacrifice tradition – in the hope that this will bring health and luck to their households. Lent rituals like this were once widespread in Europe's farming communities; perhaps because of its oddness the *Kurenti* procession is one of few to survive in anything like its original form.

Practicalities

Ptuj is linked by (painfully slow) train to Ljubljana and Varaždin: the **train station** is 500m northeast of the centre on Osojnikova Cesta, the **bus station** 100m nearer town on the same road. From both points, walk down Osojnikova to its junction with Ulica Heroja Lacka: a right turn here lands you straight in Trg Mladinskih Brigad. **Private rooms** in Ptuj aren't cheap or central – and for about the same price you might as well stay at the *Hotel Poetovio* at Trstenjakova 13 (☎062/772-640; ⑦). If this is full the **tourist office** in the clocktower on Slovenski Trg (Mon–Sat 8am–1pm & 2–6pm, Sun 8am–1pm) will put you on to the rooms. For **food** you fare better: in ascending order *Zlatorog* at Bezjakova 10 is cheap and ordinary, the *Evropa Gostilna* on Trg Mladinskih Brigad varied and boozy, and best of all, the *Restavracija Ribič*, specializes in fish on the riverfront.

Around Ptuj: Ptujska Gora and the wine regions

Twelve kilometres to the southeast of Ptuj the village of **PTUJSKA GORA** is worth visiting if you're into things Gothic. Its pocket-sized **Church of Sv Marika** was built around 1415, and though altered over the years retains some of its fine original carvings, most likeable of which is a relief above the high altar showing the *Virgin as Protectress of the World*. Seven angels lift her cloak to reveal ranks of figures, each drawn with the detail and attention of a portrait; which is indeed what they were, depicting the assembled families of the Counts of Celje. The church itself is one of the loveliest in Slovenia.

The rolling hills east of Ptuj form Slovenia's extensive wine-growing region, centred around two small towns that give their name to the local white wines: Ljutomer and Jeruzalem. *Ljutomer* Rizling is well known in Britain as party plonk, but some of the wines made here are in a much higher league: as a rule of thumb go for the bottles with a numbered circular black label, indication of a sort of Slovenian *appellation controlé*. *Sipon* and *Halozan* are among the best, and try the *Renski Rizling* – smooth, dry and not too fruity.

SLOVENE ISTRIA

Istria was always Yugoslavia at its most developed. Many of the towns here were tourist resorts back in the last century, and in recent years their proximity to northern Europe has proved a tempting target for exploitation, although through all the crowds, concrete and tourist settlements, the region has managed to retain some charm and identity.

The basis of this is Italian, coming from the 400 years of Venetian rule that preceded the region's incorporation into the Austro-Hungarian Empire, and eventually into the Yugoslav federation. There's still a fair-sized Italian minority community here, and Italian is very much the second language, although many of the Italian-speakers left Istria after the last war, afraid of what might happen once the communists took control. In response, the Yugoslav government encouraged emigration to Istria from the rest of the country, and today there are a fair number of Macedonians, Albanians and Bosnians here too, many of them living on the coast and coining their fortune out of the tourist industry.

The northern part of Istria, which is partly Slovenian, has long been a contentious area. The subject of bitter postwar wrangles between the Italians and Yugoslavia, it didn't become part of Yugoslavia until 1954. Until then, it had been divided by the Allies into two zones: "Zone A", Trieste and around, which came under a temporary Anglo-American administration; and "Zone B" – Koper, Piran, Umag and Novigrad – which for the time being fell under Yugoslav control. In a compromise designed to appease both parties, "Zone A" was finally handed over to the Italians (principally to keep the crucial port of Trieste from falling into Soviet hands) and "Zone B" formally became part of Yugoslavia. It was the sort of diplomatic fudging which pleased no one; indeed both parties were incensed at losing pieces of territory to which they believed they had a historic right. Tito had always regarded Trieste as a Yugoslav city, and the Italians found it hard to renounce their claims on Istria as a whole.

Perhaps not surprisingly, Slovene Istria is one of the most Italianate parts of the entire region: there's a steady flow of traffic to and fro across the border, Italian is fairly widely spoken, and road signs are in Italian as well as Slovene. Along the coast, diminutive towns like Piran, with their cobbled piazzas, shuttered houses and back alleys laden with laundry, are almost overwhelmingly pretty. Koper, too, is worth a look, more port than resort and a good base for exploring northern Istria.

Koper and around

Arriving from Italy, KOPER, or *Capodistria* in Italian, is the first large town you reach, a prosperous place and one of the largest Istrian centres, sited on what was originally a small island but is now incorporated into the mainland. From the main road, it's an unalluring spectacle, dominated by tower blocks, cranes and industrial estates. But within this surge of development, Koper is a rickety old Venetian town, crowded with a dense lattice of narrow streets.

Arrival and accommodation

Koper's **bus** and **train stations** are located next door to each other, twenty minutes' walk from the town centre, or a short ride on one of the frequent yellow buses. These drop you just outside the city centre, inside which only residents are allowed to drive.

Accommodation is pricy in Koper but if you're keen to stay, **private rooms** are plentifully available through *Kompas*, Pristanička 15–17 (daily 8am–7pm), or *Slovenijatourist*, Trg Anton Ukmarja (daily 8am–noon & 2–6pm), both of which are by the harbour. The least expensive **hotel** is the *Žustarna* (☎066/34-112; ⑦). The closest **campsite** is in Izola about 5km west, ten minutes away by half-hourly bus from the station, though it's said to be noisy.

The Town

All of Koper's streets and paved alleys lead to **Titov Trg**, the fulcrum of the old city, flanked by a Venetian **Loggia**, dating from 1463 and now a café. At the opposite end is the **Praetor's Palace**, Koper's most enduring symbol, with its battlements, balconies, busts and coats of arms like the stage backdrop for a Renaissance drama. Built originally in the thirteenth century, and added to and adapted 200 years later (the battlements were actually added in 1664 and only ever served a decorative purpose), this was the seat of the mayor and Venetian governor, evidenced by the facade's Lion of St Mark. Also on the square, Koper's **Cathedral** is a mixture of architectural styles, its facade blending a Venetian Gothic lower storey with an upper level completed a hundred years later in Renaissance fashion. Dedicated to Saint Nazarius, an unknown martyr who is patron saint of the town, the interior is large and imposing, and holds several paintings by Vittore Carpaccio, said to be a native of Koper – though this is disputed. Two of these, a *Massacre of the Innocents* and a *Presentation in the Temple*, hang on the high altar, the latter oddly shaped due to its originally having been painted for an organ panel.

Behind the cathedral, the Romanesque **Rotunda Carmine**, from the thirteenth century, is the cathedral baptistery. On the other side of the square, an arch through the Praetor's Palace leads on to **Čevljarska** or "shoemakers," street, the main shopping thoroughfare of the city. This eventually joins up with the **Prešernov Trg** on the southern fringe of the centre, where there's a Renaissance well from 1423, shaped like a bridge, and the only surviving town gate, the **Vrata Muda**, from 1516. In the other direction from Titov Trg, following Kidričeva, the **Civic Museum** (Tues–Fri 9am–1pm, Sat 9am–noon) holds more paintings, including works by Correggio, together with archeological fragments, ancient maps and the like.

Eating and drinking

Several **snack bars and restaurants** catering for the tourist trade are clustered around the harbour area; one of the biggest is *Taverna* at Pristanička 1, offering a wide choice of international and Istrian cuisine. In the centre of town, *Pizzeria Marko*, Prešernov Trg, is youthful and cheap, while *Okrepčevalnica Diana*, Čevljarska, is a lively bar with tasty *burek* and other snacks. *Karvarna Loggia* on the main square is a plush venue for an evening drink, complete with ivory-tinkling live musicians. Smaller, more intimate **bars** lie in the backstreets; *Bistro 6* on Gortanov Trg is one of the best.

Portoroz and Piran

Heading west from Koper the road veers right soon after Izola onto a long, tapering peninsula that projects like a lizard's tail north into the Adriatic. **PORTOROŽ** ("Port of Roses") appears almost without warning, a sprawling resort that by the end of the last century was already known for its mild climate and the health-inducing properties of its salty mud baths. Maladied middle-aged Austrians flocked here by the thousands to be smothered with murky balm dredged up from the nearby salt pans. Up went the *Palace Hotel*, in came the opportunists – and so began Portorož, a town entirely devoted to the satisfaction of its visitors. After the last war, the transition from health to package resort wasn't hard to make, and it's now one of the ugliest, most developed stretches of coast in all Istria, a horrible ghetto of bars, chalets, hotels and autocamps. The bay on which it stands preserves a kind of sheltered appeal, and **rooms** are available from both *Generalturist* and the tourist office on the main waterfront, close to where the buses stop. If you want nightlife, too, Portorož can provide it. But otherwise it's a depressing piece of development, worth hurrying on from fast.

PIRAN, at the very tip of the peninsula three or four kilometres from Portorož's bus station, couldn't be more different. There are tourists here too, lots of them, thronging the main square, packing the ranks of restaurants, milling around the souvenir-stacked harbour. But few actually stay (most are in fact from Portorož's hotel complexes) and the town preserves tangible remnants of atmosphere in its sloping web of arched alleys and little Italianate squares.

The centre of town, a couple of hundred metres around the harbour from where the buses stop, is **Tartinijev Trg**, named after the eighteenth-century Italian violinist and composer, Giuseppe Tartini, who was born in a house on the square and is remembered by a bronze statue in the centre. Tartinijev Trg is one of the loveliest squares on this coast, fringed by a mix of Venetian palaces and a portentous Austrian town hall. The red-painted fifteenth-century palace now houses the tourist office and bears the inscription "lassa pur dir" or "let them talk", which legend explains as a retort to nosey townspeople who didn't approve of the owner's more dubious romantic liaisons.

Just off the square there's a small **Aquarium** (daily 9am–1pm), with a rather sad set of tanks full of the local marine life. Opposite, across the bay of the harbour, the **Maritime Museum** (daily 9am–noon & 4–7pm) pays further homage to Tartini with a copy of his violin and assorted genuine memorabilia, along with an interesting display on Piran's salt industry and a scatter of paintings that includes native ex-votive works by Piran sailors and a ropey portrait of the local authorities by Tintoretto. Behind here – follow Rožmanova Ulica – the town's formidable sixteenth-century **walls** stagger across the hill, perforated with the same fairy-tale "Vs" as Koper's Praetor's Palace and with seven towers remaining. You can walk most of the way along these, descending afterward to follow Ulica IX Korpusa to the barnlike Baroque church of **Sv Jurij**, which crowns a commanding spot on the far side of Piran's peninsula. The campanile is visible from just about everywhere in the town and may seem familiar – it's a replica of the one in St Mark's square in Venice. A few dinars gets you a view of the broad swing of the Italian coastline, and behind, green Istria, enclosing the town with clumps of soldierly cypresses. There's nothing much inside, though, and after a quick inspection you may just as well walk further along the path to the edge of Piran's jut of land and down into the old part of town, picking a way through the dense maze of streets to emerge once again on Tartinijev Trg.

Practicalities

The **tourist office** is on Tartinijev Trg, housed in the red Venetian Gothic palace on the corner (Mon–Sat 9am–1pm & 4–8pm, Sun 9am–1pm). **Rooms** here can be in desperately short supply in high season. Of the town's **hotels**, the *Sidro* on Tartinijev Trg (☎066/75-292; ④) is, amazingly, the cheapest. The nearest **campsite** is the *Jezero*, 2km east of the town, which also has rooms in a small pension (☎066/73-473; ②). Numerous seafood **restaurants** line Piran's seafront and the backstreets of the old town. *Fontana*, Trg 1 Maja, and *Delfin*, Kosovelova 4, are among the best places for sampling Istrian specialities, although neither is cheap. The more upmarket *Pavel*, Gregorčičeva 3, is renowned for its lobster and clam dishes if you fancy a £15-a-head blowout.

travel details

Buses

Ljubljana to: Bled (hourly; 1hr 30min); Bohinj (hourly; 2hr); Divača (8 daily; 1hr 30min); Koper (8 daily; 2hr); Maribor (6 daily; 3hr 45min); Piran (8 daily; 2hr 30min); Postojna (8 daily; 1hr); Ptuj (3 daily; 4hr).

Maribor to: Ptuj (every 30min; 40min).

Koper to: Bled (1 daily; 3hr); Piran (every 20min; 30min); Portorož (every 20min; 20min).

Trains

Ljubljana to: Divača (hourly; 1hr 20min); Koper (3 daily; 2hr 30min); Maribor (6 daily; 2hr 20min); Postojna (hourly; 1hr); Ptuj (3 daily; 2hr 30min).

SPAIN

Introduction

Spain might appear from the tourist brochures to be no more than a clichéd whirl of bullfights and crowded beaches, castles and Moorish palaces. Travel for any length of time, however, and the sheer variety of this huge country, which in the north can look like Ireland and in the south like Morocco, cannot fail to impress. The separate kingdoms which made up the original Spanish nation remain very much in evidence, in a diversity of language, culture and artistic traditions incorporating personalities from Cervantes to Dalí, and Goya to Miró.

While great monuments still survive from a history which takes in Romans, Moors and the Renaissance, modern Spain broke out in innumerable – and often unpredictable – ways. The sheer pace of change, barrelling into the twentieth century in the wake of the thirty-year dictatorship of Franco, is one of the country's most stimulating aspects. Early in the 1990s, Spain enjoyed the fastest economic growth in Europe (now slowed by an acute slump), and a vitality which is almost palpable; for the first time in centuries, there is a feeling of political stability. At the same time Spanish culture has been allowed off the leash. Already in the past two decades, virtually every aspect of life has been radically transformed; there is a belief here that northern Europe has had its day, and that in future the south will lead the way. 1992, Spaniards believe, was the year which restored them to their rightful place among Europe's leading nations: Barcelona hosted the Olympics, Sevilla the World Fair, and Madrid was official "Cultural Capital of Europe".

In the **cities** there is always something happening – in clubs, on the streets, in fashion, in politics – and even in the most out-of-the-way places there's nightlife, music and entertainment, not to mention the more traditional fiestas. In the **countryside** you can still find villages which have been decaying steadily since Columbus set sail: rural areas are more and more depopulated as the young head for the cities. Yet for the visitor the landscape retains its fascination; even local variations can be so extreme that a journey of just a few hours can take you through scenes of total contrast. Spain is as mountainous a nation as any in Europe and the *sierras* have always formed formidable barriers to centralization or unification. The deserted *rías* of the northwest – green and damp – could hardly be more

different from the endless windswept plains of Castile, the great Moorish cities of the south or the eerie desert landscapes of Almería.

It's almost impossible to summarize Spain as a single country. **Catalunya** is vibrant and go-ahead; **Galicia** rural and underdeveloped; the **Basque** country suffering post-industrial depression; **Castile** and the south still, somehow, quintessentially "Spanish". There are definite highlights to Spanish travel: the three great cities of **Barcelona**, **Madrid** and **Sevilla**; the Moorish monuments of **Andalucía** and the Christian ones of **Old Castile**; beach-life in **Ibiza** or on the more deserted sands around **Cádiz** and in the north; and, for some of the best hiking in Europe, the **Pyrenees** and the Asturian **Picos de Europa**. To get the most of Spain, though, you should escape the throngs for at least some of your visit.

Information and Maps

The **Spanish National Tourist Office** (locally called *Informació* or *Iniciativo de turismo*) has a branch in virtually every major town, giving away a variable array of maps, accommodation lists and leaflets – in the busiest towns they often run out. Offices are often supplemented by provincial or municipal **Turismo** bureaux, which also vary enormously in quality – the Basque and Catalan ones are superb. Both types of office usually function Mon–Fri 9am–1pm & 3.30–7pm, Sat 9am–1pm.

Among the best **road maps** are those published by *Editorial Almax*, which also produces reliable indexed street plans of the main cities. Good alternatives are the 1:800,000 map produced by *RV* (*Reise- und Verkehrsverlag*, Stuttgart) and packaged in Spain by *Plaza & Janes*, and the less detailed offerings from *Michelin*, *Firestone* or *Rand McNally*. Serious **hikers** should look for topographical maps issued by two government agencies: the *IGN* (*Instituto Geográfico Nacional*) and the *SGE* (*Servicio Geográfico del Ejército*), although in the northern alpine areas, *Editorial Alpina* is more practical.

Money and Banks

The Spanish **peseta** circulates in coins of 1, 5, 10, 25, 50, 100, 200 and 500ptas, and notes of 1000, 2000, 5000 and 10,000ptas. **Banks** and *cajas de ahorro* (equivalent to a building society or savings and loan) have branches in all but the smallest towns. The *Banco Central* has generally the lowest rate of commission on exchange. **Hours** are Mon–Fri 9am–2pm in summer, plus Sat 9am–1pm in winter. Outside these times it's usually possible to change cash at larger hotels (generally bad rates, but low commission) or, in the cities and big resorts, with travel agents. In tourist areas you'll also find *casas de cambio*, with more convenient hours, though their rates vary a lot. Cash machines which accept Eurocheque or credit cards are widespread throughout Spain and, depending on the fee charged for withdrawals, are probably more convenient than travellers' cheques.

Communications

You can have your letters sent **poste restante** to any Spanish post office: they should be addressed to *Lista de Correos* followed by the name of the town and province. *American Express* in Madrid and Barcelona will hold mail for a month. **Post offices** (*Correos*) are open Mon–Fri 8am–2pm and Sat 9am–noon, though big branches in large cities have longer hours. Queues can be long, but stamps are also sold at tobacconists (look for the brown and yellow *Tabacos* sign).

You can make **international phone calls** direct from almost any phone box marked *teléfono internacional* or from *Telefónica* offices, where you pay afterwards. Phone boxes take 5-, 25- or 100-peseta pieces – for international calls, make sure you have a good stock of 200- and 500-peseta pieces; phones in Spain are very expensive, and there is now a bewildering range of phone boxes accepting new coins, old coins and 100 peseta telecards. The **operator** number is ☎009 for domestic calls, ☎008 for calls within Europe, ☎089 for other international calls.

Getting Around

Most of Spain is well covered by both bus and rail networks and for journeys between major towns there's often little to choose between them in cost or speed. On shorter or minor routes buses tend to be quicker and will normally take you closer to your destination. Car hire is worth considering, with costs among the lowest in Europe if you book in advance from home.

■ Trains

RENFE, the Spanish rail company, operates a horrendously complicated variety of **train** services. An ordinary train, much the same speed and cost as the bus, will be described as an *expreso*, *regional* or *rápido*. *Semi-directos* and *tranvías* (mostly short-haul) are slower, while anything described as a *correo* (mail train) will be excruciatingly slow. Expresses, in ascending order of speed and luxury, are known as *Delta*, *Electrotren*, *TER*, *Talgo* or *Pendular*. The last two categories can cost twice as much as standard second-class. The high-speed *AVE* service (supposedly up to 190mph) between Madrid and Seville has cut travelling time down to two and a half hours from the usual seven hours. In recent years many train services have been phased out in favour of **rail buses** operated jointly by *RENFE* and a private company. Fares are the same as on trains, and services usually leave and arrive from the bus stations/stops of the towns concerned.

A good way to avoid the queues is to buy tickets at travel agents which display the *RENFE* sign – they have a sophisticated computer system which can also make seat reservations (about 200ptas extra); the cost is the same as at the station. Most larger towns also have a *RENFE* office in the centre.

InterRail and *Eurail* **passes** are valid on all *RENFE* trains, but a bewildering number of supplements are charged. If you're using trains extensively in Spain but not outside the country, you might consider a *RENFE* **rail pass**, which seems to be accepted on all trains without question. They cost far less if bought in Spain: 11,500ptas for 8 days, 18,500ptas for 15. Flexitickets allow 4 days travel in any 15-day period for 9000ptas, or 9 in any 30 for 14,000ptas. *RENFE* also offers a range of discount fares on its *días azules* ("blue days"), covering most of the year with the exception of peak holiday weekends.

■ Buses

Unless you're travelling on a rail pass, **buses** will probably meet most of your transport needs; many smaller villages are accessible only by bus, almost always leaving from the capital of their province. Service varies in quality, but the buses are reliable and comfortable enough, with prices pretty standard at around 1000ptas per 100 kilometres. Many towns still have no main station, and buses may leave from a variety of places. All public transport, and the bus service especially, is drastically reduced on **Sundays and holidays** – it's best to avoid travelling to out-of-the-way places on these days.

■ Driving and Hitching

You obviously have much more freedom if you have your **own car**. Major roads are generally good, and traffic, while a little hectic in the cities, is generally well behaved. Speed limits are 60kph in built-up areas, 120kph on motorways and 90–100kph on other roads. The national **breakdown service**, the *Ayuda en Carretera*, is run by the Guardia Civil. Roadside phones on major routes are connected to the local police station, who will arrange assistance. On minor routes, contact the nearest police station via the operator.

You'll find a choice of **car rental** firms in all major towns, with the biggest ones represented at the airports and in town centres. These all charge about the same, upwards of £180/$270 a week, but you can usually get a deal from local operators (*Atesa* is the main Spanish company). If you know in advance that you'll need a car, it's still a lot cheaper to fix it up before you leave.

Hitching in Spain is not a reliable means of long-distance travel. The road down the east coast is notoriously difficult, and trying to get out of either Madrid or Barcelona can prove to be a nightmare; on the other hand, thumbing on back roads can be surprisingly productive. The Basque country, and the north in general, often prove quite easy, whereas Andalucía involves long, hot waits. From the big cities you're best off taking a bus out to a smaller place on the relevant road.

Accommodation

Simple, reasonably priced rooms are widely available in Spain, and in almost any town you'll be able to get a double for around 2000–3000ptas, a single for 1200–2500ptas. Only in major resorts and a handful of tourist cities need you pay more. In Spain, unlike most countries, you don't seem to pay extra for a central location, though you do tend to can a comparatively bad deal if you're travelling on your own as there may be few single rooms. It's always worth bargaining over room prices, and although they're officially regulated this doesn't necessarily mean much. In high season you're unlikely to have much luck, but at quiet times you may get quite a discount. If there are more than two of you, most places have rooms with three or four beds at not a great deal more than the double room price. There is a basic accommodation information service for tourists at reduced rate in English on ☎901/300 600, available between 10am–8pm from anywhere in Spain.

■ Hotel-type accommodation

The one thing all travellers need to master is the elaborate variety of types and places to stay. Cheapest of all are **fondas** (identifiable by a square blue sign with a white **F** on it), closely followed by **casas de huéspedes (CH** on a similar sign), **pensiones (P)** and, less commonly, **hospedajes**. Distinctions between all of these are rather blurred, but in general you'll find food served at both *fondas* and *pensiones* (some of which may offer rooms only on a meals-inclusive basis). *Casas de huéspedes* – literally "guest houses" – were traditionally for longer stays, and to some extent they still are.

Slightly more expensive than all these, but far more common are **hostales** (marked **Hs**) and **hostal-residencias** (**HsR**). These are categorized from one to three stars, but prices vary enormously according to location. Most *hostales* offer good functional rooms, usually with private shower, and, for doubles at least, they can be excellent value. The *residencia* designation means that no meals other than perhaps breakfast are served.

ACCOMMODATION PRICE CODES

Throughout this guide, accommodation is priced on a scale of ① to ⑧, the number indicating the lowest price per night a single person could expect to pay in that establishment in high season. With hostels this is the nightly rate per person; with hotels, the price is arrived at by dividing the cost of the cheapest double room by two. The prices indicated by the codes are as follows

① = under £5 / $8   ② = £5–10 / $8–16   ③ = £10–15 / $16–24   ④ = £15–20 / $24–32

⑤ = £20–25 / $32–40   ⑥ = £25–30 / $40–48   ⑦ = £30–35 / $48–56   ⑧ = over £35 / $56

Moving up the scale you finally reach **hoteles** **(H)**, again star-graded by the authorities. One-star hotels cost no more than three-star *hostales* – sometimes they're actually cheaper – but at three stars you pay a lot more, at four or five you're in the luxury class with prices to match. Near the top end of this scale there are also state-run **paradores**: beautiful places, often converted from castles, monasteries and other minor Spanish monuments

■ Private rooms and hostels

Outside all of these categories you will some-times see **camas** (beds) and **habitaciones** (rooms) advertised in private houses or above bars, often with the phrase "*camas y comidas*" (beds and meals) – these can be the cheapest of all options. **Youth hostels** (*Albergues Juveniles*), on the other hand, are rarely very practical, except in northern Spain where it can be difficult for solo travellers to find any other bed in summer. Few stay open all year, and in towns they are often inconveniently located. They tend to have curfews, are often block-reserved by school groups, and demand production of an *IYHF* card (though this is generally available on the spot). At 700–900ptas a person, you can easily pay more than for sharing a cheap double room in a *fonda* or *casa de huéspedes*. It is sometimes possible to stay at Spanish **monasteries**, which may let empty cells for around 450ptas a person, but if you want to be sure of a reception it's best to approach the local Turismo first, and phone ahead. In northern Spain, the Basque Country's *agroturismo* and Navarra's *casa rural* programmes offer excellent cheap accommodation in rural areas, usually in beautifully-preserved and well-maintained private houses. Full lists are available from the relevant tourist offices.

■ Camping

There are over 350 authorized **campsites** in Spain, mostly on the coast. They usually work out at about 350ptas plus the same again for a tent and a similar amount for each car or caravan. If you plan to camp extensively pick up the free *Mapa de Campings* from the National Tourist Board or the more complete *Guía de Campings* (400ptas). **Rough camping** is legal, but in prac-tice you can't camp on tourist beaches – though you can nearby, and with some sensitivity you can pitch a tent almost anywhere in the countryside.

Food and Drink

There are two ways to eat in Spain: you can go to a *restaurante* or *comedor* (dining room) and have a full meal, or you can have a succession of *tapas* (small snacks) or *raciones* (larger ones) at one or more bars.

■ Food

For **breakfast** you're probably best off in a bar or café, though some *hostales* and *fondas* will serve the "continental" basics. Traditionally, it's *chur-ros con chocolate* – long tubular doughnuts with thick drinking chocolate – but most places also serve *tostadas* (toasted rolls) with oil (*con aceite*) or butter and jam (*con mantequilla y mermelada*), or more substantial egg dishes. Cold *tortilla* (omelette) also makes an excellent breakfast. **Coffee and pastries** (*pastas*) or doughnuts are available at most cafés, too, though for a wider selection of cakes you should head for one of the many excellent *pastelerías* or *confiterías*.

One of the advantages of eating in **bars** is being able to experiment. **Tapas** are small portions, three or four small chunks of fish or meat, or a dollop of salad, which traditionally used to be served up free with a drink. These days you have to pay for anything more than a few olives, but a single helping rarely costs more than 250ptas. In the Basque Country and Navarra bars often have on offer a mouth-watering selec-tion of *pinchos* – meat, fish or just about anything else on a cocktail stick – on the bar. **Raciones** are simply bigger plates of the same for 400–600ptas, and can be enough in themselves for a light meal. If you're pushed for money, or just hungry, you can also order most *tapa/racion* fare as **bocadillos** (sandwiches in French bread).

Tascas, **bodegas**, **cervecerías** and **taber-nas** are all types of bar where you'll find *tapas* and *raciones*. Most have separate prices depend-ing on whether you eat at the bar or at a table (up to fifty percent more expensive – more if you sit out on a terrace).

For main meals, ***comedores*** are the places to seek out if your main criteria are price and quan-tity. Sometimes they're attached to a bar, *pensión* or *fonda*, but as often as not they're virtually unmarked. Since they're essentially workers' cafés they tend to serve more substan-tial meals at lunchtime and may be closed alto-gether in the evening. When you can find them – the tradition is on the way out – you'll pay around

700–1100ptas for a *menú del día* or *cubierto*, a three-course meal (usually) with wine.

Replacing *comedores* to some extent are **cafeterías**, which are graded from one to three cups (the ratings seem to be based on facilities offered rather than the quality of the food). These can be good value, especially the self-service places, but their emphasis is more northern European and light snack-meals tend to be dull. Food often comes as a *plato combinado* – literally a combined plate – something like egg and chips or *calamares* and salad, often with bread and a drink included. This usually costs 500–900ptas. *Cafeterías* often serve some kind of *menú del día* as well. You may prefer to get your *plato combinado* at a bar, which in small towns with no *comedores*, may be the only way to eat inexpensively.

Moving up the scale there are **restaurantes** (designated by one to five forks) and **marisquerías**, the latter serving exclusively fish and seafood. Cheaper *restaurantes* are often not much different in price to *comedores*. A fixed-price *cubierto*, *menú del día* or *menú de la casa* (all of which mean the same) is often the best value here: two or three courses plus wine and bread for 700–1500ptas. *IVA* (a value added tax) may be charged separately at 6 percent. Above two forks, however, prices can escalate rapidly. In all but the cheapest places it is usual to leave a tip: ten percent is quite sufficient.

Fish and seafood form the basis of a vast variety of *tapas* and are fresh and excellent even hundreds of miles from the sea; though it's not cheap, you really should make the most of what's on offer. Fish stews (*zarzuelas*) and rice-based *paellas* (which also contain meat, usually rabbit or chicken) are often memorable. **Meat** is most often grilled and served with a few fried potatoes and salad, or cured and served as a starter or in sandwiches. *Jamón Serrano*, the Spanish version of Parma ham, is superb. **Vegetarians** have a fairly hard time of it in Spain: there's always something to eat, but you may get weary of eggs and omelettes (*tortilla francesa* is a plain omelette, *con champiñones* with mushrooms).

■ Drink

Wine, either *tinto* (red), *blanco* (white) or *rosado/clarete* (rosé), is the invariable accompaniment to every meal and is extremely cheap. The most common bottled variety is *Valdepeñas*, from New Castile; *Rioja*, from the area around Logroño, is better but more expensive. Other good wines

include *Penedes* and *Bach* from Catalunya, and *Mendizabal*, a wonderful, light *Rioja* rosé.

The classic Andalucían wine is **sherry** – *Vino de Jerez*. This is served chilled or at *bodega* temperature and, like everything Spanish, comes in a perplexing variety of forms. Order *fino* or *Jerez seco* (dry sherry), *amontillado* (medium), or *oloroso* or *Jerez dulce* (sweet). **Cerveza**, lager-type beer, is generally pretty good, though more expensive than wine. Local brands, such as *Cruz Campo* in Sevilla or *Alhambra* in Granada, are often better than the national ones. Equally refreshing, though often deceptively strong, is **sangría**, a wine-and-fruit punch which you'll come across at fiestas and in tourist bars. **Sidra**, a dry farmhouse cider is most typical in the Basque Country and Asturias.

In mid-afternoon – or even at breakfast – many Spaniards take a *copa* of **liqueur** with their coffee, or else tip the liqueur or brandy into the coffee, calling the concoction *carajillo*. The best are *anís* (like Pernod) or *coñac*, excellent local brandy with a distinct vanilla flavour. Most **spirits** are ordered by brand name, since there are generally cheaper Spanish equivalents for standard imports. Specify *nacional* to avoid getting an expensive foreign brand.

Coffee – served in cafés, *heladerías* and bars – is invariably espresso, slightly bitter and served black, unless you specify *cortado* (with a drop of milk) or *con leche* (a more generous dollop). **Tea** is also available at most bars, although Spaniards usually drink it black. If you want milk, ask afterwards: ordering *té con leche* might well get you a glass of milk with a teabag floating on top.

Opening Hours and Holidays

Almost everything in Spain – shops, museums, churches, tourist offices – closes for a **siesta** of at least two hours in the hottest part of the day. There's a lot of variation, and certain **shops** now stay open all day, but basic summer working hours are Mon–Sat 9.30am–1.30pm & 5–8pm. **Museums**, with few exceptions, take a break between 1 and 4pm, and are closed Sunday afternoon and all day Monday. The really important **churches**, including most cathedrals, operate similarly; others open only for worship in the early morning and/or the evening.

There are fourteen national **holidays** and scores of local ones. The national ones are: Jan 1; Jan 6; Good Friday; Easter Sunday and

Monday; May 1; Corpus Christi (early or mid-June); June 24; July 25; Aug 15; Oct 12; Nov 1; Dec 6; Dec 8; Dec 25.

Emergencies

Though their role has been cut back since the days when they operated as Franco's right hand, the **Guardia Civil** (green uniforms and patent-leather hats or green kepis) are the most officious of Spain's police, and the ones to avoid. If you do need the police, you should always go instead to the more sympathetic **Policía Municipal**, or **Patrulla Rural** in outlying areas.

A common source of trouble is **petty theft**, which has risen to almost epidemic proportions in cities like Sevilla and Barcelona. If you take normal precautions, and don't wave money around, you've little to worry about, though fiestas seem to be a particularly dangerous time. Should you be arrested on any charge, you have the right to contact your consulate, and they are required to assist you to some degree if you have your passport stolen or lose your money.

For minor **health** complaints it's easiest to go to a *farmacia*, which you'll find in almost any town. In more serious cases you can get the address of an English-speaking doctor from the nearest relevant consulate, or from a *farmacia*, the local police or Turismo.

EMERGENCY NUMBERS

Dial ☎091 for police, fire and ambulance service.

MADRID

Madrid became Spain's capital simply through its geographical position at the centre of Iberia. When Felipe II moved the seat of government here in 1561 his aim was to create a symbol of the unification and centralization of the country. The city itself had few natural advantages – it is 300km from the sea on a 650-metre-high plateau, freezing in winter, burning in summer – and it was only the determination of successive rulers to promote a strong central capital that ensured its survival and development.

Today, Madrid is a vast, predominantly modern city, with a population of some five million and growing: pretty it isn't, especially on the journey in, through an ugly stream of concrete-block suburbs. However, the streets at the heart of the city are a pleasant surprise, with odd pockets of medieval buildings and narrow atmospheric alleys, dotted with the oddest of shops and bars, and interspersed with eighteenth–century Bourbon squares. By comparison with the historic cities of Spain – Toledo, Salamanca, Sevilla, Granada – there may be few sights of great architectural interest, but the monarchs did acquire outstanding picture collections, which formed the basis of the **Prado** museum. This has long ensured Madrid a place on the European art-tour, and the more so since the 1990s arrival – literally down the street – of the **Reina Sofia** and **Thyssen-Bornemisza** galleries, state-of-the-art homes to fabulous arrays of modern Spanish painting (including Picasso's *Guernica*) and European and American masters.

Galleries and sights aside, though, the capital has enough going for it in its own city-life and style to ensure a diverting stay. As you get to grips with the place you soon real-ise that it's the inhabitants – the Madrileños – that are the capital's key attraction: hanging out in the traditional cafés and *chocolaterías* or the summer *terrazas*, packing the lanes of the Sunday Rastro flea market, or playing hard and very, very late in a thou-sand **bars**, clubs, discos and *tascas*. Whatever Barcelona or San Sebastian might claim, the Madrid scene, immortalized in the movies of Pedro Almodovar, remains the most vibrant and fun in the country.

The area telephone code for Madrid is ☎91.

Arrival and information

Barajas airport is 16km out of town but connected with the centre by bus at least every half hour (4.45am–1.15am; 300ptas); the journey takes about half an hour and the terminal is the underground car park in the Plaza Colón. Taxis from the airport take four people and cost about 1500ptas unless you get caught in rush hour traffic.

Trains from the north arrive at the **Estación de Chamartín**, rather isolated in the north of the city. A metro line connects it with the centre and a suburban train line runs to the much more central **Estación de Atocha** – for travel to and from the south, east, west, Andalucía and Portugal. If you're coming from Galicia, Salamanca or points en route, you'll arrive at **Estación del Norte**, close to the centre near the Royal Palace. **Bus terminals** are scattered throughout the city, but the largest – used by all international services – is the **Estación Sur de Autobuses** at c/Canarias 17 (metro *Palos de la Frontera*), five blocks south of Atocha down the Paseo de las Delicias.

Tourist offices can be found at various locations: in the Torre de Madrid in Plaza de España (Mon–Sat 9am–7pm; ☎5412325); at c/Duque de Medinaceli 2 near the Prado (Mon–Fri 9am–7pm, Sat 9.30am–1.30pm; ☎4294951); at the airport (Mon–Sat 9am–8pm; ☎3058656); and in Chamartín station (Mon–Sat 9am–8pm; ☎3159976). There's also a municipal tourist office at Plaza Mayor 3 (Mon–Sat 10am–2pm & 4–8pm). All supply free maps and leaflets on Madrid and – if you're lucky – other Spanish cities.

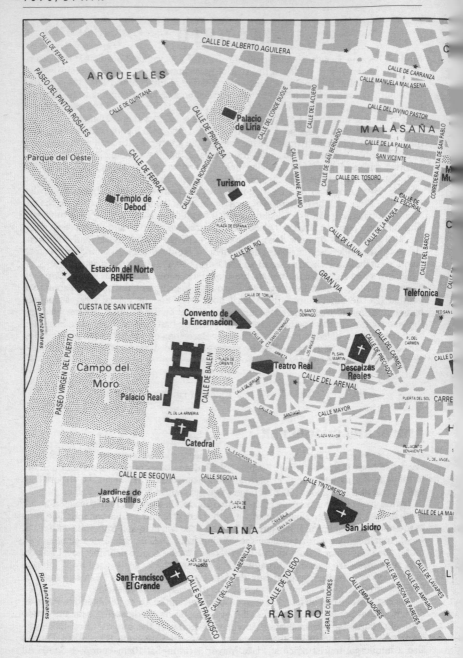

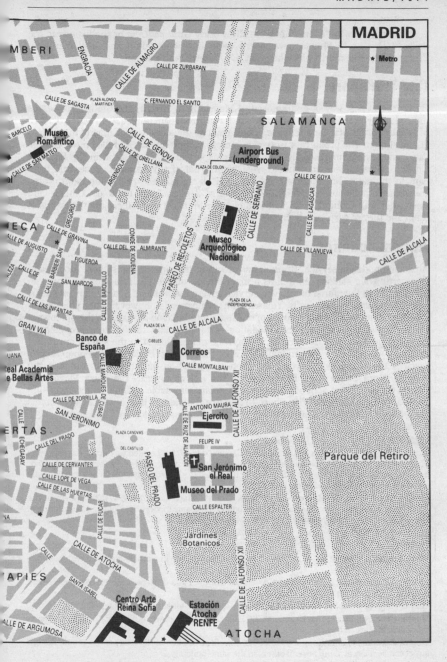

MADRID

★ Metro

MBERI

ENGRACIA

CALLE DE ALMAGRO

CALLE DE ZURBARAN

CALLE DE SAGASTA

PLAZA ALONSO MARTINEZ

C. FERNANDO EL SANTO

SALAMANCA

BARCELO

Museo Romántico

CALLE DE GENOVA

CALLE DE SAN MATEO

CALLE DE ORELLANA

Airport Bus (underground)

PLAZA DE COLON

CALLE DE GOYA

CALLE DE SERRANO

CALLE DE LAGASCAR

NECA

GREGORIO

CALLE DE GRAVINA

ARGENSOLA

CONDE DE XIQUENA

ALMIRANTE

CALLE DE ALCALA

CALLE DE AUGUSTO

CALLE DEL

Museo Arqueológico Nacional

CALLE DE VILLANUEVA

FIGUEROA

CALLE DE BARBIERI SAN

SAN MARCOS

CALLE DE BARQUILLO

CALLE DE LAS INFANTAS

GRAN VIA

PLAZA DE LA INDEPENDENCIA

PLAZA DE LA

CALLE DE ALCALA

UANA

Banco de España

CIBELES

Correos

Real Academia e Bellas Artes

CALLE MARQUES DE CUBAS

CALLE MONTALBAN

CALLE DE ZORRILLA

SAN JERONIMO

ANTONIO MAURA

Ejercito

CALLE

ERTAS

ECHEGARAY

CALLE DEL PRADO

PLAZA CANOVAS

FELIPE IV

CALLE DE CERVANTES

DEL CASTILLO

Parque del Retiro

CALLE LOPE DE VEGA

CALLE DE LAS HUERTAS

San Jerónimo el Real

Museo del Prado

CALLE DE FUCAR

CALLE ESPALTER

VA

PASEO DEL PRADO

CALLE DE ALFONSO XII

CALLE DE ALFONSO XII

Jardines Botanicos

CALLE DE ATOCHA

APIES

SANTA ISABEL

Centro Arte Reina Sofia

Estación Atocha RENFE

ALLE DE ARGUMOSA

ATOCHA

CALLE DE RUIZ DE ALARON

PASEO DE RECOLETOS

For details of **what's on**, check out the weekly *Guía del Ocio* or the listings in the daily *El Pais* or El Mundo newspapers (both have entertainments supplements on Fridays). The free tourist office handout, *En Madrid*, is also useful.

City Transport

By far the easiest way of getting around Madrid is by **metro**, and the system serves most places you're likely to want to get to. It runs from 6am until 1.30am with a flat fare of 125ptas, or 550ptas for a ten-ride ticket. You can get a free colour map of the system at any station. The urban **bus network** is more comprehensive but also more complicated and slightly more costly. There's a transport information stand in the Plaza de Cibeles, whose advice you should trust before that of any handout. Buses run from 6am to midnight, but there are also several all-night lines around the central area (departures half-hourly midnight–2am, hourly 2–6am, from Plaza de Cibeles and Puerta del Sol). At night, though, it's much safer to take a **taxi** – there are thousands of them and they're surprisingly cheap.

Accommodation

An accommodation service, *Brujula*, has offices at the airport, bus station, Atocha and Chamartín train stations, as well as a main branch on the sixth floor of the Torre de Madrid, above the tourist office. The service covers the whole of Spain and is free apart from long-distance phone calls. You shouldn't really need it, however; once you start to look there's an astonishing amount of cheap accommodation available in the old town.

Much of the cheapest accommodation is to be found in the area immediately **around the Estación de Atocha**, though the places closest to the station are rather grim and at night the area can feel somewhat threatening. Better to head up c/Atocha towards the centre, where you'll find better pickings in the streets surrounding the elegant **Plaza Santa Ana**. Prices rise as you get up towards the Plaza Mayor and Puerta del Sol (metro *Sol*), but even here there are affordable options. Other promising areas are along the **Gran Vía**, where the huge old buildings hide a vast array of hotels and *hostales* at all prices, and north of here up **c/Fuencarral** towards Malasaña.

Hostels

Hostel Richard Schirmann, in the Casa del Campo (☎4635699). Located way out in the park west of the centre, but friendly, comfortable, clean and cheap, and an enjoyably noisy bar. Metro Lago or bus #33; you can call and they'll pick you up at the metro station, roughly 1km away – you certainly shouldn't walk there alone after dark. ②

Hostel Santa Cruz de Marcenado, c/Santa Cruz de Marcenado 28 (☎2474532). North of the Plaza de España near the Palacio Liria; reasonably pleasant, modern and quiet. 1.30am curfew. Often full, so arrive early morning if possible. Metro Argüelles. ③

Hotels

Hostal Aguilar, Carrera San Jerónimo 32 (☎4295926). Just one in a building packed with possibilities. ④

Hostal Alcázar Regis, Gran Vía 61 (☎5479317). Near the Plaza de España, deservedly popular and often full. Others in the same building. ③

Hostal Alonso, c/Espoz y Mina 17 (☎5315679). Good value for so central a hotel. ②

Hostal Cruz Sol, Plaza Santa Cruz 6 (☎5327197). Slightly run-down, but in great, quiet position at other side of Plaza Mayor. ③

Hostal Escadas, c/Echegaray 5 (☎4296381). Excellent position at the heart of the action, though street can be noisy at night. Several others in the same building. ②

Casa de Huéspedes Marcelino, c/Cruz 27. Cheap, central, pleasant and friendly. ②

Hostal Lisboa, c/Ventura de la Vega 17 (☎4299894). Good three-star *hostal*, central but not too hectic. ⑤

Pensión Mollo, c/Atocha 104 (☎5287176). Close to the station on the way up; convenient if you're heavily laden. ②

Hostal Regional, c/del Príncipe 18 (☎5223373). Comfortable place in elegant old building off Plaza Santa Ana; several others share the same building. ③

Hostal Ribadavia, c/Fuencarral 25 (☎5311058). Clean, friendly place in building which also houses *Breogán* and *Krise* (both ☎5228153). ③

Hostal Riosol, c/Mayor 5 (☎5323142). Just off Puerta del Sol towards Plaza Mayor. A few cheaper rooms without bath. ③

Hostal Sil, c/Fuencarral 95 (☎4488972). Slightly quieter area near metro Tribunal and the Municipal Museum: *Serrano* (☎4488987) is in the same building. ③

Pensión Romero, c/León 13 (☎4295139). Comfortable and cheap. ②

Hostal Sud-Americana, Paseo del Prado 12 (☎4292564). Surprisingly reasonable considering it's almost opposite the Prado; some excellent rooms, others less good. ②

Campsites

Osuna, Avenida de Logroño, out near the airport. Friendly, with good facilities, reasonable prices and plenty of shade, but the ground is rock-hard and, with planes landing and taking off overhead, it's extremely noisy. Metro to Canillejas, then bus #105.

Madrid, on the N1 Burgos road at kilometre 7. Theoretically a second-class site, hence slightly cheaper than *Osuna*, but facilities are almost as good – there's a swimming pool and it s qu... Metro Plaza de Castilla followed by bus #129.

The City

The **Puerta del Sol**, with its crowds and traffic, may not be the most attractive place in the city but it's a suitable starting point. This is officially the centre of the capital and of the nation: a stone slab in the pavement outside the main building on the south side shows **Kilometre Zero**, from where six of Spain's National Routes begin, while beneath the streets, three of the city's twelve metro lines converge. On the north side, at the bottom of c/del Carmen, is a statue of a bear pawing a bush; this is both the emblem of the city and a favourite meeting place.

Immediately **north** of Sol, c/de Preciados and c/del Carmen head towards the Gran Vía; both have been pedestrianized and constitute the most popular **shopping** area in Madrid. **West**, c/del Arenal heads directly towards the Opera and Royal Palace, but there's more interest along Calle Mayor, one of Madrid's oldest and most important thoroughfares, which runs southwest, through the heart of the medieval city, also to end close to the Royal Palace.

Plaza de la Villa and Plaza Mayor

About two-thirds of the way along c/Mayor is the **Plaza de la Villa**, almost a casebook of Spanish architectural development. The oldest survivor here is the **Torre de los Lujanes**, a fifteenth-century building in Mudéjar style; next in age is the **Casa de Cisneros**, built by a nephew of Cardinal Cisneros in sixteenth-century Plateresque style; and to complete the picture the **Ayuntamiento** was begun in the seventeenth century, but later remodelled in Baroque mode. Baroque is taken a stage further, around the corner in c/San Justo, where the church of **San Miguel** shows the unbridled imagination of the eighteenth-century Italian architects who designed it.

Walking straight from the Puerta del Sol to the Plaza de la Villa, you could easily miss altogether the **Plaza Mayor**, the most important architectural and historical landmark in Madrid. This almost perfectly preserved, extremely beautiful, seventeenth-century arcaded square, set back from the street, was planned by Felipe II and Juan Herrera (architect of El Escorial) as the public meeting place of the new capital and finished thirty years later in 1619, during the reign of Felipe III, who sits astride the stallion in the central statue. In its time the square has witnessed some of the momentous events of Madrid's history: *autos-da-fé* were held by the Inquisition here, kings were crowned, festivals and demonstrations passed through, bulls were fought, and gossip was spread.

The more important of these events would be watched by royalty from the **Casa Panadería**, named after the bakery which it replaced. Nowadays it's mostly tourists who wander around the statue and pack out the expensive cafés, but an air of grandeur still clings to the place, and even today the plaza performs several public functions. In the summer months it becomes an outdoor theatre and music stage; in the autumn there's a book fair; and in the winter, just before Christmas, it becomes a bazaar for festive decorations and religious regalia.

The Palacio Real

Calle del Arenal ends at the Plaza Isabel II opposite the **Teatro Real** or Opera House, which is separated from the Palacio Real by the **Plaza de Oriente**. In the centre of the square is a superb statue of Felipe IV on horseback; it was based on designs by Velázquez, and Galileo is said to have helped with the calculations to make it balance.

The chief attraction of this otherwise rather barren area, however, is the **Palacio Real** or Royal Palace (Mon–Sat 9am–5.15/6.15pm, Sun 9am–2.15pm; 400ptas). Built after an earlier building burned down on Christmas Day 1734, this was the principal royal residence until Alfonso XIII went into exile in 1931; both Joseph Bonaparte and the Duke of Wellington lived here briefly. The present royal family inhabits a more modest residence on the western outskirts of the city, using the Palacio Real only on state occasions. The building scores high on statistics: it claims more rooms than any other European palace; a **library** with one of the biggest collections of books, manuscripts, maps and musical scores in the world; an **armoury** with an unrivalled collection of weapons dating back to the fifteenth century; and an original **pharmacy**, a curious mixture of alchemist's den and early laboratory, its walls lined with jars labelled for various remedies.

Times for guided tours (in English, Spanish, German and French), which are compulsory for the main apartments, are posted. This grand tour is long, but even so barely allows time to contemplate the extraordinary opulence: acres of Flemish and Spanish tapestries, endless Rococo decoration, bejewelled clocks and pompous portraits of the monarchs. In the **Sala del Trono** (Throne Room) there's a magnificent frescoed ceiling by Tiepolo representing the glory of Spain – an extraordinary achievement for an artist by then in his seventies.

The same ticket admits you to all the outbuildings and annexes of the palace except the **Museo de Carruajes** (Tues–Sat 10am–1.30pm, Sun 9am–3.30pm; 75ptas), a collection of state coaches and the like from the sixteenth century to the present. This is situated to the rear of the palace in the **Campo del Moro**, a small park accessible only from the far west side, off the Paseo de la Virgen del Puerto.

Facing the Palacio Real, to the south, across the shadeless Plaza Armería, is Madrid's brand new **Catedral** (closed 1.30–5pm). This was planned centuries ago and worked upon for decades but opened for business only in 1993 with an inauguration by Pope John Paul II. Its neoclassical bulk is as indistinguished inside as out, though the boutique-like Opus Dei chapel has, at least, novelty value.

The Gran Vía

North from the palace, c/Bailén runs into the **Plaza de España**, home to a couple of ageing skyscrapers, for long the city's tallest. These look over an elaborate monument to Cervantes in the middle of the square, which in turn overlooks the bewildered bronze figures of Don Quixote and Sancho Panza. The square, however, is not a place to linger – the area is popular with junkies – and it's best to head off smartly along the **Gran Vía**, the capital's major thoroughfare, which effectively divides the old city to the south from the newer parts. Permanently crowded with shoppers and sightseers, this Gran Vía is appropriately named, with splendidly quirky Art Nouveau and Art Deco facades fronting its banks, offices and apartments, and huge hand-painted posters on the cinemas. At its far end, by the golden-balled **Banco de España**, the street joins with c/Alcalá on the approach to Plaza de la Cibeles (see below). Just across the junction is the majestic old **Círculo de Bellas Artes**, a contemporary art exhibition space with a rather formal-looking but very trendy bar (100ptas for non-members).

On an entirely different plane, the **Convento de las Descalzas Reales** (Tues, Wed, Thurs & Sat 10.30am–12.30pm & 4–5.15pm, Fri & Sun 10.30am–12.30pm; 300ptas), one of the hidden treasures of the city, lies just south of the Gran Vía on the Plaza de las Descalzas. This convent was founded by Juana de Austria, daughter of Carlos V, sister of Philip II and, at nineteen, already the widow of Prince Don Juan of Portugal. In her wake came a succession of titled ladies (the name means the Convent of the Barefoot Royals) who brought fame and, above all, fortune. The place is unbelievably rich and also quite beautiful, the tranquillity within its thick walls making an extraordinary contrast to the frenzied commercialism all around. You're taken on another of those whistle-stop guided tours through the cloisters and up a ridiculously fancy stairway to a series of chambers packed with art and treasures of every kind.

The **Convento de la Encarnación**, back towards the Palacio Real and covered by the same ticket (same hours), is nowhere near as impressive, and of the hundreds of paintings the place contains, only the frescoed chapel ceiling is of much interest.

Santa Ana and Huertas

Although there are few sights here, the area east of the Puerta del Sol, a rough triangle bordered to the east by the Paseo del Prado, on the north by c/Alcalá, and along the south by c/Atocha, is likely to claim more of your time than any conventional tourist attraction, due to its superb concentration of bars and restaurants. This area developed in the nineteenth century and has a strong literary past: there are streets named after **Cervantes** and **Lope de Vega** (where one lived and the other died), the *Atheneum* club is here, as is the *Círculo de las Bellas Artes* (see Gran Vía, above) and the *Teatro Nacional*. The *Cortes,* Spain's parliament, also sits here.

The **Paseo del Prado** is part of one of the city's great avenues, running from Atocha station (opposite which is the Centro Reina Sofía), past the Prado and Thyssen galleries, to the **Plaza de la Cibeles**, named after a fountain and statue of the goddess Cibeles awash in a sea of traffic in the middle. Dominating this square is Madrid's fabulously ornate central post office, the **Palacio de Comunicaciones** – a much more convincing cathedral than the real one by the Palacio Real. To the north of Cibeles, the *paseo* continues, with name-changes first to **Recoletos** and then **Castellana**, past the major shopping and business areas. In summer, the centre of Paseo de Castellana becomes an almost continuous line of *terrazas*, where Madrid's sleepless society comes to talk, drink and be seen from midnight to dawn.

The Prado

The **Museo del Prado** (Tues–Sat 9am–7pm, Sun 9am–2pm; 400ptas) has been one of Europe's key art galleries ever since it was opened to the public in 1819. It houses all the finest works collected by Spanish royalty – for the most part avid, discerning, and wealthy buyers – as well as standout items from other Spanish sources: over 3000 paintings in all, including the world's finest collections of Goya, Velázquez and Bosch.

Even in a full day you couldn't hope to do justice to everything in the Prado, and it's much more enjoyable to make short visits with a clear idea of what you want to see. Perhaps the best approach to the museum is through the Puerta de Goya, the side entrance on c/Felipe IV. In the first rooms on the ground floor are early Spanish paintings, mostly religious subjects, then in a series of rooms to your left the early **Flemish masters** are displayed. The great triptychs of **Hieronymus Bosch** – the early *Hay Wain*, the middle-period *Garden of Earthly Delights* and the late *Adoration of the Magi* – are familiar from countless reproductions but infinitely more chilling in the original, and there's much more of his work here, along with that of **Pieter Bruegel the Elder**, Rogier van der Weyden, Memling, Bouts, Gerard David and Massys. The few German paintings are dominated by four Dürers.

The long, central downstairs gallery houses the **early Spanish collection**, and beyond this is a vast collection of works by Rubens, van Dyck and their contemporaries – not the most exciting part of the museum. At the very far end, past the cafeteria and the English and French schools are **Goya's black Paintings**, probably best seen after visiting the rest of his work on the floor above.

Upstairs, to the left of the Puerta de Goya entrance, the Italian paintings include a series of panels by **Botticelli** illustrating a story from the *Decameron*. The long central galleries beyond are usually given over to temporary exhibitions, while the Prado's greatest treasures, the collections from Spain's Golden Age, are in a series of rooms to the left. Among them are the superb **Titian** portraits of Charles V and Philip II, as well as works by Tintoretto, Bassano, Caravaggio and Veronese. Continuing on the first floor you come to the great Spanish painters, where the outstanding presence is **Velázquez**, court painter of Felipe IV, whose family is represented in many of the works. His masterpiece *Las Meninas* has a room to itself, along with its preliminary studies. In the adjacent rooms are important works by Zurbarán and Murillo, and a dazzling array of portraits and religious paintings by the Cretan-born **El Greco**, among them his mystic and hallucinatory *Crucifixion* and *Adoration of the Shepherds*.

The far end of the building is devoted almost entirely to **Francisco de Goya**, whose many portraits of his patron, Charles IV, are remarkable for their lack of any attempt at flattery while those of Queen María Luisa, whom he despised, are downright ugly. He was an enormously versatile artist: contrast the voluptuous *Majas* with the horrors depicted in *The Second of May* and *The Third of May*, on-the-spot portrayals of the rebellion against Napoléon and the subsequent reprisals. Then again, there are the series of pastoral cartoons – designs for tapestries – and, downstairs, the extraordinary *Black Paintings*, a series of murals painted on the walls of his home by the deaf and embittered painter in his old age.

South of the Prado is the **Casón del Buen Retiro**, which used to house Picasso's *Guernica* (now in the Reina Sofia – see below) but is now devoted to nineteenth-century Spanish art. It is included in the entrance ticket to the main museum.

The Thyssen-Bornemisza collection

The **Fundación Thyssen-Bornemisza** (Tues–Sun 10am–7pm; 600ptas) occupies the old Palacio de Villahermosa, diagonally opposite the Prado, at the end of the Carrera de San Jerónimo. This prestigious site played a large part in Spain's acquisition – for a knock-down $300m (£230m) in June 1993 – of what was perhaps the world's greatest private art trove, 700-odd paintings accumulated by father-and-son Swiss steel magnates. Another trump card was Baron Thyssen's current (5th) wife, "Tita" Cervera, a former Miss Spain, once married to Tarzan, who steered the works to Madrid and Barcelona against the efforts of Prince Charles and other society suitors.

Tita's portrait – a kitsch stunner – hangs in the great hall of the museum, alongside her husband and the Spanish monarchs, Juan Carlos and Sofia. Pass beyond, however, and you are into seriously premier league art: **medieval to seventeenth-century** on the top floor, **Rococo and Neoclassicism to Fauves and Expressionists** on the first floor, and **Surrealists, Pop Art and the Avant Garde** on ground level. Highlights are legion in a collection that has an almost stamp-collecting mentality in its examples of every major artist and movement, but how the Thyssens got hold of classic works by everyone from Duccio and Holbein, through El Greco and Caravaggio, to Schiele and Rothko, takes your breath away. Surprises include a strong showing of nineteenth-century Americans, some very early and very late van Goghs, and side-by-side hanging of parallel Cubist studies by Picasso, Braque and Mondrian.

The museum has a handy **bar and cafeteria** in the basement and allows re-entry, so long as you get your hand u-v stamped at the exit desk.

Centro de Arte Reina Sofia

It is fortunate that the **Centro de Arte Reina Sofia** (Mon, Tues, Thurs–Sat 10am–9pm, Sun 10am–2.30pm, closed Tues; 400ptas), facing Atocha station at the end of Paseo del Prado, keeps different opening hours and days to its neighbours. For this permanent collection of modern Spanish art, and leading exhibition space, is another essential stop on the Madrid art scene – and one that really mustn't be seen after a Prado–Thyssen overdose.

The museum, a massive former convent and hospital, is a kind of Madrid response to the Pompidou centre in Paris. Transparent lifts shuttle visitors up the outside of the building, whose levels feature a cinema, excellent art book and design shops, a print, music and photographic library, restaurant, bar and café, as well as the exhibition halls (top floor) and the collection of twentieth-century art (second floor).

It is for **Picasso's Guernica** that most visitors come to the Reina Sofia, and rightly so. Superbly displayed, along with its preliminary studies, this icon of twentieth-century Spanish art and politics – a response to the German bombing of the Basque town of Guernica in the Spanish Civil War – carries a shock that defies all familiarity. The painting is in Room 7, midway around, after strong rooms on **Cubism** and the **Paris School**. In the post-Guernica halls, Dalí's Surrealism seems trite and Miró less engaging than usual. However, the final rooms are stimulating: entitled **"Proposals"**, they comprise an evolving display of contemporary art, both Spanish and foreign.

Retiro and other parks

When you get tired of sightseeing, Madrid's many parks provide great places to escape for a few hours. The most central and most popular is the **Parque del Buen Retiro** behind the Prado, a delightful mix of formal gardens and wider spaces. Originally the grounds of a royal retreat (*retiro* in Spanish), it has been public property for more than a hundred years; the palace itself burned down in the eighteenth century. In its 330 acres you can jog, row a boat, picnic, have your fortune told, and above all promenade – on Sunday half of Madrid turns out for the *paseo*. Travelling art exhibitions are frequently housed in the beautiful **Palacio de Velázquez** and the nearby **Palacio de Cristal** (both Tues–Sat 10am–2pm & 5–7pm, Sun 10am–2pm; free). The nearby **Jardines Botanicos** (daily 10am–8pm; 100ptas), whose entrance faces the southern end of the Prado, are also delightful.

El Retiro is definitely the best of the parks for a casual wander, but over to the west of the city are a couple of others you might want to visit. The **Parque del Oeste** lies northwest of the Plaza de España, stretching up from the railway tracks of the Estación del Norte. At its southeastern end is the **Templo de Debod**, a fourth-century BC Egyptian temple that was given to Spain in recognition of the work done by Spanish engineers on the Aswan High Dam. Walking through the long, narrow park there are great views westwards, especially if you take the *teleférico*, about halfway up, which takes you high over the river to the middle of the Casa del Campo.

Casa del Campo is a huge expanse of heath and scrub that can be surprisingly wild for somewhere so accessible. In the tamer parts are an outdoor swimming pool (10am–7pm daily), picnic tables and café/bars, a **zoo** (10am–8pm daily), and a large but rather dull amusement park. The lakeside *Rockodromo* often stages free summertime concerts.

The Rastro

The area south of the Plaza Mayor and c/Atocha has traditionally been a tough, working-class district. In many places the old houses survive, huddled together in narrow streets, but the character of **Latina** and **Lavapiés** is beginning to change as their inhabitants, and the districts themselves, become younger and more fashionable.

Part of the reason for this rise in status must be the **Rastro**, which is as much part of Madrid's weekend ritual as a mass or a *paseo*. This gargantuan, thriving, thieving shambles of a street market sprawls south from metro Latina to the Ronda de Toledo, especially along Ribera de Curtidores. Through it, crowds flood between 10am and 3pm every Sunday and to a modest degree on Fridays and Saturdays too. Don't expect to find fabulous bargains, or the hidden Old Masters of popular myth; the serious antique trade has mostly moved off the streets and into the shops, while the real junk is now found only on the fringes. It's definitely worth a visit, though, if only to see the locals out in their thousands and to drop into traditional bars for *tapas*. On the streets, keep a tight grip on your bags, pockets, cameras and jewellery.

North of Gran Vía: Chueca, Malasaña and beyond

The chief reason to explore the quarters **north of Gran Vía** is for restaurants and nightlife. Although the late-late-nightclubs and discos are scattered around the city, and some even a few kilometres out from the centre, it is in **Chueca** and **Malasaña** that you'll find by far the heaviest concentration of bars and clubs downtown. Heading up in this direction by day, you might stop off at the **Museo Municipal** (c/Fuencarral 78; metro Tribunal; Tues–Fri 10am–2pm & 5–8.45pm, Sat & Sun 10am–2pm; free). Better known for its superb Churrigueresque facade than its contents, this eighteenth-century building houses exhibits tracing the development of Madrid from prehistoric times, with some fascinating scale models of the city as it used to be.

Malasaña, centred on the Plaza Dos de Mayo, was the focus of the *"movida Madrileña"*, the "happening scene" of the late 1970s and early 1980s after the death of Franco. Then it was the mecca of the young: bars appeared behind every doorway, drugs were sold openly in the streets, and there was an extraordinary atmosphere of new-found freedom. To some extent it still is like this – at night there are crowds of young people on the streets and the atmosphere is raucous (even at times threatening), yet the shops and restaurants reflect increasingly upmarket tastes. **Chueca**, at least in the centre around the Plaza Chueca, is much less respectable, but here, as you walk east towards the expensive shopping areas around the Paseo Recoletos are some of the city's most enticing streets. Offbeat restaurants, small private art galleries, and odd corner shops are to be found here in abundance and c/Almirante has some of the city's most fashionable clothes shops too.

Salamanca, across the Paseo Recoletos from Chueca, is full of fashionable apartments and expensive shops. A stroll up **c/Serrano** will take you past many of these and past a trio of museums and galleries. At no. 13 is the dusty and chaotic **Museo Arqueológico** (Tues–Sat 9.30am–8.30pm, Sun 9.30am–2.30pm; 200ptas), which contains the celebrated Celto-Iberian bust known as *La Dama de Elche*, the slightly later *Dama de Baza*, and a wonderfully rich hoard of Visigothic treasures found at Toledo. In the gardens you can visit a replica of the Altamira Caves complete with convincing copies of their prehistoric wall paintings. At no. 60 is the Fundación La Caixa, a superb exhibition space maintained by the Barcelona savings bank. And finally, at no. 122 is the **Museo Lazaro Galdiano** (Tues–Sun 10am–2pm; closed Aug; 150ptas), the pick of Madrid's smaller museums. This originally private collection donated to the state by José Galdiano, spreads over the four floors of his former home, its jumble of artworks including paintings by Bosch, Rembrandt, Velázquez, El Greco and Goya.

Eating and drinking

Madrid is a superb place to eat and, above all, drink: there can be few places in the world which rival the area around **Puerta del Sol** in either quantity or variety of outlets, from bars with spectacular seafood displays to old-time canteens offering modest-priced *menús del día*, from haute Spanish (or French, or Moroccan) cuisine to drinkers' dive bars and traditional *chocolate con churros* cafés. And the feasts continue in all directions: around **Plaza Santa Ana** and along **c/de las Huertas** to Atocha, south in the neighbourhood haunts of Latina and Lavapiés, or north in the funkier districts of **Chueca** and **Malasaña**.

In summer, all areas of the city spring forth *terrazas* – pavement café-bars – where coffees are taken by day and drinks pretty much all night. Prime areas include **Paseo Castellana**, where many of the top discos encamp (and charge accordingly), and the slightly more modest and relaxed **Las Vistillas**, on the south side of the vía duct on c/ Bailén, due south of the royal palace.

Tapas bars

El Abuelo, c/Nuñez de Arce 5. Excellent selection of *tapas* and *raciones*. Another branch on c/de la Victoria is a stand-up bar serving just four delicious prawn dishes.

El Anciano Rey de los Vinos, c/Bailén. Wine and sherry in the traditional manner straight from the barrel.

Las Bravas, c/Espoz y Mina. One of many straightforward *tapas* bars here – stand at the bar to sample the *tortillas* and *patatas bravas*.

Café Comercial, Glorieta de Bilbao. Traditional café and meeting place to linger over coffee, *coñac* and cakes.

Casa Alberto, c/de las Huertas. One of the most traditional Huertas bars: very friendly, lots of tables and huge portions. Also a restaurant at the back.

Casa Rúa, c/Ciudad Rodrigo 3, just off Plaza Mayor. Stand-up seafood *tapas* bar, popular and family/shopper-oriented.

Café Gijón, Paseo de Recoletos 21 north of Plaza de Cibeles. Traditional nineteenth-century café, tremendously atmospheric. Lunchtime *menú* and summer terrace.

Bar Gil, Paseo del Prado down towards Atocha. One of the few places near the Prado to head for a simple, inexpensive meal.

Mejillonera El Pasaje, Pasaje Matheu, off Espoz y Mina. Just one of the many places here – this specializes in mussels served in every way conceivable.

La Menorquina, c/Mayor, right on Puerta del Sol. Good for breakfast or snacks – try one of their *napolitanas* (filled croissants).

Museo del Jamón, Carrera San Jerónimo 6, Puerta del Sol end. Extraordinary place where hundreds of hams hang from the ceiling, and you can sample the different (expensive) varieties over a glass or two. Restaurant upstairs.

Café de Oriente, Plaza de Oriente. A rich kids' haunt with expensive food, but a lovely old café with a small summer *terraza*, a nice place to rest over a coffee.

Los Pepinillos, c/Hortaleza 59, Malasaña. Wonderfully seedy bar with vermouth straight from the barrel.

Taberna de Quintana, c/Quintana, off c/Princesa up towards Argüelles. Pleasant bar with excellent *tapas*.

Mainly for drinking bars

Cervecería Alemána, Plaza Santa Ana. One of Hemingway's favourite haunts and consequently full of Americans; good traditional atmosphere nonetheless.

Bodega Ángel Sierra, Plaza Chueca. Great old bar, just the place for an aperitif.

La Fidula, c/Huèrtas 57. The *grande dame* of the dozens on this street: here you can sip *fino* to the accompaniment of classical tunes performed from the tiny stage.

Los Gabrieles, c/Echegaray 17. One of the most spectacular **tiled bars** in Madrid, with fabulous nineteenth-century *azulejo* drinking scenes including a great version of Velázquez's *Los Borrachos* (the drunkards).

La Luna, c/León. A perennially popular dive.

La Venencia, c/Echegaray 7. Marvellous old wooden bar, serving only Jerez (sherry) and the most basic of *tapas* – cheese and pressed tuna. A must.

Viva Madrid, c/Manuel Gonzales. More splendid tiles and a great atmosphere.

Restaurants

Artemisa, c/Ventura de la Vega 4. Decent vegetarian restaurant.

Biotika, Amor de Diós 3 just off c/Huertas. Excellent, cheap vegetarian place.

Casa Alberto, c/Huertas 18. Small traditional *taberna* where you can eat at the bar or a small dining room at the back.

Casa Ciriaco, c/Mayor 84 (☎2480620). Good, traditional restaurant, not too expensive for the area.

Casa Mingo, Paseo de la Florida next to the chapel of San Antonio de la Florida. An Asturian place where you eat roast chicken washed down with cider. Good value and great fun. You can also buy picnic supplies here.

Creperie Ma Bretagne, c/San Vicente Ferrer. Tiny place with good pancakes, open until after midnight.

Fernández, c/Palma 6. Simple, cheap restaurant, always packed with locals and adventurous low-budget travellers.

El Gambón, c/Barbieri 1, Chueca. Excellent African food: more expensive than many of its basic neighbours, but worth it.

El Garabatu, c/Echegaray 5. Reasonably priced Asturian food and *tapas*.

Goffredo's, c/Martín de los Heros 4. A very popular pizza place.

El Granero de Lavapiés, c/Argumosa 10, near metro Lavapiés (weekdays 1–4pm only). Macrobiotic and vegetarian fare.

El Nuevo, Plaza San Miguel, immediately east of Plaza Mayor. Nice-looking place, with very good value *menú*.

Sabatini, c/Bailén 15, opposite Jardines Sabatini. Outdoor tables looking towards the palace; the food's significantly less expensive than you might expect.

La Trucha, c/Manuel Fernández y González, between Echegaray and Ventura de la Vega. Not the cheapest, but excellent meals in very Madrileño atmosphere.

Nightlife

The **bars, clubs and discos** of **Chueca** and **Malasaña**, or down south in **Huertas**, could easily occupy your whole stay in Madrid, with the most serious clubs starting around 1am and staying open until well beyond dawn. The names and styles change constantly but even where a place has closed down a new alternative usually opens up at the same address. To supplement our listings, invest in a copy of the quarterly *Madrid-Concept* magazine and check out its entries for *terrazas* (open-air terrace bars), *bares de noche* (nightclubs), *discotecas* and *actuaciones* (where you'll often be able to find live music).

Music concerts – classical, flamenco, salsa, jazz and rock – are advertised on posters around Sol and are also listed in the *Guia del Ocio* and in the newspaper, *El Pais*. In July and especially in August there's not too much happening inside, but the city council sponsors a "Veranos de la Villa" programme in some attractive outside venues.

If you find that you've somehow stayed out all night and feel in need of early morning sustenance, a final station on the clubbers' circuit is to take *chocolate con churros* at the *Chocolatería San Ginés* on c/de Coloreros, just off c/Mayor; its opening hours are midnight to 8am.

Discos, music bars and clubs

Discos and music bars can be found all over the city. Of the big **discos**, *Pacha*, c/ Barcelo 11, is the eternal survivor – it's exceptionally cool during the week, less so at weekends when the out-of-towners take over. Other high-fashion discos include *Archy*, c/Marqués de Riscal 11; *Hanoi*, c/Hortaleza by the junction with c/Fernando VI; *Joy Eslava* at c/Arenal 11, Sol; *Stella*, Arlabán 7, which is owned by singer Alaska; and *Aqualung*, Paseo de la Ermita del Santo 40 (out of town – 600ptas by taxi), where you can party poolside.

El Morocco, c/Marqués de Leganes 7, north of Gran Vía, is perhaps the **nightclub** of the moment, with an exotic decor, art-trendy clientele and nightly cabaret (at around 2am). For diving in and out of clubs, however, as Madrileños like to do, Chueca and Malasaña hold most promise. **Chueca** is the livelier area these days, with c/Pelayo a good point to start out. This street includes the quarter's most eclectic bar, *Torito*, at no. 4 and several gay bars (Chueca grafiti proclaims the area to be a *zona gay*), including *Leather* at no. 42 and *LL* at no. 71. Be aware that Chueca is also a big drug-dealing centre, especially around the central Plaza de Chueca. Over in **Malasaña**, there are drugs, too, mainly around Plaza Dos de Mayo, while the music in the clubs is often a few decibels higher. A key street to start off explorations is c/San Vicente Ferrer, where *King Creole* at no. 7 plays rockabilly, and *La Habana* at no. 23 has a great mix of salsa and reggae. For more of a chance to talk, try *Café Manuela* or *Estar*, both in c/ San Vicente Ferrer, or three pubs in the Plaza Dos de Mayo: *El Arco*, *El Sol de Mayo* and *Pepe Botella*.

Finally, the **Lavapiés** area, south of Sol, is an emerging bar and club locale and features two **lesbian** stops: a disco, *Medea* (closed Mon), at c/de la Cabeza 33; and *Fragil* (closed Mon), a good-time club at c/Lavapiés 11.

Live music

The music scene in Madrid sets the pattern for the rest of the country, and the best **rock bands** either come from Madrid or make their name here. For live bands many of the venues are in Salamanca, northeast of the centre: for example, *Sala Universal*, Dr. Esquerdo 2, and *Jacara*, Príncipe de Vergara 90. For chancing a band you've never heard of, *El Revólver* at c/Galileo 16, Argüelles, is a good bet – a club with an eclectic audience and music policy (including flamenco on Monday nights). Bigger rock concerts are usually held in one of the football stadiums.

A good array of **jazz bars** include the top-notch *Café Central*, Plaza del Ángel 10, near Sol, *Clamores* in c/Albuquerque, and *Populart* at c/de las Huertas 22. **South American** music is also on offer at various venues, especially during summer festivals; the best year-round club is the *Café del Mercado* in the Mercado Puerta de Toledo, which puts on live salsa more or less every night.

Flamenco can also be heard at its best in the summer festivals, especially at the *noches de flamenco* in the beautiful courtyard of the old barracks on c/de Conde Duque. Promising year-round venues include *Caracol*, c/Bernardino Obregón 18; *Café de Chinitas*, c/Torija 7; *La Solea*, Cava Baja 27; *Casa Patas*, Cañizares 10; and Mondays at *Revolver* (see above).

Film and theatre

Cinemas can be found all over the central area, with the biggest on Gran Vía. The Spanish routinely dub foreign movies, but a few cinemas specialize in original language screenings. These include the *Alphaville* and *Renoir* at c/Martín de los Heros 14 and 12, near Plaza de España, and the six-screen *Multicinés Ideal* at c/Doctor Cortezo 6. A *v.o.* programme of classic films is shown at the very pleasant *Filmoteca* at c/Santa Isabel 3, which in summer has an outdoor *cine-terraza*.

Classical Spanish **theatre** performances can be seen at the *Teatro Español*, Plaza Santa Ana, and more modern works in the *Centro Cultural de la Villa*, Plaza de Colón, and in the beautiful *Círculo de Bellas Artes*, Marqués de Casa Riera 2. Cultural events in English are held from time to time at the **British Institute**, c/Almagro 5, metro Alonso Martínez, which can also be a useful point for contacts.

Listings

Airlines Almost all have their offices along the Gran Vía or on c/de la Princesa, its continuation beyond the Plaza de España. Exceptions are *Iberia*, Plaza Canovas de Castillo 4 (☎5639966), and *British Airways*, c/Serrano 60 5° (☎900/177777; toll-free).

American Express Plaza de las Cortes 2 (Mon–Fri 9am–5.30pm, Sat 9am–noon; ☎3225500).

Books There's a good stock of English titles at *Booksellers S.A.*, c/José Abascal 48 (metro Iglesias or Ríos Rosas) and *Turners* on c/Genova (metro Alonso Martínez).

Bullfights Madrid's Plaza de Toros, known as *Las Ventas*, hosts some of the year's most prestigious events, especially during the June San Isidro festivities. Tickets are available at a couple of stalls on c/Victoria, just south of Sol; you pay around 50 percent more than the printed prices, which are for season tickets sold en bloc.

Car rental *Atesa*, Rosario Pino 18 (☎5720159); *Europcar*, Oreuse 29 (☎5559931); *Hertz*, Gran Vía 88 (☎5425805); *Rent Me*, Plaza de Herradores 6 (☎5590822).

Embassies *Australia*, Paseo de la Castellana 143 (☎5790428); *Canada*, Nuñez de Balboa 35 (☎431 4300); *Great Britain* and *New Zealand*, Fernando el Santo 16 (☎3190200); *Ireland*, c/Claudio Coello 73 (☎5763500); *Netherlands*, Paseo Castellana 178 (☎452100); *USA*, c/Serrano 75 (☎5774000).

Exchange 24hr at the airport. Branches of *El Corte Inglés* department store all have exchange offices with long hours and highly competitive rates and commissions.

Football Real Madrid and the Spanish national team play at the Estadio Bernabeu in the north of the city; bus #5 or #M12 from the centre.

Hospitals *Anglo-Americano*, c/Juan XXIII 1 (metro Moncloa); *Ciudad Sanitaria La Paz*, c/Dr. Esquerdo 52. For an ambulance, dial ☎7344794 or ☎2523264.

Laundry C/Marcenado 15 (metro Prosperidad); c/Donoso Cortés 17 (metro Quevedo); c/Hermosilla 121 (metro Goya); c/Palma 2 (metro Tribunal).

Left luggage at the *Estación Sur de Autobuses* (c/Canarias 17), at the *Auto-Res* and *Continental Auto* stations, at the airport bus terminal beneath Plaza Colón, and lockers at Atocha and Chamartín stations.

Post office *Palacio de Comunicaciones* in the Plaza de las Cibeles (Mon–Fri 9am–10pm, Sat 9am–2pm, Sun 10am–1pm for stamps and telegrams; Mon–Fri 9am–8pm, Sat 9am–2pm for poste restante and registered delivery).

Telephones 24-hr *Telefónica* at Gran Vía 28.

Travel agencies *Viajes Zeppelin*, Plaza Santo Domingo 2 (☎5477903), are very efficient and offer some excellent deals.

AROUND MADRID

Circling the capital are some of Spain's most fascinating cities, all making an easy day trip from Madrid, but also lying on the main routes out. From **Toledo** you can turn south to Andalucía or strike west towards Extremadura. To the northwest the roads lead past **El Escorial** through the dramatic scenery of the **Sierra de Guadarrama**, with Madrid's weekend ski resorts, to Ávila and Segovia. From **Ávila** it's just a short way on to Salamanca, or there are beautiful routes down through the **Sierra de Gredos** into Extremadura. From **Segovia** the routes north to Valladolid, Burgos and beyond await. To the east there's less of interest, but **Alcalá de Henares** and **Guadalajara** can both offer a worthwhile break in the journey into Aragón and Catalunya.

Toledo

For sheer concentration of attractions **TOLEDO** ranks with anywhere in Europe. Capital of medieval Spain until 1560, it remains the seat of the Catholic Primate and a city redolent of past glories. Set in a landscape of abrasive desolation, Toledo sits on a rocky mound isolated on three sides by a looping gorge of the Río Tajo (Tagus). Every available inch of this outcrop has been built on: houses, synagogues, churches and mosques are heaped upon one another in a haphazard spiral which the cobbled lanes infiltrate as best they can. Despite the extraordinary number of day-trippers, and the intense summer heat, Toledo is one of the most extravagant of Spanish experiences. The sightseeing crowds are in any case easy enough to avoid; simply slip into the back streets or stay the night, for by 6pm the coaches will have all gone home.

Arrival and accommodation

Toledo's **train station** is some way out on the Paseo de la Rosa, a beautiful twenty-minute walk or a bus ride (#5 or #6) to the heart of town. The **bus station** is on Avenida de Castilla la Mancha in the modern, lower part of the city; buses run frequently to the central Plaza Zocódover. The main **tourist office** (Mon–Fri 9am–2pm & 4–6pm, Sat 9am–3pm & 4–7pm, Sun 9am–3pm), outside the walls between the Puerta de Bisagra and the Hospital de Tavera, has full lists of places to stay, maps, and an information board outside; there's also a more central branch office in the Plaza de Zocódover (Mon–Sat 10am–6pm, Sun 10am–3pm).

If your first concern is **accommodation**, head directly for the old town. In summer rooms can be very hard to find, so it's worth arriving early; you may be picked up by a guide who'll earn commission for taking you to a particular place – but should at least know where there's space. Among the more central cheap establishments are *Pensión Lumbreras*, Juan Labrador 7 (☎925/221571; ②), *Fonda Segovia*, Recoletos 2 (☎925/221124; ①), and *Pensión Virgen de la Estrella*, Real del Arrabal 18 (☎925/211234; ②), on the main road uphill from the Puerta de Bisagra. Moving up a notch, you could try the *Hostal las Armas* on the corner of Plaza Zocódover at c/Armas 7 (☎925/221668; ②), the *Hostal Labrador* at Juan Labrador 16 (☎925/222620; ②), or the comfortable new *Pensión Madrid*, c/Marqués de Mendigorría 7 (☎925/221114; ③). The **youth hostel** is on the outskirts of town in a wing of the Castillo San Servando (☎925/224554; ②). The nearest campsite, *El Greco*, is a ten-minute walk from the Puerta de Bisagra on the road to Puebla de Montalbán and enjoys great views of the city. Sometimes there are also rooms available in the **university** – ask at the *Oficina de Información Juvenil* in c/Trinidad, by the cathedral.

The City

Right at the heart of the city sits the **Cathedral**. In a country so overflowing with massive religious institutions, the most powerful of them all has to be something special, and it is. A robust Gothic construction which took over 250 years (1227–1493) to complete, it has a richness of internal decoration in almost every conceivable style, with masterpieces of the Gothic, Renaissance and Baroque periods. The exterior is best appreciated from outside the city, where the 100-metre spire and the weighty buttressing can be seen to advantage. The main entrance is through the Puerta de Mollete beside the main tower, which leads into the cloister and the ticket office (daily 10.30am–1pm & 3.30–6/7pm; 350ptas; the *coro* is closed Sun morning, the New Museums are closed Mon). At the heart of the church, blocking the nave, is the **Coro**, with two tiers of magnificently carved wooden stalls. Directly opposite stands the gargantuan altarpiece of the **Capilla Mayor**, one of the triumphs of Gothic art, overflowing with intricate detail; it contains a synopsis of the entire New Testament, culminating in a Calvary at the summit. Directly behind the main altar is perhaps the most extraordinary piece of fantasy in the cathedral, the **Transparente**. Wonderfully Baroque, with marble cherubs sitting on fluffy marble clouds, it's especially magnificent when the sun reaches through the hole punched in the roof specifically for that purpose. Over twenty chapels are dotted around the walls, all of them of interest. In the **Capilla Mozárabe** mass is still celebrated daily according to the ancient Visigothic rites; if you want to look inside, get there at 9.30am, when the mass is celebrated. You should also see the Capilla de San Juan, housing the riches of the cathedral **Treasury**; the **Sacristía**, with the Cathedral's finest paintings, including works by El Greco, Velázquez and Goya; and the **New Museums**, with more work from El Greco, who was born in Crete but settled in Toledo in about 1577.

Toledo is physically dominated by the bluff, imposing **Alcázar** (Tues–Sun 9.30am–1.30pm & 4–5.30/6.30pm; 125ptas), to the east of the cathedral. There has probably always been a fortress in this commanding location, though it has been burned and bombarded so often that almost nothing is original. The most recent destruction was in 1936, during one of the most symbolic and extraordinary episodes of the Civil War, when some 600 Nationalists barricaded themselves in and held out for over two months against everything that the Republican-held town could throw at them, until finally relieved by one of Franco's armies. Franco's regime completely rebuilt the fortress as a monument to the glorification of its defenders, and their propaganda models and photos are still displayed.

An excellent collection of El Grecos can be seen to the north of here in the **Hospital de Santa Cruz** (Mon 10am–2pm & 4.30–6.30pm, Tues–Sat 10am–6.30pm, Sun 10am–2pm), a superlative Renaissance building which also boasts outstanding works by Goya and Ribera, a huge collection of ancient carpets and faded tapestries, sculpture and a small archeological collection. The **Museo de Arte Visigótico** (Tues–Sat 10am–2pm & 4–6.30pm, Sun 10am–2pm; 100ptas), in the Mudéjar church of **San Román** – a short way northwest of the cathedral – is also well worth a visit. The Visigothic jewellery and other artefacts are perhaps outshone by the building – a delightful combination of Moorish and Christian elements.

The masterpiece of El Greco, *The Burial of the Count of Orgaz*, is housed in an annexe to the nearby church of **Santo Tomé** (daily 10am–1.45pm & 3.30–5.45/6.45pm; 100ptas). It depicts the count's funeral, at which Saint Stephen and Saint Augustine appeared to lower him into the tomb, and combines his genius for the mystic – exemplified in the upper half of the picture where the count's soul is being received into heaven – with his great powers as a portrait painter and master of colour. From Santo Tomé the c/de los Amarillos leads down to the old Jewish quarter and to the **Casa del Greco** (Tues–Sat 10am–2pm & 4–6/7pm, Sun 10am–2pm; 200ptas), part of the house where the artist lived for much of his time in Toledo. The apartments themselves have been restored in a completely bogus, quaint style, but the museum displays many fine El Grecos, among them his famous *View of Toledo*.

Almost next door to the El Greco house, on c/Reyes Católicos, is the synagogue of **El Tránsito**, built along Moorish lines by Samuel Levi in 1366. Nowadays it houses a small **Sephardic Museum** (Tues–Sat 10am–1.45pm & 4–5.45pm, Sun 10am–1.45pm), tracing the distinct traditions and development of Jewish culture in Spain, though restoration is restricting the numbers of visitors allowed. The only other surviving synagogue, **Santa María la Blanca** (10am–2pm & 3.30–6/7pm; 100ptas), is a short way down the same street. Like El Tránsito, which it predates by over a century, it has been both church and synagogue, though it looks more like a mosque.

Continuing down c/Reyes Católicos, you come to the superb church of **San Juan de los Reyes** (daily 10am–2pm & 3.30–6/7pm; 100ptas), with its magnificent double-storey cloister. If you leave the city here by the **Puerta de Cambrón** you can follow the Paseo de Recaredo, which runs alongside a stretch of Moorish walls to the **Hospital de Tavera** (10.30am–1.30pm & 3.30–6pm; 300ptas), a Renaissance palace with beautiful twin patios, housing a number of fine paintings. Heading back to town, you can pass through the main city gate, the **Nueva Puerta de Bisagra**, marooned in a constant swirl of traffic. The main road bears to the left, but on foot you can climb towards the centre of town by a series of stepped alleyways, past the intriguing Mudéjar church of **Santiago del Arrabal** and the tiny mosque of **Santo Cristo de la Luz**. Built by Musa Ibn Ali in the tenth century on the foundations of a Visigothic church, this is one of the oldest Moorish monuments surviving in Spain. Only the nave, however, with its nine different cupolas, is the original Arab construction. According to legend, as King Alfonso rode into the town in triumph after the defeat of the Moors, his horse stopped and knelt before the mosque. Excavations revealed a figure of Christ, still illuminated by a lamp which had burned throughout three and a half centuries of Muslim domination – hence the name *Cristo de la Luz*.

Eating and drinking

Food is relatively expensive in Toledo, but at least it's easy to find. *La Bisagra*, c/ Arrabal 14, just uphill from the Puerta Bisagra, and *Arrabal*, opposite, are touristy but not too expensive; similar tourist places surround the Plaza Magdalena, southeast of Zocódover, and the surrounding alleys. One of the best here is *Bar Ludeña* at Plaza Magdalena 10, with a cheap *menú* and the local meat speciality, *carcamusa*. The other way from Zocódover, to the northwest, c/Santa Fe has several outdoor cafés popular with young people in the evenings. Less obvious places, all with good value lunchtime *menús*, include *Posada del Estudiante*, c/de San Pedro 2 behind the cathedral, *Restaurante Palacios*, c/Alfonso X El Sabio, *Mesón El Greco* at Bajada de Descalzas 10, and *Restaurante Plácido* at c/Santo Tomé 6. At night there's not a whole lot of action, but there are a couple of late **bars** worth a look along c/de la Sillería and c/de los Alfileritos; try *La Abadía* which caters for an older crowd. *Broadway Jazz Club* on Plaza Marrón and the nearby *Boîte de Garcilaso* usually offer live music.

El Escorial

Northwest of Madrid extends the line of mountains formed by the Sierra de Guadarrama and the Sierra de Gredos, snowcapped and forbidding even in summer. Beyond them lie Ávila and Segovia, but on the near side, in the foothills of the Guadarrama, is San Lorenzo del Escorial and the bleak **Real Monasterio del Escorial** (Tues–Sun 10am–1.30pm & 3.30–6pm; 500ptas).

An enormous building, rectangular, overbearing and severe, it looks more like a prison than a palace outside. Planned by Philip II as a monastery and mausoleum, it was a place from which he boasted he could "rule the world with two inches of paper". Later monarchs had less ascetic lifestyles, enlarging and richly decorating the palace quarters, but Philip's simple rooms, with the chair that supported his gouty leg and the deathbed from which he could look down into the church where mass was constantly celebrated, remain the most fascinating. The whole place, in the words of nineteenth-century traveller Augustus Hare, is "a stone image of the mind of its founder".

Through much of the complex you have no choice but to be shepherded by officious guides in groups of up to a hundred at a time: you can avoid the worst by coming just before lunch, and by not going straight to the royal apartments, where everyone heads when the bus or train arrives. Go instead to the **west gateway**, facing the mountains, and through the traditional main entrance. It leads into the **Patio de los Reyes**, where to the left is a school, to the right the monastery, both of them still in use, and straight ahead the **church**. In here, notice above all the flat vault of the *coro* above your head as you enter, apparently entirely without support, and the white marble Christ carved by Benvenuto Cellini. This is one of the few things permanently illuminated in the cold, dark interior, but put some money in the slot to light up the main altarpiece and the whole aspect of the church is brightened.

Back outside and around to the left are the **Sacristía** and the **Salas Capitulares** (Chapterhouses) which contain many of the monastery's religious treasures, including paintings by Titian, Velázquez and Ribera. Beside the sacristy a staircase leads down to the **Panteón de los Reyes**, the final resting place of virtually all Spanish monarchs since Charles V. Just above the entry is the *Pudrería*, a separate room in which the bodies rot for twenty years or so before the cleaned-up skeletons are moved here. Their many children are laid in the **Panteón de los Infantes**. Nearby are the **Library** with probably the most valuable collection of books in Spain, and the so-called **New Museums**, where much of the Escorial's art collection – works by Bosch, Gerard David, Dürer, Titian, Zurbarán and many others – is kept in an elegant suite of rooms.

Finally, there's the **Palace** itself – apartments crammed with treasures – for which you have to join the official convoys. Don't miss the quarters inhabited by Philip II, but unless you're profoundly interested in inlaid wood it's not worth paying extra to see the **Maderas Finas** rooms. Afterwards, you can wander at will in some of the courtyards and in the **Jardín de los Frailes** on the south side (open only during lunch).

Practicalities

There are well over twenty trains a day from Madrid and ten buses, which are faster, slightly cheaper and take you right to the monastery. If you arrive by train get immediately on the local bus which shuttles up to the centre of town; they leave promptly and it's a long uphill walk. There are several *hostales* here, among the cheapest of which are *Jardín*, c/Leandro Rubio 2 (☎91/8961007; ②) and *Malagón*, San Francisco 2 (☎91/8901576; ③). There's also a **campsite** 2km out on the road to Ávila and a **youth hostel** usually crowded with school groups in Finca de la Herreria (☎91/8903640; ②). Really it's preferable to arrive early, spend the day here, and continue in the evening to Ávila or head back to Madrid.

Eating is expensive everywhere, but try the bar just inside the gate. Farther up the hill on c/Reina Victoria, near the bus and train arrival point from Madrid, there are a few affordable restaurants. *Restaurante Cubero* on c/Don Juan Delegraz has cheap *menús*. The **tourist office** (Mon–Fri 10am–2pm & 3–6pm, Sat 10am–1.30pm) is at c/Floridablanca 10.

Ávila

Two things distinguish **ÁVILA**: its medieval walls and Saint Teresa, who was born here and whose spirit still dominates the city. It's the **walls** (Tues–Sun 10.30am–3pm; free; access from steps just inside Puerta del Alcázar) which first impress, especially if you time it right and approach the city with the evening sun highlighting their golden tone and the details of the 88 towers around the ramparts. At closer quarters they're more of a hollow facade – the old city within is more or less in ruins, and modern life takes place almost exclusively in the new developments outside the fortifications.

The legacy of **Santa Teresa**, as expressed in the many convents and churches with which she was associated, seems almost as solid as the walls. An extraordinary number of places in Ávila claim some connection with the saint, who was born here to a noble family in 1515. By the age of seven she was already deeply religious, running away with her brother to be martyred by the Moors. The spot where they were recaptured and brought back, **Las Cuatro Postes**, 1.5km along the Salamanca road, is a fine vantage point from which to admire the walls. She went on to reform the Carmelite order, found many convents of her own and become one of the most important figures of the Counter-Reformation. Perhaps the most interesting of the monuments associated with the saint is the **Convento de las Madres** (daily 10am–1pm & 4–7pm; free), the first one she founded, in 1562. Its museum contains relics and memorabilia including the coffin in which she once slept and assorted personal possessions. The **Convento de Santa Teresa** (daily 9am–1pm & 3.30–8.30pm), built over the saint's birthplace, is less interesting, although the reliquary beside the gift shop contains not only her rosary beads, but one of the fingers she used to count them with. The third major point of pilgrimage is the **Convento de la Encarnación** (Wed–Mon 9.30am–1pm & 3.30/4–6/7pm; 75ptas), where she spent 27 years as a nun. The rooms are labelled with the various things the saint did in each of them, and everything she touched and looked at or could have used is on display.

The most beautiful churches in Ávila – the cathedral, San Vicente and the convent of Santo Tomás – are less directly associated with its most famous resident. The **Cathedral** (daily 10am–1pm & 3–5/6pm; 200ptas) was started in the twelfth century but has never been finished: the earliest parts were as much fortress as church, and the apse actually forms an integral part of the city walls. Inside, the succeeding changes of style are immediately apparent; the old parts are Romanesque in design and made of a strange red-and-white mottled stone, but then there's an abrupt break and the rest of the main structure is pure white and Gothic. The basilica of **San Vicente** (Tues–Sun 10am–1pm & 4–6/7pm; 50ptas, like the cathedral, is a mixture of architectural styles. Its twelfth-century doorways and the portico which protects them are magnificent examples of Romanesque art, while the church itself shows the influence of later trends. Saint Vincent was martyred on this site, and his tomb depicts a series of particularly gruesome deaths.

El Real Monasterio de Santo Tomás (Mon–Sat 10am–1pm & 4–7pm, Sun closes 6pm) is a Dominican monastery founded in 1482, but greatly expanded over the following decade by Ferdinand and Isabella, whose summer palace it became. Inside are three exceptional cloisters, the largest of which contains an **oriental collection**, a strangely incongruous display accumulated by the monks over centuries of missionary work in the Orient. On every available surface is carved the yoke-and-arrows motif of the *Reyes Católicos*, surrounded by pomegranates, symbol of the newly conquered kingdom of Granada (*granada* means "pomegranate" in Spanish), and in the **church** is the elaborate tomb of Prince Juan, Ferdinand and Isabella's only son, whose early death opened the way for Charles V's succession. Notorious inquisitor Torquemada is buried in the sacristy. Santo Tomás is quite a walk (downhill) from the south part of town – you can get back up by the #1 bus, whose circular route takes in much of the old city.

Practicalities

There are fifteen **trains** a day from Madrid via El Escorial to Ávila, with onward connections to Salamanca and Valladolid. The **train station** is at the bottom of Avda José Antonio, to the east below the new part of town. **Buses** to and from Madrid and Segovia use a terminal on the Avda de Madrid. The **tourist office** (Mon–Fri 9.30am–2pm & 4–7pm, Sat 9.30am–1.30pm; ☎918/211387) is in the Plaza de la Catedral, directly opposite the cathedral entrance.

Cheap **rooms** are easy enough to come by, though many of them are around the train station or at the end of Avda José Antonio, which is neither the most central nor the most pleasant place to be based. *Fonda San Francisco,* Trav. José Antonio 2 (☎918/220298; ②), is one of the best around here. Nearer the centre, *Hostel Santa Anna,* c/ Alfonso de Montalvo 2 (☎918/220063; ②), is a good-value place near the church of the same name. Within the walls, places are likely to be more expensive, but the *Hostal Continental* at Plaza de la Catedral 6 (☎918/211502; ②) and *Hostal el Rastro* at Plaza del

Rastro 1 (☎918/211218; ③) are pleasant and not too exorbitant; *Hostal Bellas*, c/ Caballeros 19 (☎918/212910; ②), is excellent value, especially out of season. There's a **youth hostel** in Avda de Juventud (☎918/221716), out past the Convento de Santo Tomás, but it's very small, with a strict 11pm curfew and is only open July and August.

For cheap **meals** you're best off in the heart of the old town around the unfinished Plaza de la Victoria or, again, down by the train station. Two places off this plaza are *Vinos y Comidas*, c/Carramolino 14, for very cheap *menús*, and the *Bar El Rincón*, Plaza Zurraquín 6, for a more expensive but generous three-course *menú*. The *Cafetería Maspalomas*, opposite the bus station, offers cheap, simple food. Other places are *Masón del Rastro*, Plaza del Rastro 1, with a good, reasonably priced restaurant, and *La Posada de la Fruta*, Plaza de Pedro Davida, with an attractive, sunny courtyard to drink in. There are excellent **bars** in c/García Villareal at the western edge of the old town.

Segovia

For such a small city, **SEGOVIA** has a remarkable number of outstanding architectural monuments. Most celebrated are the Roman aqueduct, the cathedral and the fairy-tale Alcázar, but the less obvious attractions – the cluster of ancient churches and the many mansions found in the lanes of the old town, all in a warm, honey-coloured stone – are what really make it worth visiting. In winter, at over 1000m, it can be very cold here.

The **Cathedral** (summer daily 9am–7pm; winter Mon–Fri 9.30am–1pm & 3–6pm, Sat & Sun 9.30am–6pm) was the last major Gothic building in Spain, probably the last anywhere. Accordingly it takes that style to its logical extreme, with pinnacles and flying buttresses tacked on at every conceivable point. Though impressive for its size alone, the interior is surprisingly bare for so florid a construction and spoiled by a great green marble *coro* at its very centre. The treasures are almost all confined to the museum which opens off the cloisters (200ptas).

Down beside the cathedral, c/de Daoiz leads past a line of souvenir shops to the church of San Andrés and on to a small park in front of the **Alcázar** (daily 10am–6/ 7pm; 350ptas). It's an extraordinary fantasy of a castle which, with its narrow towers and many turrets, looks like something out of Disneyland. And indeed it is a sham – originally built in the fourteenth and fifteenth centuries but almost completely destroyed by a fire in 1862, it was rebuilt as a deliberately hyperbolic parody of the original. Still, it should be visited, if only for the magnificent panoramas from the tower.

Keep left on the way back into the centre and you'll come to the **Plaza San Esteban** and the first of the city's Romanesque churches, with a superb, five-storeyed, twelfth-century tower. A little further, the church of **La Trinidad** preserves perhaps the purest Romanesque style in Segovia: another with the typical local characteristics is **San Millán**, which lies between the aqueduct and the bus station, and whose interior has been restored to its original form. **San Martín**, in the Plaza Juan Bravo, again demonstrates all the local stylistic peculiarities, though the best of none of them. It has the characteristic covered portico and a fine arched tower. Overlooking the same plaza, the **Torre de Lozoya** is typical of the fine secular buildings.

The **Aqueduct**, over 800m long and at its highest point towering some 30m above the Plaza de Azoguejo, stands up without a drop of mortar or cement. No one knows exactly when it was built, but it was probably around the end of the first century AD under the Emperor Trajan. If you climb the stairs beside the aqueduct you can get a view looking down over it from a surviving fragment of the city walls; though frankly it's more impressive from a distance.

Segovia is an excellent city for walking, with some fine views and beautiful churches to be enjoyed just outside the city. Perhaps the most interesting of all the ancient churches here is **Vera Cruz** (Tues–Sun 10.30am–1.30pm & 3.30–7pm; winter closes

6pm; 125ptas), a remarkable twelve-sided building outside town in the valley facing the Alcázar. It was built by the Knights Templar in the early thirteenth century on the pattern of the church of the Holy Sepulchre in Jerusalem, and once housed part of the True Cross. Inside, the nave is circular, and its heart is occupied by a strange two-storeyed chamber – again twelve-sided – in which the knights, as part of their initiation, stood vigil over the cross. Climb the tower for a highly photogenic vista of the city. While you're over here you could also visit the prodigiously walled monastery of **San Juan de la Cruz** (daily 10am–1.30pm & 4–7pm; free), with the gaudy mausoleum of its founder-saint and the rather damp, ramshackle **Monasterio del Parral** (Mon–Fri 10am–12.30pm & 3–6.30pm, Sat & Sun 9am–noon; free).

Practicalities

You can get here by **train** from Madrid or **bus** and there are onward connections by bus to Ávila and Valladolid, and by train to Valladolid. The **train station** is some distance out of town; take bus #3 to the central Plaza Mayor. Surprisingly, this main square, right by the cathedral and surrounded by pricy cafés, is the place to start looking for somewhere to stay. There are two cheap **fondas** – *Cubo* (☎911/436386; ①) and *Aragón* (☎911/433527; ①) – on different floors of the same building at Plaza Mayor 4; *Hostal Juan Bravo*, on c/Juan Bravo 12 (☎911/435521; ②) has lots of big comfortable rooms, while there are other cheap possibilities in the streets behind the plaza or down near the aqueduct. The **youth hostel** (☎911/420226; ②) is on Paseo Conde de Sepulveda near the train station, or there's a **campsite**, *Camping Acueducto* (July–Sept), a couple of kilometres out on the road to La Granja.

The **tourist office** (summer Mon–Fri 9.30am–2pm & 5–7pm, Sat 10am–2pm & 5–7pm, Sun 10am–3pm; winter closed Sat pm & Sun) is also in the Plaza Mayor. The Calle de la Infanta Isabella, which opens off the plaza beside the *turismo*, is packed with noisy **bars** and cheap **places to eat**. Segovia's culinary speciality is roast suckling pig (*cochinillo asado*) and you'll see the little pink creatures hanging in the windows of restaurants. But it's very expensive unless you're in a large group, and to many tastes overrated. *Mesón del Campesino* is one of the best in c/Infanta Isabella, with decent value *menús*. *Casa Duque*, at Cervantes 12 on the way down to the aqueduct, is much more expensive but well worth it, with excellent *paella*. Other recommended places include *José María* at c/Cronista Lecea 11, *Santa Bárbara* at c/Ezequiel Gonzáles 33, *Narízotas* in Plaza de San Martin, and the *Cocina de San Millán* at c/San Millán 3.

NEW CASTILE AND EXTREMADURA

New Castile is at first sight Spain at its least welcoming: a vast, bare plain that is the agricultural heartland of the country, burning hot in summer, chillingly exposed in winter. Most people see it only as they thunder through on their way from Madrid to Andalucía – but in the northeast of the province, where the mountains start, is the extraordinary cliff-hanging city of **Cuenca**, a place really worth going out of your way for. **Extremadura**, east of Madrid, has far more to offer. This harsh environment was the cradle of the *conquistadores*, men who opened up a new world for the Spanish empire. Remote before and forgotten since, Extremadura enjoyed a brief golden age when the heroes returned with their gold to live in a flourish of splendour. **Trujillo**, the birthplace of Pizarro, and **Cáceres** both preserve entire towns built with *conquistador* wealth, the streets crowded with the ornate mansions of returning empire builders, and there is also **Mérida**, the most completely preserved Roman city in Spain.

Cuenca

The mountainous country of the northeastern corner of New Castile, as dramatic as any in Spain, is in complete contrast to the majority of the province. The romantic city of **CUENCA**, surrounded by a startling craggy landscape, is a fitting centre. The river Huécar, and the Júcar into which it flows, enclose the old city on three sides, and their deep gorges lend the place its extraordinary character. Cross one of the many bridges and you start to climb steeply towards the Plaza Mayor, a part of town almost impossible to avoid. Entered through the arches of the baroque **Ayuntamiento**, this is the heart of the medieval quarter.

Ahead of you is the ugly unfinished facade of the **Cathedral** (daily 9am–2pm & 4–6.30pm), someone's misguided attempt to beautify a simple Gothic building. The cathedral **museum** (200ptas) is worth a look, as is the excellent new **Archeological Museum** (Tues–Sat 10am–2pm & 4–7pm, Sun 10am–2pm; 200ptas), opposite. But the artistic highlight of Cuenca is beyond doubt the **Museo de Arte Abstracto** (Tues–Fri 11am–2pm & 4–6pm, Sat 11am–2pm & 4–8pm, Sun 11am–2pm; 300ptas), housed in the finest of the city's hanging houses or *Casas Colgadas*. This wonderful museum is run by a group of leading artists of Spain's "abstract generation" and displays their work in a house that, cantilevered over the cliff edge, is almost as absorbing as the exhibition.

There are other sights in Cuenca, but the chief attraction is the place itself. Have a drink in one of the bars opposite the cathedral in the Plaza Mayor and you can appreciate what it must feel like to live in one of the houses hanging off the cliff edge – then walk along the gorge of the Huécar to look up at the *Casas Colgadas* and the other less secure-looking buildings above the river. At night the effect is magical.

Whether you arrive by **train** (unbearably slow) or **bus** you'll be at the bottom of the modern part of town: the bus station is just beyond the train terminal. There are **hostales** and **fondas** in the side streets to either side of c/Ramón y Cajal and c/18 de Julio, which lead up towards the old town, but very few in the old town itself. *Pensión Maria*, c/Ramón y Coyal 53 (☎966/221978; ②), or *Posada San Julian*, c/de las Torres 1 (☎966/211704; ②), are among the most pleasant budget options, but if you're prepared to pay a little more for one of the most attractive *hostal* buildings in the country, try the *Posada de San José* at c/Julián Romesco 4 near the cathedral (☎966/211300; ③) for which you should book.

For **food**, there's a fair choice in the Plaza Mayor right at the heart of the old town, although these places are inevitably rather touristy – *Mangana* is worth a try at Plaza Mayor 3. In the new town, the *mesones* on c/San Francisco are good for snacks; there are a few cheap places at the bottom of c/de las Torres like the *Posada San Julian*, or stretch to the excellent but expensive *Restaurante Figón de Pedro*, c/Cervantes 13. Cuenca's **tourist office** (Mon–Fri 9am–2pm & 4.30–6.30pm, Sat 10am–1pm) is at c/García Izeara 8, on the way into town from the bus and train stations.

Trujillo

TRUJILLO is the first place you're likely to want to stop on the main road from Madrid to Extremadura and Portugal. At its heart – on a rise dominating the surrounding plains – is a walled town virtually untouched since the sixteenth century, redolent above all of the exploits of the conquerors of the Americas; Francisco Pizarro was born here, as were many of the tiny band who with such extraordinary cruelty defeated the Incas with him.

From the bus station work your way uphill through the narrow streets to the huge Plaza Mayor, where a statue of the town's most famous son bars the way to the monuments on the hill behind. In the southwest corner is the **Palacio de la Conquista** (daily 10.30am–2pm & 4.30–7pm), perhaps the grandest of Trujillo's mansions, and just one of the many built by the Pizarro clan. It was originally inhabited by Francisco's half-brother and son-in-law Hernando, who returned from the conquests to live here with his half-Inca bride, Francisco's daughter. Diagonally opposite is the bulky church of **San Martín** with the tomb, among others, of the Orellana family; Francisco de Orellana was the first explorer of the Amazon. From here you can begin to climb into the walled town – where much restoration work is going on as people move into and do up the old houses – and towards the Moorish castle at its highest point.

From the plaza, c/de Ballesteros leads up to the walls, past the domed **Torre Del Alfiler** with its coats of arms and storks' nests, and through the gateway known as the Arco de Santiago. Here, to the left, is **Santa María Mayor** (daily 9am–2pm & 4.30–7pm), the most interesting of the town's many churches. Of the many remaining mansions, or *solares*, the most interesting is the **Palacio de Orellana-Pizarro**, which nowadays houses the local school. The **castle** itself is now virtually in open countryside; for the last hundred metres of the climb you see nothing but the occasional broken-down remnant of a wall clambered over by sheep and dogs. The fortress, though, its original Moorish towers much reinforced by later defenders, has recently been restored. Below the castle, the **Casa Museo Pizarro** commemorates the conquistador's life and exploits in Peru, but is a dull, overpriced affair (Tues–Sun 11am–2pm & 4.30–6.30pm; 300ptas).

Plaza Mayor is the site of the **tourist office** (Tues–Fri 9am–2pm & 5–7pm, Sat & Sun 9.15am–2pm), and a couple of **hostales**. *La Cadena* at no. 8 (☎927/321463; ③) and *Hostal Nuria* at no. 29 (☎927/320907; ③) offer a degree of luxury, while *Pensión Boni*, c/Domingo de Ramos 7, off the northeast corner (☎927/321604; ②), is a clean, well-run budget choice. There are plenty of places to eat in the Plaza Mayor: perhaps the best is *La Troya*, with its huge *menús*; the *Pizarro* is a rather more fancy restaurant, or there are excellent *tapas* at the *Bar Las Cigüeñas* and *Bar La Pata*, around the corner.

Cáceres

CÁCERES is in many ways remarkably like Trujillo: its centre is an almost perfectly preserved medieval town adorned with mansions built on the proceeds of American exploration, and every available tower and spire is crowned by a clutch of storks' nests. Cáceres has perhaps been over-restored, and it can be very commercial – on the other hand it's a much larger and livelier place, a rapidly growing provincial capital which is also home to the University of Extremadura.

Even with a map you'll probably get lost among the winding alleys of the old town, so as a preliminary orientation try standing in the Plaza Mayor opposite the tourist office. To your left is the **Torre del Bujaco** – whose foundations date back to Roman times – with a chapel next to it and steps leading up to the low **Arco de la Estrella**, piercing the walls. To the right is the **Torre del Horno**, one of the best-preserved Moorish mud-brick structures surviving in Spain. A staircase leads up to another gateway, and beyond this is the most intact stretch of the ancient walls with several more of the original towers. Though basically Moorish in construction, the walls have been added to, altered and built against ever since. Around the other side of the old town, one Roman gateway, the **Arco del Cristo**, can still be seen.

Inside the walls, almost every building is magnificent – look out in particular for the family crests adorning many of the mansions. Through the Estrella gate, the **Casa de Toledo-Montezuma** with its domed tower is immediately to the left. To this house a follower of Cortés brought back one of the New World's more exotic prizes – a daughter of the Aztec emperor as his bride. Directly ahead is the **Plaza Santa María** with an impressive group of buildings around a refreshingly unencumbered Gothic church. The church of **San Mateo**, on the site of the ancient mosque at the town's highest point, is another Gothic structure with several attractive chapels. Next to it is the **Casa** de las **Cigüeñas** (House of the Storks) whose narrow tower was the only one allowed to preserve its original battlements when the rest were shorn by royal decree; it is now a military installation.

In the Plaza San Mateo is the **Museo Provincial** (Tues–Sat 9.30am–2.30pm, Sun 10.15am–2.30pm; 200ptas), worth visiting as much for the chance to see inside one of the finer mansions as for its well displayed local collection. Its highlight is the cistern of the original Moorish Alcázar with fine rooms of excellent horseshoe arches. The same ticket admits you to the **Fine Arts** section in the Casa de los Caballos behind it, where the work is all religious in inspiration; the same building also has the two floors dedicated to contemporary art and sculpture, with work by Miró and Picasso as well as younger, up-and-coming artists.

Practicalities

The **train station** and the new **bus station** face each other across the Carretera Sevilla, some way out: buses run from here every half-hour to a square in the new part of town near the centre, with signs leading on towards the Plaza Mayor and the **tourist office** (Mon–Fri 9am–2pm & 4/5–6/7pm, Sat & Sun 9am–2pm).The best **places to stay** are all in its immediate vicinity – try the basic but clean and convenient *Pensión Carretero* at no. 22 (☎927/247482; ②) – or if you have no luck round here, the *Hostal Princesa*, c/Camiro Llano 34 (☎927/227000; ②), is good value, down the hill out of the gate and to the left. Right on the plaza the cheapest **meals** are served at *El Puchero*, though the food is nothing special; the slightly more expensive *El Pato Blanco* is probably worth the extra. *El Figón*, in Plaza San Juan just off c/Pintores, is another step up in class. Calle de Pizarro, just outside the walls on the west side of the old town, is a good place for **bars**, or try *Lancelot*, off Cuesta del Marqués in the old town, run by an Englishman and classy but fun.

Mérida

Former capital of the Roman province of Lusitania, **MÉRIDA** contains one of the most remarkable assemblages of Roman monuments to be found anywhere – scattered in the midst of the modern city are remains of everything from engineering works to domestic villas. With the aid of a map and a little imagination, it's not hard to reconstruct the Roman city within the not especially attractive modern town.

Start your tour by the magnificent **Puente Romano**, the Roman bridge across the islet-strewn Guadiana – sixty arches long, though seven in the middle where replaced in the fifteenth century. It is defended by an enormous, plain **Alcazaba**, built by the Moors to replace a Roman construction (daily 9am–1.45pm & 5–7.15pm; 200pta ticket also includes theatre, amphitheatre and the villas). The interior is a rather barren archeological site, though you can descend into the impressive cistern. Nearby is the sixteenth-century **Plaza de España**, the heart of the modern town, while on c/Romero Leal Sagasta east of here is the so-called **Templo de Diana**, currently the object of an overzealous restoration project. In the other direction you'll find the **Arco Trajano**, an unadorned triumphal arch 15m high and 9m across.

By far the most important site, however, is that containing the **Teatro Romano** and **Anfiteatro** (daily 8am–10pm). The theatre, a present to the city from Agrippa around 15 BC, is one of the best preserved anywhere, and one of the most beautiful monuments of the entire Roman world. The stage is in a particularly good state of repair, while many of the seats have been rebuilt to offer more comfort to the audiences of the annual July season of classical plays. The adjacent amphitheatre is a slightly later and much plainer construction which in its day could accommodate as many as 15,000 people – almost half the current population of Mérida.

Just across from these buildings is the vast, red-brick bulk of the **Museo Nacional de Arte Romano** (Tues–Sat 10am–2pm & 4/5–6/7pm, Sun 10am–2pm; 200ptas), a magnificent new museum which does full justice to its high-class collection, including portrait statues of Augustus, Tiberius and Drusus, and some glorious mosaics. One of two Roman villas in Mérida, the **Casa Romana Anfiteatro** (daily 9am–1.45pm & 5–7pm), lies immediately below the museum: the other, the **Mithraeo** is situated in the shadow of the Plaza de Toros, but is closed for renovations. Both have good mosaics – especially the Casa Romana. The remaining monuments are further out, near the rail lines. A feat of imagination is required to re-create the **circus** in one's mind, as almost nothing of the masonry is left. The **Acueducto de los Milagros** is more satisfying, with a good portion surviving in the midst of vegetable gardens. Its tall arches of granite with brick courses brought water to the city in its earliest days from the reservoir at Proserpina, 5km away.

Practicalities

Mérida is a lively place for its size, and the whole area between the train station and the Plaza de España is full of **bars and cheap restaurants**. There are good value four-course *menús* at the *Restaurante Naya*, Cardero 7, close to the station, and better food for slightly more money at the *Restaurante Briz*, Félix Valverde Lillo 5, just off the plaza. Budget **accommodation**, on the other hand, is not plentiful. Best bet is the popular *Pensión El Arco*, c/Sta Beatriz de Silva 4 (☎924/310107; ②), near the Arco Trajaro. Otherwise there is good value at the *Hostal Nueva España*, Avda Extremadura 6 (☎924/313356; ②), the *Hostal Salud*, c/Vespasiano 41 (☎924/312259; ③), or the *Hostal Bueno*, c/Calvario 9 (☎924/311013; ③). There's a **campsite** not far out of town on the highway, or a much more attractive summer-only site at Proserpina, some 5km north, where you can swim in the reservoir. The **tourist office** is at the entrance to the Roman theatre site (Mon–Fri 9am–2pm & 4/5–6/7pm, Sat & Sun 9.15am–2pm).

ANDALUCÍA

Above all else – and there is plenty – it is the great Moorish monuments that vie for your attention in **Andalucía**. The Moors, a mixed race of Berbers and Arabs who crossed into Spain from North Africa, occupied *al-Andalus* for over seven centuries. Their first forces landed at Tarifa in 710 AD and within four years they had conquered virtually the whole of Spain; their last kingdom, Granada, fell to the Christian Reconquest in 1492. Between these dates they developed the most sophisticated civilization of the Middle Ages, centred in turn on the three major cities of **Córdoba**, **Sevilla** and **Granada**. Each one preserves extraordinarily brilliant and beautiful monuments, of which the most perfect is Granada's **Alhambra palace**.

On **the coast** it's easy to despair. Extending to either side of **Málaga** is the **Costa del Sol**, Europe's most developed resort area, with its beaches hidden behind a remorseless curtain of concrete hotels and apartment complexes. However, there is life beyond the Costa del Sol, especially the beaches of the Costa de la Luz towards Cádiz on the Atlantic coast, and those around Almería in the southeast corner of Spain.

Inland, and in the cities away from the tourist gaze, this is still an undeveloped, often extremely poor part of the country. For all its poverty, however, Andalucía is also Spain at its most exuberant: the home of *flamenco* and the bullfight, and the traditional images of exotic Spain. These are best absorbed at one of the hundreds of annual **ferias** and **romerías**. The best of them include the giant April Fair in Sevilla, the pilgrimage to El Rocío near Huelva in late May, and the Easter celebrations at Málaga and Sevilla.

The Costa del Sol

Perhaps the outstanding feature of the **Costa del Sol** is its ease of access. Hundreds of charter flights arrive here every week, and it's often possible to get an absurdly cheap ticket from London. **Málaga airport** is positioned midway between Málaga, the main city on the coast, and Torremolinos, its most grotesque resort. You can get to either town, cheaply and easily, by taking the electric railway which runs every half-hour along the coast between Málaga and Fuengirola. Granada, Córdoba and Sevilla are all within easy reach of Málaga; so too are Ronda and the "White Towns". In some ways then, this coast's enormous popularity is not surprising: what is surprising is that the **beaches** are generally grit-grey rather than golden and the sea is none too clean.

Málaga

MÁLAGA seems at first just a rather large and ugly town. It's the second city of the south, after Sevilla, and also one of the poorest. Yet though many people get no further than the rail or bus stations, and though the clusters of high-rises look pretty grim as you approach, it can be a surprisingly attractive place. Around the old fishing villages of El Palo and Pedregalejo, now absorbed into the suburbs, are a series of small beaches and a *paseo* lined with some of the best fish and seafood cafés in the province. And overlooking the town and port are the Moorish citadels of the Alcazaba and Gibralfaro – excellent introductions to the architecture before pressing on to the main sites at Córdoba and Granada.

The **Alcazaba** (Mon–Sat 10am–1pm & 4–7pm, Sun 10am–2pm; 100ptas) is the place to make for if you're killing time between connections. It lies just fifteen minutes' walk from the train or bus stations, and can be clearly seen from most central points. The palace near the top of the hill was the residence of the Arab Emirs of Málaga, who briefly ruled an independent kingdom from here: it has been restored as an archeological museum. Above the Alcazaba, and connected to it by a long double wall, is the **Gibralfaro castle** (free access), with enjoyable gardens, fine views and a café.

These monuments aside, Málaga's greatest claim to fame is undoubtedly its **fried fish**, acknowledged as the best in Spain. It's served everywhere, especially around the Alameda, or you can take bus #11 (from the Paseo del Parque) out to **Pedregalejo**, where the seafront **paseo** begins. Almost any of the cafés and restaurants here will serve terrific fish, though you'll have to watch the price. There are plenty of reasonably priced **rooms** if you want to stay in Málaga, above all in the grid of streets north of the Alameda. You're likely to get an offer of somewhere to stay as you arrive – if not a couple to try are *Hostal La Palma*, c/Martínez 3 (☎952/226772; ②), or *La Macarena* at c/San Agustín 9, not far from the cathedral (②). The closest **campsite** is the *Balneario del Carmen*, a gritty affair 3km out of town on Avda Juan Sebastián Elcano, well positioned for the Pedregalejo *paseo* – get there on bus #11.

Bus #3 connects the centre to the main **train and bus stations**, which are very close to each other; the main **tourist office** is at c/Marqués de Larios 5 (Mon–Fri 9.30am–1.30pm & 4–6pm, Sat 9.30am–1pm), with a branch at the bus station.

Along the coast

The **eastern stretch of the Costa del Sol**, from Málaga to Almería, is generally not too inspiring. Though far less developed than the wall-to-wall concrete from Torremolinos to Marbella in the west, it is not exactly unspoiled. If you're desperate for a swim, head for **SALOBREÑA**. The white hilltop town is set back 2km from the sea and comparatively little developed; the beach is a fair sandy strip, only partially flanked by hotels. There's a good **campsite** by the sea, and there are rooms available too – try the *Hostal López*, Camino de la Playa 18 (☎610053; ②).

To the west the real **Costa del Sol** gets going. It's estimated that 300,000 foreigners live on the Costa del Sol, the richest and fastest-growing resort area in the Mediterranean, with marina developments like ritzy Puerto Banús attracting Arab as well as European and North American money. Approached in the right kind of spirit it's possible to have fun in **TORREMOLINOS**, a resort so over-the-top it's magnificent, and with furious competition keeping prices down. A good time costs more in chic **MARBELLA**, where there are bars and nightclubs galore alongside a surprisingly well preserved old village and some wonderfully conspicuous consumption. But if you've come to Spain to be in Spain, put on the shades and stay on the coach at least until you reach **ESTEPONA** – it may be somewhat drab, but at least it's restrained, and there's space to breathe. The long dark-pebbly beach has been enlivened a little by a promenade studded with flowers and palms, and, away from the seafront, the old town is very pretty, with cobbled alleyways and two delightful plazas. There's a **campsite** here, and a number of **hostales**, like the *Hostal Vista al Mar*, c/Real 154 (☎2803247; ②).

Gibraltar

The interest of **GIBRALTAR** is essentially its novelty: the genuine appeal of the strange, looming physical presence of its rock, and the increasingly dubious one of its preservation as one of Britain's last colonies. It's a curious place to visit, not least to witness the bizarre process of its opening to mass tourism from the Costa del Sol – a sign of movement on the political future of the rock after years when the Spanish sealed the border. Ironically, this threatens to destroy Gibraltar's highly individual society and at the same time to make it much more British, after the fashion of the expatriate communities and huge resorts of the Costa. Beware that the **currency** used here is the Gibraltar pound (the same value as the British pound, but different notes and coins); if you pay in pesetas, you generally pay about five percent more.

Town and rock have a necessarily simple layout. **Main Street** (La Calle Real) runs for most of the town's length a couple of blocks back from the port; from the frontier it's a short bus ride or about a fifteen-minute walk. From near the end of Main Street you can hop on a **cable car** (Mon–Sat 9.30am–7.15pm) which will carry you up to the summit of Gibraltar – **The Top of the Rock** as it's logically known – via **Apes' Den** halfway up. This is a fairly reliable viewing point to see the tailless monkeys and hear the guides explain their legend. From The Top you can look over to the Atlas Mountains and down to the town and nearby beaches. From the Apes' Den it's an easy walk south along Queens Road to **Saint Michael's Cave**, an immense natural cavern which led ancient people to believe the rock was hollow and gave rise to its old name of *Mons Calpe* (Hollow Mountain).

Although you can be lazy and take the cable car both ways, you might instead walk up via Williss Road to visit the **Tower of Homage**. Dating from the fourteenth century, this is the most visible survival from the old **Moorish Castle**. Further up you'll find the **Upper Galleries**, blasted out of the rock during the Great Siege of 1779–82, in order to point guns down at the Spanish lines. To walk down, take the **Mediterranean Steps** – a very steep descent most of the way down the east side, turning the southern corner of the Rock. You'll pass through the Jews' Gate and into Engineer Road. From here, return to town through the Alameda Gardens and the **Trafalgar Cemetery**. This grand tour takes a half to a full day and shows you almost all there is to see: all sites on it are open Monday to Saturday from 10am to 7pm in summer (5.30pm in winter); if you visit all the attractions, buy a reduced-price ticket which includes the cave as well.

Back in town, incorporated into the **Gibraltar Museum** (Mon–Fri 10am–6pm), are two well-preserved, beautiful fourteenth-century **Moorish Baths**. This, along with the casino and the miniature golf, is about the extent of it.

Practicalities

The main **tourist office** is in Cathedral Square, and there are also offices at the airport, the Gibraltar Museum, Market Place and the Waterport coach park. If you have a car, don't attempt to bring it to Gibraltar – the queues at the border are always atrocious, and parking is a nightmare.

Shortage of space also means that **accommodation** is at a premium.. The only remotely cheap beds are at the *Toc H Hostel* on Line Wall Road (☎350/73431; ③) or the tiny *Seruya's Guest House* in Irish Town (☎350/73220; ②), both invariably full. **Camping** is strictly forbidden. **Food and drink** are by Spanish standards relatively expensive, though pub snacks or fish and chips are reliable standbys. Main Street is crowded with touristy places, among which *Smith's Fish and Chip Shop*, near the Convent, is worth a try. Elsewhere, try the *Penny Farthing* on King Street, *Happy Eater* in Cornwall's Lane, *Corks Wine Bar* in Irish Town, the *Market Café* in the public market, or *Splendid Bar* in George's Lane. **Pubs** all tend to mimic traditional English styles (and prices), the difference being that they are open all day and often into the wee hours. Places on Main Street tend to be rowdy at night – full of squaddies and visiting sailors.

A functional attraction of Gibraltar is its role as a **port for Morocco**. The timetable seems to change every few weeks, but in season there should be a catamaran to Tangier daily (1hr) as well as ferries to Tangier and occasionally to Mdiq. Tickets are sold at *Beagle Travel*, 9B Georges Lane, or *Tourafrica* in the International Commercial Centre, Casemates Square.

Algeciras

The main reason to visit **ALGECIRAS**, on the far side of the bay to Gibraltar, is for the **ferry to Morocco** – and the number of people passing through guarantees plenty of rooms. If you have trouble finding space, pick up a plan and check out the list in the **tourist office** on c/Juan de la Cierva, towards the river and railway line from the port. The port/harbour area also has plenty of **places to eat** – among them, down by the tourist office and invariably crowded, the very good value *Casa Alfonso*.

There are three or four **crossings to Tangier** each day (2hr 30min), and six or seven to the Spanish *presidio* of **Ceuta** (1hr 30min). Tickets are available at scores of travel agents all along the waterside and on most approach roads. Wait till Tangier – or if you're going via Ceuta, Tetouan – before buying any Moroccan currency. Local **buses** connect La Línea (the frontier town for Gibraltar) and Algeciras every half-hour, and there are equally regular direct services between Algeciras and Gibraltar.

Ronda

Andalucía is dotted with small, brilliantly whitewashed settlements known as the **Pueblos Blancos** or "White Towns", most often straggling up hillsides towards a castle or towered church. Perhaps the best lie in a roughly triangular area between Málaga, Algeciras and Sevilla, at whose centre is the spectacular town of **RONDA**, connected by a marvellous rail line to Algeciras. The full natural drama of Ronda, rising amid a ring of dark, angular mountains, is best appreciated as you enter the town. Built on an isolated ridge of the sierra, it's split in half by a gaping river gorge that drops sheer for 130m. Still more spectacular, the gorge is spanned by a stupendous eighteenth-century arched **bridge**, while tall whitewashed houses lean from its precipitous edges. Much of the attraction lies in this extraordinary view, but the town itself is fascinating to wander around and has sacrificed surprisingly little of its character to the flow of day-trippers from the Costa.

It divides neatly into three parts: on the near (northwest) side of the gorge, where you'll arrive, is the largely modern **Mercadillo** quarter; across the new bridge is the old Moorish town, the **Ciudad**, and its **San Francisco** suburb. Entering the Ciudad you'll cross c/Marqués de Parada, where at no. 17 is the **Casa del Rey Moro**, an early eighteenth-century mansion built on Moorish foundations, from whose garden a remarkable underground stairway descends to the river; these 365 steps, guaranteeing a water supply in times of siege, were cut by Christian slaves in the fourteenth century. Further down the same street is the splendid Renaissance **Palacio del Marqués de Salvatierra** (tours Mon–Wed & Fri–Sat 11am–2pm & 4–6pm, Sun 11am–2pm; 150ptas), and just down the hill the two old bridges – the **Puente Viejo** of 1616 and the single-span Moorish **Puente de San Miguel**. Nearby, on the southeast bank of the river, are the distinctive **Baños Árabes**, which – if not closed for restoration – you can usually visit for a small tip.

At the centre of the Ciudad quarter stands the cathedral church of **Santa María Mayor**, originally the Arab town's Friday mosque, while across the square is the **Casa de Mondragón**, probably the palace of the Moorish kings (daily 8am–2pm). Near the end of the Ciudad are the ruins of the **Alcázar**, destroyed by the French in 1809. Once it was virtually impregnable – as indeed was this whole fortress capital, which ruled an independent and isolated Moorish kingdom until 1485, just seven years before the fall of Granada – now it's full of litter and stray sheep. The principal gate of the town, through which passed the Christian conquerors, stands to the southeast of the Alcázar at the entrance to the suburb of San Francisco.

Over in **Mercadillo** quarter, look out for the **bullring** – one of the most prestigious in Spain – and the beautiful clifftop *paseo* from which you get good views of the old and new bridges.

Practicalities

All the **places to stay** are in the Mercadillo quarter, two of the cheapest very close to the bridge near the Plaza de España: an unnamed *casa de huéspedes* is in the square itself, and the *Huéspedes La Española*, c/José Aparicio 3 (☎952/871052; ②), is in the alleyway behind the **tourist office** (Mon–Fri 10am–2.30pm). Another cheap bet is the *Hostal Ronda Sol* (☎952/874497; ②) at c/Cristo 11, near the intersection with c/Sevilla.

As for **eating**, most of the bargain options are grouped round the far end of the Plaza del Socorro. As you leave it on c/Almendra, the *Restaurante Faroles* is very popular, as is the adjacent *Las Cañas*; there are a couple of good *tapas* bars in a modern arcade just behind, or try *La Rosalejo*, on the street running off the square towards c/Sevilla. The **bar** in the middle of the bridge – reached by a stairway in the Plaza de España, and operating only seasonally – is perhaps the most spectacular option.

Sevilla

SEVILLA is the great city of the Spanish south, intensely hot in summer and with an abiding reputation for theatricality and intensity. There are three important monuments – the **Giralda tower**, the **Cathedral** and the **Alcázar** – and an illustrious history to go with them, but it's the living self of this city of Carmen, Don Juan and Figaro that remains the great attraction. It is expressed on a phenomenally grand scale at the city's two great festivals – the **Semana Santa**, during the week before Easter, and the **April Feria**, which lasts a week at the end of the month. Sevilla is also Spain's second most important centre for **bullfighting**, after Madrid.

The birthplace of prime minister **Felipe González**, Sevilla has benefited considerably from his time in office – above all through gaining the **Expo 92** world fair, with all the attendant benefits for the infrastructure. Nonetheless it remains poor: petty crime is a big problem, especially in the form of bag-snatching and breaking into cars. The fairgrounds for Expo 92 are at **La Isla de la Cartuja**, northwest of the centre across the river, where Columbus' remains are said to have rested before finally being moved to the Dominican Republic; free buses take visitors from the centre.

Arrival and information

The new **train station**, Santa Justa, is a long way out of the centre on Avda Kansas City, which is also the airport road; bus #70 connects it to the main bus station. Bus #EA, the **airport** service, also passes the station, and terminates in the centre at the Puerta de Jerez, at the top of Avda Roma between the tourist office and the Fábrica de Tabacos. The **main bus station** is at the Prado de San Sebastián. Most companies and destinations go from here: exceptions include buses for Badajoz and Extremadura (*La Estrella* terminal in c/Arenal, by the bullring), and the province of Huelva (*Empresa Damas*, c/Segura, near Plaza de Armas, aka Plaza de la Legíon, near the Puente de Isabel II). The **tourist office** is at Avda de la Constitución 21 (Mon–Sat 9.30am–7.30pm; ☎4221404).

> The area telephone code for Sevilla is ☎95.

Accommodation

The most attractive **area to stay** in town is undoubtedly the **Barrio Santa Cruz**, near the cathedral, although this is generally reflected in the prices you have to pay. Rooms are relatively expensive everywhere, in fact, and almost impossible to find during the big festivals. If you can't find anything in the Barrio, try on its periphery or slightly further out to the north of the Plaza Nueva, over towards the river and the old Córdoba station.

HOSTELS AND HOTELS

Albergue Juvenil Sevilla, c/Isaac Peral 2 (☎4613150). Crowded youth hostel some way out in the University district; take bus #34 from Puerta de Jerez or Plaza Nueva. ②

Pensión Alcázar, c/Deán Miranda 12. Tiny place in a tiny street beside the Alcázar, good value if they have space. ②

Hostal Bienvenido, c/Archeros 14 (☎4413655). Another fairly small place; small rooms but nice roof terrace. ④

Casa Diego, Plaza Curtidores 7 (☎4413552). Probably the best value of several around here. ②

Casa de Huéspedes Buen Dormir, c/Farnesio 8 (☎4217492). Friendly place in a street with several possibilities; check the room. ③

Casa Moreno, Avda Cádiz 15 (☎4421460). Not the prettiest, but very close to the bus station. ②

Hostal Galatea, c/San Juan de la Palma 4, near the Iglesia de San Pedro (☎4563564). Friendly new *hostal* in a restored town house. ③

Hostal Goya, c/Mateos Gagos 31 (☎4211170). Good value, with a range of rooms, in another street with several choices. ③

Pensión Pérez Montilla, Plaza Curtidores 13 (☎4421854). Many facilities including air-conditioning. ⑤

Hostal Santa María, c/Hernando Colón 19; ☎4228505). Small place on a noisy street, but in the Giralda's shadow and cheap. ②

Hotel Simón, c/García de Vinuesa 19 (☎4226660). Well-restored mansion with excellent position across from the cathedral. Can be a bargain out of season. ④

Hostal Suiza, c/Méndez Núñez 16 (☎4220813). Just off Plaza Nueva – a range of rooms and prices, so look first. ④

CAMPSITES

Camping Sevilla (☎4514379). Right by the airport, so very noisy but otherwise not a bad site. The airport bus will get you there.

Club de Campo (☎4720520). 12km out in Dos Hermanas, a pleasant shady site with a pool. Half-hourly buses from the bus station.

The City

Sevilla was one of the earliest **Moorish conquests** (in 712) and, as part of the Caliphate of Córdoba, became the second city of *al-Andalus*. When the Caliphate broke up in the early eleventh century it was the most powerful of the independent states to emerge, extending its power over the Algarve and eventually over Córdoba itself. This period, under a series of three Arabic rulers from the Abbadid dynasty (1023–91), was something of a golden age for Sevilla, and it enjoyed a second under the Almohads, as capital of this last real Moorish empire in Spain from 1170 until 1212. In this period the Almohads rebuilt the Alcázar, enlarged the principal **mosque** and erected a new and brilliant minaret, topped with four copper spheres that could be seen from miles round. This minaret, the **Giralda**, was the culmination of Almohad architecture: it was used by the Moors both for calling the faithful to prayer and as an observatory, and was so venerated that they wanted to destroy it before the Christian conquest of the city. Instead the Giralda became the bell tower of the Christian **Cathedral**, and continues to dominate the skyline. You can ascend to the bell chamber for a remarkable view of the city and of the Gothic details of the cathedral's buttresses and statuary. But most impressive of all is the tower's inner construction, a series of 35 gentle ramps wide enough to allow two mounted guards to pass.

Originally the mosque itself was also preserved, reconsecrated as the cathedral. But in 1402 the cathedral chapter dreamt up plans for a new monument to Christian glory: "a building on so magnificent a scale that posterity will believe we were mad." From the old structure only the Giralda and the Moorish entrance court, the **Patio de los Naranjos**, were spared. The Cathedral (Mon–Sat 10am–4pm, Sun 2–4pm; 500ptas), the largest Gothic church in the world, was completed in just over a century. The central nave rises to 42 metres, and even the side chapels seem tall enough to contain an ordinary church. The total area covers 11,520 square metres, making it the third largest church in the world after Saint Paul's in London and Saint Peter's in Rome. However, recent calculations based on cubic measurements have now placed it in the number one spot.

In the centre of the church, an impressive choir opens on to the Capilla Mayor, dominated by a vast Gothic **retable** composed of 45 carved scenes from the life of Christ. The lifetime's work of a single craftsman, Pierre Dancart, this is the supreme masterpiece of the cathedral – the largest altarpiece in the world and one of the finest examples of Gothic woodcarving. You can also visit the domed Renaissance **Capilla Real**, built on the site of the original royal burial chapel, the **Sala Capitular**, with paintings by Murillo, and the the grandiose **Sacristía Mayor**, which houses the treasury.

Rulers of Sevilla have occupied the site of the **Alcázar** (Tues–Sat 10.30am–6pm, Sun 10am–2pm; 600ptas, free with *ISIC* card) from the time of the Romans. Here was built the great court of the Abbadids, which reached a peak of sophistication and exaggerated sensuality under the cruel and ruthless al-Mu'tadid – a ruler who enlarged the palace in order to house a harem of 800 women, and who decorated the terraces with flowers planted in the skulls of his enemies. Later, under the Almohads, the complex was turned into a citadel, forming the heart of the town's fortifications. Its extent was enormous, stretching to the Torre del Oro on the bank of the Guadalquivir. Parts of the Almohad walls survive, but the present structure of the palace dates almost entirely from the Christian period. Sevilla was a favoured residence of the Spanish kings for some four centuries after the reconquest – most particularly of **Pedro the Cruel** (1350–69) who lived in and ruled from the Alcázar. Pedro embarked upon a complete rebuilding of the palace, employing workmen from Granada and utilizing fragments of earlier Moorish buildings in Sevilla, Córdoba and Valencia. His works, some of the best surviving examples of **Mudéjar architecture**, form the nucleus of the Alcázar today. Later additions include a wing in which early expeditions to the Americas were planned, and the huge Renaissance apartments of Charles V. On a more mundane level, kitchens were installed to provide for General Franco, who stayed in the royal apartments whenever he visited Sevilla. Don't miss either the beautiful and rambling **Alcázar gardens**, the confused but enticing product of several eras.

Just ten minutes' walk to the east of the cathedral and centre, the **Plaza de España** and adjoining **María Luisa Park**, laid out in 1929 for an abortive "Fair of the Americas", are an ideal place to spend the middle part of the day. En route you pass by the **Fábrica de Tabacos**, the old tobacco factory that was the setting for Bizet's *Carmen*. Nowadays it's part of the university. Towards the end of the María Luisa Park, the grandest surviving pavilions from the fair (which was scuppered by the Wall Street Crash) have been adapted as **museums**. The furthest contains the city's **archeology** collections (Tues–Sun 10am–2pm), and opposite is the **Popular Arts Museum** (same hours), with interesting displays relating to the April *feria*.

After the park, perhaps the two best areas of Sevilla in which to wander – stopping for the occasional drink – are the Barrio Santa Cruz and the banks of the Guadalquivir. **Santa Cruz** is very much in character with the city's romantic image, its streets narrow and tortuous to keep out the sun, the houses brilliantly whitewashed and barricaded with iron grilles. One of the most beautiful is within the Baroque **Hospicio de los Venerables Sacerdotes**, near the centre in a plaza of the same name – one of the few buildings in the Barrio to actively seek out.

Down by the **Guadalquivir** the main landmark is the twelve-sided **Torre del Oro**, built in 1220 as part of the Alcázar fortifications. The tower later stored the gold brought back to Sevilla from the Americas – hence its name. It now houses a small **naval museum** (Tues–Sat 10am–1pm, Sun 10am–1pm; 20ptas). One block away is the **Hospital de la Caridad** (10am–1pm & 3–6pm; 200ptas) founded in 1676 by Don Miguel de Manara, the inspiration for Byron's Don Juan. Having repented his youthful excesses, he joined the Brotherhood of Charity and set up this hospital for the relief of the dying and destitute, for which purpose it is still used. There are some magnificent paintings by Murillo and Valdés Leal inside. There's more art further along at the **Museo de Bellas Artes** on Plaza del Museo (Tues–Sun 10am–2pm; 250ptas, free with EC passport), housed in a beautiful former convent. Outstanding are the paintings by Zurbarán of Carthusian monks at supper and El Greco's portrait of his son.

Eating, drinking and nightlife

Sevilla is a tremendously atmospheric place, and the city is packed with lively bars. Remember, though, that it can also can be very expensive. If you want to **eat** well and cheaply you'll generally have to steer clear of the sights and of the Barrio Santa Cruz. A couple of exceptions are the *Bodegón Pez Espada*, c/Hernando Colón (near the cathedral), and the *Buffet Libre* and *Bar-Pizzeria El Artesano* on c/Mateus Gagos. These apart, the two most promising central areas are down towards the bullring and north of here towards the Plaza del Duque de la Victoria, where you'll find cheap *comidas* at places on c/Marqués de Paradas, c/Canalejas and particularly c/San Eloy.

For straight drinking and occasional *tapas* you can be much less selective. There are **bars** all over town – a high concentration of them with barrelled sherries from nearby Jerez and Sanlúcar (the locals drink the cold, dry *fino* with their *tapas*, especially shrimp). One of the liveliest places in **Santa Cruz** is *La Gitanilla* in c/Ximénez de Enciso (cheap drinks, expensive *tapas*), but perhaps the best *tapas* bar in the city, with just about every imaginable snack, is the *Bar Modesto* at c/Cano y Cuento 5, up at the north corner of the quarter by Avda Menéndez Pelayo. *Bar Giralda* at c/Mateus Gagol is also excellent, and Plaza Santa Teresa has a couple of bars worth searching out, particularly *Las Teresas*. Up around the Alfalfa area near the Alameda de Hércules is a lively, young area with loud **music** in many of the bars: *Sopa de Ganso* and *El Lamentable* in c/Pérez Galdos, *Alcaicería* in c/Empinado and *Trama* in c/Siete Revueltas are all worth a look.

Flamenco – or more accurately *sevillanas* – music and dance are offered at dozens of places in the city, some of them extremely tacky and expensive. Unless you've heard otherwise, avoid the fixed "shows" or *tablaos* and stick to bars – an excellent bar which often has spontaneous *sevillanas* is *La Carbonería* at c/Levías 18, tricky to find but slightly to the northeast of the Iglesia de Santa Cruz.

Listings

American Express Represented by *Viajes Alhambra*, c/Coronel Segui 3, off Pl. Nueva; (☎4212923).

Car rental Most agents are along the Avda de la Constitución. One of the cheapest operators, represented in the foyer of the *Hotel Alfonso XIII* (by the tobacco factory), is *Atesa*.

Consulates *Canada*, Avda de la Constitución 30, 2° (☎4229413); *Great Britain*, Plaza Nueva 8 (☎4228875); *US*, Paseo de las Delicias 7 (☎4231884).

Hospital English-speaking doctors available at the *Hospital Universidad*, Avda Dr. Fedriani (☎378400).

Police The main station is on Plaza de la Gavidia (☎4228840).

Post Office Avda de la Constitución 32, by the cathedral; poste restante stays open Mon–Fri 9am–8pm, Sat 9am–1pm.

Telephones Plaza de la Gavidia 7, near Plaza Concordia (Mon–Sat 9am–1pm & 5.30–9pm).

Train tickets *RENFE* office at c/Zaragoza 29, off Plaza Nueva (☎4414111 for information; ☎4421562 for reservations).

Cádiz and around

CÁDIZ, the first major town to the west of Algeciras, is among the oldest settlements in Spain, founded about 1100 BC by the Phoenicians and one of the country's principal ports ever since. Its greatest period, however, and the era from which the central part of town takes most of its appearance, was the eighteenth century. Then, with the silting up of the river to Sevilla, the port enjoyed a virtual monopoly on the Spanish-American trade in gold and silver, and on its proceeds were built the cathedral, the public halls and offices, and the smaller churches. Inner Cádiz, built on a peninsula-island, remains much as it must have looked in those days, with its grand open squares, sailors' alleyways and high, turreted houses. Crumbling from the effect of the sea air on its soft limestone, it has a tremendous atmosphere – slightly seedy, definitely in decline, but still full of mystique.

Arriving by **train** you'll find yourself on the periphery of the old town, close to the Plaza de San Juan de Dios, busiest of the many squares. By **bus** you'll be a few blocks further north, along the water. With its blind alleys, cafés and backstreets, Cádiz is fascinating to wander around, even though there's not a great deal specifically to see. A couple of things to look out for, however, are the **Museo de Bellas Artes** (Mon–Fri 10am–2pm & 5.30–8pm, Sat 10am–2pm), at Plaza de Mina 5, just across from the **tourist office**, and the cathedrals. The huge **Catedral Nueva** is High Baroque, but decorated entirely in stone, with no gold or white in sight and absolutely perfect proportions. The "Old" Cathedral, **Santa Cruz**, is worth a look mainly for an interior studded with coin-in-the-slot votive candles. There are also two churches noteworthy for the paintings they contain: the chapel of the **Hospital de Mujeres** (daily 9am–6pm) has a brilliant El Greco of *St Francis in Ecstasy*; and the oval, eighteenth-century chapel of **Santa Cueva** (Mon–Sat 10am–1pm & 4–6pm) has three frescoes by Goya.

Plaza de San Juan de Dios, protruding across the neck of the peninsula from the port, has several cafés and cheap **restaurants**. *La Caleta*, whose interior is built like the bow of a ship, is particularly good. Arrayed around the square is a dense network of alleyways crammed with **hostales**, fondas and straightforward dosshouses. *El Sardinero*, right on the square at the junction of c/Fernando (☎956/285301; ②), is a reasonable place to stay, though in general the more salubrious places are to be found a couple of blocks away, towards the cathedral or Plaza de Candelaria. Near the latter, try *Hostal Colombia*, c/Colón (☎956/287629; ③), or *Hostal Barcelona* at 10 c/Montañés (☎956/213949; ②).

Jerez de la Frontera

JEREZ DE LA FRONTERA, inland towards Sevilla, is the home and heartland of sherry and also, less known but equally important, of Spanish brandy. It seems a tempting place to stop, arrayed as it is round the scores of wine *bodegas*. But you're unlikely to want to make more than a quick visit (and tasting) between buses; the town itself is hardly distinctive unless you happen to arrive during one of the two big **festivals** – the May Horse Fair, or the celebration of the vintage towards the end of September.

The **tours of the sherry and brandy processes**, however, can be interesting, and provided you don't arrive in August when most of the industry closes down (check with *Turismo* for *bodegas* that stay open), there are a great many firms and *bodegas* to choose from. The most central, next to the large but derelict ruins of a Moorish *alcázar*, is **González Byass**. Tours are given here (and at most others) from Monday to Saturday, 9am to 1pm, and are conducted in English – the second language of Jerez's sherry fraternities. Many of the firms were founded by British Catholic refugees, barred from careers at home by the sixteenth-century Supremacy Act, and even now they form a kind of Anglo-Andalucían aristocracy. The González cellars – the *soleras* – are perhaps the oldest in Jerez, and though it's no longer used, preserve an old circular chamber designed by Eiffel.

Most of the other *bodegas* are on the outskirts of town; pick up a plan of them from the **tourist office** at Alameda Cristina 7. The **train** and **bus stations** are more or less next door to each other, eight blocks east of the González *bodega* and the central Plaza de los Reyes Católicos. For **accommodation**, head for c/Medina (left out of the bus station and three blocks along) or c/Higueras, off Medina: cheaper ones to try include *Pensión Los Amarillos* (②) on Medina and *Las Palomas* (☎956/343773; ②) on Higueras.

Córdoba

CÓRDOBA stands northeast of and upstream from Sevilla beside a loop of the Guadalquivir, which was once navigable all the way up here. It is today a minor provincial capital, prosperous in a modest sort of way. Once, however, it was the largest city of Roman Spain, and for three centuries it formed the heart of the Western Islamic Empire, the great medieval Caliphate of the Moors. For visitors, it's attraction comes down to a single building, the **Mezquita** – the grandest and most beautiful mosque ever constructed by the Moors. This stands right in the centre of the city, surrounded by the old Jewish and Moorish quarters, and is a building of extraordinary mystical and aesthetic power. The Mezquita apart, Córdoba itself is a place of considerable, if introverted charm.

Arrival and accommodation

From the **train station** the broad Avda del Gran Capitán leads down to the old quarters and the Mezquita. **Bus terminals** are numerous and scattered. The main company, *Alsina Graells*, is at Avda de Medina Azahara 29, two or three blocks to the west of the Paseo de la Victoria gardens; they run services to and from Sevilla, Granada and Málaga. For Sevilla and Granada, however, you're better off on the train.

The best **places to stay** are concentrated in the narrow maze of streets above the Mezquita. C/Rey Heredia has three *fondas*, including the reasonable *Fonda Rey Heredia* at no. 26 (☎957/474182; ②), and there are many more in the streets just off here. Less obvious, less savoury, but likely to have room, are the cheap and run-down *fondas* in the wonderfully ramshackle **Plaza de la Corredera**: *Hostal Plaza Corredera* (②), at the corner of the plaza and c/Rodríguez Marin, is clean and friendly, with great views over the plaza from some rooms. There's a brand new **youth hostel** with double rooms in the Plaza Judá Leví (☎957/290166; ②) and a **campsite** – *Campamento Municipal* – 2km north on the road to Villaviciosa, with regular bus service. The **tourist office** (Mon–Fri 9.30am–2.30pm & 5–7pm, Sat 9.30am–1.30pm) is at the Palacio de Congresos y Exposiciones in c/Torrijos alongside the Mezquita.

The City

Córdoba's domination of Moorish Spain began thirty years after the conquest, in 756, when the city was placed under the control of **Abd ar-Rahman I**, who established control over all but the north of Spain. It was he who commenced the building of the Great Mosque – **La Mezquita**, in Spanish – which was enlarged by **Abd ar-Rahman II** (822–52) as an alternative to Mecca. Possessing an original script of the Koran and a bone from the arm of Muhammad, it ranked third in sanctity after the Kaaba of Mecca and the Al Aksa mosque of Jerusalem. In the tenth century Córdoba reached its zenith under **Abd ar-Rahman III** (912–67), one of the great rulers of Islamic history. Assuming power after a period of internal strife, he re-established order and settled Córdoba firmly at the head of a caliphate that took in much of Spain and North Africa: the city itself was a serious rival to Byzantium and Baghdad. His son **al-Hakam II** virtually doubled the mosque's extent, demolishing the south wall to add fourteen extra rows of columns, and employing Byzantine craftsmen to construct a new *mihrab* or prayer niche; this remains complete and is perhaps the most beautiful example of all Moorish religious architecture. The final enlargement of the building, under the chamberlain-usurper **al-Mansur** (977–1002), involved adding seven rows of columns to the whole east side. This spoiled the symmetry of the mosque, depriving the *mihrab* of its central position, but it meant there was a bay for every day of the year.

The **Mezquita** (daily April–Sept 10am–1.30pm & 4–7pm; Oct–March 10am–1.30pm & 3.30–5.30pm; free entrance at side doors 8.30am–10am; prayer niche and cathedral accessible 11am onwards; 600ptas) is approached through the **Patio de los Naranjos**, a classic Islamic court which preserves both its orange trees and the fountains for ritual purification before prayer. Originally all nineteen naves of the mosque were open to this court, allowing the rows of interior columns to appear an extension of the trees. Inside, the twin layers of red and white pillars do seem forest-like, their uniformity broken only at the culminating point of the mosque – the domed cluster of pillars surrounding the sacred **Mihrab**.

Originally the whole design of the mosque would have directed worshippers naturally towards the *mihrab*. Today, though, you almost stumble upon it, for in the centre of the mosque squats a Renaissance **choir**. This was built in 1523 in spite of fierce opposition from the town council: on seeing the work completed, Charles V told the chapter, "You have built what you or others might have built anywhere, but you have destroyed something that was unique in the world." To the left of the choir stands an earlier and happier Christian addition – the Mudéjar **Capilla de Villaviciosa**, built by Moorish craftsmen in 1371. Beside it are the dome and pillars of the earlier *mihrab*, constructed under Abd ar-Rahman II.

After the Mezquita, the rest of Córdoba can only be anticlimactic, though there are plenty of pleasant strolls to be had. The **river** with its great **Arab waterwheels** and its **bridge** built on Roman foundations, is perhaps the most attractive area. Down behind the **Episcopal Palace** you can visit the **Alcázar de los Reyes** (daily 9.30am–1.30pm & 4–7pm; 200ptas), a fortified palace built by Ferdinand and Isabella and later occupied by the Inquisition: the gardens are more enjoyable than the interior.

North of the Mezquita lies the **Judería**, Córdoba's old Jewish quarter, a fascinating network of lanes that are more atmospheric and less commercialized than Sevilla's.

Near the heart of the quarter, at c/Maimonides 18, is a **synagogue** (Tues–Sat 10am–2pm & 3.30–5.30pm, Sun 10am–1.30pm; 50ptas), one of only three in Spain – the other two are in Toledo – that survived the Jewish expulsion of 1492. Nearby is a rather bogus **Zoco** – an Arab *souk* turned into a crafts arcade – and, adjoining this, a small but fabulously kitschy **bullfighting museum** (Tues–Sat 9.30am–1.30pm & 4–7pm, Sun 9.30am–1.30pm; 200ptas).

East of the Judería, the **Museo Arqueológico** occupies a small Renaissance mansion in which Roman foundations were discovered during conversion: these have been incorporated into an imaginative and enjoyable display. A couple of blocks below, back towards the river, you'll come upon the **Plaza del Potro**, a fine old square named after the colt (*potro*) which adorns its fountain. This, as local guides proudly point out, is mentioned in *Don Quixote*, and indeed Cervantes himself is reputed to have stayed at the inn opposite, the **Mesón del Potro**. On the other side of the square is the **Museo de Bellas Artes** (Tues–Sat 10am–2pm & 6–8pm; 250ptas) with paintings by Ribera, Valdés Leal and Zurbarán.

Eating and drinking

Bars and **restaurants** are on the whole reasonably priced – you need only to avoid the touristy places round the Mezquita. Loads of alternatives can be found not too far away in the Judería and in the old quarters off to the east, above the Paseo de la Ribera. One of the best – and most expensive – in the former is *El Churrasco* at c/Romero 16; more reasonable is *El Extremeño* at Plaza Benevente 1 just north of the Mesquita. *Taberna Salinas*, c/Tundidores 3 just off the Plaza Corredera, is also excellent.

For **drinking** and *tapas*, try *Bar La Mezquita*, a tiny place near the top corner of the mosque. The local barrelled **wine** is mainly *Montilla* or *Moriles* – both are magnificent, vaguely resembling mellow, dry sherries. The *Solar Plateros* at c/San Francisco 6, just north of the Plaza del Potro, specializes in *Montilla* and also has great *tapas*. **Flamenco** performances take place at *La Buleria*, c/Pedro López 3, from 10pm every night; there's no entrance fee, but food and drink are expensive to compensate.

Granada

If you see only one town in Spain it should be **GRANADA**. For here, extraordinarily well preserved and in a tremendous natural setting, stands the **Alhambra** – the spectacular and serene climax of Moorish art in Spain. Granada was established as an independent kingdom in 1238 by **Ibn Ahmar**, a prince of the Arab Nasrid tribe which had been driven south from Zaragoza. The Moors of Granada survived only through paying tribute and allegiance to Ferdinand III of Castile – whom they were forced to assist in the conquest of Muslim Sevilla – and by the time of Ibn Ahmar's death in 1275 theirs was the only surviving Spanish Muslim kingdom.

By a series of shrewd manoeuvres Granada maintained its autonomy for two and a half centuries, but by the mid-fifteenth century a pattern of coups and internal strife had become established and a rapid succession of rulers did little to stem Christian inroads. In 1479 the kingdoms of Aragón and Castile were united by the marriage of Ferdinand and Isabella and within ten years the city of Granada stood completely alone, tragically preoccupied in a civil war between supporters of the sultan's two favourite wives. In 1490 war broke out: **Boabdil**, the last Moorish king, appealed in vain for help from his fellow Muslims in Morocco, Egypt and Ottoman Turkey, and in the following year Ferdinand and Isabella marched on Granada with an army said to total 150,000 troops. For seven months, through the winter of 1491, they laid siege to the city. On January 2, 1492, Boabdil surrendered: the Christian Reconquest of Spain was complete.

> The area telephone code for Granada is ☎958.

Arrival and information

Virtually everything of interest in Granada – including the hills of **Alhambra** (to the east) and **Sacromonte** (to the north) – is within easy walking distance of the centre. The only times you'll need a bus are when arriving and leaving, since bus and train stations are both some way out. The **train station** is a kilometre or so out on the Avda de Andaluces, and is connected to the centre by buses #11 and #4. For the **main bus station** – the *Alsina Graells* terminal on the Camino de Ronda – the #11 bus is also your best bet. If you **fly** in, there's a bus connecting the airport with Plaza Isabel la Católica, by the cathedral. Full details and timetables of the buses – and much else besides – are posted on the walls of the **tourist office** at c/Libreros 2, by the cathedral (Mon–Fri 10am–1pm & 4–7pm, Sat 10am–1pm).

Accommodation

The **Gran Vía** is Granada's main street, cutting through the middle of town. It forms a "T" at its end with **c/Reyes Católicos**, which runs east to the **Plaza Nueva** and west to the **Puerta Real**, the city's two main squares. Finding a **place to stay** in this area is easy except at the very height of season (Semana Santa is impossible). You may well be greeted by touts at the train or bus stations, and on the whole it seems safe to take their offers, though check the address. Otherwise, try the streets to either side of the Gran Vía, at the back of the Plaza Nueva, around the Puerta Real and Plaza de Carmen (particularly c/de Navas), the Plaza de la Trinidad in the university area, or along the Cuesta de Gomérez, which leads up from the Plaza Nueva towards the Alhambra.

HOTELS AND HOSTELS

Hotel América, Real de la Alhambra 53 (☎227471). Simple one-star hotel, in the Alhambra grounds: you pay for the location, but it's worth it. Booking is essential. ⑤

Pensión Atenas, Gran Vía de Colón 38 (☎278750). Large place, so worth a try, though rooms vary in quality. ③

Hostal Britz, Cuesta de Gomérez 1 (☎223652). Noisy, but otherwise very comfortable and well placed. Some rooms with bath. ③

Hostal Europa, c/de la Cruz, a couple of blocks south of the above. Friendly, cheap and small. ②

Casa de Huéspedes González, c/Buensuceso, between Plaza de Trinidad and Plaza de Gracia east of the cathedral. Perfectly good rooms, very good value. ②

Hostal Lisboa, Plaza del Carmen 27 (☎221413). Noisy at the front, but clean and comfortable. ③

Pensión Olympia, off Gran Vía de Colón opposite *Banco de Jeréz*. Central, good value place, nice people. ②

Hotel La Perla, c/Reyes Católicos 2 (☎223415). Simple hotel right in the centre, near the cathedral. ②

Hostal Terminus, Avda de Andaluces 10, on the right outside the train station (☎201424). Absolutely no frills, but cheap and right by the station if you arrive late. ②

Youth Hostel, Camino de Ronda 171 (☎272638). Handy for the train or bus stations (from *RENFE*, turn left onto Avda de la Constitución, left again onto Camino de Ronda), with lots of facilities including a pool, but insititutional and unfriendly. ②

CAMPSITES

Camping Sierra Nevada, Avda de Madrid 107. The closest site to the centre and probably the best too; easily reached on bus #3. March–Oct.

Camping El Último, Camino Huetor Vega 22. Not much further out, along Avda de Cervantes, with a pool.

The City

There are three distinct groups of buildings on the **Alhambra** hill: the **Casa Real** (Royal Palace), the palace gardens of the **Generalife**, and the **Alcazaba**. The last was all that existed when Ibn Ahmar made Granada his capital, but from its reddish walls the hilltop had already taken its name; *al-Hamra* in Arabic means literally "the red". Ibn Ahmar rebuilt the Alcazaba and added to it the huge circuit of walls and towers. Within the walls he began a palace, which he supplied with running water by diverting the river Darro; water is an integral part of the Alhambra and this engineering feat was Ibn Ahmar's greatest contribution. The Palace was essentially the product of his four-teenth-century successors, particularly Mohammed V. After their conquest of the city, Ferdinand and Isabella lived for a while in the Alhambra. They restored some rooms and converted the mosque but left the palace structure unaltered. As at Córdoba and Sevilla, it was their grandson Charles V who wreaked the most destruction: he demol-ished a whole wing to build yet another grandiose Renaissance palace. This and the Alhambra itself were simply ignored by his successors and by the eighteenth century the Royal Palace was in use as a prison. In 1812 it was taken and occupied by Napoléon's forces, who looted and damaged whole sections of the palace, and on their retreat from the city tried (but fortunately failed) to blow up the entire complex.

The standard **approach** to the Alhambra (summer Mon–Sat 9am–7.45pm, Sun 9am–5.30pm; winter 9.30am–5.45pm, Sun 9.30am–5.30pm; 600ptas, free Sun after 3pm; tick-ets can be used over two consecutive days) is along the Cuesta de Gomérez, the road that climbs uphill from the Plaza Nueva. After a few hundred metres you reach the **Puerta de las Granadas**, a massive Renaissance gateway erected by Charles V. Here two paths diverge to either side of the road: the one on the right climbs up towards a group of fortified towers, the **Torres Bermejas**, which may date from as early as the eighth century. The left-hand path leads through the woods to the main entrance, the magnificent tower gateway known as the **Puerta de la Justicia**.

Ideally you should start with the earliest, most ruined, part of the fortress – the **Alcazaba**. Arriving early is usually the best tactic to avoid huge queues – likewise, 4 to 8pm is not a bad time, since many tours have left. At the summit of the Alcazaba is the **Torre de la Vela**, named after a huge bell on its turret, where you get a fine overview of the whole area. It's in the **Casa Real**, however, that the real wonders start: the first being that the place itself has survived, since it was built from wood, brick and adobe, and was designed not to last but to be renewed and redecorated by succeeding rulers. Its buildings show a brilliant use of light and space but they are principally a vehicle for ornamental stucco decoration, in rhythmic repetitions of supreme beauty. Arabic inscriptions feature prominently: some are poetic eulogies of the buildings and rulers, but most are taken from the Koran.

The palace is in three parts, each arrayed round an interior court and with a specific function. The sultans used the **Mexuar**, the first series of rooms, for business and judi-cial purposes, and this is as far as most people would have penetrated. In the **Serallo**, beyond, they received embassies and distinguished guests: here is the royal throne room, known as the **Hall of the Ambassadors**, the largest room of the palace. The last section, the **Harem**, formed their private living quarters and would have been entered by no one but their family or servants. These are the most beautiful rooms of the palace, including the **Court of the Lions**, which has become the archetypal image of Granada.

The usual exit from the Casa Real is through the courtyard of **Charles V's palace**, where bullfights were once held. The palace is a distinguished piece of Renaissance design, but it seems totally out of place here – better to pass on to the **Generalife**. Paradise is described in the Koran as a shaded, leafy garden refreshed by running water where the "fortunate ones" may take their rest under tall canopies. It is an image which perfectly describes the Generalife, the gardens and summer palace of the sultans. Its name means literally "garden of the architect" and the grounds consist of a luxuriantly imaginative series of patios, enclosed gardens and walkways.

From just below the entrance to the Generalife the **Cuesta del Rey Chino** winds down towards the river Darro and the old Arab quarter of the Albaicín. Here the little-visited **Baños Árabes** at 31 Corredera del Darro (Tues–Sat 10am–2pm) are marvellous, and the church of **San Nicolás** offers probably the best view of the Alhambra in town. To the south of the Albaicín, opposite the Capilla Real, is the strangely painted **Palacio Madraza**, a fourteenth-century Islamic college that retains part of its old prayer hall, including a magnificently decorated *mihrab*.

The **Capilla Real** (daily March–Sept 10.30am–1pm & 4–7pm; Oct–Feb 11am–1pm & 3.30–6pm; 200ptas) is itself an impressive building, flamboyant late Gothic in style and built in the first decades of Christian rule as a mausoleum for Ferdinand and Isabella. Their tombs are as simple as could be imagined, but above them is a fabulously elaborate monument erected by their grandson Charles V. For all its stark Renaissance bulk, Granada's **Cathedral**, adjoining the Capilla Real and entered from the door beside it (same hours), is a disappointment. It was begun in 1521, just as the chapel was finished, but left uncompleted well into the eighteenth century, and still lacks a tower.

Eating and drinking

You don't come to Granada for food and nightlife, and it's certainly not one of the gastronomic centres of Spain. On the other hand, like so many Spanish cities, the centre has plenty of animated bars serving good, cheap **food** and staying open late. The open-air places on Plaza Nueva are great to while away some time, but pricy if you eat. Better value can be found in the warren of streets between here and the Gran Vía: good-value choices include the *Nueva Bodega* at c/Cetti Merién 3, the excellent *Gargantua* at Placeta Sillería 7 (near c/Reyes Católicos), and *Cafetería-Restaurante La Riviera* at c/Cetti Merién 5, whose *menú económico* includes a vegetarian option. Another nucleus of cheap eateries is the area around Plaza del Carmen (near the *Ayuntamiento*) and along c/Navas leading away from it.

One of the best **bars** in the centre is *Bodegas Castañeda*, on the corner of c/Elvira and c/Almireceros opposite the cathedral; there's no sign outside. On c/Sillería nearby *La Buhardilla* (again no sign) is about the only bar in the central area that stays open really late, so if you want to go on drinking through the early hours, head out to the student areas round the university. C/Gran Capitán, c/San Juan de Dios and c/Pedro Antonio de Alarcón are all extremely lively. In term time, students also gather in **pubs** near the bus station around the Campo del Príncipe, a square on the eastern slopes of the Alhambra, where there are often great *tapas*.

Almería province

The **province of Almería** is a strange corner of Spain. Inland it has an almost lunar landscape of desert, sandstone cones and dried-up riverbeds. On the coast it's still largely unspoiled; lack of water and roads frustrated development in the 1960s and 1970s and it is only now beginning to take off. A number of good beaches are accessible by bus, and they are worth considering during what would be the "off-season" elsewhere, since Almería's summers start well before Easter and last into November. In midsummer it frequently touches 100°F in the shade, and all year round there's an intense, almost luminous, sunlight. This and the weird scenery have made Almería one of the most popular film locations in Europe – much of *Lawrence of Arabia* was shot here, along with scores of spaghetti westerns.

Almería city

ALMERÍA itself is a pleasant modern city, spread at the foot of a stark grey mountain at whose summit is a tremendous **Alcazaba** (daily 10am–2pm & 4–7pm). From here there's a superb view of the coast, of Almería's cave quarter – the *Barrio de la Chanca* on a low hill to the left – and of the city's strange fortified **Cathedral**. There's little else to do in town, and your time is probably best devoted to strolling between the cafés, bars and *terrazas* on the main Paseo de Almería, which runs from the central Puerta de Purchena down towards the harbour, and taking day trips out to the beach. The city's own **beach**, southeast of the centre beyond the railway lines, is long but dismal.

Best for **accommodation** is the area between the bus and train stations and the centre. Possibilities include *Casa La Francesca*, c/Narvaez 18 (☎951/237554; ②), west of the cathedral, with simple clean rooms, or *Hostal Maribel*, Avda Lorca 115 (☎951/235173; ②); the nearest **campsite** is on the coast at La Garrofa, 5km west, reached by buses to Aguadulce and Roquetas de Mar (where there's another, giant site). The **tourist office** is on c/Hermanos Machado, between the harbour and the stations.

The beaches

Almería's best **beaches** lie on its eastern coast, on the strip between Carboneras and La Garrucha, centred on the town of Mojácar. This is some way up the coast and to get there you'll have to travel through some of Almería's distinctive desert scenery. There are two possible routes: via Níjar to Carboneras, or via Tabernas and Sorbas to Mojácar. **MOJÁCAR** – Almería's chief resort – lies a couple of kilometres back from the sea, a striking town of white cubist houses wrapped round a harsh outcrop of rock. There's plenty of development here, and prices can seem inflated, but it's still pleasant. There's a handful of small **hostales** in town, but you're probably best off down at the beach where there's a cheap **campsite**, lots of fine beach bars, rooms to let and several hostales – try the *Puntazo*, c/El Cantal (☎951/478229; ②), or the similarly priced *Africano* (②). The **beach** itself is excellent and the water warm and brilliantly clear.

OLD CASTILE

The foundations of modern Spain were laid in the kingdom of **Castile**. A land of frontier fortresses – the *castillos* from which it takes its name – it became the most powerful and centralizing force of the Reconquest, extending its domination through military gains and marriage alliances. The monarchs of this triumphant and expansionist age were enthusiastic patrons of the arts, endowing their cities with superlative monuments above which, quite literally, tower the great Gothic cathedrals of **Salamanca**, **León** and **Burgos**. The most impressive of the castles are at **Coca**, **Gormaz** and **Berlanga de Duero**, and there's also a wealth of Romanesque churches spread along the **Pilgrim Route to Santiago** which cut across the top of the province.

Over the past decades these and the other historic cities of Old Castile have grown to dominate the region more than ever. Although its soil is fertile, the harsh extremes of land and climate don't encourage rural settlement, and the vast central plateau is given over almost entirely to grain. The sporadic and depopulated villages are rarely of interest – travel consists of getting quickly from one grand town to the next.

Salamanca

SALAMANCA is probably the most graceful city in Spain. For four centuries it was the seat of one of the most prestigious universities in the world and despite losing this reputation in the seventeenth century, it has kept the unmistakable atmosphere of a seat of learning. It's still a small place, untouched by the piles of suburban concrete which blight so many of its contemporaries, and given a gorgeous harmony by the golden sandstone from which almost the entire city seems to be constructed. The architectural hoard is endless: two cathedrals, one Gothic, the other Romanesque, vie for attention with Renaissance palaces and gems of Plateresque decoration; the Plaza Mayor is the finest in Spain; and the surviving university buildings are tremendous.

Two great architectural styles were developed, and see their finest expression, in Salamanca. **Churrigueresque**, a particularly florid form of Baroque, takes its name from José Churriguera (1665–1723), the dominant member of a prodigiously creative family. **Plateresque** came earlier, a decorative technique of shallow relief and intricate detail named for its alleged resemblance to the art of the silversmith (*platero*).

The City

If on arrival you'd like to get a picture-perfect overall view of Salamanca, go to the extreme south of the city and cross its oldest surviving monument, the much-restored **Puente Romano** (Roman Bridge), some 400m long and itself worth seeing. Otherwise make for the grand **Plaza Mayor**, its bare central expanse completely enclosed by one continuous four-storey building decorated with iron balconies and medallion portraits. Nowhere is the Churrigueras' inspired variation of Baroque so refined as here, where the restrained elegance of the designs is heightened by the changing strength and angle of the sun. From the south side, Rua Mayor leads to the vast Baroque church of **La Clericía**, seat of the Pontifical University (Mon–Fri 9am–1.30pm & 4.30–8.30pm, Sat 9am–1pm), and the celebrated **Casa de las Conchas** (House of Shells), so-called because its facades are decorated with rows of carved scallop shells, symbol of the pilgrimage to Santiago.

From the Casa de las Conchas, c/Libreros leads to the **Patio de las Escuelas** and the Renaissance entrance to the **University** (Mon–Sat 9.30am–1.30pm & 4–6.30pm, Sun 10am–1pm). The ultimate achievement of Plateresque art, this reflects the tremendous reputation of Salamanca in the early sixteenth century, when it was one of Europe's greatest universities. Columbus sought support for his voyages of discovery from the enlightened faculty of astronomy, and for a while it was powerful enough to resist even the Inquisition. Eventually, though, decline set in: books were banned as being dangerous to the Catholic faith, and mathematics and medicine disappeared from the curriculum. Today it's socially prestigious, academically no great shakes. It does, however, run a highly successful summer language school – nowhere in Spain will you see so many young Americans.

As a further declaration of Salamanca's prestige, and in a glorious last-minute assertion of Gothic, the **Catedral Nueva** (June–Sept Mon–Sat 10am–2pm & 4–8pm, Sun 10am–2pm & 4–7pm; Oct–May daily 10am–1pm & 4–6pm) was begun in 1512. It was built within a few yards of the university and acted as a buttress for the Old Cathedral which was in danger of collapsing. The main Gothic-Plateresque facade is contemporary with that of the university and equally dazzling in its wealth of ornamental detail. Alberto Churriguera and his brother Joaquín both worked here – the former on the choirstalls, the latter on the dome. Entry to the **Catedral Vieja** (200ptas) is through the first chapel on the right. Tiny by comparison and stylistically entirely different, its most striking feature is the massive fifteenth-century retable. In the chapterhouse there's a small **museum** with a fine collection of works by Fernando Gallego, Salamanca's most famous painter.

Another faultless example of Plateresque art, the **Convento de San Esteban** (9am–1pm & 4–8pm), is a short walk down c/del Tostado from the Plaza de Anaya at the side of the Catedral Nueva. Its golden facade is divided into three horizontal sections and covered in a veritable tapestry of sculpture, while the east end of the church is occupied by a huge Baroque retable by José Churriguera himself. The monastery's cloisters, through which you enter, are magnificent too, but the most beautiful cloisters in the city stand across the road in the **Convento de las Dueñas** (10am–1pm & 4–7pm). Built on an irregular pentagonal plan in the Renaissance-Plateresque style, it has upper-storey capitals wildly carved with human heads and skulls. You should also see the **Convento de Santa Clara** (Mon–Fri 9am–2pm & 4–7pm, Sat & Sun 9.30am–2pm; 100ptas), outwardly plain but with interior features in virtually every important Spanish style; most fascinating is the original fourteenth-century ceiling hidden for years above a false baroque replacement in the chapel.

Most of the remaining interest lies in the western part of the city. If you follow c/de la Compañía from the Casa de las Conchas, you pass the Plaza San Benito, which has some fine houses, and come to the Plaza Agustinas. Buildings to look out for here include the large sixteenth-century **Palacio de Monterrey**, the seventeenth-century Augustinian monastery of **La Purísima**, opposite, and another interesting convent, **Las Ursulinas** (9.30am–1pm & 4.30–7.30pm), behind the Palacio. Facing the east wall of its church is the impressive facade of the **Casa de las Muertes**, and following c/de Fonseca leads to the magnificent Plateresque palace known as the **Colegio de los Irlandeses**.

Practicalities

The **bus and train stations** are on opposite sides of the city, each about fifteen minutes' walk from the centre. There's a small **tourist office** at the edge of Plaza Mayor, or the main office at Gran Vía 39 (both closed Sat pm & Sun). Prices for **accommodation** are reasonable, but it can be hard to find in high season – especially at fiesta time in September. Touts tend to be out in force at the *RENFE* station during the summer. On the way into town from here, there are a few choices around Plaza de España – try the *Hostal Internacional*, Avda de Mirat 15 (☎923/262799; ②). Otherwise, the Plaza Mayor is the most obvious place to head for – in the small streets surrounding it you'll find scores of small *fondas* and *hostales*, most of a high standard: *Pensión Lisboa*, on one of the best streets, c/Meléndez (☎923/214333; ②), is particularly good. The cheapest option of all is a room in a *casa particular*, available outside university terms. There are a couple of **campsites** nearby, the best at Santa Marta, about 5km out but served by regular local buses.

The **cafés** in Plaza Mayor are nearly twice the usual price but worth every peseta. Close by in Plaza del Mercado (by the **market**, itself a good source of provisions), there's a row of lively *tapas* bars, while the university area has loads of good value **bars and restaurants** catering to student budgets. Good-value food places include *Restaurante Roma* on c/Ruíz Aguilera, behind Plaza Mayor (a street that has other cheapies too), *El Trigal*, near the university entrance on c/de Serranos, which has cheap vegetarian food but no smoking or drinking, and *El Bardo*, c/Compañía 8. **Late-night bars** include *El Corrillo*, in the plaza of the same name, for jazz, and *El Callejón* at c/España 68. *El Savor*, c/San Justo 34, has good Latin music, while *El Gran Café Moderno* at Gran Vía 65 has an excellent DJ in between sets of live music. Two popular **discos** are *Sergeant Pepper*, c/de San Pablo, and *Titan*, c/Bretón; *Camelot*, c/Bordadores, and *El Puerto de Chus*, Plaza de San Julian, are favourites for foreign students.

Zamora

Leaving Salamanca to the north, you can be in **ZAMORA** within an hour by rail or road. The quietest of the great historic cities of the heartland, with a population of 60,000, it was known in medieval times as *la bien cercada* (the closed one) on account of its strong fortifications: one siege here lasted seven months. Its old quarters, medieval in appearance, are spread out along the sloping banks of the Río Duero (known as the Douro once it crosses into Portugal) and there are a dozen **Romanesque churches** within ten minutes' walk of the centre. Apart from the cathedral with its superlative collection of tapestries (11am–2pm & 5–8pm; closed Sun pm & Mon am; 200ptas), no single church stands out above the others, but their unassumingly beautiful architecture is the city's most distinctive feature.

There's a **tourist office** at c/Santa Clara 20, and plenty of **places to stay**. Among the best are the *Hostal La Reina*, c/la Reina 1 (☎988/533939; ②), and the *Pensión Balborraz*, c/Balborraz 25–29 (☎988/515519; ①), both close to the Plaza Mayor.

Burgos

BURGOS has always been a military town. For some five centuries of the Middle Ages the city was the capital of Old Castile: in the eleventh century it was the home of El Cid; in the thirteenth century of Ferdinand III, reconqueror of Murcia, Córdoba and Sevilla. It was Ferdinand who began the city's famous Gothic **cathedral**, one of the greatest in all Spain, though it seems somehow to share in the forceful solemnity and severity of Burgos' history. More recently Burgos was a Francoite stronghold – his temporary capital during the Civil War and strongly loyal to the end, with an abiding reputation for conservatism. Don't, however, be put off – it is certainly worth seeing, with the cathedral set in an atmospheric, compact old quarter of impressive grey stone buildings and two superb monasteries within walking distance.

The City

Orientation in Burgos could not be simpler, since wherever you are the **Cathedral's** profile of spires and pinnacles makes its presence felt. The church is so large and varied that it's hard to appreciate as a whole, but it's magnificent from almost any angle, with an unbelievable wealth of detail. Inside, you're immediately struck by the size and number of side chapels, the greatest of which, the Capilla del Condestable, is almost a cathedral in itself. The most curious, though, is the Capilla del Santo Cristo (first right) which contains the *Cristo de Burgos*, a cloyingly realistic image of Christ endowed with real human hair and nails and covered with the withered hide of a water buffalo, still popularly believed to be human skin. Legend has it that the icon requires a shave and a manicure every eighth day. There are superb star-shaped vaults in the adjacent Capilla de la Consolación, in the cathedral's central dome, beneath which is the tomb of El Cid, marked by a simple slab in the floor below, and the octagonal Capilla del Condestable, behind the high altar; and don't miss either the glorious Escalera Dorada, a double stairway in the north transept. To get into some of these smaller chapels you'll have to buy a treasury ticket (350ptas), which also admits you to the cloisters, the diocesan museum inside them, and the choir at the heart of the cathedral, which affords the best view into the dome.

Overlooking the plaza in front of the cathedral stands the fifteenth-century church of **San Nicolás**. Unassuming from the outside, it has an altarpiece within by Francisco de Colonia, which is as rich as anything in the city. At the side of San Nicolás, c/Pozo Seco ascends to the early Gothic church of **San Esteban**, which is now being refitted as a museum. Beyond San Esteban lies the ruinous castle with a fine view of the city and the surrounding countryside.

Inevitably these lesser churches tend to be eclipsed by the cathedral, but on the outskirts are two monasteries which are by no means overshadowed. The closer is the Cistercian **Monasterio de las Huelgas** on the "new side" of the river, about twenty minutes' walk from the city centre: cross the bridge, turn right and follow the signs along the riverbank (Mon–Sat 11am–1.15pm & 4–5.15pm, Sun 11am–1.15pm, 400ptas includes guided tour). Founded in 1187, the convent grew to extraordinary wealth and power, and is remarkable for its wealth of Mudéjar craftsmanship. Priceless embroidery, jewellery and weaponry of regal splendour are exhibited in a small museum, but the highlight is the Mudéjar-Gothic cloister.

The **Cartuja de Miraflores** lies in a secluded spot about 4km from the centre: this time turn left from the bridge along c/de Valladolid. It's still in use as a monastery and most of it is closed – you can, however, visit the **church** (Mon–Sat 10.15am–3pm & 4–7pm, Sun 11.20am–12.45pm), where in front of the high altar lies the exceptionally beautiful star-shaped tomb of John II and Isabel of Portugal, by Gil de Siloé. The same sculptor carved the magnificent altarpiece, which was plated with the first gold shipped back from America, and the tomb of the Infante Alfonso.

Practicalities

The **bus station** is south of the Puente de Santa María at c/ Mirandor 4; the **train station** a short walk away at the bottom of Avda Conde Guadalhorre. The main **tourist office** (Mon–Fri 9am–2pm & 4.30–6.30pm, Sat 10am–1.30pm) is at Plaza de Alonso Martínez 7, around the side of the cathedral and up c/Lain Calvo.

For **rooms**, the best area to try is around the Plaza de Vega, and any road off to the left as far as c/de San Pablo: *Niza* at c/General Mola 12 (☎947/261917; ②) and the cheaper *Arribas* behind the bus station at c/Defensives de Oviedo 6 (☎947/266292; ②) are both reliable. There's a **youth hostel** (☎947/220362; ②) in c/General Vigón, open July to September, and a good **campsite**, *Camping Fuentes Blancas* (April–Sept), out by the Cartuja, 45 minutes' walk or a bus ride from the Cid statue (buses hourly). There are several good **bars** serving *tapas* along c/Avellanos off Plaza Alonso Martínez: *Mesón Astorga* and *La Flor* are both lively. More formal **restaurants** include the *Rincón de España* between the river and the cathedral, and *Gaona* on c/Virgen de la Paloma, next to the cathedral.

León

The stained glass in the cathedral of **LEÓN** and the Romanesque wall paintings in its Royal Pantheon are reason enough for many people to visit the city, but León is also – unusually for this part of the country – as attractive and enjoyable in its modern quarters as it is in those areas that remain from its heyday. In 914, as the Reconquest edged its way south from Asturias, the Christian capital moved to León. Despite being sacked by al-Mansur in 996, the new capital and its territories grew rapidly: in 1035 the county of Castile matured into a fully fledged kingdom, and for the next two centuries León and Castile jointly spearheaded the war against the Moors until by the thirteenth century Castile had come to dominate her mother kingdom.

León's Gothic **Cathedral** (Mon–Sat 9.30am–1pm & 4–6.30pm, Sun 9.30am–1pm) dates from the final years of greatness. Its stained-glass **windows**, a stunning kaleidoscope of light, present one of the most magical and harmonious spectacles in Spain and the colours used – reds, golds and yellows – could only be Spanish. The glass screen added to the choir this century to give a clear view up to the altar enhances the sensation of light with its bewildering refractions. Outside, the west facade, dominated by a massive rose window, is also magnificent.

The other great attraction is the church of **San Isidoro** and the Royal Pantheon of the early kings of León and Castile. Ferdinand I, who united the two kingdoms in 1037, commissioned the complex as a shrine for the bones of Saint Isidore and a mausoleum for himself and his successors. The bones of the patron saint lie in a reliquary on the high altar: the **Pantéon** (July & Aug Mon–Sat 9am–2pm & 3–8pm, Sun 9am–2pm; Sept–June Tues–Sat 10am–1.30pm & 4–6.30pm, Sun 10am–3pm; 300ptas), two small crypt-like chambers, is in front of the west facade. One of the earliest Romanesque buildings in Spain (1054–1063), it was decorated towards the end of the twelfth century with some of the most imaginative and impressive paintings of Romanesque art. They are extraordinarily well preserved and their biblical and everyday themes are perfectly adapted to the architecture of the vaults. Eleven kings and twelve queens were laid to rest here, but the chapel was desecrated during the Peninsular War and their tombs command little attention in such a marvellous setting.

Also worth seeing is the opulent **Monasterio de San Marcos**, built in 1168 for the Knights of Santiago, one of several chivalric orders founded in the twelfth century to protect pilgrims on their way to Santiago and lead the Reconquest. In the sixteenth century the monastery was rebuilt as a palatial headquarters for the order, its massive facade lavishly embellished with Plateresque designs. Fittingly, it has been converted into a *parador*, where the guests enjoy the luxury of a magnificent church of their own – though it can be visited by non-patrons too. This is the **Iglesia San Marcos**, whose sacristy (Tues–Sat 10am–2pm & 4–7.30pm, Sun 10am–2pm) houses a small **museum** of beautiful and priceless exhibits, grouped in a room separated from the lobby of the hotel by a thick pane of glass.

Practicalities

León's modern sectors are laid out with wide, straight streets radiating like spokes from three focal plazas. One of these is the Glorieta Guzmán el Bueno near the river and the **train station**. Just south of the *RENFE* station, but on the same side of the river, León has a brand-new **bus station** on Paseo Ingeniero Miera. From the Glorieta one can see straight down the Avenida de Ordoño II and across the Plaza de Santo Domingo to the cathedral. Directly opposite the cathedral's west facade stands the town's main **tourist office** (Mon–Fri 9am–2pm & 4–6pm, Sat 10am–1pm; ☎987/237082).

Places **to stay** are numerous and spread out between the station and the cathedral. Good possibilities include the *Hostal Americana*, Avda Ordoño II 25 (☎987/251654; ②), *Hostal Londres,* Avda de Roma 1 (☎987/222274; ②), and the very cheap *Pensión Roma*, Avda de Roma 4 (☎987/224663; ①). There's a **youth hostel** with a pool, open July and August only, at c/de la Corredera 4 (☎987/202201; ②); follow Avda de Independencia from Plaza de Santo Domingo.

For sheer enjoyment, *the* time of year to be in León is for the **fiesta** of Saint Peter in the last week of June. The rest of the year, the liveliest **bars and restaurants** tend to be those in the small square of San Martín and the dark narrow streets which surround it. You'll find good food at the *Restaurante Fornos*, c/Cid 8, *Mesón Leones Racimo de Oro*, Caño Vadillo 2, and *Bar Restaurante Real*, c/Mariano D. Berrueta 7, near the cathedral.

THE NORTH COAST

Spain's **Atlantic coast** is very different from the popular image of the country, with a rocky, indented coastline full of cove beaches and fjord-like *rías*. It's an immensely beautiful region – mountainous, green and thickly forested. It rains often, and much of the time the countryside is shrouded in a fine mist. But the summers, if you don't mind the occasional shower, are a glorious escape from the unrelenting heat of the south.

In the east, butting against France, is **Euskadi** – the **Basque country** – which, despite some of the heaviest industrialization on the peninsula, remains remarkably unspoiled – neat and quiet inland, rugged and enclosed along the coast, with easy, efficient transport everywhere. **San Sebastián** is the big draw on the coast, a major resort with superb but crowded beaches, but there are any number of lesser-known, equally attractive villages along the coast all the way to **Bilbao** and beyond. Note that the Basque **language**, which bears almost no relation to Spanish, is very widespread (we've given the alternative Basque names where popularly used) and the most obvious sign of Spain's strongest separatist movement.

To the west lies **Cantabria**, centred on the port of **Santander**, with more good beaches and superb hiking in the mountains of the **Picos de Europa**. The mountains extend into **Asturias**, the one part of Spain never to be conquered by the Moors. It remains today an idiosyncratic principality standing slightly apart from the rest of the nation. Its high, remote valleys are mining country, providing the raw materials for the heavy industry of the three cities: **Gijón**, **Avilés** and **Oviedo**.

In the far west, **Galicia** looks like Ireland, and there are further parallels in its climate, culture and – despite its fertile appearance – its history of famine and poverty. While right-wing Galicia may not share the radical traditions of the Basque country or of industrial Asturias it does treasure its independence, and Gallego is still spoken by around 85 percent of the population – again, we've given Gallego place names in parentheses. For travellers, the obvious highlight is **Santiago de Compostela**, the greatest goal for pilgrims in medieval Europe. There are smaller and equally charming old stone towns throughout Galicia, and those that have retained a vibrant sense of life and atmosphere, such as **Pontevedra** and **Betanzos**, can be enjoyable bases for touring.

Once you leave the Basque country, communications in this region are generally slow. If you're not in a great hurry, you may want to make use of the independent **FEVE rail line** (rail passes are not valid). The railway begins at Bilbao and follows the coast, with an inland branch to Oviedo, all the way to El Ferrol in Galicia. It has for some time been undergoing major repairs – with services drastically reduced and occasionally replaced by buses – but despite this it's a terrific journey, skirting beaches, crossing *rías* and snaking through a succession of limestone gorges.

Irún

You're likely to approach the north coast through **IRÚN**, a major border crossing from France. Like most border towns, its chief concern is how to make a quick buck from passing travellers, and the main point in its favour is the ease with which you can leave; there are trains to Hendaye in France and to San Sebastián throughout the day, and regular long-distance and international connections. For one night, though, it's not a bad place to stay; prices are much lower than in France, and San Sebastián is no place to arrive late at night without a reservation. The train station is surrounded by small **hostales**, none of them expensive, and **bodegas and restaurants** specializing in surprisingly good "typical" Spanish food. *Fonda Algorta* and *Bar Pensión los Fronterizos*, both along c/Estación leading from the main station, have some of the cheapest rooms; for more comfort go to the nearby *Hostal Irún*, c/Zubiaurre 5 (☎943/612283; ②), or *Lizaso*, c/Aduana 5–7 (☎943/611600; ②).

San Sebastián

The undisputed queen of the Basque resorts, **SAN SEBASTIÁN** (Donostia), just half an hour down the coast from Irún, is a picturesque – though expensive – town with excellent beaches. Along with Santander, it has always been the most fashionable place to escape the heat of the southern summers, and in July and August it's always packed. Though it tries hard to be chic, San Sebastián is still too much of a family resort to compete with the south of France. Set around the deep, still bay of La Concha and enclosed by rolling low hills, it's beautifully situated; the old town sits on the eastern promontory, its back to the wooded slopes of Monte Urgull, while newer development has spread inland along the banks of the Urumea river and around the edge of the bay to the foot of Monte Igüeldo.

The **old quarter** is the centre of interest – cramped and noisy streets where crowds congregrate in the evenings to wander among the small bars and shops or sample the shellfish from the traders down by the fishing harbour. Prices tend to reflect the popularity of the area, especially in the waterside restaurants, but it's no hardship to survive on the delicious *tapas* which are laid out in all but the fanciest bars – check the prices first, as it's quite easy to run up a sizeable bill; around 100ptas per *pincho* is now the norm. Here too are the town's chief sights: the gaudy Baroque facade of the church of **Santa María**, and the more elegantly restrained sixteenth-century **San Vicente**. The centre of the old part is the Plaza de la Constitución, know locally as "La Consti"; the numbers on the balconies of the buildings around the square refer to the days when it was used as a bullring. Just behind San Vicente, the excellent **Museo de San Telmo** (Mon–Sat 9.30am–1.30pm & 3.30–7.30pm, Sun 10.15am–2pm) is a jumble of Basque folklore and assorted artworks. Behind this, **Monte Urgull** is crisscrossed by winding footpaths. From the mammoth figure of Christ on its summit there are great views out to sea and back across the bay to the town; up here too are the dilapidated remains of the castle and a few relics of forgotten sieges on display in what calls itself a military museum (Tues–Sat 10am–1pm & 3.30–5.30pm, Mon 3.30–5pm). On the way down you can stop at the **Aquarium** (May–Sept daily 10am–1.30pm & 3.30–8pm; Oct–April Tues–Sat 10am–1.30pm & 3.30–7.30pm) on the harbour – not many fish but an extensive history of Basque navigation. Still better views across the bay can be had from the top of **Monte Igüeldo**: take the bus or walk around the bay to its base, from where a funicular will carry you to the summit.

There are three **beaches** in San Sebastián: the Playa de la Concha, Ondaretta and the Playa de Gros. **La Concha** is the most central and the most celebrated, a wide crescent of yellow sand stretching round the bay from the town. Despite the almost impenetrable mass of flesh here during most of the summer, this is the best of the beaches. Out in La Concha bay is a small island, **Isla de Santa Clara**, which makes a good spot for picnics; a boat leaves from the port every half-hour in the summer until 8.30pm. **Ondaretta**, considered the best beach for swimming and never quite as packed as La Concha, is a continuation of the same strand beyond the rocky outcrop which supports the **Palacio Miramar**, once a summer home of Spain's royal family. The atmosphere here is rather more staid – it's known as *La Diplomática* for the number of Madrid's "best" families who vacation here. Though it's far less crowded, don't bother with the aptly named **Playa de Gros**. Outside the shelter of the bay it's very exposed, and it's the repository for all the filth that comes floating down the river.

Practicalities

Most **buses** use the terminal at Plaza Pío XII, fifteen minutes' walk inland along the river, the rest from the Plaza de Guipúzcoa. The main-line **train station** is across the river Urumea on the Paseo de Francia, although local lines to Hendaye and Bilbao have their terminus on c/Easo. The **tourist office**, on c/Reina Regente beside the Puente Kursaal in the old town (Mon–Sat 9am–2pm & 3.30–7pm; closed Sat afternoon out of season), is very helpful in finding a place to stay and providing accommodation, although for a greater selection of pamphlets, there is a useful Basque Government tourist office at Paseo de los Fuieros 1, just off Avenida de la Libertad (Mon–Thurs 9.30am–1.30pm & 3.30–6pm, Fri & Sat 9.30am–1.30pm).

Accommodation, though plentiful, is not cheap and can be very hard to come by in season. In the old town, there's better value around the cathedral, especially Calles Easo, San Martin, Loyola, San Bartolomé and Urdaneta, or on the other side of the river behind the Plaza de Cataluña, where you'll also find excellent *tapas* bars. Places to try in the old part include *Pensión San Jeromino*, c/San Jeromino 25 (☎943/286434 or 281689; ②), *Pensión Kaia*, c/Puerto 12 (☎943/431342; ②), and *Pensión Aussie*, c/San Jeromino 23 (☎943/422874; ③); in the central area around the cathedral, try the *Hostal Easo*, c/San Bartolomé 24 (☎943/466892; ②), *Pensión La Perla*, c/Loyola 10 (☎943/428123; ②), *Hostal Comercio*, c/Urdaneta 24 (☎943/464414; ③), *Eder II*, Alameda del Boulevard 16 (☎943/426449; ③), or *Pensión Donostiarra*, c/San Martin 6 (☎943/426167; ③). San

Sebastián's **campsite** is excellent, but it's a long way from the centre on the landward side of Monte Igüeldo, reached by bus #16 from the Alameda del Boulevard. The new **youth hostel** (☎943/310256; ②), known as "La Sirena", is located on Paseo de Igueldo, just a few minutes' walk back from the end of Ondarreta Beach.

If you're in the mood for some spectacularly expensive **food**, San Sebastián has some of the best restaurants in Spain. Less exalted cuisine is easy enough to find, though nowhere very cheap: if you want a meal rather than *tapas*, try the *menú* at places such as *Restaurante La Maitia*, c/Easo 31; *La Barranquesa*, c/Larramendi 21; *Bar Etxadi*, c/Reyes Católicos 9; or *Morgan Jatetxea*, c/Narrika Kalea 7. Alternatively, order some well-priced *raciones* at either *Gaztelu*, c/31 de Agosto 22, or *Anahi*, c/Narrika, both in the old part.

In the evenings you'll find no shortage of action, with **clubs** and **bars** wherever the tourists congregate. The fanciest are along the promenade by the beach, Paseo de la Concha; cheaper places are mostly in the old town where people normally start the evening off – later everyone heads to the area along c/Reyes Católicos behind the cathedral or c/San Bartolomé for the young crowd. For late nights, head for *Tenis* at the far end of Ondarreta Beach, where there is no entrance charge and salsa blares well into the night – it's much less posy than in the city's chic and expensive discos. Throughout the summer, too, there are constant **festivals**, many involving Basque sports including the annual rowing races between the villages along the coast. The *International Jazz Festival*, at different locations throughout the town for ten days of July, invariably attracts top performers as well as hordes of people on their way home from the fiesta in Pamplona.

Bilbao

Stretching for some 14km along the narrow valley of the heavily polluted Río Nervión, **BILBAO** (Bilbo) is a large, industrial city that rarely feels like one, its urban sprawl having gradually engulfed a series of once-separate communities. It's not a place of grand sights or glamorous tourism, but it has an unmistakable feel, incredibly friendly inhabitants, and some of the best places to eat and drink cheaply in all of Euskadi.

The main point of interest is the **Casco Viejo**, the old quarter on the east bank of the river. It's here that you'll find the best bars and restaurants among the narrow streets and antiquated shops. Here, too, are the sights that Bilbao does have to offer: the beautiful **Teatro Arriaga**, the elegantly arcaded **Plaza Nueva**, the Gothic **Catedral de Santiago** and an interesting **Historical Museum** in Plaza Miguel Unamuno (Tues–Sat 10.30am–1.30pm & 4–7pm, Sun 10.30am–1pm; free). The one sight not in this part of town is the **Museo de Bellas Artes** (Tues–Sat 10.30am–1.30pm & 4–7.30pm, Sun 10am–2pm; free), in the Parque de Doña Casilda de Iturriza on the northern edge of the new town off the Gran Vía. This is considered one of Spain's most important collections, but it's a shame that its handful of fine canvases – including works by El Greco, Zurbarán and Goya – are swamped by a host of mediocre ones.

Arriving in Bilbao can be confusing, since there's a welter of different **bus and train stations**. Most of them, however, are near the bridge which links the Plaza de España, in the new part of town, with the Casco Viejo. The **tourist office** (Mon–Fri 9am–1.30pm & 4–8pm) is adjacent to the Teatro Arriaga. The best **places to stay** are almost all in the Casco Viejo – especially along and around the streets leading off c/Bidebarrieta, which leads from Plaza Arriaga to the cathedral. Good possibilities over the river are *Hostal Gurea*, c/Bidebarrieta 14 (☎94/4163299; ②), *Hostal La Estrella*, c/María Muñoz 6, off Plaza Miguel Unamuno (☎94/4164066; ②), *Hostal Casco Viejo*, c/Santa Maria 14 (☎94/4166736; ②), *Hostal Arana*, c/Bidebarrieta 2 (☎94/4156411; ③), and *Hostal Roquefort*, c/Loteria 2–4 (☎94/4150755; ②).

Eating and drinking are also best in the Casco Viejo, and this is one of those cities where the most enjoyable way to eat is to move from bar to bar, snacking on *tapas*. Bilbao can be very lively indeed at night – and totally wild during the August **fiesta**, with scores of open-air bars, live music and impromptu dancing everywhere, and incredible atmosphere. Try especially around c/Barrencalle and c/Santa María.

Santander and around

Long a favourite summer resort of Madrileños, **SANTANDER** has a French feel – an elegant, reserved resort in a similar vein to San Sebastián. Some people find it a clean, restful base for a short stay; for others it is dull and snobbish. On a brief visit, the balance is tipped in its favour by its excellent (and no longer polluted) beaches, and the sheer style of its setting. The narrow **Bahía de Santander** is dramatic, with the city and port on one side in clear view of open countryside and high mountains on the other; a great first view of Spain if you're arriving on the **ferry** from Plymouth.

Santander was severely damaged by fire in 1941, and what's left of the city divides into two parts: the **town and port**, which are still quite a tangle, having been reconstructed on the old grid around the cathedral; and the beach suburb of **El Sardinero**, a twenty-minute walk (or bus #1 or #2) from the centre, more if you follow the coast around the wooded headland of **La Magdalena**. There are few real sights to distract you: the **Cathedral**, with its Gothic crypt, is of passing interest; the pick of the museums is the **Museo Provincial de Prehistoria**, c/Juan de la Costa 1 (Tues–Sat 9am–1pm & 4–7pm, Sun 11am–2pm; free), where finds from the province's numerous prehistorically inhabited caves are exhibited. The chief pleasures lie on the **beaches**. The first of these, **Playa de la Magdalena**, begins on the near side of the headland. The beautiful yellow strand, sheltered by cliffs and flanked by a summer windsurfing school, is deservedly popular, as is **El Sardinero** itself. If you find both beaches too crowded for your taste, there are long stretches of dunes across the bay at **Somo** (which has windsurfing boards for hire and a summer campsite) and **Pedreña**; to get to them, jump on the cheap taxi-ferry which leaves every fifteen minutes from the central dock.

Practicalities

The *RENFE* and *FEVE* **train stations** are side by side, just off the waterside; the **bus station** is directly across the square. The **tourist office**, in the arcades of the main Plaza de Velarde (Mon–Fri 9am–1.30pm & 4–7pm, Sat 9am–1.30pm), has a 24-hour computer system that gives accommodation information even when the office is closed; there's a branch office in the Jardines de Perada on the seafront. Good places to start looking for **rooms** are c/de Rodríguez in front of the station – *San Miguel* at no. 9 (☎942/210881; ③) – and c/de Hernán Cortés near the main square – *La Corza* at no. 25 (☎942/212950; ③) is recommended. If you want to be by the beach, there are some very popular cheapish places on the Avda de los Castros at Sardinero, including the *Hostal-Residencial Luisito* at no. 11 (☎942/271971; ②), and a **campsite** a short walk further down the coast. As far as **food** is concerned, try the same streets, along with c/San Simón and c/Río de la Pila, above Plaza de Velarde. If you're after seafood, wander down to the fishing port, to the east of the ferry port and stations. There's no shortage of places along the c/Marqués de la Ensanada here, but check prices before ordering.

Santillana and prehistoric caves

SANTILLANA DEL MAR, half an hour by bus to the west of Santander, is outrageously picturesque. The village is all ochre-coloured stone houses, mansions, and farms – and despite much day-trip tourism it retains a disarming charm. There are some wonderful fifteenth- to eighteenth-century mansions and a couple of fascinating churches, but the main reason to come is the atmosphere, which you'll appreciate best if you stay; there are some rooms in the village (check with the tourist office in Plaza Ramón Pelayo) and several *hostales* on the main road just outside the village; there's also a campsite a short way west. The coast near Santillana itself is rocky; the nearest **beaches** are those at Suances (8km) and Comillas (17km). Buses for both leave from opposite the town museum.

The celebrated prehistoric caves of Altamira, with their magnificent wall paintings, lie just off the main road, west of Santillana. Unfortunately they are now closed to casual visitors, but you can see lesser paintings in the caves at **PUENTE VIESGO**, 29km out of Santander on the road to Logroño – take the *SA Continental* bus from the main station in Santander. Around the village, set amid magnificent green countryside, are four separate **caves**, the most important of which is **Castillo**, its paintings clear precursors of the developments at Altamira (Tues–Sat 10am–1pm & 3–7pm, Sun 10am–1pm; free).

Oviedo and around

The principal reason for visiting **OVIEDO** is to see three small churches. They are perhaps the most remarkable in Spain, built in a unique style that emerged here in the wake of the Visigoths and before Romanesque had spread from France. All of them date from the first half of the ninth century, a period of almost total isolation for the tiny Asturian Kingdom, which was then the only part of Spain under Christian rule.

Oviedo, the modern capital of Asturias, became the centre of this outpost in 810. Here king Alfonso II built a chapel, the Cámara Santa, to house the holy relics rescued from Toledo when it fell to the Moors. Remodelled in the twelfth century, this now forms the inner sanctuary of the **Cathedral** (daily 9am–1pm & 3.30–6pm), a fine Gothic structure at the heart of the modern city. Around the cathedral, enclosed by scattered sections of the medieval town walls, is what remains of **old Oviedo**: a compact, attractive quarter in what is a fairly bleak industrial city. Some of the **palaces** – not least the archbishop's, opposite the cathedral – are worth a look, though none are open to visitors. Of interest, too, is the **Archeological Museum**, immediately behind the cathedral in the former convent of San Vicente (Mon–Sat 10am–1.30pm & 4.30–6.30pm, Sun 11am–1pm), which displays various pieces of sculpture from the "Asturian-Visigoth" churches.

The nearest of these churches, **Santullano**, lies ten minutes' walk to the northeast along c/de Gijón, right next to a busy main road. Built around 830, it's considerably larger and more spacious than the other Asturian churches, with an unusual "secret chamber" built into the outer wall. It is kept locked but the keys are available at the priest's house to the left; there are original frescoes inside, executed in similar style to Roman villas. The most impressive of the churches is **Santa María del Naranco** (Mon–Sat 10am–1pm & 3–5/7pm, plus Sun 10am–1pm in summer), majestically located on a wooded slope 3km above the city. It's a 45-minute walk from the centre along a beautiful marked route, or half an hour from the station. This perfectly harmonious little building was designed not as a church but as a royal palace or hunting lodge: the present structure was just the main hall. A couple of hundred metres beyond Santa María is the palace chapel, **San Miguel de Lillo** (same hours), built with soft golden sandstone and red tiles. This is generally assumed to be by the same architect as Santa María, though its design, the Byzantine cross-in-square, is quite different.

Practicalities

Central Oviedo is easy enough to find your way around, but transport can be confusing. Most **buses** use the underground station in the Plaza Primo de Rivera, but it's worth checking departures with the **tourist office** (Mon–Fri 9am–2pm & 4–6pm, Sat 10am–

2pm) in the cathedral square. For trains, there are two *FEVE* **stations** in addition to the regular *RENFE* one serving León. The *FEVE Asturias*, next to the *RENFE*, is for the line to Santander; the so-called *FEVE Basque*, oddly enough, serves stations west to El Ferrol. They're fifteen minutes apart, so don't try to make too tight a connection.

Accommodation is plentiful, with many **hostales** on c/de Uría alongside San Francisco park, including *México at* no. 25 (☎985/5240404; ②). Other promising areas are c/Jovellanos north of the cathedral (the *Pomar* is friendly), and c/9 de Mayo or c/ de Caveda near the main train stations. For **food**, try any of the places along c/de Altamira, such as *Casa Muñiz* or *La Caleya*. And lastly, whether you stay or not, don't leave without ordering at least one glass of Asturian *sidra* (cider) – if only for bewilderment's sake. Onlookers will show you the correct drinking protocol.

Santiago de Compostela

SANTIAGO DE COMPOSTELA, built in a warm golden granite, is one of the most beautiful of all Spanish cities. The medieval city has been declared a national monument in its entirety, and remains a remarkably integrated whole, all the better for being almost completely pedestrianized. The **pilgrimage** to Santiago captured the imagination of medieval Christian Europe on an unprecedented scale. At the height of its popularity, in the eleventh and twelfth centuries, the city was receiving over half a million pilgrims each year. People of all classes came to visit the supposed shrine of Saint James the Apostle (Santiago to the Spanish), making this the third holiest site in Christendom, after Jerusalem and Rome. The atmosphere of the place is much as it must have been in the days of the pilgrims, though tourists are now as likely to be attracted by art and history as by religion, but it's by no means a dead city – Santiago is the seat of Galicia's regional government and there's a large student population too. It's also a manageable size – you can wander fifteen minutes out of town and reach wide open countryside.

The City

All roads to Santiago lead to the **Cathedral**, whose sheer grandeur you first appreciate upon venturing into the vast expanse of the Plaza de Obradoiro. Directly ahead stands a fantastic Baroque pyramid of granite, flanked by immense bell towers and everywhere adorned with statues of Saint James in his familiar pilgrim guise with staff, broad hat and scallop-shell badge. This **Obradoiro facade** was built in the mid-eighteenth century by an obscure Santiago-born architect, Fernando Casas y Novoa, and no other work of Spanish Baroque can compare with it.

The main body of the cathedral is Romanesque, rebuilt in the eleventh and twelfth centuries after a devastating raid by the Moors. The building's highlight is the **Pórtico de Gloria**, the original west front, which now stands inside the cathedral behind the Obradoiro. This was both the culmination of all Romanesque sculpture and a precursor of the new Gothic realism, with a host of wonderfully carved figures. Saint James sits on the central column, beneath Christ and just above eye level: the pilgrims would give thanks at journey's end by praying with the fingers of one hand pressed into the roots of the *Tree of Jesse* below the saint. So many millions have performed this act of supplication that five deep and shiny holes have been worn into the solid marble.

The spiritual climax of the pilgrimage was the approach to the **High Altar**. This remains a peculiar experience. You climb steps behind the altar, embrace the Most Sacred Image of Santiago, kiss his bejewelled cape, and are handed, by way of certification, a document in Latin called a *Compostela*. The altar is a riotous creation of eighteenth-century Churrigueresque, but the statue has stood there for seven centuries and the procedure is quite unchanged. You'll notice an elaborate pulley system in front of the altar. This is for moving the immense incense-burner which, operated by eight priests, is swung in a vast ceiling-to-ceiling arc across the transept. It is stunning to watch, but takes place only at certain services – Saturday evening mass, around 5pm, is a good possibility, but check with the tourist office.

You can visit the treasury, cloisters, archeological museum and the beautiful crypt (Mon–Sat 10.30am–1.30pm & 4–6.30pm, Sun 10.30am–1.30pm; 300ptas joint ticket). The late Gothic **cloisters** in particular are well worth seeing; from the plain, mosque-like courtyard you get a wonderful view of the riotous mixture of the exterior, crawling with pagodas, domes, obelisks, battlements, scallop shells and cornucopias.

The north side of the cathedral is occupied by the **Palace of Archbishop Gelmirez** (10am–1.30pm & 3.30–7pm). Gelmirez was one of the seminal figures in Santiago's development: he rebuilt the cathedral in the twelfth century, raised the see to an arch-bishopric, and most importantly made the place extremely rich. In his palace, suitably luxuriant, are a vaulted kitchen and some fine Romanesque chambers.

The elegant Renaissance **Hostal de los Reyes Católicos** fills the northern side of the plaza, and was founded to house poor and sick pilgrims. It's now a *parador*, which means that unless you're staying here, it's not easy to get in to see the four superb patios, the chapel with magnificent Gothic stone carving and vaulted crypt. However, you can always stop in for a drink at the bar or browse around the exhibition hall.

Further afield, the main interest lies in the multifarious monasteries and convents. The enormous Benedictine **San Martín** stands close to the cathedral, the vast altar-piece in its church depicting its patron riding alongside Saint James. Nearby is **San Francisco**, reputedly founded by the saint himself during his pilgrimage to Santiago. In the north of the city are Baroque **Santa Clara**, with a unique curving facade, and a little beyond it, **Santo Domingo**. This last is perhaps the most interesting of the build-ings, featuring a magnificent seventeenth-century triple stairway, each spiral leading to different storeys of a single tower, and a fascinating museum of Gallego crafts and traditions, the **Meso do Pobo Gallego** (Mon–Sat 10am–1pm & 4–7pm; free).

Practicalities

Arriving at the **bus station** you are 1km or so north of the town centre; bus #10 will take you in to the Plaza de Galicia at the southern edge of the old city. The **train station** is a walkable distance south of this plaza along c/del Horreo. The **tourist office** is at Rua del Villar 43 (Mon–Fri 9am–2pm & 4–7pm, Sat 9am–1pm), and can provide complete lists of accommodation and facilities. The ticket office for concerts is to be found close by on the same side of the street; on the other side near the cathedral is the Sargadelos shop, a Galician institution.

You should have no difficulty finding an inexpensive **room** in Santiago, though note that *pensiones* here are often called *hospedajes*. The biggest concentration of places is on the three parallel streets leading down from the cathedral: Rua Nueva, Rua del Villar and c/del Franco. Good places to start looking are *Hospedaje Lalin*, c/Azabachería 31 (☎981/582123; ②), with rooms overlooking the back of the cathedral; *Hostal Residencia La Estela*, Avda Rajoy 1 (☎981/582796; ③), just off Plaza Obradoiro; and *Hostal Barbantes*, c/del Franco 3 (☎981/581077; ③). The nearest decent **campsite**, *Camping Santiago* (summer only), can be found on the north side of town, about 5km towards La Coruña (take the La Coruña bus from the station).

Thanks, perhaps, to the students there are plenty of cheap **places to eat** here, along with excellent **bars**; it's also the best place in Galicia to hear local Breton-style **music**, played on *gaitas* (bagpipes). For food, try the famous *El Asesino* at Plaza Universidad 16, where three elderly (and rather eccentric) sisters serve lunches so cheap and popular that they don't bother with a sign – just ask to be directed. Another student haunt is the *Casa Manolo* at Rua Traviesa 27, while c/del Franco is full of bars such as *El Bombero* and *Tacita de Oro* with reliable *tapas*. *Bodegón de Xulio* here is a really good seafood restaurant. Livelier places to drink include *Bar Ourense* and *O'Barril* on c/del Franco, *O Gato Negro* on Rua Nueva, and *O'Galo d'Ouro*, in a cellar on the Cuesta Conga.

Rías Bajas

The best of Galicia's coast lies to the south of Santiago: the **Rías Bajas**. The archetype of them all is the long narrow **Ría de Pontevedra**, closely resembling a Scandinavian fjord with its steep and forested sides, while the **Ría de Vigo** is one of the most sublime natural harbours in the world.

Pontevedra

PONTEVEDRA is the definitive old Gallego town, a maze of cobbled alleyways and colonnaded squares, with granite crosses and squat stone houses with floral balconies. There are some "sights" to see – the museum is good and there are several interesting churches – but the real joy of visiting Pontevedra is to spend time in an ancient town so lively and lived-in. It's perfect for a night out; the traditional local food and drink are both at their best.

The **bus** and **train stations** are side by side about a kilometre from the centre, served by intermittent buses which will drop you next to **La Peregrina**. This is a small pilgrim chapel built in the shape of a scallop shell, standing next to a square which is known locally as the **Herrería**. This paved plaza, lined by arcades on one side and rose trees on the other, is the border between the old and new quarters of Pontevedra.

All the twisting streets of the *Zona Monumental* are packed with tiny **bars** and jammed late into the night with drinkers and revellers. You'd probably do best to eat in the bars, rather than look for a restaurant. Platters of fish and jugs of rich white wine are available everywhere, with c/Isabel II being the epicentre of the activity. Budget **accommodation** is limited: two *fondas* standing opposite each other on the charming Plaza Teucro and a couple more in c/Charino; plus a couple of affordable *hostales* – *Madrid* at Andrés Mellado 11 (☎986/851006; ②) and *Avenida* at Eduardo Pondal 46, formerly Virgen de Comino 70 (☎986/851298; ③). If you can't find a room, consult the lists at the **tourist office** at c/General Mola 3 (Mon–Fri 9am–2pm & 5–7pm, Sat 10am–12.30pm).

Ría de Pontevedra

Pontevedra is a good base for expeditions along either shore of its *ría* – expeditions made necessary by the fact that the town itself doesn't have a beach. The **north coast** is the more popular, its best-known resort at SANGENJO boasting well over fifty hotels, often full of British and German visitors. It's also the best place to stay, with a market on Monday mornings right by the sea and plenty of pricy **hostales**. A few kilometres beyond begins the vast beach of **La Lanzada**, a favourite with strong swimmers and windsurfers. In the summer there are temporary enclaves of cafés and restaurants and a couple of **campsites**.

The less developed **south coast** is the better choice for exploring, heading out past lovely beaches towards the rugged headland, although the industrial development along the first stretch is offputting. A very frequent and very slow **trolleybus** service rattles as far as Marín from the Plaza de Galicia in Pontevedra, and there are faster buses right around the headland from the bus station. Beyond Marín, a busy naval port, the scenery rapidly improves, the bay broadening into a whole series of breathtaking and virtually deserted sandy coves. BUEU is a quiet market town and port about 12km from Marín, with a stupendous strip of **beach** stretching away from its rambling waterfront. The two **hostales**, *A Centoleira*, Playa de Beluso (☎986/320896; ④), and *Incamar* (☎986/320067; ⑤), are reasonably priced for the area. The main road turns away from the sea at Bueu, towards Cangas, but if you make your own way along the coast, towards the village of ALDAN and the cape of HIO, you'll find an unspoiled expanse of pine trees and empty beaches – an ideal place to go **camping** if you stock up in advance.

Cangas

Following the main road south from Bueu, you cross a steep ridge to astonishing views on the far side over the **Ría de Vigo**. CANGAS, where the road descends, is a small resort, at its most lively during the Friday **market**, when the seafront gardens are filled with stalls. The town spreads perhaps a kilometre along the coast to reach **Rodeira beach**. There are **rooms** available at the far end, next to the beach: try *Playa* at Avda de Ourense 76 (☎986/301363; ④) or closer to town in the *Jucamar* at Avda de Marin 5 (☎986/300694; ④). **Bars** and **places to eat** are mainly around the port. *O Pote* at Avda Castelao 13, opposite the derelict former fish market, and *Bar Celta* at c/A. Saralegui, a *tapas* bar up some steps slightly to the left of the jetty as you face the town, are both good. A **ferry** for foot passengers leaves Cangas for Vigo every half-hour from 6am to 10pm (Sun 9am–10.30pm), a pleasant twenty-minute trip.

Vigo

VIGO is a large and superbly situated city, so well sheltered from the Atlantic that the wharves and quays which make it Spain's chief fishing port stretch along the shore for nearly 5km. The cobbled streets around the **c/López Puigcerver** are a focal point: along the seafront early in the morning, kiosks revive fishermen with strong coffee, while their catch is sold here and in the nearby **market**; and all day long women stand in **Real Teófilo Llorente** with plates of fresh oysters set out for passers-by. In the evening the myriad bars on all the tiny streets come alive.

As you cross the road from the port, you can't miss the **tourist office**, whose free map has all the **accommodation** available marked on it. The choice is basically between staying down here in the old streets, such as the Rua Carral, or in the more modern areas where the **trains and buses** come in, further up the hill, where you get a bit more for your money. Possibilities on Rua Carral include the very friendly, family-run *Hostal Bienvenido* at the top of the street (☎986/228657; ②) – if the hostel is closed, go the *Bar El Pasillo* just off Rua Carral which is owned by the family, or the newly renovated hostel *Carral* at no. 18 (☎986/224927; ③). The best places near the station are the comfortable *Hostal Norte*, right beside it (☎986/223805; ③), and *La Nueva* at c/Lepanto 26 (☎986/439311; ④).

The modern **RENFE station** has direct services to Santiago, Barcelona and Madrid, and down into Portugal. **Buses** to all major destinations use a new terminal, a little way out of the centre at the junction of Avda de Madrid and Avda Gregorio Espiño.

The Islas Cíes

The most irresistible sands of the Ría de Vigo are those of the **ISLAS CÍES**. These three islands protect the entrance to the *ría*, and can be reached by boats from the Estación Marítima in Vigo or from the harbour in Bayona (6 daily from each, mid-June to mid-Sept; 1600ptas return). One island is an off-limits bird sanctuary; the other two are joined by a narrow causeway of sand, which forms a beach open on one side to the Atlantic and on the other to a placid lagoon. Most visitors stay on the beach, with its sprinkling of bars and a **campsite** in the trees, so it's easy to escape the crowds and find a deserted spot – particularly on the Atlantic side of the islands. The campsite is the only legal **accommodation** on the islands, so if you want to stay in midseason, phone ahead to make sure there's room (☎986/278501). There's a small shop, as well as a couple of restaurants – not bad, but expensive.

Bayona

BAYONA (Baiona) is situated just before the open sea at the head of a miniature *ría*, the last and the smallest in Galicia. It is arguably the region's best resort, not yet over-exploited for all its popularity with the Spanish. The town is full of reasonably priced **hostales** such as the *Mesón del Burgo*, Barrio del Burgo (☎986/355309; ④), a terrific place to stay; there are also a number of *hostal-residencias*, like *La Anunciada*, Elduayen 16 (☎986/355590; ②). Visit the great bars in the cobbled alleyway just behind the seafront, and **restaurants** all around the Plaza de Castro feature enticing window displays of lobsters and assorted shellfish.

Medieval walls surround the wooded promontory which is Bayona's most prominent feature, and it's worth paying the nominal fee to walk around the parapet, with an unobstructed view in every direction, across the *ría* and along the chain of rocky islets which leads to the Islas Cíes. There's a barely used footpath beneath the walls at sea level which gives access to several diminutive **beaches**.

The Río Miño

The **Río Miño** (Minho in Portuguese and Gallego), the border between Spain and Portugal, is only about 100m wide at its mouth and is barely navigable. The first place you can cross is a few miles upstream at Goyan (Goian), where a very cheap car ferry makes hourly journeys to the delightful walled village of Vila Nova da Cerveira. The main crossing, however, is via **TUY** (Tui), staring across to the neat ramparts of Portuguese Valença. Tuy has the usual border-crossing street of tacky wares, but also an old town, tiered amid trees and stretches of ancient walls above the fertile riverbank. Sloping lanes, paved with huge slabs of granite, climb to an imposing fortress-like **Cathedral** dedicated to San Telmo, patron saint of fishermen; its military aspect is a distinctive mark of Tuy, scene of sporadic skirmishes with the Portuguese throughout the Middle Ages. There are a couple of enticing little river beaches. Nobody seems to mind if you camp beside them; otherwise there's a good **fonda** at the end of a small rectangular plaza, just off the main road at the base of the "monumental zone." The small bar and restaurant downstairs are the best value in town.

It's a twenty-minute walk to the Portuguese border, across an iron bridge designed by Eiffel; the little town of **VALENÇA**, dwarfed behind its mighty ramparts, lies a similar distance beyond. A ferry, from Salvaterra do Minho further upstream, crosses to the similarly attractive old Portuguese town of Monção.

THE PYRENEES

With the singular exception of **Pamplona** at the time of its bull-running fiesta, the area around the Spanish Pyrenees is little visited – most people who come here at all travel straight through. In doing so they miss out on some of the most wonderful scenery in Spain, and some of the country's most attractive hiking. You'll also be struck by the slower pace of life, especially in **Navarra** (in the west, a partly Basque region) and **Aragón** (in the centre) – the **Catalan** Pyrenees, along with **Andorra**, are more developed. There are few cities here – Pamplona itself and **Zaragoza**, with its fine Moorish architecture, are the only large centres – but there are plenty of attractive small towns and of course the mountains themselves, with several beautiful **national parks** as a focus for exploration.

Pamplona

PAMPLONA (Iruña) has been the capital of Navarra since the ninth century, and long before that was a powerful fortress town defending the northern approaches to Spain. Even now it has something of the appearance of a garrison city, with its hefty walls and elaborate pentagonal citadel.

There's plenty to look at in Pamplona – the fine **Cathedral** with its magnificent cloister (the Cathedral is expected to be closed for restoration until late 1994) and interesting **Museo Diocesano** (mid-May to mid-Oct daily 9am–2pm), the sturdy **city walls** and **citadel**, the display of regional archeology, history and art in the **Museo de Navarra** (Tues–Sat 10am–2pm & 5–7pm, Sun 11am–2pm; 200ptas), and much more – but ninety percent of visitors come here for just one thing: the thrilling week of the **Fiesta of San Fermín**. From midday on July 6 until midnight on July 14 the city gives itself up to riotous nonstop celebration. The centre of the festivities is the **encierro**, or running of the bulls, which draws tourists from all over the world, but you could have a great time here for a week without ever seeing a bull, and even if you are violently opposed to bullfighting, the *encierro* – in which the animals decisively have the upper hand – is a spectacle not to miss.

Six bulls are released each morning at eight to run from their corral near the Plaza San Domingo to the bullring. In front, around and occasionally under them run the hundreds of locals and tourists who are foolish or drunk enough to test their daring against the horns. It was Hemingway's *The Sun Also Rises* that really put "Los San Fermines" on the map and the area in front of the Plaza de Toros has been renamed Plaza Hemingway by a grateful council. To watch the *encierro* it's essential to arrive early – crowds have already formed an hour before it starts. The best **vantage points** are near the starting point or on the wall leading to the bullring. The event divides into two parts: there's the actual running of the bulls; and then after the bulls have been through the streets, bullocks with padded horns are let loose on the crowd in the bullring. If you watch the actual running, you won't be able to get into the bullring, so go on two separate mornings to see both things. **Bullfights** take place daily at 6.30pm, with the bulls that ran that morning; tickets are expensive (2000–3500ptas). At the end of the week (midnight on July 14) there's a mournful candlelit procession, the **Pobre De**, at which the festivities are officially wound up for another year.

Practicalities

The **train station** is a long way from the old part of town, but bus #9 runs every ten minutes to the end of Paseo de Sarasate, a few minutes' walk from the central Plaza del Castillo – there is a *RENFE* ticket office at c/Estella 8 (Mon–Fri 10am–2pm & 4–7pm, Sat 10am–2pm). The **bus station** is more central, on c/Conde Oliveto in front of the citadel, while the **tourist office** (summer daily 10am–7pm; winter Mon–Fri 10am–2pm & 4–7pm, Sat 10am–2pm) is found at c/Duque de Ahumada 3, just off Plaza del Castillo.

You'll find most of the cheap **hostales** and **fondas** in c/San Nicolás and its continuation c/San Gregorio, off Plaza del Castillo. Rooms are in short supply during summer, and at fiesta time you've virtually no chance of a place on spec. Ones to try include *Hostal Otano*, c/San Nicolás 5 (☎948/225095; ④), *Fonda La Montañesa*, c/San Gregorio 2 (☎948/224380; ④), *Casa García*, c/San Gregorio 12 (☎948/223893; ④), and *Hostal Beatán*, c/San Nicolás 25 (☎948/223428; ④). There's a **campsite**, *Ezcaba*, 7km out of town on the road to France; again it fills several days before the fiesta. During fiesta there are also two free campsites, one by the river just below *Ezcaba*, and another nearer town along the France road. Security at these is doubtful, however. The bus service, which goes to all the campsites, is poor, but it's easy to hitch or get a lift on one of the tour buses that stay at the official campsite.

The best and rowdiest **bars** are on and around c/San Nicolás but there's not much in the way of particularly cheap **food** here. Try instead the streets around c/Major; in particular *Bar la Cepa*, *Bar Piskolaris* and *Restaurante Lanzale* on c/San Lorenzo and *Bar la Campana* on c/de la Campana, all of which offer a combination of *bocadillos* and good, cheap *menús*. *Café Roch* on c/de las Comedias is great for tapas or, to get away from the crowds, go to the elegant *Meson del Caballo Blanco* on c/Redin up above the ramparts behind the cathedral where you can order cheap *raciones* upstairs. The elegant *Café Iruña*, on Plaza del Castillo, is the place to sit over a leisurely coffee as you take in the action, as is the modern yet equally enjoyable *Café Niza* opposite the tourist office on c/Duque de Ahumada.

Zaragoza

Zaragoza is the capital of Aragón, and easily its largest and liveliest city, with over half the province's one million people and the majority of its industry. There are some excellent bars and restaurants tucked in among its remarkable monuments, and it's also a handy transport centre, with good connections into the Pyrenees and east towards Barcelona.

The most imposing of the city's churches, majestically fronting the River Ebro, is the **Basilica de Nuestra Señora del Pilar** (daily 5.45am–9.30pm), one of Zaragoza's two cathedrals. It takes its name from a pillar on which the Virgin is said to have descended from heaven in an apparition before Saint James the Apostle. The pillar, topped by a diminutive image of the Virgin, forms the centrepiece in the Holy Chapel and is the focal point for pilgrims, who line up to touch an exposed piece of the pillar, encased in a marble surround. The cathedral also has a couple of small museums – the more worthwhile of which contains a good tapestry collection – but the building itself is something of a Baroque monstrosity. In terms of beauty it can't compare with the nearby Gothic-Mudéjar old cathedral – **La Seo** (currently closed for restoration) – at the far end of the pigeon-thronged Plaza del Pilar.

The highlight of Zaragoza, which you should see even if you plan to do no more than change trains or buses here, is the city's only surviving legacy from Moorish times. Moorish Spain was never very unified, and from the tenth to the eleventh century Zaragoza was the centre of an independent dynasty, the Beni Kasim. Their palace, the **Aljafería** (Tues–Sat 10am–2pm & 4/4.30–6.30/8pm, Sun 10am–2pm; free), was built in the heyday of their rule in the mid-eleventh century, and thus predates the Alhambra in Granada and Sevilla's Alcázar. Much was added later, after the Reconquest, when the palace was adapted and used by the kings of Aragón. From the original design the fore-most relic is a tiny and beautiful **mosque** adjacent to the ticket office. Further on, and currently under restoration, is an intricately decorated court, the Patio de Santa Isabella. Crossing from here, the Grand Staircase (added in 1492) leads to a succession of mainly fourteenth-century rooms, remarkable chiefly for their carved ceilings.

If you're interested in chasing the Moorish influence further, four **Mudéjar towers** survive in Zaragoza, perhaps the finest of which is the square tower of the church of **Santa María Magdalena**.

Practicalities

Points of arrival in Zaragoza are rather scattered. From the **train station** (*Estación Portillo*), walk down the short c/General Mayandia, turn right onto Paseo María Agustín and take bus #21 to Plaza del Pilar – or walk it in about 25 minutes. There are various **bus terminals**, but virtually all long-distance services leave from the Agreda terminal at Paseo María Agustín 7 (right from the train station). For local destinations check with one of the city's three **tourist offices**. There's one in the train station (Mon–Fri 10am–2pm & 4–7pm), a second in the Torreón de la Zuda (Mon–Fri 8am–2.30pm & 4.30–7.30pm, Sat 9am–2pm), part of the city fortifications overlooking the river, and, most useful, a third in the Plaza del Pilar (Mon–Sat 10am–1.30pm & 4.30–7.30/8pm, Sun 10am–1.30pm).

There are **rooms** – and several cheap **restaurants** – close to the train station, down the side streets off Paseo María Agustín. However there's more atmosphere, better accommodation possibilities and most of the city's nightlife crowded into an area known as **El Tubo**, between c/de Alfonso I and c/Don Jaime I, close to the Plaza del Pilar. There are upwards of a dozen cheap *fondas* and *pensiones* here, rarely full; try particularly c/Estébares. Other recommended lodgings include *Hostal Cumbre*, Avenida de Cataluña 24 (☎976/291148; ②), *Hostal Estrella*, Avenida de Clave 27 (☎976/238053; ②), and *Hostal Las Torres*, Plaza del Pilar 11 (☎976/394250; ④), where all rooms have bath. You can also **camp** at the large, barren *Camping Casablanca* (April to mid-Oct), on Avenida de Madrid, 2km outside the city.

Jaca and around

Heading towards the Pyrenees from Zaragoza, **JACA** is the northernmost town of any size in Aragón and an obvious staging post. It's also a place of considerable interest – an early capital of the kingdom of Aragón that lay astride one of the main medieval pilgrim routes to Santiago. Accordingly, a magnificent **Cathedral**, the first in Spain to be built in the Romanesque style, dominates the centre of town from its position at the north edge of the old quarter. It remains impressive despite much internal remodelling over the centuries, and there's a powerful added attraction in its **Museo Diocesano** (daily in summer 10am–2pm & 4–8.30pm). This should not be missed, the dark cloisters adapted as home to a beautiful collection of twelfth to fifteenth-century frescoes, gathered from village churches in the area and from higher up in the Pyrenees.

Although barely 800 metres up, Jaca ranks as a Pyrenean resort, becoming crowded in August; even at other times of the year, accommodation prices tend to be pushed up by the ski- and cross-border trade. But Jaca is foremost an army town, with a mass of conscripts attending the local mountain warfare academy. The military connection is nothing new: the **Ciudadela**, a sixteenth-century fort built to the stellar ground plan in vogue at the time, still offers good views of surrounding peaks. You can visit the interior (daily 11am–12.30pm & 5–6.30pm; free guided tours), but it's hardly worth it, as the outside, with slumbering deer in the dry moat, is by far the most interesting part.

Arriving in Jaca by rail, you'll find yourself more than a kilometre's walk out of town; move quickly and take the city bus which connects with most trains. The more central **bus station** is on Avenida Jacetania, 200 metres northwest of the cathedral. The **tourist office** (Mon–Fri 9am–2pm & 4.30–8pm, Sat 9am–1.30pm & 5–8pm, Sun 10am–1.30pm) – worth a browse for its noticeboards offering all sorts of sport- and mountaineering-related services – is off on the west side of town on Avenida Regimiento Galicia, just downhill from the Ciudadela.

All of Jaca's budget **accommodation** can be found on the northeast edge of the old town, with two good, quiet choices being *Casa Paco*, c/Mayor 57 (☎974/361618; ②), and *Hostal Paris* by the cathedral, Plaza de San Pedro 5 (☎974/361020; ②). There's also a **youth hostel** (☎974/360536; ①) on Avenida Perimetral, at the southern end of town, and two **campsites** – the closer but more basic of these the *Victoria*, 1500m west of town by the Pamplona road. Good-value **eating** is found in that same part of the old district: carnivores will appreciate *La Fragua* at c/Gil Berges 4 (shut Weds), while *La Cabaña* at c/del Pez 10 and *La Abuela Primera* at c/de la Población 3 both offer cheap but filling *menús*.

The Aragónese Pyrenees

If you're not a keen hiker or skier, than the foothill villages of **ANSÓ** and **HECHO** set in their beautiful namesake valleys are perhaps your best single target in the **Aragónese Pyrenees**; they're noted for their distinctive, imposing architecture, and accessible by a daily (not Sun) late-afternoon bus from Jaca. Hecho, on the east, is more visited and inevitably more expensive for **accommodation and food**; try *Casa Blasquico*, Plaza de la Fuente (☎974/375007; ②), and the *comedor* at the *Fonda Lo Foratón* respectively. In the westerly valley, less frequented Ansó offers several reasonable places to **stay** and **eat**, including the *Posada Veral,* in the heart of town at c/ Cocorro 6 (☎974/370119; ②), and *Hostal Aisa* (☎974/370009; ②) on Plaza Domingo Miral; both serve meals as well.

A worthwhile target for a winter visit to alpine Aragón are the adjacent ski resorts of **ASTÚN-CANDANCHU**, north of Jaca and easily reached by bus. *Hostales* are uniformly pricy; if your budget is limited and/or you're primarily interested in nordic skiing, than either of the two year-round *albergues*, the highly considered *El Aguila* (☎974/373291; ③) or *Valle del Aragón* (☎974/373222; ①), should suit you nicely. Between Jaca and the slopes lies **CANFRANC**, the final stop on the rail line up from Zaragoza since the French discontinued the onward section of track in a fit of pique over the success of the Spanish ski resorts. The small village is rather forlorn now, and you wouldn't come especially, but you can stay at *Hostal Casa Marraco* at c/Fernando el Católico 31 (☎974/373005; ③), and eat next door at *Casa Flores*.

For a summertime walking visit, there's no better taster for the Aragónese Pyrenees than the **Parque Nacional de Ordesa**, centred on a vast, trough-like valley flanked by imposingly striated limestone palisades. A morning bus from Jaca serves Sabiñanigo, from where there's a daily morning **bus** (plus an evening service in high season) to Torla, the best base for the park. Approaching Sabiñanigo by bus or train from Zaragoza, you'll need departures before 9am and 3pm respectively to make the connection.

TORLA itself, formerly a sleepy, stone-built village, has since the 1980s been overwhelmed in its role as gateway to the park, but the older corners remain visually attractive. Don't hope for a **room** or refuge bed from late July to late August, however, without reserving well in advance – even the two **campsites** 2km and 3km north reportedly fill up. At other times of the year you can usually find space at the central *Fonda Ballarín* (☎974/486155; ②) or the thirty-bunk *Albergue Lucien Briet* (☎974/486221; ①). Both the *Fonda* and the *Bar Brecha*, which manages the *albergue*, serve good-value **meals**.

If you've a vehicle, than the entrance to the **park** itself lies just five road-kilometres beyond Torla, but hikers should opt instead for the lovely hour-and-a-half trail-walk on the far side of the river, well marked as part of the Pyrenean GR (long-distance path) system. Once actually in Ordesa, further **hikes** can be as gentle or as strenuous as you like, the most popular outing being the all-day trip to the **Circo de Soaso** waterfalls.

Several valleys east of Torla and Ordesa and cradled between the two highest summits in the Pyrenees, **BENASQUE** serves as another favourite jump-off point for mountain rambles. There is a twice-daily bus service from Barbastro on the road from Huesca to Lleida, and a marginally better chance of finding a **bed** during high season. *Fonda Barrabes*, c/Mayor 5 (☎974/551654) is the budget standby, with ① dorm beds and ② rooms; try also the unmarked *Hostal Valero* (②), managed by the pricier *Hostal Aneto* next door (☎974/551079; ③). Best **meals**, strangely, are above the *Disco Ñaka* near the church, vernerable focus of the very attractive backstreets.

CATALUNYA

With its own language, culture and, to a degree, government, **Catalunya** (Cataluña in Castilian Spanish, traditionally Catalonia in English) has a unique identity. **Barcelona**, the capital, is very much the main event. One of the most vibrant and exciting cities in Europe, it is one of those places where you stay far longer than planned. Inland, the monastery of **Montserrat**, Catalunya's main "sight," is perched on one of the most unusual rock formations in Spain, and there are provincial cities too – **Tarragona**, **Girona** and **Lleida** – of considerable charm and historic interest. Sadly, most of the coastline is a disaster, with much of the **Costa Brava** in particular a turgid sprawl of concrete. There are parts of the northernmost stretch, from **Cadaqués** to **Port Bou** on the French border, which have managed to retain some attraction but on the whole if it's beaches you're after you'd do better to keep going south – or take a ferry from Barcelona for the Balearics. Since the use of the Catalan language is so widespread, we've used Catalan spellings, with Castilian equivalents in parentheses where relevant.

Barcelona

BARCELONA, the self-confident and progressive capital of Catalunya, is a tremendous place to be. Though it boasts outstanding Gothic and Art Nouveau buildings, and some great museums – most notably those dedicated to Picasso and Catalan art – it is above all a place where there's enjoyment simply in walking the streets, stopping in at bars and cafés, drinking in the atmosphere. A thriving port and the most prosperous commercial centre in Spain, it has a sophistication and cultural dynamism way ahead of the rest of the country. In part this reflects the city's proximity to France, whose influence is apparent in the elegant boulevards and imaginative cooking. But Barcelona has also evolved an individual and eclectic cultural identity, most perfectly and eccentrically expressed in the architecture of Antoni Gaudí. The planning for the 1992 Olympics led to a new wave of civic pride, culminating in gleaming, renovated monuments and some spectacular modern buildings too. There are, however, darker sides to this prosperity and confidence; there is a great deal of poverty and a considerable drug problem, which means that the **petty crime rate** is high. It's not unusual for tourists to feel threatened in the seedier areas flanking the Ramblas. It's wise to take a few precautions; leave passports and tickets locked up in your hotel, don't be too conspicuous with expensive cameras and, if attacked, don't offer any resistance.

Arrival and information

The **airport**, 12km southwest of the city, is linked by a half-hourly train service (240ptas) with the main **Estació de Sants**, where you can take the metro to the city centre (line #3 to Liceu for the Ramblas). Many trains from the airport also run on to Plaça de Catalunya, a more direct way of reaching the Barri Gòtic. Alternatively, there's the efficient **Airbus** (*Aerobus*; every 15–30min; 5.30am–10pm; 400ptas), which departs from outside the terminals on a circular route and runs into the centre via Plaça España, Gran Vía, Plaça de Catalunya and Passieg de Grácia. A **taxi** will cost around 2000ptas to Estació de Sants, 2500ptas to somewhere more central in the old town.

Estacío de Sants is the city's main **train station**, for national and some international arrivals. The **Estació de França** (or Estació Terminal), next to the Parc de la Ciutadella, is the terminal for long-distance Spanish and European express and intercity trains. From França you can take the metro (line #4) from nearby Barceloneta, or simply walk into the Barri Gòtic, up via Laietana and into c/Ferran. The main **bus terminal** is the **Estació del Nord** (three blocks north of the Parc de la Ciutadella; metro Arc de Triomf), to which all bus companies are in the process of moving: if, by chance, you don't arrive here, you'll be dropped at a central point within easy reach of a metro station. Arriving by **ferry** from the Balearics, you'll dock at the Estació Marítima at the bottom of the Ramblas.

The **tourist offices** in Barcelona are very well organized: any of them will give you a free, large-scale **map** of the city and a public transport map too – invaluable for sorting out the complex bus routes. The main offices are at the airport (Mon–Sat 9.30am–8pm, Sun 9.30am–3pm); Estació de Sants (daily 8am–8pm); Gran Vía 658 (Mon–Fri 9am–7pm, Sat 9am–2pm); and Estacío de França (summer daily 8am–8pm; rest of the year Mon–Fri 8am–2pm & 4–10pm, Sat & Sun 8am–2pm). There's also a 24-hour, English-speaking **municipal information service**: call ☎ 010.

City Transport

The quickest way of getting around is by the modern and efficient **metro**; stations are marked by a red diamond sign. The metro starts at 5am (6am on Sun) and shuts down at 11pm – just when most people in Barcelona are thinking of going out. It's extended to 1am on Friday, Saturday, and the evening before a holiday, and to midnight on Sunday. **Bus** routes (in operation 6am–11pm) are far more complicated, but every bus stop also displays a comprehensive route map. A limited number of **night buses** fill the gap; they're yellow and most of them start in or pass through Plaça de Catalunya. There's a flat **fare** on both metro and buses of 115ptas; if you're staying a couple of days or more it's better to buy a ticket strip, or **tarja** from metro station ticket offices, which gives you ten journeys at a discounted price. The T1 costs 590ptas and covers buses and the metro; the T2 costs 560ptas and just covers the metro. Night buses cost 120ptas; a *tarja* for these costs 600ptas.

The **cable cars** across the harbour and up to Montjuïc require separate tickets and are a little expensive, though well worth taking at least once for the views. Expect to pay 700ptas one-way, 750ptas return for the cross-harbour trip. Black and yellow **taxis** (with a green roof-light lit when available for hire) are inexpensive, plentiful and very useful late at night. There's a minimum charge of 270ptas, and after that it's 100ptas per kilometre depending on the time of day.

> The area telephone code for Barcelona is ☎93.

Accommodation

Accommodation in Barcelona is among the most expensive in Spain and unless you stay in a youth hostel, you'll be hard pushed to find a room for under 3000ptas double. The tourist offices dish out lists of **hotels** and **hostales**, but these are hardly necessary as a walk through the streets of the old town reveals heavy concentrations of places to stay and it's easy to stroll around comparing rooms. Most of the **cheapest accommodation** is to be found in the side streets off and around the Ramblas, a convenient and atmospheric area in which to base yourself. The further down towards the port you get, the less salubrious and noisier the surroundings: as a very general rule, anything above c/Escudellers tends to be all right. Perhaps the best hunting ground for cheap rooms is between the Ramblas and the Plaça de Sant Jaume, in the area bordered by c/Escudellers and c/de la Boqueria. A **hotel reservations office** at the airport and at Sants station (daily 8am–10pm) will book you a place to stay on arrival (there's a fee of 100ptas), but they won't book the very cheapest places and, of course, you won't get to see the room beforehand.

There are several official and not-so-official **youth hostels** in Barcelona, where accommodation is in multi-bedded dorm rooms. Prices are around 850–900ptas each in a private hostel, a little less in an *IYHF* hostel. There are hundreds of **campsites** on the coast in either direction, but none less than 7km from the city; we've detailed the two closest, which are out towards the airport.

HOSTELS

Albergue Pere Tarres, c/Numancia 149 (☎4102309). Near Sants station (metro Les Corts). Open 4–10pm. ①

Albergue Verge de Montserrat, Passeig de la Mare del Coll 41–51, metro Vallcarca (☎2138633). An *IYHF* hostel a long way out of the city, open 7.30am–midnight. ①

Hostal de Joves, Passeig de Pujades 29 (☎3003104). An *IYHF* hostel right by the Parc de la Ciutadella and handy for the Nord bus terminal and Estació de França. Open 7.30–10am and 3pm–midnight. ①

Pensión Colom 3, c/Colom 3 (☎3180631; entrance inside Plaça Reial). The better hostel choice in Plaça Reial, with single and double rooms available too. ①

HOTELS

Residencia Australia, Ronda Universitat 11 (☎3174177). Just off Plaça Catalunya and very popular; reserve in advance. ④

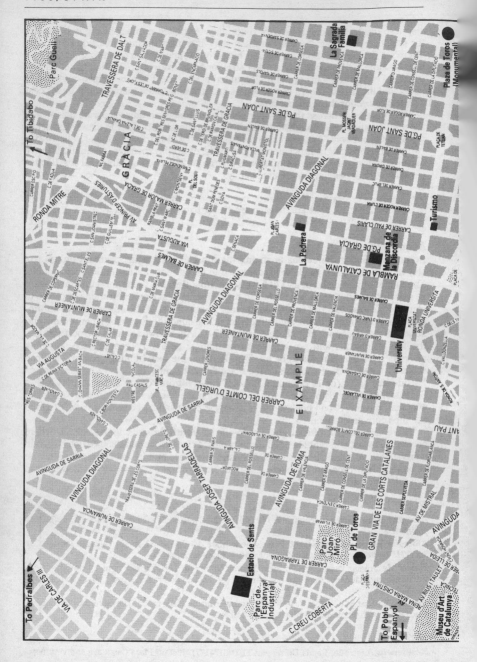

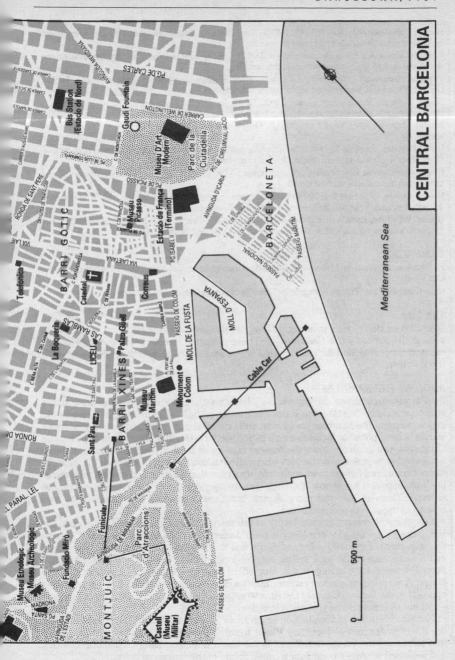

CENTRAL BARCELONA

Mediterranean Sea

Bus Station
(Estació de Nord)

Gaudi Fountain

Museu D'Art
Modern

PG. DE CARLES

CARRER DE WELLINGTON

Parc de la
Ciutadella

PG. DE PICASSO

Museu
Picasso

Estació de França
(Termino)

PG ISABEL II

VIA LAIETANA

BARRI GÒTIC

Telefònica

Catedral

Correus

Museu
Marítim

Monument
a Colom

MOLL DE LA FUSTA

PASSEIG DE COLOM

MOLL D'ESPANYA

BARCELONETA

PASSEIG NACIONAL

PASSEIG MARÍTIM

LAS RAMBLAS

La Boqueria

LICEU

Palau Güell

BARRI XINES

Sant Pau

Cable Car

RONDA DE

PARAL·LEL

Funicular

Fundació Miró

Museu Etnològic

Museu Archeologic

MADRONA

Parc
d'Atraccions

MONTJUIC

Castell
(Museu
Militar)

PASSEIG DE COLOM

0   500 m

Hostal Canaletes, Ramblas 133 (☎3015660). Near Plaça de Catalunya (and at the top of the building); fair rooms, though hot and noisy in summer. ②

Pensión Europa, c/de la Boqueria 18 (☎3187620). Some rooms have a balcony overlooking the street; cheaper rooms without bath available too. ③

Pensión Fernando, c/Arc del Remei 4 (☎2210358). Welcoming place, in a side street of c/Ferran, close to Plaça Reial. Basic rooms with separate showers. ②

Hostal Levante, Baixada Sant Miquel 2 (☎3179565). Just off the Plaça de Sant Miquel, this friendly place has decent, plain rooms in a well-kept block. ③

Hostal Mayoral, Plaça Reial 2 (☎3179534). Longtime favourite on the Plaça Reial. Cheaper out of season. ③

Hotel Oriente, Ramblas 45 (☎3022558). Stylish three-star hotel on the Ramblas; attractive turn-of-the-century decor and modern rooms with bath are worth the splurge. ⑦

Hostal-Residencia Rembrandt, c/Portaferrissa 23 (☎3181011). Spotless rooms with shower and balcony; cheaper rooms without too. ②

Hostal Opera, c/de Sant Pau 20 (☎3188201). Close enough to the Ramblas to make you overlook the rather unkempt rooms. Cheaper rooms without shower too. ②

Hostal Windsor, Rambla de Catalunya 84, metro Pg. de Gràcia (☎2151198). Small *hostal* on the Eixample's nicest avenue with well-kept and reasonably priced doubles. ④

CAMPSITES

El Barcino, Esplugas de Llobregat (☎3728501). Open all year, bus from Plaça d'Espanya or metro Can Vidalet.

Cala-Gogo-El Prat, Prat de Llobregat (☎3794600). Open Feb–Nov, bus as above.

The City

Scattered as Barcelona's main sights may be, the greatest concentration of interest is around the old town (*La Ciutat Vella*). These cramped streets above the harbour are easily manageable, and far more enjoyable, on foot. Start, as everyone else does, with the Ramblas.

AROUND THE RAMBLAS

It is a telling comment on Barcelona's character that one can recommend a single street (or strictly streets) – **the Ramblas** – as a highlight. The heart of Barcelona's life and self-image, the Ramblas are littered with cafés, shops, restaurants and newspaper stands, a focal point for locals as much as for tourists. Heading down from the Plaça de Catalunya, you gradually leave the opulent facades of the banks and department stores for a seedier area towards the port where the Ramblas cut right through the heart of the notorious red-light district, with side streets at the harbour end packed with dimly lit clubs, bars and sex shops. It's much less threatening than it once was, however: the Olympic clean-up saw the more dismal buildings renovated (or demolished) and several of the streets pedestrianized.

On your way down there are plenty of interesting buildings, some of them open for visits: don't miss the glorious **Mercat Sant Josep**, the city's main food market (Mon–Sat 8am–8pm), a splendid gallery of sights and smells with several excellent snack bars and a restaurant at the back selling market-fresh dishes. Beyond is the **Liceu** (tours Mon–Fri twice-daily; check at the box office inside), Barcelona's celebrated opera house. A surprisingly modest exterior hides a riot of gilt, glass and velvet. More or less opposite is the famous *Café de l'Òpera*, a wonderful and very fashionable meeting place – and not as expensive as you might imagine.

Not much further, hidden behind an archway just off the Ramblas and easy to miss, lies the elegant nineteenth-century **Plaça Reial**. It's decorated with tall palm trees and iron lamps (by the young Gaudí) and is the haunt of punks, bikers, Catalan eccentrics and bemused tourists stopping for a coffee at one of the pavement cafés.

Gaudí's magnificent **Palau Güell** stands just off the Ramblas, towards the bottom, at c/Nou de la Rambla 3. Much of Gaudí's early career was spent constructing elaborate follies for wealthy patrons, the most important of whom was Don Eusebio Güell, a ship-owner and industrialist. In 1885 he commissioned this mansion which is now used as a **theatre museum** (Mon–Sat 10am–1pm & 5–7pm, Sun 10am–1pm; 100ptas) so you can see the interior. Here, Gaudí's feel for different materials is remarkable – at a time when architects sought to conceal the iron supports within buildings, he turned them to his advantage.

Right at the harbour end of the Ramblas, Columbus stands pointing out to sea from the top of a tall, grandiose column: the **Monument a Colom**. You can get inside if the renovations are complete (June–Sept daily 9am–9pm; Oct–May Tues–Sat 10am–2pm & 3.30–6.30pm, Sun 10am–7pm; free) and risk the elevator to his head (it fell down in 1976) for a fine view of the city.

The whole port district has been spruced up, most notably by the construction of the harbourside *passeig*, the **Moll de la Fusta**, stretching from the Colom statue to the post office. The benches and trees are a pleasant place to sit, there are some fancy new bar-restaurants, and from a couple of points along the quayside you can take one of the regular **sightseeing boats**, *Las Golondrinas* (Nov–March daily 11am–4pm; April–June & Oct Mon–Fri 11am–5pm, Sat & Sun 11am–8pm; July–Sept daily 11am–9pm; 330ptas return, children 180ptas), across the port to the modern docks; there are also two-hour return cruises from here to the Port Olimpic (daily 11am, 1pm & 4pm; 1100ptas, children 500ptas). A more dramatic view of the city is offered by the **cable car** (noon–8pm daily; 700ptas single, 750ptas return) which sweeps right across the harbour from the base of Montjuïc to the middle of the docks and on to Barceloneta.

THE BARRI GÒTIC

A remarkable concentration of beautiful medieval Gothic buildings, just a couple of blocks off the Ramblas, the **Barri Gòtic** forms the very heart of the old city. Once it was entirely enclosed by fourth-century Roman walls, but what you see now dates principally from the fourteenth and fifteenth centuries, when Catalunya reached the height of its commercial prosperity before being absorbed into the burgeoning kingdom of Castile. Parts of the ancient walls are still visibly incorporated into later structures, especially around the Cathedral.

The quarter is centred on the **Plaça de Sant Jaume**, on one side of which stands the restored Town Hall, the **Ajuntament**. Despite appearances you are usually free to wander in and have a look around the spacious interior courtyard. Across the square rises the **Palau de la Generalitat**, home of the Catalan government (only open April 23; massive queues); restored during the sixteenth century in Renaissance style, it has a beautiful cloister on the first floor with superb coffered ceilings.

Just behind the square, the **Cathedral** (daily 8am–1.30pm & 2–7.30pm) is one of the great Gothic buildings of Spain. Modern lighting shows off the soaring airiness of the interior superbly. Outside, the magnificent **cloisters** look over a lush tropical garden with soaring palm trees and white geese, and open into, among other things, the small **cathedral museum** (Mon–Fri 11am–1pm; 50ptas). Nearby, next to the Palau Episcopal and at various points in and near Vía Laietana, you can see some of the remaining **Roman walls**.

The cathedral and its associated buildings aside, the most concentrated batch of historic monuments in the Barri Gòtic is the grouping around the nearby **Plaça del Rei**. Barcelona's finest Roman remains were uncovered beneath the former Palace of the Counts of Barcelona (the **Palau Reial**) which now houses the **Museu d'Història de la Ciutat** (Tues–Sat 10am–2pm & 4–8pm, Sun 10am–2pm; 300ptas, Wed 150ptas, free Sun). Underground, both Roman and Visigothic remains have been preserved where they were discovered during works in the 1930s. The museum also gives access to the beautiful fourteenth-century **Capella Reial de Santa Àgata** with its tall single nave and unusual stained glass, and to an extension of the royal palace known as the **Saló de Tinell**, a fine spacious example of fourteenth-century secular Gothic architecture. It was on the steps leading from the Saló de Tinell into the Plaça del Rei that Ferdinand and Isabella stood to receive Columbus on his triumphant return from America. The extraordinary **Museu Marès** (Tues–Sat 10am–3pm & 4–7pm, Sun 10am–2pm; 200ptas) occupies another wing of the palace, behind the plaça. The bulk of the museum consists of religious sculpture, including a vast number of wooden crucifixes showing the stylistic development of this form from the twelfth to the fifteenth centuries. This is infinitely more interesting than it might sound, but in case boredom should set in, the upper floors house the **Museu Sentimental** of local sculptor Federico Marès, an incredible retrospective jumble gathered during fifty years of travel. Don't miss it.

PICASSO AND THE CARRER DE MONTCADA

Heading west from the palace, you'll cross Vía Laietana and reach the Carrer de Montcada, crowded with beautifully restored old buildings. One of these houses the **Museu Picasso** (Tues–Sun 10am–8pm; 500ptas, Wed 250ptas, free 1st Sun of month), one of the most important collections of Picasso's work in the world and the only one of any significance in his native country. Although born in Málaga, **Picasso** spent much of his youth in Barcelona. He maintained close links with Barcelona and his Catalan friends even when he left for Paris in 1904, and is said always to have thought of himself as Catalan. The time Picasso spent in Barcelona encompassed most of his "Blue Period" (1901–04) and was the occasion for many of the formative influences on his art. The museum covers his entire career, though the early periods are the best represented and there are few really famous works. Nonetheless it's an essential stop, and all extremely well laid out in a strikingly beautiful medieval palace converted specifically for the museum.

Continue down the street and you'll come out opposite the great basilica of **Santa María del Mar** (Mon–Sat 9am–12.30pm & 5–8.15pm, Sun 9am–2pm), built on what was the seashore in the fourteenth century. Its soaring lines were the symbol of Catalan supremacy in Mediterranean commerce and it is still much dearer to the heart of the average local than the cathedral. The stained glass is especially beautiful.

ANTONI GAUDÍ AND THE SAGRADA FAMÍLIA

Besides modern art, Barcelona offers – above all through the work of **Antoni Gaudí** (1852–1926) – some of the most fantastic and exciting modern architecture to be found anywhere in the world. Without doubt his most famous creation is the **Temple Expiatori de la Sagrada Família** (daily 9am–8pm; 600ptas, metro Sagrada Família), a good way northeast of the Plaça de Catalunya. This has become a kind of symbol for the city, and was one of the few churches left untouched by the orgy of church burning which followed the 1936 revolution. Today the church remains unfinished, though amid great controversy work has restarted based on Gaudí's last known plans. Some maintain that the structure should be left incomplete as a memorial to Gaudí's untimely death (he was run over by a tram in 1926), others that he intended it to be the work of several generations, each continuing in its own style. The current work seems to infringe the original spirit in either case, but it still ranks as one of the most extraordinary buildings in the world.

The size alone is startling, with eight spires rising to over 100m. For Gaudí these were metaphors for the Twelve Apostles; he planned to build four more above the main facade and to add a 180-metre tower topped with a lamb (representing Jesus) over the transept, itself to be surrounded by four smaller towers symbolizing the Evangelists.

Take the lift which runs up one of the towers, and you can enjoy a dizzy view down over the whole complex and climb still further round the walls and into the towers.

Inside the Temple a small **Gaudí museum** traces the career of the architect and the history of the building. It is likely to set you on the trail of his earlier work, all of which, astonishingly, dates from before 1911 when he finished the Parc Güell and vowed to devote himself solely to the Sagrada Família: the tourist offices also issue a handy leaflet describing all his works, with a map of their locations. Above all, check out the **Parc Güell** (daily summer 9am–8pm; winter 10am–5pm; free), his most ambitious project apart from the Sagrada Família. This almost hallucinatory experience, with giant decorative lizards and a vast Hall of Columns contains another small **museum** (daily except Sat 10am–2pm & 4–7pm; 150ptas) with some of the furniture Gaudí designed. To get there, take the metro to Lesseps or bus #24 from the Plaça de Catalunya to Travesera de Dalt, from where it's a half-kilometre walk to the main gates on c/d'Olot.

CIUTADELLA

It's easy enough, even in the middle of Barcelona, to escape for a few hours into greenery and relative peace. For a quick respite from the centre nip into the **Parc de la Ciutadella**, which is within easy walking distance of the Barri Gòtic. Its attractions include a lake, Gaudí's monumental fountain and the city zoo (daily 10am–7pm; 850ptas), and you'll also find the meeting place of the Catalan parliament and the **Museu d'Art Modern** (daily except Tues 9am–9pm; 300ptas), which ranges from the eighteenth century to the 1980s. The last two occupy parts of the old citadel from which the park takes its name.

MONTJUÏC

The hill of **Montjuïc** has far more varied attractions – five museums, an amusement park, the "Spanish Village", the Olympic arena and a castle with grand views of the city. The most obvious way to approach is to take a bus or metro to the Plaça d'Espanya and walk from there up the imposing Avenida de la Reina María Cristina, past the 1929 International Fair buildings and the rows of fountains. If you'd rather start with the castle, there's the dramatic **cable car** ride from Barceloneta or from near the Colom monument (out of season it runs only at weekends), over the harbour to Jardins de Miramar, just beyond which you can pick up a second cable car to the amusement park and castle. Or there's a **funicular railway** (summer daily every 15min; 150ptas) which runs from *Paral.lel* metro station to the start of the cable car. And lastly there are **buses**: #61 from Plaça d'Espanya to the amusement park, or a free bus from the plaça to the Poble Espanyol.

If you tackle the stiff climb from the Plaça d'Espanya you'll arrive at the **Palau Nacional**, centrepiece of Barcelona's 1929 International Fair and now home to one of Spain's great museums, the **Museu d'Art de Catalunya**, with its two enormous main collections; the Gothic collection is fascinating, but it's the Romanesque section that is the more remarkable, perhaps the best collection of its kind in the world: 35 rooms of eleventh- and twelfth-century frescoes, meticulously removed from a series of small Pyrenean churches and beautifully displayed. Sadly, the museum has been closed for several years while renovation work is carried out, though by now three rooms of exhibits are to open to the public.

Barcelona's important **Museu Arqueològic** (Mon 9am–2pm, Tues–Sat 9am–8.30pm, Sun 9am–2pm; 200ptas) stands to the east of the Palau Nacional, lower down the hill. Nearby is the **Fundació Joan Miró** (Tues–Sat 11am–7pm, Thurs until 9pm, Sun 10.30am–2.30pm; 500ptas), the most adventurous of Barcelona's art museums, devoted to one of the greatest Catalan artists. A beautiful white building houses a permanent collection of paintings, graphics, tapestries and sculptures donated by Miró himself and covering the period from 1914 to 1978.

A short walk over to the other side of the Palau Nacional will bring you to the **Poble Espanyol** or "Spanish Village" (daily except Mon 9am–late-night; Mon closes 8pm 650ptas, children 325ptas), consisting of replicas of famous or characteristic buildings from all over Spain. As a crash-course introduction to Spanish architecture it's not bad – everything is well labelled and at least reasonably accurate – but inevitably the place swarms with tourists. Prices, especially for products of the "genuine Spanish workshops" (and in the bars), are exorbitant. Just down the road, the reconstruction of the **Mies van der Rohe Pavilion** (daily 10am–6pm) is a far greater treat.

From the Poble Espanyol, the main road climbs around the hill to what was the principal **Olympic arena**, passing some dazzling new buildings – the Picornell swimming pools and the Japanese-designed Palau Sant Jordi. These are overshadowed only by the Olympic Stadium itself, the **Estadi Olimpic** (daily 10am–6pm; free), built originally for the 1929 Exhibition and completely refitted by Catalan architects to accommodate the 1992 opening and closing ceremonies. The new Olympic museum, the **Galeria Olímpica**, on Passeig Olimpic (Tues–Sat 10am–2pm & 4–8pm, Sun 10am–2pm), is a hands-on affair covering the staging of the Games in the city. Far above this complex of museums and sports arenas, and offering magnificent views across the city, stands the eighteenth-century **Castell de Montjuïc**, built on seventeenth-century ruins.

TIBIDABO

If the views from the Castell de Montjuïc are good, those from the top of **Mount Tibidabo** – which forms the northwestern boundary of the city – are legendary. On one of those mythical clear days you can see across to Montserrat and the Pyrenees, and out to sea even as far as Mallorca. The very name is based on this view, taken from the Temptations of Christ in the wilderness, when Satan led him to a high place and offered him everything which could be seen: *Haec omnia tibi dabo si cadens adoraberis me* (All these things will I give thee, if thou wilt fall down and worship me). At the summit there's a wonderfully old-fashioned **Parc d'Atraccions**, and all around there are pleasant walks through the woods. To get there, take the *Ferrocarriles Catalanes* rail line from Plaça de Catalunya to Avenida Tibidabo; from there a bus connects with the funicular railway to the top.

Eating, Drinking and Nightlife

There's a huge variety of **food** available in Barcelona and even low-budget travellers can do well for themselves. The most serious problems that you're likely to encounter are that a lot of places close on Sundays and throughout August, and that the cheaper ones often have no written menu, the waiter reeling off the day's dishes at bewildering speed. Also note that the *menú del día* is rarely available in the evening. If you want to buy picnic material the covered **market** (*Mercat Sant Josep/La Boqueria*) off the Ramblas is the place to go. A couple of **supermarkets** to know about are *Centro Comercial Simago*, Ramblas 113 (food department in the basement), and *Drugstore*, Passeig de Gràcia 71, the latter open all night.

Amusing yourself in Barcelona is unlikely to be a problem. There are hundreds of excellent **bars** and **cafés** in the city centre to start your evening, including the lively *tapas* places in the Barri Gòtic. Around the Museu Picasso is a particularly good area: the Passeig del Born, the square at the end of c/Montcada behind Santa María del Mar, is crowded with popular bars. Gràcia, north of the centre, is full of little squares; the main one, Plaça del Sol, is bordered by café terraces. It's the most studenty area in Barcelona and ideal for low-key, lateish drinking. Barcelona's **nightlife** is some of Europe's most exciting. It keeps going all night too, the music bars closing at 3am, the discos at 4 to 5am, and (for the seriously dissipated) some clubs opening between 5am and 9am on weekends. Among the more expensive, trendier places, *bars modernos* are in fashion at the moment, high-tech theme palaces concentrated mainly in the

Eixample, or in the rich kids' stamping ground bordered by c/Ganduxer, Avenida Diagonal and Vía Augusta, west of Gràcia. Drinks are expensive, the music echoes the often elaborate decorations, and the "in" places change rapidly, with new ones starting up all the time. **Clubbing** can be more expensive still; in the most exclusive places even a beer is going to cost you roughly ten times what it costs in the bar next door.

For **listings** of almost anything you could want in the way of entertainment and culture, buy a copy of the weekly *Guía del Ocio* (75ptas) from any newsstand. There's a thriving **gay scene** in Barcelona; *SexTienda*, at c/Rauric 11 (very near Plaça Reial), sells a map of gay Barcelona with a list of bars, clubs and contacts.

TAPAS BARS

La Bodega, c/del Regomir 11, Barri Gòtic. Great barn of a place with long wooden benches and delicious *tapas*. Closed Mon and Aug.

Bar Celta, c/de la Mercè 16, Barri Gòtic. Galician *tapas* specialities, including excellent fried *calamares*, and heady Galician wine. Very popular. Open until 1am. Closed Aug.

La Soccarena, c/de la Mercè 21. Asturian cider bar serving goat's cheese, cured meats and excellent Asturian cider – which the waiter pours into glasses from over the back of his head to aereate the cider.

El Xampanayet, c/de Montcada 22. Terrific blue-tiled champagne bar with fine seafood *tapas*, *cava* by the glass and local *sidra*. Closed Mon, Sun night and Aug.

RESTAURANTS

Amaya, Ramblas 20–24. Busy, smoke-filled *tapas* bar on one side, mid-range (around 3000ptas) restaurant on the other, the *Amaya* serves Basque specialities.

Bar Cal Kiko, c/del Pelau (junction with c/Cervantes), Barri Gòtic. Local workers' dining room where the 675pta *menú* is filling and the atmosphere jovial. Meals 1–4pm only, *tapas* at other times; open until 10pm.

Bar-Restaurant Candanchu, Plaça Rius i Taulet 9, Gràcia; metro Fontana. Sit outside and enjoy a sandwich or *tortilla*, or go for the 800ptas *menú del dia*. Closed Tues.

La Cuina, c/Sombrerers 7, Barri Gòtic. A friendly joint down the side of Santa María del Mar, with competently cooked *platos combinados*. Around 1200ptas. Closed Mon.

Drugstore, Passeig de Gràcia 71, Eixample; metro Passeig de Gràcia. Bar-restaurant and shopping complex, open 24hr. The Mon–Fri lunch *menú* is a good buy.

Egipte, c/Jerusalem 12, Barri Xines. Long-standing favourite restaurant, with an extensive Catalan menu. You can eat well for 2500–3000ptas. There are two other branches (at c/Jerusalem 3 and Ramblas 79). Closed Sun.

Els Tres Nebots, c/de Sant Pau 42, Barri Xines. An extensive list of Catalan favourites served quickly at tables at the back of the bar. The *menú del dia* is great value at 800ptas or put together a nourishing meal for well under 1500ptas.

Restaurant España, c/Sant Pau 9–11, Barri Xines. Eat fine food in *modernista* splendour in a building designed by Domenèch i Montaner. The *menú del día* is good value at 1200ptas, but not available at night when a full meal costs around 4000ptas a head.

Restaurant Garduña, c/Morera 17–19, Barri Xines. At the back of the Sant Josep market, this offers one of the city's best *paellas* and good, fresh market produce. Lunch menú for 1000ptas; dinner more like 2500ptas. Closed Sun.

Les Corts Catalanes, Gran Vía 603 (corner Rambla de Catalunya), Eixample; metro Catalunya. Vegetarian restaurant that doubles as a health food store. An 950ptas *menú del día* (Mon–Fri lunch only), otherwise 2000–2500ptas a head to fill up on Catalan vegetarian dishes, pizzas and salads.

Los Caracoles, c/Escudellers 14, Barri Gòtic. Barcelona landmark restaurant whose name means "snails", the house speciality, along with the spit-roast chicken on display in the street outside. Around 3500ptas if you include both as part of a big meal; call in during the day to reserve a table.

Restaurant Perú, Passeig de Bourbó 10, Barceloneta. Barcelona's best seafood is served in Barceloneta. This is one of the few there that has a *menú del día*, good value at around 1100–1500ptas depending on when you eat.

Restaurant Pitarra, c/d'Avinyó 56, Barri Gòtic. A Catalan cookery in operation since 1890, lined with paintings and serving good, reasonably priced food. 2000–3500ptas a head. Closed Sun.

Pollo Rico, c/Sant Pau 31, Barri Xines. Spit-roasted chicken, chips and glass of *cava* for under 600ptas make this one of the area's most popular budget spots. Closed Wed.

Self Naturista, c/Santa Ana 15, Barri Gòtic. Popular self-service vegetarian restaurant with a 725pta *menú* and dishes that change daily. Open Mon–Sat until 10pm.

Las Siete Puertas, Passeig d'Isabel II 14, Barri Gòtic (☎3194462). Wood-panelled classic whose decor has barely changed in 150 years. Elegant but not exclusive, though you will need to book ahead. The seafood is excellent, particularly the dark *paella*. 4000ptas a head and up.

CAFÉS AND BARS

Ambos Mundos, Plaça Reial 10, Barri Gòtic. Touristy choice in the plaça, but a good vantage point for taking in some of the stranger local characters. Closed Tues.

Berimbau, Passeig del Born 17, Barri Gòtic. Cool bar with Brazilian sounds and cocktails.

Horchatería Fillol, Plaça de la Universitat 5, Eixample. *Horchata* as well as enormous milk shakes and other delights. Breakfast is coffee and croissant for 220ptas.

Café de l'Òpera, Ramblas 74. Elegant turn-of-the-century café-bar with fine coffee and a range of cakes and snacks. Open daily until 3am.

El Paraigua, Plaça Sant Miquel, Barri Gòtic. Expensive café-bar, with a chic Art Nouveau interior. Closed Sun.

Els Quatre Gats, c/Montsió 5, Barri Gòtic. *Modernista*-designed, haunt of Picasso and his contemporaries, still an interesting and arty place for a drink. Closed Sun lunch.

Café del Sol, Plaça del Sol 29, Gràcia. Trendy hang-out, just one of several similar places in this square.

Café Zurich, Plaça de Catalunya 1 (top of the Ramblas). Traditional meeting place for trendies and foreigners; its position makes it *the* place to sit and watch passing crowds.

DESIGNER BARS AND DISCOS

Apolo-Friday, c/Nou de la Rambla 113, Barri Xines. Disco with eclectic mix of music and a gay/straight crowd, old town location; open until 3am.

ARS Studio, c/Atenas 25 (junction with Ronda del General Mitre), Gràcia. Large modern bar, with a young rich kid clientele. A former cinema, it still shows old films on Sun afternoons; nights there's dancing until 4am.

La Fira, c/Provença 171, Eixample, metro Provença. A museum-bar with seats in turn-of-the-century fairground rides, plus a bar under a circus awning. Open until 3am, Sun until midnight.

Nick Havanna, c/Rosselló 208, Eixample, metro Diagonal. One of the most futuristic bars in town, enormous, yet packed to the gills at weekends. Open 8pm–4am.

Karma, Plaça Reial 10, Barri Gòtic. Good, studenty dance place with home-grown pop and rock sounds.

KGB, c/Alegre de Dalt 55, Gràcia. The closest thing the city has to a punk club, with live music Wed–Sat and weekend "shift" until 8am.

Otto Zutz, c/Lincoln 15, Gràcia. A three-storey warehouse converted into a nocturnal shop window of everything that's for sale or hire in Barcelona. With the right rags and face you're in (you may or may not have to pay depending on how impressive you are, the day of the week, etc.). The disco starts at 2am; it's a bar before that.

SiSiSi, Avda Diagonal 442, Eixample; metro Diagonal. One of the first *bars modernos*, and still one of the most elegant and laid-back. Open until 4am.

Soweto, c/Socrates 68, Eixample, metro Fabra i Puig. Reggae and African dance sounds, and late hours at the weekend.

Torres de Avila, Avda Marqués de Comillas, Poble Espanyol, Montjuïc. The city's newest and most fantastic bar yet – see it to believe it. Open 11pm–4am.

Universal, c/Mariano Cubí 184, Gràcia, metro Fontana. Post-modern bar, long one of the trendiest. Open until 3am.

Yabba Dabba Club, c/Avenir 63, Gràcia. Haunt of the spiky-haired crowd, with Gothic decor including candelabras and a sculpted torso protruding from the wall. Open until 3am, closed Sun.

Listings

Airlines *Air France*, Pg. de Gràcia 63 (☎4872526); *British Airways*, Pg. de Gràcia 85 (☎4872112); *Iberia*, Pg. de Gràcia 30 (☎3013993); *TWA*, Pg. de Gràcia 55 (☎2152382).

American Express c/Rosselló 259 (Mon–Fri 9.30–6pm, Sat 10am–noon; ☎2170070).

Books In English from *Itaca*, Rambla de Catalunya 81, *Come-In*, c/Provença 203, *The Book Store*, c/la Granja 13, and from newspaper stands down the Ramblas.

Buses The main bus station is the *Estació del Nord* on Avda Vilanova for departures throughout Catalunya, Spain and beyond. The tourist offices or travel agencies can assist with timetables. On long-distance routes, book at least a day in advance if possible.

Car rental Most rental agencies are represented at the airport. In town, contact *Atesa*, c/Balmes 141 (☎2378140); *Ital*, Traversera de Gràcia 71 (☎2012199); *Hertz*, c/Tuset 10 (☎2173248); *Avis*, c/ Casanova 209 (☎2099533).

Consulates *Australia*, Gran Vía Carles III (☎3309496); *Britain*, Avda Diagonal 477 (☎4199044); *Canada*, Vía Augusta 125 (☎2090634); *Ireland*, Gran Vía Carles III 94 (☎3309652); *Netherlands*, Pg. de Gracia 111 (☎2173700); *New Zealand*, Trav. de Grácia 64 (☎2090399); *US*, Passeig de la Reina Elisenda 23 (☎2802227).

Exchange Main banks are mostly located in Plaça de Catalunya and Pg. de Gràcia. Money can also be changed at the airport (daily 7.30am–10.45pm), Estacío de Sants (daily 8am–10pm), *Víajes Marsans*, Ramblas 134 (Mon–Fri 9am–1.30pm & 4–7.30pm), and at *Casas de Cambio* throughout the centre.

Ferries Tickets for Balearic ferries from *Transmediterránea*, at the Estacío Maritima(☎4122524). Book in advance in July and August.

Hospitals *Hospital de la Creu Roja*, c/Dos de Maig 301 (☎2359285); *Hospital Clinic*, c/Casanovas 143 (☎4546000). For emergency doctors dial ☎061; for an ambulance dial ☎3002020.

Left luggage Lockers at Sants station (6.30am–midnight; 200ptas a day) and Estacío Maritima (9am–1pm & 4–10pm).

Police Central stations at c/Ample 23 (☎3183689) and Vía Laietana 43 (☎2903000).

Post office *Correus*, Plaça Antoni Lòpez at the bottom of Vía Laietana (Mon–Sat 8.30am–10pm, Sun 10am–noon); poste restante at Window 17 (Mon–Fri 9am–9pm, Sat 9am–2pm).

Telephones *Telefónica* offices at Sants station (daily 8am–10pm) and c/Fontanella 4, off Plaça de Catalunya (Mon–Sat 8.30am–9pm).

Travel agencies Very useful (and not just for students) is the *TIVE* office at Gran Vía 1, between the Rambla and Plaça de la Universitat. Other general travel firms can be found around the Gran Via, Pg. de Gràcia, Vía Laietana and the Ramblas.

Montserrat

The extraordinary mountain of **Montserrat**, with its weirdly shaped crags of rock, its monastery and its ruined hermitage caves, stands just 40km northwest of Barcelona, off the road to Lleida. This saw-toothed outcrop is one of the most spectacular of all Spain's natural sights, and legends hang easily upon it. Saint Peter is said to have deposited a carving of the Virgin by Saint Luke in one of the mountain caves, fifty years after the birth of Christ; another tale claims this as the spot where Parsifal discovered the Holy Grail. Inevitably it's no longer remote, but the place itself is still magical and you can avoid the crowds by striking out along well-marked paths to deserted hermitages. Another option is to stay the night, since the crowds disperse by early evening.

It is the **Black Virgin** (La Moreneta), the icon supposedly hidden by Saint Peter, which is responsible for the monastery's existence: over 150 churches were dedicated to her in Italy alone, as were the first chapels of Mexico, Chile and Peru – even a Caribbean island bears her name. According to the story it was lost after being hidden during the Moorish invasion and reappeared here in 880: in the first of its miracles, it could not be moved. The chapel built to house it was the predecessor of the present monastic structures, about three-quarters of the way up the mountain.

The **monastery** itself is of no particular architectural interest, except in its monstrous bulk. Only the sixteenth-century **Basilica** is open to the public. La Moreneta, blackened by the smoke of countless candles, stands above the high altar, reached from behind, up a stairway. Near the entrance to the basilica is a **museum** (daily 10.30am–1.30pm & 3–5.30pm; 250ptas) containing paintings by Caravaggio and El Greco. The **walks** around the woods and mountainside of Montserrat are a greater attraction, with tracks to caves and hermitages in every direction. You can also take funicular railways to the hermitages of **Sant Joan** and **Sant Jeronimo**, near the summit of the mountain at 1300m.

Practicalities
The most thrilling approach is by train and cable car, about an hour and a half from Barcelona. The *Ferrocarriles Catalanes* **trains** leave from beneath the Plaça de Espanya at 9.10am, 11.10am, 1.10pm, 3.10pm and 5.10pm, each train connecting at Montserrat Aeri with a cable car (every 15min Mon–Sat 10am–5.45pm, Sun 10am–6.45pm) for an exhilarating ride. Combined return tickets, bought at Plaça d'Espanya, cost 1040ptas. There are also **tour buses** from Barcelona, leaving the Plaça de la Universitat mid-morning and returning late afternoon – enquire at any travel agent.

There's a **campsite** up by the funicular railways and a couple of **hotels**, the cheaper of which is *Colonia Puig* (☎8350268; ③); alternatively there's the *Hostal-Residencia El Monasterio* (☎8350201; ⑤) where it's best to book in advance. The **bar** in the square outside the monastery gates serves sandwiches, and there are a couple of high-priced **restaurants** and gift shops too.

The Catalan Pyrenees

The Catalan Pyrenees, every bit as spectacular as their Aragónese neighbours, have been exploited for far longer. While this has resulted in numerous less-than-aesthetic ski resorts and hydroelectric projects, it also means good public transport to the villages and a well-developed tourism infrastructure. In the less frequented corners, such as the westerly **Parc Nacional**, the scenery is the equal of any in Europe, while even the touristy train ride up to **Núria** to the east rarely fails to impress. The principality of **Andorra**, between these two attractions, has considerably less going for it, though **La Seu d'Urgell**, on the approach from the south, is a bit more worthwhile.

The Parc Nacional and around
After Ordesa, the most popular target of hikers in the Pyrenees is the **Parc Nacional de Sant Maurici and Aigües Tortes**, covering nearly 200 square kilometres of forest, lakes and cirques, presided over by 300-metre snow-capped peaks. For the less adventurous, there are lower-altitude track walks through fine scenery and visits to several villages around the park. Initial access in all cases is by once-daily bus from Pobla de Segur, itself reached by dawn bus from Barcelona, or by morning train from Lleida.

The two main "base" villages are Boí and Espot, west and east of the park boundaries respectively, with Capdella to the south a less busy alternative; all are set in their own gorgeous valleys. **BOÍ** is 21km from Pont de Suert on the main road up to the Viella tunnel, but served by daily bus. Up close, however, the tiny old quarter is dwarfed by modern construction, and tourism facilities are expensive. Exceptions include the nameless *habitaciones* (②) in the old quarter for **staying** and *Casa Higinio* for **eating**. If you draw a blank here, the more handsome neighbouring village of **TAÜLL**, uphill and east, has several possibilities in its *cases de pagès* (rural home-stays; ②) and an attractive **campsite**; although further from the park entrance, Taüll also boasts the Romanesque **church of Sant Climent**, one of several in the area. **ESPOT** lies only 7km off the main road between Pobla and the overrated Vall d'Aran (see below), but there's no bus service, and failing a lift, you'll face a steep two-hour climb. Once there, the place is appealing enough, with *Residencia Felip* (☎973/624093; ②) and *Hotel Roya* (☎973/624040; ③) providing the least expensive **accommodation**. One of the three local **campsites**, *Solau* (☎973/624068) also has a few rooms (②) to let. **Restaurants** are generally expensive, but best of these is *L'Isard*. **CAPDELLA** is served by a single afternoon bus, and boasts two **hostales**, each of which provides meals: *Leo* (☎973/663157; ②) and *Montseny* (☎973/663079; ②).

Within the park itself, camping is forbidden and accommodation is limited to four **mountain refuges** (①), but there are as many more in nearly as impressive alpine areas just outside the park boundaries. Trails or cross-country routes are not surprisingly well marked, and you rarely have to walk more than four hours between the huts.

North of the park, the long, narrow **Vall d'Aran** was once a sort of Pyrenean Shangri-La, where summer hay-reapers picturesquely wielded scythes against a backdrop of stone-built villages with pointy-steepled churches, but the giant Baqueira-Beret ski complex, phalanxes of holiday condos and swarms of French trippers have put paid to that. It's now easily the most expensive corner of Catalunya outside of Barcelona, and only worth passing through on your way to or from Aigës Tortes.

Near the top of the valley, **SALARDÚ** will be your most likely target, the meeting point of two walking routes serving the national park. There are several reasonable places to **stay**, among which the *Albergue Juli Soler Santaló* (☎973/645016; ①) and the *Refugi Rosti* (☎973/654308; ① dorms, ③ rooms) can be singled out. Both have **restaurants**, the *Santaló*'s being particularly good value. **VIELLA**, 9km west and much lower, is the capital of the region and cross point for the two bus routes from Pobla: one (summer only) via Baqueira-Beret and Salardú, the other through the namesake tunnel. It's not a particularly memorable town, but if you're forced by the bus schedules to **overnight**, there are *habitaciones* (②) at Carrer Major no. 5 and 9, and the *Pension Puig* north of the main drag at c/Camí Reiau 6 (☎973/640031; ②).

Andorra and La Seu

As recently as 1960, **ANDORRA** was virtually cut off from the rest of the world, a semi-autonomous principality conceived late in the thirteenth-century to resolve a quarrel between the counts of Foix in France and the bishops of La Seu. There are still no planes or trains, but any quaintness has been banished by Andorra's current role as a drive-in, duty-free supermarket: the main highway through the tiny country is clogged with French and Spanish tourists after the cheap electronic and sports gear, the (not especially) cheap booze in the restaurants and a tankful of discounted petrol. Andorra has no currency of its own, so both francs and pesetas are accepted. The capital, **ANDORRA LA VELLA**, must once have been an attractive town, but it's now a seething mass of cars, touristy restaurants (six-language menus a specialty) and shopfronts. For travellers, Andorra's bazaar ethic makes it a foolproof spot to cheaply replace lost or worn-out trekking or skiing items – otherwise you're best off moving on. Fortunately, not all of Andorra is like this, and with the good local bus service it's easy to escape to the resort-villages of Arsinal, Ordino and El Serrat, all close to trailheads for summer hiking.

Andorra is directly accessible by bus from Barcelona – the coaches continue on to France if you just want a behind-glass view of the place – but the most regular service starts from **LA SEU D'URGELL**, 18km south. Named after its imposing twelfth-century cathedral, La Seu is still fairly sleepy despite having hosted the 1992 Olympic canoeing competitions, which scarcely affected its compact but atmospheric old quarter. The **Cathedral** itself, at the end of c/Major, has been restored over the years but retains some graceful interior decoration and an exceptional cloister with droll column capitals; the **Cloister**, along with the adjacent **Museu Diocesano**, has controlled admission (Mon–Sat 10am–1pm & 4–7pm, Sun 10am–1pm). The **tourist office** (Mon–Sat 10am–2pm & 5–8pm; closed Sun) is on Avenida de Valira, 400m west of the **bus station** on Avenida Joan Garriga Masso, just north of the old quarter. This offers a rather limited number of inexpensive places to **stay**: closest to the terminal are *Fonda Urgel* at c/Capdevila 30 (☎973/351078; ②) and *Ignasi* on the same street at no. 30 (☎973/351036; ②). **Eating** is best at *Cal Pacho*, c/del Font.

Núria and beyond

For a beautiful but easy way to see the Pyrenees, look no further than the *Ferrocarril Cremallera* (**rack-and-pinion railway**) up to the cirque and shrine at NÚRIA. After a leisurely start from Ribes de Freser (see below), the tiny two-carriage train lurches up into the mountains, following a river between great crags. Occasionally it stops, the track only inches away from a terrifying drop, a sheer rock face soaring way above you. Once through a final tunnel, the train emerges alongside a small lake (dry in summer), at the other side of which is the one giant building that constitutes Núria. A severe stone structure, it combines church, tourist office, café, hotel and ski centre all in one; behind it is an official **campsite**.

The **hotel** is expensive (☎972/730326; ⑥), but it maintains a few simple former cells as a kind of hostel. There are also several dorm-style **refuges** around, though they are often full of Spanish groups, in which case you'll have to use the **campsite**. You'll need good equipment, even in summer, since it gets cold at night. As for **food**, you can buy hot snacks or breakfast at the *Bar Finestrelles*; there's a self-service place for midday or evening meals; and the hotel dining room is another modestly priced possibility. The privately-owned Núria train (rail passes not valid) **runs** from July to September on the quarter-hour from 9am to 5pm, plus 9.30pm, from Ribes-Enllaç, or at 23 minutes past the hour from Ribes-Vila, in the centre of Ribes de Freser. If you're coming up from Barcelona on the train, you change at Ribes-Enllaç, where the *Cremallera* platform is just two hops over from the main *RENFE* track.

Mainline trains continue to Puigcerdà, right on the **French frontier**, astride the only surviving rail link over the Pyrenees to France. Four trains a day currently leave for La Tour de Carol, 3km over the border, but if you miss them it's easy enough to walk a slightly shorter distance east to Bourg-Madame, the actual border town. PUIGCERDÀ is a lot cheaper than anywhere in France, should schedules compel an **overnight stay**: try the *Hostal La Muntanya*, c/Coronel Morera 1 (☎972/880202; ②), or *Pension Fonda Lorens*, c/Alfons Primero 1 (☎972/880486; ②). **Restaurant** prices are slightly inflated by the cross-border trade, but good bets include *La Cantonada*, c/Major 48 (beyond the bell tower), or *Bar-Restaurant Kennedy*, c/Espanya 33.

The Costa Brava

The **Costa Brava** (Rugged Coast), stretching from **Blanes** to **Port Bou** and the French border, was once the most beautiful part of the Spanish coast with its wooded coves, high cliffs, pretty beaches and deep blue water. Today, although the natural beauty cannot be entirely disguised, it's an almost total disaster, with a density of concrete tourist developments greater even than the Costa del Sol. The southern part, including the monstrous resort of **Lloret de Mar**, is the worst: further up the main road runs inland and coastal development is relatively low-key. An added attraction here is the ancient Greek site of **Empuries**. In the northernmost stretch, picturesque **Cadaqués** is becoming trendier and more expensive by the year, while nearby **Figueres**, birthplace of Salvador Dalí, is home to his museum – surreal in itself and infectiously funny.

Buses in the region are almost all operated by the *SARFA* company, with an office in every town. Although they are reasonably efficient in the summer months, it can be frustrating either trying to get to some of the smaller coastal villages or simply attempting to stick to the coast. A car or bike solves all your problems; otherwise it's worth considering using Figueres or Girona as a base for lateral trips to the coast – both are big bus termini. There is also an expensive private **boat service** (*Cruceros*) which runs in the summer from Calella (south of Blanes) to Palamos, calling chiefly at Blanes, Lloret, Tossa, Sant Feliu and Platja d'Aro. It's worth taking at least once, since the rugged coastline makes for an extremely beautiful ride.

Tossa de Mar

Leaving Barcelona, there's really nowhere to tempt you to stop before **TOSSA DE MAR**. Out of season it's a really attractive place to spend some time, and even in high summer, arriving at Tossa by boat is one of the Costa Brava's highlights, the medieval walls and turrets pale and shimmering on the hill above the modern town. The walls themselves still surround an **old quarter**, all cobbled streets and flower boxes, offering terrific views over beach and bay, and there are a couple of good beaches. If you're going to stay, pick up a free map and accommodation lists from the **tourist office**, in the same building as the **bus station**, and then head straight down the road in front of you and turn right at the roundabout for "downtown" and beaches. There is cheapish **accommodation** to be had in the maze of tiny streets around the church and below the old city walls – try *Pensión Moré*, c/San Telon 9 (☎972/340339; ②) – and there are also five **campsites** within half an hour's walk of the centre. **Eating and drinking** is not cheap in Tossa – this is package tourist land – but there are some good deals around, as well as endless "Full English Breakfast" bargains.

Palafrugell and Empuries

Tossa is something of an aberration. The coast immediately to the north is thoroughly spoiled, with another immense concentration of cement in the area around La Platja d'Aro. **PALAFRUGELL**, an old town at its liveliest during the morning market, is little to get excited about either, but it has been overlooked by most tourists and hence remains pleasant even if there's little to see. It's also a convenient and relatively cheap place to base yourself if you're aiming for the delightful coastline a few kilometres away: pine-covered slopes and some quiet little coves with scintillatingly turquoise waters. The *Pensión Familiar*, c/Sant Sebastian 29, just off the central square (☎972/300043; ②), is the cheapest **accommodation** in Palafrugell, very clean and attached to an excellent *bar/comedor*. Such is the popularity of the nearby **beaches** that in summer a virtual shuttle service runs from the **bus station** to Calella and then on to Llafranc. You might as well get off at Calella – a beautiful fishing port with tiny, crowded beaches – since Llafranc is only a twenty-minute walk away and you can get a return bus from there. Other, less frequent services run to the even lovelier Tamariu (a 90-min walk from Calella, with a campsite) and to Begur.

From Palafrugell you're within striking distance of **EMPURIES**, one of the most interesting archeological sites in Spain. It started life in 550 BC as Greek *Emporion* (literally "Trading Station") and for three centuries conducted a vigorous trade throughout the Mediterranean. Later a splendid Roman city with an amphitheatre, fine villas and a broad marketplace grew up above the old Greek town. The Romans were replaced in turn by the Visigoths, who built several basilicas and made it the seat of a bishopric. The **site** (daily spring & summer 10am–8pm; autumn & winter 10am–5pm; 400ptas) lies behind a sandy bay about 2km north of L'Escala. The remains of the original Greek colony occupy the lower ground, where remains of temples, the town gate, *agora* and several streets can easily be made out, along with a mass of house foundations (some with mosaics) and the ruins of the Visigoth basilicas. A small **museum** stands above, and beyond it stretches the vast but only partly excavated Roman town.

There are buses to **L'ESCALA** from Palafrugell (2–3 daily) and Figueres (5 daily), arriving and leaving from the *SARFA* company's office just down the road from the combined tourist office/post office at the top of town. L'Escala usually has **rooms** available but it's an expensive and unattractive place, where you're still a fair walk from the ruins and the good beaches. You could instead **camp** out on the beaches and in the woods around the archeological site, where there's little development apart from the one-star *Empuries* (☎972/770207; ③) and a few villas. Alternatively there's a **youth hostel** (☎972/771200; ②), with camping, right on the beach by the ruins; unfortunately it's often full.

Figueres

The northernmost resorts of the Costa Brava are reached via **FIGUERES**, a provincial Catalan town which would pass almost unnoticed were it not for the **Museu Dalí** (July–Sept daily 9am–8pm & 10pm–12.15am; Oct–June Tues–Sun 10.30am–5.15pm; 900ptas) installed by the artist in a building as surreal as the exhibits within. The most visited museum in Spain after the Prado, the Museu Dalí is a treat, appealing to everyone's innate love of fantasy, absurdity and participation. Although it does contain paintings and piles of sculpture, the thematically arranged display is not a collection of Dalí's "greatest hits" – those are scattered far and wide. Nonetheless, the museum defies description and is not to be missed. Dalí was born in Figueres and, on January 23, 1989, died there; his embalmed body now lies in a glass case inside the museum.

Figueres itself remains a pleasing town with a lively Rambla and plenty of cheap food and accommodation. After the museum, the main sight is the huge seventeenth-century **castle** to the northeast of town, now occupied by the military; its five-kilometre circuit of walls makes a good walk.

To make your way into the middle of town, simply follow the "Museu Dalí" signs from the **train station**. The cheapest **rooms** are at the comfortable *Pensión Bartis*, c/ Méndez Núñez 2 (☎972/501473; ①). There's a good all-year **youth hostel** (☎972/501213; ②) at c/Anicet Pages 2, off the Plaça del Sol; the town **campsite** is on the way to the castle. There's a gaggle of cheap tourist **restaurants** in the narrow streets around the Dalí museum and, although a little more expensive, some nice pavement cafés lining the Rambla. The **tourist office** (Mon–Fri 9am–7/9pm, Sat 9am–2pm) is in front of the post office building by the Plaça del Sol, and dishes out timetables for all onward transport.

Cadaqués and Port Bou

With whitewashed houses lining the narrow, hilly streets, and craggy bays on either side of the village, **CADAQUÉS** is a picturesque place. Sitting on the seafront, you can watch the fishermen take their live catches from the boats straight to the restaurant kitchens. The one minus to the place is the tiny, pebbly beaches. In the 1960s Salvador Dalí built a house on the outskirts of town and for some years Cadaqués became a distinctly hip place to be: over the last few years it has been "discovered" and has now become too trendy for its own good – and too expensive. Still, it's a lot less snobby than the south of France and can be fun for a while. Finding **rooms** is likely to be a big problem unless you're here outside peak season; check the town plan posted at the bus stop, which marks all the possibilities. The **campsite** – on the road to Port Lligat, a steep 1km out of town – is expensive and noisy. The **tourist office** (Mon–Sat 10am–1.30pm & 4/5–7/9pm, Sun 10am–noon) is close to the main beach and square on c/ des Cotxe.

PORT BOU, the last resort before the border, is also beautiful: green hills, deep blue water and a small coarse sand beach. The railway across the border made the place, but surprisingly few people stop here, and away from the station it remains tranquil and low-key. There are also some excellent outdoor **restaurants** lining the quay, none of them outrageously expensive, and a handful of modest **hostales** along the main street and on the seafront (mostly ②). The **tourist office** at the harbour should be able to help if you have difficulty.

Girona

The ancient walled town of **GIRONA** stands on a fortress-like hill, high above the unusually active Riu Onyar. It's a fine place, full of interest and oddly devoid of tourists considering that the town's airport serves most of the Costa Brava's resorts. As with so many Spanish towns, much of the pleasure of being in Girona is simply wandering around. The streets are narrow and medieval, the churches are cool and fascinating, while above the river high rows of houses lean precipitously on the banks.

Centrepoint of the old town is the **Cathedral** (daily 10am–6pm), a mighty Gothic building approached by a magnificent seventeenth-century flight of Baroque steps. Inside it is equally awesome, just one tremendous single-naved vault with a span of 22m, the largest in the world. This emphasis on width and height is a feature of Catalan Gothic with its "hall churches", of which, unsurprisingly, Girona's is the perfect example. Buy a ticket to visit the superb cloisters, the sacristy and the **Museu Capitular** (Tues–Sat 10am–2pm & 4–7pm, Sun 10am–2pm; 300ptas), with an excellent small collection of religious art. If you find the collection interesting, the **Museu d'Art** (Tues–Sun 10am–6/7pm, Sun 10am–2pm; 100ptas) contains further examples; it's housed alongside in the Episcopal Palace.

The well-preserved **Banys Arabs** (same hours and price), built by Moorish craftsmen in the thirteenth century, long after the Moors' occupation of Girona had ended, are also well worth a look, as is the surviving portion of the **Jewish quarter**, *El Call*. This was centred on c/de la Força, off which a steep alley leads up to the **Centre Bonastruc Ça Porta** (June–Oct Mon–Sat 10am–6pm, Sun 10am–2pm; Nov–May Tues–Sun 10am–2pm; free), a little complex of rooms, staircases and adjoining buildings restored in an attempt to give expression to the cultural and social life of Catalunya's Jews in medieval times.

Practicalities

If you're using **Girona airport**, 13km from the city centre, bear in mind that there's no bus service from the town and a taxi will end up being pretty expensive; most charters coming from England are linked directly by bus with the Costa Brava. The large **bus station** (behind the **train station**) is well connected with most of Catalunya. From here it's a ten-minute walk up to the river and the Pont de Pedra, just over which on the left is the **tourist office**, at Rambla de Llibertat 1 (Mon–Fri 8am–8pm, Sat 8am–2pm & 4–8pm). There's a second information office at the train station (Mon–Sat 9am–2pm).

There's plenty of cheap **accommodation** in Girona, with all the best places to stay found in the old town. The *Hostal Reyma*, c/Rey Don Martín 15, near the cathedral (☎972/200228; ②), is excellent and good value; the *Bellmirall* is also near the cathedral, at c/Bellmirall 3 (☎972/204009; ③). For cheaper rooms, the *Fonda Barnet*, c/Santa Clara 16 (☎972/200003; ②), just to the left before you cross the Pont de Pedra, is not up to the same standard but has some rooms overlooking the river. There's a new **youth hostel**, very central at c/dels Ciutadans 9, off Plaça del Vi (☎972/218003; ②).

There are several good, reasonably priced **restaurants** on c/de la Força, near the cathedral, best value being the *Bar-Restaurant Los Jara* at no. 4. *L'Arcada*, underneath the arches at Rambla de Llibertat 38, is a nice bar-restaurant with a pleasant old-time interior and good breakfast fixings. There are also some good *menús* to be had at the terraces on Plaza Independencia.

The Costa Daurada

The **Costa Daurada** – the coastline from Barcelona to south of Tarragona – is far less exploited than the Costa Brava. Sadly, it is easy enough to see why it has been neglected by the developers. With one or two exceptions – notably **Sitges** and **Tarragona** – it's a rather dull, drab expanse. Beaches can be long but they're often narrow and character-less, while the few towns are overwhelmed by pockets of villas. However, if you just want to relax by a beach for a while there are perfectly functional possibilities. Most village-resorts have small hotels and *hostales* and there are plentiful campsites dotted along the shore – albeit mostly huge and full to the brim with caravans and families.

Sitges

SITGES, 40km from Barcelona, is definitely the highlight as far as the beach towns go. It's the great weekend escape for young Barcelonans, who have created a resort very much in their own image, and is also now a major **gay** summer resort. Sitges is expensive – particularly the bars – and finding accommodation can be difficult. If you're offered a room by someone as you get off the train, take it.

There's a loose, vibrant feel to the place, with a lot of action, a sophisticated night scene, and crowded but unoppressive **beaches**. There are two beaches right in town, divided by a promontory and scattered with a series of *balnearios* (bathing stations), although recent reports suggest that the seawater here has become a bit dubious. You can walk a couple of kilometres south, towards Vilanova, where you'll come to the **Playas del Muerto**. These are both nude and the second, reached by following the railway line, is exclusively gay.

Trains to Sitges leave Barcelona's Estació de Sants roughly half-hourly throughout the day; the station in Sitges is about ten minutes' walk from the town centre. The **tourist office** (summer daily 9am–9pm; winter Mon–Fri 9.30am–2pm & 4am–6.30pm, Sat 10am–1pm) is a right turn out of the station and a short walk downhill to the *Oasis* shopping mall – you can pick up free maps and accommodation lists. **Rooms** can be scarce but the old town streets back from the sea have dozens of possibilities and should yield something. *Residencia Parellades*, c/Parellades 11 (☎93/8940801; ③), and *Hostal Mariangel* at no. 78 (☎93/8941357; ②) are both cheap and reliable; *Hostal Julian* (☎93/8940306; ②), further down from the station, isn't brilliantly located but is worth trying as it often has room. There's the *El Róca* **campsite** too, five minutes' walk behind the station (☎93/8940043).

There are many reasonable **restaurants**, above all in the side streets around the church and back from the sea: try especially c/Sant Pau and c/Sant Pere for good *menús del día*. The main street for all the **bar** action is c/1er de Maig (and its continuation, c/Marqués de Montroig), running back from the sea, crammed with places trying to blast each other out. You'll find more genteel bars, some serving excellent seafood, along the seafront promenade.The **gay scene**, mainly along c/Sant Bonaventura, is frenetic. The owners of the stylish *Parrots Pub*, at the top of c/1er de Maig in Plaça Industria, can give free advice about gay hotels, apartments and restaurants.

Tarragona

Majestically sited on a rocky bluff rising sheer above the sea, **TARRAGONA** was the most elegant city of Roman Spain. At its peak, it boasted a quarter of a million inhabitants, and was the base for Scipio's conquest of the peninsula. Later, the emperors Hadrian and Augustus both adopted it as a resort, the latter building himself a number of temples around the city. This distinguished past asserts itself throughout the modern city. Today Tarragona is the second largest port in Catalunya and its ugly outskirts are home to a huge concentration of chemical industries, oil refineries and a nuclear power plant.

The city divides clearly into two parts: a predominantly medieval, walled upper town, and a prosperous modern extension below. Walking into town from the **train station** sets you at the very top of the sweeping **Rambla Nova**, lined with fashionable cafés and restaurants (the **bus station** is at the end, at Plaça Imperial Tarraco). Parallel, and to the east, lies the **Rambla Vella**, marking the start of the old town. On either side of the *ramblas* are scattered a profusion of relics from Tarragona's Roman past, including various temples, and parts of the forum, theatre and amphitheatre.

The most interesting remains are of the ancient **Necropolis** (Tues–Sat 10am–1.30pm & 4/4.30–7/8pm, Sun 10am–2pm; 100ptas), at the end of c/Ramón i Cajal, signposted off the Rambla Nova. Here both pagan and Christian tombs have been uncovered, spanning a period from the third to the sixth centuries AD and including rare examples of Visigothic sculpture. The Roman forum has survived too. Or rather forums, since Tarragona sustained both a provincial forum (by the cathedral) and a **local forum** (Tues–Sat 10am–5.30/8pm, Sun 10am–3pm; free), whose remains (signposted) are very near the market hall and square.

At the corner of the upper town, on the Plaça de Rei near the cathedral, is an excellent **Museu Arqueológic**, open the same hours as the necropolis (100ptas). Right next door, the **Museu d'Història** or Pretori Romà (Tues–Sat 10am–6.30/8pm, Sun 10am–2pm) occupies the former residence of the Aragónese kings, built over Roman vaults and blessed with unusually good interpretive displays. The 400ptas ticket is also valid for the other Roman remains mentioned and for the **Passeig Arqueològic** (Tues–Sat 10am–5.30pm/8pm/midnight, Sun 10am–3pm), a promenade running between Roman walls of the third century BC and outer fortifications erected by the British in 1707. The focal point of the old town, however, is the **Cathedral** (daily except Sun summer 10am–12.30pm & 4–7pm; winter 10am–2pm; 300ptas), which you enter through the cloisters. This magnificent building is the most perfect example in Spain of the transition from Romanesque to Gothic forms.

Practicalities

The main **tourist office** is at Rambla Nova 46 (Mon–Sat 9.30am–8.30pm) and has a town map and accommodation lists. The best **rooms** in town, or at least the nicest location, are in the Plaça de la Font, just in the old town off the Rambla Vella. The *Pensión Marsal*, no. 26 (☎977/224069; ②), above the *Restaurante Turia*, is a good choice here. Otherwise, there are a couple of places close to the train station in the new part of town: the *Abella* at c/Apodaca 26 (☎977/234224; ②), and the *Mar i Flor* at c/Gral Contreras 29 (☎977/238231; ②). The **youth hostel** (☎977/210195; reception open 7am–8pm; ②) is at c/Marqués Guad-El-Jelu, off Avda President Companys (at the end of Rambla Nova) and is closed during September. If these offer no hope wander down towards the town beach, Platja Miraclo, below Rambla Vella, and take Vía Augusta for about 2km to Platja Rabassada; here there are three **campsites** and a number of small hotels. For somewhere to **eat**, stick to Plaça de la Font where there's a good outdoor pizzeria, the *Mistral*, or the filling, cheap *menú del día* at *Restaurante Turia*. For cakes and ice cream, Rambla Nova is bursting with pavement **cafés** all doing a roaring trade.

Lleida

LLEIDA (Lérida), at the heart of a fertile plain near the Aragónese border, lies on almost any route west from Barcelona, and it's an enjoyable place to break your journey. The city has a rich history: first a *municipium* under the Roman Empire and later the capital of a small Arab kingdom, it was reconquered by the Catalans and became the seat of a bishopric in 1149. There's little of those periods extant in today's city, although there is one building of outstanding interest.

The **old cathedral** (Tues–Sat 9.30am–1.30pm & 3–5.30/6.30pm, Sun 9.30am–1.30pm; 150ptas) lies enclosed within ruined castle walls high above the Riu Segre, a twenty-minute climb from the centre of town. It's a peculiar fortified building, which in 1707 was deconsecrated and taken over by the military. Enormous damage was inflicted over the years (documented by photos in a side chapel) but the church remains a notable example of the Transitional style, similar in many ways to the cathedral of Tarragona. Once again the Gothic cloisters are masterful, and the views from the walls are stupendous. You can climb back down towards the river by way of the **new cathedral**, a grimy eighteenth-century building enlivened only by a series of high, matchbox-sized stained-glass windows.

If you're staying, there's a cluster of **hostales and habitaciones** on the right as you leave the train station, down c/Anselmo Clavé. Continuing straight ahead, the pedestrian streets of Carrer de Carme or Magdalena blend into Carrer Major; when the name changes you have covered about half the distance between the train station and the bus station on Avda de Blondel. You can also walk from the train station along the wide Rambla Ferrán, where there are more places to stay. Taking this route you'll pass the Puerta Antigua (Old Gate) opposite the main bridge over the river. There's a **tourist office** (June–Sept Mon–Sat 9am–8pm, Sun 9am–2pm; Oct–May Mon–Fri 9am–7pm, Sat 9am–2pm) just inside the gate, while to the right is the **Plaça Sant Joan** with a few more places to stay, best being the *Residencia Mundial* at no. 4 (☎973/242700; ②). The **campsite** (April–Oct) is a couple of kilometres out of town on the Huesca road. For **eating and drinking**, c/de Cavallers – off c/Major, leading up to the castle – has several bars, all serving *tapas* and food, and you'll also find cheap restaurants in the streets leading uphill from Plaça Sant Joan.

VALENCIA AND THE EAST COAST

The area known as the **Levante** (the East) is a bizarre mixture of ancient and modern, of beauty and beastliness. The rich *huerta* of **Valencia** is said to be the most fertile slab of land in Europe, crowded with orange, lemon and peach groves, and with rice fields still irrigated by systems devised by the Moors. Yet **Murcia**, to the south, could hardly provide a more severe contrast, with some of the driest land in Europe, some of it virtually a desert. Despite a few fine beaches, much of the region's **coast** – with the exception of the coastline from Jávea to Altea – is marred by the highway to the south, the industrial development which has sprouted all around it, and of course the heavy over-development of villas and vacation homes.

Valencia

VALENCIA, the third largest city in Spain, may not approach the vitality of Barcelona or the cultural variety of Madrid, but it does at least have a lively night scene, and its clothes and furniture designers are renowned throughout Spain – a Valencian studio designed the logo for the Barcelona Olympics. It has always been an important city, fought over for the agricultural wealth of its surrounding countryside. After the Romans and Visigoths, it was occupied by the Moors for over four centuries with only a brief interruption when El Cid recaptured it. He died here in 1099 but his body, propped on a horse and led out through the gates, was still enough to cause the Moorish armies – previously encouraged by news of the death – to flee in terror. It wasn't until 1238 that James I of Aragón permanently wrested Valencia back. It has remained one of Spain's largest and richest cities ever since.

Nobody could claim that this is one of Spain's most attractive townscapes. There are some exquisite corners away from the crowds, a few really fine buildings and a couple of excellent museums, but as a whole the city is sprawling and confused, marred by unthinking modernization. Probably the most attractive features are the relaxed pavement café scene around the Plaza San Jaime and the colourful markets – Central Market, Mercado Colon and Ruzafa Market. The most interesting area for wandering around is undoubtedly the mazelike **Barrio del Carmen**, the oldest part of town, roughly between c/de Caballeros and the Río Turia around the Puerta de Serranos.

The area telephone code for Valencia is ☎96.

Arrival and information
Valencia's **train station** is reasonably central: Avenida Marqués de Sotelo leads from opposite the entrance towards the main Plaza del Ayuntamiento, beyond which lie the old parts of the city. The **bus station** is further out, at Avenida Menéndez Pidal 13, on the far bank of the dried-up river from the centre. From here it's easier to take a local bus (#28) into the centre; allow fifteen minutes if you decide to walk. The **Balearic ferry terminal** is connected to a terminus by the Ayuntamiento by the #19 bus.

The **Plaza del Ayuntamiento** is home to the **post office** as well as the municipal **tourist office** (Mon–Fri 9am–1.30pm & 4.30–7pm, Sat 9.30am–1.30pm). There's another tourist office in c/de la Paz (Mon–Fri 9am–2pm & 5–7pm, Sat 9am–1pm), and an information point inside the **train station**.

Accommodation
Most of the cheaper **places to stay** are very near the train station, in c/Bailén and c/Pelayo, which run parallel to the tracks off c/Játiva. This area, however, is pretty sleazy; you may feel more comfortable spending more in the centre, or much further out near the beach. Just about the cheapest recommendable **hotel** is the *Hostal Gran Glorieta*, c/Conde Montornes 22, just off Plaza Tetuán (☎3527885; ②), a friendly, popular place away from the noise of the station. Slightly more pricy are the basic *Hostal Residencial Don Pelayo*, c/Pelayo 7 (☎3521135; ②), the *Hostal Residencial San Vicente*, c/San Vicente 57 (☎3527061; ②), the excellently sited and very popular *El Rincón*, c/Carda 11, near Plaza del Mercado (☎3316083; ②), or the cheap *Hospedería de l Pilar*, Plaza del Mercada 19 (☎3916600; ②). More upmarket, the *Hotel Alcázar*, c/Mosén Femades 11 (☎3529575; ⑤), is a dependable and well cared for town centre establishment, near the post office, while the *Hotel La Pepica*, Avda Neptuno 2, near the beach (☎3714111; ③), offers good-value rooms with bath, and an excellent restaurant. The **youth hostel** at Avenida del Puerto 69 (July & Aug; ☎3590152; ②) is inexpensive but not too attractive, with a midnight curfew; it's halfway to the port, on the route of bus #19 from Plaza del Ayuntamiento. The most convenient **campsite** is the all-year *El Salér*, on a good beach, 10km south of the city; a regular bus goes there from the Puerta del Mar at the end of Glorieta Park. The same bus goes to the *El Palmar* site (June–Sept), 16km out, by La Albufera.

The City
The distinctive feature of Valencian architecture is its wealth of elaborate Baroque facades – you'll see them on almost every old building in town, but none so extraordinary or rich as the **Palacio del Marqués de Dos Aguas**, a short walk north of the train station. Hipólito Rovira, who designed its amazing alabaster doorway, died insane in 1740, which should come as no surprise to anyone who's seen it. Inside is the **Museo Nacional de Cerámica** (closed for restoration) with a vast collection of ceramics from all over Spain. In the same decorative vein is the church of **San Juan de la Cruz** next door. Nearby, in the Plaza Patriarca, is the Neoclassical former

university – with its beautiful cloisters and a series of classical concerts in July – and the beautiful Renaissance **Colegio del Patriarca**, whose small **art museum** (daily 11am–1pm) includes excellent works by El Greco, Morales and Ribalta.

It's not far from here, up c/de la Paz, to the **Plaza Zaragoza** and Valencia's **Cathedral**. The plaza is dominated by two octagonal towers, the florid spire of the church of Santa Catalina and the **Miguelete**, the unfinished tower of the cathedral itself. You can make the long climb up to the roof (75ptas) for a fantastic view over the city with its many blue-domed churches – a view that reaffirms the impression of haphazard development. The church's attractive and unusual feature is the lantern above the crossing, its windows glazed with sheets of alabaster. Among the exhibits in the **museum** (Mon–Sat 1–2pm & 4–6pm) is a gold and agate cup (the Santo Cáliz) said to be the one used by Christ at the Last Supper – the Holy Grail itself; it's certainly old and, while hidden away during the Dark Ages in a northern Aragón monastery, it really did inspire many of the legends associated with the Grail. Also here are two Goyas and a 2300kg gold tabernacle which is carried through the city at Corpus Christi.

A side exit leads from the cathedral to the **Plaza de la Virgen**, where you'll find the Archbishop's Palace and the tiny chapel of **Nuestra Señora de los Desamparados**. Here, thousands of candles constantly burn in front of the image of the Virgin, patron of Valencia. A secular and stylistic contrast is offered by the elegant Gothic **Lonja de la Seda** or Silk Exchange (Tues–Fri 10am–2pm & 4–6pm, Sat & Sun 10am–1pm), which still operates as a commercial exchange and exhibition centre, and by the enormous **Mercado Central**, opposite, a modernist iron and glass structure. This is one of the biggest markets in Europe, replete with amazing local fruit, fish and vegetables; it closes around 2pm every day. Other museums worth visiting include **IVAM**, the modern art museum on c/Guillem de Castro 118 (Tues–Sun 11am–8pm, 500ptas, Sun free), and the **Museo de Bellas Artes** on c/San Pío V (Tues–Sun 10am–2pm, Tues–Sat 4–6pm; free).

Also worth a look are the town's defences, including the fourteenth-century **Torres de Serranos**, an impressive gateway defending the entrance to the town across the Río Turia. The river itself, diverted after serious flooding in 1956 which damaged much of the old part of the city, is no more than a trickle now, and a huge park has been landscaped in the riverbed; the park has been grassed and planted, and includes a sports stadium, football pitches and even a huge Gulliver to climb on. Near here stands the **Palau de la Música**, a futuristic glass structure venue for concerts.

Eating, drinking and nightlife

Food in the **restaurants** in Valencia can be poor, especially considering that this is the home of *paella*. Decent mid-range possibilities include *Bar Ancoa*, Plaza San Lorenzo at c/Novellos, for cheap *platos*; *Bar Almuoín* on the street of the same name behind the cathedral, for good seafood *raciones*; and two restaurants, *La Utielana*, Plaza Picadero de los Aguas, with good roast lamb and *cocido*, even though you may have to wait for a table, and *Bar Odín*, Avenida Antic Regne de Valencia, for good *tapas* and pizzas. For bistros and cheap restaurants the best general area is the Barrio del Carmen – c/ Roteros in particular. A traditional place to go for *mejillones* (mussels) is the *Bar Pilar* on the corner of c/Moro Zeit, just off Plaza del Espart. A good vegetarian option is *La Lluna*, San Ramón 23, and for carnivores, *Barbacoa*, Plaza del Carmen, is good value. For paella, go to either Malvarossa's *La Pepica* on Paseo Neptuno, or go out of town on the El Saler bus down the south coast road to the villages of El Palmar or El Perellonet.

If you don't know where to go, Valencia can seem dead at night: the action is widely dispersed, with many locations across the Turia. To get back late at night you'll have to walk or taxi. In summer everyone is in the **bars** lining the polluted Malvarrosa Beach, like the *Genaro* and *Tropical*, large bar-discos on c/Eugenio Vines (the beach road). To get there, take bus #1, #2 or #19 – the last from Plaza del Ayuntamiento, the others from the bus station. Back in town, the youngest and loudest bars are on c/Bailén and c/Pelayo, towards the bottom end. The best of the nightlife, though, is around the Barrio del Carmen (Caballeros and c/Quart), and behind the Gran Vía de Fernando el Católico (along c/Juan Llorens and c/Calixto). In the latter area, the *Café Carioca* and *Café La Habana*, at c/Juan Llorens 52 and 41 are currently in favour, as are *La Torna* at c/Carmen 12 and *Bésame Mucho* in Ciudad Jardín at c/Explorador Andrés 6, which features live music. The new university area, around Avenida Blasco Ibáñez, is also popular: try *Público* (no. 111), the *Metro* (no. 97), *Hipódromo* and *El Asesino*, or the bars on Plaza Xuquer, just off Blasco Ibáñez. Another fashionable zone is the Plaza Cánovas Castillo and the side streets off it, full of *pubs* (music bars) where people go to see and be seen. Most **gay bars** like *Dakota* or *Balkiss* are around or in the c/Quart.

Many of the **discos** are in the university area – they include *Woody* at Menéndez y Pelayo 3 and *Público*, Blasco Ibañez 111. In the centre, there's *La Marxa* and *Calcata* off c/Caballeros, *Unsur*, c/Maestro Gozalbo, and *Jerusalem*, c/Jerusalem, off Plaza España. For more details about **what's on**, buy the weekly listings guide, *Qué y Dónde*.

Listings

Airlines *Iberia* and *Aviaco*, c/de la Paz 14 (☎3520500); *British Airways*, Plaza Rodrigo Botet 6 (☎3512284).

Airport Manises, 12km away; bus #15 (hourly); enquiries ☎3709500.

Balearic ferries Information and tickets from *Transmediterránea*, Avda Manuel Soto 19, or from any of the half-dozen travel agents on Plaza del Ayuntamiento.

Car rental Cheapest is probably *Cuñat Car Hire*, c/Burriana 51 (☎3748561). Otherwise, there's *Avis* at c/Isabel la Católica 17 (☎3510734), *Hertz* at c/Segorbe 7 (☎3415036), and *Atesa* at Avda del Cid 64 (☎3799108).

Consulates *Netherlands*, *Belgium* and *Luxembourg*, c/G.V. Germanias 18 (☎3414633); *USA*, c/ Ribera 3 (☎3516973).

Exchange Main branches of most banks are around the Pl. del Ayuntamiento or along c/Játiva. Outside banking hours, two branches of the *Caja de Ahorros* are open Mon–Sat 9am–8pm: one at c/ Játiva 14, to the left as you come out of the train station, and the other in the *Nuevo Centro*, near the bus station. The División Internacional in the *Banco de Valencia*, c/Colon 20, currently charges the lowest commission.

Hospitals Provincial hospital on Avda Cid, at the Tres Cruces junction (☎3791600).

Left luggage Self-store lockers at *RENFE*; 24-hr access, 150ptas a day.

Police Headquarters at Gran Vía Ramón y Cajal 40 (☎3510862).

Post office Main *Correos* at Plaza del Ayuntamiento 1 (Mon–Sat 9am–9pm & Sun am).

Telephones Plaza del Ayuntamiento 27 (Mon–Sat 9am–1pm & 5–9pm).

The Costa Blanca

South of Valencia stretches the **Costa Blanca**, a long strip of country with, between Gandía and Benidorm, some of the best beaches on this coast. Much of it, though, suffers from the worst excesses of package tourism and in the summer it's hard to get a room anywhere – in August virtually impossible. Campers have it somewhat easier – there are hundreds of campsites – but driving can be a nightmare unless you stick to the dull highway. Gandía is the first of the big resorts, and one of the best bets for a room, since the quiet and provincial old town lies a few kilometres inland. Oliva, 8km south, is a much lower-key development. Again the village is set back from the coast and although the main road charges through its centre, it's relatively unspoiled and there's a number of *hostales* and *fondas*.

DENIA is a far bigger place, a sizable town even without its summer visitors, and less appealing. You might though be tempted to take the daily **boat to Palma**, Mallorca. A rattling narrow-gauge railway (*FEVE*) runs down the coast from here to

Alicante, with hourly services throughout the day. Beneath the wooded capes beyond, bypassed by the main road, stretch probably the most beautiful beaches on this coastline, centred on Javea – but you'll need a car to get to any of them, and even if you have a vehicle there's barely a cheap room to be found. If you want to stay, try first the *Hostal Residencial Llacer*, Barrio de la Xara (☎96/5785104; ②), which is cheapest in the area.

Back on the main road again, **ALTEA** is set on a small hill overlooking this whole stretch of coastline. Restrained tourist development is centred on the seafront, and being so close to Benidorm it does receive some overspill. In character, however, it's a world apart. The old village up the hill is picturesquely attractive with its white houses, blue-domed church and profuse blossoms.

Beyond Altea there's nothing between you and the crowded beaches at **BENIDORM**. If you want hordes of British and Scandinavian sunseekers, scores of "English" pubs, at least seventy discos and bacon and eggs for breakfast, this is the place to come. The beach – nearly 6km of it, regularly topped up with imported Moroccan sand – is undeniably impressive, when you can see it through the roasting flesh. Surprisingly, except in August, you can usually find a room in Benidorm, though it takes a lot of walking. The cheaper places are all near the centre and away from the sea, but out of season many of the giant hotels and apartment blocks slash their prices drastically. Check with the **tourist office**, at the bottom of c/Martínez Alejos, near the old village (☎96/5853224).

Alicante

Locals describe **ALICANTE** as *la millor terra del mond* and while that's a gross exaggeration it is at least a living city, thoroughly Spanish, and a relief after some of the places you may have been passing through. There are good beaches nearby, too, a lively nightlife in season and plenty of cheap places to stay and to eat. Wide esplanades such as the Rambla de Méndez Núñez and Avenida Alfonso Sabio give the town an elegant air, and around the Plaza de Luceros and along the seafront *paseo* you can relax in style at terrace cafés – paying a bit extra for the palm tree setting, of course. The most interesting area is around the Ayuntamiento, where, among the bustle of small-scale commerce, you'll see plenty of evidence of Alicante's large Algerian community – the links with Algeria have always been strong, and boats depart from here for Oran twice a week.

The rambling **Castillo de Santa Bárbara** on the bare rock behind the town beach, is Alicante's only real "sight" – with a tremendous view from the top. It's best approached from the seaward side where a lift shaft has been cut straight up through the hill to get you to the top; the lift is directly opposite Meeting Point 5 on the other side of the road from Playa Postiguet. For the best local **beaches** head for San Juan de Alicante, 6km out, reached either by half-hourly bus from the Plaza del Mar or the *FEVE* railway. Still better, take a trip to the **island of Cantera (Tabarca)** to the south – boats leave from Explanada de España daily in summer, weather permitting.

Practicalities

The main **train station** is on Avda Salamanca, but trains on the private *FEVE* line to Benidorm and Denia leave from the small station at the far end of the Playa del Postiguet. The **bus station** for local and international services is in c/Portugal. There are daily **summer boat services** to Ibiza; tickets and information for these and the Denia or Valencia services from any travel agent in the harbour area. The **airport**, 12km west, is connected to the bus station by a regular service. The very helpful **tourist office** is on Explanada de España (summer daily 10am–9pm; winter daily except Sun 10am–7pm). There are also information desks at the bus station (closed weekends) and at the airport.

Except in August you should have little problem finding a **room**, with the bulk of the possibilities concentrated at the lower end of the old town, above the Explanada de España and around the Plaza Gabriel – especially on c/San Fernando, c/San Francisco, c/Jorge Juan and c/Castaño. Places to try include the *Olimpia*, c/San Francisco 60 (☎96/5214037; ②), the *Bosch* at c/San Francisco 12 (☎96/5206300; ②), and marginally pricier *Larensana* (☎96/5207820; ②) and *París* (☎96/5207378; ②) at c/San Fernando 10 and 56. There's a **youth hostel** on Avda Orihuela 59 (☎96/5281211; ②) and several **campsites**; two in the Albufereta to the north, and one at La Marina, south of town in woods on a good beach.

Cheap **restaurants** are clustered around the *Ayuntamiento*, including a couple of places where you can eat couscous on c/Miquel Saler. Over on the other side of town c/San Francisco, leading off a square near the bottom end of the Rambla, has a group of cheap restaurants with seats outside. For *tapas* try the *Taberna Castellana* on c/Loaces, on the other side of Avda Dr Gadea. For **bars** and the best **nightlife**, head into the Barrio Santa Cruz, whose narrow streets lie roughly between the cathedral, Plaza Carmen and Plaza San Cristóbal. At night *El Barrio*, as it's called, is avoided by many of the locals, but it's really not too rough, and there are so many bars here that you can easily steer clear of the questionable places. For **dancing**, try *Histeria*, c/de Colón, or *Bugati*, c/San Fernando.

THE BALEARIC ISLANDS

The four chief **Balearic islands** – Ibiza, Formentera, Mallorca and Menorca – maintain a character distinct from the mainland and from each other. **Ibiza**, firmly established among Europe's trendiest resorts, has an intense, outrageous street life and a floating summer population that seems to include every club-going Spaniard from Sevilla to Barcelona. It can be fun, if this sounds your idea of island activity, and above all if you're gay – Ibiza is a very tolerant place. **Formentera**, small and a little desolate, is something of a beach-annexe to Ibiza, though it struggles to present its own alternative image of reclusive artists and "in the know" tourists. **Mallorca**, the largest and best-known Balearic, also battles with its image, popularly reckoned as little more than sun, booze and beach parties. In reality you'll find all the clichés, most of them crammed into the mega-resorts of the Bay of Palma, but there's certainly much else besides: mountains, lively fishing ports, some beautiful coves and the Balearics' one real city, **Palma**. Mallorca is in fact the one island in the group you might come to other than for beaches and nightlife, with scope to explore, walk and travel about. And last, to the east, there is windswept **Menorca** – more conservative in its development, more modest in its clientele and, after the others, a little dull.

Ferries from mainland Spain (and Marseilles) are severely overpriced considering the distances involved; likewise, monopolies keep rates high for inter-island ferries, and for journeys like Ibiza–Mallorca or even Mallorca–Menorca it can be cheaper to fly. The catch here is that in mid-season flights are often booked out: the solution is to get up before dawn, head for the airport and get yourself on a waiting list for the first flight.

Expense and overdemand can be crippling in other areas too. As "holiday islands", each with a buoyant international tourist trade, the Balearics charge considerably above mainland prices for **rooms** – which from mid-June to mid-September are in very short supply. If you go at these times, and you're not into camping, it's sensible to try to fix up some kind of reservation in advance. Something you may want to do, and which will alleviate accommodation problems to some extent, is to hire transport: **cars** (also in short supply in season) can be driven off and slept in, and **mopeds** will get you and a sleeping bag to some tempting and acceptable spots.

Ibiza

IBIZA (Eivissa) is an island of excess. Beautiful and indented with scores of barely accessible cove beaches, it's nevertheless the islanders and their visitors who make it special. However outrageous you may want to be (and outrageousness is the norm), the locals have seen it all before. By day thousands of Nivea-smeared tourists spread themselves across the nudist beaches, preparing for the nightly flounce through bars and clubs. For years it was *the* European hippie escape, but nowadays is as popular with modern youth and sociable gays as with its 1960s denizens (who keep coming back).

Ibiza Town

In physical, as well as atmospheric terms, **IBIZA TOWN** is the most attractive place on the island. Most people stay in rented apartments or small *pensiones* which means fewer hotels to ruin the skyline and no package incursions. Approach by sea and you'll get the full frontal effect of the old town's walls rising like a natural extension of the rocky cliffs which protect the port. Within the walls, the ancient quarter is topped by a sturdy **cathedral**, whose illuminated clock shines out across the harbour throughout the night.

The capital is a simple enough place to find your way around. From the **ferry terminal**, the old streets of the **Sa Peña** quarter lead straight ahead towards the walls of the ancient city – **D'Alt Vila**. A waterside walk will take you from here – past bars and restaurants which at night give front-row viewing for the fashion display – round to the harbour wall from where the entire bay can be surveyed. Continue past the port and you'll be in the new town, below the old to the west. If you fly in you'll arrive at the **airport** about 6km out; there's a regular bus from here, or you can take a taxi for around 1200ptas. In the airport there's an efficient **tourist office** (daily 8am–midnight) which can provide maps and lists of accommodation as well as details on vehicle hire.

The principal **tourist office**, at Vara de Rey 13, can offer more extensive lists of **hotels and hostales** for the whole island, as well as details of apartments for stays of a week or more – not cheap, but abundant and usually pleasant. Most of the cheaper hotels are in the area around the tourist office. Even if you stay a kilometre or so east of town in Talamanca, or on the other side of the port in Figueretas, you're not that far removed from the action. A couple of starter possibilities are *Hostal Sol y Brisa*, Avenida Bartolomeu Vicente Ramón 15 (☎971/310818; ③), near the port in the street parallel to Vara de Rey, which has many others; *Hostal Las Nieves*, c/Juan de Austria 18 (☎971/315822; ③), in the street below Vicente Ramón; and *Hostal Estrella del Mar*, c/ Philip II (☎971/312212; ③), with a choice of rooms from basic to relative luxury.

Daylight hours are usually spent on the **beaches** at Las Salinas/Es Cabellet (both a short bus ride away) or the nearer but not as nice Figueretas. At night, before the discos open their doors, the shops stay open until 11pm to provide entertaining window-shopping on the way to supper. Most of the cheaper **places to eat** are in the Sa Peña quarter. One of the best bets is smoky *C'an Costa* at c/Cruz 19; along the road on the corner, *La Victoria*, c/Rimbau 1, is another popular and long-established eatery. Down by the waterside, or up in the walled town, you'll be paying a lot more; *Sam's Hamburger Bar* by the port is popular among the less adventurous (and passing US marines), while *San Juan*, c/Montgri 8, is cheap but surly.

The bulk of the **bars** in which to begin your night out are in the area around the port and c/D'Enmig. There are a few **gay bars** here too (*Bobby's, Teatro, JJ's* and *Movie*), but the most crowded ones are found up by the city walls – *Incognito's* and *Angelo's* are neighbours nestling by the Portal de las Tablas. As for **discos**, even if you haven't heard of *Pacha* or the gay *Amnesia*, you'll certainly be made aware of them during your wanderings round the port in the evening. Each – and many of their younger rivals – employs teams of PR artistes to drum up business; competition is fierce. None of them really gets going much before midnight, and the dancing goes on until dawn.

Around the island

Nowhere else can compare to the capital, certainly not the second city, San Antonio Abad, which is a highly avoidable package resort nightmare. SANTA EULALIA, the only other real town, retains a certain charm in its hilltop church looking down over the sprawling old town and modern seafront, while close by the persistent can find a number of relatively empty beaches. The same holds true for most of the rest of the coast – plenty of golden sands but a good deal of effort required to reach them. The one major exception is the northern bay of **Portinatx**, connected by a relatively major road and, despite hotel development, with a number of clean, not overly populated beaches. **Inland** there's little of anything – a few villages and holiday homes that are exceedingly pretty to drive through but offer little if you stop.

There is good **bus service** between Ibiza town, San Antonio Abad, Santa Eulalia, Portinatx and a few of the larger beaches, but hiring a vehicle will widen your options no end. It should prove particularly useful on Ibiza for finding accommodation – as difficult here as on any of the other islands and even more expensive. You may well be reduced to one of the **campsites**. Only one of these – *Camping d'en Bossa* on the road to Playa d'en Bossa – is at all near the capital; the tourist office can provide details of the others.

Formentera

Just three nautical miles south of Ibiza, **FORMENTERA** (population 4000) is the smallest of the inhabited Balearics and is thoroughly barren, the few crops having to be protected, as on Menorca, against the lashing of winter winds. Most of the island is covered in rosemary, growing wild everywhere and crawling with thousands of brilliant green lizards. Its income is derived from tourism (especially German and British), taking advantage of some of Spain's longest, whitest and least-crowded beaches. The shortage of fresh water, fortunately, continues to keep away the crowds and for the most part visitors are seeking escape with little in the way of sophistication. It is, however, becoming more popular, and is certainly not the paradise it once was.

The crossing from Ibiza is short, but strong currents ensure that it's slow – over an hour – and rough. Fares are about 2140ptas (3200ptas on the hydrofoil) and there are usually rival sailings to choose from: check the return times before deciding. Boats dock at the tiny but functional harbour of **LA SABINA**, where the two waterside streets are lined with places offering cars, mopeds or bicycles for hire, interspersed with the odd bar and café. This is the place to get yourself mobile, but if possible phone ahead, certainly if you want a car – try *Moto Rent Mar Blau* (☎971/328403), *Moto Rent Pujol* (☎971/322488), or *Autos Formentera* (☎971/322156). Check with the **tourist office** by the harbour if you need help with this, or with island accommodation (see below). The capital, **SAN FRANCISCO JAVIER**, is just a couple of kilometres away, easily reached on foot or by local bus or taxi. As well as the whitewashed fortified church – now stripped of its defensive cannon – this metropolis has several restaurants and cafés, at least three banks, four bars, a hotel, supermarkets, a pharmacist, a doctor and a *Telefónica* for international calls. An open-air market adds a touch of interest.

Formentera's main road continues from San Francisco to the island's easternmost point at La Mola. Along it, or just off it, are concentrated almost all of the island's habitation and most of the beaches. The next largest town, **SAN FERNANDO** – with a bar, a church and a *hostal* or two – serves the beach of Es Pujols where the package tour industry, such as it is, is concentrated. Despite relative crowding, it's a beautiful coast with clear water and pure white sand dunes backed by low pines. Playa Mitjorn, on the south side of this narrow stretch of the island, is an enormous stretch of sand broken only by the occasional bar or hotel. Formentera's strict regulations on new building mean that this area will remain relatively undeveloped: rather soulless, but definitely the place to head for total isolation, and the main area for nude sunbathing.

Practicalities

Most people treat Formentera as a day trip from Ibiza, and if you want to be one of the few who **stay** you may have difficulty finding anywhere not given over entirely to agency reservations. Among the better deals are *Hostal La Sabina* (☎971/320279; ④), just outside La Sabina; *Casa Rafal* in San Francisco Javier(☎971/322205; ④); *Hostal Pepe* (☎971/328033; ④) in San Fernando; *Hostal Bar Los Rosales* (☎971/320123; ⑤) and *Tahiti* (☎971/328122; ⑤) on Playa Pujols; and *Hostal Sol y Mar* (☎971/328122; ⑤) on Playa Mitjorn. Although there's no official **campsite**, finding a secluded spot should not prove too difficult. There's a basic bus service from La Sabina but journeys rarely keep to timetables, and they connect only the towns, leaving you long, hot walks to the beaches. **Taxis** are cheap with ranks at La Sabina, San Francisco and Es Pujols.

There aren't many cheap places to eat on the island. All the *hostales* mentioned above serve **food** – particularly good value at *Casa Rafal* – or you can get your own supplies from the market and supermarket in San Francisco. Es Pujols has the most restaurants; generally speaking, though, **beach bars** serve better food.

Mallorca

MALLORCA, perhaps more than anywhere in Spain, has a split identity. So much so, in fact, that there's a long-standing joke here about a fifth Balearic island, *Majorca*, a popular sort of place that pulls in an estimated three million tourists a year. There are sections of coast where high-rise hotels and shopping centres are continuous, wedged beside and upon one another and broken only by a dual carriageway down to more of the same. But the spread of development, even after twenty-five years, is surprisingly limited: "Majorca" occupies only the Bay of Palma, a forty-kilometre strip flanking the island capital. Beyond, to the north and east, things are very different. Not only are there good cove beaches, but there's a really startling variety and physical beauty to the land itself. It's this which drew the original Mallorcan tourists – the nineteenth-century Habsburg archdukes, George Sand and Chopin – and it's this which makes the island many people's favourite in the group.

Palma

You may arrive by boat from Menorca at Puerto de Alcúdia in the north of the island, but the odds are you'll find yourself in **PALMA DE MALLORCA**, the capital and the only real "city" in the Balearics. Palma is in some ways like a mainland Spanish city – lively, solid and industrious – though it is immediately set apart by its insular, Mediterranean aura. The port is by far the largest in the Balearics, the evening *paseo* the most ingrained, and, in the evenings at least, you feel the city has only passing relevance to the tourist enclaves around its bay. Arriving by sea, it is also beautiful and impressive, with the grand limestone bulk of the cathedral towering above the old town and the remnants of medieval walls.

The **ferry port** is some 3.5km west of Palma, connected to the centre by the half-hourly bus #1; Palma **airport**, 7km east of the city, is served by bus #17 to the Plaza de España. Finding your way around is fairly straightforward once you're in the centre. Around the **cathedral** is the **Portela quarter**, "Old" Palma, a cluster of alleyways and lanes that become more spacious and ordered as you move towards the zigzag of avenues built beside or in place of the city walls. Cutting up from the sea, beside the cathedral, is **Paseo Borne**, garden promenade as well as boulevard, and way up the hill to the northeast lies the **Plaza Mayor**, target for most of the day-tripping tourists.

There are hundreds of *pensiones* and hotels, and your first move in the summer should be to pick up the official lists of these from the **tourist office** at Avda Rey Jaime III 10 (Mon–Fri 9am–8pm, Sat 10am–1.30pm). They can also supply various maps, bus schedules and leaflets, and, if you can afford full hotel prices, will try to book you a

room. Best initial areas to look for yourself are around the Plaza Mayor (more expensive), on c/Apuntadores or c/San Felio running west from Paseo Borne (cheaper), and on c/San Jaime at the top of the Paseo Borne (mid-range). Specific recommendations are probably futile in summer, but some to try are *Hostal Borne*, c/San Jaime 3 (☎971/712942; ④), very popular, with a courtyard café; *Hostal Ritzi*, c/Apuntadores 6 (☎971/714610; ③); and *Hostal Terramar*, Plaza Mediterráneo 8 (☎971/233968; ④), between the waterfront and the Plaza Gomilla and perhaps the best value. There's also a **youth hostel** at c/Costa Brava 13 in El Arenal (☎971/260892; ①), but it's well out of town and invariably booked en masse by school groups; take bus #15 from Plaza de España.

Eating in Palma can be cheaper than anywhere else in the Balearics. Some of the least expensive places are on or near c/Apuntadores at the lower end of Paseo Borne – *La Zamorana* is a good place here. Elsewhere, there are varied *bocadillos* and cheapish meals at *Bodega Casa Payesa*, c/Molineros 3 – an alley off San Miguel, above Plaza Mayor – and at the friendly *Bodega Bellver* in c/Serinya, off c/de la Unió. If you want really low-price *tapas* try *Meriendas Neska*, c/de la Riera opposite the Teatro Principal. Surprisingly, the restaurants aimed at tourists along Avenida Antoni Mauri, at the bottom of Paseo Borne, often have extremely good-value *menús* too: try the *Iska*, the *Almudaina* or *Mobby Dyk*, or try the *Cafetería El Rey* on Avenida Rey Jaime III, more or less opposite the tourist office.

Most **nightlife** takes place at Terreno along the hotel mile of Avda Joan Miró. This is not very promising, and can be ludicrously expensive, but there's a fair selection of **discos** – both straight and gay – amid the souvenir shops and *hamburguesa* bars. Many of these are free to get in, though they make up for it behind the bar.

Around the island

When you feel you've exhausted the city's possibilities move across to Sóller/Deyá, Puerto Pollensa, Puerto de Alcúdia or one of the small resorts around Porto Cristo on the southeast coast. **Accommodation** is reasonable at each of these towns, though in July or August it'll be almost impossible to find. **Camping** is an alternative but not particularly provided for – there's only one "official" campsite (at Platja Brava) and a scattering of private ones registered with the Palma tourist office. You can survive by discreet use of a tent at many of the island's best beaches: pick a spot near a hotel and, again discreetly, make use of the outside showers they generally provide for guests.

Mallorca's **bus service** is reasonably good and there are even a couple of **train lines** – one, a beautiful ride up through the mountains from Palma to Sóller, is an attraction in itself. Transport of your own, though, is a strong advantage – the Palma tourist office can again advise on rental.

Menorca

Second largest of the Balearics, **MENORCA** is littered with stone reminders of its prehistoric past; rock mounds known as *talayots*, megalithic *taulas* (huge stones topped with another to form a T, around four metres high) and *navetas*, stone slab constructions shaped like an inverted loaf tin. These, and the incessant wind, are the island's most characteristic features. There's not much in the way of excitement, and only a few developed resorts, but if you're looking for peace and for some beautiful, relatively isolated beaches, Menorca is probably your best Balearic bet.

The island is boomerang shaped, stretching from Mahón in the east to the smaller, pretty port of Ciudadela in the west. **Bus routes** are limited, adhering mostly to the main central road between these two, occasionally branching off to the major coastal towns. You'll need your own vehicle to get to any of the more attractive beaches. There are one or two points to remember, though. To reach any of the emptier sands you'll probably have to drive down a track fit only for four-wheel drive – and the wind, which can be very helpful when it's blowing behind you, is distinctly uncomfortable if you're trying to ride into it on a moped. Bear in mind too that petrol stations are widely scattered. After 10pm and on Sundays and fiestas only a few pumps are open; take note of the rota posted outside and keep a full tank.

Accommodation is at a premium, with little of anything outside the bigger coastal towns. Once you find something reasonable, stay there. There's just one fairly pricy **campsite**, at Cala Santa Galdana on the coast south of Ferrerías.

Mahón

If you arrive by ferry from Barcelona or Palma you'll sail into the vast natural harbour of **MAHÓN** (Maó), the island capital. (The airport, 5km out, is served only by taxi.) It's a respectable, almost dull little town: the people are restrained and polite, and the architecture is a strange hybrid of classical Georgian bay-windowed town houses and tall, gloomy Spanish apartment blocks shading the narrow streets.

Four adjacent squares form a hub close to the docks. The **Plaza España** is reached by a twisting flight of steps from the pier and offers great views right across the port and bay; there's a fish market here in the early mornings. Immediately behind is the **Plaza Carmen**, with a simple Carmelite church whose cloisters have been adapted to house a small museum. Wander on from here up c/Virgen del Carmen and take any of the streets to the left to reach one of the oldest and most atmospheric parts of town, overlooking the port from on high. In the other direction from Plaza España lie the **Plaza de la Conquista**, with the town's main church, and the Plaza de la Constitución.

Mahón's main square is actually the **Plaza Explanada**, some way above all these along c/Hanover and c/Dr Orfila. The main **tourist office** (Mon–Fri 9am–2pm & 5–7pm, Sat 9.30am–1pm) is here and it's also home to a bunch of overfed pigeons and a military barracks. Otherwise the only excitement is on Sunday, when crowds converge on its bars and ice cream parlours, and street entertainers play to the strolling multitudes. The **port area** is considerably more interesting, and you can walk the entire length of the quayside from the *Xoriguer* gin distillery (free samples in the shop) to the suburb of Villacarlos, passing through Cala Figuera and Castelfons. By day this makes a relaxed stroll past any number of small restaurants and bars; at night it's slightly more animated, but not much.

Mahón is the best bet for **accommodation** on the island, and those possibilities that exist are all fairly central. The best place to start looking is around Plaza Reial: try the *Hostal Orsi* at 19 c/Infanta (☎971/364751; ③) or the nearby *Hostal Reynes* at 26 c/Comercio (☎971/364059; ③). Another good choice is the *Hostal Roca*, Carre del Carmen 37, off Plaza Princep (☎971/350839; ②).

Mahón has a place in culinary history as the birthplace of mayonnaise (*mahonesa*), and though it's hardly at the forefront of things these days you should have no problem finding somewhere to **eat**. In the Plaza Bastión there are two friendly bar-restaurants serving basic fare at reasonable prices. *Alfabrega*, just below here at c/San Jerónimo 31, is also very reasonably priced, as is the basic place known simply as *Comidas Económicas* at c/Rosario 27. Other than these, the majority of restaurants are down by the port, where expensive French cuisine, local *tapas*, good seafood and the standard steak and french fries are all available.

travel details

Trains

Madrid to: Algeciras (2 daily; 11hr); Alicante (4 daily; 9hr); Barcelona via Tarragona (4 daily; 10–12hr); Bilbao (3 daily; 7–8hr); Burgos (14 daily; 4); Cáceres (5 daily; 3hr 30min–4hr 30min); Cádiz (3 daily; 8–11hr); Córdoba (6 daily; 5–7hr); La Coruña (2 daily; 11hr); Cuenca (4 daily; 2hr 30min); Granada (2 daily; 7–10hr); León (5 daily;

4–6hr); Málaga (7 daily; 7–9hr); Oviedo (3 daily; 7–9hr); Pamplona (1 daily; 6hr); Pontevedra (2 daily; 9–11hr); Salamanca via Ávila (4 daily; 3hr 30min–4hr); San Sebastián (14 daily; 8hr); Santander (3 daily; 8–10hr); Santiago (2 daily; 9hr); Segovia (9 daily; 2–3hr); Sevilla (6 daily; 6–9hr); Valencia (8 daily; 5–8hr); Vigo (2 daily; 8–10hr); Zaragoza (4 daily; 5–7hr).

Algeciras to: Córdoba (4 daily; 5–6hr); Granada (1 daily; 6hr); Madrid (3 daily; 12hr 30min–15hr).

Barcelona to: Figueres (hourly; 2hr); Girona (hourly; 1hr 30min); Lleida (8 daily; 2–3hr); Puigcerdà (4 daily; 3hr 15min); Ripoll (4 daily; 2hr); Sitges (half-hourly; 35 min); Tarragona (half-hourly; 1hr 30min); La Tour de Carol (4 daily; 3hr 30min); Valencia (7 daily; 4–5 hr); Zaragoza (16 daily; 3hr 45min–4hr 30min).

Bilbao to: Barcelona (2 daily; 10–12hr); Madrid (3 daily; 8hr); Salamanca (2 daily; 9hr); Santander (5 daily; 2hr).

Burgos to: Bilbao (6 daily; 3–3hr 30min); Irún (10 daily; 3hr 30min–4hr) via San Sebastián (3–4hr).

Córdoba to: Madrid (6 daily; 7hr).

Granada to: Madrid (3 daily; 6hr 30min–10hr); Ronda (1 daily; 5hr); Valencia (2 daily; 12hr).

León to: Burgos (7 daily; 2–3hr); Barcelona (4 daily; 9hr 30min–11hr); Madrid (8 daily; 4–6hr); Oviedo (9 daily; 2hr 30min); Valladolid (13 daily; 1hr 30min–2hr 30min).

Málaga to: Córdoba (10 daily; 2hr 30min–3hr 30min); Granada (3 daily; 3hr 30min); Madrid (5 daily; 8–10hr); Ronda (3 daily; 3hr); Sevilla (3 daily; 3hr 30min–4hr).

Salamanca to: Ávila (1hr 45min); Madrid (4 daily; 3hr); Valladolid (9 daily; 2hr).

San Sebastián to: Bilbao (9 daily; 2hr 30min–3hr); Burgos (12 daily; 4hr); Madrid (4 daily; 6hr 30min–8hr 30min); Pamplona (6 daily; 2–3hr); Salamanca (2 daily; 9hr); Valencia (1 daily; 12hr); Zaragoza (4 daily; 4–5hr).

Santiago to: La Coruña (12 daily; 2hr); Madrid (2 daily; 8–10hr); Pontevedra (11 daily; 1hr 15min); Vigo (9 daily; 2hr).

Sevilla to: Cádiz (13 daily; 1hr 30min–2hr); Córdoba (2 daily; 1hr 30min–2hr); Madrid (6 daily; 6hr 30min–9hr 30min).

Valencia to: Alicante (5 daily; 2–3hr); Barcelona (8 daily; 5hr); Madrid (8 daily; 6–7hr); Zaragoza (3 daily; 6hr).

Zaragoza to: Barcelona (16 daily; 3hr 45min–4hr 30min); Canfranc (3 daily; 4hr); Huesca (3 daily;

1hr 10min); Jaca (3 daily; 3hr); Lleida (9 daily; 1hr 45min–2hr 45min); Madrid (13 daily; 3hr 30min–5hr 30min);.

Buses

Madrid to: Albacete (3 daily; 4hr); Alicante (3 daily; 6hr); Ávila (3 daily; 1hr 30min); Barcelona (4 daily; 10hr); Bilbao (4 daily; 7hr); Burgos (4 daily; 4hr); Cáceres (8 daily; 4–5hr); Córdoba (1 daily; 8hr); Cuenca (8 daily; 2hr 30min); Gijón (3 daily; 7hr); Granada (1 daily; 8hr); León (4 daily; 4hr 30min); Málaga (1 daily; 8hr); Pamplona (2 daily; 6hr); Salamanca (12 daily; 2hr 30min–3hr 30min); San Sebastián (3 daily; 8hr); Santander (2 daily; 7hr); Sevilla (1 daily; 10hr); Toledo (24 daily; 1hr 30min); Trujillo (7 daily; 4–5hr); Valencia (14 daily; 5–6hr); Valladolid (2 daily; 3hr 30min); Zamora (5 daily; 3hr 15min); Zaragoza (4 daily; 5hr).

Alicante to: Almería (2 daily; 7hr); Barcelona (5 daily; 10hr); Granada (4 daily; 9hr); Málaga (4 daily; 12hr); Madrid (3 daily; 6hr).

Barcelona to: Alicante (5 daily; 9hr); Andorra (2 daily; 5hr 30min); Girona (6–8 daily; 1hr 30min); Madrid (4 daily; 10hr); Seu d'Urgell (2 daily; 5hr); Tarragona (18 daily; 1hr 30min); Valencia (7 daily; 6hr); the Vall d'Aran (1 daily; 7hr); Zaragoza (4 daily; 5hr).

Burgos to: Bilbao (2 daily; 3hr); León (2 daily; 3hr 30min); Madrid (4 daily; 4hr); Salamanca (1 daily; 3hr 30min); Santander (2 daily; 3hr); San Sebastián (2 daily; 3hr 30min).

Córdoba to: Granada (3 daily; 4hr); Madrid (1 daily; 8hr).

Figueres to: Cadaqués (4 daily; 1hr 15min); L'Escala (3 daily; 45min); Palafrugell (3 daily; 1hr 30min).

Granada to: Alicante (3 daily; 5hr 30min); Almería (2 daily; 4hr); Madrid (1 daily; 8hr); Valencia (3 daily; 7hr 30min).

León to: Madrid (4 daily; 4hr 30min); Oviedo (4 daily; 2hr); Santander (1 daily; 3hr).

Málaga to: Algeciras (9 daily; 3hr 30min); Córdoba (2 daily; 4hr); Granada (8 daily; 2hr 30min); Osuna (2 daily; 3hr); Ronda (5 daily; 3hr 30min); Sevilla (2 daily; 4hr 30min).

Oviedo to: León (8 daily; 2hr); Madrid (8 daily; 5hr 30min).

Salamanca to: Ávila (5 daily; 1hr 30min); León (4 daily; 2hr 30min–4hr); Madrid (13 daily; 2hr 30min–3hr 30min); Mérida (3 daily; 4hr); Santander (1 daily; 5hr 30min); Sevilla (3 daily; 7hr); Zamora (13 daily; 1hr 15min).

Santander to: Bilbao (7 daily); Burgos (3 daily; 4hr); Madrid (4 daily; 8hr); Oviedo (6 daily; 3hr 30min).

Santiago to: Madrid (2 daily; 10hr); Pontevedra (15 daily; 1hr 30min); Vigo (15 daily; 2hr 30min).

Sevilla to: Cádiz (8 daily; 1hr 30min–2hr 30min); Córdoba (3 daily; 3hr 15 min); Madrid (1 daily; 10hr).

Valencia to: Alicante (6–10 daily; 4hr); Barcelona (7 daily; 6hr); Cuenca (3 daily; 4hr); Madrid (6 daily; 6hr); Sevilla (1 daily; 12hr).

Zaragoza to: Barcelona (6 daily; 4–5hr); Lleida (4 daily; 3 hr); Valladolid (3 daily; 8hr).

Ferries
Barcelona to: Ibiza (6 weekly; 9–10hr); Mahón (6 weekly; 9hr); Palma (10 weekly; 8hr).

Ibiza to: Formentera (9 daily; 1hr); Palma (2 weekly; 4hr 30min).

Palma to: Mahón (1 weekly; 6hr 30min).

Santander to: Plymouth (2 weekly; 24hrs).

Valencia to: Ibiza (2 weekly; 7hr); Palma (6 weekly; 8–9hr).

CHAPTER 22

SWEDEN

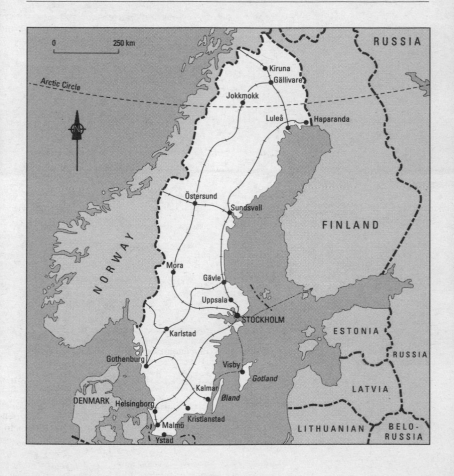

Introduction

Sweden is a large, remote and contented country whose sense of space is perhaps its most remarkable feature. Away from the relatively densely populated south, travelling without seeing a soul is not uncommon. The **south and southwest** of the country are flat holiday lands, long disputed Danish territory and harbouring a host of historic ports – **Gothenburg, Helsingborg** and **Malmö**. Off the **southeast** coast, the Baltic islands of **Öland** and **Gotland** are the country's most hyped resorts, and with good reason, supporting a lazy beach-life to match that of the best southern European spots but without the hotel blocks and crowds.

Stockholm, the capital, is of course the country's supreme attraction, a bundle of islands which houses monumental architecture, fine museums and the country's most active culture and nightlife. The two university towns, **Uppsala** and **Lund**, demand a visit, too, while, moving northwards, **Gävle, Gällivare** and **Kiruna**, still further north, all make justified demands on your time. This area, **central and northern** Sweden, is the country of tourist brochures: great swathes of forest, inexhaustible – around 96,000 – lakes and some of the best wilderness hiking in Europe. Two train routes link it with the south. The eastern run, close to the **Bothnian coast**, passes old wood-built towns and planned new ones, and ferry ports for connections to Finland. In the centre, the trains of the **Inlandsbanan** strike off through lakelands and mountains, clearing reindeer off the track as they go. Both routes meet in Sweden's **far north** – home of the *Same*, the oldest indigenous Scandinavian people.

Information and Maps

Most towns in Sweden have some kind of **tourist office**, giving out maps, timetables and other bumph, and sometimes booking private rooms, renting bikes and changing money. Some also sell discount cards during the summer which give reductions on local travel, museum entry and other freebies. They're normally open daily in high season, shorter hours during the rest of the summer, and infrequently in winter. As for maps, the best general map of Sweden is the *Hallwag* one.

Money and Banks

Swedish **currency** is the *krona* (plural *kronor*), made up of 100 öre. It comes in coins of 50öre, 1kr, 5kr and 10kr; and notes of 20kr, 50kr, 100kr, 500kr, 1000kr and 10,000kr. You can change money in **banks** all over Sweden, which are open Mon–Fri 9.30am–3pm, though branches in Stockholm and Gothenburg have longer summer hours. Outside normal banking hours you can change money in exchange offices at airports and ferry terminals, and in post offices (look for the "PK Exchange" sign), as well as at *Forex* exchange offices, which usually offer the best rates – expect to pay a minimum 20kr commission or 15kr per travellers' cheque. *Bankomat* machines give *Visa* and *Mastercard* cash advances.

Communications

Post and phones in Sweden are good, and as most people speak at least some English you won't go far wrong in the post or telephone office. **Post offices** open Mon–Fri 9am–6pm, Sat 10am–1pm, with some branches closed on Saturday throughout July, Sweden's holiday month. You can buy stamps at post offices, in addition to most newspaper kiosks, tobacconists and hotels.

For international **telephone calls** there are a few telephone offices (*Tele* or *Telebutik*), usually open outside normal business hours until around 9pm daily, or you can dial direct from public phones. These take 1kr and 5kr coins (minimum charge 2kr) and operators all speak English (domestic directory enquiries ☎07975; international ☎0019). A new service, the *Turist Telefon*, offers half-price calls from pay phones in the major cities between mid-June and mid-August; the kiosks are clearly marked. The international access code is ☎009. In addition, card phones (*Telefonkort*) are becoming more common and can work out cheaper. Cards (available from *Pressbyrån*) are charged at local rate.

Getting Around

Sweden's internal transport system is quick and efficient and runs through all weathers. Services are often reduced in the winter (especially on northern bus routes), but it's unlikely you'll ever get stranded. In summer, when everyone is on holiday,· trains and buses are packed: on long journeys it's a good idea to make reservations. All train, bus and ferry schedules are contained within the giant **Restider** (50kr), or pick up specific route information from train station offices on the new computerized information boards.

■ Trains

Swedish State Railways (**SJ** – *Statens Järnvägar*) have an extensive network, running right into the north of the country above the Arctic Circle and on into Norway. **Tickets** are expensive but happily it's almost never necessary to pay the full rate. Full second-class **fares** only apply on Friday and Sunday, and on all other days there's a 25 percent discount. Buying a *Reslust* card (150kr, valid for two people for one calendar year) entitles you to a 25 percent discount on Tuesday, Wednesday, Thursday and Saturday trains, 50 percent off red departures (marked "Röd avgång on the timetables). *InterRail* and *Eurail* passes are valid, as is the *Nordturist* pass. Available from *NSR Travel*, 21–24 Cockspur Street, London SW1Y 5DA, and throughout Scandinavia, this pass costs £189/$300 (£140/$220 for under-26s), and gives you 21 days' unlimited travel in the four main Scandinavian countries, plus free travel or large discounts on many ferry crossings and bus journeys. *NSR Travel* also sells the *Scandrail* pass, costing £93/$150 for 4 days travel in 15, £151/$240 for 9 days out of 21 and £217/$350 for 21 days travel out of 30, and again valid throughout Scandinavia. Under-26s can also buy a pass giving 14 days travel from June 20–July 4 for 435kr.

Fares are calculated by the kilometre and there's a second-class maximum of 594kr for all journeys of 881km or over. Also, from mid-June to mid-August (and certain holiday periods) a supplement of 50kr lets you travel first class on most trains. To ensure a seat, you might want to make a **reservation**; on some trains – indicated by an "R" or "IC" in the timetable – this is in theory compulsory and costs 20kr; further supplements are payable on the high-speed X2000 trains between Stockholm and Gothenburg. One booklet worth picking up is the quarterly *SJ Tågtider* **timetable** from any train station (10kr), an accurate and comprehensive list of the most useful train services in the country, except for those of the Inlandsbanan up to northern Sweden

(*InterRail* 50 percent discount) and the Pågatågen private rail line in the south (*InterRail* valid; *Nordturist* 50 percent discount).

■ Buses

Complementing the rail system are **long-distance buses** (*Expressbussar*), operated by *Swedbus* between large towns, and to and from Stockholm. *Expressbuss* often only run at weekends (usually Fri & Sun), and tend to be cheaper and slower than the equivalent train ride. In the north, buses are more frequent since they're used to carry mail to isolated regions. Several companies operate daily services, and fares are broadly similar. You can pick up a comprehensive **timetable** at any *Expressbuss* terminal, which will normally be adjacent to the train station.

■ Ferries

Unlike Norway and Finland, domestic **ferry** services in Sweden are few. The various archipelagos on the southeast coast are served by small ferries, the most comprehensive network being within the Stockholm archipelago, for which you can buy an island-hopping boat pass. The other major link is between the Baltic island of **Gotland** and the mainland at Nynäshamn and Oskarshamn, very popular routes in summer for which you should really book ahead.

■ Driving and hitching

Driving presents few problems since roads are good and generally reliable. The only real dangers are the reindeer and elk which wander onto roads in the north. To drive, you need a full licence and the vehicle registration document. Speed limits are 110kph on motorways, 90kph and 70kph on other roads, 50kph in built-up areas – although between mid-June and mid-August the 110kph limit drops to 90kph on most roads. It's compulsory to use dipped headlights during daylight hours. Swedish drink-driving laws are among the toughest in Europe and random breath-tests the norm. For **emergency assistance** on the road call *Larmtjänst* on ☎020/91 00 40.

Car hire is uniformly expensive, though most hire companies have special weekend tourist rates – from around 450kr. Otherwise, expect to pay upwards of 2500kr a week, with unlimited mileage. Lead-free petrol is widely available at around 7kr per litre. Most petrol stations are self-service and lots of them have automatic pumps where you fill up using 100kr notes.

Despite the amount of holiday traffic and the number of young Swedes with cars, **hitching** is rarely worth the effort as lifts are so few and far between. Shorter hops are a little easier to find, especially when travelling along the coasts and in the north. If you do try it though, always use a sign.

Accommodation

Finding somewhere cheap to sleep is not the hassle that might be expected in what is an otherwise expensive country, provided you're prepared to do some advance planning. There's an excellent network of youth hostels and campsites, while in the cities private rooms and bed and breakfast places are a common alternative to hotels.

■ Hotels and private rooms

Hotels come cheaper than you'd think in Sweden, especially in Stockholm and the bigger cities during the summer, when many Swedes are out of the country. The rest of the year, rooms at weekends are much cheaper than midweek: on average, for a room with TV and bathroom you can expect to pay from 500kr a double. Nearly all hotels include breakfast in the price, which can be a useful bonus. **Package deals** operated in Malmö, Stockholm and Gothenburg get you a hotel bed for one night, breakfast and the relevant city discount card from around 300kr per person. These schemes are generally valid from mid-June to mid-August and at weekends throughout the year. Further details are available in the free booklet *Hotels in Sweden*, available from the National Tourist Board, which also lists every hotel in the country. A further option is the **private rooms** that tourist offices often book for 90–140kr per person, with access to showers and sometimes a kitchen.

■ Hostels

The biggest choice lies with the country's huge chain of **youth hostels**, operated by the *Svenska Turistföreningen*, Drottninggatan 31–33, Stockholm (☎08/790 31 00). There are 280 hostels in the country, usually with single and double rooms too. Virtually all have well-equipped self-catering kitchens and serve a buffet breakfast. Prices are low (60–90kr); non-members pay an extra 35kr a night. The *STF* publish a comprehensive handbook for 60kr, available from hostels, tourist offices and large bookshops. Always ring ahead in the summer, and bear in mind that hostels usually close between 10am and 5pm, with curfews around midnight.

■ Campsites and cabins

Practically every town or village has at least one **campsite**, generally of a high standard. Pitching a tent costs around 40kr a night, plus a small charge per person, though all costs are considerably higher near the big cities. Most sites are open June to September, some throughout the year. The bulk of the sites are approved and classified by the Swedish Tourist Board and a comprehensive listings book, *Camping Sverige*, is available at larger sites and most Swedish bookshops. The Swedish National Tourist Board also puts out a short free list. Note that at most sites you'll need a camping carnet (45kr from your first stop) and that camping gaz is tricky to get hold of in Sweden. Many campsites also boast **cabins**, usually decked out with bunk beds, kitchen and equipment but not sheets. They're an excellent alternative to camping for a group or couple; cabins go for around 200–300kr for a four-bedded affair. It's wise to ring ahead to secure one. It's also possible to **camp rough** throughout the country, without asking permission, provided you stay a reasonable distance away from other dwellings.

ACCOMMODATION PRICE CODES

Throughout this guide, accommodation is priced on a scale of ① to ⑧, the number indicating the lowest price per night a single person could expect to pay in that establishment in high season. With hostels this is the nightly rate per person; with hotels, the price is arrived at by dividing the cost of the cheapest double room by two. The prices indicated by the codes are as follows

① = under £5 / $8   ② = £5–10 / $8–16   ③ = £10–15 / $16–24   ④ = £15–20 / $24–32

⑤ = £20–25 / $32–40   ⑥ = £25–30 / $40–48   ⑦ = £30–35 / $48–56   ⑧ = over £35 / $56

Food and Drink

Eating and drinking is going to take up a large slice of your daily budget in Sweden, though you'll always get good value for money. At its best, Swedish food is excellent, largely meat, fish and potato based, but varied and generally tasty and filling. Specialities include the northern Swedish delicacies – reindeer and elk meat, and wild berries – and herring in many different guises. On a budget, ethnic restaurants and pizzerias often provide better value; be sure also to fuel up on breakfast and lunch, both of which offer good-value options.

■ Food

Breakfast (*frukost*) is invariably a help-yourself buffet served in most youth hostels and some restaurants for around 40–50kr, free in hotels, consisting of juice, cereals, bread, boiled eggs, jams, salami, tea and coffee on even the most limited tables. Something to watch out for is the jug of *filmjölk* next to the ordinary milk, a thicker, sour milk for pouring on cereals. **Coffee** in Sweden is always good, often free after the first cup. **Tea** is weak as a rule but costs around the same – 10–14kr. For **snacks** and lighter meals the choice expands. A *Gatukök* (street kitchen) or *Korvstånd* (hot-dog stall) will serve a selection of hot dogs, burgers, chips and the like for around 30kr. **Burger bars** are spreading like wildfire and a hefty burger and chips meal will set you back a shade over 40kr: the local *Clockburger* is cheaper than *McDonalds* and *Wimpy*, but all are generally the source of the cheapest coffee in town. It's often nicer to hit the **konditori**, a coffee shop with succulent pastries and cakes. They're not particularly cheap (coffee and cake for 20–35kr) but are generally good, also serving *smörgåsar*, open **sandwiches** piled high with an elaborate variety of toppings for 25kr a time. For the cheapest eating, it's hard to beat the **supermarkets** and **markets**. National chains to watch for are *Åhlens* and *Domus*.

Eating in a **restaurant** is cheapest at lunchtime, when most places offer something called the *Dagens Rätt* at 45–60kr, often the only affordable way to sample real Swedish cooking. Served between 11am and 2pm, it consists of a main dish with bread and salad, sometimes a drink, and coffee. Other cheapish places for lunch are **cafeterias**, usually self-service with cheaper snacks and hot meals; large department stores

and train stations are good places to look. More expensive but good for a blowout, are restaurants and hotels that put out the **Smörgåsbord** at lunchtime for 100–150kr, where you help yourself to unlimited portions of herring, hot and cold meats, eggs, potatoes, salad, cheese and fruit. A variation on the buffet theme is the **Sillbricka**, a specialist buffet for around the same price where the dishes are all based on cured and marinaded herring.

If you don't eat the set lunch, meals in restaurants, especially at **dinner** (*middag*), can be very expensive: 150–200kr for a three-course affair, plus 30–50kr for a beer, 100kr for a bottle of house plonk. Otherwise pizzerias and Chinese restaurants offer better value. Large pizzas cost 40–50kr, usually with free salad and bread, and the price is generally the same at lunch and dinner. Chinese restaurants nearly always offer a set lunch for around 50kr, though they're pricier in the evening. Middle Eastern kebab takeaways and cafés are also widespread, where you'll get something fairly substantial in pitta bread for around 30kr.

■ Drink

Drinking is notoriously pricy. The cheapest choice is probably **beer**, which costs 30–40kr for 400ml of lager-type drink – a "stör stark". Unless you specify, it will be *starköl*, the strongest Class III beer or the slightly weaker *Mellanöl*; *folköl* is the Class II and cheaper and weaker brew; cheapest (around half the price) is *lättöl*, a Class I concoction that is virtually non-alcoholic. Classes I and II are available in supermarkets; Class III stuff is only on sale in the state licensed liquor stores, where it's around a third of the price you'll pay in a bar. *Pripps* and *Spendrups* are the two main brands. A glass of **wine** in a bar or restaurant costs around 30kr. For experimental drinking, **aquavit** is a good bet, served ice-cold in tiny shots and washed down with beer. There are various different "flavours", too, with spices and herbs added.

You'll find **bars** in all towns and cities and most villages, though they're not the focus of the social scene. In Stockholm and the larger cities the move is towards brasserie-type places; elsewhere there are more down-to-earth drinking dens, where the clientele is normally male and drunk. Wherever you drink, you'll find that things close down around 11pm or midnight, though not in Gothenburg and Stockholm where you can keep drinking into the small hours. The **Systembolaget** (state off-licence) is a deliberately unattractive place to buy booze, and apart from strong beer (12kr for a third-litre) the only bargain is the imported wine at 50kr a bottle. The shops are open Mon–Fri 9am–6pm, the minimum age for being served is 20, and you may need to show ID.

Opening Hours and Holidays

Shops are open Mon–Fri 9am–6pm, Sat 9am–1pm or 4pm. Some larger department stores stay open until 8–10pm in cities, and open on Sunday afternoons as well. Banks, offices and shops close on the following days and may close early on the preceding day: Jan 1; Jan 6; Good Friday; Easter Monday; May 1; Ascension (around mid-May); Whit Monday; the Saturday nearest Midsummer's Day (June 22); All Saint's Day (the Sat between Oct 31 and Nov 6); Dec 24, 25 & 26.

Emergencies

You're unlikely to encounter too many problems with **crime** in Sweden, and thus will have little need to contact the police. If you do, you'll find them courteous and generally able to speak English. In case of **health problems**, there is no GP system and you should instead go direct to a hospital with your passport, where for 60kr you'll receive treatment. If you need medicine, take your prescription to a chemist – *Apotek* in Swedish – which will be open shop hours, although Stockholm has a 24-hour pharmacy. Larger towns operate a rota system of late opening, with the address of the nearest late-opener posted on the door of each chemist.

EMERGENCY NUMBERS

☎90 000 for Police (*Polis*), Fire brigade (*Brandkår*) or Ambulance (*Ambulans*).

STOCKHOLM AND AROUND

STOCKHOLM comes lauded as Sweden's most beautiful city, and apart from a couple of sticky modern developments and a tangled road junction or two, it lives up to it – it's delightful, not least as a contrast to the apparently endless lakes and forests of the rest of the country. It's also a remarkably disparate capital, one whose tracts of water and range of monumental buildings give it an ageing, lived-in feel and an atmosphere quite at odds with its status as Sweden's most contemporary, forward-looking city.

Built on fourteen small islands, Stockholm was a natural site for the fortifications erected by one Birger Jarl in 1255 that grew into the current city. In the sixteenth century, the city fell to King Gustav Vasa, a century later becoming the centre of the Swedish trading empire that covered present-day Scandinavia. Following the waning of Swedish power it entered something of a quiet period, only rising to prominence again last century when industrialization sowed the seeds of the Swedish economic miracle.

The Stockholm area telephone code is ☎08.

Arrival and information

By **train**, you arrive at **Central Station**, a cavernous structure on Vasagatan in Norrmalm. All branches of the Tunnelbana, Stockholm's underground system, meet at T-Centralen, the station directly below Central Station. **Cityterminalen**, adjacent, handles all the **bus** services, both domestic and international, including the airport bus. *Viking Line* **ferries** arrive at Tegelvikshamnen in Södermalm, in the south of the city, a thirty-minute walk from the modern centre, or connected by bus to Slussen and then by Tunnelbana to T-Centralen. *Åland Line* and *Birka Cruises* services dock in Södermalm, too, just up the quayside at Stadsgården. The *Silja Line* terminal is in the northeastern reaches of the city, a short walk from Gärdet or Ropsten, from where you can take the Tunnelbana. **Arlanda airport** is 45km north of Stockholm; buses run every ten to fifteen minutes to Cityterminalen from 4.30am to 10pm (50min; 50kr). Until the direct rail link to Arlana is complete, you can make the journey by local train (*Stockholm Card* valid) or *SJ* train (rail passes valid) to Märsta, then a local bus (10min).

You should be able to pick up a map of the city at most points of arrival, but it's worth making your way to one of the **tourist centres**, which hand out fistfuls of free information and sell decent maps for 10kr. The **main office** is in Norrmalm, on the ground floor of *Sverigehuset*, at the northwestern corner of Kungsträdgården (June–Aug Mon–Fri 9am–7pm, Sat & Sun 9am–5pm; Sept–May Mon–Fri 9am–6pm, Sat & Sun 9am–3pm; ☎789 24 90), and sells the invaluable **Stockholm Card** (150kr for 24hrs, valid for 1 adult and 2 children), which gives unlimited travel on city transport, free museum entry and discounts on boat trips and tours. They are **not valid** on the direct buses to the airport or on the connecting night bus to the Nynäshamn ferry terminal. An independent *InterRail* information point at Central Station keeps long hours and distributes budget-oriented literature.

City transport

The best way to explore Stockholm's initially confusing centre is to **walk**: it takes about twenty-five minutes to cross central Stockholm on foot. You'll have to use some form of **transport** to reach the more distant sights. *Storstockholms Lokaltrafik (SL)* operates a comprehensive system of buses and trains (underground and local) reaching well out of the city centre. The **SL-Center** information office, inside T-Centralen station at Sergels

Torg (Mon–Thurs 9am–6pm, Fri 9am–5.30pm), doles out timetables and sells a useful transport map (42kr). Quickest of the transport systems is the **Tunnelbana** (T-bana) underground, based on three main lines. **Buses** can be less direct due to the nature of Stockholm's islands and central pedestrianization, though the *Turistlinjen* (Tourist Route) buses can be useful, following a continuous loop through the city between mid-June and mid-August. **Ferries** also link some of the central islands: Djurgården is connected with Nybroplan in Norrmalm in summer, and Skeppsbron in Gamla Stan (all year), and there's a summer service from Stadshuset to Långholmen. Ferry trips cost 15kr one-way, while land transport costs 13kr within one zone, 6.50kr for each additional zone – so you're normally better off investing in a **pass**. Apart from the *Stockholm Card*, there's a **tourist card** valid for 24 hours (60kr for the city) or 72 hours (115kr), which gives unlimited travel on public transport and on the ferries to Djurgården. Alternatively, you can buy a strip of twenty transferable *SL* **ticket coupons** (85kr), using two per person for each journey. Buy *SL* tickets and cards from the tourist office and *SL* offices inside T-Centralen or Central Station. **Taxis** can be hailed in the street or summoned by ringing ☎15 00 00. If you ring, it will cost 25kr for the taxi to get to you; a trip across the city centre costs around 80kr (5–10 percent less if you are all women).

Accommodation

There's plenty of **accommodation** in Stockholm, especially for budget travellers, but don't turn up late in summer and expect to get a cheap bed. Booking your first night's accommodation in advance is always a good idea, either through the *Sverigehuset* tourist centre or by phoning direct. The cheapest choices, on the whole, are found to the north of Cityterminalen, in the streets to the west of Adolf Fredriks Kyrka. There's also **Hotellcentralen**, a booking service on the lower level of Central Station (May & Sept daily 8am–7pm; June–Aug 8am–9pm; Oct–April Mon–Fri 8am–5pm; ☎24 08 80), which charges a fee of 30kr per room, 12kr for a youth hostel. *Hotellcentralen* also broker special deals, like cheaper rate packages from 305kr between mid-June and mid-August that include a free *Stockholm Card*. For **private rooms**, contact *Hotelltjänst*, Vasagatan 15–17 (☎10 44 57), who can fix you up with a double room for around 330kr.

Hostels

af Chapman, Skeppsholmen (☎679 50 15). Official hostel on a ship moored at Skeppsholmen. Without a reservation, the chances of a space in summer are negligible, although queuing from around 7am has been known to yield a bed. It is now linked to the *IYHF*'s growing worldwide computer booking system. Open April to mid-Dec. ②

Balettakademien, Döbelnsgatan 56 (☎612 38 36). A dance academy with cheap summer dorms. Open July & Aug. T-bana Rådmandgatan. ②

City Backpackers, Barnhusgatan 16, Norrmalm (☎20 69 20). New curfewless hostel with four-bed rooms ten minutes' walk from Central Station. ③

Columbus Hotell & Vandrarhem, Tjärhovsgatan 11, Södermalm (☎644 17 17). A friendly hostel with cheap beds. Open all year. T-bana Medborgarplatsen. ③

Gustav af Klimt, Stadsgårdskayen 153, Södermalm (☎640 40 77). Singles, doubles and four-bedded cabins in this floating hotel-hostel. ③

Hantverkshuset, Skeppsholmen (☎679 50 17). Dead central official hostel, at the foot of the *af Chapman*'s gangplank and better for speculative arrivals. Open all year. ②

Kista InterRail Point, Jyllandsgatan 16 (☎752 64 56). A fair distance out, but with bargain beds. Open mid-July to mid-Aug; midnight curfew. T-bana line #11 to Kista. ②

Långholmen, Kronohäktet, Långholmen (☎668 05 10). Stockholm's newest and grandest official hostel, in an old prison on Långholmen island, with ordinary doubles in summer as well as hostel beds. There's a summer ferry from Stadshusbron, or T-bana to Hornstull and follow the signs. ②

Zinken, Zinkens väg 20, Södermalm (☎668 57 86). T-bana Zinkensdamm. Huge official hostel, open all year, with kitchen facilities. Nicely situated by the water. ②

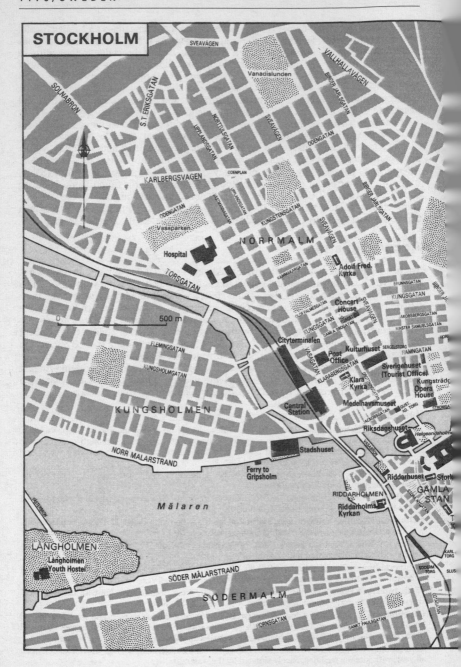

STOCKHOLM

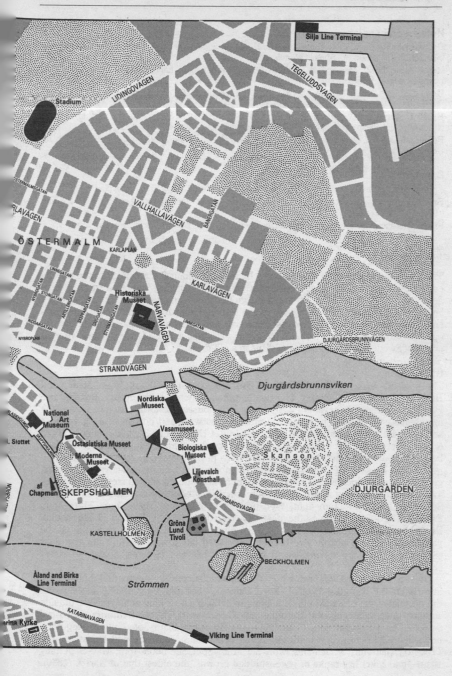

Hotels and pensions

Gustavsvikshemmet, Västmannagatan 15 (21 44 50). Same street and prices as the *Gustav Vasa* but exclusive of breakfast. T-bana Odenplan. ④

Hotell Anno 1647, Mariagränd 3 (☎644 04 80). Near Slussen, a handy location for the old town. Drops a category in summer. ⑤

Hotel Danielsson, Wallingatan 31 (☎11 10 76). Small place off Drottninggatan, north of Central Station. ④

Hotell Gustav Vasa, Västmannagatan 61 (☎34 38 01). Not a bad location, in the northern part of Norrmalm, and cheap enough, especially in summer. T-bana Odenplan. ④

Pensionat Oden, Odengatan 38 (☎612 43 49). Good Norrmalm location. Small, so ring first. T-bana Odenplan. ②

Campsites

Ängby. West of the city near beach. Open all year. T-bana line #18 or #19 to Ängbyplan.

Bredäng. 10km southwest of the centre and near the beach. Open all year, but pricey. T-bana line #13 and #15 to Bredäng.

Flaten.One star place 15km southeast of city; open May–Sept. Bus #401 from Slussen.

The City

The **Stadhuset** (June–Aug guided tours 10am, 11am, noon & 2pm; 25kr) at the water's edge near Central Station, and particularly its gently-tapering red-brick tower (May–Sept daily 10am–4pm; 10kr, included on guided tour) give the best fix on the city's layout. The building itself, a flagship of the National Romantic movement in the 1910s and 1920s, draws heavily on Swedish materials and themes exemplified in the cavernous Blue Room where the Nobel prize-givings are held and the Golden Room where a precis of Swedish history covers the walls in a gilt mosaic.

Gamla Stan

Three islands make up **Gamla Stan** or **Old Stockholm** – Riddarholmen, Staden and Helgeandsholmen – a clutter of seventeenth- and eighteenth-century Renaissance buildings, hairline medieval alleys and tall, dark houses, the former homes of wealthy merchants, still picked out today by intricate doorways and portals bearing coats of arms. On Helgeandsholmen, the **Riksdagshuset** (July to mid-Sept Mon–Fri 12.30pm & 2pm; rest of year Sat & Sun 1.30pm) is the Swedish parliament building, which can be visited on free guided tours which leave from the glassed-in rear. Being Sweden rather than Westminster, the seating for members is in healthy non-adversarial rows, grouped by constituency and not by party. In front of the Riksdagshuset, accessible by a set of steps leading down from Norrbro, the **Medeltidsmuseum** (Jan–May & Sept–Dec Tues–Sun 11am–5pm, Wed until 9pm; June–Aug Tues–Thurs 11am–7pm, Fri–Sun 11am–5pm; 30kr) is the best city-related historical collection in Stockholm. Ruins of medieval tunnels and walls were discovered during excavations under the parliament building and they've been incorporated into a walk-through underground exhibition. There are reconstructed houses, models and pictures, boats and street scenes.

Over a second set of bridges is the most distinctive monumental building in Stockholm, the **Kungliga Slottet** (Royal Palace), a beautiful Renaissance successor to the original castle of Stockholm. Finished in 1760, it's a striking achievement, outside sombre, inside a magnificent Baroque and Rococo swirl. The **Apartments** (Jan–April & Sept–Dec Tues–Sun noon–3pm; May–Aug Tues–Sat 10am–3pm; July & Aug Mon noon–3pm; 30kr) form a relentlessly linear collection of furniture and tapestries; the **Treasury** (Jan–April & Oct–Dec Mon–Sat 11am–3pm, Sun noon–4pm; May–Sept daily 10am–4pm, 25kr) has ranks of jewel-studded crowns, the oldest that of Karl X (1650).

Also worth catching is the **Armoury** (Jan–April & Sept–Dec Tues–Sun 11am–4pm; May–Aug daily 11am–4pm; 40kr), less to do with weapons and more to do with ceremony – suits of armour, costumes and horse-drawn coaches from the sixteenth century onwards, most notably the stuffed horse and mud-spattered garments of King Gustav II Adolf who died in the Battle of Lützen in 1632. For those with the energy, the **Palace Museum** (June–Aug daily noon–3pm; 5kr) contains parts of the older castle, its ruins underneath the present building.

Beyond the palace lies Gamla Stan proper, the streets suddenly narrower and darker. The first major building is the **Storkyrkan**, a rectangular brick church, consecrated in 1306, that is technically Stockholm's cathedral – the monarchs of Sweden are married and crowned here. The Baroque interior is marvellous, with an animated fifteenth-century sculpture of *St George and the Dragon*, and – perhaps more impressive – the royal pews, more like golden billowing thrones, and a monumental black and silver altarpiece. **Stortorget**, Gamla Stan's main square, is handsome and elegantly proportioned, crowded with eighteenth-century buildings and well placed for access to the surrounding narrow shopping streets, a succession of art and craft shops, restaurants and discreet fast food outlets, clogged by summer buskers and evening strollers. Just off Västerlånggatan, on Tyska Brinken, the **Tyska kyrkan**, or "German Church" (daily noon–4pm), belonged to Stockholm's medieval German merchants, a copper-topped red-brick church that was also richly fashioned in the Baroque period.

Keep right on as far as the handsome Baroque **Riddarhuset** (Mon–Fri 11.30am–12.30pm; 20kr), in whose Great Hall the Swedish aristocracy met during the seventeenth-century Parliament of the Four Estates. Their coats of arms – around 2500 of them – are splattered across the walls. Take a look downstairs, too, in the Chancery, which stocks heraldic bone china by the shelf-load and racks of fancy signet rings. From here it's a matter of seconds across the bridge onto **Riddarholmen** ("Island of the Knights"), and to **Riddarholmskyrkan** (May–Aug Mon–Sat 10am–3pm, Sun noon–3pm; Sept Wed, Sat & Sun noon–3pm; 10kr), originally a Franciscan monastery and long the burial place of Swedish royalty. Among others, you'll find the tomb of the unfortunate Gustav II Adolf in the green marble sarcophagus.

Skeppsholmen

Off Gamla Stan's eastern reaches, but unconnected by bridge, the island of **Skeppsholmen** is home to an eclectic clutch of museums, not least the **Moderna Museet** (June–Aug Tues–Thurs 11am–8pm, Fri, Sat & Sun 11am–5pm; Sept–Dec Tues–Thurs noon–8pm, Fri–Sun noon–5pm; 40kr, free Thurs), one of the best modern art museums in Europe, with a collection representing many of the twentieth century's greatest artists – Dalí, Matisse and Picasso, and an impressive stream of Warhol, Lichtenstein, Man Ray and Francis Bacon works. A steep climb up the nearby hill, to the northern tip of the island, leads to the **Östasiatiska Museet** (Tues–Sun Jan–Aug 11am–5pm; Sept–Dec noon–5pm, Tues closes 8pm; 30kr), whose Eastern antiquities display incredible craftsmanship – fifth-century Chinese tomb figures, delicate jade amulets, an awesome assembly of sixth-century Buddhas, Indian watercolours and gleaming bronze Krishnas. By the bridge to the island is the waterfront **National Art Museum** (Tues–Sun Jan–Aug 11am–5pm, Tues 11am–9pm; Sept–Dec noon–5pm, Tues 11am–8pm; 30kr), another impressive collection of applied art – beds slept in by kings, cabinets leaned on by queens, plates eaten off by nobles – from the time when Sweden was a great power, alongside Art Nouveau coffee pots and vases, and examples of Swedish furniture design. Upstairs there is a plethora of European sculpture, mesmerizing sixteenth- and seventeenth-century Russian Orthodox icons, and, among a quality selection of paintings, Rembrandt's *Conspiracy of Claudius Civilis*, one of his largest paintings. There are also minor works by other, later masters, notably Renoir, and canvases by Swedish artists.

Norrmalm and Östermalm

Modern Stockholm lies immediately to the north of Gamla Stan. It's split into two distinct sections: the central **Norrmalm** and the classier, residential streets of **Östermalm** to the east – though there's not much apart from a couple of specialist museums to draw you here. On the waterfront, at the foot of Norrbro, is **Gustav Adolfs Torg**, more a traffic island than a square, with the eighteenth-century **Opera House** its proudest and most notable building. It was here at a masked ball in 1792 that King Gustav III was shot by one Captain Ankarström, an admirer of Rousseau and member of the aristocratic opposition. The story is recorded in Verdi's opera *Un Ballo in Maschera*, and you'll find Gustav's ball costume, as well as the assassin's pistols and mask, displayed in the palace armoury in Gamla Stan. Gustav's statue marks the centre of the square, where, apart from the views, the only affordable entertainment is to rent a fishing rod and try and land a fish in the **Strömmen**, which flows through the centre of the city – a right Stockholmers have enjoyed since the seventeenth century.

Just off the square, at Fredsgatan 2, the **Medelhavsmuseet** is devoted to Mediterranean and Near Eastern Antiquities (Tues–Sun 11am–4pm, Tues closes 9pm; 30kr), with an enormous Egyptian display showing just about every aspect of Egyptian life up to the Christian era. The Cypriot collections are also huge, the largest such gathering outside Cyprus itself, depicting life through a period spanning 6000 years. North of here Klarabergsgatan leads to the **Klara kyrka** (Mon–Fri 10am–6pm, Sat 10am–7pm, Sun 8.30am–6pm), typical of Stockholm's hidden churches, hemmed in on all sides and with a light and flowery eighteenth-century painted interior and an impressive golden pulpit. Back towards the water, Norrmalm's eastern boundary is marked by **Kungsträdgården**, the most fashionable and central of the city's numerous parks – once a royal kitchen garden and now Stockholm's main meeting place, especially in summer when there's almost always something going on. Kungsträdgården reaches north as far as **Hamngatan**, at the western end of which, past the enormous *NK* department store, **Sergels Torg** is modern Stockholm at its most blatant, an unending free show centred around the five seething floors of the **Kulturhuset** (Mon ground floor only 10am–8pm, Tues 11am–10pm, Wed–Fri 11am–6pm, Sat & Sun 11am–5pm), where you'll find exhibitions on contemporary Swedish culture, a reading room, free concerts and a café on the top floor that has the best views of central Stockholm you'll find. North, **Hötorget** has an open-air fruit and veg market and the wonderful indoor **Hötorgshallen** – rambling, gluttonous food halls with ethnic snacks.

From Hötorget parallel streets run north to the **Strindbergsmuseet** (Tues–Fri 10am–4pm, Sat & Sun noon–4pm, Tues also 6–8pm; 20kr), housed in Strindberg's last residence, the so-called "Blue Tower" at Drottninggatan 85, and preserved to the extent that you must put plastic bags on your feet to protect the floors. The study is as he left it on his death, a dark and gloomy place – he wrote with venetian blinds and heavy curtains closed against the sunlight; upstairs is his library, a musty room with all the books behind glass. Close by, set in secluded gardens between Drottninggatan and Sveagatan, the **Adolf Fredrik's kyrka** is an otherwise ordinary eighteenth-century church that was the original burial spot of the French philosopher Descartes, who died in Stockholm in 1650, and is the current resting place of the Swedish prime minister, Olof Palme, who was gunned down in Stockholm in February 1986.

On the opposite side of Norrmalm in Östermalm, is the **Historiska Museet** (April–Dec Tues–Sun 11am–5pm, Thurs closes 8pm; 50kr, gives 20kr reduction to Nordiska Museet), Stockholm's most wide-ranging historical display, comprising the museums of National Antiquity and Monetary History. Ground-floor highlights include a Stone Age household and a mass of Viking weapons, coins and boats, while upstairs there's a worthy collection of medieval church art and architecture, evocatively housed in massive vaulted rooms, including some rare reassembled bits of stave churches uncovered on the Baltic island of Gotland. To get there, take the T-bana to Karlaplan.

Djurgården

Djurgården is Stockholm's nearest large expanse of park. A royal hunting ground throughout the sixteenth to eighteenth centuries, it is actually two distinct park areas separated by the water of Djurgårdsbrunnsviken, which freezes over in winter to provide some central skating. You could walk to the park from Central Station, but it's quite a hike: take the bus instead – #44 from Karlaplan or #47 from Nybroplan – or in summer the ferry from Nybroplan, or Slussen on Skeppsbron (all year).

From the northeast of the park are excellent views from 160-metre-high **Kaknäs TV tower** (mid-April to mid-Sept daily 9–10.30am; mid-Sept to mid-April 9am–6pm; 20kr), Scandinavia's highest building. South over Djurgårdsbron, are numerous museums. Palatial **Nordiska Museet** (late March to Dec Tues, Thurs & Fri noon–5pm, Wed noon–8pm, Sat & Sun 10am–5pm; 50kr, gives 20kr reduction to Hisorika Museet) is a good attempt to represent Swedish cultural history in an accessible fashion, with a particularly good *Same* section. On the ground floor of the cathedral-like interior is Carl Milles' statue of Gustav Vasa, the sixteenth-century king who drove out the Danes. Close by, the **Vasa Museet** (daily mid-June to mid-Aug 9.30am–7pm; rest of year 10am–5pm, Wed also until 8pm; 40kr) is an essential stop, displaying the *Vasa* warship which sank in Stockholm harbour on her maiden voyage in 1628. Preserved in mud for over 300 years, the ship was raised along with 12,000 objects in 1961 and now forms the centrepiece of a startling, purpose-built hall on the water's edge, fully rigged in a cradle of mechanical tackle – surrounding walkways bring you nose to nose with the cannon hatches and restored decorative relief. Adjacent exhibition halls and presentations on several levels take care of all the retrieved bits and pieces, along with displays relating to contemporary social and political life, films and videos – all with excellent English notes. East of here, **Skansen** (daily Jan–April & Sept–Dec 9am–5pm; May–Aug 9am–10pm; 40kr) is a thoughtful and surprisingly enjoyable open-air museum with 150 recon-structed buildings, from a whole town to windmills and farms, laid out on a region-by-region basis, with each section having its own daily activities that anyone can join in. Best of the buildings are the small *Same* dwellings, warm and functional, and the crafts-men's workshops in the old town quarter; and you can also potter around a small zoo and a bizarre aquarium (35kr). Immediately opposite Skansen's main gates, **Gröna Lund Tivoli** (May to mid-Sept daily noon–10/11pm/midnight; June closed Mon; restricted hours in winter; 40kr) is not a patch on its more famous namesake in Copenhagen, though it's decidedly cleaner and less seedy.

Södermalm and Långholmen

It's worth venturing beyond Slussen's traffic interchange for the heights of **Södermalm**'s crags, an area largely neglected by most visitors to the city. The perched buildings are vaguely forbidding, but get beyond the speeding main roads skirting the island and a lively and surprisingly green area unfolds – one that's still, at heart, emphati-cally working-class. By bus, take the #48 or #53 from Tegelbacken, or use the T-bana and get off at either Slussen or Medborgarplatsen. Walking, you reach the island over a double bridge from Gamla Stan, just to the south of which is the rewarding **Stadsmuseet** (Tues–Thurs 11am–7/9pm, Fri–Mon 11am–5pm; 15kr), hidden in a base-ment courtyard, which houses a set of collections relating to the city's history as a sea port and industrial centre. Nearby, take a look at the **Katarina kyrka**, rebuilt in Renaissance style in the eighteenth century. On this site the victims of the so-called "Stockholm Blood Bath" were buried in 1520, the betrayed nobility of Sweden who had opposed King Christian II's Danish invasion, burned as heretics outside the city walls.

Whether you stop in Södermalm or not, the buses and T-bana trains come this way for the island of **Långholmen**, just off its western side. There's a popular **beach** here, which gets packed in the summer, a chance to swim and plenty of shady walks through the island's trees, as well as the city's best youth hostel. You don't have to come through

Södermalm to reach Långholmen – though if you do, get off the T-bana at Hornstull and follow the signs. In summer there's a more direct **ferry** from Stadshuset, which drops you right by the hostel.

Eating and drinking

Self-catering, the *Hötorgshallen* in Hötorget is a cheap and varied indoor market, awash with small cafés and ethnic snacks. The three main areas for decent eating, day or night, are Norrmalm, Gamla Stan and Södermalm. It's most expensive to eat in the old town, but **set lunch** deals make even that affordable. Drinking in **bars** is expensive, though competition makes Stockholm more affordable. Wherever there's live music you'll pay a cover charge of 30–50kr, as well as 5–6kr to leave your coat at the cloakroom. There's a fairly fine line between cafés, restaurants and bars in Stockholm, many offering music and entertainment in the evening and food during the day.

Cafés and restaurants

Café Art, Västerlånggatan 60–62, Gamla Stan. A fifteenth-century cellar-café with massive sandwiches, good coffee and cakes.

Daily News Café, Kungsträdgården, by *Sverigehuset* tourist centre, Norrmalm. A swish bar/restaurant serving a tasty 50kr lunch and a late-night menu for 50–80kr a dish.

Hard Rock Café, Sveavägen 75, Norrmalm. Loud rock music, hefty burger meals from around 70kr and the obligatory queue.

Hermans, Stora Nygatan 11. Non-earthy vegetarian place; 50kr lunches and 60kr dinners until 7.30pm.

Kaffegillet, Trångsund, Gamla Stan. Fourteenth-century cellar-restaurant with traditional Swedish food. Lunches around the 50kr mark.

Lasse i Parken, Högalidsgatan 56, Södermalm. Café housed in an eighteenth-century house with a pleasant garden. T-bana Hornstull.

Lilla Budapest, Götgatan 27, Södermalm. A good stop for weighty Hungarian lunches, and with a bar whose drinks are a few crowns cheaper than most other places.

Markurells, Vasagatan 26, Norrmalm. Popular and cheap, mainly Swedish menu – lunch 50kr.

Operakällaren, Gustav Adolfs Torg, Norrmalm. Pricy restaurant but with a fabulous daily *smörgåsbord* for 250kr per person. Lunch in the attached *Café Opera* is 100kr.

Pelikan, Blekingegatan 40, Södermalm. Atmospheric pub with good traditional food.

Samborombon, Stora Nygatan 28, Gamla Stan. Argentinian restaurant serving steaks with excellent home-made sauce as well as South American wines.

Slingerbulten, Stora Nygatan 24, Gamla Stan. Traditional Swedish food – good lunches from 55kr.

Soldaten Svejk, Östgötagatan 15, Södermalm. Lively Czech-run joint popular with students. Cheap (40kr) evening meals Mon & Tues.

Teatercafeet, Stadsteater, Sergels Torg, Norrmalm. A daily 45–50kr set lunch Monday to Friday, always including a vegetarian dish, and a reasonably priced à la carte menu.

Bars, brasseries and pubs

Brasserie Vau de Ville, Hamngatan 17, Kungsträdgården, Norrmalm. Popular brasserie with snacks and drinks, as well as a regular menu.

Fenix, Götgatan 40, Södermalm. Trendy and lively American-style bar. Good selection of beers and cheapish food.

Gråmunken, Västerlånggatan 18, Gamla Stan. Cosy café with live jazz several nights a week.

Halfway Inn, Wollmar Yxkullsgatan, opposite T-bana Maria Torget, Södermalm. Best of several English-style pubs on Södermalm with decent bar lunches.

Kristina, Västerlånggatan 68, Gamla Stan. Café by day (with a 50kr lunch); happy hour 4–8pm when beer is only 30kr, and live jazz after 8pm.

Söders Hjärta, Bellmansgatan 22, Södermalm. Swanky restaurant with a less intimidating and friendly bar on the mezzanine floor.

Nightlife

There's plenty to keep you occupied at night in Stockholm but the drawback, again, is the price. As well as the weekend, Wednesday night is an active time, with usually plenty going on and queues at the more popular places. At specifically **live music venues** you'll pay 60–80kr entrance. For up-to-date **what's on information**, check the Friday supplement of the *Dagens Nyheter* newspaper or the latest issue of *Stockholm This Week*, free from the tourist centre. Popular venues in the summer are Kungsträdgården and Skansen, where there's always something going on.

Live music

Cityhallen, Drottninggatan 28, Norrmalm. A big, bright bar/restaurant with live rock and R&B nightly; cheapish food and drink too.

Engelen, Kornhamnstorg 59, Gamla Stan. Jazz, rock and blues nightly until 3am.

Fasching, Kungsgatan. Stockholm's premier jazz venue, with local acts and big names.

Kaos, Stora Nygatan 21, Gamla Stan. Live music from 9pm nightly; rock bands on Fridays and Saturdays in the cellar and reasonable late-night food.

Stampen, Stora Nygatan 5, Gamla Stan. Long-established and rowdy jazz club.

Tre Backar, Tegnérgatan 12–14, Norrmalm; T-bana Rådmansgatan. Good, cheap pub with a live cellar venue. Music every night; open until midnight (closed Sun).

Discos and clubs

Daily News Café, Kungsträdgården, Norrmalm. Called *Melody* at night, there are two discos inside this café/restaurant, both doing good business. A fairly young crowd.

La Isla, Fridhemsplan. Latin platters into the small hours underground in the Fridhemsplan T-bana station complex.

Pride, Sveavägen. Central Stockhom's premier gay venue with a large restaurant, bookshop and regular live music.

Listings

Airlines *British Airways*, Norrmalmstorg 1 (☎679 78 00); *Delta*, Kungsgatan 18 (☎796 94 00); *Finnair*, Norrmalmstorg 1 (☎679 93 30); *KLM*, Sveavägen 24–26 (☎676 08 80); *Lufthansa*, Norrmalmstorg 1 (☎611 22 88); *SAS*, Klarabergsviadukten 72 (☎020/91 01 50).

American Express Birger Jarlsgatan 1 (Mon–Fri 8.30am–5pm, Sat 10am–1pm).

Bicycle rental *Cykelspecializten Hoj In*, Karlsbergsvägen 55.

Car rental *Avis*, Sveavägen 61 (☎34 99 10); *Budget*, Sveavägen 155 (☎33 43 83); *Europcar/ InterRent*, Lindhagensplan (☎657 25 75).

Doctor *Medical Care Information* (☎44 92 00).

Embassies *Australia*, Sergels Torg 12 (☎613 29 00); *Canada*, Tegelbakken 4 (☎613 99 00); *Great Britain*, Skarpögatan 6–8 (☎667 01 40); *Ireland*, Östermalmsgatan 97 (☎661 80 05); *Netherlands*, Götgatan 16a (☎24 71 80); *USA*, Strandvägen 101 (☎783 53 00).

Exchange Bank at Arlanda airport is open daily 7am–10pm; *Forex* offices at Central Station (daily 7am–9pm) and Cityterminalen (Mon–Fri 8am–9pm, Sat 8am–4pm).

Ferries Tickets for Finland from *Silja Line*, Kungsgatan 2 at Stureplan (☎22 21 40); *Viking Line*, Central Station (☎714 56 00); *Birka Cruises*, Södermalmstorg 2 (☎714 55 20).

Gay Stockholm The *Gay Community Centre*, Sveavägen 59 (T-bana Rådmansgatan), has a restaurant, café, bar, disco and bookshop, counselling and meeting facilities.

Laundry Self-service laundries at Sturegatan 4 and St Eriksgatan 97.

Left luggage On the lower level at Central Station (daily 7am–11.30pm; 40kr); there are safe lockers, too, all over Central Station (25kr, 20kr or 15kr), at the *Hantverkshuset* youth hostel and the *Silja* and *Viking* ferry terminals.

Pharmacy 24-hr service from *C.W Scheele*, Klarabergsgatan 64.

Police HQ at Agnegatan 33–37 (☎769 30 00).
Post office Vasagatan 28–34 (Mon–Fri 8am–6.30pm, Sat 10am–4pm).
Telephones *TeleCentre* at Central Station (daily 8am–9pm).
Travel agency *Kilroy Travels*, Kungsgatan 4 (☎23 45 15).

Millesgarden and Drottningholm

Just a short way to the northeast of the city centre, on the mainly residential island of
Lindingö, the **Millesgarden** (Jan–April & Oct–Dec Tues–Sun 11am–4pm; May–Sept
daily 10am–5pm; June–Aug Wed closes 9pm; 30kr) is the outdoor sculpture garden of
Carl Milles (1875–1955), one of the greatest of Sweden's sculptors. Arranged on a
number of terraces carved from the steep cliffs, this is one of the most enticing visual
attractions within easy reach of central Stockholm – to get there, take the T-bana to
Ropsten and then go on by train one stop to Torvikstorg. Milles' animated, classical
figures perch precariously on pillars, overlooking the distant harbour, while the
sculptor's former home houses his staggeringly rich collection of Greek and Roman
antiquities.

Try also to visit the harmonious royal palace of **Drottningholm** (May–Aug daily
11am–4.30pm; Sept Mon–Fri 1–3.30pm, Sat & Sun noon–3.30pm; 30kr), beautifully
located on the shores of leafy Lovön island, 11km west of the centre. It's a lovely
fifty-minute boat trip there, costing 70kr return; ferries leave every thirty minutes from
Stadshusbron to coincide with the opening times. You could also take the T-bana to
Brommaplan and then bus #301 from there – a less thrilling ride, but free with the
Stockholm Card. Modelled in a thoroughly French style, Drottningholm is perhaps the
greatest achievement of the architects Tessin – father and son – and was begun in 1662
on the orders of King Karl X's widow, Eleonora. Inside the palace itself, good English
notes are available to help you sort out each room's detail, a riot of Rococo decoration
which largely dates from the time when the palace was bestowed as a wedding gift on
Princess Louisa Ulrika; since 1981 the Swedish royal family has been using the palace
as their permanent home, a move that has accelerated efforts to restore parts of the
palace to their original appearance. Though it's an expensive extra, try not to miss the
Court Theatre (tours daily May–Aug noon–4.30pm; Sept 1–3.30pm; 30kr) in the
grounds, which dates from 1766. The original backdrops and stage machinery are still
in place, complete with a display of the eighteenth-century special effects – wind and
thunder machines, trapdoors and simulated lightning. With time to spare, the
extensive palace grounds also yield the **Chinese Pavilion** (April & Sept daily
1–3.30pm; May–Aug daily 11am–4.30pm; 20kr), a sort of eighteenth-century royal
summer house.

Uppsala

An hour north of Stockholm, **UPPSALA** is regarded as the historical and religious
centre of the country, and it's a tranquil daytime alternative to the capital, with a
delightful river-cut centre, not to mention an active student-geared nightlife. Centre of
the medieval town, a ten-minute walk from the train station, is the great **Domkyrkan**
(daily June–Aug 8am–8pm; Sept–May 8am–6pm; free), Scandinavia's largest cathedral,
built as a Gothic brag to the people of Trondheim that even their mighty church could
be overshadowed. The echoing interior remains impressive, particularly the French
Gothic ambulatory, sided by tiny chapels, one of which contains a lively set of
fourteenth-century wall paintings that tell the legend of Saint Erik, Sweden's patron
saint, while another contains his relics. Poke around and you'll also find the tombs of
Reformation rebel Gustav Vasa and his son Johan III, and that of Linnaeus, the greatest

of all botanists, who lived in Uppsala. Opposite, the onion-domed **Gustavianum** (early June to late Aug daily 11am–3pm; March to early June & late Aug–Nov Sat & Sun noon–3pm; 10kr per museum, 20kr for combined ticket to four sites) was built in 1625 as part of the university, and is much touted for its tidily preserved anatomical theatre. The same building houses a couple of small collections of Egyptian, Classical and Nordic antiquities. The current **University** building is the imposing nineteenth-century Renaissance edifice over the way, among whose alumni are Anders Celsius, inventor of the temperature scale. No one will mind if you stroll in for a quick look, but to see the locked rooms – including the glorious Augsberg Art Cabinet, an ebony treasure chest presented to Gustav II Adolf – you have to ask someone in the office inside or catch a guided tour (July to late Aug 11am, 1pm & 2pm; 20kr). A little way beyond is the **Carolina Rediviva** (mid-June to mid-Aug Mon–Fri 9am–7.30pm, Sat 9am–6pm, Sun 1–3.30pm; rest of year Mon–Fri 9am–8.30pm, Sat 9am–5.30pm; 5kr charge Sat afternoon & Sunday only), one of Scandinavia's largest libraries, with a collection of rare letters and other paraphernalia, including a beautiful sixth-century Silver Bible and Mozart's manuscript for *The Magic Flute*. After this, the **castle** (late-June to mid-Aug Mon–Fri 10am–6pm, Sat & Sun 10am–5pm; April to late June and last two weeks of Aug Mon–Sat 11am–3pm, Sun 11am–4pm; 15kr) is a disappointment. In 1702 a fire that destroyed three-quarters of the city did away with much of the castle, and only one side and two towers remain of what was once an opulent palace.

Practicalities

Uppsala's **train** and **bus station** are adjacent to each other, not far from the **tourist office** at Fyris Torg 8 (Mon–Fri 10am–6pm), which hands out an English guide to the town, with a map inside. On summer weekends the tourist office inside the castle is a better bet. There are two **youth hostels**: the *YMCA Interpoint* (July to mid-Aug; ☎018/27 66 35; ②) 2km from the centre at the corner of Svartbäcksgatan and Torbjörnsgatan – take bus #10 from Stora Torget or #25 from Dragarbrunnsgatan; the beautifully sited official hostel is 6km south at Sunnerstavägen 24 (May–Aug; ☎018/32 42 20; ②) – bus #14 from Dragarbrunnsgatan. There are a few cheapish **hotels** in the centre, like the *Samariterhemt* on Hamnpladsen (☎018/13 03 45; ⑤). For **camping**, there's a site 7km out by Lake Mälaren at Graneberg (May–Aug), which also has two to four berth cabins for 200–250kr a night; take bus #14 from Dragarbrunnsgatan. For **snacks**, try the *Alma* café in the basement of the university building, though it's difficult to beat lunch at *Barowiak*, a large wooden house immediately below the castle off Nedre Slottsgatan, with a good range of vegetarian and meat-based dishes during the day, and live bands in the evening. Similar and equally popular is the *Café Katalin* on Svartbäcksgatan, with sporadic jazz nights. The summer brings a glut of open-air cafés around town, the most popular on the river: *Åkanten* below St Erik's Torg is among the best.

Gamla Uppsala

Five kilometres north of town three huge **barrows**, royal burial mounds dating back to the sixth century, mark the original site of Uppsala, **GAMLA UPPSALA** – reached on bus #14 (hourly Mon–Sat) or #54 (Sun) from Dragarbrunnsgatan. This was a pagan settlement, and a place of ancient sacrificial rites: every ninth year the festival of *Fröblot* demanded the death of nine people, hanged from a nearby tree until their corpses rotted. The pagan temple where this took place is marked by the Christian **Gamla Uppsala kyrka** (daily April–Aug 9.30am–8pm; Sept–March 9.30am–dusk), built when the Swedish kings first took baptism in the new faith. Look in for the faded wall paintings and the tomb of Celsius. There's little else to Gamla Uppsala, which is perhaps the reason the site remains so atmospheric.

SOUTHERN SWEDEN

The **south** of Sweden is a mixed bag, a nest of coastal provinces, extensive lake and forest regions and gracefully ageing cities, much of the area, especially the southwest coast, the target of Swedish holidaymakers, which means it's chock-full of campsites, beaches and cycle tracks, though rather thin on specific sights. But there is also real historical interest to the southern provinces, not least in the cities that line the coast, grandest of which is **Gothenburg**, Sweden's second city and, beyond its gargantuan shipyards, worth more time than the traditional post-ferry exodus allows. South of here, **Helsingborg**, a stone's throw from Denmark, and **Malmö**, still solidly sixteenth-century at its centre, are both worth at least a stopoff, and **Lund**, a medieval cathedral and university town, is an obvious and enjoyable point between the two. To the east, Renaissance **Kristianstad** is a less obvious target than the south coast resorts, but repays a stop on the southern routes to and from Stockholm, as does **Kalmar**, a historic fortress town further north towards the capital. Close by, the island of **Gotland** has long been a domestic tourist haven for its climate, beaches and medieval Hanseatic capital, **Visby**, and is easy and inexpensive to reach by ferry from the Småland port of Västervik, as well as from Nynäshamn, south of Stockholm.

Gothenburg

Arriving in **GOTHENBURG** by ship provides an abrupt, if misleading, introduction to Scandinavia's largest port. Ferry arrivals from Harwich are shuttled in alongside the dock-strewn river, a ride offering glimpses of colossal industrial concentration. Coming from Denmark, the images are less fleeting as the ship or catamaran pulls up right in the centre of the port and shipyards. Although the occasional rusting and abandoned dry dock bears witness to the effects of the recession in the shipping industry, it's difficult to remain unimpressed by the sheer bulk of the surviving and working hardware. And beyond the shipyards Gothenburg is the prettiest of Sweden's cities, with traffic-free streets and broad avenues split and ringed by a canal system of simple elegance.

Arrival and information

You're likely to arrive in Gothenburg by **ferry**. *Scandinavian Seaways* ferries from England dock well out of the centre at Skandiahamn. A special bus waits outside to fill up and then shuttles into the city, to Nils Ericsonsplatsen – tickets 35kr, valid one hour. (For *DFDS* departures, catch the bus from Nils Ericsonsplatsen 90min before the ship leaves.) Other arrival points string out along the docks. *Stena* line ferries from Frederikshavn in Denmark dock within twenty minutes' walk of the centre, their direct competition, *Sea Catamarans*, a further ten minutes out, and the Kiel ferries another ten (3km from the centre in all). Bus #86 runs past all three to the centre, as does tram #3 which continues on to the Nordengården **youth hostel**. **Trains** arrive at Central Station on Drottningtorget. **Buses** from destinations north of Gothenburg use Nils Ericsonsplatsen, immediately behind; those from the south, and Stockholm and Malmo, use the Heden terminal, behind Trädgårdsföreningen at the junction of Parkgatan and Södra Vägen. The **airport** is east of the city, linked by bus with Drottningtorget every fifteen minutes (30min; 50kr; 12 units – see below).

Gothenburg has two **tourist offices**: a kiosk in *Nordstan*, the shopping centre next to Central Station (Mon–Fri 9.30am–6pm, Sat 9.30am–3pm), and a **main office** on the canal front at Kungsportsplatsen 2 (Jan–April & Sept–Dec Mon–Fri 9am–5pm, Sat 10am–2pm; May Mon–Fri 9am–6pm, Sat & Sun 10am–2pm; June–Aug daily 9am–6/8pm). Both have free maps and a room booking service (25kr fee). They also sell the **Gothenburg Card**, giving unlimited bus and tram travel, free or half-price museum entry and other concessions, including a free day trip to Fredrikshavn on the *Stena Line* ferry. The card is valid for 24 hours (120kr), 48 hours (200kr) or 72 hours (250kr).

Gothenburg is perhaps the most immediately attractive Swedish city around which to **walk**, though you can't avoid using the **public transport** system, made up of trams and buses. Each city journey costs two 7kr units (*kuponger*), available from the driver, who can also sell you the magnetic *Value Card* (120kr) which drops the unit price to 5.5kr (4.4kr from 9am–3pm) and can be used for several people. Just get on and punch "2" for city rides and "BYTE" if you are continuing on another bus or tram. To further reduce costs, buy the same card for 100kr or a 50kr card from *Tid Punkten* offices (see listings) which also sell the **24-hour pass** for 35kr.

Accommodation

Of the **hostels**, the private *Nordengården*, Stockholmsgatan 16 (☎031/19 66 31; ②), is most central, reached on tram #1 or #3 to Stockholmsgatan or #6 to Redbergplatsen. *Ostkupan*, Mejerigatan 2 (June–Aug; ☎031/40 10 50; ②), is a large and slightly pricier official hostel, reached by bus #64 from Brunnsparken to Gräddgatan, or tram #1, #3 or #6 to Redbergsplatsen and bus #62 to Gräddgatan. The *M/S Seaside*, on Packhuskajen (☎031/10 10 35; ④), is a moored ship with cabin beds, 45kr for breakfast and 45kr extra for sheets; this may soon move into one of the nearby Maritime Museum ships. If it's vital to stay right in the middle of things, take advantage of the tourist office's special **hotel** deal, whereby 310–550kr per person gets you a room in a central hotel, with breakfast and free Gothenburg Card. The package operates every weekend, and daily from mid-June to mid-August. If this is beyond your budget, the tourist office can book **private rooms** for 130kr a head, plus a 50kr fee. Of **hotels**, *Aveny Turist*, Södravägen 2 (☎031/20 52 86; ③), and the *Hotel Allén*, Parkgatan 10 (☎031/10 14 50; ④), are both near the Heden bus terminal. The *M.E. Pensionat*, Chalmersgatan 27a (☎031/20 70 30; ⑤), is another good bet and the *City Hotel*, Lorensbergsgatan 6 (☎031/18 00 25; ④), has a good location on a street parallel to Avenyn. All these drop a category or two at weekends. The all-year *Kärralunds* **campsite** (140kr per pitch) is 4km out (tram #5 to Welandergatan) and has four-bed cabins for 400kr and an attached **hostel** for 90kr a night. For beaches, the two **campsites** at ASKIM, 12km out, are better; notably *Askims*, open May to mid-August, which has cabins. Catch the *Blå Express* (every 15mins from 5am–midnight; 25mins; 3units) from Drottningtorget.

The City

King Gustav II Adolf, looking for western trade, founded Gothenburg in the early seventeenth century as a response to the high tolls charged by the Danes for using the narrow sound between the two countries. As a Calvinist and businessman, Gustav much admired Dutch merchants, inviting them to trade and live in Gothenburg, and it's their influence that shaped the city, parts of which have an oddly Dutch feel about them. The area defined by the central canal represents what's left of old Gothenburg, centring on **Gustav Adolfs Torg**, a windswept square flanked by the nineteenth-century **Börshuset**, or Exchange building, and the fine **Rådhus**, originally built in 1672. Around the corner, the **Kronhuset**, off Kronhusgatan, is a typical seventeenth-century Dutch construction, built in 1643, and looking like the backdrop to a Vermeer. The cobbled courtyard outside is flanked by the mid-eighteenth-century **Kronhusbodarna** (Tues–Sun 11am–4pm), now togged up as period craft shops selling sweets and souvenirs. The **Historical Museum**, Norra Hamngatan 12 (Jan–April & Sept–Dec Tues–Sat noon–4pm, Tues also 6–9pm, Sun 11am–5pm; May–Aug Mon–Sat noon–4pm, Sun 11am–5pm; 20kr), is comprehensive and particularly strong on local matters, housed in the eighteenth-century headquarters of the *East India Company*, although it's only rescued from mediocrity by the archeological collections and displays on seventeenth-century Gothenburg. Close by, the **Maritima Centrum** (March, April, Oct & Nov Sat & Sun 11am–5pm; May–Aug daily 11am–5pm; 35kr) allows you to clamber aboard a destroyer and submarine moored at the quayside and is due for major expansion in 1994. It is still worth coming down here to have a look around, the shipyards beyond like a rusting Meccano set put into sharp perspective by the new technology industries.

Crossing the canal from Kungsportsplatsen, Kungsportsavenyn runs all the way up to Götaplatsen, a wide strip known simply as **Avenyn** that is Gothenburg's showiest thoroughfare, once lined by private houses fronted by gardens and now by a length of pavement restaurants and brasseries. About halfway down, the excellent **Röhsska Museum of Arts and Crafts** at Vasagatan 37–39 (May–Aug Mon–Fri 11am–4pm, Sat & Sun 10am–5pm; Sept–April Wed–Fri 11am–4pm, Tues 11am–9pm, Sat & Sun 10am–5pm; 25kr) celebrates among other things Swedish design through the ages. At the top end, **Götaplatsen** is the modern cultural centre of Gothenburg, home to a concert hall, theatre and **Art Museum** (daily Mon–Fri 11am–4pm, Sat & Sun 10am–5pm; Sept–April closed Mon, Wed until 9pm; 25kr), whose enormous collections include a good selection of Impressionist paintings, Pop Art and Swedish works. Beyond here, on the edge of the centre, five minutes' walk away, **Liseberg** (daily mid-April to Sept; 35kr) is an amusement park with some high-profile rides and acres of gardens, restaurants and fast food. In the opposite direction, great views of the harbour and around can be had from the excursion boats that run from Stenpiren to the **Nya Elfsborg Fortress** (early May to early Sept daily 9.45am–5.30pm), a seventeenth-century island defence guarding the harbour entrance whose surviving buildings have been turned into a museum and café.

Eating and drinking

There's no shortage of places to **eat** in Gothenburg, and the city's range of ethnic restaurants is particularly good, reflecting its trading past. For **picnic food**, the *Stora Saluhallen*, the indoor market in Kungstorget (Mon–Fri 9.30am–6pm, Sat 9.30am–2pm), is tempting beyond words and it houses the two cheapest snack bars in town and *Torg Köket*, a no-nonsense cafeteria with kebabs, felafel and fish and chips for 30–35kr. Many of the most stylish and glitzy places to eat flank Avenyn; less obvious but more interesting and usually cheaper areas to ferret around are the streets clustered on Haga Nygatan and further west off Linnégatan. *Vasa Pizzabutik*, Föreninsgatan 34, and *Pizzabutik Rimini* at Långgatan 1, are both good targets for budget pizza to eat in or take away. For **sit-down food**, the student canteen, *Kåren*, Götabergsgatan 17, has the cheapest deal in town, with set lunches for 30kr, though if you can do without meat you can't beat the vegetarian and vegan meals for 45–55kr at *Solrosen*, Kaponjärgatan 4a, which turns into a lively drinking venue at night. *Krakow*, Karlgustavsgatan 28, a central, cheap Polish eatery, with good Polish nosh and booze, challenges the reasonably-priced Czech food at *Gyllene Prag*, Sveagatan 25, for the students' attentions. *Hemma Hos*, Haga Nygatan 12, serves some of the best lunches along this street for 55kr, or you could settle for huge open sandwiches at *Fröken Olssens Kafe*, Östra Latmgatan 14, serving equally well as a stop for cake and great coffee.

There's an excellent choice of places to **drink** in Gothenburg, some staying open well into the small hours. Avenyn is the focal point of much of night-time Gothenburg, with *Brasserie Lipp* at no. 8 one of the smartest hang-outs, and *Junggrens Café* at no. 37 filling a more low-key slot complete with pastoral murals. At the junction of Avenyn and Kristinelundsgatan, *Tvåkanten* is an amiable coffee bar with seats outside in the summer. *C Van*, Linnegatan 23, is an excellent watering hole with cheap drinks, a small restaurant and occasional live music. More centrally, there's no alcohol but an amiable neo-Bohemian atmosphere until late and occasional live bands at *Café Norrlands*, Västra Hamngatan 20, and a sharper edge at *Kompaniet* a block away at Kyrkogatan 21.

Listings

Car rental *Avis*, at Central Station (☎031/80 57 80); *Europcar*, Stampgatan 220 (☎031/80 53 90); *Hertz*, Stampgatan 16 (☎031/80 37 30).

Exchange *Forex* exchange office inside Central Station (daily 8am–9pm).

Pharmacy *Apoteket Vasen*, Götagatan 10, in the *Nordstan* shopping centre; open 24hr.

Police Skånegatan 5 (☎031/61 80 00).

Post office Main office in Drottningtorget (Mon–Fri 8am–6pm, Sat 9am–noon).

Telephones Hvitfeldsplatsen 9 (Mon–Fri 9am–6pm, Sat 10am–1pm).

Transport offices *Tid Punkten*, Drottningtorget, Nils Ericsonsplatsen and Norra Hamngatan 18. Generally open Mon–Fri 7am–7/10pm, Sat & Sun 9am–6pm.

Travel agent *Kilroy Travels*, Berzeliigatan 5 (☎031/20 08 60). *Stena Lines* and *Sea Catamaran* both have offices in Nordstan and the *Scandinavian Seaways* building is opposite the main tourist office.

Helsingborg

At **HELSINGBORG** only a narrow sound separates Sweden from Denmark; indeed, Helsingborg was Danish for most of the Middle Ages, with a castle controlling the southern regions of what is now Sweden. The town's enormously important strategic position meant that it bore the brunt of repeated attacks and rebellions, the Swedes conquering the town on six separate occasions, only to lose it back to the Danes each time. Finally, in 1710, a terrible battle saw off the Danes for the last time, and the battered town lay dormant for almost two hundred years, depopulated and abandoned. Only in the nineteenth century, when the harbour was expanded and the railway constructed, did Helsingborg find new prosperity, though today the town finds it hard to persuade people to stay for longer than it takes to make their train connections.

The **waterfront** is the obvious place to begin explorations, though admittedly beyond the busy harbours there's not much to see. Up from Hamntorget and the harbours, the massive, neo-Gothic **Rådhus** marks the bottom of **Stortorget**, the long thin square sloping up to the lower battlements of what's left of Helsingborg's castle, the **kärnan** or keep (daily June–Aug 10am–8pm; Sept–March 10am–3pm; April & May 10am–5pm; 10kr), a fourteenth-century brick tower, only survivor from the original fortress. The views from the top are worth the entrance fee although you don't miss much from the lower (free) battlements. Off Stortorget, **Norra Storgatan** contains Helsingborg's oldest buildings, attractive seventeenth- and eighteenth-century merchants' houses with quiet courtyards. On Södra Storgatan, the **Stadsmuseet** (May–Aug Mon–Fri 10am–5pm, Sat & Sun noon–5pm; Sept–April Tues–Sat 11am–4pm, Sun noon–4pm; 10kr) is a glorious mess of bric-a-brac – dolls, clothes, paintings, frying pans and stuffed animals.

Apart from the Sundbussern passenger ferry to Helsingør which pulls up across an arm of the docks, all **ferries**, **trains** and **buses** arrive in a spanking new harbourside **central terminal**, also home to the **tourist office** (June–Aug Mon–Fri 9am–8pm, Sat 10am–5pm, Sun 11am–5pm; Sept–May Mon–Fri 8am–6pm), which books **private rooms** for 125kr per person plus a steep 70kr booking fee. Otherwise, cheapest central **hotels** are *Linnea*, Prästgatan 4 (☎042/11 46 60; ⑥), which drops prices in summer and at weekends, and *Bristol*, Prästgatan 4 (☎042/11 46 80; ②). The *Thalassa* **youth hostel** (☎042/11 03 84; ②) is open all year – four kilometres' walk north along Drottninggatan or get a #7 bus (#44 after 7pm) from outside the ferry terminal. For **camping**, try the waterfront site at Råå, 5km southeast; bus #1A or #1B from outside the Rådhus.

You shouldn't have any difficulty at all in finding somewhere to eat. *La Pikant*, Nedre Holländeregatan (junction with Södergatan), serves 45kr meals all day, and back towards the centre there's the *Tex Mex Bar*, Södra Storgatan 10, with Mexican and vegetarian food. *Bläckfisken* at Billeplatsen 1, the cobbled square leading up from St Maria kyrka, serves a pizza lunch for 45kr. For no-frills **drinking**, the *Charles Dickens Pub* at Södergatan 43 has an English pub menu and the cheapest beer in town.

Lund

Just forty minutes south of Helsingborg and fifteen minutes from Malmö, **LUND** is the most obvious target for a trip, a beautiful university town with a quiet medieval centre and some of the best nightlife of the region. Its weather-beaten **Domkyrkan** (Mon–Fri 8am–6pm, Sat 9.30am–5pm, Sun 9.30am–6pm), consecrated in 1145, is considered by many to be Scandinavia's finest medieval building, with a plain interior that's home to a delicate, semicircular apse with a gleaming fifteenth-century altarpiece and a mosaic of Christ surrounded by angels – although what draws most attention is a fourteenth-century astronomical clock, revealing an ecclesiastical Punch and Judy show daily at noon and 3pm. Look into the crypt, underneath the apse, littered with tombs and elaborately carved tombstones and a blaze of low pillars, sculpted with a vivid imagination.

Outside the cathedral, **Kyrkogatan**, lined with staunch, solid, nineteenth-century civic buildings, leads into the main square, **Stortorget**, off which **Kattesund** is home to an excavated set of glassed-in medieval walls. Adjacent is the **Drottens Kyrkoruin** (Mon–Thurs 10.30am–12.30pm, Sat & Sun 10am–2pm; June–Aug also Thurs 4–6pm), the remains of a medieval church in the basement of another modern building, but the real interest is in the powerful atmosphere of the old streets behind the Domkyrkan. **Kiliansgatan**, directly behind the cathedral's apse, is a lovely cobbled street, whose fine houses sport tiny courtyards and gardens. In this web of streets, **Kulturen** (daily May–Sept 11am–5pm; Oct–April noon–4pm; 30kr) is a mixture of indoor and open-air collections of southern Swedish art, silverware, ceramics, musical instruments, etc. Finish off your meanderings with a visit to the **Botaniska Trädgård** (daily 6am–8pm) just beyond, an extensive botanical garden with some shaded pathways.

Trains arrive on the western edge of town, an easy walk from the centre. The **tourist office** opposite the Domkyrkan (June–Aug Mon–Fri 10am–6pm, Sat & Sun 10am–2pm, also Thurs 4–6pm; Sept–May Mon–Fri 9am–5pm;) hands out maps. Lund makes an appealing alternative stopover to Malmö or Helsingborg by virtue of private rooms which the tourist office can book from around 130kr plus a 40kr booking fee. Its unusual **youth hostel**, *Tåget*, Vävaregatan 22 (☎046/14 28 20; ②) packs you into three-tiered sleeping compartments of six 1940s carriages parked on a branch line behind the train station; turn right and follow the signs. There are plenty of cheap places to eat. *Brasserie Lundia*, on Knut den Storesgatan near the station, is cheap and atmospheric; *Café Grädd Hyllan* a couple of doors further up serves 50kr lunches in a wicker chair-filled conservatory; *Gloria's*, and the neighbouring *Petri Bar* are two of the foci of termtime student revelry on St Petrikyrkosgatan. *Chrougen*, the student union café in the university grounds, does a 45kr lunch, or you could try the vegetarian equivalent at *Magasin Wåhlin*, Bredgatan 28.

Malmö

The third largest city in Sweden, **MALMÖ**, won back for Sweden from Denmark by Karl X in the seventeenth century, was a handsome city then and now, with a cobbled medieval core that has a lived-in, workaday feel worlds apart from the museum-piece quality of most other Swedish town centres. If you're planning to come from Copenhagen by catamaran, a quick and easy crossing, Malmö will be your first sight of Sweden – and it's not a bad introduction at all.

Arrival and accommodation

Ferries and catamarans from Copenhagen dock at various terminals along Skeppsbron. Shop around as prices vary from 29kr to 90kr one way, depending on the time of year and company; *Pilen* are usually the cheapest. Just up from here, **Central**

Station is where **trains** arrive, including the private *Pågatåg* services (to and from Helsingborg, Lund and Ystad; rail passes valid). The main **bus terminal** is outside Central Station, in Centralplan, though buses from Stockholm, Helsingborg and Gothenburg arrive at Slussplan, east of Central Station, at the end of Norra Vallgatan. The **ferry** from Dragör to Limhamn , just south of Copenhagen (25kr one way), drops you at the southwestern edge of town – bus #12 (1hr; 12kr) runs up nearby Strandgatan to Central Station.

From Central Station, cross the road and you'll find the **tourist office** at Skeppsbron 2 (June–Aug Mon–Fri 9am–7pm, Sat 9am–5pm, Sun 11am–4pm; Sept–May Mon–Fri 9am–5pm, Sat 9am–1pm). This stocks the handy *Malmö This Month* and sells the **Malmö Card**, which gives free museum entry, plus discounts on the crossings to Copenhagen, though, unusually, no discount on public transport; it costs 110kr for 24 hours and is also available for 48 hours (200kr) and 72 hours (280kr). The tourist office also sells a good-value **round trip ticket** (145kr), valid for the train to Lund and Helsingborg, the crossing to Helsingør, travel on to Copenhagen (museum discounts in Copenhagen and Malmö) and then return by catamaran to Malmö. For more budget oriented information, pop along to the *InterRail Centre*, Stortorget 25 (mid-June to Aug 10am–6/10pm), where you can also leave your bags, grab a shower and eat cheaply.

Malmö is one of the easier places in the south to find good cheap **accommodation**. *City Room*, Adelgatan 19 (☎040/795 94), will book **private rooms** for 125–200kr a head, or sell you a **Malmö Package**, providing a double room in a central **hotel**, breakfast and Malmö Card, for 260–435kr per person. The *Prize Hotel*, Carlsgatan 10c (☎040/11 25 11; ④), is the cheapest hotel in this scheme, behind the train station. As for **hostel** accommodation, the *YMCA Interpoint*, Betoniaplan 4 (☎040/211 55; ②), fifteen minutes' walk from the centre (bus #11), and *Kirsebergs Fritidsgård*, Dalhemsgatan 5 (☎040/212 24; ②), both open July to late-August, are the cheapest options. The official *IYHF* hostel at Backavägen 18 (☎040/822 20; ②) is well equipped but a bit of a jaunt, 5km from the centre – take bus #21 from Centralplan, get off at Vandrarhemmet, cross over the traffic lights and take the first right. Nearest **campsite** is *Sibbarps Camping* on Strandgatan, open all year; bus #11A from Centralplan.

The City

The largely pedestrianized streets and squares of Malmö are conducive to a leisurely stroll, and, with the canals and central parks, there are few places in Sweden more enjoyable. Most of the medieval centre was taken apart in the early sixteenth century to make way for **Stortorget**, a vast market square, as impressive today as it must have been when it first appeared, flanked on one side by the **Rådhus**, built in 1546 and popping with statuary and spiky accoutrements; there are tours of the well-preserved interior. **Södergatan** runs off south from here towards the canal, Malmö's main pedestrianized shopping street. Behind the Rådhus sits the **St Petri Kyrka** (Mon–Fri 8am–4pm, Sat 10am–3pm), a fine Gothic church with an impressively decorative pulpit and a four-tiered altarpiece. **Lilla Torget** is everyone's favourite part of the city, a late sixteenth-century spin-off from an overcrowded Stortorget, usually full and doing a roaring trade from jewellery stalls and summer buskers. The southern side of the square is formed by a row of brick and timber mid-nineteenth-century warehouses, unremarkable given the other preserved buildings around, except that they contain the **Form Design Centre** (Tues–Fri 11am–5pm, Sat 10am–4pm; free), a kind of yuppies' Habitat Museum. The shops around here sell books, antiques and gifts, though the best place to drop into is the **Saluhallen**, an excellent indoor market. Further west still lie the **Kungsparken** and the **Malmöhus** (Tues–Sat noon–4pm, Sun noon–4.30pm; June–Aug also Mon noon–4pm), a low fortified castle defended by a wide moat, two circular keeps and grassy ramparts, raised by Danish king Christian III in 1536. For a time a prison (Bothwell, third husband of Mary, Queen of Scots, its most notable occupant), the castle and its outbuildings now constitute a series of terrific museums with city-related, art, natural history, technical and military collections. Entrance, on the canal side, is 35kr, the ticket then valid for all Malmö's other museums for the rest of that day. There's a good café inside, too, and the grounds are good for a stroll, peppered with small lakes and an old windmill.

Eating, drinking and nightlife

The Saluhalle on Landbygatan by Lilla Torget stocks a marvellous array of picnic supplies. Failing that, the youth café *Suck*, Stortorget 25, houses the *InterRail Centre* and is the cheapest place to fill up with hearty snacks. For lunch, *Kocksa Krogen*, also on Stortorget, dishes up a good range of Swedish foods in a sixteenth-century cellar, prices from around 60kr; *Ki-Ling Court*, Södra Tullgatan 4, is about the cheapest Chinese joint in town with set lunches from 50kr; and *Casa Mia*, Södergatan 12, serves the best pizzas from around 60kr. In the **evening**, *Le Coeur*, Södergatan 7, is a brasserie with averagely priced beer and a pleasant atmosphere; *Gustav Adolf*, Gustav Adolfs Torg is similar to and a little cheaper than *Jim's Bar*, Västergatan 16, at the junction with Gråbrödersgatan, open until midnight and with cabaret on Tuesdays. *Hype*, the nightclub in the basement of the *Hotel Kramer*, Stortorget, runs from Thursday to Saturday (around 30kr), though early revelers often make for the free disco at Central Station; *Suck*, Stortorget 25, hosts live bands. Otherwise the best place for occasional live music is *Matssons Musikpub*, Göran Olsgatan 1, behind the Rådhus. A twenty-minute walk south from the docks is Möllevångens Torget, where *Retro* at the Ångenholmsgatan corner is one of the more appealing of the bar/restaurants which litter the area.

Ystad

An hour by train from Malmö, **YSTAD** sits at the end of a coasting ride through rolling farmland. The train station is by the docks, a murky area that gives no hint of the cosy little town to come. In the nineteenth century, its inhabitants made a mint from smuggling, a profitable occupation in the days of Napoléon's Continental Blockade. Quite apart from coming to see the crumbling medieval market town, you might well be leaving Sweden from here: ferries depart for the Danish island of Bornholm and for Poland.

The streets wind up to **Stortorget**, a well-proportioned square, at the back of which sits the grand **Sta Maria Kyrka**, a church which has been added to continually since its original foundation in the fourteenth century. The red-brick interior displays heavy, decorative tablets lining the aisle walls and enclosed wooden pews – the end-pieces sculpted with flowers and emblems. The green box-pews at either side of the entrance were reserved for women who hadn't yet been received back into the church after childbirth. From the church, take a walk down **Lilla Västergatan**, the main street in Ystad in the seventeenth and eighteenth centuries, with neat pastel-coloured houses. Walk back through Stortorget and it's not far down to the old **Greyfriars Monastery** and museum (daily noon–4pm; 10kr), a thirteenth-century survival which contains the usual local cultural and historical collections.

From the **train station**, cross the tracks to St Knuts Torg, where you'll find the **tourist office** (mid-June to mid-Aug Mon–Fri 9am–7pm, Sat 9am–6pm, Sun 2–6pm; rest of year Mon–Fri 9am–5pm). The square is also where **buses** from Lund, Malmö and Kristianstad will drop you. There are several **hotels** in town, but nothing that's a better bargain than in nearby Malmö. Try the **youth hostel** (✆0411/772 97; ②), 2km from the station at Sandskogen, where there's also a **campsite**, open May to mid-September, with cabins for rent – take bus #572 or #573. For **eating**, try *Café Diana*, Stora Östergatan 31, with cheap coffee and snacks, though it closes early evening.

Kristianstad

Located about 95km northeast of Mälmo, **KRISTIANSTAD** is the creation of Christian IV, seventeenth-century builder-king of Denmark. It's a shining example of the king's architectural preoccupations, the central squares and broad gridded streets flanking a wide river. There are other towns in Scandinavia built by Christian (notably Kristiansand in southern Norway), but Kristianstad is the earliest and most evocative – and a good place to hang around and do nothing in particular.

The town's most striking building is directly opposite the train station, the **Trefaldighetskyrkan** (daily 9am–5pm) – a symbol of all that was glorious about Christian's Renaissance ideas. A forest of pews fills the cool white church from back to front, their high sides and carved gargoyles obstructing a clear view of altar and pulpit. Kristianstad also attracts interest among movie enthusiasts, since Sweden's first films were made here between 1909 and 1911; they flicker to life at the **Film Museum** in a former studio at Östra Strandgatan 53 (Tues–Fri & Sun 1–4pm; free).

The **tourist office** on Stora Torg (June–Aug Mon–Fri 9am–8pm, Sat 9am–5pm, Sun 1–6pm; Sept–May Mon–Fri 10am–6pm) is down Nya Boulevarden, right from the station, then second left. The **campsite** *Charlottsborg Camping*, open all year, is 2km west and also has a small **hostel** (②) to get there, take bus #22 or #23 to VÄ from Busstorget, near Lilla Torget.

Kalmar

Bright **KALMAR** had much to do with Sweden's medieval development. It was the scene of the first meeting of the *Riksdag* called by failing king Magnus Eriksson in the mid-fourteenth century, and played host to the formation of the Kalmar Union, the agreement of 1397 uniting Sweden, Norway and Denmark as one – a history manifest in the surviving **Kalmar Slott** (May to mid-June & mid-Aug to Sept Mon–Sat 10am–4pm, Sun 1–4pm; mid-June to mid-Aug Mon–Sat 10am–6pm, Sun 10am–5pm; Oct & April daily 1–3pm; Nov–March Sun 1–3pm; 15kr), beautifully set on a tiny island a few minutes' walk away from the bus and train stations. Defended by a range of steep embankments and gun emplacements, the fourteenth-century buildings survived eleven sieges virtually unscathed, a record not respected by King Johan III who rebuilt the structure in the late sixteenth century. The castle is now a storybook confection, with turrets, ramparts, moat and drawbridge. The spruce interior repays a long dawdle; highlights include the intricately panelled Lozenge Hall and a dark dungeon.

If the castle seems to defend nothing in particular it's because the town was shifted to Kvarnholmen, an island to the north, in the mid-seventeenth century following a fire. This is modern Kalmar, a graceful, straightforward grid settlement which centres on the Baroque **Domkyrkan** (Mon–Sat 10am–6pm, Sun 1–6pm) on Stortorget. Time is best spent wandering the streets around **Lilla Torget**: there's not a great deal left – some seventeenth-century buildings and city walls – but what remains is authentic and atmospheric enough. The one place really worth making a beeline for is the **Kronan Exhibition**, the main attraction of the **Länsmuseum**, Skeppsbrogatan (mid-June to mid-Aug Mon–Sat 10am–6pm, Sun 1–5pm; rest of year Tues–Fri 10am–4pm, Sat & Sun 1–4pm; 25kr). The *Kronan* was one of the three biggest ships in the world – twice the size of the *Vasa* – when it went down after an explosion in the gunpowder magazine in 1676, lying undisturbed until 1980. There's an inventive walk-through reconstruction of the gun decks and admiral's cabin, as well as a swag of gold coins, clothing, sculpture, jewellery and weapons – in fact, a complete picture of seventeenth-century maritime life and a remarkable insight into a society at the height of its political powers.

The **tourist office** at Larmgatan 6, a spit away from the **train station** and **bus terminal**, doles out a decent map of Kalmar and arranges **private rooms** from around

200kr a double. Or stay at the **youth hostel** at Rappegatan 1c (☎0480/129 28; ②), 1500m away on Ängo, the next island north. The *Sjöfartsklubben* on Skeppsbrogatan (a seaman's mission but open to all) has doubles from around 200kr and cheaper dorm accommodation, while there's a **campsite** on Stensö island, 3km from the centre, with a few cheap cabins. For **food**, *Hamncafeet* at Skeppsbron opens at 6am for the harbour workers and continues to sell good-value sandwiches and coffee until the afternoon.

Gotland

The rumours about good times on **Gotland** are rife. You'll hear that the short summer season really motors like nowhere else in Sweden, and it's hot, fun and cheap. Largely, these rumours are true: the island has a youthful feel as young, mobile Stockholmers desert the capital for a boisterous summer on its beaches. But it's not all just brochure fodder. The island was an important trading post during Viking times, and later a powerbase of the Hanseatic League, under whose influence its capital Visby became one of the great cities of medieval Europe: nowhere else in Scandinavia is there such a concentration of unspoilt medieval country churches, most of them displaying a unique Baltic Gothic style and providing a permanent reminder of Gotland's former wealth.

Numerous **ferries** to Gotland, operated by *Gotlandslinjen*, run from Nynäshamn and Oskarshamn, but are packed in summer, so try to plan ahead. In Stockholm, *Gotland City* at Kungsgatan 48 (☎08/23 61 70) can provide plenty of information and sell advance tickets. One-way **fares** cost from 130kr in high season, 170kr on Friday, Saturday and Sunday. Students are entitled to a thirty percent discount and under-26s may find flying a competitive option with one-way fares from around 200kr.

Visby

Undoubtedly the finest approach to **VISBY** is by ship, seeing the old trading centre as it should be seen. The magnificent **defensive wall** is the most obvious manifestation of Visby's previous importance, a three-kilometre circuit enclosing the entire settlement. Thrown up around the end of the thirteenth century, it was actually aimed at isolating the city's foreign traders from the island's own locals. The old Hanseatic **harbour** at Almedalen is now a public park and nothing is much more than a few minutes' walk from here. Close by, pretty **Packhusplan**, the oldest square in the city, is bisected by curving Strandgatan which runs south to the fragmentary ruins of **Visborg Castle**, overlooking the harbour. Built in the fifteenth century by Erik of Pomerania, it was blown up by the Danes in the seventeenth century. In the opposite direction, Strandgatan runs towards the sea and the lush **Botanical Gardens**, just beyond which is the **Jungfrutornet** (Maiden's Tower) where a local goldsmith's daughter was walled up alive – reputedly for betraying the city to the Danes. Strandgatan is the best place to view the merchants' houses looming over the narrow streets, and is also home to the **Gotlands Fornsal Museum** at no. 14 (mid-May to Aug daily 11am–6pm; Sept to mid-May Tues–Sun noon–4pm; 20kr), which, along with the usual Viking and medieval relics, claims the largest collection of painted windows in Scandinavia. The museum also tells the tale of the slaughter of thousands of Swedes by the Danes in 1361 – an event remembered by **Valdemar's Cross**, a few hundred metres east of Söderport, where excavations earlier this century revealed a mass grave. The strikingly towered **Domkyrkan**, a short walk west of the museum (daily 10am–4pm), was built between 1190 and 1225 and as such dates from just before the great age of Gothic church building on the island. Used both as warehouse and treasury, it's been heavily restored and about the only original fixture left is the thirteenth-century sandstone font.

Ferries serving Visby dock just outside the city walls; turn left and keep walking for the centre, where the **tourist office** (mid-April to May Mon–Fri 8am–5pm, Sat & Sun 10am–4pm; June to mid-Aug Mon–Fri 8am–8pm, Sat & Sun 10am–7pm; mid-Aug to mid-April Mon–Fri 9am–4pm) is in Burmeister House on Donnersplats and sells excellent *Turistkarta Gotland* (20kr) describing all points of interest. Alternatively, a short way to the right along the harbour front leads to *Gotlandsresor* at Färjeledon 3, which has a room booking service. For getting around the island it's best to hire a **bike** and there are plenty of places to do this, all charging about 40kr a day. The tourist office can book **private rooms** in town from as little as 70kr a head, and advise on the latest location of the itinerant **youth hostel**. A popular, hostel-type alternative is *Kneippbyn* (☎0498/26 41 23; ④), 3km south of Visby, reached on a red London bus which runs from Österpost and the harbour until 11pm, and only open May to August. Gotland is a great place for **camping**; *Nordenstrands* is the closest site, 1km outside the city walls and open from May to September – follow the cycle path that runs through the Botanical Gardens along the seafront. For **eating**, Adelsgatan is lined with cafés and snack bars and has a couple of cheap kebab takeaways. Best place for sit-down drinking is the café-terrace *Vardklockan*; Strandgatan is the focus of Visby's evening parade.

The rest of the island

There is a real charm to the rest of Gotland – rolling green countryside, forest-lined roads, fine beaches and small fishing villages. And everywhere churches dominate the rural skyline, the remnants of medieval settlements destroyed in the Danish invasion. Thirteen kilometres north of Visby, the **Lummelundagrottarna** (May–Aug daily 9am–7pm; Sept daily 9am–4pm; 30kr) is a series of limestone caves, stalagmites and stalactites that form a disappointingly dull and damp stop. Far better to press on further into the eminently picturesque north, where many of the secluded cottages are summer holiday homes for urban Swedes, though much of the peninsula north of Lärbro is a military zone and prohibited to foreign tourists. You can go as far as **BUNGE** with its bright fourteenth-century fortified church and **open-air museum** (mid-May to mid-Sept daily 10am–6pm; 25kr), then take the Farosund ferry (half-hourly; free) to the island of Fårö, ringed with popular beaches and some of the island's finest limestone stacks. **SLITE**, just to the south, has a sandy beach and a campsite. There's another coastal campsite, open June to August, at Aminne, further south, and, a few kilometres away at **DAHLEM** perhaps the best example of a church in the Gotland Gothic style. Its chancel and nave date from the mid-thirteenth century, and the interior detail – like the decorative woodcarvings on the fourteenth-century choirstalls – is delicate and precise. For **beaches**, head for the east coast around **LJUGARN**, about the closest thing to a resort in Gotland, with a small **youth hostel** (June to mid-Aug; ☎0498/29 31 84; ②). At **KATTHAMMARSVIK**, to the north, there's another lengthy beach with jetties.

CENTRAL AND NORTHERN SWEDEN

In many ways, the long wedge of land that comprises **central and northern Sweden** – from the northern shores of Lake Vänern to the Norwegian border – encompasses all that is most popular and typical of the country. Rural and underpopulated counties without exception, this is Sweden as seen in the brochures – lakes, holiday cottages, forests and reindeer. Essentially the region divides into two. On the eastern side, Sweden's coast forms one edge of the **Gulf of Bothnia**, a corridor of land that, with its jumble of erstwhile fishing towns and squeaky-clean contemporary urban planning, is quite unlike the rest of the country – worth stopping off in if you're travelling north or have just arrived from Finland by ferry. Though the weather isn't as reliable as further south, you're at least guaranteed clean beaches, crystal-clear waters and fine hiking. To the west, folklorish **Dalarna** county is the most intensely picturesque region, with sweeping green countryside and inhabitants who maintain a cultural heritage (echoed in contemporary handicrafts and traditions) that goes back to the Middle Ages. And the county is *the* place in which to spend midsummer, particularly Midsummer's Night, when the whole region erupts in a frenzy of celebration. The **Inlandsbanan**, the great Inland Railway, cuts right through this area, from Lake Vänern to **Gällivare**, above the Arctic Circle, and ranks with the best European train journeys, an enthralling 1300km in three days – certainly a preferable route north to the Bothnian option. **Östersund** marks the halfway point, a shimmering, modern lakeside town.

Gävle

It's only two hours north by train from Stockholm to **GÄVLE**, principal city of the county of Gästrikland and communications hub for the west and north. Gävle is an old city, its town charter granted in the mid-fifteenth century, although this knowledge doesn't prepare you for its large squares, broad avenues and proud monumental buildings. Almost completely redesigned after a fire in 1869, the layout of the modern town, centring on the roomy Stortorget, reflects the success of its late nineteenth-century industry when Gävle was the export centre for the timber and metal produced locally. Only one part of the old town remains, Gamla Gefle, on the other side of the river from the modern town, and this is the place to head for, an area of wooden cottages and narrow cobbled streets. For a more realistic glimpse of social conditions a century ago, visit the **Joe Hill-Gården** at Nedre Bergsgatan 28 (summer daily 10am–3pm; free), the birthplace of one Joe Hill, born Joel Hägglund in 1879, who emigrated to the United States in 1902 and became a working-class hero, his songs and speeches rallying cries to comrades in the International. Framed for murder in Salt Lake City, he was executed in 1915; the museum is a collection of standard memorabilia, given piquancy by the telegram announcing his execution and his last testament. The heart of Gamla Gefle is bounded at one end by the canalized river that runs through the centre of town. On the canal side at Södra Strandgatan 20 is the **Länsmuseet** (Tues, Thurs & Fri 10am–4pm, Wed 10am–9pm, Sat & Sun 1–5pm; free), a thoughtful museum whose displays concentrate on the role of the ironworks and fisheries in the locality, as well as on strange, child-like paintings by another local hero, Johan Erik Olson.

The **train** and **bus station** are at the east end of the city, only a few minutes from the centre or Gamle Gefle. The **tourist office** is at Norra Strandgatan 13, off Stortorget (summer Mon–Fri 9am–6pm, Sat 10am–2pm, Sun 11am–4pm; winter Mon–Fri 9am–5pm), with maps and information about furnished **apartments** in central Gävle, from 250kr a night per person. The **youth hostel** is well placed in the old town at Södra Rådmansgatan 1 (☎026/12 17 45; ②), or you can try for a summer price at the central **hotels** like the *Aveny*, Södra Kungsgatan 31 (☎026/61 55 90; ②). As a rule, places round Nygatan and Stortorget are good for basic daily **lunch** offers: for a change, *Bali Garden*, Nygatan 37, is Indonesian, while the *Roma* next door does takeaway pizzas from 45kr.

Sundsvall

Known as the "Stone City", **SUNDSVALL** – the largest centre in northern Sweden – is immediately and obviously different. Once home to a rapidly expanding nineteenth-century sawmill industry, the whole city burned down in 1888 and a new centre built completely of stone emerged within ten years. The result is a living document of turn-of-the-century urban architecture, designed by architects who were engaged in rebuilding Stockholm's residential areas at the same time, though their work – 573 residential buildings in four years – was achieved at a price. The workers who had laboured on the stone buildings were shifted from their old homes in the centre, victims of their own success in refurbishing the city, and moved south to a poorly serviced suburb.

The style is simple limestone and brick, the size often overwhelming. The **Esplanaden**, a wide central avenue, cuts the grid in two, itself crossed by **Storgatan**, the widest street. The area around **Stortorget** is still the roomy commercial centre that was envisaged. Of buildings you can actually enter, the mock-Baroque exterior of the **Sundsvall Museum** (summer Mon–Thurs 10am–7pm, Fri 10am–6pm, Sat & Sun 11am–4pm; free) houses a rather second-rate collection of art; the **Gustav Adolfs Kyrkan** (daily June–Aug 11am–4pm; Sept–May 11am–2pm) marks one end of the new town, a soaring red-brick structure whose interior looks like a large Lego set. To get the best perspective on the city's plan, climb to the heights of **Gaffelbyn** and the **Norra Bergets Hantyerks Och Friluttsmuseum** (summer Mon–Fri 9am–6pm, Sat noon–4pm, Sun 11am–4pm; winter Mon–Fri 9am–4pm; free), an open-air crafts museum down Storgatan and over the main bridge.

From the **train station** the centre is five minutes' walk away, with the **tourist office** in the main Stortorget (June–Aug daily 9am–9pm; Sept–May Mon–Fri 9am–5pm). The **bus station** is at the bottom of Esplanaden. The **youth hostel** (☎060/11 21 19; ②), open May to August, is a cheap and grotty camping and cabin affair at Norra Stadsberget, and you might prefer the **private rooms** from 125kr per person plus a 60kr booking fee; otherwise *Hotel Ritz*, Esplanaden 4 (☎060/15 08 60; ④), has doubles. For **eating**, Storgatan is lined with restaurants, most offering daily lunch menus, or *Spezia*, Sjögatan 6, has bargain basement pizzas for around 40kr.

Dalarna

It's fruitless to dwell too much on the agreed beauty of **Dalarna**. It holds a special, misty-eyed place in the Swedish heart and should certainly be seen, though not to the exclusion of points further north. And anyway, despite its charms, it's conceivable you'll soon tire of the prominent folksy image. One small lakeside town looks pretty much like another, as do the ubiquitous handicrafts and souvenirs. Dalarna actually spreads further north and west than most brochures ever acknowledge. They, like most tourists, prefer to concentrate on the area immediately surrounding Lake Siljan – which on the whole isn't a bad idea. Most of the towns are connected by rail, and there are ferries across the lake at Mora and Leksand; you also don't need to worry unduly about accommodation, of which there is plenty. North of Orsa, the county becomes more mountainous and less populous, and access is tricky for an independent trip.

Lake Siljan is why many tourists come to Sweden, its gentle surroundings, traditions and local handicrafts weaving a subtle spell. There's a lush feel to much of the region, the vegetation enriched by the lake, which adds a pleasing dimension to what are, essentially, small, low-profile towns and villages. If you've only got time to see part of the lake, **MORA** is as good a place as any, and a starting point for the *Inlandsbanan* rail route (see below), but unfortunately has no youth hostel. At the northwestern corner of Lake Siljan, the little town is more or less a showcase for the work of Anders Zorn, the Swedish painter who lived in Mora and whose work is exhibited in the **Zorn Museum** (Mon–Sat 9/10am–5pm, Sun 11am/1pm–5pm; 20kr), along with his small but well-chosen personal collection. Zorn's oils reflect a passion for Dalorna's pastoral lifestyle but it's his earlier watercolours of Southern Europe and North Africa that really stand out. It's also possible to see his former home and studio, **Zorngården** (frequent guided tours in English; 25kr). The **tourist office** (summer Mon–Sat 11am–8pm, Sun noon–8pm; winter Mon–Fri 9am–5pm, Sat 9am–1pm) is down on the quayside and can point you to **private rooms** from 270kr a double and book them for 25kr.

At **RÄTTVIK**, on the eastern bulge of the lake, there's an introductory spread of museums and craft exhibitions, the **Gammelgård** (mid-June to mid–Aug Mon–Sat 11am–6pm, Sun noon–6pm), 2km from town, with reconstructed buildings, period furniture and traditional costumes. The **tourist office** is in Torget, across from the station (summer Mon–Sat 9am–8pm, Sun 11am–8pm; winter Mon–Fri 9am–5pm, Sat noon–4pm), the **youth hostel** in Knektplatsen, a few hundred metres away at the end of Järnvägsgatan (☎0248/105 66; ②), open June to August; and there's a **campsite** (☎0248/116 91) on the lakeside.

LEKSAND is perhaps the most popular and traditional of the Dalarna villages and certainly worth making the effort to reach at midsummer, when the festivals recall age-old maypole dances, the celebrations culminating in the **church boat races**, an aquatic procession of decorated longboats which the locals once rowed to church every Sunday. The **tourist office** in Norsgatan has bikes for hire, as does the **youth hostel** (☎0247/101 86; ②), 2km south of the centre at Parkgården and open all year.

Nearby **FALUN** was prosperous in the seventeenth and eighteenth centuries due to its **copper mines** (May–Aug daily 10am–4.30pm; Sept to mid-Nov, March & April Sat & Sun only 12.30–4.30pm; 50kr). Two-thirds of the world's copper ore was mined here, and Falun acquired buildings and a proud layout in line with its status as Sweden's second largest town. An unnerving element of eighteenth-century mining was the omnipresence of copper vitriol fumes, a strong preservative. One case records the body of a young man found in the mines in 1719, who died 49 years previously in an accident; his corpse was so well preserved that his erstwhile fiancée, by then an old woman, recognized him immediately. Falun's **tourist office** is in the main square (June–Aug Mon–Sat 9am–8pm, Sun 1–8pm) and there's a **youth hostel** (☎023/105 60; ②) 4km away at Haraldsbro, open all year except for the last two weeks of December (bus #703). The **campsite** is at the National Ski Stadium at Lugnet, also open all year.

The Inlandsbanan

The most charismatic of the Scandinavian rail routes, linking central Sweden with Gällivare, 1300km further north, the **Inlandsbanan** (Inland Railway) has long been the trip in northern Sweden everyone wants to make. Long under threat of closure, the line has now been privatized and looks like surviving for the moment, at least between early June and late August. *InterRail* and *Nordturist* pass holders get a fifty percent discount on the full fare which, travelling second class from Mora–Östersund ranges from 300kr in mid-June to 600kr during early July, dropping to 400kr off season. Cunning timetabling on the single daily service allows unlimited breaks on your journey but enforces stops at Östersund, Storuman, Sorsele or Arvidsjaur (the preferrable of the three) and Gällivare whichever way you travel; planning avoids a fourth at Mora. For up-to-date information on the line, contact the *Inlandståget*, Kyrkgatan 56, Östersund (Mon–Fri 8am–6pm; ☎020/53 53 53).

Mora to Östersund

Though there are connections on from places further south, the *Inlandsbanan* officially begins in **MORA** (see above), making its first stop at **ORSA**, fifteen minutes down the line, where the nearby **Grönklitt bear park** (late May to Sept; 15kr) provides the best chance to see the bears that roam the increasingly wild countryside. The **youth hostel** at the park (☎0250/462 00; ②) has fine facilities.

Several hours north of here, the line's halfway point is marked by **ÖSTERSUND**, the largest town until Kiruna in the far north, and a welcoming place, lent a holiday atmosphere unusual this far north by its **Storsjön** or Great Lake. You can make a tour of the lake on a **steamboat cruise** (late June–early Aug Tues–Sun; reduced service two weeks either side; 100kr), a two-hour passage. Otherwise, the main thing to do in town is to visit **Jamtli** (park open all year; buildings and activities mid-June to mid-Aug daily 11am–5pm; 50kr), an impressive open-air museum, fifteen minutes' walk north along Rådhusgatan, full of volunteers milling around in traditional country costume. They live here throughout the summer and everyone is encouraged to join in – baking, tree felling, grass cutting. For kids it's ideal, and you'd have to be pretty hard-bitten not to enjoy the enthusiastic atmosphere. On the way in, the **Länsmuseum** (summer Mon–Fri 9am–4pm, Sat & Sun noon–4pm; winter Mon–Fri 9am–4pm, Tues until 9pm, Sat & Sun noon–3pm; free) shows off the county collections, a rambling houseful of local exhibits that includes monster-catching gear from the last century. Back in the centre, the town slopes steeply down to the water and it's tiring work strolling the pedestrianized streets that run around Stortorget. Apart from the **Stadmuseum** (mid-June to early Aug daily 1–4pm; free), a crowded 200 years of history in a house the size of a shoebox, there's not a vast amount in the way of sights. The **harbour** is a better bet, from where you can take the bridge over the lake to **Frösön** island – the site of the original Viking settlement here.

The **tourist office** is at Rådhusgatan 44 (June to mid-Aug Mon–Sat 9am–9pm, Sun 11am–7pm; rest of year Mon–Fri 9am–5pm) and sells the *Storsjökortet* (mid-May to mid-Aug; 105kr), giving free public transport and access to the town's sights, and half price on the steamboat cruise for nine days. For a central **hotel**, try either *City Hotellet*, Artillerigatan 4 (☎063/10 84 15; ④), or *Hotell Linden*, Storgatan 64 (☎063/11 73 35; ⑤). The **youth hostel** is close to the train station at Tingsgatan 12 (mid-June to mid-Aug; ☎063/10 23 43) with single rooms. More atmospheric is the **hostel** at Jamtli (②), the tourist office will book rooms there for a fee and, although slightly more expensive, staying there saves on entrance fees to the museum. **Campers** can stay at either *Östersunds Camping*, 2km down Rådhusgatan, or on Frösön island at *Frösö camping* (June–Aug) – bus #3 from the centre. For **food**, try the young and trendy *Brunkullans* restaurant at Postgränd 5, or the daily specials at *Lilla Paris*, Storgatan 29.

Storuman, Sorsele, Arvidsjaur and the Arctic Circle

If you are travelling on the *Inlandsbanan*, you may well spend the night at **STORUMAN**, five miles north of Östersund and ten hours from Gällivare. You can pick up mountain hiking details from the **tourist office** at Skolgatan 20 or just sleep in one of the private rooms or at the **youth hostel** (☎0951/113 20; ②) from mid-June to mid-August, about three kilometres out on the E79 to Tärnaby. **SORSELE** is the next major stop on the *Inlandsbanan*, a pint-sized town that became a *cause célèbre* amongst conservationists in Sweden, causing the government to abandon its plans to regulate the flow of the River Vindel here by building a hydroelectric station. It remains wild, untouched and seething with rapids, with a **campsite** on the river bank, open all year. There's a **youth hostel** (☎0952/100 48; ②), too, a small place open from mid-June to early August. **ARVIDSJAUR** contains Sweden's oldest surviving *Same* village, dating from the late eighteenth century, a huddle of houses that was once the centre of a great winter market. They were not meant to be permanent homes, but rather a meeting place during festivals, and the last weekend in August is still taken up by a great celebratory shindig. There's a cosy private **youth hostel** at Västra Skolgatan 9 (☎0960/124 13; ②), and for cabins *Camp Gielas* lies beside one of the lakes 1km south of the station. A couple of hours north of Arvidsjaur the *Inlandsbanan* finally crosses the **Arctic Circle**, signalled by a bout of whistle-blowing as the train pulls up. Painted white rocks curve away over the hilly ground, a crude but popular representation of the Circle.

Jokkmokk

In the midst of remote densely forested, marshy country, **JOKKMOKK** is a welcome oasis. Once a wintertime *Same* quarters, the town is today a renowned handicraft centre, a *Same* high school keeping the language and culture alive. The town **museum** (daily 9/11am–6pm; 20kr) on Kyrkegatan is the place to see some of the intricate work. Have a glance, too, at the so-called **Lapp kyrka**, in which corpses were interned in wall vaults during winter, waiting for the thaw when the *Same* could go out and dig graves – the temperatures in this part of Sweden plunge below -35°C in winter. The great winter market still survives, now nearly 400 years old, held on the first Thursday, Friday and Saturday of each February, when 30,000 people gather in town. It's the best time to be in Jokkmokk, and staying means booking accommodation a good six months in advance. A smaller, less traditional autumn fair at the end of August is an easier though poorer option. The **tourist office** is at Stortorget 4 (summer daily 9am–7pm; winter Mon–Fri 8am–5pm). In summer there should be no problem getting a place at the **youth hostel** (mid-June to mid-Aug; ☎0971/119 77; ②); just follow the signs from the station. The **campsite** is open all year, 3km east on route 97.

Gällivare

GÄLLIVARE is one of Europe's most important sources of iron ore, and the modern **mines** and **works** (June–Aug daily 10am; 160kr) are distant, dark blots down which the tourist office ferries relays of tourists. Europe's largest open-cast copper mine sears the landscape 20km south of Gällivare, its gargantuan bucket-shovels and dump trucks just dots 250m down. Astounding statistics – 300 tonnes of high explosives are used for each blast – pepper the tour (June–Aug daily 1.30pm; 135kr), which also takes in Kåkstan, a rebuilt shantytown on the site of the original iron ore mine; you at least stop long enough to sample local delicacies like reindeer, salmon and lingonberry juice, all for 65kr at *Café Endast för Nyktra*. If you have any interest in seeing a working mine, this is a far better bet than the tame tourist tour at Kiruna, further north.

There's not much to Gällivare itself. Little remains of the seventeenth-century *Same* village, and the river and surrounding mountains are really the nicest feature of the town. You can walk up to **Björnfällän**, a four-kilometre hike on a well-marked path, and the views are magnificent. Buses make the journey (135kr return) to the summit 3km north beyond Björnfällan to see the Midnight Sun daily between June 2 and July 12, leaving from Lasarettegatan near the tourist office at 11pm, returning at 1am.

The **tourist office** is at Storgatan 16 (June–Aug daily 9am–8pm; Sept–May Mon–Fri 9am–4.30pm). Its long summer hours are aimed at late *Inlandsbanan* arrivals and the office has a café downstairs and a museum upstairs dealing with *Same* history. The **youth hostel** (☎0970/143 80; ②) is behind the train station and open all year, with accommodation in small cabins. There's also a small **private hostel**, *Lapphärbärget* (☎0970/125 34; ②; a category down if you provide your own sheets), next to the Lappkyrkan by the river, and the *Hotell Dundret*, Per Högströmsgatan 1 (☎0970/110 40; ④), close to the station. The **campsite** is by the river, open mid-May to mid-September; for snacks or an evening coffee and cakes by the river, make for the *Strand Café* near the campsite beside resited vernacular buildings and a few captive reindeer.

Kiruna

KIRUNA was the hub of the battle for control of the iron ore supply during World War II. From here ore was transported north by train to Narvik, over the border in Norway. Much German firepower was expended in an attempt to break the supply to the Allies, and in the process both towns suffered considerably. The **mines** still dominate the town, ugly, brooding reminders of Kiruna's prosperity, and despite the new central buildings and parks, the town retains something of a frontier feel. *Kiruna Guidetor*, Vänortsgatan 2, around the corner from the tourist office, runs guided tours (June–Aug daily at 10am, noon, 2pm & 4pm; 85kr); a coach takes visitors underground and stops off at a "tourist" mine, part of a leviathan structure containing service stations, restaurants, trains and crushing mills.

The other sights in town are also wedded to the all-important metal in one way or another. The tower of the **Rådhus** (summer Mon–Sat 9.45am–5pm, Sun 11am–5pm; winter Mon–Fri 9am–5pm) is obvious even from the train station, a strident metal pillar harbouring an intricate latticework, clock face and sundry bells which chime raucously at noon. Inside, there's a tolerable art collection, *Same* handicraft displays and a small tourist information stall. A few minutes up the road, the **Kiruna kyrka** (daily 11am–4.30pm; free) is built in the style of a *Same* hut, a massive creation of oak beams and rafters the size of a small aircraft hangar. *LKAB*, the iron ore company that paid for its construction, was also responsible for **Hjalmar Lundbohmsgården** (June–Aug daily 10am–8pm; free), a country house once used by the managing director of the company and "founder" of Kiruna. Displays inside mostly consist of turn-of-the-century photographs featuring the man himself and assorted *Same* in their winter gear. The **Kiruna Samegård** at Brytaregatan 14 (mid-June to Sept Mon–Fri 10am–6pm; also weekends in July; 10kr) is the most rewarding exhibition of *Same* culture in town, with a good art display and a general store where visiting *Same* buy basic handicraft materials – antler bone, reindeer skin and rope sold by the metre.

The **tourist office** in the Folketshus, Lars Janssongatan 17 (June–Aug Mon–Fri 9am–8pm, Sat & Sun 9am–6pm; Sept–May Mon–Fri 9am–4pm) has **private rooms** for around 150kr a double. The **youth hostel**, Skyttegatan 16 (mid-June to Aug; ☎0980/171 95; ②) is a well-signposted twenty-minute walk across town. Similar-styled accommodation is also on offer for a touch more at *Yellow House*, Hantverkaregatan 25 (☎0980/137 50; ②), the continuation of Vänortsgatan. The **campsite** is a twenty-minute walk from the centre on Campingvägen and has expensive cabins.

travel details

Trains

Stockholm to: Gällivare (2 daily; 16hr 25min); Gävle (roughly hourly; 1hr 45min); Gothenburg (10–12 daily; 3hr 10min–4hr 25min); Helsingborg (8–9 daily; 6hr 30min); Kalmar, change at Alvesta (8 daily, 3Sun; 6hr); Kiruna (2 daily; 17hr 40min); Kristianstad (7 daily; 6hr); Lund (6 daily; 4hr 35min); Malmö (6 daily; 4hr 50min); Mora (3–4 daily; 4hr 30min); Narvik (2 daily; 20hr); Östersund (4–6 daily; 6hr); Sundsvall (7 daily; 4–5hr); Uppsala (2–4 hourly; 50min).

Gothenburg to: Copenhagen (5–8 daily; 5hr); Helsingborg (6–9 daily; 2hr 40min); Kalmar (3–5 daily; 4hr 40min); Lund (6–9 daily; 3hr 30min); Malmö (6–9 daily; 3hr 45min); Oslo (4 daily; 4hr 40min).

Malmö to: Helsingborg (at least hourly; 1hr); Lund (at least hourly; 15min); Ystad (Mon–Fri hourly, Sat & Sun 4–6 daily; 1hr).

Uppsala to: Gävle (roughly hourly; 1hr 15min); Mora (3–4 daily; 3hr 20min).

Sundsvall to: Gävle (8–10 daily; 2hr 30min); Östersund (4–7 daily; 2hr–2hr 30min).

Gällivare to: Kiruna (2 daily, 1hr 15min); Narvik (4hr 40min).

Buses

Stockholm to: Gävle (3 Fri, 1 Sat, 4 Sun; 1hr 30min); Gothenburg (4 Fri, 3 Sun; 9hr 20min); Helsingborg (1 Fri, 1 Sun; 9hr); Kalmar (2–5 daily; 6hr 30min); Malmö (1 Fri, 1 Sun; 10hr); Nynäshamn (for Gotland) 90min before ferry's departure, from Vattugatan close to Central Station (30kr single); Oskarshamn (2–5 daily; 4hr 30min); Oslo (1 Fri, 1 Sun; 9hr); Sundsvall (3 Fri, 1 Sat, 4 Sun; 6hr); Uppsala (3 Fri, 1 Sat, 4 Sun; 1hr).

Gothenburg to: Gävle (1–2 daily; 10hr); Kalmar (1 Fri, 1 Sun; 6hr 30min); Kristianstad (1 Fri, 1 Sun; 5hr); Malmö (3 Fri, 3 Sun; 4hr 40min); Oslo (3–4 daily; 4hr 50min); Uppsala (1 Fri, 1 Sun; 8hr).

Ferries

Nynäshamn to: Visby (mid-June to mid-Aug 2 daily; 5hr).

Oskarshamn to: Visby (mid-June to mid-Aug 2 daily; 4hr).

International ferries

Stockholm to: Helsinki (Helsingsfors), Finland (2 daily; 15hr); St Petersburg, Russia (1 weekly; 26hr); Turku (Åbo), Finland (4 daily; 13hr).

Gothenburg to: Frederikshavn (6–8 daily; 3hr 15min); Harwich (April–Oct 4 weekly; 24hr); Newcastle (mid-June to mid-Aug 1 weekly; 24hr); Kiel (1 daily; 14hr).

Malmö to: Travemünde (June–Aug 2 daily; 8–10hr).

Sundsvall to: Vasa, Finland (1 daily; 8hr).

CHAPTER 23

SWITZERLAND

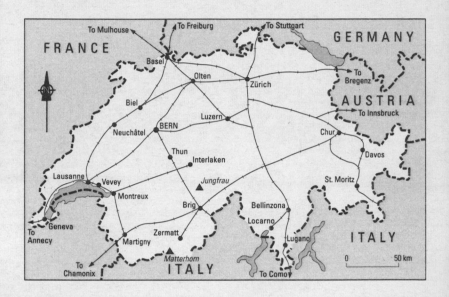

To Mulhouse
To Freiburg
To Stuttgart
GERMANY
FRANCE
Basel
Olten
To Bregenz
Zürich
AUSTRIA
Biel
Luzern
To Innsbruck
Neuchâtel
BERN
Chur
Thun
Interlaken
Davos
Lausanne
Jungfrau
St. Moritz
Vevey
Montreux
Brig
Bellinzona
Geneva
Locarno
To Annecy
Zermatt
Lugano
ITALY
Martigny
To Chamonix
Matterhorn
ITALY
To Como
0   50 km

Introduction

The renowned Swiss obsessiveness for cleanliness, punctuality and hard work, coupled with the highest standard of living in Europe, makes **Switzerland** one of the most expensive but also most problem-free of countries to travel. The tourist infrastructure is highly developed, and the Swiss themselves, although hard to get to know, are unfailingly courteous.

Pick up any Swiss newspaper and you will normally read several pages of foreign news before you come across any local stories of significance. However, it's important to remember that this quatrilingual confederation of 23 partly autonomous cantons, regarded by many as an island of stability in a turbulent Europe, spent the first 500 years of its existence rent by conflict, and it experienced a limited civil war as recently as 1847. Dating back to 1291, when the freeholding peasantry of central Switzerland formed an alliance to defend themselves against the House of Habsburg, the Confederation grew in strength as people here saw the benefits of mutual alliances. Up until the early 1500s Switzerland was an expanding military superpower feared throughout Europe, and it was only with the deep social divisions of the Reformation that the Swiss turned in on themselves and began to earn the reputation for neutrality which endures to this day. This neutrality served the Swiss well during the boom years after World War II; only now, with Switzerland lying outside the dynamics of European integration set in motion by the EC, is it beginning to look a little complacent.

Most Swiss speak English, and usually at least one of the other Swiss languages — French, German, Italian, or, in the extreme southeast, Romansch. As for **where to go**, the country's breathtaking concentration of mountainous scenery has drawn travellers since the beginning of the nineteenth century, and these days it's not always easy to avoid the crowds. The advantage is that the country is so small you can cross it by train in as little as five hours, and you can see a fair bit from one central base. Of the northern German-speaking cities, **Zürich** provides a wealth of sightseeing and nightlife possibilities as well as a base for venturing south towards the Alps. **Basel** and **Bern** — the capital — are quieter, but both have a historical pedigree which merits investigation, while **Luzern** combines the advantages of a cosmopolitan urban setting with close proximity to lakes and mountains. The most visited **Alpine** area is perhaps the central **Berner Oberland**, which has the highest concentration of picturesque peaks and mountainside villages, although the loftiest Alps are those of the **Valais** in the southwest, where the small but crowded resort of **Zermatt** provides access to the country's most distinctive peak, the **Matterhorn**. The isolated mountain valleys of **Graubunden**, in the eastern corner of the country, provide the setting for quality winter resorts like **St Moritz** and **Davos**. In the west, the cities lining the northern shore of **Lake Geneva** — notably **Geneva** itself, and **Montreux** and **Lausanne** — make up the bulk of French Switzerland, while the mild climate of Switzerland's southernmost canton, Italian-speaking **Ticino**, can seem a world apart from the rest of the country, especially the lakeside resorts of **Lugano** and **Locarno**, which can appear bathed in a subtropical, riviera atmosphere.

Information and Maps

Most places have a **tourist office**, also known as a *Verkehrsbüro* in German areas or *Office du Tourisme* in French Switzerland. Outside large cities, opening hours often allow for a long lunch and beyond the peak season can be limited. Most staff speak English and are scrupulously helpful, if sometimes a touch bemused by the notions of budget travel. Tourist offices often have maps, but otherwise there are plenty of good general **maps** of the country: the *Freytag & Berndt* 1:460,000 and *Bartholomew* 1:300,000 are both more than adequate. The *Office fédérale de topographie/ Bundesamt für Landestopographie* produce a series of more detailed 1:100,000 regional maps as well as 1:50,000 and 1:25,000 Walker's maps, all widely available in Swiss bookshops.

Money and Banks

Switzerland's unit of **currency** is the Swiss franc, divided into 100 centimes (or *Rappen* in German areas), coming in coins of 5, 10, 20 and 50 centimes and Sfr1, Sfr2 and Sfr5, and notes of Sfr10, Sfr20, Sfr50, Sfr100, Sfr500 and Sfr1000. Banks are usually open Mon–Fri 8.30am–4.30pm, although those outside major cities close between noon and 2pm. Some city and tourist resort branches open Sat 9am–4pm, although times vary. Money can also be changed at post offices and most train stations.

Communications

Post offices tend to open Mon–Fri 7.30am–noon & 1.30–6.30pm, Sat 7.30–11am, although watch out for regional variations and restricted hours in smaller branches. **Public telephones** are widespread and accept 10c, 20c, 50c, Sfr1 and Sfr5 coins; an increasing number take *Taxcards*, available from post offices to the value of Sfr10 or Sfr20. International calls can be made from most public phones; otherwise most large post offices have booths. Dialling ☎114 gets you an international operator or simply dial ☎00 followed by the code for the country you are calling. The domestic operator is ☎111.

Getting Around

The punctuality of Swiss **public transport** remains one of the wonders of the modern world. Train services usually depart on time, and rail timetables are well integrated with those of the post bus system, which operates on routes not covered by rail, serving the remoter villages and valleys.

■ Trains and buses

Travelling through Switzerland by **train** is invariably comfortable, hassle-free and often extraordinarily scenic, the higher mountain routes an attraction in their own right. The main state-run network, *SBB-CFF* (*Schweizerische Bundesbahn, Chemin de Fer Fédérale*), covers much of the country, but a large number of routes, especially Alpine lines, are operated by the privately owned rail companies who pioneered them. One-way fares work out at roughly Sfr30 per 100km. The 26+ *InterRail* ticket is currently not valid in Switzerland. Where the trains don't penetrate, buses take over, usually yellow **post buses**, serving the remoter mountain villages. Rail passes are once again sometimes valid on these but not always. The **Swiss Pass**, obtainable from the Swiss National Tourist Offices before you leave home or at train stations in Switzerland, allows unlimited travel on all state and most private railways, as well as buses and lake steamers, for 4, 8, 15 or 30 days. A second-class 8-day pass costs Sfr250, a 15-day pass Sfr290. There's also a **Half-Fare Pass**, which costs Sfr85 a month and entitles you to fifty percent off all trains, buses and lake ferries. If you plan to concentrate on one region, there are also regional passes, usually giving 5 days' travel in 15. Timetable leaflets covering specific routes are free from train stations; the three-volume official timetable, covering all rail and bus services, costs Sfr15.

■ Lake transport

Switzerland's lakes are all crossed by **ferry services** of one sort or another, but most are restricted to the summer season and are primarily tourist-oriented, duplicating routes which can be covered much more cheaply and quickly by rail. Only on lakes such as Luzern and Lugano, where hilly coastal terrain makes other forms of transport difficult, do ferries run throughout the year (albeit with limited services in winter), and are used by the locals as a way of getting about. Holders of the *Swiss Pass* are entitled to free travel on all lake ferries.

■ Driving, hitching and cycling

Switzerland's **road network** is as comprehensive and well-planned as you'd expect, and although the mountainous terrain can make for some circuitous routes there is, of course, the compensation of some superb – if sometimes hair-raising – mountain scenery. If you're planning to drive on any motorways, you have to pay a tax of about Sfr30 – a *vignette* or tax-disc can be bought from Swiss National Tourist Offices abroad, at the border or at petrol stations around the country. Speed limits are 50kph in built-up areas, 80kph on main roads, 120kph on motorways. The *Touring Club Suisse* operates a 24-hour breakdown service – call ☎140. **Car rental** costs upwards of Sfr45 a day, for a small hatchback, plus about Sfr1 per kilometre, or about Sfr700 a week with unlimited mileage. Most firms require the driver to be over 21.

Hitching is feasible on the fast routes linking the major cities of the north and east, but the really scenic bits of Switzerland are so widely scattered, and the terrain so fundamentally awkward, that it's usually difficult to get a direct ride.

Given the nature of the landscape, **cycling** is not the best way of exploring the country, though you can always avoid the nastier passes by taking your bike on regional trains (ie. not *InterCity*) for Sfr6. Cycling is recommended around the lakes and in cities, where bike lanes are usually provided. Bikes can be hired at all major train stations for around Sfr19 a day.

Accommodation

As with most things in Switzerland, accommodation is expensive. All tourist offices can help with hotel bookings, and outside office hours they normally display a board with details of the region's hotels, complete with courtesy telephone, outside. In many cases you'll find these at the end of train station platforms too.

■ Hotels and private rooms

Hotel accommodation is at least of a uniformly high standard, but as with everything in Switzerland it's not cheap. Double rooms start at about Sfr80; you won't find much below this and you should expect to pay around Sfr100 on average. There are occasionally **private rooms**, and these cost a little less, but they aren't as widespread as in other parts of Europe, and are mainly confined to rural and Alpine resort areas (look for signs offering *Zimmer frei*). Tourist offices tend not to help with private room bookings, although they may dole out long lists of addresses and telephone numbers; an additional snag is that many private rooms are only let on a Saturday to Saturday basis.

■ Hostels and campsites

If travelling on a budget, you'll need to rely a great deal on **youth hostels** (*Jugendherbergen/ Auberges de Jeunesse/Alberghi per la Gioventù*), though they can get very full between June and September, when you should book in advance. The hostels are of a high standard, and feature a high proportion of double rooms as well as small dorms. Prices depend on the category of hostel, and range from Sfr9 for a dorm bed at the lowest grade to Sfr25 at the highest, with the average running around Sfr18 including breakfast and sheet sleeping bag hire; non-*IYHF* members pay at least Sfr5 on top, sometimes more. Note that under-25s are given priority and that in towns there's sometimes a three-night maximum stay in summer. Meals, where available, are around Sfr9. There are over eighty hostels in Switzerland altogether; for more details contact the Swiss hostelling association, the *Schweizerischer Bund für Jugendherbergen*, Postfach, 3001 Bern (☎031/24 55 03).

The typical Swiss **campsite** is similarly clean and well-equipped, although the higher the altitude the more limited the opening times; many close altogether outside the main May–September season. Prices tend to hover around Sfr7 per person plus Sfr6–10 per pitch and per vehicle. Many sites require an international camping carnet.

Food and Drink

In general, **eating and drinking** will inflict another fairly massive hole in your budget. Food prices are more expensive across the board than in the rest of Europe – you may find yourself falling back on self-catering if you're travelling on a tight budget.

■ Food

Snack food is widely available and consists mainly of the ubiquitous international standbys of burgers, pizza slices and kebabs. In German areas you'll also find plentiful streetstands serving *Würste*, while French Switzerland rejoices in a wide range of delicious patisserie fare. More substantially, the few important native **dishes** are simple peasant fare on the whole. In French Switzerland cheese is the basic ingredient of both *fondue*, molten cheese and wine into which cubes of bread are dipped, and *raclette* – melted cheese scooped up with potatoes or bread. The staple in German Switzerland is *Rösti*, boiled potatoes which are grated, fried, then grilled or baked, the

---

ACCOMMODATION PRICE CODES

Throughout this guide, accommodation is priced on a scale of ① to ⑧, the number indicating the lowest price per night a single person could expect to pay in that establishment in high season. With hostels this is the nightly rate per person; with hotels, the price is arrived at by dividing the cost of the cheapest double room by two. The prices indicated by the codes are as follows

① = under £5 / $8	② = £5–10 / $8–16	③ = £10–15 / $16–24	④ = £15–20 / $24–32
⑤ = £20–25 / $32–40	⑥ = £25–30 / $40–48	⑦ = £30–35 / $48–56	⑧ = over £35 / $56

resulting golden brown hash often topped with cheese or chopped ham – each establishment has its own variant. Another native dish found in German areas is *Berner Platte*, a cold dish of mixed meats and sauerkraut.

In French Switzerland, daytime **cafés** serve food and are often the best places in which to sample an inexpensive *plat du jour*. Bars and pubs are less likely to have food, although the *Bierstuben* of the German cities often serve hearty evening meals. **Restaurants** are fairly pricy, although *fondue, raclette* and *Rösti* are common and not too expensive, especially at lunchtime when you can usually get a *plat du jour* or *Mittagsmenü* for between Sfr12 and Sfr18. Evening meals in inexpensive restaurants hover around the Sfr25–30 mark, although pizzas and pastas are often a more economical choice. The *Migros* chain of department stores, invariably to be found in the centre of all major towns, has reasonable self-service restaurants inside. Another good standby is the *Mövenpick* chain of mid-priced family restaurants – much like burger joints inside but offering reliable food and service. Watch out for *sinalco*, or *alkohol-frei* restaurants, as well as an increasing number of establishments with smoking bans.

■ Drink

The Swiss display distinctly Anglophile tendencies in their **drinking** habits: cafés are often called tearooms, bars are normally "pubs" – though these are only superficially similar to their English counterparts, most featuring waitress service. Other than pubs, drinking venues vary according to region. Cosy *Bierstuben* and *Weinkeller* are regular features of the urban scene in German-speaking Switzerland, while in the Francophone cities pavement cafés offering a range of both food and drink are more common. The local **beer** is invariably excellent, and not too expensive at Sfr2.50–3.50 for a third-litre, and you frequently encounter *Guinness* on tap, as well as more expensive imported bottled beers. **Wine** is prohibitively costly; try whites from Lake Geneva, or reds from the Rhône valley, which work out a little cheaper. Finding somewhere to drink late at night is no longer a problem in the big cities, although prices sometimes go up after the clock strikes twelve. By using supermarkets, you can

drop drinking costs dramatically. Litres of *vin de table* start from as little as Sfr3 a litre, with some quantity of beer available from Sfr2.

Opening Hours and Holidays

Opening hours are customarily Mon–Fri 8am–noon & 2–6.30pm, Sat 8am–noon & 2–5pm. In the larger cities you'll find that the lunch break is seldom taken these days. Some shops may stay open on Saturday afternoons, but these will stay closed on Monday morning to compensate, a practice that is particularly common in Geneva. Late-opening of shops is virtually unknown: usually the only places where you'll be able to buy food after 6.30pm, even in larger towns, are the vast vending machines in subterranean train station concourses.

You'll find shops, banks and many museums closed on the following **public holidays:** Jan 1; Good Friday; Easter Monday; May 1; Ascension Day; Whitsun; Dec 25 & 26. In addition, some shops and banks close for all or part of Swiss National Day, Aug 1.

Emergencies

The Swiss are an extraordinarily law-abiding people and have an endless capacity for mutual surveillance, rendering the **police** presence almost superfluous at times. You are more likely to be harassed by an upright citizen instructing you on the correct way to cross a road than by anyone with criminal intent. Many Swiss cities can seem eerily quiet after about 9pm, but the streets are safe enough. Regarding **health problems**, all hospitals have some kind of 24-hour service, although you will have to either pay or show your insurance policy. Each area has a rota system whereby one local **pharmacy** (*Apotheke/pharmacie*) stays open outside normal shopping hours. Each pharmacy will have a sign in the window telling you where the nearest open one is; local newspapers also have details.

EMERGENCY NUMBERS
Police ☎117; Ambulance ☎144; Fire ☎118.

LAKE GENEVA

The shores of **Lake Geneva** – Lac Léman in French, Genfersee in German – form the economic and cultural focus of French-speaking Switzerland, or *la Suisse romande*, as well as being the prime destination for most travellers to the western end of the country. The French Swiss belong in the cultural orbit of their French neighbours, but differ from them in their deep-rooted Calvinism, which, despite the austerity of its doctrines, established the area's reputation as a safe haven for refugees. A host of free-thinking Europeans set up home here: Voltaire found Geneva more amenable than his native France; Catholic convert and later renegade Edward Gibbon wrote a great deal of his *Decline and Fall* in Lausanne; and local-born philosopher Jean-Jacques Rousseau, although he spent so little time here, proclaimed himself "citoyen de Genève" on the frontispiece of his books, as if that in itself were sufficient proof of anti-establishment thinking. Nowadays the atmosphere couldn't be more conservative. French Switzerland's main city **Geneva** is a sterile bankers' town, albeit one enlivened by its role as headquarters of many an international organization. The so-called "Swiss Riviera", further along the lake around **Lausanne** and **Montreux**, has an air every bit as exclusive as its namesake in France, dotted with opulent lakeside villas and providing a very different picture to the unspoilt paradise which inspired Byron and Shelley to spend time here (Mary Shelley produced Frankenstein during their sojourn just outside Geneva). However, the scenery remains a powerful draw, and the view across the lake from the Swiss side towards the French Alps is one of the most invigorating in Europe.

Geneva

The puritanism of **GENEVA** (Genève) is inextricably linked with the city's struggle for independence. Long ruled by the Dukes of Savoy, who regarded the local bishopric as their private property, sixteenth-century Genevans saw the Reformation in neighbouring Switzerland as a useful ally in their struggles to rid themselves of Savoyard influence. The city of Bern played a large part in encouraging Genevan independence, despatching the reformist preacher Guillaume Farel here in 1532, and sending troops to protect the town when the city fathers finally declared their loyalty to the Reformation in 1536. However, Geneva remained outside the confederation for another 300 years (the Catholic cantons opposed their entry), and continued to be a vulnerable enclave in Savoyard soil. Its independence from Savoy was finally recognized in 1602, by which time it had established itself as the "Protestant Rome", largely due to the influence of Farel's successor Jean Calvin, under whom Geneva developed a reputation for joylessness which colours the place to this day.

> The Geneva area telephone code is ☎022.

Arrival and accommodation

Geneva's **airport** is at Cointrin, 3km north of the town, linked to the main **train station**, Gare Cornavin, by train every twenty minutes. The station is ten minutes north of the lake front at the head of rue Mont Blanc; buses #9, #5 or #6 take you into the centre. If you're coming from the Annecy/Chamonix direction you'll arrive at the **SNCF station** in Eaux-Vives on the other side of town (tram #12 into the centre). The **tourist office** (Mon–Sat 9am–6pm) is at the train station and handles accommodation bookings.

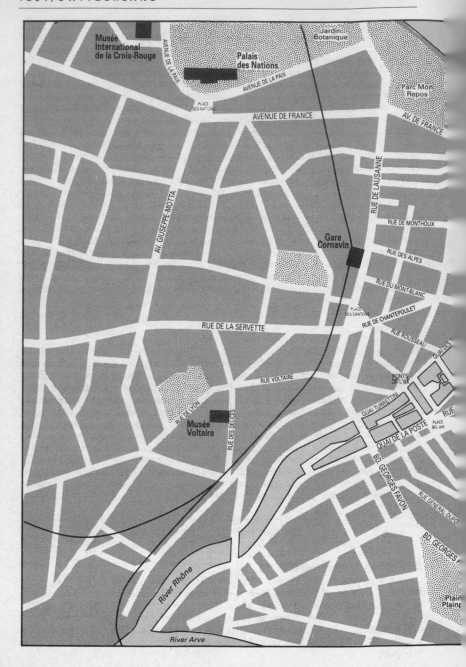

Musée
International
de la Croix-Rouge

Jardin
Botanique

Palais
des Nations

Parc Mon
Repos

AVENUE DE LA PAIX

AVENUE DE LA PAIX

PLACE
DES NATIONS

AVENUE DE FRANCE

AV. DE FRANCE

AVENUE DE LA PAIX

RUE DE LAUSANNE

AV. GIUSEPPE-MOTTA

RUE DE MONTHOUX

Gare
Cornavin

RUE DES ALPES

RUE DU MONT-BLANC

PLACE
DES CANTONS

RUE DE CHANTEPOULET

RUE DE LA SERVETTE

RUE ROUSSEAU

QUAI DES

PONTS
DE L'ILE

RUE VOLTAIRE

QUAI TURRETTIN

RUE

RUE DE LYON

PLACE
BEL-AIR

Musée
Voltaire

RUE DES DÉLICES

QUAI DE LA POSTE

BD. GEORGES-FAVON

RUE GENERAL-DUFO

BD. GEORGES

River Rhône

Plain
Plainp

River Arve

Lake Geneva

QUAI DE COLOGNY

QUAI WILSON

QUAI DU MONT-BLANC

Jet d'Eau

QUAI GUSTAVE-ADOR

AVENUE WILLIAM FAVRE

ROUTE DE FRONTENEX

PONT DU MONT-BLANC

Jardin Anglais

Gare des
Eaux-Vives

QUAI GÉNÉRAL-GUISAN

RUE DU RHÔNE

U RHÔNE

MARCHE   CROIX-D'OR   RUE DE RIVE

RÔTISSERIE MADELEINE   VIEUX-COLLÈGE

CITÉ

RUE FERDINAND-HODLER

Cathedral

GRAND RUE

DALCROZE

HELVETIQUE

Russian
Church

HÔTEL-DE-VILLE

PLACE
DU BOURG
DE FOUR

RUE CHARLES-GALLAND

PL
NEUVE

CROIX ROUGE

BD. JACLIES

Reformation
Monument

RUE DE L'ATHÉNÉE

RUE ST. VICTOR

Baur
Collection

University
Library

BD. JACQUES DALCROZE

Petit
Palais

RUE DE CANDOLLE

BD HELVETIQUE

RUE DE L'ATHÉNÉE

AVON

BD. DES

RUE DE CAROUGE

PHILOSOPHES

Parc
Bertrand

e de
alais

GENEVA

Geneva's essential sights are best explored on foot, but for longer journeys local **trams and buses** are quick and efficient. A single journey of up to three stops costs a flat fare of Sfr1.20; Sfr2 gets you an hour's validity with unlimited changes. Geneva is short on inexpensive hotels, but has a wide range of decent **hostel** accommodation, often with private rooms. The *Nouvelle Auberge de la Jeunesse*, rue Rothschild 28–30 (☎732 62 60; ②), also has swish doubles with ensuite showers for a little more; the *Cité Universitaire*, av Miremont 46 (☎346 23 55; ②), has double rooms, dormitory bunks and rock-bottom breakfast – free; *Centre Masaryk*, av de la Paix 11 (☎733 07 72; ③), in the "international" part of town near the Palais des Nations, also runs to less expensive dormitory accommodation; *Interpoint*, av Ste-Clotilde 9 (☎321 83 13; ②), is close to the *Hôtel le Grenil*, but only has dormitory accommodation and requires a Sfr65 membership fee. Among the cheaper **pensions and hotels**, *Hôtel le Grenil*, av Ste-Clotilde 7 (☎328 30 55; ⑥), offers doubles without bath for less, as does *Hôtel Lido*, rue Chantepoulet 8 (☎731 55 30; ⑤), between Gare Cornavin and the town centre. The nearest **campsite** is *Sylvabelle*, 4km away at 10 chemin de Conches; (take bus #8 from Gare Cornavin), although *Camping Pointe-à-la-Bise TCS* (☎752 12 86), 7km along bus route E beside the lake, is more pleasant.

The City

Genevans divide their city into the *rive gauche* and *rive droite*. The former, on the south bank of the river Rhône, includes the high ground of the old town grouped around its hill-top cathedral and the greyish grid of streets below, which forms the main shopping and business districts of the city. The latter takes in the hillside suburbs that are home to most of Geneva's international community. Linking the two are a series of bridges, most important of which is the central **pont du Mont Blanc**. On the *rive gauche* side, the ornamental flowerbeds of the **Jardin Anglais** are renowned for the **Horloge Fleurie** or floral clock, beyond which is the lakefront's most visible feature, the 140-metre-high plume of the **Jet d'Eau** erupting from the end of a jetty just off Quai Gustave Ador. Immediately right of the bridge, **Rousseau Island** bears a seated statue of the philosopher. Rousseau's relations with his native Geneva were always problematic: he ran away at the age of sixteen and converted to Catholicism, only returning in 1754 as a way of demonstrating his hostility towards the degeneracy of Parisian culture. His affection for the Genevan republic soon soured, and he began supporting those in the city who protested at the closed nature of its oligarchic government. The city repaid him by banning all his books in 1756 and issuing a warrant for his arrest; Rousseau renounced Genevan citizenship and never came back.

Three blocks upriver, the **Pont de l'Île** is a more attractive crossingpoint , its thirteenth-century tower dominating another island in the Rhône. On the southern side, rue de la Monnaie leads up to the main thoroughfare of the old city, the cobbled, steeply ascending **Grande Rue**, on which – among the secondhand bookshops, antique shops and galleries – the seventeenth-century **Hôtel de Ville**, and the arcaded front of the old city **armoury** opposite, stand out. A few steps beyond, the **Maison Tavel**, rue Puits-St-Pierre 6 (Tues–Sun 10am–5pm; free), is an old patrician house holding the town museum, with several floors of period furniture and material depicting the various trades of Geneva, culminating in a model of the town as it was in 1850, the virtual life's work of local architect Auguste Magnin, who wanted to capture the atmosphere of Geneva prior to the destruction of the town walls. A block away, the **Cathédrale St-Pierre** (June–Sept daily 9am–7pm; Oct daily 9am–noon & 2–6pm; Nov–Feb daily 9am–noon & 2–5pm; March–May daily 9am–noon & 2–6pm) was originally a late Romanesque structure with a slightly incongruous eighteenth-century portal. It's bare inside save for the dazzling frescoes of the *Chapelle des Maccabées* to the right of the main entrance, whose intricate floral patterns and lute-strumming angels are in fact modern versions of much-faded fifteenth-century originals – now to be found in

Geneva's main museum. The north tower (daily 9–11.30am & 2–5.30pm; Sfr2.50) offers commanding views of the old town, while outside the main entrance, steps descend to the **Site Archéologique** (Tues–Sun 10am–1pm & 2–6pm; Sfr5), a modern crypt built over the foundations of the old cathedral containing bits of medieval sculpture. Below the cathedral, the old town focuses on the **place du Bourg du Four**, a picturesque split-level square perched on the hillside, somehow preserving its small-town charm.

West of here, rue de la Croix Rouge, occupying a bastion of the old city fortifications, looks down on the **Reformation Monument** on promenade des Bastions, built in 1917 and serving as a pictorial history of Protestantism. Four main figures dominate the centre, Geneva's principal sixteenth-century preachers Farel, Calvin, Bèze and Knox, flanked by reliefs of other people or events important to the history of the reformed church – the Pilgrim Fathers, Oliver Cromwell, even Stefan Bocskay of Transylvania, who won freedom of worship for his far-flung branch of the Calvinist commonwealth in 1606. A tree-lined park separates the monument from the university library, home to a small **Musée Jean-Jacques Rousseau** (Mon–Fri 9am–noon & 2–5pm, Sat 9am–noon; free), with a smattering of manuscripts and mementoes. Immediately north is **Place Neuve**, at the far end of which the **Musée Rath** (Tues & Thurs–Sun 10am–5pm, Wed noon–9pm; Sfr5) hosts a changing programme of high-profile art exhibitions.

Geneva's municipal art collection, the **Musée d'Art et d'Histoire**, is a short walk east of here at rue Charles Galland 2 (Tues–Sun 10am–5pm; free), just south of the old town in a pleasant residential district. The ground floor contains many ancient remains – Egyptology, Greek vases, fragments from Roman Geneva and a large room full of paintings by local artist Felix Valloton, probably better known in the English-speaking world for his Art Nouveau-ish woodcuts. Upstairs a lot of space is devoted to local nine-teenth- and twentieth-century painters of dubious merit, although there's a sizeable collection of works by the Bern-born symbolist Ferdinand Hodler, whose luminous blue Genevan lakescapes display tentative steps towards Expressionism. Elsewhere there are a few Impressionists and pieces by twentieth-century artists, including an abstract painting by Le Corbusier, born at nearby La Chaux de Fonds in 1887. The star attraction is, however, Konrad Witz's altarpiece of 1444, commissioned for the cathedral by Genevan bishop François de Metz. The bishop is shown kneeling at the feet of the Virgin Mary on one of the panels, while another panel shows Christ walking on water that is unmistakeably Lake Geneva. The museum's collection of prints and drawings is around the corner in the **Cabinet des Estampes**, promenade du Pin (Tues–Sun 10am–noon & 2–6pm; free), while the nearby **Petit Palais** on Terrasse St-Victor (Mon 2–6pm, Tues–Sun 10am–noon & 2–6pm; Sfr10) offers a comprehensive summing-up of turn-of-the-century art from Impressionism through to Surrealism, including some vibrant work from Monet, Cézanne and Chagall.

The *rive droite* is by comparison a drab area of town, although it's worth heading up rue de Lyon from the station to the **Musée Voltaire** at rue des Délices 25 (Mon–Fri 2–5pm; free), the writer's former residence. A dummy dressed in Voltaire's old clothes sits at a writing desk and presides over pictures, books and manuscripts documenting the various controversies his presence here invited. Further north lie a good proportion of Geneva's many international organizations, concentrated around place des Nations (buses #5 and #8 from place Cornavin). The cavernous interiors of the **Palais des Nations** at av de la Paix 14, headquarters of the short-lived League of Nations and now home to the European section of the United Nations, can be visited on guided tours (daily July & Aug 9am–noon & 2–6pm; rest of year 10am–noon & 2–4pm; Sfr8), although the surrounding parks, situated high above the lake, are reason enough to visit. Virtually next door, the **Musée Internationale de la Croix-Rouge**, av de la Paix 17 (10am–5pm; closed Tues; Sfr8), is a state-of-the-art attempt to portray the Red Cross's good works. Below is the most beautiful part of the lakefront, an extensive area of lawns, shrubs and leafy walks, parks and botanical gardens.

A twenty-minute #12 tram ride across the River Arve is the late-Baroque suburb of CAROUGE, originally a separate town beyond the city walls built by the the King of Savoy in the eighteenth century. A fine example of eighteenth-century town planning, with a network of elegantly proportioned streets around place du Temple and place du Marché, and now largely inhabited by fashion designers and small galleries, its reputation as an outpost of hedonism beyond Geneva's jurisdiction lives on in its numerous cafés and bars.

Eating, drinking and nightlife

Though you need to tread carefully among Geneva's battery of pricy restaurants, there are plenty of centrally located cafés and bars offering lunchtime *plats du jour*, as well as inexpensive evening eats. *Le Zofage*, rue des Voisins 6, is a university cafeteria open to non-students; *Manora*, on rue de Cornavin, is a high-quality self-service restaurant with plentiful vegetarian selections. *Au Jardin des Crêpes*, av du Mail 25, serves a wide selection of sweet and savoury crêpes from around Sfr9; *Café Helvetique*, rue de Carouge 56, has filling pizzas for Sfr10–14, with *La Trattoria* on rue de la Servette near the station adding an authentic Italian touch for a couple of francs more. *Brasserie Lipp*, rue de la Confédération 8, is a fashionable but more costly place to be seen enjoying an evening meal. The train station buffet is good, too, and not at all expensive. As for **drinking**, the pavement cafés of the old city, around place du Bourg du Four and the adjoining rue de la Fontaine, are good places to drink during the day; night-time drinking centres around a scattering of English-style pubs and bars on both sides of the river, especially in the southern suburb of Carouge. The *Planteur*, on rue du Molard, is a lively bar below the old city; *First National City Café*, place des Eaux-Vives 2, is bright, stylish and rather chic. In Carouge, *La Bourse*, on place du Marché, is a stylish brasserie with cheap pizzas and other food, while *Chat Noir*, on rue Vautier, is a popular bar with frequent live jazz. The tables outside *L'Auberge Sarde*, rue Joseph Girade 5, have become a youthful hangout for both eating and drinking.

Listings

Airlines *British Airways*, rue Chantepoulet 13 (☎731 21 25); *Swissair*, rue de Lausanne (☎799 31 11).
Bicycle rental At the train station or from *Procycle* on place Montbrillant.
Books *Centre Naville*, rue Levrier 5–7, has a large choice of English-language books.
Bus station place Dorsière (☎731 41 40). Buses to Annecy and Chamonix.
Consulates *Australia*, rue de Moillebeau 56–58 (☎734 62 00); *Canada*, 1 chemin de la Bichette (☎733 90 00); *Great Britain*, rue de Vermont 37–39 (☎734 12 04); *New Zealand*, chemin du Petit-Saconnex 28A (☎734 38 00); *USA*, av de la Paix 1 (☎738 50 95).
Ferries *CGN*, quai du Mont Blanc (☎311 25 21), operate a regular service to Lausanne and Montreux between May and September.
Hospital *Hôpital Cantonal*, rue Micheli-du-Crest 24 (☎372 33 11).
Post office Main office at rue Mont Blanc (Mon–Fri 7.30am–noon & 1.45–6pm, Sat 7.30–11am).
Telephones At the main post office.
Train enquiries ☎731 64 50.

The Riviera: Lausanne, Vevey and Montreux

The eastern end of Lake Geneva, from the large conurbation of Lausanne to the end of the lake, is known as the **Riviera**, a never-ending stretch of villas and lakeside properties which often leaves little public access to the lake shore itself. The flora-lined lakeside promenades in the major resorts are, however, deftly manicured, and, coupled with the view across to the southern shore and the French Alps, make this one of the most beautiful places in the country to spend a couple of restful days. It's also well within reach of higher altitudes, the gently rising hills north of Lausanne and the loftier hill stations up behind Montreux providing an early taste of Alpine pleasures further east.

Lausanne

Capital city of the canton of Vaud, **LAUSANNE** was brought into the Swiss orbit due to the military expansionism of the Bernese, who "liberated" the area from the Dukes of Savoy in the 1530s, bringing Protestantism and abolition of serfdom in their wake. The bulk of the city is perched on lumpy terrain above the lake, with the suburban resort of Ouchy on the shoreline a mile or so below.

Arriving in Lausanne by train, the station is on a plateau below the city centre proper, reached by following the steeply ascending rue du Petit Chêne to **place St François**. From here rue St François leads over the hump of a hill to a busy shopping street, **rue Centrale**. To the left, market stalls scatter across the cobbles of **place de la Palud**, an ancient, fountained square flanked by the arcades of the Renaissance town hall, from where a stairway leads up to the **Cathedral**, a fine Romanesque-Gothic jumble straddling the eleventh to thirteenth centuries, its clean lines only peripherally adorned with memorials to past prominent citizens and a few fifteenth-century frescoes. The turreted tower (May–Sept Mon–Sat 8.30–11.30am & 1.30–5.30pm, Sun 2–5.30pm; Oct–April closes at 4.30pm; Sfr 25) gives fabulous views over the town and lake to the Savoy Alps. **The Musée Historique de Lausanne** (Tues–Sun 11am–6pm, Thurs until 8pm; Sfr4), in the former bishop's palace opposite, has episcopal treasures and an archeological collection dating back to the Neolithic era. North, a fourteenth-century château overlooks **place de la Riponne**, an arid expanse of concrete save for its dominating feature, the splendidly ostentatious **Palais de Rumine**, home to various cantonal institutions and museum collections. The **Musée Cantonal des Beaux-Arts** (Tues & Wed 11am–6pm, Thurs 11am–8pm, Fri–Sun 11am–5pm; Sfr7) has the odd Renoir and Utrillo submerged among local works, though the natural history collection is more entertaining (daily 10am–noon & 2–5pm; free) – endless cabinets crammed with bones of extinct beasts (including an entire mammoth) or the stuffed skins of their descendants. Steps at the northwest end of the place ascend to av Vinet, from where it's ten minutes' walk or a couple of stops on bus #2 to the **Musée de l'Art Brut** (Tues–Fri 10am–noon & 2–6pm, Sat & Sun 2–6pm; Sfr5), a gargantuan black pyramid filled with the work of naive, untrained "outsider" artists, passionately collected by their champion Jean Dubuffet.

Half an hour's walk uphill from the centre (or a short ride on bus #16 from place Madeleine, just above place de la Riponne) is **Le Signal**, a hill-top observation point which offers a magnificent panorama across the lake. Immediately above, the **Bois de Sauvebelin** has a few walking possibilities. Paths lead to a small lake with a surrounding wild fowl and deer reserve, and onwards to the wilder beasts of the **Vivarium**, a small zoo (Mon & Wed–Fri 2–6.30pm, Sat & Sun 10am–noon & 2–6.30pm; Sfr6). Returning to Lausanne down avenue Vulliemin you pass the **Fondation de l'Hermitage** (Tues–Sun 10am–1pm & 2–6pm, Thurs until 10pm; Sfr13), an imposing villa built in 1841 for the wealthy local Buignon family, and packed with the then fashionable English furniture and fittings, preserved along with the surrounding park as a cultural monument hosting high-profile touring exhibitions of contemporary art.

OUCHY, Lausanne's fashionable lakeside suburb, is a short hop by funicular (known locally as the metro) from the main station, or a pleasant stroll down avenue d'Ouchy. It's worth it for the lakeside gardens and view across to Evian-les-Bains in France, to which at least five ferries a day make the half-hour journey. With the headquarters of the International Olympic Committee in Lausanne, the town had no problem gaining consent for the glistening new Olympic Museum, quai d'Ouchy 1 (May–Sept Tues–Sun 10am–7pm, Thurs to 8pm; Oct–April Tues–Sun 10am–6pm, Thurs to 8pm; Sfr12), five minutes' walk east on quai de Belgique. Overlooked by sculpted symbols of supreme human endeavour, you wander the various levels – linked by a central spiral ramp – packed with interactive displays, where you can get an expert opinion on your pet Olympic controversy. Masses of memorabilia, including Carl Lewis' sweaty track shoes, round out a memorable visit.

PRACTICALITIES
The **tourist office** is in Ouchy, 100m west of the funicular terminal, at av de Rhodanie 2 (April–mid-Oct Mon–Sat 8am–7pm, Sun 9am–noon & 1–6pm; Oct–March Mon–Fri 8am–6pm, Sat 8.30am–noon & 1–5pm). There are a couple of low-cost places to stay: a **youth hostel** at chemin du Muguet 1 (☎021/26 57 82; ②), six stops west on bus #1 from the station, and the new *Jeunotel*, Chemin du Bois-de-Vaux 36 (☎021/626 02 22; ②), with 4-bed dorms – catch bus #2 five stops west from Ouchy. Closer to the action, there are a couple of small **hotels** – *Hôtel du Raisin*, place de la Palud 19 (☎021/312 27 56; ⑤), and *Hôtel du Port*, place du Port 5 (☎021/26 49 30; ⑥) – though you need to book well in advance. Most useful campsite is *Camping Vidy*, chemin du Camping 3 (☎021/24 20 31), by the lakeside close to the *Jeunotel* (bus #18).

Central Lausanne is full of touristy **restaurants** offering pasta, pizza and medium-priced international fare. *Goya*, rue Grande St-Jean 18, is one standby, or a branch of the self-service chain *Manora* at place St-François 17 offers better food in less salubrious surroundings. *Café de l'Evêché*, below the cathedral at the beginning of rue Curtat 4, has various affordable eats, regulars like fondue sharing the menu with good horse steaks. *Crêperie le Chandeleur*, rue Mercerie 9, has a nice, youthful atmosphere and a reasonably affordable selection of sweet and savoury crêpes. *Brasserie Bonaparte*, rue St Pierre 3, is equally youthful but more expensive, the food coming in daintier portions. For **nightlife**, *Le Grand Café* in the fine old *Casino de Montbenon*, allée E. Ansermet 3, five minutes west of place St François, is a popular late-night haunt offering good food and live music. *Dolce Vita*, rue Dr César Roux 30, is better for raw alternative music than the trendy *MAD* (Moulin à Danse) at rue de Genève 23, which plays less audacious stuff to a youthful crowd. There's jazz on Friday and Saturday nights at *Jazz du Boulevard*, 51 boulevard de Grancy, and at the stylish *Café Saxo*, at the bottom of rue de la Grotte.

Vevey

The small-town atmosphere of **VEVEY**, a vine-growing and market centre five miles west of Montreux, may prove a welcome change from the more cosmopolitan conurbations on either side. On a terrace just east of the station, the twelfth-century **Church of St Martin** is worth peeping inside for a glimpse of the tombs of Edmund Ludlow and Andrew Broughton. Among those responsible for sentencing Charles I to death after the English Civil War, the pair sought sanctuary in Vaud after the Restoration. Below, the collection of the **Musée Jenisch** on rue de la Gare (Tues–Sun 10.30am–noon & 2.30–5.30pm; Sfr6) features a Gustave Courbet lakescape and graphics by Le Corbusier. Touring exhibitions, which are almost always present, bump up the price to Sfr12.

Vevey's charm centres on the lakeside **Grande Place**, packed with market stalls at weekends, and the narrow streets which lead off into the old town to the east. Among the curiosities here, there's a **Swiss Camera Museum** at rue des Anciens Fosses (Tues–Sun 10.30am–noon & 2–5.30pm; Sfr4), packed with photographic ephemera, and a **Town Museum** (Musée de la Confrérie des Vignerons) at rue du Château 2 (Tues–Sun 10.30am–noon & 2–5.30pm; Sfr4), devoted to the local Confrérie des Vignerons and the meticulously organized harvest festivals they mount four times a century. Further on, the **Alimentarium** (Tues–Sun 10am–noon & 2–5pm; Sfr4), sponsored by local chocolate giants *Nestlé*, is a museum devoted to foodstuffs with a strongly educative tone.

Despite Vevey's relative quiet, you won't save too much money by **staying** here instead of Montreux or Lausanne. If you don't mind walking down the hall for a shower, the cheapest place to stay is the *Pension Famille*, rue Louis Meyer 16 (☎021/ 921 40 23; ③). Otherwise, there are a couple of **hotels**, *Des Negociants*, rue du Conseil 27 (☎021/922 70 11; ⑤), and *Hostellerie de Genève*, place du Marché 11 (☎021/921 45 77; ⑥), both in the centre near the lake. The **tourist office** (Mon–Fri 8.30am–noon & 1.30–6pm, or 8pm in July & Aug, Sat 8.30am–noon), immediately outside the station on place de la Gare, may be able to help with other options.

Trolley bus #1 regularly plies the coast road between Vevey and Montreux, but it's a good idea to walk along the lakeside promenade at least as far as Vevey's sister town of **LA TOUR DU PEILZ**, site of a colourful port beside a whitewashed château, which now hosts the Swiss **Toy Museum** (Tues–Sun 2–6pm; Sfr6). Away from the lakefront there's little of interest save for the fountain in the **place du Temple** one block beyond, topped by a head of Liberty sculpted by Gustave Courbet. Another political exile, Courbet laid low in these parts after several acts of vandalism committed during the Paris Commune. Vevey's campsite, *La Maladaire* (021/944 31 37), is by the lake half way to La Tour de Peilz.

Montreux

MONTREUX is fairly drab by the standards of the Riviera, although coachloads of visitors happily shuffle along its promenade, passing examples of Swiss horticultural perfection as they go. Nevertheless, it's a handy place from which to visit the neighbouring Château de Chillon or the mountain resorts above before pressing on towards higher altitudes to the east.

The town clings tenaciously to an outstretched arm of the Vaud Alps, and the zigzagging streets and hillside terraces of the old quarter above the train station provide marginally more interest than the thronging lakeside thoroughfare of rue de Casino below. A modest **Museum of Old Montreux** at rue de la Gare 40 (Easter–Oct daily 10am–noon & 2–5pm; Sfr4) is filled with objects illustrating the town's history, especially the impact of tourism on the local environment, explained in the "Ecomusée" on the upper floors. The nearby **Maison Visinand**, a fine old piece of vernacular architecture, now serves as Montreux's cultural centre, with regular exhibitions of local arts and crafts (Tues–Sun 3–6pm; free).

Whether you opt for the 45-minute walk along the lake, or the quicker journey on the #1 trolley bus, your first sight of the **Château de Chillon** (daily July & Aug 9am–6.15pm; April–June & Sept 9am–5.45pm; Oct 10am–4.45pm; Nov–Feb 10am–12.45pm, last entry noon & 1.30–4pm; March 10am–12.45pm, last entry noon & 1.30–4.45pm; Sfr5.50) is an unforgettable one, an elegant, turreted pile of rock jutting out into the lake, with the craggy ridge of the Dents du Midi serving as a backdrop. The château owes much of its fame to Lord Byron, who after a sailing trip here with Shelley in 1816 retreated to nearby Ouchy to dash off his prose poem *Prisoner of Chillon*. The prisoner of the title was the real-life reformist preacher François Bonivard, who was incarcerated by the castle's Savoyard masters before the Bernese conquest of the Vaud under General Naegli set him free in 1536. The influence of the Bernese bailiffs who henceforth occupied Chillon can be seen in the many wood-panelled and finely decorated halls which make up the tour of the château, although its distinctive outer appearance owes more to the much earlier efforts of thirteenth-century Duke of Savoy Peter II. Diving through the heavy stone passageways of the château (including a dungeon whose central pillar bears the dubiously attributed signature of Byron) gives some idea of the harsher side of fortress life.

PRACTICALITIES

Montreux's **tourist office** is below the station on the lakefront (Mon–Fri 8am–noon & 2–6pm, Sat 8am–noon). There's a new **youth hostel** by the lake at passage de l'Auberge 8 (☎021/963 49 34; ②) – trolleybus #1 to Territet gate or a twenty minute walk east. Among **hotels**, the *Elite*, av du Casino 25 (☎021/963 67 33; ③ – rooms without showers), and *Villa Germaine,* av de Collonges 3 (☎021/963 15 28; ③), are the cheapest. The nearest **campsite**, *Les Horizons Bleues*, is at the end of the lake in Villeneuve, near the terminus of trolley bus #1. Montreux's **Jazz Festival** takes place in mid-July, but it's hard to get tickets without writing well in advance to *Festival du Jazz*, Service de Location, Case Postale 1451, 1820 Montreux.

Beyond Montreux

Hourly trains from Montreux (*InterRail* and *Eurail* 50 percent off) wind their laborious way up to the hill stations of **GLION** (10min) and·**CAUX** (25min), popular local skiing destinations during winter. Outside of that time there's little to do at either place, but the rarefied mountain air and views are reward enough. From Caux, trains continue towards the mountain vantage point of **LES ROCHERS DE NAYE** (30min more, *Swiss Pass* not valid; *InterRail* and *Eurail* 50 percent off). Twenty minutes outside Montreux, the popular mountain resort of **LES AVANTS** is accessible by the hourly *MOB* private rail service, as is the exclusive Alpine resort of **GSTAAD**, an hour beyond – a route which leads eventually to the central Alpine region of the Berner Oberland within a couple of hours. Otherwise, the main line up the Rhône valley leads towards the high mountains of the Valais canton and the region's best known peak, the **Matterhorn**.

THE NORTHERN CITIES

Northern Switzerland, much of it known as the *Mitteland* – the country between the high Alps to the south and the Jura to the north – is the site of most agricultural, commercial and industrial activity. It's a hilly region cut by deep valleys and lakes, although the scenery is by no means as grandiose as the mountain peaks further south. That said, there's a wealth of cultural and historical interest in the German-speaking cities of **Bern, Basel, Zürich** and **Luzern**. And, wherever you choose to base yourself, the high mountains are never more than a couple of hours away by train.

Zürich

Although lacking the political and diplomatic clout of the federal capital Bern, **ZÜRICH** is perhaps the country's most important metropolis, certainly as far as economic and financial considerations are concerned. It's not a large city, its population of around a third of a million making it a lightweight among European urban centres, but it lies at the centre of a vast built-up area, known locally as the *agglomeration*, which stretches along both shores of Lake Zürich – the Zürichersee – and extends north to swallow the satellite town of Winterthur. Zürich is surprisingly cosmopolitan – over twenty percent of the population is made up of immigrants, originally Spaniards and Italians, more recently Portuguese, Turks and Sri Lankans – although it is known primarily as a bankers' and stockbrokers' city. However, Switzerland's reputation as a place to hide one's dubiously acquired assets has provoked a certain amount of local embarrassment, and the notorious numbered bank accounts are no more – they were finally withdrawn in 1991. Indeed, despite being the centre of one of the most highly developed capitalist cultures in the world, Zürich has a strong socialist tradition and is currently governed by a red–green coalition. The city council's reformist thrust is most visible in a revolutionary transport policy, which promotes public transport interests above those of private car-owners, especially now that the enlightened attitude towards drugs which made Zürich the narcotics capital of Switzerland has undergone some changes. The park behind the Kunstmuseum, where addicts were once free from police harassment, is now closed, forcing them back onto the streets of the country's larger cities, and the local council has stopped providing clean needles daily.

Arrival and accommodation

Zurich's **Hauptbahnhof** is located bang in the centre of the city. The **tourist office**, immediately outside at Bahnhofplatz 15 (April–Oct Mon–Fri 8.30am–9.30pm, Sat & Sun 8.30am–8.30pm; Nov–March Mon–Fri 8.30am–7.30pm, Sat & Sun 8.30am–8.30pm), will

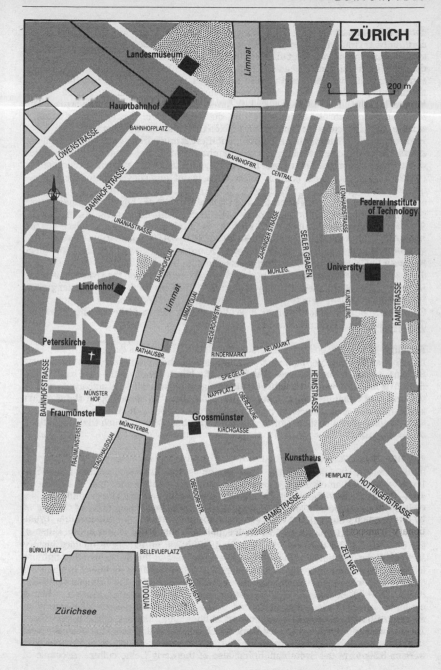

ZÜRICH

Landesmüseum

Hauptbahnhof

BAHNHOFPLATZ

LÖWENSTRASSE

BAHNHOFSTRASSE

URANIASTRASSE

BAHNHOFQUAI

Lindenhof

Limmat

Peterskirche

RATHAUSBR.

BAHNHOFSTRASSE

MÜNSTER
HOF

Fraumünster

FRAUMÜNSTERSTR.

STADTHAUSQUAI

MÜNSTERBR.

BÜRKLI PLATZ

Zürichsee

BELLEVUEPLATZ

UTOQUAI

Limmat

BAHNHOFBR.

CENTRAL

ZÄHRINGER STRASSE

SEILER GRABEN

MÜHLEG.

LIMMATQUAI

NIEDERDORFSTR.

RINDERMARKT

NEUMARKT

SPIEGELG.

NAPFPLATZ

OBERE ZÄUNE

Grossmünster

KIRCHGASSE

OBERDORFSTR.

THEATERSTR.

LEONHARDSTRASSE

Federal Institute
of Technology

University

KUNSTLERG.

RAMISTRASSE

HEIMSTRASSE

Kunsthaus

HEIMPLATZ

RAMISTRASSE

HOTTINGERSTRASSE

ZELT WEG

0   200 m

book a room and can provide maps, both for a small fee. Trains link the **airport**, 10km north in KLOTEN, with the station every twenty minutes. There are plenty of through-trains linking the airport direct to other regional centres, so there's no need to stop off in the city itself if you want to head straight on towards the Alps. Most sightseeing is easy enough on foot, but the famed **public transport** system is easy to use. Tickets are purchased in advance from machines, single journeys costing Sfr1.90 (press *Kurzstecke*), a 24-hour *Tageskarte*, Sfr6.40 (press *Stadnetz*, then double the arrow). The most important hubs are Bahnhofplatz on the west bank of the river, and Central, a small square just across the Bahnhofsbrücke on the far side of the Limmat.

Hotel prices in Zürich can be frightful, but there's much more choice than you'll see elsewhere in the country and a far greater chance of finding something that comes within your price range. Of **hostels**, the official *Jugendherberge*, Mutschellenstrasse 114 (☎482 35 44; ②), south of Zürich in Wollishofen, is not very convenient for the centre – tram #6 or #7 from the Hauptbahnhof to Morgenthal, then either one stop on bus #66 or a five-minute walk. More central is the private *Marthahaus* hostel, Zähringerstrasse 36 (☎251 45 50; ③), in the heart of the Niederdorf,with dorm beds. As for **hotels**, *Scheuble*, Mülegasse 17 (☎251 87 95; ⑦), is a nice old three-star place in the Niederdorf; the *Splendid*, Rosengasse 5 (☎252 58 50; ⑤), is a good-value two-star, also in the Niederdorf not far from *Villette*, Kruggasse 4 (☎251 23 35; ⑥), near Bellevueplatz, where the Niederdorf meets the lake. Also the *Italia*, Zeughausstrasse 61 (☎241 05 55; ④), is a short distance west of the centre beyond the river Sihl and the *Hirschen*, Niederdorfstrasse 13 (☎251 42 52; ⑤). The *Pension St Josef*, Hirschengraben 64 (☎251 27 57; ⑤), between the university and the Niederdorf, is very convivial. **Campers** should head for *Seebucht*, in Wollishofen, a pleasant lakeside site, reachable on bus #161 or #165 from Bürkliplatz.

The City

Zürich straddles the river Limmat at its junction with the Zürichersee, with the narrow pedestrian-only streets of the medieval town, the **Niederdorf**, on the east bank of the river. The western bank is the site of most business and commercial activity, as well as the city's main shopping area, although here, too, there's a sprinkling of sights. Don't forget the lake; shoreline promenades extend from central Zürich along both sides, leading past a sequence of *Strandbäder* (pay beaches) to which the people flock on summer days.

THE WEST BANK

Immediately to the north of the train station is the **Landesmuseum** (Tues–Sun 10am–5pm; free), an eccentric nineteenth-century pile built in the style of a medieval castle that is home to the country's foremost historical museum. The ground floor is a veritable treasure-trove of medieval religious art, including a panorama of the city of Zürich painted around 1500 by a local artist, Hans Leu the Elder, showing the grisly ends of the city's patron saints, Regula, Exuperantus and Felix, who were decapitated, put on a wheel and then collectively boiled. Upstairs, an extensive military history section serves as a timely reminder of the warlike past of the Swiss, whether fighting for their homeland or serving as mercenaries in foreign armies – one set of uniforms on display is from a Swiss regiment serving with the British in the Crimean campaign of the 1850s. Centrepiece is a re-creation of the 1476 Battle of Murten, when a predominantly Bernese army put an end to the expansionist designs of Burgundian monarch Charles the Bold. The archeological finds filling the rest of the upper storey are less well displayed, but motley Dark-Age burial finds and religious objects reveal something not only of the culture of the Burgundian, Aleman and Lombard tribes who were to later form the Swiss nation, but also of the early Celtic culture. A couple of rooms are devoted to pieces from the eighteenth to twentieth centuries and to the renovations currently underway at Château Pragins, midway between Geneva and Lausanne, which from 1998 will be their permanent home in the *Romand* wing of the National Museum.

The narrow streets between Bahnhofstrasse and the Limmat lead up to the **Lindenhof**, an old bastion overlooking the river which initially provided the site for a late Roman fortress and customs post. A short distance south, the **Peterskirche** (Mon–Sat 8am–6pm) is renowned for the enormous sixteenth-century clock face adorning its medieval tower, and a simple yet beautiful interior that is more like a ballroom than a church. Immediately south, the Münsterhof is overlooked by the Gothic **Fraumünster** (Mon–Sat 9am–12.30pm & 2pm–6pm), an ancient church which began life as a convent in 853 before its voluntary disbandment during the Reformation. The interior is predictably bare save for traces of thirteenth-century frescoes in the choir, and some remarkable stained glass by Marc Chagall adorning the eastern end.

THE EAST BANK

From the Münsterhof, the Münsterbrücke crosses the Limmat to **Niederdorf**, the zone of narrow cobbled thoroughfares which stretch about 1km to the north. During the day it's a tranquil area of small squares and fountains, enlivened by the occasional antique or secondhand book shop. Come the evening, it's transformed into a bustling pleasure quarter of cafés and bars. The waterfront is lined by fine Baroque *Zunfthäuser* or guildhalls, their arcaded lower storeys fronting the quayside. Built by the wealthier of Zürich's professional associations in the seventeenth and eighteenth centuries, their extravagantly decorated dining rooms are now mainly restaurants. At the eastern end of Münsterbrücke are the eighteenth-century **Helmhaus** and the Gothic **Wasserkirche**, although the scene is dominated by the twin-towered **Grossmünster** (April–Sept Mon–Sat 9am–6pm; Oct–March Mon–Sat 10am–4pm), where Huldrych Zwingli, father of Swiss Protestantism, began preaching in 1519. Originally developing his ideas in parallel with Luther, Zwingli set the Swiss church on a more extreme course after breaking with his German comrade on the nature of the Eucharist. By and large, his regime in Zürich was not noted for its tolerance, decreeing the drowning of Anabaptists in 1526; it also provoked the wrath of Switzerland's rural cantons by calling for an end to military service abroad – the prime source of income for many highland families – and the resulting civil war cost Zwingli his own life. The exterior of the Münster is largely late fifteenth-century, although the towers were topped with distinctive octagonal domes 300 years later. Inside, the scene is as austere as you would expect, but for the Romanesque crypt below the choir which contains a fifteenth-century statue of Charlemagne, who was popularly associated with the foundation of the church in the early ninth century.

Alleys behind the church lead to the **Kunsthaus** (Mon 2–5pm, Tues–Thurs 10am–9pm, Fri–Sun 10am–5pm; Sfr4), one of Switzerland's principal collections, with some fascinating late Gothic paintings, a roomful of Venetian masters and fine Flemish work. A great deal of space is devoted to native artists, pride of place going to several deranged canvases from nineteenth-century symbolist Arnold Böcklin, notably an 1892 painting of Saint Anthony preaching to the fishes. There are also rooms packed with works by Füssli, a melodramatic eighteenth-century Swiss painter who spent most of his career in London, and – in contrast – the restrained classicism of Angelika Kauffmann, another Swiss expatriate in London around the same time. A modern annexe holds a definitive collection of Alberto Giacometti sculpture and a thorough overview of the rest of twentieth-century art, strong on geometric and constructivist periods as well as abundant paintings by Chagall, Picasso, and a handful of late

Monets, including the popular *Houses of Parliament at Sunset* and two of his finest lily pond canvases. From here Rämistrasse leads around the back of Zürich's monumental university building, where the **University Archeological Museum**, Rämistrasse 73 (Tues–Fri 1–6pm, Sat & Sun 11am–5pm; free), has a small but worthwhile collection of ancient fragments – Assyrian tablets, Greek pottery and Minoan sarcophagi. Up the street at no. 101, the Federal Technological School contains a valuable **Collection of Graphics** (Mon–Fri 10am–5pm, Wed 10am–8pm; free), including drawings by Dürer and Rembrandt.

Tram #3 from Central leads to Römerhofplatz and the terminal of the **Dolderbahn**, a funicular railway which winds through hillside streets before reaching an area of wooded parkland far above the city. Better walking possibilities can be found on the **Zürichberg** (terminus of tram #6 from Central), site of the city zoo and more wooded paths. Also a little way out of the centre, Zürich has two more worthwhile museums: the **Museum Rietberg**, Gablerstrasse 18 (Tues–Sun 10am–5pm, Wed until 9pm; Sfr3; free on Wed evening & Sun) – tram #6 from Central – which specializes in non-European artefacts, with beautiful pieces from China, India and Japan; and the **Bührle Collection**, Zollikerstrasse 172 (Tues & Fri 2–5pm; Sfr6.60), accessible by tram #2 or #4 to Wildbachstrasse, displaying the collection of industrialist Emil Bührle, rich in Impressionists and nineteenth-century Parisian painters.

Eating, drinking and nightlife

The cheapest **eating** in Zürich is at the train station *Rösti Bar*, which has ten varieties from about Sfr6, or there is the self-service *Migros*, on Lowenstrasse. *Commercio*, Muhlerbachstrasse 2, serves good Italian food at reasonable prices; *Turm*, Obere Zaune, is a more fashionable restaurant in the Niederdorf, though you'll get more for your money in the shady courtyard at *Zunfthaus am Neumarkt*, tucked away down an alley at Neumarkt 5. There are also plenty of cheap eateries in Zürich's principal **drinking** area around the Niederdorf, which extends all along Limmatquai and continues onto Schifflände. There's something here to suit all tastes. Among the bars, *Pigalle*, Marktgasse 14, is popular with a youngish crowd, or there is *Ba Ba Lu*, on Schmidgasse; *Café Philosophes*, on Nägelihof behind Rüdenplatz; and *Café Bistro des Arts* on Oberdorfstrasse. The *Cabaret Voltaire*, where the original Dadaists met, closed some years ago, but the *Café Odéon* bar, Limmatquai 2, which has long had a literary and artistic clientele, is still going strong. One of the best of the many *Bierhallen* is *Rheinfelderbierhalle*, on Limmatquai, which also serves solid cheap food. Two English-style watering holes with a wide choice of beers are *Castel Pub*, Spiegelgasse 1, and *Oliver Twist*, Rindermarkt 6. *Barfuss* and *Wild*, both on Spitalgasse, tend to attract a gay clientele. On the other side of the Limmat, Zürich is quieter at night. The *Bierhalle zum Kropf*, just in front of the Peterskirche, is a lively place with filling, reasonably priced food. The *Jules Verne Bar*, on the top floor of *Brasserie Lipp* on Uraniastrasse, is a more sedate, upmarket drinking venue in atmospheric surroundings — the building (known popularly as Urania) used to be the public observatory.

As regards the more cultural types of **nightlife**, *Reithalle*, located in what used to be the barracks stables on Gessner Allee, hosts a wide variety of alternative theatre and has a lively *alfresco* restaurant/bar. *Rote Fabrik*, which you'll find at Seestrasse 395 (bus #161 or #165 from Bürkliplatz), is a more rough-and-ready gig venue, with good food in the adjoining café/bar. *Miller's Studio*, in Mühle Tiefenbrunnen, a converted nineteenth-century brewery at Seefeldstrasse 225 (trams #2 and #4 from Central), has regular live jazz. For details of what's on, the newspapers *Neue Zürcher Zeitung* and *Tages Anzeiger* have listings, and the latter has a free listings supplement, "Züri Tip", every Friday.

Listings

Airlines *British Airways*, Talacker 42 (☎211 40 90); *Swissair*, in the train station (☎251 34 34).

Bookshop *Travel Bookshop*, Rindermarkt 20, stocks guides in English (including *Rough Guides* to France, Germany and Italy).

Car rental *Avis*, Gartenhofstrasse 17 (☎242 20 40); *Europcar*, Josefstrasse 53 (☎432 24 24); *Hertz*, Morgartenstrasse 5 (☎242 84 84).

Consulates *UK*, Doufourstrasse 56 (☎363 06 44); *USA*, Reidtilstrasse 15 (☎55 25 66).

Exchange Outside banking hours, try the exchange office at the main railway station, open daily 6.15am–10.45pm.

Hospital In case of emergency dial ☎261 61 00.

Pharmacy 24-hr service at *Bellevue Apotheke*, Theaterstrasse 14.

Post office Main post office is at Kasernstrasse 95-99 (Mon–Fri 6.30am–10.30pm, Sat 6.30am–8pm, Sun 11am–10.30pm).

Telephones at the main post office on Kasernstrasse, or the train station.

Travel agent *SSR*, Leonhardstrasse 10, are youth travel specialists.

Basel

An industrial city straddling the Rhine, **BASEL** (Bâle) is often bypassed by travellers, which is a pity, since they miss out on its historic medieval centre. The University of Basel was a famed centre of learning in the late Middle Ages, and the presence here of Renaissance man of letters Erasmus was a great inspiration to the Reformation throughout the rest of Switzerland. Basel remains an enlightened place. The city authorities have a reputation for arts sponsorship which dates back to their first forays into the art market in the mid-seventeenth century, and the city's museums offer the best assemblage of art treasures in the country.

The City

One of the best of Basel's galleries is the **Kunstmuseum**, St Alban-Graben 16 (Tues-Sun 10am–5pm; Sfr6, free on first Sun of month), with a dazzling array of twentieth-century work, including paintings by Léger, Chagall, Munch, Braque and others; the Impressionists are amply represented, as are earlier works acquired for the municipality when the city council bought up the collection of sixteenth-century connoisseur Basilius Amerbach. The studio of Konrad Witz is well represented, and there are roomfuls of works by the prolific Holbein family, documenting the lives of local burghers and scholars and including a portrait of Erasmus. The nearby **Antikenmuseum**, St Alban-Graben 5 (Tues–Sun 11am–5pm; Sfr5, free on first Sun of month), is also worth a look, with a comprehensive collection of ancient Greek objects including some particularly fine vases. Down to the river by some steps, then right along St Alban-Rheinweg is the almost continually rejuvenated **Museum of Contemporary Art** at no. 60 (Tues–Sun 11am–5pm; Sfr5, free on first Sun of month, often more during special exhibitions) – equally rich in modern works, installations by Frank Stella and Joseph Beuys sharing space with a good selection of German painting from the 1980s.

Back at the Kunstmuseum, Rittergasse leads you past concentrated clumps of sixteenth-century buildings down towards the **Münster** (Mon–Fri 10am–5pm, Sat 10am–noon & 2–5pm, Sun 1–5pm), an impressive lump of red sandstone with an exterior that features some very impressive examples of medieval stone carving, most notably a series of figures sited just above the main portal that includes a depiction of the cathedral's eleventh-century founder, the Holy Roman Emperor Heinrich II, holding a model of the church. Inside the building, behind one of the pillars in the north aisle is the marble tomb of Erasmus, whose Greek New Testament, with Latin translation, published in 1516, rubbished the version of the Bible which everyone had been using up until then, and was the inspiration for future reformers like Luther and Zwingli. The ninth-century remains of the Cathedral's predecessor can still be seen tucked away in the crypt below the apse. Around the south side of the cathedral, cloisters lead through to the **Pfalz**, a square high above the river from which you can look down on the terraced banks of the Rhine and the suburb of Kleinbasel on the other side.

Close by are two more worthwhile museums that have been integrated into the same building at Augustinergasse 2 (May–Oct Tues–Sun 10am–5pm; Nov–April Tues–Sat 10am–noon & 2–5pm, Sun 10am–5pm; Sfr6, free on first Sun of month). The **Museum für Völkerkunde** displays a wide range of folk art from India, Indonesia and Africa, as well as concentrating on aspects of Swiss and Central European ethnography including a fascinating collection of masks; next door the **Naturhistorisches Museum** features the customary assembly of dinosaur skeletons and minerals. Rheinsprung continues northwards past the old **university** at no. 11, founded by Pope Pius II in 1459 and remaining stubbornly pro-Catholic for years despite the torrent of reformist scholars who were drawn here by its humanist reputation. From the bottom of Rheinsprung the curiously named Elftausend Jungfern-Gässlein ("Little Alley of the 11,000 Virgins") leads up to the fifteenth-century **St Martinskirche**, and then continues through to Marktplatz and the extravagantly decorated facade of the sixteenth-century **Rathaus** from where it's just a short stroll along the shop-lined Gerbergasse to the lively market stalls of Barfüsserplatz. Basel's **Historical Museum**, housed in the splendid Gothic Barfüsserkirche (10am–5pm; closed Tues; Sfr5, free on first Sun of month), offers more evidence of Basel's cultural pre-eminence in the fifteenth and sixteenth centuries, not least the sumptuous tapestries of the city's weavers. Behind both Marktplatz and Barfüsserplatz a hive of alleyways and quiet old streets climb steeply towards Graben, the trench which originally surrounded the fortifications, and the Gothic **Peterskirche** (Tues–Sat 9am–5pm, Sun 10am–5pm) on Petersgraben, whose deceptively plain exterior harbours colourful late medieval frescoes inside. In one chapel the 1527 tomb of Johann Froben recalls the printer who was central to Basel's intellectual life in the early sixteenth century. It was Froben who published Erasmus' Bible in 1516, and went on to print works by Luther and other reformers. The tomb bears an inscription in Latin, Hebrew and Greek, prepared by Erasmus himself.

Practicalities

Basel's **train station** is fifteen minutes south of the city centre; walk diagonally across Elisabethenanlage, then down Elisabethenstrasse towards the old centre – trams #1 and #8 will take you there, though not by the same route. There's a **tourist office** at the station (Mon–Fri 8.30am–7pm, Sat 8.30am–noon & 1.30–6pm), and another in the centre at Schifflande 5 (Mon–Fri 8.30am–6pm, Sat 8.30am–1pm). Both handle room bookings, although there's a scarcity of affordable **hotels**. The cheapest is *Badischer Hof*, Riehenring 109 (☎061/692 41 44; ⑤), a good fifteen-minute walk into Kleinbasel. The two-star *Rochat*, Petersgraben 23 (☎061/261 81 40; ⑥), by Peterskirche, is closer and only marginally more expensive, as is the *Bristol*, Centralbahnstrasse 15 (☎061/271 38 22; ⑥), by the train station, or the city's lively **youth hostel** at St Alban-Kirchrain 10 (☎061/272 05 72; ②) in the pleasant riverside neighbourhood of St Alban-Tal. There are plenty of small *Bierstuben* offering cheap lunchtime **food** in the streets behind Marktplatz; more salubrious is the *Restauration zur Harmonie*, catering to a young and stylish crowd on Petersgraben, opposite the university. The *Stadtkeller*, Marktgasse 11, has solid evening menus and a beery clientele; *Café Florian*, Totentanz 1, boasts a terrace overlooking the Rhine, a pleasant place for lunch or a daytime drink. For night-time **drinking** there are a host of *Bierstuben* in the backstreets of Kleinbasel, on the right bank over the river, especially Rheingasse, though some are a bit rough. *Fischerstube*, Rheingasse 45, is one that definitely isn't, offering excellent beers and fresh fish from the Rhine. The *Sommercasino*, Münchenstrasse 1, has a popular café featuring live jazz and sporadic (teenage) discos. *Kulturwerkstatt Kaserne*, Klybechsteinstrasse 1b, is an occasional venue for gigs.

Bern

The federal capital and centre of political power, if not always of political influence, **BERN**, like Geneva, is full of foreign envoys, endowing the place with both a cosmopolitan atmosphere and a high cost of living. The compact, picturesque streets of its centre have preserved a great deal of their medieval feel, and lying roughly midway on the fast route between French-speaking Geneva to the west and the more urbane charm of Zürich to the east, it makes an easy stopoff.

Despite the present-day tranquillity of the capital, the ancestors of the Bernese were surprisingly bellicose. Founded in 1191 by powerful local family the Zähringens, Bern began life as a fortress town peopled with a colony of knights. This community of ambitious soldier-aristocrats developed a dynamic of outward expansion, and the growth of the Swiss confederation in subsequent centuries owed a great deal to the westward conquests of the warlike Bernese.

The City
A historic pile of sandstone on a bend in the River Aare, Bern's ancient heart is best explored from **Spitalgasse**, the main street, which becomes Marktgasse, Kramgasse, then Gerechtigkeitsgasse, lined with seventeenth- and eighteenth-century houses, fountains and arcaded shops. A couple of hundred metres down, it crosses **Bärenplatz**, site of much outdoor daytime drinking and a vibrant Saturday morning market, to the right of which is the **Bundeshaus** or federal parliament building, a domed neo-Renaissance edifice. Beyond Bärenplatz, Marktgasse continues through the oft-rebuilt **Käfigturm** or prisoner's tower, originally marking the western entrance to the thirteenth-century town, to an eleventh-century town gate, converted in the sixteenth century into the **Zeitglockenturm** – a clocktower adorned with brightly coloured figures which judder into movement four minutes before each hour. To the left, in Kornhausplatz, is the most renowned of Bern's many fountains, the **Kindlifresserbrunnen**, above which a child is swallowed whole by an ogre-like form. Further along the main street, the **Albert-Einstein-Haus**, Kramgasse 49 (Feb–Nov Tues–Fri 10am–5pm, Sat 10am–4pm; Sfr2), preserves the study occupied by the famous physicist for two short but productive years from 1903. Münstergasse, one block south, leads to the **Münster** (Mon–Sat 10am–noon & 2–5pm, Sun 11am–noon & 2–5pm), a fifteenth-century Gothic structure noted for the magnificently gilded high-relief *Last Judgement* above the main entrance; its tower (Mon–Sat 10am–11.30am & 2–4.30pm, Sun 11–11.30am & 2–4.30pm; Sfr3) is the highest in the country and offers marvellous views – as does the so-called **Plattform**, a leafy square behind. At the eastern end of the city centre, the Nydeggbrücke crosses the Aare to the **Bärengraben**, Bern's famed bear pits – basically stone pits with live bears in them. Legend has it that the town's founder Berchtold V of Zähringen named Bern after killing one of the beasts during a hunt, and the animal has understandably remained a symbol of the town ever since. Representatives of the species have been confined to the pits here since the fifteenth century. The **Rosengarten**, up the hill on the opposite side of the road to the bear pits, offers the best view of the city.

Bern's **Kunstmuseum**, Hodlerstrasse 8–12 (Tues 10am–9pm, Wed–Sun 10am–5pm; Sfr4), is another comprehensive collection of art, spanning everything from Fra

Angelico to works by Matisse, Léger, Kandinsky, Braque and Picasso. Whole rooms are devoted to Paul Klee, who was born in Bern and, after spending most of his career in Germany, returned here after the rise of Nazism. The museums grouped around Helvetiaplatz on the south side of the Aare are less interesting, with the exception of the **Swiss Alpine Museum** at no. 4 (Mon 2–5pm, Tues–Sun 10am–noon & 2–5pm; Sfr4) whose archetypal images of folk culture, tourism and ecology are put into perspective. A couple of dozen immaculately executed relief sculptures give you a fix on resort locations and help illustrate the work of the early nineteenth-cntury glacier researchers who devised Ice Age Theory. The **Historisches Museum** across the square (Tues–Sun 10am–5pm; Sfr4) is good on Switzerland's prehistory, as well as displaying some fine late medieval Flemish tapesteries. The **Naturhistorisches Museum** immediately behind, at Bernastrasse 15 (Mon 2–5pm, Tues–Sat 9am–5pm, Sun 10am–5pm; Sfr3), has a notable selection of stuffed African animals, and can be relied upon to include something on the subject of bears, as well as Barry, the St Bernard credited with saving over forty lives. The other building on Helvetiaplatz, the **Kunsthalle** (Tues 10am–9pm, Wed–Sun 10am–5pm; Sfr4), is the site of big contemporary art exhibitions.

Practicalities

Bern's main **train station** is at the western end of the old centre; cross Bahnhofplatz and turn left into Spitalgasse. The **tourist office** is in the station (June–Sept daily 9am–8.30pm; Oct–May Mon–Sat 9am–6.30pm, Sun 10am–5pm). There's a **youth hostel** at Weihergasse 4 (☎031/22 63 16; ②), just below the Bundeshaus. Other cheap accommodation options include *Hotel Marthahaus*, Wyttenbachstrasse 22a (☎031/42 41 35; ⑤; bus #20), over the Lorrainebrücke from the Bahnhof, and the *National*, Hirschengraben 24 (☎031/25 19 88; ⑤), south of the station. The most convenient campsite is *Eichholz*, Stadzentrum (☎031/961 26 02), a fifteen-minute #9 tram ride towards Warbern. For **eating**, the self-service buffet in the station is a good standby, with tasty curries from Sfr10, and the local branch of *Manora*, Budenbergplatz 5a, has filling wholefood dishes. The *Klötzlikeller*, Gerechtigkeitsgasse 62, offers moderately priced food in a wine-cellar atmosphere, as does the converted granary, the *Kornhauskeller* at Kornhausplatz 18.

Details of the city's **cultural** calendar appear in *Berner Agenda*, free with the local daily *Berner Zeitung* every Thursday, and in *This Week in Bern* available free from the tourist office. *ISC*, Neubruckstrasse 10, is a small gig venue primarily for students, with discos on Fridays and Saturdays; likewise *Bierhübeli*, Neubruckstrasse 43.

Luzern

Barely an hour south of Zürich, **LUZERN** sits at the northwestern end of the **Vierwaldstättersee** or lake of the four forest cantons, historical heart of Switzerland. The communities dotted around the lake guarded the northern approaches to the St Gotthard, one of the main routes between central Europe and northern Italy. When Habsburg overlords tried to encroach on the privileges of the locals, the communities formed an alliance at Grütli on the southern shores of the lake in 1291 – which was to prove the cornerstone of the nascent Swiss confederation. Luzern, as the principal market town for the lakeside communities, was drawn into the confederation four decades later.

Evidence of Luzern's medieval prosperity is manifest in the painted houses of the town centre, and the wooden bridges which cross the river Reuss as it flows into the lake. Largest of these was the fourteenth-century **Kapellbrücke**, a wooden-roofed structure which dog-legged its way across the river until August 1993, when it was wrecked by a fire; the paintings that hung from the roof beams were reduced to ashes, but there are plans to build a replica of the bridge. The north bank is home to a compact cluster of medieval houses, with Mühlenplatz, Weinmarkt, Hirschenplatz and Kornmarkt forming an ensemble of cobbled, fountained squares ringed by colourful facades. Kornmarkt is the site of the Renaissance town hall, next door to which the **Am Rhyn-Haus**, Furrengass 21 (April–Oct daily 10am–6pm; Nov–March daily 11am–1pm & 2–4pm; Sfr5), contains a small Picasso collection, strong on later works, amassed by local art dealers the Rosengarts. Northwest of the centre, St Karli Quai hugs the riverbank as far as the **Nölliturm**, a fortified gate marking the southwestern extent of a lengthy stretch of surviving town walls. Pass through the gate and turn right up the hill to gain access to the **battlements** (daily 8am–7pm) and their extensive views of the town.

Luzern's more modern eastern end is home to three notable curiosities. The **Bourbaki Panorama**, Löwenstrasse 18 (daily May–Sept 9am–6pm; Oct–April 9am–5pm; Sfr3), is a mural depicting the retreat of the French army under General Bourbaki into Switzerland during the Franco-Prussian war of 1871. The nearby **Löwendenkmal** or lion monument, on Denkmalstrasse, is a monumental beast carved out of the cliff-face in honour of the Swiss guards who met their deaths defending the French monarch at Versailles in 1789. Immediately above, the **Gletschergarten** or glacial garden, at Denkmalstrasse 4 (May–mid-Oct 8am–6pm; mid-Oct–mid-Nov 9am–5pm; mid-Nov–Feb Tues–Sun 10.30am–4.30pm; March & April 9am–5pm; Sfr6.60), is an area of hollowed-out rock formations etched millennia ago by the Reuss glacier.

There are two further attractions towards the outskirts of town. Located in the villa the composer lived in between 1866 and 1872 at Richard-Wagner-Weg 27, the **Richard-Wagner-Museum**, (mid-April–Oct Tues–Sun 10am–noon & 2–5pm; Feb–mid-April Tues, Thurs, Sat & Sun only; Sfr5), has a lakeside site 1500m southeast of the centre, two zones away on bus #8 or #6. It's filled with sundry furniture, original scores and Wagner's old piano. On the opposite side of the bay, 2km east of town, is Switzerland's main transport museum, the **Verkehrshaus**, Lidostrasse 5 (March–Oct daily 9am–6pm; Nov–Feb Mon–Sat 10am–4pm, Sun 10am–5pm; Sfr15, 30 percent discount with *Swiss Pass*) – take bus #2 from the train station or it's a pleasant lakeside walk. Packed with railway locomotives, cable cars and other monuments to Swiss engineering skill, the museum also includes a Cosmorama, which, with the help of a Mercury capsule, tells the story of space travel.

Practicalities

Luzern's **train station** is on the south bank of the Reuss where the river meets the lake, a few paces away from the Kappelbrücke. There's a **tourist office** just east of the station at Frankenstrasse 1 (April–Oct Mon–Fri 8.30am–6pm, Sat 9am–5pm; Nov–March Mon–Fri 8.30am–noon & 2–6pm, Sat 9am–1pm), and a **youth hostel** by Lake Rotsee northwest of the town at Sedelstrasse 12 (☎041/36 88 00; ②) – bus #18 to Goplismoos. Alternative dormitory accommodation is on offer – if you arrive early enough – at the *Tourist Hotel*, St Karli Quai 12 (☎041/51 24 74; ③), or there are a couple of nice old places on the south side of the Reuss: *Goldener Stern*, Burgerstrasse 35 (☎041/23 08 91; ④), and *Schlüssel*, Franziskanerplatz 12 (☎041/23 10 61; ④). *Camping Lido*, Lidostrasse 8 (☎041/31 21 46), which also has non-reservable dorm beds in bungalows for Sfr12, is a half-hour walk east along the lake beside the Transport Museum. **Drinking and eating** venues congregate along the Rathausquai on the north bank of the Reuss. The *Pickwick Pub* is among the most popular. *Zum Storchen*, Rathausplatz, features a smart bar downstairs, a plush and expensive brasserie upstairs.

ALPINE SWITZERLAND

South and east of Bern and Luzern lies the grand Alpine heart of Switzerland, a massively impressive region of classic Swiss scenery – high peaks, sheer valleys and cool lakes – that makes great hiking and good gentle walking, not to mention winter sports. Even if you're only spending a little time in the country, it would be a mistake not to experience a little of what Switzerland has to offer beyond its major cities. The **Berner Oberland** is perhaps the most obvious and accessible place to head for. But consider, too, the **Valais** and the high peaks around the **Matterhorn**, further south towards the Italian border, and the canton of **Graubunden** in the southeastern corner of Switzerland, whose more undiscovered – almost remote – peaks and valleys provide a welcome contrast to the sometimes sanitized feel of the rest of the country.

The Berner Oberland

The most spectacular of the Alpine regions, the **Berner Oberland** lies within comfortable striking distance of both Zürich and Bern. The area is best known for the grandiose mountain ridge formed by the Eiger, Mönch and Jungfrau, and their surrounding areas of pasture. A number of resorts nestle on the shoulders of the mountains – Wengen, Grindelwald and Mürren – and provide excellent skiing in winter and walking in summer, while the valley of Lauterbrunnen below is one of the most breathtaking in the Alps. The transport hub of Interlaken is the main springboard for the area, but the sheer volume of tourist traffic passing through the town can make it a less than restful place to stay and you may prefer instead to rest up on the shores of either the Brienzersee or Thunersee. Because it's such a touristy area there are plenty of private rooms – though beware that the majority close up during May and November.

Thun

Set back from the lake which bears its name, on the banks of the River Aare, **THUN** is worth a quick stop on the way to the Oberland from Bern. The train station is ten minutes' walk from the town centre, with a **tourist office** (Mon–Fri 9am–noon & 1–6pm, Sat 9am–noon) just left of the exit. The town is renowned for the two-level arcading of its main street, the **Obere Hauptgasse**, and the arcaded **Rathausplatz** at its northwestern end. From here steps lead up to the **Castle**, built by Berthold V of Zähringen in 1190 and subsequently passing through various hands before being occupied by the Bernese in 1386. It now contains a **museum** (daily May, Oct & Nov 10am–5pm; June–Sept 9am–6pm; Sfr4) with the usual period furniture collections and militaria. If you're in Thun during the evening, check out *Café Bar Mokka*, Alserstrasse 14, a surprisingly exciting hang-out with a regular programme of live music.

Interlaken

INTERLAKEN is little more than its long main street, **Höheweg**, with a train station at each end. Interlaken Ost is the terminus of most mainline trains, and the departure point for branch lines into the mountains. Arriving from the Bern direction, it's better to alight at Interlaken West, where there's a small **tourist office** (Mon–Sat 7.30am–7pm, Sun 7.30am–noon & 1.30–6pm), the main branch of which is at Höheweg 37 (July & Aug Mon–Fri 8am–noon & 1.30–6pm, Sat 8am–noon & 1.30–4.30pm; Sept–June Mon–Fri 8am–noon & 1.30–5.30pm, Sat 8am–noon). Both offices have details of plenty of **private rooms**, although they disappear very quickly at the height of both winter and summer seasons. Interlaken's **youth hostel** is 2km east towards the Brienzersee in the village of Böningen, Aareweg 21 (☎036/22 43 53; ②); bus #1 from either of Interlaken's stations. A more raucous alternative is *Balmer's Herberge*, a private hostel a little nearer town in the suburb of Matten, Hauptstrasse 23 (☎036/22 19 61; ③), popular with North Americans. The nearest **campsite** is *Tiefenau*, on Brienzstrasse, just out of town beyond Interlaken Ost; there's also a site in Matten. Interlaken has little to amuse the trippers passing through on their way towards the mountains, save for the cafés and hotel bars lining Höheweg. The town's only real sights are the **Kursaal** on Höheweg, an elegant colonnaded building in Alpine style built in 1859, and the views towards the Jungfrau massif which can be savoured from Höhematte, a grassy rectangle of parkland just opposite.

Below the Jungfrau: Lauterbrunnen, Wengen and Grindelwald

Half-hourly trains climb from Interlaken Ost towards Lauterbrunnen and Grindelwald, the first of many possible excursions – the most popular (and most expensive) of which takes you all the way to the **Jungfraujoch** – an icy, windswept col beneath the summit of the **Jungfrau** itself – by way of a spectacular mountain railway which tunnels through the granite of the Eiger, complete with a window part way up its sheer north face, before emerging to climb up the other side. Jungfraujoch isn't the usual restaurant and viewing platform, but a complete tourist circus of ice sculptures, husky sleigh rides, a film presentation, a short ski run (hire and tows Sfr25) and a post office, all 3454m **über Meer** (above sea), and, on a clear day, worth the expense. The full journey involves two possible routes, both requiring several changes. You can either go Interlaken–Lauterbrunnen–Wengen–Kleine Scheidegg–Jungfraujoch, or Interlaken–Grindelwald–Kleine Scheidegg–Jungfraujoch. The popular practice is to go up one way and come down the other, but be warned that summer crowds create an ugly scrap for seats at every stage of the journey, and that the entire round-trip is the most expensive of Switzerland's mountain excursions, costing about Sfr140 in all, though by catching the first train of the day, you save Sfr40 on the final leg (no further reductions): *Eurail* isn't valid for any of the routes out of Interlaken; *InterRail* gets a 50 percent reduction right to Jungfraujoch; and *Swiss Pass* is valid as far as Mürren, Wengen or Grindelwald, with a 25 percent reduction thereafter. It's all very confusing, but the network linking these villages does mean that with judicious use of a railway timetable you can see a great deal in a day and still get back to Interlaken, or even Bern or Zürich, before nightfall.

The village of **LAUTERBRUNNEN** lies at the bottom of an immense U-shaped valley, famous for the waterfalls cascading down its sides. There's a **tourist office** 200m up from the **train station** (Mon–Fri 9am–noon & 3–5.30pm, Sat 9–11am), with a range of **private rooms**. Hotels include *Horner*, beyond the tourist office (☎55 16 73; ④), *Sternen*, opposite the station (☎55 12 31; ④), and *Bären*, 200m beyond the tourist office (☎036/55 16 54; ③). There are two **campsites**, *Camping Jungfrau*, 500m past the tourist office, which also has dormitory and bungalow accommodation, the latter at Sfr17 per person, and the quieter and slightly cheaper *Schützenbach*, which also has beds in huts and double rooms for Sfr255 per person. Three kilometres up the valley are the **Trümmelbachfälle** (April–Oct daily 9am–5pm; Sfr10), a series of waterfalls cutting tunnels through the rock of the valley sides – a scenic thirty-minute walk from Lauterbrunnen or an hourly post bus trip from the train station. The same bus continues past Trümmelbach to Stechelberg at the head of the valley where there is a *Naturfreundhaus* (☎036/55 12 02; ②). From here a cable car ascends first to Gimmelwald and the basic self-catering *Mountain Hostel* (no reservations; ①) by the post office, then to **MÜRREN** – also accessible from Lauterbrunnen via a funicular and narrow-gauge rail line – on a shelf of pasture land high above the valley. Mürren has a **tourist office** in its sports centre, but the main reason for visiting is the dramatic unrestricted view across to the imposing north face of the Jungfrau, a mere 6km southeast. Mürren is also the base for another cable car ride, to the 2970-metre-high **Schilthorn** to the west, where you can enjoy more panoramic views of the Jungfrau range.

Half-hourly trains make the laborious climb from Lauterbrunnen to the village of **WENGEN** lying directly above, a skiing resort that stays busy well into April, and ideal hiking territory once the snows begin to recede. Many of the walks in the vicinity have superb views down towards the Lauterbrunnen valley and across to the Jungfrau group. There's a **tourist office** around the corner from the train station (mid-June to mid-Oct & mid-Dec to March Mon–Fri 8am–noon & 2–6pm, Sat 8.30–11.30am & 4–6pm, Sun 4–6pm; mid-Oct to mid-Dec & April to mid-June Mon–Fri 8am–noon & 2–6pm, Sat 8.30–11.30am), handling private rooms and pensions. Several of the hotels offer dormitory beds for under Sfr20, the cheapest being *Bernerhof* (☎036/55 27 21; ③) just beyond the tourist office. There's a wider range of accommodation in the larger village of **GRINDELWALD**, nestling under its own lumpish mountain, the Wetterhorn. The local sports centre once again houses the **tourist office** (July–Sept Mon–Sat 8am–6pm, Sun 10am–noon & 3–5pm; Oct–June Mon–Fri 8am–noon & 2–6pm, Sat 9am–noon) with plentiful **private rooms**, although many insist on weekly lettings; if stuck, the *Bellevue* (☎036/53 12 34; ⑤) is 200m up the main street from the station. There's also a **youth hostel** fifteen minutes' steep walk up to Terrassenweg (☎036/53 10 09; ②), and hostel-type accommodation at the *Naturfreundhaus*, Terrassenweg (☎036/53 13 33; ②).

Brienz

Hourly trains – and, between June and September, hourly ferries (fewer in spring and autumn) – leave Interlaken Ost for **BRIENZ**, a tranquil lakeside town with a sprinkling of tearooms, sleepy *Gasthöfe*, and a sizeable collection of wooden architecture. It's also starting point of the **Brienzer-Rothornbahn** (25 percent discount with *Swiss Pass*), a mountain steam train departing for the Rothorn, which overlooks the town, from opposite the station hourly between June and October. The town's other attraction is the open-air museum of **Ballenberg** (mid- April to Oct daily 10am–5pm; Sfr12), which gathers together examples of vernacular architecture from all over Switzerland, peopled by appropriately costumed members of the museum staff, who demonstrate long-forgotten Alpine domestic skills. Buses leave for Ballenberg roughly hourly from Brienz train station; otherwise it's a 3km walk east. Brienz's **tourist office** is opposite the station (July & Aug Mon–Fri 8am–noon & 2–7pm, Sat 8am–noon & 2–6pm; Sept–June Mon–Fri 8am–noon & 2–6pm, Sat 8am–noon), and there's a **youth hostel** 500m west along the lake at Strandweg 10 (☎036/51 11 52; ②). **Hotel** accommodation here is a touch less expensive than in the Interlaken area; expect to find a few good-value doubles at the *Garni Hotel Schönegg* on Trachtlistrasse east of the train station (☎036/51 11 13; ④) or *Hotel Bären* on the main street ten minutes' walk through town (☎036/51 24 12; ④).

Zermatt and the Matterhorn

The **Matterhorn** is the most famous, if not the highest, of Switzerland's peaks, and climbing it is a serious business. But the land around it is perfect walking country, numerous potential trails stemming from the bustling village of Zermatt, main point of access to the Matterhorn range. The area is accessible from the Lake Geneva direction by way of the main rail line through from the vineyards of the Rhône valley, or by another line coming down from Bern. From Zürich and the northeast you need to use the Furka-Oberalp railway from Andermatt to Brig (*Eurail/InterRail* not valid, closed in winter), which operates the central section of the St Moritz–Zermatt *Glacier Express* taking in some of Switzerland's finest scenery in one day-long journey. This service excepted, you'll need to change at Brig, where the train leaves from Bahnhofplatz outside the main station, or Visp, from where a narrow-gauge service (*Eurail* not valid, *InterRail* 50 percent reduction) heads up the Mattertal towards Zermatt.

An hour away from Visp, **ZERMATT** is a pedestrian-only town, thronging with fiacres and electricity-powered minibuses. It comprises little more than a main street, which threads its way between chalets from the train station at the northern end to the cable car terminus at the south. The British contribution to both mountaineering and the region's tourist industry is documented in an **Alpine Museum** (daily summer 10am–noon & 4–6pm; winter 8am–noon & 2–6pm; Sfr3), commemorating the first ascent of the Matterhorn, led by Edward Whymper in 1865 – a feat marred by the loss of three of his companions on the way down. Zermatt is still dominated by the English and English-speaking travellers; a nineteenth-century English church immediately above the museum ministers to their needs.

Opposite the train station, the **Gornergrat-Bahn** (*Eurail* not valid, *InterRail* 50 percent reduction, *Swiss Pass* 25 percent reduction) departs every half-hour or so between 7am and 8pm in high summer to the **Gornergrat**, a vantage point with a magnificent panorama of Valaisian Alps and glacial ice below. The Monte Rosa massif, with Switzerland's highest peak, the Doufourspitze, is 10km southeast. At the south end of the village a cable car heads up to the **Schwarzsee**, the most popular point from which to view the pyramidal Matterhorn, and, when the snow clears, the start of a hairy two-hour walk to **HÖRLIHÜTTE**, at 3260m right below the mountain. From Schwarzsee, or Zermatt, further cable cars lead to Trockener Steg and a station below Klein Matterhorn, a smaller peak which looks across at its more grandiose namesake.

There's a list of **hotels** and a courtesy phone at the end of the station platform if you arrive late; otherwise the overworked **tourist office** by the station (summer & winter peak seasons Mon–Sat 8am–noon & 1.30–7pm, Sun 8.30am–noon & 4–7pm; off season Mon–Fri 8.30am–noon & 1.30–6pm, Sat 8.30am–noon) has literally thousands of addresses of **private rooms** but isn't keen to handle bookings. The **youth hostel** on the east side of the village is full of hearty hiking types (☎028/67 23 20; ④). Dinner and breakfast are included, but the hostel is closed mid-April to the end of May. *Camping Zermatt*, below the station on the road back down the valley, is open May to September; *Camping Alpbühel* is 5km away at Täsch, where drivers have to leave their vehicles.

About the cheapest restaurant in town is *Walliserkanne*, 100m up the main street from the tourist office, which, unless you buy at the Euro-pop *Channa Pub* nightclub downstairs, also has the least pricy beer.

Graubünden

Graubünden – literally the "Grey Leagues" (Grisons in French, Grigioni in Italian) – is Switzerland's largest canton, and despite world-renowned top-notch resorts such as **St Moritz** and **Davos**, is in many ways its most mysterious, its desolate mountain valleys and pine forests a sometimes stark contrast with the lush greenery of central Switzerland. It's this isolation that has in part facilitated the survival of Switzerland's fourth official language, Romansch: although threatened by the encroachment of German – a process heightened by tourism – and weakened by the lack of a single unifying dialect, this modern descendant of the Latin tongue is still spoken in the mountain valleys of the southeast. The cantonal capital **Chur** is easily reached by rail from Zürich. From here, the privately run Rätische Bahn heads south into the mountains towards St Moritz. Another line operated by the same company leaves the Chur–Zürich line at Landquart, 20km north, for Davos.

Chur

Sitting in a deep valley carved by the Rhine, **CHUR** has been a powerful ecclesiastical centre since the earliest times, and its most imposing monument is still the **Cathedral**, occupying high ground just east of the town centre. Inside there are fragments of frescoes, a fifteenth-century altarpiece depicting Christ stumbling under the weight of the cross surrounded with scenes from the life of St Catherine, and, below the choir, four carved stone figures of the Apostles dating from around 1200. The treasury, too, is worth a look (daily 10am–noon & 2–4pm) for its set of ancient reliquaries and statuary. The cathedral is surrounded by the eighteenth-century buildings of the **Hof**, the Bishop's palace. Steps descend to the **Rätisches Museum** (Tues–Sun 10am–noon & 2–5pm; Sfr5), largely devoted to folk costumes and domestic utensils from the Graubünden region. A picturesque town centre nestles below, a succession of fountained squares bisected by the main north–south thoroughfare, the **Poststrasse**, which leads past the arcaded courtyard of the fifteenth-century town hall. On Postplatz at Poststrasse's northern end, Chur's **Kunstmuseum** (Tues–Sun 10am–noon & 2–5pm, Thurs until 8pm; Sfr5) features paintings by Graubünden natives Angelika Kauffmann and Giovanni Segantini.

Chur's **train station** is ten minutes northwest of the town centre at the head of Bahnhofstrasse, a continuation of Poststrasse. The **tourist office** is at Grabenstrasse 5, east of Postplatz (Mon–Fri 8am–noon & 1.30–6pm, Sat 9am–noon), and there is a **youth hostel** (☎081/22 65 63; ②) ten minutes' walk along Steinbruchstrasse, the continuation of Grabenstrasse.

Davos

Stretched along the banks of the Landwasser river, **DAVOS** is in fact two villages, Davos-Platz and Davos-Dorf, linked by a four-kilometre ribbon of chalet-type buildings. Although primarily known as a winter resort, it's surrounded by beautiful walking territory and can be very restful in summer when the skiing hordes have departed. Most of the town's central amenities are in Davos-Platz, which stretches 2km along Promenade, the main street running between the two towns to the **Kirchner Museum** (Tues–Sun 2–6pm; Sfr7), a vibrant collection of works by the German Expressionist painter from the "Brücke" school. Davos-Dorf, at the northeastern end of the settlement, is the starting point for the **Parsennbahn**, a funicular which heads up the slopes of the **Weissfluh**, the mountain which dominates the village and whose snowfields provide some of Switzerland's best ski-runs. The funicular terminates at the **Weissfluhjoch**, a col below the summit, from where a cable car completes the journey. You can savour panoramic views here, and the invigorating walk down takes a couple of hours. There are over 400km of easier walks, especially in the meadows and woods around the Davoser See, a small lake just beyond the northern end of town.

Trains stop at both Davos-Platz and Davos-Dorf. The latter is more convenient for the **tourist office** directly opposite (May–Nov Mon–Fri 8.30am–noon & 1.45–6pm, Sat 8.30am–noon; Dec–April same hours plus Sat 4–6pm & Sun 9–11pm), although there is another (same hours) at Promenade 67 in Davos-Platz. The town's free public transport system – covering buses and trains along 15km of the valley floor – makes it easy to get to the **youth hostel** (☎081/46 14 84; closed May; ②), 2km northeast of Davos-Dorf (bus #6) overlooking Davos See. There is also a riverside campsite (☎081/46 10 43) ten minutes' walk or half-hourly bus #4 from Davos-Dorf.

St Moritz

Favoured winter retreat of the international élite, **ST MORITZ** is another modern conurbation built around two villages — St Moritz-Bad, on the shores of the St Moritz lake, and St Moritz-Dorf, on the hillside above. The **train station**, where you can also catch the PTT bus to Lugano, is directly below St Moritz-Dorf. Via Serlas winds up to a central square and the **tourist office** (July, Aug & Dec–April Mon–Sat 9am–6pm; rest of year Mon–Fri 9am–noon & 2–6pm, Sat 9am–noon) which doles out **rooms**. There's a **youth hostel** at Via Surpunt 60 in St Moritz-Bad (☎082/339 69; ②), thirty minutes' walk around the lake or a ride on one of the Dorf-Bad-Dorf buses. The same methods get you to the campsite (☎082/340 90) just beyond St Moritz-Bad.

Via del Bagn runs down the hill from Dorf to Bad, passing on the way the **Engadiner Museum** (Mon–Fri 9.30am–noon & 2–5pm, Sun 10am–noon; Sfr5), housed in a solid stone building that is one of the few surviving pieces of vernacular architecture in the town. Alongside local Bronze Age finds, the ethnographical treasures inside include a great deal of furniture, and examples of the once-ubiquitous ceramic stoves which used to warm Alpine farmhouses. Immediately above, a curious domed structure holds the **Giovanni Segantini Museum** (June–Oct Tues–Sat 9am–12.30pm & 2.30–5pm, Sun 10.30am–12.30pm & 2.30–4.30pm; Dec–May Tues–Sat 10am–12.30pm & 3–5pm, Sun 3–5pm; Sfr5), which displays the work of the largely self-taught, local-born painter. Segantini was perhaps the definitive painter of Alpine life, capturing the light of the highland pastures and the quiet dignity of the region's hardy, stoical inhabitants, and investing it with a spiritual quality that is eloquently manifest in the mountainscapes on view here, notably the three-painting series *To Be, To Pass, To Become*.

TICINO

The Italian-speaking canton of **Ticino** (Tessin to German and French speakers) occupies the southern slopes of the great Alpine chain which crosses central Switzerland. Ticino became part of the confederation in the early 1500s, when the Swiss moved to secure the southern approaches of the St Gotthard pass against the Milanese. For the next three and a half centuries, although the Ticinese were subjects of German-speaking cantons to the north, there's quite a lot of evidence to suggest that Swiss domination wasn't overly resented by the inhabitants – the abolition of feudal restrictions was often one of the results of Swiss rule. Nowadays the main attractions of the area are the lakeside resorts of **Locarno** and **Lugano**, where mountain scenery merges with the subtropical plant life encouraged by the warm climate. Ticino is also known for its ancient churches, many containing original medieval frescoes. Both Locarno and Lugano have their fair share of these, as does the cantonal capital, **Bellinzona**.

Bellinzona

Guarding the southern approaches to the San Bernadino and St Gotthard passes, **BELLINZONA** is the point through which most southbound traffic flows. It initially comes across as quite a harsh, forbidding place, especially with its three medieval fortresses thrusting violently up from a parched valley floor, but it's worth spending time to make a closer inspection before continuing towards the warm climate and lush vegetation of the lakes. The town centre, around the elegant Renaissance buildings of **Piazza Collegiata**, lies squeezed between two of the castles. On the eastern side of the square, a pathway climbs up to the **Castello de Montebello** (daily 8am–6pm) in which the **Museo Civico** (Tues–Sun 9.30/10am–noon & 2–5/5.30pm; Sfr2) houses a small collection of weaponry in a former dungeon. The church of **Santa Maria delle Grazie** (daily 6.15–11.45am & 2–6.45pm), ten minutes south of the town centre along Via Lugano, is also worth a peek for the enormous sixteenth-century *Crucifixion* on one wall, surrounded by scenes from the life of Christ. The thirteenth-century basilica of

San Bagio (daily 7.30–11.30am & 2.30–5.30pm), immediately east on the other side of the rail tracks, has more frescoes, both inside and out.

Bellinzona's **train station** is ten minutes north of the centre. There's no hostel, but the **tourist office** (Mon–Fri 8am–noon & 1.30–6.30pm, Sat 9am–noon), just south of Piazza Collegiata in the town hall, has **rooms** if you want to stay.

Locarno

The main rail line heads south towards Lugano, while another route branches west to Lake Maggiore and its principal resort, **LOCARNO**. Focus of town is the **Piazza Grande**, a busy arcaded square with the lakefront and ferry station immediately to the east. A shoreline promenade heads south to the **Bosco Isolino**, five minutes away, an area of palm-studded parkland. Most of the town's sights, however, lie in the narrow streets of the old town, ranged on gently rising ground behind the main piazza. Via Rusca leaves the western end of the square for the fifteenth-century **Castello Visconti**, housing an archeological museum (Tues–Sun 10am–noon & 2–5pm; Sfr5) strong on Bronze Age and Roman relics. Via Ripa Canova, beside the castle heads uphill to the fourteenth-century church of **San Francesco**, with faded wall decorations from the Baroque period, and, beyond, along Via Citadella, the richly Baroque **Chiesa Nuova**, with a sumptuously stuccoed ceiling held up by a gaggle of fleshy cherubs. Via Sant'Antonio leads up to a piazza of the same name, dominated by its seventeenth-century church. The most impressive feature of the town is perhaps the austere Romanesque basilica of **San Vittore**, a twelfth-century lump of stone, with an earlier crypt, languishing by the side of the main Locarno–Bellinzona road, Via della Collegiata. Take also the funicular from nearby Via delle Stazione (every 15min between 7am and 10pm) to the **Monastery of Madonna del Sasso**, an impressive ochre pile perched precariously above the town. The richly decorated pilgrimage church contains an effigy of the Madonna – the monastery was founded after a monk saw visions of the Virgin in 1480. The walk downhill through a wooded ravine is refreshing.

Practicalities

Locarno's **train station** is five minutes west of Piazza Grande down Via Ramogna. The **tourist office** is close by on Largo Zorzi (March–Oct Mon–Fri 8am–7pm, Sat & Sun 9am–noon & 1–5pm; Nov–Feb Mon–Fri 8am–noon & 2–6pm). The *Pensione Città Vecchia*, Via Toretta 10, just north of the Piazza Grande (☎093/31 45 54; ③), has **dorm accommodation** from Sfr20 per person, and *Tai Fu Quai*, Piazza Sant'Antonio (☎093/31 84 98; ④), has the cheapest rooms. There are some more atmospheric **hotels** in the old town, including the *Vecchia Locarno* on Via Catedrale (☎093/31 65 02; Sfr90), and the *Fiorentina* on Via Sant'Antonio (☎093/31 99 14; ⑤). The town's campsite (☎093/31 60 81) is a fifteen-minute walk south along the lake shore. The Piazza Grande is full of cafés, pizzerias and the like, although **eating and drinking** venues tend to be cheaper and more atmospheric in the streets of the old town behind. The *Fiorentina* hotel restaurant has affordable Italian dishes; *Bar del Pozzo*, on Piazza Sant'Antonio, is a friendly place to drink until late. Perhaps the cheapest of all, though with little style, is the *Inqua* self-service place on Piazza Stazione.

Lugano

With its compact cluster of Italianate piazzas and extensive tree-lined promenades, **LUGANO** is the most alluring of Ticino's lake resorts. There isn't much to see, but it's peaceful, with a pleasant, welcoming feel. Overlooking the town from the west, the **Cattedrale San Lorenzo** (daily 6.30am–6.30pm), characterized by its Renaissance portal, sports a few fading fresco remnants; five minutes south of the centre, down the lakeside Riva V. Vela, the church of **Santa Maria degli Angioli** contains a stunning *Crucifixion* painted by Renaissance artist Bernardino Luini. You might also look in on the cantonal **Art Gallery**, Via Canova 10 (Tues 2–5pm, Wed–Sun 10am–5pm; Sfr6), which has work by Klee and Renoir among many local pieces – look out for the depictions of early twentieth-century Ticino peasant life by Luigi Rossi and Eduardo Berti.

Thirty minutes' walk along the coast road, Via Rivera (bus #2), the **Villa Favorita** (April–late June Fri–Sun 10am–5pm; late June–Oct Tues–Sun 10am–5pm; Sfr12) is perhaps the town's most crucial attraction: home, since the departure to Madrid of earlier works of the nineteenth- and twentieth-century sections of the Thyssen-Bornemisza collection of paintings, one of Europe's richest private art collections. Displays primarily concentrate on American and European oils and watercolours, covering every major genre this century as well as the earlier Hudson River school, all well displayed in the recently renovated galleries. A kilometre across the bay to the west is **CASTAGNOLA**, a wealthy suburb of lush lakeside gardens, while a funicular from the nearby suburb of Cassarate climbs to **Monte Brè** (daily 7.30am–6.30pm); south of the town centre, another funicular departs from the suburb of Paradiso to **San Salvatore**, a rugged rock pinnacle offering fine views of the lake and surrounding countryside.

Practicalities

Lugano's **train station** overlooks the town from the west, linked to the centre by funicular or by steps down to the steep incline of Via Cattedrale. The **tourist office** is on the lakeside Riva Albertolli 5 (April–Oct Mon–Sat 9am–5/6pm; Nov–March Mon–Fri 9am–6pm). Possibly Switzerland's best, and one of its cheapest, **youth hostels** (complete with swimming pool), is at Via Cantonale 13 in the northern suburb of Crocifisso (☎091/56 27 28; ②) – take bus #5 from Piazza Manzoni, or walk 200m left out of the train station; there is more dormitory-style accommodation at *Montarina*, Via Montarina 1 (☎091/56 72 72; ②), across the tracks from the train station. Among the most characterful of the cheaper **hotels** are *Stella*, up behind the station at Via Borromini 5 (☎091/56 33 70; ④), and *Zurigo*, Corso Pestalozzi 13 (☎091/23 43 41; ④). Lugano doesn't have a campsite, but Agno, a short train tride away, has several lakeside locations. Lugano is blessed with a proliferation of reasonably priced **eateries**: Piazza Ciocarro, the lower terminus of the funicular, is home to *Savonara*, while the more compact *Commercio* is a couple of streets to the left on Via Ariosto, both serving cheap pizzas and pasta. *Pizzeria Mary* on Piazza Rezzonico is another popular choice, while *La Tinèra*, off Via dei Gorini, just behind Piazza della Riforma, is the place to go for tasty Ticinese chicken stews. Most evening **drinking** takes place in the cafés and bars around Piazza della Riforma – *Bar Argentino* on the eastern side is the most lively.

travel details

Trains

Zürich to: Basel (every 30min; 1hr 10min); Bellinzona (hourly; 2hr 30min–2hr 50min); Bern (half-hourly; 1hr 10min); Chur (hourly; 1hr 30min); Geneva (hourly; 3hr); Lausanne (hourly; 2hr 30min); Lugano (hourly; 3hr–3hr 20min); Luzern (hourly; 50min).

Bellinzona to: Locarno (every 30min; 20–30min); Lugano (every 30min; 25min).

Bern to: Basel (hourly; 1hr 10min); Brig (hourly; 1hr 45min); Interlaken (hourly; 50min); Thun (every 30min; 30min).

Brig to: Zermatt (hourly; 1hr 20min).

Chur to: Davos (hourly; 1hr 35min – change at Landquart); St Moritz (hourly; 2hr 10min).

Geneva to: Bern (hourly; 1hr 55min); Brig (better than hourly); Lausanne (3 an hour; 40 min); Montreux (hourly; 1hr); 2hr 10min–2hr 40min).

Interlaken to: Grindelwald (hourly; 40min); Jungfraujoch (hourly; 2hr 20min) Kleine Scheidegg (hourly; 1hr 20min); Lauterbrunnen (hourly; 20min); Wengen (hourly; 50min);.

Lausanne to: Montreux (every 30min; 20min); Vevey (every 30min; 15min).

Luzern to: Brienz (hourly; 1hr 35min); Interlaken (hourly; 1hr 50min).

Buses

St Moritz to: Lugano (2 daily; 20hr).

Ferries

Basel to: Geneva (half-hourly; 2hr 40min–3hr); Lausanne (hourly; 2hr 25min).

Davos to: St Moritz (hourly; 1hr 35min).

Interlaken to: Brienz (hourly June–Sept, less frequently spring & autumn; 1hr 20min); Thun (hourly June—Sept, less frequently spring & autumn; 2hr).

CHAPTER 24

TURKEY

BULGARIA

Black Sea

RUSSIA

To Sofia

Edirne

Sinop

İstanbul

Zonguldak

GREECE

To
Thessaloniki

Samsun

Trabzon

Kars

Çanakkale

Bursa

Troy

Bergama

ANAKARA

Sivas

Erzurum

Ayvalık

Manisa

İzmir

Nevşehir

Van

Çeşme

Kuşadası

Denizli

Konya

Malatya

Diyarbakir

Bodrum

Marmaris

Antalya

Adana

Gaziantep

Fethiye

Side

Alanya

Kaş

Mediterranean
Sea

CYPRUS

SYRIA

IRAQ

0   100 km

LEBANON

Introduction

Turkey is a country with a multiple identity, poised uneasily between East and West. The country is now keen to be accepted on equal terms by the West – it has aspirations to EC membership and is the only NATO ally in the Middle East region. But it is by no stretch of the imagination a Western nation, and the contradictions persist: mosques co-exist with churches; remnants of the Roman Empire crumble alongside ancient Hittite sites. Politically, modern Turkey was a bold experiment, founded on the remaining Anatolian kernel of the Ottoman Empire and almost entirely the creation of a single man, Kemal Atatürk. An explicitly secular republic, though one in which almost all of the inhabitants are at least nominally Muslim, it's a vast country and incorporates large disparities in levels of development. But it's an immensely rewarding place to travel, not least because of the people, whose reputation for friendliness and hospitality is richly deserved.

Western Turkey is the most visited and economically developed part of the country. **İstanbul**, straddling the Black and Marmara seas, is touted as Turkish mystique *par excellence*, and understandably so: it would take months to even scratch the surface of the old imperial capital, still the cultural and commercial centre of the country. Flanking it on opposite sides of the **Sea of Marmara** are the two prior seats of the Ottoman Empire, **Bursa** and **Edirne**, and, just beyond, the **Dardanelles**, with their World War I battlefields. Moving south, the **Aegean Coast** comes to the fore in the olive-swathed country around **Bergama** and **Ayvalık**. Beyond the functional city of **İzmir** are ancient sites, notably **Ephesus**, that have been a magnet for travellers since the eighteenth century, and these days this is Turkey at its most developed, with large numbers of visitors drawn to resorts like **Çeşme**, **Bodrum** and **Marmaris**, beyond which the Mediterranean Coast begins. There are remnants of the Lycians at **Xanthos**, and more resorts in **Kaş** and **Fethiye**, along the aptly-named "Turquoise Coast". Further along, **Antalya** is Turkey's fastest-growing city, a sprawling place that is the best starting point on the stretch of shoreline that reaches as far as the Syrian border, with extensive sands and archeological sites – most notably at **Perge** and **Aspendos** – until castle-topped **Alanya**, where

the tourist numbers begin to diminish. It's worth heading inland from here for the spectacular attractions of **Cappadocia**, with its famous rock churches, subterranean cities and tufa-pinnacle landscapes, and the Selçuk architecture and dervish associations of **Konya**. Further north, towards Istanbul, **Ankara**, Turkey's capital, is a planned city whose contrived Western feel gives some indication of the priorities of the modern Turkish Republic.

Information and Maps

Most Turkish towns of any size will have a *Turizm Danişma Bürosu* or **tourist office**, although outside the larger cities and resorts there's often very little actual information available and no guarantee that anyone will speak English. They are generally open Mon–Fri 8.30am–12.30pm & 1.30–5.30pm with extended evening and weekend hours in big resorts and cities.

The best available **maps** – though still rife with errors – are the *Geo Centre/RV* ones, "Turkey, West" and "Turkey, East", widely on sale at major resorts. City tourist offices normally stock reasonable **street plans**. If you're spending much time in Istanbul, the *A–Z Atlas of Istanbul* published by *Asya* is a worthwhile investment. Otherwise *Hallwag* or *Falk* do a good central street map.

Money and Banks

Turkish **currency** is the lira, abbreviated as TL. Coins come in denominations of 50, 100, 500, 1000, 2500 and 5000TL, although the smallest two have strictly nuisance value except in paying for public toilets. Notes comes as 5000, 10,000, 20,000, 50,000, 100,000 and 250,000TL. **Rates** for foreign currency are always better inside Turkey. Because of the TL's constant devaluation you should only change money as you need it, every few days.

Banks are open Mon–Fri 8.30am–noon & 1.30–5pm, and most charge a commission of about $2.50 for travellers' cheques. Between April and October many coastal resorts between Çanakkale and Alanya have weekend and evening hours at specific *nöbetçi* banks; a list is posted in the window or door of each branch. You can also use the **exchange booths** run by banks in coastal resorts, airports and ferry docks, where service is usually quicker and commissions always nonexistent. The cashpoint machines of the *Yapi Kreoi* and a few other banks will accept Visa, plus Cirrus system cards, provided you know your PIN. The **post office**, particularly in a sizeable town, is also often able to change currency and cheques, both travellers' and Euro, for 1 percent commission.

Communications

The Turkish **postal and telephone service** is run by the **PTT**. In larger towns and resorts the phone division of the main PTT is open 24 hours, with mail accepted from 8am until 7pm. Elsewhere expect both facilities to be open Mon–Sat 8am–10pm & Sun 9am–7pm. Post boxes are clearly labelled with categories of destination – "yurtdışı" means overseas.

The PTT is the best place to make **phone calls**. For local calls, you can buy *jetons*; for trunk or overseas calls, **phone cards** (available in denominations of 30, 60 and 120 units) or **metered booths** are better value. Direct-dial long-distance calls can also be made at any phone box labelled *Şehirlerarası* (Inter-city) or *Milletlerarası* (International). For Turkish **trunk calls**, dial 0 (wait for a change in tone), and then the city code plus the subscriber number. To make an **international call**, dial 00, then the country/area codes and the local number. The **operator** numbers are ☎118 for local directory assistance, ☎161 for long-distance and ☎528 2303 for the English-speaking international operator.

Getting Around

Public transport is fairly comprehensive in Turkey. Where a destination is not part of the skeletal train network, private bus companies more than compensate, in a system that is cheap and efficient. Short stretches are best covered by dolmuş – either shared taxis in towns or minibuses linking rural villages.

■ Trains

Turkey's **train network**, run by the *TCDD* or Turkish State Railways, is far from exhaustive, best used to span the distances between the three largest cities and the main provincial centres. Trains often follow ludicrously tortuous

routes and take up to twice as long as buses, although west of Ankara the best services, denoted *mavi tren* or *ekspresi*, almost match long-distance buses in speed and frequency. Reservations for most journeys can be made in İzmir, İstanbul or Ankara, though are only really necessary for the major routes. Basic prices are about the same per kilometre as the buses; students with an ISIC card get a ten percent discount. *InterRail* passes are valid, *Eurail* are not.

■ Buses and dolmuşes

Long-distance bus is the best way of getting around. There is no national bus company; most routes are covered by several firms, all of whom have ticket booths at the *otogars* (bus stations) from which they operate and (more conveniently) at offices in the town centre. There's also no such thing as a comprehensive timetable, although individual companies often provide their own. Stations are full of touts waiting to take you to the company of their choice – though it may not have the soonest departure, or the best service; **fares** vary only slightly between the best and scruffiest companies – as a broad example, İstanbul to Antalya costs around $8. It's worth the bit extra in comfort and safety to travel with the top names such as *Varun, Ulusoy, Pamukkale* or *Kamil Koç*.

For short hops you're most likely to use a **dolmuş**, a car or minibus that runs along a set route, picking passengers up along the way. On busy urban routes it's better to take the dolmuş from the start of its run; sometimes the destination will be posted on a sign at the kerbside, though generally you'll have to ask, or look at the dolmuş windshields themselves. Otherwise, to stop a dolmuş, hail it like a taxi. It's always difficult to know how much to pay if you're only going part-way, but **fares** are in any case very low; traditionally passengers make up change between themselves and pass the total up to the driver.

■ Driving and hitching

Given the excellent bus services, you don't need to **drive** in Turkey, but it can make it possible to see more of the country more quickly. Roads are usually adequate, although often dangerously narrow. You drive on the right, and give priority to the right, even on roundabouts. Speed limits are 50kph in towns, 90kph on main roads and motorways. Foreigners are rarely stopped by the police at the frequent checkpoints, but if you are you will be required to produce your driving licence and proof of ownership of the car (or car rental papers). You may also be stopped and given an on-the-spot fine for not wearing a seatbelt or for speeding; of late, highway police have become less polite – it things get tense, it's best to demonstrate (or feign) ignorance of any Turkish. A full driving licence is valid and Green Card insurance carries an expensive extra supplement to become valid in Turkey. The Turkish motoring organization, *TTOK*, have a **breakdown service**, contactable on ☎1/131 4631, free to members of most foreign motoring organizations. **Car rental** is expensive, with rates from $500 a week with unlimited mileage. Local chains tend to charge twenty to thirty percent less than the multinationals.

Hitching is a viable option where public transport is scarce or unavailable, and lifts tend to be frequent and friendly. You may be expected to share a glass of tea with the driver on reaching your destination. It is polite to offer a little money, though it will almost always be refused.

■ Ferries

Nearly all of Turkey's **ferries** are run by the *Türkiye Denizcilik İşletmesi* (Turkish Maritime Lines or *TML*), who operate everything from shuttle city services and inter-island lines to international services. All overnight services are enormously popular, and reservations must be made in advance through authorized *TML* agents. There are five classes of cabin on long-haul ferries; it's also possible to reserve a *pulman koltuk* or reclining chair, but if you leave bookings to the last minute you won't even get one of these. No one will mind if you sleep up on on deck but you do need a confirmed seat booking to be allowed on the boat in the first place. Fares are reasonable – about $40 in a third-class double cabin from İstanbul to İzmir, for example – and students up to age 28 (inclusive) with ISIC

enjoy a fifty percent discount. Cars cost almost as much again as a passenger berth.

■ Planes

Turkey's internal air network is now fairly comprehensive, but full-fare prices (eg. İzmir–Ankara at $70) are roughly five times that of ground transport. Still, the country's size means that you will probably want to use services at least once to make the most of a short, non-package visit. Besides the state-run *THY* and its subsidiary *THT*, there are private lines like *İstanbul Hava Yollari* and *Sultan Air* who often have advantageous rates undercutting *THY* – though the latter offers a healthy student discount.

Accommodation

Finding a bed for the night is generally no problem in Turkey, except in high season at the busier coastal resorts and larger towns. Prices, while still cheap by northern European standards, are no longer rock-bottom, however.

■ Hotels and pensions

Turkish **hotels** are officially graded by the tourism ministry on a scale of one to five stars; there is also a lower tier of unstarred establishments licensed by municipalities. Most one-star places cost $10–20 a double in season, with breakfast sometimes included. Unrated hotels can be as good as the lower end of the one-star class, though on average expect spartan rooms with possibly a washbasin and shower, and a squat toilet down the hall, for $4–8 a head. Often the pleasantest places to stay are **pansiyons** (pensions), small guesthouses which proliferate anywhere large numbers of holidaymakers do. If there are vacancies in season, touts in the coastal resorts and other tourist targets descend

---

ACCOMMODATION PRICE CODES

Throughout this guide, accommodation is priced on a scale of ① to ⑧, the number indicating the lowest price per night a single person could expect to pay in that establishment in high season. With hostels this is the nightly rate per person; with hotels, the price is arrived at by dividing the cost of the cheapest double room by two. The prices indicated by the codes are as follows

① = under £5 / $8   ② = £5–10 / $8–16   ③ = £10–15 / $16–24   ④ = £15–20 / $24–32

⑤ = £20–25 / $32–40   ⑥ = £25–30 / $40–48   ⑦ = £30–35 / $48–56   ⑧ = over £35 / $56

on every incoming bus, dolmuş or boat; at other times, look for signs saying *Boş oda var* ("rooms free"). Rooms tend to be sparse but clean, though places in general will be friendlier than hotels. Expect to pay $10–20 a double with en suite bath, $5–15 without.

■ Campsites and hostels

Wherever *pansiyons* are found, there will also be **campsites**, often run by the same people. Charges per head run from a couple of dollars for the most basic places to $7 in a well-appointed site at a major resort in season, plus $3–4 per tent. You may also be charged for your vehicle – anything from $5 to $20. Campsites often rent out tents or provide **chalet** accommodation, for which you'll pay $10–20. **Camping rough** is not illegal, but hardly anybody does it except when trekking in the mountains.

There are few **hostels** outside İstanbul. Most hostels – called *yurts* – are poky dormitories aimed at local students on summer holiday.

Food and Drink

At its finest, Turkish **food** is some of the best in the world, and prices won't break your budget. Unadventurous travellers are prone to get stuck in a kebab rut, but in fact all but the strictest vegetarians should find enough variety.

■ Food

The usual Turkish **breakfast** (*kahvaltı*) served at hotels and *pansiyons* is invariably a pile of bread slices accompanied by a pat of margarine, cheese, jam and a couple of olives. Only the tea is likely to be available in quantity, and you're often better off using street stands or snack joints. Many workers start the morning with a *börek*, a rich, flaky, layered pastry containing bits of mince or cheese, sold at a tiny *büfe* (stall-café) or from street carts. Others content themselves with a simple *simit* (bread rings speckled with sesame seeds), or a bowl of *çorba* (soup) with lemon.

Later in the day, vendors hawk *lahmacun*, small pizzas with meat-based toppings, and, in coastal cities *midye tava* (deep-fried mussels). Not to be confused with *lahmacun* is *pide*, Turkish pizza – flat bread with various toppings, served in a *pideci* or *pide salonu*. Another snack speciality is *mantı* – meat-filled ravioli drenched in yoghurt and oil.

For **more substantial food**, a *lokanta* is a restaurant; a *çorbaci* is a soup kitchen; and a *kebabcı* specializes in the preparation of kebab. Most budget-priced restaurants are alcohol-free; any place marked *içkili* (licensed) is likely to be more expensive. A useful exception is a *meyhane* (tavern), a smoky dive where eating is considered secondary to drinking, though these can be fairly rough.

Prices vary widely according to the type of establishment: from $2–3 a head at a simple soup kitchen up to $10–12 at the flashier resort restaurants. Many places don't have **menus**; you'll need to ascertain the prices of most main courses beforehand. A good thing to try is **mezes** or appetizers, usually a bewildering array of dishes that, along with dessert, are really the core of Turkish cuisine. Ones you'll find everywhere are *imam bayıldı* (cold baked aubergine with onion and tomato) and *dolma* (any stuffed vegetable). **Main courses** include a number of **vegetable** standbys, though they're often prepared with lamb- or chicken-based stock. Full-on **meat** dishes include several variations on the kebab, for example *İskender kebab*, heavy on the flat bread and yoghurt, *köfte* (meatballs), *şiş* (stewed meat chunks) and *çöp* (bits of lamb or offal). **Fish and seafood** are good, if usually pricey, and sold by weight more often than by item. Budget mainstays include freshly grilled *sardalya* (sardines), *palamut* (tuna), *iskumru* (mackerel), *küpes* (bogue) and *kefal* (grey mullet).

Finally, those with a sweet tooth will find every imaginable concoction at the *pastane* (sweet-shop), best the syrup-soaked **baklava**-type items and a variety of **milk puddings**, most commonly *sütlaç* (rice pudding) – one dessert that's consistently available in ordinary restaurants. Other **sweets** include *aşure*, a sort of rose-water jelly laced with pulses, raisins and nuts, and, the best-known Turkish sweet, *lokum* or "Turkish Delight" – solidified sugar and pectin, flavoured with rosewater and sometimes pistachios and sprinkled with powdered sugar.

■ Drink

Tea (*çay*) is the Turkish national drink, served in tiny tulip-shaped glasses, with sugar on the side but no milk. **Coffee** (*kahve*) is not as common, although instant coffee is increasingly popular. **Fruit juice** or *meyva suyu* can be excellent if it's pulp in a bottle, available in unusual flavours. The good stuff is so thick you might want to cut it with *memba suyu* (spring water), found at the tableside in most restaurants, or fizzy *maden suyu* (mineral water). *Meşrubat* is the generic term for all carbonated **soft drinks** such as Coca Cola, Fanta and the like – available pretty much everywhere now. You'll also come across *Ayran* or watered-down yoghurt.

Despite inroads made by Islamic fundamentalists, **alcoholic drinks** (*içkiler*) are available virtually without restriction in resorts, though you may have some thirsty moments in interior towns. **Beer** (*bira*), sold principally in bottles, comes in two main brands, *Efes Pilsen* and *Tuborg*. Turkish **wine** (*şarap*), can be very good; names to watch for include *Kavaklıdere*, *Doluca*, and *Kavalleros*. The Turkish national **aperitif** is *rakı*, not unlike Greek ouzo but rougher and stronger. It's usually drunk with ice, topped up with water.

Opening Hours & Holidays

Ordinary **shops** are open continuously from around 9am until 7pm or 8pm, depending on the owner. **Museums** are generally open from 8am or 8.30am until 5pm or 6pm, closed on Monday and often at lunchtime (usually 12.30–1.30pm). **Archeological sites** have variable opening hours, but are generally open daily from just after sunrise until just before sunset. **Mosques** frequented by tourists are kept open all the time; others open only for *namaz*, or Muslim prayer, five times a day. It's a courtesy for women to cover their heads before entering a mosque, and for both men and women to cover their legs – shorts are considered particularly offensive. Shoes should always be removed.

Emergencies

Despite popular stereotypes, you're unlikely to encounter any trouble in Turkey. Violent street crime is uncommon, theft is rare and the authorities usually treat tourists with courtesy. Keep your wits about you and an eye on your belongings and you shouldn't have any problems. **Civilian police** come in a variety of subdivisions: the green-uniformed *Polis* are the everyday security force in the towns and cities; there's the *Trafik Polis*, recognizable by their white caps; the *Belediye Zabitası*, navy-clad market police, patrol the markets and bazaars; and, in rural areas, you'll find the *Jandarma*, a division of the regular army.

For **minor health complaints** head for the nearest *eczane* or pharmacist, where you'll be able to obtain cheap remedies for ailments like diarrhoea, sunburn and flu, though you may find it difficult to find exact equivalents to any home prescriptions. Night-duty pharmacists are known as *nöbet(ci)*; a list of the current rota is posted in every chemist's front window. For more **serious ailments**, your consulate or the tourist office may be able to provide you with the address of an English-speaking doctor. Otherwise it's best to go direct to a hospital (*klinik*) – either public (*Devlet Hastane* or *SSK Hastanesi*), or private (*Özel Hastane*). The latter are far preferable in terms of cleanliness and standard of care, and since all foreigners must pay for medical attention, you may as well get the best available.

EMERGENCY NUMBERS
Police ☎155; Fire ☎111; Ambulance☎112. These all cost one small jeton.

İSTANBUL

Arriving in İSTANBUL comes as a shock. You may still be in Europe, but a walk down any backstreet will be enough to convince you that you have entered a completely alien environment. Traders with handcarts, stevedores carrying burdens twice their size, limbless beggars and shoeshine boys all frequent the streets around the city centre. Men monopolize public bars and teahouses, while women scurry about their business, heads often covered and gaze downcast. In summer, dust tracks take the place of pavements, giving way in winter to a slurry of mud. Where there are pavements, they are punctuated at intervals with unmarked pits large enough to swallow you without trace. And this is before you even begin to cross any bridges into Asia.

Yet İstanbul is the only city in the world to have played capital to consecutive Christian and Islamic empires, and retains features from all its eras, often in congested proximity to each other. **Byzantium**, as the city was formerly known, was an important centre of commerce, but only gained real power in the fourth century AD, when Constantine chose it as the new capital of the **Roman Empire**. Later it became increasingly disassociated from Rome, adopting the Greek language and Christianity and becoming, in effect, the capital of an independent empire. At the beginning of the thirteenth century, the city was sacked by the Crusaders, and by the time the Byzantines, led by Michael Palaeologus, had regained control, many of the major buildings had fallen into disrepair and the empire itself had greatly diminished in size. As the Byzantines declined, the **Ottoman Empire** prospered, and in 1453 the city was captured by Mehmet the Conqueror, who shortly after began to rebuild the city. In the following century, the victory was reinforced by the great military achievements of Selim the Grim, and by the reign of Süleyman the Magnificent, whose conquests helped fund the greatest of all Ottoman architects, Mimar Sinan. The city prospered throughout the next century but by the nineteenth century the glory days of Ottoman domination were firmly over, leading to the **War of Independence**, after which Atatürk created a new capital in Ankara – although İstanbul retained its importance as a centre of trade and commerce. In **recent years**, the population of the city has risen to some ten million, almost a fifth of the country's total, and is still on the increase, the effects of which have only added to the cacophony and congestion of the place.

> The İstanbul area telephone code is ☎1.

Arrival and information

İstanbul's **airport**, 24km southwest of the city, splits between two terminals, international and domestic, 500m apart and connected by bus. The same buses run into the city at Şişhane, near Taksim Square ($1.50). **Taxis** into town cost $10–15. There are two **train stations**, one for trains from other parts of Europe, at **Sirkeci**, the other, **Haydarpaşa**, for trains from Asian Turkey. From Sirkeci station it's easy to find a taxi to the hotels in Sultanahmet or Lâleli, and there are any number of buses – #80, #84 and #86 – from the Eminönü bus terminal on the nearby waterfront. Ferries cross the Bosphorus from Haydarpaşa station to Karaköy, from where buses run across to Sultanahmet. Arriving by bus, there are two main **bus stations**, one situated at Harem in Asia and the other at Topkapı in Europe (an outlying suburb of the city taking its name from a gate in the city walls), in one of the city's most chaotic, dirty areas – it's best to head for the tram platform via the maze of underpasses, buy a ticket on the platform and board a Sinkeci tram heading towards the city walls. Buses from European cities generally terminate at Topkapı, though some carry on to Harem; most Asian buses call at both. From Topkapı the #84 bus goes via Lâleli and Sultanahmet to Eminönü. From Harem there are dolmuşes every few minutes to Kadıköy. The most central **tourist office** is in Sultanahmet near the Hippodrome on Divanyolu Caddesi (daily 9am–5pm; ☎522 4903); they're not very helpful but might be able to spare a map.

City transport

The city's **public transport system** is undergoing modernization, and the underground system should reduce traffic congestion; meanwhile, you must rely on **buses**, of which there are two kinds – **private** (orange) buses, and municipally run **belediye** buses. You need to buy **tickets** in advance, from bus station ticket offices, newspaper stands or fast-food booths, or from touts who sell at slightly inflated prices around some bus terminals. Tickets are sold in blocks of ten for around 40¢ each. On certain buses, identified with the sign *"iki bilet gecilir"*, you need two tickets; buses for which only one ticket is required have a sign saying *"tam bilet gecilir"*. Tickets should be deposited next to the driver on boarding, although on orange buses you can usually pay the driver in cash. A recent innovation on the European side are two **tram lines**, one running from Eminönü through Sultanahmet to Topkapı and outlying suburbs; the other runs the length of İsytikal Caddesi from Beyoğlu to Taksim using turn-of-the-century trams with the conductor dressed appropriately. Both lines require tickets, purchased from booths on the platforms. There is a **municipal train network**, consisting of two lines, one on each side of the Bosphorus, but it's hardly comprehensive. Tickets, which cost the same as for buses, are bought on the platform and should be retained until leaving. There are also **dolmuşes** or shared taxis – usually cars rather than the minibuses you'll see in other parts of Turkey. They have their point of departure and destination displayed somewhere about the windscreen and you can board and alight where you want en route – flag them down as you would a taxi. Many useful routes are covered by the **passenger boats** up and down the waterways and between Europe and Asia; you need a small *jeton* (40¢), available from the dockside kiosks.

Accommodation

Finding **somewhere to stay** in İstanbul is rarely a problem, but it's best to phone ahead to avoid a lot of trudging from one full *pansiyon* to the next, and in mid-season anything up to a week's advance booking wouldn't go amiss. Some of the city's nicest small hotels and *pansiyons* are situated in **Sultanahmet**, right at the heart of İstanbul, particularly around Yerebatan Caddesi and in the less prominent but equally atmospheric backstreets between the Sultan Ahmet mosque and the sea. Failing that, there's another concentration of hotels about a mile up Ordu Caddesi, in the areas of **Aksaray** and **Lâleli** – handy if you're arriving late at night. **Taksim** is also a convenient base from which to sightsee, and comes into its own at night, when it becomes the centre of cultural and culinary activity.

Sultanahmet

Alp Guesthouse, Adliye Sok 4, Sultanahmet (☎517 9570). Very clean and pleasant with terrace and garden breakfast room. ④

Anadolu, Yerebatan Cad, Salkım Söğüt Sok 3 (☎512 1035). Small rooms without private showers, but very quiet. ②

Hipodrom Pansiyon, Üçler Sok 9 (☎516 0902). Cheap, convenient, clean rooms & friendly staff. ③

Optimist, Atmeydanı 68 (☎516 2398). Basic hotel (④) with lovely views of Sultanahmet. Book well in advance. They also have a pansiyon (②) behind.

Orient International Youth Hostel, Akbıyık Cad 13 (☎516 0171). Campbeds and no carpets but clean. ①

CENTRAL ISTANBUL

Yavuz Selim Camii

TABAK YUNUS SOK

AYKAPI C.

HALIÇ CAD

ABDÜLEZEL PAŞA CAD

ATATÜR

FEVZI PAŞA CAD

YAVUZ SELIM CAD

HALIÇ CAD

OBALI CAD

OBALI CAD

UNKAPANI

ATATÜRK BUL

RAG.

ATLAMATAŞI CAD

İSLAM C.

ÇUKUR C.

HAYDAR C.

BADEM KAP SOK

Zeyrek Camii

ATLAMATAŞI CAD

FEVZI PAŞA CAD

Fatih Camii

ZEYREK

Si Ca

FETTA

BALI PAŞA CAD

FATIH

Çinili Hamami

ATATÜRK BUL

CAD

SÜR BEY YAZICI

KATIP VEFA CAD

MIMAR SINAN CAD

Aqueduct of Valens

MACARKARDEŞLER CAD

İTFAIYE

CEMAL YENER TOSYALI CAD

KIRAZLI MESCIT S.

L

HESAP ÇEŞ.

VATAN CAD

SOFULAR TEKKESI

HORHOR CAD

ŞEHZADEBAŞI CAD

Şehzade Camii

SÜLEYMANIYE CAD

TAVUKHANE CAD

Beyazit Kulesi

VATAN CAD

ATATÜRK BUL

16 MART ŞEH. C.

BOZDOĞAN KEM

AĞA YOKUŞU

YEŞILTULUMBA SOK

VEZNECILER C.

Beyaz Camii

MILLET CAD

LÂLELI

Lâleli Camii

FETHIBEY C.

YAĞLIKÇILAR SOK

VIDINLI TEVIF P.C.

BÜYÜK REŞIT P.C.

BEYAZIT

ORDU CAD

ORDU CAD

YEN

HASEKI CAD

AKSARAY

AKSARAY C.

LÂLELI CAD

KOYSA CAD

KOCA RAGIP SOK

MITHAT PAŞA C.

TIYATRO

NAMIK KEMAL CAD

MUSTAK CAD

HAYRIYE TUCCARI CAD

CERRAHPAŞA CAD

BEYA

KUMKAPI

IBR. PAŞAY.

MOLATAŞI CAD

MOLATAŞI CAD

KUÇUKLANGA CAD

Yenikapı Train Station

LANGAHISARI SOK

ALIŞAN SOK

BABAYIĞIT SOK

Kumk Train S

ALIŞAN SOK

KENNEDY CAD

Sea of Marr

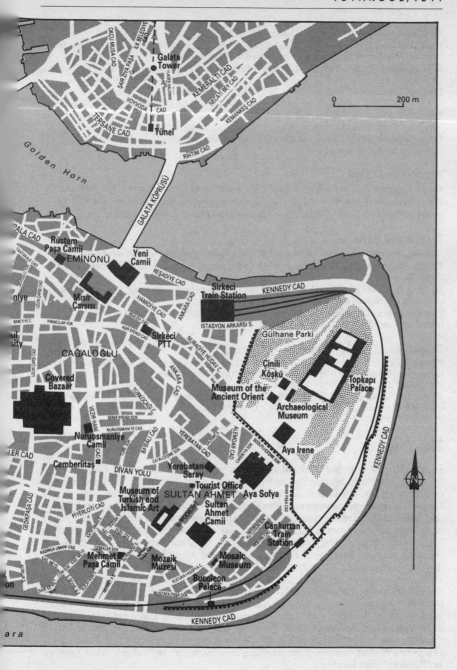

Park, Utangaç Sok 26 (☎517 6596). Clean and friendly. ④

Rose Pansiyon, Ishakpasha Mah Aksakal Sok 20, off Küçük Ayasofya Sok (☎518 9705). Small, clean and friendly new place in a quiet quarter off the Hippodrome. ④

Side Pansiyon, Utangaç Sok 20 (☎512 8175). Friendly staff, with clean rooms and a pleasant tea garden. ①

Topkapı, Işakpaşa Cad, Kutluğun Sok 1 (☎527 2433). Simply furnished but with an excellent location. ②

True Blue Pansiyon, Akbiyik Cad 2 (☎516 0545). Dormitory and triple-room accommodation. Very popular with budget travellers. ①

Uğur Pansiyon, Kasap Osman Sok 22 (☎516 0138). Clean pension off the Hippodrome. Excellent views from rooftop terrace. ③

Aksaray and Lâleli

Burak, Fethi Bey Cad, Ağa Yokuşu 1 (☎511 8679 or 522 7904). Quite ordinary but well situated. ②

Mine Pansiyon, Gençturk Cad 54 (☎511 2375). Clean rooms, shared facilities, friendly staff. ①

Neşet, Harikzadeler Sok 23 (☎526 7412 or 522 4474). Old place, but friendly and good value. ①

Taksim and Beyoulu

Alibaba, Meşrutiyet Cad 119, Tepebaşı (☎144 0781). Plain and simple but a bit scruffy. ②

Dünya, Meşrutiyet Cad 79, Tepebaşi (☎144 0940). Run-down and peeling but clean and quite cheap. ①

Hotel Gezi, Mete Cad 42 (☎251 7430). Well-run and quite classy with Bosphorus views from the restaurant and some of the rooms. ⑥

Virginie Apart Hotel, İstiklâl Cad 100, Beyoğlu (☎251 7856). Self-catering apartments in very central position. ⑦

Campsites

Ataköy Tatil Köyü, Rauf Orbay Cad, Ataköy. Ten minutes from the airport (taxi $3), with an attractive setting on the Marmara Sea, 16km from city centre. Lots of facilities. #82 bus connects with the city centre.

Florya Tourist Camping, Yeşilköy Halkalı Cad, Florya. Pleasant and leafy, well served by public transport, and cheap. About 25km from the city by #73 bus from Taksim, Florya–Topkapı dolmuş, or train from either Eminönü or Ataköy.

The City

İstanbul is divided in two by the **Bosphorus**, which runs between the Black Sea and the Sea of Marmara, dividing Europe from Asia. At right angles to it, the **Golden Horn** cuts through the city centre, on the European side of the Bosphorus. This is split between the old imperial centre in the **Sultanahmet** district and around, and **Galata** and **Taksim**, the modern centre of culture and commerce. The old centre is a hustly place, especially for women, and first impressions can be negative. Yet Sultanahmet is home to the main sightseeing attractions – the Topkapı Palace, the church of Aya Sofya, the covered bazaar – and many people spend all their time here; west, too, are more great attractions in the Süleymaniye mosque complex and the remains of the city walls. Across the Golden Horn, the modern city, connected to the historic centre by the Galata Bridge, leads up to the large and ugly Taksim Square, the heart of İstanbul's restaurant and nightlife. Down below, the old Levantine areas of **Galata** and **Pera** are home to one of the city's most famous landmarks, the Galata tower, not far from which is the entrance to the **Tünel**, İstanbul's underground, running up to the start of İstiklâl Caddesi, which runs through to Taksim. Any number of **buses** cross the Horn via the Galata and Atatürk bridges. Take ones marked "Beyoğlu" or "Taksim" from Aksaray, or "Karaköy" from Eminönü.

Sultanahmet

Perhaps the single most compelling sight in Sultanahmet is the former church of **Aya Sofya** (Tues–Sun 9.30am–5pm, galleries 1–5pm; $5), which was commissioned in the sixth century by the Emperor Justinian, and remained a symbol of Byzantine power long after the empire itself had been destroyed; the building is presently filled with scaffolding in preparation for a massive renovation programme, but this does little to mar the effects of its decoration. It was converted to a mosque in 1453, which it remained until 1932, soon after which it opened as a museum, and inside there are a few features left over from this time – a *mihrab*, a *mimber* and the enormous wooden plaques which bear sacred Islamic names of God, the Prophet Mohammed and the first four caliphs – but the most interesting elements are the original ones. Upstairs in the western gallery a large circle of green Thessalian marble marks the position of the throne of the empress. There are also remains of abstract mosaics – some of the prettiest of which can be seen under the arches of the south gallery and in the narthex – and figurative works, most impressive in the south gallery. One, beyond a pair of false marble doors on the west face of the pier, depicts Christ, the Virgin and St John the Baptist; another, on the east wall of the gallery, shows Christ flanked by an emperor and empress – believed to be Constantine IX Monomachus and the Empress Zoë. A third, dating from 1118, depicts the Virgin and Child between the Emperor John II Comnenus and the Empress Irene, and their son Prince Alexius, added later – a livelier, less conventional work. There's also a Virgin and Child in the apse, and, one of the most beautiful of all the mosaics, a Virgin and Child flanked by two emperors in the Vestibule of Warriors. Dated to the last quarter of the tenth century, it shows Justinian, to the right of the Virgin, offering a model of the church, while Constantine offers a model of the city.

Immediately to the north of Aya Sofya, the **Topkapı Palace** (9am–5pm; closed Tues; $5) is the other unmissable sight in this part of town, the centre of the Ottoman Empire for nearly four centuries until the removal of the retinue to Dolmabahçe in 1853. Built between 1459 and 1465, it consists of a collection of buildings arranged around a series of courtyards. The first courtyard, as service area of the palace, was always open to the general public and is today home to the ticket office. The second courtyard is the site of the **Divan**, although this is currently closed to the public and all you can do is peer through the windows at the Council Chamber and the couch which gave the institution its name. The **Divan tower**, visible from many vantage points all over the city, was rebuilt in 1825 by Mahmut II, replacing a squat-looking version with a pyramidal cap. Next door is the **Inner Treasury**, a six-domed hall that holds an exhibition of arms and armour. Across the courtyard are the **palace kitchens**, with their magnificent rows of chimneys, the furthest of which have been restored complete with a fascinating array of utensils, while others house a collection of some of the finest porcelain in the world – an ever-changing display continually replenished from the Topkapı collection.

Around the corner, you have to pay extra for a guided tour of the **Harem** (hourly 10am–4pm; $2.50), but it's worth it, as more rooms are gradually being opened to the public. The word *harem* means "forbidden" in Arabic; in Turkish it refers to the suite of apartments in a palace or private residence where the head of the household lived with his wives, odalisques (female slaves) and children. The harem in Topkapı consists of over four hundred rooms; the only men that were allowed to enter were the black eunuchs and the imperial guardsmen, who were only employed at certain hours and even then were blinkered. The black eunuchs were responsible for running the harem, but only allowed to enter in daylight hours; at night the female housekeepers took charge, and reported any unusual occurrences to the Chief Black Eunuch. Tours take in a good part of the complex, including the Court of the Black Eunuch, the apartments of the Valide Sultan, rebuilt after 1665, which include a particularly lovely domed dining room, and, beyond, some of the most attractive rooms in the whole palace – the apartments and reception rooms used by the sultan himself, the grandest of which is the **Hünkar Sofası** or Imperial Hall, where the sultan entertained his visitors. Another important room is a masterwork of the architect Sinan – the bedchamber of Murat III, covered in sixteenth-century İznik tiles and kitted out with a marble fountain and bronze fireplace. Below this is a large indoor swimming pool, into which Murat is supposed to have thrown gold to the women that pleased him. On the floor above was the so-called Cage, where the brothers of the ruling sultan would be incarcerated with a harem of concubines and deaf mutes until the time came for them to assume power – by which time they were frequently crazed. More highlights of the palace include the beautifully decorated dining room of Ahmet III and the newly refurbished odalisques' apartments.

Back in the main body of the palace, in the third courtyard, the **throne room**, mainly dating from the reign of Selim I, was where the sultan awaited the outcome of sessions of the Divan in order to give his assent or otherwise to their proposals. On the southwest side of the court are the rooms of the **Palace School**, where boys recruited from Christian families were converted to Islam and educated to become members of the janissary corps. The room to the left of the entrance houses a collection of embroidery and a small selection from the imperial costume collection. Nearby, the **Pavilion of the Conqueror** houses the Topkapı treasury, filled with excesses like the Topkapı Dagger, decorated with three enormous emeralds, and the Spoonmaker's Diamond, the fifth largest diamond in the world. Across the courtyard from the treasury, the **Pavilion of the Holy Mantle** houses the holy relics brought home by Selim the Grim after his conquest of Egypt in 1517, including a footprint, hair and a tooth of the Prophet Mohammed as well as his mantle and standard. Next door, the former **Hall of the Treasury** holds a selection from Topkapı's collection of paintings and miniatures, the earliest dating from the reign of Süleyman the Magnificent and showing events like the circumcision ceremony of the sultan's son, as well as a small selection of the unique works of Siyah Kalem ("the Black Pen"). Beyond, the fourth courtyard consists of gardens graced with pavilions where sultans would take their pleasure. Take a look at the pool and marble fountain on the terrace, scene of debauched revels between İbrahim I – also known as "İbrahim the Mad" – and the women of his harem. In one of his calmer moments İbrahim had built the **İftariye Köşkü**, the little balcony with a bronze canopy set into the white marble balustrade of the terrace. The **Mecidiye Köşkü** – the last building to be erected at Topkapı – commands the best view of any of the Topkapı pavilions and has been opened as a terrace café.

Just north of Topkapi, **Gülhane Parkı**, once the gardens of the palace, is the location of the graceful **Çinili Köşk**, the oldest secular building in İstanbul, built in 1472 as a kind of grandstand from which the sultan could watch sporting activities and now a **museum of ceramics** (Tues, Thurs & Sat 9.30am–5pm; $2.50). Close by, the **Museum of the Ancient Orient** (Wed, Fri & Sun 9.30am–5pm; $2.50) contains a small but dazzling collection of Anatolian, Egyptian and Mesopotamian artefacts, including the oldest peace treaty known to man, the Treaty of Kadesh (1280–1269 BC), uncovered during excavations at the site of the Hittite capital of Hattuşaş – a recent copy of it decorates the entrance to the UN building in New York. Across the courtyard, the newly refurbished **Archeological Museum** (Tues–Sun 9.30am–5pm; $2.50) has been commended for services to European culture with the 1993 Council of Europe prize for best museum. Well-lit and attractive displays with comprehensive explanatory audiovisual effects enhance exhibits of spectacular jewellery uncovered at Troy, and a video playing upstairs (10am, 11.30am, 1.30pm & 3.30pm) explains the continuation of traditions in Anatolia in building, storage and nutrition from 10,000 BC. Other displays include biographies of archeologists or descriptions and photos of sites where exhibits were uncovered, all lending greater perspective to the displays.

South of Aya Sofya, the arena of the **Hippodrome**, originally constructed by Septimus Severus in 200 AD, is now the site of a narrow and rather unprepossessing municipal park. At its southern end, the **Egyptian Obelisk** was originally 60m tall, but only the upper third survived shipment from Egypt in the fourth century. Though originally commissioned to commemorate the campaigns of Thutmos III in Egypt during the sixteenth century BC, the scenes on its base record its erection in Constantinople under the direction of Theodosius I. Nearby, the **Serpentine Column** comes from the Temple of Apollo at Delphi and was brought here by Constantine.

The **Sultan Ahmet Camii**, or Blue Mosque, on the Hippodrome's southeast side, is undeniably impressive, and instantly recognizable due to its six minarets – though inside it's rather clumsy, its four "elephant foot" pillars obscuring parts of the building and tending to dwarf the modest dome they support. The main attraction is the tiles which give the mosque its name, over twenty thousand of them, still with the clear, bright colours of late sixteenth-century İznik ware, including flower and tree panels as well as more abstract designs – though as part of the mosque is sectioned off to non-Muslims, they can be difficult to see. Outside the precinct wall is the **tomb of Sultan Ahmet** (9.30am–4.30pm; closed Tues), where the sultan is buried along with his wife and three of his sons; like the mosque, its tiled with seventeenth-century İznik tiles.

On the other side of the Hippodrome, the former palace of İbrahim Paşa, completed in 1524 for the grand vizier of Süleyman the Magnificent, is a fitting home for the **Museum of Turkish and Islamic Art** (Tues–Sun 10am–5pm; $2.50), a well-planned museum containing what is probably the best-exhibited collection of Islamic artefacts in the world, with examples of Selçuk, Mameluke and Ottoman Turkish art. İbrahim Paşa's magnificent audience hall is devoted to a collection of Turkish carpets; on the ground floor, in rooms off the central courtyard, is an exhibition of the folk art of the Yörük tribes of Anatolia. There is also an invaluable if rather faded exhibition on the dyes used in Turkish kilims and carpets, as well as sixteenth-century Persian miniatures and various Selçuk ceramics. North of here, along Yerebatan Caddesi, the **Yerebatan Saray** or "Sunken Palace" (daily 9am–5pm; $4) is one of several underground cisterns which riddle the foundations of the city but the only one to have been extensively excavated. Probably built by Constantine and enlarged by Justinian, the cistern supplied the Great Palace and later Topkapı Saray. Restorations were undertaken in 1987, and concrete pathways have been constructed to facilitate a leisurely examination. In the opposite direction from Sultan Ahmet, the **Mosaic Museum** (daily except Tues; 9.30am–5pm; $1), on Torun Sokak, contains magnificent pieces from the Palace of Bucolcon, the Great Palace of the Byzantine emperors, which once covered an enormous area from the Hippodrome down to the sea walls. The mosaics, some of which are viewed from a catwalk, probably date from Justinian's rebuilding programme of the sixth century, and include various portrayals of animals in their natural habitats, as well as domestic scenes. Further down the hill, by the waterfront, the half-hidden facade of the Bucoleon is the only surviving fragment of its walls.

Beyazit and Eminönü

West of Sultanahmet, along the run-down and busy **Divanyolu**, lies the district of **Beyazit**, centring on the **covered bazaar** (Mon–Sat 9am–7pm), said to be the largest in the world, with a huge web of streets given over to different kinds of shops. To get to it, turn off the main street by the **Column of Constantine**, erected in 330 AD to mark the city's dedication as capital of the Roman Empire. Nowadays the bazaar extends much further than the limits of the covered area, sprawling into the streets which lead down to the Golden Horn. It's a wonderful place to wander through, and there are several good carpet shops around the fountain at the intersection of Keseciler and Takkeciler Caddesis, as well as cheaper, rather scruffier places on Halıcılar Çarşısı Caddesi. When you need a break, the *Şark Kahvesi*, on Yağlıkçilar Sokak almost opposite Zenneciler Sokak, is a good place to drink strong tea while gloating over hard-won booty. West of the bazaar, peek into the **Beyazit Camii**, completed in 1506 and the oldest surviving imperial mosque in the city, with a beautiful, sombre courtyard full of richly coloured marble. The interior of the mosque is a perfect square of exactly the same proportions as the courtyard, its plan basically a simplified version of Aya Sofya, with highly crafted sixteenth-century fittings.

The area around the bazaar and the streets sloping steeply down to the river is known as **Eminönü**, adjacent to which lies **Sirkeci**, home to the main train station and ferry docks. Close by, on the waterfront, **Yeni Cami** is a large, grey and rather ugly building that was the last of İstanbul's imperial mosques to be built in the classical era. A synagogue and church had to be demolished to make room for it, which seems a shame, as it's one of the least impressive of the city centre's mosques, partly owing to the heavy layer of soot from the nearby ferry port which covers its walls and windows. Next door, the **Mısır Çarşısı** or Egyptian Bazaar, also known as the **Spice Bazaar**, is a good place to buy anything from saffron to aphrodisiacs. A short walk west, the **Rüstem Paşa Cami** is one of the most attractive of İstanbul's smaller mosques, built for Süleyman the Magnificent's grand vizier Rüstem Paşa. Designed by Sinan on a particularly awkward site, above a tangle of streets that seem to offer no room for such a building, it is barely detectable as you wander about in the streets below. But it's a successful, dramatic structure, with tiles that are among the most profuse in Turkey, from the finest period of İznik tile production.

Back on the front, the most prominent landmark is the **Galata Bridge**, which floats on pontoons, so that early every morning the central section can be towed out to allow ships a passageway. Its two tiers have long provided a marketplace for hawkers and a perch for fishermen. Few locals will eat in the restaurants on the lower level, but they are popular with those with an eye for a romantic setting. Sadly, it is soon to be replaced by a two-tier, six-lane bridge, though this will also have shops and restaurants.

West of the centre: Süleymaniye to Kariye Camii

West of Beyazit is a collection of buildings considered to be the finest of all the Ottoman mosque complexes, the **Süleymaniye Cami**, built in the 1550s by Mimar Sinan in honour of his most illustrious patron, Süleyman the Magnificent, and arguably his greatest achievement. The dome of the light and spacious mosque collapsed during the earthquake of 1766, and in the nineteenth century further damage was done by the Fossati brothers, whose attempt at Ottoman Baroque redecoration jars with the simplicity of other aspects of the building. But the original stained glass of İbrahim the Mad remains, above a simply graceful marble *mimber*, along with a few İznik tiles – a first cautious use of tiling by Sinan. Outside, the **cemetery** (Wed–Sun 9.30am–4.30pm) holds the tombs of Süleyman the Magnificent and of Roxelana, his powerful wife. Süleyman's tomb is particularly impressive, with doors inlaid with ebony and ivory, silver and jade and a peristyle supported by four antique columns leading through to the huge turban of the sultan. The rest of the complex is made up of the famous **Süleymaniye library**, established by Süleyman in an effort to bring together collections of books scattered throughout the city, and the **Tomb of Mimar Sinan**, a simple tomb except for a magnificent carved turban, a measure of the architect's high rank.

Continuing west, you can follow the line of the magnificent **Aqueduct of Valens**, part of a late fourth-century waterworks rebuilding programme carried out by the Emperor Valens. It was in use right up to the end of the nineteenth century, having been kept in good repair by successive rulers, who maintained a constant supply of water to the city in the face of both drought and siege, and six of its original ten kilometres are still standing. On the far side of the aqueduct, **Şehzade Camii**, "The Mosque of the Sultan's Son", was commissioned in 1543 on the death of Şehzade Mehmet, the 21-year-old heir of Süleyman the Magnificent. It was the first major commission of

Mimar Sinan, and only the fourth imperial mosque in the city. Again, the exterior of the mosque is its strength, with a courtyard bordered by an arched portico and two minarets decorated in relief, and the interior can seem rather charmless. Also, its most impressive feature, the imperial tombs, are closed to the public, despite the fact that they are supposed to contain one of the finest collections of İznik tiles in the country.

Across Atatürk Bulvarı, the aqueduct continues into **Zeyrek**, an attractively tatty area notable for its steep, cobbled streets and ramshackle wooden houses. Off Atatürk Bulvarı, **Zeyrek Camii** is a twelfth-century church that was converted into a mosque at the time of the Conquest and is officially open only at prayer times, though you may be able to persuade the *imam* to open the door for you. The building originally consisted of two churches and a connecting chapel, built between 1118 and 1136 as a mausoleum for the Comneni dynasty. Although the tombs have been removed, there is still evidence of the graves beneath the pavement. The mosque, which occupies the south church, is unfortunately in an advanced state of dilapidation.

Beyond Zeyrek, **Fatih** ("the Conqueror"), reachable direct from Sultanahmet on any bus going to Edirnekapı, is a fundamentalist area of the city, where even the language spoken on the streets is different, full of Arabic borrowings long ago discarded elsewhere in Turkey. In the centre of the district, the **Fatih Camii** on İslambol Caddesi was begun ten years after the conquest of İstanbul, in 1463, and completed in 1470 – although much of it was destroyed in an eighteenth-century earthquake. Despite this, its inner courtyard is one of the most beautiful in the city, porphyry columns supporting a domed portico with polychrome edges. The inscription over the door gives the date and dedication of the mosque, and the name of the architect, Atık Sinan, who was supposedly executed the year after the completion of the mosque on the orders of Mehmet, because its dome wasn't as large as that of Aya Sofya.

Twenty minutes' walk north of here, **Yavuz Selim Camii**, on Yavuz Selim Caddesi, holds a commanding position over the surrounding suburbs, begun in the reign of Selim the Grim, after whom it is named, and completed by Süleyman. Close up, the exterior is rather bleak, a fitting memorial to a man with such a reputation for cruelty, but once inside, it's a simple, restrained building, one of the most attractive of all the imperial mosques, its long pendentives alternating with tall arches to support the great shallow dome, which is hardly painted at all – an appealing lack of decoration that combines nicely with paintwork in designs reminiscent of the delicacy of Turkish carpets or ceramics. The **Tomb of Selim the Grim** (Wed–Sun 9.30am–4.30pm), next door, has lost its original decoration inside but retains two beautiful tiled panels on either side of the door.

About twenty-five minutes' walk northwest of the Selim mosque is one of the city's most compelling sights, **Kariye Camii** (9.30am–5pm; closed Tues; $2.50). This is the former church of Saint Saviour in Chora, built in the early twelfth century on the site of a building which predated the walls, hence the name – "in chora" meaning "in the country". The building contains a series of superbly preserved fourteenth-century frescoes and mosaics that are among the most evocative of all the city's Byzantine treasures. Most prominent of the mosaics are those in the narthex, the largest of which are a Christ Pantocrator and another showing the builder of the church, Metochites, offering a model of the building to a seated Christ. The frescoes in the burial chapel are equally eloquent, the most spectacular being the *Resurrection*, a dramatic representation of Christ trampling the gates of Hell underfoot and forcibly dragging Adam and Eve from their tombs.

The Walls

Six kilometres long in total, İstanbul's **land walls** are among the most fascinating Byzantine remains in Turkey. Raised by the Emperor Theodosius, they are the result of a hasty rebuilding to repel Attila the Hun's forces in 447 AD; an ancient edict was brought into effect whereby all citizens, regardless of rank, were required to help in the labour, and 16,000 men finished the project in just two months. They originally consisted of an inner wall, 5m thick and 12m high, plus an outer wall of 2m by 8m, and a 20m-wide moat. Most of the outer wall and its 96 towers are still standing, and their construction can be examined in detail if you are dressed to clamber in the dirt and brick dust. Be warned, though, that nowadays the remains provide shelter for many of İstanbul's homeless, and there are also gypsy encampments in the localities of Topkapı and Edirnekapı; you'll probably be left to your own devices but to be sure of being safe, don't go alone. Plenty of buses run from Eminönü and Sultanahmet, including the #80 to Yedikule, #84 to Topkapı and #86 to Edirnekapı, although the best way of reaching the walls is probably to take a local *banliyö* train to Yedikule, on the Marmara shore.

At the extreme southern end, **Yedikule** is an attractive quarter, home to a concentration of Greek-influenced houses and Orthodox churches, as well as a few reasonable restaurants and cafés where you can stop before setting off on your exploration of the walls. The most impressive sections of wall here have been designated the **Yedikule Museum** (Tues–Sun 9.30am–5pm; $1.50), off Yedikule Caddesi. The **Golden Gate**, flanked by two marble towers, was constructed on this site by Theodosius I in 390, before even the walls themselves. Nowadays the shape of the three arches is still visible on both sides of the wall, but it takes a degree of imagination to invest the structure with the glamour and dignity it must once have possessed. The other five towers of the Yedikule fortifications were added by Mehmet the Conqueror, and with their 12-metre-high curtain walls form an enclave which can be seen today, including two prison towers covered with inscriptions carved into the walls by prisoners.

Across the Golden Horn: Galata, Beyoğlu, Taksim and beyond

Across the Galata Bridge from the old centre, the settlement at **Galata** is as ancient as the city itself. In the fifth century the area already had city walls, and towards the end of the century Tiberius is said to have built a fortress on this side of the Horn, to facilitate the closure of the water to enemy shipping. Later the area became the main stronghold of the Genoese, and during the early centuries of Ottoman rule it became established as the city's European quarter, home to Jewish, Moorish, Greek and Armenian refugees and a popular haunt of visiting merchants, seamen and dignitaries. As Galata became crowded so the Europeans spread, gradually taking over the district above Galata, **Beyoğlu**. By the nineteenth and early twentieth centuries, the area had become fashionable for its music halls, taverns, cinemas and restaurants, and it was only after the exodus of the Greek population from İstanbul in the 1920s that Galata and Pera began to lose much of the cosmopolitan flavour on which they had thrived. The area has been cleaned up of late, although there's plenty remaining of the district's seamier side, brothels and"adult" cinemas existing alongside bars, *meyhanes* and restaurants.

The **Galata Tower** (daily 10am–6pm; $1), built in 1348, is the area's most obvious landmark, and one of the first places to head for on a sightseeing tour, since its viewing galleries, reached by means of a modern lift, offer the best panoramas of the city. Up towards Taksim from here, an unassuming doorway leads to the courtyard of the **Galata Mevlevihane** (Tues–Sun 9.30am–4.30pm), a former monastery and ceremonial hall of the "Whirling Dervishes" and now a museum of the Mevlevi sect, which was banned by Atatürk along with other Sufi organizations because of its political affiliations. Exhibits include instruments and dervish costumes, and the building itself has been beautifully restored to late eighteenth-century splendour. Continuing to the bottom of **İstiklâl Caddesi**, Beyoğlu's main boulevard, which was once known as the Grand Rue de Pera, is now a pedestrian precinct, with İstanbul's only tram line running along its 1200m length to **Taksim Square** – an undeniably impressive open space, if only for its size. The **Military Museum** (Wed–Sun 9am–5pm; 40¢), about 1500m north along Cumhuriyet Caddesi, is worth visiting mainly for the traditional Mehter band who play Ottoman music outside every afternoon that it's open, although its assortment of Ottoman armour and weaponry, along with various campaign memorabilia including the tent used by campaigning sultans, may appeal to military buffs.

Beyond Taksim, along the European shore of the Bosphorus, the most obvious place to head for is **Beşiktaş** (best reached direct by ferry from Eminönü), where the **Dolmabahçe Palace** (daily 9am–4pm; guided tours; only $8) is the largest and most sumptuous of all the palaces on the river, built in the mid-nineteenth century to replace Topkapı as the imperial residence of the Ottoman sultans. To the contemporary eye it's not so much magnificent as grotesque, a grossly excessive display of ornament and ostentatious wealth, suggesting that good taste suffered along with the fortunes of the Ottoman Empire. But it retains an Oriental feel in the organization of its rooms, divided into *selâmlık* and harem by the enormous throne room – where the ceremonies were watched by women of the harem through grilles.The four-ton chandelier in the throne room, one of the largest ever made, was a present from Queen Victoria. In the east wing of the palace, the former apartments of the heir to the throne now house a **Museum of Fine Arts** (Wed–Sun noon–4pm), with paintings from the late nineteenth and early twentieth centuries that give an intriguing insight into the lifestyle and attitudes of the late Ottoman Turks, notably in the European-style works of Osman Hamdi and the Impressionist Ruhi.

Back towards the ferry landing, the **Maritime Museum** (Wed–Sun 9.30am–noon & 1–5pm; bus #25, #25a) is one of the city's most interesting, with a collection divided between two buildings, the one facing the water housing seagoing craft, and the other, on Cezayir Caddesi, devoted to the maritime history of the Ottoman Empire and the Turkish Republic. A short walk from the main square is the **Yıldız Parkı** (daily 9am–5.30/6pm), a vast wooded area dotted with lakes and gardens that was centre of the Ottoman Empire for thirty years during the reign of Abdül Hamid. The buildings in and around the park constitute **Yıldız Palace**, a collection of structures in the old Ottoman style, and a total contrast to Dolmabahçe. Most of the pavilions date from the reign of Abdül Aziz, but it was Abdül Hamid – a reforming sultan whose downfall was brought about by his intense paranoia – who transformed Yıldız into a small city and power base. The most important surviving building is **Şale Köşkü** (daily 9.30am–5pm; $2.50), built to resemble a Swiss chalet for the first visit of Kaiser Wilhelm II in 1889.

Eating

The Sultanahmet and Beyazit districts are unfortunately thin on decent **restaurants**, especially for evening eating, and although there are a few worthwhile options in Lâleli and Aksaray, most of İstanbul's best places are located around Taksim and Galata. The **Balık Pazar** behind the Çiçek Pasajı off İstiklâl Caddesi in Beyoğlu has now become one of the city's most popular evening haunts for fish eaters, but even more atmospheric are the waterside fish restaurants in newly-gentrified Kumkapı. If you're just after a **snack**, you can find it almost anywhere. Street-food options vary from the excellent fish sandwiches served off boats by fishermen in Kadıköy, Karaköy and Eminönü, to the piles of sheep's innards – *kokoreç* – sold from booths in less salubrious areas.

Ahtapot, Köyiçi Kilise Meydanı 50, Beşiktaş. Small, friendly fish restaurant near the market that's less pricy than establishments right on the Bosphorus.

Aksu Oçakbaşi, Aksaray Cad, Azımkar Sok 5, Lâleli. Well-prepared, interesting food, not too expensive; friendly service.

Altın Sofrası, Süleymaniye Cad 33. A good bet for lunch on a visit to Süleymaniye; certainly much better than any of the touristy restaurants that face the mosque.

Borsa Lokantasi, İstiklâl Cad 87; Yalıköşkuşkü Işhanı 60/62, Eminönü. Excellent restaurants, part of a chain, serving perhaps the best Turkish meat dishes in the country.

Burç Pastanesi, İstiklâl Cad 463–465, Beyoğlu. Good breakfasts and midday snacks.

Cafe Süt, Sıraselviler Cad 24, Taksim. Clean, functional place serving cheap snacks like *menemen* and *köfte*.

Çatı Restaurant and Bar, İstiklâl Cad, A. Apaydın Sok 20, Baro Han, floor 7, Tünel, Beyoğlu (☎251 0000). Well established among İstanbul's intelligentsia but unknown to tourists, this attractive restaurant deserves its reputation for good food – you can eat for around $10 a head. Live entertainment is usually jazz. Book a window seat for good views of the city lights. Open Mon–Sat.

Demgâh Restaurant, Nevizade Sok 15, Balik Pasar, Beyoğlu. One of the best pavement-cafés for *mezze* and fish in this street full of good eateries, which has now replaced the Çiçek Pasajı in popularity.

Hacı Abdullah, Sakızağacı Cad 19, Beyoğlu. Excellent place, well-known among locals as a cheap alternative to the flashier places nearby. No alcohol, however.

Han Restaurant, Kartçinar Sok 16, Karaköy. A good, cheap lunchtime option in the Galata Tower region.

Hasır I, Kalyoncu Kulluğu Cad 94/1, Tarlabaşı, Beyoğlu. Very popular Turkish *meyhane*. Excellent food, lots of vegetarian options. Order a minimal selection from the menu as the best food will periodically be brought around on a large tray.

Havuzlu Lokantası, Gani Çelebi Sok 3, Kapalı Çarşı. Probably the best eating establishment in the bazaar.

Konyali, Ankara Cad 233, Sirkeci. Excellent pastry shop frequented by the quarter's businesspeople, who eat their breakfast standing at the counter. Also operates a decent self-service restaurant around the back in Mimar Kemalettin Cad.

Mini Express Bar-café, Tumacıbaşı Sok 12 (opposite Çiçek Pasajı). A cheap eatery popular with students, and serving *manti* (Turkish ravioli).

Pafuli Restaurant, Arnavutköy (263 6638). Specializes in Black Sea foods like *hamsi* (anchovy) bread and swordfish kebab, and is wise to book. $20 a head.

Saray, on İstiklâl Cad just above Çiçek Pasajı. Good, cheap place for sweets and snacks, the emphasisis on milk-based desserts.

Subaşı Restaurant, Kılıçlar Sok 48/2. A spit-and-sawdust place near the bazaar. Excellent lunchtime food, far better than anything else in the area. Go early as it gets packed.

Tegik Restaurant, Recep Paşa Cad 20, Taksim. Good-value Chinese, Japanese and Korean cuisine.

Tuncel, Meşrutiyet Cad 129/1, Tepebaşı, Beyoğlu. Reasonably priced and open from midday to midnight.

Zencefil, Kurabıye Sok 3, İstiklâl Cad, behind Fitaş Cinema. Health food with some vegetarian options.

Nightlife

Traditional İstanbul **nightlife** centres around restaurants and *gazinos* – clubs where *meze* are served, accompanied by singers and Oriental dancers. However, new Western-style bars and clubs are gaining in popularity – they're often no more than pastiches, but sometimes have the charm of a good location or attract an interesting clientele. Locations tend to centre around Taksim and its nearby suburbs, and along the Bosphorus, particularly the district of Ortaköy, just beyond Beşiktaş.

Bars

Cartoon Bar, Maçka Bronz Sok 4–2, Nişantaş. Decorated with cartoons and video monitors that double as tables, this bar epitomizes the İstanbul afterwork scene. Packed early evening.

Cep Sanat Evi, Tünel Müayyet Sok 11, Beyoğlu. Low-key bar in a building filled with artists' studios – although rather dead early in the week.

Cheers, Nispetiye Cad 27, Levent, Etiler. English pub open till 3am on Wednesday, Friday, and Saturday, otherwise 1am.

Gulet Café-bar, Yelkovan Sok 2, Ortaköy. A good Turkish night out with no belly dancing; upstairs has more of a taverna atmosphere.

Naima, Arnavutköyderesi Sok 1, Arnavutköy. A dark and intimate jazz bar that tends to become unbearably crowded at weekends. The bar snacks on offer are American style, burgers, sandwiches, etc.

Taksim Sanat Evi, Sıraselviler Cad 69/1, Taksim. Looks like an airport lounge but has a good view of Cihangir and decent food.

Taş Bar, Salih Efendi Sok 4, Barbaros Bulvarı, Beşiktaş. Live music every night, and Monday night is Russian night. Closes 2/3am.

Yelkovan, Muallim Naci Cad 71/3, top floor, Ortaköy. Furnished with throw cushions and low tables, a hang-out for the hippy types that have made Ortaköy their own in recent years. The outside terrace has great views of the mosque and there is live music most nights.

Ziya Bar, Muallim Naci Cad, just past Ortaköy. One of the older, more established bars, great in summer when you can use the big garden and outdoor bar.

Clubs and discos

Caz Bar, Korukent Recreation Centre, Levent, Ortaköy. Not especially trendy, but a good place to dance. Open 9pm–4am daily.

Cinema Bar, Maçka Bronz Sok 4-2, Nişantaşi. Newly opened, sultry disco with cinema theme, and old cinema seats at the back. Music is live salsa. Daily except Sun 10.30pm–3am.

Hydromel, Cumhuriyet Cad, Elmadağ. Small, intimate and reasonably priced – attracts a young crowd. Daily 9.30pm–4am; $8.

Nostalji, Tayyareci Suphi Sok 44, Arnavutköy. Tiny bar decorated with kilims and work by local painters. Music is jazzy records and at weekends there is live music. No admission charge but the drinks aren't cheap. Daily except Sun 6pm–1am, Sat 6pm–2am.

29, located in winter at Nispetiye Cad 29, Etiler; in summer in Çubuklu, reached by frequent launch from Istinye. Winter 29, which is also known for its excellent downstairs restaurant, was designed with the help of the owner's cousin, Rıfat Özbek. Summer 29 is a large outdoor club right on the water, with tables shaded by canvas umbrellas and lit by flaming torches. Music is basically disco; the crowd is all ages and very energetic. The best in town.

Listings

Airlines Aeroflot, Tarlabaşı Bulvarı, Taksim (☎252 3997); Azebaıycan Airlines, Cumhuriyet Cad 39/1, Harbiye (☎237 4200); British Airways, Cumhuriyet Cad 10, Harbiye (☎134 1300); Olympic Airways, Cumhuriyet Cad 171/A, Harbiye (☎132 9426); THY Turkish Airlines, Cumhuriyet Cad 109, Harbiye (☎145 2454).

Banks The Garanti Bankası in Sultanahmet stays open through lunchtime, and the İşbank at the airport remains open 24 hours a day. The change window in Sirkeci station is open at weekends 9am–5pm. You can change money in the bazaar, or in Tahtakale, the streets below the bazaar, at a better rate than you'll get in the banks, but for cash you'll get a better deal at the Döviz offices throughout the city, which are open at weekends and during the evenings, although few take cheques.

Books Most second-hand and English language outlets are around İstiklâl Cad in Beyoğlu. Metro Kilabevi, İstiklâl Cad 513, Librarie de Pera, Galip Dele Cad 22, Tünel, and Literatür, Sakızağaci Sok 1/1, off İstiklâl Cad, all have English books.

Bosphorus Ferry journeys up the Bosphorus are regarded by many as one of the city's highlights. There are special sightseeing boats throughout the year from Eminönü – $6 for the 1hr 40min journey to Anadolu Kavaqı. Otherwise the normal ferries are reasonably frequent, and if you get stranded (the last one from Anadolu Kavaqı in summer is at 5pm) you can always resort to a bus or dolmuş.

Buses Two of the better bus companies are Pamukkale (☎582 2934) and Ulusoy (☎582 6845); Kâmul Koç (☎249 2510) serves western and southern destinations.

Car rental Airtour, Cumhuriyet Cad, Dr Celal Öker Sok 1/1, Harbiye (☎132 8486); Europcar, Topçu Cad 1 (☎254 7788); Master Rent a Car, Ordu Cad, Ceylan Sok 2/1, Aksaray (☎527 4821); Step Rent a Car, Cumhuriyet Cad 287, Harbiye (☎140 3577); Thrifty, Recep Peker Cad Sani Sitesi 40/C, Kızıltoprak (☎345 0102).

Consulates *Australia*, Apt. 3, Tepecik Yolu Cad, Etiler (☎257 7050); *Canada*, Buyukdere Cad 101/3 Begun Han, Gayrettepe (☎272 5174); *Great Britain*, Meşrutiyet Cad 34, Tepebaşı, Beyoğlu (☎252 6436); *Ireland*, Cumhuriyet Cad 26/A, Elmadağ (☎246 6025); *Netherlands*, İstiklâl Cad 393, Galatasaray, Beyoğlu (☎251 5030); *USA*, Meşrutiyet Cad 104–108, Tepebaşı, Beyoğlu (☎251 3602).

Hamams Most central, and most frequented by tourists, are *Çemberlitaş Hamam*, on Divanyolu, and *Cağaoğlu Hamam*, Hilali Ahmed Cad 34 (daily 7am–10pm men, 8am–8pm women), the latter famous for its beautiful eighteenth-century steam rooms.

Hospitals The city's best hospitals are the foreign-funded establishments: the American *Admiral Bristol Hospital*, Güzelbahçe Sok 20, Nişantaşı (☎231 4050), *German Hospital*, Sıraselviler Cad 119, Taksim (☎251 7100), or *International Hospital*, İstanbul Cad 82, Yeşilköy (☎574 7802); also *Florence Nightingale Hospital*, Abidei Hürriyet Cad 290, Çağlayan, Şişli (☎224 4950).

Laundry *Active*, Dr Eminpasa Sok 14, off Diovanyuolu; the *Hobby*, at Caferiya Sok 6/1, Sultanahmet (9am–8pm).

Left luggage Left luggage offices (*Emanet* in Turkish) can be found in both Sirkeci and Haydarpaşa train stations.

Police The tourist police are at Alemdar Cad 6 (☎527 4503), and there are *Zabita* offices all over, including a handy one at the far end of the Hippodrome from Sultan Ahmet. Tourist police wear beige uniforms and maroon berets, and should speak English.

Post office The main post office is on Yeni Posthane Cad in Sirkeci (daily 9am–5.30pm, 8am–8pm for stamps).

Train stations Haydarpaşa (☎336 0475), Sirkeci (☎527 0051).

Travel agents For plane and bus tickets try *Marco Polo*, Divanyolu Cad 54/11, Sultanahmet (☎519 2804), or *Imperial*, Divanyolu Cad 30, Sultanahmet (☎513 9430).

Turkish Maritime Lines Rihtim Cad, Karaköy (☎249 9222).

AROUND THE SEA OF MARMARA

Despite their proximity to İstanbul, the shores and hinterland of the Sea of Marmara are relatively neglected by foreign travellers. This is not altogether surprising; here the country is at its most Balkan, and, at first glance, least exotic. But it may well be your first view of the country and it is not entirely without charm or interest. The border town of **Edirne**, at the end of the Roman and Byzantine Via Egnatia, later the medieval route to the Ottoman parts of Europe, is home to some superb early Ottoman architecture, and the early Ottoman centre of **Bursa**, which you may pass through on your way to the Aegean coast, has one of the country's most exquisite centres. Many visitors, also, justifiably, stop off at the extensive World War I battlefields and cemeteries of the **Gelibolu (Gallipoli) peninsula**, either using the north Marmara port of **Gelibolu** as a base, or, more commonly, **Çanakkale** – a town which is also a good centre for seeing the ruins of ancient **Troy** a little further south.

Edirne

More than just a border town, **EDİRNE** makes an impressive and easily digestible introduction to Turkey. It's a lively and attractive city, its life in part derived from day-tripping foreigners and truck drivers, and it boasts a clutch of elegant, early Ottoman monuments. Best of these, crowning the town hillock and reason itself for a detour, is the architect Sinan's culminating achievement, the Selimiye Camii, a testament to the time when it was Ottoman capital and, later, a favourite haunt of the sultans.

You can see the main sights of Edirne on foot, but they're widely scattered and you'll need a full day. Best starting point is the **Eski Cami** bang in the centre, the oldest mosque in town and a boxy structure begun in 1403 that's a more elaborate version of Bursa's Ulu Cami. The interior is now rather a mess as restoration proceeds, and a gaudy late-Ottoman paint job threatens to overshadow the giant calligraphy for which the mosque is famous. Just across the way, the **Bedesten** was Edirne's first covered market, though the tatty plastic goods inside nowadays are no match for the building. Nearby, the **Semiz Ali Paşa Çarşısı** is the other main bazaar, begun by Sinan in 1568 at the behest of Semiz Ali, one of the most able of the Ottoman grand viziers. A short way north of here, the name of the **Üç Şerefeli Cami**, dating from 1447, means "three-balconied", derived from the presence of three galleries for the muezzin on the tallest of the four idiosyncratic minarets, up which it is sometimes possible to climb. A little way west, the masterly **Selimiye Camii** was designed by the eighty-year-old Sinan in 1569 at the command of Selim II. The work of a confident craftsman at the height of his powers, it is virtually the municipal symbol. Its four slender **minarets** also have three balconies, and at 71m are the second tallest in the world after those in Mecca, although it's the interior which is most impressive, the dome planned to surpass that of Aya Sofya in İstanbul – which, at 31.5m in diameter, it manages by a few centimetres. Next door, the **Museum of Turkish and Islamic Arts** (Mon 10am–2pm, Tues–Sun 8am–5.30pm; 50¢) houses assorted wooden, ceramic and martial knick-knacks from the province, plus a portrait gallery of grease-wrestling champions – a speciality of Edirne. The main **Archeological Museum** (Tues–Sun 8.30am–noon & 1–5.30pm; $1), just east of the mosque, contains a predictable assortment of Greco-Roman fragments, and an ethnographic section that focuses on carpet-weaving and other local crafts. Ten minutes' further on, along Mimar Sinan Caddesi, the **Muradiye Camii** was built as a sanctuary for Mevlevi dervishes by the pious Murat II in 1435, and is distinguished inside by some of the best İznik tiles outside Bursa.

Practicalities

From elsewhere in Turkey, you'll most likely arrive at Edirne's **bus station**, just over 2km southeast of the centre, from where red city buses or dolmuşes whisk you to the centre of town. The **train station** is 1km further out in the same direction. There are two **tourist offices**, both on Talat Paşa Cad: the main one about 500m west toward the Gazi Mihal bridge at no. 76/A, and an annexe up near Hürriyet Meydanı, by the traffic signals (daily summer 8am–6.30pm ; winter 8.30am–5.30pm).

Edirne has few genuinely budget **hotels**, and those that exist are either substandard or booked solid by truck drivers. The tourist office usually points backpackers to nearby Maarif Cad, where the *Otel Anıl*'s deceptive exterior at no. 8 (①) fronts a grim dosshouse and the *Konak* next door is little better (①). The *Aksaray*, Alipaşa Ortakapı Cad 8 (☎284/212 6035; ①), is cleaner and more salubrious, but there are better options further south, along and across Saraçlar Cad: *Otel Açikgöz*, Tüfekçiler Çarşısı, Sümerbank Arkası 74 (☎284/213 1944; ①), is probably the best deal. More comfortable is the calm *Park Hotel*, Maarif Cad 7 (☎284/223 5276; ③). **Campsites** are liberally sprinkled around Edirne, though strongly oriented toward caravanners. Try *Fifi Mocamp*, 8km along the road to İstanbul, or *BP Kervansaray*, near the bus station.

Restaurants are adequate but not especially cheap. For snack lunches, look out for the tiny *ciğerci* booths serving the city speciality, deep-fried liver. Otherwise, some of the eateries on Saraçlar Cad aren't bad – the *Şark Köftecisi* and the *Serhad Köftecisi*, on the south side of Hürriyet Meydanı, are fine if cramped; try also the *Şehir*, further down the street, or the *Saray Ciğer ve Çorba Salonu*, near the post office, though the latter only serves liver and soup. The *Çimen Lokanta*, on one side of the Bedesten, is also good and affordable, as are two *meyhanes*, the *Agora* and *Emin'in Yeri*, near the *Otel Açikgöz*.

Crossing the borders

The closest crossing into **Greece** from Edirne is 7km away at Pazarkule, separated from the Greek frontier post at Kastaniés by a kilometre-wide no-man's-land. Opening times, though, are only Monday to Friday from 9am to 1pm, and 9am to 11am at weekends. Red **city buses** run from Edirne to Karağac, the nearest village, every twenty minutes, as do **dolmuşes** from behind the town hall. The alternative is to take a **taxi** ($5) all the way from Edirne to Pazarkule, and from there a Greek taxi to the Kastaniés post – $5 per car for the 1km gap. On the Greek side three daily trains, and about as many buses, make the three-hour run down to Alexandhroúpoli, the first major Greek city, between 8am and 1pm, with a couple more later in the day.

The **Bulgarian** border is less problematic. The vast complex at Kapikule, 18km northwest of Edirne, straddles the busy E5/100 expressway and is open around the clock. Most nationals need a **visa** of some kind: it costs $18 for a transit visa obtained from the Edirne consulate, $20 for one issued at the border, and $28 for a tourist visa with a more generous time limit. Red **city buses** serve the frontier eleven times daily between 6.30am and 9pm, and *Yıldırım Ko-op* **dolmuşes** ply the route half-hourly from 6.30am to 9pm. A taxi costs well over $10.

The Gelibolu Peninsula

Though endowed with some fine scenery and beaches, the slender **Gelibolu peninsula**, which forms the northwest side of the **Dardanelles**, is mainly known for its grim military history. In April 1915 it was the site of a plan (devised by Winston Churchill) to land Allied troops, many of them Australian and New Zealand units, with a view to their linking up to neutralize the Turkish shore batteries controlling the Dardanelles. It was a harebrained scheme and failed miserably, with massive casualties. The fate of the Australian and New Zealand forces was particularly horrific; they were dug in here for around six months, and suffered a carnage which engendered a bitterness and suspicion of the big Western powers that endures to this day.

Gelibolu

If you're keen to visit the battle sites and cemeteries, the peninsula's principal town, GELİBOLU, connected with the Marmara's southern shore at Lapseki, is a good base, an inviting place perched just where the Dardanelles begin to narrow, with a colourful fishing harbour, ringed by cafés and restaurants, at its heart. The **ferry jetty** is right at the inner harbour entrance; the **bus terminal** is on the opposite side next to the old tower. There's a good range of **accommodation**. At one corner of the port on Liman Caddesi is the *Anzac Pension* at no. 2 (☎286/566 3596; ①); roughly opposite and owned by the same people is the *Hotel Yılmaz* (☎286/566 1256; ②) at no. 6. Out by the lighthouse is the *Motel Anzac* (☎286/566 3591; ①). Between the lighthouse and an army camp is a serviceable beach, with a **campsite**. You can join morning and afternoon **tours** of the World War I sites for about $12 per person – ask in the hotels for details. For **eating out**, the *İmren Restaurant* on the waterfront is cheap, licensed and does excellent local sardines.

The battlefields, cemeteries and beaches

The **World War I battlefields** and **Allied cemeteries** scattered along the Gelibolu peninsula are by turns moving and numbing in the sheer multiplicity of graves, memorials and obelisks. It's difficult to imagine the bare desolation of 1915 in the lush landscape of much of the area, but the final 20km has been designated a **national park**, and some effort has been made by the Turkish authorities to signpost road junctions and sites. The open-air sites have no admission fees or restricted hours, but since there's little public transport through the area you should take a **tour** unless you have your own vehicle. The first stop on most tours is the **Kabatepe Orientation Centre and Museum**, 6km along (40¢), beyond which are the **Beach, Shrapnel Valley** and **Shell Green** cemeteries, followed by **Anzac Cove** and **Arıburnu**, site of the bungled ANZAC landing and ringed by more graves. Looking inland, you'll see the murderous badlands that gave the defenders such an advantage. Beyond Arıburnu, a left fork leads towards the beaches and salt lake at **Cape Suvla**, today renamed Kemikli Burnu; most tourists bear right for Büyük Anafartalar village and **Çonkbayırı hill**, where there's a massive New Zealand memorial and a Turkish memorial describing Atatürk's words and deeds. The spot where the Turkish leader's pocket watch stopped a fragment of shrapnel is highlighted, as is the grave of a Turkish soldier discovered in 1990 when the trenches were reconstructed. Working your way back down toward the visitors' centre, you pass **The Nek, Walker's Ridge** and **Quinn's Post**, where the trenches of the opposing forces lay within a few metres of each other – the modern road corresponds to no-man's-land. From here the single, perilous supply line ran down-valley to the present location of **Beach Cemetery**.

KABATEPE is 2km south of the orientation centre and has a good beach, although **KUM LİMANI**, 5km south of the museum, is probably more pleasant. Except for the *Kum Motel* (☎286/214 1466; ②) with its cabins and rooms, there's been little development of this beautiful setting. It's also easily accessible on public transport, since dolmuşes between Eceabat and Alçitepe pass a junction just over a kilometre away. On the other side of the peninsula, the tiny village of **KİLİTBAHİR**, dwarfed by its massive **castle**, is connected by ferry with Çanakkale, as is **ECEABAT**, a few kilometres north. There's a **PTT booth** by the jetty here, changing money, and all kinds of snack **food** within a short distance of the dock, but you wouldn't want to patronize the handful of noisy hotels overlooking it.

Bursa

Draped along the leafy lower slopes of Uludağ, which towers more than 2000 metres above, **BURSA** – first capital of the Ottoman Empire and the burial place of several sultans – does more justice to its setting than any other Turkish city besides İstanbul. Gathered here are some of the finest early Ottoman monuments in the Balkans, in a city centre that's one of the most appealing in Turkey. Although sometimes touted as a day out from İstanbul, it really deserves at least an overnight stay.

The City

The compact **Koza Parkı** is, with its fountains, benches, strolling crowds and cafés, the real heart of Bursa. On the far side looms the **Ulu Cami**, built between 1396 and 1399 by Yıldırım Beyazit I, from the proceeds of booty won from the Crusaders at Macedonian Nicopolis. Before the battle Yıldırım had vowed to construct twenty mosques if victorious. The present building of twenty domes was his rather free interpretation of this promise. The interior is dominated by a huge *şadırvan* pool in the centre, whose skylight was once open to the elements, and an intricate walnut *mimber* pieced together, it's claimed, without nails or glue. Close by is Bursa's **covered market**, the **Bedesten**, given over to the sale of jewellery and precious metals, and the **Koza Hanı**, flanking the park, still entirely occupied by silk and brocade merchants. Across the river, the **Yeşil Cami** is easily the most spectacular of Bursa's imperial mosques – though never completed, as you can see from the entrance. The hundreds of tiles inside give the mosque its name, which means "Green Mosque". Tucked above the foyer, and usually closed to visits, the imperial loge is the most extravagantly decorated chamber of all, the work attributed to a certain Al-Majnun, which translates most accurately as "intoxicated on hashish". The nearby hexagonal **Yeşil Türbe** (daily 8.30am–noon & 1–5.30pm; free) contains the sarcophagus of Çelebi Mehmet I and assorted offspring, though otherwise the immediate environs of the mosque are twee in the extreme, busy with tourists and souvenir shops. The *medrese*, the largest surviving dependency of the mosque, now houses Bursa's **Museum of Turkish and Islamic Art** (Mon 10am–1pm, Tues–Sun 8am–noon & 1–5pm; $1) – not a bad ethnographic collection, with İznik ware, Çanakkale ceramics, glass items and a mock-up of an Ottoman circumcision chamber, not to mention a collection of Karagöz puppets, the painted camel-leather props used in the Turkish national shadow play purportedly born in Bursa.

In the opposite direction from the centre of town, the **Hisar** district was Bursa's original nucleus, though it nowadays retains just a few clusters of dilapidated Ottoman housing along its warren of narrow lanes, and a few stretches of rampart, given over to ribbons of park and tea gardens. The best-preserved dwellings are a little way west in medieval **Muradiye**, where the **Muradiye Külliyesi** mosque and *medrese* complex was begun in 1424 by Murat II, the last imperial foundation in Bursa – although it's most famous for its tombs, set in lovingly tended gardens. Best of these are that of Şehzade Ahmet and his brother Şehinşah, both murdered in 1513 by their cousin Selim the Grim to preclude any succession disputes, covered with İznik tiles and contrasting sharply with the adjacent austerity of Murat II's tomb, where Roman columns inside and a wooden awning are the only superfluities. Murat was the last sultan to be interred at Bursa, and one of the few who died in his bed: in accordance with his wishes, both the coffin and the dome were originally open to the sky "so that the rain of heaven might wash my face like any pauper's".

From Muradiye it's a short walk down to Çekirge Caddesi and the southeast gate of the **Kültür Parkı**, where there's a popular tea garden, a small boating lake and three pricy restaurants. At the far end there's also an **Archeological Museum** (Tues–Sun 8.30am–noon & 1–5.30pm; $1), whose exhibits include metal jewellery from all over Anatolia, a collection of Roman glass items, and Byzantine and Roman bronzes. Just beyond the Kültür Parkı, the **Yeni Kaplıca** (daily 6am–10pm; $2), accessible by a steep driveway, are the closest of Bursa's baths, a faded reminder of the days when the town was patronized as a spa. Legend states that Süleyman the Magnificent was cured of gout after a dip in the baths and had his vizier Rüstem Paşa overhaul the building.

Practicalities

Bursa's **bus station** is a kilometre north of the centre at the top of Fevzi Cakmak Cad; there's a summer-only **tourist booth** close by, from where it's a ten-minute walk or short dolmuş ride into town. Bursa's main **tourist office** (Mon–Fri 8.30am–5.30pm) is in a subterranean mall at one corner of the Koza Parkı, well-signposted on the north side of Atatürk Cad. There are plenty of reasonably priced **hotels**, including a cluster of modest establishments south of Atatürk Cad – the hotels around the bus station are mostly pretty grim. *Hotel Bilgiç*, Ressam Şefik Bursalı Cad 30 (☎224/220 3190; ②), is perhaps the best-value in town. The *Lâl Otel*, Maksem Cad 79 (☎224/221 1710; ①), is a rambling old building with clean rooms. The *Saray*, İnönü Cad, Matbaa Çıkmazı 1 (☎224/221 2820; ①), is noisy but you can't get more central. The *İpekçi*, Çancılar Cad 38, in the bazaar west of İnönü Cad (☎224/221 1935; ②), has bright, airy rooms and is quiet despite the location. The *Belkis*, Gazcılar (Celal Bayar) Cad 168, within sight of Fevzi Çakmak Cad (☎224/254 8322; ①), has plain but relatively peaceful rooms.

There's a fair amount of culinary variety to be had in Bursa. The *Hacı İlyas*, İnebey Cad 89, is good for breakfast as well as soups. For lunch, the *İnci Lokantası*, in the inner court of the Koza Hanı, is the most atmospheric of a dozen *pide* places and tiny restaurants scattered through the bazaar. The *Kebapci Iskender*, Atatürk Caddesi 60, claims to be the place where the local speciality, *Iskender kebab*, was invented, and that's all they serve – again at lunchtime only. The *For Canlı Balık*, Yeni Balık Pazarı 14, in the fish market, is a licensed and cheap fish restaurant; *Çiçek İzgara*, Belediye Cad 15, is more elegant but still reasonable, while *Kıvılcım*, İnönü Cad 26, serves the best puddings in town. In the evening, head for Kuruçeşme Mh. Sakarya Caddesi at the foot of the citadel, where you'll find a street of lively fish restaurants. *Arap Sükrü* at number 6 is reasonably priced and not quite as male-dominated as some of the others. For **drinking**, the *Tino Bar*, at the end of Atatürk Cad, by the Setbaşı Bridge, is the only decent bar that serves booze, and it has an outdoor terrace.

Çanakkale

Though celebrated for its setting on the Dardanelles, **ÇANAKKALE** has little to detain you. However, it is a possible base for visiting the Gallipoli sites on the European side of the Dardanelles straits and for the sparse ruins of Troy. Among things to see in the town, the **Çimenlik Park** (daily 9am–10pm), southwest of the bazaar, is home to a replica of the minelayer *Nusrat*, which stymied the Allied fleet by re-mining zones at night that the French and British had swept clean by day. It's festooned inside with rather forgettable newspaper clippings of the era. The **Naval Museum** nearby (Tues–Wed & Fri–Sun 9am–noon & 1.30–5pm; free) is more worthwhile, featuring photos – parts of Gelibolu in ruins after Allied shelling, Atatürk's funeral – and military paraphernalia, including Atatürk's pocket watch which stopped a shell fragment at Gelibolu and saved his life. Two kilometres from the centre of town, the **Archeological Museum** (daily 8.30am–noon & 1–5.30pm; $1) is accessible by any dolmuş along Atatürk Caddesi labelled "Kepez" or "Güzelyalı" and has exhibits from all over the area, including brass implements, delicate glass and pottery, a coin collection, and – the most exquisite items – gold, jewellery and ivory work.

Everything you'd want to see or do in Çanakkale, except for the archeological museum, is within walking distance of the **ferry docks**, close to the start of the main Demircioğlu Caddesi. The nearby **tourist office** (daily summer 8am–8pm; winter 8.30am–5.30pm) is worth a stop if only for their free map of the Gallipoli battlefields. Arriving by bus, the **bus station** is out on Atatürk Caddesi, the local name for the coastal İzmir–Bursa highway, a fifteen-minute walk from the waterfront – though, if you ask, most drivers will drop you near the tourist office. If you're seeing the **Gallipoli battlefields** from here, the principal **tour operators** are *Anatur*, Cumhuriyet Meydani Özay İşhani (☎196/75482), and nearby *Troy Anzac* (☎196/75047), whose four-hour outings leave at 9.45am. To get your $12 or so's worth, make sure your driver-guide speaks good English.

Except for a crowded couple of weeks during mid-August when the Çanakkale/Troy Festival is being staged, you'll have little trouble finding a room. Just to the south of the tourist office, the Saat Kulesi (clocktower) signals the entrance to a warren of alleys that's home to various inexpensive **hotels and pansiyons**. Adjacent are two quite basic, budget choices: the *Kervansaray*, Fetvahane Sok 13 (②), and the *Otel Efes* just behind (☎196/73256; ②). The *Avrupa Pansiyon*, Matbaa Sok 8, tucked in between Fetvahane Sokaği and the water (☎196/74084; ②), is a step up, still fairly spartan but able to offer cleaner doubles with baths. Across Demircioğlu Cad, the *Yaldız*, Kızılay Sok 20 (☎196/71793; ③), offers relative luxury. For **camping**, the closest reasonable site is the *Şen* at **KEPEZ**, 7km south, accessible by dolmuş. Of the quayside **restaurants** south of the ferry jetty, the *Entellektüel* has the widest range of *meze* and fish. The *Şehir Lokantası*, at the southern end of the esplanade, has the quietest and most sheltered outdoor seating. Inland, the food is more modest and cheaper. Best and friendliest of the bunch in the bazaar is the *Yılmaz Restaurant*, one street back from the water; near the *Yaldiz Hotel*, the *Trakya Restaurant* serves steam-tray food at no less than three separate premises.

Troy

Although by no means the most spectacular archeological site in Turkey, **TROY** (Truva), thanks to Homer, is probably the most celebrated. The remains of the ancient city, just west of the main road around 20km south of Çanakkale, consist of some fortification remains and a few vague piles of stone with the catch-all label "Defensive Wall" – and a lot of visitors come away disappointed. But if you lower your expectations and use your imagination, you may well be impressed.

Until 1871 Troy was generally thought to have existed in legend only. The Troad Plain, where the ruins now lie, was known to be associated with the Troy that Homer wrote about in the *Iliad*, but all traces of the city had vanished completely and it was a German businessman, Heinrich Schliemann, who excavated what you see now. Schliemann's work actually caused a certain amount of damage to the site, and he removed many of his discoveries to Germany without Turkish permission. But his digging uncovered nine layers of remains, representing distinct and consecutive city developments spanning four millennia. The oldest, Troy I, dates back to about 3600 BC and was followed by four similar settlements. Troy VI or VII are thought to have been the cities described by Homer: the former is known to have been destroyed by an earthquake in about 1275 BC, while the latter shows signs of having been destroyed by fire about a quarter of a century later, around the time historians generally estimate the Trojan War to have taken place. Troy VIII, which thrived from 700 to 300 BC, was a Greek city, while the final layer of development, Troy IX, was built between 300 BC and 300 AD, during the heyday of the Roman Empire.

The **site** (daily summer 8am–8pm; winter 8am–5pm; $2) is signalled by the ticket office opposite the bus drop-off point, from where a road leads to a giant wooden horse and the **house** that Schliemann stayed in while working at Troy, containing the tools the archeologist worked with, alongside pictures of his wife wearing the jewels he pillaged and other bits and pieces. Just beyond is the ruined city itself, a craggy outcrop overlooking the plain, which stretches about 8km to the sea. It's a bleak sight, and leaves you in no doubt as to the thinness of Troy's remains, but as you stand on what's left of the ramparts and look out across the plain, it's not too difficult to imagine a besieging army, legendary or otherwise, camped out below. Walking around the site, the **walls** of Troy VI are the most obvious feature, curving around in a crescent from the entrance; there are also more definite and visible remains from Troys VIII–IX, including a council chamber and a small theatre a little way north.

Practicalities

Çanakkale is the most sensible base for seeing Troy, since its bus station is connected to the site by fairly frequent dolmuşes – a half-hour journey through olive groves and cotton fields. Failing that, you can stay in the nearby village of Tevfikıye, although the only accommodation is at the none-too-luxurious *Yarol Pension* (①). The dolmuş to the site drops you off just beyond the village in front of a cluster of shops and eateries, highlight of which is the reasonably decent *Helen Restaurant*.

THE AEGEAN COAST

Turkey's **Aegean coast** is the country at its most visited. But it is also, in many ways, its most enticing region, home to some of the best of its classical antiquities and the most appealing resorts. The north shore sees the fewest visitors: a quiet, rocky region, not over-endowed with fine beaches and with a much shorter summer season, but reasonably rich in Hellenistic remains. **Ayvalık**, the north's longest-established resort, makes an excellent place to stop for a few days, with good beaches and easy access to **Bergama** a little inland, with its unmissable ruins. Further south, **İzmir** is for most travellers an obstacle on the way to more compelling destinations. But you may arrive here, and, on closer examination, the city is not without charm and serves as a base for day trips to adjacent sights and beaches. The territory to the south is home to the best concentration of classical, Hellenistic and Roman ruins, notably **Ephesus**, usually first on everyone's list of dutiful pilgrimages, and remains at **Aphrodisias** and **Hierapolis**, inland – although the latter is more often visited for the pools and rock formations of adjacent **Pamukkale**. The **coast** itself is better down here, too, and although the larger resorts – Çeşme, Kuşadası, **Marmaris** and **Bodrum** – are beginning to be lost to the developers, Bodrum and Çeşme still have a certain amount of charm.

Ayvalık and around

AYVALIK, a couple of kilometres west of the main coast road, is a small fishing port that also makes a living from olive-oil production and tourism. But the latter is reasonably low-key and the town makes a nice base for beach-lounging and ruin-spotting at Bergama, 70km southeast. Re-founded during the 1400s on ancient ruins, Ayvalık has suffered two serious earthquakes this century, though the most devastating effect on the town occurred when its mainly Greek inhabitants were kicked out during the exchange of populations that followed the Greek-Turkish war of 1920–22. There's not a lot specifically to see, though its tangle of central streets, lined with terraces of sumptuous Greek houses and a-clatter with speeding horsecarts, is worth a wander, and there are some decent beaches in the surrounding area.

About 6km south, **SARIMSAKLI** (literally "Garlic Beach") is a resort development accessible by dolmuş or municipal bus. Across the bay from Ayvalık, the island of **CUNDA** is also a good day trip destination, with a couple of stretches of beach on its west and north edges and some harbour fish restaurants. The best way to get here in summer is by boat, though at other times you'll have to rely on the roughly hourly bus service from Atatürk Square or a taxi across the causeway connecting the island to the mainland. **Accommodation** possibilities on the island include the *Altay Pansiyon* (☎663/71024; ①), a couple of blocks inland; the *İlker Pansiyon* (no sign out; ☎663/ 71034; ①); and the *Özlem Aile Pansiyon* (☎663/71109; ①). There's also the *Günay Motel* (☎663/71048; ②). The main **campsite**, *Ortunç Camping*, about 4km southwest of town, also has a restaurant and some rooms. The *Günay*'s restaurant is reckoned about the best, though you've several more to choose from on the quay itself.

Practicalities

Ayvalık is a fairly small town, with a centre concentrated around a small square 1500m south of the main **bus station**. The **tourist office** (summer Mon–Sat 9am–noon & 1– 5pm) is ten to fifteen minutes' walk south of the town centre on the main coast road. There is a handful of cheap **hotels** in the centre of town, but few are very savoury: try the dead-central *Yurt* (☎663/22109; ②) or the *Hotel Canlı Balik*, on Gümrük Cad (☎663/22292; ②); for a little more, it's worth patronizing the *Kaptan*, Balikhane Sok 7 (☎633/28834; ③), which has doubles with bathrooms in a restored seaside soap mill. **Eating and drinking** possibilities include the touristy *Öz Canli Balik* on the quayside, and, cheaper, the *Sedef* or *Nuri'nin Yeri* inland in the bazaar.

Tickets to the Greek island of **Lesvos** are sold at *Jale Turizm*, Gümrük Cad 41/A (☎663/22740), or *Eressos Tur* (☎663/26123). Ferries run roughly three mornings a week in spring and autumn, daily except Sunday in summer. Bear in mind, though, that you may only be allowed to travel on the afternoon Greek boat if you arrived on it. Fares are $30 single, $35 open return.

Bergama

Though frequently touted as a day trip from Ayvalık, **BERGAMA** is the site of the Hellenistic – and later Roman – city of Pergamon, ruled for several centuries by a powerful local dynasty. Excavations were completed here in 1886, but unfortunately much of what was found has since been carted off to Germany. However, the acropolis of Eumenes II remains a major attraction, and there are a host of lesser sights and an old quarter of chaotic charm to detain you for a day or so.

The old town lies at the foot of the acropolis, about ten minutes' walk from the bus station. Its foremost attraction is the **Kızıl Avlu** or "Red Basilica" (daily 8.30am–5.30pm; $1), a huge edifice on the river not far from the acropolis, originally built as a temple to the Egyptian god Osiris and converted to a basilica by the early Christians, when it was one of the Seven Churches of Asia Minor addressed by Saint John in the book of Revelation – though sadly it's now a crumbling ruin with a mosque in one of its towers. The area around the basilica is a jumble of ramshackle buildings, carpet and antique shops, mosques and maze like streets. On the way from the bus station you'll pass the **Archeological Museum** (daily 8.30am–5.30pm; $1), which has a large collection of locally unearthed booty, including a statue of Hadrian from the Asclepion (see below), and various busts of figures like Zeus and Socrates. There's also a model of the Zeus altar, complete with the Berlin-resident reliefs.

The Ruins

The **Acropolis** (daily 8.30am–5.30pm, summer closes 7pm; $2.50), the ancient city of the kings of Pergamon, is set on top of a rocky bluff towering over modern Bergama, accessible by taxi from the bus station (they'll ferry you around all Bergama's ruins for a somewhat inflated $12) or on foot – a fair walk up a path from the old town, but quite manageable if it's not too hot. The first main attraction up here is the huge horseshoe-shaped **Altar of Zeus**, built during the reign of Eumenes II to commemorate his father's victory over the Gauls, and formerly decorated with reliefs depicting the battle between the giants and the gods. Even today its former splendour is apparent, though it has been much diminished by the removal of the reliefs to Berlin.

North of the Zeus altar lie the sparse remains of a **Temple of Athena**, above which loom the restored columns of the **Temple of Trajan**, where the deified Roman emperor and his successor Hadrian were revered in the imperial era. From the Temple of Athena a narrow staircase leads down to the **theatre**, the most spectacular part of the ruined acropolis, capable of seating 10,000 spectators, and a **Temple of Dionysus**, just off-stage to the northwest.

Bergama's other significant archeological site is the **Asclepion** (daily 8.30am–5.30pm; $2), a Greco-Roman medical centre which can be reached on foot from the road beginning at the Kursunlu Cami in the modern town. Much of what can be seen today was built during the first- and second-century heyday of the centre, when its function was similar to that of the nineteenth-century spa. The main features are a **Propylon** or monumental entrance gate, built during the third century AD, and a circular **Temple of Asclepios**, dating from 150 AD and modelled on the Pantheon in Rome. At the western end of the northern colonnade is a **theatre** with a seating capacity of 3500, while at the centre of the open area a **sacred fountain** still gushes mildly radioactive drinking water, near to which an underground passage leads to the two-storey circular **Temple of Telesphorus**.

Practicalities

Bergama's **tourist office** is on the town's main thoroughfare at İzmir Cad 54, ten minutes' walk from the **bus station**. The town's cheapest **hotels** tend to be in the old town, although there are a few reasonable possibilities near the bus station. Just around the corner, the basic but comfortable *Park Otel*, Park Otel Sok 6 (☎541/31246; ②), has doubles with bath. Some 400m from the otogar, *Pansiyon Mandlya*, Tanpinar Sok 5 (☎541/34488; ②), is well appointed and good value. In the old town, the *Acroteria*, Bankalar Cad 11 (☎541/32469; ①), has clean, comfortable doubles, a restaurant and terrace. Next to the police station on the same street is the *Pergamon Pansiyon*, Bankalar Cad 3 (☎541/32395; ①), crowded in the summer but clean. Perhaps the best option is the *Nike Pansiyon*, Talatpaşa Mahallesi, Tabak Köprü Çıkmazi 2, an old family-run pension on the far bank of a river, in the shadow of the acropolis. There are no en suite facilities, but there is a marvellous garden. For **food**, the *Meydan Restaurant* is the most obvious place, with a terrace and foreign-language signs making it a sure draw for tourists. The *Kervan Döner Salonu*, opposite, also has a roof terrace but is a little less touristy. Next door are the *Çiçek Birahanesi*, and the slightly cheaper *Yüksel Birahanesi*, where you can sit outside and have a beer with your meal.

İzmir

Turkey's third city and its second port after İstanbul, **İZMİR** – ancient Smyrna – is home to nearly three million people. It is blessed with a mild climate and an enviable position, straddling the head of a 50-km-long gulf fed by several streams and flanked by mountains on all sides. But despite an illustrious history, most of the city is relentlessly modern, and even enthusiasts will concede that a couple of days here are plenty.

İzmir was the Ottoman Empire's window to the west, but after World War I Greece was given an indefinite mandate over İzmir and its hinterland. This lasted until the entry into Smyrna of the Turkish army on September 9, 1922, and three days of murder and plunder in which seventy percent of the city burned to the ground. The modern city has been built pretty much from scratch, its central boulevards wide and tree-lined, and is nowadays booming; yet it is also home to some of the more persistent street hustlers in Turkey, a consequence of the disparity between the chi-chi waterfront and the grim shantytowns, further aggravated by the large numbers of foreign servicemen around due to the city's role as headquarters of NATO Southeast.

The İzmir area telephone code is ☎232.

Arrival and accommodation

Ferries anchor at the **Alsancak terminal**, 2km north of the centre; take a taxi into town (for around $2), or walk 250m south and pick up a #2 blue and white bus from the nearby suburban train station. Most **trains** pull in at **Basmane station**, at the end of Fevzipaşa Bulvari. If you **fly**, use either the frequent shuttle train from the **airport** to Alsancak train station (for the #2 bus), or, for around $1.50, the special *Havaş* airport bus will deposit you by the *Büyük Efes* hotel on Gaziosmanpaşa Bulvarı. The main **bus station** is about 2km northeast of the centre, from where you should flag down one of the blue-and-white buses labelled "Çankaya–Mersinli" – these drop you at a terminal on Hürriyet Bulvarı, two blocks east of Şair Eşref Bulvarı. İzmir has three **tourist offices**, the most central and popular of which is on Gaziosmanpaşa Bulvarı next to the *THY* office (summer daily 8.30am–7pm; ☎842 147). The modern city is somewhat confusing to negotiate but most points of interest are close together, and the most enjoyable way of exploring is on foot. Using **public transport**, on the few remaining blue and white dolmuşes, you pay the driver in cash; for the municipality's red and white services you need to buy a ticket from booths on Konak Meydanı – the well-organized centre of most routes around the city.

The main area for budget **hotels** is Yenigün, which straddles Fevzipaşa Bulvarı immediately in front of Basmane train station. There are also a couple of excellent choices closer to Konak, and, if you can stand the street noise, along Gaziosmanpaşa Bulvarı. At the bottom end of the price range, the *Saray*, Anafartalar Cad 635 (☎836 946; ①), is a pleasant place, and the nearby *Imperial*, 1296 Sok 54 (☎256 883; ②), is better than most in this area. Between these two amenity-wise, the *Meseret*, Anafartalar Cad 66 (☎255 533; ①), has clean, well-furnished doubles but less savoury shared baths.

Most travellers, though, will feel more comfortable north of Fevzipaşa Bulvarı, where a recent pedestrianization programme has made hotels quieter and more appealing.

Here, the *Bayburt*, 1370 Sok 1, on the corner of 1369 Sok (☎722 013; ②), is a huge barn of a place around a roofed-over courtyard; the newly-renovated *Oba* at 1369 Sok 27 (☎835 474; ②) with near-identical rates is also worth trying, as is the somewhat shabbier *Işik* at 1364 Sok 11 (☎831 029; ③).

The City

İzmir cannot really be said to have a single centre, although **Konak**, the busy park, bus terminal and shopping centre on the waterfront, is the spot where visitors spend most time. It's marked by the ornate **Saat Kulesi** (clock tower), the city's official symbol, and the **Konak Camii**, distinguished by its facade of enamelled tiles. Southwest of here, the **Archeological Museum** (daily 9am–5.30pm; $2) features an excellent collection of finds from all over İzmir province and beyond, including the showcased bronze statuette of a runner and a large Roman mosaic, as well as a graceful Hellenistic statuette of Eros clenching a veil in his teeth. The **Ethnographic Museum** (daily 9am–noon & 1–5.30pm; $1), opposite the archeological museum, is a more enjoyable and certainly more interesting collection, with reconstructions of local mansions and the first Ottoman pharmacy in the area, a nuptial chamber, a sitting room and circumcision recovery suite, along with vast quantities of household utensils and Ottoman weaponry.

Immediately east of Konak, İzmir's **bazaar** warrants a stroll. Anafartalar Caddesi, the main drag, is lined with clothing, jewellery and shoe shops; Fevzipaşa Bulvarı and the alleys just south are strong on leather garments, for which the city is famous. Still further east, across Gaziosmanpaşa Bulvarı, the **agora** (daily 9am–5pm; $1) is the most accessible of İzmir's ancient sites, and the most visited, dating back to the early second century BC, although what you see now are the remains of the later reconstruction, financed during the reign of the Roman emperor Marcus Aurelius. Above this, the **Kadifekale** (Velvet Castle) is perhaps the one sight in the city you shouldn't miss. The less energetic can take a red and white city bus from Konak, but the best introduction to the citadel is to walk up from the agora, the route threading through a once-elegant district of narrow streets and dilapidated pre-1922 houses. The irregularly shaped fortress dates from Byzantine and Ottoman times, and gives great views over the city from its pine-shaded tea garden.

Eating and drinking

For a city of İzmir's size, **restaurants** are remarkably thin on the ground. The obvious clutch of eateries within sight of Basmane station are undistinguished, and as so often in Turkey there's a far better choice in the bazaar area, although unfortunately most of them close up early evening. The *Aksüt*, 873 Sok 113, does excellent dairy products and breakfast pastries. The *Halikarnass Balık Lokantası*, overlooking the fountain at the junction of 870, 871 and 873 Sokaks, is a simple unlicensed fish restaurant; the *Yigit Çorba ve Kebap Salonu*, 873 Sok 117, does large portions and has good views of the adjacent mosque, though it's only open at lunchtime. The *Öz Ezo Gelin*, on the corner of 848 Sok and Anafartalar Cad, serves soups, kebabs and puddings, though no alcohol, in an elegant dining room. For pudding or ice cream only, try *Bolulu Hasan Usta*, 853 Sok 13/B, which does the best in town. *Çagdas*, Anafartalar Cad 606, is the least intimidating and cheapest of several *meyhanes* west of the station, serving a lot of food and beer for about $5 a person. *Ömür*, Anafartalar Cad 794, is cheap and friendly, serving ready-prepared dishes but no alcohol. Heading north across Fevzipaşa into Alsancak district, you're entering posher territory, but even here are some affordable options: the *Vegetarian Restaurant*, a small but cheerful place at 1375 Sok 11, and *Bizim Ev*, corner of Cumhuriyet Bulvarı and 1479 Sok, serving home cooking until 9pm. The north end of Alsancakis is also the trendy **nightlife** quarter; a stroll along the various inland alleys will turn up possibilities, which tend to change yearly.

Listings

Airlines *British Airways*, Şehit Fethi Bey Cad 120 (☎841 788).

Car rental A good local outfit is *MAC*, Akdeniz Cad 8/B (☎192 262).

Consulates *Great Britain*, Mahmut Esat Bozkurt Cad 49 (☎211 795); *Netherlands*, Cumhuriyet Meydanı 11/2 (☎634 960); *USA*, Birinci Kordon 92/3 (☎831 369).

Exchange 24-hr exchange at the PTT on Cumhuriyet Meydanı; also numerous, reputable *döriz* (foreign note dealers) in Çankaya.

Ferries Tickets and information on international services to Venice and the domestic line to İstanbul from the *Turkish Maritime Lines* facilities at the Alsancak dock (☎211 484).

Hospitals Most central is the *Konak Hastanesi*, over the road from the ethnographic and archeological museums, though the *Özel Sağlık Hastanesi* in Alsancak is preferrable.

Left luggage On the left side of Basmane station as you face it (daily 6am–9pm).

Post office There's a 24-hour office on Cumhuriyet Meydanı, with quiet phones.

Çeşme and around

A sleepy town of old Greek houses wrapped around a Genoese castle, **ÇEŞME** is the most relaxed of the southern Aegean resorts, an agreeable stopover on the way to Hios in Greece. The town's two main streets are **İnkilap Caddesi**, the main bazaar thoroughfare, and **Çarşı Caddesi**, its continuation, which saunters south along the waterfront. Çeşme's **sights** are, however, soon exhausted. You're free to clamber about every perilous inch of the waterfront **castle** (daily 8.30am–noon & 1–5.30pm; $1), and a **museum** of finds from the nearby site of Erythrae. The **kervansaray**, a few paces south, dates from the reign of Süleyman the Magnificent but is now a luxury hotel.

Coming by **ferry** from Hios, you arrive at the small jetty in front of the castle. Arriving by **bus** from İzmir, you'll be set down at the **bus station**, 1km south. **Dolmuşes** to Dalyan leave from the roundabout at the northeast of İnkilap Cad; those to other nearby attractions depart from next to the **tourist office** (Mon–Fri 8.30am–5.30pm, Sat & Sun 9am–5pm). If you're **staying**, try the *Anıt Pansiyon* (①), directly opposite the castle gate, or if it's full, the *Çelik* (①) or *Kısaoğlu* (①), adjacent about 100m beyond. Moving up in price, the *Tarhan Pansiyon* (☎549/26599; ②), behind the *kervansaray*, offers a few rooms with bath; down in the flatlands the *Alim Pansiyon*, Müftü Sok 3 (☎549/27828; ②), has bath and breakfast. Best among Çeşme's restaurants are the waterfront *Rıhtım* and *Muhsin*, the latter more reasonable, both past the PTT. More centrally, try the *Sevim Kafe*, home cooking from a tiny booth near the *kervansaray*, *Café Müller* for German waffle breakfasts and *Rumeli Pastanesi*, serving some of the best ice cream on the Aegean.

For **ferry tickets to Hios**, contact the *Ertürk* agency, in front of the tourist office, or *Karavan*, next door. Ferries go Thursday morning and Saturday evening in winter, at least once a day from July to September, and with middling frequency in spring and autumn. Current rates are $25 single, £35 open return, with no taxes applicable.

Around Çeşme: some beaches

The closest beach to Çeşme is at **BOYALIK**, 1500m east of town, but the sand is painfully exposed to cold winds and washed-up rubbish, like most beaches on this side of the peninsula. Far better to bypass it in favour of **ILICA**, 4km further on, where there's an excellent long beach but mostly package accommodation. Southeast of Çeşme, **ALAÇATI** is a fine old Greek town, built on a slope overlooking a plain, with two or three **restaurants** between several windmills and the main square, and one very simple *pansiyon*, the *Sarı* (☎549/68315; ①). The sea is 4km distant at **Çınar Plajı**, where there's a sandy beach, one simple restaurant and the *Çark Pansiyon* (☎549/67309; ①). **OVACIK**, 5km due south of Çeşme, is dusty and half-inhabited, but 4km beyond there's a small beach at **ÇATAL AZMAK**, and a better, more isolated beach five minutes' walk west. The best beaches, though, are at **ALTINKUM**, a series of sun-baked coves 9km southwest of Çeşme, easily accessible by dolmuş.

Kuşadası

KUŞADASI is Turkey's most bloated resort, a brash coastal playground which extends along several kilometres of seafront. In just three decades its population has swelled from about 6000 to almost 40,000, though how many of these are year-round inhabitants is debatable. The town is many people's introduction to the country: efficient ferry services link it with the Greek islands of Sámos and Míkonos, plus the resort is an obligatory port of call for Aegean cruise ships, which disgorge vast numbers in summer, who delight the local souvenir merchants after a visit to the ruins of Ephesus just inland.

Liman Caddesi runs from the ferry port up to **Atatürk Bulvarı**, the main harbour esplanade, from which pedestrianized **Barbaros Hayrettin Bulvarı** ascends the hill. To the left of here, the **Kale** district, huddled inside the town walls, is the old and most appealing part of town, with a namesake mosque and some fine traditional houses. If you want to **swim**, Kuşadası's most famous **beach**, the **Kadınlar Denizi** (Ladies' Beach), just over 2km southwest of town, is a popular strand, usually too crowded for its own good in season. **Güvercin Island**, closer to the centre, is mostly landscaped terraces, dotted with tea gardens and snack bars, but the swimming is rocky. For the closest decent sand, head 500m further south to the small beach north of **Yılancı Burnu**, or to **Tusan** beach, 5km north of town; all Kuşadası–Selçuk dolmuşes pass by, as well as more frequent ones labelled "Şehir İçi". Much the best beach in the area, though, is **Pamucak**, at the mouth of the Küçük Menderes River 15km north, an exposed, four-kilometre-long stretch of sand that is as yet little developed. There are regular dolmuşes from both Kuşadası and Selçuk in season.

Practicalities

Ferries arrive at Liman Cad, right by the **tourist office** (Nov–April Mon–Fri 8am–noon & 1.30–5.30pm; May & June, Sept & Oct daily 8am–6pm; July & Aug daily 7.30am–8pm), which hands out a good town plan and has exhaustive lists of accommodation. The combined **dolmuş** and **long-distance bus station**, where you'll be left if coming from the south, is over a kilometre out, past the end of Kahramanlar Cad on the ring road to Söke. Coming from the north, ask the driver to set you down on Atatürk Bulvarı, at the corner of İnönü Bulvarı.

There are plenty of **places to stay**. The best area to look is just south of the core of the town, uphill from Barbaros Hayrettin Bulvarı, particularly the upper reaches of Yıldırım, Arslanlar and Kıbrıs Cads. The *Cennet Pansiyon*, Yayla Sok 1, on the corner of Yıldırım Cad, (☎636/44893; ②), is new and spotless, as is the *Özhan*, Kıbrıs Cad 5 (☎636/42932; ②), a small but immaculately kept pension. The *Hotel Harbour* (☎636/41242; ②), between Bezirgan Sok and the Sheil station, is leafily set and has doubles with baths; on or near Arslanlar Cad are the peaceful *Golden Bed* (☎636/48708; ②) and the *Su Pansiyon* (☎636/41453; ②), both with decent doubles. For **campers**, the *BP Mocamp* out at Tusan beach is well-appointed but expensive. The *Önder* and *Yat*, both behind the yacht marina, are marginally cheaper, well kept and popular.

The *Önder* has a decent restaurant – perhaps the best in town – but with that honourable exception, value for money is not the order of the day as far as **food** goes in Kuşadası. In the Kale area, at the intersection of Yeni and Bozkurt Sok, the *Meşhur Dede Pide Salonu* is reasonable and has outdoor seating. Much further inland, at Kahramanlar Cad 45, *Cengiz* serves good steam-tray fare, while the *Yörük Firini*, İnönü Bul 19/A, is worth mentioning for its filling turnovers and brown bread. If you want to eat by the water without blasting away your entire wallet, you might try the *Ada Restaurant-Paj-Café*, on Güvercin Adası, where you can also dive off their private dock. For a **drink**, you might look in at *Bebop*, Cephane Sok 20 in the Kale, or *She*, corner of Bahar and Sakarya Sokaks; there are half-a-dozen more along Kişla Sok close by. Rather more down-market and livelier are the dozen-plus "Irish" and "English" pubs along an inland alley officially renamed Barlar Sok (Pub Lane).

Agent for most of the **ferries to Samos**, including the Greek afternoon boat, is *Diana*, on Klibis Cad (☎636/44900); one or two of the morning Turkish boats are handled by *Azim*, Liman Cad Yayla Pasajı (☎636/41553). Frequencies vary from twice monthly in winter to one or two daily from late April to late October; fares are $20 single, $35 open return, plus $10 tax each time you leave or enter Kuşadası. The once-weekly *Minoan Lines* ferry to Greece and Italy is handled exclusively by *Karavan*, Kıbrıs Cad 2/1 (☎636/41279).

Selçuk and around

SELÇUK has been catapulted into the limelight of first-division tourism by its proximity to the ruins of Ephesus, and a number of other attractions within the city limits or just outside. The flavour of tourism here, though, is different from that at nearby Kuşadası, its inland location and ecclesiastical connections making it a haven for a disparate mix of rucksackers and Bible Belters from every corner of the globe.

The **hill of Ayasoluk** (daily 8am–6.30pm; $1.50) is the first point you should head for, the traditional burial place of Saint John the Evangelist, who died here around 100 AD. Justinian built a basilica here that was one of the largest Byzantine churches in existence, various colonnades and walls from which have been re-erected, giving just a hint of the building's magnificence in its prime. The tomb of the evangelist is marked by a slab at the former site of the altar; beside the nave is the baptistery, where religious tourists pose in the act of dunking as friends' cameras click. The **castle**, 200m past the church and included in the same admission ticket, is virtually empty inside but you're allowed to make a full circuit on the ramparts – worth it for the views. Just behind the tourist office, the **archeological museum** (daily except Mon 8.30am–noon & 1–5.15/6.30pm; $2.50) has galleries of finds from Ephesus, including the famous Artemis room, with two renditions of the goddess studded with multiple testicles (not breasts, as is commonly believed) and tiny figurines of real and mythical beasts, honouring her role as mistress of animals. Beyond the museum, 600m along the road toward Ephesus, are the scanty remains of the **Artemision** or sanctuary of Artemis, a massive Hellenistic structure that was considered one of the Seven Wonders of the Ancient World, though this is hard to believe today. Within sight of here, the fourteenth-century İsa Bey Camii is the most distinguished of various Selçuk monuments.

At the base of the castle hill a **pedestrian precinct** leads east to the **train station**. Following the main highway a bit further south brings you to the **bus and dolmuş terminal**, opposite which the **tourist office** (daily May–Sept 8.30am–6.30pm) has exhaustive lists of **accommodation**. Of reasonably priced downtown choices, *Otel Aksoy*, Namık Kemal Cad 2 (☎5451/6040; ②), has doubles, as does the *Hotel Subaşı*, Cengiz Topel Cad 10 (☎5451/6359; ②), across from the *PTT*. West of the highway and closer to the tourist office, the *Barım*, Turgut Reis Sok 34 (☎5451/6927; ②), a rambling old house, is reasonable, and there's a group of pensions a block west: the *Australian*, Miltner Sok 17 (☎5451/6050; ②), run by a family of returned Turkish-Australians, is good value, as is the similarly priced *İlayda* at no. 15 (☎5451/3278; ①). Selçuk's **campsite**, *Garden*, lies just beyond the Isa Bay Camii and is well rated; alternatively, there's the *Blue Moon/Develi*, 9km out at Pamucak Beach. Best and least expensive of numerous **restaurants** along pedestrianized Cengiz Topel Caddesi are the *Seçkin*, the *Mine* and *Köfteci Turhan*.

Efes (Ephesus)

With the exception of Pompeii and some inaccessible Libyan ruins, **EPHESUS** is the largest and best-preserved ancient city around the Mediterranean, and is justifiably one of the most visited attractions in Turkey. Originally situated close to a temple devoted to the goddess Artemis, its location by a fine harbour was the secret of its success in ancient times, eventually making it wealthy capital of Roman Asia, ornamented with magnificent public buildings by a succession of emperors. Later, after Christianity took root, Saint John the Evangelist arrived here, and Saint Paul spent the years 51 to 53 AD in the city. Under the Byzantines, Ephesus was the venue for two of the councils of the early church, although the general tenor of the Byzantine era was one of decline, owing to the abandoning of Artemis-worship following the establishment of state Christianity, Arab raids, and (worst of all) the final closing off of the harbour, leading the population to siphon off to the nearby hill crowned by the tomb and church of St John, future nucleus of the town of Selçuk.

Approaching the **site** (daily summer 8am–6.30pm; winter 8am–5.30pm; $5) from Kuşadası, get the dolmuş to drop you at the *Tusan Motel* junction, a kilometre from the gate. From Selçuk it's a three-kilometre walk. In the centre of the site, the **Arcadian Way** (currently closed) is a forlorn echo of the era when it was lined with hundreds of shops and illuminated at night – although its neglect is refreshing when compared to the nearby **theatre**, recently and brutally restored to give more seating for the various summer festivals. It is, however, worth the climb to the top for the views over the surrounding countryside. From the theatre the **Marble Street** heads south, passing the main **agora**, currently closed for excavations, and a **temple of Serapis** where the city's Egyptian merchants would have worshipped. About halfway along is an alleged signpost (a footprint and a female head etched into the rock) for a **brothel**, at the junction with the Street of the Curetes, the other main street. Inside are some fine floor mosaics denoting the four seasons. Across the intersection looms the **Library of Celsus**, erected by the consul Gaius Julius Aquila between 110 and 135 AD as a memorial to his father Celsus Polemaeanus, entombed under the west wall. The elegant, two-storey facade was fitted with niches for statues of the four personified intellectual virtues, today filled with plaster copies (the originals are in Vienna). Just uphill from here, a **Byzantine fountain** looks across the Street of the Curetes to the **public latrines**, a favourite of visitors owing to the graphic obviousness of their function. Continuing along the same side of the street, you'll come to the so-called **Temple of Hadrian**, actually donated in 118 AD by a wealthy citizen in honour of Hadrian, Artemis and the city in general. Behind sprawl the **baths of Scholastica**, so named after a fifth-century Byzantine woman whose headless statue adorns the entrance and who restored the complex, which was actually 400 years older. On the far side of the street from the Hadrian shrine lies a huge pattern **mosaic**, which once fronted a series of shops. Nearby, a sign points to the **terrace houses** (admission only by application to the Selçuk Museum) which give a good idea of everyday life during imperial and early Byzantine times, with well-preserved mosaics and murals. Further up Curetes, you pass the **Temple of Domitian**, the lower floor of which houses a marginally interesting **Museum of Inscriptions** (daily 8am–5pm; free), to the large, overgrown upper agora, fringed by a colonnade to the north, and a restored *Odeion* and *Prytaneum* or civic office.

Bodrum and its peninsula

In the eyes of its devotees, **BODRUM** – ancient Halicarnassos – with its whitewashed square houses and subtropical gardens, is the most attractive and most versatile Turkish resort, a quality outfit in comparison to its upstart Aegean rivals. And it is a pleasant town in most senses, despite having no real beach – although development has proceeded apace over the last couple of decades, spreading beyond the town boundaries into the until recently little-disturbed peninsula.

The centrepiece of Bodrum is the **Castle of St Peter** (Tues-Sun 8am-noon & 2-6pm; $2.50), built by the Knights of St John over a Selçuk fortress between 1437 and 1522. The castle was subsequently neglected until the nineteenth century, when the chapel was converted to a mosque and a hamam installed, though the place was not properly refurbished until the 1960s, when it was turned into a museum. Inside, there are bits of ancient masonry incorporated into the walls, coats of arms, and a chapel housing a local Bronze Age and Mycenaean collection. The various towers house collections of underwater archeology, (including a coin and jewellery room), Classical and Hellenistic statuary and Byzantine relics retrieved from two wrecks, alongside a diorama explaining salvage techniques. Immediately north of the castle lies the **bazaar**, most of which is pedestrianized along the main thoroughfares of Kale Caddesi and Dr Alim Bey Caddesi and given over to souvenir stores and the like. From here, stroll up Türkkuyusu Caddesi and turn left to the town's other main sight, the **Mausoleum** (Tues-Sun 8am-noon & 1-5pm; 50¢), the burial place of Mausolus, the most renowned member of the Hecatomnid dynasty which ruled for the city for centuries. Mausolus greatly increased the power and wealth of Halicarnassos, and his tomb, completed by Artemisia II, his sister and wife, came to be regarded as one of the Seven Wonders of the Ancient World, decorated with friezes and standing nearly 60m high – though its present condition is disappointing, with little left besides the precinct wall, assorted column fragments and some subterranean vaults. By way of contrast, the ancient **amphitheatre**, just above the main highway to the north, has been almost overzealously restored and is used during the September festival. Begun by Mausolus, it was modified in the Roman era and originally seated 13,000, though it has a present capacity of about half that.

Practicalities

Ferries dock at the jetty west of the castle, quite close to the well-equipped **tourist office** on İskele Meydanı (Mon-Fri 8am-8pm, Sat 9am-7.30pm), though a new international terminal will soon open across the mouth of the harbour, near the expanding yacht marina. The **bus station** is 500m up Cevat Şakir Cad, which divides the town roughly in two. Desirable **accommodation** includes the *Ataer*, down an alley off Neyzen Tevfik Cad, though it can get full in season, and the *Bahçeli Ağar*, behind the marina (☎252/316 1648; ①). There's also the *Belmi*, Yangı Sokağı 6 (☎252/316 1132; ①), or the *Menekşe*, (☎252/316 3416; ①), again off Neyzen Tevfik Cad, which are little cheaper. There are three small **campsites** on Gelence Sokağı, west of Türkkuyusu Cad .

You don't come to Bodrum to ease your budget, and **eating out** is no exception. Absolute rock-bottom is the *Uslu Büfe* on Neyzen Tevfik, with tables outside but no alcohol. More cheerful is the *Çakır Ali* pizza and kebab joint, at the foot of Cevat Şakir Cad, up which the *Uğrak Lokantası* has the best-value puddings in town. On 2 Sokak off Kale Cad, you might try the *Üsküdarlı* or the *Sakallı Köfteci*. The *Ağan Bolu Turkish Kitchen* in Çarşi Mah between Çarşi and Alim Bey Caddesis is a spit-and-sawdust affair with good-value meat stews, and waiters set plates alight to heat them up. The cheapest place to **drink** is the *Piknik Bar*, midway along pedestrianized Dr Alim Bey Cad. On the Cumhuriyet Cad strip, *Meltem* is good, though plays deafening music.

Several companies handle ferry tickets to **Kos**. Try *Motif*, Neyzen Tevfik Cad 72 (☎252/316 2309); *Karya Tur*, İskele Meydanı (☎252/316 1914); *Gino Tur*, Neyzen Tevfik Cad 200/9 (☎252/316 5026); or *Fahri Kaptan*, Neyzen Tevfik Cad 190 (☎252/316 2870). Fares are the least expensive of the Greek crossings: singles $10, day returns $15, open returns $20, plus $8 tax on the Greek side. Domestic ferries also run south to **Datça**, just west of Marmaris.

Around the peninsula

There is more of interest and beauty in the rest of the **Bodrum peninsula** than is promised by the often dreary immediate environs of the town. The north side of the peninsula is greener with patches of pine forest, the more arid south studded with tall crags and a sandier coast. There is a relatively high concentration of serviceable beaches, and virtually every resort is served by dolmuşes from Bodrum's bus station.

Roughly 3km west of Bodrum, **GÜMBET** is the closest resort to the town, and the 600-metre, tamarisk-lined gritty beach is usually jam-packed. **BITEZ**, the next cove west and reached by a different side road, is a little more upmarket, but the beach is negligible. Better to continue along the south peninsular trunk road to **ORTAKENT**, an inland village, from where a road winds down several kilometres to the longest **beach** on the peninsula, its two-kilometre extent fringed by a clutter of shops, camp-sites and motels. **BAĞLA**, the next cove, has lovely sand and clean water, just one tea house and a snack bar. **KARAİNCİR**, the next bay with public access, is nearly as good – 700m of sand guarded by a pair of headlands. Of the handful of eateries, the *Ceylan* is okay; of a similar number of pensions, the *Tinaztepe* is the best. **AKYARLAR**, an old Greek port just around the bend, is more of an actual village, with a stone jetty, mosque, many pensions and a campsite. The beach is small, but with both Karaincir and a nameless bay in the opposite direction within walking distance, it's no great loss. Around the point, **TURGUTREIS** is the second resort in the area after Bodrum itself, with nearly fifty pensions, but the town is a sterile grid and the small, exposed beach closely pressed by the luckiest half-dozen of the hotels. A side road leads north to better things, through a fertile landscape to sleepy **KADIKALESİ**, with a long, partly protected sand beach and unbeatable views over to assorted islets. Besides the lone luxury hotel there are a couple of pensions, a campsite and a handful of restaurants.

Marmaris

MARMARİS rivals Kuşadası as the largest and most developed Aegean resort, its huge marina and proximity to Dalaman airport meaning that tourists pour in more or less non-stop during the warmer months. According to legend, the place was named when Süleyman the Magnificent, not finding the castle here to his liking, was heard to mutter "*Mimarı as*" (Hang the architect), later corrupted to "Marmaris" – a command which ought perhaps still apply to the designers of the seemingly endless tower blocks. Ulusal Egemenlik Bulvarı cuts Marmaris in half, and the maze of narrow streets east of it is home to most things of interest to the average tourist, though little is left of the sleepy fishing village that Marmaris was a mere two decades ago. The bazaar has been ruthlessly commercialized, and only the **Kaleiçi** district, the warren of streets at the base of the tiny castle, offers a pleasant wander.

The **bus station** is two blocks behind the marina on the east side of town, a few minutes from the town centre. The main bus companies all have offices at the Kordon Cad end of Ulusal Egemenlik Bulvarı and run free services from here to the bus station to coincide with bus departures. Arriving by **ferry**, the dock abuts İskele Meydanı, on one side of which stands the **tourist office** (summer daily 8am–8pm; winter Mon–Fri 8am–noon & 1–5pm), dispensing town plans and **accommodation** details. *Dilek*, Hacı Mustafa Sok 108 (☎252/412 3591; ①), and *Işıksal*, Hacı Mustafa Sok 89 (☎252/412 1391; ①), are two similar, plain pensions one street back from the marina; the *Can Pansiyon*, 53 Sok 17 (☎252/412 1233; ①), is another simple affair. More central is the *Kordon Pansiyon*, Yeni Kordon Sok 24 (☎252/412 4762; ①), behind the *PTT*. The *Interyouth Hostel* (☎252/412 6432; ①), 300m past the hospital on the road to Datça, is a new three-storey youth hostel with all mod cons, and the *Suat*, Hamdi Yuzak Sok 48 (☎252/412 3961; ①), *Onay*, next door (☎252/412 1330; ①), and the *Emrah* a little way down (☎252/412 3881; ①), are three relatively quiet old-fashioned pensions.

Getting a decent **meal** at a reasonable price is a challenge. *Ay Yıldız*, on a small plaza near the bazaar mosque, is okay; try also *Can Restaurant*, on the ground floor of the namesake pension, or *İstanbul Pide Salonu* across the street. Not surprisingly, most of Marmaris' **drinking** happens on the Netsel Marina, where yachties wreck their livers during happy hour at *Scorpio*. There's also an upmarket restaurant, the *Okimo*, here with a good open buffet – eat as much of their mainly Turkish and French quality cuisine as you can manage for $15 a head. The tiny *Bar Ivy* seems to get a younger, more back-packing crowd. *Palm Tree*, Hacı Mustafa Sok 97, is a fine garden pub with music.

Authorized agents for the morning ferry to **Rhodes** include *Yexil Marmaris*, Barbaros Cad 11 (☎252/412 2290), and *Anadolu Turizm*, on the corner of 53 Sok and Kordon (☎252/412 3514).

Datça

Though too manicured these days, **DATÇA**, 30km west of Marmaris, is still many times calmer than Bodrum or Marmaris. It's essentially the shore annexe of inland Reşadiye village, but under the ministrations of visiting yachtspeople and package operators has outgrown its parent. Carpet shops are big news here, with prices still relatively low. The town is principally a single high street meandering between two sheltered bays separated by a hillock and then a narrow isthmus. As far as things to do go, it's really a matter of picking your swimming and sunbathing spot. The **east beach**, part sand, part cement quay with cafés, is quieter but the cleanliness is suspect. The **west beach**, mixed pebble and sand, is acceptable and becomes better the further you get from the yachts.

Two **bus** companies currently serve Datça, so there's no bus station. Bodrum-bound **ferries**, operated by *Karya Tours*, run from Körmen Limanı, 9km north, connected by a short bus ride. The best place to stay is the hillock separating the two bays, where the *Huzur* (☎252/712 1052; ②) is the most modern; the reasonable *Sadık* (☎252/712 1196; ②), and the *Karaöglu* (☎252/712 1079; ②), with the best view and a pleasant café, have affordable rooms. There's also an attractive **campsite**, *Camping Ilıca*, at the far end of the western beach. For **food**, try the *Durak*, on the main road near the bus stop.

Aphrodisias

Situated on a high plateau around 100km inland, **APHRODISIAS** is one of the more isolated of Turkey's major archeological sites. It was one of the earliest occupied centres in Anatolia, but remained for many centuries only a shrine, and never really grew into a town until the second century BC, when it became a major cultural centre. It was renowned in particular for its school of sculpture, benefiting from nearby quarries of high-grade marble, examples of which adorned every corner of the empire.

A loop path around the site (daily 8am–5.30pm; $2.50) passes all of the major monuments, beginning with the virtually intact **theatre**, founded in the first century BC but extensively modified by the Romans three centuries later. Further on you pass the **double agora**, two squares ringed by Ionic and Corinthian stoas, and the fine **baths of Hadrian**, well preserved right down to the floor tiles and the odd mosaic. North of the baths, several columns sprout from a multi-roomed structure commonly known as the **bishop's palace**, east of which is the appealing Roman **odeon**, with nine rows of seats. Perhaps the most impressive feature of the site is, however, the 30,000-seat **stadium**, a little way north, one of the largest and best-preserved in Anatolia. The **museum** (daily 8am–5.30pm; $2.50) consists almost entirely of sculpture recovered from the ruins, which, given that Aphrodisias met most of the demand for effigies under the empire, makes for a considerable collection. On display is statuary related to the cult of Aphrodite, a joyous satyr carrying the child Dionysus in his arms, and a quasi-satirical portrait of Flavius Palmatus, Byzantine governor of Asia.

Aphrodisiás is situated 13km east of Karacasu, the nearest sizeable town, which is connected by frequent **dolmuş** to **NAZILLI**, 50km away. If you're staying in Pamukkale, it's tempting to try and devise a loop back to Denizli through Tavas, but you must get to Tavas in time for the last dolmuş back to Denizli, and thence to Pamukkale, which is difficult. Whatever happens, try to avoid getting stranded at Aphrodisias or Karacasu. If you are going to get stuck, you're better off doing so at **GEYRE**, where there are two pension/campsites, *Chez Mestan* and *Chez Bayar*.

Denizli, Pamukkale and Hierapolis

Devastated by earthquakes in 1710 and 1899, **DENİZLİ**, 50km east of Nazilli, is a gritty agricultural town of just under 200,000 inhabitants. It has little appeal itself, but you may well pass through, especially if you're heading on to Pamukkale, to which there are regular buses and dolmuşes. If you do need to **stay**, the *Pension Temiz* (☎258/264 0342; ②), in the block opposite the police station on Enverpaşa Caddesi, and the *Arar Otel*, İstiklâl Cad, Delıki Çinar Meydanı 9 (☎258/263 7195; ②), are reasonable. Near the bus station, the *Grand Hotel Keskin*, Istasyon Cad 11 (☎258/263 3565; ③), is luxuriously comfortable. You can **eat** well at one of several places just southeast of the bus stand; there are also numerous kebab and *pide* places around Delıki Çinar Meydanı.

The rock formations of **PAMUKKALE**, 10km or so north – literally "Cotton Castle" – are perhaps the most visited attraction in this part of Turkey, a series of white terraces saturated with dissolved calcium bicarbonate, bubbling up from the feet of the Çal Dağı mountains beyond. As the water surges over the edge of the plateau and cools, carbon dioxide is given off and calcium carbonate precipitated as hard chalk or travertine. The spring emerges in what once was the exact middle of the ancient city of **Hierapolis**, the ruins of which would merit a stop even if they weren't coupled with the natural phenomenon. As things are, you can often hardly see them for the tour buses, souvenir hawkers and motels.

Most travellers stay in **PAMUKKALE KÖYÜ**, above which the **travertine terraces** are deservedly the first item on their agenda, although the pools are very shallow and a foot-soak is all that's possible – original water levels are depleted by the diversion of water to pools of nearby hotels. There is talk of closing some of these and stopping tourists walking on the terraces at all. Present restrictions require removal of shoes.

If you want to take a bath in the springs, *Pammukkale Motel* (☎258/272 2024) up on the plateau encloses the **sacred pool** of the ancients, with mineral water bubbling from its bottom at 95°F (open to public 9am–6pm; $2, free if eating at poolside restaurant at around $10 a head).

The **archeological zone** of Hierapolis lies west of Pamukkale Köyü, via a narrow road winding up past the *Turism Motel*. Its main features include a **temple of Apollo** and the adjacent **Plutonium** – the latter a cavern emitting a toxic gas, probably a mixture of sulphur compounds and carbon dioxide, capable of killing man and beast alike. There's also a restored **Roman theatre**, just east of here, dating from the second century AD and in exceptionally good shape, with most of the stage buildings and their elaborate reliefs. Arguably the most interesting part of the city, though, is the colonnaded street which once extended for almost one kilometre from a gate 400m southeast of the sacred pool, terminating in monumental portals a few paces outside the walls – only the most northerly of which, a triple arch flanked by towers and dedicated to the emperor Domitian in 84 AD, still stands. Just south of the arch is the elaborate tomb of Flavius Zeuxis – the first of more than a thousand tombs constituting the **necropolis**, the largest in Asia Minor, extending for nearly 2km along the road. There's also a **museum** (daily 9am–noon & 1.30–5pm), housed in the restored, second-century AD baths, whose disappointing collection consists of statuary, sarcophagi, masonry fragments and smaller knick-knacks recovered during excavations.

Practicalities

With over a hundred pensions, there's no shortage of **accommodation** in Pamukkale Köyü. One of the best and friendliest is the *Kervansaray* (☎258/272 2209; ②), with its good rooftop restaurant. If they're full, you'll be pointed a few metres further out of town to the *Aspawa* (☎258/272 2094; ②). In the northern part of the village, the oldest pension, *Ali's* (☎258/272 2065; ②), charges slightly more but the view of the terraces compensates. **Eating out**, the situation is dire; the exceptions are the *Kervansaray* and the *Pammukkale Motel* poolside restaurant.

THE MEDITERRANEAN COAST

The first stretch of Turkey's **Mediterranean Coast**, dominated by the Arkdağ and Bey mountain ranges of the Taurus chain and known as the "Turquoise Coast", is perhaps its most popular, famed for its pine-studded shore, minor ruins and beautiful scenery. Most of this is connected by Highway 400, which winds precipitously above the sea from Marmaris to Antalya. In the west of the region, **Dalyan** is renowned for its beach – a breeding ground of loggerhead turtles – as well as being a characterful small resort. West, **Fethiye**, along with the nearby lagoon of **Ölüdeniz**, is a full-blown regional centre, and gives good access to some of the pick of the region's Lycian ruins, the best of which – **Xanthos** and **Patara** – are close to one of the coast's nicest beaches. The region's second major resort, **Kaş**, smaller than Fethiye but no less popular, is a good base for scenery which becomes increasingly spectacular until you reach the site of **Olympos**, close to another fine beach. Further along, past the port and major city of **Antalya**, the landscape becomes less dramatic but is home to yet more impressive ruins, notably those of the old Pamphylian cities of **Perge** and **Aspendos**. **Side**, too, has its share of antiquities, although it's better known as a tourist resort, as is the former pirate refuge of **Alanya**, set on a spectacular headland topped by a stunning Selçuk citadel. Beyond here you're entering the relatively undiscovered reaches of eastern Turkey.

Dalyan and around

DALYAN, 7km off Highway 400, is one of the calmer resorts along this stretch of coast, and a good base for surrounding attractions. Life here centres on the Dalyan River, which flows past the village – the one drawback in the summer months is mosquitos, especially along the riverbank, for which the area has been notorious since antiquity. Go armed with a good repellent, and buy an *esenmat*, a machine that plugs into the electricity supply, from any good chemist in Turkey. **Pension** prices are fixed by the municipality: all doubles without baths ①, with bath ②. There is a string of pleasant places on the riverbank, one of the nicest being *Midas Pansiyon* (☎6116/2195; ②), which has camping facilities as well; other good options are *Aktaş Pansiyon* (☎6116/2042; ②), or its friendly neighbour, *Miletos Pansiyon* (☎6116/2532; ①). **Restaurants** in Dalyan are fairly undistinguished, though the *Gelgör* at the road's end across from the fish plant is well-set and reasonably priced; long-established *Denizati* in the town centre is better but expensive.

Boats run up and down the river to the nearby attractions of Kaunos, İstuzu Beach and Köyceğiz Lake; most leave by 10.30am, returning by 6pm. Most people settle for the standard, somewhat rushed, all-in tour of Köyceğiz Lake, Kaunos and İstuzu Beach at $3 a head, though you can also charter a boat for about $60 per day, choosing your pace and itinerary. **İstuzu Beach**, a 12km drive south, is the breeding ground of the loggerhead turtle, which means entry is banned at night between May and October. During the day the beach is open to the public, and is a good place to swim and sunbathe, although you should be careful of disturbing the turtle eggs and nests, which are easily disrupted.

North of Dalyan, **KÖYCEĞIZ** is a sleepy little town whose position on the ten-metre-deep **Köyceğiz Golü** gives it a source of income from the fish who swim up the Dalyan Çayı from the sea to spawn here. There's no real point in staying here, but it's connected with Dalyan by regular buses, and you may want to stop over for a night to visit the mud baths or view the ruins of the Carian city of **KAUNOS** on the opposite side of the lake. Kaunos (daily 8.30am–6pm; $1) was famous for the bad health of its inhabitants, who probably suffered from the malarial mosquitoes that thrived in the marshy lowlands around the city. Much of Kaunos is still below ground, despite long-running excavation, and only the most obvious sites, like the **agora**, a **Doric Temple** and the **fort**, are labelled. The **amphitheatre** is the most impressive structure, predominantly Greek in style and resting against the hillside to the south. Northeast of the theatre, the city's baths and a Byzantine basilica are also in good condition.

Fethiye and around

FETHİYE is well situated for access to some of the region's ancient sites, many of which date from the time when this was the independent kingdom of Lycia. And although the region's best beaches, around the Ölüdeniz Lagoon, are now much too crowded for comfort, Fethiye still has qualities which set it above many other Mediterranean resorts. It's a real market town, soon perhaps to be capital of a newly designated province; there are other nearby attractions and beaches besides Ölüdeniz; and, unlike Kaş, which is confined by its sheer rock backdrop, Fethiye has been able to spread to accommodate the increase in tourist traffic.

Fethiye occupies the location of the Lycian city of **Telmessos**, the remains of which, in the shape of a number of Lycian rock tombs, cover the hillside above the bus station. Most notable is the **Amyntas Tomb**, carved in close imitation of the facade of a temple. There's not all that much else to see in Fethiye, although you can visit the remains of the medieval **fortress**, on the hillside behind the harbour area of town. In the centre of town, off Atatürk Caddesi, Fethiye's **museum** (Tues–Sun 8am–5pm; $1) is badly labelled and very small, but some of the exhibits help to enhance the nearby archeological sights. The most interesting piece is the stelae found at the Letoön, dating from 358 BC, which was important in translating the Lycian language.

One of the most dramatic sights in the area is the ghost village of **KAYA KÖYÜ** (Levissi), 7km out of town, served by dolmuşes from behind the PTT. The village was abandoned in 1923, when its Anatolian Greek population were relocated, along with more than a million others, to a country which had never been their homeland, and whose language many of them couldn't speak. All you see now is a hillside covered with more than 2000 ruined cottages and an attractive **basilica**, to the right of the main path 200m up the hill from the road, one of three churches here – but the general state of neglect only serves to highlight the plight of the former inhabitants. There are plans to make an international "peace and friendship" conference centre here, but ordinary travellers must still stay at a couple of *pansiyons* at the edge of Kaya. You can walk from Kaya Köyü to **Ölüdeniz** – about two hours, through the village, over the hill and down to the lagoon – although it is also served by frequent **dolmuşes** from Fethiye. The warm waters of the lagoon make for pleasant swimming if you don't mind paying the small entrance fee, although the crowds can reach saturation level in high season – in which case the nearby, more prosaic beaches of **Belceğiz** and **Kidrak** are better bets.

Practicalities

Fethiye's new **bus station** is about 1km southeast of the centre; dolmuşes to Ölüdeniz, Çalış beach and Kaya village arrive and leave from the old otogar, east of the central market. The **tourist office**, near the harbour at İskele Meydanı 1 (summer daily 8am–8pm), can point you in the right direction for **hotels**, which are distributed throughout the town centre and the suburbs of Karagözler and Çaliş. Downtown, try the *Ülgen Pansiyon* (☎615/43491; ①), up the stairs beyond Paspatir Cad, or the *Kaya Otel*, Cumhuriyet Cad 6 (☎615/42469; ②). In the quieter Karagözler, the *Savaşci* (☎615/44108; ③) and the *Pinara* (☎615/42151; ①) are backpacker favourites. Out in **Çaliş**, actually a beach resort served by dolmuş from town, two inland, adjacent pensions are good budget choices: the *Oykun* (☎615/31605; ①) and the *Beşik* (①). For **camping**, one of the best sites is the *Ölüdeniz*, which has its own beach and restaurant; it's just past the official entrance to Ölüdeniz Lagoon on the left.

The best **eating** in Fethiye is done at *Meğri*, with two premises: a touristy one at Likya Sok 8, and a more down-home outlet at Çarşi Cad 13, best for lunch. Another excellent option is a cheap *pide* place, *Nefis Pide İki*, at Tütün Sok 21, though this gets thronged at lunchtimes. Other good choices include *Özlem İzgara* and *Pide* on Çarşi Cad, and the *meyhane* under the Kent Oteli.

Around Fethiye: the Lycian sites

East of Fethiye lies the heartland of ancient Lycia, home to a number of archeological sites, all within easy reach of Fethiye. The closest is the **LETOÖN**, accessible by taking a dolmuş from Fethiye to Kumluova, the site lying 4km off the main highway. The Letoön was the official sanctuary of the Lycian Federation, and the extensive **ruins** ($1 admission when warden present) to be seen today bear witness to its importance. The low ruins of three **temples** occupy the centre of the site, the westernmost of which bears a dedication to Leto. The central temple, dating from the fourth century, is identified by a dedication to Artemis, while the easternmost temple has a floor mosaic of a lyre, bow and quiver, suggesting a dedication to Artemis and Apollo, who were apparently the region's most revered deities. Beyond the temple, to the southwest, is a **nymphaeum**, though it's now permanently flooded. There is also a large, well-preserved **theatre** on the right, entered through a vaulted passage.

On the other side of the valley, the remains of the hilltop city of **XANTHOS** are perhaps the most fascinating of the Lycian sites, though sadly the most important relic discovered at the site, the fourth-century Nereid Monument, is now in the British Museum. However, there is still enough to see here to reward a lengthy visit. Buses between Fethiye and Patara drop you off in Kinik, from where it's a twenty-minute walk up to the ruins ($1 admission when attended). West of the car park are the acropolis and agora and a Roman theatre, beside which are two Lycian tombs – the so-called **Harpy Tomb**, a cement cast of the original decorated with pairs of bird-woman figures carrying children in their arms, and a Lycian-type **sarcophagus** standing on a pillar tomb, thought to date from the third century BC. Northeast of the agora looms a structure known popularly as the **Xanthian obelisk** – in fact the remains of a pillar tomb covered on all four sides by the longest known Lycian inscription, running to 250 lines and including 12 lines of Greek verse. The nearby Roman **theatre** is pretty complete, only missing the upper seats which were incorporated into the Byzantine city wall.

PATARA, a little way south and reachable by regular dolmuş from Fethiye, was the principal port of Lycia, famed for its oracle of Apollo and as the birthplace of Saint Nicholas, the Western Santa Claus. Two kilometres from the modern village, the site entrance is marked by a triple-arched Roman gateway, almost completely intact. The site itself has some well-preserved **baths** and a small **temple** lodged in a course of boundary wall. To the south, close to the beach, is a **theatre**, the cavea of which is now half full of sand – although the stage building is partly intact. The hill to the south of the theatre is the city's **acropolis**, worth climbing to view the pit at the top, once thought to be a lighthouse but in fact a cistern.

Nowadays Patara is best known for its white sand beach, served by dolmuş from the village of Gelemiş. It can get a bit crowded in season, but the walk along the dunes towards the river mouth, 7km northwest, turns up more than enough solitary spots.

For **accommodation**, the Otlu brothers' long-running *Golden Pansiyon* (☎3215/5184; ②)) has recently been joined by their posher *Patara View Point Hotel* (③) on the ridge east of the main crossroads. Near this is the *Libya Pansiyon* (☎3215/5211; ②), and on the western rise of the village, the *Terah* is another good choice (☎3215/5180; ②). **Eating** possibilities aren't scintillating, though the *Golden Pansiyon's* diner often has trout, and the two cafés down at the beach feature *manti* or Turkish ravioli.

Kaş and around

KAŞ around 25km further east from Patara, is beautifully situated, nestled in a curving bay against a backdrop of vertical, 500-metre-high cliffs. However, what was a quaint fishing village as recently as 1983 has grown to become a tourist metropolis. There's no beach to speak of in Kaş itself, but there's plenty to see in the countryside around, and the town does get lively at night. It's also the site of ancient **Antiphellos**, the ruins of which litter the streets of the modern town, as well as covering the peninsula to the west. Most interesting of these is the **lion tomb**, a towering structure that had two burial chambers, at the top of Uzun Çarşi. Half a kilometre from the main square, along Hastane Caddesi, a small, almost complete Hellenistic **theatre** looks out to sea; on a nearby hilltop stands a unique rock-cut **Doric tomb**, also almost completely intact. The closest decent **beach** near Kaş is **Kaputaş**, on the way to Kalkan, a small stretch of pebbles and sand which understandably gets crowded.

The **tourist office** is at Cumhuriyet Meydanı 5 (Mon–Fri 8.30am–noon & 1–8pm, Sat & Sun 10am–noon & 1pm–8pm). They have lists of **hotel** and **pansiyon** prices, but, looking, you're strictly on your own. Doing this, it's best to avoid the noisy main streets and head east or west. East, try the *Yayla* or *Köşk pansiyons* (②), while above Kastane Caddesi on the west, *Kale* (☎322/63226; ②) and *Ay* (☎322/61562; ②) even have sea views. The *Toros Hotel*, behind the market square (☎322/61923; ③), is more comfortable, with a roof terrace and bar. There are two **campsites** close to Kaş. The *Büyükçakıl* site on the east side of town along Hükümet Caddesi rents out tents with beds for around $10 per person, and is pleasantly shaded by olive trees. *Kaş Camping* is on the west side of town, a kilometre out on Kastane Caddesi, and has its own seaside diving platform, restaurant and bar. Of many **restaurants**, the *Çınar Restaurant*, on Çukurbağlı Caddesi, serves reasonable *meze* and fish; the strangely-named *Sebastian Kalamar*, at no. 11 of the same street, has a pleasant garden setting and occasional live music in the evenings. The *Eriş*, 20m inland behind the tourist office, is a long established restaurant and okay for a splurge.

East of Kaş: Demre, Myra and Andriake

A winding 45-minute drive beyond Kaş lies the river delta town of **DEMRE** (officially Kale), a rather scruffy citrus- and tomato-growing town, too far away from the coast to be worthy of the "seaside" tag and afforded more attention by tour parties than it can really deal with. However, it is worth visiting for its **Church of St Nicholas** (daily summer 8am–7pm; $2), in the centre of town on Müze Caddesi, highly evocative of the life and times of its patron saint – even if the saint's sarcophagus, left of the entrance, is not considered the real one (which lies under the floor), and its atmosphere is diminished by an outsized protective cover. The remains of the ancient Lycian city of **Myra** (daily 8am–7pm; $1), 2km north of the centre, make up one of the most beautiful Lycian sites, consisting mainly of a large theatre and some of the best examples of house-style rock tombs to be seen in Lycia. And the site of the ancient city's port, **Andriake**, now known as Çayağzı, 2km beyond Demre, is also worth a visit, and is close to a minimally-developed sandy **beach**. The substantial remains of the so-called **Hadrian's granary** are the most prominent feature of the site, built between 119 and

139 AD by the emperor Hadrian and consisting of eight rooms constructed of well-fitting blocks, the outer walls still standing to their original height on the far bank of the stream running parallel to the road to the beach. Above the main gate are busts of Hadrian and a woman who is thought to be the empress Sabina.

Few travellers stay in Demre, and the choice available is less than inspiring. Best value are *pansiyons* on the road to Myra, such as the *Kent* (☎3224/2042; ①) and the *Lykia* (☎3224/2579; ①), and best in the town centre is the *Şahin* on Müze Cad (☎3224/5686; ②). Closest campsite, on route Andriahe, is the *Ocak başi*, near some mineral springs; for eating, try the *İpek* downtown on Müze Cad, where two can eat and drink for less than $13.

Olympos

Around 50km east of Demre, fifteen minutes' walk from the hamlet of Çirali, is another Lycian city, **OLYMPOS**, an idyllic site ($1 admission when gates are staffed), located on a beautiful sandy bay and the banks of a river which nearly dries up in summer. On the south bank is part of a quay wall and a warehouse; to the east on the same side lie the walls of a Byzantine church; while further back, in the undergrowth, there is a theatre, most of whose seats have gone. On the north side of the river are more striking ruins, namely a well-preserved marble door frame, and, at its foot, a statue base with an inscription to Marcus Aurelius. Beyond is a Byzantine *hamam* with mosaic floors, and a Byzantine canal which would have carried water to the heart of the city.

About an hour's well-marked stroll above the citrus groves of nearby Çirali flickers **Chimaera**, a series of eternal flames issuing from cracks in the bare rock which can be extinguished but will always re-ignite. It's not known what causes the phenomenon; a survey by oil prospectors in 1967 detected traces of methane in the gas but otherwise its make-up is unique to this spot. What is known, however, is that the fire has been burning since antiquity, and inspired the Lycians to worship the god Hephaestos (the Roman Vulcan) here. The mountain was also associated with a fire-breathing monster, also known as the Chimaera, with a lion's head, a goat's rear and a snake for a tail.

There is one daily minibus from Çıralı to Antalya and back; otherwise, hitch the 8km down the most northerly of three side turnings from the main highway. More than a dozen fairly basic *pansiyons* (①) hide in the citrus groves behind the beach; few, except the *Aygün* (☎3185/7144; ②) have phones or much space, so it's a matter of chancing on vacancies in season. Rough camping on the beach is frowned on now that an official campsite, *Green Point*, has begun operating. Beach restaurants are simple and short-lived, owing to battles with the forest service (the area is officially a National Park); most durable lately seem to be *Olympos Yavuz*, the *Star* and the *Om* pudding shop.

Antalya and around

Turkey's fastest growing city, **ANTALYA** is also the one metropolis besides İstanbul that's simultaneously a major tourist destination. Blessed with an ideal climate and a stunning setting, Antalya has seen the annual tourist influx grow to almost match its permanent population, which now stands at just under half a million. Despite the appearance of its grim concrete sprawl, it's an agreeable place, although the main area of interest for visitors is confined to the relatively tiny old quarter; it also makes a good base for visiting the nearby ancient sites of Perge and Aspendos.

The Antalya telephone code is ☎242.

Arrival and accommodation

The central **bus station** is at the top of Kazım Özalp Cad, still universally referred to by its old name of Sarampol, which runs for just under a kilometre down to the Saat Kulesi on the fringe of the old town. A little way east, 800m down Ali Çetinkaya Cad, is the **Doğu Garaj** (Eastern Dolmuş Station), linked to the bus terminal by dolmuş. About 5km west of the centre is the **ferry dock**, also connected by dolmuş. Antalya's **airport** is around 10km northeast of the city centre; *THY* buses make the fifteen-minute trip into town and city centre-bound dolmuşes pass nearby. There are two central **tourist offices**, one beside *THY* on Cumhuriyet Cad (Mon–Fri 8am–5.30pm, Sat & Sun 9am–5pm), the other in the old town next to the *Hotel Aspen* (Mon–Fri 8am–noon & 1.30–5.30pm). Both hand out city maps.

Most travellers **stay** in the old town, called Kaleiçi, although there's also a nucleus of hotels between the bus station and the bazaar. The *Sabah Pansiyon*, Hesapçı Sok 60/A (☎247 5345; ②), is clean and well-run and its patron speaks good English. *Pansiyon Falez*, Hıdırlık Sok 48 (☎227 0985; ②), has great views, and the *Adler Pansiyon*, Barbaros Mahalle Civelek Sok 16 (☎321 7818; ①), is one of the least expensive of the old town pensions – basic but characterful. The *Antique Pansiyon*, Tuzcular Mah, Paşa Cami Sok 28 (☎242 4615; ②), is original old Anatolian with a shady courtyard, or there's the *Kumluca Oteli*, 457 Sok 21 (☎321 1123; ②). The *Kaya*, 459 Sok 12 (☎321 1391), is a spotless place. *Bambas Hotel and Camping* on the Lara road out of town just before the beach (☎215 263) is pleasant and well-equipped with its own rocky cove for swimming.

The City

The intersection of Cumhuriyet Caddesi and Sarampol is the most obvious place to begin a tour of Antalya, dominated by the **Yivli Minare** or "Fluted Minaret", erected in the thirteenth century and today something of a symbol of the city. Downhill from here is the **old harbour**, recently restored and site of the evening promenade for half of Antalya. North is the disappointing bazaar, while south, beyond the Saat Kalesi, lies **Kaleiçi** or the old town, currently succumbing to tweeness as every house is redone as a carpet shop, café or pension. On the far side, on Atatürk Caddesi, the triple-arched **Hadrian's Gate** recalls a visit by the emperor in 130 AD, while Hesapçı Sokak leads south past the **Kesik Minare** (Broken Minaret) to a number of tea gardens and the **Hıdırlık Kulesi**, of indisputable Roman vintage but ambiguous function – it could have been a lighthouse, bastion or tomb. The one thing you shouldn't miss while in Antalya is the **Archeological Museum** (Tues–Sun 9am–6pm; $2), one of the top five archeological collections in the country; it's on the western edge of town at the far end of Kenan Evren Bulvarı, reachable by dolmuş. Highlights include an array of Bronze Age urn burials from near Elmalı, and finds from an unusually southerly Phrygian tumulus. There's also second-century statuary from Perge, an adjoining sarcophagus wing with an almost undamaged coffer depicting the life of Hercules, a number of mosaics and a reliquary containing some purported bones of Saint Nicholas – not to mention an ethnography section with ceramics, household implements, weapons and embroidery and a small but well thought out children's section.

Antalya's **beaches** don't rate much consideration. **Konyaltı**, 3km west of Kalekapısı, is divided into paying sections and free zones but all are shadeless, pebbly and polluted. **Lara**, 10km distant in the opposite direction and reached by dolmuşes running along Atatürk Caddesi, has fine sand but is accessible only for a fee.

Eating, drinking and nightlife

Many *pansiyons* have their own restaurant in Kaleiçi, and you may prefer to eat in rather than attempt to explore the limited and overpriced options. Otherwise a couple of suggestions are *Portakal Çiçeği*, an atmospheric courtyard restaurant at Mexcit Sok 13/A, Kaleiçi, or *Ünal Restaurant*, Imaret Sok, Kalekapısı 8. Upmarket are *Ahtapot* for fish at the marina, and *Blue Parrot's Café*, İzimirli Ali Efendi Sok 10, serving international cuisine. *Tektat*, Sarampol 84, has the best puddings in town and a garden to shield you from the traffic. Cumhuriyet Cad is the location of a number of cafés and restaurants with terraces offering excellent views of the harbour – good for leisurely breakfasts – and, southwest of the junction of Cumhuriyet Cad and Atatürk Bulvarı, the covered pedestrian precinct, Eski Sebzeciler İçi Sokak, is crammed with tiny restaurants. The twin *Gaziantep 1 & 2* eateries, 200m from each other at the edge of the bazaar through the *pasaj* at İsmet Paşa Cad 3, are excellent. To all intents and purposes **nightlife** is down at the harbour, where the *Café İskele*, its tables grouped around a fountain, is pleasant and not overpriced, while the mainstay of the town's nightlife, *Club 29*, nearby at the harbour is expensive, but offers disco, terrace, pool and restaurant.

East of Antalya: Perge and Aspendos

East of Antalya lies an area known in ancient times as **Pamphylia**, a remote region that was home to four great cities – Perge, Sillyon, Aspendos and Side. The closest to Antalya is **PERGE**, about 15km east, reachable by taking a dolmuş to the village of Aksu on the main eastbound road, from where it's a fifteen-minute walk to the site (daily 8am–6.30pm; $2.50). Perge was founded around 1000 BC and is an enticing spot nowadays, the ruins expansive and impressive. Just beyond the site entrance, the **theatre** was originally constructed by the Greeks but substantially altered by the Romans in the second century AD; built into the side of a hill, it could accommodate 14,000 people on 42 seating levels. Northeast of here is Perge's massive horseshoe-shaped **stadium**, the largest in Asia Minor and excellently preserved. East of the stadium is the city proper, marked by a cluster of souvenir and soft drinks stands. Just in front of the outer gates is the **tomb of Plancia Magna**, a benefactress of the city, whose name appears later on a number of inscriptions. Inside is a **Byzantine basilica**, beyond which lies the fourth-century AD **agora**; southwest are some **Roman baths**, a couple of whose pools have been exposed. At the northwest corner of the agora is Perge's **Hellenistic Gate**, with its two mighty circular towers, the only building to have survived from the period. Behind, there's a 300-metre-long colonnaded street, with a water channel running down the middle and shells of shops on either side.

The next best Pamphylian site is **ASPENDOS** (daily 8am–6.30pm; $2), off the main road close to the villages of Serik and Belkos and accessible from Antalya by regular dolmuş during summer. The principal feature is the well-preserved **theatre**, built in the second century AD to a Roman design, with an elaborate stage behind which the scenery could be lowered. The stage, auditorium and arcade above are all intact, and what you see today is pretty much what the spectators saw during the theatre's heyday – a state of preservation due in part to Atatürk, who after a visit declared that it should be preserved and used for performances rather than as a museum. Later, the theatre was used as a Selçuk *kervanseray*, and restoration work from that period – plasterwork decorated with red zigzags – is visible over the stage. There's also a small museum, left of the entrance, exhibiting pictures of theatre "entrance tickets" and coins.

Side

About 25km east of Aspendos, **SİDE**, a ruined Hellenistic port and one-time trysting place of Antony and Cleopatra, was perhaps the foremost of the Pamphylian cities, and the ruins of the ancient port survive. Over the last few years or so, however, Side has changed almost unrecognizably due to indiscriminate tourist development. If it's sun, sand and surf you're after, you may want to spend some time here – the beaches are superb. If you're more interested in the ruins, try and visit out of season.

Fortunately even the inroads of mass tourism have been unable to smother the grandeur of ancient Side's buildings and monuments. The **city walls** are particularly well preserved, with a number of towers still in place, and the **agora** is today fringed with the stumps of many remaining columns. Opposite the agora is the site of the former **Roman baths**, now restored to house a **museum** (Tues–Sun 8am–noon & 1.30–5pm; $2.50) with a cross-section of locally unearthed objects – mainly Roman statuary, reliefs and sarcophagi. South of here, a still-intact monumental gateway serves as an entrance to the modern resort and to Side's 20,000-seat **theatre** (daily 8am–7pm; $1), the largest in Pamphylia, and supported by arched vaults rather than built into a hillside, unlike those at Perge and Aspendos. At the back of the theatre, reached via the agora, is a row of ancient **toilets**, complete with niches for statues facing the cubicles.

Side has some fine sandy **beaches**. To the **west** the beach stretches for about 10km, lined by hotels and beach clubs, though the crowds can be heavy during high season. To the **east** the sands are emptier and stretch all the way to Alanya, though there's less in the way of facilities. **Buses and dolmuşes** arrive and depart from a large car park north of the town's main drag, just inside the monumental gateway.

The **tourist office** (Mon–Fri 9am–5pm) is on the main road into town just before the first city gate. **Accommodation** possibilities are endless. At the bottom end of the price scale are the *Kader Pansiyon* and *Cizmeci Pansiyon* (☎753 1291; ②), both west of the main street. A little more upmarket are the *Hanimeli Pansiyon* (☎753 1789; ④) and the *Şen Pansiyon* (☎753 3645; ③), just west of the square at the bottom of the main street. For **camping**, there are a number of sites along the western beach, beginning about 500m from the theatre. There's no shortage of places to **eat and drink**; try the *Toros Restaurant* near the harbour, where you can sample reasonably priced fish dishes on the terrace, or the *Aphrodite*, which has excellent swordfish. A good cheapie is the *Bademalti* on the main drag.

Alanya

Until a little over ten years ago **ALANYA** was a sleepy coastal town with no more than a handful of flyblown hotels. Now it's one of the Mediterranean coast's major resorts, a booming place but one that has fortunately managed to hold on to much of its character and is much less crowded than Side, even in midsummer.

Most of old Alanya lies on the great rocky promontory that juts out into the sea, dominating the modern town, the bulk of which is occupied by the **castle** – an hour's winding climb or a short ride on an hourly bus from the tourist office. At the end of the road is the **İç Kale**, or inner fortress (daily 8am–8pm; $2), built in 1226, pretty much intact, with the shell of a Byzantine **church**, decorated with fading frescoes, in the centre. In the northwestern corner of the fortress, a platform gives fine views of the western beaches and the mountains, though it originally served as a springboard from which prisoners were thrown to their deaths on the rocks below. On the opposite side of the promontory, the **Kızılkule** – "Red Tower"'– is a 35-metre-high defensive tower that today houses a pedestrian **ethnographic museum** (Tues–Sun 8am–noon & 1.30–5pm; 75¢), and has a roof terrace that overlooks the town's eastern harbour. Back down at sea level, apart from the hotels and restaurants, modern Alanya has little to offer. On the western side of the promontory, the **Alanya Museum** (Tues–Sun 8am–noon & 1.30–5.30pm; $1) is filled with local archeological finds and ethnological ephemera, though the best thing about it is the garden, a former Ottoman graveyard. Nearby, the **Damlataş** or "Cave of Dripping Stones" (daily 10am–sunset; 25¢) is a stalactite- and stalagmite-filled cavern with a moist, warm atmosphere said to benefit asthma sufferers. It's accessible from behind the *Dalmataş Restaurant*.

Ananya's **beaches**, though not particularly clean, are at least extensive, stretching 3km west and 8km east. Finer sand and fewer crowds can be found 23km away on he Side road at **Incekum** (meaning "fine sand"), which is practically devoid of development and backed by pine forests.

Alanya's **bus station** is a twenty-minute walk from the centre, but if you come in by dolmuş you'll probably be able to get off in the middle of town. The **tourist office** is at Çarşı Mahallesi, Kalearkası (Mon–Fri 9am–5.30pm), opposite the town museum. **Accommodation** possibilities take in the full price range, though the best places can be block-booked in summer. The *Pension Best* near the museum off Damlatas Cad (☎513 0446; ②) has cheap B&B or clean, spacious apartments for families. The *Otel Melbo* (☎513 6451; ③) off Keykubat Cad on Altin Sak, behind the eastern beach, has an English patron and rooms with balconies. The *Alanya Palas*, İskele Cad 6 (☎513 1016; ①), and the *Baba Hotel*, next door (☎513 1032; ①), are similar in price and standards. There are a couple of **campsites** west of Alanya on the Side road: the *Alanya-Motorcamp*, about 25km out just before a large hotel complex, newly built and with a restaurant and shops, and the *BP-Kervansaray Motorcamp*, a little closer, where you get roughly the same deal. For **food**, the small streets running between Gazipaşa Cad and Hükümet Cad have lots of cheap *pide* and kebab places, and restaurants on Müftüler Cad include the excellent *Saray Lokantasi*, the *Sultan* and the *Tuna Kebap ve Yemek Salonu*.

THE HATAY

The **Hatay** only became part of modern Turkey in 1939, having been apportioned to the French Protectorate of Syria since the dismemberment of the Ottoman Empire; it was handed over to Turkey in a move calculated to buy support, or at least neutrality in the imminent World War. The majority of people here speak Arabic as their first language and there's some backing for union with Syria, which has led to ongoing border tension.

Arab influence in the Hatay goes back to the seventh century, when Arab raiders began hacking at the edges of the collapsing Byzantine Empire. They were never able to secure long-lasting political control over the region, but were able to establish themselves as permanent settlers – before them the area was held by Romans, and before that, by the Seleucids, who prized its position straddling trading routes into Syria.

Antakya is the Hatay's main centre and best starting point for exploring the region. Though little survives from the city's Seleucid and Roman past, it has enough attractions to make it worth at least a full day, notably an excellent archeological museum and a cave church where Saint Peter is said to have preached. From Antakya there are frequent dolmuş connections to **Harbiye**, site of the Roman resort of Daphne.

İskenderun and around

South of Yakacik, the build-up of wayside industry and pollution is the signal for **İSKENDERUN**, founded by Alexander the Great as Alexandria ad Issum to commemorate his victory over the Persians. Already a major trade nexus during Roman times, under the Ottomans Askenderun became the main port for Halab (Aleppo), now in Syria, from where trade routes fanned out to Persia and the Arabian peninsula. Today there's nothing of historical interest here, but the harbour town is a pleasant base with good hotels and a palm-lined seaside promenade.

The local **tourist information office**, Atatürk Bulvarı 49/B (Mon–Fri 8am–noon & 1.30–5.30pm, Sat & Sun 9am–noon & 1.30–6pm; ☎326/614 1620), is on the waterfront by the town pier, in an area where the town's cheaper **pensions and hotels** lie. The best of the inexpensive places is the plain *Kavaklı Pansiyon*, Şehit Pamir Cad 52, Sok 14 (☎326/617 4606; ①). Another even cheaper option with showers down the corridor but clean, quiet rooms is the *Erzin Otel*, Kanatti Cad 28 (☎326/617 4456; ①); also worth investigating is the *Hotel Açikalin*, Şehit Pamir Cad 13 (☎326/617 3732; ①), which has ceiling fans. The *Belediye* **campsite** is out to the southwest of the town, reached by dolmuş (displaying 49 Evler/Sahil Evler on the front) from Şehit Pamir Cad.

Uluçınar and Belen

Dolmuşes run from İskenderun to the small resort and fishing town of ULUÇINAR (also called Arsuz) about 40km to the southwest, where there are some decent stretches of beach, though often charging for entry – very popular with Syrian tourists and people from İskenderun. Of a number of **hotels** and **pensions** in the town, best is probably the *Motel Yunus*, Akdeniz Cad (②), opposite the post office. The best place to eat is the waterfront *Plaj Restaurant*, which does good fish and seafood dishes. Beyond Uluçınar, if you can be bothered to follow the road south for a few kilometres, you'll come across some more undiscovered **beaches**.

South of İskenderun the road rises up into the mountains, passing through the small hill town of **BELEN**, where a pair of cafés make a good place to break a long journey. It's a quiet, unspoilt place, with a few springs gushing curative water. From here the road strains and curves through the **Belen Pass** – of great strategic importance during Roman times, when it was known as the *Pylae Syriae* or Gates of Syria. The pass is perhaps not quite as dramatic as the name suggests, mainly bare hillside with few distinctive features, and the road descending gradually into the lush Amık plain below.

Antakya and around

ANTAKYA, 25km south, stands on the site of ancient Antioch, and although there's little sense of historical continuity, the city's laid-back pace and heavily Arab atmosphere make it unique in Turkey. Flanked by mountains to the north and south, it sits in the bed of a broad river valley planted with olive trees – a welcome visual relief if you have travelled down from the drab flatlands surrounding Adana.

The city was founded as Antioch in the fourth century BC by one of the four generals among whom the empire of Alexander the Great was divided. It soon grew into an important commercial centre, and by the second century BC had developed into one of the largest cities of the ancient world, a major staging post on the newly opened trade routes from the Mediterranean to Asia, and a centre of learning; it was here that Saint Peter chose as location of one of the world's first Christian communities.

Despite being razed by a series of earthquakes during the sixth century AD, Antioch maintained its prosperity after the Roman era, and only with the rise of Constantinople did the city decline, passing through the hands of various occupiers before finally falling to the Mamelukes of Egypt, who sacked it in 1268. By the time the Ottomans took over in 1516, Antioch had long since vanished from the main stage of world history, and by the turn of last century was little more than a village, squatting amid the ruins of the ancient metropolis. After World War I, Antakya and most of the rest of the Hatay passed into the hands of the French, who laid the foundations of the modern city.

The Antakya area telephone code is ☎326.

The City

Antakya is cut in two by the Asi River, known in ancient times as Orontes. At the heart of the city, spanning the river, is the much-renovated **Rana Köprüsü** or "Old Bridge" which dates from the third century AD. The eastern bank is home to **old Antakya** – a maze of narrow streets, backed by the rocky cliffs of the Ziyaret Dağı range – and the **bazaar and market areas** north of Kemal Paşa Caddesi are easily worth an hour or two of wandering. At the eastern end of Kemal Paşa Caddesi is the **Habibi Naccar Camii**, a mosque incorporated into the shell of a former Byzantine church, which was in turn built on the site of an ancient temple. The distinctive pointed minaret was added during the seventeenth century and is not – as you might imagine – a former church tower.

From the Rana Köprüsü, it's a quick hop across to the western side of the river and the **Archeological Museum** (Tue–Sun 8am–noon & 1.30–5.30pm, Mon 1.30–5.30pm; $2), whose collection of locally unearthed Roman **mosaics** ranks among the best of its kind in the world. The first four rooms of the museum are in a state of near-immaculate preservation and mostly depict scenes from Roman mythology. Most of the mosaics were unearthed at the suburb of Daphne, now known as Harbiye (see below), which was Antioch's main holiday resort in Roman times. Depictions range from the Rape of Ganymede, to a well-endowed hunchback grinning wickedly and a drunken Dionysus leering at a green-clad nymph.

Right at the northeastern edge of town lies the **Saint Pierre Kilisesi** or St Peter's Church (Tues–Sun 8am–noon & 1.30–6pm; 50c), the cave church of Saint Peter, from which the story has it, the apostle once preached to the Christian population of Antioch; the slightly kitsch-looking facade of the church was constructed by the Crusaders during the twelfth century. Inside water drips down the cave-walls and the cool atmosphere provides a welcome break from the heat of summer. Beneath your feet you'll be able to discern traces of mosaic work thought to date from the fifth century AD, while to the right of the altar is a kind of font set in the floor and fed by a spring with reputed curative properties. A passageway leads from the church through the rock and emerges on the other side of the hill, serving as an escape route for beleaguered early Christians. A special service is held here on 29 June to mark the anniversary of Saint Peter's death, attended by members of Antakya's small Christian community. More regular masses are celebrated in a nineteenth-century church just off Kurtuluş Caddesi.

At the southeast edge of town, near the hospital, is the **Aqueduct of Trajan**, a surviving fragment of the city's Roman water supply system. Some way to the north of here is the **Habibi Neccar Cave,** once home to a solitary prophet.

Practicalities

From the otogar it's a ten-to-fifteen-minute walk to the town centre. Antakya's **tourist office** is in the new town at Atatürk Caddesi 41 (Mon–Fri 8am–noon & 1.30–6.30pm, ☎891/12636). There's a dearth of good, cheap hotels in Antakya, and you're really stuck with cheapies around the bus station or paying more for a couple of good options on Hurriyet Caddesi. The best of the cheapies is the *Hotel Güney* at İstiklâl Sok 28 (☎215 1778; ①) behind İstiklâl Cad. The *Divan Otel*, İstiklâl Cad 62 (☎215 1548; ①) is just as cheap but none too clean. Best value in Antakya at present is the newly-opened *Saray*, Hurriyet Cad 3 (☎212 5437; ②), which is spotless, with some good views of the old town mosque and *hamam*. With a little more money, try the *Atahan Hotel*, Hürriyet Caddesi 28 (☎891/11407,11408; ②).

The best places to **eat and drink** are on Hürriyet Caddesi, notably the *Han*, 19/1 Hurriyet Cad, where traditional Hatay spicy *mezze* and grills are served upstairs in a walled courtyard. There are plenty of other options, including a number along İstiklâl Caddesi. Local delicacies and specialities worth sampling include the crystallized squashes sold by weight in many of the *pastanes*.

Harbiye

About 10km south of Antakya is **HARBİYE,** the ancient and celebrated suburb of Daphne, a beautiful gorge to which revellers and holidaymakers flocked in Roman times, drawn by shady cypress and laurel groves dotted with waterfalls and pools. Today Antakya's modern citizens follow their example, and there is a regular dolmuş service from the city otogar. From the dolmuş drop-off point follow a road uphill past modern houses until you come to a waterfall. From here follow the path down into the gorge, where a number of shady tea gardens await amid a landscape that can have hardly altered since Roman times.

> ### ACCESS TO SYRIA
>
> A number of bus companies operating out of Antakya otogar offer services to cities in Syria; several buses depart for Halab (Aleppo) every day and the four hour journey costs $6. There are also daily departures for the eight hour journey to Damascus ($10). At present, visa regulations are erratic, so enquire at the Syrian Embassy in your home country before departure, or either the Syrian Embassy in Ankara, at Abdullah Cevdet Sok 7, Çankaya (☎4/138 8704), or the Syrian consulate in İstanbul, at Silâhhane Cad 59/9, Ralli Apt, Teşvikiye, Şişli (☎1/148 3284). If you have a visa, remember that you have to change $100 into Syrian currency at the official rate at the border. Inside the country, you'll get about four times this rate on the black market.

The Romans built a temple to Apollo in Daphne, since it was generally held to be the setting for the god's pursuit of her. According to the myth, Daphne, when seized by Apollo, prayed for deliverance; in answer to her prayers Peneus transformed her into a laurel tree. Another legend relates that the resort was venue of Paris' gift of the golden apple to Aphrodite, which gesture indirectly precipitated the Trojan War. Later, and with possibly more basis in fact, Mark Antony and Cleopatra are said to have married here.

CENTRAL TURKEY

When the first Turkish nomads arrived in Anatolia during the tenth and eleventh centuries, the landscape must have been strongly reminiscent of their Central Asian homeland. The terrain that so pleased the tent-dwelling herdsmen of a thousand years ago, however, has few attractions for modern visitors: monotonous, rolling vistas of stone-strewn grassland, dotted with rocky outcrops, hospitable only to sheep. In winter it can be numbingly cold here, while summer temperatures can rise to unbearable levels.

It seems appropriate that the heart of original Turkish settlement should be home to the political and social centre of modern Turkey, **Ankara**, a modern European-style capital, symbol of Atatürk's dream of a secular Turkish republic. The south central part of the country draws more visitors, not least for **Cappadocia** in the far east of the region, where water and wind have created a land of fantastic forms from the soft tufa rock, including forests of cones, table mountains and canyon-like valleys, all further hewn by civilizations that have found the area sympathetic to their needs. Further south still, **Konya** is best-known as the birthplace of the Sufi Muslim sect and is a good place to stop over between Cappadocia and the coast.

Ankara

Modern **ANKARA** is really two cities, a double identity that is due to the breakneck pace at which it has developed since being declared capital of the Turkish Republic in 1923. Until then Ankara – known as Angora – had been a small provincial city, known chiefly for the production of soft goat's wool. This city still exists, in and around the old citadel that was the site of the original settlement. The other Ankara is the modern metropolis that has grown up around a carefully planned attempt to create a seat of government worthy of a modern, Western-looking state. It's worth visiting just to see how successful this has been, although there's not much else to the place, and its museums and handful of other sights need only detain you for a day or two at most.

Arrival and information

Ankara's Essenboğa **airport** is 33km north of town and buses into the centre tend to depart about half an hour after flights land; a taxi will set you back about $15. Arriving at the city's **bus station** on Hipodrom Cad, 2km west of the city centre, it's usually easy enough to pick up city buses: a #44 will take you to Kızılay, a #64 to Ulus. The **train station** is also on Hipodrom Cad, closer in, and the same buses pass by.

Getting around the city is no problem, with plentiful **buses** running the length of the main Atatürk Bulvarı. Bus tickets are bought in advance from kiosks next to the main bus stops. There are **tourist offices** at Gazi Mustafa Kemal Bulvarı 121 (daily 8.30am–5.30pm) and Gazi Mustafa Kemal Bulvarı 33 (Mon–Fri 8am–8pm, Sat & Sun 9am–5pm). They will be able to provide you with a useful map but not much else.

The Ankara area telephone code is ☎312.

Accommodation

Most of the cheaper **hotels** are in the streets east of Atatürk Bulvarı between Ulus and Opera Meydanı; north of Ulus, on and around Çankırı Cad, are a few more upmarket places. There are also clusters along Gazi Mustafa Kemal Bulvarı in Maltepe and on Atatürk Bulvarı south of Kızılay, with prices increasing as you move south.

Buhara, Sanayi Cad 13, Ulus (☎324 5245). One of the better ones for this price. ②
Çoruh, Denizciler Cad 47, near Opera Meydanı (☎312 4113). A reasonable family-run hotel which has doubles with showers. ②
Hisar, Hisarparkı Cad 6, Ulus (☎311 9889). Washbasins only, but the rooms are clean and presentable. ①
Mithat, İtfaiye Meydanı, Tavus Sok 2 (☎311 5410). Decent double rooms with bathrooms. ②
Olimpiyat, Rüzgarlı Eşdost Sok 18, Ulus (☎243 331). Good rooms at a reasonable price. ②
Sıpahı, İtfaiye Meydanı, Kosova Sok 1 (☎324 0235). Clean, homely rooms with washbasins. ①
Turan Palas, Çankırı Cad, Beşık Sok 3, Ulus (☎312 5225). Reasonable enough for a budget place. ①
Zümrüt Palas, Posta Cad 16, Ulus (☎310 3210). Good value for money. ①

The City

Finding your way around Ankara is fairly easy. The city is bisected north–south by **Atatürk Bulvarı**, and everything you need is in easy reach of this broad and busy street. At the northern end, **Ulus Meydanı** (known simply as Ulus), a large square and an important traffic intersection marked by a huge equestrian Atatürk statue, is the best jumping-off point for the old part of the city, a village of narrow cobbled streets and ramshackle wooden houses centring on the **Hisar**, Ankara's old fortress and citadel. It was the Gauls who built the first fortifications on this site, but most of what can be seen today dates from Byzantine times, with substantial Selçuk and Ottoman additions. There are tremendous views of the rest of the city from inside, as well as an unexceptional twelfth-century mosque, the **Alâeddin Camii**. The **Aslanhane Camii**, in the **bazaar** area to the south, is more impressive, built by the Selçuks during the thirteenth century, with a carved wooden ceiling supported by 24 wooden columns and a distinctive blue-tiled *mihrab*.

Follow Kadife Sokak from here towards the modern city and you come to the **Museum of Anatolian Civilizations** (Tues–Sun 8.30am–5.30pm; $2), which boasts an incomparable collection of archeological objects housed in a restored Ottoman *bedesten* or covered market. Hittite carving and relief work form the most compelling section of the museum, mostly taken from Carchemish, a city which occupied a site near the present Syrian border. There are also Neolithic finds from Çatal Höyük, 52km south-

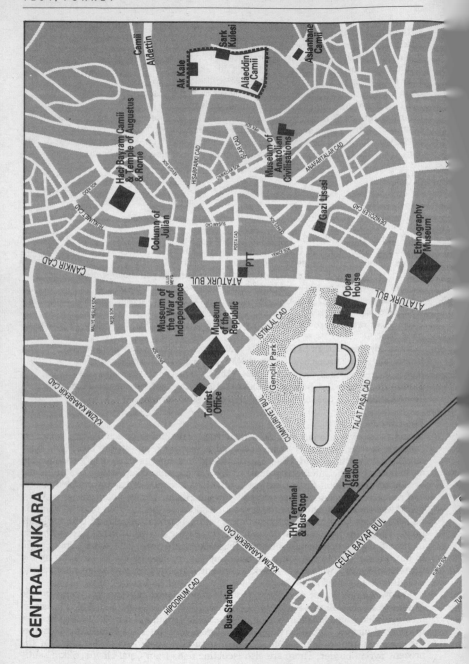

CENTRAL ANKARA

Camii
Aldettin

Ak Kale
Şark
Kulesi
Alâeddin
Camii

Aslanhane
Camii

Museum of
Anatolian
Civilisations

Haçı Bayram Camii
& Temple of Augustus
& Rome

Gazi Lisesi

Column of
Julian

Ethnography
Museum

ÇANKIR CAD

ATATÜRK BUL

PTT

Opera
House

ATATÜRK BUL

Museum of
the War of
Independence

Museum
of the
Republic

Gençlik Park

İSTIKLAL CAD

Tourist
Office

KAZIM KARABEKIR CAD

Train
Station

THY Terminal
& Bus Stop

TALAT PAŞA CAD

KAZIM KARABEKIR CAD

CELAL BAYAR BUL

HIPODRUM CAD

Bus Station

east of Konya, the site of one of Anatolia's oldest settlements; early Bronze Age stag figures, pottery figures and vessels unearthed at Kültepe, near Kayseri; examples of Urartian metalwork; and Phrygian finds from the royal tombs at Gordion, many of which have a distinctly Hellenistic feel.

North of Ulus Meydanı is what's left of Roman Ankara, namely the **Column of Julian** on Hükümet Meydanı, erected in honour of a visit to Ankara by Julian the Apostate, who reigned briefly from 361. Close by, the **Hacıbayram Cami** was erected on the ruins of the **Temple of Augustus and Rome**, built by the Phrygians during the second century BC in honour of Cybele. Today the remains of the temple wall on the square next to the mosque are about all that's left. The Hacıbayram Camii itself was built in 1400 by Hacı Bayram Veli, the founder of an order of dervishes, whose tomb in front is a popular place of pilgrimage. South down Atatürk Bulvar, the **Gençlik Parkı** was built on the orders of Atatürk to provide a recreational spot for the hard-toiling citizens of his model metropolis; it features an artificial lake, funfair, cafés and an **Opera House** near the entrance – Atatürk developed a taste for opera while serving in Sofia in 1905. Further down Atatürk Bulvarı, the **Ethnography Museum** (Tues–Sun 8.30am–12.30pm & 1.30–5.30pm; 50¢) boasts rooms used as an office by the great man, as well as the usual collection of folk costumes and Ottoman art and artefacts.

Across the main west–east rail line lies **Sıhhıye Meydanı** and the real heart of modern Ankara, which focuses on the large square of **Kızılay**, the main transport hub of the city. A few streets east rise the four minarets of the **Kocatepe Camii**, a modern mosque built in Ottoman style that ranks as one of the biggest in the world. Beyond lies Turkey's parliament building, a strip of embassies and the **Presidential Palace**, whose grounds are home to the **Çankaya Atatürk Museum**.

Northeast of here, **Anıt Kabir** is the site of Atatürk's mausoleum (daily 9am–4/5pm; bus #63 from Ulus), at the end of a long colonnaded avenue lined by Hittite lions. A twentieth-century reworking of a Hellenistic temple, it's almost bare inside except for the 40,000 kilogramme sarcophagus and the guards who keep an eye on visitors to make sure they evince an appropriate degree of respect. Outside, on the left of the courtyard, is the **sarcophagus of İsmet İnönü**, Atatürk's friend and prime minister, who succeeded him as president of the republic. At the southeastern end of the courtyard is a **museum** containing various pieces of Atatürk memorabilia, including a number of Lincoln limousines which served as his official transport.

Eating

Standard *pide* and kebab places can be found on just about every street in Ankara and there's an abundance of good sweet and cake shops, though really good **restaurants** are surprisingly rare, and, outside of the big hotel **bars**, you'll find few places to get a drink other than gloomy male-dominated "pubs". Ulus, particularly along Çankırı Cad, is a good place to look, with a broad range of places which are among the cheapest in town. At the Kızılay end of Karanfil Sokak and on Selânik Sokak you'll find some slightly more upmarket but still easily affordable alternatives. Restaurants on Tunalı Hilmi Caddesi in Kavaklidere tend to be more expensive and not necessarily better than those elsewhere – you're paying for the chance to rub shoulders with the city's more affluent inhabitants.

Akman Boza ve Pasta Salonu, Atatürk Bulvarı 3, Ulus. In a shopping plaza just south of the Atatürk statue, serving light meals, pastries and *boza*, a refreshing millet-based drink.

Alaros Chicken, Tunalı Hilmi Caddesi, Bestekar Sok 86/A, Kavaklidere. Upmarket fast food joint with good chicken dishes.

Altin Şiş, Karanfil Sok 17, Kızılay. A reasonably priced kebab place which does good puddings.

Ankara Sofrasi, Hoşdere Cad 76, Çankaya. Traditional Turkish dishes including excellent *manti*. A little off the beaten track but worth the effort.

Boyacizâde Konaği, Berrak Sok 7–9. One of a crop of new restaurants in restored houses in the old citadel. Though obviously aimed at tourists, it's very pleasant and a meal here won't break the bank.

Cambo, Karanfil Sok 15, Kızılay. Moderately priced sit-down place, good for kebabs and snacks.

Hacı Mehmet Özlek, Sanayi Cad 7, Ulus. A pleasant, friendly place with a decently priced menu. Ask to be seated upstairs.

Kebabıstan, Karanfil Sok/Yüksel Cad, Kızılay. Plush kebab restaurant, offering all kinds of kebab including excellent mushroom *şiş*.

Körfez Lokantası, Bayındır Sok 24. Arguably the best restaurant in town, always packed, and serving good-sized portions of excellent, moderately priced Turkish food.

Pizza Pino, Tunalı Hilmi Cad 111/B, Kavaklidere. Authentic, though pricey, pizza in glossy surroundings.

Rema Lokantası, Posta Cad/Sanayi Cad, Ulus. Basic *lokanta* serving just about the cheapest eats in the area.

Santral Kefiterya, Çankırı Cad, Ulus. A beer hall serving simple kebab dishes.

Uğrak Piknik and **Uğrak Lokantası,** Çankırı Cad, Ulus. A cafeteria with fixed meals for about $2.50 along with a proper restaurant.

Bars and cafés

Outside of the big hotel bars you'll find few places to drink other than gloomy male-dominated pubs. There are some possibilities in the more affluent parts of town towards the southern end of Atatürk Bulvarı.

Café Seven, Reşit Galip Cad 57/A, Gaziosmanpaşa. A café/bar student hang-out with live music in the evening. Snack food available.

Galeri Nev, Horasan Sok 14. A combined café-gallery with a garden in summer.

Jazz Bar, Tunali Hilmi Cad 4/1, Kavaklidere. A bar run by Alpay, a famous Turkish musician, who also performs there.

Nightlife

Cinema Foreign language films are usually shown in the original with Turkish subtitles. Most cinemas show mainsteam releases with regularly changing programmes. Try the *Metropol,* Selanik Cad 76, Lizilay.

Opera The Opera House at Opera Meydanı is great value. Admission is usually less than $4 for lively and well-attended performances of works like *Madame Butterfly* and *La Bohème.*

Discos *Timeout,* Simon Bolivar Cad 28. More a restaurant with a big dance floor but worth checking out.

Listings

Airlines *THY,* Atatürk Bul 167/A (☎117 6499).

Buses Most bus companies have offices on Gazi Mustafa Kemal Bulvarı, Ziya Gökalp Cad, İzmir Cad and Menekşe Sok, where you can buy tickets in advance.

Car rental *Akatur,* Cinnah Cad 28/2, Çankaya (☎126 0603); *Avis,* Tunus Cad 68/2, Kavaklıdere (☎167 2313); *Europcar,* Küçük Esat Cad 25/C, Bakanlıkar (☎118 3430); *Hertz* Kızılırmak Sok 1 (☎118 8440).

Embassies *Australia,* Nenehatun Cad 83, Gaziosmanpaşa (☎136 1240); *Canada,* Nenehatun Cad 75, Gaziosmanpaşa (☎136 1275); *Great Britain,* Şehit Ersan Cad 46/A, Çankaya (☎127 4310); *Netherlands,* Köroğlu Sok 6, Gaziosmanpaşa (☎136 1074); *USA,* Atatürk Bulvarı 110, Çankaya (☎126 5470).

Exchange Outside banking hours use the train station PTT (daily 7am–11pm), or the main PTT, which is open 24hr.

Hospital The *Hacettepe Hastanesı,* just west of Hasırcılar Sok in Sihhiye, normally has an English-speaking doctor available.

Left luggage There's an office at the bus station where they'll charge about $1 per piece.

PTT Main *PTT* is the *Merkez Postahane,* on Atatürk Bulvarı just up from the Opera House in Ulus.

Cappadocia

A land created by the complex interaction of natural and human forces over vast spans of time, **Cappadocia**, around 150km southeast of Ankara, is initially a disturbing place, the great expanses of bizarrely eroded volcanic rock giving an impression of barrenness. It's in fact an exceedingly fertile region, and one whose weird formations of soft, dusty rock have been adapted over millennia by many varying cultures, from Hittites to later Christians hiding away from Arab marauders. Indeed, the most fascinating aspect of a visit to the area is the impression of continuity. There are more than a thousand rock-churches in Cappadocia, dating from the earliest days of Christianity to the thirteenth century, and some caves are still inhabited; the fields are still fertilized with guano collected in rock-cut pigeon houses; and pottery is still made from the clay of the Kızılırmak river. It's a popular area with tourists, and getting more so, but the crowds are largely confined to a few areas.

The **best-known sites** are located within the triangle delimited by the roads connecting Nevşehir, Avanos and Ürgüp. Within this region are the greater part of the valleys of fairy chimneys, the rock-cut churches of the **Göreme** open-air museum, with their amazing selection of frescoes, and the **Zelve** monastery, a complex of troglodyte dwellings and churches hewn out of the rock. **Nevşehir** itself isn't much of a town, but it's an important travel centre, and while **Ürgüp** makes perhaps a more attractive base from which to tour the surrounding valleys, it isn't as well served by public transport. Outside the triangle to the south are the underground cities of **Derinkuyu** and **Kaymaklı**, fascinating warrens attesting to the ingenuity of the ancient inhabitants.

The telephone code for Nevşehir, including Avanos, Ürgüp and Derinkuyu, is ☎384.

Nevşehir

Though said to be Turkey's richest town, **NEVŞEHİR**, at the very heart of Cappadocia, can hardly be accused of an ostentatious display of wealth. However, it is a useful base for the region. Frequent bus services all over Cappadocia run from here, and in some cases it's necessary to make a wide detour to the city in order to travel between two neighbouring towns.

The Ottoman castle stands at the heart of the old city, southwest of the modern centre, and is a good landmark. The new city below is divided by two main streets, **Atatürk Bulvarı**, on which are situated most of the hotels and restaurants, and **Lale** Caddesi, turning into Gülşehir Caddesi to the north, where you'll find the main dolmuş station. The remains of the citadel are no big deal in themselves but the views are good. On the side of the hill, the eighteenth-century **Damat İbrahim Paşa Camii** is set in a large precinct made all the more impressive by the surrounding cramped streets, and has a cool, dark interior further enhanced by small decorative details. Opposite, the **Damat İbrahim Paşa Hamamı** (7.30am–9pm; Sat women only, other days men only; $4) is also in good working order and well run. The **Nevşehir Museum**, on Yeni Kayseri Caddesi (daily 8am–noon & 1–5pm; 50¢), is well worth the twenty-minute walk from the tourist office, with a collection that includes three terracotta sarcophagi dating from the third to fourth century AD, finds from the Phrygian and Byzantine periods, and Turkish carpets, kilims and looms.

The **tourist office** (daily 8am–5pm), on Atatürk Bulvarı on the right as you head downhill towards Ürgüp, can arm you with a hotel price list and a map. Two companies run **organized tours** of the area – *Tulip*, opposite the tourist office on Atatürk Bulvarı (☎213 1303), and *Neşe*, Aksaray Cad 5/A (☎213 3484), which is reputedly better.

Pensions in Nevşehir are neither as cheap nor as good as elsewhere in Cappadocia. Two places not far from the tourist office are the reasonably priced *Hotel Kaymak*, Eski Sanayi Meydanı 11 (☎213 5427; ①), and the clean, cheap *Kemer Pansiyon* (☎213 1751; ①), 100m above Lâle Park at Aksaray Cad 3/1. A ten-minute walk away off the Ankara road at Hasimi Sok 3 is a cheap pension called the *Maison du Turc*, with clean, if rather spartan rooms. The nicest of the **campsites** in the region, the *Koru Mocamp*, is signposted off to the right as you turn from Nevşehir into Üçhisar. For **food**, the *Aspava Restaurant*, Atatürk Bulvarı 29, serves well-prepared dishes, and the *Astro*, Lâle Cad 22/1 serves cheap, well-prepared stews and kebabs in pleasant surroundings.

Derinkuyu and Kaymaklı

Among the most extraordinary phenomena of the Cappadocia region are the remains of a number of underground settlements, some of them large enough to have accommodated up to 30,000 people. The cities are though to date back to Hittite times and it is possible that they were used as shelters during the attacks of 1200 BC, when the Hittite empire was destroyed by invaders from Thrace. However, the complexes were enlarged by later civilizations, the presence of missionary schools, churches and wine cellars indicating that they were most probably used by Christian communities. A total of forty such settlements, from villages to vast cities, have been discovered, but only a few have so far been opened to the public.

The most thoroughly excavated is in the village of **DERİNKUYU**, (daily May–Sept 8am–7pm; Oct–April 8am–5pm; $2.50, students $1.25), 29km from Nevşehir and accessible by dolmuş. The city is well-lit and the original ventilation system still functions remarkably well, but some of the passages are small and cramped. The size of this rock-cut warren is difficult to comprehend even on a thorough exploration, since only part of what has been excavated is open, and even this is thought to comprise only a quarter of the original city. The area consists of a total of eight floors reaching to a depth of 55 metres. What you'll see includes – on the first two floors – stables, wine presses and a dining hall or school room with two long, rock-cut tables; living quarters, churches, armouries and tunnels on the third and fourth floors; and a crucifix-shaped church, a meeting hall, a dungeon and a grave on the lower levels.

Nine kilometres north of Derinkuyu on the Nevşehir–Niğde highway you'll have passed **KAYMAKLI** (March–Sept 8am–7pm; Oct–Feb 8.30am–5pm; $2). Smaller and consequently less popular than Derinkuyu, only five of its underground levels have been excavated to date. The layout is very similar, networks of streets with small living spaces leading off into underground plazas with various functions, the more obvious of which are stables, smoke-blackened kitchens, storage space and wine presses.

Göreme and around

The small town of **GÖREME** is of central importance to Cappadocian tourism, principally because it is the best-known of the few remaining Cappadocian villages whose rock-cut houses and fairy chimneys are still inhabited. The number of visitors has expanded remarkably in the last decade or so, but despite this it retains a degree of charm, and the tufa landscapes are just a short stroll away. Public transport is adequate and hitching relatively easy, so if you are intending to spend some time in the region, this is not a bad place to base your explorations.

There are two **churches** in the hills above, the **Durmuş Kadir Kilisesi**, clearly visible across the vineyard next to a cave house with rock-cut steps, and the two-domed **Karşıbucak Yusuf Koç Kilisesi**, which houses frescoes in very good condition. About 2km outside the village, the **Göreme Open-Air Museum** (daily 8.30am–5.30pm; $2.50), up a steep hill on the road to Ürgüp, is the best known and most visited of all the monastic settlements in the Cappadocia region, the site of over thirty churches, mainly dating from the ninth to the end of the eleventh century and containing some of the best of all the frescoes in Cappadocia. Most are barely discernible from the outside, apart from a few small holes serving as windows or air shafts. But inside the churches re-create many of the features of Byzantine buildings, with domes, barrel-vaulted ceilings and cross plans supported by mock pillars, capitals and pendentives. The best-preserved church is the **Tokalı Kilise**, "the Church with the Buckle", located away from the others on the opposite side of the road about 50m back towards the village. It's two churches, in fact, both frescoed, an **Old Church**, dating from the second decade of the tenth century, and a **New Church**, whose frescoes represent some of the finest examples of tenth-century Byzantine art. The best-known of the churches in the main complex are the three columned churches, the **Elmalı Kilise** (Church of the Apple), the **Karanlık Kilise** (Dark Church) and the **Çarıklı Kilise** (Church of the Sandals) – eleventh-century churches heavily influenced by Byzantine forms and painted with superb skill. Look, too, at the church of **St Barbara**, named after the depiction of the saint on the north wall, although most famous for the strange insect figure on the wall – the significance of which can only be guessed at.

If staying, there are plenty of **pensions** in Göreme, with carefully controlled prices. Among the best places are the *Paradise* (☎271 2248; ②), which has constant hot water and is very friendly, and the *Rock Valley Pansiyon* (☎271 2474; ②), comfortable and clean, with one of the best-value restaurants in town. The *Peri Pansiyon* (☎271 2136; ②) is good, too, unique and pretty with its high-rise fairy chimneys. The *Paradise* and the *Peri* are situated at the beginning of the road to the Open-Air Museum and the *Rock Valley* is in the other direction. You could also try the newly opened *L'Elysee Pension*; ②, which has clean simple rooms. There are several **campsites** on the fringes of Göreme, best the *Cappadocia*, on the Kayseri road, and *Dilek*, on the Ürgüp road near the *Peri Pansiyon* – more sheltered and with a nice little restaurant. Both have swimming pools. Apart from the **restaurant** at *Rock Valley*, which serves vegetarian food and good breakfasts, the best place to eat is the *Ataman*, back through the village; although pricy, everything is immaculately prepared from local specialities like Kayseri *pastırma* (cured meat baked in paper) to French soufflés; alternatively, try the *Konak Evi*, a restored Ottoman mansion with a variety of lovely settings in which to enjoy dishes.

Zelve

The deserted **monastery complex** in the three valleys of ZELVE (daily 8.30am–6pm; $2.50), a few kilometres north of Göreme off the Avanos–Çavuşin road, is one of the most fascinating remnants of Cappadocia's troglodyte past. The churches here date back to before the ninth century, but the valley was inhabited by Turkish Muslims who hacked their dwellings out of the tuff rock face until about thirty years ago). On the left-hand side of the first valley, about halfway up, are the remains of a small Ottoman mosque, the prayer hall and *mihrab* of which are partly hewn from the rock; and a large number of chapels and medieval oratories are scattered up and down the valleys, many of them decorated with carved crosses. A thorough exploration really requires a torch and old clothes: some of the rooms are entered by means of precarious steps, others by swinging up through holes in the floors, and, on occasion, massive leaps to a lower floor – good fun if you're reasonably energetic and have a head for heights.

Ürgüp

Around 5km east of Göreme, **ÜRGÜP** is perhaps Cappadocia's most tourist-friendly town, a formerly Greek community that has somehow managed to absorb the increase in tourists with more dignity than most of the rest of the region. There are still many distinctive and beautiful houses of Greek and Ottoman origin scattered around the town, and the cliffs above are riddled with man-made cave dwellings, now put to use as storage space and stabling – though until fairly recently they were lived in. There isn't much to see apart from the **museum** (daily 8am–5pm; 50¢), tiny and not particularly well labelled, with exhibits that include a selection of prehistoric ceramics, figurines, lamps and ornaments found during excavations in the area.

The **bus station** is in the centre of town, a little way south of Kayseri Cad, the main shopping street (one of the best places in Turkey to buy carpets and kilims), where you'll also find the **tourist office** at no. 37 (daily 8.30am–5.30pm), next to the museum in a park. Ürgüp is full of **hotels and pensions**. There are several decent places on the road to Nevşehir: the *Asia Minor*, İstiklâl Cad 38 (☎341 2741; ②), is comfortable, and the *Born Hotel* on Ahmet Refik Cad (☎341 4756; ①) is smaller and rather chaotic, but good fun. There's also the friendly and quiet *Seymen Pansiyon* (☎341 2380; ①), above the hamam on İstiklâl Cad, and the *Cappadoce Hotel* (☎341 4714; ①), an old Greek monastery with a pleasant courtyard and a variety of rooms ranging from four-person dorms to doubles with bathrooms. Just up the road from here is the *Elvan* (☎341 4191; ①). On the other side of town, beyond the tourist office on Kayseri Cad, the *Göreme Otel* (☎341 4022; ①) is pleasant and has camping space in the garden. The *Çamlık* **campsite**, across the river on the Kayseri road about 1km out of town, has good facilities and plenty of shade. Ürgüp's best **restaurant** is the *Hanedan*, opposite the *Türkerler Motel* on the Nevşehir road, and although its international evening menu is pricy it does a great lunchtime *mezes* buffet for $5 a head. The *Sömine Café and Restaurant* in Ürgüp's central square, Cumhuriyet Meydanı (above the taxi rank on Suat Hayrı Ürgüplu Cad) has a good atmosphere inside and out on the massive patio, and the food is Turkish specialities, well prepared. Cheaper options include the popular *Cappadocia Restaurant* at Cumhuriyet Meydanı 16, and the *Kardeşler Pide Salonu*, Dumlupınar Cad 13, which serves good *pide*.

For seeing the rest of Cappadocia, there are regular buses to Nevşehir and **dolmuşes** to Göreme and Kayseri from the bus station – although it's often quicker to hitch. *Magic Valley* (☎341 2145) and *Hiro Tours* (☎341 4857) at the bus station run tours of the area and rent **cars** and **mopeds**. Haydour Haykir's *Prestige Touristic Services* (☎341 8077) on Suat Hayrı Ürgüplu Cad do trekking tours in Cappadocia and can provide mountain guides. They also rent out cars.

Konya

The home of Celalledin Rumi or the **Mevlâna** ("Our Master"), the mystic who founded the Mevlcvi or "Whirling Dervish" sect, and the centre of Sufic mystical practice and teaching, **KONYA** is a place of pilgrimage for the entire Muslim world. It was also something of a capital during the Selçuk era, many of the buildings from which are still standing, along with examples of their highly distinctive crafts and applied arts on display in Konya's museums. As a result, although initially not a very appealing city of over half a million, it's well worth a stop for a night at least, especially if you're making your way down to the coast from Cappadocia.

The City

The **Mevlâna Müzesi** (Mon 10am–5.30pm, Tues–Sun 9am–5.30pm; $2.50 for foreigners) is among Turkey's more rewarding sights, housed in the first lodge (*tekke*) of the Mevlevi dervish sect, at the eastern end of Mevlâna Bulvarı, and easily recognizable by its distinctive fluted turquoise dome. The teachings of the Mevlâna, which emphasized tolerance, love and charity, were an exciting departure from Islamic orthodoxy, and they're still one of the most attractive aspects of the religion to Westerners and liberal Muslims alike. The *tekke* is thought to have been presented as a gift to the Mevlâna's father, Bahaeddin Veled, by the Selçuk sultans, and it served as a place of teaching, meditation and ceremonial dance from shortly after Rumi's death in 1273 until 1925, when Atatürk banned all Sufic orders. The main building of the museum holds the **mausoleum** containing the tombs of the Mevlâna, his father and other notables. You should leave your shoes at the door and shuffle along in a queue of pilgrims; women must cover their heads, and if you're wearing shorts you'll be given a skirt-like affair to cover your legs, regardless of gender. In the adjoining room, the original **semahane** (or ceremonial hall), exhibits include some of the musical instruments of the first dervishes, the original illuminated *Mathnawi* – the poetical work of the Mevlâna – and silk and woollen carpets, including one 500-year-old silk carpet from Selçuk Persia that is supposedly the finest ever woven. The latticed gallery above was for women spectators, a modification introduced by the followers of the Mevlâna after his death. In the adjoining room, a casket containing hairs from the beard of the Prophet Mohammed is displayed alongside illuminated medieval Korans.

At the opposite end of Mevlâna Caddesi (later Alâeddin Caddesi, once west of Aziziye Caddesi) from the Mevlâna Müzesi, the **Alâeddin Parkı** is a nice place to stroll, this is the site of the original Selçuk acropolis and the source of finds dating back to 7000 BC, most of which are now in the museum in Ankara. At the foot of the hill to the north are the scant remains of a Selçuk palace, although you'd do better to head straight for the imposing **Alâeddin mosque**, begun in 1130 and completed in 1221, with an odd facade graced with bits of masonry from an earlier construction. Assuming it's open again after a long restoration, the interior has distinctly Selçuk features like a network of wooden beams, and the remains of eight Selçuk sultans are enshrined in the courtyard. The nearby **Karatay Medrese** on Alâeddin Bulvarı (daily 8am–noon & 1.30–5.30pm; $1) is another important Selçuk monument, built in 1251 and combining elements such as Arabic striped stonework and Greek Corinthian columns with a structure which is distinctly Selçuk, its tall doorway surmounted by a pointed stalactite arch. Inside, the symmetrical design of the famed dome of stars is a stylized representation of the solar system in tiles, a perfect backdrop for the Selçuk **ceramics** on display, which are covered with striking images of birds, animals and even angels. Behind its fine Selçuk portal the **İnce Minare Medrese** (Tues–Sun 8am–noon & 1.30–5.30; 50¢), below the park on Alâeddin Bulvarı, is also now a museum, featuring stone and woodcarving, with exhibits from the palace on the present site of the Alâeddin Parkı. The other museum worthy of note is the **Museum of Archeology** (Tues–Sun 8.30am–5pm; $1) in the south of the city, containing the only pre-Selçuk remains in the city, including a few Hittite artefacts and three well-preserved Roman sarcophagi from Pamphylia.

Practicalities

Konya's **bus station** is over 2km out on Ankara Cad – take the *Konak–Otogar* dolmuş into town; the **train station** is around the same distance out from the centre at the far end of İstasyon Cad, connected to the centre by bus every half-hour. The **tourist office** is at Mevlâna Cad 21 (Mon–Fri 8.30am–5pm). Konya's better **hotels** are on or just north of Mevlâna Cad; the ones south of here, around the bazaar, are cheaper but a bit rough. The *Suat* right in the bazaar, and the *Şeref Palas*, Şerefşirin Sok 8 (☎33/113543; ①), are about the cheapest you'll find. The *Çatal Aile Pansiyon* on Naci Fikret Sok, behind the tourist office (☎33/114981; ①), is small, friendly and central; the *Otel Çeşme* at Akifpaşa Sok 35, off İstanbul Cad (☎33/512 426; ③), has rooms with baths which can be bargained down except in December during the annual Mevlâna festival when many hotels fill. It's worth also keeping in mind the *Bella Hotel*, Aziziye Cad 19 (☎33/514070; ③, again ② at slow times). As for **eating**, the *Damla*, reached from a small arcade off Alâeddin Bulvarı, is okay and has alcohol, though the food is much better at the *Şifa Lokantası*, Mevlâna Cad 29/30, and still very reasonably priced. The *Marmaris*, on the corner of Alâeddin and Mazhar Babalık Sok, is a decent kebab and *pide* place; so also is the *Hanedan Et Lokantasi*, near the *Şifa* on Aziziye Cad.

travel details

Trains

İstanbul to: Ankara (5 daily; 8hr); Edirne (1 daily; 6hr 30min); Denizli (1 daily; 14hr 30min); İzmir (2 daily; 11hr); Konya (3 daily; 14hr).

Ankara to: İzmir (2 daily; 14hr).

İzmir to: Selçuk (3 daily; 2hr).

Buses and dolmumes

İstanbul to: Ankara (half-hourly; 10hr); Alanya (hourly; 14hr); Antalya (4 daily; 12hr); Ayvalık (hourly; 9hr); Bodrum (4 daily; 12hr); Bursa (hourly; 5hr); Çanakkale (hourly; 5hr 30min); Datça (1 daily; 17hr); Denizli (hourly; 15hr); Fethiye (hourly; 15hr); İzmir (hourly; 10hr); Göreme (5 daily; 12hr 30min); Kuşadası (3 daily; 11hr); Marmaris (4 daily; 13hr); Nevşehir (3 daily; 12hr); Side (1 daily; 13hr); Ürgüp (5 daily; 12hr 30min); Konya (7 daily; 11hr).

Ankara to: Antalya (12 daily; 10hr); Bodrum (10 daily; 12hr); Bursa (hourly; 7hr); İstanbul (every 30min; 8hr); İzmir (hourly; 9hr); Konya (14 daily; 3hr 30min); Nevşehir (12 daily; 4hr 30min).

Antalya to: Alanya (hourly; 2hr); Denizli (6 daily; 5hr 30min); Fethiye, by inland route (3 daily; 4hr); İzmir (6 daily; 9hr 30min); Kaş (7 daily; 4hr 30min); Konya (6 daily; 6hr 30min); Side (3 an hour; 1hr 15min).

Ayvalık to: Bergama (4 daily; 1hr); Bursa (10 daily; 4hr 30min); Çanakkale (hourly; 3hr); İzmir (hourly; 2hr 30min).

Bergama to: Ayvalık (4 daily; 1hr); İzmir (12 daily; 2hr).

Bursa to: Çanakkale (hourly; 6hr); Ankara (hourly; 7hr); İstanbul (hourly; 5hr); İzmir (15 daily; 7hr).

Bodrum to: Marmaris (8 daily; 3hr 15min; Ankara (several daily; 13hr)); Fethiye (6 daily; 4hr 30min).

Çanakkale to: Bursa (16 daily; 6hr); Ayvalık (hourly; 3hr); İzmir (hourly; 5hr 30min).

Datça to: Marmaris (13 daily; 2hr 15min); Ankara (3 daily; 13hr).

Denizli to: Bodrum (2–3 daily; 4hr 30min); Antalya (8 daily; 5hr 30min–4hr 15min); Konya (several daily; 7hr 15min); Marmaris (2–3 daily; 3hr 30min).

Edirne to: Çanakkale (2 daily; 4hr 30min).

Fethiye to: İzmir (every 30min; 7hr); Ankara (2 daily; 12hr); Antalya (8 daily; 4hr); Bodrum (6 daily; 5hr); Denizli (5 daily; 4hr); Kaş (15 daily; 2hr 30min); Marmaris (10 daily; 3hr); Patara (10 daily; 1hr 30min).

Kuşadası to: Bodrum (3 daily; 3hr); Pamukkale (12 daily; 3hr 30min).

İzmir to: Selçuk (every 20min; 1hr 20min); Ankara (8 daily; 9hr); Antalya (8 daily; 8hr 30min); Ayvalık (every 30min; 2hr 30min); Bergama (hourly; 2hr); Bodrum (hourly; 4hr); Bursa (6 daily; 7hr); Çanakkale (4 daily; 5hr 30min); Çeşme (every 15–20min; 1hr 30min); Datça (hourly; 7hr); Denizli (hourly; 4hr); Fethiye (12–18 daily; 7hr); Kuşadası (half-hourly; 1hr 40min); Marmaris (hourly; 5hr);

Kaş to: Fethiye (8 daily; 2hr 30min); Antalya (6 daily; 5hr); Bodrum (3 daily; 7hr); Marmaris (4 daily; 4hr 30min); Patara (10 daily; 1hr); Pamukkale (2 daily; 10hr).

Marmaris to: Dalaman (hourly; 1hr 30min); Ankara (14 daily; 13hr); Bodrum (4 daily; 3hr 15min); Denizli (6 daily; 3hr 30min); Fethiye (10 daily; 3hr).

Nevşehir to: Marmaris (1 daily; 14hr); Antalya (1 daily; 11hr); İzmir (1 daily; 12hr); Konya (4 daily; 3hr).

Domestic ferries

Çanakkale to: Eceabat (hourly; 20min).

Datça to: Bodrum (April–Oct 2 daily; 1hr 30min).

Eceabat to: Çanakkale (hourly; 20min).

Gelibolu to: Lapseki (15 daily; 20min).

İzmir to: İstanbul (1 weekly; 19hr).

Kilitbahir to: Çanakkale (hourly; 10min).

INDEX

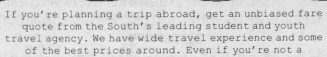

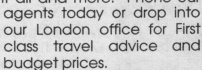

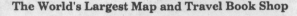

You are
A STUDENT

You travel
THE WORLD

You want
TO SAVE MONEY

Here's how

The International Student Identity Card

Available at Student Travel Offices Worldwide.

Entitles you to discounts and special services worldwide.

WHATEVER CORNER YOU'RE OFF TO, YOU CAN AFFORD IT WITH STA TRAVEL.

At STA Travel we're all seasoned travellers, so wherever you're bound, we're bound to have been. We offer the best deals on fares with the flexibility to change your mind as you go.
There are even better deals for students.

Call 071-937 1221 for your free copy of The STA Travel Guide.
117 Euston Road, NW1. 86 Old Brompton Road, SW7.
North America 071-937 9971, Europe 071-937 9921, Long Haul 071-937 9962,
Round the World 071-937 1733, or 061-834 0668 (Manchester).
USA freephone 1-800-777-0112.
Manchester, Leeds, Cambridge, Bristol, Oxford, London.

ABTA (99209) IATA

STA
STA TRAVEL

WHEREVER YOU'RE BOUND, WE'RE BOUND TO HAVE BEEN.